The EUROPEAN Book of FOOTBALL
2006/2007

A Comprehensive Guide to the Continental Game

in association with

edited by *Mike Hammond*   published by *m press (media) ltd*

ISBN 0-9550943-3-X

The European Book of Football 2006/2007

A Comprehensive Guide to the Continental Game

in association with

WORLD SOCCER

edited by *Mike Hammond*   published by *m press (media) ltd*

The European Book of Football 2006/2007

The European Book of Football 2006/2007
First Published in Great Britain
by m press (media) ltd, 2006

Copyright m press (media) ltd
Unit 4, Ashton Gate, Harold Hill, Romford, Essex,
England RM3 8UF

ISBN 0-9550943-3-X

All rights reserved. No part of this publication may be reproduced, stored in any retrieval system or transmitted, in any form or by any means, without the written consent of the publisher.

Further copies available from:

www.calmproductions.com

orders@calmproductions.com

UK hotline 0845 408 2606

EDITORIAL TEAM

Editor
MIKE HAMMOND (mrhhammo@aol.com)

Correspondents and Researchers
Mert Aydin (Turkey), Nikolai Belov (Russia), José Del Olmo (Spain), Tamás Dénes (Hungary), Mike Dryomin (Azerbaijan), Elred Faisst (Austria), Marco Gatta (Italy), Marshall Gillespie (Northern Ireland, Republic of Ireland), Miron Goihman (Kazakhstan, Moldova), Michael Hansen (Denmark), Peter Hekkema (Holland), Romeo Ionescu (Romania), Michel Jambonet (France), Valery Karpushkin (Latvia), Mikael Kirakosyan (Armenia), Jean-Paul & Daniel Kolbusch (Luxembourg), Jesper Krogshede Sørensen (Faroe Islands, National Team Kits), Fuad & Fedja Krvavac (Bosnia-Herzegovina), Zdenek Kucera (Czech Republic), Tarmo Lehiste (Estonia), Dag Lindholm (Norway), Ewan Macdonald (Scotland), Ian McNaughtan (Club Colours), Goran Mancevski (Macedonia), Giovanni Nappi (Albania), Kazimierz Oleszek (Poland), Olexandr Pauk (Belarus, Ukraine), Humberto Pereira Silva (Portugal), Ivan & Zdravko Reic (Croatia), Mike Ritter (Germany), Revaz Shengelia (Georgia), Vídir Sigurdsson (Iceland), Martin Sohlström (Sweden), Dusan Stamenkovic (Serbia & Montenegro), Andrej Stare (Slovenia), Algis Staskevicius (Lithuania), Edouard Stutz (Switzerland), Matej Széher (Slovakia), Mel Thomas (Wales), Vesa Tikander (Finland), Akis Tsopelas (Greece), Serge Van Hoof (Belgium), Victor Vassallo (Malta), Jacob Zelazo (Bulgaria, Cyprus, Israel).

Club crests sourced with the aid of High Quality Football Logos (www.hqfl.dk) and The Best Brands of the World (www.brandsoftheworld.com).

Photographs
EMPICS Sports Photo Agency, Getty Images

Designed and Printed by
m press (sales) ltd, England
+44 (0)1708 379 979

CONTENTS

Section 1

Introductions 6
Welcomes from the Publisher, the Editor and Gavin Hamilton of *World Soccer*

WORLD CUP FINALS 2006 12
Comprehensive coverage of the global extravaganza in Germany, with a complete narrative and pictorial review plus all the important stats

World Cup Qualifiers 60
A round-up of all the groups and games from the European qualifying zone

Euro 2008 72
All the fixtures for the qualifying tournament

UEFA Champions League 2005/06 74
How the Cup was won – a detailed round-by-round review of the world's most prestigious club competition

UEFA Cup 2005/06 105
All the important facts, figures and stories

Section 2

NATION-BY-NATION 126
Everything you need to know about the 52 European nations and their top-division clubs – in words, pictures and a compendium of statistics you won't find anywhere else
(A separate Index for this section can be found on page 127)

Section 3

THE DIRECTORY 783
Up to date for 2006/07, an exhaustive reference of contact details, coaches, championships and cups

Section 4

***THE EUROPEAN BOOK OF FOOTBALL* TOP 100 PLAYERS OF THE SEASON** 849
Is your favourite included? We list the best players of 2006/07 – and provide profiles and stats to explain why

…and in the centre of the Book

THE COLOUR SECTION
Logos, Crests, Kits, Maps and Club Locations in full colour, with special pages for the non-European World Cup teams

Section 1

Welcome

It's been quite a year for European football, with a World Cup dominated by the continent's leading teams. Now, after the world party, the focus returns firmly and squarely to the European game and the hard graft of the domestic leagues, continental club competitions and qualifying for the next major international tournament, the 2008 European Championship finals in Austria and Switzerland.

Even though the globalisation of football means more people know more about the game's leading players and clubs than ever before, there is still a need for printed media that reach the parts that others do not reach. The European Book of Football is one such publication, and it deserves recognition for the valuable resource that it has become.

The diversification of the football media over the past decade, particularly via the internet, has actually made it harder to find reliable statistics on European football. The efforts of Mike Hammond and his team of contributors mean everything is brought together in one place - comprehensively and, most importantly, accurately.

World Soccer is again very happy to endorse the European Book of Football as it becomes established as a standard reference work across the continent.

Gavin Hamilton
Editor, World Soccer

After the success of last year's inaugural publication, we are delighted to bring you the second edition of the European Book of Football, which of course features full, unrivalled coverage of the 2006 World Cup.

The tournament featured the usual high drama and controversy, with some moments bordering on the truly bizarre, but it was excellently run by the Germans, who deserve the highest praise for their outstanding organisation.

Congratulations also to Italy for winning the trophy for the fourth time, their magnificent team spirit shining through despite all the problems back home.

Barcelona are the new champions of Europe and they, too, were worthy winners, although it was a pity that the controversial sending-off of Arsenal goalkeeper Jens Lehmann rather spoiled the final as a spectacle.

The Champions League is off and running again, but the main focus for international teams over the next two years is Euro 2008. It promises to be an interesting ride for the continent's 52 participating nations along the road to Vienna.

This publication, I trust, will continue to be a vital tool of reference for those of you who follow the European game with more than a passing interest.

My thanks, once again, go to Mike Hammond and his team for producing the wealth of invaluable information, much of it exclusive, contained within these pages.

Cliff Moulder
Publisher, m press (media) ltd

Editor's Comment

Twenty years ago, when I first started compiling yearbooks on European football like this one, it was easy to know when the season began and ended.

Nowadays, no sooner is one competition over than another is immediately underway. Who was it that first uttered those immortal words: "Stop the world, I want to get off"?

Football's supercharged, rolling fixture list is a modern reality, but it makes it increasingly difficult for everyone associated with the game to take stock, consider and progress.

If England had reached the 2006 World Cup final – which, as an Englishman, I have to confess would have been nice – then Steven Gerrard's season would have stopped just four days short of the full year.

One of the most extraordinary images of the 2005/06 season, for me, was watching Gerrard and many of his fellow competitors falling to the turf with fatigue and cramp during extra-time of the FA Cup final. These were highly trained, finely honed athletes appearing in what, for most of them, was the biggest game of the season, yet they were dropping like flies – or, as one writer cleverly observed, "like Subbuteo players" – before our very eyes.

When Gerrard, who had just given the greatest performance of his career, was interviewed after the match, he looked like someone who had just emerged from the wreckage of a motorway pile-up. "I'm OK," he assured a worried interviewer.

On hearing those words a whole country sighed with relief. Why? Because in a few weeks' time he would have to go through it all again, at the World Cup.

FIFA made a sensible move when they imposed a four-week break between the end of the domestic season and the start of 'The Greatest Show on Earth' in Germany. But whether there were any benefits is questionable.

It was not a good World Cup.

It started off all right, and the Germans, as we knew they would, organised it brilliantly. But as the tournament progressed, the quality of the football gradually got worse. The coaches became more circumspect, the increasingly fatigued players more fearful of failure.

Italy, as the winners, will forever remember the tournament with fondness – as, too, will the overachieving hosts. But, for just about every other team, the overriding feeling on departure was of what might have been. Most will have wondered how things could have turned out had they been just a bit more daring and adventurous.

Italy were worthy winners, but only because they were the best of a fairly moderate bunch. They were brilliantly organised and prepared by Marcello Lippi and they defended with all the skill and determination one has come to expect from Italian sides down the years. But although they were the best team, they weren't a great team.

For me, the only true greatness on display in Germany was the defending of Fabio Cannavaro. I watched every one of Italy's matches and, ranking each player's performance as I do, had the Italy captain down as the man of the match in three of the Azzurri's games – the opener against Ghana, the quarter-final against Ukraine and the semi-final against Germany. He scored pretty highly in all the others too.

When you also consider that he played all the knockout games without his regular partner, Alessandro Nesta, it was a month of genuine majesty for Cannavaro. If any other player even comes near to winning the 2006 Ballon d'Or or World Player of the Year award, it will be a scandal almost on a par with the one the new Real Madrid galáctico left behind him at Juventus.

In a way it is a shame to have to extol the virtues of a defender. But the 2006 World Cup was a tournament in which the art of stopping goals was far more in evidence than that of scoring them.

There was not one great attacking player on show in Germany. With the exception of Cameroon's Samuel Eto'o, all the best strikers in the world were there, but none of them shone like they should have done. Alas, the best performances we saw from them were in the half-time adverts.

Maybe that's the problem. Or maybe it was because most of them were ordered to play up front on their own. Thierry Henry, Wayne Rooney, Andriy Shevchenko, Luca Toni. There they were, all selflessly ploughing a lone furrow, wearing themselves out to such a degree that when a rare chance did fall to them, they barely had the energy to muster a shot. The more fashionable alternative was to wait for a challenge, fall over and claim a penalty.

The most irksome aspect of Germany 2006 was, needless to say, the cheating and the diving. In my opinion, the reason players go to ground so easily is that they know it is worth their while to do so. If referees didn't blow their whistle for a free-kick at every slightest physical contact, then the players would stay on their feet. It's as simple as that.

Refereeing is a difficult, perhaps impossible, job. But it would help considerably if those rulemakers and taskmasters who programme the match officials how to act realised that football is, and

always has been, a contact sport. There are legal limits to that bodily contact, of course, but generally the main reason why the game is not allowed to flow as it should do these days is because referees will not permit fifty-fifty tussles for the ball.

As soon as one player feels he is losing out in the physical contest, he hits the deck, knowing that there is a more than even chance that the referee, or one of his assistants, will take the easy option of signalling for a foul.

This persistent interruption to the play was probably even more responsible for the shortage of quality matches at the World Cup than the cautious, negative tactics of the coaches. Fortunately, the Mexican official who handled the Germany v Italy semi-final ran to a different agenda and was happy to keep the action flowing. The result was a fine game. Not a great game – there wasn't enough goalmouth action for that – but certainly an enjoyable and absorbing one.

Argentina v Mexico was the only one of the 64 matches that could be described as a five-star classic, although the final group encounter between Australia and Croatia was just as pulsating. At the World Cup, where all of the game's finest footballers are gathered in search of sport's ultimate prize, you expect a bit more.

Perhaps the saddest aspect of the whole tournament, though, was the folly of Zinedine Zidane.

Bizarrely, and embarrassingly, he was awarded the Golden Ball as the official player of the tournament the day after his moment of utter madness in the Olympiastadion. French apologists, led by President Chirac, sprang to the player's defence, even scraping the barrel by offering up some sort of politically correct pretext for Zidane's misdeed. But as Marco Materazzi, his agent provocateur, bluntly stated, everyone saw what Zidane did. Whatever the Italian defender had said, the French captain's violent reaction was inexcusable.

Football followers the world over will be forever grateful for what Zidane offered the game. He was the best footballer on the planet for the best part of a decade. And he also gave the most bewitching individual performance of the 2006 World Cup, in the quarter-final against Brazil. But sadly he chose to depart in disgrace – on the biggest stage of all.

Just as Italy, not France, will always be the world champions of 2006, Zidane's reputation will always be stained by what he did in Berlin.

Sad, very sad. But true.

Everyone else does it, so here you are – my Team of the Tournament for the 2006 World Cup:

Buffon
(Italy)

Zambrotta   **Cannavaro**   **Márquez**   **Lahm**
(Italy)   *(Italy, capt)*   *(Mexico)*   *(Germany)*

        Gattuso   **Pirlo**
        (Italy)   *(Italy)*

Maxi Rodríguez   **Riquelme**   **Robben**
(Argentina)   *(Argentina)*   *(Holland)*

                    Klose
                    (Germany)

Please note that I wanted to pick two strikers but couldn't find them.

As I write this, another summer slog is about to come to an end. No, not the InterToto tournament or cricket's Twenty20 Cup, but the compilation of this Book.

Attentive readers will notice that there have been a few slight changes to the contents and layout this year. On customer demand we have put each club's League Results and Appearances next to each other rather than on separate pages. We have also added club colours in The Directory (and made room for them by removing the names of secretaries and the like). In order to accommodate our extensive coverage of the World Cup (which also amounts to including the logos and kits of the non-European participants in the Colour Section), we have had to trim down the statistical content of the Top 100 Players of the Season section.

There are a number of people I need to thank for making the European Book of Football a reality. Firstly, Cliff Moulder of m press (media) ltd for daring to go where others feared to tread and publishing it. Secondly, Keith Jackson and Chas Dickenson for their diligence in making up the pages, and application in meeting the tight deadlines. Thirdly, all the many Europe-wide contributors who provided the information (their names are listed - in order of the alphabet rather than merit – on page 4). My particular gratitude here goes to Jesper Krogshede Sørensen for the hours he put in for free checking and double-checking the National Team Appearances.

Thanks are also of course due to my family for putting up with my hermit-like existence during the summer – particularly to Rebecca for taking some time off from being a teenager and helping out with the work, and to Charlie for providing his Grumpy Old Dad with some much needed youthful sporting insight.

And last, but not least, to whoever brought us computers, emails and the internet. How I managed 20 years ago, I really do not know.

MIKE HAMMOND (mrhhammo@aol.com)
August, 2006

Glossary

Country Codes, Abbreviations, Symbols

There are many instances throughout the Book where country names are abbreviated using three-letter Codes.

Here is a list of those Codes, ranged alphabetically by country and split into Europe and Rest of the World

EUROPE

ALB	Alb	Albania
AND	And	Andorra
ARM	Arm	Armenia
AUT	Aut	Austria
AZB	Azb	Azerbaijan
BLS	Bls	Belarus
BEL	Bel	Belgium
BOS	Bos	Bosnia-Herzegovina
BUL	Bul	Bulgaria
CRO	Cro	Croatia
CYP	Cyp	Cyprus
CZE	Cze	Czech Republic
DEN	Den	Denmark
ENG	Eng	England
EST	Est	Estonia
FAR	Far	Faroe Islands
FIN	Fin	Finland
FRA	Fra	France
GEO	Geo	Georgia
GER	Ger	Germany
GRE	Gre	Greece
HOL	Hol	Holland
HUN	Hun	Hungary
ISL	Isl	Iceland
ISR	Isr	Israel
ITA	Ita	Italy
KAZ	Kaz	Kazakhstan
LAT	Lat	Latvia
LIE	Lie	Liechtenstein
LIT	Lit	Lithuania
LUX	Lux	Luxembourg
MAC	Mac	Macedonia
MLT	Mlt	Malta
MOL	Mol	Moldova
NIR	Nir	Northern Ireland
NOR	Nor	Norway
POL	Pol	Poland
POR	Por	Portugal
IRL	Irl	Republic of Ireland
ROM	Rom	Romania
RUS	Rus	Russia
SMR	Smr	San Marino
SCO	Sco	Scotland
SCG	Scg	Serbia & Montenegro
SVK	Svk	Slovakia
SLO	Slo	Slovenia
ESP	Esp	Spain
SWE	Swe	Sweden
SUI	Sui	Switzerland
TUR	Tur	Turkey
UKR	Ukr	Ukraine
WAL	Wal	Wales

REST OF THE WORLD

ALG	Alg	Algeria
ANG	Ang	Angola
ARG	Arg	Argentina
AUS	Aus	Australia
BAH	Bah	Bahrain
BNG	Bng	Bangladesh
BAR	Bar	Barbados
BEN	Ben	Benin
BER	Ber	Bermuda
BOL	Bol	Bolivia
BRA	Bra	Brazil
BFA	Bfa	Burkina Faso
BUR	Bur	Burundi
CMR	Cmr	Cameroon
CAN	Can	Canada
CAF	Caf	Central African Republic

Glossary

CHD	Chd	Chad	STK	Stk	St. Kitts & Nevis
CHL	Chl	Chile	STV	Stv	St. Vincent
CHN	Chn	China	SAU	Sau	Saudi Arabia
COL	Col	Colombia	SEN	Sen	Senegal
CON	Con	Congo	SRL	Srl	Sierra Leone
CRC	Crc	Costa Rica	SNG	Sng	Singapore
CVD	Cvd	Cape Verde Islands	SOL	Sol	Solomon Islands
CUB	Cub	Cuba	RSA	Rsa	South Africa
DRC	Drc	Democratic Republic of Congo	KOR	Kor	South Korea
DOM	Dom	Dominican Republic	SYR	Syr	Syria
ECU	Ecu	Ecuador	TAD	Tad	Tadjikistan
EGY	Egy	Egypt	TAH	Tah	Tahiti
SAL	Sal	El Salvador	THA	Tha	Thailand
ETH	Eth	Ethiopia	TOG	Tog	Togo
FIJ	Fij	Fiji	TRI	Tri	Trinidad & Tobago
GAB	Gab	Gabon	TUN	Tun	Tunisia
GAM	Gam	Gambia	TRK	Trk	Turkmenistan
GHA	Gha	Ghana	UGA	Uga	Uganda
GUA	Gua	Guatemala	UAE	Uae	United Arab Emirates
GUI	Gui	Guinea	USA	Usa	United States
GBS	Gbs	Guinea-Bissau	URU	Uru	Uruguay
HAI	Hai	Haiti	UZB	Uzb	Uzbekistan
HON	Hon	Honduras	VEN	Ven	Venezuela
HKG	Hkg	Hong Kong	VIE	Vie	Vietnam
IND	Ind	India	ZAM	Zam	Zambia
IRN	Irn	Iran	ZIM	Zim	Zimbabwe
IRQ	Irq	Iraq			
CIV	Civ	Ivory Coast			
JAM	Jam	Jamaica			
JOR	Jor	Jordan			
JPN	Jpn	Japan			
KEN	Ken	Kenya			
KRG	Krg	Krygystan			
KUW	Kuw	Kuwait			
LBN	Lbn	Lebanon			
LIB	Lib	Liberia			
LBY	Lby	Libya			
MAD	Mad	Madagascar			
MWI	Mwi	Malawi			
MLY	Mly	Malaysia			
MLI	Mli	Mali			
MEX	Mex	Mexico			
MAR	Mar	Morocco			
MOZ	Moz	Mozambique			
NAM	Nam	Namibia			
NZL	Nzl	New Zealand			
NGR	Ngr	Niger			
NGA	Nga	Nigeria			
NKO	Nko	North Korea			
OMN	Omn	Oman			
PAN	Pan	Panama			
PAR	Par	Paraguay			
PER	Per	Peru			
QTR	Qtr	Qatar			
RWA	Rwa	Rwanda			

ABBREVIATIONS/SYMBOLS

Here are some other general Abbreviations and Symbols that are used throughout the Book

TABLES
Pld = Played
W = Won
D = Drawn
L = Lost
F = Goals For
A = Goals Against
Pts = Points
– – – – – – – – = promotion line (at the top)
• • • • • • • • • • • • • • • = play-off line
– – – – – – – – = relegation line (at the bottom)

RESULTS
H or h = home
A or a = away
og = own-goal
(p) or p = penalty

APPEARANCES/GOALS
G = Goalkeeper
D = Defender
M = Midfielder
A = Attacker
Aps = Number of Appearances in Starting XI
(s) = Number of Appearances as a Substitute
Gls = Number of Goals scored

World Cup 2006

Group A:
Germans quickly into their stride

The 18th FIFA World Cup, possibly the most eagerly awaited of them all, kicked off in the early evening of Friday, June 9 at the futuristic and magnificent Allianz-Arena in the outskirts of Munich.

For the first time in 36 years the Opening Match featured the hosts rather than the holders. So while Brazil had to sit and wait another four days before getting their show on the road, Germany, staging the tournament for the second time (after West Germany had done the honours in 1974), strode out to take on unfancied Concacaf qualifiers Costa Rica.

They did so without their talisman, captain and one genuine global superstar, Michael Ballack, who had picked up a calf strain in a warm-up game and was deemed by Germany coach Jürgen Klinsmann and his medical staff to be short of sufficient fitness to lead his country into World Cup battle. With former skipper Oliver Kahn having been demoted to the position of deputy goalkeeper, behind long-time rival Jens Lehmann, the captaincy was passed temporarily to midfielder Bernd Schneider, one of four survivors from the team that had lost 2-0 to Brazil in the 2002 final in Japan.

Although the German public had been led to believe, following a series of unconvincing performances in the build-up, that their team had little or no chance of lifting the trophy for the fourth time, the fact that they had lost just one game at home in the two years under Klinsmann – a run of 15 matches – suggested to neutral observers that they were anything but also-rans.

Explosive start

The match, and the competition, got off to an explosive start when, with just five minutes and nine seconds on the clock, Germany scored. The raucous adulation the goal received was intensified by its beauty. Local hero Philipp Lahm, the Bayern Munich left-back, cut inside his marker and curled a spectacular and precise right-foot shot into the top corner of the net via the inside of the post. It was an early candidate for Goal of the Tournament and it set the tone for what was to be an enthralling and entertaining match – totally out of keeping with the tradition of stodgy, angst-ridden World Cup openers.

Within six minutes of Lahm's wonder strike, Costa Rica, with their first notable attack, had stunned the crowd by drawing level. A lack of communication in the German defence enabled the Central Americans' all-time record scorer, Paulo Wanchope, to spring the offside trap, keep his composure and steer his shot wide of the advancing Lehmann.

Five minutes later Germany were back in front when their centre-forward, Miroslav Klose, pounced from close range following good work from wingers Schneider and Bastian Schweinsteiger. It was Klose's 28th birthday and the Bundesliga's top scorer was to give himself double cause for celebration early in the second half when he stabbed in at the second attempt to make it 3-1.

That should have been that for the Germans, but while they looked strong going forward, voraciously exploiting the space given to them by their defensively disorganised opponents, they had their own problems at the back. With 17 minutes remaining Wanchope once again found a way through the German reargaurd. Collecting Walter Centeño's deft through-ball, he beat Lehmann for the second time with a carefully aimed finish.

German anxiety resurfaced for a while but Costa Rica could fashion no more openings and an excellent match was concluded in fitting fashion with a fourth German goal that was perhaps even more spectacular than their first – a delicious first-time shot from distance by midfielder Torsten Frings that swerved majestically beyond Costa Rican keeper José Porras.

Group A

Germany deserved their victory. They had scored four goals and played attractive football. Costa Rica had also played their part in what was the highest-scoring Opening Match of all time, and the officiating from Argentine referee Horacio Elizondo and his two assistants was practically flawless. The 2006 World Cup had got off to a flying start.

Later that evening there was another Europe-Latin America showdown as Poland took on Ecuador in Gelsenkirchen. Like Costa Rica, both teams had attended the 2002 World Cup but exited after the first round. This was an opportunity to make amends, and it was Ecuador who rose to the challenge in the first half, taking the lead midway through it with a glancing header from striker Carlos Tenorio and almost doubling their advantage shortly afterwards when Agustín Delgado lifted the ball just over the bar.

Unyielding defence

Throughout the first period the Poles seemed determined to live up to their billing as the weakest of the 14 European teams at the finals, but they did show greater commitment and enthusiasm after the interval. Their problem was that Iván Hurtado and Giovanny Espinoza were unyielding at the back for Ecuador, and it was no great surprise when the South Americans made it 2-0 ten minutes from time, Delgado tapping home his 30th international goal following a hairline offside break from substitute Iván Kaviedes.

The Poles launched a spirited late rally, with substitute strikers Ireneusz Jelen and Pawel Brozek both unluckily striking the frame of the goal, but at the final whistle there could be no doubt that the better team had won.

Poland had lost their first two games in Korea four years earlier, and with Germany, a team they had never beaten, up next, it looked as if history was about to repeat itself. The venue for the fixture, Dortmund's Westfalenstadion, also hindered Polish chances as Germany had never lost an international there. Plus, Michael Ballack was back from injury to captain the hosts. Having been goal shy against Ecuador, Poland could be forgiven for enviously eyeing up the two opposition strikers, Miroslav Klose and Lukas Podolski, both born in Poland but raised in Germany.

As the match progressed, it appeared that Klose and Podolski both retained some sympathy for the land of their fathers. The former headed an inviting Lahm cross wide of an empty net after 21 minutes, and at the very end of an eventful first half the latter squandered another chance set up by Lahm when he scuffed badly wide.

Although Germany dominated, Poland were up for the fight, showing real heart and commitment as they strove to keep the hosts at bay. Goalkeeper Artur Boruc was in inspired form, producing one athletic save to deny Klose, while skipper Jacek Bak was a consistently authoritative and courageous leader of the defence. Both players were forced to work overtime as the pressure on Poland's goal intensified in the closing stages following the dismissal of midfielder Radoslaw Sobolewski for a second yellow card. Desperate for the point that would keep alive their hopes of making the second round, the Poles repeatedly repelled Germany's advances. It was heroic stuff, but in the first minute of stoppage time, just after Klose and Ballack had both struck the woodwork from close range, the Poles' resistance was finally broken. Slack defending on the left enabled Germany's speedy young substitute David Odonkor to gallop to the byline, and his perfect low cross was met with a brilliant, and dramatic, half-volleyed finish by another substitute, veteran striker Oliver Neuville.

It was typical Germany – a late winner scored by a substitute – but while the home fans celebrated wildly, it was hard not to feel sorry for their Polish counterparts who ill deserved such a cruel fate.

Germany speedster David Odonkor gets the better of Poland's Ireneusz Jelen

Group A

Qualification confirmed

It was the next day before Poland's exit and Germany's qualification were confirmed. Ecuador carried on where they had left off against the Poles by comprehensively beating Costa Rica 3-0 in Hamburg. It was a largely uneventful contest, but the South Americans took command with an early headed goal from Carlos Tenorio and finished off their feeble opponents with a second, powerfully rifled home by Agustín Delgado, shortly after the interval. With their first-ever qualification for the knockout phase of a World Cup now assured, and a superior goal difference to Germany's placing them at the top of the group, Ecuador took their foot off the gas for the final half-hour. Costa Rica's Alvaro Saborio shook the woodwork with a brilliant 87th-minute strike but the final say went to Ecuador who concluded the match in style with a brilliant third goal, volleyed home on the run by substitute Kaviedes from Edison Méndez's superb right-wing cross.

That was effectively that. Ecuador and Germany were through, Poland and Costa Rica out. The only unresolved issue was which team would top the group. Ecuador's Colombian coach Luis Fernández Suárez demonstrated with his decision to rest several key players that he was not unduly concerned about the outcome of the final game against Germany in Berlin, and after Klose had expertly put the hosts 1-0 up after just four minutes, it was plain for all to see that Jürgen Klinsmann's side would get the win they needed to finish first. Klose made it 2-0 just before time after collecting Michael Ballack's exquisite pass and rounding the keeper before Lukas Podolski netted his first goal of the competition, at the end of a sumptuous counter-attack, to decide the outcome once and for all on 57 minutes.

In the other match Poland came from behind to beat Costa Rica with two set-piece goals from defender Bartosz Bosacki, a player who had never previously scored for his country and had only been drafted into the squad as a late replacement.

But as Poland and Costa Rica trooped home, Germany marched menacingly forward - with maximum points, with the tournament's leading scorer (Klose, on four goals) and with the growing support of a nation that had suddenly fallen madly in love with their team.

GROUP A

RESULTS

9/6/06, Munich
GERMANY 4 *(Lahm 6, Klose 19, 62, Frings 87)*
COSTA RICA 2 *(Wanchope 12, 73)*
Referee – Elizondo (ARG)
GERMANY – Lehmann; Friedrich, Mertesacker, Metzelder, Lahm; Schneider (Odonkor 90), Frings, Borowski (Kehl 72), Schweinsteiger; Klose (Neuville 79), Podolski.
COSTA RICA – Porras; Umana, Sequeira, Marín; Martínez (Drummond 67), Solís (Bolaños 78), Fonseca, González; Centeño; Gómez (Azofeifa 90), Wanchope.

9/6/06, Gelsenkirchen
POLAND 0
ECUADOR 2 *(Tenorio C. 24, Delgado 80)*
Referee – Kamikawa (JPN)
POLAND – Boruc; Baszczynski, Jop, Bak, Zewlakow; Radomski, Sobolewski (Jelen 67); Smolarek, Szymkowiak, Krzynowek (Kosowski 77); Zurawski (Brozek 84).
ECUADOR – Mora; De la Cruz, Hurtado (Guagua 69), Espinoza, Reasco; Valencia, Castillo, Tenorio E., Méndez; Delgado (Urrutia 83), Tenorio C. (Kaviedes 65).

14/6/06, Dortmund
GERMANY 1 *(Neuville 90)*
POLAND 0
Referee – Medina Cantalejo (ESP)
GERMANY – Lehmann; Friedrich (Odonkor 64), Mertesacker, Metzelder, Lahm; Schneider, Frings, Ballack, Schweinsteiger (Borowski 77); Klose, Podolski (Neuville 71).
POLAND – Boruc; Baszczynski, Bosacki, Bak, Zewlakow (Dudka 83); Smolarek, Sobolewski, Radomski, Krzynowek (Lewandowski 77); Jelen (Brozek 90), Zurawski.
Sent off: Sobolewski (75)

15/6/06, Hamburg
COSTA RICA 0
ECUADOR 3 *(Tenorio C. 8, Delgado 55, Kaviedes 90)*
Referee – Codjia (BEN)
COSTA RICA – Porras; Sequeira, Marín, Umana; Wallace, Solís, Fonseca (Saborio 29), Centeño (Bernard 83), González (Hernández 56); Gómez, Wanchope.
ECUADOR – Mora; De la Cruz, Hurtado, Espinoza (Guagua 69), Reasco; Valencia (Urrutia 74), Castillo, Tenorio E., Méndez; Tenorio C. (Kaviedes 46); Delgado.

20/6/06, Berlin
GERMANY 3 *(Klose 4, 44, Podolski 57)*
ECUADOR 0
Referee – Ivanov (RUS)
GERMANY – Lehmann; Friedrich, Huth, Mertesacker, Lahm; Schneider (Asamoah 72), Frings (Borowski 67), Schweinsteiger; Ballack; Klose (Neuville 67), Podolski.
ECUADOR – Mora; De la Cruz, Guagua, Espinoza, Ambrossi; Méndez, Ayovi (Urrutia 69), Tenorio E., Valencia (Lara 63); Borja (Benítez 46), Kaviedes.

20/6/06, Hanover
COSTA RICA 1 *(Gómez 25)*
POLAND 2 *(Bosacki 33, 66)*
Referee – Maidin (SNG)
COSTA RICA – Porras; Umana, Marín, Badilla; Drummond (Wallace 70), Solís, Centeño, González; Bolaños (Saborio 78), Gómez (Hernández 82); Wanchope.
POLAND – Boruc; Baszczynski, Bosacki, Bak, Zewlakow; Szymkowiak, Radomski (Lewandowski 64), Krzynowek; Smolarek (Rasiak 85), Zurawski (Brozek 46), Jelen.

FINAL TABLE

		Pld	W	D	L	F	A	Pts
1	Germany	3	3	0	0	8	2	9
2	Ecuador	3	2	0	1	5	3	6
3	Poland	3	1	0	2	2	4	3
4	Costa Rica	3	0	0	3	3	9	0

TOP GOALSCORERS

4 Miroslav KLOSE (Germany)
2 Agustín DELGADO (Ecuador)
   Carlos TENORIO (Ecuador)
   Bartosz BOSACKI (Poland)
   Paulo WANCHOPE (Costa Rica)

World Cup 2006

Group B:
England struggle through

England entered the 2006 World Cup with high hopes. It was to be their final tournament under Swedish coach Sven Göran Eriksson, who promised to bow out in glory. A talented pool of individuals – arguably the best since the country's one and only World Cup victory, on home soil in 1966 – strengthened the belief of an expectant nation that 40 years of suffering and soul-searching might indeed be brought to an end

The team's build-up to the tournament had been soured by an injury to Wayne Rooney, who broke a bone in his right foot in the penultimate match of the Premiership season six weeks before the team's opening match against Paraguay. It was a massive blow to England's ambitions, but the young Manchester United striker made an extraordinary recovery, and on the eve of the tournament he was passed fit to take part – if not for the first game against the South Americans.

England had blamed the sweltering heat for their timid quarter-final exit to Brazil in 2002, so there was some trepidation when they took the field in Frankfurt on a baking hot Saturday afternoon in temperatures of well over 30°C. Those fears were soon allayed, however, when a free-kick from skipper David Beckham was headed into his own net by counterpart Carlos Gamarra with less than four minutes on the clock. It was the perfect start for the men in white, and for the first half-hour, with Paraguay having lost their goalkeeper Justo Villar to a freak early injury, a dominant England appeared to be cruising. A second goal seemed inevitable, but despite creating several openings, the lack of a killer instinct up front, where Michael Owen posed very little threat, left the game hanging in the balance.

Paraguay, who almost equalised just before the interval, came at England with renewed vigour, and Eriksson's team, not for the first time, began to wilt as the match progressed. Unable to keep the ball for any length of time, England invited the Paraguayans on to them. But the opposition were poor, and with Rio Ferdinand repeating his flawless 2002 World Cup form at the back, there was scant danger to England's goal. Even so, the final whistle was greeted more with relief than jubilation by the England players and their many thousands of supporters. The three points were welcome and probably deserved, but it was certainly not the performance of prospective champions. The absent Rooney, it seemed, could not come back soon enough.

Later the same day Trinidad & Tobago faced Sweden in Dortmund. The Caribbean side, competing in their first World Cup and as the least populous nation ever to grace the finals, were viewed by all and sundry as whipping boys. The Swedes, however, had failed to win a match since qualifying and went into the game short not only of confidence but also of their first-choice goalkeeper, Andreas Isaksson, who

David Beckham feels the heat in Frankfurt

Group B

had suffered concussion in training.

Emergency keeper

Trinidad & Tobago were also forced into emergency action in goal when Kelvin Jack injured himself in the pre-match warm-up. This enabled the veteran Shaka Hislop to take position between the posts. He would go on to have the match of his life.

Sweden, as expected, were the dominant team but Hislop made two good saves in quick succession just before half-time to keep the score at 0-0. The underdogs' efforts appeared to be all in vain, however, when, with the second half barely underway, they were reduced to ten men following a reckless foul by left-back Avery John, who had already been booked for a similar lunge in the first half. It was backs-to-the-wall stuff for the West Indians from then on, but coach Leo Beenhakker's illogical decision to bring on a second striker almost paid dividends when substitute Cornell Glen smashed a shot against the bar. The last half-hour was played almost exclusively in the T & T half, but with the Swedish forwards lacking precision and Hislop playing out of his skin, the goal simply would not come. The match ended 0-0, but to all intents and purposes it was a victory for Trinidad & Tobago and a defeat for Sweden – as the contrasting expressions of the two sets of players and fans at the final whistle graphically demonstrated.

The result in Dortmund was good news indeed for England, who not only topped the group but could secure qualification for the second phase with what appeared to be a routine victory against Trinidad & Tobago in Nuremberg. If only football were that simple!

In the event England and their vast legion of followers were to suffer another 90 minutes of torture. Spared the bright sunshine and heat of Frankfurt, Eriksson's team, given their reputation, should have made easy meat of their limited opponents, many of whom earned their living in the lower leagues of English football. But the fare they served up for the first hour was ponderous, predictable and at times utterly embarrassing – symbolised by one spectacularly off-target volley from Peter Crouch just before half-time. Indeed, only a last-ditch clearance from under the crossbar by England's best player, John Terry, kept his team from going into the interval 1-0 down.

Late breakthrough

The replacement of the out-of-form Owen by Rooney after 58 minutes brought an understandable roar of approval from the terraces,

Hugs all round for Trinidad & Tobago keeper Shaka Hislop after his heroic display against Sweden

but ironically it was the introduction, at the same time, of another substitute, 19-year-old winger Aaron Lennon, that sparked some much-needed energy into England's play. Nevertheless, it was a long and anxious wait before the breakthrough finally came, Crouch redeeming himself with a towering header to despatch a David Beckham cross firmly past Hislop seven minutes from time. Remarkably, it was the first second-half goal England had scored at the World Cup finals in nine matches. In stoppage time they added another, beautifully rifled home left-footed from the edge of the area by Steven Gerrard. Victory – England's eighth in succession - was secure. So, too, was a place in the last 16. But it had all been a desperate struggle.

The second qualifying place was up for grabs as Paraguay faced Sweden an hour or so later in Berlin. Victory was a must for both teams after their opening-game disappointments, but with the Paraguayans unambitious and the Swedes once again toothless in attack, a 0-0 draw looked inevitable. Sweden went close twice through substitute Marcus Allbäck in the second half but it was not until the 89th minute that the Scandinavians' moment of deliverance arrived, Allbäck cleverly nodding a cross into the path of Freddie Ljungberg, who directed his header accurately into the far corner. It was a crushing blow

Group B

for Paraguay, now eliminated, and a momentous goal for the Swedes, now all but qualified barring an unforeseen combination of results on the final day.

Trinidad & Tobago were never likely to claim the victory they needed over Paraguay after conceding an early own-goal. They duly bowed out with a second successive 2-0 defeat, which meant that the key issue at stake in the England-Sweden encounter was which team would win the group and therefore avoid playing Germany in the last 16. To meet that objective England required only a point whereas Sweden had to win.

Cole cracker

For the first 45 minutes in Cologne, England were clearly the better side. Playing in late evening at a ground with the stands close to the pitch seemed to invigorate them – and this despite the horrendous injury that forced Michael Owen to leave the field after only a couple of minutes with what was later diagnosed as a cruciate ligament tear. With Wayne Rooney starting the match, England had more presence up front, but it was the skill of Joe Cole that particularly caught the eye, none more so than after 34 minutes when he let fly with a dipping volley from 30 yards that flew into the top corner of the Swedish net to give England a deserved lead.

If the first 45 minutes belonged to England, the second period was practically all Sweden's. An early equaliser, glanced in from a left-wing corner from Marcus Allbäck (who thus proudly claimed the 2,000th goal in World Cup finals history), exposed a hitherto glaring weakness in England's defending at set-pieces, and twice in the next ten minutes Sweden were denied a second goal only by the crossbar. The siege eventually subsided, but not before Steven Gerrard had cleared a Kim Källström shot off the line, and it was the Liverpool superstar who would restore England's lead, five minutes from time, with an excellent header from a carefully judged Joe Cole cross. A first win over Sweden since 1968 beckoned, but England could not protect their lead. A long throw caused further panic in defence and Henrik Larsson slipped in to equalise.

It was a bad way for England to finish the game, and the group, but the goal was largely irrelevant. The result meant that they topped the group and booked themselves a date with Ecuador in Stuttgart, whereas Sweden faced the less appetising prospect of a last-16 showdown with the Germans in Munich.

GROUP B
RESULTS

10/6/06, Frankfurt
ENGLAND 1 *(Gamarra 4og)*
PARAGUAY 0
Referee – *Rodríguez (MEX)*
ENGLAND – *Robinson; Neville, Ferdinand, Terry, Cole A.; Beckham, Gerrard, Lampard, Cole J. (Hargreaves 83); Owen (Downing 56), Crouch.*
PARAGUAY – *Villar (Bobadilla 8); Caniza, Cáceres, Gamarra, Toledo (Núñez 82); Bonet (Cuevas 68), Paredes, Acuña, Riveros; Santa Cruz, Haedo Valdez.*

10/6/06, Dortmund
TRINIDAD & TOBAGO 0
SWEDEN 0
Referee – *Maidin (SNG)*
TRINIDAD & TOBAGO – *Hislop; Gray, Sancho, Lawrence, John A.; Yorke; Edwards, Birchall, Theobald (Whitley 67); Samuel (Glen 53); John S. Sent off: John A. (46)*
SWEDEN – *Shaaban; Alexandersson, Mellberg, Lucic, Edman; Linderoth (Källström 79); Wilhelmsson (Jonson 79), Svensson (Allbäck 62); Ljungberg; Ibrahimovic, Larsson.*

15/6/06, Nuremberg
ENGLAND 2 *(Crouch 83, Gerrard 90)*
TRINIDAD & TOBAGO 0
Referee – *Kamikawa (JPN)*
ENGLAND – *Robinson; Carragher (Lennon 58), Ferdinand, Terry, Cole A.; Beckham, Gerrard, Lampard, Cole J. (Downing 74); Owen (Rooney 58), Crouch.*
TRINIDAD & TOBAGO – *Hislop; Edwards, Sancho, Lawrence, Gray; Whitley, Birchall, Yorke, Theobald (Wise 84); Jones (Glen 69), John S.*

15/6/06, Berlin
SWEDEN 1 *(Ljungberg 89)*
PARAGUAY 0
Referee – *Michel (SVK)*
SWEDEN – *Isaksson; Alexandersson, Mellberg, Lucic, Edman; Wilhelmsson, Linderoth, Källström, Ljungberg; Larsson, Ibrahimovic (Allbäck 46).*
PARAGUAY – *Bobadilla; Caniza, Gamarra, Cáceres, Núñez; Bonet, Acuña, Paredes, Riveros (Dos Santos 62); Santa Cruz (López 63), Haedo Valdez.*

20/6/06, Cologne
SWEDEN 2 *(Allbäck 51, Larsson 90)*
ENGLAND 2 *(Cole J. 34, Gerrard 85)*
Referee – *Busacca (SUI)*
SWEDEN – *Isaksson; Alexandersson, Mellberg, Lucic, Edman; Linderoth (Andersson 90); Jonson (Wilhelmsson 52), Källström, Ljungberg; Allbäck (Elmander 74), Larsson.*
ENGLAND – *Robinson; Carragher, Ferdinand (Campbell 55), Terry, Cole A.; Hargreaves; Beckham, Lampard, Cole J.; Owen (Crouch 4), Rooney (Gerrard 67).*

20/6/06, Kaiserslautern
PARAGUAY 2 *(Sancho 25og, Cuevas 86)*
TRINIDAD & TOBAGO 0
Referee – *Rosetti (ITA)*
PARAGUAY – *Bobadilla; Caniza, Cáceres (Manzur 78), Gamarra, Núñez; Barreto, Acuña, Paredes, Dos Santos; Santa Cruz, Haedo Valdez (Cuevas 66).*
TRINIDAD & TOBAGO – *Jack; Edwards, Lawrence, Sancho, John A. (Jones 31); Birchall, Whitley (Latapy 66), Yorke, Theobald (Wolfe 66); Glen (Wise 41), John S.*

FINAL TABLE

		Pld	W	D	L	F	A	Pts
1	England	3	2	1	0	5	2	7
2	Sweden	3	1	2	0	3	2	5
3	Paraguay	3	1	0	2	2	2	3
4	Trinidad & Tobago	3	0	1	2	0	4	0

TOP SCORER
2 Steven GERRARD (England)

World Cup 2006

Group C:
Awesome Argentina throw down gauntlet

Every World Cup has its Group of Death, and Group C was the obvious candidate to claim that billing in 2006. Headed by Argentina, one of the pre-tournament favourites, and also containing two impressive European qualifiers in Holland and Serbia & Montenegro plus African vice-champions the Ivory Coast, it was possibly the toughest section imaginable given the pre-draw seedings.

Hamburg's AOL-Arena was the setting for the group's opening fixture, between Argentina and World Cup freshmen the Ivory Coast. Those present in the capacity crowd were to witness a high-class encounter between two excellent sides. Staged on the second evening of the tournament, the match whetted the appetite for the four weeks of competition ahead.

Argentina, industrious and zestful from the off, ought to have been ahead after only 14 minutes when a header from defender Roberto Ayala was palmed by Ivorian goalkeeper Jean-Jacques Tizié against the inside of the post and apparently just over the line. But with the officials' visibility obscured and no goal-line technology in place, the goal was not given. Ten minutes later, though, the South Americans duly went in front as Hernán Crespo stabbed the ball home from close range following indecision in defence at a Juan Román Riquelme corner.

The African side gamely fought back, but shortly after their best clear opening was squandered by Kader Keita they fell two goals behind. It was a rapier thrust from Riquelme that sliced through them, his perfect pass playing in Javier Saviola, who took the chance unerringly, poking the ball under the body of the advancing Tizié.

Riquelme in control

Given the quality of Argentina's play, with Riquelme at the hub of almost everything, there appeared to be no way back for the men in orange. But as the South Americans eased off in the last 20 minutes, the Africans launched a concerted effort to get back into the game. They were rewarded eight minutes from time when skipper Didier Drogba halved the deficit with a fine left-foot shot on the turn. But that was all they could muster. Argentina defended without undue concern for the remainder of the game and would have had a third goal but for an offside flag that debatably denied Maxi Rodríguez after he had followed up a Riquelme shot to score.

The following afternoon Holland and Serbia & Montenegro locked horns in the first all-European encounter of the competition. It was stiflingly hot in Leipzig, but the Dutch were on their game from the start and took the lead after 18 minutes when Arjen Robben scampered through the middle on to fellow winger Robin van Persie's clipped pass, held off an attempt at a shirt-tug by defender Goran Gavrancic and deftly drove the ball past Dragoslav Jevric. For the rest of the first half Robben was a constant danger, his dribbling and shooting causing the Serbian defence far greater problems than they had encountered during a qualifying campaign in which they conceded just one goal. However, at 1-0 and with Predrag Djordjevic looking lively for the Eastern Europeans, the game was far from over.

Like England against Paraguay a day earlier, Holland began to suffer in the intense heat as the second half wore on, but although Serbia & Montenegro improved thanks to the introduction of lively substitutes Ognjen Koroman and Danijel Ljuboja, they created next to nothing in terms of goalscoring chances. The Dutch defence remained secure, and at the other end Robben continued to conjure up moments of magic. By the final whistle Holland had the three points they desperately wanted, and in the irrepressible young Chelsea left-winger the World Cup had a new star.

Group C

Serbia & Montenegro had given their all in Leipzig, but five days later, under the closed roof of Gelsenkirchen's AufSchalke Arena, their World Cup hopes were to be torn to shreds by a masterclass performance from Argentina.

José Pekerman's side, cheered from the VIP seats by Diego Maradona, were in inspired form from the very start. One-nil up after only six minutes thanks to a finely crafted goal from right-winger Maxi Rodríguez, they used that early breakthrough as a springboard to a riveting first-half display, the highlight of which was a majestic second goal that is sure to go down in World Cup legend as one of the very best in the tournament's long history. Finished off with a rising left-foot shot from Estebán Cambiasso (an early substitute for the injured Lucho González), it came at the end of a patient, precise build-up involving 24 passes, during which no opposition player came close to ridding the Argentinians of the ball. The penultimate touch, a back-heel from Hernán Crespo right into Cambiasso's path, was the best of all.

Flamboyant finish

Argentina extended their lead to 3-0 before half-time with another fine goal, set up by Javier Saviola and finished, via the inside of the post, by Maxi Rodríguez. That was the game as good as won. There was an understandable lull in the action for the first 20 minutes of the second period, but after Mateja Kezman had harshly received a straight red card for sliding in on Javier Mascherano, Argentina decided to go for the jugular. With sprightly young attackers Carlos Tévez and Lionel Messi introduced to the fray, the Albiceleste concluded the match in flamboyant and destructive style, adding three further goals, one from Crespo (after a brilliant cross by Messi) and one apiece from the two dynamic substitutes.

With a five-star, six-goal performance under their belt and so much top-class individual talent to call upon, both in the starting XI and on the bench, it was little wonder that Argentina were now firmly installed as the new favourites to lift the trophy.

With Argentina virtually qualified and Serbia & Montenegro all but out, the fixture between Holland and the Ivory Coast in Stuttgart was now pivotal. The Gottlieb-Daimler-Stadion was transformed into a sea of orange for the occasion, and it was the Dutch segment that was rocking and rolling midway through the first half after two goals in the space of four minutes – the first a

Maxi Rodríguez enjoys putting Argentina in front against Serbia & Montenegro

stunning free-kick from Robin van Persie, the second a sharp finish from Ruud van Nistelrooy after he had been fed through by Arjen Robben.

As against Argentina, however, the Africans reacted positively to their two-goal deficit. Before long they had reduced the arrears thanks to a wonderful diagonal strike on the run by diminutive winger Bakary Koné. It was the first goal conceded by Dutch keeper Edwin van der Sar in 11 competitive matches, and there might have been another before the interval as the Africans began to exert ceaseless pressure. There was more to come from Henri Michel's adventurous side in the second half, but despite continuing to force the issue, the second goal they needed to remain in the competition frustratingly eluded them. The Dutch defended stoutly and withstood everything

Group C

the Ivorians could hurl at them. The final whistle came as a relief to Marco van Basten and his team, but, for the tournament as a whole, the early exit of the Ivory Coast was as unwarranted as it was unwelcome. Had they been drawn in a more favourable group, they would surely have made it through to the last 16.

Key men rested

It was also a disappointment to the neutral observer that Group C had been settled in advance of the final round of matches. That meant Argentina and Holland going head to head with deliberately understrength starting XIs as they rested key players for the knockout phase. Two regulars who did appear for Holland were veterans Edwin van der Sar and Phillip Cocu, the former joining Frank de Boer as his country's all-time record international on his 112th appearance, the latter winning his 100th cap.

The Dutch needed a third successive win to leapfrog the buoyant Argentinians and top the group, but with Robben rested they rarely looked like scoring. There was more action at the other end, where the ever-inventive Riquelme secured his status as the standout player of the first round and youngsters Messi and Tévez, both selected from the start, again looked lively. But Holland's defence, impressive in the previous two games, again stood firm and defiant. The outcome was a goalless draw – a predictable, if fair, outcome to a match that had largely been rendered irrelevant by what had gone before.

There was more gripping entertainment in the wooden spoon play-off at the Allianz-Arena, where Ivory Coast fell two goals behind for the third game in succession but on this occasion succeeded completely with their comeback bid, claiming a heart-warming 3-2 victory thanks to a late winning penalty from Bonaventure Kalou, surprisingly chosen for the task ahead of Aruna Dindane, who had scored the previous two goals, one of them from the spot. While the Africans went home with their heads held high, it was an undignified exit from the competition for Serbia & Montenegro in what was their last ever international as a unified nation.

GROUP C
RESULTS

10/6/06, Hamburg
ARGENTINA 2 *(Crespo 24, Saviola 38)*
IVORY COAST 1 *(Drogba 82)*
Referee – De Bleeckere (BEL)
ARGENTINA – Abbondanzieri; Burdisso, Ayala, Heinze, Sorín; Mascherano; Maxi Rodríguez, Cambiasso, Riquelme (Aimar 90); Saviola (Lucho González 76), Crespo (Palacio 64).
IVORY COAST – Tizié; Eboué, Touré K., Meïté, Boka; Keita (Koné A. 77), Zokora, Touré Y., Akalé (Koné B. 62); Kalou (Dindane 56), Drogba.

11/6/06, Leipzig
SERBIA & MONTENEGRO 0
HOLLAND 1 *(Robben 17)*
Referee – Merk (GER)
SERBIA & MONTENEGRO – Jevric; Dragutinovic, Gavrancic, Djordjevic N. (Koroman 43), Krstajic; Duljaj, Stankovic, Djordjevic P., Nadj; Kezman (Ljuboja 66), Milosevic (Zigic 46).
HOLLAND – Van der Sar; Heitinga, Ooijer, Mathijsen (Boulahrouz 86), Van Bronckhorst; Cocu; Sneijder, Van Bommel (Landzaat 60); Van Persie, Van Nistelrooy (Kuijt 69), Robben.

16/6/06, Gelsenkirchen
ARGENTINA 6 *(Maxi Rodríguez 6, 41, Cambiasso 31,*
Crespo 78, Tévez 84, Messi 88)
SERBIA & MONTENEGRO 0
Referee – Rosetti (ITA)
ARGENTINA – Abbondanzieri; Burdisso, Ayala, Heinze, Sorín; Mascherano; Lucho González (Cambiasso 17), Maxi Rodríguez (Messi 75); Riquelme; Saviola (Tévez 58), Crespo.
SERBIA & MONTENEGRO – Jevric; Duljaj, Gavrancic, Dudic, Krstajic; Koroman (Ljuboja 49), Nadj (Ergic 46), Djordjevic P., Stankovic; Milosevic (Vukic 70), Kezman.
Sent off: Kezman (65)

16/6/06, Stuttgart
HOLLAND 2 *(Van Persie 23, Van Nistelrooy 27)*
IVORY COAST 1 *(Koné B. 38)*
Referee – Ruiz (COL)
HOLLAND – Van der Sar; Heitinga (Boulahrouz 46), Ooijer, Mathijsen, Van Bronckhorst; Sneijder (Van der Vaart 50), Van Bommel, Cocu; Van Persie, Van Nistelrooy (Landzaat 72), Robben.
IVORY COAST – Tizié; Eboué, Touré K., Meïté, Boka; Koné B. (Dindane 61), Touré Y., Zokora, Romaric (Yapi Yapo 61); Koné A. (Akalé 73), Drogba.

21/6/06, Frankfurt
HOLLAND 0
ARGENTINA 0
Referee – Medina Cantalejo (ESP)
HOLLAND – Van der Sar; Jaliens, Boulahrouz, Ooijer, De Cler; Cocu, Sneijder (Maduro 86), Van der Vaart; Van Persie (Landzaat 67), Van Nistelrooy (Babel 56), Kuijt.
ARGENTINA – Abbondanzieri; Burdisso (Coloccini 24), Ayala, Milito, Cufré; Maxi Rodríguez, Mascherano, Cambiasso; Riquelme; Messi (Cruz 69), Tévez.

21/6/06, Munich
IVORY COAST 3 *(Dindane 37p, 67, Kalou 86p)*
SERBIA & MONTENEGRO 2 *(Zigic 10, Ilic 20)*
Referee – Rodríguez (MEX)
IVORY COAST – Barry; Eboué, Domoraud, Kouassi, Boka; Touré Y., Keita (Kalou 72), Zokora, Akalé (Koné B. 16); Koné A., Dindane.
Sent off: Domoraud (90)
SERBIA & MONTENEGRO – Jevric; Gavrancic, Djordjevic N., Dudic, Krstajic (Nadj 16); Ergic, Duljaj, Stankovic, Djordjevic P.; Ilic, Zigic (Milosevic 66).
Sent off: Nadj (44)

FINAL TABLE

		Pld	W	D	L	F	A	Pts
1	Argentina	3	2	1	0	8	1	7
2	Holland	3	2	1	0	3	1	7
3	Ivory Coast	3	1	0	2	5	6	3
4	Serbia & Montenegro	3	0	0	3	2	10	0

TOP SCORERS

2   MAXI RODRÍGUEZ (Argentina)
     Hernán CRESPO (Argentina)
     Aruna DINDANE (Ivory Coast)

World Cup 2006

Group D:
Scolari retains his magic touch

Whereas Group C was devoid of makeweights, Group D appeared to have two of them in the shape of Asian qualifiers Iran and African first-timers Angola. It all looked fairly plain sailing at the outset for group seeds Mexico and European vice-champions Portugal, the latter led into battle by Luiz Felipe Scolari, the triumphant coach of his native Brazil at the 2002 World Cup in Korea/Japan.

However, the early moments of the group's opening encounter, between Mexico and Iran in Nuremberg, suggested that there might be a surprise in store. The Iranians twice came close to snatching an early advantage, through Vahid Hashemian, one of several German-based players in their team, but brilliant goalkeeping by Óscar Sánchez, who had only just returned to the Mexican training camp following the sudden death of his father, kept the scores level.

By half-time it was still all-square, but at 1-1, after both sides had scored from well worked set-pieces. Mexico netted first, through an unmarked Omar Bravo at a free-kick, before Iran equalised through defender Yahya Golmohammadi following a corner. As the second half progressed, Iran were plainly happy with the draw. Mexico, however, were anything but, and with their captain Rafael Márquez, fresh from his Champions League success with Barcelona, inspiring his team from all over the pitch, there was a sense of justice when the Central Americans killed the contest with two goals in three minutes. The first came about after a couple of disastrous errors in the Iranian defence, with Bravo skilfully converting substitute Zinha's neat pass. The second was a flying header from Zinha himself after the little Brazilian-born playmaker had played a delightful one-two with Mario Méndez.

Portugal set about joining Mexico on three points later that evening in their eagerly anticipated encounter with former colony Angola. They almost took the lead after just 15 seconds when Pauleta pulled his left-foot shot fractionally wide of goal, but the man who had overtaken Eusébio as his country's all-time record marksman during the qualifying campaign had only a few more minutes to wait before registering his 47th international goal and putting Portugal 1-0 up.

Figo on song

Luís Figo, the veteran skipper, set up Pauleta's goal and he was to be the game's outstanding individual.

Luís Figo – back to his brilliant best against Angola

Group D

With Deco injured, Figo was deployed in an unfamiliar central midfield role and he seemed to relish the extra responsibility. Twice towards the end of the half he set up chances for his protégé, Cristiano Ronaldo, but the young winger's first effort, a header, crashed against the crossbar and his second, a powerful first-time strike, was brilliantly saved by Angolan keeper João Ricardo.

Angola's resistance was impressive but they offered precious little in attack, and the game went dead for a lengthy period in the second half as Portugal, with Cristiano Ronaldo surprisingly replaced by the defensively-minded Costinha, sensed that one goal would be sufficient for them to win the game. It almost cost them as Angola came on strong in the closing minutes, but the Africans' lack of ruthlessness in the final third put paid to their chances of an upset.

Mexico's bid to reach the second round for the fourth World Cup running suffered a hiccup in their second match, against Angola in Hanover, as the African side's defence carried on the good work they had displayed against Portugal. Despite creating the only opportunities in a drab game, the Mexicans were wasteful in front of goal. They badly missed the predatory skills of injured striker Jared Borgetti, whose record goal haul for his country incorporated a tournament-best 14 in the qualifying campaign, and it was the Angolan keeper, João Ricardo, a player without a club, who claimed the man-of-the-match honours as the Africans resiliently held out for the 0-0 draw that kept their qualification hopes alive.

The following afternoon Portugal faced Iran in Frankfurt and for an hour of the game they went through the same ordeal as Mexico, pressing hard to break down a dogged defence but failing to do so largely as a result of poor finishing and stout goalkeeping. Unlike the Mexicans, however, the breakthrough did finally arrive. Just when it seemed as if they had completely run out of ideas, the Portuguese were indebted to a piece of individual brilliance from the outstanding player on the pitch, Barcelona midfielder Deco. Moving on to a square ball from Luís Figo just outside the area, he drilled a brilliant first-time shot low into the corner of the net, leaving goalkeeper Ebrahim Mirzapour rooted to the spot.

Confident penalty

Although Iran briefly threatened to equalise, the match was concluded in Portugal's favour when Figo was tripped just inside the area by Yahya Golmohammadi and Cristiano Ronaldo confidently thumped in the ensuing penalty. The Manchester

Angola goalkeeper João Ricardo – defiant against Mexico

United player had the ball in the net again in time added on but was denied by the offside flag. It mattered not. Portugal, with two wins, were through to the next round while Iran, with two defeats, were eliminated.

Portugal's premature qualification afforded them the luxury of sending out a depleted team for their final group fixture, against Mexico in Gelsenkirchen. Coach Scolari seemed unconcerned about registering a tenth successive World Cup finals win (a sequence carried forward from the seven straight victories he had recorded as Brazil's coach in 2002) as he left out all of his players burdened by a yellow card – including Pauleta, Deco and Cristiano Ronaldo – to ensure their eligibility for the second round.

Mexico's chief incentive was to claim the point that would guarantee their progress into the last 16, but they were also aware that victory would see them qualify as group winners. The only way they could be eliminated was if they lost and Angola simultaneously beat Iran. Even then, there would have to be a four-goal swing in the Africans' favour.

It was never realistically on the cards, and although Angola took an unexpected lead against the Iranians with their first real chance of the game, after an hour's play, through substitute Flávio, the Middle

Group D

Easterners equalised soon afterwards. As against Mexico, their goal came from a defender at a corner, with centre-back Sohrab Bakhtiarizadeh adding his (unpronounceable) name to the competition's growing list of one-goal wonders.

Sidefoot finish

Mexico's welfare was threatened only briefly, at the start of the game in Gelsenkirchen, when Portugal raced into an early 2-0 lead. Maniche, a class act for his country at Euro 2004, finished off a lovely pass from Simão with a deft sidefoot shot to make it 1-0 after just six minutes, and Simão converted Portugal's second penalty of the tournament to double their advantage after Mexico skipper Márquez had bizarrely fielded the ball with his hand at a corner.

The remainder of the game, however, belonged to Mexico. Back in the hunt five minutes after Simão's penalty when Francisco Fonseca glanced in Pavel Pardo's corner at an unattended far post, they continued to make positive inroads into the Portuguese defence both before and after the interval. But a succession of chances came and went, the best of them when Bravo, the two-goal hero against Iran, blasted a generously awarded 57th-minute penalty kick over the bar. If Mexico were lucky to get that spot-kick – Miguel's handling of the ball on the ground was purely unintentional – then they were dealt an extremely harsh blow a few minutes later when Slovakian referee Lubos Michel ruled that Luis Pérez had dived to obtain another penalty – in fact, he simply lost his footing – and showed him his second yellow card of the evening.

The catalogue of refereeing aberrations continued as Michel wrongly booked Márquez for a supposed foul on Simão – the Portuguese winger clearly dived – and then denied Mexico a second penalty after Paulo Ferreira had plainly taken out Bravo. It was to Mexico's great credit that they continued to dominate, and create chances, with ten men, but ultimately they could not find the equaliser they merited and Portugal clung on to maintain their 100 per cent record – and prolong the remarkable winning run of their coach. Portugal's reward for winning the group would be an all-European tie against Holland while Mexico, with just four points gained from nine, would have to do battle with the new tournament favourites, Argentina.

GROUP D
RESULTS

11/6/06, Nuremberg
MEXICO 3 *(Bravo 28, 76, Zinha 79)*
IRAN 1 *(Golmohammadi 36)*
Referee – *Rosetti (ITA)*
MEXICO – *Sánchez; Márquez, Osorio, Salcido; Méndez, Bravo, Pardo, Torrado (Pérez 46); Pineda; Franco (Zinha 46), Borgetti (Fonseca 52).*
IRAN – *Mirzapour; Kaabi, Golmohammadi, Rezaei, Nosrati (Borhani 81); Mahdavikia, Teymourian, Nekounam, Karimi (Madanchi 63); Hashemian, Daei.*

11/6/06, Cologne
ANGOLA 0
PORTUGAL 1 *(Pauleta 4)*
Referee – *Larrionda (URU)*
ANGOLA – *João Ricardo; Jamba, Kali, Delgado, Loco; Mendonca, Figueiredo (Miloy 80), André, Mateus, Zé Kalanga (Edson 70) ; Akwá (Mantorras 59).*
PORTUGAL – *Ricardo; Miguel, Fernando Meira, Ricardo Carvalho, Nuno Valente; Tiago (Hugo Viana 83), Petit (Maniche 72); Cristiano Ronaldo (Costinha 60), Figo, Simão; Pauleta.*

16/6/06, Hanover
MEXICO 0
ANGOLA 0
Referee – *Maidin (SNG)*
MEXICO – *Sánchez; Márquez, Osorio, Salcido; Méndez, Pardo, Zinha (Arellano 52), Torrado, Pineda (Morales 78); Franco (Fonseca 74), Bravo.*
ANGOLA – *João Ricardo ; Jamba, Kali, Delgado, Loco ; Figueiredo (Rui Marques 73), André, Mateus (Mantorras 68), Mendonca, Zé Kalanga (Miloy 83) ; Akwá.*
Sent off : *André (79)*

17/6/06, Frankfurt
PORTUGAL 2 *(Deco 63, Cristiano Ronaldo 80p)*
IRAN 0
Referee – *Poulat (FRA)*
PORTUGAL – *Ricardo; Miguel, Fernando Meira, Ricardo Carvalho, Nuno Valente; Costinha, Maniche (Petit 67); Figo (Simão 88), Deco (Tiago 81), Cristiano Ronaldo; Pauleta.*
IRAN – *Mirzapour; Kaabi, Rezaei, Golmohammadi (Bakhtiarizadeh 88), Nosrati; Mahdavikia, Nekounam, Karimi, Teymourian; Madanchi (Khatibi 67), Hashemian.*

21/6/06, Gelsenkirchen
PORTUGAL 2 *(Maniche 6, Simão 24p)*
MEXICO 1 *(Fonseca 29)*
Referee – *Michel (SVK)*
PORTUGAL – *Ricardo; Miguel (Paulo Ferreira 61), Fernando Meira, Ricardo Carvalho, Caneira; Petit, Maniche; Figo (Boa Morte 80), Tiago, Simão; Hélder Postiga (Nuno Gomes 69).*
MEXICO – *Sánchez; Rodríguez (Zinha 46), Osorio, Salcido; Méndez (Franco 80), Pardo, Márquez, Pérez, Pineda (Castro 69); Bravo, Fonseca.*
Sent off: *Pérez (61)*

21/6/06, Leipzig
IRAN 1 *(Bakhtiarizadeh 75)*
ANGOLA 1 *(Flávio 60)*
Referee – *Shield (AUS)*
IRAN – *Mirzapour; Bakhtiarizadeh, Rezaei, Kaabi (Borhani 67), Nosrati (Shojaei 13); Mahdavikia, Zandi, Teymourian, Madanchi; Hashemian (Khatibi 39), Daei.*
ANGOLA – *João Ricardo; Jamba, Kali, Loco, Delgado; Miloy, Figueiredo (Rui Marques 72), Mateus (Love 23), Mendonca, Zé Kalanga; Akwá (Flávio 51).*

FINAL TABLE

		Pld	W	D	L	F	A	Pts
1	Portugal	3	3	0	0	5	1	9
2	Mexico	3	1	1	1	4	3	4
3	Angola	3	0	2	1	1	2	2
4	Iran	3	0	1	2	2	6	1

TOP SCORER
2   Omar BRAVO (Mexico)

World Cup 2006

Group E: Azzurri advance as Czechs check out

Italy came to their 12th successive World Cup finals with a massive black cloud hovering over the domestic game. A widespread match-fixing scandal in which a number of top Serie A clubs were implicated had overshadowed the Azzurri's build up to the finals in Germany. There was huge pressure on coach Marcello Lippi and his players to put a smile back on the face of Italian football, but in a tough opening group containing Euro 2004 semi-finalists the Czech Republic, 2002 quarter-finalists the USA and African dark horses Ghana, their first task was simply to ensure qualification for the second round.

Unlike most group seeds, the Italians were not the first into action. That honour was reserved for the Czechs and the Americans, who met in Gelsenkirchen. The USA had never beaten a European team at the World Cup and after five minutes that sorry sequence looked likely to continue as their opponents took the lead, beanpole striker Jan Koller thudding in an unstoppable header from Zdenek Grygera's perfect right-wing cross.

American skipper Claudio Reyna was unfortunate to see his well struck shot come back off the post, but the Czechs were the stronger, more inventive side and cemented their superiority with a wonderful second goal, struck with venom and accuracy from distance by midfielder Tomas Rosicky. But although they were in control of proceedings, the half ended on a low for the European side as Koller, his country's record scorer, pulled up with a hamstring injury. With Milan Baros absent with an injured foot, the Czechs had to approach the second half without both of their recognised strikers.

Rosicky rules

Fortunately, the Americans displayed little resolve to get back into the game, and the Czech midfield continued to rule the roost. Rosicky, who had just left Borussia Dortmund for Arsenal, revelled in the home of Dortmund's rivals Schalke, smacking another powerful long-range shot against the crossbar and then adding a splendid third goal for his team when he collected Pavel Nedved's astute through ball, raced goalwards and calmly clipped the ball past the USA's veteran goalkeeper Kasey Keller. The 3-0 scoreline was everything the Czechs had hoped for, but the loss of their star striker, probably for the rest of the tournament, undoubtedly tempered their celebrations.

Italy's campaign began later that evening in Hanover against Ghana. It was the African side's finals debut, and they came to Germany with the youngest squad of any of the 32 competing teams. But if they were nervous, they didn't show it. Like the Ivory Coast against Argentina 48 hours earlier, the Ghanaians were to play their part in a riveting contest. The Italians, unbeaten in 18 matches, lined up without injured duo Gianluca Zambrotta and Gennaro Gattuso, but there was a place in the starting XI for Francesco Totti, back in double-quick time from a broken leg and sporting a new short-back-and-sides haircut.

The first half was evenly contested, with Luca Toni, the prolific Fiorentina striker, rattling the crossbar and Ghanaian full-back Emmanuel Pappoe blazing over with the goal at his mercy. It was anybody's game, but Italy made the breakthrough just before half-time when Andrea Pirlo fired home through a crowded penalty area following a corner. Traditionally the Azzurri opt to protect one-goal leads, but on this occasion they continued to go forward at every opportunity. With Ghana increasingly having to resort to long-range pot-shots in their bid to equalise, the more measured football came from the Italians.

Justice done

On 76 minutes Ghana's experienced centre-back Samuel Kuffour got lucky when he hauled down

Group E

goalbound Italian substitute Vincenzo Iaquinta but was rescued by a debatable offside flag. However, justice of a sort was done a few minutes later when Kuffour made a sloppy backpass and Iaquinta pounced on it before drawing the goalkeeper and slotting the ball into the empty net. Two-nil was about right, although Ghana left the field complaining that they might have been awarded a couple of penalties.

Kuffour was dropped for Ghana's next game, against the Czechs, and he wasn't missed as the African side made up for their opening defeat with a colossal display in Cologne. A goal up inside 75 seconds when young striker Asamoah Gyan confidently drove the ball past Petr Cech, Ghana were to give the Chelsea goalkeeper one of the busiest matches of his career as they poured forward continually during the course of the 90 minutes.

The Czechs, so strong in their opening game, seemed shellshocked by the Ghanaian approach. With their own attack blunted through injury – reserve target man Vladislav Lokvenc looked lost up front on his own – and their defence all at sea, they could not get into the game. When Tomás Ujfalusi was red-carded midway through the second half for conceding a penalty, the game appeared to be over. But Gyan, who was booked for taking the spot-kick too early, then struck his next effort against the post. It didn't seem to matter, though, because for the remainder of the game, with the Czech defence depleted and disintegrated, Ghana created chance after chance, only to be denied repeatedly by the brilliant Cech. A second goal had to come, though, and with eight minutes to go, midfielder Sulley Ali Muntari, the best player on the pitch, rasped a left-foot shot high into the corner of the net to secure victory once and for all.

Next up was Italy against the USA, and there was to be no let-up in the Group E fireworks on an evening of high drama in Kaiserslautern. The USA began brilliantly, taking the game to their illustrious opponents with some measured football. But on 22 minutes, on their first excursion into the American penalty area, Italy scored, Albert Gilardino glancing in Andrea Pirlo's perfectly flighted free-kick. It was tough on the Americans, but in two crazy minutes they were right back in the game, and then some. First they equalised as Italy right-back Cristian Zaccardo sliced a free-kick horribly into his own net, then they claimed a one-man advantage as Italian midfielder Daniele De Rossi was red-carded for a violent elbow on US striker Brian McBride, who left the field temporarily, his face splattered with blood.

Foolishly, however, the Americans threw away a

Take that! Italy's Daniele De Rossi elbows American striker Brian McBride in the face

golden opportunity to claim an historic victory when they lost two players of their own in a couple of minutes either side of the interval. Pablo Mastroeni was the first to go, for a reckless lunge, and then the dunce's cap was passed to centre-back Eddie Pope, who, already yellow-carded for one foul on Gilardino, earned another one for taking away the feet of the same player. It seemed certain that the USA's lack of discipline would cost them, but the remaining nine men were to show extraordinary grit during the second half. They might even have taken the lead had the officials not ruled out a DaMarcus Beasley goal for a questionable offside. The last quarter of the game was played almost exclusively in the American half, but as Italy probed and probed, with the brilliant Pirlo to the fore, the USA came under enormous pressure. They withstood it manfully, and by the final whistle their exhaustion

Group E

was mixed with joyous relief that they were still in the competition, albeit with just one point rather than the three they looked like getting during the first half.

All four in contention

Going into the final round of matches, all four teams were still in contention for a second-round place. Italy, with four points, were in the driving seat, needing a win or draw against the Czechs to be certain of progressing. As for the Czech Republic and Ghana, they had to win to be sure of going through whereas the Americans needed victory both for themselves and the Czechs.

Most of the decisive moments occurred in the first half. Ghana and Italy both went 1-0 up, the Africans through winger Haminu Draman after an error by Claudio Reyna, the Azzurri through a header from defender Marco Materazzi, who had only been on the field for ten minutes after replacing the injured Alessandro Nesta. Although the Americans equalised just before half-time with an excellent goal from Clint Dempsey, they fell victim to a shocking refereeing decision by German Markus Merk, who awarded a non-existent penalty that was confidently despatched by Ghana skipper Stephen Appiah.

No further goals in Nuremberg meant that Ghana celebrated another win and a well-earned qualification. There was victory and progress also for Italy. Having been given a one-man advantage for the whole of the second half yet again after an idiotic second yellow-card offence by Czech midfielder Jan Polák in first-half stoppage time, Marcello Lippi's men controlled the remainder of the game against a disappointing Czech side who offered little other than the extraordinary will and skill of their captain, Pavel Nedved. The game was decided three minutes from time when substitute Filippo Inzaghi, who had missed two good chances, broke away from the halfway line, skipped past Petr Cech and tapped the ball home for his 22nd international goal.

All in all, the two best teams had made it through, but the Czechs and the Americans had both contributed to what was unquestionably the most exciting and eventful of the eight first-round groups.

GROUP E

RESULTS

12/6/06, Gelsenkirchen
UNITED STATES 0
CZECH REPUBLIC 3 *(Koller 5, Rosicky 36, 76)*
Referee – *Amarilla (PAR)*
UNITED STATES – *Keller; Cherundolo (Johnson 46), Pope, Onyewu, Lewis; Beasley, Mastroeni (O'Brien 46), Reyna, Convey; Donovan, McBride (Wolff 77).*
CZECH REPUBLIC – *Cech; Grygera, Ujfalusi, Rozehnal, Jankulovski; Galásek; Poborsky (Polák 83), Rosicky (Stajner 86), Nedved, Plasil; Koller (Lokvenc 44).*

12/6/06, Hanover
ITALY 2 *(Pirlo 40, Iaquinta 83)*
GHANA 0
Referee – *Simon (BRA)*
ITALY – *Buffon; Zaccardo, Nesta, Cannavaro, Grosso; Perrotta, Pirlo, De Rossi; Totti (Camoranesi 56); Gilardino (Iaquinta 64), Toni (Del Piero 82).*
GHANA – *Kingston; Paintsil, Kuffour, Mensah, Pappoe (Shilla 46); Addo E.; Appiah, Essien, Muntari; Amoah (Pimpong 68), Gyan (Tachie-Mensah 89).*

17/6/06, Cologne
CZECH REPUBLIC 0
GHANA 2 *(Gyan 2, Muntari 82)*
Referee – *Elizondo (ARG)*
CZECH REPUBLIC – *Cech; Grygera, Ujfalusi, Rozehnal, Jankulovski; Galásek (Polák 46); Poborsky (Stajner 55), Rosicky, Nedved, Plasil (Sionko 68); Lokvenc.*
Sent off: *Ujfalusi (65)*
GHANA – *Kingston; Paintsil, Mensah, Shilla, Mohamed; Addo O. (Boateng 46); Essien, Appiah, Muntari; Gyan (Pimpong 85), Amoah (Addo E. 80).*

17/6/06, Kaiserslautern
ITALY 1 *(Gilardino 22)*
UNITED STATES 1 *(Zaccardo 27og)*
Referee – *Larrionda (URU)*
ITALY – *Buffon; Zaccardo (Del Piero 54), Nesta, Cannavaro, Zambrotta; Perrotta, Pirlo, Totti (Gattuso 35), De Rossi; Gilardino, Toni (Iaquinta 62).*
Sent off: *De Rossi (28)*
UNITED STATES – *Keller; Cherundolo, Onyewu, Pope, Bocanegra; Dempsey (Beasley 62), Reyna, Mastroeni, Convey (Conrad 52); Donovan; McBride.*
Sent off: *Mastroeni (45), Pope (47)*

22/6/06, Hamburg
ITALY 2 *(Materazzi 26, Inzaghi 87)*
CZECH REPUBLIC 0
Referee – *Archundia (MEX)*
ITALY – *Buffon; Zambrotta, Cannavaro, Nesta (Materazzi 17), Grosso; Camoranesi, Perrotta, Pirlo, Gattuso; Totti; Gilardino (Inzaghi 60).*
CZECH REPUBLIC – *Cech; Grygera, Kovác (Heinz 78), Rozehnal, Jankulovski; Polák; Poborsky (Stajner 46), Nedved, Rosicky, Plasil; Baros (Jarolim 64).*
Sent off: *Polák (45)*

22/6/06, Nuremberg
GHANA 2 *(Draman 22, Appiah 45p)*
UNITED STATES 1 *(Dempsey 43)*
Referee – *Merk (GER)*
GHANA – *Kingston; Paintsil, Mensah, Shilla, Mohamed; Boateng (Addo O. 46), Essien, Appiah, Draman (Tachie-Mensah 80); Amoah (Addo E. 59), Pimpong.*
UNITED STATES – *Keller; Cherundolo (Johnson 61), Onyewu, Conrad, Bocanegra; Reyna (Olsen 40); Dempsey, Donovan, Beasley, Lewis (Convey 74); McBride.*

FINAL TABLE

	Pld	W	D	L	F	A	Pts
1 Italy	3	2	1	0	5	1	7
2 Ghana	3	2	0	1	4	3	6
3 Czech Republic	3	1	0	2	3	4	3
4 United States	3	0	1	2	2	6	1

TOP SCORER

2 Tomás ROSICKY (Czech Republic)

World Cup 2006

Group F: Socceroos seize the day

The fascination in Group G was not so much how Brazil, the holders and overwhelming pre-tournament favourites, would perform but which of their challengers, Croatia, Australia and Japan, would accompany them into the last 16.

Australia and Japan got the group underway on a roasting hot afternoon in Kaiserslautern. As expected, there was little to choose between the two teams. Chances were split fifty-fifty in the first half but it was Japan who led, in highly controversial circumstances, at the interval after the Egyptian referee had allowed their goal to stand when there was a clear foul on Australian keeper Mark Schwarzer, baulked as he tried to catch Shunsuke Nakamura's inswinging free-kick.

The Aussies, as is their wont, came out fighting after the break and Mark Viduka forced a brilliant save out of Yoshikatsu Kawaguchi with a well-struck free-kick, but as the heat began to sap the energy of the players, it looked as if the Japanese would hold on to their priceless, if ill-gotten, three points. The game was petering out when suddenly it came leaping back to life. Tim Cahill, the Australian substitute, pounced in a goalmouth mêlée and swept his shot through the crowd to make it 1-1. Moments later the Everton midfielder almost went from hero to villain when he made a rash challenge on Japan full-back Yuichi Komano in his own penalty area, but scandalously the referee waved play on.

Then, as if to add insult to injury, Cahill went up the other end and rifled in another goal – a stunning right-foot shot that entered the net spectacularly via the inside of the post. From being down and seemingly out, Australia, remarkably, were now in the lead. Their first ever World Cup finals victory was in reach, and in stoppage time they sealed it when another substitute, John Aloisi, took on his marker and drilled the ball home with his left foot to make it 3-1. It was a stunning late, late show by the Socceroos and another World Cup coup for their coach, Dutchman Guus Hiddink, whose canny use of substitutes in the baking conditions had effectively won the game.

Magic Quartet

An oddity in the fixture list meant that the Brazil-Croatia game did not take place until the following evening, with four matches from other groups having been played in between. The Brazilians are usually worth waiting for at the World Cup, and there was particular expectation ahead of this game in Berlin, with coach Carlos Alberto Parreira having declared several weeks in advance that he would be lining up his so-called 'Magic Quartet' of Ronaldo, Adriano, Kaká and freshly crowned Champions League winner Ronaldinho.

But as the great Pelé kept reminding everyone in the build-up, Brazil do not sit easily with the tag of favourites. Despite a fantastic atmosphere in the Olympiastadion, the Seleção found it difficult to assert themselves against resilient and well

Tim Cahill starts Australia's late rally with the equaliser against Japan

Group F

Ronaldo of Brazil – not the fittest player at the World Cup

organised opponents. The focus of attention inevitably kept switching to the tubby figure leading the Brazilian attack. He wore the no. 9 and the name 'Ronaldo' on the back of his shirt, but this was a player far removed from the World Cup-winning super striker of 2002. It seemed remarkable that in the four weeks he had been in training with Brazil, the coaching staff had been unable to get him anything like match-fit. Ronaldo's presence was on reputation alone, of that there was no doubt.

For 44 minutes Brazil, in the image of their once great centre-forward, huffed and puffed. But then, with one elegant swipe of his left foot, Kaká brought Brazil, and the game, to life. It was a goal out of nothing, beautifully executed by the one member of the Magic Quartet actually living up to the hype.

Croatia tried to restore parity in the second half, but although they played with patience and fluidity, every time they carved out a half-chance, the shot went straight at goalkeeper Dida. Brazil also had opportunities to seal the win but Ronaldo blasted over, Ronaldinho had a header well saved by Stipe Pletikosa and Adriano sidefooted wide. Ronaldo was whistled as he waddled off midway through the first half, to be replaced by the considerably more mobile Robinho. Brazil held out for the 1-0 win, but they did nothing to substantiate the pre-tournament predictions that they would cruise to a sixth world title.

Brazil travelled from Berlin to Munich for their next game, against Australia. As the two teams took the field in the Allianz-Arena, they were both in a very strong position to qualify. This was because Japan and Croatia could manage only a 0-0 draw between them in Nuremberg. Once again the Japanese were forced to play in sweltering mid-afternoon temperatures, at which their Brazilian coach, Zico, launched a vehement protest. He would have been even angrier had his team lost the match, which might have been the case had goalkeeper Kawaguchi not brilliantly saved a first-half penalty from Croatian set-piece expert Darijo Srna.

Ronaldo unfit

With the other two teams drawing a blank, the victors in Munich were guaranteed qualification while the losers would still require only a draw in their final game to be sure of progressing. To some extent the pressure was off. It should have been the chance for Brazil to remove the shackles and show their true colours, but once again their play was fitful rather than fluent and hurried rather than harmonious. As for Ronaldo, he again looked desperately unfit, failing to make any impression on a very well organised and disciplined Australian defence.

Goalless at half-time, Brazil went ahead early in the second period when Adriano, hitherto anonymous, stroked in an accurate left-foot shot from Ronaldo's square pass on the edge of the area. This might have been the signal for Brazil to ram home their supposed superiority, but instead it was Australia who came hard at them, missing two gilt-edged opportunities through Marco Bresciano and – a minute after his introduction as a substitute - Harry Kewell. From then on in Australia matched Brazil in every department, but it was the holders who finished the stronger, and they made it 2-0 a minute from time when substitute Fred tapped in after a Robinho shot had rebounded back off the post. Kaká had a simple chance to extend Brazil's lead in stoppage time but he put it wide. Still, at least the Milan midfielder had made a contribution to the game, which was more than could be said for World Footballer of the Year Ronaldinho, strangely and disappointingly peripheral throughout the 90 minutes.

Nevertheless, six points out of six guaranteed Brazil a place in the next round, and they were to make it ten World Cup wins out of ten when they came from behind to beat Japan 4-1 in Dortmund. It was an improved performance from the world champions and certainly from Ronaldo, who suddenly came alive after heading in the equaliser just before half-time. His second goal, and Brazil's fourth, was reminiscent of the Ronaldo of old and brought him level with Gerd Müller as the most prolific World Cup finals marksman of all time, with a total of 14 goals.

While Brazil sent Japan, and Zico, home, the real drama took place down in Stuttgart, where Croatia and Australia played out a momentous match, arguably the best of the entire first round. It was a white-knuckle ride from first minute to last,

Group F

concluding in the most extraordinary fashion as English referee Graham Poll completely lost the plot, dishing out yellow and red cards in such profusion that he actually displayed three yellows to one player, Croatian defender Josip Simunic, before despatching him to the touchline – and this after he had mysteriously blown for the end of the game.

Croatia, needing a win to progress, struck early, a brilliant free-kick from their swaggering wing-back Darijo Srna soaring past the giant frame of Australian goalkeeper Zeljko Kalac, oddly selected by Guus Hiddink ahead of regular custodian Mark Schwarzer. Kalac was to have a dreadful game, continually undermining the excellent efforts of those in front of him. It was his glaring error that enabled Croatia to retake the lead, through skipper Niko Kovac's weakly struck shot, after the Socceroos had drawn level with a penalty from defender Craig Moore just before half-time.

Kewell strikes

For 20 minutes Australia were facing elimination, but they kept pressing for an equaliser, only to find Stipe Pletikosa, the Croatia keeper, in defiant and courageous form. Australia's first penalty had been awarded after a gratuitous handball by defender Stjepan Tomas. Now, with 15 minutes remaining, he committed exactly the same offence, but incredibly referee Poll failed to see it. No matter. Within a minute Australia got their equaliser, Harry Kewell calmly turning and shooting home with his weaker right foot. Had the linesman been more observant, he would have disallowed the goal for offside, but it was a tight decision and the Aussies, who had also been denied a clear penalty for a rugby tackle on Viduka early in the game, deserved their moment of good fortune.

The last few minutes were played amidst utter chaos. Red cards for Dario Simic, Brett Emerton and, belatedly, Simunic heightened the drama as Croatia strove in vain for the winning goal. One big chance fell to Igor Tudor, but he dallied too long and was crowded out by three Australian defenders. When the final whistle sounded, it was just as the Aussies were putting the ball in the net for the third time. Confusion reigned, but ultimately the realisation dawned that Australia, deservedly, were through – to play Italy - while Croatia, as in 2002, were out after just three matches.

GROUP F
RESULTS

12/6/06, Kaiserslautern
AUSTRALIA 3 *(Cahill 84, 89, Aloisi 90)*
JAPAN 1 *(Nakamura 27)*
Referee – Abdel Fatah (EGY)
AUSTRALIA – *Schwarzer; Moore (Kennedy 61), Neill, Chipperfield; Wilkshire (Aloisi 75), Emerton, Grella, Bresciano (Cahill 53), Culina; Viduka, Kewell.*
JAPAN – *Kawaguchi; Nakazawa, Miyamoto, Tsuboi (Moniwa 56); Oguro 90); Komano, Nakata H., Fukunishi, Nakamura, Alex; Takahara, Yanagisawa (Ono 79).*

13/6/06, Berlin
BRAZIL 1 *(Kaká 44)*
CROATIA 0
Referee – Archundía (MEX)
BRAZIL – *Dida; Cafú, Lúcio, Juan, Roberto Carlos; Kaká, Émerson, Zé Roberto, Ronaldinho; Ronaldo (Robinho 69), Adriano.*
CROATIA – *Pletikosa; Simic, Kovac R., Simunic; Srna, Kovac N. (Leko J. 40), Tudor, Babic; Kranjcar; Prso, Klasnic (Olic 57).*

18/6/06, Nuremberg
JAPAN 0
CROATIA 0
Referee – De Bleeckere (BEL)
JAPAN – *Kawaguchi; Kaji, Nakazawa, Miyamoto, Alex;* *Nakamura, Nakata H., Fukunishi (Inamoto 46), Ogasawara; Yanagisawa (Tamada 62), Takahara (Oguro 85).*
CROATIA – *Pletikosa; Simic, Kovac R., Simunic; Srna (Bosnjak 87), Kovac N., Tudor (Olic 70), Babic; Kranjcar (Modric 78); Prso, Klasnic.*

18/6/06, Munich
BRAZIL 2 *(Adriano 49, Fred 89)*
AUSTRALIA 0
Referee – Merk (GER)
BRAZIL – *Dida; Cafú, Lúcio, Juan, Roberto Carlos; Émerson (Gilberto Silva 72), Zé Roberto, Kaká, Ronaldinho; Adriano (Fred 88), Ronaldo (Robinho 72).*
AUSTRALIA – *Schwarzer; Neill, Moore (Aloisi 68), Popovic (Bresciano 38), Chipperfield; Emerton, Cahill (Kewell 56), Grella, Culina, Sterjovski; Viduka.*

22/6/06, Dortmund
JAPAN 1 *(Tamada 34)*
BRAZIL 4 *(Ronaldo 45, 81, Juninho 52, Gilberto 60)*
Referee – Poulat (FRA)
JAPAN – *Kawaguchi; Kaji, Tsuboi, Nakazawa, Alex; Inamoto; Nakamura, Ogasawara, Nakata H.; Maki (Takahara 66), Tamada.*
BRAZIL – *Dida (Rogério Ceni 81); Cicinho, Lúcio, Juan, Gilberto, Kaká (Zé Roberto 71), Juninho, Gilberto Silva, Ronaldinho (Ricardinho 71); Ronaldo, Robinho.*

22/6/06, Stuttgart
CROATIA 2 *(Srna 2, Kovac N. 56)*
AUSTRALIA 2 *(Moore 38p, Kewell 79)*
Referee – Poll (ENG)
CROATIA – *Pletikosa; Simic, Tomas, Simunic; Srna, Tudor, Kovac N., Babic; Kranjcar (Leko J. 65); Prso, Olic (Modric 73).*
Sent off: *Simic (85), Simunic (90)*
AUSTRALIA – *Kalac; Emerton, Moore, Neill, Chipperfield (Kennedy 75); Culina, Sterjovski (Bresciano 71), Grella (Aloisi 63), Cahill, Kewell; Viduka.*
Sent off: *Emerton (87)*

FINAL TABLE

	Pld	W	D	L	F	A	Pts
1 Brazil	3	3	0	0	7	1	9
2 Australia	3	1	1	1	5	5	4
3 Croatia	3	0	2	1	2	3	2
4 Japan	3	0	1	2	2	7	1

TOP SCORERS

2 RONALDO (Brazil)
Tim CAHILL (Australia)

World Cup 2006

Group G:
Les Bleus leave it late

France and Switzerland had little to complain about after the first-round draw had paired them with South Korea and Togo. Although the Koreans had reached the semi-finals in 2002, that was largely down to the fringe benefits of home advantage. As for the African first-timers, they could hardly have endured a more chaotic build-up. Not content with changing their coach just a few months before the finals, they almost lost the services of the new man in charge, German veteran Otto Pfister, when he offered his resignation as a result of a wage row only days before their opening match.

Less than 24 hours before their game with South Korea in Frankfurt, rumblings of discontent remained in the Togolese camp, with some voices suggesting the situation was so serious that the team might even fail to fulfil the fixture. Thankfully, however, common sense prevailed and they did turn up, although the players might have felt like walking straight out of the stadium when the South Korean national anthem was mistakenly played twice instead of their own.

Neutral interest in the match was minimal at the outset and the first half of the game was so devoid of quality that when Togo took the lead with a superb goal from striker Mohammed Kader after 31 minutes, the moment almost seemed surreal. But Togo's dreams of victory were effectively buried nine minutes into the second half when defender Yaovi Abalo was sent off for a second yellow-card offence after fouling Park Ji-sung on the edge of the penalty area. From the ensuing free-kick, Lee Chun-soo found the top corner with a beautiful strike to make it 1-1. It had taken a long time but now the Koreans began to play and on 72 minutes they got the winning goal, 2002 hero Ahn Jung-hwan, a half-time substitute, crisply shooting into the far corner via a slight deflection to send the noisy red-clad hordes in the stands into a state of frenzied delirium. It was South Korea's first ever World Cup victory on foreign soil – at the 15th time of asking.

Dreary draw

Three good goals had lit up a generally dismal affair in Frankfurt, but later in the day there was to be precious little illumination as France and Switzerland played out a dreary goalless draw in Stuttgart. The two teams had cancelled each other out twice in the qualifying tournament so it was not wholly surprising that they did so again at the finals. France were marginally the better side but appeared lethargic in attack, where Thierry Henry ploughed a lone furrow. Chances did come and go, for both teams, but while Alexander Frei and Daniel Gygax both squandered big opportunities for the Swiss, youngster Franck Ribéry, making his first international start, was the biggest culprit for the French. By the end both teams seemed reasonably happy with the point, but for the neutral spectator there was little to treasure from either side, save a fine display (on his home ground) from Swiss left-back Ludovic Magnin.

France's next game, against South Korea in Leipzig, was as one-sided as any in the first round, but incredibly Raymond Domenech's side were unable to mark their utter domination of proceedings with a victory. Ahead early through Thierry Henry's precise finish, they should have gone on to destroy their limited opponents. Perhaps they would have done had a 32nd-minute header from Patrick Vieira that clearly went over the line been officially registered as the goal it evidently was. It was an awful decision by the officials, but France, to their credit, barely raised a complaint. Maybe they felt that the game was so clearly theirs for the taking that other chances, and goals, would surely follow.

Unfortunately, those chances never came. With South Korea – despite relentless booming support from the stands - unable to get anywhere near the

Group G

French goal, 1-0 looked safe and secure. But then, with nine minutes to go, the unbelievable happened. The Koreans not only launched a meaningful attack but actually scored a goal from it, Park Ji-sung bundling the ball inelegantly over the line via Fabien Barthez's fingertips. Now France had to alter their strategy completely. They raced downfield and lay siege to the Korean goal. Vieira skied embarrassingly high and wide, Henry, fed through by Zinedine Zidane, brought a brilliant save out of Lee Woon-jae, and further half-chances went begging as the Koreans, who had defended resolutely throughout, held on for a remarkable draw. With four points on the board to France's two, the Koreans were firmly in contention for a place in the last 16.

Togo, still smarting over their wage dispute, made it to Dortmund for their second game, against Switzerland, and for the first 45 minutes they were much the better team. Unfortunately for them, it was the Swiss who went into the interval 1-0 up, a 16th-minute tap-in from Alexander Frei giving the European side an unjust lead. Togo had strong claims for a penalty when Emmanuel Adebayor went over Patrick Müller's trailing leg but their luck was out, and insult was added to injury when Müller made a brilliant saving tackle to deny Mohammed Kader just a few seconds later.

Swiss go top

The second half was a very different story as Switzerland, with Hakan Yakin introduced to add more creativity, began to run the show in midfield. Although victory was their first priority, they knew that a win by two goals would put them on top of the group and leave them needing only a draw against the Koreans to ensure qualification for the last 16. With Togo looking increasingly dispirited, Switzerland saw their chance and went for it. But it was not until the 88th minute that they finally made the breakthrough, a fine square ball from substitute Mauro Lustrinelli feeding young winger Tranquillo Barnetta, whose right-foot shot was firm and true, fizzing into the corner of the Togolese net.

Switzerland's 2-0 win spelt elimination for Togo, but the Africans still had a role to play in the Group G finale. If they could deny France victory in Cologne, the 1998 champions would be out of the competition. On the other hand, Raymond Domenech and his players were aware that a win by two goals would ensure their progress at the expense of the losers of the Switzerland-South Korea showdown in Hanover – or, in the event of a draw, the Koreans.

There was huge pressure on the French to deliver,

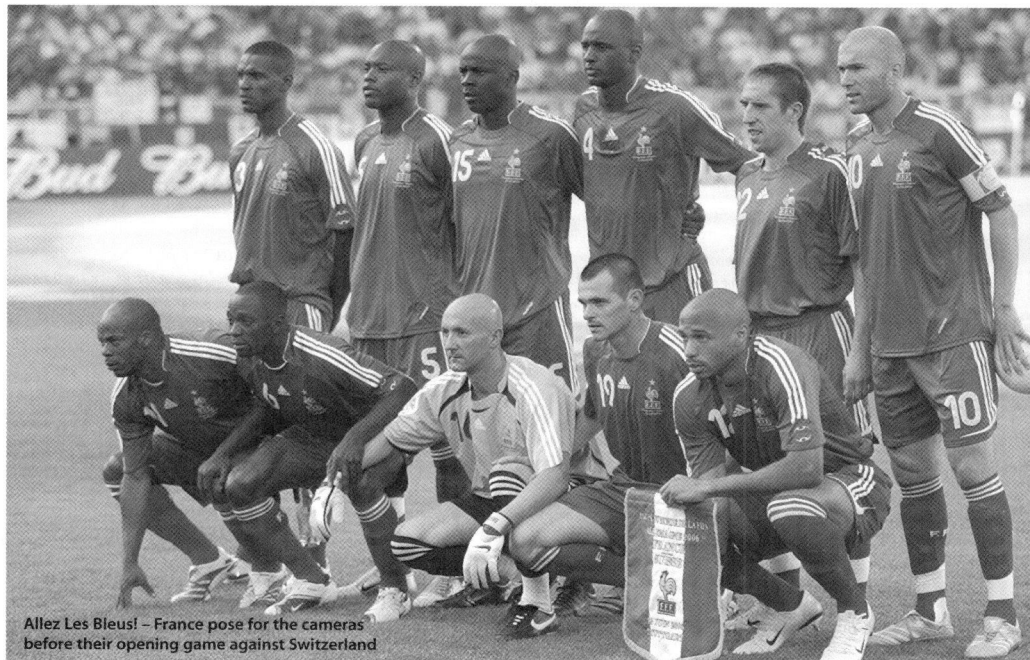

Allez Les Bleus! – France pose for the cameras before their opening game against Switzerland

Group G

but with Zinedine Zidane suspended after picking up yellow cards in each of the first two games and confidence eroded by their embarrassing failure to kill off the Koreans, nothing was guaranteed. For the first 45 minutes France created a multitude of chances, but none of them were taken, with David Trezeguet, the replacement for Zidane, spurning the majority of them. Such was France's superiority, however, that it seemed impossible for Togo to survive for the full 90 minutes. And, sure enough, the goal Les Bleus craved arrived ten minutes after the interval when Patrick Vieira, playing on his 30th birthday, drilled his team into the lead. A second goal, rapped in by Thierry Henry, followed shortly afterwards and France, albeit in extremis, were through.

Power header

Now the attention switched to Hanover, where Switzerland were in the driving seat after a tremendous header from defender Philippe Senderos from a Yakin free-kick had powered them ahead on 22 minutes. The Koreans closed the first half strongly but without scoring, and after the interval, as the bad news filtered through from Cologne, they began to lose their self-belief. They had come back to beat Togo 2-1 but the Swiss, who had yet to concede a goal, were a different proposition entirely. The match, and South Korea's elimination, was settled on 77 minutes when Switzerland went 2-0 up. It was a contentious goal from the Korean perspective, with the linesman raising his flag for offside as Alexander Frei raced through to squeeze his shot into the net from a tight angle, but quite correctly the Argentine referee, Horacio Elizondo, overruled his assistant, having spotted that the through-ball was actually played by a Korean defender.

So, for the first time in their history, Switzerland went through to the second round of the World Cup as group winners – and with three clean sheets into the bargain. It was an impressive feat, and it earned them the right to meet Ukraine in the last 16 while France faced the much more daunting prospect of taking on in-form Group H winners Spain.

GROUP G

RESULTS

13/6/06, Frankfurt
SOUTH KOREA 2 *(Lee Chun-soo 54, Ahn Jung-hwan 72)*
TOGO 1 *(Kader 31)*
Referee – Poll (ENG)
SOUTH KOREA – Lee Woon-jae; Choi Jin-cheul, Kim Young-chul, Kim Jin-kyu (Ahn Jung-hwan 46); Song Chong-gug, Lee Ho, Lee Eul-yong (Kim Nam-il 68), Lee Young-pyo; Park Ji-sung, Lee Chun-soo; Cho Jae-jin (Kim Sang-sik 84).
TOGO – Agassa; Tchangai, Abalo, Nibombe, Assemoassa (Forson 55); Senaya (Touré 55), Mamam, Romao, Salifou (Aziawonou 87); Kader, Adebayor.
Sent off: Abalo (53).

13/6/06, Stuttgart
FRANCE 0
SWITZERLAND 0
Referee – Ivanov (RUS)
FRANCE – Barthez; Sagnol, Thuram, Gallas, Abidal; Ribéry (Saha 70), Makelele, Vieira, Wiltord (Dhorasoo 85); Zidane; Henry.
SWITZERLAND – Zuberbühler; Degen P. (Gygax 56), Müller (Djourou 75), Senderos, Magnin; Barnetta, Cabanas, Vogel, Wicky (Margairaz 82); Frei, Streller.

18/6/06, Leipzig
FRANCE 1 *(Henry 9)*
SOUTH KOREA 1 *(Park Ji-sung 81)*
Referee – Archundia (MEX)
FRANCE – Barthez; Sagnol, Thuram, Gallas, Abidal; Wiltord (Ribéry 60), Vieira, Makelele, Malouda; Zidane (Trezeguet 90); Henry.
SOUTH KOREA – Lee Woon-jae; Kim Dong-jin, Young-chul, Choi Jin-cheul, Lee Young-pyo; Kim Nam-il; Park Ji-sung, Lee Eul-yong (Seol Ki-hyeon 46), Lee Ho (Kim Sang-sik 69); Lee Chun-soo (Ahn Jung-hwan 72), Cho Jae-jin.

19/6/06, Dortmund
TOGO 0
SWITZERLAND 2 *(Frei 17, Barnetta 88)*
Referee – Amarilla (PAR)
TOGO – Agassa; Touré, Tchangai, Nibombe, Forson; Dossevi (Senaya 69), Romao, Agboh (Salifou 25), Mamam (Malm 87); Adebayor, Kader.
SWITZERLAND – Zuberbühler; Degen P., Müller, Senderos, Magnin; Barnetta, Vogel, Cabanas (Streller 77), Wicky; Gygax (Yakin 46), Frei (Lustrinelli 88).

23/6/06, Cologne
TOGO 0
FRANCE 2 *(Vieira 55, Henry 61)*
Referee – Larrionda (URU)
TOGO – Agassa; Tchangai, Abalo, Nibombe, Forson; Senaya, Aziawonou, Salifou, Mamam (Olufade 59); Adebayor (Dossevi 75), Kader.
FRANCE – Barthez; Sagnol, Thuram, Gallas, Silvestre; Ribéry (Govou 77), Vieira (Diarra 81), Makelele, Malouda (Wiltord 74); Trezeguet, Henry.

23/6/06, Hanover
SWITZERLAND 2 *(Senderos 23, Frei 77)*
SOUTH KOREA 0
Referee – Elizondo (ARG)
SWITZERLAND – Zuberbühler; Degen P., Müller, Senderos (Djourou 53), Spycher, Barnetta, Vogel, Cabanas, Wicky (Behrami 88); Yakin (Margairaz 71); Frei.
SOUTH KOREA – Lee Woon-jae; Lee Young-pyo (Ahn Jung-hwan 63), Choi Jin-cheul, Kim Jin-kyu, Kim Dong-jin; Lee Ho, Kim Nam-il; Park Ji-sung, Lee Chun-soo, Park Chu-young (Seol Ki-hyeon 66); Cho Jae-jin.

FINAL TABLE

		Pld	W	D	L	F	A	Pts
1	Switzerland	3	2	1	0	4	0	7
2	France	3	1	2	0	3	1	5
3	South Korea	3	1	1	1	3	4	4
4	Togo	3	0	0	3	1	6	0

TOP SCORERS

2   Alexander FREI (Switzerland)
     Thierry HENRY (France)

World Cup 2006

Group H:
Spain sail through

Spain don't generally get the rub of the green at the World Cup, but they had no reason to curse their luck after being grouped with Ukraine, Tunisia and Saudi Arabia in the opening round. Of all the eight seeded teams, they probably had the most straightforward route into the last 16. Although Ukraine had been the first European team to qualify for the finals, they were on virgin territory. Saudi Arabia, with their 100 per cent home-based squad, were the least fancied of the four Asian representatives, while Tunisia, despite a good recent record in Africa, had never progressed beyond the first phase in three previous attempts.

Spain's first match was ostensibly their most difficult – against Ukraine – but on a hot, sunny afternoon in Leipzig, Luis Aragonés's side were to prove their Cup-winning credentials with a confident and lively performance that simply blew their nervous, stagestruck opponents away. Not that they were short of luck. The key refereeing decisions virtually all went their way, not least when Ukrainian superstar Andriy Shevchenko, feeling his way back to fitness after a knee injury, was denied a clear run on goal by a faulty offside decision with the score at 0-0.

Within a couple of minutes Spain were in front, Liverpool midfielder Xabi Alonso deflecting a left-wing corner inside the near post with a stooping header. Four minutes later it was 2-0 as David Villa's free-kick took a wicked deflection and flew past the helpless Olexandr Shovkovskyi. Now Spain were in complete control, and with Ukraine looking overawed on their World Cup debut, a rout was on the cards.

First red card

Although there were no further goals in the first half, Spain received another big slice of good fortune when, two minutes after the interval, the Swiss referee awarded them a highly contentious penalty after Fernando Torres had received the slightest tug on his shorts – outside the penalty area – from Vladyslav Vashchuk. To make matters worse for Ukraine, the centre-back was sent off. It was the first straight red card of the tournament and also, in the 15th game, the first penalty. David Villa drove the spot-kick low into the corner to kill the game as a contest. The second half saw sporadic efforts by Ukraine to make a game of it, but the last word, fittingly, fell to the best player on the pitch, the rampant Fernando Torres, who finished off some terrific build-up work by defender Carles Puyol with a fierce right-foot shot.

At 4-0, Spain could hardly have wished for a better start. For Ukraine it was a debut to forget. But the day wasn't an entire disaster for the World Cup debutants, because a few hours later Tunisia and Saudi Arabia shared the spoils in an eventful 2-2 draw in Munich.

It was the classic game of two halves. Tunisia, who

Fernando Torres strikes a fourth goal for Spain to complete the drubbing of Ukraine

Group H

were hoping to restore some African pride after all of the continent's other four representatives had lost their opening game, bossed a low-quality first half, taking a deserved lead through diminutive striker Ziad Jaziri's confident, athletic finish on 23 minutes. But the Saudis sprang to life after the break. Their prolific forward Yasser Al Qahtani equalised with a strike every bit as aesthetic as Jaziri's, lifting in Mohammed Noor's fine cross, and from then on they were on top. Saudi Arabia's dream scenario appeared to be realised when veteran striker Sami Al Jaber, participating in his fourth World Cup, came off the bench to replace Al Qahtani and scored with a fine breakaway goal just a couple of minutes after his arrival. But in a breathlessly exciting climax Tunisia salvaged a draw – and the avoidance of an African whitewash – when defender Radhi Jaidi, thrown forward in desperation as an extra attacker, headed Jaziri's clever clipped cross powerfully into the net.

The concession of that late equaliser appeared still to be haunting the Saudis when they took on Ukraine on a drizzly evening in Hamburg five days later. The Ukrainians, on the other hand, showed no ill-effects at all of their humbling by Spain. One-nil up after just three minutes when defender Andriy Rusol bundled the ball home with his knee from a Maxym Kalynychenko corner, they gave their bedraggled opponents the runaround for the whole 90 minutes.

Superb set-pieces

Kalynychenko, who had been overlooked against Spain, was the catalyst, his superb set-piece deliveries repeatedly causing havoc in the Saudi defence. There was a sumptuous second goal before the interval – a long-range screamer from Serhiy Rebrov – but the moment the Ukrainan fans had really been waiting for arrived 45 seconds after the break when Andriy Shevchenko, who had endured a frustrating first half, got his World Cup up and running by heading in Kalynychenko's left-wing free-kick, albeit with the aid of a discreet shove on his marker. Intriguingly, the Milan striker was winning his 66th cap and this was his first international against non-European opposition.

The goal liberated Shevchenko, but it was Kalynychenko who continued to shine the brightest and there could be no more appropriate conclusion to the game than when, six minutes from time, the blond Spartak Moscow midfielder raced through the middle and blasted Shevchenko's unselfish pull-back high into the net. It was the end of an utter annihilation for the Saudis, who failed to create a single chance all

Maxym Kalynychenko – Ukraine's star performer against Saudi Arabia

game, but Ukraine were now firmly back in contention for a place in the last 16…on the assumption that Spain would beat Tunisia later that evening.

For over an hour in Stuttgart, however, a huge shock was in the offing as the Tunisians scored early, through midfielder Jawher Mnari, then defended their lead with remarkable courage and discipline. As the match wore on, it became a straightforward game of attack against defence. Spain's lack of penetration forced coach Luis Aragonés to introduce two half-time substitute in Cesc Fábregas and Raúl, and both would eventually make a telling impact, the former with a tremendously influential midfield performance, the latter by smartly bringing Spain level in the 71st minute after Tunisian keeper Ali Boumnijel could only parry a Fábregas shot.

Boumnijel, at 40 the oldest player competing at the finals, had been outstanding up to that point, but five minutes later he was responsible for the goal that gave Spain the lead, inadvisedly leaving his line in pursuit of a long ball and allowing Fernando Torres to clip the ball into the unguarded net. Tunisia were a beaten side now and Spain, to chants of 'olé' from the stands, saw out the game with ease, adding a third goal in stoppage time from the penalty spot when Fernando Torres converted – albeit with a weak kick that Boumnijel should have saved – after he had been hauled down by Alaeddine Yahia.

Group H

All four Group H matches had yielded four goals and Spain, with a maximum six points, were through already to the second phase. That allowed Aragonés to rest his entire first XI for the final group fixture against Saudi Arabia. The Saudis, who could still mathematically qualify with a big win, never really believed in that possibility and theirs was largely an exercise in damage limitation in Kaiserslautern. In that respect they succeeded, restricting Spain to a solitary goal, a header by centre-back Juanito, thanks in the main to a resilient goalkeeping display from Mabrouk Zaid.

There was much more to play for up in Berlin, where Ukraine needed a draw and Tunisia a win to join Spain in the second phase. The expectation was for an encounter as exciting as the one between Australia and Croatia the previous evening, but instead, for no apparent reason, the World Cup endured arguably its poorest match to date – a lifeless, tepid affair played at a snail's pace and with an extraordinary lack of desire from both sets of players.

Awful decision

Tunisia's hopes of advancement were effectively dashed just before half-time when their lone striker, Ziad Jaziri, was red carded for a second bookable offence. Ukraine went on to win the game 1-0 but only thanks to an awful decision by the Paraguayan referee, who gifted the men in yellow a non-existent penalty after Andriy Shevchenko had tripped over his own foot. The Chelsea-bound striker picked himself up to convert the spot-kick and book his country's place in the next round.

The victory meant that Ukraine were the only one of the five Eastern European participants to qualify, but they had hardly done so in style. Tunisia, for their part, only had themselves to blame for their third successive first-round exit. Ukraine had been there for the taking, but the lack of ambition that saw the Tunisians' best, albeit injured, forward – Brazilian-born Santos – introduced only when it was too late to matter left few neutrals bemoaning their departure.

GROUP H

RESULTS

14/6/06, Leipzig
SPAIN 4 *(Xabi Alonso 13, David Villa 17, 48p, Fernando Torres 81)*
UKRAINE 0
Referee – Busacca (SUI)
SPAIN – Casillas; Sergio Ramos, Pablo, Puyol, Pernia; Xabi Alonso (Albelda 55); Senna, Xavi, Luis García (Fábregas 77); David Villa (Raúl 55), Fernando Torres.
UKRAINE – Shovkovskyi; Yezerskyi, Rusol, Vashchuk, Nesmachnyi; Gusev (Vorobei 46), Gusin (Shelayev 46), Tymoshchuk, Rotan (Rebrov 64); Shevchenko, Voronin.
Sent off: Vashchuk (47)

14/6/06, Munich
TUNISIA 2 *(Jaziri 23, Jaidi 90)*
SAUDI ARABIA 2 *(Al Qahtani 57, Al Jaber 84)*
Referee – Shields (AUS)
TUNISIA – Boumnijel; Trabelsi, Jaidi, Hagui, Jemmali; Bouazizi (Nafti 55), Namouchi, Mnari, Chedli (Ghodhbane 69); Jaziri, Chikhaoui (Essediri 82).
SAUDI ARABIA – Zaid; Al Dokhi, Tukar, Al Montashari; Al Ghamdi, Aziz, Khariri, Al Temyat (Al Hawsawi 68), Sulimani; Noor (Ameen 75), Al Qahtani (Al Jaber 82).

19/6/06, Hamburg
SAUDI ARABIA 0
UKRAINE 4 *(Rusol 4, Rebrov 36, Shevchenko 46, Kalynychenko 84)*
Referee – Poll (ENG)
SAUDI ARABIA – Zaid; Al Dokhi (Khathran 55), Tukar, Al Montashari, Sulimani; Al Ghamdi, Ameen (Al Hawsawi 55), Noor (Al Jaber 76), Khariri, Aziz; Al Qahtani.
UKRAINE – Shovkovskyi; Gusev, Rusol, Sviderskyi, Nesmachnyi; Rebrov (Rotan 71), Shelayev, Tymoshchuk, Kalylnychenko; Voronin (Gusin 78), Shevchenko (Milevskyi 85).

19/6/06, Stuttgart
SPAIN 3 *(Raúl 71, Fernando Torres 76, 90p)*
TUNISIA 1 *(Mnari 8)*
Referee – Simon (BRA)
SPAIN – Casillas; Sergio Ramos, Pablo, Puyol, Pernía; Senna (Fábregas 46), Xabi Alonso, Xavi; Luis García (Raúl 46); David Villa (Joaquín 56), Fernando Torres.
TUNISIA – Boumnijel; Trabelsi, Jaidi, Hagui, Ayari (Yahia 57); Bouazizi (Ghodhbane 57), Nafti, Mnari, Namouchi, Chedli (Guemamdia 79); Jaziri.

23/6/06, Kaiserslautern
SAUDI ARABIA 0
SPAIN 1 *(Juanito 36)*
Referee – Codjia (BEN)
SAUDI ARABIA – Zaid; Al Dokhi, Tukar, Al Montashari, Sulimani (Massad 81); Khathran, Noor, Khariri, Aziz (Al Temyat 13); Al Jaber (Al Hawsawi 68), Al Harthi.
SPAIN – Cañizares; Míchel Salgado, Marchena, Juanito, Antonio López; Joaquín, Iniesta, Albelda, Fábregas (Xavi 66), Reyes (Fernando Torres 69); Raúl (David Villa 46).

23/6/06, Berlin
UKRAINE 1 *(Shevchenko 70p)*
TUNISIA 0
Referee – Amarilla (PAR)
UKRAINE – Shovkovskyi; Gusev, Rusol, Sviderskyi, Nesmachnyi; Rebrov (Vorobei 54), Shelayev, Tymoshchuk, Kalynychenko (Gusin 75); Shevchenko (Milevskyi 88), Voronin.
TUNISIA – Boumnijel; Trabelsi, Hagui, Jaidi, Ayari; Bouazizi (Ben Saada 79), Mnari, Nafti (Ghodhbane 90), Namouchi, Chedli (Santos 79); Jaziri.
Sent off: Jaziri (45)

FINAL TABLE

		Pld	W	D	L	F	A	Pts
1	Spain	3	3	0	0	8	1	9
2	Ukraine	3	2	0	1	5	4	6
3	Tunisia	3	0	1	2	3	6	1
4	Saudi Arabia	3	0	1	2	2	7	1

TOP SCORERS

3 FERNANDO TORRES (Spain)
2 DAVID VILLA (Spain)
   Andriy SHEVCHENKO (Ukraine)

World Cup 2006

Second Round:
Big guns blast their way through

The round of the last 16 – to use official FIFA parlance – contained ten of the original 14 entrants from Europe. Half of the other six places were taken by South American sides, with Mexico, Australia and Ghana filling the other three. Of the six global confederations, only Asia was unrepresented (although with Australia set to move there from Oceania, the AFC could also claim a continuing involvement).

The first of the second-round matches featured hosts Germany in an all-European tie with Sweden. There was no doubt which team started out as favourites. Germany had taken maximum points from their group games and built up an ominous head of steam whereas the Swedes had yet to produce a performance of any sustained quality. It took only four minutes before the German crowd were up on their feet acclaiming an opening goal. Lukas Podolski was credited with it, although his shot actually cannoned into the net off a Swedish defender. The architect of the goal was Podolski's strike-partner Miroslav Klose, and eight minutes later it was even better work from the tournament's leading scorer that set up Podolski for his second goal. Klose's lovely reverse ball into the area took out three defenders, allowing the young Bayern Munich-bound striker to fire the ball into the net with a sweet left-foot shot.

The gate to the quarter-finals was open, but Jürgen Klinsmann's side were in no mood to ease up. A gaping hole in the Swedish midfield allowed Germany to drive forward repeatedly and fire in a succession of shots. Only resilient goalkeeping from Andreas Isaksson prevented a rout. When defender Teddy Lucic was red-carded after two fouls in quick succession on Klose, it looked all over for the Swedes, but miraculously they were given a lifeline early in the second half when Henrik Larsson had his ankle tapped and went to ground in the area. Oddly Swedish coach Lars Lagerbäck made a substitution just before Larsson was about to take the penalty. Possibly distracted by the delay, the veteran striker ballooned his kick wildly and embarrassingly over the bar.

Convincing win

That was Sweden's last hope extinguished. The remainder of the game was played almost entirely in and around the Swedish penalty area. There should have been further goals, but Isaksson's continued heroics kept the score at 2-0. No matter. Germany were through to the quarter-finals, and in convincing, confident style.

Argentina, the most impressive team in the first round, were up against Mexico in Leipzig. A year earlier the two teams had met in the Confederations Cup semi-final, with the Argentinians winning on penalties. Mexico captain Rafael Márquez had been red-carded in that game but he wasted no time in making amends, stabbing the ball home at the far post with just four minutes on the clock after his marker, Gabriel Heinze, had allowed him to escape at a free-kick. It was a brilliant start for Mexico, but within a few minutes Argentina were level. A corner swung in from the right by birthday boy Juan Román Riquelme was met by the head of Jared Borgetti, but unfortunately Mexico's fit-again striker succeeded only in deflecting it into his own net. Hernán Crespo, who dangled his foot near to the ball in the challenge, was officially credited with the goal but that seemed an extremely generous decision by the FIFA technical panel.

The two early goals made for a wonderful game, the best of the tournament in terms of the quality of the football and the excitement generated. Chances were created at both ends, and there was high controversy, too, especially in the closing seconds of the first half when Mexico's Francisco Fonseca became the victim of a 'professional' foul by Heinze. He would have been clean through on goal, but the Swiss referee preposterously decreed that Heinze

Second Round

was not the 'last man' and showed him a yellow card rather than red.

It was not the only big mistake from referee Busacca. Later in the game he booked the wrong Mexican player – an error that would have led to Gerardo Torrado being sent off in extra-time. That the extra 30 minutes were needed also came down to a terrible decision, right at the end of normal time, when Lionel Messi, a lively late substitute for Javier Saviola, scored what should have been a momentous winning goal, only to have it chalked off for an incorrect, if admittedly tight, offside decision. In truth, Mexico had played so well that for them to lose in such circumstances would have been cruel in the extreme.

Wonder goal

The Mexicans deserved a shot at extra-time, and the match deserved to be decided by something special. Fortunately, that glorious moment arrived eight minutes into the first extra period when Argentine winger Maxi Rodríguez, stationed on the right hand corner of the penalty area, gathered a long crossfield pass by Juan Pablo Sorín on his chest and, without allowing the ball to bounce, smashed it with his left foot high into the far corner of the net. It was a wonderful goal, and although the excitement continued throughout the remainder of extra-time, it proved to be decisive. Argentina just about earned the right to march forward into the next round, but Mexico, for whom the back three of Márquez, Carlos Salcido and Ricardo Osorio had been majestic, were desperately unfortunate losers. It was their fourth successive second-round exit but undoubtedly their most gallant.

The following afternoon it was England's turn to make it three out of three for the group winners. Despite their mediocrity in the first phase, and the oppressive heat and humidity in Stuttgart's Gottlieb-Daimler-Stadion, they were heavily fancied to overcome Ecuador. Sven Göran Eriksson decided to introduce the previously unused Michael Carrick into central midfield, in place of Peter Crouch, which left Wayne Rooney playing up front on his own. Ecuador, needless to say, restored all of the first-choice players they had rested for the game against Germany.

One of those players, striker Carlos Tenorio, should have had his third goal in as many games when he seized on an uncharacteristically sloppy header from John Terry. But with only the goalkeeper to beat, he took a fraction too long and Ashley Cole heroically raced back to challenge, his slightest deflection helping the ball up on to the crossbar and away to safety. That early scare should have jolted

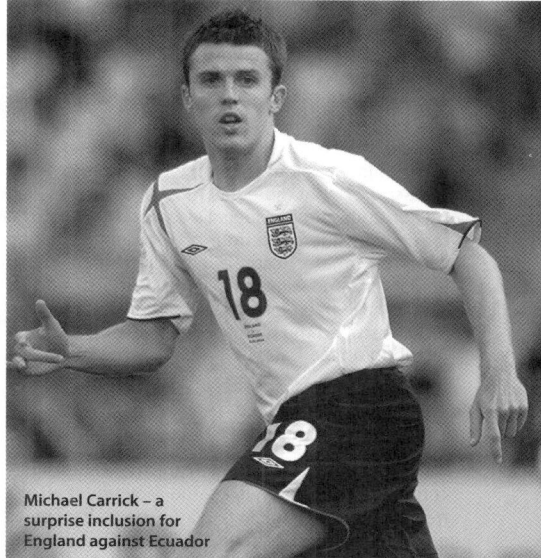

Michael Carrick – a surprise inclusion for England against Ecuador

England into life but once again they struggled to create openings in attack.

Beckham free-kick

The outcome was in the balance until the hour mark when David Beckham, who had done nothing up to that point, curled in one of his trademark free-kicks, just eluding goalkeeper Cristián Mora at his near post. It made him the first Englishman to score in three World Cups – all three of the goals, curiously, coming against South American opposition. Ecuador's heads went down after this and England should have finished them off, but despite the best efforts up front of Rooney the second goal wouldn't come. Frank Lampard, whose shooting had been woeful in the group games, continued to misfire badly, squandering three good chances to kill off the opposition. Fortunately for England, Ecuador had nothing to offer in reply, so their quarter-final place was never seriously in jeopardy after they had gone ahead, but it was another laboured performance from Eriksson's team.

England's quarter-final opponents were to be decided later that day as Portugal took on Holland in Nuremberg. It was a repeat of the Euro 2004 semi-final, which Portugal had won 2-1. Luiz Felipe Scolari's side were to triumph again but in shambolic fashion. It was one of the most eagerly anticipated ties of the round but ultimately it was destroyed by Russian referee Vladimir Ivanov, whose apparent belief that every indiscretion, however

Second Round

slight, merited some form of sanction led to no fewer than 16 yellow cards and four red – a World Cup record – being brandished. The players hardly helped matters, with their lack of self control and, worse still, blatant gamesmanship.

It all made for a lousy, ill tempered 90 minutes. There was no flow at all to the game. Occasionally there were some bright moments, most of them provided by Portuguese midfielders Deco and Maniche. The former was one of the four players sent off (along with team-mate Costinha and Dutchmen Khalid Boulahrouz and Giovanni van Bronckhorst), and he should have been joined by captain Luís Figo, who luckily escaped the ultimate censure after a blatant headbutt on Mark van Bommel.

Maniche strikes

The game was decided by a fine goal midway through the first half from Maniche, who skilfully controlled and shot in the same movement after a neat set-up by Pauleta. Holland had chances to equalise, the best of them falling to Phillip Cocu, who instinctively turned a shot against the bar just after half-time, but with ace marksman Ruud van Nistelrooy strangely kept on the bench throughout – he was neither injured nor suspended – it could be argued that the Oranje got what they deserved. With just three goals scored in four games, their problem was plain for all to see.

The fifth of the eight second-round ties saw Italy take on Australia in Kaiserslautern. Both teams had played at the venue in the first round, with the Socceroos beating Japan there and the Azzurri being held by the United States. Not surprisingly, there was a recall for Australia keeper Mark Schwarzer, but Guus Hiddink, whose South Korea side had knocked Italy out at the same stage of the competition four years earlier, had to make do without the injured Harry Kewell, goalscoring hero of the final group game against Croatia. As for Italy, there was a surprise recall for Alessandro Del Piero in place of Francesco Totti.

Possession was shared fifty-fifty in the first half, but Italy, predictably, were the better, more purposeful side. Twin strikers Luca Toni and Alberto Gilardino both spurned chances, and when, six minutes after the interval, the Spanish referee ruled that Marco Materazzi merited instant dismissal after a clattering foul on Marco Bresciano, it seemed as if the Italians would be left to rue those missed opportunities. Toni was sacrificed to make way for another defender, Andrea Barzagli, and Italy regrouped. Australia, badly missing Kewell's invention, could make no inroads into a backline brilliantly marshalled by Fabio Cannavaro, and with Gianluigi Buffon looking unbeatable in goal, the stalemate continued.

Grosso injustice

With Italy's attacking ambition blunted, extra-time, and penalties, seemed inevitable. But with added time almost up, Italy left-back Fabio Grosso bravely ventured forward down the left. He beat one defender and made his way into the penalty area. Lucas Neill, who had enjoyed a superb tournament at the heart of the Aussie defence, stood before him but needlessly went to ground, allowing Grosso to fall over his body and con the inept referee into giving Italy a penalty. Totti, on as a substitute and impressive in his 20 minutes on the field, duly smashed the spot-kick home. It was the

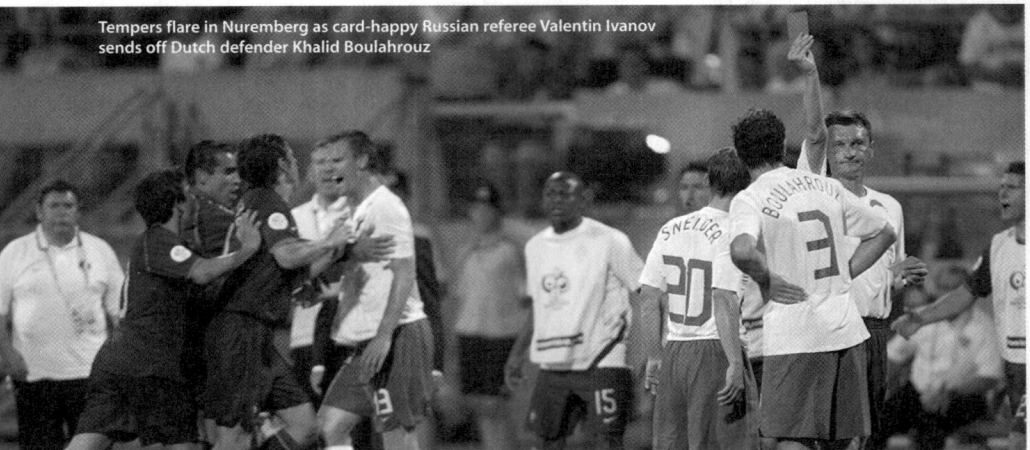

Tempers flare in Nuremberg as card-happy Russian referee Valentin Ivanov sends off Dutch defender Khalid Boulahrouz

Second Round

last kick of the game. Italy had sneaked through to the quarter-finals. Australia, cruelly, were out.

Totti's penalty was to be the only goal of the day. The evening game between Switzerland and Ukraine, two of the more unlikely prospective quarter-finalists, produced no goals and hardly any entertainment during two horribly tedious hours in Cologne. Apart from one effort apiece against the crossbar midway through the first half – a header from Andriy Shevchenko and a free-kick from Alexander Frei – neither side looked likely to score. The fear factor ruled. It was risk-free football of the worst kind. The competition's first penalty shoot-out was unavoidable, and even then the first two efforts – from Shevchenko and Marco Streller – failed to find the target. Ukraine's lively young substitute, Artem Milevskyi, finally found the net with an audacious chip, but with Tranquillo Barnetta and Ricardo Cabanas also missing, successful conversions from Serhiy Rebrov and Oleh Gusev sent Ukraine through to the quarter-finals. Switzerland were out – despite becoming the first team in World Cup history to be eliminated without conceding a goal.

Record-breaker Ronaldo

Brazil faced Ghana with the advantage of playing their second successive game in Dortmund's Westfalenstadion. They had beaten Japan there, now they were fully expected to overcome Ghana. Ronaldo, who had scored twice against the Japanese, needed just one more goal to become the World Cup finals' all-time top scorer, and it took him only five minutes to dethrone Gerd Müller, latching on to Kaká's delightful through-ball and using his familiar stepover routine to weave past the keeper and stroke the ball into the empty net. It was an historic goal and an important one, too, because Ghana were determined to give the world champions a fight. Indeed, for the second quarter of the game they took the game to Brazil and created several openings. They should have equalised in 42 minutes when a point-blank header from John Mensah hit goalkeeper Dida's legs, and it was a cruel twist of the knife that saw them concede a second goal – and an offside one at that – on the stroke of half-time. Adriano's inelegant finish – off his knee – gave Brazil their 200th goal at the World Cup finals. It had been a half of momentous goals but the defending champions were extremely fortunate to be 2-0 up as they headed for the dressing-rooms.

Ghana, to their credit, continued to pose problems for the Brazilian defence after the break, but Dida made a couple of tidy saves, and when striker

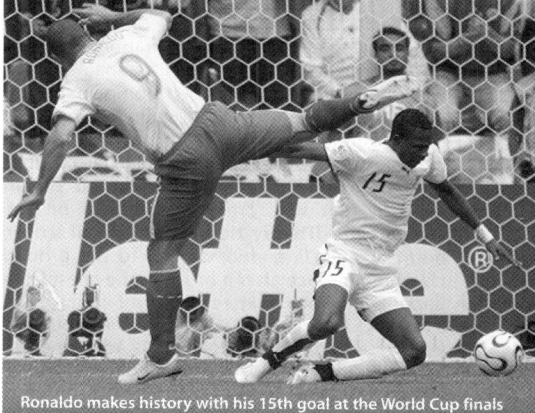
Ronaldo makes history with his 15th goal at the World Cup finals

Asamoah Gyan was rightly red-carded as he sought to dive for a penalty (he had already been booked), Brazil made the Africans pay with a third goal. Again it resulted from Ghana playing a high line in defence and having their offside trap sprung. Zé Roberto, Brazil's best player on the night, scored it, cleverly clipping the ball over the goalkeeper before walking it into the empty net. It was the sort of goal that might have been scored by Ronaldinho, but yet again the Barcelona megastar had a quiet evening. Barring a sudden metamorphosis in the latter stages of the competition, this was clearly not going to be his World Cup.

The second round concluded with a battle of heavyweights as Spain locked horns with France in Hanover. Spain had never previously beaten France in a competitive international, but their form had been far superior to that of their opponents in the group games and they were favoured to progress. Luis Aragonés's decision to field Raúl from the start enabled the Spain skipper to celebrate his 29th birthday by collecting his 99th cap.

There was a cagey opening to the game, with little activity in either penalty area, until the 27th minute when Spain won a soft penalty after Lilian Thuram caught defender Pablo's heel as he was going away from goal. David Villa drilled in his third goal of the competition, low and via the inside of the post, to put the Spaniards in front. But with France defending in numbers, Spain were unable to capitalise on their lead and by half-time the scores were level at 1-1 thanks to an individual goal from the youngest member of the French side, Franck Ribéry, who broke the Spanish offside trap, took the ball past Iker Casillas and just squeezed it into the net before two backtracking defenders could intervene.

Second Round

Henry histrionics

Now it was anyone's game. Aragonés, whose unbeaten record in two years as Spain's coach was under threat, tried to pep up Spain's attack with three substitutions but France were sturdy and resolute, allowing no way through. Incursions into Spain's penalty area were equally rare. Unfortunately, the game turned on an incident that will forever cast a slur on the reputation of Thierry Henry. The Arsenal striker, normally such a gentleman, fell to the ground clutching his face after a brush in the chest from Carles Puyol. The Italian referee not only awarded a free-kick for France in a dangerous area but also yellow-carded Puyol. Worse was to come for Spain as Zinedine Zidane's ensuing free-kick was flicked on by a Spanish head to the far post where Patrick Vieira, the man of the match, headed it into the net off the flailing leg of Spanish defender Sergio Ramos. Spain could not respond, and in the dying moments of the game Zidane broke free down the left, cut inside and swept the ball low past Casillas to seal France's place in the quarter-finals.

Yet again Spain had flattered to deceive at a major tournament. Of all the eight teams heading for home at this stage, they had the biggest cause for regret. France and Ukraine were the only two non-group winners to go through. The rest of the line-up for the quarter-finals was pretty much as expected, with four European teams – Germany, England, Italy and Portugal - joining South American heavyweights Brazil and Argentina. Now the 2006 World Cup could begin in earnest..

SECOND ROUND

RESULTS

24/6/06, Munich
GERMANY 2 *(Podolski 4, 12)*
SWEDEN 0
Referee – *Simon (BRA)*
GERMANY – *Lehmann; Friedrich, Metzelder, Mertesacker, Lahm; Schneider, Frings (Kehl 85), Ballack, Schweinsteiger (Borowski 72); Podolski (Neuville 74), Klose.*
SWEDEN – *Isaksson; Alexandersson, Mellberg, Lucic, Edman; Linderoth, Jonson (Wilhelmsson 52), Källström (Hansson 39), Ljungberg; Ibrahimovic (Allbäck 72), Larsson.*
Sent off: *Lucic (35)*

24/6/06, Leipzig
ARGENTINA 2 *(Crespo 10, Maxi Rodríguez 98)*
MEXICO 1 *(Márquez 5)*
(aet)
Referee – *Busacca (SUI)*
ARGENTINA – *Abbondanzieri; Scaloni, Ayala, Heinze, Sorín; Cambiasso (Aimar 75), Mascherano, Maxi Rodríguez; Riquelme; Crespo (Tévez 75), Saviola (Messi 84).*
MEXICO – *Sánchez; Márquez, Osorio, Salcido; Castro, Méndez, Guardado (Pineda 66), Pardo (Torrado 38), Morales (Zinha 74); Borgetti, Fonseca.*

25/6/06, Stuttgart
ENGLAND 1 *(Beckham 60)*
ECUADOR 0
Referee – *De Bleeckere (BEL)*
ENGLAND – *Robinson; Hargreaves, Ferdinand, Terry, Cole A.; Carrick; Beckham (Lennon 87); Gerrard (Downing 90), Lampard, Cole J. (Carragher 76); Rooney.*
ECUADOR – *Mora; De la Cruz, Hurtado, Espinoza, Reasco; Valencia, Castillo, Tenorio E. (Lara 69), Méndez; Tenorio C. (Kaviedes 71), Delgado.*

25/6/06, Nuremberg
PORTUGAL 1 *(Maniche 23)*
HOLLAND 0
Referee – *Ivanov (RUS)*
PORTUGAL – *Ricardo; Miguel, Ricardo Carvalho, Fernando Meira, Nuno Valente; Maniche, Costinha; Figo (Tiago 85), Deco, Cristiano Ronaldo (Simão 34); Pauleta (Petit 46).*
Sent off: *Costinha (45), Deco (78)*
HOLLAND – *Van der Sar; Boulahrouz, Ooijer, Mathijsen (Van der Vaart 56), Van Bronckhorst; Van Bommel (Heitinga 67), Cocu (Vennegoor of Hesselink 85), Sneijder; Van Persie, Kuijt, Robben.*
Sent off: *Boulahrouz (63), Van Bronckhorst (90)*

26/6/06, Kaiserslautern
ITALY 1 *(Totti 90p)*
AUSTRALIA 0
Referee – *Medina Cantalejo (ESP)*
ITALY – *Buffon; Zambrotta, Cannavaro, Materazzi, Grosso; Perrotta, Pirlo, Gattuso, Del Piero (Totti 75); Gilardino (Iaquinta 46), Toni (Barzagli 56).*
Sent off: *Materazzi (51)*
AUSTRALIA – *Schwarzer; Moore, Neill, Chipperfield; Sterjovski (Aloisi 81), Culina, Grella, Wilkshire, Bresciano; Cahill; Viduka.*

26/6/06, Cologne
SWITZERLAND 0
UKRAINE 0
(aet; 0-3 on pens)
Referee – *Archundia (MEX)*
SWITZERLAND – *Zuberbühler; Degen P., Djourou (Grichting 33), Müller, Magnin; Barnetta, Vogel, Cabanas, Wicky; Yakin (Streller 64); Frei (Lustrinelli 116).*
UKRAINE – *Shovkovskyi; Gusev, Vashchuk, Gusin, Nesmachnyi; Vorobei (Rebrov 93), Tymoshchuk, Shelayev, Kalynychenko (Rotan 75); Voronin (Milevskyi 110), Shevchenko.*

27/6/06, Dortmund
BRAZIL 3 *(Ronaldo 5, Adriano 45, Zé Roberto 84)*
GHANA 0
Referee – *Michel (SVK)*
BRAZIL – *Dida; Cafú, Lúcio, Juan, Roberto Carlos; Émerson (Gilberto Silva 46), Zé Roberto; Kaká (Ricardinho 83), Ronaldinho; Ronaldo, Adriano (Juninho 61).*
GHANA – *Kingston; Paintsil, Mensah, Shilla, Pappoe; Draman, Appiah, Addo E. (Boateng 60), Muntari; Amoah (Tachie-Mensah 69), Gyan.*
Sent off: *Gyan (81)*

27/6/06, Hanover
SPAIN 1 *(David Villa 28p)*
FRANCE 3 *(Ribéry 41, Vieira 83, Zidane 90)*
Referee – *Rosetti (ITA)*
SPAIN – *Casillas; Sergio Ramos, Pablo, Puyol, Pernía; Fábregas, Xabi Alonso, Xavi (Senna 72); Raúl (Luis García 54); David Villa (Joaquín 54), Fernando Torres.*
FRANCE – *Barthez; Sagnol, Thuram, Gallas, Abidal; Ribéry, Vieira, Makelele, Malouda (Govou 74); Zidane, Henry (Wiltord 88).*

World Cup 2006

Quarter-Finals:
South American challenge bites the dust

Germany against Argentina was the first and most eagerly awaited of the quarter-final ties. The hosts and the new tournament favourites, they were the two teams that had done the most to bring the tournament to life in the early stages of the competition. The contention of some was that this was a final before the final. It certainly had an appropriate venue – the Olympiastadion in Berlin.

With so much mutual respect and such a huge prize to play for, it was no great surprise that the game began in a slow, cautious fashion with a lot of square, unadventurous passes. It didn't make for much of a spectacle. The first half brought just one notable attempt on goal – a header from Michael Ballack that he should have put into the net but planted agonisingly wide of the post.

The game was crying out for a goal, and four minutes after the interval it got one. A corner swung in from the right by Argentine creator-in-chief Juan Román Riquelme was met with a brave, powerful and accurate header from centre-back Roberto Ayala that flew past the helpless Jens Lehmann on the line. For the first time in the competition Germany were behind. Now they had to take risks. The game, inevitably, began to open up, but Argentina's defence looked solid enough even after goalkeeper Roberto Abbondanzieri was forced to leave the field with an injury of his own making as he clattered into Miroslav Klose after misjudging a corner. It was only a block from the outstanding Ayala that prevented a Ballack shot from causing further embarrassment to the keeper.

Cautious Pekerman

The enforced substitution of Abbondanzieri was swiftly followed by the unenforced, ultra-defensive replacement of Riquelme by Estebán Cambiasso. Argentina coach José Pekerman was clearly intent on holding on to what he had, but it was a risk, and one he compounded a few minutes later when he took off Hernán Crespo for Julio Cruz. Not only had Pekerman now denied the team the services of their playmaker and most reliable goalscorer, but it meant he could no longer bring on teenage supersub Lionel Messi. Argentina's eggs were all in one basket: they could not afford for Germany to score and take the match into extra-time.

But Germany, as every football follower is well aware, never give up, and, sure enough, with just ten minutes of normal time remaining, they grabbed an equaliser. Ballack floated in a cross from the left, Tim Borowski flicked it on and Miroslav Klose got in front of Juan Pablo Sorín to

Argentina coach José Pekerman – a bad day at the office in Berlin

Quarter-Finals

place a superb header past replacement keeper Leo Franco. It was the Werder Bremen striker's tenth goal in World Cup finals, but his first outside the group phase. Klose, too, was soon withdrawn from the fray, and as the match entered extra-time, both coaches had used up all their substitutes. Furthermore, as the extra period progressed, it was obvious that Ballack was struggling for fitness. The additional 30 minutes produced little goalmouth activity, so the contest had to be decided on penalties.

Both teams had a perfect record in World Cup shoot-outs (three wins apiece), but it was Germany who always looked likely to triumph once Ayala had allowed Jens Lehmann to save his weak sidefoot effort. With Germany 2-1 up at that stage thanks to successful strikes from Oliver Neuville and Ballack (as against one from Cruz), they needed only to keep scoring, which they did in confident manner through Lukas Podolski and Borowski. Their fifth taker was not needed because although Maxi Rodríguez kept Argentina's hopes alive by successfully converting his team's third kick, Cambiasso, like Ayala, was denied by a fine Lehmann save and that was that. The Germans, to cacophonous acclaim from the stands, were through to the semi-finals.

Post-match brawl

Argentina's World Cup was over, but some of their players could not live with the reality, and there was an almighty scuffle between the two sets of players and officials on the pitch as the South Americans completely lost their heads. For such a fine team, it was a wholly undignified way for them to bow out. Individual fines and suspensions would later follow – four games for Leandro Cufré, two for Maxi Rodríguez - but it was the damage done to Argentina's reputation that would hurt them the most. Although they had won many friends during the competition for the fluent style of their play, nobody likes bad losers.

Germany's semi-final opponents were to be decided later in the evening as Italy took on Ukraine in Hamburg – the venue for the Azzurri's group win over another Eastern European side, the Czech Republic. Both teams made changes in personnel, with a recall for Italy's second-round matchwinner Francesco Totti and a first international start for highly-rated Ukrainian young gun Artem Milevskyi, given his chance up front alongside Andriy Shevchenko in place of the injured Andriy Voronin.

The two sides had drawn 0-0 in a friendly on Swiss soil on the eve of the finals, but fortunately a repeat scoreline was made impossible after just six minutes when Italy full-back Gianluca Zambrotta galloped forward and let fly with a low left-foot shot that goalkeeper Olexandr Shovkovskyi could only help into the net. The goal was to be the only highlight of a mediocre first half. Italy were content to sit on their lead and defend in numbers, denying the Ukrainians the opportunity to feed their forwards.

Fortunately, Oleh Blokhin's team showed a bit more get-up-and-go after the interval, and for a ten-minute spell the men in yellow attacked Gianluigi Buffon's goal with real purpose. A number of chances were created, and in the 58th minute a great save by Buffon from Oleh Gusev was swiftly followed by a clearance off the line from Zambrotta. Ukraine were cursing their luck, but it got a whole lot worse within a few seconds when the action switched to the other end and Italy, with what was their first real chance since the goal, made it 2-0 with a header from Luca Toni that should have been discounted for a blatant offside.

Toni seals it

The game had turned within a minute but Ukraine did not give up, Andriy Gusin heading against the crossbar in his team's next attack. The gods, however, were smiling on the Azzurri, and on 69 minutes their semi-final place was sealed when Toni tapped in his second goal after fine work on the left from Zambrotta. It was tough on Ukraine, but by the final whistle the 3-0 scoreline brooked no argument. Although they had been forced to survive a number of scares, Italy had largely controlled the match. They

Jens Lehmann makes the first of his two penalty saves against Argentina

Quarter-Finals

also boasted yet another clean sheet, their fourth in five games - a tribute to the remarkably consistent defensive work of Buffon, Zambrotta, Gennaro Gattuso and, especially, the flawless Azzurri skipper Fabio Cannavaro.

With Germany and Italy safely through, it was England's turn to become the third European heavyweight to reach the semi-finals. Standing between them and that prize were Portugal, led by Luiz Felipe Scolari, the man who had masterminded the downfall of Sven Göran Eriksson's team in the quarter-finals of both the 2002 World Cup (when he coached Brazil) and Euro 2004 and who had now totted up a personal record of 11 successive World Cup finals victories. Could it be third time lucky for the Swede? Portugal's loss of the suspended Deco and Costinha was a factor that appeared to aid England's chances, as did the return from injury of experienced right-back Gary Neville, an absentee since the opening game against Paraguay.

England owed their fans a much improved performance, and, as ever, there were legions of them in attendance, their massive vocal and visual support almost turning the Arena AufSchalke into a home ground for the Three Lions. It was up to Eriksson and his much-trumpeted team to show their true colours, but with Wayne Rooney again selected up front on his own – a position that hardly maximised the natural strengths of the 20-year-old – they again struggled to create any clear-cut chances in an even, largely uneventful first half.

Portugal looked half the team without the craft of Deco, but defensively they were solid. England needed something different to break them down, and they got it when speedy teenage winger Aaron Lennon was introduced for the injured – and hitherto invisible – David Beckham early in the second half. His pace and trickery set up an excellent chance which Joe Cole wastefully put over the bar.

Rooney sees red

But just when it seemed that England were getting on top, disaster struck. Rooney, eagerly battling for possession with a couple of opponents on the halfway line, was pulled up by the Argentine referee, Horacio Elizondo, as Ricardo Carvalho, the Portuguese centre-back, lay writhing on the ground. It was not immediately obvious what had happened, but Rooney's Manchester United colleague Cristiano Ronaldo charged up to the scene of the incident with words of 'advice' for the referee. Rooney warded him off with a playful shove. Seconds later Elizondo pulled Rooney aside and, to the youngster's obvious shock and horror,

Wayne Rooney can't believe his eyes as referee Horacio Elizondo brandishes the red card

thrust out his red card. Video replays showed that Rooney had planted his foot in Ricardo Carvalho's groin during their tangle for the ball, but it did not appear to be a deliberate gesture, just the action of a player trying – unlike many of his peers – to stay on his feet and retain his balance. Whether the punishment was for the alleged stamp or the push – some comments from the referee before he saw the TV replay would have been interesting - the fact was that Rooney was off the field and England, as in 1998 against Argentina when Beckham had been dismissed, were forced to play the rest of the game with ten men.

The whole scenario now changed. Peter Crouch was sent on to lead the line, with Joe Cole sacrificed. Inevitably Portugal began to have more of the play, but with the totally ineffectual Pauleta withdrawn and replaced by a winger, Simão, there was no focal point to their attack. Luís Figo tested the reflexes of Paul Robinson with a fine chip but, that moment apart, England's defence stood steadfast and resolute. In fact, the best chance of all fell to Lennon, who failed to connect properly with his left foot after Ricardo had made a meal of saving a Frank Lampard free-kick.

And so the match moved into extra-time. It was tense and nerve-racking but pitifully short of

Quarter-Finals

quality football. The best players on the field were England's stout defenders and their super-fit German-based holding midfielder Owen Hargreaves. There was a brief scare when Hélder Postiga, the man belatedly introduced by Scolari to play centre-forward, headed the ball into Robinson's net, but England fans breathed again as the linesman raised his flag for offside. One final chance in the last embers of extra-time was wasted as Maniche lifted the ball over the net. Immediately afterwards the final whistle sounded. England had done extremely well to survive for almost an hour, but now came the ultimate test of their nerve and one which they had failed so many times previously in big tournaments, most recently against Portugal at Euro 2004. It was time for penalties.

Simão, decisively, put Portugal ahead with the first kick. England's first taker, surprisingly, was Lampard – a man whose confidence at putting the ball in the net had been eroded by a succession of missed chances throughout the tournament and who walked to the spot as if to the gallows. Predictably, he missed, allowing Ricardo to save easily to his left. But then Portugal's Hugo Viana hit the post, and after Hargreaves had brought England level at 1-1, Petit also failed to find the target with his effort, driving his shot wide via the outside of the post.

Paying the penalty

Now was England's time to strike. Up stepped Steven Gerrard. He had to score. The whole of England implored him. But the Liverpool captain, visibly gripped by nerves, didn't listen. He put his shot in the same place as Lampard and again Ricardo guessed right, pushing the ball to safety. Hélder Postiga then made it 2-1 to Portugal. Jamie Carragher, who had been brought on for Lennon at the end of extra-time presumably for this task alone, looked focused enough as he strode forward for his spot-kick. But he was too focused and drove his shot into the net before the referee's whistle. Forced to go again, his second effort was inevitably more hesitant, and this time he put it too close to Ricardo, who tipped the ball up against the crossbar. Criminally, England had missed three kicks out of four. They now watched in dread as the pantomime villain himself, Cristiano Ronaldo, stepped forward to deliver the coup de grâce and end England's World Cup dream. The whistles were deafening, the pressure intense, but the young winger struck his shot firm and true, giving Robinson no chance. Portugal's World Cup would

Glum faces and bowed heads – it's another penalty shoot-out failure for England

Quarter-Finals

go on. England's had ended. For the fifth time at a major tournament and the third in four World Cups they had been eliminated on penalties. They had nobody to blame but themselves.

After three quarter-finals of drama and tension but little memorable football, the tournament was crying out for some genuine star quality, for an individual or a team to shed the nerves and put on a proper show. Surely it was time for Brazil and their so-called Magic Quartet to come out of their shell and deliver against France.

Return of Zidane

But in Frankfurt, in a repeat of the 1998 final, it was the man who had conquered Brazil in Paris eight years earlier, Zinedine Zidane, who would roll back the years with a virtuoso performance as memorable as any in his brilliant heyday. The veteran French skipper not only played Ronaldinho off the park but he must have made every other player on the pitch feel terribly inadequate as he treated the crowd and millions of televiewers worldwide to the full repertoire of his skills.

Brazil, frankly, made it easy for him. Carlos Alberto Parreira's side were woeful, and they got what was coming to them after 57 minutes when Zidane's beautifully flighted free-kick from the left was volleyed past Dida at the far post by an unmarked Thierry Henry. France might have extended their lead, twice, through Franck Ribéry, shortly afterwards, but their defence was so solid that it didn't really matter. It was only in the closing minutes of the game, when it suddenly seemed to dawn on Brazil that they were losing grip of their trophy, that they finally began to apply some sustained pressure. But the will and hunger just wasn't there – as characterised by a very inviting 89th-minute free-kick that Ronaldinho casually wafted over the bar.

Brazil were out with a whimper. France, surprisingly but gloriously, had rediscovered the genius of Zinedine Zidane just in time. They were in the semi-finals, completing an all-European quartet for the first time since 1982. Three of the big pre-tournament favourites – Argentina, England and Brazil – were gone. Now it was anybody's Cup…

Zinedine Zidane bamboozles Brazil

QUARTER-FINALS

RESULTS

30/6/06, Berlin
GERMANY 1 *(Klose 80)*
ARGENTINA 1 *(Ayala 49)*
(aet; 4-2 on pens)
Referee – Michel (SVK)
GERMANY – Lehmann; Friedrich, Mertesacker, Metzelder, Lahm; Schneider (Odonkor 62), Frings, Ballack, Schweinsteiger (Borowski 74); Klose (Neuville 85), Podolski.
ARGENTINA – Abbondanzieri (Leo Franco 71); Coloccini, Ayala, Heinze, Sorín ; Maxi Rodríguez, Mascherano, Lucho González; Riquelme (Cambiasso 72); Crespo (Cruz 78), Tévez.

30/6/06, Hamburg
ITALY 3 *(Zambrotta 6, Toni 59, 69)*
UKRAINE 0
Referee – De Bleeckere (BEL)
ITALY – Buffon; Zambrotta, Cannavaro, Barzagli, Grosso; Camoranesi (Oddo 68), Gattuso (Zaccardo 76), Pirlo (Barone 68), Perrotta; Totti; Toni.
UKRAINE – Shovkovskyi; Sviderskyi (Vorobei 20), Rusol (Vashchuk 45), Gusin, Nesmachnyi; Gusev, Tymoshchuk, Shelayev, Kalynynchenko; Milevskyi (Belik 72), Shevchenko.

1/7/06, Gelsenkirchen
ENGLAND 0
PORTUGAL 0
(aet; 1-3 on pens)
Referee – Elizondo (ARG)
ENGLAND – Robinson; Neville, Terry, Ferdinand, Cole A.; Hargrevaes; Beckham (Lennon 51; Carragher 118), Gerrard, Lampard, Cole J. (Crouch 65); Rooney.
Sent off: Rooney (62)
PORTUGAL – Ricardo; Miguel, Fernando Meira, Ricardo Carvalho, Nuno Valente; Maniche, Petit; Figo (Hélder Postiga 86), Tiago (Hugo Viana 74), Cristiano Ronaldo; Pauleta (Simão 63).

1/7/06, Frankfurt
BRAZIL 0
FRANCE 1 *(Henry 57)*
Referee – Medina Cantalejo (ESP)
BRAZIL – Dida; Cafú (Cicinho 76), Lúcio, Juan, Roberto Carlos; Gilberto Silva, Juninho (Adriano 63), Zé Roberto, Kaká (Robinho 79); Ronaldinho; Ronaldo.
FRANCE – Barthez; Sagnol, Thuram, Gallas, Abidal; Vieira, Makelele; Ribéry (Govou 76), Zidane, Malouda (Wiltord 81); Henry (Saha 85).

World Cup 2006

Semi-Finals:
Blue is the colour

The portents for the first semi-final, between Germany and Italy in Dortmund, were intriguing. While Italy had never previously lost to Germany in a major tournament, the Germans were unbeaten in 14 matches at the Westfalenstadion. Their latest victory at the venue had come in the group phase when they overcame Poland 1-0 with a stoppage-time winner. Perhaps of even greater relevance was Italy's 4-1 victory over Jürgen Klinsmann's team in Florence only a few months earlier – a result that had led to questions being raised in the German parliament about Klinsmann's suitability to lead the team at the World Cup.

Now, after steering the team to four successive victories and a penalty shoot-out win over Argentina, Klinsmann was being widely festooned with praise by his fellow countrymen. Germany were just one match away from appearing in their eighth World Cup final. The last time they had been eliminated from the competition at the semi-final stage was in 1970...by Italy. Since then they had won five in a row.

The Italians, now unbeaten in 23 matches, restored Marco Materazzi to their miserly defence, replacing Andrea Barzagli, the other deputy for the injured Alessandro Nesta. Otherwise they were unchanged from the team that had overcome Ukraine 3-0. Germany were without midfield do-it-all Torsten Frings, suspended retrospectively by FIFA for his part in the post-match fracas with Argentina. Into his place came local lad Sebastian Kehl, while Klinsmann made another change in his midfield, replacing the out-of-form Bastian Schweinsteiger with Tim Borowski.

Superior Italy

Right from the start it was clear that the Italians meant business. There was a determination and a fluency to their play that suggested Germany would have to surpass everything they had done before if they were to fulfil their World Cup dream. For the first 45 minutes Marcello Lippi's team played the superior football, fashioning three or four half-chances that all came to nought only through resilient German defending. The best opportunity of the first period came at the other end, where Bernd Schneider found space on the right-hand side of the penalty area but drove over after a poor first touch. With just one goal in 70 internationals, perhaps it was no surprise that he missed the target.

Although chances were at a premium, the match was attractive and entertaining, largely thanks to the excellence of the Mexican referee, Benito Archundía, who authoritatively ignored any efforts to feign injury and allowed the game to flow freely with few unnecessary stoppages. A goal at either end would have improved things, but there was much to admire in the class of both defences. Gianluigi Buffon was called into action when Lukas Podolski spun cleverly in the area and fired in a shot, but otherwise the two goalkeepers were brilliantly protected. The best player on the field, yet again, was Azzurri skipper Fabio Cannavaro, so it was something of a double paradox when, after 82 minutes, the referee spoiled his flawless evening by gifting the Germans a free-kick right on the edge of the area for a non-existent foul by Cannavaro on Podolski (which, if it had been one, actually took place inside the area). Fortunately, justice was done when Michael Ballack, who was having a poor game, fired the free-kick harmlessly over the bar.

Riveting stuff

If normal time was absorbing rather than exciting, the additional 30 minutes were to be absolutely riveting. They got off to an explosive start when Italy struck the woodwork twice in as many minutes, substitute Alberto Gilardino outmanoeuvring Ballack inside the area before clipping the inside the post and Gianluca Zambrotta hammering a snapshot from distance against the top of the crossbar.

Semi-Finals

Germany's two big chances in the extra period both fell to Podolski. He should have scored with a header that he sent hopelessly wide, but he was denied in his next attempt by a fine save from Buffon. Italy, evidently fearing penalties, kept going forward. With strikers Vincenzo Iaquinta and Alessandro Del Piero having been added in extra-time, coach Lippi's intention was clear. As the final whistle drew ever nearer, the level of tension and excitement rose. Twice Del Piero had chances, then, with two minutes remaining the outstanding Andrea Pirlo unleashed a stunning left-foot shot that Lehmann acrobatically pushed for a corner. Seconds later, with Germany ambushed in front of their own goal, Pirlo again collected the ball just outside the area. Another shot was anticipated, but the wily Milan midfielder fooled everyone by slotting a delicious pass into the area. What happened next will remain etched in the minds of all Italian football followers forever more. Full-back Fabio Grosso swung his left foot at the ball and made perfect contact, curling it exquisitely into the net, beyond Lehmann's grasp, at the far post.

It was a stunning strike. While Grosso reeled away in ecstasy, his face contorted à la Marco Tardelli in the 1982 final (against the same opposition), the German crowd fell silent, dumbfounded by what had just taken place. There were only seconds left in which to rescue the World Cup dream. Time enough for Ballack to get in a shot - but to the collective grief of a nation, the ball was ballooned way off target. Then another German attack was broken up by the majestic Cannavaro. The ball was swiftly despatched downfield to Gilardino. With only a few seconds left, everyone expected him make a bee-line for the corner flag. Instead, thrillingly, he held the ball up and laid it to his left for the onrushing Del Piero, who positioned his body perfectly to lift the ball beautifully into the top corner of Lehmann's net. Two-nil to Italy. Game over.

An excellent match, brilliantly refereed, had produced a fitting, extraordinary climax. For once Italy had thrown caution to the wind, and they had been rewarded. They had dared and won. Their place in the final was amply merited. As for Germany, there were many tears. Their hopes had been crushed right at the death, but they had no reason to reproach themselves. A team of limited ability but great heart, they had exceeded expectations and done themselves proud. A lack of fitness in extra-time might have been their downfall, but they could have no complaints about the outcome. They had been beaten by the better side.

Twenty-four hours later France, the conquerors of Brazil, met Portugal - and their Brazilian coach Luiz Felipe Scolari - in Munich. Although the two

Full-back Fabio Grosso finally breaks the deadlock against Germany with a sumptuous strike

Semi-Finals

France coach Raymond Domenech mocks the grounded Cristiano Ronaldo

countries had never met in World Cup combat, they had faced each other twice in European Championship semi-finals, in 1984 and 2000, with the French prevailing on both occasions before going on to win the trophy.

Yellow peril

Les Bleus, who had now adopted all white as their lucky strip after their victories over Spain and Brazil, were also unchanged in personnel. The main concern in the French camp centred around the yellow cards against the names of key performers Patrick Vieira and Zinedine Zidane. Portugal, too, had several players with a yellow to their name but they did have both Deco and Costinha back from suspension. Also in their line-up was Cristiano Ronaldo, who was to discover that his unsporting behaviour against England had not gone unnoticed by the World Cup public at large when, at every touch, he was roundly booed by the Allianz-Arena crowd.

In truth, the youngster never let the abuse affect him and he was arguably the most eye-catching player on the field as Portugal threatened to take control early in the first half. Before long, though, the young colt would be upstaged by France's two thoroughbreds, Thierry Henry and Zidane. Raymond Domenech's team had done very little in the first half-hour, but when Henry's leg was caught by Ricardo Carvalho in the penalty area, the Uruguayan referee pointed to the spot. Goalkeeper Ricardo had demonstrated his spot-kick heroics against England, but although he again correctly anticipated the direction of the shot, Zidane's right-foot strike was too well placed in the corner for him to get a full hand on it.

One-nil up at half-time, France went for the killer second goal early in the second period but shots from Henry and Franck Ribéry were both repelled by Ricardo. Portugal tried to respond, but the neat approach work they had shown in the early stages of the game increasingly gave way to fatigue and frustration – and then, in consequence, diving and cheating - as they struggled to breach the fortress-like French rearguard. Ronaldo found a way through to test Fabien Barthez with a stunning free-kick. The veteran keeper reacted with a thoroughly unconvincing scoop-like save, but his blushes were spared when Luís Figo could only head the rebound on to the roof of the net.

From that moment on France, looking worn and weary, retreated ever deeper into defence. It was not the best of spectacles, but with Portugal so lame and clueless in attack – they had not scored for over four and a half hours – the policy paid off.

The final whistle brought understandable jubilation from the French players and fans – as well as some undignified moaning at the officials from Scolari – but for the neutrals it was another big game that had failed to deliver. The tournament was sagging. If the 2006 World Cup was to be remembered with any real fondness, it desperately needed a great final.

SEMI-FINALS

RESULTS

4/7/06, Dortmund
GERMANY 0
ITALY 2 *(Grosso 119, Del Piero 120)*
(aet)
GERMANY – Lehmann; Friedrich, Mertesacker, Metzelder, Lahm; Schneider (Odonkor 82), Ballack, Kehl, Borowski (Schweinsteiger 71); Klose (Neuville 111), Podolski.
ITALY – Buffon; Zambrotta, Cannavaro, Materazzi, Grosso; Camoranesi (Iaquinta 91), Pirlo, Gattuso, Perrotta (Del Piero 103); Totti; Toni (Gilardino 73).

5/7/06, Munich
PORTUGAL 0
FRANCE 1 *(Zidane 33p)*
Referee – Larrionda (URU)
PORTUGAL – Ricardo; Miguel (Paulo Ferreira 62), Fernando Meira, Ricardo Carvalho, Nuno Valente; Costinha (Hélder Postiga 74), Maniche; Figo, Deco, Cristiano Ronaldo; Pauleta (Simão 67).
France – Barthez; Sagnol, Thuram, Gallas, Abidal; Makelele, Vieira; Ribéry (Govou 71), Zidane, Malouda (Wiltord 67); Henry (Saha 83).

World Cup 2006

Third Place Play-Off:
Hosts sign off with a bang

Generally speaking the Third Place Play-off is a waste of time – an irrelevant contest between two teams who, having suffered the trauma of losing a semi-final, would rather be elsewhere. But when the host nation is involved, the fixture does serve a useful function, enabling the team to bid an emotional farewell to their supporters and – if things go to plan – provide an appropriate send-off with a victory.

South Korea were unable to manage that four years earlier when they lost to Turkey, but this time, in front of a raucous sell-out crowd in Stuttgart, Jürgen Klinsmann's Germany duly did the business.

For most of the first half Portugal looked as if they might spoil the party. With Deco pulling the strings in central midfield and Cristiano Ronaldo (despite the howls of derision that continued to greet his every touch) running at the German defence, the prospects looked bright for Luiz Felipe Scolari's side. Or at least they would have done had Pauleta's major-tournament malaise in front of goal not continued to haunt him. He should have scored after 15 minutes but Oliver Kahn, given his opportunity at last (allegedly at rival Jens Lehmann's behest), saved diligently. Kahn, wearing the captain's armband in Michael Ballack's injury-induced absence, would go on to perform with distinction all evening in what was believed to be his 86th and final international appearance.

Show-stealer Schweinsteiger

Apart from an optimistic penalty appeal and one well struck Lukas Podolski free-kick, the Germans did little in the first 45 minutes. But the match came alive early in the second period when Bastian Schweinsteiger, one of Germany's more disappointing performers during the tournament, cut inside from the left and unleashed a powerful swerving shot that deceived the flailing Ricardo to put the hosts 1-0 up. The blond Bayern Munich midfielder was to steal the show from then on in. A few minutes later he drove in a free-kick, which Portuguese midfielder Petit deflected into the net with his shin like a cricketer edging a catch to slip. Schweinsteiger couldn't possibly claim that goal – his shot was going well wide – but he duly got his second 12 minutes from time with what was almost a replica of his first, only better placed, in the corner, giving Ricardo absolutely no chance.

The German party was in full swing now, but a dampener was put on proceedings when, two minutes from time, substitute Nuno Gomes headed in arguably the cross of the tournament from Luís Figo to reduce the deficit to 3-1. The Portugal skipper was a substitute himself, having been mysteriously 'dropped' by Scolari for what was definitely his farewell appearance on the international stage. Still, that glorious assist was a fine way in which to bow out, even if the goal, Portugal's first in over six hours of football, denied Kahn a worthy clean sheet.

The honours, and the bronze medals, went to Germany, and there could be no argument that Klinsmann and his players deserved something tangible out of a tournament to which they – and the German public – had given so much.

THIRD PLACE PLAY-OFF

RESULT

8/7/06, Stuttgart

GERMANY 3 *(Schweinsteiger 56, 78, Petit 60og)*
PORTUGAL 1 *(Nuno Gomes 88)*
Referee – *Kamikawa (JPN)*

GERMANY – Kahn; Lahm, Nowotny, Metzelder, Jansen; Schneider, Frings, Kehl, Schweinsteiger (Hitzlsperger 79); Klose (Neuville 64), Podolski (Hanke 71).

PORTUGAL – Ricardo; Paulo Ferreira, Ricardo Costa, Fernando Meira, Nuno Valente (Nuno Gomes 70); Costinha (Petit 46), Maniche; Cristiano Ronaldo, Deco, Simão; Pauleta (Gigo 77).

World Cup 2006

Final:
Italy triumph as Zidane bows out in disgrace

The first all-European World Cup final since 1982 – and the first without Brazil since 1990 – took place on the evening of Sunday, July 9 in the imposing, majestic Olympiastadion in Berlin.

Neither Italy nor France, the two finalists, had played at the venue in the earlier rounds. Largely on the strength of their superior performance in the semi-final Italy were quoted as slight favourites to win, but recent history favoured the French, who had knocked their neighbours out of the 1998 World Cup on penalties and dramatically come from behind to defeat them with a 'golden goal' in the final of Euro 2000.

The match had an extra special meaning for the two captains, Fabio Cannavaro of Italy and Zinedine Zidane of France, by common consent the tournament's two outstanding individual performers. While Cannavaro was winning his 100th cap for Italy, Zidane was playing the final game of his entire career.

The two coaches, who had each been in charge for just two years, both had long-running records to preserve. Marcello Lippi was on a 24-match unbeaten run, whereas Raymond Domenech had yet to lose a competitive game. With such impressive statistics, it was perhaps surprising that few people had tipped either team to reach the final at the start of the tournament.

But the fancied front-runners had all fallen by the wayside, and the stage was now set for the Azzurri and Les Bleus. The colour clash meant that Italy came out in all blue, with France, quite contentedly, wearing the all-white kit that had served them so well in each of the three knockout rounds.

Dramatic start

The match got off to a scrappy but dramatic start. Thierry Henry, the last realistic contender to deprive Germany's five-goal Miroslav Klose of the Golden Shoe, looked as if his evening might be over after less than a minute's play when he ran into Cannavaro and suffered what appeared to be a mild case of concussion. The Arsenal striker looked decidedly groggy for a few minutes, but the recovery appeared complete when, with his next meaningful touch of the ball, he played a pass through to Florent Malouda in the inside-left channel. Two Italian defenders converged on the French left-winger as he entered the penalty area. Anticipating a collision, he began to fall to ground, and as he did so Marco Materazzi made the slightest of contact with him. It was clear from video replays that the big Italian centre-back was trying to get the offending leg out of the way, but Argentine referee Horacio Elizondo did not have that luxury. He saw contact and pointed to the spot. Malouda's dive,

Thierry Henry is led off the field after an early blow to the head

Final

simulation, professionalism – call it what you will – had, like so many before him in the 2006 World Cup, duped the referee into awarding him a foul.

It was a bad decision but France were not complaining. Zidane, who had scored the winner in the semi-final against Portugal from the penalty spot, stepped forward to try to become the first opponent to score past Gianluigi Buffon in seven matches. It was a moment of high tension, yet Zidane went for an audacious 'falling leaf' chip – as patented by the Czech, Antonin Panenka, in a European Championship final 30 years earlier. With Buffon fooled into moving to his right, the ball floated high into the centre of the goal. But Zidane hadn't made a perfect connection and it struck the underside of the crossbar, bounced down and then back into play. Luckily for the French skipper, it landed just over the goal-line – by half a yard at most. More luckily still, the officials saw that it did and signalled a goal.

Materazzi heads home

The hope among neutrals was that such a contentious goal would not ultimately decide the match. Fortunately a dozen minutes later Italy struck back to level the scores. Ironically it was Materazzi, the man who had conceded the penalty, who got the goal, outleaping his marker Patrick Vieira to head home Andrea Pirlo's exquisitely flighted right-wing corner.

The two early goals promised much, and Italy, in particular, seemed keen to make the match an entertaining one. With their full-backs, Gianluca Zambrotta and Fabio Grosso, continually unleashed to assist in attack, the Azzurri confidently surged forward in search of victory. Set-pieces were a particular concern for the French defence. Materazzi powered in another header, only to be penalised for a push, then Luca Toni connected with another Pirlo corner and sent the ball thudding against the top of the crossbar. The one disappointment in the Italy ranks was Francesco Totti, who couldn't get into the game. Neither, despite his early goal, could Zidane.

The start of the second half brought a renewed assault on the Italian goal from France that appeared to catch Lippi and his players by surprise. Henry and Malouda, in particular, began to worry the Azzurri with their direct running, and there might have been a second penalty when Malouda went tumbling again under a less than convincing challenge from Zambrotta.
Eventually, with Vieira having been forced out of the action with a hamstring strain, the wave of French

The World Cup Final ball feels the full force of Marco Materazzi's forehead as Italy equalise

attacks subsided. Italy almost seized the moment in spectacular fashion when Toni brilliantly headed in a Pirlo free-kick, but correctly, if only marginally, the linesman disallowed the goal for offside.

There was still another half-hour of normal time remaining, but as fear and fatigue took over – Zidane even looked as if he might have to depart with a shoulder injury after a collision with the ever-rugged Cannavaro – neither team was willing to risk pushing extra men forward and go all out for the winner.

And so, for the fifth time in history, the World Cup final went into extra-time. The pace had slowed almost to walking pace, but France, the better team in the second half, continued to hold sway. They created a couple of chances, too, with Franck Ribéry stabbing a shot fractionally wide after a neat one-two with Malouda, and Zidane finding rare space in the Italian penalty area to send in a powerful header, from Willy Sagnol's cross, that Buffon athletically tipped over the bar.

Zidane's moment of madness

Zidane was so close to being the hero then, but a few minutes later his world came crashing down on him in the most extraordinary, inexplicable fashion. The French captain had just had a brief verbal altercation off the ball with Materazzi when, without any obvious provocation, he turned round and launched himself at the Italian defender, headbutting him

Final

violently in the upper torso. A TV camera recorded the incident in graphic detail. There was absolutely no doubt. Zidane, in the final match of his glorious career, had lost control completely and had to be sent off. Referee Elizondo did not see the incident, but eventually, after a minute or so of deliberation during which presumably one of the touchline officials caught a glimpse of the damning televisual evidence (although FIFA later denied this), the message got through to the man in the middle as to what had taken place and he promptly reached for his pocket and – as he had done to Wayne Rooney in the England-Portugal quarter-final – showed Zidane the red card.

The rest of extra-time was played out in an atmosphere of stunned disbelief. The French fans, who had clearly not witnessed the incident, jeered intensely whenever the Italians had possession. But the advantage of having one extra man was nullified by the evident exhaustion of the players in the blue shirts. Clearly, there would be no late drive to avoid penalties as there had been a few days earlier against Germany in Dortmund. As for France, deprived so ignominiously of their captain, they looked equally content to take football's greatest showpiece to penalties.

From every perspective, it was a sad and sorry end to the tournament, and there was a widespread feeling of deflation at Elizondo's final whistle. Not only because of how Zidane's career had ended, but also because, for the second time in history, the World Cup winners would have to be determined by a penalty shoot-out.

Italy had lost the previous final shoot-out, against Brazil, in 1994, and also failed from the spot in the World Cups of 1990 and 1998 (the latter to France). It was time for redemption.

Pirlo stepped up first and smashed his shot nervelessly into the roof of the net. Sylvain Wiltord, an extra-time substitute for Henry, replied with an equally confident effort that gave Buffon no chance. Next up was Materazzi, the central figure in all of the evening's dramatic turns, and he drove low and hard to make it 2-1. David Trezeguet, the man whose 'golden goal' had sunk Italy in the Euro 2000 final, strode forward next for France. He put his foot through the ball but watched in horror as it struck the underside of the crossbar and bounced down – unlike Zidane's effort in normal play - the wrong side of the goalline.

Now it was advantage Italy. Could they hold their nerve? It was desperately tense. Another substitute, Daniele De Rossi, back from his four-match ban, fired home. 3-1. Then Eric Abidal sent Buffon the wrong way to make it 3-2. Alessandro Del Piero maintained Italy's advantage with a sumptuous strike, and suddenly Sagnol had to score to keep the contest alive. He did, with absolute conviction. All eyes now turned to the centre circle to see who would take Italy's fifth penalty. If this one went in, the World Cup would be theirs. It was Fabio Grosso, the left-back who had turned the semi-final against Germany.

Glorious Grosso

Under the most intense pressure imaginable Grosso strode forward and without hesitation smashed a glorious left-footer high into the top corner way beyond Barthez's reach. Five penalties out of five, each more emphatic than the other. Italy had won. They were world champions for the fourth time.

After a few unforgettable minutes cavorting across the pitch with unbridled glee, the Italian players went up to collect their gold medals and Fabio Cannavaro, the man of the tournament, the Azzurri

A stern-faced Zinedine Zidane surveys his victim after his shameful final act as a professional footballer

Group A

Fabio Cannavaro lives the ultimate football dream – Italy are the new world champions

skipper, eventually pushed through the throng, raised himself on to the podium and, with flashbulbs, flares and tickertape going off all around him, lifted the most treasured trophy in sport high into the Berlin sky.

Italy had not played particularly well in the final – indeed, there was a strong case for arguing that France were the better team on the day – but over the whole tournament they were worthy winners. Collectively they were extremely strong and tough to beat, and in Buffon, Pirlo, Zambrotta, Grosso, Gennaro Gattuso and the peerless Cannavaro they possessed six individuals whose consistency of performance merited inclusion in every observer's Team of the Tournament.

Italy were a good team but not a great one. But then there were no great teams at the 2006 World Cup. Superbly coached by Marcello Lippi, they were the best of a moderate bunch and, as such, they deserved their title. Argentina, Brazil, England, Germany and France had not delivered when it really mattered. Italy had.

That is why for the next four years they can proudly proclaim themselves as the Champions of the World.

FINAL

RESULT

9/7/06, Berlin
ITALY 1 *(Materazzi 19)*
FRANCE 1 *(Zidane 7p)*
(aet; 5-3 on pens)
Referee – *Elizondo (ARG)*
ITALY – *Buffon; Zambrotta, Cannavaro, Materazzi, Grosso; Camoranesi (Del Piero 86), Gattuso, Pirlo, Perrotta (De Rossi 61); Totti (Iaquinta 61); Toni.*
FRANCE – *Barthez; Sagnol, Thuram, Gallas, Abidal; Makelele, Vieira (Diarra 56); Ribéry (Trezeguet 100), Zidane, Malouda; Henry (Wiltord 107).*
Sent off: *Zidane (109)*

TOP GOALSCORERS

5	Miroslav KLOSE (Germany)
3	Thierry HENRY (France)
	Zinedine ZIDANE (France)
	Lukas PODOLSKI (Germany)
	Hernán CRESPO (Argentina)
	MAXI RODRÍGUEZ (Argentina)
	RONALDO (Brazil)
	FERNANDO TORRES (Spain)
	DAVID VILLA (Spain)

World Cup 2006

GERMANY
Coach – Jürgen KLINSMANN

No	Name	Pos	Aps	(s)	Gls
1	Jens LEHMANN	G	6		
2	Marcell JANSEN	D	1		
3	Arne FRIEDRICH	D	6		
4	Robert HUTH	D	1		
5	Sebastian KEHL	M	2	(2)	
6	Jens NOWOTNY	D	1		
7	Bastian SCHWEINSTEIGER	M	6	(1)	2
8	Torsten FRINGS	M	6		1
9	Mike HANKE	A		(1)	
10	Oliver NEUVILLE	A		(7)	1
11	Miroslav KLOSE	A	7		5
12	Oliver KAHN	G	1		
13	Michael BALLACK	M	5		
14	Gerald ASAMOAH	A		(1)	
15	Thomas HITZLSPERGER	M		(1)	
16	Philipp LAHM	D	7		1
17	Per MERTESACKER	D	6		
18	Tim BOROWSKI	M	2	(4)	
19	Bernd SCHNEIDER	M	7		
20	Lukas PODOLSKI	A	7		3
21	Christoph METZELDER	D	6		
22	David ODONKOR	M		(4)	
23	Timo HILDEBRAND	G			

COSTA RICA
Coach – Alexandre GUIMARÃES

No	Name	Pos	Aps	(s)	Gls
1	Álvaro MESEN	G			
2	Jervis DRUMMOND	D	1	(1)	
3	Luis MARÍN	D	3		
4	Michael UMAÑA	D	3		
5	Gilberto MARTÍNEZ	D	1		
6	Daniel FONSECA	M	2		
7	Cristián BOLAÑOS	M	1	(1)	
8	Mauricio SOLÍS	M	3		
9	Paulo WANCHOPE	A	3		2
10	Walter CENTENO	M	3		
11	Ronald GÓMEZ	A	3		1
12	Leonardo GONZÁLEZ	D	3		
13	Kurt BERNARD	A		(1)	
14	Randall AZOFEIFA	M		(1)	
15	Harold WALLACE	D	1	(1)	
16	Carlos HERNÁNDEZ	M		(2)	
17	Gabriel BADILLA	D	1		
18	José Francisco PORRAS	G	3		
19	Álvaro SABORIO	A		(2)	
20	Douglas SEQUEIRA	D	2		
21	Víctor NÚÑEZ	A			
22	Michael RODRÍGUEZ	D			
23	Wardy ALFARO	G			

POLAND
Coach – Pawel JANAS

No	Name	Pos	Aps	(s)	Gls
1	Artur BORUC	G	3		
2	Mariusz JOP	D	1		
3	Seweryn GANCARCZYK	D			
4	Marcin BASZCZYNSKI	D	3		
5	Kamil KOSOWSKI	M		(1)	
6	Jacek BAK	D	3		
7	Radoslaw SOBOLEWSKI	M	2		
8	Jacek KRZYNOWEK	M	3		
9	Maciej ZURAWSKI	A	3		
10	Miroslaw SZYMKOWIAK	M	2		
11	Grzegorz RASIAK	A		(1)	
12	Tomasz KUSZCZAK	G			
13	Sebastian MILA	M			
14	Michal ZEWLAKOW	D	3		
15	Euzebiusz SMOLAREK	A	3		
16	Arkadiusz RADOMSKI	M	3		
17	Dariusz DUDKA	D		(1)	
18	Mariusz LEWANDOWSKI	D		(2)	
19	Bartosz BOSACKI	D	2		2
20	Piotr GIZA	M			
21	Ireneusz JELEN	A	2	(1)	
22	Lukasz FABIANSKI	G			
23	Pawel BROZEK	A		(3)	

ECUADOR
Coach – Luis Fernández SUÁREZ (COL)

No	Name	Pos	Aps	(s)	Gls
1	Edwin VILLAFUERTE	G			
2	Jorge GUAGUA	D	1	(2)	
3	Iván HURTADO	D	3		
4	Ulises DE LA CRUZ	D	4		
5	José Luis PERLAZA	D			
6	Patricio URRUTIA	M		(3)	
7	Cristián LARA	M		(2)	
8	Edison MÉNDEZ	M	4		
9	Félix BORJA	A	1		
10	Iván KAVIEDES	A	1	(3)	1
11	Agustín DELGADO	A	3		2
12	Cristián MORA	G	4		
13	Paul AMBROSSI	D	1		
14	Segundo CASTILLO	M	3		
15	Marlon AYOVI	M	1		
16	Luis Antonio VALENCIA	M	4		
17	Giovanny ESPINOZA	D	4		
18	Neicer REASCO	D	3		
19	Luis SARITIMA	M			
20	Edwin TENORIO	M	4		
21	Carlos TENORIO	A	3		2
22	Damián LANZA	G			
23	Christián BENÍTEZ	A		(1)	

ENGLAND
Coach – Sven Göran ERIKSSON (SWE)

No	Name	Pos	Aps	(s)	Gls
1	Paul ROBINSON	G	5		
2	Gary NEVILLE	D	2		
3	Ashley COLE	D	5		
4	Steven GERRARD	M	4	(1)	2
5	Rio FERDINAND	D	5		
6	John TERRY	D	5		
7	David BECKHAM	M	5		1
8	Frank LAMPARD	M	5		
9	Wayne ROONEY	A	3	(1)	
10	Michael OWEN	A	3		
11	Joe COLE	M	5		1
12	Sol CAMPBELL	D		(1)	
13	David JAMES	G			
14	Wayne BRIDGE	D			
15	Jamie CARRAGHER	D	2	(2)	
16	Owen HARGREAVES	M	3	(1)	
17	Jermaine JENAS	M			
18	Michael CARRICK	M	1		
19	Aaron LENNON	M		(3)	
20	Stewart DOWNING	M		(3)	
21	Peter CROUCH	A	2	(2)	1
22	Scott CARSON	G			
23	Theo WALCOTT	M			

PARAGUAY
Coach – Anibal RUIZ (URU)

No	Name	Pos	Aps	(s)	Gls
1	Justo VILLAR	G	1		
2	Jorge NÚÑEZ	D	2	(1)	
3	Delio TOLEDO	D	1		
4	Carlos GAMARRA	D	3		
5	Julio César CÁCERES	D	3		
6	Carlos BONET	M	2		

World Cup 2006

No	Name	Pos	Aps	(s)	Gls
7	Salvador CABAÑAS	M			
8	Edgar BARRETO	M	1		
9	Roque SANTA CRUZ	A	3		
10	Roberto ACUÑA	M	3		
11	Diego GAVILÁN	M			
12	Derlis GÓMEZ	G			
13	Carlos PAREDES	M	3		
14	Paulo DA SILVA	D			
15	Julio MANZUR	D		(1)	
16	Cristián RIVEROS	M	2		
17	José MONTIEL	M			
18	Nélson HAEDO VALDEZ	A	3		
19	Julio DOS SANTOS	M	1	(1)	
20	Dante LÓPEZ	A		(1)	
21	Denis CANIZA	D	3		
22	Aldo BOBADILLA	G	2	(1)	
23	Nélson CUEVAS	A		(2)	1

TRINIDAD & TOBAGO
Coach – Leo BEENHAKKER (HOL)

No	Name	Pos	Aps	(s)	Gls
1	Shaka HISLOP	G	2		
2	Ian COX	D			
3	Avery JOHN	D	2		
4	Marvin ANDREWS	D			
5	Brent SANCHO	D	3		
6	Dennis LAWRENCE	D	3		
7	Chris BIRCHALL	M	3		
8	Cyd GRAY	D	2		
9	Aurtis WHITLEY	M	2	(1)	
10	Russell LATAPY	M		(1)	
11	Carlos EDWARDS	M	3		
12	Collin SAMUEL	M	1		
13	Cornell GLEN	A	1	(2)	
14	Stern JOHN	A	3		
15	Kenwyne JONES	A	1	(1)	
16	Evans WISE	M		(2)	
17	Atiba CHARLES	D			
18	Densill THEOBALD	M	3		
19	Dwight YORKE	A	3		
20	Jason SCOTLAND	A			
21	Kelvin JACK	G	1		
22	Clayton INCE	G			
23	Anthony WOLFE	D		(1)	

SWEDEN
Coach – Lars LAGERBÄCK

No	Name	Pos	Aps	(s)	Gls
1	Andreas ISAKSSON	G	3		
2	Mikael NILSSON	D			
3	Olof MELLBERG	D	4		
4	Teddy LUCIC	D	4		
5	Erik EDMAN	D	4		
6	Tobias LINDEROTH	M	4		
7	Niclas ALEXANDERSSON	D	4		
8	Anders SVENSSON	M	1		
9	Fredrik LJUNGBERG	M	4		1
10	Zlatan IBRAHIMOVIC	A	3		
11	Henrik LARSSON	A	4		1
12	John ALVBAGE	G			
13	Petter HANSSON	D		(1)	
14	Fredrik STENMAN	D			
15	Karl SVENSSON	D			
16	Kim KÄLLSTRÖM	M	3	(1)	
17	Johan ELMANDER	A		(2)	
18	Mattias JONSON	M	2	(2)	
19	Daniel ANDERSSON	M		(1)	
20	Marcus ALLBÄCK	A	1	(3)	1
21	Christian WILHELMSSON	M	2	(2)	
22	Markus ROSENBERG	A			
23	Rami SHAABAN	G	1		

ARGENTINA
Coach – José PEKERMAN

No	Name	Pos	Aps	(s)	Gls
1	Roberto ABBONDANZIERI	G	5		
2	Roberto AYALA	D	5		1
3	Juan Pablo SORÍN	D	4		
4	Fabricio COLOCCINI	D	1	(1)	
5	Esteban CAMBIASSO	M	3	(2)	1
6	Gabriel HEINZE	D	4		
7	Javier SAVIOLA	A	3		1
8	Javier MASCHERANO	M	5		
9	Hernán CRESPO	A	4		3
10	Juan Román RIQUELME	M	5		
11	Carlos TÉVEZ	A	2	(2)	1
12	LEO FRANCO	G		(1)	
13	Lionel SCALONI	D	1		
14	Rodrigo PALACIO	A		(1)	
15	Gabriel MILITO	D	1		
16	Pablo AIMAR	M		(2)	
17	Leandro CUFRÉ	D	1		
18	MAXI RODRÍGUEZ	M	5		3
19	Lionel MESSI	A	1	(2)	1
20	Julio CRUZ	A		(2)	
21	Nicolás BURDISSO	D	3		
22	LUCHO GONZÁLEZ	M	2	(1)	
23	Óscar USTARI	G			

IVORY COAST
Coach – Henri MICHEL (FRA)

No	Name	Pos	Aps	(s)	Gls
1	Jean-Jacques TIZIE	G	2		
2	Kanga AKALE	M	2	(1)	
3	Arthur BOKA	D	3		
4	Kolo TOURE	D	2		
5	Didier ZOKORA	M	3		
6	Blaise KOUASSI	D	1		
7	Emerse FAE	M			
8	Bonaventure KALOU	A	1	(1)	1
9	Arouna KONE	A	2	(1)	
10	Gilles YAPI YAPO	M		(1)	
11	Didier DROGBA	A	2		1
12	Abdoulaye MEITE	D	2		
13	Marc ZORO	D			
14	Bakary KONE	A	1	(2)	1
15	Aruna DINDANE	A	1	(2)	2
16	Gérard GNANHOUAN	G			
17	Cyrille DOMORAUD	D	1		
18	Kader KEITA	A	2		
19	Yaya TOURE	M	3		
20	Guy DEMEL	M			
21	Emmanuel EBOUE	D	3		
22	ROMARIC Ndri	M	1		
23	Boubacar BARRY	G	1		

SERBIA & MONTENEGRO
Coach – Ilija PETKOVIC

No	Name	Pos	Aps	(s)	Gls
1	Dragoslav JEVRIC	G	3		
2	Ivan ERGIC	M	1	(1)	
3	Ivica DRAGUTINOVIC	D	1		
4	Igor DULJAJ	M	3		
5	Nemanja VIDIC	D			
6	Goran GAVRANCIC	D	3		
7	Ognjen KOROMAN	M	1	(1)	
8	Mateja KEZMAN	A	2		
9	Savo MILOSEVIC	A	2	(1)	
10	Dejan STANKOVIC	M	3		
11	Predrag DJORDJEVIC	M	3		
12	Oliver KOVACEVIC	G			
13	Dusan BASTA	D			
14	Nenad DJORDJEVIC	D	2		
15	Milan DUDIC	D	2		

World Cup 2006

No	Name	Pos	Aps	(s)	Gls
16	Dusan PETKOVIC	D			
17	Albert NADJ	M	2	(1)	
18	Zvonimir VUKIC	M		(1)	
19	Nikola ZIGIC	A	1	(1)	1
20	Mladen KRSTAJIC	D	3		
21	Danijel LJUBOJA	A		(2)	
22	Sasa ILIC	M	1		1
23	Vladimir STOJKOVIC	G			

HOLLAND
Coach – Marco VAN BASTEN

No	Name	Pos	Aps	(s)	Gls
1	Edwin VAN DER SAR	G	4		
2	Kew JALIENS	D	1		
3	Khalid BOULAHROUZ	D	2	(2)	
4	Joris MATHIJSEN	D	3		
5	Giovanni VAN BRONCKHORST	D	3		
6	Denny LANDZAAT	M		(3)	
7	Dirk KUIJT	A	2	(1)	
8	Phillip COCU	M	4		
9	Ruud VAN NISTELROOY	A	3		1
10	Rafael VAN DER VAART	M	1	(2)	
11	Arjen ROBBEN	A	3		1
12	Jan KROMKAMP	D			
13	André OOIJER	D	4		
14	Johnny HEITINGA	D	2	(1)	
15	Tim DE CLER	D	1		
16	Hedwiges MADURO	M		(1)	
17	Robin VAN PERSIE	A	4		1
18	Mark VAN BOMMEL	M	3		
19	Jan VENNEGOOR OF HESSELINK	A		(1)	
20	Wesley SNEIJDER	M	4		
21	Ryan BABEL	A		(1)	
22	Henk TIMMER	G			
23	Maarten STEKELENBURG	G			

MEXICO
Coach – Ricardo LA VOLPE (ARG)

No	Name	Pos	Aps	(s)	Gls
1	Oswaldo SÁNCHEZ	G	4		
2	Claudio SUÁREZ	D			
3	Carlos SALCIDO	D	4		
4	Rafael MÁRQUEZ	D	4		1
5	Ricardo OSORIO	D	4		
6	Gerardo TORRADO	M	2	(1)	
7	ZINHA	M	1	(3)	1
8	Pavel PARDO	M	4		
9	Jared BORGETTI	A	2		
10	Guillermo FRANCO	A	2	(1)	
11	Ramón MORALES	M	1	(1)	
12	José Jesús CORONA	G			
13	Guillermo OCHOA	G			
14	Gonzalo PINEDA	M	3	(1)	
15	José Antonio CASTRO	D	1	(1)	
16	Mario MÉNDEZ	D	4		
17	Francisco FONSECA	A	2	(2)	1
18	Andrés GUARDADO	M	1		
19	Omar BRAVO	A	3		2
20	Rafael GARCÍA	M			
21	Jesús ARELLANO	M		(1)	
22	Francisco RODRÍGUEZ	D	1		
23	Luís PÉREZ	M	1	(1)	

IRAN
Coach – Zdravko IVANKOVIC (CRO)

No	Name	Pos	Aps	(s)	Gls
1	Ebrahim MIRZAPOUR	G	3		
2	Mehdi MAHDAVIKIA	M	3		
3	Sohrab BAKHTIARIZADEH	D	1	(1)	1
4	Yahya GOLMOHAMMADI	D	2		
5	Rahman REZAEI	D	3		
6	Javad NEKOUNAM	M	2		
7	Feridoon ZANDI	M	1		
8	Ali KARIMI	M	2		
9	Vahid HASHEMIAN	A	3		
10	Ali DAEI	A	2		
11	Rasoul KHATIBI	A		(2)	
12	Hassan ROUDBARIAN	G			
13	Hossein KAABI	D	3		
14	Andranik TEYMOURIAN	M	3		
15	Arash BORHANI	A		(2)	
16	Reza ENAYATI	A			
17	Java KAZEMEIAN	M			
18	Moharram NAVIDKIA	M			
19	Amir Hossein SADEQI	D			
20	Mohamad NOSRATI	D	3		
21	Mehrzad MADANCHI	M	2	(1)	
22	Vahid TALEBLOO	G			
23	Masoud SHOJAEI	D		(1)	

ANGOLA
Coach – Luís Oliveira GONÇALVES

No	Name	Pos	Aps	(s)	Gls
1	JOÃO RICARDO	G	3		
2	MARCO AIROSA	D			
3	JAMBA	D	3		
4	LEBO LEBO	D			
5	KALI	D	3		
6	MILOY	D	1	(2)	
7	FIGUEIREDO	M	3		
8	ANDRÉ	M	2		
9	MANTORRAS	A		(2)	
10	AKWÁ	A	3		
11	MATEUS	A	3		
12	LAMA	G			
13	EDSON	M		(1)	
14	MENDONCA	M	3		
15	RUI MARQUES	D		(2)	
16	FLÁVIO	A		(1)	1
17	ZÉ KALANGA	M	3		
18	LOVE	A		(1)	
19	ANDRÉ TITI BUENGO	A			
20	LOCO	D	3		
21	DELGADO	D	3		
22	MÁRIO	G			
23	MARCO ABREU	D			

PORTUGAL
Coach – Luiz Felipe SCOLARI (BRA)

No	Name	Pos	Aps	(s)	Gls
1	RICARDO	G	7		
2	PAULO FERREIRA	D	1	(2)	
3	Marco CANEIRA	D	1		
4	RICARDO COSTA	D	1		
5	FERNANDO MEIRA	D	7		
6	COSTINHA	M	4	(1)	
7	Luís FIGO	M	6	(1)	
8	PETIT	M	3	(3)	
9	PAULETA	A	6		1
10	HUGO VIANA	M		(2)	
11	SIMÃO Sabrosa	M	3	(4)	1
12	QUIM	G			
13	MIGUEL	D	6		
14	NUNO VALENTE	D	6		
15	Luís BOA MORTE	A		(1)	
16	RICARDO CARVALHO	D	6		
17	CRISTIANO RONALDO	M	6		1
18	MANICHE	M	6	(1)	2
19	TIAGO	M	3	(2)	
20	DECO	M	4		1
21	NUNO GOMES	A		(2)	1
22	PAULO SANTOS	G			
23	HÉLDER POSTIGA	A	1	(2)	

World Cup 2006

ITALY
Coach – Marcello LIPPI

No	Name	Pos	Aps	(s)	Gls
1	Gianluigi BUFFON	G	7		
2	Cristian ZACCARDO	D	2	(1)	
3	Fabio GROSSO	D	6		1
4	Daniele DE ROSSI	M	2	(1)	
5	Fabio CANNAVARO	D	7		
6	Andrea BARZAGLI	D	1	(1)	
7	Alessandro DEL PIERO	A	1	(4)	1
8	Gennaro GATTUSO	M	5	(1)	
9	Luca TONI	A	6		2
10	Francesco TOTTI	A	6	(1)	1
11	Alberto GILARDINO	A	4	(1)	1
12	Angelo PERUZZI	G			
13	Alessandro NESTA	D	3		
14	Marco AMELIA	G			
15	Vincenzo IAQUINTA	A		(5)	1
16	Mauro CAMORANESI	M	4	(1)	
17	Simone BARONE	M		(2)	
18	Filippo INZAGHI	A		(1)	1
19	Gianluca ZAMBROTTA	D	6		1
20	Simone PERROTTA	M	7		
21	Andrea PIRLO	M	7		1
22	Massimo ODDO	D		(1)	
23	Marco MATERAZZI	D	3	(1)	2

GHANA
Coach – Ratomir DUJKOVIC (SCG)

No	Name	Pos	Aps	(s)	Gls
1	Sammy ADJEI	G			
2	Hans SARPEI	D			
3	Asamoah GYAN	A	3		1
4	Samuel KUFFOUR	D	1		
5	John MENSAH	D	4		
6	Emmanuel PAPPOE	D	2		
7	Illiasu SHILLA	D	3	(1)	
8	Michael ESSIEN	M	3		
9	Derek BOATENG	M	1	(2)	
10	Stephen APPIAH	M	4		1
11	Sulley Ali MUNTARI	M	3		1
12	Alex TACHIE-MENSAH	A		(3)	
13	Habib MOHAMED	D	2		
14	Matthew AMOAH	A	4		
15	John PAINTSIL	D	4		
16	George OWU	G			
17	Daniel QUAYE	D			
18	Eric ADDO	M	2	(2)	
19	Razak PIMPONG	A	1	(2)	
20	Otto ADDO	M	1	(1)	
21	Ahmed ISSAH	D			
22	Richard KINGSTON	G	4		
23	Haminu DRAMAN	M	2		1

UNITED STATES
Coach – Bruce ARENA

No	Name	Pos	Aps	(s)	Gls
1	Tim HOWARD	G			
2	Chris ALBRIGHT	D			
3	Carlos BOCANEGRA	D	2		
4	Pablo MASTROENI	M	2		
5	John O'BRIEN	M		(1)	
6	Steve CHERUNDOLO	D	3		
7	Eddie LEWIS	D	2		
8	Clint DEMPSEY	M	2		1
9	Eddie JOHNSON	M		(2)	
10	Claudio REYNA	M	3		
11	Brian CHING	A			
12	Cory GIBBS	D		(1)	
13	Jimmy CONRAD	D	1	(1)	
14	Ben OLSEN	M		(1)	
15	Bobby CONVEY	M	2	(1)	
16	Josh WOLFF	A		(1)	
17	DaMarcus BEASLEY	M	2	(1)	
18	Kasey KELLER	G	3		
19	Marcus HAHNEMANN	G			
20	Brian McBRIDE	A	3		
21	Landon DONOVAN	M	3		
22	Oguchi ONYEWU	D	3		
23	Eddie POPE	D	2		

CZECH REPUBLIC
Coach – Karel BRÜCKNER

No	Name	Pos	Aps	(s)	Gls
1	Petr CECH	G	3		
2	Zdenek GRYGERA	D	3		
3	Pavel MARES	D			
4	Tomás GALÁSEK	M	2		
5	Radoslav KOVÁC	D	1		
6	Marek JANKULOVSKI	D	3		
7	Libor SIONKO	M		(1)	
8	Karel POBORSKY	M	3		
9	Jan KOLLER	A	1		1
10	Tomás ROSICKY	M	3		2
11	Pavel NEDVED	M	3		
12	Vratislav LOKVENC	A	1	(1)	
13	Martin JIRÁNEK	D			
14	David JAROLÍM	M		(1)	
15	Milan BAROS	A	1		
16	Jaromír BLAZEK	G			
17	Jiri STAJNER	A		(3)	
18	Marek HEINZ	A		(1)	
19	Jan POLÁK	M	1	(2)	
20	Jaroslav PLASIL	M	3		
21	Tomás UJFALUSI	D	2		
22	David ROZEHNAL	D	3		
23	Antonin KINSKY	G			

BRAZIL
Coach – CARLOS ALBERTO Parreira

No	Name	Pos	Aps	(s)	Gls
1	DIDA	G	5		
2	CAFÚ	D	4		
3	LÚCIO	D	5		
4	JUAN	D	5		
5	ÉMERSON	M	3		
6	ROBERTO CARLOS	D	4		
7	ADRIANO	A	3	(1)	2
8	KAKÁ	M	5		1
9	RONALDO	A	5		3
10	RONALDINHO	M	5		
11	ZÉ ROBERTO	M	4	(1)	1
12	ROGÉRIO CENI	G		(1)	
13	CICINHO	D	1	(1)	
14	LUISÃO	D			
15	CRIS	D			
16	GILBERTO	D	1		1
17	GILBERTO SILVA	M	2	(2)	
18	MINEIRO	M			
19	JUNINHO	M	2	(1)	1
20	RICARDINHO	M		(2)	
21	FRED	A		(1)	1
22	JÚLIO CÉSAR	G			
23	ROBINHO	A	1	(3)	

CROATIA
Coach – Zlatko KRANJCAR

No	Name	Pos	Aps	(s)	Gls
1	Stipe PLETIKOSA	G	3		
2	Darijo SRNA	M	3		1
3	Josip SIMUNIC	D	3		
4	Robert KOVAC	D	2		
5	Igor TUDOR	M	3		
6	Jurica VRANJES	M			

World Cup 2006

No	Name	Pos	Aps	(s)	Gls
7	Dario SIMIC	D	3		
8	Marko BABIC	M	3		
9	Dado PRSO	A	3		
10	Niko KOVAC	M	3		1
11	Mario TOKIC	D			
12	Joey DIDULICA	G			
13	Stjepan TOMAS	D	1		
14	Luka MODRIC	M		(2)	
15	Ivan LEKO	M			
16	Jerko LEKO	M		(2)	
17	Ivan KLASNIC	A	2		
18	Ivica OLIC	A	1	(2)	
19	Niko KRANJCAR	M	3		
20	Anthony SERIC	M			
21	Bosko BALABAN	A			
22	Ivan BOSNJAK	M		(1)	
23	Tomislav BUTINA	G			

AUSTRALIA
Coach – Guus HIDDINK (HOL)

No	Name	Pos	Aps	(s)	Gls
1	Mark SCHWARZER	G	3		
2	Lucas NEILL	D	4		
3	Craig MOORE	D	4		1
4	Tim CAHILL	M	3	(1)	2
5	Jason CULINA	M	4		
6	Tony POPOVIC	D	1		
7	Brett EMERTON	M	3		
8	Josip SKOKO	M			
9	Mark VIDUKA	A	4		
10	Harry KEWELL	M	2	(1)	1
11	Stan LAZARIDIS	M			
12	Ante COVIC	G			
13	Vince GRELLA	M	4		
14	Scott CHIPPERFIELD	M	4		
15	John ALOISI	A		(4)	1
16	Michael BEAUCHAMP	D			
17	Archie THOMPSON	A			
18	Zeljko KALAC	G	1		
19	Josh KENNEDY	A		(2)	
20	Luke WILKSHIRE	M	2		
21	Mile STERJOVSKI	M	3		
22	Mark MILLIGAN	D			
23	Marco BRESCIANO	M	2	(2)	

JAPAN
Coach – ZICO (BRA)

No	Name	Pos	Aps	(s)	Gls
1	Seigo NARAZAKI	G			
2	Teruyuki MONIWA	D		(1)	
3	Yuichi KOMANO	D	1		
4	Yasuhito ENDO	M			
5	Tsuneyasu MIYAMOTO	D	2		
6	Koji NAKATA	D			
7	Hidetoshi NAKATA	M	3		
8	Mitsuo OGASAWARA	M	2		
9	Naohiro TAKAHARA	A	2	(1)	
10	Shunsuke NAKAMURA	M	3		1
11	Seiichiro MAKI	A	1		
12	Yoichi DOI	G			
13	Atsushi YANAGISAWA	A	2		
14	ALEX dos Santos	D	3		
15	Takahashi FUKUNISHI	M	2		
16	Masashi OGURO	A		(2)	
17	Junichi INAMOTO	M	1	(1)	
18	Shinji ONO	M		(1)	
19	Keisuke TSUBOI	D	2		
20	Keiji TAMADA	A	1	(1)	1
21	Akira KAJI	D	2		
22	Yuji NAKAZAWA	D	3		
23	Yoshikatsu KAWAGUCHI	G	3		

FRANCE
Coach – Raymond DOMENECH

No	Name	Pos	Aps	(s)	Gls
1	Mickaël LANDREAU	G			
2	Jean-Alain BOUMSONG	D			
3	Eric ABIDAL	D	6		
4	Patrick VIEIRA	M	7		2
5	William GALLAS	D	7		
6	Claude MAKELELE	M	7		
7	Florent MALOUDA	M	6		
8	Vikash DHORASOO	M		(1)	
9	Sidney GOVOU	A		(4)	
10	Zinedine ZIDANE	M	6		3
11	Sylvain WILTORD	A	2	(5)	
12	Thierry HENRY	A	7		3
13	Mikaël SILVESTRE	D	1		
14	Louis SAHA	A		(3)	
15	Lilian THURAM	D	7		
16	Fabien BARTHEZ	G	7		
17	Gaël GIVET	D			
18	Alou DIARRA	M		(2)	
19	Willy SAGNOL	D	7		
20	David TREZEGUET	A	1	(2)	
21	Pascal CHIMBONDA	D			
22	Franck RIBERY	M	6	(1)	1
23	Grégory COUPET	G			

SWITZERLAND
Coach – Jakob "Köbi" KUHN

No	Name	Pos	Aps	(s)	Gls
1	Pascal ZUBERBÜHLER	G	4		
2	Johan DJOUROU	D	1	(2)	
3	Ludovic MAGNIN	D	3		
4	Philippe SENDEROS	D	3		1
5	Xavier MARGAIRAZ	M		(2)	
6	Johann VOGEL	M	4		
7	Ricardo CABANAS	M	4		
8	Raphaël WICKY	M	4		
9	Alexander FREI	A	4		2
10	Daniel GYGAX	M	1	(1)	
11	Marco STRELLER	A	1	(2)	
12	Diego BENAGLIO	G			
13	Stéphane GRICHTING	D		(1)	
14	David DEGEN	M			
15	Blerim DZEMAILI	M			
16	Tranquillo BARNETTA	M	4		1
17	Christoph SPYCHER	D	1		
18	Mauro LUSTRINELLI	A		(2)	
19	Valon BEHRAMI	M		(1)	
20	Patrick MÜLLER	D	4		
21	Fabio COLTORTI	G			
22	Hakan YAKIN	M	2	(1)	
23	Philipp DEGEN	D	4		

SOUTH KOREA
Coach – Dick ADVOCAAT (HOL)

No	Name	Pos	Aps	(s)	Gls
1	LEE Woon-jae	G	3		
2	KIM Young-chul	D	2		
3	KIM Dong-jin	D	2		
4	CHOI Jin-cheul	D	3		
5	KIM Nam-il	M	2	(1)	
6	KIM Jin-kyu	D	2		
7	PARK Ji-sung	M	3		1
8	KIM Do-heon	M			
9	AHN Jung-hwan	A		(3)	1
10	PARK Chu-young	A	1		
11	SEOL Ki-hyeon	A		(2)	
12	LEE Young-pyo	D	3		
13	LEE Eul-yong	M	2		
14	LEE Chun-soo	M	3		1
15	BAEK Ji-hoon	M			

World Cup 2006

No	Name	Pos	Aps	(s)	Gls
16	CHUNG Kyung-ho	A			
17	LEE Ho	M	3		
18	KIM Sang-sik	D		(2)	
19	CHO Jae-jin	A	3		
20	KIM Yong-dae	G			
21	KIM Young-kwang	G			
22	SONG Chong-gug	D	1		
23	CHO Won-hee	D			

TOGO
Coach – Otto PFISTER (GER)

No	Name	Pos	Aps	(s)	Gls
1	Ouro-Nimini TCHAGNIROU	G			
2	Dare NIBOMBE	D	3		
3	Jean-Paul ABALO	D	2		
4	Emmanuel ADEBAYOR	A	3		
5	Massamesso TCHANGAI	D	3		
6	Yao AZIAWONOU	M	1	(1)	
7	Moustapha SALIFOU	M	2	(1)	
8	Kuami AGBOH	D	1		
9	Thomas DOSSEVI	M	1	(1)	
10	Chérif-Touré MAMAM	M	3		
11	Robert MALM	A		(1)	
12	Eric AKOTO	D			
13	Richmond FORSON	D	2	(1)	
14	Adekamni OLUFADE	M		(1)	
15	Alaixys ROMAO	M	2		
16	Kossi AGASSA	G	3		
17	Mohamed KADER	A	3		1
18	Yao Junior SENAYA	M	2	(1)	
19	Ludovic ASSEMOASSA	D	1		
20	Affo ERASSA	D			
21	Franck ATSOU	D			
22	Kodjovi OBIALLE	G			
23	Assimiou TOURE	D	1	(1)	

SPAIN
Coach – Luis ARAGONÉS

No	Name	Pos	Aps	(s)	Gls
1	Iker CASILLAS	G	3		
2	MÍCHEL SALGADO	D	1		
3	Mariano PERNÍA	D	3		
4	Carlos MARCHENA	D	1		
5	Carles PUYOL	D	3		
6	David ALBELDA	M	1	(1)	
7	RAÚL	A	2	(2)	1
8	XAVI	M	3	(1)	
9	FERNANDO TORRES	A	3	(1)	3
10	José Antonio REYES	M	1		
11	LUIS GARCÍA	M	2	(1)	
12	ANTONIO LÓPEZ	D	1		
13	Andrés INIESTA	M	1		
14	XABI ALONSO	M	3		1
15	SERGIO RAMOS	D	3		
16	Marcos SENNA	M	2	(1)	
17	JOAQUÍN	M	1	(2)	
18	Cesc FÁBREGAS	M	2	(2)	
19	Santiago CAÑIZARES	G	1		
20	JUANITO	D	1		1
21	DAVID VILLA	A	3	(1)	3
22	PABLO	D	3		
23	José Manuel REINA	G			

UKRAINE
Coach – Oleh BLOKHIN

No	Name	Pos	Aps	(s)	Gls
1	Olexandr SHOVKOVSKYI	G	5		
2	Andriy NESMACHNYI	D	5		
3	Olexandr YATSENKO	D			
4	Anatoliy TYMOSHCHUK	M	5		
5	Volodymyr YEZERSKYI	D	1		
6	Andriy RUSOL	D	4		1
7	Andriy SHEVCHENKO	A	5		2
8	Oleh SHELAYEV	M	4	(1)	
9	Oleh GUSEV	M	5		
10	Andriy VORONIN	A	4		
11	Serhiy REBROV	A	2	(2)	1
12	Andriy PYATOV	G			
13	Dmytro CHIGRINSKYI	D			
14	Andriy GUSIN	M	3	(2)	
15	Artem MILEVSKYI	A	1	(3)	
16	Andriy VOROBEI	A	1	(3)	
17	Vladislav VASHCHUK	D	2	(1)	
18	Serhiy NAZARENKO	M			
19	Maxym KALYNYCHENKO	M	4		1
20	Olexiy BELIK	A		(1)	
21	Ruslan ROTAN	M	1	(2)	
22	Vyacheslav SVIDERSKYI	D	3		
23	Bohdan SHUST	G			

TUNISIA
Coach – Roger LEMERRE (FRA)

No	Name	Pos	Aps	(s)	Gls
1	Ali BOUMNIJEL	G	3		
2	Karim ESSEDIRI	D		(1)	
3	Karim HAGUI	D	3		
4	Alaeddine YAHIA	D		(1)	
5	Ziad JAZIRI	A	3		1
6	Hatem TRABELSI	D	3		
7	Haykel GUEMAMDIA	A		(1)	
8	Mehdi NAFTI	M	2	(1)	
9	Yassine CHIKHAOUI	A	1		
10	Kaies GHODHBANE	M		(3)	
11	Francileudo dos SANTOS	A		(1)	
12	Jawher MNARI	M	3		1
13	Riadh BOUAZIZI	M	3		
14	Adel CHEDLI	M	3		
15	Radhi JAIDI	D	3		1
16	Adel NEFZI	G			
17	Chaouki BEN SAADA	A		(1)	
18	David JEMMALI	D	1		
19	Anis AYARI	D	2		
20	Hamed NAMOUCHI	M	3		
21	Karim SAIDI	D			
22	Hamdi KASRAOUI	G			
23	Sofiane MELLITI	M			

SAUDI ARABIA
Coach – Marcos PAQUETA (BRA)

No	Name	Pos	Aps	(s)	Gls
1	Mohammed AL DEAYEA	G			
2	Ahmad AL DOKHI	D	3		
3	Redha TUKAR	D	3		
4	Hamad AL MONTASHARI	D	3		
5	Naif AL QADI	D			
6	Omar AL GHAMDI	M	2		
7	Mohammed AMEEN	M	1	(1)	
8	Mohammed NOOR	M	3		
9	Sami AL JABER	A	1	(2)	1
10	Mohammed AL SHLHOUB	M			
11	Saad AL HARTHI	A	1		
12	Abdulaziz KHATHRAN	D	1	(1)	
13	Hussein SULIMANI	D	3		
14	Suad KHARIRI	M	3		
15	Ahmed AL BAHRI	D			
16	Khaled AZIZ	M	3		
17	Mohammed AL BISHI	M			
18	Nawaf AL TEMYAT	M	1	(1)	
19	Mohammad MASSAD	D		(1)	
20	Yasser AL QAHTANI	A	2		1
21	Mabrouk ZAID	G	3		
22	Mohammad KHOJAH	G			
23	Malek AL HAWSAWI	A		(3)	

World Cup 2006

European Qualifying Tournament:
Big Battalions all through to Germany

The final stages of European qualifying for the World Cup finals in Germany provided differing degrees of drama and excitement over the eight groups. But when the dust had settled, following the three two-legged play-offs in November, there were no major surprises among the list of 13 nations (a quarter of the UEFA membership) that would join the hosts and 22 other countries from planet football at the Greatest Show on Earth the following summer.

GROUP 1

Holland and the Czech Republic, familiar foes from the previous European Championship, during which they met on three occasions, twice in the qualifiers and once at the finals in Portugal, went into their final four fixtures well placed to qualify in tandem, with the team that failed to win the group having a strong chance of claiming one of the two 'best runners-up' berths,

The Dutch had dropped just two points in their opening eight matches (away to Macedonia), whereas the Czechs had strung together seven successive victories following their opening 2-0 defeat in Amsterdam. There seemed no apparent threat from below – third-placed Romania were five points adrift of the Czechs and had played a game more – but the scenario altered when the Romanians followed up a routine 2-0 victory at home to Andorra with another win by the same scoreline at home to the Czechs. Adrian Mutu, who had missed a large chunk of the qualifying campaign as a result of a drugs ban, netted all four of Romania's goals.

Momentarily Romania were ahead of the Czechs in second place, but four days later Karel Brückner's side restored their two-point lead with a 4-1 win over Armenia in Olomouc, albeit after a nervy, goalless first half. Holland, meanwhile, sped clear at the top with back-to-back wins over Armenia (1-0 in Yerevan) and Andorra (4-0 in Eindhoven).

With a four-point advantage, Marco van Basten's team travelled to Prague for their penultimate fixture knowing that a win or draw would secure their qualification as group winners and that even a defeat would leave them needing only a home win over Macedonia four days later to secure top spot.

Double Dutch

Despite the absence of veteran midfielder Phillip Cocu, expelled against Andorra for an elbowing incident, Holland maintained their winning run with an impressive display in the Czech capital. After surviving an early scare, when Tomás Rosicky had a penalty brilliantly saved by Edwin van der Sar, the Dutch took control with two goals in quick succession. In-form midfielder Rafael van der Vaart

Two Dutchmen with Germany in their sights – Ruud van Nistelrooy and Rafael van der Vaart

European Qualifying Tournament

GROUP 1

RESULTS
Macedonia 3, Armenia 0
Finland 3, Andorra 0
Andorra 1, Romania 5
Holland 2, Czech Republic 0
Finland 3, Armenia 1
Andorra 1, Macedonia 0
Holland 3, Finland 1
Armenia 1, Romania 1
Macedonia 0, Andorra 0
Czech Republic 4, Finland 3
Andorra 0, Czech Republic 4
Macedonia 1, Romania 2
Czech Republic 8, Andorra 1
Czech Republic 6, Macedonia 1
Romania 3, Armenia 0
Romania 2, Finland 1
Romania 2, Macedonia 1
Armenia 0, Finland 2
Czech Republic 1, Romania 0
Macedonia 2, Holland 2
Armenia 0, Czech Republic 3
Andorra 0, Holland 3
Macedonia 0, Czech Republic 2
Armenia 2, Andorra 1
Romania 0, Holland 2
Holland 2, Armenia 0
Armenia 1, Macedonia 2
Holland 2, Romania 0
Finland 0, Holland 4

(17/8/05)
Macedonia 0, Finland 3 *(Eremenko 8, 45, Roiha 87)*
Romania 2 *(Mutu 29, 41)*, Andorra 0

(3/9/05)
Andorra 0, Finland 0
Armenia 0, Holland 1 *(Van Nistelrooy 63)*
Romania 2 *(Mutu 28, 58)*, Czech Republic 0

(7/9/05)
Czech Republic 4 *(Heinz 47, Polák 52, 76, Baros 58)*, Armenia 1 *(Hakobyan Ara 85)*
Finland 5 *(Forssell 10, 12, 61, Tihinen 41, Eremenko 54)*, Macedonia 1 *(Maznov 48)*
Holland 4 *(Van der Vaart 22, Lima A. 27og, Van Nistelrooy 42, 88)*, Andorra 0

(8/10/05)
Czech Republic 0, Holland 2 *(Van der Vaart 32, Opdam 39)*
Finland 0, Romania 1 *(Mutu 41p)*

(12/10/05)
Andorra 0, Armenia 3 *(Sonejee 39og, Hakobyan Aram 52, Hakobyan Ara 62)*
Finland 0, Czech Republic 3 *(Jun 6, Rosicky 51, Heinz 58)*
Holland 0, Macedonia 0

FINAL TABLE

		Pld	Home W D L F A	Away W D L F A	Total W D L F A	Pts
1	Holland	12	5 1 0 13 1	5 1 0 14 2	10 2 0 27 3	32
2	Czech Republic	12	5 0 1 23 8	4 0 2 12 4	9 0 3 35 12	27
3	Romania	12	5 0 1 11 4	3 1 2 9 6	8 1 3 20 10	25
4	Finland	12	3 0 3 11 10	2 1 3 10 9	5 1 6 21 19	16
5	Macedonia	12	1 2 3 6 9	1 1 4 5 15	2 3 7 11 24	9
6	Armenia	12	1 1 4 4 10	1 0 5 5 15	2 1 9 9 25	7
7	Andorra	12	1 1 4 2 15	0 1 5 2 19	1 2 9 4 34	5

TOP GOALSCORERS
8 Jan KOLLER (Czech Republic)
Alexei EREMENKO (Finland)
7 Ruud VAN NISTELROOY (Holland)
Adrian MUTU (Romania)
6 Milan BAROS (Czech Republic)
Tomás ROSICKY (Czech Republic)
5 Vratislav LOKVENC (Czech Republic)
Goran PANDEV (Macedonia)
4 Jan POLÁK (Czech Republic)
Mikael FORSSELL (Finland)

scored the first, driving in with his left from Arjen Robben's craftily disguised pull-back, and defender Barry Opdam made it 2-0 with a towering header from a Robben corner. Milan Baros struck the bar for the Czechs in the second half, but Holland held on in some comfort to protect an eighth successive clean sheet. Their place in Germany was now secure, but with Romania winning 1-0 in Finland on the same day (with yet another Mutu goal), the Czechs were not just out of the running for one of the best runners-up spots; they now had to win themselves in Finland four days later simply to reach the play-offs at Romania's expense.

It was a tricky assignment in Helsinki, but Rosicky made amends for his penalty miss against the Dutch by creating an early goal for Tomás Jun and then netting the all-important second just after the interval with a firm half-volley from the edge of the area. Marek Heinz ensured there would be no Finnish comeback by rattling in the third goal with a superb 25-yard left-footer.

So the Czech Republic, who had never reached the World Cup finals as an independent nation, were through to the play-offs, while Romania, despite their impressive finish, had to contemplate qualifying failure for the third major tournament in a row. On top of the table, with impressive statistics of ten wins, two draws (they were held again by Macedonia, in their final match), no defeats and just three goals conceded stood Holland, back in the World Cup big time after missing out on the 2002 tournament in the Far East.

GROUP 2

This appeared to be the most competitive of the eight groups at the outset, but Ukraine, who had never previously qualified for a major tournament, surprisingly took charge with a run of seven straight victories that enabled them to build up a virtually impregnable seven-point lead with three matches remaining, leaving 2002 bronze medallists Turkey, European champions Greece and regular tournament qualifiers Denmark to scrap it out for the runners-up spot and a place in the play-offs.

Ukraine knew that a victory in any of their final three fixtures would seal their qualification. The last two

European Qualifying Tournament

Ukraine midfielder Ruslan Rotan – a goalscorer in Georgia

games were at home, but Oleh Blokhin's side were keen to get the job done at the first attempt, in Georgia, and when they took the lead just before half-time with a dipping right-foot shot from midfielder Ruslan Rotan, their prospects of doing so looked extremely bright, particularly as they had not conceded a goal in their previous six matches. But with a place in Germany almost in their grasp, they let it slip, conceding a dramatic 89th-minute equaliser – a stunning left-footed free-kick from Giorgi Gakhokidze.

Airport announcement

Help, though, was soon at hand from elsewhere. As the Ukrainians were waiting for their flight home at Tbilisi airport, word reached them that in the night's other game, in Istanbul, Denmark had denied Turkey victory with a stoppage-time equaliser. It was the perfect outcome for Ukraine as it kept their seven-point lead intact and meant that with two games remaining they could no longer be caught. As such, they became the first of the European qualifiers to book their place at the finals.

Denmark's late, late show in Istanbul kept alive their play-off hopes, but paradoxically Søren Larsen's goal

GROUP 2

RESULTS
Albania 2, Greece 1
Turkey 1, Georgia 1
Greece 0, Turkey 0
Albania 0, Denmark 2
Ukraine 1, Greece 1
Kazakhstan 0, Albania 1
Georgia 2, Denmark 2
Turkey 0, Ukraine 3
Greece 2, Denmark 1
Georgia 1, Greece 3
Georgia 2, Turkey 5
Ukraine 1, Denmark 0
Turkey 0, Greece 0
Denmark 3, Albania 1
Kazakhstan 0, Turkey 6
Denmark 1, Ukraine 1
Georgia 2, Albania 0
Kazakhstan 1, Ukraine 2
Turkey 4, Kazakhstan 0
Denmark 1, Turkey 1
Ukraine 2, Georgia 0
Greece 3, Kazakhstan 1
Albania 0, Ukraine 2
Denmark 3, Kazakhstan 0
Turkey 2, Albania 0
Greece 2, Albania 0
Albania 3, Georgia 2
Ukraine 2, Kazakhstan 0
Greece 0, Ukraine 1

(17/8/05)
Kazakhstan 1 *(Kenzhekhanov 23)*, Georgia 2 *(Demetradze 50, 82)*

(3/9/05)
Albania 2 *(Myrtaj 54, Bogdani 56)*, Kazakhstan 1 *(Nizovtsev 64)*
Georgia 1 *(Gakhokidze 89)*, Ukraine 1 *(Rotan 44)*
Turkey 2 *(Okan Buruk 48, Tümer 81)*, Denmark 2 *(Jensen C. 41, Larsen 90)*

(7/9/05)
Denmark 6 *(Jensen C. 9, Poulsen 30, Agger 42, Tomasson 54, Larsen 79, 83)*, Georgia 1 *(Demetradze 36p)*
Kazakhstan 1 *(Zhumaskaliyev 53)*, Greece 2 *(Giannakopoulos 79, Liberopoulos 90)*
Ukraine 0, Turkey 1 *(Tümer 55)*

(8/10/05)
Denmark 1 *(Gravgaard 39)*, Greece 0
Georgia 0, Kazakhstan 0
Ukraine 2 *(Shevchenko 45, Rotan 86)*, Albania 2 *(Bogdani 75, 82)*

(12/10/05)
Albania 0, Turkey 1 *(Tümer 57)*
Greece 1 *(Papadopoulos 17)*, Georgia 0
Kazakhstan 1 *(Kuchma 86)*, Denmark 2 *(Gravgaard 46, Tomasson 49)*

FINAL TABLE

		Pld	Home W D L F A	Away W D L F A	Total W D L F A	Pts
1	Ukraine	12	3 2 1 8 4	4 2 0 10 3	7 4 1 18 7	25
2	Turkey	12	2 3 1 9 6	4 2 0 14 3	6 5 1 23 9	23
3	Denmark	12	4 2 0 15 4	2 2 2 9 8	6 4 2 24 12	22
4	Greece	12	4 1 1 8 3	2 2 2 7 6	6 3 3 15 9	21
5	Albania	12	3 0 3 7 9	1 1 4 4 11	4 1 7 11 20	13
6	Georgia	12	1 3 2 8 11	1 1 4 6 14	2 4 6 14 25	10
7	Kazakhstan	12	0 0 6 4 15	0 1 5 2 14	0 1 11 6 29	1

TOP GOALSCORERS
7 FATIH Tekke (Turkey)
6 Andriy SHEVCHENKO (Ukraine)
  Jon Dahl TOMASSON (Denmark)
5 Søren LARSEN (Denmark)
  Giorgi DEMETRADZE (Georgia)
4 Erjon BOGDANI (Albania)

European Qualifying Tournament

also damaged their chances because it left Ukraine with nothing to play for the following week at home to Turkey, and the Turks duly bagged three improbable points thanks to Tümer Metin's second-half strike.

A month later the same player would secure Turkey's play-off berth in almost identical fashion as Fatih Terim's side prevailed 1-0 in Albania. Greece and Denmark also won their final-day fixtures, but with the Danes having beaten the European champions 1-0 in Copenhagen a few days earlier, there was nothing either team could do to prevent the triumphant Turks (who ended up unbeaten on their travels) from moving forward into the play-offs.

GROUP 3

Portugal, the European vice-champions, had World Cup qualification effectively sewn up as Group 3 entered its final phase. Three points above second-placed Slovakia (against whom they had a superior head-to-head record) and with three of their final four fixtures at home against modest opposition –

Luxembourg, Liechtenstein and Latvia – it was only a matter of time before Luiz Felipe Scolari's side secured their place in Germany as group winners.

The only obstacle in their path was a testing match in Moscow against a Russian side vying with Slovakia for second place. Portugal journeyed to the Russian capital on the back of a 6-0 thrashing of Luxembourg. They would not add to their goal tally in Moscow but they did manage to keep a clean sheet of their own, helped in no small part by the sending-off of Russian midfielder Alexei Smertin for a second bookable offence just before half-time.

Blushes spared

Portugal duly clinched their place at the finals a month and a day later, but for the second time in the competition they found it a real struggle against Liechtenstein. Held to a humiliating 2-2 draw in the first game in Vaduz, Scolari's men found themselves a goal down at home in Aveiro and their fightback proved anything but straightforward as Luís Figo fired a penalty over the bar with the score at 1-1 in

GROUP 3

RESULTS

Liechtenstein 1, Estonia 2
Estonia 4, Luxembourg 0
Russia 1, Slovakia 1
Portugal 4, Estonia 0
Liechtenstein 2, Portugal 2
Slovakia 4, Latvia 1
Luxembourg 0, Liechtenstein 4
Liechtenstein 1, Latvia 3
Russia 4, Estonia 0
Liechtenstein 1, Russia 2
Latvia 4, Luxembourg 0
Estonia 2, Liechtenstein 0
Russia 2, Latvia 0
Latvia 1, Liechtenstein 0

Slovakia 3, Luxembourg 1
Latvia 0, Portugal 2
Luxembourg 3, Latvia 4
Slovakia 7, Liechtenstein 0
Luxembourg 0, Russia 4
Latvia 2, Estonia 2
Portugal 7, Russia 1
Luxembourg 0, Portugal 5
Estonia 1, Slovakia 2
Estonia 1, Russia 1
Slovakia 1, Portugal 1
Portugal 2, Slovakia 0
Estonia 0, Portugal 1
Luxembourg 0, Slovakia 4

(17/8/05)
Latvia 1 *(Astafjevs 6)*, Russia 1 *(Arshavin 24)*
Liechtenstein 0, Slovakia 0

(3/9/05)
Estonia 2 *(Oper 11, Smirnov 71)*, Latvia 1 *(Laizans 90)*
Portugal 6 *(Jorge Andrade 23, Ricardo Carvalho 30, Pauleta 37, 56, Simão 79, 83)*, Luxembourg 0
Russia 2 *(Kerzhakov 27, 65)*, Liechtenstein 0

(7/9/05)
Latvia 1 *(Laizans 74)*, Slovakia 1 *(Vittek 35)*
Liechtenstein 3 *(Frick M. 38, Fischer 77, Beck T. 90)*, Luxembourg 0
Russia 0, Portugal 0

(8/10/05)
Portugal 2 *(Pauleta 49, Nuno Gomes 86)*, Liechtenstein 1 *(Fischer 32)*

Russia 5 *(Izmailov 7, Kerzhakov 18, Pvalyuchenko 69, Kirichenko 75, 90)*, Luxembourg 1 *(Reiter 52p)*
Slovakia 1 *(Hlinka 76)*, Estonia 0

(12/10/05)
Luxembourg 0, Estonia 2 *(Oper 7, 79p)*
Portugal 3 *(Pauleta 19, 21, Hugo Viana 85)*, Latvia 0
Slovakia 0, Russia 0

FINAL TABLE

		Home					Away					Total					
	Pld	W	D	L	F	A	W	D	L	F	A	W	D	L	F	A	Pts
1 Portugal	12	6	0	0	24	2	3	3	0	11	3	9	3	0	35	5	30
2 Slovakia	12	4	2	0	16	3	2	3	1	8	5	6	5	1	24	8	23
3 Russia	12	4	2	0	14	2	2	3	1	9	10	6	5	1	23	12	23
4 Estonia	12	3	1	2	10	5	2	1	3	6	12	5	2	5	16	17	17
5 Latvia	12	2	3	1	9	6	2	0	4	9	15	4	3	5	18	21	15
6 Liechtenstein	12	1	2	3	8	9	1	0	5	5	14	2	2	8	13	23	8
7 Luxembourg	12	0	0	6	3	23	0	0	6	2	25	0	0	12	5	48	0

TOP GOALSCORERS

11 PAULETA (Portugal)
7 CRISTIANO RONALDO (Portugal)
6 Róbert VITTEK (Slovakia)
   Andres OPER (Estonia)
5 Andrei ARSHAVIN (Russia)
   Maris VERPAKOVSKIS (Latvia)
4 Miroslav KARHAN (Slovakia)
   Dmitriy SYCHOV (Russia)
   Alexandr KERZHAKOV (Russia)
   Jurijs LAIZANS (Latvia)
   Mario FRICK (Liechtenstein)

European Qualifying Tournament

the second half. Fortunately, Nuno Gomes's late header spared the team's blushes, sealing the win they needed to guarantee back-to-back World Cup qualification for the first time in Portugal's history. Four days later they celebrated by beating Latvia in rather more convincing fashion, with Pauleta scoring twice in a 3-0 win to become not only Portugal's all-time top scorer (ahead of Eusébio) but also to secure his place as the best marksman in the entire European qualifying zone with a final tally of 11 goals.

The battle between Slovakia and Russia for second place went to the wire, with the two teams coming head to head on the final day. Slovakia's better goal difference meant that they could afford a draw, and that is what they got, in front of a rare full house in Bratislava, as a game of few chances ended goalless. It was the first time Slovakia had ever reached the play-offs of a major competition. Russia's elimination brought the curtain down on the brief reign of coach Yuriy Syomin, recruited to the position less than six months earlier.

A clash of heads in Bratislava between Russia defender Vasiliy Berezutskiy and Slovakia striker Róbert Vittek

GROUP 4

With the top four countries having cancelled each other out with a non-stop succession of draws, everything was still to play for as Group 4 entered the final straight. There were just three points separating the Republic of Ireland, Switzerland, Israel and France during the summer hiatus.

The situation looked particularly worrying for group seeds France, who had drawn all three of their home games 0-0 and faced the prospect of difficult away fixtures in Ireland and Switzerland. An urgent remedy was required, and it was provided by the return from international exile of midfield maestro Zinedine Zidane, who had been voluntarily absent from the team for 12 months. His unexpected U-turn inspired two other experienced players, Lilian Thuram and Claude Makelele, to offer up their services again.

Suitably reinforced, France made light work of beating the Faroe Islands in Lens, winning 3-0, but the big test for the remodelled side came four days later in Dublin, a place where they had not won for over 50 years. It was a critical encounter for both teams and it proved to be as tightly contested as all the other head-to-head clashes between the top four. The difference on this occasion, though, was that the game didn't end up all square. A stunning 25-yard shot from Thierry Henry midway through the second half silenced the capacity Lansdowne Road crowd, bringing France three vital points and enabling them to leapfrog their vanquished opponents and join Switzerland, 3-1 winners in Cyprus, at the top of the table.

Close contest

Switzerland met France the following month in Berne knowing that victory for either side would ensure that they finished above the other. Another close contest was anticipated and that was what transpired in the Stade de Suisse. France took the lead with a disputed goal from Djibril Cissé, who exploited a mix-up in the Swiss defence, but they lost it 11 minutes from time when left-back Ludovic Magnin curled in a dangerous free-kick that was deflected into the net off the head of Thuram. The 1-1 draw, coupled with Ireland's scrappy 1-0 win in Cyprus, left all permutations open going into the final day.

Once the calculations had been made, France knew that unless Switzerland won in Dublin a victory at home to Cyprus would give them first place in the group. A win by four goals would put them out of reach whatever occurred in Dublin. It was a gripping conclusion to the group and the outcome remained unresolved right to the end. Switzerland were the superior side in Dublin, but two gilt-edged chances for top scorer Alex Frei went begging and by the end, with news coming through that France, inspired by Zidane, had got the four goals they required in the Stade de France to clinch top spot (albeit after a frustratingly long delay between goals three and four), the Swiss eased off and decided to protect the point that ensured their unbeaten record and a place in the play-offs on goal difference ahead of Israel, whose programme was already complete.

European Qualifying Tournament

GROUP 4

RESULTS

France 0, Israel 0
Switzerland 6, Faroe Islands 0
Israel 2, Cyprus 1
Cyprus 2, Faroe Islands 2
Israel 2, Switzerland 2
Republic of Ireland 2, Faroe Islands 0
France 0, Switzerland 0
Israel 1, France 1
Faroe Islands 1, Switzerland 3
Faroe Islands 0, Republic of Ireland 2
Republic of Ireland 3, Cyprus 0
Faroe Islands 0, France 2
Switzerland 1, Republic of Ireland 1
France 0, Republic of Ireland 0
Cyprus 0, France 2
Cyprus 1, Israel 2
Israel 1, Republic of Ireland 1
Switzerland 1, Cyprus 0
Republic of Ireland 2, Israel 2

(17/8/05)
Faroe Islands 0, Cyprus 3 *(Konstantinou M. 39, 77p, Krassas 90)*

(3/9/05)
France 3 *(Cissé 13, 76, Olsen 18og)*, Faroe Islands 0
Switzerland 1 *(Frei 5)*, Israel 1 *(Keissy 20)*

(7/9/05)
Cyprus 1 *(Aloneftis 34)*, Switzerland 3 *(Frei 15, Senderos 70, Gygax 86)*
Faroe Islands 0, Israel 2 *(Nimni 55, Katan 80)*
Republic of Ireland 0, France 1 *(Henry 68)*

(8/10/05)
Cyprus 0, Republic of Ireland 1 *(Elliott 6)*
Israel 2 *(Benayoun 1, Zandberg 89)*, Faroe Islands 1 *(Samuelsen 90)*
Switzerland 1 *(Magnin 79)*, France 1 *(Cissé 52)*

(12/10/05)
France 4 *(Zidane 29, Wiltord 31, Dhorasoo 44, Giuly 84)*, Cyprus 0
Republic of Ireland 0, Switzerland 0

FINAL TABLE

		Home					Away					Total					Pts
	Pld	W	D	L	F	A	W	D	L	F	A	W	D	L	F	A	
1 France	10	2	3	0	7	0	3	2	0	7	2	5	5	0	14	2	20
2 Switzerland	10	2	3	0	10	3	2	3	0	8	4	4	6	0	18	7	18
3 Israel	10	2	3	0	8	6	2	3	0	7	4	4	6	0	15	10	18
4 Republic of Ireland	10	2	2	1	7	3	2	3	0	5	2	4	5	1	12	5	17
5 Cyprus	10	0	1	4	4	10	1	0	4	4	10	1	1	8	8	20	4
6 Faroe Islands	10	0	0	5	1	12	0	1	4	3	15	0	1	9	4	27	1

TOP GOALSCORERS

6   Alexander FREI (Switzerland)
4   Djibril CISSE (France)
     Johan VONLANTHEN (Switzerland)
     Robbie KEANE (Reublic of Ireland)
     Yossi BENAYOUN (Israel)
     Michalis KONSTANTINOU (Cyprus)

Ireland's weak finish to the campaign – they had led the table after seven matches but finished up fourth – heralded the end of Brian Kerr's reign as manager. For France, however, that win in Dublin – the only one of the 12 games between the leading four teams that yielded a victor – had ultimately proved crucial. The return of Zidane and co had provided the spark to reignite Les Bleus' campaign, and now, having survived it unscathed, the 1998 world champions could make plans to regain their crown in Germany.

GROUP 5

Italy's bid to make a 12th successive appearance at the World Cup finals suffered a nasty jolt early in the campaign when they lost in Slovenia, but thereafter things improved for the Azzurri, and with all of their rivals dropping points right, left and centre, Marcello Lippi's side appeared to be in a position of some security as Group 5 entered its decisive phase.

Their run-in began in Glasgow against a Scotland side that had found a new lease of life under coach Walter Smith. A grand occasion at Hampden Park was matched by an excellent game. Scotland took an early lead when Kenny Miller headed in Paul Hartley's superb cross and for a while, with the home side producing one of their best performances in years, a shock result appeared to be on the cards. But Italy applied persistent pressure in the second half and were rewarded when half-time substitute Fabio Grosso volleyed in a scrambled equaliser 15 minutes from time.

Toni hat-trick

Scotland's rising hopes of a play-off berth had been checked by Grosso's goal but they were dented even more by Norway's last-gasp win in Slovenia. Four days later, while Italy were getting back to winning ways – and taking complete command of the group - with a 4-1 destruction of Belarus in Minsk (thanks to a Luca Toni hat-trick), Scotland impressively beat the Norwegians 2-1 in Oslo with Miller again providing the goals. But ultimately it would prove too little, too late. On the penultimate matchday a trio of 1-0 wins – for Italy against Slovenia, Norway against Moldova and, surprisingly, Belarus in Scotland – settled all the key issues.

Italy, who needed only a draw in Palermo to secure top spot, won the game with a late goal from local favourite Cristian Zaccardo, while Norway put themselves out of reach in second place thanks to Sigurd Rushfeldt's strike in Oslo and to Scotland's sudden fall from grace against a depleted Belarus in Glasgow, during the first half of which the visitors, who had switched several of their regular first-

European Qualifying Tournament

GROUP 5

RESULTS

Italy 2, Norway 1
Moldova 0, Italy 1
Scotland 0, Slovenia 0
Scotland 0, Norway 1
Italy 4, Belarus 3
Norway 3, Slovenia 0
Moldova 0, Norway 0
Belarus 1, Slovenia 1
Scotland 2, Moldova 0

Slovenia 3, Moldova 0
Norway 1, Belarus 1
Belarus 4, Moldova 0
Slovenia 1, Italy 0
Moldova 1, Scotland 1
Italy 2, Scotland 0
Slovenia 1, Belarus 1
Norway 0, Italy 0
Belarus 0, Scotland 0

(3/9/05)
Moldova 2 *(Rogaciov 15, 49)*, Belarus 0
Scotland 1 *(Miller 12)*, Italy 1 *(Grosso 75)*
Slovenia 2 *(Cimerotic 5, Zlogar 83)*, Norway 3 *(Carew, Lundekvam 24, Gamst Pedersen 90)*

(7/9/05)
Belarus 1 *(Kutuzov 4)*, Italy 4 *(Toni 6, 14, 55, Camoranesi 45)*
Moldova 1 *(Rogaciov 30)*, Slovenia 2 *(Lavric 46, Mavric M. 57)*
Norway 1 *(Årst 89)*, Scotland 2 *(Miller 21, 31)*

(8/10/05)
Italy 1 *(Zaccardo 78)*, Slovenia 0
Norway 1 *(Rushfeldt 50)*, Moldova 0
Scotland 0, Belarus 1 *(Kutuzov 6)*

(12/10/05)
Belarus 0, Norway 1 *(Helstad 70)*
Italy 2 *(Vieri 71, Gilardino 85)*, Moldova 1 *(Gatcan 76)*
Slovenia 0, Scotland 3 *(Fletcher 4, McFadden 47, Hartley 84)*

FINAL TABLE

		Pld	Home W D L F A	Away W D L F A	Total W D L F A	Pts
1	Italy	10	5 0 0 11 5	2 2 1 6 3	7 2 1 17 8	23
2	Norway	10	2 2 1 6 3	3 1 1 6 4	5 3 2 12 7	18
3	Scotland	10	1 2 2 3 3	2 2 1 6 4	3 4 3 9 7	13
4	Slovenia	10	2 1 2 7 7	1 2 2 3 6	3 3 4 10 13	12
5	Belarus	10	1 2 2 6 6	1 2 2 6 8	2 4 4 12 14	10
6	Moldova	10	1 2 2 4 4	0 0 5 1 12	1 2 7 5 16	5

TOP GOALSCORERS

4 Luca TONI (Italy)
   Vitaliy KUTUZOV (Belarus)

teamers to the Under-21 side, ran riot, with early marksman Vitaliy Kutuzov left cursing himself for not scoring a hat-trick.

There were different fortunes for Belarus and Scotland four days later, but Italy ended their campaign with yet another win, maintaining their perfect home record thanks to a late winning goal from Alberto Gilardino against Moldova in Lecce.

Alberto Gilardino – the Milan striker sealed Italy's campaign with a late winner against Moldova

GROUP 6

England and Poland, World Cup rivals so often in the past, had a firm grip on the top two places in Group 6 going into the closing stages of the campaign. Although England had won the head-to-head 2-1 in Chorzow, the Poles had been victorious in each of their other six matches and, having played one game more than Sven Göran Eriksson's team, led the table by two points over the summer break.

England faced two awkward games in early September away to local rivals Wales and Northern Ireland. The first match, in Cardiff, saw Eriksson fiddle with his usual formation, using Wayne Rooney up front on his own in a 4-5-1 system as a result of Michael Owen's suspension. Although they dominated possession and defended well, England could only manage a stuttering 1-0 win thanks to a deflected shot by the otherwise ineffective Joe Cole and a world-class save by Paul Robinson from a John Hartson header.

Later that day Poland kept the pressure on by defeating Austria 3-2 in a thrilling contest in Chorzow. The home side were in complete control during the first half, but the Austrians responded brilliantly in the second, scoring twice through substitute striker Roland Linz, who was cruelly deprived of a hat-trick – and his team of a valuable point - when he headed against the bar in the final minute.

Four days later Austria's outside chance of a play-off

European Qualifying Tournament

place ended when they were held 0-0 in Azerbaijan, but although that result guaranteed both front-runners at least a play-off spot, there was to be a rude awakening later in the day for England as they fell to one of the most embarrassing defeats in their World Cup history, beaten 1-0 in Belfast by a euphoric Northern Ireland.

Historic Healy

If the whole evening was a shambles for Eriksson and his highly paid players, with only skipper David Beckham, operating in central midfield, performing to anything like his normal standard, it was a truly unforgettable occasion for their hosts, who exploited England's patternless, chaotic play by scoring a memorable winning goal, from all-time top scorer David Healy, 16 minutes from time. England had no response. It was Eriksson's first defeat in a qualifying game, and, even more incredibly, Northern Ireland's first home win over England since 1927.

On the same evening Poland looked to have secured qualification with a 1-0 home win over Wales as, at worst, one of the two 'best runners-up', but minutes after the final whistle in Warsaw a late winner from Sweden in Hungary agonisingly denied them that prize.

A month and a day later, however, the Poles' place in Germany was duly clinched – without their having

England captain David Beckham congratulates Northern Ireland goalscorer David Healy

to kick a ball. It was the same scenario for England. After an unconvincing 1-0 win at Old Trafford over Austria, during which Beckham was harshly sent off for two mild yellow-card offences in rapid succession, England returned to their Manchester hotel and awaited news of the Czech Republic-Holland clash in Group 1. The news was good. Holland's 2-0 win meant that Poland or England would definitely qualify automatically as one of the best runners-up.

For a long time it had seemed that the meeting at Old Trafford between the top two would be decisive.

GROUP 6

RESULTS

Austria 2, England 2
Northern Ireland 0, Poland 3
Poland 1, England 2
Austria 1, Poland 3
England 2, Wales 0
Northern Ireland 3, Austria 3
England 4, Northern Ireland 0
Wales 0, Austria 2
England 2, Azerbaijan 0
Azerbaijan 0, Poland 3

Azerbaijan 1, Wales 1
Austria 2, Azerbaijan 0
Wales 2, Northern Ireland 2
Azerbaijan 0, Northern Ireland 0
Azerbaijan 0, England 1
Wales 2, Poland 3
Poland 8, Azerbaijan 0
Austria 1, Wales 0
Poland 1, Northern Ireland 0

(3/9/05)
Northern Ireland 2 *(Elliott 60, Feeney 85p)*, Azerbaijan 0
Poland 3 *(Smolarek 12, Kosowski 22, Zurawski 68)*, Austria 2 *(Linz 61, 80)*
Wales 0, England 1 *(Cole J. 54)*

(7/9/05)
Azerbaijan 0, Austria 0
Northern Ireland 1 *(Healy 74)*, England 0
Poland 1 *(Zurawski 54p)*, Wales 0

(8/10/05)
England 1 *(Lampard 25p)*, Austria 0

Northern Ireland 2 *(Gillespie 46, Davis 50)*, Wales 3 *(Davies 27, Robinson 38, Giggs 61)*

(12/10/05)
Austria 2 *(Aufhauser 44, 90)*, Northern Ireland 0
England 2 *(Owen 44, Lampard 80)*, Poland 1 *(Frankowski 45)*
Wales 2 *(Giggs 3, 51)*, Azerbaijan 0

FINAL TABLE

		Pld	Home W D L F A	Away W D L F A	Total W D L F A	Pts
1	England	10	5 0 0 11 1	3 1 1 6 4	8 1 1 17 5	25
2	Poland	10	4 0 1 14 4	4 0 1 13 5	8 0 2 27 9	24
3	Austria	10	3 1 1 8 5	1 2 2 7 7	4 3 3 15 12	15
4	Northern Ireland	10	2 1 2 8 9	0 2 3 3 2 9	2 3 5 10 18	9
5	Wales	10	1 1 3 6 8	1 1 3 4 7	2 2 6 10 15	8
6	Azerbaijan	10	0 3 2 1 5	0 0 5 0 16	0 3 7 1 21	3

TOP GOALSCORERS

7 Tomasz FRANKOWSKI (Poland)
  Maciej ZURAWSKI (Poland)
5 Frank LAMPARD (England)
4 Jacek KRZYNOWEK (Poland)

European Qualifying Tournament

Now, with both teams safely qualified, its only relevance was to determine the group winners. England, with Rooney back from a one-match suspension, played far better than they had against the Austrians and deservedly ran out winners, although it took a fabulous late strike from Frank Lampard, the team's leading scorer in the competition with five goals, to claim the three points that secured a 100 per cent home record and catapulted them above their opponents into first place in the final group standings.

GROUP 7

Spain's struggle to score goals had left the perennial World Cup qualifiers under threat from Serbia & Montenegro in the battle to win Group 8, and when the team formerly known as Yugoslavia registered a seventh successive clean sheet in beating Lithuania 2-0 to move two points clear at the top of the table, there was understandable anxiety among Spanish fans in the build-up to the clash of the top two on September 7 in Madrid.

Those fears seemed misplaced when Raúl gave the home side an early lead in the Vicente Calderón stadium and Spain went on to dominate the first half, but with local hero Fernando Torres firing blanks the job was not yet done, and after the interval it was another Atlético Madrid striker, new recruit Mateja Kezman, who drew Serbia & Montenegro level after a rare error from Real Madrid goalkeeper Iker Casillas. Kezman later had a glorious chance to win the game for the visitors and all but ensure their qualification but he put his shot wide. Nevertheless, the 1-1 draw was good news for Serbia & Montenegro, who remained two points in front of Spain with two games remaining. It would have been even better had FIFA adopted the policy used in European club competitions of applying the away-goals rule as a factor in determining classification by head-to-head results. But they didn't, so instead of needing four points from their final two games to be sure of first place, Ilija Petkovic's side were obliged to win both of them – away to Lithuania and at home to Bosnia-Herzegovina.

Back in the hunt

The Bosnians had won only one of their first six matches, but suddenly, after back-to-back 1-0 wins over Belgium and Lithuania, in each of which veteran midfielder Sergej Barbarez grabbed the winning goal, they were right back in the hunt. As for Belgium, their last lingering hopes of a seventh successive World Cup qualification were crushed by a 2-0 home defeat by Spain, in which the visitors' two outstanding performers were Casillas, who made two excellent saves, and Fernando Torres, who scored both goals, the first of them an exquisite volley from José Antonio Reyes' equally impressive long diagonal pass.

With Serbia & Montenegro also winning 2-0 in Lithuania and Bosnia-Herzegovina's long-serving striker Elvir Bolic helping himself to a hat-trick in a 3-0 win over San Marino, the battle lines were drawn for the final day. If Spain, as expected, were to win in San Marino, that would secure them at least a play-off place. But they could only win the group if Serbia & Montenegro failed to beat Bosnia-Herzegovina in Belgrade. A win for Bosnia would put them above their hosts on the head-to-head rule and earn them at least a play-off spot.

Spain's victory over San Marino was never in doubt after they went ahead in the first minute. Fernando Torres went on to score a hat-trick, but it was the one goal scored by his club strike partner Kezman in the seventh minute of the game in Belgrade that would prove to be of greater value. Kezman's fourth goal in as many games – a tap-in from giant centre-forward Nikola Zigic's knockdown – was all Serbia & Montenegro, and their miserly defence, needed to win the game and book their passage to Germany. With just one goal conceded in ten matches, there could be no argument that they deserved their automatic qualification, although that didn't stop Spain boss Luis Aragonés from defiantly claiming that his team had been the best in the group. One look at the final table, however, showed that while Serbia & Montenegro could advance to Germany, Spain, as in their Euro 2004 campaign, would have to seek qualification via the back-door entry of the play-offs.

Mateja Kezman – his goals took Serbia & Montenegro to the World Cup finals

European Qualifying Tournament

GROUP 7

RESULTS
Belgium 1, Lithuania 1
Bosnia-Herzegovina 1, Spain 1
Bosnia-Herzegovina 0, Serbia & Montenegro 0
Spain 2, Belgium 0
Serbia & Montenegro 5, San Marino 0
San Marino 0, Lithuania 1
Belgium 4, Bosnia-Herzegovina 1
San Marino 1, Belgium 2
San Marino 1, Bosnia-Herzegovina 3
Spain 1, Lithuania 0
San Marino 0, Serbia & Montenegro 3
Lithuania 4, San Marino 0
Lithuania 0, Spain 0
Belgium 0, Serbia & Montenegro 2
Spain 5, San Marino 0
Bosnia-Herzegovina 1, Lithuania 1
Serbia & Montenegro 0, Spain 0
Serbia & Montenegro 0, Belgium 0
Spain 1, Bosnia-Herzegovina 1

(3/9/05)
Bosnia-Herzegovina 1 *(Barbarez 62)*, Belgium 0
Serbia & Montenegro 2 *(Kezman 18, Ilic 75)*, Lithuania 0

(7/9/05)
Belgium 8 *(Simons 32p, Daerden 39, 67, Buffel 44, Mpenza M. 52, 71, Vandenbergh 53, Van Buyten 83)*, San Marino 0
Lithuania 0, Bosnia-Herzegovina 1 *(Barbarez 33)*
Spain 1 *(Raúl 18)*, Serbia & Montenegro 1 *(Kezman 68)*

(8/10/05)
Belgium 0, Spain 2 *(Fernando Torres 56, 59)*

Bosnia-Herzegovina 3 *(Bolic 48, 75, 85)*, San Marino 0
Lithuania 0, Serbia & Montenegro 2 *(Kezman 43, Vukic 88)*

(12/10/05)
Lithuania 1 *(Deschacht 38og)*, Belgium 1 *(Geraerts 17)*
San Marino 0, Spain 6 *(Antonio López 1, Fernando Torres 10, 78p, 89, Sergio Ramos 30, 38)*
Serbia & Montenegro 1 *(Kezman 7)*, Bosnia-Herzegovina 0

FINAL TABLE

		Pld	Home W D L F A	Away W D L F A	Total W D L F A	Pts
1	Serbia & Montenegro	10	3 2 0 8 0	3 2 0 8 1	6 4 0 16 1	22
2	Spain	10	3 2 0 10 2	2 3 0 9 1	5 5 0 19 3	20
3	Bosnia-Herzegovina	10	2 3 0 6 2	2 1 2 6 7	4 4 2 12 9	16
4	Belgium	10	2 1 2 13 6	1 2 2 3 5	3 3 4 16 11	12
5	Lithuania	10	1 2 2 5 4	1 2 2 3 5	2 4 4 8 9	10
6	San Marino	10	0 0 5 2 15	0 0 5 0 25	0 0 10 2 40	0

TOP GOALSCORERS
6   FERNANDO TORRES (Spain)
5   Mateja KEZMAN (Serbia & Montenegro)
     Elvir BOLIC (Bosnia-Herzegovina)
4   Zvonimir VUKIC (Serbia & Montenegro)

GROUP 8

With 60 per cent of Group 8's fixtures completed, it was fairly obvious that Croatia and Sweden would finish in the top two. The only question was in which order. And even then that might prove irrelevant given that both teams were in a strong position to withstand the disappointment of failing to win the group by qualifying automatically as one of the two 'best runners-up'.

Both teams posted convincing wins on matchday seven to reinforce their positions of strength. Croatia came from behind to win 3-1 in Iceland thanks to a brace from Bruges hitman Bosko Balaban while Sweden also netted three goals in the second half to overcome Bulgaria, thus killing off any lingering challenge from Hristo Stoichkov's team.

Matchday eight proved rather more problematic for the two pace-setters. As Croatia surrendered their perfect away record by stumbling to an ignominious 1-1 draw in Malta, the Swedes left it extremely late before taking all three points in Hungary, Zlatan Ibrahimovic's rather fortuitous winning goal arriving deep into stoppage-time. That win enabled Sweden to vault into a one-point lead in advance of the following month's showdown in Zagreb.

Srna spot on

Although the game had been switched to Split because of concerns about the Zagreb crowd's heckling of Croatia boss Zlatko Kranjcar's son, playmaker Niko, in an earlier game, the Croatian FA eventually reversed the decision and returned the fixture to the Maksimir stadium. Kranjcar junior, who had controversially moved from Dinamo Zagreb to Hajduk Split the previous season, duly took the field and it was his cross that was handled by Swedish skipper Olof Mellberg early in the second half, allowing Darijo Srna, the matchwinner against the Swedes in Gothenburg earlier in the campaign, the opportunity to score from the penalty spot, which he accomplished in style, sending goalkeeper Andreas Isaksson the wrong way. It proved to be the winning goal, enabling Croatia to wrest back group leadership from their rivals and secure their fifth major tournament qualification in just six attempts.

Sweden, however, had no need to be unduly disheartened by their first qualifying defeat away from home for eight years, because a few hundred miles to the north, in Prague, the Czech Republic's home defeat to Holland left the Scandinavians requiring only a point from their final fixture at home to Iceland to claim automatic qualification for the finals as one of the best runners-up.

While Croatia duly secured top spot four days later by maintaining their unbeaten record with a goalless draw in Hungary, Sweden signed off with a 3-1 victory over Iceland that not only clinched their qualification but also kept up their impressive strike-rate of three goals per game – the highest average figure of any of the teams in the European qualifying zone.

European Qualifying Tournament

GROUP 8

RESULTS

Croatia 3, Hungary 0
Malta 0, Sweden 7
Sweden 0, Croatia 1
Malta 0, Iceland 0
Bulgaria 4, Malta 1
Malta 0, Hungary 2
Croatia 4, Iceland 0
Hungary 1, Bulgaria 1
Iceland 2, Hungary 3
Iceland 4, Malta 1

Iceland 1, Bulgaria 3
Hungary 3, Iceland 2
Croatia 2, Bulgaria 2
Sweden 3, Hungary 0
Iceland 1, Sweden 4
Bulgaria 0, Sweden 3
Croatia 3, Malta 0
Bulgaria 1, Croatia 3
Sweden 6, Malta 0

(3/9/05)
Hungary 4 *(Torghelle 35, Said 57og, Takács Á. 65, Rajczi 83)*, Malta 0
Iceland 1 *(Gudjohnsen 24)*, Croatia 3 *(Balaban 56, 61, Srna 82p)*
Sweden 3 *(Ljungberg 60, Mellberg 75, Ibrahimovic 90)*, Bulgaria 0

(7/9/05)
Bulgaria 3 *(Berbatov 21, Iliev G. 69, Petrov M. 86)*, Iceland 2 *(Steinsson 9, Hreidarsson 16)*
Hungary 0, Sweden 1 *(Ibrahimovic 90)*
Malta 1 *(Wellman 74)*, Croatia 1 *(Kranjcar 19)*

(8/10/05)
Bulgaria 2 *(Berbatov 30, Lazarov 55)*, Hungary 0

Croatia 1 *(Srna 56p)*, Sweden 0

(12/10/05)
Hungary 0, Croatia 0
Malta 1 *(Barbara 78)*, Bulgaria 1 *(Yankov 67)*
Sweden 3 *(Ibrahimovic 29, Larsson 42, Källström 90)*, Iceland 1 *(Arnason 25)*

FINAL TABLE

	Pld	Home W D L F A	Away W D L F A	Total W D L F A	Pts
1 Croatia	10	4 1 0 13 2	3 2 0 8 3	7 3 0 21 5	24
2 Sweden	10	4 0 1 15 2	4 0 1 15 2	8 0 2 30 4	24
3 Bulgaria	10	3 0 2 10 9	1 3 1 7 8	4 3 3 17 17	15
4 Hungary	10	2 2 1 8 4	2 0 3 5 10	4 2 4 13 14	14
5 Iceland	10	1 0 4 9 14	0 1 4 5 13	1 1 8 14 27	4
6 Malta	10	0 3 2 2 11	0 0 5 2 21	0 3 7 4 32	3

TOP GOALSCORERS

8 Zlatan IBRAHIMOVIC (Sweden)
7 Fredrik LJUNGBERG (Sweden)
   Dimitar BERBATOV (Bulgaria)
6 Eidur GUDJOHNSEN (Iceland)
5 Dado PRSO (Croatia)
   Henrik LARSSON (Sweden)
4 Darijo SRNA (Croatia)

PLAY-OFFS

The draw for the qualifying play-offs, held two days after the conclusion of the group phase, split the three seeded teams – Spain, Turkey and the Czech Republic. Of the trio, Spain, in being paired with Slovakia, looked to have been given the easiest ride to Germany, while the Czechs, despite their sagging form, looked strongly fancied to dispose of Norway. On the other hand, Switzerland, unbeaten in ten group games, against Turkey, the 2002 bronze medallists, looked too close to call.

Spain were quickly into their stride in the first leg at the Vicente Calderón stadium in Madrid. Liverpool mdfielder Luis Enrique, who had never previously found the net for his country, scored two fine goals, the first with a finely placed header, the second on the volley from Xavi's chipped pass. There was only one team in it but just after half-time Slovakia landed a sucker punch when substitute Szilárd Németh latched on to a dreadful backpass from – of all people – Luis García before nutmegging Iker Casillas with his shot.

Double trouble

The match, and the tie, was effectively settled on 63 minutes, however, when Spain were awarded a highly controversial penalty for handball and, to double Slovakia's misery, Marián Had, already on a yellow card, earned a second for contesting the decision and was sent off. Fernando Torres smashed in the penalty to restore Spain's two-goal lead, and before long the home side had doubled that advantage as Luis García redeemed himself with another fine finish to complete his hat-trick and substitute Fernando Morientes made it 5-1 with a typically assured header.

The second leg, in Bratislava, was virtually a dead rubber. Luis García was absent with a heel injury but it was another player who had never previously scored at international level, Valencia striker David Villa, who ensured that Spain travelled to Germany with an unbeaten record thanks to his well-taken 71st-minute equaliser after Slovakia had taken a surprise lead, with a low left-footed drive from striker Filip Holosko, just after the interval.

The Czech Republic travelled north to Oslo for the first leg of their play-off buoyed by the return from international exile, after 16 months, of their former captain and inspiration, Pavel Nedved. As expected, the Juventus midfielder had a strong impact on the game but it was another old-timer, Vladimír Smicer, who won the game, smartly heading in an excellent right-wing cross from yet another veteran campaigner, Karel Poborsky.

European Qualifying Tournament

First finals

The Czechs fully deserved their win on a very poor surface in the Ullevaal stadium. The playing conditions were better in Prague four days later, and once again Karel Brückner's side ran the show. Qualification was all but secured after 35 minutes when Tomás Rosicky drove home a powerful shot on the run after a strong surge down the right by Milan Baros. Smicer later had a goal questionably ruled out for offside, but it didn't matter. One goal in each leg had been enough. The Czech Republic were through to the World Cup finals for the very first time.

There was a terrific atmosphere in the Stade de Suisse as Switzerland expectantly hosted Turkey. Köbi Kuhn's team were on top throughout the first half and the home fans had something to cheer at the end of it when Philippe Senderos flicked in a header from Ludovic Magnin's deep, pacy free-kick. Marco Streller missed a great opportunity to double Switzerland's lead early in the second half but was denied by a point-blank save from Volkan. The home side pushed for a second goal and were rewarded late in the game when substitute Valon Behrami, with his very first touch, swept the ball in at the far post from a slightly deflected right-wing cross.

The extra protection of that second goal made Switzerland slight favourites ahead of the second leg in Istanbul, but when Turkey's experienced defender Alpay handled in the area to gift Switzerland an early penalty, from which Alexander Frei scored, the likelihood of a Turkish comeback seemed remote. They now required four goals without reply to turn the tie.

But come back Turkey did. Two headed goals from Tuncay Sanli – playing in his home Fenerbahçe stadium – brought the home fans back to life, and when Necati sent Pascal Zuberbühler the wrong way from the penalty spot early in the second half, Switzerland were in real trouble. Turkey pressed repeatedly for the all-important fourth goal but six minutes from time the noisy home fans fell eerily silent as the Swiss broke away on the counter-attack and Streller skilfully took the ball round keeper Volkan before slotting it left-footed into the empty net. There was still time for Turkey to strike back, Tuncay completing a hat-trick of headers five minutes later, but the Swiss defence eventually held on to their priceless away-goals advantage.

Violent brawl

At the final whistle there was rage and disappointment in the stands and absolute

It's all kicking off in Istanbul – Turkey defender Alpay puts the boot in as Switzerland striker Marco Streller heads for sanctuary

pandemonium on the field and in the tunnel, where rival players and members of the coaching staff attacked each other with violent kicks and punches. A full-scale brawl ensued, which would lead to a FIFA investigation and swingeing punishments for the perpetrators, most of them Turkish. Switzerland could not get out of Istanbul quickly enough, but when they arrived home, they were met by thousands of exultant fans. The team's unbeaten run may have ended but it didn't matter. While Turkey would be staying at home the following summer, Switzerland would be in neighbouring Germany playing World Cup finals football for the first time in 12 years.

And thus Europe's line-up for the 2006 finals was complete, with Switzerland, Spain and the Czech Republic joining group winners Holland, Ukraine, Portugal, France, Italy, England, Serbia & Montenegro and Croatia plus best runners-up Poland and Sweden alongside tournament hosts Germany. A 14-strong task force fit to take on the world.

PLAY-OFFS

Norway 0, Czech Republic 1 *(Smicer 31)*
Czech Republic 1 *(Rosicky 35)*, Norway 0
(Czech Republic 2-0)

Spain 5 *(Luis García 8, 16, 72, Fernando Torres 65p, Morientes 78)*, Slovakia 1 *(Németh 49)*
Slovakia 1 *(Holosko 50)*, Spain 1 *(David Villa 71)*
(Spain 6-2)

Switzerland 2 *(Senderos 41, Behrami 86)*, Turkey 0
Turkey 4 *(Tuncay 24, 38, 89, Necati 52p)*, Switzerland 2 *(Frei 2p, Streller 84)*
(4-4; Switzerland on away goals)

Euro 2008

Qualifying Fixtures

GROUP A

Portugal, Poland, Serbia, Belgium, Finland, Armenia, Azerbaijan, Kazakhstan

2006
16/8	Belgium v Kazakhstan
2/9	Poland v Finland; Serbia v Azerbaijan
6/9	Armenia v Belgium; Azerbaijan v Kazakhstan; Finland v Portugal ; Poland v Serbia
7/10	Armenia v Finland; Kazakhstan v Poland; Portugal v Azerbaijan; Serbia v Belgium
11/10	Belgium v Azerbaijan; Kazakhstan v Finland; Poland v Portugal; Serbia v Armenia
15/11	Belgium v Poland; Finland v Armenia; Portugal v Kazakhstan

2007
24/3	Kazakhstan v Serbia; Poland v Azerbaijan; Portugal v Belgium
28/3	Azerbaijan v Finland; Poland v Armenia; Serbia v Portugal
2/6	Azerbaijan v Poland; Belgium v Portugal; Finland v Serbia; Kazakhstan v Armenia
6/6	Armenia v Poland; Finland v Belgium; Kazakhstan v Azerbaijan
22/8	Armenia v Portugal; Belgium v Serbia; Finland v Kazakhstan
8/9	Azerbaijan v Armenia; Portugal v Poland; Serbia v Finland
12/9	Armenia v Azerbaijan; Finland v Poland; Kazakhstan v Belgium; Portugal v Serbia
13/10	Armenia v Serbia; Azerbaijan v Portugal; Belgium v Finland; Poland v Kazakhstan
17/10	Azerbaijan v Serbia; Belgium v Armenia; Kazakhstan v Portugal
17/11	Finland v Azerbaijan; Poland v Belgium; Portugal v Armenia; Serbia v Kazakhstan
21/11	Armenia v Kazakhstan; Azerbaijan v Belgium; Portugal v Finland; Serbia v Poland

GROUP B

France, Italy, Ukraine, Scotland, Lithuania, Georgia, Faroe Islands

2006
16/8	Faroe Islands v Georgia
2/9	Georgia v France; Italy v Lithuania; Scotland v Faroe Islands
6/9	France v Italy; Lithuania v Scotland; Ukraine v Georgia
7/10	Faroe Islands v Lithuania; Italy v Ukraine; Scotland v France
11/10	France v Faroe Islands; Georgia v Italy; Ukraine v Scotland

2007
24/3	Lithuania v France; Scotland v Georgia
28/3	Georgia v Faroe Islands; Italy v Scotland; Ukraine v Lithuania
2/6	France v Ukraine; Lithuania v Georgia; Faroe Islands v Italy
6/6	Faroe Islands v Scotland; France v Georgia; Lithuania v Italy
22/8	Faroe Islands v Ukraine
8/9	Georgia v Ukraine; Italy v France; Scotland v Lithuania
12/9	France v Scotland; Lithuania v Faroe Islands; Ukraine v Italy
13/10	Faroe Islands v France; Italy v Georgia; Scotland v Ukraine
17/10	France v Lithuania; Scotland v Georgia; Ukraine v Faroe Islands
17/11	Lithuania v Ukraine; Scotland v Italy
21/11	Georgia v Lithuania; Italy v Faroe Islands; Ukraine v France

GROUP C

Greece, Turkey, Norway, Bosnia-Herzegovina, Hungary, Moldova, Malta

2006
2/9	Hungary v Norway; Malta v Bosnia-Herzegovina; Moldova v Greece
6/9	Bosnia-Herzegovina v Hungary; Norway v Moldova; Turkey v Malta
7/10	Greece v Norway; Hungary v Turkey; Moldova v Bosnia-Herzegovina
11/10	Bosnia-Herzegovina v Greece; Malta v Hungary; Turkey v Moldova

2007
24/3	Greece v Turkey; Moldova v Malta; Norway v Bosnia-Herzegovina
28/3	Hungary v Moldova; Malta v Greece; Turkey v Norway
2/6	Bosnia-Herzegovina v Turkey; Greece v Hungary; Norway v Malta
6/6	Greece v Moldova; Bosnia-Herzegovina v Malta; Norway v Hungary
8/9	Hungary v Bosnia-Herzegovina; Malta v Turkey; Moldova v Norway
12/9	Bosnia-Herzegovina v Moldova; Norway v Greece; Turkey v Hungary
13/10	Greece v Bosnia-Herzegovina; Hungary v Malta; Moldova v Turkey
17/10	Bosnia-Herzegovina v Norway; Malta v Moldova; Turkey v Greece
17/11	Greece v Malta; Moldova v Hungary; Norway v Turkey
21/11	Hungary v Greece; Malta v Norway; Turkey v Bosnia-Herzegovina

Euro 2008

GROUP D

Czech Republic, Germany, Slovakia, Republic of Ireland, Wales, Cyprus, San Marino

2006
2/9	Czech Republic v Wales; Germany v Republic of Ireland; Slovakia v Cyprus
6/9	San Marino v Germany; Slovakia v Czech Republic
7/10	Cyprus v Republic of Ireland; Czech Republic v San Marino; Wales v Slovakia
11/10	Republic of Ireland v Czech Republic; Slovakia v Germany; Wales v Cyprus
15/11	Cyprus v Germany; Republic of Ireland v San Marino

2007
7/2	San Marino v Republic of Ireland
24/3	Cyprus v Slovakia; Czech Republic v Germany; Republic of Ireland v Wales
28/3	Czech Republic v Cyprus; Republic of Ireland v Slovakia; Wales v San Marino
2/6	Germany v San Marino; Wales v Czech Republic
6/6	Germany v Slovakia
22/8	San Marino v Cyprus
8/9	San Marino v Czech Republic; Slovakia v Republic of Ireland; Wales v Germany
12/9	Cyprus v San Marino; Czech Republic v Republic of Ireland; Slovakia v Wales
13/10	Cyprus v Wales; Republic of Ireland v Germany; Slovakia v San Marino
17/10	Germany v Czech Republic; Republic of Ireland v Cyprus; San Marino v Wales
17/11	Czech Republic v Slovakia; Germany v Cyprus; Wales v Republic of Ireland
21/11	Cyprus v Czech Republic; Germany v Wales; San Marino v Slovakia

GROUP E

England, Croatia, Russia, Israel, Estonia, Macedonia, Andorra

2006
16/8	Estonia v Macedonia
2/9	England v Andorra; Estonia v Israel
6/9	Israel v Andorra; Macedonia v England; Russia v Croatia
7/10	Croatia v Andorra; England v Macedonia; Russia v Israel
11/10	Andorra v Macedonia; Croatia v England; Russia v Estonia
15/11	Israel v Croatia; Macedonia v Russia

2007
24/3	Croatia v Macedonia; Estonia v Russia; Israel v England
28/3	Andorra v England; Israel v Estonia
2/6	Estonia v Croatia; Macedonia v Israel; Russia v Andorra
6/6	Andorra v Israel; Croatia v Russia; Estonia v England
22/8	Estonia v Andorra
8/9	Croatia v Estonia; England v Israel; Russia v Macedonia
12/9	Andorra v Croatia; England v Russia; Macedonia v Estonia
13/10	England v Estonia
17/10	Croatia v Israel; Macedonia v Andorra; Russia v England
17/11	Andorra v Estonia; Israel v Russia; Macedonia v Croatia
21/11	Andorra v Russia; England v Croatia; Israel v Macedonia

GROUP F

Sweden, Spain, Denmark, Latvia, Iceland, Northern Ireland, Liechtenstein

2006
2/9	Latvia v Sweden; Northern Ireland v Iceland; Spain v Liechtenstein
6/9	Iceland v Denmark; Northern Ireland v Spain; Sweden v Liechtenstein
7/10	Denmark v Northern Ireland; Latvia v Iceland; Sweden v Spain
11/10	Iceland v Sweden; Liechtenstein v Denmark; Northern Ireland v Latvia

2007
24/3	Liechtenstein v Northern Ireland ; Spain v Denmark
28/3	Liechtenstein v Latvia ; Northern Ireland v Sweden ; Spain v Iceland
2/6	Denmark v Sweden ; Iceland v Liechtenstein ; Latvia v Spain
6/6	Latvia v Denmark ; Liechtenstein v Spain ; Sweden v Iceland
22/8	Northern Ireland v Liechtenstein
8/9	Iceland v Spain ; Latvia v Northern Ireland ; Sweden v Denmark
12/9	Denmark v Liechtenstein; Iceland v Northern Ireland; Spain v Latvia
13/10	Denmark v Spain; Iceland v Latvia ; Liechtenstein v Sweden
17/10	Denmark v Latvia ; Liechtenstein v Iceland ; Sweden v Northern Ireland
17/11	Latvia v Liechtenstein ; Northern Ireland v Denmark ; Spain v Sweden
21/11	Denmark v Iceland ; Spain v Northern Ireland ; Sweden v Latvia

GROUP G

Holland, Romania, Bulgaria, Slovenia, Albania, Belarus, Luxembourg

2006
2/9	Belarus v Albania; Luxembourg v Holland; Romania v Bulgaria
6/9	Albania v Romania; Bulgaria v Slovenia; Holland v Belarus
7/10	Bulgaria v Holland; Romania v Belarus; Slovenia v Luxembourg
11/10	Belarus v Slovenia; Luxembourg v Bulgaria; Holland v Albania

2007
24/3	Albania v Slovenia; Luxembourg v Belarus; Holland v Romania
28/3	Bulgaria v Albania; Romania v Luxembourg; Slovenia v Holland
2/6	Albania v Luxembourg; Belarus v Bulgaria; Slovenia v Romania
6/6	Bulgaria v Belarus; Luxembourg v Albania; Romania v Slovenia
8/9	Belarus v Romania; Luxembourg v Slovenia; Holland v Bulgaria
12/9	Albania v Holland; Bulgaria v Luxembourg; Slovenia v Belarus
13/10	Belarus v Luxembourg; Romania v Holland; Slovenia v Albania
17/10	Albania v Bulgaria; Luxembourg v Romania; Holland v Slovenia
17/11	Albania v Belarus; Bulgaria v Romania; Holland v Luxembourg
21/11	Belarus v Holland; Romania v Albania; Slovenia v Bulgaria

N.B. Top two from each group qualify for finals (June 7-29, 2008). Co-hosts Austria and Switzerland qualify automatically.

European Cups

Barcelona back in business

FIRST/SECOND QUALIFYING ROUNDS

The opening two qualifying rounds of the UEFA Champions League are generally seen as a weeding-out process, with few, if any, of the participants expected to make it all the way through to the group phase.

In 2005/06, however, there was more interest in this embryonic stage of the competition than usual thanks to the enforced presence of the Cup holders themselves, Liverpool.

The Merseysiders' memorable triumph over Milan in the 2005 final had given UEFA a massive headache. Because they had finished outside the top four in the English Premiership, strictly speaking Liverpool had not officially qualified for the 2005/06 competition. That, of course, was a nonsense. It is a given in any sporting competition that the holders have a right to defend their trophy. UEFA, acknowledging this, decided to allow Liverpool back in but only under special conditions – firstly, that they would enjoy no seeded privileges or 'country protection' at any stage of the competition; secondly, and rather insultingly, that they would have to enter right at the start, in the first qualifying round.

So, a mere 49 days after they had triumphed in Istanbul, the European champions were back on the Champions League treadmill alongside the Continent's rank and file, rubbing shoulders with the reigning champions of Albania, Armenia and Azerbaijan. The good news for Rafa Benítez's side, however, was that they avoided a trip to any of those far-flung places. Instead, the draw for the first qualifying round very kindly, and romantically, pitted them against a team just one hour's coach drive away from Anfield - Welsh champions Total Network Solutions.

Dream come true

Naturally, the team from the mid-Wales village of Llansantffraid were ecstatic with the draw. It was a dream come true for a club whose average gate in the Welsh Premiership was not much more than 300. Naturally, they had no chance of progressing but plenty of opportunity to make money. In the event, they performed with plenty of endeavour and pride in both games – at Anfield and Wrexham's Racecourse Ground – but were slain by the special talent of Istanbul hero Steven Gerrard, who, having seemed set to leave Liverpool for Chelsea in the short close-season, returned with a

Liverpool's Djibril Cissé battles for the ball against Total Network Solutions

UEFA Champions League 2005/2006

defiant statement of his loyalty to the club by scoring five of the tie's six goals.

Elsewhere, another local derby of sorts saw Dubliners Shelbourne decisively beat Belfast side Glentoran 6-2 on aggregate, with ace striker Jason Byrne netting two goals in each game. Rabotnicki Kometal Skopje and Sheriff Tiraspol also netted six goals in eliminating Skonto Riga and Sliema Wanderers, respectively, but the most free-scoring team of the round were Lithuanian champions FBK Kaunas, who scored four goals in each game to trounce HB of the Faroe Islands 8-2 on aggregate and book themselves a date in the next round with…Liverpool.

The second qualifying round invariably proves to be the final resting place for those who have come through the first preliminary stage, but there was never much chance of the holders falling into that category. Although they fell a goal behind in Lithuania, Liverpool quickly retrieved the situation and eventually went on to take the tie 5-1 on aggregate, with the irrepressible Gerrard adding another two goals to his total

Celtic thrashed

Only two other teams managed to survive the opening two rounds – Anorthosis, of Cyprus, who knocked out Turkish side Trabzonspor despite playing the last 15 minutes of the second leg with ten men, and Slovakian debutants Artmedia Bratislava, who produced one of the most remarkable results in European Cup history, thrashing Scottish giants Celtic, newly managed by Gordon Strachan, 5-0 in the first leg. It was a very different story, of course, at Parkhead the following week, but Celtic's comeback fell one goal short and, remarkably, their European campaign was over by the second day of August.

Another astonishing 5-0 victory was posted by Hungarian champions Debrecen away to their Croatian counterparts Hajduk Split, who, having lost the first leg 3-0, slumped humiliatingly out of the second qualifying round for the second successive year. Shelbourne, who had eliminated Hajduk 12 months earlier, could not repeat their feat against Steaua Bucharest despite holding the former champions to a goalless draw in Dublin.

One major upset to compare with Celtic's exit saw Champions League perennials Dynamo Kiev come a cropper against Swiss 'unknowns' FC Thun, while Malmö needed a late goal in Israel to knock out Maccabi Haifa, who paid the price for earlier goalscorer Shlomi Arbeitman's 70th-minute red card.

FIRST QUALIFYING ROUND RESULTS

(12/7/05 & 19/7/05)
FC Levadia Tallinn 1 *(Nahk 45p)*, Dinamo Tbilisi 0
Dinamo Tbilisi 2 *(Melkadze 48, Orbeladze 50)*, FC Levadia Tallinn 0
(Dinamo Tbilisi 2-1)

(12/7/05 & 20/7/05)
Dinamo Minsk 1 *(Lentsevich 58)*, Anorthosis 1 *(Frousos 44)*
Anorthosis 1 *(Samaras 71)*, Dinamo Minsk 0
(Anorthosis 2-1)

Kairat Almaty 2 *(Fomenko 39, Artemov 70)*, Artmedia Bratislava 0
Artmedia Bratislava 4 *(Borbély 21, Tchur 32, Kozák 94p, Stano 120)*, Kairat Almaty 1 *(Bogomolov 91)* *(aet)*
(Artmedia Bratislava 4-3)

Neftçi Baku 2 *(Mämmädov 20, Misura 90)*, FH 0
FH 1 *(Borgvardt 60)*, Neftçi Baku 2 *(Misura 51, Mämmädov 77)*
(Neftçi Baku 4-1)

Rabotnicki Kometal Skopje 6 *(Kralevski 30, Ignatov 57p, Nuhiji 65, 85, Trajcov 69, Maznov 76)*, Skonto Riga 0
Skonto Riga 1 *(Pereplyotkin 90)*, Rabotnicki Kometal Skopje 0
(Rabotnicki Kometal Skopje 6-1)

Sliema Wanderers 1 *(Bogdanovic 72)*, Sheriff Tiraspol 4 *(Epureanu 21, 62, Kuchuk 25, Florescu 51)*
Sheriff Tiraspol 2 *(Derme 78, Cocis 83)*, Sliema Wanderers 0
(Sheriff Tiraspol 6-1)

(13/7/05 & 19/7/05)
HB 2 *(Lag 29, 62)*, FBK Kaunas 4 *(Velicka 2, 25, Klimek 35, Zelmikas 63)*
FBK Kaunas 4 *(Velicka 44, Rimkevicius 64, 82, Zelmikas 90)*, HB 0
(FBK Kaunas 8-2)

Liverpool 3 *(Gerrard 8, 21, 89)*, Total Network Solutions 0
Total Network Solutions 0, Liverpool 3 *(Cissé 26, Gerrard 82, 83)*
(Liverpool 6-0)

(13/7/05 & 20/7/05)
F91 Dudelange 0, Zrinjski Mostar 1 *(Maric B. 15)*
Zrinjski Mostar 0, F91 Dudelange 4 *(Gruszczynski 90, 105, Di Gregorio 96, Hug 112)* *(aet)*
(F91 Dudelange 4-1)

Glentoran 1 *(Ward 77)*, Shelbourne 2 *(Byrne J. 55, 65p)*
Shelbourne 4 *(Heary 13, Byrne J. 32p, 71, Crowe 58)*, Glentoran 1 *(McCann 21)*
(Shelbourne 6-2)

ND Gorica 2 *(Kovacevic M. 66, Birsa 82)*, SK Tirana 0
SK Tirana 3 *(Rraklli 38, Dabulla 42, Salihi 45)*, ND Gorica 0
(SK Tirana 3-2)

FC Haka 1 *(Pasoja 26)*, Pyunik Yerevan 0
Pyunik Yerevan 2 *(Pachajyan 3, Diawara 30)*, FC Haka 2 *(Mattila 38, Fowler 63)*
(FC Haka 3-2)

UEFA Champions League 2005/2006

SECOND QUALIFYING ROUND RESULTS

(26/7/05 & 2/8/05)
FBK Kaunas 1 *(Barevicius 21)*, Liverpool 3 *(Cissé 27, Carragher 30, Gerrard 55p)*
Liverpool 2 *(Gerrard 77, Cissé 86)*, FBK Kaunas 0
(Liverpool 5-1)

(26/7/05 & 3/8/05)
RSC Anderlecht 5 *(Tihinen 21, Jetsrovic 24, Mpenza 32, Goor 35, Vanderhaeghe 77)*, Neftçi Baku 0
Neftçi Baku 1 *(Boret 5p)*, RSC Anderlecht 0
(RSC Anderlecht 5-1)

Anorthosis 2 *(Nikolaou 25, Frousos 83, Tsitaishvili 90)*, Trabzonspor 1 *(Fatih Tekke 75)*
Trabzonspor 1 *(Fatih Tekke 40)*, Anorthosis 0
(Anorthosis 3-2)

Dinamo Tbilisi 0, Brøndby IF 2 *(Skoubo 59, Elmander 83)*
Brøndby IF 3 *(Lorentzen 9, 42, Kamper 86)*, Dinamo Tbilisi 1 *(Iashvili 65)*
(Brøndby IF 5-1)

Dynamo Kiev 2 *(Gusev 20, Shatskikh 45)*, FC Thun 2 *(Rodolfo 38og, Aegerter 66)*
FC Thun 1 *(Bernardi 90)*, Dynamo Kyiv 0
(FC Thun 3-2)

Vålerenga Fotball 1 *(Dos Santos 50p)*, FC Haka 0
FC Haka 1 *(Lehtinen 9)*, Vålerenga Fotball 4 *(Waehler 26, Flo 28, 74, Iversen 59)*
(Vålerenga Fotball 5-1)

(27/7/05 & 2/8/05)
Artmedia Bratislava 5 *(Halenár 43, 76, 89, Vascák 57, Mikulic 78)*, Celtic 0
Celtic 4 *(Thompson 21p, Hartson 44, McManus 54, Beattie 82)*, Artmedia Bratislava 0
(Artmedia Bratislava 5-4)

(27/7/05 & 3/8/05)
Debreceni VSC 3 *(Bogdanovic 26, 40, Kerekes 58)*, Hajduk Split 0
Hajduk Split 0, Debreceni VSC 5 *(Halmosi 1, 27, Kerekes 22, Sidibe 75, Kiss 90)*
(Debreceni VSC 8-0)

F91 Dudelange 1 *(Martine 8)*, SK Rapid Wien 6 *(Lawarée 2, 65, Akagündüz 3, 15, Hofmann 5, Kienast 84)*
SK Rapid Wien 3 *(Lawarée 47, 81, Dollinger 86)*, F91 Dudelange 2 *(Tosun 7og, Gruszczynski 37)*
(SK Rapid Wien 9-3)

Malmö FF 3 *(Osmanovski 33, Andersson D. 48p, Mattisson 68)*, Maccabi Haifa 2 *(Harazi 2, Colautti 44)*
Maccabi Haifa 2 *(Colautti 10, Arbeitman 60)*, Malmö FF 2 *(Afonso Alves 21, Abelsson 88)*
(Malmö FF 5-4)

Partizan Beograd 1 *(Odita 63)*, Sheriff Tiraspol 0
Sheriff Tiraspol 0, Partizan Beograd 1 *(Odita 74)*
(Partizan Beograd 2-0)

Rabotnicki Kometal Skopje 1 *(Nuhiji 12)*, Lokomotiv Moskva 1 *(Sychov 90)*
Lokomotiv Moskva 2 *(Sychov 75, Asatiani 85)*, Rabotnicki Kometal Skopje 0
(Lokomotiv Moskva 3-1)

Shelbourne 0, Steaua Bucuresti 0
Steaua Bucuresti 4 *(Nicolita 18, Iacob 27, Dinita 61, Oprita 90p)*, Shelbourne 1 *(Byrne J. 38)*
(Steaua Bucuresti 4-1)

SK Tirana 0, CSKA Sofia 2 *(Gueye 89, Gargorov 90)*
CSKA Sofia 2 *(Zadi 2, Todorov 90)*, SK Tirana 0
(CSKA Sofia 4-0)

THIRD QUALIFYING ROUND

Among those entering the third qualifying round were five former winners of the European Cup and another five runners-up. Because of Liverpool's bonus participation, England had three entrants, all from the North West. Manchester United were familiar contestants, whereas Everton, Liverpool's local rivals, were bidding to compete in the Champions League proper for the very first time.

It was Everton's misfortune, however, to be drawn against another team with the same hunger and ambition – Villarreal – and the Spaniards proved their class in winning the first leg 2-1 at Goodison Park before a tight second leg at El Madrigal was decided in the last minute by a breakaway goal from Diego Forlán. Everton had good reason for grievance, however, when, shortly after Mikel Arteta had scored with a free-kick, Duncan Ferguson had a perfectly good goal ruled out by soon-to-retire Italian referee Pierluigi Collina.

Manchester United had no trouble disposing of Debrecen, 6-0 on aggregate, while Liverpool also overcame Eastern European opposition, knocking out Bulgarian champions CSKA Sofia despite a dispiriting 1-0 second-leg defeat at Anfield.

Artmedia advance

Liverpool thus became the first club to reach the Champions League group phase from the first qualifying round, but they had to share the honour with the resilient Slovakians of Artmedia Bratislava, who edged through on penalties after two goalless draws against Partizan Belgrade. Club Bruges also required spot-kicks to eliminate Vålerenga of Norway and join Anderlecht, conquerors of Slavia Prague, in the last 32, while the most exciting tie of the round saw Polish champions Wisla Krakow cruelly eliminated after extra-time in Athens against Panathinaikos having had a valid goal disallowed by English referee Mike Riley with the score at 2-1.

FC Thun also made it through, with astonishing ease, against Malmö, but there was no joy for the team that had finished above them in the previous season's Swiss Super League, FC Basel. Their dreams of a shock win over Werder Bremen died with the concession of three goals in eight second-half minutes at the Weserstadion.

In eliminating Monaco, Real Betis joined Villarreal as Champions League debutants, ensuring a full participation for Spain in the group phase. Italy also took a full complement through as Inter

UEFA Champions League 2005/2006

comfortably saw off Shakhtar Donetsk and Udinese reached the promised land for the first time at the expense of Portugal's Sporting.

Rangers ensured a continuing Scottish presence by overcoming surprise qualifiers Anorthosis, while Rapid Vienna kept the Austrian flag flying thanks to a crucial late winning header against Lokomotiv in Moscow from Slovakian defender Jozef Valachovic. Ajax's edgy victory over Danish champions Brøndby, in which Swedish striker Johan Elmander, formerly of Feyenoord, was outstanding, meant that just one Scandinavian team made it through – Champions League regulars Rosenborg. They survived a late scare to eliminate Steaua Bucharest, one of seven teams from Eastern Europe that would now have to trade in the promise of fame and fortune in the Champions League for dreams of lesser glory in the UEFA Cup.

GROUP PHASE

There were 16 countries represented in the draw for the group phase of the UEFA Champions

New signing Park Ji-sung helps Manchester United ease past Debrecen

THIRD QUALIFYING ROUND RESULTS

(9/8/05 & 23/8/05)
Real Betis 1 *(Edú 90)*, AS Monaco FC 0
AS Monaco FC 2 *(Gerard 33, Maoulida 63)*, Real Betis 2 *(Ricardo Oliveira 17, 75)*
(Real Betis 3-2)

Wisla Krakow 3 *(Brozek Pa. 13, Uche 52, Frankowski 70)*, Panathinaikos 1 *(Olisadebe 4)*
Panathinaikos 4 *(Morris 62, Olisadebe 65, Papadopoulos 87, Kotsios 114)*, Wisla Krakow 1 *(Sobolewski 78) (aet)*
(Panathinaikos 5-4)

(9/8/05 & 24/8/05)
Anorthosis 1 *(Frousos 72)*, Rangers 2 *(Novo 64, Ricksen 71)*
Rangers 2 *(Buffel 39, Prso 58)*, Anorthosis 0
(Rangers 4-1)

Everton 1 *(Beattie 42)*, Villarreal CF 2 *(Figueroa 27, Josico 45)*
Villarreal CF 2 *(Sorín 21, Forlán 90)*, Everton 1 *(Arteta 69)*
(Villarreal CF 4-2)

Manchester United 3 *(Rooney 7, Van Nistelrooy 49, Cristiano Ronaldo 63)*, Debreceni VSC 0
Debreceni VSC 0, Manchester United 3 *(Heinze 20, 60, Richardson 65)*
(Manchester United 6-0)

Vålerenga Fotball 1 *(Iversen 57)*, Club Brugge KV 0
Club Brugge KV 1 *(Balaban 79)*, Vålerenga Fotball 0 *(aet)*
(1-1; Club Brugge KV 4-3 on pens)

(10/8/05 & 23/8/05)
Artmedia Bratislava 0, Partizan Beograd 0
Partizan Beograd 0, Artmedia Bratislava 0 *(aet)*
(0-0; Artmedia Bratislava 4-3 on pens)

CSKA Sofia 1 *(Dimitrov V. 45)*, Liverpool 2 *(Cissé 25, Morientes 31, 58)*
Liverpool 0, CSKA Sofia 1 *(Iliev 14)*
(Liverpool 3-2)

Malmö FF 0, FC Thun 1 *(Adriano 34)*
FC Thun 3 *(Bernardi 26, Lustrinelli 40, 66)*, Malmö FF 0
(FC Thun 4-0)

SK Rapid Wien 1 *(Valachovic 75p)*, Lokomotiv Moskva 1 *(Samedov 10)*
Lokomotiv Moskva 0, SK Rapid Wien 1 *(Valachovic 84)*
(SK Rapid Wien 2-1)

Sporting CP 0, Udinese 1 *(Iaquinta 27p)*
Udinese 3 *(Iaquinta 23p, 90, Natali 35)*, Sporting CP 2 *(Douala 38, Pinilla 90)*
(Udinese 4-2)

Steaua Bucuresti 1 *(Iacob 30)*, Rosenborg BK 1 *(Helstad 85)*
Rosenborg BK 3 *(Solli 38, Ødegaard 57, Radoi 60og)*, Steaua Bucuresti 2 *(Radoi 74, Iacob 76)*
(Rosenborg BK 4-3)

(10/8/05 & 24/8/05)
RSC Anderlecht 2 *(Goor 7, Mpenza 38)*, SK Slavia Praha 1 *(Jarolim 21)*
SK Slavia Praha 0, RSC Anderlecht 2 *(Serhat 69, Mpenza 83)*
(RSC Anderlecht 4-1)

FC Basel 2 *(Degen 27, Rossi 52)*, SV Werder Bremen 1 *(Klose 73)*
SV Werder Bremen 3 *(Klasnic 64, 72, Borowski 67p)*, FC Basel 0
(SV Werder Bremen 4-2)

Brøndby IF 2 *(Skoubo 33, Escudé 90og)*, Ajax 2 *(Rosenberg 30, Babel 73)*
Ajax 3 *(Babel 50, Sneijder 80, 88)*, Brøndby IF 1 *(Elmander 44)*
(Ajax 5-3)

Shakhtar Donetsk 0, Internazionale 2 *(Martins 68, Adriano 79)*
Internazionale 1 *(Recoba 12)*, Shakhtar Donetsk 1 *(Elano 24)*
(Internazionale 3-1)

UEFA Champions League 2005/2006

League. The 32 clubs included five newcomers – Villarreal, Betis, Udinese, FC Thun and Artmedia Bratislava – and, almost without exception, all of Europe's most prestigious and decorated clubs.

The only non-winners among the first band of seeds were Arsenal, and they landed the easiest draw of all when they were grouped with Ajax, Sparta Prague and Thun. The complex mechanics of the draw procedure meant that a number of teams were 'placed', including pre-tournament favourites Chelsea, who, because of Liverpool's lack of 'country protection', found themselves in the same group as the team that had controversially beaten them in the previous season's semi-final.

Milan and PSV, the other two semi-finalists in 2004/05, were also immediately re-acquaintanted, while Juventus and Bayern Munich were coupled together in the group phase for the second year running.

Group A

Although the overall draw was fair and balanced, there was little doubt which two teams were fancied to progress in Group A – despite the fact that it was the only one of the eight pools containing four reigning domestic champions. Right from the outset the only issues at stake appeared to be which of Juventus and Bayern Munich would top the group and which of Club Bruges and Rapid Vienna would prolong their European adventure in the UEFA Cup.

The opening two Matchdays went mostly to plan for the Big Two. Bayern scraped two 1-0 wins with a couple of scruffy goals while Juventus provided more entertaining fare in winning 2-1 away to Bruges (where new signing Patrick Vieira was sent off) and 3-0 at home to Rapid Vienna in Turin (where Zlatan Ibrahimovic finally scored his first Champions League goal for the club).

The eagerly awaited mid-October showdown in the Allianz-Arena lived up to the billing, with Bayern deservedly extending their 100 per cent record at their fabulous new stadium with a 2-1 win thanks to a couple of first-half goals from Sebastian Deisler and Martín Demichelis. Two weeks later, though, the Italian champions reaped their revenge – despite a pitiful attendance of only 16,000 in the Stadio delle Alpi. Frenchman David Trezeguet was the man of the match, deciding the contest with two classy finishes, the second late in the game after Deisler had equalised with a long-range free-kick.

While Juve and Bayern were trading victories, Bruges sneaked up to within three points of the leading duo by taking maximum points off Rapid. Having been beaten 1-0 at home in the first game by a lucky Bosko Balaban goal, the Austrians took the lead in Belgium after just 25 seconds with a diving header from Czech striker Marek Kincl, but that served only to spark the Belgians into life and they went on to win 3-2.

Rapid routed

Matchday Five saw Bruges's faint hopes of splitting the top two fade and die as they went down 1-0 to Juve in Turin. Alessandro Del Piero made up for a couple of earlier misses by heading in the only goal of the game ten minutes from time, equalling in the process the club's all-time goalscoring record. Meanwhile in Munich, Bayern contemptuously dismissed Rapid 4-0 to go top of the table on goal difference. Deisler once again opened the scoring, with a low diagonal shot, and the Germans closed the deal in the second half with a goal on his Champions League debut from Iranian midfielder Ali Karimi and two late strikes from Dutchman Roy Makaay, who thus brought a lengthy personal goal drought to an end.

Qualification was thus settled, as was Bruges's transfer to the UEFA Cup. The important question of group leadership was still at stake, though, and it proved to be a close-run thing. Juve, thanks to a brace from record-breaking marksman Del Piero, eventually won the battle as they completed Rapid's whitewash with a 3-1 in Vienna, but Bayern were denied victory in Bruges only by a controversial incident at the end when French

Alessandro Del Piero – two more goals in Vienna to add to his Champions League haul

UEFA Champions League 2005/2006

GROUP A RESULTS

(14/9/05)
Club Brugge KV 1 *(Yulu-Matondo 85)*, Juventus 2 *(Nedved 66, Trezeguet 75)*
SK Rapid Wien 0, FC Bayern München 1 *(Guerrero 60)*

(27/9/05)
FC Bayern München 1 *(Demichelis 32)*, Club Brugge KV 0
Juventus 3 *(Trezeguet 27, Mutu 82, Ibrahimovic 85)*, SK Rapid Wien 0

(18/10/05)
FC Bayern München 2 *(Deisler 32, Demichelis 39)*, Juventus 1 *(Ibrahimovic 90)*
SK Rapid Wien 0, Club Brugge KV 1 *(Balaban 75)*

(2/11/05)
Club Brugge KV 3 *(Portillo 8, Balaban 25, Verheyen 63)*, SK Rapid Wien 2 *(Kincl 1, Adamski 81)*
Juventus 2 *(Trezeguet 61, 85)*, FC Bayern München 1 *(Deisler 66)*

(22/11/05)
FC Bayern München 4 *(Deisler 21, Karimi 54, Makaay 72, 76)*, SK Rapid Wien 0
Juventus 1 *(Del Piero 80)*, Club Brugge KV 0

(7/12/05)
Club Brugge KV 1 *(Portillo 32)*, FC Bayern München 1 *(Pizarro 21)*
SK Rapid Wien 1 *(Kincl 52)*, Juventus 3 *(Del Piero 35, 45, Ibrahimovic 41)*

FINAL TABLE

	Pld	Home					Away					Total					Pts
		W	D	L	F	A	W	D	L	F	A	W	D	L	F	A	
1 Juventus	6	3	0	0	6	1	2	0	1	6	4	5	0	1	12	5	15
2 FC Bayern München	6	3	0	0	7	1	1	1	1	3	3	4	1	1	10	4	13
3 Club Brugge KV	6	1	1	1	5	5	1	0	2	1	2	2	1	3	6	7	7
4 SK Rapid Wien	6	0	0	3	1	5	0	0	3	2	10	0	0	6	3	15	0

referee Laurent Duhamel ruled out Paolo Guerrero's last-ditch winner on the pretext that he had already blown for time as the Peruvian was about to shoot. It was a weird decision but it didn't really matter. Even if the goal had been given, Juve would still have topped the group.

Group B

Arsenal's first step on the road to Paris looked to be a straightforward one as they entertained Swiss minnows FC Thun at Highbury, but it would prove to be a night of some frustration and discomfort for Arsène Wenger's team after Robin van Persie was harshly dismissed for supposed dangerous play in the closing moments of the first half. Even after the Gunners had finally broken Swiss resistance with a superb headed goal from Gilberto Silva, they could not hold on to their lead for more than two minutes, a cross-cum-shot from Portuguese midfielder Nélson Ferreira subsequently flying in at the far post. But with time almost up the Gunners were rescued by substitute Dennis Bergkamp, who held off a defender's challenge, possibly illegally, before slotting his shot wide of the goalkeeper. It was tough luck on Thun but a huge relief for Arsenal.

There was also an important late goal from a Dutchman in the other opening tie as Ajax gained a deserved 1-1 draw away to Sparta Prague thanks to a stunning long-range right-foot shot from Wesley Sneijder. It was the second wondergoal of the evening, the first having flown into the Ajax net off the right boot of Sparta striker Miroslav Matusovic midway through the second half.

Two weeks later Sparta were undone by another late goal as Thun made amends for their Highbury torment with an 89th-minute winner from Bosnian defender Selver Hodzic. It was an early strike from Arsenal's Freddie Ljungberg in Amsterdam, with just 80 seconds on the clock, that set Arsenal en route to a precious victory over Ajax. With several key players missing, including Van Persie, Bergkamp, Gilberto and Thierry Henry, the Gunners' 2-1 win was an impressive achievement.

Hooray Henry!

Although Wenger's team were struggling away from home on the domestic front, they maintained their perfect start in Europe with a 2-0 victory in Prague. It was an especially memorable night for Henry, who, having come on as an early substitute following a five-week injury lay-off, scored two wonderful goals, his 185th and 186th for the club, to equal, then break, Ian Wright's Arsenal goalscoring record. Two weeks later the Frenchman punctured the Sparta defence again with another glorious goal before Van Persie added two late strikes to complete a 3-0 win that clinched Arsenal's place in the last 16 with two games to spare.

Ajax's home and away victories over Thun – 2-0 in Holland, 4-2 in Switzerland (with not one, but two late goals) – put the Amsterdammers in a commanding position to claim the second qualifying spot, and they duly sealed their place in the last 16 on Matchday Five with a 2-1 victory at home to Sparta Prague. Youngster Nigel de Jong, the matchwinner in Switzerland, again proved decisive, coming off the bench to score both Ajax goals, but in this group of dramatic finishes there was a late scare for Danny Blind's side when Sparta scrambled a 90th-minute goal to make it 2-1 and should have had a stoppage-time penalty after Ajax defender Urby Emanuelson had recklessly taken out Jan Simák.

The group concluded with two goalless draws. A

UEFA Champions League 2005/2006

Arsenal manager Arsène Wenger – a study in concentration at the Amsterdam ArenA

missed penalty from Henry against Ajax not only prevented Arsenal from going through with maximum points but also ended the team's 100 per cent home record in all competitions in their final season at Highbury. Sparta's failure to beat Thun in Prague enabled the Swiss side to finish third and take the consolation prize of a UEFA Cup place.

Group C

Barcelona, the Spanish champions, got their tenth Champions League campaign off to a winning start with a fine 2-0 victory in Bremen. Deco opened the scoring early on with his speciality – a deflected shot – but Werder had their chances to equalise before Ronaldinho applied the decisive blow from the penalty spot after teenage wonderboy Lionel Messi, on as a substitute, had been hauled down by Christian Schulz.

Udinese's Champions League debut could hardly have gone better as star striker Vincenzo Iaquinta scored the perfect hat-trick – header, right foot, left foot – to give the provincial Italian side a thumping 3-0 victory over Panathinaikos. Iaquinta could even have added to his tally with two further opportunities late on, but he had done more than enough to warrant the adulation that rained down on him from the Stadio Friuli terraces.

Unfortunately, a contract wrangle meant that Iaquinta was not selected for Udinese's next game, away to Barcelona, and without him the Serie A side fell to a comprehensive 4-1 defeat. Deco scored for the second game in a row, from a lovely free-kick, but the undisputed man of the match was Ronaldinho, who gave a stellar performance, scoring a wonderful hat-trick. Serse Cosmi, the Udinese coach, was so impressed with the Brazilian that he asked for his shirt…at half-time! Ronaldinho kept his promise and handed it over at the end of the game.

Another lively game, in Athens, ended with Panathinaikos scraping a 2-1 win over a Werder Bremen side that finished the contest with ten men after Ivan Klasnic's late dismissal. Things were not looking good for the Germans, and on Matchday Three they suffered more disappointment when they conceded a late equaliser in Udine after largely dominating the match. Panathinaikos were also outplayed on home soil, but they managed to scramble a welcome point against Barcelona on a night when Samuel Eto'o did everything but score.

Eto'o hat-trick

The Cameroonian striker made up for it two weeks later at the Nou Camp when he destroyed the

GROUP B RESULTS

(14/9/05)
Arsenal 2 *(Gilberto Silva 51, Bergkamp 90)*, FC Thun 1 *(Ferreira 53)*
AC Sparta Praha 1 *(Matusovic 66)*, Ajax 1 *(Sneijder 90)*

(27/9/05)
Ajax 1 *(Rosenberg 71)*, Arsenal 2 *(Ljungberg 2, Pires 69p)*
FC Thun 1 *(Hodzic 89)*, AC Sparta Praha 0

(18/10/05)
Ajax 2 *(Anastasiou 36, 55)*, FC Thun 0
AC Sparta Praha 0, Arsenal 2 *(Henry 21, 74)*

(2/11/05)
Arsenal 3 *(Henry 28, Van Persie 81, 86)*, AC Sparta Praha 0
FC Thun 2 *(Lustrinelli 56, Adriano 74)*, Ajax 4 *(Sneijder 26, Deumi 63og, De Jong 90, Boukhari 90)*

(22/11/05)
Ajax 2 *(De Jong 68, 89)*, AC Sparta Praha 1 *(Petrás 90)*
FC Thun 0, Arsenal 1 *(Pires 88p)*

(7/12/05)
Arsenal 0, Ajax 0
AC Sparta Praha 0, FC Thun 0

FINAL TABLE

		Home					Away					Total					
	Pld	W	D	L	F	A	W	D	L	F	A	W	D	L	F	A	Pts
1 Arsenal	6	2	1	0	5	1	3	0	0	5	1	5	1	0	10	2	16
2 Ajax	6	2	0	1	5	3	1	2	0	5	3	3	2	1	10	6	11
3 FC Thun	6	1	0	2	3	5	0	1	2	1	4	1	1	4	4	9	4
4 AC Sparta Praha	6	0	2	1	1	3	0	0	3	1	6	0	2	4	2	9	2

UEFA Champions League 2005/2006

Greeks with a hat-trick of the highest class. Barcelona looked to be in the mood from the start after taking the lead with just 40 seconds on the clock through Dutchman Mark van Bommel. From then on it was the Eto'o show. He made it 2-0 with a flying header, and after Lionel Messi had exploited hesitant defending in the Greek defence to score his first Champions League goal, Eto'o added to Panathinaikos's woe with a finely crafted goal, set up jointly by Messi and Ronaldinho, just before half-time. The best, however, was saved till last as the African Footballer of the Year completed his hat-trick with a wondrous first-time lob on the run. It capped a sensational team performance by Barcelona, who, with ten points from four games, found themselves six points ahead of all the other three teams.

Werder Bremen boosted their hopes of a second-round berth with a thrilling 4-3 win at home to Udinese. At one stage they were 3-0 up, but the Italians launched a magnificent comeback, à la Liverpool in the previous season's final, by scoring three goals in six minutes, only for the Germans to snatch victory with French midfielder John Micoud's second goal of the evening.

Thomas Schaaf's side urgently needed those three points because their next fixture took them to Camp Nou. Barça were without a number of key players, including Eto'o, Messi and Xavi, but with Ronaldinho once again in sublime form, the Catalans proved far too hot to handle. The Brazilian magician scored one goal – from a free-kick that goalkeeper Andreas Reinke should have saved – and brilliantly created two others, for Gabi and Henrik Larsson, as Barcelona made mathematically certain of their qualification, as group winners, for the last 16.

Udinese looked set to join them after they scored two late goals, the second of them a belter from former French international Vincent Candela, to come from behind and win 2-1 in the pouring rain of Athens. The Italians now required only a point at home to already-qualified Barça to go through. Panathinaikos were out but needed a draw away to Bremen to claim a UEFA cup place. The Germans had to win to stay in Europe and if Barcelona won in Udine, victory would keep them in the Champions League.

As was their privilege, Barça sent an understrength team to Italy. Even coach Frank Rijkaard failed to make the trip after being told by doctors to stay at home after contracting a lung infection. But even

GROUP C RESULTS

(14/9/05)
Udinese 3 *(Iaquinta 28, 73, 76)*, Panathinaikos 0
SV Werder Bremen 0, FC Barcelona 2 *(Deco 13, Ronaldinho 77p)*

(27/9/05)
FC Barcelona 4 *(Ronaldinho 13, 32, 90p, Deco 41)*, Udinese 1 *(Felipe 24)*
Panathinaikos 2 *(González 5p, Mantzios 8)*, SV Werder Bremen 1 *(Klose 41)*

(18/10/05)
Panathinaikos 0, FC Barcelona 0
Udinese 1 *(Di Natale 86)*, SV Werder Bremen 1 *(Felipe 64og)*

(2/11/05)
FC Barcelona 5 *(Van Bommel 1, Eto'o 14, 40, 65, Messi 34)*, Panathinaikos 0
SV Werder Bremen 4 *(Klose 15, Baumann 24, Micoud 51, 67)*, Udinese 3 *(Di Natale 54, 57, Schulz 60og)*

(22/11/05)
FC Barcelona 3 *(Gabri 14, Ronaldinho 26, Larsson 71)*, SV Werder Bremen 1 *(Borowski 22p)*
Panathinaikos 1 *(Charalambides 45)*, Udinese 2 *(Iaquinta 80, Candela 83)*

(7/12/05)
Udinese 0, FC Barcelona 2 *(Ezquerro 86, Iniesta 90)*
SV Werder Bremen 5 *(Micoud 2p, Haedo Valdez 28, 32, Klose 51, Frings 90)*, Panathinaikos 1 *(Morris 53)*

FINAL TABLE

		Pld	Home W	D	L	F	A	Away W	D	L	F	A	Total W	D	L	F	A	Pts
1	FC Barcelona	6	3	0	0	12	2	2	1	0	4	0	5	1	0	16	2	16
2	SV Werder Bremen	6	2	0	1	9	6	0	1	2	3	6	2	1	3	12	12	7
3	Udinese	6	1	1	1	4	3	1	0	2	6	9	2	1	3	10	12	7
4	Panathinaikos	6	1	1	1	3	3	0	0	3	1	13	1	1	4	4	16	4

The first of three – Samuel Eto'o scores a spectacular header against Panathinaikos

UEFA Champions League 2005/2006

without all their big hitters the Catalans dominated the game. Udinese clung on desperately for the 0-0 draw that would see them through, but two late strikes from the visitors sent them crashing out. The despair in Udine contrasted hugely with the elation in Bremen, where Panathinaikos were humbled on their travels once again as Werder punctured their feeble defence five more times. The Germans' fifth goal, drilled home by Torsten Frings, came just as the news of Barça's two late goals reached the Weserstadion, ensuring a euphoric climax to the evening's entertainment in northern Germany.

Group D

Manchester United, having sailed through their qualifying tie, were not expected to have any difficulty negotiating a safe passage through a group comprising Villarreal, Lille and Benfica. Having reached the knockout phase in each of the previous nine seasons, a record tenth successive qualification looked almost assured for Sir Alex Ferguson's team once the draw had been made.

United made a decent start, in terms of the result, when they drew 0-0 with Villarreal at El Madrigal but the point came at a price, with defender Gabriel Heinze, who had scored twice in the qualifying round, being carried off with a serious injury and Wayne Rooney stupidly earning himself a red card for ironically clapping the referee – experienced Danish official Kim Milton Nielsen – just moments after he had been booked.

Another goalless draw looked on the cards in the other game until Benfica's diminutive Italian striker Fabrizio Miccoli sunk Lille with a powerful header two minutes into stoppage-time. The Portuguese champions thus travelled to Manchester a fortnight later as leaders of the group. It was their first meeting with United since the 1968 European Cup final at Wembley, but Old Trafford was not a happy place following a shock home defeat by Blackburn in the Premiership the previous weekend and there were even boos aimed at United's illustrious manager. It was not the most auspicious of occasions for Ryan Giggs' 100th European game, but the Welshman improved the atmosphere by putting his team ahead with a deflected free-kick at the end of the first half. Fourteen minutes into the second period the groans rang out again as Simão, the Benfica skipper, curled in a superb free-kick to make it 1-1, but United subsequently took the game to their opponents and were ultimately rewarded for their endeavour when Ruud van Nistelrooy pounced on a lucky deflection in the penalty box to tap the ball across the line and give United victory.

With Lille and Villarreal sharing a goalless draw in the Ligue 1 side's temporary home of the Stade de France, United were on top of the table. And with the French side visiting Old Trafford next, it seemed as if the Premiership side would consolidate their position. But with Rooney still suspended, United again looked short of firepower. A bad night turned worse when Paul Scholes was sent off and Giggs carried off in the second half, and by the end of the 90 minutes a goalless draw – the third of the group – did not appear too harmful.

United beaten

A fortnight later, however, the group seeds were indeed in trouble when they fell to an improbable defeat at the Stade de France. Lille's first goal in four games came towards the end of the first half when Slovenian international Milenko Acimovic received a neat pass inside from full-back Grégory Tafforeau and beat Edwin van der Sar with a rising right-foot shot. United could not respond in the second half and Lille, backed by the biggest crowd in their history (66,470), celebrated a famous victory.

The new group leaders after four matches were Villarreal. After a third successive draw, 1-1 at home to Benfica, they claimed their first win in the return match thanks to a single goal from midfielder Marcos Senna. With just eight goals scored in eight games, this was a punishing group for the spectators, and there was no improvement on Matchday Five as both games again finished

Benfica's Beto celebrates the goal that knocks out Manchester United

UEFA Champions League 2005/2006

GROUP D RESULTS

(14/9/05)
SL Benfica 1 *(Miccoli 90)*, Lille OSC 0
Villarreal CF 0, Manchester United 0

(27/9/05)
Lille OSC 0, Villarreal CF 0
Manchester United 2 *(Giggs 39, Van Nistelrooy 85)*, SL Benfica 1 *(Simão 59)*

(18/10/05)
Manchester United 0, Lille OSC 0
Villarreal CF 1 *(Riquelme 73p)*, SL Benfica 1 *(Manuel Fernandes 77)*

(2/11/05)
SL Benfica 0, Villarreal CF 1 *(Senna 82)*
Lille OSC 1 *(Acimovic 38)*, Manchester United 0

(22/11/05)
Lille OSC 0, SL Benfica 0
Manchester United 0, Villarreal CF 0

(7/12/05)
SL Benfica 2 *(Geovanni 16, Beto 34)*, Manchester United 1 *(Scholes 6)*
Villarreal CF 1 *(Guayre 67)*, Lille OSC 0

FINAL TABLE

	Pld	Home W	D	L	F	A	Away W	D	L	F	A	Total W	D	L	F	A	Pts
1 Villarreal CF	6	1	2	0	2	1	1	2	0	1	0	2	4	0	3	1	10
2 SL Benfica	6	2	0	1	3	2	0	2	1	2	3	2	2	2	5	5	8
3 Lille OSC	6	1	2	0	1	0	0	1	2	0	2	1	3	2	1	2	6
4 Manchester United	6	1	2	0	2	1	0	1	2	1	3	1	3	2	3	4	6

goalless. Even with Rooney back from suspension and Villarreal's two stars, Juan Román Riquelme and ex-United striker Diego Forlán, missing, the English side could find no way through the Spanish team's well-manned defence.

With Lille and Benfica also drawing a blank in Saint-Denis, all things remained possible with one game to go. The permutations were endless, but the bottom line was that a last-day victory for any of the four teams would guarantee their progress into the last 16.

Benfica bounce back

Manchester United took on Benfica in the Estádio da Luz sporting the all-blue kit they had famously worn in the 1968 final. If it was intended as a lucky charm, it seemed to work initially as Scholes ended their goal drought by bundling home Gary Neville's cross after just six minutes. But it proved to be a false dawn for the visitors. Benfica fought back, Brazilian midfielder Geovanni headed them level and Beto, with his first goal for the club, put them ahead with a powerful low shot that deflected past goalkeeper Edwin van der Sar.

Could United respond? The answer was an emphatic no. For the rest of the game they were dreadful, creating nothing at all. Benfica simply coasted to victory and into the next round where they were joined, as group winners, by Villarreal, 1-0 victors over Lille.

United did not even have the consolation of a UEFA Cup place. That went to the French side thanks to their superior head-to-head record. With just three goals scored in six games, it was utter humiliation for United as they contemplated a second half of the season without Champions League football for the first time in a decade.

Group E

Veteran Milan defender Paolo Maldini had not been particularly kind to his own club as he assisted UEFA officials in making the draw for the group phase. Although the previous season's beaten finalists were firm favourites to win Group E, they knew that they would not be able to take it easy against PSV, Schalke and Fenerbahçe, a trio of opponents that all had their sights trained on a place in the last 16.

The Rossoneri made a convincing enough start, with Kaká scoring two superb goals in a 3-1 home win over Fenerbahçe. The Turkish champions were on level terms with only a few minutes remaining but a sensational solo goal from the young Brazilian schemer and a tap-in from Andriy Shevchenko enabled Carlo Ancelotti's side to claim three well-earned points. PSV also began with a home win, beating Schalke 1-0 with a header from Jan Vennegoor of Hesselink.

The PSV centre-forward turned villain two weeks later in Istanbul, however, when he conceded a penalty and received a second yellow card shortly afterwards. Brazilian trickster Alex was the main man for Fenerbahçe, scoring twice and setting up a late third goal for Ghanaian midfielder Stephen Appiah as his team raced to a 3-0 win. Schalke twice came from behind at home to Milan to record their first point in a 2-2 draw. The visitors opened the scoring after just 21 seconds when goalkeeper Frank Rost fumbled Clarence Seedorf's speculative long-range strike, but the German side battled hard for the draw and scored a wonderful second equaliser through substitute Hamit Altintop.

Matchday Three brought no change to the standings as Milan were held 0-0 in the San Siro by PSV while Fenerbahçe and Schalke shared six

UEFA Champions League 2005/2006

Andriy Shevchenko finishes off Fenerbahçe in Milan – he would score four more against the Turks in Istanbul

goals in Istanbul. There was a late blow for the Turks when Alex was red-carded for a second caution, and two more of Fenerbahçe's Brazilian contingent, Fábio Luciano and Marco Aurélio, were to receive their marching orders in the return fixture two weeks later as coach Christoph Daum made an unhappy return to Germany. A headed goal in each half, from Kevin Kuranyi and Søren Larsen, brought Schalke their first victory of the competition, which put them level on points with Milan, surprisingly beaten 1-0 in Eindhoven by an early goal from PSV's in-form Peruvian striker Jefferson Farfán.

Shevchenko shines

With no wins in three games, Milan were now in danger of going out. And their next fixture was in Istanbul, scene of their Champions League final nightmare six months earlier. One man who particularly needed to get that game against Liverpool out of his system was Andriy Shevchenko, and the Ukrainian marksman did so with one of the great Champions League performances, bludgeoning Fenerbahçe into submission – and out of the tournament – with a one-man masterclass. Milan won 4-0 and Shevchenko scored all the goals, becoming the first player in Champions League history to strike four times in an away fixture. The Ukrainian's efforts rather overshadowed another individual exploit on the same evening as Schalke's Georgian international Levan Kobiashvili scored all three of his team's goals, including two from the penalty spot, to overcome PSV and ensure a dramatic conclusion to the group.

Despite their defeat in Gelsenkirchen, which dropped them to third place, PSV were still in control of their destiny. A third successive home win, against eliminated Fenerbahçe, would guarantee their progress to the knockout phase, leaving Milan and Schalke to contest the other qualification place. Sure enough, the Dutch champions got their three points, thanks to an early goal from Phillip Cocu and a late one from Farfán. Milan, meanwhile, were struggling to see off Schalke at the San Siro. A victory or a low-scoring draw was all they needed, but even after Kaká had notched his second brace of the competition to put them 3-1 up, a quick reply from Schalke's star Brazilian, Lincoln, left the Germans with a quarter of the game in which to score the equaliser that would take them through at Milan's expense on the head-to-head away-goals rule. But the Italians survived – just – and the 3-2 victory was enough to see them qualify as group winners and send Schalke tumbling into the UEFA Cup.

Group F

Real Madrid, the Champions League's top seeds, appeared to have been handed a favourable draw when they were grouped with Lyon, Olympiakos

GROUP E RESULTS

(13/9/05)
Milan 3 *(Kaká 18, 86, Shevchenko 89)*, Fenerbahçe 1 *(Alex 63p)*
PSV 1 *(Vennegoor of Hesselink 33)*, FC Schalke 04 0

(28/9/05)
Fenerbahçe 3 *(Alex 40p, 68, Appiah 90)*, PSV 0
FC Schalke 04 2 *(Larsen 3, Altintop 70)*, Milan 2 *(Seedorf 1, Shevchenko 59)*

(19/10/05)
Fenerbahçe 3 *(Luciano 14, Márcio Nobre 73, Appiah 79)*, FC Schalke 04 3 *(Lincoln 59, 62, Kuranyi 77)*
Milan 0, PSV 0

(1/11/05)
PSV 1 *(Farfán 12)*, Milan 0
FC Schalke 04 2 *(Kuranyi 32, Sand 90)*, Fenerbahçe 0

(23/11/05)
Fenerbahçe 0, Milan 4 *(Shevchenko 16, 52, 70, 76)*
FC Schalke 04 3 *(Kobiashvili 18p, 73, 79p)*, PSV 0

(6/12/05)
Milan 3 *(Pirlo 42, Kaká 52, 60)*, FC Schalke 04 2 *(Poulsen 49, Lincoln 66)*
PSV 2 *(Cocu 14, Farfán 85)*, Fenerbahçe 0

FINAL TABLE

		Home				Away				Total				
	Pld	W	D	L	F A	W	D	L	F A	W	D	L	F A	Pts
1 Milan	6	2	1	0	6 3	1	1	1	6 3	3	2	1	12 6	11
2 PSV	6	3	0	0	4 0	0	1	2	0 6	3	1	2	4 6	10
3 FC Schalke 04	6	2	1	0	7 2	0	1	2	5 7	2	2	2	12 9	8
4 Fenerbahçe	6	1	1	1	6 7	0	0	3	1 7	1	1	4	7 14	4

UEFA Champions League 2005/2006

and Rosenborg. Although all three opponents were competition regulars, only Lyon, with two successive quarter-final placings, had achieved anything of note. The prospects did not look good for the Greeks or the Norwegians.

Real, though, had opened with a 3-0 defeat at Bayer Leverkusen the previous season, and the Galácticos' early nerves were ruthlessly exposed again at the Stade Gerland as Lyon, newly coached by ex-Liverpool boss Gérard Houllier, ripped them to shreds with a breathtaking first-half display. Goalkeeper Iker Casillas was beaten three times in ten minutes, and the damage to his team would have been even greater had he not saved a penalty from Juninho just before the interval. It was a stunning effort from the French champions, and there was simply no way back for Real in the second half. Another Champions League campaign, another opening 3-0 defeat.

There was an even bigger surprise in the other game as Olympiakos, normally so assured at home, were beaten 3-1 in Piraeus by Rosenborg, a team that had not won away in the competition for six years – a run of 16 matches. Comical defending brought about the Greek side's downfall, although the visitors were deeply indebted to their goalkeeper Espen Johnsen for a series of heroic saves before the game was settled with a late breakaway goal from visiting striker Øyvind Storflor.

Raúl's record

There was a return to normality on Matchday Two as Lyon beat Rosenborg 1-0 in Trondheim and Real Madrid, assisted by an awesome display of right-wing crossing from David Beckham, beat Olympiakos 2-1 at the Bernabéu. Raúl headed home one of the Englishman's deliveries after just nine minutes to put Real in front and simultaneously make history with his 50th goal in Europe's premier club competition – one more than the previous record tally held by another Real legend, Alfredo Di Stéfano. Olympiakos threatened to spoil Raúl's, and Real's, evening when Pantelis Kafes, a midfielder wearing the no.1 shirt, rifled in a shock equaliser early in the second half. But Beckham kept testing the Greek defence with his deadly crosses and finally he got his second assist of the evening when substitute Roberto Soldado headed home the winner four minutes from time.

The England captain was in prime form once again three weeks later as Real delivered a stupendous second-half display against Rosenborg. A goal down at the interval, the Spaniards swept all before them in the second half. Beckham created two goals for defenders Jonathan Woodgate and Iván Helguera before rounding off the scoring himself with a trademark free-kick, but the best of Real's four goals was the second one, delightfully finished by Raúl after equally skilful set-up play by new Brazilian recruit Robinho.

Olympiakos suffered a case of déjà vu in Lyons as they again went down 2-1 to a late winner after levelling the game through an excellent Kafes goal. Whereas Beckham had shot them down in the Bernabéu, it was Juninho who tormented them in the Stade Gerland, opening the scoring early on with a wonderful free-kick (his Champions League speciality) and providing an immaculate assist for Sidney Govou's late winner. Two weeks later the brilliant Brazilian was at it again, scoring another excellent free-kick and inspiring the team to a 4-1 win that sealed their place in the last 16 with a 100 per cent success rate.

Real Madrid also confirmed their qualification by completing the double over Rosenborg in Trondheim, although it was largely down to the excellence of Casillas that they secured maximum points from their visit. Three weeks later it took something special to beat the Spanish international keeper at the Bernabéu as John Carew, the Lyon striker, deceived him, and defender Roberto Carlos, with a brilliant back-heeled finish. It earned the French side a 1-1 draw and confirmed their qualification as group winners.

On the same night Rosenborg denied Olympiakos

Real Madrid's Raúl is quietly pleased with his record 50th Champions League goal

UEFA Champions League 2005/2006

GROUP F RESULTS

(13/9/05)
Olympique Lyonnais 3 *(Carew 21, Juninho 26, Wiltord 31)*, Real Madrid 0
Olympiakos 1 *(Lago 19og)*, Rosenborg BK 3 *(Ciljan Skjelbred 43, Mavrogenidis 48og, Storflor 90)*

(28/9/05)
Real Madrid 2 *(Raúl 9, Soldado 86)*, Olympiakos 1 *(Kafes 48)*
Rosenborg BK 0, Olympique Lyonnais 1 *(Cris 45)*

(19/10/05)
Olympique Lyonnais 2 *(Juninho 4, Govou 89)*, Olympiakos 1 *(Kafes 84)*
Real Madrid 4 *(Woodgate 48, Raúl 52, Helguera 68, Beckham 82)*, Rosenborg BK 1 *(Strand 40)*

(1/11/05)
Olympiakos 1 *(Babangida 3)*, Olympique Lyonnais 4 *(Juninho 41, Carew 43, 57, Diarra 55)*
Rosenborg BK 0, Real Madrid 2 *(Dorsin 26og, Guti 41)*

(23/11/05)
Real Madrid 1 *(Guti 41)*, Olympique Lyonnais 1 *(Carew 72)*
Rosenborg BK 1 *(Helstad 88)*, Olympiakos 1 *(Rivaldo 25)*

(6/12/05)
Olympique Lyonnais 2 *(Benzema 33, Fred 90)*, Rosenborg BK 1 *(Braaten 68)*
Olympiakos 2 *(Bulut 50, Rivaldo 87)*, Real Madrid 1 *(Sergio Ramos 7)*

FINAL TABLE

	Pld	Home W	D	L	F	A	Away W	D	L	F	A	Total W	D	L	F	A	Pts
1 Olympique Lyonnais	6	3	0	0	7	2	2	1	0	6	2	5	1	0	13	4	16
2 Real Madrid	6	2	1	0	7	3	1	0	2	3	5	3	1	2	10	8	10
3 Rosenborg BK	6	0	1	2	1	4	1	0	2	5	7	1	1	4	6	11	4
4 Olympiakos	6	1	0	2	4	8	0	1	2	3	5	1	1	4	7	13	4

a first ever away win in the Champions League when Thorstein Helstad scrambled in a late equaliser. It gave Rosenborg their first home goal, and first home point, of the competition and was good enough to ensure that the Norwegians, rather than the Greeks, would go forward into the UEFA Cup. Olympiakos would win their final match, at home to a Real Madrid side led by caretaker coach Juan Ramón López Caro, with a late winning goal from ex-Barcelona man Rivaldo, and Rosenborg would lose by the same 2-1 scoreline to a last-minute winner away to Lyon, but it didn't matter. The die was already cast thanks to the Norwegians' head-to-head superiority.

Group G

The inclusion of two clubs from the same country in a Champions League group was a first for the competition. Neither Chelsea nor Liverpool were especially pleased to be in each other's company, but with fallen Belgian giants Anderlecht and Spanish first-timers Real Betis joining them in Group G, the odds were heavily stacked in favour of a Premiership one-two.

Liverpool made a particularly strong statement of intent in their opening game, away to Betis, when they scored two fine goals in the opening 15 minutes and impressively beat the Seville side 2-1 – despite manager Rafa Benítez's strange decision to leave captain Steven Gerrard, the star of the qualifying adventure, on the bench. Chelsea also claimed maximum points on Matchday One, but theirs was nothing more than a workmanlike performance at home to Anderlecht, with Frank Lampard's 19th-minute indirect free-kick proving conclusive against an ultra-defensive Belgian side.

That was Anderlecht's eighth successive Champions League defeat, and the sorry run continued a fortnight later when they lost 1-0 at home to Betis. The Spanish side rattled the woodwork no fewer than four times in the first half before Brazilian striker Ricardo Oliveira made the deserved breakthrough with a beautifully placed shot. Meanwhile, at Anfield, the two Premiership giants were not unexpectedly cancelling each other out in a dull, scrappy goalless encounter of very few chances. Chelsea were probably the happier at the final whistle, if only because the 0-0 draw brought to an end a run of four successive Champions League defeats away from home.

There would be no end to Anderlecht's misery, however, in their two matches against Liverpool. A magnificent volley from Djibril Cissé gave the Merseysiders a 1-0 win in Brussels and they followed that up with an easy 3-0 win at Anfield, the Frenchman again finding the target – albeit from an offside position – after excellent goals from Spaniards Fernando Morientes and Luis García. Anderlecht's Serbian striker Nenad Jestrovic was sent off for racist comments made to Liverpool midfielder Momo Sissoko that were overheard by the referee.

Stamford blitz

Chelsea eclipsed Betis at Stamford Bridge with a 4-0 win that incorporated some splendid goals, the best of them from Hernán Crespo, but it was a different story in Seville two weeks later as Betis bounced back with a surprise 1-0 victory. The winning goal came in the first half from Dani, who had only been on the field a couple of minutes after substituting Ricardo Oliveira, carried off with a serious knee injury that was to put him out for the rest of the season. Chelsea's new signing Michael Essien came close to equalising in the second half but his shot struck one post, rolled

UEFA Champions League 2005/2006

across the goal-line and hit the other before rebounding to safety.

The defeat was Chelsea's first of the season in any competition and it put them under pressure for their next fixture, away to Anderlecht, but the Belgians proved as obliging as ever, and two early volleyed goals from Crespo and Ricardo Carvalho brought José Mourinho and his team a long overdue overseas victory. With Liverpool and Betis simultaneously drawing 0-0 at Anfield, it meant that both English teams were safely through to the last 16, with the Spaniards claiming the UEFA Cup spot.

Matchday Six would see Anderlecht finally break their Champions League duck – after 12 successive defeats - with a 1-0 win in Seville, but in the big game at Stamford Bridge to determine which of the two English qualifiers would go into the last-16 draw as group winners, Chelsea and Liverpool played out yet another tepid goalless draw, a result that enabled the visitors to remain at the top of the table. The match was lifted from the mundane only by a shocking challenge by Essien on Liverpool midfielder Didi Hamann. The

Hernán Crespo strikes early for Chelsea in Brussels

Ghanaian escaped immediate censure but video evidence would later bring him a two-game ban, excluding him from both legs of their second-round tie.

GROUP H

With Celtic removed from the competition in mid-summer, Rangers were the only Scottish team in the group phase. Among their opponents were Celtic's surprise conquerors, Artmedia Bratislava, but the greater threat to the Glasgow side's continued progress came from the Italians of Inter and 2004 European champions FC Porto.

Rangers made a grand start, beating Porto 3-2 in a thrilling encounter at Ibrox. Twice they led, the second time through a controversial goal from Dado Prso, but twice the Portuguese side came back to equalise, through Brazilian defender Pepe. There were just five minutes remaining when Rangers' Greek defender Sotiris Kyrgiakos got the back of his head to a long punt from Barry Ferguson and angled it into the net off the post.

While Rangers' winning goal came late, Inter's, away to Artmedia, came early, Julio Cruz steering in Adriano's pass after just 17 minutes. Cruz's fellow Argetine, Juan Sebastián Verón was later red-carded, but despite some late pressure from the Slovakians, the Serie A side hung on for their win.

One-nil was also Inter's margin of victory on Matchday Two at home to Rangers. The San Siro was empty – as it would be for all three of the Nerazzurri's group games – as punishment for the crowd disturbances at the previous season's quarter-final against Milan, but Roberto Mancini's

GROUP G RESULTS

(13/9/05)
Real Betis 1 *(Arzu 51)*, Liverpool 2 *(Sinama-Pongolle 2, Luis García 14)*
Chelsea 1 *(Lampard 19)*, RSC Anderlecht 0

(28/9/05)
RSC Anderlecht 0, Real Betis 1 *(Ricardo Oliveira 69)*
Liverpool 0, Chelsea 0

(19/10/05)
RSC Anderlecht 0, Liverpool 1 *(Cissé 20)*
Chelsea 4 *(Drogba 24, Ricardo Carvalho 44, Cole J. 59, Crespo 64)*, Real Betis 0

(1/11/05)
Real Betis 1 *(Dani 28)*, Chelsea 0
Liverpool 3 *(Morientes 34, Luis García 61, Cissé 89)*, RSC Anderlecht 0

(23/11/05)
RSC Anderlecht 0, Chelsea 2 *(Crespo 8, Ricardo Carvalho 15)*
Liverpool 0, Real Betis 0

(6/12/05)
Real Betis 0, RSC Anderlecht 1 *(Kompany 44)*
Chelsea 0, Liverpool 0

FINAL TABLE

		Home				Away				Total				
	Pld	W	D	L	F A	W	D	L	F A	W	D	L	F A	Pts
1 Liverpool	6	1	2	0	3 0	2	1	0	3 1	3	3	0	6 1	12
2 Chelsea	6	2	1	0	5 0	1	1	1	2 1	3	2	1	7 1	11
3 Real Betis	6	1	0	2	2 3	1	1	1	1 4	2	1	3	3 7	7
4 RSC Anderlecht	6	0	0	3	0 4	1	0	2	1 4	1	0	5	1 8	3

UEFA Champions League 2005/2006

side did not let it deter them. Despite a missed penalty by Cruz, the points were secured by a deflected free-kick from Chilean schemer David Pizarro. Inter would have made it 2-0 but for an incredible miss from Santiago Solari with the goal gaping. Luckily for him, there were no spectators there to see it.

Slovakian shock

FC Porto did have a crowd to play to against Artmedia, but by the end of the game in the Estádio do Dragão the noises raining down from the stands were far from supportive. After taking a 2-0 lead, Co Adriaanse's team criminally underestimated their opponents' powers of recovery, and the Slovakian outsiders turned the game around in dramatic style with goals from Peter Petrás, Jan Kozák and Balázs Borbély, three players whose names would have been wholly unfamiliar to 99 per cent of the Porto fans at the start of the game.

To their credit, Porto bounced back in their next home game, beating Inter 2-0 with a freak own-goal from Marco Materazzi and a deflected shot from Benni McCarthy. There were no goals at all at Ibrox, where Artmedia Bratislava continued to surprise. Rangers should have won the return match, in Slovakia, two weeks later but dreadful defending from Alex McLeish's side enabled their hosts to equalise not once but twice, and on this occasion, unlike against Porto, Rangers could not find a third goal. They had their chance, but Peter Løvenkrands put a simple header wide in the closing stages.

Porto were also unable to potect their lead in the deserted San Siro as two Cruz goals, the first from the penalty spot, turned the match around for Inter. But Porto did have the satisfaction of scoring arguably the goal of the tournament – a glorious free-kick from youngster Hugo Almeida that left his left boot 35 yards from goal and was still rising at great velocity as it thundered into the roof of the net.

Inter confirmed their qualification three weeks later with a comprehensive 4-0 win at home to Artmedia. For the first time in their history Inter took the field without an Italian in their line-up. In fact, there was just one European, Luís Figo, and he opened the scoring before Adriano ended his personal goal drought in spectacular style with a hat-trick of typically clinical left-foot finishes. In Portugal, Porto had a glorious opportunity to move above Rangers into second position, especially after Lisandro López had headed them in front on the hour. But the Scots found an unlikely equaliser from an even unlikelier source as substitute Ross McCormack, who had only just come on for his Champions League debut, tucked the ball home from an assist by another youngster, Chris Burke. An incredible double save at the death from Ronald Waterreus kept the score at 1-1 and left Rangers in a strong position to become the first Scottish side ever to progress to the Champions League knockout phase.

Going into their final game, at home to already-qualified Inter, Rangers required a win to be certain of qualification or a draw if Artmedia failed to beat Porto in Bratislava. Even a defeat would suffice if the other game ended in a draw. Of course, Rangers had blown far better opportunities in the past – as in the UEFA Cup a year earlier – so nobody was counting any chickens at Ibrox. Furthermore, the team was struggling badly at domestic level and manager McLeish was on the brink of the sack. After a run of nine games without a win in all competitions, only Champions League progress, it seemed, could save him.

Impending doom

An air of impending doom descended on Ibrox when Adriano headed Inter in front after 30 minutes, but the stadium came alive again soon

Alex McLeish lives out borrowed time at Rangers

UEFA Champions League 2005/2006

GROUP H RESULTS

(13/9/05)
Artmedia Bratislava 0, Internazionale 1 *(Cruz 17)*
Rangers 3 *(Løvenkrands 35, Prso 59, Kyrgiakos 85)*, FC Porto 2 *(Pepe 47, 71)*

(28/9/05)
Internazionale 1 *(Pizarro 49)*, Rangers 0
FC Porto 2 *(Lucho González 32, Diego 39)*, Artmedia Bratislava 3 *(Petrás 45, Kozák 54, Borbély 74)*

(19/10/05)
FC Porto 2 *(Materazzi 22og, McCarthy 35)*, Internazionale 0
Rangers 0, Artmedia Bratislava 0

(1/11/05)
Artmedia Bratislava 2 *(Borbély 8, Kozák 59)*, Rangers 2 *(Prso 3, Thompson 44)*
Internazionale 2 *(Cruz 75p, 82)*, FC Porto 1 *(Hugo Almeida 16)*

(23/11/05)
Internazionale 4 *(Figo 28, Adriano 41, 59, 74)*, Artmedia Bratislava 0
FC Porto 1 *(Lisandro López 60)*, Rangers 1 *(McCormack 83)*

(6/12/05)
Artmedia Bratislava 0, FC Porto 0
Rangers 1 *(Løvenkrands 38)*, Internazionale 1 *(Adriano 30)*

FINAL TABLE

| | | Pld | \multicolumn{5}{c}{Home} | \multicolumn{5}{c}{Away} | \multicolumn{5}{c}{Total} | Pts |

		Pld	W	D	L	F	A	W	D	L	F	A	W	D	L	F	A	Pts
1	Internazionale	6	3	0	0	7	1	1	1	1	2	3	4	1	1	9	4	13
2	Rangers	6	1	2	0	4	3	0	2	1	3	4	1	4	1	7	7	7
3	Artmedia Bratislava	6	0	2	1	2	3	1	1	1	3	6	1	3	2	5	9	6
4	FC Porto	6	1	1	1	5	4	0	1	2	3	5	1	2	3	8	9	5

afterwards when Løvenkrands raced through on to Thomas Buffel's excellent through-ball, outpaced the veteran Sinisa Mihajlovic and clipped the ball past Francesco Toldo. Cristiano Zanetti's red card helped Rangers' cause in the second half, but they rarely looked like getting a winner and the game ended 1-1.

Fortunately, that was enough to see the Scots through, but only because Artmedia Bratislava missed a succession of big chances on a quagmire of a pitch against Porto. Just one goal would have brought the Slovakian champions a sensational qualification, but it wasn't to be their day. Their only consolation was that the 0-0 draw earned them a UEFA Cup place. The way they had battered Porto, that was the very least they deserved.

SECOND ROUND

Surprisingly, just one country, Holland, managed to take its full complement of teams forward into the knockout phase of the competition. While PSV and Ajax, the only two Dutch representatives, remained in contention, England had surprisingly lost the services of Manchester United, Spain had relinquished Real Betis, Italy had left behind Udinese and Germany had surrendered Schalke. Even so, there was a still a heavyweight presence from the leading nations, with three teams each from England, Italy and Spain and two from Germany. The remaining three places were taken up by one team apiece from France, Portugal and Scotland. Eastern Europe was completely unrepresented, as was Scandinavia.

The draw for the last 16, which kept apart group winners and (Liverpool aside) those teams from the same country, produced two plum Anglo-Spanish ties. For the second year in a row Chelsea were paired at this stage of the competition with Barcelona, while Real Madrid and Arsenal were drawn together for the first time ever in official European competition. There were a couple of interesting Bundesliga-Serie A match-ups as well, especially the one between Bayern Munich and Milan. PSV against Lyon was a repeat of the previous season's quarter-final while Liverpool, the holders, were given the chance to avenge Manchester United as they were paired with Benfica.

Holders bow out

Liverpool travelled to Lisbon for the first leg in good heart, having knocked United out of the FA Cup the previous weekend, but with Steven Gerrard again 'rested' by Rafa Benítez, the Merseysiders seemed content to defend and hold out for a 0-0 draw. They were almost there until, out of the blue, Benfica won the game with a fine header from their giant Brazilian centre-back Luisão six minutes from time. Now the holders were under pressure. They attacked ceaselessly throughout the first half at Anfield but spurned a host of chances and were made to pay for their errant finishing just before the interval when Simão rifled a fantastic right-foot shot into the top corner. Liverpool needed three goals without reply in the second half. That had been their speciality, of course, the previous season, but this time they never looked likely to retrieve the situation and their defence of the trophy was finally ended when Benfica scored a second goal, spectacularly hooked home by Fabrizo Miccoli, at the end of the game.

Arsenal went to the Bernabéu to face Real Madrid beset with injuries, but nobody would have known it as they produced one of their greatest ever European performances, completely outplaying the Spanish aristocrats from first moment to last and winning the game with a majestic individual goal, early in the second half, from Thierry Henry. The Frenchman, playing up front on his own, decided to take on the Real defence from the

UEFA Champions League 2005/2006

centre circle. He went past three opponents before steering an immaculate left-foot shot wide of Iker Casillas. It was his 40th European goal for Arsenal and undoubtedly one of his best. It also enabled the Gunners to become the first English club ever to beat Real at the Bernabéu – even if there weren't actually any Englishmen in the team.

Penalty scare

The same Arsenal XI lined up for the second leg at Highbury. With the away goal and a lead to protect, the Londoners were favourites to progress. They survived an early penalty scare but should have extended their lead at the end of an absorbing first half when José Antonio Reyes struck the crossbar with the goal at his mercy. Real came at Arsenal after the interval, and Raúl hit the post, but Arsenal's defending was exceptional and Henry, as ever, was a constant threat up front, forcing one fine save from Casillas and showing wonderful skill before stroking another shot just wide. The match finished with Jens Lehmann saving dramatically from Robinho, and that was that. A terrific game had ended 0-0, and Arsenal, with one of the most prized European scalps of all, were through to the quarter-finals.

PSV, like Real Madrid, were unable to recover from a home defeat in their tie with Lyon. A Juninho free-kick – does he score any other type of goal? – did the damage at the Philips Stadion, where PSV had been unbeaten in all competitions for 31 matches, but the Dutch champions had only themselves to blame for a host of missed chances, the worst of them late in the game from Arouna Koné in front of an open goal. The French side, seeking revenge for their quarter-final elimination on penalties the previous season, ripped PSV to shreds in the return. Two first-half goals from Portuguese midfielder Tiago, between which the visitors had Phillip Cocu sent off for a violent challenge, paved the way to a comfortable 4-0 win. It was concluded by a sumptuous strike from Brazilian striker Fred, who celebrated the fact that his wife had given birth to a daughter earlier in the day by reeling away with a baby's dummy in his mouth.

Bayern Munich were hoping to give German football a lift at the start of World Cup year against Milan but they were always in trouble after failing to win the home leg at the Allianz-Arena. Michael Ballack put the home side ahead with a magnificent dipping volley, but Andriy Shevchenko levelled from the penalty spot after a needless hand-ball from Valérien Ismaël. The French defender was to make amends by scoring in the San Siro two weeks later but his goal would prove to be a mere consolation as Milan battered Bayern into submission with an outstanding display. It was a particularly bad night for Oliver Kahn – and his hopes of keeping goal for Germany at the World Cup – as the Rossoneri smashed four goals past him. Particularly unnerving for the Bayern keeper was the second of them, glanced in by Shevchenko just 90 seconds after Kahn had aggressively confronted the Ukrainian, who had just put his penalty wide of the post.

Italian double

Milan's win completed an Italian double over Germany. Twenty-four hours earlier Juventus had sneaked past Werder Bremen thanks to a goalkeeping howler of the worst possible kind by Werder's young stand-in keeper Tim Wiese. The German side had come from behind to win an exciting first leg at the Weserstadion 3-2 with two late goals from Tim Borowski and Johan Micoud. When the Frenchman extended that lead with another goal early in the second leg, Juve were right up against it. They peppered the Bremen goal but Wiese, who was deputising for the injured Andreas Reinke, made save after fabulous save to protect his team's advantage. Eventually he was beaten, by David Trezeguet, but Werder still led, and there were just two minutes of the match remaining when Wiese made the error that will probably haunt him forever. Collecting a cross from the right, he went to ground and, seemingly

Thierry Henry silences the Bernabéu

UEFA Champions League 2005/2006

to waste a bit of time, rolled over a couple of times. But as he did so, the ball slipped from his grasp. It fell right at the feet of Juve's Brazilian midfielder Émerson, who gratefully rolled it into the empty net to put the Italian champions through on the away-goals rule.

Inter ensured a three-pronged Italian presence in the quarter-finals when, a week after all the other ties had been completed, they beat Ajax 1-0 at home in a San Siro stadium that, for the first time in the competition, was allowed to open its turnstiles to spectators. After coming back from a two-goal deficit to draw 2-2 in Amsterdam, Roberto Mancini's team knew that they only had to keep a clean sheet to progress, and with Ajax desperately short of firepower that seemed the most likely outcome when Adriano screwed a 27th-minute penalty wide of the post. But the game would get its goal, and a beauty it was too, as Serbian midfielder Dejan Stankovic, who had scored in the first leg, cut inside from the left and curled a wonderful shot just inside the far post. For the fourth time in five seasons Inter were through to the Champions League quarter-finals.

Offside goal

The first leg of the Rangers-Villarreal tie also ended 2-2 as the Scottish side, still led by Alex McLeish, came twice from behind against a Spanish team that had not scored more than one goal in any of their group games. There was a strong case for arguing that their second goal, from Diego Forlán, should have been disallowed for offside (it certainly would have been under the old rule of 'interfering with play') but a freak own-goal from Villarreal's Bolivian defender Juan Manuel Peña near the end at least ensured that it did not decide the game. Unfortunately for Rangers, however, it would ultimately decide the tie, because the second leg at El Madrigal finished 1-1, enabling the Spanish debutants to go through on that very away goal. Rangers, backed by huge travelling support, led early through Peter Løvenkrands' fourth goal of the competition, but poor marking enabled the home side to equalise, through Argentine left-back Rodolfo Arruabarrena, early in the second half. Thereafter it was all Villarreal, with newly signed Mexican striker Guillermo Franco missing a succession of chances. Rangers did get one big opportunity to pull off a momentous win, only for Kris Boyd, their prolific new striker, to squander it. So, Rangers' sixth successive Champions League draw was not enough. They were out. Villarreal, unbeaten so far in their debut campaign, were through to the quarter-finals.

Crucial but controversial – Diego Forlán nets for Villarreal at Ibrox

The biggest tie of the round, for the second season running, was Chelsea versus Barcelona. As in the previous season, the two teams were on top of their domestic tables. The Premiership side had edged through in dramatic, controversial circumstances 12 months earlier. This time, the fixtures were reversed, with Barcelona, as group winners, having the advantage of hosting the second leg. Before the draw José Mourinho, the abrasive Chelsea manager, had professed an ambivalence towards finishing first or second in the group, but privately he would surely have preferred to avoid such a quick reunion with Frank Rijkaard's in-form team.

The previous season's encounter at Stamford Bridge, won 4-2 by Chelsea, had gone down in legend as one of the Champions League's great games. A repeat seemed unlikely, however, given the disgraceful state of the pitch. One player who looked as if he could cope with any surface was Barcelona's teenage winger Lionel Messi. The 18-year-old left-footer, stationed on the right flank, repeatedly turned Chelsea left-back Asier Del Horno inside-out in the early passage of play, and the Spaniard's frustration was eventually to result in his expulsion when he clumsily, if not maliciously, clattered into the young Argentine by the corner flag. With Messi exaggerating the impact by rolling around on the floor and referee Rune Hauge besieged by a gang of Barcelona players demanding retribution from his top

UEFA Champions League 2005/2006

pocket, it was perhaps inevitable that the red card would appear. Even so it was an extremely harsh decision. Two thirds of the match remained, and Chelsea would have to play with just ten men.

Own-goals galore

Remarkably, it was the Londoners who took the lead, 14 minutes into the second half, when a Frank Lampard free-kick was deflected into his own net by Barcelona's Thiago Motta. Twelve minutes later, though, the visitors were level when Chelsea put through their own net, captain John Terry inadvertently glancing a dangerous Ronaldinho free-kick past Petr Cech. Now Barça scented blood and they swamped the Chelsea goal for the next ten minutes, creating chance after chance. Messi hit the bar and was then denied a clear penalty after being baulked by Terry, who had just cleared a Ronaldinho effort off the line. A goal was inevitable and it duly came after a swift counter-attack, with Rafael Márquez chipping in a cross that Samuel Eto'o headed powerfully into the net. Ten minutes remained but Barça eased off, happy with their lot. At 2-1 up and the home game to come, they were in a commanding position to reach the quarter-finals.

Only one English team – Liverpool, some 30 years earlier – had ever won at Camp Nou. And as Chelsea had to score at least twice to retrieve the tie, the proverbial mountain was theirs to climb. Barcelona never gave them a chance. Content to retain possession and keep the English side well away from goal, the Catalans were in complete control. The game itself was fairly tedious, but the capacity crowd didn't care. Ronaldinho did, though, and on 78 minutes he scored a wonderful individual goal, wriggling into the area before driving low past Cech. That should have been Barça's victory signed and sealed. But deep into stoppage-time Chelsea were awarded an extremely generous penalty, which Lampard converted. It was the final kick of the game. Mourinho would later claim – and factually he was correct – that Barça had not beaten his team in any of the four games when it was 11 against 11, but there could be no doubt that on this occasion the better team – and by some distance - had won the tie.

QUARTER-FINALS

The draw for the quarter-finals, staged amidst much pomp and ceremony in Paris's Hôtel de Ville, managed to keep apart the three surviving teams from Italy as well as the two remaining representatives from La Liga. With the pairings for the semi-finals also decided immediately afterwards, the road to Paris was mapped out for all eight teams.

Although the prospect of a Milan-Barcelona semi-final was enticing, the most attractive quarter-final tie was undoubtedly Arsenal against Juventus. Having eliminated the record champions of Spain, the Gunners were now obliged to overcome the record champions of Italy. Arsenal had never previously progressed beyond the quarter-finals of the competition. To do so now, they had to reprise what another English team, Liverpool, had done 12 months earlier.

The first leg, in North London, saw the return to Highbury of former favourite Patrick Vieira, but it would not be a happy homecoming at all for the French international midfielder. Instead the game would be dominated by the young Spaniard who had replaced him in the heart of the Arsenal midfield, 18-year-old Cesc Fábregas.

SECOND ROUND RESULTS

(21/2/06 & 8/3/06)
FC Bayern München 1 *(Ballack 23)*, Milan 1 *(Shevchenko 57p)*
Milan 4 *(Inzaghi 8, 47, Shevchenko 25, Kaká 59)*, FC Bayern München 1 *(Ismaël 36)*
(Milan 5-2)

SL Benfica 1 *(Luisão 84)*, Liverpool 0
Liverpool 0, SL Benfica 2 *(Simão 36, Miccoli 89)*
(SL Benfica 3-0)

PSV 0, Olympique Lyonnais 1 *(Juninho 64)*
Olympique Lyonnais 4 *(Tiago 26, 45, Wiltord 71, Fred 90)*, PSV 0
(Olympique Lyonnais 5-0)

Real Madrid 0, Arsenal 1 *(Henry 47)*
Arsenal 0, Real Madrid 0
(Arsenal 1-0)

(22/2/06 & 7/3/06)
Chelsea 1 *(Motta 59og)*, FC Barcelona 2 *(Terry 71og, Eto'o 80)*
FC Barcelona 1 *(Ronaldinho 79)*, Chelsea 1 *(Lampard 90p)*
(FC Barcelona 3-2)

Rangers 2 *(Løvenkrands 21, Peña 81og)*, Villarreal CF 2 *(Riquelme 7p, Forlán 34)*
Villarreal CF 1 *(Arruabarrena 49)*, Rangers 1 *(Løvenkrands 11)*
(3-3; Villarreal CF on away goals)

SV Werder Bremen 3 *(Schulz 39, Borowski 87, Micoud 90)*, Juventus 2 *(Nedved 74, Trezeguet 82)*
Juventus 2 *(Trezeguet 65, Émerson 88)*, SV Werder Bremen 1 *(Micoud 13)*
(4-4; Juventus on away goals)

(22/2/06 & 14/3/06)
Ajax 2 *(Huntelaar 16, Rosales 20)*, Internazionale 2 *(Stankovic 49, Cruz 86)*
Internazionale 1 *(Stankovic 57)*, Ajax 0
(Internazionale 3-2)

UEFA Champions League 2005/2006

There were other outstanding individual performances on the night from the team in the redcurrant shirts – notably from the two Ivorian defenders, Kolo Touré and Emmanuel Eboué, and the incomparable (ex-Juventino) Thierry Henry – but it was Fábregas who stole the show and he, too, who opened the scoring, five minutes before halftime, with a low shot that wrong-footed goalkeeper Gianluigi Buffon after Vieira had crucially been dispossessed by Robert Pires at the start of the move.

All over them

Juventus, with so many players underperforming, were there for the taking, and Arsenal continued to dominate in the second half. In fact, they were all over the Italians, whose shoddiness on the ball and absence of team spirit utterly belied their position at the top of Serie A. Henry doubled Arsenal's lead on 69 minutes, finishing off an exquisite move involving Alexandr Hleb and the ubiquitous Fábregas with an assured close-range finish.

Juventus, utterly outplayed, lost the plot completely towards the end. With Vieira already out of the second leg after collecting a yellow card, Mauro Camoranesi – with a scything late challenge on Robin van Persie – and Jonathan Zebina – with a malicious chop on Henry – were both red-carded. Arsenal never really threatened to get a third goal but at 2-0 they had given themselves a glorious opportunity to make history. Surely, after one of the club's greatest ever performances, they would not waste it.

Eight days later the two teams met again in Turin. Juve's influential Czech midfielder Pavel Nedved, who had been suspended for the first leg, was back in the team, but for the first 45 minutes in the Stadio delle Alpi the Italian league leaders were just as toothless and unthreatening up front as they had been for the whole game at Highbury. Arsenal should have killed the tie stone dead when Fábregas was played in by Hleb on 64 minutes, but he fired his shot straight at Buffon. That incident seemed to spark a bit of urgency into Juve's play but apart from a well struck shot by Nedved that Jens Lehmann repelled with a fine save, their pressure brought no reward, and when the Czech midfielder was red-carded for a second foul in quick succession on Eboué, the game was up for Fabio Capello's side. Arsenal, fittingly, finished the game on top. They had bossed the tie completely and now had eight successive clean sheets in the competition. A first ever semi-final

Pavel Nedved – suspended for the first game against Arsenal, sent off in the second

appearance in Europe's premier competition was their just reward.

Dutch reunion

Benfica against Barcelona brought together two former team-mates in the Dutch national side, Ronald Koeman and Frank Rijkaard, the two clubs' respective coaches. Barça travelled across the Iberian peninsular to Lisbon without wonderboy Lionel Messi, injured in the second leg of the Chelsea tie, but even without his flamboyant talent they were able to pick numerous holes in the Benfica defence. Unfortunately, for all their dominance, they couldn't find a way past Benfica's inspired Brazilian keeper Moretto. The mid-season signing from Nacional of Madeira had the game of his life, albeit aided and abetted by some wayward Barcelona finishing, and there might even have been a twist in the tale similar to the previous round's home tie against Liverpool when Benfica came on strong at the end, having one convincing penalty claim for handball turned down (by English referee Steve Bennett) and then forcing Barcelona keeper Víctor Valdés into a fine save

UEFA Champions League 2005/2006

from skipper (and ex-Barça player) Simão.

Despite all the excitement and the goalmouth action, the scoreline somehow remained 0-0, which left the tie wide open for the return in Camp Nou. Moretto proved unbeatable again five minutes into the second leg when he brilliantly saved a Ronaldinho penalty, but not long afterwards the Brazilian maestro finally got the better of his defiant compatriot, sidefooting home a Samuel Eto'o pull-back from the byline. With the spectre of the away-goals rule looming, Barça needed a second goal, but Benfica were resolute in defence and it proved to be a tense, anxious evening for the big Catalan crowd. Simão caused a few palpitations when he put a good chance fractionally wide and Giorgos Karagounis tested Víctor Valdés with a long-range strike, but the home side resisted well and finally secured their semi-final place late in the game when Eto'o finished a fine move with a typically explosive right-foot finish.

After failing at the quarter-final hurdle two years running, Lyon were hoping to make it third time lucky against Milan. Their cause was not helped in the first leg, at home, by the absence of their best player, Juninho, through suspension, and without his set-piece skills Gérard Houllier's side rarely troubled the Milan rearguard. The better chances in a tight contest fell to visiting striker Andriy Shevchenko, all in the first half, but three times he was denied by Lyon keeper Grégory Coupet. The game finished goalless. It was a fair result but a surprising one as it was the first time in 20 Champions League games that Lyon had failed to score.

QUARTER-FINAL RESULTS

(28/3/06 & 5/4/06)
Arsenal 2 *(Fàbregas 40, Henry 69)*, Juventus 0
Juventus 0, Arsenal 0
(Arsenal 2-0)

SL Benfica 0, FC Barcelona 0
FC Barcelona 2 *(Ronaldinho 19, Eto'o 88)*, SL Benfica 0
(FC Barcelona 2-0)

(29/3/06 & 4/4/06)
Internazionale 2 *(Adriano 7, Martins 54)*, Villarreal CF 1 *(Forlán 1)*
Villarreal CF 1 *(Arruabarrena 56)*, Internazionale 0
(2-2; Villarreal CF on away goal)

Olympique Lyonnais 0, Milan 0
Milan 3 *(Inzaghi 25, 88, Shevchenko 90)*, Olympique Lyonnais 1 *(Diarra 31)*
(Milan 3-1)

Full house

A sell-out crowd of 83,000 packed the San Siro for the return six days later. Lyon, who had not lost away from home all season in any competition, played exceptionally well in the first half, but Milan scored from virtually their only worthwhile opportunity, through Filippo Inzaghi, and although Lyon midfielder Mahamadou Diarra exploited uncharacteristically poor defending from the Italians at a Juninho free-kick to head his team level soon afterwards, the French side should really have been ahead at the interval. On the away-goal rule, of course, they were indeed in front. Milan now had to score. The second half saw the home side gradually build up a head of steam, but it looked as if Lyon might survive. Just two minutes of normal time remained when the French side's hearts were broken. Although Inzaghi got the goal, it was Shevchenko who made it with a superb shot that struck Coupet's fingertips and both posts before his strike-partner applied the final tap-in. In stoppage-time the Ukrainian got a goal for himself – his ninth of the competition and his 43rd in the Champions League – to twist the knife and prove yet again the value to any team of a great striker.

As Milan progressed, Inter went out, beaten by Villarreal. The Nerazzurri recovered from the shock of conceding a goal after just 45 seconds of the home leg to win the match 2-1 with goals from strikers Adriano and Obafemi Martins, but Juan Román Riquelme finished the game at the San Siro very strongly, thudding a free-kick against the crossbar, and the brilliant Argentine playmaker was to enhance his burgeoning reputation with a magnificent individual display at El Madrigal the following week. It was Riquelme's floated free-kick into the penalty area that brought about the only goal of the game, a header from Rodolfo Arruabarrena (also the match-winner in the previous round against Rangers), and after helping his team into the lead, the crafty schemer was all over the place, driving Inter to distraction with his mesmerising ball skills, perceptive passes and thunderous shots. Although they had required the away-goals rule to take them through for the second round running, Villarreal thoroughly deserved their place in the semi-finals. For a team competing in their first Champions League campaign, it was some feat.

SEMI-FINALS

The semi-finals began with Milan hosting Barcelona in the San Siro. The popular consensus was that the winner of this superheavyweight clash would go on

UEFA Champions League 2005/2006

to lift the trophy in Paris. Both clubs had brought the previous weekend's domestic fixture forward to the Friday night in order to give themselves the best possible preparation. Barça travelled without Deco, who was suspended, and Lionel Messi and Henrik Larsson, who were injured, while Milan brought in Alberto Gilardino up front for Pippo Inzaghi, who was ill.

After a cagey start Milan threatened twice in quick succession, with Gilardino, yet to score in the Champions League, striking the inside of the post and Andriy Shevchenko, seeking his tenth goal of the competition, forcing a good save with a firm downward header. The game sagged after that and for the rest of the first half Ronaldinho, in particular, really struggled to get his game together.

After the interval, though, the excitement perked up. Kaká and Gilardino between them messed up an excellent chance created by Shevchenko and a few minutes later they were left to rue that missed opportunity when Ronaldinho came alive at last and fed a beautiful pass into the area, which Ludovic Giuly smashed home from a tight angle with a superb left-foot shot. Once ahead, Barcelona, and Ronaldinho in particular, began to show their class. The Catalans' ability to keep the ball and frustrate Milan worked a treat. Although they were behind on their own ground, the Rossoneri couldn't raise their game. They created just one decent chance, which substitute Massimo Ambrosini hurriedly and horribly screwed wide from Kaká's delightful reverse pass.

Ton up for Barça

With a 1-0 lead, Barcelona were in the driving seat, but although Milan had been poor in the San Siro, all was still to play for at Camp Nou the following week. It was Barcelona's 100th Champions League match, and surprisingly the Catalans played quite an adventurous open game at the start, with Samuel Eto'o twice being denied by the awareness of Milan keeper Dida. As in Milan, however, the defences were on top, and as the match wore on without much incident in the second half, it looked as if Barcelona's plans were simply to hold on to their first-leg advantage. On 69 minutes, however, Barça, and in particular their captain, Carles Puyol, got incredibly lucky. A cross into the Barcelona box was headed home by Shevchenko, but although the sound of Markus Merk's whistle was heard before the ball entered the net, there was simply no foul. Puyol had just lost his footing. It was a huge call, and one the German referee got totally wrong.

Milan goalkeeper Dida – his clean sheet in Camp Nou was not enough

In fairness, however, Milan barely deserved anything out of the game. It was Barça who finished it on the front foot, with Larsson and Deco both testing Dida, and at the final whistle, after a disappointing 0-0 draw – the first time in 13 months the Catalans had failed to score at home - it was Barça who could justly claim to have been the superior side over the two legs. They, not Milan, would be in Paris on May 17.

Arsenal against Villarreal did not have quite the prestige of the other semi-final, but there was a massive incentive for the two clubs, neither of whom had ever come close to a European Cup final before. The odds favoured Arsenal, but only slightly. The first leg was in London, and it was an emotional night for the Gunners, making their final floodlit appearance at Highbury before their summer move to the new Emirates Stadium.

Touré strikes

The appearance of a squirrel on the pitch brought some early jollity to proceedings, but the Highbury faithful were up in arms shortly

UEFA Champions League 2005/2006

Jens Lehmann keeps out Juan Román Riquelme's penalty to put Arsenal in the final

afterwards when Thierry Henry had a goal wrongly disallowed for offside (he was level with the defender when the ball was played to him). It was a tight, evenly balanced contest but Arsenal found a way through the Spanish rearguard in the 41st minute when Henry slipped the ball through to Alexandr Hleb, the Belarussian squared it perfectly across from the left and Kolo Touré, still upfield after an earlier corner, rammed it into the net from close range. Before the half was over, however, Villarreal were denied a clear penalty when Gilberto Silva upended José Mari on the edge of the area. But the referee saw it as a dive by the Spaniard and waved play on. Juan Román Riquelme was so incensed that he was booked for his protests.

Riquelme was not enjoying his evening. Arsenal policed him brilliantly and he had little impact on the game. Both he and his team in general were non-existent as an attacking force in the second half, but it was clear that the priority of Villarreal's Chilean coach Manuel Pellegrini was simply to keep the score at 1-0. They achieved that with a fair degree of comfort as Arsenal, for all their possession, were unable to work Villarreal's stand-in keeper Mariano Barbosa more than once or twice throughout the entire half.

Although Villarreal's regular keeper, Sebastián Viera, was fit again for the second leg, Barbosa surprisingly kept his place. Arsenal, however, knew that they did not need to beat Barbosa to reach the final. A tenth successive clean sheet would do, and with their no.1 keeper, Jens Lehmann, yet to concede a Champions League goal all season, they were entitled to have every confidence in their own defensive capabilities. The problem, however, was that Philippe Senderos, Touré's regular central defensive partner, was injured, and when Mathieu Flamini, the team's long-running makeshift left-back (in the absence of England international Ashley Cole), pulled a hamstring after only nine minutes, suddenly only half of the back-four that had kept out Real Madrid and Juventus – and Villarreal in the first leg – were now in situ.

For the first hour of the contest all Arsenal did was defend. Perhaps their mindset was wrong, but they kept giving the ball away, allowing Villarreal to come on to them at every opportunity. Thierry Henry, all alone up front, was frustrated and disillusioned, a mere passenger. Villarreal, cautious themselves in the first half, began to attack with greater purpose after the interval. Guillermo Franco twice headed wide, then the Mexican forward set up Diego Forlán, who sidefooted fractionally over. The Villarreal fire appeared to have been doused when, out of nothing and with just a minute of normal time remaining, they were gifted a penalty. Gaël Clichy, the early substitute for Flamini, made a careless, if innocuous, challenge on José Mari, who predictably flung himself to the ground. It was a theatrical dive but the experienced Russian referee, Valentin Ivanov, fell for it hook, line and sinker and pointed to the spot.

Hero Lehmann

It was a huge moment, both for the penalty-taker, Juan Román Riquelme, and the goalkeeper, Jens Lehmann. It was a battle of nerves, and the German won it, protecting his invincible record with a superb save to his left before his team-mates mobbed him with congratulatory hugs and handshakes. Riquelme was evidently distraught. His big moment had come and gone. It was Villarreal's last chance to rescue the tie, and he had blown it. Lehmann, who had been a figure of authority throughout the game, setting a new Champions League record for keeping his goal intact, was the Arsenal hero. He deserved all the adulation that came his way. His team had played poorly but he had rescued them, and now, for the first time in their history, Arsenal were through to the final of the European Cup.

UEFA Champions League 2005/2006

SEMI-FINAL RESULTS

(18/4/06 & 26/4/06)
Milan 0, FC Barcelona 1 *(Giuly 58)*
FC Barcelona 0, Milan 0
(FC Barcelona 1-0)

(19/4/06 & 25/4/06)
Arsenal 1 *(Touré 41)*, Villarreal CF 0
Villarreal CF 0, Arsenal 0
(Arsenal 1-0)

FINAL

The 51st European Cup final, staged in Paris to commemorate the 50th anniversary of the first one, brought together two of the Continent's most progressive, attractive teams.

Arsenal, who had never won club football's most prestigious trophy, had reached the Stade de France showpiece on the back of a remarkable defensive record, but in their Parisian front man, Thierry Henry, they possessed arguably the world's best striker. Barcelona, kings of Europe only once previously, back in 1992, had been billed as the competition favourites ever since their victory over another London team, Chelsea, in the second round, and they too possessed a superstar with Parisian connections, ex PSG playmaker, and reigning European and World Footballer of the Year, Ronaldinho.

The Catalans, who had already won La Liga for the second year in succession, came into the game with a team that was practically full strength. Teenage wonderboy Lionel Messi was not yet fully recovered from the thigh injury he had picked up against Chelsea, while Barça boss Frank Rijkaard selected Frenchman Ludovic Giuly (the semi-final match-winner against Milan) ahead of veteran Swedish striker Henrik Larsson. Arsenal welcomed back left-back Ashley Cole after a long injury lay-off, and his England international colleague Sol Campbell was also included in central defence to replace the injured Philippe Senderos.

Lively start

The match began at a lively pace, strangely but encouragingly open and adventurous for a Champions League final. Henry worked a good chance for himself after only three minutes but was denied by Víctor Valdés's leg, while Samuel Eto'o and Deco both tested Jens Lehmann with a couple of snapshots.

The German goalkeeper, who, remarkably, had not conceded a Champions League goal all season, was to become the game's key figure on 19 minutes when he came off his line fractionally late and advanced on a goalbound Eto'o, who had been played through the Arsenal offside trap by Ronaldinho. The Cameroonian striker sidestepped to his right as the two players met just outside the penalty area. Lehmann stretched out to block the ball but caught the man instead, sending him tumbling to the turf. The ball, meanwhile, ran on to the right where Giuly was waiting to stroke it into the net.

Norwegian referee Rune Hauge had a massive decision to make. The sensible one would have been to award Barcelona the goal and book Lehmann, but instead he decided to disallow the goal, award a free-kick to Barça on the edge of the area and show the Arsenal goalkeeper the red card. In whistling for the foul before Giuly received the ball to score, Hauge had acted too soon. It meant bad news for both teams. With Ronaldinho curling the ensuing free-kick over, Barcelona had been deprived of a 1-0 lead. Arsenal, on the other hand, had lost their goalkeeper (and Robert Pires, sacrificed to make way for deputy keeper Manuel Almunia) with 70 minutes (and possibly more) still to play. As for any neutrals watching, the game, which had begun so brightly, had been ruined as a spectacle.

Or had it? After 15 humdrum minutes, during which the two teams struggled to re-organise their tactics and formation, Arsenal were awarded a hugely contentious free-kick just wide of the Barcelona area on the right. Action replays showed that Emmanuel Eboué, who had already received a yellow card, had conned Hauge with a blatant dive. The Ivorian full-back should have received a second one for his deception, but instead Henry swung in the free-kick and Campbell, soaring above a static defence, headed Arsenal powerfully into the lead. Now the match really was interesting. If Arsenal could maintain their long run of clean sheets, the European crown would be theirs.

Refereeing errors

Just before half-time Almunia made a tremendous fingertip save to deny Eto'o a quick equaliser, and the young Spaniard would be called on time and time again as the rain teemed down in the second half. Hauge continued to make wrong decisions, booking Henry for a perfectly judged sliding tackle and Barça's Oleguer for another foul that wasn't on Freddie Ljungberg. Henry was given a glorious opportunity to kill the game when sent clean through on 70 minutes, but the normally assured

UEFA Champions League 2005/2006

finish just wasn't there when it mattered most, and he fired his shot straight at Víctor Valdés.

That was a huge let-off for Barcelona, and their reaction was to intensify the pressure at the other end. Ronaldinho, though, was not having the best of games, and Arsenal's defence continued to look solid. But then, with one exquisite touch from substitute Larsson, deflecting on Andrés Iniesta's pass, Eto'o was through. Was he offside when the ball was played on to him? Possibly, but the linesman gave the African striker the benefit of the doubt, and he seized his opportunity by sliding the ball past Almunia through the tiniest of gaps at his near post.

Arsenal's resistance had finally crumbled - after 16 hours and 35 minutes without conceding a Champions League goal. Worse, though, was soon to follow. Five minutes later Larsson again opened up the Arsenal defence, laying the ball inside for another substitute, Brazilian full-back Juliano Belletti, who smashed the ball across goal and jumped for joy as it flew into the net up off Almunia's legs. As with the first goal, the keeper was slightly at fault. Would Lehmann have saved both goals? Nobody will ever know. What was certain, though, was that Barcelona, thanks to the unlikeliest of goalscorers, were now 2-1 up with less than ten minutes remaining.

No way back

There was no way back for Arsenal. The Catalans simply played keepball for the remainder of the game. The English side would later bemoan the referee, but Henry and his manager Arsène Wenger did not do themselves any favours with their charmless post-match comments. Granted, the Norwegian official had had a poor night, but it was difficult to work out how he had allegedly favoured Barcelona.

Not that the Catalans had anything to complain about. For the second year running the winners had dramatically come from behind to take the trophy. Frank Rijkaard's classy use of substitutions had won his team an historic victory. Carles Puyol had the honour and privilege of becoming only the second Barça captain to lift the European Cup. Not surprisingly, he and his team-mates milked the moment dry. Fourteen years of hurt had ended. FC Barcelona, the champions of Spain, could now also proclaim themselves officially as the best team in Europe.

FINAL

(17/5/06)
Stade de France, Saint-Denis
FC BARCELONA 2 *(Eto'o 77, Belletti 81)*
ARSENAL 1 *(Campbell 37)*
Referee – *Hauge (NOR)*
FC BARCELONA – *Víctor Valdes, Oleguer (Belletti 71), Puyol, Márquez, Van Bronckhorst, Edmílson (Iniesta 46), Deco, Van Bommel (Larsson 61), Giuly, Ronaldinho, Eto'o.*
ARSENAL – *Lehmann, Eboué, Touré, Campbell, Cole, Gilberto Silva, Hleb (Reyes 84), Pires (Almunia 19), Fàbregas (Flamini 74), Ljungberg, Henry.*
Sent off: *Lehmann (19)*

The Champions League trophy belongs to Barcelona

TOP GOALSCORERS

9	Andriy SHEVCHENKO (Milan)
7	RONALDINHO (FC Barcelona)
6	Samuel ETO'O (FC Barcelona)
	David TREZEGUET (Juventus)
5	Thierry HENRY (Arsenal)
	KAKÁ (Milan)
	ADRIANO (Internazionale)
	Johan MICOUD (SV Werder Bremen)
4	Julio CRUZ (Internazionale)
	JUNINHO (Olympique Lyonnais)
	John CAREW (Olympique Lyonnais)
	Filippo INZAGHI (Milan)
	Peter LØVENKRANDS (Rangers)
	Vincenzo IAQUINTA (Udinese)

UEFA Champions League 2005/2006

APPEARANCES/GOALS 2005/06

AJAX (Holland)

No	Name	Nat	Pos	Aps	(s)	Gls
17	Yannis ANASTASIOU	GRE	A	3		2
11	Ryan BABEL		A	3	(4)	
28	Nourdin BOUKHARI	MAR	A	5	(2)	1
9	Angelos CHARISTEAS	GRE	A	1	(2)	
19	Urby EMANUELSON		D	6		
6	Tomás GALÁSEK	CZE	M	5		
3	Zdynek GRYGERA	CZE	D	6		
4	John HEITINGA		D	3	(2)	
25	Klaas-Jan HUNTELAAR		A	2		1
16	Nigel DE JONG		M	3	(2)	3
22	JUANFRAN	ESP	D	2	(1)	
21	Olaf LINDENBERGH		M	5		
8	Hedwiges MADURO		M	7		
27	Edgar MANUCHARYAN	ARM	A		(1)	
10	Steven PIENAAR	RSA	M	7		
7	Mauro ROSALES	ARG	A	3	(1)	1
24	Markus ROSENBERG	SWE	A	4	(2)	1
18	Wesley SNEIJDER		M	5		2
1	Maarten STEKELENBURG		G	6		
2	Hatem TRABELSI	TUN	D	5	(1)	
15	Thomas VERMAELEN	BEL	D	5		
12	Hans VONK	RSA	G	2		

RSC ANDERLECHT (Belgium)

No	Name	Nat	Pos	Aps	(s)	Gls
10	Walter BASEGGIO		M	1	(3)	
31	Mark DE MAN		D	4		
19	Laurent DELORGE		M	1	(1)	
3	Olivier DESCHACHT		D	5		
20	Fabrice EHRET	FRA	M		(1)	
14	Bart GOOR		M	6		
8	Nenad JESTROVIC	SCG	A	2	(2)	
5	Roland JUHÁSZ	HUN	D	3		
27	Vincent KOMPANY		D	2		1
7	Goran LOVRE	SCG	N	1		
9	Mbo MPENZA		A	5		
13	Silvio PROTO		G	5		
11	Grégory PUJOL	FRA	A	1	(1)	
24	SERHAT Akin	TUR	A	3	(2)	
30	Hannu TIHINEN	FIN	D	5	(1)	
41	Cheik Ismael TIOTE	CIV	D	1		
34	Lamine TRAORE	BUR	D		(1)	
37	Anthony VAN DEN BORRE		D	4		
4	Yves VANDERHAEGHE		M	5		
17	Christian WILHELMSSON	SWE	M	4	(1)	
22	Oleh YASHCHUK	UKR	A	1		
21	Pär ZETTERBERG	SWE	M	3	(2)	
6	Michael ZEWLAKOW	POL	D	3	(1)	
1	Daniel ZITKA	CZE	G	1		

ARSENAL (England)

No	Name	Nat	Pos	Aps	(s)	Gls
24	Manuel ALMUNIA	ESP	G	5	(1)	
10	Dennis BERGKAMP	HOL	A	1	(3)	1
23	Sol CAMPBELL		D	6		1
22	Gaël CLICHY	FRA	D	2	(2)	
3	Ashley COLE		D	3		
18	Pascal CYGAN	FRA	D	2	(1)	
2	Abou DIABY	FRA	M		(2)	
27	Emmanuel EBOUE	CIV	D	9	(2)	
15	Cesc FÁBREGAS	ESP	M	10	(3)	1
16	Mathieu FLAMINI	FRA	M	11	(1)	
19	GILBERTO SILVA	BRA	M	10	(1)	1
14	Thierry HENRY	FRA	A	10	(1)	5
13	Alexandr HLEB	BLS	M	9	(1)	
29	Sebastian LARSSON	SWE	M	1		
12	LAUREN	CMR	D	5	(1)	
1	Jens LEHMANN	GER	G	8		
8	Fredrik LJUNGBERG	SWE	M	9		1
42	Quincy OWUSU-ABEYIE	HOL	M	1	(3)	
7	Robert PIRES	FRA	M	7	(5)	2
9	José Antonio REYES	ESP	M	11	(1)	
20	Philippe SENDEROS	SUI	D	7		
17	Alexandre SONG	CMR	M	1	(1)	
28	Kolo TOURE	CIV	D	12		1
11	Robin VAN PERSIE	HOL	A	3	(4)	2

ARTMEDIA BRATISLAVA (Slovakia)

No	Name	Nat	Pos	Aps	(s)	Gls
17	Balázs BORBÉLY		M	5		2
24	Peter BURÁK		D	1		
1	Juraj COBOS		G	6		
2	Ondrej DEBNÁR		D	6		
4	Ján DURICA		D	6		
20	Branislav FODREK		A	6		
9	Luís Fábio GOMES	BRA	A		(1)	
14	Juraj HALENÁR		A	3	(3)	
16	Lukás HARTIG		A	5		
23	Roman KONECNY		D		(1)	
25	Ján KOZÁK		M	6		2
10	Martin MIKULIC		A		(2)	
12	Branislav OBZERA		A	3	(2)	
21	Peter PETRÁS		D	6		1
3	Pavol STANO		M	2	(4)	
13	Daniel TCHUR		M		(3)	
22	Ales URBANEK		D	6		
8	Blazej VASCÁK		M	5	(1)	

FC BARCELONA (Spain)

No	Name	Nat	Pos	Aps	(s)	Gls
2	Juliano BELLETTI	BRA	D	7	(3)	1
20	DECO	POR	M	11		2
15	EDMÍLSON	BRA	M	7	(2)	
9	Samuel ETO'O	CMR	A	11		6
14	Santiago EZQUERRO		A	1	(3)	1
18	GABRI		M	2	(2)	1
8	Ludovic GIULY	FRA	M	6	(2)	1
24	Andrés INIESTA		M	5	(5)	1
25	Albert JORQUERA		G	1		
7	Henrik LARSSON	SWE	A	5	(5)	1
4	Rafael MÁRQUEZ	MEX	D	8		
11	MAXI LÓPEZ	ARG	A		(1)	
30	Lionel MESSI	ARG	A	4	(2)	1
3	Thiago MOTTA	BRA	M	4	(3)	
23	OLEGUER		D	11		
5	Carles PUYOL		D	12		
10	RONALDINHO	BRA	A	12		7
16	SYLVINHO	BRA	D		(1)	
17	Mark VAN BOMMEL	HOL	M	7	(2)	1
12	Giovanni VAN BRONCKHORST	HOL	D	13		
1	VÍCTOR VALDES		G	12		
6	XAVI		M	4		

FC BAYERN MÜNCHEN (Germany)

No	Name	Nat	Pos	Aps	(s)	Gls
13	Michael BALLACK		M	6		1

UEFA Champions League 2005/2006

No	Name	Nat	Pos	Aps	(s)	Gls
26	Sebastian DEISLER		M	5	(1)	3
6	Martín DEMICHELIS	ARG	M	7	(1)	2
33	José Paolo GUERRERO	PER	A	1	(6)	1
23	Owen HARGREAVES	ENG	M	2		
25	Valérien ISMAEL	FRA	D	8		1
16	Jens JEREMIES		M		(1)	
1	Oliver KAHN		G	7		
8	Ali KARIMI	IRN	M	2	(1)	1
21	Philipp LAHM		D	2	(1)	
69	Bixente LIZARAZU	FRA	D	6		
3	LÚCIO	BRA	D	7		
10	Roy MAKAAY	HOL	A	8		2
14	Claudio PIZARRO	PER	A	6		1
22	Michael RENSING		G	1		
2	Willy SAGNOL	FRA	D	7		
20	Hasan SALIHAMIDZIC	BOS	M	1		
24	Roque SANTA CRUZ	PAR	A	1	(1)	
7	Mehmet SCHOLL		M	1	(5)	
31	Bastian SCHWEINSTEIGER		M	4	(3)	
11	ZÉ ROBERTO	BRA	M	6	(2)	

SL BENFICA (Portugal)

No	Name	Nat	Pos	Aps	(s)	Gls
13	ALCIDES	BRA	D	4		
3	ANDERSON	BRA	D	8	(1)	
16	BETO	BRA	M	7	(1)	1
11	GEOVANNI	BRA	M	7	(1)	1
27	JOÃO PEREIRA		D		(3)	
10	Giorgos KARAGOUNIS	GRE	M	2	(5)	
17	Andrei KARYAKA	RUS	M		(1)	
5	LÉO	BRA	D	9		
4	LUISÃO	BRA	D	10		1
9	MANTORRAS	ANG	A		(5)	
14	MANUEL FERNANDES		M	8		1
19	MARCEL	BRA	A		(1)	
30	Fabrizio MICCOLI	ITA	A	4	(2)	2
1	MOREIRA		G	2		
31	MORETTO	BRA	G	4		
22	NÉLSON		D	6		
15	NUNO ASSIS		A	1	(1)	
21	NUNO GOMES		A	8		
6	PETIT		M	9		
12	QUIM		G	3		
33	RICARDO ROCHA		D	6	(3)	
34	Laurent ROBERT	FRA	M	3	(1)	
43	RUI NEREU		G	1	(1)	
20	SIMÃO		M	8		2

REAL BETIS (Spain)

No	Name	Nat	Pos	Aps	(s)	Gls
8	ARZU		M	3		1
14	CAPI		M	2	(2)	
22	Paolo CASTELLINI	ITA	D	1	(1)	
1	Pedro CONTRERAS		G	1		
6	DANI		A		(2)	1
13	Antonio DOBLAS		G	5		
24	EDÚ	BRA	A	2		
9	FERNANDO		A	3	(2)	
26	ISRAEL		A	1	(1)	
17	JOAQUÍN Sánchez		M	5	(1)	
31	JUANDE		M	1		
4	JUANITO		D	5		
19	JUANLU		A	1		
3	Daniel LEMBO	URU	D	1		
20	MARCOS ASSUNÇÃO	BRA	M	2	(3)	

No	Name	Nat	Pos	Aps	(s)	Gls
27	MELLI		D	5		
25	MIGUEL ANGEL		M	2		
15	NANO		D	1	(1)	
16	ÓSCAR LÓPEZ		D	5		
12	RICARDO OLIVEIRA	BRA	A	4		1
5	David RIVAS		D	5		
18	Alberto RIVERA		M	5		
7	Fernando VARELA		M	4		
21	XISCO		A	2	(3)	

CLUB BRUGGE KV (Belgium)

No	Name	Nat	Pos	Aps	(s)	Gls
10	Bosko BALABAN	CRO	A	4		2
11	Jonathan BLONDEL		M	3	(1)	
1	Tomislav BUTINA	CRO	G	5		
6	Philippe CLEMENT		D	4		
2	Olivier DE COCK		D	2		
14	Grégory DUFER		M	3	(1)	
8	Gaëtan ENGLEBERT		M	3	(3)	
17	Ivan GVOZDENOVIC	SCG	D	1	(1)	
19	Rune LANGE	NOR	A	1	(1)	
18	Ivan LEKO	CRO	M	4	(1)	
26	Birger MAERTENS		D	6		
22	Javier PORTILLO	ESP	A	5	(1)	2
3	Kevin ROELANDTS		M	1	(3)	
16	Serhiy SEREBRENNIKOV	UKR	M		(1)	
15	Marek SPILAR	SVK	D	5		
23	Stijn STIJNEN		G	1		
4	Joos VALGAEREN		D	1		
32	Jason VANDELANNOITE		D	2		
32	Günther VANDENAERDE		D	4	(1)	
7	Gert VERHEYEN		M	3	(1)	1
3	Sven VERMANT		M	6		
30	VICTOR	BRA	A		(2)	
34	Jeanvion YULU-MATONDO		A	2	(1)	1

CHELSEA (England)

No	Name	Nat	Pos	Aps	(s)	Gls
1	Petr CECH	CZE	G	7		
12	Carlton COLE		A		(2)	
10	Joe COLE		M	5	(1)	1
9	Hernán CRESPO	ARG	A	2	(3)	2
23	Carlo CUDICINI	ITA	G	1		
3	Asoer DEL HORNO	ESP	D	3	(1)	
19	Lassana DIARRA	FRA	M		(2)	
15	Didier DROGBA	CIV	A	5	(2)	1
11	Damien DUFF	IRL	M	5	(1)	
5	Michael ESSIEN	GHA	M	6		
13	William GALLAS	FRA	D	7		
14	GEREMI Njitap	CMR	M		(2)	
22	Eidur GUDJOHNSEN	ISL	A	4	(2)	
29	Robert HUTH	GER	D		(3)	
8	Frank LAMPARD		M	8		2
4	Claude MAKELELE	FRA	M	6		
20	PAULO FERREIRA	POR	D	6		
6	RICARDO CARVALHO	POR	D	8		2
16	Arjen ROBBEN	HOL	M	6		
26	John TERRY		D	8		
24	Shaun WRIGHT-PHILLIPS		M	1	(5)	

FENERBAHÇE (Turkey)

No	Name	Nat	Pos	Aps	(s)	Gls
20	ALEX	BRA	M	4		3
39	Nicolas ANELKA	FRA	A	6		
4	Stephen APPIAH	GHA	M	6		2

UEFA Champions League 2005/2006

No	Name	Nat	Pos	Aps	(s)	Gls
24	DENIZ Baris		D	1		
2	FÁBIO LUCIANO	BRA	D	5		
27	KEMAL Aslan		M		(3)	
11	MÁRCIO NOBRE	BRA	A	4	(2)	1
15	MARCO AURÉLIO	BRA	M	5		
7	MEHMET Yogatli		M	1	(3)	
19	ÖNDER Turaci		D	6		
21	SELÇUK Sahin		M	5		
23	SEMIH Sentürk		A		(1)	
30	SERKAN Balci		D	6		
3	SERVET Çetin		D	1		
10	TUNCAY Sanli		A	4	(1)	
5	ÜMIT Özat		D	6		
1	VOLKAN Demirel		G	6		

INTERNAZIONALE (Italy)

No	Name	Nat	Pos	Aps	(s)	Gls
10	ADRIANO	BRA	A	8	(1)	5
49	Marco ANDREOLLI		D	1		
55	Daniel BOUMSONG	CMR	M		(1)	
3	Nicolás BURDISSO	ARG	D	3	(1)	
19	Estebán CAMBIASSO	ARG	M	7	(1)	
31	CÉSAR	BRA	M	2		
2	Iván CÓRDOBA	COL	D	7		
9	Julio CRUZ	ARG	A	4	(2)	4
16	Giuseppe FAVALLI		D	2		
7	Luís FIGO	POR	M	8		1
12	JÚLIO CÉSAR	BRA	G	5		
18	KILY GONZÁLEZ	ARG	M		(2)	
30	Obafemi MARTINS	NGA	A	5	(4)	1
23	Marco MATERAZZI		D	7	(1)	
11	Sinisa MIHAJLOVIC	SCG	D	1	(2)	
44	Matteo MOMENTE		A		(1)	
8	David PIZARRO	CHL	M	4	(2)	1
20	Álvaro RECOBA	URU	A	2	(3)	
25	Walter SAMUEL	ARG	D	9		
21	Santiago SOLARI	ARG	M	4		
5	Dejan STANKOVIC	SCG	M	5	(1)	2
1	Francesco TOLDO		G	5		
14	Juan Sebastián VERÓN	ARG	M	7		
33	Pierre WOME	CMR	D	7		
6	Cristiano ZANETTI		M	2	(2)	
4	Javier ZANETTI	ARG	D	5	(1)	
13	ZÉ MARIA	BRA	M		(2)	

JUVENTUS (Italy)

No	Name	Nat	Pos	Aps	(s)	Gls
32	Christian ABBIATI		G	6		
14	Federico BALZARETTI		D	2	(2)	
20	Manuele BLASI		M	4	(1)	
1	Gianluigi BUFFON		G	4		
16	Mauro CAMORANESI		M	8	(1)	
28	Fabio CANNAVARO		D	9		
3	Giorgio CHIELLINI		D	4	(2)	
10	Alessandro DEL PIERO		A	3	(4)	3
8	ÉMERSON	BRA	M	9		1
23	Giuliano GIANNICHEDDA		M	3	(2)	
9	Zlatan IBRAHIMOVIC	SWE	A	9		3
6	Robert KOVAC	CRO	D	4		
18	Adrian MUTU	ROM	A	3	(5)	1
11	Pavel NEDVED	CZE	M	7	(1)	2
7	Gianluca PESSOTTO		D	1	(1)	
21	Lilian THURAM	FRA	D	8		
17	David TREZEGUET	FRA	A	9		6
4	Patrick VIEIRA	FRA	M	7		

25	Marcelo ZALAYETA	URU	A		(6)	
19	Gianluca ZAMBROTTA		D	8		
27	Jonathan ZEBINA	FRA	D	2		

LILLE OSC (France)

No	Name	Nat	Pos	Aps	(s)	Gls
11	Hicham ABOUCHEROUANE	MAR	A		(1)	
15	Milenko ACIMOVIC	SLO	M	4	(1)	1
12	Mathieu BODMER		M	6		
7	Yohan CABAYE		M	1	(1)	
21	Mathieu CHALME		D	5		
2	Mathieu DEBUCHY		M	3	(1)	
8	Geoofrey DERNIS		M	4	(2)	
29	Stéphane DUMONT		M	1	(1)	
13	Nicolas FAUVERGUE		A		(2)	
10	Daniel GYGAX	SUI	M	1	(1)	
23	Abdul Kader KEITA	CIV	A		(1)	
26	Stefan LICHTSTEINER	SUI	D	3	(1)	
17	Jean MAKOUN	CMR	M	6		
27	Kevin MIRALLAS	BEL	A		(2)	
9	Matt MOUSSILOU		A	4	(2)	
14	Peter ODEMWINGIE	NGA	A	3	(2)	
25	Nicolas PLESTAN		D	2		
5	Rafael SCHMITZ	BRA	D	5		
1	Tony SYLVA	SEN	G	6		
20	Grégory TAFFOREAU		D	6		
4	Efstathiou TAVLARIDIS	GRE	D	4		
22	Milivoje VITAKIC	SCG	D	2		

LIVERPOOL (England)

No	Name	Nat	Pos	Aps	(s)	Gls
23	Jamie CARRAGHER		D	8		
9	Djibril CISSE	FRA	A	2	(5)	2
15	Peter CROUCH		A	6		
3	Steve FINNAN	IRL	D	6		
11	Robbie FOWLER		A	1	(1)	
8	Steven GERRARD		M	5	(2)	
16	Dietmar HAMANN	GER	M	4	(2)	
4	Sami HYYPIÄ	FIN	D	7		
17	JOSEMI	ESP	D	2		
7	Harry KEWELL	AUS	M	2	(4)	
10	LUIS GARCÍA	ESP	M	7		2
19	Fernando MORIENTES	ESP	A	4	(1)	1
34	Darren POTTER	IRL	M		(1)	
25	José Manuel REINA	ESP	G	8		
6	John Arne RIISE	NOR	M	5	(1)	
24	Florent SINAMA-PONGOLLE	FRA	A	1	(2)	1
22	Mohamed SISSOKO	MLI	M	6		
21	Djimi TRAORE	MLI	D	5		
28	Stephen WARNOCK		D	1	(1)	
14	XABI ALONSO	ESP	M	6		
30	Boudewijn ZENDEN	HOL	M	2	(2)	

OLYMPIQUE LYONNAIS (France)

No	Name	Nat	Pos	Aps	(s)	Gls
20	Eric ABIDAL		D	6		
18	Hatem BEN ARFA		A	1		
19	Karim BENZEMA		M	1		1
23	Jérémy BERTHOD		D	2		
32	Romain BEYNIE		M		(1)	
5	Cláudio CAÇAPA	BRA	D	7		
9	John CAREW	NOR	A	8	(2)	4
6	Jérémy CLEMENT		M	1	(5)	
31	François CLERC		D	4	(1)	
1	Grégory COUPET		G	9		

UEFA Champions League 2005/2006

No	Name	Nat	Pos	Aps	(s)	Gls
3	CRIS	BRA	D	10		1
7	Mahamadou DIARRA	MLI	M	9		2
15	Lamine DIATTA	SEN	D	1		
11	FRED	BRA	A	2	(7)	2
14	Sidney GOVOU		A	6	(1)	1
8	JUNINHO	BRA	M	8		4
10	Florent MALOUDA		A	9		
24	Sylvain MONSOREAU		D	2		
4	Patrick MÜLLER	SUI	D	2		
26	Benoît PEDRETTI		M	2	(3)	
12	Anthony REVEILLERE		D	6	(1)	
21	TIAGO	BRA	M	8		2
30	Rémy VERCOUTRE		G	1		
22	Sylvain WILTORD		A	5	(5)	2

MANCHESTER UNITED (England)

No	Name	Nat	Pos	Aps	(s)	Gls
26	Phil BARDSLEY		D	2		
6	Wes BROWN		D	2		
7	CRISTIANO RONALDO	POR	M	6		
5	Rio FERDINAND		D	6		
24	Darren FLETCHER	SCO	M	5		
11	Ryan GIGGS	WAL	M	3	(1)	1
4	Gabriel HEINZE	ARG	D	1		
2	Gary NEVILLE		D	1	(1)	
22	John O'SHEA	IRL	D	6		
13	PARK Ji-sung	KOR	M		(5)	
23	Kieran RICHARDSON		M	2	(2)	
8	Wayne ROONEY		A	4		
42	Giuseppe ROSSI	ITA	A		(1)	
9	Louis SAHA	FRA	A		(2)	
18	Paul SCHOLES		M	5		1
27	Mikaël SILVESTRE	FRA	D	5		
14	Alan SMITH		M	6		
19	Edwin VAN DER SAR	HOL	G	6		
10	Ruud VAN NISTELROOY	HOL	A	6		1

MILAN (Italy)

No	Name	Nat	Pos	Aps	(s)	Gls
23	Massimo AMBROSINI		M	1	(3)	
2	CAFÚ	BRA	D	3	(2)	
5	Alessandro COSTACURTA		D	2	(1)	
1	DIDA	BRA	G	12		
8	Gennaro GATTUSO		M	11		
11	Alberto GILARDINO		A	6	(4)	
9	Filippo INZAGHI		A	4	(2)	4
18	Marek JANKULOVSKI	CZE	D		(2)	
22	KAKÁ	BRA	M	12		5
16	Zeljko KALAC	AUS	G		(1)	
4	Kakha KALADZE	GEO	D	10	(1)	
3	Paolo MALDINI		D	6	(3)	
13	Alessandro NESTA		D	10		
21	Andrea PIRLO		M	12		1
10	RUI COSTA	POR	M		(4)	
20	Clarence SEEDORF	HOL	M	11		1
27	SERGINHO	BRA	D	8	(3)	
7	Andriy SHEVCHENKO	UKR	A	11	(1)	9
17	Dario SIMIC	CRO	D	1	(1)	
31	Jaap STAM	HOL	D	8	(1)	
32	Christian VIERI		A	3	(2)	
14	Johann VOGEL	SUI	M	1	(4)	

OLYMPIAKOS (Greece)

No	Name	Nat	Pos	Aps	(s)	Gls
32	Giorgos ANATOLAKIS		D	5		
40	Haruna BABANGIDA	NGA	M	3	(2)	1
22	Erol BULUT	TUR	M	3	(1)	1
18	Alexandre D'ACOL	BRA	A		(1)	
20	DANI	ESP	A	2	(1)	
11	Predrag DJORDJEVIC	SCG	M	5		
21	Grigoris GEORGATOS		D	3		
34	Kleopas GIANNOU		G	1		
1	Pantelis KAFES		M	5	(1)	2
5	Michalis KAPSIS		D	2	(1)	
23	Michalis KONSTANTINOU	CYP	A	2	(1)	
19	Thanasis KOSTOULAS		D	4	(1)	
8	Milos MARIC	SCG	M		(1)	
14	Dimitris MAVROGENIDIS		D	3		
71	Antonis NIKOLAIDIS		G	5		
9	Giannis OKKAS	CYP	A	2	(4)	
30	Tasos PANTOS		D	3		
10	RIVALDO	BRA	M	5		2
12	Gabriel SCHÜRRER	ARG	D	2		
6	Ieroklis STOLTIDIS		M	5	(1)	
15	Yaya TOURE	CIV	M	6		

PANATHINAIKOS (Greece)

No	Name	Nat	Pos	Aps	(s)	Gls
15	Srdjan ANDRIC	CRO	M		(1)	
25	Igor BISCAN	CRO	D	4		
21	Kostantinos CHARALAMBIDES	CYP	M	2		1
31	Filippos DARLAS		D	5		
6	FLÁVIO CONCEIÇÃO	BRA	M	5		
1	Mario GALINOVIC	CRO	G	6		
7	Theofanis GEKAS		A		(2)	
8	Ezequiel GONZÁLEZ	ARG	M	6		1
8	Giannis GOUMAS		D	3		
4	Elias KOTSIOS		D	2	(3)	
27	Sotirios LEONTIOU		M	2	(2)	
26	Evangelos MANTZIOS		A	3	(1)	1
5	Nasief MORRIS	RSA	D	6		1
29	Mikael NILSSON	SWE	M	5		
11	Dimitris PAPADOPOULOS		A	3	(1)	
19	Anthony SERIC	CRO	M	4		
40	Sándor TORGHELLE	HUN	A	4	(1)	
22	Alexandros TZIOLIS		M	1	(2)	
24	Loukas VINTRA		D	4		
14	Nordin WOOTER	HOL	M	1	(3)	

FC PORTO (Portugal)

No	Name	Nat	Pos	Aps	(s)	Gls
27	ALAN	BRA	A	2	(2)	
12	José BOSINGWA		D	4	(1)	
13	BRUNO ALVES		D	1	(2)	
35	Marek CECH	SVK	D	2		
21	CÉSAR PEIXOTO		D	4		
20	DIEGO	BRA	M	4		1
22	FATIH Sonkaya	TUR	D		(1)	
39	HUGO ALMEIDA		A	2	(4)	1
6	IBSON	BRA	M	2	(1)	
25	IVANILDO		A		(1)	
9	JORGINHO	BRA	D	5		
11	LISANDRO LÓPEZ	ARG	A	2		1
8	LUCHO GONZÁLEZ	ARG	M	6		1
9	Benni McCARTHY	RSA	A	3	(1)	1
18	PAULO ASSUNÇÃO	BRA	M	4		
4	PEDRO EMANUEL		D	5		
14	PEPE	BRA	D	5		2
16	RAUL MEIRELES		M		(1)	
3	RICARDO COSTA		D	3		
7	RICARDO QUARESMA		M	5	(1)	
19	Tomislav SOKOTA	CRO	A	1		

UEFA Champions League 2005/2006

99	VÍTOR BAÍA		G	6	

PSV (Holland)

No	Name	Nat	Pos	Aps	(s)	Gls
18	Eric ADDO	GHA	D	3	(1)	
20	Ibrahim AFELLAY		M	8		
37	Ismail AISATTI		A	2	(4)	
4	ALEX	BRA	D	7		
11	DaMarcus BEASLEY	USA	M	4	(1)	
8	Phillip COCU		M	8		1
15	Jason CULINA	AUS	M	2		
17	Jefferson FARFÁN	PER	A	8		2
14	Osmar FERREYRA	ARG	M		(1)	
1	Heurelho GOMES	BRA	G	8		
10	Arouna KONE	CIV	A	1	(1)	
19	Michael LAMEY		D	5	(1)	
16	Theo LUCIUS		D	4	(1)	
2	André OOIJER		D	7		
3	Michael REIZIGER		D	5	(2)	
29	ROBERT	BRA	A	3	(1)	
35	Gerald SIBON		A		(1)	
6	Timmy SIMONS	BEL	M	8		
7	Mika VÄYRYNEN	FIN	M		(1)	
9	Jan VENNEGOOR OF HESSLINK		A	5	(1)	1

RANGERS (Scotland)

No	Name	Nat	Pos	Aps	(s)	Gls
5	Marvin ANDREWS	TRI	D	2	(1)	
3	Olivier BERNARD	FRA	D	4		
27	Kris BOYD		A		(2)	
4	Thomas BUFFEL	BEL	A	3	(2)	
17	Chris BURKE		M	3	(2)	
6	Barry FERGUSON		M	8		
7	Brahim HEMDANI	FRA	M	5		
20	Alan HUTTON		D	3		
21	Francis JEFFERS	ENG	A	2	(2)	
14	Sotiris KYRGIAKOS	GRE	D	8		1
26	Peter LØVENKRANDS	DEN	A	8		4
44	Ross McCORMACK		A		(1)	1
12	Robert MALCOLM		D	1		
24	Ian MURRAY		D	5	(1)	
31	Hamed NAMOUCHI	TUN	M	7		
23	Federico NIETO	ARG	A	1	(1)	
10	Nacho NOVO	ESP	A		(3)	
9	Dado PRSO	CRO	A	5		2
8	Alex RAE		M	1		
2	Fernando RICKSEN	HOL	D	6		
16	Julien RODRIGUEZ	FRA	D	6		
34	Steven SMITH		D	1		
19	Steven THOMPSON		A	1	(3)	1
25	Ronald WATERREUS	HOL	G	8		

SK RAPID WIEN (Austria)

No	Name	Nat	Pos	Aps	(s)	Gls
2	Marcin ADAMSKI	POL	D	4		1
10	Muhammet AKAGÜNDÜZ		A	3	(3)	
22	Radek BEJBL	CZE	D	5		
23	Andreas DOBER		D	5		
17	Matthias DOLLINGER		M	1	(2)	
12	György GARICS		D		(2)	
1	Raimund HEDL		G	1		
4	Martin HIDEN		D	3	(1)	
7	Peter HLINKA	SVK	M	6		
11	Steffen HOFFMANN	GER	M	6		
6	Andreas IVANSCHITZ		M	5		
13	Markus KATZER		D	2		
20	Roman KIENAST		A		(1)	
25	Marek KINCL	CZE	A	6		2
6	György KORSÓS	HUN	M	6		
9	Axel LAWAREE	BEL	A	3	(1)	
16	Sebastian MARTINEZ		M		(6)	
24	Helge PAYER		G	5		
26	Jozef VALACHOVIC	SVK	D	5		

REAL MADRID (Spain)

No	Name	Nat	Pos	Aps	(s)	Gls
40	ADRIAN MARTÍN		M		(1)	
35	Javier BALBOA		M	1		
23	David BECKHAM	ENG	M	7		1
1	Iker CASILLAS		G	7		
19	Antonio CASSANO	ITA	A		(1)	
11	CICINHO	BRA	D	1		
28	Rubén DE LA RED		M	1	(1)	
13	DIEGO LÓPEZ		G	1		
21	Carlos DIOGO	URU	D	4	(1)	
16	Thomas GRAVESEN	DEN	M	4	(2)	
14	GUTI		M	5	(2)	2
6	Iván HELGUERA		D	4		1
34	JAVI GARCÍA		A		(1)	
8	JÚLIO BAPTISTA	BRA	A	4	(3)	
29	José Manuel JURADO		M		(1)	
24	Álvaro MEJÍA		D		(3)	
2	MÍCHEL SALGADO		D	4	(1)	
12	PABLO GARCÍA	URU	M	4		
22	Francisco PAVÓN		D	3		
7	RAÚL		A	5	(1)	2
15	RAÚL BRAVO		D	2	(1)	
3	ROBERTO CARLOS	BRA	D	7		
10	ROBINHO	BRA	A	7	(1)	
9	RONALDO	BRA	A	2		
4	SERGIO RAMOS		D	7		1
27	Roberto SOLDADO		A	1	(1)	1
18	Jonathan WOODGATE	ENG	D	3		1
5	Zinedine ZIDANE	FRA	M	4		

ROSENBORG BK (Norway)

No	Name	Nat	Pos	Aps	(s)	Gls
5	Christer BASMA		D	4	(1)	
7	Ørjan BERG		M	2		
25	Daniel BRAATEN		A	5	(1)	1
33	Mikael DORSIN	SWE	D	6		
14	Sebastian EGUREN	URU	M		(1)	
20	Thorstein HELSTAD		A	4	(2)	1
1	Espen JOHNSEN		G	6		
9	Frode JOHNSEN		M	3	(3)	
26	Bjørn Tore KVARME		D	6		
18	Alejandro LAGO	URU	D	2		
10	Vidar RISETH		D	5	(1)	
15	Per Ciljan SKJELBRED		M	5		1
11	Jan Gunnar SOLLI		M	5		
21	Ståle STENSAAS		D		(1)	
17	Øyvind STORFLOR		A	6		1
6	Roar STRAND		M	5		1
19	Alexander TETTEY		M		(2)	
4	Fredrik WINSNES		M	2	(2)	
13	Alexander ØDEGAARD		A		(4)	

FC SCHALKE 04 (Germany)

No	Name	Nat	Pos	Aps	(s)	Gls
6	Hamit ALTINTOP	TUR	M	5	(1)	1
14	Gerald ASAMOAH		A		(2)	
25	Zlatan BAJRAMOVIC	BOS	M		(4)	

UEFA Champions League 2005/2006

No	Name	Nat	Pos	Aps	(s)	Gls
5	Marcelo José BORDON	BRA	D	6		
8	Fabian ERNST		M	5		
3	Levan KOBIASHVILI	GEO	M	6		3
20	Mladen KRSTAJIC	SCG	D	6		
22	Kevin KURANYI		A	5	(1)	2
9	Søren LARSEN	DEN	A	2	(2)	1
10	LINCOLN	BRA	M	6		3
2	Christian Bager POULSEN	DEN	M	6		1
18	RAFINHA	BRA	D	5		
16	Daró RODRÍGUEZ	URU	D	5		
1	Frank ROST		G	6		
11	Ebbe SAND	DEN	A	2	(4)	1
19	Gustavo VARELA	URU	M	1	(2)	

AC SPARTA PRAHA (Czech Republic)

No	Name	Nat	Pos	Aps	(s)	Gls
29	Jaromír BLAZEK		G	6		
9	Libor DOSEK		A	2	(3)	
2	Martin HASEK		M	4		
12	Ondrej HERZAN		M	1	(2)	
26	Jiří JESLINEK		A		(2)	
23	Michal KADLEC		D	6		
18	Karol KISEL	SVK	M	3		
15	Petr LUKÁS		D	4		
28	Miroslav MATUSOVIC		A	1	(3)	1
4	Pavel PERGL		D	2		
19	Martin PETRÁS	SVK	D	6		1
11	Adam PETROUS		D	5		
8	Karel POBORSKY		M	1		
21	Tomás POLACEK		M	6		
20	Zdenek POSPECH		D	6		
16	Jan SIMÁK		M	1	(1)	
6	Tomás SIVOK		M	2		
10	Miroslav SLEPICKA		A	4	(2)	
7	Lukás ZELENKA		M	6		

FC THUN (Switzerland)

No	Name	Nat	Pos	Aps	(s)	Gls
9	ADRIANO	BRA	M	5	(1)	1
19	Silvan AEGERTER		M	6		
6	Tiago BERNARDI	BRA	M	3	(1)	
12	Armand DEUMI	CMR	D	4		
7	Grégory DURUZ		D	1	(1)	
21	Nélson FERREIRA	POR	M	5		1
8	GÉLSON	BRA	M	1	(3)	
11	Andres GERBER		M	1	(2)	
3	José GONÇALVES		D	6		
26	Selver HODZIC	BOS	D	5		1
1	Eldin JAKUPOVIC	BOS	G	6		
2	LEANDRO	BRA	M	5	(1)	
20	Mauro LUSTRINELLI		A	6		1
5	Ljubo MILICEVIC	AUS	D	5		
13	Pape OMAR	SEN	A		(2)	
17	Alen ORMAN	AUT	D	6		
14	Nenad SAVIC		M		(1)	
15	Eren SEN	GER	A		(5)	
10	Adriano SPADOTO	BRA	M	1		

UDINESE (Italy)

No	Name	Nat	Pos	Aps	(s)	Gls
31	Paulo BARRETO	BRA	A	1	(2)	
4	Valerio BERTOTTO		D	5		
32	Vincent CANDELA	FRA	M	6		1
1	Morgan DE SANCTIS		G	6		
17	David DI MICHELE		A	3	(3)	
10	Antonio DI NATALE		A	4	(2)	3
19	FELIPE	BRA	D	5		1
9	Vincenzo IAQUINTA		A	5		4
39	JUAREZ	BRA	D	2	(1)	
23	Stefano MAURI		M		(5)	
27	Marco MOTTA		D		(1)	
18	Sulley Ali MUNTARI	GHA	M	6		
14	Cesare NATALI		D	2		
5	Christian OBODO	NGA	M	6		
13	Giampiero PINZI		M	2	(1)	
20	Fausto ROSSINI		A		(1)	
6	Roberto Néstor SENSINI	ARG	D	4	(1)	
16	Fernando TISSONE	ARG	M		(1)	
8	José Luís VIDIGAL	POR	M	3		
7	Damiano ZENONI		M	6		

VILLARREAL CF (Spain)

No	Name	Nat	Pos	Aps	(s)	Gls
3	Rodolfo ARRUABARRENA	ARG	D	11		2
4	César ARZO		D	3	(1)	
25	Mariano BARBOSA		G	4		
11	Javier CALLEJA		M	1	(3)	
9	Luciano FIGUEROA	ARG	A	2	(3)	
5	Diego FORLÁN	URU	A	11		2
99	Guillermo FRANCO	MEX	A	1	(4)	
2	GONZALO RODRÍGUEZ	ARG	D	8	(1)	
7	Antonio GUAYRE		A	1	(3)	1
14	HÉCTOR FONT		M	1	(3)	
17	JAVI VENTA		D	8		
23	JOSÉ MARI		A	9	(1)	
6	JOSICO		M	7	(4)	
15	Jan KROMKAMP	HOL	D	4		
22	Juan Manuel PEÑA	BOL	D	8	(1)	
16	QUIQUE ÁLVAREZ		D	6	(1)	
8	Juan Román RIQUELME	ARG	M	10		2
10	ROGER García		M	1	(5)	
21	SANTI CAZORLA		M	1	(1)	
19	Marcos SENNA	BRA	M	10	(1)	1
12	Juan Pablo SORÍN	ARG	M	10		
18	Alessio TACCHINARDI	ITA	M	7	(1)	
13	Sebastián VIEIRA	URU	G	8		
30	XISCO Nadal		A		(1)	

SV WERDER BREMEN (Germany)

No	Name	Nat	Pos	Aps	(s)	Gls
16	Leon ANDREASEN	DEN	D	4		
6	Frank BAUMANN		M	8		1
24	Tim BOROWSKI		M	7		2
2	Frank FAHRENHORST		D	4	(1)	
22	Torsten FRINGS		M	8		1
9	Nélson HAEDO VALDEZ	PAR	A	5	(3)	2
14	Aaron HUNT		A		(6)	
20	Daniel JENSEN	DEN	M		(2)	
12	Ivan KLASNIC	CRO	A	4		
11	Miroslav KLOSE		A	7		3
10	Johan MICOUD	FRA	M	8		5
4	NALDO	BRA	D	7		
15	Patrick OWOMOYELA		D	8		
3	Petri PASANEN	FIN	D	1	(2)	
1	Andreas REINKE		G	6		
27	Chrisian SCHULZ		D	8		1
7	Jurica VRANJES	CRO	M	1	(1)	
18	Tim WIESE		G	2		

European Cups

Sevilla burst Boro bubble

QUALIFYING ROUNDS

With European football's governing body having closed their ears to criticism and maintained the controversial and cluttered new format that had been introduced to their secondary club competition the previous season, the 2005/06 UEFA Cup got underway a couple of days after the Champions League, in early-July, with the opening legs of the first qualifying round.

No fewer than fifty clubs, from the lower-ranked nations of UEFA's five-year performance chart, entered the competition at this stage, with another 37 set to join the 25 winners at the second stage of pre-qualifying in August.

There were a lot of matches to get through before the competition proper could begin in September, and a lot of teams to filter out. Of UEFA's 52 member nations, only Kazakhstan, the most recent to join, did not supply any clubs as neither FK Taraz nor Irtysh Pavlodar, who had both qualified by right, could meet UEFA's licensing requirements.

As usual, for reasons that remain mysterious, the champions of Andorra and San Marino were not permitted to play in the Champions League. Instead they flew the flag alone for their respective principalities in the UEFA Cup, along with FC Vaduz, the perennial winners of the Liechtenstein Cup.

Domagnano, of San Marino, were predictably thrashed 8-0 on aggregate, by the Slovenians of Domzale, but Andorra's Sant Julià outdid them, going down 10-0 over their two games with Rapid Bucharest.

Double figures

The Romanians were the only team to reach double figures in the first qualifying round, but many other ties were extremely one-sided. There were some that went to the wire, with both Linfield of Northern Ireland and Rhyl of Wales benefiting from the away-goals rule. Vaduz also sneaked through, 2-1 on aggregate over Dacia Chisinau of Moldova, but there was an alarming exit for once-great Ferencváros, who crashed out to the up-and-coming Belarussians of MTZ-RIPO Minsk.

The majority of the 25 teams that made it through the first qualifying round went no further. Among the handful of exceptions were Irish side Cork City, who did well to eliminate Swedish high-fliers Djurgårdens IF on the away-goals rule. Domzale also used that method to overcome MS Ashdod after scoring a last-minute equaliser in the second leg, but while another Israeli side, Maccabi Tel Aviv, surprisingly crashed out, after extra-time, to Mediterranean rivals APOEL of Cyprus, their near-namesakes Maccabi Petach Tikva posted the highest winning margin of the round by thrashing Macedonian side Baskimi Kumanovo 11-0 on aggregate.

It was a good round for Bulgaria, with all three of their representatives – Levski Sofia, Litex Lovech and Lokomotiv Plovdiv – getting through potentially tricky ties against fellow Balkan opposition. Norway, too, managed to advance on three fronts, with Brann, Viking and – after the only penalty shoot-out of the round – Tromsø all making progress. Tromsø's victory over Esbjerg denied Denmark a clean sweep and also prevented the three Fair Play qualifiers from going through in concert. Viking and Mainz, the other two wildcard entrants, made it through, with the German club's easy win over Keflavík ensuring a five-pronged Bundesliga presence in the first round thanks to Hamburg's qualification from the InterToto Cup.

France, too, would have five clubs in the first round, with InterToto Cup 'winners' Lens and Marseille joining regular qualifiers Auxerre, Strasbourg and Rennes.

UEFA Cup 2005/2006

FIRST QUALIFYING ROUND RESULTS

(14/7/05 & 28/7/05)

AC Allianssi 3 *(Vajanne 34, Cleaver 42, Poulsen 85)*, CS Pétange 0
CS Pétange 1 *(Kefert 55)*, AC Allianssi 1 *(Poulsen 63)*
(AC Allianssi 4-1)

FK Baki 1 *(Sultanov 79)*, MSK Zilina 0
MSK Zilina 3 *(Straka 7, Cisovsky 37, Labant 85)*, FK Baki 1 *(Stolcers 71)*
(MSK Zilina 3-2)

Banants Yerevan 2 *(Hakobyan 82, Gharabaghtsyan 89)*, Lokomotivi Tbilisi 3 *(Alaverdashvili 41, Kebadze 48, Oniani 53p)*
Lokomotivi Tbilisi 0, Banants Yerevan 2 *(Hakobyan 22, Khachatryan 81)*
(Banants Yerevan 4-3)

Baskimi Kumanovo 3, Zepce 0 *(w/o) (original result 0-0)*
Zepce 1 *(Mesic 80)*, Baskimi Kumanovo 1 *(Gjurcevski 49)*
(Baskimi Kumanovo 4-1)

Birkirkara 0, APOEL 2 *(Georgiou 72, Jovanovic 80)*
APOEL 4 *(Kaklamanos 38, 59, Neophytou 53, Georgiou 90)*, Birkirkara 0
(APOEL 6-0)

Domagnano 0, Domzale 5 *(Stevanovic 14, Zavril 47, Nikezic 63, 86, Kacicnik 82)*
Domzale 3 *(Juninho 20, Nikezic 45, Zeljkovic 88p)*, Domagnano 0
(Domzale 8-0)

Ekranas Panevezys 0, Cork City 2 *(O'Donovan 25, O'Callaghan 90)*
Cork City 0, Ekranas Panevezys 1 *(Klimavicius 60)*
(Cork City 2-1)

Elbasani 1 *(Dalipi K. 28)*, Vardar Skopje 1 *(Trickovski 65)*
Vardar Skopje 0, Elbasani 0
(1-1; Vardar Skopje on away goal)

Esbjerg FB 1 *(Berglund 90)*, FC Flora Tallinn 2 *(Sirevicius 57, Sidorenkov 60)*
FC Flora Tallinn 0, Esbjerg FB 6 *(Poulsen 15, Kristiansen 16, Berglund 23, Andreasen 41, Murcy 56, 86)*
(Esbjerg FB 7-2)

Etzella Ettelbruck 0, Keflavík 4 *(Sveinsson 17, 59, 76, 80)*
Keflavík 2 *(Sveinsson 75, Kristinsson 88)*, Etzella Ettelbruck 0
(Keflavík 6-0)

Ferencváros 0, MTZ-RIPO Minsk 2 *(Mkhitaryan 38, Tarashchik 90)*
MTK-RIPO Minsk 1 *(Kontsevoi 48)*, Ferencváros 2 *(Lipcsei 45, Rósa 90)*
(MTZ-RIPO Minsk 3-2)

ÍBV 1 *(Sigurdsson P. 25)*, B36 1 *(Midjord 7)*
B36 2 *(Mørkøre 2, Midjord 59)*, ÍBV 1 *(Jeffs 41)*
(B36 3-2)

Linfield 1 *(Mouncey 6)*, FK Ventspils 0
FK Ventspils 2 *(Rekhviashvili 39, Rimkus 90)*, Linfield 1 *(Thompson 8)*
(2-2; Linfield on away goal)

Longford Town 2 *(Paisley 35, Ferguson 54)*, Carmarthen Town 0
Carmarthen Town 5 *(Thomas 16, 75, Lloyd 49, 65p, Cotterrall 80)*, Longford Town 1 *(Myler 20p)*
(Carmarthen Town 5-3)

FSV Mainz 4 *(Ruman 11, Auer 36, 67, Noveski 58)*, Mika Ashtarak 0
Mika Ashtarak 0, FSV Mainz 0
(FSV Mainz 4-0)

Nistru Otaci 3 *(Pancovici 12, Matiura 69p, Blajco 88)*, Xäzär Länkäran 1 *(Ramazanov 25)*
Xäzär Länkäran 1 *(Äliyev 74)*, Nistru Otaci 2 *(Lichioiu 19, 41)*
(Nistru Otaci 5-2)

NSÍ 0, Metalurgs Liepaja 3 *(Petersen 23og, Karlsons 67, Grebis 72)*
Metalurgs Liepaja 3 *(Dobrecovs 4, 35, Klava 81)*, NSÍ 0
(Metalurgs Liepaja 6-0)

Omonia 3 *(Mguni 30, Kozlej 47, Vakouftsis 85p)*, Hibernian 0
Hibernians 0, Omonia 3 *(Grozdanovski 5, 63, Vakouftsis 44p)*
(Omonia 6-0)

Portadown 1 *(Arkins 90p)*, Viking FK 2 *(Østenstad 53p, Kopteff 79)*
Viking FK 1 *(Nhleko 57)*, Portadown 0
(Viking FK 3-1)

Rhyl 2 *(Hunt 11, 70)*, Atlantas Klaipeda 1 *(Zvingilas 77)*
Atlantas Klaipeda 3 *(Zernys 12p, Laurisas 68, Petreikis 78)*, Rhyl 2 *(Stones 33, Powell 62)*
(4-4; Rhyl on away goals)

UE Sant Juliá 0, Rapid Bucuresti 5 *(Niculae 10, 34, 66, Félix 62og, Vasilache 76)*
Rapid Bucuresti 5 *(Buga 1, 17, 21, 29, Maldarasanu 79)*, UE Sant Juliá 0
(Rapid Bucuresti 10-0)

Teuta Durrës 3 *(Mançaku 32, 58, Xhafa 48)*, Siroki Brijeg 1 *(Abramovic 82)*
Siroki Brijeg 3 *(Medvid 33, Erceg 42, Wagner 70)*, Teuta Durrës 0
(Siroki Brijeg 4-3)

Torpedo Kutaisi 0, FC BATE Borisov 1 *(Baga 26p)*
FC BATE Borisov 5 *(Molosh 10, Lebedev 21, 37, Rubnenko 39, 43)*, Torpedo Kutaisi 0
(FC BATE Borisov 6-0)

FC TVMK Tallinn 1 *(Teever 37)*, MyPa 1 *(Kuparinen 77)*
MyPa 1 *(Rimas 56og)*, FC TVMK Tallinn 0
(MyPa 2-1)

FC Vaduz 2 *(Gohouri 33, Gaspar de Souza 72)*, Dacia Chisinau 0
Dacia Chisinau 1 *(Japalau 64)*, FC Vaduz 0
(FC Vaduz 2-1)

FIRST ROUND

Eighty clubs converged from various directions to make up the first round. These included 16 disappointed refugees from the Champions League, among them such notables as Monaco, Everton, Steaua Bucharest and, from Portugal, the previous season's UEFA Cup runners-up Sporting.

The holders of the trophy, CSKA Moscow, were also present, and they moved through into the second round group phase thanks to a brace of 3-1 wins against Danish club FC Midtjylland, in each of which the man of the match in the previous season's final, Brazilian Daniel Carvalho, helped himself to a couple of goals.

Sporting, however, went crashing out of the competition after another sensational blow-out in the Estádio Alvalade. Two-one up from the first leg against Swedish side Halmstad, they were within a couple of minutes of qualification on home soil

UEFA Cup 2005/2006

SECOND QUALIFYING ROUND RESULTS

(11/8/05 & 25/8/05)

APOEL 1 *(Neophytou 65)*, Maccabi Tel Aviv 0
Maccabi Tel Aviv 2 *(Nimni 63, Mesika 117)*, APOEL 2 *(Makridis 93, Neophytou 95)* (aet)
(APOEL 3-2)

MS Ashdod 2 *(Rajovic 18, Dika Dika 34)*, Domzale 2 *(Stevanovic 2, De Souza 27)*
Domzale 1 *(Nikezic 90)*, MS Ashdod 1 *(Ebiede 70)*
(3-3; Domzale on away goals)

Banants Yerevan 2 *(Hakobyan 24, 43)*, Dnipro Dnipropetrovsk 4 *(Yezerskyi 49, Kornilenko 82, 83, Balabanov 85)*
Dnipro Dnipropetrovsk 4 *(Shelayev 10p, 45, Rykun 32, Balabanov 70)*, Banants Yerevan 0
(Dnipro Dnipropetrovsk 8-2)

Baskimi Kumanovo 0, Maccabi Petach Tikva 5 *(Magomedov 5, Toema 13, Mashiach 22p, Ederi 70, Sarsour 90)*
Maccabi Petach Tikva 6 *(Golan 9, 39, 89, Ganon 41, Sarsour 64, 66)*, Baskimi Kumanovo 0
(Maccabi Petach Tikva 11-0)

SK Brann 0, AC Allianssi 0
AC Allianssi 0, SK Brann 2 *(Ludvigsen 58, Miller 88)*
(SK Brann 2-0)

Dinamo Bucuresti 3 *(Munteanu V. 12p, Zicu 25, 43)*, Omonia 1 *(Konnafis 4)*
Omonia 2 *(Kaiafas 28, Christou 31)*, Dinamo Bucuresti 1 *(Niculescu 55)*
(Dinamo Bucuresti 4-3)

Djurgårdens IF 1 *(Amoah 80)*, Cork City 1 *(Fenn 8)*
Cork City 0, Djurgårdens IF 0
(1-1; Cork City on away goal)

Esbjerg FB 0, Tromsø IL 1 *(Strand 10)*
Tromsø IL 0, Esbjerg FB 1 *(Lucena 17)* (aet)
(1-1; Tromsø IL 3-2 on pens)

Grasshopper-Club Zürich 1 *(Eduardo 68)*, Wisla Plock 0
Wisla Plock 3 *(Gesior 35, 38, Zilic 69)*, Grasshopper-Club Zürich 2 *(Dos Santos 30, Eduardo 83)*
(3-3; Grasshopper-Club Zürich on away goals)

Groclin Dyskobolia Grodzisk 4 *(Rocki 46, Wozniak 55og, Porázik 68, Slusarski 83)*, Dukla Banská Bystrica 1 *(Bazik 72)*
Dukla Banská Bystrica 0, Groclin Dyskobolia Grodzisk 0
(Groclin Dyskobolia Grodzisk 4-1)

Halmstads BK 1 *(Johansson A. 32)*, Linfield 1 *(Kearney 73)*
Linfield 2 *(Mouncey 54, Ferguson 82)*, Halmstads BK 4 *(Thorvaldsson 10, Jönsson 33, Preko 45, Djuric 74)*
(Halmstads BK 5-3)

Inter Zapresic 1 *(Pecelj S. 41)*, Crvena Zvezda Beograd 3 *(Zigic 20, 49, Pantelic 80)*
Crvena Zvezda Beograd 4 *(Jankovic 6, Pantelic 42, 85, Zigic 44p)*, Inter Zapresic 0
(Crvena Zvezda Beograd 7-1)

FC København 2 *(Álvaro Santos 48, Gravgaard 55)*, Carmarthen Town 0
Carmarthen Town 0, FC København 2 *(Møller 38, 40)*
(FC København 4-0)

Krylya Sovetov Samara 2 *(Baba Adamu 8, Husin 74p)*, FC BATE Borisov 0
FC BATE Borisov 0, Krylya Sovetov Samara 2 *(Bulyga 5, Vinogradov 50)*
(Krylya Sovetov Samara 4-0)

Legia Warszawa 0, FC Zürich 1 *(Rafael 90)*
FC Zürich 4 *(Keita 35, 65, Dzemaili 30, César 78p)*, Legia Warszawa 0 *(Szalachowski 20)*
(FC Zürich 5-1)

Litex Lovech 1 *(Zhelev 83)*, Rijeka 0
Rijeka 2 *(Krpan 64p, Rendulic 90)*, Litex Lovech 1 *(Caillet 44p)*
(2-2; Litex Lovech on away goal)

FSV Mainz 2 *(Auer 10, Babatz 70p)*, Keflavík 0
Keflavík 0, FSV Mainz 2 *(Thurk 26, Geissler 85)*
(FSV Mainz 4-0)

Metalurgs Liepaja 2 *(Kalonas 16, Dobrecovs 83p)*, KRC Genk 3 *(Vandenbergh 47, Daerden 59, Stojanovic 80)*
KRC Genk 3 *(Vandenbergh 6, Daerden 18, Stojanovic 28)*, Metalurgs Liepaja 0
(KRC Genk 6-2)

FC Midtjylland 2 *(Kristensen 39, 71)*, B36 1 *(Højsted 79)*
B36 2 *(Midjord 3, Mørkøre 85)*, FC Midtjylland 2 *(Pimpong 17, Sørensen 33)*
(FC Midtjylland 4-3)

MTZ-RIPO Minsk 1 *(Kontsevoi 70)*, FK Teplice 1 *(Rilke 34)*
FK Teplice 2 *(Rilke 56, Masek 90)*, MTZ-RIPO Minsk 1 *(Mkhitaryan 69)*
(FK Teplice 3-2)

MyPa 0, Dundee United 0
Dundee United 2 *(Kerr 15, Samuel 29)*, MyPa 2 *(Adriano 72p, 87)*
(2-2; MyPa on away goals)

Nistru Otaci 0, Grazer AK 2 *(Schrott 54, Ehmann 57)*
Grazer AK 1 *(Jurkuzovic 33)*, Nistru Otaci 0
(Grazer AK 3-0)

OFK Beograd 2 *(Kirovski 32, Ivanovic 39)*, Lokomotiv Plovdiv 1 *(Kamburov 55)*
Lokomotiv Plovdiv 1 *(Stoinev 75)*, OFK Beograd 0
(2-2; Lokomotiv Plovdiv on away goal)

CMC Publikum Celje 1 *(Bersnjak 68)*, Levski Sofia 0
Levski Sofia 3 *(Yovov 41, 65, Domovchiyski 69)*, CMC Publikum Celje 0
(Levski Sofia 3-1)

Rapid Bucuresti 3 *(Niculae 44, 50, Maldarasanu 67)*, Vardar Skopje 0
Vardar Skopje 1 *(Naumov 39)*, Rapid Bucuresti 1 *(Vasilache 58)*
(Rapid Bucuresti 4-1)

Rhyl 0, Viking FK 1 *(Kopteff 11)*
Viking FK 2 *(Nhleko 8, 26)*, Rhyl 1 *(Adamson 35)*
(Viking FK 3-1)

FC Sopron 0, Metalurg Donetsk 3 *(Shyshchenko 53, Oleksiyenko 85, 90)*
Metalurg Donetsk 2 *(Zotov 56, Oleksiyenki 89p)*, FC Sopron 1 *(Florea 98og)*
(Metalurg Donetsk 5-1)

FC Superfund Pasching 2 *(Chaile 33, Wisio 87)*, Zenit Sankt-Peterburg 2 *(Kerzhakov 15, Arshavin 73)*
Zenit Sankt-Peterburg 1 *(Spivak 12p)*, FC Superfund Pasching 1 *(Gilewicz 88)*
(3-3; Zenit Sankt-Peterburg on away goals)

FC Vaduz 0, Besiktas 1 *(Okan 12)*
Besiktas 5 *(Ailton 35, Ahmed Hassan 61, Ahmet 83, Adem 89, Pancu 90)*, FC Vaduz 1 *(Gaspar de Souza 29)*
(Besiktas 6-1)

Zeta Golubovci 0, Siroki Brijeg 1 *(Erceg 90)*
Siroki Brijeg 4 *(Lukacevic 16, Juricic 18, Ronielle 26, Bubalo 64)*, Zeta Golubovci 2 *(Vukovic 4, 44)*
(Siroki Brijeg 5-2)

MSK Zilina 1 *(Barcos 40)*, FK Austria Wien 2 *(Sebo 89, Linz 90)*
FK Austria Wien 2 *(Linz 65, 70)*, MSK Zilina 2 *(Cisovsky 26, Gottwald 31)*
(FK Austria Wien 4-3)

UEFA Cup 2005/2006

when Lithuanian defender Tomas Zvirgzdauskas levelled the aggregate scores and sent the game into extra-time. Zvirgzdauskas then put Sporting in front with an own-goal before Patrik Ingelsten pounced with the tie-deciding goal for the Swedes.

Feyenoord, the 2002 UEFA Cup winners, also came a cropper, losing 2-1 on aggregate to Rapid Bucharest, who had joined the competition at the first qualifying round stage. Rapid were one of three clubs from the Romanian capital to power their way into the group phase. Steaua, who had been eliminated from the Champions League by Rosenborg, got their revenge on Norwegian opposition by outclassing Vålerenga (the team poised to end Rosenborg's long sequence of Norwegian title successes) with a 6-1 aggregate triumph, while Dinamo made mincemeat of Champions League outcasts Everton, demolishing the Premiership club with a brilliant second-half display in Bucharest to run out 5-2 winners over the two legs.

England looked like losing another representative when Bolton trailed on the away-goals rule to Lokomotiv Plovdiv in Bulgaria. But, as in the first leg, Sam Allardyce's team came from a goal behind to win the game with two late goals, the first of them gift-wrapped by a Bulgarian defender. Middlesbrough, the other Premiership entrants, were never in serious danger against Greek club Xanthi, comfortably winning the tie 2-0.

Auxerre ousted

France lost just one of their five teams as Auxerre, the French Cup winners, fell on the away-goals rule to Levski Sofia. The other club from the Bulgarian capital, CSKA, also helped to ensure that the German Bundesliga would not take a full complement through to the next round by beating Bayer Leverkusen (and their prolific ex-CSKA striker Dimitar Berbatov) 1-0 home and away. Leverkusen were not the only German fallers. Mainz, the country's Fair Play qualifiers, went out to Sevilla – despite holding the Spanish side to a creditable first-leg 0-0 draw in Andalusia.

The three InterToto qualifiers all progressed, although only Lens did so with any great ease. Marseille needed penalties after two goalless games against Belgium's GBA, while Hamburg were indebted to a late penalty from in-form Dutch international Rafael van der Vaart as they struggled to overcome FC København. It was a late spot-kick from another Dutch international midfielder, Denny Landzaat, that eventually settled the most freescoring and exciting tie of the round as AZ, the previous season's semi-finalists, managed to peg

FIRST ROUND RESULTS

(15/9/05 & 29/9/05)

APOEL 0, Hertha BSC Berlin 1 *(Marcelinho 90p)*
Hertha BSC Berlin 3 *(Marcelinho 15, Rafael 25, Cairo 52)*, APOEL 1 *(Makridis 76)*
(Hertha BSC Berlin 4-1)

AJ Auxerre 2 *(Poyet 55, Pieroni 84)*, Levski Sofia 1 *(Bardon 35)*
Levski Sofia 1 *(Koprivarov 26)*, AJ Auxerre 0
(2-2; Levski Sofia on away goal)

FC Baník Ostrava 2 *(Klimpl 28, Magera 45p)*, SC Heerenveen 0
SC Heerenveen 5 *(Samaras 3, Nilsson 44, Huntelaar 59, 67, Yildirim 66)*, FC Baník Ostrava 0
(SC Heerenveen 5-2)

FC Basel 5 *(Delgado 10, 79, 88, Ergic 70, Eduardo 85)*, Siroki Brijeg 0
Siroki Brijeg 0, FC Basel 1 *(Petric 7)*
(FC Basel 6-0)

Bayer 04 Leverkusen 0, CSKA Sofia 1 *(Todorov 15)*
CSKA Sofia 1 *(Hdiouad 67)*, Bayer 04 Leverkusen 0
(CSKA Sofia 2-0)

Besiktas 0, Malmö FF 1 *(Afonso 71)*
Malmö FF 1 *(Afonso 61)*, Besiktas 4 *(Youla 28, 34, 52, Tümer 90)*
(Besiktas 4-2)

Bolton Wanderers 2 *(Diouf 72, Borgetti 90)*, Lokomotiv Plovdiv 1 *(Jancevski 28)*
Lokomotiv Plovdiv 1 *(Iliev 51)*, Bolton Wanderers 2 *(Tunchev 79og, Nolan 86)*
(Bolton Wanderers 4-2)

SK Brann 1 *(Winters 44)*, Lokomotiv Moskva 2 *(Ruopolo 70, Lebedenko 76)*
Lokomotiv Moskva 3 *(Loskov 61, Asatiani 77, Bilyaletdinov 90)*, SK Brann 2 *(Macallister 47, Miller 74)*
(Lokomotiv Moskva 5-3)

Brøndby IF 2 *(Skoubo 45, Johansen 74)*, FC Zürich 0
FC Zürich 2 *(Rafael 14, 80)*, Brøndby IF 1 *(Elmander 47)*
(Brøndby IF 3-2)

Crvena Zvezda Beograd 0, Sporting Braga 0
Sporting Braga 1 *(Jaime 86)*, Crvena Zvezda Beograd 1 *(Purovic 10)*
(1-1; Crvena Zvezda Beograd on away goal)

CSKA Moskva 3 *(Gusev 21, Daniel Carvalho 76, 79)*, FC Midtjylland 1 *(Pimpong 23)*
FC Midtjylland 1 *(Nielsen D. 14)*, CSKA Moskva 3 *(Daniel Carvalho 61, 77, Samodin 76)*
(CSKA Moskva 6-2)

Dinamo Bucuresti 5 *(Niculescu 27, Zicu 51, Petre 74, Bratu 76, 90)*, Everton 1 *(Yobo 30)*
Everton 1 *(Cahill 28)*, Dinamo Bucuresti 0
(Dinamo Bucuresti 5-2)

Feyenoord 1 *(Kuijt 40)*, Rapid Bucuresti 1 *(Vasilache 74p)*
Rapid Bucuresti 1 *(Buga 12)*, Feyenoord 0
(Rapid Bucuresti 2-1)

UEFA Cup 2005/2006

Germinal Beerschot Antwerpen 0, Olympique Marseille 0
Olympique Marseille 0, Germinal Beerschot Antwerpen 0 *(aet)*
(0-0; Olympique Marseille 4-1 on pens)

Grasshopper-Club Zürich 1 *(Rogério 1)*, MyPa 1 *(Manso 20)*
MyPa 0, Grasshopper-Club Zürich 3 *(Touré 74, Salatic 80, Rogério 86)*
(Grasshopper-Club Zürich 4-1)

Grazer AK 0, RC Strasbourg 2 *(Pagis 1, Lacour 45)*
RC Strasbourg 5 *(Haggui 6, Farnerud A. 40, Farnerud P. 50, Le Pen 60, Hosni 68)*, Grazer AK 0
(RC Strasbourg 7-0)

Halmstads BK 1 *(Thorvaldsson 43p)*, Sporting CP 2 *(Wender 44, Deivid 47)*
Sporting CP 2 *(Wender 34, Zvirgzdauskas 102og)*, Halmstads BK 3 *(Thorvaldsson 15, Zvirgzdauskas 89, Ingelsten 113) (aet)*
(4-4; Halmstads BK on away goals)

Hamburger SV 1 *(Van der Vaart 37)*, FC København 1 *(Van Heerden 40)*
FC København 0, Hamburger SV 1 *(Van der Vaart 89p)*
(Hamburger SV 2-1)

Hibernian 0, Dnipro Dnipropetrovsk 0
Dnipro Dnipropetrovsk 5 *(Nazarenko 1, Shershun 26, Shelayev 39p, Melashchenko 87, 90)*, Hibernian 1 *(Riordan 10)*
(Dnipro Dnipropetrovsk 5-1)

Krylya Sovetov Samara 5 *(Leilton 12, Baba Adamu 45, Kovba 50, Husin 62, Bober 90)*, AZ 3 *(Vlaar 18, Perez 56, Van Galen 85)*
AZ 3 *(Van Galen 45, Koevermans 80, Landzaat 86p)*, Krylya Sovetov Samara 1 *(Baba Adamu 16)*
(6-6; AZ on away goals)

RC Lens 1 *(Hilton 12)*, Groclin Dyskobolia Grodzisk 1 *(Lachor 13og)*
Groclin Dyskobolia Grodzisk 2 *(Sedlácek 57p, Sablík 79)*, RC Lens 4 *(Cousin 23, 53, Dindane 30, Lachor 90)*
(RC Lens 5-3)

Litex Lovech 2 *(Venkov 65, Novakovic 90)*, KRC Genk 2 *(Daerden 55, Stojanovic 87)*
KRC Genk 0, Litex Lovech 1 *(Sandrinho 56)*
(Litex Lovech 3-2)

Maccabi Petach Tikva 0, Partizan Beograd 2 *(Vukcevic 33, Radonjic 46)*
Partizan Beograd 2 *(Radonjic 12p, 41)*, Maccabi Petach Tikva 5 *(Mashiach 3p, Golan 20, 44, 48, Edrei 88)*
(Maccabi Petach Tikva 5-4)

Middlesbrough 2 *(Boateng 28, Viduka 82)*, Xanthi 0
Xanthi 0, Middlesbrough 0
(Middlesbrough 2-0)

AS Monaco FC 2 *(Kapo 24, Adebayor 48)*, Willem II 0
Willem II 1 *(Hadouir 84)*, AS Monaco FC 3 *(Maicon 48, Adebayor 55, Chevantón 89)*
(AS Monaco FC 5-1)

Palermo 2 *(Corini 6, Brienza 30p)*, Anorthosis 1 *(Ketsbaia 76)*
Anorthosis 0, Palermo 4 *(Caraccioli 5, Makinwa 46, 68, Santana 53)*
(Palermo 6-1)

PAOK 1 *(Salpigidis 25)*, Metalurg Donetsk 1 *(Shyshchenko 68)*
Metalurg Donetsk 2 *(Kosyrin 39, Shyshchenko 57)*, PAOK 2 *(Salpigidis 42, Konstantinidis 45)*
(3-3; PAOK on away goals)

Stade Rennais FC 3 *(Frei 27, 74, Hadji 83)*, CA Osasuna 1 *(Milosevic 50)*
CA Osasuna 0, Stade Rennais FC 0
(Stade Rennais FC 3-1)

Roma 5 *(Aquilani 1, Panucci 22, 44, Montella 28, Totti 53)*, Aris 1 *(Sanjurjo 39)*
Aris 0, Roma 0
(Roma 5-1)

Sevilla FC 0, FSV Mainz 0
FSV Mainz 0, Sevilla FC 2 *(Kanouté 9, 40)*
(Sevilla FC 2-0)

Shakhtar Donetsk 4 *(Elano 1, Brandão 34, 45p, Vorobei 73)*, Debreceni VSC 1 *(Sidibe 89)*
Debreceni VSC 0, Shakhtar Donetsk 2 *(Brandão 20, Elano 24)*
(Shakhtar Donetsk 6-1)

SK Slavia Praha 2 *(Hrdlicka 62, Piták 78)*, Cork City 0
Cork City 1 *(O'Callaghan 73p)*, SK Slavia Praha 2 *(Piták 27, Vlcek 63)*
(SK Slavia Praha 4-1)

VfB Stuttgart 2 *(Tomasson 7, Gentner 89)*, Domzale 0
Domzale 1 *(Stevanovic 16)*, VfB Stuttgart 0
(VfB Stuttgart 2-1)

FK Teplice 1 *(Jirsák 48)*, RCD Espanyol 1 *(Luis García 84)*
RCD Espanyol 2 *(Fredson 81, Jofre 89)*, FK Teplice 0
(RCD Espanyol 3-1)

Tromsø IL 1 *(Szekeres 77)*, Galatasaray 0
Galatasaray 1 *(Hakan 78)*, Tromsø IL 1 *(Ademolu 33)*
(Tromsø IL 2-1)

Viking FK 1 *(Mambo-Mumba 71)*, FK Austria Wien 0
FK Austria Wien 2 *(Rushfeldt 20, Lasnik 46)*, Viking FK 1 *(Nygaard 12)*
(2-2; Viking FK on away goal)

Vitória Guimarães 3 *(Cléber 21p, Mário Sérgio 70, Benachour 71)*, Wisla Krakow 0
Wisla Krakow 0, Vitória Guimarães 1 *(Saganowski 82)*
(Vitória Guimarães 4-0)

Vitória Setúbal 1 *(Fábio 46)*, Sampdoria 1 *(Flachi 14)*
Sampdoria 1 *(Gasbarroni 8)*, Vitória Setúbal 0
(Sampdoria 2-1)

Vålerenga Fotball 0, Steaua Bucuresti 3 *(Radoi 24, Iacob 35, Goian 74)*
Steaua Bucuresti 3 *(Dica 30, Bostina 41, Iacob 48)*, Vålerenga Fotball 1 *(Hulsker 56)*
(Steaua Bucuresti 6-1)

Zenit Sankt-Peterburg 0, AEK 0
AEK 0, Zenit Sankt-Peterburg 1 *(Arshavin 89)*
(Zenit Sankt-Peterburg 1-0)

UEFA Cup 2005/2006

back a 6-3 deficit against Russian provincials Krylya Sovetov Samara.

PAOK also used the away-goals rule to get past Metalurg Donetsk, but they were the only one of four Greek teams to reach the group phase. Their city rivals Aris, now a second division team, were no match for Roma while AEK were eliminated at the death by Zenit Sankt-Peterburg, who owed them one after the Athens side had semi-conspired to send them out of the group phase the previous season.

The highest scorers of the round, oddly, were French Ligue 1 strugglers Strasbourg, who put seven goals without replay past the Austrians of GAK. FC Basel managed six for and none against in their tie with Bosnian survivors Siroki Brijeg, with Argentine import Matías Delgado helping himself to a hat-trick at the St. Jakob Park. Palermo and Shakhtar Donetsk both posted 6-1 aggregate wins, while there was a surprisingly easy 4-0 victory for Vitória Guimarães over Polish champions Wisla Krakow.

The success-rate of the Champions League drop-outs was exactly 50 per cent, with only eight of the 16 progressing. The most galling exit was that of Serbia & Montenegro champions Partizan Belgrade. Not content with having subjected their supporters to a penalty shoot-out defeat against Artmedia Bratislava in the Champions League qualifiers, they imploded dramatically on the same ground against Maccabi Petach Tikva, going down to an astonishing 5-2 defeat in Belgrade after a handsome 2-0 win in Israel.

SECOND ROUND (GROUP PHASE)

The experiment of the previous season was repeated as the UEFA Cup branched off into a group phase. With 40 teams playing matches spread over five Matchdays between late October and mid-December, the action was fairly intense.

The 40 teams were split into eight groups of five. Each side played four games – two at home, two away – and the top three teams in each group (i.e. 24 in all) qualified for the third round alongside eight further cast-offs from the Champions League.

Group A

There was an interesting mix to Group A and a surprise outcome on Matchday One as Monaco, the beaten finalists in the Champions League less than 18 months earlier, lost their opening tie 1-0 in Norway to Viking.

The Monégasques had to sit on that result for over a month before they were next called into action, but on their return they found inspiration from their Togolese striker Emmanuel Adebayor, who scored one goal and made the other in a 2-0 win over Hamburg. As the German club had won each of their opening two matches without conceding a goal, they were effectively through to the third round already.

Viking, who lost their second game in Hamburg, almost made it two home wins out of two, but a late equaliser in Stavanger from Slavia Prague's star man Karel Piták proved crucial in the final reckoning. On Matchday Four the Czech side had a number of chances to gain victory at home to Monaco, but the visitors, decked out in an unfamiliar all yellow (both clubs traditionally wear red and white halves), showed them how to finish with two excellent goals from man of the match Toifilou Maoulida. With CSKA Sofia recovering from two opening defeats to end Viking's programme (and Englishman Roy Hodgon's tenure at the club) with a 2-0 win in the Bulgarian capital, the group remained wide open with one round of matches still to play.

Although Viking needed an unlikely combination of results to stay in contention, the other four teams all

Viking's Brede Paulsen Hangeland tussles with Monaco's Olivier Kapo in Stavanger – the Norwegians won 1-0

UEFA Cup 2005/2006

headed optimistically into their final fixture. For Hamburg and Monaco, both at home, a draw would suffice, but Slavia knew that if they matched or bettered CSKA's result they would go through as well. In the event, the battle for third place went right to the wire. Slavia, though 2-0 down in Hamburg, looked comfortable as, with ten minutes to play, the Bulgarians were trailing by the same score in Monaco. But then CSKA reduced the deficit through playmaker Velizar Dimitrov and in the third minute of stoppage-time they very nearly made it 2-2. But a fine save from Monaco keeper Guillaume Warmuz kept the final score at 2-1. Had CSKA equalised, they would have gone through in Slavia's place and HSV would have topped the group. Instead, CSKA finished last and Monaco first.

Group B

Group B opened with a couple of away wins. Espanyol set the ball rolling by overcoming Russian champions Lokomotiv Moscow with a goal from Spanish international striker Raúl Tamudo while Palermo triumphed several hundred miles to the south in Israel, beating Maccabi Petach Tikva 2-1.

The Israelis, who had come through so spectacularly against Partizan Belgrade in the previous round, would soon discover that they were out of their depth. That goal against the Sicilian club was to be their only one in the group. Three further defeats followed, with confirmed elimination coming after two of them.

Lokomotiv had the better of a goalless draw in Palermo and would have won the game but for a startling miss by Russian international Marat Izmailov. However, the Russian side more than made up for the disappointment of two goalless outings by scoring four apiece in their next two fixtures – at home to Brøndby, away to Maccabi – and that was enough to secure their place in the third round before the other four teams wrapped up the proceedings in mid-December.

Espanyol scored a late equaliser to draw 1-1 at home to Palermo, and they repeated that scoreline the following week in Denmark against an abrasive Brøndby side that finished up with nine men. Michael Laudrup's side travelled to Sicily needing a win in their final game to qualify at their opponents' expense but with the suspensions aggravated by an injury to key striker Johan Elmander, the Danes' task always looked forlorn, and Palermo, despite minimal support, cruised to a 3-0 win. Having begun the day with an identical record to that of Espanyol, the Serie A side finished ahead of the Catalan side, who could only manage

GROUP A RESULTS

(20/10/05)
CSKA Sofia 0, Hamburger SV 1 *(Van der Vaart 56)*
Viking FK 1 *(Nhleko 18)*, AS Monaco FC 0

(2/11/05)
Hamburger SV 2 *(Van der Vaart 21, Lauth 66)*, Viking FK 0
SK Slavia Praha 4 *(Fort 5, 75, Vlcek 36, Piták 56)*, CSKA Sofia 2 *(Gargorov 10, Sakaliev 58)*

(24/11/05)
AS Monaco FC 2 *(Adebayor 44, Veigneau 90)*, Hamburger SV 0
Viking FK 2 *(Nhleko 26, Gaarde 55)*, SK Slavia Praha 2 *(Vlcek 51, Piták 83)*

(30/11/05)
CSKA Sofia 2 *(Yanev 35p, Zadi 47)*, Viking FK 0
SK Slavia Praha 0, AS Monaco FC 2 *(Maoulida 11, 71)*

(15/12/05)
Hamburger SV 2 *(Barbarez 9, Mpenza 57)*, SK Slavia Praha 0
AS Monaco FC 2 *(Kapo 50, Squillaci 75)*, CSKA Sofia 1 *(Dimitrov V. 84)*

FINAL TABLE		Home					Away					Total					Pts
	Pld	W	D	L	F	A	W	D	L	F	A	W	D	L	F	A	
1 AS Monaco FC	4	2	0	0	4	1	1	0	1	2	1	3	0	1	6	2	9
2 Hamburger SV	4	2	0	0	4	0	1	0	1	1	2	3	0	1	5	2	9
3 SK Slavia Praha	4	1	0	1	4	4	0	1	1	2	4	1	1	2	6	8	4
4 Viking FK	4	1	1	0	3	2	0	0	2	0	4	1	1	2	3	6	4
5 CSKA Sofia	4	1	0	1	2	1	0	0	2	3	6	1	0	3	5	7	3

GROUP B RESULTS

(19/10/05)
Lokomotiv Moskva 0, RCD Espanyol 1 *(Tamudo 53)*

(20/10/05)
Maccabi Petach Tikva 1 *(Golan 45)*, Palermo 2 *(Brienza 11, Terlizzi 77)*

(2/11/05)
Brøndby IF 2 *(Lantz 67, Absalonsen 83)*, Maccabi Petach Tikva 0
Palermo 0, Lokomotiv Moskva 0

(23/11/05)
Lokomotiv Moskva 4 *(Loskov 60, 64, 84, Lebedenko 63)*, Brøndby IF 2 *(Retov 11, Skoubo 28)*

(24/11/05)
RCD Espanyol 1 *(Luis García 90)*, Palermo 1 *(González 45)*

(30/11/05)
Brøndby IF 1 *(Skoubo 66)*, RCD Espanyol 1 *(Tamudo 42)*
Maccabi Petach Tikva 0, Lokomotiv Moskva 4 *(Loskov 27, Lebedenko 47, 48, Ruopolo 52)*

(15/12/05)
RCD Espanyol 1 *(Pochettino 83)*, Maccabi Petach Tikva 0
Palermo 3 *(Makinwa 24, Rinaudo 44, 88)*, Brøndby IF 0

FINAL TABLE		Home					Away					Total					Pts
	Pld	W	D	L	F	A	W	D	L	F	A	W	D	L	F	A	
1 Palermo	4	1	1	0	3	0	1	1	0	3	2	2	2	0	6	2	8
2 RCD Espanyol	4	1	1	0	2	1	1	1	0	2	1	2	2	0	4	2	8
3 Lokomotiv Moskva	4	1	0	1	4	3	1	1	0	4	0	2	1	1	8	3	7
4 Brøndby IF	4	1	1	0	3	1	0	0	2	2	7	1	1	2	5	8	4
5 Maccabi Petach Tikva	4	0	0	2	1	6	0	0	2	0	3	0	0	4	1	9	0

UEFA Cup 2005/2006

Steaua Bucharest's Nicolae Dica – on target twice against Lens

one goal, from defender Mauricio Pochettino, in beating Maccabi Petach Tikva at a deserted Estadio Montjuic.

Group C

Swedish side Halmstad were unable to follow up their shock elimination of 2004/05 semi-finalists Sporting. Beaten 1-0 at home by Hertha Berlin on Matchday One, they were crushed 5-0 by InterToto qualifiers Lens a couple of weeks later. Further heavy defeats by Sampdoria and Steaua Bucharest sent them crashing out of the competition without a point.

Hertha, like Halmstad, would score just one goal – Andreas Neuendorf's winner in Sweden – but as the German side conceded none in four games, that was sufficient to take them into the next round. Romanian champions Steaua drew both of their away fixtures 0-0, but at home they were lethal, routing Lens 4-0 and qualifying for the last 32 with a game to spare after beating Halmstad 3-0. Their 0-0 draw in Berlin on Matchday Five ensured that they, like their hosts, qualified with their goal intact. More importantly, the result enabled them to top the group.

While Hertha and Steaua were helping each other out in Berlin, Lens and Sampdoria fought out a thriller at the Stade Bollaert. The Italians needed a draw to progress whereas Lens required a win. It was evenly matched throughout, but the French side claimed a memorable victory when, a minute into stoppage-time, young Tunisian striker Issam Jemaa, who had never previously scored for the club, drove in a superb left-foot cross-shot past Samp keeper Luca Castellazzi. It was the Italian side's only defeat in the group, yet it was enough to send them spinning out of the competition.

GROUP C RESULTS

(20/10/04)
Halmstads BK 0, Hertha BSC Berlin 1 *(Neuendorf 67)*
Steaua Bucuresti 4 *(Iacob 13, Goian 16, Dica 43, 63)*, RC Lens 0

(2/11/05)
RC Lens 5 *(Cousin 16, 23, 47, Jemaa 73, Lachor 90)*, Halmstads BK 0
Sampdoria 0, Steaua Bucuresti 0

(24/11/05)
Halmstads BK 1 *(Djuric 18)*, Sampdoria 3 *(Volpi 31, Diana 67, 86)*
Hertha BSC Berlin 0, RC Lens 0

(30/11/05)
Sampdoria 0, Hertha BSC Berlin 0
Steaua Bucuresti 3 *(Radoi 11, Goian 63, Iacob 71)*, Halmstads BK 0

(15/12/05)
Hertha BSC Berlin 0, Steaua Bucuresti 0
RC Lens 2 *(Thomert 10, Jemaa 90)*, Sampdoria 1 *(Flachi 23)*

FINAL TABLE	Pld	Home W D L F A	Away W D L F A	Total W D L F A	Pts
1 Steaua Bucuresti	4	2 0 0 7 0	0 2 0 0 0	2 2 0 7 0	8
2 RC Lens	4	2 0 0 7 1	0 1 1 0 4	2 1 1 7 5	7
3 Hertha BSC Berlin	4	0 2 0 0 0	1 1 0 1 0	1 3 0 1 0	6
4 Sampdoria	4	0 2 0 0 0	1 0 1 4 3	1 2 1 4 3	5
5 Halmstads BK	4	0 0 2 1 4	0 0 2 0 8	0 0 4 1 12	0

Group D

AZ, the previous season's semi-finalists, and Middlesbrough, who had reached the last 16 on their debut European campaign, were the favourites to progress in a group made up of opposition from Bulgaria, Switzerland and Ukraine. They both made a dream start. An early goal from Dutchman Jimmy Floyd Hasselbaink was enough to secure three points for Boro away to Grasshopper, while a Georgian, Shota Arveladze, and a Moroccan, Tarik Sektioui, got the goals that brought the Alkmaar club three points in Dnipropetrovsk.

Two goals in quick succession from Australian striker Mark Viduka enlivened a dull game at the Riverside to give Boro three further points at home

UEFA Cup 2005/2006

to Dnipro, and when they followed that up with a 0-0 draw in the wind and rain of Alkmaar three weeks later, their place in round three was assured.

In fact, the group was sewn up completely on Matchday Four when AZ won 2-0 away to Litex Lovech and Dnipro finally woke up after three successive defeats with a farewell 3-2 victory in Zurich. The result in Switzerland meant that the Bulgarians, who had earlier beaten both Grasshopper and Dnipro, celebrated qualification despite the home defeat. It was the first time Lovech had ever prolonged their European involvement beyond Christmas.

Middlesbrough and AZ both completed their programme with a win, but it was the English side who topped the group, on goal difference, thanks to two wonderful late strikes from Italian striker Massimo Maccarone. After six UEFA Cup games, Steve McClaren's side had yet to concede a goal.

Group E

As in Groups B and D, the two opening games in Group E resulted in away victories. It was no surprise that Roma, the competition favourites, won in Tromsø – even if conditions up in the Arctic Circle were somewhat alien to the Italians – but Strasbourg's 2-0 victory in nearby Basle was wholly unexpected given that the French side had yet to win a game in Ligue 1 while their hosts were leading the Swiss Super League.

FC Basel redeemed themselves a couple of weeks later by winning away themselves, 2-1 in Belgrade against Red Star, but there was no stopping the team from the Alsace. After running up another three points at home to Tromsø, they went to the Italian capital and held Roma to a 1-1 draw, clinching qualification in the process.

Red Star looked out for the count when they lost their second game 3-1 in Norway, but a tremendous rally at home to Roma in their next match, in which giant striker Nikola Zigic scored two excellent goals and the visitors' Antonio Cassano missed a penalty, put them back in the hunt with one game to play.

Basel's 4-1 home win over Tromsø eliminated the Norwegians, but with the Swiss champions visiting Roma on Matchday Five, it meant that Red Star could clinch a second-round berth if they won at already-qualified Strasbourg. The French side, still struggling badly at home, put out a second-string XI and Red Star appeared to be cruising towards their objective when they went 2-0 up midway through the second half. But a bad miss by Zigic

GROUP D RESULTS

(20/10/05)
Dnipro Dnipropetrovsk 1 (Matyukhin 67), AZ 2 (Arveladze 13, Sektioui 53)
Grasshopper-Club Zürich 0, Middlesbrough 1 (Hasselbaink 10)

(2/11/05)
Litex Lovech 2 (Novakovic 13, Sandrinho 81), Grasshopper-Club Zürich 1 (Dos Santos 90)
Middlesbrough 3 (Yakubu 36, Viduka 50, 56), Dnipro Dnipropetrovsk 0

(24/11/05)
AZ 0, Middlesbrough 0
Dnipro Dnipropetrovsk 0, Litex Lovech 2 (Novakovic 72, Nazarenko 90og)

(30/11/05)
Grasshopper-Club Zürich 2 (Touré 85, Rençgli 90), Dnipro Dnipropetrovsk 3 (Nazarenko 39, Kravchenko 62, Mykhailenko 83)
Litex Lovech 0, AZ 2 (Van Galen 10, Sektioui 82)

(15/12/05)
AZ 1 (Koevermans 70), Grasshopper-Club Zürich 0
Middlesbrough 2 (Maccarone 80, 86), Litex Lovech 0

FINAL TABLE		Home					Away					Total					
	Pld	W	D	L	F	A	W	D	L	F	A	W	D	L	F	A	Pts
1 Middlesbrough	4	2	0	0	5	0	1	1	0	1	0	3	1	0	6	0	10
2 AZ	4	1	1	0	1	0	2	0	0	4	1	3	1	0	5	1	10
3 Litex Lovech	4	1	0	1	2	3	1	0	1	2	2	2	0	2	4	5	6
4 Dnipro Dnipropetrovsk	4	0	0	2	1	4	1	0	1	3	5	1	0	3	4	9	3
5 Grasshopper-Club Zür.	4	0	0	2	2	4	0	0	2	1	3	0	0	4	3	7	0

GROUP E RESULTS

(20/10/05)
FC Basel 0, RC Strasbourg 2 (Diané 15, Bokc 25)
Tromsø IL 1 (Årst 42), Roma 2 (Kuffour 35, Cufré 84)

(2/11/05)
Crvena Zvezda Beograd 1 (Purovic 25), FC Basel 2 (Delgado 30p, Rossi 88)
RC Strasbourg 2 (Pagis 38, Arrache 66), Tromsø IL 0

(24/11/05)
Roma 1 (Cassano 73), RC Strasbourg 1 (Belaid 52)
Tromsø IL 3 (Kibebe 22, Årst 37, 74p), Crvena Zvezda Beograd 1 (Zigic 24)

(1/12/05)
FC Basel 4 (Petric 17, Delgado 61, Chipperfield 67, Degen 75), Tromsø IL 3 (Strand 2, 29, Årst 19)
Crvena Zvezda Beograd 3 (Zigic 37, 86, Purevic 77), Roma 1 (Nonda 23)

(14/12/05)
Roma 3 (Taddei 14, Totti 45, Nonda 49), FC Basel 1 (Petric 78)
RC Strasbourg 2 (Gameiro 79, 90), Crvena Zvezda Beograd 2 (Basta 34, Djokaj 64)

FINAL TABLE		Home					Away					Total					
	Pld	W	D	L	F	A	W	D	L	F	A	W	D	L	F	A	Pts
1 RC Strasbourg	4	1	1	0	4	2	1	1	0	3	1	2	2	0	7	3	8
2 Roma	4	1	1	0	4	2	1	0	1	3	4	2	1	1	7	6	7
3 FC Basel	4	1	0	1	4	5	1	0	1	3	4	2	0	2	7	9	6
4 Crvena Zvezda Beograd	4	1	0	1	4	3	0	1	1	3	5	1	1	2	7	8	4
5 Tromsø IL	4	1	0	1	4	3	0	0	2	3	6	1	0	3	7	9	3

UEFA Cup 2005/2006

was to herald a nightmare finish for Walter Zenga's side as young Strasbourg striker Kevin Gameiro, making his first start for the club, scored not once but twice, his second goal coming four minutes into stoppage-time.

The Strasbourg players and fans celebrated wildly, but it was Basel, not they, who were the chief beneficiaries of Gameiro's timely header. Beaten 3-1 in Rome, the Swiss side were on their way out of the competition on goal difference, but Red Star's collapse enabled them to qualify in extremis alongside Strasbourg and Roma.

Group F

CSKA Moscow discovered that being the holders of the UEFA Cup brought no favours when they were drawn in the toughest of the eight second-round groups. With Olympique Marseille, Heerenveen, Dinamo Bucharest and Levski Sofia making up the quintet, there was little margin for error, but the Russians gave themselves a steep uphill climb when they lost their opening game 2-1 at home to InterToto qualifiers Marseille, a penalty save by Fabien Barthez from Sergei Ignashevich not helping their cause.

Marseille's Nigerian international Taye Ismaila Taiwo – his late penalty brought victory over Heerenveen

GROUP F RESULTS

(20/10/05)
CSKA Moskva 1 *(Vágner Love 80)*, Olympique Marseille 2 *(Lamouchi 23, Niang 38)*
Dinamo Bucuresti 0, SC Heerenveen 0

(2/11/05)
SC Heerenveen 0, CSKA Moskva 0
Levski Sofia 1 *(Angelov E. 90)*, Dinamo Bucuresti 0

(24/1/105)
CSKA Moskva 2 *(Vágner Love 49, 73)*, Levski Sofia 1 *(Domovchiyski 90)*
Olympique Marseille 1 *(Taiwo 90p)*, SC Heerenveen 0

(1/12/05)
Dinamo Bucuresti 1 *(Munteanu V. 72)*, CSKA Moskva 0
Levski Sofia 1 *(Yovov 54)*, Olympique Marseille 0

(14/12/05)
SC Heerenveen 2 *(Samaras 54, Hanssen 90)*, Levski Sofia 1 *(Ivanov 52)*
Olympique Marseille 2 *(Cesar 39, Delfim 45)*, Dinamo Bucuresti 1 *(Niculescu 52)*

CSKA picked up a useful away point at Heerenveen and then three at home to Levski Sofia – thanks to a brace from Vágner Love – but a 1-0 defeat away to Dinamo Bucharest – in which the Brazilian striker missed countless chances - left them exposed to the will of others as they sat out the final round of matches.

Marseille beat Heerenveen at the Stade Vélodrome with a lucky late penalty, driven home by 20-year-old Nigerian left-back Ismaila Taiwo, and although they then lost 1-0 in Bulgaria to Levski Sofia, results elsewhere meant that both the French side and the Bulgarians, who had also beaten Dinamo Bucharest in Sofia, were both safely qualified in advance of Matchday Five.

With Marseille and Levski both through, there was just one qualifying place up for grabs, and Heerenveen, Dinamo and CSKA were all still in contention. There were a number of permutations, but the holders could only hope that Marseille beat Dinamo, preferably by more than one goal, and that Heerenveen failed to win at home to Levski.

An exciting final day was anticipated but nobody could have imagined the drama and heartache that would unfold in the final seconds of both games. In

FINAL TABLE

	Pld	Home W	D	L	F	A	Away W	D	L	F	A	Total W	D	L	F	A	Pts
1 Olympique Marseille	4	2	0	0	3	1	1	0	1	2	2	3	0	1	5	3	9
2 Levski Sofia	4	2	0	0	2	0	0	0	2	2	4	2	0	2	4	4	6
3 SC Heerenveen	4	1	1	0	2	1	0	1	1	0	1	1	2	1	2	2	5
4 CSKA Moskva	4	1	0	1	3	3	0	1	1	0	1	1	1	2	3	4	4
5 Dinamo Bucuresti	4	1	1	0	1	0	0	0	2	1	3	1	1	2	2	3	4

UEFA Cup 2005/2006

Holland, Heerenveen beat Levski with literally the last kick of the game – as the Bulgarians had done themselves to Dinamo in an earlier fixture – while in Marseille the Romanian side thought they had levelled the game at 2-2 with their final kick only to discover to their horror that the referee had already blown for full-time. It was an amazing climax. Heerenveen's last-gasp winner, from Norwegian substitute André Hanssen, put them through at CSKA's expense, but if Dinamo's goal had counted, the Romanians would have progressed instead.

Group G

The thrills of Group F would not be replicated in Group G. The three qualifiers from this section were all settled in advance of the final fixtures, with French club Rennes and lone Greek representatives PAOK both losing each of their first three games.

Shakhtar Donetsk, the Ukrainian champions, were the first team to reach six points, beating PAOK 1-0 at home and then Stuttgart 2-0 away, but their 100 per cent record was brought to an end on Matchday Three when Rapid Bucharest, coached by Razvan Lucescu, beat the team coached by his father, Mircea, 1-0 in Donetsk. It was a late goal from Marius Maldarasanu that earned Lucescu junior the family bragging rights, and the midfielder was to earn Rapid another three points seven days later when his immaculately executed one-step free-kick proved enough to see off PAOK and eliminate the Greeks from the competition.

Shakhtar joined Rapid on nine points by winning 1-0 at Rennes, and Stuttgart also made it to that total when a couple of goals from homegrown striker Mario Gomez enabled them to beat the Romanians in the Gottlieb-Daimler-Stadion. It was a late 'consolation' goal, however, from one of Rapid's young strikers, Lucian Burdujan, that would eventually establish the final placings in the group. Without that goal Rapid would have finished third and Stuttgart first. With it, the positions were reversed, Shakhtar remaining unmoved in second place.

Group H

Five teams from the furthest extremes of Europe's boundaries contested Group H – Bolton from the north-west, Zenit St. Petersburg from the north-east, Besiktas from the south-east and two teams, Sevilla and Vitória Guimarães, from the south-west. With the exception of Guimarães's relatively short hop from northern Portugal to Andalusia, all of the teams racked up plenty of air miles in their quest to reach the round of the last 32.

GROUP G RESULTS

(20/10/05)
Stade Rennais FC 0, VfB Stuttgart 2 *(Tomasson 87, Ljuboja 90p)*
Shakhtar Donetsk 1 *(Brandão 68p)*, PAOK 0

(2/11/05)
Rapid Bucuresti 2 *(Niculae 42, Buga 67)*, Stade Rennais FC 0
VfB Stuttgart 0, Shakhtar Donetsk 2 *(Fernandinho 31, Marica 88)*

(24/11/05)
PAOK 1 *(Karipidis 48)*, VfB Stuttgart 2 *(Ljuboja 85, 90p)*
Shakhtar Donetsk 0, Rapid Bucuresti 1 *(Maldarasanu 87)*

(1/12/05)
Rapid Bucuresti 1 *(Maldarasanu 45)*, PAOK 0
Stade Rennais FC 0, Shakhtar Donetsk 1 *(Elano 38p)*

(14/12/05)
PAOK 5 *(Rochat 4og, Christoudopoulos 38, Yiasoumi 79, 89, Salpigidis 83p)*,
Stade Rennais FC 1 *(Briand 70)*
VfB Stuttgart 2 *(Gomez 20, 37)*, Rapid Bucuresti 1 *(Burdujan 80)*

FINAL TABLE		Home					Away					Total					
	Pld	W	D	L	F	A	W	D	L	F	A	W	D	L	F	A	Pts
1 Rapid Bucuresti	4	2	0	0	3	0	1	0	1	2	2	3	0	1	5	2	9
2 Shakhtar Donetsk	4	1	0	1	1	1	2	0	0	3	0	3	0	1	4	1	9
3 VfB Stuttgart	4	1	0	1	2	3	2	0	0	4	1	3	0	1	6	4	9
4 PAOK	4	1	0	1	6	3	0	0	2	0	2	1	0	3	6	5	3
5 Stade Rennais FC	4	0	0	2	0	3	0	0	2	1	7	0	0	4	1	10	0

Unsurprisingly, the ten matches yielded just one away win – and unfortunately for Besiktas, who beat Guimarães in Portugal on Matchday Five, their victory would prove to be academic. Bolton Wanderers' 1-1 draw at home to Sevilla the same evening confirmed the Turks' elimination – despite their respectable final haul of five points.

Bolton, playing European football for the very first time, ended up third in the table but as the only team in the group to go through their four matches unbeaten. The ability to come from behind that had helped the Premiership side through the first round continued to serve them well as they claimed 1-1 draws away in Istanbul and Guimarães, the latter with a tremendous late equaliser from Portuguese youngster Ricardo Vaz Té, who had entered as a substitute only seconds earlier.

Bolton's only win came on a sodden pitch at home to Zenit, and that was the Russians' only defeat. They beat both Iberian sides 2-1 in St. Petersburg and clinched qualification with a 1-1 draw at Besiktas. Sevilla confirmed their presence in round three on the same night as they beat Vitória Guimarães 3-1, with Argentine striker Javier Saviola, on loan from Barcelona, adding to his earlier goals against Besiktas and Zenit with an impressive first-

UEFA Cup 2005/2006

GROUP H RESULTS

(20/10/05)
Besiktas 1 *(Aílton 7)*, Bolton Wanderers 1 *(Borgetti 29)*
Zenit Sankt-Peterburg 2 *(Spivak 39p, Arshavin 54)*, Vitória Guimarães 1 *(Neca 59)*

(2/11/05)
Bolton Wanderers 1 *(Nolan 24)*, Zenit Sankt-Peterburg 0
Sevilla FC 3 *(Saviola 64, Kanouté 65, 89)*, Besiktas 0

(24/11/05)
Vitória Guimarães 1 *(Saganowski 86)*, Bolton Wanderers 1 *(Vaz Té 88)*
Zenit Sankt-Peterburg 2 *(Kerzhakov 11, 89)*, Sevilla FC 1 *(Saviola 90)*

(1/12/05)
Besiktas 1 *(Ibrahim Akin 23)*, Zenit Sankt-Peterburg 1 *(Horshkov 30)*
Sevilla FC 3 *(Saviola 10, 27, Adriano 39)*, Vitória Guimarães 1 *(Benachour 44)*

(14/12/05)
Bolton Wanderers 1 *(N'Gotty 65)*, Sevilla FC 1 *(Adriano 74)*
Vitória Guimarães 1 *(Saganowski 12)*, Besiktas 3 *(Ibrahim Toraman 9, 60, Youla 18)*

FINAL TABLE		Home					Away					Total					
	Pld	W	D	L	F	A	W	D	L	F	A	W	D	L	F	A	Pts
1 Sevilla FC	4	2	0	0	6	1	0	1	1	2	3	2	1	1	8	4	7
2 Zenit Sankt-Peterburg	4	2	0	0	4	2	0	1	1	1	2	2	1	1	5	4	7
3 Bolton Wanderers	4	1	1	0	2	1	0	2	0	2	2	1	3	0	4	3	6
4 Besiktas	4	0	2	0	2	2	1	0	1	3	4	1	2	1	5	6	5
5 Vitória Guimarães	4	0	1	1	2	4	0	0	2	2	5	0	1	3	4	9	1

European novices Bolton Wanderers gave as good as they got against former European champions Marseille. They were refused several penalty claims in the first leg at the Reebok, which ended 0-0, and took the lead in the Stade Vélodrome, only to be undone by an equaliser on the stroke of half-time from French starlet Franck Ribéry and an own-goal midway through the second period.

Bolton's exit left Middlesbrough as the lone Premiership survivors. They conceded their first goals of the competition in overcoming a VfB Stuttgart side that had just parted company with their high-profile Italian coach Giovanni Trapattoni. Boro won the first game at the Gottlieb-Daimler-Stadion 2-1 but the Germans finished that game strongly and carried that momentum into the return at the Riverside the following week, scoring early and making life extremely difficult for Steve McClaren's team on a wet, dreary evening. It was only dogged defending that took Boro through on the away-goals rule.

Palermo also found the going tough against Slavia Prague, the team that came through the group phase with only four points. The Czechs won the first leg but were ousted by an excellent goal from youngster Denis Godeas in the return.

half brace. The Spanish side's 1-1 draw at the Reebok Stadium on Matchday Five enabled them to finish on top of the group ahead of Zenit on goal difference. Unlike in the Champions League, the head-to-head rule (which would have favoured the Russians) was not applicable in the UEFA Cup.

THIRD ROUND (ROUND OF LAST 32)

The draw for the third round – or round of the last 32, as officially termed by UEFA – was carefully structured. The eight winners from the group phase were all paired with the eight teams that had come through in third place, while the eight runners-up took on the eight new arrivals from the Champions League.

The privilege of playing the second leg at home was accorded to the group winners and runners-up. In the case of the former, it proved to be a telling advantage, with only one of the second-round table-toppers, Monaco, failing to make further progress. But as they were struggling in Ligue 1, it was not a huge shock that they should be eliminated by Swiss league leaders FC Basel.

Although Basel were the only third-placed survivors, a number of others put up a good fight.

Away-day joy

The other four group winners all made life easy for themselves by winning their away legs. A scrappy goal from Jordi – it went in off his thigh – brought Sevilla a 1-0 win away to Lokomotiv Moscow, which set up a 3-0 aggregate triumph. Rapid Bucharest advanced in precisely the same manner against a Hertha Berlin side that exited the competition after five successive games without a goal. Steaua ensured a Bucharest double-act in the next round with an impressive 3-1 win at Heerenveen, and Strasbourg knocked out Litex Lovech after a 2-0 win in Bulgaria.

As in the first round of the competition, the success rate of the Champions League infiltrators was exactly 50 per cent. While Artmedia Bratislava, Club Bruges, Rosenborg and FC Thun went out, Real Betis, Lille, Schalke and Udinese all progressed.

Schalke racked up the biggest winning margin of the round. They were in real trouble for much of the first leg against Espanyol but two excellent second-half performances, especially in Barcelona, where they scored there goals without reply, saw the 1997 winners safely through. Hamburg joined their Bundesliga rivals in the last 16 thanks to a couple of goals from Belgian defender Daniel Van Buyten at home to Thun, but Lens became the first of the

UEFA Cup 2005/2006

three InterToto winners to go out as they fell 3-1 on aggregate to Udinese.

In-form Roma did well to beat Bruges 2-1 in Belgium after losing midfielder Daniele De Rossi to a red card midway through the first half. They were also without skipper Francesco Totti for the return leg after he broke his leg a few days earlier in a Serie A game, but despite that and a surprising lack of support from the stands (Roma had just run up ten successive league wins but the Olimpico was half-empty), they repeated the scoreline of the first leg thanks to a deflected winning goal from full-back Cesare Bovo.

Zenit St. Petersburg, led by their Russian international strikeforce of Alexandr Kerzhakov and Andrei Arshavin, played splendidly in the freezing February temperatures to see off fellow out-of-season northern Europeans Rosenborg. An eventful season in Europe ended for Artmedia Bratislava as the Slovakians were well beaten by Levski Sofia, for whom striker Emil Angelov netted all three goals in a 3-0 aggregate win. And there was further UEFA Cup extra-time heartbreak for the previous season's semi-finalists AZ as they went out at home to Real Betis.

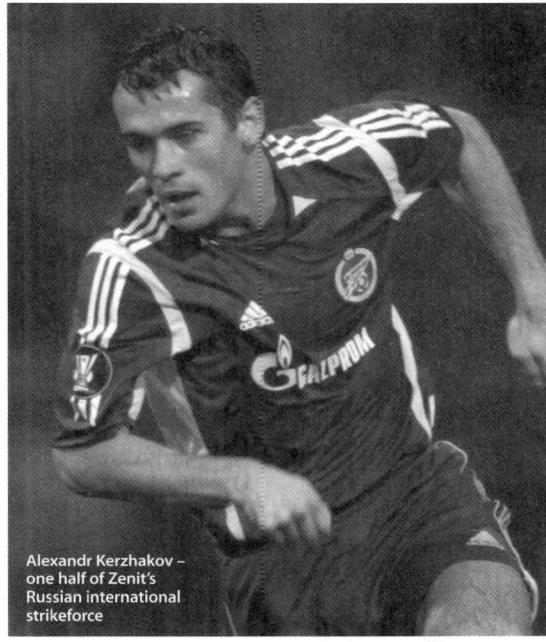

Alexandr Kerzhakov – one half of Zenit's Russian international strikeforce

THIRD ROUND RESULTS

(15/2/06 & 23/2/06)

Artmedia Bratislava 0, Levski Sofia 1 *(Angelov E. 9)*
Levski Sofia 2 *(Angelov E. 14, 27)*, Artmedia Bratislava 0
(Levski Sofia 3-0)

FC Basel 1 *(Degen 78)*, AS Monaco FC 0
AS Monaco FC 1 *(Vieri 21p)*, FC Basel 1 *(Majstorovic 56)*
(FC Basel 2-1)

Real Betis 2 *(Tardelli 70, Robert 79)*, AZ 0
AZ 2 *(Arveladze 26, Jaliens 35)*, Real Betis 1 *(Melli 93) (aet)*
(Real Betis 3-2)

Bolton Wanderers 0, Olympique Marseille 0
Olympique Marseille 2 *(Ribéry 45, Ben Haim 68og)*, Bolton Wanderers 1 *(Giannakopoulos 25)*
(Olympique Marseille 2-1)

Club Brugge KV 1 *(Portillo 60)*, Roma 2 *(Vanaudenaerde 44og, Perrotta 74)*
Roma 2 *(Mancini 55, Bovo 71)*, Club Brugge KV 1 *(Verheyen 60)*
(Roma 4-2)

SC Heerenveen 1 *(Bruggink 24)*, Steaua Bucuresti 3 *(Dica 29, Goian 76, Paraschiv 78)*
Steaua Bucuresti 0, SC Heerenveen 1 *(Bruggink 86)*
(Steaua Bucuresti 3-2)

Hertha BSC Berlin 0, Rapid Bucuresti 1 *(Negru 68p)*
Rapid Bucuresti 2 *(Niculae 50, Buga 79)*, Hertha BSC Berlin 0
(Rapid Bucuresti 3-0)

Lille OSC 3 *(Fauvergue 19, Dernis 57, Odemwingie 77)*, Shakhtar Donetsk 2 *(Brandão 89, Marica 90)*
Shakhtar Donetsk 0, Lille OSC 0
(Lille OSC 3-2)

Litex Lovech 0, RC Strasbourg 2 *(Le Pen 2, Diané 82)*
RC Strasbourg 0, Litex Lovech 0
(RC Strasbourg 2-0)

Lokomotiv Moskva 0, Sevilla FC 1 *(Jordi 74)*
Sevilla FC 2 *(Maresca 33, Puerta 89)*, Lokomotiv Moskva 0
(Sevilla FC 3-0)

Rosenborg BK 0, Zenit Sankt-Peterburg 2 *(Arshavin 22, Kerzhakov 32)*
Zenit Sankt-Peterburg 2 *(Kerzhakov 55, Denisov 87)*, Rosenborg BK 1 *(Riseth 45)*
(Zenit Sankt-Peterburg 4-1)

FC Schalke 04 2 *(Bordon 67, Ernst 89)*, RCD Espanyol 1 *(Luis García 34)*
RCD Espanyol 0, FC Schalke 04 3 *(Kuranyi 54, Sand 70, Lincoln 73)*
(FC Schalke 04 5-1)

Udinese 3 *(Di Natale 35, Barreto 61, 82)*, RC Lens 0
RC Lens 1 *(Frau 55)*, Udinese 0
(Udinese 3-1)

(16/2/06 & 23/2/06)

SK Slavia Praha 2 *(Jarolím 29, Barzagli 48og)*, Palermo 1 *(Conteh 40)*
Palermo 1 *(Godeas 51)*, SK Slavia Praha 0
(2-2; Palermo on away goal)

VfB Stuttgart 1 *(Ljuboja 86)*, Middlesbrough 2 *(Hasselbaink 20, Parnaby 46)*
Middlesbrough 0, VfB Stuttgart 1 *(Tiffert 13)*
(2-2; Middlesbrough on away goals)

FC Thun 1 *(Adriano 30)*, Hamburger SV 0
Hamburger SV 2 *(Van Buyten 2, 33)*, FC Thun 0
(Hamburger SV 2-1)

UEFA Cup 2005/2006

FOURTH ROUND (ROUND OF LAST 16)

The composition of the UEFA Cup's last 16 was fairly predictable, with no fewer than 11 of the teams coming from the Continent's Big Five of England, France, Germany, Italy and Spain. Romania still had two representatives, and the line-up was completed by one club apiece from Bulgaria, Russia and Switzerland.

By the end of the fourth round, however, there would be a far more even and cosmopolitan spread. This would be the round of shocks and surprises.

Of the eight ties, it could be argued that as many as six went against the form book. The three Italian clubs all went out, as did the surviving trio from France. The other two casualties were from Germany and Spain. By the end of the fourth-round action only one country remained with multiple representation, and that was Romania.

Rapid Bucharest, who, alone among the final 16, had entered the competition back in July at the first qualifying stage, beat Hamburg 2-0 at home in the first leg with a couple of sensational goals, one at the end of each half, from Daniel Niculae (a rocket 30-yard shot into the top corner) and Mihai Buga (a perfect glancing header). The Germans came back strongly in the AOL-Arena, but another Buga goal earned Razvan Lucescu's side their second German scalp in successive rounds. Steaua joined their local rivals in the quarter-finals with a breathtaking 3-0 win in Seville (scene of their 1986 European Cup final victory) against Real Betis. Cosmin Olaroiu's side were unlucky not to win the first leg in front of a large and vocal crowd at the national stadium in Bucharest, but they certainly made amends in the return, with midfielder Banel Nicolita scoring twice to lead a second-half rout of the Champions League outcasts.

Udinese, another club that had lived the Champions League high life in the autumn, crashed out to Levski Sofia. Lucky to draw the home leg 0-0 after surviving possibly the worst miss of the tournament (a close-range header over an open goal from Levski's leading marksman Emil Angelov), the Serie A side hardly helped their chances by fielding a virtual second XI for the following week's return leg in Sofia. The gamble looked to be paying off when Argentine midfielder Fernando Tissone exploited disorganised Bulgarian defending at a free-kick to give Udinese a precious away goal. It was the first time Levski had conceded at home in six games but, with the confidence of a team that had won each of their previous five home games, they turned the tie

Levski Sofia's evergreen veteran, Daniel Borimirov

around in the second half, scoring twice, through veteran utility man Daniel Borimirov and Croatian defender Igor Tomasic, to win the game and stride through to the quarter-finals.

Just desserts

In treating the competition with disdain, Udinese had got their just desserts, and it was a not dissimilar tale for Palermo. The Sicilians beat Schalke 1-0 at home but went to Gelsenkirchen with a deliberately weakened side and paid the price. The tie turned in the Germans' favour at the end of the first half when Palermo captain Eugenio Corini handled on the line and was sent off. Levan Kobiashvili levelled the aggregate score from the ensuing penalty, and as Schalke dominated the second half they were rewarded with two fine goals, both set up brilliantly by German international winger Gerald Asamoah.

Roma, riven with injuries, especially up front, could not afford to dabble too much with their team selection against Middlesbrough. The Premiership side were deserved 1-0 victors in the first leg at

UEFA Cup 2005/2006

the Riverside, with Yakubu's early penalty (after a foul on his strike-partner Jimmy Floyd Hasselbaink) proving decisive, and when they took the lead six days later at the Stadio Olimpico in their first attack, with a superb Hasselbaink header from a Stewart Downing cross, Roma, the competition favourites, were up against it. A quick response from makeshift striker Mancini set up a thrilling second half. The Brazilian made it 2-1 on the night with a questionable penalty (after a rash challenge from Ray Parlour), but Boro defended superbly after that, with goalkeeper Mark Schwarzer to the fore, and they eventually held out to go through on the away-goals rule for the second round in succession. Middlesbrough's achievement was all the more creditworthy for the fact that Roma, despite missing talisman Totti and several other forwards, had played really well. The red card shown to defender Philippe Mexès in stoppage-time for a foul on Downing merely compounded the Italian club's disappointment.

If Italy's whitewash was partly self-induced, the same couldn't be said about France's. The three Ligue 1 survivors – Lille, Marseille and Strasbourg – were all fully committed to the competition but simply found themselves ousted by superior opposition.

Lille beat Sevilla 1-0 at home but lost 2-0 in Andalusia and seldom looked like getting the away goal they required to survive. Strasbourg, who had won 2-0 away to 'local rivals' FC Basel in their opening group game, now lost by the same score in the St. Jakob Park. Basel's Argentine playmaker Matías Delgado netted his sixth goal of the competition from a free-kick and finished the game by setting up a second goal late on for 18-year-old substitute Zdravko Kuzmanovic. The tie was effectively sealed when Basel's Brazilian striker Eduardo made it 3-0 on aggregate with a close-range tap-in after just three minutes. He later added another as Basel drew the match 2-2 and added Strasbourg's scalp to that of Monaco, their Ligue 1 victims a few weeks earlier.

Marseille's hopes of a second UEFA Cup final appearance in three seasons evaporated when they lost their home leg 1-0 to Zenit St. Petersburg and had playmaker Franck Ribéry sent off. The Russians played superbly in the Stade Vélodrome, with goalscorer Andrei Arshavin a constant menace, but they were less impressive at home on a dreadful pitch and nervously sneaked through in the end after a deflected free-kick from OM defender Frédéric Déhu had put the visitors in sight of an improbable away-goals win.

FOURTH ROUND RESULTS

(9/3/06 & 15/3/06)

Lille OSC 1 *(Dernis 24)*, Sevilla FC 0
Sevilla FC 2 *(Kanouté 29, Luis Fabiano 45)*, Lille OSC 0
(Sevilla FC 2-1)

Middlesbrough 1 *(Yakubu 12p)*, Roma 0
Roma 2 *(Mancini 43, 66p)*, Middlesbrough 1 *(Hasselbaink 32)*
(2-2; Middlesbrough on away goal)

Rapid Bucuresti 2 *(Niculae 45, Buga 88)*, Hamburger SV 0
Hamburger SV 3 *(Lauth 24, Barbarez 36, Van der Vaart 63)*, Rapid Bucuresti 1 *(Buga 51)*
(3-3; Rapid Bucuresti on away goal)

(9/3/06 & 16/3/06)

FC Basel 2 *(Delgado 8, Kuzmanovic 88)*, RC Strasbourg 0
RC Strasbourg 2 *(Carlier 10, Kanté 78)*, FC Basel 2 *(Eduardo 3, 26)*
(FC Basel 4-2)

Olympique Marseille 0, Zenit Sankt-Peterburg 1 *(Arshavin 51)*
Zenit Sankt-Peterburg 1 *(Kerzhakov 69)*, Olympique Marseille 1 *(Déhu 74)*
(Zenit Sankt-Peterburg 2-1)

Palermo 1 *(Brienza 15)*, FC Schalke 04 0
FC Schalke 04 3 *(Kobiashvili 44p, Larsen 72, Azaouagh 80)*, Palermo 0
(FC Schalke 04 3-1)

Steaua Bucuresti 0, Real Betis 0
Real Betis 0, Steaua Bucuresti 3 *(Nicolita 54, 82, Iacob 78)*
(Steaua Bucuresti 3-0)

Udinese 0, Levski Sofia 0
Levski Sofia 2 *(Borimirov 51, Tomasic 63)*, Udinese 1 *(Tissone 22)*
(Levski Sofia 2-1)

QUARTER-FINALS

As in the Champions League, the draw for the quarter-finals was swiftly followed by the draw for the semi-finals. With seven countries represented and most of the fancied teams having fallen, it was anybody's Cup. The toughest half of the draw comprised Schalke, Sevilla and Zenit, while Middlesbrough, having knocked out Stuttgart and Roma, optimistically eyed up a quarter-final clash with FC Basel and a potential semi-final confrontation with one of the two Romanian clubs, Steaua and Rapid, who had been drawn together.

There was an electric atmosphere in Rapid's Valentin Stanescu stadium for the first leg of the Bucharest derby. Rapid had won all seven of their previous home games in the competition without conceding a goal, whereas Steaua had not lost

UEFA Cup 2005/2006

QUARTER-FINAL RESULTS

(30/3/06 & 6/4/06)

FC Basel 2 *(Delgado 43, Degen 45)*, Middlesbrough 0
Middlesbrough 4 *(Viduka 33, 57, Hasselbaink 79, Maccarone 90)*, FC Basel 1 *(Eduardo 22)*
(Middlesbrough 4-3)

Levski Sofia 1 *(Borimirov 6)*, FC Schalke 04 3 *(Varela 48, Lincoln 69, Asamoah 79)*
FC Schalke 04 1 *(Lincoln 58)*, Levski Sofia 1 *(Angelov E. 24)*
(FC Schalke 04 4-2)

Rapid Bucuresti 1 *(Moldovan 50)*, Steaua Bucuresti 1 *(Nicolita 5)*
Steaua Bucuresti 0, Rapid Bucuresti 0
(1-1; Steaua Bucuresti on away goal)

Sevilla FC 4 *(Saviola 15, 80, Martí 54p, Adriano 90)*, Zenit Sankt-Peterburg 1 *(Kerzhakov 45)*
Zenit Sankt-Peterburg 1 *(Hyun 50)*, Sevilla FC 1 *(Kepa 63)*
(Sevilla FC 5-2)

Game on! Mark Viduka starts the Middlesbrough fightback against FC Basel

away. Something had to give, and in the fifth minute of play it was Rapid's defence that was finally breached as Banel Nicolita, Steaua's two-goal hero against Betis, cleverly controlled Daniel Oprita's excellent pull-back and drilled the ball low into the net with his left foot. Steaua might have gone further ahead in the first half – they had a second goal ruled out after an outswinging corner was adjudged to have curled out of play in flight – but Rapid struck back just after the interval when veteran striker Viorel Moldovan tapped home from close range following a ghastly error from Steaua's imported goalkeeper Carlos.

At 1-1, all was to play for the following week at the Lia Manoliu stadium. Steaua had not scored at their temporary home in each of the previous two rounds, and they would again find it a struggle. But the away-goal factor was in their favour and it was Rapid who had to score if they, not Steaua, were to be Romania's first UEFA Cup semi-finalists since Universitatea Craiova in 1983. It was another tight encounter, largely bereft of chances. Rapid turned up the heat towards the end but they couldn't get the breakthrough. It ended 0-0, and Steaua's fans celebrated as if the UEFA Cup was already theirs.

Basel entertained Middlesbrough on a night of driving rain at the St. Jakob Park The Swiss side took a firm grip on the tie with two goals at the end of the first half. Boro keeper Mark Schwarzer was deceived by a speculative bouncing shot from the competition's top scorer Matías Delgado for the first, and it was the Argentine schemer whose brilliant pass set up David Degen for a second just a couple of minutes later. Boro offered little in response after the interval other than a late header from Ugo Ehiogu (a replacement for injured skipper Gareth Southgate) that was grabbed on the goal-line by Pascal Zuberbühler.

Barnstorming Boro

The Swiss international keeper was to have a far busier night at the Riverside the following week. The tie looked over when Basel striker Eduardo rifled the ball home to make the aggregate score 3-0 midway through the first half. Boro now needed four goals to stay in the competition. Mark Viduka made it 1-1 soon afterwards, but when Yakubu was denied by Zuberbühler's fine one-handed save just before the interval, any chance of a comeback looked to have gone. English teams are renowned for their fighting spirit, however, and in the second half Middlesbrough threw everything they had at Basel. Viduka scored an excellent second goal on 57 minutes, sliding in with his left after rounding the keeper. Then, shortly after the Swiss had been

UEFA Cup 2005/2006

reduced to ten men following Swedish defender Daniel Majstorovic's red card, Jimmy Floyd Hasselbaink smashed in an unstoppable right-foot drive to make it 3-1. Now it really was game on. The crowd roared Boro forward in the last ten minutes and finally got their reward when substitute Massimo Maccarone squeezed in a shot off Zuberbühler at the near post. It was an incredibly exciting finish. There was even time for Basel to get forward and almost score themselves, but Schwarzer denied Delgado with a crucial save. Moments later the final whistle sounded and Boro's amazing comeback was complete.

While Steaua and Boro had to live on their nerves, progress into the semi-finals was rather more serene for Schalke and Sevilla.

The Germans profited from an outrageous decision by English referee Mike Riley in the first leg of their tie with Levski Sofia. The Bulgarians, looking to record a seventh straight home win, took the lead with a brilliant individual goal from Daniel Borimirov after just six minutes and, with an excited crowd behind them, were comfortably in control. But ten minutes before half-time Levski's French striker Cédric Bardon was shown a second yellow card for a supposed foul on Schalke's Georgian international Levan Kobiashvili when he clearly didn't touch him. It was a terrible decision and it completely changed the course of the game. After the interval Schalke exploited their one-man advantage to the full, scoring three goals without reply, with Brazilian playmaker Lincoln scoring one – a brilliant curling shot – and setting up the other two. The second leg, in Gelsenkirchen, was largely rendered irrelevant by Schalke's 3-1 win. Levski gallantly took the lead, with Emil Angelov's fifth goal of the competition, but once again it was Lincoln, with another splendid goal, who delivered for Schalke in their time of need.

Sevilla also effectively won their tie with Zenit St. Petersburg in the first leg. Two goals from the lively Javier Saviola – his fifth and sixth of the competition – and a crucial last-minute strike from Adriano helped Juande Ramos's side to a decisive 4-1 victory at the Estádio Sánchez Pizjuán. With Zenit reduced to nine men at the end after the expulsions of Norwegian defender Erik Hagen and star striker Andrei Arshavin, any hopes of a Russian comeback in the city formerly known as Leningrad appeared to be compromised.

Zenit had beaten Sevilla 2-1 at home in a second round group game, but now they had to win by a much greater margin. Zenit's excuse for a pitch (brown, bare and stodgy), allied to the falling snow,

Javier Saviola – the Argentine striker set Sevilla on the road to victory against Zenit

might have been considered as advantageous, but Sevilla were making their third trip to Russia and were suitably prepared. Zenit dominated the first half but had to wait until early in the second before their new signing from Korea, Hyun Young-min, put them 1-0 up. The next goal, however, went to the Spaniards – set up on the counter-attack by full-back Daniel Alves, scored by substitute Kepa – and although the goalscorer was immediately sent off, Zenit also went down to ten men shortly afterwards when Croatian defender Ivica Krizanac was red-carded for a scything challenge on Sevilla's Italian midfielder Enzo Maresca. Sevilla should have won the game but Daniel Alves had a penalty (which he had earned himself) brilliantly saved by Vyacheslav Malafeyev. Not that it was remotely consequential. With their 5-2 lead, Sevilla were safely through to the last four.

SEMI-FINALS

The two-legged semi-finals, played, as in the previous three knockout rounds, on successive weeks, may have been lacking in glamour compared to the Champions League, but they

UEFA Cup 2005/2006

would be just as keenly contested.

Schalke, the only former UEFA Cup winners still in contention, were expected to win their home leg against Sevilla, but a defiant display of goalkeeping from Andrés Palop kept the German attackers at bay. With playmaker Lincoln and German international striker Kevin Kuranyi surprisingly demoted to the bench by Schalke boss Mirko Slomka, Sevilla's task was apparently made easier. Certainly, Schalke were much improved after the pair's introduction in the second half, and it was from a Lincoln corner, powerfully headed goalwards by his compatriot Marcelo Bordon, that Palop made the best of his many saves seven minutes from time.

It was Schalke keeper Frank Rost's turn to steal the limelight the following week in Seville. Again there was nothing to choose between two evenly-matched teams. Schalke only occasionally threatened to score the goal that would leave Sevilla needing to score twice, but Rost was frequently called into action and ensured the game went into extra-time with a fine one-handed save to deny Javier Saviola. Something special was needed to end the stalemate, and 11 minutes into extra-time the home side found an unlikely hero in substitute Antonio Puerta, who curled a superb left-foot shot past Rost and into the far corner. It was the only goal of the tie and probably the most important in Sevilla's history as it propelled them into their first European final.

Middlesbrough travelled to Romania to play Steaua Bucharest without injured duo Gareth Southgate and Mark Viduka and the suspended Chris Riggott. There was a makeshift look to their defence, and Steaua's Nicolae Dica found a way through it on 30 minutes, turning adroitly in a crowded penalty area before rifling an excellent shot high and wide of Mark Schwarzer. As in Basle a few weeks earlier, Boro rarely threatened to score. Even after going a goal down, their objective seemed to be one of containment. By the end of the game, after Dica and full-back Petre Marin had spurned chances to stretch Steaua's advantage, the final scoreline of 1-0 flattered the visitors.

In between the two legs Middlesbrough were beaten in the semi-final of the FA Cup by West Ham, with goalkeeper Schwarzer adding to their woes by fracturing a cheekbone. Now the UEFA Cup was the only silverware in sight for Steve McClaren's team. For the first time during their European run the Riverside was sold out. The game began in an atmosphere of cheery optimism, but midway through the half a dark cloud of gloom had

Schalke keeper Frank Rost – finally beaten in extra-time

descended on the stadium. Two goals from Steaua, both the result of handling errors from Schwarzer's deputy Brad Jones, appeared to have secured the Romanians' place in the Eindhoven final.

No way back?

Steaua had not lost any of their previous away fixtures, winning and drawing three apiece and conceding just two goals in the process. Now, thanks to Dica and defender Dorin Goian, they were 2-0 up. There seemed no possible way back for Middlesbrough – not least because with a quarter of the game gone they hadn't created a single chance.

But with Massimo Maccarone, the match-winning hero against Basel, introduced early as a replacement for injured skipper Gareth Southgate, there was suddenly hope. With almost his first touch the Italian smashed in a right-foot cross-shot to make it 2-1. But with Mark Viduka having two efforts saved by Carlos before half-time, Boro began the second period, as against Basel, requiring three further goals to win the tie.

The second half was one-way traffic. Steaua, understandably, were intent only on defending

UEFA Cup 2005/2006

their lead, but the more Middlesbrough attacked, the more edgy the Romanians became. On 64 minutes a superb left-wing cross by Stewart Downing was headed in by Viduka. 2-2. Fábio Rochemback then fizzed a shot over the bar, and soon afterwards Boro were ahead on the night, defender Riggott turning the ball in from close range after Downing's shot had been parried by the increasingly desperate Carlos.

It was attack versus defence from now on as the home side sought a second miraculous comeback. With George Boateng driving Boro on from midfield and Downing looking a threat whenever he gained possession on the left, the home side pressed forward ceaselessly. Time appeared to be running out, but then Downing whipped over another delicious cross from the left and there, waiting at the far post to head the ball joyously into the net, was…Maccarone. Incredibly, the Italian had done it again. History had repeated itself. It was Basel all over again. There was absolute bedlam in the stands. The Romanians tried to rouse themselves and, like the Swiss before them, so very nearly scored. But time was on Boro's side. Slovakian referee Lubos Michel blew his whistle and the Riverside Stadium erupted in joy. For the second time in three weeks the Middlesbrough supporters had witnessed a footballing miracle. Next stop Eindhoven.

FINAL

With Arsenal and Barcelona set to face each other in the Champions League final a week later, Middlesbrough against Sevilla in Einhoven was inevitably billed as England v Spain Part 1. More specifically, it was Teesside against Andalusia, a contest between two provincial clubs who had never previously reached a European final, nor indeed ever come close.

It was a particularly poignant occasion for Middlesbrough manager Steve McClaren. It was his 250th and final game in charge before he moved on to become the head coach of England – a position to which he had been appointed only six days earlier. McClaren's opposite number, Juande Ramos, had no such lofty pretensions. His only concern was with steering Sevilla to their first major trophy success in 58 years.

After all the high drama of their victories over Basel and Steaua, Middlesbrough should have been full of confidence. But they began nervously with lots of misplaced passes, and before long Sevilla had taken a stranglehold on the match. All the action was at the Boro end. Mark Schwarzer

SEMI-FINAL RESULTS

(20/4/06 & 27/4/06)

FC Schalke 04 0, Sevilla FC 0
Sevilla FC 1 *(Puerta 101)*, FC Schalke 04 0 *(aet)*
(Sevilla FC 1-0)

Steaua Bucuresti 1 *(Dica 30)*, Middlesbrough 0
Middlesbrough 4 *(Maccarone 33, 89, Viduka 64, Riggott 73)*, Steaua Bucuresti 2 *(Dica 16, Goian 24)*
(Middlesbrough 4-3)

wearing a transparent mask to protect his broken cheekbone, easily saved a low shot from Luís Fabiano, but within a couple of minutes the Brazilian striker had beaten the Australian goalkeeper, meeting Daniel Alves's perfectly flighted cross with a superb glancing header that entered the net off the inside of the far post.

Sevilla thoroughly deserved their half-time lead, but seven minutes into the second period Middlesbrough were presented with a glorious chance to equalise. Chris Riggott, who had allowed Luís Fabiano to get away from him for Sevilla's goal, looked to have made amends when he headed the

Boro boss Steve McClaren – an unhappy last night in Eindhoven

UEFA Cup 2005/2006

ball across goal right into the path of Mark Viduka. But although the Australian connected well with his shot, he fired it straight at Andrés Palop, who made a point-blank save with his legs. The game started to open up, but with Boro's Dutchmen George Boateng and Jimmy Floyd Hasselbaink looking completely out of sorts on their native soil and half-fit captain Gareth Southgate really struggling at the back, there was no flow or stealth to the Premiership side's game. With four strikers on the field, McClaren had decided to go for broke. If Sevilla skipper Javi Navarro had been punished with a penalty kick for his clear barge on Viduka in the 76th minute, the gamble might well have paid off. But referee Herbert Fandel waved play on and, to add insult to injury, Sevilla promptly moved the ball up to the other end of the field and made it 2-0.

Lethal counter-attack

Youngster Jesús Navas led the counter-attack, Frédérick Kanoute (a half-time substitute for the ineffective Javier Saviola) forced a save from Schwarzer, but the ball fell to Enzo Maresco, and the young Italian midfielder gleefully drove the ball across the line from close range.

The game was now up for Boro. Sevilla, though, were in no mood for mercy. Six minutes later Maresca grabbed another goal, bouncing in a left-foot shot just beyond Schwarzer's reach. There was still time for a fourth, clipped in by Kanouté after the overworked Aussie keeper could only parry another Maresca shot. Middlesbrough had disintegrated. Sevilla were in seventh heaven. With 15 minutes to go the match had still been in the balance. Now the Spanish side had posted the biggest winning margin in the short history of one-off UEFA Cup finals and, more importantly, had a trophy to show off for the first time since their Spanish Cup triumph of 1948.

As captain Javi Navarro lifted the Cup, Sevilla became the competition's 23rd different winner and only the third from Spain (after Real Madrid and Valencia). Their victory was uncontested. All of the best players on the field – Daniel Alves, Jesús Navas, Maresca and Luís Fabiano – wore white. It was a great night for Juande Ramos and his team but a desperately disappointing way for McClaren to take his leave. Middlesbrough had enjoyed a fantastic run to the final, but on the night it really mattered, they had been second best – something which, to the club's considerable credit, the players, manager and chairman duly, and sportingly, acknowledged after the game.

A big smile from Sevilla skipper Javi Navarro as he lifts the UEFA Cup

FINAL

(10/5/06)
Philips Stadion, Eindhoven
SEVILLA FC 4 *(Luís Fabiano 26, Maresca 78, 84, Kanouté 89)*
MIDDLESBROUGH 0
Referee – Fandel (GER)
SEVILLA FC – *Palop, Alves, Javi Navarro, Escudé, David, Jesús Navas, Martí, Maresca, Adriano (Puerta 86), Saviola (Kanouté 46), Luís Fabiano (Renato 72).*
MIDDLESBROUGH – *Schwarzer, Parnaby, Riggott, Southgate, Queudrue (Yakubu 70), Morrison (Maccarone 46), Boateng, Rochemback, Downing, Viduka (Cattermole 85), Hasselbaink.*

TOP GOALSCORERS

7	Matias DELGADO (FC Basel)
6	Frédéric KANOUTE (Sevilla FC)
	Javier SAVIOLA (Sevilla FC)
	Mark VIDUKA (Middlesbrough)
	Nicolae DICA (Steaua Bucuresti)
	Alexandr KERZHAKOV (Zenit Sankt-Peterburg)
5	Massimo MACCARONE (Middlesbrough)
	Dorin GOIAN (Steaua Bucuresti)
	Victoras IACOB (Steaua Bucuresti)
	Mihai BUGA (Rapid Bucuresti)
	Emil ANGELOV (Levski Sofia)
	BRANDÃO (Shakhtar Donetsk)
	Rafael VAN DER VAART (Hamburger SV)
	Daniel COUSIN (RC Lens)
	Dmitriy LOSKOV (Lokomotiv Moskva)
	Karel PITÁK (SK Slavia Praha)

Ballon d'Or/International Cups

2005 BALLON D'OR

Pts	Player
225	**RONALDINHO (BRA) – FC Barcelona**
148	Frank LAMPARD (ENG) – Chelsea
142	Steven GERRARD (ENG) – Liverpool
41	Thierry HENRY (FRA) – Arsenal
33	Andriy SHEVCHENKO (UKR) – Milan
23	Paolo MALDINI (ITA) – Milan
22	ADRIANO (BRA) – Internazionale
21	Zlatan IBRAHIMOVIC (SWE) – Juventus
19	KAKÁ (BRA) – Milan
18	Samuel ETO'O (CMR) – FC Barcelona
	John TERRY (ENG) – Chelsea
15	JUNINHO Pernambucano (BRA) – Olympique Lyonnais
8	Claude MAKELELE (FRA) – Chelsea
7	Michael BALLACK (GER) – FC Bayern München
	Petr CECH (CZE) – Chelsea
	Didier DROGBA (CIV) – Chelsea
	Juan Román RIQUELME (ARG) – Villarreal CF
5	Zinedine ZIDANE (FRA) – Real Madrid
4	Gianluigi BUFFON (ITA) – Juventus
3	Jamie CARRAGHER (ENG) – Liverpool
	CRISTIANO RONALDO (POR) – Manchester United
2	Michael ESSIEN (GHA) – Olympique Lyonnais & Chelsea
1	LUIS GARCÍA (ESP) – Liverpool
	Pavel NEDVED (CZE) – Juventus

The following nominees received no votes:
David BECKHAM (ENG) – Real Madrid
Mauro CAMORANESI (ITA) – Juventus
Fabio CANNAVARO (ITA) – Juventus
Grégory COUPET (FRA) – Olympique Lyonnais
CRIS (BRA) – Olympique Lyonnais
DECO (POR) – FC Barcelona
DIDA (BRA) – Milan
ÉMERSON (BRA) – Juventus
Luís FIGO (POR) – Real Madrid & Internazionale
Diego FORLÁN (URU) – Villarreal CF
Roy MAKAAY (HOL) – FC Bayern München
Michael OWEN (ENG) – Real Madrid & Newcastle United
PARK Ji-sung (KOR) – PSV & Manchester United
Andrea PIRLO (ITA) – Milan
RAÚL (ESP) – Real Madrid
Arjen ROBBEN (HOL) – Chelsea
ROBERTO CARLOS (BRA) – Real Madrid
ROBINHO (BRA) – Real Madrid
RONALDO (BRA) – Real Madrid
Wayne ROONEY (ENG) – Manchester United
Lilian THURAM (FRA) – Juventus
David TREZEGUET (FRA) – Juventus
Mark VAN BOMMEL (HOL) – PSV & FC Barcelona
Ruud VN NISTELROOY (HOL) – Manchester United
Patrick VIEIRA (FRA) – Arsenal & Juventus
XAVI (ESP) – FC Barcelona

2005 CLUB WORLD CHAMPIONSHIP

FIRST ROUND
(11/12/05)
Al Ittihad 1 *(Noor 78)*, Al Ahly 0
(12/12/05)
Saprissa 1 *(Bolaños 47)*, Sydney FC 0

SEMI-FINALS
(14/12/05)
FC São Paulo 3 *(Amoroso 16, 47, Rogério Ceni 57p)*, Al Ittihad 2 *(Noor 33, Al Montashari 68)*
(15/12/05)
Liverpool 3 *(Crouch 3, 58, Gerrard 32)*, Saprissa 0

FIFTH-PLACE PLAY-OFF
(16/12/05)
Sydney FC 2 *(Yorke 35, Carney 66)*, Al Ahly 1 *(Moteab 45)*

THIRD-PLACE PLAY-OFF
(18/12/05)
Saprissa 3 *(Saborio 13, 85p, Gómez 89)*, Al Ittihad 2 *(Kallon 28, Job 53p)*

FINAL
(18/12/05)
International Stadium, Yokohama
FC SÃO PAULO 1 *(Mineiro 27)*
LIVERPOOL 0
Referee – *Archundia (MEX)*
FC SÃO PAULO – Rogério Ceni, Cicinho, Fábio Santos, Edcarlos, Lugano, Júnior, Mineiro, Josué, Danilo, Amoroso, Aloísio *(Grafite 75)*.
LIVERPOOL – Reina, Finnan, Carragher, Hyypiä, Warnock *(Riise 79)*, Luis García, Gerrard, Sissoko *(Sinama-Pongolle 79)*, Xabi Alonso, Kewell, Morientes *(Crouch 85)*.

2005 UEFA SUPER CUP

(26/8/05)
Stade Louis II, Monaco
LIVERPOOL 3 *(Cissé 82, 103, Luis García 109)*
CSKA MOSKVA 1 *(Daniel Carvalho 28)*
(aet)
Referee – *Temmink (HOL)*
LIVERPOOL – Reina, Josemi, Hyypiä, Carragher, Riise *(Cissé 79)*, Finnan *(Sinama-Pongolle 55)*, Hamann, Xabi Alonso *(Sissoko 71)*, Zenden, Luis García, Morientes.
CSKA MOSKVA – Akinfeev, Berezutskiy V., Odiah *(Gusev 90)*, Ignashevich, Berezutskiy A., Zhirkov *(Semberas 66)*, Aldonin, Pahimic, Krasic *(Dudu Cearense 83)*, Daniel Carvalho, Vágner Love.

Section 2

Nation-by-Nation

Welcome to the Main Section of the Book.

Here you will find separate chapters, alphabetically arranged, on each of the 52 UEFA-affiliated countries.

Included for each Nation is a narrative Review of the Season accompanied by the following statistics:

NATIONAL TEAM RESULTS

Information on all internationals played between July 1, 2005 and July 9, 2006, including Dates, Opponents, Venues, Results and Scorers

Key: H = home; A = away; N = Neutral; og = own-goal; (p) = penalty; (WCQ) = World Cup Qualifier; (WCF) = World Cup Finals

NATIONAL TEAM APPEARANCES

Details of the participants in the above matches (coaches and players), including, for each player, Name, Date of Birth, Club, match-by-match Appearances, and all-time Caps and Goals

Opponents are ranged across the top and abbreviated with the appropriate three-letter code – three capital letters indicate a competitive match

Foreign clubs are indicated with the appropriate three-letter code

Key to Appearances: G = Goalkeeper; D = Defender; M = Midfielder; A = Attacker; s = substitute
The number appearing after a letter indicates the time of a substitution

EUROPEAN CUPS

Full details, including line-ups, of all matches played by the country's clubs in the UEFA Champions League and the UEFA Cup

FINAL LEAGUE TABLE

The final classification of the country's top division, including Home, Away and Total records

Key: Pld = Played; W = Won; D = Drawn; L = Lost; F = Goals For; A = Goals Against; Pts = Points
.... = play-off line
- - - - - - - - = relegation line

TOP GOALSCORERS

A list of the top ten goalscorers (with clubs) in the country's top division

LEAGUE RESULTS/ SCORERS

Information on each top-division club's League fixtures, including Dates, Opponents, Results and Scorers. Also included are all Coaches (Managers) used during the season and, in the case of new ones, the dates of their appointments

Key: h = home; a = away; og = own-goal; (p) = penalty; (w/o) = walkover

LEAGUE APPEARANCES/ GOALS

Information on all the players used by each top-division club in the League campaign, including Name, Nationality, Playing Position, Appearances and Goals. Where applicable, and known, Squad Numbers are also included

Nation-by-Nation

Key to headings:

No = Squad (shirt) number

Name = Full name (these are listed alphabetically)

Nat = Nationality (home-based unless indicated with three-letter code)

Pos = Playing Position. Key: G = Goalkeeper; D = Defender; M = Midfielder; A = Attacker

Aps = Number of Appearances in Starting XI

(s) = Number of Appearances as a Substitute

Gls = Number of Goals scored

DOMESTIC CUP

Results from the country's main domestic knockout competition, beginning with the round at which the top-division teams (or some of them) enter. Goalscorers/times are indicated in the quarter-finals and semi-finals, with full details, including line-ups, for the Final

SECOND LEVEL FINAL TABLE

The final classification of the country's second level (i.e. feeder league to the top division) table(s). Play-off details, where applicable, are also indicated

Key: Pld = Played; W = Won; D = Drawn; L = Lost; F = Goals For; A = Goals Against; Pts = Points

– – – – – – – – = promotion line (at the top)

• • • • • • • • • • • • • • • = play-off line

– – – – – – – – = relegation line (at the bottom)

N.B. A key to all the three-letter codes can be found on pages 10/11

INDEX

Summary of European Cup Qualifiers 2006/07	128
Summary of Relegated/Promoted Clubs	130
Albania	132
Andorra	142
Armenia	145
Austria	153
Azerbaijan	165
Belarus	176
Belgium	188
Bosnia-Herzegovina	204
Bulgaria	217
Croatia	231
Cyprus	244
Czech Republic	255
Denmark	270
England	282
Estonia	305
Faroe Islands	315
Finland	323
France	335
Georgia	356
Germany	370
Greece	389
Holland	403
Hungary	421
Iceland	434
Israel	442
Italy	453
Kazakhstan	475
Latvia	486
Liechtenstein	494
Lithuania	496
Luxembourg	506
Macedonia	516
Malta	527
Moldova	535
Northern Ireland	543
Norway	556
Poland	569
Portugal	584
Republic of Ireland	601
Romania	612
Russia	627
San Marino	641
Scotland	644
Serbia & Montenegro	657
Slovakia	671
Slovenia	682
Spain	692
Sweden	713
Switzerland	725
Turkey	737
Ukraine	753
Wales	768

European Cup Qualifiers 2006/07

Country	UEFA Champions League	UEFA Cup
Albania	Elbasani*	SK Tirana+, Dinamo Tiranë
Andorra		Ranger's FC*
Armenia	Pyunik Yerevan*	Mika Ashtarak+, Banants Yerevan
Austria	FK Austria Wien*+, Red Bull Salzburg	SV Mattersburg, FC Superfund Pasching, (SV Ried)
Azerbaijan	FK Baki*	Qarabag Agdam+, Karvan Yevlax
Belarus	Shakhter Soligorsk*	FC BATE Borisov+, Dinamo Minsk
Belgium	RSC Anderlecht*, R Standard Liège	SV Zulte-Waregem+, Club Brugge KV, [KSV Roeselare]
Bosnia-Herzegovina	Siroki Brijeg*	Orasje+, Sarajevo
Bulgaria	Levski Sofia*	CSKA Sofia+, Litex Lovech, Lokomotiv Sofia
Croatia	Dinamo Zagreb*	Rijeka+, Varteks Varazdin
Cyprus	Apollon*	APOEL+, Omonia, (Ethnikos)
Czech Republic	FC Slovan Liberec*, FK Mladá Boleslav	AC Sparta Praha+, SK Slavia Praha
Denmark	FC København*	Randers FC+, Brøndby IF, (OB)
England	Chelsea*, Manchester United, Liverpool+, Arsenal	West Ham United, Tottenham Hotspur, Blackburn Rovers, (Newcastle United)
Estonia	FC TVMK Tallinn*+	FC Flora Tallinn, FC Levadia Tallinn
Faroe Islands	B36*	GÍ+, Skála
Finland	MyPa*	FC Haka+, HJK
France	Olympique Lyonnais*, Girondins de Bordeaux, Lille OSC	Paris Saint-Germain+, AS Nancy-Lorraine, RC Lens, (Olympique Marseille), (AJ Auxerre)
Georgia	Sioni Bolnisi*	Ameri Tbilisi+, WIT Georgia Tbilisi
Germany	FC Bayern München*+, SV Werder Bremen, Hamburger SV	Eintracht Frankfurt, FC Schalke 04, Bayer 04 Leverkusen, (Hertha BSC Berlin)
Greece	Olympiakos*+, AEK	Panathinaikos, Iraklis, Xanthi, Atromitos
Holland	PSV*, Ajax+	FC Groningen, AZ, Feyenoord, SC Heerenveen, (FC Twente)

Hungary	Debreceni VSC*	FC Fehérvár+, Újpest FC
Iceland	FH*	Valur+, ÍA
Israel	Maccabi Haifa*	Hapoel Tel Aviv+, Beitar Jerusalem, Bnei Yehuda Tel Aviv
Italy	Internazionale*+, Roma, Milan, Chievo	Palermo, Livorno, Parma
Kazakhstan	Aktobe Lento*	Tobol Kostanai, Kairat Almaty
Latvia	Metalurgs Liepaja*	FK Ventspils+, Skonto Riga
Liechtenstein		FC Vaduz+
Lithuania	Ekranas Panevezys*	FBK Kaunas+, Suduva Marijampole
Luxembourg	F91 Dudelange*+	Jeunesse Esch, Etzella Ettelbruck
Macedonia	Rabotnicki Kometal Skopje*	Makedonija GP Skopje+, Vardar Skopje
Malta	Birkirkara*	Hibernians+, Sliema Wanderers
Moldova	Sheriff Tiraspol*+	Nistru Otaci, Zimbru Chisinau
Northern Ireland	Linfield*+	Glentoran, Portadown
Norway	Vålerenga Fotball*	Molde FK+, IK Start, FC Lyn Oslo, [SK Brann]
Poland	Legia Warszawa*	Wisla Plock+, Wisla Krakow, Zaglebie Lubin
Portugal	FC Porto*+, Sporting CP, SL Benfica	Vitória Setúbal, Sporting Braga, CD Nacional
Republic of Ireland	Cork City*	Drogheda United+, Derry City
Romania	Steaua Bucuresti*	Rapid Bucuresti+, Dinamo Bucuresti
Russia	CSKA Moskva*+, Spartak Moskva	Lokomotiv Moskva, Rubin Kazan
San Marino		Murata
Scotland	Celtic*, Heart of Midlothian+	Gretna, Rangers
Serbia	Crvena Zvezda Beograd*+	OFK Beograd, Partizan Beograd, Hajduk Rodic MB Kula
Slovakia	MFK Ruzomberok*+	Spartak Trnava, Artmedia Bratislava
Slovenia	ND Gorica*	Koper+, Domzale, (Maribor)
Spain	FC Barcelona*, Real Madrid, Valencia CF, CA Osasuna	Sevilla FC, RCD Espanyol+, RC Celta
Sweden	Djurgårdens IF*+	Åtvidabergs FF, IFK Göteborg, [Gefle IF]
Switzerland	FC Zürich*	FC Sion+, FC Basel, BSC Young Boys Bern, (Grasshopper-Club Zuurich)
Turkey	Galatasaray*, Fenerbahçe	Besiktas+, Trabzonspor, (Kayserispor)
Ukraine	Shakhtar Donetsk*, Dynamo Kyiv+	Metalurg Zaporizhzhya, Chornomorets Odesa
Wales	The New Saints*	Rhyl+, Llanelli

Key: * Champions
+ Cup winners
Teams in brackets – e.g. (SV Ried) – InterToto Cup qualifiers
Teams in square brackets – e.g. [KSV Roeselare] – Fair Play qualifiers

Relegated/Promoted Clubs 2005/06

Country	Relegated	Promoted
Albania	Lushnja, Skënderbeu Korçë	Flamurtari Vlorë, Apolonia Fier, Kastrioti Krujë, Luftëtari Gjirokastër
Andorra	UE Extremenya	FC Encamp
Armenia	Lernayin Artsakh Yerevan	Gandzasar Kapan
Austria	VfB Admira Wacker Mödling	SC Rheindorf Altach
Azerbaijan	MOIK Baki, Göyäzän Qazax	Gilan Xanlar, Simurq Zaqatala
Belarus	Zvezda-VA-BGU Minsk, Slaviya Mozyr	Belshina Bobruisk, Lokomotiv Vitebsk
Belgium	RAA La Louvière	RAEC Mons
Bosnia-Herzegovina	Buducnost Banovici, Travnik	Velez Mostar, Borac Banja Luka
Bulgaria	Naftex Bourgas, Pirin 1922 Blagoevgrad	Spartak Varna, Rilski sportist Samokov, Conegliano German
Croatia	Inter Zapresic	Sibenik
Cyprus	ENTHOI, APEP, APOP/Kinyras	AEP, Aris, Ayia Napa
Czech Republic	FK Chmel Blsany, FC Vysocina Jihlava	SK Kladno, Dynamo Ceské Budejovice
Denmark	AGF, SønderjyskE	Vejle BK, Randers FC
England	Sunderland, West Bromwich Albion, Birmingham City	Reading, Sheffield United, Watford
Estonia	JK Dünamo Tallinn, FC Kuressaare	JK Vaprus Pärnu, FC Ajax Lasnamäe
Faroe Islands	TB	B68
Finland	TP-47, RoPS	FC Honka, VPS
France	FC Metz, AC Ajaccio, RC Strasbourg	Valenciennes FC, CS Sedan Ardennes, FC Lorient
Georgia	Spartaki Tbilisi, Dinamo Sokhumi Kolkheti 1913 Poti, FC Tbilisi, FC Tskhinvali	Chikhura Sachkhere, Merani Tbilisi, Olimpi Rustavi
Germany	MSV Duisburg, 1.FC Köln, 1.FC Kaiserslautern	VfL Bochum, Alemannia Aachen, FC Energie Cottbus
Greece	Akratitos, Kallithea, Levadiakos	Kerkira, Ergotelis, Aris
Holland	RBC Roosendaal	Excelsior
Hungary	Lombard-Pápa TFC, Ferencváros	Dunakanyar-Vác FC, Paksi SE

Summary

Iceland	Thróttur, Fram	Breidablik, Víkingur
Israel	Hapoel Bnei Sakhnin, Hapoel Nazareth Ilit	Maccabi Herzliya, Hakoah Amidar Ramat Gan
Italy	Treviso, Lecce, Juventus	Atalanta, Catania, Torino
Kazakhstan	Bolat Temirtau, Zhetysu Taldykorgan	Energetik Pavlodar, Kaisar Kyzylorda
Latvia	Venta Kuldiga, Olimps Riga	Dizvanagi Rezekne, Ditton Daugavpils
Lithuania	–	–
Luxembourg	US Rumelange, Avenir Beggen	FC Differdange 03, Progrès Niedercorn, FC Mondercange, FC Mamer 32
Macedonia	Belasica Strumica, Cementarnica 55 Skopje	Peliser Bitola, Napredak Kicevo
Malta	Hamrun Spartans, Mosta	St. George's, Marsa
Moldova	–	Olimpia Balti, Iskra-Stali Ribnita
Northern Ireland	Ards, Institute	Crusaders, Donega Celtic
Norway	FK Bodø/Glimt, Aalesunds FK	Stabaek Fotball, Sandefjord Fotball
Poland	Polonia Warszawa	Widzew Lodz, Lodzki KS
Portugal	FC Penafiel, Vitória Guimarães, Rio Ave FC, CF Os Belenenses	SC Beira Mar, Desportivo Aves
Republic of Ireland	Finn Harps, Shamrock Rovers	Sligo Rovers, Dublin City
Romania	FCM Bacau, Sportul Studentesc Bucuresti	Cehlaul Piatra Neamt, Universitatea Craiova, UTA Arad, Unirea Urziceni
Russia	Terek Groznyi, Alania Vladikavkaz	Luch-Energia Vladivostok, Spartak Nalchik
Scotland	Livingston	St. Mirren
Serbia	Jedinstvo Bijelo Polje, Obilic Beograd, Buducnost Podgorica, Rad Beograd, Habitpharm Ivanjica, Zeta Golubovci	Bezanija Beograd, Mladost Apatin
Slovakia	Matador Púchov	MFK Kosice, Slovan Bratislava, FC Senec
Slovenia	Rudar Velenje	Factor Ljubljana
Spain	Málaga CF, Cádiz CF, Deportivo Alavés	RC Recreativo, Club Gimnàstic, Levante UD
Sweden	Assyriska FF, GIF Sundsvall, Landskrona BoIS	AIK, Östers IF, GAIS
Switzerland	Yverdon-Sport FC, Neuchâtel Xamax FC	FC Luzern, FC Sion
Turkey	Diyarbakirspor, Samsunspor, Malatyaspor	Bursaspor, Antalyaspor, Sakaryaspor
Ukraine	Zakarpattya Uzhgorod, Volyn Lutsk	Zorya Lugansk, Karpaty Lviv
Wales	Grange Harlequins	–

Albania

Seamless transition for Elbasani

Runners-up one year, champions the next.

On the face of it, there is a progressive logic to Elbsani's 2005/06 Albanian title triumph. The truth, however, is that the club's first championship win for 22 years took everybody by surprise.

Elbasani had impressed everyone by finishing second to Tirana in 2004/05. But their hopes of going one better seemed forlorn when they lost the architect of that achievement, coach Artan Bushati (to the national Under-21 team), as well as several key players, notably newly-capped defenders Armend Dallku and Teufik Osmani and captain Julian Ahmataj.

Another key defender, Albanian international Nevil Dede, looked set to return to his former club Tirana, but there was a late hitch in the deal so he decided to stay in Elbasan and skipper a team newly led by inexperienced coach Ilir Daja, a former Dinamo Tirana star whose career had been cut short by serious injury. With Daja and Dede at the helm Elbasani began the season strongly and never relented. They led the 36-match campaign almost without interruption, continually holding off the challenge from the capital and ultimately completing the season with a handsome 11-point victory margin.

There was nothing spectacular about Elbasani's style of play. Defensive rigour and tactical nous were their two chief attributes. Also crucial was their invincibility against Tirana, the champions for the previous three seasons and still the most technically gifted team in the land. For the second successive season Elbasani were unbeaten in all four matches against Tirana. Furthermore, they won three of them, the most memorable victory coming in the capital on May 6 when an ill-tempered match, held up for ten minutes by the over-excited visiting fans, was decided 3-2 in Elbasani's favour thanks to a winning penalty from…goalkeeper Elvis Kotorri. Elbasani had needed only a point to secure the title but they got all three, the first two goals coming from Skerdi Bejzade (the club's runaway leading scorer) and skipper Dede (the next highest marksman, with five goals).

Looking for Mr Right

Tirana's title hopes were scuppered by their poor results against Elbasani, but off the field they did themselves no favours. Despite their sound finances a lack of harmony in the boardroom led to four different coaches being used. Mr Right finally arrived when Mirel Josa was brought in from Skënderbeu Korçë. He led the club to seven wins in his first eight games (the only stain was defeat in Elbasan) before Skënderbeu – of all clubs – halted him and his team in their tracks. Skënderbeu had endured a dreadful run following Josa's departure and would eventually be relegated after a play-off defeat against Teuta Durrës, but for one match only they raised their game and effectively released Tirana's grip on the title.

NATIONAL TEAM RESULTS 2005/06

17/8/05	Azerbaijan		H	Tirana	2-1 Bushi (37), Cana (72)
3/9/05	Kazakhstan (WCQ)	H	Tirana	2-1 Myrtaj (54), Bogdani (56)
8/10/05	Ukraine (WCQ)	A	Dnipropetrovsk	2-2 Bogdani (75, 82)
12/10/05	Turkey (WCQ)		H	Tirana	0-1
1/3/06	Lithuania		H	Tirana	1-2 Aliaj (32p)
22/3/06	Georgia		H	Tirana	0-0

Albania

NATIONAL TEAM APPEARANCES 2005/06

Coach – Hans-Peter BRIEGEL (GER)			Azb	KAZ	UKR	TUR	Lit	Geo	Caps	Goals
Isli HIDI	15/10/80	SK Tirana	G						2	-
Tefik OSMANI	17/4/84	Metalurg Zaporizhzhya (UKR)	D						6	-
Elvis SINA	14/11/78	SK Tirana	D80						4	-
Elvin BEQIRI	27/9/80	Metalurg Donetsk (UKR)	D	D	D	D				
		/Maccabi Tel Aviv (ISR)						D	29	-
Besnik HASI	29/11/71	RSC Anderlecht (BEL)	D	D	M	M				
		/KSC Lokeren OV (BEL)						D	38	1
Lorik CANA	27/7/83	Paris Saint-Germain (FRA)	M							
		/Olympique Marseille (FRA)		M	M	M	M63		20	1
Edvin MURATI	12/11/75	Iraklis (GRE)	M46	M	s86	s50	M69		45	4
Bledi SHKËMBI	13/8/79	Metalurg Zaporizhzhya (UKR)	M46						13	-
Altin LALA	18/2/74	Hannover 96 (GER)	M46	M	M	M	M	M	49	2
Alban BUSHI	24/8/73	Levadiakos (GRE)	A46	s85			A46		59	14
Edmond KAPLLANI	31/7/82	Karlsruher SC (GER)	A46	s89	s70	s73		s46	9	-
Ervin SKELA	17/11/76	1.FC Kaiserslautern (GER)	s46	M	M	M	s46	M46	38	6
Altin HAXHI	7/6/75	Anorthosis (CYP)	s46	M46	M86	M50		M75	52	2
Redi JUPI	30/4/74	Diyarbakirspor (TUR)	s46	M		s63		M	19	-
Florian MYRTAJ	15/9/76	Catanzaro (ITA)	s46	A89						
		/Perugia (ITA)						s46	25	3
Erjon BOGDANI	14/4/75	Siena (ITA)	s46	A85	A	A	s46	A82	30	5
Armend DALLKU	16/6/83	Vorskla Poltava (UKR)	s80		D	D63	s63	D	9	-
Ilion LIKA	17/5/80	Dinamo Tiranë		G	G	G		G	12	-
Ansi AGOLLI	11/10/82	Neuchâtel Xamax FC (SUI)	s46					s75	2	-
Ardian ALIAJ	24/9/76	Stade Brestois 29 (FRA)			D	D	D		25	8
Igli TARE	25/7/73	Lazio (ITA)			A70	A73	A46		63	9
Arjan BEQAJ	20/8/75	Ionikos (GRE)					G		18	-
Klodian DURO	21/12/77	SK Tirana					M	s46	34	1
Dorian BYLYKBASHI	8/8/80	Partizani Tiranë					M46		2	-
Endrit VRAPI	23/5/83	Elbasani					s69	D	2	-
Admir TELI	2/6/81	Vllaznia Shkodër						D46	1	-
Debatik CURRI	28/12/83	Vorskla Poltava (UKR)						M46	1	-
Bekim KASTRATI	25/3/79	Borussia Mönchengladbach (GER)						A46	1	-
Erjon XHAFA	31/5/82	Dinamo Tiranë						s46	1	-
Ardit BEQIRI	13/2/79	Partizani Tiranë						s46	12	-
Hamdi SALIHI	19/1/84	SK Tirana						s82	1	-

Albania

By way of compensation Josa did lead the Blue and Whites to victory in the Albanian Cup. Beaten on penalties in the previous year's final, Tirana redeemed themselves by taking the trophy with a 1-0 victory over Elbasani's semi-final conquerors Vllaznia Shkodër. Midfielder Klodian Duro scored the decisive goal from a free-kick midway through the second half.

Tirana's Cup win enabled city rivals Dinamo to qualify for the UEFA Cup. Although Dinamo lost their final league game – staged three days after the Cup final – 1-0 to relegation-threatened Teuta, Tirana did them another favour by holding Partizani to a 2-2 draw. A win would have enabled Partizani, and their ex-Tirana coach Sulejman Starova, to leapfrog Dinamo into third place, but early goals from Tirana's Hamdi Salihi (his 29th of the season) and Rezart Dabulla gave the home side too much to do. Apart from the acquisition of an InterToto place, Partizani's only satisfaction was the ten points they took from Elbasani.

Dinamo did well to finish third given all the administrative chaos at the club, which saw coaches being hired and fired every few weeks. They started the season with several Argentine players (brought in by coach Ramón Cabrera, sacked in pre-season after InterToto elimination) and ended it with a heavy Croatian influence (thanks to the mid-season reign of ex-Hajduk Split boss Ivan Katalinic).

Briegel bows out

Every club in the Kategoria Pare bar Elbasani switched coach at least once, and there was also a change for the national team in May following the Albanian FA's failure to agree a new deal with Hans-Peter Briegel. The German, three years in charge, had led the team to four victories in the World Cup qualifiers – an unprecedented achievement – but had nevertheless been widely criticised for not doing even better.

His replacement is 74-year-old Otto Baric, a vastly experienced Croatian who led his country to the finals of Euro 2004. Much of Baric's career has been spent in Austria, which of course is where half of Euro 2008 will be staged. Should he take Albania to those finals, it would undoubtedly be the greatest achievement of his long career – not least because with several stalwarts (Altin Lala, Igli Tare, Alban Bushi etc) now entering the twilight of their careers, the team is in urgent need of regeneration.

EUROPEAN CUPS 2005/06

UEFA CHAMPIONS LEAGUE

SK TIRANA
1st qualifying round ND GORICA (SLO)
A 0-2
Hidi, Sina, Dabulla, Pisha, Bulku E., Hajdari, Bakalli, Ahmataj, Rraklli, Muka, Salihi.
H 3-0 *Rraklli (38), Dabulla (42), Salihi (45)*
Hidi, Sina, Dabulla, Pisha, Bulku E., Muka, Hajdari, Ahmataj (Tafaj A. 85), Patushi (Bakalli 75), Salihi, Rraklli (Merkoçi 78).

2nd qualifying round CSKA SOFIA (BUL)
H 0-2
Hidi, Sina (Fagu 90), Dabulla, Pisha, Bulku E., Rraklli (Merkoçi 46), Muka, Salihi, Hajdari (Behari 70), Ahmataj, Patushi.
A 0-2
Hidi, Pisha, Behari, Dabulla, Bulku E., Rraklli, Salihi (Fagu 82), Sina, Ahmataj (Tafaj A. 63), Patushi, Merkoçi (Bakalli 58).

UEFA CUP

TEUTA DURRËS
1st qualifying round SIROKI BRIJEG (BOS)
H 3-1 *Mançaku (32, 58), Xhafa (48)*
Kapllani, Tetova, Zëre, Brahja, Kotja (Hodo 43), Sakaj (Kovac 88), Gjondeda, Babamusta, Mançaku, Xhafa, Xhihani (Curri 24).
A 0-3
Kapllani, Tetova, Zëre, Brahja, Kotja, Sakaj, Gjondeda (Xhai 65), Curri (Hodo 38), Mançaku, Xhafa, Xhihani (Hasho 72).

ELBASANI
1st qualifying round VARDAR SKOPJE (MAC)
H 1-1 *Dalipi K. (28)*
Kotorri, Dallku, Dede, Teli, Belisha, Osja, Merxha (Çapja 83), Bejzade, Asllani (Dalipi E. 83), Dalipi K., Kaçi (Nora 65).
A 0-0
Kotorri, Dede, Teli, Balisha, Osja, Merxha (Mehmetaj 89), Bejzade, Dalipi E., Dalipi K. (Memelli 70), Nora (Kaçi 70), Vrapi.

TOP GOALSCORERS 2005/06

29	Hamdi SALIHI (SK Tirana)
16	El Hadji GOUDJABI (Dinamo Tiranë)
15	Skerdi BEJZADE (Elbasani)
13	Vioresin SINANI (Vllaznia Shkodër)
12	Orjand ABAZAJ (Shkumbini Peqin)
10	Hervé FORTUNAT (Besa Kavajë)
9	Olgert STAFA (Shkumbini Peqin)
8	Arbër ABILALIAJ (Shkumbini Peqin)
	Migen MEMELLI (Skënderbeu Korçë)
7	Dorian BYLYKBASHI (Partizani Tiranë)
	Pavlin DHËMBI (Dinamo Tiranë/Partizani Tiranë)
	Bledar MANÇAKU (Teuta Durrës)
	Devi MUKA (SK Tirana)
	Emiliano VELIAJ (Besa Kavajë)

Albania

FINAL LEAGUE TABLE 2005/06

		Pld	Home					Away					Total					Pts
			W	D	L	F	A	W	D	L	F	A	W	D	L	F	A	
1	Elbasani	36	15	2	1	31	7	6	8	4	19	15	21	10	5	50	22	73
2	SK Tirana	36	11	5	2	31	15	6	6	6	23	18	17	11	8	54	33	62
3	Dinamo Tiranë	36	10	6	2	35	15	7	4	7	18	20	17	10	9	53	35	61
4	Partizani Tiranë	36	15	3	0	39	9	3	3	12	12	26	18	6	12	51	35	60
5	Besa Kavajë	36	10	2	6	29	15	3	5	10	20	27	13	7	16	49	42	46
6	Vllaznia Shkodër	36	10	4	4	28	17	3	2	13	11	28	13	6	17	39	45	45
7	Shkumbini Peqin	36	10	3	5	18	14	2	4	12	13	35	12	7	17	31	49	43
8	Teuta Durrës	36	8	6	4	19	16	3	3	12	13	29	11	9	16	32	45	42
9	Skënderbeu Korçë	36	12	3	3	22	12	0	3	15	11	38	12	6	18	33	50	42
10	Lushnja	36	4	7	7	17	25	1	3	14	5	33	5	10	21	22	58	25

Relegation Play-off

(17/5/06) Skënderbeu Korçë 0, Teuta Durrës 1

LEAGUE RESULTS/ SCORERS/APPEARANCES/ GOALS 2005/06

BESA KAVAJË

Coach – Ilir Duro; (28/8/05) Agim Canaj; (3/12/05) Ilir Shulku; (5/4/06) Përparim Daiu

2005

Date	Opponent	H/A	Score	Scorers
27/8	Elbasani	a	0-1	
7/9	Partizani Tiranë	h	4-1	Fortunat 2, Salihu 2
10/9	SK Tirana	a	1-1	Fortunat
16/9	Shkumbini Peqin	h	2-1	Fortunat, Dragusha
24/9	Vllaznia Shkodër	a	3-0	Veliaj, Fortunat, Arapi
1/10	Dinamo Tiranë	a	2-2	Hamzaj (p), Veliaj
15/10	Skënderbeu Korçë	h	4-0	Dragusha, Fortunat, Salihu (p), Hamzaj
23/10	Teuta Durrës	a	2-0	Veliaj 2
29/10	Lushnja	h	0-0	
5/11	Elbasani	h	0-1	
9/11	Partizani Tiranë	a	1-1	Kraja
19/11	SK Tirana	h	1-1	Veliaj
26/11	Shkumbini Peqin	a	0-1	
30/11	Vllaznia Shkodër	h	0-1	
4/12	Dinamo Tiranë	h	3-0	Rraklli, Veliaj, Salihu
11/12	Skënderbeu Korçë	a	0-2	
18/12	Teuta Durrës	h	1-0	Fortunat
22/12	Lushnja	a	1-1	Salihu

2006

Date	Opponent	H/A	Score	Scorers
15/1	Elbasani	a	1-2	Nana Bikoula
21/1	Partizani Tiranë	h	2-1	Lila, Fortunat
27/1	SK Tirana	a	1-1	og (Andaveris)
15/2	Shkumbini Peqin	h	2-0	Kasollja, Nana Bikoula
18/2	Vllaznia Shkodër	a	2-5	Hamzaj 2
25/2	Dinamo Tiranë	a	2-3	Rrakli, Fortunat
4/3	Skënderbeu Korçë	h	2-0	Rrakli, Bubeqi
11/3	Teuta Durrës	a	1-2	Bubeqi
18/3	Lushnja	h	6-0	Bubeqi 3, og (Lamaj), Hamzaj, Rrakli
25/3	Elbasani	h	0-2	(w/o)
1/4	Partizani Tiranë	a	1-3	Fortunat
4/4	SK Tirana	h	0-2	
8/4	Shkumbini Peqin	a	0-1	

Date	Opponent	H/A	Score	Scorers
15/4	Vllaznia Shkodër	h	1-0	Hamzaj (p)
22/4	Dinamo Tiranë	h	0-1	
29/4	Skënderbeu Korçë	a	2-0	Veliaj, Salihu
6/5	Teuta Durrës	h	1-4	Hasalliu
13/5	Lushnja	a	0-1	

Name	Nat	Pos	Aps	(s)	Gls
Renato ARAPI		M	10	(9)	1
Shpetim BABAJ	KOS	D	31		
Timothe BENISSON	SEN	D	1	(2)	
Gentian BRATJA		D	2	(9)	
Dorian BUBEQI		A	10	(8)	5
Gentian ÇELA		D	7	(6)	
Selim DAIU		D		(1)	
Enik DHIMA		D	6	(7)	
Alban DRAGUSHA	KOS	M	21	(1)	2
Bledar DURA		G	34		
Hervé FORTUNAT	FRA	A	25	(2)	10
Taulant GUMA		G	2		
Romeo HAMZAJ		A	13	(14)	6
Erind HASALLIU		A		(2)	1
Renato HYSENAJ		M		(1)	
Rigers HYSO		M	3	(3)	
Dritan ISLAMAJ	KOS	D		(2)	
Artan KARAPICI		M	19	(8)	
Merdian KASOLLJA		D	15	(8)	1
Ervis KRAJA		D	34		1
Dritan KRASNIQI	KOS	D	5	(8)	
Aldo KULI		M	1		
Andi LILA		D	29		1
Luan MEHMETI		M	2		
Olgert MUKA		D		(1)	
Ismet MUNISHI	KOS	M	12	(1)	
Emanuel NANA BIKOULA	NGA	M	22		2
Korab NELA		M		(1)	
Malek PIKO BINOGOL	CMR	M	10	(2)	
Altin RRAKLLI		A	14		4
Abdulla Isshaka SALIHU	NGA	M	27	(1)	6
Mamadou SISSOKO	SEN	D	1		
Emiliano VELIAJ		A	33	(1)	7
Ymer XHAFERRI	KOS	D	1	(1)	
Fatjon YMERI		A	4	(1)	
Emanuel ZEIRAHO	NGA	M	2		

Albania

DINAMO TIRANË

Coach – Luka Bonacic (CRO); (29/8/05) Vasil Bici; (15/11/05) Ivan Katalinic (CRO); (15/2/06) Vasil Bici; (15/3/06) Sulejman Demollari; (25/3/06) Vasil Bici

2005
27/8	Lushnja	a	2-2	Goudjabi 2
7/9	Elbasani	h	0-0	
10/9	Partizani Tiranë	a	1-2	Dhëmbi
17/9	SK Tirana	h	3-3	Goudjabi, Ahmataj, Poçi (p)
24/9	Shkumbini Peqin	a	2-0	Xhafa F., Deliallisi
1/10	Besa Kavajë	h	2-2	Dhëmbi, Goudjabi
15/10	Vllaznia Shkodër	a	1-1	Deliallisi
22/10	Skënderbeu Korçë	a	1-0	Mariño
30/10	Teuta Durrës	h	4-0	Goudjabi, Vincetic, Mile, Ahmataj
4/11	Lushnja	h	3-0	Goudjabi, Asllani, Kastel
9/11	Elbasani	a	0-3	
19/11	Partizani Tiranë	h	1-2	og (Dhëmbi)
26/11	SK Tirana	a	1-1	Deliallisi
30/11	Shkumbini Peqin	h	3-1	Diop, Poçi, Pema
4/12	Besa Kavajë	a	0-3	
10/12	Vllaznia Shkodër	h	3-0	Escudero, og (Kelmendi), Asllani
18/12	Skënderbeu Korçë	h	3-1	Kastel, Goudjabi, Mariño
22/12	Teuta Durrës	a	1-0	Goudjabi

2006
13/1	Lushnja	a	4-1	Ahmataj, Poçi (p), Pema, Vincetic
21/1	Elbasani	h	1-1	Diop
28/1	Partizani Tiranë	a	0-1	
15/2	SK Tirana	h	1-1	Pema
18/2	Shkumbini Peqin	a	1-0	Goudjabi
25/2	Besa Kavajë	h	3-2	Goudjabi, Ahmataj (p), Diop
4/3	Vllaznia Shkodër	a	2-0	Goudjabi 2
10/3	Skënderbeu Korçë	a	0-1	
18/3	Teuta Durrës	h	2-0	Pema, Goudjabi
25/3	Lushnja	h	0-1	
1/4	Elbasani	a	1-1	Goudjabi
5/4	Partizani Tiranë	h	3-0	Xhafa E., Ahmataj, Goudjabi
8/4	SK Tirana	a	0-3	
15/4	Shkumbini Peqin	h	0-0	
22/4	Besa Kavajë	a	1-0	Caval
29/4	Vllaznia Shkodër	h	2-1	Deliallisi, Asllani
6/5	Skënderbeu Korçë	h	1-0	Goudjabi
13/5	Teuta Durrës	a	0-1	

Name	Nat	Pos	Aps	(s)	Gls
Julian AHMATAJ		M	31	(1)	5
Enkeleid ALIKAJ		M	11	(13)	
Klodian ASLLANI		A	8	(11)	3
Vasian BALLÇO		M		(4)	
Ditmar BICI		D	1		
Kristijan CAVAL	CRO	D	9	(7)	1
Erald DELIALLISI		M	23	(6)	4
Pavlin DHËMBI		M	6	(1)	2
Ablaye Papa DIOP	SEN	M	26	(5)	3
Verhas DOMAGOJ	CRO	M	10	(3)	
Leandro ESCUDERO	ARG	D	11	(4)	1
Nertil FERRAJ		A		(8)	
El Hadji GOUDJABI	SEN	A	33		16
Branimir IVANISEVIC	SCG	M	8	(1)	
Zoran KASTEL	CRO	D	21	(2)	2
Aba Ibrahim KONE	MLI	D	17	(4)	
Héctor LEDESMA	ARG	A		(2)	
Ilion LIKA		G	36		
Juan Carlos MARIÑO	PER	M	13	(1)	2
Vangjell MILE		M	2	(6)	1
Néstor Emanuel MOIRAGHI	ARG	D	13	(1)	
Eleandro PEMA		A	19	(8)	4
Artion POÇI		M	26	(5)	3
Ilir QORRI		A	4	(3)	
Zekrija RAMADANI	MAC	D	1		
Indrit THAÇI		M		(1)	
Goran VINCETIC	CRO	D	31	(1)	2
Erjon XHAFA		D	32		1
Fjodor XHAFA		D	4		1

ELBASANI

Coach – Ilir Daja

2005
27/8	Besa Kavajë	h	1-0	Dede (p)
7/9	Dinamo Tiranë	a	0-0	
11/9	Skënderbeu Korçë	h	3-1	Bejzade, Nora, Tetova
17/9	Teuta Durrës	a	1-1	Tetova
25/9	Lushnja	h	4-0	og (Lamaj), Bejzade, Osja, Çapja
30/9	Vllaznia Shkodër	h	2-0	Bejzade, Tetova
15/10	Partizani Tiranë	a	0-1	
22/10	SK Tirana	h	1-0	Dede
29/10	Shkumbini Peqin	a	2-1	Bejzade 2
5/11	Besa Kavajë	a	1-0	Brahja
9/11	Dinamo Tiranë	h	3-0	Çapja, Vrapi, Bejzade (p)
18/11	Skënderbeu Korçë	a	0-1	
26/11	Teuta Durrës	h	2-1	Vrapi, Qorri
30/11	Lushnja	a	2-0	Bejzade, Dalipi K.
3/12	Vllaznia Shkodër	a	0-0	
10/12	Partizani Tiranë	h	0-1	
16/12	SK Tirana	a	1-1	Devolli
22/12	Shkumbini Peqin	h	2-0	Dede, Dalipi K.

2006
15/1	Besa Kavajë	h	2-1	Brahja, Rizvanolli
21/1	Dinamo Tiranë	a	1-1	Qorri
28/1	Skënderbeu Korçë	h	2-1	Brahja, Qorri
15/2	Teuta Durrës	a	0-0	
19/2	Lushnja	h	1-0	Dede
26/2	Vllaznia Shkodër	h	1-0	Dalipi K.
4/3	Partizani Tiranë	a	0-2	
11/3	SK Tirana	h	1-0	Kaçi
19/3	Shkumbini Peqin	a	0-0	
25/3	Besa Kavajë	a	2-0	(w/o)
1/4	Dinamo Tiranë	h	1-1	Bejzade
5/4	Skënderbeu Korçë	a	0-0	
8/4	Teuta Durrës	h	2-0	Çapja, Kotorri (p)
15/4	Lushnja	a	4-2	Qorri, Bejzade 3
22/4	Vllaznia Shkodër	a	2-3	Rizvanolli, Tetova
29/4	Partizani Tiranë	h	1-1	Bejzade
6/5	SK Tirana	a	3-2	Bejzade, Dede, Kotorri (p)
13/5	Shkumbini Peqin	h	2-0	Bejzade 2

Name	Nat	Pos	Aps	(s)	Gls
Abraham ALECHENWU	NGA	D	33	(1)	
Olsi BEJOLLARI		D		(3)	
Skerdi BEJZADE		A	31	(2)	15
Julian BRAHJA		D	35		3
Hetlen ÇAPJA		M	31	(3)	3
Endri DALIPI		M		(2)	
Klevis DALIPI		A	20	(7)	3
Nevil DEDE		D	33		5

Albania

Name	Nat	Pos	Aps	(s)	Gls
Bledar DEVOLLI		A	11	(4)	1
Ertil DUKA		M		(1)	
Fisnik GASHI	KOS	M		(2)	
Sokol ISHKA		M	2	(2)	
Albert KAÇI		A	5	(6)	1
Elvis KOTORRI		G	36		2
Egert KUÇI		M	1	(10)	
Armando MEHMETAJ		M		(1)	
Eriol MERXHA		M	11	(3)	
Arlind NORA		M	21	(4)	1
Safet OSJA		D	35		1
Oltion OSMANI		M		(5)	
Tefik OSMANI		D	2	(2)	
Ilir QORRI		A	25	(2)	4
Erion RIZVANOLLI		A	4	(10)	2
Gentian STOJKU		D	7	(10)	
Xhevair SUKAJ		A		(4)	
Erind TETOVA		M	19	(12)	4
Endrit VRAPI		D	34		2

LUSHNJA
Coach – Perlat Sevo; (20/1/06) Artan Bano; (15/2/06) Sulejman Demollari; (10/3/06) Artan Bano

2005
27/8	Dinamo Tiranë	h	2-2	Gjyla, Dervishi R.	
6/9	Skënderbeu Korçë	a	1-1	Dervishi R. (p)	
10/9	Teuta Durrës	h	0-0		
18/9	Vllaznia Shkodër	h	1-3	Ceno	
25/9	Elbasani	a	0-4		
2/10	Partizani Tiranë	h	2-1	Ceno, Dervishi R. (p)	
14/10	SK Tirana	a	0-1		
22/10	Shkumbini Peqin	h	3-2	Ceno 2 (1p), Shtrepi	
29/10	Besa Kavajë	a	0-0		
4/11	Dinamo Tiranë	a	0-3		
9/11	Skënderbeu Korçë	h	2-1	Idrizi, Xhagalliu	
20/11	Teuta Durrës	a	0-1		
26/11	Vllaznia Shkodër	a	0-3		
30/11	Elbasani	h	0-2		
4/12	Partizani Tiranë	a	0-2		
10/12	SK Tirana	h	0-1		
18/12	Shkumbini Peqin	a	0-1		
22/12	Besa Kavajë	h	1-1	Lamaj	

2006
13/1	Dinamo Tiranë	h	1-4	Ohadero	
20/1	Skënderbeu Korçë	a	1-2	Çela G.	
28/1	Teuta Durrës	h	0-0		
15/2	Vllaznia Shkodër	h	0-1		
19/2	Elbasani	a	0-1		
25/2	Partizani Tiranë	h	1-1	Eboh	
3/3	SK Tirana	a	0-1		
10/3	Shkumbini Peqin	h	0-1		
18/3	Besa Kavajë	a	0-6		
25/3	Dinamo Tiranë	a	1-0	Kuli	
1/4	Skënderbeu Korçë	h	1-1	Kuli	
5/4	Teuta Durrës	a	1-1	Gjyla	
8/4	Vllaznia Shkodër	a	0-1		
15/4	Elbasani	h	2-4	Kuli, Çela G.	
22/4	Partizani Tiranë	a	0-3		
29/4	SK Tirana	h	0-0		
6/5	Shkumbini Peqin	a	1-2	Ndoni	
13/5	Besa Kavajë	h	1-1	Boriçi	

Name	Nat	Pos	Aps	(s)	Gls
Ermal ARRA		D	8	(1)	
Amarildo BORIÇI		A	3	(10)	1
Gentian BYLYKBASHI		A	4		
Albano BYZHYTI		D	24	(1)	
Mikel ÇANKO		A	1	(4)	
Rigers ÇEKAJ		D	7	(8)	
Ervis ÇELA		M		(1)	
Gentian ÇELA		D	16		2
Elton CENO		A	19	(1)	4
Erton DERVISHI		M	3	(13)	
Roland DERVISHI		M	12	(1)	3
Enik DHIMA		D	16		
Ilir DIBRA		M	11	(1)	
Elton DURI		M	14	(8)	
John EBOH	NGA	A	13		1
ELEZI		M		(1)	
Judmir GAZHELI		D	24	(2)	
Viktor GJYLA		D	31		2
Sherif IDRIZI		M	17	(2)	1
Bekim KULI		A	15		3
Vasiljevsk LAMAJ		M	26	(1)	1
Ervin LIKA		M	14		
Laert NDONI		D	31	(1)	1
Ambrose OHADERO	NGA	A	10	(3)	1
Hektor PREMÇE		G	14	(2)	
Fatmir SEFA		M	2	(2)	
Andi SHTREPI		M	4	(9)	1
SPAHIU		D		(3)	
Mikel SPAHO		G	23		
SULA		A	3		
SULI		M		(1)	
Erion XHAFA		D	6	(4)	
Saimir XHAGALLIU		M	25	(7)	1
Erjon ZENELI		M		(3)	

PARTIZANI TIRANË
Coach – Neptun Bajko; (17/9/05) Sulejman Mema; (16/11/05) Sulejman Starova

2005
27/8	Shkumbini Peqin	h	1-0	Wander	
7/9	Besa Kavajë	a	1-4	Drobnjak	
10/9	Dinamo Tiranë	h	2-1	Wander 2	
17/9	Skënderbeu Korçë	a	1-2	Bylykbashi D.	
24/9	Teuta Durrës	h	3-0	Bylykbashi D. 2 (1p), Karder	
2/10	Lushnja	a	1-2	Wander	
15/10	Elbasani	h	1-0	Berisha	
22/10	Vllaznia Shkodër	h	2-0	Wander, Hallaçi	
29/10	SK Tirana	a	0-1		
5/11	Shkumbini Peqin	h	1-2	Halili	
9/11	Besa Kavajë	h	1-1	Halili	
19/11	Dinamo Tiranë	a	2-1	Dhëmbi 2	
25/11	Skënderbeu Korçë	h	3-0	Delain, Abilaliaj, Muzaka	
30/11	Teuta Durrës	a	2-1	Dhëmbi, Bylykbashi D.	
4/12	Lushnja	h	2-0	Abilaliaj, Bylykbashi D.	
10/12	Elbasani	a	1-0	Bylykbashi D.	
18/12	Vllaznia Shkodër	a	0-1		
22/12	SK Tirana	h	1-0	Abilaliaj	

2006
14/1	Shkumbini Peqin	h	3-0	Delain, Abilaliaj, Bylykbashi D.	
21/1	Besa Kavajë	a	1-2	Abilaliaj	
28/1	Dinamo Tiranë	h	1-0	Muzaka	
15/2	Skënderbeu Korçë	a	0-0		
18/2	Teuta Durrës	h	4-1	Abilaliaj 2, Dhëmbi 2	
25/2	Lushnja	a	1-1	Delain	

Albania

4/3	Elbasani	h	2-0	Halili, Allmuça
11/3	Vllaznia Shkodër	h	2-2	Delain, Karder
19/3	SK Tirana	a	0-1	
25/3	Shkumbini Peqin	a	0-2	
1/4	Besa Kavajë	h	3-1	Bakaj El., Muzaka 2
5/4	Dinamo Tiranë	a	0-3	
8/4	Skënderbeu Korçë	h	3-1	Rodrigo, Qose, Muzaka (p)
15/4	Teuta Durrës	a	0-1	
22/4	Lushnja	h	3-0	Delain, Abilaliaj, Berisha
29/4	Elbasani	a	1-1	Bakaj El.
6/5	Vllaznia Shkodër	a	0-1	
13/5	SK Tirana	h	2-2	Bakaj El., Rodrigo (p)

Name	Nat	Pos	Aps	(s)	Gls
Arbër ABILALIAJ		A	19	(4)	8
Igli ALLMUÇA		M	31	(2)	1
Edvan BAKAJ		G	1		
Elis BAKAJ		A	11	(15)	3
Ardit BEQIRI		D	32	(2)	
Arjan BERISHA	GER	M	11	(14)	2
Sokol BULKU		D		(1)	
Dorian BYLYKBASHI		M	21	(2)	7
Gentian BYLYKBASHI		A		(2)	
Sasa DELAIN	DRC	D	32		5
Pavlin DHËMBI		M	22		5
Armando DODA		M		(1)	
Jovan DROBNJAK	SCG	A	4	(3)	1
Alpin GALLO		D	32		
Mahir HALILI		A	15	(11)	3
Rahman HALLAÇI		M	25	(6)	1
Gerard HASMETA		D		(1)	
JOSETA De Trinidade	BRA	M		(2)	
JURIANDER de Rodrigues	BRA	D	2	(3)	
Edward KANGWA	ZAM	A		(1)	
Alan KARDER de Sousa	BRA	D	25		2
Claudio LÓPEZ	ARG	D	4		
Gjergji MUZAKA		M	29	(5)	5
Premislaw NORKO	POL	G	11		
Luan PINARI		D	2	(3)	
Rigels QOSE		A	10	(5)	1
RODRIGO do Nascimento	BRA	D	10	(7)	2
Orges SHEHI		G	24		
Arjan SHETA		D	13	(6)	
WANDER dos Santos	BRA	A	10		5

SHKUMBINI PEQIN
Coach – Faruk Sejdini; (24/9/05) Alfred Ferko; (3/11/05) Sulejman Demollari; (22/1/06) Faruk Sejdini

2005

27/8	Partizani Tiranë	a	0-1	
6/9	SK Tirana	h	1-1	Stafa
10/9	Vllaznia Shkodër	a	0-5	
16/9	Besa Kavajë	h	1-2	Abazaj
24/9	Dinamo Tiranë	h	0-2	
1/10	Skënderbeu Korçë	a	0-3	
15/10	Teuta Durrës	h	2-1	Nabubwane, Gjata
22/10	Lushnja	a	2-3	Abazaj, Stafa
29/10	Elbasani	h	1-2	Stafa
5/11	Partizani Tiranë	h	2-1	Stafa, Abazaj
11/11	SK Tirana	a	4-4	Stafa, Ishka, Ymeri 2
19/11	Vllaznia Shkodër	h	0-0	
26/11	Besa Kavajë	h	1-0	Abazaj
30/11	Dinamo Tiranë	a	1-3	Muça A.
3/12	Skënderbeu Korçë	h	2-1	Abazaj, og (Osusi)
10/12	Teuta Durrës	a	1-2	Magani (p)
18/12	Lushnja	h	1-0	Pashaj
22/12	Elbasani	a	0-2	

2006

14/1	Partizani Tiranë	a	0-3	
21/1	SK Tirana	h	0-1	
28/1	Vllaznia Shkodër	a	0-0	
15/2	Besa Kavajë	a	0-2	
18/2	Dinamo Tiranë	h	0-1	
25/2	Skënderbeu Korçë	a	2-0	Dervishi, Abazaj
4/3	Teuta Durrës	h	0-2	(w/o)
10/3	Lushnja	a	1-0	Abazaj
19/3	Elbasani	h	0-0	
25/3	Partizani Tiranë	h	2-0	Abazaj, Stafa
1/4	SK Tirana	a	1-3	Stafa
5/4	Vllaznia Shkodër	h	1-0	Abazaj
8/4	Besa Kavajë	h	1-0	Abazaj
15/4	Dinamo Tiranë	a	0-0	
22/4	Skënderbeu Korçë	h	2-1	Abazaj, Stafa
29/4	Teuta Durrës	a	0-0	
6/5	Lushnja	h	2-1	Stafa, Abazaj
13/5	Elbasani	a	0-2	

Name	Nat	Pos	Aps	(s)	Gls
Orjand ABAZAJ		A	33	(3)	12
Rubin BAÇI		D		(1)	
Endri DALIPI		M	17		
Roland DERVISHI		A	16		1
Alirjan GJATA		M		(7)	1
Lazi GJIKA		G	1		
Renato HYSENAJ		M	1		
Sokol ISHKA		A	26		1
Renaldo KALARI		D	17	(4)	
Alket KRUJA		M		(2)	
Ervin LLANI		G	26		
Gugash MAGANI		D	32	(2)	1
Rezart MAHO		M	7	(9)	
Alban MUÇA		D	10	(4)	1
Dashamir MUÇA		D	5	(4)	
Tochukwu NABUBWANE	NGA	M	3	(1)	1
Astrit NEXHA		M	1	(2)	
OLIVEIRA de Rodrigues	BRA	D	9	(6)	
Valentin ONIEKA	NGA	M	5	(5)	
Alfred OSMANI		G	9		
Lorenc PASHAJ		D	36		1
Daniel RAMAZANI		D		(2)	
Serhiy ROMANISHIN	UKR	M	13		
Andi SALLATA		D	10		
Alfred SALLIU		D	8	(14)	
Admir SEJFULLAI		A	5	(2)	
Olgert STAFA		M	28	(4)	9
Ervis TAFAJ		D	5	(1)	
Fatjon TAFAJ		D	32		
Indrit THAÇI		M	6		
Ermal VARFI		M	6		
Klement XHYRA		M	22	(4)	
Fatjon YMERI		A	7	(17)	2
Bledar ZYBA		D		(1)	

SKËNDERBEU KORÇË
Coach – Mirel Josa; (18/2/06) Gjergji Ballço; (22/2/06) Agim Canaj

2005

27/8	Teuta Durrës	a	1-1	Memelli
6/9	Lushnja	h	1-1	Mërtiri

Albania

11/9	Elbasani	a	1-3	Pandong	
17/9	Partizani Tiranë	h	2-1	Pandong 2	
24/9	SK Tirana	a	0-3		
1/10	Shkumbini Peqin	h	3-0	Arberi 2, Liçi	
15/10	Besa Kavajë	a	0-4		
22/10	Dinamo Tiranë	h	0-1		
29/10	Vllaznia Shkodër	a	1-2	Liçi	
5/11	Teuta Durrës	h	1-0	Memelli	
9/11	Lushnja	a	1-2	Memelli	
18/11	Elbasani	h	1-0	Memelli	
25/11	Partizani Tiranë	a	0-3		
30/11	SK Tirana	h	4-3	Liçi, Memelli, Osusi, Arberi	
3/12	Shkumbini Peqin	a	1-2	Ngjela	
11/12	Besa Kavajë	h	2-0	Memelli, Pandong	
18/12	Dinamo Tiranë	a	1-3	Memelli (p)	
22/12	Vllaznia Shkodër	h	1-0	Memelli	
2006					
14/1	Teuta Durrës	a	1-1	Ballço	
20/1	Lushnja	h	2-1	Ballço, Rustemi	
28/1	Elbasani	a	1-2	Liçi	
15/2	Partizani Tiranë	h	0-0		
18/2	SK Tirana	a	0-2		
25/2	Shkumbini Peqin	h	0-2		
4/3	Besa Kavajë	a	0-2		
10/3	Dinamo Tiranë	h	1-0	Arberi	
18/3	Vllaznia Shkodër	a	0-1		
25/3	Teuta Durrës	h	1-0	Arberi	
1/4	Lushnja	a	1-1	Arberi	
5/4	Elbasani	h	0-0		
8/4	Partizani Tiranë	a	1-3	Ngjela	
15/4	SK Tirana	h	1-0	Liçi	
22/4	Shkumbini Peqin	a	1-2	Osusi	
29/4	Besa Kavajë	h	0-2		
6/5	Dinamo Tiranë	a	0-1		
13/5	Vllaznia Shkodër	h	2-1	Pandong 2	

Name	Nat	Pos	Aps	(s)	Gls
Restiald AGOLLI		M	30		
Olgert AMETLLI		G	3	(1)	
Klodian ARBERI		A	28	(2)	6
Gabriel AWIA	NGA	D	21	(4)	
Vasian BALLÇO		M	8	(3)	2
Endri ÇAJKU		M	19	(5)	
Bledar DEVOLLI		A	15		
Daniel DRABAJ		M	1		
FRASHËRI		D	1	(1)	
Blerim HASALLA		D	14	(5)	
HASANAJ		D		(2)	
Lewis ITEANYCHUKWU	NGA	M	16	(4)	
Bledi KADIU		A	16	(12)	
Stavrion LAKO		D	31	(1)	
Klajdi LARDI		D	4	(6)	
Gentian LIÇI		M	31		5
Migen MEMELLI		A	11	(1)	8
Ilirjan MËRTIRI		M	16	(8)	1
Arion MUSTAFA		G	33		
Marius NGJELA		M	6	(20)	2
James OSUSI	NGA	M	34		2
Roger PANDONG	CMR	M	25	(9)	6
Kastriot RUSTEMI		D	27		1
Eugen VEIZI		M	6	(7)	

TEUTA DURRËS
Coach – Hasan Lika; (24/2/06) Stavri Nica; (19/3/06) Alfred Ferko

2005					
27/8	Skënderbeu Korçë	h	1-1	Pashaj	
6/9	Vllaznia Shkodër	h	3-0	Mançaku 2, Buna	
10/9	Lushnja	a	0-0		
17/9	Elbasani	h	1-1	Xhihani	
24/9	Partizani Tiranë	a	0-3		
1/10	SK Tirana	h	1-0	Xhihani	
15/10	Shkumbini Peqin	a	1-2	Mançaku	
23/10	Besa Kavajë	h	0-2		
30/10	Dinamo Tiranë	a	0-4		
5/11	Skënderbeu Korçë	a	0-1		
9/11	Vllaznia Shkodër	a	1-3	Zëre	
20/11	Lushnja	h	1-0	Ezeriaha	
26/11	Elbasani	a	1-2	Shaqiri	
30/11	Partizani Tiranë	h	1-2	Mançaku	
3/12	SK Tirana	a	1-2	Tiko	
10/12	Shkumbini Peqin	h	2-1	Xhihani, Zëre	
18/12	Besa Kavajë	a	0-1		
22/12	Dinamo Tiranë	h	0-1		
2006					
14/1	Skënderbeu Korçë	h	1-1	Babamusta	
21/1	Vllaznia Shkodër	h	3-1	Mançaku, Zëre, Gjondeda	
28/1	Lushnja	a	0-0		
15/2	Elbasani	h	0-0		
18/2	Partizani Tiranë	a	1-4	Mançaku	
24/2	SK Tirana	h	0-4		
4/3	Shkumbini Peqin	a	2-0	(w/o)	
11/3	Besa Kavajë	h	2-1	Kotja, Gega	
18/3	Dinamo Tiranë	a	0-2		
25/3	Skënderbeu Korçë	a	0-1		
1/4	Vllaznia Shkodër	h	1-1	Ziambo	
5/4	Lushnja	h	1-1	Xhihani	
8/4	Elbasani	a	0-2		
15/4	Partizani Tiranë	h	1-0	Tiko	
22/4	SK Tirana	a	1-0	Mançaku	
29/4	Shkumbini Peqin	h	0-0		
6/5	Besa Kavajë	a	4-1	Buna (p), Gega, Xhihani, Hodo	
13/5	Dinamo Tiranë	h	1-0	Babamusta	

Name	Nat	Pos	Aps	(s)	Gls
Alert ALCANI		M	1	(1)	
Dritan BABAMUSTA		M	14	(3)	2
Ervin BARDHI		M		(4)	
Justin BESPALLA		M	4	(3)	
Qazim BUNA		M	30	(1)	2
Eduart CURRI		M	8	(3)	
Ilir DIBRA		D	5	(2)	
Marlond DOLLAKU		D	11		
Albert DURO		D	17		
Emanuel EZERIAHA	NGA	M	5	(3)	1
Ilir GEGA		A	1	(5)	2
Gentian GJONDEDA		M	14	(2)	1
Alban HASANI-NEZIRI		D	3	(2)	
Bledar HODO		D	25	(3)	1
Jeton JAKUPI	KOS	M	20	(4)	
Marenglen KAPAJ		M	25		
Xhevair KAPLLANI		G	35		
Oerd KOTJA		M	15	(8)	1
Aleksandar KOVAC	SCG	M	22	(4)	
Arben LIKMETA		M	7	(4)	
Bledar MANÇAKU		A	32		7
Olgert MUKA		D	4	(2)	
Entonio PASHAJ		D	21		1

Albania

Jeton QERIMI		KOS	D	6		
Sadat SHAHINI		BOS	M		(4)	
Ardit SHAQIRI		MAC	M	3	(11)	1
Gledis TAFAJ			G	1		
Ligor TIKO			A	10	(8)	2
Ergen VEIZI			M	3	(4)	
Parid XHIHANI			A	23	(7)	5
Arjan ZËRE			D	24		3
January ZIAMBO		ZAM	A	7	(4)	1

SK TIRANA
Coach – Leonardo Menichini (ITA); (11/11/05) (Shkelqim Muça); (15/11/05) Krenar Alimehmeti; (20/2/06) Mirel Josa

2005
27/8	Vllaznia Shkodër	a	2-1	Salihi, Muka
6/9	Shkumbini Peqin	a	1-1	Salihi
10/9	Besa Kavajë	h	1-1	og (Salihu)
17/9	Dinamo Tiranë	a	3-3	Salihi 2, Bulku
24/9	Skënderbeu Korçë	h	3-0	Salihi 2, Merkoçi
1/10	Teuta Durrës	a	0-1	
14/10	Lushnja	h	1-0	Duro K. (p)
22/10	Elbasani	a	0-1	
29/10	Partizani Tiranë	h	1-0	Muka (p)
5/11	Vllaznia Shkodër	h	2-0	Duro K. (p), Muzzachi
11/11	Shkumbini Peqin	a	4-4	Salihi 3, Xhafa
19/11	Besa Kavajë	a	1-1	Muka
26/11	Dinamo Tiranë	h	1-1	Salihi
30/11	Skënderbeu Korçë	a	3-4	Salihi 3
3/12	Teuta Durrës	h	2-1	Muka, Salihi
10/12	Lushnja	a	1-0	Dabulla
16/12	Elbasani	h	1-1	Hajdari
22/12	Partizani Tiranë	a	0-1	

2006
14/1	Vllaznia Shkodër	a	2-0	Muka, Salihi
21/1	Shkumbini Peqin	a	1-0	Salihi
27/1	Besa Kavajë	h	1-1	Salihi
15/2	Dinamo Tiranë	a	1-1	Salihi
18/2	Skënderbeu Korçë	h	2-0	Salihi, og (Hasalla)
24/2	Teuta Durrës	a	4-0	Dabulla, Salihi 2, Andaveris
3/3	Lushnja	h	1-0	Peña
11/3	Elbasani	a	0-1	
19/3	Partizani Tiranë	h	1-0	Salihi
25/3	Vllaznia Shkodër	h	2-1	Salihi 2
1/4	Shkumbini Peqin	h	3-1	Peña, Muka, Salihi (p)
5/4	Besa Kavajë	a	2-0	Salihi 2
8/4	Dinamo Tiranë	h	3-0	Duro K. (p), Bakalli, Muka
15/4	Skënderbeu Korçë	a	0-1	
22/4	Teuta Durrës	h	0-0	
29/4	Lushnja	a	0-0	
6/5	Elbasani	h	2-3	Duro K. (p), Salihi
13/5	Partizani Tiranë	a	2-2	Salihi, Dabulla

Name		Nat	Pos	Aps	(s)	Gls
Augusto ANDAVERIS		BOL	A	6	(11)	1
Egert BAKALLI			M	23	(5)	1
Ervin BULKU			D	24		1
Percy COLQUE		BOL	D	2	(3)	
Rezart DABULLA			D	29		3
Klodian DURO			M	29		4
Albert DURO			D		(1)	
Erbim FAGU			A		(1)	
Gentian HAJDARI			D	28	(4)	1
Adnand HALITI			D	8	(2)	
Isli HIDI			G	20		
Rinush KARAJ			A		(1)	
Eldorado MERKOÇI			A	13	(16)	1
Alban MUÇA			D		(3)	
Devi MUKA			M	32	(1)	7
Cristian MUZZACHI		ITA	M	9	(1)	1
Blendi NALLBANI			G	16		
Joni NDOJA			A		(4)	
Saimir PATUSHI			M	25		
Diómedes PEÑA		COL	D	15		2
Arjan PISHA			D	29	(3)	
Altin RRAKLLI			A	4	(2)	
Hamdi SALIHI			A	35		29
Jetmir SEFA			M	8	(6)	
Elvis SINA			M	33		
Alban TAFAJ			D	2	(12)	
Fjodor XHAFA			A	6	(17)	1

VLLAZNIA SHKODËR
Coach – Dervis Hadziosmanovic; (5/10/05) Hysen Dedja

2005
27/8	SK Tirana	h	1-2	Patushi
6/9	Teuta Durrës	a	0-3	
10/9	Shkumbini Peqin	h	5-0	Sinani 2, Ndreka, Hoti, Beqiri A.
18/9	Lushnja	a	3-1	Sinani 2 (1p), Patushi
24/9	Besa Kavajë	h	0-3	
30/9	Elbasani	a	0-2	
15/10	Dinamo Tiranë	h	1-1	Rinaldo
22/10	Partizani Tiranë	a	0-2	
29/10	Skënderbeu Korçë	h	2-1	Rinaldo, Sinani
5/11	SK Tirana	a	0-2	
9/11	Teuta Durrës	h	3-1	Rinaldo 2, Ahi
19/11	Shkumbini Peqin	a	0-0	
26/11	Lushnja	h	3-0	Sinani, Doçi, Teli
30/11	Besa Kavajë	a	1-0	Doçi
3/12	Elbasani	h	0-0	
10/12	Dinamo Tiranë	a	0-3	
18/12	Partizani Tiranë	h	1-0	Geraldo Júnior
22/12	Skënderbeu Korçë	a	0-1	

2006
14/1	SK Tirana	h	0-2	
21/1	Teuta Durrës	a	1-3	Sinani
28/1	Shkumbini Peqin	h	0-0	
15/2	Lushnja	a	1-0	og (Xhafa)
18/2	Besa Kavajë	h	5-2	Sinani 4, Ahi
26/2	Elbasani	a	0-1	
4/3	Dinamo Tiranë	h	0-2	
11/3	Partizani Tiranë	a	2-2	Bokatola-Lossombo, Leandro
18/3	Skënderbeu Korçë	h	1-0	Sinani
25/3	SK Tirana	a	1-2	Cani
1/4	Teuta Durrës	h	1-2	Leandro (p)
5/4	Shkumbini Peqin	a	0-1	
8/4	Lushnja	h	1-0	Leandro
15/4	Besa Kavajë	a	0-1	
22/4	Elbasani	h	3-2	Sinani (p), Beka, Bokatola-Lossombo
29/4	Dinamo Tiranë	a	1-2	Lika G.
6/5	Partizani Tiranë	h	1-0	og (Kardek)
13/5	Skënderbeu Korçë	a	1-2	Cani

Name	Nat	Pos	Aps	(s)	Gls
Franc AHI		M	19	(13)	2
Rudi BEKA		A	2	(10)	1

Albania

Amarildo BELISHA		M	25	(3)	
Arsen BEQIRI		D	4	(7)	1
Edmir BEQIRI		M	1		
Olti BISHANI		G	2		
Richard BOKATOLA-LOSSOMBO	CDR	M	10	(1)	2
Nevian CANI		M	4	(14)	2
Besmir DANI		M		(1)	
Edmond DOÇI		M	26	(5)	2
Jovan DROBNJAK	SCG	A	2	(1)	
GERALDO JÚNIOR	BRA	M	2	(9)	1
Armir GRIMA		G	6	(1)	
GURI		M		(1)	
Alban HASANI-NEZIRI		D	16	(1)	
Arion HOTI		M	19	(9)	1
Marenglen KAPAJ		M	4	(3)	
Shkëlzen KELMENDI		D	13	(3)	
Bekim KULI		A	5	(2)	
LEANDRO da Silva	BRA	M	29		3
Suad LICI		M	12	(2)	
Gilman LIKA		A	25	(3)	1
Harris LIKA		D	1		
Tochukwu NABUBWANE	NGA	M	2	(1)	
Gasper NDOJA		G	23		
Henri NDREKA		D	21	(1)	1
NIMANI		D		(1)	
Saimir PATUSHI		M	6		2
Ranko RADONJIC	SCG	M	2		
Igor RADUSCINOVIC	SCG	D	30		
RINALDO do Macendo	BRA	A	12		4
K. SEMINA		D	1		
Orges SHEHI		G	5		
Vioresin SINANI		A	33		13
Erkan SULEJMANI	KOS	A	5	(5)	
Alsid TAFILI		A	2	(3)	
Admir TELI		D	28		1
Devis ZMIJANI		D	2		

DOMESTIC CUP 2005/06

SECOND ROUND
(20/9/05 & 28/9/05)
Ada Velipojë v Partizani 0-2; 1-3 *(1-5)*
(21/9/05 & 27/9/05)
Iliria Fushë-Krujë v SK Tirana 0-3; 2-3 *(2-6)*
Veleçiku Koplik v Vllaznia Shkodër 1-4; 0-7 *(1-11)*
Turbina Cërrik v Elbasani 2-6; 0-0 *(2-6)*
(21/9/05 & 28/9/05)
Besëlidhja Lezhë v Teuta Durrës 1-1; 1-3 *(2-4)*
Egnatia Rrogozhinë v Besa Kavajë 1-1; 0-3 *(1-4)*
Erzeni Shijak v Shkumbini Peqin 0-1; 0-3 *(w/o)* *(0-4)*
Kastrioti Krujë v Laçi 2-0; 0-0 *(2-0)*
Tepelena v Apolonia Fier 2-3; 0-3 *(2-6)*
Burreli v Dinamo Tiranë 1-1; 0-4 *(1-5)*
Cakrani v Flamurtari Vlorë 1-2; 0-7 *(1-9)*
Sopoti Librazhd v Pogradeci 0-2; 0-5 *(0-7)*
Tomori Berat v Lushnja 1-2; 0-2 *(1-4)*
Delvina v Butrinti Sarandë 1-2; 0-2 *(1-4)*
Devolli Bilisht v Skënderbeu Korçë 1-0; 0-1 *(aet; 3-4 on pens)*
Përmeti v Luftëtari Gjirokastër 3-1; 0-3 *(3-4)*

THIRD ROUND
(19/10/05 & 26/10/05)
Besa Kavajë v Vllaznia Shkodër 1-1; 1-2 *(2-3)*
Kastrioti Krujë v Partizani Tiranë 1-0; 0-3 *(1-3)*
Skënderbeu Korçë v Dinamo Tiranë 0-2; 1-6 *(1-8)*

Apolonia Fier v SK Tirana 0-1; 2-5 *(2-6)*
Pogradeci v Elbasani 2-0; 1-4 *(3-4)*
Flamurtari Vlorë v Teuta Durrës 0-2; 1-1 *(1-3)*
Butrinti Sarandë v Shkumbini Peqin 1-0; 0-4 *(1-4)*
Luftëtari Gjirokastër v Lushnja 0-1; 0-2 *(0-3)*

QUARTER-FINALS
(15/3/06 & 29/3/06)
Partizani Tiranë 2 *(Cardec 17, Gallo 55)*, SK Tirana 3 *(Muka 37, Patushi 57, Salihi 90)*
SK Tirana 1 *(Muka 9)*, Partizani Tiranë 1 *(Bakaj El. 29)*
(SK Tirana 4-3)
Teuta Durrës 3 *(Zëre 28, Xhihani 73, 90)*, Elbasani 3 *(Dede 23, Qorri 54, Doçi 65)*
Elbasani 3 *(Stojku 55, Nora 59, Rizvanolli 81)*, Teuta Durrës 1 *(Gega 60)*
(Elbasani 6-4)
Lushnja 0, Dinamo Tiranë 2 *(Goudjabi 35, 57)*
Dinamo Tiranë 4 *(Ivanisevic 38, Pema 51, Goudjabi 70, Vincetic 75)*, Lushnja 0
(Dinamo Tiranë 6-0)
Shkumbini Peqin 0, Vllaznia Shkodër 2 *(Sinani 25, Lika 54)*
Vllaznia Shkodër 1 *(Ahi 11)*, Shkumbini Peqin 0
(Vllaznia Shkodër 3-0)

SEMI-FINALS
(12/4/06 & 26/4/06)
SK Tirana 4 *(Duro 30p, Salihi 38, 67, Muka 86)*, Dinamo Tiranë 2 *(Pema 28, Goudjabi 75)*
Dinamo Tiranë 1 *(Xhafa 58p)*, SK Tirana 0
(SK Tirana 4-3)
Vllaznia Shkodër 2 *(Sinani 47, Leandro 89)*, Elbasani 0
Elbasani 2 *(Rizvanolli 34, Qorri 37)*, Vllaznia Shkodër 1 *(Ahi 43)*
(Vllaznia Shkodër 3-2)

FINAL
(10/5/06)
Roza Haxhiu stadium, Lushnjë
SK TIRANA 1 *(Duro 65)*
VLLAZNIA SHKODËR 0
Referee - *Farina (ITA)*
SK TIRANA - Nallbani, Sina, Pisha, Penja, Dabulla, Bakalli, Duro, Patushi, Bulku E., Muka *(Xhafa 72)*, Salihi *(Merkoçi 87)*.
VLLAZNIA SHKODËR - Grima, Hoti *(Beka 70)*, Teli, Ndreka, Radusinovic, Leandro, Belisha, Ahi, Doci *(Lici 67)*, Lika *(Cani 87)*, Sinani.

SECOND LEVEL FINAL TABLE 2005/06

		Pld	W	D	L	F	A	Pts
1	Flamurtari Vlorë	26	20	1	5	52	16	61
2	Apolonia Fier	26	16	7	3	47	20	55
3	Kastrioti Krujë	26	15	7	4	35	14	52
4	Luftëtari Gjirokastër	26	15	3	8	37	25	48
5	Pogradeci	26	14	5	7	34	28	47
6	Tomori Berat	26	11	4	11	42	40	37
7	Turbina Cërrik	26	9	8	9	30	29	35
8	Erzeni Shijak	26	9	6	11	29	34	33
9	Tepelena	26	8	5	13	27	31	29
10	Acia Velipojë	26	9	2	15	25	40	29
11	Besëlidhja Lezhë	26	7	7	12	31	27	28
12	Laçi	26	7	7	12	16	23	28
13	Egnatia Rrogozhinë	26	8	4	14	27	38	28
14	Butrinti Sarandë	26	1	0	25	10	77	3

Andorra

Ranger's feast on first title

A new name was added to the Andorran Primera Divisio's roll of honour as Ranger's FC, rogue apostrophe and all, celebrated their 25th anniversary by winning the national title for the first time.

There was never much doubt that Vicenç Marqués's side, sponsored by a local pizzeria, possessed all the ingredients to make it a happy birthday for the club from the capital. Victorious in each of their first six matches, Ranger's led with 28 points from 11 games at the winter break and added three further wins in the early spring to lead by five points at the end of the First Phase.

Their closest pursuers, defending champions Sant Julià, gave up the ghost completely at the start of the six-match play-off series when they lost their opening two games. This handed the title to Ranger's on a plate, and on April 9, with a 2-0 victory over Championship Group also-rans FC Lusitans, the championship was secure.

Ranger's further extended their lead to a massive 12 points by the finish. It was a fitting climax to the career of the club's 36-year-old striker and captain, Andorran international Justo Ruiz, although there was major disappointment to follow for both him and the rest of the side when they failed to add the Copa Constitucio to their Primera Divisio crown.

One-nil up in the Cup final against FC Santa Coloma with the final whistle about to blow, Ranger's conceded a stoppage-time equaliser. That was only the start of the agony as they went on to be defeated on penalties by Xavi Roura's side, who thus collected the trophy for the second season in succession. It was a case of the biter being bit in the shoot-out as Ranger's had also used that method of advancement to see off Lusitans in the semi-final. Unsurprisingly, the other beaten semi-finalists were Sant Julià.

Worst team in Europe

Sant Julià had begun the season by losing 10-0 on aggregate in the first qualifying round of the UEFA Cup. Although that was the biggest losing margin of the round, their conquerors, Rapid Bucharest, went on to reach the quarter-finals, so Sant Julià could use that in their defence against accusations of being the worst team in Europe. In any case, they were hardly that given what happened to UE Extremenya in their first season in Andorra's top division. The newly promoted club's exercise in damage limitation succeeded only in the twin objectives of avoiding a complete whitewash (they drew one game and lost the other 17) and preventing the concession of 100 goals (the counter stopped at 98, although as the team didn't show up for their final game, at Atlétic d'Escaldes, and were thus penalised by a statutory 3-0 defeat, they rather cunningly dodged that issue).

Extremenya were replaced in the top flight by the team that had swapped places with them at the end of the previous season, FC Encamp, who won the second division at a canter, undefeated in their 18 games. The introduction of a play-off between the top two divisions meant that Encamp might

NATIONAL TEAM RESULTS 2005/06

17/8/05	Romania (WCQ)	A	Constanta	0-2
3/9/05	Finland (WCQ)	H	Andorra La Vella	0-0
7/9/05	Holland (WCQ)	A	Eindhoven	0-4
12/10/05	Armenia (WCQ)	H	Andorra la Vella	0-3

Andorra

NATIONAL TEAM APPEARANCES 2005/06

Coach – David RODRIGO

Player	DOB	Club	ROM	FIN	HOL	ARM	Caps	Goals
Jesús Álvarez "KOLDO"	4/9/70	FC Andorra (ESP)	G	G	G	G	55	-
Josep Manel AYALA	8/4/80	UE Luzenac (ESP)	D		M	M	21	-
Ildefons LIMA	10/11/78	Triestina (ITA)	D	D		D	44	4
Jordi ESCURA	19/4/80	CFJ Mollerusa (ESP)	D46	D	s30		41	-
Antoni SIVERA	13/4/78	UE Luzenac (ESP)	D	D89	D	D18	15	-
Oscar SONEJEE	26/3/76	FC Andorra (ESP)	M	M	M	M	58	2
Alberto RODRIGUES	12/2/86	FC Santa Coloma	M90				2	-
Marc PUJOL	21/8/82	UE Santboià (ESP)	M	M84			21	1
Marc BERNAUS	2/2/77	Elche CF (ESP)	M		M	M	8	1
Gabriel RIERA	5/6/85	Ranger's FC	A81	s73	s54	A82	9	1
Fernando SILVA	16/5/77	CF Quintanar del Rey (ESP)	A		A54		17	1
Javi MARTIN	21/12/75	FC Andorra (ESP)	s46	M	D	M	5	-
Sergi MORENO	25/11/87	Getafe CF (ESP)	s81	A73			7	-
Genís GARCÍA	18/5/78	Ranger's FC	s90	s84			21	-
Antoni LIMA	22/9/70	FC Palamós (ESP)		D	D	D	46	1
Manolo JIMÉNEZ	12/8/76	FC Andorra (ESP)		M	M76	s82	47	1
Justo RUIZ	31/8/69	Ranger's FC		A	A30	A	54	2
Juli FERNÁNDEZ	19/11/74	FC Santa Coloma		s89	D		30	-
Juli SÁNCHEZ	20/6/78	CF Balaguer (ESP)			s76	s18	53	1
Marcio VIEIRA	10/10/80	FC Marco (ESP)				M56	1	-
Ludovic CLEMENTE	9/5/86	FC Andorra (ESP)				s56	1	-

have had company on their ascent, but Principat, another former champion club, retained their top-flight place at the expense of second division runners-up Engordany.

The Andorran national team ended their 2006 World Cup qualifying campaign in October 2005 with a 3-0 home defeat by Armenia. It was an extremely disappointing way in which to conclude their programme. Had they won or drawn the game, David Rodrigo's side would have avoided finishing bottom of the Group One table, leaving Armenia to the wooden spoon instead. Even so, the five points they collected were five points more than they had managed in any of their previous World Cup and European Championship campaigns. A worthy goalless draw at home to Finland added to the four points they had taken off Macedonia, and the final balance sheet was considered good enough by the Andorran FA to earn Rodrigo a new four-year contract. Should he see it out, the 38-year-old will complete a decade in charge of the team, having been recruited to the post in June 1999.

Rodrigo is hardly the busiest national team coach around. Andorra played no further friendly internationals in 2005/06 after the final World Cup qualifier with Armenia. Much of his spare time was spent profitably, however, as he laid the

Andorra

foundations for a national Under-21 side with the help of his two veteran internationals, Justo Ruiz and goalkeeper Koldo Álvarez.

Wembley date cancelled

When the Euro 2008 draw was made and the fixtures arranged, it looked as if Andorra would have the honour and privilege of being the first competitive opposition to play at the new Wembley. But the major delays in the reconstruction of English football's national stadium sadly put paid to that idea. A first ever European Championship point will be the team's number one priority on the road to Austria/Switzerland, and with the Macedonians once again drawn in their group, Rodrigo and his players will be gravely disappointed if they don't fulfil that particular objective.

EUROPEAN CUPS 2005/06

UEFA CUP

UE SANT JULIÁ
1st qualifying round RAPID BUCURESTI (ROM)
H 0-5
Guillermo, Gerardo, Alex, Felix, Lucho, Chinho, Gerard (Nico 78), Pacha, Leo (Mario 57), Alejandro, Luis (Flávio 51).
A 0-5
Guillermo, Lucho, Gerardo, Cristián, Flávio, Alejandro, Gerard, Chinho, Luis (Leo 61), Pacha (Mario 47), Filipe (Joel 76).

DOMESTIC CUP 2005/06

SECOND ROUND
(5/2/06)
FC Encamp 3, Inter d'Escaldes 4
FC Casa Benfica 2, Atlètic d'Escaldes 3
FC Lusitans B 0, UE Extremenya 2
UE Engordany 2, CE Principat 1

QUARTER-FINALS
(7/5/06)
Inter d'Escaldes 2, Ranger's FC 3 *(aet)*
Atlètic d'Escaldes 0, FC Lusitans 0 *(aet; 6-7 on pens)*
FC Santa Coloma w/o UE Extremenya
UE Engordany 0, UE Sant Julià 5

SEMI-FINALS
(10/5/06)
Ranger's FC 0, FC Lusitans 0 *(aet; 4-2 on pens)*
FC Santa Coloma 1, UE Sant Julià 0

FINAL
(13/5/06)
FC SANTA COLOMA 1 *(Leo 90)*
RANGER'S FC 1 *(Pareja 61)*
(aet; 5-3 on pens)

FINAL LEAGUE TABLES 2005/06

Championship Group

		Pld	W	D	L	F	A	Pts
1	Ranger's FC	20	16	3	1	73	12	51
2	UE Sant Julià	20	12	3	5	61	19	39
3	FC Santa Coloma	20	11	3	6	47	17	36
4	FC Lusitans	20	9	1	10	30	41	28

Relegation Group

		Pld	W	D	L	F	A	Pts
5	Inter d'Escaldes	20	11	3	6	36	28	36
6	Atlètic d'Escaldes	20	8	4	8	21	27	28
7	CE Principat	20	3	2	15	18	55	11
8	UE Extremenya	20	0	1	19	11	98	1

First Phase

		Pld	W	D	L	F	A	Pts
1	Ranger's FC	14	12	1	1	62	7	37
2	UE Sant Julià	14	10	2	2	53	12	32
3	FC Santa Coloma	14	9	1	4	41	12	28
4	FC Lusitans	14	8	0	6	26	29	24
5	Inter d'Escaldes	14	7	2	5	22	23	23
6	Atlètic d'Escaldes	14	3	3	8	10	24	12
7	CE Principat	14	1	2	11	12	45	5
8	UE Extremenya	14	0	1	13	9	83	1

SECOND LEVEL FINAL TABLE 2005/06

First Phase

		Pld	W	D	L	F	A	Pts
1	FC Encamp	12	10	2	0	50	6	32
2	FC Casa Benfica	12	7	2	3	23	18	23
3	UE Engordany	12	7	1	4	33	26	22
4	FC Santa Coloma B	12	6	1	5	24	19	19
5	Sporting Escaldes	12	3	2	7	14	36	11
6	CE Principat B	12	2	1	9	11	30	7
7	FC Lusitans B	12	2	1	9	8	28	7

Play-Offs

		Pld	W	D	L	F	A	Pts
1	FC Encamp	18	14	4	0	64	12	46
2	UE Engordany	18	11	1	6	44	35	34
3	FC Casa Benfica	18	7	4	7	26	29	25
4	FC Santa Coloma B	18	7	3	8	33	30	24

PROMOTION/RELEGATION PLAY-OFF
(14/5/06)
CE Principat 3, UE Engordany 0

Armenia

Numbers game doesn't add up

The Armenian Premier Division is a difficult beast to control.

What should have been an eight-team competition in 2005 began with nine participants, only to be reduced back to the original number when one of the clubs, newly-promoted Lernayin Artsakh Yerevan, decided in mid-term that they didn't fancy top-flight football after all and withdrew, turning all of their subsequent matches into 3-0 victories for the opposition.

Then, at the end of the season, plans to turn the 2006 championship into a ten-club affair fell into further confusion due to a number of factors, most of them finance-driven, including the withdrawal of precious foreign sponsorship. Ultimately it had to kick off with just eight teams, including one, Ararat Yerevan, which was actually the club's second XI. Elsewhere, Yerevan United, belatedly offered promotion, disbanded, while Dinamo-Zenit changed their name to Ulis. The one genuine newcomer to the top tier was Gandzasar Kapan, and they had come up despite losing their promotion/relegation play-off 5-1 to Shirak Gyumri – a club that had avoided relegation the previous season simply because the league authorities decided that the Premier Division could not do without them.

Five in a row

Amidst this chaos at least one club provided some continuity and stability as Pyunik Yerevan won the Armenian championship for the fifth year in succession.

It was not the free run to the title they had enjoyed in previous campaigns. Although, as ever, they led from the front all season, they were never completely in the clear, and had the season lasted a little longer, their end-of-season stutter, in which they lost three matches, might have been fatal. Led by Dutchman Henk Wisman, who also doubled up as the Armenian national team coach, Pyunik were never able to shake off Mika Ashtarak and Banants Yerevan, who ended up in second and third place, respectively - just as they had done in 2004.

The injury and mid-season sale to Ajax of teenage wonderboy Edgar Manucharyan (the league's joint-top scorer in 2004) was a big factor in Pyunik's relative decline, as was the unexplained mid-season departure of three of the team's imported players, Mamadou Diawara, Carl Lombé and Apula Bete. When the league campaign took a month's break in August at the end of the first phase of competition (a format change, incidentally, that was devised in mid-season), this trio jetted off on holiday, never to return.

It was actually on the day that Pyunik suffered their only home defeat of the season – 1-0 to bogey side Esteghlal-Kotayk Abovyan – that they were confirmed as champions. This was because Banants, their closest pursuers, simultaneously went down 4-1 to Mika – a result that enabled the club from Ashtarak to clinch runners-up spot for the second season running.

Mika, coached by Armen Adamyan, also claimed the Armenian Cup two years running when, six months

NATIONAL TEAM RESULTS 2005/06

17/8/05	Jordan	A	Amman	0-0	
3/9/05	Holland (WCQ)	H	Yerevan	0-1	
7/9/05	Czech Republic (WCQ)	A	Olomouc	1-4	Hakobyan Ara (85)
12/10/05	Andorra (WCQ)	A	Andorra La Vella	3-0	Sonejee (39og), Hakobyan Aram (52), Hakobyan Ara (62)
28/2/06	Romania	N	Nicosia	0-2	
1/3/06	Cyprus	A	Limassol	0-2	

Armenia

NATIONAL TEAM APPEARANCES 2005/06

Coach – Henk WISMAN (HOL)

Player	DOB	Club	Jor	HOL	CZE	AND	Rom	Cyp	Caps	Goals
Apula Edima BETE	17/6/86	Pyunik Yerevan	G						6	-
Sergis HOVSEPYAN	2/11/72	Pyunik Yerevan	D	D	D		D	D	78	-
Robert ARZUMANYAN	24/7/85	Pyunik Yerevan	D	D	D	D	D	D	10	-
Alexander TADEVOSYAN	9/8/80	Pyunik Yerevan	D	D	D63	D	D	s74	17	-
Romik KHACHATRYAN	23/8/78	OFI (GRE)	M46	M	M71	M			42	1
Karen ALEKSANYAN	17/6/80	Zimbru Chisinau (MOL)	M	M	M	M	M85	M63	15	-
Aghvan MKRTCHYAN	27/2/81	Pyunik Yerevan	M80	M	M		M	M	13	-
Valeri ALEKSANYAN	4/9/84	Pyunik Yerevan	M	s84	M	M78	M63	s74	10	-
Hamlet MKHITARYAN	24/11/73	MTZ-RIPO Minsk (BLS)	M66			M83	M	M	42	1
Ara HAKOBYAN	4/11/80	Stal Alchevsk (UKR) /Metalurg Donetsk (UKR)	A60	s17	A	A	A85	s58	26	4
Aram HAKOBYAN	15/8/79	Banants Yerevan	A75	A80	A57	A81	A76	s63	14	1
Rafael NAZARYAN	26/3/75	Pyunik Yerevan	s46						19	1
Armen SHAHGELDYAN	23/8/73	Mika Ashtarak	s60						44	6
Aram VOSKANYAN	26/8/75	Yesil-Bogatyr Petropavlovsk (KAZ)	s66	s80		s81	s85	M58	11	-
Nshan ERZRUMYAN	17/12/79	Kilikia Yerevan	s75						1	-
Eghishe MELIKYAN	13/8/79	Metalist Donetsk (UKR)	s80		s63	D			19	-
Roman BEREZOVSKI	15/8/74	Dinamo Moskva (RUS) /FK Khimki (RUS)		G	G		G	G	45	-
Karen DOKHOYAN	6/11/76	Krylya Sovetov Samara (RUS)		D	D	D			34	2
Samvel MELKONYAN	15/3/84	Banants Yerevan		M84		s78	M	M74	4	-
Edgar MANUCHARYAN	19/1/87	Ajax (HOL)		A17					9	1
Galust PETROSYAN	5/9/81	Zimbru Chisinau (MOL)			s57		s76	A	6	-
Armen TIGRANYAN	16/8/85	Pyunik Yerevan			s71				1	-
Gevorg KASPAROV	25/7/80	Pyunik Yerevan				G			1	-
Artur VOSKANYAN	13/8/70	Pyunik Yerevan				s83	s85	s46	31	-
Levan PACHAJYAN	20/9/83	Pyunik Yerevan					s63	A74	7	-
Artashes BAGHDASARYAN	11/2/84	Kilikia Yerevan						D46	1	-

after the 2005 league campaign had ended, they 'double-booked' a UEFA Cup place by retaining the trophy at Pyunik's expense, winning the final 1-0 thanks to a goal from much-travelled veteran Armenian international striker Armen Shahgeldyan, who had been playing in Lebanon when Mika won the 2005 Cup final.

Timid exit

Armenian football made little impression outside the national borders in 2005/06. Pyunik's below-par performances on the domestic front were aggravated by a timid aggregate defeat to FC Haka of Finland in the first qualifying round of the Champions League, while Mika and Banants both failed to reach the first round proper of the UEFA Cup. As for the national side, they spared themselves the absolute humiliation of finishing below Andorra in their World Cup qualifying group by beating the minnows 3-0 in the Pyrenees in their final fixture, but there was little of a positive nature to report from the team's visit to the Cyprus international tournament the following spring nor from the draw for Euro 2008, which saw Wisman and his players placed in Group One, the only pool containing eight teams, one of whom was Azerbaijan.

Sour relations between the two nations resulted in Pyunik withdrawing from the 2006 CIS Cup in Moscow when faced with the alternative of confronting their counterparts from Azerbaijan in the semi-final. UEFA will be hoping that things have settled down between the two neighbouring countries by the time they are scheduled to come face to face, twice in four days, in September 2007.

Armenia

EUROPEAN CUPS 2005/06

UEFA CHAMPIONS LEAGUE

PYUNIK YEREVAN
1st qualifying round FC HAKA (FIN)
A 0-1
Bete, Tigranyan (Alexanyan 88), Tadevosyan, Hovsepyan, Mkrtchyan, Voskanyan, Diawara (Pachajyan 70), Arzumanyan, Nazaryan, Davtyan, Lombe (Sahakyan 84).
H 2-2 *Pachajyan (3), Diawara (30)*
Gasparyan, Tigranyan, Tadevosyan, Hovsepyan, Mkrtchyan, Voskanyan (Alexanyan 75), Diawara, Arzumanyan, Pachajyan, Nazaryan, Davtyan (Petrosyan 75).

UEFA CUP

MIKA ASHTARAK
1st qualifying round FSV MAINZ (GER)
A 0-4
Hovhannisyan G., Hovhannisyan V., Magdyev, Tahmazyan (Shevchenko 77), Mekoyan, Mikayelyan, Morozov, Asatryan (Beglaryan 66), Davtyan, Adamyan Artashes (Petikyan 46), Adamyan Artyom.
H 0-0
Hakobyan, Magdyev, Petikyan, Mikayelyan, Hovhannisyan, Harutyunyan (Davtyan 56), Marozov, Adamyan Artashes (Meloyan 63), Asatryan, Shahgeldyan, Adamyan Artyom (Beglaryan 83).

BANANTS YEREVAN
1st qualifying round LOKOMOTIVI TBILISI (GEO)
H 2-3 *Hakobyan (82), Gharabaghtsyan (89)*
Ivardava, Grigoryan H., Grigoryan A.(Khachatryan 59), Simonyan, Seku, Karapetyan, Dudnik, Jenebyan (Hayrapetyan 55), Hakobyan, Melkonyan, Gusila (Gharabaghtsyan 51).
A 2-0 *Hakobyan (22), Khachatryan (81)*
Ganiyev, Oseyan (Hayrapetyan 69), Melkonyan (Gharabaghtsyan 55), Simonyan, Hakobyan, Gusila, Grigoryan A., Dudnik, Seku (Khachatryan 58), Jenebyan, Arakelyan.

2nd qualifying round DNIPRO DNIPROPETROVSK (UKR)
H 2-4 *Hakobyan (24, 43)*
Ganiyev, Grigoryan A., Simonyan, Khachatryan, Arakelyan, Melkonyan, Jenebyan (Hayrapetyan 83), Dudnik (Tadevosyan 71), Oseyan, Gusila (Gharabaghtsyan 55), Hakobyan.
A 0-4
Ganiyev, Grigoryan A., Simonyan, Khachatryan, Dudnik, Gusila (Grigoryan H. 46), Garabaghtsyan (Tadevosyan 46), Arakelyan, Oseyan, Melkonyan (Hayrapetyan 69), Hakobyan.

TOP GOALSCORERS 2005

18	Nshan ERZRUMYAN	(Kilikia Yerevan)
13	Artyom M. ADAMYAN	(Mika Ashtarak)
12	Aram HAKOBYAN	(Banants Yerevan)
11	Samvel PETROSYAN	(Esteghlal-Kotayk Abovyan)
9	Tigran DAVTYAN	(Pyunik Yerevan)
8	Armen SHAHGELDYAN	(Mika Ashtarak)
	Aghvan MKRTCHYAN	(Pyunik Yerevan)
	Vahe TADEVOSYAN	(Banants Yerevan)
7	Tigran GHARABAGHTSYAN	(Banants Yerevan)
	Sargis MOVSISYAN	(Kilikia Yerevan)

LEAGUE RESULTS/ SCORERS/APEARANCES/ GOALS 2005

ARARAT YEREVAN
Coach – Sevada Arzumanyan

2005
13/4	Kilikia Yerevan	a	0-5	
18/4	Pyunik Yerevan	h	0-3	
1/5	Dinamo-Zenit Yerevan	a	1-0	Atabekyan
6/5	Mika Ashtarak	h	0-1	
18/5	Esteghlal-Kotayk Abovyan	a	1-1	Ekuchukwu
23/5	Lernayin Artsakh Yerevan	h	0-2	
29/5	Shirak Gyumri	a	0-2	
11/6	Banants Yerevan	h	1-2	Atabekyan
15/6	Mika Ashtarak	a	0-1	
29/6	Esteghlal-Kotayk Abovyan	h	1-3	Nersisyan
3/7	Kilikia Yerevan	h	0-5	
6/7	Pyunik Yerevan	a	0-5	
13/7	Dinamo-Zenit Yerevan	h	0-4	
18/7	Shirak Gyumri	h	1-0	Navoyan
24/7	Lernayin Artsakh Yerevan	a	3-0	(w/o)
31/7	Banants Yerevan	a	1-4	Abrahamyan
8/9	Shirak Gyumri	a	1-1	Atabekyan
15/9	Shirak Gyumri	h	1-0	Ouzouher (p)

No	Name	Nat	Pos	Aps	(s)	Gls
11	Vardan ABRAHAMYAN		M	16	(1)	1
6	Artak ANTONYAN		M		(2)	
14	Khachik ARAMYAN		M		(1)	
13	Gor ATABEKYAN		A	8	(2)	3
7	Gagik AVAGYAN		M	12	(2)	
15	Karapet BAGHDASARYAN		A		(2)	
9	Levon BEGLARYAN		A	1	(1)	
2	Aram BENIAMINYAN		D	2	(3)	
21	Garik BOYAKHCHYAN		G	6		
8	Arkadi CHILINGARYAN		M	15		
6	Arsen DALLAKYAN		M	9	(2)	
12	Banyi Paul EKUCHUKWU	NGA	A	5	(3)	1
5	Karen GRIGORYAN		D	12		
20	Vakhtang HAKOBYAN	GEO	D	9		
3	Narek HARUTYUNYAN		D	2		
16	Hovhannes L. HOVHANNISYAN		M	2		
24	Musa Idovu IRUNMENHAY	NGA	M	6	(1)	
4	Hayk MKHITARYAN		M	7	(5)	
5	Hayk MURADYAN		M	4	(2)	
19	Hayk NARIMANYAN		D	13	(2)	
10	Karen NAVOYAN		M	12		1
18	Artur NAZARYAN		A	6	(5)	
9	Albert NERSISYAN		A	6	(2)	1
17	Basden OUZOUHER		A	11	(2)	1
8	Artur SARGSYAN		M	1	(2)	
1	Slavik SUKIASYAN		G	11	(1)	
26	Giorgi SULABERIDZE	GEO	A	6		
15	Vahan TOPALYAN		M	4	(6)	
14	Rafayel VARDANYAN		A	1	(7)	

BANANTS YEREVAN
Coach – Hovhannes Zanazanyan; (/6/05) Ashot Barsegyan

2005
12/4	Esteghlal-Kotayk Abovyan	h	1-0	Solodyannikov
17/4	Lernayin Artsakh Yerevan	a	3-2	Tadevosyan, Hakobyan,

Armenia

FINAL LEAGUE TABLES 2005

FINAL ROUND
TOP SIX

		Pld	Home					Away					Total					Pts
			W	D	L	F	A	W	D	L	F	A	W	D	L	F	A	
1	Pyunik Yerevan	20	5	4	1	17	7	6	2	2	18	8	11	6	3	35	15	39
2	Mika Ashtarak	20	3	5	2	16	13	6	3	1	14	3	9	8	3	30	16	35
3	Banants Yerevan	20	6	0	4	17	15	3	6	1	14	12	9	6	5	31	27	33
4	Esteghlal-Kotayk Abovyan	20	4	5	1	9	6	4	2	4	13	13	8	7	5	22	19	31
5	Kilikia Yerevan	20	2	2	6	8	16	2	3	5	12	16	4	5	11	20	32	17
6	Dinamo-Zenit Yerevan	20	1	1	8	6	20	1	1	8	6	21	2	2	16	12	41	8

RELEGATION GROUP

		Pld	W	D	L	F	A	W	D	L	F	A	W	D	L	F	A	Pts
7	Ararat Yerevan	18	2	0	7	4	20	2	2	5	7	19	4	2	12	11	39	14
8	Shirak Gyumri	18	2	3	4	12	18	1	0	8	7	18	3	3	12	19	36	12
9	Lernayin Artsakh Yerevan	16	1	0	7	5	21	2	0	6	9	16	3	0	13	14	37	9

FIRST PHASE

		Pld	W	D	L	F	A	W	D	L	F	A	W	D	L	F	A	Pts
1	Pyunik Yerevan	16	6	2	0	18	4	5	3	0	14	2	11	5	0	32	6	38
2	Mika Ashtarak	16	4	4	0	15	8	6	1	1	12	3	10	5	1	27	11	35
3	Banants Yerevan	16	6	0	2	16	9	4	4	0	16	8	10	4	2	32	17	34
4	Esteghlal-Kotayk Abovyan	16	3	5	0	11	4	4	2	2	17	11	7	7	2	28	15	28
5	Kilikia Yerevan	16	4	1	3	14	11	2	2	4	15	14	6	3	7	29	25	21
6	Dinamo-Zenit Yerevan	16	3	1	4	10	12	1	2	5	10	14	4	3	9	20	26	15
7	Shirak Gyumri	16	2	2	4	11	17	1	0	7	7	17	3	2	11	18	34	11
8	Ararat Yerevan	16	1	0	7	3	20	2	1	5	6	18	3	1	12	9	38	10
9	Lernayin Artsakh Yerevan	16	1	0	7	5	21	2	0	6	9	16	3	0	13	14	37	9

N.B. *The top six teams from the First Phase qualify for the Final Round, carrying forward only their head-to-head results against the other five qualified teams.*

30/4	Shirak Gyumri	h	1-0		Simonyan
12/5	Kilikia Yerevan	a	1-0		Melkonyan
17/5	Pyunik Yerevan	h	2-5		Tadevosyan
					Tadevosyan, Grigoryan A. (p)
23/5	Dinamo-Zenit Yerevan	a	0-0		
11/6	Ararat Yerevan	a	2-1		Jenebyan, Hakobyan (p)
20/6	Kilikia Yerevan	h	2-0		Gharabaghtsyan, Hakobyan
25/6	Mika Ashtarak	h	0-2		
29/6	Pyunik Yerevan	a	0-0		
2/7	Esteghlal-Kotayk Abovyan	a	1-1		Gharabaghtsyan
9/7	Lernayin Artsakh Yerevan	h	3-0		(w/o)
18/7	Mika Ashtarak	a	4-4		Gusila, Arakelyan, Hakobyan, Gharabaghtsyan
23/7	Dinamo-Zenit Yerevan	h	3-1		Davtyan, Gharabaghtsyan, Jenebyan
31/7	Ararat Yerevan	h	4-1		Tadevosyan, Arakelyan, Gharabaghtsyan 2
4/8	Shirak Gyumri	a	5-0		Hakobyan 2, Melkonyan, Dudnik, Bareghamyan
29/8	Esteghlal-Kotayk Abovyan	a	0-0		
12/9	Kilikia Yerevan	h	1-3		Tadevosyan
18/9	Pyunik Yerevan	a	2-2		Arakelyan, Khachatryan
25/9	Mika Ashtarak	h	1-2		Gharabaghtsyan
2/10	Dinamo-Zenit Yerevan	h	1-0		Tadevosyan
6/10	Esteghlal-Kotayk Abovyan	h	4-1		Tadevosyan, Hakobyan 3
16/10	Kilikia Yerevan	a	1-0		Arakelyan
23/10	Pyunik Yerevan	h	2-1		Hakobyan 2
30/10	Mika Ashtarak	a	1-4		og (Antonyan)
6/11	Dinamo-Zenit Yerevan	a	4-1		Melkonyan, Hakobyan (p), Tadevosyan, Arakelyan

No	Name	Nat	Pos	Aps	(s)	Gls
17	Ararat ARAKELYAN		M	11	(5)	5
11	Aram BAREGHAMYAN		M		(17)	1
2	Oleksandr BOZHENKOV	UKR	D	5		
15	Besik CHIKHLADZE	GEO	D	7		
16	Andriy DANAYEV	UKR	M	9		
12	Vahe DAVTYAN		M	5	(7)	1
8	Yuriy DUDNIK	UKR	M	5		1
1	Temur GANIYEV	UZB	G	18	(1)	
24	Tigran GHARABAGHTSYAN		M	11	(8)	7
3	Ashot GRIGORYAN		D	17	(3)	1
6	Grigor GRIGORYAN		M	1	(4)	
4	Hovhannes GRIGORYAN		M	13	(1)	
9	Dmitri GUSILA	MOL	A	3		1
10	Aram HAKOBYAN		A	22	(2)	12
16	Artur HARUTYUNYAN		G	1		
29	Aghvan HAYRAPETYAN		M	3	(9)	
5	Manuchar IVARDAVA	GEO	G	6		
7	Romeo JENEBYAN		M	14	(3)	2

Armenia

No	Name	Nat	Pos	Aps	(s)	Gls
14	Eduard KAKOSYAN		M	2	(3)	
26	Ara KARAPETYAN		M	3	(4)	
7	Ara KHACHATRYAN		M	16	(1)	1
25	Narek MANUKYAN		M		(3)	
21	Samvel MELKONYAN		A	21	(1)	3
20	Artak OSEYAN		M	9	(6)	
9	Artur A. PETROSYAN		M	1	(5)	
23	Giorgi PURTSELADZE	GEO	M	5	(3)	
7	Suren SARGSYAN		M	5	(5)	
2	Serghei SECU	MOL	D	3		
5	Karen SIMONYAN		D	22	(1)	1
8	Vladislav SOLODYANNIKOV	UKR	A	6		1
19	Vahe TADEVOSYAN		A	21	(2)	8
5	Edgar TOROSYAN		M	2	(2)	
18	Artyom YEVLANOV	UKR	D	8		

DINAMO-ZENIT YEREVAN
Coach – Ashot Kirakosyan

2005

Date	Opponent	h/a	Score	Scorers
18/4	Mika Ashtarak	a	1-2	Khachatryan
1/5	Ararat Yerevan	h	0-1	
6/5	Esteghlal-Kotayk Abovyan	a	0-1	
13/5	Lernayin Artsakh Yerevan	h	3-2	Hakobyan S., Nersisyan, Mkrtchyan R.
18/5	Shirak Gyumri	a	3-3	Avanesyan, Aghasyan, Khachatryan
23/5	Banants Yerevan	h	0-0	
29/5	Kilikia Yerevan	a	0-0	
12/6	Pyunik Yerevan	h	0-1	
17/6	Esteghlal-Kotayk Abovyan	h	1-3	Aghasyan
22/6	Lernayin Artsakh Yerevan	a	0-1	
27/6	Shirak Gyumri	h	2-1	Tbilashvili, Galstyan
9/7	Mika Ashtarak	h	0-2	
13/7	Ararat Yerevan	a	4-0	Khachatryan 2, Tbilashvili, Mkrtchyan R.
19/7	Kilikia Yerevan	h	4-2	Mkrtchyan R. 2, Khachatryan, Aghasyan
23/7	Banants Yerevan	a	1-3	Mkrtchyan R.
30/7	Pyunik Yerevan	a	1-4	Tbilashvili (p)
27/8	Pyunik Yerevan	a	0-5	
12/9	Esteghlal-Kotayk Abovyan	h	0-2	
18/9	Mika Ashtarak	a	2-1	Tbilashvili 2 (2p)
25/9	Kilikia Yerevan	h	0-2	
2/10	Banants Yerevan	a	0-1	
6/10	Pyunik Yerevan	h	0-1	
16/10	Esteghlal-Kotayk Abovyan	a	0-1	
23/10	Mika Ashtarak	h	0-3	
30/10	Kilikia Yerevan	a	1-3	Petrosyan
6/11	Banants Yerevan	h	1-4	Hakobyan H.

No	Name	Nat	Pos	Aps	(s)	Gls
19	Albert AFYAN		D	25		
16	Nikolay AGHASYAN		A	12		3
3	Grigor S. ARAKELYAN		D		(1)	
2	Aram AVANESYAN		D	17	(1)	1
10	Artur GALSTYAN		A	18	(6)	1
5	Hrant GHUKASYAN		M	10	(5)	
20	Hayk HAKOBYAN		M		(5)	1
17	Stepan HAKOBYAN		M	14	(7)	1
18	Vahagn HARUTYUNYAN		M	12	(5)	
13	Vachagan KARAPETYAN		D	21		
19	Vahagn KARAPETYAN		M		(1)	
9	Never KHACHATRYAN		A	15	(3)	5
4	Aleksandre KHAVTASI	GEO	M		(2)	
15	Mikael KMENTONI	SLO	M	3	(13)	
12	Gerasim MARGARYAN		D		(2)	

No	Name	Nat	Pos	Aps	(s)	Gls
6	Gevorg MIRIJANYAN		D	19		
14	Babken MKRTCHYAN		D		(3)	
21	Khoren MKRTCHYAN		D	7	(6)	
11	Rafayel MKRTCHYAN		A	20		5
18	Hayk MURADYAN		D	9		
13	Albert NERSISYAN		A	8	(4)	1
17	Vardan K. PETROSYAN		A	5	(3)	1
14	Robert SAHAKYAN		M	9	(6)	
7	Armen G. SARGSYAN		M	11		
8	Lyova SARGSYAN		M	2	(2)	
1	Vahan SHMAVONYAN		G	2	(2)	
17	Karen SUKIASYAN		M		(1)	
20	Gaga TBILASHVILI	GEO	A	22		5
10	Artyom VARDANYAN		M		(1)	
16	Edik YERITSYAN		G	24		
4	Ghazar YUZBASHYAN		M	1	(1)	

ESTEGHLAL-KOTAYK ABOVYAN
Coach – Arsen Chilingaryan

2005

Date	Opponent	h/a	Score	Scorers
12/4	Banants Yerevan	a	0-1	
17/4	Kilikia Yerevan	h	2-2	Petrosyan, Minosyan V.
1/5	Pyunik Yerevan	a	1-1	Babayan
6/5	Dinamo-Zenit Yerevan	h	1-0	Petrosyan
13/5	Mika Ashtarak	a	1-1	Harutyunyan
18/5	Ararat Yerevan	h	1-1	og (Beniaminyan)
30/5	Lernayin Artsakh Yerevan	a	4-1	Petrosyan 2, Barseghyan (p), Mirzakhanyan
12/6	Shirak Gyumri	h	3-0	Minasyan A. 2, Babayan
17/6	Dinamo-Zenit Yerevan	a	3-1	Babayan, Minasyan A., Petrosyan
21/6	Mika Ashtarak	h	0-0	
29/6	Ararat Yerevan	a	3-1	Balabekyan 2, Petrosyan
2/7	Banants Yerevan	h	1-1	Minasyan A.
8/7	Kilikia Yerevan	a	3-4	Minasyan A. 2, Mirzakhanyan (p)
21/7	Lernayin Artsakh Yerevan	h	3-0	(w/o)
30/7	Shirak Gyumri	a	2-1	Barseghyan, Sukiasyan
4/8	Pyunik Yerevan	h	0-0	
29/8	Banants Yerevan	h	0-0	
12/9	Dinamo-Zenit Yerevan	a	2-0	Balabekyan, Petrosyan
18/9	Kilikia Yerevan	h	1-0	Petrosyan
24/9	Pyunik Yerevan	h	2-1	Petrosyan, Babayan
2/10	Mika Ashtarak	a	0-1	
6/10	Banants Yerevan	a	1-4	Sukiasyan
16/10	Dinamo-Zenit Yerevan	h	1-0	Barseghyan (p)
23/10	Kilikia Yerevan	h	2-0	Petrosyan 2
30/10	Pyunik Yerevan	a	1-0	Aghasyan
6/11	Mika Ashtarak	h	0-2	

No	Name	Nat	Pos	Aps	(s)	Gls
1	Harutyun ABRAHAMYAN		G	6		
11	Zohrab ADARYAN		M		(1)	
16	Nikolay AGHASYAN		M	9	(1)	1
27	Arsen AYVAZYAN		M	11		
20	Armen BABAYAN		A	19	(2)	4
11	Arsen BALABEKYAN		A	3	(15)	3
3	Karen BARSEGHYAN		D	23		3
18	Arkadi CHILINGARYAN		D	7	(1)	
25	Hovhannes DEMIRCHYAN		D	6	(2)	
2	Norayr GRIGORYAN		D	20	(1)	
6	Tigran HAKHNAZARYAN		D		(4)	
19	Ararat HARUTYUNYAN		M	10	(3)	1
8	Harutyun HARUTYUNYAN		M	3	(12)	
23	Nikolay KAKOSYAN		M	1		
13	Avetik KIRAKOSYAN		M	22	(1)	

Armenia

No	Name	Nat	Pos	Aps	(s)	Gls
18	Arman MINASYAN		A	12	(1)	6
5	Vahagn MINASYAN		D	14		1
9	Gor MIRZAKHANYAN		M	10	(8)	2
15	Karen NAVOYAN		M	10		
10	Samvel PETROSYAN		A	16	(7)	11
28	Arman POGHOSYAN		D	7	(3)	
22	Nikolay SARGSYAN		G	19		
15	Mikheil SIMONYAN	GEO	M	10	(4)	
14	Gagik SUKIASYAN		M	17	(7)	2
19	Gevorg TUMANYAN		M		(3)	
7	Hrachya VARDAZARYAN		M	18	(5)	
15	Ghazar YUZBASHYAN		M	2		

KILIKIA YEREVAN
Coach – Samvel Darbinyan

2005

13/4	Ararat Yerevan	h	5-0	Nazaryan, Movsisyan 2, Mkrtchyan, Erzrumyan N.
17/4	Esteghlal-Kotayk Abovyan	a	2-2	Movsisyan, Erzrumyan N. (p)
30/4	Lernayin Artsakh Yerevan	h	1-0	Baghdasaryan
5/5	Shirak Gyumri	a	1-3	Erzrumyan N.
12/5	Banants Yerevan	h	0-1	
29/5	Dinamo-Zenit Yerevan	h	0-0	
11/6	Mika Ashtarak	a	2-2	Erzrumyan S., Erzrumyan N.
16/6	Shirak Gyumri	h	4-2	Erzrumyan S., Erzrumyan N. 2, Movsisyan
20/6	Banants Yerevan	a	0-2	
25/6	Pyunik Yerevan	a	0-1	
3/7	Ararat Yerevan	a	5-0	Movsisyan, Erzrumyan N. 3 (2p), Atoyan S.
8/7	Esteghlal-Kotayk Abovyan	h	4-3	Movsisyan, Erzrumyan N. 2 (1p), Hovhannisyan A.G.
14/7	Lernayin Artsakh Yerevan	a	3-0	(w/o)
19/7	Dinamo-Zenit Yerevan	a	2-4	Erzrumyan S., Zakaryan
23/7	Pyunik Yerevan	h	0-3	
31/7	Mika Ashtarak	h	0-2	
28/8	Mika Ashtarak	a	0-0	
12/9	Banants Yerevan	a	3-1	Erzrumyan N.2, Erzrumyan S.
18/9	Esteghlal-Kotayk Abovyan	h	0-1	
25/9	Dinamo-Zenit Yerevan	a	2-0	Erzrumyan N. 2
1/10	Pyunik Yerevan	a	1-2	Stepanyan
6/10	Mika Ashtarak	a	0-0	
16/10	Banants Yerevan	h	0-1	
23/10	Esteghlal-Kotayk Abovyan	a	0-2	
30/10	Dinamo-Zenit Yerevan	h	3-1	Erzrumyan N. 2, Movsisyan
6/11	Pyunik Yerevan	h	1-4	Erzrumyan N.

No	Name	Nat	Pos	Aps	(s)	Gls
2	Mamikon ATOYAN		D	14	(2)	
24	Suren ATOYAN		M	9	(7)	1
13	Hayk AVETISYAN		A		(6)	
12	Mayis AZIZYAN		G	17	(1)	
18	Vahan BABAYAN		M	8	(5)	
4	Artashes BAGHDASARYAN		M	21		1
7	Vahagn BAGHOYAN		M	14	(6)	
20	Khachatur DEMIRCHYAN		M		(1)	
10	Nshan ERZRUMYAN		A	22	(1)	18
9	Sergey ERZRUMYAN		M	22		4
25	Garnik GHASABYAN		A		(1)	
5	Aram A. HAKOBYAN		M	19	(3)	
26	Artak G. HOVHANNISYAN		M	18	(1)	1
14	Harutyun HOVHANNISYAN		A	4	(7)	
29	Armen KIRAKOSYAN		G	8	(1)	
26	Vahram LOBYAN		M	6	(4)	
19	Artavazd MKRTCHYAN		D	4	(12)	1
23	Sargis MOVSISYAN		A	16	(6)	7
25	Sargis NAZARYAN		M	18	(4)	1
6	Vram PETOYAN		M	19	(1)	
27	Karen STEPANYAN		M	7		1
17	Eduard VARDANYAN		M	8		
13	Karen ZAKARYAN		D	21		1

LERNAYIN ARTSAKH YEREVAN
Coach – Arkadi Andreasyan

2005

12/4	Shirak Gyumri	a	4-1	Minasyan A.S. 2, Safaryan, Renato
17/4	Banants Yerevan	h	2-3	Renato, Sargsyan
30/4	Kilikia Yerevan	a	0-1	
5/5	Pyunik Yerevan	h	0-2	
13/5	Dinamo-Zenit Yerevan	a	2-3	Ghazaryan, Yesayan
17/5	Mika Ashtarak	h	1-3	Mkrtchyan L.
23/5	Ararat Yerevan	a	2-0	Safaryan, Renato
30/5	Esteghlal-Kotayk Abovyan	h	1-4	Yesayan (p)
16/6	Pyunik Yerevan	a	1-3	Renato
22/6	Dinamo-Zenit Yerevan	h	1-0	Minasyan A.S.
28/6	Mika Ashtarak	a	0-2	
1/7	Shirak Gyumri	h	0-3	(w/o)
9/7	Banants Yerevan	a	0-3	(w/o)
14/7	Kilikia Yerevan	h	0-3	(w/o)
21/7	Esteghlal-Kotayk Abovyan	a	0-3	(w/o)
24/7	Ararat Yerevan	h	0-3	(w/o)

No	Name	Nat	Pos	Aps	(s)	Gls
8	Albert ACHEMYAN		A	5	(1)	
24	Artur A. AVAGYAN		M	1	(1)	
12	Artur S. AVAGYAN		G	5	(2)	
14	Karen AVOYAN		M		(3)	
7	Hakob BADALYAN		M	2	(4)	
17	Artur V. GABRIELYAN		M	7	(3)	
13	David Zh. GEVORGYAN		A		(3)	
10	Ararat GHAZARYAN		A	5	(1)	1
19	Harutyun N. HARUTYUNYAN		A	3	(2)	
5	Tigran L. HOVHANNISYAN		M	5	(4)	
18	Karen N. KHACHATRYAN		M	3	(4)	
23	Artak MINASYAN		M	1		
5	Artur H. MINASYAN		M	2		
15	Artur S. MINASYAN		M	8		3
3	Levon MKRTCHYAN		D	10		1
23	Sergey MKRTCHYAN		D	7	(1)	
21	Nenad RADACA	SCG	G	6	(1)	
8	RENATO de Moraes	BRA	A	10	(1)	4
9	Edgar SAFARYAN		A	9		2
20	Arsen SARGSYAN		A	6	(3)	1
14	Gagik SIMONYAN		D	3		
11	Karen STEPANYAN		D	6		
13	Khdr TAMOYAN		M	3	(1)	
7	Ara VOSKANYAN		M		(2)	
2	Arkadi YEPREMYAN		D	5		
6	Tigran YESAYAN		A	9		2

MIKA ASHTARAK
Coach – Armen Adamyan

2005

13/4	Pyunik Yerevan	a	0-1	
18/4	Dinamo-Zenit Yerevan	h	2-1	Shevchenko, Adamyan A.M.
6/5	Ararat Yerevan	a	1-0	Hovhannisyan V.G.
13/5	Esteghlal-Kotayk Abovyan	h	1-1	Adamyan A.M.
17/5	Lernayin Artsakh Yerevan	a	3-1	Petikyan, Adamyan A.M. (p), Davtyan
24/5	Shirak Gyumri	h	3-0	Adamyan A.M. 2 (1p),

Austria

form young striker Mark Janko (nine goals in seven games), looked ready to pounce. But when push came to shove, it was Austria who held their nerve and Salzburg who wilted under the pressure. As Schinkels' men won 3-1 away at Sturm Graz, Salzburg were defeated 3-2 at Wacker Tirol. Now Austria needed only to win their penultimate fixture, at home to Tirol, and the title was theirs for the 23rd time. They did not disappoint the expectant crowd at the Franz Horr stadium, winning the game 2-1 thanks to a deflected 18th-minute shot from Czech import Libor Sionko and, after the Tyroleans had equalised, a close-range winner from Slovakian striker Filip Sebo.

Three days later Sebo would open the scoring as the Violetten went on to complete the tenth Double in their history by overcoming Mattersburg 3-0 in the Austrian Cup final. It was the club's record-extending 25th Cup triumph but the first time they had successfully defended the trophy for 43 years.

Stronach withdraws

If there was joy for FK Austria on the field, celebrations were rather tempered off it by an impending financial crisis following billionaire owner Frank Stronach's decision to end his patronage of the club in 2007. The Austro-Canadian businessman stood down as Bundesliga president in the autumn of 2005 (to be replaced at the controls by Mattersburg's Martin Pucher) and announced at the same time that he would gradually sever his ties with the Violetten. A controversial, often unpopular figure, some FK Austria fans may not be too disheartened to see him go but they will certainly miss his money. No sooner had the Double been won than the club's accountants were putting players up for sale and proposing stringent budget cuts. On the other hand, it was pointed out that for the first time since Stronach had arrived at the club, in 1998, Austria had started and finished the season with the same coach – Schenkels – and consequently benefited from the club president's more withdrawn approach by collecting both domestic trophies.

While Schenkels, and Stöger, gained plenty of plaudits for the club's Double triumph, there were several unsung heroes among the playing staff. Veteran French midfielder Jocelyn Blanchard proved to be an inspirational captain and was voted the Bundesliga's Player of the Year by the presidents and coaches of the ten top-division clubs. Roland Linz topped the league's scoring charts (alongside Sanel Kuljic of SV Ried) with 15 goals, while Slovenian playmaker Nastja Ceh proved to be a fine acquisition from Club Bruges and the two Croatian internationals, goalkeeper Joey Didulica and centre-back Mario Tokic, contributed greatly towards the club's impressive defensive statistics.

Jocelyn Blanchard – Bundesliga Player of the Year

Ambitious plans

While FK Austria ended the season facing an uncertain future, with several of those key players set to leave, Red Bull Salzburg were drawing up even more ambitious plans. Having added Austrian national team playmaker Andreas Ivanschitz to their ranks at the start of the year, they created big international headlines by announcing that their new coaching team for 2006/07 would be Giovanni Trapattoni and Lothar Matthäus. Clearly, with this high-profile appointment, owner Mateschitz was aiming higher than mere domestic supremacy. With Salzburg's runners-up spot having earned them a place in the qualifying stages of the Champions League, his big wish was to see the club rubbing

Austria

NATIONAL TEAM APPEARANCES 2005/06

Coach – Hans KRANKL
/(8/9/05) (Willi RUTTENSTEINER & Andreas HERZOG)
/(1/1/06) Josef HICKERSBERGER

Player	DOB	Club	Sco	POL	AZB	ENG	NIR	Can	Cro	Caps	Goals
Helge PAYER	9/8/79	SK Rapid Wien	G46					G	G	9	-
Ernst DOSPEL	8/10/76	FK Austria Wien	D54							19	-
Anton EHMANN	17/12/72	Grazer AK	D	D81						13	-
Emanuel POGATETZ	16/1/83	Middlesbrough (ENG)	D	D	D		D	D	D	20	1
Ronald GERCALIU	12/2/86	SK Sturm Graz /Red Bull Salzburg	D		D83		s78		s73	4	-
Markus SCHOPP	22/2/74	Red Bull Salzburg	M69	M81		M65	M55			56	6
Dietmar KÜHBAUER	4/4/71	SV Mattersburg	M79	M						55	5
René AUFHAUSER	21/6/76	Red Bull Salzburg	M	M		M	M	M	M66	31	5
Andreas IVANSCHITZ	15/10/83	SK Rapid Wien /Red Bull Salzburg	M	M	M	M	M	M80	M	20	3
Christian MAYRLEB	8/6/72	Red Bull Salzburg	A63	A	A61					29	6
Ivica VASTIC	19/9/69	LASK Linz	A63							45	12
Andreas SCHRANZ	2/5/79	Grazer AK	s46	G	G					5	-
Joachim STANDFEST	30/5/80	Grazer AK	s54	D46			s55	M85	D	11	1
Muhammet AKAGÜNDÜZ	11/1/78	SK Rapid Wien	s63					A61		5	1
Sanel KULJIC	10/10/77	SV Ried	s63	s81	s61	s65				4	-
Andreas IBERTSBERGER	27/7/82	SC Freiburg (GER)	s69		D	D81	s46		D	7	1
Jürgen SÄUMEL	8/9/84	SK Sturm Graz	s79		s83					2	-
Mario HIEBLINGER	5/7/77	Grazer AK		D	s48					12	-
Martin STRANZL	16/8/80	VfB Stuttgart (GER) /Spartak Moskva (RUS)		M	D48	D	D		D	30	2
Roland LINZ	9/8/81	FK Austria Wien		s46	A	A	A	A	s64	15	2
Markus KIESENEBNER	21/4/79	FK Austria Wien		s81	M	M	M	M73		11	1
Michael MÖRZ	2/4/80	SV Mattersburg			M			s80	s73	3	-
Martin AMERHAUSER	23/7/74	Grazer AK			M					12	3
Jürgen MACHO	24/8/77	1.FC Kaiserslautern (GER)				G	G			4	-
Andreas DOBER	31/3/86	SK Rapid Wien				D	D46	D		3	-
Paul SCHARNER	11/3/80	SK Brann (NOR) /Wigan Athletic (ENG)				D	D	D	D	14	-
Markus WEISSENBERGER	8/3/75	Eintracht Frankfurt (GER)			M46					22	1
Yüksel SARIYAR	1/8/79	FC Superfund Pasching			s46			s85		3	1
Andreas LASNIK	9/11/83	FK Austria Wien			s81					1	-
Roman WALLNER	4/2/82	VfB Admira Wacker Mödling				A78				20	5
Martin HIDEN	11/3/73	SK Rapid Wien						D46		33	1
Ferdinand FELDHOFER	23/10/79	FC Wacker Tirol						s46	s66	6	-
Zlatko JUNUZOVIC	26/9/87	Grazer AK						s61		1	-
Thomas PRAGER	13/9/85	SC Heerenveen (HOL)							M	1	-
Christoph LEITGEB	14/4/85	SK Sturm Graz							M73	1	-
Stefan LEXA	1/11/76	Eintracht Frankfurt (GER)							M84	5	-
Mark JANKO	25/6/83	Red Bull Salzburg							A64	1	-
Christoph FUCHS	7/4/86	SV Mattersburg							s84	1	-

Austria

shoulders with Europe's elite in the most prestigious club competition of them all.

Money, of course, isn't everything in football, as Admira Wacker Mödling discovered to their cost by dropping out of the Bundesliga at the end of a campaign that had begun with such optimism following the arrival of an Iranian investor and a number of well known players from home and abroad. They never recovered from a catastrophic start – just two points from their first nine matches – and were rooted in bottom place all season. Furthermore, they went down in disgrace following a mass brawl after a game against Wacker Tirol, with several Admira players subsequently being punished with lengthy bans.

Admira's top-flight place was taken, surprisingly, by village club SC Rheindorf Altach, who won the second division in only their second season at that level, having successfully fended off the twin challenge of LASK Linz and Austria Lustenau. Ex-Austrian international Michael Streiter was the coach who took Altach up, ensuring top-flight football once again for the western province of Vorarlberg after Bregenz's relegation in 2005.

Arnie snubbed

It looked as if there might be complications in the promotion/relegation issue when both Graz clubs, GAK and Sturm, were initially refused a licence for 2006/07. However, political intervention eventually rescued both clubs from enforced demotion. Neither had performed with any distinction during the 2005/06 campaign, in the midst of which the name of local boy-made-good Arnold Schwarzenegger was officially removed from their shared stadium in response to the Hollywood actor-turned-California-governor's refusal to grant a pardon to three death-row prisoners.

The best performances from the provinces came from Upper Austrian duo Pasching and Ried. The former made it into Europe for the third season in a row despite losing long-serving coach Georg Zellhofer to Rapid Vienna midway through the season. A fine run in the spring under ex-national team boss Dietmar Constantini concluded with a last-day victory over champions FK Austria that secured third place and a UEFA Cup spot alongside Cup runners-up Mattersburg. The InterToto place went to Heinz Hochhauser's Ried, whose fourth-place finish just two years after promotion constituted the season's biggest surprise.

EUROPEAN CUPS 2005/06

UEFA CHAMPIONS LEAGUE

SK RAPID WIEN

2nd qualifying round F91 DUDELANGE (LUX)
A 6-1 *Lawarée (2, 65), Akagündüz (3, 15), Hofmann (5), Kienast (84)*
Payer, Dober (Martinez 38), Valachovic, Hlinka, Adamski, Korsós, Hoffmann (Dollinger 46), Ivanschitz, Bejbl, Akagündüz (Kienast 72), Lawarée.
H 3-2 *Lawarée (47, 81), Dollinger (86)*
Hedl, Garics, Hlinka, Prenner, Adamski, Dollinger, Martinez (Kavlak 70), Tosun (Valachovic 63), Korsós, Lawarée, Kienast (Kincl 63).

3rd qualifying round LOKOMOTIV MOSKVA (RUS)
H 1-1 *Valachovic (75p)*
Payer, Adamski (Dollinger 77), Hlinka, Valachovic, Korsós (Dober 77), Martinez, Bejbl, Hofmann, Ivanschitz, Kincl, Akagündüz.
A 1-0 *Valachovic (84)*
Payer, Dober, Hlinka, Valachovic, Adamski, Bejbl, Hoffmann, Korsós (Martinez 74), Ivanschitz, Kincl, Akagündüz (Lawarée 54).

1st round Group A
Match 1 FC BAYERN MÜNCHEN (GER)
H 0-1
Payer, Dober, Valachovic, Bejbl, Adamski, Hofmann, Korsós (Martinez 65), Hlinka, Ivanschitz (Dollinger 84), Kindl, Lawaree (Akagündüz 74).

Match 2 JUVENTUS (ITA)
A 0-3
Payer, Dober (Martinez 76), Valachovic, Bejbl, Adamski, Hofmann, Korsós, Hlinka, Ivanschitz, Kindl, Akagündüz (Lawarée 53).

Match 3 CLUB BRUGGE KV (BEL)
H 0-1
Payer, Dober (Hiden Mart. 54), Valachovic, Bejbl (Martinez 73), Adamski, Hofmann, Korsós, Hlinka, Ivanschitz, Kindl, Lawaree (Akagündüz 73).

Match 4 CLUB BRUGGE KV
A 2-3 *Kincl (1), Adamski (81)*
Hedl, Dober (Garics 83), Hiden Mart., Bejbl, Adamski, Hofmann, Korsós, Hlinka, Dollinger (Martinez 70), Kincl, Lawarée (Akagündüz 71).

Match 5 FC BAYERN MÜNCHEN
A 0-4
Payer, Korsós, Hiden Mart., Bejbl, Katzer, Hofmann, Valachovic (Martinez 67), Hlinka (Garics 80), Ivanschitz (Dollinger 90), Akagündüz, Kincl.

Match 6 JUVENTUS
H 1-3 *Kincl (52)*
Payer, Dober, Hiden Mart., Valachovic, Katzer, Korsós (Martinez 80), Hlinka, Hofmann, Ivanschitz, Kincl, Akagündüz (Kienast 86).

UEFA CUP

FK AUSTRIA WIEN

2nd qualifying round MSK ZILINA (SVK)
A 2-1 *Sebo (89), Linz (90)*
Sáfár, Dospel, Tokic, Papac, Dheedene, Sionko (Sebo 79), Blanchard, Kiesenebner, Ceh (Linz 46), Rushfeldt, Mila (Lasnik 64).
H 2-2 *Linz (65, 70)*
Sáfár, Troyansky, Tokic, Papac, Dheedene, Sebo (Sionko 62), Radomski, Ceh (Kiesenebner 73), Lasnik (Rushfeldt 46), Linz, Mila.

Austria

1st round VIKING FK (NOR)
A 0-1
Didulica, Troyansky, Tokic, Hill (Antonsson 90), Dospel, Sionko, Radomski, Blanchard, Lasnik (Dos Santos 64), Linz (Sebo 46), Mila.
H 2-1 *Rushfeldt (20), Lasnik (46)*
Didulica, Dospel, Tokic, Antonsson, Lasnik (Kiesenebner 64), Sionko (Sebo 78), Radomski, Blanchard, Ceh (Mila 54), Linz, Rushfeldt.

GRAZER AK
2nd qualifying round NISTRU OTACI (MOL)
A 2-0 *Schrott (54), Ehmann (57)*
Schranz, Ehmann, Standfest, Plassnegger, Schrott, Bleidelis, Muratovic (Demo 81), Sick, Amerhauser (Kujbali 66), Skoro, Bazina (Junuzovic 66).
H 1-0 *Junuzovic (33)*
Schranz, Ehmann, Standfest, Hielbinger (Sonnleitner 66), Schrott, Pötscher, Bleidelis, Demo (Muratovic 46), Kujbali, , Skoro, Junuzovic (Bazina 70).

1st round RC STRASBOURG (FRA)
H 0-2
Schranz, Ehmann, Standfest, Hielbinger, Plassnegger, Majstorovic, Demo (Junuzovic 56), Muratovic (Bleidelis 59), Amerhauser (Kujabi 80), Oboriah, Bazina.
A 0-5
Schranz, Ehmann, Standfest, Sonnleitner, Plassnegger, Majstorovic, Demo (Sick 54), Bleidelis, Amerhauser, Kollmann (Junzovic 64), Bazina (Muratovic 74).

FC SUPERFUND PASCHING
2nd qualifying round ZENIT SANKT-PETERBURG (RUS)
H 2-2 *Chaile (33), Wisio (87)*
Schicklgruber, Chaile (Kovacevic 90), Baur, Vorisek, Wisio, M'Bock (Karatay 76), Bubenik, Sariyar, Schoppitsch, Glieder, Pichlmann.
A 1-1 *Gilewicz (88)*
Schicklgruber, Chaile, Baur, Vorisek, Wisio, M'Bock, Bubenik, Kovacevic, Sariyar, Schoppitsch, Pichlmann.

TOP GOALSCORERS 2005/06

15	Sanel KULJIC (SV Ried)
	Roland LINZ (FK Austria Wien)
11	Mark JANKO (Red Bull Salzburg)
	Mario BAZINA (Grazer AK/SK Rapid Wien)
	Marek KINCL (SK Rapid Wien)
	Michael MÖRZ (SV Mattersburg)
9	Sigurd RUSHFELDT (FK Austria Wien)
	Alexander ZICKLER (Red Bull Salzburg)
	Muhammet AKAGÜNDÜZ (SK Rapid Wien)
	Ilco NAUMOSKI (SV Mattersburg)
	Thomas PICHLMANN (FC Superfund Pasching)
	Olivier NZUZI (SK Sturm Graz)

LEAGUE RESULTS/SCORERS/APPEARANCES/GOALS 2005/06

VFB ADMIRA WACKER MÖDLING
Coach – Dominik Thalhammer; (17/8/05) Robert Pflug; (23/2/06) Hubert Baumgartner & Ernst Baumeister

2005

Date	Opponent	H/A	Score	Scorers
13/7	FK Austria Wien	h	1-2	Bule
20/7	SK Sturm Graz	a	1-2	Bule
23/7	Grazer AK	h	1-2	Bule
30/7	FC Wacker Tirol	a	0-1	
6/8	SV Mattersburg	h	1-2	Horvath
14/8	FC Superfund Pasching	a	0-5	
20/8	SV Ried	h	2-2	Bule, Bjelica
27/8	Red Bull Salzburg	a	2-3	Bjelica (p), Akoto
10/9	SK Rapid Wien	h	1-1	Egressy
17/9	SK Rapid Wien	a	1-0	og (Gavrics)
21/9	FK Austria Wien	a	1-2	Faraji
24/9	SK Sturm Graz	h	2-3	Thonhofer, Wallner
2/10	Grazer AK	a	1-4	Saglik
15/10	FC Wacker Tirol	h	5-2	Bjelica 2, Saglik, Thonhofer, Pashazadeh
22/10	SV Mattersburg	a	1-3	Bjelica
26/10	FC Superfund Pasching	h	1-2	Horvath
29/10	SV Ried	a	0-4	
5/11	Red Bull Salzburg	h	0-4	
19/11	FK Austria Wien	h	0-1	
26/11	SK Sturm Graz	a	1-1	Bozkurt
3/12	Grazer AK	h	2-0	Pashazadeh, Thonhofer
8/12	FC Wacker Tirol	a	0-4	

2006

Date	Opponent	H/A	Score	Scorers
25/2	FC Superfund Pasching	a	3-0	Horvath, Bjelica, og (Ortlechner)
11/3	Red Bull Salzburg	a	1-0	Landerl
13/3	SV Ried	h	0-0	
22/3	SV Mattersburg	h	0-1	
25/3	SK Rapid Wien	h	2-1	Bule, Saglik
29/3	SK Rapid Wien	a	1-0	Flögel
1/4	FK Austria Wien	a	4-4	Bule, Landerl, Wagner 2 (1p)
8/4	SK Sturm Graz	h	2-0	Bjelica, Hoffer
12/4	Grazer AK	a	0-3	
15/4	FC Wacker Tirol	h	1-1	Bule
22/4	SV Mattersburg	a	2-3	Vishaj, Hoffer
29/4	FC Superfund Pasching	h	2-1	Hoffer 2
06/5	SV Ried	a	0-2	
13/5	Red Bull Salzburg	h	0-3	

No	Name	Nat	Pos	Aps	(s)	Gls
26	Eric AKOTO	TOG	D	15	(2)	1
29	Valter ANDROSIC	CRO	D	6	(3)	
10	Nenad BJELICA	CRO	A	26	(2)	7
31	Osman BOZKURT	TUR	A	2	(3)	1
9	Nino BULE	CRO	A	25	(2)	7
32	Daniel DUNST		M	1	(5)	
15	Gábor EGRESSY	HUN	A	1	(10)	1
28	Moshen FARAJI	IRN	M	8	(3)	1
8	Thomas FLÖGEL		M	21	(4)	1
4	Mario FÜRTHALER		D	5	(3)	
14	Ákos FÜZI	HUN	D	3	(1)	
18	Michael HORVATH		M	30		3
16	Erwin HOFFER		D	10	(7)	4
12	Miroslaw HYLL	SVK	G	1		
19	Rolf LANDERL		M	13		2
1	Thomas MANDL		G	35		
12	Bernhard MORGENTHALER		M	6	(5)	
2	Patrick OSOINIK		M	8	(1)	
6	Jürgen PANIS		M	32		
3	Thomas PANNY		D	1		
7	Mehdi PASHAZADEH	IRN	M	18	(2)	2
21	Srdjan PECELY	BOS	D	15	(1)	
	Patrick PIRCHER		D	12	(2)	
27	Mahir SAGLIK	TUR	A	15	(8)	3
13	Bernhard SCHACHNER		M	1	(6)	
17	Christian THONHOFER		M	20	(8)	3

Austria

11	Butrint VISHAJ	M	4	(2)	1
5	Michael WAGNER	M	25	(1)	2
20	Roman WALLNER	A	10	(5)	1
23	Gerd WIMMER	M	23	(2)	
25	Daniel WOLF	M	4	(10)	

FK AUSTRIA WIEN
Coach – Frenk Schinkels (HOL)

2005
13/7	VfB Admira Mödling	a	2-1	Linz 2
19/7	Grazer AK	h	3-2	Sionko, Dospel, Tokic
23/7	SV Mattersburg	a	2-1	Mila, Rushfeldt
30/7	SV Ried	h	2-0	Rushfeldt, Lasnik
6/8	SK Rapid Wien	a	1-3	Ceh
14/8	SK Sturm Graz	h	2-1	Kiesenebner, Lasnik
20/8	FC Wacker Tirol	a	2-2	Rushfeldt (p), Ceh
28/8	FC Superfund Pasching	h	0-2	
11/9	Red Bull Salzburg	h	2-0	Linz 2
18/9	Red Bull Salzburg	a	0-1	
21/9	VfB Admira Mödling	a	2-1	Rushfeldt 2 (1p)
24/9	Grazer AK	a	0-1	
2/10	SV Mattersburg	h	3-0	Rushfeldt 2, Kiesenebner
16/10	SV Ried	a	0-0	
22/10	SK Rapid Wien	h	0-2	
26/10	SK Sturm Graz	a	0-0	
29/10	FC Wacker Tirol	h	0-0	
6/11	FC Superfund Pasching	a	1-0	Linz
19/11	VfB Admira Mödling	a	1-0	Rushfeldt (p)
3/12	SV Mattersburg	a	2-0	Linz 2
8/12	SV Ried	h	3-0	Linz, Sebo (p), Mila

2006
18/2	FC Wacker Tirol	a	2-0	Tokic, Sebo
25/2	SK Sturm Graz	h	0-0	
5/3	SK Rapid Wien	a	3-0	Linz 2, Dos Santos
11/3	FC Superfund Pasching	h	1-1	Sebo
15/3	Grazer AK	h	2-1	Linz (p), Sionko
19/3	Red Bull Salzburg	a	0-3	
26/3	Red Bull Salzburg	h	2-2	Blanchard, Rushfeldt
1/4	VfB Admira Mödling	h	4-4	Linz, Ceh, Sebo, Janocko (p)
8/4	Grazer AK	a	0-0	
12/4	SV Mattersburg	h	1-0	Vachousek
16/4	SV Ried	a	0-0	
23/4	SK Rapid Wien	h	3-1	Sionko 2, Linz
30/4	SK Sturm Graz	a	3-1	Sionko, Linz 2
06/5	FC Wacker Tirol	h	2-1	Sionko, Sebo
13/5	FC Superfund Pasching	a	0-2	

No	Name	Nat	Pos	Aps	(s)	Gls
4	Mikael ANTONSSON	SWE	D	12		
15	Jocelyn BLANCHARD	FRA	M	33		1
19	Nastja CEH	SLO	M	28	(4)	3
17	Didier DHEEDENE	BEL	D	17	(1)	
1	Joseph DIDULICA	CRO	G	29		
6	Ernst DOSPEL		D	15	(2)	1
26	Maicon DOS SANTOS	BRA	M	6	(2)	1
14	Delano HILL	HOL	D	4	(2)	
10	Vladimir JANOCKO	SVK	M		(2)	1
20	Markus KIESENEBNER		M	12	(8)	2
16	Andreas LASNIK		M	11	(10)	2
29	Roland LINZ		A	25	(6)	15
18	Florian METZ		D	3	(9)	
32	Sebastian MILA	POL	M	7	(6)	2
30	Sasa PAPAC	BOS	D	17	(3)	
22	Jocachim PARAPATITS		A		(5)	
8	Arek RADOMSKI	POL	M	25		
21	Sigurd RUSHFELDT	NOR	A	22	(11)	9
23	Szabolcs SÁFÁR		G	7		
24	Franz SCHIEMER		M	2	(3)	
28	Christian SCHRAGNER		D	9	(2)	
9	Filip SEBO	SVK	A	17	(15)	5
7	Libor SIONKO	CZE	M	23	(8)	6
5	Mario TOKIC	CRO	D	29		2
3	Fernando Ariel TROYANSKY	ARG	D	27	(1)	
11	Stepan VACHOUSEK	CZE	M	13		1
31	Roman WALLNER		A	3	(6)	

GRAZER AK
Coach – Walter Schachner; (9/1/06) Lars Søndergaard (DEN)

2005
12/7	Red Bull Salzburg	h	3-1	Bazina 2, Kollmann
20/7	FC Austria Wien	a	2-3	Plassnegger, Ehmann
23/7	VfB Admira Mödling	a	2-1	Bazina (p), Ehmann
30/7	SV Mattersburg	h	1-0	Ehmann
6/8	SV Ried	a	1-2	Plassnegger
14/8	SK Rapid Wien	h	1-1	Bazina (p)
22/8	SK Sturm Graz	a	2-0	Hieblinger, Skoro
28/8	FC Wacker Tirol	h	1-1	Bazina
10/9	FC Superfund Pasching	a	0-1	
17/9	FC Superfund Pasching	h	0-0	
21/9	Red Bull Salzburg	a	0-1	
24/9	FK Austria Wien	h	1-0	Kollmann (p)
2/10	VfB Admira Mödling	h	4-1	Bazina 2, Kollmann, Lienhart
15/10	SV Mattersburg	a	1-3	Kollmann (p)
22/10	SV Ried	h	2-2	Sick, Skoro
25/10	SK Rapid Wien	a	2-3	Bazina, Standfest
30/10	SK Sturm Graz	h	2-0	Sonnleitner, Skoro
5/11	FC Wacker Tirol	a	1-0	Bazina
20/11	Red Bull Salzburg	h	3-1	Junuzovic, Bazina, Schrott
3/12	VfB Admira Mödling	a	0-2	
8/12	SV Mattersburg	h	3-0	Skoro 2, Kollmann

2006
18/2	SK Sturm Graz	a	0-0	
25/2	SK Rapid Wien	h	3-1	Standfest, Kollmann 2
11/3	FC Wacker Tirol	a	0-1	
15/3	FK Austria Wien	a	1-2	Standfest
18/3	FC Superfund Pasching	a	0-1	
25/3	FC Superfund Pasching	h	1-2	Schenk
29/3	SV Ried	a	1-2	Skoro
2/4	Red Bull Salzburg	a	0-5	
8/4	FK Austria Wien	h	0-0	
12/4	VfB Admira Mödling	a	3-0	Hassler 2, og (Panis)
15/4	SV Mattersburg	a	0-1	
22/4	SV Ried	h	1-4	Junuzovic
29/4	SK Rapid Wien	h	0-2	
06/5	SK Sturm Graz	h	2-3	Junuzovic, Skoro
13/5	FC Wacker Tirol	a	3-1	og (Knabel), Junuzovic, Hassler

No	Name	Nat	Pos	Aps	(s)	Gls
11	Martin AMERHAUSER		M	32	(3)	
20	René AUFHAUSER		M	3		
22	Mario BAZINA	CRO	A	17	(2)	10
9	Imants BLEIDELIS	LAT	M	7	(11)	
18	Igor DEMO	CRO	D	14		
5	Anton EHMANN		D	16		3
6	Dominic HASSLER		A	6	(2)	3
33	Mario HIEBLINGER		D	15	(4)	1
16	Zlatko JUNUZOVIC		A	29	(4)	4
28	Roland KOLLMANN		A	18	(7)	7
3	Pa Saikou KUJJABI	GAM	A	3	(21)	
27	Thomas LECHNER		M	6	(1)	

Austria

FINAL LEAGUE TABLE 2005/06

		Pld	Home W	D	L	F	A	Away W	D	L	F	A	Total W	D	L	F	A	Pts
1	FK Austria Wien	36	11	5	2	32	18	8	5	5	19	15	19	10	7	51	33	67
2	Red Bull Salzburg	36	15	0	3	42	12	5	3	10	20	30	20	3	13	62	42	63
3	FC Superfund Pasching	36	10	4	4	25	12	6	6	6	18	20	16	10	10	43	32	58
4	SV Ried	36	10	7	1	30	12	3	6	9	18	35	13	13	10	48	47	52
5	SK Rapid Wien	36	10	1	7	35	22	3	9	6	16	19	13	10	13	51	41	49
6	Grazer AK	36	9	5	4	31	18	4	1	13	16	30	13	6	17	47	48	45
7	SV Mattersburg	36	7	7	4	25	20	5	1	12	15	34	12	8	16	40	54	44
8	SK Sturm Graz	36	5	8	5	19	17	5	4	9	25	34	10	12	14	44	51	42
9	FC Wacker Tirol	36	7	4	7	26	25	3	8	7	18	30	10	12	14	44	55	42
10	VfB Admira Mödling	36	5	4	9	23	28	4	2	12	19	41	9	6	21	42	69	33

No	Name		Pos	Aps	(s)	Gls
19	Andreas LIENHART		D	4	(8)	1
25	Mario MAJSTOROVIC		D	17	(1)	
8	Samir MURATOVIC	BOS	M	26	(3)	
20	James Chibuzor OBIORAH	NGA	A	3	(2)	
18	Daniel PIRKER		M	2	(1)	
26	Gernot PLASSNEGGER		D	31		2
2	Gregor PÖTSCHER		D	7	(4)	
15	Philipp SCHENK		M	2	(8)	1
1	Andreas SCHRANZ		G	36		
14	Andreas SCHROTT		D	22	(4)	1
23	Gernot SICK		M	6	(2)	1
10	Alen SKORO	BOS	A	11	(12)	7
24	Mario SONNLEITNER		D	25		1
17	Ralph SPIRK		M	6	(2)	
7	Joachim STANDFEST		D	32		3

SV MATTERSBURG
Coach – Franz Lederer

2005
13/7	FC Superfund Pasching	h	0-0	
20/7	Red Bull Salzburg	a	0-4	
23/7	FK Austria Wien	h	1-2	Patocka
30/7	Grazer AK	a	0-1	
6/8	VfB Admira Mödling	a	2-1	Wagner T., Patocka
14/8	SV Ried	h	4-3	Naumoski 2, Mörz, Patocka
20/8	SK Rapid Wien	a	2-1	Naumoski, Hanikel
27/8	SK Sturm Graz	h	1-1	Naumoski
10/9	FC Wacker Tirol	a	2-4	Naumoski, Mössner
17/9	FC Wacker Tirol	h	0-0	
21/9	FC Superfund Pasching	a	0-2	
24/9	Red Bull Salzburg	h	0-1	
2/10	FK Austria Wien	a	0-3	
15/10	Grazer AK	h	3-1	Naumoski, Mörz, Wagner T.
22/10	VfB Admira Mödling	h	3-1	Mörz, Wagner T. 2
26/10	SV Ried	a	2-3	Wagner R., Pauschenwein
29/10	SK Rapid Wien	h	0-0	
5/11	SK Sturm Graz	a	2-0	Mörz, Hanikel
19/11	FC Superfund Pasching	h	1-2	Mörz
26/11	Red Bull Salzburg	a	1-3	Kühbauer (p)
3/12	FK Austria Wien	h	0-2	
8/12	Grazer AK	a	0-3	

2006
18/2	SK Rapid Wien	a	0-2	
25/2	SV Ried	h	3-1	Wagner T., Mörz 2 (1p)
11/3	SK Sturm Graz	h	1-1	Wagner T.
18/3	FC Wacker Tirol	a	0-2	
22/3	VfB Admira Mödling	a	1-0	Fuchs
25/3	FC Wacker Tirol	h	2-2	Mörz, Wagner T.
1/4	FC Superfund Pasching	a	0-2	
9/4	Red Bull Salzburg	h	2-1	Wagner T., Mravac
12/4	FK Austria Wien	a	0-1	
15/4	Grazer AK	h	1-0	Mörz
22/4	VfB Admira Mödling	h	3-2	Naumoski 2, Mörz (p)
29/4	SV Ried	a	2-2	Mörz, og (Glasner)
06/5	SK Rapid Wien	h	0-0	
13/5	SK Sturm Graz	a	1-0	Naumoski

No	Name	Nat	Pos	Aps	(s)	Gls
27	Cem ATAN		M	7	(6)	
1	Thomas BORENITSCH		G	31		
22	Markus BÖCSKÖR		G	5	(1)	
12	Patrick BÜRGER		A	3	(4)	
25	Christian FUCHS		M	34	(1)	1
14	Marcus HANIKEL		A	10	(13)	2
23	Clemens IVANSCHITZ		M		(6)	
20	Bernd KAINTZ		M	30	(3)	
8	Marek KAUSICH	SVK	M	18	(2)	
11	Enrico KULOVITS		M	14	(5)	
10	Dietmar KÜHBAUER		M	32		1
17	Martin LANG		D	7	(4)	
18	Julian LEIDL		M		(2)	
5	Michael MÖRZ		M	35		11
26	Lukas MÖSSNER		A	3	(9)	1
7	Adnan MRAVAC		D	32		1
24	Ilco NAUMOSKI	MAC	A	26	(4)	9
13	Jürgen PATOCKA		D	32	(1)	3
6	Anton PAUSCHENWEIN		M	11	(4)	1
16	Krzysztof RATAJCZYK	POL	D	34		
19	Markus SCHMIDT		M	5	(2)	
15	René WAGNER	CZE	A	1	(17)	1
9	Thomas WAGNER		M	26	(5)	8

SK RAPID WIEN
Coach – Josef Hickersberger; (1/1/06) Georg Zellhofer

2005
13/7	SK Sturm Graz	h	2-3	Kincl 2
19/7	FC Wacker Tirol	a	3-0	Kincl, Akagündüz, Ivanschitz
23/7	FC Superfund Pasching	h	2-0	Valachovic, Lawareé
30/7	Red Bull Salzburg	a	2-0	Kincl, Ivanschitz
6/8	FK Austria Wien	h	3-1	Hlinka, Valachovic (p), Hofmann

Austria

14/8	Grazer AK	a	1-1	Kincl	
20/8	SV Mattersburg	h	1-2	Hlinka	
27/8	SV Ried	a	2-2	Lawarée, Kincl	
10/9	VfB Admira Mödling	a	1-1	Kienast	
17/9	VfB Admira Mödling	h	0-1		
20/9	SK Sturm Graz	a	2-2	Bejbl, Valachovic	
24/9	FC Wacker Tirol	h	2-0	Hlinka, Akagündüz	
1/10	FC Superfund Pasching	a	0-2		
15/10	Red Bull Salzburg	h	2-3	Hofmann, Kincl	
22/10	FK Austria Wien	a	2-0	Lawarée, Kincl	
25/10	Grazer AK	h	3-2	Ivanschitz 2, Martinez	
29/10	SV Mattersburg	a	0-0		
5/11	SV Ried	h	2-2	Bejbl, Akagündüz	
19/11	SK Sturm Graz	h	3-1	Akagündüz, Kincl, Martinez	
26/11	FC Wacker Tirol	a	0-0		
3/12	FC Superfund Pasching	h	3-1	Hofmann, Ivanschitz (p), Akagündüz	
10/12	Red Bull Salzburg	a	0-2		
2006					
18/2	SV Mattersburg	h	2-0	Akagündüz, Bazina	
25/2	Grazer AK	a	1-3	Kincl	
5/3	FK Austria Wien	h	0-3		
12/3	SV Ried	a	0-0		
25/3	VfB Admira Mödling	a	1-2	Akagündüz	
29/3	VfB Admira Mödling	h	0-1		
1/4	SK Sturm Graz	a	0-0		
8/4	FC Wacker Tirol	h	2-1	Akagündüz, Valachovic	
11/4	FC Superfund Pasching	a	0-1		
15/4	Red Bull Salzburg	h	0-1		
23/4	FK Austria Wien	a	1-3	Martinez	
29/4	Grazer AK	h	2-0	Valachovic, Lawarée	
06/5	SV Mattersburg	a	0-0		
13/5	SV Ried	h	6-0	Kavlak 2, og (Berger M.), Akagündüz, Kincl, Dober	

No	Name	Nat	Pos	Aps	(s)	Gls
2	Marcin ADAMSKI	POL	D	18	(3)	
10	Muhammet AKAGÜNDÜZ		M	25	(9)	9
8	Mario BAZINA	CRO	A	9	(1)	1
22	Radek BEJBL	CZE	M	29	(3)	2
14	Thomas BURGSTALLER		D	4	(1)	
23	Andreas DOBER		D	18	(5)	1
19	Matthias DOLLINGER		M	4	(10)	
12	György GARICS		D	18	(10)	
1	Raimund HEDL		G	4		
18	Markus HIDEN		D	4	(1)	
4	Martin HIDEN		D	19		
7	Peter HLINKA	SVK	M	23	(5)	3
11	Steffen HOFMANN	GER	M	19	(1)	3
8	Andreas IVANSCHITZ		M	18		5
13	Markus KATZER		D	12	(1)	
17	Veli KAVLAK		M	9	(5)	2
20	Roman KIENAST		A	1	(9)	1
25	Marek KINCL	CZE	A	28	(7)	11
6	György KORSÓS	HUN	M	21	(5)	
15	Stefan KULOVITS		M	8	(2)	
3	Vladimír LABANT	SVK	D	7	(1)	
9	Axel LAWAREE	BEL	A	14	(12)	4
16	Sebastian MARTINEZ		M	23	(9)	3
24	Helge PAYER		G	32		
27	Helmut PRENNER		M		(2)	
26	Jozef VALACHOVIC	SVK	D	29	(1)	5

RED BULL SALZBURG
Coach – Kurt Jara

2005					
13/7	Grazer AK	a	1-3	Knavs	
20/7	SV Mattersburg	h	4-0	Zickler 2, Carboni, Mayrleb	
24/7	SV Ried	a	0-3		
30/7	SK Rapid Wien	h	0-2		
7/8	SK Sturm Graz	a	0-0		
14/8	FC Wacker Tirol	h	2-0	Schopp, Aufhauser	
20/8	FC Superfund Pasching	a	0-1		
27/8	VfB Admira Mödling	h	3-2	Schopp, Zickler, Kirchler	
11/9	FK Austria Wien	a	0-2		
18/9	FK Austria Wien	h	1-0	Jezek	
21/9	Grazer AK	h	1-0	Zickler (p)	
24/9	SV Mattersburg	a	1-0	Pichorner	
1/10	SV Ried	h	2-0	Schopp 2	
15/10	SK Rapid Wien	a	3-2	Mayrleb 2, Linke	
23/10	SK Sturm Graz	h	3-0	Zickler 2, Jezek	
26/10	FC Wacker Tirol	a	0-3		
29/10	FC Superfund Pasching	h	1-0	Scharrer	
5/11	VfB Admira Mödling	a	4-0	Schopp, Carboni, Kirchler, Janko	
20/11	Grazer AK	a	1-3	Aufhauser	
26/11	SV Mattersburg	h	3-1	Mayrleb, Jezek, Scharrer	
4/12	SV Ried	a	1-2	Linke	
10/12	SK Rapid Wien	h	2-0	Suazo, Schopp	
2006					
19/2	FC Superfund Pasching	a	0-0		
26/2	FC Wacker Tirol	h	5-2	Zickler, Linke, Ivanschitz, Mayrleb, Aufhauser	
4/3	SK Sturm Graz	a	0-4		
11/3	VfB Admira Mödling	h	0-1		
19/3	FK Austria Wien	h	3-0	Zickler 2, Janko	
26/3	FK Austria Wien	a	2-2	Janko, Mayrleb	
2/4	Grazer AK	h	5-0	Janko 2, Aufhauser 2, Jezek	
9/4	SV Mattersburg	a	1-2	Pöllhuber	
12/4	SV Ried	h	3-0	Janko, Jezek 2	
15/4	SK Rapid Wien	a	1-0	Janko	
22/4	SK Sturm Graz	h	3-2	Janko 3	
29/4	FC Wacker Tirol	a	2-3	Aufhauser 2	
06/5	FC Superfund Pasching	h	1-2	Jezek	
13/5	VfB Admira Mödling	a	3-0	Janko, Aufhauser, Mayrleb	

No	Name	Nat	Pos	Aps	(s)	Gls
22	Heinz Dieter ARZBERGER		G	20		
28	René AUFHAUSER		M	30	(1)	8
3	László BODNÁR	HUN	D	4	(4)	
5	Alejo Ezequiel CARBONI	ARG	M	33		2
25	Ronald GERCALIU		D	2		
23	Pascal GRÜNWALD		G		(1)	
10	Andreas IVANSCHITZ		M	9	(3)	1
2	Christoph JANK		D	13	(4)	
21	Mark JANKO		A	13	(4)	11
11	Patrik JEZEK	CZE	M	27	(3)	7
8	Roland KIRCHLER		M	23	(4)	2
15	Aleksander KNAVS	SLO	D	28		1
4	Thomas LINKE	GER	D	24		3
9	Vratislav LOKVENC	CZE	A	4	(1)	
16	Mario Wolfgang MAIR		A	6	(17)	
1	Alexander MANNINGER		G	16		
19	Christian MAYRLEB		A	11	(17)	7
3	Sebastian MIRANDA	CHL	D	3	(1)	
26	Ernst ÖBSTER		M	1	(6)	
30	Péter OROSZ	HUN	A		(1)	
17	Jürgen Gerhard PICHORNER		M	28	(1)	1
14	Alexander PÖLLHUBER		D	6	(1)	1
20	Markus SCHARRER		M	4	(11)	2
18	Markus SCHOPP		M	31		6
12	Maynor Rene SUAZO	HON	M	5	(10)	1
6	Alex von SCHWEDLER	CHL	D	5	(1)	

Austria

31	Thomas WINKLHOFER		D	26	(1)	
7	Alexander ZICKLER	GER	A	24	(7)	9

SV RIED
Coach – Heinz Hochhauser

2005
13/7	FC Wacker Tirol	h	0-0	
20/7	FC Superfund Pasching	a	0-0	
24/7	Red Bull Salzburg	h	3-0	Kuljic, Angerschmid, Eder
31/7	FK Austria Wien	a	0-2	
6/8	Grazer AK	h	2-1	Rasinger, Wolf
14/8	SV Mattersburg	a	3-4	Seo, Dabac, Kuljic
22/8	VfB Admira Mödling	h	2-2	Kuljic 2
27/8	SK Rapid Wien	h	2-2	Seo, Kuljic
10/9	SK Sturm Graz	a	1-3	Seo
17/9	SK Sturm Graz	h	2-1	Sulimani, Seo
21/9	FC Wacker Tirol	a	1-1	Kuljic (p)
25/9	FC Superfund Pasching	h	0-0	
1/10	Red Bull Salzburg	a	0-2	
16/10	FK Austria Wien	h	0-0	
22/10	Grazer AK	a	2-2	Drechsel 2
26/10	SV Mattersburg	h	3-2	Drechsel 2, Kuljic
29/10	VfB Admira Mödling	h	4-0	Seo, Berchtold, Glasner, Kuljic
5/11	SK Rapid Wien	a	2-2	Seo, og (Bejbl)
19/11	FC Wacker Tirol	h	3-0	Seo, Glasner, Berchtold
26/11	FC Superfund Pasching	a	1-0	Drechsel
4/12	Red Bull Salzburg	h	2-1	Kablar, Kuljic
8/12	FK Austria Wien	a	0-3	

2006
25/2	SV Mattersburg	a	1-3	Drechsel
12/3	SK Rapid Wien	h	0-0	
13/3	VfB Admira Mödling	a	0-0	
18/3	SK Sturm Graz	a	0-1	
25/3	SK Sturm Graz	h	2-0	Rasinger, Kuljic (p)
29/3	Grazer AK	a	2-1	Kuljic 2
1/4	FC Wacker Tirol	a	1-0	Kuljic
8/4	FC Paschnig	h	1-2	Kuljic
12/4	SV Salzburg	a	0-3	
16/4	FK Austria Wien	h	0-0	
22/4	Grazer AK	a	4-1	Kastner 2, Michalík, Brenner
29/4	SV Mattersburg	h	2-2	Dabac, Kastner
06/5	VfB Admira Mödling	h	2-0	Kastner, Kuljic (p)
13/5	SK Rapid Wien	a	0-6	

No	Name	Nat	Pos	Aps	(s)	Gls
17	Michael ANGERSCHMID		D	21	(1)	1
1	Hans-Peter BERGER		G	35		
4	Markus BERGER		D	15	(3)	
7	Dietmar BERCHTOLD		M	26	(1)	2
18	Ewald BRENNER		M	33		1
11	Ronald BRUNMAYR		A		(3)	
3	Dario DABAC	CRO	D	29	(2)	2
16	Herwig DRECHSEL		M	27	(2)	6
8	Thomas EDER		M	2	(9)	1
9	Günter FRIESENBICHLER		A		(9)	
5	Oliver GLASNER		M	30		2
21	Davorin KABLAR	CRO	D	31		1
20	Daniel KASTNER		A	5	(12)	4
27	Sanel KULJIC		A	34		15
26	Henrique Lenta LIMA	BRA	D	10	(15)	
15	Rastislav MICHALÍK	SVK	M	17	(3)	1
24	Andreas MICHL		G	1	(2)	
19	Milan RASINGER		M	15	(14)	2
6	Andreas SCHICKER		D	27	(5)	
14	SEO Jung-won	KOR	M	28		7

10	Daniel SOBKOVA		M		(1)	
23	Emin SULIMANI		A	9	(11)	1
25	Dubrovka TESEVIC		M		(1)	
	Miodrag VUKOTIC	SCG	D	1	(1)	
22	Patrick WOLF		M		(6)	1

SK STURM GRAZ
Coach – Michael Petrovic

2005
13/7	SK Rapid Wien	a	3-2	Mujiri, Silvestre, Tsimba
20/7	VfB Admira Mödling	h	2-1	Mujiri 2
23/7	FC Wacker Tirol	h	0-0	
31/7	FC Superfund Pasching	a	2-2	Filipovic, Sarac
7/8	Red Bull Salzburg	h	0-0	
14/8	FK Austria Wien	a	1-2	Sarac
22/8	Grazer AK	h	0-2	
27/8	SV Mattersburg	a	1-1	Mujiri
10/9	SV Josko Ried	h	3-1	Nzuzi, Filipovic, Sarac
17/9	SV Ried	a	1-2	Sarac
20/9	SK Rapid Wien	h	2-2	Mujiri, Filipovic (p)
24/9	VfB Admira Mödling	a	3-2	Filipovic, Tsimba, Sarac
1/10	FC Wacker Tirol	h	2-0	Nzuzi, Rauter
15/10	FC Superfund Pasching	h	2-0	Filipovic, Säumel J.
23/10	Red Bull Salzburg	a	0-3	
26/10	FK Austria Wien	h	0-0	
30/10	Grazer AK	a	0-2	
5/11	SV Mattersburg	h	0-2	
19/11	SK Rapid Wien	a	1-3	Nzuzi
26/11	VfB Admira Mödling	h	1-1	Mujiri
3/12	FC Wacker Tirol	h	2-3	Nzuzi 2
8/12	FC Superfund Pasching	a	1-3	Nzuzi

2006
18/2	Grazer AK	h	0-0	
25/2	FK Austria Wien	a	0-0	
4/3	Red Bull Salzburg	h	4-0	Filipovic, Salmutter 3
11/3	SV Mattersburg	a	1-1	Amadou
18/3	SV Ried	h	1-0	Amadou
25/3	SV Ried	a	0-2	
1/4	SK Rapid Wien	h	0-0	
8/4	VfB Admira Mödling	a	0-2	
12/4	FC Wacker Tirol	a	4-2	Salmutter, Verlaat (p), Nzuzi 2
15/4	FC Superfund Pasching	h	1-1	Krammer
22/4	Red Bull Salzburg	a	2-3	Leitgeb, Nzuzi
30/4	FK Austria Wien	h	1-3	Salmutter
06/5	Grazer AK	a	3-2	Verlaat, Filipovic, Salmutter
13/5	SV Mattersburg	h	0-1	

No	Name	Nat	Pos	Aps	(s)	Gls
17	Dangadji Rabihou AMADOU	CMR	A	18	(9)	2
18	Johannes ERTL		D	19	(8)	
26	Bojan FILIPOVIC	SCG	M	29		7
15	Ronald GERCALIU		D	21		
14	Thomas KRAMMER		M	12	(3)	1
5	Adam LEDWON	POL	M	24		
7	Christoph LEITGEB		M	19	(1)	1
2	Sandro LINDSCHINGER		D		(2)	
4	Mitja MÖREC	SLO	D	16		
20	David MUJIRI	GEO	M	20		6
3	Günther NEUKIRCHNER		D	35		
12	Olivier Niati Polo NZUZI	DRC	A	21	(6)	9
10	Ozren PERIC	BOS	A		(1)	
8	Herbert RAUTER		D	1	(25)	1
9	Diego ROTTENSTEINER		D		(10)	
16	Dragan SARAC	SCG	M	33		5
21	Klaus SALMUTTER		A	13	(3)	6

Austria

FC SUPERFUND PASCHING
Coach – Georg Zellhofer; (31/12/05) Andreas Heraf; (6/3/06) Dietmar Constantini

2005			
13/7	SV Mattersburg	a	0-0
20/7	SV Ried	h	0-0
23/7	SK Rapid Wien	a	0-2
31/7	SK Sturm Graz	h	2-2	Pichlmann, Chaile
6/8	FC Wacker Tirol	a	2-2	Sariyar, Pichlmann
14/8	VfB Admira Mödling	h	5-0	Chiquinho, Bubenik, Pichlmann, Vorísek, Glieder
20/8	Red Bull Salzburg	h	1-0	og (Knavs)
28/8	FK Austria Wien	a	2-0	og (Tokic), Vorísek
10/9	Grazer AK	h	1-0	Sariyar
18/9	Grazer AK	a	0-0	
21/9	SV Mattersburg	h	2-0	Sariyar, Bubenik
25/9	SV Ried	a	0-0	
1/10	SK Rapid Wien	h	2-0	Baur, og (Adamski)
15/10	SK Sturm Graz	a	0-2	
22/10	FC Wacker Tirol	h	2-3	Gilewicz, og (Aigner)
26/10	VfB Admira Mödling	a	2-1	Baur, Karatay
29/10	Red Bull Salzburg	a	0-1	
6/11	FK Austria Wien	h	0-1	
19/11	SV Mattersburg	a	2-1	Kabát, Pichlmann
26/11	SV Ried	h	0-1	
3/12	SK Rapid Wien	a	1-3	Baur
8/12	SK Sturm Graz	h	3-1	Pichlmann, Gilewicz, Karatay
2006				
19/2	Red Bull Salzburg	h	0-0	
25/2	VfB Admira Mödling	a	0-3	
4/3	FC Wacker Tirol	a	0-1	
11/3	FK Austria Wien	a	1-1	Kabát
18/3	Grazer AK	h	1-0	Pichlmann
25/3	Grazer AK	a	2-1	Gilewicz 2
1/4	SV Mattersburg	h	2-0	Ketelaer, Kabát
8/4	SV Ried	a	2-1	Pichlmann, Karatay
11/4	SK Rapid Wien	h	1-0	Vorísek
15/4	SK Sturm Graz	a	1-1	Pichlmann
22/4	FC Wacker Tirol	h	1-1	Chiquinho
29/4	VfB Admira Mödling	a	1-2	Gilewicz
06/5	Red Bull Salzburg	a	2-1	Kovacevic, Ketelaer
13/5	FK Austria Wien	h	2-0	Pichlmann, Ketelaer

No	Name	Nat	Pos	Aps	(s)	Gls
18	Michael BAUR		D	34		3
15	Mario BOLTER		D	7	(1)	
11	Erich BRABEC	CZE	D	12	(4)	
12	Wolfgang BUBENIK		M	21	(2)	2
2	Carlos CHAILE	ARG	D	34		1
8	Alexandre da Silva "CHIQUINHO"	BRA	M	24	(5)	2
19	Radoslaw GILEWICZ	POL	A	18	(8)	5
9	Eduard GLIEDER		A	5	(9)	1
25	Michael GSPURNING		G	2		
28	Manuel HARTL		M	1		
13	Alexander HAUSER		M		(4)	
29	Markus HERMES		A		(1)	
23	Péter KABÁT	HUN	A	13	(4)	3
21	Volkan KAHRAMAN		M	2	(3)	
25	Gerald SÄUMEL		M	1	(11)	
24	Jürgen SÄUMEL		M	18		1
10	Franck SILVESTRE	FRA	D	21		1
1	Grzegorz SZAMOTULSKI	POL	G	36		
27	Cedrik Kinzumbi TSIMBA	SUI	A	8	(7)	2
28	Frank VERLAAT	HOL	D	31		2
10	Dursun KARATAY		M	5	(18)	3
7	Marcel KETELAER	GER	A	11	(2)	3
4	Bozo KOVACEVIC		M	25	(4)	1
3	Patrice MBOCK	FRA	D	6	(5)	
27	Daniel MILOJEVIC		A	2	(7)	
22	Manuel ORTLECHNER		M	25	(2)	
9	Thomas PICHLMANN		A	24	(8)	9
24	Mario REITER		D		(1)	
20	Yüksel SARIYAR		M	23	(1)	3
1	Josef SCHICKLGRUBER		G	34		
14	Kai Walter SCHOPPTISCH		M	21	(6)	
6	Peter VORÍSEK	CZE	D	30	(1)	3
5	Tomasz WISIO	POL	M	17	(6)	
16	Michael WOJTANOWICZ		M		(1)	

FC WACKER TIROL
Coach – Stanislav Cherchesov (RUS)

2005				
13/7	SV Ried	a	0-0	
19/7	SK Rapid Wien	h	0-3	
23/7	Sk Sturm Graz	a	0-0	
30/7	VfB Admira Mödling	h	1-0	Aganun
6/8	FC Superfund Pasching	h	2-2	Aganun, Aigner
13/8	Red Bull Salzburg	a	0-2	
20/8	FK Austria Wien	h	2-2	Pacanda, Aganun
28/8	Grazer AK	a	1-1	Aganun
10/9	SV Mattersburg	h	4-2	Brzeczek, Grüner, Aigner 2
17/9	SV Mattersburg	a	0-0	
21/9	SV Ried	h	1-1	Pacanda
24/9	SK Rapid Wien	a	0-2	
1/10	SK Sturm Graz	h	0-2	
15/10	VfB Admira Mödling	a	2-5	Aganun, Schroll
22/10	FC Superfund Pasching	a	3-2	Brzeczek, Aganun, Schreter
26/10	Red Bull Salzburg	h	3-0	Hattenberger, Feldhofer, Schreter
29/10	FK Austria Wien	a	0-0	
5/11	Grazer AK	a	0-1	
19/11	SV Ried	a	0-3	
26/11	SK Rapid Wien	h	0-2	
3/12	SK Sturm Graz	a	3-2	Pacanda 3
8/12	VfB Admira Mödling	a	4-0	Hattenberger, Eder, Pacanda, Hölzl
2006				
18/2	FK Austria Wien	h	0-2	
26/2	Red Bull Salzburg	a	2-5	Kolousek, Hölzl
4/3	FC Superfund Pasching	h	1-0	Brzeczek
11/3	Grazer AK	a	1-0	Hattenberger
18/3	SV Mattersburg	h	2-0	Pacanda, Aigner
25/3	SV Mattersburg	a	2-2	Kolousek, Eder
1/4	SV Ried	a	0-1	
8/4	SK Rapid Wien	a	1-2	Sturm
12/4	SK Sturm Graz	h	2-4	Knabel, Aigner
15/4	VfB Admira Mödling	a	1-1	Eder
22/4	FC Superfund Pasching	a	1-1	Hölzl
29/4	Red Bull Salzburg	h	3-2	Brzeczek, og (Manninger), Mimm
06/5	FK Austria Wien	a	1-2	Gruber
13/5	Grazer AK	a	1-3	Aganun

No	Name	Nat	Pos	Aps	(s)	Gls
12	Olumuyiwa Olushola AGANUN	NGA	A	20	(12)	7
14	Hannes AIGNER		A	16	(13)	5
14	Benedict AKWUEGBU	NGA	A	1		
18	Jerzy BRZECZEK	POL	M	24	(4)	4
24	Martin DOLLINGER		M		(2)	
2	Hannes EDER		M	17	(2)	3

Austria

3	Ferdinand FELDHOFER		D	30		1
22	Alexander GRUBER		D	17	(9)	1
25	Theo GRÜNER		M	19	(8)	1
5	Matthias HATTENBERGER		M	19	(3)	3
11	Andreas HÖLZL		M	35		3
23	Alexander HÖRTNAGL		M	13	(2)	
4	Torsten KNABEL		D	16	(8)	1
8	Václav KOLOUSEK	CZE	M	13	(1)	2
10	Florian MADER		M	3	(14)	
7	Dennis MIMM		M	26	(5)	1
9	Milan PACANDA	CZE	A	17	(5)	7
19	Zeljko PAVLOVIC	CRO	G	31		
1	Harald PLANER		G	5	(1)	
13	Marcel SCHRETER		D	8	(5)	2
8	Harald SCHROLL		D	7	(1)	1
26	Florian STURM		M	3	(3)	1
6	Filip TAPALOVIC	CRO	M	28	(3)	
17	Bernd WINDISCH		M	28	(3)	

DOMESTIC CUP 2005/06

FIRST ROUND
(13/9/05)
SV Donau 6, FC Kufstein 0
(20/9/05)
Wiener Sportklub 3, PSV Team für Wien 2
(26/9/05)
FC Waidhofen/Ybbs 5, SK St. Magdalena 3
SV Spittal/Drau 3, FC Kelag Kärnten 1
(27/9/05)
SV Würmla 0, FC Gratkorn 1
TSV Hartberg 0, SC Austria Lustenau 1
OSV Schwarz Weiss Salzburg 0, SCR Altach 10
Erster FC Vöcklabruck 0, LASK Linz 2
ATSV Sattledt 0, FC Wacker Tirol 3
FC Koblach 0, SV Kapfenberg 8
Köflach Askö 1, SC Schwannenstadt 2
WSG Wattens 6, DSV Leoben 8 *(after pens)*
Vienna 2, Red Bull Salzburg 3
SV Hall in Tirol 0, VfB Admira Wacker Mödling 5
SC Eisenstadt 1, FK Austria Wien Amateure 2
DSG Union Perg 2, 1.SC Ebner Sollenau 0
SK St. Andrä 5, Union Vöcklamarkt 2
SK Sturm Graz Amateure 2, Red Bull Salzburg Amateure 1
(28/9/05)
Kremser SC 3, SK Sturm Graz 5 *(aet)*
SV Tondach Gleinstätten 0, SV Ried 2
Grazer AK Amateure 1, SV Mattersburg 2
SPG Götzens 1, SV Langenrohr 2

SECOND ROUND
(17/10/05)
SV Spittal/Drau 1, SC Rheindorf Altach 4
(18/10/05)
Wiener Sportklub 1, SV Kapfenberg 5
SAK Klagenfurt 0, FC Gratkorn 1
SV Donau 0, SC Schwannenstadt 4
FC Waidhofen/Ybbs 1, SV Mattersburg 3
DSG Union Perg 0, LASK Linz 3
SK Sturm Graz Amateure 0, FC Wacker Tirol 3
SV Langenrohr 4, SK Sturm Graz 5
SC Austria Lustenau 2, DSV Leoben 0
FK Austria Wien Amateure 1, Red Bull Salzburg 0
(19/10/05)
SK St. Andrä 1, SV Ried 3
SKN St. Pölten 6, VfB Admira Wacker Mödling 5 *(after pens)*

THIRD ROUND
(7/3/06)
SV Mattersburg 3, SC Schwannenstadt 0
FC Superfund Pasching 3, Grazer AK 1
SV Kapfenberg 2, LASK Linz 0
(8/3/06)
SC Austria Lustenau 3, SK Rapid Wien 5 *(after pens)*
(21/3/06)
FK Austria Wien Amateure 0, SV Ried 5
SC Rheindorf Altach 2, SK Sturm Graz 0
SKN St. Pölten 1, FC Gratkorn 2
(22/3/06)
FK Austria Wien 2, FC Wacker Tirol 0

QUARTER-FINALS
(4/4/06)
SC Rheindorf Altach 2 *(Jagne 36p, Sara 96)*, FC Superfund Pasching 3 *(Kabát 23, 93, Milojevic 119) (aet)*
FC Gratkorn 1 *(Panagiotoloulos 42)*, SV Ried 2 *(Kuljic 37, Brunmayr 70)*
SV Kapfenberg 0, FK Austria Wien 1 *(Prettenthaler 58og)*
SV Mattersburg 1 *(Wagner T. 90)*, SK Rapid Wien 0

SEMI-FINALS
(18/4/06)
FC Superfund Pasching 2 *(Vorisek 41, Gilewicz 64)*, SV Mattersburg 3 *(Patocka 27, Mörz 31, 68)*
(19/4/06)
FK Austria Wien 4 *(Sebo 25, Troyansky 57, Dheedene 69, Papac 90)*, SV Ried 0

FINAL
(9/5/06)
Ernst-Happel-Stadion, Vienna
FK AUSTRIA WIEN 3 *(Sebo 27, Rushfeldt 45, Troyansky 82)*
SV MATTERSBURG 0
Referee – Hofmann
FK AUSTRIA WIEN – Sáfár, Troyansky, Tokic, Papac, Dheedene, Sionko, Kiesenebner *(Radomski 46)*, Blanchard, Janocko *(Ceh 63)*, Sebo *(Wallner 76)*, Rushfeldt.
SV MATTERSBURG – Borenitsch, Mravac, Patocka, Ratajczyk, Atan *(Kaintz 86)*, Kühbauer, Mörz, Lang, Fuchs, Wagner T. *(Wagner R. 75)*, Naumoski *(Bürger 84)*.

SECOND LEVEL FINAL TABLE 2005/06

		Pld	W	D	L	F	A	Pts
1	SC Rheindorf Altach	36	20	8	8	61	35	68
2	LASK Linz	36	19	9	8	51	30	66
3	SC Austria Lustenau	36	17	11	8	54	32	62
4	FK Austria Wien Amateure	36	16	10	10	58	40	58
5	FC Gratkorn	36	14	12	10	47	40	54
6	DSV Leoben	36	14	9	13	59	49	51
7	FC Kärnten	36	15	6	15	57	50	51
8	SV Kapfenberg	36	10	9	17	51	69	39
9	SC Schwanenstadt	36	9	6	21	33	57	33
10	FC Kufstein	36	4	4	28	23	92	16

Azerbaijan

Thrilling conclusion to title race

After several years of disorder, the Azeri national championship finally appears to have found some stability. In 2005/06 the top division was reduced from 18 teams to 14 and the outcome was a riveting contest that remained undecided right until the final second of the season.

In the end the competition had a brand new winner as FK Baku (or Baki, as the locals refer to their capital city) timed their run to perfection with victories, and clean sheets, in each of their final eight games. They needed every point, too, because in the final standings they stood just one ahead of Karvan Yevlax.

Amazingly, the champions' eight-match surge came immediately after they had appointed a new coach. When the experienced Äsgär Abdullayev was sacked in late March following an embarrassing 1-1 draw at bottom-placed Göyäzan Qazax, little-known Böyükaga Haciyev was brought in as a replacement. It was a bold move, but one that would bring extraordinary dividends.

The key victory was the 1-0 win at defending champions Neftçi. FK Baku were under siege for most of the game but defended brilliantly and won it with a breakaway goal from Brazilian striker Leandro Gomes. It was with another backs-to-the-wall 1-0 win, away to city rivals Inter, that Haciyev's team clinched their maiden title on the final day. Azeri international midfielder Emi Imamäliyev put FK Baku in front after 26 minutes but they had to defend for their lives during the last 20 minutes after Gomes had been sent off.

Qarabag's Cup

Runners-up Karvan were left to rue goalless draws in each of their previous two games against Neftçi and Turan Tovuz. The team were cruelly denied the services of their Ivorian striker Yacouba Bamba in the run-in, and the man who topped the league scoring charts was still injured when Karvan took on Qarabag Agdam in the Cup final. Without him Karvan lost 2-1. Qarabag's leading marksman Samir Musayev netted the winner three minutes from time to bring the Agdam club their first Cup win in 13 years.

It was a bad season for Azerbaijan's wealthiest club, Xäzär Länkäran. The 2004/05 runners-up finished a lowly seventh after a catastrophic start that also included defeat to Moldova's Nistru Otaci in the UEFA Cup. Xäzär have taken the lead in the recruitment of foreign footballers (and coaches) to Azerbaijan. Such has been the influx, however, that the AFFA has been forced to impose a limit on imported players. To counteract this, clubs have endeavoured to naturalise players by providing Azeri citizenship. Two such players – Yuriy Muzyka (a Ukrainian) and Sergei Sokolov (a Russian) – have even been capped by Azerbaijan, although a national scandal erupted when the Azeri passport of another Ukrainian, Yevhen Shyman, was found to be fake, prompting a wider investigation into other cases.

Certainly, the national side could do with an improvement in fortunes after a World Cup qualifying campaign in which they managed just one goal in ten games. A new coach, Sahin Diniyev, has been appointed to oversee a Euro 2008 campaign that will involve 'interesting' clashes with fellow ex-Soviet republics Armenia and Kazakhstan.

NATIONAL TEAM RESULTS 2005/06

17/8/05	Albania	A	Tirana	1-2	Tagizadä (2)
3/9/05	Northern Ireland (WCQ)	A	Belfast	0-2	
7/9/05	Austria (WCQ)	H	Baku	0-0	
12/10/05	Wales (WCQ)	A	Cardiff	0-2	
28/2/06	Ukraine	H	Baku	0-0	
12/4/06	Turkey	H	Baku	1-1	Sadiqov R.F. (64p)
18/5/06	Moldova	A	Chisinau	0-0	

Azerbaijan

NATIONAL TEAM APPEARANCES 2005/06

Coach – Vaqif SADIQOV
/(29/11/05) Sahin DINIYEV

Player	DOB	Club	Alb	NIR	AUT	WAL	Ukr	Tur	Mol	Caps	Goals
Dmitriy KRAMARENKO	12/9/75	Karvan Yevlax	G	G	G	G				33	-
Rafael ÄMIRBÄYOV	23/2/76	FK Baki	D85	D	D	D				16	-
Räsad F. SADIQOV	16/6/82	Kayserispor (TUR) /Neftçi Baki	D	D		D	D	D		37	2
Aftandil HACIYEV	13/8/81	Turan Tovuz /Neftçi Baki	D	D	D		s76		D	23	-
Mahir SÜKÜROV	12/12/82	Karvan Yevlax	M85	s74	M	M				20	-
Emin QULIYEV	12/4/77	Xäzär Länkäran	M	M	M					42	3
Aslan KÄRIMOV	7/1/73	Qarabag Agdam	M	M	M	M	M46	M	M	60	-
Mahmud QURBANOV	10/5/73	Xäzär Länkäran	M72	M65						63	-
Emin IMAMÄLIYEV	7/8/80	FK Baki	M82	M		M89	M86	M88	M69	29	-
Qurban QURBANOV	13/4/72	Inter Baki	A84		A90					64	12
Zaur TAGIZADÄ	21/2/79	Neftçi Baki	A80	M84	A86	A				37	6
Yuriy MUZYKA	10/8/82	Karvan Yevlax	s72	M	M78	M				4	-
Färrux ISMAYILOV	30/8/78	Karvan Yevlax	s80			A69			A69	28	5
Alim QURBANOV	5/12/77	Xäzär Länkäran	s82							4	1
Ilqar QURBANOV	25/4/86	Xäzär Länkäran	s84				M68	M75		14	1
Ramin QULIYEV	22/6/81	FK Baki	s85				s83	s88	s69	4	-
Zaur HÄSIMOV	24/10/81	Inter Baki	s85					s83	s75	6	-
Samir ÄLIYEV	14/4/79	Xäzär Länkäran		A74	s90	s69				30	1
Anatoliy PONOMARYOV	12/6/82	Kalmar FF (SWE)		s65						13	1
Nadir NÄBIYEV	18/7/80	Neftçi Baki		s84	s86		A83	A70		25	1
Tärlan ÄHMÄDOV	17/1171	Karvan Yevlax			D					73	-
Kamal QULIYEV	14/11/76	Xäzär Länkäran			M					46	-
Elmar BAXSIYEV	3/8/80	Inter Baki			s78	s80	M76	M90	M85	8	-
Emin AGAYEV	10/8/73	NoSta Novotroitsk (RUS)			D80					65	1
Vüqar QULIYEV	20/11/78	Olimpik Baki			M					4	-
Ruslan POLADOV	30/11/79	Inter Baki			s89					1	-
Färhad VÄLIYEV	1/11/80	Inter Baki				G	G	G		3	-
Sergei SOKOLOV	12/6/79	Qarabag Agdam				D	D	D		3	-
Azär MÄMMÄDOV	7/2/76	Qarabag Agdam				D	D	D		13	-
Ramazan ABBASOV	1/2/78	FK Baki				M	M83	M75		3	-
Ceyhun SULTANOV	12/6/79	FK Baki				M68	M62	M60		5	1
Cämsid MÄHÄRRÄMOV	3/10/83	Karvan Yevlax				s46				1	-
Elsän MÄMMÄDOV	4/5/80	Inter Baki				s68	s70	A46		3	-
Vüqar NADIROV	17/8/87	Xäzär Länkäran				s68	s62	s46		7	-
Elvin NURIYEV	18/7/80	Inter Baki				s86	s90	s85		3	-
Räsad Ä. SADIQOV	8/10/83	Neftçi Baki					s75	s60		2	-
Vaqif CAVADOV	25/5/89	CSKA Moskva (RUS)						s69		1	-

Azerbaijan

EUROPEAN CUPS 2005/06

UEFA CHAMPIONS LEAGUE

NEFTÇI BAKI
1st qualifying round FH (ISL)
H **2-0** *Mämmädov A. (20), Misura (90)*
Häsänzadä, Abramidze, Sadiqov R.F., Abbasov, Tagizadä, Chertohanov, Cordas (Musayev 82), Boret, Mämmädov A. (Misura 60), Adamia, Näbiyev.
A **2-1** *Misura (51), Musayev (77)*
Häsänzadä, Abramidze, Sadiqov R.F., Abbasov, Tagizadä, Chertohanov, Boret, Mämmädov A. (Qafitullin 90), Adamia, Näbiyev (Rähmanov 85), Misura (Musayev 71).

2nd qualifying round RSC ANDERLECHT (BEL)
A **0-5**
Häsänzadä (Micovic 46), Abramidze, Sadiqov R.F., Abbasov, Cordas, Adamia, Qafitullin (Getman 9), Boret, Mämmädov A., Näbiyev, Misura (Subasic 74).
H **1-0** *Boret (5p)*
Micovic, Getman, Sadiqov R.F., Abbasov, Cordas, Tagizadä, Abramidze, Mämmädov A., Boret, Sadiqov R.Ä. (Musayev 69), Näbiyev (Cordas 90), Subasic (Misura 76).

UEFA CUP

FK BAKI
1st qualifying round MSK ZILINA (SVK)
H **1-0** *Sultanov (79)*
Cissokho, Mälikov, Ämirbäyov, Quliyev R., Ladaga, Lici (Qurbanov 89), Gogoberishvili, Abuzärov (Sultanov 59), Imamäliyev, Gomes, Stolcers (Vasilyev 66).
A **1-3** *Stolcers (71)*
Cissokho, Mälikov, Ämirbäyov, Quliyev R., Ladaga, Suleap (Qurbanov 75), Lici (Stolcers 58), Gogoberishvili, Imamäliyev, Vasilyev (Mehdiyev 41), Gomes.

XÄZÄR LÄNKÄRAN
1st qualifying round NISTRU OTACI (MOL)
A **1-3** *Ramazanov (25)*
Martsyoshkin, Stankov, Savic, Mämmädov F., Quliyev K., Qurbanov M., Quliyev E., Qurbanov A., Abdullayev (Mämmädov X. 75), Äliyev, Ramazanov (Qurbanov I. 78).
H **1-2** *Äliyev (74)*
Korac, Stankov, Savic, Niftäliyev Ä. (Qurbanov A. 46), Mämmädov F. (Qurbanov I. 76), Quliyev K., Qurbanov M., Quliyev E., Abdullayev (Mämmädov X. 46), Äliyev, Ramazanov.

TOP GOALSCORERS 2005/06

16	Yacouba BAMBA (Karvan Yevlax)	
15	Ahmed TIJANI (Sahdag Qusar)	
12	Pathé BANGOURA (Gänclärbirliyi Sumqayit)	
	Nadir NÄBIYEV (Neftçi Baki)	
11	Branimir SUBASIC (Neftçi Baki)	
10	Samir MUSAYEV (Qarabag Agdam)	
9	Samir ÄLIYEV (Xäzär Länkäran/Inter Baki)	
	Irakli BERAIA (FK Gäncä/Qarabag Agdam)	
	Tomislav MISURA (Neftçi Baki)	
8	Leandro Melino GOMES (FK Baki)	
	Färrux ISMAYILOV (Karvan Yevlax)	
	JUNIVAN de Mello Soäres (Turan Tovuz)	

LEAGUE RESULTS/ SCORERS/APPEARANCES/ GOALS 2005/06

FK BAKI
Coach – Äsgär Abdullayev; (28/3/06) Böyükaga Haciyev

2005

Date	Opponent	H/A	Score	Scorers
12/8	Karvan Yevlax	h	1-0	Vasilyev
22/8	Xäzär Länkäran	a	1-0	Imamäliyev
28/8	Sahdag Qusar	h	0-1	
11/9	Qarabag Agdam	a	4-2	Suleap, Vasilyev, Gomes 2
17/9	Göyäzän Qazax	h	3-0	Pérez 2, Gomes
2/10	MOIK Baki	a	4-0	Stolcers, og (Qasimov), Gomes, Abuzärov
22/10	FK Gäncä	h	0-0	
30/10	MKT-Araz Imisli	a	1-2	Stolcers
13/11	Gänclärbirliyi Sumqayit	h	2-0	Stolcers, Pérez
26/11	Turan Tovuz	a	0-1	
3/12	Neftçi Baki	h	2-2	Stolcers, Abuzärov
10/12	Olimpik Baki	a	1-0	Pérez
17/12	Inter Baki	h	1-0	Gogoberishvili

2006

Date	Opponent	H/A	Score	Scorers
12/2	Karvan Yevlax	a	0-1	
17/2	Xäzär Länkäran	h	1-1	Gomes
22/2	Sahdag Qusar	a	3-0	Vasilyev (p), Sultanov, Pérez
12/3	Qarabag Agdam	h	2-1	Sultanov, Loban
25/3	Göyäzän Qazax	a	1-1	Vasilyev
30/3	MOIK Baki	h	3-0	Gogoberishvili, Pérez, Gomes
6/4	FK Gäncä	a	2-0	Gomes, Vasilyev
17/4	MKT-Araz Imisli	h	3-0	Imamäliyev, Vasilyev, Gogoberishvili
21/4	Gänclärbirliyi Sumqayit	a	2-0	Sultanov 2
29/4	Turan Tovuz	h	1-0	Abbasov R.
7/5	Neftçi Baki	a	1-0	Gomes
14/5	Olimpik Baki	h	2-0	Sultanov, Vasilyev
29/5	Inter Baki	a	1-0	Imamäliyev

No	Name	Nat	Pos	Aps	(s)	Gls
18	Asif ABBASOV		D	10	(2)	
17	Ramazan ABBASOV		M	11	(1)	1
6	Elnur ABDULLAYEV		M		(4)	
4	Samir ÄBDÜRRÄHMANOV		D		(2)	
77	Yasar ABUZÄROV		M	13	(6)	2
27	Pasa ÄLIYEV		A		(3)	
3	Rafael ÄMIRBÄYOV		D	17	(1)	
14	Aleksandre GOGOBERISHVILI	GEO	M	26		3
55	Leandro Melino GOMES	BRA	A	22		8
19	Emin IMAMÄLIYEV		M	24	(1)	3
2	André Luís LADAGA	BRA	M	22		
11	Stanislav LOBAN	UKR	M	1	(8)	1
21	Rail MÄLIKOV		D	23	(1)	
1	Rauf MEHDIYEV		G	8		
33	Orxan MIRZÄYEV		G		(1)	
20	Ruslan MUSAYEV		M	1	(4)	
12	Fernando Néstor PÉREZ	ARG	A	14	(4)	6
7	Ramin QULIYEV		D	24	(1)	
22	Ilyas QURBANOV		D		(2)	
8	Aleksandre REKHVIASHVILI	GEO	M	7	(1)	
23	Khalidou SISSOKO	SEN	G	18		
11	Andrejs STOLCERS	LAT	A	9	(1)	4
20	Marius Mircea SULEAP	ROM	M	8	(3)	1

Azerbaijan

FINAL LEAGUE TABLE 2005/06

		Pld	Home					Away					Total					Pts
			W	D	L	F	A	W	D	L	F	A	W	D	L	F	A	
1	FK Baki	26	9	3	1	21	5	9	1	3	21	7	18	4	4	42	12	58
2	Karvan Yevlax	26	11	2	0	29	3	6	4	3	21	6	17	6	3	50	9	57
3	Neftçi Baki	26	5	6	2	22	9	10	3	0	29	7	15	9	2	51	16	54
4	Inter Baki	26	10	1	2	20	4	4	7	2	15	10	14	8	4	35	14	50
5	Qarabag Agdam	26	7	4	2	18	14	5	0	8	14	18	12	4	10	32	32	40
6	Turan Tovuz	26	8	1	4	18	11	3	4	6	9	10	11	5	10	27	21	38
7	Xäzär Länkäran	26	5	5	3	15	6	4	4	5	12	12	9	9	8	27	18	36
8	Sahdag Qusar	26	5	3	5	12	15	5	2	6	14	21	10	5	11	26	36	35
9	MKT-Araz Imisli	26	7	3	3	20	16	2	5	6	11	20	9	8	9	31	36	35
10	FK Gäncä	26	5	2	6	22	20	2	5	6	13	26	7	7	12	35	46	28
11	Gänclärbirliyi Sumqayit	26	3	2	8	15	24	3	7	3	10	13	6	9	11	25	37	27
12	Olimpik Baki	26	2	4	7	5	15	3	4	6	10	12	5	8	13	15	27	23
13	MOIK Baki	26	1	2	10	3	27	1	1	11	10	40	2	3	21	13	67	9
14	Göyäzän Qazax	26	0	9	4	13	21	0	0	13	1	31	0	9	17	14	52	9

| 10 | Ceyhun SULTANOV | M | 15 | (9) | 5 |
| 9 | Vadim VASILYEV | A | 13 | (9) | 7 |

FK GÄNCÄ

Coach – Sahin Diniyev; (9/1/06) Mehman Allahverdiyev; (13/2/06) Fuad Ismayilov; (4/4/06) (Äläddin Hüseynov); (11/4/06) Fuad Ismayilov

2005
12/8	Inter Baki	h	2-2	Beraia I., Sokolov
21/8	MKT-Araz Imisli	h	5-0	Beraia I. 2, Qurbanov, Xankisiyev, Mämmädov E.
28/8	Gänclärbirliyi Sumqayit	a	2-2	Akhtyamov, og (Gogoladze)
11/9	Turan Tovuz	h	0-0	
18/9	Neftçi Baki	a	2-1	Beraia I. 2
1/10	Olimpik Baki	h	0-1	
22/10	FK Baki	a	0-0	
30/10	Karvan Yevlax	h	1-0	Beraia G.
13/11	Xäzär Länkäran	a	1-1	Beraia I.
27/11	Sahdag Qusar	h	3-1	Beraia I., Mämmädov E. 2
4/12	Qarabag Agdam	a	0-0	
11/12	Göyäzän Qazax	h	3-0	Akhtyamov 2, Xankisiyev
18/12	MOIK Baki	a	3-0	Akhtyamov, Beraia I., Beraia G.

2006
17/2	MKT-Araz Imisli	a	1-3	Mämmädov S.
22/2	Gänclärbirliyi Sumqayit	h	1-2	Yeremeyev
12/3	Turan Tovuz	a	1-2	Mämmädov E.
25/3	Neftçi Baki	h	0-5	
29/3	Inter Baki	a	0-5	
2/4	Olimpik Baki	a	0-1	
6/4	FK Baki	h	0-2	
16/4	Karvan Yevlax	a	1-7	Qämbärov E.
21/4	Xäzär Länkäran	h	1-2	Märdanov
29/4	Sahdag Qusar	a	0-2	
7/5	Qarabag Agdam	h	1-2	Äliyev
14/5	Göyäzän Qazax	a	2-2	Äliyev 2
29/5	MOIK Baki	h	5-3	Äliyev 2, Märdanov, Mämmädov M., Mämmädov S.

No	Name	Nat	Pos	Aps	(s)	Gls
6	Samir AGAYEV		M	1		
22	Daniel AKHTYAMOV		A	13		4
10	Pasa ÄLIYEV		A	8	(2)	5
7	Goga BERAIA	GEO	M	11		2
9	Irakli BERAIA	GEO	A	12	(1)	8
19	Serhiy HORDUN	UKR	A	8	(4)	
15	Ilqar HÜSEYNOV		M	15	(3)	
17	Ramiz HÜSEYNOV		D	5	(4)	
12	Tariyel HÜSEYNOV		G	3	(1)	
5	Abuzär IBRAHIMOV		M	7	(1)	
4	Färhad ISGÄNDÄROV		M	5	(2)	
8	Samir ISMAYILOV		A	1	(1)	
55	Eduard KOKOYEV	RUS	G	21		
4	Azär MÄMMÄDOV		D	13		
18	Eldäniz MÄMMÄDOV		M	6	(12)	4
7	Mätläb MÄMMÄDOV		M	19	(1)	1
14	Säbuhi MÄMMÄDOV		A	10	(8)	2
8	Xaliq MÄRDANOV		M	21		2
10	Vügar NAMAZOV		M		(1)	
16	Anar NÄZIROV		G	2		
6	Vadar NURIYEV		D	11		
11	Elsän QÄMBÄROV		M	12		1
10	Saleh QÄMBÄROV		A	1		
10	Etimad QURBANOV		M	8	(3)	1
2	Ruslan SADIQOV		M	7	(5)	
11	Elçin SEYIDOV		D	1	(1)	
5	Sergei SOKOLOV		D	13		1
17	Adil SÜKÜROV		M	7	(3)	
15	Ceyhun TANRIVERDIYEV		M	2	(6)	
2	Vasif VÄLIYEV		D	10	(1)	
3	Xälil XÄLILOV		A	1	(1)	
8	Elmir XANKISIYEV		M	4	(2)	2
3	Ilham YADULLAYEV		D	23		
19	Dmitriy YEREMEYEV		M	5	(2)	1

Azerbaijan

GÄNCLÄRBIRLIYI SUMQAYIT
Coach – Äfqan Talibov

2005
13/8	Göyäzän Qazax	h	2-0	Bangoura 2
21/8	MOIK Baki	a	1-1	Bangoura
28/8	FK Gäncä	h	2-2	Mehmet Ali (p), Bangoura
11/9	MKT-Araz Imisli	h	2-3	Äliyev N., Bangoura (p)
18/9	Inter Baki	h	1-2	Bangoura
2/10	Turan Tovuz	h	2-2	Nuriyev, Eminov
23/10	Neftçi Baki	a	1-1	Nuriyev
29/10	Olimpik Baki	h	1-3	Ämiraslanov
13/11	FK Baki	a	0-2	
27/11	Karvan Yevlax	h	0-3	
4/12	Xäzär Länkäran	a	0-0	
10/12	Sahdag Qusar	h	3-2	Bangoura 2, Xälilov
18/12	Qarabag Agdam	a	1-1	Äliyev N.

2006
12/2	Göyäzän Qazax	a	1-1	Mehmet Ali
17/2	MOIK Baki	h	1-0	Sahbazov
22/2	FK Gäncä	a	2-1	Muradov, Bangoura (p)
11/3	MKT-Araz Imisli	a	1-1	Bangoura
25/3	Inter Baki	a	0-0	
1/4	Turan Tovuz	a	1-0	Sahbazov
5/4	Neftçi Baki	h	1-2	Bangoura
16/4	Olimpik Baki	a	1-0	Bangoura
21/4	FK Baki	h	0-2	
29/4	Karvan Yevlax	a	1-3	Äliyev N.
14/5	Sahdag Qusar	a	0-2	
26/5	Xäzär Länkäran	h	0-1	
30/5	Qarabag Agdam	h	0-2	

No	Name	Nat	Pos	Aps	(s)	Gls
20	Orxan AGAYARZADÄ		D	10	(1)	
15	Amil ÄHMÄDOV		M		(2)	
10	Namiq ÄLIYEV		M	24	(1)	3
9	Vasif ÄLIYEV		M	1	(6)	
24	Emin ÄMIRASLANOV		M	7	(4)	1
7	Zaur ÄSÄDOV		M	7	(4)	
14	Hikmät BAGIROV		M	1		
22	Pathé BANGOURA	GUI	A	21	(2)	12
1	Saliou DIALLO	GUI	G	17		
18	Ähmäd EMINOV		M	5	(4)	1
3	Goderdzi GOGOLADZE	GEO	D	14	(4)	
6	Ramin HÜSEYNOV		D	11	(2)	
24	Elnur IMANQULIYEV		A		(9)	
12	Davud KÄRIMI		G	9		
15	Bureima MAIGA	BFA	M	1	(1)	
14	Elçin MÄMMÄDOV		M		(1)	
23	Räsad MÄMMÄDOV		D	22		
21	Azär MEHDIYEV		M	11	(6)	
11	MEHMET ALI Arslan	TUR	A	25		2
5	Räsad MURADOV		M	10		1
19	Issa NIKIEMA	BFA	A	9	(2)	
15	Elvin NURIYEV		M	6	(4)	2
8	Emil PASAYEV		D	23	(1)	
27	Elnur RÜSTÄMOV		M	11	(14)	
18	Fäqan SAHBAZOV		A	8	(3)	2
5	Nicat TAGIYEV		A		(1)	
2	Moussa TRAORÉ	GUI	D	11	(1)	
26	Tärlan XÄLILOV		M	22	(1)	1

GÖYÄZÄN QAZAX
Coach – Mäqsäd Yaqubäliyev

2005
13/8	Gänclärbirliyi Sumqayit	a	0-2	
22/8	Turan Tovuz	h	1-4	Sariyev
27/8	Neftçi Baki	a	0-6	
10/9	Olimpik Baki	h	2-2	Abadov, Äliyev
17/9	FK Baki	a	0-3	
1/10	Karvan Yevlax	h	0-2	
23/10	Xäzär Länkäran	a	0-2	
30/10	Sahdag Qusar	h	1-1	Kärimov N.
13/11	Qarabag Agdam	a	1-2	Mädätov
27/11	Inter Baki	a	0-1	
3/12	MOIK Baki	h	2-2	Mädätov (p), Animofoshe
11/12	FK Gäncä	a	0-3	
17/12	MKT-Araz Imisli	h	1-1	Tanriverdiyev

2006
12/2	Gänclärbirliyi Sumqayit	h	1-1	Tanriverdiyev
17/2	Turan Tovuz	a	0-1	
21/2	Neftçi Baki	h	0-1	
12/3	Olimpik Baki	a	0-2	
25/3	FK Baki	h	1-1	Välädov K.
1/4	Karvan Yevlax	a	0-5	
5/4	Xäzär Länkäran	h	0-0	
16/4	Sahdag Qusar	a	0-1	
21/4	Qarabag Agdam	h	1-3	Animofoshe
29/4	Inter Baki	h	1-1	Animofoshe
6/5	MOIK Baki	a	0-1	
14/5	FK Gäncä	h	2-2	Hüseynov, Abadov
30/5	MKT-Araz Imisli	a	0-2	

No	Name	Nat	Pos	Aps	(s)	Gls
15	Elsän ABADOV		D	21	(5)	2
4	Fisayo ABAYOMI	NGA	M	20	(3)	
7	Namiq ADILOV		M	1		
12	Elxan AGAYEV		G	5		
18	Kamil ÄHMÄDOV		M	7	(4)	
9	Fuad ÄLIYEV		A	8	(4)	1
10	Ghani ANIMOFOSHE	NGA	A	22	(1)	3
1	Namiq BAYRAMOV		G	12		
20	Ruslan HÜSEYNOV		M	15	(1)	1
3	Dimitri KAPANADZE	GEO	D	20	(1)	
7	Namiq KÄRIMOV		M	11	(6)	1
12	Ramiz KÄRIMOV		G	9		
17	Ülfät MÄDÄTOV		D	19	(2)	2
19	Sämäd MAHMUDOV		D		(2)	
19	Elbrus S. MÄMMÄDOV		D	13		
16	Emmanuel OLUKAYODE	NGA	A	12	(2)	
6	Müsfiq QÄMBÄROV		D	19	(3)	
5	Elxan SAHNIYAROV		D	20	(4)	
21	Qosqar SARIYEV		M	8	(6)	1
22	Ramin TANRIVERDIYEV		M	17	(1)	2
11	Elçin VÄKILOV		A	4	(11)	
8	Babäk VÄLÄDOV		M	11	(3)	
14	Koroglu VÄLÄDOV		M	12	(5)	1

INTER BAKI
Coach – Anatoliy Konkov (UKR); (22/3/06) Oleh Smolyanynov (UKR); (28/4/06) Valentyn Khodukin (UKR)

2005
12/8	FK Gäncä	a	2-2	Levin, Chernyak
22/8	Karvan Yevlax	h	2-1	Qurbanov (p), Zagorac
27/8	MKT-Araz Imisli	a	2-2	Poladov R., Idahor
11/9	Xäzär Länkäran	h	2-0	Makovskiy M., Makovskiy V.
18/9	Gänclärbirliyi Sumqayit	a	2-1	Idahor, Mämmädov Els.

Azerbaijan

Date	Opponent	H/A	Score	Scorers
1/10	Sahdag Qusar	h	2-1	Lychkin, Idahor
22/10	Turan Tovuz	a	1-0	Lychkin
30/10	Qarabag Agdam	h	2-0	Lychkin (p), og (Musayev R.)
12/11	Neftçi Baki	a	1-1	Mämmädov Els.
27/11	Göyäzän Qazax	h	1-0	Idahor
4/12	Olimpik Baki	a	0-0	
10/12	MOIK Baki	h	3-0	Levin, Chernyak, Lychkin
17/12	FK Baki	a	0-1	
2006				
17/2	Karvan Yevlax	a	0-0	
22/2	MKT-Araz Imisli	h	1-0	Äliyev S.
12/3	Xäzär Länkäran	a	1-1	Häsimov
25/3	Gänclärbirliyi Sumqayit	h	0-0	
29/3	FK Gäncä	h	5-0	Zagorac, Äliyev S. 4 (1p)
2/4	Sahdag Qusar	a	2-0	Ismayilov, Makovskiy V.
6/4	Turan Tovuz	h	1-0	Mämmädov Els.
16/4	Qarabag Agdam	a	0-1	
21/4	Neftçi Baki	h	0-1	
29/4	Göyäzän Qazax	a	1-1	Häsimov
6/5	Olimpik Baki	h	1-0	Idahor
14/5	MOIK Baki	a	3-0	Häsimov 2, Mämmädov Els.
29/5	FK Baki	h	0-1	

No	Name	Nat	Pos	Aps	(s)	Gls
3	Ayxan ABBASOV		M	6	(4)	
12	Samir ÄLIYEV		A	12		5
72	Ilkin BAGIYEV		G		(1)	
8	Elmar BAXSIYEV		M	21	(1)	
23	Serhiy CHERNYAK	UKR	M	22		2
1	Igor DIMITRIJEVIC	SCG	G	5		
2	Zaur HÄSIMOV		D	12	(2)	4
22	Lucky IDAHOR	NGA	A	16	(3)	5
6	Äliyar ISMAYILOV		M	10		1
14	Serhiy KONOVALOV	UKR	M	4	(3)	
18	Yevhen KOTOV	UKR	D	13		
15	Volodymyr LEVIN	UKR	D	26		2
19	Vyacheslav LYCHKIN		M	13	(5)	4
4	Mikhail MAKOVSKIY	BLS	M	23		1
21	Vladimir MAKOVSKIY	BLS	A	22	(1)	2
11	Elnur MÄMMÄDOV		M	6	(3)	
9	Elsän MÄMMÄDOV		A	9	(13)	4
14	Aleksandar NEDOVIC	SCG	M	4	(2)	
16	Elvin NURIYEV		M		(2)	
10	Aqsin ÖMÄROV		M	3	(13)	
72	Oleh OSTAPENKO	UKR	G	1		
1	Elsän POLADOV		G	1		
7	Ruslan POLADOV		M	13	(1)	1
13	Qurban QURBANOV		A	3		1
17	Orxan RÄCÄBOV		M		(5)	
20	Ramil SAYADOV		M	3	(5)	
11	Marius Mircea SULEAP	ROM	M	2	(2)	
42	Färhad VÄLIYEV		G	19		
5	Milan ZAGORAC	SCG	D	17	(1)	2

KARVAN YEVLAX
Coach – Fuad Yaman (TUR); (13/8/05) Yunis Hüseynov

2005

Date	Opponent	H/A	Score	Scorers
12/8	FK Baki	a	0-1	
22/8	Inter Baki	a	1-2	Trapaidze
27/8	Xäzär Länkäran	h	1-0	Bamba
11/9	Sahdag Qusar	a	2-1	Bamba, Muzyka
18/9	Qarabag Agdam	h	1-0	Bamba
1/10	Göyäzän Qazax	a	2-0	Bamba, Ismayilov
22/10	MOIK Baki	h	5-1	Mämmädov, Bamba, Kärimov K. 2, Ismayilov
30/10	FK Gäncä	a	0-1	
12/11	MKT-Araz Imisli	h	1-0	Bayramow
27/11	Gänclärbirliyi Sumqayit	a	3-0	Bamba 2, Mämmädov
3/12	Turan Tovuz	h	1-0	Bamba
10/12	Neftçi Baki	a	0-0	
17/12	Olimpik Baki	h	1-0	Mämmädov
2006				
12/2	FK Baki	h	1-0	Bamba
17/2	Inter Baki	h	0-0	
22/2	Xäzär Länkäran	a	0-0	
11/3	Sahdag Qusar	h	3-0	Ferreira, Ismayilov, Mougadi
26/3	Qarabag Agdam	a	0-0	
1/4	Göyäzän Qazax	h	5-0	Bamba 3, Bayramow, Kärimov K.
5/4	MOIK Baki	a	5-0	Mämmädov, og (Qasimov), Bamba, Abbasov S., og (Qasimov)
16/4	FK Gäncä	h	7-1	Bamba 2, og (Väliyev), Pereira, Akhalkatsi, Abdulov, Ismayilov
21/4	MKT-Araz Imisli	a	3-1	Ismayilov, Bamba, Sükürov
29/4	Gänclärbirliyi Sumqayit	h	3-1	Bayramow, Ismayilov 2
14/5	Neftçi Baki	h	0-0	
22/5	Turan Tovuz	a	0-0	
30/5	Olimpik Baki	a	5-0	Kärimov K., Bayramow, Ismayilov, Mougadi, Mämmädov

No	Name	Nat	Pos	Aps	(s)	Gls
21	Elnur ABBASOV		D	1		
26	Samir ABBASOV		D	2	(5)	1
9	Samir ABDULOV		A		(4)	1
4	Tärlan ÄHMÄDOV		D	10	(1)	
35	Romani AKHALKATSI	GEO	M	12	(1)	1
18	Ruslan ÄMIRCANOV		M	3	(3)	
28	Yacouba BAMBA	CIV	A	21	(1)	16
32	Nazar BAYRAMOW	TRK	M	25		4
11	Souleymane CAMARA	CIV	A		(1)	
33	CLEYTON Dias	BRA	M	1		
22	Marcos FERREIRA	BRA	M	19	(2)	1
1	Elxan HÄSÄNOV		G	14		
24	Aleksandre INTSKIRVELI	GEO	D	17		
16	Färrux ISMAYILOV		A	13	(8)	8
10	Känan KÄRIMOV		A	17	(6)	4
12	Sahil KÄRIMOV		G		(1)	
99	Dmitriy KRAMARENKO		G	12		
5	Cämsid MÄHÄRRÄMOV		M	1	(8)	
23	Ismayil MÄMMÄDOV		M	26		5
20	Cavad MIRZÄYEV		M		(3)	
8	Bachir MOUGADI	TUN	M	5	(7)	2
6	Samir MÜTÄLLIMOV		D		(1)	
17	Yuriy MUZYKA		M	10	(6)	1
14	Mäkan NÄSYROW	TRK	M	1	(4)	
15	Ernani PEREIRA	BRA	D	26		
25	Mahir SÜKÜROV		D	25		1
7	Gocha TRAPAIDZE	GEO	M	25		1
3	Mehman YUNUSOV		D		(2)	

MKT-ARAZ IMISLI
Coach – Ihor Nakonechnyi (UKR)

2005

Azerbaijan

14/8	MOIK Baki	h	3-1		Fábio Luís (p), Zeynalov, Maurilho
21/8	FK Gäncä	a	0-5		
27/8	Inter Baki	h	2-2		og (Häsimov), Agakisiyev (p)
11/9	Gänclärbirliyi Sumqayit	a	3-2		Fábio Luís (p), Parkhomenko, Agakisiyev
17/9	Turan Tovuz	a	1-3		Muradov
1/10	Neftçi Baki	h	0-5		
23/10	Olimpik Baki	a	0-0		
30/10	FK Baki	h	2-1		Baldovaliev, Muteba
12/11	Karvan Yevlax	a	0-1		
26/11	Xäzär Länkäran	h	2-1		Fábio Luís, Baldovaliev
3/12	Sahdag Qusar	a	1-1		Yunisoglu
11/12	Qarabag Agdam	h	1-0		Agakisiyev
17/12	Göyäzän Qazax	a	1-1		Agakisiyev
2006					
12/2	MOIK Baki	a	3-0		Makovei, Zeynalov, Agakisiyev
17/2	FK Gäncä	h	3-1		Äbdürähmanov, Fábio Luís, Baldovaliev
22/2	Inter Baki	a	0-1		
11/3	Gänclärbirliyi Sumqayit	h	1-1		Fábio Luís
26/3	Turan Tovuz	h	0-1		
1/4	Neftçi Baki	a	1-1		Baldovaliev
6/4	Olimpik Baki	h	0-0		
17/4	FK Baki	a	0-3		
21/4	Karvan Yevlax	h	1-3		Usubov
7/5	Sahdag Qusar	h	3-0		Makovei 2, Muteba
14/5	Qarabag Agdam	a	1-2		Makovei
22/5	Xäzär Länkäran	a	0-0		
30/5	Göyäzän Qazax	h	2-0		Agakisiyev, Zeynalov

No	Name	Nat	Pos	Aps	(s)	Gls
19	Ramil ABDASOV		M		(1)	
15	Renat ABDASOV		D	6	(3)	
55	Ilqar ÄBDÜRRÄHMANOV		D	8		1
5	Ceyhun ADISIRINOV		D	20	(4)	
9	Murad AGAKISIYEV		M	21	(2)	6
17	Hüseyn ÄLIYEV		M	1	(1)	
12	Sadiq ÄLIYEV		G	2		
99	Oleksandr BABAK	UKR	G	6		
20	Samir BABAYEV		M	1		
29	Zoran BALDOVALIEV	MAC	A	14	(2)	4
18	Sinisa BRANKOVIC	SCG	D	21		
4	Monday ETOVE	NGA	D	1		
11	FÁBIO LUÍS Ramim	BRA	A	21	(2)	5
1	Allahverdi FÄRZÄLIYEV		G		(1)	
5	Zaur HIDAYÄTOV		D	6	(2)	
14	Valeh KÄRIMOV		M	5	(8)	
21	Ihor MAKOVEI	UKR	M	9	(1)	4
7	Thomas MAURILHO	BRA	M	12	(4)	1
77	Xalid MURADOV		A	6	(13)	1
22	Maurice Pedro MUTEB	DRC	M	9	(8)	2
2	Dmytro PARKHOMENKO	UKR	D	23		1
4	Aqsin SALAHOV		D	4	(3)	
3	Yevhen SHYMAN	UKR	M	3		
8	Tengizi SICHINAVA	GEO	D	11		
3	Zoran STERJOVSKI	MAC	A	6		
1	Nadir SÜKÜROV		G	6		
12	Etibar TARIVERDIYEV		G	12	(1)	
6	Ruhid USUBOV		D	1	(2)	1
16	Valentyn VYSHTALYUK	UKR	D	13	(1)	

25	Rämzi XUBALIYEV		A	(3)	
33	Sasa YUNISOGLU		D	18	1
10	Zeynal ZEYNALOV		M	20 (3)	3

MOIK BAKI
Coach – Akif Ibadov; (21/8/05) Samil Üseynov; (15/3/06) Ramil Äliyev

2005

14/8	MKT-Araz Imisli	a	1-3		Abbasov (p)
21/8	Gänclärbirliyi Sumqayit	h	1-1		Abbasov
28/8	Turan Tovuz	a	1-5		Abbasov
10/9	Neftçi Baki	h	0-1		
17/9	Olimpik Baki	a	1-0		Ämiraslanov
2/10	FK Baki	h	0-4		
22/10	Karvan Yevlax	a	1-5		Imanquliyev
29/10	Xäzär Länkäran	h	0-0		
12/11	Sahdag Qusar	a	0-1		
26/11	Qarabag Agdam	h	0-2		
3/12	Göyäzän Qazax	a	2-2		Abbasov 2 (2p)
10/12	Inter Baki	a	0-3		
18/12	FK Gäncä	h	0-3		
2006					
12/2	MKT-Araz Imisli	h	0-3		
17/2	Gänclärbirliyi Sumqayit	a	0-1		
22/2	Turan Tovuz	h	1-2		Ämiraslanov
11/3	Neftçi Baki	a	0-4		
25/3	Olimpik Baki	h	0-2		
30/3	FK Baki	a	0-3		
5/4	Karvan Yevlax	h	0-5		
16/4	Xäzär Länkäran	a	0-6		
21/4	Sahdag Qusar	h	0-1		
29/4	Qarabag Agdam	h	1-2		Häsänov H.
6/5	Göyäzän Qazax	h	1-0		Mämmädov F.Q.
14/5	Inter Baki	h	0-3		
29/5	FK Gäncä	a	3-5		Hümbätov, Häsänov H., Bagirov

No	Name	Nat	Pos	Aps	(s)	Gls
17	Ramazan ABBASOV		M	13		5
2	Namiq ADILOV		M	23	(1)	
26	Rövsän ÄMIRASLANOV		A	17	(7)	2
3	Siyasät ÄSGÄROV		D	17	(1)	
20	Vüqar ÄSGÄROV		M	14	(8)	
14	Mähämmad ASLANOV		D	7	(1)	
11	Elgün BAGIROV		A		(3)	1
21	Hikmät BAGIROV		M	9	(1)	
1	Anar BAYRAMOV		G	21		
15	Teymur DADASOV		M	1		
20	Elvin HÄMIDOV		M		(1)	
7	Hüseyn HÄSÄNOV		A	21	(3)	2
5	Rähim HÄSANOV		D	8		
6	Akif HÜMBÄTOV		M	14	(4)	1
19	Cavid HÜSEYNOV		A		(3)	
9	Elnur IMANQULIYEV		A	11	(1)	1
8	Cavid ISMAYILOV		D	2	(5)	
9	Tärlan MAHMUDOV		A	7	(2)	
14	Vüqar MÄMMÄD		D	6		
19	Cavid MÄMMÄDOV		M	1		
18	Färid K. MÄMMÄDOV		M	4	(1)	
10	Färid Q. MÄMMÄDOV		M	15	(2)	1
22	Ruslan S. MÄMMÄDOV		G	5	(3)	
11	Ruslan MÄMMÄDOV		D	1	(1)	
4	Zaur MÄMMÄDOV		M	1	(7)	
15	Natiq NÄCÄFOV		D	12		

Azerbaijan

16	Elvin QAFAROV		M	1	(6)		5	Ruslan QAFITULLIN		D	9		
15	Natiq QASIMOV		D	21			9	Elçin RÄHMANOV		M	2	(5)	
2	Araz QULAMOV		D	1			6	Räsad Ä. SADIQOV		M	11	(12)	2
14	Samir QULIYEV		M	19	(1)		14	Räsad F. SADIQOV		D	12	(1)	
17	Äli SÄFÄROV		M	10	(4)		20	Branimir SUBASIC	SCG	A	15	(9)	11
16	Cälaläddin TAGIYEV		M	1			22	Zaur TAGIZADÄ		M	12	(5)	3
5	Samir XAIROV		D	3									

NEFTÇI BAKI
Coach – Agasälim Mircavadov

OLIMPIK BAKI
Coach – Stjepan Cordas (CRO); (9/9/05) Cämaläddin Äliyev; (7/10/05) Petar Kurcubic (SCG)

2005
13/8	Sahdag Qusar	h	3-1	Näbiyev 3
22/8	Qarabag Agdam	a	2-2	Misura, Tagizadä
27/8	Göyäzän Qazax	h	6-0	Misura 2 (1p), Tagizadä, Abramidze, Sadiqov R.Ä., Näbiyev
10/9	MOIK Baki	a	1-0	Abramidze
18/9	FK Gäncä	h	1-2	Boret
1/10	MKT-Araz Imisli	a	5-0	Abramidze, Misura 3, Adamia
23/10	Gänclärbirliyi Sumqayit	h	1-1	Näbiyev
29/10	Turan Tovuz	a	2-0	Getman, Misura
12/11	Inter Baki	h	1-1	Misura
26/11	Olimpik Baki	h	0-0	
3/12	FK Baki	a	2-2	Näbiyev, Misura (p)
10/12	Karvan Yevlax	h	0-0	
18/12	Xäzär Länkäran	a	1-0	Näbiyev

2006
11/2	Sahdag Qusar	a	4-1	Subasic 2 (1p), Näbiyev, Adamia (p)
16/2	Qarabag Agdam	h	2-0	Subasic, Adamia
21/2	Göyäzän Qazax	a	1-0	Subasic
11/3	MOIK Baki	h	4-0	Näbiyev 3, Subasic
25/3	FK Gäncä	a	5-0	Subasic 2, Boret, Petrov, Tagizadä
1/4	MKT-Araz Imisli	h	1-1	Näbiyev
5/4	Gänclärbirliyi Sumqayit	a	2-1	Abramidze, Subasic
16/4	Turan Tovuz	h	1-0	Boret
21/4	Inter Baki	a	1-0	Subasic
29/4	Olimpik Baki	h	3-1	Subasic, Petrov, Sadiqov R.Ä.
7/5	FK Baki	h	0-1	
14/5	Karvan Yevlax	a	0-0	
30/5	Xäzär Länkäran	h	2-2	Subasic, Petrov

2005
12/8	Xäzär Länkäran	h	0-2	
21/8	Sahdag Qusar	a	0-0	
27/8	Qarabag Agdam	h	1-2	Rzayev V. (p)
10/9	Göyäzän Qazax	a	2-2	Baljak, Quliyev
17/9	MOIK Baki	h	0-1	
1/10	FK Gäncä	a	1-0	Baljak
23/10	MKT-Araz Imisli	h	0-0	
29/10	Gänclärbirliyi Sumqayit	a	3-1	Sadiqov, Baljak, Mustafayev X.
13/11	Turan Tovuz	h	0-0	
26/11	Neftçi Baki	a	0-0	
4/12	Inter Baki	h	0-0	
10/12	FK Baki	h	0-1	
17/12	Karvan Yevlax	a	0-1	

2006
12/2	Xäzär Länkäran	a	0-1	
17/2	Sahdag Qusar	h	0-0	
22/2	Qarabag Agdam	a	2-3	Kovacevic, Nduka
12/3	Göyäzän Qazax	h	2-0	Quliyev, Mitrovic (p)
25/3	MOIK Baki	a	2-0	Haciyev, Ismayilov
2/4	FK Gäncä	h	1-0	Haciyev
6/4	MKT-Araz Imisli	a	0-0	
16/4	Gänclärbirliyi Sumqayit	h	0-1	
21/4	Turan Tovuz	a	0-1	
29/4	Neftçi Baki	h	1-3	Kovacevic
6/5	Inter Baki	a	0-1	
14/5	FK Baki	a	0-2	
30/5	Karvan Yevlax	h	0-5	

No	Name	Nat	Pos	Aps	(s)	Gls
19	Ruslan ABBASOV		D	9	(2)	
4	Valeri ABRAMIDZE	GEO	D	23		4
10	Giorgi ADAMIA	GEO	M	23	(1)	3
18	Elvin ÄLIYEV		M	4	(3)	
55	Elnur ALLAHVERDIYEV		D	6	(3)	
16	Orxan BABAYEV		A		(1)	
7	Vadim BORET	MOL	M	21	(1)	3
8	Oleksandr CHERTOHANOV	UKR	M	24	(1)	
24	Darko CORDAS	CRO	M	2	(5)	
2	Iqor GETMAN		D	13	(2)	1
3	Aftandil HACIYEV		D	12		
17	Aqil MÄMMÄDOV		M	10	(7)	
1	Vladimir MICOVIC	SCG	G	26		
15	Tomislav MISURA	SLO	A	12	(6)	9
11	Bäxtiyar MUSAYEV		M	4	(2)	
21	Nadir NÄBIYEV		A	23	(1)	12
77	Svetoslav Stefanov PETROV	BUL	M	13		3

No	Name	Nat	Pos	Aps	(s)	Gls
17	Elnur ABDULLAYEV		M	7	(5)	
1	Amil AGACANOV		G	16		
11	Daniel AKHTYAMOV		A	7	(1)	
20	Elmir ALIYEV		M	12	(2)	
21	Emin ÄMIRASLANOV		A	2	(7)	
77	Mirko BABIC	SCG	M	7		
4	Raso BABIC	SCG	D	21		
21	Srdjan BALJAK	SCG	A	10		3
36	Dalibor DRAGIC	SCG	D	11		
18	Nizami HACIYEV		A	10	(5)	2
55	Zaur ISMAYILOV		M	12	(6)	1
23	Emil KITELMAN	ISR	D	3		
19	Domagoj KOSIC	CRO	M	2		
9	Aleksandar KOVACEVIC	SCG	M	9		2
12	Hüseyn MÄHÄMMÄDOV		G	10		
15	Semjon MILOSEVIC	BOS	D	2		
8	Marko MITROVIC	SCG	M	24		1
44	Nurmagomed MURTUZALIYEV	RUS	M	2	(1)	
11	Shährüz MUSTAFAYEV		M	3	(3)	
2	Xäyal MUSTAFAYEV		D	20	(2)	1
22	Samir MÜTÄLLIMOV		D	12		
55	Äfqan NAGIYEV		M		(3)	

Azerbaijan

No	Name	Nat	Pos	Aps	(s)	Gls
3	Charlie Usim NDUKA	NGA	D	22		1
23	Abdülkadir ÖZ	TUR	D	2	(1)	
21	Bosko PERAICA	CRO	A	3		
11	Elsän QÄMBÄROV		M	2	(6)	
6	Vüqar QULIYEV		D	22		2
11	Ähmäd QURBANOV		D	1	(8)	
16	Tähmuraz RZAYEV		A	2	(1)	
7	Vidadi RZAYEV		M	13	(2)	1
9	Säbuhi SADIQOV		M		(9)	1
9	Yusif SAMILOV		M	1		
12	Vagif SIRINBÄYOV		G		(1)	
7	Anar VÄLIYEV		D	5	(4)	
85	Tomislav VISEVIC	BOS	M	11		

QARABAG AGDAM
Coach – Elxan Abdullayev; (30/12/05) Böyükaga Agayev

2005
12/8	Turan Tovuz	a	1-2	Kravchenko
22/8	Neftçi Baki	h	2-2	Hüseynov M., Kravchenko
27/8	Olimpik Baki	a	2-1	Hüseynov M., Sokolovskyi (p)
11/9	FK Baki	h	2-4	Voskoboinyk, Kravchenko
18/9	Karvan Yevlax	a	0-1	
2/10	Xäzär Länkäran	h	2-1	Hüseynov M., Musayev S. (p)
22/10	Sahdag Qusar	a	1-3	Cabbarov
30/10	Inter Baki	a	0-2	
13/11	Göyäzän Qazax	h	2-1	Musayev S. 2
26/11	MOIK Baki	a	2-0	Musayev S. (p), Sokolovskyi
4/12	FK Gäncä	h	0-0	
11/12	MKT-Araz Imisli	a	0-1	
18/12	Gänclärbirliyi Sumqayit	h	1-1	Musayev S.

2006
12/2	Turan Tovuz	h	1-0	Beraia I.
16/2	Neftçi Baki	a	0-2	
22/2	Olimpik Baki	h	3-2	Orucov, Musayev S. (p), og (Nduka)
12/3	FK Baki	a	1-2	Quliyev
26/3	Karvan Yevlax	h	0-0	
1/4	Xäzär Länkäran	a	0-2	
6/4	Sahdag Qusar	h	0-1	
16/4	Inter Baki	h	1-0	Xankisiyev
21/4	Göyäzän Qazax	a	3-1	Musayev S. 3
29/4	MOIK Baki	h	2-1	Haqverdiyev, Hüseynov M.
7/5	FK Gäncä	a	2-1	Haqverdiyev, Musayev S.
14/5	MKT-Araz Imisli	h	2-1	Beraia G., Sokolov
30/5	Gänclärbirliyi Sumqayit	a	2-0	Hüseynov M., Sokolov

No	Name	Nat	Pos	Aps	(s)	Gls
13	Eltay ASLANOV		M	2	(3)	
21	Goga BERAIA	GEO	M	13		1
20	Irakli BERAIA	GEO	A	3		1
5	Blazenko BEKOVAC	CRO	D	8		
20	Azär CABBAROV		M	8	(1)	1
6	Zoran CILINSEK	SCG	D	5	(2)	
7	Mustafa ENGIN ÖZMAN	TUR	M	7	(1)	
4	Vasif HAQVERDIYEV		D	20	(2)	2
12	Cahangir HÄSÄNZADÄ		G	13		
10	Müsfiq HÜSEYNOV		A	15	(6)	5
18	Ramiz HÜSEYNOV		M	3	(5)	
7	Romal HÜSEYNOV		M	8	(2)	
17	Bojan ILIC	SLO	M	12		
2	Hüseyn ISGÄNDÄROV		D	10	(2)	
13	Egidijus JUSKA	LIT	A	4		
8	Aslan KÄRIMOV		M	20		
1	Vital KAVALYOU	BLS	G	13	(1)	
21	Serhiy KRAVCHENKO	UKR	M	11	(1)	3
16	Tärlan MAHMUDOV		A		(2)	
3	Azär MÄMMÄDOV		D	13		
17	Räsad MURADOV		M		(1)	
18	Ruslan MUSAYEV		M	3	(6)	
9	Samir MUSAYEV		A	19	(3)	10
15	Mübariz ORUCOV		M	16	(4)	1
16	Färid QULIYEV		A	4	(3)	1
14	Fäqan SAHBAZOV		A		(5)	
5	Sergei SOKOLOV		D	13		2
91	Denys SOKOLOVSKYI	UKR	M	12	(1)	2
3	Dmitriy SPIRIN		D	10	(1)	
11	Oleksandr VOSKOBOINYK	UKR	A	5	(6)	1
11	Elmir XANKISIYEV		M	9	(4)	1
6	Dmitriy YEREMEYEV		M		(1)	
14	Namiq YUSIFOV		D	7	(4)	

SAHDAG QUSAR
Coach – Sabir Äliyev

2005
13/8	Neftçi Baki	a	1-3	Tijani
21/8	Olimpik Baki	h	0-0	
28/8	FK Baki	a	1-0	Agayev
11/9	Karvan Yevlax	h	1-2	Tijani
17/9	Xäzär Länkäran	a	2-1	Tijani, Ämirquliyev R.
1/10	Inter Baki	a	1-2	Tijani
22/10	Qarabag Agdam	h	3-1	Tijani 3
30/10	Göyäzän Qazax	a	1-1	Tijani
12/11	MOIK Baki	h	1-0	Tijani
27/11	FK Gäncä	a	1-3	Ämirquliyev R.
3/12	MKT-Araz Imisli	h	1-1	Ämirquliyev R.
10/12	Gänclärbirliyi Sumqayit	a	2-3	Tijani 2
17/12	Turan Tovuz	h	0-0	

2006
11/2	Neftçi Baki	h	1-4	Tijani (p)
17/2	Olimpik Baki	a	0-0	
22/2	FK Baki	h	0-3	
11/3	Karvan Yevlax	a	0-3	
26/3	Xäzär Länkäran	h	0-2	
2/4	Inter Baki	h	0-2	
6/4	Qarabag Agdam	a	1-0	Äsgärov
16/4	Göyäzän Qazax	h	1-0	Äsgärov
21/4	MOIK Baki	a	1-0	Dasdämirov
29/4	FK Gäncä	h	2-0	Sidoryuk, Tijani
7/5	MKT-Araz Imisli	a	0-3	
14/5	Gänclärbirliyi Sumqayit	h	2-0	Äsgärov, Tijani
29/5	Turan Tovuz	a	3-2	Äsgärov, Tijani, Dasdämirov

No	Name	Nat	Pos	Aps	(s)	Gls
8	Sahmar ABDULLAYEV		A		(6)	
6	Äli ABUSOV		M	8	(2)	
16	Häbib AGAYEV		M	21	(1)	1
13	Kamran ÄLIBABAYEV		D	23	(1)	
19	Fair ÄMIRQULIYEV		M	1	(6)	
10	Rahid ÄMIRQULIYEV		M	14	(1)	3
7	Zahir ÄSGÄROV		M	26		4
20	Pärviz BAGIROV		M	1	(3)	
8	Arif DASDÄMIROV		M	18	(1)	2
1	Igor DIMITRIJEVIC	SCG	G	9		
18	Marius HUMENICHE	ROM	A	17	(3)	

Azerbaijan

No	Name	Nat	Pos	Aps	(s)	Gls
34	Vüqar ISMAYILOV		D	10		
9	Isabala ISRAFILOV		M	1	(3)	
20	Timur ISRAFILOV		D	11	(3)	
22	Pärvin MÄDÄTOV		M		(2)	
14	Nodar MÄMMÄDOV		M	11	(1)	
22	Taqim NOVRUZOV		M		(2)	
55	Aleksandr NURÄLIYEV		M	6	(8)	
66	Ruslan QULIYEV		G	10	(1)	
11	Sänan QURBANOV		A	5	(4)	
11	Bähram SAHQULIYEV		A	10		
66	Said SALADOYE	NGA	G	4	(1)	
4	Vyacheslav SIDORYUK	RUS	D	26		1
3	Abdul Shittu TAURED	NGA	D	23		
17	Ahmed TIJANI	NGA	A	26		15
90	Osman UMAROV	RUS	G	3	(1)	
2	Alik YUNUSOV		D	2	(3)	

TURAN TOVUZ
Coach – Naci Sensoy (TUR); (22/1/06) Sakit Aliyev

2005
12/8	Qarabag Agdam	h	2-1	Junivan, Allahverdiyev
22/8	Göyäzän Qazax	a	4-1	Junivan 3, Nikiema
28/8	MOIK Baki	h	5-1	Junivan 3, Medoevi, Äläkbärov
11/9	FK Gäncä	a	0-0	
17/9	MKT-Araz Imisli	h	3-1	Nikolov A. (p), Sichinava, Abbasov A.
2/10	Gänclärbirliyi Sumqayit	a	2-2	Nikiema, Nikolov A.
22/10	Inter Baki	h	0-1	
29/10	Neftçi Baki	h	0-2	
13/11	Olimpik Baki	a	0-0	
26/11	FK Baki	h	1-0	Junivan
3/12	Karvan Yevlax	a	0-1	
11/12	Xäzär Länkäran	h	1-0	Kovacevic
17/12	Sahdag Qusar	h	0-0	

2006
12/2	Qarabag Agdam	a	0-1	
17/2	Göyäzän Qazax	h	1-0	Hüseynov C.
22/2	MOIK Baki	a	2-1	Qurbanov E., Qarayev
12/3	FK Gäncä	h	2-1	Qurbanov E., Hüseynov C.
26/3	MKT-Araz Imisli	a	1-0	Mämmädov E.
1/4	Gänclärbirliyi Sumqayit	h	0-1	
6/4	Inter Baki	a	0-1	
16/4	Neftçi Baki	a	0-1	
21/4	Olimpik Baki	h	1-0	Qädiri
29/4	FK Baki	a	0-1	
14/5	Xäzär Länkäran	a	0-1	
22/5	Karvan Yevlax	h	0-0	
29/5	Sahdag Qusar	h	2-3	Äliyev H. 2

No	Name	Nat	Pos	Aps	(s)	Gls
5	Ayxan ABBASOV		M	10	(1)	1
15	Elnur ABBASOV		D	9	(1)	
2	Elxan ABDIYEV		D	3	(1)	
14	Sahmar ABDULLAYEV		A		(1)	
1	Kamran AGAYEV		G	12		
7	Kamal ÄLÄKBÄROV		M	12	(7)	1
18	Hafiz ÄLIYEV		M	18	(4)	2
6	Ramin ÄLIYEV		G		(1)	
2	Elnur ALLAHVERDIYEV		D	9	(1)	1
5	Eltay ASLANOV		M	12		
4	Dalibor DRAGIC	SCG	D	12		
14	Ilqar FÄRHADOV		M	7	(2)	
15	Vüqar FÄRHADOV		M	1	(5)	
3	Aftandil HACIYEV		D	6		
11	Cavid HÜSEYNOV		M	5	(3)	2
12	Eldäniz HÜSEYNOV		G	1		
7	Romal HÜSEYNOV		M	9		
3	Vurgun HÜSEYNOV		D	6	(1)	
9	JUNIVAN de Mello Soäres	BRA	A	12		8
16	Aleksandar KOVACEVIC	SCG	M	8	(3)	1
14	Zaza LATSABIDZE	GEO	M	9	(2)	
77	Pärvin MÄDÄTOV		M	1	(5)	
8	Camal MÄMMÄDOV		M	13	(3)	
6	Elvin MÄMMÄDOV		A	11	(1)	1
21	Zaza MEDOEVI	GEO	A		(6)	1
20	Aqil NÄBIYEV		D	12	(2)	
77	Issa NIKIEMA	BFA	A	5	(7)	2
10	Asen NIKOLOV	BUL	M	12		2
16	Kiril NIKOLOV	BUL	D	3		
96	Elsän POLADOV		G	13		
21	Asäf QÄDIRI		M	10	(3)	1
9	Vüsal QARAYEV		A	5	(5)	1
9	Rüfät QULIYEV		M	3	(4)	
10	Etimad QURBANOV		M	12		2
11	Tengizi SICHINAVA	GEO	M	12		1
4	Irakli VASHAKIDZE	GEO	D	13		

XÄZÄR LÄNKÄRAN
Coach – Rasim Kara (TUR); (12/9/05) Nazim Süleymanov; (28/11/05) (Senol Fidan (TUR)); (7/12/05) Viktor Pasulko (UKR)

2005
12/8	Olimpik Baki	a	2-0	Ramazanov, Petkovic
22/8	FK Baki	h	0-1	
27/8	Karvan Yevlax	a	0-1	
11/9	Inter Baki	a	0-2	
17/9	Sahdag Qusar	h	1-2	Qurbanov M.
2/10	Qarabag Agdam	a	1-2	Äliyev
23/10	Göyäzän Qazax	h	2-0	Äliyev (p), Nadirov
29/10	MOIK Baki	a	0-0	
13/11	FK Gäncä	h	1-1	Äliyev (p)
26/11	MKT-Araz Imisli	a	1-2	Äliyev
4/12	Gänclärbirliyi Sumqayit	h	0-0	
11/12	Turan Tovuz	a	0-1	
18/12	Neftçi Baki	h	0-1	

2006
12/2	Olimpik Baki	h	1-0	Mämmädov X.
17/2	FK Baki	a	1-1	Ilyes
22/2	Karvan Yevlax	h	0-0	
12/3	Inter Baki	h	1-1	Savu
26/3	Sahdag Qusar	a	2-0	Ramazanov, Savu
1/4	Qarabag Agdam	h	2-0	Qurbanov A., Ilyes
5/4	Göyäzän Qazax	a	0-0	
16/4	MOIK Baki	h	6-0	Qurbanov I., Nadirov 2, Quliyev E., Qurbanov A., Lita
21/4	FK Gäncä	a	2-1	Lita (p), Munteanu
14/5	Turan Tovuz	h	1-0	Lita
22/5	MKT-Araz Imisli	h	0-0	
26/5	Gänclärbirliyi Sumqayit	a	1-0	Lita
30/5	Neftçi Baki	a	2-2	Qurbanov M., Mämmädov X.

No	Name	Nat	Pos	Aps	(s)	Gls
27	Räsad ABDULLAYEV		M	22	(2)	
14	Ramin AGAYEV		D	5		
7	Samir ÄLIYEV		A	8	(3)	4

Azerbaijan

4	Kingsley ATAKORAH	GHA	D	3	(1)	
20	Vüsal HÜSEYNOV		M	5	(4)	
9	Robert ILYES	ROM	M	13		2
22	Ramiz KÄRIMOV		M	2	(1)	
33	Milorad KORAC	SCG	G	2		
30	Catalin Nicolae LITA	ROM	M	7		4
6	Füzuli MÄMMÄDOV		D	13	(6)	
10	Xaqani MÄMMÄDOV		A	6	(11)	2
1	Alyaksandr MARTSYOSHKIN	BLS	G	13		
19	Daniel Gheorghe MUNTEANU	ROM	D	11		1
17	Vüqar NADIROV		A	7	(10)	3
2	Mikayil NAMAZOV		D	7	(3)	
3	Ädahim NIFTÄLIYEV		D	11	(4)	
22	Marinko PETKOVIC	SCG	A	3		1
5	Emin QULIYEV		M	22	(1)	1
66	Kamal QULIYEV		M	4		
18	Alim QURBANOV		M	13	(7)	2
8	Ilqar QURBANOV		A	12	(9)	1
7	Mahmud QURBANOV		M	23	(2)	2
29	Zaur RAMAZANOV		A	13	(7)	2
73	Miroslav SAVIC	SCG	D	20	(1)	
15	Ionut Cristian SAVU	ROM	A	8		2
23	Martin STANKOV	BUL	D	20		
9	Slaven STANKOVIC	SCG	M	2		
16	Mikayil YUSIFOV		G	11		

DOMESTIC CUP 2005/06

FIRST ROUND
(24/9/05 & 15/10/05)
ABN Bärdä v Gänclärbirliyi Sumqayit 0-2; 1-2 *(1-4)*
Simurq Zaqatala v Turan Tovuz 1-1; 1-2 *(2-3)*
Viläs Masalli v Qarabag Agdam 0-5; 1-1 *(1-6)*
Energetik Mingäçevir v Olimpik Baki 1-3; 1-3 *(2-6)*
ANSAD-Petrol Neftçala v Xäzär-2 Länkäran 0-3; 0-0 *(0-3)*
Göy-Göl Xanlar v MOIK Baki 2-0; 4-0 *(6-0)*
Särur Baki v Xäzär Länkäran 0-5; 0-9 *(0-14)*
(25/9/05 & 16/10/05)
Sahdag-2 Qusar v MKT-Araz Imisli 0-3; 2-4 *(2-7)*
Ädliyyä Baki v Karvan Yevlax 0-3; 0-3 *(0-6)*
Rote Fahne Tovuz v Göyäzän Qazax 0-1; 0-2 *(0-3)*
Gänclärbirliyi-2 Sumqayit v Sahdag Qusar 2-5; 0-3 *(2-8)*
Yeni Yevlax v Bakili Baki 1-3; 1-1 *(2-4)*
(9/10/05 & 16/10/05)
Neftçi-2 Baki v FK Gäncä 0-2; 1-3 *(1-5)*

SECOND ROUND
(4/11/05 & 19/11/05)
Neftçi Baki v Gänclärbirliyi Sumqayit 1-2; 2-0 *(3-2)*
(5/11/05 & 19/11/05)
Göy-Göl Xanlar v Turan Tovuz 0-0; 0-1 *(0-1)*
Xäzär-2 Länkäran v Qarabag Agdam 0-0; 1-2 *(1-2)*
Olimpik Baki v FK Baki 0-0; 0-3 *(0-3)*
(5/11/05 & 20/11/05)
MKT-Araz Imisli v Bakili Baki 5-1; 2-0 *(7-1)*
Sahdag Qusar v Xäzär Länkäran 0-2; 0-1 *(0-3)*
FK Gäncä v Karvan Yevlax 1-3; 1-1 *(2-4)*
Göyäzän Qazax v Inter Baki 1-1; 0-1 *(1-2)*

QUARTER-FINALS
(4/3/06 & 18/3/06)
Neftçi Baki 3 *(Petrov 5, Subasic 12, Näbiyev 27)*, Turan Tovuz 0
Turan Tovuz 0, Neftçi Baki 0
(Neftçi Baki 3-0)

Qarabag Agdam 3 *(Juska 30, Musayev S. 56, 68)*, FK Baki 2 *(Pérez 45, Vasilyev 89p)*
FK Baki 0, Qarabag Agdam 0
(Qarabag Agdam 3-2)

(5/3/06 & 19/3/06)
MKT-Araz Imisli 0, Xäzär Länkäran 0
Xäzär Länkäran 1 *(Ramazanov 29)*, MKT-Araz Imisli 1 *(Muradov 90)*
(1-1; MKT-Araz Imisli on away goals)

Karvan Yevlax 1 *(Bamba 75)*, Inter Baki 1 *(Makouski U. 78)*
Inter Baki 1 *(Äliyev S. 90)*, Karvan Yevlax 4 *(Päsimov 2og, Sükürov 45, Mämmädov 47, Ferreira 59)*
(Karvan Yevlax 5-2)

SEMI-FINALS
(25/4/06 & 3/5/06)
Neftçi Baki 0, Qarabag Agdam 0
Qarabag Agdam 1 *(Musayev S. 30)*, Neftçi Baki 0
(Qarabag Agdam 1-0)

(25/4/06 & 7/5/06)
Xäzär Länkäran 1 *(Lita 87)*, Karvan Yevlax 0
Karvan Yevlax 3 *(Kärimov 20, Ismayilov 28, Mämmädov 79)*, Xäzär Länkäran 0
(Karvan Yevlax 3-1)

FINAL
(3/6/06)
Säfa Stadionu, Baku
QARABAG AGDAM 2 *(Haqverdiyev 45, Musayev S. 87)*
KARVAN YEVLAX 1 *(Akhalkatsi 1)*
Referee – Äliyev V.
QARABAG AGDAM – Häsänzadä, Mämmädov A., Haqvediyev *(Orucov 85)*, Sokolov, Yusifov *(Hüseynov M. 66)*, Hüseynov Ram., Kärimov A., Ilic, Hüseynov Ram., Beraia G., Musayev S.
KARVAN YEVLAX – Kramarenko, Pereira, Intskirveli, Sükürov, Trapaidze, Mougadi, Mämmädov I., Bayramow, Akhalkatsi *(Abbasov 59)*, Kärimov K., Ismayilov.

SECOND LEVEL FINAL TABLE 2005/06

		Pld	W	D	L	F	A	Pts
1	Gilan Xanlar	30	22	6	2	72	14	72
2	Xäzär-2 Länkäran	30	22	3	5	60	18	69
3	Simurq Zaqatala	30	19	8	3	67	14	65
4	ANSAD-Petrol Neftçala	30	20	2	8	56	30	62
5	Ädliyyä Baki	30	16	8	6	63	30	56
6	Bakili Baki	30	16	8	6	32	23	56
7	ABN Bärdä	30	13	9	8	50	30	48
8	Rote Fahne Tovuz	30	13	6	11	49	46	45
9	Neftçi-2 Baki	30	12	4	14	29	34	40
10	Energetik Mingäçevir	30	10	5	15	41	52	35
11	Gänclärbirliyi-2 Sumqayit	30	9	5	16	35	53	32
12	Sahdag-2 Qusar	30	6	10	14	37	80	28
13	Azärbaycan U-17	29	6	4	19	33	49	22
14	Yeni Yevlax	29	4	6	19	23	54	18
15	Viläs Masalli	30	4	6	20	30	71	18
16	Särur Baki	30	2	2	26	12	91	8

N.B. Xäzär-2 Länkäran ineligible for promotion.

Belarus

Shakhter shake 'em up

The Belarus national championship's reputation as the most democratic in Europe was further enhanced in 2005 as yet another first-time winner was added to the competition's roll of honour. Shakhter Soligorsk became the eighth different club in ten years to take the title and the sixth among that group of champions to be crowned for the first time.

With top-five finishes in every season since 1999 and a first domestic Cup win in 2004, Shakhter's triumph was not entirely unexpected. But their complete domination of the title race took everybody by surprise. A run of seven straight victories from mid-May to the end of June enabled Yuriy Vergeichik's side to take a firm grip on proceedings, and by the halfway point they were seven points in front of the chasing pack and yet to taste defeat.

Things got even better in the second half of the campaign as Shakhter continued to pile up the points. Vergeichik, at 37 the youngest coach in the division, demanded that his team show no mercy in the run-in, repeatedly insisting that the title was not assured until it was arithmetically impossible for any other club to overhaul them. His players dutifully obeyed his command, securing a sensational maiden triumph with two games to spare thanks to a comprehensive 4-0 victory at home to Torpedo Zhodino.

Most of Shakhter's best performances had actually come away from their ramshackled Stroitel stadium, but eight days after sealing the title the club disappointingly lost 1-0 away to outgoing champions Dinamo Minsk. It was their first, and only, defeat of the season and prevented them from becoming the first club ever to take the Belarussian title with an unbeaten record.

Collective effort

Shakhter's victory was a collective effort. There were no stars in the team, no foreigners either. Defender Anatoliy Budayev was an inspirational captain, and there were important contributions also from other experienced men like defender Alexandr Yurevich, midfielder Andrei Leonchik and striker Sergei Nikiforenko. Youth also played its part, with Pavel Plaskonnyi, Mikhail Martinovich and especially top scorer Alexandr Klimenko all exceeding expectations. A last-day 1-0 win over 2003 champions FC Gomel stretched Shakhter's final margin of victory to a remarkable 13 points. In a league reduced from 16 teams to 14, that was no mean feat.

Dinamo Minsk's victory over Shakhter in the penultimate round proved crucial in helping the country's most popular and decorated club to qualify for the UEFA Cup as league runners-up. Dinamo had made a terrible start to the season,

NATIONAL TEAM RESULTS 2005/06

17/8/05	Lithuania	A	Vilnius	0-1	
3/9/05	Moldova (WCQ)	A	Chisinau	0-2	
7/9/05	Italy (WCQ)	H	Minsk	1-4	Kutuzov (4)
8/10/05	Scotland (WCQ)	A	Glasgow	1-0	Kutuzov (6)
12/10/05	Norway (WCQ)	H	Minsk	0-1	
12/11/05	Latvia	H	Vitebsk	3-1	Korytko (27), Kornilenko (52, 90)
28/2/06	Greece	N	Limassol	0-1	
1/3/06	Finland	N	Paphos	2-2	Kornilenko (34), Shkabara (54) (aet; 6-7 on pens)
30/5/06	Tunisia	A	Tunis	0-3	
2/6/06	Libya	A	Tunis	1-1	Shtanyuk (13) (aet; 1-3 on pens)

Belarus

which cost 2004 title-winning coach Yuriy Shukanov his job, and it was only after the appointment of the club's third coach of the campaign, Ukrainian Olexandr Ryabokon, that things began to change for the better. They did so dramatically, with the disappointment of an early exit from the Champions League being swept away by a stunning run of ten successive domestic league victories. There was never any realistic chance of Dinamo recovering the lost ground on Shakhter and becoming the first club to retain the Belarussian title in over a decade, but that surge of form eventually proved sufficient to lift Dinamo ahead of their three rivals for the runners-up spot – MTZ-RIPO Minsk, Torpedo Zhodino and FC BATE Borisov.

Puntus doubles up

MTZ-RIPO, the club owned by Lithuanian entrepreneur Vladimir Romanov (of Heart of Midlothian fame), enjoyed a spectacular improvement from the previous season, when they had only clung on to their top-flight place after a play-off. Winners also of the 2005 Belarussian Cup, they were deeply indebted to the talents of coach Yuriy Puntus, lured to the club on an attractive salary from FC BATE Borisov, where he had been a successful kingmaker for many years. Puntus would stay on at MTZ-RIPO in 2006 despite being appointed as the new head coach of the Belarus national team. As he had combined his previous duties as Under-21 coach with a club job, the Belarus Football Federation were happy for him to remain concurrently at the helm of MTZ-RIPO.

One of the highlights of MTZ-RIPO's 2005 campaign was their European debut, when they beat Hungarian giants Ferencváros 2-0 in Budapest. Although they lost the home leg 2-1, they made it through the first qualifying round of the UEFA Cup and also put up a valiant fight in the next round against Czech side Teplice. There would be no return to Europe in 2006, however. MTZ-RIPO's third-place finish would only have earned them a return visit to the UEFA Cup had second-placed Dinamo Minsk gone on to win the 2005/06 Belarussian Cup. But that prospect went out of the window when Dinamo were beaten in the quarter-finals by Shakhter.

The newly-anointed champions were favourites to complete a delayed Double when they subsequently ousted FC Gomel on away goals to meet FC BATE Borisov in the final. Their opponents had twice been beaten in previous finals, including 12 months previously by MTZ-RIPO, but they were to make it third time lucky in 2006, taking the trophy for the first time after an exciting, incident-packed encounter in the Dinamo stadium thanks to two late extra-time goals from Dmitry Platonov (a new signing from their relegated semi-final victims, Zvezda-BGU Minsk) and Belarus international Gennadiy Bliznyuk.

FC BATE's UEFA Cup place was assured after their semi-final win and provided compensation for a disappointing 2005 league campaign, in which they finished outside the top three for the first time since promotion in 1997. That it was also their first season without coach Puntus in charge was clearly no coincidence. His replacement, Igor Kriushenko, did a reasonable job but too many draws (11 in total) proved to be their downfall.

Stripeikis strikes

One interesting sideshow to the league campaign was the contest to win the league's top-scorer crown. It was finally won, for the second season running, by Naftan Novopolotsk's Valeriy Stripekis, the league's all-time leading marksman, but only thanks to a highly charitable gesture from his club colleague Igor Chumachenko, who, despite being only one goal behind his club colleague, provided a generous assist for Stripeikis (rather than going for goal himself) in the final game of the season

MTZ-RIPO Minsk owner Vladimir Romanov – a collector of European clubs

Belarus

NATIONAL TEAM APPEARANCES 2005/06

Coach – Anatoliy BAIDACHNYI / (24/2/06) Yuriy PUNTUS

Player	DoB	Club	Lit	MOL	ITA	SCO	NOR	Lat	Gre	Fin	Tun	Lby	Caps	Goals
Yuriy ZHEVNOV	17/4/81	FK Moskva (RUS)	G46	G	G			s46				G	10	-
Sergei YASKOVICH	11/1/72	Tom Tomsk (RUS)	D39	D	D33								31	-
Sergei OMELYANCHUK	8/8/80	Lokomotiv Moskva (RUS) /Shinnik Yaroslavl (RUS)	D	D	D		D	D	D			D	28	1
Sergei SHTANYUK	13/8/73	Shinnik Yaroslavl (RUS) /Metalurg Zaporizhzhya (UKR)	D	D	D		D	D	D		D	D	63	3
Sergei GURENKO	30/9/72	Lokomotiv Moskva (RUS)	D	D									78	3
Andrei LAVRIK	7/12/74	Amkar Perm (RUS)	M46		M	M		M46					37	1
Denis KOVBA	6/9/79	Krylya Sovetov Samara (RUS)	M		M	M	M58		M57	M	M67	M	29	1
Valentin BYALKEVICH	27/1/73	Dynamo Kyiv (UKR)	M80	M	M								56	10
Alexandr HLEB	1/5/81	Arsenal (ENG)	M	M	M	M			M				22	3
Vitaliy BULYGA	12/1/80	Krylya Sovetov Samara (RUS)	M46	s56	M	M88	M	M46	M57	s66			22	4
Vitaliy KUTUZOV	20/3/80	Sampdoria (ITA)	A	A	A76	A	A	A					30	9
Oleg SHKABARA	15/2/83	Dinamo Moskva (RUS) /FC Gomel	s39					M46	s57	s46			5	2
Vasiliy KHOMUTOVSKIY	30/8/78	Steaua Bucuresti (ROM) /Tom Tomsk (RUS)	s46			G	G	G46	G		G		17	-
Sergei KORNILENKO	14/6/83	Dnipro Dnipropetrovsk (UKR)	s46 /75					s46	A46	A46	A85	s46	9	3
Timofei KALACHEV	1/5/81	FC Khimki (RUS) /FK Rostov (RUS)	s46	M56			M	M82	s46	M	M	M53	13	-
Vyacheslav HLEB	12/2/83	MTZ-RIPO Minsk	s75	s67	s76			s72	s46				10	2
Denis SASHCHEKO	3/10/81	Halmstads BK (SWE)	s80			s88	M64						5	-
Alexandr KULCHIY	1/11/73	Tom Tomsk (RUS)			M	M80	M	M	M				56	5
Vladimir KORYTKO	6/7/79	Terek Groznyi (RUS) /Metalurg Zaporizhzhya (UKR)			M67	s80	M	M72	M46	s64	M59	A73	16	1
Igor TARLOVSKIY	21/9/74	Fakel Voronezh (RUS)				s33	D	D					22	1
Andrei OSTROVSKIY	13/5/73	Chornomorets Odesa (UKR)					D	D					52	1
Pavel KIRILCHIK	4/1/81	Kryvbas Kryvyi Rih (UKR) /Chornomorets Odesa (UKR)					s58	s46	D46				3	-
Yevgeniy LOSHANKOV	2/1/79	Chornomorets Odesa (UKR)					s64						1	-
Yan TIGOREV	10/3/84	Dinamo Minsk					D	s46	s46				3	-
Artem CHELYADINSKIY	29/12/77	Metalurg Zaporizhzhya (UKR)						s46			s85	D	5	-
Alexei SUCHKOV	21/3/81	Karpaty Lviv (UKR)						s82	M72	s55	s46	s46	7	-
Alexandr YUREVICH	8/8/79	Shakhter Soligorsk						D		D	D		3	-
Artem KONTSEVOI	20/5/83	MTZ-RIPO Minsk						s57	s46	s63	s46		4	-
Vitaliy VOLODENKOV	25/4/76	Dinamo Minsk						s72	M55				12	-
Vladimir GAYEV	28/10/77	Dinamo Bucuresti (ROM)							G46				1	-
Alexandr SHAGOIKO	27/8/80	FC Gomel							D	D	s73		3	-
Dmitriy LENTSEVICH	20/6/83	Torpedo Moskva (RUS)							D	D	s53		3	-
Alexei PANKOVETS	18/4/81	FC Gomel							D	s67			2	-
Nikolai KASHEVSKIY	5/10/80	Kryvbas Kryvyi Rih (UKR)							M64	M46	M46		3	-
Oleg STRKHANOVICH	13/10/79	MTZ-RIPO Minsk							M46				1	-
Vladimir MAKOVSKIY	23/4/77	Inter Baki (AZB)							A66				28	4
Alexandr SULIMA	1/8/79	MTZ-RIPO Minsk							s46				6	-
Roman VASILYUK	23/11/78	FC Gomel								A63	A46		18	7
Vitaliy LANKO	4/4/77	Spartak Nalchik (RUS)									s59	M46	3	-

Belarus

away to Lokomotiv Minsk. Stripeikis thus topped the goal charts for the fourth time in his career (he also achieved the feat for Slaviya Mozyr in 1999 and Belshina Bobruisk in 2002), his 16-goal tally edging out Chumachenko and Shakhter Soligorsk's Klimenko, who both managed 14.

One goal further back was the remarkable Roman Vasilyuk, who returned in mid-season from a sorry spell in Israel with Hapoel Tel Aviv yet still found the net 13 times in as many games for his new club, FC Gomel. The journeyman striker, who once netted all four goals for Belarus in a World Cup qualifier against Poland, was a 31-goal top scorer for Slaviya Mozyr when they won the league in 2000, and he finished second to Stripeikis in the 2004 listings with 17 goals for Dinamo Brest. He was also the leading marksman in the 2005/06 Belarussian Cup with six goals.

If there was excitement in the race for the Golden Boot, there was none at all in the relegation and promotion issues. Slaviya and Zvezda-BGU finished way off the pace at the foot of the First Division while the two teams relegated 12 months earlier, Belshina Bobruisk and Lokomotiv Vitebsk, returned to the top flight with consummate ease.

Sixth seeds

Belarus's disappointing finish to the 2006 World Cup qualifying campaign – three defeats in their last four games overshadowed an excellent 1-0 win in Scotland – brought the curtain down on Analtoliy Baidachnyi's two-year reign. It also demoted the country into the sixth band of seeds for the Euro 2008 qualifying draw. There is little chance of the team ending their major-tournament duck and qualifying for the finals in Austria/Switzerland, but with Puntus now at the controls and the talismanic Alexandr Hleb, Belarus's Player of the Year (for the third time) in 2005, continuing to improve following a fine debut season at Arsenal which climaxed with his appearance in the Champions League final, considerable improvement is anticipated.

Puntus was unable to lead the team to victory in his first four official engagements, but the team's confidence was boosted considerably by a 2-1 victory over an England 'B' side in Reading at the end of May, with Sergei Kornilenko's superb late winning goal offering further proof that the gifted young Dnipro Dnipropetrovsk striker is a man who can score goals in any company.

EUROPEAN CUPS 2005/06

UEFA CHAMPIONS LEAGUE

DINAMO MINSK
1st qualifying round ANORTHOSIS (CYP)
H 1-1 *Lentsevich (58)*
Lesko, Tigorev, Lentsevich, Pavlyukovich, Chalei, Volodenkov, Kozyr, Edu, Razin (Kovel 26), Zoubek (Kachuro 58), Kislyak (Rozhkov 86).
A 0-1
Lesko, Chalei, Lentsevich, Pavlyukovich, Tigorev, Volodenkov, Kislyak, Edu (Rozhkov 76), Kozyr, Zoubek (Kachuro 64), Kovel.

UEFA CUP

MTZ-RIPO MINSK
1st qualifying round FERENCVÁROS (HUN)
A 2-0 *Mkhitaryan (38), Tarashchik (90)*
Sulima, Bylina, Stashchenyuk, Popel, Mikhnyuk, Zhilavec, Shchegrikovich, Afanasiyev (Maltsev 68), Mkhitaryan (Tarashchik 80), Todua (Yeremchuk 55), Kontsevoi.
H 1-2 *Kontsevoi (48)*
Sulima, Bylina, Stashchenyuk, Popel, Mikhnyuk, Zhilavec (Maltsev 80), Shchegrikovich, Mkhitaryan (Yeremchuk 78), Afanasiyev, Kontsevoi, Todua (Tarashchik 66).

2nd qualifying round FK TEPLICE (CZE)
H 1-1 *Kontsevoi (70)*
Sulima, Tarashchik, Stashchenyuk, Mikhnyuk, Bylina, Afanasiyev, Popel, Mkhitaryan, Zhilavec (Todua 46), Hleb, Kontsevoi.
A 1-2 *Mkhitaryan (69)*
Sulima, Mikhnyuk, Stashchenyuk, Popel, Bylina, Afanasiyev, Tarashchik, Mkhitaryan, Zhilavec (Maltsev 46), Hleb (Yeremchuk 79), Kontsevoi.

FC BATE BORISOV
1st qualifying round TORPEDO KUTAISI (GEO)
A 1-0 *Baga (26p)*
Fedorovich, Baga, Radkov, Garkusha, Molosh, Kobets, Likhtarovich, Yermakovich, Stasevich (Zhavnerchik 72), Lebedev (Baranov 81), Rubnenko (Vishnyakov 62).
H 5-0 *Molosh (10), Lebedev (21, 37), Rubnenko (39, 43)*
Fedorovich, Molosh, Radkov, Baga, Garkusha, Likhtarovich (Baranov 64), Yermakovich, Kobets, Stasevich, Rubnenko (Skripchenko 46), Lebedev (Vishnyakov 62).

2nd qualifying round KRYLYA SOVETOV SAMARA (RUS)
A 0-2
Fedorovich, Baga, Khaletskiy, Rdakov, Garkusha, Molosh (Stasevich 64), Likhtarovich, Yermakovich, Kobets, Lebedev (Zhavnerchik 68), Vishnyakov (Rubnenko 52).
H 0-2
Fedorovich, Baga, Radkov, Garkusha, Likhtarovich, Molosh, Skripchenko (Shorokh 55), Kobets (Shmigero 54), Rubnenko, Lebedev (Zhavnerchik 75), Vishnyakov.

Belarus

TOP GOALSCORERS 2005

16	Valeriy STRIPEIKIS (Naftan Novopolotsk)	
14	Alexandr KLIMENKO (Shakhter Soligorsk)	
	Igor CHUMACHENKO (Naftan Novopolotsk)	
13	Roman VASILYUK (FC Gomel)	
	Vitaliy RODIONOV (Torpedo Zhodino)	
12	Vadim BOIKO (Dinamo Brest)	
	Sergei NIKIFORENKO (Shakhter Soligorsk)	
11	Alexandr KOBETS (FC BATE Borisov)	
10	Artem KONTSEVOI (MTZ-RIPO Minsk)	
	Alexandr PAVLOV (Dnepr-Transmash Mogilev)	

LEAGUE RESULTS/ SCORERS/APPEARANCES/ GOALS 2005

FC BATE BORISOV
Coach – Igor Kriushenko

2005				
16/4	Shakhter Soligorsk	a	2-2	Lebedev, Beganskiy
24/4	Darida Mikashevichi	h	1-1	Baranov
29/4	Dnepr-Transmash Mogilev	a	1-1	Kobets
8/5	Naftan Novopolotsk	h	3-0	Shorokh, Beganskiy (p), Vishnyakov
14/5	MTZ-RIPO Minsk	a	1-0	Kobets
18/5	Zvezda-VA-BGU Minsk	h	4-0	Lebedev, og (Zayats), Beganskiy, Stasevich
28/5	Slaviya Mozyr	a	2-2	Beganskiy 2 (2p)
12/6	Torpedo Zhodino	h	0-1	
17/6	Lokomotiv Minsk	a	3-3	Rubnenko, Beganskiy, Kobets
22/6	Dinamo Minsk	h	1-0	Kobets
30/6	Neman Grodno	a	1-1	Beganskiy
6/7	FC Gomel	h	1-1	Lebedev
19/7	Dinamo Brest	a	2-1	Skripchenko, Kobets
1/8	Shakhter Soligorsk	h	0-2	
6/8	Darida Mikashevichi	a	1-1	Kobets
15/8	Dnepr-Transmash Mogilev	h	2-1	Kobets, Zhavnerchik
20/8	Naftan Novopolotsk	a	2-1	Kobets, Rubnenko
29/8	MTZ-RIPO Minsk	h	0-1	
11/9	Zvezda-VA-BGU Minsk	a	2-2	Bliznyuk 2 (p)
17/9	Slaviya Mozyr	h	2-0	Skripchenko, Radkov
25/9	Torpedo Zhodino	a	1-1	Kobets (p)
1/10	Lokomotiv Minsk	h	1-0	Yermakovich (p)
21/10	Neman Grodno	h	2-0	Baga, Lebedev
26/10	Dinamo Minsk	a	2-2	Kobets, Bliznyuk
30/10	FC Gomel	a	3-2	Lebedev, Bliznyuk, Kobets
5/11	Dinamo Brest	h	2-1	Bliznyuk, Shmigero

Name	Nat	Pos	Aps	(s)	Gls
Alexei BAGA		D	17		1
Alexandr Vasiliyevich BARANOV		M	9	(4)	1
Pavel BEGANSKIY		A	7	(5)	7
Gennadiy BLIZNYUK		A	8		5
Alexandr FEDOROVICH		G	21		
Roman GARKUSHA		D	8	(2)	
Alexei KHALETSKIY		D	16		
Dmitriy KLIMOVICH		D	4	(4)	
Alexandr KOBETS		M	22	(3)	11
Alexandr LEBEDEV		A	17	(7)	5
Dmitriy LIKHTAROVICH		M	21	(1)	
Dmitriy MOLOSH		D	22	(1)	
Roman OVCHINNIKOV	RUS	A		(1)	
Boris PANKRATOV		G	5		
Artem RADKOV		D	25	(1)	1
Dmitriy RUBNENKO		M	14	(4)	2
Pavel SHMIGERO		M	1	(6)	1
Andrei SHOROKH		M	5	(5)	1
Mikhail SIVAKOV		M		(2)	
Vadim SKRIPCHENKO		D	17	(3)	2
Igor STASEVICH		M	6	(8)	1
Alexandr VISHNYAKOV		M	6	(11)	1
Alexandr YERMAKOVICH		M	25		1
Maxim ZHAVNERCHIK		M	10	(9)	1

DARIDA MIKASHEVICHI
Coach - Ludas Rumbutis

2005				
17/4	Dinamo Brest	a	2-0	Dovgulevets, Lukashenko
24/4	FC BATE Borisov	a	1-1	Kabelskiy
29/4	Naftan Novopolotsk	h	0-0	
9/5	Zvezda-VA-BGU Minsk	a	4-0	Trubilo, Kuzmenok 2, Sokolov
14/5	Torpedo Zhodino	h	0-3	
20/5	Dinamo Minsk	a	1-0	Dovgulevets
29/5	FC Gomel	h	1-1	Muradyan
11/6	Shakhter Soligorsk	a	1-3	Muradyan
17/6	Dnepr-Transmash Mogilev	h	4-1	Muradyan 2, Pyatrauskas, Kuzmenok
22/6	MTZ-RIPO Minsk	a	1-5	Terentiyev
30/6	Slaviya Mozyr	h	1-2	Misyuk
7/7	Lokomotiv Minsk	a	0-0	
17/7	Neman Grodno	h	0-1	
31/7	Dinamo Brest	h	1-0	Kondrashuk
6/8	FC BATE Borisov	h	1-1	Muradyan
13/8	Naftan Novopolotsk	a	2-3	Trubilo, Muradyan
20/8	Zvezda-VA-BGU Minsk	h	1-2	Kovalenok
27/8	Torpedo Zhodino	a	0-0	
11/9	Dinamo Minsk	h	0-1	
17/9	FC Gomel	a	1-3	Kovalenok
25/9	Shakhter Soligorsk	h	0-2	
1/10	Dnepr-Transmash Mogilev	a	3-3	Kovalenok 3
17/10	MTZ-RIPO Minsk	h	1-3	Misyuk
22/10	Slaviya Mozyr	a	1-0	Monakhov
30/10	Lokomotiv Minsk	h	0-0	
5/11	Neman Grodno	a	3-1	Milevskiy, Syropyatov, Kovalenok

Name	Nat	Pos	Aps	(s)	Gls
Dmitriy ASNIN		G		(1)	
Ivan DENISEVICH		M	24	(1)	
Andrei DEREVYAGO		D		(1)	
Alexei DOBROVOLSKIY		M	2	(5)	
Pavel DOVGULEVETS		D	9		2
Igor GEITSMAN	RUS	G	5		
Dmitriy KABELSKIY		D	23	(1)	1
Ruslan KONDRASHUK		M	15	(3)	1
Dmitriy KOVALENOK		A	10	(2)	6
Oleg KUZMENOK		A	6	(3)	3
Andrei LAPSHIN		D		(1)	
Denis LAVSHUK		M	1	(3)	
Fedor LUKASHENKO		M	8	(3)	1
Andrei MILEVSKIY		M	9	(3)	1

Belarus

FINAL LEAGUE TABLE 2005

		Pld	Home W	Home D	Home L	Home F	Home A	Away W	Away D	Away L	Away F	Away A	Total W	Total D	Total L	Total F	Total A	Pts
1	Shakhter Soligorsk	26	9	4	0	30	8	10	2	1	29	6	19	6	1	59	14	63
2	Dinamo Minsk	26	10	1	2	29	10	5	4	4	21	16	15	5	6	50	26	50
3	MTZ-RIPO Minsk	26	9	1	3	20	11	7	0	6	23	19	16	1	9	43	30	49
4	Torpedo Zhodino	26	7	4	2	23	11	7	1	5	17	14	14	5	7	40	25	47
5	FC BATE Borisov	26	8	2	3	19	8	4	9	0	23	19	12	11	3	42	27	47
6	Dnepr-Transmash Mogilev	26	6	7	0	27	10	6	0	7	21	26	12	7	7	48	36	43
7	FC Gomel	26	8	0	5	23	18	4	3	6	11	14	12	3	11	34	32	39
8	Dinamo Brest	26	7	1	5	17	11	4	2	7	22	22	11	3	12	39	33	36
9	Naftan Novopolotsk	26	7	0	6	28	24	3	3	7	15	20	10	3	13	43	44	33
10	Darida Mikashevichi	26	2	4	7	10	17	5	4	4	20	19	7	8	11	30	36	29
11	Lokomotiv Minsk	26	4	3	6	22	20	3	2	8	8	23	7	5	14	30	43	26
12	Neman Grodno	26	4	2	7	12	20	3	1	9	8	30	7	3	16	20	50	24
13	Zvezda-BGU Minsk	26	1	3	9	16	31	2	2	9	8	29	3	5	18	24	60	14
14	Slaviya Mozyr	26	0	3	10	7	34	2	2	9	7	26	2	5	19	14	60	11

Name	Nat	Pos	Aps	(s)	Gls
Andrei MISYUK		M	19	(2)	2
Vasiliy MONAKHOV	RUS	A	11	(1)	1
Karen MURADYAN	ARM	M	19	(7)	6
Artem OSMOLOVSKIY		G	3	(1)	
Mindaugas PUODZIUNAS	LIT	D	1		
Ionas PYATRAUSKAS		D	21	(2)	1
Anton RYABTSEV		D	18	(6)	
Andrei SAMOILENKO		A	1	(6)	
Igor SARASEK		M	8	(10)	
Sergei SHALAI		G	18	(1)	
Vitaliy SHEPETOVSKIY		M	6	(3)	
Alexandr SOKOLOV	RUS	A	8	(1)	1
Alexei SYROPYATOV	RUS	D	24		1
Alexandr TERENTIYEV		M	1	(6)	1
Vitaliy TRUBILO		M	16	(4)	2

DINAMO BREST
Coach – Mikhail Markhel

2005

Date	Opponent	H/A	Score	Scorers
17/4	Darida Mikashevichi	h	0-2	
23/4	Naftan Novopolotsk	a	1-2	Boiko
30/4	Zvezda-VA-BGU Minsk	h	3-0	Boiko, Demidovich, Ishmakov
8/5	Torpedo Zhodino	a	2-0	Boiko, Naumov
14/5	Dinamo Minsk	h	1-1	Boiko
21/5	FC Gomel	a	1-2	Boiko
28/5	Shakhter Soligorsk	h	0-1	
12/6	Dnepr-Transmash Mogilev	a	2-2	Naumov, Sokol
17/6	MTZ-RIPO Minsk	h	1-0	Sokol
22/6	Slaviya Mozyr	a	3-1	Boiko, Sukhoveyev, Sokol (p)
29/6	Lokomotiv Minsk	h	1-2	Sokol
6/7	Neman Grodno	a	2-2	Boiko, Sheryakov
19/7	FC BATE Borisov	h	1-2	Sheryakov
31/7	Darida Mikashevichi	a	0-1	
6/8	Naftan Novopolotsk	h	1-0	Sokol
13/8	Zvezda-VA-BGU Minsk	a	4-1	Sokol (p), Sukhoveyev, Boiko 2
20/8	Torpedo Zhodino	h	0-1	
28/8	Dinamo Minsk	a	0-2	
11/9	FC Gomel	h	1-0	Mozolevskiy
17/9	Shakhter Soligorsk	a	0-4	
25/9	Dnepr-Transmash Mogilev	h	2-1	Sheryakov, Kalachev
30/9	MTZ-RIPO Minsk	a	4-0	Sheryakov, Bespanskiy, Boiko, Mozolevskiy
16/10	Slaviya Mozyr	h	2-0	Mozolevskiy 2
23/10	Lokomotiv Minsk	a	2-3	Dvoretskiy, Mozolevskiy
30/10	Neman Grodno	h	4-1	Boiko, Mozolevskiy, Sokol (p), Lukashenko
5/11	FC BATE Borisov	a	1-2	Boiko

Name	Nat	Pos	Aps	(s)	Gls
Yuriy AFANASENKO		G	18		
Roman ASTAPENKO		G	1		
Serhiy BERBAT	UKR	M	6	(3)	
Dmitriy BESPANSKIY		M	12	(4)	1
Vadim BOIKO		A	24	(2)	12
Oleg CHEREPNEV		D	15	(1)	
Alexandr DEMESHKO		M		(1)	
Vadim DEMIDOVICH		M		(4)	1
Alexei DVORETSKIY		D	17	(5)	1
Alexei FILCHAGIN	RUS	M		(1)	
Alexandr GOLOVCHIK		D	6	(1)	
Vadym ISHMAKOV	UKR	D	20	(4)	1
Dmitriy KALACHEV		M	22	(1)	1
Fedor LUKASHENKO		M	10	(1)	1
Dmitriy MOZOLEVSKIY		A	8	(14)	6
Alexei NAUMOV	RUS	D	24		2
Vladimir NEVINSKIY		M	6	(3)	
Sergei SAKHARUK		G	7		
Andrei SHERYAKOV		A	10	(8)	4
Kirill SHREITOR		A		(2)	
Viktor SOKOL		M	20	(3)	7
Vladimir SOROCHINSKIY		D	21		
Maxim SUKHOVEYEV		A	17	(2)	2
Roman TREPACHKIN		M	7	(1)	
Andrei TSEVAN		A	2	(3)	
Eduard VALUTA	MOL	D	10	(1)	
Alexandr VOINAKH		M		(1)	

Belarus

Alexandr VOLODKO		M	3	(6)	

DINAMO MINSK
Coachs – Yuriy Shukanov; (16/5/05) Alexandr Bashmakov; (2/7/05) Olexandr Ryabokon (UKR)

2005
Date	Opponent	h/a	Score	Scorers
16/4	MTZ-RIPO Minsk	a	1-0	Chalei
24/4	Slaviya Mozyr	h	1-0	Volodenkov
1/5	Lokomotiv Minsk	a	2-3	Razin (p), Zoubek
9/5	Neman Grodno	h	0-1	
14/5	Dinamo Brest	a	1-1	Gigevich
20/5	Darida Mikashevichi	h	0-1	
28/5	Naftan Novopolotsk	a	2-3	Volodenkov, Chalei
12/6	Zvezda-VA-BGU Minsk	h	3-0	Lentsevich, Pavlyukovich, Kovel
17/6	Torpedo Zhodino	a	2-2	Razin, Pavlyukovich
22/6	FC BATE Borisov	a	0-1	
29/6	FC Gomel	h	3-1	Edu, Razin 2
6/7	Shakhter Soligorsk	a	1-1	Zoubek
16/7	Dnepr-Transmash Mogilev	h	5-2	Volodenkov 2, Kislyak, Kovel 2
1/8	MTZ-RIPO Minsk	h	3-1	Kislyak (p), Kovel 2
7/8	Slaviya Mozyr	a	4-0	Volodenkov 2, Kislyak (p), Khatskevich
14/8	Lokomotiv Minsk	h	4-0	Kislyak 2, Kovel 2
21/8	Neman Grodno	a	2-1	Kislyak (p), Volodenkov
28/8	Dinamo Brest	h	2-0	og (Bespanskiy), Gigevich
11/9	Darida Mikashevichi	a	1-0	Pavlyuchek
17/9	Naftan Novopolotsk	h	3-2	Edu 2, og (Skinderis M.)
25/9	Zvezda-VA-BGU Minsk	a	4-2	Pavlyukovich, Razin, Kovel, Volodenkov
1/10	Torpedo Zhodino	h	2-0	Razin 2 (1p)
22/10	FC Gomel	a	1-2	Chalei
26/10	FC BATE Borisov	h	2-2	Kovel, Kislyak
30/10	Shakhter Soligorsk	h	1-0	Pavlyuchek
5/11	Dnepr-Transmash Mogilev	a	0-0	

Name	Nat	Pos	Aps	(s)	Gls
Dmitriy CHALEI		D	20	(2)	3
Andrei CHUKHLEI		M		(2)	
Alexei DOBROVOLSKIY		M	1		
Eduardo Moreira Arauju "EDU"	BRA	A	20	(1)	3
Sergei GIGEVICH		M	1	(14)	2
Petr KACHURO		A	1		
Alexandr KHATSKEVICH		M	5	(1)	1
Sergei KISLYAK		M	13	(2)	7
Sergei KONTSEVOI		D		(3)	
Leonid KOVEL		A	21	(2)	9
Serhiy KOZYR	UKR	M	4		
Dmitriy LENTSEVICH		D	22	(2)	1
Artur LESKO		G	22		
Alexandr LUKHVICH		D	5	(1)	
Denis NARKOVICH		M		(1)	
Dmitriy PARKHACHEV		A		(5)	
Kirill PAVLYUCHEK		D	17	(1)	2
Sergei PAVLYUKOVICH		M	22		3
Anton PUTILO		M	7	(8)	
Andrei RAZIN		M	17	(1)	7
Igor ROZHKOV		M	20	(3)	
Pavel SHISHEYA		G		(1)	
Yan TIGOREV		D	24		
Alexandr TISHKEVICH		M	3	(11)	
Yuriy TSYGALKO		G	4		
Vitaliy VOLODENKOV		A	23	(1)	8
Alexei YANUSHKEVICH		D		(1)	

Petar ZLATINOV	BUL	M	5	(4)	
David ZOUBEK	CZE	M	9	(3)	2

DNEPR-TRANSMASH MOGILEV
Coach – Valeriy Streltsov

2005
Date	Opponent	h/a	Score	Scorers
16/4	FC Gomel	h	1-0	Baranov A.
23/4	Shakhter Soligorsk	a	0-3	
29/4	FC BATE Borisov	h	1-1	Baranov V.
9/5	MTZ-RIPO Minsk	h	2-1	Bondarev, Baranov V.
14/5	Slaviya Mozyr	a	3-0	Baranov V., Pavlov, Voronkov
21/5	Lokomotiv Minsk	h	5-1	Pavlov, Bondarev 2, Baranov V., Ogorodnik
28/5	Neman Grodno	a	3-1	Baranov V., Pavlov, Bondarev
12/6	Dinamo Brest	h	2-2	Pavlov, Baranov A.
17/6	Darida Mikashevichi	a	1-4	Baranov V.
22/6	Naftan Novopolotsk	h	1-1	Bychenok
29/6	Zvezda-VA-BGU Minsk	a	2-0	Pavlov, Bondarev
6/7	Torpedo Zhodino	h	1-0	Voronkov
16/7	Dinamo Minsk	a	2-5	Pavlov, Ogorodnik
31/7	FC Gomel	a	2-1	Galyuza I., Bondarev
7/8	Shakhter Soligorsk	h	1-1	Voronkov
15/8	FC BATE Borisov	a	1-2	Bondarev
21/8	MTZ-RIPO Minsk	a	1-2	Galyuza I.
27/8	Slaviya Mozyr	h	0-0	
10/9	Lokomotiv Minsk	a	1-0	Ogorodnik
17/9	Neman Grodno	h	6-0	Ogorodnik 2 (1p), Bychenok, Voronkov, Pavlov, Baranov V.
25/9	Dinamo Brest	a	1-2	Galyuza I.
1/10	Darida Mikashevichi	h	3-3	Galyuza I., Baranov A., Pavlov
16/10	Naftan Novopolotsk	a	4-3	Bondarev 2 (1p), Galyuza I., Chaika
22/10	Zvezda-VA-BGU Minsk	h	4-0	Pavlov 2, Ogorodnik, Voronkov
30/10	Torpedo Zhodino	a	0-3	
5/11	Dinamo Minsk	h	0-0	

Name	Nat	Pos	Aps	(s)	Gls
Dmytro ANTYPOV	UKR	D		(1)	
Alexandr Vladimirivich BARANOV		D	25		3
Vasyl BARANOV	UKR	M	15	(4)	7
Sergei BEKISH		G	23		
Vitaliy BONDAREV	UKR	A	19	(7)	9
Viktor BOROVITSKIY		D	18	(4)	
Alexandr BYCHENOK		M	19	(7)	2
Alexandr CHAIKA		M	7	(1)	1
Yevhen CHERNYAVSKYI	UKR	M		(1)	
Danylo CHUPRYNA	UKR	M		(2)	
Olexandr FESHCHEKO	UKR	D		(1)	
Illya GALYUZA	UKR	M	25		5
Serhiy GALYUZA	UKR	D	13	(2)	
Alexandr GAVRYUSHKO		M		(2)	
Andrei GORBUNOV		G	3	(1)	
Andriy HONCHAR	UKR	D	9	(3)	
Yevgeniy KAPOV		D	25		
Ruslan KOPANTSOV		G		(1)	
Anton MATVEYENKO		M		(5)	
Dmitriy OGORODNIK		A	10	(12)	6
Alexandr PAVLOV		M	23		10
Alexei TISHCHENKO		M	24		
Olexiy TUPCHIY	UKR	M	3	(14)	

Belarus

Ihor VORONKOV UKR M 25 5

FC GOMEL
Coach – Alexandr Kuznetsov (RUS); (12/8/05) Nikolai Goryunov

2005
Date	Opponent	h/a	Score	Scorers
16/4	Dnepr-Transmash Mogilev	a	0-1	
24/4	MTZ-RIPO Minsk	h	1-0	Pankovets
30/4	Slaviya Mozyr	a	1-1	Tikhonchik
9/5	Lokomotiv Minsk	h	0-1	
14/5	Neman Grodno	a	2-1	Denisyuk, Razumov
21/5	Dinamo Brest	h	2-1	Tikhonchik, Pankovets
29/5	Darida Mikashevichi	a	1-1	Kozak
11/6	Naftan Novopolotsk	h	1-2	Kozak
16/6	Zvezda-VA-BGU Minsk	a	1-0	Denisyuk
22/6	Torpedo Zhodino	h	2-1	Gorovtsov, Zabolotskiy
29/6	Dinamo Minsk	a	1-3	Shagoiko
6/7	FC BATE Borisov	a	1-1	Tikhonchik
17/7	Shakhter Soligorsk	h	0-3	
31/7	Dnepr-Transmash Mogilev	h	1-2	Markhel
6/8	MTZ-RIPO Minsk	a	1-3	Sinchuk
13/8	Slaviya Mozyr	h	2-1	Vasilyuk 2 (1p)
21/8	Lokomotiv Minsk	a	1-0	Razumov
27/8	Neman Grodno	h	3-0	Vasilyuk 2 (1p), Razumov
11/9	Dinamo Brest	a	0-1	
17/9	Darida Mikashevichi	h	3-1	Pankovets, Razumov, Vasilyuk (p)
25/9	Naftan Novopolotsk	a	2-0	Vasilyuk 2
1/10	Zvezda-VA-BGU Minsk	h	4-2	Vasilyuk 4 (1p)
16/10	Torpedo Zhodino	a	0-1	
22/10	Dinamo Minsk	h	2-1	Vasilyuk, Shagoiko
30/10	FC BATE Borisov	h	2-3	Pankovets, Vasilyuk
5/11	Shakhter Soligorsk	a	0-1	

Name	Nat	Pos	Aps	(s)	Gls
Anton AMELCHENKO		G	15		
Georgi BIZHEV	BUL	A		(1)	
Dmitriy DENISYUK		M	25		2
Andrei GOROVTSOV		M	14	(6)	1
Dmitriy KAMZOLOV		D		(1)	
Sergei KOZAK		M	23	(1)	2
Alexei KRAVCHENKO		D	7	(7)	
Alexandr LENTSEVICH		G	11		
Andrei LUKASHEVICH		D	14	(1)	
Yuriy MARKHEL		A	12	(11)	1
Rustam MUSTAFIN	RUS	D	21	(1)	
Awua-Siaw Léo NÉLSON	BRA	D	12		
Alexei PANKOVETS		D	25		4
Sergei PYRKH		M	2	(10)	
Maxim RAZUMOV		A	25	(1)	4
Alexandr SHAGOIKO		D	25		2
Denys SINCHUK	UKR	M	15	(11)	1
Valeriy TARASENKO		D	15	(1)	
Anatoliy TIKHONCHIK		A	12	(10)	3
Alexei TIMOSHENKO		M		(2)	
Roman VASILYUK		A	13		13
Sergei ZABOLOTSKIY		M		(6)	1

LOKOMOTIV MINSK
Coach – Anatoliy Yurevich

2005
Date	Opponent	h/a	Score	Scorers
17/4	Zvezda-VA-BGU Minsk	h	0-0	
23/4	Torpedo Zhodino	a	1-3	Rybak
1/5	Dinamo Minsk	h	3-2	Krot, Mikhnovets, Zenin
9/5	FC Gomel	a	1-0	Krot
15/5	Shakhter Soligorsk	h	0-2	
21/5	Dnepr-Transmash Mogilev	a	1-5	Mikhnovets
28/5	MTZ-RIPO Minsk	h	2-3	Atangana, Krivets
11/6	Slaviya Mozyr	a	2-0	Linev 2
17/6	FC BATE Borisov	h	3-3	Atangana 3
22/6	Neman Grodno	h	4-1	Shvydakov, Kukharenok, Krivets, Atangana
29/6	Dinamo Brest	a	2-1	Krot (p), Zenin
7/7	Darida Mikashevichi	h	0-0	
16/7	Naftan Novopolotsk	a	0-4	
30/7	Zvezda-VA-BGU Minsk	a	1-1	Krivets
7/8	Torpedo Zhodino	h	2-3	Linev, Krot (p)
14/8	Dinamo Minsk	a	0-4	
21/8	FC Gomel	h	0-1	
27/8	Shakhter Soligorsk	a	0-1	
10/9	Dnepr-Transmash Mogilev	h	0-1	
17/9	MTZ-RIPO Minsk	a	0-1	
25/9	Slaviya Mozyr	h	5-0	Volkov 2, Dragun, Zenin 2 (1p)
1/10	FC BATE Borisov	a	0-1	
16/10	Neman Grodno	a	0-2	
23/10	Dinamo Brest	h	3-2	Linev, Volkov, Zenin
30/10	Darida Mikashevichi	a	0-0	
5/11	Naftan Novopolotsk	h	0-2	

Name	Nat	Pos	Aps	(s)	Gls
Aram Abdukader AL MADZHID	SAU	D		(1)	
Igor ANTSYPOV		D	17	(2)	
Simon Pierre ATANGANA	CMR	A	10		5
Pavel BAGRYANTSEV	RUS	M	2	(9)	
Georgi BERIANIDZE	GEO	D	4		
Alexei DENISENYA		A	2	(2)	
Stanislav DRAGUN		M	3	(12)	1
Sergei KABELSKIY		D	21		
Dmitriy KALECHITS		D		(1)	
Sergei KRASNIKOV		G	1		
Sergei KRIVETS		M	26		3
Sergei KROT		A	13	(5)	4
Andrei KUKHARENOK		A	5	(11)	1
Yevgeniy LINEV		D	23		4
Vitaliy MAKAVCHIK		G	25		
Maxim MANENOK		A		(1)	
Alexandr MIKHNOVETS		M	22	(3)	2
Khurshed RAKHIMOV	RUS	M		(1)	
Pavel RYBAK		D	16	(4)	1
Vladimir SHELEG		D	5	(1)	
Vladimir SHIBEKO		D	13	(2)	
Sergei SHUMANOV		M	5	(7)	
Nikolai SHVYDAKOV		M	14	(1)	1
Yevgeniy SMIRNOV	RUS	M	1	(6)	
Igor SUBOCHEV		D	3		
Konstantin VASHKO		D	19	(3)	
Roman VOLKOV		A	8	(4)	3
Arkadiy ZENIN	RUS	M	26		5
Yevgeniy ZHUK		D	2	(2)	

MTZ-RIPO MINSK
Coach - Yuriy Puntus

2005
Date	Opponent	h/a	Score	Scorers
16/4	Dinamo Minsk	h	0-1	
24/4	FC Gomel	a	0-1	
30/4	Shakhter Soligorsk	h	1-1	Mkhitaryan (p)
9/5	Dnepr-Transmash Mogilev	a	1-2	Tarashchik
14/5	FC BATE Borisov	h	0-1	
18/5	Slaviya Mozyr	h	2-0	Vaskin, Fedorov
28/5	Lokomotiv Minsk	a	3-2	Mkhitaryan (p),

Belarus

12/6	Neman Grodno	h	1-0		Stashchenyuk, Kontsevoi
17/6	Dinamo Brest	a	0-1		Kontsevoi
22/6	Darida Mikashevichi	h	5-1		Tarashchik 2, Mkhitaryan 2, Stashchenyuk
29/6	Naftan Novopolotsk	a	3-2		Kontsevoi 3
6/7	Zvezda-VA-BGU Minsk	h	3-1		Kontsevoi 3
19/7	Torpedo Zhodino	a	1-3		Mkhitaryan
1/8	Dinamo Minsk	a	1-3		Hleb
6/8	FC Gomel	h	3-1		Yeremchuk 2, Todua
15/8	Shakhter Soligorsk	a	1-3		Afanasiev
21/8	Dnepr-Transmash Mogilev	h	2-1		Strakhanovich, Hleb
29/8	FC BATE Borisov	a	1-0		Hleb
11/9	Slaviya Mozyr	a	5-0		Tarashchik, Todua 3, Strakhanovich
17/9	Lokomotiv Minsk	h	1-0		Kontsevoi
25/9	Neman Grodno	a	2-0		Kontsevoi, Hleb
30/9	Dinamo Brest	h	0-4		
17/10	Darida Mikashevichi	a	3-1		Strakhanovich 2, Yeremchuk
22/10	Naftan Novopolotsk	h	1-0		Bylina
30/10	Zvezda-VA-BGU Minsk	a	2-1		Stashchenyuk, Yeremchuk
5/11	Torpedo Zhodino	h	1-0		Zapalau

Name	Nat	Pos	Aps	(s)	Gls
Mikhail AFANASIEV		M	19	(3)	1
Alexandr BYLINA		D	26		1
Karen EGIZARYAN	ARM	M		(6)	
Denys FEDOROV	UKR	A	5	(4)	1
Alexandr GORBACHEV	RUS	D	2	(4)	
Vyacheslav HLEB		A	11		4
Pavlo IVANOV	UKR	D		(1)	
Sergei KISLYI		A		(2)	
Artem KONTSEVOI		A	21	(1)	10
Vasiliy KUZNETSOV	RUS	G	1	(2)	
Igor MALTSEV		M	9	(9)	
Sergei MIKHNYUK		D	19	(1)	
Gamlet MKHITARYAN	ARM	M	18		5
Oleg POPEL		D	25		
Stanislav SHAKHRAYEV		M	2	(7)	
Dmitriy SHCHEGRIKOVICH		M	13	(3)	
Alexandr STASHCHENYUK		D	22	(1)	3
Oleg STRAKHANOVICH		M	10		4
Alexandr SULIMA		G	25		
Vitaliy TARASHCHIK		M	23	(3)	4
Gia TODUA	GEO	A	7	(1)	4
Sergei TSVETINSKIY		D	5	(2)	
Andrei VASKIN		D		(1)	1
Mikhail YEREMCHUK		A	11	(14)	4
Serghei ZAPALAU	MOL	M	9		1
Denis ZHILAVEC	SLO	M	3	(3)	

NAFTAN NOVOPOLOTSK
Coach – Vyacheslav Akshayev

2005

17/4	Neman Grodno	a	0-1	
23/4	Dinamo Brest	h	2-1	Kakabadze, Stripeikis (p)
29/4	Darida Mikashevichi	a	0-0	
8/5	FC BATE Borisov	a	0-3	
14/5	Zvezda-VA-BGU Minsk	h	3-1	Stepanov, Stripeikis (p), Chumachenko
21/5	Torpedo Zhodino	a	0-1	
28/5	Dinamo Minsk	h	3-2	Stepanov, Chumachenko, Kakabadze
11/6	FC Gomel	a	2-1	Stripeikis 2
16/6	Shakhter Soligorsk	h	1-4	Chumachenko

22/6	Dnepr-Transmash Mogilev	a	1-1		Chumachenko
29/6	MTZ-RIPO Minsk	h	2-3		Stripeikis, Pakulin
6/7	Slaviya Mozyr	a	3-1		Chumachenko, Deikalo, Pakulin
16/7	Lokomotiv Minsk	h	4-0		Chumachenko 2 (1p), Stripeikis 2
30/7	Neman Grodno	h	3-0		Kakabadze, Chumachenko, Stripeikis
6/8	Dinamo Brest	a	0-1		
13/8	Darida Mikashevichi	h	3-2		Chumachenko 2 (1p), Deikalo
20/8	FC BATE Borisov	h	1-2		Chumachenko (p)
27/8	Zvezda-VA-BGU Minsk	a	3-5		Chumachenko, Stripeikis, Gerashchenko
11/9	Torpedo Zhodino	h	0-2		
17/9	Dinamo Minsk	a	2-3		Stripeikis 2
25/9	FC Gomel	h	0-2		
1/10	Shakhter Soligorsk	a	2-2		Stripeikis, Gerashchenko
16/10	Dnepr-Transmash Mogilev	h	3-4		Stripeikis 2, Chumachenko
22/10	MTZ-RIPO Minsk	a	0-1		
30/10	Slaviya Mozyr	h	3-1		Chumachenko, Stripeikis (p), Kakabadze
5/11	Lokomotiv Minsk	a	2-0		Verkhovtsev, Stripeikis

Name	Nat	Pos	Aps	(s)	Gls
Valeriy APANAS		D	1	(2)	
Igor CHUMACHENKO		M	26		14
Ruslan DANILYUK		D	2	(1)	
Vitaliy DEIKALO		A	9	(6)	2
Alexandr DOLENKO		A	6	(3)	
Alexei DUBINA		D	10	(1)	
Vyacheslav GERASHCHENKO		M	15	(2)	2
Vasiliy GLUSHANKOV		M	8	(4)	
Suliko KAKABADZE	GEO	A	20	(6)	4
Maxim KARPOVICH		M	9	(8)	
Serhiy KHISTEV	UKR	D	1		
Dmitriy KOVALENOK		A	2	(5)	
Vladimir KRUGLOV		M		(1)	
Artur MATVEICHIK		M	10	(10)	
Artem PAKULIN		M	21	(3)	2
Alexei POGE		G	12		
Andrei PUSHKAREV	RUS	M		(1)	
Vitaliy ROGOZHKIN		D	23	(1)	
F RUDDIKRUS		M		(1)	
Alexandr SEDNEV		D	23		
Vladimir SHAKOV		M		(1)	
Marius SKINDERIS	LIT	D	19		
Simas SKINDERIS	LIT	G	14	(1)	
Sergei STEPANOV	RUS	M	13	(7)	2
Valeriy STRIPEIKIS		A	26		16
Dmitriy VERKHOVTSEV		D	8	(2)	1
Konstantin YAKUBOVSKIY		M	8	(7)	

NEMAN GRODNO
Coach – Sergei Solodovnikov; (30/6/05) Sergei Nefedov

2005

17/4	Naftan Novopolotsk	h	1-0	Nadiyevskiy
23/4	Zvezda-VA-BGU Minsk	a	1-0	Parfenov
30/4	Torpedo Zhodino	h	0-2	
9/5	Dinamo Minsk	a	1-0	Parfenov
14/5	FC Gomel	h	1-2	Lyasyuk
21/5	Shakhter Soligorsk	a	0-3	
28/5	Dnepr-Transmash Mogilev	h	1-3	Lyasyuk
12/6	MTZ-RIPO Minsk	a	0-1	
16/6	Slaviya Mozyr	h	1-0	Lyasyuk

Belarus

22/6	Lokomotiv Minsk	a	1-4	Kirenya	
30/6	FC BATE Borisov	h	1-1	Parfenov	
6/7	Dinamo Brest	h	2-2	Korzhuk, Zedelashvili	
17/7	Darida Mikashevichi	a	1-0	Narkovich	
30/7	Naftan Novopolotsk	a	0-3		
6/8	Zvezda-VA-BGU Minsk	h	1-0	Parfenov	
13/8	Torpedo Zhodino	a	2-3	Korzhuk, Lukashov	
21/8	Dinamo Minsk	h	1-2	Parfenov	
27/8	FC Gomel	a	0-3		
11/9	Shakhter Soligorsk	h	0-3		
17/9	Dnepr-Transmash Mogilev	a	0-6		
25/9	MTZ-RIPO Minsk	h	0-2		
1/10	Slaviya Mozyr	a	1-1	Lyasyuk (p)	
16/10	Lokomotiv Minsk	h	2-0	Parfenov, Grigorov	
21/10	FC BATE Borisov	a	0-2		
30/10	Dinamo Brest	a	1-4	Zedelashvili	
5/11	Darida Mikashevichi	h	1-3	Gorbach	

Name	Nat	Pos	Aps	(s)	Gls
Andrei ASHIKHMIN		G	15		
Maxim BORDACHEV		M	11	(1)	
Dmitriy DOLYA		M		(1)	
Vyacheslav DUSMANOV	RUS	G	7		
Dmitriy GINTOV		M	14	(4)	
Andrei GORBACH		A	3	(6)	1
Vyacheslav GRIGOROV		M	15	(5)	1
Alexandr KARPOVICH		A	1		
Oleg KIRENYA		M	4	(5)	1
Andrei KORZHUK		D	17	(1)	2
Mikhail KOTIN		D	5	(3)	
Artur KRIVONOS		D	4	(1)	
Sergei KURGANSKIY		G	4		
Alexandr LAVRISH		A		(1)	
Yuriy LUKASHOV		M	24		1
Andrei LYASYUK		A	9	(13)	4
Ihor MALYSH	UKR	M	12	(10)	
Yuriy MAMIDO		D	12	(1)	
Gennadiy MARDAS		D	22		
Sergei METELITSA	RUS	A	1	(10)	
Dmitriy MITT	RUS	D	1	(1)	
Vitaliy NADIYEVSKIY		D	15	(1)	1
Denis NARKOVICH		A	9	(3)	1
Vadim NARUSHEVICH		D	3		
Dmitriy PARFENOV		A	22	(2)	6
Dmitriy RADKOV		D	22		
Nikolai YEZERSKIY		D	19	(2)	
Nikolas ZEDELASHVILI	GEO	A	15	(5)	2

SHAKHTER SOLIGORSK
Coach – Yuriy Vergeichik

2005

16/4	FC BATE Borisov	h	2-2	Patsko, Borel	
23/4	Dnepr-Transmash Mogilev	h	3-0	Goncharik (p), Nikiforenko, Novik	
30/4	MTZ-RIPO Minsk	a	1-1	Klimenko	
8/5	Slaviya Mozyr	h	0-0		
15/5	Lokomotiv Minsk	a	2-0	Plaskonnyi, Martinovich	
21/5	Neman Grodno	h	3-0	Martinovich 2, Nikiforenko	
29/5	Dinamo Brest	a	1-0	Martinovich	
11/6	Darida Mikashevichi	h	3-1	Nikiforenko 3	
16/6	Naftan Novopolotsk	a	4-1	Yurevich, Klimenko, Goncharik 2	
22/6	Zvezda-VA-BGU Minsk	h	3-1	Nikiforenko, Yurevich, Selitskiy (og)	
29/6	Torpedo Zhodino	a	1-0	Klimenko	
6/7	Dinamo Minsk	h	1-1	Klimenko	
17/7	FC Gomel	a	3-0	Martinovich, Nikiforenko, Klimenko	
1/8	FC BATE Borisov	h	2-0	Klimenko, Goncharik	
7/8	Dnepr-Transmash Mogilev	a	1-1	Goncharik	
15/8	MTZ-RIPO Minsk	h	3-1	Goncharik 2 (1p), Nikiforenko	
20/8	Slaviya Mozyr	a	6-1	Klimenko 2, Nikiforenko 2, Borel, Goncharik	
27/8	Lokomotiv Minsk	h	1-0	Kovalchuk (p)	
11/9	Neman Grodno	a	3-0	Plaskonnyi, Kovalchuk, Klimenko	
17/9	Dinamo Brest	h	4-0	Krot, Klimenko 3	
25/9	Darida Mikashevichi	a	2-0	Sobol, Klimenko	
1/10	Naftan Novopolotsk	h	2-2	Budayev, Sobol	
16/10	Zvezda-VA-BGU Minsk	a	3-1	og (Losik), Nikiforenko, Goncharik	
22/10	Torpedo Zhodino	h	4-3	Nikiforenko, Martinovich 2, Grenkov	
30/10	Dinamo Minsk	a	0-1		
5/11	FC Gomel	h	1-0	Klimenko	

Name	Nat	Pos	Aps	(s)	Gls
Alexei BELOUSOV		D	11		
Viktor BOREL		A	2	(13)	2
Anatoliy BUDAYEV		D	24		1
Artem GONCHARIK		A	6	(15)	9
Alexandr GRENKOV		M	23	(3)	1
Maxim GUKAILO		M	3	(7)	
Alexandr KLIMENKO		A	25	(1)	14
Sergei KOVALCHUK		M	13		2
Sergei KROT		A	3	(5)	1
Leonid LAGUN		M		(1)	
Vadim LASOVSKIY		M	12	(2)	
Andrei Ivanovich LEONCHIK		M	25		
Igor LOGVINOV		G	26		
Dmitriy MAKAR		M		(2)	
Mikhail MARTINOVICH		M	19	(2)	7
Sergei NIKIFORENKO		A	26		12
Alexandr NOVIK		M	4	(11)	1
Mikhail PATSKO		M	4	(10)	1
Pavel PLASKONNYI		D	24		2
Andrei PORYVAYEV		D		(3)	
Alexandr SOBOL		D	10	(2)	2
Alexandr YUREVICH		D	26		2

SLAVIYA MOZYR
Coach – Andrei Sosnovskiy; (10/8/'05) Ilie Carp (MOL)

2005

16/4	Torpedo Zhodino	h	0-2		
24/4	Dinamo Minsk	a	0-1		
30/4	FC Gomel	h	1-1	Krokhan	
8/5	Shakhter Soligorsk	a	0-0		
14/5	Dnepr-Transmash Mogilev	h	0-3		
18/5	MTZ-RIPO Minsk	a	0-2		
28/5	FC BATE Borisov	h	2-2	Branovitskiy, Ledenev	
11/6	Lokomotiv Minsk	h	0-2		
16/6	Neman Grodno	a	0-1		
22/6	Dinamo Brest	h	1-3	Korotkevich (p)	
30/6	Darida Mikashevichi	a	2-1	Krokhan, Azarov	
6/7	Naftan Novopolotsk	h	1-3	Korotkevich	
16/7	Zvezda-VA-BGU Minsk	a	2-1	Salbiyev, Kosak	
31/7	Torpedo Zhodino	h	1-6	Korotkevich	
7/8	Dinamo Minsk	h	0-4		
13/8	FC Gomel	a	1-2	Salbiyev	

Belarus

20/8	Shakhter Soligorsk	h	1-6	Korotkevich
27/8	Dnepr-Transmash Mogilev	a	0-0	
11/9	MTZ-RIPO Minsk	h	0-5	
17/9	FC BATE Borisov	a	0-2	
25/9	Lokomotiv Minsk	a	0-5	
1/10	Neman Grodno	h	1-1	Salbiyev
16/10	Dinamo Brest	a	0-2	
22/10	Darida Mikashevichi	h	0-1	
30/10	Naftan Novopolotsk	a	1-3	Khamitov
5/11	Zvezda-VA-BGU Minsk	h	0-1	

Name	Nat	Pos	Aps	(s)	Gls
Sergei ASTAPCHIK		G	5		
Vitaliy AZAROV	UKR	M	14	(6)	1
Igor BALIN		D	24	(1)	
Yevgeniy BRANOVITSKIY		D	11	(4)	1
Dmitriy CHUMAK		M	7	(3)	
Serghei CONDREA	MOL	D	9		
Alexandr DAVIDOVICH		D	15	(3)	
Andrei DOVNAR		M	1	(6)	
Ilya FEDORENKO		A		(2)	
Sergei KISEL		M	3	(1)	
Timur KHAMITOV	RUS	M	7		1
Alexandr KOBENKO	RUS	M	4		
Stanislav KOROTKEVICH		A	15	(4)	4
Artem KOSAK		A	24	(1)	1
Igor KOVALEVICH		M	14		
Vadym KROKHAN	UKR	A	23	(3)	2
Vitaliy LEDENEV		A	9		1
Alexandr LUZHANKOV		A	2	(4)	
Yevgeniy NOVAK		D	18	(1)	
Nikolai ROMANYUK		G	2		
Vladimir SALBIYEV	RUS	A	15	(9)	3
Olexandr SAVENCHUK	UKR	M	6	(2)	
Alexei TARABANOV		M	4	(2)	
Sergei TRUNIN		A	4	(4)	
Yevgeniy VEREVKA		M	10	(1)	
Yuriy VODOVOZOV		M	9	(9)	
Alexei ZAITSEV		M	3	(10)	
Andrei ZAROVSKIY		G	9	(1)	
Alexandr ZAZIMKO		D	9		
Vyacheslav ZHIGAILOV	MOL	G	10		

TORPEDO ZHODINO
Coach – Yuriy Maleyev

2005

16/4	Slaviya Mozyr	a	2-0	Karolik, og (Balin)
23/4	Lokomotiv Minsk	h	3-1	Karolik (p), Zuyev, Rodionov
30/4	Neman Grodno	a	2-0	Karolik 2 (1 p)
8/5	Dinamo Brest	h	0-2	
14/5	Darida Mikashevichi	a	3-0	Rodionov, Moroz, Trukhov
21/5	Naftan Novopolotsk	h	1-0	Litvinchuk
28/5	Zvezda-VA-BGU Minsk	a	2-2	Karolik, Rodionov
12/6	FC BATE Borisov	a	1-0	Irkha
17/6	Dinamo Minsk	h	2-2	Trukhov, Irkha
22/6	FC Gomel	a	1-2	Rodionov
29/6	Shakhter Soligorsk	h	0-1	
6/7	Dnepr-Transmash Mogilev	a	0-1	
19/7	MTZ-RIPO Minsk	h	3-1	Kolomyts, Rodionov, Doroshkevich
31/7	Slaviya Mozyr	h	6-1	Rodionov 3, Divakov, Zuyev, Irkha
7/8	Lokomotiv Minsk	a	3-2	Zuyev, Trukhov, Rodionov
13/8	Neman Grodno	h	3-2	Shumanskiy, Zuyev, Kiriyevich
20/8	Dinamo Brest	a	1-0	Trukhov
27/8	Darida Mikashevichi	h	0-0	
11/9	Naftan Novopolotsk	a	2-0	Rodionov 2
17/9	Zvezda-VA-BGU Minsk	h	0-0	
25/9	FC BATE Borisov	h	1-2	Rodionov
1/10	Dinamo Minsk	a	0-2	
16/10	FC Gomel	h	1-0	Trukhov
22/10	Shakhter Soligorsk	a	0-4	
30/10	Dnepr-Transmash Mogilev	h	3-0	Kolomyts, Rodionov, Karolik
5/11	MTZ-RIPO Minsk	a	0-1	

Name	Nat	Pos	Aps	(s)	Gls
Alexei ADAMITSKIY		D	19	(2)	
Alexandr BULOICHIK		D	26		
Vladimir BUSHMA		G	3		
Andrei DIVAKOV		D	19		1
Yuriy DOROSHKEVICH		M		(2)	1
Sergei IRKHA		M	22	(1)	3
Denis KAROLIK		A	25		6
Alexandr KIRIYEVICH		A		(4)	1
Yuriy KOLOMYTS	RUS	D	25		2
Mikhail LITVINCHUK		A		(15)	1
P LUTKO		M	1		
Vladimir MOROZ		M	13	(10)	1
Vitaliy RODIONOV		A	26		13
Vladimir SELKIN		G	23		
Yuriy SHUMANSKIY		D	14	(7)	1
Serhiy STARENKYI	UKR	M	1	(3)	
Vitaliy STAROVYK	UKR	M	1	(4)	
Igor TRUKHOV		M	26		5
Daler TUKHTASUNOV	TAD	M	1	(4)	
Sergei ZENEVICH		D	25		
Maxim ZINOVIYEV		D	8		
Yevgeniy ZUYEV		A	8	(17)	4

ZVEZDA-VA-BGU MINSK
Coach – Sergei Gomonov; (10/7/05) Yuriy Antonovich

2005

17/4	Lokomotiv Minsk	a	0-0	
23/4	Neman Grodno	h	0-1	
30/4	Dinamo Brest	a	0-3	
9/5	Darida Mikashevichi	h	0-4	
14/5	Naftan Novopolotsk	a	1-3	Sidko
18/5	FC BATE Borisov	a	0-4	
28/5	Torpedo Zhodino	h	2-2	Kamzolov, Verzhbitskiy
12/6	Dinamo Minsk	a	0-3	
16/6	FC Gomel	h	0-1	
22/6	Shakhter Soligorsk	a	1-3	Shepetovskiy
29/6	Dnepr-Transmash Mogilev	h	0-2	
6/7	MTZ-RIPO Minsk	a	1-3	Sosnovskiy
16/7	Slaviya Mozyr	h	1-2	Sosnovskiy
30/7	Lokomotiv Minsk	h	1-1	og (Antsypov)
6/8	Neman Grodno	a	0-1	
13/8	Dinamo Brest	h	1-4	Verzhbitskiy
20/8	Darida Mikashevichi	a	2-1	Grits, Prokopchik (p)
27/8	Naftan Novopolotsk	h	5-3	D. Platonov 3, Verzhbitskiy, Prokopchik
11/9	FC BATE Borisov	h	2-2	Verzhbitskiy 2
17/9	Torpedo Zhodino	a	0-0	
25/9	Dinamo Minsk	h	2-4	D. Platonov 2
1/10	FC Gomel	a	2-4	D. Platonov 2
16/10	Shakhter Soligorsk	h	1-3	Khomutovskiy
22/10	Dnepr-Transmash Mogilev	a	0-4	
30/10	MTZ-RIPO Minsk	h	1-2	Losik
05/11	Slaviya Mozyr	a	1-0	Leonchik

Belarus

Name	Nat	Pos	Aps	(s)	Gls
Mikhail ATRASHKEVICH		G	14	(2)	
Sergei AVRAMCHIKOV		M	5	(3)	
Sergei DUBOYENKO		M	2	(3)	
Alexandr GERASIMOVICH		G	12		
Yegor GRITS		M	19	(5)	1
Pavel KALENYUK		D	4		
Dmitriy KAMZOLOV		D	11		1
Yuriy KHOMUTOVSKIY		A	3	(9)	1
Dmitriy KOZLOV		D	11		
Ilya KUZMENKO		D		(1)	
Andrei Leonidovich LEONCHIK		M	21	(5)	1
Igor LOSIK		D	14	(2)	1
Vladislav PETKEVICH		M	14	(7)	
Dmitriy PLATONOV		M	22	(1)	7
Pavel PLATONOV		M	14	(2)	
Yuriy PROKOPCHIK		M	21		2
Andrei SAMOILENKO		A	11	(2)	
Alexei SELITSKIY		D	12	(1)	
Vitaliy SHEPETOVSKIY		M	7	(3)	1
Pavel SIDKO		A	1	(6)	1
Alexandr SOROKIN		M		(1)	
Sergei SOSNOVSKIY		D	25		2
Dmitriy VERZHBITSKIY		M	21	(5)	5
Yuriy YAKIMENKO		M	1	(3)	
Denis ZAYATS		D	21	(1)	
Dmitriy ZHDANYUK		M		(15)	

DOMESTIC CUP 2005/06

SECOND ROUND
(23/7/05)
Spartak Shklov 0, FC BATE Borisov 1
Smena Minsk 1, MTZ-RIPO Minsk 2
(24/7/05)
Khimik Svetlogorsk 2, Darida Mikashevichi 0
Lokomotiv Vitebsk 2, Dinamo Minsk 4
FC Gorki 1, Neman Grodno 3
Kommunalnik Slonim 0, Shakhter Soligorsk 2
DYuSSh Kirovsk 0, Lokomotiv Minsk 4
Veras Nesvizh 1, Dnepr-Transmash Mogilev 0
FC Bereza 1, Zvezda-BGU Minsk 3
Vedrich-97 Rechitsa 1, Naftan Novopolotsk 4
FC Orsha 2, Torpedo Zhodino 8
FC Lida 1, FC Gomel 2
FC Smorgon 0, Slaviya Mozyr 1
Torpedo-Kadino Mogilev 0, Dinamo Brest 1

THIRD ROUND
(21/9/05)
Khimik Svetlogorsk 1, Veras Nesvizh 0
FC Gomel 1, Torpedo Zhodino 2
Zvezda-BGU Minsk 3, Neman Grodno 1
Dinamo Brest 2, Lokomotiv Minsk 0 *(aet)*
Naftan Novopolotsk 0, Dinamo Minsk 4
MTZ-RIPO Minsk 2, Shakhter Soligorsk 3
FC BATE Borisov 2, Slaviya Mozyr 2 *(aet; 12-11 on pens)*
FC Baranovichi 2, FC Polotsk 1

QUARTER-FINALS
(1/4/06 & 5/4/06)
FC Gomel 5 *(Stripeikis 11, 53, Vasilyuk 50, 57, 63)*, Khimik Svetlogorsk 1 *(Gavrilovich 34)*
Khimik Svetlogorsk 0, FC Gomel 0
(FC Gomel 5-1)

Dinamo Minsk 0, Shakhter Soligorsk 1 *(Goncharik 90)*
Shakhter Soligorsk 1 *(Martinovich 19)*, Dinamo Minsk 0
(Shakhter Soligorsk 2-0)

Dinamo Brest 0, FC BATE Borisov 0
FC BATE Borisov 1 *(Bliznyuk 22)*, Dinamo Brest 0
(FC BATE Borisov 1-0)

Zvezda-BGU Minsk 4 *(Samoilenko 16, 64, Sidko 67p, Sosnovschi 90)*, FC Baranovichi 1 *(Gitselev 69)*
FC Baranovichi 0, Zvezda-BGU Minsk 2 *(Samoilenko 13, Sidko 38)*
(Zvezda-BGU Minsk 6-1)

SEMI-FINALS
(10/4/06 & 14/4/06)
Shakhter Soligorsk 0, FC Gomel 0
FC Gomel 1 *(Vasilyuk 51)*, Shakhter Soligorsk 1 *(Klimenko 60)*
(1-1; Shakhter Soligorsk on away goal)

FC BATE Borisov 3 *(Stasevich 56, 90, Rodionov 58)*, Zvezda-BGU Minsk 1 *(Avramchikov 9)*
Zvezda-BGU Minsk 0, FC BATE Borisov 4 *(Platonov 13, Kobets 31, Lebedev 89, 90)*
(FC BATE Borisov 7-1)

FINAL
(27/5/06)
Dinamo Stadium, Minsk
FC BATE BORISOV 3 *(Molosh 26, Platonov 115, Bliznyuk 117)*
SHAKHTER SOLIGORSK 1 *(Klimenko 65)*
(aet)
Referee – Shmolik
FC BATE BORISOV – Pankratov, Likhtarovich, Molosh, Radkov, Baga, Yermakovich, Bliznyuk *(Lebedev 118)*, Kobets, Khaletskiy, Rodionov *(Platonov 77)*, Stasevich *(Zhavnerchik 60)*.
SHAKHTER SOLIGORSK – Logvinov, Budayev, Yurevich, Leonchik, Klimenko, Nikiforenko *(Bychenok 46)*, Martinovich, Lasovskiy *(Novik 53)*, Plaskonnyi, Kovalchuk, Beganskiy *(Borel 94)*.
Sent off: Plaskonnyi (116)

SECOND LEVEL FINAL TABLE 2005

		Pld	W	D	L	F	A	Pts
1	Belshina Bobruisk	30	23	4	3	61	19	73
2	Lokomotiv Vitebsk	30	21	7	2	76	23	70
3	FC Smorgon	30	15	9	6	57	35	54
4	ZLIN Gomel	30	14	12	4	35	17	54
5	Smena Minsk	30	14	8	8	31	23	50
6	Granit Mikashevichi	30	13	7	10	39	35	46
7	Khimik Svetlogorsk	30	14	3	13	42	34	45
8	Vedrich-97 Rechitsa	30	11	6	13	37	41	39
9	FC Baranovichi	30	11	5	14	38	43	38
10	FC Lida	30	10	7	13	41	43	37
11	Veras Nesvizh	30	9	10	11	31	33	37
12	Torpedo-Kadino Mogilev	30	7	8	15	22	45	29
13	Kommunalnik Slonim	30	8	4	18	35	43	28
14	FC Bereza	30	8	4	18	36	58	28
15	FC Orsha	30	6	6	18	33	74	24
16	Dnepr-DYuSSh-1 Mogilev	30	4	4	22	22	70	16

Belgium

Adding insult to injury

Belgian football is stuck in a trough from which there appears to be no imminent escape. For the first time in 28 years the World Cup finals took place without Belgian participation. The country's top club, Anderlecht, set a new record of successive defeats in the UEFA Champions League. And as if the impoverished performances of the nation's top teams were not enough, insult was added to injury when details emerged of a match-fixing scandal involving a shady Chinese businessman and one of the country's top-division clubs, Lierse.

It was hardly corruption on an Italian scale – in fact, the alleged rigging was restricted to one game only, an Eerste Klasse encounter between Lierse and Anderlecht in February 2004, and was not actually carried through – but the mere revelation that such dark deeds were being committed in the name of sport inevitably stretched the tolerance level of some Belgian football followers beyond breaking point.

If a way is to be found out of the present malaise, a good starting point would be an improvement in the performances of the national team. The Rode Duivels/Diables Rouges have now missed two major tournaments in a row. They were on a record run of six successive World Cup qualifications, but a continuation of that impressive sequence was never really likely as Aimé Anthuenis's side blundered from one mediocre display to another. Belgium veered off the road to Germany at an early stage and their fate was effectively sealed when they lost 1-0 in Bosnia-Herzegovina. A home defeat by Spain confirmed the team's demise, and when the campaign ended with a 1-1 draw in Lithuania, Anthuenis, at long last, was given the sack.

Vandereycken takes over

The poisoned chalice was subsequently passed on to 52-year-old René Vandereycken, a former Red Devil who won 50 caps for his country between 1975 and 1986. The former Anderlecht and Genk boss announced on his arrival that he intended to return to the counter-attacking tactics that had served Belgium well in the (increasingly distant) past. His first match in charge, a nice gentle opener across the border in Luxembourg, had to be abandoned midway through the second half because of a snow blizzard, but as Belgium had just gone 2-0 up at the time at least Vandereycken could claim to have got off to a positive start, if not strictly speaking a winning one. Three further internationals in May brought one win (against Germany-bound Saudi Arabia) and two draws (against Slovakia, away, and Turkey, at home), although it was only a last-ditch equaliser against the Turks in Genk's Feniksstadium that preserved the coach's unbeaten start.

Perhaps more significantly, Vandereycken gave debut caps to a dozen players. It remains to be seen how many of them, if any, can make the grade at international level. They will certainly have plenty of opportunities as Belgium have been drawn in the only Euro 2008 group containing eight teams. Portugal, the World Cup semi-finalists, are widely expected to win the group, but Belgium, even in their current state of transition, should be able to compete on an even footing with Poland and Serbia, who are also under new management after bombing out of the World Cup early.

It will be no encouragement whatsoever to Vandereycken, however, that most of the best players in the 2005/06 Eerste Klasse championship were non-Belgian. The 2005 Golden Shoe was collected by Standard Liège's Portuguese winger Sérgio Conceição, the 2005/06 Player of the Season gong and the Ebony Shoe (for the best player of African descent) went to Gent's Dutch-Moroccan starlet Mbark Boussoufa, while the first four positions in the top-scorer list were filled by

Belgium

foreigners – GBA's Tosin Dosunmu (Nigeria) with 18 goals, Standard's Mohammed Tchité (Congo) with 16, Lokeren's Aristide Bancé (Burkina Faso) with 15 and Club Bruges's Bosko Balaban (Croatia) with 13.

The qualification of both Club Bruges and Anderlecht for the Champions League provided a rare positive note for the Belgian game, but there was little to cheer in the competition proper. Bruges took third place in a group containing Bayern Munich and Juventus (which was about the best they could hope for), but Anderlecht's Champions League horror show continued as they prolonged their run of consecutive defeats in the competition to 12. There was no joy in the UEFA Cup, either, as both Genk and GBA failed to reach the group phase. The latter lost to Marseille on penalties after two goalless draws, having sacked Marc Brys, their Belgian Cup-winning coach of only a few months earlier, midway through the tie. Although Bruges managed to hitch a ride into the third round of the UEFA Cup, they also fell at the first hurdle, beaten home and away by Roma. Their consolation goal at the Stadio Olimpico, from Gert Verheyen, did however enable the veteran winger to become Bruges's record scorer in Europe, with 23 goals, bypassing the tally of club legend Raoul Lambert.

Verheyen milestone

Verheyen, who would retire from football, aged 35, at the end of the season, also reached another milestone when he scored his 150th Eerste Klasse goal in Bruges's 2-2 draw against Anderlecht in October. In fact, he scored both Bruges goals in the game, having never previously found the net against his former club. Overall, though, it would be a fairly anti-climatic farewell season for Verheyen. Bruges, who had appointed club icon Jan Ceulemans as their new coach, were hoping to make a successful title defence for the first time since 1978 but despite the goals of Balaban, ex-Real Madrid youth team prodigy Javier Portillo and Verheyen himself, an uncharacteristic inconsistency plagued the team all season. After back-to-back defeats by Anderlecht (0-2 at home) and Gent (1-4 away, with a hat-trick from Boussoufa), Ceulemans was shown the door and replaced by Emilio Ferrera. The new boss, who had been sacked by La Louvière in the early autumn after no wins in eight games, led Bruges through their final five matches unbeaten, but it was good enough only to earn third place – the club's lowest final placing for more than a decade.

The title went to Anderlecht – for the 28th time in

NATIONAL TEAM RESULTS 2005/06

17/8/05	Greece	H	Brussels	2-0	Mpenza E. (19), Mpenza M. (24)
3/9/05	Bosnia-Herzegovina (WCQ)	A	Zenica	0-1	
7/9/05	San Marino (WCQ)	H	Antwerp	8-0	Simons (32p), Daerden (39, 67), Buffel (44), Mpenza M. (52, 71), Vandenbergh (53), Van Buyten (83)
8/10/05	Spain (WCQ)	H	Brussels	0-2	
12/10/05	Lithuania (WCQ)	A	Vilnius	1-1	Geraerts (17)
1/3/06	Luxembourg	A	Luxemburg	2-0	Vandenbergh (43), Pieroni (62) (abandoned after 64 minutes)
11/5/06	Saudi Arabia	A	Sittard	2-1	Caluwé (3), Vandenborre (55)
20/5/06	Slovakia	A	Trnava	1-1	Geraerts (77)
24/5/06	Turkey	H	Genk	3-3	Ibrahim Toraman (27og), Sonck (43), Hoefkens (90)

their history – but many people will probably look back on 2005/06 as the season when Standard Liège lost the championship as opposed to Anderlecht winning it.

Without a title since 1983, Standard began the season in strident form, winning their first four games, beating Club Bruges and Anderlecht 2-0 at home and packing up for the Christmas break at the top of the table. Dominique D'Onofrio's team was a multi-national, multi-cultural concoction, but there was a nice balance to the side, with Tchité scoring the goals, Sérgio Conceição driving the midfield, experienced Belgian internationals Eric Deflandre and Philippe Léonard manning the defensive flanks alongside American international Oguchi Onyewu, and Croatian Vedran Runje confidently keeping goal.

Standard self-destruct

However, as the business end of the season approached, Standard began to self-destruct. It had happened the previous season when they lost a UEFA Cup play-off to Genk, and now there would be a doubly traumatic conclusion to their campaign. The start of the collapse could be traced back to the first leg of their Belgian Cup semi-final, at home to newly promoted Zulte-Waregem. Not only did they lose the game 2-1 (and also ultimately the tie, on

Belgium

away goals) but they also lost the services of Sérgio Conceição who, after being red-carded for spitting, reacted by pushing referee Peter Vervecken. The Golden Shoe winner was further punished with a long suspension that ruled him out of the final few weeks of the season.

Standard managed to hold it together in the league until the title decider away to Anderlecht on April 21. Topping the table by a point, D'Onofrio's team went to Brussels with a sole purpose – to avoid defeat. Having gone 12 matches unbeaten, a more positive approach might have been expected, but Standard timidly surrendered the initiative and were deservedly beaten 2-0.

Nine days later, while Anderlecht were dropping two points at Gent, Standard had a glorious chance to regain first place, with a win away at Roeselare, but a dramatic stoppage-time save from Roeselare's second-string goalkeeper, Wouter Biebauw, kept the scoreline at 0-0. That was Standard's last chance gone. The following weekend Anderlecht wrapped up the title with an easy 3-0 home win against Zulte-Waregem, a team whose minds were on the upcoming Belgian Cup final against Excelsior Mouscron.

Anderlecht's title

Standard's consolation prize was a place in the Champions League qualifying round – and the opportunity to compete among Europe's elite 32 for the first time – but there could be no escaping the fact that they had thrown away a marvellous opportunity to make history. Instead it was Anderlecht, in coach Franky Vercauteren's first full season in charge, who claimed the championship crown.

With only 25 points collected out of a possible 51 away from home, it was not the most emphatic of the Brussels club's 28 titles. But they were rarely troubled in the Constant Vanden Stock stadium, winning 14 of their 17 games and drawing the other three. It was also to the team's credit that while they were coming apart at the seams in Europe and also suffering a humiliating exit from the Belgian Cup at the hands of second division strugglers Verbroedering Geel, they kept things ticking over in the league.

Anderlecht made several changes of personnel in mid-season, with fans' favourite Walter Baseggio departing for Italy and the previous season's top scorer, Nenad Jestrovic, absconding to Qatar. Into Jestrovic's boots came Argentine striker Nicolás Frutos, and he was to hit the ground running with nine goals in his first ten matches. Anderlecht also had to make do without their best defender, Vincent Kompany, for the second half of the season after the highly-rated teenager suffered a serious shoulder injury. But there were excellent performances in the spring from two Belgian internationals at the other end of the age scale, Bart Goor and Yves Vanderhaeghe, as well as a dynamic farewell season from veteran Swedish playmaker Pär Zetterberg.

While Anderlecht and Standard qualified for the Champions League, Club Bruges were joined in the UEFA Cup by Zulte-Waregem, who crowned an outstanding first season in the top flight by winning the Belgian Cup, the first newly promoted club to do so. Having failed to win any of their last eight league games, they were the underdogs going into the final against Mouscron, but a dramatic last-minute winner from 22-year-old Tim Matthijs earned the club a first ever trophy – and secured Francky Dury the Coach of the Season award into the bargain. Remarkably, both promoted clubs would find themselves playing in Europe in 2006/07 as Roeselare joined Zulte-Waregem in the UEFA Cup after winning a place in the competition through the Fair Play lottery.

There was only one club promoted to the Eerste Klasse in 2006 – Mons, who came straight back up after one season to replace La Louvière. A restructuring of the play-off system enabled Lierse, the 17th-placed team in the top flight, to enter a six-game post-championship series with three teams from the Tweede Klasse. They had scored only 22 goals in 34 regular league fixtures but managed 13 in their play-off encounters to preserve their top-flight status – albeit temporarily pending further investigation into the match-fixing scandal.

Nicolás Frutos – off to a flier with Anderlecht

Belgium

NATIONAL TEAM APPEARANCES 2005/06

Coach – Aimé ANTHEUNIS / (1/1/06) René VANDEREYCKEN

Player	DOB	Club	Gre	BOS	SMR	ESP	LIT	Lux	Sau	Svk	Tur	Caps	Goals
Silvio PROTO	23/5/83	RSC Anderlecht	G	G	G	G	G	G46				11	-
Olivier DESCHACHT	16/2/81	RSC Anderlecht	D	D	D	D	D					14	-
Daniel VAN BUYTEN	7/2/78	Hamburger SV (GER)	D	D	D	D						31	3
Vincent KOMPANY	10/4/86	RSC Anderlecht	D	D	D12							14	-
Anthony VANDEN BORRE	24/10/87	RSC Anderlecht	D88	D78	D68	D61	s46	s46	M	D69	s68	11	1
Jelle VAN DAMME	10/10/83	SV Werder Bremen (GER)	D90	M78					D	D86		11	-
Timmy SIMONS	11/12/76	PSV (HOL)	M	M	M	M	M	D	M	M	M	46	2
Yves VANDERHAEGHE	30/1/70	RSC Anderlecht	M90	M	M68	M	M					48	2
Luigi PIERONI	8/9/80	AJ Auxerre (FRA)	A74	A		s75		A		A46	s86	16	1
Mbo MPENZA	4/12/76	RSC Anderlecht	A76	A	A	A75	A	M46				51	3
Emile MPENZA	4/7/78	Hamburger SV (GER)	A80			A	A					49	17
Roberto BISCONTI	21/7/73	OGC Nice (FRA)	s74		s68							13	-
Kevin VANDENBERGH	16/5/83	KRC Genk	s76	s68	A			A46	A75		s46	9	2
Karel GERAERTS	5/1/82	R Standard Liège	s80	s78			M46		M46	s69	M	6	2
Olivier DOLL	9/6/73	KSC Lokeren OV	s88									6	-
Philippe LEONARD	14/2/74	R Standard Liège	s90					D	D	D	D	24	-
Philippe CLEMENT	22/3/74	Club Brugge KV	s90					D				35	1
Thomas BUFFEL	19/2/81	Rangers (SCO)		M68	M	M61			s46	M77	M46	28	6
Koen DAERDEN	8/3/82	KRC Genk		s78	s12							8	3
Bart GOOR	9/4/73	RSC Anderlecht			M	M	M	M		s77	M	66	13
Carl HOEFKENS	6/10/78	Stoke City (ENG)			s68	D	D46		s46	D	D	10	1
Eric DEFLANDRE	2/8/73	R Standard Liège				s61	D					57	-
Jonathan WALASIAK	23/10/82	R Standard Liège				s61	M					4	-
Birger MAERTENS	28/6/80	Club Brugge KV					s46					1	-
Thomas VERMAELEN	14/11/85	Ajax (HOL)						D	D46			2	-
Gil SWERTS	23/9/82	Vitesse (HOL)						D46		M	D68	3	-
Peter VAN DER HEYDEN	16/7/76	VfL Wolfsburg (GER)						M46		M		19	1
Geert DE VLIEGER	16/10/71	Manchester City (ENG)						s46				43	-
Stein HUYSEGEMS	16/6/82	AZ (HOL)						s46	s75	s83	A46	6	-
Gabi MUDINGAYI	1/10/81	Lazio (ITA)						s46				2	-
Wesley SONCK	9/8/78	Borussia M'gladbach (GER)						s46		A83	A46	37	15
Stijn STIJNEN	7/4/81	Club Brugge KV							G	G62	G46	3	-
Pieter COLLEN	20/6/80	Feyenoord (HOL)							D46			1	-
Tom CALUWE	11/4/78	FC Utrecht (HOL)							M46			1	1
Steven DEFOUR	15/4/88	KRC Genk							M89		s46	2	-
Wim DE DECKER	6/4/82	Germinal Beerschot Antw.							s46			1	-
Nathan D'HAEMERS	26/1/78	SV Zulte-Waregem							s46			1	-
Nicolas LOMBAERTS	20/3/85	KAA Gent							s89			1	-
Mousa DEMBELE	16/7/87	Willem II (HOL)								s46	s46	2	-
Brian VANDENBUSSCHE	24/9/81	SC Heerenveen (HOL)								s62		1	-
Davy SCHOLLEN	28/2/78	NAC Breda (HOL)									s46	1	-

Belgium

EUROPEAN CUPS 2005/06

UEFA CHAMPIONS LEAGUE

CLUB BRUGGE KV
3rd qualifying round VÅLERENGA FOTBALL (NOR)
A 0-1
Butina, De Cock, Clément, Maertens (Ishiaku 78), Valgaeren, Klukowski, Englebert, Vermant, Leko, Verheyen, Balaban (Blondel 82).
H 1-0 *Balaban (79)*
(aet; 4-3 on pens)
Butina, Vanaudenaerde (Dufer 69), Maertens, Valgaeren, Klukowski, Englebert, Clément, Vermant, Leko (Van Tornhout 78), Verheyen (Blondel 110), Balaban.

1st round Group A
Match 1 JUVENTUS (ITA)
H 1-2 *Yulu-Matondo (85)*
Stijnen, Spilar, Maertens, Valgaeren (Victor 74), De Cock, Vermant (Leko 83), Englebert, Vanaudenaerde, Yulu-Matondo, Portillo (Blondel 52), Balaban.

Match 2 FC BAYERN MÜNCHEN (GER)
A 0-1
Butina, Dufer, Vandelannoite, Maertens, De Cock, Blondel, Vermant, Englebert (Roelandts 84), Leko (Portillo 68), Verheyen (Yulu-Matondo 75), Balaban.

Match 3 SK RAPID WIEN (AUT)
A 1-0 *Balaban (75)*
Butina, Vanaudenaerde, Maertens (Englebert 69), Spilar, Blondel, Clément, Vermant, Leko, Dufer (Roelandts 90), Portillo (Verheyen 69), Balaban.

Match 4 SK RAPID WIEN
H 3-2 *Portillo (8), Balaban (25), Verheyen (63)*
Butina, Vanaudenaerde, Maertens, Spilar, Blondel, Verheyen, Clément, Vermant, Leko (Roelandts 85), Portillo (Victor 89), Balaban (Englebert 82).

Match 5 JUVENTUS
A 0-1
Butina, Vanaudenaerde, Maertens, Spilar, Gvozdenovic (Lange 84), Clément (Englebert 50), Dufer (Serebrennikov 80), Leko, Vermant, Verheyen, Portillo.

Match 6 FC BAYERN MÜNCHEN
H 1-1 *Portillo (32)*
Butina, Maertens, Clément, Spilar, Vandelanoitte, Englebert (Vanaudenaerde 90), Vermant, Roelandts, Yulu-Matondo (Dufer 88), Portillo, Lange (Gvozdenovic 76).

RSC ANDERLECHT
2nd qualifying round NEFTÇI BAKU (AZB)
H 5-0 *Tihinen (21), Jestrovic (24), Mpenza (32), Goor (35), Vanderhaeghe (77)*
Zitka, Deschacht, Kompany, Tihinen, Vanden Borre, Goor, Vanderhaeghe, Wilhelmsson, Zetterberg (Baseggio 80), Jestrovic (Serhat 73), Mpenza (Zewlakow 63).
A 0-1
Zitka, Deschacht, Kompany (Deman 82), Tihinen, Vanden Borre, Zewlakow, Goor (Serhat 64), Hasi, Vanderhaeghe, Wilhelmsson, Mpenza (Jestrovic 69).

3rd qualifying round SK SLAVIA PRAHA (CZE)
H 2-1 *Goor (7), Mpenza (38)*
Zitka, Tihinen, Kompany, Deschacht, Vanden Borre, Vanderhaeghe, Zetterberg (Baseggio 81), Goor, Serhat, Jestrovic (Wilhelmsson 62), Mpenza.
A 2-0 *Serhat (69), Mpenza (83)*
Zitka, Vanden Borre (Zewlakow 89), Tihinen, Kompany, Deschacht, Wilhelmsson (Zetterberg 87), Vanderhaeghe, De Man, Goor, Mpenza, Serhat (Delorge 85).

1st round Group G
Match 1 CHELSEA (ENG)
A 0-1
Zitka, Zewlakow (Jestrovic 81), Juhász, Tihinen, De Man, Deschacht, Vanden Borre, Vanderhaeghe (Delorge 89), Goor, Serhat (Wilhelmsson 70), Mpenza.

Match 2 REAL BETIS (ESP)
H 0-1
Proto, Deschacht, Tihinen (Serhat 79), De Man, Vanden Borre, Vanderhaeghe (Baseggio 85), Goor, Zetterberg; Wilhelmsson, Jestrovic, Mpenza.

Match 3 LIVERPOOL (ENG)
H 0-1
Proto, Vanden Borre, De Man, Tihinen (Traoré 50), Deschacht (Serhat 74), Wilhelmsson, Vanderhaeghe (Baseggio 61), Zetterberg, Goor, Mpenza, Jestrovic.

Match 4 LIVERPOOL
A 0-3
Proto, Zewlakow, Tihinen, De Man, Juhász, Wilhelmsson, Zetterberg, Vanderhaeghe (Jestrovic 69), Goor, Serhat (Pujol 69), Mpenza (Baseggio 81).

Match 5 CHELSEA
H 0-2
Proto, Zewlakow, Tihinen, Kompany, Deschacht, Wilhelmsson, Vanden Borre, Vanderhaeghe (Yashchuk 46), Goor, Mpenza (Zetterberg 60), Serhat (Ehret 75).

Match 6 REAL BETIS
A 1-0 *Kompany (44)*
Zitka, Delorge, Juhász, Kompany, Deschacht, Tioté (Zetterberg 84), Lovre (Tihinen 68), Baseggio (Zewlakow 68), Goor, Pujol, Yashchuk.

UEFA CUP

GERMINAL BEERSCHOT ANTWERPEN
1st round OLYMPIQUE MARSEILLE (FRA)
H 0-0
Luciano, De Wree, Van Dooren, Cvitanovic, Monteyne, Snoeckx (Van der Weerden 83), Chimedza, De Decker, Hendrikx, Oztürk, N'Diefi (Cavens 72).
A 0-0
(aet; 1-4 on pens)
Luciano, De Wree, Cvitanovic, Van Dooren, Monteyne, Snoeckx (Lolo 84), De Decker, Dickson, Hendrikx (Oztürk 64), N'Diefi, Josemar (Chimedza 101).

KRC GENK
2nd qualifying round METALURGS LIEPAJA (LAT)
A 3-2 *Vandenbergh (47), Daerden (59), Stojanovic (80)*
Moons, Cornelis, Priske, Matoukou, Mikulic, Beslija, Seyfo, Daerden, Engelaar, Soetaers (Sigurdsson 82), Vandenbergh (Stojanovic 69).
H 3-0 *Vandenbergh (6), Daerden (18), Stojanovic (28)*
Moons, Cornelis, Matoukou, Mikulic, Sigurdsson, Beslija (Remacle 78), Wamfor, Daerden (Haroun 68), Soetaers, Stojanovic, Vandenbergh (Ogunjimi 68).

1st round LITEX LOVECH (BUL)
A 2-2 *Daerden (55), Stojanovic (87)*
Moons, Cornelis, Matoukou, Mikulic, Vandooren, Beslija, Oliseh, Haroun, Daerden, Soetaers (Wamfor 82), Peeters (Stojanovic 76).
H 0-1
Moons, Cornelis, Matoukou (Beslija 61), Soley, Mikulic, Sigurdsson, Wamfor (Defour 70), Oliseh, Soetaers, Vandenbergh, Peeters, Stojanovic.

CLUB BRUGGE KV
3rd round ROMA (ITA)
H 1-2 *Portillo (60)*

Belgium

Butina (Stijnen 16), Vanaudenaerde (Gvozdenovic 86), Maertens, De Cock, Klukowski, Vermant, Roelandts (Ishiaku 53), Leko, Dufer, Portillo, Balaban.
A 1-2 Verheyen (60)
Stijnen, De Cock, Maertens, Clément, Klukowski (Roelandts 61), Englebert, Vermant (Leko 61), Gvozdenovic, Yulu-Matondo, Balaban, Verheyen (Portillo 61).

TOP GOALSCORERS 2005/06

18	Tosin DOSUNMU (Germinal Beerschot Antwerpen)
16	Mohammed TCHITE (R Standard Liège)
15	Aristide BANCE (KSV Lokeren OV)
13	Bosko BALABAN (Club Brugge KV)
12	Kevin VANDENBERGH (KRC Genk)
11	Wagneau ELOI (KSV Roeselare)
	Mbo MPENZA (RSC Anderlecht)
10	SERHAT Akin (RSC Anderlecht)
	Jackson COELHO (KVC Westerlo)
	Mahamadou DISSA (KSK Beveren)
	Tony SERGEANT (SV Zulte-Waregem)

LEAGUE RESULTS/ SCORERS/APPEARANCES 2005/06

RSC ANDERLECHT
Coach – Frank Vercauteren

2005				
6/8	RAA La Louvière	h	6-0	Mpenza, Serhat 2, Zetterberg, Goor, Mitu
14/8	KSV Cercle Brugge	a	2-0	Serhat (p), Mpenza
20/8	Germinal Beerschot	h	3-1	Jestrovic 2 (1p), Mpenza
28/8	KRC Genk	a	3-3	Mpenza 3
10/9	R Excelsior Mouscron	h	3-1	Jestrovic 2, Mpenza
17/9	FC Brussels	a	1-1	og (Culek)
21/9	KSV Roeselare	h	5-1	Vanden Borre, Baseggio, Serhat, Jestrovic 2 (1p)
25/9	K Lierse SK	a	0-0	
1/10	K St.-Truidense VV	h	3-0	Jestrovic, Mpenza, Baseggio
15/10	KSK Beveren	a	1-0	Jestrovic
23/10	Club Brugge KV	h	2-2	Serhat 2
28/10	KSC Lokeren	a	2-2	Serhat, Wilhelmsson
5/11	RSC Charleroi	h	3-1	Vanden Borre, Wilhelmsson, Tihinen
20/11	KVC Westerlo	a	1-2	Zetterberg (p)
2/12	KAA Gent	h	3-0	Tihinen, Mpenza 2
10/12	SV Zulte-Waregem	a	2-1	Kompany, Wilhelmsson
14/12	R Standard Liège	a	0-2	
18/12	RAA La Louvière	h	0-0	
2006				
21/1	KSV Cercle Brugge	h	2-2	Vanden Borre, Frutos
27/1	Germinal Beerschot	a	0-2	
4/2	KRC Genk	h	4-1	Goor 2, Zetterberg (p), Frutos
11/2	R Excelsior Mouscron	a	1-0	Frutos
17/2	FC Brussels	h	2-0	Frutos, Zetterberg
24/2	KSV Roeselare	a	2-0	Wilhelmsson, Frutos
5/3	K Lierse SK	h	3-0	Goor, Frutos, Zetterberg (p)
10/3	K St.-Truidense VV	a	0-3	
18/3	KSK Beveren	h	4-0	Zetterberg (p), Wilhelmsson, Frutos, Serhat
26/3	Club Brugge KV	a	2-0	Frutos 2
31/3	KSC Lokeren	h	1-1	Serhat
7/4	RSC Charleroi	a	1-1	Pujol
14/4	KVC Westerlo	h	5-0	Pujol 3, Zetterberg (p), Mpenza
21/4	R Standard Liège	h	2-0	Serhat, Zetterberg
30/4	KAA Gent	a	0-0	
5/5	SV Zulte-Waregem	h	3-0	Traoré, Tihinen, og (Dindeleux)

No	Name	Nat	Pos	Aps	(s)	Gls
28	Sami ALAGUI	GER	A		(1)	
10	Walter BASEGGIO		M	6	(4)	2
19	Laurent DELORGE		D	1	(11)	
31	Mark DEMAN		D	22	(6)	
3	Olivier DESCHACHT		D	32	(1)	
20	Fabrice EHRET	FRA	M	2		
29	Nicolás FRUTOS	ARG	A	12	(2)	9
14	Bart GOOR		M	30	(2)	4
15	Besnik HASI	ALB	M	1	(2)	
8	Nenad JESTROVIC	SCG	A	10	(3)	8
5	Roland JUHÁSZ	HUN	D	9	(2)	
27	Vincent KOMPANY		D	12		1
7	Goran LOVRE	SCG	M	1	(1)	
99	Marius MITU	ROM	M	1	(1)	1
9	Mbo MPENZA		A	16	(13)	11
13	Silvio PROTO		G	27		
11	Grégory PUJOL	FRA	A	6	(5)	4
24	SERHAT Akin	TUR	A	21	(6)	10
42	Sébastien SIANI	CMR	A		(3)	
30	Hannu Olavi TIHINEN	FIN	D	29		3
41	Cheik Isamel TIOTE	CIV	M		(2)	
34	Lamine TRAORE	BFA	D	4	(3)	1
37	Anthony VANDEN BORRE		D	13	(9)	3
4	Yves VANDERHAEGHE		M	26	(1)	
17	Christian WILHELMSSON	SWE	A	31		5
22	Oleh YASHCHUK	UKR	A	2	(7)	
21	Pär ZETTERBERG	SWE	M	28	(2)	8
6	Michal ZEWLAKOW	POL	D	25	(6)	
1	Daniel ZITKA	CZE	G	7		

KSK BEVEREN
Coach - Vincent Dufour; (9/3/06) Eddy De Bolle

2005				
6/8	FC Brussels	h	0-2	
14/8	KSV Roeselare	a	0-1	
20/8	K Lierse SK	h	4-1	Zézéto, Diallo 2, Gervinho
26/8	K St.-Truidense VV	a	0-1	
11/9	R Standard Liège	a	3-1	Sanogo 2, Né
18/9	Club Brugge KV	h	0-1	
21/9	KSC Lokeren	a	2-1	Sanogo, Dissa
24/9	RSC Charleroi	h	1-1	Zézéto
1/10	KVC Westerlo	a	1-4	Dissa
15/10	RSC Anderlecht	h	0-1	
22/10	KAA Gent	a	0-3	
29/10	SV Zulte-Waregem	h	2-1	Dissa, Zézéto
5/11	RAA La Louvière	a	0-2	
19/11	KSV Cercle Brugge	h	5-1	Junior, Dissa 2, Seka, Gervinho
4/12	KRC Genk	h	0-2	
10/12	R Excelsior Mouscron	a	3-1	Dissa 2, Seka
14/12	Germinal Beerschot	a	1-3	Dissa
17/12	FC Brussels	a	1-3	Joseph-Augustin
2006				
21/1	KSV Roeselare	h	1-1	Gervinho

Belgium

FINAL LEAGUE TABLE 2005/06

		Pld	W	D	L	F	A	W	D	L	F	A	W	D	L	F	A	Pts
			Home					**Away**					**Total**					
1	RSC Anderlecht	34	14	3	0	54	10	6	7	4	18	17	20	10	4	72	27	70
2	R Standard Liège	34	12	2	3	30	13	7	6	4	21	15	19	8	7	51	28	65
3	Club Brugge KV	34	14	1	2	32	10	4	9	4	19	23	18	10	6	51	33	64
4	KAA Gent	34	9	4	4	26	15	9	3	5	22	19	18	7	9	48	34	61
5	KRC Genk	34	12	4	1	30	12	4	5	8	18	26	16	9	9	52	38	57
6	SV Zulte-Waregem	34	7	4	6	25	22	7	3	7	26	27	14	7	13	51	49	49
7	Germinal Beerschot	34	8	6	3	28	14	5	2	10	17	31	13	8	13	45	45	47
8	KSC Lokeren OV	34	7	5	5	28	24	5	6	6	20	25	12	11	11	48	49	47
9	KVC Westerlo	34	7	6	4	24	22	6	1	10	18	26	13	7	14	42	48	46
10	FC Brussels	34	6	7	4	18	14	6	3	8	12	16	12	10	12	30	30	46
11	RSC Charleroi	34	9	4	4	24	13	2	8	7	15	26	11	12	11	39	39	45
12	KSV Roeselare	34	8	4	5	28	15	2	7	8	16	27	10	11	13	44	42	41
13	KSV Cercle Brugge	34	7	4	6	23	20	3	4	10	15	36	10	8	16	38	56	38
14	R Excelsior Mouscron	34	8	1	8	27	16	3	3	11	16	27	11	4	19	43	43	37
15	K St.-Truidense VV	34	4	7	6	21	23	4	3	10	15	26	8	10	16	36	49	34
16	KSK Beveren	34	6	4	7	21	19	3	2	12	14	36	9	6	19	35	55	33
17	K Lierse SK	34	6	5	6	14	18	2	3	12	8	34	8	8	18	22	52	32
18	RAA La Louvière	34	2	9	6	14	22	2	5	10	12	30	4	14	16	26	56	26

28/1	K Lierse SK	a	0-2	
4/2	K St.-Truidense VV	h	1-1	Gervinho
11/2	R Standard Liège	h	0-2	
19/2	Club Brugge KV	a	0-1	
25/2	KSC Lokeren	h	1-3	Tokpa
3/3	RSC Charleroi	a	0-4	
11/3	KVC Westerlo	h	4-1	Dissa 2, Agboh, Gervinho
18/3	RSC Anderlecht	a	0-4	
25/3	KAA Gent	h	0-1	
1/4	SV Zulte-Waregem	a	2-2	Diallo, Fontenette
8/4	RAA La Louvière	h	1-0	Gervinho
15/4	KSV Cercle Brugge	a	1-1	Joseph-Augustin
22/4	Germinal Beerschot	h	0-0	
30/4	KRC Genk	a	0-2	
5/5	R Excelsior Mouscron	h	1-0	Diallo

No	Name	Nat	Pos	Aps	(s)	Gls
3	Kuami AGBOH	FRA	M	4	(5)	1
18	ARUNINA Alain Koudou	CIV	A	5	(6)	
8	BADJAN Kante Seydou	CIV	D	14	(3)	
1	COPA Barry Boubacar	CIV	G	27		
19	Mohamed DIALLO	CIV	M	27	(6)	4
4	Diabis Abdoulaye DIAWARA	CIV	D	31		
23	Mahamadou DISSA	MLI	A	28	(4)	10
15	Olivier FONTENETTE	FRA	D	27		1
27	Gervais GERVINHO	CIV	A	20	(12)	6
13	Jonathan JOSEPH-AUGUSTIN	CIV	D	25		2
23	JUNIOR Abdoulaye Djire	CIV	M	29		1
9	KAIPER Constant Kipre	CIV	A	4	(8)	
3	Kristof LARDENOIT		D		(3)	
2	MAHAN Armand Mondakan	CIV	D	29	(2)	
9	Akin MURAT		M		(1)	
16	Marco NE	CIV	M	9	(1)	1
14	Sekou OUATARRA	CIV	A	3	(3)	
11	PACHECO Herman Ahiba	CIV	M	12	(3)	
20	Moussa SANOGO	CIV	A	10	(4)	3
10	SEKA Roméo Affessi	CIV	M	14	(8)	2

6	Alexandre TOKPA	CIV	M	23	(4)	1
1	Davino VERHULST		G	7	(1)	
25	Vénance ZEZETO	CIV	A	9	(11)	3
5	ZITO Tamla Ladji Mekerme	CIV	A	17	(2)	

KSV CERCLE BRUGGE
Coach - Harm van Veldhoven

2005
6/8	KVC Westerlo	a	0-2	
14/8	RSC Anderlecht	h	0-2	
20/8	KAA Gent	a	0-1	
27/8	SV Zulte-Waregem	h	2-4	Pivaljevic, Boi
10/9	RAA La Louvière	a	0-0	
17/9	R Standard Liège	h	0-3	
21/9	Germinal Beerschot	h	3-0	Pivaljevic, De Smet 2
24/9	KRC Genk	a	1-3	Roiha
2/10	R Excelsior Mouscron	h	1-0	Dekelver
15/10	FC Brussels	a	2-1	Dekelver 2
22/10	KSV Roeselare	h	2-2	Pinas, Milosevic
29/10	K Lierse SK	a	4-0	Pinas 2, De Smet, Dekelver
5/11	K St.-Truidense VV	h	2-1	Pivaljevic, Boi
19/11	KSK Beveren	a	1-5	Valenta
27/11	Club Brugge KV	h	0-1	
3/12	KSC Lokeren	a	1-2	Dekelver
10/12	RSC Charleroi	h	2-0	De Smet, Pinas
17/12	KVC Westerlo	h	2-2	Boi, Meyssen
21/1	RSC Anderlecht	a	2-2	Meyssen, Dekelver

2006
28/1	KAA Gent	h	1-2	Dekelver
4/2	SV Zulte-Waregem	a	1-3	Dekelver
11/2	RAA La Louvière	h	1-0	Pivaljevic
18/2	R Standard Liège	a	1-7	Muhamadu
25/2	Germinal Beerschot	a	0-0	
4/3	KRC Genk	h	1-1	Dekelver
11/3	R Excelsior Mouscron	a	0-6	
18/3	FC Brussels	h	0-5	
26/3	KSV Roeselare	a	0-1	

Belgium

1/4	K Lierse SK	h	3-0	De Smet, Pivaljevic (p), Muhamadu
8/4	K St.-Truidense VV	a	1-1	Pinas
15/4	KSK Beveren	h	1-1	De Smet
23/4	Club Brugge KV	a	0-2	
30/4	KSC Lokeren	h	2-0	Pivaljevic, Pinas
5/5	RSC Charleroi	a	1-0	De Smet

No	Name	Nat	Pos	Aps	(s)	Gls
12	Frederik BOI		M	21	(8)	3
11	Dieter DEKELVER		A	24	(6)	9
19	Stijn DE SMET		A	24	(5)	7
16	Jimmy DEWULF		D	31		
30	Matthias FEYS		A		(3)	
5	Christophe GRONDIN	FRA	D	23	(6)	
2	Luke JONES	ENG	D	8		
20	Jan MASUREEL		D	20	(3)	
10	Harold MEYSSEN		M	19	(5)	2
17	Milenko MILOSEVIC	SCG	M	15	(4)	1
14	Ibad MUHAMADU	HOL	M	7	(5)	2
22	Brian PINAS	HOL	A	17	(12)	6
9	Darko PIVALJEVIC	SCG	A	28	(1)	6
3	Anthony PORTIER		D	13	(1)	
14	Paulus ROIHA	FIN	A	4	(7)	1
8	Slobodan SLOVIC	SCG	D	13	(12)	
13	Djordje SVETLICIC	SCG	D	19	(1)	
15	Vit VALENTA	CZE	M	1	(12)	1
21	Bram VANDENBUSSCHE		D	10	(7)	
1	Francky VANDENDRIESSCHE		G	34		
6	Tom VAN MOL		M	29		
4	Denis VIANE		M	14		

CLUB BRUGGE KV
Coach – Jan Ceulemans; (3/4/06) Emilio Ferrera

2005

5/8	R Excelsior Mouscron	h	2-0	Leko, Balaban
13/8	FC Brussels	a	1-1	Ishiaku
20/8	KSV Roeselare	h	1-0	Balaban
27/8	K Lierse SK	a	1-1	Balaban
10/9	K St.-Truidense VV	h	2-1	Balaban 2
18/9	KSK Beveren	a	1-0	Yulu-Matondo
21/9	R Standard Liège	a	0-2	
24/9	KSC Lokeren	h	0-1	
30/9	RSC Charleroi	a	3-3	Leko, Portillo, Víctor
15/10	KVC Westerlo	h	2-1	Balaban (p), Verheyen
23/10	RSC Anderlecht	a	2-2	Vermant, Verheyen
29/10	KAA Gent	h	2-1	Portillo 2
6/11	SV Zulte-Waregem	a	1-2	Lange
19/11	RAA La Louvière	h	4-0	Portillo, Leko, Lange, Dufer
27/11	KSV Cercle Brugge	a	1-0	Balaban
3/12	Germinal Beerschot	h	2-0	Balaban 2
11/12	KRC Genk	a	2-2	Verheyen, Clément
17/12	R Excelsior Mouscron	a	1-0	Verheyen

2006

20/1	FC Brussels	h	3-0	Portillo 2, Roelandts
29/1	KSV Roeselare	a	1-1	Ishiaku
3/2	K Lierse SK	h	3-1	Leko, Clément 2
11/2	K St.-Truidense VV	a	2-2	Clément, Dufer
19/2	KSK Beveren	h	2-1	Roelandts
26/2	R Standard Liège	h	1-1	Leko
4/3	KSC Lokeren	a	0-2	
11/3	RSC Charleroi	h	2-1	Verheyen, Portillo
18/3	KVC Westerlo	a	0-0	
26/3	RSC Anderlecht	h	0-2	
1/4	KAA Gent	a	1-4	Portillo
7/4	SV Zulte-Waregem	h	2-1	og (Salou), Verheyen
16/4	RAA La Louvière	a	1-0	Balaban

23/4	KSV Cercle Brugge	h	2-0	Balaban, Verheyen
30/4	Germinal Beerschot	a	1-1	Ishiaku
5/5	KRC Genk	h	3-0	Balaban 2 (1p), Clément

No	Name	Nat	Pos	Aps	(s)	Gls
14	Bosko BALABAN	CRO	A	26	(4)	13
1	Tomislav BUTINA	CRO	G	19		
11	Jonathan BLONDEL		M	4	(7)	
6	Philippe CLEMENT		D	21	(1)	5
2	Olivier DE COCK		D	16	(3)	
14	Grégory DUFER		M	7	(12)	2
8	Gaëtan ENGLEBERT		M	21	(7)	
17	Ivan GVOZDENOVIC	SCG	D	10	(2)	
9	Manaseh ISHIAKU	NGA	A	8	(9)	3
18	Michael KLUKOWSKI	CAN	D	17	(1)	
19	Rune LANGE	NOR	A		(2)	2
18	Ivan LEKO	CRO	M	30		5
26	Birger MAERTENS		D	33		
22	Javier PORTILLO	ESP	A	21	(3)	8
27	Vincent PROVOOST		M		(1)	
31	Kevin ROELANDTS		M	10	(11)	2
16	Serhiy SEREBRENNIKOV	UKR	M	1	(1)	
15	Marek SPILAR	SVK	D	11	(1)	
23	Stijn STIJNEN		G	15		
32	Gunther VANAUDENAERDE		D	22		
33	Jason VANDELANOITTE		D	10	(5)	
16	Elrio VAN HEERDEN	RSA	M	4	(6)	
29	Dieter VAN TORNHOUT		A		(1)	
4	Joos VALGAEREN		D	3	(2)	
7	Gert VERHEYEN		A	30	(2)	7
3	Sven VERMANT		M	30	(2)	1
30	VÍCTOR Simões de Oliveira	BRA	A	1	(5)	1
34	Jeanvion YULU-MATONDO		A	4	(9)	1

FC BRUSSELS
Coach – Albert Cartier

2005

6/8	KSK Beveren	a	2-0	Sels, De Camargo
13/8	Club Brugge KV	h	1-1	De Camargo
21/8	KSC Lokeren	a	0-1	
27/8	RSC Charleroi	h	2-2	De Camargo, Culek
10/9	KVC Westerlo	a	0-3	
17/9	RSC Anderlecht	h	1-1	Sels (p)
20/9	KAA Gent	a	1-2	Kargbo
24/9	SV Zulte-Waregem	h	1-1	De Camargo
1/10	RAA La Louvière	a	3-0	Culek, De Camargo 2
15/10	KSV Cercle Brugge	h	1-2	Culek
22/10	Germinal Beerschot	a	1-0	Niçoise
29/10	KRC Genk	h	1-0	De Camargo
5/11	R Excelsior Mouscron	a	1-1	Niçoise
19/11	R Standard Liège	h	3-1	og (Léonard), Gorius, Niçoise
3/12	K Lierse SK	a	1-1	Espartero
10/12	K St.-Truidense VV	h	0-0	
14/12	KSV Roeselare	h	1-0	Zaaboub
17/12	KSK Beveren	h	3-1	De Camargo 2, Culek

2006

20/1	Club Brugge KV	a	0-3	
28/1	KSC Lokeren	h	1-1	Snelders
4/2	RSC Charleroi	a	0-1	
17/2	RSC Anderlecht	a	0-2	
22/2	KVC Westerlo	h	1-0	Andersen
26/2	KAA Gent	h	0-1	
4/3	SV Zulte-Waregem	a	0-0	
11/3	RAA La Louvière	h	0-0	
18/3	KSV Cercle Brugge	a	1-0	Petö
25/3	Germinal Beerschot	h	0-1	

Belgium

1/4	KRC Genk	a	0-1	
7/4	R Excelsior Mouscron	h	0-1	
16/4	R Standard Liège	a	0-1	
22/4	KSV Roeselare	a	1-0	Selemani
30/4	K Lierse SK	h	2-1	Bruno, Selemani
5/5	K St.-Truidense VV	a	1-0	Culek (p)

No	Name	Nat	Pos	Aps	(s)	Gls
15	Kristoffer ANDERSEN	DEN	A	7	(4)	1
	Patricio BENGUI		M		(1)	
7	Christ BRUNO		D	29	(1)	1
3	Alexandere CLEMENT	FRA	D	5	(2)	
19	Steve COLPAERT		D	28		
5	Richard CULEK	CZE	M	32	(1)	5
10	Igor DE CAMARGO	BRA	A	14	(1)	9
26	Cédric DELLEVOET		M		(3)	
12	István DUDAS	HUN	G		(1)	
18	Mario ESPARTERO	FRA	M	20	(2)	1
14	Julien GORIUS	FRA	M	23	(7)	1
8	Alan HAYDOCK		M	28	(1)	
2	Michael JONCKHEERE		D	4	(5)	
4	Ibrahim KARGBO	SRL	D	25	(1)	1
22	Gert-Jan MARTENS		M		(2)	
23	Mickaël NIÇOISE	FRA	A	17	(9)	3
1	Patrick NYS		G	33		
15	Fabrice OMONGA Djadi		A	8	(8)	
24	Zoltán PETÖ	HUN	M	25	(3)	1
25	Moussa SANOGO	CIV	A	6	(1)	
21	Musa SELEMANI	RWA	M	16	(10)	2
9	Werry SELS		M	20	(3)	2
13	Kristof SNELDERS		A	19	(10)	1
11	Davy THEUNIS		M	4		
16	Sofiane ZAABOUB	FRA	D	10	(10)	1
20	Isa ZIGI		G	1		

RSC CHARLEROI
Coach – Jacky Mathijssen

2005

7/8	Germinal Beerschot	h	2-0	Christ, Reina
14/8	KRC Genk	a	0-0	
20/8	R Excelsior Mouscron	h	1-0	Christ
27/8	FC Brussels	a	2-2	Sterchele, Christ
10/9	KSV Roeselare	h	1-1	Sterchele
17/9	K Lierse SK	a	0-0	
20/9	K St.-Truidense VV	h	0-1	
24/9	KSK Beveren	a	1-1	Chabaud
30/9	Club Brugge KV	h	3-3	Camus, Siquet, Sterchele
15/10	KSC Lokeren	a	2-4	Chabaud, Forschelet
21/10	R Standard Liège	a	0-1	
29/10	KVC Westerlo	h	2-1	Sterchele, Orlando
5/11	RSC Anderlecht	a	1-3	Sterchele
19/11	KAA Gent	h	2-0	Defays, Sterchele
3/12	RAA La Louvière	h	0-2	
10/12	KSV Cercle Brugge	a	0-2	
14/12	SV Zulte-Waregem	a	0-3	
17/12	Germinal Beerschot	a	1-0	Sterchele

2006

22/1	KRC Genk	h	2-1	Akgül, Serebrennikov
28/1	R Excelsior Mouscron	a	1-0	Orlando
4/2	FC Brussels	h	1-0	Ciman
18/2	K Lierse SK	h	0-1	
21/2	KSV Roeselare	a	0-2	
25/2	K St.-Truidense VV	h	1-1	Sterchele
3/3	KSK Beveren	h	4-0	Orlando, Akgül, Defays, Brogno (p)
11/3	Club Brugge KV	a	1-2	og (Valgaeren)
18/3	KSC Lokeren	h	3-1	Sterchele, Akgül, Camus

24/3	R Standard Liège	h	0-0	
2/4	KVC Westerlo	a	1-1	Akgül
7/4	RSC Anderlecht	h	1-1	Akpala
15/4	KAA Gent	a	2-2	Oulmers, Keré
22/4	SV Zulte-Waregem	h	2-0	Akpala, Christ
30/4	RAA La Louvière	a	2-2	Oulmers, Dante
5/5	KSV Cercle Brugge	h	0-1	

No	Name	Nat	Pos	Aps	(s)	Gls
13	AKGÜL Izzet		A	9	(8)	4
27	Joseph AKPALA	NGA	A	3	(5)	2
14	Ousmane BANGOURA	GUI	A		(4)	
10	Toni BROGNO		A	12	(11)	1
15	Fabien CAMUS	FRA	M	16	(7)	2
6	Sébastien CHABAUD	FRA	M	14		2
24	Grégory CHRIST	FRA	M	22	(7)	4
26	Laurent CIMAN		D	18		1
18	DANTE Bonfim	BRA	D	11	(1)	1
2	Frank DEFAYS		D	27		2
20	Thibaut DETAL		M	14	(8)	
7	Gérald FORSCHELET	FRA	D	7	(7)	1
23	Márcio GIOVANNINI	BRA	D		(1)	
16	Mamahoudou Badou KERE	BFA	M	29		1
30	Nasredine KRAOUCHE	ALG	M	21	(6)	
1	Damien LAHAYE		G	1		
28	Bertrand LAQUAIT	FRA	G	33		
22	ORLANDO dos Santos Costa	BRA	A	25	(5)	3
21	Abdelmajid OULMERS	MAR	M	20	(7)	2
4	Loris REINA	FRA	D	14	(4)	1
5	Rémi RIBAULT	FRA	D	9	(2)	
5	Serhiy SEREBRENNIKOV	UKR	M	12		1
25	Thierry SIQUET		D	11		1
9	François STERCHELE		A	26	(5)	9
9	Steeve-Alain THEOPHILE	FRA	M		(1)	
3	Velimir VARGA	SLO	D	20		

KRC GENK
Coach – Hugo Broos

2005

6/8	KSC Lokeren	a	1-1	Vandenbergh (p)
14/8	RSC Charleroi	h	0-0	
20/8	KVC Westerlo	a	1-1	Vandenbergh
28/8	RSC Anderlecht	h	3-3	Vandooren, Cornelis, Mikulic
10/9	KAA Gent	a	0-2	
18/9	SV Zulte-Waregem	h	3-1	Mikulic, Stojanovic 2
21/9	RAA La Louvière	a	3-2	Stojanovic, Peeters, Vandenbergh
24/9	KSV Cercle Brugge	h	3-1	Seyfo, Peeters, Vandenbergh
2/10	Germinal Beerschot	a	2-2	Soetaers, Peeters
16/10	R Standard Liège	h	0-1	
22/10	R Excelsior Mouscron	h	1-0	Sigurdsson
29/10	FC Brussels	a	0-1	
5/11	KSV Roeselare	h	4-1	Vandenbergh 2, Defour, Engelaar
20/11	K Lierse SK	a	2-1	Engelaar, Soetaers
27/11	K St.-Truidense VV	h	2-0	Soetaers, Peeters
4/12	KSK Beveren	a	2-0	Beslija, Chatelle
11/12	Club Brugge KV	h	2-2	Beslija, Peeters
17/12	KSC Lokeren	h	2-2	Peeters, Vandenbergh (p)

2006

22/1	RSC Charleroi	a	1-2	Vandenbergh
28/1	KVC Westerlo	h	2-0	Peeters, Pocognoli
4/2	RSC Anderlecht	a	1-4	Vandenbergh
12/2	KAA Gent	h	2-1	Peeters, og (Lombaerts)
18/2	SV Zulte-Waregem	a	0-1	
25/2	RAA La Louvière	h	5-0	(w/o ; original result 1-0 Peeters)

Belgium

4/3	KSV Cercle Brugge	a	1-1	og (Masureel)
11/3	Germinal Beerschot	h	1-0	Engelaar
17/3	R Standard Liège	a	0-1	
26/3	R Excelsior Mouscron	a	0-1	
1/4	FC Brussels	h	1-0	Stojanovic
9/4	KSV Roeselare	a	2-1	Matoukou, Daerden
15/4	K Lierse SK	h	1-0	Vandenbergh
22/4	K St.-Truidense VV	a	2-2	Vandenbergh, Seyfo
30/4	KSK Beveren	h	2-0	Vandenbergh, Daerden
5/5	Club Brugge KV	a	0-3	

No	Name	Nat	Pos	Aps	(s)	Gls
6	Mirsad BESLIJA	BOS	M	12	(2)	2
12	Thomas CHATELLE		M	10	(8)	1
8	Gert CLAESSENS		D	7	(1)	
23	Hans CORNELIS		D	21		1
13	Wouter CORSTJENS		D		(1)	
20	Koen DAERDEN		M	13	(1)	2
25	Steven DEFOUR		M	25	(1)	1
21	Orlando ENGELAAR	HOL	M	22	(4)	3
17	Faris HAROUN		M	7	(13)	
5	Eric MATOUKOU	CMR	D	12	(3)	1
4	Tomislav MIKULIC	CRO	M	24	(1)	2
1	Jan MOONS		G	34		
16	Marvin OGUNJIMI		A		(8)	
17	Sunday OLISEH	NGA	M	16		
19	Bob PEETERS		A	17	(4)	9
15	Sébastien POCOGNOLI		D	12	(3)	1
19	Brian PRISKE	DEN	D	3		
14	Jordan REMACLE		M	2	(5)	
3	Soley SEYFO	GAM	D	23	(1)	2
2	Indridi SIGURDSSON	ISL	D	18	(7)	1
10	Tom SOETAERS		M	12	(6)	3
33	Nenad STOJANOVIC	SCG	A	12	(9)	4
11	Kevin VANDENBERGH		A	23	(8)	12
11	Gonzague VANDOOREN		M	16	(5)	1
24	Kenneth VAN GOETHEM		M	6		
29	Sven VERDONCK		M	9		
22	Justice WAMFOR	CMR	M	18	(2)	

KAA GENT
Coach – Georges Leekens

2005

6/8	SV Zulte-Waregem	h	1-3	De Beule
12/8	RAA La Louvière	a	1-1	Datti
20/8	KSV Cercle Brugge	h	1-0	Vrancken
27/8	Germinal Beerschot	a	1-2	Boussoufa
10/9	KRC Genk	h	2-0	Thompson, Vrancken
16/9	R Excelsior Mouscron	a	2-1	Grégoire, Mamouni
20/9	FC Brussels	h	2-1	Boussoufa, Grégoire
25/9	KSV Roeselare	a	1-1	Cooreman
1/10	K Lierse SK	h	1-1	Vrancken
16/10	K St.-Truidense VV	a	1-1	Vrancken
22/10	KSK Beveren	h	3-0	Foley, Datti, Boussoufa
29/10	Club Brugge KV	a	1-2	Foley
4/11	KSC Lokeren	h	1-2	Martens
19/11	RSC Charleroi	a	0-2	
2/12	RSC Anderlecht	a	0-3	
11/12	R Standard Liège	h	2-1	Grégoire, Zoko
14/12	KVC Westerlo	h	0-1	
18/12	SV Zulte-Waregem	a	2-1	Zoko, Grégoire

2006

21/1	RAA La Louvière	h	3-0	Zoko, Boussoufa, Lombaerts
28/1	KSV Cercle Brugge	a	2-1	Vrancken, Zoko
4/2	Germinal Beerschot	h	2-1	Grégoire, Martens
12/2	KRC Genk	a	1-2	Smoje (p)
18/2	R Excelsior Mouscron	h	0-0	
26/2	FC Brussels	a	1-0	Vrancken
4/3	KSV Roeselare	h	1-2	Boussoufa
11/3	K Lierse SK	a	3-1	Grégoire, Foley, Vrancken
19/3	K St.-Truidense VV	h	1-0	De Beule
25/3	KSK Beveren	a	1-0	Grégoire
1/4	Club Brugge KV	h	4-1	Boussoufa 3, De Beule
8/4	KSC Lokeren	a	2-1	Foley 2
15/4	RSC Charleroi	h	2-2	Boussoufa, Zoko
23/4	KVC Westerlo	a	1-0	Foley
30/4	RSC Anderlecht	h	0-0	
5/5	R Standard Liège	a	2-0	Grégoire, Pavlovic

No	Name	Nat	Pos	Aps	(s)	Gls
4	Anyanwu BLESSING		D	12	(3)	
9	Mbark BOUSSOUFA	MAR	A	28		9
16	Steve COOREMAN		M	8	(7)	1
10	Aliyu DATTI	NGA	A	14	(9)	2
21	Davy DE BEULE		M	30	(1)	3
22	Mamadou DIOP	SEN	A		(1)	
18	Dominic FOLEY	IRL	A	25		6
14	Christophe GREGOIRE		M	26	(1)	8
15	Yngvar HÅKONSEN	NOR	M	3	(7)	
23	Frédéric HERPOEL		G	34		
7	Stephen LAYBUTT	AUS	D	26		
6	Nicolas LOMBAERTS		D	31		1
17	Maâmar MAMOUNI	ALG	M	16	(7)	1
11	Sandy MARTENS		A	21	(7)	2
3	Daniel MIRVIC	BOS	D	6	(11)	
13	Nenad MLADENOVIC	SCG	A	5	(5)	
13	Ernest NFOR	CMR	A			
8	Nebojsa PAVLOVIC	SCG	M	10	(1)	1
2	Dario SMOJE	CRO	D	29	(1)	1
17	Kenny THOMPSON		M	8	(10)	1
8	Jovica TRAJCEV		M	1	(2)	
20	Wouter VRANCKEN		M	30		7
12	Zéphirin ZOKO	CIV	A	11	(9)	5

GERMINAL BEERSCHOT ANTWERPEN
Coach – Marc Brys; (22/9/05) Jos Daerden

2005

7/8	RSC Charleroi	a	0-2	
13/8	KVC Westerlo	h	0-1	
20/8	RSC Anderlecht	a	1-3	Dosunmu
27/8	KAA Gent	h	2-1	Öztürk, Dosunmu
10/9	SV Zulte-Waregem	a	1-2	Camara
18/9	RAA La Louvière	h	1-1	De Wree
21/9	KSV Cercle Brugge	a	0-3	
25/9	R Standard Liège	h	2-2	De Wree, Dickson
2/10	KRC Genk	h	2-2	Dosunmu 2
15/10	R Excelsior Mouscron	a	1-4	Dosunmu
22/10	FC Brussels	h	0-1	
30/10	KSV Roeselare	a	1-5	Van der Weerden
5/11	K Lierse SK	h	4-0	Dosunmu 3, Josemar
19/11	K St.-Truidense VV	a	2-1	De Roeck, Dosunmu
3/12	Club Brugge KV	a	0-2	
9/12	KSC Lokeren	h	2-1	Dosunmu, Lolo
14/12	KSK Beveren	h	3-1	De Wree, Dosunmu, Dickson
17/12	RSC Charleroi	h	0-1	

2006

21/1	KVC Westerlo	a	3-1	De Roeck, Dosunmu 2
27/1	RSC Anderlecht	h	2-0	Cavens 2
4/2	KAA Gent	a	1-2	Lolo
11/2	SV Zulte-Waregem	h	2-0	Van der Weerden, Dosunmu
19/2	RAA La Louvière	a	1-1	Dosunmu
25/2	KSV Cercle Brugge	h	0-0	
5/3	R Standard Liège	a	1-3	Messoudi
11/3	KRC Genk	h	0-1	

Belgium

18/3	R Excelsior Mouscron	h	1-0	Cvitanovic
25/3	FC Brussels	a	1-0	Hendrikx
1/4	KSV Roeselare	h	2-2	Messoudi, Dosunmu
8/4	K Lierse SK	a	2-0	Dosunmu, Hendrikx
15/4	K St.-Truidense VV	h	4-0	De Roeck, Cavens 2, Josemar
22/4	KSK Beveren	a	0-0	
30/4	Club Brugge KV	h	1-1	Cavens
5/5	KSC Lokeren	a	2-1	Dosunmu, Cavens

No	Name	Nat	Pos	Aps	(s)	Gls
22	Brian BADZA	ZIM	A		(2)	
24	Kader Mohamed CAMARA	GUI	M		(6)	1
9	Jurgen CAVENS		A	9	(4)	6
13	Cephas CHIMEDZA	ZIM	M	9	(2)	
10	Daniel CRUZ	COL	M	12	(2)	
17	Mario CVITANOVIC	CRO	D	17	4	1
12	Wim DE DECKER		D	33		
6	Jonas DE ROECK		D	23		3
8	Kris DE WREE		M	17		3
25	DICKSON Agyeman		M	12	(9)	2
15	Tosin DOSUNMU	NGA	A	31		18
27	JOSEMAR dos Santos Gil	BRA	A	11	(7)	2
16	Marc HENDRIKX		M	15	(9)	2
10	Julien KEMAJOU		M		(2)	
18	Alexis KUBILSKIS		M		(2)	
21	Igor LOLO	CIV	D	21	(1)	2
26	LUCIANO da Silva Moura	BRA	G	30		
19	Mohamed MESSOUDI		M	23	(1)	2
89	Ninoslav MILENKOVIC	BOS	D	1	(6)	
5	Pieter-Jan MONTEYNE		D	33		
23	Pius N'DIEFI	CMR	A	4	(2)	
3	Edwin OUON		D	2	(4)	
11	Sezer ÖZTÜRK	GER	A	5	(3)	1
14	PRINCE Asubonteng		A	3	(5)	
7	Karel SNOECKX		M	9	(4)	
2	Chris VAN DER WEERDEN	HOL	D	13	(5)	2
4	Kurt VAN DOOREN		D	33		
1	Bram VERBIST		G	4	(1)	
23	VÍCTOR Simões de Oliveira	BRA	A	4	(9)	

K LIERSE SK
Coach – Paul Put; (7/11/05) René Trost

2005
6/8	R Standard Liège	a	1-3	Imschoot
14/8	K St.-Truidense VV	h	1-0	Nunes
20/8	KSK Beveren	a	1-4	Imschoot
27/8	Club Brugge KV	h	1-1	Nunes
17/9	RSC Charleroi	h	0-0	
21/9	KVC Westerlo	a	0-0	
25/9	RSC Anderlecht	h	0-0	
1/10	KAA Gent	a	1-1	Yakovenko
15/10	SV Zulte-Waregem	h	0-2	
22/10	RAA La Louvière	a	0-1	
29/10	KSV Cercle Brugge	h	0-4	
5/11	Germinal Beerschot	a	0-4	
9/11	KSC Lokeren	a	0-1	
20/11	KRC Genk	h	1-2	Fassotte
3/12	FC Brussels	h	1-1	Tohoua
11/12	KSV Roeselare	a	0-2	
14/12	R Excelsior Mouscron	a	0-5	
18/12	R Standard Liège	h	0-2	

2006
21/1	K St.-Truidense VV	a	1-1	Nunes
28/1	KSK Beveren	h	2-0	Yakovenko, Mujanovic
3/2	Club Brugge KV	a	1-3	og (Clément)
11/2	KSC Lokeren	h	2-0	Nunes (p), Wils

18/2	RSC Charleroi	a	1-0	Mrdja (p)
25/2	KVC Westerlo	h	2-1	Tohoua, Mujanovic
5/3	RSC Anderlecht	a	0-3	
11/3	KAA Gent	h	1-3	Mujanovic
17/3	SV Zulte-Waregem	a	1-0	Imschoot
25/3	RAA La Louvière	h	0-0	
1/4	KSV Cercle Brugge	a	0-3	
8/4	Germinal Beerschot	h	0-2	
15/4	KRC Genk	a	0-1	
22/4	R Excelsior Mouscron	h	2-0	Imschoot, Develer
30/4	FC Brussels	a	1-2	Elberkani
5/5	KSV Roeselare	h	1-0	Mrdja

No	Name	Nat	Pos	Aps	(s)	Gls
3	Marko ANDIC	SCG	D	22	(1)	
18	Creedence Clearwater COUTO	BRA	A	6	(6)	
20	Daniel CRUZ	COL	M	11	(2)	
30	Thomas DE CORTE		M	5	(1)	
26	Kane DEVELER		A	3	(6)	1
16	Timothy DREESEN		M	15	(1)	
10	Mohammed ELBERKANI	HOL	A	2	(8)	1
4	Laurent FASSOTTE		D	21		1
8	Kristof IMSCHOOT		M	23	(4)	4
24	Hasan KACIC	CRO	D	21		
10	Krunoslav LOVREK	CRO	M	6	(1)	
22	Cliff MARDULIER		G	13	(1)	
17	Ninoslav MILENKOVIC	BOS	M	12		
33	Dragan MRDJA	SCG	A	16	(4)	2
15	Goran MUJANOVIC	CRO	M	18	(2)	3
5	Michael Chidiebere NNAJI	NGA	D	29	(1)	
9	Alessandro NUNES	BRA	A	19	(9)	4
19	Jurgen RAEYMAEKERS		A	8	(14)	
14	Jimmy SMET		D	4		
16	Karel SNOECKX		M	13	(1)	
	Jochem TANGHE		G	3		
2	Adolph TOHOUA	CIV	M	14	(3)	2
26	Goran TOMIC	CRO	A	1		
11	Tony VAIRELLES	FRA	A	13	(2)	
18	Sven VANDENBROECK		M	7	(2)	
	Sven VAN DER JEUGT		G	3		
1	Yves VAN DER STRAETEN		G	15		
	Jérome VAN DER ZIJL		D	3	(3)	
16	Ognjen VUKOJEVIC	CRO	D	8	(1)	
6	Stef WILS		M	28		1
13	Oleksandr YAKOVENKO	UKR	A	12	(13)	2

KSC LOKEREN OV
Coach – Slavoljub Muslin (SCG); (23/12/05) Aimé Antheunis; (27/2/06) Rudy Cossey

2005
6/8	KRC Genk	h	1-1	Bancé
13/8	R Excelsior Mouscron	a	2-0	Vidarsson A,, Van Handenhoven
21/8	FC Brussels	h	1-0	Bancé
28/8	KSV Roeselare	a	0-4	
17/9	K St.-Truidense VV	a	2-1	Bouchouari, Jukic
21/9	KSK Beveren	h	1-2	Jukic
24/9	Club Brugge KV	a	1-2	Kristinsson
1/10	R Standard Liège	a	1-2	Zanzan
15/10	RSC Charleroi	h	4-2	Bouchouari (p), Drulic, Bancé, Grétarsson
22/10	KVC Westerlo	a	1-1	Bouchouari
28/10	RSC Anderlecht	h	2-2	João Carlos, Diallo
4/11	KAA Gent	a	2-1	Drulic 2
9/11	K Lierse SK	h	1-0	Kristinsson
19/11	SV Zulte-Waregem	h	2-3	Kristinsson (p), João Carlos
3/12	KSV Cercle Brugge	h	2-1	Krsitinsson, Camara

Belgium

9/12	Germinal Beerschot	a	1-2	Bouchouari	
14/12	RAA La Louvière	a	1-1	Jukic	
17/12	KRC Genk	a	2-2	Bancé, Drulic	
2006					
21/1	R Excelsior Mouscron	h	1-1	Bancé	
28/1	FC Brussels	a	1-1	Overmeire	
4/2	KSV Roeselare	h	2-2	Bancé, Bouchouari	
11/2	K Lierse SK	a	0-2		
18/2	K St.-Truidense VV	h	1-2	Kristinsson	
25/2	KSK Beveren	a	3-1	Bancé 3	
4/3	Club Brugge KV	h	2-0	Camara, Bancé	
12/3	R Standard Liège	h	0-0		
18/3	RSC Charleroi	a	1-3	Kristinsson	
25/3	KVC Westerlo	h	3-2	Bancé 3	
31/3	RSC Anderlecht	a	1-1	og (Tihinen)	
8/4	KAA Gent	h	1-2	Bouchouari	
16/4	SV Zulte-Waregem	a	1-1	Bancé	
22/4	RAA La Louvière	h	3-2	Vukomanovic 2, Bancé	
30/4	KSV Cercle Brugge	a	0-2		
5/5	Germinal Beerschot	h	1-2	Hasi	

No	Name	Nat	Pos	Aps	(s)	Gls
25	Aristide BANCE	BFA	A	19	(9)	15
22	Ali BOUABE	MAR	M	1		
31	Hakim BOUCHOUARI		A	29	(1)	6
15	Aboubacar CAMARA	GUI	M	16	(10)	2
25	Kwinten CLAPPAERT		M		(1)	
11	Victor CORRIA	GUI	M	2	(5)	
23	Xavier DESCHACHT		A		(4)	
32	Benjamin DE WILDE		D		(1)	
28	Frederik DE WINNE		D	4	(6)	
16	Mamadou Alimou DIALLO	GUI	D	13	(4)	1
30	Lezou DOBA	CIV	D	1		
4	Olivier DOLL		D	27		
14	Goran DRULIC	SCG	A	10	(3)	4
2	Hassan EL MOUATAZ	MAR	D	5		
19	Predrag FILIPOVIC	SCG	D	16		
8	Arnar GRÉTARSSON	ISL	M	5	(4)	
6	Besnik HASI	ALB	M	15		1
3	JOÃO CARLOS Pinto Chaves	BRA	D	24		2
9	Ivica JOVANOVIC	SCG	A		(1)	
20	Stepjan JUKIC	CRO	A	3	(13)	3
29	Jean-Paul KIELO LEZI	CON	M	1	(5)	
10	Rúnar KRISTINSSON	ISL	M	31		6
12	Jugoslav LAZIC	SCG	G	18		
1	Zvonko MILOJEVIC	SCG	G	16		
13	Kilian OVERMEIRE		M	18	(7)	1
26	Madi Saidou PANADETIGIURI	BFA	M	28	(1)	
13	Gunther VAN HANDENHOVEN		M	10		1
15	Michaël VAN HOEY		D	17	(2)	
6	Arnar VIDARSSON	ISL	M	15		
27	David VIDARSSON	ISL	M	2		
5	Ivan VUKOMANOVIC	SCG	M	17	(6)	2
21	ZANZAN Mohama Atte-Oudeyi	TOG	D	11	(1)	1

RAA LA LOUVIERE
Coach – Emilio Ferrera; (3/10/05) (Frédéric Tilmant); (21/10/05) Gilbert Bodart; (20/2/06) Frédéric Tilmant

2005					
6/8	RSC Anderlecht	a	0-6		
12/8	KAA Gent	h	1-1	Sánchez	
20/8	SV Zulte-Waregem	a	0-0		
27/8	R Standard Liège	h	2-3	Guilmot, Sánchez	
10/9	KSV Cercle Brugge	h	0-0		
18/9	Germinal Beerschot	a	1-1	Oulai	
21/9	KRC Genk	h	2-3	Stojkov, Pinelli	
24/9	R Excelsior Mouscron	a	1-2	Jbari	
1/10	FC Brussels	h	0-3		
15/10	KSV Roeselare	a	1-4	Stojkov	
22/10	K Lierse SK	h	1-0	Potier	
29/10	K St.-Truidense VV	a	3-1	Stojkov, Brahami, Potier	
5/11	KSK Beveren	h	2-0	og (Fontenette), Jbari	
19/11	Club Brugge KV	a	0-4		
3/12	RSC Charleroi	a	2-0	Guilmot, Sánchez	
10/12	KVC Westerlo	h	0-3		
14/12	KSC Lokeren	h	1-1	Emeran	
18/12	RSC Anderlecht	h	0-0		
2006					
21/1	KAA Gent	a	0-3		
28/1	SV Zulte-Waregem	h	2-2	Mazurkiewicz, Oliseh (p)	
11/2	KSV Cercle Brugge	a	0-1		
19/2	Germinal Beerschot	h	1-1	Lecomte	
22/2	R Standard Liège	a	1-1	Durieux	
25/2	KRC Genk	a	0-5	(w/o; original result 0-1)	
4/3	R Excelsior Mouscron	h	0-0		
11/3	FC Brussels	a	0-0		
18/3	KSV Roeselare	h	0-0		
25/3	K Lierse SK	a	0-0		
1/4	K St.-Truidense VV	h	0-2		
8/4	KSK Beveren	a	0-1		
16/4	Club Brugge KV	h	0-1		
22/4	KSC Lokeren	a	2-3	Stojkov, Bozak	
30/4	RSC Charleroi	h	2-2	Stojkov 2	
5/5	KVC Westerlo	a	1-2	Stojkov	

No	Name	Nat	Pos	Aps	(s)	Gls
11	Rony BAYNON		A		(3)	
1	Asmir BEGOVIC	CAN	G	2		
14	George BLAY	GHA	D	25	(1)	
17	Frédéric BOZAK		A	6	(5)	1
8	Mohammed Fadel BRAHAMI	ALG	M	19	(2)	1
22	Mickaël CORDIER		G	30		
7	Bob COUSIN	FRA	A	9	(1)	
24	Benoit DANIEL		G	2		
15	Quentin DURIEUX		D	11	(2)	1
26	Martin EKANI	FRA	D	15	(3)	
13	Fritz EMERAN	FRA	D	27		1
9	Stavros GLOUFTSIS	GRE	A	1	(2)	
3	Olivier GUILMOT		D	34		2
18	Nordin JBARI		A	26	(1)	2
	Benoit LADRIERE		A	1	(1)	
27	Alexandre LECOMTE	FRA	A	6	(2)	1
23	Dimitri LEURQUIN		D	1		
2	Trésor LUNTALA	FRA	D	11	(12)	
19	Jaroslav MAZURKIEWICZ	POL	D	22	(5)	1
5	Laurent MONTOYA	FRA	D	8	(5)	
	Blaise N'GOMA		A	1		
12	Egutu OLISEH	NGA	M	28	(3)	1
21	Jules César OULAI	CIV	M	9	(3)	1
16	Julien PINELLI		A	15	(2)	1
25	Alexandre POTIER		A		(7)	2
10	ROGÉRIO de Oliveira	BRA	D	6	(6)	
9	Sergio SÁNCHEZ	ARG	A	4	(8)	3
10	Youssef SOFIANE	FRA	A	6	(2)	
11	Geraldo SPRIO		A	1	(1)	
23	Aco STOJKOV	MAC	A	9	(5)	7
6	Alexandre TEKLAK		D	32		
4	TIAGO	BRA	D	1	(7)	
7	Yannick VERVALLE		D	6	(2)	

R EXCELSIOR MOUSCRON
Coach - Geert Brouckaert; (21/11/05) Gil Vandenbrouck; (9/1/06) Paul Put; (10/2/06) Gil Vandenbrouck

2005

Belgium

Date	Opponent	H/A	Score	Scorers
5/8	Club Brugge KV	a	0-2	
13/8	KSC Lokeren	h	0-2	
20/8	RSC Charleroi	a	0-1	
27/8	KVC Westerlo	h	1-0	Oussalah
10/9	RSC Anderlecht	a	1-3	Tailson
16/9	KAA Gent	h	1-2	Tailson
21/9	SV Zulte-Waregem	a	1-4	Siljak
24/9	RAA La Louvière	h	2-1	Siljak, Filekovic
2/10	KSV Cercle Brugge	a	0-1	
15/10	Germinal Beerschot	h	4-1	Oussalah, og (Monteyne), Custovic (p), Tailson
22/10	KRC Genk	a	0-1	
30/10	R Standard Liège	h	2-1	Noukeu, Fellahi
5/11	FC Brussels	h	1-1	Fellahi
20/11	KSV Roeselare	a	0-5	
3/12	K St.-Truidense VV	a	6-3	Tailson, Custovic 3, Noukeu, Oussalah
10/12	KSK Beveren	h	1-3	Oussalah
14/12	K Lierse SK	h	5-0	Hatchi, Noukeu, Custovic 2, Dimbala
17/12	Club Brugge KV	h	0-1	
2006				
21/1	KSC Lokeren	a	1-1	Sanchez d'Avolio
28/1	RSC Charleroi	h	0-1	
4/2	KVC Westerlo	a	5-0	Filekovic, Siljak 2 (1p), Custovic 2
11/2	RSC Anderlecht	h	0-1	
18/2	KAA Gent	a	0-0	
25/2	SV Zulte-Waregem	h	0-1	
4/3	RAA La Louvière	a	0-0	
11/3	KSV Cercle Brugge	h	6-0	og (Masureel), Dugardein, Zewlakow 3, Fellahi
18/3	Germinal Beerschot	a	0-1	
26/3	KRC Genk	h	1-0	Dorothée
1/4	R Standard Liège	a	1-2	Santos
8/4	FC Brussels	h	1-0	og (Bruno)
15/4	KSV Roeselare	h	0-1	
22/4	K Lierse SK	a	0-2	
30/4	K St.-Truidense VV	h	3-0	Tailson, Fellahi, Noukeu
5/5	KSK Beveren	a	0-1	

No	Name	Nat	Pos	Aps	(s)	Gls
22	Yassine BENAJIBA		M	3	(4)	
12	Olivier BESENGEZ		D	17	(1)	
3	Jean-Philippe CHARLET		D	17	(8)	
7	Adnan CUSTOVIC	BOS	A	27		8
28	Benjamin DELACOURT	FRA	D		(1)	
26	Patrice DIMBALA		A	20	(6)	1
25	Jean-Félix DOROTHEE	FRA	D	16	(9)	1
4	Steve DUGARDEIN		M	30		1
13	Karim FELLAHI	FRA	M	12	(5)	4
27	Suad FILEKOVIC	SLO	M	16	(4)	2
6	Sébastien GRIMALDI	FRA	D	5		
20	David GRONDIN	FRA	M	23	(5)	
	Julien HAGHEDOOREN		M		(1)	
24	Kevin HATCHI	FRA	D	27	(1)	1
1	Patrice LUZI	FRA	G	26		
9	Ricardo MAGRO		A	1	(1)	
21	Christophe MARTIN		G	8	(1)	
17	Patrice NOUKEU	CMR	M	30	(1)	4
14	Mustapha OUSSALAH		M	17		4
16	Francisco SANCHEZ D'AVOLIO		M	21	(4)	1
29	Giba Dos SANTOS Tavares	BRA	M	1	(6)	1
19	Ermin SILJAK	BOS	A	5	(10)	4
8	Stjepan SKOCIBUSIC	CRO	D		(7)	
9	José TAILSON	BRA	A	13	(7)	5
18	Geoffrey TOYES	FRA	D	22	(3)	

15	Daan VAN GYSEGHEM		M	5	(1)	
10	Marcin ZEWLAKOW	POL	A	12		3

KSV ROESELARE
Coach - Dennis Van Wijk

Date	Opponent	H/A	Score	Scorers
2005				
6/8	K St.-Truidense VV	a	0-1	
14/8	KSK Beveren	h	1-0	Eloi
20/8	Club Brugge KV	a	0-1	
28/8	KSC Lokeren	h	4-0	Peeters 3, Coquelet
10/9	RSC Charleroi	a	1-1	De Vleeschauwer
18/9	KVC Westerlo	h	0-2	
21/9	RSC Anderlecht	a	1-5	De Vleeschauwer
25/9	KAA Gent	h	1-1	Vandamme
1/10	SV Zulte-Waregem	a	1-2	Peeters
15/10	RAA La Louvière	h	4-1	De Coninck, De Vleeschauwer, og (Durieux), Eloi
22/10	KSV Cercle Brugge	a	2-2	Annys, Dufoor
30/10	Germinal Beerschot	h	5-1	Vaesen, Dufoor, Eloi 2, Vandamme
5/11	KRC Genk	a	1-4	Soumare
20/11	R Excelsior Mouscron	h	5-0	Eloi 4, Coquelet
3/12	R Standard Liège	a	0-0	
11/12	K Lierse SK	h	2-0	Peeters, Dufoor
14/12	FC Brussels	a	0-1	
17/12	K St.-Truidense VV	h	1-1	Peeters
2006				
21/1	KSK Beveren	a	1-1	Eloi
29/1	Club Brugge KV	h	1-1	Eloi
4/2	KSC Lokeren	a	2-2	Lahousse, Vandamme
18/2	KVC Westerlo	a	2-3	Eloi, Smits
21/2	RSC Charleroi	h	2-0	Smits, Vaesen
24/2	RSC Anderlecht	h	0-2	
4/3	KAA Gent	a	2-1	Smits, Malki
11/3	SV Zulte-Waregem	h	0-3	
18/3	RAA La Louvière	a	0-0	
26/3	KSV Cercle Brugge	h	1-0	Vandamme
1/4	Germinal Beerschot	a	2-2	Dufoor, Vaesen
9/4	KRC Genk	h	1-2	Lahousse
15/4	R Excelsior Mouscron	a	1-0	Vaesen
22/4	FC Brussels	h	0-1	
30/4	R Standard Liège	h	0-0	
5/5	K Lierse SK	a	0-1	

No	Name	Nat	Pos	Aps	(s)	Gls
14	Maxime ANNYS		M	19	(9)	1
8	Steve BARBE		M	8	(2)	
12	Wouter BIEBOUW		G	3	(1)	
13	Christian BOUCKENOOGHE	NZL	A		(6)	
18	Emmanuel COQUELET		A	8	(4)	2
20	Björn DE CONINCK		D	13		1
2	Cyril DETREMMERIE		D	2	(6)	
6	Koen DE VLEESCHAUWER		M	27	(2)	3
29	Sebastien DUFOOR		A	18	(6)	4
17	Chemcedine EL ARAICHI		D	23	(3)	
73	Wagneau ELOI	HAI	A	25		11
21	Eric JOLY	FRA	M	9	(3)	
15	James LAHOUSSE		D	34		2
19	Christophe LAUWERS		A	3	(10)	
22	Sanharib MALKI		F	5	(8)	1
3	Martijn MONTEYNE		D	27	(1)	
7	Rocky PEETERS		A	15	(1)	6
1	Jurgen SIERENS		G	31		
18	Bjorn SMITS		D	16		3
9	Abdoulaye SOUMARE	FRA	M	6	(7)	1
4	Daan VAESEN		D	33		4

Belgium

16	Jamaïque VANDAMME		A	17	(13)	4
10	Frederik VANDERBIEST		M	32		
	Sergio VAN KANTEN		M		(1)	
11	Bas VERVAEKE		A		(8)	
7	Bart VLAEMINCK		M		(1)	

K ST.-TRUIDENSE VV
Coach – Herman Vermeulen; (9/2/06) Thomas Caers

2005
6/8	KSV Roeselare	h	1-0	Stolica
14/8	K Lierse SK	a	0-1	
21/8	R Standard Liège	a	0-2	
26/8	KSK Beveren	h	1-0	Simaeys
10/9	Club Brugge KV	a	1-2	Simaeys
17/9	KSC Lokeren	h	1-2	Simaeys
20/9	RSC Charleroi	a	1-0	Stolica
24/9	KVC Westerlo	h	0-1	
1/10	RSC Anderlecht	a	0-3	
16/10	KAA Gent	h	1-1	Mbonabucya
22/10	SV Zulte-Waregem	a	5-1	Stolica 3, Hajnal, Mbonabucya
29/10	RAA La Louvière	h	1-3	Mbonabucya
5/11	KSV Cercle Brugge	a	1-2	Mbonabucya
19/11	Germinal Beerschot	h	1-2	Stolica
27/11	KRC Genk	a	0-2	
3/12	R Excelsior Mouscron	h	3-6	og (Van Gyseghem), Stolica, Hajnal
10/12	FC Brussels	a	0-0	
17/12	KSV Roeselare	a	1-1	Simaeys

2006
21/1	K Lierse SK	h	1-1	Mbonabucya
28/1	R Standard Liège	h	0-0	
4/2	KSK Beveren	a	1-1	De Condé
11/2	Club Brugge KV	h	2-2	Buvens, Peeters
18/2	KSC Lokeren	a	2-1	Stolica (p), Buvens
25/2	RSC Charleroi	h	1-1	Hajnal (p)
4/3	KVC Westerlo	a	1-2	Peeters
10/3	RSC Anderlecht	h	3-0	Mbonabucya 2, Hajnal
19/3	KAA Gent	a	0-1	
25/3	SV Zulte-Waregem	h	2-0	Mbonabucya, Peeters
1/4	RAA La Louvière	a	2-0	Hajnal, Stolica
8/4	KSV Cercle Brugge	h	1-1	Nijs
15/4	Germinal Beerschot	a	0-4	
22/4	KRC Genk	h	2-2	Debroux, Simaeys
30/4	R Excelsior Mouscron	a	0-3	
5/5	FC Brussels	h	0-1	

No	Name	Nat	Pos	Aps	(s)	Gls
23	Christopher BARATTO		D	2	(2)	
1	Dusan BELIC	SCG	G	12		
20	Frank BOECKX		G	7	(1)	
	Jonas BOGAERTS		M	1	(1)	
11	Kris BUVENS		M	21	(7)	2
2	Sander DEBROUX		D	29	(1)	1
14	Dimitri DE CONDÉ		M	14	(3)	1
1	Bart DEELKENS		G	15		
4	Kristof DELORGE		M		(1)	
17	Peter DELORGE		M	30		
30	Tamás HAJNAL	HUN	M	10	(11)	5
3	Nicky HAYEN		D	29		
26	Kristof LARDENOIT		D	5	(1)	
18	Désiré MBONABUCYA	RWA	A	19	(8)	8
16	Landry MULEMO		D	22	(2)	
9	Jari NIEMI	FIN	A	10	(17)	
12	Marco NIJS		A	10	(7)	1
23	Rocky PEETERS		A	14		3
10	Nils PRUD'HOMME		M		(7)	

8	Cyril RAMOND	FRA	D	17		
6	Jurgen RUTTEN		A		(4)	
7	Brendan SANTALAB	AUS	A	2	(7)	
16	Jeroen SIMAEYS		M	29	(2)	5
27	Asanda SISHUBA	RSA	M	3	(2)	
21	Ilija STOLICA	CRO	A	27	(5)	9
33	Ibrahim TANKARY	NGA	A	1	(2)	
24	David VAN HOYWEGHEN		D	22		
15	Egon WISNIOWSKI		D	23	(2)	

R STANDARD LIEGE
Coach – Dominique D'Onofrio

2005
6/8	K Lierse SK	h	3-1	Tchité, Geraerts, Sérgio Conceição
14/8	SV Zulte-Waregem	a	2-1	Tchité, Garbini
21/8	K St.-Truidense VV	h	2-0	Sérgio Conceição, Bangoura
27/8	RAA La Louvière	a	3-2	Tchité 3
11/9	KSK Beveren	h	1-3	Tchité
17/9	KSV Cercle Brugge	a	3-0	Tchité, Sérgio Conceição, Walasiak
21/9	Club Brugge KV	h	2-0	Onyewu, Léonard
25/9	Germinal Beerschot	a	2-2	Sérgio Conceição, og (Cvitanovic)
1/10	KSC Lokeren	h	2-1	Tchité 2
16/10	KRC Genk	a	1-0	Tchité
21/10	RSC Charleroi	h	1-0	Sérgio Conceição
30/10	R Excelsior Mouscron	a	1-2	Tchité
6/11	KVC Westerlo	h	1-0	Moreira
19/11	FC Brussels	a	1-3	Sérgio Conceição
3/12	KSV Roeselare	h	0-0	
11/12	KAA Gent	a	1-2	Rapaic
14/12	RSC Anderlecht	h	2-0	Moreira, og (Juhász)
18/12	K Lierse SK	a	2-0	Geraerts, Tchité

2006
21/1	SV Zulte-Waregem	h	1-2	Niculae
28/1	K St.-Truidense VV	a	0-0	
11/2	KSK Beveren	h	2-0	Rapaic, Niculae
18/2	KSV Cercle Brugge	h	7-1	Rapaic 3 (1p), De Camargo, Tchité 2, Kovalenko
22/2	RAA La Louvière	h	1-1	Niculae
26/2	Club Brugge KV	a	1-1	Onyewu
5/3	Germinal Beerschot	h	3-1	Sérgio Conceição, Tchité, Vulin
12/3	KSC Lokeren	a	0-0	
17/3	KRC Genk	h	1-0	Niculae
24/3	RSC Charleroi	a	0-0	
1/4	R Excelsior Mouscron	h	2-1	Négouai, Tchité
8/4	KVC Westerlo	a	2-0	Négouai, Rapaic
16/4	FC Brussels	h	1-0	Rapaic
21/4	RSC Anderlecht	a	0-2	
30/4	KSV Roeselare	a	0-0	
5/5	KAA Gent	h	0-2	

No	Name	Nat	Pos	Aps	(s)	Gls
6	Matthieu ASSOU-EKOTTO	FRA	M	10	(1)	
17	Sambegou BANGOURA	GUI	A	2	(1)	1
28	Mathieu BEDA	FRA	D	13	(1)	
21	Igor DE CAMARGO	BRA	A	4		1
2	Eric DEFLANDRE		D	29		
30	Siramana DEMBELE	FRA	D	15		
3	Ivica DRAGUTINOVIC	SCG	D	3		
20	Michel GARBINI Pereira	BRA	M	9	(5)	1
22	Karel GERAERTS		M	33		2
3	JORGE COSTA	POR	D	13		
29	Serhiy KOVALENKO	UKR	A	5	(17)	1
14	Philippe LEONARD		D	29	(1)	1

Belgium

10	Da Silva MOREIRA Almani	POR	M	20	(6)	2
4	Aleksandar MUTAVDZIC	SCG	M	1	(2)	
13	Christian NEGOUAI		M	12	(11)	2
9	Marius NICULAE	ROM	A	11	(15)	4
5	Oguchi ONYEWU	USA	D	29		2
11	Milan RAPAIC	CRO	M	17	(1)	7
27	Cédric ROUSSEL		A	2	(3)	
1	Vedran RUNJE	CRO	G	34		
19	Mohammed SARR	SEN	D	11	(1)	
7	SÉRGIO Paulo CONCEIÇÃO	POR	M	25		7
25	Mohammed TCHITE	CON	A	32	(1)	16
4	Lovre VULIN	CRO	D	1		1
15	Jonathan WALASIAK		M	11	(13)	1
8	WAMBERTO Souza Campos	BRA	A	3	(7)	

3	Wim MENNES		M	22	(8)	2
14	Michael MODUBI	RSA	L	2	(1)	
16	Pule Jeffrey NTUKA	RSA	D	23	(5)	3
23	John OWOERI	NGA	A	7	(3)	
25	Jonathan RUTTENS		G		(1)	
10	Emanuel SARKI	NGA	M	3	(4)	
13	Michal SCASNY	CZE	D	9	(8)	
9	Peter UTAKA	NGA	A	25	(5)	5
12	Jochen VAN ARWEGEN		M	4	(13)	
	Bram VAN GEEL		A	1	(1)	
15	Tom VAN IMSCHOOT		M	33		1
11	Nico VANKERCKHOVEN		D	29		1
4	Mario VERHEYEN		D	26		
	Toon VERVOORT		A		(1)	
2	Marc WAGEMAKERS		D	24		

KVC WESTERLO
Coach – Herman Helleputte

2005

Date	Opponent	h/a	Score	Scorers
6/8	KSV Cercle Brugge	h	2-0	Coelho, Janssens
13/8	Germinal Beerschot	a	1-0	De Wilde
20/8	KRC Genk	h	1-1	Coelho
27/8	R Excelsior Mouscron	a	0-1	
10/9	FC Brussels	h	3-0	Coelho 2, Delen
18/9	KSV Roeselare	a	2-0	Janssens, Ntuka
21/9	K Lierse SK	h	0-0	
24/9	K St.-Truidense VV	a	1-0	Delen
1/10	KSK Beveren	h	4-1	Utaka 2, Janssens, Coelho
15/10	Club Brugge KV	a	1-2	Delen
22/10	KSC Lokeren	h	1-1	Coelho (p)
29/10	RSC Charleroi	a	1-2	Utaka
6/11	R Standard Liège	a	0-1	
20/11	RSC Anderlecht	h	2-1	Utaka, Coelho (p)
3/12	SV Zulte-Waregem	h	2-2	Coelho 2
10/12	RAA La Louvière	a	3-0	Ntuka, Coelho, De Wilde
14/12	KAA Gent	a	1-0	De Wilde
17/12	KSV Cercle Brugge	a	2-2	De Wilde, Janssens

2006

Date	Opponent	h/a	Score	Scorers
21/1	Germinal Beerschot	h	1-3	Janssens (p)
28/1	KRC Genk	a	0-2	
4/2	R Excelsior Mouscron	h	0-5	
18/2	KSV Roeselare	h	3-2	Van Kerckhoven, Janssens, Evens
22/2	FC Brussels	a	0-1	
25/2	K Lierse SK	a	1-2	Van Imschoot
4/3	K St.-Truidense VV	h	2-1	Kolar, Delen
11/3	KSK Beveren	a	1-4	Utaka
18/3	Club Brugge KV	h	0-0	
25/3	KSC Lokeren	a	2-3	Janssens, Evens
2/4	RSC Charleroi	h	1-1	Ntuka
8/4	R Standard Liège	h	0-2	
14/4	RSC Anderlecht	a	0-5	
23/4	KAA Gent	h	0-1	
30/4	SV Zulte-Waregem	a	2-1	Delen, Mennes
5/5	RAA La Louvière	a	2-1	Janssens, Mennes

No	Name	Nat	Pos	Aps	(s)	Gls
33	Samir BELOUFA	FRA	D	5	(3)	
19	Mosia BOY-BOY	RSA	M		(9)	
10	Jackson COELHO	BRA	A	18		10
	Gianno CONALLE		M		(1)	
18	Jef DELEN		M	20	(2)	5
21	Björn DE WILDE		A	2	(15)	4
7	Bossam ELEJIKO	NGA	D	12	(5)	
5	Bernt EVENS		D	28		2
1	Ronny GASPERCIC		G	34		
6	Christiaan JANSSENS		M	34		8
8	Martin KOLAR	CZE	M	13		1

SV ZULTE-WAREGEM
Coach - Francky Dury

2005

Date	Opponent	h/a	Score	Scorers
6/8	KAA Gent	a	3-1	Sergeant, Leleu, Van Nieuwenhuyze
14/8	R Standard Liège	h	1-2	Meert
20/8	RAA La Louvière	h	0-0	
27/8	KSV Cercle Brugge	a	4-2	Dupré, D'Haemers, Meert, Salou
10/9	Germinal Beerschot	h	2-1	Matthijs, Salou
18/9	KRC Genk	a	1-3	Sergeant
21/9	R Excelsior Mouscron	h	4-1	Dupré (p), Meert, Sergeant, Matthijs
24/9	FC Brussels	a	1-1	De Brul
1/10	KSV Roeselare	h	2-1	Dupré, Matthijs
15/10	K Lierse SK	a	2-0	Sergeant, Salou
22/10	K St.-Truidense VV	h	1-5	Salou
29/10	KSK Beveren	a	1-2	Van Nieuwenhuyze
6/11	Club Brugge KV	h	2-1	Salou, Dupré
19/11	KSC Lokeren	a	3-2	Meert 2, Salou
3/12	KVC Westerlo	a	2-2	Meert, Leleu
10/12	RSC Anderlecht	h	1-2	Sergeant
14/12	RSC Charleroi	h	3-0	Sergeant, D'Haemers 2
18/12	KAA Gent	h	1-2	Matthijs

2006

Date	Opponent	h/a	Score	Scorers
21/1	R Standard Liège	a	2-1	D'Haemers, Sergeant
28/1	RAA La Louvière	a	2-2	Sergeant, Meert
4/2	KSV Cercle Brugge	h	3-1	Sergeant, Salou 2
11/2	Germinal Beerschot	a	0-2	
18/2	KRC Genk	h	1-0	Sergeant
25/2	R Excelsior Mouscron	a	1-0	Matthijs
4/3	FC Brussels	h	0-0	
11/3	KSV Roeselare	a	3-0	Breleur, Meert, Matthijs
17/3	K Lierse SK	h	0-1	
25/3	K St.-Truidense VV	a	0-2	
1/4	KSK Beveren	h	2-2	Salou, Thiebaut
7/4	Club Brugge KV	a	1-2	Matthijs
16/4	KSC Lokeren	h	1-1	Dindeleux
22/4	RSC Charleroi	a	0-2	
30/4	KVC Westerlo	h	1-2	Matthijs
5/5	RSC Anderlecht	a	0-3	

No	Name	Nat	Pos	Aps	(s)	Gls
14	Silvio BRELEUR	FRA	A	2	(2)	1
12	Tjorven DE BRUL		D	29	(1)	1
15	Nathan D'HAEMERS		M	31		4
11	Frederik D'HOLLANDER		A	1	(6)	
24	Frédéric DINDELEUX	FRA	D	13	(4)	1
3	Frédéric DUPRE		D	29	(1)	4
4	Stefan LELEU		D	28		2
7	Tim MATTHIJS		A	16	(14)	8

Belgium

10	Stijn MEERT		M	29	(2)	8
1	Pieter MERLIER		G	25		
2	Stijn MINNE		D	29		
20	Ibrahim SALOU	GHA	A	29		9
25	Bjorn SENGIER		G	9		
8	Tony SERGEANT		M	31	(1)	10
22	Ibrahim TANKARY	NGA	A		(3)	
23	Gunther THIEBAUT		A	2	(12)	1
16	Wouter VANDENDRIESSCHE		M	4	(11)	
11	Jonas VANDERMARLIERE		M	1	(5)	
6	Ludwin VAN NIEUWENHUYZE		M	30		2
21	Sven VAN RYCKEGHEM		G		(1)	
17	Lander VAN STEENBRUGGHE		M	3	(5)	
5	Guy VELDEMAN		D	5	(2)	
19	Jo VERMAST		A		(1)	
9	Matthieu VERSCHUERE	FRA	M	27	(1)	
18	Michaël WIGGERS		M	1	(5)	

DOMESTIC CUP 2005/06

1/16 FINALS
(10/11/05)
RSC Anderlecht 0, KFC Verbroedering Geel 0 *(aet; 5-6 on pens)*
(11/11/05)
FCV Dender 0, K St.-Truidense VV 1
KFC Zwarte Leeuw 0, KAA Gent 3
R Standard Liège 2, ROC Charleroi-Marchienne 0
(12/11/05)
RAEC Mons 1, RAA La Louvière 0
KV Red Star Waasland 0, KSK Beveren 1
RFC Tournai 1, KRC Genk 2
R Excelsior Mouscron 2, Tornhout 1992 KM 1
KVC Westerlo 4, KRC Mechelen 0
KSC Lokeren OV 2, Sprimont Sporting 1
VG Oostende 0, SC Charleroi 1
(13/11/05)
SK Lierse 1, SV Roeselare 1 *(aet; 3-2 on pens)*
FC Brussels 0, Oud-Heverlee Leuven 1
(30/11/05)
WS Woluwe FC 2, KSV Cercle Brugge 3
SV Zulte-Waregem 2, Club Brugge KV 1
(06/12/05)
RFC Union Kelmis 0, Germinal Beerschot Antwerpen 2

1/8 FINALS
(21/12/05)
K St.-Truidense VV 2, KRC Genk 1
KSK Beveren 5, KSC Lokeren OV 1
KAA Gent 1, KSV Cercle Brugge 1 *(aet; 4-2 on pens)*
R Excelsior Mouscron 2, RAEC Mons 1 *(aet)*
K Lierse SK 1, KVC Westerlo 2
RSC Charleroi 2, Oud-Heverlee Leuven 0
KFC Verbroedering Geel 0, SV Zulte-Waregem 1
R Standard Liège 1, Germinal Beerschot Antwerpen 0

QUARTER-FINALS
(25/1/06 & 8/2/06)
K St.-Truidense VV 0, RSC Charleroi 0
RSC Charleroi 2 *(Sterchele 23, Orlando 84)*, K St.-Truidense VV 0
(RSC Charleroi 2-0)

R Excelsior Mouscron 0, KSK Beveren 0
KSK Beveren 0, R Excelsior Mouscron 2 *(Custovic 15, Noukeu 41)*
(R Excelsior Mouscron 2-0)

SV Zulte-Waregem 3 *(Salou 17, 63, 87)*, KVC Westerlo 0
KVC Westerlo 3 *(Ntuka 30, Janssens 49, 63)*, SV Zulte-Waregem 1 *(Salou 95) (aet)*
(SV Zulte-Waregem 4-3)

KAA Gent 2 *(Grégoire 56, De Beule 90)*, R Standard Liège 1 *(Kovalenko 44)*
R Standard Liège 4 *(Tchité 35, 56, 59, Rapaic 80)*, KAA Gent 2 *(Foley 21, Sarr 50og)*
(R Standard Liège 5-4)

SEMI-FINALS
(21/3/06 & 12/4/06)
R Standard Liège 1 *(Léonard 63)*, SV Zulte-Waregem 2 *(D'Haemers 7, Sergeant 80)*
SV Zulte-Waregem 0, R Standard Liège 1 *(Onyewu 73)*
(2-2; SV Zulte-Waregem on away goals)

(22/03/06 & 11/4/06)
RSC Charleroi 0, R Excelsior Mouscron 1 *(Zewlakow 60)*
R Excelsior Mouscron 1 *(Dimbala 60)*, RSC Charleroi 1 *(Akpala 81)*
(R Excelsior Mouscron 2-1)

FINAL
(13/5/06)
Koning Boudewijnstadion, Brussels
SV ZULTE-WAREGEM 2 *(Leleu 11, Matthijs 90)*
R EXCELSIOR MOUSCRON 1 *(Custovic 61)*
Referee - *Allaerts*
SV ZULTE-WAREGEM - Merlier, Dupré, Leleu, De Brul, Minne, Matthijs, Van Nieuwenhuyze, Verschuere (Vandendriessche 69), Meert, Sergeant, Salou.
R EXCELSIOR MOUSCRON - Luzi, Grondin, Toyes, Besengez (Hatchi 59), Charlet (Dimbala 59), Sánchez, Dugardein, Noukeu, Dorothée, Custovic, Zewlakow.

SECOND LEVEL FINAL TABLE 2005/06

		Pld	W	D	L	F	A	Pts
1	RAEC Mons (*3)	32	18	9	5	58	29	63
2	KVSK United (*1)	32	17	10	5	59	35	61
3	KFC Verbroedering Geel	32	16	6	10	43	29	54
4	KV Red Star Waasland	32	14	11	7	55	45	53
5	KV Kortrijk	32	14	10	8	50	40	52
6	Oud-Heverlee Leuven	32	14	8	10	48	36	50
7	R Antwerp FC	32	14	7	11	53	50	49
8	KAS Eupen	32	12	8	12	46	47	44
9	KFC VW Hamme (*2)	32	12	7	13	48	47	43
10	KV Oostende	32	10	11	11	44	46	41
11	KSK Ronse	32	11	6	15	47	60	39
12	AFC Tubize	32	11	5	16	42	48	38
13	KV Mechelen	32	9	9	14	38	44	36
14	R Excelsior Virton	32	8	12	12	27	39	36
15	R Union Saint-Gilloise	32	8	9	15	37	53	33
16	KFC Dessel Sport	32	8	7	17	33	48	31
17	KMSK Deinze	32	6	5	21	33	65	23

N.B. (*) = period winners; K Beringen-Heusden-Zolder withdrew after 23 matches.

PROMOTION/RELEGATION PLAY-OFF FINAL TABLE

		Pld	W	D	L	F	A	Pts
1	K Lierse SK	6	4	0	2	13	7	12
2	KVSK United	6	3	1	2	11	9	10
3	KFC VW Hamme	6	3	0	3	8	9	9
4	KFC Verbroedering Geel	6	1	1	4	8	15	4

Bosnia-Herzegovina

Two more years for Sliskovic

Bosnia-Herzegovina did not qualify for the 2006 World Cup but they came much closer to doing so than most people expected, and that achievement earned long-serving coach Blaz Sliskovic another two-year extension to his contract.

As in the Euro 2004 qualifiers, Bosnia-Herzegovina were still in contention going into their final group fixture. A run of three successive victories, against Belgium, Lithuania and San Marino, sent Sliskovic's men into their final group game, away to Serbia & Montenegro, requiring a victory to eliminate their hosts and accede into the play-offs. It wasn't to be, an early Mateja Kezman goal puncturing that particular dream, but with a final balance of four wins, four draws and two defeats, the country had much to be proud of.

Despite a couple of discouraging performances in Asia during the spring, there should be no shortage of confidence for Sliskovic and his players as they bid for a place at the Euro 2008 finals, having been drawn in a group that contains title holders Greece but not one participant from the World Cup in Germany. Veteran skipper Sergej Barbarez initially announced his retirement from international football after the defeat in Belgrade but his excellent club form for Hamburg persuaded him to carry on. Should the 35-year-old maintain that high standard, he will continue be an invaluable asset to the team.

Sliskovic has been permitted by the Bosnia and Herzegovina Fotball Federation to operate concurrently as a club coach while also serving the national team. Previously at Hajduk Split, he was brought in by his hometown club Zrinjski Mostar as an emergency measure on the eve of the 2005/06 season following a catastrophic 4-0 extra-time defeat at home to F91 Dudelange of Luxembourg in the first qualifying round of the UEFA Champions League. That humiliation – after a 1-0 first-leg win – inevitably cost the previous season's championship-winning coach, Franjo Dzidic, his job.

Euro calamity

With the 2004/05 Cup winners Sarajevo and league runners-up Zeljeznicar having both been refused entry into European competition because of their failure to obtain a UEFA licence, Zrinjski were the country's only bona fide Euro representatives. Zepce, who had been coerced into taking Zeljeznicar's place, made a complete hash of their European debut, fielding an ineligible player against Baskimi Kumanovo and forfeiting the first leg 3-0 en route to a 4-1 aggregate defeat. In contrast Siroki Brijeg, the Cup runners-up, made excellent progress through both UEFA Cup qualifying rounds before meeting their match in Swiss champions FC Basel.

That European mini-adventure was to have a positive knock-on effect in domestic competition as Siroki Brijeg sought to regain the domestic championship they had won in 2003/04. In fact,

NATIONAL TEAM RESULTS 2005/06

17/8/05	Estonia	A	Tallinn	0-1	
3/9/05	Belgium (WCQ)	H	Zenica	1-0	Barbarez (62)
7/9/05	Lithuania (WCQ)	A	Vilnius	1-0	Barbarez (33)
8/10/05	San Marino (WCQ)	H	Zenica	3-0	Bolic (48, 75, 85)
12/10/05	Serbia & Montenegro (WCQ)	A	Belgrade	0-1	
28/2/06	Japan	N	Dortmund	2-2	Misimovic (56p), Spahic (70)
26/5/06	South Korea	A	Seoul	0-2	
31/5/06	Iran	A	Teheran	2-5	Misimovic (5), Barbarez (17)

Bosnia-Herzegovina

NATIONAL TEAM APPEARANCES 2005/06
Coach – Blaz SLISKOVIC

Player	DOB	Club	Est	BEL	LIT	SMR	SCG	Jpn	Kor	Irn	Caps	Goals
Kenan HASAGIC	1/2/80	Gaziantepspor (TUR)	G82	G	G		G	G			17	-
Dzemo BERBEROVIC	5/11/81	Sarajevo /Litex Lovech (BUL)	D63	D	D	D	D	D			11	-
Emir SPAHIC	18/8/80	Torpedo Moskva (RUS) /Lokomotiv Moskva (RUS)	D	D			D	D	D89		17	1
Velimir VIDIC	12/10/79	Zrinjski Mostar	D46					s87	D	D	8	-
Vedin MUSIC	11/3/73	Modena (ITA) /Torino (ITA)	D		D	D64	D	D66	D71		35	-
Zlatan BAJRAMOVIC	12/8/79	FC Schalke 04 (GER)	M	M	M		M	M87	M68	M	25	2
Sergej JAKIROVIC	23/12/76	Zagreb (CRO) /CSKA Sofia (BUL)	M		s88	s64		M	s75		5	-
Sergej BARBAREZ	17/9/71	Hamburger SV (GER)	M	M	M	M78	M	M76	M87	M46	46	15
Vladan GRUJIC	17/5/81	Alania Vladikavkaz (RUS) /Litex Lovech (BUL)	M	M		M81			D75		19	-
Elvir BOLIC	10/10/71	Malatyaspor (TUR) /Istanbulspor (TUR)	A	A72	A87	A	A71				50	24
Zvjezdan MISIMOVIC	5/6/82	VfL Bochum (GER)	A72	s72	s87	s78	s71	A68	A	A	18	5
Ninoslav MILENKOVIC	31/12/77	K Lierse SK (BEL) /Germinal Beerschot (BEL)	s46	D77	D		D	s89	s58	s60	14	-
Almir GREDIC	27/4/76	Zeljeznicar Sarajevo	s63								4	-
Zajko ZEBA	22/5/83	Maribor (SLO)	s72								1	-
Goran BRASNIC	26/9/73	Zepce	s82								6	-
Sasa PAPAC	7/2/80	FK Austria Wien (AUT)		D	D		D	D	D	D	29	-
Mladen BARTOLOVIC	10/4/77	Zagreb (CRO)		A88	s59	A	s46	A	A76	A59	9	-
Mirko HRGOVIC	5/2/79	VfL Wolfsburg (GER) /Hajduk Split (CRO)		s77		s70		s71	s76	M60	16	-
Branimir BAJIC	19/10/79	Partizan Beograd (SCG) /Al Wahda (UAE)			D	D		D76	D37		12	-
Ivica GRLIC	6/8/75	MSV Duisburg (GER)			M	M	M46	M58	s37		13	1
Mirsad BESLIJA	6/7/79	KRC Genk (BEL) /Heart of Midlothian (SCO)			M59		s66	M76			36	3
Almir TOLJA	25/10/74	Saba Battery Teheran (IRN)				G					14	-
Hasan SALIHAMIDZIC	1/1/77	FC Bayern München (GER)				M70	M				41	6
Albin PELAK	9/4/81	Sarajevo				s81					3	-
Senijad IBRICIC	26/9/86	Zagreb (CRO)						s68	s68	s63	4	-
Admir VLADAVIC	29/6/82	Zeljeznicar Sarajevo						s76	M68	s59	3	-
Admir RASCIC	16/9/81	Zeljeznicar Sarajevo						s76			1	-
Romeo MITROVIC	12/7/79	Zrinjski Mostar							G	G	7	-
Dalibor SILIC	23/1/79	Siroki Brijeg							M	s79	7	-
Petar JELIC	18/10/86	Modrica Maxima							s68	s46	2	-
Edin HUSIC	10/11/85	Orasje							s76		1	-
Nikola VASILJEVIC	19/12/83	Modrica Maxima							s87	D63	2	-
Nedim HALILOVIC	1/7/79	Varteks Varzadin (CRO)								M79	15	-

competing on two fronts brought the best out of Ivica Barbaric's side. They won six of their opening seven fixtures and drew the other. Their first defeat – away to Celik Zenica in early October – only arrived after their European campaign was over.

By the time the winter break arrived in late November, Siroki Brijeg had a three-point lead. The key to their consistency was the prolific goalscoring of Croatian striker Domagoj Abramovic, who scored 11 of their 19 goals. In mid-season the squad was

Bosnia-Herzegovina

reinforced by an influx of Brazilians as well as a high-profile new goalkeeper in ex-Croatian international Vladimir Vasilj. Clearly, Siroki Brijeg meant business.

Siroki Brijeg seal it

Although Abramovic's goals dried up in the spring, the team continued to add consistently to their points haul, and with the challenge fading from elsewhere, notably from early pace-setters Modrica Maxima and defending champions Zrinjski, the contest soon developed into a duel between Siroki Brijeg and Sarajevo. With a meeting between the two sides in the national stadium scheduled for the penultimate round, it was in Siroki Brijeg's interests to get the title wrapped up before then. Thanks to the two clubs' respective away form, they managed just that. While Siroki Brijeg won 2-1 at Posusje, Sarajevo were going down 2-1 at struggling Celik Zenica. Then, two weeks later, it was all over as Sarajevo lost away to another relegation candidate, Travnik, while Siroki Brijeg easily beat Slavija Sarajevo 3-0 at home.

Five days after their title triumph, Siroki Brijeg strove to complete the Double by winning the domestic Cup. They had already drawn the home leg of the final 0-0 against Orasje so, with home advantage such an overriding consideration in Bosnia-Herzegovina, their chances of going to the other side of the country and collecting a win were no greater than even. In the event, Orasje eclipsed them with three second-half goals, two of them from skipper Ivo Pejic, to celebrate their ten-year anniversary with a first major trophy. Orasje's UEFA Cup place had already been booked by Siroki Brijeg's championship triumph.

Siroki Brijeg would lose 3-0 again three days later – in the now meaningless league summit away to Sarejevo – and then throw away their unbeaten home record with a 2-0 defeat to Zepce. It was a disappointing end to the season, but Barbaric and his players could console themselves in the knowledge that 15 other teams in the division would gladly have swapped places with them. Two in particular were Travnik and Buducnost Banovici, who both dropped out of the top flight after Celik escaped with a 3-1 win over Leotar Trebinje on the final day. Their places were taken by Borac Banja Luka – who thus came straight back up after a year away – and Velez Mostar – who finally made it third time lucky after agonising near-misses in each of the previous two seasons.

EUROPEAN CUPS 2005/06

UEFA CHAMPIONS LEAGUE

ZRINJSKI MOSTAR
1st qualifying round F91 DUDELANGE (LUX)
A **1-0** *Maric B. (15)*
Mitrovic, Vidic, Dzidic, Papic, Zurzinov, Mulina, Smajic, Maric B. (Zizovic 62), Avdic (Vasilj 46), Karadza, Djuric (Semren 89).
H **0-4** *(aet)*
Mitrovic, Vidic, Dzidic, Papic, Zurzinov, Mulina, Smajic, Maric B. (Avdic 54), Zizovic (Semren 77), Karadza, Djuric (Landeka 54).

UEFA CUP

SIROKI BRIJEG
1st qualifying round TEUTA DURRËS (ALB)
A **1-3** *Abramovic (82)*
Basic, Anic (Kozul 63), Medvid, Bajkusa (Galic 65), Rezic, Landeka, Bubalo, Kovacic, Erceg (Lukacevic 75), Silic, Abramovic.
H **3-0** *Medvid (33), Erceg (43), Wagner (70)*
Basic, Anic, Medvid, Landeka, Rezic, Wagner, Silic, Lukacevic (Ivic 90), Ronielle, Erceg (Bubalo 85), Abramovic (Juricic 91).

2nd qualifying round ZETA GOLUBOVCI (SCG)
A **1-0** *Erceg (90)*
Basic, Anic, Medvid, Landeka, Rezic, Tabi, Wagner, Lukacevic (Galic 63), Ronielle (Ivankovic 92), Abramovic (Juricic 79), Erceg.
H **4-2** *Lukacevic (16), Juricic (18), Ronielle (26), Bubalo (64)*
Basic, Anic, Medvid, Landeka, Rezic, Tabi, Lukacevic (Galic 84), Juricic (Bajkusa 59), Silic, Abramovic (Bubalo 47), Ronielle.

1st round FC BASEL (SUI)
A **0-5**
Basic, Anic, Kozul, Renato, Landeka, Rezic, Silic, Abramovic (Galic 84), Lukacevic (Bubalo 69), Gomes, Erceg (Bajkusa 57).
H **0-1**
Basic, Anic, Medvid, Landeka, Renato, Silic, Tabi, Bubalo (Ivankovic 78), Lukacevic (Kovacic 56), Abramovic, Erceg.

ZEPCE
1st qualifying round BASKIMI KUMANOVO (MAC)
A **0-3** *(w/o)*
Brasnic, Doci, Kraisnik (Dragicevic 68), Mikelini, Hasanovic, Juric, Sirovica, Rako, Selimbegovic (Imamovic 46), Kurtic, Maksimovic.
H **1-1** *Mesic (80)*
Brasnic, Doci, Kraisnik, Mikelini, Kurtic, Hasanovic, Juric, Sirovica (Rako 52; Ivesic K. 75), Mesic, Imamovic, Niverge (Duspara 85).

TOP GOALSCORERS 2005/06

18	Petar JELIC (Modrica Maxima)
13	Mirza MESIC (Zepce/Posusje)
12	Damir TOSUNOVIC (Orasje)
	Domagoj ABRAMOVIC (Siroki Brijeg)
10	Rasid AVDIC (Zrinjski Mostar/Zeljeznicar Sarajevo)
9	Bojan GOLUBOVIC (Leotar Trebinje)
	Stevo NIKOLIC (Modrica Maxima)
	Milanko DJERIC (Slavija Sarajevo)
	Nenad ZECEVIC (Radnik Bijeljina/Leotar Trebinje)
	Slaven DAMJANOVIC (Orasje)

Bosnia-Herzegovina

FINAL LEAGUE TABLE 2005/06

		Pld	Home W	D	L	F	A	Away W	D	L	F	A	Total W	D	L	F	A	Pts
1	Siroki Brijeg	30	13	1	1	26	7	6	5	4	12	12	19	6	5	38	19	63
2	Sarajevo	30	13	2	0	37	6	5	4	6	20	20	18	6	6	57	26	60
3	Zrinjski Mostar	30	13	2	0	31	6	4	1	10	16	23	17	3	10	47	29	54
4	Modrica Maxima	30	14	1	0	36	7	3	1	11	17	23	17	2	11	53	30	53
5	Slavija Sarajevo	30	10	3	2	26	12	2	2	11	15	35	12	5	13	41	47	41
6	Zeljeznicar Sarajevo	30	9	2	4	26	14	2	5	8	12	19	11	7	12	38	33	40
7	Jedinstvo Bihac	30	12	0	3	31	11	1	1	13	7	30	13	1	16	38	41	40
8	Zepce	30	9	4	2	17	9	2	3	10	12	31	11	7	12	29	40	40
9	Leotar Trebinje	30	11	2	2	33	18	1	1	13	10	30	12	3	15	43	48	39
10	Posusje	30	11	2	2	28	11	1	1	13	10	35	12	3	15	38	46	39
11	Sloboda Tuzla	30	10	3	2	24	13	1	3	11	7	27	11	6	13	31	40	39
12	Orasje	30	11	1	3	37	14	1	1	13	14	37	12	2	16	51	51	38
13	Radnik Bijeljina	30	10	2	3	28	16	1	3	11	9	36	11	5	14	37	52	38
14	Celik Zenica	30	9	4	2	24	12	1	1	13	9	33	10	5	15	33	45	35
15	Travnik	30	10	2	3	27	12	0	2	13	6	29	10	4	16	33	41	34
16	Buducnost Banovici	30	9	3	3	22	13	1	0	14	7	35	10	3	17	29	48	33

LEAGUE RESULTS/ SCORERS/APPEARANCES/ GOALS 2005/06

BUDUCNOST BANOVICI
Coach – Nermin Garic; (5/4/06) Rasim Mujezinovic

2005
6/8	Zepce	h	0-2	
14/8	Radnik Bijeljina	a	0-2	
20/8	Zrinjski Mostar	h	1-0	Kavazovic
27/8	Leotar Trebinje	a	3-1	Kavazovic 2, Omerbegovic
10/9	Jedinstvo Bihac	h	1-0	Kavazovic
17/9	Orasje	a	0-1	
24/9	Zeljeznicar Sarajevo	h	2-1	Dedic, Bojic
1/10	Sloboda Tuzla	a	0-3	
15/10	Celik Zenica	h	2-1	Mehmedovic, Suljic
22/10	Modrica Maxima	a	1-4	Alibasic
29/10	Travnik	h	1-0	Suljic
5/11	Siroki Brijeg	a	0-1	
12/11	Posusje	h	1-0	Mehmedovic
19/11	Slavija Sarajevo	h	1-3	Kavazovic
26/11	Sarajevo	a	1-2	Mehmedovic

2006
25/2	Zepce	a	1-2	Kavazovic
4/3	Radnik Bijeljina	h	5-0	Cergic, Smajic 2, Mehmedovic 2
12/3	Zrinjski Mostar	a	0-2	
16/3	Leotar Trebinje	h	1-1	Cardaklija
19/3	Jedinstvo Bihac	a	0-2	
22/3	Orasje	h	3-1	Mehmedovic 2, Slisko
25/3	Zeljeznicar Sarajevo	a	1-3	Omerbegovic
1/4	Sloboda Tuzla	h	0-1	
5/4	Celik Zenica	a	0-3	
8/4	Modrica Maxima	h	1-0	Alibasic
15/4	Travnik	a	0-5	
22/4	Siroki Brijeg	h	0-0	
29/4	Posusje	a	0-1	
6/5	Slavija Sarajevo	a	0-3	
13/5	Sarajevo	h	3-3	Bojic, Mehmedovic, Zoletic

Name	Nat	Pos	Aps	(s)	Gls
Elvis ALIBASIC		M	2	(14)	2
Vedran BOJIC		M	23	(1)	2
Mirel CAMRKOVIC		D	11	(4)	
Anes CARDAKLIJA		A	14	(9)	1
Elvis CERGIC		M	25	(1)	1
Nedim COLIC		D	8	(5)	
Mehmedalija COVIC		D	8	(3)	
Dino DEDIC		D	27		1
Jasmin HIDIC		D		(2)	
Almir HUSANOVIC		M	20	(2)	
Muris HUSIC		G	28		
Eldar IKANOVIC		M	7	(6)	
Emir IKANOVIC		M	2	(10)	
Zehrudin KAVAZOVIC		M	23	(1)	6
Edin MEHMEDOVIC		A	23		8
Mirnes MULAVDIC		M		(1)	
Elvis OMERBEGOVIC		D	5	(1)	2
Munever RIZVIC		D	14		
Nermin SAHBAZOVIC		G	2	(1)	
Mensudin SERIFOVIC		D	1		
Igor SLISKO		M	18	(1)	1
Semir SLOMIC		A	1	(9)	
Kabir SMAJIC		D	15	(3)	2
Samid SULJIC		D	25		2
Darko VOJVODIC		D	6	(1)	
Muamer ZOLETIC		D	12	(1)	1
Dilaver ZRNANOVIC		D	10		

CELIK ZENICA
Coach – Esher Hadziadic; (4/8/05) Omer Kopic; (26/8/05) Nelson Moura Mourão (BRA); (10/11/05) Esher Hadziabdic; (19/3/06) Kemal Hafizovic

2005
6/8	Jedinstvo Bihac	h	3-0	Dzidic, Mahmutovic, Bajramovic A.
13/8	Orasje	a	2-3	Beganovic, Mahmutovic
20/8	Zeljeznicar Sarajevo	h	0-0	

Bosnia-Herzegovina

Date	Opponent	H/A	Score	Scorers
27/8	Sloboda Tuzla	a	0-3	
11/9	Posusje	h	2-1	Dzidic 2
17/9	Modrica Maxima	h	1-0	Sousa
24/9	Travnik	a	2-0	Ljevakovic, Dzidic
2/10	Siroki Brijeg	h	2-0	Bajramovic S., Ljevakovic
15/10	Buducnost Banovici	a	1-2	Dzidic (p)
22/10	Slavija Sarajevo	h	1-4	Ljevakovic
29/10	Sarajevo	a	1-6	Mahmutovic
5/11	Zepce	h	1-1	Dzidic (p)
13/11	Radnik Bijeljina	a	0-3	
29/11	Zrinjski Mostar	h	0-2	
26/11	Leotar Trebinje	a	0-1	
2006				
25/2	Jedinstvo Bihac	a	1-4	Mahmutovic
4/3	Orasje	h	4-1	Hrustanovic 2, Sirovica, Mahmutovic
12/3	Zeljeznicar Sarajevo	a	0-0	
16/3	Sloboda Tuzla	h	0-0	
19/3	Posusje	a	0-3	
22/3	Modrica Maxima	a	0-1	
25/3	Travnik	h	1-1	Sirovica
2/4	Siroki Brijeg	a	0-2	
5/4	Buducnost Banovici	h	3-0	Silva, Beganovic, Sirovica
9/4	Slavija Sarajevo	a	1-2	Vrsajevic
15/4	Sarajevo	h	2-1	Djalac, Vrsajevic
22/4	Zepce	a	0-1	
29/4	Radnik Bijeljina	h	1-0	Marciano (p)
6/5	Zrinjski Mostar	a	1-2	Sirovica
13/5	Leotar Trebinje	h	3-1	Tica 2, Djalac

Name	Nat	Pos	Aps	(s)	Gls
Eldin ADILOVIC		M	2	(11)	
Asmir AVDUKIC		G	11		
Admir BAJRAMOVIC		D	8	(3)	1
Sead BAJRAMOVIC	SCG	D	19		1
Elvedin BEGANOVIC		D	24		2
Senad BRKIC		A	1	(1)	
Jasmin BURIC		G	19		
Milos DJALAC		A	15		2
Ermin DZANANOVIC		D	1	(1)	
Admir DZIDIC		A	12	(1)	6
Suad GRABUS		A	6	(3)	
Serif HASIC		M	1	(4)	
Rusmir HRUSTANOVIC		M	4	(3)	2
Armin IMAMOVIC		M	14		
Admir LJEVAKOVIC		A	24	(1)	3
Izudin KAMBEROVIC		M	26	(2)	
Mahir KARIC		M		(3)	
Ajdin MAHMUTOVIC		M	14	(10)	5
MARCIANO do Nascimento	BRA	M	26		1
Kenan NEMALJAKOVIC		M	1		
Daglas NUMANOVIC		M	9	(1)	
Gavrilo PETROVIC		M	11		
Fenan SALCINOVIC		D	6	(12)	
Narcsio de SILVA	BRA	M	16	(2)	1
Damir SIROVICA		M	13		4
António de SOUSA	BRA	M	9	(7)	1
Sergej TICA		M	2	(1)	2
Samir VRBAN		D	2	(6)	
Avdija VRSAJEVIC		M	18	(2)	2
Haris ZATAGIC		M	16	(3)	

JEDINSTVO BIHAC
Coach – Besim Sabic; (20/8/05) Ahmet Kecalovic; (10/9/05) Miralem Ibrahimovic

Date	Opponent	H/A	Score	Scorers
2005				
6/8	Celik Zenica	a	0-3	
13/8	Modrica Maxima	h	1-3	Mujadzic
20/8	Travnik	a	0-2	
30/8	Siroki Brijeg	h	0-2	
10/9	Buducnost Banovici	a	0-1	
17/9	Slavija Sarajevo	h	5-0	Dedic, Mirvic 2, Hodzic, Dujmovic
24/9	Sarajevo	a	0-2	
1/10	Zepce	h	3-0	Mirvic, Mesic, Mehadzic
16/10	Radnik Bijeljina	a	0-3	
23/10	Zrinjski Mostar	h	1-3	Susnjar El.
30/10	Leotar Trebinje	a	0-2	
8/11	Posusje	a	1-1	Mirvic
12/11	Orasje	h	2-0	Lihovac, Cahtarevic
20/11	Zeljeznicar Sarajevo	a	1-2	Stambolija
26/11	Sloboda Tuzla	h	2-1	Cahtarevic 2
2006				
25/2	Celik Zenica	h	4-1	Susnjar El. 2 (1p), Mehadzic, Dujmovic
4/3	Modrica Maxima	a	2-3	Mehadzic, Selimovic
11/3	Travnik	h	1-0	Selimovic
16/3	Siroki Brijeg	a	0-1	
19/3	Buducnost Banovici	h	2-0	Dujmovic, Mirvic
22/3	Slavija Sarajevo	a	1-0	Mehadzic
25/3	Sarajevo	h	1-0	Hodzic
2/4	Zepce	a	0-1	
5/4	Radnik Bijeljina	h	2-0	Hodzic, Mesic
9/4	Zrinjski Mostar	a	0-2	
15/4	Leotar Trebinje	h	2-1	Mehadzic (p), Hodzic
22/4	Posusje	h	3-0	Susnjar El., Selimovic 2
29/4	Orasje	a	1-5	Vuklisevic
6/5	Zeljeznicar Sarajevo	h	2-0	Cahtarevic 2
13/5	Sloboda Tuzla	a	1-2	Mirvic

Name	Nat	Pos	Aps	(s)	Gls
Igor ABDIHOZIC		D	4	(3)	
Damir ARNAUTOVIC		D		(1)	
Izet ARSLANOVIC		D	12		
Vahidin CAHTAREVIC		M	20	(1)	5
Alen DEDIC		M	24	(2)	1
Miroslav DUJMOVIC		A	16	(1)	3
Adis DZAFEROVIC		D	11	(2)	
Sanid HALILOVIC		M	2	(8)	
Ekrem HODZIC		D	25	(1)	4
Elvis KAHRIMANOVIC		M	15	(6)	
Petar KUS		M	3	(3)	
Faruk LIHOVAC		D	9	(3)	1
Elvis MEHADZIC		M	24	(1)	5
Elvis MESIC		D	27		2
Admir MIRVIC		A	21	(7)	6
Damir MUJADZIC		M	7	(12)	1
Elmedin MUJNOVIC		M	1	(1)	
Denis MUJKIC		G	29		
Adin MULAOSMANOVIC		D	11		
Emir MULIC		M	12	(4)	
Stjepan RUZAN		M	6	(4)	
Damir SAHINOVIC		D		(3)	
Edin SEJDIC		D	4		
Vernes SELIMOVIC		M			4
Vernes SMAJLOVIC		M	15		
Adis STAMBOLIJA		M	5	(2)	1
Edin SUSNJAR		G	1		
Elvir SUSNJAR		M	15	(6)	4
Ivan VELIC		D	7	(2)	

Bosnia-Herzegovina

LEOTAR TREBINJE
Coach – Obren Vukicevic; (20/10/05) Vladimir Pecelj

2005
Date	Opponent	H/A	Score	Scorers
6/8	Modrica Maxima	a	1-2	Jankovic (p)
13/8	Travnik	h	1-1	Jankovic (p)
20/8	Siroki Brijeg	a	0-3	
27/8	Buducnost Banovici	h	1-3	Stupic
10/9	Slavija Sarajevo	a	0-1	
17/9	Sarajevo	h	1-1	Jankovic
25/9	Zepce	a	0-2	
1/10	Radnik Bijeljina	h	1-3	Miljanovic (p)
16/10	Zrinjski Mostar	a	0-2	
23/10	Posusje	a	2-4	Stupic 2
30/10	Jedinstvo Bihac	h	2-0	Jankovic, Boskovic
5/11	Orasje	a	0-3	
12/11	Zeljeznicar Sarajevo	h	1-0	Jankovic (p)
19/11	Sloboda Tuzla	a	0-1	
26/11	Celik Zenica	h	1-0	Drec

2006
Date	Opponent	H/A	Score	Scorers
25/2	Modrica Maxima	h	2-1	Golubovic, Ramic (p)
4/3	Travnik	a	1-3	Seslija
11/3	Siroki Brijeg	h	3-1	Zecevic, Jankovic, Mulina (p)
16/3	Buducnost Banovici	a	1-1	Golubovic
19/3	Slavija Sarajevo	h	3-2	Zecevic 2, Pecelj
22/3	Sarajevo	a	0-1	
25/3	Zepce	h	5-1	Golubovic 2, Pecelj, Corlija, Boskovic
2/4	Radnik Bijeljina	a	1-2	Jankovic
5/4	Zrinjski Mostar	h	2-1	Zecevic, Mulina (p)
8/4	Posusje	h	5-2	Mulina 3 (2p), Golubovic 2
15/4	Jedinstvo Bihac	a	1-2	Golubovic
21/4	Orasje	h	4-2	Mulina (p), Golubovic, Boskovic 2
29/4	Zeljeznicar Sarajevo	a	2-0	Zecevic 2
6/5	Sloboda Tuzla	h	1-0	Boskovic
13/5	Celik Zenica	a	1-3	Golubovic

Name	Nat	Pos	Aps	(s)	Gls
Savo ANDRIC		M	7	(2)	
Srdjan ANDRIC		A	6	(15)	
Dusan BERAK		G	9		
Novica BERAK		G		(1)	
Rade BOSKOVIC		D	18	(8)	5
Nikola BRATIC		D	2	(3)	
Gavrilo CORLIJA		M	20		1
Oleg CURIC		M	7	(7)	
Darko DREC		D	19		1
Bojan GOLUBOVIC		A	15		9
Ilija GRKAVAC		D	1		
Pajo JANKOVIC		M	23	(1)	7
Igor JOKSIMOVIC		D	5	(3)	
Aleksandar JOVANOVIC		M	6		
Slobodan KOKIC		D	7	(3)	
Rajko KOMNENIC		A	14		
Vukmir MIJANOVIC		G	14		
Goran MILICEVIC		D		(1)	
Sasa MILJANOVIC		D	8	(4)	1
Sinisa MULINA		M	12		6
Milivoje NOZICA		D	1	(2)	
Miljan PECELJ		D	8		2
Dejan PIKIC		M	6		
Zeljko RADOVIC		M	10		
Anel RAMIC		D	19	(5)	1
Bojan VUKLISEVIC		M	4	(3)	1
Damjan RATKOVIC		D	9	(2)	
Srdjan RATKOVIC		D		(1)	
Branko SESLIJA		M		(8)	1
Bosko STUPIC		A	13	(1)	3
Vladimir SUDAR		G	7		
Vladimir TODOROVIC		D	5	(3)	
Miljan VICO		A	16	(8)	
Danilo VLACIC		M	6	(8)	
Bojan VUCINIC		M	3		
Predrag VUKICEVIC		D	20	(1)	
Nenad ZECEVIC	SCG	M	14		6

MODRICA MAXIMA
Coach – Mitar Lukic

2005
Date	Opponent	H/A	Score	Scorers
6/8	Leotar Trebinje	h	2-1	Bajic Ma. 2 (1p)
13/8	Jedinstvo Bihac	a	3-1	Nikolic, Jelic, Kusljic
20/8	Orasje	h	3-1	Stojic (p), Jelic, Tadic
27/8	Zeljeznicar Sarajevo	a	2-1	Magazin, Jelic
10/9	Sloboda Tuzla	h	2-0	Bajic Ma., Kusljic
17/9	Celik Zenica	a	0-1	
24/9	Posusje	h	1-0	Jelic (p)
1/10	Travnik	h	4-0	Jelic 2, Puric, Tadic
15/10	Siroki Brijeg	a	1-2	Bajic Ma.
22/10	Buducnost Banovici	h	4-1	Nikolic 2, Jelic (p), Kusljic
29/10	Slavija Sarajevo	a	1-3	Nikolic
5/11	Sarajevo	h	2-0	Nikolic 2
12/11	Zepce	a	0-0	
19/11	Radnik Bijeljina	h	4-1	Bajic Ma., Magazin, Nikolic, Puric
27/11	Zrinjski Mostar	a	0-1	

2006
Date	Opponent	H/A	Score	Scorers
25/2	Leotar Trebinje	a	1-2	Stojic
4/3	Jedinstvo Bihac	h	3-2	Vasic S., Magazin, Jelic
11/3	Orasje	a	0-1	
16/3	Zeljeznicar Sarajevo	h	1-1	Jelic
19/3	Sloboda Tuzla	a	4-0	Jelic 2, Dimitrijevic, Jeftic
22/3	Celik Zenica	h	1-0	Jelic
26/3	Posusje	a	0-2	
1/4	Travnik	a	0-1	
5/4	Siroki Brijeg	h	1-0	Jelic
8/4	Buducnost Banovici	a	0-1	
15/4	Slavija Sarajevo	h	1-0	Vasic S.
22/4	Sarajevo	a	1-2	Jeftic
29/4	Zepce	h	4-0	Puric, Vasic S., Jelic, Nikolic
6/5	Radnik Bijeljina	a	4-5	Nikolic, Jelic 2 (1p), Bajic Ma.
13/5	Zrinjski Mostar	h	3-0	Jelic 2 (1p), Vasiljevic

Name	Nat	Pos	Aps	(s)	Gls
Marko BAJIC	SCG	A	25	(1)	6
Mladen BAJIC		D		(1)	
Tomislav BAJUNOVIC		D	14	(4)	
Niksa DIMITRIJEVIC		M	6	(3)	1
Predrag DJUKIC		M		(1)	
Miroslav JEFTIC		M	11	(3)	2
Petar JELIC		A	29		18
Nedjeljko JOKSIMOVIC		D		(1)	
Dragan JOLOVIC	SCG	M	16	(2)	
Goran KUSLJIC		D	3	(11)	3
Bojan MAGAZIN		M	22	(1)	3
Bojan MAKSIMOVIC		D	12	(6)	
Stevo NIKOLIC		A	17	(7)	9
Velibor PAVLOVIC		M	2	(4)	
Milan PETROVIC		G	9	(1)	

Bosnia-Herzegovina

Name	Nat	Pos	Aps	(s)	Gls
Dario PURIC		M	27	(2)	3
Danijel SAVIC		M		(1)	
Djordje SAVIC		A	13	(15)	
Nemanja STJEPANOVIC		M	27		
Marko STOJIC		M	20	(1)	2
Aleksandar STOJKOVIC	SCG	M	1		
Joco STOKIC		D		(3)	
Danijel TADIC		M		(18)	2
Bojan TRIPIC		G	21		
Marko VASIC		M		(3)	
Sreten VASIC	SCG	M	27		3
Nikola VASILJEVIC		D	28		1
Sinisa ZERIC		D		(2)	

ORASJE
Coach – Ivo Knezevic; (26/11/05) Davor Mladina (CRO)

2005
6/8	Sloboda Tuzla	a	0-0	
13/8	Celik Zenica	h	3-2	Pejic I., Miskovic, Ibricic
20/8	Modrica Maxima	a	1-3	Damjanovic
27/8	Travnik	h	3-0	Pejic I. 2 (1p), Coskovic
10/9	Siroki Brijeg	a	1-2	Pejic I. (p)
17/9	Buducnost Banovici	h	1-0	Djuric M.
24/9	Slavija Sarajevo	a	0-3	
1/10	Sarajevo	h	1-1	Husic
16/10	Zepce	a	3-1	Damjanovic, Tosunovic 2
22/10	Radnik Bijeljina	h	6-1	Pejic I., Tosunovic 3, Brasnic L., Damjanovic
30/10	Zrinjski Mostar	a	0-1	
5/11	Leotar Trebinje	h	3-0	Brasnic V., Tosunovic, Markovic
12/11	Jedinstvo Bihac	a	0-2	
20/11	Posusje	a	0-1	
26/11	Zeljeznicar Sarajevo	h	1-0	Djuric M.

2006
25/2	Sloboda Tuzla	h	4-1	Damjanovic, Husic, Brasnic V., Tosunovic
4/3	Celik Zenica	a	1-4	Tosunovic
11/3	Modrica Maxima	h	1-0	Babic
16/3	Travnik	a	2-4	Tosunovic, Djuric M.
19/3	Siroki Brijeg	h	1-3	Damjanovic
22/3	Buducnost Banovici	a	1-3	Djuric P.
25/3	Slavija Sarajevo	h	4-1	Pejic I. (p), Damjanovic, Husic 2
1/4	Sarajevo	a	1-5	Tosunovic
5/4	Zepce	h	2-0	Pejic I. (p), Djuric M.
9/4	Radnik Bijeljina	a	0-1	
15/4	Zrinjski Mostar	h	1-2	Damjanovic
21/4	Leotar Trebinje	a	2-4	Zivkovic G. 2
29/4	Jedinstvo Bihac	h	5-1	Babic 2, Damjanovic, Brasnic V., Tosunovic
6/5	Posusje	a	2-3	Damjanovic, Ristanic
13/5	Zeljeznicar Sarajevo	h	1-2	Tosunovic

Name	Nat	Pos	Aps	(s)	Gls
Sabit ALIMANOVIC		M	3	(5)	
Ivica BABIC		A	17	(3)	3
Zdenko BAOTIC		G	18		
Luka BRASNIC		D	18	(3)	1
Velimir BRASNIC		A	7	(5)	3
Ivan BRESKIC		M	2	(3)	
Stamenko COSKOVIC		A	18	(2)	1
Slaven DAMJANOVIC		A	17	(6)	9
Marko DJURIC	CRO	A	14	(4)	4
Pavle DJURIC	CRO	M	11	(3)	1
Armin DZANANOVIC		D	3	(3)	
Edin HUSIC		M	18	(5)	4
Besim IBRICIC		M	2	(5)	1
Miro KLAIC		D	22		
Luka KOBAS		G	12		
Slavko KOBAS		M	21	(3)	
Ivan MARKOVIC		D	11	(6)	1
Marjan MAROSEVIC		D	1		
Drago MISKOVIC		M	22		1
Fedja OMERAGIC		D	2	(1)	
Igor ORSOLIC		M	3	(1)	
Ivo PEJIC		D	24	(2)	7
Matijas PEJIC		M	2	(2)	
Ilija RISTANIC		M	20	(3)	1
Raif SMAJIC		G		(1)	
Mijo STUDENOVIC		M	9	(1)	
Damir TOSUNOVIC		M	12	(7)	12
Antonio VIDOVIC		M		(1)	
Anto ZIVKOVIC		D	1	(1)	
Goran ZIVKOVIC		D	22		2

POSUSJE
Coach – Vjekoslav Lokica (CRO); (18/9/05) Ivo Istuk

2005
6/8	Zeljeznicar Sarajevo	a	0-3	
13/8	Sarajevo	h	0-1	
20/8	Sloboda Tuzla	a	2-3	Vranjkovic, Dolic
28/8	Zepce	h	4-1	Idrizovic 2, Dolic, De Oliveira
11/9	Celik Zenica	a	1-2	Dolic
18/9	Radnik Bijeljina	h	0-0	
24/9	Modrica Maxima	a	0-1	
2/10	Zrinjski Mostar	h	2-1	Andonov, Celiscak
15/10	Travnik	a	0-1	
23/10	Leotar Trebinje	h	4-2	Ceric, Bisaku L. 2 (2p), Idrizovic
30/10	Siroki Brijeg	a	1-1	Ceric
8/11	Jedinstvo Bihac	h	1-1	Milanovic
12/11	Buducnost Banovici	a	0-1	
20/11	Orasje	h	1-0	Divkovic
26/11	Slavija Sarajevo	a	0-4	

2006
25/2	Zeljeznicar Sarajevo	h	1-0	Mesic (p)
4/3	Sarajevo	a	0-3	
13/3	Sloboda Tuzla	h	3-2	Mesic (p), Coric, Visevic
16/3	Zepce	a	0-1	
19/3	Celik Zenica	h	3-0	Peraica, Coric, Mesic
22/3	Radnik Bijeljina	a	1-4	Peraica
26/3	Modrica Maxima	h	2-0	Mesic, Vranjkovic
2/4	Zrinjski Mostar	a	0-1	
5/4	Travnik	h	1-0	Dzidic
8/4	Leotar Trebinje	a	2-5	Coric, Milosevic
15/4	Siroki Brijeg	h	1-2	Milosevic
22/4	Jedinstvo Bihac	a	0-3	
29/4	Buducnost Banovici	h	1-0	Peraica
6/5	Orasje	a	3-2	Mesic 2 (1p), DJairon
13/5	Slavija Sarajevo	h	4-1	Milosevic, Coric 2, Serdarusic

Name	Nat	Pos	Aps	(s)	Gls
Marian ANDONOV	MAC	M	1	(5)	1
Zvonko BAKULA		D	4	(3)	
Dejan BANDOVIC		G	11		
Leonardo BISAKU	CRO	D	4	(1)	2
Manuel BISAKU	CRO	M	8	(2)	
Vedran CELISCAK	CRO	M	12		1
Tarik CERIC		D	24		2

Bosnia-Herzegovina

Name	Nat	Pos	Aps	(s)	Gls
Elvis CORIC		M	13	(2)	5
Eric Matos DE OLIVEIRA	BRA	M	9		1
Denis DIVKOVIC		A	4	(6)	1
Velimir DOLIC		A	10	(3)	3
Aldin DZIDIC		A	20	(1)	1
Boze GALIC		M	1	(3)	
Andro HRKAC		M		(4)	
Ferid IDRIZOVIC		M	21	(2)	3
Damásio Feliciano JAIRON	BRA	M	8	(4)	1
Stipe MATIC		M	22	(1)	
Mirza MESIC		A	12		6
Damir MILANOVIC		D	23		1
Semjon MILOSEVIC		D	13	(1)	3
Danijel PANDZIC		D		(1)	
Bosko PERAICA		A	12		3
Goran RADNIC		D	16	(5)	
Kaja ROGULJ	CRO	D	8	(1)	
Nikola SCHRENG	CRO	G	19		
Ante SERDARUSIC		M	2	(12)	1
Daniel STOJANOVIC		D	13	(10)	
Josip TOPIC		M	5		
Tomislav VISEVIC		D	13		1
Mladen VRANJKOVIC		M	17	(3)	2
Ivan ZOVKO		D	5	(5)	

RADNIK BIJELJINA
Coach – Nikola Bala; (28/11/05) Mile Jovin (SCG); (22/3/06) Dusan Jevric (SCG)

2005
7/8	Siroki Brijeg	a	1-2	Pivac
14/8	Buducnost Banovici	h	2-0	Savic, Pivac
20/8	Slavija Sarajevo	a	0-0	
28/8	Sarajevo	h	0-3	
11/9	Zepce	a	0-1	
18/9	Posusje	a	0-0	
25/9	Zrinjski Mostar	h	1-3	Pivac (p)
1/10	Leotar Trebinje	a	3-1	Pivac, Mijailovic, Sivcevic
16/10	Jedinstvo Bihac	h	3-0	Matic 2, Kisjuhas
22/10	Orasje	a	1-6	Vukasinovic
30/10	Zeljeznicar Sarajevo	h	3-1	Zecevic 2, Matic
5/11	Sloboda Tuzla	a	0-3	
13/11	Celik Zenica	h	3-0	Matic 2, Trifkovic
19/11	Modrica Maxima	a	1-4	Kisjuhas
27/11	Travnik	h	2-1	Zecevic, Vukasinovic

2006
25/2	Siroki Brijeg	h	0-1	
4/3	Buducnost Banovici	a	0-5	
12/3	Slavija Sarajevo	h	1-0	Stojanovic
16/3	Sarajevo	a	1-4	Pivac (p)
19/3	Zepce	h	1-1	Railic
22/3	Posusje	a	4-1	Rankic 2, Savic, Vidic (p)
26/3	Zrinjski Mostar	a	0-4	
2/4	Leotar Trebinje	h	2-1	Stojanovic 2 (1p)
5/4	Jedinstvo Bihac	a	0-2	
9/4	Orasje	h	1-0	Pivac
15/4	Zeljeznicar Sarajevo	a	0-0	
22/4	Sloboda Tuzla	h	0-0	
29/4	Celik Zenica	a	0-1	
6/5	Modrica Maxima	h	5-4	Stojanovic, Kojic, Pivac (p), Trifkovic, Savic
13/5	Travnik	a	2-3	Kojic, Petricevic

Name	Nat	Pos	Aps	(s)	Gls
Darko ALEKSIC	SCG	D	19		
Dragan ANDJELIC		D	3	(5)	
Miladin ANDRIC		M		(1)	
Delimir BAJIC		D	24	(2)	
Aleksandar BRDJANIN		D	6	(3)	
Dragan DJORDJIC		G	1		
Zeljko GARVRILOVIC		M	8	(2)	
Igor JAMBREK		M		(1)	
Marko JEVTIC	SCG	D	19	(2)	
Predrag KISJUHAS		M	4	(7)	2
Ziko KOJIC		M	8	(6)	2
Nikola LAZAREVIC		D		(1)	
Jovica LUKIC		M	2	(2)	
Goran MAKSIMOVIC	SCG	G	18		
Goran MARKOVIC		D	3	(3)	
Dragan MATIC		M	8	(2)	5
Darko MIJAILOVIC	SCG	M	22	(1)	1
Sasa NOVAKOVIC		D	12	(4)	
Damir OPACIC		M	5	(4)	
Dejan PANTELIC		G	11		
Mladen PETRICEVIC		M	11	(3)	1
Gojko PIVAC		A	27	(1)	7
Aleksandar RAILIC		D	9	(2)	1
Vladimir RANKIC		D	13	(9)	2
Srdjan SAVIC		M	21	(4)	3
Milomir SIVCEVIC	SCG	M	4	(9)	1
Milos STOJANOVIC		M	10	(1)	4
Ivica TONKOVIC		M		(3)	
Perica TRIFKOVIC		D	28	(1)	2
Sasa VIDIC		M		(3)	1
Filip VUJIC		D	1	(3)	
Svetozar VUKASINOVIC		M	20	(4)	2
Nenad ZECEVIC	SCG	M	13		3

SARAJEVO
Coach – Husref Musemic

2005
6/8	Slavija Sarajevo	a	1-1	Hasancic
13/8	Posusje	a	1-0	Hasancic
20/8	Zepce	h	2-0	Avdija, Avdic
28/8	Radnik Bijeljina	a	3-0	Avdic, Hadzic, Muharemovic
11/9	Zrinjski Mostar	h	1-0	Hadzic
17/9	Leotar Trebinje	a	1-1	Avdic
24/9	Jedinstvo Bihac	h	2-0	Pelak, Hasancic
1/10	Orasje	a	1-1	Avdic
15/10	Zeljeznicar Sarajevo	h	0-0	
22/10	Sloboda Tuzla	a	3-1	Avdic 2, Muharemovic
29/10	Celik Zenica	h	6-1	Trivunovic 2, Repuh 2 (1p), Obuca 2
5/11	Modrica Maxima	a	0-2	
12/11	Travnik	h	3-0	Avdic 2, Pelak
20/11	Siroki Brijeg	a	1-2	Pelak (p)
26/11	Buducnost Banovici	h	2-1	Pelak 2 (1p)

2006
25/2	Slavija Sarajevo	h	1-1	Maksumic
4/3	Posusje	h	3-0	Matko, Obuca, Muharemovic
12/3	Zepce	a	3-1	Obuca, Muharemovic (p), Matko
16/3	Radnik Bijeljina	h	4-1	Muharemovic (p), Saric 2, Matko
19/3	Zrinjski Mostar	a	1-3	Obuca
22/3	Leotar Trebinje	h	1-0	Mackic (p)
25/3	Jedinstvo Bihac	a	0-1	
1/4	Orasje	h	5-1	Duro, Obuca 2, Hasancic, Matko
5/4	Zeljeznicar Sarajevo	a	1-0	Matko

Bosnia-Herzegovina

Date	Opponent	h/a	Score	Scorers
8/4	Sloboda Tuzla	h	2-0	Mackic (p), Saric
15/4	Celik Zenica	a	1-2	Matko
22/4	Modrica Maxima	h	2-1	Ihtijarevic, Trivunovic
29/4	Travnik	a	0-2	
6/5	Siroki Brijeg	h	3-0	Hadzic, Repuh, Saric
13/5	Buducnost Banovici	a	3-3	Saric, Obuca, Hasancic

Name	Nat	Pos	Aps	(s)	Gls
Muhamed ALAIM		G	26		
Almir ALIC		D		(1)	
Alen AVDIC		A	12		8
Arben AVDIJA		M	7	(6)	1
Semir COMAGA		D		(1)	
Samir DURO		M	15		1
Muhamed DZAKMIC		D	12	(5)	
Armin DZANANOVIC		M	2	(2)	
Damir HADZIC		D	18	(4)	3
Admir HASANCIC		A	9	(8)	5
Faruk IHTIJAREVIC		M	12	(5)	1
Elvis IMSIROVIC		M	5	(4)	
Aldin JANJOS		M	1	(3)	
Emir JANJOS		M	4	(10)	
Adi KAPETANOVIC		D		(1)	
Adis KAPETANOVIC		D		(1)	
Vladimir KARALIC		A		(3)	
Elvis KARIC		G	4		
Marinko MACKIC		D	26		2
Ajdin MAKSUMIC		D	14	(6)	1
Matija MATKO	CRO	A	13	(1)	6
Veldin MUHAREMOVIC		M	23		5
Dalibor NEDIC		D	2	(1)	
Emir OBUCA		A	17	(8)	8
Albin PELAK		M	12		5
Senad REPUH		M	27		3
Albin PELAK		M	12		5
Samir SARIC		A	15	(12)	5
Mirza SELIMOVIC		M		(3)	
Elvedin SPAHIC	SCG	D	2	(2)	
Vule TRIVUNOVIC		D	28		3
Muhidin ZUKIC		D	24		

SIROKI BRIJEG
Coach – Ivica Barbaric

2005

Date	Opponent	h/a	Score	Scorers
7/8	Radnik Bijeljina	h	2-1	Lukacevic, Erceg
14/8	Zrinjski Mostar	a	0-0	
20/8	Leotar Trebinje	h	3-0	Rezic, Abramovic 2 (1p)
30/8	Jedinstvo Bihac	a	2-0	Ronielle, Abramovic
10/9	Orasje	h	2-1	Abramovic 2
20/9	Zeljeznicar Sarajevo	a	1-0	Abramovic
25/9	Sloboda Tuzla	h	1-0	Abramovic
2/10	Celik Zenica	a	0-2	
15/10	Modrica Maxima	h	2-1	Bubalo, Landeka
22/10	Travnik	a	1-0	Abramovic
30/10	Posusje	h	1-1	Abramovic
5/11	Buducnost Banovici	h	1-0	Abramovic (p)
12/11	Slavija Sarajevo	a	1-1	Ronielle
20/11	Sarajevo	h	2-1	Juricic, Abramovic (p)
27/11	Zepce	a	0-0	

2006

Date	Opponent	h/a	Score	Scorers
25/2	Radnik Bijeljina	a	1-0	Rezic
5/3	Zrinjski Mostar	h	1-0	Silic
11/3	Leotar Trebinje	a	1-3	Ronielle
16/3	Jedinstvo Bihac	h	1-0	Ronielle
19/3	Orasje	a	3-1	Celson, Wagner, Erceg
22/3	Zeljeznicar Sarajevo	h	2-0	Erceg, Ronielle
25/3	Sloboda Tuzla	a	0-0	
2/4	Celik Zenica	h	2-0	Abramovic, Bubalo
5/4	Modrica Maxima	a	0-1	
9/4	Travnik	h	3-0	Celson, Wagner 2
15/4	Posusje	a	2-1	Lukacevic, Silic
22/4	Buducnost Banovici	a	0-0	
29/4	Slavija Sarajevo	h	3-0	Celson 2, Landela
6/5	Sarajevo	a	0-3	
13/5	Zepce	h	0-2	

Name	Nat	Pos	Aps	(s)	Gls
Domagoj ABRAMOVIC	CRO	A	26		12
Branimir ANIC		D	26	(1)	
Danijel BAJKUSA		D	11	(6)	
Tomislav BASIC		G	18		
Spomenko BOSNJAK		M	12	(1)	
Ivan BUBALO		M	9	(13)	2
Ricardo CELSON Borges	BRA	A	8	(4)	4
Nenad DZIDIC		G	1	(1)	
Hrvoje ERCEG	CRO	A	14	(5)	3
Ivica GALIC		M	4	(13)	
Jure IVANKOVIC		M		(3)	
Nikola JURICIC		A	7	(6)	1
Marko KOVACIC		D	6	(9)	
Dalibor KOZUL		D	1	(5)	
Danijel KOZUL		M		(1)	
Ivica LANDEKA		D	23		2
Josip LUKACEVIC		M	15	(7)	2
Ivan MEDVID	CRO	D	14		
Boris PANDZA		M	8	(1)	
RENATO Alves	BRA	M	10	(8)	
Stipe REZIC	CRO	M	25		2
RONIELLE Faria Gomes	BRA	M	26		5
Dalibor SILIC		M	28		2
Etsan William TABY	CMR	M	18	(2)	
Vladimir VASILJ	CRO	G	11		
WAGNER Santos Lago	BRA	M	9	(4)	3

SLAVIJA SARAJEVO
Coach – Milomir Odovic

2005

Date	Opponent	h/a	Score	Scorers
6/8	Sarajevo	h	1-1	Stefanovic (p)
13/8	Zepce	a	1-1	Vuksanovic
20/8	Radnik Bijeljina	h	0-0	
28/8	Zrinjski Mostar	a	0-3	
10/9	Leotar Trebinje	h	1-0	Djeric
17/9	Jedinstvo Bihac	a	0-5	
24/9	Orasje	h	3-0	Vuksanovic, Djeric 2
30/9	Zeljeznicar Sarajevo	a	2-4	Bjelica, Muminovic
15/10	Sloboda Tuzla	h	1-0	Radovanovic
22/10	Celik Zenica	a	4-1	Radovanovic 2, Sreco, Stefanovic
29/10	Modrica Maxima	h	3-1	Stefanovic (p), Atanackovic, Stankovic
5/11	Travnik	a	0-2	
12/11	Siroki Brijeg	h	1-1	Muminovic
19/11	Buducnost Banovici	a	3-1	Radovanovic, Stefanovic, Djeric
26/11	Posusje	h	4-0	Vuksanovic (p), Bjelica, Sreco, Djeric

2006

Date	Opponent	h/a	Score	Scorers
25/2	Sarajevo	a	1-1	Muminovic
3/3	Zepce	h	1-0	Injac
12/3	Radnik Bijeljina	a	0-1	

Bosnia-Herzegovina

16/3	Zrinjski Mostar	h	2-1	Radovanovic 2	
19/3	Leotar Trebinje	a	2-3	Vitkovic, Sreco	
22/3	Jedinstvo Bihac	h	0-1		
25/3	Orasje	a	1-4	Radovanovic	
2/4	Zeljeznicar Sarajevo	h	1-4	Radovanovic	
5/4	Sloboda Tuzla	a	0-1		
9/4	Celik Zenica	h	2-1	Djeric, Vuksanovic (p)	
15/4	Modrica Maxima	a	0-1		
22/4	Travnik	h	3-2	Vuksanovic 2 (1p), Djeric	
29/4	Siroki Brijeg	a	0-3		
6/5	Buducnost Banovici	h	3-0	Djeric 2, Vuksanovic	
13/5	Posusje	a	1-4	Vuksanovic (p)	

Name	Nat	Pos	Aps	(s)	Gls
Branislav ATANACKOVIC	SCG	A	11	(1)	1
Dragan BJELICA		D	21		2
Aleksandar BOZOVIC		G	20		
Dragan CICOVIC		M		(3)	
Milanko DJERIC		M	28		9
Nemanja DJUROVIC		M		(2)	
Djordje GRUBACIC		D	6	(6)	
Dimitrije INJAC	SCG	A	16	(7)	1
Zoran KOKOT		M	2	(5)	
Aleksandar KOSORIC		M	2	(2)	
Nemanja KRESTALICA		M	1		
Vladimir MARIC		G	10	(1)	
Milan MUMINOVIC		A	27		3
Predrag PAPAZ		M	11	(1)	
Ilija PRODANOVIC		D	1	(1)	
Miljan RADONJA		M	2	(9)	
Igor RADOVANOVIC		A	23	(1)	8
Bojan REGOJE		D	24		
Nemanja SESLIJA		M		(1)	
Aleksandar SIMIC		M	3	(18)	
Goran SIMIC		M	24	(2)	
Milan SRECO		A	7	(10)	3
Ivan STANKOVIC		M	27		1
Miodrag STEFANOVIC	SCG	M	27		4
Ostoja STJEPANOVIC	MAC	M	13	(5)	
Srdjan VITKOVIC		D	1	(6)	1
Sretko VUKSANOVIC	FRA	M	23	(1)	8

SLOBODA TUZLA
Coach – Sakib Malkocevic; (18/8/05) Nihad Mujezinovic; (22/3/06) Ibrahim Crnkic

2005

6/8	Orasje	h	0-0	
13/8	Zeljeznicar Sarajevo	a	1-5	Kasapovic
20/8	Posusje	h	3-2	Krupinac, Mujic, Kasapovic
27/8	Celik Zenica	h	3-0	Mesanovic 2, Okanovic
10/9	Modrica Maxima	a	0-2	
18/9	Travnik	h	1-0	Krupinac
25/9	Siroki Brijeg	a	0-1	
1/10	Buducnost Banovici	h	3-0	Mesanovic, Kasapovic (p), Mujic
15/10	Slavija Sarajevo	a	0-1	
22/10	Sarajevo	h	1-3	Mesanovic
30/10	Zepce	a	0-0	
5/11	Radnik Bijeljina	h	3-0	Mujic, Mesanovic (p), Osmanhodzic
13/11	Zrinjski Mostar	a	1-4	Osmanhodzic
19/11	Leotar Trebinje	h	1-0	Mujic
26/11	Jedinstvo Bihac	a	1-2	Osmanhodzic

2006

25/2	Orasje	a	1-4	Osmanhodzic
4/3	Zeljeznicar Sarajevo	h	1-1	Osmanhodzic
13/3	Posusje	a	2-3	Matic 2
16/3	Celik Zenica	a	0-0	
19/3	Modrica Maxima	h	0-4	
22/3	Travnik	a	0-2	
25/3	Siroki Brijeg	h	0-0	
1/4	Buducnost Banovici	a	1-0	Osmanhodzic
5/4	Slavija Sarajevo	h	1-0	Mujic
8/4	Sarajevo	a	0-2	
15/4	Zepce	h	3-1	Karic, Salamovic, Mujic
22/4	Radnik Bijeljina	a	0-0	
29/4	Zrinjski Mostar	h	2-1	Kuduzovic, Karic
6/5	Leotar Trebinje	a	0-1	
13/5	Jedinstvo Bihac	h	2-1	Krupinac, Hadzic (p)

Name	Nat	Pos	Aps	(s)	Gls
Nedzad BAJROVIC		D	1	(1)	
Emir BORIC		D	6	(5)	
Jasminko BRCINOVIC		M	5	(7)	
Admir BRDJANOVIC		M	4	(1)	
Kenan CEJVANOVIC		M	16	(2)	
Mirza CEJVANOVIC		D	7	(3)	
Dino CRNKIC		M		(1)	
Ratko DUJKOVIC		G	12		
Senad HADZIC		M	24	(4)	1
Almir HALILOVIC		M	13	(6)	
Adnan JAHIC		M	9	(2)	
Bojan JOVIC		G	14		
Denis KARIC		M	21		2
Emir KASAPOVIC		A	17	(1)	3
Vedran KOVACEVIC		D		(1)	
Mirzet KRUPINAC		D	23		3
Samir KUDUZOVIC		M	22		
Adnan LIKIC		D	14		
Njegos MATIC		M	6	(5)	2
Almir MEDIC		G	3		
Enes MESANOVIC		M	14		5
Senad MUJIC		M	15	(9)	6
Stanisa NIKOLIC		M	13		
Tarik OKANOVIC		A	14	(4)	1
Muhamed OMIC		D	20	(2)	
Adnan OSMANHODZIC		M	16	(4)	6
Senedin OSTROKOVIC		G	1		
Aleksandar PANTIC		D	8	(2)	
Adnan POZEGIC		D		(2)	
Semir SALAMOVIC		M		(9)	1
Adnan SMAJLOVIC		A		(5)	
Amir SPAHIC		M	2	(1)	
Dario TOMIC		M	2		
Darko VOJVODIC		D	8	(1)	

TRAVNIK
Coach – Dragan Jovic; (22/4/06) Ado Pindjo

2005

6/8	Zrinjski Mostar	h	1-1	Siljak
13/8	Leotar Trebinje	a	1-1	Kevric
20/8	Jedinstvo Bihac	h	2-0	Siljak, Biloglavic
27/8	Orasje	a	0-3	
10/9	Zeljeznicar Sarajevo	h	0-2	
18/9	Sloboda Tuzla	a	0-1	
24/9	Celik Zenica	h	0-2	
1/10	Modrica Maxima	a	0-4	
15/10	Posusje	h	1-0	Terzic
22/10	Siroki Brijeg	h	0-1	
29/10	Buducnost Banovici	a	0-1	

Bosnia-Herzegovina

Date	Opponent	H/A	Score	Scorers
5/11	Slavija Sarajevo	h	2-0	Siljak, Kevric
12/11	Sarajevo	a	0-3	
19/11	Zepce	h	1-1	Varupa
27/11	Radnik Bijeljina	a	1-2	Siljak
2006				
25/2	Zrinjski Mostar	a	1-3	Siljak
4/3	Leotar Trebinje	h	3-1	Zeric 3
11/3	Jedinstvo Bihac	a	0-1	
16/3	Orasje	h	4-2	Zeric, Smajic, Ibricic, Caluk
19/3	Zeljeznicar Sarajevo	a	0-1	
22/3	Sloboda Tuzla	h	2-0	Varupa (p), Ibricic
25/3	Celik Zenica	a	1-1	Ibricic
1/4	Modrica Maxima	h	1-0	Varupa
5/4	Posusje	a	0-1	
9/4	Siroki Brijeg	a	0-3	
15/4	Buducnost Banovici	h	5-0	Varupa (p), Hadziahmetovic, Dolic, Ibricic, Siljak
22/4	Slavija Sarajevo	a	2-3	Varupa, Alic
29/4	Sarajevo	h	2-0	Hadziahmetovic, Ibricic
6/5	Zepce	a	0-1	
13/5	Radnik Bijeljina	h	3-2	Dolic 2, Ibricic

Name	Nat	Pos	Aps	(s)	Gls
Adi ADILOVIC		G	26		
Almir ALIC		A	9	(4)	1
Nermin BASIC		M	1	(9)	
Boris BILJESKO		A	4	(1)	
Luka BILOBRK		G	4		
Albin BILOGLAVIC		M	8	(2)	1
Zikret BULJINA		M	29		
Haris CALUK		M		(5)	1
Alen CURIC		M		(7)	
Velimir DOLIC		A	14		3
Zeljko FRLJIC		M	5		
Izudin HADZIAHMETOVIC		M	10	(2)	2
Mustafa HASANSPAHIC		M	4	(7)	
Besim IBRICIC		A	12	(2)	6
Elvedin KARADZA		D	1		
Jasmin KEVRIC		M	12	(1)	2
Adin KUNDIC		M		(4)	
Adin LIHOVAC		D	3	(15)	
Mirza MEHANOVIC		D		(1)	
Kristijan PANTIC		M	7	(1)	
Samir PINJO		D	11		
Ermin POTURAK		D	4	(4)	
Nihad RIBIC		D	24		
Midhat SARAJCIC		D	26		
Nedzad SELIMOVIC		D	5	(4)	
Mirsad SILJAK		M	23	(1)	6
Edin SMAJIC		M	19		1
Sinbad TERZIC		M	13	(7)	1
Elvedin VARUPA		D	26		5
Nedzad ZERIC		M	30		4

ZELJEZNICAR SARAJEVO
Coach – Ratko Ninkovic; (12/3/06) Almir Memic

Date	Opponent	H/A	Score	Scorers
2005				
6/8	Posusje	h	3-0	Vladavic, Hadzic, Dudo
13/8	Sloboda Tuzla	h	5-1	Vladavic, Hadzic, Rascic Ad. 2, Memisevic
20/8	Celik Zenica	a	0-0	
27/8	Modrica Maxima	h	1-2	Gredic (p)
10/9	Travnik	a	2-0	Gredic, Vladavic
20/9	Siroki Brijeg	h	0-1	
24/9	Buducnost Banovici	a	1-2	Kajtaz
30/9	Slavija Sarajevo	h	4-2	Gredic (p), Pjanic, Muharemovic, Rascic Ad.
17/10	Sarajevo	a	0-0	
22/10	Zepce	h	2-1	Memisevic, Sinanovic
30/10	Radnik Bijeljina	a	1-3	Rascic Ad.
5/11	Zrinjski Mostar	h	3-1	Vladavic, Kajtaz (p), Rascic Ad.
12/11	Leotar Trebinje	a	0-1	
20/11	Jedinstvo Bihac	h	2-1	Alagic, Rascic Ad.
26/11	Orasje	a	0-1	
2006				
25/2	Posusje	a	0-1	
4/3	Sloboda Tuzla	a	1-1	Sinanovic
12/3	Celik Zenica	h	0-0	
16/3	Modrica Maxima	a	1-1	Vladavic
19/3	Travnik	h	1-0	Avdic
22/3	Siroki Brijeg	a	0-2	
25/3	Buducnost Banovici	h	3-1	Avdic 2, Zeric
2/4	Slavija Sarajevo	a	4-1	Pelak 2, Avdic, Rascic Al.
5/4	Sarajevo	h	0-1	
8/4	Zepce	a	1-3	Muharemovic
14/4	Radnik Bijeljina	h	0-0	
22/4	Zrinjski Mostar	a	1-1	Vladavic
29/4	Leotar Trebinje	h	0-2	
6/5	Jedinstvo Bihac	a	0-2	
13/5	Orasje	h	2-1	Vladavic, Avdic

Name	Nat	Pos	Aps	(s)	Gls
Mirzet ALAGIC		A	16	(3)	1
Rasid AVDIC		A	12	(1)	5
Haris BESLIJA		A	12	(4)	
Josip BOJO		D		(1)	
Edin COCALIC		M	6		
Boubacar DIALIBA	SEN	M	1	(8)	
Juonouss DIATTA	SEN	M	2	(3)	
Edin DUDO		M	16	(5)	1
Haris EFENDIC		G	21		
Branko GRAHOVAC		G	9		
Almir GREDIC		M	19	(1)	3
Emir HADZIC		A	11	(2)	2
Nermin JAMAK		M	1	(3)	
Admir KAJTAZ		M	20		2
Adi KAPETANOVIC		D	1		
Nedim KUDRA		M	3	(4)	
Elmir KUDUZOVIC		M	8	(2)	
Damir MEMISEVIC		M	24	(1)	2
Dino MUHAREMOVIC		M	16	(3)	2
Edis MULALIC		D	12		
Sanjin ORTAS		A	2	(1)	
Albin PELAK		A	5	(1)	2
Anel PJANIC		A	2	(11)	1
Aleksandar RAILIC		D	4	(3)	
Admir RASCIC		A	22	(2)	6
Almir RASCIC		M	18		1
Nermin SEJFOVIC		D	1	(1)	
Mersad SELIMBEGOVIC		M	22		
Mensur SINANOVIC		M	5	(1)	2
Alen SPAHIC		M		(2)	
Amir SPAHIC		M	8		
Semir STILIC		A	1	(5)	
Admir VLADAVIC		A	21	(1)	7
Amanaka ZABLON	KEN	M	1		
Senad ZERIC		A	6	(3)	1
Ermin ZUKANOVIC		M	2	(6)	

Bosnia-Herzegovina

ZEPCE
Coach – Nikola Nikic; (22/10/05) Tado Tomas

2005
Date	Opponent	H/A	Score	Scorers
6/8	Buducnost Banovici	a	2-0	Mesic 2
14/8	Slavija Sarajevo	h	1-1	Mesic
20/8	Sarajevo	a	0-2	
28/8	Posusje	a	1-4	Mesic
11/9	Radnik Bijeljina	h	1-0	Mesic
18/9	Zrinjski Mostar	a	1-2	Thomas
25/9	Leotar Trebinje	h	2-0	Juric, Sirovica
1/10	Jedinstvo Bihac	a	0-3	
16/10	Orasje	h	1-3	Juric
22/10	Zeljeznicar Sarajevo	a	1-2	Mesic
30/10	Sloboda Tuzla	h	0-0	
5/11	Celik Zenica	a	1-1	Mesic
12/11	Modrica Maxima	h	0-0	
19/11	Travnik	a	1-1	Masic
27/11	Siroki Brijeg	h	0-0	

2006
Date	Opponent	H/A	Score	Scorers
25/2	Buducnost Banovici	h	2-1	Krajisnik, Blagojevic (p)
3/3	Slavija Sarajevo	a	0-1	
12/3	Sarajevo	h	1-3	Doci
16/3	Posusje	h	1-0	Imamovic
19/3	Radnik Bijeljina	a	1-1	Obrenovic
22/3	Zrinjski Mostar	h	2-0	Blagojevic, Pejovic
25/3	Leotar Trebinje	a	1-5	Hasanovic M.
2/4	Jedinstvo Bihac	h	1-0	Blagojevic
5/4	Orasje	a	0-2	
8/4	Zeljeznicar Sarajevo	h	3-1	Blagojevic, Papic, Mikelini
15/4	Sloboda Tuzla	a	1-3	Juric
22/4	Celik Zenica	h	1-0	Blagojevic
29/4	Modrica Maxima	a	0-4	
6/5	Travnik	h	1-0	Doci
13/5	Siroki Brijeg	a	2-0	Imamovic 2

Name	Nat	Pos	Aps	(s)	Gls
Sefik BESIC		M	1	(8)	
Zoran BLAGOJEVIC		A	12		5
Dejan BOZOVIC	SCG	M	6	(1)	
Goran BRASNIC		G	13		
Patrik DOCI	SCG	D	25		2
Ivan DRAGICEVIC		D	3	(1)	
Petar DUSPARA		A	4	(4)	
Almir HASANOVIC		M	20		
Mirza HASANOVIC		M	5	(1)	1
Vahidin IMAMOVIC		A	18	(3)	3
Boris IVESIC		M	1	(1)	
Kristijan IVESIC		A	11	(7)	
Vitomir JELIC		D	21	(1)	
Goran JURIC		M	22		3
Dzenan KRAJISNIK		D	25	(3)	1
Rafael KURAJA	SLO	D	2	(1)	
Edis KURTIC		D	20	(1)	
Dragan MAKSIMOVIC		G	6		
Srdjan MARCETIC		D	4	(4)	
Eldin MASIC		M	8	(8)	1
Emir MEMIC		M	4	(5)	
Mirza MESIC		A	12		7
Nikola MIKELINI		M	21		1
Nikolas NJUKEN	CMR	M	10		
Aleksandar OBRENOVIC	SCG	A	7	(3)	1
Ermin ORUC		M		(1)	
Josip PAPIC		M	12		1
Milos PEJOVIC		M	2	(4)	1
Josip RAKO		M	6	(3)	
Damir SIROVICA		A	14	(1)	1
Issa THOMAS	SFL	M	3	(3)	1
Nikola TROGRLIC		G	11		
Mladen VIDOVIC		M	1	(4)	

ZRINJSKI MOSTAR
Coach – Blaz Sliskovic

2005
Date	Opponent	H/A	Score	Scorers
6/8	Travnik	a	1-1	Papic
14/8	Siroki Brijeg	h	0-0	
20/8	Buducnost Banovici	a	0-1	
28/8	Slavija Sarajevo	h	3-0	Avdic 2, Maric
11/9	Sarajevo	a	0-1	
18/9	Zepce	h	2-1	Smajic, Djuric
25/9	Radnik Bijeljina	a	3-1	Djuric, Avdic, Smajic
2/10	Posusje	a	1-2	Avdic
16/10	Leotar Trebinje	h	2-0	Zizovic, Djuric
21/10	Jedinstvo Bihac	a	3-1	Avdic, Zizovic, Papic
30/10	Orasje	h	1-0	Dzidic I.
5/11	Zeljeznicar Sarajevo	a	1-3	Sliskovic
13/11	Sloboda Tuzla	h	4-1	Kordic, Smajic, Vasilj, Vidic
19/11	Celik Zenica	a	2-0	Kordic, Smajic
27/11	Modrica Maxima	h	1-0	Kordic

2006
Date	Opponent	H/A	Score	Scorers
25/2	Travnik	h	3-1	Zizovic (p), Diarra, Joldic
5/3	Siroki Brijeg	a	0-1	
12/3	Buducnost Banovici	h	2-0	Kresic, Kordic
16/3	Slavija Sarajevo	a	1-2	Biscevic
19/3	Sarajevo	h	3-1	Joldic, Zizovic (p), Diarra
22/3	Zepce	a	0-2	
26/3	Radnik Bijeljina	h	4-0	Djuric, Gagro (p), Joldic, Maric
2/4	Posusje	h	1-0	Kordic
5/4	Leotar Trebinje	a	1-2	Vasilj
9/4	Jedinstvo Bihac	h	2-0	Zizovic (p), Djuric
15/4	Orasje	a	2-1	Biscevic, Zurzinov
22/4	Zeljeznicar Sarajevo	h	1-1	Vasilj
29/4	Sloboda Tuzla	a	1-2	Diarra
6/5	Celik Zenica	h	2-1	Diarra, Smajic
13/5	Modrica Maxima	a	0-3	

Name	Nat	Pos	Aps	(s)	Gls
Rasid AVDIC	SCG	A	10	(3)	5
Aleksandar BAJIC		M		(1)	
Bulend BISCEVIC		M	7	(5)	2
Denis CORIC		M	5	(5)	
Mario COSIC		M	2	(5)	
Rikardo de COSTA	BRA	M	1		
Laminne DIARRA	SEN	M	6	(7)	4
Velibor DJURIC		A	27	(1)	5
Damir DZIDIC		D	11	(2)	
Ivica DZIDIC		D	17		1
Nenad GAGRO		M	20	(2)	1
Admir JOLDIC		A	5	(2)	3
Alvin KARADZA		M	8	(4)	
Kresimir KORDIC		M	11	(2)	5
Teo KRESIC		M	7	(5)	1
Davor LANDEKA		D	27	(2)	
Boris MARIC		M	4	(9)	2
Nikola MARIC		G	7	(1)	
Romeo MITROVIC		G	23		
Sinisa MULINA		M	3	(6)	
Ilija PRODANOVIC		M	8		

Bosnia-Herzegovina

Josip PAPIC		D	7	(4)	2
Demir RAMOVIC	SCG	M	7	(9)	
Ante SEMREN		M	1		
Vladimir SLISKOVIC		A	1	(7)	1
Sulejman SMAJIC		M	28		5
Stanislav VASILJ		M	7	(7)	3
Velimir VIDIC		D	27		1
Mladen ZIZOVIC		M	26	(3)	5
Igor ZURZINOV	SCG	M	17	(2)	1

DOMESTIC CUP 2005/06

1/16 FINALS
(21/9/05)
Odzak 102 0, Siroki Brijeg 3 *(w/o)*
Radnik Bijeljina 2, Igman Konjic 3
Sloga Doboj 0, Modrica Maxima 2
Sloboda Tuzla 0, Zeljeznicar Sarajevo 1
Borac Banja Luka 4, Travnik 0
Celik Zenica 0, SASK Napredak Sarajevo 1
Orasje 3, Velez Mostar 1
Rudar Ugljevik 1, Ljubic 0
Slavija Sarajevo 4, Jedinstvo Bihac 4 *(8-7 on pens)*
Buducnost Banovici 1, Bosna Visoko 0
Rudar Kakanj 3, Vogosca 1
Zrinjski Mostar 5, Kozara Bosanska Gradiska 0
Sarajevo 2, Leotar Trebinje 0
MIS Kresevo 3, Tomislav Tomislavgrad 0
Zepce 7, OFK Tuzla 0
Posusje 3, Jedinstvo Brcko Distrikt 0 *(w/o)*

1/8 FINALS
(19/10/05 & 26/10/05)
Orasje v Buducnost Banovici 2-1; 0-0 *(2-1)*
Siroki Brijeg v Rudar Kakanj 2-0; 0-1 *(2-1)*
MIS Kresevo v Igman Konjic 3-0; 0-1 *(3-1)*
SASK Napredak Sarajevo v Slavija Sarajevo 0-1; 0-4 *(0-5)*
Posusje v Zepce 0-0; 0-1 *(0-1)*
Zrinjski Mostar v Modrica Maxima 3-1; 0-2 *(3-3; Modrica Maxima on away goal)*
Zeljeznicar Sarajevo v Rudar Ugljevik 2-0; 0-1 *(2-1)*
Sarajevo v Borac Banja Luka 4-0; 3-1 *(7-1)*

QUARTER - FINALS
(9/11/05 & 17/11/05)
Sarajevo 1 *(Avdic 68)*, Zeljeznicar Sarajevo 1 *(Alagic 59)*
Zeljeznicar Sarajevo 1 *(Rascic Ad. 42)*, Sarajevo 0 *(abandoned after 50 minutes)*
Zeljeznicar Sarajevo 3, Sarajevo 0 *(w/o)*
(Zeljeznicar Sarajevo 4-1)

Zepce 1 *(Mikelini 40)*, MIS Kresevo 0
MIS Kresevo 2 *(Pavlovic 40, 89)*, Zepce 2 *(Imamovic 43, Niverge 90)*
(Zepce 3-2)

Siroki Brijeg 4 *(Rezic 25, Lukacevic 65, Juricic 89, Landeka 90)*, Slavija Sarajevo 0
Slavija Sarajevo 1 *(Vuksanovic 19p)*, Siroki Brijeg 1 *(Erceg 16)*
(Siroki Brijeg 5-1)

Modrica Maxima 0, Orasje 5 *(Djuric P. 6, Damjanovic 41, Brasnic V. 61, 88, Pejic I. 76)*,
Orasje 1 *(Djuric M. 60)*, Modria Maxima 1 *(Vasic 48)*
(Orasje 6-1)

SEMI-FINALS
(29/3/06 & 12/4/06)
Zeljeznicar Sarajevo 1 *(Zeric 47)*, Siroki Brijeg 0
Siroki Brijeg 2 *(Celson 52, Abramovic 73p)*, Zeljeznicar Sarajevo 0
(Siroki Brijeg 2-1)

Orasje 2 *(Tosunovic 84, 87)*, Zepce 1 *(Imamovic 47)*,
Zepce 1 *(Marcetic 57)*, Orasje 1 *(Miskovic 26)*
(Orasje 3-2)

FINAL
(19/4/06)
Pecara Stadium, Siroki Brijeg
SIROKI BRIJEG 0
ORASJE 0
Referee – *Panic*
SIROKI BRIJEG – Vasilj, Pandza, Anic, Bajkusa, Landeka, Wagner, Bosnjak *(Kovacic 71)*, Galic *(Juricic 46)*, Celson, Lukacevic *(Samic 56)*, Silic.
ORASJE – Kobas L., Miskovic, Klaic, Zivkovic, Brasnic L., Damjanovic *(Kobas S. 60)*, Pejic I., Coskovic, Husic, Tosunovic *(Breskic 88)*, Brasnic V. *(Orsolic 82)*.

(3/05/06)
NC Goal Stadium, Orasje
Referee – *Efendic*
ORASJE 3 *(Pejic I. 54, 90, Kobas S. 78)*
SIROKI BRIJEG 0
ORASJE – Kobas L., Miskovic, Klaic, Zivkovic, Brasnic L., Tosunovic *(Babic 82)*, Coskovic, Pejic I., Husic, Damjanovic *(Kobas S. 46)*, Brasnic V. *(Ristanic 87)*.
SIROKI BRIJEG – Vasilj, Anic, Silic, Rezic, Landeka, Bajkusa, Lukacevic 51), Ronielle, Bosnjak, Celson, Wagner *(Juricic 64)*, Tabi.

(ORASJE 3-0)

SECOND LEVEL FINAL TABLES 2005/06

	Bosnia	Pld	W	D	L	F	A	Pts
1	Velez Mostar	30	19	7	4	52	21	64
2	Rudar Kakanj	30	15	5	10	48	27	50
3	Brotnjo Citluk	30	15	3	12	59	33	48
4	MIS Kresevo	30	15	3	12	42	41	48
5	SASK Napredak	30	14	5	11	38	25	47
6	Troglav Livno	30	13	8	9	45	42	47
7	Gradina Srebrenik	30	14	4	12	58	40	46
8	GOSK Gabela	30	14	4	12	38	29	46
9	Bosna Visoko	30	14	4	12	39	38	46
10	Mramor	30	15	1	14	30	37	46
11	Radnicki Lukavac	30	14	3	13	29	29	45
12	Vitez FIS	30	12	7	11	34	35	43
13	Iskra Bugojno	30	12	6	12	34	33	42
14	Podgrmec Sanski Most	30	9	4	17	30	49	31
15	Olimpik Sarajevo	30	6	7	17	28	48	25
16	Ljubuski	30	3	1	26	9	86	10

	Srpska	Pld	W	D	L	F	A	Pts
1	Borac Banja Luka	30	19	5	6	50	19	62
2	Ljubic Prnjavor	30	16	5	9	45	28	53
3	Drina Zvornik	30	15	5	10	39	28	50
4	Kozara B. Gradiska	30	14	5	11	38	34	47
5	BSK Banja Luka	30	14	5	11	36	34	47
6	Rudar Prijedor	30	14	2	14	36	39	44
7	Sloga Doboj	30	13	4	13	38	32	43
8	Glasinac Sokolac	30	12	7	11	32	28	43
9	Mladost Gacko	30	14	1	15	39	43	43
10	Rudar Ugljevik	30	12	7	11	40	34	43
11	Jedinstvo Brcko	30	11	7	12	38	38	40
12	Sloboda Novi Grad	30	13	1	16	36	51	40
13	Famos Vojkovici	30	11	6	13	34	35	39
14	Laktasi	30	12	3	15	44	48	39
15	Sloga Trn	30	9	7	14	27	37	34
16	Nikos Kambera	30	4	4	22	18	57	16

Bulgaria

Levski lead Euro charge

Bulgaria didn't go to the World Cup. In fact, Hristo Stoichkov's team were eliminated from the running long before their qualifying programme came to an end. But the country did make its mark internationally with a string of impressive performances in the 2005/06 European club competitions.

Although Champions League qualification remained elusive, there were no fewer than three Bulgarian clubs involved at the group phase of the UEFA Cup. Furthermore, two of them – Levski Sofia and Litex Lovech – made it through to the latter stages, with the other – CSKA Sofia – coming excruciatingly close to joining them. Levski continued their fabulous run all the way through to the quarter-finals, becoming the most successful Bulgarian club in Europe since CSKA reached the last eight of the Champions Cup in 1989/90.

It was an outstanding collective effort and one that considerably boosted the country's UEFA coefficient. In all, the four clubs (including Lokomotiv Plovdiv, who exited the UEFA Cup in the first round) played 38 matches – a national record – against opposition from 17 different countries. There were many highlights – CSKA's 1-0 victory at Anfield against Champions League holders Liverpool; Levski posting six successive home wins, the first five of them without conceding a goal; and Litex Lovech reaching the group phase with a fine win in Belgium. The low point, undoubtedly, was Levski's quarter-final home defeat by Schalke – a game totally transformed by an outrageous red card for Levski's French import Cédric Bardon.

Brave fightback

Levski were Bulgaria's team of the season on two fronts. The Sofia Blues regained the championship title from CSKA, so ending a four-year wait, and they did so with a tremendous fightback in the second half of the season. Buoyed by their European exploits, Stanimir Stoilov's side recovered from a seven-point deficit on CSKA at the winter break with such speed and determination that it took them just five games to unseat their city rivals from top spot. The fifth of those games was the head-to-head clash in the Bulgarska Armia stadium, which Levski won with a second-half penalty from ex-Bulgarian international striker Georgi 'Gonzo' Ivanov, who had returned to the club in mid-season from Turkish side Trabzonspor.

Having moved into the driving seat with that win, Levski kept a straight line right through to the finish. The victory over CSKA came slap bang in the middle of a decisive nine-game winning run. The championship was secured with two games to spare after a 2-1 victory at Botev Plovdiv, coupled with a shock defeat by CSKA at struggling Rodopa Smolyan, gave Stoilov's men an unbridgeable eight-point lead.

It was Levski's 24th title, taking them to within six of CSKA's record. With the UEFA Cup run thrown in, it was arguably the most successful season in the club's history. The manner of their championship triumph was also deeply satisfying. The team celebrated in their final home game of the season, against Litex Lovech, with each of the players sporting blue hair and entering the pitch carrying 24 balloons (one for each title).

Thanks to the excellence of coach Stoilov, Levski were a team that amounted to much more than the sum of their parts. There were no star individuals, although veteran utility man Daniel Borimirov, a survivor of Bulgaria's World Cup side at

Bulgaria

USA 94, enjoyed a momentous campaign. Georgi Petkov was an excellent goalkeeper and left-back Elin Topuzakov a fine captain. The team's joint-top scorers, with 11 goals apiece, were Dimitar Telkiyski and Valeri Domovchiyski. The latter, who turned 20 only in May, was the revelation of the season and the key man in the Levski attack during the second half of the campaign. Despite his youth and the fact that he started only half of the league matches, Domovchiyski was voted the Bulgarian A Division's official Player of the Season. With his refined talent on the ball and his cool head, he could be Bulgarian football's next big thing.

Jesic jettisoned

Levski's joy meant misery, of course, for CSKA. The Sofia Reds were irresistible during the autumn, winning 13 of their 14 matches and drawing the other, 1-1 away to Levski. They scored an incredible 53 goals in doing so, and with a seven-point lead at the winter break, they looked near-certainties to retain their title. But after the team's UEFA Cup exit and a three-month winter break during which there was a surprisingly large volume of transfer activity, CSKA's form slipped from the sublime to the ridiculous. They went into the big match against Levski without a win in three games, and after the defeat, CSKA's first at home in almost two years, the club's Serbian coach Miodrag Jesic was sacked – after a year in charge - and replaced by ex-Bulgarian national team boss Plamen Markov.

CSKA won their next two games but they couldn't live with Levski, and a couple of costly draws against Marek Dupnitsa and Cherno More Varna left them with too many points to claw back. The defeat by Rodopa that put the final nail in their coffin – and rescued their opponents from relegation - was partly explained by the fact that Markov's men had a Cup final against Cherno More to play four days later.

Remarkably, CSKA had gone seven years without winning the domestic knockout trophy, and with Cup final defeats in each of the previous two seasons there was a fierce determination at the club to make it third time lucky against the first-time finalists from the Black Sea coast. The outcome was never in doubt after CSKA skipper Emil Gargorov shot his team ahead on 12 minutes. A thunderous strike from the same player made it 2-0 midway through the first half, and soon afterwards the club's Ivorian striker Guillaume Dah Zadi finished the game as a contest with a superb header. Violence erupted at half-time as the two sets of supporters clashed on the Vasil Levski stadium terraces, and those incidents rather overshadowed the remainder of the game, although there was more dismay for the Cherno More fans when Brazilian Daniel Morales missed a penalty and was then sent off before Nigerian striker Masena Moke scored a late consolation, also from the penalty spot.

Markov considered CSKA's Cup final performance the best since he had taken over, and the team went on to win their last two league fixtures and reduce the gap on Levski to just three points. They also finished five points clear of third-placed Litex Lovech, who thus finished one place higher than the previous season. Astutely coached by Ljupko Petrovic, the man who led Red Star Belgrade to European Cup victory in 1991, Lovech finished the season with an 11-match unbeaten run to move ahead of Lokomotiv Sofia. They also possessed the league's joint-top scorer in 16-goal Slovenian striker Milivoje Novakovic. He shared the honour with CSKA's Portuguese striker José Furtado, a mid-season acquisition from Vihren Sandanski (for whom he netted ten of his 16 goals), although both players would probably have had to play second fiddle to the Golden Boot winner of the previous two seasons, Lokomotiv Plovdiv's Martin Kamburov, had he not departed for the Middle East while heading the listings again (on 13 goals) at Christmas.

NATIONAL TEAM RESULTS 2005/06

Date	Opponent	H/A/N	Venue	Score	Scorers
17/8/05	Turkey	H	Sofia	3-1	Berbatov (25, 42), Petrov M. (37)
3/9/05	Sweden (WCQ)	A	Solna	0-3	
7/9/05	Iceland (WCQ)	H	Sofia	3-2	Berbatov (21), Iliev G. (69), Petrov M. (86)
8/10/05	Hungary (WCQ)	H	Sofia	2-0	Berbatov (30), Lazarov (55)
12/10/05	Malta (WCQ)	A	Ta' Qali	1-1	Yankov (67)
12/11/05	Georgia	H	Sofia	6-2	Yankov (2, 28), Berbatov (35, 47), Todorov S. (63, 90p)
16/11/05	Mexico	N	Houston	3-0	Valkanov (4), Bojinov (33), Berbatov (80)
1/3/06	Macedonia	A	Skopje	1-0	Petrov M. (29)
9/5/06	Japan	A	Osaka	2-1	Todorov S. (1), Yanev (90)
11/5/06	Scotland	N	Kobe	1-5	Todorov Y. (26)

Bulgaria

NATIONAL TEAM APPEARANCES 2005/06
Coach – Hristo STOICHKOV

Player	DOB	Club	Tur	SWE	ISL	HUN	MLT	Geo	Mex	Mac	Jpn	Sco	Caps	Goals
Georgi PETKOV	14/3/76	Levski Sofia	G							s46			3	-
Valentin ILIEV	16/9/80	CSKA Sofia	D82	D	D	D	D			D	s46		8	-
Radostin KISHISHEV	30/7/74	Charlton Athletic (ENG)	D	D	D	D	D87			D			63	-
TIAGO SILVA	4/4/79	CSKA Sofia	D										1	-
Elin TOPUZAKOV	5/2/77	Levski Sofia	D	D	D	D	D			D	D	D	23	-
Chavdar YANKOV	6/8/84	Hannover 96 (GER)	M63	M78	M46	M74	M	M		M12			18	4
Blagoi GEORGIEV	21/12/81	Slavia Sofia	M60	M		s62	s63	M57	s85				14	-
Zdravko LAZAROV	20/2/76	Gaziantepspor (TUR)	M	M78	M76	M62	s46	s54	M62				22	2
Martin PETROV	15/1/79	Atlético Madrid	A65	A	A	A	A46	A37	A85	A62	A86	A	59	10
Martin KAMBUROV	13/10/80	Lokomotiv Plovdiv	A71	s78		s46	s87						11	-
Dimitar BERBATOV	30/1/81	Bayer 04 Leverkusen (GER)	A68	A	A	A		A66	A86	A85			49	32
Georgi ILIEV	5/9/81	Lokomotiv Plovdiv /CSKA Sofia	s60	s78	s46	D	D	s37	D	s12	s26	s72	11	1
Emil GARGOROV	15/2/81	CSKA Sofia	s63	s58	M90	s74	M						10	1
Milan KOPRIVAROV	20/7/83	Levski Sofia	s65										1	-
Tsvetan GENKOV	8/2/84	Lokomotiv Sofia	s68		s76			s66	s86	s85		s72	6	-
Asen KARASLAVOV	8/6/80	Slavia Sofia	s71		s90			D	D		s90	D55	9	-
Aleksander TUNCHEV	10/7/81	Lokomotiv Plovdiv	s82					D57	s79				4	-
Dimitar IVANKOV	30/10/75	Kayserispor (TUR)		G	G	G				G46			37	-
Ivailo PETKOV	7/12/75	Ankaragücü (TUR)		D	D					D			63	3
Stilian PETROV	5/7/79	Celtic (SCO)		M	M	M46		A54	A89	M			63	7
Georgi IVANOV	2/7/76	Samsunspor (TUR)		A58									34	4
Mihail VENKOV	28/7/83	Litex Lovech				D	D						4	-
Stoyan KOLEV	3/2/76	Lokomotiv Plovdiv					G	G68	G		G	G71	10	-
Valeri BOJINOV	15/2/86	Fiorentina (ITA)					A63	A56	A	A46			12	2
Daniel BOZHKOV	27/4/83	Botev Plovdiv						D	D	s62			3	-
Nikolai DOMAKINOV	11/7/80	Botev Plovdiv						D	D				2	-
Svetoslav TODOROV	30/8/78	Portsmouth (ENG)						s56	s62	s46	A63	A72	36	7
Yanko VALKANOV	25/7/82	Slavia Sofia						s57	D79				2	1
Kloyan KARADZHINOV	25/1/77	Lokomotiv Sofia						s57					1	-
Yordan LINKOV	26/1/78	Vihren Sandanski						s68					1	-
Marcho DAFCHEV	12/5/78	Lokomotiv Sofia							s89				1	-
Velizar DIMITROV	13/4/79	CSKA Sofia								A46			15	2
Emil ANGELOV	17/6/80	Levski Sofia								s46			1	-
Stanislav ANGELOV	12/4/78	Levski Sofia									D	D	2	-
Zivko MILANOV	15/6/84	Levski Sofia									D	D	2	-
Rosen KIRILOV	4/6/73	Litex Lovech									D	D	51	-
Zoran JANKOVIC	8/2/84	Dalian Shide (CHN)								M26			22	2
Lúcio VAGNER	15/6/76	Levski Sofia								M46			1	-
Dimitar TELKIYSKI	5/5/77	Levski Sofia								M90	M		4	-
Yordan TODOROV	27/7/81	CSKA Sofia									A	A	2	1
Valeri DOMOVCHIYSKI	10/5/86	Levski Sofia									s63	M72	2	-
Hristo YANEV	4/5/79	CSKA Sofia									s86	s55	7	3
Borislav MIHAYLOV	28/8/88	Levski Sofia										s71	1	-

Bulgaria

Assassination

Kamburov's departure was one of many during the winter break from Lokomotiv Plovdiv, a club thrown into turmoil by the assassination, in August 2005, of their popular president Georgi Iliev. He was gunned down in cold blood just after watching his team beat OFK Belgrade to book a place in the first round of the UEFA Cup. Coach Eduard Eranosian, who had led the club to the Bulgarian title in 2004, was sacked by Iliev's widow in early October after a 4-2 defeat at Lokomotiv Sofia. With ex-Bulgarian international midfielder Ayan Sadakov in charge, the team did remarkably well to finish the season in fifth place – albeit 28 points behind champions Levski.

There were two matches fewer than expected during the league season following the early withdrawal of Pirin Blagoevgrad, who, having failed to settle their debts, were excluded after just two games, both of which (defeats by Slavia Sofia and Vihren) were subsequently annulled. Pirin were not to be confused with Pirin 1922, also from Blagoevgrad, who had just been promoted to the top division for the first time. By the end of the season, however, they too found themselves relegated. It was a close call, but a goalless draw on the final day away to their relegation rivals Botev Plovdiv condemned them to join bottom club Naftex Bourgas in the B Division. In a desperate bid for survival Naftex recruited the services of one of Bulgaria's most esteemed coaches, multi-title-winner Georgi Vasilev, but he was unable to save them. Shortly after their relegation was confirmed, Naftex merged with the other Bourgas club, Chernomorets.

Bulgaria's national side ended their 2006 World Cup qualifying campaign with a tame 1-1 draw against Malta. However, they did manage to finish third, well behind dual qualifiers Croatia and Sweden, thanks to a couple of home wins over Iceland and Hungary. Dimitar Berbatov found the net in both of those games, and the pin-up boy of Bulgarian football scored five more times in friendlies during the season to boost his all-time international tally to an impressive 32 goals (in 49 appearanecs), putting him third in the all-time listings just behind his coach, Stoichkov, whose 37 goals came in 83 games. Berbatov, now of Tottenham Hotspur, will be the figurehead of Bulgaria's Euro 2008 qualifying campaign in which they are likely to be challenged strongly by neighbours Romania for a place in Austria/Switzerland alongside group seeds and favourites Holland.

EUROPEAN CUPS 2005/06

UEFA CHAMPIONS LEAGUE

CSKA SOFIA

2nd qualifying round SK TIRANA (ALB)
A 2-0 *Gueye (89), Gargorov (90)*
Hmaruc, Zabavník, Iliev, Gueye, Tiago Silva (Matic 90), Hidiouad, Yanev, Gargorov, Todorov, Sakaliev (Zadi 61), Matko (Dimitrov P. 70).
H 2-0 *Zadi (2), Todorov (90)*
Hmaruc, Zabavník, Iliev (Matic 57), Gueye, Tiago Silva, Todorov, Yanev, Hidiouad, Gargorov (Yurukov 77), Sakaliev (Dimitrov P. 57), Zadi.

3rd qualifying round LIVERPOOL (ENG)
H 1-3 *Dimitrov V. (45)*
Hmaruc, Zabavník, Tiago Silva, Gueye, Matic, Hidiouad, Yanev (Dimitrov P. 35), Gargorov, Dimitrov V. (Sakaliev 58), Zadi (Yordanov 79), Todorov.
A 1-0 *Iliev (14)*
Maksic, Dimitrov V., Zabavník, Zadi (Dimitrov P 84), Iliev, Hidiouad, Yurukov (Sakaliev 71), Gargorov, Tiago Silva, Gueyev, Todorov.

UEFA CUP

LEVSKI SOFIA

2nd qualifying round CMC PUBLIKUM CELJE (SLO)
A 0-1
Petkov, Tomasic, Eromoigbe, Borimirov, Angelov S. (Ivanov 62), Telkiyski, Jayeoba, Vagner, Angelov E. (Ivanov 62), Koprivarov (Yovov 76), Topuzakov.
H 3-0 *Yovov (41, 65), Domovchiyski (69)*
Petkov, Milanov, Tomasic, Eromoigbe (Angelov E. 30; Bukarev 80), Borimirov, Yovov (Domovchiyski 65), Angelov S., Telkiyski, Jayeoba, Vagner, Koprivarov

1st round AJ AUXERRE (FRA)
A 1-2 *Bardon (35)*
Mihaylov, Milanov, Tomasic, Eromoigbe, Borimirov, Domovchiyski, Angelov S. (Koprivarov 69), Telkiyski, Vagner, Bardon (Bukarev 87), Topuzakov.
H 1-0 *Koprivarov (26)*
Petkov, Tomasic, Eromoigbe, Borimirov, Topuzakov Domovchiyski, Angelov S. (Koprivarov 69), Telkiyski, Vagner, Bardon (Bukarev 87), Koprivarov

2nd round Group F
Match 1 DINAMO BUCURESTI (ROM)
H 1-0 *Angelov E. (90)*
Petkov, Milanov, Tomasic, Topuzakov (Angelov S. 67), Vagner, Eromoigbe, Borimirov, Telkiyski, Domovchiyski (Angelov E. 77), Bardon, Koprivarov (Yovov 66).

Match 2 CSKA MOSKVA (RUS)
A 1-2 *Domovchiyski (90)*
Petkov, Milanov, Tomasic, Vagner, Topuzakov, Eromoigbe, Borimirov, Telkiyski (Bukarev 86), Angelov E. (Yovov 64), Domovchiyski, Bardon (Koprivarov 74).

Match 3 OLYMPIQUE MARSEILLE (FRA)
H 1-0 *Yovov (54)*
Petkov, Vagner, Milanov, Tomasic, Eromoigbe, Borimirov, Telkiyski (Bukarev 90), Yovov (Angelov S. 70), Domovchiyski (Angelov E. 59), Bardon.

Match 4 SC HEERENVEEN (HOL)
A 1-2 *Ivanov (52)*
Petkov, Milanov, Eromoigbe, Yovov, Topuzakov, Bukarev, Ivanov (Domovchiyski 69), Angelov S., Telkiyski (Vergilov 89), Vagner, Angelov E. (Koprivarov 82).

3rd round ARTMEDIA BRATISLAVA (SVK)
A 1-0 *Angelov E. (9)*

Bulgaria

Petkov, Topuzakov, Tomasic, Angelov S., Vagner, Eromoigbe, Borimirov, Telkiyski (Koprivarov 71), Yovov (Domovchiyski 86), Bardon, Angelov E.
H 2-0 *Angelov E. (14, 27)*
Petkov, Topuzakov, Tomasic, Angelov S., Vagner, Eromoigbe, Borimirov, Telkiyski, Yovov (Domovchiyski 85), Bardon (Ivanov 88), Angelov E. (Koprivarov 76).

4th round UDINESE (ITA)
A 0-0
Petkov, Milanov, Topuzakov, Eromoigbe, Borimirov, Angelov E. (Domovchiyski 64), Telkiyski, Vagner, Bardon (Hristov 90), Yovov (Bukarev 82), Angelov S.
H 2-1 *Borimirov (51), Tomasic (63)*
Petkov, Tomasic, Eromoigbe, Borimirov, Topuzakov, Angelov S., Telkiyski, Vagner, Bardon (Bukarev 85), Yovov, Angelov E. (Domovchiyski 46)

Quarter-final FC SCHALKE 04 (GER)
H 1-3 *Borimirov (6)*
Petkov, Milanov, Topuzakov, Tomasic, Borimirov, Domovchiyski (Angelov E. 58), Angelov S, Telkiyski (Bukarev 75), Vagner, Yovov (Koprivarov 70), Bardon.
A 1-1 *Angelov E. (24)*
Petkov, Tomasic, Milanov, Borimirov, Hristov (Bukarev 5), Domovchiyski, Angelov S., Koprivarov (Yovov 72), Ivanov M. (Telkiyski 65), Vagner, Angelov E.

LOKOMOTIV PLOVDIV
2nd qualifying round OFK BEOGRAD (SCG)
A 1-2 *Kamburov (55)*
Kolev, Ivanov, Kotev, Jordani, Dimitrov, Petrov, Mihaylov (Jancevski 46), Krizmanic (Halimi 66), Hristev, Stoynev (Zlatinov 46), Kamburov.
H 1-0 *Stoynev (75)*
Kolev, Ivanov, Tunchev, Jordani, Dimitrov, Petrov, Halimi, Jancevski, Vandev (Stoynev 55), Hristev (Georgiev 51), Krizmanic (Iliev 46).

1st round BOLTON WANDERERS (ENG)
A 1-2 *Jancevski (28)*
Kolev, Ivanov, Tunchev, Kotev, Jordani, Dimitrov, Petrov, Halimi (Georgiev 46), Jancevski (Stoynev 90), Iliev (Vandev 80), Krizmanic.
H 1-2 *Iliev (51)*
Kolev, Ivanov, Tunchev, Kotev, Jordani, Dimitrov, Petrov, Jancevski, Vandev (Stoynev 63), Iliev, Krizmanic (Halimi 80).

LITEX LOVECH
2nd qualifying round RIJEKA (CRO)
H 1-0 *Zhelev (83)*
Vutov, Popov (Hazurov B. 72), Cichero, Caillet, Venkov, Berberovic, Jelenkovic, Genchev, Zlatinov (Zhelev 79), Sandrinho (Lyubenov 58), Hazurov K.
A 1-2 *Caillet (44p)*
Gospodinov, Popov, Cichero, Caillet, Venkov, Berberovic, Jelenkovic, Genchev, Zlatinov (Palankov 74), Hazurov B. (Kirilov 89), Sandrinho (Zanev 68).

1st round KRC GENK (BEL)
H 2-2 *Venkov (65), Novakovic (90)*
Vutov, Popov, Cichero, Caillet, Venkov, Berberovic, Jelenkovic, Genchev, Zlatinov, Sandrinho, Novakovic.
A 1-0 *Sandrinho (56)*
Vutov, Popov (Berberovic 60), Cichero, Caillet, Venkov, Kirilov, Jelenkovic, Genchev, Zlatinov (Lyubenov 85), Sandrinho, Novakovic.

2nd round Group D
Match 1 GRASSHOPPER-CLUB ZÜRICH (SUI)
H 2-1 *Novakovic (13), Sandrinho (81)*
Vutov, Popov, Cichero, Caillet, Venkov, Kirilov, Jelenkovic, Genchev (Berberovic 80), Zlatinov (Palankov 86), Novakovic (Lyubenov 89).

Match 2 DNIPRO DNIPROPETROVSK (UKR)
A 2-0 *Novakovic (72), Nazarenko (90og)*
Vutov, Popov, Cichero, Caillet, Venkov, Jelenkovic, Genchev, Zlatinov (Lyubenov 85), Berberovic, Sandrinho (Palankov 90), Novakovic.

Match 3 AZ (HOL)
H 0-2
Vutov, Popov, Cichero, Caillet, Venkov, Genchev (Lyubenov 58), Sandrinho (Manolev 82) Jelenkovic, Zlatinov, Berberovic (Palankov 46), Novakovic.

Match 4 MIDDLESBROUGH (ENG)
A 0-2
Vutov, Cichero, Venkov, Gaillet, Ganchev, Palankov (Kirilov 76), Sandrinho (Hazurov B. 86), Jelenkovic, Zlatinov (Lyubenov 73), Berberovic, Novakovic.

3rd round RC STRASBOURG (FRA)
H 0-2
Vutov, Cichero, Kirilov, Caillet, Zanev, Genchev (Lyubenov 62), Grujic, Zlatinov (Zhelev 80), Sandrinho (Hazurov B. 46), Jelenkovic, Novakovic.
A 0-0
Vutov, Cichero, Kirilov, Zanev, Berberovic, Grujic, Jelenkovic, Palankov (Hazurov B. 83), Popov (Lyubenov 62), Sandrinho (Zlatinov 62), Novakovic.

CSKA SOFIA
1st round BAYER 04 LEVERKUSEN (GER)
A 1-0 *Todorov (15)*
Maksic, Zabavník, Iliev, Gueye, Tiago Silva, Hidiouad, Jakirovic, Gargorov (Sakaliev 90), Todorov (Matic 89), Dimitrov V., Zadi (Yurkov 68).
H 1-0 *Hidiouad (67)*
Maksic, Zabavník, Iliev, Gueye, Tiago Silva, Hidiouad, Jakirovic, Gargorov, Yanev (Zadi 90), Todorov (Yurukov 79), Dimitrov V. (Sakaliev 86).

2nd round Group A
Match 1 HAMBURGER SV (GER)
H 0-1
Maksic, Zabavník, Iliev, Tiago Silva, Gueye, Jakirovic (Zadi 66), Hidiouad, Gargorov, Todorov, Yanev (Sakaliev 66), Dimitrov V. (Yurukov 82).

Match 2 SK SLAVIA PRAHA (CZE)
A 2-4 *Gargorov (10), Sakaliev (58)*
Maksic, Zabavník, Gueye, Yurukuv (Ivanov 46), Tiago Silva, Jakirovic, Todorov, Gargorov, Yanev (Zadi 71), Sakaliev, Dimitrov V. (Matko 90).

Match 3 VIKING FK (NOR)
H 2-0 *Yanev (35p), Zadi (47)*
Maksic, Zabavník, Iliev, Tiago Silva, Gueye, Jakirovic, Todorov (Yurukov 80), Gargorov, Yanev (Branekov 90), Sakaliev (Zadi 45), Dimitrov V..

Match 4 AS MONACO FC (FRA)
A 1-2 *Dimitrov V. (84)*
Maksic, Zabavník, Iliev, Gueye (Yurukov 64), Tiago Silva, Jakirovic, Hidiouad (Branekov 74), Todorov, Gargorov, Yanev (Zadi 23), Dimitrov V..

TOP GOALSCORERS 2005/06

16	José FURTADO (Vihren Sandanski/CSKA Sofia)
	Milivoje NOVAKOVIC (Litex Lovech)
13	Martin KAMBUROV (Lokomotiv Plovdiv)
	Sasa ANTUNOVIC (Lokomotiv Sofia)
11	Valeri DOMOVCHIYSKI (Levski Sofia)
	Tsvetan GENKOV (Lokomotiv Sofia)
	Emil GARGOROV (CSKA Sofia)
	Dimitar TELKIYSKI (Levski Sofia)
10	Guillaume Dah ZADI (CSKA Sofia)
	Stoyko SAKALIEV (CSKA Sofia)

Bulgaria

LEAGUE RESULTS/SCORERS/APPEARANCES/GOALS 2005/06

BELASITSA PETRICH
Coach – Petar Mikhtarski; (3/10/05) (Ilia Karadaliev & Rumen Popov); (11/10/05) Stevica Kuzmanovski (MAC)

2005
Date	Opponent	h/a	Score	Scorers
6/8	Naftex Bourgas	h	2-1	Stoilov, Petrov (p)
14/8	Pirin 1922 Blagoevgrad	a	1-1	Dianu
20/8	CSKA Sofia	h	1-5	Dianu
27/8	Beroe Stara Zagora	a	1-2	Stoilov
17/9	Cherno More Varna	a	0-4	
24/9	Lokomotiv Sofia	h	0-1	
1/10	Rodopa Smolyan	a	1-2	Arnaudov
15/10	Slavia Sofia	h	2-0	Lichkov, Nakov B.
22/10	Vihren Sandanski	a	0-2	
2910	Botev Plovdiv	h	4-1	Daskalov, Stoilov 2, Ivanov (p)
6/11	Litex Lovech	a	1-2	Ivanov
19/11	Marek Dupnitsa	h	1-0	Daskalov
27/11	Lokomotiv Plovdiv	h	1-1	Vavá
4/12	Levski Sofia	a	0-2	

2006
Date	Opponent	h/a	Score	Scorers
4/3	Naftex Bourgas	a	0-0	
11/3	Pirin 1922 Blagoevgrad	h	1-0	Daskalov
19/3	CSKA Sofia	a	2-2	Ivanov, Júlio César
25/3	Beroe Stara Zagora	h	4-0	Marquinhos (p), Ivanov 3
8/4	Cherno More Varna	h	0-0	
15/4	Lokomotiv Sofia	a	1-0	Marquinhos
19/4	Rodopa Smolyan	h	0-1	
23/4	Slavia Sofia	a	0-1	
29/4	Vihren Sandanski	h	2-0	Marquinhos, Ivanov
6/5	Botev Plovdiv	a	0-0	
16/5	Litex Lovech	h	1-2	Dubala
20/5	Marek Dupnitsa	a	3-1	Ivanov, Dubala 2
28/5	Lokomotiv Plovdiv	a	2-1	Ivanov, Dubala
31/5	Levski Sofia	h	2-1	Dubala, Júlio César

No	Name	Nat	Pos	Aps	(s)	Gls
14	Vladimir ARNAUDOV		D	5	(2)	1
13	Fábio BAHIA	BRA	A	5	(3)	
	Daniel CHERVENKOV		M		(1)	
	Marian DAMYANOV		A		(3)	
9	Georgi DASKALOV		A	11	(7)	3
	Cláudio DIANU	BRA	D	24		2
7	Petro DINKOV		D	19	(5)	
2	Claudinel DOS SANTOS	BRA	A	3	(2)	
	Santos DUBALA	BRA	A	11	(2)	5
	Daniel GADZHEV		M		(2)	
12	Kostadin GEORGIEV		G	4	(2)	
1	Ivailo IVANIKOV		G	10		
17	Yuri IVANIKOV		M		(4)	
18	Ventsislav IVANOV		A	23	(2)	9
5	JÚLIO CÉSAR	BRA	A	5		2
19	Vladimir KABRANOV		A	4	(4)	
	Joël KIQI	FRA	D	12	(1)	
10	Svetlan KONDEV		A	6	(4)	
8	Anton KOSTADINOV		D	19	(4)	
4	Anton LICHKOV		D	20	(2)	1
1	Angel MANOLOV		G	14	(1)	
23	António MARQUINHOS	BRA	M	12		3
	Ivo MIHAYLOV		M		(1)	
7	Blagoi NAKOV		D	12	(6)	1

No	Name	Nat	Pos	Aps	(s)	Gls
14	Dimitar NAKOV		M	9	(3)	
5	Dobrin ORLOVSKI		A	11	(1)	
	Ivan PENELOV		D	1		
6	Georgi PETROV		D	22	(1)	1
	Zakiri RAMADAN	MAC	M	10		
	Vangel STOICHEV		M		(1)	
9	Yordan STOILOV		M	17	(3)	4
18	Stefan TODOROV		A	1	(6)	
11	Marcelo VAVÁ	BRA	A	18	(2)	1

BEROE STARA ZAGORA
Coach – Hans Kodric (CRO); (10/11/05) Petko Petkov

2005
Date	Opponent	h/a	Score	Scorers
7/8	Vihren Sandanski	a	1-3	Tanchovski
13/8	Botev Plovdiv	h	2-0	Minchev, Mitev
20/8	Litex Lovech	a	0-1	
27/8	Belasitsa Petrich	h	2-1	Minchev, Dimitrov
10/9	Lokomotiv Plovdiv	a	1-2	Tanchovski
18/9	Levski Sofia	h	4-4	Kwoki 3, Mitev (p)
24/9	Naftex Bourgas	a	0-0	
1/10	Pirin 1922 Blagoevgrad	h	3-0	Kwoki, Tanchovski 2
15/10	CSKA Sofia	a	0-7	
22/10	Marek Dupnitsa	a	0-1	
5/11	Cherno More Varna	a	0-1	
19/11	Lokomotiv Sofia	h	1-2	Kwoki
26/11	Rodopa Smolyan	a	2-2	Kirov, Kwoki
3/12	Slavia Sofia	h	3-2	Dimitrov 2, Mitev (p)

2006
Date	Opponent	h/a	Score	Scorers
4/3	Vihren Sandanski	h	2-1	Dimitrov, Kolev (p)
11/3	Botev Plovdiv	a	2-2	Kolev (p), Dimitrov
18/3	Litex Lovech	h	3-1	Ivanov I., Djeferovic, Dimitrov
25/3	Belasitsa Petrich	a	0-4	
1/4	Lokomotiv Plovdiv	h	1-1	Kolev (p)
9/4	Levski Sofia	a	0-2	
15/4	Naftex Bourgas	h	2-1	Dimitrov, Mitev
19/4	Pirin 1922 Blagoevgrad	a	0-0	
23/4	CSKA Sofia	h	1-4	Dimitrov
29/4	Marek Dupnitsa	h	0-0	
16/5	Cherno More Varna	h	0-4	
20/5	Lokomotiv Sofia	a	1-4	Spisic
28/5	Rodopa Smolyan	h	3-0	Kirov, Mitev 2
31/5	Slavia Sofia	a	2-4	Mitev, Tonchev

No	Name	Nat	Pos	Aps	(s)	Gls
14	BRUNO FERNANDES	POR	D	12		
9	Zahari DIMITROV		A	15	(6)	8
5	Vanja DJEFEROVIC	CRO	D	24		1
20	Marcel ELAME	CMR	D	2		
13	Dino EZE	NGA	A		(1)	
15	Ivo IVANOV		D	22	(1)	1
	Koycho IVANOV		D	6	(3)	
6	Lyudmil KIROV		M	21	(9)	2
3	Peter KOLEV		D	23		3
26	Ivelin KOSTOV		A	3	(9)	
24	Pavel KOVACHEV		D	5	(3)	
19	Isaac KWOKI	GHA	M	24	(1)	6
28	Simeon MINCHEV		M	19	(2)	2
10	Daniel MITEV		A	15	(9)	7
22	Daniel Bekano N'DENE	CMR	G	10	(2)	
27	Eduard RATNIKOV	EST	M	4	(5)	
2	Ivan SPAHIEV		D	24	(2)	
8	Viktor SPISIC	CRO	M	27		1

Bulgaria

FINAL LEAGUE TABLE 2005/06

| | | Pld | \multicolumn{5}{c}{Home} | \multicolumn{5}{c}{Away} | \multicolumn{5}{c}{Total} | Pts |

#	Team	Pld	W	D	L	F	A	W	D	L	F	A	W	D	L	F	A	Pts
1	Levski Sofia	28	12	2	0	44	6	9	3	2	27	17	21	5	2	71	23	68
2	CSKA Sofia	28	11	2	1	43	11	9	3	2	30	11	20	5	3	73	22	65
3	Litex Lovech	28	12	1	1	32	10	6	5	3	19	12	18	6	4	51	22	60
4	Lokomotiv Sofia	28	11	0	3	32	11	7	0	7	17	18	18	0	10	49	29	54
5	Lokomotiv Plovdiv	28	9	1	4	26	15	2	6	6	17	27	11	7	10	43	42	40
6	Belasitsa Petrich	28	8	2	4	21	13	3	4	7	12	20	11	6	11	33	33	39
7	Slavia Sofia	28	9	2	3	22	11	3	1	10	11	23	12	3	13	33	34	39
8	Cherno More Varna	28	7	4	3	17	7	3	3	8	12	20	10	7	11	29	27	37
9	Vihren Sandanski	28	8	2	4	24	21	2	0	12	11	34	10	2	16	35	55	32
10	Beroe Stara Zagora	28	8	3	3	27	21	0	5	9	9	32	8	8	12	36	53	32
11	Marek Dupnitsa	28	7	3	4	18	15	1	4	9	5	22	8	7	13	23	37	31
12	Rodopa Smolyan	28	4	3	7	14	18	3	1	10	9	34	7	4	17	23	52	25
13	Botev Plovdiv	28	4	8	2	14	13	0	4	10	6	25	4	12	12	20	38	24
14	Pirin 1922 Blagoevgrad	28	3	5	6	14	19	2	3	9	9	27	5	8	15	23	46	23
15	Naftex Bourgas	28	3	5	6	6	11	1	1	12	8	32	4	6	18	14	43	18

No	Name	Nat	Pos	Aps	(s)	Gls
1	Stoyan STAVREV		G	18		
29	Ivan TANCHOVSKI		M	18		4
21	Emil TODOROV		A		(5)	
7	Zdravko TODOROV		A	3	(14)	
18	Ivan TONCHEV		A	2	(6)	1
11	Stoian ZHELEV		M	10	(1)	
	Zhelio ZHELEV		M	1	(1)	

BOTEV PLOVDIV
Coach – Yasen Petrov; (Trifon Pachev); (23/1/06) Atanos Marinov

2005
Date	Opp	H/A	Score	Scorers
6/8	CSKA Sofia	h	1-4	Saidhodzha
13/8	Beroe Stara Zagora	a	0-2	
27/8	Cherno More Varna	a	0-2	
11/9	Lokomotiv Sofia	h	1-0	Andonov
17/9	Rodopa Smolyan	a	0-0	
25/9	Slavia Sofia	h	0-0	
1/10	Vihren Sandanski	a	2-3	Vargov, Andonov
15/10	Marek Dupnitsa	h	1-0	Vidolov
23/10	Litex Lovech	h	0-0	
29/10	Belasitsa Petrich	a	1-4	Minev V.
5/11	Lokomotiv Plovdiv	h	1-1	Dimitrov
20/11	Levski Sofia	a	1-4	Andonov
26/11	Naftex Bourgas	h	3-3	Vidolov (p), Kakalov 2
4/12	Pirin 1922 Blagoevgrad	a	0-0	

2006
Date	Opp	H/A	Score	Scorers
5/3	CSKA Sofia	a	0-1	
11/3	Beroe Stara Zagora	h	2-2	Vidolov 2 (1p)
25/3	Cherno More Varna	h	0-0	
1/4	Lokomotiv Sofia	a	0-1	
8/4	Rodopa Smolyan	h	1-0	Minev Y.
15/4	Slavia Sofia	a	1-2	Ivanov
19/4	Vihren Sandanski	h	3-1	Vidolov (p), Kakalov 2
23/4	Marek Dupnitsa	a	0-3	
30/4	Litex Lovech	a	0-2	
6/5	Belasitsa Petrich	h	0-0	
16/5	Lokomotiv Plovdiv	a	0-0	
20/5	Levski Sofia	h	1-2	Andonov
28/5	Naftex Bourgas	a	1-1	Krastev
31/5	Pirin 1922 Blagoevgrad	h	0-0	

No	Name	Nat	Pos	Aps	(s)	Gls
7	Georgi ANDONOV		M	24	(3)	4
	Mauro ANEGRE	BRA	A	2	(3)	
1	Lilcho ARSOV		G	20		
18	Georgi AVRAMOV		M	10	(5)	
	Boris BLAGOIEV		A	1	(4)	
3	Daniel BOZHKOV		D	26		
24	Borislav DIMITROV		A	3	(7)	1
5	Nikolai DOMAKINOV		D	26		
20	Grisha IVANOV		A	2	(7)	
21	Georgi KAKALOV		A	13	(8)	4
23	Borislav KARAMATEV		M	21	(3)	
9	Stefan KOSTADINOV		M	8	(13)	
17	Krasimir KRASTEV		M	7	(5)	1
	Georgi KURTEV		A		(2)	
19	Nedko MILENOV		A	22	(1)	
14	Veselin MINEV		D	25	(1)	1
25	Yordan MINEV		D	26		1
	Dimitar PASHEV		D	4	(3)	
15	Dormushali SAIDHODZHA		A	11	(5)	1
12	Pavel STANEV		G	7	(2)	
	Stefan STOYCHEV		G	1		
	Todor TIMONOV		M	1	(6)	
	Emil URUMOV		A		(3)	
10	Atanas VARGOV		A	10		1
2	Vasil VASILEV		D	12	(1)	
11	Kostadin VIDOLOV		M	26	(1)	5

CHERNO MORE VARNA
Coach – Ilian Iliev; (Krasen Karlev); (21/3/06) Yasen Petrov

2005
Date	Opp	H/A	Score	Scorers
7/8	Rodopa Smolyan	a	1-0	Genchev
13/8	Slavia Sofia	h	1-0	Kostadinov P.
21/8	Vihren Sandanski	a	1-2	Timnev
27/8	Botev Plovdiv	h	2-0	Vachev, Vladimirov
10/9	Litex Lovech	a	2-5	Vachev, Vladimirov
17/9	Belasitsa Petrich	h	4-0	Milosevic, Vladimirov 2, Todorov
24/9	Lokomotiv Plovdiv	a	0-2	
2/10	Levski Sofia	h	0-1	

The European Book of Football 2006/2007 - 223

Bulgaria

15/10	Naftex Bourgas	a	0-1	
22/10	Pirin 1922 Blagoevgrad	h	3-1	Kosturkov, Genchev (p), Georgiev
29/10	CSKA Sofia	a	0-3	
5/11	Beroe Stara Zagora	h	0-0	
26/11	Marek Dupnitsa	a	1-1	Zhekov
2/12	Lokomotiv Sofia	h	0-2	
2006				
4/3	Rodopa Smolyan	h	0-1	
11/3	Slavia Sofia	a	0-1	
18/3	Vihren Sandanski	h	3-1	Kostadinov P., Hristov, Morales (p)
25/3	Botev Plovdiv	a	0-0	
2/4	Litex Lovech	h	1-1	Donigio
8/4	Belasitsa Petrich	a	0-0	
15/4	Lokomotiv Plovdiv	h	0-0	
19/4	Levski Sofia	a	1-3	Zhekov
23/4	Naftex Bourgas	h	1-0	Vladimirov
29/4	Pirin 1922 Blagoevgrad	a	1-0	Alexandrov
6/5	CSKA Sofia	h	0-0	
16/5	Beroe Stara Zagora	a	4-0	Moke, Simov, Vladimirov 2
28/5	Marek Dupnitsa	h	2-0	Moke (p), Zhekov
31/5	Lokomotiv Sofia	a	1-2	Genchev (p)

No	Name	Nat	Pos	Aps	(s)	Gls
15	Alexandar ALEXANDROV		D	20	(1)	1
	Detelin DIMITROV		D	6	(2)	
21	Inzaghi DONIGIO	GBS	M	7	(7)	1
16	Ivan GEORGIEV		M	1	(8)	1
	Dean GENCHEV		M	12	(3)	3
27	Martin HRISTOV		A	11	(8)	1
	Marko ILIC	SCG	M	5	(4)	
	Adilson KASAMA	GUI	M	4	(2)	
1	Krasimir KOLEV		G	15	(1)	
8	Petar KOSTADINOV		D	23	(2)	2
16	Vladimir KOSTADINOV		A	5		
7	Yanko KOSTURKOV		M	13	(7)	1
2	Kuncho KUNCHEV		D	5	(3)	
25	Adelino LOPES	GUY	D	10	(1)	
	MARCOS da Silva	BRA	M	3	(5)	
23	Miroslav MILOSEVIC	SCG	D	20		1
	Konstantin MIRCHEV		M	11	(1)	
19	Masena Mateta MOKE	NGA	A	3	(2)	2
32	Daniel MORALES	BRA	D	8		1
	Atanas PASHKULEV		D		(1)	
22	Ivailo PETROV		G	13		
9	Todor SIMOV		A	9	(4)	1
20	Stanislav STOYANOV		D	21	(2)	
11	Plamen TIMNEV		A	6	(5)	1
	Emil TODOROV		A	10	(3)	1
5	Veselin VACHEV		D	24		2
11	Georgi VLADIMIROV		A	21	(5)	7
14	Slavi ZHEKOV		D	22	(3)	3

CSKA SOFIA
Coach – Miodrag Jesic (SCG); (4/4/06) Plamen Markov

2005				
6/8	Botev Plovdiv	a	4-1	Zadi, Gargorov 2, Sakaliev
14/8	Litex Lovech	h	2-1	Zadi, Hidiouad (p)
20/8	Belasitsa Petrich	a	5-1	Yurukov 2, Todorov, Tiago Silva 2
11/9	Levski Sofia	a	1-1	Dimitrov V.
18/9	Naftex Bourgas	h	3-0	Sakaliev 2, Todorov
24/9	Pirin 1922 Blagoevgrad	a	3-0	Sakaliev 2, Gargorov
2/10	Marek Dupnitsa	a	4-1	Hidiouad (p), Gargorov, Sakaliev, Dimitrov V.
15/10	Beroe Stara Zagora	h	7-0	Hidiouad 3, Zadi 2, Sakaliev, Todorov
26/10	Lokomotiv Plovdiv	h	4-3	Sakaliev, Zabavník, Dimitrov V., Jakirovic
29/10	Cherno More Varna	h	3-0	Gargorov, Yurukov, Dimitrov V.
6/11	Lokomotiv Sofia	a	2-1	Branekov, Tiago Silva (p)
19/11	Rodopa Smolyan	h	7-0	Yanev 2 (2p), Sakaliev 2, Zadi 2, Gargorov
26/11	Slavia Sofia	a	2-1	Zadi, Iliev V.
4/12	Vihren Sandanski	h	6-0	Gueye 2, Zadi, Yanev, Dimitrov V. 2
2006				
5/3	Botev Plovdiv	h	1-0	Hidiouad
12/3	Litex Lovech	a	1-1	Zadi
19/3	Belasitsa Petrich	h	2-2	Furtado, Dimitrov V.
26/3	Lokomotiv Plovdiv	a	0-1	
2/4	Levski Sofia	h	0-1	
9/4	Naftex Bourgas	a	1-0	Gargorov
15/4	Pirin 1922 Blagoevgrad	h	2-0	Furtado, Jakirovic
19/4	Marek Dupnitsa	h	1-1	Furtado
23/4	Beroe Stara Zagora	a	4-1	Trica, Gargorov 2, Furtado
6/5	Cherno More Varna	a	0-0	
16/5	Lokomotiv Sofia	h	3-2	Hidiouad (p), Zadi, Furtado
20/5	Rodopa Smolyan	a	0-1	
28/5	Slavia Sofia	h	2-1	Tiago Silva, Gargorov
31/5	Vihren Sandanski	a	3-1	Tunchev, Furtado, Gargorov

No	Name	Nat	Pos	Aps	(s)	Gls
24	Stoyan ABRASHEV		A		(5)	
16	Alexandar BRANEKOV		D	7	(6)	1
15	Petar DIMITROV		M		(6)	
8	Velizar DIMITROV		M	16	(3)	7
77	José FURTADO	POR	A	5	(9)	6
23	Emil GARGOROV		M	24	(1)	11
34	Daniel GEORGIEV		M	3	(4)	
29	Ibrahima GUEYE	SEN	D	14		2
18	Mourad HIDIOUAD	MAR	M	19		7
31	Evgheni HMARUC	MOL	G	2		
10	Georgi ILIEV		M	11	(2)	
14	Valentin ILIEV		D	23		1
25	Ivan IVANOV		D	5	(1)	
6	Sergej JAKIROVIC	BOS	M	18	(2)	2
5	Kiril KOTEV		D	7		
1	Oliver KOVACEVIC	SCG	G	9		
12	Todor KYUCHUKOV		G	1		
1	Dejan MAKSIC	SCG	G	8		
17	Slavko MATIC	SCG	A	2	(4)	
	Mateja MATKO	CRO	A		(1)	
	Alexandar MLADENOV		A		(1)	
17	Aleksandar MUTAVDZIC	BOS	D	1	(2)	
4	Adrian OLEGOV		D		(3)	
22	Ilko PIRGOV		G	8	(1)	
21	Stoyko SAKALIEV		A	10	(3)	10
27	TIAGO SILVA		D	21		4
30	Yordan TODOROV		D	28		3
19	Eugen TRICA	ROM	A	5	(4)	1
3	Alexandar TUNCHEV		D	10		1
7	Hristo YANEV		M	15	(7)	3
	Evgeni YORDANOV		A	1		
20	Yordan YURUKOV		M	7	(14)	3
2	Radoslav ZABAVNÍK	SVK	D	12		1
11	Guillaume Dah ZADI	CIV	A	16	(5)	10
5	Vladimir ZAFIROV		M		(1)	

Bulgaria

LEVSKI SOFIA
Coach – Stanimir Stoilov

2005

Date	Opponent	H/A	Score	Scorers
7/8	Lokomotiv Plovdiv	a	4-2	Koprivarov, Telkiyski, Borimirov, Jayeoba
14/8	Marek Dupnitsa	a	3-2	Jayeoba 2, Koprivarov
20/8	Naftex Bourgas	h	6-0	Borimirov (p), Yovov 2, Jayeoba 2, Koprivarov
28/8	Pirin 1922 Blagoevgrad	a	1-1	Milanov
11/9	CSKA Sofia	h	1-1	Telkiyski
18/9	Beroe Stara Zagora	a	4-4	Bardon 2, Angelov S., Angelov E.
2/10	Cherno More Varna	a	1-0	Angelov E.
16/10	Lokomotiv Sofia	h	3-1	Domovchiyski 2 (1p), Telkiyski
23/10	Rodopa Smolyan	a	2-1	Koprivarov, Tomasic
28/10	Slavia Sofia	h	5-0	Borimirov 2, Domovchiyski 2, Telkiyski
7/11	Vihren Sandanski	a	2-1	Angelov E., Telkiyski
20/11	Botev Plovdiv	h	4-1	Yovov 2, Bardon (p), Borimirov
4/12	Belasitsa Petrich	h	2-0	Bardon, Domovchiyski
9/12	Litex Lovech	a	0-1	

2006

Date	Opponent	H/A	Score	Scorers
4/3	Lokomotiv Plovdiv	h	4-0	Telkiyski 2, Domovchiyski, Angelov E.
12/3	Marek Dupnitsa	h	2-0	Domovchiyski, Telkiyski
19/3	Naftex Bourgas	a	2-0	Telkiyski, Ivanov Ge.
26/3	Pirin 1922 Blagoevgrad	h	3-0	Ivanov Ge., Angelov E., Domovchiyski
2/4	CSKA Sofia	a	1-0	Ivanov Ge. (p)
9/4	Beroe Stara Zagora	h	2-0	Ivanov Ge., Angelov E.
19/4	Cherno More Varna	h	3-1	Bardon, Borimirov, Angelov S.
23/4	Lokomotiv Sofia	a	2-0	Domovchiyski 2
30/4	Rodopa Smolyan	h	6-1	Borimirov, Bardon, Domovchiyski, Dimitrov 2, Ivanov M.
6/5	Slavia Sofia	a	2-2	Topuzakov, Bardon
16/5	Vihren Sandanski	h	2-0	Borimirov, Telkiyski (p)
20/5	Botev Plovdiv	a	2-1	Ivanov Ge. (p), Borimirov
27/5	Litex Lovech	h	1-1	Telkiyski (p)
31/5	Belasitsa Petrich	a	1-2	Pavlov

No	Name	Nat	Pos	Aps	(s)	Gls
28	Emil ANGELOV		A	11	(10)	6
20	Stanislav ANGELOV		D	19	(3)	2
30	Lachezar BALTANOV		D	1		
27	Cédric BARDON	FRA	A	18	(2)	7
7	Daniel BORIMIROV		M	22		9
13	Asen BUKAREV		M	3	(9)	
19	Georgi CHILIKOV		A		(1)	
24	Nikolai DIMITROV		A	1	(5)	2
17	Valeri DOMOVCHIYSKI		A	14	(10)	11
8	Bogomil DYAKOV		D	9	(1)	
6	Richard EROMOIGBE	NGA	M	26		
17	Galin IVANOV		A		(1)	
9	Georgi IVANOV		A	9	(2)	5
18	Miroslav IVANOV		M	6	(13)	1
23	Egundayo JAYEOBA	NGA	A	1	(2)	5
77	Milan KOPRIVAROV		A	13	(8)	4
88	Nikolai MIHAYLOV		G	5	(1)	
3	Zhivko MILANOV		M	17	(2)	1
16	Marian OGNEANOV		M	1	(2)	
6	Antonio PAVLOV		A		(1)	1
1	Georgi PETKOV		G	23		

14	Cetin SADUA		A		(1)	
2	Todor STOEV		D	1		
5	Borislav STOYCHEV		D		(1)	
21	Dimitar TELKIYSKI		M	25	(1)	11
5	Ivan TODOROV		D	1		
4	Igor TOMASIC	CRO	D	23		1
11	Elin TOPUZAKOV		D	23		1
25	Lúcio VAGNER		D	22	(1)	
	Anton VERGILOV		D		(2)	
10	Hristo YOVOV		A	14	(5)	4

LITEX LOVECH
Coach – Ljupko Petrovic (SCG)

2005

Date	Opponent	H/A	Score	Scorers
6/8	Pirin 1922 Blagoevgrad	h	0-2	
14/8	CSKA Sofia	a	1-2	Popov R.
20/8	Beroe Stara Zagora	h	1-0	Sandrinho
10/9	Cherno More Varna	h	5-2	Caillet, Zlatinov, Sandrinho 2, Novakovic
18/9	Lokomotiv Sofia	a	0-1	
24/9	Rodopa Smolyan	h	3-0	Novakovic, Cichero, Caillet (p)
2/10	Slavia Sofia	a	0-0	
16/10	Vihren Sandanski	h	4-1	Zlatinov, Zhelev, Novakovic, Genchev
23/10	Botev Plovdiv	a	0-0	
29/10	Marek Dupnitsa	h	4-0	Sandrinho 2, Lyubenov (p), Novakovic
6/11	Belasitsa Petrich	h	2-1	Hazurov B., Novakovic
20/11	Lokomotiv Plovdiv	a	2-1	Hazurov B., Zlatinov
4/12	Naftex Bourgas	a	2-0	Hazurov B. 2
9/12	Levski Sofia	h	1-0	Novakovic

2006

Date	Opponent	H/A	Score	Scorers
5/3	Pirin 1922 Blagoevgrad	a	3-1	Novakovic 2, Jelenkovic
12/3	CSKA Sofia	h	1-1	Novakovic
18/3	Beroe Stara Zagora	a	1-3	Novakovic
2/4	Cherno More Varna	a	1-1	Sandrinho
9/4	Lokomotiv Sofia	h	3-1	Zlatinov, Zhelev (p), Popov I.
15/4	Rodopa Smolyan	a	1-0	Zhelev (p)
19/4	Slavia Sofia	h	2-1	Novakovic, Zhelev
23/4	Vihren Sandanski	a	5-1	Sandrinho, Zhelev 2, Novakovic, Popov I.
30/4	Botev Plovdiv	h	2-0	Popov I, Novakovic
6/5	Marek Dupnitsa	a	0-0	
16/5	Belasitsa Petrich	a	2-1	Popov I. 2
20/5	Lokomotiv Plovdiv	h	3-1	Novakovic 2, Zhelev (p)
27/5	Levski Sofia	a	1-1	Novakovic
31/5	Naftex Bourgas	h	1-0	Zhelev

No	Name	Nat	Pos	Aps	(s)	Gls
33	Dzemo BERBEROVIC	BOS	M	20	(4)	
18	Jean-Philippe CAILLET	FRA	D	17	(2)	2
4	Alejandro CICHERO	VEN	D	14		1
7	Stanislav GENCHEV		M	20	(7)	1
22	Yordan GOSPODINOV		G	3	(1)	
21	Vladan GRUJIC	BOS	A	10		
	Borislav HAZUROV		M	4	(14)	4
9	Kostadin HAZUROV		A	2	(4)	
23	Nebojsa JELENKOVIC	SCG	M	26		1
	JOÃOZINHO Correa	BRA	A	1		
6	Rosen KIRILOV		D	19	(1)	
13	Abdelkrim KISSY	MAR	D	1		
	Martin KOVACHEV		D	1		
8	Lyubomir LYUBENOV		M	4	(20)	1
16	Stanislav MANOLEV		A	1	(2)	

Bulgaria

No	Name	Nat	Pos	Aps	(s)	Gls
11	Milivoje NOVAKOVIC	SLO	A	24		16
	Orlin ORLINOV		A		(1)	
28	Todor PALANKOV		M	7	(6)	
32	Ivelin POPOV		A	8	(2)	5
2	Robert POPOV	MAC	D	9	(8)	1
10	Alessandro SANDRINHO	BRA	A	26		7
26	TIAGO SILVA	BRA	D	2	(3)	
12	Todor TODOROV		G	1		
5	Mihail VENKOV		D	12	(1)	
1	Vitomir VUTOV		G	24		
29	Petar ZANEV		D	9	(2)	
3	Zhivko ZHELEV		D	17	(5)	8
24	Petar ZLATINOV		A	26	(1)	4

LOKOMOTIV PLOVDIV
Coach – Eduard Eranosian; (3/10/05) Ayan Sadakov

2005
Date	Opponent	h/a	Score	Scorers
7/8	Levski Sofia	h	2-4	Stoynev, Kamburov M.
14/8	Naftex Bourgas	a	1-1	Halimi
20/8	Pirin 1922 Blagoevgrad	h	3-1	Kamburov M. (p), Vandev 2
10/9	Beroe Stara Zagora	h	2-1	Kamburov M. 2 (1p)
24/9	Cherno More Varna	h	2-0	Kamburov M. 2
2/10	Lokomotiv Sofia	a	2-4	Krizmanic, Kamburov M.
16/10	Rodopa Smolyan	h	3-1	Kamburov M. 2, Iliev G.
23/10	Slavia Sofia	a	1-0	Kamburov M.
26/10	CSKA Sofia	a	3-4	Tunchev 2, Kamburov M.
30/10	Vihren Sandanski	h	2-1	Kamburov M. (p), Iliev G.
5/11	Botev Plovdiv	a	1-1	Kotev
20/11	Litex Lovech	h	1-2	Georgiev D.
27/11	Belasitsa Petrich	a	1-1	Stoynev
4/12	Marek Dupnitsa	h	2-0	Vandev, Kamburov M.

2006
Date	Opponent	h/a	Score	Scorers
4/3	Levski Sofia	a	0-4	
12/3	Naftex Bourgas	h	3-1	og (Krastev), Vandev 2
18/3	Pirin 1922 Blagoevgrad	a	2-3	Halimi, Vandev
26/3	CSKA Sofia	h	1-0	Zlatinov
1/4	Beroe Stara Zagora	a	1-1	Zlatinov
15/4	Cherno More Varna	a	0-0	
18/4	Lokomotiv Sofia	h	1-2	Zlatkovski
23/4	Rodopa Smolyan	a	2-1	Zlatinov, Zlatkovski (p)
29/4	Slavia Sofia	h	3-0	Elame, Vandev, Halimi
6/5	Vihren Sandanski	a	1-1	Zlatkovski
16/5	Botev Plovdiv	h	0-0	
20/5	Litex Lovech	a	1-3	Zlatinski (p)
28/5	Belasitsa Petrich	h	1-2	Zlatkovski
31/5	Marek Dupnitsa	a	1-3	Vandev

No	Name	Nat	Pos	Aps	(s)	Gls
20	Radoslav ANEV		M	5	(6)	
19	Krasimir DIMITROV		M	25		
	Marcel ELAME	CMR	D	10		1
	Dino EZE	NGA	A	1	(6)	
	Daniel GEORGIEV		M	8	(3)	1
21	Mario GEORGIEV		D		(7)	
9	Ilami HALIMI	MAC	M	14	(4)	3
	Nedyalko HUBENOV		A	1		
22	Velko HRISTEV		D	22	(3)	
	Marko ILIC	SCG	M		(1)	
	Dimitar ILIEV		M	4	(7)	
7	Georgi ILIEV		M	12	(1)	2
2	Vladimir IVANOV		D	26		
10	Boban JANCEVSKI	MAC	A	3	(8)	
	Vladimer JORDANI	GEO	D	5	(3)	
11	Martin KAMBUROV		A	12	(1)	13
1	Vasil KAMBUROV		G	9	(1)	

No	Name		Pos	Aps	(s)	Gls
12	Stoyan KOLEV		G	19		
6	Kiril KOTEV		D	13		1
25	Ivan KRIZMANIC	SCG	A	2	(4)	1
16	Atanas KRUSHKOV		D		(1)	
4	Saso LAZAREVSKI	MAC	D	1		
16	Ivo MIHAYLOV		M	1	(2)	
	Dobrin ORLOVSKI		M	10	(2)	
24	Robert PETROV	MAC	D	20		
3	Georgi SAMOKISHEV		D	12	(1)	
13	Metodi STOYNEV		A	10	(1)	2
3	Alexandar TUNCHEV		D	11		2
18	Yavor VANDEV		A	20	(3)	8
	Georgi VELICHKOV		M		(1)	
30	Vladislav ZLATINOV		A	16	(5)	3
15	Hristo ZLATINSKI		M	14	(2)	1
	Zorav ZLATKOVSKI		A	2	(6)	4

LOKOMOTIV SOFIA
Coach – Stefan Grozdanov

2005
Date	Opponent	h/a	Score	Scorers
6/8	Marek Dupnitsa	h	4-0	Orachev, Antunovic 2, Rumenov
13/8	Rodopa Smolyan	h	3-1	Genkov, Antunovic, Dobrev
21/8	Slavia Sofia	a	0-2	
27/8	Vihren Sandanski	h	2-0	Dafchev, Genkov
11/9	Botev Plovdiv	a	0-1	
18/9	Litex Lovech	h	1-0	Trenchev
24/9	Belasitsa Petrica	a	1-0	Rumenov
2/10	Lokomotiv Plovdiv	h	4-2	Antunovic, Genkov 2, Rumenov
16/10	Levski Sofia	a	1-3	Antunovic
22/10	Naftex Bourgas	h	3-0	og (Krastev), Karadzhinov, Kondev
29/10	Pirin 1922 Blagoevgrad	a	2-0	Antunovic 2
6/11	CSKA Sofia	h	1-2	Genkov
19/11	Beroe Stara Zagora	a	2-1	Genkov, Antunovic
3/12	Cherno More Varna	a	2-0	Karadzhinov, Dafchev

2006
Date	Opponent	h/a	Score	Scorers
5/3	Marek Dupnitsa	a	2-0	Antunovic (p), Kondev
11/3	Rodopa Smolyan	a	1-2	Paskov
17/3	Slavia Sofia	h	2-1	Dafchev, Antunovic
25/3	Vihren Sandanski	a	0-2	
1/4	Botev Plovdiv	h	1-0	Dafchev
9/4	Litex Lovech	a	1-3	Dafchev
15/4	Belasitsa Petrica	h	0-1	
18/4	Lokomotiv Plovdiv	a	2-1	Koilov, Karadzhinov
23/4	Levski Sofia	h	0-2	
29/4	Naftex Bourgas	a	1-0	Paskov
6/5	Pirin 1922 Blagoevgrad	h	5-0	Genkov 3, Antunovic, Paskov
16/5	CSKA Sofia	a	2-3	Karadzhinov, Paskov (p)
20/5	Beroe Stara Zagora	h	4-1	Paskov, Antunovic, Genkov 2 (1p)
31/5	Cherno More Varna	h	2-1	Antunovic, Paskov (p)

No	Name	Nat	Pos	Aps	(s)	Gls
14	Sasa ANTUNOVIC	SCG	A	20	(5)	13
30	Dimo ATANASOV		M	10	(6)	
9	Marcho DAFCHEV		A	25		5
11	Kristiyan DOBREV		M	11	(3)	1
3	Dean DONCHEV		D	22		
28	Stefan DONCHEV		D	8	(2)	
8	Tsvetan GENKOV		A	27		11
1	Uros GOLUBOVIC	SCG	G	28		
18	Kaloyan KARADZHINOV		A	25		4

Bulgaria

16	Hristo KOILOV		M	21	(3)	1
23	Boris KONDEV		A	1	(4)	2
20	Hristo MARKOV		M	1	(19)	
17	Malon ORACHEV		M	27		1
24	Ivan PASKOV		A	12	(1)	6
6	Yulian PETKOV		M	11	(4)	
	Svetoslav PETROV		M	3	(7)	
5	Mlen RADUKANOV		D	4	(4)	
22	Stanislav RUMENOV		A	4	(14)	3
19	Darko SAVIC	SCG	D	26		
	Mladen STOEV		A		(2)	
4	Ivo TRENCHEV		D	13		1
	Ivailo TSVETKOV		M		(3)	
4	Yordan VARBANOV		D	9	(1)	

MAREK DUPNITSA
Coach – Rumen Stoyanov; (Sasho Pargov); (22/12/05) Stoyan Kostev

2005
6/8	Lokomotiv Sofia	a	0-4		
14/8	Levski Sofia	h	2-3		Bizhev, Bachev
20/8	Rodopa Smolyan	a	0-0		
27/8	Naftex Bourgas	h	2-0		Petrov, Krastovchev (p)
11/9	Slavia Sofia	a	0-1		
18/9	Pirin 1922 Blagoevgrad	h	0-0		
25/9	Vihren Sandanski	a	2-3		Bizhev 2
2/10	CSKA Sofia	h	1-4		Georgiev D.
15/10	Botev Plovdiv	a	0-1		
22/10	Beroe Stara Zagora	h	1-0		Krastovchev
29/10	Litex Lovech	a	0-4		
19/11	Belasitsa Petrich	a	0-1		
26/11	Cherno More Varna	h	1-1		Iliev
4/12	Lokomotiv Plovdiv	a	0-2		

2006
5/3	Lokomotiv Sofia	h	0-2		
12/3	Levski Sofia	a	0-2		
19/3	Rodopa Smolyan	h	1-0		Georgiev D.
25/3	Naftex Bourgas	a	0-0		
1/4	Slavia Sofia	h	1-0		Kyuchukov Y.
9/4	Pirin 1922 Blagoevgrad	a	2-1		Kyuchukov A., Pargov
15/4	Vihren Sandanski	h	2-1		Kyuchukov A., Pargov
19/4	CSKA Sofia	a	1-1		Mitov
23/4	Botev Plovdiv	h	3-0		Pargov 3
29/4	Beroe Stara Zagora	a	0-0		
6/5	Litex Lovech	h	0-0		
20/5	Belasitsa Petrich	h	1-3		Pargov (p)
28/5	Cherno More Varna	a	0-2		
31/5	Lokomotiv Plovdiv	h	3-1		Karakanov 2, Pargov

No	Name	Nat	Pos	Aps	(s)	Gls
	Ventsislav ALDEV		M	2	(5)	
20	Kemal ALOMEROVIC	MAC	M	3	(6)	
4	Radoslav BACHEV		D	23	(1)	1
	Nikolai BLAGOEV		A	1	(3)	
10	Georgi BIZHEV		A	12	(1)	3
15	Ventsislav BONEV		D	23	(2)	
12	Nikolai CHAVDAROV		G	13	(2)	
14	Stoyan DRAMOV		D	4	(1)	
	Todor HRISTOV		M	2	(2)	
8	Dimitar GEORGIEV		M	17	(9)	2
11	Svetoslav GEORGIEV		D	12	(1)	
7	Ilia ILIEV		M	28		1
3	Velik IRMIEV		D	19	(2)	
13	Radoslav IVANOV		M	19	(1)	
6	Rumen KALCHEV		A	14	(7)	
2	Dimitar KOEMDZHIEV		D	17	(4)	

	Georgi KARAKANOV		M	12	(1)	2
	Enyo KRASTOVCHEV		A	11		2
	Angelo KYUCHUKOV		M	9		2
10	Yanek KYUCHUKOV		D	12		1
5	Dobromir MITOV		D	11	(7)	1
14	Georgi NIKOLOV		D	10	(6)	
9	Ivo PARGOV		A	13	(1)	7
19	Hristo PETROV		A	3	(8)	1
19	Svetoslav RIZOV		A		(5)	
	Ivailo SIMEONOV		M		(1)	
1	Tihomir TODOROV		G	15		
	Veselin VELIKOV		D	3		

NAFTEX BOURGAS
Coach – Ivan Tsvetanov; (30/10/05) (Blagomir Mitrev); (23/11/05) Ivan Kyuchukov; (25/4/06) Georgi Vasilev

2005
6/8	Belasitsa Petrich	a	1-2		Krumov
14/8	Lokomotiv Plovdiv	h	1-1		Krumov
20/8	Levski Sofia	a	0-6		
27/8	Marek Dupnitsa	a	0-2		
10/9	Pirin 1922 Blagoevgrad	h	1-2		Krumov (p)
18/9	CSKA Sofia	a	0-3		
24/9	Beroe Stara Zagora	h	0-0		
15/10	Cherno More Varna	h	1-0		Krastev
22/10	Lokomotiv Sofia	a	0-3		
29/10	Rodopa Smolyan	h	0-1		
5/11	Slavia Sofia	a	0-1		
19/11	Vihren Sandanski	h	1-0		Starokin
26/11	Botev Plovdiv	a	3-3		Todorov 2 (1p), Sarmov
4/12	Litex Lovech	h	0-2		

2006
4/3	Belasitsa Petrich	h	0-0		
12/3	Lokomotiv Plovdiv	a	1-3		Krumov
19/3	Levski Sofia	h	0-2		
25/3	Marek Dupnitsa	h	0-0		
1/4	Pirin 1922 Blagoevgrad	a	0-2		
9/4	CSKA Sofia	h	0-1		
15/4	Beroe Stara Zagora	a	1-2		Abedi
23/4	Cherno More Varna	a	0-0		
29/4	Lokomotiv Sofia	h	0-1		
6/5	Rodopa Smolyan	a	2-1		Todorov (p), Radulovic
16/5	Slavia Sofia	h	1-0		Dzhambazov
20/5	Vihren Sandanski	a	0-2		
28/5	Botev Plovdiv	h	1-1		Dzhambazov
31/5	Litex Lovech	a	0-1		

No	Name	Nat	Pos	Aps	(s)	Gls
	Prince ABEDI	NGA	A	4	(8)	1
	Atanas BORNOSUZOV		M	1		
7	Georgi BOZHILOV		D	5	(5)	
2	Liubomir BOZHINOV		M	5	(6)	
3	Veselin BRANIMIROV		D	11		
1	Ivan CVOROVIC	CRO	G	10		
3	Peycho DELIMINKOV		D		(1)	
6	Kostadin DZHAMBAZOV		D	16	(5)	2
9	Dean HRISTOV		A	4	(9)	
	Boyan ILIEV		D	4		
22	Stoicho KOLEV		M	6	(5)	
23	Nikolai KOSTOV		D	9	(4)	
	Nikolai KRASTEV		D	21		1
25	Plamen KRUMOV		A	14		4
11	Tomás MICA	CZE	M	12	(1)	
	Goran MLADJENOVIC	SCG	D		(1)	
	Dean MOLDOVANOV		D	2		

Bulgaria

No	Name	Nat	Pos	Aps	(s)	Gls
19	Veselin PENEV		D	16	(4)	
26	Zoran RADULOVIC	SCG	A	9	(8)	1
	Georgi SARMOV		A	19	(3)	1
23	Dario SERRA	ITA	M	15	(2)	
12	Svilen SIMEONOV		G	14		
	Hristo SPASOV		A		(1)	
	Orlin STAROKIN		A	9	(10)	1
1	Vladislav STOYANOV		G	4	(1)	
	Plamen TIMNEV		A	6	(1)	
18	Radomir TODOROV		D	27		3
	Marin TSENOV		M	16	(3)	
	Tsvetomir VALERIEV		M	7		
20	Ivelin YANEV		D	1		
13	Kostadin YANEV		D	13		
4	Stanislav ZHEKOV		D	28		

No	Name	Nat	Pos	Aps	(s)	Gls
21	Stanislav MANOLEV		A	10		3
10	Atanas NIKOLOV		A	17	(8)	4
	Vasil OGNEANOV		M	4	(1)	
14	Dimitar PARASKOV		A		(5)	
7	Ivan PAVLOV		M	20	(1)	3
2	Tsvetelin RALCHOVSKI		D	15	(3)	
13	Miroslav RIZOV		M	25	(1)	
19	Petar SHOPOV		A	13		2
1	Lachezar SOTIROV		G	9		
16	Ivan STOYCHEV		M	22	(1)	
19	Stanko STOYCHEV		A	5	(5)	2
9	Pavlin TODOROV		A	13	(7)	4
12	Ilian VASILIEV		G	19		
24	Lyubomir VITANOV		M	12	(8)	

PIRIN 1922 BLAGOEVGRAD
Coach – Boris Nikolov; (23/11/05) Kiril Kachamanov; (9/5/06) Petar Mihtarski

2005
Date	Opponent	h/a	Score	Scorers
6/8	Litex Lovech	a	2-0	og (Cichero), Georgiev A.
14/8	Belasitsa Petrich	h	1-1	Shopov
20/8	Lokomotiv Plovdiv	a	1-3	Georgiev A.
28/8	Levski Sofia	h	1-1	Nikolov
10/9	Naftex Bourgas	a	2-1	Pavlov, Todorov
18/9	Marek Dupnitsa	a	0-0	
24/9	CSKA Sofia	h	0-3	
1/10	Beroe Stara Zagora	a	0-3	
22/10	Cherno More Varna	a	1-3	Shopov
29/10	Lokomotiv Sofia	h	0-2	
5/11	Rodopa Smolyan	a	1-2	Todorov
20/11	Slavia Sofia	h	0-1	
26/11	Vihren Sandanski	a	1-1	Krastev
4/12	Botev Plovdiv	h	0-0	

2006
Date	Opponent	h/a	Score	Scorers
5/3	Litex Lovech	h	1-3	Todorov (p)
11/3	Belasitsa Petrich	a	0-1	
18/3	Lokomotiv Plovdiv	h	3-2	Nikolov, Manolev 2
26/3	Levski Sofia	a	0-3	
1/4	Naftex Bourgas	h	2-0	Pavlov 2
9/4	Marek Dupnitsa	h	1-2	Nikolov
15/4	CSKA Sofia	a	0-2	
19/4	Beroe Stara Zagora	h	0-0	
29/4	Cherno More Varna	h	0-1	
6/5	Lokomotiv Sofia	a	0-5	
16/5	Rodopa Smolyan	h	2-2	Todorov (p), Georgiev G.
20/5	Slavia Sofia	a	1-3	Stoychev S.
28/5	Vihren Sandanski	h	3-1	Manolev, Nikolov, Stoychev S.
31/5	Botev Plovdiv	a	0-0	

No	Name	Nat	Pos	Aps	(s)	Gls
	Blagoi ANDONOV		D	3	(2)	
6	Anton BACHEV		D	16	(6)	
3	Nikolai BODUROV		D	10	(3)	
15	Olgin CHOBAN		A	3	(1)	
18	Svetoslav DYAKOV		D	12		
11	Asen GEORGIEV		A	8	(5)	2
15	Georgi GEORGIEV		D	10	(2)	1
	Svetoslav GEORGIEV		D	11	(1)	
7	Konstantin GERGANCHEV		M	8	(5)	
17	Zdravko IVANOV		M	22	(3)	
8	Konstantin KATSIMERSKI		M	12	(4)	
14	Kiril KRASTEV		M	6	(4)	1
32	Boyan MAKAVEEV		A	3	(3)	

RODOPA SMOLYAN
Coach – Angel Slavkov; (16/4/06) Antoni Zdravkov

2005
Date	Opponent	h/a	Score	Scorers
7/8	Cherno More Varna	h	0-1	
13/8	Lokomotiv Sofia	a	1-3	Staev
20/8	Marek Dupnitsa	h	0-0	
27/8	Slavia Sofia	h	1-3	Peev
11/9	Vihren Sandanski	a	1-2	Rusev
17/9	Botev Plovdiv	h	0-0	
24/9	Litex Lovech	a	0-3	
1/10	Belasitsa Petrich	h	2-1	Kikyov, Chipchev
16/10	Lokomotiv Plovdiv	a	1-3	Rusev
23/10	Levski Sofia	h	1-2	Karamanov
29/10	Naftex Bourgas	a	1-0	Staev
5/11	Pirin 1922 Blagoevgrad	h	2-1	Rusev, Petkov
19/11	CSKA Sofia	a	0-7	
26/11	Beroe Stara Zagora	h	2-2	Rusev, Kikyov (p)

2006
Date	Opponent	h/a	Score	Scorers
4/3	Cherno More Varna	a	1-0	Rusev
11/3	Lokomotiv Sofia	h	2-1	Peev, Dimitrov
19/3	Marek Dupnitsa	a	0-1	
26/3	Slavia Sofia	a	0-3	
1/4	Vihren Sandanski	h	1-2	Rusev (p)
8/4	Botev Plovdiv	a	0-1	
15/4	Litex Lovech	h	0-1	
19/4	Belasitsa Petrich	a	1-0	og (Nakov)
23/4	Lokomotiv Plovdiv	h	1-2	Rusev
30/4	Levski Sofia	A	1-6	Lyaskov
6/5	Naftex Bourgas	h	1-2	Rusev (p)
16/5	Pirin 1922 Blagoevgrad	a	2-2	Chipchev, Peev
20/5	CSKA Sofia	h	1-0	Peev
28/5	Beroe Stara Zagora	a	0-3	

No	Name	Nat	Pos	Aps	(s)	Gls
	Lyubomir BOZHANKOV		M	8	(2)	
	Valentin CHAUSHEV		D		(1)	
1	Zdravko CHAVDAROV		G	10	(2)	
18	Filip CHIPCHEV		A	4	(10)	2
9	Dimitar DAMIANOV		M	4	(7)	
9	Borislav DIMITROV		A	9	(3)	1
3	Martin DIMOV		D	20		
21	Vladimir DRAMANLIEV		A	1	(2)	
6	Kostadin DYAKOV		D	11	(5)	
8	Kiril DZHOROV		M	21		
	Atanas FIDANIN		D	2	(1)	
15	Ivan KARAMANOV		M	10	(6)	1
	Lyubomir KEKHAIOV		A		(1)	
5	Atanas KIKYOV		D	9	(2)	2
	Georgi KURTEV		A	2	(2)	
20	Mihail LAZAROV		D	26	(1)	

Bulgaria

No	Name		Nat	Pos	Aps	(s)	Gls
16	Atanas LYASKOV			M	3	(6)	1
	Dimitar MUTAFOV			D	12	(1)	
4	Lyuben NIKOLOV			D	4	(7)	
10	Daniel PEEV			M	16	(8)	4
21	Emil PETKOV			M	25	(1)	1
11	Desislav RUSEV			A	27		8
19	Kalin SHTARKOV			M	2	(5)	
19	Simeon STEREV			A	1	(4)	
14	Todor SIMEONOV			D	24		
7	Hristo STAEV			A	21		2
	Dimitar TSENOVSKI			A	4	(4)	
4	Yavor VALCHINOV			D	5	(2)	
26	Vasil VASILIEV			G	18		
	Anton VERGILOV			D	9		

SLAVIA SOFIA
Coach – Petar Hubchev; (10/11/05) Aliosha Andonov

2005
13/8	Cherno More Varna	a	0-1	
21/8	Lokomotiv Sofia	h	2-0	Kolev T., Rangelov D.
27/8	Rodopa Smolyan	a	3-1	Speranza, Georgiev, Kolev T.
11/9	Marek Dupnitsa	h	1-0	Kolev T.
17/9	Vihren Sandanski	h	1-2	Gjocevski
25/9	Botev Plovdiv	a	0-0	
2/10	Litex Lovech	h	0-0	
15/10	Belasitsa Petrich	a	0-2	
23/10	Lokomotiv Plovdiv	h	0-1	
28/10	Levski Sofia	a	0-5	
5/11	Naftex Bourgas	h	1-0	Georgiev
20/11	Pirin 1922 Blagoevgrad	a	1-0	Rangelov D.
26/11	CSKA Sofia	h	1-2	Ivanovic
3/12	Beroe Stara Zagora	a	2-3	Georgiev, Rangelov R. (p)

2006
11/3	Cherno More Varna	h	1-0	Ivanovic
17/3	Lokomotiv Sofia	a	1-2	og (Genkov)
26/3	Rodopa Smolyan	h	3-0	Rangelov D., Kolev T. 2
1/4	Marek Dupnitsa	a	0-1	
9/4	Vihren Sandanski	a	2-0	Kolev T. 2 (1p)
15/4	Botev Plovdiv	h	2-1	Rangelov D., Kolev T.
19/4	Litex Lovech	a	1-2	og (Genchev)
23/4	Belasitsa Petrich	h	1-0	Petkov
29/4	Lokomotiv Plovdiv	a	0-3	
6/5	Levski Sofia	h	2-2	Valkanov, Kyumyurdzhiev
16/5	Naftex Bourgas	a	0-1	
20/5	Pirin 1922 Blagoevgrad	h	3-1	Rangelov D. 2 (1p), Valkanov
28/5	CSKA Sofia	a	1-2	Stefanov D.
31/5	Beroe Stara Zagora	h	4-2	Stoykov, Pavlov 2, Kerchev

No	Name	Nat	Pos	Aps	(s)	Gls
1	Armen AMBARTSUMYAN	ARM	G	23		
	Ignat DAMIANOV		A	1	(1)	
11	Tanko DYAKOV		M	9	(6)	
	Blagoi GEORGIEV		M	14		3
	Baldo DI GREGORIO	ITA	M	1	(4)	
21	Daniel GJOCEVSKI	MAC	D		(12)	1
	Nikolai HARIZANOV		D	1	(4)	
23	Velimir IVANOVIC	SCG	M	5	(2)	2
6	Asen KARASLAKOV		D	26		
17	Martin KERCHEV		A	7	(3)	1
	Petar KOLEV		M		(2)	
10	Todor KOLEV		A	25	(1)	8
	Dimitar KRASTEV		M	1		
3	Petar KYUMYURDZHIEV		D	22	(2)	1
25	Georgi MECHEDZHIEV		M	18		

No	Name		Nat	Pos	Aps	(s)	Gls
20	Ivan NAIDENOV			M	1	(2)	
	Borislav PAVLOV			D	3	(5)	2
24	Yordan PETKOV			D	11		1
	Emil PETROV			D		(1)	
9	Dimitar RANGELOV			A	24		6
4	Radoslav RANGELOV			M	21	(2)	1
8	Giovanni SPERANZA		GER	M	23	(2)	1
26	Dimitar STEFANOV			D	5	(3)	1
27	Martin STEFANOV			A	3	(11)	
18	Angel STOYKOV			D	27		1
	Slavcho TOSHEV			G	5	(1)	
16	Ilian TRIFONOV			M	10	(4)	
	Ivailo TSVETKOV			D		(1)	
5	Yanko VALKANOV			D	22	(3)	2
19	Dimitar VODENICHAROV			A		(3)	

VIHREN SANDANSKI
Coach – Georgi Bachev; (9/11/05) (Kiril Vangelov); (23/1/06) Petar Zhekov

2005
7/8	Beroe Stara Zagora	h	3-1	Sofroniev, Furtado, Bachev
21/8	Cherno More Varna	h	2-1	Bachev, Furtado
27/8	Lokomotiv Sofia	a	0-2	
11/9	Rodopa Smolyan	h	2-1	Bachev 2 (1p)
17/9	Slavia Sofia	a	2-1	Furtado 2
25/9	Marek Dupnitsa	h	3-2	Furtado, Bachev, Simonovic
1/10	Botev Plovdiv	h	3-2	Simonovic, Furtado 2
16/10	Litex Lovech	a	1-4	Simonovic
22/10	Belasitsa Petrich	h	2-0	Bachev, Furtado
30/10	Lokomotiv Plovdiv	a	1-2	Furtado
7/11	Levski Sofia	h	1-2	Sofroniev
19/11	Naftex Bourgas	a	0-1	
26/11	Pirin 1922 Blagoevgrad	h	1-1	Furtado
4/12	CSKA Sofia	a	0-6	

2006
4/3	Beroe Stara Zagora	a	1-2	Stoynev
18/3	Cherno More Varna	a	1-3	Stoynev
25/3	Lokomotiv Sofia	h	2-0	Bachev, Ododji
1/4	Rodopa Smolyan	a	2-1	Stoynev, Simonovic
9/4	Slavia Sofia	h	0-2	
15/4	Marek Dupnitsa	a	1-2	Simonovic
19/4	Botev Plovdiv	a	1-3	Simonovic (p)
23/4	Litex Lovech	h	1-5	Ododji (p)
29/4	Belasitsa Petrich	a	0-2	
6/5	Lokomotiv Plovdiv	h	1-1	Stoynev
16/5	Levski Sofia	a	0-2	
20/5	Naftex Bourgas	h	2-0	Serginho, Ododji
28/5	Pirin 1922 Blagoevgrad	a	1-3	Ododji
31/5	CSKA Sofia	h	1-3	Stoynev

No	Name	Nat	Pos	Aps	(s)	Gls
	Marian ANDONOV	MAC	M		(5)	
	Kiril ANDREEV		M	3	(6)	
	Nuno Miguel ALMEIDA	POR	D	16	(3)	
	Georgi BACHEV		A	20	(1)	7
	Youssef Omar BELO	NGA	G	6		
23	Rumen BOSILKOV		M	2	(4)	
5	Zoran CVETKOVIC	SCG	D	21		
	Alessandro DOS SANTOS	BRA	A		(2)	
	José FURTADO	POR	A	12		10
	Valentin GEORGIEV		D	10	(2)	
	Slavko GEORGIEVSKI	MAC	A	10		
33	Stanimir GOSPODINOV		D	15	(3)	
21	Krasimir IVANOV		A	3	(5)	
6	Yuri IVANOV		M	1	(8)	

Bulgaria

77	Yordan LINKOV		G	16	(3)	
26	Marko MARKOV		A	12	(14)	
	Vedran MURATOVIC	CRO	A		(1)	
1	Shaloze ODODJI	NGA	A	21	(3)	4
	SEMEDO	POR	A	2	(4)	
9	SERGINHO	POR	A	22	(2)	1
	Georgi SHEITANOV		G	6	(1)	
28	Bruno SIKLIC	CRO	M	19	(1)	
15	Sasa SIMONOVIC	SCG	A	19	(1)	6
17	Victor SOFRONIEV		A	26		2
	Metodi STOYNEV		A	13		5
18	Emil TRENKOV		D	23	(2)	
	Marko VUKOJEVIC	CRO	D	1		
16	Tsvetan ZAREV		D	9	(4)	

DOMESTIC CUP 2005/06

FOURTH ROUND
(6/11/05)
Spartak Pleven 4, Spartak–S94 Plovdiv 1
Mynior Pernik 0, Beroe Stara Zagora 2
Arkus Lyaskovats 2, Pirin Gotse Delchev 0
Rilski Sportist Samokov 1, Slavia Sofia 0
Chernomorets Bourgas 1, Naftex Bourgas 1 *(aet; 3-4 on pens)*
Lokomotiv Plovdiv 1, Marek Dupnitsa 2
Pirin 1922 Blagoevgrad 2, Lokomotiv Sofia 1
Vadima-Rakovski Sevlievo 4, Minyor Bobov Dol 0
Nesebar 0, Rodopa Smolyan 2 (aet)
Yantra Gabrovo 0, AKB Minyor Radnevo 1
(10/11/05)
Koneliano German 0, Litex Lovech 2
Pomorie 0, Shumen 2001 0 *(aet; 4-5 on pens)*
(11/11/05)
Belasitsa Petrich 1, CSKA Sofia 2
Haskovo 0, Levski Sofia 2
(30/11/05)
Botev Plovdiv 1, Vihren Sandanski 1 *(aet; 2-3 on pens)*
Bye - Cherno More Varna

FIFTH ROUND
(10/12/05)
Arkus Lyaskovats 0, Naftex Bourgas 4
Rodopa Smolyan 0, Pirin 1922 Blagoevgrad 2 *(aet)*
Vadima-Rakovski Sevlievo 0, Beroe Stara Zagora 1 *(aet)*
Shumen 2001 3, Spartak Pleven 0
Rilski Sportist Samokov 5, AKB Minyor Radnevo 0
(14/12/05)
Vihren Sandanski 2, Marek Dupnitsa 1
(22/3/06)
CSKA Sofia 1, Litex Lovech 0
Cherno More Varna 3, Levski Sofia 2 *(aet)*

QUARTER-FINALS
(12/4/06)
Prin 1922 Blagoevgrad 1 *(Nikolov 52)*, Naftex Bourgas 1 *(Krastev 87)* *(aet; 3-4 on pens)*
CSKA Sofia 4 *(Tunchev 11, Trica 37, Hidiouad 56, Todorov 90)*, Beroe Stara Zagora 1 *(Todorov 67)*
Shumen 2001 2 *(Hrystyanov 56, 104p)*, Rilski Sportist Samokov 1 *(Adzhov 84)* *(aet)*
Vihren Sandanski 0, Cherno More Varna 2 *(Georgiev G. 98, 115)* *(aet)*

SEMI-FINALS
(3/5/06)
Shumen 2001 1 *(Hrystyanov 26)*, Cherno More Varna 2 *(Moke 11, Kostadinov 95)* *(aet)*
CSKA Sofia 4 *(Gargorov 45, Tiago Silva 52, Trica 61, Hidiouad 88)*, Naftex Bourgas 1 *(Serra 43)*

FINAL
(24/5/06)
Vasil Levski National Stadium, Sofia
CSKA SOFIA 3 *(Gargorov 12, 28, Zadi 35)*
CHERNO MORE VARNA 1 *(Moke 90p)*
Referee – *Rodríguez (ESP)*
CSKA SOFIA – Pirgov, Tunchev, Kotev *(Ivanov 61)*, Jakirovic *(Iliev G. 80)*, Dimitrov V. *(Yanev 76)*, Zadi, Iliev V., Hidiouad, Gargorov, Tiago Silva, Trica.
CHERNO MORE VARNA – Kolev, Lopes, Vachev, Stoyanov, Milosevic, Donigio *(Hristov 70)*, Morales, Zhekov, Kostadinov P. *(Kostadinov V. 63)*, Moke, Georgiev.
Sent off: Morales *(81)*.

SECOND LEVEL FINAL TABLES 2005/06

WEST		Pld	W	D	L	F	A	Pts
1	Rilski sportist Samokov	26	20	3	3	54	25	63
2	Conegliano German	26	19	5	2	54	15	62
3	Spartak Pleven	26	19	2	5	58	18	59
4	Vidima-Rakovski Sevlievo	26	12	7	7	39	26	43
5	Beli orli Pleven	26	11	5	10	34	32	38
6	Pirin Gotse Delchev	26	10	6	10	39	27	36
7	Hebar Pazardzhik	26	10	3	13	35	35	33
8	Etar 1924 Veilko Tranovo	26	9	3	14	31	39	30
9	Minior Bobov dol	26	8	5	13	34	37	29
10	Lokomotiv Mezdra	26	7	6	13	25	46	27
11	Montana	26	6	8	12	23	47	26
12	Minior Pernik	26	6	6	14	25	43	24
13	Yantra Gabrovo	26	5	7	14	23	52	22
14	Balkan Botevgrad	26	5	4	17	11	43	19

EAST		Pld	W	D	L	F	A	Pts
1	Spartak Varna	26	17	5	4	34	12	56
2	Maritsa 1921 Plovdiv	26	14	7	5	41	21	49
3	Haskovo	26	15	3	8	37	19	48
4	Spartak-s94 Plovdiv	26	12	7	7	32	26	43
5	AKB Minior Radnevo	26	11	6	9	30	32	39
6	Dunav Ruse	26	10	6	10	27	35	36
7	Shumen 2001	26	10	4	12	32	33	34
8	Nesebar	26	10	4	12	37	37	34
9	Dobrudzha Dobrich	26	10	4	12	27	26	34
10	Kaliakra Kavarna	26	9	5	12	27	36	32
11	Svetkavista Targovishte	26	8	7	11	26	26	31
12	Sliven 2000	26	9	4	13	22	30	31
13	Pomorie	26	6	6	14	22	38	24
14	Zagorets Nova Zagora	26	3	8	15	21	44	17

PROMOTION PLAY-OFF
(7/6/06)
Conegliano German 3, Maritsa 1921 Plovdiv 2

Croatia

Unfulfilled expectations

Maybe there was too much expectation, too much complacency. Croatia travelled to Germany for the World Cup finals with high hopes, but as in 2002 they flew home after just three matches. They failed to win any of them. Gallantly beaten 1-0 by pre-tournament favourites Brazil in Berlin, they missed a penalty in a 0-0 draw against Japan in Nuremberg and were eventually made to pay for sloppy defending and indiscipline in a dramatic 2-2 draw against Australia in Stuttgart.

With Euro 2004 thrown into the mix, it was the third major tournament in which Croatia had failed to progress beyond their opening group. There was enormous disappointment for the thousands of fans who had followed the team across Germany and the millions back home. Things had looked very promising when Zlatko Kranjcar's side completed their qualifying campaign unbeaten, topping Group Eight after doing the double over Sweden. A memorable 3-2 victory over Argentina in Basle inevitably heightened the mood of optimism, but when the Kovac brothers, Niko and Robert, rashly predicted that they would be contesting the final in their native Berlin, the bonfire of expectancy was suddenly raging out of control.

The team did not play badly in any of their three games, yet they didn't play particularly well either. They scored only two goals, and one of those – Niko Kovac's against Australia – was purely down to atrocious goalkeeping. All three strikers – Dado Prso, Ivan Klasnic and Ivica Olic – were either out of form or out of their depth, while the manager's son, Niko Kranjcar, did precious little to justify his reputation as the 'new Zvonimir Boban'.

Star man Srna

The team's most threatening player going forward was right wing-back Darijo Srna. Although he had a penalty saved against Japan, the Shakhtar Donetsk player scored a terrific free-kick to open the scoring against Australia and was a bundle of energy and set-piece creativity in every game. On the other flank Marko Babic had a fine game against Brazil but did little thereafter, while the three central defenders and midfield anchorman Igor Tudor all sullied their reputations for one reason or another in the final game against Australia. The team's most consistent defender was goalkeeper Stipe Pletikosa, who justified his selection ahead of Tomislav Butina, the regular

NATIONAL TEAM RESULTS 2005/06

17/8/05	Brazil	H	Split	1-1	Kranjcar (32)
3/9/05	Iceland (WCQ)	A	Reykjavík	3-1	Balaban (56, 61), Srna (82p)
7/9/05	Malta (WCQ)	A	Ta' Qali	1-1	Kranjcar (19)
8/10/05	Sweden (WCQ)	H	Zagreb	1-0	Srna (56p)
12/10/05	Hungary (WCQ)	A	Budapest	0-0	
12/11/05	Portugal	A	Coimbra	0-2	
29/1/06	South Korea	N	Hong Kong	0-2	
1/2/06	Hong Kong	A	Hong Kong	4-0	Knezevic (15), Leko J. (30), Eduardo (64), Bosnjak (71)
1/3/06	Argentina	N	Basle	3-2	Klasnic (3), Srna (52), Simic (90)
23/5/06	Austria	A	Vienna	4-1	Klasnic (11, 35), Babic (55), Balaban (69)
28/5/06	Iran	H	Osijek	2-2	Prso (31), Babic (90p)
3/6/06	Poland	N	Wolfsburg	0-1	
7/6/06	Spain	N	Geneva	1-2	Pablo (15og)
13/6/06	Brazil (WCF)	N	Berlin	0-1	
18/6/06	Japan (WCF)	N	Nuremberg	0-0	
22/6/06	Australia (WCF)	N	Stuttgart	2-2	Srna (2), Kovac N. (56)

Croatia

custodian during the qualifying campaign.

Dario Simic, who became Croatia's most-capped international during the tournament, overtaking Robert Jarni's total of 81, has now withdrawn his services, and striker Prso, Croatia's Footballer of the Year for the past three seasons, has decided to follow suit. Whether that diminishes Croatia's chances of making it six major tournament qualifications out of seven as they strive to reach Euro 2008 remains to be seen, but one thing is certain. Zlatko Kranjcar will not have the opportunity to redeem himself in Austria and Switzerland. He was sacked in mid-July by the executive committee of the Croatian Football Federation and replaced by Slaven Bilic.

Dario Simic – a man with more Croatian caps than anyone else

Despite the disappointment of Germany 2006, the Croatian public will continue to show passionate support for those wearing the red and white checked shirts. There is nothing else that quite unites the nation. The domestic game has now become so bereft of quality that in the summer of 2005 all three of Croatia's European representatives – and there are only three these days – were eliminated after just one qualifying round tie.

Hajduk humiliation

While Rijeka and Inter Zapresic came a cropper in the UEFA Cup, the most humiliating exit was that of Hajduk Split, who suffered the worst aggregate defeat in their 40-year European history when they followed up a 3-0 first-leg defeat away to Hungarian champions Debrecen by losing the return leg 5-0 in Split.

It was the second year in a row that Hajduk's Champions League campaign had hit the buffers in the second qualifying round, but whereas a year earlier the club had taken positives out of their shock early exit against Shelbourne and gone on to make a successful defence of the domestic league title, in 2005/06 the team were psychologically beyond repair. Miroslav Blazevic, the veteran coach who had led Croatia to third place at the 1998 World Cup, was Hajduk's man in charge for the Debrecen debacle. Only just recruited from Varteks Varazdin, he offered to resign but was absolved of blame and asked to stay on. Within a few weeks, though, after a run of four league games without a win, Blazevic was duly dismissed and replaced by ex-club legend Ivan Gudelj.

Hajduk's season would never get going. Despite the playmaking talent of Niko Kranjcar and the return to the club, on a year's loan, of goalkeeper Pletikosa, the Dalmatians were never in with a chance of winning a third successive title. In fact, as the weeks went by with no sign of improvement, their chief objective was simply to qualify for the top group after the 22-match split. They made it, by a single point, but not before another new coach had been appointed, Gudelj making away for Luka Bonacic (in charge once before, in the 1997/98 season) after a home defeat to arch-rivals Dinamo Zagreb in a match held over until the start of the spring campaign.

Bonacic was very open and honest about Hajduk's shortcomings, but a month into his reign he was

Croatia

NATIONAL TEAM APPEARANCES 2005/06

Coach – Zlatko KRANJCAR

Player	DOB	Club	Bra	ISL	MLT	SWE	HUN	Por	Kor	Hkg	Arg	Aut	Irn	Pol	Esp	BRA	JPN	AUS	Caps	Goals
Tomislav BUTINA	30/3/74	Club Brugge KV (BEL)	G46		G	G	G							G					28	-
Stjepan TOMAS	6/3/76	Galatasaray (TUR)	D46		D	D	D				D46	D	D46					D	49	1
Robert KOVAC	6/4/74	Juventus (ITA)	D	D		D	D	D46				D61	D	D	D46	D	D		58	-
Josip SIMUNIC	18/2/78	Hertha BSC (GER)	D	D	D	D		D						D	D85	D	D	D	45	3
Darijo SRNA	1/5/82	Shakhtar D'sk (UKR)	M	M	M	M	M	M46			M	M70	M64	M46		M	M87	M	39	10
Igor TUDOR	16/4/78	Siena (ITA)	M	M		D	M				D	D	M46		M	M	M70	M	55	3
Niko KOVAC	15/10/71	Hertha BSC (GER)	M87	M	M	M		M			M82	M57	M23		M67	M40	M	M	61	9
Marko BABIC	28/1/81	B Leverkusen (GER)	M	M	M	M					M	M	M	M	M	M	M	M	36	3
Niko KRANJCAR	13/8/84	Hajduk Split	M83	M	M	M		M	M	M	M90	M	M	M46	M70	M	M78	M65	24	3
Ivan KLASNIC	29/1/80	Werder Bremen (GER)	A78		s80	A70	A63				A75	A46	A75	A	A89	A57	A		22	7
Ivica OLIC	14/9/79	CSKA Moskva (RUS)	A51						s75		s46	s58	A46			s57	s70	A73	39	6
Stipe PLETIKOSA	8/1/79	Shakhtar D'sk (UKR) /Hajduk Split	s46	G	G						G	G46	G		G	G	G	G	53	-
Dario SIMIC	12/11/75	Milan (ITA)	s46	D	D80	s90	s90		D	D	D	D87	D	D	D	D	D		83	3
EDUARDO da Silva	25/2/83	Dinamo Zagreb	s51					A	A83										5	1
Bosko BALABAN	15/10/78	Club Brugge KV (BEL)	s78	A	A68		A	A77				s57	s75	s73	s89				28	8
Anthony SERIC	15/1/79	Panathinaikos (GRE)	s83		M68														14	-
Jurica VRANJES	31/1/80	Werder Bremen (GER)	s87				M						s23	M63	s67				24	-
Dado PRSO	5/11/74	Rangers (SCO)		A84	A	A90	A				A90	A57	A58		A76	A	A	A	32	9
Ivan BOSNJAK	6/9/79	Dinamo Zagreb		s84	s68	s70	s63/90	s46	M	M				s46	s76		s87		14	1
Mario TOKIC	23/7/75	FK Austria Wien (AUT)		D		D		s46	D	D	s46	s61	s46	s87	s85				28	-
Jerko LEKO	9/4/80	Dynamo Kyiv (UKR)			s68		s63	M	M	M	s82	s70	s64	s63	M	s40		s65	38	2
Ivan LEKO	7/2/78	Club Brugge KV (BEL)				M63	s77				s84			s46	s70				13	-
Joey DIDULICA	14/9/77	FK Austria Wien (AUT)						G	G46		s46								4	-
Vedran JESE	3/2/81	Inter Zapresic						D70	s83										2	-
Mato NERETLJAK	3/6/79	Suwon Samsung (KOR)						D	D46										10	1
Josip BALATINAC	7/3/79	Osijek						M46											1	-
Leon BENKO	11/11/83	Varteks Varazdin						A	A69										2	-
Davor VUGRINEC	24/3/75	Rijeka						A70	s46										27	7
Mladen PETRIC	1/1/81	FC Basel (SUI)						s46		s90									7	1
Neven VUKMAN	14/10/85	Varteks Varazdin						s70	D46										2	-
Nikola SAFARIC	11/3/81	Varteks Varazdin						s70	s77										2	-
Dario KNEZEVIC	20/4/82	Rijeka							D										1	1
Sinisa LINIC	23/8/82	Rijeka							M										1	-
Ivan TURINA	3/10/80	Dinamo Zagreb							s46										1	-
Mladen BARTULOVIC	5/10/86	Hajduk Split							s46/77										1	-
Srebrenko POSAVEC	19/3/80	Varteks Varazdin							s69										1	-
Luka MODRIC	9/9/85	Dinamo Zagreb									M84	s57	s46	M73	s46		s78	s73	7	-
Marijan BULJAT	12/9/81	Dinamo Zagreb							s90			s46							2	-

Croatia

accosted in front of his house by a couple of masked men and beaten up with baseball bats. It was a serious assault and left Bonacic with severe head wounds. Although it was believed to be the handiwork of a couple of disaffected Hajduk fans, no positive identification of the attackers meant that the case remained open. Bonacic defiantly returned to work but he was unable to lift Hajduk any higher than fifth place in the final table, and with the club exiting the Croatian Cup at the semi-final stage (beaten by Rijeka, their conquerors in the 2005 final), that left them without a trophy for the first time in four years and out of Europe for the first time since Croatian independence.

Dinamo back on top

Dinamo Zagreb had endured an equally traumatic season in 2004/05, but the country's most popular club turned things around in a big way, romping home virtually uncontested to their eighth Croatian title. Zdravko Mamic returned to his post as the club's executive vice-president and virtually ran the show for Dinamo, providing the club's new coach, Josip Kuze, with pretty much everything he wanted, both in terms of playing personnel and training schedules.

Dinamo started the campaign with a number of high-scoring victories and were soon out of sight at the top of the table. By the winter break their lead had grown to eight points with a game in hand, and there was an even bigger cushion to protect them at the 22-match cut-off. Even though they took it easy in the ten-match play-off series, losing twice – to sole pursuers Rijeka and down-and-out Hajduk – they still managed to finish with an 11-point victory margin.

The title was secured with a 1-0 home win over Osijek. Fittingly, the scorer of the only goal was midfielder-cum-striker Ivan Bosnjak. Four days later he would grab two more goals in a celebratory 5-3 victory at Varteks Varazdin to boost his season's tally to 22 – the best in the division. Two goals behind him was team-mate Eduardo da Silva. The Brazilian-born Croatian international doubled his tally from the previous season and, like Bosnjak, scored his first international goal in a mid-season friendly away to Hong Kong. Unlike Bosnjak and Dinamo's highly promising young playmaker Luka Modric, he would not be selected for Croatia's World Cup squad.

Another player surprisingly omitted from Zlatko Kranjcar's selection was Davor Vugrinec. The 30-year-old forward returned from Italy to join Rijeka on transfer deadline day at the end of August and became the star attraction of the entire league, earning himself another move, to Dinamo, at the end of the season. Vugrinec scored 15 goals to help Rijeka finish second to Dinamo in the league and he also made a telling contribution towards the club's second successive Croatian Cup triumph, scoring an important goal away to Hajduk in the semi-final and adding three more in the two-legged final against Varteks.

Cup final drama

After a 4-0 win in the first leg, at home, Rijeka looked to have the Cup in their pocket, but by the end of an extraordinary second leg, in which Varteks scored three times in the last few minutes, the visitors were left hanging on to Vugrinec's away goal for their victory. It finished 5-5 on aggregate, and Rijeka were pressed so tightly against the ropes by the end that Varteks almost snatched a crucial sixth goal deep into stoppage-time.

Rijeka's defence of the trophy was assisted by the early exit of Dinamo at the hands of second division outfit Naftas Ivanic Grad. The match was originally scheduled to take place in Zagreb but Dinamo offered home advantage to their opponents under the fair assumption that they would run up a handsome victory wherever the fixture was played. But the league leaders were made to pay dearly for their generosity as Naftas pulled off a sensational 3-2 victory.

Eliminated in the quarter-final by Varteks, Naftas struggled to make an impression in the league, finishing mid-table in the Second Division South, which was won by Sibenik. They were scheduled to meet Second Division North winners Belisce, but after the latter failed to obtain a licence to compete in the upper tier, Sibenik were promoted automatically. The team they replaced, surprisingly, were Inter Zapresic, title challengers only a year earlier.

Although the top division retained its 12-club complement for 2006/07, the league organisers decided to bring an end to the two-phase championship, reintroducing instead the previous 33-match format in which each club plays the others three times.

Croatia

EUROPEAN CUPS 2005/06

UEFA CHAMPIONS LEAGUE

HAJDUK SPLIT
2nd qualifying round DEBRECENI VSC (HUN)
A 0-3
Kale, Zilic, Granic, Dolonga, Damjanovic, Blatnjak, Pralija, Bartulovic, Kranjcar, Grgurovic (Makarin 80), Busic.
H 0-5
Kale, Zilic, Granic, Dolonga, Biscevic (Makarin 85), Damjanovic, Hrman, Blatnjak (Munhoz 46), Kranjcar, Bartulovic, Busic.

UEFA CUP

RIJEKA
2nd qualifying round LITEX LOVECH (BUL)
A 0-1
Zilic, Ivancic, Tkalcevic, Knezevic, Saric (Prpic 83), Tadic (Kerekez 76), Prisc, Rendulic, Linic, Novakovic, Krpan.
H 2-1 *Krpan (64p), Rendulic (90)*
Zilic, Ivancic, Lerant (Prpic 70), Knezevic, Saric, Tadic (Sharbini Ah. 84), Linic (Prisc 60), Rendulic, Novakovic, Zekic, Krpan.

INTER ZAPRESIC
2nd qualifying round CRVENA ZVEZDA BEOGRAD (SCG)
H 1-3 *Pecelj S. (41)*
Miskovic, Radeljic, Pecelj S., Polovanec, Skulic, Ceraj (Babic 66) Cizmek, Janjetovic, Poljak (Gondzic 55), Gulic (Pecelj M. 55), Piskor.
A 0-4
Kranjcec, Pecelj S., Radeljic, Polovanec, Cicak (Cizmek 66), Ceraj, Skulic, Janjetovic (Gondzic 66), Poljak, Piskor (Babic 56), Pecelj M.

TOP GOALSCORERS 2005/06

22	Ivan BOSNJAK (Dinamo Zagreb)
20	EDUARDO da Silva (Dinamo Zagreb)
15	Davor VUGRINEC (Rijeka)
	Ahmed SHARBINI (Rijeka)
13	Leon BENKO (Varteks Varazdin)
	Srdan LAKIC (Kamen Ingrad Velika)
12	Stiven RIVIC (Pula)
11	Igor MOSTARLIC (Medimurje Cakovec)
	Ivan JOLIC (Varteks Varazdin)
10	Niko KRANJCAR (Hajduk Split)
	Dino KRESINGER (Medimurje Cakovec)

LEAGUE RESULTS/SCORERS/APPEARANCES/GOALS 2005/06

CIBALIA VINKOVCI
Coach – Davor Mladina; (26/9/05) Branko Karacic; (8/4/06) Igor Stimac

2005
23/7	Dinamo Zagreb	h	0-4	
30/7	Rijeka	a	1-4	*Knezevic*
6/8	Inter Zapresic	h	1-0	*Andricevic A.*
13/8	Varteks Varazdin	a	0-4	
20/8	Slaven Belupo	h	1-0	*Bagaric*
27/8	Hajduk Split	a	1-1	*Ratkovic*
10/9	Zagreb	h	1-1	*Krizanovic*
17/9	Kamen Ingrad Velika	a	0-2	
24/9	Medimurje Cakovec	h	0-2	
1/10	Pula	a	3-2	*Ratkovic, Pavlicic (p), Stojanovski*
15/10	Osijek	h	3-1	*Krizanovic (p), Prijic, Stojanovski*
22/10	Dinamo Zagreb	a	0-1	
26/10	Rijeka	h	4-0	*Krizanovic, Stojanovski, Andricevic A., Pavlicic*
29/10	Inter Zapresic	a	0-1	
5/11	Varteks Varazdin	h	1-0	*Prijic*
19/11	Slaven Belupo	a	2-4	*og (Crnac), Prijic*
26/11	Hajduk Split	h	1-0	*Zgela*
3/12	Zagreb	a	0-1	

2006
18/2	Kamen Ingrad Velika	h	1-1	*Zgela*
25/2	Medimurje Cakovec	a	3-3	*Zgela, Stojanovski, Jukan*
4/3	Pula	h	0-2	
11/3	Osijek	a	1-1	*Knezevic*
18/3	Slaven Belupo	h	1-1	*Pletikosic*
25/3	Inter Zapresic	a	3-4	*Zgela, Tadic, Knezevic*
1/4	Pula	h	0-0	
8/4	Zagreb	a	0-0	
15/4	Medimurje	h	0-0	
22/4	Slaven Belupo	a	0-1	
29/4	Inter Zapresic	h	1-1	*Krizanovic*
6/5	Pula	a	2-0	*Ratkovic, Keric*
10/5	Zagreb	h	2-1	*Andricevic A., Jukan*
13/5	Medimurje	a	0-4	

Name	Nat	Pos	Aps	(s)	Gls
Antun ANDRICEVIC		D	28		3
Mario ANDRICEVIC		M	5	(8)	
Davor BAGARIC		M	23	(1)	1
Mario BARISIC		M	4	(8)	
Mario BILEN		D	4	(2)	
Davor BURCSA		G	11	(1)	
Amer JUKAN		M	10	(4)	2
Matko KALINIC		G	20		
Andrej KERIC		A	7	(8)	
Kristijan KNEZEVIC		A	9	(12)	3
Mladen KRIZANOVIC		D	31		3
Danijel KUZMANOVIC		A	1	(3)	
Danijel KUZMIC		D	5	(3)	
Boris LEUTAR		D	31		
Frane LOJIC		M	9	(2)	
MARIC		G	1		
Ivan MAROSLAVAC		M	28		
Dejan PAVLICIC		M	11	(2)	2
Jozo PLETIKOSIC		M	9	(10)	1
Dejan PRIJIC		M	21	(2)	3
Zoran RATKOVIC		A	24	(7)	3
Aleksandar STOJANOVSKI		A	15	(8)	4
Mario TADIC		D	29		1
Ivan ZGELA		M	15	(5)	4
Ante ZORE		D	1	(3)	

Croatia

FINAL LEAGUE TABLES 2005/06

Championship Group

		Pld	\multicolumn{5}{c}{Home}	\multicolumn{5}{c}{Away}	\multicolumn{5}{c}{Total}	Pts
			W	D	L	F	A	W	D	L	F	A	W	D	L	F	A	
1	Dinamo Zagreb	32	13	2	1	34	7	11	2	3	44	14	24	4	4	78	21	76
2	Rijeka	32	10	5	1	36	15	10	0	6	25	21	20	5	7	61	36	65
3	Varteks Varazdin	32	8	1	7	30	26	7	1	8	21	22	15	2	15	51	48	47
4	Osijek	32	9	4	3	17	11	4	1	11	14	37	13	5	14	31	48	44
5	Hajduk Split	32	8	4	4	30	17	2	6	8	10	18	10	10	12	40	35	40
6	Kamen Ingrad Velika	32	6	2	8	16	20	5	3	8	17	27	11	5	16	33	47	38

Relegation Group

		Pld	W	D	L	F	A	W	D	L	F	A	W	D	L	F	A	Pts
7	Pula	32	11	1	4	31	14	2	5	9	13	22	13	6	13	44	36	45
8	Slaven Belupo Koprivnica	32	7	7	2	26	17	3	4	9	20	31	10	11	11	46	48	41
9	Cibalia Vinkovci	32	7	6	3	17	14	2	4	10	16	33	9	10	13	33	47	37
10	Zagreb	32	10	1	5	18	14	1	3	12	8	29	11	4	17	26	43	37
11	Medimurje Cakovec	32	6	4	6	27	28	3	5	8	13	23	9	9	14	40	51	36
12	Inter Zapresic	32	6	2	8	19	29	2	5	9	11	24	8	7	17	30	53	31

First Phase

		Pld	W	D	L	F	A	W	D	L	F	A	W	D	L	F	A	Pts
1	Dinamo Zagreb	22	9	2	0	27	4	9	0	2	34	7	18	2	2	61	11	56
2	Rijeka	22	7	3	1	25	10	7	0	4	17	18	14	3	5	42	28	45
3	Osijek	22	7	3	1	14	6	3	1	7	11	26	10	4	8	25	32	34
4	Varteks Varazdin	22	5	1	5	20	19	5	0	6	14	16	10	1	11	34	35	31
5	Hajduk Split	22	5	3	3	20	10	2	5	4	8	11	7	8	7	28	11	29
6	Kamen Ingrad Velika	22	4	2	5	12	14	4	3	4	14	16	8	5	9	26	30	29
7	Pula	22	7	1	3	22	10	1	3	7	7	16	8	4	10	29	26	28
8	Zagreb	22	7	0	4	13	10	1	3	7	6	17	8	3	11	19	27	27
9	Cibalia Vinkovci	22	6	2	3	13	11	1	3	7	11	24	7	5	10	24	35	26
10	Slaven Belupo Koprivnica	22	5	4	2	19	14	0	3	8	10	24	5	7	10	29	38	22
11	Inter Zapresic	22	4	2	5	12	19	2	2	7	5	15	6	4	12	17	34	22
12	Medimurje Cakovec	22	3	3	5	14	22	2	3	6	12	21	5	6	11	26	43	21

N.B. The top six and bottom six clubs split into two groups after 22 matches.

DINAMO ZAGREB
Coach – Josip Kuze

2005
23/7	Cibalia Vinkovci	a	4-0	Bosnjak, Corluka, Modric, Eduardo (p)
30/7	Osijek	a	0-1	
6/8	Rijeka	h	5-1	Bosnjak, Mamic, Chago 2, Cesar
14/8	Inter Zapresic	a	6-0	Eduardo 3, Modric, Corluka, Bosnjak
20/8	Varteks Varazdin	h	1-0	Cesar
27/8	Slaven Belupo	a	2-0	Bosnjak, Eduardo
11/9	Hajduk Split	h	0-0	
18/9	Zagreb	a	4-0	Buljat, Modric, Etto, Eduardo
24/9	Kamen Ingrad Velika	h	5-0	Mamic, Ljubojevic, Eduardo 2, Maric
1/10	Medimurje Cakovec	a	5-1	Etto, Eduardo, Bosnjak 2 (1p), Corluka
15/10	Pula	h	1-0	Chago
22/10	Cibalia Vinkovci	h	1-0	Mamic (p)
26/10	Osijek	h	3-1	Eduardo 2 (1p), Etto
29/10	Rijeka	a	1-0	Mitu
2/11	Inter Zapresic	h	0-0	
20/11	Varteks Varazdin	a	5-2	Eduardo 2, Etto, Bosnjak 2
26/11	Slaven Belupo	h	4-1	Eduardo, Bosnjak 2, Cale

2006
12/2	Hajduk Split	a	1-0	Modric
18/2	Zagreb	h	4-1	Bosnjak (p), Eduardo 2, Anderson
25/2	Kamen Ingrad Velika	a	5-1	Bosnjak 2 (2p), Anderson, Cale, Drpic
4/3	Medimurje Cakovec	h	3-0	Anderson, Bosnjak 2
11/3	Pula	a	1-2	Bosnjak
18/3	Kamen Ingrad Velika	h	2-0	Bosnjak, Modric
25/3	Rijeka	h	1-2	Etto
2/4	Osijek	a	0-0	

Croatia

8/4	Varteks Varazdin	h	2-1	Eduardo 2 (1p)
15/4	Hajduk Split	a	0-1	
22/4	Kamen Ingrad Velika	a	3-1	Bosnjak 2 (1p), Modric
29/4	Rijeka	a	2-2	Tomic, Modric
6/5	Osijek	h	1-0	Bosnjak
10/5	Varteks Varazdin	a	5-3	Bosnjak 2, Eduardo 2, Carlos
13/5	Hajduk Split	h	1-0	Modric

No	Name	Nat	Pos	Aps	(s)	Gls
9	ANDERSON Costa	BRA	A	4	(9)	3
23	Eddy BOSNAR	AUS	D	7	(3)	
12	Ivan BOSNJAK		A	27		22
2	Marijan BULJAT		D	27	(2)	1
3	Hrvoje CALE		D	22	(3)	2
	CARLOS Santos de Jesus	BRA	D	5	(2)	1
21	Bostjan CESAR	SLO	D	5		2
13	Mathias CHAGO		M	26	(2)	3
5	Vedran CORLUKA		D	31		3
26	Dino DRPIC		D	29		1
24	EDUARDO da Silva		A	27	(2)	20
7	Oelilton Araújo dos Santos ETTO	BRA	D	23	(1)	5
6	Vedran JESE		D		(1)	
	JÚNIOR	BRA	M		(5)	
18	Teo KARDUM		A		(1)	
16	Dejan LOVREN		M		(1)	
14	Mario LUCIC		D	2	(5)	
	Goran LJUBOJEVIC		A	5	(5)	1
28	Zoran MAMIC		M	30		3
4	Silvio MARIC		M	5	(17)	1
	Dumitru MITU	ROM	M	7	(4)	1
10	Luka MODRIC		M	32		8
17	Miroslav SARIC		M		(11)	
8	Ante TOMIC		M	5	(7)	1
1	Ivan TURINA		G	32		
20	Ognjen VUKOJEVIC		M	1	(5)	
11	Dario ZAHORA		A		(4)	

HAJDUK SPLIT
Coach – Miroslav Blazevic; (19/9/05) Ivan Gudelj; (13/2/06) Luka Bonacic

2005

20/7	Osijek	h	6-0	Biscevic, Bartulovic, Busic 2, Kranjcar
30/7	Zagreb	h	3-1	Kranjcar 2 (1p), Busic
6/8	Kamen Ingrad Velika	a	1-2	Suto
13/8	Medimurje Cakovec	h	1-0	Kranjcar (p)
20/8	Pula	a	0-2	
27/8	Cibalia Vinkovci	h	1-1	Makarin
11/9	Dinamo Zagreb	a	0-0	
17/9	Rijeka	h	0-1	
24/9	Inter Zapresic	a	2-2	Vucko, Kranjcar (p)
1/10	Varteks Varazdin	h	3-0	Busic, Blatnjak, Deranja
15/10	Slaven Belupo	a	0-0	
22/10	Osijek	a	1-1	Kranjcar
26/10	Zagreb	a	2-1	Marcic, Vucko
29/10	Kamen Ingrad Velika	h	1-2	Dolonga
5/11	Medimurje Cakovec	a	1-1	Blatnjak
19/11	Pula	h	1-1	Kranjcar (p)
26/11	Cibalia Vinkovci	a	0-1	

2006

12/2	Dinamo Zagreb	h	0-1	
18/2	Rijeka	a	0-1	
25/2	Inter Zapresic	h	3-2	Dolonga, Erceg, Kranjcar (p)
4/3	Varteks Varazdin	a	1-0	Blatnjak
11/3	Slaven Belupo	h	1-1	Hrgovic
18/3	Rijeka	a	1-1	Hrgovic
25/3	Osijek	h	3-0	Jelavic 2, Kranjcar
1/4	Varteks Varazdin	a	0-2	
8/4	Kamen Ingrad Velika	a	0-1	
15/4	Dinamo Zagreb	h	1-0	Cimerotic
22/4	Rijeka	h	0-4	
29/4	Osijek	a	1-2	
6/5	Varteks Varazdin	h	2-2	Bartulovic, og (Pokrivac)
10/5	Kamen Ingrad Velika	h	4-1	Hrgovic, Kranjcar, Busic, Jelavic
13/5	Dinamo Zagreb	a	0-1	

No	Name	Nat	Pos	Aps	(s)	Gls
12	Vladimir BALIC		G	4		
13	Mladen BARTULOVIC		M	15	(2)	2
	Bulend BISCEVIC	BOS	M	7	(1)	1
8	Dragan BLATNJAK	BOS	A	22		3
	BUDIMIR		M		(2)	
	Jurica BULJAT		D	2	(1)	
30	Tomislav BUSIC		A	12	(8)	5
5	Frane CACIC		M	6	(7)	
14	Sebastjan CIMEROTIC	SLO	M	4	(1)	1
22	Josip CUTUK		D	6	(1)	
4	Dario DAMJANOVIC	BOS	M	22	(2)	
	Zvonimir DERANJA		A	4	(4)	1
6	Vlatko DOLONGA		D	15	(1)	2
	Mate DRAGICEVIC		A		(3)	
9	Tomislav ERCEG		A	8	(5)	1
27	Igor GAL		D	14		
	Goran GRANIC		D	15	(1)	
24	Mario GRGUROVIC		M	8	(7)	
18	Mirko HRGOVIC		M	13	(1)	3
28	Danijel HRMAN		D	3	(2)	
23	Nikica JELAVIC	BOS	A	6	(3)	3
	Tvrtko KALE		G	6		
11	Nikola KALINIC		A	2	(4)	
3	Igor KRALEVSKI	MAC	D	12	(1)	
10	Niko KRANJCAR		M	32		10
	Marin LJUBICIC		M		(2)	
16	Kresimir MAKARIN		A	2	(6)	1
7	Filip MARCIC		M	17	(3)	1
21	Darko MILADIN		D	22		
26	Pablo MUNHOZ	URU	A	6	(6)	
	PEZO		M	2	(1)	
1	Stipe PLETIKOSA		G	22		
	Nenad PRALIJA		M	3	(2)	
20	Ivan REZIC		D	5	(3)	
15	Mate SELAK		M	1	(2)	
2	Petar SUTO		M	8	(4)	1
	Luka VUCKO		D	11		2
17	Tonci ZILIC		D	15		

INTER ZAPRESIC
Coach – Srecko Bogdan; (28/8/05) Djuro Bago

2005

23/7	Medimurje Cakovec	a	2-1	Poljak, Pecelj S.
30/7	Pula	h	2-0	Piskor, Cizmek
6/8	Cibalia Vginkovci	a	0-1	
14/8	Dinamo Zagreb	h	0-6	

Croatia

Date	Opponent	H/A	Score	Scorers
20/8	Rijeka	a	0-0	
28/8	Osijek	a	0-1	
10/9	Varteks	h	1-2	Gulic
17/9	Slaven Belupo	a	0-3	
24/9	Hajduk Split	h	2-2	Jese, Gulic
1/10	Zagreb	a	0-1	
15/10	Kamen Ingrad Velika	h	0-0	
22/10	Medimurje Cakovec	h	1-3	Gondzic
26/10	Pula	a	0-3	
29/10	Cibalia Vinkovci	h	1-0	Skulic
5/11	Dinamo Zagreb	a	0-0	
19/11	Rijeka	h	0-2	
26/11	Osijek	h	2-3	Strok, Jese (p)
3/12	Varteks Varazdin	a	0-2	
2006				
17/2	Slaven Belupo	h	2-1	Karic, Zekic
25/2	Hajduk Split	a	2-3	Gondzic, Karic
4/3	Zagreb	h	1-0	Karic (p)
11/3	Kamen Ingrad Velika	a	1-0	Strok
18/3	Zagreb	a	1-3	Strok
25/3	Cibalia Vinkovci	h	4-3	Jese, Karic 2 (1p), Skulic
1/4	Slaven Belupo	a	1-1	Gondzic
8/4	Medimurje Cakovec	a	2-2	Gondzic, Piskor
14/4	Pula	h	1-4	Jese
21/4	Zagreb	h	1-0	Piskor
29/4	Cibalia	a	1-1	Piskor
6/5	Slaven Belupo	h	1-2	Gondzic
10/5	Medimurje Cakovec	h	0-1	
13/5	Pula	a	1-2	Gondzic

Name	Nat	Pos	Aps	(s)	Gls
Ivan BABIC		A	4	(4)	
Goran BRASNIC		G	14		
Stipe BRNAS		D	12		
Igor CAGALJ		D	18	(2)	
Tomislav CERAJ		M	13	(5)	
Krunoslav CICAK	BOS	M	1		
Mario CIZMEK		M	18	(3)	1
Tomislav GONDZIC		A	19	(7)	6
Bernard GULIC		A	7	(10)	2
IVEKOVIC		D	1		
Marko JANJETOVIC		M	12	(2)	
Drazen JELIC	BOS	M	2	(4)	
Josip JERNEIC		M	11		
Vedran JESE		D	23		4
Veldin KARIC		A	10	(1)	5
Domagoj KRANJCEC		G	5	(1)	
Damir KRZNAR		M	18	(2)	
Davor KUKEC		M	10	(2)	
Petr LAGA		D	12	(1)	
MADARIC		M		(1)	
Mario MISKOVIC		G	13		
Milan PECELJ	BOS	M	3	(4)	
Srdjan PECELJ	BOS	D	6		1
Davor PISKOR		A	19	(9)	4
Stjepan POLJAK		M	14	(10)	1
Kristijan POLOVANEC		D	14		
Ivan RADELJIC		D	18		
Ernad SKULIC		M	16	(8)	2
Hrvoje STROK		M	13	(1)	3
Ivan UDAREVIC		M	4	(1)	
Krunoslav VIDAK		D	10	(4)	
Zoran ZEKIC		A	12	(2)	1

KAMEN INGRAD VELIKA
Coach – Ivica Matkovic

Date	Opponent	H/A	Score	Scorers
2005				
20/7	Varteks Varazdin	h	0-1	
30/7	Slaven Belupo	a	1-1	Lakic
6/8	Hajduk Split	h	2-1	Lakic, Brajkovic
13/8	Zagreb	a	1-2	Papa
20/8	Osijek	h	2-0	Mujcin, Brajkovic
27/8	Medimurje Cakovec	h	2-2	Lakic, Kralj
10/9	Pula	a	2-1	Lakic (p), Mujcin
17/9	Cibalia Vinkovci	h	2-0	Lakic 2
24/9	Dinamo Zagreb	a	0-5	
1/10	Rijeka	h	0-1	
15/10	Inter Zapresic	a	0-0	
22/10	Varteks Varazdin	a	3-1	Parmakovic, Brajkovic, Lakic
26/10	Slaven Belupo	h	0-0	
29/10	Hajduk Split	a	2-1	Papa, Lakic
5/11	Zagreb	h	1-2	Tomic
19/11	Osijek	a	0-1	
26/11	Medimurje Cakovec	a	3-0	Parmakovic, Sivonjic, Lakic
3/12	Pula	h	2-1	Tomic, Sivonjic
2006				
18/2	Cibalia Vinkovci	a	1-1	Lakic
25/2	Dinamo Zagreb	h	1-5	Brajkovic (p)
4/3	Rijeka	a	1-3	Stipkovic
11/3	Inter Zapresic	h	0-1	
18/3	Dinamo Zagreb	h	0-2	
25/3	Varteks Varazdin	h	0-1	
1/4	Rijeka	a	0-3	
8/4	Hajduk Split	h	1-0	Lakic
15/4	Osijek	a	0-1	
22/4	Dinamo Zagreb	h	1-3	Lakic
29/4	Varteks Varazdin	a	2-1	Papa, Lakic
6/5	Rijeka	h	1-0	Sest
10/5	Hajduk Split	a	1-4	Parmakovic
13/5	Osijek	h	1-2	Brajkovic

Name	Nat	Pos	Aps	(s)	Gls
AVDUKIC		M	2		
Matej BOGDANOVIC		M	1	(3)	
Tomislav BOZIC		D	6	(4)	
Vasko BOZINOVSKI	MAC	D	13	(2)	
Mate BRAJKOVIC		A	24	(3)	5
BRKANAC		M		(1)	
Kristijan CAVAL		M	7	(1)	
Silvije CAVLINA		G	18		
Jusuf DAJIC	BOS	A	1	(4)	
Mario DARMOPIL	BOS	M	28	(1)	
GOLIK		M		(1)	
Mario KRALJ		M	19	(3)	1
Srdan LAKIC		A	30		13
Ivica MATAS		G	12		
Edin MUJCIN	BOS	M	25		2
Jasmin MUJDZA	BOS	M	17	(2)	
Braslav OSTOJIC		M	5	(7)	
Drago PAPA		M	28		3
Ninoslav PARMAKOVIC		M	28		3
Filip PEIC		A		(4)	

Croatia

Name	Nat	Pos	Aps	(s)	Gls
Vanja PETROVIC		M	15	(1)	
Kreso POLETI		D	28	(1)	
Sasa SEST		A	6	(5)	1
Ilija SIVONJIC		M	2	(14)	2
SKARICIC		D	2	(3)	
Mladen STIPKOVIC		M	8	(13)	1
Petar TOMIC		M	19	(2)	2
Nikola ZEBA		D		(1)	
Marko ZELENIKA		M	8	(9)	

MEDIMURJE CAKOVEC
Coach – Miljenko Dovecer; (2/3/06) (Albert Pobor); (25/3/06) Stanko Mrsic

2005
Date	Opponent	h/a	Score	Scorers
23/7	Inter Zapresic	h	1-2	Kresinger
30/7	Varteks Varazdin	a	2-3	Vincetic, Sesar
6/8	Slaven Belupo	h	2-0	Katic, Sesar
13/8	Hajduk Split	a	0-1	
20/8	Zagreb	h	0-0	
27/8	Kamen Ingrad Velika	a	2-2	Kresinger, Guvo
10/9	Osijek	h	1-0	Guvo
17/9	Pula	h	2-0	Zurak, Sesar
24/9	Cibalia Vinkovci	a	2-0	Balaskovic (p), Mostarlic
1/10	Dinamo Zagreb	h	1-5	Mesic
15/10	Rijeka	a	1-4	Mostarlic
22/10	Inter Zapresic	a	3-1	Kresinger, Mostarlic, Krivic
26/10	Varteks Varazdin	h	1-4	Mostarlic
29/10	Slaven Belupo	a	1-1	Mostarlic
5/11	Hajduk Split	h	1-1	Kresinger
19/11	Zagreb	a	0-1	
26/11	Kamen Ingrad Velika	h	0-3	
3/12	Osijek	a	1-1	Mostarlic

2006
Date	Opponent	h/a	Score	Scorers
18/2	Pula	a	0-4	
25/2	Cibalia Vinkovci	h	3-3	Pirija, Mostarlic, Kresinger
4/3	Dinamo Zagreb	a	0-3	
11/3	Rijeka	h	2-4	Mostarlic, Cicero Lima
18/3	Pula	a	0-1	
25/3	Slaven Belupo	h	3-4	Kresinger 2, Racki
1/4	Zagreb	a	0-1	
8/4	Inter Zapresic	h	2-2	Mostarlic, Celiscak
15/4	Cibalia Vinkovci	a	0-0	
22/4	Pula	h	2-0	Mostarlic 2 (2p)
29/4	Slaven Belupo	a	0-0	
6/5	Zagreb	h	2-0	Bratkovic, Cicero Lima
10/5	Inter Zapresic	a	1-0	Kresinger
13/5	Cibalia Vinkovci	h	4-0	Cicero Lima, Balaskovic, Kresinger 2

Name	Nat	Pos	Aps	(s)	Gls
Andre BATISTA SILVA	BRA	D	21	(3)	
Valerio BALASKOVIC		M	28		2
Dalibor BOZAC		D	8	(1)	
Krunoslav BRATKOVIC		D	11	(4)	1
Tihomir BULAT		G	26		
CELISCAK		M	10		1
CICERO LIMA	BRA	A	10	(2)	3
Davor CONKAS		G	1		
Vjekoslav CVEK		M		(1)	
Tomislav DUJMOVIC		M	17		
FISER		M		(2)	
Jure GUVO		A	9	(4)	2
Ivan HABUS		D	9	(4)	
Hrvoje JANCETIC		M	16		
Miro KATIC	BOS	M	8	(5)	1
Mario KOVACEVIC		M	27		
Dino KRESINGER		A	26	(3)	10
Danijel KRIVIC		M	9	(3)	1
Stjepan KRZNAR		M	2	(3)	
MIDENJAK		M		(2)	
MEDARIC		M		(1)	
Robert MESIC		A	4	(11)	1
Igor MOSTARLIC		A	27	(2)	11
PIRIJA		A	4	(6)	1
RACKI		A	2	(2)	1
RICARDO da Costa	BRA	M	9		
Mario SARIC		D	10	(9)	
Sinisa SESAR		D	30		3
Vjekoslav TOMIC		G	5		
Goran VINCETIC		M	4		1
Marko ZAVRTNIK		M		(2)	
ZUPAN		D	6	(3)	
Ante ZURAK		D	13	(3)	1

OSIJEK
Coach – Ivo Susak

2005
Date	Opponent	h/a	Score	Scorers
20/7	Hajduk Split	a	0-6	
30/7	Dinamo Zagreb	h	1-0	Balatinac
6/8	Zagreb	a	1-0	Primorac
14/8	Rijeka	h	0-1	
20/8	Kamen Ingrad Velika	a	0-2	
28/8	Inter Zapresic	h	1-0	Ruzak
10/9	Medimurje Cakovec	a	0-1	
17/9	Varteks Varazdin	h	2-0	Balatinac, Vojnovic A.
24/9	Pula	a	2-2	Vojnovic A. 2
1/10	Slaven Belupo	h	4-2	Balatinac 2 (1p), Primorac, Vojnovic A.
15/10	Cibalia Vinkovci	a	1-3	Smoje
22/10	Hajduk Split	h	1-1	Balatinac
26/10	Dinamo Zagreb	a	1-3	Turkovic
29/10	Zagreb	h	1-0	Vitajic A.
5/11	Rijeka	a	1-4	Milardovic
19/11	Kamen Ingrad Velika	h	1-0	Dinjar
26/11	Inter Zapresic	a	3-2	Turkovic, Smoje, Balatinac
3/12	Medimurje Cakovec	h	1-1	og (Batista)

2006
Date	Opponent	h/a	Score	Scorers
18/2	Varteks Varazdin	a	1-0	Milardovic
25/2	Pula	h	1-0	Turkovic
4/3	Slaven Belupo	a	1-3	Vuica
11/3	Cibalia Vinkovci	h	1-1	Barisic
18/3	Varteks Varazdin	h	0-2	
25/3	Hajduk Split	a	0-3	
2/4	Dinamo Zagreb	h	0-0	
8/4	Rijeka	a	1-3	Barisic
15/4	Kamen Ingrad Velika	h	1-0	Primorac
22/4	Varteks Varazdin	a	0-3	
29/4	Hajduk Split	h	2-1	Milardovic, Barisic
6/5	Dinamo Zagreb	a	0-1	
10/5	Rijeka	h	0-2	
13/5	Kamen Ingrad Velika	a	2-1	Dinjar, Smoje

No	Name	Nat	Pos	Aps	(s)	Gls
22	Valentin BABIC		M	27		

Croatia

No	Name	Pos	Aps	(s)	Gls
18	Josip BALATINAC	M	16		6
	Josip BARISIC	A	8	(10)	3
2	Hrvoje BUBALO	D	10	(5)	
7	Anton DEDAJ	M	31		
23	Marko DINJAR	M	28	(3)	2
26	Josip KNEZEVIC	M	4	(1)	
15	David Junior LOPES	D	16	(1)	
	MIKAC	M		(3)	
6	Josip MILARDOVIC	M	29	(2)	3
21	Ante MILAS	A	8	(5)	
19	Josip MISIC	M	1	(1)	
5	Mijo NADJ	D	18	(9)	
27	Vedran NIKSIC	A	7	(2)	
	Igor OSTOPANJ	D	1		
9	Karlo PRIMORAC	A	24	(2)	3
21	Igor RUZAK	A		(3)	1
1	Mario SKENDER	G	32		
24	Ivo SMOJE	D	18	(1)	3
12	Filip SUSNJARA	G		(1)	
8	Slaven TOKIC	M	3	(6)	
10	Almir TURKOVIC	A	18	(9)	3
	Ante VITAJIC	D	18	(1)	1
3	Frane VITAJIC	M	3	(2)	
20	Aljosa VOJNOVIC	A	10	(14)	4
	Hrvoje VOJNOVIC	M		(1)	
14	Mario VRATOVIC	D	4		
4	Damir VUICA	D	18	(1)	1

PULA
Coach – Igor Pamic; (2/10/05) Milivoj Bracun; (11/3/06) Krunoslav Jurcic

2005
Date	Opponent	h/a	Score	Scorers
23/7	Rijeka	a	2-2	Jerneic, Pilipovic
30/7	Inter Zapresic	a	0-2	
6/8	Varteks Varazdin	h	0-3	
13/8	Slaven Belupo	a	1-1	Rivic
20/8	Hajduk Split	h	2-0	Sehic, Rivic
27/8	Zagreb	a	0-2	
10/9	Kamen Ingrad Velika	h	1-2	Pamic
17/9	Medimurje Cakovec	a	0-2	
24/9	Osijek	h	2-2	Sehic (p), Iftic
1/10	Cibalia Vinkovci	h	2-3	Sehic, Jerneic
15/10	Dinamo Zagreb	a	0-1	
22/10	Rijeka	h	3-0	Sehic 2, Jerneic
26/10	Inter Zapresic	h	3-0	Stosic, Rivic, Fucek
29/10	Varteks Varazdin	a	0-2	
5/11	Slaven Belupo	h	1-0	Sehic
19/11	Hajduk Split	a	1-1	Sehic
26/11	Zagreb	h	2-0	Kontesic 2
3/12	Kamen Ingrad Velika	a	1-2	Starcevic

2006
Date	Opponent	h/a	Score	Scorers
18/2	Medimurje Cakovec	h	4-0	Starcevic, Ramadani 2 (1p), Rivic
25/2	Osijek	a	0-1	
4/3	Cibalia Vinkovci	a	2-0	Rivic, Babic
11/3	Dinamo Zagreb	h	2-1	Pamic, Rivic (p)
18/3	Medimurje Cakovec	h	1-0	Starcevic
25/3	Zagreb	a	4-1	Halilovic, Raic-Sudar, Pamic, Babic
1/4	Cibalia Vinkovci	a	0-0	
8/4	Slaven Belupo	h	2-0	Rivic, Juric
14/4	Inter Zapresic	a	4-1	Raic-Sudar, Rivic 3 (1p)
22/4	Medimurje Cakovec	a	0-2	
29/4	Zagreb	a	0-1	
6/5	Cibalia Vinkovci	h	0-2	
10/5	Slaven Belupo	a	2-2	Rivic (p), Raic-Sudar
13/5	Inter Zapresic	h	2-1	Halilovic, Rivic (p)

Name	Nat	Pos	Aps	(s)	Gls
Ivan BABIC		M	4	(6)	2
Agron BARLECAJ		A		(2)	
BARUKCIC		M	1	(1)	
Silvio CAVRIC		M	4	(2)	
Sandi DOBRIC		D	13		
Zoran DRACA		D	3	(2)	
FUCEK		M	2	(7)	1
GRIZELJ		A	2	(9)	
Almir HALILOVIC	BOS	A	13	(1)	2
Mahir IFTIC	BOS	D	25		1
Vanja IVESA		G	26		
Josip JERNEIC		A	13	(1)	3
Marko JURIC		M	22	(3)	1
Mario JURIN		M		(1)	
Almir KAPETAN		M		(6)	
Sasa KOLIC		D	4	(4)	
Ljupko KONTESIC		M	3	(3)	2
Igor LOZO		D	20	(2)	
Josip LUKUNIC		D	4	(4)	
Marko MAKSIMOVIC	BOS	M	19	(5)	
Dario MIJATOVIC		D	10		
Andre Emanuel OTTOU		D	1	(3)	
Manuel PAMIC		M	22	(2)	3
Renato PILIPOVIC		M	3		1
Marko RADAS		D	15	(1)	
Ervin RADULOVIC		G	6		
Darko RAIC-SUDAR		M	31	(1)	3
Zedi RAMADANI		M	11	(6)	2
Stiven RIVIC		A	28		12
SAKOTA		M		(4)	
Asim SEHIC	BOS	A	9	(2)	7
STAMBOLIJA		M	4	(1)	
Dalibor STARCEVIC		D	28		3
Vedran STOSIC		A	6	(12)	1

RIJEKA
Coach – Elvis Scoria; (30/10/05) Dragan Skocic

2005
Date	Opponent	h/a	Score	Scorers
23/7	Pula	h	2-2	Zekic, Krpan (p)
30/7	Cibalia Vinkovci	h	4-1	Prpic 3, Krpan
6/8	Dinamo Zagreb	a	1-5	Krpan
14/8	Osijek	a	1-0	Ivancic
20/8	Inter Zapresic	h	0-0	
28/8	Varteks Varazdin	a	4-1	Sharbini Ah. 3, Krpan
10/9	Slaven Belupo	h	4-2	Vugrinec 2, og (Kurilic), Sharbini Ah.
17/9	Hajduk Split	a	1-0	Sharbini Ah.
24/9	Zagreb	h	0-0	
1/10	Kamen Ingrad Velika	a	1-0	Vugrinec
15/10	Medimurje Cakovec	h	4-1	Sharbini Ah., Novakovic 2, Vugrinec
22/10	Pula	a	0-3	
26/10	Cibalia Vinkovci	a	0-4	
29/10	Dinamo Zagreb	h	0-1	
5/11	Osijek	h	4-1	Sharbini Ah. 2, Vugrinec,

Croatia

19/11	Inter Zapresic	a	2-0		Novakovic Sharbini Ah., Vugrinec
26/11	Varteks Varazdin	h	3-1		Novakovic, Ivancic, Vugrinec
3/12	Slaven Belupo	a	3-1		Novakovic, Linic 2
2006					
18/2	Hajduk Split	h	1-0		Novakovic
25/2	Zagreb	a	0-2		
4/3	Kamen Ingrad Velika	h	3-1		Prisc, Novakovic, Sharbini Ah.
11/3	Medimurje Cakovec	a	4-2		Vugrinec 3 (1p), Sharbini Ah.
18/3	Hajduk Split	h	1-1		Vugrinec (p)
25/3	Dinamo Zagreb	a	2-1		og (Drpic), Vugrinec
1/4	Kamen Ingrad Velika	h	3-0		Bobic, Novakovic 2
8/4	Osijek	h	3-1		Rendulic, Linic, Sharbini Ah.
15/4	Varteks Varazdin	a	0-1		
22/4	Hajduk Split	a	4-0		Vugrinec 3, Sharbini Ah.
29/4	Dinamo Zagreb	h	2-2		Linic, Sharbini Ah
6/5	Kamen Ingrad Velika	a	0-1		
10/5	Osijek	a	2-0		Linic 2
13/5	Varteks Varazdin	h	2-1		Sharbini Ah., Bobic

No	Name	Nat	Pos	Aps	(s)	Gls
9	Fredi BOBIC	GER	A	4	(4)	2
24	Eddy BOSNAR	AUS	D	8		
8	Kresimir BRKIC		M		(1)	
16	Fausto BUDICIN		D	5	(3)	
19	Sandi DOBRIC		M	1		
4	Zoran IVANCIC		D	13	(3)	2
23	Dusan KERKEZ	BOS	M	9	(13)	
5	Dario KNEZEVIC		D	28		
13	Petar KRPAN		A	13	(5)	4
6	Peter LERANT	SVK	D	19	(1)	
25	Sinisa LINIC		M	29		6
21	Igor NOVAKOVIC		A	20		9
14	Goran PARACKI		M		(1)	
22	Mario PRISC		M	20	(5)	1
3	Marin PRPIC		M	4	(2)	3
	RADAS		M		(1)	
1	Velimir RADMAN		G	1	(2)	
20	Krunoslav RENDULIC		M	28		1
18	Goran RUBIL		M	1	(2)	
15	Danijel SARIC		M	25	(3)	
10	Ahmed SHARBINI		A	22	(5)	15
17	Anas SHARBINI		M	2	(7)	
7	Dragan TADIC		M	27	(5)	
2	Igor TKALCEVIC		D	14	(8)	
30	Davor VUGRINEC		A	23	(1)	15
	Zoran ZEKIC		A	5	(4)	1
12	Dragan ZILIC	SCG	G	31		

SLAVEN BELUPO KOPRIVNICA
Coach – Branko Karacic; (19/8/05) Nikola Jurcevic; (4/12/05) Elvis Scoria

2005				
20/7	Zagreb	a	1-3	Musa (p)
30/7	Kamen Ingrad Velika	h	1-1	Musa (p)
6/8	Medimurje Cakovec	a	0-2	
13/8	Pula	h	1-1	Jambrusic
20/8	Cibalia Vinkovci	a	0-1	
27/8	Dinamo Zagreb	h	0-2	
10/9	Rijeka	a	2-4	Karabogdan, Musa (p)
17/9	Inter Zapresic	h	3-0	Dodik, Musa (p), Mumlek
24/9	Varteks Varazdin	a	2-2	Karabogdan, Musa
1/10	Osijek	a	2-4	Pejic, Musa
15/10	Hajduk Split	h	0-0	
22/10	Zagreb	h	1-0	Vrucina
26/10	Kamen Ingrad Velika	a	0-0	
29/10	Medimurje Cakovec	h	1-1	Kurilic
5/11	Pula	a	0-1	
19/11	Cibalia Vinkovci	h	4-2	Karabogdan 2, Karabatic, Dodik
26/11	Dinamo Zagreb	a	1-4	Vrucina
3/12	Rijeka	h	1-3	Dodik
2006				
17/2	Inter Zapresic	a	1-2	Saranovic (p)
25/2	Varteks Varazdin	h	4-3	Vrucina 2, Dodik, Musa
4/3	Osijek	h	3-1	Vrucina, Pejic, Mumlek (p)
11/3	Hajduk Split	a	1-1	Mumlek (p)
18/3	Cibalia Vinkovci	a	1-1	Mumlek
25/3	Medimurje Cakovec	a	4-3	Dodik 2, Vrucina, Pejic
1/4	Inter Zapresic	h	1-1	Mumlek (p)
8/4	Pula	a	0-2	
15/4	Zagreb	h	3-0	Mumlek, Pejic, Vrucina
22/4	Cibalia Vinkovci	h	1-0	Vrucina
29/4	Medimurje Cakovec	a	0-0	
6/5	Inter Zapresic	a	2-1	Saranovic, Dodik
10/5	Pula	h	2-2	Musa, Pejic
13/5	Zagreb	a	3-0	Mumlek, Dodik, Jambrusic

Name	Nat	Pos	Aps	(s)	Gls
Dario BODRUSIC		D	28	(1)	
Petar BOSNJAK		D	16	(4)	
Dalibor BOZAC		D	13		
Pavo CRNAC		D	4		
Marijo DODIK		A	24	(3)	8
Ante DUNKOVIC		M	21	(16)	
Ivan ELEZ		D	6	(2)	
Igor GAL		D	8		
Krunoslav JAMBRUSIC		A		(3)	2
Jurica KARABATIC		D	7	(2)	1
Ivica KARABOGDAN		A	15	(2)	4
Antonio KOVAC		M	8	(11)	
Sime KURILIC		D	28		1
LEE Jeong-young	KOR	M	13	(1)	
Robert LISJAK		G	18		
Miljenko MUMLEK		M	19		7
Igor MUSA		D	30		8
Jane NIKOLOSKI		G	4		
Petar PEJIC		A	17	(6)	5
Dalibor POLDRUGAC		M	24		
Ivan RADELJIC		D	14		
Edin SARANOVIC	BOS	A	9	(15)	2
Dejan SOMOCI		A	1	(4)	
Dalibor VISKOVIC	SLO	D	9		
Bojan VRUCINA		A	16	(10)	8

VARTEKS VARAZDIN
Coach – Zlatko Dalic

2005				
20/7	Kamen Ingrad Velika	a	1-0	Safaric
30/7	Medimurje Cakovec	h	3-2	Safaric 2, Jolic

Croatia

6/8	Pula	a	2-0	Plantic, Mujanovic
13/8	Cibalia Vinkovci	h	4-0	Safaric 2, Jolic 2
20/8	DinamoZagreb	a	0-1	
28/8	Rijeka	h	1-4	Jolic
10/9	Inter Zapresic	a	2-1	Halilovic, Benko
17/9	Osijek	a	0-2	
24/9	Slaven Belupo	h	2-2	Jolic 2
1/10	Hajduk Split	a	0-3	
15/10	Zagreb	h	3-1	Jolic 2, Jertec
22/10	Kamen Ingrad Velika	h	1-3	Benko
26/10	Medimurje Cakovec	a	4-1	Benko 2, Posavec, Jolic
29/10	Pula	h	2-0	Benko 2
5/11	Cibalia Vinkovci	a	0-1	
20/11	Dinamo Zagreb	h	2-5	Benko, Posavec
26/11	Rijeka	a	1-3	Benko
3/12	Inter Zapresic	h	2-0	Benko, Jolic
2006				
18/2	Osijek	h	0-1	
25/2	Slaven Belupo	a	3-4	Novinic, Benko, Safaric
4/3	Hajduk Split	h	0-1	
11/3	Zagreb	a	1-0	Jolic
18/3	Osijek	a	2-0	Pavlicic, Halilovic
25/3	Kamen Ingrad Velika	a	1-0	Benko
1/4	Hajduk Split	h	2-0	Ipsa 2
8/4	Dinamo Zagreb	a	1-2	Kardum
15/4	Rijeka	h	1-0	Novinic
22/4	Osijek	h	3-0	Safaric, Novinic, Benko
29/4	Kamen Ingrad Velika	h	1-2	Benko
6/5	Hajduk Split	a	2-2	Ipsa, Safaric (p)
10/5	Dinamo Zagreb	h	3-5	Safaric (p), Posavec, Novinic
13/5	Rijeka	a	1-2	Posavec

Name	Nat	Pos	Aps	(s)	Gls
Marko BASIC		D	1		
BEGOVIC		M	1		
Leon BENKO		A	27		13
Gordan GOLIK		M	2	(6)	
Nedim HALILOVIC	BOS	A	23	(7)	2
Kristijan IPSA		D	27	(1)	3
Darijo JERTEC		M	24	(6)	1
Ivan JOLIC	BOS	A	27	(3)	11
Mladen JURCEVIC		D	4	(5)	
Teo KARDUM		A	1	(10)	1
Zoran KASTEL		M	10		
Miroslav KOPRIC		G	10		
Mario LUCIC		D	10	(2)	
Ivan MANCE		G	2		
MALEC		M		(1)	
Nikola MELNJAK		M	19	(2)	
Dominik MOHOROVIC		A	1	(8)	
Goran MUJANOVIC		M	6		1
Enes NOVINIC		A	4	(18)	4
Milan PAVLICIC		A	12	(4)	1
Mirko PLANTIC		D	5	(8)	1
Nikola POKRIVAC		M	28		
Srebrenko POSAVEC		D	25	(4)	4
Zedi RAMADANI		A		(1)	
Nikola SAFARIC		M	29		9
Tomislav VRANJIC		G	20		
Vladimir VUK		D	17	(4)	
Neven VUKMAN		D	17		

ZAGREB
Coach – Mile Petkovic; (10/12/05) Milos Rus

2005				
20/7	Slaven Belupo	h	3-1	Bartolovic, Jakirovic, Vidovic
30/7	Hajduk Split	a	1-3	Mandukic
6/8	Osijek	h	0-1	
13/8	Kamen Ingrad Velika	h	2-1	Vidovic, Mandukic
20/8	Medimurje Cakovec	a	0-0	
27/8	Pula	h	2-0	Custic, Pelajic
10/9	Cibalia Vinkovci	a	1-1	Cutura
18/9	Dinamo Zagreb	h	0-4	
24/9	Rijeka	a	0-0	
1/10	Inter Zapresic	h	1-0	Pelajic
15/10	Varteks Varazdin	a	1-3	Pelajic
22/10	Slaven Belupo	a	0-1	
26/10	Hajduk Split	h	1-2	Pelajic
29/10	Osijek	a	0-1	
5/11	Kamen Ingrad Velika	h	2-1	Ivankovic, Brkljaca
19/11	Medimurje Cakovec	h	1-0	Mandukic
26/11	Pula	a	0-2	
3/12	Cibalia Vinkovci	h	1-0	Ivankovic
2006				
18/2	Dinamo Zagreb	a	1-4	Parlov
25/2	Rijeka	h	2-0	Pelajic, Ibricic
4/3	Inter Zapresic	a	0-1	
11/3	Varteks Varazdin	h	0-1	
18/3	Inter Zapresic	h	3-1	Ibricic, Brkljaca, Pelajic
25/3	Pula	a	1-4	Bartolovic
1/4	Medimurje Cakovec	h	1-0	Bartolovic
8/4	Cibalia Vinkovci	h	0-0	
15/4	Slaven Belupo	a	0-3	
22/4	Inter Zapresic	a	0-1	
29/4	Pula	h	1-0	Ibricic
6/5	Medimurje Cakovec	a	0-2	
10/5	Cibalia Vinkovci	a	1-2	Jurendic
13/5	Slaven Belupo	h	0-3	

Name	Nat	Pos	Aps	(s)	Gls
Mladen BARTOLOVIC	BOS	M	26		3
Ivan BJELOBRADIC		M	2		
Franjo BOZIC		A	1	(6)	
Mario BRKLJACA		D	24	(3)	2
Stipe BRNAS		D	11		
Ivan CUNCIC		M	8	(7)	
Hrvoje CUSTIC		A	7	(12)	1
Mario CUTURA		D	24		1
Senijad IBRICIC	BOS	M	19	(6)	3
Vedran IVANKOVIC		D	12	(2)	2
Sergej JAKIROVIC	BOS	M	2		1
JURENDIC		A	1		1
Tomislav LABUDOVIC		D	17		
Ivan LAJTMAN		M	12	(9)	
Mario MANDUKIC		A	18	(9)	3
Vladimir MARKOTIC	BOS	G	13		
Dejan MISKOVIC		D	3	(2)	
Mensur MUJDZA	BOS	D	14	(1)	
Safet NADAREVIC	BOS	D	26	(3)	
ORSULIC		M		(1)	
PARLOV		D	17	(5)	
Mladen PELAJIC		D	27	(2)	6
PETRICEVIC		A		(6)	

Croatia

SOPIC		D	16	(3)
SPICIC		M	1	(1)
Dragan STOJKIC	BOS	G	19	
Rajko VIDOVIC		A	7	(4) 2
Ivica VRDOLJAK	SCG	D	25	

DOMESTIC CUP 2005/06

1/16 FINALS
(21/9/05)
HASK 0, Dinamo Zagreb 8
Hrvace 0, Hajduk Split 3
Ogulin 2, Varteks Varazdin 3
Jedinstvo Omladinac Kapra 0, Rijeka 2
Vodice 0, Osijek 5
ZET 1, Pula 0
Moslavina 1, Zagreb 0
Slavonija Slavonska Pozega 1, Kamen Ingrad Velika 3
Samobor 1, Cibalia Vinkovci 4
Vinogradar 2, Pomorac Kostrena 1
Vukovar 91 0, Slaven Belupo Koprivnica 3
Cakovec 0, Inter Zapresic 4
Medimurje Cakovec 2, Zadar 0
Zagorec 0, Hrvatski dragovoljac Zagreb 3
Segesta Sisak 1, Belisce 0
Naftas Ivanic Grad 2, Sibenik 0

1/8 FINALS
(19/10/05)
Naftas Ivanic Grad 3, Dinamo Zagreb 2
Segesta Sisak 1, Hajduk Split 2 *(aet)*
Hrvatski dragovoljac Zagreb 0, Varteks Varazdin 2
Rijeka 3, Medimurje Cakovec 1
Osijek 2, Inter Zapresic 0
Slaven Belupo Koprivnica 5, ZET 0
Vinogradar 3, Moslavina 2
Cibalia Vinkovci 1, Kamen Ingrad Velika 3

QUARTER-FINALS
(9/11/05 & 15/11/05)
Vinogradar 1 *(Buckovic 14)*, Rijeka 2 *(Zekic 34, Sharbini Ah. 41p)*
Rijeka 8 *(Linic 8, 14, 42, 53, 56, Novakovic 10, 90, Sharbini Ah. 61)*, Vinogradar 0
(Rijeka 10-1)

Slaven Belupo Koprivnica 1 *(Dodik 53)*, Kamen Ingrad Velika 0
Kamen Ingrad Velika 4 *(Brajkovic 4, Tomic 28, Paramakovic 42, Simunic 43)*, Slaven Belupo Koprivnica 1 *(Dodik 74)*
(Kamen Ingrad Velika 4-2)

Varteks Varazdin 4 *(Jolic 3, Benko 23, 47, Melnjak 27)*, Naftas Ivanic Grad 1 *(Cingel 88)*
Naftas Ivanic Grad 1 *(Domic 79)*, Varteks Varazdin 1 *(Jolic 23)*
(Varteks Varazdin 5-2)

Osijek 1 *(Vojnovic A. 16)*, Hajduk Split 1 *(Marcic 41)*
Hajduk Split 2 *(Kranjcar 9, 11p)*, Osijek 1 *(Balatinac 22)*
(Hajduk Split 3-2)

SEMI-FINALS
(29/3/06 & 5/4/06)
Hajduk Split 1 *(Kranjcar 21p)*, Rijeka 1 *(Vugrinec 55)*
Rijeka 1 *(Novakovic 23)*, Hajduk Split 0
(Rijeka 2-1)

Varteks Varazdin 3 *(Pokrivac 50, Benko 53, 70)*, Kamen Ingrad Velika 3 *(Parmakovic 30, Lakic 61, Brajkovic 81)*

Kamen Ingrad Velika 1 *(Zelenika 88)*, Varteks Varazdin 2 *(Pavlicic 10, Jolic 25)*
(Varteks Varazdin 5-4)

FINAL
(26/4/06)
Stadion na Kantridi, Rijeka
RIJEKA 4 *(Vugrinec 20, 69, Linic 43, Bobic 81)*
VARTEKS VARAZDIN 0
Referee – Kovacic
RIJEKA – Zilic, Saric *(Tkalcevic 83)*, Knezevic, Lerant, Rendulic, Tadic *(Bobic 72)*, Prisc, Novakovic, Linic, Vugrinec, Sharbini Ah. *(Rubil 57)*.
VARTEKS VARAZDIN – Kopric, Ipsa, Lucic, Vuk, Jertec *(Kardum 61)*, Posavec, Halilovic, Safaric, Pokrivac, Jolic, Benko *(Pavlicic 90)*.

(3/5/06)
Gradski stadion, Varazdin
VARTEKS VARAZDIN 5 *(Lucic 23, Benko 54, Safaric 84p, Novinic 89, 90)*
RIJEKA 1 *(Vugrinec 71)*
Referee – Supraha
VARTEKS VARAZDIN – Kopric, Lucic *(Mohorovic 78)*, Vuk *(Jolic 61)*, Pokrivac, Melnjak *(Posavec 66)*, Halilovic, Safaric, Pavlicic, Jertec, Jolic, Benko.
RIJEKA – Zilic, Saric, Lerant, Knezevic, Rendulic, Prisc, Kerkez *(Tadic 38)*, Novakovic, Linic, Vugrinec, Sharbini Ah. *(Tkalcevic 68)*.

(5-5; Rijeka on away goal)

SECOND LEVEL FINAL TABLES 2005/06

NORTH		Pld	W	D	L	F	A	Pts
1	Belisce	22	14	6	2	41	14	48
2	Graficar Vodovod Osijek	22	11	6	5	38	21	39
3	Bjelovar	22	11	4	7	25	26	37
4	Vukovar 91	22	11	2	9	36	21	35
5	Koprivnica	22	10	5	7	34	23	35
6	Metalac Osijek	22	9	6	7	28	16	33
7	Marsonia Slavonski Brod	22	9	4	9	25	30	31
8	Cakovec	22	7	7	8	33	40	28
9	Granicar Zupanja	22	7	4	11	28	28	25
10	Dilj Vinkovci	22	6	6	10	28	44	24
11	Slavonija Slavonska Pozega	22	5	7	10	30	42	22
12	Mladost Molve	22	2	3	17	23	64	9

SOUTH		Pld	W	D	L	F	A	Pts
1	Sibenik	22	14	5	3	47	25	47
2	Pomorac Kostrena	22	10	10	2	45	22	40
3	Croatia Sesvete	22	11	2	9	39	30	35
4	Novalja	22	10	3	9	36	29	33
5	Hrvatski dragovoljac Zagreb	22	8	8	6	30	29	32
6	Imotski	22	8	8	6	27	26	32
7	Naftas Ivanic Grad	22	8	8	6	31	33	32
8	Zadar	22	7	6	9	29	27	27
9	Mosor Zrnovnica	22	6	7	9	21	36	25
10	Solin Grada	22	5	6	11	37	39	21
11	Segesta Sisak	22	6	2	14	21	41	20
12	Karlovac	22	4	5	13	18	44	17

N.B. Promotion play-off between Belisce and Sibenik cancelled as Belisce could not obtain licence to play in top division. Sibenik promoted automatically.

Cyprus

Apollon hold their nerve

An exciting three-way tussle for the Cypriot championship ended in a well deserved victory for Apollon of Limassol, who thus became the fourth different club to take the title in as many years.

Pursued, hounded and, once or twice, overtaken by the Big Two from the capital, APOEL and Omonia, the team from the southern coastal town showed remarkable resilience and stamina to keep going from start to finish and eventually emerge triumphant. Apollon's first title in 12 years, and third in all, was clinched under severe pressure on the final day as they beat outgoing champions Anorthosis 3-1 in front of an ecstatic home crowd.

With Omonia and APOEL both cruising to easy victories elsewhere, it was imperative that Apollon won the game. But as they had drawn each of their previous five encounters with Omonia, APOEL and Anorthosis, it was far from a foregone conclusion. When the visitors took the lead inside the first 15 minutes, the Apollon fans understandably feared the worst, but the league's top scorer, Polish striker Lukasz Sosin, soon levelled, and by half-time a second Apollon goal, from Portuguese import João Pedro Paiva, had put the Limassol side in front. Midway through the second half the three points – and the title – were secured as Sosin coolly despatched a penalty to make it 3-1.

Sharpshooter Sosin

It was the Pole's 28th goal of the season. In 2004/05 he had also topped the scorers' charts with 21 goals as Apollon finished a lowly seventh. Now, at the end of German coach Bernd Stange's first full season in charge, Sosin had a championship winner's medal to add to his Golden Boot.

Apollon ended the 26-match campaign undefeated – the only European domestic champions to achieve that feat in 2005/06. Stange, who had arrived at the club midway through the previous season, was the chief architect of their success. A former head coach of East Germany, he also worked in Iraq and led that war-torn country to a surprise fourth place at the Athens Olympics. Using his contacts in Baghdad, he brought three Iraqi players to Apollon, and they all played a big part in the team's title triumph. There was barely a Cypriot presence in the side. No fewer than 14 foreigners, from eight different countries, represented the club during the season. Tragically, however, one of them, Hungarian midfielder Gábor Zavadszky, did not live to see the team triumph. The 31-year-old died suddenly in January. Needless to say, the championship victory was dedicated to him.

Omonia finished one point adrift of Apollon to claim the runners-up spot and a place in the UEFA Cup. They switched coaches in mid-season, with Romanian Ioan Andone arriving from Dinamo Bucharest to replace Belgian Henk Houwaart. They also added Brazilian-born ex-Germany international striker Paulo Roberto Rink to their

NATIONAL TEAM RESULTS 2005/06

13/8/05	Iraq	H	Limassol	2-1	Yiasoumi (63, 79)
17/8/05	Faroe Islands (WCQ)	A	Toftir	3-0	Konstantinou M. (39, 77p), Krassas (90)
7/9/05	Switzerland (WCQ)	H	Nicosia	1-3	Aloneftis (34)
8/10/05	Republic of Ireland (WCQ)	H	Nicosia	0-1	
12/10/05	France (WCQ)	A	Saint-Denis	0-4	
16/11/05	Wales	H	Limassol	1-0	Michael (42p)
28/2/06	Slovenia	H	Larnaca	0-1	
1/3/06	Armenia	H	Nicosia	2-0	Okkas (18), Michael (61)

Cyprus

NATIONAL TEAM APPEARANCES 2005/06

Coach – Angelos ANASTASIADIS

Name	DOB	Club	Irq	FAR	SUI	IRL	FRA	Wal	Slo	Arm	Caps	Goals
Michalis MORFIS	15/1/79	APOEL	G	G	G		G	G72	G		13	-
Nicos NICOLAOU	5/8/73	Anorthosis	D46		s64		s81				28	1
Elias CHARALAMBOUS	25/9/80	PAOK (GRE)	D46	s79	D		D	s59	s63	D52	20	-
Stelios OKKARIDES	17/11/77	APOEL	D58	s62	D46			D	D54	D79	25	-
Loukas LOUKA	17/4/78	Anorthosis	D	D	D	D	D	s79	D	s82	14	-
Costas CHARALAMBIDES	25/7/81	Panathinaikos (GRE)	M	M	M	M	M	M	M54	M	24	5
Stavros GEORGIOU	14/3/72	APOEL	M53								11	1
Stathis ALONEFTIS	29/3/83	Larisa (GRE)	M63		M	M	M	s59	M63	M	10	1
Alexandros GARPOZIS	5/9/80	Xanthi (GRE)	M	M62		M	M46	M59	M		11	-
Yiasemakis YIASOUMI	31/5/75	PAOK (GRE)	A	s86	s82	s68	A63	A76	A	s81	42	5
Eleftherios ELEFTHERIOU	2/6/74	Paralimni	A46	A							14	-
Christos MARANGOS	9/5/83	Anorthosis	s46			s73	s46		s65		4	-
Costas MAKRIDES	13/1/82	APOEL	s46	M		M	M81	M	M65	M82	19	-
Chrysis MICHAEL	26/5/77	APOEL	s46	M	M82	M30		M	D68	M69	31	4
Georgios THEODOTOU	1/1/74	Omonia	s53	D79						D	60	-
Andreas KONSTANTINOU	12/10/80	AEK	s58								1	-
Georgios NIKOLAOU	21/5/82	Omonia	s63								4	-
Simon KRASSAS	10/7/82	AEK (GRE)			M	M64	s30	M	M59		13	1
Yiannakis OKKAS	11/2/77	Olympiakos (GRE)		A	A	A68		A	A54	A74	70	14
Michalis KONSTANTINOU	19/2/78	Olympiakos (GRE)		A86	A	A			s54	A81	51	22
Lambros LAMBROU	9/9/77	Ethnikos			s46	D73	D	D79	s54	s52	19	-
Marios ELIA	14/4/79	APOEL			D	D	D	D70	D		18	1
Nicos PANAYIOTOU	16/12/70	Panahaiki (GRE)				G				s81	77	-
Petros FILANIOTIS	13/4/80	AEL					s63				4	-
Anthonis GEORGIALLIDES	30/1/82	Anorthosis						s72		G81	4	-
Alekos ALEKOU	13/12/83	Aris						s76			1	-
Christis THEOFILOU	30/4/80	Apollon						s70	s68	D	3	-
Marinos SATSIAS	24/5/78	APOEL						s54	s69		30	-
Giorgos MERKIS	30/7/84	Apollon							s79		1	-
Nektarios ALEXANDROU	19/12/83	APOEL							s74		1	-

ranks. He had scored prolifically in the first half of the season for Nicosia rivals Olympiakos, but neither he nor his team-mates could find the net in the big game away to Apollon two rounds from the end, which meant that his back-to-back hat-tricks in the final two games were of only token value. Omonia were the only one of the top four teams to lose at home, and it was that 1-0 defeat to Paralimni in early February that eventually cost the Greens the title.

APOEL's Cup

APOEL effectively gave up on the title when they lost 1-0 to Omonia in round 23. They did, however, gain revenge on their arch-rivals a few weeks later by beating them 3-1 away to clinch a place in the final of the Cypriot Cup, against AEK. Although the final was played at AEK's home ground in Larnaca, APOEL ensured a fifth successive season in Europe by beating their 'hosts' 3-2 with an extra-time

Cyprus

winner from Serbian striker Sasa Jovanovic.

It was APOEL's first Cup win in seven years but their record 18th victory in all. The man who led them to victory was ex-Poland national team boss Jerzy Engel. He had arrived at the end of October in place of the unfortunate Marios Constandinou, sacked for disappointing performances rather than results (which included the elimination of Maccabi Tel Aviv from the UEFA Cup), but the Cup final proved to be the Pole's final game in charge after the club failed to agree new contract terms.

Anorthosis, still led by Georgian player-coach Temuri Ketsbaia, had a frustrating season on all fronts. It started with a bang when they sensationally knocked Trabzonspor out of the Champions League preliminaries, thus becoming the first Cypriot club ever to defeat Turkish opposition in official European competition. But subsequent disappointments in Europe against Rangers (in the Champions League) and Palermo (in the UEFA Cup) were matched by poor results at home. Ultimately Ketsbaia's side would pay the price for an abundance of draws, but at no stage did the defending champions ever really threaten to intervene in the three-horse race for the title.

With Cyprus's membership of the European Union enabling the country's top clubs to flood their playing staffs with overseas acquisitions, these are tough times for homegrown players and, in consequence, for the Cyprus national side. It is symbolic that the island's best players almost all now play on mainland Greece. But even with stars of the Hellenic league like Panathinaikos midfielder Costas Charalambides and Olympiakos striker Michalis Konstantinou in their ranks, Cyprus had a very poor 2006 World Cup qualifying series, collecting four meagre points – and all of those from the Faroe Islands.

Angelos Anastasiadis (a Greek) took over as coach midway through that campaign but the team will almost certainly have to improve during the Euro 2008 qualifiers if he is to hang around for the duration. Not so long ago Cyprus provided awkward opposition for even the most illustrious visitors to Limassol and Nicosia, but the team's confidence looked shot during the World Cup qualifiers, and with the Cypriot fans looking increasingly disaffected, the consequence was lethargy, apathy and a rather sad state of affairs all round.

EUROPEAN CUPS 2005/06

UEFA CHAMPIONS LEAGUE

ANORTHOSIS

1st qualifying round DINAMO MINSK (BLS)
A 1-1 *Frousos (44)*
Georgallides, Xenidis, Nikolaou (Konstantinou 85), Katsavakis, Poursaitidis, Ketsbaia, Haber, Louka, Tsitaishvili, Kinkladze (Maragos 76), Frousos (Tsolakides 46).
H 1-0 *Samaras (71)*
Georgallides, Katsavakis, Nikolaou (Konstantinou 88), Haber, Poursaitidis (Tsolakides 64), Tsitaishvili, Maragos, Ketsbaia, Louka, Kinkladze (Kampantais 46), Samaras.

2nd qualifying round TRABZONSPOR (TUR)
H 3-1 *Nikolaou (25), Frousos (83), Tsitaishvili (90)*
Georgallides, Kampantais (Frousos 77), Poursaitidis, Haber, Maragos, Ketsbaia (Kinkladze 54), Nikolaou, Tsitaishvili, Xenidis, Samaras (Haxhi 20), Katsavakis.
A 0-1
Georgallides, Frousos (Xenidis 75), Poursaitidis, Haber, Maragos (Kinkladze 57), Ketsbaia (Konstantinou 66), Louka, Nikolaou, Tsitaishvili, Haxhi, Katsavakis.

3rd qualifying round RANGERS (SCO)
H 1-2 *Frousos (72)*
Georgallides, Poursaitidis (Tsolakides 74), Haxhi, Louka, Xenidis, Maragos (Konstantinou 83), Frousos, Kinkladze, Ketsbaia, Tsitaishvili (Kampantais 70), Nikolaou.
A 0-2
Georgallides, Poursaitidis, Maragos, Ketsbaia (Kinkladze 54), Haber, Nikolaou, Tsitaishvili, Xenidis, Samaras (Haxhi 20), Katsavakis, Frousos,

UEFA CUP

OMONIA

1st qualifying round HIBERNIANS (MLT)
H 3-0 *Mguni (30), Kozlej (47), Vakouftsis (85p)*
Leoni, Kittos, Georgiou, Konnafis, Papaioannou, Kaiafas, Grozdanovski (Dobrasinovic 79), Theodotou, Korolovszky (Ioakim 79), Mguni (Kozlej 46), Vakouftsis.
A 3-0 *Grozdanovski (5, 63), Vakouftsis (44p)*
Leoni, Kittos, Georgiou, Konnafis, Papaioannou (Kakoyiannis 66), Theodotou, Korolovszky, Kaiafas (Ioakim 75), Grozdanovski, Kozlej, Vakouftsis (Dobrasinovic 56).

2nd qualifying round DINAMO BUCURESTI (ROM)
A 1-3 *Konnafis (4)*
Leoni, Kittos (Vakouftsis 23), Konnafis, Papaioannou, Georgiou, Kaiafas, Korolovszky, Grozdanovski, Theodotou, Magno (Mguni 67), N'Diaye (Kakoyiannis 57).
H 2-1 *Kaiafas (28), Christou (31)*
Leoni, Konnafis, Papaioannou (Kozlej 67), Kakoyiannis, Theodotou (Grozdanovski 64), Korolovszky, Dobrasinovic (Mguni 72), Kittos, Kaiafas, Magno, Vakouftsis.

APOEL

1st qualifying round BIRKIRKARA (MLT)
A 2-0 *Georgiou (72), Jovanovic (80)*
Morphis, Elia, Okkarides, Daskalakis, Georgiou, Michael, Makridis, Jovanovic, Alexandrou (Sampson 60), Neophytou (Kaklamanos 56), Nasiopoulos.
H 4-0 *Kaklamanos (38, 59), Neophytou (53), Georgiou (90)*
Morphis, Elia, Okkarides, Daskalakis, Georgiou, Michael, Makridis, Jovanovic, Alexandrou (Efstathiou 65), Neophitou (Eleftheriou 76), Kaklamanos (Sampson 80).

Cyprus

2nd qualifying round MACCABI TEL AVIV (ISR)
H 1-0 *Neophytou (65)*
Morphis, Elia, Okkarides, Kenedy, Daskalakis, Georgiou (Jovanovic 51), Michael, Fernandes, Makridis, Neophytou (Alexandrou 79), Kaklamanos (Nasiopoulos 58).
A 2-2 *Makridis (93), Neophytou (95)*
(aet)
Morphis, Elia, Okkarides, Kenedy, Daskalakis, Michael, Fernandes, Makridis, Jovanovic (Georgiou 52) Neophytou (Jamroz 102), Nasiopoulos (Alexandrou 70).

1st round HERTHA BSC BERLIN (GER)
H 0-1
Morphis, Okkarides, Okon, Daskalakis, Kenedy, Michael, Georgiou (Solari 76), Fernandes, Makridis (Jovanovic 65), Kaklamanos (Neophytou 62), Alexandrou.
A 1-3 *Makridis (76)*
Morphis, Okkarides, Daskalakis, Okon (Kenedy 36), Elia, Georgiou, Makridis, Michael, Fernandes (Jovanovic 72), Alexandrou, Neophytou (Nasiopoulos 56).

ANORTHOSIS
1st round PALERMO (ITA)
A 1-2 *Ketsbaia (76)*
Georgallides, Poursaitidis, Katsavakis, Louka, Xenidis, Maragos (Tsitaishvili 45; Bryce 60), Haber, Konstantinou, Haxhi (Samaras 46), Ketsbaia, Frousos.
H 0-4
Georgallides, Louka, Poursaitidis, Katsavakis, Xenidis, Haxhi (Maragos 58), Nikolaou, Haber, Tsitaishvili (Maragos 68), Frousos, Kampantais (Tököli 46).

TOP GOALSCORERS 2005/06

28	Lukasz SOSIN (Apollon)	
23	Paulo Roberto RINK (Olympiakos/Omonia)	
16	Nikos FROUSSOS (Anorthosis)	
15	Kyriakos CHAILIS (Nea Salamina)	
	Alexis ALEXANDRIS (APOP/Kinyras)	
14	Esteban SOLARI (APOEL)	
13	Kostas ELIA (Paralimni)	
	Nemanja COROVIC (AEL)	
12	Giorgos VAKOUFTSIS (Omonia)	
	Julius WOBAY (Nea Salamina)	

LEAGUE RESULTS/SCORERS/APPEARANCES/GOALS 2005/06

AEK
Coach – Nikolai Kostov (BUL); (5/12/05) Marios Constandinou

2005
27/8	Ethnikos	a	1-2	Raducan
11/9	Paralimni	a	0-1	
17/9	Omonia	h	2-3	Datoru, Oliseh
25/9	AEL	a	1-1	Bah
3/10	Anorthosis	h	1-1	Datoru
16/10	ENTHOI	a	4-1	Bah 2, Moita, Pavlou
22/10	Olympiakos	h	2-1	Moita, Oliseh (p)
30/10	APOP	a	2-1	Siligardakis, Osterc
5/11	APOEL	h	1-2	Bah
13/11	Apollon	a	0-3	
26/11	Nea Salamina	h	0-0	
4/12	APEP	a	1-2	Traoré
17/12	Dighenis	h	1-1	Bah

2006
8/1	Ethnikos	h	3-0	Siligardakis, Raducan, Bah
14/1	Paralimni	h	1-0	Raducan
21/1	Omonia	a	1-3	Bah
5/2	AEL	h	2-0	Pavlou 2
11/2	Anorthosis	a	0-1	
25/2	ENTHOI	h	2-0	Raducan, Bah
12/3	Olympiakos	a	2-3	Konstantinou 2 (1p)
19/3	APOP	h	5-0	Datoru 2, Raducan, Pavlou, Moita
25/3	APOEL	a	0-3	
8/4	Apollon	h	2-3	Siligardakis, Moita
15/4	Nea Salamina	a	2-3	Ceesay, Raducan
29/4	APEP	h	3-1	Raducan og (Bastida), Ceesay, Datoru
6/5	Dighenis	a	0-1	

No	Name	Nat	Pos	Aps	(s)	Gls
10	Ismalia BAH	SEN	M	22	(2)	8
7	Jatto CEESAY	GAM	M	8		2
21	Paraskevas CHRISTOU		D	16		
25	Savvas CHRISTOU		M	3	(10)	
9	George DATORU	NGA	A	22	(3)	5
5	Yiannos DIMSTHENOUS		D	12	(4)	
7	Christophe-Antoine ETTORI	FRA	M	4	(2)	
40	Angelos GEORGIOU	GRE	G	7		
18	Stefanos GEORGIOU		M	1	(3)	
24	Andreas KONSTANTINOU		D	17		2
15	Panayiotis KYTHRAIOTIS		G	12	(2)	
23	Konstantinos MINA		D	22	(2)	
27	Pedro Joaquim MOITA	POR	A	16	(8)	4
30	Cristian MUNTEANU	ROM	G	7		
6	Kennedy NAGOLI	ZIM	M		(2)	
4	Azubike OLISEH	NGA	D	20		2
29	Milan OSTERC	SLO	A	4	(3)	1
20	Christos PANAYIOTOU		D	3	(9)	
11	Kyriakos PAVLOU		D	11	(8)	4
28	Michalis PRODROMOU		M	1		
8	Narcis RADUCAN	ROM	M	23	(1)	6
22	Haralambos SILIGARDAKIS	GRE	M	15	(6)	3
26	Amar TRAORE	SEN	M	21	(2)	1
17	Christos XENOFONDOS		A	1	(1)	
3	José Gonçalves "ZÉ NANDO"	POR	D	18	(1)	

AEL
Coach – Andreas Michaelides; Bojan Prasnikar (SLO); (11/2/06) Louzos Mayroydis

2005
27/8	APEP	a	2-1	Sebök, og (Andreou)
11/9	Dighenis	h	3-0	Corovic, Sebök 2
17/9	Ethnikos	a	0-0	
25/9	AEK	h	1-1	Karic
1/10	Omonia	a	0-2	
15/10	Paralimni	a	5-3	Zahana-Oni, William 3, Sebök
22/10	Anorthosis	h	3-0	Christodoulou 2, Corovic
30/10	ENTHOI	a	2-1	Corovic 2
6/11	Olympiakos	h	2-2	Sebök, William
12/11	APOP	a	3-1	Corovic 2, William
26/11	APOEL	h	1-1	Corovic
4/12	Apollon	a	0-2	
17/12	Nea Salamina	h	0-3	

2006
8/1	APEP	h	4-0	Corovic 2, William 2

Cyprus

FINAL LEAGUE TABLE 2005/06

		Pld	Home W	Home D	Home L	Home F	Home A	Away W	Away D	Away L	Away F	Away A	Total W	Total D	Total L	Total F	Total A	Pts
1	Apollon	26	11	2	0	39	7	8	5	0	29	17	19	7	0	68	24	64
2	Omonia	26	10	2	1	30	11	10	1	2	29	9	20	3	3	59	20	63
3	APOEL	26	11	2	0	37	12	8	3	2	26	10	19	5	2	63	22	62
4	Anorthosis	26	8	5	0	25	7	7	3	3	30	19	15	8	3	55	26	53
5	Paralimni	26	5	5	3	27	19	7	2	4	13	9	12	7	7	40	28	43
6	Nea Salamina	26	8	1	4	30	20	4	4	5	23	28	12	5	9	53	48	41
7	AEL	26	6	3	4	27	22	4	2	7	17	26	10	5	11	44	48	35
8	AEK	26	7	3	3	25	12	2	1	10	14	25	9	4	13	39	37	31
9	Ethnikos	26	5	2	6	21	19	3	2	8	21	24	8	4	14	42	43	28
10	Dighenis	26	4	4	5	15	19	3	3	7	18	26	7	7	12	33	45	28
11	Olympiakos	26	4	3	6	26	25	2	6	5	14	25	6	9	11	40	50	27
12	APOP/Kinyras	26	3	2	8	22	24	2	1	10	13	41	5	3	18	35	65	18
13	APEP	26	1	2	10	8	26	0	3	10	9	46	1	5	20	17	72	8
14	ENTHOI	26	0	2	11	5	43	1	2	10	10	32	1	4	21	15	75	7

15/1	Dighenis	a	2-2	Corovic, Filaniotis
22/1	Ethnikos	h	2-3	Christodoulou, Corovic
5/2	AEK	a	0-2	
12/2	Omonia	h	1-2	og (Grozdanovski)
25/2	Paralimni	h	2-1	og (Sotiriou), Corovic
12/3	Anorthosis	a	0-5	
18/3	ENTHOI	h	3-2	Filaniotis 2 (1p), Tököli
26/3	Olympiakos	a	2-3	William, Charalambous C.
8/4	APOP	h	4-3	Vattis, Charalambous K., Corovic, Filaniotis
15/4	APOEL	a	0-2	
29/4	Apollon	h	1-4	Bulajic
6/5	Nea Salamina	a	1-2	og (Bolohan)

No	Name	Nat	Pos	Aps	(s)	Gls
4	Marios ANDONIOU		D	12	(2)	
22	Kyriakos ANDREOU		M			
5	Spasoje BULAJIC	SLO	D	25		1
11	Christos CHARALAMBOUS		A	10	(7)	1
29	Kyriakos CHARALAMBOUS		M	3	(1)	1
2	Christos CHRISTODOULOU		D	8		3
9	Nemanja COROVIC	SCG	A	19	(1)	13
7	Giorgos DEMETRIADIS		M	5	(6)	
33	Petros FILANIOTIS		A	16	(8)	4
77	Christos GERMANOS		D	14	(5)	
3	Miha GOLOB	SLO	D	21	(1)	
19	Amir KARIC	SLO	M	10	(1)	1
35	Antonis KAVAZIS		D	2	(5)	
40	Antonis KEZOS		D	9	(3)	
35	Antonis KONNARIS		D	13		
70	Panos KONSTANTINOU		G	5		
12	Xenios KYRIAKOU		M	5	(5)	
6	Liasos LOUKA		M	17	(4)	
37	Giorgos NEOCLEOUS		A	1		
15	Neofytos NEOFYTOU		M	2	(1)	
10	József SEBŐK	HUN	M	11	(0)	5
77	Simon SESLAR	SLO	M	5	(1)	
1	Marko SIMEUNOVIC	SLO	G	8		
20	Dimitris STYLIANOU		G	13	(2)	
55	Attila TÖKÖLI	HUN	A	6		1
38	Elias VATTIS		A	2	(3)	1
44	Muamer VUGDALIC	SLO	D	11	(1)	

| 8 | Boaventura WILLIAM | BRA | A | 19 | (1) | 8 |
| 30 | Landry ZAHANA-ONI | CIV | A | 14 | (2) | 1 |

ANORTHOSIS
Coach – Temuri Ketsbaia (GEO)

2005

29/8	Nea Salamina	a	5-2	Froussos 2, Tsitaishvili, Louka, Ketsbaia
10/9	APEP	h	1-1	Louka
18/9	Dighenis	a	1-1	Katsavakis
24/9	Ethnikos	h	2-0	Ketsbaia, Kabantais
3/10	AEK	a	1-1	Nikolaou
16/10	Omonia	h	2-1	Froussos 2
22/10	AEL	a	0-3	
29/10	Paralimni	a	1-0	Froussos
7/11	ENTHOI	h	1-0	Nikolaou (p)
13/11	Olympiakos	a	2-1	Haber, Tsitaishvili
26/11	APOP	h	6-1	Kabantais, Xenidis, Marangos, Froussos 2, Tököli
3/12	APOEL	a	3-5	Froussos, Nikolaou 2 (1p)
17/12	Apollon	h	1-1	Froussos

2006

7/1	Nea Salamina	h	2-0	Tsitaishvili, Nikolaou
15/1	APEP	a	1-0	Froussos
21/1	Dighenis	h	1-0	Ketsbaia
5/2	Ethnikos	a	5-0	Katsavakis, Froussos, Kiassos, Mujiri, Xenidis
11/2	AEK	h	1-0	Katsavakis
25/2	Omonia	a	2-2	Froussos, Ketsbaia
12/3	AEL	h	5-0	Ketsbaia 3, Tsitaishvili, Fabinho
18/3	Paralimni	h	0-0	
26/3	ENTHOI	a	6-0	Froussos 4 (1p), Mujiri, Kiassos
9/4	Olympiakos	h	1-1	Tsitaishvili
15/4	APOP	a	2-1	Fabinho, Tsitaishvili (p)
29/4	APOEL	h	2-2	Nikolaou 2
6/5	Apollon	a	1-3	Kiassos

No	Name	Nat	Pos	Aps	(s)	Gls
17	Steven BRYCE	CRC	M		(5)	
10	Stelian CARABAS	ROM	M	10	(1)	

Cyprus

No	Name	Nat	Pos	Aps	(s)	Gls
8	FABINHO	BRA	M	3	(3)	2
11	Nikos FROUSSOS	GRE	A	21	(4)	16
3	Giorgi GABIDAURI	GEO	M	1	(1)	
1	Antonis GIORGALLIDES		G	23		
6	Marco HABER	GER	M	19	(5)	1
22	Altin HAXHI	ALB	D	16		
3	Leonidas KABANTAIS	GRE	A	5	(4)	2
4	Nikos KATSAVAKIS	GRE	M	22		3
14	Temuri KETSBAIA	GEO	A	18	(1)	7
26	Kostas KIASSOS	GRE	M	10	(1)	3
12	Kostas KONSTANTINOU		M	3	(1)	
78	Loukas LOUKA		D	17	(2)	2
16	Christos MARANGOS		M	16	(8)	1
21	Amiran MUJIRI	GEO	M	7	(3)	2
31	Zoltán NAGY	HUN	G	3		
5	Nikos NIKOLAOU		D	21	(1)	7
7	Savvas POURSAITIDIS	GRE	M	26		
23	Konstantinos SAMARAS		D	4	(4)	
55	Attila TÖKÖLI	HUN	A	3	(7)	1
9	Klimenti TSITAISHVILI	GEO	A	18	(5)	6
18	Iacovos TSOLAKIDIS		D		(2)	
20	Giorgos XENIDIS	GRE	D	17	(2)	2
80	Nikos ZAPROPOULOS	GRE	D	3	(3)	

APEP
Coach – Tasos Kyriakou; (Nicky Papavasiliou)

2005
Date	Opp		Res	Scorers
27/8	AEL	h	1-2	Kontolefteros L.
10/9	Anorthosis	a	1-1	Jovanovic
17/9	ENTHOI	h	1-1	Sepér
25/9	Olympiakos	a	0-8	
1/10	APOP	h	1-2	og (Ignatiou)
16/10	APOEL	a	0-2	
23/10	Apollon	h	1-2	Stylianou
29/10	Nea Salamina	a	0-5	
6/11	Paralimni	h	0-2	
12/11	Dighenis	h	1-2	Jefferson
26/11	Ethnikos	a	0-4	
4/12	AEK	h	2-1	Solomou, Beress
18/12	Omonia	a	1-2	Jefferson

2006
Date	Opp		Res	Scorers
8/1	AEL	a	0-4	
15/1	Anorthosis	h	0-1	
21/1	ENTHOI	a	0-0	
4/2	Olympiakos	h	0-0	
11/2	APOP	a	1-3	Jefferson
25/2	APOEL	h	0-3	
11/3	Apollon	a	1-5	Evandro
18/3	Nea Salamina	h	1-3	Kenedy
25/3	Paralimni	a	1-6	Evandro
8/4	Dighenis	a	3-3	Bastida S. 2, Gari
15/4	Ethnikos	h	0-2	
29/4	AEK	a	1-3	Houche
6/5	Omonia	h	0-5	

No	Name	Nat	Pos	Aps	(s)	Gls
2	Andreas ANDREOU		D	9	(2)	
69	Nikos AVGOUSTI		G	1		
40	Paulinho BASTIDA	BRA	M	6		
33	Sergio BASTIDA	ARG	M	25		2
99	Ferenc BERESS	HUN	M	1	(2)	1
82	Maurice CHRISTOPHE	FRA	M	10		
88	Tomis CHRYSOSTOMOU		M	8	(2)	
86	Yiannis DEMETRIOU		D	7	(6)	
22	Franck DIA	FRA	M	5	(3)	
21	Michalis EFTHYMIOU		D	5	(3)	
10	EVANDRO Russo	BRA	A	18	(4)	2
87	Marc GARI	FRA	A	8	(4)	1
15	Boussad HOUCHE	FRA	M	14	(1)	1
9	Rubim JEFFERSON	BRA	A	16	(6)	3
45	Taso JOVANOVIC	SCG	M	4	(2)	1
23	Daniel KENEDY	POR	M	7		1
22	Katanga KIBIKULA	DRC	D	8		
4	Giorgos KONTOLEFTEROS		D	2		
55	Lefteris KONTOLEFTEROS		A	7	(4)	1
6	Marios KYRIAKOU		M	11		
16	Hilaire MUNOZ	FRA	G	9		
77	Anastasias SALONIDIS	GRE	D	10	(1)	
5	Akós SEPÉR	HUN	D	21		1
11	Andreas SOFOKLEOUS		D	1		
7	Kostas SOLOMOU		M	15	(2)	1
18	Marios STAVRINIDIS		G	4		
25	Giorgos STYLIANOU		M	16	(4)	1
13	Vit TURTENWALD	CZE	D	23	(2)	
1	Ryan WUEST	RSA	G	12		

APOEL
Coach – Marios Constandinou; (31/10/05) Jerzy Engel (POL)

2005
Date	Opp		Res	Scorers
28/8	Olympiakos	h	2-2	Elia, Nasiopoulos
10/9	APOP	a	1-0	Alexandrou
18/9	Paralimni	h	2-0	Makrides, Fernandes (p)
24/9	Apollon	h	2-2	Alexandrou, Jovanovic
3/10	Nea Salamina	a	2-0	Kaklamanos, Fernandes
16/10	APEP	h	2-0	Neophytou, Georgiou
22/10	Dighenis	a	1-0	Neophytou (p)
30/10	Ethnikos	h	1-0	Eleftheriou
5/11	AEK	a	2-1	Solari, Makrides
12/11	Omonia	h	2-1	Solari, Georgiou
26/11	AEL	a	1-1	Neophytou
3/12	Anorthosis	h	5-3	Solari, Neophytou 2 (2p), Alexandrou, Jovanovic
18/12	ENTHOI	a	7-0	Alexandrou 2, Solari 3, Neophytou (p), Jovanovic

2006
Date	Opp		Res	Scorers
7/1	Olympiakos	a	3-1	Fernandes 2, Georgiou
14/1	APOP	h	5-0	Solari 3, Fernandes, Michael (p)
21/1	Paralimni	a	1-2	Neophytou
5/2	Apollon	a	1-1	Solari
11/2	Nea Salamina	h	5-3	Makrides, Solari 2, Neophytou, Fernandes
25/2	APEP	a	3-0	Neophytou, Fernandes, Makrides
11/3	Dighenis	h	1-0	Kaklamanos
19/3	Ethnikos	a	2-1	Solari, Kaklamanos
25/3	AEK	h	3-0	Solari, Michael, Fernandes
8/4	Omonia	a	0-1	
15/4	AEL	h	2-0	Daskalakis, Michael
29/4	Anorthosis	a	2-2	Michael (p), Fernandes
6/5	ENTHOI	h	5-1	Alexandrou 2, Udarevic, Elia, Michael

No	Name	Nat	Pos	Aps	(s)	Gls
4	Jean-Paul Yavoi ABALO	TOG	D	2		
11	Nektarios ALEXANDROU		A	18	(7)	7
18	Dimitris DASKALAKIS		D	19	(1)	1
27	Giorgios ELEFTHERIOU		M	2	(8)	1
19	Marios ELIA		D	20	(1)	2
10	Ricardo Ribeiro FERNANDES	POR	M	21	(1)	9
14	Stevros GEORGIOU		M	7	(12)	3
31	Costas HANIOTAKIS	GRE	G	1		
8	Bartlomiej JAMROZ	POL	M	2	(2)	

Cyprus

No	Name	Nat	Pos	Aps	(s)	Gls
5	Sasa JOVANOVIC	SCG	A	6	(15)	3
9	Alexandros KAKLAMANOS	GRE	A	13	(7)	3
55	Daniel KENEDY	POR	M	9	(1)	
20	Constantinos MAKRIDES		M	24		4
33	Chrysis MICHAEL		M	24	(1)	5
1	Michalis MORFIS		G	25		
7	Giorgios NASIOPOULOS	GRE	A	3	(4)	1
99	Marios NEOPHYTOU		A	16	(3)	9
6	Stelios OKKARIDIS		D	12	(1)	
4	Paul OKON	AUS	D	11		
3	Jaroslaw POPIELA	POL	M	12		
22	Yiannis SAMPSON		D	11	(3)	
29	Estebán SOLARI	ARG	A	16	(4)	14
17	Marinos SATSIAS		M	9	(2)	
21	Aleksandar TODOROVSKI	SCG	D	2		
25	Ivan UDAREVIC	CRO	D	1		1

APOLLON
Coach – Bernd Stange (GER)

2005
28/8	ENTHOI	h	4-0	Sosin 2, Christofi (p), Andone
11/9	Olympiakos	a	3-2	Paiva, Pinto, Sosin
17/9	APOP	h	4-0	Merkis, Sosin 2, Demetriou
24/9	APOEL	a	2-2	Moustakas, Paiva
1/10	Paralimni	h	3-0	Karim 2, Sosin
16/10	Nea Salamina	h	5-1	Paiva, Sosin 3, Pinto
23/10	APEP	a	2-1	Sosin, Paiva
29/10	Dighenis	h	3-2	Sosin, Theofilou, Moustakas
5/11	Ethnikos	a	2-1	Christofi, Sosin
13/11	AEK	h	3-0	Christofi, Theofilou, Arig
27/11	Omonia	a	1-1	Moustakas
4/12	AEL	h	2-0	Sosin, Christofi
17/12	Anorthosis	a	1-1	Paiva

2006
9/1	ENTHOI	a	4-1	og (Adamou), Merkis, Karim, Sosin
14/1	Olympiakos	h	4-0	Karim 2, Sosin, Nasser
22/1	APOP	a	1-0	Sosin
5/2	APOEL	h	1-1	Sosin
12/2	Paralimni	a	1-1	Nasser
25/2	Nea Salamina	a	2-2	Sosin 2
11/3	APEP	h	5-1	Sosin 2 (1p), Christofi, Arig, Andone
18/3	Dighenis	a	3-2	Andone, Sosin, Theofilou
25/3	Ethnikos	h	2-1	Sosin, Paiva
8/4	AEK	a	3-2	Sosin, Barun, Theofilou
15/4	Omonia	h	0-0	
29/4	AEL	a	4-1	Nasser 2, Sosin 2
6/5	Anorthosis	h	3-1	Sosin 2 (1p), Paiva

No	Name	Nat	Pos	Aps	(s)	Gls
6	Bogdan ANDONE	ROM	M	24		3
11	Jassim ARIG	IRQ	D	19	(2)	2
22	Sofronis AUGOUSTI		G	1		
2	Marko BARUN	SLO	D	24		1
33	Christoforos CHRISTOFI		A	7	(6)	5
17	Ales CHVALOVSKY	CZE	G	25		
27	Michalis DEMETRIOU		M		(5)	1
39	Filipe DUARTE		D		(3)	
19	Craig HIGNETT	ENG	A	4	(8)	
18	Mahdi KARIM	IRQ	M	20	(3)	5
55	Gábor KOROLOVSZKY	HUN	D	8		
20	Lambros LAMBROU		A		(4)	
5	Vassos MELANARKITIS		D	2		
16	Giorgos MERKIS		M	14	(5)	2
8	Radoslaw MICHALSKI	POL	M	21		
21	Pericles MOUSTAKAS		D	16	(8)	3
25	Mohammad NASSER	IRQ	A	3	(7)	4
89	João Pedro PAIVA	POR	A	14	(7)	7
10	Hélio José PINTO	POR	M	22	(3)	2
4	Pawel SIBIK	POL	M	2	(1)	
26	Athos SOLOMOU		M	8	(8)	
9	Lukasz SOSIN	POL	A	26		28
21	Christis THEOFILOU		D	25		4
7	Gábor ZAVADSZKY	HUN	M	1	(2)	

APOP/KINYRAS
Coach – Pythos Neophytou; (21/9/05) (Sofocles Sofocleous); (6/10/05) Alecos Alexandris

2005
28/8	Paralimni	h	0-2	
10/9	APOEL	h	0-1	
17/9	Apollon	a	0-4	
24/9	Nea Salamina	h	1-1	Ioannou
1/10	APEP	a	2-1	Belic, Mihalache
16/10	Dighenis	h	1-3	Ioannou
23/10	Ethnikos	a	0-2	
30/10	AEK	h	1-2	Belic
5/11	Omonia	a	0-4	
12/11	AEL	h	1-3	Ignatiou
26/11	Anorthosis	a	1-6	Alexandris
3/12	ENTHOI	h	7-1	Pest, Alexandris 3, Belic, Konstandinou 2
17/12	Olympiakos	a	2-3	Belic, Ndikumana

2006
7/1	Paralimni	a	0-4	
14/1	APOEL	a	0-5	
22/1	Apollon	h	0-1	
4/2	Nea Salamina	a	1-2	Alexandris
11/2	APEP	h	3-1	Ndikumana, Alexandris, Belic
25/2	Dighenis	a	1-1	Mineiro
11/3	Ethnikos	h	3-2	Alexandris, Pest, Ipirotis
19/3	AEK	a	0-5	
26/3	Omonia	h	1-2	Alexandris
8/4	AEL	a	3-4	Alexandris 2, Belic
15/4	Anorthosis	h	1-2	Alexandris
29/4	ENTHOI	a	3-0	Alexandris 2 (1p), Konstandinou
6/5	Olympiakos	h	3-3	Alexandris 2, Ndikumana

No	Name	Nat	Pos	Aps	(s)	Gls
44	Michalis AGATHANGELOU		M	5	(1)	
99	Alexis ALEXANDRIS	GRE	A	17		15
77	Hugo ALVES	BRA	M		(1)	
32	Milan BELIC	SCG	A	15	(3)	6
48	Ivan DJUROVIC	SCG	D	3		
29	Radislav DRAGICEVIC	SCG	M	9		
15	Angelos GEORGIOU	GRE	G	8		
4	Koullis IGNATIOU		D	15	(2)	1
79	Giorgos IOANNOU		D	13		2
31	Thodosis IOSIF		G	6		
12	Costas IPIROTIS	GRE	M	15	(2)	1
19	KATSONOURIS		M	4	(1)	
16	Vangelis KONSTANDINOU		D	9	(4)	3
6	David KUTYAURIPO	ZIM	D	19	(2)	
51	Christos LABAKIS	GRE	G	5		
30	Charis LOIZOU		M	7	(9)	
10	Antonis MAKRIS		A	5	(2)	
82	Andreas MELANARKITIS		M	13	(2)	
8	Dragos MIHALACHE	ROM	M	5	(3)	1

Cyprus

No	Name	Nat	Pos	Aps	(s)	Gls
26	Leo MINEIRO	BRA	M	8		1
3	Hamed NDIKUMANA	RWA	D	23		3
10	Yiannis PACHTALIAS		M	3	(4)	
32	Giannis PALATES		M	1		
7	Krisztian PEST	HUN	M	18	(4)	2
17	Ioannis RETSAS		M	8		
9	Balazs SCHRANCZ	HUN	A	4	(6)	
1	Kostas SOKRATOUS		D	6	(1)	
24	Kostas SOLOMOU		A	1	(5)	
11	Andreas STEFANOU		D	8		
23	Simeon STEVICA	SVK	A		(2)	
22	Admir SUHONJIC	SLO	G	7		
2	Michael VAN ZUNDERT	HOL	D		(1)	
5	Leonidas VOKOLOS	GRE	M	12		
20	Vryonis VRYONI		D	14	(3)	

DIGHENIS
Coach – Savvas Constantinou

2005
Date	Opponent		Score	Scorers
28/8	Omonia	h	0-4	
11/9	AEL	a	0-3	
18/9	Anorthosis	h	1-1	Mujamba
24/9	ENTHOI	a	1-1	Novakovic
2/10	Olympiakos	h	0-1	
16/10	APOP	a	3-1	Achilleos, Novakovic, Dimitriadis
22/10	APOEL	h	0-1	
29/10	Apollon	a	2-3	Dimitriadis 2
6/11	Nea Salamina	h	2-1	Dimitriadis 2
12/11	APEP	a	2-1	Novakovic, Dimitriadis
27/11	Paralimni	h	0-2	
3/12	Ethnikos	h	2-0	Lambrou, Maris
17/12	AEK	a	1-1	Domocos

2006
Date	Opponent		Score	Scorers
8/1	Omonia	a	0-3	
15/1	AEL	h	2-2	Novakovic, Domocos
21/1	Anorthosis	a	0-1	
4/2	ENTHOI	h	1-0	Kountouris
12/2	Olympiakos	a	4-1	Mujamba 3, Novakovic
25/2	APOP	h	1-1	Domocos
11/3	APOEL	a	0-1	
18/3	Apollon	h	2-3	Maris, Vayer
25/3	Nea Salamina	a	1-4	Maris
8/4	APEP	h	3-3	Mujamba 2, Novakovic
15/4	Paralimni	a	2-2	Mujamba, Novakovic
29/4	Ethnikos	a	2-4	Vayer, Laban
6/5	AEK	h	1-0	Vayer

No	Name	Nat	Pos	Aps	(s)	Gls
6	Stelios ACHILLEOS		M	22	(1)	1
3	Andonis ANDONIOU		D	12		
24	Stefan APOSTOL	ROM	D	20	(1)	
2	Nektarios ARTEME		G	8		
11	Petros DIMITRIADIS	GRE	A	10	(3)	6
10	Viorel DOMOCOS	ROM	M	9	(6)	3
4	Adrian FALUB	ROM	D	21		
21	Dimitris FYLAKTIOU		M	1		
15	Takis FYLAKTOU		M	3	(2)	
30	Constantinos GEORGIADIS		A	2	(6)	
22	Stefanos GEORGIOU		D	24	(1)	
29	Giorgos KAKOULIS		G	3		
17	Chrystofomos KALOS		A	1	(1)	
1	Savvas KONSTANDINOU		G	15		
8	Christos KOUNTOURIS		D	7	(16)	1
23	Vincent LABAN	FRA	M	22		1
5	Lambrou LAMBROU		D	11	(2)	1
7	Dimitris MARIS	GRE	M	21	(4)	3
19	Michalis MARKOU		D	6		
16	Jack MUJAMBA	CON	A	4	(13)	7
9	Zoran NOVAKOVIC	SCG	A	20	(6)	7
5	Andreas PANAYIOTU		D	4	(1)	
33	Costas TSIRONIS	GRE	D	20	(2)	
28	Gábor VAYER	HUN	A	20	(4)	3

ENTHOI
Coach – Mikulás Komanicky (CZE); (29/9/05) Savas Paraskevas; (6/12/05) Georgi Petkov (BUL)

2005
Date	Opponent		Score	Scorers
28/8	Apollon	a	0-4	
11/9	Nea Salamina	h	1-2	Ioannou
17/9	APEP	a	1-1	Fasouliotis (p)
24/9	Dighenis	h	1-1	Angeli
1/10	Ethnikos	a	1-1	Angeli
16/10	AEK	h	1-4	Gibro
22/10	Omonia	a	1-2	Iona
30/10	AEL	h	1-2	Panayiotou
7/11	Anorthsis	a	0-1	
12/11	Paralimni	a	1-2	Gibro
26/11	Olympiakos	h	0-2	
3/12	APOP	a	1-7	Ioannou
18/12	APOEL	h	0-7	

2006
Date	Opponent		Score	Scorers
9/1	Apollon	h	1-4	Fabula
15/1	Nea Salamina	a	1-3	Panayiotou
21/1	APEP	h	0-0	
4/2	Dighenis	a	0-1	
11/2	Ethnikos	h	0-6	
25/2	AEK	a	0-2	
11/3	Omonia	h	0-5	
18/3	AEL	a	2-3	Ioannou 2 (1p)
26/3	Anorthsis	h	0-6	
9/4	Paralimni	h	0-1	
16/4	Olympiakos	a	1-0	Gibro
29/4	APOP	h	0-3	
6/5	APOEL	a	1-5	Apostolou

No	Name	Nat	Pos	Aps	(s)	Gls
21	Adamos ADAMOU		D	19	(1)	
25	Athos ANGELI		A	10	(3)	2
3	Akis APOSTOLOU		D	10		1
27	Reinaldo APPOLINARIO	BRA	M	23	(3)	
20	Aristos ARISTOCLEOUS		D	8	(5)	
77	Aristodimos ARISTODIMOU		M	16	(4)	
23	Andrew ESELUKE	NGA	A	4	(4)	
5	Marek FABULA	SVK	M	24	(1)	1
10	Panagiotis FASOULIOTIS		A	9	(1)	1
11	George GIBRO	LIB	M	20	(3)	3
12	Andreas HATZINIKOLAU		M	2	(2)	
17	Akis IOANNOU		M	13	(2)	4
28	Frixos IOANNOU		D	8		
33	Michalis IONA		A	14	(8)	1
9	Giorgos KONSTANDINIDIS		D	14	(5)	
7	Dimitris KYRIAKOU		M	7	(1)	
4	Kostas LOIZOU		D	12		
15	Georgos MALAIS		G		(1)	
99	Andreas MAYRIS		G	11		
30	Martin MISCIK	SVK	G	4		
1	Vassilis MYTILINEOS	GRE	G	11		
12	Andreas NIKOLAOU		M	2	(1)	
19	Marios PANAYIOTOU		A	12	(2)	2
16	Giorgos PETROU		M	15	(1)	
31	Yaw RUSH	GHA	M	3	(4)	

Cyprus

26	Andreas SAOUROS		M	6	(3)
44	Nikos STAVROU		D	4	
22	Marios THEOFANOUS		D	5	(4)

ETHNIKOS
Coach – Mironas Sifakis

2005
27/8	AEK	h	2-1	Kotsonis, Kebadze
10/9	Omonia	a	2-3	Kmetec, Lambrou
17/9	AEL	h	0-0	
24/9	Anorthosis	a	0-2	
1/10	ENTHOI	h	1-1	Kebadze
15/10	Olympiakos	a	1-1	Kmetec
23/10	APOP	h	2-0	Gjurev, Kmetec
30/10	APOEL	a	0-1	
5/11	Apollon	h	1-2	Lambrou
12/11	Nea Salamina	a	1-2	Lerinc
26/11	APEP	h	4-0	Isailovic 2, Lambrou, Stefanovic
3/12	Dighenis	a	0-2	
18/12	Paralimni	h	0-1	

2006
8/1	AEK	a	0-3	
14/1	Omonia	h	0-1	
22/1	AEL	a	3-2	Kebadze 2, Maranhão
5/2	Anorthosis	h	0-5	
11/2	ENTHOI	a	6-0	Kebadze 2, Kmetec 3, Iordache (p), Kafalis
25/2	Olympiakos	h	4-0	Stjepanovic 2, Kmetec, Poyiatzis
11/3	APOP	a	2-3	Stjepanovic 2
19/3	APOEL	h	1-2	Stjepanovic
25/3	Apollon	a	1-2	Kebadze
8/4	Nea Salamina	h	2-4	Kebadze, Stjepanovic
15/4	APEP	a	2-0	Kmetec, Stjepanovic (p)
29/4	Dighenis	h	4-2	Stjepanovic 2 (1p), Kebadze, Kmetec
6/5	Paralimni	a	3-3	Stjepanovic, Kmetec 2

No	Name	Nat	Pos	Aps	(s)	Gls
22	Panayiotis CHARALAMBOUS		G	6	(1)	
14	Kyriakos CHATZIAROS		A	1	(6)	
13	Petros CHATZIAROS		D	1	(2)	
2	Dimos DIMOSTHENOUS		D	8		
16	Elpidoporos ELIA		M	2	(11)	
11	Borce GJUREV	MAC	M	19	(3)	1
5	Giorgos IOANNOU		D	9		
26	Marius IORDACHE	ROM	D	9		1
28	Dragan ISAILOVIC	SCG	A	8	(4)	2
21	Kostas KAFALIS		M	15	(5)	1
18	Andreas KATZIS		M	10	(2)	
29	Levan KEBADZE	GEO	A	19		8
9	Marko KMETEC	SLO	A	17	(5)	11
1	Aleksander KOCIC	MAC	G	20		
6	Christos KOTSONIS		M	19	(4)	1
3	Lambrous LAMBROU		D	18		3
23	Leo LERINC	SCG	M		(5)	1
23	MARANHÃO	BRA	M	3	(3)	1
17	Christas PASHIALIS		M	14	(4)	
10	Christos POYIATZIS		A	16	(3)	1
19	Artemis SAVVA		M	1		
8	Lars SCHLICHTING	GER	M	11	(3)	
4	Christos SIAILIS		D	10		
15	Dimitris SIMOF		D	10	(1)	
20	Nokolai SOFOCLEOUS		D	1		
7	Zoran STJEPANOVIC	SCG	M	20	(3)	11

| 5 | Petr VLCEK | CZE | D | 13 | |

NEA SALAMINA
Coach – Imre Gellei (HUN); (24/10/05) Andreas Michaelides

2005
29/8	Anorthosis	h	2-5	Chailis, Wobay
11/9	ENTHOI	a	2-1	Chailis, Wobay
17/9	Olympiakos	h	5-1	Wobay, Louka (p), Chailis, Bükszegi 2
24/9	APOP	a	1-1	Chailis
3/10	APOEL	h	0-2	
16/10	Apollon	a	1-5	Wobay
23/10	Paralimni	h	0-2	
29/10	APEP	h	5-0	Louka 2 (1p), Chailis 3
6/11	Dighenis	a	1-2	Chailis
12/11	Ethnikos	h	2-1	Chailis 2
26/11	AEK	a	0-0	
3/12	Omonia	h	0-1	
17/12	AEL	a	3-0	Chailis (p), Szamosi, Wobay

2006
7/1	Anorthosis	a	0-2	
15/1	ENTHOI	h	3-1	Wobay 2, Varnava
22/1	Olympiakos	a	1-1	Panagi G.
4/2	APOP	h	2-1	Juhár, N'Diaye
11/2	APOEL	a	3-5	Wobay, Stere, Louka
25/2	Apollon	h	2-2	Wobay, Stere
11/3	Paralimni	a	2-2	Louka, Juhár
18/3	APEP	a	3-1	Wobay, Chailis 2
25/3	Dighenis	h	4-1	Szamosi, Wobay, Chailis, De Souza
8/4	Ethnikos	a	4-2	Bükszegi, Panagi A, Chailis, N'Diaye
15/4	AEK	h	3-2	Louka 2, Christodoulou
29/4	Omonia	a	2-6	N'Diaye 2
6/5	AEL	h	2-1	Wobay, Kargbo

No	Name	Nat	Pos	Aps	(s)	Gls
7	Cristian BOLOHAN	ROM	M	23	(1)	
29	Zoltán BÜKSZEGI	HUN	A	10	(8)	3
9	Kyriakos CHAILIS		A	22	(1)	15
19	Mrios CHRISTODOULOU		M	16	(4)	1
18	Ulusoy COSKUN	TUR	A	1	(5)	
20	José DE SOUZA	BRA	M	2	(8)	1
2	Paris ELIA		D	11	(6)	
30	Andreas IOANNIDES		D	9	(2)	
5	Tamás JUHÁR	HUN	D	26	(1)	2
16	Jamil KARGBO	SRL	D	4	(9)	1
4	Andreas KITTOS		D	1	(6)	
11	Marios LOUKA		A	14	(6)	7
26	Syeni N'DIAYE	SEN	A	8	(1)	4
24	Marios NIKOLAOU		D	11	(1)	
10	Andonis PANAGI		M	2	(9)	1
15	Giorgos PANAGI		M	15	(3)	1
28	Miroslav SEMAN	SLO	G	26		
21	Mihai STERE	ROM	M	19		2
74	Tamás SZAMOSI	HUN	D	22	(1)	2
14	Andreas THODOSIOU		D	2		
12	Andreas VARNAVA		A		(4)	1
77	Julius WOBAY	SRL	M	23		12
6	Bogdan ZAJAC		D	19		

OLYMPIAKOS
Coach – Rainer Rauffmann

2005
| 28/8 | APOEL | a | 2-2 | Pittas, Rink |
| 11/9 | Apollon | h | 2-3 | Rink 2 (1p) |

Cyprus

17/9	Nea Salamina	a	1-5	Rink	
25/9	APEP	h	8-0	Moyo 2, Rink 2, Polking, Filippou, Themistocleous, Ablordey	
2/10	Dighenis	a	1-0	Rink	
15/10	Ethnikos	h	1-1	Rink	
22/10	AEK	a	1-2	Moyo	
29/10	Omonia	h	1-3	Rink	
6/11	AEL	a	2-2	Pelagias, Polking	
13/11	Anorthosis	h	1-2	Rink	
26/11	ENTHOI	a	2-0	Polking, Themistocleous	
4/12	Paralimni	a	1-1	Rink (p)	
17/12	APEP	h	3-2	Themistocleous, Rink 2	
2006					
7/1	APOEL	h	1-3	Pittas	
14/1	Apollon	a	0-4		
22/1	Nea Salamina	h	1-1	Pittas	
4/2	APEP	a	0-0		
12/2	Dighenis	h	1-4	Pittas	
25/2	Ethnikos	a	0-4		
12/3	AEK	h	3-2	Malekkos (p), Polking, Pittas	
18/3	Omonia	a	0-1		
26/3	AEL	h	3-2	Moyo, Pittas 2	
9/4	Anorthosis	a	1-1	Moyo	
16/4	ENTHOI	h	0-1		
29/4	Paralimni	h	1-1	Pittas	
6/5	APOP	a	3-3	Konstandinou 3	

No	Name	Nat	Pos	Aps	(s)	Gls
16	Godwin ABLORDEY	GHA	M	15	(4)	1
18	Alex BECERRA	PER	M	6	(1)	
22	Christos CHADZEPANDELIDIS		D	10	(3)	
17	Evangelos CHRISTODOULOU		M	3		
14	Alessandro DE BARTOLO	ARG	M	8	(1)	
2	Filippos FILIPPOU		D	20	(1)	1
28	Christos GENETHLIOU		M	2	(2)	
25	Giorgos GEORGIADIS		M	7	(2)	
27	Mohamad KAMARA	SRL	A	1	(1)	
13	Kostandinos KONSTANDINOU		A	1	(1)	3
9	Robert LEKE	CMR	A	7	(4)	
11	Kostakis MALEKKOS		M	4	(4)	1
17	Evangelos MAYARIS		M	3		
3	Dimitris MEIDANIS	GRE	D	17	(2)	
19	Thabai MOYO	ZIM	A	13	(6)	5
4	Nikos NIKOLAOU		M	20	(1)	
24	Nikos NIKOLAOU		M	8	(3)	
30	Feidias PANAYIOTOU		M	2		
6	Giorgos PEGLIS	GRE	M	13	(5)	
5	Giorgos PELAGIAS		D	9	(1)	1
8	Alexis PITTAS		M	17	(2)	8
7	Alexander POLKING	GER	M	21	(1)	4
27	Jorge RAMIREZ	PER	A	3	(1)	
27	Paulo Roberto RINK	GER	A	12		13
20	Loukas STYLIANOU		D	16	(4)	
10	Marios THEMISTOCLEOUS		M	22	(4)	3
23	Tesos YIALLOURIS		G	26		

OMONIA
Coach – Henk Houwaart (BEL); (28/12/05) Ioan Andone (ROM)

2005

28/8	Dighenis	a	4-0	Konnafis, Vakouftsis, Mguni 2	
10/9	Ethnikos	h	3-2	Dobrasinovic, Mguni, Kakoyiannis	
17/9	AEK	a	3-2	Magno, Dobrasinovic, Kaiafas	
25/9	Paralimni	a	1-0	Kaiafas	
1/10	AEL	h	2-0	Mguni, Ioakim	
16/10	Anorthosis	a	1-2	Vakouftsis (p)	
22/10	ENTHOI	h	2-1	Magno, Grozdanovski	
29/10	Olympiakos	a	3-1	N'Diaye, Vakouftsis 2	
5/11	APOP	h	4-0	Magno 2, Grozdanovski, N'Diaye	
12/11	APOEL	a	1-2	Vakouftsis (p)	
27/11	Apollon	h	1-1	Vakouftsis (p)	
3/12	Nea Salamina	a	1-0	Vakouftsis (p)	
18/12	APEP	h	2-1	Dobrasinovic, Grozdanovski	
2006					
8/1	Dighenis	h	3-0	Kozlej, Magno (p), Vakouftsis	
14/1	Ethnikos	a	1-0	Rink	
21/1	AEK	h	3-1	Kakoyiannis, Rink, Mguni	
4/2	Paralimni	h	0-1		
12/2	AEL	a	2-1	Kaiafas, Rink (p)	
25/2	Anorthosis	h	2-2	Mguni, Konstanti (p)	
11/3	ENTHOI	a	5-0	Konnafis, Theodotou, Rink (p), Mguni, Vakouftsis	
18/3	Olympiakos	h	1-0	Konnafis	
26/3	APOP	a	2-1	Konnafis, Vakouftsis	
8/4	APOEL	h	1-0	Vakouftsis	
15/4	Apollon	a	0-0		
29/4	Nea Salamina	h	6-2	Rink 3, Magno, Vakouftsis, Dobrasinovic	
6/5	APEP	a	5-0	Rink 3 (1p), Mguni, Kaiafas (p)	

No	Name	Nat	Pos	Aps	(s)	Gls
11	Sinisa DOBRASINOVIC	SCG	M	23		4
21	Nikolas GEORGIOU		M	25		
7	Vlatko GROZDANOVSKI	MAC	M	11	(11)	3
3	Akis IOAKIM		M	5	(5)	1
20	Kostas KAIAFAS		D	22		4
81	Loizos KAKOYIANNIS		D	19		2
	Ljubisa KEKIC	SCG	A		(1)	
79	Stelios KITTOS		D	18	(4)	
99	Petros KONNAFIS		D	26		4
55	Georgious KONSTANTI		D	1	(8)	1
5	Gábor KOROLOVSZKY	HUN	D	1	(5)	
9	Jozef KOZLEJ	SVK	A	11	(7)	1
1	Demitris LEONIS		G	7		
30	MAGNO Mocelin		M	24	(1)	6
70	Musa MGUNI	ZIM	A	11	(6)	8
33	Seyni N'DIAYE	SEN	A	4	(4)	2
8	Charis NIKOLAOU		M	3	(6)	
6	Makis PAPAIOANNOU		D	9	(7)	
27	Paulo Roberto RINK	GER	A	11	(2)	10
22	Khalid SINOUH	MAR	G	11		
2	Giorgos THEODOTOU		D	9	(1)	1
10	Giorgos VAKOUFTSIS	GRE	A	22	(4)	12
14	Ádám VEZÉR	HUN	G	8	(1)	
24	Stijn VREVEN	BEL	M	5	(1)	

PARALIMNI
Coach – Eli Gutman (ISR)

2005

28/8	APOP	a	2-0	Eleftheriou (p), Elia	
11/9	AEK	h	1-0	Zlogar	
18/9	APOEL	a	0-2		
25/9	Omonia	h	0-1		
1/10	Apollon Limassol	a	0-3		
15/10	AEL	h	3-5	Elia 2, Tanjic	
23/10	Nea Salamina	a	2-0	Zlogar, Elia	

The European Book of Football 2006/2007 - 253

Cyprus

Date	Opponent	H/A	Score	Scorers
29/10	Anorthosis	h	0-1	
6/11	APEP	a	2-0	Ipavec, Goumenos
12/11	ENTHOI	h	2-1	Elia, Eleftheriou
27/11	Dighenis	a	2-0	Goumenos, Eleftheriou
4/12	Olympiakos	h	1-1	Ipavec
18/12	Ethnikos	a	1-0	Goumenos
2006				
7/1	APOP	h	4-0	Eleftheriou 2, Zlogar, Elia
14/1	AEK	a	0-1	
21/1	APOEL	h	2-1	Elia 2
4/2	Omonia	a	1-0	Zlogar
12/2	Apollon Limassol	h	1-1	Kaseke
25/2	AEL	a	1-2	Eleftheriou
11/3	Nea Salamina	h	2-2	Elia, Guvo
18/3	Anorthosis	a	0-0	
25/3	APEP	h	6-1	Ipavec, Guvo, Zlogar 2, Elia 2
9/4	ENTHOI	a	1-0	Guvo
15/4	Dighenis	h	2-2	Ipavec 2 (1p)
24/9	Olympiakos	a	1-1	Elia
6/5	Ethnikos	h	3-3	Guvo, Elia, Ipavec

No	Name	Nat	Pos	Aps	(s)	Gls
15	Ishmael ADDO	GHA	A		(1)	
15	Eric EJIOFOR	NGA	D	25		
10	Lefteris ELEFTHERIOU		M	15	(2)	6
7	Kostas ELIA		A	21	(2)	13
17	Dimos GOUMENOS		M	18	(6)	3
9	Jure GUVO	CRO	A	7	(1)	4
8	Patrik IPAVEC	SLO	A	20	(6)	6
10	Amer JUKAN	BOS	M	3	(7)	
5	Bekim KAPIC	SLO	D	26		
4	Marios KARAS		M	3	(6)	
16	Noel KASEKE	ZIM	D	25		1
21	Giorgos KOLANIS		M	6	(14)	
30	Lefteris MERTAKAS		D		(2)	
22	Bojan MILIC	SLO	G	2		
1	Petar MILOSEVSKI	MAC	G	24		
3	Nikos NIKOLAOU		M	9	(1)	
6	Petros SOTIRIOU		D	3	(5)	
33	Panikos SPYROU		D	16	(3)	
2	Almir TANJIC	SLO	M	22		1
31	Lajos TERJÉK	HUN	M	17	(6)	
28	Giorgos TOFA		A		(2)	
11	Pavlos TSOLAKIS		M	2	(7)	
36	Anton ZLOGAR	SLO	A	22	(1)	6

DOMESTIC CUP 2005/06

SECOND ROUND
(played in groups of four)
Group A
1 Anorthosis 11 pts; 2 AEP 11; 3 Dighenis 6; 4. ENTHOI 1
Group B
1 APOEL 15 pts; 2 Apollon 13; 3 APEP 5; 4 ASIL 1
Group C
1 Olympiakos 13 pts; 2 Nea Salamina 3; 3 AEL 5; 4 Ethnikos 3
Group D
1 Omonia 15 pts; 2 AEK 9; 3 Paralimni 9; 4. Aris 3

QUARTER-FINALS
(7/3/06 & 31/3/06)
Nea Salamina 2 *(Wobay 10, Christodoulou 19)*, APOEL 1 *(Fernandes 90)*
APOEL 4 *(Kaklamanos 25, Solari 63, Fernandes 80, Ilia 90p)*, Nea Salamina 0
(APOEL 5-2)

(8/3/06 & 1/4/06)
Apollon 0, Omonia 2 *(Mguni 45, Rink 63p)*
Omonia 0, Apollon 0
(Omonia 2-0)

(8/3/06 & 2/4/06)
AEP 2 *(Vozehnal 19, Foti 33p)*, Olympiakos 0
Olympiakos 2 *(Themistokleous 72p, Pittas 83)*, AEP 1 *(Foti 23)*
(AEP 3-2)

(8/3/06 & 19/4/06)
AEK 2 *(Datoru 43, Oliseh 56)*, Anorthosis 0
Anorthosis 3 *(Kabantais 23, Frousos 32p, Xenidis 76)*, AEK 1 *(Datou 87)*
(3-3; AEK on away goal)

SEMI-FINALS
(26/4/06 & 3/5/06)
AEP 1 *(Kostis 17p)*, AEK 1 *(Raducan 37)*
AEK 0, AEP 0
(AEK 1-1)

APOEL 3 *(Jovanovic 35, 55, 83)*, Omonia 3 *(Rink 30, 86, 90p)*
Omonia 1 *(Rink 8)*, APOEL 3 *(Kaklamanos 15, Georgiou 48, Neophytou 85)*
(APOEL 6-4)

FINAL
(13/5/06)
Zenon Stadium, Larnaca
APOEL 3 *(Neophytou 15p, Kaklamanos 17, Jovanovic 107)*
AEK 2 *(Ceesay 19, Raducan 42p)*
(aet)
Referee – Tryfonos
APOEL – Morfis, Popiela *(Todorovski 90)*, Elia, Daskalakis, Satsias, Michael, Fernandes, Makrides, Alexandrou *(Jovanovic 76)*, Neophytou *(Solari 59)*, Kaklamanos.
AEK – Georgiou A., Mina, Zé Nando, Christou P., Oliseh, Siligardakis, Pavlou *(Panayiotou 76)*, Raducan *(Moita 87)*, Ceesay, Bah *(Christou S. 104)*, Datoru.

SECOND LEVEL FINAL TABLE 2005/06

		Pld	W	D	L	F	A	Pts
1	AE Paphos	26	17	6	3	69	23	57
2	Aris	26	18	2	6	66	36	56
3	Ayia Napa	26	14	6	6	48	27	48
4	Alki	26	12	5	9	48	34	41
5	Omonia Aradippou	26	9	10	7	33	29	37
6	MEAP	26	9	9	8	38	36	36
7	Doxa Katakopia	26	8	11	7	37	30	35
8	Helkanoras	26	9	7	10	37	35	34
9	Anagennisi	26	9	5	12	39	45	32
10	Onisillos	26	8	8	10	33	42	32
11	Iraklis	26	8	7	11	33	50	31
12	Elpida	26	8	3	15	41	50	27
13	Ethnikos Assias	26	7	5	14	41	50	26
14	SEK Athanasiou	26	1	6	19	19	85	9

Czech Republic

Age, injuries and indiscipline

The Czech Republic's first World Cup appearance ended disappointingly early. The team went into the tournament ranked third in the world by FIFA but failed to make it even into the last 16 – despite the boost of winning their opening match 3-0.

As Karel Brückner's side made mincemeat of the United States in Gelsenkirchen, fears that the Czechs might have peaked at Euro 2004, where they reached the semi-finals, seemed completely unfounded. Jan Koller, back from a long-term knee injury, rammed in an early header – his record 43rd international goal – and Tomás Rosicky completed a resounding victory with two sumptuous goals. It was the most convincing start by any team at the finals bar Spain, yet ten days later, following a pair of 2-0 defeats to Ghana and Italy, the Czechs were packing their bags for the journey home.

The schizophrenic nature of the team's displays had something to do with the quality of the opposition – the Americans were woeful, whereas Ghana played out of their skin and Italy were, well, Italy – but there were other decisive factors.

Firstly, age. The Czechs had the oldest team at the finals, and it was obvious that some of their stalwart performers of the past, such as Karel Poborsky and Tomás Galásek, were well past their best. When they took on the youngest team at the finals, Ghana, the difference in energy and athleticism was plain for all to see.

Secondly, injuries. The hamstring pull that Koller picked up in the opening game was a hammer blow. His replacement, Vratislav Lokvenc, who had also missed most of the season following knee surgery, was not up to the task, and with Milan Baros, the leading marksman at Euro 2004, also injured on the eve of the tournament, and Vladimír Smicer deemed insufficiently fit even to make the squad, that left the Czech attack completely decimated.

Thirdly, indiscipline. Against both Ghana and Italy the Czechs played a large chunk of the game with just ten men. Key defender Tomás Ujfalusi was sent off midway through the second half in conceding a penalty against the Ghanaians, and holding midfielder Jan Polák was idiotically red-carded on the stroke of half-time after committing a second cautionable offence against the Italians. According to coach Brückner, these two dismissals were the major cause of his team's premature elimination.

Brückner carries on

Although Brückner surprisingly announced his intention to stay on as coach for Euro 2008, the post mortem did seem to indicate that the Czech Republic had reached the end of an era. Poborsky, the country's record-cap holder with 118 appearances, was the first of the 'veterans' to confirm that he had played his last game for the team, and he was later followed into international retirement – for good this time - by Pavel Nedved, who had previously withdrawn his services after Euro 2004 only to return for the World Cup qualifying play-off against Norway and then, of course, for the finals.

Nedved's outstanding farewell performance against Italy was one of the few positives to be taken from the World Cup. There were excellent individual displays also from Rosicky (against the

Czech Republic

USA) and goalkeeper Petr Cech (against Ghana), but as a team they fell a long way short of the form displayed two years earlier in Portugal.

The Czechs have long been European Championship specialists, but they could find it something of a struggle in a Euro 2008 qualifying group containing Germany, the Republic of Ireland, Wales and improving ex-fellow nationals Slovakia – especially as there is little top-class talent coming through.

The 2005/06 Gambrinus Liga showed up the dearth of quality at local level. It was a very poor championship, almost wholly devoid of star players. Defensive football dominated, goals were in short supply, and only four players in the entire league managed individual goal tallies in double figures. Little-known young Slovakian striker Milan Ivana, of 1.FC Slovácko Uherské Hradiste, was the competition's leading marksman with just 11 goals – the lowest winning total in the history of not only the Czech but also the Czechoslovakian top division.

In 2004/05 the top scorer had been Sparta Prague's young Czech international striker Tomás Jun (with 14 goals). He quit the perennial champions at the end of the campaign for a new career in Turkey, and although he struggled to make his mark there, lasting only half a season at Trabzonspor before a switch to Besiktas, the move sparked a flurry of transfer activity from the Gambrinus Liga to the Turkish Super Lig, much of it during the winter break.

The flight from the Czech Republic of the country's top players was reflected in Brückner's World Cup squad. Only two home-based players made it into the chosen 23, and one of those, Sparta Prague goalkeeper Jaromír Blazek, didn't get on to the field in Germany whereas the other, Poborsky, was playing second division football with Dynamo Ceské Budejovice. The only Gambrinus Liga player to taste any World Cup action in Germany was Sparta's mid-season signing Mauro Lustrinelli, who got a few minutes of action for Switzerland.

Sparta soap opera

Blazek, Poborsky and Lustrinelli all played a part in the soap opera that was Sparta Prague's season. The defending champions were widely expected to defend their title but they came apart at the seams early on and could not be stitched back together again. Unpopular coach Jaroslav Hrebík had a big falling-out with club skipper Poborsky over tactics in September, and the club surprisingly sided with the coach. Thus Poborsky was farmed out on loan to Ceské Budejovice, a club he part-owned. But without their captain Sparta's performances got even worse, and after three successive league defeats, Hrebík was finally given the boot.

Into his place came ex-Sparta and Czechoslovakia striker Stanislav Griga. The Slovakian had coached Slovan Liberec the previous season before leaving in a huff citing lack of ambition. Now, ironically, it was Liberec, led by Griga's former assistant (and ex-Sparta boss) Vitezslav Lavicka, who were galloping clear at the top of the table while Sparta lunged from one calamity to another, both at home and in Europe.

Sparta were granted automatic access to the group stages of the Champions League, but they never remotely looked like living up to their seeded status. A brilliant goal from Miroslav

NATIONAL TEAM RESULTS 2005/06

Date	Opponent	H/A/N	Venue	Score	Scorers
17/8/05	Sweden	A	Gothenburg	1-2	Koller (22p)
3/9/05	Romania (WCQ)	A	Constanta	0-2	
7/9/05	Armenia (WCQ)	H	Olomouc	4-1	Heinz (47), Polák (52, 76), Baros (58)
8/10/05	Holland (WCQ)	H	Prague	0-2	
12/10/05	Finland (WCQ)	A	Helsinki	3-0	Jun (6), Rosicky (51), Heinz (58)
12/11/05	Norway (WCQ)	A	Oslo	1-0	Smicer (31)
16/11/05	Norway (WCQ)	H	Prague	1-0	Rosicky (35)
1/3/06	Turkey	A	Izmir	2-2	Poborsky (20p), Stajner (61)
26/5/06	Saudi Arabia	N	Innsbruck	2-0	Baros (15), Jankulovski (90p)
30/5/06	Costa Rica	H	Jablonec nad Nisou	1-0	Lokvenc (82)
3/6/06	Trinidad & Tobago	H	Prague	3-0	Koller (6, 40), Nedved (22)
12/6/06	United States (WCF)	N	Gelsenkirchen	3-0	Koller (5), Rosicky (36, 76)
17/6/06	Ghana (WCF)	N	Cologne	0-2	
22/6/06	Italy (WCF)	N	Hamburg	0-2	

Czech Republic

Matusovic at home to Ajax almost brought them an opening win, but Wesley Sneijder's equally spectacular last-minute equaliser denied them victory and it was all downhill thereafter, with even Swiss first-timers FC Thun (with Lustrinelli in their ranks) embarrassingly edging them out of a UEFA Cup spot.

In the league Sparta fared even worse, losing 4-1 away to arch-rivals Slavia Prague – their first derby defeat for six years – and then three times more before the winter break. At the halfway point Sparta had been beaten eight times and conceded more goals than any other team. They lay ninth in the table 15 points adrift of leaders Liberec. With elimination from Europe sealed by a timid 0-0 draw with Thun, their season was in complete disarray.

Comings and goings

Sparta carried out major surgery during the winter break, with several players coming and going. The new arrivals included Lustrinelli in attack and, more importantly, four new defenders in Václav Drobny, Slovakian duo Radoslav Zabavník and Michal Hanek and, after eight years in exile, ex-Czech international Tomás Repka. Despite another defeat, 2-1 at home to high-flying Liberec, in their first fixture of 2006, Sparta gradually began to climb up the table. A nine-match unbeaten run, during which only three goals were conceded, helped them up into a final position of fifth. That was still desperately disappointing by their standards, but the season did end on a happy note when Griga's men salvaged a place in Europe by winning the Czech Cup. A penalty shoot-out victory over holders Baník Ostrava after 90 goalless minutes (there is no extra-time in the Czech Cup) was enough to maintain the club's 23-year unbroken run in Europe. Goalkeeper Blazek was not even required to make a save in the shoot-out as Ostrava's Lukás Magera and Radek Sloncík both missed the target. Sparta's four successful marksmen were Tomás Sivok, Matusovic, Michal Kadlec and, decisively, Ondrej Herzán.

The Cup final took place at the Stadion U Nisy in Liberec, which three weeks earlier had been the setting for joyous celebrations among the local populace as Slovan Liberec clinched their second Czech title in four years with a 1-1 draw at home to SIAD Most. It was a thoroughly comprehensive

Tomás Repka – back in Prague after eight years in exile

but wholly unexpected triumph. Irrespective of the trials and tribulations at Sparta, Slovan had been written off as title candidates following the departure of coach Griga and several key players, including Czech international Polák to Germany, striker Michal Pospísil to Scotland and defender Petr Lukás, midfielder Karol Kisel and striker Miroslav Slepicka, all to Sparta.

Liberec's title

Victories in each of their first five matches propelled Liberec to the top of the table in September and, to widespread disbelief, they managed to stay there for the rest of the season. Even the mid-season sale – to Turkey – of their top-scoring Slovakian international striker Filip Holosko did not deflect them from their course. By the time they claimed the title, with two games to spare, Lavicka's team had been beaten only twice and recorded clean sheets in exactly half of their 28 matches. Goalkeeper Marek Cech (no relation to Petr) had an excellent season, as did the relentlessly consistent quartet in front of him – Slovakian right-back Peter Singlar, skipper Tomás Zápotocny, giant stopper Pavel Kostál and long-

Czech Republic

NATIONAL TEAM APPEARANCES 2005/06

Coach – Karel BRÜCKNER

Player	DOB	Club	Swe	ROM	ARM	HOL	FIN	NOR	NOR	Tur	Sau	Crc	Tri	USA	GHA	ITA	Caps	Goals
Petr CECH	20/5/82	Chelsea (ENG)	G	G		G	G	G	G	G	G	G		G	G	G	G	44	-
Zdenek GRYGERA	14/5/80	Ajax (HOL)	D	D	D	D	D	D	D		D	s46	D	D	D	D	D	44	1
David ROZEHNAL	5/7/80	Paris St-Germain (FRA)	D46		D70	D	D	D	D	D	D	D	D	D	D	D	D	25	-
Tomáš HÜBSCHMAN	4/9/81	Shakhtar D. (UKR)	D46															20	-
Tomáš UJFALUSI	24/3/78	Fiorentina (ITA)	D	D	D	D	D	D	D	D	D	D		D	D	D		50	2
Tomáš GALÁSEK	15/1/73	Ajax (HOL)	M69		M	M	M	M						M		M46		51	1
Vladimír SMICER	24/5/73	Gir. Bordeaux (FRA)	M46	M		s46	s44	M60	A79	A75								81	27
Marek HEINZ	4/8/77	Bor. M'gladbach (GER) /Galatasaray (TUR)	M78		M75	M	s58	A	s79		s68		M	s61			s78	29	5
Libor SIONKO	1/2/77	FK Austria Wien (AUT)	M46								s46	s46			s68			20	1
Milan BAROS	28/10/81	Liverpool (ENG) /Aston Villa (ENG)	A	A	A80	A		A61	A90	A89	A89	s46	A46				A64	50	27
Jan KOLLER	30/3/73	Bor. Dortmund (GER)	A	A	A								A71	A61	A44			69	43
René BOLF	25/2/74	AJ Auxerre (FRA)	s46	D59														34	-
Zdenek POSPECH	14/12/78	AC Sparta Praha	s46	s14														2	-
Rudolf SKÁCEL	17/7/79	Hearts (SCO)	s46		M46													3	1
Jan POLÁK	14/3/81	1.FC Nürnberg (GER)	s46	M		M	M58	s60	s61	M	M	M	M46	M61	s83	s46	M	21	5
Lukáš ZELENKA	5/10/79	AC Sparta Praha /V. Manisaspor (TUR)	s69								s85							3	-
Tomáš JUN	17/1/83	Trabzonspor (TUR) /Besiktas (TUR)	s78	s75	s80		A73				s89							10	2
Marek JANKULOVSKI	9/5/77	Milan (ITA)		D14			D	D	D	D		s46	D79	D	D	D		51	8
Karel POBORSKY	30/3/72	AC Sparta Praha /Dyn. Ceske Budejovice		M	M	M	M	M	M	M	M	M64	s46	M61	M83	M55	M46	118	8
Tomáš SIVOK	15/9/83	AC Sparta Praha		s59	s70													2	-
Jaromír BLAZEK	29/12/72	AC Sparta Praha			G							G						11	-
Martin JIRÁNEK	25/5/79	Spartak Moskva (RUS)			D44				D53	s89	D46	s83						24	-
Tomáš ROSICKY	4/10/80	Bor. Dortmund (GER)			M	M86	M88	M68	M68	M46				M86	M	M		57	17
Jirí STAJNER	27/5/76	Hannover 96 (GER)			M77	s86		s75	A85	s56	A46	s61	s86	s55	s46			24	3
David JAROLÍM	17/5/79	Hamburger SV (GER)			s77				s64	M46				s64				4	-
Pavel MARES	18/1/76	Zenit St- P'burg (RUS)			D					D46	s79							10	-
Radoslav KOVÁC	27/11/79	Spartak Moskva (RUS)			s73		s68		D					D78				7	-
Pavel NEDVED	30/8/72	Juventus (ITA)				M	M		M			M83	M	M	M			90	18
Jirí JAROSÍK	27/10/77	Birmingham C. (ENG)				s88												23	-
Jaroslav PLASIL	5/1/82	AS Monaco FC (FRA)				s90	M90	s46	M	M	M	M68	M					17	1
Karel PITÁK	28/1/80	SK Slavia Praha				s53												1	-
Stepán VACHOUSEK	26/7/79	FK Austria Wien (AUT)				s90												23	2
Vratislav LOKVENC	27/9/73	RB Salzburg (AUT)					A56	s71	s61	s44	A							74	14

Czech Republic

serving veteran left-back Tomás Janú. The latter was one of only three survivors from the club's 2002 championship win, the others being midfielders Petr Papousek and Ivan Hodúr.

There was a controversial end to Liberec's season, however, when they lost their final league fixture 3-2 at home to the season's surprise package FK Mladá Boleslav, surrendering their unbeaten home record to a last-minute winner from Marek Kulic, who had already scored two (dubious) penalties in the first half. Kulic's hat-trick gave Mladá Boleslav the win they needed to finish second to Liberec and join them in the qualifying round of the 2006/07 Champions League.

The team that missed out – because of an inferior record in the two head-to-head meetings with Mladá Boleslav - were the previous season's runners-up, Slavia Prague. They completed their season with a fourth successive victory – 3-0 at Vysocina Jihlava – but despite scoring more goals than any other team in the league – 56 – and possessing the player of the season in ten-goal midfielder and captain Karel Piták, Slavia's efforts were only good enough for a return to the UEFA Cup (a competition in which they had reached the third round in 2005/06, following Champions League exclusion at the qualifying stage). However, with the Slovan Liberec-Mladá Boleslav fixture subsequently coming under a joint FA and police investigation over allegations of match-rigging, Slavia's long-standing claims that they were the victims of biased refereeing (their 3-1 defeat at Liberec a few weeks earlier had been interrupted by a mid-game walk-off by the Slavia players) appeared to have some foundation.

There was further speculation of foul play on the final day as Sparta lost 3-1 at home to Viktoria Plzen, a result that enabled the visitors to avoid relegation, condemning Vysocina Jihlava instead. Like Mladá Boleslav, Plzen, who had only been promoted by default a year earlier, were awarded two contentious penalties en route to their first away win at Sparta for 65 years.

Village club Chmel Blsany finished bottom of the table and also went down, while there was a quick return to the Gambrinus Liga for Poborsky's Dynamo Ceské Budejovice as well as a welcome one for second division champions SK Kladno, a club of great tradition that had been absent from the top flight for 36 years.

EUROPEAN CUPS 2005/06

UEFA CHAMPIONS LEAGUE

AC SPARTA PRAHA
1st round Group B
Match 1 AJAX (HOL)
H 1-1 *Matusovic (66)*
Blazek, Pospech, Petrás, Lukás, Kadlec, Kisel, Poborsky, Sivok, Zelenka, Polácek (Dosek 79), Slepicka (Matusovic 49).

Match 2 FC THUN (SUI)
A 0-1
Blazek, Pospech, Petrás, Lukás, Kadlec, Kisel, Hasek, Sivok, Polácek, Zelenka (Dosek 84), Slepicka (Herzán 60).

Match 3 ARSENAL (ENG)
H 0-2
Blazek, Pergl (Matusovic 70), Petrous, Lukás, Kadlec, Pospech, Kisel, Petrás, Zelenka, Polácek, Slepicka (Dosek 77)

Match 4 ARSENAL
A 0-3
Blazek, Pergl, Petrás, Lukás, Kadlec, Pospech, Hasek, Petrous (Jeslínek 80), Zelenka, Polácek (Slepicka 58), Matusovic.

Match 5 AJAX
A 1-2 *Petrás (90)*
Blazek, Petrás, Petrous, Lukás, Kadlec, Pospech, Herzán (Simák 85), Zelenka (Slepicka 70), Hasek, Polácek, Dosek.

Match 6 FC THUN (SUI)
H 0-0
Blazek, Pospech, Petrás, Petrous, Kadlec, Simák (Jeslínek 60), Zelenka, Hasek (Herzán 82), Polácek, Dosek, Slepicka (Matusovic 66).

SK SLAVIA PRAHA
3rd qualifying round RSC ANDERLECHT (BEL)
A 1-2 *Jarolím (21)*
Kozácik, Kovác, Latka, Holenák, Zboncák, Piták, Suchy, Gedeon, Jarolím, Hrdlicka, Vlcek.
H 0-2
Kozácik, Svec (Fort 46), Latka, Holenák, Zboncák, Piták, Suchy, Gedeon (Zábojník 65), Jarolím, Hrdlicka (Svento 90), Vlcek.

UEFA CUP

FC BANÍK OSTRAVA
1st round SC HEERENVEEN (HOL)
H 2-0 *Klimpl (28), Magera (45p)*
Raska, Hoffmann, Klimpl, Besta, Cízek, Rajtoral, Bystron, Magera, Metelka (Coupek 55), Papadopulos (Stanek 83), Zeher (Sloncík 63).
A 0-5
Raska, Hoffmann, Klimpl, Besta, Cízek (Zeher 81), Rajtoral (Racko 60), Stanek, Bystron, Magera (Zurek 64), Metelka, Papadopulos.

FK TEPLICE
2nd qualifying round MTZ-RIPO MINSK (BLS)
A 1-1 *Rilke (34)*
Postulka, Ryska, Rada, Hunal, Krmas, Dolezal (Fenin 81), Sabou, Benát, Verbír, Masek (Varadi 69), Rilke.
H 2-1 *Rilke (56), Masek (90)*

Czech Republic

Postulka, Ryska, Rada, Hunal, Krmas, Dolezal, Benát, Sabou, Verbír, Masek, Rilke (Fenin 67).

1st round RCD ESPANYOL (ESP)
H 1-1 *Jirsák (48)*
Postulka, Kaufman, Rada, Hunal, Krmas, Dolezal, Jirsák (Varadi 81), Sabou, Verbír, Rilke (Fenin 77), Masek.
A 0-2
Kolár, Kaufman (Karlík 81), Rada, Hunal, Krmas, Benát, Jirsák (Dolezal 81), Sabou, Verbír, Rilke (Varadi 74), Masek.

SK SLAVIA PRAHA
1st round CORK CITY (IRL)
H 2-0 *Hrdlicka (62), Piták (78)*
Kozácik, Zábojník, Latka, Hubácek, Krajcík, Jarolím (Fort 69), Suchy, Hrdlicka, Svento, Piták, Pesír (Kratochvíl 79).
A 2-1 *Piták (27), Vlcek (63)*
Kozácik, Krajcík, Latka, Suchy, Zboncák, Piták, Jarolím, Hrdlicka (Cernoch 90), Svento, Vlcek (Kratochvíl 90), Fort (Pesír 82).

2nd round Group A
Match 1 CSKA SOFIA (BUL)
H 4-2 *Fort (5, 75), Vlcek (36), Piták (56)*
Kozácik, Krajcík, Latka, Suchy, Hubácek, Piták, Jarolím (Kratochvíl 90), Hrdlicka, Svento, Fort (Pesír 87), Vlcek (Svec 90).

Match 2 VIKING FK (NOR)
A 2-2 *Vlcek (51), Piták (83)*
Kozácik, Krajcík, Latka, Suchy, Hubácek (Zábojník 79), Piták, Jarolím, Hrdlicka, Svento, Vlcek (Gedeon 90), Fort (Pesír 68).

Match 3 AS MONACO FC (FRA)
H 0-2
Kozácik, Krajcík, Latka (Zábojník 46), Suchy, Hubácek, Piták, Jarolím, Hrdlicka, Svento, Vlcek (Svec 78), Fort (Pesír 72).

Match 4 HAMBURGER SV (GER)
A 0-2
Kozácik, Krajcík, Latka, Suchy, Holenák, Vlcek (Pesír 80), Jarolím, Gedeon, Hrdlicka (Svec 86), Svento, Fort (Seliga 30).

3rd round PALERMO (ITA)
H 2-1 *Jarolím (29), Barzagli (48og)*
Vorel, Krajcík, (Svec 77), Dosoudil, Suchy, Hubácek, Piták, Hrdlicka

TOP GOALSCORERS 2005/06

11	Milan IVANA (1.FC Slovácko Uherské Hradiste)
10	Karel PITÁK (SK Slavia Praha)
	Stanislav VLCEK (SK Slavia Praha)
	Marek KULIC (FK Mladá Boleslav)
9	Horst SIEGL (FK SIAD Most)
8	Rudolf OTEPKA (FK Marila Príbram)
	Libor DOSEK (FC Slovan Liberec/AC Sparta Praha)
	Lubos PECKA (FK Mladá Boleslav)
	Adam VARADI (FK Teplice/FC Baník Ostrava)
7	Filip HOLOSKO (FC Slovan Liberec)
	Tomás MICHÁLEK (FK Jablonec 97)
	Pavel FORT (SK Slavia Praha)
	Rogerio Botelho GAÚCHO (SK Sigma Olomouc/SK Slavia Praha)

(Holenák 46), Svento, Vlcek, Fort (Hercegfalvi 82).
A 0-1
Vorel, Krajcík, Suchy, Dosoudil, Hubácek, Vlcek, Piták, Svec (Kratochvíl 52), Holenák, Svento (Janda 78), Fort (Hercegfalvi 78).

LEAGUE RESULTS/ SCORERS/APPEARANCES/ GOALS 2005/06

FC BANÍK OSTRAVA
Coach – Jozef Jarabinsky; (29/8/05) Pavel Hapal

2005				
8/8	SK Sigma Olomouc	a	0-1	
13/8	FC Tescoma Zlín	h	4-1	Magera 2, Papadopulos, Zurek
22/8	FK SIAD Most	a	0-4	
27/8	FK Mladá Boleslav	h	1-3	Magera
9/9	1.FC Brno	a	1-1	Zurek
18/9	FC Slovan Liberec	h	1-1	og (Janu)
24/9	AC Sparta Praha	a	2-0	Papadopulos, Racko
3/10	FK Marila Príbram	h	0-1	
15/10	1.FC Slovácko U.H.	a	0-0	
22/10	FC Vysocina Jihlava	h	1-0	Papadopulos
30/10	FK Chmel Blsany	h	0-0	
6/11	FK Teplice	a	2-0	Cízek, Papadopulos
19/11	FK Jablonec 97	h	2-1	Zurek, Papadopulos
28/11	FC Viktoria Plzen	a	0-0	
3/12	SK Slavia Praha	h	1-3	Metelka
10/12	FC Tescoma Zlín	a	0-1	
2006				
26/2	FK Mladá Boleslav	a	1-2	Magera
11/3	FC Slovan Liberec	h	0-1	
20/3	AC Sparta Praha	h	0-2	
23/3	FK SIAD Most	h	0-0	
1/4	1.FC Slovácko U.H.	h	2-0	Lukes, Zurek
8/4	FC Vysocina Jihlava	a	1-0	Varadi
16/4	FK Chmel Blsany	a	1-1	Coupek
19/4	FK Marila Príbram	a	2-2	Lukes, Bystron
22/4	FK Teplice	h	0-0	
27/4	FK Jablonec 97	a	2-1	Varadi, Magera
30/4	FC Viktoria Plzen	h	6-0	Lukes 2, Strihavka, Zurek, Varadi, Hoffmann
3/5	1.FC Brno	h	1-1	Varadi
10/5	SK Slavia Praha	a	0-4	
13/5	SK Sigma Olomouc	h	4-1	Varadi 2 (1p), Strihavka, Tomasák

No	Name	Nat	Pos	Aps	(s)	Gls
8	Pavel BESTA		D	30		
6	David BYSTRON		M	24	(3)	1
12	Petr CIGÁNEK		D	2	(3)	
7	Martin CÍZEK		M	16		1
15	Petr COUPEK		M	17	(2)	1
9	Josef HOFFMANN		D	22		1
5	Maros KLIMPL	SVK	D	29		
2	Michal LESÁK		D	9		
4	Martin LUKES		A	10	(5)	4
29	Lukás MAGERA		A	14	(15)	5
24	Frantisek METELKA		M	19	(3)	1
28	Vladimír MISINSKY		A	3	(5)	
14	Michal PAPADOPULOS		A	14	(1)	5
21	Filip RACKO		M	1	(2)	1
15	Frantisek RAJTORAL		M	23	(3)	
22	Martin RASKA		G	25		

Czech Republic

FINAL LEAGUE TABLE 2005/06

		Pld	Home W	D	L	F	A	Away W	D	L	F	A	Total W	D	L	F	A	Pts
1	FC Slovan Liberec	30	9	5	1	22	9	7	6	2	21	13	16	11	3	43	22	59
2	FK Mladá Boleslav	30	11	2	2	30	13	5	4	6	20	23	16	6	8	50	36	54
3	SK Slavia Praha	30	10	4	1	29	12	5	5	5	27	22	15	9	6	56	34	54
4	FK Teplice	30	9	5	1	22	14	3	11	1	16	10	12	16	2	38	24	52
5	AC Sparta Praha	30	8	3	4	25	17	5	3	7	18	22	13	6	11	43	39	45
6	FC Baník Ostrava	30	6	5	4	23	14	4	5	6	12	18	10	10	10	35	32	40
7	1.FC Slovácko Uherské Hradiste	30	8	6	1	19	8	1	5	9	10	20	9	11	10	29	28	38
8	FK Jablonec 97	30	8	3	4	21	13	2	4	9	14	26	10	7	13	35	39	37
9	SK Sigma Olomouc	30	6	5	4	21	20	4	2	9	13	24	10	7	13	34	44	37
10	FK SIAD Most	30	9	2	4	24	18	1	4	10	10	23	10	6	14	34	41	36
11	FC Tescoma Zlín	30	8	6	1	21	10	0	5	10	6	23	8	11	11	27	33	35
12	1.FC Brno	30	6	6	3	18	13	1	8	6	17	23	7	14	9	35	36	35
13	FK Marila Príbram	30	6	8	1	27	16	2	2	11	9	20	8	10	12	36	36	34
14	FC Viktoria Plzen	30	5	6	4	17	16	2	4	9	13	27	7	10	13	30	43	31
15	FC Vysocina Jihlava	30	4	5	6	10	15	2	6	7	10	21	6	11	13	20	36	29
16	FK Chmel Blsany	30	4	7	4	13	17	1	4	10	9	27	5	11	14	22	44	26

10	Radek SLONCÍK		M	12	(6)
13	Zdenek STANEK		M	14	(6)
17	David STRIHAVKA		A	11	2
20	Petr TOMASÁK		M	6	(7) 1
14	Adam VARADI		A	9	(4) 6
1	Petr VASEK		G	5	
27	Róbert ZEHER	SVK	A	5	(8)
26	Libor ZUREK		A	10	(13) 5

1.FC BRNO
Coach – Jirí Kotrba; (17/10/05) Josef Mazura

2005
7/8	FK Marila Príbram	a	1-2	Zelenka
15/8	FC Slovan Liberec	h	0-1	
21/8	FC Vysocina Jihlava	h	1-2	Zelenka (p)
29/8	AC Sparta Praha	a	1-1	Cerny
9/9	FC Baník Ostrava	h	1-1	Baláz
18/9	FK Chmel Blsany	a	2-2	Svancara, Mezlík P.
23/9	FK Teplice	h	1-2	Svancara
1/10	1.FC Slovácko U.H.	a	1-1	Svancara
16/10	FK Jablonec 97	h	1-1	Svancara
23/10	SK Sigma Olomouc	a	2-3	Zelenka, Cerny
31/10	SK Slavia Praha	h	1-0	Mezlík P.
5/11	FC Tescoma Zlín	a	0-2	
20/11	FC Viktoria Plzen	h	3-1	Zelenka 2, Siegl
27/11	FK Mladá Boleslav	a	1-2	Svancara
4/12	FK SIAD Most	h	1-0	Besta
10/12	FC Slovan Liberec	a	0-0	

2006
18/2	FC Vysocina Jihlava	a	0-0	
25/2	AC Sparta Praha	h	1-1	Simr
19/3	FK Teplice	a	1-1	Trousil
26/3	1.FC Slovácko U.H.	h	0-0	
2/4	FK Jablonec 97	a	2-0	Mezlík P., Siegl
9/4	SK Sigma Olomouc	h	1-0	Holek
20/4	FK Chmel Blsany	h	1-0	Baláz

23/4	FC Tescoma Zlín	h	1-1	Holek
26/4	FC Viktoria Plzen	a	1-2	Besta
30/4	FK Mladá Boleslav	h	4-2	Simr, Zelenka, Horejs, Besta
3/5	FC Baník Ostrava	a	1-1	Pavlík (p)
6/5	SK Slavia Praha	a	1-3	Vrána
10/5	FK SIAD Most	a	3-3	Besta 2, Simr
13/5	FK Marila Príbram	h	1-0	Svancara

No	Name	Nat	Pos	Aps	(s)	Gls
7	Libor BALÁZ		M	12	(9)	2
14	Ales BESTA		A	15	(8)	5
17	Petr BREZOVAN	SVK	G	6	(1)	
26	Jaroslav CERNY		M	28		2
28	Filip CHLUP		M	8	(7)	
4	Marián HAD	SVK	D	11		
6	Lukás HLAVATY		M	4	(1)	
5	Mario HOLEK		M	23	(1)	2
19	David HOREJS		D	19	(2)	1
4	Zdenek HOUST		D	1	(2)	
8	Petr KRÁTKY		D	3		
18	Martin KUNCL		D	9	(2)	
20	Martin LEJSAL		G	12		
25	Pavel MEZLÍK		A	15	(9)	3
3	Radek MEZLÍK		D	1	(3)	
11	Petr MUSIL		M		(2)	
24	Petr PAVLÍK		M	13		1
23	Zdenek PARTYS		M	9	(2)	
2	Ales SCHUSTER		D	16	(3)	
10	Patrik SIEGL		M	25	(2)	2
8	Pavel SIMR		A	6	(10)	3
21	Roman SMUTNY		M		(1)	
15	Marek STRESÍK		A	1		
9	Petr SVANCARA		A	16	(5)	6
22	Jan TROUSIL		D	28		1
1	Michal VÁCLAVÍK		G	12		
12	Karel VECERA		M	11	(4)	

Czech Republic

30	Pavel VRÁNA		A	2	(4)	1
29	Ludek ZELENKA		A	24	(2)	6
13	Martin ZIVNY		D		(4)	

FK CHMEL BLSANY
Coach – Michal Bílek

2005

6/8	FC Tescoma Zlín	a	1-0	Polodna
14/8	FC Viktoria Plzen	h	0-3	
21/8	FK Mladá Boleslav	a	1-4	Kolár
28/8	FK Marila Príbram	h	1-0	Bílek
11/9	FK SIAD Most	a	1-3	Kolár
18/9	1.FC Brno	h	2-2	Deváty, Strihavka
24/9	FC Slovan Liberec	a	0-2	
2/10	FC Vysocina Jihlava	h	2-2	Strihavka, Dort
15/10	AC Sparta Praha	a	2-5	Selicha, Polodna
23/10	1.FC Slovácko U.H.	h	1-1	Kolár
30/10	FC Baník Ostrava	a	0-0	
6/11	SK Sigma Olomouc	a	2-3	Dirnbach, Selicha
21/11	FK Teplice	h	0-0	
27/11	SK Slavia Praha	a	0-0	
4/12	FK Jablonec 97	h	1-0	Polodna
11/12	FC Viktoria Plzen	a	0-2	

2006

5/3	FK SIAD Most	h	0-1	
19/3	FC Slovan Liberec	h	0-0	
22/3	FK Mladá Boleslav	h	1-0	Polodna
25/3	FC Vysocina Jihlava	a	0-0	
2/4	AC Sparta Praha	h	0-0	
5/4	FK Marila Príbram	a	1-1	Deváty
8/4	1.FC Slovácko U.H.	a	0-2	
16/4	FC Baník Ostrava	h	1-1	Deváty
20/4	1.FC Brno	a	0-1	
23/4	SK Sigma Olomouc	h	0-2	
26/4	FK Teplice	a	1-2	Sindelár (p)
30/4	SK Slavia Praha	h	1-3	Sindelár
10/5	FK Jablonec 97	a	0-2	
13/5	FC Tescoma Zlín	h	3-2	Brunclík, Vorel (p), Klasna

No	Name	Nat	Pos	Aps	(s)	Gls
25	Jirí BÍLEK		M	15		1
15	Jan BROCHINSKY		M	15	(6)	
6	David BRUNCLÍK		M	8		1
31	Antonín BUCEK		G	1	(1)	
3	Tomás BULDRA		M	1	(2)	
1	Michal DANEK		G	16		
20	Pavel DEVÁTY		M	26	(1)	3
6	Marian DIRNBACH		D	8	(2)	1
17	Filip DORT		M	15		1
18	Martin HORÁCEK		D	5	(1)	
16	Jakub HOTTEK		M	4	(4)	
22	Stepán KACAFÍREK		A		(3)	
26	Jan KLASNA		M		(1)	1
11	Daniel KOLÁR		M	14		3
6	Vlastimil KOZÍSEK		M		(1)	
12	Jirí KREJCÍ		D	11		
5	Karel KREJCÍK		D	7		
11	Petr LOOS		D	2	(4)	
14	Lukás MICHAL		M	13	(3)	
9	Martin MÜLLER		D	13		
23	Lukás NACHTMAN		D	3	(5)	
23	Tomás PESÍR		A	10		
26	Lukás PLESKO		D	4	(6)	
10	Michal POLODNA		A	21	(9)	4
8	Radek SELICHA		M	9	(6)	2

18	Radek SINDELÁR		M	13		2
30	Martin SLAVÍK		G	13		
2	Radek SOUREK		D	23		
27	David STRIHAVKA		A	8	(2)	2
3	Jakub SÜSSER		D		(1)	
11	Petr TRAPP		D	14		
16	Zdenek VOLEK		M	6	(7)	
7	Jan VOREL		D	29		1
8	Róbert ZEHER	SVK	A	3	(8)	

FK JABLONEC 97
Coach – Petr Rada

2005

7/8	1.FC Slovácko U.H.	h	2-1	M. Baránek, Senkerík
14/8	SK Sigma Olomouc	h	1-2	og (Gaúcho)
20/8	SK Slavia Praha	a	2-3	Senkerík, Nesvadba
28/8	FC Viktoria Plzen	h	3-1	Loucka, Senkerík, Kordula
10/9	FC Tescoma Zlín	a	1-3	Husek
18/9	FK Marila Príbram	h	3-1	Klapka, og (Formánek), Senkerík
25/9	FK Mladá Boleslav	a	1-2	Michálek
1/10	FC Slovan Liberec	h	1-0	Michálek
16/10	1.FC Brno	a	1-1	Senkerík
30/10	FC Vysocina Jihlava	a	1-1	Smísek
5/11	AC Sparta Praha	h	2-1	Michálek, Smísek
19/11	FC Baník Ostrava	a	1-2	Michálek
23/11	FK SIAD Most	h	3-0	Michálek 2, Smísek
27/11	FK Teplice	h	0-0	
4/12	FK Chmel Blsany	a	0-1	
11/12	SK Sigma Olomouc	a	2-0	Senkerík, Michálek

2006

19/2	SK Slavia Praha	h	0-2	
25/2	FC Viktoria Plzen	a	2-1	Lafata 2
5/3	FC Tescoma Zlín	h	2-0	Lafata, Kisa
19/3	FK Mladá Boleslav	h	1-1	Kisa
25/3	FC Slovan Liberec	a	0-2	
29/3	FK Marila Príbram	a	2-2	Lafata, Svátek
2/4	1.FC Brno	h	0-2	
9/4	FK SIAD Most	a	0-3	
15/4	FC Vysocina Jihlava	h	0-0	
24/4	AC Sparta Praha	a	0-3	
27/4	FC Baník Ostrava	h	1-2	Weber
30/4	FK Teplice	a	1-1	Baránek
10/5	FK Chmel Blsany	h	2-0	Jindrísek (p), Smísek
13/5	FC Slovácko U.H.	a	0-1	

No	Name	Nat	Pos	Aps	(s)	Gls
11	Miroslav BARÁNEK		M	20	(4)	2
20	Jirí BOBOK		G	3		
25	Václav DROBNY		D	15		
13	Tomás GLOS		D	6	(1)	
10	Ladislav GRUBHOFFER		A		(6)	
18	Richard HROTEK		D	23		
2	Tomás HUBER		D	1		
8	Lubos HUSEK		M	23		1
16	Josef JINDRÍSEK		M	7	(9)	1
6	Rastislav KISA		M	7	(4)	2
12	Filip KLAPKA		M	23		1
24	Michal KORDULA		M	16	(9)	1
25	Stepán KUCERA		D	7	(1)	
26	Jaroslav LACIGA		D	4	(2)	
14	David LAFATA		A	14		4
15	Lubos LOUCKA		D	4		1
23	Tomás MICHÁLEK		M	14	(2)	7
7	Petr MUSIL		M	1	(5)	

Czech Republic

5	Jaroslav NESVADBA		D	15	1
19	Dusan NULÍCEK		A	1	(7)
21	Vladimír PONCÁK	SVK	D	17	(2)
14	Zdenek SENKERÍK		A	15	6
9	Petr SMÍSEK		A	17	(8)	4
1	Michal SPIT		G	27	
23	Jan SVÁTEK		A	4	(7)	1
17	Jiri SVOJTKA		D	9	(7)
22	Karel VRABEC		M	1	(2)
3	Jozef WEBER		M	29	1
5	Petr ZÁBOJNÍK		D	7	

FK MARILA PRÍBRAM
Coach – Pavel Tobiás

2005
7/8	1.FC Brno	h	2-1	Pilík, Otepka (p)
14/8	FC Vysocina Jihlava	a	3-2	Cupr, Formánek, og (Heide)
21/8	FK Teplice	h	1-1	Otepka (p)
28/8	FK Chmel Blsany	a	0-1	
11/9	SK Sigma Olomouc	h	3-0	Otepka 2, Straceny
18/9	FK Jablonec 97	a	1-3	Buryán
24/9	SK Slavia Praha	h	2-2	Riegel 2
3/10	FC Baník Ostrava	a	0-1	Riegel
16/10	FC Tescoma Zlín	h	3-0	Riegel, Klesa, Huna
23/10	FC Viktoria Plzen	a	1-2	Mendy
30/10	FK Mladá Boleslav	a	0-0	
7/11	FC Slovan Liberec	h	2-2	Straceny, Navrátil
20/11	FK SIAD Most	a	0-1	
27/11	1.FC Slovácko U.H.	h	1-1	Otepka (p)
3/12	AC Sparta Praha	a	1-1	Riegel
11/12	FC Vysocina Jihlava	h	2-0	Mendy, Frejlach

2006
20/2	FK Teplice	a	1-2	Buryán
5/3	SK Sigma Olomouc	a	1-2	Divecky
29/3	FK Jablonec 97	h	2-2	Riegel, Divecky
18/3	SK Slavia Praha	a	0-1	
2/4	FC Tescoma Zlín	a	0-1	
5/4	FK Chmel Blsany	h	1-1	Otepka (p)
8/4	FC Viktoria Plzen	h	2-0	Otepka, Frejlach
15/4	FK Mladá Boleslav	h	1-2	Buryán
19/4	FC Baník Ostrava	h	2-2	Plesko, Divecky
22/4	FC Slovan Liberec	a	0-1	
26/4	FK SIAD Most	h	1-0	Frejlach
29/4	1.FC Slovácko U.H.	a	0-2	
10/5	AC Sparta Praha	h	2-2	Otepka, Frejlach
13/5	1.FC Brno	a	0-1	

No	Name	Nat	Pos	Aps	(s)	Gls
4	Jan BURYÁN		D	24	(3)	3
8	Martin CUPR		M	21	(5)	1
10	Radek DIVECKY		A	12		3
12	Tomás FENYK		D	1		
14	René FORMÁNEK		D	29		1
20	Tomás FREJLACH		M	12	(5)	4
18	Jan GRUBER		A	10		
7	Pavel HASEK		M	4	(9)	
12	Nedim HIROS	SCG	D		(2)	
11	Daniel HUNA		A	3	(9)	1
25	Petr JAVOREK		M	1	(1)	
27	Michal KLESA		A	10	(17)	1
8	Václav KOLOUSEK		M	14		
2	Marcel MÁCHA		D	29		
16	Alexandre MENDY	FRA	A	12	(1)	2
4	Jirí MLIKA		A	1		
3	Jakub NAVRÁTIL		D	20	(4)	1

9	Rudolf OTEPKA		M	22		8
1	Oldrich PARÍZEK		G	27		
17	Miroslav PENNER		D	24		
13	Tomás PILÍK		A		(12)	1
6	Lukás PLESKO		D	7	(3)	1
16	Miroslav PODRAZKY		M		(4)	
5	Jan RIEGEL		D	28		6
30	Radek SNOZÍK		G	3	(1)	
10	Ludek STRACENY		M	16		2
19	Jan VOSAHLÍK		A		(8)	

FK MLADÁ BOLESLAV
Coach – Dusan Uhrin jr

2005
7/8	FC Slovan Liberec	h	2-4	Vít, Svejdík
21/8	FK Chmel Blsany	h	4-1	Matejovsky (p), Sevínsky, Pecka, Holub
27/8	FC Baník Ostrava	a	3-1	Cáp, Matejovsky, Kulic
1/9	1.FC Slovácko U.H.	a	1-1	Matejovsky
11/9	FK Teplice	h	0-2	
18/9	SK Sigma Olomouc	a	3-2	Holub, Vít, Kysela
25/9	FK Jablonec 97	h	2-1	Holub 2
3/10	SK Slavia Praha	a	1-2	Sevínsky
16/10	FC Viktoria Plzen	h	2-2	Kysela, Holub
22/10	FC Tescoma Zlín	a	0-2	
30/10	FK Marila Príbram	h	0-0	
6/11	FK SIAD Most	h	1-0	Palát
19/11	AC Sparta Praha	a	2-4	Simr, Pecka
27/11	1.FC Brno	h	2-1	Kulic, og (Trousil)
11/12	1.FC Slovácko	h	1-0	Rychlík

2006
26/2	FC Baník Ostrava	h	2-1	Matejovsky (p), Vaculík
5/3	FK Teplice	a	1-1	Kulic
12/3	SK Sigma Olomouc	h	2-0	Vít, Sviták
19/3	FK Jablonec 97	a	1-1	Palát
22/3	FK Chmel Blsany	a	0-1	
27/3	SK Slavia Praha	h	4-1	Kulic 2, Sevínsky, Pecka
2/4	FC Viktoria Plzen	a	1-0	Ordos
9/4	FC Tescoma Zlín	a	2-0	Vaculík, Matejovsky (p)
12/4	FC Vysocina Jihlava	a	0-0	
15/4	FK Marila Príbram	a	2-1	Pecka 2
23/4	FK SIAD Most	a	0-1	
27/4	AC Sparta Praha	h	2-0	Pecka, Vaculík
30/4	1.FC Brno	a	2-4	Sedlácek, Ordos
10/5	FC Vysocina Jihlava	h	4-0	Kulic 2 (1p), Pecka 2
13/5	FC Slovan Liberec	a	3-2	Kulic 3 (2p)

No	Name	Nat	Pos	Aps	(s)	Gls
9	Milos BREZINSKY	SVK	D	18	(1)	
22	David BRUNCLÍK		M	2	(4)	
4	Tomás CÁP		D	15	(2)	1
7	Radim HOLUB		A	7	(5)	5
2	Petr KRÁTKY		M	4	(2)	
1	Pavel KUCERA		G	17		
10	Marek KULIC		A	27	(1)	10
20	Jan KYSELA		A	19	(7)	2
8	Marek MATEJOVSKY		M	26		5
27	Miroslav MILLER		G	13	(1)	
18	Michal ORDOS		A	2	(11)	2
6	Marián PALÁT		D	19	(2)	2
16	Lubos PECKA		A	26	(3)	8
12	Jose Diego PIRES	BRA	M	1	(5)	
17	Jirí RYCHLÍK		D	16	(8)	1
11	Tomás SEDLÁCEK		A		(7)	1
3	Frantisek SEVÍNSKY		D	29		3

Czech Republic

18	Pavel SIMR		A	2	(5)	1
18	Jirí SKÁLA		D	1		
23	Jaromír SMERDA		D	17		
14	Ondrej SVEJDÍK		D	24		1
25	Martin SVITÁK		M	4	(14)	1
5	Lukás VACULÍK		M	15	(2)	3
21	Jirí VÍT		D	26	(2)	3

FK SIAD MOST
Coach – Premysl Bicovsky; (1/1/06) Zdenek Scasny

2005

7/8	FK Teplice	h	2-1	Polácek, og (Hunal)
13/8	AC Sparta Praha	a	1-2	Pilar
22/8	FC Baník Ostrava	h	4-0	Siegl 2, Bocek, Macek
27/8	1.FC Slovácko U.H.	a	1-2	Pilar
11/9	FK Chmel Blsany	h	3-1	Skoda, Siegl, Brzezina
18/9	FC Vysocina Jihlava	a	0-1	
26/9	SK Sigma Olomouc	h	0-2	
2/10	FC Viktoria Plzen	a	1-2	Cízek
15/10	SK Slavia Praha	h	0-3	
30/10	FC Tescoma Zlín	h	0-0	
6/11	FK Mladá Boleslav	a	0-1	
20/11	FK Marila Príbram	h	1-0	Brzezina
23/11	FK Jablonec 97	a	0-3	
26/11	FC Slovan Liberec	h	1-2	Brzezina (p)
4/12	1.FC Brno	a	0-1	
12/12	AC Sparta Praha	h	0-3	

2006

26/2	1.FC Slovácko U.H.	h	3-2	og (Svejnoha), Siegl, Hainault
5/3	FK Chmel Blsany	a	1-0	Siegl
12/3	FC Vysocina Jihlava	h	2-1	Pikl (p), Brzezina
19/3	SK Sigma Olomouc	a	1-1	Pikl
23/3	FC Baník Ostrava	a	0-0	
26/3	FC Viktoria Plzen	h	1-0	Jendruscák
1/4	SK Slavia Praha	a	0-3	
9/4	FK Jablonec 97	h	3-0	Mendy 2, Pikl
15/4	FC Tescoma Zlín	a	1-1	Procházka
23/4	FK Mladá Boleslav	h	1-0	Pikl
26/4	FK Marila Príbram	a	0-1	
29/4	FC Slovan Liberec	a	1-1	Siegl (p)
10/5	1.FC Brno	h	3-3	Siegl 2, Jendruscák
13/5	FK Teplice	a	3-4	Gasparík, Siegl, Mendy

No	Name	Nat	Pos	Aps	(s)	Gls
24	Martin BOCEK		A		(11)	1
11	Adam BRZEZINA		A	10	(16)	4
7	Radek CÍZEK		M	8	(15)	1
3	Michal GASPARÍK	SVK	A	9	(4)	1
4	André HAINAULT	CAN	D	13		1
3	Zdenek HOUST		D	13		
6	Martin HRUSKA		M	6	(1)	
18	Ladislav JAMRICH		D	3	(1)	
21	Petr JENDRUSCÁK		M	21	(7)	2
25	Gbalou Ange KOUYO	CIV	D	2	(2)	
25	Tomás KULVAJT		A	3	(4)	
9	Michal MACEK		M	18	(4)	1
13	Alexandre MENDY	FRA	A	14		3
16	Jirí NOVOTNY		A	26		
23	Ales PIKL		M	11		4
8	Tomás PILAR		M	27	(2)	2
6	Tomás POLÁCEK		M	4		1
14	Jan PROCHÁZKA		D	22		1
17	Lukás SCHUT		M		(1)	
10	Horst SIEGL		A	28	(1)	9

4	Richard SITARCÍK		D	7	(2)	
12	Ales SKERLE		D	27	(2)	
19	Jaroslav SKODA		M	17	(1)	1
5	Václav STÍPEK		A		(2)	
2	Gratien Gaël SUARES	FRA	D		(1)	
1	Martin SVOBODA		G	30		
13	Roman SVRCEK		D		(2)	
5	Vitali TRUBILA	BLS	A		(1)	
15	Martin ZBONCÁK		D	11		

SK SIGMA OLOMOUC
Coach – Petr Ulicny

2005

8/8	FC Baník Ostrava	h	1-0	Schulmeister J.
14/8	FK Jablonec 97	a	2-1	Melinho, Gaúcho
21/8	FC Viktoria Plzen	a	0-1	
27/8	SK Slavia Praha	h	4-3	Rojka 2, Melinho, Hudec
11/9	FK Marila Príbram	a	0-3	
18/9	FK Mladá Boleslav	h	2-3	Onofrej, Hudec (p)
26/9	FK SIAD Most	a	2-0	Onofrej, Randa
2/10	FC Tescoma Zlín	h	0-0	
17/10	FC Slovan Liberec	a	0-2	
23/10	1.FC Brno	h	3-2	Hubník M. 2, Hudec (p)
29/10	AC Sparta Praha	a	2-1	Gaúcho, Hubník M.
6/11	FK Chmel Blsany	h	3-2	Melinho, Onofrej, Hubník R.
19/11	1.FC Slovácko U.H.	a	2-2	Rojka, Hubník M.
27/11	FC Vysocina Jihlava	h	1-2	Hubník M.
5/12	FK Teplice	a	0-1	
11/12	FK Jablonec 97	h	0-2	

2006

27/2	SK Slavia Praha	a	1-2	Babnic
5/3	FK Marila Príbram	h	2-1	Chmelícek, Hubník M.
12/3	FK Mladá Boleslav	a	0-2	
19/3	FK SIAD Most	h	1-1	Kovár (p)
22/3	FC Viktoria Plzen	h	1-1	Hubník R.
3/4	FC Slovan Liberec	h	1-0	Horácek
9/4	1.FC Brno	a	1-1	Horácek
15/4	AC Sparta Praha	h	1-2	Chmelícek
19/4	FC Tescoma Zlín	a	0-1	
23/4	FK Chmel Blsany	a	2-0	Onofrej, Chmelícek
26/4	1.FC Slovácko U.H.	h	1-1	Babnic
29/4	FC Vysocina Jihlava	a	0-3	
10/5	FK Teplice	h	0-0	
13/5	FC Baník Ostrava	a	1-4	Rydel

No	Name	Nat	Pos	Aps	(s)	Gls
19	Peter BABNIC	SVK	A	11	(6)	2
16	Ales BEDNÁR		A		(2)	
30	Martin BLAHA		G	2	(1)	
11	Ales CHMELÍCEK		A	9	(1)	3
8	Rogério Botelho GAÚCHO	BRA	A	6		2
25	Tomás GLOS		M	1	(3)	
13	Martin HORÁCEK		D	18	(4)	2
10	Michal HUBNÍK		A	19	(1)	6
5	Roman HUBNÍK		D	27		2
15	Martin HUDEC		D	22	(1)	3
7	Tomás JANOTKA		M		(2)	
7	Marek KASCÁK		M	5	(8)	
9	Radim KÖNIG		M	11	(3)	
4	Radim KOPECKY		D	1	(2)	
22	Michal KOVÁR		D	25		1
25	Ivo KRAJCOVIC		D	2	(3)	
13	Radim KUCERA		D	2		
1	Tomás LOVÁSIK	SVK	G	28		
21	Tarciso Rogério Pereira MELINHO	BRA	M	14	(1)	3

Czech Republic

No	Name	Nat	Pos	Aps	(s)	Gls
6	Ladislav ONOFREJ	SVK	M	27	(1)	4
14	Andrej PECNIK	SLO	D	9	(4)	
2	Tomás RANDA		D	26		1
27	David ROJKA		A	2	(10)	3
24	Filip RYDEL		M	19	(8)	1
7	Jan SCHULMEISTER		A	3	(8)	1
21	Vojtech SCHULMEISTER		A		(1)	
3	Radek SPILÁCEK		M	18		
16	Pavel SULTÉS		A	3	(6)	
17	Kamil VACEK		M	7	(2)	
12	Michal VEPREK		D	2	(1)	
18	Martin VYSKOCIL		A	11	(10)	

SK SLAVIA PRAHA
Coach – Karel Jarolím

2005
Date	Opponent	h/a	Score	Scorers
5/8	FC Vysocina Jihlava	h	1-1	Piták
14/8	FK Teplice	a	0-1	
20/8	FK Jablonec 97	h	3-2	Krajcík, Piták, Svento
27/8	SK Sigma Olomouc	a	3-4	Piták, Svento, Hrdlicka
10/9	FC Viktoria Plzen	a	1-1	Krajcík
18/9	FC Tescoma Zlín	h	1-0	Fort
24/9	FK Marila Príbram	a	2-2	Latka, Vlcek
3/10	FK Mladá Boleslav	h	2-1	Jarolím, Hrdlicka
15/10	FK SIAD Most	a	3-0	Fort, Hrdlicka, Jarolím (p)
23/10	AC Sparta Praha	h	4-1	Svento, Latka, Vlcek, Krajcík
31/10	1.FC Brno	a	0-1	
6/11	1.FC Slovácko U.H.	h	2-0	Svento, Vlcek
19/11	FC Slovan Liberec	a	3-3	Hrdlicka, Pesír, Fort
27/11	FK Chmel Blsany	h	0-0	
3/12	FC Baník Ostrava	a	3-1	Piták, Holenák, Jarolím
10/12	FK Teplice	h	1-1	Piták

2006
Date	Opponent	h/a	Score	Scorers
19/2	FK Jablonec 97	a	2-0	Fort, Piták
27/2	SK Sigma Olomouc	h	2-1	Jarolím (p), Holenák
4/3	FC Viktoria Plzen	h	1-0	Fort
18/3	FK Marila Príbram	h	1-0	Piták
27/3	FK Mladá Boleslav	a	1-4	Vlcek
1/4	FK SIAD Most	h	3-0	Fort, Piták (p), Kalivoda
8/4	AC Sparta Praha	a	1-2	Vlcek
12/4	FC Tescoma Zlín	a	2-2	Gaúcho, Kalivoda (p)
22/4	1.FC Slovácko U.H.	a	0-0	
26/4	FC Slovan Liberec	h	1-3	Janda
30/4	FK Chmel Blsany	a	3-1	Vlcek 2, Piták (p)
6/5	1.FC Brno	h	3-1	Vlcek, Piták, Gaúcho
10/5	FC Baník Ostrava	h	4-0	Gaúcho 2, Svento, Fort
13/5	FC Vysocina Jihlava	a	3-0	Vlcek 2, Gaúcho

No	Name	Nat	Pos	Aps	(s)	Gls
36	Evandro da Silva ADAUTO	BRA	A		(2)	
27	Ante ARACIC	CRO	D	9	(2)	
26	Martin CERNOCH		A		(4)	
9	Milan CERNY		M	2	(4)	
33	Radek DOSOUDIL		D	8	(1)	
24	Pavel ELIÁS		M	3		
16	Pavel FORT		A	15	(6)	7
10	Rogério Botelho GAÚCHO	BRA	A	7	(3)	5
14	Patrik GEDEON		M	5		
26	Zoltán HERCEGFALVI	HUN	A	1	(8)	
11	Miroslav HOLENÁK		D	17		2
28	Tomás HRDLICKA		M	12	(6)	4
4	David HUBÁCEK		D	16	(2)	
8	Petr JANDA		M	9	(4)	1
20	Lukás JAROLÍM		M	29		4
25	David KALIVODA		M	4	(7)	2

No	Name	Nat	Pos	Aps	(s)	Gls
12	Ivan KOVÁC	SVK	D	4		
29	Matús KOZÁCIK	SVK	G	16		
19	Matej KRAJCÍK	SVK	D	22	(1)	3
2	Karel KRATOCHVÍL		D	4	(7)	
6	Martin LATKA		D	12	(1)	2
25	Tomás PESÍR		A	6	(9)	1
23	Karel PITÁK		M	22	(2)	10
35	Aleksander SELIGA	SLO	G	1	(1)	
3	Jirí STUDÍK		D	2	(2)	
17	Marek SUCHY		M	21	(1)	
5	Michal SVEC		M	7	(4)	
18	Dusan SVENTO		M	20	(2)	5
10	Cesaro VICTORINO	MEX	M	2	(2)	
7	Stanislav VLCEK		A	26	(3)	10
13	Michal VOREL		G	13		
24	Petr ZÁBOJNÍK		D	6	(4)	
21	Martin ZBONCÁK		M	9		

1.FC SLOVÁCKO UHERSKÉ HRADISTE
Coach – Ladislav Molnár; (27/10/05) Stanislav Levy

2005
Date	Opponent	h/a	Score	Scorers
7/8	FK Jablonec 97	a	1-2	Kúdela
22/8	FC Tescoma Zlín	a	1-3	Czinege
27/8	FK SIAD Most	h	2-1	Malár, Ivana
1/9	FK Mladá Boleslav	h	1-1	Malár
12/9	FC Slovan Liberec	a	1-2	Ivana
17/9	AC Sparta Praha	h	2-0	Sowunmi, Malár
25/9	FC Vysocina Jihlava	a	0-1	
1/10	1.FC Brno	h	1-1	Licka
15/10	FK Baník Ostrava	h	0-0	
23/10	FK Chmel Blsany	a	1-1	Róth
29/10	FK Teplice	h	1-1	Pavlík (p)
6/11	SK Slavia Praha	a	0-2	
19/11	SK Sigma Olomouc	h	2-2	Sowunmi, Ivana
27/11	FK Marila Príbram	a	1-1	Ivana
3/12	FC Viktoria Plzen	h	1-0	Ivana
11/12	FK Mladá Boleslav	a	0-1	

2006
Date	Opponent	h/a	Score	Scorers
18/2	FC Tescoma Zlín	h	2-0	Ivana 2
26/2	FK SIAD Most	a	2-3	Polách (p), Svejnoha
4/3	FC Slovan Liberec	h	1-2	Sowunmi
13/3	AC Sparta Praha	a	0-1	
18/3	FC Vysocina Jihlava	h	1-0	Sowunmi
26/3	1.FC Brno	a	0-0	
1/4	FC Baník Ostrava	h	0-2	
8/4	FK Chmel Blsany	h	2-0	Ivana 2 (1p)
15/4	FK Teplice	a	0-0	
22/4	SK Slavia Praha	h	0-0	
26/4	SK Sigma Olomouc	a	1-1	Brezny
29/4	FK Marila Príbram	h	2-0	Rajnoch, Ivana
10/5	FC Viktoria Plzen	a	2-0	Suskavcevic, Ivana
13/5	FK Jablonec 97	h	1-0	Rajnoch

No	Name	Nat	Pos	Aps	(s)	Gls
28	Daniel BREZNY		M	5	(2)	1
13	Jakub BURES		D	1	(1)	
3	Petr COUPEK		M		(1)	
7	Ondrej CTVRTNÍCEK		A		(1)	
16	Juraj CZINEGE	SVK	M	3	(4)	1
1	Petr DROBISZ		G	29		
8	Petr FILIPSKY		M	2	(1)	
22	Milan IVANA	SVK	A	28	(1)	11
13	Jirí KOWALÍK		A		(1)	
6	Ondrej KÚDELA		M	5	(7)	1
15	Mario LICKA		M	21	(5)	1

Czech Republic

No	Name	Nat	Pos	Aps	(s)	Gls
25	Ondrej LYSONEK		D	15		
9	Vladimír MALÁR		A	22	(5)	3
5	Pavel MALCHÁREK		A	4	(15)	
12	Pavel NEMCICKY		D	17	(1)	
2	Rudolf OBAL		A	1	(11)	
30	Miroslav ONDRUSEK		G	1		
17	Michal ORDOS		A	2	(10)	
10	Jan PALÍNEK		D	10		
24	Petr PAVLÍK		M	16		1
4	Milan PETRZELA		M	18	(3)	
21	Tomás POLÁCH		M	19	(2)	1
11	Zbynek POSPECH		A	1		
27	Jan RAJNOCH		D	28		2
2	Ferenc RÓTH	HUN	M	16	(1)	1
11	Thomas SOWUNMI	HUN	A	14	(10)	4
19	Darko SUSKAVCEVIC		D	29		1
20	Martin SVEJNOHA		D	23	(2)	1

FC SLOVAN LIBEREC
Coach – Vítezslav Lavicka

2005

Date	Opponent		Score	Scorers
7/8	FK Mladá Boleslav	a	4-2	Hodúr, Dosek, Pudil, Holenda
15/8	1.FC Brno	a	1-0	Ancic
20/8	AC Sparta Praha	h	2-0	Hodúr, Matula
28/8	FC Vysocina Jihlava	a	2-0	Pospech, Hodúr
12/9	1.FC Slovácko U.H.	h	2-1	Pudil, Holosko
18/9	FC Baník Ostrava	a	1-1	Zápotocny (p)
24/9	FK Chmel Blsany	h	2-0	Hodúr, Singlár
1/10	FK Jablonec 97	a	0-1	
17/10	SK Sigma Olomouc	h	2-0	Papousek, Holosko
24/10	FK Teplice	a	0-0	
29/10	FC Viktoria Plzen	h	2-0	Holosko 2
7/11	FK Marila Príbram	a	2-2	Holenda, Pudil
19/11	SK Slavia Praha	h	3-3	Holenda, Holosko, Pospech
26/11	FK SIAD Most	a	2-1	Holosko 2
3/12	FC Tescoma Zlín	h	1-0	Zápotocny (p)
10/12	1.FC Brno	h	0-0	

2006

Date	Opponent		Score	Scorers
18/2	AC Sparta Praha	a	2-1	Dort, Holenda
25/2	FC Vysocina Jihlava	h	0-0	
4/3	1.FC Slovácko U.H.	a	2-1	Dort, Kostál
11/3	FC Baník Ostrava	h	1-0	Zápotocny
19/3	FK Chmel Blsany	a	0-0	
25/3	FK Jablonec 97	h	2-0	Kostál, Janu
3/4	SK Sigma Olomouc	a	0-1	
10/4	FK Teplice	h	1-1	Pospech
16/4	FC Viktoria Plzen	a	1-1	Pospech
22/4	FK Marila Príbram	h	1-0	Bílek
26/4	SK Slavia Praha	a	3-1	Papousek, Zápotocny (p), Abrahám
29/4	FK SIAD Most	h	1-1	Blazek
10/5	FC Tescoma Zlín	a	1-1	Pospech
13/5	FK Mladá Boleslav	h	2-3	Matula, Abrahám

No	Name	Nat	Pos	Aps	(s)	Gls
26	Martin ABRAHÁM		M	17	(4)	2
9	Juraj ANCIC	SVK	M	2	(13)	1
7	Jirí BÍLEK		M	11	(1)	1
28	Jan BLAZEK		A	1	(5)	1
24	Marek CECH		G	28		
25	Jakub DOHNÁLEK		M		(2)	
27	Filip DORT		M	13		2
7	Libor DOSEK		A	1		1
6	Josef HAMOUZ		D	5	(15)	

No	Name		Pos	Aps	(s)	Gls
1	Zbynek HAUZR		G	2		
12	Radek HOCHMEISTER		D	4	(15)	
10	Ivan HODÚR	SVK	M	23	(2)	4
29	Jan HOLENDA		A	15	(3)	4
13	Filip HOLOSKO	SVK	A	14	(1)	7
17	Tomás JANU		D	29		1
14	Pavel KOSTÁL		D	27		2
8	József MAGASFÄLDI	HUN	M		(3)	
2	Jan MATULA		D	12	(9)	2
23	Petr PAPOUSEK		M	25	(2)	2
11	Zbynek POSPECH		A	18	(6)	5
3	Daniel PUDIL		M	28	(1)	3
18	Tomas RADZINEVICIUS	LIT	A	2	(2)	
19	Peter SINGLÁR	SVK	D	26		1
20	Josef TUMA	GER	M	3	(3)	
5	Tomás ZÁPOTOCNY		D	24		4

AC SPARTA PRAHA
Coach – Jaroslav Hrebík; (12/10/05) Stanislav Griga

2005

Date	Opponent		Score	Scorers
6/8	FC Viktoria Plzen	a	2-1	Kisel, Zelenka
13/8	FK SIAD Most	h	2-1	Poborsky (p), Sivok
20/8	FC Slovan Liberec	a	0-2	
29/8	1.FC Brno	h	1-1	Sivok
10/9	FC Vysocina Jihlava	h	2-0	Zelenka 2
17/9	1.FC Slovácko U.H.	a	0-2	
24/9	FC Baník Ostrava	h	0-2	
2/10	FK Teplice	a	1-2	Polácek
15/10	FK Chmel Blsany	h	5-2	Polácek, Dosek, og (Vorel), Matusovic, Petrás
23/10	SK Slavia Praha	a	1-4	Matusovic
29/10	SK Sigma Olomouc	h	1-2	Matusovic (p)
5/11	FK Jablonec 97	a	1-2	Polácek
19/11	FK Mladá Boleslav	h	4-2	Dosek, Polácek, Herzán, Slepicka
26/11	FC Tescoma Zlín	a	2-3	Dosek 2
3/12	FK Marila Príbram	h	1-1	Petrás (p)
12/12	FK SIAD Most	a	3-0	Zelenka, Matusovic, Pospech

2006

Date	Opponent		Score	Scorers
18/2	FC Slovan Liberec	h	1-2	Lustrinelli
25/2	1.FC Brno	a	1-1	Zabavník
13/3	1.FC Slovácko U.H.	h	1-0	Matusovic (p)
20/3	FC Baník Ostrava	a	2-0	Pospech, Dosek
25/3	FK Teplice	h	0-0	
2/4	FK Chmel Blsany	a	0-0	
8/4	SK Slavia Praha	h	2-1	Pospech, Slepicka
15/4	SK Sigma Olomouc	a	2-1	Loucka, Lustrinelli
19/4	FC Vysocina Jihlava	a	1-0	Sivok
24/4	FK Jablonec 97	h	3-0	Lustrinelli, Pospech, Kisel
27/4	FK Mladá Boleslav	a	0-2	
1/5	FC Tescoma Zlín	h	1-0	Kisel
10/5	FK Marila Príbram	a	2-2	Dosek 2
13/5	FC Viktoria Plzen	h	1-3	Kolár

No	Name	Nat	Pos	Aps	(s)	Gls
29	Jaromír BLAZEK		G	29		
9	Libor DOSEK		A	20	(8)	7
22	Václav DROBNY		D	10		
31	Tomás GRIGAR		G	1	(1)	
13	Michal HANEK	SVK	D	2		
2	Martin HASEK		M	15	(3)	
12	Ondrej HERZÁN		A	2	(5)	1
17	Jirí JESLÍNEK		A	1	(2)	
5	Marek JUNGR		A		(1)	

Czech Republic

No	Name	Nat	Pos	Aps	(s)	Gls
23	Michal KADLEC		D	28	(1)	
18	Karol KISEL	SVK	M	24		3
11	Daniel KOLÁR		A		(7)	1
7	Tomás KÓNA	SVK	M	5	(5)	
14	Lubos LOUCKA		D	3	(2)	1
15	Petr LUKÁS		D	16	(2)	
30	Mauro LUSTRINELLI	SUI	A	10	(3)	3
28	Miroslav MATUSOVIC		A	20	(8)	5
4	Pavel PERGL		D	4	(5)	
19	Martin PETRÁS	SVK	D	12	(2)	2
11	Adam PETROUS		D	13		
8	Karel POBORSKY		M	5	(1)	1
21	Tomás POLÁCEK		M	12	(5)	4
20	Zdenek POSPECH		D	29		4
2	Tomás REPKA		D	13		
16	Jan SIMÁK		M	11	(7)	
6	Tomás SIVOK		M	13	(2)	3
10	Miroslav SLEPICKA		A	8	(8)	2
8	Radoslav ZABAVNÍK	SVK	D	13	(1)	1
7	Lukás ZELENKA		M	11	(3)	4

FK TEPLICE
Coach – Vlastislav Marecek

2005

Date	Opponent	h/a	Score	Scorers
7/8	FK SIAD Most	a	1-2	Verbír
14/8	SK Slavia Praha	h	1-0	Verbír (p)
21/8	FK Marila Príbram	a	1-1	Dolezal
28/8	FC Tescoma Zlín	h	2-1	Masek, Varadi
11/9	FK Mladá Boleslav	a	2-0	Verbír 2
19/9	FC Viktoria Plzen	h	2-1	Hunal, og (Knákal)
23/9	1.FC Brno	a	2-1	Dolezal, Varadi
2/10	AC Sparta Praha	h	2-1	Benát, Rilke
16/10	FC Vysocina Jihlava	a	4-0	og (Pernis), Masek 2, Dolezal
24/10	FC Slovan Liberec	h	0-0	
29/10	1.FC Slovácko U.H.	a	1-1	Masek
6/11	FC Baník Ostrava	h	0-2	
21/11	FK Chmel Blsany	a	0-0	
27/11	FK Jablonec 97	a	0-0	
5/12	SK Sigma Olomouc	h	1-0	Sabou
10/12	SK Slavia Praha	a	1-1	Jirsák

2006

Date	Opponent	h/a	Score	Scorers
20/2	FK Marila Príbram	h	2-1	Dolezal (p), og (Penner)
25/2	FC Tescoma Zlín	a	0-0	
5/3	FK Mladá Boleslav	h	1-1	Krmas
12/3	FC Viktoria Plzen	a	3-3	Fenin, Dzeko, Rada (p)
19/3	1.FC Brno	h	1-1	Dolezal (p)
25/3	AC Sparta Praha	a	0-0	
2/4	FC Vysocina Jihlava	h	3-1	Sabou, Jirsák, Dzeko
10/4	FC Slovan Liberec	a	1-1	Sabou
15/4	1.FC Slovácko U.H.	h	0-0	
22/4	FC Baník Ostrava	a	0-0	
26/4	FK Chmel Blsany	h	2-1	Dzeko, Krmas
30/4	FK Jablonec 97	h	1-0	Klein
10/5	SK Sigma Olomouc	a	0-0	
13/5	FK SIAD Most	h	4-3	Verbír 2, Krmas, Fenin

No	Name	Nat	Pos	Aps	(s)	Gls
19	Petr BENÁT		M	18	(5)	1
10	Ariel COLZERA	ARG	A		(2)	
12	Michal DOLEZAL		M	21	(5)	5
23	Edin DZEKO	BOS	A	9	(4)	3
16	Martin FENIN		A	3	(13)	2
18	Tomás HUNAL		D	27		1
6	Tomás JIRSÁK		M	21	(4)	2
2	Pavel KARLÍK		A		(1)	
3	Josef KAUFMAN		D	17	(4)	
4	Martin KLEIN		D	9	(10)	1
25	Zdenek KOUKAL		M		(5)	
10	Jirí KOWALÍK		A		(2)	
8	Pavel KRMAS		D	29		3
20	Karel KROUPA		A	5	(3)	
23	Jirí MASEK		A	15		4
1	Tomás POSTULKA		G	30		
5	Karel RADA		D	29		1
17	Emil RILKE		A	22	(6)	1
22	Antonín ROSA		D	1	(1)	
15	Vlastimil RYSKA		D	2	(1)	
11	Jirí SABOU		M	26		3
24	Jan STOHANZL		M	3	(2)	
14	Ondrej SZABÓ		M	5	(4)	
7	Dusan TESARÍK		M	6	(6)	
24	Adam VARADI		A	3	(8)	2
9	Pavel VERBÍR		M	29		6

FC TESCOMA ZLÍN
Coach – Lubomír Blaha

2005

Date	Opponent	h/a	Score	Scorers
6/8	FK Chmel Blsany	h	0-1	
13/8	FC Baník Ostrava	a	1-4	Cincala
22/8	1.FC Slovácko U.H.	h	3-1	Svach, Cincala, Lukastík
28/8	FK Teplice	a	1-2	Kraus
10/9	FK Jablonec 97	h	3-1	Kraus, Vrtelka, Zapletal
18/9	SK Slavia Praha	a	0-1	
24/9	FC Viktoria Plzen	h	0-0	
2/10	SK Sigma Olomouc	a	0-0	
16/10	FK Marila Príbram	a	0-3	
22/10	FK Mladá Boleslav	h	2-0	Baca, Lukastík
30/10	FK SIAD Most	a	0-0	
5/11	1.FC Brno	h	2-0	Kroca, Cincala
20/11	FC Vysocina Jihlava	a	0-0	
26/11	AC Sparta Praha	h	3-2	Kraus 2, Kroca
3/12	FC Slovan Liberec	a	0-1	
10/12	FC Baník Ostrava	h	1-0	Baca

2006

Date	Opponent	h/a	Score	Scorers
18/2	1.FC Slovácko U.H.	a	0-2	
25/2	FK Teplice	h	0-0	
5/3	FK Jablonec 97	a	0-2	
19/3	FC Viktoria Plzen	a	1-1	og (Rada)
2/4	FK Marila Príbram	h	1-0	Kraus
9/4	FK Mladá Boleslav	a	0-2	
12/4	SK Slavia Praha	h	2-2	Zemlík 2
15/4	FK SIAD Most	h	1-1	Zbozínek
19/4	SK Sigma Olomouc	h	1-0	Cincala
23/4	1.FC Brno	a	1-1	Svach
26/4	FC Vysocina Jihlava	h	1-1	Cincala
1/5	AC Sparta Praha	a	0-1	
10/5	FC Slovan Liberec	h	1-1	Zbozínek
13/5	FK Chmel Blsany	a	2-3	Zapletal, Kraus

No	Name	Nat	Pos	Aps	(s)	Gls
27	Martin BACA		A	14	(11)	2
1	Vít BARÁNEK		G	20		
8	Marek CELUSTKA		D		(1)	
13	Bronislav CERVENKA		M	24	(1)	
11	Václav CINCALA		A	22	(3)	5
21	Roman DOBES		M	7	(5)	
16	Tomás DUJKA		M	8	(5)	
18	Tomás JANÍCEK		D	18	(6)	
19	Jan JELÍNEK		M		(5)	

Czech Republic

No	Name	Nat	Pos	Aps	(s)	Gls
30	Ales KORÍNEK		G	2		
26	Jan KRAUS		A	24	(4)	6
5	Zdenek KROCA		D	28	(1)	2
8	Edvard LASOTA		M	1	(4)	
28	Josef LUKASTÍK		M	21	(4)	2
22	Otakar NOVÁK		G	8		
23	Lukás OPIELA	SVK	A	11	(9)	
14	Ales PIKL		M	9		
9	Juraj SKRIPEC	SVK	A	7	(11)	
25	Jaroslav SVACH		A	28		2
24	Vlastimil VIDLICKA		D	26		
12	Vít VRTELKA		M	26	(1)	1
2	Václav ZAPLETAL		M	13	(9)	2
15	Ivo ZBOZÍNEK		D	10		2
7	Jan ZEMLÍK		A	3	(7)	2

FC VIKTORIA PLZEN
Coach – Zdenek Michálek; (12/4/06) Frantisek Straka

2005
Date	Opponent	H/A	Score	Scorers
6/8	AC Sparta Praha	h	1-2	Smejkal
14/8	FK Chmel Blsany	a	3-0	Zakopal, Fillo, Kousal
21/8	SK Sigma Olomouc	h	1-0	Vágner
28/8	FK Jablonec 97	a	1-3	Smejkal
10/9	SK Slavia Praha	h	1-1	Vágner (p)
19/9	FK Teplice	a	1-2	Fillo
24/9	FC Tescoma Zlín	a	0-0	
2/10	FK SIAD Most	h	2-1	Vágner, Limbersky
16/10	FK Mladá Boleslav	a	2-2	Vágner, Limbersky
23/10	FK Marila Príbram	h	2-1	Zakopal, Vágner
29/10	FC Slovan Liberec	a	0-2	
6/11	FC Vysocina Jihlava	h	0-0	
20/11	1.FC Brno	a	1-3	Knákal M.
28/11	FK Baník Ostrava	h	0-0	
3/12	1.FC Slovácko U.H.	a	0-1	
11/12	FK Chmel Blsany	h	2-0	Fillo, Kousal

2006
Date	Opponent	H/A	Score	Scorers
25/2	FK Jablonec 97	h	1-2	Zakopal
4/3	SK Slavia Praha	a	1-1	Barteska (p)
12/3	FK Teplice	h	3-3	Fillo 2, Limbersky
19/3	FC Tescoma Zlín	h	1-1	Kousal
22/3	SK Sigma Olomouc	a	1-1	Procházka
26/3	FK SIAD Most	a	0-1	
2/4	FK Mladá Boleslav	h	0-1	
8/4	FK Marila Príbram	a	0-2	
16/4	FC Slovan Liberec	h	1-1	Rada
22/4	FC Vysocina Jihlava	a	0-2	
26/4	1.FC Brno	h	2-1	Barteska, Krbecek
30/4	FK Baník Ostrava	a	0-6	
10/5	1.FC Slovácko U.H.	h	0-2	
13/5	AC Sparta Praha	a	3-1	Kousal 2 (2p), Fillo

No	Name	Nat	Pos	Aps	(s)	Gls
10	Milan BARTESKA		M	25	(1)	2
14	Ales BEDNÁR		A	15	(9)	
31	David BICÍK		G	3		
23	Tomás BOREK		M	1		
11	Martin FILLO		A	27	(2)	6
16	Ondrej HONKA		A		(4)	
23	Marek JAROLÍM		M		(5)	
2	Martin KNAKAL		D	19	(8)	1
3	Petr KNAKAL		D	6	(1)	
7	Miloslav KOUSAL		A	13	(11)	5
9	Tomás KRBECEK		A	3	(1)	1
8	David LIMBERSKY		M	22	(1)	3
19	Ján MUCHA	SVK	G	9		
12	Radek PILAR		M	25		
6	Václav PROCHÁZKA		D	26	(2)	1
4	Tomás RADA		D	20	(3)	1
16	Jiri SÍMA		M	1	(7)	
15	Petr SÍMA		M	6	(7)	
13	Ondrej SIML		M		(1)	
21	Michal SMEJKAL		D	1	(8)	2
22	Marek SMOLA		D	29		
20	Jan SVÁTEK		A	5	(2)	
1	Martin TICHÁCEK		G	18		
24	Robert VÁGNER		A	18	(9)	5
20	Petr VLCEK		D	9	(1)	
18	Jan ZAKOPAL		D	29		3

FC VYSOCINA JIHLAVA
Coach – Karel Vecera

2005
Date	Opponent	H/A	Score	Scorers
5/8	SK Slavia Praha	a	1-1	Vladyka
14/8	FK Marila Príbram	h	2-3	Vladyka, Kaplan
21/8	1.FC Brno	a	2-1	Demeter, Vladyka
28/8	FC Slovan Liberec	h	0-2	
10/9	AC Sparta Praha	a	0-2	
18/9	FK SIAD Most	h	1-0	Pernis
25/9	1.FC Slovácko U.H.	h	1-0	Vojtísek
2/10	FK Chmel Blsany	a	2-2	Kaplan, Vladyka
16/10	FK Teplice	h	0-4	
22/10	FC Baník Ostrava	a	0-1	
30/10	FK Jablonec 97	h	1-1	Vladyka
6/11	FC Viktoria Plzen	a	0-0	
20/11	FC Tescoma Zlín	h	0-0	
27/11	SK Sigma Olomouc	a	2-1	Vesely, Demeter
11/12	FK Marila Príbram	a	0-2	

2006
Date	Opponent	H/A	Score	Scorers
18/2	1.FC Brno	h	0-0	
25/2	FC Slovan Liberec	a	0-0	
12/3	FK SIAD Most	a	1-2	Lovetínsky
18/3	1.FC Slovácko U.H.	a	0-1	
25/3	FK Chmel Blsany	h	0-0	
2/4	FK Teplice	a	1-3	Svoboda
8/4	FC Baník Ostrava	h	0-1	
12/4	FK Mladá Boleslav	h	0-0	
15/4	FK Jablonec 97	a	0-0	
19/4	AC Sparta Praha	a	0-1	
22/4	FC Viktoria Plzen	h	2-0	Lovetínsky, Pernis
26/4	FC Tescoma Zlín	a	1-1	Peska
29/4	SK Sigma Olomouc	h	3-0	Kopic, Peska, Pernis
10/5	FK Mladá Boleslav	a	0-3	
13/5	SK Slavia Praha	h	0-3	

No	Name	Nat	Pos	Aps	(s)	Gls
2	Pavel BARTOS		D	8	(5)	
25	Michal DEMETER	SVK	M	12	(1)	2
12	Petr HEIDE		D	5	(1)	
3	Michal KADLEC		D	29		
10	Tomás KAPLAN		A	19	(9)	2
15	Milan KOPIC		D	9		1
7	Jiri LISKA		M	22	(1)	
9	Michal LOVETÍNSKY		M	24	(3)	2
20	Libor MACHÁCEK		G		(1)	
21	Jiri MALÍNEK		M	21	(7)	
14	Michal PACHOLÍK		M	2	(12)	
8	Lubos PERNIS	SVK	A	13	(13)	3
19	Vladimír PESKA		A	5	(3)	2
20	Branislav RZESZOTO	SVK	G	20		
26	Ondrej SOUREK		D	19	(5)	

Czech Republic

6	Jan STOHANZL	M	5	(8)	
6	Ivo SVOBODA	A	11	(1)	1
13	Petr TULIS	G	1		
22	Vladimír VÁCHA	A	6	(11)	
18	Michal VESELY	M	19	(4)	1
11	Petr VLADYKA	M	28	(1)	5
5	Pavel VOJTÍŠEK	D	15	(1)	1
1	Michal VOREL	G	9	(1)	
4	Marek ZÚBEK	M	28		

DOMESTIC CUP 2005/06

SECOND ROUND
(31/8/05)
FC Zenit Cáslav 0, AC Sparta Praha 6
Trinec Fotbal 1, FC Baník Ostrava 1 *(4-5 on pens)*
Tatran Prachatice 2, FC Viktoria Plzen 1
1.HFK Olomouc 1, SK Sigma Olomouc 1 *(4-1 on pens)*
SK Kladno 2, FK SIAD Most 1
TJ Dvur Králové 0, SK Slavia Praha 3
FK Pencín-Turnov 0, FC Slovan Liberec 3
SK Spartak MAS Sezimovo Ústí 3, FK Marila Príbram 6
FK Baník Sokolov 0, FK Teplice 5
FC Velké Karlovice 2, FC Tescoma Zlín 2 *(4-5 on pens)*
SK DEKORA Zdírec nad Doubravou 0, FC Vysocina Jihlava 3
SK Buldoci Karlovy Vary-Dvory 0, FK Chmel Blsany 2
FK DOBET Ostrozská Nová Ves 0, 1.FC Brno 8
SK Slovan Varnsdorf 2, SC Xaverov Horní Pocernice 1
FC Tatran Kohoutovice Brno-Kohoutovice 0, FC DOSTA Bystrc-Knínicky 1
Mestsky FK Karviná 0, Jakubcovice Fotbal 1
FK OEZ Letohrad 1, FC Hradec Králové 1 *(5-6 on pens)*
1.SC Znojmo 0, FK Kunovice 2
SK SULKO Zábreh 0, SK Hanácká Slavia Kromeríz 0 *(7-8 on pens)*
FK Litvínov 2, FC Chomutov 0
FK Králuv Dvur 1, SK Dynamo Ceské Budejovice 4
FK Kolín 4, FC Dragoun Brevnov Praha-Brevnov 1
Bohemians Praha 1, FK AS Pardubice 2
FK STAFFIN Holysov 0, SK Strakonice 1908 3
FC Morkovice 1, FK Mutenice 1 *(5-6 on pens)*
FK AVÍZO Mesto Albrechtice 0, FC Hlucín 3
SK Horovice 2, SK Union Celákovice 2 *(2-3 on pens)*
(6/9/05)
FK Ústí nad Labem 2, FK Jablonec 97 1
FK Náchod-Destné 2, FK Mladá Boleslav 0
Mestsky SK Breclav 0, 1.FC Slovácko Uherské Hradiste 1
FK Novy Bydzov 0, FK Viktoria Zizkov 1
FC MSA Dolní Benesov 0, FC Vítkovice 2

THIRD ROUND
(21/9/05)
FK Litvínov 1, AC Sparta Praha 7
SK Slovan Varnsdorf 0, SK Kladno 1
FK Viktoria Zizkov 4, FC Slovan Liberec 3
SK Strakonice 1908 1, FK Chmel Blsany 3
FK Kunovice 2, FC Tescoma Zlín 1
Tatran Prachatice 1, SK Dynamo Ceské Budejovice 2
FK Mutenice 1, 1.FC Slovácko Uherské Hradiste 2
1.HFK Olomouc 0, SK Hanácká Slavia Kromeríz 0 *(5-4 on pens)*
FK Kolín 0, FK Marila Príbram 2
FK AS Pardubice 0, FK Ústí nad Labem 1
FC Vítkovice 2, FK Vysocina Jihlava 0
FC Hlucín 0, SK Slavia Praha 4
(4/10/05)
FK Náchod-Destné 2, FC Hradec Králové 3
(5/10/05)
FC DOSTA Bystrc-Knínicky 0, 1.FC Brno 1
(11/10/05)
Jakubcovice Fotbal 0, FC Baník Ostrava 1
SK Union Celákovice 0, FK Teplice 5

FOURTH ROUND
(26/10/05)
SK Kladno 0, AC Sparta Praha 2
FK Kunovice 1, SK Dynamo Ceské Budejovice 0
FK Ústí nad Labem 0, 1.FC Brno 1
FC Vítkovice 0, SK Slavia Praha 1
FC Hradec Králové 2, 1.HFK Olomouc 1
FC Marila Príbram 1, FC Baník Ostrava 2
FK Viktoria Zizkov 2, FK Chmel Blsany 2 *(6-5 on pens)*
(1/11/05)
1.FC Slovácko Uherské Hradiste 2, FK Teplice 0

QUARTER-FINALS
(12/4/06)
AC Sparta Praha 2 *(Lustrinelli 16, Kisel 21)*, FK Viktoria Zizkov 0
FK Kunovice 0, FC Baník Ostrava 2 *(Bystron 3, Varadi 41)*
(18/4/06)
1.FC Slovácko Uherské Hradiste 0, 1.FC Brno 0 *(4-1 on pens)*
(19/4/06)
FC Hradec Králové 1 *(Rolko 28)*, SK Slavia Praha 0

SEMI-FINALS
(16/5/06)
FC Baník Ostrava 2 *(Varadi 15, 90)*, FC Hradec Králové 0
AC Sparta Praha 2 *(Lustrinelli 38, Kóna 63)*, 1.FC Brno 0

FINAL
(19/5/06)
Stadion U Nisy, Liberec
AC SPARTA PRAHA 0
FC BANÍK OSTRAVA 0
(4-2 on pens)
Referee - Damková
AC SPARTA PRAHA – Blazek, Zabavník, Repka, Lukás, Kadlec, Kolár (Herzán 74), Sívok, Kóna, Pospech, Dosek, Lustrinelli (Matusovic 66).
FC BANÍK OSTRAVA – Raska, Hoffmann, Klimpl, Besta, Tomasák, Varadi, Lukes (Sloncík 77), Stanek, Bystron, Rajtoral (Zurek 90), Strihavka (Magera 85).

SECOND LEVEL FINAL TABLE 2005/06

		Pld	W	D	L	F	A	Pts
1	SK Kladno	30	17	6	7	45	21	57
2	SK Dynamo Ceské Budejovice	30	17	4	9	55	26	55
3	FK Ústí nad Labem	30	14	7	9	47	39	49
4	FC Hradec Králové	30	13	10	7	31	28	49
5	FK Viktoria Zizkov	30	12	10	8	42	33	46
6	1.HFK Olomouc	30	9	14	7	27	31	41
7	SC Xaverov Horní Poăernice	30	11	7	12	40	35	40
8	SK Hanácká Slavia Kromeríz	30	10	9	11	32	36	39
9	FC Vítkovice	30	9	9	12	26	33	36
10	FC Hlucín	30	10	6	14	31	47	36
11	FK Kunovice	30	9	8	13	35	43	35
12	FK AS Pardubice	30	9	7	14	35	38	34
13	SK Sigma Olomouc „B"	30	9	7	14	33	40	34
14	1.FK Drnovice	30	7	13	10	24	40	34
15	AC Sparta Praha „B"	30	8	10	12	32	37	34
16	1.FC Brno „B"	30	7	11	12	24	32	32

Denmark

FC København regain Superliga title

For the sixth year in a row the quest for the Danish Superliga title turned out to be a private power struggle between the country's two biggest and most popular clubs, FC København and Brøndby IF.

Both clubs began the season strongly. While Brøndby, the defending champions, kicked off with four straight victories to take an early lead, FC København overhauled them at the end of August with six wins and one draw in their first seven matches.

Once in front, FCK would stay put, but the challenge from Michael Laudrup's Brøndby would be ever present. By the winter shutdown in early December, 20 of the 33 matches had been played and FCK had won 15 of them, losing only one – a surprise 3-1 defeat at Esbjerg. Yet Brøndby were still only four points back, and given the recent tradition for the team in second place to launch a spring offensive, the title was anything but a foregone conclusion.

Besides which, FCK were on the point of losing their long-serving Swedish coach Hans Backe. Despite the club's lofty standing in the league, not to mention their continued participation in both the Danish Cup and the Scandinavian Royal League, he insisted that the time was right for him to leave.

The club found a popular successor for Backe in ex-player Ståle Solbakken, a Norwegian who had been working in his homeland with Ham-Kam, but there was trouble in store for the new coach at the start of the spring resumption when FCK were beaten on successive weekends by their great rivals, losing a Cup quarter-final 1-0 in extra-time and then the big league encounter (in front of 26,018 spectators) 3-0. Now there was just one point separating them.

Winter sale

While FCK had lost their coach during the winter, Brøndby had sold two of their best players to foreign clubs, centre-back Dan Agger to Liverpool and eight-goal striker Morten Skoubo to Real Sociedad. Although that proved to be no handicap whatsoever in those first two games against FCK, as time went by the club would feel the effects. A home win against Silkeborg while their rivals' game against Nordsjaelland was called off because of snow enabled Brøndby to take up interim residence at the top of the table but a week later, after defeat at Viborg, FCK were back in control. With their Swedish international duo of Marcus Allbäck and Tobias Linderoth striking a rich vein of form, FCK reeled off six successive victories, and by the time Brøndby came to visit Parken at the end of April, their advantage had grown to six points.

Michael Laudrup – the Superliga will miss him

Denmark

A season's record crowd of 41,201 came to see if FCK could obtain the win that would effectively clinch the championshup; or if Brøndby could get the victory that would re-open the title race with three games remaining. In the event neither side managed a goal, let alone a win. The 0-0 draw clearly favoured FC København, and seven days later, after both teams had won in midweek, the club from the capital's fourth title in six seasons was duly wrapped up – despite a 1-0 defeat in Odense against OB. With Brøndby also falling to defeat, 4-1 at newly promoted Horsens, FCK had an unbreachable six-point lead with one game remaining.

It was a double celebration for Solbakken and his players. A few weeks earlier the club had retained the Royal League trophy, with flamboyant Ghanaian international Razak Pimpong, a mid-season signing from FC Midtjylland, scoring a late winning goal in the final against Solbakken's former club, Lillestrøm. Pimpong's contributions in the Superliga were overshadowed by those of FCK's other two winter arrivals, Norwegian Brede Hangeland and Canadian Atiba Hutchison, who both strengthened the team's defence and midfield, respectively. The team's main men in attack were also foreigners – Allbäck, the Swede, and Brazilian striker Álvaro Santos, both of whom struck 15 goals, one fewer than the Superliga's top marksman for the third year running, Steffen Højer.

Transferred from OB to Viborg the previous summer, Højer's 16 goals helped his new club to an impressive fourth-place finish. But his old club, coached by ex-Arsenal manager Bruce Rioch, finished a place higher thanks to a powerful surge at the end that brought them six wins and two draws from their last nine games.

Laudrup bows out

While OB's reward was qualification for the InterToto Cup, runners-up Brøndby took their place in the UEFA Cup – a tournament in which they had competed in 2005/06 after a valiant defeat to Ajax in the third qualifying round of the Champions League. Eliminated from the UEFA Cup just before Christmas at the completion of the group phase, Brøndby's bid to retain the Danish Cup ended in late April when they lost their two-legged semi-final to Esbjerg. A disappointing campaign finished on an embarrassing low when the team surrendered their unbeaten home record to already relegated SønderjyskE in the final league game. The Brøndby fans jeered their team from the field, with some even calling for the head of coach Laudrup. Their wish was soon granted as the former Danish national team hero stood down, along with his assistant John "Faxe" Jensen, after failing to agree terms over a contract renewal.

Laudrup's absence from the Superliga scene will, one suspect, be sorely felt. Attendances in the Danish top flight were down by 7.4 per cent in 2005/06, with the average gate at 7,954. As usual, FC København had the best home crowds, with an average of 21,551 spectators turning up to watch at Parken. The loss of a popular figurehead like Laudrup could see the figures tumble still further in 2006/07.

On the other hand, interest would surely be reignited if a Danish club could finally make some headway in Europe. Recent performances from the Superliga clubs in UEFA competition have varied between disappointing and disastrous, with the result that, InterToto and Fair Play qualification notwithstanding, there are just three places open to Danish representatives. Brøndby won a few important coefficient points by playing in the UEFA Cup group phase in 2005/06, and there would have been a few more collected by FC København but for a highly contentious penalty decision awarded against them in their first-round tie against Hamburg. FCK were on the verge of claiming a memorable away-goals triumph against the high-flying Bundesliga side when Dutchman Rafael van der Vaart's last-ditch spot-kick in Copenhagen controversially knocked them out.

Denmark's 2006/07 European task force had an unfamiliar third member alongside FCK and

NATIONAL TEAM RESULTS 2005/06

17/8/05	England	H	Copenhagen	4-1	Rommedahl (60), Tomasson (63), Gravgaard (67), Larsen (90)
3/9/05	Turkey (WCQ)	A	Istanbul	2-2	Jensen C. (41), Larsen (90)
7/9/05	Georgia (WCQ)	H	Copenhagen	6-1	Jensen C. (9), Poulsen (30), Agger (42), Tomasson (54), Larsen (79, 83)
8/10/05	Greece (WCQ)	H	Copenhagen	1-0	Gravgaard (39)
12/10/05	Kazakhstan (WCQ)	A	Almaty	2-1	Gravgaard (46), Tomasson (49)
1/3/06	Israel	A	Tel Aviv	2-0	Perez (7), Skoubo (19)
27/5/06	Paraguay	H	Aarhus	1-1	Tomasson (51)
31/5/06	France	A	Lens	0-2	

Denmark

NATIONAL TEAM APPEARANCES 2005/06

Coach – Morten OLSEN

Name	DOB	Club	Eng	TUR	GEO	GRE	KAZ	Isr	Par	Fra	Caps	Goals
Thomas SØRENSEN	12/6/76	Aston Villa (ENG)	G	G	G	G	G46	G			54	-
Brian PRISKE	14/5/77	KRC Genk (BEL) /Portsmouth (ENG)	D		D46		D	D	s46	D	21	-
Daniel AGGER	12/12/84	Brøndby IF	D	D	D						4	1
Per NIELSEN	15/10/73	Brøndby IF	D46			D	D				9	-
Niclas JENSEN	17/8/74	Fulham (ENG)	D	D85	D	D	D89	D46			49	-
Thomas GRAVESEN	11/3/76	Real Madrid (ESP)	M	M	M	M		M69	M84		63	5
Christian Bager POULSEN	28/2/80	FC Schalke 04 (GER)	M86	M	M60	M	M	M90	M46	M	39	2
Claus JENSEN	29/4/77	Fulham (ENG)	M73	M	M63	M86					41	8
Jesper GRØNKJAER	12/8/77	VfB Stuttgart (GER)	M46	s79		s72		M78	M72		60	5
Martin JØRGENSEN	6/10/75	Fiorentina (ITA)	M46	M79	M	M	M	M	M	M	71	11
Jon Dahl TOMASSON	29/8/76	VfB Stuttgart (GER)	A64	A	A68	A	M		A84	A87	81	39
Michael GRAVGAARD	3/4/78	FC København	s46	s46	D	D	D	D			6	3
Thomas KAHLENBERG	20/3/83	AJ Auxerre (FRA)	s46		s60		s46				6	-
Dennis ROMMEDAHL	22/7/78	Charlton Athletic (ENG)	s46	M	M	M72	M46				58	11
Søren LARSEN	6/9/81	FC Schalke 04 (GER)	s64	s85	s63	s86	A		s84	s72	9	6
Kenneth PEREZ	29/8/74	AZ (HOL)	s73		s68			A78	s67	s87	19	2
Daniel JENSEN	25/6/79	SV Werder Bremen (GER)	s86				M	s69	s46	M72	20	-
Thomas HELVEG	24/6/71	Borussia Mönchengladbach (GER)		D	D		s89		D	D	100	2
Jesper CHRISTIANSEN	24/4/78	FC København					s46		G	G	4	-
Lars JACOBSEN	20/9/79	FC København						D	D	s64	3	-
Per KRØLDRUP	31/7/79	Fiorentina (ITA)						D		D64	15	-
Morten SKOUBO	30/6/80	Real Sociedad (ESP)							A87	A67	4	1
Michael SILBERBAUER	7/7/81	FC København						s78	s72	M	8	1
Peter LØVENKRANDS	29/1/80	Rangers (SCO)						s78			14	-
Søren BERG	15/5/76	OB						s87			2	-
Nicolai STOKHOLM	1/4/76	OB						s90	s84		2	-
Bo SVENSSON	4/8/79	Borussia Mönchengladbach (GER)							D		1	-
Jan KRISTIANSEN	4/8/81	1.FC Nürnberg (GER)							D	D77	5	-
Allan Kierstein JEPSEN	4/7/77	Vålerenga Fotball (NOR)								s77	2	-

Denmark

Brøndby as Jutland minnows Randers FC booked their UEFA Cup spot with an unlikely win in the Danish Cup. It was the club's fourth victory in as many finals, but as their most recent triumph had come 33 years earlier and they went into the final at Parken, against Esbjerg, as a First Division team, it was a considerable surprise to most of the 23,825 spectators in attendance that they came through to win.

Esbjerg became Randers' fourth Superliga scalp of the competition thanks to top scorer Karsten Johansen's low drive five minutes from the end of extra-time. Johansen was naturally overjoyed with his historic goal, but by removing his shirt in the post-goal celebrations he picked up his second yellow card of the game and was sent off. Fortunately, his team-mates, including charismatic veteran midfielder Stif Tøfting, survived the remaining five minutes without him, and Randers' remarkable exploit was complete.

Randers return

A few weeks later the team coached by ex-Danish international defender Lars Olsen were popping the champagne corks again as they celebrated promotion to the Superliga. Relegated the season before, Randers made an immediate return to the top flight as runners-up to Vejle BK, back among the big boys after a four-year absence. The big surprise of the season was the relegation of AGF, from Denmark's second city of Aarhus. They finished rock bottom of the Superliga, 15 points from safety, and thus ended a record 31-year stint in the country's top division.

Another run brought to an end was that of the Danish national team, whose failure to qualify for the 2006 World Cup interrupted a sequence of five successive major tournament qualifications. Although they finished the campaign strongly, winning their final three matches, the 2-2 draw in Turkey that preceded those victories over Georgia, Greece and Kazakhstan was not enough to carry them into the play-offs. Initially there was some doubt as to whether Morten Olsen would stay on as coach, but eventually he was persuaded to put pen to paper on a new deal that will see him carry on until the next World Cup in 2010. His first objective, though, is to ensure that Denmark make it seven European Championship appearances out of seven by qualifying for a place at the 2008 finals in Austria and Switzerland. To do so, they will probably have to eliminate arch-rivals Sweden.

EUROPEAN CUPS 2005/06

UEFA CHAMPIONS LEAGUE

BRØNDBY IF

2nd qualifying round DINAMO TBILISI (GEO)
A 2-0 Skoubo (59), Elmander (83)
Ankergren, Johansen, Nielsen, Agger, Sennels, Retov, Daugaard, Jørgensen (Lorentzen 78), Lantz (Absalonsen 55), Elmander, Skoubo (Kamper 70).
H 3-1 Lorentzen (9, 42), Kamper (86)
Ankergren, Johansen (Schmidt 74), Nielsen, Agger, Sennels, Lorentzen, Daugaard, Lantz, Jørgensen (Absalonsen 65), Elmander (Kamper 56), Skoubo.

3rd qualifying round AJAX (HOL)
H 2-2 Skoubo (33), Escudé (90og)
Ankergren, Rytter, Nielsen, Agger, Sennels, Jørgensen (Kamper 39), Lantz (Absalonsen 80), Retov, Lorentzen (Daugaard 67), Elmander, Skoubo.
A 1-3 Elmander (44)
Ankergren, Rytter, Nielsen, Agger, Sennels, Jørgensen (Absalonsen 74), Lantz (Daugaard 81), Retov, Lorentzen (Kamper 57), Elmander, Skoubo.

UEFA CUP

FC MIDTJYLLAND

2nd qualifying round B36 (FAR)
H 2-1 Kristensen (39, 71)
Tidman, Daugaard, Nielsen K-B., Traoré, Jørgensen, Sørensen (Kaergaard 76), Thygesen (Oluwafemi 76), Hansen M., Poulsen Sv. (Jessen 64), Nielsen D., Kristensen.
A 2-2 Pimpong (17), Sørensen (33)
Tidman, Daugaard, Nielsen K-B., Mikkelsen, Jessen (Poulsen Sv. 87), Sørensen, Thygesen, Hansen, Pimpong (Lindkvist 57), Nielsen D. (Kaergaard 46), Kristensen.

1st round CSKA MOSKVA (RUS)
A 1-3 Pimpong (23)
Tidman, Daugaard, Nielsen K-B., Mikkelsen, Lindkvist, Sørensen, Hansen, Traoré (Thygesen 62), Pimpong (Poulsen Si. 74), Nielsen D. (Madsen 83), Kristensen.
H 1-3 Nielsen D. (14)
Tidman, Daugaard, Nielsen K-B., Mikkelsen, Lindkvist, Sørensen, Thygesen (Madsen 82), Hansen (Traoré 42), Pimpong (Poulsen Si. 54), Kristensen, Nielsen D.

FC KØBENHAVN

2nd qualifying round CARMARTHEN TOWN (WAL)
H 2-0 Álvaro Santos (48), Gravgaard (55)
Christiansen, Jacobsen, Svensson, Gravgaard, Bergdølmo, Silberbauer, Linderoth, Allbäck, Van Heerden, Ijeh (Saarinen 89), Álvaro Santos (Møller 80).
A 2-0 Møller (38, 40)
Christiansen, Jacobsen, Svensson, Gravgaard, Bergdølmo, Silberbauer, Linderoth (Saarinen 64), Larsen, Van Heerden, Allbäck (Ijeh 64), Møller (Álvaro Santos 75).

1st round HAMBURGER SV (GER)
A 1-1 Van Heerden (40)
Christiansen, Jacobsen, Svensson, Gravgaard, Bergdølmo, Van Heerden (Thomassen 89), Silberbauer, Linderoth, Fredgaard (Saarinen 78), Allbäck (Larsen 56), Álvaro Santos.
H 0-1
Christiansen, Jacobsen, Svensson (Thomassen 83), Gravgaard, Bergdølmo, Van Heerden (Larsen 87), Silberbauer, Linderoth, Fredgaard, Álvaro Santos, Møller.

Denmark

ESBJERG FB

1st qualifying round FC FLORA TALLINN (EST)
H 1-2 *Berglund (90)*
Winde, Afriyie, Christensen, Høgh, Jensen M. (Kryger 65), Poulsen, Lucena, Jørgensen J. (Andreasen 65), Kristiansen (Jensen M-F. 74), Berglund, Murcy.
A 6-0 *Poulsen (15), Kristiansen (16), Berglund (23), Andreasen (41), Murcy (56, 86)*
Winde, Afriyie, Nielsen, Høgh, Poulsen, Andreasen (Jørgensen J. 46), Lucena (Nøhr 60), Kristiansen, Berglund (Jensen M. 46), Pedersen, Murcy.

2nd qualifying round TROMSØ IL (NOR)
H 0-1
Winde, Afriyie, Christensen, Høgh, Jensen (Pedersen 56), Poulsen, Andreasen (Hansen 46), Lucena, Kristiansen, Berglund, Murcy (Nøhr 81).
A 1-0 *Lucena (17)*
(aet; 2-3 on pens)
Winde, Afriyie (Hansen 119), Christensen, Høgh, Poulsen, Andreasen, Lucena, Kristiansen, Pedersen (Jensen 91), Berglund, Murcy (Jørgensen L. 103).

BRØNDBY IF

1st round FC ZÜRICH (SUI)
H 2-0 *Skoubo (45), Johansen (74)*
Ankergren, Skarbalius, Johansen, Hansen, Sennels, Jørgensen (Daugaard 76), Lantz, Retov, Rasmussen T., Elmander (Christensen 65), Skoubo (Lorentzen 79).
A 1-2 *Elmander (47)*
Ankergren, Johansen, Andersen, Nielsen, Sennels, Jørgensen (Daugaard 34), Retov (Lorentzen 72), Lantz, Rasmussen T., Elmander, Skoubo (Kamper 62).

2nd round Group B
Match 1 MACCABI PETACH TIKVA (ISR)
H 2-0 *Lantz (67), Absalonsen (83)*
Ankergren, Johansen, Andersen, Nielsen, Sennels, Jørgensen (Kamper 46), Daugaard, Lantz, Rasmussen T. (Absalonsen 81), Lorentzen, Elmander (Bagger 86).

Match 2 LOKOMOTIV MOSKVA (RUS)
A 2-4 *Retov (12), Skoubo (28)*
Ankergren, Rytter, Johansen, Nielsen, Sennels, Lorentzen (Christensen 74), Lantz, Retov (Kamper 46), Daugaard, Rasmussen T. (Absalonsen 80), Skoubo.

Match 3 RCD ESPANYOL (ESP)
H 1-1 *Skoubo (66)*
Ankergren, Rytter (Daugaard 71), Johansen, Nielsen, Sennels, Lorentzen, Retov (Jørgensen 78), Elmander, Lantz, Rasmussen T., Skoubo (Christensen 75).

Match 4 PALERMO (ITA)
A 0-3
Ankergren, Rytter, Nielsen (Agger 55), Andersen, Sennels (Jørgensen 60), Lorentzen (Christensen 72), Lantz, Retov, Daugaard, Rasmussen T., Skoubo.

TOP GOALSCORERS 2005/06

16	Steffen HØJER (Viborg FF)
15	Marcus ALLBÄCK (FC København)
	Mads JUNKER (FC Nordsjaelland)
	ÁLVARO SANTOS (FC København)
14	Fredrik BERGLUND (Esbjerg FB)
13	Johan ELMANDER (Brøndby IF)
	José Roberto Rodrigues MOTA Júnior (Viborg FF)
11	Besart BERISHA (AC Horsens)
	Morten "Duncan" RASMUSSEN (AGF/Brøndby IF)
	Peter SAND (SønderjyskE)
10	Jacob OLESEN (SønderjyskE/Viborg FF)

LEAGUE RESULTS/ SCORERS/APPEARANCES/ GOALS 2005/06

AAB
Coach – Erik Hamrén (SWE)

2005				
20/7	FC København	h	0-1	
24/7	OB	a	1-2	Augustinussen
30/7	FC Midtjylland	h	1-1	Braemer
6/8	Brøndby IF	a	1-3	Hübertz
14/8	Esbjerg FB	h	2-0	Risgård, Enevoldsen
21/8	Silkeborg IF	h	1-1	Braemer
28/8	AC Horsens	a	0-0	
11/9	FC Nordsjaelland	h	1-1	Augustinussen
17/9	AGF	a	4-2	Ericsson, Tobiasen, Braemer, Augustinussen
21/9	SønderjyskE	h	3-2	Ericsson, Lindström, Braemer
25/9	Viborg FF	a	0-2	
2/10	FC Midtjylland	h	2-2	Braemer, Curth
16/10	Esbjerg FB	a	1-2	Curth
23/10	AGF	h	1-1	Ericsson
26/10	OB	a	2-0	Kristensen, Braemer
29/10	Viborg FF	a	0-2	
6/11	Brøndby IF	h	3-0	Sakiri 2, Ericsson
20/11	FC Nordsjaelland	a	1-0	Curth
27/11	FC København	h	0-2	
4/12	Silkeborg IF	a	4-1	Würtz, Braemer, Curth 2
2006				
12/3	AC Horsens	h	2-2	Winsnes, Würtz (p)
19/3	SønderjyskE	a	2-2	Caca, og (From)
26/3	SønderjyskE	h	2-2	Caca 2
29/3	FC København	a	0-1	
2/4	FC Nordsjaelland	a	2-4	Würtz 2 (2p)
8/4	Brøndby IF	a	3-4	Sakiri, Jacobsen, Caca
13/4	Viborg FF	h	1-1	Augustinussen
17/4	OB	h	0-0	
23/4	AGF	a	1-1	Kortegaard
30/4	AC Horsens	a	1-0	Hübertz
4/5	Silkeborg IF	h	1-0	Hübertz
7/5	FC Midtjylland	a	4-2	Jakobsen, Risgård, Braemer, Hoch
14/5	Esbjerg FB	h	1-0	Curth

No	Name	Nat	Pos	Aps	(s)	Gls
8	Trond ANDERSEN	NOR	D	7		
9	Thomas AUGUSTINUSSEN		M	27		4
20	Simon BRAEMER		A	19	(10)	8
18	Lucas CACA de Deus Santos	BRA	M	11	(1)	4
4	Danny CALIFF	USA	D	8	(1)	
14	Jeppe CURTH		A	16	(7)	6
23	Thomas ENEVOLDSEN		M		(5)	1
18	Martin ERICSSON	SWE	A	20		4
25	Daniel HOCH	SWE	A	1	(3)	1
11	Poul HÜBERTZ		A	13	(13)	3
5	Jón Rói JACOBSEN	FAR	D	5		1
2	Michael JAKOBSEN		D	27		1
15	Allan Kierstein JEPSEN		D	20		
36	Thomas KORTEGAARD		D	17	(11)	1
27	Patrick KRISTENSEN		A	2		1
7	Mattias LINDSTRÖM	SWE	M	23	(1)	1
1	Jimmy NIELSEN		G	33		
16	Allan OLESEN		D	29		
19	Suni OLSEN	FAR	M	7	(10)	

Denmark

FINAL LEAGUE TABLE 2005/06

		Pld	Home W	D	L	F	A	Away W	D	L	F	A	Total W	D	L	F	A	Pts
1	FC København	33	11	5	1	35	15	11	2	3	27	12	22	7	4	62	27	73
2	Brøndby IF	33	15	1	1	46	11	6	3	7	14	23	21	4	8	60	34	67
3	OB	33	10	1	6	26	16	7	6	3	23	12	17	7	9	49	28	58
4	Viborg FF	33	8	5	3	30	17	7	4	6	32	26	15	9	9	62	43	54
5	AaB	33	5	9	3	23	20	6	3	7	25	24	11	12	10	48	44	45
6	Esbjerg FB	33	9	4	4	31	20	3	2	11	12	25	12	6	15	43	45	42
7	FC Midtjylland	33	5	6	6	20	22	5	5	6	22	30	10	11	12	42	52	41
8	Silkeborg IF	33	8	3	5	19	19	3	3	11	14	31	11	6	16	33	50	39
9	FC Nordsjaelland	33	6	4	6	28	24	3	7	7	21	31	9	11	13	49	55	38
10	AC Horsens	33	5	7	4	16	13	3	6	8	13	28	8	13	12	29	41	37
11	SønderjyskE	33	3	3	10	18	34	3	5	9	23	38	6	8	19	41	72	26
12	AGF	33	2	4	10	18	33	2	6	9	18	30	4	10	19	36	63	22

4	Marco REDA	CAN	D	5	(5)	
21	Kasper RISGÅRD		M	5	(9)	2
17	Artim SAKIRI	MAC	M	9	(3)	3
26	Jacob SØRENSEN		M	5	(7)	
24	Jens-Kristian SØRENSEN		M		(1)	
5	Ole TOBIASEN		D	12	(1)	1
8	Fredrik WINSNES	NOR	M	13		1
22	Rasmus WÜRTZ		M	29	(1)	4

AGF
Coach – Sören Åkeby (SWE); (5/10/05) (Brian Steen Nielsen); (1/1/06) Ove Pedersen

2005
20/7	Silkeborg IF	a	1-2	Lindrup
24/7	SønderjyskE	a	1-2	Rasmussen M.
31/7	Viborg FF	h	2-3	Rasmussen M. 2
7/8	FC København	a	1-1	Kure K.
13/8	OB	h	0-4	
21/8	FC Midtjylland	a	3-3	Cansdell-Sherriff, Rasmussen M., George (p)
28/8	Brøndby IF	h	3-0	Hanssen (p), Rasmussen M. 2
11/9	Esbjerg FB	a	1-0	Rasmussen M.
17/9	AaB	h	2-4	George, Rasmussen M.
21/9	AC Horsens	a	1-1	Rasmussen M.
25/9	FC Nordsjaelland	h	0-2	
2/10	Esbjerg FB	h	2-2	Kaagh 2
16/10	OB	a	1-3	Rasmussen M.
23/10	AaB	a	1-1	og (Reda)
26/10	Viborg FF	h	3-3	George, og (Alvbåge), Grahn
30/10	Brøndby IF	a	0-4	
6/11	FC Nordsjaelland	h	1-3	George
20/11	FC København	a	1-1	Hanssen
27/11	Silkeborg IF	h	2-0	George, Hanssen (p)
4/12	AC Horsens	a	1-2	George (p)

2006
11/3	SønderjyskE	h	1-1	Graulund
19/3	FC Midtjylland	a	0-2	
26/3	FC Midtjylland	h	1-2	George
29/3	Silkeborg IF	a	0-1	
1/4	FC København	h	0-4	
9/4	FC Nordsjaelland	a	1-3	og (Olsen D.)
13/4	Brøndby IF	h	0-1	

17/4	Viborg FF	a	2-2	Pleidrup, Krabbe
23/4	AaB	h	1-1	Risholt
29/4	SønderjyskE	a	0-1	
4/5	AC Horsens	h	0-1	
7/5	Esbjerg FB	a	3-1	Tullberg, Grahn, Kure A.
14/5	OB	h	0-2	

No	Name	Nat	Pos	Aps	(s)	Gls
25	Tuomas AHO	FIN	D	6		
20	Danilo ARRIETA		M	6	(9)	
6	Shane CANSDELL-SHERIFF	AUS	D	24	(3)	1
30	Navid DAYYANI		D	13	(1)	
10	Peter FOLDGAST		A	5	(1)	
16	Mads FROST		M	4	(2)	
11	Christer GEORGE	NOR	A	25		7
19	Jens GJESING		D	13	(8)	
17	Tobias GRAHN	SWE	M	22	(3)	2
23	Peter GRAULUND		A	9		1
4	Thomas HANSEN		D	12		
24	Jonny HANSSEN	NOR	M	20		3
5	Carsten HEMMINGSEN		M		(5)	
31	Richard HENDRIKSSON	SWE	D	3		
33	Morten HYLDGAARD		G	4		
14	Jimmi HØYER		M	8	(1)	
15	Jesper JØRGENSEN		A		(2)	
34	Anders KAAGH		A	5	(5)	2
36	Frederik KRABBE		D	6	(4)	1
27	Anders KURE		D	15	(5)	1
21	Kasper KURE		D	11	(4)	1
9	Thomas LINDRUP		M	12	(1)	1
28	Michael LUMB		A	2	(9)	
15	Jamie McMASTER	ALS	M	3	(3)	
7	Lars PLEIDRUP		M	11	(1)	1
5	Jacob RASMUSSEN		D	15		
18	Morten „Duncan" RASMUSSEN		A	19		10
1	Steffen RASMUSSEN		G	29		
3	Roger RISHOLT	NCR	M	18	(2)	1
22	Cheikh SARR		D	8		
7	Helgi SIGURDSSON	ISL	A	4	(11)	
8	Jesper SØRENSEN		D	29	(1)	
18	Mike TULLBERG		A	2	(4)	1
35	Michael VESTER		M		(1)	

Denmark

BRØNDBY IF
Coach – Michael Laudrup

2005				
20/7	FC Midtjylland	h	3-0	Skoubo 2, Nielsen
23/7	Silkeborg IF	h	2-0	Lorentzen, Skoubo
31/7	Esbjerg FB	a	3-2	Jørgensen, Christensen 2
6/8	AaB	h	3-1	Retov, Jørgensen, Kamper
14/8	AC Horsens	a	0-0	
20/8	FC Nordsjaelland	h	2-1	Elmander, Lorentzen
28/8	AGF	a	0-3	
10/9	SønderjyskE	h	3-0	Skoubo 2, Johansen (p)
18/9	Viborg FF	a	1-3	Retov
21/9	FC København	h	1-1	Elmander
24/9	OB	a	3-1	Skoubo 2, Elmander
2/10	AC Horsens	h	4-1	Elmander 2, Daugaard, Hansen
16/10	SønderjyskE	a	2-1	Andersen, Rasmussen T.
23/10	FC Midtjylland	h	5-0	Elmander 3 (1p), Lorentzen 2
26/10	Esbjerg FB	a	0-0	
30/10	AGF	h	4-0	Jørgensen, Lorentzen, Daugaard, Johansen (p)
6/11	AaB	a	0-3	
19/11	Viborg FF	h	1-0	Skoubo
26/11	OB	a	1-0	Rasmussen T.
4/12	FC Nordsjaelland	a	2-0	Lorentzen, Nielsen
2006				
12/3	FC København	h	3-0	Rasmussen T., Ericsson, Retov
18/3	Silkeborg IF	a	0-2	
26/3	Silkeborg IF	h	3-1	Elmander, Rasmussen T. 2
29/3	OB	h	1-0	Lantz
2/4	Viborg FF	a	0-2	
8/4	AaB	h	4-3	og (Olesen), Elanga, Ericsson, Elmander
13/4	AGF	a	1-0	Ericsson
17/4	Esbjerg FB	h	3-0	Rasmussen T., Elmander, Absalonsen
23/4	FC Midtjylland	a	0-2	
30/4	FC København	a	0-0	
4/5	FC Nordsjaelland	h	3-1	Nielsen, Rasmussen M., Elmander
7/5	AC Horsens	a	1-4	Elmander
14/5	SønderjyskE	h	1-2	Rasmussen M. "Duncan"

No	Name	Nat	Pos	Aps	(s)	Gls
24	Johan ABSALONSEN		A	2	(16)	1
22	Daniel AGGER		D	8		
23	Trond ANDERSEN	NOR	D	18		1
16	Casper ANKERGREN		G	18		
25	Kim CHRISTENSEN		A	8	(8)	2
8	Kim DAUGAARD		M	14	(11)	2
14	Joseph ELANGA	CMR	D	12		1
19	Johan ELMANDER	SWE	A	31		13
10	Martin ERICSSON	SWE	M	13		3
14	Thomas HANSEN		D	3	(1)	1
32	Mike JENSEN		M		(2)	
5	Dan Anton JOHANSEN		D	13	(5)	2
26	Mads JØRGENSEN		M	10	(3)	3
12	Jonas KAMPER		M	10	(9)	1
18	Henrik KILDENTOFT		D	6	(7)	
6	Marcus LANTZ	SWE	M	28	(1)	1
7	Kasper LORENTZEN		A	15	(4)	6
4	Per NIELSEN		D	25		3
29	Morten RASMUSSEN		D	7	(1)	1
17	Morten "Duncan" RASMUSSEN		A	4	(2)	1
21	Thomas RASMUSSEN		M	27		6
9	Martin RETOV		M	28	(3)	3
3	Thomas RYTTER		D	16	(2)	
13	Stefan SCHMIDT		M	2	(11)	
20	Asbjørn SENNELS		D	19		
2	Aurelijus SKARBALIUS	LIT	D	1	(2)	
17	Morten SKOUBO		A	10	(2)	8
34	Martin SPELMANN		D		(1)	
1	Karim ZAZA	MAR	G	15		

ESBJERG FB
Coach – Ove Pedersen; (1/1/06) Troels Bech

2005				
20/7	OB	h	2-2	Kristiansen, Berglund
24/7	FC Midtjylland	a	1-2	Poulsen
31/7	Brøndby IF	h	2-3	Berglund 2
7/8	Silkeborg IF	h	4-0	Murcy 2, Kristiansen, Berglund
14/8	AaB	a	0-2	
21/8	AC Horsens	h	0-0	
28/8	FC Nordsjaelland	a	0-2	
11/9	AGF	h	0-1	
18/9	SønderjyskE	a	1-0	Lucena
21/9	Viborg FF	h	1-4	Kristiansen
25/9	FC København	a	1-5	Kryger
2/10	AGF	a	2-2	Kryger, Poulsen
16/10	AaB	h	2-1	Kryger, Demba-Nyrén
23/10	Viborg FF	a	0-1	
26/10	Brøndby IF	h	0-0	
30/10	FC Nordsjaelland	a	2-0	Berglund 2
5/11	FC København	h	3-1	Poulsen, Kristiansen, Berglund
20/11	Silkeborg IF	a	1-2	Berglund
27/11	AC Horsens	h	1-1	Zimling
4/12	SønderjyskE	a	3-1	Kryger, Berglund, Poulsen
2006				
12/3	FC Midtjylland	a	2-0	Berglund 2
19/3	OB	a	0-1	
25/3	OB	h	1-0	Murcy
29/3	AC Horsens	a	0-1	
2/4	Silkeborg IF	a	2-0	Berglund 2
9/4	FC København	h	1-2	Zimling
13/4	FC Nordsjaelland	a	4-0	Zimling, Klarström, Demba-Nyrén 2
17/4	Brøndby IF	a	0-3	
23/4	Viborg FF	h	3-2	Nøhr, Demba-Nyrén, Afriyie
30/4	FC Midtjylland	a	0-0	
4/5	SønderjyskE	h	3-2	Demba-Nyrén 2, Berglund
7/5	AGF	h	1-3	Nøhr
14/5	AaB	a	0-1	

No	Name	Nat	Pos	Aps	(s)	Gls
4	Kolja AFRIYIE	GER	D	15	(5)	1
20	Hans Henrik ANDREASEN		M	5	(1)	
11	Fredrik BERGLUND	SWE	A	29	(1)	14
3	Anders Møller CHRISTENSEN		D	26		
9	Njogu DEMBA-NYRÉN	SWE	A	13	(6)	6
26	Anders EGHOLM		D		(1)	
2	Frank HANSEN		D	20	(5)	
1	Jan HOFFMANN		G	19	(2)	
24	Nicolai HØGH		D	8		
13	Martin JENSEN		D	32		
18	Morten Friis JENSEN		A		(5)	
19	Jesper JØRGENSEN		M	7	(14)	
15	Andreas KLARSTRÖM	SWE	M	11	(2)	1

Denmark

15	Jan KRISTIANSEN		M	20		4
8	Lasse KRYGER		A	19	(5)	4
21	Jerry LUCENA		M	31	(2)	1
7	Tommy LØVENKRANDS		M	1	(11)	
25	Michaël MURCY	FRA	A	16	(10)	3
17	Lars Christian NIELSEN		D	26		
5	Anders NØHR		M	5	(14)	2
12	Simon Azoulay PEDERSEN		A	2	(3)	
22	Jakob POULSEN		M	20		4
31	Søren RIEKS		M		(1)	
26	Mikkel VENDELBO		M		(2)	
14	Martin VINGAARD		M		(2)	
16	Lars WINDE		G	14		
6	Niki ZIMLING		M	24	(2)	3

AC HORSENS
Coach – Kent Nielsen

2005
20/7	Viborg FF	h	0-3	
24/7	FC København	a	0-2	
31/7	OB	h	0-0	
7/8	FC Midtjylland	a	1-2	Søgaard
14/8	Brøndby IF	h	0-0	
21/8	Esbjerg FB	a	0-0	
28/8	AaB	h	0-0	
11/9	Silkeborg IF	a	1-0	Berisha
18/9	FC Nordsjaelland	a	0-5	
21/9	AGF	h	1-1	Berisha
25/9	SønderjyskE	a	3-1	Berisha 2, Klausen
2/10	Brøndby IF	a	1-4	og (Nielsen)
16/10	FC Nordsjaelland	h	0-0	
22/10	FC København	a	0-1	
26/10	Silkeborg IF	h	0-0	
30/10	OB	h	0-0	
6/11	SønderjyskE	a	1-1	Gade
20/11	FC Midtjylland	h	3-4	Klausen, Akonnor, og (Sørensen)
27/11	Esbjerg FB	a	1-1	Lodberg
4/12	AGF	h	2-1	Berisha, Lodberg

2006
12/3	AaB	a	2-2	Berisha 2
19/3	Viborg FF	h	3-1	Berisha, Akonnor, Lodberg
26/3	Viborg FF	a	1-1	Friis
29/3	Esbjerg FB	h	1-0	Lodberg
2/4	FC Midtjylland	a	0-0	
9/4	SønderjyskE	h	2-0	Tchami, Berisha
13/4	OB	a	0-3	
16/4	Silkeborg IF	a	1-2	Rasmussen
22/4	FC København	h	0-1	
30/4	AaB	h	0-1	
4/5	AGF	a	1-0	Berisha
7/5	Brøndby IF	h	4-1	Akonnor 2, Ernemann, Berisha
14/5	FC Nordsjaelland	a	0-3	

No	Name	Nat	Pos	Aps	(s)	Gls
26	Charles AKONNOR	GHA	M	20	(4)	4
5	Steffen ALGREEN		D	9	(1)	
16	Besart BERISHA	ALB	A	25	(7)	11
19	Steffen ERNEMANN		M	18	(14)	1
14	Søren FRIIS		M	24	(4)	1
2	Per GADE		D	31		1
3	Martin HALLE		D	20		
6	Johan Byrial HANSEN	FAR	D	14	(3)	
12	Martin HEINZE		M	9	(11)	
7	Lasse HOLMGAARD		M	9	(10)	
9	Simon Elbaek JENSEN		A	1	(9)	
1	Søren JOCHUMSEN		G	33		
15	Kasper KLAUSEN		M	24	(6)	2
11	Niels LODBERG		A	25	(4)	4
20	Rasmus MARVITS		D	31		
18	Miki RASMUSSEN		A		(3)	1
4	Mads RIEPER		D	27		
8	Abdul SULE	NGA	A	11	(12)	
10	Allan SØGAARD		M	29		1
23	Joël TCHAMI	CMF	A	3	(3)	1

FC KØBENHAVN
Coach – Hans Backe (SWE); (1/1/06) Ståle Solbakken (NOR)

2005
20/7	AaB	a	1-0	Álvaro Santos
24/7	AC Horsens	h	2-0	Jacobsen (p), Álvaro Santos
31/7	FC Nordsjaelland	a	2-1	Álvaro Santos, Allbäck
7/8	AGF	h	1-1	Ijeh
14/8	SønderjyskE	a	1-0	Bergdølmo
21/8	Viborg FF	h	2-1	Jacobsen (p), Ijeh
28/8	Silkeborg IF	h	2-0	Jacobsen (p), Gravgaard
11/9	OB	a	2-0	Allbäck 2
18/9	FC Midtjylland	h	3-1	Álvaro Santos 2, Møller
21/9	Brøndby IF	a	1-1	Van Heerden
25/9	Esbjerg FB	h	5-1	og (Hoffmann), Van Heerden, Møller, Allbäck 2
2/10	OB	h	1-1	Álvaro Santos
16/10	Silkeborg IF	a	3-0	Allbäck, Álvaro Santos, Møller
22/10	AC Horsens	h	1-0	Møller
26/10	SønderjyskE	a	4-1	Álvaro Santos 2, Van Heerden, Møller
30/10	FC Midtjylland	h	2-0	Møller 2
5/11	Esbjerg FB	a	1-3	Gravgaard
20/11	AGF	h	1-1	Álvaro Santos
27/11	AaB	a	2-0	Bergdølmo (p), Allbäck
4/12	Viborg FF	h	3-1	Álvaro Santos 2, Allbäck

2006
12/3	Brøndby IF	a	0-3	
19/3	FC Nordsjaelland	h	3-3	Ijeh, Bergvold, Allbäck
29/3	AaB	h	1-0	Linderoth
1/4	AGF	a	4-0	Allbäck 2, og (Hansen), Hutchinson
9/4	Esbjerg FB	h	2-1	Allbäck, Bergvold
13/4	FC Midtjylland	a	3-1	Allbäck, Álvaro Santos 2 (1p)
17/4	SønderjyskE	h	4-1	Allbäck, Silberbauer, og (Stolberg), Álvaro Santos
22/4	AC Horsens	a	1-0	Ijeh
26/4	FC Nordsjaelland	a	1-1	Silberbauer
30/4	Brøndby IF	h	0-0	
4/5	Viborg FF	a	1-0	Allbäck
7/5	OB	a	0-1	
14/5	Silkeborg IF	h	2-3	Silberbauer, Hangeland

No	Name	Nat	Pos	Aps	(s)	Gls
11	Marcus ALLBÄCK	SWE	A	27	(3)	15
7	ÁLVARO SANTOS	BRA	A	28	(2)	15
15	André BERGDØLMO	NOR	D	27		2
28	Martin BERGVOLD		M	19	(3)	2
22	Morten BERTOLT		M		(8)	
26	Jeppe BRANDRUP		M		(1)	
1	Jesper CHRISTIANSEN		G	33		
18	Carsten FREDGAARD		M	5	(2)	
14	Michael GRAVGAARD		D	26		2

Denmark

No	Name	Nat	Pos	Aps	(s)	Gls
5	Brede HANGELAND	NOR	D	13		1
13	Atiba HUTCHISON	CAN	M	13		1
9	Peter IJEH	NGA	A	4	(12)	4
2	Lars JACOBSEN		D	33		3
23	William Kvist JØRGENSEN		M	5	(16)	
12	Thomas Røll LARSEN		M	5	(4)	
6	Tobias LINDEROTH	SWE	M	29		1
32	Peter MØLLER		A	7	(8)	7
20	Razak PIMPONG	GHA	M	2	(6)	
3	Urmas ROOBA	EST	D	2		
5	Janne SAARINEN	FIN	D	4	(3)	
8	Michael SILBERBAUER		M	32		3
4	Bo SVENSSON		D	18		
16	Dan THOMASSEN		D	10	(8)	
17	Ole TOBIASEN		D	2		
26	Elrio VAN HEERDEN	RSA	M	19		3
18	Klaus KAERGAARD		A	6	(1)	
23	Frank KRISTENSEN		A	20	(6)	7
31	Ulrik LINDKVIST		D	6	(4)	
7	Claus MADSEN		M	8	(5)	1
12	Jesper MIKKELSEN		D	27	(2)	5
28	Marc Søgaard MØLLER		D	3	(4)	
8	David NIELSEN		A	15	(5)	6
32	Kristian Bak NIELSEN		D	27		4
26	Ajilore OLUWAFEMI	NGA	M	19	(3)	2
11	Razak PIMPONG	GHA	M	8	(3)	1
17	Kwadko POKU	GHA	A	3	(1)	
11	Simon POULSEN		M	15	(2)	1
20	Svenne POULSEN		M	1	(13)	1
1	Anders RASMUSSEN		G	16		
29	Winston REID	NZL	D	4	(5)	
24	Dennis SØRENSEN		M	31	(1)	6
21	Mikkel THYGESEN		M	29	(1)	2
16	Ola TIDMAN	SWE	G	17		
5	Christian TRAORE		M	25	(6)	
2	Magnus TROEST		D	15	(1)	2

FC MIDTJYLLAND
Coach – Erik Rasmussen

2005

Date	Opponent	H/A	Score	Scorers
20/7	Brøndby IF	a	0-3	
24/7	Esbjerg FB	h	2-1	Kristensen 2
30/7	AaB	a	1-1	Pimpong
7/8	AC Horsens	a	2-1	Poulsen Sv., Nielsen D.
14/8	FC Nordsjaelland	a	2-3	Daugaard, Sørensen
21/8	AGF	h	3-3	Nielsen D., Poulsen Si., Kristensen
28/8	SønderjyskE	a	4-2	Mikkelsen 3 (2p), Nielsen D.
11/9	Viborg FF	h	1-1	Nielsen K-B.
18/9	FC København	a	1-3	Nielsen D.
21/9	OB	h	0-1	
25/9	Silkeborg IF	h	1-0	Mikkelsen
2/10	AaB	a	2-2	Kristensen, Nielsen D.
15/10	Viborg FF	h	0-1	
23/10	Brøndby IF	a	0-5	
26/10	FC Nordsjaelland	h	1-1	Nielsen K-B.
30/10	FC København	h	0-2	
6/11	Silkeborg IF	h	0-2	
20/11	AC Horsens	a	4-3	Thygesen 2, Madsen, Sørensen
27/11	SønderjyskE	h	2-2	Nielsen K-B. (p), Sørensen
3/12	OB	h	1-2	Sørensen

2006

Date	Opponent	H/A	Score	Scorers
12/3	Esbjerg FB	a	0-2	
19/3	AGF	h	2-0	Nielsen K-B., Daugaard
26/3	AGF	a	2-1	Troest 2
29/3	SønderjyskE	a	2-0	Oluwafemi, Mikkelsen
2/4	AC Horsens	h	0-0	
9/4	Silkeborg IF	a	0-0	
13/4	FC København	h	1-3	Nielsen D.
17/4	FC Nordsjaelland	a	2-2	Sørensen, Agbetu
23/4	Brøndby IF	h	2-0	Agbetu, Oluwafemi
30/4	Esbjerg FB	h	0-0	
4/5	OB	a	1-0	Kristensen
7/5	AaB	h	2-4	Kristensen 2
14/5	Viborg FF	a	1-1	Sørensen

No	Name	Nat	Pos	Aps	(s)	Gls
35	Akeem AGBETU	NGA	A	4	(1)	2
9	Rasmus DAUGAARD		D	33		2
3	Nikola GJOSEVSKI	MAC	D	1		
10	Michael HANSEN		M	15	(3)	
22	Rasmus HANSEN		M		(3)	
19	Leon JESSEN		M	9	(5)	
33	Martin JUNGBLOOT		A		(2)	
15	Nicolai JØRGENSEN		D	6	(2)	

FC NORDSJAELLAND
Coach – Johnny Petersen

2005

Date	Opponent	H/A	Score	Scorers
20/7	SønderjyskE	h	1-1	Olsen T.
24/7	Viborg FF	a	1-3	Hansen
31/7	FC København	h	1-2	Junker
7/8	OB	a	0-0	
14/8	FC Midtjylland	h	3-2	Junker, Kristensen, Dickoh og (Agger)
20/8	Brøndby IF	a	1-2	
28/8	Esbjerg FB	h	2-0	Junker, Olsen T.
11/9	AaB	a	1-1	Junker
18/9	AC Horsens	h	5-0	Kristensen, Junker 3 (1p), Olsen T.
21/9	Silkeborg IF	a	1-1	Olsen T.
25/9	AGF	a	2-0	Junker, Dickoh
1/10	Silkeborg IF	h	2-2	Olsen T., Junker
16/10	AC Horsens	a	0-0	
23/10	SønderjyskE	a	4-2	Andreasen, Junker 2 (1p), Hansen
26/10	FC Midtjylland	a	1-1	Petersen
30/10	Esbjerg FB	h	0-2	
6/11	AGF	a	3-1	Junker 3
20/11	AaB	h	0-1	
27/11	Viborg FF	a	1-4	Junker
4/12	Brøndby IF	h	0-2	

2006

Date	Opponent	H/A	Score	Scorers
12/3	OB	a	0-2	
19/3	FC København	a	3-3	Hansen, Kamwendo, Olsen T.
29/3	Viborg FF	h	1-3	Olsen D.
2/4	AaB	a	4-2	Santala, og (Jacobsen J-R.), Ribers, Pearce
9/4	AGF	h	3-1	Santala 2, Olsen D.
13/4	Esbjerg FB	a	0-4	
17/4	FC Midtjylland	h	2-2	Kamwendo, Olsen D.
23/4	SønderjyskE	a	2-2	Olsen D., Santala
26/4	FC København	h	1-1	Kamwendo
30/4	OB	h	0-3	
4/5	Brøndby IF	a	1-3	Ribers
7/5	Silkeborg IF	a	0-2	
14/5	AC Horsens	h	3-0	Olsen D., Hansen, Richter J.

No	Name	Nat	Pos	Aps	(s)	Gls
28	Emmanuel AKE	KEN	A		(6)	
14	Thomas ANDREASEN		M	14	(4)	1

Denmark

No	Name	Nat	Pos	Aps	(s)	Gls
3	Bosun AYENI	NGA	M	17	(5)	
1	Kim CHRISTENSEN		G	33		
5	Francis DICKOH	GHA	D	30		2
18	Henrik EGGERTS		M	7	(4)	
17	Anders Due HANSEN		M	31		4
23	Daniel JENSEN		D		(7)	
10	Mads JUNKER		A	20		15
9	Joseph KAMWENDO	MWI	A	8		3
6	Morten KARLSEN		M	19	(9)	
16	Thomas KRISTENSEN		M	22	(4)	2
7	Søren KROGH		M		(5)	
27	Dennis Bo MORTENSEN		A		(4)	
8	Allan OLESEN		D	23		
29	Danny OLSEN		M	10	(1)	5
15	Tommy OLSEN		A	21	(8)	6
12	Heath PEARCE	USA	D	31		1
20	Stephan PETERSEN		M	13	(6)	1
8	Jacob RASMUSSEN		D		(1)	
2	Michael RIBERS		D	33		2
26	Jonathan RICHTER		M	8	(6)	1
21	Simon RICHTER		D	14	(7)	
32	Jukka SANTALA	FIN	A	9	(3)	4
13	Kris STADSGAARD		D		(7)	

OB
Coach – Bruce Rioch (SCO)

2005

20/7	Esbjerg FB	a	2-2	Berg, og (Løvenkrands)
24/7	AaB	h	2-1	Miti, Berg
31/7	AC Horsens	a	0-0	
7/8	FC Nordsjaelland	h	0-0	
13/8	AGF	a	4-0	Miti 2, Borre, Berg
21/8	SønderjyskE	h	2-3	Laursen, Miti
27/8	Viborg FF	a	2-1	og (Andersen), Vinzents
11/9	FC København	h	0-2	
18/9	Silkeborg IF	h	3-1	Miti 2, Ophaug
21/9	FC Midtjylland	a	1-0	Miti
24/9	Brøndby IF	h	1-3	Hansen
2/10	FC København	a	1-1	Sørensen (p)
16/10	AGF	h	3-1	Stokholm (p), Miti, og (Kure A.)
23/10	Silkeborg IF	a	0-1	
26/10	AaB	h	0-2	
30/10	AC Horsens	a	0-0	
6/11	Viborg FF	h	3-0	Aas, Júnior, Berg
20/11	SønderjyskE	a	4-2	Hansen, Laursen, Berg, Bouden
26/11	Brøndby IF	h	0-1	
3/12	FC Midtjylland	a	2-1	Berg, Júnior

2006

12/3	FC Nordsjaelland	h	2-0	Fevang, Júnior
19/3	Esbjerg FB	h	1-0	Berg
25/3	Esbjerg FB	a	0-1	
29/3	Brøndby IF	a	0-1	
2/4	SønderjyskE	h	3-0	Júnior 3
9/4	Viborg FF	a	2-2	Berg, Stokholm
13/4	AC Horsens	h	3-0	Hansen, Júnior, Sørensen
17/4	AaB	a	0-0	
23/4	Silkeborg IF	h	2-1	Bouden, Fevang
30/4	FC Nordsjaelland	a	3-0	Sørensen 2, Júnior
4/5	FC Midtjylland	h	0-1	
7/5	FC København	h	1-0	Júnior
14/5	AGF	a	2-0	Fevang, Stokholm

No	Name	Nat	Pos	Aps	(s)	Gls
6	Alexander AAS	NOR	D	31	(1)	1
10	Søren BERG		A	33		8
17	Martin BORRE		M	26	(3)	1
29	Jonas BORRING		M	14	(5)	
24	Bouabid BOUDEN	MAR	A	4	(11)	2
9	Denni CONTEH		A	1	(3)	
4	Morten FEVANG	NOR	M	6	(1)	3
14	Esben HANSEN		M	30		3
16	Søren JENSEN		D	4		
20	Anders JOCHUMSEN		A	1	(1)	
11	José Luiz Guimarães Sanábio JÚNIOR	BRA	A	15	(1)	9
26	Jesper LANGE		A		(1)	
19	Michael LARSEN		D	9	(5)	
3	Ulrik LAURSEN		D	27	(1)	2
7	Mwape MITI	ZAM	A	15		8
1	Arkadiusz ONYSZKO	POL	G	33		
2	Jan Tore OPHAUG	NOR	D	22	(7)	1
28	Lasse ROSTHOLM		A		(2)	
25	Nicolai STOKHOLM		M	29		3
18	Magne STURØD	NOR	M	4	(5)	
15	Chris SØRENSEN		D	33		4
12	Andrew TEMPO	ZAM	M	6	(7)	
8	Ulrich VINZENTS		D	20		1

SILKEBORG IF
Coach – Viggo Jensen

2005

20/7	AGF	h	2-1	Degn, Akinci
23/7	Brøndby IF	a	0-2	
31/7	SønderjyskE	h	3-2	Nagel, Raun, Askou
7/8	Esbjerg FB	a	0-4	
14/8	Viborg FF	h	1-1	Schnedler (p)
21/8	AaB	a	1-1	Vestergaard
28/8	FC København	a	0-2	
11/9	AC Horsens	h	0-1	
18/9	OB	a	1-3	Akinci
21/9	FC Nordsjaelland	h	1-1	Olsen T.
25/9	FC Midtjylland	a	0-1	
1/10	FC Nordsjaelland	a	2-2	Degn (p), Fetai
16/10	FC København	h	0-3	
23/10	OB	h	1-0	Alkhag
26/10	AC Horsens	a	0-0	
30/10	SønderjyskE	h	0-1	
6/11	FC Midtjylland	a	2-0	Flinta, Raun
20/11	Esbjerg FB	h	2-1	Alkhag 2
27/11	AGF	a	0-2	
4/12	AaB	h	1-4	Nagel

2006

12/3	Viborg FF	a	3-2	Sveinsson 2, Flinta
18/3	Brøndby IF	h	2-0	Sveinsson 2
26/3	Brøndby IF	a	1-3	Alkhag
29/3	AGF	h	1-0	Askou
2/4	Esbjerg FB	a	0-2	
9/4	FC Midtjylland	a	0-0	
13/4	SønderjyskE	a	0-2	
16/4	AC Horsens	h	2-1	og (Marvits), Flinta
23/4	OB	a	1-2	Hansen (p)
30/4	Viborg FF	h	1-3	Sveinsson
4/5	AaB	a	0-1	
7/5	FC Nordsjaelland	h	2-0	Olsen K., Hansen
14/5	FC København	a	3-2	Sveinsson, Olsen K. 2

No	Name	Nat	Pos	Aps	(s)	Gls
10	Muhammed AKINCI		M	21	(4)	2
9	Iddi ALKHAG		A	12	(8)	4
15	Lasse ANKJAER		M		(1)	
3	Jens Berthel ASKOU		D	32	(1)	2

Denmark

No	Name	Nat	Pos	Aps	(s)	Gls
8	Anders CLAUSEN		A		(2)	
7	Peter DEGN		M	20	(1)	2
6	Bjarni Olafur EIRIKSSON	ISL	D	13		
14	Bajram FETAI		A	8	(4)	1
18	Dennis FLINTA		A	17	(9)	3
8	Michael HANSEN		M	13		2
1	Henrik IPSEN		G	2		
24	Simon NAGEL		M	22	(10)	2
25	Jesper NIELSEN		D	3	(2)	
22	Martin Ørnskov NIELSEN		M	17	(3)	
19	Kim OLSEN		A		(5)	3
20	Thomas OLSEN		M	26	(3)	1
11	Ulrik Baerholm PEDERSEN		D	16	(1)	
12	Thomas POULSEN		M	20	(3)	
1	David PREECE	ENG	G	31		
5	Kasper Vandborg RASMUSSEN		D	8	(4)	
23	Thomas RAUN		M	16	(14)	2
21	Henrik SCHNEDLER		D	21	(3)	1
27	Hördur SVEINSSON	ISL	A	13		6
17	Morten SØNDERGAARD		A	5		
2	Jonas TROEST		D	18		
4	Anders VELLER		D	9	(1)	
29	Søren Ulrik VESTERGAARD		A		(9)	1

SØNDERJYSKE
Coach – Søren Kusk; (26/8/05) (Peter Sand); (14/9/05) Morten Bruun; (1/5/06) Ole Schwennesen

2005
Date	Opponent	h/a	Result	Scorers
20/7	FC Nordsjaelland	a	1-1	Mazurkiewicz
24/7	AGF	h	2-1	Hansen, Johansen
31/7	Silkeborg IF	a	2-3	Sand, Jørgensen
7/8	Viborg FF	a	1-3	Poulsen
14/8	FC København	h	0-1	
21/8	OB	a	3-2	Sand 2, Johansen
28/8	FC Midtjylland	h	2-4	Sand, og (Mikkelsen)
10/9	Brøndby IF	a	0-3	
18/9	Esbjerg FB	h	0-1	
21/9	AaB	a	2-3	Olesen 2
25/9	AC Horsens	h	1-3	Nonbo
2/10	Viborg FF	a	1-1	Olesen
16/10	Brøndby IF	h	1-2	Stolberg
23/10	FC Nordsjaelland	a	2-4	Olesen 2
26/10	FC København	h	1-4	Hansen
30/10	Silkeborg IF	a	1-0	Álvaro Santos
6/11	AC Horsens	h	1-1	Olesen
20/11	OB	h	2-4	Olesen, Johansen
27/11	FC Midtjylland	a	2-2	Mikkelsen, Olesen
4/12	Esbjerg FB	h	1-3	Sand

2006
Date	Opponent	h/a	Result	Scorers
11/3	AGF	a	1-1	Danry
19/3	AaB	h	2-2	Sand, Pedersen
26/3	AaB	a	2-2	Sand, Mikkelsen
29/3	FC Midtjylland	h	0-2	
2/4	OB	a	0-3	
9/4	AC Horsens	a	0-2	
13/4	Silkeborg IF	h	2-0	Sand, Pedersen
17/4	FC København	a	1-4	Gregersen
23/4	FC Nordsjaelland	h	2-2	Sand 2
29/4	AGF	h	1-0	Pedersen
4/5	Esbjerg FB	a	2-3	Mosquera, Nonbo
7/5	Viborg FF	h	0-4	
14/5	Brøndby IF	a	2-1	Sand, Pedersen

No	Name	Nat	Pos	Aps	(s)	Gls
14	Mads BEIERHOLM		M	3	(6)	
19	Michael CHRISTENSEN		D	9		
21	Dennis DANRY		D	10	(6)	1
1	Kim DREJS		G	14		
18	Kenneth FROM		D	30	(1)	
4	Thomas GORMSEN		A		(1)	
13	Jacob GREGERSEN		D	30		1
8	Henrik HANSEN		M	32		2
25	Henrik IPSEN		G	8		
6	Rógvi JACOBSEN	FAR	A		(5)	
12	Rasmus JOHANSEN		A	7	(5)	3
3	Henrik JØRGENSEN		D	28	(3)	1
11	Tomasz MAZURKIEWICZ	POL	M	2	(2)	1
20	Peter Nymann MIKKELSEN		M	25	(4)	2
16	Jesper MORTENSEN		G	11		
27	John Jairo MOSQUERA	COL	A	1	(6)	1
23	Michael NONBO		M	17	(7)	2
9	Jacob OLESEN		A	13	(6)	8
2	Martin PEDERSEN		D	18	(7)	
9	Simon Azoulay PEDERSEN		A	13		4
6	Simon POULSEN		M	5		1
7	Thomas RATHE		M	10	(10)	
17	Peter SAND		M	30	(1)	11
22	Leandro de Deus SANTOS	BRA	A		(4)	1
15	Jacob STOLBERG		D	12	(4)	1
10	Jacob SØRENSEN		M	11	(2)	
6	Johnny THOMSEN		M	2	(3)	
5	Martin THOMSEN		D	22	(1)	
10	Nicolai WAEL		A		(1)	

VIBORG FF
Coach – Ove Christensen

2005
Date	Opponent	h/a	Result	Scorers
20/7	AC Horsens	a	3-0	Mota 2, Højer
24/7	FC Nordsjaelland	h	3-1	Andie, Frandsen, Fabricius
31/7	AGF	a	3-2	Mota (p), Andersen, Højer
7/8	SønderjyskE	h	3-1	Højer, Mota, Fabricius
14/8	Silkeborg IF	a	1-1	Mota
21/8	FC København	a	1-2	Frandsen (p)
27/8	OB	h	1-2	Åslund
11/9	FC Midtjylland	a	1-1	Åslund
18/9	Brøndby IF	h	3-1	Frandsen 2, Højer
21/9	Esbjerg FB	a	4-1	Åslund, Højer, Frandsen, Fabricius
25/9	AaB	h	2-0	Højer 2 (1p)
2/10	SønerjyskE	h	1-1	Mota
15/10	FC Midtjylland	a	1-0	Mota
23/10	Esbjerg FB	h	1-0	Frandsen
26/10	AGF	a	3-3	Nørlund, Højer, Jensen
29/10	AaB	h	2-0	Poulsen, Mota
6/11	OB	a	0-3	
19/11	Brøndby IF	a	0-1	
27/11	FC Nordsjaelland	h	4-1	Højer, og (Dickoh), Rosén, Fabricius
4/12	FC København	a	1-3	Højer

2006
Date	Opponent	h/a	Result	Scorers
12/3	Silkeborg IF	h	2-3	Rasmussen, Olesen
19/3	AC Horsens	a	1-3	Mota
26/3	AC Horsens	h	1-1	Højer (p)
29/3	FC Nordsjaelland	a	3-1	Mota 2, Rask
2/4	Brøndby IF	h	2-0	Mota, Frandsen
9/4	OB	h	2-2	Nørlund, Højer
13/4	AaB	a	1-1	Højer
17/4	AGF	h	2-2	Nørlund 2

Denmark

Date	Opponent		Score	Scorers
23/4	Esbjerg FB	a	2-3	Højer, Andie
30/4	Silkeborg IF	a	3-1	Poulsen, Olesen, Rask
4/5	FC København	h	0-1	
7/5	SønderjyskE	a	4-0	Frandsen, Mota, Højer, Fabricius
14/5	FC Midtjylland	h	1-1	Højer

No	Name	Nat	Pos	Aps	(s)	Gls
1	John ALVBÅGE	SWE	G	33		
2	Jesper ANDERSEN		D	30		1
3	Thomas ANDIE		D	25	(3)	2
20	Stefan BIDSTRUP		M		(3)	
17	Christian Flindt BJERG		M	2	(5)	
8	Thomas G. CHRISTENSEN		D	2	(4)	
28	John DYRING		M		(1)	
21	Kenneth FABRICIUS		A	1	(15)	5
15	Thomas FRANDSEN		M	31		8
22	Søren FREDERIKSEN		A		(3)	
24	Steffen HØJER		A	31		16
26	Søren JENSEN		D	11	(4)	1
9	José Roberto Rodrigues MOTA Júnior	BRA	A	19	(9)	13
14	Jakob Glerup NIELSEN		M	32		
7	Alex NØRLUND		M	25	(3)	4
11,26	Paul OBIEFULE	NGA	M	5	(13)	
19	Jacob OLESEN		A	2	(6)	2
6	Christopher POULSEN		M	28		2
4	Mikkel RASK		M	7	(9)	2
18	David RASMUSSEN		M	4	(4)	1
25	Mikael ROSÉN	SWE	D	32		1
5	Thomas TENGSTEDT		D	23	(1)	
16,11	Martin ÅSLUND	SWE	M	20	(3)	3

DOMESTIC CUP 2005/06

FOURTH ROUND
(14/9/05)
B1909 1, HIK 1 *(aet; 3-0 on pens)*
Dalum IF 0, Silkeborg IF 1 *(aet)*
Døllefjelde Musse IF 2, Lyngby BK 5
BK Frem 2, AB 1 *(aet)*
FC Nordsjaelland 0, Viborg FF 3
Naestved BK 1, Herfølge BK 3
Randers FC 2, AGF 0
Slagelse B & I 2, Hjørring IF 1
SønderjyskE 1, AC Horsens 2
(21/9/05)
B93 3, Kolding FC 5
Byes – Brøndby IF, Esbjerg FB, FC København, FC Midtjylland, OB, AaB

FIFTH ROUND
(13/10/05)
Randers FC 2, AC Horsens 0
(19/10/05)
AaB 2, FC Midtjylland 1 *(aet)*
B1909 5, Herfølge BK 2
Brøndby IF 2, Silkeborg IF 1
BK Frem 2, Viborg FF 2 *(aet; 6-5 on pens)*
Kolding FC 1, OB 1 *(aet; 5-6 on pens)*
Lyngby BK 0, Esbjerg FB 0 *(aet; 4-5 on pens)*
Slagelse B & I 2, FC København 2 *(aet; 4-5 on pens)*

QUARTER-FINALS
(5/3/06)
AaB 2 *(Jakobsen 43, Curth 87)*, OB 2 *(Berg 74, Jonior 90)* *(aet; 7-6 on pens)*
Brøndby IF 1 *(Elmander 103)*, FC København 0 *(aet)*
(12/3/06)
Randers FC 3 *(Fabinho 50, Da Silva 80, Johansen 85)*, BK Frem 0
(15/3/06)
B1909 1 *(Zewe 12)*, Esbjerg FB 3 *(Berglund 1, 73, Klarström 54)*

SEMI-FINALS
(20/4/06 & 27/4/06)
Esbjerg FB 5 *(Zimling 11, Lucena 31, Hansen 33), Berglund 80, 90)*, Brøndby IF 2 *(Rasmussen T. 35, Absalonsen 86)*
Brøndby IF 1 *(Ericsson 76)*, Esbjerg FB 0
(Esbjerg FB 5-3)

Randers FC 0, AaB 0
AaB 1 *(Curth 13)*, Randers FC 1 *(Jakobsen 73og)*
(1-1; Randers FC on away goal)

FINAL
(11/5/06)
Parken, Copenhagen
RANDERS FC 1 *(Johansen 115)*
ESBJERG FB 0
(aet)
Referee – Milton Nielsen
RANDERS FC – Jensen, Pedersen S., Pedersen R., Sandberg, Damborg, Da Silva *(Hansen 71)*, Tøfting, Pedersen K-M., Fredgaard *(Holdgaard 110)*, Johansen, Larsen *(Christiansen 77)*.
Sent off: Johansen *(115)*
ESBJERG FB – Winde, Hansen, Christensen *(Afriyie 86)*, Nielsen, Jensen M., Murcy *(Kryger 67)*, Zimling, Lucena, Nøhr *(Klarström 80)*, Demba-Nyrén, Berglund.

SECOND LEVEL FINAL TABLE 2005/06

		Pld	W	D	L	F	A	Pts
1	Vejle BK	30	19	6	5	62	32	63
2	Randers FC	30	19	4	7	64	30	61
3	Lyngby BK	30	18	5	7	68	44	59
4	Køge BK	30	17	8	5	59	35	59
5	BK Fremad Amager	30	15	4	11	54	55	49
6	Kolding FC	30	14	4	12	50	50	46
7	FC Fredericia	30	12	5	13	48	40	41
8	Ølstykke FC	30	12	5	13	41	40	41
9	Herfølge BK	30	11	7	12	51	41	40
10	BK Frem	30	11	7	12	47	42	40
11	HIK	30	9	11	10	44	44	38
12	AB	30	11	4	15	43	54	37
13	Brabrand IF	30	10	5	15	32	54	35
14	Lolland Falster Alliancen	30	9	7	14	51	53	34
15	BK Skjold	30	4	6	20	27	75	18
16	Brønshøj BK	30	1	8	21	28	80	11

England

The same old story

Another major tournament. Another quarter-final exit. Another defeat on penalties.

England's performance at the 2006 World Cup was entirely predictable. Yet the level of expectation placed upon Sven Göran Eriksson and his team both before and during the tournament demanded that they do far more than just conform to stereotype. This, we were told, would be England's year: the perfect opportunity for the 'golden generation' – the country's best collection of footballers since 1966 - to end 40 years of agony and frustration and regain the game's biggest prize.

Those who believed, or simply wanted to believe, the hype were to suffer a let-down of monstrous proportions. England did not just fail to win the World Cup. They never came remotely close. They blundered and burgled their way to the last eight of the competition, and when they finally came face to face with half-decent opposition (although that might be a slightly flattering description of Portugal), they were unable to raise their game.

Was it all down to unfulfilled potential and an uninspirational, uninventive manager, or were England never really that good in the first place? Certainly, they are no good at taking penalties. To lose one shoot-out is excusable, to lose two is careless, to lose five out of six at major tournaments (including all three at the World Cup) is pathetic.

There were some who felt England were 'unlucky' to lose to Portugal after having Wayne Rooney controversially sent off and valiantly keeping their goal intact for the best part of an hour with reduced numbers. But by allowing the Portuguese goalkeeper to save three of their four spot-kicks, they undid all of their previous good work at a stroke.

Magnificent fans

While England's magnificent fans certainly deserved better from their team, it is fair to say that few neutrals mourned the team's passing. England were supposed to be one of the teams to watch in Germany, yet the moments of genuine quality they provided were few and far between. That isn't to say the football played by any of the other teams was especially spellbinding, but England played five

The best thing about England in Germany was the support

England

matches and did not deliver one good performance. Their best half was the first 45 minutes against Sweden, but that was immediately followed by their worst, in which they conceded two goals – albeit their only ones of the tournament – to two set-pieces. Against Paraguay, Trinidad & Tobago and Ecuador – three low-grade opponents that were there for the taking – England won the Eriksson way, by tediously doing just enough and no more.

The Swede had fuelled the pre-tournament expectation by announcing that England were World Cup winners-in-waiting, yet in no match did his team look like world-beaters. There were, of course, mitigating factors. Wonderboy Rooney had succumbed to the 'curse of the metatarsal', breaking his foot six weeks before the tournament, and although he made a miraculous recovery, he was certainly not at his sharpest. Michael Owen tore knee ligaments early in the game against Sweden, ruling him out of action for months. And then there was the freak heatwave that descended over Germany for the duration of England's stay, slowing down their traditional tempo.

But if he had problems, then Eriksson compounded them with some daft decisions. To select only four strikers, two of whom (Rooney and Owen) were recovering from injury and another (17-year-old Theo Walcott) nobody, not even apparently Eriksson himself, had ever seen play a 90-minute match, was a frivolous temptation of fate. Then, having waited so patiently for Rooney, Eriksson put him up front on his own – a role that was not just unfamiliar to the youngster but which criminally wasted his talents. That his frustration got the better of him against Portugal was not entirely a surprise (although those who rushed to blame and condemn him for stamping on Ricardo Carvalho should have given credence to the player's insistence that he did not so deliberately).

The game against Portugal was Eriksson's last in charge. His post-World Cup departure had been rubber-stamped a few months earlier after an elaborate 'sting' by the unscrupulous English tabloid press that not only exposed his greed and disloyalty but also compromised the spirit within the squad as a result of the indiscreet comments he made about some of his key players.

Expensive failure

Most England fans were happy for Eriksson to be given one last chance, but after Germany the near-unanimous verdict on his five-and-a-half-year reign is that he was an expensive failure. His tactics were inherently negative and cautious, anti-English almost, and when required to take a risk, he would generally do it with reluctance; sometimes, as in the Walcott case, with downright recklessness. Given the quality of personnel at his disposal, three quarter-finals do not constitute a success, although, in fairness, unlike previous incumbents, he always ensured that the team qualified for the major tournaments – even if, as on the road to Germany 2006, they invariably did so without flair or panache.

Before England had even flown home from Germany, David Beckham called a press conference to announce that he was standing down from the captaincy. It was not unusual for Beckham to have the last word – media manipulation is as much his stock in trade as those inswinging free-kicks – but the reality is that he would have been forced to relinquish the armband in any case by Eriksson's successor, and erstwhile assistant, Steve McClaren.

Beckham enjoyed special treatment from Eriksson for far too long. He captained England at each of the three tournaments for which the Swede was in charge yet never imposed himself, never lived up to the billing. He scored one goal and made two others in Germany but in open play he was a passenger, a

NATIONAL TEAM RESULTS 2005/06

Date	Opponent	H/A/N	Venue	Score	Scorers
17/8/05	Denmark	A	Copenhagen	1-4	Rooney (87)
3/9/05	Wales (WCQ)	A	Cardiff	1-0	Cole J. (54)
7/9/05	Northern Ireland (WCQ)	A	Belfast	0-1	
8/10/05	Austria (WCQ)	H	Manchester	1-0	Lampard (25p)
12/10/05	Poland (WCQ)	H	Manchester	2-1	Owen (44), Lampard (80)
12/11/05	Argentina	N	Geneva	3-2	Rooney (39), Owen (86,90)
1/3/06	Uruguay	H	Liverpool	2-1	Crouch (75), Cole J. (90)
30/5/06	Hungary	H	Manchester	3-1	Gerrard (47), Terry (51), Crouch (84)
3/6/06	Jamaica	H	Manchester	6-0	Lampard (11), Taylor (16og), Crouch (28, 66, 88), Owen (31)
10/6/06	Paraguay (WCF)	N	Frankfurt	1-0	Gamarra (3og)
15/6/06	Trinidad & Tobago (WCF)	N	Nuremberg	2-0	Crouch (83), Gerrard (90)
20/6/06	Sweden (WCF)	N	Cologne	2-2	Cole J. (34), Gerrard (85)
25/6/06	Ecuador (WCF)	N	Stuttgart	1-0	Beckham (60)
1/7/06	Portugal (WCF)	N	Gelsenkirchen	0-0	(aet; 1-3 on pens)

England

one-paced, one-footed luxury whose only real attribute was his dead-ball delivery. Frank Lampard was even worse, his uncharacteristically inaccurate shooting eroding his confidence to such an extent that it was an absurdity for him to elect – or be elected - to take the first penalty against Portugal. Michael Owen was inept before his injury, while Steven Gerrard, despite scoring two fine goals, never looked convincing in tandem with Lampard. Had Eriksson been braver, or shrewder, he would have dropped Beckham and Lampard, but his allegiance to his star players – an apparent blind faith in their ability to come good when it mattered – proved to be a fatal own-goal.

On the positive side, Joe Cole played well in most games and scored a wonderful goal against Sweden; the much-derided Owen Hargreaves blossomed into an indefatigable holding midfielder; the central defensive axis of Rio Ferdinand and John Terry was consistently solid; and young Aaron Lennon looked lively and threatening whenever he came off the bench. Eriksson deserved praise for persisting with Hargreaves and selecting Lennon, but even he must now secretly be wondering how things might have turned out if he had played Lennon and Hargreaves instead of Beckham and Lampard and selected Peter Crouch – another semi-success – alongside Rooney.

McClaren's mission

But that is history. And so is Eriksson. The future belongs to McClaren, whose first mission is to ensure that England qualify for the Euro 2008 finals. Croatia and Russia will be tricky adversaries, but, injures and suspensions notwithstanding, the new head coach should be able to carry on working with the same players who generally breezed through qualifying under Eriksson. The hope is that McClaren – despite his long association with the Swede – will be his own man and give the team the freedom to express themselves, playing exciting, fast-paced football – just as they do for their clubs in the Premiership.

Although the FA claimed that McClaren was their first choice, it was an open secret that they made contact with Portugal's Brazilian boss Luiz Felipe Scolari in Lisbon just before the appointment was announced. Another strong non-English candidate was ex-Leicester and Celtic manager Martin O'Neill, but, as with his mentor, Brian Clough, in the 1970s, he was seen as too unconventional and eccentric. McClaren was the safe choice and, in an Englishman-only field, unarguably the one with the best credentials. Rival candidates Alan Curbishley and Sam Allardyce had never won anything, and although McClaren's only silverware was the English League Cup, he did himself no harm by steering Middlesbrough through to the final of the 2005/06 UEFA Cup.

Alas, McClaren's final game for Boro would be a calamitous one as the Teesside club were routed 4-0 by Sevilla in Eindhoven. In the previous two rounds, however, McClaren's team did English football proud with two miraculous, almost identical, comebacks. Needing to score four goals at the Riverside to retrieve the tie against FC Basel and Steaua Bucharest, they did so on each occasion, with the decisive goal coming from Italian supersub Massimo Maccarone.

It was only the second time Boro had competed in Europe. Their first had been in the previous season's UEFA Cup, when they reached the last 16, so there was no denying the credentials of England's head coach-elect. Even so, a farewell victory in Eindhoven would have been opportune, to say the least, given that he had been officially sworn in at FA headquarters just six days previously.

Middlesbrough against Sevilla was the first of two Anglo-Spanish European finals. The more important one took place the following week in Paris, and once again there was grave disappointment for the travelling fans from England as Arsenal were beaten by Barcelona in the Stade de France. Despite taking the lead with a powerful header from Sol Campbell after goalkeeper Jens Lehmann had been sent off early for a professional foul, the Gunners were eventually shot down by the Catalans, who ran in two goals in quick succession to turn the game and take the trophy.

Awesome Arsenal

It was Arsenal's first appearance in the final of Europe's premier club competition. They had never previously gone beyond the quarter-finals, but with things not going well on the domestic front, the North London club crowned their final season at Highbury – in their one-season-only 'redcurrant' shirts - with a string of exceptional Champions League performances. They hit the heights in the first knockout round with an awesome diaplay against Real Madrid and were even more imperious in the quarter-finals against Juventus, playing the record Italian champions off the park in an utterly

England

Another goal for the irrepressible Thierry Henry – this one against Liverpool

one-sided 2-0 win at Highbury. Villarreal proved more difficult to shift in the semis, but Lehmann's heroic late penalty save ensured that the team went to Paris with a record ten successive clean sheets.

The remarkable thing about Arsenal's defensive record was the fact that three members of their first-choice back four – Ashley Cole, Sol Campbell and Lauren – were missing for most of the campaign. Instead mainstay Kolo Touré was joined by his exuberant compatriot Emmanuel Eboué at right-back, Swiss youngster Philippe Senderos in the centre and French midfielder Mathieu Flamini as a makeshift left-back. Goalkeeper Lehmann did not concede a Champions League goal all season (a record he involuntarily protected with his early dismissal in the final), and there were outstanding contributions elsewhere from young Cesc Fábregas in central midfield and, of course, the brilliant Thierry Henry in attack.

The Frenchman's most memorable goal of another prolific campaign was undoubtedly his solo strike in the Bernabéu, but there were many more gems sprinkled among his 27-goal haul in the Premiership. There could be no more fitting curtain call for Highbury than when Henry scored a hat-trick in the final league game of the season against Wigan. It was a hat-trick not just of symbolic value, because the 4-2 victory enabled Arsenal to leapfrog their local rivals Tottenham, finish fourth and return to the Champions League – in their brand new Emirates Stadium - in 2006/07. At the time it was not known whether Henry, courted by Barcelona, would remain with the club, but two days after the Champions League final defeat the club's new all-time record goalscorer cheered up the Arsenal fans by signing a new four-year contract.

Henry's brilliance earned him a third Footballer of the Year title to go with his fourth Premiership Golden Shoe in five seasons. His decision to stay in England is an enormous boost to the Premiership, although both he and his club will be keen to put up a more spirited fight on the domestic front in 2006/07. Finishing 24 points behind London rivals Chelsea was certainly not on the Gunners' agenda for 2005/06.

Champions Chelsea

Defending the Premiership title proved to be a piece of cake for Chelsea. Victories in each of their first nine matches swept José Mourinho's side into a commanding position, and although their year-long run without defeat in the Premiership was halted by

England

NATIONAL TEAM APPEARANCES 2005/06

Coach – Sven Göran ERIKSSON (SWE)

Player	DOB	Club	Den	WAL	NIR	AUT	POL	Arg	Uru	Hun	Jam	PAR	TRI	SWE	ECU	POR	Caps	Goals
Paul ROBINSON	15/10/79	Tottenham Hotspur	G46	G	G	G	G	G	G	G	G46	G	G	G	G	G	26	-
Gary NEVILLE	18/2/75	Manchester United	D46						D	D46		D				D	81	-
Rio FERDINAND	7/1/78	Manchester United	D	D	D	s64	D	D	D	D	D	D	D	D55	D	D	52	1
John TERRY	7/12/80	Chelsea	D46		D	D	D	D	D46	D75	D31	D	D	D	D	D	29	1
Ashley COLE	20/12/80	Arsenal	D	D	D					D	D35	D	D	D	D	D	51	-
David BECKHAM	2/5/75	Real Madrid (ESP)	M	M	M	M		M	M64	M	M68	M	M	M	M87	M51	94	17
Steven GERRARD	30/5/80	Liverpool	M82	M84	M75	M		M	M66	A65	M78	M	M	s67	M90	M	47	9
Frank LAMPARD	20/6/78	Chelsea	M64	M	M84	M	M	M		M	M68	M	M	M	M	M	45	11
Joe COLE	8/11/81	Chelsea	M	M77	s52	M61	M86	s57	M	M	M	M83	M74	M	M76	M65	37	6
Wayne ROONEY	24/10/85	Manchester United	A	A	M		A	A	A64				s58	A67	A	A	33	11
Jermain DEFOE	7/10/82	Tottenham Hotspur	A46	s68	s75			s82									16	1
David JAMES	1/8/70	Manchester City	s46								s46						34	-
Glen JOHNSON	23/8/84	Chelsea	s46														5	-
Jamie CARRAGHER	28/1/78	Liverpool	s46	D	D	D	D		s31	M	D		D58	D	s76	s118	29	-
Michael OWEN	14/12/79	Real Madrid (ESP) /Newcastle United	s46		A	A80	A83	A		A65	A	A56	A58	A4			80	36
Owen HARGREAVES	20/1/81	FC Bayern (GER)	s64	s77	s84					s46		s83		M	D	M	34	-
Jermaine JENAS	18/2/83	Newcastle United /Tottenham Hotspur	s82					s83		s66							15	-
Luke YOUNG	19/7/79	Charlton Athletic		D	D	D	D	D81									7	-
Shaun WRIGHT-PHILLIPS	25/10/81	Chelsea		M68	M52		M67	s64									8	1
Kieran RICHARDSON	21/10/84	Manchester United		s84		s80											4	2
Sol CAMPBELL	18/9/74	Arsenal				D64			s75	s31			s55				69	1
Peter CROUCH	30/1/81	Liverpool			A	s67	s81	s64	s65	A	A	A	s4		s65		11	6
Ledley KING	12/10/80	Tottenham Hotspur				s61	M	M57	s46								16	1
Alan SMITH	28/10/80	Manchester United					s86										16	1
Wayne BRIDGE	5/8/80	Chelsea					D46	D31	s35								23	1
Paul KONCHESKY	15/5/81	West Ham United					s46										2	-
Michael CARRICK	28/7/81	Tottenham Hotspur								M	s68			M			7	-
Darren BENT	6/2/84	Charlton Athletic								A82							1	-
Theo WALCOTT	16/3/89	Arsenal									s65						1	-
Aaron LENNON	16/4/87	Tottenham Hotspur									s68		s58		s87	s51 /118	4	-
Stewart DOWNING	22/7/84	Middlesbrough									s78	s56	s74		s90		5	-

England

Manchester United, unlike Arsenal the previous season the West Londoners did not allow defeat at Old Trafford to knock them out of their stride. Quite the contrary. Mourinho's men responded by reeling off another ten consecutive wins. By the first week of the New Year, Chelsea's lead had escalated to 13 points. The race for the Premiership was all but run.

Chelsea eased off in the early spring, but that was largely because they had other fish to fry. Their Champions League journey came to a premature end, however, when, having failed to win their group (they were beaten to first place by Liverpool), they were drawn against Barcelona. Triumphant against the Catalans 12 months earlier, they bit the dust this time, although once again Chelsea lost the first leg after having a player controversially sent off. Asier Del Horno's early dismissal at Stamford Bridge shaped the tie – and also left Mourinho with a ready-made excuse for his team's failure (despite the Catalans' superiority over the two legs).

Chelsea's hopes of a domestic Double disappeared when Liverpool beat them at Old Trafford in the FA Cup semi-final., but there was no stopping them in the Premiership. A week later they secured back-to-back titles by hammering their closest pursuers Manchester United 3-0 at fortress Stamford Bridge, where they had dropped just two points all season. The match was overshadowed by the injury to United's Wayne Rooney, but the comprehensive victory encapsulated Chelsea's Premiership superiority and enabled skipper John Terry to lift the championship trophy at the end of the game.

Terry was a colossus all season long in central defence, and there was sustained excellence also from his two England colleagues Frank Lampard (the club's top scorer in the league with 16 goals) and Joe Cole. Frenchmen William Gallas and Claude Makelele rarely had an off day, while Petr Cech was a figure of great authority in goal. Didier Drogba and Arjen Robben also had their moments, although both had their reputations scarred by persistent accusations of diving. Of the new signings, Michael Essien slotted in well, but Shaun Wright-Phillips was a complete flop. As for manager Mourinho, he cut an increasingly irascible figure as the season progressed. Unwilling to take criticism but always ready to dish it out, his eccentric charm gradually gave way to a me-against-the-world-type arrogance that alienated a lot of his previous admirers.

Thanks to Russian owner Roman Abramovich's bottomless pit of money, Chelsea were able to strengthen their squad still further during the summer with the acquisition of several new players, foremost among them Andriy Shevchenko and Michael Ballack. Blue, rather than red, it seems, could be the dominant colour in England for several years yet.

Changing of the guard

For the third year running Manchester United failed to win the Premiership. They did apply a bit of pressure on Chelsea with a Rooney-inspired nine-match winning run, in the midst of which they also lifted the League Cup, but generally it was another season in which Sir Alex Ferguson's side stagnated rather than progressed. The old guard started to unravel. Skipper Roy Keane upped and left in the autumn; replacement captain Gary Neville struggled to stay fit; Paul Scholes suffered a complicated eye injury that cut short his season at Christmas; Ryan Giggs showed increasing signs of wear and tear. Furthermore, ace marksman Ruud van Nistelrooy had a major falling-out with Ferguson. Dropped from the League Cup final against Wigan (which United won 4-0 without him), he never regained his place from Frenchman Louis Saha – despite a Premiership tally of 21 goals that was second only to Henry.

The death of Old Trafford legend George Best brought great sadness to the club, and there was a ghastly injury to Alan Smith to compound an FA Cup exit at Anfield, but the real low point of United's season was their early elimination from the Champions League. They made desperately difficult work of a straightforward group, scoring only three goals and eventually finishing bottom of the pile after a 2-1 defeat away to Benfica. It was the first time in a decade that United had failed to extend their Champions League involvement beyond Christmas, and the shellshocked expression on Ferguson's face after the game in Lisbon told its own story.

Liverpool's Champions League adventure lasted a round longer than United's but was also prematurely ended by Benfica. It was an ignominious exit for the holders of the trophy, who had been forced by UEFA to defend it from the very start of the competition, in mid-July. Rafa Benítez's side were much improved on the domestic front, although they made life difficult for themselves in the Premiership with a poor start that included a 4-1 defeat at Anfield by Chelsea. There would be no more home defeats in the league, and Liverpool went on to finish third, just one point behind

England

runners-up Manchester United and nine (as opposed to 37 the previous season) adrift of Chelsea.

The Gerrard Final

Better still, Liverpool eliminated both United and Chelsea en route to winning the FA Cup. The final, played once again in Cardiff's Millennium Stadium because of interminable delays in the construction of the New Wembley, was a classic. West Ham played magnificently, but the game will go down in history as the Steven Gerrard Final. The Liverpool captain, majestic all season, scored two magnificent goals, the second in the last minute of normal time, to rescue his team from defeat. It was 3-3 after 90 minutes, and after a gruelling extra-time, during which Gerrard was one of many players to be grounded by cramp, Liverpool finally prevailed in a penalty shoot-out, with an exhausted Gerrard driving home one of their spot-kicks.

West Ham's heartbreaking defeat was tempered by the knowledge that they had already qualified for the UEFA Cup (which they did by overcoming Middlesbrough in the semi-final). A week earlier the Hammers had ensured that Tottenham, rather than Arsenal, joined them in the secondary European competition by beating them 2-1 in the Premiership. Spurs, led by amiable Dutchman Martin Jol, had held fourth place for most of the season, even after a controversial 1-1 draw at Highbury, only to be denied right at the last as their local rivals vaulted over them. Nevertheless, it was a fine season for Spurs, who sent four players - Paul Robinson, Michael Carrick, Jermaine Jenas and Aaron Lennon - to the World Cup with England. It would have been six if Ledley King had not been injured (yet another metatarsal break) and Jermain Defoe not foolishly left at home.

The third UEFA Cup place was taken by Blackburn Rovers, who made good progress under ex-Wales boss Mark Hughes, while the one InterToto spot on offer went to Newcastle United. The Magpies had another fraught campaign, with Graeme Souness being sacked, new signing Michael Owen missing the second half of the season through injury (yes, a metatarsal break) and Alan Shearer retiring. Glenn Roeder did so well in the caretaker manager role (six wins in the last seven games) that he was given the job permanently.

Bolton Wanderers didn't quite make it back into Europe following a debut fling in the competition that ended at the third-round stage in Marseilles, but Sam Allardyce's rugged team again stood their ground well. There was also an amazing top-half-of-the-table finish for newly promoted Wigan Athletic, whose team of lower-league journeymen were Chelsea's closest challengers in the early weeks of the season. Manager Paul Jewell did a magnificent job, even taking the club to the League Cup final after a thrilling victory over Arsenal.

Doomed to the drop

If West Ham and Wigan enjoyed life at the top, the same couldn't be said of the other promoted club, Sunderland. Doomed early on, it took them until their final fixture at the Stadium of Light, against Fulham, to record their one and only home win, and they were relegated with a lowest-ever points tally. Two Midlands clubs, West Bromwich Albion and (surprisingly) Birmingham City accompanied them down to the 'Championship' after Portsmouth were rescued by Harry 'Houdini' Redknapp, re-recruited from Southampton midway through the campaign.

Reading, managed by ex-England winger Steve Coppell, reached the top flight for the first time after a stunning season in the Championship, scoring 99 goals in their 46 games and recording 106 points – 16 more than runners-up Sheffield United. Third-placed Watford ensured further Home Counties presence in the top flight with a convincing victory in the play-offs, posting 3-0 wins over both Crystal Palace in the semis and once-mighty Leeds United in the final.

Steven Gerrard smashes home the first of his two goals in the FA Cup final

England

EUROPEAN CUPS 2005/06
UEFA CHAMPIONS LEAGUE

LIVERPOOL
1st qualifying round TOTAL NETWORK SOLUTIONS (WAL)
H 3-0 *Gerrard (8, 21, 89)*
Reina, Finnan, Hyypiä, Carragher, Riise, Gerrard, Xabi Alonso, Warnock (Zenden 64), Potter (Cissé 76), Le Tallec, Morientes.
A 3-0 *Cissé (26), Gerrard (82, 83)*
Reina, Finnan, Hyypiä, Carragher (Whitbread 53), Riise, Xabi Alonso (Gerrard 68), Hamann, Zenden, Potter, Cissé, Le Tallec (Luis García 58).

2nd qualifying round FBK KAUNAS (LIT)
A 3-1 *Cissé (27), Carragher (30), Gerrard (55p)*
Reina, Josemi, Hyypiä, Carragher, Riise, Gerrard (Sissoko 60), Xabi Alonso, Zenden, Potter (Luis García 63), Crouch (Morientes 75), Cissé.
H 2-0 *Gerrard (77), Cissé (86)*
Carson, Finnan, Hyypiä, Whitbread, Warnock, Hamann (Gerrard 75), Sissoko, Zenden, Luis García, Crouch (Potter 55), Morientes (Cissé 46).

3rd qualifying round CSKA SOFIA (BUL)
A 3-1 *Cissé (25), Morientes (31, 58)*
Reina, Finnan, Hyypiä, Carragher, Warnock, Luis García, Xabi Alonso (Hamann 64), Gerrard (Sissoko 70), Riise, Cissé, Morientes (Barragán 79).
H 0-1
Carson, Finnan, Josemi, Hyypiä, Warnock (Zenden 64), Potter (Luis García 46), Hamann, Sissoko, Riise, Cissé (Sinama-Pongolle 83), Morientes.

1st round Group G
Match 1 REAL BETIS (ESP)
A 2-1 *Sinama-Pongolle (2), Luis García (14)*
Reine, Josemi, Carragher, Hyypiä, Traoré, Sinama-Pongolle (Gerrard 73), Xabi Alonso, Sissoko, Zenden (Riise 65), Luis García, Crouch (Cissé 58).

Match 2 CHELSEA (ENG)
H 0-0
Reina, Finnan, Carragher, Hyypiä, Traoré, Hamann, Xabi Alonso, Gerrard, Luis García, Cissé (Sinama-Pongolle 77), Crouch.

Match 3 RSC ANDERLECHT (BEL)
A 1-0 *Cissé (20)*
Reina, Josemi, Carragher, Hyypiä, Traoré, Sissoko (Zenden 82), Xabi Alonso, Hamann, Riise (Warnock 88), Luis García, Cissé (Kewell 75).

Match 4 RSC ANDERLECHT
H 3-0 *Morientes (34), Luis García (61), Cissé (89)*
Reina, Finnan, Carragher, Hyypiä, Riise, Gerrard (Kewell 78), Xabi Alonso, Sissoko, Luis García, Crouch (Cissé 71), Morientes (Zenden 52).

Match 5 REAL BETIS
H 0-0
Reina, Finnan, Carragher, Hyypiä, Riise, Gerrard (Potter 89), Sissoko, Hamann, Zenden, Crouch (Kewell 84), Morientes (Cissé 67).

Match 6 CHELSEA
A 0-0
Reina, Finnan, Carragher, Hyypiä, Traoré, Gerrard, Hamann, Sissoko, Riise (Kewell 60), Luis García (Sinama-Pongolle 80), Crouch (Morientes 69).

2nd round SL BENFICA
A 0-1
Reina, Finnan, Carragher, Hyypiä, Riise, Luis García, Xabi Alonso, Sissoko (Hamann 35), Kewell, Fowler (Cissé 66), Morientes (Gerrard 78)
H 0-2
Reina, Finnan, Carragher, Traoré, Warnock (Hamann 70), Luis García, Gerrard, Xabi Alonso, Kewell (Cissé 63), Morientes (Fowler 70), Crouch.

CHELSEA
1st round Group G
Match 1 RSC ANDERLECHT (BEL)
H 1-0 *Lampard (19)*
Cech, Paulo Ferreira, Terry, Ricardo Carvalho, Gallas, Makelele, Essien (Huth 90), Lampard, Duff (Cole J. 76), Robben (Wright-Phillips 67), Drogba.

Match 2 LIVERPOOL (ENG)
A 0-0
Cech, Paulo Ferreira, Ricardo Carvalho, Terry, Gallas, Makelele, Essien, Lampard, Duff (Crespo 74), Robben (Wright-Phillips 64), Drogba (Huth 90).

Match 3 REAL BETIS (ESP)
H 4-0 *Drogba (24), Ricardo Carvalho (44), Cole J. (59), Crespo (64)*
Cudicini, Gallas, Ricardo Carvalho, Terry, Del Horno, Makelele (Diarra 75), Essien, Lampard, Wright-Phillips (Gudjohnsen 66), Cole J., Drogba (Crespo 46).

Match 4 REAL BETIS
A 0-1
Cech, Paulo Ferreira, Ricardo Carvalho, Terry, Gallas, Essien, Makelele, Lampard, Coel J. (Wright-Phillips 46), Gudjohnsen (Drogba 46), Robben (Duff 65).

Match 5 RSC ANDERLECHT
A 2-0 *Crespo (8), Ricardo Carvalho (15)*
Cech, Gallas, Terry, Ricardo Carvalho, Del Horno, Essien, Cole J. (Diarra 63), Lampard, Gudjohnsen (Geremi 78), Duff, Crespo (Cole C. 86).

Match 6 LIVERPOOL
H 0-0
Cech, Paulo Ferreira (Del Horno 46), Ricardo Carvalho, Terry, Gallas, Essien, Gudjohnsen, Lampard, Robben (Cole C. 73), Duff (Wright-Phillips 73), Drogba.

2nd round FC BARCELONA (ESP)
H 1-2 *Motta (59og)*
Cech, Paulo Ferreira, Ricardo Carvalho, Terry, Del Horno, Makelele, Gudjohnsen, Lampard, Cole J. (Geremi 38), Robben (Wright-Phillips 77), Crespo (Drogba 46).
A 1-1 *Lampard (90p)*
Cech, Paulo Ferreira, Ricardo Carvalho, Terry, Gallas, Cole J. (Huth 83), Makelele, Lampard, Duff (Gudjohnsen 58), Robben, Drogba (Crespo 58).

ARSENAL
1st round Group B
Match 1 FC THUN (SUI)
H 2-1 *Gilberto Silva (51), Bergkamp (90)*
Almunia, Lauren, Touré, Campbell, Cole, Ljungberg (Hleb 81), Fábregas (Bergkamp 72), Gilberto Silva, Pires, Van Persie, Reyes (Owusu-Abeyie 81).

Match 2 AJAX (HOL)
A 2-1 *Ljungberg (2), Pires (69p)*
Almunia, Lauren, Touré, Campbell, Cole, Hleb (Cygan 90), Fábregas, Flamini, Pires (Clichy 88), Ljungberg, Reyes (Owusu-Abeyie 81).

Match 3 AC SPARTA PRAHA (CZE)
A 2-0 *Henry (21, 74)*
Lehmann, Lauren, Touré, Cygan, Clichy, Fábregas (Owusu-Abeyie 89), Flamini, Gilberto Silva, Pires, Van Persie (Eboué 72), Reyes (Henry 15).

Match 4 AC SPARTA PRAHA
H 3-0 *Henry (28), Van Persie (81, 86)*
Almunia, Lauren, Touré, Campbell, Clichy, Pires (Fábregas 73), Gilberto Silva, Flamini, Reyes (Eboué 82), Bergkamp, Henry (Van Persie 67).

Match 5 FC THUN
A 1-0 *Pires (88p)*

England

Almunia, Eboué, Senderos, Campbell, Cygan (Lauren 67), Ljungberg, Song (Fábregas 56), Flamini, Reyes, Van Persie, Henry (Pires 70).

Match 6 AJAX
H 0-0
Almunia, Eboué, Touré, Senderos, Lauren (Gilbert 73), Owusu-Abeyie, Flamini, Larsson, Hleb (Fábregas 62), Reyes (Van Persie 65), Henry.

2nd round REAL MADRID (ESP)
A 1-0 *Henry (47)*
Lehmann, Eboué, Touré, Senderos, Flamini, Hleb (Pires 75), Fábregas (Song 90), Gilberto Silva, Ljungberg, Reyes (Diaby 78), Henry.
H 0-0
Lehmann, Eboué, Touré, Senderos, Flamini, Hleb (Bergkamp 86), Fábregas, Gilberto Silva, Ljungberg, Reyes (Pires 67), Henry.

Quarter-final JUVENTUS (ITA)
H 2-0 *Fábregas (40), Henry (69)*
Lehmann, Eboué, Touré, Senderos, Flamini, Hleb, Gilberto Silva, Fábregas, Reyes (Van Persie 81), Pires, Henry.
A 0-0
Lehmann, Eboué, Touré, Senderos, Flamini, Gilberto Silva, Hleb (Diaby 85), Ljungberg, Fábregas, Reyes (Pires 63), Henry.

Semi-final VILLARREAL CF (ESP)
H 1-0 *Touré (41)*
Lehmann, Eboué, Touré, Senderos, Flamini, Hleb (Bergkamp 79), Fábregas, Gilberto Silva, Pires, Ljungberg (Van Persie 79), Henry.
A 0-0
Lehmann, Eboué, Touré, Campbell, Flamini (Clichy 8), Gilberto Silva, Hleb, Fábregas, Ljungberg, Reyes (Pires 69), Henry.

Final FC BARCELONA (ESP)
Saint-Denis
1-2 *Campbell (37)*
Lehmann, Eboué, Touré, Campbell, Cole, Gilberto Silva, Hleb (Reyes 84), Pires (Almunia 19), Fábregas (Flamini 74), Ljungberg, Henry.

MANCHESTER UNITED
3rd qualifying round DEBRECENI VSC (HUN)
H 3-0 *Rooney (7), Van Nistelrooy (49), Cristiano Ronaldo (63)*
Van der Sar, Neville, Ferdinand, Silvestre, O'Shea, Fletcher, Keane (Park 67), Scholes, Cristiano Ronaldo (Smith 67), Rooney, Van Nistelrooy.
A 3-0 *Heinze (20, 60), Richardson (65)*
Van der Sar, Neville (Richardson 13), Brown, Ferdinand, Heinze, Cristiano Ronaldo, Fletcher (Miller 61), Scholes (Bardsley 46), Giggs, Smith, Van Nistelrooy.

1st round Group D
Match 1 VILLARREAL CF (ESP)
A 0-0
Van der Sar, O'Shea, Ferdinand, Silvestre, Heinze (Richardson 33), Fletcher, Smith, Scholes, Cristiano Ronaldo (Giggs 80), Rooney, Van Nistelrooy (Park 80).

Match 2 SL BENFICA (POR)
H 2-1 *Giggs (39), Van Nistelrooy (85)*
Van der Sar, Bardsley, Ferdinand, O'Shea, Richardson, Fletcher, Smith, Cristiano Ronaldo, Scholes, Giggs, Van Nistelrooy.

Match 3 LILLE OSC (FRA)
H 0-0
Van der Sar, Bardsley, Ferdinand, Silvestre, O'Shea, Cristiano Ronaldo, Fletcher, Smith, Giggs (Park 84), Scholes, Van Nistelrooy.

Match 4 LILLE OSC
A 0-1
Van der Sar, O'Shea, Ferdinand, Brown, Silvestre, Cristiano Ronaldo (Rossi 89),
Fletcher, Smith, Richardson (Park 65), Rooney, Van Nistelrooy.

Match 5 VILLARREAL CF
H 0-0
Van der Sar, Brown (Neville 73), Ferdinand, Silvestre, O'Shea, Fletcher (Park 53) Smith (Saha 82), Scholes, Cristiano Ronaldo, Rooney, Van Nistelrooy.

Match 6 SL BENFICA
A 1-2 *Scholes (6)*
Van der Sar, Neville, Ferdinand, Silvestre, O'Shea (Richardson 85), Cristiano Ronaldo (Park 67), Smith, Scholes, Giggs (Saha 60), Rooney, Van Nistelrooy.

EVERTON
3rd qualifying round VILLARREAL CF (ESP)
H 1-2 *Beattie (42)*
Martyn, Hibbert, Weir, Yobo, Pistone (McFadden 80), Neville, Arteta, Cahill, Davies, Kilbane (Ferguson 62), Beattie (Bent 63).
A 1-2 *Arteta (69)*
Martyn, Hibbert, Yobo, Weir, Neville, Arteta, Davies (McFadden 78), Cahill, Kilbane (Osman 60), Bent, Ferguson.

UEFA CUP
BOLTON WANDERERS
1st round LOKOMOTIV PLOVDIV (BUL)
H 2-1 *Diouf (72), Borgetti (90)*
Jääskeläinen, Hunt, Jaidi, N'Gotty, Iván Campo, Gardner, Giannakopoulos (Fernandes 66), Nakata, Okocha (Nolan 66), Diouf, Pedersen (Borgetti 57).
A 2-1 *Tunchev (79og), Nolan (86)*
Walker, O'Brien (Nakata 66), Ben Haim, N'Gotty, Pedersen, Faye, Fernandes (Nolan 56), Giannakopoulos, Okocha, Borgetti (Davies 56), Diouf.

2nd round Group H
Match 1 BESIKTAS (TUR)
A 1-1 *Borgetti (29)*
Walker, O'Brien, Ben Haim, Jaidi, Gardner, Faye, Fernandes (Nolan 59), Nakata, Fadiga, Borgetti, Diouf.

Match 2 ZENIT SANKT-PETERBURG (RUS)
H 1-0 *Nolan (24)*
Jääskeläinen, O'Brien, Ben Haim, N'Gotty, Gardner, Faye, Giannakopoulos, Nakata (Okocha 66), Nolan (Diouf 85), Speed, Davies (Borgetti 74).

Match 3 VITÓRIA GUIMARÃES (POR)
A 1-1 *Vaz Té (88)*
Jääskeläinen, O'Brien, Ben Haim, N'Gotty, Gardner, Faye, Nolan, Nakata (Speed 58), Giannakopoulos, Okocha (Vaz Té 86), Borgetti (Diouf 63).

Match 4 SEVILLA FC (ESP)
H 1-1 *N'Gotty (65)*
Walker, Hunt, Ben Haim, Jaidi, Gardner (N'Gotty 46), Faye (Speed 55), Nakata, Okocha, Diouf, Fadiga, Davies (Vaz Té 65).

3rd round OLYMPIQUE MARSEILLE (FRA)
H 0-0
Jääskeläinen, O'Brien, Ben Haim, N'Gotty, Gardner, Faye, Giannakopoulos, Nolan, Okocha (Speed 60), Davies, Borgetti (Vaz Té 67).
A 1-2 *Giannakopoulos (25)*
Jääskeläinen, O'Brien, Ben Haim, N'Gotty, Gardner, Faye (Pedersen 73; Borgetti 88), Giannakopoulos, Speed (Vaz Té 84), Okocha, Nolan, Davies.

MIDDLESBROUGH
1st round XANTHI (GRE)
H 2-0 *Boateng (28), Viduka (82)*
Schwarzer, Abel Xavier, Ehiogu, Bates, Pogatetz, Parlour (Morrison 74), Doriva, Boateng, Johnson (Queudrue 61), Viduka, Maccarone (Yakubu 74).
A 0-0

England

Jones, Abel Xavier, Southgate, Riggott, Pogatetz, Queudrue (Parnaby 79), Doriva, Boateng, Morrison, Maccarone (Németh 71), Hadsselbaink (Yakubu 71).

2nd round Group D
Match 1 GRASSHOPPER-CLUB ZÜRICH (SUI)
A 1-0 *Hasselbaink (10)*
Schwarzer, Parnaby, Riggott, Southgate, Pogatetz, Boateng, Doriva, Mendieta (Queudrue 79), Németh (Morrison 67), Hasselbaink, Viduka (Yakubu 85).

Match 2 DNIPRO DNIPROPETROVSK (UKR)
H 3-0 *Yakubu (36), Viduka (50, 56)*
Schwarzer, Bates, Riggott, Pogatetz, Queudrue, Parnaby, Mendieta (Kennedy 60), Doriva, Morrison, Viduka (Németh 64), Yakubu (Maccarone 57).

Match 3 AZ (HOL)
A 0-0
Jones, Bates, Ehiogu, Riggott, Pogatetz, Morrison (Parnaby 63), Boateng, Doriva, Németh (Queudrue 73), Hasselbaink, Viduka (Yakubu 63).

Match 4 LITEX LOVECH (BUL)
H 2-0 *Maccarone (80, 86)*
Jones, Bates, Ehiogu, Riggott, Pogatetz, Morrison, Doriva, Kennedy, Johnson, Hasselbaink (Cattermole 83), Maccarone.

3rd round VFB STUTTGART (GER)
A 2-1 *Hasselbaink (20), Parnaby (46)*
Schwarzer, Davies, Riggott, Southgate, Pogatetz, Parnaby, Rochemback, Doriva, Boateng (Kennedy 79), Downing (Johnson 70), Hasselbaink (Yakubu 84).
H 0-1
Schwarzer, Davies, Riggott, Southgate, Queudrue, Parnaby, Cattermole, Mendieta (Ehiogu 86), Boateng, Downing (Taylor 90), Hasselbaink (Yakubu 86).

4th round ROMA (ITA)
H 1-0 *Yakubu (12p)*
Schwarzer, Davies, Riggott, Southgate, Pogatetz, Mendieta, Cattermole, Boateng, Downing (Queudrue 90), Yakubu (Viduka 81), Hasselbaink.
A 1-2 *Hasselbaink (32)*
Schwarzer, Davies (Queudrue 46), Riggott, Southgate, Pogatetz, Mendieta, Boateng, Cattermole, Downing, Yakubu (Parlour 59), Hasselbaink.

Quarter-final FC BASEL (SUI)
A 0-2
Schwarzer, Parnaby, Riggott, Pogatetz (Ehiogu 68), Queudrue, Mendieta (Rochemback 75), Parlour, Doriva, Downing, Viduka, Hasselbaink (Yakubu 75).
H 4-1 *Viduka (33, 57), Hasselbaink (79), Maccarone (90)*
Schwarzer, Parnaby, Riggott, Southgate, Queudrue (Maccarone 67), Morrison (Hasselbaink 46), Rochemback, Boateng, Downing, Yakubu (Taylor 90), Viduka.

Semi-final STEAUA BUCURESTI (ROM)
A 0-1
Schwarzer, Parnaby, Bates, Ehiogu, Queudrue, Morrison (Parlour 70), Rochemback, Boateng, Downing, Hasselbaink, Yakubu (Maccarone 70).
H 4-2 *Maccarone (33, 89), Viduka (64), Riggott (73)*
Jones, Riggott, Southgate (Maccarone 26), Queudrue, Parnaby, Rochemback, Downing, Boateng, Taylor (Yakubu 56), Hasselbaink, Viduka.

Final SEVILLA FC (ESP)
Eindhoven
0-4
Schwarzer, Parnaby, Riggott, Southgate, Queudrue (Yakubu 70), Morrison (Maccarone 46), Boateng, Rochemback, Downing, Viduka (Cattermole 85), Hasselbaink.

EVERTON
1st round DINAMO BUCURESTI (ROM)
A 1-5 *Yobo (30)*

Martyn, Hibbert, Yobo, Weir, Nuno Valente, Davies (Kilbane 72), Cahill, Osman, Neville, Bent, McFadden (Freguson 78).
H 1-0 *Cahill (28)*
Martyn, Hibbert (Weir 24), Yobo, Ferrari, Nuno Valente (Bent 68), Arteta, Cahill, Neville, Kilbane (Beattie 68), McFadden, Ferguson.

TOP GOALSCORERS 2005/06

27	Thierry HENRY (Arsenal)
21	Ruud VAN NISTELROOY (Manchester United)
18	Darren BENT (Charlton Athletic)
16	Frank LAMPARD (Chelsea)
	Wayne ROONEY (Manchester United)
	Robbie KEANE (Tottenham Hotspur)
14	Marlon HAREWOOD (West Ham United)
13	YAKUBU (Middlesbrough)
	Craig BELLAMY (Blackburn Rovers)
12	Didier DROGBA (Chelsea)
	Henri CAMARA (Wigan Athletic)

LEAGUE RESULTS/ SCORERS/APPEARANCES/ GOALS 2005/06

ARSENAL
Manager – Arsène Wenger (FRA)

2005				
14/8	Newcastle United	h	2-0	Henry (p), Van Persie
21/8	Chelsea	a	0-1	
24/8	Fulham	h	4-1	Cygan 2, Henry 2
10/9	Middlesbrough	a	1-2	Reyes
19/9	Everton	h	2-0	Campbell 2
24/9	West Ham United	a	0-0	
2/10	Birmingham City	h	1-0	og (Clemence)
15/10	West Bromwich Albion	a	1-2	Senderos
22/10	Manchester City	h	1-0	Pires (p)
29/10	Tottenham Hotspur	a	1-1	Pires
5/11	Sunderland	h	3-1	Van Persie, Henry 2
19/11	Wigan Athletic	a	3-2	Van Persie, Henry 2
26/11	Blackburn Rovers	h	3-0	Fàbregas, Henry, Van Persie
3/12	Bolton Wanderers	a	0-2	
10/12	Newcastle United	a	0-1	
18/12	Chelsea	h	0-2	
26/12	Charlton Athletic	a	1-0	Reyes
28/12	Portsmouth	h	4-0	Bergkamp, Reyes, Henry 2 (1p)
31/12	Aston Villa	a	0-0	
2006				
3/1	Manchester United	h	0-0	
14/1	Middlesbrough	h	7-0	Henry 3, Senderos, Pires, Gilberto Silva, Hleb
21/1	Everton	a	0-1	
1/2	West Ham United	h	2-3	Henry, Pires
4/2	Birmingham City	a	2-0	Adebayor, Henry
11/2	Bolton Wanderers	h	1-1	Gilberto Silva
14/2	Liverpool	a	0-1	
25/2	Blackburn Rovers	a	0-1	

England

FINAL LEAGUE TABLE 2005/06

		Pld	Home					Away					Total					Pts
			W	D	L	F	A	W	D	L	F	A	W	D	L	F	A	
1	Chelsea	38	18	1	0	47	9	11	3	5	25	13	29	4	5	72	22	91
2	Manchester United	38	13	5	1	37	8	12	3	4	35	26	25	8	5	72	34	83
3	Liverpool	38	15	3	1	32	8	10	4	5	25	17	25	7	6	57	25	82
4	Arsenal	38	14	3	2	48	13	6	4	9	20	18	20	7	11	68	31	67
5	Tottenham Hotspur	38	12	5	2	31	16	6	6	7	22	22	18	11	9	53	38	65
6	Blackburn Rovers	38	13	3	3	31	17	6	3	10	20	25	19	6	13	51	42	63
7	Newcastle United	38	11	5	3	28	15	6	2	11	19	27	17	7	14	47	42	58
8	Bolton Wanderers	38	11	5	3	29	13	4	6	9	20	28	15	11	12	49	41	56
9	West Ham United	38	9	3	7	30	25	7	4	8	22	30	16	7	15	52	55	55
10	Wigan Athletic	38	7	3	9	24	26	8	3	8	21	26	15	6	17	45	52	51
11	Everton	38	8	4	7	22	22	6	4	9	12	27	14	8	16	34	49	50
12	Fulham	38	13	2	4	31	21	1	4	14	17	37	14	6	18	48	58	48
13	Charlton Athletic	38	8	4	7	22	21	5	4	10	19	34	13	8	17	41	55	47
14	Middlesbrough	38	7	5	7	28	30	5	4	10	20	28	12	9	17	48	58	45
15	Manchester City	38	9	2	8	26	20	4	2	13	17	28	13	4	21	43	48	43
16	Aston Villa	38	6	6	7	20	20	4	6	9	22	35	10	12	16	42	55	42
17	Portsmouth	38	5	7	7	17	24	5	1	13	20	38	10	8	20	37	62	38
18	Birmingham City	38	6	5	8	19	20	2	5	12	9	30	8	10	20	28	50	34
19	West Bromwich Albion	38	6	2	11	21	24	1	7	11	10	34	7	9	22	31	58	30
20	Sunderland	38	1	4	14	12	37	2	2	15	14	32	3	6	29	26	69	15

4/3	Fulham	a	4-0	Henry 2, Adebayor, Fàbregas
12/3	Liverpool	h	2-1	Henry 2
18/3	Charlton Athletic	h	3-0	Pires, Adebayor, Hleb
1/4	Aston Villa	h	5-0	Adebayor, Henry 2, Van Persie, Diaby
9/4	Manchester United	a	0-2	
12/4	Portsmouth	a	1-1	Henry
15/4	West Bromwich Albion	h	3-1	Hleb, Pires, Bergkamp
22/4	Tottenham Hotspur	h	1-1	Henry
1/5	Sunderland	a	3-0	og (Collins), Fàbregas, Henry
4/5	Manchester City	a	3-1	Ljungberg, Reyes 2
7/5	Wigan Athletic	h	4-2	Pires, Henry 3 (1p)

No	Name	Nat	Pos	Aps	(s)	Gls
25	Emmanuel ADEBAYOR	TOG	A	12	(1)	4
10	Dennis BERGKAMP	HOL	A	8	(16)	2
23	Sol CAMPBELL		D	20		2
22	Gaël CLICHY	FRA	D	5	(2)	
3	Ashley COLE		D	9	(2)	
18	Pascal CYGAN	FRA	D	11	(1)	2
2	Abou DIABY	FRA	M	9	(3)	1
36	Johan DJOUROU	SUI	D	6	(1)	
27	Emmanuel EBOUE	CIV	D	11	(7)	
15	Cesc FÀBREGAS	ESP	M	30	(5)	3
16	Mathieu FLAMINI	FRA	M	19	(12)	
38	Kerrea GILBERT		D	2		
19	GILBERTO SILVA	BRA	M	33		2
14	Thierry HENRY	FRA	A	30	(2)	27
13	Alexandr HLEB	BLS	M	17	(8)	3
29	Sebastian LARSSON	SWE	D	2	(1)	
12	LAUREN	CMR	D	22		
1	Jens LEHMANN	GER	G	38		
8	Fredrik LJUNGBERG	SWE	M	21	(4)	1
41	Arturo LUPOLI	ITA	A		(1)	
26	Quincy OWUSU-ABEYIE	HOL	A		(4)	
7	Robert PIRES	FRA	M	23	(10)	7
9	José Antonio REYES	ESP	M	22	(4)	5
20	Philippe SENDEROS	SUI	D	19	(1)	2
17	Alexandre SONG	CMR	M	3	(2)	
28	Kolo TOURE	CIV	D	33		
11	Robin VAN PERSIE	HOL	A	13	(11)	5

ASTON VILLA
Manager – David O'Leary (IRL)

2005				
13/8	Bolton Wanderers	h	2-2	Phillips, Davis
20/8	Manchester United	a	0-1	
23/8	Portsmouth	a	1-1	og (Hughes)
27/8	Blackburn Rovers	h	1-0	Baros
12/9	West Ham United	a	0-4	
17/9	Tottenham Hotspur	h	1-1	Milner
24/9	Chelsea	a	1-2	Moore
2/10	Middlesbrough	h	2-3	Moore, Davis
16/10	Birmingham City	a	1-0	Phillips
22/10	Wigan Athletic	h	0-2	
31/10	Manchester City	a	1-3	Ridgewell
5/11	Liverpool	h	0-2	
19/11	Sunderland	a	3-1	Phillips, Barry, Baros
26/11	Charlton Athletic	h	1-0	Davis
3/12	Newcastle United	a	1-1	McCann
10/12	Bolton Wanderers	a	1-1	Angel
17/12	Manchester United	h	0-2	
26/12	Everton	h	4-0	Baros 2, Delaney, Angel
28/12	Fulham	a	3-3	Moore, Ridgewell 2
31/12	Arsenal	h	0-0	
2006				
2/1	West Bromwich Albion	a	2-1	Davis, Baros (p)

England

Date	Opponent	H/A	Score	Scorers
14/1	West Ham United	h	1-2	Hendrie
21/1	Tottenham Hotspur	a	0-0	
1/2	Chelsea	h	1-1	Moore
4/2	Middlesbrough	a	4-0	Moore 3, Phillips
11/2	Newcastle United	h	1-2	Moore
25/2	Charlton Athletic	a	0-0	
4/3	Portsmouth	h	1-0	Baros
11/3	Blackburn Rovers	a	0-2	
18/3	Everton	a	1-4	Agbonlahor
25/3	Fulham	h	0-0	
1/4	Arsenal	a	0-5	
9/4	West Bromwich Albion	h	0-0	
16/4	Birmingham City	h	3-1	Baros 2, Cahill
18/4	Wigan Athletic	a	2-3	Angel, Ridgewell
25/4	Manchester City	h	0-1	
29/4	Liverpool	a	1-3	Barry
7/5	Sunderland	h	2-1	Barry, Ridgewell

No	Name	Nat	Pos	Aps	(s)	Gls
30	Gabriel AGBONLAHOR		A	3	(6)	1
9	Juan Pablo ANGEL	COL	A	11	(19)	3
24	Eirik BAKKE	NOR	M	8	(5)	
10	Milan BAROS	GZE	A	24	(1)	8
6	Gareth BARRY		M	36		3
23	Patrik BERGER	CZE	M	3	(5)	
16	Wilfred BOUMA	HOL	D	20		
21	Gary CAHILL		D	6	(1)	1
12	Steven DAVIS	NIR	M	34	(1)	4
15	Ulises DE LA CRUZ	ECU	D	4	(3)	
2	Mark DELANEY	WAL	D	12		1
14	Eric DJEMBA-DJEMBA	CMR	M		(4)	
26	Craig GARDNER		M	3	(5)	
7	Lee HENDRIE		M	7	(9)	1
18	Aaron HUGHES	NIR	D	35		
5	Martin LAURSEN	DEN	D	1		
8	Gavin McCANN		M	32		1
4	Olof MELLBERG	SWE	D	27		
11	James MILNER		M	27		1
22	Luke MOORE		A	16	(11)	8
20	Kevin PHILLIPS		A	21	(3)	4
19	Liam RIDGEWELL		D	30	(2)	5
3	JLloyd SAMUEL		D	14	(5)	
11	Nolberto SOLANO	PER	M	2	(1)	
1	Thomas SØRENSEN	DEN	G	36		
13	Stuart TAYLOR		G	2		
17	Peter WHITTINGHAM		M	4		

BIRMINGHAM CITY
Manager – Steve Bruce

2005

Date	Opponent	H/A	Score	Scorers
13/8	Fulham	a	0-0	
20/8	Manchester City	h	1-2	Butt
23/8	Middlesbrough	h	0-3	
27/8	West Bromwich Albion	a	3-2	Heskey 2, Jarosik
10/9	Charlton Athletic	h	0-1	
17/9	Portsmouth	a	1-1	Jarosík
24/9	Liverpool	h	2-2	og (Warnock), Pandiani
2/10	Arsenal	a	0-1	
16/10	Aston Villa	h	0-1	
22/10	Blackburn Rovers	a	0-2	
29/10	Everton	h	0-1	
5/11	Newcastle United	a	0-1	
26/11	Sunderland	a	1-0	Gray
5/12	West Ham United	h	1-2	Heskey
10/12	Fulham	h	1-0	Butt
17/12	Manchester City	a	1-4	Jarosík
26/12	Tottenham Hotspur	a	0-2	
28/12	Manchester United	h	2-2	Clapham, Pandiani
31/12	Chelsea	a	0-2	

2006

Date	Opponent	H/A	Score	Scorers
2/1	Wigan Athletic	h	2-0	Pennant, Melchiot
14/1	Charlton Athletic	a	0-2	
21/1	Portsmouth	h	5-0	Jarosík, Pennant, Upson, Forssell (p), Dunn
1/2	Liverpool	a	1-1	og (Xabi Alonso)
4/2	Arsenal	h	0-2	
13/2	West Ham United	a	0-3	
25/2	Sunderland	h	1-0	Heskey
4/3	Middlesbrough	a	0-1	
11/3	West Bromwich Albion	h	1-1	Forssell (p)
18/3	Tottenham Hotspur	h	0-2	
26/3	Manchester United	a	0-3	
1/4	Chelsea	h	0-0	
4/4	Bolton Wanderers	h	1-0	Jarosík
8/4	Wigan Athletic	a	1-1	Dunn
16/4	Aston Villa	a	1-3	Sutton
19/4	Blackburn Rovers	h	2-1	Butt, Forssell
22/4	Everton	a	0-0	
29/4	Newcastle United	h	0-0	
7/5	Bolton Wanderers	a	0-1	

No	Name	Nat	Pos	Aps	(s)	Gls
36	Mathew BIRLEY		M		(1)	
24	Alex BRUCE		M	3	(2)	
20	Nicky BUTT		M	22	(2)	3
28	DJ CAMPBELL		A	4	(7)	
3	Jamie CLAPHAM		D	13	(3)	1
25	Stephen CLEMENCE		M	13	(2)	
4	Kenny CUNNINGHAM	IRL	D	31		
10	David DUNN		M	8	(7)	2
9	Mikael FORSSELL	FIN	A	10	(17)	3
21	Julian GRAY		M	18	(3)	1
16	Emile HESKEY		A	34		4
6	Muzzy IZZET	TUR	M	10	(6)	
14	Jiri JAROSÍK	CZE	M	19	(5)	5
22	Damien JOHNSON	NIR	M	31		
15	Neil KILKENNY		M	6	(12)	
8	Martin LATKA	CZE	D	6		
11	Stan LAZARIDIS	AUS	M	11	(6)	
29	Mario MELCHIOT	HOL	D	22	(1)	1
19	Clinton MORRISON	IRL	A		(1)	
12	Mehdi NAFTI	TUN	M	1		
31	Marcos PAINTER		D	2	(2)	
8	Walter PANDIANI	URU	A	7	(10)	2
7	Jermaine PENNANT		M	35	(3)	2
23	Matthew SADLER		D	8		
40	Chris SUTTON		A	10		1
1	Maik TAYLOR	NIR	G	34		
2	Martin TAYLOR		D	20	(1)	
26	Olivier TEBILY	CIV	D	12	(4)	
5	Matthew UPSON		D	24		1
18	Nico VAESEN	BEL	G	4		

BLACKBURN ROVERS
Manager – Mark Hughes (WAL)

2005

Date	Opponent	H/A	Score	Scorers
13/8	West Ham United	a	1-3	Todd
20/8	Fulham	h	2-1	Gamst Pedersen, Tugay
24/8	Tottenham Hotspur	h	0-0	
27/8	Aston Villa	a	0-1	
11/9	Bolton Wanderers	a	0-0	
18/9	Newcastle United	h	0-3	

England

Date	Opponent	H/A	Score	Scorers
24/9	Manchester United	a	2-1	Gamst Pedersen 2
1/10	West Bromwich Albion	h	2-0	Kuqi 2
15/10	Liverpool	a	0-1	
22/10	Birmingham City	h	2-0	Dickov (p), Bellamy
29/10	Chelsea	a	2-4	Bellamy 2 (1p)
5/11	Charlton Athletic	h	4-1	Emerton, Dickov, Gamst Pedersen, Bellamy
19/11	Manchester City	a	0-0	
26/11	Arsenal	a	0-3	
3/12	Everton	h	0-2	
10/12	West Ham United	h	3-2	Dickov 2 (1p), Kuqi
17/12	Fulham	a	1-2	og (Knight)
26/12	Middlesbrough	a	2-0	Kuqi 2
31/12	Wigan Athletic	a	3-0	Gamst Pedersen, Reid, Bellamy
2006				
2/1	Portsmouth	h	2-1	Gamst Pedersen, Dickov
14/1	Bolton Wanderers	h	0-0	
21/1	Newcastle United	a	1-0	Gamst Pedersen
1/2	Manchester United	h	4-3	Bentley 3, Neill (p)
4/2	West Bromwich Albion	a	0-2	
11/2	Everton	a	0-1	
15/2	Sunderland	h	2-0	Bellamy 2
25/2	Arsenal	h	1-0	Gamst Pedersen
5/3	Tottenham Hotspur	a	2-3	Sinama-Pongolle, Bellamy
11/3	Aston Villa	h	2-0	Todd, Bellamy
18/3	Middlesbrough	h	3-2	Bellamy 2, Gamst Pedersen
25/3	Sunderland	a	1-0	Reid
3/4	Wigan Athletic	h	1-1	Kuqi
8/4	Portsmouth	a	2-2	Bellamy 2
16/4	Liverpool	h	0-1	
19/4	Birmingham City	a	1-2	Savage
29/4	Charlton Athletic	a	2-2	Reid, og (Powell)
2/5	Chelsea	h	1-0	Reid
7/5	Manchester City	h	2-0	Khizanishvili, Kuqi

No	Name	Nat	Pos	Aps	(s)	Gls
11	Craig BELLAMY	WAL	A	22	(5)	13
29	David BENTLEY		M	23	(6)	3
10	Paul DICKOV	SCO	A	17	(4)	5
7	Brett EMERTON	AUS	M	17	(13)	1
5	Garry FLITCROFT		M	1	(1)	
1	Brad FRIEDEL	USA	G	38		
19	Paul GALLAGHER	SCO	A		(1)	
12	Morten GAMST PEDERSEN	NOR	M	34		9
33	Michael GRAY		D	30		
18	Vratislav GRESKO	SVK	D	1	(2)	
17	Matt JANSEN		A	1	(3)	
25	Jemal JOHNSON	USA	A		(2)	
3	Zurab KHIZANISHVILI	GEO	D	24	(2)	1
9	Shefki KUQI	FIN	A	15	(18)	7
21	Dominic MATTEO	SCO	D	6		
15	Aaron MOKOENA	RSA	M	4	(16)	
2	Lucas NEILL	AUS	D	35		1
6	Ryan NELSEN	NZL	D	31		
21	Sergio PETER	GER	M	1	(7)	
14	Steven REID	IRL	M	31	(3)	4
8	Robbie SAVAGE	WAL	M	34		1
17	Florent SINAMA-PONGOLLE	FRA	A	8	(2)	1
19	David THOMPSON		M	2	(4)	
4	Andy TODD		D	20	(2)	2
16	TUGAY Kerimoglu	TUR	M	23	(4)	1

BOLTON WANDERERS
Manager – Sam Allardyce
2005

Date	Opponent	H/A	Score	Scorers
13/8	Aston Villa	a	2-2	Davies, Iván Campo
21/8	Everton	h	0-1	
24/8	Newcastle United	h	2-0	Diouf, Giannakopoulos
27/8	West Ham United	a	2-1	Nolan, Iván Campo
11/9	Blackburn Rovers	h	0-0	
18/9	Manchester City	a	1-0	Speed (p)
24/9	Portsmouth	h	1-0	Nolan
2/10	Wigan Athletic	a	1-2	Jaidi
15/10	Chelsea	a	1-5	Giannakopoulos
23/10	West Bromwich Albion	h	2-0	Nakata, Nolan
29/10	Charlton Athletic	a	1-0	Nolan
7/11	Tottenham Hotspur	h	1-0	Nolan
27/11	Fulham	a	1-2	og (Legwinski)
3/12	Arsenal	h	2-0	Diagne-Faye, Giannakopoulos
10/12	Aston Villa	h	1-1	Diouf
17/12	Everton	a	4-0	Davies, Giannakopoulos 2, Speed (p)
26/12	Sunderland	a	0-0	
31/12	Manchester United	a	1-4	Speed
2006				
2/1	Liverpool	h	2-2	Jaidi, Diouf
14/1	Blackburn Rovers	a	0-0	
21/1	Manchester City	h	2-0	Borgetti, Nolan
1/2	Portsmouth	a	1-1	Fadiga
4/2	Wigan Athletic	h	1-1	Giannakopoulos
11/2	Arsenal	a	1-1	Nolan
26/2	Fulham	h	2-1	og (Helguson), Nolan
4/3	Newcastle United	a	1-3	Davies
11/3	West Ham United	h	4-1	Giannakopoulos 2, Speed, Pedersen
18/3	Sunderland	h	2-0	Davies, Nolan
26/3	Middlesbrough	a	3-4	Giannakopoulos, Okocha, Jaidi
1/4	Manchester United	h	1-2	Davies
4/4	Birmingham City	a	0-1	
9/4	Liverpool	a	0-1	
15/4	Chelsea	h	0-2	
17/4	West Bromwich Albion	a	0-0	
22/4	Charlton Athletic	h	4-1	Vaz Té, Davies 2, Borgetti
30/4	Tottenham Hotspur	a	0-1	
3/5	Middlesbrough	h	1-1	Vaz Té
7/5	Birmingham City	h	1-0	Vaz Té

No	Name	Nat	Pos	Aps	(s)	Gls
26	Tal BEN HAIM	ISR	D	32	(3)	
18	Jared BORGETTI	MEX	A	5	(13)	2
14	Kevin DAVIES		A	37		7
25	Abdoulaye DIAGNE-FAYE	SEN	M	23	(4)	1
21	El-Hadji DIOUF	SEN	A	17	(3)	3
12	Martin DJETOU	FRA	M	1	(2)	
32	Jaroslaw FOJUT	POL	D		(1)	
39	Khalilou FADIGA	SEN	M	5	(3)	1
23	Fabrice FERNANDES	FRA	M		(1)	
11	Ricardo GARDNER	JAM	D	27	(3)	
7	Stelios GIANNAKOPOULOS	GRE	M	29	(5)	9
2	Nicky HUNT		D	12	(8)	
8	IVÁN CAMPO	ESP	D	8	(7)	2
22	Jussi JÄÄSKELÄINEN	FIN	G	38		
15	Radhi JAIDI	TUN	D	15	(1)	3
17	Matt JANSEN		A	3	(3)	
16	Hidetoshi NAKATA	JPN	M	14	(7)	1
5	Bruno N'GOTTY	FRA	D	27	(2)	
4	Kevin NOLAN		M	35	(1)	9
24	Joey O'BRIEN	IRL	D	22	(1)	
10	Jay-Jay OKOCHA	NGA	M	18	(9)	1

England

9	Henrik PEDERSEN	DEN	D	15	(6)	1	
6	Gary SPEED	WAL	M	29	(2)	4	
20	Ricardo VAZ TÉ	POR	A	6	(16)	3	

CHARLTON ATHLETIC
Manager – Alan Curbishley

2005
13/8	Sunderland	a	3-1	Bent D. 2, Murphy
20/8	Wigan Athletic	h	1-0	Bent D.
28/8	Middlesbrough	a	3-0	Rommedahl, Perry, Bent D.
10/9	Birmingham City	a	1-0	Bent D.
17/9	Chelsea	h	0-2	
24/9	West Bromwich Albion	a	2-1	Murphy 2 (1p)
1/10	Tottenham Hotspur	h	2-3	Bent D. 2
17/10	Fulham	h	1-1	Murphy
22/10	Portsmouth	a	2-1	Ambrose, Rommedahl
29/10	Bolton Wanderers	h	0-1	
5/11	Blackburn Rovers	h	1-4	Hughes
19/11	Manchester United	h	1-3	Ambrose
26/11	Aston Villa	a	0-1	
4/12	Manchester City	h	2-5	Bent D., Bothroyd
10/12	Sunderland	h	2-0	Bent D., Ambrose
17/12	Wigan Athletic	a	0-3	
26/12	Arsenal	h	0-1	
31/12	West Ham United	h	2-0	Bartlett, Bent D.

2006
2/1	Everton	a	1-3	Holland
14/1	Birmingham City	h	2-0	Hughes, Bent D.
22/1	Chelsea	a	1-1	Bent M.
31/1	West Bromwich Albion	h	0-0	
5/2	Tottenham Hotspur	a	1-3	Thomas
8/2	Liverpool	h	2-0	Bent D. (p), Young
12/2	Manchester City	a	2-3	Bent D., Bent M.
22/2	Newcastle United	a	0-0	
25/2	Aston Villa	h	0-0	
4/3	Liverpool	a	0-0	
12/3	Middlesbrough	h	2-1	Bent D. 2
18/3	Arsenal	a	0-3	
26/3	Newcastle United	h	3-1	Bent D. (p), og (Bowyer), Bothroyd
2/4	West Ham United	a	0-0	
8/4	Everton	h	0-0	
15/4	Fulham	a	1-2	Euell
17/4	Portsmouth	h	2-1	Hughes, Bent D.
22/4	Bolton Wanderers	a	1-4	Bent D. (p)
29/4	Blackburn Rovers	h	0-2	
7/5	Manchester United	a	0-4	

No	Name	Nat	Pos	Aps	(s)	Gls
18	Darren AMBROSE		M	19	(9)	3
16	Stephan ANDERSEN	DEN	G	15		
17	Shaun BARTLETT	RSA	A	6	(10)	1
10	Darren BENT		A	36		18
6	Marcus BENT		A	12	(1)	2
38	Jay BOTHROYD		A	3	(15)	2
15	Talal EL-KARKOURI	MAR	M	4	(6)	
9	Jason EUELL		M	5	(5)	1
24	Jonathan FORTUNE		D	7	(4)	
8	Matt HOLLAND	IRL	M	20	(3)	1
3	Hermann HREIDARSSON	ISL	D	34		
20	Bryan HUGHES		M	22	(11)	3
21	Jonatan JOHANSSON	FIN	A	1	(3)	
1	Dean KIELY	IRL	G	3		
7	Radostin KISHISHEV	BUL	M	34	(3)	
12	Kevin LISBIE		A		(6)	
13	Danny MURPHY		M	17	(1)	4

36	Thomas MYHRE	NOR	G	20		
5	Chris PERRY		D	27	(1)	1
12	Chris POWELL		D	25	(2)	
19	Dennis ROMMEDAHL	DEN	M	19	(2)	2
29	Lloyd SAM		M		(2)	
28	Osei SANKOFA		D	3	(1)	
25	Aleksei SMERTIN	RUS	M	18		
4	Gonzalo SORONDO	URU	D	7		
23	Jonathan SPECTOR	USA	D	13	(7)	
14	Jerome THOMAS		M	16	(9)	1
2	Luke YOUNG		D	32		1

CHELSEA
Manager – José Mourinho (POR)

2005
14/8	Wigan Athletic	a	1-0	Crespo
21/8	Arsenal	h	1-0	Drogba
24/8	West Bromwich Albion	h	4-0	Lampard 2, Cole J., Drogba
27/8	Tottenham Hotspur	a	2-0	Del Horno, Duff
10/9	Sunderland	h	2-0	Geremi, Drogba
17/9	Charlton Athletic	a	2-0	Crespo, Robben
24/9	Aston Villa	h	2-1	Lampard 2 (1p)
2/10	Liverpool	a	4-1	Lampard (p), Duff, Cole J., Geremi
15/10	Bolton Wanderers	h	5-1	Drogba 2, Lampard 2, Gudjohnsen
23/10	Everton	a	1-1	Lampard
29/10	Blackburn Rovers	h	4-2	Drogba, Lampard 2 (1p), Cole J.
6/11	Manchester United	a	0-1	
19/11	Newcastle United	h	3-0	Cole J., Crespo, Duff
26/11	Portsmouth	h	2-0	Crespo, Lampard (p)
3/12	Middlesbrough	h	1-0	Terry
10/12	Wigan Athletic	h	1-0	Terry
18/12	Arsenal	a	2-0	Robben, Cole J.
26/12	Fulham	h	3-2	Gallas, Lampard, Crespo
28/12	Manchester City	a	1-0	Cole J.
31/12	Birmingham City	h	2-0	Crespo, Robben

2006
2/1	West Ham United	a	3-1	Lampard, Crespo, Drogba
15/1	Sunderland	a	2-1	Crespo, Robben
22/1	Charlton Athletic	h	1-1	Gudjohnsen
1/2	Aston Villa	a	1-1	Robben
5/2	Liverpool	h	2-0	Gallas, Crespo
11/2	Middlesbrough	a	0-3	
25/2	Portsmouth	h	2-0	Lampard, Robben
4/3	West Bromwich Albion	a	2-1	Drogba, Cole J.
11/3	Tottenham Hotspur	h	2-1	Essien, Gallas
19/3	Fulham	a	0-1	
25/3	Manchester City	h	2-0	Drogba 2
1/4	Birmingham City	a	0-0	
9/4	West Ham United	h	4-1	Drogba, Crespo, Terry, Gallas
15/4	Bolton Wanderers	a	2-0	Terry, Lampard
17/4	Everton	h	3-0	Lampard, Drogba, Essien
29/4	Manchester United	h	3-0	Gallas, Cole J., Ricardo Carvalho
2/5	Blackburn Rovers	a	0-1	
7/5	Newcastle United	a	0-1	

No	Name	Nat	Pos	Aps	(s)	Gls
1	Petr CECH	CZE	G	34		
12	Carlton COLE		A		(9)	
10	Joe COLE		M	26	(8)	8
9	Hernán CRESPO	ARG	A	20	(10)	10
23	Carlo CUDICINI	ITA	G	3	(1)	
3	Asier DEL HORNO	ESP	D	25		1

England

No	Name	Nat	Pos	Aps	(s)	Gls
19	Lassana DIARRA	FRA	M	2	(1)	
15	Didier DROGBA	CIV	A	20	(9)	12
11	Damien DUFF	IRL	M	18	(10)	3
5	Michael ESSIEN	GHA	M	27	(4)	2
13	William GALLAS	FRA	D	33	(1)	5
14	GEREMI Njitap	CMR	M	8	(7)	2
22	Eidur GUDJOHNSEN	ISL	M	16	(10)	2
29	Robert HUTH	GER	D	7	(6)	
2	Glen JOHNSON		D	4		
8	Frank LAMPARD		M	35		16
4	Claude MAKELELE	FRA	M	29	(2)	
7	MANICHE	POR	M	3	(5)	
20	PAULO FERREIRA	POR	D	18	(3)	
40	Lenny PIDGELEY		G	1		
6	RICARDO CARVALHO	POR	D	22	(2)	1
16	Arjen ROBBEN	HOL	M	21	(7)	6
46	Jimmy SMITH		M		(1)	
26	John TERRY		D	36		4
24	Shaun WRIGHT-PHILLIPS		M	10	(17)	

EVERTON
Manager – David Moyes (SCO)

2005
13/8	Manchester United	h	0-2	
21/8	Bolton Wanderers	a	1-0	Bent
27/8	Fulham	a	0-1	
10/9	Portsmouth	h	0-1	
19/9	Arsenal	a	0-2	
24/9	Wigan Athletic	h	0-1	
2/10	Manchester City	a	0-2	
15/10	Tottenham Hotspur	a	0-2	
23/10	Chelsea	h	1-1	Beattie (p)
29/10	Birmingham City	a	1-0	Davies
6/11	Middlesbrough	h	1-0	Beattie
19/11	West Bromwich Albion	a	0-4	
27/11	Newcastle United	h	1-0	Yobo
3/12	Blackburn Rovers	a	2-0	McFadden, Arteta
11/12	Manchester United	a	1-1	McFadden
14/12	West Ham United	h	1-2	Beattie
17/12	Bolton Wanderers	h	0-4	
26/12	Aston Villa	a	0-4	
28/12	Liverpool	h	1-3	Beattie
31/12	Sunderland	a	1-0	Cahill

2006
2/1	Charlton Athletic	h	3-1	Beattie, Cahill 2
14/1	Portsmouth	a	1-0	Osman
21/1	Arsenal	h	1-0	Beattie
31/1	Wigan Athletic	a	1-1	og (Thompson)
4/2	Manchester City	h	1-0	Weir
11/2	Blackburn Rovers	h	1-0	Beattie
25/2	Newcastle United	a	0-2	
4/3	West Ham United	a	2-2	Osman, Beattie
11/3	Fulham	h	3-1	Beattie 2 (1p), McFadden
18/3	Aston Villa	h	4-1	McFadden, Cahill 2, Osman
25/3	Liverpool	a	1-3	Cahill
1/4	Sunderland	h	2-2	Osman, McFadden
8/4	Charlton Athletic	a	0-0	
15/4	Tottenham Hotspur	h	0-1	
17/4	Chelsea	a	0-3	
22/4	Birmingham City	h	0-0	
29/4	Middlesbrough	a	1-0	McFadden
7/5	West Bromwich Albion	h	2-2	Anichebe, Ferguson

No	Name	Nat	Pos	Aps	(s)	Gls
38	Victor ANICHEBE	NGA	A		(2)	1
6	Mikel ARTETA	ESP	M	27	(2)	1
8	James BEATTIE		A	29	(3)	10
7	Marcus BENT		A	7	(11)	1
17	Tim CAHILL	AUS	M	32		6
16	Lee CARSLEY	IRL	M	3	(2)	
10	Simon DAVIES	WAL	M	22	(8)	1
20	Matteo FERRARI	ITA	D	6	(2)	
9	Duncan FERGUSON	SCO	A	7	(20)	1
22	Tony HIBBERT		D	29		
14	Kevin KILBANE	IRL	M	21	(13)	
2	Per KRØLDRUP	DEN	D	1		
11	James McFADDEN	SCO	A	24	(8)	6
25	Nigel MARTYN		G	20		
3	Gary NAYSMITH	SCO	D	7		
18	Phil NEVILLE		M	34		
19	NUNO VALENTE	POR	D	20		
21	Leon OSMAN		M	28	(7)	4
23	Alessandro PISTONE	ITA	D	2		
30	John RUDDY		G		(1)	
15	Alan STUBBS		D	13	(1)	
13	Iain TURNER	SCO	G	2	(1)	
27	Andy VAN DER MEYDE	HOL	M	7	(3)	
29	James VAUGHAN		A		(1)	
5	David WEIR	SCO	D	32	(1)	1
26	Sander WESTERVELD	HOL	G	2		
1	Richard WRIGHT		G	14	(1)	
4	Joseph YOBO	NGA	D	29		1

FULHAM
Manager – Chris Coleman (WAL)

2005
13/8	Birmingham City	h	0-0	
20/8	Blackburn Rovers	a	1-2	McBride
24/8	Arsenal	a	1-4	Jensen C.
27/8	Everton	h	1-0	McBride
10/9	Newcastle United	a	1-1	McBride
17/9	West Ham United	h	1-2	Boa Morte
26/9	Tottenham Hotspur	a	0-1	
1/10	Manchester United	h	2-3	John, Jensen C.
17/10	Charlton Athletic	a	1-1	John
22/10	Liverpool	h	2-0	John, Boa Morte
29/10	Wigan Athletic	a	0-1	
5/11	Manchester City	h	2-1	Malbranque 2
20/11	Middlesbrough	a	2-3	John, Diop
27/11	Bolton Wanderers	h	2-1	McBride 2
3/12	West Bromwich Albion	a	0-0	
10/12	Birmingham City	a	0-1	
17/12	Blackburn Rovers	h	2-1	Diop, Boa Morte
26/12	Chelsea	a	2-3	McBride, Helguson (p)
28/12	Aston Villa	h	3-3	McBride 2, Helguson (p)
31/12	Portsmouth	a	0-1	

2006
2/1	Sunderland	h	2-1	John 2
14/1	Newcastle United	h	1-0	Malbranque
23/1	West Ham United	a	1-2	Helguson
31/1	Tottenham Hotspur	h	1-0	Bocanegra
4/2	Manchester United	a	2-4	McBride, Helguson
11/2	West Bromwich Albion	h	6-1	Helguson 2, Radzinski, og (Davies), John 2
26/2	Bolton Wanderers	a	1-2	Helguson
4/3	Arsenal	h	0-4	
11/3	Everton	a	1-3	John (p)
15/3	Liverpool	a	1-5	John
19/3	Chelsea	h	1-0	Boa Morte
25/3	Aston Villa	a	0-0	
1/4	Portsmouth	h	1-3	Malbranque
15/4	Charlton Athletic	a	2-1	Boa Morte 2

England

24/4	Wigan Athletic	h	1-0	Malbranque
29/4	Manchester City	a	2-1	John, Malbranque
4/5	Sunderland	a	1-2	Radzinski
7/5	Middlesbrough	h	1-0	Helguson (p)

No	Name	Nat	Pos	Aps	(s)	Gls
11	Luís BOA MORTE	POR	A	35		6
3	Carlos BOCANEGRA	USA	D	20	(1)	1
31	Wayne BRIDGE		D	12		
9	Michael BROWN		M	6	(1)	
19	Philippe CHRISTANVAL	FRA	D	7	(7)	
1	Mark CROSSLEY	WAL	G	13		
14	Pape Bouba DIOP	SEN	M	21	(1)	2
27	Simon ELLIOTT	NZL	M	12		
18	Ahmad ELRICH	AUS	M	2	(2)	
24	Alain GOMA	FRA	D	13		
10	Heidar HELGUSON	ISL	A	15	(11)	8
8	Claus JENSEN	DEN	M	11		2
23	Niclas JENSEN	DEN	D	14	(2)	
15	Collins JOHN	HOL	A	16	(17)	11
6	Zat KNIGHT		D	29	(1)	
22	Dean LEACOCK		D	5		
5	Sylvain LEGWINSKI	FRA	M	10	(3)	
10	Brian McBRIDE	USA	A	34	(4)	9
4	Steed MALBRANQUE	FRA	M	32	(2)	6
29	Antti NIEMI	FIN	G	9		
35	Ian PEARCE		D	10		
7	Mark PEMBRIDGE	WAL	M	5		
13	Tomasz RADZINSKI	CAN	A	23	(10)	2
21	Zesh REHMAN		D	3		
17	Liam ROSENIOR		D	22	(2)	
2	Moritz VOLZ	GER	D	23		
30	Tony WARNER	TRI	G	16	(2)	

LIVERPOOL
Manager – Rafael Benítez (ESP)

2005

13/8	Middlesbrough	a	0-0	
20/8	Sunderland	h	1-0	Xabi Alonso
10/9	Tottenham Hotspur	a	0-0	
18/9	Manchester United	h	0-0	
24/9	Birmingham City	a	2-2	Luis García, Cissé (p)
2/10	Chelsea	h	1-4	Gerrard
15/10	Blackburn Rovers	h	1-0	Cissé
22/10	Fulham	a	0-2	
29/10	West Ham United	h	2-0	Xabi Alonso, Zenden
5/11	Aston Villa	a	2-0	Gerrard (p), Xabi Alonso
19/11	Portsmouth	h	3-0	Zenden, Cissé, Morientes
26/11	Manchester City	a	1-0	Riise
30/11	Sunderland	a	2-0	Luis García, Gerrard
3/12	Wigan Athletic	h	3-0	Crouch 2, Luis García
10/12	Middlesbrough	h	2-0	Morientes 2
26/12	Newcastle United	h	2-0	Gerrard, og (Given)
28/12	Everton	a	3-1	Crouch, Gerrard, Cissé
31/12	West Bromwich Albion	h	1-0	Crouch

2006

2/1	Bolton Wanderers	a	2-2	Gerrard (p), Luis García
14/1	Tottenham Hotspur	h	1-0	Kewell
22/1	Manchester United	a	0-1	
1/2	Birmingham City	h	1-1	Gerrard
5/2	Chelsea	a	0-2	
8/2	Charlton Athletic	a	0-2	
11/2	Wigan Athletic	a	1-0	Hyypiä
14/2	Arsenal	h	1-0	Luis García
26/2	Manchester City	h	1-0	Kewell
4/3	Charlton Athletic	h	0-0	
12/3	Arsenal	a	1-2	Luis García
15/3	Fulham	h	5-1	Fowler, og (Brown), Morientes, Crouch, Warnock
19/3	Newcastle United	a	3-1	Crouch, Gerrard, Cissé (p)
25/3	Everton	h	3-1	og (Neville), Luis García, Kewell
1/4	West Bromwich Albion	a	2-0	Fowler, Cissé
9/4	Bolton Wanderers	h	1-0	Fowler
16/4	Blackburn Rovers	a	1-0	Fowler
26/4	West Ham United	a	2-1	Cissé 2
29/4	Aston Villa	h	3-1	Morientes, Gerrard 2
7/5	Portsmouth	a	3-1	Fowler, Crouch, Cissé

No	Name	Nat	Pos	Aps	(s)	Gls
5	Daniel AGGER	DEN	D	4		
5	Milan BAROS	CZE	A		(2)	
23	Jamie CARRAGHER		D	36		
9	Djibril CISSE	FRA	A	19	(14)	9
15	Peter CROUCH		A	27	(5)	7
1	Jerzy DUDEK	POL	G	5	(1)	
3	Steve FINNAN	IRL	D	33		
11	Robbie FOWLER		A	9	(5)	5
8	Steven GERRARD		M	32		10
16	Dietmar HAMANN	GER	M	13	(4)	
4	Sami HYYPIÄ	FIN	D	35	(1)	1
17	JOSEMI	ESP	D	3	(3)	
7	Harry KEWELL	AUS	M	22	(4)	3
2	Jan KROMKAMP	HOL	D	6	(7)	
10	LUIS GARCÍA	ESP	M	15	(15)	7
19	Fernando MORIENTES	ESP	A	20	(8)	5
25	José Manuel REINA	ESP	G	33		
6	John Arne RIISE	NOR	M	24	(8)	1
24	Florent SINAMA-PONGOLLE	FRA	A	3	(4)	
22	Momo SISSOKO	MLI	M	21	(5)	
21	Djimi TRAORE	MLI	D	9	(6)	
28	Stephen WARNOCK		D	15	(5)	1
14	XABI ALONSO	ESP	M	29	(6)	3
30	Boudewijn ZENDEN	HOL	M	5	(2)	2

MANCHESTER CITY
Manager – Stuart Pearce

2005

13/8	West Bromwich Albion	h	0-0	
20/8	Birmingham City	a	2-1	Barton, Cole
23/8	Sunderland	a	2-1	Vassell, Sinclair
27/8	Portsmouth	h	2-1	Reyna, Cole
10/9	Manchester United	a	1-1	Barton
18/9	Bolton Wanderers	h	0-1	
24/9	Newcastle United	a	0-1	
2/10	Everton	h	2-0	Mills D., Vassell
16/10	West Ham United	a	2-1	Cole 2
22/10	Arsenal	a	0-1	
31/10	Aston Villa	h	3-1	Vassell 2, Cole
5/11	Fulham	a	1-2	Croft
19/11	Blackburn Rovers	h	0-0	
26/11	Liverpool	h	0-1	
4/12	Charlton Athletic	a	5-2	Cole 2, Sinclair, Barton, Vassell
10/12	West Bromwich Albion	a	0-2	
17/12	Birmingham City	h	4-1	Sommeil, Barton (p), Sibierski, Wright-Phillips
26/12	Wigan Athletic	a	3-4	Sibierski, Barton, Cole
28/12	Chelsea	h	0-1	
31/12	Middlesbrough	a	0-0	

2006

4/1	Tottenham Hotspur	h	0-2	

England

Date	Opponent	H/A	Score	Scorers
14/1	Manchester United	h	3-1	Sinclair, Vassell, Fowler
21/1	Bolton Wanderers	a	0-2	
1/2	Newcastle United	h	3-0	Riera, Cole, Vassell
4/2	Everton	a	0-1	
12/2	Charlton Athletic	h	3-2	Dunne, Samaras, Barton
26/2	Liverpool	a	0-1	
5/3	Sunderland	h	2-1	Samaras 2
11/3	Portsmouth	a	1-2	Dunne
18/3	Wigan Athletic	h	0-1	
25/3	Chelsea	a	0-2	
2/4	Middlesbrough	h	0-1	
8/4	Tottenham Hotspur	a	1-2	Samaras
15/4	West Ham United	a	0-1	
25/4	Aston Villa	a	1-0	Vassell
29/4	Fulham	h	1-2	Dunne
4/5	Arsenal	h	1-3	Sommeil
7/5	Blackburn Rovers	a	0-2	

No	Name	Nat	Pos	Aps	(s)	Gls
8	Joey BARTON		M	31		6
9	Andrew COLE		A	20	(2)	9
40	Lee CROFT		M	4	(17)	1
5	Sylvain DISTIN	FRA	D	31		
22	Richard DUNNE	IRL	D	31	(1)	3
44	Willo FLOOD	IRL	M	1	(4)	
7	Robbie FOWLER		A		(4)	1
38	Stephen IRELAND	IRL	M	13	(11)	
1	David JAMES		G	38		
41	Stephen JORDAN		D	18		
43	Ishmael MILLER		A		(1)	
18	Danny MILLS		D	18		1
26	Matthew MILLS		D		(1)	
14	Kiki MUSAMPA	HOL	M	24	(3)	
16	Nedum ONUOHA		D	8	(2)	
6	Claudio REYNA	USA	M	22		1
45	Micah RICHARDS		D	11	(1)	
19	Alberto RIERA	ESP	M	12	(3)	1
20	Giorgos SAMARAS	GRE	A	10	(4)	4
10	Antoine SIBIERSKI	FRA	M	12	(12)	2
28	Trevor SINCLAIR		M	29	(2)	3
2	David SOMMEIL	FRA	D	14	(2)	2
17	SUN Jihai	CHN	D	16	(13)	
3	Ben THATCHER	WAL	D	18		
11	Darius VASSELL		A	36		8
42	Bradley WRIGHT-PHILLIPS		M	1	(16)	1

MANCHESTER UNITED
Manager – Sir Alex Ferguson (SCO)

2005

Date	Opponent	H/A	Score	Scorers
13/8	Everton	a	2-0	Van Nistelrooy, Rooney
20/8	Aston Villa	h	1-0	Van Nistelrooy
28/8	Newcastle United	a	2-0	Rooney, Van Nistelrooy
10/9	Manchester City	h	1-1	Van Nistelrooy
18/9	Liverpool	a	0-0	
24/9	Blackburn Rovers	h	1-2	Van Nistelrooy
1/10	Fulham	a	3-2	Van Nistelrooy 2 (1p), Rooney
15/10	Sunderland	h	3-1	Rooney, Van Nistelrooy, Rossi
22/10	Tottenham Hotspur	h	1-1	Silvestre
29/10	Middlesbrough	a	1-4	Cristiano Ronaldo
6/11	Chelsea	h	1-0	Fletcher
19/11	Charlton Athletic	a	3-1	Smith, Van Nistelrooy 2
27/11	West Ham United	h	2-1	Rooney, O'Shea
3/12	Portsmouth	h	3-0	Scholes, Rooney, Van Nistelrooy
11/12	Everton	h	1-1	Giggs
14/12	Wigan Athletic	h	4-0	Ferdinand, Rooney 2, Van Nistelrooy (p)
17/12	Aston Villa	a	2-0	Van Nistelrooy, Rooney
26/12	West Bromwich Albion	h	3-0	Scholes, Ferdinand, Van Nistelrooy
28/12	Birmingham City	a	2-2	Van Nistelrooy, Rooney
31/12	Bolton Wanderers	h	4-1	og (Ngotty), Saha, Cristiano Ronaldo 2

2006

Date	Opponent	H/A	Score	Scorers
3/1	Arsenal	a	0-0	
14/1	Manchester City	a	1-3	Van Nistelrooy
22/1	Liverpool	h	1-0	Ferdinand
1/2	Blackburn Rovers	a	3-4	Saha, Van Nistelrooy 2
4/2	Fulham	h	4-2	Park, Cristiano Ronaldo 2, Saha
11/2	Portsmouth	a	3-1	Van Nistelrooy, Cristiano Ronaldo 2
6/3	Wigan Athletic	a	2-1	Cristiano Ronaldo, og (Chimbonda)
12/3	Newcastle United	h	2-0	Rooney 2
18/3	West Bromwich Albion	a	2-1	Saha 2
26/3	Birmingham City	h	3-0	og (Taylor Maik), Giggs, Rooney
29/3	West Ham United	h	1-0	Van Nistelrooy
1/4	Bolton Wanderers	a	2-1	Saha, Van Nistelrooy
9/4	Arsenal	h	2-0	Rooney, Park
14/4	Sunderland	h	0-0	
17/4	Tottenham Hotspur	a	2-1	Rooney 2
29/4	Chelsea	a	0-3	
1/5	Middlesbrough	h	0-0	
7/5	Charlton Athletic	h	4-0	Saha, Cristiano Ronaldo, og (Euell), Richardson

No	Name	Nat	Pos	Aps	(s)	Gls
26	Phil BARDSLEY		D	3	(5)	
6	Wes BROWN		D	17	(2)	
7	CRISTIANO RONALDO	POR	M	24	(9)	9
3	Patrice EVRA	FRA	D	7	(4)	
5	Rio FERDINAND		D	37		3
24	Darren FLETCHER	SCO	M	23	(4)	1
11	Ryan GIGGS	WAL	M	22	(5)	2
4	Gabriel HEINZE	ARG	D	2	(2)	
1	Tim HOWARD	USA	G		(1)	
16	Roy KEANE	IRL	M	4	(1)	
17	Liam MILLER		M		(1)	
2	Gary NEVILLE		D	24	(1)	
22	John O'SHEA	IRL	D	34		1
13	PARK Ji-sung	KOR	M	23	(11)	2
28	Gerard PIQUÉ	ESP	D	1	(2)	
23	Kieron RICHARDSON		M	12	(10)	1
8	Wayne ROONEY		A	34	(2)	16
42	Giuseppe ROSSI	ITA	A	1	(4)	1
9	Louis SAHA	FRA	A	12	(7)	7
18	Paul SCHOLES		M	18	(2)	2
27	Mikaël SILVESTRE	FRA	D	30	(3)	1
14	Alan SMITH		M	15	(6)	1
20	Ole Gunnar SOLSKJAER	NOR	A		(3)	
19	Edwin VAN DER SAR	HOL	G	38		
10	Ruud VAN NISTELROOY	HOL	A	28	(7)	21
15	Nemanja VIDIC	SCG	D	9	(2)	

MIDDLESBROUGH
Manager – Steve McClaren

2005

Date	Opponent	H/A	Score
13/8	Liverpool	h	0-0

England

20/8	Tottenham Hotspur	a	0-2		
23/8	Birmingham City	a	3-0	Viduka 2, Queudrue	
28/8	Charlton Athletic	h	0-3		
10/9	Arsenal	h	2-1	Yakubu, Maccarone	
18/9	Wigan Athletic	a	1-1	Yakubu	
25/9	Sunderland	h	0-2		
2/10	Aston Villa	a	3-2	Yakubu 2 (1p), Boateng	
15/10	Portsmouth	h	1-1	Yakubu	
23/10	West Ham United	a	1-2	Queudrue	
29/10	Manchester United	h	4-1	Mendieta 2, Hasselbaink, Yakubu (p)	
6/11	Everton	a	0-1		
20/11	Fulham	h	3-2	Morrison, Yakubu, Hasselbaink	
27/11	West Bromwich Albion	h	2-2	Viduka, Yakubu (p)	
3/12	Chelsea	a	0-1		
10/12	Liverpool	a	0-2		
18/12	Tottenham Hotspur	h	3-3	Yakubu 2, Queudrue	
26/12	Blackburn Rovers	h	0-2		
31/12	Manchester City	h	0-0		
2006					
2/1	Newcastle United	a	2-2	Yakubu, Hasselbaink	
14/1	Arsenal	a	0-7		
21/1	Wigan Athletic	h	2-3	Hasselbaink, Yakubu	
31/1	Sunderland	a	3-0	Pogatetz, Parnaby, Hasselbaink	
4/2	Aston Villa	h	0-4		
11/2	Chelsea	h	3-0	Rochemback, Downing, Yakubu	
26/2	West Bromwich Albion	a	2-0	Hasselbaink 2	
4/3	Birmingham City	h	1-0	Viduka	
12/3	Charlton Athletic	a	1-2	Viduka	
18/3	Blackburn Rovers	a	2-3	Viduka, Rochemback	
26/3	Bolton Wanderers	h	4-3	Hasselbaink 2 (1p), Viduka, Parnaby	
2/4	Manchester City	a	1-0	Cattermole	
9/4	Newcastle United	h	1-2	Boateng	
15/4	Portsmouth	a	0-1		
17/4	West Ham United	h	2-0	Hasselbaink, Maccarone (p)	
29/4	Everton	h	0-1		
1/5	Manchester United	a	0-0		
3/5	Bolton Wanderers	a	1-1	Johnson	
7/5	Fulham	a	0-1		

No	Name	Nat	Pos	Aps	(s)	Gls
2	ABEL XAVIER	POR	D	4		
26	Matthew BATES		D	12	(4)	
7	George BOATENG	HOL	M	25	(1)	2
39	Lee CATTERMOLE		M	10	(4)	1
11	Malcolm CHRISTIE		A	3	(3)	
23	Colin COOPER		D		(1)	
42	Tom CRADDOCK		M		(1)	
24	Andrew DAVIES		D	4	(8)	
17	DORIVA	BRA	M	19	(8)	
19	Stewart DOWNING		M	11	(1)	1
4	Ugo EHIOGU		D	16	(2)	
30	Danny GRAHAM		A	1	(2)	
9	Jimmy Floyd HASSELBAINK	HOL	A	12	(10)	10
16	Joseph-Desiré JOB	CMR	A		(1)	
37	Adam JOHNSON		M	8	(5)	1
22	Brad JONES	AUS	G	9		
34	Jason KENNEDY		A	1	(2)	
18	Massimo MACCARONE	ITA	A	6	(11)	2
29	Tony McMAHON		D	3		
14	Gaizka MENDIETA	ESP	M	15	(2)	2
25	James MORRISON		M	21	(3)	1
8	Szilárd NÉMETH	SVK	A	1	(4)	
15	Ray PARLOUR		M	11	(2)	
21	Stuart PARNABY		D	19	(1)	2
12	Emanuel POGATETZ	AUT	D	21	(3)	1
3	Franck QUEUDRUE	FRA	D	26	(3)	3
2	Michael REIZIGER	HOL	D	4		
5	Chris RIGGOTT		D	22		
10	Fábio ROCHEMBACK	BRA	M	22		2
1	Mark SCHWARZER	AUS	G	27		
6	Gareth SOUTHGATE		D	24		
33	Andrew TAYLOR		D	7	(6)	
27	Ross TURNBULL		G	2		
36	Mark VIDUKA	AUS	A	19	(8)	7
41	Josh WALKER		M		(1)	
31	David WHEATER		D	4	(2)	
20	YAKUBU Aiyegbeni	NGA	A	29	(5)	13

NEWCASTLE UNITED
Manager – Graeme Souness (SCO); (2/2/06) (Glenn Roeder)

2005					
14/8	Arsenal	a	0-2		
20/8	West Ham United	h	0-0		
24/8	Bolton Wanderers	a	0-2		
28/8	Manchester United	h	0-2		
10/9	Fulham	h	1-1	N'Zogbia	
18/9	Blackburn Rovers	a	3-0	Shearer, Owen, N'Zogbia	
24/9	Manchester City	h	1-0	Owen	
1/10	Portsmouth	a	0-0		
15/10	Wigan Athletic	a	0-1		
23/10	Sunderland	h	3-2	Ameobi, og (Caldwell), Emre	
30/10	West Bromwich Albion	a	3-0	Owen 2, Shearer	
5/11	Birmingham City	h	1-0	Emre	
19/11	Chelsea	a	0-3		
27/11	Everton	a	0-1		
3/12	Aston Villa	h	1-1	Shearer (p)	
10/12	Arsenal	h	1-0	Solano	
17/12	West Ham United	a	4-2	Owen 3, Shearer	
26/12	Liverpool	h	0-2		
31/12	Tottenham Hotspur	a	0-2		
2006					
2/1	Middlesbrough	h	2-2	Solano, Clark	
14/1	Fulham	a	0-1		
21/1	Blackburn Rovers	h	0-1		
1/2	Manchester City	a	0-3		
4/2	Portsmouth	h	2-0	N'Zogbia, Shearer	
11/2	Aston Villa	a	2-1	Ameobi, N'Zogbia	
22/2	Charlton Athletic	h	0-0		
25/2	Everton	a	2-0	Solano 2	
4/3	Bolton Wanderers	h	3-1	Solano, Shearer, Ameobi	
12/3	Manchester United	a	0-2		
19/3	Liverpool	h	1-3	Ameobi	
26/3	Charlton Athletic	a	1-3	Parker	
1/4	Tottenham Hotspur	h	3-1	Bowyer, Ameobi, Shearer (p)	
9/4	Middlesbrough	a	2-1	og (Boateng), Ameobi	
15/4	Wigan Athletic	h	3-1	Shearer 2 (1p), Bramble	
17/4	Sunderland	a	4-1	Chopra, Shearer (p), N'Zogbia, Luque	
22/4	West Bromwich Albion	h	3-0	Solano, Ameobi 2 (1p)	
29/4	Birmingham City	a	0-0		
7/5	Chelsea	h	1-0	Bramble	

No	Name	Nat	Pos	Aps	(s)	Gls
23	Shola AMEOBI		A	25	(5)	8
33	Celestine BABAYARO	NGA	D	26	(2)	
6	Jean-Alain BOUMSONG	FRA	D	30	(3)	

England

No	Name	Nat	Pos	Aps	(s)	Gls
11	Lee BOWYER		M	18	(10)	1
19	Titus BRAMBLE		D	21	(3)	2
2	Stephen CARR	IRL	D	19		
28	Michael CHOPRA		A	6	(7)	1
21	Lee CLARK		M	8	(14)	1
8	Kieron DYER		M	4	(7)	
3	Robbie ELLIOTT		D	14	(3)	
5	EMRE Belözoglu	TUR	M	19	(1)	2
15	Amdy FAYE	SEN	M	14	(8)	
1	Shay GIVEN	IRL	G	38		
7	Jermaine JENAS		M	3	(1)	
20	Albert LUQUE	ESP	A	6	(8)	1
16	James MILNER		M	1	(2)	
18	Craig MOORE	AUS	D	8		
14	Charles N'ZOGBIA	FRA	M	27	(5)	5
37	Alan O'BRIEN	IRL	M		(3)	
10	Michael OWEN		A	10	(1)	7
17	Scott PARKER		M	26		1
35	Matthew PATTISON	RSA	M	2	(1)	
26	Peter RAMAGE		D	23		
9	Alan SHEARER		A	31	(1)	10
4	Nolberto SOLANO	PER	M	27	(2)	6
27	Steven TAYLOR		D	12		

PORTSMOUTH
Manager – Alain Perrin (FRA); (24/11/05) (Joe Jordan); (7/12/05) Harry Redknapp

2005

Date	Opponent		Score	Scorers
13/8	Tottenham Hotspur	h	0-2	
20/8	West Bromwich Albion	a	1-2	Robert
23/8	Aston Villa	h	1-1	LuaLua
27/8	Manchester City	a	1-2	Viafara
10/9	Everton	a	1-0	og (Ferguson)
17/9	Birmingham City	h	1-1	LuaLua
24/9	Bolton Wanderers	a	0-1	
1/10	Newcastle United	h	0-0	
15/10	Middlesbrough	a	1-1	O'Neil
22/10	Charlton Athletic	h	1-2	Darío Silva
29/10	Sunderland	a	4-1	Vukic, Taylor 2, Darío Silva
5/11	Wigan Athletic	h	0-2	
19/11	Liverpool	a	0-3	
26/11	Chelsea	h	0-2	
3/12	Manchester United	a	0-3	
12/12	Tottenham Hotspur	a	1-3	LuaLua
17/12	West Bromwich Albion	h	1-0	Todorov
26/12	West Ham United	h	1-1	O'Neil
28/12	Arsenal	a	0-4	
31/12	Fulham	h	1-0	O'Neil

2006

Date	Opponent		Score	Scorers
2/1	Blackburn Rovers	a	1-2	Taylor
14/1	Everton	h	0-1	
21/1	Birmingham City	a	0-5	
1/2	Bolton Wanderers	h	1-1	Karadas
4/2	Newcastle United	a	0-2	
11/2	Manchester United	h	1-3	Taylor
25/2	Chelsea	a	0-2	
4/3	Aston Villa	a	0-1	
11/3	Manchester City	h	2-1	Pedro Mendes 2
18/3	West Ham United	a	4-2	LuaLua, Davis, Pedro Mendes, Todorov
1/4	Fulham	a	3-1	O'Neil 2, LuaLua
8/4	Blackburn Rovers	h	2-2	LuaLua, Todorov
12/4	Arsenal	h	1-1	LuaLua
15/4	Middlesbrough	h	1-0	O'Neil
17/4	Charlton Athletic	a	1-2	D'Alessandro
22/4	Sunderland	h	2-1	Todorov, Taylor (p)
29/4	Wigan Athletic	a	2-1	Benjani, Taylor (p)
7/5	Liverpool	h	1-3	Koroman

No	Name	Nat	Pos	Aps	(s)	Gls
15	Jamie ASHDOWN		G	17		
25	BENJANI Mwaruwari	ZIM	A	16		1
18	Aliou CISSE	SEN	M	2	(1)	
4	Andrés D'ALESSANDRO	ARG	M	13		1
31	DARÍO SILVA	URU	A	13		2
28	Sean DAVIS		M	16	(1)	1
40	Salif DIAO	SEN	M	7	(4)	
16	Andy GRIFFIN		D	20	(2)	
22	Richard HUGHES	SCO	M	21	(5)	
8	Azar KARADAS	NOR	A	4	(13)	1
33	Dean KIELY	IRL	G	15		
20	Ognjen KOROMAN	SCG	M	1	(1)	1
32	Lomana Trésor LUALUA	DRC	A	24	(1)	7
19	Collins MBESUMA	ZAM			(4)	
10	Ivica MORNAR	CRO	A	1	(1)	
5	Andy O'BRIEN	IRL	D	29		
26	Gary O'NEIL		M	36		6
23	Emmanuel OLISADEBE	POL	A		(2)	
11	Noé PAMAROT	FRA	D	4	(4)	
30	PEDRO MENDES	POR	M	14		3
17	Vincent PERICARD	FRA	A	3	(3)	
2	Linvoy PRIMUS		D	20		
6	Brian PRISKE	DEN	D	26	(4)	
11	Laurent ROBERT	FRA	M	13	(4)	1
24	Wayne ROUTLEDGE		M	3	(10)	
20	Giannis SKOPELITIS	GRE	M		(5)	
21	Frank SONGO'O		M		(2)	
3	Dejan STEFANOVIC	SCG	D	27	(1)	
14	Matthew TAYLOR		M	32	(2)	6
9	Svetoslav TODOROV	BUL	A	6	(19)	4
4	John VIAFARA	COL	M	10	(4)	1
7	Grégory VIGNAL	FRA	D	13	(1)	
38	Zvonimir VUKIC	SCG	M	6	(3)	1
1	Sander WESTERVELD	HOL	G	6		

SUNDERLAND
Manager – Mick McCarthy (IRL); (6/3/05) (Kevin Ball)

2005

Date	Opponent		Score	Scorers
13/8	Charlton Athletic	h	1-3	Gray
20/8	Liverpool	a	0-1	
23/8	Manchester City	a	1-2	Le Tallec
27/8	Wigan Athletic	a	0-1	
10/9	Chelsea	a	0-2	
17/9	West Bromwich Albion	h	1-1	Breen
25/9	Middlesbrough	a	2-0	Miller, Arca
1/10	West Ham United	h	1-1	Miller
15/10	Manchester United	h	1-3	Elliott
23/10	Newcastle United	a	2-3	Lawrence, Elliott
29/10	Portsmouth	h	1-4	Whitehead (p)
5/11	Arsenal	a	1-3	Stubbs
19/11	Aston Villa	h	1-3	Whitehead (p)
26/11	Birmingham City	a	0-1	
30/11	Liverpool	h	0-2	
3/12	Tottenham Hotspur	a	2-3	Whitehead, Le Tallec
10/12	Charlton Athletic	a	0-2	
26/12	Bolton Wanderers	h	0-0	
31/12	Everton	h	0-1	

2006

Date	Opponent		Score	Scorers
2/1	Fulham	a	1-2	Lawrence
15/1	Chelsea	h	1-2	Lawrence
21/1	West Bromwich Albion	a	1-0	og (Watson)

England

31/1	Middlesbrough	h	0-3	
4/2	West Ham United	a	0-2	
12/2	Tottenham Hotspur	h	1-1	Murphy
15/2	Blackburn Rovers	a	0-2	
25/2	Birmingham City	a	0-1	
5/3	Manchester City	a	1-2	Kyle
11/3	Wigan Athletic	h	0-1	
18/3	Bolton Wanderers	a	0-2	
25/3	Blackburn Rovers	h	0-1	
1/4	Everton	a	2-2	Stead, Delap
14/4	Manchester United	a	0-0	
17/4	Newcastle United	h	1-4	Hoyte
22/4	Portsmouth	a	1-2	Miller
1/5	Arsenal	h	0-3	
4/5	Fulham	h	2-1	Le Tallec, Brown
7/5	Aston Villa	a	1-2	Collins

No	Name	Nat	Pos	Aps	(s)	Gls
13	Ben ALNWICK		G	5		
33	Julio ARCA	ARG	M	22	(2)	1
31	Christian BASSILA	FRA	M	12	(1)	
5	Gary BREEN	IRL	D	33	(2)	1
20	Chris BROWN		A	10	(3)	1
6	Steven CALDWELL	SCO	D	23	(1)	
15	Danny COLLINS	WAL	D	22	(1)	1
1	Kelvin DAVIS		G	33		
4	Rory DELAP	IRL	M	5	(1)	1
10	Stephen ELLIOTT	IRL	A	11	(4)	2
18	Andy GRAY	SCO	A	13	(8)	1
32	Justin HOYTE		D	27		1
16	Kevin KYLE	SCO	A	9	(3)	1
7	Liam LAWRENCE		M	19	(10)	3
17	Anthony LE TALLEC	FRA	M	12	(15)	3
23	Grant LEADBITTER		M	8	(4)	
3	George McCARTNEY	NIR	D	13		
14	Tommy MILLER		M	27	(2)	3
26	Daryl MURPHY	IRL	A	5	(13)	1
12	Nyron NOSWORTHY		D	24	(6)	
4	Carl ROBINSON	WAL	M	3	(2)	
28	Dan SMITH		D	1	(2)	
9	Jonathan STEAD		A	21	(9)	1
22	Alan STUBBS		D	8	(2)	1
11	Andrew WELSH		M	12	(2)	
8	Dean WHITEHEAD		M	37		3
19	Martin WOODS		M	1	(6)	
2	Stephen WRIGHT		D	2		

TOTTENHAM HOTSPUR
Manager – Martin Jol (HOL)

2005

13/8	Portsmouth	a	2-0	og (Griffin), Defoe
20/8	Middlesbrough	h	2-0	Defoe, Mido
24/8	Blackburn Rovers	a	0-0	
27/8	Chelsea	h	0-2	
10/9	Liverpool	h	0-0	
17/9	Aston Villa	a	1-1	Keane
26/9	Fulham	h	1-0	Defoe
1/10	Charlton Athletic	a	3-2	King, Mido, Keane
15/10	Everton	h	2-0	Mido, Jenas
22/10	Manchester United	a	1-1	Jenas
29/10	Arsenal	h	1-1	King
7/11	Bolton Wanderers	a	0-1	
20/11	West Ham United	h	1-1	Mido
26/11	Wigan Athletic	a	2-1	Keane, Davids
3/12	Sunderland	h	3-2	Mido, Keane, Carrick
12/12	Portsmouth	h	3-1	King, Mido (p), Defoe
18/12	Middlesbrough	a	3-3	Keane, Jenas, Mido
26/12	Birmingham City	h	2-0	Keane (p), Defoe
28/12	West Bromwich Albion	a	0-2	
31/12	Newcastle United	h	2-0	Tainio, Mido

2006

4/1	Manchester City	a	2-0	Mido, Keane
14/1	Liverpool	a	0-1	
21/1	Aston Villa	h	0-0	
31/1	Fulham	a	0-1	
5/2	Charlton Athletic	h	3-1	Defoe 2, Jenas
12/2	Sunderland	a	1-1	Keane
19/2	Wigan Athletic	h	2-2	Mido, Defoe
5/3	Blackburn Rovers	h	3-2	Keane 2, Mido
11/3	Chelsea	a	1-2	Jenas
18/3	Birmingham City	a	2-0	Lennon, Keane
27/3	West Bromwich Albion	h	2-1	Keane 2 (1p)
1/4	Newcastle United	a	1-3	Keane
8/4	Manchester City	h	2-1	Stalteri, Carrick
15/4	Everton	a	1-0	Keane (p)
17/4	Manchester United	h	1-2	Jenas
22/4	Arsenal	a	1-1	Keane
30/4	Bolton Wanderers	h	1-0	Lennon
7/5	West Ham United	a	1-2	Defoe

No	Name	Nat	Pos	Aps	(s)	Gls
37	Lee BARNARD		A		(3)	
11	Michael BROWN		M	2	(7)	
23	Michael CARRICK		M	35		2
27	Callum DAVENPORT		D	1	(3)	
5	Edgar DAVIDS	HOL	M	28	(3)	1
20	Michael DAWSON		D	31	(1)	
18	Jermain DEFOE		A	23	(12)	9
14	Erik EDMAN	SWE	D	3		
30	Anthony GARDNER		D	16		
22	Tom HUDDLESTONE		D		(4)	
32	Johnnie JACKSON		M		(1)	
28	Jermaine JENAS		M	30		6
9	Frédéric KANOUTE	MLI	A		(1)	
10	Robbie KEANE	IRL	A	25	(11)	16
3	Stephen KELLY	IRL	D	9		
26	Ledley KING		D	26		3
16	LEE Young-pyo	KOR	D	31		
25	Aaron LENNON		M	21	(6)	2
15	Ahmed Hossam "MIDO"	EGY	A	24	(3)	11
8	Danny MURPHY		M	2	(8)	
2	Noureddine NAYBET	MAR	D	2	(1)	
17	Noé PAMAROT	FRA	D		(2)	
8	PEDRO MENDES	POR	M	3	(3)	
9	Grzegorz RASIAK	POL	A	4	(4)	
19	Andy REID	IRL	M	7	(6)	
1	Paul ROBINSON		G	38		
21	Wayne ROUTLEDGE		M	2	(1)	
7	Paul STALTERI	CAN	D	33		1
6	Teemu TAINIO	FIN	M	22	(2)	1

WEST BROMWICH ALBION
Manager – Bryan Robson

2005

13/8	Manchester City	a	0-0	
20/8	Portsmouth	h	2-1	Horsfield 2
24/8	Chelsea	a	0-4	
27/8	Birmingham City	h	2-3	Horsfield 2
10/9	Wigan Athletic	h	1-2	Greening
17/9	Sunderland	a	1-1	Gera

England

24/9	Charlton Athletic	h	1-2	Davies	
1/10	Blackburn Rovers	a	0-2		
15/10	Arsenal	h	2-1	Kanu, Carter	
23/10	Bolton Wanderers	a	0-2		
30/10	Newcastle United	h	0-3		
5/11	West Ham United	a	0-1		
19/11	Everton	h	4-0	Ellington 2 (1p), Clement, Earnshaw	
27/11	Middlesbrough	a	2-2	Ellington, Kanu	
3/12	Fulham	h	0-0		
10/12	Manchester City	h	2-0	Kamara, Campbell	
17/12	Portsmouth	a	0-1		
26/12	Manchester United	a	0-3		
28/12	Tottenham Hotspur	h	2-0	Kanu 2	
31/12	Liverpool	a	0-1		
2006					
2/1	Aston Villa	h	1-2	Watson	
15/1	Wigan Athletic	a	1-0	Albrechtsen	
21/1	Sunderland	h	0-1		
31/1	Charlton Athletic	a	0-0		
4/2	Blackburn Rovers	h	2-0	Campbell, Greening	
12/2	Fulham	a	1-6	Campbell	
26/2	Middlesbrough	h	0-2		
4/3	Chelsea	h	1-2	Kanu	
11/3	Birmingham City	a	1-1	Ellington	
18/3	Manchester United	h	1-2	Ellington	
27/3	Tottenham Hotspur	a	1-2	Davies	
1/4	Liverpool	h	0-2		
9/4	Aston Villa	a	0-0		
15/4	Arsenal	a	1-3	Quashie	
17/4	Bolton Wanderers	h	0-0		
22/4	Newcastle United	a	0-3		
1/5	West Ham United	h	0-1		
7/5	Everton	a	2-2	Gera, Martínez	

No	Name	Nat	Pos	Aps	(s)	Gls
14	Martin ALBRECHTSEN	DEN	D	26	(5)	1
21	Kevin CAMPBELL		A	19	(10)	3
17	Darren CARTER		M	11	(8)	1
12	Richard CHAPLOW		A	4	(3)	
6	Neil CLEMENT		D	29	(2)	1
19	Curtis DAVIES		D	33		2
23	Robert EARNSHAW	WAL	A	4	(8)	1
22	Nathan ELLINGTON		A	15	(16)	5
4	Thomas GAARDSØE	DEN	D	7		
11	Zoltán GERA	HUN	M	12	(3)	2
8	Jonathan GREENING		M	37	(1)	2
28	Jared HODGKISS		D		(1)	
9	Geoff HORSFIELD		A	10	(7)	4
1	Russell HOULT		G		(1)	
33	Junichi INAMOTO	JPN	M	16	(6)	
10	Andy JOHNSON	WAL	M	8		
15	Diomansy KAMARA	SEN	A	21	(5)	1
25	Nwankwo KANU	NGA	A	17	(8)	5
20	Chris KIRKLAND		G	10		
13	Jan KOZÁK	SVK	M	4	(2)	
29	Tomasz KUSZCZAK	POL	G	28		
5	Williams MARTÍNEZ	URU	D	1	(1)	
5	Darren MOORE		D	3	(1)	
31	Stuart NICHOLSON		A		(4)	
3	Paul ROBINSON		D	33		
7	Nigel QUASHIE	SCO	M	9		1
2	Riccardo SCIMECA		D	2		
24	Ronnie WALLWORK		M	31		
16	Steve WATSON		D	28	(2)	1

WEST HAM UNITED
Manager – Alan Pardew

2005					
13/8	Blackburn Rovers	h	3-1	Sheringham, Reo-Coker, Etherington	
20/8	Newcastle United	a	0-0		
27/8	Bolton Wanderers	h	1-2	Sheringham (p)	
12/9	Aston Villa	h	4-0	Harewood 3, Benayoun	
17/9	Fulham	a	2-1	Harewood, og (Warner)	
24/9	Arsenal	h	0-0		
1/10	Sunderland	a	1-1	Benayoun	
16/10	Manchester City	a	1-2	Zamora	
23/10	Middlesbrough	h	2-1	Sheringham, og (Riggott)	
29/10	Liverpool	a	0-2		
5/11	West Bromwich Albion	h	1-0	Sheringham	
20/11	Tottenham Hotspur	a	1-1	Ferdinand	
27/11	Manchester United	h	1-2	Harewood	
5/12	Birmingham City	a	2-1	Zamora, Harewood	
10/12	Blackburn Rovers	a	2-3	Zamora, Harewood	
14/12	Everton	a	2-1	og (Weir), Zamora	
17/12	Newcastle United	h	2-4	og (Solano), Harewood (p)	
26/12	Portsmouth	a	1-1	Collins	
28/12	Wigan Athletic	h	0-2		
31/12	Charlton Athletic	a	0-2		
2006					
2/1	Chelsea	h	1-3	Harewood	
14/1	Aston Villa	a	2-1	Zamora, Harewood (p)	
23/1	Fulham	h	2-1	Ferdinand, Benayoun	
1/2	Arsenal	a	3-2	Reo-Coker, Zamora, Etherington	
4/2	Sunderland	h	2-0	Ashton, Konchesky	
13/2	Birmingham City	h	3-0	Harewood 2, Ashton	
4/3	Everton	h	2-2	Harewood, Ashton	
11/3	Bolton Wanderers	a	1-4	Sheringham	
18/3	Portsmouth	h	2-4	Sheringham, Benayoun	
25/3	Wigan Athletic	a	2-1	Harewood, Reo-Coker	
29/3	Manchester United	a	0-1		
2/4	Charlton Athletic	h	0-0		
9/4	Chelsea	a	1-4	Collins	
15/4	Manchester City	h	1-0	Newton	
17/4	Middlesbrough	a	0-2		
26/4	Liverpool	h	1-2	Reo-Coker	
1/5	West Bromwich Albion	a	1-0	Reo-Coker	
7/5	Tottenham Hotspur	h	2-1	Fletcher, Benayoun	

No	Name	Nat	Pos	Aps	(s)	Gls
39	Jérémie ALIADIERE	FRA	A	1	(6)	
9	Dean ASHTON		A	9	(2)	3
21	David BELLION	FRA	A	2	(6)	
15	Yossi BENAYOUN	ISR	M	30	(4)	5
13	Stephen BYWATER		G		(1)	
1	Roy CARROLL	NIR	G	19		
30	Clive CLARKE		D	2		
19	James COLLINS	WAL	D	13	(1)	2
7	Christian DAILLY	SCO	D	6	(16)	
11	Matthew ETHERINGTON		M	33		2
5	Anton FERDINAND		D	32	(1)	2
6	Carl FLETCHER	WAL	M	6	(6)	1
4	Danny GABBIDON	WAL	D	31	(1)	
10	Marlon HAREWOOD		A	31	(6)	14
34	Shaka HISLOP	TRI	G	16		
18	Yaniv KATAN	ISR	A	2	(3)	
3	Paul KONCHESKY		D	36	(1)	1
17	Hayden MULLINS		M	35		
26	Shaun NEWTON		M	8	(17)	1
24	Mark NOBLE		M	4	(1)	

England

No	Name	Nat	Pos	Aps	(s)	Gls
35	Kyle REID		M	1	(1)	
20	Nigel REO-COKER		M	31		5
2	Tomás REPKA	CZE	D	19		
2	Lionel SCALONI	ARG	D	13		
8	Teddy SHERINGHAM		A	15	(11)	6
23	Jimmy WALKER		G	3		
22	Elliott WARD		D	3	(1)	
25	Bobby ZAMORA		A	17	(17)	6

WIGAN ATHLETIC
Manager – Paul Jewell

2005
Date	Opponent	H/A	Score	Scorers
14/8	Chelsea	h	0-1	
20/8	Charlton Athletic	a	0-1	
27/8	Sunderland	h	1-0	Roberts (p)
10/9	West Bromwich Albion	a	2-1	Connolly, Bullard
18/9	Middlesbrough	h	1-1	Camara
24/9	Everton	a	1-0	Francis
2/10	Bolton Wanderers	h	2-1	Camara, McCulloch
15/10	Newcastle United	h	1-0	Roberts
22/10	Aston Villa	a	2-0	og (Hughes), Mahon
29/10	Fulham	h	1-0	Chimbonda
5/11	Portsmouth	a	2-0	Chimbonda, Roberts
19/11	Arsenal	h	2-3	Camara, Bullard
26/11	Tottenham Hotspur	h	1-2	McCulloch
3/12	Liverpool	a	0-3	
10/12	Chelsea	a	0-1	
14/12	Manchester United	h	0-4	
17/12	Charlton Athletic	h	3-0	Camara 3
26/12	Manchester City	h	4-3	Roberts 2, McCulloch, Camara
28/12	West Ham United	a	2-0	Roberts, Camara
31/12	Blackburn Rovers	h	0-3	

2006
Date	Opponent	H/A	Score	Scorers
2/1	Birmingham City	a	0-2	
15/1	West Bromwich Albion	h	0-1	
21/1	Middlesbrough	a	3-2	Roberts, Thompson, Mellor
31/1	Everton	h	1-1	Scharner
4/2	Bolton Wanderers	a	1-1	Johansson
11/2	Liverpool	h	0-1	
19/2	Tottenham Hotspur	a	2-2	Johansson 2
6/3	Manchester United	h	1-2	Scharner
11/3	Sunderland	a	1-0	Camara
18/3	Manchester City	a	1-0	McCulloch
25/3	West Ham United	h	1-2	McCulloch
3/4	Blackburn Rovers	a	1-1	Roberts
8/4	Birmingham City	h	1-1	Johansson
15/4	Newcastle United	a	1-3	Bullard
18/4	Aston Villa	h	3-2	Bullard, Camara 2
24/4	Fulham	a	0-1	
29/4	Portsmouth	h	1-2	Camara
7/5	Arsenal	a	2-4	Scharner, Thompson

No	Name	Nat	Pos	Aps	(s)	Gls
26	Leighton BAINES		D	35	(2)	
21	Jimmy BULLARD		M	35	(1)	4
7	Henri CAMARA	SEN	A	25	(4)	12
2	Pascal CHIMBONDA	FRA	D	37		2
22	David CONNOLLY	IRL	A	4	(12)	1
16	Arjan DE ZEEUW	HOL	D	31		
1	John FILAN	AUS	G	15		
17	Damien FRANCIS		M	16	(4)	1
6	Stéphane HENCHOZ	SUI	D	26		
4	Matt JACKSON		D	11	(5)	
8	Andreas JOHANSSON	SWE	M	6	(10)	4
11	Graham KAVANAGH	IRL	M	32	(3)	
10	Lee McCULLOCH	SCO	M	27	(3)	5
3	Stephen McMILLAN		D		(2)	
14	Alan MAHON	IRL	M	5	(1)	1
33	Neil MELLOR		A	3		1
12	Mike POLLITT		G	23	(1)	
30	Jason ROBERTS	GRE	A	34		8
18	Paul SCHARNER	AUT	D	14	(2)	3
24	Josip SKOKO	AUS	M	3	(2)	
19	Ryan TAYLOR		D	3	(8)	
20	Gary TEALE	SCO	M	20	(4)	
27	David THOMPSON		M	7	(3)	2
15	David WRIGHT		D	1	(1)	
23	Reto ZIEGLER	SUI	M	5	(5)	

DOMESTIC CUP 2005/06

THIRD ROUND
(6/1/06)
Port Vale 2, Doncaster Rovers 1
(7/1/06)
Arsenal 2, Cardiff City 1
Barnsley 1, Walsall 1
Blackburn Rovers 3, Queens Park Rangers 0
Brighton & Hove Albion 0, Coventry City 1
Chelsea 2, Huddersfield Town 1
Cheltenham Town 2, Chester City 2
Crystal Palace 4, Northampton Town 1
Derby County 2, Burnley 1
Hull City 0, Aston Villa 1
Ipswich Town 0, Portsmouth 1
Luton Town 3, Liverpool 5
Manchester City 3, Scunthorpe United 1
Millwall 1, Everton 1
Newcastle United 1, Mansfield Town 0
Norwich City 1, West Ham United 2
Nuneaton Borough 1, Middlesbrough 1
Preston North End 2, Crewe Alexandra 1
Sheffield United 1, Colchester United 2
Sheffield Wednesday 2, Charlton Athletic 4
Southampton 4, Milton Keynes Dons 3
Stockport County 2, Brentford 3
Stoke City 0, Tamworth 0
Torquay United 0, Birmingham City 0
Watford 0, Bolton Wanderers 3
West Bromwich Albion 1, Reading 1
Wigan Athletic 1, Leeds United 1
Wolverhampton Wanderers 1, Plymouth Argyle 0
(8/1/06)
Burton Albion 0, Manchester United 0
Fulham 1, Leyton Orient 2
Leicester City 3, Tottenham Hotspur 2
Sunderland 3, Northwich Victoria 0

Replays
(17/1/06)
Birmingham City 2, Torquay United 0
Chester City 0, Cheltenham Town 1
Leeds United 3, Wigan Athletic 3 *(aet; 2-4 on pens)*
Middlesbrough 5, Nuneaton Borough 2
Reading 3, West Bromwich Albion 2 *(aet)*
Tamworth 1, Stoke City 1 *(aet; 4-5 on pens)*
Walsall 2, Barnsley 0
(18/1/06)

England

Everton 1, Millwall 0
Manchester United 5, Burton Albion 0

FOURTH ROUND
(28/1/06)
Aston Villa 3, Port Vale 1
Bolton Wanderers 1, Arsenal 0
Brentford 2, Sunderland 1
Charlton Athletic 2, Leyton Orient 1
Cheltenham Town 0, Newcastle United 2
Colchester United 3, Derby County 1
Coventry City 1, Middlesbrough 1
Everton 1, Chelsea 1
Leicester City 0, Southampton 1
Manchester City 1, Wigan Athletic 0
Preston North End 1, Crystal Palace 1
Reading 1, Birmingham City 1
Stoke City 2, Walsall 1
West Ham United 4, Blackburn Rovers 2
(29/1/06)
Portsmouth 1, Liverpool 2
Wolverhampton Wanderers 0, Manchester United 3

Replays
(7/2/06)
Birmingham City 2, Reading 1
Crystal Palace 1, Preston North End 2
(8/2/06)
Chelsea 4, Everton 1
Middlesbrough 1, Coventry City 0

FIFTH ROUND
(18/2/06)
Bolton Wanderers 0, West Ham United 0
Charlton Athletic 3, Brentford 1
Liverpool 1, Manchester United 0
Newcastle United 1, Southampton 0
(19/2/06)
Aston Villa 1, Manchester City 1
Chelsea 3, Colchester United 1
Preston North End 0, Middlesbrough 2
Stoke City 0, Birmingham City 1

Replays
(14/3/06)
Manchester City 2, Aston Villa 1
(15/3/06)
West Ham United 2, Bolton Wanderers 1 (aet)

QUARTER-FINALS
(20/3/06)
Manchester City 1 *(Musampa 85)*, West Ham United 2 *(Ashton 41, 69)*
(21/3/06)
Birmingham City 0, Liverpool 7 *(Hyypiä 3, Crouch 5, 38, Morientes 59, Riise 70, Tébily 77og, Cissé 89)*
(22/3/06)
Chelsea 1 *(Terry 4)*, Newcastle United 0
(23/3/06)
Charlton Athletic 0, Middlesbrough 0

Replay
(12/4/06)
Middlesbrough 4 *(Rochemback 11, Morrison 26, Hasselbaink 73, Viduka 77)*, Charlton Athletic 2 *(Hughes 13, Southgate 76og)*

SEMI-FINALS
(22/4/06)
(Old Trafford, Manchester)
Chelsea 1 *(Drogba 70)*, Liverpool 2 *(Riise 21, Luis García 53)*
(23/4/06)
(Villa Park, Birmingham)
Middlesbrough 0, West Ham United 1 *(Harewood 78)*

FINAL
(13/5/06)
Millennium Stadium, Cardiff
LIVERPOOL 3 *(Cissé 32, Gerrard 54, 90)*
WEST HAM UNITED 3 *(Carragher 21og, Ashton 28, Konchesky 64)*
(aet; 3-1 on pens)
Referee – Wiley
LIVERPOOL – Reina, Finnan, Carragher, Hyypiä, Riise, Gerrard, Xabi Alonso *(Kromkamp 67)*, Sissoko, Kewell *(Morientes 48)*, Cissé, Crouch *(Hamann 71)*.
WEST HAM UNITED – Hislop, Scaloni, Ferdinand, Gabbidon, Konchesky, Benayoun, Fletcher *(Dailly 77)*, Reo-Coker, Etherington *(Sheringham 85)*, Ashton *(Zamora 71)*, Harewood.

SECOND LEVEL FINAL TABLE 2005/06

		Pld	W	D	L	F	A	Pts
1	Reading	46	31	13	2	99	32	106
2	Sheffield United	46	26	12	8	76	46	90
3	Watford	46	22	15	9	77	53	81
4	Preston North End	46	20	20	6	59	30	80
5	Leeds United	46	21	15	10	57	38	78
6	Crystal Palace	46	21	12	13	67	48	75
7	Wolverhampton Wanderers	46	16	19	11	50	42	67
8	Coventry City	46	16	15	15	62	65	63
9	Norwich City	46	18	8	20	56	65	62
10	Luton Town	46	17	10	19	66	67	61
11	Cardiff City	46	16	12	18	58	59	60
12	Southampton	46	13	19	14	49	50	58
13	Stoke City	46	17	7	22	54	63	58
14	Plymouth Argyle	46	13	17	16	39	46	56
15	Ipswich Town	46	14	14	18	53	66	56
16	Leicester City	46	13	15	18	51	59	54
17	Burnley	46	14	12	20	46	54	54
18	Hull City	46	12	16	18	49	55	52
19	Sheffield Wednesday	46	13	13	20	39	52	52
20	Derby County	46	10	20	16	53	67	50
21	Queens Park Rangers	46	12	14	20	50	65	50
22	Crewe Alexandra	46	9	15	22	57	86	42
23	Millwall	46	8	16	22	35	62	40
24	Brighton & Hove Albion	46	7	17	22	39	71	38

PROMOTION PLAY-OFFS
Leeds United 1, Preston North End 1
Preston North End 0, Leeds United 2
(Leeds United 3-1)

Crystal Palace 0, Watford 3
Watford 0, Crystal Palace 0
(Watford 3-0)

(21/5/06)
Watford 3, Leeds United 0

Estonia

Records tumble to TVMK

With the Meistriliiga increased from eight clubs to ten, and the number of matches from 28 to 36, it was a long season in Estonia. It was also a record-breaking one for FC TVMK of Tallinn, who not only won their first championship title since independence but did so in record-breaking style.

Perhaps the most impressive statistic of all was the 41 goals scored by TVMK's Estonian international striker Tarmo Neemelo. The 23-year-old had found the net a mere 13 times in 2004, but he more than trebled his output in 2005. The goals flowed from his boots all season long, and with goals in each of the last three games he bypassed the record tally of 39 set two years earlier by Norwegian striker Tor Henning Hamre of FC Flora Tallinn. Fittingly, it was Neemelo's 40th goal – a majestic left-foot volley against FC Flora in the season's penultimate match – that secured TVMK's title, putting them six points clear of defending champions FC Levadia Tallinn with just one game remaining.

As a team TVMK also set a new goalscoring record for the Meistriliiga, finding the net 138 times – an average of just under four goals per game. No matter that 33 of those goals came in the four games against whipping boys Dünamo Tallinn (who conceded 157 in all); even without those, TVMK would still have amassed a ton. Almost as impressive were TVMK's defensive figures. In a free-scoring league they conceded just 21 goals, never more than two in any game, and kept clean sheets in more than half of their matches.

This mixture of a prolific attack and a mean defence enabled TVMK to win 30 of their 36 games. They won 17 of their 18 away fixtures and were unbeaten at home. But despite all this they still had company at the top of the table, from FC Levadia, for most of the campaign. It was not until the fourth meeting between the two clubs that TVMK finally managed to beat their city rivals. Surprise, surprise, it was Neemelo who scored the winning goal in a 2-1 victory that effectively put TVMK in the clear.

Russian coach

TVMK took the title with a head coach, 59-year-old Russian Vjatsheslav Bulavin, who was not officially recognised as such by the Estonian football authorities because he lacked the necessary qualifications. Although he was assisted by Sergei Ratnikov throughout the league campaign, the latter had absconded to become the 'number one' at Tammeka Tartu by the time TVMK added the Estonian Cup to their trophy cabinet the following spring. Also gone from the team by then were Neemelo, who had signed a contract with Swedish Allsvenskan club Helsingborg, and the team's second top scorer, 19-goal Ingemar Teever, who had also moved to Sweden to sign for Östers IF.

TVMK's match-winner in the Cup final against FC

NATIONAL TEAM RESULTS 2005/06

17/8/05	Bosnia-Herzegovina	H	Tallinn	1-0	Viikmäe (35)
3/9/05	Latvia (WCQ)	H	Tallinn	2-1	Oper (11), Smirnov (71)
8/10/05	Slovakia (WCQ)	A	Bratislava	0-1	
12/10/05	Luxembourg (WCQ)	A	Luxembourg	2-0	Oper (7, 79p)
12/11/05	Finland	A	Helsinki	2-2	Kruglov (62p), Lindpere (85)
16/11/05	Poland	A	Ostrowiec Swietokrzyski	1-3	Teever (68)
1/3/06	Northern Ireland	A	Belfast	0-1	
28/5/06	Turkey	N	Hamburg	1-1	Neemelo (87)
31/5/06	New Zealand	H	Tallinn	1-1	Klavan (3)

Estonia

Flora was 18-year-old Latvian winger Vladislavs Gabovs, who struck with his first touch after being introduced as an 83rd-minute substitute. TVMK goalkeeper Vitali Telesh had kept his side in the game with several fine saves before Bulavin's timely substitution turned the game and enabled TVMK to make amends for their 1-0 defeat to FC Levadia in the 2005 Cup final (which had also been decided by a late goal).

Although FC Flora lost the Cup final, their semi-final victory over Maag (formerly Merkuur) Tartu, coupled with TVMK's over Trans Narva, guaranteed their re-qualification for the UEFA Cup at the expense of Trans, who had finished ahead of them, third to fourth, in the league. Trans also set a new league record during the season as goalkeeper Sergei Ussoltsev went 889 minutes without conceding a goal, beating the previous mark set by Estonian national team legend Mart Poom.

Dünamo Tallinn and FC Kuressaare, the two teams promoted to the Meistriliiga at the end of the 2004 season – despite finishing only fourth and fifth, respectively, in Division One – were both relegated. Rock bottom Dünamo were replaced by JK Vaprus Pärnu while Kuressaare lost their place on the away-goals rule in a play-off against FC Ajax Lasnamäe. It was the first time in the top flight for both newcomers.

Estonia's three representatives in European club competition all lasted just one round, although TVMK might have stood a better chance of getting past the Finns of MyPa had they not lost star striker Neemelo to a red card in the second leg. Even more disappointed were FC Flora, who recorded a famous 2-1 win in Denmark against Esbjerg, only to be thrashed 6-0 at home in the return.

Historic victory

There were joyous scenes in the A.Le Coq Arena a few weeks later, however, when the Estonian national side beat Latvia 2-1 in a World Cup qualifier. It was the country's first victory over their Baltic neighbours since 1940 and it also enabled Estonia to finish above their arch-rivals in the Group Two final table. Estonia secured fourth place with a 2-0 victory in Luxembourg, both goals coming from the country's all-time record scorer Andres Oper, who with that brace lifted his cumulative haul to 30.

Oper was voted Estonian Player of the Year for

Andres Oper (right), Estonia's record scorer, puts himself about in the historic 2-1 win over neighbours Latvia

Estonia

2005 – the third time he had earned that particular commendation – and by the end of the international season the 28-year-old striker would find himself stuck on 99 international caps. Bypassing him to the century mark was FC Flora striker Kristen Viikmäe, who thus became the fifth Estonian player to reach three figures. Out in front, on 147 caps, just three shy of Lothar Matthäus's European record, was the indefatigable Martin Reim, still going strong for club and country at 35.

Having guided Estonia through the second part of the World Cup qualifying campaign, the team's Dutch coach Jelle Goes was rewarded for his efforts with a new contract that will keep him in charge until the end of the Euro 2008 qualifiers. The match that every Estonian fan is looking forward to is scheduled for June 6, 2007 in Tallinn – the country's first ever meeting with England.

NATIONAL TEAM APPEARANCES 2005/06

Coach – Jelle GOES (HOL)

Name	DOB	Club	Bos	LAT	SVK	LUX	Fin	Pol	Nir	Tur	Nzl	Caps	Goals
Artur KOTENKO	20/8/81	FC Levadia Tallinn	G	G	G	G	G				G	14	-
Enar JÄÄGER	18/11/84	Torpedo Moskva (RUS)	D	D	D	D	D	s15	D	D	D	36	-
Raio PIIROJA	11/7/79	Fredrikstad FK (NOR)	D	D	D	D	s84	D	D			61	4
Andrei STEPANOV	16/3/79	Torpedo Moskva (RUS)	D	D	D	D	D	D15	D	D	D	60	1
Urmas ROOBA	8/7/78	FC København (DEN)	D51						D			64	1
Sergei TEREHHOV	18/4/75	Shinnik Yaroslavl (RUS)	M	M	M74	M60	M	M		M58	s73	85	5
Kristen VIIKMÄE	10/2/79	FC Flora Tallinn	A72	A57	A37					A80	M73	100	14
Liivo LEETMA	20/1/77	FC KooTeePee (FIN)	M	M	M87							34	-
Ragnar KLAVAN	30/10/85	Heracles Almelo (HOL)	M				M			M	M	27	1
Dmitri KRUGLOV	24/5/84	Lokomotiv Moskva (RUS)	M	D	D	D	D			D	D	18	1
Andres OPER	7/11/77	Torpedo Moskva (RUS) /Roda JC (HOL)	A	A	A	A				s54		99	30
Maksim SMIRNOV	28/12/79	FC TVMK Tallinn /FC Levadia Tallinn	s51	M78	M	s60				s58		39	2
Tarmo NEEMELO	10/2/82	FC TVMK Tallinn /Helsingborgs IF (SWE)	s72	s57	s37	A	A	A	A	s80	A	10	1
Aleksandr DMITRIJEV	18/2/82	FC Levadia Tallinn		M	M	M	M	M	M	M	M	10	-
Ingemar TEEVER	24/2/83	FC TVMK Tallinn /Östers IF (SWE)		s78			M84	M81		M72		20	4
Taavi RÄHN	16/05/81	Volyn Lutsk (UKR)				s87	M60	M	s54	M77		28	-
Joel LINDPERE	5/10/81	FC Flora Tallinn			s74		A	A	A54	A64	M	44	4
Martin REIM	14/5/71	FC Flora Tallinn				s60		M54	s77	M80		147	14
Erko SAVIAUK	20/10/77	FC TVMK Tallinn					D					60	1
Teet ALLAS	2/6/77	FC Flora Tallinn						D		D	D	67	2
Mart POOM	3/2/72	Arsenal (ENG)						G	G	G		104	-
Jürgen KURESOO	11/2/87	FC Flora Tallinn						s81	s72			2	-
Andrei SIDORENKOV	12/2/84	FC Flora Tallinn							M82			2	-
Jarmo AHJUPERA	13/4/84	FC Flora Tallinn							s82			3	-
Vjatsheslav ZAHOVAIKO	29/12/81	FC Flora Tallinn								s64	A66	29	4
Vladislav GUSSEV	26/8/86	FC TVMK Tallinn								s80		1	-
Konstantin VASSILJEV	16/8/84	FC Levadia Tallinn									s66	1	-

Estonia

EUROPEAN CUPS 2005/06

UEFA CHAMPIONS LEAGUE

FC LEVADIA TALLINN
1st qualifying round DINAMO TBILISI (GEO)
H 1-0 *Nahk (45p)*
Kotenko, Cepauskas, Hohlov-Simson, Shishov, Kalimullin, Dovydenas, Dmitrijev, Nahk, Teniste (Kasimir 46), Vassiljev, Leitan (Purje 60).
A 0-2
Kotenko, Cepauskas, Hohlov-Simson, Shishov, Kalimullin, Dovydenas (Purje 64), Dmitrijev (Shadrin 60), Nahk, Kasimir, Vassiljev, Zelinski (Leitan 46).

UEFA CUP

FC TVMK TALLINN
1st qualifying round MYPA (FIN)
H 1-1 *Teever (37)*
Telesh, Sarajev, Skiperski, Rimas (Seero 84), Saviauk, Jushka (Kisseljov 86), Borissov, Smirnov, Shirmelis, Teever, Neemelo.
A 0-1
Telesh, Seero, Skiperski (Malov 77), Rimas, Saviauk, Jushka, Kisseljov (Shirmelis 59), Borissov (Paitsev 86), Smirnov, Teever, Neemelo.

FC FLORA TALLINN
1st qualifying round ESJBERG FB (DEN)
A 2-1 *Sirevicius (57), Sidorenkov (60)*
Kaalma, Jääger (Dupikov 82), Sirevicius, Bärengrub, Tölpus, Reinumäe, Reim, Haavistu, Saharov, Vunk, Kosemets (Sidorenkov 15; Kureso 77).
H 0-6
Kaalma, Jääger, Sirevicius, Bärengrub, Tölpus, Reinumäe, Reim, Haavistu (Antonov 83), Viikmäe (Dupikov 73), Vunk, Sidorenkov (Kureso 62).

TOP GOALSCORERS 2005

41	Tarmo NEEMELO	(FC TVMK Tallinn)
26	Maksim GRUZNOV	(JK Trans Narva)
19	Vjatsheslav ZAHOVAIKO	(FC Flora Tallinn)
	Ingemar TEEVER	(FC TVMK Tallinn)
18	Indrek ZELINSKI	(FC Levadia Tallinn)
17	Egidijus JUSKA	(FC TVMK Tallinn)
16	Vitali LEITAN	(FC Levadia Tallinn)
15	Kristjan TIIRIK	(JK Tammeka Tartu)
14	Anton SEREDA	(JK Merkuur Tartu/JK Trans Narva)
13	Dmitri USTRITSKI	(JK Tulevik Viljandi)

LEAGUE RESULTS/SCORERS/APPEARANCES/GOALS 2005

JK DÜNAMO TALLINN
Coach – Viktor Neshtsheretnõi

2005

Date	Opponent	H/A	Score	Scorers
6/3	JK Tammeka Tartu	a	0-9	
13/3	JK Trans Narva	h	0-6	
16/3	FC Levadia Tallinn	a	0-5	
20/3	FC Valga	a	1-2	Krivoshein
3/4	FC Kuressaare	h	1-0	Krõlov
10/4	JK Merkuur Tartu	a	1-3	Krõlov
17/4	FC TVMK Tallinn	h	0-7	
24/4	FC Flora Tallinn	a	1-3	Krõlov
1/5	JK Tulevik Viljandi	h	0-0	
8/5	JK Tulevik Viljandi	a	1-4	Krõlov
15/5	FC Flora Tallinn	h	0-3	
22/5	FC TVMK Tallinn	a	1-5	Krivoshein
29/5	JK Merkuur Tartu	h	1-6	Butajev
12/6	FC Kuressaare	a	0-2	
15/6	JK Tammeka Tartu	a	0-3	
19/6	FC Valga	h	3-6	Butajev 2, Sorga
22/6	FC Levadia Tallinn	h	0-4	
6/7	JK Trans Narva	a	3-7	Burov, Harutjunjan, Butajev (p)
10/7	JK Tammeka Tartu	h	2-7	Harutjunjan, Butajev (p)
24/7	JK Trans Narva	h	0-5	
31/7	FC Levadia Tallinn	a	1-3	Steinberg
7/8	FC Valga	a	0-5	
14/8	FC Kuressaare	h	3-4	Butajev 2 (1p), Zidkov D.
21/8	JK Merkuur Tartu	a	0-4	
28/8	FC TVMK Tallinn	h	0-12	
11/9	FC Flora Tallinn	a	0-7	
14/9	JK Tulevik Viljandi	h	2-0	Harutjunjan, Butajev (p)
18/9	JK Tulevik Viljandi	a	1-1	Harutjunjan
21/9	FC Flora Tallinn	h	0-2	
25/9	FC TVMK Tallinn	a	1-9	Butajev
2/10	JK Merkuur Tartu	h	2-1	Steinberg, Butajev
16/10	FC Kuressaare	a	1-8	Zidkov M.
23/10	FC Valga	h	1-1	Harutjunjan
26/10	FC Levadia Tallinn	h	0-4	
30/10	JK Trans Narva	a	0-7	
6/11	JK Tammeka Tartu	h	1-2	Gussev

Name	Nat	Pos	Aps	(s)	Gls
Mihail ANDREJEV	RUS	D	22	(2)	
Anatoli BOZHKO		D	1	(2)	
Sergei BUROV		A	12	(2)	1
Konstantin BUTAJEV		A	27		10
Aleksandr FALJOV		D	5	(2)	
Nicolas-Rogen GOMES DE CARVALHO	POR	A		(2)	
Sergei GULKO		D	2	(1)	
Aleksandr GUSSEV		M	14	(2)	1
Avetis HARUTJUNJAN		M	23	(5)	5
Janek HEPNER		D	32	(1)	
Elvis HRUPA		M	6	(6)	
Artur KASHITSKI		A	1	(2)	
Paul KIRSIPUU		M	22		
Sergei KOSTIN		D	36		
Ilja KRIVOSHEIN		D	19	(2)	2
Andrei KRÕLOV		A	9		4
Sergei KUBÕSHKIN	RUS	D	9	(1)	
Mihhail LISSENKOV		G	16	(5)	
Grigori OSHOMKOV		G	16	(4)	
Aleksei PANIN		M	1	(3)	
Andres PASNITSHENKO		D	2	(1)	
Arvidas RUKSHENAS		M	1	(2)	
Andrei RUSAK		A	5	(4)	
Andrei SEMKO		A	11	(7)	
Urmas SORGA		M	23	(1)	1
Jevgeni SPIRIDONOV	RUS	D	4		
Erik SHTEINBERG		A	30	(1)	2
Sergei TOMAILÕ	RUS	G	4		
Dmitri ZHIDKOV		D	13	(11)	2
Maksim ZHIDKOV		D	30		1

Estonia

FINAL LEAGUE TABLE 2005

		Pld	Home					Away					Total					Pts
			W	D	L	F	A	W	D	L	F	A	W	D	L	F	A	
1	FC TVMK Tallinn	36	13	5	0	68	13	17	0	1	70	8	30	5	1	138	21	95
2	FC Levadia Tallinn	36	15	1	2	51	10	13	4	1	46	15	28	5	3	97	25	89
3	JK Trans Narva	36	12	1	5	56	22	11	5	2	43	12	23	6	7	99	34	75
4	FC Flora Tallinn	36	12	2	4	42	13	9	4	5	39	23	21	6	9	81	36	69
5	JK Tulevik Viljandi	36	7	6	5	25	21	5	5	8	21	27	12	11	13	46	48	47
6	JK Merkuur Tartu	36	9	2	7	34	36	2	5	11	18	50	11	7	18	52	86	40
7	JK Tammeka Tartu	36	5	3	10	32	36	3	2	13	18	52	8	5	23	50	88	29
8	FC Valga	36	4	2	12	18	40	4	2	12	20	38	8	4	24	38	78	28
9	FC Kuressaare	36	4	5	9	25	41	3	1	14	15	55	7	6	23	40	96	27
10	JK Dünamo Tallinn	36	3	2	13	16	70	0	1	17	12	87	3	3	30	28	157	12

FC FLORA TALLINN
Coach – Janno Kivisild

2005

Date	Opponent	H/A	Score	Scorers
6/3	JK Merkuur Tartu	h	0-0	
13/3	FC TVMK Tallinn	a	2-4	Bärengrub, Post
16/3	FC Valga	h	2-0	Zahovaiko (p), Tölpus
20/3	JK Tulevik Viljandi	h	3-0	Jääger, Zahovaiko 2
3/4	JK Tammeka Tartu	a	2-0	Jääger, Saharov
10/4	JK Trans Narva	h	2-1	Bärengrub, Zahovaiko
17/4	FC Levadia Tallinn	a	2-0	Sidorenkov, Ishtshuk
24/4	JK Dünamo Tallinn	h	3-1	Saharov, Post, Tölpus
1/5	FC Kuressaare	a	3-1	Zahovaiko 2 (1p), Ishtshuk
8/5	FC Kuressaare	h	6-0	Sidorenkov, Zahovaiko 5
15/5	JK Dünamo Tallinn	a	3-0	Zahovaiko 3
22/5	FC Levadia Tallinn	h	0-2	
29/5	JK Trans Narva	a	2-2	Zahovaiko 2
12/6	JK Tammeka Tartu	h	3-0	Zahovaiko, Bärengrub, Vunk
19/6	JK Tulevik Viljandi	a	1-1	Sidorenkov
22/6	FC Valga	a	3-1	Zahovaiko 2, Jääger
6/7	FC TVMK Tallinn	h	1-3	Reim
10/7	JK Merkuur Tartu	a	1-1	Jääger
17/7	JK Merkuur Tartu	h	1-0	Saharov
24/7	FC TVMK Tallinn	a	2-4	Vunk 2 (1p)
31/7	FC Valga	h	1-0	Berge
7/8	JK Tulevik Viljandi	h	2-1	Tölpus, Viikmäe
14/8	JK Tammeka Tartu	a	3-1	Taska, Viikmäe 2
21/8	JK Trans Narva	h	0-0	
28/8	FC Levadia Tallinn	a	0-2	
11/9	JK Dünamo Tallinn	h	7-0	Berge 3, Haavistu, Viikmäe, Allas, Frolov
14/9	FC Kuressaare	a	1-1	Ishtshuk
18/9	FC Kuressaare	h	7-0	Reinumäe, Haavistu, Viikmäe 3 (1p), Ishtshuk, Lindpere
21/9	JK Dünamo Tallinn	a	2-0	Lindpere, Ishtshuk
25/9	FC Levadia Tallinn	h	1-3	Sirevicius
2/10	JK Trans Narva	a	0-2	
16/10	JK Tammeka Tartu	h	3-1	Viikmäe, Lindpere, Sirevicius
23/10	JK Tulevik Viljandi	a	2-3	Bärengrub, Haavistu
26/10	FC Valga	a	4-0	Berge, Lindpere, Viikmäe, Kuresoo
30/10	FC TVMK Tallinn	h	0-1	
6/11	JK Merkuur Tartu	a	6-0	Jääger 4, og (Lössanov), Senjesh

Name	Nat	Pos	Aps	(s)	Gls
Mihkel AKSALU		G	8		
Teet ALLAS		D	21	(1)	1
Andrei ANTONOV		A	2	(6)	
Alo BÄRENGRUB		D	30		4
Alfred BERGE	NOR	A	3	(7)	5
Alo DUPIKOV		D	2	(9)	
Andre FROLOV		D		(2)	1
Kert HAAVISTU		A	18	(3)	3
Mihail ISHTSHUK		M	1	(8)	5
Enver JÄÄGER		A	12	(16)	8
Martin KAALMA		G	24		
Rene KAAS		G	3		
Andres KOOGAS		D	7	(3)	
Märt KOSEMETS		M	11	(4)	
Jürgen KURESOO		A	12	(10)	1
Joel LINDPERE		A	10	(1)	4
Karl PALATU		D	8		
Sander POST		D	13		2
Martin REIM		M	27	(1)	1
Ott REINUMÄE		M	21	(4)	1
Henri RÜÜTLI		M		(1)	
Aleksander SAHAROV		A	11	(5)	3
Lauri SENJESH		A	2	(1)	1
Andrei SIDORENKOV		D	23	(6)	3
Kauri SIIM		D	11		
Tomas SIREVICIUS	LIT	M	30	(1)	2
Martin TASKA		D	13		1
Rain TÖLPUS		D	27	(1)	3
Keijo TOMSON		M	1	(3)	
Jürgen VEBER		G	1		
Kristen VIIKMÄE		A	13	(3)	9
Martin VUNK		M	16	(1)	3
Vjatsheslav ZAHOVAIKO		A	15		19

FC KURESSAARE
Coach – Jan Vazinski

2005

Date	Opponent	H/A	Score	Scorers
6/3	JK Tulevik Viljandi	a	0-1	
13/3	JK Tammeka Tartu	h	1-0	Kulikov
16/3	JK Trans Narva	a	1-4	Kriska
20/3	FC Levadia Tallinn	h	0-2	
3/4	JK Dünamo Tallinn	a	0-1	
10/4	FC Valga	a	1-0	Alonen (p)
17/4	JK Merkuur Tartu	h	1-2	Pukk

Estonia

Date	Opponent	H/A	Score	Scorers
24/4	FC TVMK Tallinn	a	1-3	Kulikov
1/5	FC Flora Tallinn	h	1-3	Kulikov
8/5	FC Flora Tallinn	a	0-6	
15/5	FC TVMK Tallinn	h	1-6	Mölder
22/5	JK Merkuur Tartu	a	0-5	
29/5	FC Valga	h	0-0	
12/6	JK Dünamo Tallinn	h	2-0	Alonen, Pukk
15/6	JK Tulevik Viljandi	h	1-1	Pukk
19/6	FC Levadia Tallinn	a	0-2	
22/6	JK Trans Narva	a	2-5	Pukk, Kulikov
6/7	JK Tammeka Tartu	a	1-3	Pukk
20/7	JK Tulevik Viljandi	a	0-1	
24/7	JK Tammeka Tartu	h	2-1	Reiska, Kulikov
31/7	JK Trans Narva	a	0-3	
7/8	FC Levadia Tallinn	h	1-3	Pukk
14/8	JK Dünamo Tallinn	a	4-3	Kulikov, Raamat, Mölder, Valuiski
21/8	FC Valga	a	4-2	Kulikov 2, Pukk, Kaljuste
28/8	JK Merkuur Tartu	h	1-1	Alonen
11/9	FC TVMK Tallinn	a	1-6	Meet (p)
14/9	FC Flora Tallinn	h	1-1	Alonen
18/9	FC Flora Tallinn	a	0-7	
21/9	FC TVMK Tallinn	h	1-8	Koplimäe
25/9	JK Merkuur Tartu	a	0-2	
2/10	FC Valga	h	0-3	
16/10	JK Dünamo Tallinn	h	8-1	Koplimäe 3, Kaljuste, Pukk 3, Õunpuu
23/10	FC Levadia Tallinn	a	0-4	
26/10	JK Trans Narva	h	1-3	Tasa
30/10	JK Tammeka Tartu	a	2-2	Pukk, Kaljuste
6/11	JK Tulevik Viljandi	h	1-1	Mölder

Name	Nat	Pos	Aps	(s)	Gls
Viktor ALONEN		M	31		4
Taavi AZAROV		M	22	(4)	
Rait HANSEN		G	10	(1)	
Kuldar KALJUSTE		M	20	(1)	3
Hendrik KARLSON		A	8	(16)	
Märt KLUGE		D	17	(3)	
Andrus KOPLIMÄE		M	29	(3)	4
Jaanis KRISKA		M	14	(7)	1
Dmitri KULIKOV		M	31		8
Kert KÜTT		G	12		
Roland KÜTT		G	12		
Kalle LEPP		M	2	(11)	
Janek MEET		M	13	(6)	1
Maikko MÖLDER		A	17	3	3
Aik ORGLA		G	2	(1)	
Indrek ÕUNPUU		M		(3)	1
Peeter PIHEL		M	9	(9)	
Martti PUKK		A	35		11
Kaarel RAAMAT		M	30	(2)	1
Margus RAJAVER		M	6	(5)	
Mikk RAJAVER		A		(2)	
Urmas RAJAVER		D	4	(5)	
Priit REISKA		M	24	(1)	1
Arli SAAR		D		(2)	
Martin SALONG		A	11	(15)	
Veiko TASA		M	2	(2)	1
Vitali VALUISKI		A	19		1
Rainer VESKIMÄE		M	16		
Sander VIIRA		D		1	

FC LEVADIA TALLINN
Coach – Tarmo Rüütli

2005

Date	Opponent	H/A	Score	Scorers
2/3	JK Trans Narva	a	4-0	Leitan, Kruglov 2, Vassiljev (p)
6/3	JK Trans Narva	a	1-3	Leitan
13/3	FC Valga	a	3-0	Karalius, Kruglov, Zelinski
16/3	JK Dünamo Tallinn	h	5-0	og (Andrejev), Leitan, Karalius, Tshelnokov 2
20/3	FC Kuressaare	a	2-0	Vassiljev (p), Zelinski
3/4	JK Merkuur Tartu	h	4-0	og (Lössanov), Dovydenas, Vassiljev, Nahk
10/4	FC TVMK Tallinn	a	2-2	Tshelnokov, Nahk
17/4	FC Flora Tallinn	h	0-2	
24/4	JK Tulevik Viljandi	a	2-2	Zelinski, Vassiljev
1/5	JK Tammeka Tartu	h	5-2	Rulkov, Zelinski, Leitan, Karalius 2
8/5	JK Tammeka Tartu	a	2-0	Cepauskas, Leitan
15/5	JK Tulevik Viljandi	h	2-0	Leitan, Dovydenas
22/5	FC Flora Tallinn	a	2-0	Zelinski, Leitan
29/5	FC TVMK Tallinn	h	2-1	Dovydenas, Nahk
12/6	JK Merkuur Tartu	a	2-2	Nahk, Teniste
19/6	FC Kuressaare	h	2-0	Zelinski, Puri S.
22/6	JK Dünamo Tallinn	a	4-0	Dovydenas, Dmitrijev, og (Hepner), Demutski
6/7	FC Valga	h	3-0	Vassiljev 2, Leitan
24/7	FC Valga	a	4-0	Dovydenas, Purje, Shadrin, Zelinski
27/7	JK Trans Narva	h	1-1	Zelinski
31/7	JK Dünamo Tallinn	h	3-0	Shadrin, Kasimir, Cepauskas
7/8	FC Kuressaare	a	3-1	Vassiljev, Teniste, Kasimir
14/8	JK Merkuur Tartu	h	8-0	Leitan 4, Zelinski 3, Shadrin
21/8	FC TVMK Tallinn	a	0-0	
28/8	FC Flora Tallinn	h	2-0	Kasimir, Puri S.
11/9	JK Tulevik Viljandi	a	3-1	Kalimullin, Zelinski 2
14/9	JK Tammeka Tartu	h	1-0	Cepauskas
18/9	JK Tammeka Tartu	a	2-1	Zelinski, Nahk (p)
21/9	JK Tulevik Viljandi	h	2-1	Zelinski, Shadrin
25/9	FC Flora Tallinn	a	3-1	Dmitrijev, Dovydenas, Puri E.
2/10	FC TVMK Tallinn	h	1-2	Cepauskas
16/10	JK Merkuur Tartu	h	3-2	Dovydenas, Saag, Vassiljev
23/10	FC Kuressaare	h	4-0	Zelinski, og (Kluge), Leitan, Shadrin
26/10	JK Dünamo Tallinn	a	4-0	Zelinski, Purje 2, Röshkevitsh
30/10	FC Valga	h	3-0	Purje, Zelinski, Röshkevitsh
6/11	JK Trans Narva	h	3-0	Leitan 3

Name	Nat	Pos	Aps	(s)	Gls
Anton ARISTOV		D		(1)	
Vaagn ARUTUNJAN		M	2	(7)	
Vitoldas CEPAUSKAS	LIT	D	29		4
Aleksei DEMUTSKI		M	2	(1)	1
Aleksandr DJATSHENKO		G	4	(1)	
Aleksandr DMITRIJEV		M	13	(6)	2
Marius DOVYDENAS	LIT	M	27	(3)	7
Jevgeni GURTSHIOGLUJANTS		A		(1)	
Sergei HOHLOV-SIMSON		D	24	(1)	
Aleksandr IVANOV		M		(2)	
Andrei KALIMULLIN		D	31	(3)	1
Martynas KARALIUS	LIT	A	13	(1)	4
Siksten KASIMIR		A	13	(4)	3
Eduard KOMAROV		M		(2)	
Dmitri KORZHINSKI		G		(1)	
Artur KOTENKO		G	32		
Dmitri KRUGLOV		D	13	(1)	3
Aleksei KUTS		M		(1)	
Vitali LEITAN		A	31	(3)	16
Konstantin NAHK		M	29		5
Eino PURI		M		(7)	1

Estonia

Sander PURI		M	3	(11)	2
Ats PURJE		A	6	(6)	4
Miroslav RÕSHKEVITSH		M	11	(8)	2
Aleksandr RULKOV		A	1	(4)	1
Kaimar SAAG		M	2	(1)	1
Andrei SHADRIN		A	7	(5)	5
Tihhon SHISHOV		D	32	(2)	
Taavi TAMMO		D	1	(1)	
Taijo TENISTE		A	9	(3)	2
Vladimir TSHELNOKOV		A	9	(2)	3
Konstantin VASSILJEV		M	24	(7)	8
Indrek ZELINSKI		A	28	(1)	18

JK MERKUUR TARTU
Coach – Grigori Jevtushenko; (1/8/05) (Sergei Zamogilnõi)

2005

Date	Opponent		Score	Scorers
6/3	FC Flora Tallinn	a	0-0	
13/3	JK Tulevik Viljandi	h	2-0	Tjunin, Gussev Vl.
16/3	JK Tammeka Tartu	a	2-2	Leitan, Gussev Vl.
20/3	JK Trans Narva	h	2-3	Starovoitov, Kasimir
3/4	FC Levadia Tallinn	a	0-4	
10/4	JK Dünamo Tallinn	h	3-1	Tjunin, Gussev Vl., Starovoitov
17/4	FC Kuressaare	a	2-1	Apalinski, Gussev Vl.
24/4	FC Valga	a	1-1	Kasimir (p)
1/5	FC TVMK Tallinn	h	1-6	Gussev Vl.
8/5	FC TVMK Tallinn	a	1-2	Sereda
15/5	FC Valga	h	2-1	Kasimir 2 (2p)
22/5	FC Kuressaare	h	5-0	Sereda, Gussev Vl., Lõssanov, Kasimir (p), Usmanov
29/5	JK Dünamo Tallinn	a	6-1	Sereda 2, og (Sorga), Dubõkin, Tjunin 2
1/6	JK Trans Narva	a	2-6	Sereda, Gussev Vl.
12/6	FC Levadia Tallinn	a	2-2	Sereda, Kasimir
22/6	JK Tammeka Tartu	h	3-0	Ivanov 2, Sereda
6/7	JK Tulevik Viljandi	a	0-0	
10/7	FC Flora Tallinn	h	1-1	Ottshik
17/7	FC Flora Tallinn	a	0-1	
24/7	JK Tulevik Viljandi	h	2-1	Ottshik (p), Leitan
31/7	JK Tammeka Tartu	a	0-2	
7/8	JK Trans Narva	h	0-7	
14/8	FC Levadia Tallinn	a	0-8	
21/8	JK Dünamo Tallinn	h	4-0	Ivanov 2, Ossipov, Russakov
28/8	FC Kuressaare	a	1-1	Mamontov
11/9	FC Valga	h	1-2	Pruttshenko
14/9	FC TVMK Tallinn	h	1-3	Ivanov
18/9	FC TVMK Tallinn	a	1-8	O'Konnel-Bronin
21/9	FC Valga	h	2-1	Usmanov, Ivanov
25/9	FC Kuressaare	h	2-0	Ottshik, Bazjukin
2/10	JK Dünamo Tallinn	a	1-2	Sirel
16/10	FC Levadia Tallinn	h	2-3	Ivanov 2
23/10	JK Trans Narva	h	0-4	
26/10	JK Tammeka Tartu	h	0-1	
30/10	JK Tulevik Viljandi	a	0-5	(w/o; original result 1-5 Ivanov)
6/11	FC Flora Tallinn	h	0-6	

Name	Nat	Pos	Aps	(s)	Gls
Rodion ALEKSEJEV		D	14		
Pavel APALINSKI		A	13		1
Maksim BAZJUKIN	RUS	M	26		1
Aleksandr DUBÕKIN		M	10	(5)	1
Dmitri FJODOROV		M	1	(1)	
Nikolai GRISHIN	RUS	G	11	(2)	
Vitali GUSSEV		M	3	(1)	
Vladislav GUSSEV		A	13	(7)	7
Vladislav IVANOV		A	24	(4)	8
Siksten KASIMIR		A	16		6
Artjom LAVJAGIN		A	1	(1)	
Jevgeni LAZERENKOV		D		(1)	
Juri LEITAN		D	20	(3)	2
Sergei LEPMETS		G	15		
Nikolai LÕSSANOV		D	27		1
Vjatsheslav LÜTTER		A			
Aleksei MAMONTOV		M	17	(6)	1
Sergei MITIN	UKR	D	13		
Ivan O`KONNEL-BRONIN		M	6		1
Artur OSSIPOV		M	25	(3)	1
Sergei OTTSHIK		D	20	(1)	3
Aleksandr PRUTTSHENKO		M	5	(7)	1
Kaspar RÕIVASSEPP		D	9	(8)	
Stanislav RUSSAKOV		D	8	(9)	1
Vadim SAMULIN		D	1	(3)	
Sergei SERDJUK		G	5		
Anton SEREDA		M	12	(5)	7
Denis SERIKOV		M	6	(2)	
Jaanus SIREL		D	29	(4)	1
Sergei STAROVOITOV		M	10	(1)	2
Andrei TJUNIN		M	14	(1)	4
Andrei USMANOV		M	20	(6)	2
Jevgeni VOITOVITSH		M		(1)	
Renars ZHARCENKO	LAT	A	2	(1)	

JK TAMMEKA TARTU
Coach – Meelis Eelmäe

2005

Date	Opponent		Score	Scorers
6/3	JK Dünamo Tallinn	h	9-0	Naaber 2, Roops 2, Konsa 2, Vaino, og (Krõlov), Tiirik
13/3	FC Kuressaare	a	0-1	
16/3	FC Merkuur Tartu	h	2-2	og (Sirel), Tiirik
20/3	FC TVMK Tallinn	a	0-9	
3/4	FC Flora Tallinn	h	0-2	
10/4	JK Tulevik Viljandi	a	1-1	Tiirik
17/4	FC Valga	h	3-4	Meerits, Tiirik 2
24/4	JK Trans Narva	h	0-3	
1/5	FC Levadia Tallinn	a	2-5	Jürgenson, Tomson
8/5	FC Levadia Tallinn	h	0-2	
15/5	JK Trans Narva	a	1-5	Tiirik
22/5	FC Valga	a	0-1	
29/5	JK Tulevik Viljandi	h	2-2	Anniste, Tiirik
12/6	FC Flora Tallinn	a	0-3	
15/6	JK Dünamo Tallinn	h	3-0	Tiirik, Tomson, Kuus
19/6	FC TVMK Tallinn	h	0-2	
22/6	FC Merkuur Tartu	a	0-3	
6/7	FC Kuressaare	h	3-1	Tomson, Roops, Anniste
10/7	JK Dünamo Tallinn	a	7-2	Roops, Tomson, Gomes 2, Tiirik 3
24/7	FC Kuressaare	a	1-2	Roops
31/7	JK Merkuur Tartu	h	2-0	Gomes, Tiirik
7/8	FC TVMK Tallinn	a	0-5	
14/8	FC Flora Tallinn	h	1-3	Vellemaa
21/8	JK Tulevik Viljandi	a	1-3	Roops
28/8	FC Valga	h	2-1	Tiirik (p), Roops
11/9	JK Trans Narva	h	0-3	
14/9	FC Levadia Tallinn	a	0-1	
18/9	FC Levadia Tallinn	h	1-2	Tiirik (p)
21/9	JK Trans Narva	a	0-6	
25/9	FC Valga	a	1-1	Anniste
2/10	JK Tulevik Viljandi	h	2-4	Tiirik, Konsa
16/10	FC Flora Tallinn	a	1-3	Anniste (p)
23/10	FC TVMK Tallinn	h	0-3	

Estonia

26/10	JK Merkuur Tartu	a	1-0	Gomes
30/10	FC Kuressaare	h	2-2	Meerits, Tamm
6/11	JK Dünamo Tallinn	a	2-1	Anniste (p), Konsa

Name	Nat	Pos	Aps	(s)	Gls
Aivar ANNISTE		M	36		5
Marcelo GOMES Inocéncio	BRA	D	13	4	4
Ando HAUSENBERG		M	2	(9)	
Janno HERMANSON		G	18		
Markus JÜRGENSON		A	25	(7)	1
Oliver KONSA		A	17	(6)	4
Kert KÜTT		G	18		
Timo KUUS		D		(6)	1
Ott MEERITS		M	34		2
Jaak NAABER		M	3	(6)	2
Mark ORAV		D		(3)	
Kristjan PAAPSI		A		(6)	
Robert PLUUM		A		(1)	
Siim ROOPS		D	34		7
Eduard SHKUNOV		A	29	(5)	
Heiko TAMM		M	2	(21)	1
Timo TENISTE		M	23	(6)	
Ragnar TIIDEBERG		D	35		
Kristjan TIIRIK		D	28	(4)	15
Rasmus TOMSON		M	17	(7)	4
Kait-Kaarel VAINO		D	32		1
Taavi VELLEMAA		M	30	(4)	1

JK TRANS NARVA
Coach – Valeri Bondarenko

2005

2/3	FC Levadia Tallinn	h	0-4	
6/3	FC Levadia Tallinn	h	3-1	Gorjatshov 2, Kulatshenko
13/3	JK Dünamo Tallinn	a	6-0	Gruznov 2, Kulatshenko 3, Kulik
16/3	FC Kuressaare	h	4-1	Kulatshenko 2, Gruznov, Gorjatshov
20/3	JK Merkuur Tartu	a	3-2	og (Kasimir), Ametov, Kulatshenko
3/4	FC TVMK Tallinn	h	0-3	
10/4	FC Flora Tallinn	a	1-2	Kitto
17/4	JK Tulevik Viljandi	h	1-2	Lipartov
24/4	JK Tammeka Tartu	a	3-0	Gruznov, Tarassenkov, Lipartov
1/5	FC Valga	h	3-1	Gruznov 2, Ametov
8/5	FC Valga	a	2-1	Lipartov, Gorjatshov
15/5	JK Tammeka Tartu	h	5-1	Lipartov 2, Gruznov 3
22/5	JK Tulevik Viljandi	a	2-0	Popov, Lipartov
29/5	FC Flora Tallinn	h	2-2	Gorjatshov, Gruznov
1/6	JK Merkuur Tartu	h	6-2	Gorjatshov 2 (1p), Popov 2, Gruznov 2
12/6	FC TVMK Tallinn	a	0-0	
22/6	FC Kuressaare	a	5-2	Tarassenkov, Kazakov, Lipartov, Gruznov, Ametov
6/7	JK Dünamo Tallinn	h	7-3	Gruznov 2, Kazakov, Tarassenkov, Kitto (p), Gorshkov, Kulatshenko
24/7	JK Dünamo Tallinn	a	5-0	Kitto, Tarassenkov, Ametov (p), Popov, Kulatshenko
27/7	FC Levadia Tallinn	a	1-1	Gruznov
31/7	FC Kuressaare	h	3-0	Kitto, Kazakov, Gruznov
7/8	JK Merkuur Tartu	a	7-0	Kazakov, Starovoitov 3, Lipartov, Sereda 2
14/8	FC TVMK Tallinn	h	0-2	
21/8	FC Flora Tallinn	a	0-0	
28/8	JK Tulevik Viljandi	h	0-0	(w/o; original result 5-0)
11/9	JK Tammeka Tartu	a	3-0	Gruznov 4, Sereda) Lipartov, Sereda 2
18/9	FC Valga	a	2-0	Dubõkin, Kazakov
21/9	JK Tammeka Tartu	h	6-0	Gruznov 2, Starovoitov 2, Sereda 2
25/9	JK Tulevik Viljandi	a	0-0	
28/9	FC Valga	h	3-0	Kazakov, Tarassenkov, Gruznov
2/10	FC Flora Tallinn	h	2-0	Gruznov, Kazakov
16/10	FC TVMK Tallinn	a	0-0	
23/10	JK Merkuur Tartu	h	4-0	Tarassenkov 2, Gruznov 2
26/10	FC Kuressaare	a	3-1	og (Pinel), Gruznov, Kazakov
30/10	JK Dünamo Tallinn	h	7-0	Ametov 2, Dubõkin, Gruznov 2, Sereda, Starovoitov
6/11	FC Levadia Tallinn	a	0-3	

Name	Nat	Pos	Aps	(s)	Gls
Irfan AMETOV	UKR	M	13	(10)	6
Pavel APALINSKI		A	2	(3)	
Ilja DJORD	RUS	D	17		
Dmitri DOBROVOLSKI	UKR	D	26		
Aleksandr DUBÕKIN		M	13	(1)	2
Oleg GORJATSHOV		M	16		7
Aleksei GORSHKOV		M	18	(5)	1
Maksim GRUZNOV		A	33		26
Sergei KAZAKOV		M	21	(13)	8
Stanislav KITTO		M	31		4
Aleksandr KULATSHENKO		M	9	(12)	9
Aleksandr KULIK		D	32		1
Oleg KUROTSHKIN		D	1	(1)	
Dmitri LIPARTOV	RUS	A	26	(3)	9
Vitas MALISHAUSKAS		G	1		
Sergei MITIN	UKR	D	4	(1)	
Sergei POPOV		M	8	(19)	4
Andrei PRUSS		D	11	(2)	
Anton SEREDA		M	2	(9)	7
Dmitri SHELEHHOV		D	23	(5)	
Sergei STAROVOITOV		M	8	(4)	6
Aleksandr TARASSENKOV		M	32	(2)	7
Andrei TJUNIN		M	14	(1)	
Sergei USSOLTSEV		G	35		
Aleksandr ZAHHARENKOV		M		(1)	

JK TULEVIK VILJANDI
Coach – Marko Lelov

2005

6/3	FC Kuressaare	h	1-0	Kudu
13/3	JK Merkuur Tartu	a	0-2	
16/3	FC TVMK Tallinn	h	0-2	
20/3	FC Flora Tallinn	a	0-3	
3/4	FC Valga	h	0-2	
10/4	JK Tammeka Tartu	h	1-1	Ustritski
17/4	JK Trans Narva	a	2-1	Ahjupera, og (Ussoltsev)
24/4	FC Levadia Tallinn	h	2-2	Palatu, Ishtshuk
1/5	JK Dünamo Tallinn	a	0-0	
8/5	JK Dünamo Tallinn	h	4-1	Hurt, Ahjupera, Kalda, Ustritski
15/5	FC Levadia Tallinn	a	0-2	
22/5	JK Trans Narva	h	0-2	
29/5	JK Tammeka Tartu	a	2-2	Ahjupera, Ustritski
12/6	FC Valga	a	2-1	Ahjupera 2
15/6	FC Kuressaare	a	1-1	Ahjupera
19/6	FC Flora Tallinn	h	1-1	Ahjupera
22/6	FC TVMK Tallinn	a	1-1	Ahjupera (p)
6/7	JK Merkuur Tartu	h	0-0	

Estonia

20/7	FC Kuressaare	h	1-0	Ahjupera
24/7	JK Merkuur Tartu	a	1-2	Haavistu
31/7	FC TVMK Tallinn	h	0-3	
7/8	FC Flora Tallinn	a	1-2	Ustritski
14/8	FC Valga	h	2-0	Ahjupera, Saar
21/8	JK Tammeka Tartu	h	3-1	Anis, Ustritski, Kudu
28/8	JK Trans Narva	a	0-0	(w/o; original result 0-5)
11/9	FC Levadia Tallinn	h	1-3	Ustritski
14/9	JK Dünamo Tallinn	a	0-2	
18/9	JK Dünamo Tallinn	h	1-1	Kalda
21/9	FC Levadia Tallinn	a	1-2	Ustritski
25/9	JK Trans Narva	h	0-0	
2/10	JK Tammeka Tartu	a	4-2	Hurt 2, Lember, Ahjupera
16/10	FC Valga	a	5-1	Ustritski 3, Saar, Hurt
23/10	FC Flora Tallinn	h	3-2	Haavistu, Hurt, Ustritski
26/10	FC TVMK Tallinn	a	0-2	
30/10	JK Merkuur Tartu	h	5-0	(w/o; original result 5-1 Ahjupera, Oja, Ustritski 2, Sirel)
6/11	FC Kuressaare	a	1-1	Laasberg

Name	Nat	Pos	Aps	(s)	Gls
Jarmo AHJUPERA		A	31	(5)	12
Andre ANIS		M	3	(5)	1
Taavi AUS		M	1	(1)	
Mikk HAAVISTU		D	31	(1)	2
Martin HURT		M	29		5
Vitali ISHTSHUK		A	15	(15)	1
Janek KALDA		M	25	(1)	2
Markko KUDU		A	4	(16)	2
Joonas LAASBERG		M	3	(1)	1
Meelis LAURIMAA		D	14	(11)	
Mati LEMBER		M	29	(2)	1
Pavel LONDAK		G	36		
Raiko MUTLE		D	35		
Armand NARIS		D		(2)	
Reimo OJA		A	2	(14)	1
Karl PALATU		D	17		1
Erkki PÄRNA		A	1		
Priit RAAMAT		M	10		
Mihkel SAAR		M	19	(3)	2
Aleksei SAVITSKI		D	19		
Priit SIREL		M	22	(1)	1
Heikki TALIMAA		A	14		
Kaarel TANI		A	1	(13)	
Theimo TARVIS		A	3		
Dmitri USTRITSKI		A	32	(1)	13

FC TVMK TALLINN
Coach – Vjatsheslav Bulavin (RUS)

2005

6/3	FC Valga	h	5-0	Rimas, Teever (p), Kisseljov, Malov, Skiperski
13/3	FC Flora Tallinn	h	4-2	Sirmelis, Teever, Juska, og (Allas)
16/3	JK Tulevik Viljandi	a	2-0	Juska, Smirnov
20/3	JK Tammeka Tartu	a	9-0	Teever 2, Juska 2, Smirnov 2, Neemelo 2, Kisseljov
3/4	JK Trans Narva	a	3-0	Neemelo 2, Smirnov
10/4	FC Levadia Tallinn	h	2-2	Teever, Malov
17/4	JK Dünamo Tallinn	h	7-0	Neemelo 4, Teever, Borissov, Kisseljov
24/4	FC Kuressaare	h	3-1	Saviauk, Teever (p), Borissov
1/5	JK Merkuur Tartu	a	6-1	Skiperski, og (Grishin), Paitsev, Saviauk, Juska (p), Kostin
8/5	JK Merkuur Tartu	h	2-1	Paitsev, Teever
15/5	FC Kuressaare	a	6-1	Neemelo 2, Paitsev 2, Malov, Juska
22/5	JK Dünamo Tallinn	h	5-1	Malov, Juska, Teever (p), Neemelo, Smirnov
29/5	FC Levadia Tallinn	a	1-2	Teever (p)
12/6	JK Trans Narva	h	0-0	
19/6	JK Tammeka Tartu	a	2-0	Juska 2
22/6	JK Tulevik Viljandi	h	1-1	Neemelo
6/7	FC Flora Tallinn	a	3-1	Saviauk, Neemelo, Teever
10/7	FC Valga	a	5-0	Neemelo 2, Smirnov, Teever, Juska
17/7	FC Valga	h	3-0	Seera, Kisseljov, Borissov
24/7	FC Flora Tallinn	h	4-2	Neemelo, Malov, og (Sirevicius), Teever
31/7	JK Tulevik Viljandi	a	3-0	Neemelo, Teever, Sirmelis
7/8	JK Tammeka Tartu	h	5-0	Neemelo 2, Kisseljov (p), Teever, Borissov
14/8	JK Trans Narva	a	2-0	Teever 2
21/8	FC Levadia Tallinn	h	0-0	
28/8	JK Dünamo Tallinn	a	12-0	Gussev 3, Neemelo 3, Juska, Sirmelis, Teever 2, Malov, Paitsev
11/9	FC Kuressaare	h	6-1	Gussev, Neemelo 3, Kacanovs, Juska
14/9	JK Merkuur Tartu	a	3-1	Smirnov, Neemelo, Malov
18/9	JK Merkuur Tartu	h	8-1	Neemelo 4, Juska, Sirmelis, Skiperski, Gussev
21/9	FC Kuressaare	a	8-1	Neemelo 3, Borissov, Skiperski, Smirnov, Paitsev, Malov
25/9	JK Dünamo Tallinn	h	9-1	Neemelo 3, Juska 3 (1p), Smirnov, Sirmelis, Skiperski
2/10	FC Levadia Tallinn	a	2-1	Juska, Neemelo
16/10	JK Trans Narva	h	0-0	
23/10	JK Tammeka Tartu	a	3-0	Paitsev, Neemelo, Malov
26/10	JK Tulevik Viljandi	h	2-0	Neemelo, Malov
30/10	FC Flora Tallinn	a	1-0	Neemelo
6/11	FC Valga	a	1-0	Neemelo

Name	Nat	Pos	Aps	(s)	Gls
Andrei BORISSOV		M	30	(2)	5
Vladislav GUSSEV		A	5	(2)	5
Egidijus JUSKA	LIT	A	26	(2)	17
Jevgenijs KACANOVS	LAT	D	14	(1)	1
Maksim KISSELJOV		M	18	(11)	5
Andrei KOSTIN		M	13	(13)	1
Dmitri MAKAREVITSH		A		(1)	
Deniss MALOV		M	15	(8)	10
Nikolai MASHITSHEV		M	2	(10)	
Tarmo NEEMELO		A	26	(7)	41
Anton PAITSEV		A	15	(4)	7
Daniil RATNIKOV		M		(3)	
Tomas RIMAS	LIT	D	30	(1)	1
Konstantin RUBTSOV		G		(2)	
Eduard SARAJEV		D	24		
Erko SAVIAUK		D	17	(3)	3
Vadim SEERO		D	18	(6)	1
Gintas SIRMELIS	LIT	M	23	(6)	5
Dmitri SKIPERSKI	RUS	D	28	(4)	5
Maksim SMIRNOV		M	31		9
Ingemar TEEVER		A	25	(3)	19
Vitali TELESH		G	35		
Antons TRIFONOVS	LAT	G	1	(1)	

FC VALGA

Estonia

Coach – Ivo Lehtmets

2005

Date	Opponent	H/A	Score	Scorers
6/3	FC TVMK Tallinn	a	0-5	
13/3	FC Levadia Tallinn	h	0-3	
16/3	FC Flora Tallinn	a	0-2	
20/3	JK Dünamo Tallinn	h	2-1	Marmor, Kams
3/4	JK Tulevik Viljandi	a	2-0	Marmor, Girishin
10/4	FC Kuressaare	h	0-1	
17/4	JK Tammeka Tartu	a	4-3	Kams, Kaukvere, og (Roops), Girishin
24/4	JK Merkuur Tartu	h	1-1	Kasterpalu
1/5	JK Trans Narva	a	1-3	Vanna
8/5	JK Trans Narva	h	1-2	Taska
15/5	JK Merkuur Tartu	a	1-2	Kasterpalu
22/5	JK Tammeka Tartu	h	1-0	Marmor
29/5	FC Kuressaare	a	0-0	
12/6	JK Tulevik Viljandi	h	1-2	Vanna
19/6	JK Dünamo Tallinn	a	6-3	Girishin 2, Kasterpalu 2, Tükk, Marmor
22/6	FC Flora Tallinn	h	1-3	Marmor
6/7	FC Levadia Tallinn	a	0-3	
10/7	FC TVMK Tallinn	h	0-5	
17/7	FC TVMK Tallinn	a	0-3	
24/7	FC Levadia Tallinn	h	0-4	
31/7	FC Flora Tallinn	a	0-1	
7/8	JK Dünamo Tallinn	h	5-0	Tükk, Kasterpalu 3, Kuusk
14/8	JK Tulevik Viljandi	a	0-2	
21/8	FC Kuressaare	h	2-4	Girishin, Minlibajev
28/8	JK Tammeka Tartu	a	1-2	Girishin
11/9	JK Merkuur Tartu	h	2-1	Girishin, Kasterpalu
18/9	JK Trans Narva	h	0-2	
21/9	JK Merkuur Tartu	a	1-2	Vanna
25/9	JK Tammeka Tartu	h	1-1	Kasterpalu
28/9	JK Trans Narva	a	0-3	
2/10	FC Kuressaare	h	3-0	Kams, Kasterpalu, Valejev
16/10	JK Tulevik Viljandi	h	1-5	Kaukvere
23/10	JK Dünamo Tallinn	a	1-0	Vanna
26/10	FC Flora Tallinn	h	0-4	
30/10	FC Levadia Tallinn	a	0-3	
6/11	FC TVMK Tallinn	h	0-1	

Name	Nat	Pos	Aps	(s)	Gls
Marko ARGE		M	24	(3)	
Dmitri GIRISHIN		A	20	(4)	7
Rene KAAS		G	13		
Norman KÄGO		D		(3)	
Gert KAMS		M	24	(1)	3
Rait KASTERPALU		M	17	(17)	10
Tõnis KAUKVERE		M	17	(10)	2
Indrek KLEIN		M	13		
Rait KUUSK		M	17		1
Reijo LEMETSAAR		G	1		
Kristian MARMOR		A	30		5
Magnus MARTINSON		A	8	(11)	
Andrei MAZURKEVITSH		A	30		
Roman MINLIBAJEV		A	13		1
Lauri NUUMA		M	4	(5)	
Harri OJAMAA		M	7	(1)	
Timo OLESK		M	10	(5)	
Henri PAAVO		M		(8)	
Sander REELO		G	7		
Andrei SAVOTSHKIN		A	30	(3)	
Martin TASKA		D	17		1
Siim TREIMUTH		D	14	(4)	
Janar TÜKK		M	28	(1)	2
Indrek VALEJEV		M	7	(9)	1
Tõnis VANNA		A	30		4
Jürgen VEBER		G	15		

DOMESTIC CUP 2005

1/8 FINALS
(9/11/05)
Merkuur Tartu 3, Lelle SK 0
JK Dünamo Tallinn 5, FCF Järva-Jaani SK 2
JK Kaitseliit/Kalev 4, FC Kuressaare 5 *(aet)*
FC TVMK Tallinn 2, FC Levadia Tallinn 1
SC Kuradid Tallinn 0, JK Trans Narva 9
FC Valga 4, JK Merkuur-Juunior Tartu 0
FC Flora Tallinn 2, JK Tulevik Viljandi 1
(10/11/05)
FC Hansa United 0, JK Kalev Tallinn 8

QUARTER-FINALS
(19/4/06)
FC Warrior Valga 1 *(Akerta 81)*, FC TVMK Tallinn 2 *(Mashitshev 32, Kacanovs 45)*
JK Trans Narva 4 *(Kitto 20, Kazakov 25, Lipartov 54, Gruznov 90)*, JK Dünamo Tallinn 1 *(Andrejev 66)*
JK Maag Tartu 7 *(Starovoitov 20, Gussev 26, 31, Kasimir 37, Mamontov 59, 85, Alonen 79og)*, FC Kuressaare 0
JK Kalev Tallinn 0, FC Flora Tallinn 5 *(Post 3, 52, Kärson 62og, Ahjupera 87, Zahovaiko 90)*

SEMI-FINALS
(3/5/06)
JK Maag Tartu 0, FC Flora Tallinn 2 *(Lindpere 26, Ahjupera 69)*
JK Trans Narva 2 *(Kitto 18p, Dubökin 25)*, FC TVMK Tallinn 3 *(Rimas 5, Borissov 29, Gussev 56)*

FINAL
(17/5/06)
Kadriorg Stadium, Tallinn
FC TVMK TALLINN 1 *(Gabovs 86)*
FC FLORA TALLINN 0
Referee – Saar
FC TVMK TALLINN – Telesh, Seero, Rimas, Saviauk, Borissov (Kisseljov 61), Sarajev, Haavistu (Gabovs 83), Shirmelis, Dobrecovs, Mashitshev, Gussev.
FC FLORA TALLINN – Londak, Ahjupera, Reinumäe, Hurt (Kams 90), Zahovaiko, Reim, Allas, Lindpere (Jääger 35), Sidorenkov, Vunk (Sirevicius 90), Post.

SECOND LEVEL FINAL TABLE 2005

		Pld	W	D	L	F	A	Pts
1	JK Vaprus Pärnu	36	26	6	4	92	39	84
2	FC Levadia Tallinn II	36	26	4	6	104	31	82
3	FC Ajax Lasnamäe	36	23	8	5	111	30	77
4	JK Tallinna Kalev	36	18	9	9	85	71	63
5	JK Tervis Pärnu	36	14	8	14	73	53	50
6	FC TMVK II Tallinn	36	12	5	19	51	80	41
7	FC Elva	36	10	6	20	42	71	36
8	Lelle SK	36	11	1	24	49	100	34
9	Tallinna JK	36	9	4	23	38	100	30
10	JK Merkuur-Juunior Tartu	36	3	5	28	27	97	14

N.B. FC Levadia Tallinn II ineligible for promotion.

PROMOTION/RELEGATION PLAY-OFFS
(13/11/05)
FC Ajax Lasnamäe 1, FC Kuressaare 0
(19/11/05)
FC Kuressaare 2, FC Ajax Lasnamäe 1
(2-2; FC Ajax Lasnamäe on away goal)

Faroe Islands

Excitement all the way to the end

There was an early start and a late finish to the 1. deild, the Faroe Islands national championship, in 2005 as, for the first time ever, 27 matches were played by the ten clubs instead of the usual 18.

Some feared that the league extension might result in one team running away with the title, but in the event quite the opposite happened. By mid-October, with a couple of matches remaining, no fewer than four clubs were still in contention for the title. There was also great excitement in the battle for survival, with three teams still under threat of relegation going into the final day.

As the season progressed, the table effectively separated into two halves, with five teams breaking away to contest the title and the other five struggling to avoid the drop. It made for some engrossing entertainment, with just about every match having something at stake.

All good stories should have an exciting ending, and the league planners certainly got their wish when the two clubs from the capital, B36 and HB, met in the Gundadalur in Tórshavn on the last day in a winner-takes-all finale. B36 were one point ahead of HB, the champions for the previous three seasons, with Skála, the season's surprise package, another point in arrears. If B36 or HB won, the title would be theirs, but if the two Tórshavn clubs drew and Skála simultaneously won at home to relegation-threatened GÍ, then Skála would take the title for the very first time.

B36 win the day

It was to be B36's day. Sigfríður Clementsen's side had drawn their previous two meetings with HB, but this time they went one better, winning the game 2-1 with goals from veteran skipper Allan Mørkøre (his 11th of the season) and another Faroe Islands international, midfielder Frode Benjaminsen. As Skála could only manage a 2-2 draw with GÍ, B36 could also have drawn and still finished first, but the title triumph tasted all the sweeter for having wrapped it up with a win over their local rivals.

It was a double blow for HB as it meant they also missed out on a European place. Although Skála, HB and NSÍ (6-5 winners over KÍ) all finished level on 50 points, it was Skála who had the best head-to-head record among the three and thus qualified for the UEFA Cup.

The other UEFA Cup place had been decided three months earlier when, in the final of the Cup, GÍ hammered fellow strugglers ÍF 4-1 at the Gundadalur to take the trophy for the sixth time. Remarkably, all of the four teams that went on to challenge for the league title were eliminated early from the Cup. B36 actually beat Skála 4-1 away in their opening tie but were later disqualified for fielding an unregistered player.

GÍ and ÍF went on to contest the final after knocking out second division opponents in the semis. GÍ's victims were B71, humbled 7-2 on aggregate, and the two teams would meet again at the end of the season, with GÍ salvaging their top-flight status thanks to an even more one-sided aggregate win (7-1).

Play-off scrapped

It was the fourth year running that the team from the 1. deild had won the play-off, so, to balance things

NATIONAL TEAM RESULTS 2005/06

17/8/05	Cyprus (WCQ)	H	Toftir	0-3	
3/9/05	France (WCQ)	A	Lens	0-3	
7/9/05	Israel (WCQ)	H	Tórshavn	0-2	
8/10/05	Israel (WCQ)	A	Tel Aviv	1-2	Samuelsen S. (90)
14/5/06	Poland	A	Wronki	0-4	

Faroe Islands

out, it was decided that the fixture would be scrapped in 2006, with two teams being promoted and relegated automatically instead. After two successive play-off failures, B71 will certainly be glad of that.

The 2. deild was won by B68, the team automatically relegated in 2004. They swapped places with the previous season's 2. deild champions, TB – condemned to an immediate relegation by their last-day 0-0 draw against B68's Cup semi-final conquerors, ÍF.

The busy domestic schedule seemed to have a positive effect on B36 in Europe as they claimed a rare win for the islands by knocking North Atlantic 'neighbours' ÍBV of Iceland out of the UEFA Cup and then putting up a courageous performance against FC Midtjylland of Denmark.

There was a change of regime for the Faroe Islands national side at the end of the World Cup qualifying campaign, with Henrik Larsen calling it a day and handing over the reins to his assistant, ex-NSÍ coach Jógvan Martin Olsen. The new man managed to fit in just one preparatory game in advance of the Euro 2008 qualifiers – a 4-0 defeat in Poland – but there should be big crowds on the islands in 2007 for the visit of new world champions Italy and World Cup runners-up France.

NATIONAL TEAM APPEARANCES 2005/06

Coach – Henrik LARSEN (DEN) / (10/10/05) Jøgvan Martin OLSEN

Player	DOB	Club	CYP	FRA	ISR	ISR	Pol	Caps	Goals
Jens Martin KNUDSEN	11/6/67	NSÍ	G				G46	65	-
Johan Byrial HANSEN	18/9/75	AC Horsens (DEN)	D79			D15		15	-
Óli JOHANNESEN	6/5/72	TB	D	D	D	D	D	77	1
Jón Rói JACOBSEN	7/4/83	BK Frem (DEN)	D	D	D	D		25	-
Atli DANIELSEN	15/8/83	Sogndal IL (NOR) /KÍ	D		s15		D80	13	-
Súni OLSEN	7/3/81	AaB (DEN)	M15	M	M		M	24	1
Jákup á BORG	26/10/79	HB	M	M55	M69		M	43	2
Rógvi JACOBSEN	5/3/79	KR (ISL)	M	s66	M	M		36	6
Claus Bech JØRGENSEN	27/4/76	Coventry City (ENG)	M	M76	M85	M		9	1
Andrew av FLØTUM	13/6/79	Fremad Amager (DEN)	A	M	s61	A66		22	1
Todi JÓNSSON	2/2/72	IK Start (NOR)	A46	A66				45	9
Mortan úr HØRG	21/9/80	VB /HB	s15	D	D	D	s80	5	-
Christian Høgni JACOBSEN	12/5/80	NSÍ	s46	s55	A61	A80	A	27	2
Hedin á LAKJUNI	19/2/78	KÍ	s79	s76	s69			16	1
Jájup MIKKELSEN	14/8/70	B36		G	G	G	s46	42	-
Ingi HØJSTED	12/11/85	B36		M	M	M		4	-
Fródi BENJAMINSEN	14/12/77	B36		M	M	M	M62	36	2
Simun SAMUELSEN	21/5/85	Keflavík (ISL)			s85	s80		3	1
Jónhard FREDERIKSBERG	27/8/80	Skála				s66		10	-
Jann Ingi PETERSEN	7/1/84	B68					D80	10	-
Janus JOENSEN	27/5/81	HB					D56	1	-
Kári NIELSEN	3/3/81	HB					M	2	-
Hans Pauli SAMUELSEN	18/10/84	EB/Streymur					A69	1	-
Hjalgrím ELTTØR	3/3/83	KÍ					s56	13	-
Bárdur OLSEN	1986	EB/Streymur					s62	1	-
Bjarni JØRGENSEN	29/8/84	Skála					s69	1	-
Rasmus NOLSØE	25/1/85	HB					s80	1	-

Faroe Islands

EUROPEAN CUPS 2005/06

UEFA CHAMPIONS LEAGUE

HB
1st qualifying round FBK KAUNAS (LIT)
H 2-4 *Lag (29, 62)*
Johannesen, Danielsen (Askelsen 61), Nielsen M.H., Joensen Jó., Joensen J.M., Borg, Nolsøe Rú., Nielsen K., Larsen, Lag (Mortensen 74), Jespersen (Mortansson 46).
A 0-4
Johannesen, Joensen Jó., Nielsen M.H. (Danielsen 59), Joensen J.M., Lag (Askelsen 59), Larsen (Mortansson 59), Nolsøe Ra., Nolsøe Rú., Nielsen K., Jacobsen, Borg.

UEFA CUP

NSÍ
1st qualifying round METALURGS LIEPAJA (LAT)
H 0-3
Knudsen, Hansen Ó., Hansen D. (Hansen K. 75), Nielsen, Johannesen, Hansen J.R. (Løkin 67), Petersen J., Petersen H.L., Onyema, Olsen A., Joensen (Dalbud 85).
A 0-3
Knudsen, Hansen Ó., Nielsen, Johannesen, Hansen J.R. (Danielsen 87), Petersen J., Petersen H.L., Jacobsen (Hansen K. 75), Onyema, Olsen A., Joensen (Hansen D. 42).

B36
1st qualifying round ÍBV (ISL)
A 1-1 *Midjord (7)*
Mikkelsen, Alex, Mørkøre, Thorsteinsson, Højsted (Joensen B.H. 90), Thomassen, Benjaminsen, Joensen N. (Hanssen 87), Jacobsen K., Matras, Midjord.
H 2-1 *Mørkøre (2), Midjord (59)*
Mikkelsen, Alex, Mørkøre, Thorsteinsson, Højsted, Thomassen, Benjaminsen, Joensen N. (Skorini 87), Jacobsen K., Matras, Midjord (Hanssen 78).

2nd qualifying round FC MIDTJYLLAND (DEN)
A 1-2 *Højsted (79)*
Mikkelsen, Alex, Mørkøre, Joensen B.H., Thorsteinsson, Højsted (Skorini 90), Thomassen, Joensen N. (Gunnarsson 80), Jacobsen K., Matras, Hanssen (Hermansen 78).
H 2-2 *Midjord (3), Mørkøre (85)*
Mikkelsen, Alex, Mørkøre, Joensen B.H., Thorsteinsson, Højsted (Onyebuchi 88), Thomassen, Benjaminsen, Joensen N. (Skorini 90), Matras, Midjord (Hanssen 78).

TOP GOALSCORERS 2005

18	Christian Høgni JACOBSEN (NSÍ)
16	Sorin ANGHEL (EB/Streymur)
13	Jónhard FREDERIKSBERG (Skála)
12	Bogi GREGERSEN (Skála)
11	Allan MØRKØRE (B36)
	Samal JOENSEN (GÍ)
	Hans á LAG (HB)
9	Súni OLSEN (GÍ)
	Hedin á LAKJUNI (KÍ)
	Hjalgrim ELTTØR (KÍ)
	Dan DJURHUUS (VB)

LEAGUE RESULTS/ SCORERS/APPEARANCES/ GOALS 2005

B36
Coach – Sigfridur Clementsen

2005				
28/3	NSÍ	h	0-1	
3/4	TB	a	0-0	
10/4	EB/Streymur	h	1-0	Onyebuchi
17/4	ÍF	a	2-0	Onyebuchi, Jacobsen K.
24/4	KÍ	h	2-1	Onyebuchi, Mørkøre
1/5	VB	a	3-0	Mørkøre, Alex, Hermansen
8/5	GÍ	h	3-0	Thomassen, Midjord, Mørkøre
11/5	Skála	a	1-1	Mørkøre
16/5	HB	h	0-0	
22/5	Skála	h	2-2	Mørkøre, Benjaminsen
29/5	NSÍ	h	2-0	Mørkøre, Højgaard
19/6	TB	h	0-0	
22/6	VB	a	2-1	Midjord, Mørkøre
27/6	ÍF	a	2-0	Midjord, Benjaminsen
3/7	EB/Streymur	h	0-1	
9/7	KÍ	a	2-0	Mørkøre, Benjaminsen
18/7	GÍ	h	3-1	Benjaminsen, Højsted, Onyebuchi
7/8	HB	a	1-1	Onyebuchi
14/8	Skála	a	2-2	Midjord, Onyebuchi
21/8	NSÍ	a	0-1	
28/8	VB	h	1-0	Thomassen
11/9	TB	a	2-1	Mørkøre, Benjaminsen
18/9	ÍF	h	1-1	Alex
25/9	EB/Streymur	a	2-1	Onyebuchi, Mørkøre
2/10	KÍ	h	0-0	
16/10	GÍ	a	2-1	Benjaminsen, Midjord
22/10	HB	h	2-1	Mørkøre, Benjaminsen

No	Name	Nat	Pos	Aps	(s)	Gls
2	ALEX dos Santos	BRA	D	27		2
10	Frodi BENJAMINSEN		M	26		7
12	Johan ELLLINSGAARD		M		(2)	
14	Johan V. GUNNARSSON		M	1	(1)	
11	Levi HANSSEN	NZL	A	4	(14)	
4	Bogi HERMANSEN		M		(10)	1
18	Eydun HØJGAARD		M	9	(2)	1
6	Ingi HØJSTED		D	24		1
28	Herbert i Lon JACOBSEN		D	15		
15	Kenneth JACOBSEN		D	22	(2)	1
13	Bardur H. JOENSEN		D	2	(11)	
14	Niels JOENSEN		M	5	(3)	
5	Danjal Petur JOHANSEN		D		(1)	
22	Klæmint MATRAS		M	17	(4)	
20	Bergur MIDJORD		A	24	(1)	5
1	Jakup MIKKELSEN		G	27		
3	Allan MØRKØRE		D	27		11
7	Okeke Obele ONYEBUCHI	RSA	A	15	(9)	7
17	Thomas H. RUBEKSEN		A		(6)	
9	Ronnie SAMUELSEN		M		(1)	
12	Heini i SKORINI		M		(1)	
8	Mikkjal THOMASSEN		M	23		2
19	Pól THORTEINSSON		D	24	(1)	
7	WELLINGTON da Silva Soares	BRA	A	5	(4)	

EB/STREYMUR
Coach – Piotr Krakowski (POL)

2005				
28/3	GÍ	a	2-1	Clementsen, Samuelsen H.P.

Faroe Islands

FINAL LEAGUE TABLE 2005

		Pld	Home					Away					Total					Pts
			W	D	L	F	A	W	D	L	F	A	W	D	L	F	A	
1	B36	27	7	5	2	17	8	8	4	1	21	9	15	9	3	38	17	54
2	Skála	27	7	6	1	33	18	6	5	2	22	12	13	11	3	55	30	50
3	HB	27	12	1	1	47	11	3	4	6	19	24	15	5	7	66	35	50
4	NSÍ	27	8	4	1	27	15	6	4	4	31	29	14	8	5	58	44	50
5	EB/Streymur	27	4	7	2	24	13	7	3	4	24	22	11	10	6	48	35	43
6	ÍF	27	3	4	6	16	22	3	5	6	16	35	6	9	12	32	57	27
7	KÍ	27	3	2	9	28	31	4	2	7	12	21	7	4	16	40	52	25
8	VB	27	4	2	8	21	26	2	4	7	15	31	6	6	15	36	57	24
9	GÍ	27	2	2	9	15	29	4	3	7	20	29	6	5	16	35	58	23
10	TB	27	4	4	5	18	15	1	3	10	8	34	5	7	15	26	49	22

Date	Opp	H/A	Score	Scorers
3/4	Skála	h	0-0	
10/4	B36	a	0-1	
17/4	NSÍ	h	2-2	Samuelsen H.P., Hansen G.
24/4	TB	a	0-3	
1/5	HB	a	0-4	
8/5	ÍF	h	2-2	Bø, Joensen T.
11/5	KÍ	a	1-0	Petersen
16/5	VB	h	1-1	Samuelsen H.P.
22/5	ÍF	a	3-2	Vesturtún 2, Anghel
29/5	KÍ	h	1-0	Samuelsen H.P.
12/6	HB	a	0-3	
18/6	NSÍ	h	2-2	Samuelsen H.P., Anghel
25/6	TB	a	1-1	Samuelsen H.P.
3/7	B36	a	1-0	Petersen
9/7	GÍ	h	1-1	Petersen
17/7	Skála	a	1-1	Anghel
7/8	VB	h	6-1	Anghel 2, Petersen 2, Olsen Bá., Samuelsen H.P.
13/8	ÍF	h	1-1	Bø
21/8	KÍ	a	4-2	Anghel 2, Samuelsen H.P., Bø
27/8	HB	h	4-0	Anghel 3, Olsen Bá.
11/9	NSÍ	a	5-2	Joensen T. 2, Samuelsen R., Anghel, Petersen
21/9	TB	h	3-0	Anghel, Hansen G., Bø
25/9	B36	h	1-2	Anghel
2/10	GÍ	a	5-1	Anghel 3, Olsen Bá., Niclasen
16/10	Skála	h	0-1	
22/10	VB	a	1-1	Hansen G.

No	Name	Nat	Pos	Aps	(s)	Gls
10	Sorin ANGHEL	ROM	A	25		16
19	Egil a BØ		D	23	(1)	4
22	Fródi CLEMENTSEN		D	16	(3)	1
7	Marni DJURHUUS		M	23		
4	Esmar EIDSIGARD		D	9	(3)	
18	Arnbjørn T. HANSEN		D		(2)	
21	Gert HANSEN		D	26	(1)	3
9	Hallur JACOBSEN		M	1	(5)	
18	Eydfinnur JOENSEN		M	1	(1)	
8	Jákup M. JOENSEN		M	10	(6)	
22/14	Teitur JOENSEN		M	7	(8)	3
14/22	Leif NICLASEN		A	1	(6)	1
15	Bárdur OLSEN		M	27		3
18	Brian OLSEN		M		(8)	
6	Andrzej PACEK	POL	D	20	(1)	

No	Name		Nat	Pos	Aps	(s)	Gls
17	Sonni L. PETERSEN			A	18	(8)	6
1	Magnus POULSEN			G	3		
13	Ólavur POULSEN			M	9	(3)	
11	Hans Pauli SAMUELSEN			M	21	(1)	8
8/5	Ronnie SAMUELSEN			M	6	(2)	1
1	Gunnar á STEIG			G	11		
12	Johan á STONGUM			M	12	(3)	
1	Rene TORGARD			G	13		
5	Knút VESTURTÚN			D	15	(2)	2
18	Finnbjørn ZACHARIASEN			M		(1)	

GÍ
Coach – Krzysztof Popczynski (POL); (2/10/05) Petur Mohr

2005

Date	Opp	H/A	Score	Scorers
28/3	EB/Streymur	h	1-2	Olsen
3/4	ÍF	a	3-4	Olsen, Popczynski, og (Petersen E.)
10/4	KÍ	h	1-2	Olsen
17/4	VB	a	1-0	Dalheim
20/4	HB	a	1-3	Jacobsen S.L.
1/5	Skála	h	2-3	Olsen 2
8/5	B36	a	0-3	
11/5	NSÍ	h	0-0	
16/5	TB	a	0-3	
22/5	VB	a	3-0	Joensen Sa., Popczynski, Olsen
29/5	ÍF	h	3-0	Olsen 2, Jacobsen S.L.
12/6	KÍ	a	2-1	Olsen, Jacobsen S.L.
19/6	HB	h	0-2	
26/6	NSÍ	a	1-1	Jacobsen S.L.
9/7	EB/Streymur	a	1-1	Joensen Sa.
14/7	TB	h	2-1	Joensen Sa. 2
18/7	B36	a	1-3	Joensen Sa.
7/8	Skála	h	1-4	Jacobsen P.Ar.
13/8	VB	h	1-1	Joensen Sa.
21/8	ÍF	a	3-1	Popczynski 2, Joensen Sa.
28/8	KÍ	h	1-2	Joensen Sa.
11/9	HB	a	1-4	Popczynski
18/9	NSÍ	h	1-5	Joensen Sa.
25/9	TB	a	1-3	Joensen Sa.
2/10	EB/Streymur	h	1-5	Joensen Sa.
16/10	B36	h	1-2	Petersen Á.R.
22/10	Skála	a	2-2	Jacobsen H., Jacobsen P.Ar.

No	Name	Nat	Pos	Aps	(s)	Gls
1	Marcin DAWID	POL	G	12		
2	Jónreid DALHEIM		M	19	(6)	1

Faroe Islands

7/18	Hans Jørgin DJURHUUS		D	9	
5	Kaj ENNIGARD		D	11	(8)
10	Atli GREGERSEN		D	16	(1)
1	Hallur HANSEN		G	5	
7	Leivur HANSEN		D	3	
3	Hanus JACOBSEN		M	24	(2)	1
11	Per JACOBSEN		A		(2)
10	Poul Andrias JACOBSEN		M		(1)
18	Poul Arni JACOBSEN		A	10	(7)	2
15	Poul H. JACOBSEN		M	10	(3)
14	Sam JACOBSEN		D	20	(2)
11	Símun Louis JACOBSEN		M	22	(1)	4
15	Sverri JACOBSEN		A		(2)
16	Magni JARNSKOR		M	11	(7)
1	Meinhardt JOENSEN		G	1	
16	Mortan JOENSEN		G	2	
1	Poul Næss JOENSEN		G	6	
4	Samal JOENSEN		M	20	(2)	11
1	Sunvard JOENSEN		G	1	
12	Bjarni JUSTINUSSEN		D	5	(2)
9	Súni OLSEN		M	13	(1)	9
6	Áslakkur R. PETERSEN		D	16	(7)	1
7	Hans Pauli PETERSEN		M	15	(1)
8	Krzysztof POPCZYNSKI	POL	A	20	(6)	5
10	Páll Rói POULSEN		D		(1)
17	Robert RZECZYCKI	POL	D	26	

HB
Coach – Heine Fernandez (DEN); (11/9/05) Julian Hansen

2005

28/3	KÍ	a	3-4	Askelsen 2, Lag
3/4	NSÍ	h	2-1	Dam, Nolsøe Rú.
10/4	VB	a	0-1	
17/4	TB	h	3-1	Lag, Dam, og (Johannesen O.)
20/4	GÍ	h	3-1	Lag, Borg, Askelsen
1/5	EB/Streymur	h	4-0	Nolsøe Rú. 3, Askelsen
8/5	Skála	a	3-4	Nolsøe Ra. 3
11/5	ÍF	h	6-0	Fernandez 2, og (Eliasen B.), Askelsen, Nolsøe Rú., Jespersen
16/5	B36	a	0-0	
23/5	NSÍ	h	3-1	Lag, Jespersen, Borg
29/5	TB	a	2-1	Askelsen, Nolsøe Rú.
12/6	EB/Streymur	h	3-0	Borg, Lag, Nolsøe Ra.
19/6	GÍ	a	2-0	Nolsøe Ra., Askelsen
22/6	Skála	h	1-2	Nolsøe Rú.
3/7	VB	a	2-2	Jespersen, Lag
10/7	ÍF	h	9-0	Lag 2, Fernandez 2, Mortansson 2, Borg, Jespersen, Danielsen
16/7	KÍ	a	3-2	Lag 2, Askelsen
7/8	B36	h	1-1	Mortensen
13/8	NSÍ	a	1-2	Jespersen
21/8	TB	h	4-1	Mortansson 2, Nolsøe Ra., Arge
27/8	EB/Streymur	a	0-4	
11/9	GÍ	h	4-1	Jespersen, Borg, Rubeksen, Arge
18/9	Skála	a	1-1	og (Rasmussen)
25/9	VB	h	2-1	Mortensen, Lag
2/10	ÍF	a	1-1	Arge
16/10	KÍ	h	2-1	Arge, Borg
22/10	B36	a	1-2	Mortansson

No	Name		Nat	Pos	Aps	(s)	Gls
8	Uni ARGE			A	2	(6)	4

6	Tor-Ingar ASKELSEN		M	22	(3)	8
9	Jákup á BORG		M	25		6
15	Rani Debes CHRISTIANSEN		D	1	(3)	
23	John Henri DAM		A	6	(3)	2
18	Hallur DANIELSEN		D	22	(2)	1
11	Heine FERNANDEZ	DEN	A	2	(5)	4
8	Svenn JACOBSEN		M	11	(9)	
10	Rókur av Fløtum JESPERSEN		M	16	(9)	6
4	Janus M. JOENSEN		D	26		
2	Johannis JOENSEN		D	19	(1)	
24	Páll Mohr JOENSEN		A	1	(4)	
1	Bárdur JOHANNESEN		G	27		
5	Hans á LAG		D	21	(3)	11
12	Emil Nolsøe LEIFSSON		M	1	(2)	
20	Bardur MORTANSSON		A	9	(5)	5
19	Vagnur M. MORTENSEN		D	11	(3)	2
23	Johan Eivind MOURITSEN		A		(1)	
14	Kári NIELSEN		M	24		
17	Rasmus NOLSØE		D	26		6
7	Rúni NOLSØE		M	25		7
22	Hendrik RUBEKSEN		A		(11)	1
16	Tróndur VATHHAMAR		G		(1)	

ÍF
Coach – Petur Simonsen

2005

28/3	VB	a	1-0	Zachariasen
3/4	GÍ	h	4-3	Eliasen H., Nielsen, Lakjuni M., Sylla
10/4	Skála	a	3-3	Ennigard, Zachariasen, Lakjuni M.
17/4	B36	h	0-2	
24/4	NSÍ	a	1-1	Eliasen S.
1/5	TB	h	1-0	Elttør
8/5	EB/Streymur	a	2-2	Elttør, Nielsen
11/5	HB	a	0-6	
16/5	KÍ	h	0-3	
22/5	EB/Streymur	h	2-3	Lakjuni M., Nielsen
29/5	GÍ	a	0-3	
12/6	Skála	h	0-0	
19/6	VB	a	2-3	Sylla, Ennigard
27/6	B36	h	0-2	
2/7	KÍ	h	3-0	Petersen E., Eliasen B. 2
10/7	HB	a	0-9	
17/7	NSÍ	h	1-2	Lakjuni M.
7/8	TB	a	1-0	Zachariasen
13/8	EB/Streymur	a	1-1	Sylla
21/8	GÍ	h	1-3	Eliasen H.
28/8	Skála	a	1-2	Sylla
11/9	VB	h	3-3	Eliasen B.,Eliasen S. 2
18/9	B36	a	1-1	Zachariasen
25/9	KÍ	a	2-0	Ryggshamar, Sylla
2/10	HB	h	1-1	Eliasen H.
16/10	NSÍ	a	1-4	Sylla
22/10	TB	h	0-0	

No	Name	Nat	Pos	Aps	(s)	Gls
16	Jakup Helgi EGHOLM		G	1		
7	Tordur EGHOLM		M		(1)	
6	Bartal ELIASEN		D	20	(5)	3
10	Hanus ELIASEN		M	20	(5)	3
15/30	Simun ELIASEN		M	25		3
3	Sverri ELLINGSGAARD		M	1	(1)	
18	Rúni ELTTØR		D	19	(1)	2
5	Poul ENNIGARD		D	20		2
4/12	Danjal Pauli HØJGAARD		M		(6)	
16/1	Allan JOENSEN		G	12		

Faroe Islands

No	Name	Nat	Pos	Aps	(s)	Gls
1	Jacob KAAS	DEN	G	10		
11/14	Bárdur á LAKJUNI		M	3	(6)	
28	Magni á LAKJUNI		A	13	(4)	4
8	Fritleif í LAMBANUM		M	15	(2)	
14	Emil Nolsøe LEIFSSON		M	9		
12	Gunnar NIELSEN		M	11	(3)	3
9	Atli PETERSEN		D	8	(17)	
2	Áki PETERSEN		M	15	(3)	
11	Eydolvur PETERSEN		M	15		1
19	Frank POULSEN		M	1	(6)	
19	Roy RÓIN		M		(1)	
6/15	Eydun RYGGSHAMAR		M	11		1
20	Ahmed Davy SYLLA	CIV	A	26	(1)	6
21	John Solheim THOMSEN		M	11	(2)	
16/1	Tordur THOMSEN		G	4		
16	Emil TOFTEGAARD		G		(1)	
17	Høgni ZACHARIASEN		M	27		4

KÍ
Coach – Ove Flindt Bjerg (DEN); (8/5/05) Oddbjørn Joensen

2005

28/3	HB	h	4-3	Fles 2, Danielsen, Elttør
3/4	VB	h	1-1	Danielsen
10/4	GÍ	a	2-1	Danielsen, Lakjuni
19/4	Skála	h	0-2	
24/4	B36	a	1-2	Elttør
1/5	NSÍ	h	2-3	Samuelsen J. 2
8/5	TB	a	0-0	
11/5	EB/Streymur	h	0-1	
16/5	ÍF	a	3-0	Lakjuni 2, Nysted
22/5	TB	h	6-1	Lakjuni 3, Danielsen, Nysted, Jacobsen K.
29/5	EB/Streymur	a	0-1	
12/6	GÍ	h	1-2	Elttør
15/6	Skála	a	0-4	
25/6	VB	a	1-5	Lakjuni
2/7	ÍF	h	0-3	
9/7	B36	h	0-2	
16/7	HB	h	2-3	Danielsen, Elttør
7/8	NSÍ	a	0-1	
13/8	TB	a	2-1	Elttør, Jacobsen K.
21/8	EB/Streymur	h	2-4	Wierzbicki, Nysted
28/8	GÍ	a	2-1	Wierzbicki, Lakjuni
11/9	Skála	h	0-0	
15/9	VB	h	5-1	Mørkøre 3, Lakjuni, Elttør
25/9	ÍF	h	0-2	
2/10	B36	a	0-0	
16/10	HB	a	1-2	Nysted
22/10	NSÍ	h	5-6	Elttør 3, Nysted, Joensen S.

No	Name	Nat	Pos	Aps	(s)	Gls
4	Jan ANDREASEN		D	21	(4)	
5	Harley BERTHOLDSEN		D	11	(1)	
2	Leon BJARTALÍD		D	18	(3)	
11	Atli DANIELSEN		M	18		5
10	Hjalgrim ELTTØR		A	26		9
17	Erling FLES		A	6	(5)	2
12	John HAMMER		A		(1)	
17	Emir HUSEINOVIC	BOS	M		(2)	
17	Jon JACOBSEN		M		(1)	
20	Kristoffur JACOBSEN		A	9	(16)	2
15	Otto JACOBSEN		M		(1)	
12	Sigmund JACOBSEN		M		(2)	
2	Allan JOENSEN		M		(1)	
6	Arnold JOENSEN		M	25	(1)	
8	Jan JOENSEN		M	3		
1	Kartin JOENSEN		G	15		
16	Meinhardt JOENSEN		G	10		
8	Símun JOENSEN		M	10		1
7	Steffan KALSØ		D		(1)	
18	Eydun KLAKSTEIN		M	14		
9	Hedin á LAKJUNI		A	27		9
15	Tórdur LERVIG		M	2	(3)	
7	Høgni MADSEN		M	22		
11	Kurt MØRKØRE		A	6		3
5	Niclas NICLASEN		D	20		
19	Ovi NYSTED		D	22	(3)	5
8	Julian SAMUELSEN		A	1	(7)	2
16	Mathias SAMUELSEN		G	2		
12	Marek WIERZBICKI	POL	M	9		2

NSÍ
Coach – Trygvi Mortensen

2005

28/3	B36	a	1-0	Jacobsen C.H.
3/4	HB	a	1-2	Olsen A.
10/4	TB	h	1-1	Olsen A.
17/4	EB/Streymur	a	2-2	Onyema, Jacobsen C.H.
24/4	ÍF	h	1-1	Jacobsen C.H.
1/5	KÍ	a	3-2	Jacobsen C.H., Hansen Ó., Hansen D.
8/5	VB	h	5-1	Petersen H.L., Olsen A., Jacobsen C.H., Onyema, Dalbud
11/5	GÍ	a	0-0	
16/5	Skála	h	1-3	Olsen A.
23/5	HB	a	1-3	Petersen H.L.
29/5	B36	a	0-2	
11/6	TB	h	2-0	Petersen J., Petersen H.L.
18/6	EB/Streymur	a	2-2	Petersen H.L., Nielsen
26/6	GÍ	h	1-1	Onyema
3/7	Skála	a	1-3	Hansen Ó.
10/7	VB	h	3-1	Jacobsen C.H.3
17/7	ÍF	a	2-1	Onyema, Joensen
7/8	KÍ	h	1-0	Joensen
13/8	HB	h	2-1	Jacobsen C.H.2
21/8	B36	h	1-0	Joensen
28/8	TB	a	4-4	Joensen, Hansen J., Jacobsen C.H., Petersen H.L.
11/9	EB/Streymur	h	2-5	Hansen J., Olsen A.
18/9	GÍ	a	5-1	Jacobsen C.H.2, Hansen Ó., Petersen J., Joensen
266/9	Skála	h	3-3	Joensen, Johannesen, Jacobsen C.H.
2/10	VB	a	3-2	Jacobsen C.H., Olsen A., Hansen J.
16/10	ÍF	h	4-1	Petersen H.L., Olsen A., Jacobsen C.H., og (Eliasen S.)
22/10	KÍ	a	6-5	Jacobsen C.H.2, Hansen D., Petersen J., Hansen Ó., Petersen H.L.

No	Name	Nat	Pos	Aps	(s)	Gls
2	Hjalmar DALBUD		A		(7)	1
20	Debes DANIELSEN		A		(4)	
2	Áki L. HANSEN		M		(1)	
4	Dánjal HANSEN		D	21	(5)	2
12	Einar HANSEN		M	14	(9)	
23	Jústinus R. HANSEN		D	20	(9)	3
5	Kári HANSEN		M	4	(9)	
3	Óli HANSEN		D	27		4
10	Christian Høgni JACOBSEN		A	25		18
18	Sjúrdur JACOBSEN		D	7	(4)	

Faroe Islands

	Name	Nat	Pos	Aps	(s)	Gls
	Pall Mohr JOENSEN		M	11	(3)	6
9	Viggo JOHANNESEN		D	24	(1)	1
	Jens Martin KNUDSEN		G	27		
	Gert LANGGAARD		M	3	(3)	
9	Bogi LØKIN		M	2	(6)	
5	Brynjólvur NIELSEN		M	27		1
1	Jan NÓNKLETT		A		(1)	
3	Andy OLSEN		M	25	(2)	7
9	Bugvi OLSEN		M		(1)	
1	Ikechukwo ONYEMA	NGA	A	12	(5)	4
	Helgi L. PETERSEN		A	23		7
	Jónstein PETERSEN		M	25	(2)	3

SKÁLA
Coach – Jóhan Nielsen

2005

Date	Opp	h/a	Score	Scorers
28/3	TB	h	5-1	Frederiksberg 2, Gregersen, Thorleifsson, Florescu
3/4	EB/Streymur	a	0-0	
10/4	ÍF	h	3-3	Frederiksberg, Gregersen 2
19/4	KÍ	a	2-0	Thorleifsson, Frederiksberg
24/4	VB	h	0-1	
1/5	GÍ	a	3-2	Jacobsen P.D. 2, Curcic
8/5	HB	h	4-3	Rasmussen, Jacobsen P.D., Curcic, Frederiksberg
11/5	B36	h	1-1	Gregersen
16/5	NSÍ	a	0-1	
22/5	B36	a	2-2	Jørgensen, Frederiksberg
29/5	VB	h	3-1	Thorleifsson 2, Gregersen
12/6	ÍF	a	0-0	
15/6	KÍ	h	4-0	Gregersen 3, Berg A.
22/6	HB	a	2-1	Berg A., Stankovic
3/7	NSÍ	h	3-1	Florescu, Jacobsen P.D., Thorleifsson
10/7	TB	a	2-0	Frederiksberg, Thorleifsson
17/7	EB/Streymur	h	1-1	Jacobsen P.D.
7/8	GÍ	a	4-1	Jørgensen, Gregersen, Rasmussen, Frederiksberg
14/8	B36	h	2-2	Gregersen 2
21/8	VB	a	5-1	Frederiksberg 2, Jørgensen 2, Jacobsen R.
28/8	ÍF	h	2-1	Rasmussen, Florescu
11/9	KÍ	a	0-0	
18/9	HB	h	1-1	Gregersen
26/9	NSÍ	a	3-3	Frederiksberg 3
2/10	TB	a	0-1	
16/10	EB/Streymur	a	1-0	Stankovic
22/10	GÍ	h	2-2	Florescu, Poulsen

No	Name	Nat	Pos	Aps	(s)	Gls
22	Arnhold BERG		D	4	(7)	2
22	Jogvan BERG		A		(1)	
19/11	Milic CURCIC	SCG	D	22	(1)	2
2	Bárdur DANIELSEN		D	11	(7)	
1	Vlada FILIPOVIC	SCG	G	19		
14	Iulian FLORESCU	ROM	D	26		4
10	Jónhard FREDERIKSBERG		A	27		13
3	Ionel Cristian GORGONARU	ROM	D	4	(4)	
17	Bogi GREGERSEN		A	25	(1)	12
16	Pauli G. HANSEN		M	23		
6	Pætur Dam JACOBSEN		M	26		5
11	Rói JACOBSEN		D	5	(8)	1
15	Teitur JOENSEN		M		(3)	
18	Alexandur JOHANSEN		M		(3)	
15	Sveinur JUSTINUSSEN		M		(11)	
8	Bjarni JØRGENSEN		A	21		4
4	Johannus MIKKELSEN		M		(2)	
18	Malmberg OLSEN		A		(1)	
22	Volmar POULSEN		D		(4)	1
5	Rúni RASMUSSEN		D	25	(2)	3
7	Nenad STANKOVIC	SCG	M	26		2
9	Hanus THORLEIFSSON		M	25		6
1	Eugen VODA	ROM	G	8	(2)	

TB
Coach – Milan Milanovic

2005

Date	Opp	h/a	Score	Scorers
28/3	Skála	a	1-5	Larby
3/4	B36	h	0-0	
10/4	NSÍ	a	1-1	Johannesen O.
17/4	HB	a	1-3	Johannesen O.
24/4	EB/Streymur	h	3-0	Abrahamsen 2, Johannesen O.
1/5	ÍF	a	0-1	
8/5	KÍ	h	0-0	
11/5	VB	a	1-0	Larby
16/5	GÍ	h	3-0	Johannesen O., Abrahamsen, Poulsen
22/5	KÍ	a	1-6	Petrovic
29/5	HB	h	1-2	Johannesen O.
11/6	NSÍ	a	0-2	
19/6	B36	a	0-0	
25/6	EB/Streymur	h	1-1	Larby
10/7	Skála	a	0-2	
14/7	GÍ	a	1-2	Larby
17/7	VB	a	1-5	Johannesen J.
7/8	ÍF	h	0-1	
13/8	KÍ	h	1-2	Tomic
21/8	HB	a	1-4	Tomic
28/8	NSÍ	h	4-4	Mortensen D. 2, Johannesen O., Tomic
11/9	B36	h	1-2	Johannesen O.
21/9	EB/Streymur	a	0-3	
25/9	GÍ	h	3-1	Christiansen 2, Petrovic
2/10	Skála	h	1-0	Tomic
16/10	VB	h	0-2	
22/10	ÍF	a	0-0	

No	Name	Nat	Pos	Aps	(s)	Gls
4	Olivur ABRAHAMSEN		A	16	(2)	3
10	Hallur CHRISTIANSEN		A	14	(9)	2
10	Bardur DIMON		M	11		
5	Mortan ENNI		M	2	(12)	
17	Jon Tordur HOLM		M	6	(3)	
6	Petur HOLM		D		(3)	
11	Jon JOHANNESEN		D	23		1
13	Oli JOHANNESEN		D	27		7
17	Aleksandar JOVOCIC	SCG	M	19	(2)	
15	Emmanuel LARBY	GHA	A	17	(1)	4
	Niclas LUDVIG		D		(2)	
18	Predrag MARKOVIC	SCG	G	26		
1	Fredrik MERKORN		G	1		
2	Bui MORTENSEN		M	10	(9)	
9	Dan MORTENSEN		M	8	(2)	2
5	Daniel NYARKO	GHA	M	4		
7	Einar PETERSEN		M	24	(3)	
6	Aca PETROVIC	SCG	D	25		2
5	Allan POULSEN		M	15	(7)	1
8	Birgir RASMUSSEN		M	11	(12)	
16	Niels RØDGAARD		D		(1)	
2	Allan SMEDEMARK	DEN	M	4	(5)	
12	Eydun SVALDBARD		M		(1)	
15	Dejan TOMIC	SCG	A	10		4
	Magnus P. WEST		A		(1)	
14	Predrag ZIVKOVIC	SCG	D	24		

Faroe Islands

VB
Coach – John Christensen; (19/6/05) Dragan Kovacevic (SCG)

2005

Date	Opponent	H/A	Score	Scorers
28/3	ÍF	h	0-1	
3/4	KÍ	a	1-1	Kulic
10/4	HB	h	1-0	Kulic
17/4	GÍ	h	0-1	
24/4	Skála	a	1-0	Zivanovic
1/5	B36	h	0-3	
8/5	NSÍ	a	1-5	Poulsen P.N.
11/5	TB	h	0-1	
16/5	EB/Streymur	a	1-1	Poulsen Jón K.
22/5	GÍ	h	0-3	
29/5	Skála	a	1-3	Djurhuus
19/6	ÍF	h	3-2	Kulic 2, Djurhuus
22/6	B36	h	1-2	Zivanovic
25/6	KÍ	h	5-1	Djurhuus 2, Ble, Samuelsen, Poulsen Jón K.
3/7	HB	h	2-2	Samuelsen, Djurhuus
10/7	NSÍ	a	1-3	Djurhuus
17/7	TB	h	5-1	Samuelsen 2, Sørensen, Djurhuus, Kulic
7/8	EB/Streymur	a	1-6	Poulsen P.N.
13/8	GÍ	a	1-1	Poulsen John
21/8	Skála	h	1-5	Poulsen P.N.
28/8	B36	a	0-1	
11/9	ÍF	a	3-3	Zivanovic 2, Djurhuus
15/9	KÍ	a	1-5	Sørensen
25/9	HB	a	1-2	Poulsen P.N.
2/10	NSÍ	h	2-3	Djurhuus, Augustinussen
16/10	TB	a	2-0	úr Hørg M., Joensen D.J.
22/10	EB/Streymur	h	1-1	Ble

No	Name	Nat	Pos	Aps	(s)	Gls
6	Palli AUGUSTINUSSEN		M	3	(1)	1
7	Evrard BLE	CIV	M	24		2
14	Dan DJURHUUS		A	27		9
3	Mortan úr HØRG		D	27		1
13	Suni úr HØRG		D	19	(1)	
6	Danjal Johan JOENSEN		M	2	(6)	1
10	Hallur Dam JOENSEN		M	1	(2)	
1	Bjarni JOHANSEN		G	27		
15	Kenneth KJÆRBO		A		(1)	
10	Milan KULIC	SCG	M	22		5
6	Birni KÆRBECH		D	3	(1)	
17	Eydstein í LÁGABØ		M	1	(3)	
4	Kári í LÁGABØ		D	10	(1)	
6	Michael í LÁGABØ		D	11		
9	Sigmund MIKKELSEN		A	1	(2)	
19	Jákup F. OLSEN		D	17		
20	Jón Pauli OLSEN		M		(1)	
19	John POULSEN		M	7		1
5	Jón Krosslá POULSEN		M	1	(18)	2
15	Poul N. POULSEN		M	26	(1)	4
8	Símun SAMUELSEN		M	17		4
5	Jacob SKAANING		A		(6)	
2	Anders SØRENSEN	DEN	D	27		2
11	Nenad ZIVANOVIC	SCG	A	24		4

DOMESTIC CUP 2005

SECOND ROUND
(20/3/05)
Skála w/o B36
MB 0, B71 2
FS Vágar 1, TB 2
Fram w/o KÍ
EB/Streymur 0, B68 1
HB 3, NSÍ 2
VB 0, ÍF 1
(22/3/05)
LÍF 2, GÍ 4

QUARTER-FINALS
(5/5/05)
GÍ 3 *(Olsen 2, Jacobsen H. 10, Jacobsen P.Ar. 74)*, Skála 1 *(Frederiksberg 60)*
TB 2 *(Johannesen J. 22, Larby 82)*, B71 4 *(Hansen 43, Clayton 50,99, Poulsen 120)* *(aet)*
B68 2 *(Poulsen 53, Johnson 60)*, Fram 1 *(Poulsen 31)*,
HB 0, ÍF 1 *(Sylla 2)*

SEMI-FINALS
(6/7/05 & 24/7/05)
B71 1 *(Hentze 10)*, GÍ 5 *(Joensen Sa. 18, Olsen 45, 76, Popczynski 89, og 90)*
GÍ 2 *(Djurhuus 64, Joensen Sa. 90)*, B71 1 *(Olsen 51)*
(GÍ 7-2)

ÍF 2 *(Eliasen H. 30, 79)*, B68 1 *(Petersen 62)*
B68 0, ÍF 1 *(Eliasen B. 13)*
(ÍF 3-1)

FINAL
(29/7/05)
Gundadalur stadium, Tórshavn
GÍ 4 *(Jacobsen H. 30, 43, 85, Petersen A. 82)*
ÍF 1 *(Nielsen 73p)*
Referee – Sondun
GÍ – Joensen Su., Dalheim, Ennigard, Gregersen, Djurhuus (Rzeczycki 89), Petersen A. (Jacobsen Sam 86), Joensen Sa., Olsen, Jacobsen H., Popczynski, Jacobsen P.Ar. (Jarnskor 58).
ÍF – Thomsen, Lambanum, Elttør, Eliasen S., Petersen Aki, Eliasen H. (Petersen Atli 76), Petersen E., Zachariasen, Leifsson (Nielsen 57), Sylla, Lakjuni M. (Lakjuni B. 67).

SECOND LEVEL FINAL TABLE 2005

		Pld	W	D	L	F	A	Pts
1	B68	18	14	3	1	71	16	45
2	B71	18	13	2	3	66	20	41
3	FS Vágar	18	12	2	4	51	18	38
4	AB	18	12	2	4	55	33	38
5	HB II	18	7	1	10	40	44	22
6	LÍF	18	6	3	9	45	48	21
7	Royn	18	6	2	10	27	52	20
8	Sumba	18	6	1	11	35	68	19
9	B36	18	4	3	11	21	47	15
10	GÍ	18	0	1	17	18	83	1

PROMOTION/RELEGATION PLAY-OFFS
(26/10/05)
GÍ 3, B71 0
(29/10/05)
B71 1, GÍ 4
(GÍ 7-1)

Finland

Not in Finland, surely...

2005 was the year when the football world at large finally took notice of the Finnish domestic championship, the Veikkausliiga. Unfortunately, it was all for the wrong reasons.

In June, the previous season's runners-up AC Allianssi announced out of the blue that they had been taken over by new Belgian owners. Before long it was disclosed that the new proprietor was actually a mysterious Chinese businessman by the name of Ye Zheyun. The new club general manager, Olivier Suray, brought with him a Belgian coach, Thierry Pister, and six new players, mostly journeymen from the lower rungs of the Belgian league ladder. For his first match, away to champions FC Haka, Pister was instructed to field all his imports and the five least experienced Finnish players. Allianssi lost 8–0 after hapless performances by the new intake, the goalkeeper in particular. The regular keeper, Henri Sillanpää, had just been dispatched to a non-existent trial at La Louvière.

The evidence of some sort of foul play was overwhelming. An investigation was launched immediately and it completely overshadowed the rest of Allianssi's season. In fact, Pister and his crew regrouped and played decent enough football to secure a mid-table position before leaving Finland for good after the end of the season. That was not enough to save the club from ignominy, when more revelations about Mr. Ye were published. In the larger scheme of things the Allianssi affair turned out to be just an exotic outgrowth of the Belgian match-fixing scandal, with Suray later confessing that the game had been rigged. For the Finnish public it was a rude lesson in globalisation. It was quite a shock to learn that their sleepy domestic football scene had been made a target of illegal gambling on the other side of the planet. For Allianssi, it proved to be the end of the road. The club's Finnish board members were accused of nothing other than naievety but they failed to convince the Veikkausliiga of the financial viability of the club. Allianssi's league licence was therefore revoked, which meant that the 2006 Veikkausliiga season would consist of only 13 clubs rather than the scheduled 14.

First title

On the happier side of things, MyPa finally won their long-overdue first Finnish championship title – after finishing second five times and third three times since their promotion in 1992. Based in the small industrial town of Anjalankoski (the club name is derived from the township of Myllykoski) and financially secured by the local paper mill, they were widely viewed as the pre-season favourites. A spell of seven victories in a row in mid-season put MyPa firmly in the driving seat, and they clinched the title with a 3-0 win over Tampere United two matches from the end.

NATIONAL TEAM RESULTS 2005/06

Date	Opponent	H/A/N	Venue	Score	Scorers
17/8/05	Macedonia (WCQ)	A	Skopje	3-0	Eremenko (8, 45), Roiha (87)
3/9/05	Andorra (WCQ)	A	Andorra La Vella	0-0	
7/9/05	Macedonia (WCQ)	H	Tampere	5-1	Forssell (10,12,61), Tihinen (41), Eremenko (54)
8/10/05	Romania (WCQ)	H	Helsinki	0-1	
12/10/05	Czech Republic (WCQ)	H	Helsinki	0-3	
12/11/05	Estonia	H	Helsinki	2-2	Sjölund (7), Arkivuo (59)
21/1/06	Saudi Arabia	A	Riyadh	1-1	Roiha (87)
25/1/06	South Korea	N	Riyadh	0-1	
18/2/06	Japan	A	Shizuoka	0-2	
28/2/06	Kazakhstan	N	Larnaca	0-0	(1-3 on pens)
1/3/06	Belarus	N	Paphos	2-2	Riihilahti (82), Forssell (90) (5-4 on pens)
25/5/06	Sweden	A	Gothenburg	0-0	

Finland

Key men in Ilkka Mäkelä's experienced squad were the wing-backs, Toni Huttunen and Tuomo Könönen, as well as defensive midfielder and captain Tuomas Haapala, who was rewarded with a trial in England at Manchester City. The acquisition of Adriano from Allianssi proved decisive, as the Brazilian striker netted 11 goals for the new champions. MyPa even managed a decent run in Europe, eliminating former finalists Dundee United from the UEFA Cup on the away-goals rule before bowing out to Grasshopper of Switzerland. There was much ado in the second leg of the Grasshopper tie when MyPa, who had drawn the first game 1-1 in Zurich, looked to have taken the lead, only for the referee, having awarded the goal, to be persuaded to disallow it by his fourth official. MyPa went on to lose the game 3-0 but that did not deter them from making an official complaint to UEFA.

For once, HJK were nobody's favourite for the title race, but English coach Keith Armstrong proved his mettle again with a youthful squad. In fact, "Klubi" gave MyPa a real run for their money and ran up 17 games without defeat through to early August. Armstrong had worn a winter coat at the start of the season and continued to wear it as a lucky charm – despite the summer heat – until the team lost a game. HJK eventually self-destructed – less because of the coach's attire than because they sold their star Swedish defender Joakim Jensen to Hammarby only days before losing their other stopper Markus Halsti to injury. Juho Mäkelä's 16 goals for HJK earned him the league top scorer's award and a transfer to Scottish Premier League challengers Hearts.

Tampere United finished third ahead of Haka, whose title defence was undone by indifferent finishing away from home. As is their habit, Haka compensated for a disappointing league season – albeit scarred by just two defeats - by winning the Finnish Cup, for a record 12th time. The evergreen Valeriy Popovich scored one and created another two of their four goals against Kari Ukkonen's TPS in the final.

The most disappointing team of the year were heavy-spending FC Lahti, who never recovered from a disastrous start. Of their much-vaunted new striking duo, Rafael delivered 14 league goals but Mika Kottila a mere four. Coach Harri Kampman was eventually sacked and replaced by the former Finland manager, Antti Muurinen. Promoted IFK Mariehamn in the sunny Åland Islands were every fan's favourite away fixture, and their blend of local talent and Swedish imports kept them comfortably clear of the drop zone. For Lapland, by contrast, it was a season to forget, as both RoPS and TP-47 were relegated. The Arctic Circle duo were replaced for 2006 by old league hands VPS of Vaasa (who overcame RoPS on the away-goals rule in the play-off) and ambitious debutants FC Honka from Espoo.

Hodgson hired

Experienced coach Jyrki Heliskoski was entrusted to salvage some pride from the remainder of Finland's World Cup qualifying fixtures following Muurinen's dismissal in June 2005. No sooner was Heliskoski appointed than the Finland FA announced that he would eventually be replaced by much-travelled Roy Hodgson - of Switzerland, Inter and Blackburn Rovers fame - for the 2008 European Championship campaign. After some wrangling, the Englishman's Norwegian employers FK Viking agreed to release him early at the turn of the year.

Heliskoski did not enjoy a happy tenure. Although there were two comfortable victories over Macedonia, the second of which featured a hat-trick for star striker Mikael Forssell – the first by a Finnish player in a fully competitive international – those wins straddled a dismal draw away to Andorra, and the World Cup campaign ended in utter gloom when first Romania and then Czech Republic outplayed the listless host team in Helsinki. Heliskoski controversially dropped his top scorer Alexei Eremenko from the game against the Czechs as he had been involved in a road accident in the centre of Helsinki in which his girlfriend, driving the car, was found to be over the alcohol limit. Eremenko, a blameless passenger, was left fuming.

By contrast, Hodgson enjoyed a quiet first spring at the helm, saving his ammunition for the Euro qualifiers in the autumn. A goalless away draw against Sweden's World Cup reserves in Gothenburg was a slightly promising but not entirely convincing start. Hodgson's major challenge in the long run will be to find replacements for ageing and alarmingly injury-prone core players. Only Liverpool defender Sami Hyypiä (voted Finland's Player of the Year for 2005) and Bolton goalkeeper Jussi Jääskeläinen saw a full season of regular action in a big league in Europe. The skipper, Jari Litmanen, enjoying semi-retirement in the Swedish league, celebrated his record-breaking 101st cap in Cyprus in a 2-2 draw against Belarus, bypassing the previous figure of 100 set by Ari Hjelm.

Finland

NATIONAL TEAM APPEARANCES 2005/06

Coach – Jyrki HELISKOSKI / (1/1/06) Roy HODGSON (ENG)

Player	DOB	Club	MAC	AND	MAC	ROM	CZE	Est	Sau	Kor	Jpn	Kaz	Bls	Swe	Caps	Goals
Jussi JÄÄSKELÄINEN	19/4/75	Bolton Wanderers (ENG)	G		G	G							G	G	27	-
Petri PASANEN	24/9/80	SV Werder Bremen (GER)	D	D									D	D46	30	1
Sami HYYPIÄ	7/10/73	Liverpool (ENG)	D	D		D	D						D		75	4
Hannu TIHINEN	1/7/76	RSC Anderlecht (BEL)	D	D	D								D	D	48	4
Toni KALLIO	9/8/78	Molde FK (NOR)	D	D	D	D	D				D	D		D	21	1
Markus HEIKKINEN	13/10/78	Luton Town (ENG)	M		M	M	M	M59		M				M77	22	-
Pekka LAGERBLOM	19/10/82	SV Werder Bremen (GER) /1.FC Köln (GER)	M79	s46		M	D58			M80	M83			s53	11	-
Teemu TAINIO	27/11/79	Tottenham Hotspur (ENG)	M	M	M80	M	M								33	5
Alexei EREMENKO Jr.	24/3/83	Lecce (ITA) /Saturn Ramenskoe (RUS)	M84	M64	A	A		M						A77	22	10
Mikael FORSSELL	15/3/81	Birmingham City (ENG)	A61	A73	A	A73	s63						A	s77	40	16
Shefki KUQI	10/11/76	Blackburn Rovers (ENG)	A	A											42	5
Paulus ROIHA	3/8/80	KSV Cercle Brugge (BEL) /ADO Den Haag (HOL)	s61				A59	A90	s60				A		16	4
Jari LITMANEN	20/2/71	Malmö FF (SWE)	s79						A73	A83			A	A	102	25
Janne SAARINEN	28/2/77	FC København (DEN) /FC Honka	s84	M	M52	M75	M12							s77	41	-
Mikko KAVÉN	19/2/75	Tampere United		G	G				G			G			15	-
Toni KUIVASTO	31/12/75	Djurgårdens IF (SWE)		D	D	D	D	D		D			D	D	66	1
Peter KOPTEFF	10/4/79	Viking FK (NOR) /Stoke City (ENG)		M46	s71	s75	s12						M	s66	39	1
Aki RIIHILAHTI	9/9/76	Crystal Palace (ENG)		s64	M71								M		63	11
Daniel SJÖLUND	22/4/83	Djurgårdens IF (SWE)		s73		s73	A63	M86			A74				9	1
Ari NYMAN	7/2/84	FC Inter Turku		s52	D62	s58	D	D82		D	D	D64			12	-
Jonatan JOHANSSON	16/8/75	Charlton Athletic (ENG) /Norwich City (ENG)		s80	s62	A						A	M66		70	12
Joonas KOLKKA	28/9/74	ADO Den Haag (HOL)				M						M	M89		68	11
Tuomo KÖNÖNEN	29/12/77	MyPa /Odd Grenland (NOR)				D			D	D					6	-
Juha PASOJA	16/11/76	FC Haka /Ham-Kam Fotball (NOR)				D	D	D46		D81	D			s46	11	-
Tuomas HAAPALA	20/4/79	MyPa /Manchester City (ENG)				M					M	M73			3	-
Kari ARKIVUO	23/6/83	FC Lahti /Sandefjord Fotball (NOR)				M				M83	M80	M			5	1
Ville TAULO	14/8/85	FC Lahti							s86	s82	s69				3	-
Tuomas UUSIMÄKI	9/7/77	Örgryte IS (SWE)							s59	M	M69	s69	M		5	-
Juho MÄKELÄ	23/6/83	HJK /Heart of Midlothian (SCO)							s59	s73	A60	s73			6	-
Henri SILLANPÄÄ	4/6/79	AC Allianssi							G	G					4	-
Juuso KANGASKORPI	4/9/75	FC Haka							M82	s69	s80				7	-
Jari ILOLA	24/11/78	IF Elfsborg (SWE)							M88	s46	M69		M53		25	1
Veli LAMPI	18/7/84	HJK							s82		s80	s64			3	-
Antti OKKONEN	6/4/83	Landskrona BoIS (SWE)							s88	M69					13	-
Jukka SAUSO	20/6/82	Örgryte IS (SWE)							s90	D	s81				5	-
Jussi KUJALA	4/4/83	Tampere United								s83	s74				3	-
Keijo HUUSKO	5/8/80	SFK Lyn (NOR) /Strømsgodset IF (NOR)								s83		A81			8	2
Tero TAIPALE	14/12/72	MyPa									s81				1	-
Peter ENCKELMAN	10/3/77	Blackburn Rovers (ENG)										G			7	-
Miika KOPPINEN	5/7/78	Rosenborg BK (NOR)										D			18	-
Mika VÄYRYNEN	28/12/81	PSV Eindhoven (HOL)										s83	M		20	-
Roni POROKARA	12/12/83	FC Honka												s89	1	-

Finland

EUROPEAN CUPS 2005/06

UEFA CHAMPIONS LEAGUE

FC HAKA
1st qualifying round PYUNIK YEREVAN (ARM)
H 1-0 *Pasoja (26)*
Vilmunen, Kangaskorpi, Pasoja, Salli, Nenonen (Okkonen 52), Kauppila, Karjalainen, Popovich, Innanen (Eerola 79), Manninen, Lehtinen (Fowler 63).
A 2-2 *Mattila (38), Fowler (63)*
Vilmunen, Kangaskorpi, Pasoja, Salli, Okkonen, Karjalainen (Fowler 46), Kauppila, Eerola, Manninen (Juuti 84), Innanen, Mattila (Rosenberg 69).

2nd qualifying round VÅLERENGA FOTBALL (NOR)
A 0-1
Vilmunen, Kangaskorpi, Okkonen, Pasoja, Salli, Fowler, Innanen (Rosenberg 90), Kauppila, Manninen (Eerola 82), Popovich, Mattila (Lehtinen 51).
H 1-4 *Lehtinen (9)*
Vilmunen, Kangaskorpi, Okkonen (Rosenberg 75), Pasoja, Salli, Eerola, Fowler, Innanen, Manninen (Nenonen 58), Popovich, Lehtinen (Mattila 68).

UEFA CUP

MYPA
1st qualifying round FC TVMK TALLINN (EST)
A 1-1 *Kuparinen (77)*
Korhonen, Könönen, Miranda, Lindström, Huttunen, Haapala, Taipale, Kuparinen, Tauriainen (Karhu 63), Helenius (Tarvajärvi 63), Adriano.
H 1-0 *Rimas (56og)*
Korhonen, Könönen, Miranda, Lindström, Huttunen, Haapala, Taipale (Tauriainen 69), Kuparinen, Karhu (Muinonen 60), Tarvajärvi, Adriano.

2nd qualifying round DUNDEE UNITED (SCO)
H 0-0
Korhonen, Könönen, Miranda, Lindström, Huttunen, Haapala, Taipale, Tauriainen (Muinonen 74), Karhu, Tarvajärvi (Kaijasilta 79), Adriano.
A 2-2 *Adriano (72p, 81)*
Korhonen, Könönen, Miranda, Lindström, Huttunen, Haapala, Taipale (Kaijasilta 73), Kuparinen, Karhu, Tarvajärvi (Manso 57), Adriano.

1st round GRASSHOPPER-CLUB ZÜRICH (SUI)
A 1-1 *Manso (20)*
Korhonen, Huttunen, Timoska, Lindström, Karhu, Taipale (Tauriainen 83), Kuparinen, Haapala, Manso (Kansikas 61), Puhakainen (Kaijasilta 73), Adriano.
H 0-3
Korhonen, Könönen, Miranda, Timoska, Huttunen, Haapala, Taipale (Helenius 77), Kuparinen (Manso 46), Tauriainen (Karhu 60), Puhakainen, Adriano.

AC ALLIANSSI
1st qualifying round CS PETANGE (LUX)
H 3-0 *Vajanne (34), Cleaver (42), Poulsen (85)*
Sillanpää, Sarajärvi, Marjamaa, Lindström, Simula, Chebaiki, Cleaver, Savolainen, Sampo (Pulkkinen 75), Vajanne (Poulsen 80), La Placa (Omelianovich 62).
A 1-1 *Poulsen (63)*
Sillanpää, Douai, Marjamaa, Lindström, Pulkkinen, Yildiz (Savolainen 58), Chebaiki (Stafsula 67), Cleaver, Omelianovich (Simula 67), La Placa, Poulsen.

2nd qualifying round SK BRANN (NOR)
A 0-0
Sillanpää, Douai, Lindström, Tuunainen, Pulkkinen, Chebaiki (Yildiz 80), Marjamaa, Omelianovich (Cleaver 55), La Placa, Vajanne, Savolainen.
H 0-2
Sillanpää, Douai, Lindström, Tuunainen, Pulkkinen (Simula 77), Chebaiki, Marjamaa, Omelianovich, Cleaver, Vajanne, (Poulsen 51), Savolainen.

TOP GOALSCORERS 2005

16	Juho MÄKELÄ (HJK)
14	RAFAEL (FC Lahti)
	David CARLSSON (IFK Mariehamn)
11	Kalle PARVIAINEN (KuPS)
	ADRIANO (MyPa)
9	Valeriy POPOVICH (FC Haka)
	Serge N'GAL (FC Inter Turku)
8	Mikko INNANEN (FC Haka)
	Toni LEHTINEN (FC Haka)
	Joakim JENSEN (HJK)
	Mikko PAATELAINEN (FF Jaro)
	Saku PUHAKAINEN (MyPa)
	Ville LEHTINEN (AC Allianssi/Tampere United)

LEAGUE RESULTS/ SCORERS/APPEARANCES/ GOALS 2005

AC ALLIANSSI
Coach – Ari Tiittanen; (30/6/05) Thierry Pister (BEL)

2005				
28/4	FC Inter	a	0-0	
5/5	RoPS	h	1-1	Lehtinen
12/5	FF Jaro	a	1-1	Simula
16/5	FC KooTeePee	h	1-2	Stafsula
22/5	FC Lahti	h	3-1	Cleaver (p), Simula, Vuorinen
29/5	TPS	a	0-0	
4/6	HJK	a	2-2	Poulsen, Ojanen
12/6	TP-47	h	1-0	Tuunainen
16/6	MyPa	a	0-0	
19/6	IFK Mariehamn	a	0-0	
29/6	Tampere United	h	1-0	Savolainen
7/7	FC Haka	a	0-8	
17/7	TPS	h	3-3	Cleaver (p), Omelianovich 2
21/7	RoPS	a	3-1	Marjamaa, Stafsula, Poulsen
31/7	TP-47	a	1-0	Marjamaa
6/8	FC Lahti	a	1-4	Savolainen
14/8	KuPS	h	1-1	Poulsen
21/8	FC Haka	h	2-2	Vajanne 2
29/8	Tampere United	a	0-2	
1/9	IFK Mariehamn	h	3-1	Vajanne 2, La Placa
8/9	FC Inter	h	2-3	Poulsen 2
11/9	MyPa	h	1-3	Cleaver
18/9	KuPS	a	2-1	Savolainen, Chebaiki
21/9	FF Jaro	h	1-2	Poulsen
1/10	HJK	h	1-2	Marjamaa
15/10	FC KooTeePee	a	2-1	Savolainen, Vajanne

No	Name	Nat	Pos	Aps	(s)	Gls

Finland

FINAL LEAGUE TABLE 2005

		Pld	Home					Away					Total					Pts
			W	D	L	F	A	W	D	L	F	A	W	D	L	F	A	
1	MyPa	26	8	3	2	28	11	9	2	2	23	7	17	5	4	51	18	56
2	HJK	26	8	3	2	23	10	7	4	2	20	16	15	7	4	43	26	52
3	Tampere United	26	7	5	1	23	9	8	1	4	15	12	15	6	5	38	21	51
4	FC Haka	26	9	3	1	32	7	4	8	1	15	12	13	11	2	47	19	50
5	FC Inter Turku	26	7	3	3	21	10	5	5	3	17	10	12	8	6	38	20	44
6	FC Lahti	26	8	2	3	26	15	3	3	7	13	21	11	5	10	39	36	38
7	AC Allianssi	26	4	4	5	21	21	4	6	3	12	20	8	10	8	33	41	34
8	FC KooTeePee	26	6	3	4	22	18	3	3	7	13	24	9	6	11	35	42	33
9	TPS	26	6	2	5	17	11	2	4	7	13	24	8	6	12	30	35	30
10	KuPS	26	4	3	6	14	22	4	2	7	18	23	8	5	13	32	45	29
11	FF Jaro	26	4	6	3	13	9	2	2	9	8	22	6	8	12	21	31	26
12	IFK Mariehamn	26	5	2	6	17	16	1	3	9	10	27	6	5	15	27	43	23
13	RoPS	26	2	5	6	9	16	1	3	9	9	34	3	8	15	18	50	17
14	TP-47	26	1	3	9	10	23	3	1	9	12	24	4	4	18	22	47	16

No	Name	Nat	Pos	Aps	(s)	Gls
25	Hocine CHEBAIKI	BEL	M	15		1
14	Chris CLEAVER	ENG	A	21	(2)	3
2	Mustapha DOUAI	BEL	D	12		
29	Grégory GOFFIN	BEL	G	1		
15	Rexhep ISLAMI		A		(1)	
18	Matti KANGAS		D		(2)	
23	Kristian KOJOLA		D	1	(1)	
24	Jean-Pierre LA PLACA	SUI	A	14		1
18	Ville LEHTINEN		A	7	(3)	1
5	Mathias LINDSTRÖM		D	17	(1)	
21	Tomi MAANOJA		G	2		
8	Timo MARJAMAA		M	18		3
22	Risto OJANEN		M	4	(5)	1
10	Serhiy OMELIANOVICH	UKR	A	7	(1)	2
6	Jon POULSEN		A	11	(10)	6
16	Heikki PULKKINEN		M	23	(1)	
3	Timo SALO		M	1	(1)	
11	Peter SAMPO		A	13	(3)	
13	Jani SARAJÄRVI		D	10		
30	Juska SAVOLAINEN		M	21	(2)	4
1	Henri SILLANPÄÄ		G	23		
19	Henri SIMELIUS		A		(1)	
7	Mikko SIMULA		M	15	(5)	2
15	Dritan STAFSULA	ALB	M	9	(7)	2
4	Jarno TUUNAINEN		D	16	(2)	1
17	Jarkko VÄHÄSARJA		D	2	(2)	
9	Justus VAJANNE		A	11	(3)	5
20	Hermanni VUORINEN		A	2	(8)	1
26	Kasim YILDIZ	FRA	D	10	(1)	

FC HAKA
Coach – Olli Huttunen

2005

28/4	KuPS	h	1-0	Popovich
5/5	TPS	a	0-0	
12/5	MyPa	h	1-0	Kauppila
17/5	RoPS	a	2-2	Karjalainen, Torkkeli
21/5	Tampere United	a	0-0	
29/5	FF Jaro	h	2-1	Karjalainen, Manninen
3/6	FC Inter	h	1-1	Innanen
12/6	FC Lahti	h	0-0	
15/6	HJK	a	0-1	
18/6	TP-47	h	2-0	Kauppila, Innanen
30/6	FC KooTeePee	a	3-3	Lehtinen 3
3/7	KuPS	a	0-0	
7/7	AC Allianssi	h	8-0	Lehtinen 2, Innanen 2, Kauppila, Karjalainen, Popovich, Salli
16/7	FF Jaro	a	1-0	Mattila
31/7	FC Lahti	a	0-0	
6/8	Tampere United	h	1-3	Pasoja
13/8	IFK Mariehamn	a	1-0	Nascimento
18/8	TPS	h	6-0	Fowler, Manninen, Innanen, Kangaskorpi (p), Popovich, Mattila
21/8	AC Allianssi	a	2-2	Kangaskorpi, Kauppila
28/8	FC KooTeePee	h	1-1	Popovich
1/9	TP-47	a	2-2	Nascimento, Innanen
10/9	HJK	h	2-0	Popovich, Lehtinen
18/9	IFK Mariehamn	h	3-1	Innanen, Popovich, Kangaskorpi
24/9	MyPa	a	3-2	Nascimento, Popovich, Lehtinen
4/10	FC Inter	a	1-0	Popovich
15/10	RoPS	h	4-0	Kangaskorpi (p), Innanen, Lehtinen, Popovich

No	Name	Nat	Pos	Aps	(s)	Gls
6	Kalle EEROLA		D	3	(4)	
20	Cheyne FOWLER	RSA	D	20	(3)	1
7	Mikko INNANEN		M	24	(2)	8
23	Jaakko JUUTI		M		(1)	
2	Juuso KANGASKORPI		M	25		4
3	Lasse KARJALAINEN		M	12	(5)	3
8	Jani KAUPPILA		M	20	(6)	4
17	Toni LEHTINEN		A	19	(4)	8
9	Mikko MANNINEN		M	12	(12)	2
18	Jarno MATTILA		A	2	(11)	2

Finland

No	Name	Nat	Pos	Aps	(s)	Gls
10	Igor NASCIMENTO	ANG	A	3	(6)	3
11	Mika NENONEN		A	19	(3)	
4	Jarkko OKKONEN		D	16	(7)	
5	Juha PASOJA		D	24	(1)	1
14	Valeriy POPOVICH	RUS	A	26		9
13	Erno ROSENBERG		M		(1)	
15	Janne SALLI		D	19	(1)	1
16	Tommi TORKKELI		M	16	(6)	1
1	Mikko VILMUNEN		G	26		

HJK
Coach – Keith Armstrong (ENG)

2005

Date	Opponent	h/a	Score	Scorers
29/4	TP-47	h	2-0	Oliveira, Mäkelä
5/5	IFK Mariehamn	h	0-0	
12/5	KuPS	a	2-1	Oravainen, Jensen
16/5	MyPa	a	1-1	Zeneli E.
19/5	TPS	h	3-1	Aalto J., Mäkelä, Jensen
28/5	FC Inter	a	0-0	
4/6	AC Allianssi	h	2-2	Mäkelä, Jensen
12/6	RoPS	a	2-0	Mäkelä 2
15/6	FC Haka	h	1-0	Savolainen
19/6	FC KooTeePee	h	2-2	Jensen 2 (1p)
29/6	FF Jaro	a	0-0	
3/7	TP-47	a	2-1	De Gregorio, Aalto J.
10/7	FC Lahti	h	2-1	Jensen (p), Mäkelä
13/7	Tampere United		1-1	Jensen (p)
24/7	IFK Mariehamn	a	4-3	Mäkelä 2, Oravainen 2
30/7	RoPS	h	7-0	Hänninen, Mäkelä 2, Jensen (p), Hetemaj, Oravainen, Halsti
6/8	TPS	a	1-0	Halsti
20/8	Tampere United	h	0-2	
28/8	FF Jaro	h	1-0	Mäkelä
31/8	FC KooTeePee	a	3-5	Nurmela, Mäkelä 2
10/9	FC Haka	a	0-2	
14/9	FC Inter	h	2-1	Aalto J., Mäkelä
17/9	FC Lahti	a	2-1	Mäkelä 2 (1p)
25/9	KuPS	h	0-1	
1/10	AC Allianssi	a	2-1	Savolainen, Koivisto
15/10	MyPa	h	1-0	Nurmela

No	Name	Nat	Pos	Aps	(s)	Gls
6	Iiro AALTO		D	24		
20	Jussi AALTO		A	7	(7)	3
2	Ilari ÄIJÄLÄ		D	2	(4)	
31	Virgile BOUMELAHA	FRA	D	1		
9	Raffaelle DE GREGORIO	NZL	M	14	(2)	1
30	Adel EID		D	1	(1)	
19	Rami HAKANPÄÄ		M	2		
22	Markus HALSTI		D	17		2
17	Mika HÄNNINEN		M	14	(5)	1
14	Perparim HETEMAJ		M	14	(12)	1
5	Joakim JENSEN	SWE	D	16		8
25	Jani KOIVISTO		A		(2)	1
11	Veli LAMPI		M	26		
18	Juho MÄKELÄ		A	23	(2)	16
32	Pablo MUÑIZ	URU	D	7		
29	Mika NURMELA		M	7		2
4	Ville NYLUND		D	17	(1)	
10	Valmir Alves OLIVEIRA	BRA	A	4	(6)	1
21	Petri ORAVAINEN		A	14	(7)	4
7	Vili SAVOLAINEN		M	23	(2)	2
26	Felix SIIVONEN		M		(1)	

27	Sebastian SORSA		M	19	(5)	
15	Aleksandar VASILJEVIC	SCG	A	1	(4)	
1	Ville WALLÉN		G	26		
24	Erfan ZENELI		M	2	(3)	1
8	Ridvan ZENELI		M	5	(6)	

FC INTER TURKU
Coach – Kari Virtanen

2005

Date	Opponent	h/a	Score	Scorers
28/4	AC Allianssi	h	0-0	
5/5	MyPa	a	1-1	N'Gal
12/5	IFK Mariehamn	h	4-0	Ilo 2, N'Gal 2
16/5	FF Jaro	a	0-0	
22/5	RoPS	h	2-0	N'Gal 2
25/5	Tampere United	a	0-1	
28/5	HJK	h	0-0	
3/6	FC Haka	a	1-1	N'Gal
12/6	FC KooTeePee	h	2-0	Otoo, Furuholm
15/6	KuPS	a	3-0	Mutumba, Ilo 2
29/6	TPS	h	2-0	Ilo, Petrescu
21/7	MyPa	h	1-4	Petrescu
27/7	FC KooTeePee	a	2-0	Gustafsson, Petrescu
3/8	RoPS	a	0-0	
10/8	FC Lahti	h	4-0	Lehtonen, Petrescu, Pertot 2
14/8	TP-47	h	1-0	Laaksonen
21/8	FC Lahti	a	0-1	
27/8	TPS	a	3-1	Pertot, Otoo, N'Gal
8/9	AC Allianssi	a	3-2	Ilo 2, Petrescu
11/9	KuPS	h	3-2	Pertot, N'Gal, Petrescu
14/9	HJK	a	1-2	N'Gal
18/9	TP-47	a	1-1	Laaksonen
21/9	IFK Mariehamn	a	2-0	Mutumba, Petrescu
26/9	Tampere United	h	0-1	
4/10	FC Haka	h	0-1	
15/10	FF Jaro	h	2-2	Tumanto, og (Luoma)

No	Name	Nat	Pos	Aps	(s)	Gls
1	Magnus BAHNE		G	26		
5	Diego CORPACHE	ARG	D	25		
2	Timo FURUHOLM		A	2	(3)	1
21	Mats GUSTAFSSON		D	25		1
18	Matti HEIMO		A	3	(4)	
9	Miikka ILO		A	19	(5)	7
27	Valtter LAAKSONEN		A	7	(7)	2
25	Joonas LAURIKAINEN		D		(3)	
29	Henri LEHTONEN		D	25		1
76	Samuli LINDELÖF		A	2		
28	Mika MÄKITALO		M	4	(3)	
10	Martin MUTUMBA	SWE	A	9	(7)	2
7	Serge N'GAL	CMR	A	18	(3)	9
20	Ari NYMAN		D	18	(1)	
24	Prince OTOO	GHA	A	22	(1)	2
19	Aristídes PERTOT	ARG	M	21	(1)	4
11	Tomi PETRESCU		A	23	(1)	7
22	Sami SANEVUORI		D	1	(1)	
14	Jukka SINISALO		D	16	(2)	
16	Jesper TÖRNQVIST		D		(5)	
8	Touko TUMANTO		M	20	(5)	1

FF JARO
Coach – Hannu Touru

2005

Date	Opponent	h/a	Score
28/4	Tampere United	a	0-3

Finland

5/5	KuPS	a	0-1	
12/5	AC Allianssi	h	1-1	Aleksandrov
16/5	FC Inter	h	0-0	
22/5	MyPa	h	0-0	
25/5	FC Lahti	a	0-4	
29/5	FC Haka	a	1-2	Eremenko R.
12/6	IFK Mariehamn	a	1-3	Eremenko R.
15/6	TP-47	a	0-0	
19/6	TPS	h	1-0	Aleksandrov
29/6	HJK	h	0-0	
10/7	RoPS	a	0-1	
16/7	FC Haka	h	0-1	
20/7	Tampere United	h	1-3	Wargh J.
23/7	KuPS	h	2-1	Aleksandrov 2
31/7	IFK Mariehamn	h	0-0	
6/8	MyPa	a	2-0	Portin Je., Storbacka
14/8	FC KooTeePee	h	6-1	Hevonkorpi, Paatelainen 5
21/8	RoPS	h	2-0	Paatelainen, Stevic
28/8	HJK	a	0-1	
31/8	TPS	a	0-2	
11/9	TP-47	h	0-2	
18/9	FC KooTeePee	a	0-2	
21/9	AC Allianssi	a	2-1	Stevic, Paatelainen
2/10	FC Lahti	h	0-0	
15/10	FC Inter	a	2-2	Paatelainen, Wargh J.

No	Name	Nat	Pos	Aps	(s)	Gls
18	Mattias AINASOJA		D	18	(2)	
7	Kiril ALEKSANDROV	BUL	A	13	(11)	4
16	Jonas EMET		M		(2)	
14	Alexei EREMENKO		M	16	(4)	
10	Roman EREMENKO		M	10	(3)	2
1	Otto FREDRIKSON		G	26		
29	Angel GINEV	BUL	D	19	(2)	
27	Mika GRANHOLM		D	1	(3)	
4	Toni HEVONKORPI		D	22		1
3	Juha LUOMA		D	23	(2)	
17	Tom MELARTI		A		(1)	
23	Mikael MUURIMÄKI		A	6	(8)	
28	Mikko PAATELAINEN		A	10		8
19	PIRACAÍA	BRA	M	14		
22	Jens PORTIN		D	17	(2)	1
20	Jonas PORTIN		D		(1)	
24	Sasa STEVIC	SCG	M	7		2
2	Niklas STORBACKA		M	18	(5)	1
26	Björn-Erik SUNDQVIST		A		(2)	
5	Jani TIMONEN		D	3	(10)	
6	Denis TUMASIAN	RUS	M	18	(3)	
11	Ville VÄISÄNEN		A	20	(1)	
9	Jimmy WARGH		M	24		2
8	Mathias WARGH		A	1	(7)	

FC KOOTEEPEE
Coach – Janne Hyppönen

2005

28/4	TPS	h	1-0	Nykänen
5/5	TP-47	h	0-3	
12/5	Tampere United	h	3-0	og (Kuoppala), Koivisto 2
16/5	AC Allianssi	a	2-1	Kinnaslampi, Liljeqvist
22/5	KuPS	h	0-2	
29/5	FC Lahti	a	1-1	Turunen Te.
5/6	RoPS	h	0-0	
12/6	FC Inter	a	0-2	
15/6	IFK Mariehamn	h	3-1	Laakso, Venäläinen, Nykänen
19/6	HJK	a	2-2	Venäläinen (p), Liljeqvist
30/6	FC Haka	h	3-3	Kinnaslampi, Turunen Tu., Venäläinen
3/7	TPS	a	1-3	Turunen Te.
9/7	MyPa	a	1-2	Helenius
16/7	FC Lahti	h	2-0	og (Järvinen), Liljeqvist
24/7	TP-47	a	2-0	Turunen Te., Venäläinen
27/7	FC Inter	h	0-2	
3/8	KuPS	a	1-2	Venäläinen
14/8	FF Jaro	a	1-6	Tyyskä
19/8	MyPa	h	2-2	og (Huttunen), Venäläinen
28/8	FC Haka	a	1-1	Liljeqvist
31/8	HJK	h	5-3	Liljeqvist 2 (1p), Vanninen, Helenius, Ikävalko
11/9	IFK Mariehamn	a	0-2	
18/9	FF Jaro	h	2-0	Liljeqvist, Turunen Te.
21/9	Tampere United	a	0-2	
2/10	RoPS	a	1-0	Leetma
15/10	AC Allianssi	h	1-2	Venäläinen

No	Name	Nat	Pos	Aps	(s)	Gls
5	Roope HEILALA		D	26		
23	Vesa HELENIUS		M	8	(10)	2
21	Niko IKÄVALKO		A	1	(8)	1
25	Tuukka KESSELI		A		(1)	
4	Jussi KINNASLAMPI		D	17		2
14	Jani KOIVISTO		A	3	(5)	2
19	Janne LAAKSO		M	9	(11)	1
6	Erkka LÄNSIMIES		D		(1)	
15	Jani LAURETSALO		M		(1)	
10	Liivo LEETMA	EST	M	13	(6)	1
18	Kim LILJEQVIST		A	19	(3)	7
1	Teuvo MOILANEN		G	14		
40	Giorgi NIKURADZE	GEO	G	11		
16	Juho NYKÄNEN		A	16	(5)	2
11	Tuomo PAAKKARI		D	20	(1)	
3	Jarkko RIIHIMÄKI		D	4	(9)	
14	Julius RIKBERG		M		(3)	
13	Ville TURA		G	1		
24	Teemu TURUNEN		M	22	(2)	4
22	Tuomo TURUNEN		D	10	(6)	1
17	Marko TYYSKÄ		M	21	(4)	1
8	Jukka VANNINEN		M	24		1
9	Ilja VENÄLÄINEN		A	24	(1)	7
7	Anssi VIREN		D	23	(1)	

KUPS
Coach – Juha Malinen

2005

28/4	FC Haka	a	0-1	
5/5	FF Jaro	h	1-0	Hartikainen
12/5	HJK	h	1-2	Ablade
16/5	TPS	a	1-3	Anyamkyegh
22/5	FC KooTeePee	a	2-0	Parviainen, Ablade
29/5	MyPa	a	0-3	
4/6	IFK Mariehamn	h	2-2	Anyamkyegh, Ablade
12/6	Tampere United	h	0-2	
15/6	FC Inter	h	0-3	
19/6	FC Lahti	a	1-2	Parviainen
29/6	RoPS	a	4-3	Kärkkäinen, Ablade, Parviainen, Gruborovics
3/7	FC Haka	h	0-0	
10/7	TP-47	h	3-1	Anyamkyegh 2, Parviainen
17/7	MyPa	h	0-3	

Finland

Date	Opponent	H/A	Score	Scorers
23/7	FF Jaro	a	1-2	Holopainen
31/7	Tampere United	a	0-0	
3/8	FC KooTeePee	h	2-1	Hartikainen, Parviainen
14/8	AC Allianssi	a	1-1	Turunen M.
21/8	TP-47	a	1-3	Ablade
28/8	RoPS	h	2-1	Parviainen, Oinonen
1/9	FC Lahti	h	1-4	Itälä
11/9	FC Inter	a	2-3	Ablade, Parviainen (p)
18/9	AC Allianssi	h	1-2	Turunen M.
25/9	HJK	a	1-0	Parviainen
2/10	IFK Mariehamn	a	4-2	Parviainen 2, Oinonen 2
15/10	TPS	h	1-1	Parviainen

No	Name	Nat	Pos	Aps	(s)	Gls
10	Seth ABLADE	GHA	A	22	(1)	6
17	Edward ANYAMKYEGH	NGA	A	24	(2)	4
12	Patrick BANTAMOI	SRL	G	11		
13	Jan BERG		D		(1)	
8	Tamás GRUBOROVICS	HUN	M	14	(7)	1
5	Jani HARTIKAINEN		D	26		2
18	Jussi HEIKELÄ		A	15	(9)	
19	Jonni HEIKKINEN		D	6	(3)	
11	Pietari HOLOPAINEN		M	17	(7)	1
3	Matti HURME		D	26		
2	Olli-Pekka ITÄLÄ		D	25		1
15	Pyry KÄRKKÄINEN		D	10	(3)	1
14	Marko KIVILÄ		M	6	(4)	
1	István MITRING	HUN	G	15		
20	Kai NYYSSÖNEN		A	14	(2)	
29	Miikka OINONEN		A	5	(7)	3
7	Kalle PARVIAINEN		A	26		11
16	Antti ROPPONEN		A	2	(6)	
26	Berat SADIK		A		(5)	
9	Tero TAHVANAINEN		A	1	(9)	
4	Miikka TURUNEN		M	21	(3)	2
23	Patrik TURUNEN		D		(3)	

FC LAHTI
Coach – Harri Kampman

2005

Date	Opponent	H/A	Score	Scorers
28/4	MyPa	h	1-4	Rafael
3/5	Tampere United	a	1-3	Rafael
12/5	RoPS	h	4-1	Rafael, Järvinen, Siikala 2
16/5	IFK Mariehamn	a	0-2	
22/5	AC Allianssi	a	1-3	Kautonen
25/5	FF Jaro	h	4-0	Siikala, Vartiainen 2, Pehkonen
29/5	FC KooTeePee	h	1-1	Rafael
12/6	FC Haka	a	0-0	
15/6	TPS	a	1-0	Kautonen (p)
19/6	KuPS	h	2-1	Taulo 2
29/6	TP-47	h	1-4	Arkivuo
2/7	MyPa	a	1-3	Rafael
10/7	HJK	a	1-2	Kottila
13/7	RoPS	a	1-1	Vartiainen
16/7	FC KooTeePee	a	0-2	
28/7	Tampere United	h	3-1	Rafael, Järvinen, Kottila
31/7	FC Haka	h	0-0	
6/8	AC Allianssi	h	4-1	Kottila, Rafael, Kemppinen, Taulo
10/8	FC Inter	a	0-4	
21/8	FC Inter	h	1-0	Rafael
28/8	TP-47	a	3-0	Rafael, Arkivuo, Kautonen
1/9	KuPS	a	4-1	Rafael 2, Taulo, Korte
11/9	TPS	h	1-0	Rafael
17/9	HJK	h	1-2	Rafael (p)
2/10	FF Jaro	a	0-0	
15/10	IFK Mariehamn	h	3-0	Kottila, Korte, Rafael

No	Name	Nat	Pos	Aps	(s)	Gls
11	Kari ARKIVUO		M	22		2
2	Heikki HAARA		D	13	(1)	
3	Mikko HAUHIA		D	20	(3)	
7	Toni JÄRVINEN		A	26		2
8	Tommi KAUTONEN		M	23	(2)	3
20	Jonne KEMPPINEN		A	5	(16)	1
17	Eero KORTE		M	1	(3)	2
6	Jarkko KOSKINEN		M	12	(2)	
4	Jukka KOSKINEN		D	5		
1	Mika KOTTILA		A	23	(2)	4
5	Lasse LAGERBLOM		D	8	(2)	
19	Matti LÄHITIE		M	4	(3)	
15	Niko LEPPÄNEN		D	10	(5)	
99	Sami MAHLIO		M	12	(1)	
21	Antti PEHKONEN		D	18	(1)	1
9	RAFAEL Pires Vieira	BRA	A	26		14
22	Ville-Veikko SAVOLAINEN		A		(5)	
14	Joonas SIIKALA		A	4	(11)	3
30	Michal SLAWUTA	POL	G	26		
18	Ville TAULO		M	22	(3)	4
24	Tommi VARTIAINEN		D	6		3

IFK MARIEHAMN
Coach – Pekka Lyyski

2005

Date	Opponent	H/A	Score	Scorers
28/4	RoPS	h	1-0	Sandvärn
5/5	HJK	a	0-0	
12/5	FC Inter	a	0-4	
16/5	FC Lahti	h	2-0	Holm, Weckström K.
22/5	TP-47	a	2-0	Ahnström, Wirtanen
29/5	Tampere United	h	0-0	
4/6	KuPS	a	2-2	Niskala, og (Itälä)
12/6	FF Jaro	h	3-1	Carlsson D. 3
15/6	FC KooTeePee	a	1-3	Carlsson D.
19/6	AC Allianssi	h	0-0	
29/6	MyPa	a	1-2	Sandvärn (p)
2/7	RoPS	a	0-1	
10/7	TPS	h	0-1	
24/7	HJK	h	3-4	Carlsson D. 2, Lyyski
31/7	FF Jaro	a	0-0	
3/8	TP-47	h	4-2	Carlsson D. 3, Wiklander
13/8	FC Haka	h	0-1	
21/8	TPS	a	1-4	Sjölund
29/8	MyPa	h	0-1	
1/9	AC Allianssi	a	1-3	Carlsson D.
11/9	FC KooTeePee	h	2-0	Carlsson D. 2
14/9	Tampere United	a	1-2	og (Sainio)
18/9	FC Haka	a	1-3	Wiklander
21/9	FC Inter	h	0-2	
2/10	KuPS	h	2-4	Carlsson D. 2
15/10	FC Lahti	a	0-3	

No	Name	Nat	Pos	Aps	(s)	Gls
6	Daniel AHNSTRÖM	SWE	M	25		1
21	Linus BLOMSTER		M		(6)	
24	Olivier BOUMELAHA	FRA	A	1	(3)	
9	David CARLSSON	SWE	A	23	(2)	14
4	Johan CARLSSON	SWE	M	10	(3)	
17	André HANSELL		D	23	(1)	
16	Nedim HIROS	BOS	A	3	(1)	

Finland

7	Peter HOLM		D	22	(2)	1
30	Antti KUISMALA		G	7		
10	Peter LUNDBERG		A	11	(11)	
1	Tommy LUNDBERG		G	6		
8	Jani LYYSKI		D	11	(2)	1
11	Mika NISKALA		M	14		1
5	Jens POLVIANDER		D	21	(1)	
23	Erik SANDVÄRN	SWE	D	23		2
2	Joakim SIGNELL		D		(1)	
13	Sami SINKKONEN		G	13		
22	Peter SJÖLUND		M	5	(10)	1
3	Mikael SUNDSTRÖM		M	6	(8)	
20	Alexander WECKSTRÖM		A		(3)	
19	Kristoffer WECKSTRÖM		M	20		1
14	Sebastian WIKLANDER	SWE	M	20	(3)	2
18	Tommy WIRTANEN		M	22	(3)	1

MYPA
Coach – Ilkka Mäkelä

2005

28/4	FC Lahti	a	4-1	Puhakainen, Tauriainen, Tarvajärvi, Adriano
5/5	FC Inter	h	1-1	Adriano
12/5	FC Haka	a	0-1	
16/5	HJK	h	1-1	Adriano
22/5	FF Jaro	a	0-0	
29/5	KuPS	h	3-0	Timoska, Adriano, Puhakainen
3/6	TP-47	a	1-0	Kuparinen
11/6	TPS	a	2-0	Puhakainen, Karhu
16/6	AC Allianssi	h	0-0	
19/6	RoPS	a	2-0	Karhu, Puhakainen
29/6	IFK Mariehamn	h	2-1	Adriano, Timoska
2/7	FC Lahti	h	3-1	Lindström, Adriano (p), Muinonen
9/7	FC KooTeePee	h	2-1	Haapala, Helenius
17/7	KuPS	a	3-0	Miranda, Adriano, Tauriainen
21/7	FC Inter	a	4-1	Helenius 2, Adriano, Muinonen
31/7	TPS	h	1-0	Tauriainen
6/8	FF Jaro	h	0-2	
21/8	FC KooTeePee	a	2-2	Adriano (p), Karhu
29/8	IFK Mariehamn	a	1-0	Puhakainen
1/9	RoPS	h	5-1	Puhakainen, Kuparinen, Manso (p), Kaijasilta, Muinonen
11/9	AC Allianssi	a	3-1	og (Douai), Karhu, Adriano (p)
18/9	Tampere United	a	1-0	Puhakainen
24/9	FC Haka	h	2-3	Taipale, Helenius
3/10	Tampere United	h	3-0	Taipale, Adriano, Haapala
6/10	TP-47	h	5-0	Mäkelä, Manso 2 (1p), Miranda, Puhakainen
15/10	HJK	a	0-1	

No	Name	Nat	Pos	Aps	(s)	Gls
30	ADRIANO Munoz	BRA	A	22		11
10	Tuomas HAAPALA		A	23		2
8	Niki HELENIUS		A	5	(6)	4
15	Mika HERNESNIEMI		M	1	(1)	
16	Toni HUTTUNEN		D	24		
26	Petteri KAIJASILTA		A	6	(1)	1
24	Aleksej KANGASKOLKKA		A		(1)	
20	Tuomas KANSIKAS		D	3	(4)	
13	Tero KARHU		M	11	(12)	4
12	Aapo KILJUNEN		G	1		
2	Tuomo KÖNÖNEN		D	24	(2)	
1	Janne KORHONEN		G	25		
7	Tuomas KUPARINEN		A	19	(2)	2
5	Jukka LINDSTRÖM		D	15	(4)	1
19	Mikko MÄKELÄ		A	2	(4)	1
25	Marco MANSO	BRA	M	3	(5)	3
18	Hugo MIRANDA	PAR	D	21		2
14	Eetu MUINONEN		M	12	(11)	3
9	Saku PUHAKAINEN		A	13	(7)	8
4	Tero TAIPALE		M	23	(2)	2
17	Niklas TARVAJÄRVI		A	10	(3)	1
11	Kimmo TAURIAINEN		M	8	(7)	3
3	Sampsa TIMOSKA		D	15	(2)	2

ROPS
Coach – Mika Lumijärvi; (1/7/05) Matti Vikman

2005

28/4	IFK Mariehamn	a	0-1	
5/5	AC Allianssi	a	1-1	Saileti
12/5	FC Lahti	a	1-4	Jalava
17/5	FC Haka	h	2-2	Mahlakaarto, Saileti
22/5	FC Inter	a	0-2	
29/5	TP-47	h	0-0	
5/6	FC KooTeePee	a	0-0	
12/6	HJK	h	0-2	
15/6	Tampere United	a	3-3	Majava, Peura, Paija
19/6	MyPa	h	0-2	
29/6	KuPS	h	3-4	Kuusela, Saileti 2 (1p)
2/7	IFK Mariehamn	h	1-0	Jalava
10/7	FF Jaro	h	1-0	Saileti
13/7	FC Lahti	h	1-1	Mahlakaarto
17/7	TP-47	a	2-0	Gigov, Saileti
21/7	AC Allianssi	h	1-3	Saileti (p)
30/7	HJK	a	0-7	
3/8	FC Inter	h	0-0	
21/8	FF Jaro	a	0-2	
28/8	KuPS	a	1-2	Avdija
1/9	MyPa	a	1-5	Avdija
11/9	Tampere United	h	0-1	
14/9	TPS	a	0-3	
18/9	TPS	h	0-0	
2/10	FC KooTeePee	h	0-1	
15/10	FC Haka	a	0-4	

No	Name	Nat	Pos	Aps	(s)	Gls
22	Lulezim AVDIJA	SCG	A	17	(4)	2
15	Zoran BOGESIC	CRO	A	11	(3)	
25	George CHILUFYA	ZAM	D	14		
8	Raphael EDEREHO	NGA	A	4	(3)	
28	Cesar GARCIA Pellegrin	URU	M	5		
26	Spas GIGOV	BUL	A	8	(1)	1
10	Dejan GODAR	CRO	M	23		
6	Jarkko HURME		D	20		
30	Vesa INKERÖINEN		D	1	(1)	
3	Petri JALAVA		D	23		2
4	Matti KILPELÄ		D	10	(6)	
17	Matti KUTILA		D	1	(8)	
2	Panu KUUSELA		D	17	(2)	1
29	Srdjan LADIC	CRO	M	5		
7	Janne MAHLAKAARTO		M	13	(4)	2
11	Juha MAJAVA		M	12	(7)	1
5	Markus PAIJA		D	20	(4)	1
27	Adrian PELKA	GER	D	2		

Finland

No	Name	Nat	Pos	Aps	(s)	Gls
18	Antti PEURA		M	12	(9)	1
9	Zeddy SAILETI	ZAM	A	25		7
12	Risto-Pekka SÖDERLUND		G		(1)	
16	Ville SYVÄJÄRVI		M	14	(7)	
24	Janne TURPEENNIEMI		A	1	(2)	
1	Jani VIANDER		G	26		
21	Ville YLIPAAVALNIEMI		M	2	(8)	

TAMPERE UNITED
Coach – Ari Hjelm

2005

Date	Opponent		Score	Scorers
28/4	FF Jaro	h	3-0	Hynynen, Wiss, Marchis
5/5	FC Lahti	h	3-1	Wiss, Kopunovic, Scheweleff
12/5	FC KooTeePee	a	0-3	
16/5	TP-47	a	1-0	Kujala
21/5	FC Haka	h	0-0	
25/5	FC Inter	h	1-0	Heinänen
29/5	IFK Mariehamn	a	0-0	
12/6	KuPS	a	2-0	Wiss, Kujala
15/6	RoPS	h	3-3	Heinänen, Kopunovic, og (Paija)
29/6	AC Allianssi	a	0-1	
13/7	HJK	h	1-1	Heinänen
20/7	FF Jaro	a	3-1	Lehtinen, Wiss, Scheweleff
28/7	FC Lahti	a	1-3	Scheweleff
31/7	KuPS	h	0-0	
6/8	FC Haka	a	3-1	Ojanperä, Lahtinen, Lehtinen
9/8	TPS	h	2-2	Lehtinen, Scheweleff
20/8	HJK	a	2-0	Scheweleff 2 (1p)
29/8	AC Allianssi	h	2-0	Kujala, Lehtinen
11/9	RoPS	a	1-0	Kujala
14/9	IFK Mariehamn	h	2-1	Kujala, Saarinen
18/9	MyPa	h	0-1	
21/9	FC KooTeePee	h	2-0	Marchis, Hynynen
26/9	FC Inter	a	1-0	Lehtinen
29/9	TPS	a	1-0	Lahtinen
3/10	MyPa	a	0-3	
15/10	TP-47	h	4-0	Lehtinen 2, Wiss, Hynynen

No	Name	Nat	Pos	Aps	(s)	Gls
19	Heikki AHO		D	23	(1)	
15	Petri HEINÄNEN		M	16		3
9	Antti HYNYNEN		M	12	(12)	3
23	Mikko-Ville HYYHÖNEN		D	1	(1)	
18	Toni JUNNILA		A	1	(8)	
1	Mikko KAVÉN		G	26		
10	Velibor KOPUNOVIC	CRO	A	12	(2)	2
7	Jussi KUJALA		M	22	(1)	5
6	Jussi KUOPPALA		D	23		
8	Mika LAHTINEN		A	5	(18)	2
24	Ville LEHTINEN		A	15		7
4	Vasile MARCHIS	ROM	D	19	(1)	2
5	Antti OJANPERÄ		M	18	(6)	1
21	Janne RÄSÄNEN		D	8		
13	Sakari SAARINEN		M	13	(8)	1
16	Kari SAINIO		M	24		
11	Jussi-Pekka SAVOLAINEN		M		(3)	
20	Henri SCHEWELEFF		A	17		6
17	Miki SIPILÄINEN		A	4	(3)	
27	Dritan STAFSULA	ALB	M	4		
47	Jukka SUIKKI		A		(4)	
14	Jarkko WISS		M	23		5

TP-47
Coach – Kari Vaalto & Oleg Eprintsev (RUS)

2005

Date	Opponent		Score	Scorers
28/4	HJK	a	0-2	
5/5	FC KooTeePee	a	3-0	Kainu (p), Isteri, Patterson
9/5	TPS	a	0-1	
16/5	Tampere United	h	0-1	
22/5	IFK Mariehamn	h	0-2	
29/5	RoPS	a	0-0	
3/6	MyPa	h	0-1	
12/6	AC Allianssi	a	0-1	
15/6	FF Jaro	h	0-0	
18/6	FC Haka	a	0-2	
29/6	FC Lahti	a	4-1	Kainu 3 (1p), Patterson
3/7	HJK	h	1-2	Tenkula
10/7	KuPS	a	1-3	Hakasalo
17/7	RoPS	h	0-2	
24/7	FC KooTeePee	h	0-2	
31/7	AC Allianssi	h	0-1	
3/8	IFK Mariehamn	a	2-4	Isteri, Kainu
14/8	FC Inter	a	0-1	
21/8	KuPS	h	3-1	Kainu, Pekkanen, Hakala
28/8	FC Lahti	h	0-3	
1/9	FC Haka	h	2-2	Bulgakov, Isteri
11/9	FF Jaro	a	2-0	Hakala, Kainu
18/9	FC Inter	h	1-1	Tenkula
21/9	TPS	h	3-5	Ikäläinen 2, Hakasalo
6/10	MyPa	a	0-5	
15/10	Tampere United	a	0-4	

No	Name	Nat	Pos	Aps	(s)	Gls
3	Anatoli BULGAKOV	RUS	D	19	(3)	1
5	Craig DEAN	ENG	D	12	(1)	
4	Jukka HAKALA		D	25		2
15	Jussi HAKASALO		M	14	(3)	2
14	Tommi HALONEN		M		(2)	
23	Jari HASA		A	3		
1	Janne HENRIKSSON		G	26		
20	Sakari HIUKKA		D	25	(1)	
19	Joonas IKÄLÄINEN		D	24		2
10	Jaakko ISTERI		M	19	(5)	3
17	Pekka KAINU		A	26		7
6	Anatoli KAKSHAROV	BLS	M	4		
26	Tarmo KOIVURANTA		M	1	(2)	
8	Mika LÄHDERINNE		M	11	(4)	
7	Alfred MAKOPA	CMR	M		(7)	
18	Marc NDIKUNADE	CMR	A	15		
7	Kyle PATTERSON	ENG	A	5	(6)	2
16	Ville PEKKANEN		A	10	(9)	1
18	Timo PELTOLA		A		(1)	
2	Pekka RÄISÄNEN		D	6	(2)	
11	Juha SAARIO		M		(12)	
12	Tapio SIHVONEN		G		(1)	
21	Anton SMITH	ENG	A	4	(2)	
22	Jarno TENKULA		M	19	(3)	2
9	Tommy TORVIKOSKI		M	11	(5)	
13	Valeri TSYGANENKA	BLS	A	5	(3)	
7	David WILLIAMSON	NIR	M	2	(2)	

TPS
Coach – Kari Ukkonen

2005

Date	Opponent		Score	Scorers
28/4	FC KooTeePee	a	0-1	

Finland

5/5	FC Haka	h	0-0		
9/5	TP-47	h	1-0	Szilágyi	
16/5	KuPS	h	3-1	Szilágyi 2, Oinonen	
19/5	HJK	a	1-3	Lehtonen	
29/5	AC Allianssi	h	0-0		
11/6	MyPa	h	0-2		
15/6	FC Lahti	h	0-1		
19/6	FF Jaro	a	0-1		
29/6	FC Inter	a	0-2		
3/7	FC KooTeePee	h	3-1	Hyyrynen 2, Hakala	
10/7	IFK Mariehamn	a	1-0	Szilágyi	
17/7	AC Allianssi	a	3-3	Auremaa, Szilágyi (p), Ady	
31/7	MyPa	a	0-1		
6/8	HJK	h	0-1		
9/8	Tampere United	a	2-2	Lehtonen 2	
18/8	FC Haka	a	0-6		
21/8	IFK Mariehamn	h	4-1	Casagrande, Surraco, Ady 2	
27/8	FC Inter	h	1-3	Hyyrynen	
31/8	FF Jaro	h	2-0	Tuomanen, Surraco	
11/9	FC Lahti	a	0-1		
14/9	RoPS	h	3-0	Surraco, Auremaa, Leino	
18/9	RoPS	a	0-0		
21/9	TP-47	a	5-3	Hyyrynen 2, Casagrande, Ady, Surraco	
29/9	Tampere United	h	0-1		
15/10	KuPS	a	1-1	Hyyrynen	

No	Name	Nat	Pos	Aps	(s)	Gls
20	Mika ÄÄRITALO		A	4		
7	ADY Pereira dos Santos	BRA	M	13	(1)	4
9	Jarno AUREMAA		A	13	(7)	2
10	Marco CASAGRANDE		M	20	(3)	2
21	Jussi HAIJANEN		M	7	(3)	
25	Antti HAKALA		A	6	(16)	1
8	Jarno HEINIKANGAS		M	18	(1)	
19	Mika HELIN		D	15		
18	Mikko HYYRYNEN		A	24	(1)	6
16	Kimmo KOTAMÄKI		A	6	(9)	
4	Ville LEHTONEN		D	12	(7)	3
5	Petri LEINO		D	21	(1)	1
2	Jussi NUORELA		D	6		
15	Miikka OINONEN		A	3	(5)	1
26	Sami RÄHMÖNEN		M		(2)	
17	Kushtrim RAMA		M		(1)	
13	Walter SURRACO	URU	A	10		4
11	Gábor SZILÁGYI	HUN	A	12		5
1	Jani TUOMALA		G	26		
14	Jukka-Pekka TUOMANEN		M	25		1
24	Joonas TURSAS		D	8	(1)	
3	Janne VELLAMO		M	16	(3)	
6	Juha VIRKKI		D	7		
28	Jani VIRTANEN		A	4	(6)	
27	Janne VUORINEN		M		(1)	

DOMESTIC CUP 2005

FOURTH ROUND
(21/4/05)
FC Kiisto 0, Tampere United 4
(23/4/05)
EuPa 0, KPV 5
FC YPA 1, FF Jaro 3
JIPPO 3, KuPS Akatemia 0
LBK 0, VaKP 5
FC Futura 3, FC Inter 6 *(aet)*
FC IKHTYS 0, HJK 15
MP 0, MyPa 3
PK-37 0, KuPS 5
FC Raahe 0, RoPS 5
FC Pathoven 1, HyPS 5
JBK 2, PoPa 3
SAPA 2, UPK 2 *(aet; 3-2 on pens)*
FC Kontu 0, TPS 4
FC City Stars 3, EIF 1
OPedot 1, SibboV 0
FCK Salamat 2 1, KäPa 2
FC VAPSI 0, FC Haka 11
Loiske 4, Lapuan Ponnistus 0
PP-70 2 1, Virkiä 1 *(aet; 9-8 on pens)*
FC KooTeePee 2 0, FC KooTeePee 6
KaDy 1, VoPpK 6
KajHa 1, TP-47 3
(25/4/05)
TiPS 2 0, TiPS 3
KaaRe 3, GrIFK 5
(26/4/05)
ÅIFK 0, KaaPo 3
MiKi 1, FC Kuusankoski 2 *(aet)*
Ilves U20 0, FJK 5
Öja-73 1, KPV U20 4
PoPo 1, JJK U20 6
Tervarit U20 0, OLS 5
(27/4/05)
TKT 0, TPV 1
SIlves 0, FC Hämeenlinna 2
FC-88 0, PS Kemi 3
Lumottu Puutarha 0, PK-35 13
PuiU 4 0, RoU 4
FC Turku-82 0, Klubi-04 8
FC Korsholm 2, Sepsi-78 1
PsInto 2, GBK 1
(28/4/05)
PK-35 U20 0, FC Honka 3
Kelohonka 0, Atlantis FC 6
FC POHU U20 0, FC Espoo 4
Zulimanit 3, FC Vaajakoski 4
(29/4/05)
LoPa 0, FC Viikingit 2
Närpes Kraft 1, TP-Seinäjoki 2 *(aet)*
VIFK U20 0, PP-70 2
HerTo 2, RIlves 5
HIFK 0, FC Salamat 0 *(aet; 5-4 on pens)*
Vilpas 0, FC Inter U20-1 3
JäPS 1, Ponnistus 0
LPS 3, PIF 2
FC Inter U20-2 1, Gnistan 3
FC Pantterit 6, SaPa 1
OuJK 2, PAVE 1
MyPa U20 3, Kings 8
JuPS 0, Huima 8
FC Kurenpojat 4, Tervarit 5 *(aet)*
(30/4/05)
FC Rauma 1, VIFK 4
JJK 1, WJK 0
LaVe 0, NIK 1
(2/5/05)
KTP 1, Kajo 2 *(aet)*
HJK U20 2, SalPa 1 *(aet; 4-3 on pens)*

Finland

FIFTH ROUND
(22/6/05)
FC Inter 0, MyPa 1
(23/6/05)
OLS 0, RoPS 1
KPV 0, KuPS 1
FC Korsholm 0, TP-47 2
NIK 0, FF Jaro 9
TiPS 0, FC Lahti 6
PK-35 2, FC Viikingit 1 *(aet)*
Loiske 0, TPS 2
FC Pantterit 0, AC Allianssi 1
KaaPo 0, Tampere United 4
RoU w/o FJK
OPedot 1, HJK 5
KäPa 0, FC Honka 3
SaPa 0, FC KooTeePee 4
Gnistan 2, FC Hämeenlinna 0
FC Inter U20-1 2, PP-70 3 *(aet)*
Atlantis FC 2, FC Haka 6
JJK 3, Kings 0 (aet)
KPV U20 1, Huima 2 *(aet)*
TPV 4, HyPS 0
PS Kemi 4, Tervarit 2
JIPPO 2, FC Vaajakoski 1
HJK U20 0, PoPa 3
Kajo 1, Klubi-04 2
PP-70 2 1, FC Kuusankoski 5
HIFK 1, GrIFK 6
City Stars 7, JJK U20 2
OuJK 1, TP-Seinäjoki 10
PsInto 0, VIFK 4
JäPS 2, LPS 2 *(aet; 6-7 on pens)*
VaKP 3, FC Espoo 5
RIlves 5, VoPpK 1

SIXTH ROUND
(24/8/05)
FC Kuusankoski 2, TPV 0
City Stars 1, LPS 0
JIPPO 0, FC Lahti 2
Huima 0, TP-47 1
PoPa 1, FF Jaro 2
RoU 0, Klubi-04 1
GrIFK 0, FC Espoo 1
TP-Seinäjoki 1, KuPS 0
PK-35 4, PP-70 2
FC Haka 4, FC KooTeePee 2
HJK 2, Tampere United 2 *(aet; 7-8 on pens)*
RIlves 1, PS Kemi 4
JJK 2, RoPS 1 (aet)
Gnistan 0, TPS 3
VIFK 0, FC Honka 3
(10/10/05)
MyPa 2, AC Allianssi 1

SEVENTH ROUND
(1/10/05)
FC Kuusankoski 2, FC Haka 5
(2/10/05)
FC Espoo 2, TP-47 7
(16/10/05)
FC Honka 2, JJK 0
(19/10/05)
City Stars 0, FC Lahti 2
PS Kemi 1, PK-35 2
FF Jaro 0, TPS 2
TP-Seinäjoki 0, Tampere United 1
Klubi-04 0, MyPa 2

QUARTER-FINALS
(22/10/05)
FC Haka 4 *(Popovich 77, Kauppila 99, Innanen 113, Karjalainen 116)*, Tampere United 1 *(Saarinen 53) (aet)*
MyPa 0, FC Lahti 1 *(Korte 80)*
TP-47 1 *(Isteri 29)*, TPS 2 *(Casagrande 57, Auremaa 75)*
FC Honka 4 *(Vasara 52, Nybäck 60, 70, Korhonen 87)*, PK-35 1 *(Markkanen 88)*

SEMI-FINALS
(25/10/05)
FC Honka 0, FC Haka 1 *(Lehtinen 57)*
TPS 1 *(Surraco 7)*, FC Lahti 1 *(Rafael 53) (aet; 5-3 on pens)*

FINAL
(29/10/05)
Finnair Stadium, Helsinki
FC HAKA 4 *(Popovich 40, Fowler 50, Innanen 59, Mattila 90)*
TPS 1 *(Auremaa 83)*
Referee - Asumaa
FC HAKA – Vilmunen, Kangaskorpi, Okkonen, Pasoja, Nenonen, Kauppila, Fowler, Popovich, Manninen *(Karjalainen 70)*, Innanen *(Salli 90)*, Lehtinen *(Mattila 85)*.
TPS – Tuomala, Heinikangas, Leino, Nuorela, Helin *(Haijanen 72)*, Casagrande *(Virtanen 59)*, Tuomanen, Ady, Rähmönen, Surraco, Hyyrynen *(Auremaa 57)*.

SECOND LEVEL FINAL TABLE 2005

		Pld	W	D	L	F	A	Pts
1	FC Honka	26	17	6	3	57	17	57
2	VPS	26	17	2	7	49	23	53
3	PK-35	26	12	9	5	28	21	45
4	KPV	26	13	2	11	36	29	41
5	Rakuunat	26	12	5	9	34	36	41
6	FC Viikingit	26	11	4	11	43	34	37
7	Atlantis FC	26	9	7	10	39	35	34
8	PP-70	26	9	5	12	32	39	32
9	MP	26	9	5	12	31	42	32
10	AC Oulu	26	8	7	11	32	33	31
11	FC Hämeenlinna	26	8	6	12	26	39	30
12	VG-62	26	8	5	13	29	41	29
13	OLS	26	8	4	14	23	42	28
14	P-Iirot	26	6	3	17	25	53	21

PROMOTION/RELEGATION PLAY-OFFS
(19/10/05)
VPS 0, RoPS 0
(22/10/05)
RoPS 1, VPS 1
(1-1; VPS on away goal)

France

The saddest adieu

In footballing terms, losing the final of the World Cup on penalties is about as heartbreaking as it gets. France's despair in Berlin's Olympiastadion on the evening of July 9, 2006 ran even deeper than that. They went into the shoot-out without their captain, the great Zinedine Zidane, sent off in extra-time for an act of premeditated violence that will haunt him for the rest of his days.

Many of the world's greatest footballers have been known to lose their cool, to respond petulantly, even physically, to provocation. But what Zidane did to Italy's Marco Materazzi may well go down in history as the single most stupid act of aggression ever witnessed on a football field.

It was the last match of the Frenchman's glorious career. It was the World Cup final. The score was 0-0. It was deep into extra-time. A shoot-out was looming, and Zidane was France's penalty expert. He had even put his team ahead from the spot earlier in the game (and won the semi-final against Portugal in the same manner). Above all, he was the captain of France, their leader.

No excuse

It doesn't really matter what Materazzi said to Zidane (and the precise wording is unlikely ever to be revealed). No amount of verbal baiting should have led him to do what he did. There could be no excuse. Quite apart from the scar his assault left on the image of football on its day of maximum global exposure, it was the damage his action did to his own team that was so extraordinarily difficult to comprehend.

This was a player on whom France's World Cup hopes so depended that he was persuaded out of international retirement a year earlier simply to rescue the team from qualifying failure. It was a mission he accomplished with characteristic commitment and panache. Then, in Germany, after Les Bleus had struggled to get through a straightforward opening group containing Switzerland, South Korea and Togo, he suddenly transformed them back into potential world-beaters

NATIONAL TEAM RESULTS 2005/06

Date	Opponent	H/A/N	Venue	Score	Scorers
17/8/05	Ivory Coast	H	Montpellier	3-0	Gallas (28), Zidane (63), Henry (67)
3/9/05	Faroe Islands (WCQ)	H	Lens	3-0	Cissé (13, 76), Olsen (18og)
7/9/05	Republic of Ireland (WCQ)	A	Dublin	1-0	Henry (68)
8/10/05	Switzerland (WCQ)	A	Berne	1-1	Cissé (52)
12/10/05	Cyprus (WCQ)	H	Saint-Denis	4-0	Zidane (29), Wiltord (31), Dhorasoo (48), Giuly (84)
9/11/05	Costa Rica	N	Fort-de-France	3-2	Anelka (49), Cissé (80), Henry (87)
12/11/05	Germany	H	Saint-Denis	0-0	
1/3/06	Slovakia	H	Saint-Denis	1-2	Wiltord (75p)
27/5/06	Mexico	H	Saint-Denis	1-0	Malouda (45)
31/5/06	Denmark	H	Lens	2-0	Henry (13), Wiltord (76p)
7/6/06	China	H	Saint-Etienne	3-1	Trezeguet (31), Wang Yun (89og), Henry (90)
13/6/06	Switzerland (WCF)	N	Stuttgart	0-0	
18/6/06	South Korea (WCF)	N	Leipzig	1-1	Henry (9)
23/6/06	Togo (WCF)	N	Cologne	2-0	Vieira (55), Henry (61)
27/6/06	Spain (WCF)	N	Hanover	3-1	Ribéry (41), Vieira (83), Zidane (90)
1/7/06	Brazil (WCF)	N	Frankfurt	1-0	Henry (57)
5/7/06	Portugal (WCF)	N	Munich	1-0	Zidane (33p)
9/7/06	Italy (WCF)	N	Berlin	1-1	Zidane (7p) (aet; 3-5 on pens)

France

with pivotal performances against Spain, Brazil and Portugal. His display against the Brazilians in the quarter-final rivalled anything he had achieved at his peak while steering France to World Cup victory on home soil in 1998 and to European Championship glory in Belgium and Holland two years later.

But with his career about to end, and with the prospect of bringing it to the perfect conclusion still very much alive, Zidane flipped.

While he sat in the French dressing-room doing Lord knows what, the team-mates he had left behind went on to lose the match on penalties. Even had they won, it is difficult to imagine that Zidane would have been allowed back to lift the trophy. It was David Trezeguet whose missed penalty proved decisive in the shoot-out, but the French fall-guy was unquestionably their absent skipper.

Golden Ball

How ironic, how perverse, that Zidane should be announced as the official Player of the Tournament the day after his grievous misdeed. FIFA, having initially considered handing the Golden Ball instead to Italy's winning captain Fabio Cannavaro on moral grounds, eventually relented. Whether the trophy provides a comfort to him as he settles into a life away from the game, only he can say. The French, clearly, will continue to idolise him, but for the rest of the world, sadly, the memory of Zinedine Zidane, one of football's genuine all-time greats, will forever be tainted by that infamous headbutt.

Now, of course, France must plan ahead without Zizou. It won't be easy because he has been so central to everything the team has achieved over the past decade. But much encouragement will be taken from the general performance of the team in Germany.

Little had been expected of Les Bleus going into the tournament. Indeed, coach Raymond Domenech was widely derided by the French public, not least for his unpopular decision to keep the experienced Fabien Barthez in goal at the expense of Grégory Coupet. After two stodgy draws against Switzerland and South Korea, his standing was at an all-time low. But the team got him, and themselves, out of a hole with a 2-0 win over Togo, and thereafter, with Zidane at the controls, they suddenly began to tick.

Lilian Thuram (now France's all-time record cap-holder) and William Gallas were consistently strong in central defence, while Bayern Munich's Willy Sagnol, playing in his adopted land, surpassed everyone's expectations with his excellence at right-back. Claude Makelele and – eventually – Patrick Vieira were rock solid in central midfield, while Thierry Henry, though never matching the splendour of his Arsenal form, foraged well in his lone front-running role and scored three goals, including the winner against Brazil.

New contract

Opinion was somewhat divided over the youngest member of the French team, 23-year-old winger Franck Ribéry, but he certainly brought something different to the party, and given that he had never started an international match prior to the tournament, he lasted the pace pretty well. It was to Domenech's credit that he selected and persisted with Ribéry, and by the end of the tournament the grey-haired, bespectacled 54-year-old had not only won over the French public but also earned himself a much-improved new contract.

Although the World Cup marked the end of an era, with Zidane and possibly some of the other veterans (Makelele, Thuram, Barthez) calling time on their international careers, there should be enough quality and experience left for Domenech's team to challenge again at Euro 2008. Intriguingly, their qualifying group pits them once again with Italy. Fortunately, there are no penalty shoot-outs in qualifying games. What's more, two teams go through to the finals.

With some of the old guard dropping out, Domenech will be increasingly casting his eye over the French domestic scene as he looks to plug the gaps in his squad. Doubtless much of his research time will be spent in the VIP box of the Stade Gerland, home to the perennial champions of France, Olympique Lyonnais.

Lyon did it again in 2005/06, and they did it with even greater style and conviction than before. Despite the departure of their coach, Paul Le Guen, and their best player, Michael Essien, the club quickly regrouped under new entraîneur Gérard Houllier and sailed unchallenged to their record-breaking fifth successive title.

No French club had ever won five championships in a row. Indeed, the achievement has been matched in the major European leagues by only three clubs –

France

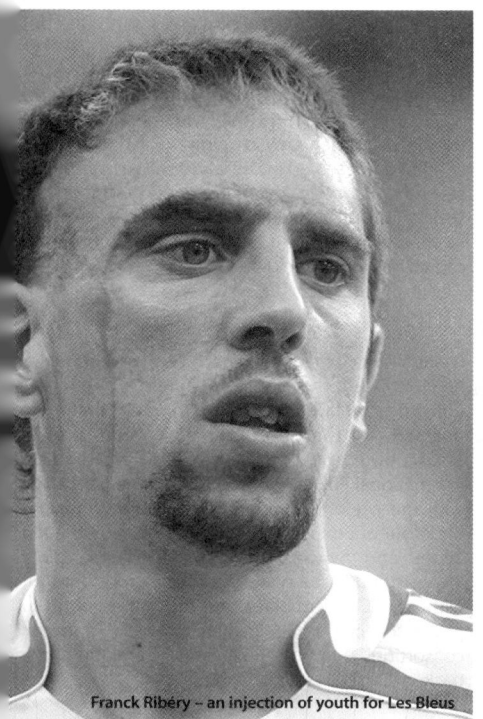

Franck Ribéry – an injection of youth for Les Bleus

Juventus and Torino in Italy, Real Madrid in Spain. But there was never any doubt that Lyon would triumph again. They showed the opposition a clean pair of heels right from the start, dropping just two points in their first six matches (in a 1-1 draw away to Marseille) and remaining unbeaten until the last round before Christmas, when they surprisingly came a cropper in a Friday night encounter at home to Lille (1-3) – and this just five days after a goalless local derby against Saint-Etienne, the first game of the season (in all competitions) in which Houllier's men had failed to score. Even then, their lead at the mid-season break was a handsome 12 points.

Leagues apart

Significantly, at that halfway point in the season, only three points separated the eight teams immediately beneath the leaders. It was one league for Lyon, another for the rest.

Nothing changed in the New Year. The defending champions resumed with a 4-0 win at Strasbourg, in which French international forward Sylvain Wiltord scored a hat-trick, and pressed on relentlessly, eventually tying up the title in mid-April with four rounds to go. Four rounds but five matches, because as they went out to play Paris Saint-Germain in the Parc des Princes the title had been mathematically secured 24 hours earlier by Lille's 3-2 win over Bordeaux.

Lyon would beat PSG 1-0 with a goal from their Brazilian striker Fred but then surrender their unbeaten away record with defeats in Monaco and Lille (who thus completed the double over them). The final two home games provided plenty of celebratory fare for the Lyon fans, however, as the team spanked Saint-Etienne 4-0 before lacerating Le Mans 8-1. Fred scored a hat-trick on the final day to edge out Wiltord as the team's top scorer (14 goals to 12), and the win took the team's final points haul to 84. That was a new Ligue 1 record, as was their 15-point margin of victory.

There were four players in the squad – goalkeeper Coupet, defender Caçapa, midfielder Juninho and striker Sidney Govou – who had taken part in all five of Lyon's championship triumphs. All four were as influential as ever in 2005/06, with free-kick maestro Juninho being voted French Player of the Year at the end of the season and Ligue 1's Best Foreign Player in the midst of it. Other key contributions came from centre-back Cris and midfield anchor Mahamadou Diarra, while youngster François Clerc was a real find at right-back and new signing Tiago a more than useful addition alongside Juninho and Diarra in central midfield.

San Siro exit

Lyon would probably not have traded that fifth consecutive domestic title for a place at the Stade de France in the final of the Champions League, but there was massive disappointment at the club when they exited the competition at the quarter-final stage for the third year in a row. They were only a few minutes away from laying that quarter-final hoodoo to rest at the San Siro when Milan struck twice to knock them out.

Even so, it was another season in which Lyon proved themselves to be genuine contenders for football's most coveted club trophy. Their campaign started with a wonderful 3-0 victory over Real Madrid, and they went on to win the group with ease, their only dropped points coming at the Bernabéu in a 1-1 draw. PSV, who had ended Lyon's European adventure on penalties the previous season, were then soundly beaten in the last 16 before Houllier's

France

men finally met their match in Milan.

A week after their European exit Lyon also came to grief at the quarter-final stage of the Coupe de France, losing 2-1 at home to an in-form Marseille. 'OM' would subsequently hammer Rennes 3-0 to book a place in the final against their arch-foes Paris Saint-Germain. There was even more spice to the fixture than usual after Marseille had sent a team of youth players and fringe first-teamers to Paris for the league game at the Parc des Princes a few weeks earlier. This was a protest against PSG's ticket allocation and security measures for the match. In the event Marseille's youngsters did extraordinarily well to hold the full PSG side to a goalless draw, but the French Football Federation took a dim view of proceedings and their ethical committee, chaired by ex-PSG favourite Dominique Rocheteau, decided to dock both clubs the point they had earned.

The sentence was later revoked on appeal, but the mutual animosity in both camps was more intense than ever in the lead-up to the Cup final. This time Marseille did send out a proper team. For a club that had not won any silverware since their 1993 Champions League victory, they could hardly do otherwise. But in front of a full house of 79,061 fans at the Stade de France it wasn't enough. The Parisians scored early, through Ivorian striker Bonaventure Kalou (the man who had netted the last-minute winner for Auxerre in the 2005 final), and when they made it 2-0 early in the second half through another new signing, Vikash Dhorasoo (who had not scored in the league all season), PSG's seventh victory in the competition was all but sealed. Toifiliou Maoulida pulled a goal back for OM to ensure an exciting finish, but the team from the capital deservedly held on to win.

Huge win

It was a huge win for PSG coach Guy Lacombe, who had replaced the popular Laurent Fournier at Christmas but failed to improve the club's mid-table position in the league. Despite the prolific goalscoring of their captain, Portuguese international Pauleta (who, with 21 goals, ran away with the Ligue 1's Golden Boot), and a consistent back four of Bernard Mendy, David Rozehnal, Mario Yepes and Sylvain Armand, PSG were wildly inconsistent. Fortunately, the Cup victory brought with it a UEFA Cup place, and that was enough to pacify the club's new owners, a North American consortium that had taken over from long-time backers Canal Plus.

Although Marseille were delighted at the time with the point their reserve side had acquired in the Parc des Princes, a victory in that game would have earned them a place alongside PSG on the 2006/07 UEFA Cup starting grid. As it was, they had to be content with another visit to the InterToto Cup. That summer tournament had been their point of entry into the UEFA Cup in 2005/06, and they made good progress in the senior competition, reaching the fourth round, where they were beaten by the Russians of Zenit St. Petersburg.

Marseille were just one of seven Ligue 1 sides who made it one way or another into the UEFA Cup. In addition to the three original qualifiers – Auxerre, Strasbourg and Rennes – there was a second InterToto qualifier in Lens while Monaco (in the first round) and Lille (in the third round) both parachuted in from the Champions League. Despite this mass participation not one team managed to reach the quarter-finals.

Auxerre, in their first season post-Guy Roux, were the first to fall, against Bulgarian side Levski Sofia – an early black mark for new coach Jacques Santini, who would be on his way at the end of the season,

PSG skipper Pauleta – French Cup winner and Ligue 1 top scorer

France

NATIONAL TEAM APPEARANCES 2005/06

Coach – Raymond DOMENECH

Player	DOB	Club	Civ	FAR	IRL	SUI	CYP	Crc	Ger	Svk	Mex	Den	Chn	SUI	KOR	TOG	ESP	BRA	POR	ITA	Caps	Goals
Grégory COUPET	31/12/72	Olympique Lyonnais	G	G	G	G	G		G												18	-
Willy SAGNOL	18/3/77	Bayern München (GER)	D	D	D		D		M	D	D	D89	D	D	D	D	D	D	D	D	45	-
Lilian THURAM	1/1/72	Juventus (ITA)	D23	D78	D	D	D	D	D	D	D50	D	D	D	D	D	D	D	D	D	121	2
Jean-Alain BOUMSONG	14/12/79	Newcastle United (ENG)	D	D	D	D	D		D	D	s50										19	1
William GALLAS	17/8/77	Chelsea (ENG)	D	D	D	D	D	D	D		D46	D	D	D	D	D	D	D	D	D	47	1
Claude MAKELELE	18/2/73	Chelsea (ENG)	M88	M	M	M			M		M48	M	M	M	M	M	M	M	M	M	50	-
Vikash DHORASOO	10/10/73	Paris Saint-Germain	M	s58	M	M46	M		M	M75	M	s52			s85						17	1
Sylvain WILTORD	10/5/74	Olympique Lyonnais	M79	s66	M	A	M59	M64		s46	s46	s57	s84	M85	M60	s74	s88	s81	s67	s107	87	26
Zinedine ZIDANE	23/6/72	Real Madrid (ESP)	M	M58	M70	M	M		M46	M52	M66	M	M	M90		M	M	M	M	M	108	31
Florent MALOUDA	13/6/80	Olympique Lyonnais	M72	M	s70	M90		M	M69	s46	M	M	M		M	M74	M74	M81	M67	M	19	2
Thierry HENRY	17/8/77	Arsenal (ENG)	A72	A66	A		A		A46	s46		A79	A	A	A	A	A88	A85	A83	A107	85	36
Sébastien SQUILLACI	11/8/60	AS Monaco FC	s23	s78																	10	-
Djibril CISSE	12/8/81	Liverpool (ENG)	s72	A	s76	s46	A		s72	s69		A	s79	A13							30	9
Jérôme ROTHEN	31/3/78	Paris Saint-Germain	s72				s72		s69												11	-
David TREZEGUET	15/9/77	Juventus (ITA)	s79						A69	A46	A75		s13		s90	A			s100		66	32
											/84											
Alou DIARRA	15/7/81	RC Lens	s88			s25	M	s75	M	s48				s81				s56			11	-
Patrick VIEIRA	23/6/76	Juventus (ITA)			M	M76	M	M25		M	M46	M	s75	M		M81	M	M	M	M56	94	6
Anthony REVEILLERE	10/11/79	Olympique Lyonnais				D		s15	D												5	-
Sidney GOVOU	24/7/79	Olympique Lyonnais				s90	M90	s64							s77	s74	s76	s71			23	3
Ludovic GIULY	10/7/76	Barcelona (ESP)				s59															17	3
Franck JURIETTI	30/3/75	Girondins de Bordeaux				s90															1	-
Fabien BARTHEZ	28/6/71	Olympique Marseille							G		G	G	G	G	G	G	G	G	G	G	87	-
Gaël GIVET	9/10/81	AS Monaco FC					D72														11	-
Eric ABIDAL	11/9/79	Olympique Lyonnais					D15		s63	D	D83	D	D	D		D	D	D	D	D	14	-
Nicolas ANELKA	14/3/79	Fenerbahçe (TUR)					A72	s46	A46												31	7
Mikaël SILVESTRE	9/8/77	Manchester Utd (ENG)					D63	s46	s83					D							40	2
Franck RIBERY	1/3/83	Olympique Marseille							s75	s66	s75	M70	s60	M77	M	M76	M71	M100			10	1
Louis SAHA	8/8/78	Manchester Utd (ENG)							A57		s70						s85	s83			12	2
Pascal CHIMBONDA	21/2/79	Wigan Athletic (ENG)							s89												1	-

France

replaced by Marseille's Jean Fernandez. Rennes, who had knocked out Spanish Cup winners Osasuna, then fell at the group phase after four defeats, while Lens and Monaco both exited in round three. Marseille were then accompanied through the exit door in round four by Strasbourg and latecomers Lille.

Monaco, Champions League finalists in 2004, failed to reach the group phase after falling to Real Betis, and within a few weeks, following some poor results in the league, coach Didier Deschamps was shown the door. His successor, Francesco Guidolin, made a bright start but the team soon drifted into mediocrity. The Italian brought in a couple of his compatriots, Marco Di Vaio and Christian Vieri, to try to lift the team, but the latter was soon injured and by the end of the season, despite a late spurt of form by another striker, Uruguayan Ernesto Chevantón, Monaco were down in tenth and out of Europe.

Another crack

Former Monaco coach Claude Puel continued to overachieve with Lille, lifting them into third place and giving them another crack at the Champions League, albeit via the qualifying round. The northerners gained automatic access to the group phase in 2005/06. They would score only one goal in six games, but as that was the winner against Manchester United in the Stade de France - their temporary European home – it was not an entirely negative experience.

Bordeaux, coached by former PSG and Brazil defender Ricardo Gomes, were the season's big surprise. Close to relegation the previous season, the Girondins surged up to second place to claim automatic Champions League qualification. They were a team short of stars and goals, but they defended superbly as a unit – one-nil wins were their speciality - and were beaten only five times.

PSG were joined in the UEFA Cup by fourth-placed Lens and League Cup winners Nancy, who overcame fellow mid-table dwellers Nice 2-1 in the Stade de France final. Relegation was a foregone conclusion, with Metz, Ajaccio and Strasbourg (despite their UEFA Cup heroics) all dropping into the bottom three early and staying there, eventually to be replaced by Ligue 2 champions Valenciennes and their two cohorts, Sedan and Lorient.

EUROPEAN CUPS 2005/06

UEFA CHAMPIONS LEAGUE

OLYMPIQUE LYONNAIS

1st round Group F
Match 1 REAL MADRID (ESP)
H **3-0** *Carew (21), Juninho (26), Wiltord (31)*
Coupet, Reveillère, Cris, Caçapa, Berthod, Tiago (Pedretti 86), Diarra, Juninho, Wiltord (Govou 80), Carew (Fred 72), Malouda.

Match 2 ROSENBORG BK (NOR)
A **1-0** *Cris (45)*
Coupet, Reveillère, Cris, Caçapa, Berthod, Govou (Wiltord 89), Tiago, Diarra, Juninho, Malouda, Carew (Fred 90).

Match 3 OLYMPIAKOS (GRE)
H **2-1** *Juninho (4), Govou (89)*
Coupet, Reveillère, Cris, Caçapa, Abidal, Govou (Clément 90), Tiago, Diarra, Juninho, Malouda (Wiltord 75), Fred (Carew 70).

Match 4 OLYMPIAKOS
A **4-1** *Juninho (41), Carew (43, 57), Diarra (55)*
Coupet, Reveillère, Cris, Caçapa, Abidal, Govou, Tiago (Clément 75), Diarra, Juninho (Pedretti 78), Malouda (Wiltord 68), Carew.

Match 5 REAL MADRID
A **1-1** *Carew (72)*
Coupet, Reveillère, Cris, Caçapa, Monsoreau (Fred 69), Tiago, Diarra, Juninho (Clément 90), Govou (Wiltord 69), Carew, Malouda.

Match 6 ROSENBORG BK (NOR)
H **2-1** *Benzema (33), Fred (90)*
Vercoutre, Reveillère (Clerc 83), Cris, Diatta, Monsoreau, Pedretti, Benzema (Beynie 90), Clément, Wiltord, Carew (Fred 55), Ben Arfa.

2nd round PSV (HOL)
A **1-0** *Juninho (64)*
Coupet, Clerc, Cris (Wiltord 46), Müller, Abidal, Tiago, Diarra, Juninho, Govou, Maloufda, Carew (Fred 62).
H **4-0** *Tiago (26, 45), Wiltord (71), Fred (90)*
Coupet, Clerc, Cris, Müller, Abidal, Tiago (Clément 80), Diarra, Juninho (Pedretti 76), Wiltord, Carew (Fred 66), Malouda.

Quarter-final MILAN (ITA)
H **0-0**
Coupet, Clerc, Cris, Caçapa, Abidal, Tiago, Diarra, Pedretti (Clément 68), Wiltord, Carew (Fred 63), Malouda.
A **1-3** *Diarra (31)*
Coupet, Clerc, Cris, Caçapa, Abidal, Juninho, Diarra, Malouda, Wiltord, Fred (Carew 71), Govou (Reveillère 83).

LILLE OSC

1st round Group D
Match 1 SL BENFICA (POR)
A **0-1**
Sylva, Chalmé, Plestan, Schmitz, Tafforeau, Cabaye, Makoun, Gygax (Debuchy 46), Bodmer, Dernis (Lichtsteiner 84), Moussilou (Odemwingie 71).

Match 2 VILLARREAL CF (ESP)
H **0-0**
Sylva, Lichtsteiner, Plestan, Schmitz, Tafforeau, Debuchy, Makoun, Bodmer (Dumont 46), Acimovic (Dernis 84), Odemwingie, Moussilou (Fauvergue 73).

France

Match 3 MANCHESTER UNITED (ENG)
A 0-0
Sylva, Chalmé, Tavlaridis, Schmitz, Vitakic, Bodmer, Makoun, Debuchy (Keita 84), Acimovic (Dernis 60), Tafforeau, Odemwingie (Moussilou 73).

Match 4 MANCHESTER UNITED
H 1-0 *Acimovic (38)*
Sylva, Debuchy, Tavlaridis, Schmitz, Tafforeau, Bodmer, Makoun, Chalmé, Acimovic (Cabaye 76), Dernis (Gygax 79), Moussilou (Odemwingie 84).

Match 5 SL BENFICA
H 0-0
Sylva, Lichtsteiner, Tavlaridis, Schmitz, Tafforeau, Chalmé (Miralals 69), Bodmer, Makoun, Dernis, Acimovic (Fauvergue 87), Moussilou (Aboucherouane 75).

Match 6 VILLARREAL CF
A 0-1
Sylva, Chalmé, Tavlaridis, Vitakic, Tafforeau, Lichtsteiner (Moussilou 70), Dumont, Bodmer, Makoun, Dernis (Acimovic 60), Odemwingie (Mirallas 75).

AS MONACO FC

3rd qualifying round REAL BETIS (ESP)
A 0-1
Roma, Maicon, Squillaci, Modesto, Evra, Sorlin (Gigliotti 82), Bernardi, Zikos, Meriem, Adebayor, Chevantón (Maoulida 68).
H 2-2 *Gerard (33), Maoulida (63)*
Warmuz, Maicon, Squillaci, Modesto, Evra, Meriem (Maoulida 62), Gerard, Bernardi, Sorlin (Gigliotti 79), Kapo, Adebayor.

UEFA CUP

AJ AUXERRE
1st round LEVSKI SOFIA (BUL)
H 2-1 *Poyet (55), Pieroni (84)*
Cool, Radet, Kalabane, Grichting, Jaurès, Diaby (Lachuer 46), Violeau, Cheyrou, Akalé (Berson 74), Benjani (Poyet 46), Pieroni.
A 0-1
Cool, Sagna, Grichting, Mignot, Radet (Bolf 76), Lachuer, Berson, Violeau, Diaby (Poyet 66), Akalé, Pieroni (Benjani 65).

RC STRASBOURG
1st round GRAZER AK (AUT)
A 2-0 *Pagis (1), Lacour (45)*
Cassard, Deroff, Hagui, Kanté, Boka, Lacour, Hosni, Keita, Le Pen (Diané 90), Pagis (Arrache 77), Farnerud A. (Gmamdia 71).
H 5-0 *Hagui (6), Farnerud A. (40), Farnerud P. (50), Le Pen (60), Hosni (68)*
Cassard, Deroff, Hagui, Kanté, Boka, Lacour (Johansen 63), Hosni, Farnerud P., Le Pen, Pagis (Gmamdia 59), Farnerud A. (Arrache 72).

2nd round Group E
Match 1 FC BASEL (SUI)
A 2-0 *Diané (15), Boka (25)*
Cassard, Deroff, Devaux, Kanté, Boka (Farnerud P. 64), Johansen, Hosni, Lacour, Farnerud A., Pagis (Faty 86), Diané (Le Pen 74).

Match 2 TROMSØ IL (NOR)
H 2-0 *Pagis (38), Arrache (66)*
Cassard, Deroff, Devaux, Bellaïd, Kanté, Lacour, Farnerud P. (Krebs 60), Faty, Arrache (Mouloungui 69), Pagis (Carlier 74), Diané.

Match 3 ROMA (ITA)
A 1-1 *Bellaid (52)*
Puydebois, Lacour, Bellaïd, Kanté (Schneider 70), Boka, Johansen, Faty (Arrache 80), Farnerud P., Farnerud A. (Krebs 46), Diané, Gmamdia.

Match 4 CRVENA ZVEZDA BEOGRAD (SCG)
H 2-2 *Gameiro (79, 90)*
Cassard, Deroff, Bellaïd (Hagui 77), Schneider, Boka, Johansen (Lacour 72), Krebs, Faty, Le Pen, Diané, Gameiro.

3rd round LITEX LOVECH (BUL)
A 2-0 *Le Pen (2), Diané (82)*
Puydebois, Lacour, Hagui, Kantee, Abou, Loué, Diané (Deroff 82), Abdessadki, Farenrud P., Le Pen, Gameiro (Farnerud A. 66).
H 0-0
Puydebois, Deroff, Devaux, Hagui, Boka, Lacour, Diané (Loué 68), Abdessadki, Krebs (Gameiro 60), Le Pen (Farnerud P. 75), Farnerud A.

4th round FC BASEL (SUI)
A 0-2
Puydebois, Deroff, Hagui (Bellaïd 87), Kanté, Abou, Loué (Abdessadki 40), Hosni, Diané, Farnerud P., Lacour (Boka 63), Farnerud A.
H 2-2 *Carlier (10), Kanté (78)*
Puydebois, Deroff, Bellaïd, Kanté, Abou, Faty, Johansen, Farnerud P., Boka, Carlier, Farnerud A.

STADE RENNAIS FC
1st round CA OSASUNA (ESP)
H 3-1 *Frei (27, 74), Hadji (83)*
Isaksson, Jeunechamp, Ouaddou, Adailton, Perrier-Doumbé, Mvuemba (Hadji 46), Didot (Gourcuff 76), Källström, Utaka (Briand 85), Frei, Monterrubio.
A 0-0
Isaksson, Perrier-Doumbé, Adailton, Faty, Edman, Bourillon, Hadji, Didot (Gourcuff 64), Källström, Monterrubio (Briand 90), Utaka (Frei 83).

2nd round Group G
Match 1 VFB STUTTGART (GER)
H 0-2
Pouplin, Mbia (Gourcuff 61), Adailton, Faty, Edman (Nguéma 90), Bourillon, Didot, Hadji (Briand 64), Monterrubio, Utaka, Frei.

Match 2 RAPID BUCURESTI (ROM)
A 0-2
Pouplin, Mbia, Adailton, Briand 71), Ouaddou, Edman, Gourcuff, Bourillon, Didot (Barbosa 76), Utaka, Frei (Sow 83), Monterrubio.

Match 3 SHAKHTAR DONETSK (UKR)
H 0-1
Pouplin, Mbia, Ouaddou, Faty (Adailton 46), Edman, Didot, Gourcuff, Utaka (Briand 67), Källström (Mvuemba 46), Monterrubio, Frei.

Match 4 PAOK (GRE)
A 1-5 *Briand (70)*
Pouplin, Perrier-Doumbé, Adailton, Rochat, Sepsi, Barbosa (Källström 72), Bourillon, Mvuemba, Sow (Frei 72), Briand, N'Guéma (Utaka 72).

RC LENS
1st round GROCLIN DYSKOBOLIA GRODZISK (POL)
H 1-1 *Hilton (12)*
Itandje, Barul, Hilton, Gillet, Lachor (Dindane 64), Carrière, Diarra, Assou-Ekotto, Thomert, Jussié, Cousin.
A 4-2 *Cousin (23, 53), Dindane (30), Lachor (90)*
Itandje, Demont (Barul 83), Coulibaly, Hilton, Assou-Ekotto, Keita, Diarra, Dindane, Jussié (Carrière 76), Cousin (Lachor 60), Thomert.

2nd round Group C
Match 1 STEAUA BUCURESTI (ROM)

France

A 0-4
Itandje, Barul, Hilton, Coulibaly (Jussié 46), Gillet, Assou-Ekotto, Demont, Diarra (Carrière 71), Keita (Leroy 45), Dindane, Thomert.

Match 2 HALMSTADS BK (SWE)
H 5-0 *Cousin (16, 23, 47), Jemaa (73), Lachor (90)*
Itandje, Demont (Lacourt 69), Gillet, Hilton, Lachor, Barul, Keita, Leroy (Jemaa 73), Carrière, Thomert, Cousin (Jussié 76).

Match 3 HERTHA BSC BERLIN (GER)
A 0-0
Itandje, Barul, Hilton, Gillet, Assou-Ekotto, Demont, Diarra, Keita, Jemaa (Thomert 82), Jussié, Dindane (Cousin 82).

Match 4 SAMPDORIA (ITA)
H 2-1 *Thomert (10), Jemaa (90)*
Itandje, Demont, Gillet, Coulibaly, Assou-Ekotto, Diarra, Keita, Dindane (Jemaa 78), Jussié (Carrière 65), Thomert, Cousin.

3rd round UDINESE (ITA)
A 0-3
Itandje, Demont, Coulibaly, Hilton, Assou-Ekotto, Diarra (Khiter 74), Keita, Frau (Jemaa 64), Jussié (Carrière 64), Thomert, Cousin.
H 1-0 *Frau (55)*
Chabbert, Barul, Feindouno (84), Coulibaly, Gillet, Assou-Ekotto, Carrière, Lacourt, Jemaa (Cousin 62), Frau, Khiter, Dindane (Demont 74).

OLYMPIQUE MARSEILLE

1st round GERMINAL BEERSCHOT ANTWERPEN (BEL)
A 0-0
Carrasso, Beye, André Luis, Déhu, Cesar, Nakata (Taiwo 64), Lamouchi, Cana, Oruma (Nasri 77), Giménez, Mendoza (Koke 60).
H 0-0
(aet; 4-1 on pens)
Carrasso, Beye, André Luis, Meïté, Nakata (Taiwo 46), Nasri, Delfim (Cana 90), Oruma, Koke, Mendoza (Giménez 46), Niang.

2nd round Group F
Match 1 CSKA MOSKVA (RUS)
A 2-1 *Lamouchi (23), Niang (38)*
Barthez, Ferreira, Cana, André Luis, Cesar, Taiwo, Ribéry (Giménez 73), Beye, Lamouchi, Oruma, Niang (Nasri 77).

Match 2 SC HEERENVEEN (HOL)
H 1-0 *Taiwo (90p)*
Barthez, Meïté, André Luis, Cesar, Taiwo, Koke (Nasri 61), Lamouchi (Mendoza 81), Delfim, Oruma, Ribéry, Niang (Cana 90).

Match 3 LEVSKI SOFIA (BUL)
A 0-1
Barthez, Ferreira (Ribéry 64), Beye, André Luis, Cesar, Nakata, Nasri (Oruma 78), Delfim, Koke (Niang 64), Giménez, Mendoza.

Match 4 DINAMO BUCURESTI (ROM)
H 2-1 *Cesar (39), Delfim (45)*
Barthez, Ferreira, André Luis, Cesar, Taiwo, Lamouchi (Oruma 71), Delfim, Cana, Nasri (Begeorgi 77), Ribéry, Giménez (Mendoza 67).

3rd round BOLTON WANDERERS (ENG)
A 0-0
Barthez, Ferreira, Beye, Déhu, Cesar, Taiwo, Nasri (Giménez 74), Cana, Oruma, Ribey, Niang (Cantareil 90).
H 2-1 *Ribéry (45), Ben Haim (68og)*
Barthez, Ferreira (Deruda 67), Beye, Déhu, Meïté, Taiwo, Nasri, Cana (Civelli 90),
Oruma, Ribéry (Cantareil 80), Niang.

4th round ZENIT SANKT-PETERBURG (RUS)
H 0-1
Barthez, Ferreira (Giménez 61), Beye, Déhu, Meïté, Taiwo, Lamouchi (Deruda 82), Oruma, Nasri (Delfim 82), Niang, Ribery.
A 1-1 *Déhu (74)*
Carrasso, Beye, Civelli (Deruda 76), Déhu, Meïté, Taiwo, Lamouchi (Begeorgi 77), Cana, Nasri, Niang, Giménez (Delfim 84).

AS MONACO FC

1st round WILLEM II (HOL)
H 2-0 *Kapo (24), Adebayor (48)*
Warmuz, Maicon, Squillaci, Modesto, Evra, Meriem (Maoulida 75), Zikos, Bernardi, Sorlin, Kapo, Adebayor (Gigliotti 71).
A 3-1 *Maicon (48), Adebayor (55), Chevantón (89)*
Warmuz, Maicon, Squillaci, Givet, Evra (Cubilier 11), Perez (Sorlin 26), Zikos, Bernardi, Meriem (Chevantón 73), Kapo, Adebayor.

2nd round Group A
Match 1 VIKING FK (NOR)
A 0-1
Warmuz, Squillaci, Modesto, Givet, Maicon, Plasil (Zikos 46), Bernardi, Evra (Gigliotti 46), Meriem, Adebayor, Kapo (Maoulida 84).

Match 2 HAMBURGER SV (GER)
H 2-0 *Adebayor (44), Veigneau (90)*
Warmuz, Cubilier, Modesto, Givet, Evra, Bernardi, Zikos, Plasil (Maurice-Belay 59), Meriem (Veigneau 76), Sorlin, Adebayor.

Match 3 SK SLAVIA PRAHA (CZE)
A 2-0 *Maoulida (11, 71)*
Warmuz, Cubilier, Modesto, Givet, Evra, Plasil (Veigneau 77), Bernardi (Zikos 59), Perez, Sorlin, Maurice-Belay (Gigliotti 83), Maoulida.

Match 4 CSKA SOFIA (BUL)
H 2-1 *Kapo (50), Squillaci (75)*
Warmuz, Cubilier, Squillaci, Modesto, Veigneau, Perez (Bernardi 46), Zikos, Plasil (Givet 67), Kapo, Adebayor, Maoulida (Maurice-Belay 46).

3rd round FC BASEL (SUI)
A 0-1
Warmuz, Maicon, Squillaci, Givet (Modesto 21), Dos Santos, Bernardi, Zikos, Gakpe, Meriem (Gigliotti 90), Plasil (Veigneau 66), Vieri.
H 1-1 *Vieri (21p)*
Roma, Maicon, Squillaci, Modesto, Dos Santos, Bernardi, Zikos, Gakpe (Maurice-Belay 62), Meriem (Kapo 76), Plasil (Chevantón 62), Vieri.

LILLE OSC

3rd round SHAKHTAR DONETSK (UKR)
H 3-2 *Fauvergue (19), Dernis (57), Odemwingie (77)*
Malicki (Pichon 51), Lichtsteiner, Tavlaridis, Schmitz, Vitakic, Dernis (Kader Keita 71), Makoun, Bodmer, Debuchy, Fauvergue (Cabaye 80), Odemwingie.
A 0-0
Sylva, Chalmé, Tavlaridis, Schmitz, Tafforeau, Cabaye (Fauvergue 68), Debuchy, Lichtsteiner (Keita 59), Bodmer, Dernis, Odemwingie (Franquart 77).

4th round SEVILLA FC (ESP)
H 1-0 *Dernis (24)*
Sylva, Chalmé, Plestan, Schmitz, Vitakic, Makoun, Dumont (Franquart 88), Keita (Lichtsteiner 75), Bodmer, Dernis, Moussilou (Mirallas 60).
A 0-2
Sylva, Chalmé, Tavlaridis, Schmitz, Tafforeau, Makoun, Dumont (Keita 59), Lichtsteiner, Bodmer, Dernis (Fauvergue 78), Moussilou (Odemwingie 46).

France

TOP GOALSCORERS 2005/06

- 21 PAULETA (Paris Saint-Germain)
- 14 Peter ODEMWINGIE (Lille OSC)
- FRED (Olympique Lyonnais)
- 13 Daniel COUSIN (RC Lens)
- 12 Luigi PIERONI (AJ Auxerre)
- Sylvain WILTORD (Olympique Lyonnais)
- 11 John UTAKA (Stade Rennais FC)
- 10 Péguy LUYINDULA (AJ Auxerre)
- Mamadou NIANG (Olympique Marseille)
- Mickaël PAGIS (RC Strasbourg/Olympique Marseille)
- Ernesto Javier CHEVANTÓN (AS Monaco FC)
- Mamadou DIALLO (FC Nantes)
- ILAN (FC Sochaux)
- Daniel MOREIRA (Toulouse FC)

LEAGUE RESULTS/SCORERS/APPEARANCES/GOALS 2005/06

AC AJACCIO
Coach – Rolland Courbis; (12/1/06) José Pasqualetti

2005
Date	Opponent	H/A	Score	Scorers
30/7	AS Saint-Etienne	a	0-0	
6/8	Lille OSC	h	3-3	Rocchi, Lucas, Saïfi
13/8	FC Nantes	a	2-0	Edson, Rocchi
20/8	Le Mans UC 72	h	0-0	
27/8	Olympique Marseille	a	1-1	Saïfi (p)
10/9	AS Nancy-Lorraine	h	1-0	Lucas
18/9	AJ Auxerre	a	0-2	
21/9	RC Strasbourg	h	0-0	
24/9	Girondins de Bordeaux	a	0-1	
16/10	Olympique Lyonnais	a	2-3	Diawara (p), og (Tiago)
23/10	Stade Rennais FC	h	0-1	
29/10	AS Monaco FC	a	0-3	
5/11	FC Metz	a	0-2	
11/11	RC Lens	h	0-0	
19/11	FC Sochaux	h	0-1	
26/11	Toulouse FC	a	0-3	
3/12	ES Troyes AC	h	0-1	
10/12	OGC Nice	a	0-1	
17/12	Paris Saint-Germain	h	1-1	Rocchi

2006
Date	Opponent	H/A	Score	Scorers
4/1	Lille OSC	a	0-2	
11/1	FC Nantes	h	0-2	
14/1	Le Mans UC 72	a	0-1	
21/1	Olympique Marseille	h	3-1	Lucas 2, N'Diaye
28/1	AS Nancy-Lorraine	a	0-0	
4/2	AJ Auxerre	h	1-0	N'Diaye
11/2	RC Strasbourg	a	2-2	N'Diaye 2
18/2	Girondins de Bordeaux	h	0-2	
25/2	RC Lens	a	0-1	
4/3	Olympique Lyonnais	h	1-3	Lucas
11/3	Stade Rennais FC	a	0-3	
18/3	AS Monaco FC	h	1-0	N'Diaye
25/3	FC Metz	h	0-1	
1/4	FC Sochaux	a	1-3	António Carlos
8/4	Toulouse FC	h	1-0	Diawara
15/4	ES Troyes AC	a	0-3	
30/4	OGC Nice	h	0-3	
6/5	Paris Saint-Germain	a	4-2	Chafni 2, Abdoun, Scarpelli
13/5	AS Saint-Etienne	h	3-1	Abdoun, Scarpelli 2

No	Name	Nat	Pos	Aps	(s)	Gls
22	Djamel ABDOUN		M	2	(5)	2
28	ANDRÉ LUIZ Moreira	BRA	M	23	(2)	
4	ANTÓNIO CARLOS dos Santos	BRA	D	19	(1)	1
	Anthony BARON		D	2		
20	Christophe BASTIEN		M	2	(8)	
29	Xavier BECAS		A		(1)	
20	Kamel CHAFNI	MAR	M	30	(4)	2
25	Xavier COLLIN		D	36		
13	Frédeeric DANJOU		D	21	(2)	
19	Kaba DIAWARA	GUI	A	16	(4)	2
18	Nenad DZODIC	SCG	D	12	(1)	
10	EDSON Marcelo	BRA	A	17	(8)	1
	Azite FRANKLIN		M		(1)	
27	Daouda JABI	GUI	D	29	(2)	
15	Fabien LAURENTI		D	30		
	Dimitri LESUEUR		A		(1)	
9	LUCAS Pereira Filho	BRA	A	20	(11)	5
	Florian LUCCHINI		G		(1)	
12	Christophe MANDRICHI		A	6	(11)	
17	Laurent MERLIN		A		(1)	
	Jean-Toussaint MORETTI		D		(1)	
	Moussa N'DIAYE	SEN	A	17		5
1	Stéphane PORATO		G	33		
5	Martial ROBIN		D	13	(9)	
7	Romain ROCCHI		M	21	(3)	3
6	RODRIGO Lacerba Ramos	BRA	M	36		
8	Rafik SAÏFI	ALG	M	16	(10)	2
11	Mathieu SCARPELLI		A	5	(7)	3
16	Stéphane TREVISAN		G	5	(2)	
14	Stéphane ZIANI		M	7		

AJ AUXERRE
Coach – Jacques Santini

2005
Date	Opponent	H/A	Score	Scorers
30/7	RC Strasbourg	a	0-0	
6/8	AS Monaco FC	a	2-0	Violeau, Pieroni
13/8	Girondins de Bordeaux	h	1-0	Pieroni
20/8	RC Lens	a	0-7	
28/8	Olympique Lyonnais	h	0-2	
10/9	Stade Rennais FC	a	1-3	Diaby
18/9	AC Ajaccio	h	2-0	Akalé, Luyindula
21/9	FC Metz	a	2-1	Mignot, Luyindula
24/9	FC Sochaux	h	3-0	Luyindula, Kahlenberg, Cheyrou
2/10	Toulouse FC	a	0-2	
15/10	ES Troyes AC	h	3-0	Lachuer, Luyindula, Benjani
22/10	OGC Nice	a	0-1	
30/10	Paris Saint-Germain	h	2-0	og (Cissé), Pieroni
5/11	AS Saint-Etienne	a	1-1	Mignot
19/11	Lille OSC	h	3-2	Lachuer, Pieroni 2 (1p)
25/11	Le Mans UC 72	a	2-0	Pieroni, Lachuer
3/12	FC Nantes	h	4-0	Luyindula 2, Pieroni, Cheyrou
10/12	Olympique Marseille	a	0-1	
17/12	AS Nancy-Lorraine	h	0-1	

2006
Date	Opponent	H/A	Score	Scorers
5/1	AS Monaco FC	h	2-1	Luyindula, Kahlenberg
11/1	Girondins de Bordeaux	a	0-1	

France

FINAL LEAGUE TABLE 2005/06

		Pld	Home					Away					Total					Pts
			W	D	L	F	A	W	D	L	F	A	W	D	L	F	A	
1	Olympique Lyonnais	38	13	4	2	40	18	12	5	2	33	13	25	9	4	73	31	84
2	Girondins de Bordeaux	38	11	7	1	23	11	7	8	4	20	14	18	15	5	43	25	69
3	Lille OSC	38	12	5	2	33	7	4	9	6	23	24	16	14	8	56	31	62
4	RC Lens	38	11	7	1	34	14	3	11	5	14	20	14	18	6	48	34	60
5	Olympique Marseille	38	10	8	1	28	13	6	4	9	16	22	16	12	10	44	35	60
6	AJ Auxerre	38	13	3	3	33	9	4	5	10	17	30	17	8	13	50	39	59
7	Stade Rennais FC	38	11	3	5	34	25	7	2	10	14	24	18	5	15	48	49	59
8	OGC Nice	38	11	4	4	22	12	5	6	8	14	19	16	10	12	36	31	58
9	Paris Saint-Germain	38	11	3	5	34	20	2	10	7	10	18	13	13	12	44	38	52
10	AS Monaco FC	38	8	7	4	23	14	5	6	8	19	22	13	13	12	42	36	52
11	Le Mans UC 72	38	9	7	3	21	8	4	6	9	12	28	13	13	12	33	36	52
12	AS Nancy-Lorraine	38	5	8	6	19	17	7	4	8	16	20	12	12	14	35	37	48
13	AS Saint-Etienne	38	6	8	5	18	15	5	6	8	11	24	11	14	13	29	39	47
14	FC Nantes	38	7	7	5	22	18	4	5	10	15	23	11	12	15	37	41	45
15	FC Sochaux	38	6	7	6	17	19	5	4	10	17	28	11	11	16	34	47	44
16	Toulouse FC	38	7	6	6	21	18	3	5	11	15	29	10	11	17	36	47	41
17	ES Troyes AC	38	6	7	6	20	18	3	5	11	17	29	9	12	17	37	47	39
18	AC Ajaccio	38	6	5	8	15	20	2	4	13	12	33	8	9	21	27	53	33
19	RC Strasbourg	38	2	8	9	15	26	3	6	10	18	30	5	14	19	33	56	29
20	FC Metz	38	5	4	10	13	24	1	7	11	13	35	6	11	21	26	59	29

Date	Opponent	H/A	Score	Scorers
14/1	RC Lens	h	1-0	Luyindula
22/1	Olympique Lyonnais	a	1-1	Luyindula
28/1	Stade Rennais FC	h	2-0	Pieroni (p), Kahlenberg
4/2	AC Ajaccio	a	0-1	
11/2	FC Metz	h	1-1	Pieroni (p)
18/2	FC Sochaux	a	0-1	
25/2	Toulouse FC	h	2-0	Akalé, Kahlenberg
5/3	ES Troyes AC	a	1-1	Kahlenberg
11/3	OGC Nice	h	2-0	Akalé, Bolf
19/3	Paris Saint-Germain	a	1-4	Mathis
25/3	AS Saint-Etienne	h	0-0	
1/4	Lille OSC	a	1-1	Luyindula
9/4	Le Mans UC 72	h	0-0	
15/4	FC Nantes	a	2-3	Akalé, Kahlenberg
3/5	Olympique Marseille	h	1-2	Mignot
6/5	AS Nancy-Lorraine	a	3-1	Pieroni, Lachuer, Kahlenberg
13/5	RC Strasbourg	h	4-0	Kahlenberg, Pieroni 2 (1p), Mathis

No	Name	Nat	Pos	Aps	(s)	Gls
11	Kanga AKALE	CIV	M	22	(9)	4
21	BENJANI Mwaruwari	ZIM	A	10	(1)	1
13	Mathieu BERSON		M	20	(7)	
5	René BOLF	CZE	D	7	(3)	1
7	Benoît CHEYROU		M	34	(1)	2
1	Fabien COOL		G	38		
17	Abou DIABY		M	3	(2)	1
	Ludovic GENEST		A		(1)	
4	Stéphane GRICHTING	SUI	D	24	(1)	
16	Sébastien HAMEL		G		(2)	
3	Jean-Sébastien JAURES		D	16	(2)	
26	Younes KABOUL		D	8	(1)	
10	Thomas KAHLENBERG	DEN	M	29	(9)	8
25	Omar KALABANE	GUI	D	8		
8	Yann LACHUER		M	22	(5)	4
20	Péguy LUYINDULA		A	26	(7)	10
34	Baptiste MARTIN		D	7	(8)	
18	Lionel MATHIS		M	11	(12)	2
12	Jean-Pascal MIGNOT		D	28		3
9	Luigi PIERONI	BEL	A	21	(12)	12
28	Romain POYET		A	2	(12)	
2	Johan RADET		D	32	(1)	
29	Bacary SAGNA		D	23		
6	Philippe VIOLEAU		M	27	(3)	1

GIRONDINS DE BORDEAUX
Coach – Ricardo Gomes (BRA)

2005

Date	Opponent	H/A	Score	Scorers
30/7	Olympique Marseille	a	2-0	Faubert, Ducasse
6/8	AS Nancy-Lorraine	h	1-0	Chamakh
13/8	AJ Auxerre	a	0-1	
20/8	AS Monaco FC	h	1-0	Cheyrou
27/8	RC Strasbourg	a	0-0	
11/9	RC Lens	a	1-1	Chamakh
17/9	Olympique Lyonnais	h	1-1	Smicer
21/9	Stade Rennais FC	a	2-2	Smicer (p), Chamakh
24/9	AC Ajaccio	h	1-0	Darcheville
1/10	FC Metz	a	1-0	Fernando
15/10	FC Sochaux	h	1-1	Alonso
22/10	Toulouse FC	a	1-1	Francia
29/10	ES Troyes AC	h	2-0	Darcheville 2
5/11	OGC Nice	a	1-0	Laslandes
20/11	Paris Saint-Germain	h	0-2	
26/11	AS Saint-Etienne	a	1-1	Faubert
3/12	Lille OSC	h	1-0	Fernando
10/12	Le Mans UC 72	a	0-1	
17/12	FC Nantes	h	0-0	

France

2006

Date	Opponent	H/A	Score	Scorers
7/1	AS Nancy-Lorraine	a	0-0	
11/1	AJ Auxerre	h	1-0	Alonso
14/1	AS Monaco FC	a	1-0	Denilson
21/1	RC Strasbourg	h	2-1	Fernando, Faubert
28/1	RC Lens	h	1-0	Laslandes (p)
1/2	Olympique Lyonnais	a	0-0	
11/2	Stade Rennais FC	h	2-0	Fernando, Smicer
8/2	AC Ajaccio	a	2-0	Chamakh, Denilson
25/2	FC Metz	h	3-3	Chamakh 2, Alonso
11/3	Toulouse FC	h	2-0	Henrique, Laslandes (p)
18/3	ES Troyes AC	a	1-1	Darcheville
26/3	OGC Nice	h	1-0	Denilson
2/4	Paris Saint-Germain	a	1-3	Perea
8/4	AS Saint-Etienne	h	0-0	
15/4	Lille OSC	a	2-3	Darcheville (p), Faubert
23/4	FC Sochaux	a	3-0	Faubert, Jemmali, Darcheville
30/4	Le Mans UC 72	h	2-2	Chamakh, Darcheville
6/5	FC Nantes	a	1-0	Darcheville (p)
13/5	Olympique Marseille	h	1-1	Fernando

No	Name	Nat	Pos	Aps	(s)	Gls
21	Kodjo AFANOU		D	18		
8	Alejandro ALONSO	ARG	M	8	(13)	3
4	Roberto Severo "BETO"	POR	D	4		
29	Marouane CHAMAKH	MAR	A	22	(7)	7
14	Bruno CHEYROU		M	22	(4)	1
9	Jean-Claude DARCHEVILLE		A	29	(5)	8
22	DENILSON de Oliveira	BRA	M	20	(11)	3
19	Pierre DUCASSE		M	1	(5)	1
18	Julien FAUBERT		M	27	(7)	5
5	FERNANDO Menegazzo	BRA	M	27	(4)	5
10	Juan Pablo FRANCIA	ARG	M	6	(11)	1
3	Carlos HENRIQUE	BRA	D	18		1
13	David JEMMALI	TUN	D	32	(2)	1
6	Franck JURIETTI		D	25	(1)	
7	Lilian LASLANDES		A	15	(13)	3
15	Ted LAVIE		M	1	(1)	
17	Laurent LEROY		A		(2)	
23	Florian MARANGE		D	14		
24	Rio MAVUBA		M	30	(7)	
12	Edixon PEREA	COL	A	8	(13)	1
27	Marc PLANUS		D	32		
16	Ulrich RAME		G	35		
1	Frédéric ROUX		G	3	(1)	
11	Vladimír SMICER	CZE	M	21	(4)	3
	Madimoussa TRAORE		A		(1)	

LE MANS UC 72
Coach – Frédéric Hantz

2005

Date	Opponent	H/A	Score	Scorers
31/7	Olympique Lyonnais	h	1-2	De Melo
6/8	FC Metz	a	0-0	
13/8	Stade Rennais FC	h	4-0	De Melo 2 (1p), Lucau, Bangoura
20/8	AC Ajaccio	a	0-0	
27/8	ES Troyes AC	h	1-0	Thomas F.
10/9	Toulouse FC	a	2-0	Lucau, Hautcoeur
17/9	FC Sochaux	h	2-1	Hautcoeur, De Melo
21/9	OGC Nice	a	0-1	
24/9	Paris Saint-Germain	h	0-0	
1/10	AS Saint-Etienne	a	0-3	
15/10	Lille OSC	h	1-1	Thomas F. (p)
23/10	RC Strasbourg	h	2-0	Hautcoeur, Matsui
29/10	FC Nantes	a	0-1	
5/11	Olympique Marseille	h	3-0	Chiumiento, Fanchone, Bangoura
19/11	AS Nancy-Lorraine	a	0-1	
25/11	AJ Auxerre	h	0-2	
3/12	AS Monaco FC	a	0-2	
10/12	Girondins de Bordeaux	h	1-0	Bangoura
18/12	RC Lens	a	0-2	

2006

Date	Opponent	H/A	Score	Scorers
4/1	FC Metz	h	2-0	De Melo 2
11/1	Stade Rennais FC	a	0-1	
14/1	AC Ajaccio	h	1-0	og (António Carlos)
21/1	ES Troyes AC	a	3-1	Matsui 2, Fauré
28/1	Toulouse FC	h	1-1	De Melo
4/2	FC Sochaux	a	0-0	
11/2	OGC Nice	h	2-0	Fanchone, Bangoura
18/2	Paris Saint-Germain	a	1-0	Fauré (p)
25/2	AS Saint-Etienne	h	0-1	
4/3	Lille OSC	a	0-4	
12/3	RC Strasbourg	a	2-1	Bangoura, Grafite
18/3	FC Nantes	h	0-0	
25/3	Olympique Marseille	a	1-1	Fanchone
2/4	AS Nancy-Lorraine	h	0-0	
9/4	AJ Auxerre	a	0-0	
15/4	AS Monaco FC	h	0-0	
30/4	Girondins de Bordeaux	a	2-2	Bangoura, Grafite
6/5	RC Lens	h	0-0	
13/5	Olympique Lyonnais	a	1-8	Grafite

No	Name	Nat	Pos	Aps	(s)	Gls
9	Ismaël BANGOURA	GUI	A	15	(8)	6
25	Marco BASA	SCG	D	32		
20	Laurent BONNART		D	35		
15	Grégory CERDAN		D	15	(6)	
27	David CHIUMIENTO	SUI	M	9	(9)	1
21	Jérémy CHOPLIN		M		(2)	
18	Túlio DE MELO	BRA	A	18	(6)	7
26	Martin DOUILLARD		A	3	(9)	
29	Edorisi EKHOUSUEHI	NGA	A	3	(7)	
17	James FANCHONE		A	30	(7)	3
27	Cédric FAURE		A	10	(4)	2
24	Yannick FISCHER		D	8	(4)	
13	Sébastien GORMOND		M	1	(2)	
	GRAFITE	BRA	A	7	(4)	3
7	Yohan HAUTCOEUR		M	31	(4)	3
2	Luigi LAVECCHIA	ITA	D	1		
	Guillaume LORIOT		M	3	(4)	
14	Chiguy LUCAU		A	8	(5)	2
22	Daisuke MATSUI	JPN	M	28	(5)	3
30	Yohann PELE		G	36		
28	Jacques-Désiré PERIATAMBEE		M	5	(7)	
23	Clément PINAULT		D	2	(2)	
19	Yoann POULARD		D	26		
16	Rodolphe ROCHE		G	2	(1)	
11	ROMARIC N'Dri	CIV	A	16	(5)	
5	Frédéric THOMAS		M	38		2
6	Olivier THOMAS		D	36		

RC LENS
Coach – François Gillot

2005

Date	Opponent	H/A	Score	Scorers
30/7	FC Nantes	a	0-2	
6/8	Olympique Marseille	h	2-0	Keita, Hilton
13/8	AS Nancy-Lorraine	a	2-1	Diarra, Dindane
20/8	AJ Auxerre	h	7-0	Cousin 2, Thomert 2,

The European Book of Football 2006/2007 - 345

France

					Jussié 2, Demont
28/8	AS Monaco FC	a	0-0		
11/9	Girondins de Bordeaux	h	1-1		Cousin
18/9	RC Strasbourg	a	1-1		Dindane
22/9	Olympique Lyonnais	a	1-1		Coulibaly
25/9	Stade Rennais FC	h	0-0		
15/10	OGC Nice	h	2-2		Diarra, Thomert
23/10	ES Troyes AC	a	1-1		Cousin
29/10	Toulouse FC	h	1-0		Cousin
6/11	FC Sochaux	a	1-1		Cousin
11/11	AC Ajaccio	a	0-0		
19/11	FC Metz	h	0-0		
27/11	Paris Saint-Germain	a	4-3		Thomert, Dindane 2, Jussié
4/12	AS Saint-Etienne	h	2-1		Thomert, Cousin
10/12	Lille OSC	a	0-0		
18/12	Le Mans UC 72	h	2-0		Dindane, Cousin
2006					
4/1	Olympique Marseille	a	1-1		Hilton
11/1	AS Nancy-Lorraine	h	1-2		Frau
14/1	AJ Auxerre	a	0-1		
22/1	AS Monaco FC	h	1-1		Gillet
28/1	Girondins de Bordeaux	a	0-1		
4/2	RC Strasbourg	h	2-1		Cousin, Khiter
11/2	Olympique Lyonnais	h	1-1		Jussié
18/2	Stade Rennais FC	a	1-4		Cousin
26/2	AC Ajaccio	h	1-0		Cousin
4/3	OGC Nice	a	0-0		
11/3	ES Troyes AC	h	1-0		Cousin
18/3	Toulouse FC	a	1-1		Frau
25/3	FC Sochaux	h	2-1		Keita, Frau
—	FC Metz	a	1-0		Frau (p)
8/4	Paris Saint-Germain	h	1-1		Jussié (p)
15/4	AS Saint-Etienne	a	0-2		
29/4	Lille OSC	h	4-2		Thomert, Cousin (p), Keita, Frau
6/5	Le Mans UC 72	a	0-0		
13/5	FC Nantes	h	3-1		Jussié, Dindane, Coulibaly

No	Name	Nat	Pos	Aps	(s)	Gls
32	Benoît ASSOU-EKOTTO	CMR	D	33	(1)	
34	Patrick BARUL		D	9	(13)	
10	Eric CARRIERE		M	13	(13)	
1	Sébastien CHABBERT		G	1	(1)	
4	Adama COULIBALY	MLI	D	33	(2)	2
9	Daniel COUSIN	GAB	A	29	(4)	13
26	Yohan DEMONT		D	34		1
23	Alou DIARRA		M	31	(1)	2
27	Aruna DINDANE	CIV	A	21	(7)	6
14	Pierre-Alain FRAU		A	16	(4)	5
5	Nicolas GILLET		D	11	(5)	1
3	HILTON da Silva	BRA	D	35		2
30	Charles ITANDJE		G	37		
22	Issam JEMAA	TUN	A		(6)	
11	JUSSIÉ Ferreira Vieira	BRA	A	29	(6)	6
8	Seydou KEITA	MLI	M	34	(1)	3
29	Seïd KHITER		M		(8)	1
15	Yoann LACHOR		D	4	(1)	
36	Jonathan LACOURT		M	6	(3)	
7	Jérôme LEROY		M	14	(1)	
7	Guillermo RODRÍGUEZ	URU	D	1	(1)	
18	Olivier THOMERT		A	27	(2)	6

LILLE OSC
Coach – Claude Puel

2005					
30/7	Stade Rennais FC	h	1-0		Makoun
6/8	AC Ajaccio	a	3-3		Makoun, Gygax, Debuchy
13/8	ES Troyes AC	h	1-2		Debuchy
20/8	FC Sochaux	a	0-0		
24/8	Toulouse FC	h	0-0		
10/9	FC Metz	a	2-0		Odemwingie 2
17/9	OGC Nice	h	4-0		Makoun, Acimovic, Odemwingie, Gygax
21/9	Paris Saint-Germain	a	1-2		Fauvergue
25/9	AS Saint-Etienne	h	2-0		Moussilou, Aboucherouane
2/10	AS Monaco FC	h	0-1		
15/10	Le Mans UC 72	a	1-1		Moussilou
22/10	FC Nantes	h	2-0		Makoun, Moussilou
29/10	Olympique Marseille	a	1-1		Acimovic
6/11	RC Strasbourg	h	2-0		Odemwingie, Lichtsteiner
19/11	AJ Auxerre	a	2-3		Bodmer (p), Cabaye
26/11	AS Nancy-Lorraine	h	1-0		Aboucherouane
3/12	Girondins de Bordeaux	a	0-1		
10/12	RC Lens	h	0-0		
16/12	Olympique Lyonnais	a	3-1		Odemwingie, Debuchy, Dumont
2006					
4/1	AC Ajaccio	h	2-0		Odemwingie, Gygax
11/1	ES Troyes AC	a	0-1		
14/1	FC Sochaux	h	3-0		Moussilou, og (Pitau), Gygax
21/1	Toulouse FC	a	0-0		
29/1	FC Metz	h	3-1		Keita, og (Monsot), Tavlaridis
4/2	OGC Nice	a	0-2		
12/2	Paris Saint-Germain	h	0-0		
18/2	AS Saint-Etienne	a	2-0		Debuchy, Keita
26/2	AS Monaco FC	a	1-0		Odemwingie
4/3	Le Mans UC 72	h	4-0		Odemwingie, Bodmer (p), Schmitz, Mirallas
12/3	FC Nantes	a	1-1		Keita
19/3	Olympique Marseille	h	0-0		
25/3	RC Strasbourg	a	2-2		Keita 2
1/4	AJ Auxerre	h	1-1		Odemwingie
8/4	AS Nancy-Lorraine	a	0-0		
15/4	Girondins de Bordeaux	h	3-2		Bodmer, Odemwingie 2
29/4	RC Lens	a	2-4		Odemwingie, Keita
6/5	Olympique Lyonnais	h	4-0		Dernis, Odemwingie 2, Makoun
13/5	Stade Rennais FC	a	2-2		Fauvergue, Bodmer

No	Name	Nat	Pos	Aps	(s)	Gls
11	Hicham ABOUCHEROUANE	MAR	M	11	(1)	2
15	Milenko ACIMOVIC	SLO	A	12		2
12	Mathieu BODMER		M	28	(7)	4
7	Yohan CABAYE		M	20	(7)	1
21	Matthieu CHALME		D	25	(5)	
6	DANTE Bonfim Costa	BRA	D	1		
2	Mathieu DEBUCHY		M	22	(5)	4
8	Geoffrey DERNIS		M	15	(6)	1
29	Stéphane DUMONT		M	8	(1)	1
13	Nicolas FAUVERGUE		A	9	(9)	2
19	Peter FRANQUART		D	1	(2)	
10	Daniel GYGAX	SUI	M	12	(10)	4
23	Kader KEITA	CIV	A	20	(7)	6
	Flavien LEPOSTOLLEC		M		(1)	
26	Stephan LICHTSTEINER	SUI	D	21	(10)	1
17	Jean MAKOUN	CMR	M	29	(2)	5
16	Grégory MALICKI		G	6		
27	Kevin MIRALLAS	BEL	A	3	(12)	1
9	Matt MOUSSILOU		A	12	(13)	4
14	Peter ODEMWINGIE	NGA	A	17	(9)	14

France

25	Nicolas PLESTAN		D	16		
5	Rafael SCHMITZ	BRA	D	26		1
1	Tony SYLVA	SEN	G	32		
20	Grégory TAFFOREAU		D	32	(1)	
4	Efstathios TAVLARIDIS	GRE	D	26		1
	Larsen TOURE		A	1	(1)	
22	Milivoje VITAKIC	SCG	D	13	(2)	

OLYMPIQUE LYONNAIS
Coach – Gérard Houllier

2005

31/7	Le Mans UC 72	a	2-1	Wiltord, Carew
7/8	RC Strasbourg	h	1-0	Carew
14/8	Olympique Marseille	a	1-1	Carew
20/8	AS Nancy-Lorraine	h	1-0	Caçapa
28/8	AJ Auxerre	a	2-0	Diarra, Juninho
10/9	AS Monaco FC	h	2-1	Fred 2
17/9	Girondins de Bordeaux	a	1-1	Wiltord
22/9	RC Lens	h	1-1	Tiago
25/9	FC Nantes	a	1-0	Fred
2/10	Stade Rennais FC	a	3-1	Juninho, Tiago, Wiltord
16/10	AC Ajaccio	h	3-2	Fred, Juninho, Wiltord
22/10	FC Metz	a	4-0	Carew, Juninho, Wiltord, Malouda
29/10	FC Sochaux	h	1-0	Malouda
5/11	Toulouse FC	a	1-0	Govou
19/11	ES Troyes AC	h	2-1	Cris 2
26/11	OGC Nice	a	1-1	Govou
3/12	Paris Saint-Germain	a	2-0	Fred, Carew
11/12	AS Saint-Etienne	a	0-0	
16/12	Lille OSC	h	1-3	Govou

2006

4/1	RC Strasbourg	a	4-0	Wiltord 3, Berthod
11/1	Olympique Marseille	h	2-0	Tiago, Govou
14/1	AS Nancy-Lorraine	a	2-0	Caçapa, Fred
22/1	AJ Auxerre	h	1-1	Diarra
5/2	Girondins de Bordeaux	h	0-0	
11/2	RC Lens	a	1-1	Wiltord
17/2	FC Nantes	h	3-1	Juninho, Diarra, Fred
25/2	Stade Rennais FC	a	1-4	Juninho (p)
4/3	AC Ajaccio	a	3-1	Juninho, Fred, Benzema
11/3	FC Metz	h	4-0	Malouda 2, Carew, Müller
18/3	FC Sochaux	a	4-0	Wiltord 2, Pedretti, Malouda
25/3	Toulouse FC	h	1-1	Carew
1/4	ES Troyes AC	a	1-0	Tiago
8/4	OGC Nice	h	2-1	Fred, Malouda
16/4	Paris Saint-Germain	a	1-0	Fred
23/4	AS Monaco FC	a	1-2	Carew
30/4	AS Saint-Etienne	h	4-0	og (Hellebuyck), Fred, Juninho (p), Pedretti
6/5	Lille OSC	a	0-4	
13/5	Le Mans UC 72	h	8-1	Fred 3, Cris, Wiltord, Juninho, Govou, Tiago

No	Name	Nat	Pos	Aps	(s)	Gls
20	Eric ABIDAL		D	14		
18	Hatem BEN ARFA		M	5	(7)	
19	Karim BENZEMA		A	4	(9)	1
23	Jérémy BERTHOD		D	14	(2)	1
5	Cláudio CAÇAPA	BRA	D	26		2
9	John CAREW	NOR	A	18	(8)	8
6	Jérémy CLEMENT		M	6	(9)	
31	François CLERC		D	13	(1)	
1	Grégory COUPET		G	37		
3	Cristiano Marques Gomes "CRIS"	BRA	D	36		3
7	Mahamadou DIARRA	MLI	M	30	(1)	3

15	Lamine DIATTA	SEN	D	7	(6)	
13	Pierre-Alain FRAU		A	2	(2)	
11	Frederico Chaves Guedes "FRED"	BRA	A	20	(11)	14
14	Sidney GOVOU		A	24	(11)	5
8	JUNINHO Pernambucano	BRA	M	30	(2)	9
10	Florent MALOUDA		M	24	(7)	6
24	Sylvain MONSOREAU		D	13	(6)	
4	Patrick MÜLLER	SUI	D	9	(3)	1
26	Benoît PEDRETTI		M	14	(7)	2
12	Anthony REVEILLERE		D	19	(1)	
21	TIAGO Mendes	POR	M	26	(3)	5
30	Rémy VERCOUTRE		G	1	(1)	
22	Sylvain WILTORD		A	26	(9)	12

OLYMPIQUE MARSEILLE
Coach – Jean Fernandez

2005

30/7	Girondins de Bordeaux	h	0-2	
6/8	RC Lens	a	0-2	
14/8	Olympique Lyonnais	h	1-1	Taiwo
20/8	Stade Rennais FC	a	2-3	Niang, Lamouchi
27/8	AC Ajaccio	h	1-1	Giménez
11/9	FC Sochaux	a	1-0	Oruma
18/9	ES Troyes AC	h	2-1	Ribéry, Lamouchi
21/9	Toulouse FC	a	0-1	
24/9	FC Metz	h	3-1	Déhu, Ribéry, Niang
2/10	OGC Nice	a	1-0	Ribéry
16/10	Paris Saint-Germain	h	1-0	Cana
22/10	AS Saint-Etienne	a	1-2	Ribéry
29/10	Lille OSC	h	1-1	Koke
5/11	Le Mans UC 72	a	0-3	
19/11	FC Nantes	h	2-1	Oruma, Ribéry
27/11	AS Monaco FC	h	2-1	Oruma, Lamouchi
4/12	AS Nancy-Lorraine	a	1-1	Niang
10/12	AJ Auxerre	h	1-0	Niang
17/12	RC Strasbourg	a	1-0	Niang

2006

4/1	RC Lens	h	1-1	Beye
11/1	Olympique Lyonnais	a	1-2	Lamouchi
15/1	Stade Rennais FC	h	1-0	Pagis
21/1	AC Ajaccio	a	1-3	Pagis
28/1	FC Sochaux	h	0-0	
5/2	ES Troyes AC	a	1-0	Lamouchi
12/2	Toulouse FC	h	0-0	
19/2	FC Metz	a	0-1	
26/2	OGC Nice	h	1-0	Maoulida
5/3	Paris Saint-Germain	a	0-0	
12/3	AS Saint-Etienne	h	2-0	Pagis 2
19/3	Lille OSC	a	0-0	
25/3	Le Mans UC 72	h	1-1	Maoulida
1/4	FC Nantes	a	3-1	Niang 2, Maoulida
8/4	AS Monaco FC	a	0-1	
15/4	AS Nancy-Lorraine	h	6-0	Niang 2, Maoulida 2, Pagis 2
3/5	AJ Auxerre	a	2-1	Niang, Civelli
6/5	RC Strasbourg	h	2-2	Nasri, Ribéry
13/5	Girondins de Bordeaux	a	1-1	Maoulida

No	Name	Nat	Pos	Aps	(s)	Gls
2	ANDRÉ LUÍS Garcia	BRA	D	11	(4)	
9	Rachmane BARRY	SEN	A	1		
16	Fabien BARTHEZ		G	24		
20	Laurent BATLLES		M	1	(3)	
23	Habib BEYE	SEN	D	25	(4)	1
	Garry BOCALY		M	1		

France

No	Name	Nat	Pos	Aps	(s)	Gls
18	Jérôme BONNISSEL		D	5		
19	Lorik CANA	ALB	M	28		1
21	Alain CANTAREIL		D	2	(4)	
1	Cédric CARRASSO		G	14	(1)	
26	Bostjan CESAR	SLO	D	17		
28	Renato CIVELLI	ARG	A	10	(1)	1
5	Frédéric DEHU		D	30		1
6	José DELFIM	POR	M	9	(4)	
	Mohamed Amine DENNOUN		A	1		
32	Thomas DERUDA		M		(2)	
	Papa Moustapha DIOP	SEN	A			
4	Demétrius FERREIRA	BRA	D	16	(7)	
	Anthony FLACHI		M		(1)	
	Vincent GASTINE		M	1		
13	Christian GIMÉNEZ	ARG	A	9	(12)	1
10	KOKE Contreras	ESP	A	4	(5)	1
14	Sabri LAMOUCHI		M	31	(1)	5
18	Péguy LUYINDULA		A	2		
9	Toifilou MAOULIDA		A	15	(1)	6
12	Abdoulaye MEÏTE	CIV	D	12	(1)	
17	Andrés MENDOZA	PER	A	2	(9)	
27	Koji NAKATA	JPN	D	3	(1)	
22	Samir NASRI		M	14	(16)	1
33	Mame N'DIAYE	SEN	A	1		
11	Mamadou NIANG	SEN	A	25	(3)	10
15	Salomon OLEMBE	CMR	M		(1)	
8	Wilson ORUMA	NGA	M	25	(5)	3
25	Mickaël PAGIS		A	13		6
	Alexis PRADIE		D	1		
7	Franck RIBERY		M	35		6
3	Taye Ismalia TAIWO	NGA	D	30		1

FC METZ
Coach – Joël Muller

2005

Date	Opponent	h/a	Score	Scorers
29/7	Paris Saint-Germain	a	1-4	Ahn
6/8	Le Mans UC 72	h	0-0	
13/8	AS Saint-Etienne	a	0-2	
20/8	RC Strasbourg	h	0-0	
27/8	FC Nantes	a	0-0	
10/9	Lille OSC	h	0-2	
17/9	AS Nancy-Lorraine	a	1-1	Renouard
21/9	AJ Auxerre	h	1-2	N'Diaye
24/9	Olympique Marseille	a	1-3	Renouard
1/10	Girondins de Bordeaux	h	0-1	
15/10	AS Monaco FC	a	0-3	
22/10	Olympique Lyonnais	h	0-4	
29/10	Stade Rennais FC	a	1-2	Tum
5/11	AC Ajaccio	h	2-0	Gueye, Djiba
19/11	RC Lens	a	0-0	
26/11	ES Troyes AC	a	0-0	
3/12	Toulouse FC	h	2-2	Proment 2 (1p)
10/12	FC Sochaux	a	1-1	Ahn
17/12	OGC Nice	h	1-0	Borbiconi

2006

Date	Opponent	h/a	Score	Scorers
4/1	Le Mans UC 72	a	0-2	
11/1	AS Saint-Etienne	h	0-1	
14/1	RC Strasbourg	a	1-2	Tum
21/1	FC Nantes	h	1-4	Proment
29/1	Lille OSC	a	1-3	Borbiconi
11/2	AJ Auxerre	a	1-1	Obraniak
19/2	Olympique Marseille	h	1-0	Gueye
25/2	Girondins de Bordeaux	a	3-3	Youla, og (Roux), Contout
4/3	AS Monaco FC	h	2-1	og (Plasil), Tum
7/3	AS Nancy-Lorraine	h	0-0	

11/3	Olympique Lyonnais	a	0-4	
18/3	Stade Rennais FC	h	0-1	
25/3	AC Ajaccio	a	1-0	Ouadah
1/4	RC Lens	h	0-1	
8/4	ES Troyes AC	h	2-4	Ouadah, Gueye
14/4	Toulouse FC	a	0-2	
30/4	FC Sochaux	h	0-1	
6/5	OGC Nice	a	1-2	Agouazzi
13/5	Paris Saint-Germain	h	1-0	Huszti

No	Name	Nat	Pos	Aps	(s)	Gls
16	Kossi AGASSA	TOG	G	1		
21	Laurent AGOUAZZI		M	5	(3)	1
19	AHN Jung-hwan	KOR	A	10	(6)	2
22	Jamal ALIOUI	MAR	D	12		
8	Samuel ALLEGRO		D	3		
31	Sébastien BASSONG		D	15	(8)	
	Flavien BELSON-BENGABER		M		(4)	
2	Frank BERIA		D	30	(2)	
	Gaëtan BONG		D	3		
5	Stéphane BORBICONI		D	38		2
33	Papiss CISSE	SEN	A		(1)	
27	Roy CONTOUT		A	8	(10)	1
	Mamadou DIAKITE		M	1		
23	Dino DJIBA	SEN	M	13	(2)	1
	Nicolas FARINA		A		(1)	
11	Babacar GUEYE	SEN	A	8	(14)	3
20	Szabolcs HUSZTI	HUN	M	13	(5)	1
	KANG Jin-Ouk	KOR	D	1	(3)	
22	Grégory LECA		M		(2)	
14	Chérif-Touré MAMAM	TOG	M	3	(7)	
15	Sylvain MARCHAL		D	2		
30	Christophe MARICHEZ		G	7		
28	Carl MEDJANI		D	21	(2)	
4	Mehdi MENIRI	ALG	D	18	(2)	
3	Hemza MIHOUBI		D	12		
29	Stéphane MORISOT		D	4	(1)	
25	Momar N'DIAYE	SEN	A	7	(6)	1
13	Ludovic OBRANIAK		M	31		1
10	Abdelnasser OUADAH	ALG	M	27	(1)	2
3	Grégory PAISLEY		D	8		
24	Ruslan PIMENOV	RUS	M	6	(1)	
12	Grégory PROMENT		M	35		3
26	Sébastien RENOUARD		M	8	(6)	2
9	Hervé TUM	CMR	A	18	(3)	3
1	Grégory WIMBEE		G	30		
8	Souleymane YOULA	GUI	A	16	(1)	1
7	Marcin ZEWLAKOW	POL	A	4	(9)	

AS MONACO FC
Coach – Didier Deschamps; (19/9/05) (Jean Petit); (4/10/05) Francesco Guidolin (ITA)

2005

Date	Opponent	h/a	Score	Scorers
30/7	AS Nancy-Lorraine	a	1-0	Kapo
6/8	AJ Auxerre	h	0-2	
14/8	RC Strasbourg	a	2-1	Squillaci, Chevantón
20/8	Girondins de Bordeaux	a	0-1	
28/8	RC Lens	h	0-0	
10/9	Olympique Lyonnais	a	1-2	Gigliotti
18/9	Stade Rennais FC	h	0-2	
21/9	ES Troyes AC	a	2-1	Adebayor, Givet
24/9	OGC Nice	h	0-0	
2/10	Lille OSC	a	1-0	Kapo
15/10	FC Metz	h	3-0	Gigliotti, Zikos, Meriem
23/10	FC Sochaux	a	1-2	Maicon
29/10	AC Ajaccio	h	3-0	Chevantón, Givet, Plasil

France

Date	Opponent	H/A	Score	Scorers
6/11	Paris Saint-Germain	a	0-0	
19/11	AS Saint-Etienne	h	1-0	Meriem
27/11	Olympique Marseille	a	1-2	Meriem
3/12	Le Mans UC 72	h	2-0	Modesto, Sorlin
11/12	FC Nantes	a	0-0	
18/12	Toulouse FC	h	1-0	Kapo (p)
2006				
5/1	AJ Auxerre	a	1-2	Di Vaio
11/1	RC Strasbourg	h	1-1	Kapo
14/1	Girondins de Bordeaux	h	0-1	
22/1	RC Lens	a	1-1	Gakpé
4/2	Stade Rennais FC	a	3-1	Vieri 2, Veigneau
11/2	ES Troyes AC	h	1-1	Vieri
18/2	OGC Nice	a	0-2	
26/2	Lille OSC	h	0-1	
4/3	FC Metz	a	1-2	Di Vaio
11/3	FC Sochaux	h	4-1	Chevantón, Di Vaio 2, Kapo
18/3	AC Ajaccio	a	0-1	
26/3	Paris Saint-Germain	h	1-1	Chevantón
1/4	AS Saint-Etienne	a	1-1	Chevantón
8/4	Olympique Marseille	h	1-0	Chevantón
15/4	Le Mans UC 72	a	0-0	
23/4	Olympique Lyonnais	h	2-1	Chevantón, Di Vaio
30/4	FC Nantes	h	1-1	Chevantón
6/5	Toulouse FC	a	3-3	Gakpé, Dos Santos, Chevantón
13/5	AS Nancy-Lorraine	h	2-2	Chevantón, Modesto

No	Name	Nat	Pos	Aps	(s)	Gls
24	Emmanuel ADEBAYOR	TOG	A	11	(2)	1
7	Lucas BERNARDI	ARG	M	29	(3)	
	André BIANCARELLI		G		(1)	
25	Souleymane CAMARA	SEN	A		(2)	
9	Ernesto Javier CHEVANTÓN	URU	A	18	(5)	10
18	Eric CUBILIER		D	10	(3)	
23	Marco DI VAIO	ITA	A	15		5
3	Manuel DOS SANTOS		D	14	(1)	1
3	Patrice EVRA		D	15		
34	Serge GAKPE		A	8	(5)	2
10	GERARD López	ESP	M	6	(1)	
22	David GIGLIOTTI		A	4	(10)	2
32	Gaël GIVET		D	32		2
17	Olivier KAPO		M	20	(5)	5
20	Arnaud LESCURE		D	1	(1)	
13	MAICON Douglas	BRA	D	28		1
14	Toifilou MAOULIDA		A	9	(7)	
	Malaury MARTIN		M	1		
28	Nicolas MAURICE-BELAY		A	6	(7)	
21	Camel MERIEM		M	25	(5)	3
4	François-Joseph MODESTO		D	21	(8)	2
26	Marco MUSLIN		D		(1)	
5	Diego PÉREZ	URU	M	15	(7)	
6	Jaroslav PLASIL	CZE	M	17	(4)	1
30	Flavi ROMA	ITA	G	15		
11	Olivier SORLIN		M	18	(2)	1
19	Sébastien SQUILLACI		D	26	(1)	1
31	Olivier VEIGNEAU		D	11	(9)	1
36	Christian VIERI	ITA	A	5	(2)	3
1	Guillaume WARMUZ		G	23		
15	Vassilis ZIKOS	GRE	M	15	(2)	1

AS NANCY-LORRAINE
Coach – Pablo Correa (URU)

Date	Opponent	H/A	Score	Scorers
2005				
30/7	AS Monaco FC	h	0-1	
6/8	Girondins de Bordeaux	a	0-1	
13/8	RC Lens	h	1-2	Zerka
20/8	Olympique Lyonnais	a	0-1	
27/8	Stade Rennais FC	h	6-0	Kroupi 3 (1p), og (Rochat), Diakhaté, Puygrenier
10/9	AC Ajaccio	a	0-1	
17/9	FC Metz	h	1-1	André Luiz
21/9	AS Saint-Etienne	a	2-0	Lécluse, Sarkisian
24/9	ES Troyes AC	h	2-1	Curbelo 2
1/10	FC Sochaux	a	2-0	Curbelo, Kroupi
15/10	Toulouse FC	h	2-0	Diakhaté, Kroupi (p)
22/10	Paris Saint-Germain	a	0-1	
30/10	OGC Nice	h	0-0	
5/11	FC Nantes	a	0-3	
19/11	Le Mans UC 72	h	1-0	Kim
26/11	Lille OSC	a	0-1	
4/12	Olympique Marseille	h	1-1	Zerka
10/12	RC Strasbourg	h	1-2	Zerka
17/12	AJ Auxerre	a	1-0	Zerka (p)
2006				
4/1	Girondins de Bordeaux	h	0-0	
11/1	RC Lens	a	2-1	Zerka, Brison
14/1	Olympique Lyonnais	h	0-2	
21/1	Stade Rennais FC	a	2-0	Brison, Duchemin
28/1	AC Ajaccio	h	0-0	
11/2	AS Saint-Etienne	h	2-0	Chrétien, Kroupi (p)
18/2	ES Troyes AC	a	1-0	Zerka
25/2	FC Sochaux	h	0-3	
4/3	Toulouse FC	a	1-1	Sarkisian
7/3	FC Metz	a	0-0	
11/3	Paris Saint-Germain	h	1-1	Brison
18/3	OGC Nice	a	0-1	
25/3	FC Nantes	h	0-0	
2/4	Le Mans UC 72	a	0-0	
8/4	Lille OSC	h	0-0	
15/4	Olympique Marseille	a	0-6	
30/4	RC Strasbourg	a	3-1	Kroupi 3 (1p)
6/5	AJ Auxerre	h	1-3	André Luiz
13/5	AS Monaco FC	a	2-2	og (Givet), André Luiz

No	Name	Nat	Pos	Aps	(s)	Gls
25	ADAILTON da Silva	BRA	D	14	(2)	
5	ANDRÉ LUIZ Silva	BRA	D	20	(9)	3
12	Dagui BAKARI	CIV	A	1		
6	Pascal BERENGUER		M	30	(5)	
8	Frédéric BIANCALANI		D	27	(4)	
1	Gennaro BRACIGLIANO		G	34		
23	Jonathan BRISON		M	19	(11)	3
	Basile CAMERLING		A	1	(4)	
	Romain CHOULEUR		M		(3)	
20	Mickaël CHRETIEN		D	29	(3)	1
17	Gaston CURBELO		A	11	(3)	3
	Manuel DA COSTA		D	7	(3)	
3	Pape DIAKHATE	SEN	D	33		2
7	Emmanuel DUCHEMIN		M	25	(1)	1
24	Benjamin GAVANON		M	24	(4)	
15	Abdoulaye KEITA	SEN	M	3		
9	Carlos Henrique Dias "KIM"	BRA	A	17	(6)	1
22	Eli KROUPI	CIV	A	15	(7)	9
4	Cédric LECLUSE		D	23	(4)	1
26	Landry N'GUEMO	CMR	M	9	(5)	
	Patrick N'TOLLA	CMR	D		(1)	
28	Sébastien PUYGRENIER		D	28	(4)	1
21	Grgely RUDOLF	HUN	A	1	(4)	
18	Adrián SARKISIAN	URU	M	24	(9)	2

France

16	Olivier SORIN		G	4		
11	Moncef ZERKA	MAR	M	19	(8)	6

FC NANTES
Coach – Serge Le Dizet

2005

30/7	RC Lens	h	2-0	Yapi Yapo, Glombard	
7/8	Stade Rennais FC	a	3-0	Faé, Diallo, Bamogo	
13/8	AC Ajaccio	h	0-2		
20/8	OGC Nice	a	1-1	Faé	
27/8	FC Metz	h	0-0		
10/9	ES Troyes AC	a	0-1		
17/9	Toulouse FC	h	2-0	Diallo 2	
21/9	FC Sochaux	a	0-1		
25/9	Olympique Lyonnais	h	0-1		
1/10	Paris Saint-Germain	a	0-2		
15/10	AS Saint-Etienne	h	1-1	Keseru	
22/10	Lille OSC	a	0-2		
29/10	Le Mans UC 72	h	1-0	Keseru (p)	
5/11	AS Nancy-Lorraine	h	3-0	Da Rocha, Signorino, Bamogo	
19/11	Olympique Marseille	a	1-2	Bamogo	
27/11	RC Strasbourg	h	4-3	Delhommeau, Bamogo, Dimitrijevic, Da Rocha	
3/12	AJ Auxerre	a	0-4		
11/12	AS Monaco FC	h	0-0		
17/12	Girondins de Bordeaux	a	0-0		

2006

4/1	Stade Rennais FC	h	0-2		
11/1	AC Ajaccio	a	2-0	Capoue, Diallo	
14/1	OGC Nice	h	0-0		
21/1	FC Metz	a	4-1	Guillon, Diallo 2, Payet	
4/2	Toulouse FC	a	0-1		
11/2	FC Sochaux	h	3-1	Diallo 3	
14/2	ES Troyes AC	h	1-1	Keseru	
17/2	Olympique Lyonnais	a	1-3	Diallo	
25/2	Paris Saint-Germain	h	0-0		
5/3	AS Saint-Etienne	a	0-1		
12/3	Lille OSC	h	1-1	Rossi	
18/3	Le Mans UC 72	a	0-0		
25/3	AS Nancy-Lorraine	a	0-0		
1/4	Olympique Marseille	h	1-3	Oliech	
8/4	RC Strasbourg	a	1-0	Capoue	
15/4	AJ Auxerre	h	3-2	Oliech, Cetto, Faé	
30/4	AS Monaco FC	a	1-1	Capoue	
6/5	Girondins de Bordeaux	h	0-1		
13/5	RC Lens	a	1-3	Faé	

No	Name	Nat	Pos	Aps	(s)	Gls
19	Habib BAMOGO		A	15	(16)	4
23	Bocundji CA	GBS	M	13	(6)	
11	Aurélien CAPOUE		M	16	(4)	3
4	Mauro CETTO	ARG	D	29		1
8	Frédéric DA ROCHA		M	31	(4)	2
	Kevin DAS NEVES		D	2		
12	Pascal DELHOMMEAU		D	17	(4)	1
13	Mamadou DIALLO	MLI	A	29	(6)	10
29	Milos DIMITRIJEVIC	SCG	M	18	(6)	1
20	Karim EL-MOURABET		D		(1)	
6	Emerse FAE	CIV	M	27	(2)	4
21	Luigi GLOMBARD		A	9	(7)	1
24	Loïc GUILLON		D	28	(3)	1
16	Tony HEURTEBIS		G	2	(1)	
28	Claudiu KESERU	ROM	A	6	(8)	3
1	Mickaël LANDREAU		G	36		
35	David LERAY		D	14	(7)	
18	Imed MHADHEBI	TUN	M	7	(2)	
9	Denis OLIECH	KEN	A	6	(3)	2
33	Dimitri PAYET		A		(3)	1
5	Jean-Jacques PIERRE		D	9		
9	Grégory PUJOL		A		(1)	
14	Olivier QUINT		M	3	(3)	
25	Julio Hernán ROSSI	ARG	A	8	(4)	1
15	Nicolas SAVINAUD		D	26	(2)	
3	Franck SIGNORINO		D	33		1
17	Jérémy TOULALAN		M	29		
10	Gilles YAPI YAPO	CIV	M	5	(4)	1

OGC NICE
Coach – Frédéric Antonetti

2005

30/7	ES Troyes AC	h	1-1	Vahirua	
6/8	Toulouse FC	a	2-0	Koné, Traoré (p)	
13/8	FC Sochaux	h	1-2	Traoré	
20/8	FC Nantes	h	1-1	Bagayoko	
27/8	Paris Saint-Germain	a	2-1	og (Rozehnal), Bagayoko	
10/9	AS Saint-Etienne	h	0-1		
17/9	Lille OSC	a	0-4		
21/9	Le Mans UC 72	h	1-0	Bagayoko	
24/9	AS Monaco FC	a	0-0		
2/10	Olympique Marseille	h	0-1		
15/10	RC Lens	a	2-2	Roudet, Camara	
22/10	AJ Auxerre	h	1-0	Vahirua	
30/10	AS Nancy-Lorraine	a	0-0		
5/11	Girondins de Bordeaux	h	0-1		
19/11	RC Strasbourg	a	0-0		
26/11	Olympique Lyonnais	h	1-1	Bagayoko	
4/12	Stade Rennais FC	a	0-1		
10/12	AC Ajaccio	h	1-0	Koné	
17/12	FC Metz	a	0-1		

2006

4/1	Toulouse FC	h	2-1	Koné, Vahirua	
11/1	FC Sochaux	a	1-1	Roudet	
14/1	FC Nantes	a	0-0		
21/1	Paris Saint-Germain	h	1-0	Traoré	
4/2	Lille OSC	h	2-0	Vahirua, Roudet	
11/2	Le Mans UC 72	a	0-2		
14/2	AS Saint-Etienne	a	1-0	Bellion	
18/2	AS Monaco FC	h	2-0	Bellion (p), Koné	
26/2	Olympique Marseille	a	0-1		
4/3	RC Lens	h	0-0		
11/3	AJ Auxerre	a	0-2		
18/3	AS Nancy-Lorraine	h	1-0	Koné	
26/3	Girondins de Bordeaux	a	0-1		
1/4	RC Strasbourg	h	3-1	Jarjat, Bagayoko, Traoré	
8/4	Olympique Lyonnais	a	1-2	Éderson	
16/4	Stade Rennais FC	h	2-1	Bellion, Abordanado	
30/4	AC Ajaccio	a	3-0	Bellion, Koné 2	
6/5	FC Metz	h	2-1	Traoré, Bellion	
13/5	ES Troyes AC	a	2-1	Vahirua, Éderson	

No	Name	Nat	Pos	Aps	(s)	Gls
3	Jacques ABARDONADO		D	30	(2)	1
9	Mamadou BAGAYOKO	MLI	A	27	(5)	5
14	Florent BALMONT		M	37		
18	David BELLION		A	13	(2)	5
27	Yoann BIGNE		M	5	(10)	
7	Roberto BISCONTI	BEL	M	7	(1)	
9	Souleymane CAMARA	SEN	A	2	(14)	1
23	Drissa DIAKITE	MLI	M	3	(2)	

France

No	Name	Nat	Pos	Aps	(s)	Gls
20	Pablo Franco DOLCI	ARG	M		(2)	
6	Olivier ECHOUAFNI		M	27	(5)	
8	ÉDERSON Honoreto	BRA	M	7	(13)	2
24	Rod FANNI		D	20	(1)	
16	Damien GREGORINI		G	33		
5	François GRENET		D		(1)	
15	Florian JARJAT		D	7	(9)	1
12	Bakari KONE	CIV	A	32		7
1	Hugo LLORIS		G	5		
26	Cyril ROOL		M	29		
18	Sébastien ROUDET		M	15	(12)	3
3	Bill TCHATO	CMR	D	20	(4)	
17	Sammy TRAORE	MLI	D	33		5
19	Marama VAHIRUA		A	23	(10)	5
2	Cédric VARRAULT		D	27	(1)	
21	Anther YAHIA	ALG	D	16	(5)	

PARIS SAINT-GERMAIN
Coach – Laurent Fournier; (27/12/05) Guy Lacombe

2005
Date	Opponent	h/a	Score	Scorers
29/7	FC Metz	h	4-1	Kalou, Cissé, Rothen, Landrin
6/8	FC Sochaux	a	1-0	Cissé
13/8	Toulouse FC	h	2-0	Pauleta 2
21/8	ES Troyes AC	a	1-1	Pauleta
27/8	OGC Nice	h	1-2	Pauleta
10/9	RC Strasbourg	h	1-0	Kalou
18/9	AS Saint-Étienne	a	0-3	
21/9	Lille OSC	h	2-1	Pauleta 2
24/9	Le Mans UC 72	a	0-0	
1/10	FC Nantes	h	2-0	Yepes, Pauleta
16/10	Olympique Marseille	a	0-1	
22/10	AS Nancy-Lorraine	h	1-0	Kalou
30/10	AJ Auxerre	a	0-2	
6/11	AS Monaco FC	h	0-0	
20/11	Girondins de Bordeaux	a	2-0	Yepes, Pauleta
27/11	RC Lens	h	3-4	Pauleta 2, Yepes
3/12	Olympique Lyonnais	a	0-2	
10/12	Stade Rennais FC	h	2-0	Pauleta 2
17/12	AC Ajaccio	a	1-1	Kalou

2006
Date	Opponent	h/a	Score	Scorers
4/1	FC Sochaux	h	3-1	Landrin, Pancrate, Pauleta
12/1	Toulouse FC	a	0-1	
15/1	ES Troyes AC	h	2-1	Pauleta (p), Pancrate
21/1	OGC Nice	a	0-1	
4/2	AS Saint-Étienne	h	2-2	Pauleta, Pancrate
8/2	RC Strasbourg	a	1-1	Pauleta
12/2	Lille OSC	a	0-0	
18/2	Le Mans UC 72	h	0-1	
25/2	FC Nantes	a	0-0	
5/3	Olympique Marseille	h	0-0	
11/3	AS Nancy-Lorraine	a	1-1	Kalou
19/3	AJ Auxerre	h	4-1	Kalou 2, og (Boli), Pauleta
26/3	AS Monaco FC	a	1-1	Paulo César
2/4	Girondins de Bordeaux	h	3-1	Pauleta 3 (1p)
8/4	RC Lens	a	1-1	Kalou
16/4	Olympique Lyonnais	h	0-1	
3/5	Stade Rennais FC	a	1-1	Kalou
6/5	AC Ajaccio	h	2-4	Yepes, Pauleta
13/5	FC Metz	a	0-1	

No	Name	Nat	Pos	Aps	(s)	Gls
16	Jérôme ALONZO		G	12	(1)	
22	Sylvain ARMAND		D	34	(1)	
17	Jean-Hugues ATEBA BILAYI	CMR	D	2		
3	Jean-Michel BADIANE		D	2	(1)	

No	Name	Nat	Pos	Aps	(s)	Gls
18	Carlos BUENO	URU	A	2	(10)	
19	Lorik CANA	ALB	M		(2)	
8	Edouard CISSE		M	29	(2)	2
10	Vikash DHORASOO		M	31	(3)	
34	Franck DJA DJEDJE	CIV	A		(2)	
26	Boukary DRAME	SEN	D	1	(3)	
14	Rudy HADDAD		M	2	(3)	
15	Bonaventure KALOU	CIV	A	24	(4)	9
24	Christophe LANDRIN		M	18	(8)	2
1	Lionel LETIZI		G	26	(1)	
23	Modeste M'BAMI	CMR	M	31	(3)	
5	Bernard MENDY		D	33	(3)	
7	Fabrice PANCRATE		A	10	(19)	3
9	Pedro Resendes "PAULETA"	POR	A	35	(1)	21
13	PAULO CÉSAR	BRA	D	7	(2)	1
2	Stéphane PICHOT		D	13	(8)	
	Hocine RAGUED		M	1		
12	Cristián RODRÍGUEZ	URU	M	4	(7)	
25	Jérôme ROTHEN		M	27	(1)	1
4	David ROZEHNAL	CZE	D	38		
11	Sergei SEMAK	RUS	M	4	(9)	
6	Mario YEPES	COL	D	32		4

STADE RENNAIS FC
Coach – Ladislau Bölöni (ROM)

2005
Date	Opponent	h/a	Score	Scorers
30/7	Lille OSC	a	0-1	
7/8	FC Nantes	h	0-3	
13/8	Le Mans UC 72	a	0-4	
20/8	Olympique Marseille	h	3-2	Utaka, Frei, Källström
27/8	AS Nancy-Lorraine	a	0-6	
10/9	AJ Auxerre	h	3-1	Hadji 2, Monterrubio
18/9	AS Monaco FC	a	2-0	Källström, Gourcuff
21/9	Girondins de Bordeaux	h	2-2	Källström, Monterrubio
25/9	RC Lens	a	0-0	
2/10	Olympique Lyonnais	h	1-3	Källström
15/10	RC Strasbourg	a	1-0	Briand
23/10	AC Ajaccio	a	1-0	Frei
29/10	FC Metz	h	2-1	Utaka, Frei
6/11	ES Troyes AC	a	1-2	Gourcuff
20/11	Toulouse FC	h	4-1	Gourcuff, Ouaddou, Frei, Monterrubio (p)
26/11	FC Sochaux	a	0-1	
4/12	OGC Nice	h	1-0	Frei
10/12	Paris Saint-Germain	a	0-2	
17/12	AS Saint-Étienne	h	0-1	

2006
Date	Opponent	h/a	Score	Scorers
4/1	FC Nantes	a	2-0	Didot, Utaka
11/1	Le Mans UC 72	h	1-0	Briand
15/1	Olympique Marseille	a	0-1	
21/1	AS Nancy-Lorraine	h	0-2	
28/1	AJ Auxerre	a	0-2	
4/2	AS Monaco FC	h	1-3	Mvuemba
11/2	Girondins de Bordeaux	a	0-2	
18/2	RC Lens	h	4-1	Utaka 3, Monterrubio
25/2	Olympique Lyonnais	a	4-1	Utaka 3, Gourcuff
4/3	RC Strasbourg	h	2-1	Källström, Briand
11/3	AC Ajaccio	h	3-0	Gourcuff, Monterrubio, Hadji
18/3	FC Metz	a	1-0	Gourcuff
25/3	ES Troyes AC	h	2-0	Utaka, Mensah
2/4	Toulouse FC	a	1-0	og (Aubey)
9/4	FC Sochaux	h	2-1	Källström 2 (1p)
16/4	OGC Nice	a	1-2	Utaka
3/5	Paris Saint-Germain	h	1-1	Källström (p)
6/5	AS Saint-Étienne	a	0-0	

France

13/5	Lille OSC	h	2-2	Frei 2	

No	Name	Nat	Pos	Aps	(s)	Gls
4	ADAILTON dos Santos	BRA	D	17	(2)	
14	Cédric BARBOSA		M	2	(11)	
6	Grégory BOURILLON		M	30	(2)	
19	Jimmy BRIAND		A	11	(18)	3
22	Etienne DIDOT		M	14	(5)	1
9	Erik EDMAN	SWE	D	26		
5	Jacques FATY		D	16	(7)	
23	Alexander FREI	SUI	A	20	(3)	7
10	Yoann GOURCUFF		M	28	(8)	6
11	Youssouf HADJI	MAR	A	14	(7)	3
1	Andreas ISAKSSON	SWE	G	24		
27	Cyril JEUNECHAMP		D	13		
8	Kim KÄLLSTRÖM	SWE	M	34		8
17	Stéphane M'BIA	CMR	M	18	(4)	
25	John MENSAH	GHA	D	12		1
18	Olivier MONTERRUBIO		M	29	(3)	5
28	Arnold MVUEMBA		M	5	(11)	1
24	Stéphane N'GUEMA	GAB	A	1	(5)	
3	Abdeslam OUADDOU	MAR	D	19		1
2	Jean-Joël PERRIER-DOUMBE	CMR	D	26	(2)	
30	Simon POUPLIN		G	14	(1)	
21	Alain ROCHAT	SUI	D	4	(5)	
24	Olivier SORLIN		M	13		
29	Moussa SOW		A	1	(6)	
7	John UTAKA	NGA	A	27	(1)	11

AS SAINT-ETIENNE
Coach – Elie Baup

2005

30/7	AC Ajaccio	h	0-0	
6/8	ES Troyes AC	a	0-0	
13/8	FC Metz	h	2-0	Piquionne 2
21/8	Toulouse FC	a	1-1	Hellebuyck
27/8	FC Sochaux	h	0-0	
10/9	OGC Nice	a	1-0	Piquionne
18/9	Paris Saint-Germain	h	3-0	Mendy, Piquionne, Feindouno
21/9	AS Nancy-Lorraine	h	0-2	
24/9	Lille OSC	a	0-2	
1/10	Le Mans UC 72	h	3-0	Perrin, Hognon, Hellebuyck
15/10	FC Nantes	a	1-1	og (Savinaud)
22/10	Olympique Marseille	h	2-1	Feindouno, Hellebuyck
29/10	RC Strasbourg	a	1-0	Gomis
5/11	AJ Auxerre	h	1-1	Hognon
19/11	AS Monaco FC	a	0-1	
26/11	Girondins de Bordeaux	h	1-1	Ilunga
4/12	RC Lens	a	1-2	Perrin
11/12	Olympique Lyonnais	h	0-0	
17/12	Stade Rennais FC	a	1-0	Feindouno

2006

4/1	ES Troyes AC	h	1-1	Hognon
11/1	FC Metz	a	1-0	Hélder Postiga
21/1	FC Sochaux	a	0-4	
1/2	Toulouse FC	h	1-3	Diawara
4/2	Paris Saint-Germain	a	2-2	Piquionne, og (Alonzo)
11/2	AS Nancy-Lorraine	a	0-2	
14/2	OGC Nice	h	0-1	
18/2	Lille OSC	h	0-2	
25/2	Le Mans UC 72	a	1-0	Hélder Postiga
5/3	FC Nantes	h	1-0	Mazure
12/3	Olympique Marseille	a	0-2	
19/3	RC Strasbourg	h	1-0	
25/3	AJ Auxerre	a	0-0	
1/4	AS Monaco FC	h	1-1	Gomis
8/4	Girondins de Bordeaux	a	0-0	
15/4	RC Lens	h	2-0	Sablé, Piquionne
30/4	Olympique Lyonnais	a	0-4	
6/5	Stade Rennais FC	h	0-0	
13/5	AC Ajaccio	a	1-3	Sablé

No	Name	Nat	Pos	Aps	(s)	Gls
3	BRUNO BASTO	POR	D	7	(1)	
6	Zoumana CAMARA		D	36		
21	Mouhamadou DABO	SEN	M	9	(9)	
22	Fousseni DIAWARA	MLI	D	31	(4)	1
14	Pascal FEINDOUNO	GUI	A	26	(2)	3
18	Bafétimbi GOMIS		A	7	(17)	2
20	HÉLDER POSTIGA	POR	A	14	(2)	2
8	David HELLEBUYCK		M	35		3
4	Vincent HOGNON		D	30		3
12	Samy HOURI		M		(3)	
23	Hérita ILUNGA	DRC	D	30		1
16	Jérémie JANOT		G	37		
17	Abdelaziz KAMARA		D	3		
10	Sébastien MAZURE		A	7	(13)	1
11	Frédéric MENDY	SEN	A	10	(6)	1
19	Damien PERQUIS		D	7	(8)	
24	Loïc PERRIN		M	18	(8)	2
25	Ignacio PIATTI	ARG	M		(1)	
9	Frédéric PIQUIONNE		A	33	(1)	6
27	Julien SABLE		M	36		2
15	Lamine SAKHO	SEN	A	3	(5)	
7	Siaka TIENE	CIV	M	2	(3)	
1	Jodi VIVIANI		G	1		
29	Allaeddine YAHIA	TUN	D	6	(4)	
5	Didier ZOKORA	CIV	M	30	(1)	

FC SOCHAUX
Coach – Dominique Bijotat

2005

30/7	Toulouse FC	h	0-1	
6/8	Paris Saint-Germain	h	0-1	
13/8	OGC Nice	a	2-1	Ilan 2 (1p)
20/8	Lille OSC	h	0-0	
27/8	AS Saint-Etienne	a	0-0	
11/9	Olympique Marseille	h	0-1	
17/9	Le Mans UC 72	a	1-2	Ilan
21/9	FC Nantes	h	1-0	Dagano
24/9	AJ Auxerre	a	0-3	
1/10	AS Nancy-Lorraine	h	0-2	
15/10	Girondins de Bordeaux	a	1-1	Ménez
23/10	AS Monaco FC	h	2-1	Ilan, Dagano
29/10	Olympique Lyonnais	a	0-1	
6/11	RC Lens	h	1-1	Ilan
19/11	AC Ajaccio	a	1-0	Erding
26/11	Stade Rennais FC	h	1-0	Genghini
3/12	RC Strasbourg	a	0-0	
10/12	FC Metz	h	1-1	Isabey
17/12	ES Troyes AC	a	1-2	Isabey

2006

4/1	Paris Saint-Germain	a	1-3	Sène
11/1	OGC Nice	h	1-1	Ménez
14/1	Lille OSC	a	0-3	
21/1	AS Saint-Etienne	h	4-0	Ménez, Ilan, Dagano 2 (1p)
28/1	Olympique Marseille	a	0-0	
4/2	Le Mans UC 72	h	0-0	
11/2	FC Nantes	a	1-3	Ilan
18/2	AJ Auxerre	h	1-0	Dagano
25/2	AS Nancy-Lorraine	a	3-0	Dagano, og (Lécluse), Ilan

France

1/3	AS Monaco FC	a	1-4	Ilan (p)	
18/3	Olympique Lyonnais	h	0-4		
25/3	RC Lens	a	1-2	og (Demont)	
1/4	AC Ajaccio	h	3-1	N'Daw, Dagano, Wéldon	
9/4	Stade Rennais FC	a	1-2	Diawara	
15/4	RC Strasbourg	h	1-1	Ilan	
23/4	Girondins de Bordeaux	a	0-3		
30/4	FC Metz	a	1-0	Isabey	
6/5	ES Troyes AC	h	1-1	Afolabi	
13/5	Toulouse FC	a	2-1	Wéldon, Erding	

No	Name	Nat	Pos	Aps	(s)	Gls
2	Rabiu AFOLABI	NGA	D	31	(1)	1
8	Fabien BOUDARENE		M	17	(2)	
10	Philippe BRUNEL		M	10	(9)	
25	Arnaud BÜHLER	SUI	D	10	(2)	
20	Jean CALVE		D	17		
27	Omar DAF	SEN	D	7		
19	Moumouni DAGANO	BFA	A	27	(5)	7
21	Souleymane DIAWARA	SEN	D	22	(1)	1
26	Mevlut ERDING		A	3	(7)	2
23	Benjamin GENGHINI		M	1	(2)	1
9	Araújo Dall'Igna "ILAN"	BRA	A	26	(1)	10
12	Michaël ISABEY		M	35	(1)	3
34	Maxime JOSSE		D	6		
17	Mohamed KADER TOURE	TOG	A	2	(9)	
14	Johann LONFAT	SUI	M	5	(2)	
1	Alexandre MARTINOVIC		G	2	(1)	
31	Mourad MEGHNI		M	10	(6)	
26	Jérémy MENEZ		A	27	(4)	3
10	Valéry MEZAGUE		M	10	(6)	
4	João MIRANDA	BRA	D	18	(2)	
18	Guirane N'DAW	SEN	M	30		1
14	Romain PITAU		M	38		
6	Lionel POTILLON		D	8		
	Julien QUERCIA		A	1	(5)	
16	Teddy RICHERT		G	36		
13	Badara SENE	SEN	M	2	(1)	1
24	Pape Habib SOW		D		(1)	
22	Dusko TOSIC	SCG	D	12	(2)	
29	WÉLDON Santos	BRA	A	2	(10)	2
29	Jaouad ZAIRI	MAR	A	3	(7)	

RC STRASBOURG
Coach – Jacky Duguépéroux

2005

30/7	AJ Auxerre	h	0-0	
7/8	Olympique Lyonnais	a	0-1	
14/8	AS Monaco FC	h	1-2	Le Pen
20/8	FC Metz	a	0-0	
27/8	Girondins de Bordeaux	h	0-0	
10/9	Paris Saint-Germain	a	0-1	
18/9	RC Lens	h	1-1	Pagis
21/9	AC Ajaccio	a	0-0	
24/9	Toulouse FC	h	2-4	Hagui 2
2/10	ES Troyes AC	a	1-1	Farnerud A.
15/10	Stade Rennais FC	h	0-1	
23/10	Le Mans UC 72	a	0-2	
29/10	AS Saint-Etienne	h	0-1	
6/11	Lille OSC	a	0-2	
19/11	OGC Nice	h	0-0	
27/11	FC Nantes	a	3-4	Pagis 2 (1p), Diané
3/12	FC Sochaux	h	0-0	
10/12	AS Nancy-Lorraine	a	2-1	Pagis (p), Diané
17/12	Olympique Marseille	h	0-1	

2006

4/1	Olympique Lyonnais	h	0-4		
11/1	AS Monaco FC	a	1-1	Kanté	
14/1	FC Metz	h	2-1	Le Pen (p), Johansen	
21/1	Girondins de Bordeaux	a	1-2	Le Pen (p)	
4/2	RC Lens	a	1-2	Gameiro	
8/2	Paris Saint-Germain	h	1-1	Diané	
11/2	AC Ajaccio	h	2-2	Farnerud A., Diané	
18/2	Toulouse FC	a	2-1	Farnerud P., Abdessadki (p)	
26/2	ES Troyes AC	h	2-0	Diané, Abdessadki	
4/3	Stade Rennais FC	a	1-2	Kanté	
12/3	Le Mans UC 72	h	1-2	Diané	
19/3	AS Saint-Etienne	a	2-0	Diané, Farnerud P.	
25/3	Lille OSC	h	2-2	Farnerud A., Diané	
_	OGC Nice	a	1-3	Johansen (p)	
8/4	FC Nantes	h	0-1		
15/4	FC Sochaux	a	1-1	Farnerud P.	
30/4	AS Nancy-Lorraine	h	1-3	Diané	
6/5	Olympique Marseille	a	2-2	Abdessadki, Carlier	
13/5	AJ Auxerre	a	0-4		

No	Name	Nat	Pos	Aps	(s)	Gls
11	Yacine ABDESSADKI		M	13		3
6	Ahmed ABOU MOSLEM	EGY	D	14		
13	Salim ARRACHE	ALG	M	7	(7)	
4	Christian BASSILA		M	1		
28	Habib BELLAÏD		D	13	(2)	
15	Arthur BOKA	CIV	D	20	(7)	
29	Rudy CARLIER		A	3	(8)	1
16	Stéphane CASSARD		G	24		
2	Yves DEROFF		D	25	(4)	
3	Jean-Christophe DEVAUX		D	16	(4)	
20	Amara DIANE	CIV	A	26	(8)	9
7	Alexander FARNERUD	SWE	M	23	(8)	3
10	Pontus FARNERUD	SWE	M	24	(8)	3
25	Ricardo FATY		D	4	(3)	
23	Kévin GAMEIRO		A	5	(3)	1
22	Haikel GMAMDIA	TUN	A	6	(7)	
21	Karim HAGUI	TUN	D	21	(2)	2
8	Abd Rabo HOSNI	EGY	M	20	(2)	
18	Pascal JOHANSEN		M	21	(4)	2
5	Cédric KANTE	MLI	D	30		2
24	Sidi Yaya KEITA	MLI	M	10	(2)	
12	Gaëtan KREBS		M		(2)	
19	Guillaume LACOUR		M	26	(1)	
14	Ulrich LE PEN		M	22	(4)	3
27	Egard Gnoleba LOUE	CIV	M	9		
17	Eric MOULOUNGUI	GAB	A		(2)	
17	Szilárd NÉMETH	SVK	A	4	(5)	
9	Mickaël PAGIS		A	16		4
1	Nicolas PUYDEBOIS		G	14	(1)	
26	Yann SCHNEIDER		D	1	(3)	
	Jean-Christophe VERGEROLLE		D		(1)	

TOULOUSE FC
Coach – Erick Mombaerts

2005

30/7	FC Sochaux	a	1-0	Santos	
6/8	OGC Nice	h	0-2		
13/8	Paris Saint-Germain	a	0-2		
21/8	AS Saint-Etienne	h	1-1	Moreira	
24/8	Lille OSC	a	0-0		
10/9	Le Mans UC 72	h	0-2		
17/9	FC Nantes	a	0-2		
21/9	Olympique Marseille	h	1-0	Bergougnoux	
24/9	RC Strasbourg	a	4-2	Batlles, Moreira, Dieuze, Santos	

France

2/10	AJ Auxerre	h	2-0	Emana, Bergougnoux	
15/10	AS Nancy-Lorraine	a	0-2		
22/10	Girondins de Bordeaux	h	1-1	Moreira	
29/10	RC Lens	a	0-1		
5/11	Olympique Lyonnais	h	0-1		
20/11	Stade Rennais FC	a	1-4	Congré	
26/11	AC Ajaccio	h	3-0	Moreira (p), Mathieu, Bonnet	
3/12	FC Metz	a	2-2	Moreira, Santos	
10/12	ES Troyes AC	h	2-1	Bergougnoux, Mathieu	
18/12	AS Monaco FC	a	0-1		
2006					
4/1	OGC Nice	a	1-2	Dao	
12/1	Paris Saint-Germain	h	1-0	Moreira	
21/1	Lille OSC	h	0-0		
28/1	Le Mans UC 72	a	1-1	Akpa-Akpro	
1/2	AS Saint-Etienne	a	3-1	Akpa-Akpro 2, Arribagé	
4/2	FC Nantes	h	1-0	Arribagé	
12/2	Olympique Marseille	a	0-0		
18/2	RC Strasbourg	h	1-2	Moreira	
25/2	AJ Auxerre	a	0-2		
4/3	AS Nancy-Lorraine	h	1-1	Emana	
11/3	Girondins de Bordeaux	a	0-2		
18/3	RC Lens	h	1-1	Mansaré	
25/3	Olympique Lyonnais	a	1-1	Moreira	
2/4	Stade Rennais FC	h	0-1		
8/4	AC Ajaccio	a	0-1		
14/4	FC Metz	h	2-0	Santos, Moreira	
30/4	ES Troyes AC	a	1-3	Batlles	
6/5	AS Monaco FC	h	3-3	Santos, Moreira (p), Dieuze	
13/5	FC Sochaux	h	1-2	Batlles	

No	Name	Nat	Pos	Aps	(s)	Gls
18	Yacine ABDESSADKI	MAR	M	7	(2)	
26	Jean-Louis AKPA-AKPRO		A	4	(10)	3
4	Dominique ARRIBAGE		D	32		2
12	Lucien AUBEY	CON	D	33		
29	Laurent BATLLES		M	28	(3)	3
21	Henri BEDIMO	CMR	D	3	(5)	
15	Bryan BERGOUGNOUX		A	18	(15)	3
23	Alexandre BONNET		M	7	(8)	1
6	Julien CARDY		M	12	(9)	
3	Daniel CONGRE		D	15	(1)	1
9	Issoumaïla DAO	CIV	D	10	(7)	1
25	Nicolas DIEUZE		M	30	(5)	2
16	Nicolas DOUCHEZ		G	13	(1)	
28	Albin EBONDO		D	25	(4)	
20	Achille EMANA	CMR	M	25	(1)	2
27	Mohamed FOFANA		D	4		
8	Thibault GIRESSE		M	2	(7)	
7	Stéphane LIEVRE		D	2	(4)	
17	Fodé MANSARE	GUI	M	15	(8)	1
5	Jérémy MATHIEU		M	35		2
10	Daniel MOREIRA		A	36	(1)	10
33	Xavier PENTECOTE		A		(4)	
1	Christophe REVAULT		G	25		
11	Francileudo SANTOS	TUN	A	17	(8)	5
14	François SIRIEIX		M	7	(1)	
19	Nabil TAÏDER		M	13	(2)	

ES TROYES AC
Coach – Jean-Marc Furlan

2005

30/7	OGC Nice	a	1-1	Dallet	
6/8	AS Saint-Etienne	h	0-0		
13/8	Lille OSC	a	2-1	Nivet (p), Dallet	
21/8	Paris Saint-Germain	h	1-1	Dallet	
27/8	Le Mans UC 72	a	0-1		
10/9	FC Nantes	h	1-0	Grax	
18/9	Olympique Marseille	a	1-2	Grax (p)	
21/9	AS Monaco FC	h	1-2	Grax	
24/9	AS Nancy-Lorraine	a	1-2	Grax	
2/10	RC Strasbourg	h	1-1	Jaziri	
15/10	AJ Auxerre	a	0-3		
23/10	RC Lens	h	1-1	Adam	
29/10	Girondins de Bordeaux	a	0-2		
6/11	Stade Rennais FC	h	2-1	Jaziri, Tourenne	
19/11	Olympique Lyonnais	a	1-2	Nivet	
26/11	FC Metz	h	0-0		
3/12	AC Ajaccio	a	1-0	Amzine	
10/12	Toulouse FC	a	1-2	Grax	
17/12	FC Sochaux	h	2-1	Boucansaud, Jaziri	
2006					
4/1	AS Saint-Etienne	a	1-1	Grax	
11/1	Lille OSC	h	1-0	Matuidi	
15/1	Paris Saint-Germain	a	1-2	Ba	
21/1	Le Mans UC 72	h	1-3	Nivet	
5/2	Olympique Marseille	h	0-1		
11/2	AS Monaco FC	a	1-1	Enza Yamissi	
14/2	FC Nantes	a	1-1	Nivet (p)	
18/2	AS Nancy-Lorraine	h	0-1		
26/2	RC Strasbourg	a	0-2		
5/3	AJ Auxerre	h	1-1	Ba	
11/3	RC Lens	a	0-1		
18/3	Girondins de Bordeaux	h	1-1	Nivet	
25/3	Stade Rennais FC	a	0-2		
1/4	Olympique Lyonnais	h	0-1		
8/4	FC Metz	a	4-2	Amzine, Dallet, Nivet (p), Grax	
15/4	AC Ajaccio	h	3-0	Tourenne, Faye, Bangoura	
30/4	Toulouse FC	h	3-1	Dallet, Grax (p), Jaziri	
6/5	FC Sochaux	a	1-1	Grax	
13/5	OGC Nice	h	1-2	Jaziri	

No	Name	Nat	Pos	Aps	(s)	Gls
11	Frédéric ADAM		M	8	(1)	1
17	Gharib AMZINE	MAR	M	29	(4)	2
29	Georges BA	CIV	A	6	(13)	2
7	Ibrahima BANGOURA	GUI	A	7	(7)	1
2	Branko BOSKOVIC	SCG	M	11	(8)	
3	Florian BOUCANSAUD		D	30		1
4	Sébastien DALLET		A	23	(6)	5
11	Gaël DANIC		M	1	(10)	
31	Stéphan DROUIN		D	5	(1)	
18	Alexandre DUJEUX		D	14	(6)	
12	Eloge ENZA YAMISSI	CAF	M	7	(11)	1
27	Cédric FAIVRE		M		(4)	
23	Ibrahima FAYE	SEN	D	32		1
24	Nicolas FLORENTIN		A		(1)	
9	Sébastien GRAX		A	20	(9)	9
21	Auriol GUILLAUME		A	3		
19	Ziad JAZIRI	TUN	A	11	(10)	5
26	Blaise KOUASSI	CIV	D	25	(1)	
1	Ronan LE CROM		G	38		
20	Blaise MATUIDI		M	30	(1)	1
28	Juan Luis MONTERO	ESP	D	30		
13	Christian NADE		A	7	(10)	
18	Benjamin NIVET		M	38		6
11	Grégory PAISLEY		D	13		
6	Carl TOURENNE		M	29	(2)	2
33	Ali ZITOUNI	TUN	A	1		

France

DOMESTIC CUP 2005/06

1/32 FINALS
(6/1/06)
Vannes OC 1, FC Lorient 2
(7/1/06)
AS Cannes 1, Agde 1 *(aet; 3-4 on pens)*
Sainte-Geneviève 5, Mulhouse 0
Longuenesse w/o SM Caen *(original result 0-4)*
Corte 2, Stade Rennais FC 3
Drancy Jeanne d'Arc 0, FC Metz 4
Lyon Duchère 2, Toulouse FC 1
AS Saint-Etienne 0, Lille OSC 1 *(aet)*
Saint-Louis Neuweg 1, Colmar 2
RC Strasbourg 4, AS Nancy-Lorraine 0
Vermelles 0, Paris Saint-Germain 4
Amiens SCF 2, Plabennec 0
LB Châteauroux 2, Yzeure 0
Dijon Football 2, Forbach 1
Montpellier HSC 2, Hyères 1
St-Pryve-St-Hilaire 0, Entente Sannois Saint-Gratien 6
Fontenay le Comte 0, Vitré 1
Calais 3, ES Troyes AC 2 *(aet)*
Moulins 2, FC Istres 2 *(aet; 5-3 on pens)*
Saint-Lô 0, AC Ajaccio 2
Brive 0, Bois-Guillaume 0 *(aet; 4-5 on pens)*
SC Bastia 3, CS Louhans-Cuiseaux 71 3 *(aet; 4-1 on pens)*
Stade Brestois 29 3, OGC Nice 0
FC Nantes 2, Valenciennes FC 1
Oissel 1, FC Sochaux 2 *(aet)*
Royê 1, Alençon 0
Le Mans UC 72 0, RC Lens 1
Wasquehal 1, Girondins de Bordeaux 3
(8/1/06)
Olympique Noisy-le-Sec 0, AJ Auxerre 1
Rhône Vallées 0, AS Monaco FC 6
Grenoble Foot 38 0, Olympique Lyonnais 4
Olympique Marseille 4, Le Havre AC 0

1/16 FINALS
(27/1/06)
Stade Brestois 29 2, Amiens SCF 0
(28/1/06)
Dijon Football 1, Moulins 0
SC Bastia 2, Agde 0 *(aet)*
(31/1/06)
Lyon Duchère 0, RC Strasbourg 0 *(aet; 5-4 on pens)*
Bois-Guillaume 0, FC Nantes 2
Girondins de Bordeaux 2, Entente Sannois Saint-Gratien 1
Stade Rennais FC 1, RC Lens 0
(1/2/06)
FC Lorient 0, Lille OSC 1
Paris Saint-Germain 1, AJ Auxerre 0
AC Ajaccio 1, Olympique Lyonnais 2 *(aet)*
Olympique Marseille 2, FC Metz 0
Colmar 1, AS Monaco FC 0 *(aet)*
(11/2/06)
Sainte-Geneviève 0, Calais 1
Vitré 3, Longuenesse 1
(14/2/06)
LB Châteauroux 1, FC Sochaux 0 *(aet)*
(22/2/06)
Montpellier HSC 6, Royê 1

1/8 FINALS
(14/3/06)
Lyon Duchère 0, Paris Saint-Germain 3
(21/3/06)
Colmar 1, Stade Rennais FC 4
Olympique Lyonnais 1, SC Bastia 0
FC Nantes 3, Dijon Football 0
(22/3/06)
Montpellier HSC 1, Girondins de Bordeaux 0
Olympique Marseille 2, FC Sochaux 0
Vitré 0, Lille OSC 2
Calais 1, Stade Brestois 28 0 *(aet)*

QUARTER-FINALS
(11/4/06)
Paris Saint-Germain 2 *(Kalou 40, Pauleta 57)* Lille OSC 1 *(Tavlaridis 30)*
Olympique Lyonnais 1 *(Fred 22)*, Olympique Marseille 2 *(Maoulida 17, Niang 65)*
(12/4/06)
Calais 0, FC Nantes 1 *(Da Rocha 88)*
Stade Rennais FC 5 *(Briand 2, Monterrubio 95, 101, Utaka 102, Källström 110)*, Montpellier HSC 3 *(Lafourcade 11, 103, 111)* *(aet)*

SEMI-FINALS
(20/4/06)
Olympique Marseille 3 *(Ribéry 1, Taiwo 19, Nicng 45)*, Stade Rennais FC 0
FC Nantes 1 *(Cetto 72)*, Paris Saint-Germain 2 *(Pancrate 68, Pauleta 86)*

FINAL
(29/4/06)
Stade de France, Saint-Denis *(Paris)*
PARIS SAINT-GERMAIN 2 *(Kalou 6, Dhorasoo 47)*
OLYMPIQUE MARSEILLE 1 *(Maoulida 67)*
Referee – Duhamel
PARIS SAINT-GERMAIN – Letizi, Mendy, Rozehnal, Yepes, Armand, M'Bami, Dhorasoo, Cissé, Rothen *(Paulo César 86)*, Kalou, Pauleta.
OLYMPIQUE MARSEILLE – Barthez, Beye *(Nasri 80)*, Déhu, Civelli, Taiwo, Cana, Ribéry, Niang, Pagis *(Oruma 37)*, Lamouchi, Maoulida

SECOND LEVEL FINAL TABLE 2005/06

		Pld	W	D	L	F	A	Pts
1	Valenciennes FC	38	21	11	6	51	28	74
2	CS Sedan Ardennes	38	19	14	5	50	32	71
3	FC Lorient	38	18	12	8	49	26	66
4	SM Caen	38	18	12	8	56	35	66
5	Dijon Football	38	16	12	10	47	32	60
6	SC Bastia	38	16	10	12	47	40	58
7	Le Havre AC	38	13	16	9	48	41	55
8	US Créteil	38	13	15	10	46	33	54
9	En Avant Guingamp	38	12	14	12	36	32	50
10	Grenoble Foot 38	38	12	12	14	42	45	48
11	FC Gueugnon	38	11	15	12	29	37	48
12	Montpellier HSC	38	12	11	15	34	43	47
13	FC Istres	38	12	11	15	33	45	47
14	Stade Reims	38	10	15	13	32	31	45
15	LB Châteauroux	38	10	14	14	48	48	44
16	Amiens SCF	38	9	16	13	32	44	43
17	Stade Brestois 29	38	9	15	14	34	48	42
18	Clermont FA	38	10	8	20	35	59	38
19	Stade Lavallois	38	9	8	21	38	59	35
20	FC Sète 34	38	4	11	23	31	60	23

Georgia

New names on the trophies

Two years after their players and fans brought shame and dishonour on the club in a violent championship play-off, village outfit Sioni Bolnisi defied all the odds to become the champions of Georgia for the first time. Ironically, it was the team that had defeated them in that infamous 2004 decider, WIT Georgia Tbilisi, who stayed with them all the way again, Sioni only clinching their maiden title on the last day of the season with a thumping 4-0 win at Torpedo Kutaisi.

It was a season of firsts all round as Ameri Tbilisi, founded only in 2002, concluded their debut season in the top division by winning the Georgian Cup. Coached by ex-Georgian international defender Giorgi Chikhradze, Ameri beat champions-elect Sioni in the semi-finals and survived a last-minute equaliser in the final against FC Zestafoni (who had eliminated WIT Georgia in the semis) before triumphing 4-3 in a penalty shoot-out. It was the second successive Cup final defeat for Zestafoni, beaten 2-0 by Lokomotivi Tbilisi 12 months earlier.

Ameri were one of half a dozen clubs promoted in 2005 as the Umaglesi Liga (Premier Division) increased its membership from ten clubs to 16 while simultaneously reducing the teams' workload from 36 games to just 30.

It was widely expected that Dinamo Tbilisi, champions and UEFA Cup protagonists in 2004/05, would dominate proceedings again, but instead Sioni and WIT Georgia reprised their duel of 2003/04, with Dinamo having to resort to a peripheral role in the title race.

Tskhadadze switch

A poor start for the defending champions ultimately led to the sacking of title-winning coach Kahaber Tskhadadze during the winter break, but while Dinamo fell further behind in the spring following the appointment of ex-Russian Under-21 coach Andrei Chernyshov, Tskhadadze moved to Bolnisi and kept Sioni on track for the title despite the mid-season departure of several of their players, including top-scoring captain Jaba Dvali, who ended a loan spell at the club by returning to Dinamo.

Sioni were greatly indebted in the spring to the goals of their other main striker, Akaki Mikuchadze. He not only scored the winner in each of the home games against Dinamo and WIT Georgia but ended the season in grand style with a hat-trick in the title-clinching 4-0 win at Torpedo. It was not quite enough to bring Mikuchadze the league's top scorer prize. That went instead to his

NATIONAL TEAM RESULTS 2005/06

Date	Opponent	H/A	Venue	Score	Scorers
17/8/05	Kazakhstan (WCQ)	A	Almaty	2-1	Demetradze (50, 82)
3/9/05	Ukraine (WCQ)	H	Tbilisi	1-1	Gakhokidze (89)
7/9/05	Denmark (WCQ)	A	Copenhagen	1-6	Demetradze (36p)
8/10/05	Kazakhstan (WCQ)	H	Tbilisi	0-0	
12/10/05	Greece (WCQ)	A	Piraeus	0-1	
12/11/05	Bulgaria	A	Sofia	2-6	Jakobia (84), Gogua (89)
16/11/05	Jordan	H	Tbilisi	3-2	Demetradze (4, 65), Arveladze (75)
1/3/06	Malta	A	Ta' Qali	2-0	Martsvaladze (9), Kankava (17)
22/3/06	Albania	A	Tirana	0-0	
27/5/06	New Zealand	N	Altenkirchen	1-3	Arveladze (44)
31/5/06	Paraguay	N	Dornbirn	0-1	

Georgia

NATIONAL TEAM APPEARANCES 2005/06

Coach – Gaioz DARSADZE /(15/1/06) Klaus TOPPMÖLLER (GER)

Player	DoB	Club	KAZ	UKR	DEN	KAZ	GRE	Bul	Jor	Mlt	Alb	Nzl	Par	Caps	Goals
Giorgi LOMAIA	8/8/79	FK Khimki (RUS) /Luch-Energie Vladivostok (RUS)	G	G	G						G46	G	G	24	-
Zurab MENTESHASHVILI	30/1/80	Skonto Riga (LAT)	D	D79	D						M35		M78	17	1
Zurab KHIZANISHVILI	6/10/81	Rangers (SCO) /Blackburn Rovers (ENG)	D	D	D		D	D	D			D	D	40	-
Kakha KALADZE	27/2/78	Milan (ITA)	D	D	D	D	D	D	D			D	D	52	-
Levan KOBIASHVILI	10/7/77	FC Schalke 04 (GER)	M	M79	M	M	M	M		M			M	61	4
Kakhaber ALADASHVILI	11/8/83	Dinamo Tbilisi /Dynamo Kyiv (UKR)	M78								M88	s46	M63	4	-
Jaba KANKAVA	18/3/86	Alania Vladikavkaz (RUS) /Arsenal Kyiv (UKR)	M	M		M	M	M	M		M	M46	M	10	1
Levan TSKITISHVILI	10/10/76	VfL Wolfsburg (GER)	M	M	M81						D			39	1
Giorgi GAKHOKIDZE	5/11/75	FC Twente (HOL)	M	M	M									20	3
Aleksandre IASHVILI	23/10/77	SC Freiburg (GER)	A67					s46				s46	s71	29	9
Giorgi DEMETRADZE	26/9/76	Alania Vladikavkaz (RUS) /Maccabi Tel Aviv (ISR)	A90	A	A67	A	A85	A55	A77			A46	s63	45	11
David MUJIRI	2/1/78	SK Sturm Graz (AUT) /Krylya Sovetov Samara (RUS)	s67	s79	s67	M	M	M46	M72	M61		s55	s74	15	-
David ODIKADZE	14/4/81	Dinamo Tbilisi	s78	M	M62									4	-
Giorgi GANUGRAVA	21/2/88	FC Zestafoni	s90		s62	M	M	M65	M82	M	s35			8	-
Malkhaz ASATIANI	4/8/81	Lokomotiv Moskva (RUS)		M87	M	D						M66	M74	20	4
Gogita GOGUA	4/10/83	FK Khimki (RUS) /Spartak Nalchik (RUS)		s79	M		M	s46	M74		M	M55	s63	11	1
Mikheil ASHVETIA	10/11/77	FK Rostov (RUS)		s87		A86		s55	s82					20	5
Lasha SALUKVADZE	21/12/81	Rubin Kazan (RUS)		s81	D	D46	D						D63	10	-
Nukri REVISHVILI	2/3/87	Torpedo Kutaisi				G	G	G68	G	G				5	-
Kakha MJAVANADZE	2/10/78	Anzhi Makhachkala (RUS) /Chornomorets Odesa (UKR)				D	D	D46	D			D46		14	-
Rati TSINAMDZGVRISHVILI	22/3/88	Ameri Tbilisi					s86	s46						2	-
Beka GOTSIRIDZE	17/8/88	FC Zestafoni						s85						1	-
Shota ARVELADZE	22/2/73	AZ (HOL)						A68	A82			A	A	57	21
Ilia KANDELAKI	26/12/81	Chornomorets Odesa (UKR)						s65	M			s66	M	5	-
Zviad STURUA	25/4/78	Dinamo Tbilisi						s68						2	-
Lasha JAKOBIA	20/8/80	Metalist Kharkiv (UKR)						s68	s72		A			7	1
David KVIRKVELIA	27/6/80	Alania Vladikavkaz (RUS) /Metalurg Zaporizhzhya (UKR)							s74			M66	s78	17	-
Vitali DARASELIA	27/9/78	Alania Vladikavkaz (RUS)							s77					10	-
Vladimer BURDULI	26/10/80	Alania Vladikavkaz (RUS)							s82					16	2
David MCHEDLISHVILI	5/4/88	Ameri Tbilisi								D55				1	-
Mate GVINIANIDZE	10/12/86	Lokomotiv Moskva (RUS)								D	D			2	-
Giorgi POPKHADZE	25/9/86	FC Tbilisi								D		s46		2	-
Revaz GOTSIRIDZE	17/1/81	KamAZ Nab. Chelny (RUS)								A82				1	-
Otar MARTSVALADZE	14/7/84	Dynamo Kyiv (UKR)								A			A71	2	1
Mirza BJALAVA	5/2/88	FC Zestafoni								s55				1	-
Kakha MAKHARADZE	20/10/87	Dinamo Tbilisi								s61				1	-
Giorgi CHELIDZE	25/10/86	Lokomotiv Moskva (RUS)								s82				1	-
Levan MAGRADZE	5/12/77	Xanthi (GRE)									D			4	-
Giorgi SHASHIASHVILI	1/9/79	Dinamo Tbilisi									D			13	-
Zaal ELIAVA	2/1/85	Skonto Riga (LAT)									D			1	-
Vasil GIGIADZE	3/6/77	Kryvbas Kryvyi Rih (UKR)									A	A46		3	-
Grigol CHANTURIA	25/9/73	FC Zestafoni										s46		3	-
Giorgi SETURIDZE	1/4/85	Dinamo Batumi										s88		1	-
Otar KHIZANEISHVILI	26/9/81	SC Freiburg (GER)											s46	13	-
Zurab IONANIDZE	2/12/71	FC Zestafoni											s66	4	1

Georgia

former strike partner Dvali, who, with four goals in Dinamo Tbilisi's final game, remained on top of the charts with a final tally of 21.

Runners-up WIT Georgia, who drew their final game 1-1 at Dinamo Batumi, had the league's leading marksman at the halfway stage in 21-year-old Otar Martsvaladze, but the form that had brought the youngster 14 goals in as many games earned him a trial at Dynamo Kiev, and the Ukrainian giants decided to take him on. His goals in the run-in could have made all the difference to the title race, but in Georgia needs must, and when big foreign clubs show an interest in a player, they are seldom rebuffed.

Toppmöller takes over

In the event, Martsvaladze barely got a kick at Dynamo, but he did score a goal nine minutes into his international debut as Georgia posted a 2-0 victory away to Malta. It was also the first match of new coach Klaus Toppmöller's reign, the ex-Bayer Leverkusen coach having been signed up by the Georgian Football Federation (GFF) a few weeks earlier.

Toppmöller's biggest claim to fame as a club coach was in the 2001/02 season when he led Leverkusen to three runners-up spots – in the Bundesliga, the German Cup and the UEFA Champions League. He can hardly be expected to steer the underachieving Georgians to the Euro 2008 finals given that only two teams qualify from a group that happens to contain both of the 2006 World Cup finalists, Italy and France, but the GFF will certainly expect to see an improvement in the team's performances.

Georgia played pitifully in the World Cup qualifiers – initially under another foreign coach, Frenchman Alain Giresse – to finish sixth out of seven teams, with only Kazakhstan below them. Toppmöller's task will be to get more, much more, out of a squad that is not short of talent. Several Georgian players performed with distinction in 2005/06, notably veteran striker Shota Arveladze at Dutch club AZ, Levan Kobiashvili at Schalke (for whom he scored a Champions League hat-trick) and Georgian Footballer of the Year Kakha Kaladze at Milan. Toppmöller has 'done a Klinsmann' by refusing to live in the country, but as in his homeland during the World Cup, that will not be a problem as long as he comes up with the right results.

EUROPEAN CUPS 2005/06

UEFA CHAMPIONS LEAGUE

DINAMO TBILISI

1st qualifying round FC LEVADIA TALLINN (EST)
A 0-1
Sturua, Aladashvili, Gigauri, Orbeladze, Kandelaki, Odikadze, Nozadze, Babunashvili, Navalovski, Melkadze, Megreladze (Bobokhidze 63).

H 2-0 *Melkadze (48), Orbeladze (50)*
Sturua, Aladashvili, Kemoklidze, Orbeladze, Kandelaki, Odikadze, Nozadze, Babunashvili (Makharadze 72), Chelidze (Gigauri 66), Bobokhidze (Akobia 80), Melkadze.

2nd qualifying round BRØNDBY IF (DEN)
H 0-2
Sturua, Aladashvili, Gigauri, Orbeladze, Amisulashvili, Kandelaki, Nozadze (Grigalashvili 80), Babunashvili, Makharadze, Bobokhidze (Akobia 46), Melkadze (Iashvili 63).

A 1-3 *Iashvili (65)*
Sturua, Kandelaki, Iashvili (Akobia 68), Orbeladze, Gigauri (Kemoklidze 46), Aladashvili, Babunashvili, Nozadze, Makharadze, Odikadze, Megreladze (Iashvili 46), Melkadze.

UEFA CUP

LOKOMOTIVI TBILISI

1st qualifying round BANANTS YEREVAN (ARM)
A 3-2 *Alaverdashvili (41), Kebadze (48), Oniani (53p)*
Shekriladze, Oniani G., Makhviladze, Oniani R., Seturidze, Kebadze, Inomov, Purtukhia (Popkhadze 60), Kakhelishvili, Alaverdashvili (Kipiani 81), Siradze (Chivadze 72).

H 0-2
Shekriladze, Oniani R., Oniani G., Makhviladze, Seturidze, Kebadze, Kakhelishvili, Inomov, Alaverdashvili (Chivadze 73), Purtukhia (Ppkhadze 46), Siradze (Tavberidze 83).

TORPEDO KUTAISI

1st qualifying round FC BATE BORISOV (BLS)
H 0-1
Revishvili, Barabadze, Gamezardashvili (Prangishvili 80), Bakradze, Rakviashvili, Soselia (Shalamberidze 52), Chkhetiani (Tekhov 46), Bolkvadze, Akhalaia, Kakaladze, Jikia.

A 0-5
Revishvili, Barabadze, Prangishvili, Janjalia (Chakhunashvili 50), Akhalaia, Shalamberidze, Tekhov, Soselia, Zivzivadze (Kvetenadze 61), Khatiashvili (Kvirikashvili 48), Gongadze.

LEAGUE RESULTS/ SCORERS/APPEARANCES/ GOALS 2005/06

AMERI TBILISI
Coach – Giorgi Chikhradze

2005				
1/8	Torpedo Kutaisi	a	1-0	Davitashvili
7/8	FC Zestafoni	h	2-0	Khvadagiani, Koshkadze
20/8	Lokomotivi Tbilisi	a	0-3	
28/8	Dinamo Tbilisi	h	1-1	Kaidarashvili
10/9	Dila Gori	a	1-0	Davitashvili
17/9	FC Tskhinvali	h	1-0	Sevastopulo

Georgia

TOP GOALSCORERS 2005/06

21	Jaba DVALI (Sioni Bolnisi/Dinamo Tbilisi)	
19	Akaki MIKUCHADZE (Sioni Bolnisi)	
17	Zurab IONANIDZE (FC Zestafoni)	
14	Otar MARTSVALADZE (WIT Georgia Tbilisi)	
	Giorgi MEGRELADZE (Dinamo Tbilisi)	
11	Saba SULTANISHVILI (Dila Gori/FC Tskhinvali)	
	Mikheil BOBOKHIDZE (Dinamo Tbilisi)	
10	Vladimer DVALISHVILI (Dinamo Tbilisi/Dinamo Batumi)	
	David IMEDASHVILI (WIT Georgia Tbilisi)	
9	Suliko DAVITASHVILI (Ameri Tbilisi)	
	Zviad KUTATELADZE (Kolkheti 1913 Poti)	
	Grigol IMETADZE (FC Zestafoni)	

Date	Opponent	H/A	Score	Scorers
25/9	Dinamo Batumi	a	0-1	
30/9	WIT Georgia Tbilisi	h	1-2	Sevastopulo
15/10	Kolheti 1913 Poti	a	1-0	Sevastopulo
22/10	FC Borjomi	h	1-0	Davitashvili
30/10	Dinamo Sokhumi	a	3-0	Sevastopulo, Tatanashvili, Koshkadze
5/11	Spartaki Tbilisi	h	1-0	Davitashvili
13/11	Kakheti Telavi	a	2-1	Davitashvili 2
19/11	Sioni Bolnisi	h	0-1	
26/11	FC Tbilisi	a	0-0	
2006				
22/2	Torpedo Kutaisi	h	5-1	Sevastopulo 2, Silagava, Dekanosidze, Davitashvili
4/3	FC Zestafoni	a	0-1	
11/3	Lokomotivi Tbilisi	h	4-1	Dolidze 3 (1p), Tsinamdzgvrishvili
15/3	Dinamo Tbilisi	a	2-1	Davitashvili 2
25/3	Dila Gori	h	1-0	Khvadagiani
29/3	FC Tskhinvali	a	0-1	
1/4	Dinamo Batumi	h	0-1	
5/4	WIT Georgia Tbilisi	a	1-3	Tsinamdzgvrishvili
12/4	Kolheti 1913 Poti	h	1-0	Tsinamdzgvrishvili
15/4	FC Borjomi	a	1-2	Silagava
19/4	Dinamo Sokhumi	h	1-0	Sevastopulo
22/4	Spartaki Tbilisi	a	1-1	Davitnidze
29/4	Kakheti Telavi	h	0-0	
6/5	Sioni Bolnisi	a	0-3	
9/5	FC Tbilisi	h	0-2	

Name	Nat	Pos	Aps	(s)	Gls
Jaba BERIANIDZE		D	16	(5)	
Mirza BJALAVA		D		(5)	
David BOLKVADZE		M	10	(2)	
Tengiz CHIKVILADZE		D	13	(1)	
Besik CHIMAKADZE		M	1	(1)	
Givi CHKHETIANI		M	1	(9)	
Konstantine DARSANIA		M	4	(5)	
Suliko DAVITASHVILI		A	26	(1)	9
Giorgi DAVITNIDZE		D	22		1
Giorgi DEKANOSIDZE		M	19	(1)	1
Denis DOBROVOLSKI		M	19	(3)	
Grigol DOLIDZE		M	12	(1)	3
Giorgi ELBAKIDZE		D	5	(4)	
Gegi GARUCHAVA		D	3	(2)	
Zurab GVADZABIA		M	4	(1)	
Mikheil JISHKARIANI		A		(1)	
Aleksandre KAIDARASHVILI		A	18	(7)	1
Amiran KEDELASHVILI		D	12	(4)	
Vakhtang KHVADAGIANI		D	26		2
Aleksandre KOSHKADZE		M	23	(2)	2
Zurab KVACHAKHIA		G	6		
Giorgi KVAKHADZE		D	20	(3)	
David MCHEDLISHVILI		M	2	(6)	
Paata METONIDZE		M		(1)	
Revaz NACHKEPIA		G	2		
Nikoloz NADIRADZE		M		(1)	
Lado NADIRASHVILI		G	19		
Giorgi NIKOLAISHVILI		M	4	(2)	
Giorgi NIKURADZE		G	3		
David SEVASTOPULO		A	20	(2)	7
Giorgi SILAGAVA		M	11	(5)	2
Dimitri TATANASHVILI		A	2	(11)	1
Rati TSINAMDZGVRISHVILI		A	7	(3)	3

FC BORJOMI
Coach – Soso Pruidze; (1/3/06) Vladimer Khachidze

Date	Opponent	H/A	Score	Scorers
2005				
30/7	Dinamo Batumi	a	0-1	
6/8	Kolheti 1913 Poti	h	1-0	Burnadze
19/8	Dinamo Sokhumi	a	3-1	Burnadze, Gabiskiria, og (Silagadze L.)
28/8	Kakheti Telavi	h	2-1	Koridze, Jikia S.
11/9	FC Tbilisi	a	5-0	Koridze 4, Getsadze
20/9	FC Zestafoni	h	1-0	Aptsiauri
24/9	Dinamo Tbilisi	a	2-1	Koridze, Getsadze
1/10	FC Tskhinvali	h	4-0	Burnadze, Gabiskiria, Jikia S., Getsadze
15/10	WIT Georgia Tbilisi	a	0-4	
22/10	Ameri Tbilisi	a	0-1	
30/10	Spartaki Tbilisi	h	5-0	Aptsiauri 2, Gabiskiria, Jikia S., Naskidashvili
5/11	Sioni Bolnisi	a	0-1	
13/11	Torpedo Kutaisi	h	1-0	Burnadze (p)
19/11	Lokomotivi Tbilisi	a	1-2	Koridze
26/11	Dila Gori	h	4-3	Aptsiauri, Gabiskiria, Koridze, Getsadze
2006				
22/2	Dinamo Batumi	h	0-1	
4/3	Kolheti 1913 Poti	a	0-0	
11/3	Dinamo Sokhumi	h	3-0	De Porras, Aptsiauri, Jikia S.
15/3	Kakheti Telavi	a	0-1	
25/3	FC Tbilisi	h	2-0	De Porras 2
29/3	FC Zestafoni	a	0-0	
1/4	Dinamo Tbilisi	h	4-2	Ceballe, Burnadze, Sajaia, Sanikidze (p)
5/4	FC Tskhinvali	a	2-1	Sanikidze (p), Gochashvili
12/4	WIT Georgia Tbilisi	h	1-0	De Porras
15/4	Ameri Tbilisi	h	2-1	De Porras, Jikia S.
19/4	Spartaki Tbilisi	a	2-3	Sanikidze (p), Gabiskiria
22/4	Sioni Bolnisi	h	1-0	Sanikidze
29/4	Torpedo Kutaisi	a	2-0	Ceballe, Getsadze
6/5	Lokomotivi Tbilisi	h	2-0	Gochashvili, De Porras
9/5	Dila Gori	a	0-2	

Name	Nat	Pos	Aps	(s)	Gls
Tornike APTSIAURI		M	17	(2)	5
David BAKRADZE		D	27	(1)	
Aleksandre BURNADZE		D	29		5
Darío Daniel CEBALLE	ARG	M	12		2
Lasha CHELIDZE		D	13		

Georgia

FINAL LEAGUE TABLE 2005/06

		Pld	Home					Away					Total					Pts
			W	D	L	F	A	W	D	L	F	A	W	D	L	F	A	
1	Sioni Bolnisi	30	14	1	0	36	5	9	3	3	21	12	23	4	3	57	17	73
2	WIT Georgia Tbilisi	30	12	2	1	29	7	9	3	3	24	10	21	5	4	53	17	68
3	Dinamo Tbilisi	30	11	2	2	32	9	9	2	4	29	13	20	4	6	61	22	64
4	FC Zestafoni	30	10	4	1	25	8	8	3	4	19	14	18	7	5	44	22	61
5	FC Borjomi	30	14	0	1	33	8	5	2	8	17	18	19	2	9	50	26	59
6	Dinamo Batumi	30	9	3	3	24	8	8	4	3	18	13	17	7	6	42	21	58
7	Ameri Tbilisi	30	9	2	4	19	9	6	2	7	13	17	15	4	11	32	26	49
8	Lokomotivi Tbilisi	30	8	2	5	25	18	3	2	10	16	30	11	4	15	41	48	37
9	Kakheti Telavi	30	9	1	5	26	18	1	3	11	7	28	10	4	16	33	46	34
10	Kolkheti 1913 Poti	30	8	3	4	21	10	1	2	12	5	26	9	5	16	26	36	32
11	Dila Gori	30	9	1	5	25	13	0	3	12	10	31	9	4	17	35	44	31
12	Torpedo Kutaisi	30	5	4	6	15	18	3	2	10	13	24	8	6	16	28	42	30
13	FC Tbilisi	30	6	1	8	17	23	3	1	11	12	21	9	2	19	29	44	29
14	FC Tskhinvali	30	5	2	8	18	24	3	1	11	12	37	8	3	19	30	61	27
15	Dinamo Sokhumi	30	4	2	9	13	26	1	1	13	13	44	5	3	22	26	70	18
16	Spartaki Tbilisi	30	3	5	7	11	26	0	1	14	1	31	3	6	21	12	57	15

Name	Nat	Pos	Aps	(s)	Gls
Givi CHKETIANI		M	7	(6)	
Gonzalo Martín DE PORRAS	ARG	A	13	(1)	6
Iuri GABISKIRIA		M	24	(1)	5
Revaz GETSADZE		A	24	(1)	5
Vladimer GOCHASHVILI		A	9	(10)	2
Paata GVIRJISHVILI		M	9	(4)	
Lasha JANGIDZE		D	1	(1)	
Revaz JIKIA		A	2	(7)	
Shota JIKIA		M	10	(13)	5
Giorgi KORIDZE		M	12	(2)	8
Levan LAZARASHVILI		M		(1)	
Nikoloz LOMIDZE		M		(2)	
Zurab MAMALADZE		G	27		
David MAMARDASHVILI		G	3	(2)	
Giorgi MEMARNISHVILI		D	25	(2)	
Levan MEREBASHVILI		D	13		
Mikheil MESKHI		M	26		
Besik MIKIASHVILI		D	8	(3)	
Tamaz NASKIDASHVILI		M		(3)	1
Edik SAJAIA		D	7	(1)	1
Levan SANIKIDZE		A	12	(1)	4
Zakaria TALAKHADZE		M		(1)	
Levan TEDIASHVILI		M		(5)	

DILA GORI
Coach – Vladimer Kachidze ; (13/2/06) Larenti Bolotashvili ; (27/3/06) Malkhaz Latsabidze

2005
30/7	Spartaki Tbilisi	h	1-0	Labadze
6/8	Sioni Bolnisi	a	0-2	
20/8	Torpedo Kutaisi	h	2-0	Takadze M., Khanishvili
29/8	Lokomotivi Tbilisi	a	1-2	Khanishvili
10/9	Ameri Tbilisi	h	0-1	
17/9	Dinamo Batumi	h	2-0	Shatakishvili, Takadze M.
25/9	Kolheti 1913 Poti	a	1-2	Khanishvili
1/10	Dinamo Sokhumi	h	5-0	Sultanishvili 4 (1p), Khanishvili
15/10	Kakheti Telavi	a	0-3	
22/10	FC Tbilisi	h	3-0	Shatakishvili 2, Tsutsunava (p)
30/10	FC Zestafoni	a	0-2	
5/11	Dinamo Tbilisi	h	0-2	
13/11	FC Tskhinvali	a	2-2	Tsutsunava, Labadze
19/11	WIT Georgia Tbilisi	h	1-3	Khanishvili
26/11	FC Borjomi	a	3-4	Labadze 2, Khanishvili

2006
23/2	Spartaki Tbilisi	a	0-1	
4/3	Sioni Bolnisi	h	0-2	
11/3	Torpedo Kutaisi	a	0-0	
15/3	Lokomotivi Tbilisi	h	0-0	
25/3	Ameri Tbilisi	a	0-1	
29/3	Dinamo Batumi	a	1-3	Jokhadze
1/4	Kolheti 1913 Poti	h	1-0	Turmanidze
5/4	Dinamo Sokhumi	a	1-1	Galogre
12/4	Kakheti Telavi	h	4-2	Tsutsunava 2, Turmanidze 2
15/4	FC Tbilisi	a	0-2	
19/4	FC Zestafoni	h	0-1	
22/4	Dinamo Tbilisi	a	1-4	Tlashadze (p)
29/4	FC Tskhinvali	h	4-2	Tsutsunava, Kurtanidze, Labadze, og (Dvali)
6/5	WIT Georgia Tbilisi	a	0-2	
9/5	FC Borjomi	h	2-0	Turmanidze, Vacheishvili

Name	Nat	Pos	Aps	(s)	Gls
Vakhtang AKOPIAN		D	3		
Aleksandre BOKUCHAVA		D	2	(2)	
Zaza CHELIDZE		M	4		
Grigol DZIDZIGURI		M		(2)	
David GALOGRE		D	13		1
Kakhaber GEGESHIDZE		G	9		
Levan GOCHASHVILI		D	12		
Lasha GVARUTSIDZE		D	11		
Tamaz ILURIDZE		G	21		
Levan JOKHADZE		M	6	(1)	1
Givi KARKUZASHVILI		M	14		
Revaz KHACHAPURIDZE		D	11		
Besik KHACHIPERADZE		M	1	(1)	
Koba KHANISHVILI		M	13		6
Aleksandre KHVICHIA		M		(1)	

Georgia

Name	Pos	Aps	(s)	Gls
Irakli KOBAKHIDZE	D	12		
Lasha KOBAKHIDZE	M	3	(3)	
Irakli KUTALIA	M	7		
Ioseb KURTANIDZE	A	5	(2)	1
Aleksandre LABADZE	A	11	(10)	5
Giorgi LATSABIDZE	M	1	(2)	
Tamaz LAVRELASHVILI	D	6	(1)	
David MAISURADZE	D	9		
Dimitri MAKASHVILI	M		(1)	
Giorgi MASURASHVILI	D	5	(9)	
Levan MCHEDLIDZE	M	1	(1)	
Galaktion MDZINARISHVILI	M		(6)	
Guram NADIRADZE	M	3	(12)	
Paata NASKIDASHVILI	G		(1)	
Archil OLGESASHVILI	M	9	(1)	
David PETRIASHVILI	M	2	(1)	
Irakli PIRANISHVILI	M	3	(1)	
Giorgi REVAZISHVILI	M	12		
Albert SAKVARELIDZE	M	18	(1)	
Kristepore SHATAKISHVILI	A	23		3
Soso SHENGELIA	M		(1)	
Saba SULTANISHVILI	A	14		4
Ivane TAKADZE	M		(1)	
Mikheil TAKADZE	M	14		2
David TLASHADZE	M	18	(7)	1
Irakli TOMASHVILI	M	2	(6)	
Mamuka TORONJADZE	M	2	(2)	
Kakhaber TSUTSUNAVA	A	13	(3)	5
Lasha TURMANIDZE	A	9	(3)	4
Kakha VACHEISHVILI	M	8	(2)	1

DINAMO BATUMI
Coach – Amiran Gogitidze; (15/9/05) Otar Gabelia

2005
30/7	FC Borjomi	h	1-0	Zirakishvili
6/8	Spartaki Tbilisi	a	0-0	
20/8	Sioni Bolnisi	h	0-1	
28/8	Torpedo Kutaisi	a	1-0	Burnadze
10/9	Lokomotivi Tbilisi	h	0-1	
17/9	Dila Gori	a	0-2	
25/9	Ameri Tbilisi	h	1-0	Mantskava
1/10	Kolheti 1913 Poti	h	2-0	Mantskava (p), Kakaladze
14/10	Dinamo Sokhumi	a	1-2	Mantskava
22/10	Kakheti Telavi	h	1-0	Gusharashvili
31/10	FC Tbilisi	a	3-1	Zirakishvili 3
5/11	FC Zestafoni	h	2-2	Jeladze, Mikadze
13/11	Dinamo Tbilisi	a	1-3	Gusharashvili
19/11	FC Tskhinvali	h	0-0	
26/11	WIT Georgia Tbilisi	a	0-0	

2006
22/2	FC Borjomi	a	1-0	Jikia
4/3	Spartaki Tbilisi	h	5-0	Jikia 2, Mantskava, Thiago Genero, Dvalishvili
11/3	Sioni Bolnisi	a	2-2	Kebadze, Jikia
15/3	Torpedo Kutaisi	h	2-0	Thiago Genero, Dvalishvili
25/3	Lokomotivi Tbilisi	a	2-1	Mantskava, Dvalishvili
29/3	Dila Gori	h	3-1	Oniani G. 2 (1p), Dvalishvili
1/4	Ameri Tbilisi	a	1-0	Kebadze
5/4	Kolheti 1913 Poti	a	1-0	Jikia
12/4	Dinamo Sokhumi	h	4-0	Dvalishvili 2, Makhvladze, Jikia
15/4	Kakheti Telavi	a	3-1	Dvalishvili, Thiago Genero (p), Jikia
19/4	FC Tbilisi	h	1-0	Dvalishvili
22/4	FC Zestafoni	a	0-0	
29/4	Dinamo Tbilisi	h	1-2	Oniani R.
6/5	FC Tskhinvali	a	2-1	Oniani G. (p), Dvalishvili
30/5	WIT Georgia Tbilisi	h	1-1	Oniani R.

Name	Nat	Pos	Aps	(s)	Gls
Irakli BALADZE		G	1	(1)	
Murtaz BURNADZE		M	6		1
Lasha CHKHAIDZE		M	1		
Vitali DARCHIDZE		M	7	(2)	
David DATVADZE		M	1	(2)	
David DIDIA		M		(1)	
Zurab DUMBADZE		D	2		
Vladimer DVALISHVILI		A	15		9
Zurab EKONIA		M	14	(5)	
David GALOGRE		D	4	(3)	
David GOGISHVILI		M	5	(2)	
Nika GUSHARASHVILI		D	10		2
Levan GVAZAVA		M	5	(2)	
Gizo JELADZE		M	13		1
Revaz JIKIA		A	15		7
Mikheil KAKALADZE		A	9	(6)	1
Kakhaber KATSARAVA		M	9	(3)	
Levan KEBADZE		M	14		2
Vasil KUNCHULIA		M		(1)	
Mamuka LOMIDZE		D	13		
Ivane MAKHARADZE		D	13	(1)	
Mikheil MAKHVILADZE		D	15		1
Giorgi MANTSKAVA		M	22	(3)	5
Giorgi MIKADZE		A	7	(4)	1
Irakli NACHKEBIA		M	1		
Giorgi ONIANI		D	15		3
Roin ONIANI		M	15		2
Archil PARTENADZE		A	1	(4)	
David PIRTSKHALAISHVILI		A	2	(4)	
Giorgi SETURIDZE		M	13		
Levan SHAVGULIDZE		M	1		
Kakhaber SIDAMONIDZE		D	12	(1)	
Giorgi SOMKHISHVILI		G	7	(1)	
Beglar TEDORADZE		M	13		
Besik TEDORADZE		D	4	(3)	
THIAGO GENERO	BRA	A	10	(2)	3
Irakli TOTLADZE		G	22		
Irakli TSANAVA		M	2	(11)	
Tengiz UGREKHELIDZE		M	4	(6)	
Robert ZIRAKISHVILI		A	7	(4)	4

DINAMO SOKHUMI
Coach – Gocha Jorjoliani

2005
30/7	FC Tskhinvali	h	0-2	
6/8	WIT Georgia Tbilisi	a	2-2	Mamporia, Rusia
19/8	FC Borjomi	h	1-3	Rusia
27/8	Spartaki Tbilisi	a	1-0	og (Elizbarashvili)
9/9	Sioni Bolnisi	h	1-2	Chomakhidze
17/9	Torpedo Kutaisi	a	2-4	Chomakhidze, Rusia
25/9	Lokomotivi Tbilisi	a	0-1	
1/10	Dila Gori	a	0-5	
14/10	Dinamo Batumi	h	2-1	Gadelia, Tsereteli (p)
22/10	Kolheti 1913 Poti	a	0-4	
30/10	Ameri Tbilisi	h	0-3	
5/11	Kakheti Telavi	a	2-0	Gadelia, Khachidze
13/11	FC Tbilisi	a	3-1	Jvania, Gadelia, Rusia
19/11	FC Zestafoni	h	0-1	
27/11	Dinamo Tbilisi	a	0-4	

2006
23/2	FC Tskhinvali	a	3-4	Gadelia 2, Gagua
4/3	WIT Georgia Tbilisi	h	0-1	

Georgia

11/3	FC Borjomi	a	0-3	
15/3	Spartaki Tbilisi	h	0-0	
25/3	Sioni Bolnisi	a	0-1	
29/3	Torpedo Kutaisi	h	0-3	
2/4	Lokomotivi Tbilisi	h	4-1	Nozadze, Gagua, Chanturia (p), Machaladze
5/4	Dila Gori	h	1-1	Nozadze
12/4	Dinamo Batumi	a	0-4	
15/4	Kolheti 1913 Poti	h	1-0	Nozadze
19/4	Ameri Tbilisi	a	0-1	
22/4	Kakheti Telavi	a	1-3	Skharulidze
29/4	FC Tbilisi	h	0-2	
6/5	FC Zestafoni	a	1-4	Kakhelashvili
9/5	Dinamo Tbilisi	h	1-6	Kakhelashvili

Name	Nat	Pos	Aps	(s)	Gls
Lasha AMBIDZE		D	9		
Gela BARTIA		M	9	(4)	
Irakli CHANTURIA		M	18	(8)	1
Gia CHKHAIDZE		D	13		
Lasha CHKHAIDZE		M	3	(2)	
Vaja CHKODZE		D	20	(2)	
Shota CHOMAKHIDZE		M	13	(1)	2
Shukri DONDOLADZE		M	4	(3)	
Lasha EGADZE		M	4	(7)	
Vladimir EKVANIA		M		(1)	
Teimuraz GADELIA		A	14		5
Mikheil GAGNIDZE		M		(2)	
Valerian GAGUA		A	18	(3)	2
Pavle GASVIANI		M	1		
Romeo GOGITADZE		D	4		
Giorgi GOROZIA		M		(1)	
Valter GUCHUA		D	2		
Giorgi GURGENIANI		M		(5)	
Giorgi JELADZE		M	1	(2)	
Zviad JELADZE		D	13		
Goga JVANIA		M	21		1
Kakhaber JINCHARADZE		G	1		
David KAKHELASHVILI		A	4	(4)	2
Merab KASHIBADZE		M		(1)	
Giorgi KHACHIDZE		M	20	(1)	1
Avtandil LABADZE		G	19	(1)	
Levan MACHALADZE		D	19	(1)	1
Gocha MAMPORIA		M	4	(9)	1
Irakli MCHEDLIDZE		M		(1)	
David MCHEDLISHVILI		M		(3)	
Giorgi MOLODINI		D	14		
Giorgi NADIRASHVILI		M	4		
Archil NOZADZE		M	12	(1)	3
Beka PARJIANI		M		(3)	
Mamuka RUSIA		A	13		4
Konstantine SEPIASHVILI		G	10	(1)	
Manuchar SHAMUGIA		M	3	(3)	
Besik SHENGELIA		M	1	(1)	
Lasha SILAGADZE		D	4	(4)	
Levan SILAGADZE		D	1		
Irakli SKHARULIDZE		M	14	(1)	1
Irakli TOLORDAVA		A		(1)	
Mamuka TSERETELI		D	9		1
Tengiz UGREKHELIDZE		M	11		

DINAMO TBILISI
Coach – Kakhaber Tskhadadze; (1/2/06) Andrei Chernyshov (RUS)

2005

30/7	Kakheti Telavi	a	3-1	Megreladze, Babunashvili, Makharadze
7/8	FC Tbilisi	h	1-0	Megreladze
20/8	FC Zestafoni	a	0-1	
28/8	Ameri Tbilisi	a	1-1	Iashvili
10/9	FC Tskhinvali	h	1-0	Megreladze
18/9	WIT Georgia Tbilisi	a	0-1	
24/9	FC Borjomi	h	1-2	Bobokhidze
2/10	Spartaki Tbilisi	a	3-0	Bobokhidze, Iashvili 2
16/10	Sioni Bolnisi	h	3-0	Iashvili, Megreladze, Melkadze
23/10	Torpedo Kutaisi	a	2-0	Megreladze, Chirikashvili
30/10	Lokomotivi Tbilisi	h	1-0	Iashvili
5/11	Dila Gori	a	2-0	Nozadze, Bobokhidze
13/11	Dinamo Batumi	h	3-1	Megreladze, Bobokhidze 2
19/11	Kolheti 1913 Poti	a	0-0	
27/11	Dinamo Sokhumi	h	4-0	Megreladze 2, Dvalishvili, Bobokhidze

2006

22/2	Kakheti Telavi	h	1-0	og (Kobaidze)
4/3	FC Tbilisi	a	3-2	Ambrósio 3
11/3	FC Zestafoni	h	2-2	Bobokhidze 2
15/3	Ameri Tbilisi	h	1-2	Iashvili (p)
25/3	FC Tskhinvali	a	2-0	Megreladze, Bobokhidze
29/3	WIT Georgia Tbilisi	h	0-0	
1/4	FC Borjomi	a	2-4	Megreladze 2 (1p)
5/4	Spartaki Tbilisi	h	3-0	Iashvili, Megreladze, Shashiashvili
12/4	Sioni Bolnisi	a	0-1	
15/4	Torpedo Kutaisi	h	2-1	Burduli, Dvali
19/4	Lokomotivi Tbilisi	a	3-0	Bobokhidze, Vatsadze, Burduli
22/4	Dila Gori	h	4-1	Burduli, Shashiashvili, Dvali 2
29/4	Dinamo Batumi	a	2-1	Megreladze 2
6/5	Kolheti 1913 Poti	h	5-0	Bobokhidze, Dvali 3, Kobakhidze
9/5	Dinamo Sokhumi	a	6-1	Dvali 4, Burduli, Daraselia

Name	Nat	Pos	Aps	(s)	Gls
Lado AKHALAIA		M	5	(2)	
Levan AKOBIA		D	10	(8)	
Kakhaber ALADASHVILI		M	11		
Aleksandre AMISULASHVILI		D	15		
Jucemar Luiz Domingos AMBRÓSIO	BRA	M	8	(2)	3
Shota BABUNASHVILI		M	6		1
Mikheil BOBOKHIDZE		A	17	(7)	11
Vladimer BURDULI		M	12		4
Giorgi CHELIDZE		M	2	(6)	
Irakli CHIRIKASHVILI		M	2	(8)	1
Vitali DARASELIA		M	10		1
Jaba DVALI		A	10	(2)	10
Vladimer DVALISHVILI		A	1	(4)	1
David GIGAURI		D	22	(2)	
Shota GRIGALASHVILI		M	3	(1)	
Soso GRISHIKASHVILI		G	13		
Sandro IASHVILI		A	11	(5)	7
Ilia KANDELAKI		D	3		
Revaz KEMOKLIDZE		D	11	(4)	
Sandro KOBAKHIDZE		M	8		1
Ucha LOBJANIDZE		D	2	(2)	
Giorgi LORIA		G		(1)	
Kakha MAKHARADZE		M	10	(4)	1
Giorgi MEGRELADZE		A	21	(1)	14
Levan MELKADZE		A	7	(5)	1
Giorgi MEREBASHVILI		M	11	(9)	
Giorgi NAVALOVSKI		M	12	(1)	
Lasha NOZADZE		M	28	(2)	1

Georgia

David ODIKADZE	M	4		
Sergo ORBELADZE	D	17	(1)	
Nikoloz PIRTSKHALAVA	D		(2)	
Archil SAKHVADZE	M	4		
Giorgi SHASHIASHVILI	D	13		2
Zviad STURUA	G	16		
Gulverd TOMASHVILI	D	2	(4)	
Mate VATSADZE	A		(4)	1
Galvan Gomes VIEIRA BRA	M	2	(1)	
Irakli ZOIDZE	G	1		

Rati IMERLISHVILI	D	9	(7)	1
Irakli IZORIA	M		(4)	
Giorgi KEVLISHVILI	M	24	(4)	
Koba KOBAIDZE	D	29		2
Vladimer KOBAKHIDZE	A	9	(3)	5
Vasil KUNCHULIA	M	3		
Merab KUPRASHVILI	M	16	(5)	1
Aleksandre KVIRKVELIA	D	8	(1)	
Zviad LABADZE	D	6		
Irakli MAGLAKELIDZE	D	13		
Konstantine METREVELI	A	2	(1)	
Gocha NADIRASHVILI	M	11		
Otar ROSTIASHVILI	M	11	(2)	1
Irakli SIKHARULIDZE	M	4	(2)	
Mikheil SOSELIA	A	20	(4)	5
Vepkhia TARUGASHVILI	D	25		
Luka TETIASHVILI	D	3	(16)	
Giorgi TSINADZE	G	13		
Dimitri TSISKARISHVILI	M		(1)	

KAKHETI TELAVI
Coach – Otar Korgalidze; (1/10/05) Jemal Makharashvili

2005

30/7	Dinamo Tbilisi	h	1-3	Kobaidze
6/8	FC Tskhinvali	a	1-0	Burduli
20/8	WIT Georgia Tbilisi	h	0-1	
28/8	FC Borjomi	a	1-2	Bedoidze
10/9	Spartaki Tbilisi	h	1-0	Burduli
17/9	Sioni Bolnisi	a	1-4	Davitashvili
25/9	Torpedo Kutaisi	h	1-0	Arudashvili (p)
2/10	Lokomotivi Tbilisi	a	0-3	
15/10	Dila Gori	h	3-0	Kobaidze, og (Khachapuridze), Arudashvili
22/10	Dinamo Batumi	a	0-1	
30/10	Kolheti 1913 Poti	h	3-2	Arudashvili, Soselia 2
5/11	Dinamo Sokhumi	a	0-2	
13/11	Ameri Tbilisi	h	1-2	Kuprashvili
19/11	FC Tbilisi	h	1-1	Soselia
27/11	FC Zestafoni	a	0-4	

2006

22/2	Dinamo Tbilisi	a	0-1	
4/3	FC Tskhinvali	h	4-0	og (Lomidze), Kobakhidze 2, Soselia
11/3	WIT Georgia Tbilisi	a	0-1	
15/3	FC Borjomi	h	1-0	Imerlishvili
25/3	Spartaki Tbilisi	a	0-0	
29/3	Sioni Bolnisi	h	1-2	Bidzinashvili
1/4	Torpedo Kutaisi	a	0-1	
5/4	Lokomotivi Tbilisi	h	4-3	Rostiashvili, Kobakhidze, Soselia (p), Davitashvili
12/4	Dila Gori	a	2-4	og (Maisuradze D.), Burduli
15/4	Dinamo Batumi	h	1-3	Kobakhidze
19/4	Kolheti 1913 Poti	a	2-2	Davitahsvili, Burduli
22/4	Dinamo Sokhumi	h	3-1	Davitashvili, Kobakhidze, Burduli
29/4	Ameri Tbilisi	a	0-0	
6/5	FC Tbilisi	a	0-3	
9/5	FC Zestafoni	h	1-0	og (Khidesheli)

Name	Nat	Pos	Aps	(s)	Gls
Valeri AMIRANIDZE		D	1	(6)	
Vasil ARUDASHVILI		M	14	(4)	3
David BEDOIDZE		M	21		1
Zakro BIDZINASHVILI		M		(6)	1
David BURDULI		M	24	(1)	5
Aleksi BURNADZE		M		(3)	
Beka BURNADZE		M	8	(4)	
Nikoloz DAVITASHVILI		A	23	(3)	4
Gela DZAMUNASHVILI		G	2		
Giorgi GAMBASHIDZE		M		(1)	
Nikoloz GELASHVILI		A	4		
Irakli GIORGOBIANI		M	11		
David GOGADZE		M	1		
Giga IASHVILI		G	15	(1)	

KOLKHETI 1913 POTI
Coach – Soso Pilia

2005

30/7	WIT Georgia Tbilisi	h	1-0	Kutateladze
6/8	FC Borjomi	a	0-1	
20/8	Spartaki Tbilisi	h	1-0	Kutateladze
28/8	Sioni Bolnisi	a	0-2	
10/9	Torpedo Kutaisi	h	1-0	Kutateladze
18/9	Lokomotivi Tbilisi	a	0-2	
25/9	Dila Gori	h	2-1	Kutateladze 2
1/10	Dinamo Batumi	a	0-2	
15/10	Ameri Tbilisi	h	0-1	
22/10	Dinamo Sokhumi	h	4-0	Krasovski, Kutateladze 2, Margalitadze
30/10	Kakheti Telavi	a	2-3	Krasovski, Janashia
5/11	FC Tbilisi	h	2-1	Shalamberidze (p), Krasovski
14/11	FC Zestafoni	a	0-3	
19/11	Dinamo Tbilisi	h	0-0	
26/11	FC Tskhinvali	a	3-1	Janashia, Kutidze, Tsikarishvili

2006

22/2	WIT Georgia Tbilisi	a	0-3	
4/3	FC Borjomi	h	0-0	
11/3	Spartaki Tbilisi	a	0-0	
15/3	Sioni Bolnisi	h	0-1	
25/3	Torpedo Kutaisi	a	0-0	
29/3	Lokomotivi Tbilisi	h	4-1	Margalitadze 2, Janashia, Kutetaladze
1/4	Dila Gori	a	0-1	
5/4	Dinamo Batumi	h	0-1	
12/4	Ameri Tbilisi	a	0-1	
15/4	Dinamo Sokhumi	a	0-1	
19/4	Kakheti Telavi	h	2-2	Krasovski, Tsikarishvili
22/4	FC Tbilisi	a	0-1	
29/4	FC Zestafoni	h	1-2	Janashia
6/5	Dinamo Tbilisi	a	0-5	
9/5	FC Tskhinvali	h	3-0	Tsikarishvili 2, Kutateladze (p)

Name	Nat	Pos	Aps	(s)	Gls
Giorgi ALASANIA		M	1		
Zurab BATIASHVILI		G	11		
Giorgi BERULAVA		M	1		
Gocha GOCHALEISHVILI		M	4	(6)	
Giorgi GOGENIA		D	2	(1)	

Georgia

Name	Pos	Aps	(s)	Gls
Nugzar GOGNADZE	M	1		
Iuri GVANIA	M		(1)	
Gela JAKHUA	M		(1)	
Zamir JANASHIA	A	22	(5)	4
David KAVTARADZE	M	1		
David KHARDZEISHVILI	G	4		
Giorgi KHIZANISHVILI	M		(1)	
Remi KHOPERIA	M		(1)	
Giorgi KILASONIA	D	21	(1)	
Mikheil KOBULADZE	D	10		
Giorgi KRASOVSKI	M	26	(1)	4
Tariel KURASHVILI	D	13	(7)	
Zviad KUTATELADZE	A	21	(4)	9
Ilo KUTIDZE	D	16		1
Levan LATARIA	G	15		
David LOLUA	M	6	(4)	
Edisher MARGALITADZE	A	27		3
David NARSIA	M	16	(2)	
Giorgi NODIA	M	1		
Teimuraz PARULAVA	D	25	(1)	
Zurab RAZMADZE	M	13	(3)	
Giorgi SAKHOKIA	D	2	(2)	
Demur SAMSEISHVILI	M	3	(4)	
Joni SHALAMBERIDZE	M	20		1
Mamuka SOLOMONIA	M		(1)	
Giorgi TKEBUCHAVA	M		(1)	
Amiran TSABRIA	M	3	(6)	
Tato TSEKVASHVILI	M	3	(5)	
Manuchar TSIKARISHVILI	M	12	(6)	4
Gela TSIKOLIA	M	1		
Kakha TURKIA	M	6		
Levan VARTAGAVA	M	23	(2)	

LOKOMOTIVI TBILISI
Coach – (25/1/06) Soso Siradze

2005
Date	Opponent	h/a	Score	Scorers
1/8	Sioni Bolnisi	h	1-1	Oniani R.
6/8	Torpedo Kutaisi	a	0-0	
20/8	Ameri Tbilisi	h	3-0	og (Nikuradze), Siradze, Kakhelishvili
29/8	Dila Gori	h	2-1	Kebadze, Siradze
10/9	Dinamo Batumi	a	1-0	Oniani R.
18/9	Kolheti 1913 Poti	h	2-0	Kakhelishvili 2
25/9	Dinamo Sokhumi	h	1-0	Alaverdishvili
2/10	Kakheti Telavi	h	3-0	Sirbiladze, De Anaía, og (Kevlishvili)
15/10	FC Tbilisi	a	2-0	Oniani G., Oniani R.
23/10	FC Zestafoni	h	0-0	
30/10	Dinamo Tbilisi	a	0-1	
5/11	FC Tskhinvali	h	3-0	Kebadze 2, Purtukhia
13/11	WIT Georgia Tbilisi	a	0-2	
19/11	FC Borjomi	h	2-1	Oniani R., Siradze
28/11	Spartaki Tbilisi	a	6-0	Sirbiladze, Siradze, og (Demetradze), Kebadze, De Anaía, Oniani R.

2006
Date	Opponent	h/a	Score	Scorers
22/2	Sioni Bolnisi	a	0-4	
4/3	Torpedo Kutaisi	h	2-3	Alaverdashvili, Ogbaidze
11/3	Ameri Tbilisi	a	1-4	Kakhelishvili
15/3	Dila Gori	a	0-0	
25/3	Dinamo Batumi	h	1-2	Alaverdashvili
29/3	Kolheti 1913 Poti	a	1-4	Chivadze (p)
2/4	Dinamo Sokhumi	a	1-4	Jgenti
5/4	Kakheti Telavi	a	3-4	Jgenti 2, Kipiani
12/4	FC Tbilisi	h	1-4	Menabde
15/4	FC Zestafoni	a	0-3	
19/4	Dinamo Tbilisi	h	0-3	
22/4	FC Tskhinvali	a	1-2	Jgenti
29/4	WIT Georgia Tbilisi	h	1-2	Chivadze
6/5	FC Borjomi	a	0-2	
9/5	Spartaki Tbilisi	h	3-1	Chivadze, Jgenti 2

Name	Nat	Pos	Aps	(s)	Gls
Giorgi ALAVERDASHVILI		A	12	(7)	3
Zurab AVALIANI		M	11	(1)	
Tornike BAKHTADZE		M	7	(2)	
Giorgi BARBAKADZE		M	7	(2)	
Giorgi BUDAGASHVILI		M		(1)	
Zviad CHALADZE		G	5		
Grigol CHANTURIA		G	14		
Giorgi CHIVADZE		A	10	(7)	3
Ramon DE ANAÍA	BRA	M	9	(9)	2
Nodar EBRALIDZE		D	9		
Vladimer GELASHVILI		D	1		
Giorgi GULORDAVA		D	10	(1)	
Islom INOMOV	UZB	M	14		
Mikheil JGENTI		A	14	(1)	6
Shota JISHKARIANI		M	1		
Giorgi KAKHELISHVILI		A	26	(1)	4
Lasha KEBADZE		M	15		4
Levan KENIA		A	2	(2)	
Irakli KHARADZE		M	1	(3)	
Lasha KHORGUASHVILI		D	3	(3)	
Giorgi KIPIANI		A	5	(7)	1
Giorgi KORIPADZE		M		(2)	
Levan LOMIDZE		G	8		
Mikheil MAKHVILADZE		D	15		
Giorgi MENABDE		M	1	(4)	1
Tornike METREVELI		M		(2)	
Giorgi MIKHAILIDI		D	3	(1)	
Archil NOZADZE		M	2	(1)	
Levan OGBAIDZE		M	11		1
Giorgi ONIANI		D	15		1
Roin ONIANI		M	10	(1)	5
Giorgi PANOV		M		(2)	
Artem PETROSIANI		D	9	(4)	
Dachi POPKHADZE		M	7	(4)	
Temur PURTUKHIA		M	9	(7)	1
Edik SAJAIA		D	13		
Giorgi SETURIDZE		D	14		
Beka SHEKRILADZE		G	1		
David SIRADZE		M	13		4
Irakli SIRBILADZE		A	8	(1)	2
Giorgi TAVBERIDZE		M	3	(1)	
Chichiko TUTBERIDZE		D	10		
Vladimer ZUKHBAIA		G	2		

SIONI BOLNISI
Coach – Khvicha Kasrashvili; (15/2/06) Kakhaber Tskhadadze

2005
Date	Opponent	h/a	Score	Scorers
1/8	Lokomotivi Tbilisi	a	1-1	Chikviladze
6/8	Dila Gori	h	2-0	Dvali 2 (1p)
20/8	Dinamo Batumi	a	1-0	Dolidze
28/8	Kolheti 1913 Poti	h	2-0	Dvali, Dolidze
9/9	Dinamo Sokhumi	a	2-1	Dvali, Mikuchadze
17/9	Kakheti Telavi	h	4-1	Dolidze, Bolkvadze, Mikuchadze 2
26/9	FC Tbilisi	a	2-1	Mikuchadze, Dvali
1/10	FC Zestafoni	h	1-0	Dolidze
16/10	Dinamo Tbilisi	a	0-3	
23/10	FC Tskhinvali	h	6-1	Dvali 2, Dolidze, Bolkvadze, Mikuchadze, Khmaladze

Georgia

Date	Opponent	H/A	Score	Scorers
30/10	WIT Georgia Tbilisi	a	1-2	Dvali (p)
5/11	FC Borjomi	h	1-0	Dvali
14/11	Spartaki Tbilisi	a	1-1	Dolidze
19/11	Ameri Tbilisi	a	1-0	Kutsurua
26/11	Torpedo Kutaisi	h	3-1	Bolkvadze (p), Dvali 2
2006				
22/2	Lokomotivi Tbilisi	h	4-0	Mikuchadze 2, Kvitaishvili, Khutsishvili
4/3	Dila Gori	a	2-0	Alavidze, Mikuchadze
11/3	Dinamo Batumi	h	2-2	Mikuchadze, Rakviashvili
15/3	Kolheti 1913 Poti	a	1-0	Khutsishvili
25/3	Dinamo Sokhumi	h	1-0	Mikuchadze
29/3	Kakheti Telavi	a	2-1	Khutsishvili, Alavidze
1/4	FC Tbilisi	h	1-0	Bajelidze
5/4	FC Zestafoni	a	0-0	
12/4	Dinamo Tbilisi	h	1-0	Mikuchadze
15/4	FC Tskhinvali	a	3-1	Mikuchadze, Kutsurua, Khmaladze
19/4	WIT Georgia Tbilisi	h	1-0	Mikuchadze
22/4	FC Borjomi	a	0-1	
29/4	Spartaki Tbilisi	h	4-0	Mikuchadze (p), Chichveishvili, Kvitaishvili, Kardava
6/5	Ameri Tbilisi	h	3-0	Khutsishvili, Mikuchadze 2 (2p)
9/5	Torpedo Kutaisi	a	4-0	Mikuchadze 3, Alavidze

Name	Nat	Pos	Aps	(s)	Gls
Archil ALAVIDZE		M	12	(4)	3
Zurab AVALIANI		M		(5)	
Levan BAJELIDZE		M	9	(7)	1
Zurab BATIASHVILI		G	12		
Mindia BOBGIASHVILI		G	17		
David BOLKVADZE		M	15		3
Levan CHACHUA		D	1	(4)	
Lasha CHELIDZE		D	13		
David CHICHVEISHVILI		D	13	(1)	1
Tengiz CHIKVILADZE		D	11		1
Grigol DOLIDZE		M	14		6
Jaba DVALI		A	15		11
Nikoloz GAVASHELI		G	1		
Oleksandr GUBRIENKO	UKR	M	6	(3)	
Besik KARDAVA		A		(13)	1
Levan KHMALADZE		M	28		2
Mikheil KHUTSISHVILI		A	11	(3)	4
Mikheil KOBAURI		D	21	(5)	
Mikheil KORSANTIA		M		(1)	
Giorgi KUTSURUA		M	12	(6)	2
Giorgi KVITAISHVILI		M	13	(10)	2
Eugene LASHYUK	UKR	M		(1)	
Levan MEREBASHVILI		D	7		
Akaki MIKUCHADZE		A	27	(1)	19
Giorgi OKROPIRIDZE		M	2	(10)	
Temur RAKVIASHVILI		D	23		1
Irakli SIRBILADZE		A	5	(2)	
David SVANIDZE		D	25	(4)	
Tornike TABATADZE		M		(2)	
Beglar TEDORADZE		D	6	(1)	
Vladimer UGREKHELIDZE		M	11	(3)	

SPARTAKI TBILISI
Coach – Gigla Imnadze; (17/1/06) Jumber Abashidze

Date	Opponent	H/A	Score	Scorers
2005				
30/7	Dila Gori	a	0-1	
6/8	Dinamo Batumi	h	0-0	
20/8	Kolheti 1913 Poti	a	0-1	
27/8	Dinamo Sokhumi	h	0-1	
10/9	Kakheti Telavi	a	0-1	
20/9	FC Tbilisi	h	1-0	Jangidze
25/9	FC Zestafoni	a	0-1	
2/10	Dinamo Tbilisi	h	0-3	
15/10	FC Tskhinvali	a	0-2	
23/10	WIT Georgia Tbilisi	h	1-4	Mchedlishvili
30/10	FC Borjomi	a	0-5	
5/11	Ameri Tbilisi	a	0-1	
14/11	Sioni Bolnisi	h	1-1	Malichava
19/11	Torpedo Kutaisi	a	0-1	
28/11	Lokomotivi Tbilisi	h	0-6	
2006				
23/2	Dila Gori	h	1-0	Khubua
4/3	Dinamo Batumi	a	0-5	
11/3	Kolheti 1913 Poti	h	0-0	
15/3	Dinamo Sokhumi	a	0-0	
25/3	Kakheti Telavi	h	0-0	
29/3	FC Tbilisi	a	0-1	
1/4	FC Zestafoni	h	1-3	Maglaperidze
5/4	Dinamo Tbilisi	a	0-3	
12/4	FC Tskhinvali	h	1-3	Jangidze
15/4	WIT Georgia Tbilisi	a	0-2	
19/4	FC Borjomi	h	3-2	Okroshiashvili 2, Mushkudiani
22/4	Ameri Tbilisi	h	1-1	Okroshiashvili
29/4	Sioni Bolnisi	a	0-4	
6/5	Torpedo Kutaisi	h	1-2	Shalamberidze
9/5	Lokomotivi Tbilisi	a	1-3	Gagnidze (p)

Name	Nat	Pos	Aps	(s)	Gls
Giorgi CHANTLADZE		D	4	(9)	
Archil DANELIA		M	2	(11)	
Tornike DEMETRADZE		M	7	(2)	
Akaki DEVADZE		G	5		
Shukri DONDOLADZE		D	1	(4)	
Tornike ELIZBARASHVILI		D	17	(1)	
Giorgi GABELIA		G		(1)	
Aleksandre GADZADZE		G	6	(2)	
Otar GAGNIDZE		M	9	(1)	1
Vasil GUCHASHVILI		A	9	(1)	
Aleksandre IMNAISHVILI		D	22		
Amiran JANELIDZE		M	1	(1)	
Lasha JANGIDZE		M	23		2
Irakli JIBLADZE		M	14		
Lasha JORBENADZE		D	2		
Levan KBILTSETSKHLASHVILI		M	1		
Abesalom KHARAISHVILI		D	1	(2)	
Gela KHUBUA		M	23		1
Koba KOBALADZE		M	6	(10)	
David KOKIASHVILI		M	4		
Mikheil KOTRIKADZE		M	11	(2)	
Vasil LIPARTELIANI		M	2		
Mikheil LOBJANIDZE		M	6	(2)	
David MAGLAPERIDZE		A	13	(8)	1
David MAISASHVILI		M	12	(1)	
Temur MALANIA		M	1		
Irakli MALICHAVA		M	16	(4)	1
Teimuraz MCHEDLISHVILI		M	26		1
Ilia MODEBADZE		D	9	(3)	
Zurab MUSHKUDIANI		A	2	(2)	1
David NAPETVARIDZE		G	19		
Koba NAZGAIDZE		D	1		
Givi OKROSHIASHVILI		A	9		3
Data PIPIA		D	1		
Paata RATIA		M		(2)	

Georgia

Onise RIJAMADZE		D	1		
Koba SHALAMBERIDZE		M	5	(1)	1
Rati TABIDZE		D	17	(1)	
Giga TABUTSADZE		D	8	(2)	
Mikheil TOPURIA		M		(2)	
Soso URUSHADZE		M	13	(7)	
Lasha VASHAKIDZE		M	1		

FC TBILISI
Coach – Giorgi Devdariani; (13/3/06) Tengiz Katsia; (27/3/06) Gocha Tkebuchava

2005
Date	Opponent	H/A	Score	Scorers
31/7	FC Zestafoni	h	0-1	
7/8	Dinamo Tbilisi	a	0-1	
21/8	FC Tskhinvali	h	0-2	
28/8	WIT Georgia Tbilisi	a	1-2	Topuria
11/9	FC Borjomi	h	0-5	
20/9	Spartaki Tbilisi	a	0-1	
26/9	Sioni Bolnisi	h	1-2	Kvaskhvadze
1/10	Torpedo Kutaisi	a	0-1	
15/10	Lokomotivi Tbilisi	h	0-2	
22/10	Dila Gori	a	0-3	
31/10	Dinamo Batumi	h	1-3	Kvaskhvadze
5/11	Kolheti 1913 Poti	a	1-2	Popkhadze (p)
13/11	Dinamo Sokhumi	h	4-3	Kvaskhvadze, Liluashvili 2, Topuria
19/11	Kakheti Telavi	a	1-1	Liluashvili
26/11	Ameri Tbilisi	h	0-0	

2006
Date	Opponent	H/A	Score	Scorers
22/2	FC Zestafoni	a	1-2	Kvaratskhelia V.
4/3	Dinamo Tbilisi	h	2-3	Kvaratskhelia V., Beridze
11/3	FC Tskhinvali	a	0-3	
15/3	WIT Georgia Tbilisi	h	0-1	
25/3	FC Borjomi	a	0-2	
29/3	Spartaki Tbilisi	h	1-0	Sakhvadze
1/4	Sioni Bolnisi	a	0-1	
5/4	Torpedo Kutaisi	h	2-1	Barabadze R., og (Beruashvili)
12/4	Lokomotivi Tbilisi	a	4-1	Barabadze R. 3, Zirakishvili
15/4	Dila Gori	h	2-0	Kvaratskhelia L. 2
19/4	Dinamo Batumi	a	0-1	
22/4	Kolheti 1913 Poti	h	1-0	Khojava
29/4	Dinamo Sokhumi	a	2-0	Miminoshvili, Barabadze R.
6/5	Kakheti Telavi	h	3-0	Barabadze R., Burnadze, Kvaratskhelia V.
9/5	Ameri Tbilisi	a	2-0	Sakhvadze, Burnadze

Name	Nat	Pos	Aps	(s)	Gls
Mikheil ALAVIDZE		G	17		
Tornike APTSIAURI		M	8		
Mikheil BARABADZE		M	5	(3)	
Revaz BARABADZE		A	14	(4)	6
Teimuraz BARAMIDZE		M	10	(5)	
Giorgi BENDELIANI		A	1		
Giorgi BERIDZE		D	12	(6)	1
Mikheil BESARASHVILI		M	10		
Gaga BOCHOIDZE		D	13		
Avtandil BUCHASHVILI		M		(1)	
Murtaz BURNADZE		M	2	(4)	2
Levan CHAGELISHVILI		D	2		
Gedevan DARASELIA		M	8	(1)	
Giorgi DARSADZE		M	4	(1)	
Shalva GODERDZISHVILI		M		(1)	
Nukri GOGOKHIA		M	6	(4)	
Nika GUSHARASHVILI		D	13		
Giorgi IASHVILI		M	3	(2)	
Irakli JGENTI		D	1	(2)	
Murtaz KAKABADZE		M	4	(3)	
Besik KHACHIPERADZE		M	6		
Gocha KHOJAVA		M	8	(1)	1
Leri KHOKHONISHVILI		D	21	(4)	
Mikheil KHUTSISHVILI		M		(2)	
Vaja KORIDZE		D	12	(3)	
Mikheil KOSTAVA		M		(2)	
Levan KVARATSKHELIA		A	11	(2)	2
Vakhtang KVARATSKHELIA		A	9	(8)	3
Nika KVASKHVADZE		M	12	(6)	4
Irakli LILUASHVILI		M	5	(1)	3
Jaba LIPARTIA		M	1	(1)	
Giorgi LOLADZE		D	3	(1)	
Nodar MACHAVARIANI		D	1		
Dimitri MAKASHVILI		M		(1)	
Giorgi MAMNIASHVILI		M	2	(1)	
Besik MIKIASHVILI		D	15		
Lasha MIMINOSHVILI		D	24	(2)	1
Ilia MODEBADZE		M	2		
Zurab MUSHKUDIANI		A	1	(1)	
Gogi J. PIPIA		M	1	(1)	
Gogi K. PIPIA		A	3		
Irakli PIRANISHVILI		M		(4)	
Giorgi POPKHADZE		D	12		2
Giorgi ROSTOMASHVILI		M	5	(3)	
Archil SAKHVADZE		M	9		2
Beka SHEKRILADZE		G	1		
Giorgi SOMKHISHVILI		G	4		
Revaz TEVDORADZE		G	8		
Mikheil TOPURIA		M	9	(1)	2
Mikheil TSNOBILADZE		M	1		
Irakli VASHAKIDZE		D	6		
Robert ZIRAKISHVILI		A	5	(2)	1

TORPEDO KUTAISI
Coach – Revaz Burkadze; (8/2/06) Mikheil Kvernadze

2005
Date	Opponent	H/A	Score	Scorers
1/8	Ameri Tbilisi	h	0-1	
6/8	Lokomotivi Tbilisi	h	0-0	
20/8	Dila Gori	a	0-2	
28/8	Dinamo Batumi	h	0-1	
10/9	Kolheti 1913 Poti	a	0-1	
17/9	Dinamo Sokhumi	h	4-2	Barabadze, Mdivnishvili, Dzodzuashvili, Svanidze
25/9	Kakheti Telavi	a	0-1	
1/10	FC Tbilisi	h	1-0	Dzodzuashvili
15/10	FC Zestafoni	a	1-1	Janashia
23/10	Dinamo Tbilisi	h	0-2	
30/10	FC Tskhinvali	a	0-0	
5/11	WIT Georgia Tbilisi	h	2-2	Popkhadze, Shalamberidze
13/11	FC Borjomi	a	0-1	
19/11	Spartaki Tbilisi	h	1-0	Janashia (p)
26/11	Sioni Bolnisi	a	1-3	Gongadze

2006
Date	Opponent	H/A	Score	Scorers
22/2	Ameri Tbilisi	a	1-5	Janashia (p)
4/3	Lokomotivi Tbilisi	a	3-2	Gongadze 2, Kvernadze R. (p)
11/3	Dila Gori	h	0-0	
15/3	Dinamo Batumi	a	0-2	
25/3	Kolheti 1913 Poti	h	0-0	
29/3	Dinamo Sokhumi	a	3-0	Dogonadze, Gamezardashvili, Dzodzuashvili
1/4	Kakheti Telavi	h	1-0	Kvernadze R.
5/4	FC Tbilisi	a	1-2	Korgalidze

Georgia

Date	Opponent	H/A	Score	Scorers
12/4	FC Zestafoni	h	2-3	Gamezardashvili (p), Dogonadze
15/4	Dinamo Tbilisi	a	1-2	Guruli
19/4	FC Tskhinvali	h	4-1	Korgalidze, Kipiani
22/4	WIT Georgia Tbilisi	a	0-1	
29/4	FC Borjomi	h	0-2	
6/5	Spartaki Tbilisi	a	2-1	Kipiani, Kvernadze R.
9/5	Sioni Bolnisi	h	0-4	

Name	Nat	Pos	Aps	(s)	Gls
Rati BARABADZE		D	16		1
Levan BERUASHVILI		D	11		
David BUKHRASHVILI		M		(1)	
Giga BURJANADZE		D	5	(7)	
David CHIGVINIDZE		A	1	(3)	
Zviad CHKHETIANI		M	24		
Sergo CHURADZE		G	11		
Konstantine DARSANIA		M	4	(4)	
Mikheil DATIASHVILI		M	1		
Armaz DOGONADZE		M	20	(3)	2
Merab DZODZUASHVILI		A	12	(5)	3
Kakha EBRALIDZE		D	7	(1)	
David GAMEZARDASHVILI		D	11		2
Mamuka GONGADZE		M	18	(8)	4
Giorgi GORGODZE		M	2	(4)	
Giorgi GURULI		M	5	(2)	1
Biktor GVETADZE		M		(1)	
David JANASHIA		A	12		3
Giorgi JASHI		D	1	(2)	
Beka KAVTELADZE		D	1	(2)	
Giorgi KETASHVILI		M		(1)	
Giorgi KIPIANI		M	9	(2)	2
David KHURTSILAVA		M	15	(5)	
Irakli KOBAKHIDZE		D	1	(3)	
Levan KORGALIDZE		M	10		2
Shota KURTSIKIDZE		A	2	(1)	
Akaki KVERNADZE		D	8	(2)	
Revaz KVERNADZE		A	14		4
Kakha KVETENADZE		M	2		
Aleksandre LAGADZE		M	16	(6)	
Irakli MAGLAKELIDZE		D	13		
Levan MDIVNISHVILI		M	5	(7)	1
Omar MIGINEISHVILI		G	8		
Nikoloz NADIRADZE		M	2	(1)	
David ONIANI		M	1		
Giga ORMOTSADZE		D	5	(1)	
Dimitri PARAMONOV		M	7	(1)	
Avtandil POPKHADZE		M	15	(2)	1
Nukri REVISHVILI		G	11		
Koba SHALAMBERIDZE		M	9	(5)	1
Giorgi SHENGELIA		A	1	(2)	
Giorgi SULABERIDZE		M	2		
Kakhaber SVANIDZE		M	7		1
Mikheil TEKHOV		M	5	(4)	

FC TSKHINVALI
Coach – Zurab Maisuradze; (15/8/05) Ivane Takadze

2005

Date	Opponent	H/A	Score	Scorers
30/7	Dinamo Sokhumi	a	2-0	Chitaia B., Bakarandze (p)
6/8	Kakheti Telavi	h	0-1	
21/8	FC Tbilisi	a	2-0	Chitaia B., Maisuradze G.
27/8	FC Zestafoni	h	0-2	
10/9	Dinamo Tbilisi	a	0-1	
17/9	Ameri Tbilisi	a	0-1	
25/9	WIT Georgia Tbilisi	h	0-3	
1/10	FC Borjomi	a	0-4	
15/10	Spartaki Tbilisi	h	2-0	Bakarandze, Chitaia B.
23/10	Sioni Bolnisi	a	1-6	Datvadze
30/10	Torpedo Kutaisi	h	0-0	
5/11	Lokomotivi Tbilisi	a	0-3	
13/11	Dila Gori	h	2-2	Bakarandze, Maisuradze D. (p)
19/11	Dinamo Batumi	a	0-0	
26/11	Kolheti 1913 Poti	h	1-3	Datvadze

2006

Date	Opponent	H/A	Score	Scorers
23/2	Dinamo Sokhumi	h	4-3	Sultanishvili 3, Chitaia B.
4/3	Kakheti Telavi	a	0-4	
11/3	FC Tbilisi	h	3-0	Khanishvili K., Chitaia B., Sultanishvili
15/3	FC Zestafoni	a	1-3	Datvadze
25/3	Dinamo Tbilisi	h	0-2	
29/3	Ameri Tbilisi	h	1-0	Chitaia B.
1/4	WIT Georgia Tbilisi	a	0-3	
5/4	FC Borjomi	h	1-2	Sultanishvili (p)
12/4	Spartaki Tbilisi	a	3-1	Khanishvili K., Datvadze, Sultanishvili
15/4	Sioni Bolnisi	h	1-3	Maisuradze G. (p)
19/4	Torpedo Kutaisi	a	1-4	Khanishvili K.
22/4	Lokomotivi Tbilisi	h	2-1	Datvadze, Chitaia B.
29/4	Dila Gori	a	2-4	Bolotashvili, Khanishvili D.
6/5	Dinamo Batumi	h	1-2	Sultanishvili (p)
9/5	Kolheti 1913 Poti	a	0-3	

Name	Nat	Pos	Aps	(s)	Gls
Giorgi AKHALKATSI		M	2	(5)	
Vakhtang AKOPIAN		D	1	(1)	
Paata BAKARANDZE		A	14	(1)	3
Otar BOBOKHIDZE		G	3		
David BOLOTASHVILI		M	2	(6)	1
David CHIGVINIDZE		A	4	(1)	
Beka CHITAIA		A	26		7
Giorgi CHITAIA		D	14	(2)	
David DATVADZE		M	20	(2)	5
Elguja DVALI		M	3	(2)	
David EJOSHVILI		M	19	(2)	
Nika GABLAIA		A	1	(1)	
Paata GAMTSEMLIDZE		M	13	(1)	
Giorgi KAIDARASHVILI		D		(2)	
Ushangi KARELI		M	1		
Givi KARKUZASHVILI		D	13		
Sergo KESANASHVILI		G	2		
Revaz KHACHAPUDZE		D	9		
Emzar KHACHATURIAN		M	1	(1)	
David KHANISHVILI		M	13	(4)	1
Koba KHANISHVILI		M	13		3
David KHOKHOBASHVILI		D	3	(5)	
Zaza KOBESASHVILI		D	14		
Giorgi LOMIDZE		D	28	(1)	
David MAISURADZE		M	13		1
Giorgi MAISURADZE		M	9	(7)	2
Glaktion MDZINARISHVILI		M	3	(10)	
Mikheil MOSIASHVILI		M	14		
Nodar NOZADZE		A	12	(8)	
Mikheil PERSAEV		D	10	(4)	
David RAJAMASHVILI		M		(1)	
Gizo SHENGELIA		G	17	(1)	
Ramaz SOGOLASHVILI		G	8		
Saba SULTANISHVILI		A	11	(1)	7
Ivane TAKADZE		M	2	(5)	
Mikheil TAKADZE		M	12		
Omar TSARITSASHVILI		M		(2)	
Beka ZEDGENIDZE		M		(1)	

Georgia

WIT GEORGIA TBILISI
Coach – Nestor Mumladze

2005

Date	Opponent	H/A	Score	Scorers
30/7	Kolheti 1913 Poti	a	0-1	
6/8	Dinamo Sokhumi	h	2-2	Martsvaladze 2 (1p)
20/8	Kakheti Telavi	a	1-0	Imedashvili
28/8	FC Tbilisi	h	2-1	Datunaishvili P, Peikrishvili
18/9	Dinamo Tbilisi	h	1-0	Martsvaladze
25/9	FC Tskhinvali	a	3-0	Imedashvili, Sakhokia, Martsvaladze
30/9	Ameri Tbilisi	a	2-1	Gelashvili 2
15/10	FC Borjomi	h	4-0	Peikrishvili, Kobiashvili, Martsvaladze, Mantskava
19/10	FC Zestafoni	a	4-0	Peikrishvili, Martsvaladze 3
23/10	Spartaki Tbilisi	a	4-1	Imedashvili, Sakhokia, Martsvaladze 2
30/10	Sioni Bolnisi	h	2-1	Martsvaladze, Gelashvili
5/11	Torpedo Kutaisi	a	2-2	Datunaishvili G., Digmelashvili (p)
13/11	Lokomotivi Tbilisi	h	2-0	Gelashvili, Martsvaladze
19/11	Dila Gori	a	3-1	Martsvaladze 2, Datunaishvili G.
26/11	Dinamo Batumi	h	0-0	

2006

Date	Opponent	H/A	Score	Scorers
22/2	Kolheti 1913 Poti	h	3-0	Digmelashvili, Imedashvili, Kvakhadze
4/3	Dinamo Sokhumi	a	1-0	Peikrishvili
11/3	Kakheti Telavi	h	1-0	Digmelashvili (p)
15/3	FC Tbilisi	a	1-0	Digmelashvili
25/3	FC Zestafoni	h	1-2	Imedashvili
29/3	Dinamo Tbilisi	a	0-0	
1/4	FC Tskhinvali	h	3-0	Datunaishvili G., Peikrishvili, Sakhokia
5/4	Ameri Tbilisi	h	3-1	Imedashvili 2, Datunaishvili G.
12/4	FC Borjomi	a	0-1	
15/4	Spartaki Tbilisi	h	2-0	Gelashvili, Imedashvili
19/4	Sioni Bolnisi	a	0-1	
22/4	Torpedo Kutaisi	h	1-0	Imedashvili
29/4	Lokomotivi Tbilisi	a	2-1	Gelashvili 2
6/5	Dila Gori	h	2-0	Peikrishvili (p), Guchashvili
9/5	Dinamo Batumi	a	1-1	Imedashvili

Name	Nat	Pos	Aps	(s)	Gls
David ABSHILAVA		D	9	(1)	
Grigol BEDIASHVILI		G	19		
Giorgi BERIASHVILI		A	3	(10)	
Giorgi DATUNAISHVILI		M	26	(2)	4
Pavle DATUNAISHVILI		D	22		1
David DIGMELASHVILI		M	29		4
Irakli EBANOIDZE		A	1	(4)	
Nikoloz GELASHVILI		A	19	(2)	7
Vasil GUCHASHVILI		M	10	(4)	1
Oleg SVELESIANI		D	23	(4)	
David IMEDASHVILI		M	22		10
Lasha JAPARIDZE		D	6	(3)	
Irakli KLIMIASHVILI		M		(1)	
Vladimer KOBAKHIDZE		M	1	(1)	
Tengiz KOBIASHVILI		D	16		1
Akaki KUKHILAVA		D	6	(1)	
Giorgi KVAGINIDZE		M		(3)	
Aleksandre KVAKHADZE		D	12	(3)	1
Levan KVARATSKHELIA		M		(2)	
David LOMAIA		D	24	(3)	
Lasha MANTSKAVA		D	1	(4)	1
Otar MARTSVALADZE		A	14		14
Giorgi MELKADZE		M	2	(11)	
Ardalion MIKABERIDZE		G	11		
Giorgi PEIKRISHVILI		M	24	(3)	6
Luka RAZMADZE		M	9	(11)	
Zaza SAKHOKIA		A	20	(6)	3
Radion TSKHOMARIA		D	1	(3)	
Revaz TSULADZE		M		(1)	

FC ZESTAFONI
Coach – Temur Makharadze; (15/10/05) Koba Jorjikashvili; (19/11/05) Temur Makharadze; (1/4/06) Koba Jorjikashvili

2005

Date	Opponent	H/A	Score	Scorers
31/7	FC Tbilisi	a	1-0	Kvernadze
7/8	Ameri Tbilisi	a	0-2	
20/8	Dinamo Tbilisi	h	1-0	Nuoni
27/8	FC Tskhinvali	a	2-0	Gongadze, Imedadze
20/9	FC Borjomi	a	0-1	
25/9	Spartaki Tbilisi	h	1-0	Khidesheli
1/10	Sioni Bolnisi	a	0-1	
15/10	Torpedo Kutaisi	h	1-1	Ionanidze (p)
19/10	WIT Georgia Tbilisi	h	0-4	
23/10	Lokomotivi Tbilisi	a	0-0	
30/10	Dila Gori	h	2-0	Imedadze, og (Karkuzashvili)
5/11	Dinamo Batumi	a	2-2	Imedadze, Ionanidze
14/11	Kolheti 1913 Poti	h	3-0	Ionanidze 2, Imedadze
19/11	Dinamo Sokhumi	a	1-0	Ionanidze (p)
27/11	Kakheti Telavi	h	4-0	Ionanidze 2 (1p), Gotsiridze, Gongadze

2006

Date	Opponent	H/A	Score	Scorers
22/2	FC Tbilisi	h	2-1	Ionanidze, Chelidze
4/3	Ameri Tbilisi	h	1-0	Gongadze
11/3	Dinamo Tbilisi	a	2-2	Ionanidze 2
15/3	FC Tskhinvali	h	3-1	Imedadze, Pipia 2
25/3	WIT Georgia Tbilisi	a	2-1	Pipia, Ionanidze (p)
29/3	FC Borjomi	h	0-0	
_	Spartaki Tbilisi	a	3-1	Imedadze 2, Ganugrava
5/4	Sioni Bolnisi	h	0-0	
12/4	Torpedo Kutaisi	a	3-2	Ionanidze, og (Gamezardashvili), Gotsiridze
15/4	Lokomotivi Tbilisi	h	3-0	Imedadze, Ionanidze 2
19/4	Dila Gori	a	1-0	Imedadze
22/4	Dinamo Batumi	h	0-0	
29/4	Kolheti 1913 Poti	a	2-1	Ionanidze 2 (1p)
6/5	Dinamo Sokhumi	h	4-1	og (Machaladze), Turmanidze, Ionanidze, Chelidze
9/5	Kakheti Telavi	a	0-1	

Name	Nat	Pos	Aps	(s)	Gls
Aleksi BENASHVILI		D	2	(9)	
Mikheil BESARASHVILI		M	6	(4)	
Mirza BJALAVA		D	5	(1)	
Grigol CHANTURIA		G	13		
Giorgi CHELIDZE		M	12	(2)	2
Kakhaber CHKHETIANI		M	28		
Murtaz DAUSHVILI		M		(2)	
Zurab DZAMSASHVILI		D	24		
Irakli DZARIA		A	1	(4)	
Giorgi GANUGRAVA		M	21	(5)	1
Giorgi GAVASHELISHVILI		D	1	(2)	
Boris GELACHEISHVILI		M		(2)	
Shalva GONGADZE		D	27		3
Tornike GORGIASHVILI		M	1		

Georgia

Beka GOTSIRIDZE		A	15	(7)	2
Grigol IMEDADZE		A	19	(7)	9
Zurab IONANIDZE		A	23	(4)	17
Giorgi IVANISHVILI		M		(2)	
David JANELIDZE		M		(2)	
Giorgi KHIDESHELI		D	14		1
Giorgi KHUMARASHVILI		D	1		
Zurab KVACHAKHIA		G	15		
Roin KVASKHVADZE		G	2	(1)	
Revaz KVERNADZE		M	1	(5)	1
Beka NOZADZE		M	17	(7)	
Sergei NUONI	MOL	M	13	(9)	1
Dimitri PARAMONOV		M	1		
Paata PEZUASHVILI		D	1		
Gogi PIPIA		A	19	(5)	3
Amiran SANAIA		M	1		
Gocha SULAKADZE		M	3	(2)	
Tornike TARKHNISHVILI		M	1		
Sevasti TODUA		D	20	(1)	
Giorgi TURMANIDZE		M	23	(2)	1

DOMESTIC CUP 2005/06

1/16 FINALS
(23/8/05 & 4/9/05)
Dila Gori v Meskheti Akhaltsikhe 3-3; 0-1 *(3-4)*
FC Zestafoni v FC Zugdidi 3-0; 4-0 *(7-0)*
Dinamo Sokhumi v FC Sagarejo 1-1; 1-1 *(2-2; Dinamo Sokhumi 3-0 on pens)*
FC Borjomi v Merani Tbilisi 2-0; 2-1 *(4-1)*
(24/8/05 & 5/9/05)
Ameri Tbilisi v Meshakre Agara 1-2; 4-1 *(5-3)*
Dinamo Batumi v Guria Lanchkhuti 3-0; 3-1 *(6-1)*
Sioni Bolnisi v Liakhvi Tamarasheni 6-1; 2-1 *(8-2)*
Kolkheti 1913 Poti v Magaroeli Chiatura 6-0; 2-0 *(8-0)*
Spartaki Tbilisi v Samgori Gardabani 3-1; 3-2 *(6-3)*
Kakheti Telavi v Chikhura Sachkhere 0-3; 1-3 *(1-6)*
FC Tbilisi v FC Rustavi 3-1; 0-1 *(3-2)*
FC Tkshinvali v FC Gagra 4-4; 3-3 *(7-7; FC Gagra on away goals)*

1/8 FINALS
(8/11/05 & 22/11/05)
Ameri Tbilisi v FC Gagra 4-1; 0-0 *(4-1)*
FC Borjomi v Dinamo Sokhumi 2-0; 2-1 *(4-1)*
Dinamo Tbilisi v Chikhura Sachkere 0-0; 2-0 *(2-0)*
Spartaki Tbilisi v FC Zestafoni 0-4; 1-3 *(1-7)*
Sioni Bolnisi v Meskheti Akhaltsikhe 2-0; 1-1 *(3-1)*
Dinamo Batumi v Kolkheti 1913 Poti 0-2; 0-1 *(0-3)*
WIT Georgia Tbilisi v Torpedo Kutaisi 1-0; 5-0 *(6-0)*
Lokomotivi Tbilisi v FC Tbilisi 1-0; 1-0 *(2-0)*

QUARTER-FINALS
(18/2/06 & 7/3/06)
Sioni Bolnisi 1 *(Alavidze 90)*, FC Borjomi 0
FC Borjomi 0, Sioni Bolnisi 1 *(Bajelidze 29)*
(Sioni Bolnisi 2-0)

WIT Georgia Tbilisi 3 *(Imedashvili 18, Gelashvili 51, Beriashvili 68)*, Lokomotivi Tbilisi 1 *(Jgenti 9)*
Lokomotivi Tbilisi 0, WIT Georgia Tbilisi 1 *(Imedashvili 3)*
(WIT Georgia Tbilisi 4-1)

Ameri Tbilisi 0, Kolkheti 1913 Poti 0
Kolkheti 1913 Poti 0, Ameri Tbilisi 1 *(Chikviladze 36)*
(Ameri Tbilisi 1-0)

(7/3/06 & 18/3/06)
FC Zestafoni 1 *(Ionanidze 73)*, Dinamo Tbilisi 0
Dinamo Tbilisi 0, FC Zestafoni 0
(FC Zestafoni 1-0)

SEMI-FINALS
(8/4/06 & 2/5/06)
WIT Georgia Tbilisi 1 *(Kvakhadze 18)*, FC Zestafoni 2 *(Dzamsashvili 45, Gotsiridze 88)*
FC Zestafoni 3 *(Ionanidze 21p, Benashvili 63, Gongadze 73)*, WIT Georgia Tbilisi 1 *(Gelashvili 7)*
(FC Zestafoni 5-2)

Sioni Bolnisi 0, Ameri Tbilisi 0
Ameri Tbilisi 1 *(Sevastopulo 68)*, Sioni Bolnisi 0
(Ameri Tbilisi 1-0)

FINAL
(13/5/06)
M. Meskhi stadium, Tbilisi
AMERI TBILISI 2 *(Davitashvili 10, Tsinamdzgvrishvili 50)*
FC ZESTAFONI 2 *(Ionanidze 29, Gongadze 90)*
(aet; 4-3 on pens)
AMERI TBILISI – Kvachakhia, Kedelashvili, Elbakidze, Davitnidze, Khvadagiani, Bolkvadze, Dekanosidze, Dobrovolski, Sevastopulo (Dolidze 60), Davitashvili *(Kvakhadze 78)*, Tsinamdzgvrishvili (Tatanashvili 73).
FC ZESTAFONI – Chanturia, Turmanidze, Gongadze, Todua, Bjalava (Nudni 62), Chkhetiani, Benashvili (Imedadze 74), Ganugrava, Nozadze (Chelidze 69), Pipia, Ionanidze.

SECOND LEVEL FINAL TABLE 2005/06

		Pld	W	D	L	F	A	Pts
1	Chikhura Sachkhere	34	24	6	4	87	34	78
2	Merani Tbilisi	34	23	5	6	59	27	74
3	FC Gagra	34	19	11	4	49	22	68
4	Dinamo 2 Tbilisi	34	18	8	8	57	27	62
5	Meshkare Agara	34	18	8	8	57	27	62
6	Meskheti Akhaltsikhe	34	17	6	11	50	30	57
7	Ameri 2 Tbilisi	34	14	9	11	40	29	51
8	FC Rustavi	34	13	10	11	50	37	49
9	Guria Lanchkhuti	34	14	5	15	50	47	47
10	WIT Georgia Tbilisi	34	13	6	15	43	45	45
11	FC Tbilisi 2	34	12	8	14	34	40	44
12	FC Zugdidi	34	12	7	15	24	33	43
13	Meshakhte Tkibuli	34	11	9	14	38	40	42
14	Magaroeli Chiatura	34	10	7	17	38	56	37
15	FC Zestafoni 2	34	9	9	16	23	44	36
16	FC Sagarejo	34	7	10	17	28	44	31
17	Imedi Tbilisi	34	6	2	26	22	85	20
18	Liakhvi Tamarasheni	34	4	1	29	24	90	13

N.B. Dinamo 2 Tbilisi ineligible for promotion.

PROMOTION/RELEGATION PLAY-OFFS
(14/5/06)
FC Tbilisi 4, Meshkare Agara 1
(15/5/06)
FC Tskhinvali 3, FC Gagra 0

Germany

Klinsmann delights a nation

Jürgen Klinsmann said all along that his goal was to win the 2006 World Cup. He didn't fulfil that objective, but curiously nobody held it against him. Almost every German supporter was quite content with third place.

The unanimous verdict was that Germany, playing on German soil, had done as well as they could. They had surpassed expectations, both by reaching the semi-finals and by playing attractive, offensive football in the process. When Italy scored those two late goals to eliminate Klinsmann's team from the tournament, the German public could have been excused for retreating into a state of deep depression, cursing their luck and wondering what might have been. Instead, they had a quick sob, picked themselves up and carried on with the World Cup party.

Although generally the 2006 tournament will not be remembered for the quality of its football, it was brilliantly organised and hosted. Germany as a nation lived up to its reputation for efficiency while at the same time offering a friendly face to the world and perhaps debunking some of the myths about the German people that have – not unreasonably – been passed through the generations since the dark days of the Second World War.

In truth, the image of Germany has not been helped over the years by the rather dour, mechanical approach of its national football team. Unlike, say, Brazil, the country's World Cup achievements have been grudgingly respected rather than wholeheartedly admired. For example, when a distinctly mediocre, workaday Nationalmannschaft scrapped its way to the 2002 final in the Far East, most of the world recoiled in horror at the prospect of the Germans actually winning the trophy.

Spirit of adventure

In 2006, however, things were different. Klinsmann's team, while not eschewing those traditional German characteristics of graft, endeavour and discipline, played with a spirit of adventure. They tried to attack in every game, they played with two out-and-out strikers, they used the full width of the pitch, they were not afraid to shoot from distance, and they scored more goals – 14 in seven games – than any of the other 31 competing teams. Perhaps the singular victory for Klinsmann's class of 06 was that neutrals actually found themselves wanting Germany to win.

Those who had written the Germans off before the

Bronze is beautiful for Jürgen Klinsmann and Germany

Germany

tournament on the basis of a catastrophic performance against Italy in Florence, where they lost 4-1 and were utterly outplayed, should have known better. Klinsmann's team had demonstrated during his two years in charge that they were a completely different beast at home. In fact, when they kicked off the World Cup against Costa Rica in Munich, their home record under Klinsmann read: won nine, drawn five, lost one.

Furthermore, the Germans had an easy first-round group, just the sort they needed to build up momentum and get a sceptical public on their side. Full-back Philipp Lahm's wonderful early goal in the Opening Game set the tone for what was to follow. From then on the home fans were treated to a series of jubilant highs – substitute Oliver Neuville's late winner against Poland; an easy 3-0 win against Ecuador; a one-sided annihilation of Sweden; a characteristically flawless penalty shoot-out to eliminate Argentina.

Who knows whether the Germans would have won another shoot-out in the semi-final had Italy not shattered their dreams at the end of an epic contest with those two last-gasp goals (after all, the Azzurri were pretty impressive themselves from the spot in the final)? But although Germany were denied their big date in Berlin, they signed off with another rapturously received victory over Portugal in the third-place play-off, two long-range piledrivers from Bastian Schweinsteiger lighting up the evening in Stuttgart and ensuring that, with their bronze medals, Klinsmann and his players had something tangible with which to recall a magical month.

Golden Shoe

Although Germany's great strength was the balance and spirit of the team, several individuals caught the eye. Miroslav Klose won the Golden Shoe as the tournament's top scorer, with five goals, and he did much more besides, notably setting up his strike partner Lukas Podolski for both goals against Sweden with fabulous assists. Lahm was industrious and inventive in every game, a right-footed left-back par excellence, while Jens Lehmann, the only non-Bundesliga player in the regular starting XI, fully justified Klinsmann's decision to choose him over Kahn as the no.1 goalkeeper, not least with his two penalty saves against Argentina. Even the hotly contested central-defensive partnership of Per Mertesacker and Christoph Metzelder looked increasingly resilient as the tournament progressed, although they were well protected by the tireless Torsten Frings, whose absence from the semi-final through suspension (for his part in the post-match mêlée against Argentina) was keenly felt.

Captain Michael Ballack was not as influential as in 2002, and he failed to score, but he never seemed fully fit. Nevertheless, he was outstanding against Sweden and heroic against Argentina. If he had been on his game against Italy, Germany would probably have won, but he had a wretched evening in Dortmund – possibly his worst performance in the white shirt of his country.

A few days after the World Cup dust had settled Klinsmann announced his resignation. It was not entirely unexpected. There had always been some doubt as to whether he would carry on. He explained that he would find it difficult to raise and motivate himself for another challenge with the team, and most people understood.

NATIONAL TEAM RESULTS 2005/06

Date	Opponent	H/A	Venue	Score	Scorers
17/8/05	Holland	A	Rotterdam	2-2	Ballack (49), Asamoah (81)
3/9/05	Slovakia	A	Bratislava	0-2	
7/9/05	South Africa	H	Bremen	4-2	Podolski (12, 48, 55), Borowski (47)
8/10/05	Turkey	A	Istanbul	1-2	Neuville (90)
12/10/05	China	H	Hamburg	1-0	Frings (51p)
12/11/05	France	A	Saint-Denis	0-0	
1/3/06	Italy	A	Florence	1-4	Huth (82)
22/3/06	United States	H	Dortmund	4-1	Schweinsteiger (46), Neuville (73), Klose (75), Ballack (79)
27/5/06	Luxembourg	H	Freiburg	7-0	Klose (5, 59), Frings (19p), Podolski (36, 65p), Neuville (90, 90)
30/5/06	Japan	H	Leverkusen	2-2	Klose (75), Schweinsteiger (80)
2/6/06	Colombia	H	Mönchengladbach	3-0	Ballack (20), Schweinsteiger (37), Borowski (69)
9/6/06	Costa Rica (WCF)	H	Munich	4-2	Lahm (6), Klose (17, 61), Frings (87)
14/6/06	Poland (WCF)	H	Dortmund	1-0	Neuville (90)
20/6/06	Ecuador (WCF)	H	Berlin	3-0	Klose (4, 44), Podolski (57)
24/6/06	Sweden (WCF)	H	Munich	2-0	Podolski (4, 12)
30/6/06	Argentina (WCF)	H	Berlin	1-1	Klose (80) (aet; 4-2 on pens)
4/7/06	Italy (WCF)	H	Dortmund	0-2	(aet)
8/7/06	Portugal (WCF)	H	Stuttgart	3-1	Schweinsteiger (56, 78), Petit (60og)

Germany

Even without their inspirational leader, this Germany team looks to have a bright future. Joachim Löw, Klinsmann's right-hand man, was swiftly appointed to replace him, thus ensuring a seamless transition into the Euro 2008 qualifiers.

Löw is only the tenth man to be appointed Bundestrainer. His target is European Championship victory across the border in Austria and Switzerland. Before the World Cup few would have bet on such an eventuality. Now, with a settled and successful side that, form and fitness permitting, is unlikely to change much, if at all, over the next two years, a record fourth European triumph has to be considered a distinct possibility.

Record crowds

Germany's love for football was plain to see at the World Cup, and thanks largely to the lure of watching the game in all those marvellous new state-of-the-art stadiums the Bundesliga registered an all-time record average attendance of 39,424 in 2005/06.

The commitment of the fans was commendable, not least from those 69,770 (on average) regular visitors to Dortmund's wonderful Westfalenstadion, where local side Borussia won just eight times and scored a mere 23 goals in 17 matches. At the end of the season the financially over-burdened club – despite those huge crowds – were forced to sell off their two Czech stars, Tomás Rosicky and Jan Koller. Even so, with World Cup fever having stoked up passions to a new level, there is talk that the club will pass the 70,000-barrier in 2006/07.

Dortmund finished seventh in 2005/06, out of Europe and some 29 points adrift of champions Bayern Munich. There were sell-out crowds for virtually every game at Bayern's new Allianz-Arena, and for good reason as Felix Magath's side went six months in their new home without dropping a point. It was not so much a title race as an exhibition march for the Bavarians as they turned the screw on the opposition right from the start. Eleven goals in their opening three matches, six of them from Dutch hitman Roy Makaay, demonstrated Bayern's appetite for a record-extending 20th Bundesliga title, and they carried that all-conquering form right through the autumn, signing off for Christmas with a 2-1 victory at the Westfalenstadion that gave them a six-point halfway lead over second-placed Hamburg.

Other than Juventus in the Champions League, HSV were the only team to beat Bayern in the autumn. Their 2-0 victory at the AOL-Arena in late September brought a halt to a Bundesliga-record run (carried over from the previous season) of 15 straight victories. In fact, Hamburg would prove to be Bayern's nemesis again in the early spring when they had the audacity not just to end Bayern's perfect record in the Allianz-Arena but to win the game – played in a snow blizzard – with a last-minute goal from new Dutch signing Nigel de Jong.

Simply the best

Bayern shrugged off those two setbacks with an air of casual disdain. They knew they were the best team in the country and they kept proving it week after week. Although the quality of their performance dipped slightly in the second half of the season, there was never any serious threat to

Michael Ballack – a fruitful farewell season in Munich

Germany

their position of supremacy. The sheer strength in depth of Bayern's squad ensured that if one or two players were off form, it didn't really matter; there were plenty more where they came from.

Ballack, as ever, was the main man, the pick of a team in which French full-back Willy Sagnol, Brazilian centre-back Lúcio and Peruvian striker Claudio Pizarro also excelled, so it must have been hard for him to stomach when, in the final game of the season, a week after Bayern had wrapped up the title with a 1-1 draw at Kaiserslautern, he was booed by a section of the Allianz-Arena crowd. Those fans could not tolerate the notion that the team's star player was about to leave them – even though it had been apparent for some time that he was set to quit the Bundesliga for the Premiership and join Chelsea. Typically, Ballack responded to the jeering by netting his 14th goal of the season.

Ballack's fourth and final season at Bayern brought victory not only in the championship but also in the German Cup. Because of the World Cup, the final of the DFB-Pokal was brought forward a few weeks from its usual slot at the end of the domestic fixture calendar. With its sense of occasion therefore somewhat diluted, it was perhaps unsurprising that the match against Eintracht Frankfurt proved to be less than riveting. Bayern won it with a header from Pizarro although they were equally indebted to a brilliant late save from Oliver Kahn.

With the Bundesliga platter being brandished a week later, Bayern ensured that coach Magath's second season in charge ended exactly as his first had done – with a domestic Double. Even though it was the sixth time that Bayern had won both trophies in the same season, neither they nor any other German club had ever won back-to-back Doubles. There was another record set by the club's veteran midfielder Mehmet Scholl who, though not a regular in the team, played often enough to collect his eighth championship winner's medal.

The one blot on Bayern's season was their failure to impose themselves in the Champions League. They sailed through an easy group but had to take the runners-up spot behind Juventus, which gave them a tough draw in the last 16, where they were comprehensively outplayed by Milan. Bayern's 4-1 defeat at the San Siro ended German interest in the Champions League. Schalke had fallen in the group phase, also at the hands of Milan, and on the day before Bayern's exit, Werder Bremen were ousted in Turin by Juventus. No wonder Germany lost to the Italians a few months later at the World Cup…

Bremen book in

Werder's Champions League departure was a cruel one – sabotaged by a dreadful late error from the otherwise excellent stand-in goalkeeper Tim Wiese at the Stadio delle Alpi – but Thomas Schaaf's side booked themselves in for another sitting at Europe's top table by finishing runners-up to Bayern in the Bundesliga. It was a close call with northern rivals Hamburg, but Werder deservedly claimed their prize with an impressive 2-1 win at the AOL-Arena on the final day. A draw would have sufficed for HSV to take second place, but Miroslav Klose's 25th goal of the season proved decisive.

Klose, whose tally earned him the title of Bundesliga Torschützenkönig (goal king) for the first time in his career, was one of many Bremen players to leave a profound imprint on the season. His fellow German internationals Torsten Frings and Tim Borowski were outstanding in midfield, while foreigners Ivan Klasnic, Johan Micoud and Nélson Haedo Valdez all helped to give Werder the Bundesliga's most prolific attack (79 goals in 34 games).

Hamburg, on the other hand, had the best defence (30 goals conceded), which was largely down to their rugged Low Countries central pairing of Dutchman Khalid Boulahrouz and Belgian Daniel Van Buyten. There were few Germans in the team, but Thomas Doll, HSV's shrewd, ever-smiling coach, made light of that potential handicap, moulding together an excellent unit that, but for the two lengthy injury breaks that curtailed the involvement of brilliant new signing Rafael van der Vaart, might have put up a stronger challenge to Bayern for the title. To beat the champions twice was a real feather in the cap of Doll and his players, although it was Bayern who ended HSV's interest in the German Cup after an absorbing pre-Christmas tie at the Allianz-Arena decided by Englishman Owen Hargreaves' memorable extra-time winner. Hamburg's other hope of a first major trophy in 19 years ended when the Romanians of Rapid Bucharest knocked them out of the UEFA Cup (which they had accessed via the InterToto Cup) on the away-goals rule.

Schalke went the furthest of the six Bundesliga sides that competed in the UEFA Cup. Edged out of the Champions League – a failure that cost coach Ralf Rangnick his job – the team from Gelsenkirchen saw off Espanyol, Palermo and Levski

Germany

NATIONAL TEAM APPEARANCES 2005/06

Coach – Jürgen KLINSMANN

Player	DOB	Club	Hol	Svk	Rsa	Tur	Chn	Fra	Ita	Usa	Lux	Jpn	Col	CRC	POL	ECU	SWE	ARG	ITA	POR	Caps	Goals
Oliver KAHN	15/6/69	FC Bayern München	G		G	G				G	s46									G	86	-
Arne FRIEDRICH	29/5/79	Hertha BSC Berlin	D74			D	D	D	D82	D		D	D	D64	D	D	D	D			42	-
Per MERTESACKER	29/9/84	Hannover 96	D66	D	D	D	D46	D	D46	D	s46	D	D	D	D	D	D	D	D		29	1
Christian WÖRNS	10/5/72	Borussia Dortmund	D	D46																	66	-
Bernd SCHNEIDER	17/11/73	Bayer 04 Leverkusen	D	M82	s46	M		M	M76	M68	M68	M		D	M62	M90	M	M72	M	M62 M82	71	1
Torsten FRINGS	22/11/76	SV Werder Bremen	M66			M46	M		M68			M46	M	M71	M		M	M67	M85	M		M	58	8
Dietmar HAMANN	27/8/73	Liverpool (ENG)	M74																		59	5
Fabian ERNST	30/5/79	FC Schalke 04	M46	M46	s68				s82												24	1
Michael BALLACK	26/9/76	FC Bayern München	M	M	M			M	M	M		M	M		M	M	M	M	M		70	31
Miroslav KLOSE	9/6/78	SV Werder Bremen	A46	A	A77		A	A	A	A63	A	A61	A79	A	A67	A	A85	A111	A64		62	29
Kevin KURANYI	2/3/82	FC Schalke 04	A	s82	s77	A46	s53	s83													35	14
Sebastian DEISLER	5/1/80	FC Bayern München	s46	M	M46	s46	M	M46	M												36	3
Gerald ASAMOAH	3/10/78	FC Schalke 04	s46	A46	s77			s46	A67	s63		s71		s72							41	6
Robert HUTH	18/8/84	Chelsea (ENG)	s66			s46	D	D		D46				D							17	2
Thomas HITZLSPERGER	5/4/82	VfB Stuttgart	s66	D46		s82	s89			s46		s86							s79		16	-
Andreas HINKEL	26/3/82	VfB Stuttgart	s74	s74																	17	-
Tim BOROWSKI	2/5/80	SV Werder Bremen	s74		M	M73	M	s76	s68	s68	M	M63	s62	M72	s77	s67	s72	s74	M71		26	2
Jens LEHMANN	10/11/69	Arsenal (ENG)		G	G			G	G		G46	G	G	G	G	G	G	G	G		38	-
Patrick OWOMOYELA	5/11/79	SV Werder Bremen		D74	D	D	s90		s82												11	-
Lukas SINKIEWICZ	9/10/85	1.FC Köln		s46	D	D															3	-
Marcell JANSEN	4/11/85	Borussia Mönchengladbach		s46	D	D		D		D46	D	s73							D		8	-
Bastian SCHWEINSTEIGER	1/8/84	FC Bayern München		s46	M68	M82	D89	s46	s68	s46	M		M	M73	M	M77	M	M72	M74	s71 M79	35	9
Lukas PODOLSKI	4/6/85	1.FC Köln		s46	A77	A	A53	A83	A46	A46	A71	A70	A71	A	A71	A	A74	A	A	A71	32	15
Oliver NEUVILLE	1/5/73	Borussia Mönchengladbach			s46	A90				s67	s71	s70	s61	s79	s71	s67	s74	s85	s111	s64	62	9
Mike HANKE	5/11/83	VfL Wolfsburg			s73														s71		7	1
Christoph METZELDER	5/11/80	Borussia Dortmund				D		s46	D	D55	D	D	D		D	D	D	D			28	-
Philipp LAHM	11/11/83	FC Bayern München					D	D			D86	D	D	D	D	D	D				25	2
Sebastian KEHL	13/2/80	Borussia Dortmund						M82	s46		s71	s72			s85		M	M			31	3
Jens NOWOTNY	11/1/74	Bayer 04 Leverkusen							s55									D			47	1
David ODONKOR	21/2/84	Borussia Dortmund							s63		s90	s64				s62	s82				5	-

Germany

Sofia en route to a semi-final with Sevilla that they lost in extra-time. That was an impressive start for the team's 'unknown' new coach Mirko Slomka (formerly Rangnick's assistant), but in the Bundesliga he could lift the side no higher than fourth place, which meant UEFA Cup football from the start for the Royal Blues in 2006/07.

First hurdle

Bayer Leverkusen also re-qualified for the UEFA Cup. They had fallen at the first hurdle against CSKA Sofia, which led to the dismissal of coach Klaus Augenthaler. Rudi Völler stepped in for a few weeks before Michael Skibbe, once of Dortmund and also Völler's former assistant with the German national side, took over. The season would be a roller-coaster ride for the Leverkusener, including a wacky 7-4 defeat at Schalke, but with Bulgarian striker Dimitar Berbatov banging in the goals, they finished strongly to vault over several challengers and take fifth place.

Hertha Berlin and VfB Stuttgart both disappointed. Hertha attracted decent crowds to the Olympiastadion but seldom entertained, failing to score in three successive home UEFA Cup games. Stuttgart's bold move to recruit illustrious Italian coach Giovanni Trapattoni backfired and he was dismissed in February. The Swabians ended the season with a Bundesliga-record 16 draws.

Sixteen goals – all of them scored by Slovakian striker Róbert Vittek and all in the second half of the season - was the extraordinary statistic that catapulted Nuremberg up from 15th place at Christmas to eighth at the close. None of the three teams below Nuremberg at the winter break managed to escape. MSV Duisburg tried out three coaches but still ended up bottom, while the efforts of World Cup stadium-dwellers Cologne and Kaiserslautern to dislodge themselves from trouble in the spring eventually came to nought. Kaiserslautern had a chance to escape on the final day in a relegation hum-dinger at Wolfsburg, but the 2-2 draw sent them down.

The Zweite Bundesliga, second division, was won by yo-yo club Bochum, who finished a point ahead of Alemannia Aachen. The third promotion place was taken by Energie Cottbus, which meant that, following Hansa Rostock's relegation in 2005, a club from the former East Germany would once again infiltrate the Bundesliga elite in 2006/07.

EUROPEAN CUPS 2005/06

UEFA CHAMPIONS LEAGUE

FC BAYERN MÜNCHEN

1st round Group A
Match 1 SK RAPID WIEN (AUT)
A **1-0** *Guerrero (60)*
Kahn, Sagnol, Lúcio, Ismaël, Lizarazu (Demichelis 52), Hargreaves, Schweinsteiger (Deisler 83), Zé Roberto, Scholl, Pizarro (Guerrero 52), Makaay.

Match 2 CLUB BRUGGE KV (BEL)
H **1-0** *Demichelis (32)*
Kahn, Sagnol, Lúcio, Ismaël, Lizarazu (Scholl 52), Demichelis, Schweinsteiger, Zé Roberto, Ballack, Makaay, Guerrero (Santa Cruz 72).

Match 3 JUVENTUS (ITA)
H **2-1** *Deisler (32), Demichelis (39)*
Kahn, Sagnol, Lúcio, Ismaël, Lizarazu (Schweinsteiger 30), Demichelis, Deisler, Zé Roberto, Ballack, Santa Cruz (Scholl 88), Makaay.

Match 4 JUVENTUS
A **1-2** *Deisler (66)*
Kahn, Sagnol, Lúcio, Ismaël, Schweinsteiger, Demichelis (Scholl 86), Deisler, Zé Roberto, Ballack, Makaay (Guerrero 88), Pizarro.

Match 5 SK RAPID WIEN
H **4-0** *Deisler (21), Karimi (54), Makaay (72, 76)*
Kahn, Sagnol, Lúcio, Ismaël, Lizarazu (Lahm 63), Demichelis, Deisler, Zé Roberto (Schweinsteiger 46), Karimi (Guerrero 82), Makaay, Pizarro.

Match 6 CLUB BRUGGE KV
A **1-1** *Pizarro (21)*
Kahn, Lahm, Ismaël, Demichelis, Lizarazu, Hargreaves (Schweinsteiger 67), Deisler, Karimi (Zé Roberto 46), Ballack, Pizarro, Makaay (Guerrero 46).

2nd round MILAN (ITA)
H **1-1** *Ballack (23)*
Rensing, Sagnol, Lúcio, Ismaël, Lahm, Demichelis, Salihamidzic (Karimi 58), Zé Roberto (Scholl 76), Ballack, Makaay (Guerrero 80), Pizarro.
A **1-4** *Ismaël (36)*
Kahn, Sagnol, Ismaël, Lúcio, Lizarazu (Zé Roberto 52), Demichelis, Deisler (Scholl 63), Schweinsteiger, Ballack, Pizarro, Makaay (Guerrero 46).

FC SCHALKE 04

1st round Group E
Match 1 PSV (HOL)
A **0-1**
Rost, Rafinha, Bordon, Rodríguez, Krstajic, Altintop (Bajramovic 87), Poulsen, Ernst (Varela 72), Kobiashvili, Kuranyi, Sand (Larsen 72).

Match 2 MILAN (ITA)
H **2-2** *Larsen (3), Altintop (70)*
Rost, Rafinha, Bordon, Rodríguez, Krstajic, Poulsen, Ernst (Bajramovic 85), Ernst (Altintop 68), Kobiashvili, Lincoln (Sand 74), Larsen.

Match 3 FENERBAHÇE (TUR)
A **3-3** *Lincoln (59, 62), Kuranyi (77)*
Rost, Altintop, Bordon, Rodríguez, Krstajic, Poulsen, Rafinha, Kobiashvili, Lincoln, Sand (Kuranyi 46), Larsen.

Match 4 FENERBAHÇE
H **2-0** *Kuranyi (32), Sand (90)*
Rost, Rafinha, Bordon, Rodríguez, Krstajic, Poulsen, Ernst (Varela 82), Altintop (Sand 64), Lincoln, Kobiashvili, Kuranyi (Bajramovic 90).

Match 5 PSV

Germany

H 3-0 *Kobiashvili (18p, 73, 79p)*
Rost, Altintop, Bordon, Rodríguez, Krstajic, Ernst, Poulsen, Lincoln, Varela (Asamoah 74), Kobiashvili (Bajramovic 89), Kuranyi (Sand 82).

Match 6 MILAN
A 2-3 *Poulsen (49), Lincoln (66)*
Rost, Rafinha, Bordon, Rodríguez, Krstajic (Larsen 84), Poulsen, Ernst (Asamoah 46), Lincoln, Altintop, Kobiashvili, Kuranyi (Sand 84).

SV WERDER BREMEN
3rd qualifying round FC BASEL (SUI)
A 1-2 *Klose (73)*
Reinke, Ümit (Owomoyela 65), Pasanen, Naldo, Van Damme (Schulz 46), Vranjes, Frings, Borowski, Micoud, Klose, Klasnic
H 3-0 *Klasnic (64, 72), Borowski (67p)*
Reinke, Owomoyela, Pasanen, Naldo, Schulz, Baumann (Jensen 46), Frings, Borowski, Micoud (Vranjes 88), Klose, Klasnic (Haedo Valdez 73).

1st round Group C
Match 1 FC BARCELONA (ESP)
H 0-2
Reinke, Owomoyela, Pasanen, Naldo, Schulz, Baumann (Jensen 63), Frings, Borowski, Micoud, Haedo Valdez (Hunt 83), Klasnic.

Match 2 PANATHINAIKOS (GRE)
A 1-2 *Klose (41)*
Reinke, Owomoyela, Andreasen, Naldo, Schulz (Haedo Valdez 75), Baumann (Hunt 63), Frings, Borowski, Micoud, Klose, Klasnic.

Match 3 UDINESE (ITA)
A 1-1 *Felipe (64og)*
Reinke, Owomoyela, Andreasen, Naldo, Schulz, Baumann, Frings, Borowski, Micoud, Klose, Haedo Valdez (Hunt 84).

Match 4 UDINESE
H 4-3 *Klose (15), Baumann (24), Micoud (51, 67)*
Reinke, Owomoyela (Fahrenhorst 68), Andreasen, Naldo, Schulz, Baumann (Vranjes 85), Frings, Borowski, Micoud, Klose, Haedo Valdez (Hunt 80).

Match 5 FC BARCELONA
A 1-3 *Borowski (22p)*
Reinke, Owomoyela, Andreasen, Fahrenhorst, Naldo, Schulz, Baumann, Frings, Micoud, Klose (Hunt 58), Haedo Valdez.

Match 6 PANATHINAIKOS
H 5-1 *Micoud (2p), Haedo Valdez (28, 32), Klose (51), Frings (90)*
Reinke, Owomoyela, Fahrenhorst, Andreasen, Schulz (Pasanen 50), Baumann (Jensen 75), Vranjes, Frings, Micoud, Klose, Haedo Valdez (Hunt 79).

2nd round JUVENTUS (ITA)
H 3-2 *Schulz (39), Borowski (87), Micoud (90)*
Wiese, Owomoyela, Fahrenhorst, Naldo, Schulz, Baumann, Frings, Borowski, Micoud, Klose (Haedo Valdez 68), Klasnic
A 1-2 *Micoud (13)*
Wiese, Owomoyela, Fahrenhorst, Naldo, Schulz, Baumann (Pasanen 73), Frings, Borowski, Micoud, Klose, Klasnic (Haedo Valdez 82).

UEFA CUP

HERTHA BSC BERLIN
1st round APOEL (CYP)
A 1-0 *Marcelinho (90p)*
Fiedler, Friedrich, Van Burik (Madlung 56), Simunic, Fathi, Kovac, Cairo (Bastürk 79), Neuendorf, Gilberto, Marcelinho, Okoronkwo (Rafael 52).
H 3-1 *Marcelinho (15), Rafael (25), Cairo (52)*
Fiedler, Friedrich (Schröder 46), Madlung, Simunic, Fathi, Dárdai, Cairo, Bastürk (Neuendorf 61), Gilberto, Marcelinho, Rafael (Okoronkwo 35).

2nd round Group C
Match 1 HALMSTADS BK (SWE)
A 1-0 *Neuendorf (67)*
Fiedler, Friedrich, Van Burik, Simunic, Fathi, Dárdai, Schröder, Neuendorf (Marx 90), Bastürk, Marcelinho, Rafael (Okoronkwo 90).

Match 2 RC LENS (FRA)
H 0-0
Fiedler, Friedrich, Van Burik, Simunic, Fathi, Dárdai (Neuendorf 73), Kovac, Bastürk, Cairo (Boateng 63), Marcelinho, Rafael (Samba 86).

Match 3 SAMPDORIA (ITA)
A 0-0
Fiedler, Friedrich, Madlung, Simunic, Fathi, Kovac, Marx, Bastürk, Boateng, Marcelinho (Neuendorf 87), Rafael (Samba 90).

Match 4 STEAUA BUCURESTI (ROM)
H 0-0
Fiedler, Chahed, Friedrich, Madlung, Fathi, Kovac, Boateng (Okoronkwo 76), Gilberto, Bastürk (Neuendorf 78), Marcelinho, Dejagah (Samba 90).

3rd round RAPID BUCURESTI (ROM)
H 0-1
Fiedler, Chahed, Friedrich, Madlung, Fathi (Dejagah 78), Boateng, Cairo, Bastürk, Gilberto, Marcelinho (Samba 78), Sverkos (Okoronkwo 70).
A 0-2
Fiedler, Chahed, Friedrich, Van Burik (Samba 76), Fathi, Schmidt, Marx (Cairo 67), Gilberto, Marcelinho (Dejagah 77), Sverkos, Okowronkwo.

VFB STUTTGART
1st round DOMZALE (SLO)
H 2-0 *Tomasson (7), Gentner (89)*
Hildebrand, Stranzl, Fernando Meira, Delpierre, Magnin, Meissner (Hitzlsperger 79), Soldo, Gentner, Grønkjaer (Tiffert 64), Ljuboja, Tomasson (Gomez 70).
A 0-1
Hildebrand, Hinkel, Fernando Meira, Delpierre, Gerber, Soldo, Gentner, Hitzlsperger, Cacau, Grønkjaer (Stranzl 85), Tomasson.

2nd round Group G
Match 1 STADE RENNAIS FC (FRA)
A 2-0 *Tomasson (87), Ljuboja (90p)*
Hildebrand, Stranzl, Fernando Meira, Delpierre, Magnin, Soldo, Tiffert, Hitzlsperger, Grønkjaer (Ljuboja 50), Cacau (Carevic 69), Tomasson.

Match 2 SHAKHTAR DONETSK (UKR)
H 0-2
Heinen, Stranzl, Fernando Meira, Delpierre, Magnin, Meissner (Grønkjaer 57), Soldo, Tiffert, Gentner (Cacau 46), Ljuboja, Tomasson (Streller 72).

Match 3 PAOK (GRE)
A 2-1 *Ljuboja (85, 90p)*
Hildebrand, Stranzl (Carevic 72), Fernando Meira, Delpierre, Magnin, Soldo, Meissner, Tiffert, Hitzlsperger, Tomasson (Gomez 61), Ljuboja.

Match 4 RAPID BUCURESTI (ROM)
H 2-1 *Gomez (20, 37)*
Heinen, Babbel, Delpierre, Hinkel, Gerber, Carevic, Hitzlsperger, Gentner, Grønkjaer (Stranzl 89), Cacau (Tiffert 77), Gomez (Streller 60).

3rd round MIDDLESBROUGH (ENG)
H 1-2 *Ljuboja (86)*
Hildebrand, Stranzl (Beck 46), Fernando Meira, Delpierre, Gerber, Soldo, Meissner (Gentner 78), Grønkjaer, Hitzlsperger (Gomez 63), Ljuboja, Tomasson.
A 1-0 *Tiffert (13)*
Hildebrand, Hinkel, Babbel, Delpierre, Magnin (Hitzlsperger 81), Soldo, Meissner (Cacau 75), Gentner, Tiffert, Grønkjaer (Gomez 63), Ljuboja.

Germany

BAYER 04 LEVERKUSEN
1st round CSKA SOFIA (BUL)
H 0-1
Butt, Fritz (Castro 46), Juan, Roque Júnior, Athirson (Lazovic 75), Ramelow, Rolfes (Barnetta 46), Schneider, Babic, Voronin, Berbatov.
A 0-1
Butt, Fritz, Ramelow, Roque Júnior, Rolfes (Babic 75), Castro (Krzynowek 46), Barnetta (Freier 65), Athirson, Schneider, Voronin, Berbatov.

FSV MAINZ
1st qualifying round MIKA ASHTARAK (ARM)
H 4-0 *Ruman (11), Auer (36, 67), Noveski (58)*
Wache, Abel (Demirtas 76), Friedrich, Noveski, Weigelt, Da Silva (Pekovic 76), Babatz, Gerber, Thurk, Ruman (Jovanovic 82) Auer.
A 0-0
Wache, Abel, Friedrich, Noveski, Weigelt, Gerber, Babatz, Da Silva (Weiland 83), Ruman (Addo 67), Thurk (Weiland 63), Auer.

2nd qualifying round KEFLAVÍK (ISL)
H 2-0 *Auer (10), Babatz (70p)*
Wache, Abel (Demirtas 46), Friedrich, Noveski, Weigelt, Gerber (Geissler 70), Babatz, Da Silva, Thurk, Ruman (Addo), Auer.
A 2-0 *Thurk (26), Geissler (85)*
Wache, Abel, Friedrich, Noveski, Rose, Gerber, Babatz, Da Silva (Pekovic 61), Ruman, Thurk (Geissler 76), Auer (Addo 71).

1st round SEVILLA FC (ESP)
A 0-0
Wache, Abel, Friedrich, Noveski, Rose, Gerber (Geissler 46), Pekovic (Demirtas 64), Da Silva (Babatz 46), Thurk, Ruman, Romulo.
H 0-2
Wache, Abel, Friedrich, Noveski, Weigelt, Pekovic, Gerber (Auer 74), Da Silva (Geissler 63), Ruman (Weiland 63), Thurk, Zidan.

HAMBURGER SV
1st round FC KØBENHAVN (DEN)
H 1-1 *Van der Vaart (37)*
Wächter, Klingbeil (Trochowski 57), Rheinhardt, Van Buyten, Atouba, Demel (Ziegler 87), Mahdavikia, Jarolím, Van der Vaart, Lauth, Takahara (Kucukovic 57).
A 1-0 *Van der Vaart (89p)*
Wächter, Demel, Boulahrouz, Van Buyten, Atouba, Wicky (Trochowski 61), Jarolím (Takahara 72), Beinlich, Van der Vaart, Mpenza (Lauth 83), Barbarez.

2nd round Group A
Match 1 CSKA SOFIA (BUL)
A 1-0 *Van der Vaart (56)*
Wächter, Wicky, Demel (Klingbeil 46), Van Buyten, Atouba, Beinlich, Jarolím, Trochowski (Mahdavikia 59), Van der Vaart, Mpenza (Ziegler 87), Barbarez.

Match 2 VIKING FK (NOR)
H 2-0 *Van der Vaart (21), Lauth (66)*
Wächter, Mahdavikia, Boulahrouz, Van Buyten, Atouba, Wicky (Laas 41), Trochowski, Beinlich (Takyi 75), Van der Vaart, Lauth, Barbarez (Kucukovic 75).

Match 3 AS MONACO FC (FRA)
A 0-2
Wächter, Demel (Mahdavikia 46), Boulahrouz, Van Buyten, Klingbeil, Wicky (Ziegler 46), Jarolím, Trochowski (Lauth 72), Van der Vaart, Mpenza, Barbarez.

Match 4 SK SLAVIA PRAHA (CZE)
H 2-0 *Barbarez (9), Mpenza (57)*
Kirschstein, Mahdavikia, Demel, Van Buyten, Wicky (Laas 60), Jarolím, Beinlich, Trochowski, Mpenza (Lauth 64), Barbarez (Lauth 70).

3rd round FC THUN (SUI)
A 0-1
Wächter, Mahdavikia, Demel (Klingbeil 77), Van Buyten, Atouba, Wicky, De Jong (Takahara 65), Jarolím (Laas 81), Trochowski, Barbarez, Lauth.

H 2-0 *Van Buyten (2, 33)*
Wächter, Mahdavikia, Boulahrouz, Van Buyten, Atouba, Wicky, Jarolim, De Jong (Demel 86), Trochowski (Van der Vaart 64), Barbarez, Takahara (Lauth 71).

4th round RAPID BUCURESTI (ROM)
A 0-2
Wächter, Mahdavikia, Boulahrouz, Van Buyten, Demel, Wicky, De Jong, Trochowski (Klingbeil 46), Van der Vaart, Takahara (Laas 71), Barbarez (Kucukovic 46).
H 3-1 *Lauth (24), Barbarez (36), Van der Vaart (63)*
Kirschstein, Demel (Takahara 54), Boulahrouz, Van Buyten, Atouba, Wicky, Mahdavikia, Jarolim, Van der Vaart, Lauth (Reinhardt 83), Barbarez.

FC SCHALKE 04
3rd round RCD ESPANYOL (ESP)
H 2-1 *Bordon (67), Ernst (89)*
Rost, Rafinha, Bordon, Krstajic, Boenisch (Varela 67), Poulsen, Ernst, Bajramovic (Asamoah 46), Lincoln, Kuranyi (Sand 80), Larsen.
A 3-0 *Kuranyi (54), Sand (70), Lincoln (73)*
Rost, Rafinha, Bordon (Kläsener 76), Krstajic, Kobiashvili, Poulsen, Ernst, Bajramovic, Lincoln, Asamoah (Sand 66), Kuranyi (Larsen 74).

4th round PALERMO (ITA)
A 0-1
Rost, Rafinha, Bordon, Krstajic, Kobiashvili, Poulsen (Rodríguez 78), Poulsen, Ernst, Bajramovic, Sand, Asamoah (Varela 81), Larsen.
H 3-0 *Kobiashvili (44p), Larsen (72), Azaouagh (80)*
Rost, Rafinha, Rodríguez, Krstajic, Kobiashvili, Poulsen, Ernst (Varela 68), Bajramovic (Sand 85), Azaouagh (Baumjohann 90), Asamoah, Larsen.

Quarter-final LEVSKI SOFIA (BUL)
A 3-1 *Varela (48), Lincoln (69), Asamoah (79)*
Rost, Altintop, Bordon, Krstajic (Rodríguez 83), Kobiashvili, Ernst, Poulsen, Lincoln, Asamoah, Larsen (Varela 46), Kuranyi (Sand 74).
H 1-1 *Lincoln (58)*
Rost, Rafinha, Bordon, Rodríguez, Krstajic, Poulsen, Bajramovic, Lincoln, Asamoah (Altintop 74), Larsen, Kuranyi (Sand 79).

Semi-final SEVILLA FC (ESP)
H 0-0
Rost, Rafinha, Bordon, Krstajic, Kobiashvili, Poulsen, Ernst (Bajramovic 74), Altintop (Lincoln 46), Asamoah, Varela (Kuranyi 65), Larsen.
A 0-1 (aet)
Rost, Rafinha, Bordon, Rodríguez (Larsen 90), Kobiashvili, Poulsen, Ernst, Bajramovic (Varela 62), Lincoln, Asamoah (Sand 90), Kuranyi.

TOP GOALSCORERS 2005/06

25	Miroslav KLOSE	(SV Werder Bremen)
21	Dimitar BERBATOV	(Bayer 04 Leverkusen)
20	Halil ALTINTOP	(1.FC Kaiserslautern)
17	Roy MAKAAY	(FC Bayern München)
16	Róbert VITTEK	(1.FC Nürnberg)
15	Ivan KLASNIC	(SV Werder Bremen)
14	Michael BALLACK	(FC Bayern München)
13	Ebi SMOLAREK	(Borussia Dortmund)
12	Diego KLIMOWICZ	(VfL Wolfsburg)
	Ioannis AMANATIDIS	(Eintracht Frankfurt)
	MARCELINHO	(Hertha BSC Berlin)
	Lukas PODOLSKI	(1.FC Köln)
	Michael THURK	(FSV Mainz 05)

Germany

LEAGUE RESULTS/ SCORERS/APPEARANCES/ GOALS 2005/06

ARMINIA BIELEFELD
Coach – Thomas von Heesen

2005

Date	Opponent	h/a	Score	Scorers
5/8	SV Werder Bremen	a	2-5	Krupnikovic, Zuma
13/8	Hamburger SV	h	0-2	
28/8	FSV Mainz 05	h	2-0	Krupnikovic 2 (2p)
10/9	VfB Stuttgart	a	1-1	Pinto
17/9	1.FC Kaiserslautern	h	0-0	
20/9	Borussia Dortmund	a	0-2	
24/9	Bor.Mönchengladbach	h	0-2	
1/10	Bayer 04 Leverkusen	a	1-1	Boakye
15/10	Hertha BSC Berlin	h	3-0	Borges, Westermann, Zuma
22/10	1.FC Nürnberg	a	3-2	Fink, Diego León, Zuma
31/10	Hannover 96	h	4-1	Fink, Zuma, Boakye 2
5/11	Eintracht Frankfurt	a	0-3	
19/11	FC Bayern München	h	1-2	Boakye
26/11	VfL Wolfsburg	a	0-0	
3/12	FC Schalke 04	h	0-1	
10/12	MSV Duisburg	a	1-1	Vata
17/12	1.FC Köln	h	3-2	Kobylík, Fink 2

2006

Date	Opponent	h/a	Score	Scorers
29/1	SV Werder Bremen	h	0-1	
4/2	Hamburger SV	a	1-2	Boakye
7/2	FSV Mainz 05	a	1-1	Boakye
11/2	VfB Stuttgart	h	2-1	Boakye 2
18/2	1.FC Kaiserslautern	a	0-2	
25/2	Borussia Dortmund	h	1-0	Kauf
5/3	Arminia Bielefeld	a	0-2	
11/3	Bayer 04 Leverkusen	h	1-0	Djalovic
19/3	Hertha BSC Berlin	a	0-1	
27/3	1.FC Nürnberg	h	0-0	
2/4	Hannover 96	a	1-0	Vata
8/4	Eintracht Frankfurt	h	1-0	Westermann
15/4	FC Bayern München	a	0-2	
22/4	VfL Wolfsburg	h	0-1	
3/5	FC Schalke 04	a	1-3	Küntzel
6/5	MSV Duisburg	h	0-2	
13/5	1.FC Köln	a	2-4	Kobylík, Djalovic

No	Name	Nat	Pos	Aps	(s)	Gls
9	Isaak BOAKYE	GHA	A	22	(3)	8
3	Márcio BORGES	BRA	D	26	(1)	1
6	Detlef DAMMEIER		M	10	(3)	
15	Tim DANNEBERG		M	1	(1)	
24	DIEGO LEÓN Ayarza	ESP	A		(4)	1
20	Radomir DJALOVIC	SCG	A	6	(15)	2
23	Dennis EILHOFF		G	1	(1)	
13	Michael FINK		M	32	(1)	4
4	Petr GABRIEL	CZE	D	6		
1	Mathias HAIN		G	33		
5	Rüdiger KAUF		M	15	(1)	1
11	David KOBYLÍK	CZE	M	19	(6)	2
19	Bernd KORZYNIETZ		D	34		
7	Nebojsa KRUPNIKOVIC	SCG	M	8		3
31	Radim KUCERA	CZE	D	12	(3)	
14	Marco KÜNTZEL		A	18	(1)	1
17	Ioannis MASMANIDIS		M	10	(6)	
30	Roberto PINTO	POR	M	3	(28)	1
21	Massimilliano PORCELLO	ITA	M	4	(2)	
8	Tobias RAU		D	7	(7)	

No	Name	Nat	Pos	Aps	(s)	Gls
2	Markus SCHULER		D	27	(1)	
25	Kamil VÁCEK	CZE	M		(1)	
10	Fatmir VATA	ALB	M	18	(4)	2
16	Heiko WESTERMANN		D	34		2
18	Artur WICHNIAREK	POL	A	5	(4)	
22	Sibusiso ZUMA	RSA	A	23	(2)	4

BAYER 04 LEVERKUSEN
Coach – Klaus Augenthaler; (16/9/05) (Rudi Völler); (10/10/05) Michael Skibbe

2005

Date	Opponent	h/a	Score	Scorers
7/8	Eintracht Frankfurt	a	4-1	Berbatov, Voronin, Schneider, Krzynowek
13/8	FC Bayern München	h	2-5	Berbatov (p), Babic
27/8	VfL Wolfsburg	a	1-2	Berbatov
10/9	FC Schalke 04	h	1-1	Berbatov
18/9	MSV Duisburg	a	3-1	Juan, Berbatov, Athirson
21/9	1.FC Köln	h	2-1	Voronin, Rolfes
24/9	SV Werder Bremen	a	1-2	Rolfes
1/10	Arminia Bielefeld	h	1-1	Voronin
15/10	FSV Mainz 05	a	1-3	Barnetta
23/10	VfB Stuttgart	h	1-1	Barnetta
29/10	1.FC Kaiserslautern	a	2-2	Barnetta, Voronin
5/11	Borussia Dortmund	h	2-1	Juan, og (Kringe)
19/11	Bor. Mönchengladbach	a	1-1	Rolfes
26/11	Hamburger SV	h	0-1	
4/12	Hertha BSC Berlin	h	1-2	Berbatov
10/12	1.FC Nürnberg	a	1-1	Schneider
17/12	Hannover 96	h	0-0	

2006

Date	Opponent	h/a	Score	Scorers
27/1	Eintracht Frankfurt	h	2-1	Freier, Butt (p)
4/2	FC Bayern München	a	0-1	
8/2	VfL Wolfsburg	h	4-0	Berbatov, Barnetta, Schneider, Madouni
11/2	FC Schalke 04	a	4-7	Voronin 2, Berbatov, Krzynowek
18/2	MSV Duisburg	h	3-2	Freier, Barnetta, Berbatov
25/2	1.FC Köln	a	3-0	Berbatov, Voronin, Krzynowek
4/3	SV Werder Bremen	h	1-1	Berbatov
11/3	Arminia Bielefeld	a	0-1	
18/3	FSV Mainz 05	h	1-2	Freier
25/3	VfB Stuttgart	a	2-0	Freier, Berbatov
1/4	1.FC Kaiserslautern	h	5-1	Barnetta, Berbatov 3 (2p), Fritz
8/4	Borussia Dortmund	a	2-1	Berbatov, Freier
15/4	Bor. Mönchengladbach	h	2-1	Rolfes 2
22/4	Hamburger SV	a	2-0	Rolfes, Freier
2/5	Hertha BSC Berlin	a	5-1	Juan, Berbatov 2, Ramelow, Schneider
6/5	1.FC Nürnberg	h	2-2	Berbatov 2 (1p)
13/5	Hannover 96	a	2-2	Rolfes, Berbatov

No	Name	Nat	Pos	Aps	(s)	Gls
13	ATHIRSON Mazolli	BRA	D	15	(3)	1
19	Marko BABIC	CRO	M	11	(6)	1
7	Tranquillo BARNETTA	SUI	M	26	(5)	6
9	Dimitar BERBATOV	BUL	A	34		21
1	Jörg BUTT		G	34		1
29	Jan-Ingwer CALLSEN-BRACKER		D		(1)	
27	Gonzalo CASTRO	ESP	M	14	(7)	
26	Sascha DUM		D		(1)	
10	Paul Slawomir FREIER		M	20	(9)	6
17	Clemens FRITZ		M	24	(5)	1
4	JUAN Silveira	BRA	D	30		3

Germany

FINAL LEAGUE TABLE 2005/06

		Pld	Home W	D	L	F	A	Away W	D	L	F	A	Total W	D	L	F	A	Pts
1	FC Bayern München	34	14	2	1	42	14	8	7	2	25	18	22	9	3	67	32	75
2	SV Werder Bremen	34	12	3	2	50	18	9	4	4	29	19	21	7	6	79	37	70
3	Hamburger SV	34	10	2	5	26	16	11	3	3	27	14	21	5	8	53	30	68
4	FC Schalke 04	34	10	6	1	32	16	6	7	4	15	15	16	13	5	47	31	61
5	Bayer 04 Leverkusen	34	7	6	4	30	23	7	4	6	34	26	14	10	10	64	49	52
6	Hertha BSC Berlin	34	8	5	4	30	22	4	7	6	22	26	12	12	10	52	48	48
7	Borussia Dortmund	34	8	4	5	23	18	3	9	5	22	24	11	13	10	45	42	46
8	1.FC Nürnberg	34	9	3	5	31	20	3	5	9	18	31	12	8	14	49	51	44
9	VfB Stuttgart	34	5	7	5	18	19	4	9	4	19	20	9	16	9	37	39	43
10	Bor. Mönchengladbach	34	8	7	2	27	18	2	5	10	15	32	10	12	12	42	50	42
11	FSV Mainz 05	34	6	7	4	31	23	3	4	10	15	24	9	11	14	46	47	38
12	Hannover 96	34	4	9	4	27	24	3	8	6	16	23	7	17	10	43	47	38
13	Arminia Bielefeld	34	8	2	7	18	15	2	5	10	14	32	10	7	17	32	47	37
14	Eintracht Frankfurt	34	5	5	7	24	22	4	4	9	18	29	9	9	16	42	51	36
15	VfL Wolfsburg	34	4	10	3	16	16	3	3	11	17	39	7	13	14	33	55	34
16	1.FC Kaiserslautern	34	5	5	7	26	33	3	4	10	21	38	8	9	17	47	71	33
17	1.FC Köln	34	5	4	8	24	29	2	5	10	25	42	7	9	18	49	71	30
18	MSV Duisburg	34	3	9	5	17	23	2	3	12	17	40	5	12	17	34	63	27

No	Name	Nat	Pos	Aps	(s)	Gls
8	Jacek KRZYNOWEK	POL	M	8	(13)	3
11	Danko LAZOVIC	SCG	A	1	(8)	
23	Ahmed MADOUNI	FRA	D	10	(4)	1
5	Jens NOWOTNY		D	13	(1)	
26	Michal PAPADOPULOS	CZE	A		(5)	
28	Carsten RAMELOW		M	23	(2)	1
6	Simon ROLFES		M	29	(3)	7
3	ROQUE JÚNIOR	BRA	D	14	(1)	
25	Bernd SCHNEIDER		M	29		4
2	Fredrik STENMAN	SWE	D	14	(1)	
14	Josip TADIC	CRO	A		(1)	
12	Andriy VORONIN	UKR	A	25	(4)	7

FC BAYERN MÜNCHEN
Coach – Felix Magath

2005
5/8	Bor. Mönchengladbach	h	3-0	Hargreaves, Makaay 2
13/8	Bayer 04 Leverkusen	a	5-2	Ballack, Makaay 3, Karimi
27/12	Hertha BSC Berlin	h	3-0	Ballack, Scholl, Makaay
10/9	1.FC Nürnberg	a	2-1	Guerrero, Ballack
17/9	Hannover 96	h	1-0	Demichelis
20/9	Eintracht Frankfurt	a	1-0	Guerrero
24/9	Hamburger SV	a	0-2	
1/10	VfL Wolfsburg	h	2-0	Santa Cruz, Lúcio
15/10	FC Schalke 04	a	1-1	Santa Cruz
22/10	MSV Duisburg	h	4-0	Ballack, Santa Cruz, Zé Roberto, Pizarro
29/10	1.FC Köln	a	2-1	Lúcio, Ballack
5/11	SV Werder Bremen	h	3-1	Schweinsteiger, Pizarro, Makaay
19/11	Arminia Bielefeld	a	2-1	Pizarro 2
26/11	FSV Mainz 05	h	2-1	Pizarro 2
3/12	VfB Stuttgart	a	0-0	
11/12	1.FC Kaiserslautern	h	2-1	Ballack, Makaay (p)
17/12	Borussia Dortmund	a	2-1	Karimi, Pizarro

2006
27/1	Bor. Mönchengladbach	a	3-1	Makaay 2, Ballack
4/2	Bayer 04 Leverkusen	h	1-0	Ballack
7/2	Hertha BSC Berlin	a	0-0	
12/2	1.FC Nürnberg	h	2-1	Makaay, Ballack
18/2	Hannover 96	a	1-1	Ballack
25/2	Eintracht Frankfurt	h	5-2	Guerrero 2, Ballack 2, Pizarro
4/3	Hamburger SV	h	1-2	Scholl
11/3	VfL Wolfsburg	a	0-0	
19/3	FC Schalke 04	h	3-0	Salihamidzic, Pizarro, Makaay
25/3	MSV Duisburg	a	3-1	Salihamidzic, Makaay, Pizarro
1/4	1.FC Köln	h	2-2	Sagnol, Makaay
8/4	SV Werder Bremen	a	0-3	
17/4	Arminia Bielefeld	h	2-0	Ballack, Scholl
23/4	FSV Mainz 05	a	2-2	Makaay 2 (1p)
3/5	VfB Stuttgart	h	3-1	Santa Cruz, Pizarro, Schweinsteiger
6/5	1.FC Kaiserslautern	a	1-1	Ottl
13/5	Borussia Dortmund	h	3-3	Makaay, Schweinsteiger, Ballack

No	Name	Nat	Pos	Aps	(s)	Gls
13	Michael BALLACK		M	26		14
26	Sebastian DEISLER		M	13	(3)	
6	Martín DEMICHELIS	ARG	D	27		1
19	Julio DOS SANTOS	PAR	M	1		
29	Bernd DREHER		M	1		
33	José Paolo GUERRERO	PER	A	6	(8)	4
23	Owen HARGREAVES	ENG	M	14	(2)	1
25	Valérien ISMAËL	FRA	D	30		
16	Jens JEREMIES		M	3	(19)	
1	Oliver KAHN		G	31		
8	Ali KARIMI	IRN	M	11	(9)	2
21	Phillip LAHM		D	12	(8)	
69	Bixente LIZARAZU	FRA	D	16	(2)	
3	LÚCIO	BRA	D	30		2
10	Roy MAKAAY	HOL	A	29	(2)	17
39	Andreas OTTL		M	2	(6)	1
14	Claudio PIZARRO	PER	A	23	(3)	11
22	Michael RENSING		G	2	(4)	
2	Willy SAGNOL	FRA	D	31		1

Germany

20	Hasan SALIHAMIDZIC	BOS	M	13	(8)	2	14	Euzebiusz SMOLAREK	POL	A	34		13
24	Roque SANTA CRUZ	ESP	A	9	(4)	4	39	Marcus STEEGMANN		M		(2)	
7	Mehmet SCHOLL		M	2	(16)	3	16	Cedric VAN DER GUN	HOL	A		(3)	
31	Bastian SCHWEINSTEIGER		M	20	(10)	3	1	Roman WEIDENFELLER		G	24		
11	ZÉ ROBERTO	BRA	M	22	(5)	1	4	Christian WÖRNS		D	28		3

BORUSSIA DORTMUND
Coach – Bert van Marwijk (HOL)

2005
Date	Opponent	H/A	Score	Scorers
5/8	VfL Wolfsburg	a	2-2	Smolarek, Koller
13/8	FC Schalke 04	h	1-2	Smolarek
28/8	MSV Duisburg	a	1-1	Ricken
11/9	1.FC Köln	h	2-1	Ricken 2 (1p)
17/9	SV Werder Bremen	a	2-3	Smolarek 2
20/9	Arminia Bielefeld	h	2-0	Koller, Smolarek
24/9	FSV Mainz 05	a	1-1	Metzelder
2/10	VfB Stuttgart	h	0-0	
15/10	1.FC Kaiserslautern	a	3-3	Smolarek 3
23/10	Hamburger SV	h	1-1	Metzelder
29/10	Bor. Mönchengladbach	h	2-1	Kehl, Smolarek
5/11	Bayer 04 Leverkusen	a	1-2	Ricken
19/11	Hertha BSC Berlin	h	2-0	Smolarek 2
26/11	1.FC Nürnberg	a	2-1	Odonkor, Nuri
3/12	Hannover 96	h	0-2	
10/12	Eintracht Frankfurt	a	0-2	
17/12	FC Bayern München	h	1-2	Kringe

2006
Date	Opponent	H/A	Score	Scorers
27/1	VfL Wolfsburg	h	3-2	Wörns, Smolarek, Gambino
4/2	FC Schalke 04	a	0-0	
7/2	MSV Duisburg	h	2-0	Brzenska, Rosicky
12/2	1.FC Köln	a	0-0	
18/2	SV Werder Bremen	h	0-1	
25/2	Arminia Bielefeld	a	0-1	
4/3	FSV Mainz 05	h	1-1	Wörns
11/3	VfB Stuttgart	a	0-0	
18/3	1.FC Kaiserslautern	h	2-1	Dedé, Kringe
25/3	Hamburger SV	a	4-2	Smolarek, Rosicky 2, Kringe
1/4	Bor. Mönchengladbach	a	1-2	Rosicky (p)
8/4	Bayer 04 Leverkusen	h	1-2	Brzenska
15/4	Hertha BSC Berlin	a	0-0	
22/4	1.FC Nürnberg	h	2-1	Kringe 2
2/5	Hannover 96	a	2-1	Rosicky, Wörns
6/5	Eintracht Frankfurt	h	1-1	Gambino
13/5	FC Bayern München	a	3-3	Koller 2, Degen

No	Name	Nat	Pos	Aps	(s)	Gls
8	Matthew AMOAH	GHA	A	4	(4)	
3	Markus BRZENSKA		D	18	(3)	2
7	Delron BUCKLEY	RSA	A	18	(10)	
24	Nizamettin CALISKAN	TUR	M	1	(1)	
17	DEDÉ	BRA	D	31		1
23	Phillip DEGEN	SUI	D	26	(5)	1
33	Salvatore GAMBINO		A	6	(9)	2
30	Dennis GENTENAAR	HOL	G	10		
27	Uwe HÜNEMEIER		D	1	(1)	
5	Sebastia KEHL		M	29		1
9	Jan KOLLER	CZE	A	6	(3)	4
6	Florian KRINGE		M	29	(1)	5
22	Marc-André KRUSKA		M	8	(16)	
2	Christoph METZELDER		D	18	(5)	2
25	NURI Sahin	TUR	M	23		1
11	David ODONKOR		A	26	(7)	1
18	Lars RICKEN		A	8	(2)	4
10	Tomás ROSICKY	CZE	M	26	(2)	5
13	Kosi SAKA	CON	M		(5)	

BORUSSIA MÖNCHENGLADBACH
Coach – Horst Köppel

2005
Date	Opponent	H/A	Score	Scorers
5/8	FC Bayern München	a	0-3	
13/8	VfL Wolfsburg	h	1-1	Bøgelund
27/8	FC Schalke 04	a	1-1	Bøgelund
10/9	MSV Duisburg	h	2-1	Neuville, Zé António
17/9	1.FC Köln	a	1-2	Neuville (p)
20/9	SV Werder Bremen	h	2-1	Broich, og (Baumann)
24/9	Arminia Bielefeld	a	2-0	Kluge, Neuville
1/10	FSV Mainz 05	h	1-0	Zé António
15/10	VfB Stuttgart	a	1-1	Kluge
22/10	1.FC Kaiserslautern	h	4-1	Strasser, El Fakiri, Kluge, Neuville
29/10	Borussia Dortmund	a	1-2	Neuville
6/11	Hamburger SV	h	0-0	
19/11	Bayer 04 Leverkusen	h	1-1	Polanski
27/11	Hertha BSC Berlin	a	2-2	Kahé, og (Friedrich)
3/12	1.FC Nürnberg	h	0-1	
10/12	Hannover 96	a	1-1	Kahé
17/12	Eintracht Frankfurt	h	4-3	Jansen, Neuville 2, Sverkos

2006
Date	Opponent	H/A	Score	Scorers
27/1	FC Bayern München	h	1-3	Sonck
5/2	VfL Wolfsburg	a	0-2	
8/2	FC Schalke 04	h	0-0	
11/2	MSV Duisburg	a	1-1	Svensson
18/2	1.FC Köln	h	2-0	og (Lell), Neuville
25/2	SV Werder Bremen	a	0-2	
5/3	Arminia Bielefeld	h	2-0	Jansen, Sonck
11/3	FSV Mainz 05	a	0-3	
18/3	VfB Stuttgart	h	1-1	Fukal
26/3	1.FC Kaiserslautern	a	0-3	
1/4	Borussia Dortmund	h	2-1	Rafael 2
9/4	Hamburger SV	a	0-2	
15/4	Bayer 04 Leverkusen	a	1-2	Neuville
22/4	Hertha BSC Berlin	h	2-2	og (Chahed), Broich
2/5	1.FC Nürnberg	a	2-5	Zé António, Sonck
6/5	Hannover 96	h	2-2	Jansen, Sonck
13/5	Eintracht Frankfurt	a	2-0	Neuville, Rafael

No	Name	Nat	Pos	Aps	(s)	Gls
20	Kaspar BØGELUND	DEN	D	12	(4)	2
11	Jörg BÖHME		M		(1)	
29	Thomas BROICH		M	19	(9)	2
33	Marvin COMPPER		D	1	(4)	
3	Filip DAEMS	BEL	D	15	(7)	
14	Hassan EL FAKIRI	NOR	M	25	(6)	1
10	Giovane ÉLBER	BRA	A		(4)	
36	Robert FLESSERS		M	2	(1)	
18	Milan FUKAL	CZE	D	21	(4)	1
28	Marek HEINZ	CZE	M	3		
4	Thomas HELVEG	DEN	D	4	(1)	
5	Marcell JANSEN		D	32		3
15	KAHÉ	BRA	A	18	(9)	2
1	Darius KAMPA		G	1		
35	Bekim KASTRATI	ALB	A		(4)	
26	Kasey KELLER	USA	G	33		
24	Peer KLUGE		M	25	(3)	3
8	Krisztián LISZTES	HUN	M	3	(2)	

Germany

No	Name	Nat	Pos	Aps	(s)	Gls
27	Oliver NEUVILLE		A	34		10
21	Niels OUDE KAMPHUIS	HOL	M	11	(1)	
19	Eugen POLANSKI		M	19	(2)	1
23	Nando RAFAEL		A	6	(8)	3
9	Wesley SONCK	BEL	A	10	(4)	4
7	Jeff STRASSER	LUX	D	25	(1)	1
2	Bo SVENSSON	DEN	D	12	(1)	1
25	Václav SVERKOS	CZE	A	2	(11)	1
16	Bernd THIJS	BEL	M	8	(7)	
13	ZÉ ANTÓNIO	POR	D	33	(1)	3

MSV DUISBURG
Coach – Norbert Meier; (8/12/05) (Heiko Scholz); (17/12/05) Jürgen Kohler; (4/4/05) Heiko Scholz

2005
Date	Opponent	h/a	Score	Scorers
5/8	VfB Stuttgart	h	1-1	Ahanfouf
13/8	1.FC Kaiserslautern	a	3-5	Möhrle 2, Ahanfouf
28/8	Borussia Dortmund	h	1-1	Kurth
10/9	Bor. Mönchengladbach	a	1-2	Möhrle
18/9	Bayer 04 Leverkusen	h	1-3	Lavric
21/9	Hertha BSC Berlin	a	2-3	Grlic, Biliskov
24/9	1.FC Nürnberg	h	1-0	Kurth
1/10	Hannover 96	a	1-1	Ahanfouf
16/10	Eintracht Frankfurt	h	0-1	
22/10	FC Bayern München	a	0-4	
29/10	VfL Wolfsburg	h	1-0	Bugera
5/11	FC Schalke 04	a	0-3	
20/11	Hamburger SV	a	0-2	
3/12	SV Werder Bremen	a	0-2	
6/12	1.FC Köln	h	1-1	Ahanfouf
10/12	Arminia Bielefeld	h	1-1	Ahanfouf
17/12	FSV Mainz 05	a	1-1	Möhrle

2006
Date	Opponent	h/a	Score	Scorers
28/1	VfB Stuttgart	a	1-0	Caligiuri
4/2	1.FC Kaiserslautern	h	2-2	Kurth, Tararache (p)
7/2	Borussia Dortmund	a	0-2	
11/2	Bor. Mönchengladbach	h	1-1	Lavric
18/2	Bayer 04 Leverkusen	a	2-3	Lavric 2
26/2	Hertha BSC Berlin	h	2-1	Tararache (p), Lavric
4/3	1.FC Nürnberg	a	0-3	
11/3	Hannover 96	h	0-0	
18/3	Eintracht Frankfurt	a	2-5	Bodzek, Lavric
25/3	FC Bayern München	h	1-3	Ahanfouf (p)
1/4	VfL Wolfsburg	a	1-1	Van Houdt
9/4	FC Schalke 04	h	1-1	og (Poulsen)
15/4	Hamburger SV	h	0-2	
22/4	1.FC Köln	a	1-3	Ahanfouf
3/5	SV Werder Bremen	h	3-5	Ahn, Ahanfouf 2
6/5	Arminia Bielefeld	a	2-0	Ahn, Caligiuri
13/5	FSV Mainz 05	h	0-0	

No	Name	Nat	Pos	Aps	(s)	Gls
15	Abdelaziz AHANFOUF		A	22	(5)	9
19	AHN Jung-hwan	KOR	M	3	(9)	2
27	Markus ANFANG		M	5	(7)	
23	Necat AYGÜN		D	2	(6)	
3	Thomas BAELUM	DEN	D	27	(1)	
26	Sven BEUCKERT		G		(3)	
5	Marino BILISKOV	CRO	D	21		1
13	Adam BODZEK		D	6	(3)	1
7	Alexander BUGERA		D	23		1
33	Marco CALIGIURI		M	11	(3)	2
14	Nasir EL KASMI		M		(2)	
20	Ivica GRLIC	BOS	M	11	(2)	1
6	Markus HAUSWEILER		M	3		
23	Josef IVANOVIC		A		(1)	
1	Georg KOCH		G	34		
18	Markus KURTH		A	26	(5)	3
10	Klemen LAVRIC	SLO	A	18	(4)	6
30	Dirk LOTTNER		M	16	(3)	
17	Alexander MEYER		D	25		
22	Kai MICHALKE		A	2	(4)	
4	Uwe MÖHRLE		D	31		4
9	Mike RIETPIETSCH		M	2	(11)	
25	Niklas STEGMANN		A		(1)	
16	Mihai TARARACHE	ROM	M	15		2
2	Razundara TJIKUZU	NAM	D	20	(3)	
21	Peter VAN HOUDT	BEL	A	14	(15)	1
29	Tobias WILLI		M	22	(3)	
11	Carsten WOLTERS		D	15	(3)	

EINTRACHT FRANKFURT
Coach – Friedhelm Funkel

2005
Date	Opponent	h/a	Score	Scorers
7/8	Bayer 04 Leverkusen	h	1-4	Vasoski
13/8	Hertha BSC Berlin	a	0-2	
27/8	1.FC Nürnberg	h	1-0	Jones
10/9	Hannover 96	a	0-2	
17/9	Hamburger SV	a	1-1	Cha
20/9	FC Bayern München	h	0-1	
24/9	VfL Wolfsburg	a	0-1	
1/10	FC Schalke 04	h	0-1	
16/10	MSV Duisburg	a	1-0	Meier
22/10	1.FC Köln	h	6-3	Amanatidis, Rehmer, Chris, Köhler, Meier, Cha
29/10	SV Werder Bremen	a	1-4	Amanatidis
5/11	Arminia Bielefeld	h	3-0	Copado, Meier 2
19/11	FSV Mainz 05	a	2-2	og (Noveski) 2
27/11	VfB Stuttgart	h	1-1	Amanatidis
10/12	Borussia Dortmund	h	2-0	Copado, Amanatidis
14/12	1. FC Kaiserslautern	a	2-1	Weissenberger, Copado
17/12	Bor. Mönchengladbach	a	3-4	Copado 2, Chris

2006
Date	Opponent	h/a	Score	Scorers
27/1	Bayer 04 Leverkusen	a	1-2	Amanatidis
4/2	Hertha BSC Berlin	h	1-1	Jones
8/2	1.FC Nürnberg	a	1-0	Amanatidis
11/2	Hannover 96	h	0-1	
19/2	Hamburger SV	h	1-2	Meier
25/2	FC Bayern München	a	2-5	Preuss, Meier
5/3	VfL Wolfsburg	h	1-1	Amanatidis
12/3	FC Schalke 04	a	0-2	
18/3	MSV Duisburg	h	5-2	Amanatidis 3, Köhler, Copado (p)
25/3	1.FC Köln	a	1-1	Rehmer
1/4	SV Werder Bremen	h	0-1	
8/4	Arminia Bielefeld	a	0-1	
15/4	FSV Mainz 05	h	0-0	
22/4	VfB Stuttgart	a	2-0	Meier, Amanatidis (p)
3/5	1.FC Kaiserslautern	h	2-2	Köhler, Amanatidis
6/5	Borussia Dortmund	a	1-1	Cha
13/5	Bor. Mönchengladbach	h	0-2	

No	Name	Nat	Pos	Aps	(s)	Gls
18	Ioannis AMANATIDIS	GRE	A	31	(1)	12
11	CHA Du-Ri	KOR	A	11	(16)	3
31	Mounir CHAFTAR		D	1		
29	CHRIS	BRA	D	20	(2)	2
17	Daniyel CIMEN		M	8	(4)	
20	Francisco COPADO	ESP	A	21	(3)	6
30	Benjamin HUGGEL	SUI	M	20	(8)	

Germany

No	Name	Nat	Pos	Aps	(s)	Gls
13	Jermaine JONES		A	20		2
7	Benjamin KÖHLER		A	25	(4)	3
8	Stefan LEXA	AUT	M	6	(7)	
14	Alexander MEIER		M	32	(1)	7
1	Oka NIKOLOV	MAC	G	30		
2	Patrick OCHS		D	25	(3)	
4	Christoph PREUSS		M	18	(5)	1
21	Markus PRÖLL		G	2		
33	Marko REHMER		D	25		2
22	Christopher REINHARD		D	5	(2)	
23	Marco RUSS		D	8	(1)	
24	Alexander SCHUR		M		(2)	
16	Christoph SPYCHER	SUI	D	24		
26	Dominik STROH-ENGEL		A		(3)	
9	Arie VAN LENT		A	2	(9)	
5	Aleksandar VASOSKI	MAC	D	33		1
10	Markus WEISSENBERGER		M	5	(9)	1
3	André WIEDENER		D		(1)	
28	Jan ZIMMERMANN		G	2		

HAMBURGER SV
Coach – Thomas Doll

2005

Date	Opponent	h/a	Score	Scorers
6/8	1.FC Nürnberg	h	3-0	Mpenza, Barbarez 2 (1p)
13/8	Arminia Bielefeld	a	2-0	Barbarez (p), Van der Vaart
27/8	Hannover 96	h	1-1	Mahdavikia
10/9	Mainz 05	a	3-1	Wicky, Mahdavikia, Van der Vaart
17/9	Eintracht Frankfurt	h	1-1	Van Buyten
21/9	VfB Stuttgart	a	2-1	Van der Vaart, Jarolím
24/9	FC Bayern München	h	2-0	Van der Vaart, Trochowski
2/10	1.FC Kaiserslautern	a	3-0	Van der Vaart 2, Barbarez
15/10	VfL Wolfsburg	h	0-1	
23/10	Borussia Dortmund	a	1-1	Trochowski
29/10	FC Schalke 04	h	1-0	Mahdavikia
6/11	Bor. Mönchengladbach	a	0-0	
20/11	MSV Duisburg	h	2-0	Barbarez, Lauth
26/11	Bayer 04 Leverkusen	a	1-0	Jarolím
3/12	1.FC Köln	h	3-1	Atouba, Lauth, Barbarez
10/11	Hertha BSC Berlin	h	2-1	og (Van Burik), Mahdavikia (p)
18/12	SV Werder Bremen	a	1-1	Kucukovic

2006

Date	Opponent	h/a	Score	Scorers
27/1	1.FC Nürnberg	a	1-2	og (Wolf)
4/2	Arminia Bielefeld	h	2-1	Trochowski, Barbarez
8/2	Hannover 96	a	1-2	Barbarez
11/2	FSV Mainz 05	h	1-0	Mahdavikia
19/2	Eintracht Frankfurt	a	2-1	Trochowski, Van Buyten
26/2	VfB Stuttgart	h	0-2	
4/3	FC Bayern München	a	2-1	Demel, De Jong
12/3	1.FC Kaiserslautern	h	3-0	Lauth, og (Schönheim), Van der Vaart (p)
18/3	VfL Wolfsburg	a	1-0	Lauth
25/3	Borussia Dortmund	h	2-4	Lauth, Aílton
2/4	FC Schalke 04	a	2-0	Van der Vaart, Aílton
9/4	Bor. Mönchengladbach	h	2-0	Van der Vaart (p), Takahara
15/4	MSV Duisburg	a	2-0	og (Möhrle), Aílton
22/4	Bayer 04 Leverkusen	h	0-2	
2/5	1.FC Köln	a	1-0	Barbarez
6/5	Hertha BSC Berlin	a	2-4	Trochowski, Lauth
13/5	SV Werder Bremen	h	1-2	Barbarez

No	Name	Nat	Pos	Aps	(s)	Gls
24	AÍLTON Gonçalves	BRA	A	9	(4)	3
3	Thimothée ATOUBA	CMR	D	31		1
10	Sergej BARBAREZ	BOS	M	33		10
22	Stefan BEINLICH		M	16		
21	Khalid BOULAHROUZ	HOL	D	28		
28	Nigel DE JONG	HOL	M	12		1
20	Guy DEMEL	FRA	D	20	(2)	1
13	Mario FILLINGER		M		(2)	
14	David JAROLÍM	CZE	M	31		2
8	Markus KAHL		M		(3)	
12	Sascha KIRSCHSTEIN		G	14		
16	René KLINGBEIL		D	6	(12)	
19	Mustafa KUCUKOVIC		A		(5)	1
27	Alexander LAAS		M		(5)	
11	Benjamin LAUTH		A	22	(9)	6
7	Mehdi MAHDAVIKIA	IRN	M	28	(3)	5
25	Emile MPENZA	BEL	A	5	(5)	1
4	Bastian REINHARDT		D	8	(6)	
32	Naohiro TAKAHARA	JPN	A	6	(15)	1
31	Charles TAKYI		A		(1)	
15	Piotr TROCHOWSKI		M	24	(8)	5
5	Daniel VAN BUYTEN	BEL	D	26	(1)	2
23	Rafael VAN DER VAART	HOL	M	18	(1)	9
1	Stefan WÄCHTER		G	20		
6	Raphaël WICKY	SUI	M	17	(1)	1
24	Reto ZIEGLER	SUI	M		(8)	

HANNOVER 96
Coach – Ewald Lienen; (9/11/05) Peter Neururer

2005

Date	Opponent	h/a	Score	Scorers
5/8	Hertha BSC Berlin	h	2-2	Dabrowski, Tarnat
13/8	1.FC Nürnberg	a	1-1	Brdaric
27/8	Hamburger SV	a	1-1	Stajner
10/9	Eintracht Frankfurt	h	2-0	Stajner, Yankov
17/9	FC Bayern München	a	0-1	
20/9	VfL Wolfsburg	h	2-4	Brdaric 2
24/9	FC Schalke 04	h	0-2	
1/10	MSV Duisburg	h	1-1	Delura
16/10	1.FC Köln	a	4-1	Stajner, Ricardo Sousa (p), Brdaric 2
22/10	SV Werder Bremen	h	0-0	
30/10	Arminia Bielefeld	a	1-4	Mertesacker
5/11	FSV Mainz 05	h	2-2	Brdaric (p), Tarnat
20/11	VfB Stuttgart	a	2-2	Hashemian, Yankov
26/11	1.FC Kaiserslautern	h	5-1	Tarnat 2, Brdaric 2, Hashemian
3/12	Borussia Dortmund	a	2-0	Cherundolo, Dabrowski
10/12	Bor. Mönchengladbach	h	1-1	Stajner
17/12	Bayer 04 Leverkusen	a	0-0	

2006

Date	Opponent	h/a	Score	Scorers
27/1	Hertha BSC Berlin	a	1-1	Dabrowski
5/2	1.FC Nürnberg	h	1-1	Stajner
8/2	Hamburger SV	h	2-1	Zuraw, Hashemian
11/2	Eintracht Frankfurt	a	1-0	Yankov
18/2	FC Bayern München	h	1-1	Brdaric
25/2	VfL Wolfsburg	a	1-2	Brdaric
4/3	FC Schalke 04	h	1-2	Christiansen
11/3	MSV Duisburg	a	0-0	
18/3	1.FC Köln	h	1-0	Hashemian
25/3	SV Werder Bremen	a	0-5	
2/4	Arminia Bielefeld	h	0-1	
8/4	FSV Mainz 05	a	0-0	
16/4	VfB Stuttgart	h	3-3	Stajner, Balitsch, Mertesacker
22/4	1.FC Kaiserslautern	a	0-1	
2/5	Borussia Dortmund	h	1-2	Mertesacker
6/5	Bor. Mönchengladbach	a	2-2	Mertesacker, Vinícius

Germany

	13/5	Bayer 04 Leverkusen		h	2-2	Mertesacker, Yankov

No	Name	Nat	Pos	Aps	(s)	Gls
14	Hanno BALITSCH		M	30	(1)	1
13	Thomas BRDARIC		A	28	(3)	10
6	Steve CHERUNDOLO	USA	D	22		1
9	Thomas CHRISTIANSEN	ESP	A		(4)	1
5	Christoph DABROWSKI		M	32		3
7	Michael DELURA		M	7	(18)	1
36	Johannes DIETWALD		M		(1)	
1	Robert ENKE		G	32		
28	Hendrik HAHNE		A	2	(5)	
35	Sören HALFAR		D	3	(2)	
16	Vahid HASHEMIAN	IRN	A	25	(4)	4
21	Mohammadou IDRISSOU	CMR	A	1	(3)	
30	Morten JENSEN		G	1		
25	Frank JURIC	CRO	G	1		
8	Altin LALA	ALB	M	28	(1)	
29	Per MERTESACKER		D	30		5
31	Fabian MONTABELL		M		(3)	
10	RICARDO SOUSA	POR	M	6	(7)	1
27	Silvio SCHRÖTER		M	5	(6)	
24	Jiri STAJNER	CZE	A	30	(3)	6
11	Daniel STENDEL		A	1	(5)	
18	Michael TARNAT		D	29		4
4	Jonas TROEST	DEN	D	3	(4)	
2	VINÍCIUS Bergantin	BRA	D	14	(9)	1
23	Chavdar YANKOV	BUL	M	15	(7)	4
3	Dariusz ZURAW	POL	D	29	(1)	1

HERTHA BSC BERLIN
Coach – Falko Götz

2005
5/8	Hannover 96	a	2-2	Marcelinho (p), Wichniarek
13/8	Eintracht Frankfurt	h	2-0	Schröder, og (Van Lent)
27/8	FC Bayern München	a	0-3	
11/9	VfL Wolfsburg	h	3-0	Friedrich, Pantelic, Gilberto
18/9	FC Schalke 04	a	0-0	
21/9	MSV Duisburg	h	3-2	Pantelic, Marcelinho (p), Rafael
25/9	1.FC Köln	a	1-0	Madlung
1/10	SV Werder Bremen	h	1-2	Dárdai
15/10	Arminia Bielefeld	a	0-3	
22/10	FSV Mainz 05	h	3-1	Marcelinho 2, Pantelic
29/10	VfB Stuttgart	a	3-3	Cairo, Rafael, Marcelinho
5/11	1.FC Kaiserslautern	h	3-0	Marcelinho, Pantelic, Rafael
19/11	Borussia Dortmund	a	0-2	
27/11	Bor. Mönchengladbach	h	2-2	Bastürk, Kovac
4/12	Bayer 04 Leverkusen	a	2-1	Bastürk, Marcelinho
10/12	Hamburger SV	a	1-2	Bastürk
18/12	1.FC Nürnberg	h	1-1	Madlung

2006
27/1	Hannover 96	h	1-1	Van Burik
4/2	Eintracht Frankfurt	a	1-1	Boateng
7/2	FC Bayern München	h	0-0	
11/2	VfL Wolfsburg	a	1-1	Marcelinho (p)
18/2	FC Schalke 04	h	1-2	Madlung
26/2	MSV Duisburg	a	1-2	Bastürk
4/3	1.FC Köln	h	2-4	Pantelic 2
11/3	SV Werder Bremen	a	3-0	Boateng, Marcelinho, Bastürk
19/3	Arminia Bielefeld	h	1-0	Pantelic
25/3	FSV Mainz 05	a	2-2	Pantelic 2
1/4	VfB Stuttgart	h	2-0	Marcelinho 2 (1p)
8/4	1.FC Kaiserslautern	a	2-0	Pantelic, Gilberto
15/4	Borussia Dortmund	h	0-0	
22/4	Bor. Mönchengladbach	a	2-2	Bastürk, Kovac
2/5	Bayer 04 Leverkusen	h	1-5	Marcelinho
6/5	Hamburger SV	h	4-2	Neuendorf, Madlung, Kovac, Pantelic
13/5	1.FC Nürnberg	a	1-2	Dárdai

No	Name	Nat	Pos	Aps	(s)	Gls
7	Yildiray BASTÜRK	TUR	M	25	(2)	6
27	Kevin-Prince BOATENG	GHA	M	17	(4)	2
11	Ellery CAIRO	HOL	A	14	(4)	1
28	Sofian CHAHED		D	12	(3)	
8	Pál DÁRDAI	HUN	M	9	(7)	2
16	Ashkan DEJAGAH		A		(3)	
29	Malik FATHI		D	26		
12	Christian FIEDLER		G	29		
3	Arne FRIEDRICH		D	31		1
6	GILBERTO da Silva Melo	BRA	M	22		2
5	Niko KOVAC	CRO	M	24	(4)	3
17	Alexander MADLUNG		D	14	(8)	4
10	MARCELINHO	BRA	M	32		12
32	Thorben MARX		M	4	(4)	
20	Andreas NEUENDORF		M	7	(18)	1
21	Solomon OKORONKWO	NGA	A	2	(9)	
9	Marko PANTELIC	SCG	A	26	(2)	11
24	Nando RAFAEL	ANG	A	7	(5)	3
35	Christopher SAMBA	FRA	D	2	(10)	
19	Andreas SCHMIDT		M	1		
22	Oliver SCHRÖDER		D	14	(4)	1
14	Josip SIMUNIC	CRO	D	18		
25	Václav SVERKOS	CZE	A	6	(4)	
1	Gerhard TREMMEL		G	5		
4	Dick VAN BURIK	HOL	D	25		1
18	Artur WICHNIAREK	POL	A	2	(1)	1

1. FC KAISERSLAUTERN
Coach – Michael Henke; (19/11/05) Wolfgang Wolf

2005
7/8	FC Schalke 04	a	1-2	Altintop
13/8	MSV Duisburg	h	5-3	Altintop 3, Lembi, Sanogo
27/8	1.FC Köln	a	3-2	Altintop 2, Skela (p)
10/9	SV Werder Bremen	h	1-5	Altintop
17/9	Arminia Bielefeld	a	0-0	
21/9	FSV Mainz 05	h	0-2	
25/9	VfB Stuttgart	a	0-1	
2/10	Hamburger SV	h	0-3	
15/10	Borussia Dortmund	h	3-3	Altintop 3
22/10	Bor. Mönchengladbach	a	1-4	Sanogo
29/10	Bayer 04 Leverkusen	h	2-2	Engelhardt, Göktan
5/11	Hertha BSC Berlin	a	0-3	
19/11	1.FC Nürnberg	h	1-3	Blank
26/11	Hannover 96	a	1-5	Sanogo
11/12	FC Bayern München	a	1-2	Sanogo
14/12	Eintracht Frankfurt	h	1-2	Seitz
17/12	VfL Wolfsburg	h	3-2	Altintop 3

2006
29/1	FC Schalke 04	h	0-2	
4/2	MSV Duisburg	a	2-2	Halfar 2
7/2	1.FC Köln	h	2-2	Sanogo (p), Schönheim
11/2	SV Werder Bremen	a	2-0	Sanogo, Skela
18/2	Arminia Bielefeld	h	2-0	Sanogo 2
25/2	FSV Mainz 05	a	2-0	Sanogo 2 (1p)
7/3	VfB Stuttgart	h	1-1	Altintop
12/3	Hamburger SV	a	0-3	
18/3	Borussia Dortmund	a	1-2	Skela

Germany

Date	Opponent	h/a	Score	Scorers
26/3	Bor. Mönchengladbach	h	3-0	Altintop 2, Skela
1/4	Bayer 04 Leverkusen	a	1-5	Pletsch
8/4	Hertha BSC Berlin	h	0-2	
16/4	1.FC Nürnberg	a	2-3	Altintop 2
22/4	Hannover 96	h	1-0	Halfar
3/5	Eintracht Frankfurt	a	2-2	Reinert, Ziemer
6/5	FC Bayern München	h	1-1	Altintop
13/5	VfL Wolfsburg	a	2-2	Altintop, Ziemer

No	Name	Nat	Pos	Aps	(s)	Gls
19	Halil ALTINTOP	TUR	A	34		20
3	Mathieu BEDA	FRA	D	16		
16	Axel BELLINGHAUSEN		M	17	(3)	
33	Stefan BLANK		D	14	(3)	1
39	Steffen BOHL		M		(2)	
30	Balázs BORBÉLY	SVK	M	6	(2)	
20	Marco ENGELHARDT		M	30	(2)	1
21	Thomas ERNST		G	3		
27	Florian FROMLOWITZ		G	11	(1)	
8	Berkant GÖKTAN	TUR	M	2	(5)	1
28	Daniel HALFAR		M	5	(13)	3
5	Ingo HERTZSCH		D	22	(4)	
40	Jon Inge HØILAND	NOR	D	8	(1)	
9	Carsten JANCKER		A	5		
2	Hervé Nzelo LEMBI	BEL	D	29		1
1	Jürgen MACHO	AUT	G	20		
32	Lucien METTOMO	FRA	D	9		
14	Mihael MIKIC	CRO	M	6	(14)	
6	Christian NERLINGER		M	3	(1)	
15	Marcelo PLETSCH		D	21	(1)	1
29	Sebastian REINERT		M	9	(5)	1
22	Torsten REUTER		D	5	(3)	
23	Thomas RIEDL		M	5	(6)	
18	Boubacar SANOGO	CIV	A	21	(3)	10
34	Fabian SCHÖNHEIM		M	17	(1)	1
17	Jochen SEITZ		M	7	(5)	1
13	Ciriaco SFORZA	SUI	M	7		
7	Ervin SKELA	ITA	M	33	(1)	4
4	Timo WENZEL		D	4		
10	Ferydoon ZANDI	IRN	M	5	(14)	
38	Marcel ZIEMER		A		(2)	2

1. FC KÖLN
Coach – Uwe Rapolder (SUI); (18/12/05) Hans-Peter Latour (SUI)

2005

Date	Opponent	h/a	Score	Scorers
5/8	FSV Mainz 05	h	1-0	Schlicke (p)
14/8	VfB Stuttgart	a	3-2	Feulner, Streit 2
27/8	1.FC Kaiserslautern	h	2-3	Scherz, Podolski
11/9	Borussia Dortmund	a	1-2	Scherz
17/9	Bor. Mönchengladbach	h	2-2	Podolski, Schlicke
21/9	Bayer 04 Leverkusen	a	1-2	Helmes
25/9	Hertha BSC Berlin	h	0-1	
1/10	1.FC Nürnberg	a	1-2	Helmes
16/10	Hannover 96	h	1-4	Streit
22/10	Eintracht Frankfurt	a	3-6	Streit, Podolski (p), Alpay
29/10	FC Bayern München	h	1-2	Scherz
5/11	VfL Wolfsburg	a	1-1	Epstein
19/11	FC Schalke 04	h	2-2	Benschneider, Epstein
3/12	Hamburger SV	a	1-3	Schlicke
6/12	MSV Duisburg	a	1-1	Podolski
11/12	SV Werder Bremen	h	1-4	Szabics
17/12	Arminia Bielefeld	a	2-3	Springer, Scherz

2006

Date	Opponent	h/a	Score	Scorers
27/1	FSV Mainz 05	a	2-4	Podolski (p), Scherz
4/2	VfB Stuttgart	h	0-0	
7/2	1.FC Kaiserslautern	a	2-2	Streller 2
12/2	Borussia Dortmund	h	0-0	
18/2	Bor. Mönchengladbach	a	0-2	
25/2	Bayer 04 Leverkusen	h	0-3	
4/3	Hertha BSC Berlin	a	4-2	Podolski 2, Streller, Scherz
11/3	1.FC Nürnberg	h	3-4	Zivkovic, Matip, Podolski
18/3	Hannover 96	a	0-1	
25/3	Eintracht Frankfurt	h	1-1	Springer
1/4	FC Bayern München	a	2-2	Feulner, Streit
8/4	VfL Wolfsburg	h	3-0	Scherz, Helmes, og (Sarpei)
15/4	FC Schalke 04	a	1-1	Podolski
22/4	MSV Duisburg	h	3-1	Streit, Feulner, Podolski
2/5	Hamburger SV	h	0-1	
6/5	SV Werder Bremen	a	0-6	
13/5	Arminia Bielefeld	h	4-2	Podolski 2, Scherz, Helmes

No	Name	Nat	Pos	Aps	(s)	Gls
27	ALPAY Özalan	TUR	D	21		1
16	Alexander BADE		G	12	(1)	
4	Roland BENSCHNEIDER		D	8	(4)	1
29	Ricardo CABANAS	SUI	M	16		
2	Carsten CULLMANN		D	9	(1)	
39	Denis EPSTEIN		M	3	(8)	2
12	EVANILSON Aparecido	BRA	D	2	(1)	
23	Markus FEULNER		M	12	(1)	3
18	Dimitrios GRAMMOZIS	GRE	M	12	(7)	
14	Rolf-Christel GUIÉ-MIEN	CON	M	3	(4)	
17	Patrick HELMES		A	3	(19)	4
30	Christian LELL		D	23	(3)	
13	Anthony LURLING	HOL	M	6	(6)	
11	Peter MADSEN	DEN	A	5	(3)	
25	Marvin MATIP		D	23		1
36	Youssef MOKHTARI	MAR	M	10	(3)	
10	Lukas PODOLSKI		A	30	(2)	12
3	Christian RAHN		D	9	(2)	
8	Matthias SCHERZ		A	17	(10)	8
21	Sebastian SCHINDZIELORZ		M	10	(6)	
22	Björn SCHLICKE		D	14	(1)	3
6	Andrew SINKALA	ZAM	M	8	(1)	
20	Lukas SINKIEWICZ		D	32	(1)	
15	Christian SPRINGER		M	12	(6)	2
7	Albert STREIT		M	28	(2)	6
28	Marco STRELLER	SUI	A	11	(3)	3
19	Imre SZABICS	HUN	A	4	(7)	1
9	Attila TÖKÖLI	HUN	A		(1)	
37	Patrick WEISER		D	1		
33	Stefan WESSELS		G	22		
24	Boris ZIVKOVIC	CRO	D	8		1

FSV MAINZ 05
Coach – Jürgen Klopp

2005

Date	Opponent	h/a	Score	Scorers
5/8	1.FC Köln	a	0-1	
14/8	SV Werder Bremen	h	0-2	
28/8	Arminia Bielefeld	a	0-2	
10/9	Hamburger SV	h	1-3	Ruman
17/9	VfB Stuttgart	h	1-2	Noveski
21/9	1.FC Kaiserslautern	a	2-0	Thurk, Auer
24/9	Borussia Dortmund	h	1-1	Zidan (p)
1/10	Bor. Mönchengladbach	a	0-1	
15/10	Bayer 04 Leverkusen	h	3-1	Ruman 2, Thurk
22/10	Hertha BSC Berlin	h	1-3	Friedrich
30/10	1.FC Nürnberg	h	4-1	og (Paulus), Auer, Da Silva, Thurk
5/11	Hannover 96	a	2-2	Friedrich, Auer
19/11	Eintracht Frankfurt	h	2-2	Noveski, Ruman

Germany

5/11	FC Bayern München	a	1-2		Auer
?/12	VfL Wolfsburg	h	5-1		Thurk 2 (1p), Auer, Ruman, Zidan
3/12	FC Schalke 04	a	0-1		
7/12	MSV Duisburg	h	1-1		Da Silva
2006					
7/1	1.FC Köln	h	4-2		Thurk 2, Zidan, Auer
?/2	SV Werder Bremen	a	2-4		Zidan, Weiland N.
?/2	Arminia Bielefeld	h	1-1		Zidan (p)
1/2	Hamburger SV	a	0-1		
9/2	VfB Stuttgart	a	1-2		Da Silva
5/2	1.FC Kaiserslautern	h	0-2		
?/3	Borussia Dortmund	a	1-1		Thurk
1/3	Bor. Mönchengladbach	h	3-0		Thurk 2, Zidan
8/3	Bayer 04 Leverkusen	a	2-1		Zidan 2
5/3	Hertha BSC Berlin	h	2-2		Thurk (p), Casey
?/4	1.FC Nürnberg	a	0-3		
?/4	Hannover 96	h	0-0		
5/4	Eintracht Frankfurt	a	0-0		
23/4	FC Bayern München	h	2-2		Zidan, Friedrich
?/5	VfL Wolfsburg	a	3-0		Thurk, Auer 2
5/5	FC Schalke 04	h	1-0		Auer
13/5	MSV Duisburg	a	0-0		

No	Name	Nat	Pos	Aps	(s)	Gls
28	Mathias ABEL		D	18	(2)	
6	Otto ADDO		M	7	(10)	
7	Benjamin AUER		A	25	(4)	9
19	Christof BABATZ		M	14	(3)	
26	Tamás BÓDOG	HUN	D		(1)	
21	Conor CASEY	USA	A	4	(6)	1
25	António DA SILVA	BRA	M	33		3
41	Tobias DAMM		M		(1)	
5	Christian DEMIRTAS		D	25	(3)	
10	Manuel FRIEDRICH		D	34		3
31	Tom GEISSLER		M		(15)	
8	Fabian GERBER		M	15	(6)	
20	Ranisav JOVANOVIC	SCG	A		(2)	
4	Nikolce NOVESKI	MAC	D	33		2
13	Milorad PEKOVIC	SCG	M	23	(1)	
15	ROMULO Marcos	BRA	A	1	(7)	
17	Marco ROSE		D	13	(6)	
11	Petr RUMAN	CZE	A	16	(8)	5
23	Jonas SELA		G		(1)	
27	Michael THURK		A	32		12
1	Dimo WACHE		G	20		
24	Benjamin WEIGELT		D	20	(3)	
9	Dennis WEILAND		M		(3)	
22	Niclas WEILAND		A	5	(9)	1
29	Christian WETKLO		G	14	(1)	
14	Mohammed ZIDAN	EGY	A	22	(4)	9

1. FC NÜRNBERG
Coach – Wolfgang Wolf; (31/10/05) (Dieter Lieberwirth); (9/11/05) Hans Meyer

2005					
6/8	Hamburger SV	a	0-3		
13/8	Hannover 96	h	1-1		Mintál
27/8	Eintracht Frankfurt	a	0-1		
10/9	FC Bayern München	h	1-2		Pínola
17/9	VfL Wolfsburg	a	1-1		Schroth
21/9	FC Schalke 04	h	1-1		Kiessling
24/9	MSV Duisburg	a	0-1		
1/10	1.FC Köln	h	2-1		Kiessling 2
15/10	SV Werder Bremen	a	2-6		Kiessling, Schroth
22/10	Arminia Bielefeld	h	2-3		Reinhardt, Banovic
30/10	FSV Mainz 05	a	1-4		Kiessling
6/11	VfB Stuttgart	h	0-1		
19/11	1.FC Kaiserslautern	a	3-1		Banovic, Müller L., Saenko
26/11	Borussia Dortmund	h	1-2		Kiessling
3/12	Bor. Mönchengladbach	a	1-0		Nikl
10/12	Bayer 04 Leverkusen	h	1-1		Schroth
18/12	Hertha BSC Berlin	a	1-1		Saenko
2006					
27/1	Hamburger SV	h	2-1		Saenko, Kiessling
5/2	Hannover 96	a	1-1		Vittek
8/2	Eintracht Frankfurt	h	0-1		
12/2	FC Bayern München	a	1-2		Vittek
18/2	VfL Wolfsburg	h	1-0		Saenko
25/2	FC Schalke 04	a	0-2		
4/3	MSV Duisburg	h	3-0		Vittek 3
11/3	1.FC Köln	a	4-3		Vittek 3 (2p), Saenko
18/3	SV Werder Bremen	h	3-1		Vittek 2, Schroth
27/3	Arminia Bielefeld	a	0-0		
1/4	FSV Mainz 05	h	3-0		Saenko, Kiessling, Vittek
8/4	VfB Stuttgart	a	0-1		
16/4	1.FC Kaiserslautern	h	3-2		Vittek 2, Paulus
22/4	Borussia Dortmund	a	1-2		Nikl
2/5	Bor. Mönchengladbach	h	5-2		Vittek 2, Polák, Saenko, Kiessling
6/5	Bayer 04 Leverkusen	a	2-2		Mnari, Kiessling
13/5	Hertha BSC Berlin	h	2-1		Vittek, Saenko

No	Name	Nat	Pos	Aps	(s)	Gls
10	Ivica BANOVIC	CRO	M	15	(8)	2
20	Bartosz BOSACKI	POL	D	3	(1)	
13	Mario CANTALUPPI	SUI	D	31	(1)	
14	Adel CHEDLI	TUN	M	3	(2)	
9	Markus DAUN		A	7	(6)	
4	GLÁUBER	BRA	D	10	(2)	
27	Stefan KIESSLING		A	20	(11)	10
19	Jan KRISTIANSEN	DEN	M	3	(5)	
2	Benjamin LENSE		D	9	(2)	
11	Marek MINTÁL	SVK	M	4		1
36	Jawher MNARI	TUN	M	21	(2)	1
17	Lars MÜLLER		M	11	(5)	1
6	Sven MÜLLER		M	10	(7)	
7	Marek NIKL	CZE	D	24	(3)	2
15	Sezer ÖZTÜRK	TUR	M		(2)	
35	Chhunly PAGENBURG		A		(1)	
31	Thomas PAULUS		D	9	(9)	1
25	Horacio Javier PÍNOLA	ARG	D	24	(1)	1
8	Jan POLÁK	CZE	M	32		1
28	Dominik REINHARDT		D	22	(2)	1
23	Ivan SAENKO	RUS	A	22	(3)	8
1	Raphael SCHÄFER		G	34		
21	Markus SCHROTH		A	20	(9)	4
34	Samuel SLOVÁK	SVK	M		(1)	
37	Sebastian SZIKAL		M		(1)	
30	Phillip TSCHAUNER		G		(1)	
33	Róbert VITTEK	SVK	A	24	(6)	16
26	Maik WAGEFELD		M		(3)	
5	Andreas WOLF		D	16	(4)	

FC SCHALKE 04
Coach – Ralf Rangnick; (12/12/05) Mirko Slomka

2005					
7/8	1.FC Kaiserslautern	h	2-1		Larsen, Krstajic
13/8	Borussia Dortmund	a	2-1		Kuranyi 2
27/8	Bor. Mönchengladbach	h	1-1		Sand
10/9	Bayer 04 Leverkusen	a	1-1		Larsen

Germany

18/9	Hertha BSC Berlin	h	0-0		
21/9	1.FC Nürnberg	a	1-1	Larsen	
24/9	Hannover 96	h	2-0	Lincoln, Kuranyi	
1/10	Eintracht Frankfurt	a	1-0	Larsen	
15/10	FC Bayern München	h	1-1	Larsen (p)	
22/10	VfL Wolfsburg	a	0-0		
29/10	Hamburger SV	a	0-1		
5/11	MSV Duisburg	h	3-0	Kuranyi, og (Meyer), Rodríguez	
19/11	1.FC Köln	a	2-2	Kuranyi, Sand	
26/11	SV Werder Bremen	h	2-1	Kuranyi 2	
3/12	Arminia Bielefeld	a	1-0	Poulsen	
10/12	FSV Mainz 05	h	1-0	Bordon	
17/12	VfB Stuttgart	a	0-2		
2006					
29/1	1.FC Kaiserslautern	a	2-0	Lincoln, Kobiashvili (p)	
4/2	Borussia Dortmund	h	0-0		
8/2	Bor. Mönchengladbacg	a	0-0		
11/2	Bayer 04 Leverkusen	h	7-4	Larsen 2, Krstajic, Bajramovic, Kuranyi, Lincoln, Asamoah	
18/2	Hertha BSC Berlin	a	2-1	Asamoah, Bajramovic	
25/2	1.FC Nürnberg	h	2-0	Kuranyi, Lincoln	
4/3	Hannover 96	a	2-1	Poulsen, Bajramovic	
12/3	Eintracht Frankfurt	h	2-0	Larsen, Sand	
19/3	FC Bayern München	a	0-3		
25/3	VfL Wolfsburg	h	2-2	Kuranyi, Lincoln	
2/4	Hamburger SV	h	0-2		
9/4	MSV Duisburg	a	1-1	Larsen	
15/4	1.FC Köln	h	1-1	Bajramovic	
23/4	SV Werder Bremen	a	0-0		
3/5	Arminia Bielefeld	h	3-1	Asamoah, Larsen, Altintop	
6/5	FSV Mainz 05	a	0-1		
13/5	VfB Stuttgart	h	3-2	Sand, Bordon, Waldoch	

No	Name	Nat	Pos	Aps	(s)	Gls
6	Hamit ALTINTOP	TUR	D	15	(7)	1
14	Gerald ASAMOAH		A	15	(9)	3
7	Mimoun AZAOUAGH		M	3	(1)	
25	Zlatan BAJRAMOVIC	BOS	M	16	(9)	4
21	Alexander BAUMJOHANN		M		(1)	
31	Sebastian BOENISCH		M		(1)	
5	Marcelo José BORDON	BRA	D	31		2
8	Fabian ERNST		M	30	(2)	
13	Christofer HEIMEROTH		G	2		
4	Thomas KLÄSENER		D		(3)	
3	Levan KOBIASHVILI	GEO	M	32		1
20	Mladen KRSTAJIC	SCG	D	29		2
22	Kevin KURANYI		A	30		10
9	Søren LARSEN	DEN	A	11	(19)	10
33	Joseph LAUMANN		M		(1)	
10	LINCOLN Cássio	BRA	M	29		5
2	Christian Bager POULSEN	DEN	D	26	(2)	2
18	RAFINHA	BRA	D	28	(1)	
16	Darío RODRÍGUEZ	URU	D	19	(3)	1
1	Frank ROST		G	32		
11	Ebbe SAND	DEN	A	12	(18)	4
19	Gustavo Antonio VARELA	URU	M	14	(13)	
15	Tomasz WALDOCH	POL	D		(2)	1

VFB STUTTGART
Coach – Giovanni Trapattoni (ITA); (9/2/06) Armin Veh

2005				
5/8	MSV Duisburg	a	1-1	Cacau
14/8	1.FC Köln	h	2-3	Streller, Tiffert
27/8	SV Werder Bremen	a	1-1	Tomasson

10/9	Arminia Bielefeld	h	1-1	Tomasson	
17/9	FSV Mainz 05	a	2-1	Tomasson, Gomez	
21/9	Hamburger SV	h	1-2	Gomez	
25/9	1.FC Kaiserslautern	h	1-0	Tomasson	
2/10	Borussia Dortmund	a	0-0		
15/10	Bor. Mönchengladbach	h	1-1	og (Strasser)	
23/10	Bayer 04 Leverkusen	a	1-1	Ljuboja (p)	
29/10	Hertha BSC Berlin	h	3-3	Ljuboja, Cacau, Gomez	
6/11	1.FC Nürnberg	a	1-0	Tiffert	
20/11	Hannover 96	h	2-2	Tomasson 2	
27/11	Eintracht Frankfurt	a	1-1	Ljuboja	
3/12	FC Bayern München	h	0-0		
10/12	VfL Wolfsburg	a	1-0	Meissner	
17/12	FC Schalke 04	h	2-0	Gomez, Ljuboja	
2006					
28/1	MSV Duisburg	h	0-1		
4/2	1.FC Köln	a	0-0		
8/2	SV Werder Bremen	h	0-0		
11/2	Arminia Bielefeld	a	1-2	Magnin	
19/2	FSV Mainz 05	h	2-1	Ljuboja, Tiffert	
26/2	Hamburger SV	a	2-0	Meissner, Gomez	
7/3	1.FC Kaiserslautern	a	1-1	Gomez	
11/3	Borussia Dortmund	h	0-0		
18/3	Bor. Mönchengladbach	a	1-1	Cacau	
25/3	Bayer 04 Leverkusen	h	0-2		
1/4	Hertha BSC Berlin	a	0-2		
8/4	1.FC Nürnberg	h	1-0	Tomasson	
16/4	Hannover 96	a	3-3	Ljuboja, Hitzlsperger, Tomasson	
22/4	Eintracht Frankfurt	h	0-2		
3/5	FC Bayern München	a	1-3	Ljuboja	
6/5	VfL Wolfsburg	h	2-1	Ljuboja (p), Gentner	
13/5	FC Schalke 04	a	2-3	Hitzlsperger, Cacau	

No	Name	Nat	Pos	Aps	(s)	Gls
5	Markus BABBEL		D	10	(2)	
32	Andreas BECK		M	4	(1)	
8	Daniel BIEROFKA		M	1		
18	Jerónimo CACAU	BRA	A	8	(12)	4
14	Mario CAREVIC	CRO	M	1	(5)	
17	Mathieu DELPIERRE	FRA	D	29		
6	FERNANDO MEIRA	POR	D	32		
40	Christian GENTNER		M	15	(8)	1
12	Heiko GERBER		D	7	(3)	
33	Mario GOMEZ		A	7	(23)	6
22	Jesper GRØNKJAER	DEN	M	16	(9)	
23	Dirk HEINEN		G	3		
1	Timo HILDEBRAND		G	31		
2	Andreas HINKEL		D	24	(2)	
11	Thomas HITZLSPERGER		M	24	(2)	2
38	Danijel LJUBOJA	SCG	A	23	(3)	8
21	Ludovic MAGNIN	SUI	D	24	(1)	1
7	Silvio MEISSNER		M	20	(5)	2
20	Zvonimir SOLDO	CRO	M	31		
3	Martin STRANZL	AUT	D	11	(4)	
9	Marco STRELLER	SUI	A	3	(4)	1
13	Christian TIFFERT		M	25	(3)	3
10	Jon Dahl TOMASSON	DEN	A	25	(1)	8

SV WERDER BREMEN
Coach – Thomas Schaaf

2005				
5/8	Arminia Bielefeld	h	5-2	Klose 2, Klasnic 2, Baumann
14/8	FSV Mainz 05	a	2-0	Klasnic, Klose
27/8	VfB Stuttgart	h	1-1	Klasnic

Germany

Date	Opponent	H/A	Score	Scorers
10/9	1.FC Kaiserslautern	a	5-1	Micoud, Klose 2, Frings, Vranjes
17/9	Borussia Dortmund	h	3-2	Klose, Klasnic, Micoud
20/9	Bor. Mönchengladbach	a	1-2	Van Damme
24/9	Bayer 04 Leverkusen	h	2-1	Klose, Klasnic
1/10	Hertha BSC Berlin	a	2-1	Borowski, Valdez
15/10	1.FC Nürnberg	h	6-2	Klose 3, Klasnic 2, Borowski
22/10	Hannover 96	a	0-0	
29/10	Eintracht Frankfurt	h	4-1	Frings, Borowski 2, Klose
5/11	FC Bayern München	a	1-3	Klose
19/11	VfL Wolfsburg	h	6-1	Baumann, Borowski 2, Klose 2, Naldo
26/11	FC Schalke 04	a	1-2	Valdez
3/12	MSV Duisburg	h	2-0	Valdez, Borowski
11/12	1.FC Köln	a	4-1	Naldo, Klose 2, Micoud
18/12	Hamburger SV	h	1-1	Micoud
2006				
29/1	Arminia Bielefeld	a	1-0	Fahrenhorst
4/2	FSV Mainz 05	h	4-2	Valdez 2, Klasnic, Micoud
8/2	VfB Stuttgart	a	0-0	
11/2	1.FC Kaiserslautern	h	0-2	
18/2	Borussia Dortmund	a	1-0	Klasnic
25/2	Bor. Mönchengladbach	h	2-0	Klose, Klasnic
4/3	Bayer 04 Leverkusen	a	1-1	Frings (p)
11/3	Hertha BSC Berlin	h	0-3	
17/3	1.FC Nürnberg	a	1-3	Klose
25/3	Hannover 96	h	5-0	Valdez 3, Micoud, Klose
1/4	Eintracht Frankfurt	a	1-0	Klose (p)
8/4	FC Bayern München	h	3-0	og (Schweinsteiger), Jensen, Borowski
15/4	VfL Wolfsburg	a	1-1	Valdez
23/4	FC Schalke 04	h	0-0	
3/5	MSV Duisburg	a	5-3	Micoud 2, Klose 2, Klasnic
6/5	1.FC Köln	h	6-0	Borowski 2, Klose 2, Klasnic 2
13/5	Hamburger SV	a	2-1	Klasnic, Klose

Date	Opponent	H/A	Score	Scorers
5/8	Borussia Dortmund	h	2-2	Klimowicz, Hofland
13/8	Bor. Mönchengladbach	a	1-1	Hanke
27/8	Bayer 04 Leverkusen	h	2-1	D'Alessandro, Thiam
11/9	Hertha BSC Berlin	a	0-3	
17/9	1.FC Nürnberg	h	1-1	Klimowicz
20/9	Hannover 96	a	4-2	Hanke 2, Klimowicz, D'Alessandro
24/9	Eintracht Frankfurt	h	1-0	Klimowicz
1/10	FC Bayern München	a	0-2	
15/10	Hamburger SV	a	1-0	Klimowicz
22/10	FC Schalke 04	h	0-0	
29/10	MSV Duisburg	a	0-1	
5/11	1.FC Köln	h	1-1	Klimowicz
19/11	SV Werder Bremen	a	1-6	Klimowicz
26/11	Arminia Bielefeld	h	0-0	
4/12	FSV Mainz 05	a	1-5	Klimowicz
10/12	VfB Stuttgart	h	0-1	
17/12	1.FC Kaiserslautern	a	2-3	Klimowicz, Hanke
2006				
27/1	Borussia Dortmund	a	2-3	Hanke, Klimowicz
5/2	Bor. Mönchengladbach	h	2-0	Klimowicz, Hanke
8/2	Bayer 04 Leverkusen	a	0-4	
11/2	Hertha BSC Berlin	h	1-1	Hofland
18/2	1.FC Nürnberg	a	0-1	
25/2	Hannover 96	h	2-1	Hanke, Menseguez
5/3	Eintracht Frankfurt	a	1-1	Hanke
11/3	FC Bayern München	h	0-0	
18/3	Hamburger SV	h	0-1	
25/3	FC Schalke 04	a	2-2	Hoogendorp, Lamprecht
1/4	MSV Duisburg	h	1-1	Marlet
8/4	1.FC Köln	a	0-3	
15/4	SV Werder Bremen	h	1-1	Hristov
22/4	Arminia Bielefeld	a	1-0	Karhan (p)
3/5	FSV Mainz 05	h	0-3	
6/5	VfB Stuttgart	a	1-2	Menseguez
13/5	1.FC Kaiserslautern	h	2-2	Makiadi, Klimowicz

No	Name	Nat	Pos	Aps	(s)	Gls
16	Leon ANDREASEN	DEN	D	11	(7)	
6	Frank BAUMANN		M	19		2
24	Tim BOROWSKI		M	31		10
2	Frank FAHRENHORST		D	22	(1)	1
22	Torsten FRINGS		M	28		3
14	Aaron HUNT		A	1	(6)	
20	Daniel JENSEN	DEN	M	12	(15)	1
17	Ivan KLASNIC	CRO	D	21	(9)	15
11	Miroslav KLOSE		A	25	(1)	25
19	Pekka LAGERBLOM	FIN	M		(3)	
10	Johan MICOUD	FRA	M	30		8
4	NALDO	BRA	D	32		2
15	Patrick OWOMOYELA		D	27	(5)	
3	Petri PASANEN	FIN	D	14	(3)	
29	Jerome POLENZ		A		(3)	
1	Andreas REINKE		G	20		
27	Christian SCHULZ		D	29	(1)	
5	ÜMIT Davala	TUR	D	1		
9	Nelson Haedo VALDEZ	PAR	A	20	(10)	9
23	Jelle VAN DAMME	BEL	D	3	(5)	1
33	Christian VANDER		G		(1)	
7	Jurica VRANJES	CRO	M	14	(15)	1
18	Tim WIESE		G	14	(1)	

VFL WOLFSBURG
Coach – Holger Fach; (29/12/05) Klaus Augenthaler

2005

No	Name	Nat	Pos	Aps	(s)	Gls
16	ABOUDA	BRA	A		(1)	
19	ALEX	POR	D	17		
10	Andrés D'ALESSANDRO	ARG	M	13		2
26	Karsten FISCHER		M	2	(3)	
33	Maik FRANZ		D	13	(3)	
11	Mike HANKE		A	25	(6)	8
29	Kevin HOFLAND	HOL	D	19		2
20	Rick HOOGENDORP	HOL	A	8	(6)	1
8	Marian HRISTOV	BUL	M	8	(1)	1
1	Simon JENTZSCH		G	34		
27	Miroslav KARHAN	SVK	M	27	(3)	1
9	Diego KLIMOWICZ	ARG	A	25	(1)	12
32	Christopher LAMPRECHT		D	3	(11)	1
4	Matthias LANGKAMP		D		(1)	
15	Cedrick MAKIADI		M		(10)	1
21	Steve MARLET	FRA	A	7	(14)	1
36	Juan Carlos MENSEGUEZ	ARG	A	29	(4)	2
22	Bojan NEZIRI	SCG	D	17	(3)	
18	Facundo QUIROGA	ARG	D	27	(1)	
31	Hans SARPEI		M	21	(7)	
5	Stefan SCHNOOR		D	10	(10)	
6	Pablo THIAM		M	19	(5)	1
14	Marko TOPIC	BOS	A		(2)	
17	Levan TSKITISHVILI	GEO	M	15		
3	Peter VAN DER HEYDEN	BEL	D	22	(2)	
14	Tom VAN DER LEEGTE	HOL	M	12	(1)	
7	Patrick WEISER		D	1	(1)	

Germany

DOMESTIC CUP 2005/06

FIRST ROUND
(19/8/05)
Wuppertaler SV 1, TSV 1860 München 2
RW Oberhausen 1, Eintracht Frankfurt 2
Holstein Kiel 0, SpVgg Unterhaching 2
Rot-Weiss Essen 2, Energie Cottbus 2 *(aet; 4-5 on pens)*
1.FC Köln II 0, Hannover 96 4
VfL Bochum II 2, Erzgebirge Aue 3
FSV Mainz 05 II 0, Karlsruher SC 3
RW Erfurt 2, LR Ahlen 1 *(aet)*
(20/8/05)
FC St.Pauli 3, Wacker Burghausen 2 *(aet)*
Jahn Regensburg 1, Alemannia Aachen 3 *(aet)*
FC Ingolstadt 04 1, 1.FC Saarbrücken 1 *(aet; 4-5 on pens)*
Kickers Offenbach 3, 1.FC Köln 1
Tennis Borussia Berlin 0, VfL Bochum 6
Stuttgarter Kickers 1, Hamburger SV 5
Eintracht Trier 0, 1.FC Kaiserslautern 3
SC Paderborn 07 0, VfL Wolfsburg 2
SG Wattenscheid 09 1, SV Werder Bremen 3
FC 08 Villingen 2, FC Hansa Rostock 5 *(aet)*
Rot-Weiss Erfurt II 0, Bayer 04 Leverkusen 8
FC Bremerhaven 0, FC Schalke 04 3
TuS Koblenz 2, Hertha BSC Berlin 3 *(aet)*
(21/8/05)
Sachsen Leipzig 1, Dynamo Dresden 1 *(aet; 3-5 on pens)*
TSG Hoffenheim 3, VfB Stuttgart 4 *(aet)*
VfL Osnabrück 2, Sp Vgg Greuther Fürth 2 *(aet; 10-9 on pens)*
Sportfreunde Siegen 0, SC Freiburg 1
1.FC Eschborn 0, 1. FC Nürnberg 4
FC Kutzhof 0, Borussia Mönchengladbach 3
VfL Wolfsburg II 0, MSV Duisburg 1
MSV 1919 Neuruppin 0, FC Bayern München 4
FC Hansa Rostock II 0, FSV Mainz 05 3
Magdeburger SV Preussen 0, Arminia Bielefeld 3
(22/8/05)
Eintracht Braunschweig 2, Borussia Dortmund 1

SECOND ROUND
(25/10/05)
FC St. Pauli 4, VfL Bochum 0
RW Erfurt 2, 1.FC Kaiserslautern 4
SpVgg Unterhaching 2, 1.FC Saarbrücken 1 *(aet)*
SV Werder Bremen 2, VfL Wolfsburg 2 *(aet; 5-4 on pens)*
Eintracht Frankfurt 6, FC Schalke 04 0
1.FC Nürnberg 3, Dynamo Dresden 0
Alemannia Aachen 1, Hannover 96 2
SC Freiburg 4, Eintracht Braunschweig 1
(26/10/05)
VfL Osnabrück 2, FSV Mainz 05 2 *(aet; 2-4 on pens)*
Hamburger SV 3, Bayer 04 Leverkusen 2
TSV 1860 München 3, MSV Duisburg 2
Arminia Bielefeld 2, Energie Cottbus 1
FC Hansa Rostock 3, VfB Stuttgart 2
Kickers Offenbach 2, Karlsruher SC 1
Hertha BSC Berlin 3, Borussia Mönchengladbach 0
Erzgebirge Aue 0, FC Bayern München 1

THIRD ROUND
(20/12/05)
Arminia Bielefeld 2, SpVgg Unterhaching 0
SC Freiburg 1, TSV 1860 München 3 *(aet)*
1.FC Kaiserslautern 1, FSV Mainz 05 1 *(aet; 3-4 on pens)*
(21/12/05)
Eintracht Frankfurt 1, 1.FC Nürnberg 1 *(aet; 4-1 on pens)*
Hannover 96 1, SV Werder Bremen 4
FC St. Pauli 4, Hertha BSC Berlin 3 *(aet)*
FC Hansa Rostock 1, Kickers Offenbach 1 *(aet; 3-4 on pens)*
FC Bayern München 1, Hamburger SV 0 *(aet)*

QUARTER FINALS
(24/1/06)
Bayern München 3 *(Pizarro 81, Guerrero 94, 115)*, FSV Mainz 05 2 *(Zidan 21p, Ruman 106) (aet)*
(25/1/06)
Arminia Bielefeld 1 *(Boakye 28)*, Kickers Offenbach 1 *(Judt 27p) (aet; 4-2 on pens)*
TSV 1860 München 1 *(Reisinger 11)*, Eintracht Frankfurt 3 *(Copado 21, Amanatidis 78, Meier 90)*
FC St. Pauli 3 *(Mazingu-Dinzey 10, Boll 59, Schultz 65)*, SV Werder Bremen 1 *(Micoud 27)*

SEMI FINALS
(11/4/06)
Eintracht Frankfurt 1 *(Amanatidis 16)*, Arminia Bielefeld 0
(12/4/06)
FC St.Pauli 0 FC Bayern München 3 *(Hargreaves 15, Pizarro 84, 89)*

FINAL
(29/4/06)
Olympiastadion, Berlin
FC BAYERN MÜNCHEN 1 *(Pizarro 59)*
EINTRACHT FRANKFURT 0
Referee – Fandel
FC BAYERN MÜNCHEN – Kahn, Sagnol, Lúcio, Ismaël, Lahm, Demichelis, Salihamidzic *(Zé Roberto 46)*, Ballack, Hargreaves *(Jeremies 81)*, Makaay *(Scholl 90)*, Pizarro.
EINTRACHT FRANKFURT – Nikolov, Rehmer *(Cimen 34; Weissenberger 82)*, Russ, Vasoski, Ochs, Huggel, Spycher, Lexa *(Copado 72)*, Meier, Köhler, Amanatidis.

SECOND LEVEL FINAL TABLE 2005/06

		Pld	W	D	L	F	A	Pts
1	VfL Bochum	34	19	9	6	55	26	66
2	Alemannia Aachen	34	20	5	9	61	36	65
3	FC Energie Cottbus	34	16	10	8	49	33	58
4	SC Freiburg	34	16	8	10	41	33	56
5	SpVgg Greuther Fürth	34	15	9	10	51	42	54
6	Karlsruher SC	34	15	8	11	55	45	53
7	FC Erzgebirge Aue	34	13	9	12	38	36	48
8	SV Wacker Burghausen	34	12	11	11	45	49	47
9	SC 07 Paderborn	34	13	7	14	46	40	46
10	FC Hansa Rostock	34	13	4	17	44	49	43
11	Kickers Offenbach	34	12	7	15	42	53	43
12	Eintracht Braunschweig	34	13	4	17	37	48	43
13	TSV 1860 München	34	11	9	14	41	44	42
14	SpVgg Unterhaching	34	12	6	16	42	48	42
15	Dynamo Dresden	34	11	8	15	39	45	41
16	1.FC Saarbrücken	34	11	5	18	37	63	38
17	LR Ahlen	34	9	8	17	36	50	35
18	Sportfreunde Siegen	34	8	7	19	35	54	31

Greece

Olympiakos all the way

They don't travel well. In fact, their record on foreign soil in the Champions League is nothing short of atrocious. But at home Olympiakos are the undisputed masters.

The Red and Whites from Piraeus collected their ninth Greek championship title in ten years, and it was probably the most comprehensive of the lot. For good measure they added victory in the Greek Cup, thus securing a double Double. It was the first time since the late 1950s that they had won the two domestic trophies back to back.

Their league triumph in 2004/05 was an edge-of-the-seat affair that remained undecided until the final whistle of their very last game. This time Olympiakos were so comfortably in command of proceedings that they secured first place with four games to spare – and, furthermore, on the day they suffered their heaviest defeat of the season, 2-0 to Iraklis.

Dream start

New coach Trond Sollied, headhunted from Belgian champions Club Bruges, got off to a dream start when Olympiakos beat arch-rivals Panathinaikos 2-0 in front of 65,000 spectators at the Olympic Stadium on the opening day of the season. Veteran skipper Predrag Djordjevic was the star of the show, creating one goal and scoring the other. The shaven-headed Serb did not stop there. His tenth season at the club would arguably be his best of all as he went on to top score with 15 goals (albeit nine of them from the penalty spot).

A few weeks after winning away to Panathinaikos, Olympiakos did likewise at AEK, beating their other chief rivals 3-1. A couple of improbable defeats temporarily halted the Olympiakos charge but from then on they were irrepressible, coursing through the winter months with a string of victories – 16 in all – to make the club's 34th title a foregone conclusion. Within that magnificent winning run came repeat victories over Panathinaikos (3-2) and AEK (3-0). It was a procession.

Olympiakos's flawless league form was transported into the Greek Cup, where they knocked out Xanthi and Larisa to book a final rendez-vous in Crete with AEK. With the championship sewn up, the team took their foot off the gas in the closing weeks, losing four away fixtures in a row, but the trip south to Crete was the away-day that really mattered and Djordjevic and co cemented their superiority over AEK with another 3-0 win to complete the Double.

Predrag Djordjevic – Olympiakos captain and star

Greece

The Cup final was won without injured Brazilian superstar Rivaldo, but the veteran World Cup winner had an outstanding season, especially in the early spring when he was back to the brilliance he showed in his prime at Barcelona. Olympiakos president Sokratis Kokkalis publicly stated that Rivaldo was the best thing ever to happen to Greek club football and put his money where his mouth was by offering the Brazilian a lucrative one-year contract extension. Rivaldo and Djordjevic, skilful left-footers both, happily co-existed in Sollied's 3-4-1-2 system, with the Brazilian playing just behind the two strikers and the Serb patrolling the left flank. Two other key players were new signings Yaya Touré (the brother of Arsenal defender Kolo) and Cypriot international striker Michalis Konstantinou, who, like goalkeeper Antonis Nikopolidis a year earlier, was audaciously recruited from Panathinaikos.

Olympiakos's brilliant domestic campaign ended with a celebration party after their final home game. The match itself, against Ionikos, was not especially memorable – it finished goalless, giving Olympiakos their only draw of the season – but afterwards skipper Djordjevic had the honour of being presented with the championship trophy by the great Diego Maradona.

The one big blot on Olympiakos's season was their failure, once again, to make any headway in the Champions League. Defeated in each of their first four matches, they were within touching distance of their first ever away win before agonisingly conceding a late equaliser to Rosenborg, which meant that their subsequent 2-1 home victory over Real Madrid carried no weight whatsoever.

Euro exit

Panathinaikos memorably, if controversially, overcame Polish champions Wisla Krakow to join Olympiakos in the Champions League group phase, but they matched their rivals' incompetence by accumulating just four points and finishing bottom of their group. The four Greek UEFA Cup representatives also went out early. PAOK, the only one of the quartet to reach the group phase, suffered three straight defeats, and although they signed off with a handsome 5-1 win at home to Rennes, their elimination meant that for the first time in 11 years there would be no Greek involvement in Europe after Christmas.

While Olympiakos's title triumph guaranteed them a return ticket to the Champions League, there was to be no seat at Europe's top table in 2006/07 for Panathinaikos. The Greens finished level on points with AEK – by the end the pair were just three behind the champions – but the Yellow and Blacks' superior head-to-head record secured them a place in the third qualifying round.

Pana had a ropey season on all fronts, plumbing the absolute depths when they were knocked out of the Greek Cup by second division Ergotelis. A last-minute penalty condemned the Athens giants to their first ever elimination from the competition by lower-division opponents. It was a surprise to many that the club's Italian coach Alberto Malesani survived that humiliation, but the board kept faith with him until the end of the season, when he was replaced by the Swede, Hans Backe.

AEK also changed coach in the summer, with Fernando Santos returning home to take charge of Benfica. He had the nerve to take AEK's best player and captain, Greek international Kostas Katsouranis, with him, although Nikos Liberopoulos, the team's other top performer, with 14 goals in the league and several more in the Cup, stayed on to spearhead the club's assault on the Champions League.

Iraklis and Xanthi finished fourth and fifth, respectively, joining Panathinaikos in the UEFA Cup, but sixth-placed PAOK were denied access as they could not meet the financial conditions required to

NATIONAL TEAM RESULTS 2005/06

17/8/05	Belgium	A	Brussels	0-2
7/9/05	Kazakhstan (WCQ)	A	Almaty	2-1 Giannakopoulos (79), Liberopoulos (90)
8/10/05	Denmark (WCQ)	A	Copenhagen	0-1
12/10/05	Georgia (WCQ)	H	Piraeus	1-0 Papadopoulos (17)
16/11/05	Hungary	H	Piraeus	2-1 Giannakopoulos (31), Kafes (90)
21/1/06	South Korea	N	Riyadh	1-1 Zagorakis (10)
25/1/06	Saudi Arabia	A	Riyadh	1-1 Zagorakis (56p)
28/2/06	Belarus	N	Limassol	1-0 Samaras (15)
1/3/06	Kazakhstan	N	Nicosia	2-0 Samaras (86), Giannakopoulos (90)
25/5/06	Australia	A	Melbourne	0-1

Greece

NATIONAL TEAM APPEARANCES 2005/06

Coach – Otto REHHAGEL (GER)

Player	DOB	Club	Bel	KAZ	DEN	GEO	Hun	Kor	Sau	Bls	Kaz	Aus	Caps	Goals
Antonis NIKOLOPIDIS	4/1/71	Olympiakos	G	G	G	G	G75	G	G46	G		G	71	-
Yourkas SEITARIDIS	4/6/81	Dinamo Moskva (RUS)	D	D	D	D	D53			D46	D	D	43	-
Michalis KAPSIS	18/10/73	Olympiakos	D	D	D	D	s90	D	D63	D			32	1
Sotiris KYRGIAKOS	23/7/79	Panathinaikos /Rangers (SCO)	D46		D		D			s69	D	D46	19	1
Panagiotis FYSSAS	12/6/73	Heart of Midlothian (SCO)	D71	D76			D86			D46	D	D79	53	4
Angelos BASINAS	3/1/76	Panathinaikos /RCD Mallorca (ESP)	M46	M	M46	M	M			s46	M	M46	69	4
Vassilis LAKIS	10/9/76	AEK	M46										35	3
Giorgos KARAGOUNIS	6/3/77	Internazionale (ITA) /SL Benfica (POR)	M	M	M				M	M46	M46	M86	53	5
Theodoros ZAGORAKIS	27/10/71	PAOK	M66	M	M	M54	M46	M46	M82	M58	M64	s46	116	3
Stelios GIANNAKOPOULOS	12/7/74	Bolton Wanderers (ENG)	M69	M	M		M90			s58	s46	M46	61	12
Angelos CHARISTEAS	9/2/80	Ajax (HOL)	A	A						A69	A46	A	51	14
Nikos LIBEROPOULOS	4/8/75	AEK	s46	s55	A62		s46	s46	s79				45	9
Giorgos ALEXOPOULOS	7/2/77	AEK	s46					s77	s63				3	-
Zisis VRYZAS	9/11/73	Fiorentina (ITA)	s46	A55	A76	s46							68	9
Pantelis KAFES	24/6/78	Olympiakos	s66	s60	s62	s54	s46	M	s82				29	3
Dimitris SALPIGIDIS	18/8/81	PAOK	s69		s46	A	A46	A	A	A46	A46	s46	9	-
Loukas VINTRA	5/2/81	Panathinaikos	s71			s53		D	D	s46	s64		9	-
Kostas KATSOURANIS	21/6/79	AEK		M60	M	M	M			M		M	29	1
Fanis GEKAS	23/5/80	Panathinaikos		s76	s76		s86	s46	A	s46		s86	10	-
Traianos DELLAS	31/1/76	AEK				D64		D58				D	29	1
Giannis GOUMAS	24/5/75	Panathinaikos				D			D77		D		38	-
Dimitris PAPADOPOULOS	20/9/81	Panathinaikos				A	s46	A46			s46		19	2
Vangelis MANTZIOS	22/4/83	Panathinaikos				A46	A46	A46	A79		s46		5	-
Giorgos ANATOLAKIS	16/3/74	Olympiakos				s64		s58	s77	A		s46	15	-
Paraskevas ANTZAS	18/8/76	Xanthi				D	D	D					15	-
Stefanos KOTSOLIS	6/5/79	Larisa					s75		s46		G46		3	-
Panagiotis LAGOS	18/7/75	Iraklis						M46	M	s46		s46	4	-
Philippos DARLAS	23/10/83	Panathinaikos						s46					1	-
Alexandros TZIOLIS	13/2/85	Panathinaikos							s46 /77				1	-
Giorgos SAMARAS	21/2/85	Manchester City (ENG)								A	s46	A46	3	2
Giannis AMANATIDIS	3/12/81	Eintracht Frankfurt (GER)									A46	s79	9	-
Kostas HALKIAS	30/5/74	Real Murcia (ESP)									s46		5	-

Greece

obtain a UEFA licence. Into their place, therefore, stepped Atromitos, a club that had played third-division football in 2004/05 but acceded to the top flight after a merger with Chalkidona.

Akratitos and Kallithea were doomed to relegation long before the end of the season, but there was a gripping finale in the scrap to avoid the other place in the drop zone. OFI hosted newly promoted Levadiakos on the final day needing to win by two clear goals to leapfrog their opponents to safety. It was 1-0 to the islanders – a result which would have led to a play-off – before the home side snatched the all-important second goal, through Nigerian striker Joseph Nwafor, four minutes into stoppage-time.

Rehhagel remains

Greece, the reigning European champions, did not make it to the World Cup finals in Germany. In fact, they finished a lowly fourth in their group after a 1-0 defeat in Denmark. But there was some good news ahead of their European Championship defence as German coach Otto Rehhagel agreed to stay on for another two years.

It would be an embarrassment if Greece were unable to defend their title in 2008. It has happened before, when 1984 winners France failed to qualify for Euro 88, but there were only eight finalists in those days. Now there are 16, and as Greece's status as holders allowed them to claim seeded status at the qualifying draw and head a none-too-difficult group containing Turkey, Norway, Bosnia-Herzegovina, Hungary, Moldova and Malta, there really can be no excuses if they fail to reach the finals.

Rehhagel acknowledged that the principal reason behind the team's World Cup qualifying failure was a lack of goals. To that end he endeavoured to find alternatives to his tried and trusted strike partnership of Angelos Charisteas and Zisis Vryzas during the remainder of the 2005/06 season. The league's top two scorers, Dimitris Salpigidis of PAOK and Fanis Gekas of Panathinaikos, were both found wanting, but 21-year-old Giorgos Samaras, who made an expensive move to Manchester City from Heerenveen in mid-season, hit the jackpot with winning goals on each of his first two appearances. The strapping striker will doubtless have a big role to play on the road to Austria and Switzerland.

EUROPEAN CUPS 2005/06

UEFA CHAMPIONS LEAGUE

OLYMPIAKOS

1st round Group F
Match 1 ROSENBORG BK (NOR)
H 1-3 *Lago (19og)*
Nikopolidis, Mavrogenidis, Anatolakis, Kostoulas, Georgatos, Rivaldo (Dani 87), Touré (Kafes 89), Stoltidis, Babangida (Okkas 80), Konstantinou, Djordjevic.

Match 2 REAL MADRID (ESP)
A 1-2 *Kafes (48)*
Nikopolidis, Mavrogenidis (Kapsis 40), Anatolakis, Kostoulas, Georgatos, Rivaldo, Stoltidis (Babangida 90), Touré, Kafes, Djordjevic, Konstantinou (Okkas 85).

Match 3 OLYMPIQUE LYONNAIS (FRA)
A 1-2 *Kafes (84)*
Nikopolidis, Pantos, Bulut, Anatolakis (Babangida 90), Kostoulas, Kapsis, Kafes, Stoltidis (Konstantinou 85), Touré, Djordjevic, Okkas.

Match 4 OLYMPIQUE LYONNAIS
H 1-4 *Babangida (3)*
Giannou, Pantos, Georgatos, Anatolakis, Kostoulas (Stoltidis 65), Rivaldo, Touré, Kafes, Djordjevic (Bulut 65), Babangida, Okkas (D'Acol 81).

Match 5 ROSENBORG BK
A 1-1 *Rivaldo (25)*
Nikopolidis, Pantos, Bulut, Anatolakis, Schürrer, Touré, Kafes, Rivaldo (Maric 86), Stoltidis, Dani, Babangida (Okkas 71).

Match 6 REAL MADRID
H 2-1 *Bulut (50), Rivaldo (87)*
Nikopolidis, Mavrogenidis, Bulut, Kapsis (Kostoulas 65), Schürrer, Touré, Kafes (Babangida 90), Rivaldo, Stoltidis, Djordjevic, Dani (Okkas 58).

PANATHINAIKOS

3rd qualifying round WISLA KRAKOW (POL)
A 1-3 *Olisadebe (4)*
Galinovic, Vintra, Seric, Morris, Kotsios, Biscan (Tziolis 62), Flávio Conceição, Wooter (Theodoridis 75), Papadopoulos (Charlambides 81), Olisadebe, Gekas.
H 4-1 *Morris (62), Olisadebe (65), Papadopoulos (87), Kotsios (114)*
(aet)
Galinovic, Vintra, Seric, Morris, Kotsios, Biscan (Leontiou 74), Flávio Conceição, Wooter (Papadopoulos 51), Charlambides, Olisadebe (Andric 69), Gekas.

1st round Group C
Match 1 UDINESE (ITA)
A 0-3
Galinovic, Nilsson, Seric, Kotsios, Goumas, Morris, Biscan, Wooter (Leontiou 76), González, Charlambides (Gekas 70), Torghelle.

Match 2 SV WERDER BREMEN (GER)
H 2-1 *González (5p), Mantzios (8)*
Galinovic, Vintra, Darlas, Goumas (Kotsios 41), Morris, Seric, Flávio Conceição, Nilsson, González, Mantzios (Gekas 72), Torghelle (Tziolis 58).

Match 3 FC BARCELONA (ESP)
H 0-0
Galinovic, Vintra, Darlas, Morris, Biscan, Seric (Wooter 88), Flávio Conceição, Nilsson, González (Papadopoulos 76), Mantzios, Torghelle (Leontiou 59).

Match 4 FC BARCELONA
A 0-5
Galinovic, Vintra, Darlas (Tziolis 61), Morris, Biscan (Kotsios 46), Seric (Wooter 79), Flávio Conceição, Nilsson, González, Leontiou, Papadopoulos.

Greece

Match 5 UDINESE
H 1-2 *Charalambides (45)*
Galinovic, Kotsios, Darlas, Goumas, Morris, Flávio Conceição, González, Charalambides, Leontiou (Torghelle 83), Papadopoulos (Andric 64), Mantzios.

Match 6 SV WERDER BREMEN
A 1-5 *Morris (53)*
Galinovic, Vintra, Darlas (Wooter 71), Morris, Biscan, Flávio Conceição, Tziolis, Nilsson (Kotsios 78), González, Papadopoulos, Torghelle (Mantzios 73).

UEFA CUP

ARIS
1st round ROMA (ITA)
A 1-5 *Sanjurjo (39)*
Pourliotopoulos, Domoraud (Velonis 56), Naidos, Gogolos, Papadopoulos, Passalis (Gougoulias 77), Nebegleras, Moisiadis, Sanjurjo, Cáceres, Nacho (Abelas 56).
H 0-0
Karatziovalis, Naidos, Koltsidas, Papadopoulos, Moisiadis, Vangelis, Descamps, Bolos (Domoraud 57), Nebegleras, Beniskos, Cáceres.

AEK
1st round ZENIT SANKT-PETERBURG (RUS)
A 0-0
Sorrentino, Kontis, Moras, Cirillo, Alexopoulos, Malbasa, Katsouranis (Kiriakidis 90), Ivic, Venhlynskyi (Lakis 84), Liberopoulos, Júlio César (Soãres 73).
H 0-1
Sorrentino, Cirillo, Kontis, Alexopoulos, Malbasa, Katsouranis, Ivic, Chanko (Krassas 83), Soãres, Liberopoulos, Venhlynskyii (Júlio César 74).

XANTHI
1st round MIDDLESBROUGH (ENG)
A 0-2
Pizanovsky, Torosidis (Quintana 67), Papadimitriou, Sikov, Paviot (Kazakis 87), Antzas, Magradze (Leonardo 76), Luciano, Labriakos, Émerson, Andrade.
H 0-0
Pizanovsky, Torosidis (Kazakis 46), Sikov, Paviot, Papadimitriou, Magradze (Garpozis 69), Antzas, Émerson, Andrade (Leonardo 60), Luciano, Labriakos.

PAOK
1st round METALURG DONETSK (UKR)
H 1-1 *Salpigidis (25)*
Tohouroglou, Udeze, Karipidis, Fatih (Sikabala 74), Megahed, Zagorakis, Vangelis (Maladenis 55), Engomitis (Feutchine 53), Charalambous, Mieciel, Salpigidis.
A 2-2 *Salpigidis (42), Konstantinidis (45)*
Fernandes, Udeze, Karipidis, Balafas, Konstantinidis, Feutchine, Iliadis (Zografakis 55), Zagorakis, Charalambous, Salpigidis (Chasiotis 71), Mieciel (Giasemi 81).

2nd round Group G
Match 1 SHAKHTAR DONETSK (UKR)
A 0-1
Fernandes, Fatih (Christodoulopoulos 88), Chasiotis, Udeze, Charalambous, Balafas (Sikabala 71), Zagorakis (Engomitis 86), Iliadis, Konstantinidis, Salpigidis, Mieciel.

Match 2 VFB STUTTGART (GER)
H 1-2 *Karipidis (48)*
Fernandes, Udeze, Karipidis, Charalambous, Zagorakis, Feutchine (Christodoulopoulos 87), Megahed (Balafas 77), Konstantinidis, Salpigidis, Chasiotis, Mieciel (Maladenis 77).

Match 3 RAPID BUCURESTI (ROM)
A 0-1
Fernandes, Karipidis, Chasiotis, Zagorakis (Vangelis 38), Feutchine (Megahed 46), Iliadis, Konstantinidis, Charalambous, Salpigidis (Sikabala 56), Mieciel, Christodoulopoulos.

Match 4 STADE RENNAIS FC (FRA)
H 5-1 *Rochat (4og), Christodoulopoulos (38), Yiasoumi (79, 89), Salpigidis (83p)*
Fernandes, Udeze, Karipidis, Engomitis (Adralas 75), Feutchine, Konstantinidis, Balafas, Maladenis (Iliadis 44), Sikabala, Yiasoumi, Christodoulopoulos (Salpigidis 73).

TOP GOALSCORERS 2005/06

17	Dimitris SALPIGIDIS (PAOK)
15	Fanis GEKAS (Panathinaikos)
	LUCIANO de Sousa (Xanthi/Panionios)
	Predrag DJORDJEVIC (Olympiakos)
14	Nikos LIBEROPOULOS (AEK)
13	Joël EPALE (Iraklis)
10	Dimitris PAPADOPOULOS (Panathinaikos)
	Michalis KONSTANTINOU (Olympiakos)
	Oliver MAKOR (Ionikos)
9	CLAYTON Silva (Apollon Kalamarias)

LEAGUE RESULTS/ SCORERS/APPEARANCES/ GOALS 2005/06

AEK
Coach – Fernando Santos

2005				
29/8	Atromitos	a	0-0	
11/9	Iraklis	h	2-0	Liberopoulos, Júlio César
18/9	Egaleo	h	1-1	Liberopoulos
25/9	Larisa	a	1-0	Venhlynskyi
2/10	Olympiakos	h	1-3	Alexopoulos
16/10	Ionikos	a	1-0	Liberopoulos
23/10	Panathinaikos	h	3-0	Liberopoulos, Tsanko, Lakis
31/10	Panionios	a	2-0	Liberopoulos, Soãres
5/11	Kallithea	h	2-0	Lakis, Liberopoulos
21/11	Akratitos	a	2-1	Lakis, Liberopoulos
27/11	Levadiakos	a	1-0	Katsouranis
4/12	PAOK	h	2-1	Cirillo, Soãres
10/12	OFI	a	1-0	Júlio César
17/12	Apollon Kalamarias	h	2-1	Liberopoulos, Alexopoulos
2006				
8/1	Xanthi	a	0-0	
14/1	Atromitos	h	2-1	Liberopoulos, Venhlynskyi
29/1	Iraklis	a	0-4	
4/2	Egaleo	a	2-0	Liberopoulos, Cirillo
12/2	Larisa	h	1-0	Katsouranis
19/2	Olympiakos	a	0-3	
26/2	Ionikos	h	2-1	Venhlynskyi, Katsouranis
5/3	Panathinaikos	a	0-1	
12/3	Panionios	h	2-0	Katsouranis, Ivic
18/3	Kallithea	a	4-1	Ivic, Alexopoulos, Émerson, Kapetanos
26/3	Akratitos	h	2-0	Liberopoulos 2
2/4	Levadiakos	h	2-0	Ivic, Liberopoulos
9/4	PAOK	a	1-2	Katsouranis (p)
16/4	OFI	h	2-0	Katsouranis, Liberopoulos
30/4	Apollon Kalamarias	a	1-0	Lakis
14/5	Xanthi	h	0-0	

Greece

FINAL LEAGUE TABLE 2005/06

		Pld	Home					Away					Total					Pts
			W	D	L	F	A	W	D	L	F	A	W	D	L	F	A	
1	Olympiakos	30	13	1	1	39	8	10	0	5	24	15	23	1	6	63	23	70
2	AEK	30	12	2	1	26	8	9	2	4	16	12	21	4	5	42	20	67
3	Panathinaikos	30	13	1	1	32	9	8	3	4	23	14	21	4	5	55	23	67
4	Iraklis	30	13	1	1	28	7	2	5	8	11	24	15	6	9	39	31	51
5	Xanthi	30	10	5	0	19	5	3	3	9	12	20	13	8	9	31	25	47
6	PAOK	30	10	2	3	28	13	3	5	7	16	18	13	7	10	44	31	46
7	Atromitos	30	8	4	3	20	12	4	2	9	16	25	12	6	12	36	37	42
8	Larisa	30	10	3	2	21	11	0	6	9	10	26	10	9	11	31	37	39
9	Apollon Kalamarias	30	6	5	4	19	14	4	3	8	13	22	10	8	12	32	36	38
10	Egaleo	30	6	4	5	11	15	2	5	8	12	26	8	9	13	23	41	33
11	Panionios	30	4	4	7	20	24	5	1	9	13	21	9	5	16	33	45	32
12	Ionikos	30	6	6	3	21	13	0	8	7	15	28	6	14	10	36	41	32
13	OFI	30	6	5	4	17	13	1	5	9	6	24	7	10	13	23	37	31
14	Levadiakos	30	8	4	3	19	13	0	3	12	5	23	8	7	15	24	36	31
15	Kallithea	30	4	5	6	20	26	0	3	12	8	23	4	8	18	28	49	20
16	Akratitos	30	3	4	8	9	19	1	2	12	10	28	4	6	20	19	47	18

No	Name	Nat	Pos	Aps	(s)	Gls
6	Giorgos ALEXOPOULOS		D	30		3
27	Louay CHANKO	SWE	M	12	(9)	1
22	Dionisis CHIOTIS		G	5		
5	Bruno CIRILLO	ITA	D	24		2
55	Traianos DELLAS		D	2	(4)	
25	ÉMERSON Moises Costa	BRA	M	13		1
31	Nikos GEORGEAS		D	24	(1)	
17	Vladan IVIC	SCG	M	23	(4)	3
99	JULIO CÉSAR da Silva Sousa	BRA	A	16	(12)	2
35	Pantelis KAPETANOS		A	1	(9)	1
21	Kostas KATSOURANIS		M	29		6
26	Elias KIRIAKIDIS		M	1	(2)	
24	Christos KONTIS		M	12	(3)	
30	Simos KRASSAS	CYP	A	1	(2)	
23	Vassilis LAKIS		M	22	(6)	4
33	Nikos LIBEROPOULOS		A	27		14
3	Nikola MALBASA	SCG	D	13	(3)	
18	Vangelis MORAS		D	7	(6)	
20	Vasilis PLIATSIKAS		M	1	(2)	
8	Miltos SAPANIS		M	5	(7)	
7	Alessandro SOÃRES	BRA	A	22	(6)	2
1	Stefano SORRENTINO	ITA	G	25		
14	Stavros TZIORTZOPOULOS		D	8	(1)	
11	Oleh VENHLYNSKYI	UKR	A	7	(8)	3

AKRATITOS
Coach – Ilie Dumitrescu (ROM) ; (2/10/05) Dimitris Barbalias;
(26/10/05) Manuel Keoseyan ; (17/4/06) Vangelis Goutis

2005
28/8	Iraklis	h	3-1	Gustavo, De Francesco, Edu Sales (p)
11/9	Egaleo	a	0-1	
17/9	Larisa	h	0-0	
24/9	Olympiakos	a	0-2	
2/10	Ionikos	h	0-0	
15/10	Panathinaikos	a	0-1	
23/10	Panionios	h	0-1	
29/10	Kallithea	a	0-2	
6/11	Levadiakos	a	1-1	Londo
21/11	AEK	h	1-2	Gustavo
27/11	PAOK	a	0-2	
4/12	OFI	h	1-1	Edu Sales
11/12	Apollon Kalamarias	a	0-3	
19/12	Xanthi	h	2-0	Edu Sales 2

2006
8/1	Atromitos	a	0-2	
14/1	Iraklis	a	0-1	
28/1	Egaleo	h	0-3	
5/2	Larisa	a	1-2	Ledesma
13/2	Olympiakos	h	0-1	
19/2	Ionikos	a	2-3	og (King), De Francesco
26/2	Panathinaikos	h	0-2	
5/3	Panionios	a	4-2	Skoufalis, Marinescu, Ledesma, De Francesco
12/3	Kallithea	h	1-0	Ledesma
19/3	Levadiakos	h	0-0	
26/3	AEK	a	0-2	
2/4	PAOK	h	0-3	
9/4	OFI	a	2-2	Gustavo, De Francesco
16/4	Apollon Kalamarias	h	1-3	De Francesco
30/4	Xanthi	a	0-2	
14/5	Atromitos	h	0-2	

No	Name	Nat	Pos	Aps	(s)	Gls
5	Kostas APOSTOLAKIS		D	12	(1)	
27	Christos ARAVIDIS		A	4	(7)	
20	Kostas BADAS		D	17		
15	Estref BILLA	ALB	G	4		
33	Sebastián DE FRANCESCO	ARG	A	14	(13)	5
24	Oumar DIENG	SEN	D	9	(1)	
11	Eduardo "EDU" SALES	BRA	A	13	(3)	4
23	GUSTAVO Nakarato Veronezi	BRA	M	20	(4)	3
40	Alexandros KARAHALIOS		M	1	(5)	
99	Nikos KOSTAKIS		G	3		
35	Froylán LEDESMA	CRC	A	12	(1)	3
77	Sotiris LIBEROPOULOS		G	9		
12	Dieudonné LONDO	GAB	A	5	(4)	1
4	Lauren Michel MACQUET	FRA	M	21	(4)	
16	Lucian MARINESCU	ROM	M	19	(8)	1

Greece

APOLLON KALAMARIAS
Coach – Dragan Kokotovic; (19/12/05) Thomas Katsavakis

No	Name	Nat	Pos	Aps	(s)	Gls
21	Roberto Ramirez MERINO	PER	M	16	(3)	
14	Mustafa MUSUMBU	BEL	M	1	(4)	
6	Milan OBRADOVIC	SCG	D	14		
19	Massimo PAGANIN	ITA	D	10		
1	Kostas PAGONIS		A	11	(5)	
18	Dimitris PATSIAVOURAS		M	2	(2)	
34	Berni Pisaro PEÑA	CRC	D	12		
3	Christos PIPINIS		M	21	(1)	
55	Giannis SFAKIANAKIS		D	9		
10	Manolis SKOUFALIS		D	16	(5)	1
9	Saba Almami SOW	SEN	A	4	(4)	
28	Bogdan STELEA	ROM	G	14		
29	William SUNSING	CRC	A	5	(4)	
25	Antonis SXIZAS		M	4	(1)	
8	Themis TZIMOPOULOS		M	12	(2)	
22	Sven VANDENBROEKE	BEL	M		(1)	
30	Paolo VANOLI	ITA	D	4		
7	Nikola VUJOVIC	SCG	A	8	(5)	
17	Christos ZIGOURIS		A		(2)	
32	Francisco ZUELA	ANG	M	14		

2005
28/8	OFI	h	2-1	Wellington, Mouzaoui
11/9	Levadiakos	h	1-1	Papadopoulos N.A. (p)
18/9	Xanthi	a	0-2	
26/9	Atromitos	h	1-2	Clayton (p)
2/10	Iraklis	a	1-0	Pappas
15/10	Egaleo	h	0-0	
24/10	Larisa	a	1-4	Wellington
29/10	Olympiakos	h	1-2	El-Omari
6/11	Ionikos	a	0-2	
19/11	Panathinaikos	a	0-3	
27/11	Panionios	h	1-0	Amponsah
3/12	Kallithea	a	0-0	
11/12	Akratitos	h	3-0	Pappas 2, Clayton
17/12	AEK	a	1-2	Orfanos

2006
9/1	PAOK	h	2-2	og (Zagorakis), Pappas
15/1	OFI	a	2-1	Pappas, Parmaxidis
1/2	Levadiakos	a	0-1	
5/2	Xanthi	h	2-1	Clayton, Karaliopoulos
12/2	Atromitos	a	1-1	Mouzaui
20/2	Iraklis	h	2-0	Mouzaui, Clayton
26/2	Egaleo	a	0-0	
5/3	Larisa	h	2-2	Pappas, Clayton
12/3	Olympiakos	a	1-2	Clayton (p)
19/3	Ionikos	h	2-1	Pappas, Clayton
26/3	Panathinaikos	h	0-1	
2/4	Panionios	a	1-2	Wellington
9/4	Kallithea	h	0-0	
16/4	Akratitos	a	3-1	Fitanidis, Wellington, Clayton
30/4	AEK	h	0-1	
14/5	PAOK	a	2-1	Wellington, Clayton

No	Name	Nat	Pos	Aps	(s)	Gls
35	AÍLTON Modesto de Oliveira	BRA	A	2	(1)	
25	Kofi AMPONSAH	GHA	D	23		1
99	Christos CHRISTOFORIDIS		A	3	(2)	
10	CLAYTON Silva	BRA	A	29		9
4	Ali EL-OMARI	MAR	D		(6)	1
6	Sokratis FITANIDIS		D	26		1
44	Aristidis GALANOPOULOS		D	11		
5	Dimtris IOANNOU		D	18	(4)	
18	Merkouris KARALIOPOULOS		D	18	(5)	1
16	Dimitris KARAMANLIS		M	12	(6)	
50	Christos KELPEKIS		G	1		
40	Giorgos KOLTSIS		D	9	(2)	
30	Pavol KOVAC	SVK	G	26		
15	Vladimir MATIJASEVIC	SCG	D	2	(2)	
3	Vasilis MIROFIDIS		D	1	(1)	
9	Karim MOUZAOUI	FRA	A	11	(13)	3
17	Maciej MURAWSKI	PCL	D	22	(4)	
24	Dimitris ORFANOS		A	17	(3)	1
33	Nikos A. PAPADOPOULOS		D	2		1
8	Nikos X. PAPADOPOULOS		D	24		
77	Charis PAPPAS		A	25	(3)	7
20	Triantafilos PARMAXIDIS		M	15	(5)	1
21	Dimitris PETKAKIS		M	14		
27	Pavel POPARA	SCG	A	1	(3)	
1	Sasa RADIVOJEVIC	SCG	G	3		
31	Nikos SAMOUILIDIS		D	4	(11)	
7	Kostas SPIROPOULOS		M		(4)	
11	Daniel Gonçalves WELLINGTON	BRA	A	11	(10)	5

ATROMITOS
Coach – Giorgos Parashos

2005
29/8	AEK	h	0-0	
10/9	PAOK	a	2-2	Zaharopoulos, og (Udeze)
18/9	OFI	h	4-0	Skarmoutsos, Katemis, Dimos, Koutsis
26/9	Apollon Kalamarias	a	2-1	Skarmoutsos, N'Doe
3/10	Xanthi	h	0-1	
15/10	Levadiakos	h	1-0	Skarmoutsos
21/10	Iraklis	a	0-2	
30/10	Egaleo	h	0-0	
5/11	Larisa	a	1-2	Katemis
19/11	Olympiakos	h	0-1	
27/11	Ionikos	a	1-3	Korakakis
3/12	Panathinaikos	h	1-0	Korakakis
11/12	Panionios	a	0-2	
18/12	Kallithea	a	3-2	N'Doe 2, Zaharopoulos (p)

2006
8/1	Akratitos	h	2-0	Dagas, N'Doe
14/1	AEK	a	1-2	Zaharopoulos (p)
29/1	PAOK	h	2-1	Katemis, Korakakis
5/2	OFI	a	0-0	
12/2	Apollon Kalamarias	h	1-1	Djebbour
19/2	Xanthi	a	0-1	
26/2	Levadiakos	a	0-1	
5/3	Iraklis	h	3-0	Zaharopoulos 3
11/3	Egaleo	a	1-0	Djebbour
19/3	Larisa	h	0-0	
27/3	Olympiakos	a	0-3	
2/4	Ionikos	h	3-2	Geladaris, Djebbour, Zaharopoulos (p)
9/4	Panathinaikos	a	3-4	Merino, Djebbour 2
16/4	Panionios	h	1-3	Zaharopoulos (p)
30/4	Kallithea	h	2-1	Merino, Karadimos
14/5	Akratitos	a	2-0	N'Doe 2

No	Name	Nat	Pos	Aps	(s)	Gls
1	Kostas ANDRIOLAS		G	1		
4	Vangelis DAGAS		D	16	(2)	1
6	Markos DIMOS		D	20	(8)	1
19	Rafik DJEBBOUR	FRA	A	12		5
18	Christos ELIOPOULOS		A		(3)	
3	Dimitris GELADARIS		D	25	(1)	1
14	Giorgos GEORGIOU		D	22	(2)	
24	Giorgos HALARIS		A	6	(3)	
11	Loukas KARADIMOS		M	16	(7)	1

Greece

No	Name	Nat	Pos	Aps	(s)	Gls
2	Giannis KATEMIS		D	22	(7)	3
27	Giorgos KORAKAKIS		M	27	(1)	3
37	Giorgos KOUTSIS		M	23	(1)	1
22	Elias MANIKAS		A		(6)	
33	Stergios MARINOS		A		(3)	
16	Roberto Ramírez MERINO	PER	M	10	(2)	2
23	Chrisostomos MICHAILIDIS		G	29		
5	Christos MIKES		D	20	(2)	
15	Francis N'DOE	LIB	A	10	(10)	6
28	Panagiotis PAPPAS		D	10	(5)	
10	Milen PETKOV	BUL	M	7	(3)	
32	Alain RAGUEL	FRA	D	11	(6)	
40	Nikos SKARMOUTSOS		A	6	(4)	3
8	Giannis SOTIRHOS		M	15	(10)	
9	Giorgos ZAHAROPOULOS		A	22	(3)	8
25	Manolis LIAPAKIS		M	5	(4)	
26	Dimosthenis MANOUSAKIS		M	17	(5)	2
24	Marko MARIC	CRO	M	23	(1)	1
16	Christos MOUSTOGIANNIS		A	6	(6)	1
17	Nikos NIKOLOPOULOS		A	16	(6)	3
23	Souleymane Akim OMO	NGA	A	24	(1)	1
5	Kostas PAPOUTSIS		D	20	(1)	2
3	Goran POPOV	MAC	D	15	(4)	
22	Manolis PSOMAS		D	24		
13	Prokopis SAGANAS		A	3	(13)	
33	Mahamadou SIDIBE	CMR	G	14		
27	Giannis SKOPELITIS		M	16		1
6	Stathis STEFANIDIS		A	4	(3)	
20	Sotiris TSATSOS		M	18	(6)	2
28	Dimitris TSITSOMITROS		D		(1)	
2	Giannis ZAPROPOULOS		D	25	(2)	1

EGALEO
Coach – Giorgos Vazakas; (13/12/05) Giorgos Hatzaras

2005
27/8	Kallithea	a	1-1	Tsatsos
11/9	Akratitos	h	1-0	Agritis
18/9	AEK	a	1-1	Cesarec
25/9	PAOK	a	0-2	
9/10	OFI	h	0-0	
15/10	Apollon Kalamarias	a	0-0	
23/10	Xanthi	h	3-2	Fotakis, Manousakis, og (Sikov)
30/10	Atromitos	a	0-0	
7/11	Iraklis	h	1-1	Chloros
20/11	Levadiakos	h	1-0	Nikolopoulos
26/11	Larisa	a	1-1	Zapropoulos
3/12	Olympiakos	h	1-3	Maric
11/12	Ionikos	a	1-4	Manousakis
18/12	Panathinaikos	h	0-2	

2006
7/1	Panionios	a	1-0	Tsatsos
22/1	Kallithea	h	1-0	Omo
28/1	Akratitos	a	3-0	Agritis, Nikolopoulos, Skopelitis
4/2	AEK	h	0-2	
12/2	PAOK	h	1-0	Nikolopoulos
18/2	OFI	a	0-1	
26/2	Apollon Kalamarias	h	0-0	
4/3	Xanthi	a	0-1	
11/3	Atromitos	h	0-1	
19/3	Iraklis	a	2-4	Moustogiannis, Agritis (p)
26/3	Levadiakos	h	1-2	Papoutsis
1/4	Larisa	h	1-0	Agritis
8/4	Olympiakos	a	1-5	Papoutsis
15/4	Ionikos	h	1-1	Kivelidis
30/4	Panathinaikos	a	0-4	
14/5	Panionios	h	0-3	

No	Name	Nat	Pos	Aps	(s)	Gls
9	Tasos AGRITIS		A	17	(4)	4
11	Giorgos BARKOGLOU		M		(3)	
29	Danijel CESAREC	CRO	A	10	(8)	1
7	Giannis CHLOROS		A	8	(6)	1
14	Giannis CHRISTOU		M	5	(3)	
21	Daniel EDUSEI	GHA	D	16		
10	Giorgos FOTAKIS		M	12	(1)	
1	Luigi GENAMO		G	11		
19	Labros HONOS		D	1	(4)	
30	Hrvoje JANCETIC	CRO	M	12	(2)	
31	Pawel KIESZEK	POL	G	5		
32	Leonidas KIVELIDIS		A	1	(1)	1
8	Giorgos LABROPOULOS		M	2	(2)	

IONIKOS
Coach – Sakis Tsiolis

2005
4/9	Levadiakos	a	1-1	og (Dimou)
11/9	Panathinaikos	h	1-1	Makor
18/9	Panionios	a	3-3	Makor (p), Da Costa, Konstantinidis
25/9	Kallithea	h	2-1	Da Costa 2
2/10	Akratitos	a	0-0	
16/10	AEK	h	0-1	
23/10	PAOK	a	1-6	Makor
30/10	OFI	h	1-1	Coimbra
6/11	Apollon Kalamarias	h	2-0	Makor 2
19/11	Xanthi	a	1-1	Perrone
27/11	Atromitos	h	3-1	Makor 2, Perrone
4/12	Iraklis	a	1-2	Coimbra
11/12	Egaleo	h	4-1	Konstantinidis, Gutman, Da Costa, King
18/12	Larisa	a	0-0	

2006
8/1	Olympiakos	h	0-1	
15/1	Levadiakos	h	2-0	Konstantinidis, Vourexakis
29/1	Panathinaikos	a	0-1	
5/2	Panionios	h	0-1	
11/2	Kallithea	a	3-3	Ukar, Makor (p), Perrone
19/2	Akratitos	h	3-2	og (Diang), Ukar, Makor (p)
26/2	AEK	a	1-2	Perrone
5/3	PAOK	h	1-1	Onouaci
12/3	OFI	a	0-3	
19/3	Apollon Kalamarias	a	1-2	Makor
26/3	Xanthi	h	0-0	
2/4	Atromitos	a	2-3	King, Triantafilou
9/4	Iraklis	h	1-1	Onouaci
15/4	Egaleo	a	1-1	Onouaci
30/4	Larisa	h	1-1	Perrone
14/5	Olympiakos	a	0-0	

No	Name	Nat	Pos	Aps	(s)	Gls
18	Fernando Martín BENÍTEZ	ARG	A		(6)	
1	Arjan BEQAJ	ALB	G	28		
9	Milton COIMBRA	BOL	A	9	(3)	2
8	Felipe DA COSTA	POR	M	23	(1)	4
28	Giorgos EFTHIMIOU		M		(1)	
19	Marcelo GUTMAN	ARG	A	20	(3)	1
12	Elias KAKARAS		M	6	(4)	
15	Giorgos KANTIMIRIS		G	2	(1)	
6	Devanir Ferreira "KING"	POR	D	22	(1)	2
17	Sotiris KONSTANTINIDIS		M	18	(3)	5
2	Efthimios KOTITSAS		D	6	(7)	
20	Gabriel Leonardo LETTIERI	ARG	M	19	(5)	

Greece

10	Oliver MAKOR	LIB	A	26	(1)	10
13	Giorgos MELABIANAKIS		M	23	(1)	
25	Kostas MENDRINOS		M	2	(5)	
4	Sokratis OFRIDOPOULOS		D		(3)	
80	Benjamin ONOUACI	NGA	A	5	(8)	3
3	Juan Luciano PAJUELO	PER	D	8	(9)	
21	Emmanuel PERRONE	ARG	A	18	(8)	5
5	Giorgos POULOPOULOS		D	28		
24	Stathis ROKAS		M	2	(2)	
27	Vasilis SAHINIDIS		A		(3)	
79	Tasos TRIANTAFILOU		A	2	(8)	1
7	Nikos TSIBLIDIS		A	20	(3)	
26	Kendal UKAR	FRA	A	18	(2)	2
16	Giorgos VOUREXAKIS		D	25		1

IRAKLIS
Coach – Savvas Kofidis

2005
28/8	Akratitos	a	1-3	Papapostolou	
11/9	AEK	a	0-2		
19/9	PAOK	h	0-0		
25/9	OFI	a	1-0	Lagos	
2/10	Apollon Kalamarias	h	0-1		
17/10	Xanthi	a	1-4	Epalle	
22/10	Atromitos	h	2-0	Epalle (p), Lawal	
30/10	Levadiakos	h	2-0	Epalle, Lagos	
7/11	Egaleo	a	1-1	Epalle	
20/11	Larisa	h	2-1	Epalle, Georgiadis	
28/11	Olympiakos	a	1-2	Herrera	
4/12	Ionikos	h	2-1	Lagos 2	
11/12	Panathinaikos	a	2-2	Epalle, Kapetanos P.	
18/12	Panionios	h	1-0	Katsiabis	

2006
8/1	Kallithea	a	0-0		
14/1	Akratitos	h	1-0	Prittas	
29/1	AEK	h	4-0	Lagos 2, Herrera, Epalle	
5/2	PAOK	a	0-1		
11/2	OFI	h	2-0	Georgiadis, Epalle	
20/2	Apollon Kalamarias	a	0-2		
25/2	Xanthi	h	2-0	og (Paviot), Herrera	
5/3	Atromitos	a	2-3	Epalle, Lagos	
12/3	Levadiakos	a	1-0	Epalle	
19/3	Egaleo	h	4-2	Epalle 2, Georgiadis, Herrera	
25/3	Larisa	a	0-0		
3/4	Olympiakos	h	2-0	Herrera, Epalle	
9/4	Ionikos	a	1-1	og (King)	
16/4	Panathinaikos	h	1-0	Herrera	
30/4	Panionios	a	0-3		
13/5	Kallithea	h	3-2	Georgiadis 2, Herrera	

No	Name	Nat	Pos	Aps	(s)	Gls
1	Giorgos ABARIS		G	25		
12	Eduardo ALEMÃO	BRA	D	1		
37	Giorgos BANTIS		G		(1)	
70	Kostas DIAMANTIDIS		M		(5)	
77	Panagiotis DILBERIS		G	4	(1)	
22	Panagiotis DROUGAS		M	25	(1)	
10	Joël EPALLE	CMR	M	29		13
31	Indrit FORTUZI	ALB	M		(4)	
17	Giorgos GEORGIADIS		A	21	(1)	5
20	José Estebán HERRERA	ARG	A	27	(2)	7
9	Kostas KAPETANOS		A	1	(13)	
11	Pantelis KAPETANOS		A	4	(10)	1
21	Fanis KATERGIANAKIS		G	1		
4	Tasos KATSIABIS		M	20	(2)	1
19	Panagiotis LAGOS		M	26	(2)	7
8	Garba LAWAL	NGA	M	12	(9)	1

7	Edvin MURATI	ALB	M	7	(9)	
18	Giannis PAPAPOSTOLOU		A	2	(7)	1
2	Grigoris PAPAZAHARIAS		D	19	(5)	
3	Charalambos PERPERIDIS		M	2	(7)	
6	Elias POURSANIDIS		M	24	(1)	
55	Thanasis PRITTAS		M	28		1
27	Bark SEGHIRI	FRA	D	19		
25	Nikos SOULIDIS		M		(1)	
5	Kostas STEFANIS		M	9	(6)	
13	Miroslaw SZNAUCNER	POL	D	24	(1)	

KALLITHEA
Coach – Stoicho Mladenov (BUL); (18/10/05) Vavgelis Goutis; (30/10/05) Ilie Dumitrescu (ROM); (20/2/06) Giorgos Vazakas; (21/3/06) Antonis Manikas

2005
27/8	Egaleo	h	1-1	Tsigas	
12/9	Larisa	a	0-2		
17/9	Olympiakos	h	0-3		
25/9	Ionikos	a	1-2	Lazanas	
1/10	Panathinaikos	h	2-4	Telkiiski, Georgiev	
16/10	Panionios	a	0-1		
23/10	Levadiakos	a	0-1		
29/10	Akratitos	h	2-0	Lazanas, Yanchev	
5/11	AEK	a	0-2		
20/11	PAOK	h	1-1	Koulakiotis	
27/11	OFI	a	0-0		
3/12	Apollon Kalamarias	h	0-0		
11/12	Xanthi	a	2-2	Koutsospiros 2	
18/12	Atromitos	h	2-3	Venetis, Lazanas	

2006
8/1	Iraklis	h	0-0		
22/1	Egaleo	a	0-1		
28/1	Larisa	h	2-1	Petkovic 2	
6/2	Olympiakos	a	1-2	Koutsospiros	
11/2	Ionikos	h	3-3	Sylla, Cléber 2	
19/2	Panathinaikos	a	0-2		
25/2	Panionios	h	1-2	Mijatovic	
4/3	Levadiakos	h	3-2	Koutsospiros, Petkovic, Cléber	
12/3	Akratitos	a	0-1		
18/3	AEK	h	1-4	Tsigas	
25/3	PAOK	a	1-2	Koutsospiros	
2/4	OFI	h	0-1		
9/4	Apollon Kalamarias	a	0-0		
16/4	Xanthi	h	2-1	Koulakiotis, Diamantis	
30/4	Atromitos	a	1-2	Radovanovic	
13/5	Iraklis	a	2-3	Cléber, Radovanovic	

No	Name	Nat	Pos	Aps	(s)	Gls
4	Achileas ANGELOPOULOS		D	5	(2)	
52	Panagiotis BARTZOKAS		G	21		
99	Alain BEHI	FRA	D	13	(1)	
18	Xenofon BELEGRINIS		D	7	(6)	
43	CLÉBER Fereira Madui	BRA	D	7	(4)	4
22	Dimitris DIAMANTIS		M	4	(11)	1
8	Radislav DRAGICEVIC	SCG	M	1	(2)	
6	Borislav GEORGIEV	BUL	D	21	(3)	1
31	Babis GONTZOS		A		(4)	
2	Vasilis KARATZAS		M	18	(1)	
5	Giorgos KOULAKIOTIS		D	25		2
9	Christos KOUTSOSPIROS		A	16	(7)	5
21	Giannis LAZANAS		A	14	(3)	3
44	Aleksandar MIJATOVIC	SCG	D	13		1
23	Amiran MUJIRI	GEO	M	7		
19	Agisilaos PASAS		M	16	(10)	
11	Goran PETKOVIC	SCG	M	19	(6)	3

Greece

No	Name	Nat	Pos	Aps	(s)	Gls
17	Grigoris PSARIS		M	1		
88	Branko RADOVANOVIC	SCG	A	10	(2)	2
32	Giorgos SOULOGIANNIS		G	9		
40	Jean-Marie SYLLA	GUI	M	21	(1)	1
20	Hristo TELKIISKI	BUL	D	10	(3)	1
3	Vaggelis TSIOLIS		M	20	(3)	
10	Thanasis TSIGAS		A		(7)	2
33	Michalis TZORBATZAKIS		D	5		
25	Tasos VENETIS		D	22	(2)	1
14	Leonidas VOKOLOS		D	8	(3)	
7	Todor YANCHEV	BUL	M	17	(3)	1

LARISA
Coach – Giorgos Donis

2005
Date	Opponent	h/a	Score	Scorers
28/8	Panionios	a	1-1	Spasic
12/9	Kallithea	h	2-0	Digozis, Aloneftis
17/9	Akratitos	a	0-0	
25/9	AEK	h	0-1	
2/10	PAOK	a	2-2	og (Karipidis), Kiparissis
16/10	OFI	a	2-3	Kiparissis, Aloneftis
24/10	Apollon Kalamarias	h	4-1	Bahramis, Digozis (p), Katsiaros, Kiparissis
30/10	Xanthi	a	0-1	
5/11	Atromitos	h	2-1	Kiparissis 2
20/11	Iraklis	a	1-2	Kiparissis
26/11	Egaleo	h	1-1	Serban
4/12	Levadiakos	h	1-0	Kiparissis
12/12	Olympiakos	a	0-4	
18/12	Ionikos	h	0-0	

2006
Date	Opponent	h/a	Score	Scorers
7/1	Panathinaikos	a	0-3	
16/1	Panionios	h	1-0	Förster
28/1	Kallithea	a	1-2	Vela Júnior
5/2	Akratitos	h	2-1	Chloros, Kalantzis
12/2	AEK	a	0-1	
18/2	PAOK	h	2-1	Chloros, Kalantzis
26/2	OFI	h	1-0	Gavrilopoulos
5/3	Apollon Kalamarias	a	2-2	Guga, Bahramis
13/3	Xanthi	h	3-1	Gavrilopoulos, Bahramis, Aloneftis
19/3	Atromitos	a	0-0	
25/3	Iraklis	h	0-0	
1/4	Egaleo	a	0-1	
9/4	Levadiakos	a	0-3	
16/4	Olympiakos	h	2-1	Digozis (p), Aloneftis
30/4	Ionikos	a	1-1	Kalantzis
14/5	Panathinaikos	h	0-3	

No	Name	Nat	Pos	Aps	(s)	Gls
34	Thierry ABOUNA	CMR			(1)	
46	Stathis ALONEFTIS	CYP	M	22	(3)	4
33	Panagiotis BAHRAMIS		M	17	(9)	3
97	Giannis CHLOROS		A	6	(1)	2
15	Spiros CHRISTOPOULOS		G	3		
14	Nikos DABIZAS		D	27		
66	Angelos DIGOZIS		M	27	(1)	3
5	Marco FÖRSTER	GER	D	6	(2)	1
7	Giorgos GALITSIOS		D	26	(1)	
55	Alexis GAVRILOPOULOS		A	11	(6)	2
6	Dimitris GIKAS		M	9	(5)	
18	José Augusto Santos GUGA	BRA	A	3	(5)	1
40	HÉLDER Marino	POR	D	8	(1)	
9	Christos KALANTZIS		A	15	(11)	3
77	Panagiotis KATSIAROS		D	27		1
11	Thomas KIPARISSIS		A	12	(13)	7
26	Stefanos KOTSOLIS		G	27		

No	Name	Nat	Pos	Aps	(s)	Gls
22	Ivan NEDELJKOVIC	SCG	A		(1)	
19	Thanasis PALAIOLOGOS		A	1		
17	Apostolos PAPAKOSTAS		M	4	(7)	
4	Giorgos PASIOS		M	2	(1)	
3	Antonis PUTAS		M	1	(1)	
10	Denis SERBAN	ROM	M	27		1
2	Giorgos SIMOS		D	17		
30	Mirnes SOSIC	SLO	M	1	(3)	
20	Sladjan SPASIC	SCG	A	5	(11)	1
32	Vaggelis STOURNARAS		D	2		
23	Dimitris TSIATSIOS		M	3	(3)	
27	Giuseppe VELA JÚNIOR	BRA	M	18	(3)	1
8	Zisis ZIAGAS		M	3	(1)	

LEVADIAKOS
Coach – Takis Lemonis

2005
Date	Opponent	h/a	Score	Scorers
4/9	Ionikos	h	1-1	Dimitropoulos
11/9	Apollon Kalamarias	a	1-1	Rusev
18/9	Panathinaikos	h	0-0	
25/9	Xanthi	a	0-1	
1/10	Panionios	h	3-2	Bushi, Rusev, Pastos
15/10	Atromitos	a	0-1	
23/10	Kallithea	h	1-0	Alex
30/10	Iraklis	a	0-2	
6/11	Akratitos	h	1-1	Rusev
20/11	Egaleo	a	0-1	
27/11	AEK	h	0-1	
4/12	Larisa	a	0-1	
10/12	PAOK	h	2-2	og (Megahed), Alex
17/12	Olympiakos	a	0-1	

2006
Date	Opponent	h/a	Score	Scorers
8/1	OFI	h	1-0	Gurma
15/1	Ionikos	a	0-2	
1/2	Apollon Kalamarias	h	1-0	Bushi (p)
4/2	Panathinaikos	a	0-2	
12/2	Xanthi	h	0-2	
19/2	Panionios	a	1-1	Bushi
26/2	Atromitos	h	1-0	og (Georgiou)
4/3	Kallithea	a	2-3	Bushi 2
12/3	Iraklis	h	0-1	
19/3	Akratitos	a	0-0	
26/3	Egaleo	h	2-1	Alex, Sosic
2/4	AEK	a	0-2	
9/4	Larisa	h	3-0	Bushi 2 (1p), Alex
16/4	PAOK	a	1-3	Pastos
30/4	Olympiakos	h	3-2	Dimitropoulos, Bushi, Rusev
14/5	OFI	a	0-2	

No	Name	Nat	Pos	Aps	(s)	Gls
14	José de Paula ALEX	BRA	A	14	(6)	4
15	ANDERSON Oliveira Almeida	BRA	M	12		
16	Paraskevas ANDRALAS		M	12	(1)	
21	Touré BASALA	MLI	M	25	(2)	
20	Alban BUSHI	ALB	A	18	(4)	8
11	Giannis CHRISAFIS		M	18	(4)	
81	Rogério CORREA	BRA	M	5	(1)	
56	Nikos DIMITROPOULOS		D	23		2
5	Pavlos DIMOU		D	18	(5)	
9	Mario GURMA	ALB	M	11	(6)	1
23	Adrian IORDACHE	ROM	M	2	(3)	
2	Kostas KALLIMANIS		D	25	(3)	
10	Loukas KARAKATSANIS		M	3	(9)	
1	Nikos KARAKOSTAS		G	4	(2)	
12	Rastislav LAZORÍK	SVK	A		(3)	
31	Panagiotis MACHAIRAS		D	11	(6)	
79	Elias MANIKAS		A		(5)	

Greece

No	Name	Nat	Pos	Aps	(s)	Gls
3	Carlos Alberto MASSARA	ARG	D	5	(2)	
50	Miguel Ángel MEA VITALI	VEN	M	15		
19	Theopistos PAPADOPOULOS		D	1		
6	Dimitris PAPPAS		M	1	(2)	
4	Tasos PASTOS		D	17	(3)	2
22	Diego Rafael PERONE	URU	A	2	(4)	
27	Danilo RIBEIRO	BRA	M		(3)	
99	Ivan RUSEV	BUL	M	23	(5)	4
32	Mirnes SOSIC	SLO	M	10	(1)	1
28	Theodosis THEODOSIADIS		M	15		
7	Nikos TIPOLIATIS		M		(1)	
8	Christos VELETANIS		D		(3)	
77	Nikos ZAFIROPOULOS		G	26		
13	Giorgos ZISOPOULOS		M	14	(2)	

OFI
Coach – Vangelis Vlahos; (13/2/06) Miron Sifakis

2005
28/8	Apollon Kalamarias	a	1-2	Triantafilou
11/9	Xanthi	h	1-1	og (Zapropoulos)
18/9	Atromitos	a	0-4	
25/9	Iraklis	h	0-1	
9/10	Egaleo	a	0-0	
16/10	Larisa	h	3-2	Mahlas 3
23/10	Olympiakos	h	1-0	Mahlas
30/10	Ionikos	a	1-1	Mahlas
6/11	Panathinaikos	h	0-2	
20/11	Panionios	a	1-1	Sfakianakis
27/11	Kallithea	h	0-0	
4/12	Akratitos	a	1-1	Mahlas
10/12	AEK	h	0-1	
18/12	PAOK	a	0-2	

2006
8/1	Levadiakos	a	0-1	
15/1	Apollon Kalamarias	h	1-2	Ofori-Quaye
29/1	Xanthi	a	0-0	
5/2	Atromitos	h	0-0	
11/2	Iraklis	a	0-2	
18/2	Egaleo	h	1-0	Deyanov (p)
26/2	Larisa	a	0-1	
5/3	Olympiakos	a	0-4	
12/3	Ionikos	h	3-0	Mahlas 2, Deyanov
19/3	Panathinaikos	a	1-3	Nwafor
26/3	Panionios	h	1-1	Nwafor
2/4	Kallithea	a	1-0	Deyanov
9/4	Akratitos	h	2-2	Issa, Chipev
16/4	AEK	a	0-2	
30/4	PAOK	h	2-1	Nwafor, Davidson
14/5	Levadiakos	h	2-0	Issa, Nwafor

No	Name	Nat	Pos	Aps	(s)	Gls
6	Pavlos ADAMOS		D		(2)	
16	Adriano ADRIANINHO	BRA	M		(5)	
3	Anestis ANASTASIADIS		D	11	(7)	
4	Dimitris ARVANITIS		D	6		
2	Gerasimos BELEVONIS		D	2	(4)	
23	Steven BRYCE	CRC	A		(3)	
36	Zvetomir CHIPEV	BUL	M	7	(2)	1
77	DAVIDSON Morais Oliveira	BRA	D	28	(1)	1
20	Tasos DENTSAS		D	7	(12)	
22	Metodi DEYANOV	BUL	M	18	(6)	3
40	Pedro Rocha Mendes EDNÍLSON	GUI	M	2	(2)	
12	Mariano Fernando GONZÁLEZ	ARG	D	11	(1)	
13	Pierre ISSA	RSA	D	10		2
99	Giorgos KAZANTZIS		A	4	(8)	
10	Romik KHACHATRYAN	ARM	M	22		
33	Giorgos KOLTZOS		M	10	(1)	

No	Name			Pos	Aps	(s)	Gls
15	Kostas KONSTANTAKIS			D	1		
24	Kostas KONSTANTINIDIS			M	13		
5	Nikos KOUNENAKIS			D	13		
9	Nikos MAHLAS			A	25		8
11	Joseph NWAFOR	NGA		A	21	(5)	4
25	Peter OFORI-QUAYE	GHA		A	14	(2)	1
8	Minas PITSOS			D	21	(2)	
28	Vasilis PLOUSIS			D	2	(1)	
17	Manolis RUBAKIS			D	19	(6)	
66	Kabba SAMURA	SRL		A	2	(4)	
19	Stelios SFAKIANAKIS			M	19	(2)	1
87	Michalis SIFAKIS			G	30		
7	Kostas STAVRAKAKIS			M	3	(5)	
30	Aleksandar TOMOVSKI-TOMASH	BUL		D	6	(2)	
18	Tasos TRIANTAFILOU			A	3	(9)	1

OLYMPIAKOS
Coach – Trond Sollied (NOR)

2005
28/8	Panathinaikos	a	2-0	Stoltidis, Djordjevic
10/9	Panionios	h	5-0	Kafes, Stoltidis, Kostoulas, Taralidis, Babangida
17/9	Kallithea	a	3-0	og (Telkiiski), Djordjevic, Castillo
24/9	Akratitos	h	2-0	Djordjevic, Konstantinou
2/10	AEK	a	3-1	Djordjevic (p), Konstantinou, Okkas
16/10	PAOK	h	1-2	Touré
23/10	OFI	a	0-1	
29/10	Apollon Kalamarias	a	2-1	Okkas, Konstantinou
6/11	Xanthi	h	2-0	og (Torosidis), Djordjevic (p)
19/11	Atromitos	a	1-0	Stoltidis
28/11	Iraklis	h	2-1	Djordjevic (p), Okkas
3/12	Egaleo	a	3-1	Touré 2, Djordjevic (p)
12/12	Larisa	h	4-0	og (Dabizas), Okkas, Djordjevic, Babangida
17/12	Levadiakos	h	1-0	Djordjevic (p)

2006
8/1	Ionikos	a	1-0	Stoltidis
15/1	Panathinaikos	h	3-2	Rivaldo 2, Konstantinou
30/1	Panionios	a	3-2	Konstantinou 2, Djordjevic (p)
6/2	Kallithea	h	2-1	Rivaldo (p), Georgatos
13/2	Akratitos	a	1-0	Rivaldo
19/2	AEK	h	3-0	Okkas, Rivaldo 2
26/2	PAOK	a	2-1	Okkas, Konstantinou
5/3	OFI	h	4-0	Konstantinou, Djordjevic (p), Rivaldo, Dani
12/3	Apollon Kalamarias	h	2-1	Dani, Djordjevic (p)
18/3	Xanthi	a	0-1	
27/3	Atromitos	h	3-0	Konstantinou, Bulut, Djordjevic (p)
3/4	Iraklis	a	0-2	
8/4	Egaleo	h	5-1	Kafes, Stoltidis, Djordjevic, Okkas, Castillo
16/4	Larisa	a	1-2	Djordjevic
30/4	Levadiakos	a	2-3	Maric, Konstantinou
14/5	Ionikos	h	0-0	

No	Name	Nat	Pos	Aps	(s)	Gls
32	Giorgos ANATOLAKIS		D	26		
40	Haruna BABANGIDA	NGA	A	11	(14)	2
22	Erol BULUT	TUR	D	17		1
7	Nery Alberto CASTILLO	URU	A	2	(15)	2
18	Alexandre Joakim D' ACOL	BRA	A		(3)	
20	Daniel Garcia "DANI"	ESP	A	8	(11)	2
11	Predrag DJORDJEVIC	SCG	M	29		15

Greece

No	Name	Nat	Pos	Aps	(s)	Gls
21	Grigoris GEORGATOS		D	17	(5)	1
34	Kleopas GIANNOU		G	1		
1	Pantelis KAFES		M	17	(5)	2
5	Michalis KAPSIS		D	3	(1)	
23	Michalis KONSTANTINOU	CYP	A	19	(2)	10
19	Thanasis KOSTOULAS		D	10	(2)	1
8	Milos MARIC	SCG	M	2	(9)	1
14	Dimitris MAVROGENIDIS		D	13	(1)	
71	Antonis NIKOPOLIDIS		G	29		
9	Yiannakis OKKAS	CYP	A	21	(6)	7
30	Tasos PANTOS		D	16	(3)	
2	Christos PATSATZOGLOU		D		(2)	
10	Vítor Borba Fereira "RIVALDO"	BRA	M	21	(1)	7
12	Gabriel SCHÜRRER	ARG	D	20		
6	Ieroklis STOLTIDIS		M	26	(1)	5
17	Giannis TARALIDIS		M	1	(4)	1
15	Yaya TOURE	CIV	M	20		3
25	Spiros VALLAS		D	1		
10	Ezequiel GONZÁLEZ	ARG	M	26	(1)	5
8	Giannis GOUMAS		D	22		4
4	Elias KOTSIOS		D	12	(6)	2
27	Sotiris LEONTIOU		M	2	(13)	
26	Vangelis MANTZIOS		A	9	(13)	8
5	Nasief MORRIS	RSA	D	24		
29	Mikael NILSSON	SWE	D	14	(2)	
9	Emmanuel OLISADEBE	POL	A	3	(3)	
11	Dimitris PAPADOPOULOS		A	24	(1)	10
19	Anthony SERIC	CRO	D	20	(1)	1
28	Giorgos THEODORIDIS		M	1	(5)	
40	Sándor TORGHELLE	HUN	A	2	(9)	
22	Alexandros TZIOLIS		M	16	(5)	1
24	Loukas VINTRA		D	22	(1)	
14	Nordin WOOTER	HOL	M	7	(2)	1

PANATHINAIKOS
Coach – Alberto Malesani (ITA)

2005
28/8	Olympiakos	h	0-2	
11/9	Ionikos	a	1-1	González (p)
18/9	Levadiakos	a	0-0	
24/9	Panionios	h	3-0	Mantzios, González, Goumas
1/10	Kallithea	a	4-2	Gekas 2, Kotsios, Wooter
15/10	Akratitos	h	1-0	Mantzios
23/10	AEK	a	0-3	
30/10	PAOK	h	1-0	Mantzios
6/11	OFI	a	2-0	Flávio Conceição, Papadopoulos
19/11	Apollon Kalamarias	h	3-0	Mantzios, Goumas, Seric
26/11	Xanthi	h	2-1	Andric, Mantzios
3/12	Atromitos	a	0-1	
11/12	Iraklis	h	2-2	González (p), Gekas
18/12	Egaleo	a	2-0	Mantzios, Biscan

2006
7/1	Larisa	h	3-0	Gekas 2, Tziolis
15/1	Olympiakos	a	2-3	González (p), Gekas
29/1	Ionikos	h	1-0	Gekas
4/2	Levadiakos	h	2-0	Goumas, Gekas
12/2	Panionios	a	4-2	Kotsios, Mantzios, Gekas, Papadopoulos
19/2	Kallithea	h	2-0	Gekas, Papadopoulos
26/2	Akratitos	a	2-0	Papadopoulos, Gekas
5/3	AEK	h	1-0	Biscan
11/3	PAOK	a	1-0	Papadopoulos
19/3	OFI	h	3-1	Papadopoulos 2, Biscan
26/3	Apollon Kalamarias	a	1-0	González (p)
2/4	Xanthi	a	1-1	Gekas
9/4	Atromitos	h	4-3	Gekas 2, Papadopoulos, Charalambides
16/4	Iraklis	a	0-1	
30/4	Egaleo	h	4-0	Gekas, og (Zaproyalos), Papadopoulos 2
14/5	Larisa	a	3-0	Goumas, Mantzios, Andric

No	Name	Nat	Pos	Aps	(s)	Gls
15	Srdjan ANDRIC	CRO	M	6	(8)	2
25	Igor BISCAN	CRO	M	19	(2)	3
21	Costas CHARALAMBIDES	CYP	M	20	(6)	1
31	Phillipos DARLAS		D	15	(4)	
6	FLÁVIO CONCEIÇÃO	BRA	M	14		1
1	Mario GALINOVIC	CRO	G	30		
7	Fanis GEKAS		A	22	(6)	15

PANIONIOS
Coach – Josef Csaplár (CZE); (12/9/05) (Nikos Pantelis); (1/10/05) Géza Farkas (HUN); (16/10/05) Josef Bubenko (SVK); (20/2/06) Vangelis Vlahos

2005
28/8	Larisa	h	1-1	Fernández (p)
10/9	Olympiakos	a	0-5	
18/9	Ionikos	h	3-3	Exouzidis, Oravec, Fernández
24/9	Panathinaikos	a	0-3	
1/10	Levadiakos	a	2-3	Breska, Makos
16/10	Kallithea	h	1-0	Nalitzis
23/10	Akratitos	a	1-0	Oravec
31/10	AEK	h	0-2	
6/11	PAOK	a	0-1	
20/11	OFI	h	1-1	Breska
27/11	Apollon Kalamarias	a	0-1	
5/12	Xanthi	h	0-2	
11/12	Atromitos	h	2-0	Makos, Fernández (p)
18/12	Iraklis	a	0-1	

2006
7/1	Egaleo	h	0-1	
16/1	Larisa	a	0-1	
30/1	Olympiakos	h	2-3	Zografakis, Luciano
5/2	Ionikos	a	1-0	Luciano
12/2	Panathinaikos	h	2-4	Luciano, og (Leontiou)
19/2	Levadiakos	h	1-1	Luciano (p)
25/2	Kallithea	a	2-1	Giannopoulos, Breska
5/3	Akratitos	h	2-4	Luciano (p), Exouzidis
12/3	AEK	a	0-2	
20/3	PAOK	h	0-1	
26/3	OFI	a	1-1	Luciano
2/4	Apollon Kalamarias	h	2-1	Luciano, Makos
9/4	Xanthi	a	0-1	
16/4	Atromitos	a	3-1	Kapandais, Breska, Luciano
30/4	Iraklis	h	3-0	Zografakis, Smiljanic, Dimitriadis
14/5	Egaleo	a	3-0	Kapandais, Luciano 2 (2p)

No	Name	Nat	Pos	Aps	(s)	Gls
29	Mario BRESKA	SVK	A	18	(9)	4
4	Thomas CHIHON	GER	D	6		
39	Petros DIMITRIADIS		A	2	(6)	1
24	Savvas EXOUZIDIS		D	22	(4)	2
23	Darío Ezequiel FERNÁNDEZ	ARG	M	17	(10)	3
5	Aristides GALANOPOULOS		D	2	(2)	
27	Josef GASPÁR	SVK	M	9	(1)	
6	Panagiotis GIANNOPOULOS		D	22	(2)	1
20	Fanouris GOUNDOULAKIS		M	17	(2)	
9	Leonidas KAPANDAIS		A	9	(3)	2
10	Kostas KIASSOS		M	9		

Greece

No	Name	Nat	Pos	Aps	(s)	Gls
3	Dimitris KONTODIMOS		M	9	(1)	
13	Vaggelis KOUTSOPOULOS		M	10	(4)	
16	Simos KRASSAS	CYP	M	3		
18	David LANGER	CZE	A	11		
30	Nikos LAZARIDIS		A	5	(3)	
38	LUCIANO de Sousa	BRA	M	14		10
7	Ahmet MAGDI	EGY	M	22	(4)	
14	Grigoris MAKOS		M	16	(7)	3
2	Giannis MANIATIS		D	7	(6)	
25	Nikos MITROU		M	2	(6)	
8	Dimitris NALITZIS		A	11	(1)	1
33	Fernando NAVAS	ARG	M	1	(1)	
32	Tomás ORAVEC	SVK	A	8	(5)	2
11	Dilon SHEPPARD	RSA	A	5	(5)	
17	Mirko SMILJANIC	SCG	D	18	(2)	1
21	Nikos SPIROPOULOS		M	10	(1)	
35	Habibou TRAORE	SEN	M		(2)	
1	Martin VANIAK	CZE	G	30		
26	Dimitris ZOGRAFAKIS		M	15		2

PAOK
Coach – Nikos Karageorgiou ; (16/9/05) Giorgos Kostikos; (20/2/06) Ilie Dumitrescu (ROM)

2005
Date	Opponent	h/a	Score	Scorers
28/8	Xanthi	a	0-1	
10/9	Atromitos	h	2-2	Mieciel, Salpigidis
19/9	Iraklis	a	0-0	
25/9	Egaleo	h	2-0	Salpigidis, Feutchine
2/10	Larisa	h	2-2	Salpigidis (p), Maladenis
16/10	Olympiakos	a	2-1	Konstantinidis 2
23/10	Ionikos	h	6-1	Udeze, Konstantinidis, Salpigidis 2, Feutchine, Christodoulopoulos
30/10	Panathinaikos	a	0-1	
6/11	Panionios	h	1-0	Salpigidis (p)
20/11	Kallithea	a	1-1	Sikabala
27/11	PAOK	h	2-0	Christodoulopoulos, Sikabala
4/12	AEK	a	1-2	Mieciel
10/12	Levadiakos	a	2-2	Salpigidis, Maladenis
18/12	OFI	h	2-0	Christodoulopoulos, Salpigidis

2006
Date	Opponent	h/a	Score	Scorers
9/1	Apollon Kalamarias	a	2-2	Yiasoumi, Charalambous
15/1	Xanthi	h	1-0	Salpigidis
29/1	Atromitos	a	1-2	Salpigidis (p)
5/2	Iraklis	h	1-0	Mieciel
12/2	Egaleo	a	0-1	
18/2	Larisa	a	1-2	Mieciel
26/2	Olympiakos	h	1-2	Sikabala
5/3	Ionikos	a	1-1	Sikabala
11/3	Panathinaikos	h	0-1	
20/3	Panionios	a	1-0	Salpigidis
25/3	Kallithea	h	2-1	Salpigidis 2 (2p)
2/4	Akratitos	a	3-0	Salpigidis, Yiasoumi 2
9/4	AEK	h	2-1	og (Alexopoulos), Salpigidis
16/4	Levadiakos	h	3-1	Salpigidis 2, Yiasoumi
30/4	OFI	a	1-2	Yiasoumi
14/5	Apollon Kalamarias	h	1-2	Mieciel

No	Name	Nat	Pos	Aps	(s)	Gls
6	Paraskevas ANDRALAS		M		(1)	
37	Nikos ARABATZIS		M	7	(2)	
25	Sotiris BALAFAS		M	12	(5)	
44	Elias CHARALAMBOUS	CYP	D	19	(3)	1
23	Dionisis CHASIOTIS		D	20	(1)	
29	Lazaros CHRISTODOULOPOULOS		M	10	(14)	3
30	Yotis ENGOMITIS	CYP	M	2	(8)	
2	FATIH Akyel	TUR	D	6		
1	Daniel Márcio FERNANDES	CAN	G	27		
22	Guy Armando FEUTCHINE	CMR	M	17	(1)	2
28	Stelios ILIADIS		M	12	(9)	
4	Christos KARIPIDIS		D	23	(2)	
31	Pantelis KONSTANTINIDIS		M	23	(2)	3
5	Christos MALADENIS		M	16	(5)	2
15	Stelios MALEZAS		D		(2)	
77	Amir Amzi MEGAHED	EGY	D	3	(5)	
20	Marcin MIECIEL	POL	A	19	(6)	5
27	Houssein MUMIN		M		(3)	
9	Dimitris SALPIGIDIS		A	29	(1)	17
10	Mahmoud Fadlalla SIKABALA	EGY	M	16	(7)	4
33	Kyriakos TOHOUROGLOU		G	3		
24	Ifeanyi UDEZE	NGA	D	25	(1)	1
18	Labros VANGELIS		M	11	(3)	
11	Yiasemakis YIAOUMI	CYP	A	8	(6)	5
7	Theodoros ZAGORAKIS		M	22		

XANTHI
Coach – Giannis Mantzourakis

2005
Date	Opponent	h/a	Score	Scorers
27/8	PAOK	h	1-0	Antzas
11/9	OFI	a	1-1	Paviot
18/9	Apollon Kalamarias	h	2-0	Labriakos, Luciano (p)
25/9	Levadiakos	h	1-0	Kazakis
3/10	Atromitos	a	1-0	Labriakos
17/10	Iraklis	h	4-1	Luciano, Labriakos 2, Torosidis
23/10	Egaleo	a	2-3	Labriakos, Luciano
30/10	Larisa	h	1-0	Luciano
6/11	Olympiakos	a	0-2	
19/11	Ionikos	h	1-1	Luciano
26/11	Panathinaikos	a	1-2	Garpozis
5/12	Panionios	a	2-0	Baykara, Émerson
11/12	Kallithea	h	2-2	De Mattia, Labriakos
19/12	Akratitos	a	0-2	

2006
Date	Opponent	h/a	Score	Scorers
8/1	AEK	h	0-0	
15/1	PAOK	a	0-1	
29/1	OFI	h	0-0	
5/2	Apollon Kalamarias	a	1-2	Barkoglou
12/2	Levadiakos	a	2-0	Paviot, Garpozis
19/2	Atromitos	h	1-0	Delgado
25/2	Iraklis	a	0-2	
4/3	Egaleo	h	1-0	Torosidis
13/3	Larisa	a	1-3	Fliskas
18/3	Olympiakos	h	1-0	Kazakis
26/3	Ionikos	h	0-0	
2/4	Panathinaikos	h	1-1	Zuela
9/4	Panionios	h	1-0	Garpozis
16/4	Kallithea	a	1-2	Barkoglou
30/4	Akratitos	h	2-0	Delgado, Garpozis
14/5	AEK	a	0-0	

No	Name	Nat	Pos	Aps	(s)	Gls
18	Paraskevas ANTZAS		D	22	(1)	1
99	Giorgos BARKOGLOU		M	6	(3)	2
20	BAYKARA Deniz	TUR	M	6	(13)	1
11	Marcos Yañez CHANGUI	ESP	M	1	(1)	
10	Stelian CARABAS	ROM	M	2	(2)	
25	Francisco Gomez CHIQUINO	BRA	D	18	(1)	
7	William DE MATTIA	BRA	D	1	(11)	1
38	Francisco DELGADO	POR	M	5	(4)	2
6	ÉMERSON Moises Costa	BRA	M	16		1
21	Kostas FLISKAS		D	6	(5)	1

Greece

19	Alexandros GARPOZIS	CYP	A	17	(6)	4
34	Vlasis KAZAKIS		A	1	(21)	2
13	Stavros LABRIAKOS		A	28		6
22	David LAFATA	CZE	A	4	(5)	
28	Leonardo Santos LEO MINEIRO	BRA	M	5	(3)	
8	LUCIANO de Sousa	BRA	M	11		5
33	Levan MAGRADZE	GEO	M	22	(3)	
44	Damián Alexandro MANSO	ARG	D	10		
5	Giannis PAPADIMITRIOU		D	24		
17	Jacques PAVIOT	FRA	D	21	(1)	2
43	Petr PIZANOVSKY	CZE	G	30		
15	Diego Jesús QUINTANA	ARG	D	16	(1)	
55	Antonis RICCA		M	4		
14	Vance SIKOV	MAC	D	16	(3)	
35	Vasilis TOROSIDIS		M	21	(3)	2
4	Nikos ZAPROPOULOS		D	5	(1)	
32	Francisco ZUELA	ANG	M	12		1

DOMESTIC CUP 2005/06

THIRD ROUND
(26/10/05)
Olympiakos Volou 0, Panionios 2
Ilisiakos 0, Egaleo 2
Niki Volou 1, OFI 1 *(aet; 3-2 on pens)*
Enosi Thrakis 0, Ionikos 0 *(aet; 4-5 on pens)*
Giannina 0, AEK 3
(27/10/05)
Veria 0, Xanthi 2
Agrotikos Asteras 1, PAOK 1 *(aet; 5-4 on pens)*
(8/11/05)
Panserraikos 0, Larisa 1
(9/11/05)
Ethnikos 1, Kallithea 1 *(aet; 4-2 on pens)*
Asteras Tripolis 0, Apollon Kalamarias 0 *(aet; 2-3 on pens)*
Pantrakikos 2, Akratitos 2 *(aet; 5-6 on pens)*
Ergotelis 1, Panathinaikos 0
Ethnikos Asteras 1, Levadiakos 0
(10/11/05)
Panahaiki 1, Iraklis 1 *(aet; 4-2 on pens)*
Paniliakos 0, Olympiakos 4
Thrasivoulos 2, Atromitos 0

FOURTH ROUND
(20/12/05)
Thrasivoulos 0, Olympiakos 2
(21/12/05)
Larisa 0, Apollon Kalamarias 0
AEK 1, Ethnikos 1
Agrotikos Asteras 2, Ergotelis 0
(22/12/05)
Ethnikos Asteras 2, Panionios 1
Ionikos 1, Niki Volou 4
Xanthi 1, Panahaiki 0
Akratitos 0, Egaleo 0

Replays
(11/1/06)
Ethnikos 1, AEK 1 *(aet; 3-4 on pens)*
(12/1/06)
Apollon Kalamarias 1, Larisa 2
(17/1/06)
Egaleo 1, Akratitos 1 *(aet; 4-5 on pens)*

QUARTER-FINALS
(31/1/06 & 8/2/06)
Larisa 1 *(Vela Junior 12)*, Akratitos 0
Akratitos 0, Larisa 1 *(Dabizas 37)*
(Larisa 2-0)

(1/2/06 & 8/2/06)
Ethnikos Asteras 1 *(Jundi 67)*, Agrotikos Asteras 1 *(Kizeridis 73)*
Agrotikos Asteras 4 *(Kaliakis 35, Iordanidis 67.75, Bekiaris 90)*, Ethnikos Asteras 0
(Agrotikos Asteras 5-1)

(2/2/06 & 9/2/06)
Olympiakos 1 *(Rivaldo 20)*, Xanthi 1 *(Labriakos 86)*
Xanthi 0, Olympiakos 1 *(Rivaldo 75)*
(Olympiakos 2-1)

(7/2/06 & 22/2/06)
Niki Volou 0, AEK 0
AEK 2 *(Liberopoulos 26, Katsouranis 68)*, Niki Volou 0
(AEK 2-0)

SEMI-FINALS
(21/3/06 & 12/4/06)
AEK 3 *(Liberopoulos 59, Moras 80, Sapanis 86)*, Agrotikos Asteras 0
Agrotikos Asteras 1 *(Tsouklis 90)*, AEK 0
(AEK 3-1)

(22/3/06 & 12/4/06)
Olympiakos 3 *(Konstantinou 31, 80, Stoltidis 42)*, Larisa 1 *(Aloneftis 72)*
Larisa 0, Olympiakos 1 *(Castillo 90)*
(Olympiakos 4-1)

FINAL
(10/5/06)
Pagritio Stadium, Iraklion, Crete
OLYMPIAKOS 3 *(Konstantinou 61, Ivic 71og, Castillo 90)*
AEK 0
Referee - Terovitsas
OLYMPIAKOS — Nikopolidis, Mavrogenidis, Bulut, Anatolakis, Schürrer, Touré (Maric 65), Kafes, Stoltidis, Okkas (Castillo 76), Djordjevic, Konstantinou (Dani 90).
AEK — Sorrentino, Georgeas, Tziortzopoulos, Cirillo, Dellas (Soares 72), Katsouranis, Emerson, Ivic, César (Kapetanos 76), Lakis, Liberopoulos (Alexopoulos 83).

SECOND LEVEL FINAL TABLE 2005/06

		Pld	W	D	L	F	A	Pts
1	Ergotelis	30	16	8	6	41	23	56
2	Kerkira	30	17	5	8	38	26	56
3	Aris	30	14	12	4	33	17	54
4	Thrasivoulos	30	15	8	7	40	25	53
5	Veria	30	10	11	9	28	27	41
6	Kastoria	30	10	10	10	28	28	40
7	Ilisiakos	30	11	7	12	43	35	40
8	Kalamata	30	9	12	9	26	28	39
9	Ethnikos Asteras	30	8	14	8	36	40	38
10	Niki Volou	30	9	11	10	32	31	38
11	Proodeftiki	30	9	11	10	31	34	38
12	Haidari	30	9	10	11	27	27	37
13	Panserraikos	30	10	7	13	28	37	37
14	Olympiakos Volou	30	10	7	13	30	37	37
15	Panahaiki	30	9	7	14	24	29	34
16	Paniliakos	30	2	4	24	16	57	9

N.B. Paniliakos — 1 pt deducted.

Holland

Oranje run out of juice

Holland's impressive qualifying statistics – ten wins, two draws, no defeats - led many to believe they could be World Cup contenders in Germany. Their record in previous major tournaments across the border – World Cup 1974, Euro 88 – further fuelled the feeling that the Dutch might come good again.

The reality, however, was that Marco van Basten's team were a work in progress rather than the finished article. They bore no comparison, for example, with the brilliant Dutch side that Guus Hiddink led to the semi-finals of the 1998 tournament in France – not to mention the thrilling teams that reached back-to-back World Cup finals in the 1970s.

Bright start

Things began brightly enough in Germany, with winger Arjen Robben inspiring the side to an opening victory in the burning heat of Leipzig against Serbia & Montenegro, but after that everything went slowly downhill. Fortunate to beat the Ivory Coast 2-1 in Stuttgart and thereby clinch their qualification for the next round, they could then afford to take it easy against Argentina in Frankfurt. A goalless draw ensued, which left Holland in second place and facing a last-16 clash with their bogey team Portugal, against whom they had claimed just one win in nine previous meetings (as opposed to five defeats, the most recent in the semi-final of Euro 2004).

The 'battle of Nuremberg' resulted in another defeat and, if truth be told, an ugly exit for the men in…not orange, but unorthodox white and blue. A brutal game, badly refereed, might have ended differently if a couple of key decisions had gone Holland's way, but with Ruud van Nistelrooy sitting idly on the bench and the hottest young striker in the Dutch game, Ajax's Klaas-Jan Huntelaar, watching on TV from his holiday home, the team's lack of firepower proved costly.

The defeat by Portugal was only the second in 25 matches under Van Basten (curiously, the other, a 3-1 friendly defeat by Italy, was also officiated by Russian referee, Valentin Ivanov) and the first during his tenure on foreign soil. A few other records were broken during Holland's stay in Germany, notably goalkeeper Edwin van der Sar bypassing former team-mate Frank de Boer to become Holland's record cap-holder (113) and midfielder Phillip Cocu joining the pair as only the third Dutchman to make a century of international appearances. Aged 35 years and 239 days when he took the field against Portugal, Cocu also became the oldest outfield player ever to represent Holland at the World Cup.

Young guns

So much for the veterans. The most encouraging feature of the tournament for Dutch fans was the performance of some of the side's younger elements. Robben confirmed his class at the highest level, as did fellow winger Robin van Persie, a surprise replacement on the right flank (like Robben, he is totally left-footed) for Dirk Kuijt. And although they are not in the first flush of youth, inexperienced defenders Khalid Boulahrouz and Joris Mathijsen proved with their assured displays that they can be relied upon for several years to come.

When Van Basten and his sidekick John van 't Schip signed their contracts with the Dutch FA (KNVB) in 2004, it was acknowledged that, with all the rebuilding work required, the World Cup would be seen merely as a stepping-stone

Holland

towards Euro 2008 and the following global extravaganza in South Africa. Anything the team could achieve in Germany, it was agreed, would be considered a bonus.

One interesting story that emerged after Holland's elimination concerned the role played by Van Basten's mentor, Johan Cruijff. It was generally understood, and accepted, that Cruijff would have an unofficial advisory role – something the great man had always wanted (a lot of influence but no burden of responsibility) – yet it was revealed, by Cruijff himself, that Van Basten had actually asked him (Cruijff) to take charge intermittently as Bondscoach during the World Cup, with Van Basten looking and learning as his assistant. Cruijff, however, had politely refused – perhaps, said some, to safeguard his own legend.

Holland have been handed a straightforward qualifying group for Euro 2008 – free of any other World Cup participants – so it will be interesting to see how the team develops over the next two years. Van Basten's eagerness to experiment with new players is unlikely to stop, particularly as Foppe de Haan's Under-21 side, with World Cup reject Huntelaar as their top-scoring star, won the 2006 European championship in Portugal – Holland's first ever major international title at junior or youth level.

Busy schedule

Because of the busy international summer, and because of the newly introduced end-of-season play-offs to determine European places, Holland's Eredivisie had a much more congested programme than usual. There was no winter break – well, one weekend off in early January – and a few midweek dates had to be taken up, leading to an earliest-ever finish in mid-April.

The play-offs, introduced as part of a new TV deal to spice up the end of the season, were hugely controversial. No fewer than 14 of the Eredivisie teams had to prolong their season. The only clubs permitted to go on holiday were the champions, the bottom-placed club and those in 14th and 15th position. The rest all had something to play for – be it a place in the Champions League, UEFA Cup or InterToto Cup, or simply staying in the Eredivisie.

Fittingly, the one club that strongly voted against the play-offs, PSV, did not have to take part in them. Once again Guus Hiddink worked the oracle and brought the Eindhoven club another title – his sixth in two spells at the Philips Stadion, a Dutch record. As at the start of the previous campaign, Hiddink was forced to remodel the side following a spate of departures. Mark van Bommel left for Barcelona, Johann Vogel to Milan and the two South Korean fliers, Park Ji-sung and Lee Young-pyo, joined defender Wilfred Bouma on the plane to England. The only significant new arrival was Belgian international Timmy Simons from Club Bruges.

Hiddink had his work cut out, but after a tentative start PSV soon found their stride. A controversial penalty, converted by Simons, brought them a 1-0 home win over Ajax, and although they lost 1-0 at Feyenoord and had their perfect home record – in all competitions – halted by FC Twente in their final game of 2005, they still led the table (by a point from Feyenoord) at the winter mini-break.

Nine in a row

It was in the first two months of 2006 that Hiddink's team really kicked on and left the rest for dead. They ruthlessly exploited a generous fixture programme to rattle off nine straight victories. Peruvian striker Jefferson Farfán was in sensational form, but it was his two strike partners, Jan Vennegoor of Hesselink and Arouna Koné,

Guus Hiddink – a record sixth Eredivisie title with PSV

Holland

who scored arguably the two most important goals of the season, in the first five minutes of the away game at Alkmaar, which PSV won 2-1 to move 11 points clear at the top. A victory for AZ, whose unbeaten home record had ended a week earlier against FC Utrecht, would have reignited the title race. Now, with their 2-1 win, PSV's 19th title was all but signed and sealed.

The victory in Alkmaar came five days after PSV had lost 1-0 at home to Lyon in the first knockout round of the Champions League. Hiddink's men had come through the group phase for the second season running thanks to a hat-trick of wins in the Philips Stadion (against Schalke, Milan and Fenerbahçe), all without conceding a goal. As they hadn't managed to find the net once on their travels, the odds were against a second-leg comeback in France, but it was quite a shock to the system when Lyon hammered them 4-0 in the Stade Gerland.

Taking that defeat as his cue, Hiddink announced that he would be quitting PSV at the end of the season. He already had his summer booked, as the head coach of Australia, whom he had qualified for the World Cup finals in thrilling style the previous November. His next engagement, it later emerged, would be as the national team coach of Russia.

Hiddink duly signed off with another title, but there would be no victorious farewell in the Dutch Cup final. Seeking to win the domestic Double for the second successive season, PSV were beaten 2-1 in the Feyenoord Stadium by Ajax. Despite having three weeks to prepare for the game while their opponents were sweating it out in the play-offs, PSV, like every other Eredivisie side, could not cope with the brilliance of Huntelaar. The young striker, who had scored 17 league goals in the first half of the season for Heerenveen and 16 in the second half for Ajax (following an internal Dutch record transfer of £6.2m), scored both goals in the final, the second in the last minute, to bring the Amsterdammers the KNVB-Beker for a record 16th time.

No faith in Blind

Hiddink's final game for PSV would also be Danny Blind's last as coach of Ajax. Despite that victory, despite the even greater achievement of leading the club into the Champions League with their play-off victories over Feyenoord and FC Groningen, and despite the continued support of the Ajax fans (who know a club legend when they see one), Blind no longer had the confidence of the club's board of directors. Ajax had finished 24 points behind PSV in the Eredivisie and were never involved in the title race. The coach might have pointed out, in his defence, that a lot of major refereeing decisions had gone against him (notably in the away games at AZ, PSV and FC Utrecht), that several key players had been out for a long time with injuries, and that his team had gone just as far as PSV in the Champions League (they were eliminated in the last 16 by Inter). But the powers that be had already made their minds up and chosen to give the job to Frank Rijkaard's assistant at Barcelona, Henk ten Cate.

Feyenoord had an unsatisfactory first season under Erwin Koeman. Eliminated early from Europe (by Rapid Bucharest), they had a strong autumn in the league but fell away badly after Christmas. Their 'K2' strike partnership of Dirk Kuijt and Salomon Kalou continued to flourish, but there were a lot of tired legs in the team for the play-off games against Ajax – as the 7-2 aggregate defeat brutally demonstrated.

It was FC Groningen, fifth in the Eredivisie, who

NATIONAL TEAM RESULTS 2005/06

Date	Opponent	H/A/N	Venue	Result	Scorers
17/8/05	Germany	H	Rotterdam	2-2	Robben (3, 46)
3/9/05	Armenia (WCQ)	A	Yerevan	1-0	Van Nistelrooy (63)
7/9/05	Andorra (WCQ)	H	Eindhoven	4-0	Van der Vaart (22), Lima A. (27og), Van Nistelrooy (42, 88)
8/10/05	Czech Republic (WCQ)	A	Prague	2-0	Van der Vaart (32), Opdam (39)
12/10/05	Macedonia (WCQ)	H	Amsterdam	0-0	
12/11/05	Italy	H	Amsterdam	1-3	Babel (37)
1/3/06	Ecuador	H	Amsterdam	1-0	Kuijt (48)
27/5/06	Cameroon	H	Rotterdam	1-0	Van Nistelrooy (23)
1/6/06	Mexico	H	Eindhoven	2-1	Heitinga (53), Babel (57)
4/6/06	Australia	H	Rotterdam	1-1	Van Nistelrooy (9)
11/6/06	Serbia & Montenegro (WCF)	N	Leipzig	1-0	Robben (18)
16/6/06	Ivory Coast (WCF)	N	Stuttgart	2-1	Van Persie (23), Van Nistelrooy (26)
21/6/06	Argentina (WCF)	N	Frankfurt	0-0	
25/6/06	Portugal (WCF)	N	Nuremberg	0-1	

Holland

took on Ajax in the play-off final. The northerners, coached by the charismatic Ron Jans, moved into their new Euroborg Stadium halfway through the season and played so well there that it was soon christened the "Green Hell". No visitors managed to beat them there in ten games, but it was an away goal from Ajax's Wesley Sneijder in the second leg of the play-off 'final' that finally scuppered the club's hopes of a miraculous qualification for the Champions League.

Wesley Sneijder – his goal in Groningen clinched Champions League qualification for Ajax

Entertaining AZ

For the second season in a row the most entertaining football in the country was played by AZ, where ex-Ajax, Barcelona and Holland coach Louis van Gaal proved himself a worthy, and classy, successor to Co Adriaanse (who went on to do the Double in Portugal with FC Porto). The Alkmaar club finished second in the regular league season – their best placing since their title-winning 1980/81 campaign – but surprisingly succumbed to Groningen in the play-offs.

No fewer than eight AZ players were selected for Holland during the season and there was a staggering return to form from Georgian veteran Shota Arveladze. The ex-Ajax striker scored 22 Eredivisie goals, including two against his old club in a memorable 4-2 win in September and the winner against Feyenoord in March. In any other season that goal might have put AZ into the Champions League, but play-off failure sent them back into the UEFA Cup. Semi-finalists under Adriaanse in 2004/05, AZ performed creditably once again in the competition under Van Gaal before crashing out in extra-time at home to Betis. That was the last European game staged at the Alkmaarderhout. The club's new DSB Stadium (named after club president Dirk Scheringa) was inaugurated in the summer with a friendly against Arsenal.

After all the play-offs were completed, the European line-up for 2006/07 looked like this: PSV in the Champions League, Ajax in the Champions League qualifiers, FC Groningen, AZ, Feyenoord and SC Heerenveen in the UEFA Cup, and FC Twente in the InterToto. The heaviest casualties of the new system were FC Utrecht, sixth in the Eredivisie but out of the European frame altogether. It was a disappointing ending to a season totally overshadowed by the sudden death, in November, of the club's much-loved 26-year-old French defender David Di Tommaso.

NAC Breda and Willem II won their respective relegation play-off groups, so the only team to come up from the Eerste Divisie was Excelsior of Rotterdam and the only team to go down was RBC Roosendaal, who rewrote the record books by accumulating just nine points from their 34 games – after conversion to the old method of two points for a win, the worst tally in Eredivisie history.

Holland

NATIONAL TEAM APPEARANCES 2005/06

Coach – Marco VAN BASTEN			Ger	ARM	AND	CZE	MAC	Ita	Ecu	Cmr	Mex	Aus	SCG	CIV	ARG	POR	Caps	Goals
Edwin VAN DER SAR	29/10/70	Man Utd (ENG)	G	G	G	G	G	G46	G	G		G	G	G	G	G	113	-
Jan KROMKAMP	17/8/80	Valencia CF (ESP) /Liverpool (ENG)	D46	D63		D84		D61		D	D	D46					11	-
Khalid BOULAHROUZ	28/12/81	Hamburg (GER)	D	D	D	D57	D			D		s86	s46	D	D		15	-
Barry OPDAM	27/2/76	AZ	D	D	D	D	D		D								8	1
Tim DE CLER	8/11/78	AZ	D46		D					D				D			4	-
Denny LANDZAAT	6/5/76	AZ	M	M51		M	M46	M		s78	M	s50	s60	s72	s67		26	1
Hedwiges MADURO	13/2/85	Ajax	M52	M	s78	M	M64		s46		M	s37			s86		12	-
Phillip COCU	29/10/70	PSV	M	M	M			M87	M46	M78		M37	M	M	M	M85	101	10
Arjen ROBBEN	23/1/84	Chelsea (ENG)	A		A		A77		A	A82		A	A		A		23	7
Ruud VAN NISTELROOY	1/7/76	Man Utd (ENG)	A46	A	A	A	A			A75		A	A69	A72	A56		54	28
Dirk KUIJT	22/7/80	Feyenoord	A46	A		A	A	A	A	s75	A		s64	s69	A	A	22	4
Rafael VAN DER VAART	11/2/83	Hamburg (GER)	s46	s75	M	M	M	M					s50	M	s56		38	6
Wilfred BOUMA	15/6/78	PSV	s46														20	1
Roy MAKAAY	9/3/75	Bayern M (GER)	s46														43	6
Robin VAN PERSIE	6/8/83	Arsenal (ENG)	s46	A75	A	s77	A86			A	A46	A	A	A	A67	A	14	2
Johnny HEITINGA	15/11/83	Ajax	s52							D		s46	D	D46		s67	21	2
Giovanni VAN BRONCKHORST	5/2/75	Barcelona (ESP)		D		D	D	D	D	D		D64	D	D		D	60	3
Wesley SNEIJDER	9/6/84	Ajax		s51	M78		s46			M	M	M50	M	M50	M86	M	27	5
Jan VENNEGOOR OF HESSELINK	7/11/78	PSV		s63	s67			s82		s46					s85		8	-
Theo LUCIUS	19/12/76	PSV			D67												3	-
Ron VLAAR	16/2/85	AZ			s57		D60										2	-
Nigel DE JONG	30/11/84	Ajax			s84	D	s61										10	-
Edgar DAVIDS	13/3/73	Tottenham (ENG)				s64											74	6
Ryan BABEL	19/12/86	Ajax				s86	A82		s82	A					s56		7	3
Joris MATHIJSEN	5/4/80	AZ					D	D	D		D	D86	D		D56		11	-
Romeo CASTELEN	3/5/83	Feyenoord					A										8	1
Henk TIMMER	3/12/71	AZ					s46			G46							2	-
André OOIJER	11/7/74	PSV					s60		D		D	D	D	D	D		23	2
George BOATENG	5/9/75	M'brough (ENG)					s87	M61									4	-
Kew JALIENS	15/9/78	AZ						D						D			2	-
Mark VAN BOMMEL	22/4/77	Barcelona (ESP)						M	M		M	M60	M		M67		40	7
Martijn MEERDINK	15/9/76	AZ						A									1	-
Nicky HOFS	17/5/83	Feyenoord						s61									1	-
Maarten STEKELENBURG	22/9/81	Ajax							s46								2	-

Holland

EUROPEAN CUPS 2005/06

UEFA CHAMPIONS LEAGUE

PSV

1st round Group E
Match 1 FC SCHALKE 04 (GER)
H **1-0** *Vennegoor of Hesselink (33)*
Gomes, Reiziger, Ooijer, Addo, Lucius, Afellay, Simons, Cocu (Lamey 82), Farfán, Vennegoor of Hesselink (Robert 86), Beasley.

Match 2 FENERBAHÇE (TUR)
A **0-3**
Gomes, Ooijer, Alex, Addo, Lucius (Ferreyra 54), Afellay, Simons, Cocu, Beasley, Vennegoor of Hesselink, Farfán.

Match 3 MILAN (ITA)
A **0-0**
Gomes, Reiziger, Alex, Ooijer, Lamey, Afellay, Simons, Cocu, Beasley, Robert (Aissati 63), Farfán.

Match 4 MILAN
H **1-0** *Farfán (12)*
Gomes, Ooijer, Alex, Lamey, Afellay (Reiziger 58), Simons, Aissati, Cocu, Farfán (Addo 86), Vennegoor of Hesselink, Beasley.

Match 5 FC SCHALKE 04
A **0-3**
Gomes, Reiziger (Sibon 77), Alex, Ooijer, Lamey, Afellay, Simons (Lucius 46), Cocu, Aissati (Vennegoor of Hesselink 46), Farfán, Robert.

Match 6 FENERBAHÇE
H **2-0** *Cocu (14), Farfán (85)*
Gomes, Lucius, Alex, Ooijer, Lamey, Afellay (Aissati 24), Simons, Cocu, Farfán, Vennegoor of Hesselink, Robert (Reiziger 67).

2nd round OLYMPIQUE LYONNAIS (FRA)
H **0-1**
Gomes, Reiziger, Alex, Ooijer, Lamey, Afellay (Koné 73), Simons, Culina (Aissati 53), Cocu, Farfán, Vennegoor of Hesselink.
A **0-4**
Gomes, Lucius, Alex (Aissati 76), Addo, Reiziger, Culina (Väyrynen 57), Simons, Afellay, Cocu, Farfán (Beasley 57), Koné.

AJAX

3rd qualifying round BRØNDBY IF (DEN)
A **2-2** *Rosenberg (30), Babel (73)*
Vonk, Trabelsi, Grygera, Escudé, Emanuelson, De Jong, Maduro, Boukhari (Sneijder 77), Pienaar, Rosenberg (Charisteas 89), Babel.
H **3-1** *Babel (50), Sneijder (80, 88)*
Vonk, Trabelsi, Grygera, Escudé, Emanuelson, De Jong, Maduro, Boukhari (Sneijder 62), Pienaar (Galásek 82), Rosenberg (Heitinga 90), Babel.

1st round Group B
Match 1 AC SPARTA PRAHA (CZE)
A **1-1** *Sneijder (90)*
Vonk, Trabelsi, Grygera, Maduro, Emanuelson, Galásek (Heitinga 90), Sneijder, Lindenbergh, Pienaar (Rosales 80), Rosenberg (Charisteas 76), Babel.

Match 2 ARSENAL (ENG)
H **1-2** *Rosenberg (71)*
Vonk, De Jong, Grygera, Vermaelen, Emanuelson (Juanfran 85), Galásek, Lindenbergh, Boukhari (Manucharyan 70), Pienaar, Charisteas (Rosales 57), Babel.

Match 3 FC THUN (SUI)
H **2-0** *Anastasiou (36, 55)*
Stekelenburg, Trabelsi, Grygera, Maduro, Emanuelson, De Jong, Galasek,
Sneijder, Pienaar (Boukhari 84), Anastasiou (Babel 82), Rosales (Heitinga 90).

Match 4 FC THUN
A **4-2** *Sneijder (26), Deumi (63og), De Jong (90), Boukhari (90)*
Stekelenburg, Heitinga, Grygera, Maduro, Emanuelson, De Jong, Galásek, Sneijder (Boukhari 89), Pienaar, Anastasiou, Babel.

Match 5 AC SPARTA PRAHA
H **2-1** *De Jong (68, 89)*
Stekelenburg, Trabelsi, Grygera, Vermaelen, Emanuelson, Maduro, Sneijder, Lindenbergh (De Jong 53), Pienaar, Anastasiou (Rosenberg 62), Boukhari.

Match 6 ARSENAL
A **0-0**
Stekelenburg, Heitinga, Grygera (Trabelsi 15), Vermaelen, Juanfran, Maduro (De Jong 27), Galasek, Sneijder, Pienaar, Rosenberg, Boukhari (Babel 80).

2nd round INTERNAZIONALE (ITA)
H **2-2** *Huntelaar (16), Rosales (20)*
Stekelenburg, Trabelsi, Heitinga, Vermaelen, Emanuelson, Maduro, Lindenbergh, Boukhari, Rosales (Babel 88), Huntelaar, Rosenberg.
A **0-1**
Stekelenburg, Trabelsi, Maduro, Vermaelen, Juanfran, Pienaar, Lindenbergh, Boukhari, Rosales (Babel 74), Huntelaar, Rosenberg (Charisteas 60).

UEFA CUP

WILLEM II

1st round AS MONACO FC (FRA)
A **0-2**
Moens, Wau, Kreek, Victoria, Smit (Delanoy 24), Caluwé, Reuser, Agustien, Ceesay (Denissen 85), Dembele (Kolsi 89), Bobson.
H **1-3** *Hadouir (84)*
Moens, Wau, Smit, Victoria (Van Nieuwstadt 50), Van der Haar, Caluwé, Reuser (Delanoy 72), Agustien, Denissen (Hadouir 71), Dembele, Kolsi.

AZ

1st round KRYLYA SOVETOV SAMARA (RUS)
A **3-5** *Vlaar (18), Perez (56), Van Galen (85)*
Timmer, Steinsson, Vlaar (Buskermolen 70), Opdam, De Cler, Landzaat, Van Galen, Schaars (De Zeeuw 70), Sektioui (Koevermans 80), Arveladze, Perez.
H **3-1** *Van Galen (45), Koevermans (80), Landzaat (86p)*
Timmer, Jaliens, De Zeeuw (Koevermans 59), Opdam, De Cler, Landzaat, Van Galen, Schaars, Sektioui (Huysegems 77), Arveladze (Steinsson 90), Perez.

2nd round Group D
Match 1 DNIPRO DNIPROPETROVSK (UKR)
A **2-1** *Arveladze (13), Sektioui (53)*
Timmer, Steinsson, Opdam, Jaliens, De Cler, Landzaat, Perez, Schaars, Sektioui (Meerdink 85), Arveladze (Ramzi 90), Huysegems.

Match 2 MIDDLESBROUGH (ENG)
H **0-0**
Timmer, Steinsson, Mathijsen, Jaliens, De Cler, Landzaat, Van Galen, Schaars, Sektioui (Meerdink 60), Arveladze (Koevermans 78), Perez.

Match 3 LITEX LOVECH (BUL)
A **2-0** *Van Galen (10), Sektioui (82)*
Timmer, Steinsson (Meerdink 73), Mathijsen, Jaliens, Buskermolen (Vlaar 86), Landzaat, Ramzi, Schaars, Sektioui, Koevermans, Van Galen (Huysegems 81).

Match 4 GRASSHOPPER-CLUB ZÜRICH (SUI)
H **1-0** *Koevermans (70)*
Timmer, Steinsson (Opdam 64), Jaliens, Mathijsen, De Cler, Landzaat, De Zeeuw (Ramzi 73), Medunjanin, Sektioui, Koevermans, Van Galen (Huysegems 64).

3rd round REAL BETIS (ESP)
A **0-2**
Timmer, Steinsson, Jaliens, Mathijsen, De Cler, Landzaat, Perez, Molhoek (De Zeeuw 32), Meerdink (Ikedia 80), Arveladze, Van Galen (Huysegems 64).

Holland

2-1 *Arveladze (26), Jaliens (35)*
(aet)
...immer, Jaliens, Mathijsen, Opdam, De Cler, Landzaat, Van Galen (Koevermans 1), Schaars (Molhoek 86), Sektioui (Meerdink 102), Arveladze, Perez.

FEYENOORD
1st round RAPID BUCURESTI (ROM)
H 1-1 *Kuijt (40)*
...odewijks, Östlund, Greene, Bahia, Bosschaart, Ghaly, Paauwe, Pardo (Owoeri ...5), Boussaboun (Castelen 67), Kuijt, Kalou.
A 0-1
...odewijks, Östlund, Greene (Vincken 65), Bahia, Bosschaart, Ghaly (De Guzmán ...6), Ono, Paauwe (Boussaboun 80), Castelen, Kuijt, Kalou.

SC HEERENVEEN
1st round FC BANÍK OSTRAVA (CZE)
A 0-2
Waterman, Bakkati, Hansson, Seip, Drost, Bosvelt, Breuer (Samaras 84), Bruggink (Steur 70), Yildirim, Huntelaar, Pranjic.
H 5-0 *Samaras (3), Nilsson (44), Huntelaar (59, 67), Yildirim (66)*
Waterman, Seip, Hansson, Breuer, Drost J., Bosvelt (Derveld 46), Bruggink (Drost H. 77), Pranjic, Yildirim, Huntelaar, Samaras (Nilsson 17).

2nd round Group F
Match 1 DINAMO BUCURESTI (ROM)
A 0-0
Waterman, Seip, Hansson, Breuer, Drost J., Kissi, Bosvelt, Pranjic, Yildirim, Huntelaar, Nilsson.

Match 2 CSKA MOSKVA (RUS)
H 0-0
Waterman, Seip, Derveld, Breuer, Drost J., Bosvelt, Kissi, Pranjic, Yildirim (Bruggink 73), Huntelaar, Nilsson (Samaras 64).

Match 3 OLYMPIQUE MARSEILLE (FRA)
A 0-1
Vandenbussche, Seip, Hansson, Derveld (Bruggink 90), Drost J., Drost H., Breuer, Pranjic, Yildirim, Huntelaar (Nilsson 31), Samaras.

Match 4 LEVSKI SOFIA (BUL)
H 2-1 *Samaras (54), Hanssen (90)*
Vandenbussche, Drost H., Hansson, Breuer, Drost J., Bosvelt (Hanssen 64), Bruggink (Derveld 84), Pranjic, Yildirim, Huntelaar, Samaras.

3rd round STEAUA BUCURESTI (ROM)
H 1-3 *Bruggink (24)*
Vandenbussche, Seip, Hansson, Breuer, Drost J. (Derveld 83), Bosvelt, Nørregaard (Hanssen 74), Pranjic, Yildirim, Bruggink (De Vries 74), Nilsson.
A 1-0 *Bruggink (86)*
Vandenbussche, Seip, Hansson, Breuer (Drost J. 46), Derveld, Prager, Nørregaard (Bruggink 46), Pranjic, Yildirim, De Vries, Nilsson (Hanssen 71).

TOP GOALSCORERS 2005/06

33 Klaas-Jan HUNTELAAR (SC Heerenveen/Ajax)
22 Shota ARVELADZE (AZ)
   Dirk KUIJT (Feyenoord)
21 Jefferson FARFÁN (PSV)
15 Salomon KALOU (Feyenoord)
13 Arouna KONE (Roda JC/PSV)
12 Rick HOOGENDORP (RKC Waalwijk)
   Markus ROSENBERG (Ajax)
   Blaise N'KUFO (FC Twente)
11 Jan VENNEGOOR OF HESSELINK (PSV)

LEAGUE RESULTS/ SCORERS/APPEARANCES/ GOALS 2005/06

ADO DEN HAAG
Coach - Frans Adelaar

2005				
20/8	Heracles Almelo	h	1-2	Den Ouden
26/8	SC Heerenveen	h	1-0	Saeijs
11/9	NAC Breda	a	1-4	Saeijs (p)
16/9	FC Twente	h	0-0	
21/9	Ajax	a	2-2	Elia, Saeijs
24/9	Willem II	a	0-1	
1/10	RKC Waalwijk	h	2-1	Den Ouden, Stroeve
16/10	Vitesse	a	1-3	Stroeve
23/10	FC Groningen	a	1-3	De Graaf
29/10	AZ	h	0-2	
6/11	FC Utrecht	a	1-1	og (Keller)
19/11	NEC	h	0-1	
27/11	PSV	a	0-3	
4/12	Sparta Rotterdam	a	3-2	Kolkka, Bodde, Verhoek
10/12	RBC Roosendaal	h	3-0	Van der Leegte, Kolkka 2
18/12	Feyenoord	h	2-1	Den Ouden (p), Saavedra
27/12	Roda JC	a	1-3	Kolkka
2006				
15/1	FC Utrecht	h	2-3	Mols, Den Ouden (p)
18/1	AZ	a	1-3	Stroeve
22/1	NEC	a	0-5	
29/1	PSV	h	0-2	
5/2	SC Heerenveen	a	0-3	
8/2	NAC Breda	h	0-3	
12/2	Ajax	h	1-2	Mols
19/2	Heracles Almelo	a	3-1	Elia, De Graaf, Den Ouden
25/2	Vitesse	h	2-0	Kolkka 2
5/3	RKC Waalwijk	a	0-3	
11/3	FC Groningen	h	2-1	Mols, Bodde (p)
18/3	Roda JC	h	1-1	Rankovic
26/3	Feyenoord	a	2-0	Kolkka 2
1/4	Willem II	h	1-1	Stroeve
9/4	FC Twente	a	0-2	
12/4	RBC Roosendaal	a	2-1	De Graaf, Stroeve (p)
16/4	Sparta Rotterdam	h	0-2	

No	Name	Nat	Pos	Aps	(s)	Gls
23	Said BAKKATI		D	13		
12	Ferry BODDE		M	12	(7)	2
29	Jaroslav DROBNY	CZE	G	12		
5	Youssef EL AKCHAOUI		D	26	(2)	
19	Eljero ELIA		A	17	(13)	2
21	Edwin DE GRAAF		M	21	(2)	3
3	Cory GIBBS	USA	D	5		
15	Spira GRUJIC	SCG	D	15	(1)	
22	Peter JUNGSCHLAGER		M	8	(4)	
14	Joonas KOLKKA	FIN	A	30	(1)	8
31	Christiaan KUM		D	2	(1)	
6	Tom VAN DER LEEGTE		M	18		1
2	Angelo MARTHA		D	1		
9	Michael MOLS		A	25	(4)	3
17	John O'BRIEN	USA	M	2	(1)	
7	Geert DEN OUDEN		A	19	(7)	5
18	Cees PAAUWE		G	1		
8	Aleksandar RANKOVIC	SCG	D	22	(4)	1
26	Raimund RIEDEWALD		D	2		
11	Paulus ROIHA	FIN	A		(9)	
2	Daniel RIJAARD		D	14		
20	Tomasz RZASA	POL	D	23	(2)	

Holland

FINAL LEAGUE TABLE 2005/06

		Pld	Home					Away					Total					Pts
			W	D	L	F	A	W	D	L	F	A	W	D	L	F	A	
1	PSV	34	14	3	0	36	8	12	3	2	35	15	26	6	2	71	23	84
2	AZ	34	11	4	2	43	18	12	1	4	35	14	23	5	6	78	32	74
3	Feyenoord	34	13	3	1	47	11	8	5	4	32	23	21	8	5	79	34	71
4	Ajax	34	9	6	2	35	15	9	0	8	31	26	18	6	10	66	41	60
5	FC Groningen	34	13	3	1	26	9	3	5	9	20	34	16	8	10	46	43	56
6	FC Utrecht	34	8	4	5	26	22	8	3	6	22	22	16	7	11	48	44	55
7	SC Heerenveen	34	10	4	3	41	25	4	4	9	22	33	14	8	12	63	58	50
8	Roda JC	34	9	2	6	30	28	6	3	8	27	26	15	5	14	57	54	50
9	FC Twente	34	9	1	7	25	17	4	7	6	19	19	13	8	13	44	36	47
10	NEC	34	7	4	6	23	20	6	4	7	20	23	13	8	13	43	43	47
11	Vitesse	34	9	2	6	33	27	4	3	10	19	27	13	5	16	52	54	44
12	RKC Waalwijk	34	7	4	6	29	26	4	2	11	19	32	11	6	17	48	58	39
13	Heracles Almelo	34	6	3	8	19	28	5	3	9	16	30	11	6	17	35	58	39
14	Sparta Rotterdam	34	8	0	9	25	23	2	7	8	9	27	10	7	17	34	50	37
15	ADO Den Haag	34	6	3	8	18	22	4	2	11	18	40	10	5	19	36	62	35
16	NAC Breda	34	6	5	6	24	31	2	4	11	21	35	8	9	17	45	66	33
17	Willem II	34	5	4	8	27	29	2	3	12	18	37	7	7	20	45	66	28
18	RBC Roosendaal	34	1	5	11	14	32	0	1	16	8	58	1	6	27	22	90	9

PLAY-OFFS

Champions League qualification
(20/4/06 & 23/4/06)
FC Groningen 3, AZ 1
AZ 2, FC Groningen 1
(FC Groningen 4-3)

Ajax 3, Feyenoord 0
Feyenoord 2, Ajax 4
(Ajax 7-2)

(26/4/06 & 3/5/06)
Ajax 2, FC Groningen 0
FC Groningen 2, Ajax 1
(Ajax 3-2)

UEFA Cup qualification
(22/4/06 & 26/4/06)
FC Twente 2, FC Utrecht 0
FC Utrecht 1, FC Twente 3
(FC Twente 5-1)

Roda JC 0, SC Heerenveen 0
SC Heerenveen 1, Roda JC 0
(SC Heerenveen 1-0)

(30/4/06 & 3/5/06)
FC Twente 0, SC Heerenveen 1
SC Heerenveen 5, FC Twente 0
(SC Heerenveen 6-0)

InterToto qualification
(19/4/06 & 23/4/06)
Heracles Almelo 0, NEC 2
NEC 2, Heracles Almelo 3
(NEC 4-3)

RKC Waalwijk 4, Vitesse 4
Vitesse 2, RKC Waalwijk 0
(Vitesse 6-4)

(26/4/06 & 3/5/06)
Vitesse 0, NEC 0
NEC 1, Vitesse 2
(Vitesse 2-1)

(11/5/06 & 14/5/06)
Vitesse 1, FC Twente 1
FC Twente 2, Vitesse 0
(FC Twente 3-1)

AJAX
Coach - Danny Blind

4	Alberto SAAVEDRA	ESP	D	25	(1)	1
3	Jan-Paul SAEIJS		D	15		3
10	Roy STROEVE		A	19	(9)	5
16	Wesley VERHOEK		A	6	(13)	1
1	Dorus DE VRIES		G	20		
30	Robert ZWINKELS		G	1		

2005
20/8	RBC Roosendaal	a	2-0	Pienaar, Rosenberg
28/8	Feyenoord	h	1-2	Charisteas
10/9	Willem II	a	2-0	Galdsek, Charisteas
18/9	AZ	a	2-4	Sneijder 2
21/9	ADO Den Haag	h	2-2	Maduro, Sneijder
24/9	Roda JC	h	4-1	Charisteas 2, Pienaar, Galdsek (p)
2/10	Sparta Rotterdam	a	2-1	De Jong 2
15/10	Heracles Almelo	h	0-0	
23/10	PSV	a	0-1	
28/10	SC Heerenveen	h	0-0	
6/11	NEC	a	0-1	
19/11	FC Twente	h	2-0	og (Majstorovic), Rosenberg
27/11	FC Utrecht	a	0-1	
4/12	RKC Waalwijk	h	4-1	Maduro, Sneijder, Rosenberg, Babel
11/12	Vitesse	a	2-0	Galdsek (p), Charisteas
18/12	NAC Breda	a	2-0	Rosenberg, Sneijder
27/12	FC Groningen	h	3-2	Rosenberg, Charisteas 2
30/12	SC Heerenveen	a	2-4	Vermaelen, Galdsek (p)

2006
15/1	NEC	h	1-1	Rosenberg
22/1	FC Twente	a	3-2	Rosenberg, Maduro, Emanuelson
29/1	FC Utrecht	h	1-4	Rosenberg
5/2	Feyenoord	a	2-3	Rosenberg, Huntelaar
8/2	Willem II	h	1-0	Rosenberg
12/2	ADO Den Haag	a	2-1	Grygera, Huntelaar
19/2	RBC Roosendaal	h	6-0	Huntelaar 4, Rosenberg 2
26/2	Heracles Almelo	a	3-1	Huntelaar, Timisela, Babel
5/3	Sparta Rotterdam	h	6-0	Boukhari 2, Huntelaar 3 (1p), Vermaelen
12/3	PSV	h	0-0	
19/3	FC Groningen	a	2-3	Huntelaar, Vermaelen

Holland

Date	Opponent	H/A	Score	Scorers
26/3	NAC Breda	h	1-1	Huntelaar
2/4	Roda JC	a	1-2	Huntelaar
9/4	AZ	h	1-0	Boukhari
12/4	Vitesse	h	2-1	Huntelaar, Charisteas
16/4	RKC Waalwijk	a	4-2	Heitinga, Huntelaar 2 (1p), Boukhari

No	Name	Nat	Pos	Aps	(s)	Gls
17	Ioannis ANASTASIOU	GRE	A	3	(3)	
32	Vurnon ANITA		M	1		
11	Ryan BABEL		A	12	(13)	2
31	Emmanuel BOAKIYE	GHA	D	3	(3)	
28	Nourdin BOUKHARI	MAR	A	17	(7)	4
9	Angelos CHARISTEAS	GRE	A	7	(10)	8
19	Urby EMANUELSON		D	22	(4)	1
5	Julien ESCUDE	FRA	D	2		
6	Tomas GALÁSEK	CZE	M	25	(1)	4
3	Zdenek GRYGERA	CZE	D	18		1
4	John HEITINGA		D	13	(6)	1
25	Klaas-Jan HUNTELAAR		A	16		16
16	Nigel DE JONG		D	12	(4)	2
22	JUANFRAN	ESP	D	11	(5)	
21	Olaf LINDENBERGH		M	16	(2)	
8	Hedwiges MADURO		D	27	(1)	3
27	Edgar MANUCHARYAN	ARM	A	2	(2)	
29	Nicolae MITEA	ROM	A		(1)	
10	Steven PIENAAR	RSA	M	14	(1)	2
7	Mauro ROSALES	ARG	A	23	(6)	
24	Markus ROSENBERG	SWE	A	28	(3)	12
38	Jeffrey SARPONG		M	4	(5)	
33	Robbert SCHILDER		M	2	(2)	
18	Wesley SNEIJDER		M	18	(1)	5
1	Maarten STEKELENBURG		G	27		
45	Michael TIMISELA		D	2	(2)	1
2	Hatem TRABELSI	TUN	D	20		
15	Thomas VERMAELEN	BEL	D	22	(2)	3
12	Hans VONK	RSA	G	7	(1)	

AZ
Coach - Louis van Gaal

2005

Date	Opponent	H/A	Score	Scorers
12/8	Sparta Rotterdam	h	3-0	Arveladze 2, Sektioui
21/8	FC Utrecht	a	2-1	Van Galen 2
27/8	Vitesse	a	5-0	Arveladze 2, Perez 3
10/9	RBC Roosendaal	h	7-0	Arveladze 3, Perez, Landzaat 2 (1p), Huysegems
18/9	Ajax	h	4-2	Arveladze 2, Perez 2
25/9	NAC Breda	a	1-2	Sektioui
2/10	NEC	h	3-2	Perez, Sektioui, Arveladze
15/10	PSV	a	0-3	
23/10	Willem II	h	5-1	Sektioui, Landzaat (p), Perez, Meerdink, Steinsson
29/10	ADO Den Haag	a	2-0	Sektioui, Arveladze
5/11	Heracles Almelo	h	2-2	Sektioui, Arveladze
20/11	FC Groningen	a	0-0	
27/11	Roda JC	h	2-0	Landzaat, Koevermans
3/12	SC Heerenveen	a	2-1	Arveladze, Landzaat
10/12	FC Twente	a	3-1	Huysegems, Koevermans, Landzaat
18/12	RKC Waalwijk	h	3-0	De Zeeuw, Huysegems, Steinsson
26/12	Feyenoord	a	0-2	

2006

Date	Opponent	H/A	Score	Scorers
14/1	Heracles Almelo	a	2-0	Landzaat, Perez
18/1	ADO Den Haag	h	3-1	Landzaat 2 (1p), Ikedia
21/1	FC Groningen	h	1-1	Arveladze
27/1	Roda JC	a	4-1	Arveladze 3, Huysegems
4/2	Vitesse	h	1-1	Steinsson
7/2	RBC Roosendaal	a	5-0	Van Galen, Meerdink, Arveladze 3
10/2	Sparta Rotterdam	a	1-0	Perez
19/2	FC Utrecht	h	2-3	og (Van Steensel), Koevermans
26/2	PSV	h	1-2	Schaars
3/3	NEC	a	2-0	Medunjanin, Koevermans
12/3	Willem II	a	3-1	Medunjanin, Steinsson, Huysegems
19/3	Feyenoord	h	1-0	Arveladze
26/3	RKC Waalwijk	a	1-0	Medunjanin
4/4	NAC Breda	h	3-2	Koevermans 2, Arveladze
9/4	Ajax	a	0-1	
12/4	FC Twente	h	0-0	
16/4	SC Heerenveen	a	4-2	Koevermans 2, Huysegems 2

Name	Nat	Pos	Aps	(s)	Gls
Shota ARVELADZE	GEO	A	30	(1)	22
Michael BUSKERMOLEN		M		(6)	
Tim DE CLER		D	30		
Barry VAN GALEN		M	21	(3)	3
Stein HUYSEGEMS	BEL	A	15	(17)	7
Pius IKEDIA	NGA	A	3	(9)	1
Kew JALIENS		D	29	(1)	
Danny KOEVERMANS		A	4	(17)	8
Denny LANDZAAT		M	29		9
Jeremain LENS		A		(1)	
Joris MATHIJSEN		D	25		
Danny MATHIJSSEN		M		(1)	
Haris MEDUNJANIN		A	6	(4)	3
Martijn MEERDINK		A	13	(6)	2
Rogier MOLHOEK		M	6	(2)	
Barry OPDAM		D	23	(1)	
Kenneth PEREZ	DEN	A	27	(4)	10
Adil RAMZI	MAR	A	2	(6)	
Juha REINI	FIN	D		(1)	
Stijn SCHAARS		M	24		1
Tarik SEKTIOUI	MAR	A	17	(1)	6
Grétar STEINSSON	ISL	D	14	(6)	4
Henk TIMMER		G	32		
Ron VLAAR		D	3	(4)	
Demi DE ZEEUW		D	19	(7)	1
Theo ZWARTHOED		G	2		

FEYENOORD
Coach - Erwin Koeman

2005

Date	Opponent	H/A	Score	Scorers
14/8	NAC Breda	h	2-0	Pardo, Kuijt
21/8	Sparta Rotterdam	a	3-1	Kuijt, Pardo, Ghaly
28/8	Ajax	a	2-1	Kalou, Kuijt
11/9	NEC	h	3-0	Kalou, Pardo, Castelen
18/9	SC Heerenveen	h	5-1	Kuijt 2, Bahia, Paauwe, Kalou
25/9	FC Twente	a	3-1	Castelen 2, Kuijt
2/10	FC Utrecht	a	1-3	og (Keller)
16/10	FC Groningen	h	4-1	Boussaboun, Kuijt, Kalou, Ghaly
23/10	RKC Waalwijk	a	1-2	Castelen
30/10	Willem II	a	3-1	De Guzmán, Castelen, Paauwe
6/11	Vitesse	h	0-0	
20/11	Roda JC	a	3-2	Kuijt, Bahia, Biseswar
27/11	Heracles Almelo	h	7-1	Boussaboun 2, Greene, Kalou, Kuijt 2, De Guzmán
3/12	RBC Roosendaal	h	2-2	Pardo, De Guzmán
11/12	PSV	h	1-0	Kuijt

Holland

18/12	ADO Den Haag	a	1-2	Kalou	
26/12	AZ	h	2-0	Paauwe, De Guzmán	
29/12	Willem II	h	6-1	Kuijt 3, Pardo, Kalou 2	
2006					
15/1	Vitesse	a	1-0	Bahia	
22/1	Roda JC	h	0-0		
29/1	Heracles Almelo	a	4-0	Kalou, Kuijt, Castelen, Paauwe	
5/2	Ajax	h	3-2	Hofs, Castelen, Kuijt	
8/2	NEC	a	2-1	og (Wisgerhof), Kuijt	
12/2	NAC Breda	a	3-3	Kalou 2, Castelen	
19/2	Sparta Rotterdam	h	4-0	Hofs 2, Kuijt, Boussaboun	
26/2	FC Groningen	a	1-1	Van Hooijdonk	
5/3	FC Utrecht	h	3-0	Kalou 2, Kuijt	
12/3	RKC Waalwijk	h	1-1	og (Van Diemen)	
19/3	AZ	a	0-1		
26/3	ADO Den Haag	h	0-2		
2/4	FC Twente	h	4-2	Kalou 2, Kuijt 2 (1p)	
7/4	SC Heerenveen	a	1-1	Van Hooijdonk	
12/4	PSV	a	1-1	Castelen	
16/4	RBC Roosendaal	h	2-0	Kuijt (p), Van Hooijdonk	

No	Name	Nat	Pos	Aps	(s)	Gls
1	Maikel AERTS		G	6	(2)	
4	André BAHIA	BRA	D	34		3
35	Diego BISESWAR		A	1	(5)	1
5	Pascal BOSSCHAART		D	23	(6)	
19	Ali BOUSSABOUN	MAR	A	14	(11)	4
28	Romeo CASTELEN		A	22	(1)	9
39	Pieter COLLEN	BEL	D	6	(2)	
27	Timothy DERIJCK	BEL	D		(1)	
24	Royston DRENTHE		D		(3)	
32	Sherif EKRAMY	EGY	G	2	(1)	
6	Hossam GHALY	EGY	M	16		2
24	Edwin DE GRAAF		M		(2)	
18	Serginho GREENE		D	32		1
33	Jonathan DE GUZMÁN	CAN	M	27	(2)	4
34	Christian GYAN	GHA	D	1	(1)	
10	Nicky HOFS		M	13	(1)	3
9	Pierre VAN HOOIJDONK		A		(11)	3
21	Salomon KALOU	CIV	A	33	(1)	15
7	Dirk KUIJT		A	33		22
20	LEONARDO	BRA	A		(1)	
30	Patrick LODEWIJKS		G	26		
8	Shinji ONO	JPN	M	2	(2)	
2	Alexander ÖSTLUND	SWE	D	17		
26	John OWOERI	NGA	A		(1)	
17	Patrick PAAUWE		M	30		4
14	Sebastián PARDO	CHL	M	11	(10)	5
3	Karim SAIDI	TUN	D	1	(3)	
16	Alfred SCHREUDER		M	1		
23	Ferne SNOYL		D	7		
29	Tim VINCKEN		A		(3)	
20	Ron VLAAR		D	16		

FC GRONINGEN
Coach - Ron Jans

2005

14/8	RBC Roosendaal	h	1-0	Cornelisse
21/8	RKC Waalwijk	a	1-2	Lindgren
28/8	Heracles Almelo	a	1-2	Van de Laak
11/9	Sparta Rotterdam	h	0-1	
18/9	PSV	h	1-0	Cornelisse
24/9	Vitesse	a	0-2	
2/10	Willem II	h	2-0	Luirink, Levchenko
16/10	Feyenoord	a	1-4	Silva
23/10	ADO Den Haag	h	3-1	Buijs 2, Cornelisse
30/10	Roda JC	h	1-0	Buijs
6/11	SC Heerenveen	a	0-4	
20/11	AZ	h	0-0	
30/11	NAC Breda	a	2-2	Cornelisse (p), Salmon
4/12	FC Twente	h	1-0	Cornelisse
11/12	FC Utrecht	a	2-0	Salmon, Cornelisse
18/12	NEC	h	3-0	Salmon 2, Fledderus
27/12	Ajax	a	2-3	Salmon, Levchenko
30/12	Roda JC	a	3-1	Buijs, Fledderus, Nevland
2006				
13/1	SC Heerenveen	h	2-0	Nevland, Buijs
21/1	AZ	a	1-1	Salmon
29/1	NAC Breda	h	3-2	Levchenko, Salmon, Lindgren
4/2	Heracles Almelo	h	0-0	
7/2	Sparta Rotterdam	a	0-1	
12/2	RBC Roosendaal	a	2-1	Nevland, Cornelisse
18/2	RKC Waalwijk	h	1-0	Fledderus
26/2	Feyenoord	h	1-1	Fledderus
4/3	Willem II	a	0-5	
11/3	ADO Den Haag	a	1-2	Nevland
19/3	Ajax	h	3-2	Levchenko (p), Nevland, Van der Linden
25/3	NEC	a	2-2	Van de Laak, Buijs
2/4	Vitesse	h	2-1	Nevland 2
9/4	PSV	a	1-1	Nevland
12/4	FC Utrecht	h	2-1	Van de Laak, Lindgren
16/4	FC Twente	a	1-1	Cornelisse

Name	Nat	Pos	Aps	(s)	Gls
Kiran BECHAN		A		(4)	
Danny BUIJS		M	32	(2)	6
Yuri CORNELISSE		A	26	(7)	8
Mark-Jan FLEDDERUS		M	12	(11)	4
Mathias FLORÉN	SWE	D	16	(9)	
Robbin KIEFT		A		(2)	
Tieme KLOMPE		D		(1)	
Arnold KRUISWIJK		D	21	(1)	
Rogier KROHNE		A		(3)	
Koen VAN DE LAAK		A	20	(4)	3
Yevgeniy LEVCHENKO	RUS	M	26	(2)	4
Antoine VAN DER LINDEN		D	24	(1)	1
Gijs LUIRINK		D	19	(1)	1
Rasmus LINDGREN	SWE	M	25	(7)	3
Paul MATTHIJS		M	29		
Erik NEVLAND	NOR	A	23	(6)	8
Marcel PANNEKOEK		M		(1)	
Bas ROORDA		G	34		
Glen SALMON	RSA	A	16	(8)	7
Gibril SANKOH	SRL	D	20	(5)	
Valery SEDOC		D	2		
Stefano SEEDORF		M	11	(8)	
Bruno SILVA	URU	D	18	(3)	1
Koert THALEN		D		(1)	

SC HEERENVEEN
Coach - Gertjan Verbeek

2005

13/8	Vitesse	a	2-2	Huntelaar, Hansson
20/8	Roda JC	h	5-4	Yildirim, Samaras, Pranjic, Huntelaar 2
26/8	ADO Den Haag	a	0-1	
10/9	Heracles Almelo	h	1-2	Huntelaar (p)
18/9	Feyenoord	a	1-5	Yildirim
23/9	NEC	h	2-1	Samaras, Pranjic
2/10	PSV	h	2-3	Bosvelt, Tarjavärvi
15/10	NAC Breda	a	3-0	Huntelaar 3
23/10	FC Utrecht	h	1-1	Tarjavärvi
28/10	Ajax	a	0-0	

Holland

6/11	FC Groningen	h	4-0	Huntelaar 2, Bosvelt, Huntelaar, Samaras
20/11	Sparta Rotterdam	a	2-1	Derveld, Huntelaar
27/11	RBC Roosendaal	h	2-0	Bruggink, .Nørregaard
3/12	AZ	a	1-2	Samaras
10/12	Willem II	h	3-3	Bruggink, Huntelaar 2
17/12	FC Twente	h	3-1	Huntelaar 2 (1p), Nilsson
27/12	RKC Waalwijk	a	2-2	Huntelaar 2
30/12	Ajax	h	4-2	Samaras 2, Huntelaar, Hanssen
2006				
13/1	FC Groningen	a	0-2	
21/1	Sparta Rotterdam	h	0-0	
28/1	RBC Roosendaal	a	2-0	Bruggink, Hansson
5/2	ADO Den Haag	h	3-0	Nilsson 3
8/2	Heracles Almelo	a	1-1	Nilsson
11/2	Vitesse	h	4-1	Yildirim 2, Bosvelt, Nilsson
18/2	Roda JC	a	1-2	Bruggink
26/2	NAC Breda	h	2-1	Nørregaard, Pranjic
4/3	PSV	a	1-4	De Vries
12/3	FC Utrecht	a	0-2	
18/3	RKC Waalwijk	h	2-1	Pranjic, Bruggink
25/3	FC Twente	a	2-1	Nilsson 2
1/4	NEC	a	1-4	Nilsson
7/4	Feyenoord	h	1-1	Tarvajärvi
12/4	Willem II	a	3-4	De Vries, Bosvelt, Bruggink
16/4	AZ	h	2-4	De Vries, Pranjic

No	Name	Nat	Pos	Aps	(s)	Gls
2	Said BAKKATI		D	6	(2)	
28	Joey VAN DEN BERG		D		(1)	
6	Paul BOSVELT		M	30		4
31	Michael BRADLEY	USA	M	1		
4	Michel BREUER		D	30		
17	Arnold BRUGGINK		A	25	(6)	6
18	Fernando DERVELD		D	8	(10)	1
22	Henrico DROST		D	6	(5)	
15	Jeroen DROST		D	24	(1)	
38	Reza GHOOCHANNEJHAD		A		(1)	
11	André HANSSEN	NOR	M	4	(6)	1
3	Petter HANSSON	SWE	D	33		2
9	Klaas-Jan HUNTELAAR		A	14	(1)	17
21	Abdelkarim KISSI	MAR	M	14	(1)	
30	Ken Ilso LARSEN	DEN	A		(1)	
10	Lasse NILSSON	SWE	A	21	(7)	9
8	Hjalte Bo NØRREGAARD	DEN	M	9	(7)	2
2	Jakob POULSEN	DEN	D	7		
14	Thomas PRAGER	AUT	M	5	(10)	
23	Danijel PRANJIC	CRO	M	32		5
20	Giorgios SAMARAS	GRE	A	13	(2)	6
5	Marcel SEIP		D	24	(4)	
16	Sebastiaan STEUR		A		(3)	
19	Niklas TARVAJÄRVI	FIN	A	2	(15)	3
25	Brian VANDENBUSSCHE	BEL	G	23	(1)	
12	Mark DE VRIES		A	1	(6)	3
24	Boy WATERMAN		G	11		
7	Ugur YILDIRIM		A	31		4

HERACLES ALMELO
Coach - Peter Bosz

2005

13/8	PSV	h	1-1	Sluijter
20/8	ADO Den Haag	a	2-1	Hirayama 2
28/8	FC Groningen	h	2-1	Tamerus, Quansah (p)
2/10	FC Twente	h	0-4	
10/9	SC Heerenveen	a	2-1	Quansah, Tamerus
17/9	RKC Waalwijk	h	0-2	
25/9	Sparta Rotterdam	a	0-2	
15/10	Ajax	a	0-0	
21/10	NEC	h	0-2	
29/10	Vitesse	a	1-5	Quansah
5/11	AZ	a	2-2	Calinkov, Pieckenhagen
20/11	RBC Roosendaal	h	3-0	Hellings, Calinkov, Hirayama
27/11	Feyenoord	a	1-7	Jansen
2/12	Roda JC	h	0-1	
10/12	NAC Breda	a	1-2	Jansen
18/12	FC Utrecht	h	1-1	Hirayama
30/12	Vitesse	h	3-1	Hirayama, Tamerus 2
2006				
11/1	Willem II	a	2-1	Sluijter, Hirayama
14/1	AZ	h	0-2	
21/1	RBC Roosendaal	a	2-1	Hirayama, Nurmela
29/1	Feyenoord	h	0-4	
4/2	FC Groningen	a	0-0	
8/2	SC Heerenveen	h	1-1	Tanghe
11/2	PSV	a	0-1	
19/2	ADO Den Haag	h	1-3	Tanghe
26/2	Ajax	h	1-3	Sluijter
5/3	FC Twente	a	0-2	
11/3	NEC	a	0-2	
18/3	Willem II	h	1-0	Nurmela
26/3	FC Utrecht	a	0-1	
1/4	Sparta Rotterdam	h	1-0	Quansah
8/4	RKC Waalwijk	a	2-0	Quansah, Tamerus
12/4	NAC Breda	h	4-2	Tamerus, Hirayama, Tanghe, Hocher
16/4	Roda JC	a	1-2	Tanghe

Name	Nat	Pos	Aps	(s)	Gls
Denis CALINKOV	MOL	A	8	(6)	2
Sergio HELLINGS		M	14	(6)	1
Sota HIRAYAMA	JPN	A	15	(16)	8
Marc HOCHER		A	27	(2)	1
Bernard HOFSTEDE		A		(1)	
Nico-Jan HOOGMA		D	29	(1)	
Rudy JANSEN		D	28		2
Ragnar KLAVAN	EST	D	15		
Brian VAN LOO		G	2		
Mark LOOMS		D	18	(5)	
Rob MAAS		M	25		
Mika NURMELA	FIN	A	21	(1)	2
Martin PIECKENHAGEN	GER	G	32		1
Kwame QUANSAH	GHA	A	24	(7)	5
Peter REEKERS		D	22	(5)	
Thijs SLUIJTER		A	26	(4)	3
Marnix SMIT		D	8	(7)	
Gert-Jan TAMERUS		A	14	(19)	6
Stefaan TANGHE	BEL	M	14		4
Remon DE VRIES		M	25	(6)	
Sander WEENK		A		(1)	
Jan WUIJTENS	BEL	M	7	(7)	

NAC BREDA
Coach - Ton Lokhoff; (2/1/06) Cees Lok; (23/4/06) John Karelse

2005

14/8	Feyenoord	a	0-2	
19/8	Willem II	h	1-0	Vonlanthen
27/8	Sparta Rotterdam	a	0-1	
11/9	ADO Den Haag	h	4-1	Zonneveld, Slot, Mendes da Silva, Rigters
17/9	NEC	a	1-1	Jenner
25/9	AZ	h	2-1	Slot, Vonlanthen
30/9	RBC Roosendaal	a	2-1	Vonlanthen, Van Hooijdonk (p)
15/10	SC Heerenveen	h	0-2	

Holland

Date	Opponent	H/A	Score	Scorers
22/10	FC Twente	h	1-1	Vonlanthen
29/10	RKC Waalwijk	a	1-4	Van Hooijdonk
5/11	Roda JC	a	3-3	Van Hooijdonk 2, Penders
19/11	FC Utrecht	h	0-1	
30/11	FC Groningen	h	2-2	Van Hooijdonk, Slot
3/12	PSV	a	0-3	
10/12	Heracles Almelo	h	2-1	Vonlanthen, Zwaanswijk
18/12	Ajax	h	0-2	
27/12	Vitesse	a	1-2	Van Gessel
2006				
11/1	RKC Waalwijk	h	1-2	Jenner
14/1	Roda JC	h	0-4	
22/1	FC Utrecht	a	2-2	Diba, Rigters
29/1	FC Groningen	a	2-3	Van Gessel, Leonardo
4/2	Sparta Rotterdam	h	0-0	
8/2	ADO Den Haag	a	3-0	Diba, Van Gessel, Leonardo
12/2	Feyenoord	h	3-3	Diba 2, Jenner
19/2	Willem II	a	0-2	
26/2	SC Heerenveen	a	1-2	Leonardo
4/3	RBC Roosendaal	h	2-1	og (Roumani), Slot
10/3	FC Twente	a	0-1	
17/3	Vitesse	h	2-2	Leonardo 2
26/3	Ajax	a	1-1	Mendes da Silva
4/4	AZ	a	2-3	Slot, Leonardo
8/4	NEC	h	2-1	Diba, Leonardo
12/4	Heracles Almelo	a	2-4	Leonardo, Stam
16/4	PSV	h	2-6	Vonlanthen, Derijck

No	Name	Nat	Pos	Aps	(s)	Gls
27	Aykut DEMIR	TUR	D	4	(4)	
29	Timothy DERIJCK	BEL	D	12		1
15	Anouar DIBA	MAR	A	17	(8)	5
2	Kurt ELSHOT		D	33		
24	Ivo VAN ENGELEN		D	3	(1)	
5	Sander VAN GESSEL		M	31		3
17	Pierre VAN HOOIJDONK		A	17		5
19	Julian JENNER		A	23	(6)	3
22	Arie JONKER		A		(2)	
12	Benny KERSTENS		D	5	(2)	
20	Wilmer KOUSEMAKER		D	1	(1)	
30	LEONARDO	BRA	A	11	(3)	8
7	David MENDES DA SILVA		D	26		2
3	Rob PENDERS		D	4		1
6	Tamás PETÖ	HUN	M	11	(3)	
11	Maceo RIGTERS		A	7	(17)	2
1	Davy SCHOLLEN	BEL	G	17		
9	Victor SIKORA		A	10	(3)	
10	Arne SLOT		M	21	(5)	5
17	Evander SNO		D	12	(2)	
23	Ron STAM		M	20	(8)	1
14	Tony VIDMAR	AUS	D	20	(1)	
18	Johan VONLANTHEN	SUI	A	19	(13)	6
8	Mike ZONNEVELD		M	4		1
4	Patrick ZWAANSWIJK		D	29	(2)	
16	Arno VAN ZWAM		G	17		

NEC
Coach - Cees Lok; (19/11/05) (Ron De Groot)

Date	Opponent	H/A	Score	Scorers
2005				
14/8	FC Utrecht	h	0-0	
20/8	FC Twente	a	1-0	Tininho
27/8	RKC Waalwijk	h	1-3	Niedzielan
11/9	Feyenoord	a	0-3	
17/9	NAC Breda	h	1-1	Van der Doelen
23/9	SC Heerenveen	a	1-2	Takak
2/10	AZ	a	2-3	Grot, Niedzielan
16/10	RBC Roosendaal	h	3-1	Denneboom, Niedzielan, Grot
21/10	Heracles Almelo	a	2-0	Barreto, Niedzielan
30/10	Sparta Rotterdam	h	0-0	
6/11	Ajax	h	1-0	Denneboom
19/11	ADO Den Haag	a	1-0	Takak
30/11	Willem II	h	2-0	Denneboom, Barreto
4/12	Vitesse	h	1-0	Worm
9/12	Roda JC	a	1-0	Boutahar
18/12	FC Groningen	a	0-3	
26/12	PSV	h	0-2	
2006				
15/1	Ajax	a	1-1	Wielaert
18/1	Sparta Rotterdam	a	3-1	Niedzielan 3
22/1	ADO Den Haag	h	5-0	Barreto, Jones 2, Denneboom, Niedzielan
28/1	Willem II	a	2-2	Jones 2 (1p)
5/2	RKC Waalwijk	a	3-1	Denneboom, Boutahar, Niedzielan
8/2	Feyenoord	h	1-2	Denneboom
12/2	FC Utrecht	a	1-1	Worm
17/2	FC Twente	h	0-3	
24/2	RBC Roosendaal	a	0-2	
3/3	AZ	h	0-2	
11/3	Heracles Almelo	h	2-0	Denneboom, Jones
18/3	PSV	a	0-1	
25/3	FC Groningen	h	2-2	Tininho, Jones
1/4	SC Heerenveen	h	4-1	Niedzielan, Pothuizen (p), Denneboom, Grot
8/4	NAC Breda	a	1-2	Boutahar
12/4	Roda JC	h	0-3	
16/4	Vitesse	a	1-1	Tininho (p)

No	Name	Nat	Pos	Aps	(s)	Gls
1	Gábor BABOS	HUN	G	29		
8	Edgar BARRETO	PAR	M	31	(1)	3
10	Said BOUTAHAR	MAR	A	25	(5)	3
7	Romano DENNEBOOM		A	29		8
17	Bjorn VAN DER DOELEN		M	26	(3)	1
9	Bart VAN DEN EEDE	BEL	A	4	(4)	
25	Raymon VAN EMMERIK		G	5		
18	Guilliano GROT		A	6	(24)	3
5	David JONES	ENG	A	13	(4)	6
4	Jeffrey LEIWAKABESSY		D	31		
14	Muslu NALBANTOGLU	TUR	D	8	(10)	
23	Andrzej NIEDZIELAN	POL	A	24	(3)	10
15	Jonas OLSSON	SWE	D	34		
6	Patrick POTHUIZEN		D	5	(6)	1
20	Alexander PRENT		A	1	(5)	
21	Jasar TAKAK		A	13	(8)	2
16	TININHO	BRA	M	25	(3)	3
19	José VALENCIA	ECU	D		(2)	
29	Sven WERKHOVEN		A		(1)	
2	Rob WIELAERT		D	29		1
3	Peter WISGERHOF		D	30	(1)	
24	Rutger WORM		A	6	(11)	2

PSV
Coach - Guus Hiddink

Date	Opponent	H/A	Score	Scorers
2005				
13/8	Heracles Almelo	a	1-1	Cocu
21/8	Vitesse	h	2-1	Farfán, Cocu
28/8	Roda JC	a	3-0	Farfán, Beasley, Cocu
10/9	FC Utrecht	h	1-0	Koné
18/9	FC Groningen	a	0-1	
24/9	RBC Roosendaal	h	2-0	Simons, Farfán
2/10	SC Heerenveen	a	3-2	Koné 3
15/10	AZ	h	3-0	Cocu 2, Vennegoor of Hesselink
23/10	Ajax	h	1-0	Simons (p)

Holland

29/10	FC Twente	a	1-0	Afellay
5/11	Sparta Rotterdam	h	3-0	Farfán 2, Beasley
19/11	RKC Waalwijk	a	4-4	Farfán 3, Robert
27/11	ADO Den Haag	h	3-0	Vennegoor of Hesselink 2, Koné
3/12	NAC Breda	h	3-0	Vennegoor of Hesselink, Farfán, Koné
11/12	Feyenoord	a	0-1	
17/12	Willem II	h	4-1	Vennegoor of Hesselink 2, Farfán, Väyrynen
26/12	NEC	a	2-0	Koné, Beasley
29/12	FC Twente	h	1-1	Cocu
2006				
15/1	Sparta Rotterdam	a	1-0	og (Gudelj)
20/1	RKC Waalwijk	h	2-0	Farfán, Beasley
29/1	ADO Den Haag	a	2-0	Farfán, Cocu
4/2	Roda JC	h	3-2	Vennegoor of Hesselink 2 (1p), Aissati
8/2	FC Utrecht	a	2-1	Farfán 2
11/2	Heracles Almelo	h	1-0	Farfán
17/2	Vitesse	a	3-1	Farfán 2, Lamey
26/2	AZ	a	2-1	Vennegoor of Hesselink, Koné
4/3	SC Heerenveen	h	4-1	Koné 2, Cocu, Alex
12/3	Ajax	a	0-0	
18/3	NEC	h	1-0	Farfán
25/3	Willem II	a	3-0	Aissati, Addo, Koné
1/4	RBC Roosendaal	a	2-1	Afellay, Alex
9/4	FC Groningen	h	1-0	Farfán
12/4	Feyenoord	h	1-1	Cocu
16/4	NAC Breda	a	6-2	Vennegoor of Hesselink 2, Farfán 2, Väyrynen, Cocu

No	Name	Nat	Pos	Aps	(s)	Gls
18	Eric ADDO	GHA	D	16	(4)	1
20	Ibrahim AFELLAY		M	18	(5)	2
37	Ismail AISSATI		M	6	(12)	2
4	ALEX	BRA	D	28		2
5	Michael BALL	ENG	D	9	(3)	
33	Roy BEERENS		A		(2)	
11	DaMarcus BEASLEY	USA	A	18	(9)	4
5	Wilfred BOUMA		D	3		
8	Phillip COCU		M	33		10
15	Jason CULINA	AUS	A	19	(4)	
17	Jefferson FARFÁN	PER	A	28	(3)	21
14	Osman Daniel FERREYRA	ARG	M	1		
1	Heurelho GOMES	BRA	G	32		
10	Arouna KONE	CIV	A	20	(1)	11
19	Michael LAMEY		D	24	(2)	1
24	Nguyen LEE	USA	M		(1)	
3	LEE Young-pyo	KOR	D	3		
16	Theo LUCIUS		M	18	(3)	
2	Andre OOIJER		D	23	(1)	
3	Michael REIZIGER		D	12	(1)	
29	ROBERT	BRA	A		(9)	1
35	Gerald SIBON		A		(2)	
6	Timmy SIMONS	BEL	M	32		2
27	Archie THOMPSON	AUS	A		(2)	
7	Mika VÄYRYNEN	FIN	M	4	(7)	2
9	Jan VENNEGOOR OF HESSELINK		A	25	(7)	11
21	Edwin ZOETEBIER		G	2	(1)	

RBC ROOSENDAAL
Coach - Dolf Roks; (4/1/06) Robert Maaskant

2005				
14/8	FC Groningen	a	0-1	
20/8	Ajax	h	0-2	
28/8	Willem II	h	1-1	Lammens (p)
10/9	AZ	a	0-7	
17/9	Sparta Rotterdam	h	1-1	Wau
24/9	PSV	a	0-2	
30/9	NAC Breda	h	1-2	De Lange (p)
16/10	NEC	a	1-3	El Khattabi
22/10	Vitesse	h	0-3	
30/10	FC Utrecht	a	1-4	Kpaka
4/11	RKC Waalwijk	h	1-1	Kpaka
20/11	Heracles Almelo	a	0-3	
27/11	SC Heerenveen	a	0-2	
3/12	Feyenoord	h	2-2	Kpaka, Loran
10/12	ADO Den Haag	a	0-3	
17/12	Roda JC	h	0-2	
26/12	FC Twente	a	1-4	Sillah
29/12	FC Utrecht	h	1-2	Sillah
2006				
14/1	RKC Waalwijk	a	1-1	Daelemans
21/1	Heracles Almelo	h	1-2	Daelemans
28/1	SC Heerenveen	h	0-2	
3/2	Willem II	a	1-3	Vos
7/2	AZ	h	0-5	
12/2	FC Groningen	h	1-2	Sillah
19/2	Ajax	a	0-6	
24/2	NEC	h	2-0	Sillah, Kpaka
4/3	NAC Breda	a	1-2	Daelemans
12/3	Vitesse	a	1-5	Kpaka
19/3	FC Twente	h	1-1	Sillah
25/3	Roda JC	a	1-5	Fleur
1/4	PSV	h	1-2	Sillah
8/4	Sparta Rotterdam	a	0-5	
12/4	ADO Den Haag	h	1-2	Sillah
16/4	Feyenoord	a	0-2	

No	Name	Nat	Pos	Aps	(s)	Gls
2	Jorge ACUÑA	CHL	M	23	(1)	
25	Richie BASOSKI		A	1	(3)	
16	Björn DAELEMANS	BEL	A	22	(6)	3
3	Arjan EBBINGE		D	9		
10	Ali EL KHATTABI	MAR	A	15	(4)	1
8	Melvin FLEUR		D	22	(4)	1
13	José FORTES RODRIGUES	ESP	D	18	(2)	
12	Erwin FRIEBEL		G	4	(1)	
9	Donny DE GROOT		A	3	(3)	
14	Danny GUIJT		A	1	(2)	
18	Paul KPAKA	SRL	A	21	(8)	5
2	Sidney LAMMENS	BEL	D	20	(3)	1
21	Paul DE LANGE		M	26		1
4	Tyrone LORAN		D	26		1
19	Fouad MAKHOUT	MAR	A	1	(10)	
11	Edgar MARCELINO	POR	A	17	(9)	
5	Robert MOLENAAR		D	14	(2)	
17	Pauwie OTTO		D		(1)	
20	Frits PAAP		A	11	(12)	
15	Akram ROUMANI	MAR	D	28	(2)	
24	Ebrima SILLAH	GAM	A	20		7
17	Tim SMOLDERS	BEL	M	19	(9)	
1	Mark VOLDERS	BEL	G	30		
9	Henk VOS		A	12	(1)	1
7	Nyron WAU		A	11	(5)	1
22	Adem YARAN	TUR	D		(1)	

RKC WAALWIJK
Coach - Adri Koster

2005				
13/8	Willem II	a	2-1	Hoogendorp 2
21/8	FC Groningen	h	2-1	De Ceulaer, Martens
27/8	NEC	a	3-1	Hoogendorp, De Ceulaer, Janssen

Holland

Date	Opponent	H/A	Score	Scorers
9/9	Roda JC	h	2-0	Hoogendorp, Molhoek
17/9	Heracles Almelo	a	2-0	Keller, Hoogendorp (p)
24/9	FC Utrecht	h	2-3	De Ceulaer, Hoogendorp (p)
1/10	ADO Den Haag	a	1-2	Van de Haar
15/10	FC Twente	a	0-2	
23/10	Feyenoord	h	2-1	Martens, Teixeira
29/10	NAC Breda	h	4-1	Hoogendorp (p), Molhoek, Van de Haar, Martens
4/11	RBC Roosendaal	a	1-1	Keller
19/11	PSV	h	4-4	De Ceulaer, Hoogendorp 2, Keller
29/11	Vitesse	a	2-4	De Ceulaer, Martens
4/12	Ajax	a	1-4	Hoogendorp
11/12	Sparta Rotterdam	h	3-2	Martens, Hoogendorp, Molhoek
18/12	AZ	a	0-3	
27/12	SC Heerenveen	h	2-2	Zuiverloon, Martens
2006				
11/1	NAC Breda	a	2-1	Janssen, Hoogendorp
14/1	RBC Roosendaal	h	1-1	De Ceulaer
20/1	PSV	a	0-2	
29/1	Vitesse	h	0-1	
5/2	NEC	h	1-3	Fuchs
8/2	Roda JC	a	0-1	
11/2	Willem II	h	1-0	Janssen
18/2	FC Groningen	a	0-1	
24/2	FC Twente	h	0-0	
5/3	ADO Den Haag	h	3-0	De Ceulaer, Van Dijk D. 2
12/3	Feyenoord	a	1-1	Berger
18/3	SC Heerenveen	a	1-2	Van Dijk D.
26/3	AZ	h	0-1	
31/3	FC Utrecht	a	1-3	Van de Haar
8/4	Heracles Almelo	h	0-2	
12/4	Sparta Rotterdam	a	2-3	Van de Haar, og (Olfers)
16/4	Ajax	h	2-4	Lurling, Peters

Name	Nat	Pos	Aps	(s)	Gls
Lion AXWIJK		D	1	(3)	
Tim BAKENS		D	14	(1)	
Martijn BARTO		A	1	(6)	
Ruud BERGER		A	5	(5)	1
Benjamin DE CEULAER	BEL	A	25		7
Patrick VAN DIEMEN		M	26		
Ryan DONK		D	4	(1)	
Dominique VAN DIJK		A	9	(20)	3
Rob VAN DIJK		G	34		
Robert FUCHS		M	15	(6)	1
Cerezo FUNG A WING		D	1	(2)	
Hans VAN DE HAAR		A	22	(1)	4
Ramon VAN HAAREN		D	27		
Rick HOOGENDORP		A	18		12
Jochen JANSSEN	BEL	A	8	(12)	3
Stephan KELLER	SUI	D	29	(1)	3
Michael KROHN-DEHLI	DEN	M	12	(5)	
Didi LONGUET		M	3	(1)	
Anthony LURLING		A	14		1
Maarten MARTENS	BEL	M	21		6
Danny MATHIJSSEN		M	11	(3)	
Rogier MOLHOEK		M	16		3
Dustley MULDER		D	9	(2)	
Tim PETERS		A		(2)	1
Touvarno PINAS		A		(1)	
Eddy PUTTER		A		(1)	
Randy RUSTENBERG		D	1	(1)	
Sjack VAN RIJSBERGEN		D		(1)	
Virgilio TEIXEIRA	POR	D	25		1
David TRIANTAFILLIDIS	BEL	D		(1)	
Gianni ZUIVERLOON		D	23	(5)	1

RODA JC
Coach - Huub Stevens

Date	Opponent	H/A	Score	Scorers
2005				
13/8	FC Twente	h	2-0	Sonko, Koné
20/8	SC Heerenveen	a	4-5	Sonko, Koné, Van Dijk (p), Sérgio
28/8	PSV	h	0-3	
9/9	RKC Waalwijk	a	0-2	
18/9	Willem II	h	0-2	
24/9	Ajax	a	1-4	Sonko
1/10	Vitesse	h	3-2	Senden, Sérgio, Oper
16/10	FC Utrecht	h	2-1	Sérgio, Oper
22/10	Sparta Rotterdam	a	3-2	og (Zoontjes), Cissé, Oper
30/10	FC Groningen	a	0-1	
5/11	NAC Breda	h	3-3	Sérgio, Oper, Bodnár
20/11	Feyenoord	h	2-3	Sérgio, Oper
27/11	AZ	a	0-2	
2/12	Heracles Almelo	a	1-0	Seergio
9/12	NEC	h	0-1	
17/12	RBC Rosendaal	a	2-0	Bodnár, Van Dijk
27/12	ADO Den Haag	h	3-1	Vicelich, Oper, Bodor
30/12	FC Groningen	h	1-3	Oper
2006				
14/1	NAC Breda	a	4-0	Vicelich, Van Dijk, Oper, Cissé
22/1	Feyenoord	a	0-0	
27/1	AZ	h	1-4	Voigt
4/2	PSV	a	2-3	Cziommer, Sérgio
8/2	RKC Waalwijk	h	1-0	Cristiano
11/2	FC Twente	a	0-1	
18/2	SC Heerenveen	h	2-1	Van Dijk (p), Cziommer
26/2	FC Utrecht	a	1-2	Van Dijk
4/3	Vitesse	a	3-1	Cziommer, Bodor 2
11/3	Sparta Rotterdam	h	1-1	Cziommer
18/3	ADO Den Haag	a	1-1	Sonko
25/3	RBC Roosendaal	h	5-1	Cziommer 3, Sonko, Rudge
2/4	Ajax	h	2-1	og (Lindenbergh), Sonko
9/4	Willem II	a	2-2	Cristiano, Rudge
12/4	NEC	a	3-0	Cristiano 2, Cissé
16/4	Heracles Almelo	h	2-1	Cissé, Cziommer (p)

No	Name	Nat	Pos	Aps	(s)	Gls
24	Kevin BEGOIS	BEL	G	2		
13	László BODNÁR	HUN	D	14	(1)	2
27	Boldizsár BODOR	HUN	D	31	(2)	3
19	Sekou CISSE	CIV	A	24	(3)	4
16	Jérôme COLINET	BEL	M		(5)	
9	CRISTIANO	BRA	A	7	(14)	4
18	Simon CZIOMMER	GER	M	15		8
12	Dirk-Jan DERKSEN		A	2	(4)	
14	Kevin VAN DESSEL	BEL	M	5	(2)	
26	Gregoor VAN DIJK		M	28		5
5	Pedrag FILIPOVIC	SCG	D	9	(3)	
20	Diego JONGEN		A		(1)	
6	Pa-Modou KAH	NOR	D	32		
11	Arouna KONE	CIV	A	2		2
1	Vladan KUJOVIC	SCG	G	32		
17	Vincent LACHAMBRE	BEL	D	28	(3)	
25	Ken LEEMANS	BEL	D	12	(8)	
11	Andres OPER	EST	A	23	(1)	8
21	Olaf ROMPELBERG		D		(1)	
20	Humphrey RUDGE		D		(5)	2
4	Jan-Paul SAEIJS		D	11		
2	Ger SENDEN		D	23	(1)	1
10	SÉRGIO	BRA	M	33		7
7	Edrissa SONKO	GAM	A	7	(11)	6
8	Ivan VICELICH	NZL	M	23	(4)	2

Holland

| | Alexander VOIGT | | GER | D | 11 | (6) | 1 |

SPARTA ROTTERDAM
Coach - Wiljan Vloet

2005
13/8	AZ	a	0-3		
20/8	Feyenoord	h	1-3	Van den Bergh	
27/8	NAC Breda	h	1-0	Van den Bergh	
10/9	FC Groningen	a	1-0	Oost (p)	
17/9	RBC Roosendaal	a	1-1	Oost	
25/9	Heracles Almelo	h	2-0	Van den Bergh 2	
2/10	Ajax	a	1-2	Polak	
15/10	Willem II	a	0-0		
22/10	Roda JC	h	2-3	De Fauw, Cvetkov	
30/10	NEC	a	0-0		
5/11	PSV	a	0-3		
19/11	SC Heerenveen	h	1-2	Rose	
30/11	FC Twente	a	0-1		
3/12	ADO Den Haag	h	2-3	Rose 2	
11/12	RKC Waalwijk	a	2-3	Polak (p), Van den Bergh	
15/12	Vitesse	h	1-0	De Fauw	
26/12	FC Utrecht	a	1-1	Cvetkov	

2006
15/1	PSV	h	0-1		
18/1	NEC	h	1-3	Van Tornhout	
21/1	SC Heerenveen	a	0-0		
28/1	FC Twente	h	1-0	Oost	
4/2	NAC Breda	a	0-0		
7/2	FC Groningen	h	1-0	De Fauw	
10/2	AZ	h	0-1		
19/2	Feyenoord	a	0-4		
25/2	Willem II	h	3-2	Rose, Obodai, Bouaouzan	
5/3	Ajax	a	0-6		
11/3	Roda JC	a	1-1	Gudde	
19/3	FC Utrecht	h	0-1		
24/3	Vitesse	a	1-3	Oost (p)	
1/4	Heracles Almelo	a	0-1		
8/4	RBC Roosendaal	h	5-0	Emnes, Cvetkov, Rose, Oost 2 (1p)	
12/4	RKC Waalwijk	h	3-2	Oost 2 (2p), Cvetkov	
16/4	ADO Den Haag	a	2-0	Van den Bergh, Cvetkov	

No	Name	Nat	Pos	Aps	(s)	Gls
25	Istvan BAX		A		(2)	
10	Ricky VAN DEN BERGH		A	19	(4)	6
14	Rachid BOUAOUZAN		A	16	(14)	1
18	Marciano BRUMA		D	3	(2)	
17	Edwin VAN BUEREN		M	13	(5)	
	Ivan CVETKOV	BUL	A	13	(14)	5
16	Marvin EMNES		A	4	(6)	1
2	Davy DE FAUW	BEL	D	32		3
22	Wouter GUDDE		D	20	(6)	1
5	Nebojsa GUDELJ	SCG	D	31		
7	Sani KAITA	NIG	M	7	(3)	
16	Cristophe KINET	BEL	M	1	(1)	
6	Jan MICHELS		M	17	(4)	
8	Anthony OBODAI	GHA	M	28		1
3	Steve OLFERS		D	17	(2)	
9	Jason OOST		A	26	(4)	8
21	Sjaak POLAK		M	22	(6)	2
1	Rene PONK		G	34		
11	Yuri ROSE		M	32		5
27	Nathan RUTJES		D		(1)	
15	Danny SCHENKEL		D	15	(1)	
25	Dieter VAN TORNHOUT	BEL	A	10	(3)	1
25	Marvin WIJKS		A		(1)	
24	Kerem YILMAZ		M		(3)	
4	Tom ZOONTJES		D	14	(2)	

FC TWENTE
Coach - Rini Coolen; (1/2/06) (Jan van Staa)

2005
13/8	Roda JC	a	0-2	
20/8	NEC	h	0-1	
28/8	FC Utrecht	a	3-1	Culina, N'Kufo, Touma
11/9	Vitesse	h	0-1	
16/9	ADO Den Haag	a	0-0	
25/9	Feyenoord	h	1-3	Zomer
2/10	Heracles Almelo	a	4-0	Majstorovic, Bakircioglü, Zomer, N'Kufo
15/10	RKC Waalwijk	h	2-0	Bakircioglü 2
22/10	NAC Breda	a	1-1	Niemeyer
29/10	PSV	h	0-1	
5/11	Willem II	h	3-1	Afonso, N'Kufo 2 (1p)
19/11	Ajax	a	0-2	
30/11	Sparta Rotterdam	h	1-0	Gerritsen
4/12	FC Groningen	a	0-1	
10/12	AZ	h	1-3	og (Meerdink)
17/12	SC Heerenveen	a	1-3	Gerritsen
26/12	RBC Roosendaal	h	4-1	Niemeyer, Zomer 2, Majstorovic
29/12	PSV	a	1-1	Bakircioglü

2006
15/1	Willem II	a	1-1	N'Kufo (p)
22/1	Ajax	h	2-3	N'Kufo 2
28/1	Sparta Rotterdam	a	0-1	
5/2	FC Utrecht	h	3-0	Bakircioglü, Touma, N'Kufo
8/2	Vitesse	a	2-1	Gerritsen, Touma
11/2	Roda JC	h	1-0	Zomer
17/2	NEC	a	3-0	N'Kufo, Bakircioglü, Gerritsen
24/2	RKC Waalwijk	a	0-0	
5/3	Heracles Almelo	h	2-0	Touma, Gerritsen
10/3	NAC Breda	h	1-0	Bakircioglü
19/3	RBC Roosendaal	a	1-1	Bakircioglü
25/3	SC Heerenveen	h	1-2	N'Kufo
2/4	Feyenoord	a	2-4	Gerritsen, N'Kufo
9/4	ADO Den Haag	h	2-0	Touma, N'Kufo
12/4	AZ	a	0-0	
16/4	FC Groningen	h	1-1	Afonso

No	Name	Nat	Pos	Aps	(s)	Gls
19	Guilherme AFONSO	SUI	A	5	(18)	2
8	Kennedy BAKIRCIOGLÜ	SWE	M	29	(3)	8
1	Sander BOSCHKER		G	28		
15	Elbekay BOUCHIBA	MAR	M	4	(7)	
26	Wout BRAMA		M	23	(6)	
10	Jason CULINA	AUS	A	6		1
24	Karim EL AHMADI	MAR	M	7	(1)	
21	Giorgi GAKHOKIDZE	GEO	A	11	(4)	
10	Anatoli GERK	RUS	M	2		
23	Patrick GERRITSEN		A	18	(6)	6
12	Jeroen HEUBACH		D	28		
25	Marcel KLEIZEN		A		(5)	
5	Konstantinos LOUMPOUTIS	GRE	D	6	(3)	
3	Daniel MAJSTOROVIC	SWE	D	19		2
17	Peter NIEMEYER	GER	M	27	(3)	2
9	Blaise N'KUFO	SUI	A	32		12
18	Rahim OUEDRAOGO	BFA	M	19	(3)	
16	Remko PASVEER		G	6		
2	Resit SCHUURMAN		D	7	(3)	
11	Dmitri SHOUKOV	RUS	A	9	(3)	
20	Bas SIBUM		M	17	(7)	
7	Sharbel TOUMA	SWE	A	23	(5)	5
6	Karim TOUZANI	MAR	D		(2)	
14	Arnar VIDARSSON	ISL	D	6	(3)	

Holland

22	Niels WELLENBERG		M	11	
4	Ramon ZOMER		D	31	5

FC UTRECHT
Coach - Foeke Booy

2005

14/8	NEC	a	0-0		
21/8	AZ	h	1-2	Di Tommaso	
28/8	FC Twente	h	1-3	Somers	
10/9	PSV	a	0-1		
18/9	Vitesse	h	1-0	Somers	
24/9	RKC Waalwijk	a	3-2	Van den Bergh, Douglas, Fortune	
2/10	Feyenoord	h	3-1	Nelisse 3	
16/10	Roda JC	a	1-2	Braafheid	
23/10	SC Heerenveen	a	1-1	Van den Bergh	
30/10	RBC Roosendaal	h	4-1	Maachi 2, Broerse, Fortune	
6/11	ADO Den Haag	h	1-1	Nelisse	
19/11	NAC Breda	a	1-0	Kruijs	
27/11	Ajax	h	1-0	Tiendalli	
11/12	FC Groningen	h	0-2		
14/12	Willem II	a	1-0	Broerse	
18/12	Heracles Almelo	a	1-1	Fortune	
26/12	Sparta Rotterdam	h	1-1	Van den Bergh	
29/12	RBC Roosendaal	a	2-1	Maachi, Tanghe	

2006

15/1	ADO Den Haag	a	3-2	Van den Bergh, Nelisse, Tiendalli	
22/1	NAC Breda	h	2-2	Keller, Nelisse	
29/1	Ajax	a	4-1	Ramzi 3, Nelisse (p)	
5/2	FC Twente	a	0-3		
8/2	PSV	h	1-2	Ramzi	
12/2	NEC	h	1-1	Caluwé	
19/2	AZ	a	3-2	Van Steensel, Ramzi, Nelisse (p)	
26/2	Roda JC	h	2-1	Van den Bergh, Ramzi	
5/3	Feyenoord	a	0-3		
12/3	SC Heerenveen	h	2-0	Nelisse, Fortune	
19/3	Sparta Rotterdam	a	1-0	Van den Bergh	
26/3	Heracles Almelo	h	1-0	Fortune	
31/3	RKC Waalwijk	h	3-1	Braafheid, Ramzi, Fortune	
9/4	Vitesse	a	0-1		
12/4	FC Groningen	a	1-2	Caluwé	
16/4	Willem II	h	1-4	Caluwé	

No	Name	Nat	Pos	Aps	(s)	Gls
19	Adnan ALISIC		M		(1)	
11	Dave VAN DEN BERGH		A	26	(4)	6
20	Edson BRAAFHEID		D	31		2
8	Joost BROERSE		D	21	(3)	2
39	Kees VAN BUUREN		D	3	(1)	
10	Tom CALUWE	BEL	M	15		3
2	Tim CORNELISSE		D	13		
4	David DI TOMMASO	FRA	D	13		1
7	Darl DOUGLAS		A	9	(17)	1
15	Marc-Antoine FORTUNE	FRA	A	15	(16)	6
16	Franck GRANDEL	FRA	G	9	(2)	
6	Jean-Paul DE JONG		M	25	(3)	
22	Sander KELLER		D	30		1
21	Rick KRUIJS		M	17	(9)	1
37	Nassir MAACHI		A	9	(1)	3
14	Robin NELISSE		A	29	(3)	9
9	Adil RAMZI	MAR	A	15		7
43	Giuseppe ROSSINI	ITA	A		(8)	
5	Etienne SHEW-ATJON		D	2	(13)	
23	Hans SOMERS	BEL	M	26	(4)	2
3	Leendert VAN STEENSEL		A	5	(9)	1
10	Stefaan TANGHE	BEL	M	7	(4)	1

1	Joost TEROL		G	25	
12	Dwight TIENDALLI		D	29	2

VITESSE
Coach - Edward Sturing

2005

13/8	SC Heerenveen	h	2-2	Esajas, Janssen	
21/8	PSV	a	1-2	og (Alex)	
27/8	AZ	h	0-5		
11/9	FC Twente	a	1-0	Amoah	
18/9	FC Utrecht	a	0-1		
24/9	FC Groningen	h	2-0	Swerts, Benson	
1/10	Roda JC	a	2-3	Janssen, Benson	
16/10	ADO Den Haag	h	3-1	Benson, og (Bodde), Hersi	
22/10	RBC Roosendaal	a	3-0	Janssen 2, Hersi	
29/10	Heracles Almelo	h	5-1	De Mul, Hersi 2, Amoah 2	
6/11	Feyenoord	a	0-0		
18/11	Willem II	a	4-3	Amoah 3, Janssen	
29/11	RKC Waalwijk	h	4-2	Janssen, Amoah, Hersi 2	
4/12	NEC	a	0-1		
11/12	Ajax	h	0-2		
16/12	Sparta Rotterdam	a	0-1		
27/12	NAC Breda	h	2-1	Amoah 2	
30/12	Heracles Almelo	a	1-3	Benson	

2006

15/1	Feyenoord	h	0-1		
21/1	Willem II	h	2-1	Benson 2	
29/1	RKC Waalwijk	a	1-0	Dingsdag	
4/2	AZ	a	1-1	Swerts	
8/2	FC Twente	h	1-2	Hersi	
11/2	SC Heerenveen	a	1-4	Junker	
17/2	PSV	h	1-3	Hersi	
25/2	ADO Den Haag	a	0-2		
4/3	Roda JC	a	1-3	og (Senden)	
12/3	RBC Roosendaal	h	5-1	Junker, Knol, Hersi, Knopper, Benson	
17/3	NAC Breda	a	2-2	Knopper, Van der Schaaf	
24/3	Sparta Rotterdam	h	3-1	Janssen, Junker, De Mul	
2/4	FC Groningen	a	1-2	Knopper	
9/4	FC Utrecht	h	1-0	Junker	
12/4	Ajax	a	1-2	Hersi	
16/4	NEC	h	1-1	Van der Schaaf	

No	Name	Nat	Pos	Aps	(s)	Gls
10	Matthew AMOAH	GHA	A	17	(1)	9
19	Fred BENSON	GHA	A	9	(19)	7
20	Peter VAN DEN BERG		D	4		
25	Siebe BLONDELLE	BEL	D	2	(1)	
22	Gino COUTINHO		G	1		
15	Michael DINGSDAG		D	33		1
11	Etienne ESAJAS		A	5	(6)	1
5	Purrel FRANKEL		D	24	(8)	
9	Igor GLUSCEVIC	SCG	A		(7)	
7	Youssouf HERSI		A	21	(4)	10
8	Theo JANSSEN		M	30		7
10	Mads JUNKER	DEN	A	16		4
26	Onur KAYA	BEL	M	5	(4)	
4	Ruud KNOL		D	25	(2)	1
17	Richard KNOPPER		M	23		3
24	Tim DE MEERSMAN	BEL	A		(1)	
6	Tom DE MUL	BEL	A	16	(11)	2
21	Eldridge ROJER		A	3	(18)	
16	Remco VAN DER SCHAAF		M	27		2
28	Gill SWERTS	BEL	D	29	(1)	2
23	Paul VERHAEGH		D	12		
2	Stijn VREVEN	BEL	D	17		
1	Harald WAPENAAR		G	33		
3	Abubakari YAKUBU	GHA	M	22		

Holland

WILLEM II
Coach - Robert Maaskant; (21/11/05) (Kees Zwamborn)

2005
Date	Opponent	H/A	Score	Scorers
13/8	RKC Waalwijk	h	1-2	Reuser
19/8	NAC Breda	a	0-1	
28/8	RBC Roosendaal	a	1-1	Caluwé
10/9	Ajax	h	0-2	
18/9	Roda JC	a	2-0	Kerekes, Caluwé
24/9	ADO Den Haag	h	1-0	Reuser
2/10	FC Groningen	a	0-2	
14/10	Sparta Rotterdam	h	0-0	
23/10	AZ	a	1-5	Agustien
30/10	Feyenoord	h	1-3	Denissen
5/11	FC Twente	a	1-3	Bobson
18/11	Vitesse	h	3-4	Smit, Fehér, Reuser
30/11	NEC	a	0-2	
10/12	SC Heerenveen	a	3-3	Caluwé, Hadouir 2
14/12	FC Utrecht	h	0-1	
17/12	PSV	a	1-4	Ceesay
29/12	Feyenoord	a	1-6	Reuser

2006
Date	Opponent	H/A	Score	Scorers
11/1	Heracles Almelo	h	1-2	Dembele
15/1	FC Twente	h	1-1	Hadouir
21/1	Vitesse	a	1-2	Dembele
28/1	NEC	h	2-2	Dembele, Van Mosselveld
3/2	RBC Roosendaal	h	3-1	Dembele, Hadouir (p), og (Lammens)
8/2	Ajax	a	0-1	
11/2	RKC Waalwijk	a	0-1	
19/2	NAC Breda	h	2-0	og (Sno), Dembele
25/2	Sparta Rotterdam	a	2-3	Redan, Agustien
4/3	FC Groningen	h	5-0	Valencia, Hadouir, Wau, Redan, Dembele
12/3	AZ	h	1-3	Redan
18/3	Heracles Almelo	a	0-1	
25/3	PSV	h	0-3	
1/4	ADO Den Haag	a	1-1	Dembele
9/4	Roda JC	h	2-2	Redan, Smit
12/4	SC Heerenveen	h	4-3	Dembele 2, Redan 2
16/4	FC Utrecht	a	4-1	Redan 2, Kerekes, Reuser

No	Name	Nat	Pos	Aps	(s)	Gls
21	Kemy AGUSTIEN		M	30	(4)	2
25	Mathieu ASSOU-EKOTTO	FRA	M	15		
11	Kevin BOBSON		A	12	(10)	1
10	Tom CALUWE	BEL	M	14	(1)	3
20	Jatto CEESAY	GAM	A	5	(7)	1
12	Sven DELANOY	BEL	M	2	(2)	
9	Moussa DEMBELE	BEL	A	25	(8)	9
23	Hans DENISSEN		A		(6)	1
30	Csaba FEHÉR	HUN	M	16	(4)	1
3	Albert VAN DER HAAR		D	16	(2)	
7	Anouar HADOUIR	MAR	A	20	(4)	5
25	Ryan HOLMAN		D		(1)	
12	Jens JANSE		D	8	(1)	
10	Joe KEENAN	ENG	M	12	(1)	
18	Zsombor KEREKES	HUN	A	11	(9)	2
14	Marko KOLSI	FIN	M	2	(1)	
5	Michel KREEK		D	4		
1	Oscar MOENS		G	11		
19	Frank VAN MOSSELVELD		D	10	(1)	1
20	Marko MUSLIN	FRA	D	5		
14	Steef NIEUWENDAAL		M		(1)	
22	Jos VAN NIEUWSTADT		D	14	(2)	
26	Tristan PEERSMAN	BEL	G	13		
15	Iwan REDAN		A	7	(4)	8
6	Martijn REUSER		A	15	(5)	5
17	Arvid SMIT		M	14	(6)	2
4	Frank VAN DER STRUIJK		D	14	(1)	
4	Arjan SWINKELS		D	1	(2)	
5	José VALENCIA	ECU	D	15		1
8	Raymond VICTORIA		M	25		
2	Nuelson WAU		D	23	(1)	1
15	Jonathan WILMET	BEL	A	5	(3)	
16	Peter ZOIS	AUS	G	10	(1)	

DOMESTIC CUP 2005/06

FIRST ROUND
(6/8/05)
HSC'21/Brein 1, Stormvogels Telstar 0
Urk 1, FC Omniworld 4
SC Joure 0, Ajax II 2
Harkemase Boys 1, Vitesse 4
Ajax *(Saturday amateurs)* 0, Go Ahead Eagles 4
WKE 1, Cambuur Leeuwarden 4
Quick Boys 0, FC Twente 2 *(aet)*
ACV 1, FC Volendam 3
IJsselmeervogels 1, BV Veendam 3
Turkiyemspor 0, Rijnsburgse Boys 1
EVV 1, FC Dordrecht 4
Westlandia 1, TOP Oss 1 *(aet)*
Nuenen 0, Helmond Sport 8
Kozakken Boys 0, RKC Waalwijk 4
SV Triborgh 0, Roda JC 5
HSV Hoek 0, FC Eindhoven 3
FC Vinkenslag 0, NAC Breda 6
VUC 1, MVV 4 *(aet)*
Caesar/Vos Holding 0, ASWH 5
UDI '19/Beter Bed 0, Capelle 0 *(aet; 4-3 on pens)*
(9/8/05)
Argon 0, Haarlem 1
AFC 0, De Graafschap 2
DCG *(Saturday amateurs)* 0, Heracles Almelo 3
Be Quick 1887 2, AGOVV Apeldoorn 3 *(aet)*
Ter Leede 0, FC Groningen 1
WHC 3, FC Emmen 4 *(aet)*
Nijenrodes 0, FC Zwolle 7
Elinkwijk 0, FC Utrecht 10
ADO '20 1, Excelsior '31 2
Drachtster Boys 0, WSV 3
Excelsior Maassluis 2, FC Den Bosch 1
Schijndel/SBA 0, Sparta Rotterdam 5
OJC Rosmalen 0, VVV Venlo 6
Groesbeekse Boys 0, ADO Den Haag 12
Gemert 2, RBC Roosendaal 1
Sparta '25 0, NEC 7
SHO 0, PSV II 1
Unitas '30 0, Fortuna Sittard 4
NEC *(amateurs)* 1, Excelsior 4
De Treffers / Kegro 2, Baronie 1

N.B. De Graafschap, Heracles Almelo and PSV II all subsequently disqualified for fielding an unregistered player.

SECOND ROUND
(20/9/05)
Ajax II 3, Cambuur Leeuwarden 1
Fortuna Sittard 1, FC Twente 3
FC Emmen 2, UDI '19/Beter Bed 1
RKC Waalwijk 4, TOP Oss 1 *(aet)*
WSV 0, Helmond Sport 2
Excelsior 2, NEC 5
AFC 1, FC Omniworld 1 *(aet)*
FC Dordrecht 3, Gemert 0

Holland

Haarlem 1, MVV 3 *(aet)*
Excelsior Maassluis 1, VVV Venlo 4
FC Volendam 3, BV Veendam 2
(21/9/05)
Vitesse 3, AGOVV 3 *(aet; 2-4 on pens.)*
Roda JC 4, Rijnsburgse Boys 0
HSC '21/Brein 0, FC Eindhoven 2
FC Groningen 2, Sparta 1
ASWH 0, FC Utrecht 4
FC Zwolle 2, NAC Breda 4
De Treffers/Kegro 4, Excelsior '31 0
DCG *(Saturday amateurs)* 1, Go Ahead Eagles 3
ADO Den Haag 11, SHO 1

THIRD ROUND
(25/10/05)
Helmond Sport 1, De Treffers/Kegro 0 *(aet)*
Ajax II 1, AGOVV Apeldoorn 0 *(aet)*
Go Ahead Eagles 0, Roda JC 1
FC Eindhoven 2, FC Emmen 0
AFC 0, MVV 2
FC Dordrecht 0, FC Volendam 4
(26/10/05)
RKC Waalwijk 1, FC Twente 2 *(aet)*
FC Utrecht 1, VVV Venlo 2 *(aet)*
FC Groningen 3, ADO Den Haag 0
NEC 2, NAC Breda 2 *(aet; 5-4 on pens)*

FOURTH ROUND
(20/12/05)
SC Heerenveen 2, VVV Venlo 0
MVV 3, Willem II 1
PSV 3, FC Twente 0
Helmond Sport 2, Ajax II 1
(21/12/05)
AZ 2, NEC 0
Roda JC 1, Feyenoord 0
(22/12/05)
FC Groningen 3, FC Volendam 0
FC Eindhoven 1, Ajax 6

QUARTER-FINALS
(31/1/06)
Helmond Sport 0, Roda JC 2 *(Oper 7, 50)*
AZ 4 *(Landzaat 19, Meerdink 36, 52, Koevermans 70)*, MVV 0
(1/2/06)
FC Groningen 2 *(Nevland 55, Fledderus 87)*, PSV 3 *(Cocu 5, 27, Farfán 25)*
(2/2/06)
SC Heerenveen 0, Ajax 3 *(Rosales 9, Huntelaar 89, Emanuelson 90)*

SEMI-FINALS
(22/3/06)
PSV 2 *(Simons 103, Farfán 119)*, AZ 0 *(aet)*
Ajax 4 *(Huntelaar 90, 109, Babel 94, 106)*, Roda JC 1 *(Oper 61) (aet)*

FINAL
(7/5/06)
Feyenoord Stadium, Rotterdam
AJAX 2 *(Huntelaar 48, 90)*
PSV 1 *(Lamey 53)*
Referee - *Vink*
AJAX - Stekelenburg, Boakye, Heitinga, Vermaelen, Emanuelson, Galásek, Sneijder, Boukhari, Charisteas (Maduro 66), Huntelaar, Rosenberg (Babel 46).
PSV - Gomes, Lamey, Ooijer, Addo, Ball, Afellay (Kone 59), Simons, Cocu, Beasley, Vennegoor of Hesselink, Farfán

SECOND LEVEL FINAL TABLE 2005/06

		Pld	W	D	L	F	A	Pts
1	Excelsior (*4)	38	22	9	7	68	25	75
2	VVV Venlo	38	20	8	10	53	34	68
3	FC Volendam (*1)	38	19	9	10	59	43	66
4	Helmond Sport	38	19	7	12	62	55	64
5	De Graafschap	38	17	11	10	63	51	62
6	FC Emmen	38	18	6	14	68	56	60
7	FC Den Bosch	38	16	11	11	62	51	59
8	Haarlem (*5)	38	17	8	13	57	51	59
9	FC Dordrecht	38	15	11	12	61	45	56
10	AGOVV Apeldoorn (*6)	38	17	5	16	64	62	56
11	TOP Oss (*3)	38	15	10	13	51	53	55
12	FC Zwolle (*2)	38	15	9	14	57	52	54
13	MVV	38	13	12	13	53	52	51
14	BV Veendam	38	14	9	15	54	60	51
15	Cambuur Leeuwarden	38	12	14	12	48	50	50
16	Stormvogels Telstar	38	9	13	16	37	53	40
17	FC Eindhoven	38	11	6	21	53	65	39
18	Go Ahead Eagles	38	8	11	19	45	70	35
19	FC Omniworld	38	7	8	23	50	87	29
20	Fortuna Sittard	38	2	11	25	35	85	17

(*) = period winners.
N.B. Cambuur Leeuwarden – 3 pts deducted.

PROMOTION/RELEGATION PLAY-OFFS
First round
(11/4/06 & 14/4/06)
FC Zwolle 1, Haarlem 1
Haarlem 1, FC Zwolle 3
(FC Zwolle 4-2)

TOP Oss 3, AGOVV Apeldoorn 0
AGOVV Apeldoorn 0, TOP Oss 2
(TOP Oss 5-0)

Second round
(21/4/06 & 24/4/06)
FC Zwolle 2, Willem II 4
Willem II 6, FC Zwolle 2
(Willem II 10-4)

De Graafschap 1, VVV Venlo 1
VVV Venlo 2, De Graafschap 4
(De Graafschap 5-3)

Helmond Sport 0, FC Volendam 1
FC Volendam 2, Helmond Sport 3
(28/4/06)
Helmond Sport 1, FC Volendam 2 *(aet)*

TOP Oss 0, NAC Breda 0
NAC Breda 2, TOP Oss 2
(28/4/06)
TOP Oss 1, NAC Breda 3

Third round
(5/5/06 & 8/5/06)
De Graafschap 0, Willem II 1
Willem II 2, De Graafschap 1
(Willem II 3-1)

FC Volendam 1, NAC Breda 2
NAC Breda 0, FC Volendam 0
(NAC Breda 2-1)

Hungary

Újpest gift title to Debrecen

Debrecen retained the Hungarian title, becoming only the second non-Budapest side to claim back-to-back championship wins (after Rába ETO, 1981-83). But the jubilation felt by the club from Hungary's second city was more than matched by the despair of Újpest FC from the capital, who threw away the chance of their first title since 1998 by wilting under the pressure during the final few weeks.

Debrecen – or Loki, as they are invariably referred to in Hungary – made a terrific start to the season, coming from behind to beat Sopron in the Super Cup and thrashing Croatian champions Hajduk Split 8-0 on aggregate in the Champions League qualifying round. That earned them another qualifying tie against Manchester United, and although they were predictably ousted by the Premiership club, the team's appetite was suitably whetted for their main goal of the season – to retain the Hungarian title.

After the team's failure to reach the Champions League group phase, club owner Gábor Szima was forced to sell off the team's top two scorers from the previous season, Zsombor Kerekes and Igor Bogdanovic, but with coach Attila Supka still expertly pulling the reins, the effect on the team's performance in attack was minimal. They scored two goals in each of their first eight league games, and by the winter break they were still unbeaten, trailing Újpest by a single point.

Storming run

Debrecen's unbeaten record ended in the first game of spring – 2-0 at Zalaegerszeg – but they soon steadied themselves, and despite losing to a late goal at Újpest they finished the campaign with a storming late run, winning all of their last nine games. As their Budapest rivals began to cave in, that surge proved good enough for the champions to make a successful defence of their title.

In many ways the second triumph was better than the first. They accumulated six points more (68 to 62), significantly increased their goal output (69 to 57) and sustained far fewer defeats (two to six). They also remained unbeaten at home, extending that record of invincibility to 25 matches since Supka took charge in November 2004. Most of Loki's best players were those who had also starred the previous season – playmaker Tamás Sándor, midfield do-it-all Péter Halmosi and, after his mid-season return from Turkey, nine-goal Bogdanovic. Of the newcomers, the stand-out player in more ways than one was beanpole Senegalese centre-forward Ibrahima Sidibe. He was a consistent menace to opposition defences all season and finished up as Debrecen's leading marksman on 15 goals – three more than new Croatian striker Bojan Brnovic, who lost his way – and his place to Bogdanovic - in the spring.

Újpest had the NB I's overall top marksman in 22-goal Péter Rajczi, but he would end the season as

NATIONAL TEAM RESULTS 2005/06

Date	Opponent	H/A/N	Venue	Score	Scorers
17/8/05	Argentina	H	Budapest	1-2	Torghelle (29)
3/9/05	Malta (WCQ)	H	Budapest	4-0	Torghelle (35), Said (57og), Takács Á. (65), Rajczi (83)
7/9/05	Sweden (WCQ)	H	Budapest	0-1	
8/10/05	Bulgaria (WCQ)	A	Sofia	0-2	
12/10/05	Croatia (WCQ)	H	Budapest	0-0	
16/11/05	Greece	A	Piraeus	1-2	Kenesei (77p)
14/12/05	Mexico	N	Phoenix	0-2	
18/12/05	Antigua & Barbuda	N	Miami	3-0	Vadócz (10), Feczesin (32), Ferenczi (80)
24/5/06	New Zealand	H	Budapest	2-0	Huszti (48), Szabics (81)
30/5/06	England	A	Manchester	1-3	Dárdai (55)

Hungary

something of a scapegoat for his team's title collapse after being sent off in the first half of their final fixture, against FC Fehérvár.

Red cards were, alas, a feature of Újpest's season. They collected no fewer than 14 in 30 matches (as opposed to Debrecen's three). Against that, they showed great mental strength with their ability to score important late goals – as in both matches against Ferencváros and at home to Debrecen. Unfortunately, the tables were dramatically turned in their penultimate home fixture against MTK. One-nil up in the 89th minute, they conceded twice before the final whistle and had two players sent off. Referee Ferenc Bede had to take defensive action as several Újpest fans ran on the pitch to confront him. The outcome of that ugly incident was a one-match ban on Újpest's stadium. It meant they had to seek alternative accommodation for the vital last game of the season against Fehérvár. Surprisingly they chose the Ferenc Puskás stadium – where they had lost the league title two years previously – and, lo and behold, lightning was to strike in the same place twice. Despite taking the lead, Újpest lost 3-1, and with Debrecen collecting an easy three points at home to relegated Pápa, the provincials ended up three points in the clear.

Successful blend

Újpest's young coach Géza Mészöly (son of ex-national team boss Kálmán Mészöly) was so upset that he decided to quit. That was a pity because he had worked wonders with a team that successfully blended the experience of Hungarian internationals past and present with a group of enthusiastic teenagers. Újpest played attractive attacking football (especially at home) and had some of the club's older supporters making comparisons with the famous free-scoring Újpest Dózsa side of the early 1970s that won seven titles in a row.

Újpest's last-day meltdown was particularly surprising because their opponents, Fehérvár, went into the game with nothing to play for. They were already safe in third place and, better still, had secured a place in the UEFA Cup by winning the Hungarian Cup a couple of weeks earlier. It was the first major trophy in the club's history. The 1985 UEFA Cup runners-up had been in a select company of three clubs (with Birmingham and Alavés) to have reached a European final but never won their domestic championship or national Cup, but a week after Middlesbrough joined that group, the club from Székesfehérvár left it. Although the form-book strongly favoured Aurél Csertöi's side to overcome league strugglers Vasas in the final, they only just prevailed, winning an extended penalty shoot-out after an exciting 2-2 draw. The Cup success capped a best-ever season for the club, rescued from financial ruin thanks to a takeover by former league president László Szieben.

If Vasas had won the Cup, it would have been a unique treble for their coach Attila Pintér, who had steered Ferencváros to the trophy in 2004 and Sopron in 2005. There was worse to come for the Budapest club ten days later when they lost 4-1 away to Kaposvári Rákóczi and were relegated.

Fradi forced out

Or so it seemed. Just four days before the 2006/07 season was about to kick off, Vasas were restored to the top division following the earth-shattering news that Ferencváros, the country's most popular and successful club, had been refused a licence to participate in the NB I because of their perilous financial situation.

'Fradi' had been ever-presents in the Hungarian top flight since 1901, so this was a momentous development. There had been concerns about their ailing finances for some time, and their frailties were all too apparent in 2005/06. The season began disastrously with a UEFA Cup qualifying defeat to Belarussian opposition, and they were close to the relegation zone when coach Csaba László was sacked after leading the team to just two wins in 11 games. Replacement coach Imre Gellei – the former Hungary manager – immediately steadied the ship as Fradi went through their next 11 fixtures without defeat, but having been banned from competing in the Hungarian Cup because of crowd misbehaviour during the previous season's final, their only possible route back into Europe was via the league. After their atrocious start, that was always out of question. They did well in the end to finish sixth, 27 points behind the champions.

It was no surprise that Hungary failed to qualify for the 2006 World Cup. They now enter their third decade without major tournament participation. In the last 20 years their qualifying record has been so poor that only once have they beaten a team that went on to reach the finals (Latvia, Euro 2004).

German legend Lothar Matthäus failed to end the misery and was not offered a new contract. It took several months before his replacement was announced. Several foreign candidates were considered, but in the end new Hungarian FA president István Kisteleki decided to go local and appoint Péter Bozsik, son of the legendary József

Hungary

NATIONAL TEAM APPEARANCES 2005/06

Coach – Lothar MATTHÄUS (GER) /(17/3/06) Péter BOZSIK

Player	DOB	Club	Arg	MLT	SWE	BUL	CRO	Gre	Mex	Atg	Nzl	Eng	Caps	Goals
Gábor KIRÁLY	1/4/76	Crystal Palace (ENG)	G	G	G	G	G	G			G	G	65	-
László BODNÁR	25/2/79	Roda JC (HOL)	D	D	D	D	M	D					31	-
László ÉGER	7/5/77	Debreceni VSC	D		D			D				D	5	-
Roland JUHÁSZ	1/7/83	MTK Budapest	D	D	D46								16	1
Vilmos VANCZÁK	20/6/83	Újpest FC	D87	D	D	D	D		D		D87	s80 s9	14	-
Zoltán BÖÖR	14/8/78	Debreceni VSC	M69	M57	M87		M	M69					21	1
Ákos TAKÁCS	14/2/82	Ferencváros	M	M	M								5	1
Zoltán GERA	22/4/79	West Bromwich Albion (ENG)	M	M76	A						M	M	35	9
Szabolcs HUSZTI	18/4/83	FC Metz (FRA)	M	s57	M	M	M				M84	M	19	5
Péter HALMOSI	25/9/79	Debreceni VSC	M69	M	s87	M46		M				D	9	-
Sándor TORGHELLE	5/5/82	Panathinaikos (GRE)	A69	A69	A	A		A			s84	s62	20	6
Krisztián KENESEI	7/1/77	Györi ETO FC	s69	A				s69					29	9
Tamás PRISKIN	27/9/86	Györi ETO FC	s69						s66		M66		3	-
Zsombor KEREKES	13/9/73	Debreceni VSC	s69		s90	s46							9	2
Norbert TÓTH	11/8/76	Újpest FC	s87										19	1
Tamás HAJNAL	15/3/81	K St.-Truidense VV (BEL)		M	M90	M	M	M90					10	-
Péter RAJCZI	3/4/81	Újpest FC		s69					A59		A46	s84	9	3
Ákos BUZSÁKY	7/5/82	Plymouth Argyle (ENG)		s76		M77	s76						3	-
Gábor GYEPES	26/6/81	Wolverhampton Wanderers (ENG)			s46	D	D	D					22	1
Péter STARK	17/8/78	Györi ETO FC				D	D						19	-
Zoltán BALOG	22/2/78	Ferencváros				D		D46		[	s87		6	-
Zoltán KOVÁCS	24/9/73	Újpest FC				s77	A						20	2
Zsolt BÁRÁNYOS	15/12/75	Vasas					M76						6	-
György KORSÓS	22/8/76	SK Rapid Wien (AUT)					M	M					33	1
Dénes RÓSA	7/4/77	Ferencváros						M	M				10	-
István FERENCZI	14/9/77	Debreceni VSC						s46	s59	s56			8	2
Attila BÖJTE	2/9/76	Újpest FC						s90	[	D			6	-
Balázs RABÓCZKI	9/1/78	FC København (DEN)							G	G85			2	-
Krisztián VERMES	7/7/85	Újpest FC							[	D39			2	-
Ákos KOLLER	4/9/74	FC Fehérvár							M	D87			2	-
Krisztián VADÓCZ	30/5/86	Budapest Honvéd /AJ Auxerre (FRA)							M	M		s83	3	1
Dániel TÖZSÉR	12/5/85	Ferencváros							M66	M			2	-
Róbert FECZESIN	22/2/86	Újpest FC							A71	M80			2	1
Csaba REGEDEI	16/1/83	Györi ETO FC							s71	s39			2	-
Illés SITKU	5/2/78	FC Fehérvár							A56				1	-
Gábor BORI	16/1/84	MTK Budapest							s46				1	-
Árpád MAJOROS	21/12/83	Vasas							s66				1	-
Vince KAPCSOS	15/10/85	Rákospalotai EAC							s80				1	-
Géza VLASZÁK	3/9/73	Újpest FC							s85				5	-
Zoltán TAKÁCS	6/11/83	Budapest Honvéd							s87				1	-
Csaba FEHÉR	2/9/75	Willem II (HOL)									D	D	35	-
Vilmos SEBÖK	13/6/73	Zalaegerszeg									D		53	9
Tamás PETÖ	8/6/74	FC Brussels (BEL)									D80		15	-
Zsolt LÖW	29/4/79	FC Hansa Rostock (GER)									D		19	1
Balázs TÓTH	24/9/81	Malatyaspor (TUR)									M75	M62	12	-
Pál DÁRDAI	16/3/76	Hertha BSC Berlin (GER)									M	M	44	4
Balázs MOLNÁR	1/7/77	Zalaegerszeg									M	M83	10	-
Imre SZABICS	22/3/81	1.FC Köln (GER)									A84	A73	18	9
Attila POLONKAI	12/6/79	Rákospalotai EAC									s75	s73	3	-
Ádám KOMLÓSI	6/12/77	Debreceni VSC										D9	8	-

Hungary

Bozsik, right-half of the world-famous Magical Magyars side of the 1950s. Bozsik junior, whose Zalaegerszeg side played Manchester United in the 2002/03 Champions League qualifiers (and beat them in Budapest), returned to Old Trafford for one of his first games in charge. The original invitation from England had been for Hungary to become the team's first opponents at the new Wembley Stadium. But with that white elephant still under construction, Bozsik took a new-look team to Manchester, where they showed plenty of promise in a 3-1 defeat.

EUROPEAN CUPS 2005/06

UEFA CHAMPIONS LEAGUE

DEBRECENI VSC
2nd qualifying round HAJDUK SPLIT (CRO)
H 3-0 *Bogdanovic (26, 40), Kerekes (58)*
Csernyánszki, Nikolov, Máté, Éger, Szatmári, Dombi, Habi (Kiss 62), Sándor, Halmosi, Kerekes (Bernáth 71), Bogdanovic (Brnovic 79).
A 5-0 *Halmosi (1, 27), Kerekes (22), Sidibe (75), Kiss (90)*
Csernyánszki, Nikolov, Éger, Máté, Szatmári, Dombi, Vukmir, Sándor, Halmosi (Böör 76), Kerekes (Sidibe 57), Bogdanovic (Kiss 56).

3rd qualifying round MANCHESTER UNITED (ENG)
A 0-3
Csernyánszki, Nikolov, Éger, Máté, Szatmári, Dombi (Böör 85), Vukmir, Sándor, Halmosi, Kerekes (Sidibe 52), Bogdanovic (Kiss 60).
H 0-3
Csernyánszki, Éger, Máté, Vukmir, Dombi (Szatmári 56), Sándor, Kiss, Böör (Madar 77), Halmosi, Kerekes, Bogdanovic (Brnovic 46).

UEFA CUP

FC SOPRON
2nd qualifying round METALURG DONETSK (UKR)
H 0-3
Balogh, Bagoly (Horváth 53), Ibric, Costisor, Hanák, Fehér (Luca 68), Vén, Lazic, Cotan, Demjén, Fülöp (Csordás 56).
A 1-2 *Florea (88og)*
Balogh, Bagoly, Ibric, Costisor, Hanák, Fehér (Györi 58), Lazic, Cotan, Demjén (Sira 64), Fülöp (Cigan 79), Csordás.

FERENCVÁROS
2nd qualifying round MTZ-RIPO MINSK (BLS)
H 0-2
Udvarácz, Bognár (Csepregi 78), Balog, Budovinszky, Grósz, Gyepes, Takács, Rósa, Tözsér (Eros 65), Bajevski (Bartha 79), Laczkó.
A 2-1 *Lipcsei (45), Rósa (90)*
Udvarácz, Takács (Szalai 78), Budovinszky, Tímár, Balog, Rósa, Keller (Nógrádi 72), Lipcsei, Tözsér, Bajevski, Laczkó (Csurka 90).

DEBRECENI VSC
1st round SHAKHTAR DONETSK (UKR)
A 1-4 *Sidibe (89)*
Csernyánszki, Bernáth, Éger, Komlósi, Szatmári, Dombi (Sidibe 46), Kiss, Sándor, Nikolov (Mészáros 46), Halmosi, Brnovic.
H 0-2
Csernyánszki, Bernáth, Éger, Máté, Nikolov (Jeremiás 68), Mészáros (Madar 54), Virág, Dzsudzsák (Szatmári 54), Halmosi, Kiss, Sidibe.

TOP GOALSCORERS 2005/06

- 22 Péter RAJCZI (Újpest FC)
- 19 Tibor MÁRKUS (FC Tatabánya)
- 18 József KANTA (MTK Budapest)
- 15 Ibrahima SIDIBE (Debreceni VSC)
- 14 Illés SITKU (FC Fehérvár)
- 13 Zoltán KOVÁCS (Újpest FC)
- 12 Bojan BRNOVIC (Debreceni VSC)
  Ádám HREPKA (MTK Budapest)
- 11 Ferenc HORVÁTH (Diósgyöri VTK/FC Fehérvár)
  Zoltán JOVÁNCZAI (Ferencváros)
  András HORVÁTH (FC Sopron)
  Tamás PRISKIN (Györi ETO FC)
  ALVES (Budapest-Honvéd/Kaposvári Rákóczi FC)
  Szabolcs GYÁNÓ (Vasas)
  Vilmos SEBÖK (Zalaegerszeg)

LEAGUE RESULTS/ SCORERS/APPEARANCES/ GOALS 2005/06

BUDAPEST-HONVÉD
Coach – Aldo Dolcetti (ITA)

2005				
30/7	FC Sopron	a	1-1	Vadócz (p)
7/8	Ferencváros	h	3-1	Alves 3
21/8	FC Fehérvár	a	0-3	
27/8	Lombard Pápa TFC	a	2-2	Csobánki, Genito
17/9	Zalaegerszeg	h	4-0	Dancs, Miro, Takács, Alves (p)
24/9	Kaposvári Rákóczi FC	a	0-0	
15/10	Györi ETO FC	a	2-1	Miro, Takács
22/10	Újpest FC	h	1-0	Takács
29/10	Diósgyöri VTK	a	0-1	
5/11	Vasas	h	2-2	Takács (p), Kovács Z.
19/11	Rákospalotai EAC	a	3-1	Alves (p), Miro, Dobos
26/11	Pécsi MFC	h	1-1	Dobos
29/11	MTK Budapest	h	2-2	Miro, Alves
3/12	Debreceni VSC	a	1-6	Dobos (p)
10/12	FC Tatabánya	h	1-3	Venczel
2006				
25/2	FC Sopron	h	0-3	
18/3	Lombard Pápa TFC	h	1-0	Bozori
25/3	Zalaegerszeg	a	0-0	
1/4	Kaposvári Rákóczi FC	h	0-2	
7/4	MTK Budapest	a	0-0	
15/4	Györi ETO FC	h	3-2	Dobos 2, Genito
12/4	Ferencváros	a	1-3	Schrancz
19/4	FC Fehérvár	h	1-1	Schrancz
22/4	Újpest FC	a	0-7	
29/4	Diósgyöri VTK	h	0-1	
5/5	Vasas	a	2-1	Csobánki, Dancs
13/5	Rákospalotai EAC	h	1-3	Baranyai
20/5	Pécsi MFC	a	0-1	
26/5	Debreceni VSC	h	0-1	
3/6	FC Tatabánya	a	1-3	Csobánki

No	Name	Nat	Pos	Aps	(s)	Gls
13	André ALVES	BRA	A	12	(2)	6

Hungary

FINAL LEAGUE TABLE 2005/06

		Pld	Home W	D	L	F	A	Away W	D	L	F	A	Total W	D	L	F	A	Pts
1	Debreceni VSC	30	11	4	0	41	15	9	4	2	28	19	20	8	2	69	34	68
2	Újpest FC	30	12	1	2	47	18	8	4	3	27	19	20	5	5	74	37	65
3	FC Fehérvár	30	10	4	1	31	11	9	3	3	21	13	19	7	4	52	24	64
4	MTK Budapest	30	10	2	3	37	15	8	4	3	28	18	18	6	6	65	33	60
5	FC Tatabánya	30	6	5	4	27	20	5	3	7	19	25	11	8	11	46	45	41
6	Ferencváros	30	6	5	4	23	18	4	6	5	20	20	10	11	9	43	38	41
7	Kaposvári Rákóczi FC	30	6	5	4	20	15	4	2	9	15	26	10	7	13	35	41	37
8	Diósgyőri VTK	30	5	6	4	17	13	5	1	9	16	31	10	7	13	33	44	37
9	Győri ETO FC	30	5	4	6	26	24	4	5	6	21	26	9	9	12	47	50	36
10	FC Sopron	30	7	4	4	22	14	2	4	9	17	25	9	8	13	39	39	35
11	Zalaegerszeg	30	7	4	4	29	17	2	4	9	13	30	9	8	13	42	47	35
12	Pécsi MFC	30	7	4	4	23	10	1	5	9	14	31	8	9	13	37	41	33
13	Budapest-Honvéd	30	5	4	6	20	22	3	5	7	13	30	8	9	13	33	52	33
14	Rákospalotai EAC	30	3	2	10	14	28	4	3	8	16	31	7	5	18	30	59	26
15	Vasas	30	3	5	7	16	20	2	5	8	16	27	5	10	15	32	47	25
16	Lombard Pápa TFC	30	4	3	8	19	35	1	4	10	11	41	5	7	18	30	76	22

No	Name	Nat	Pos	Aps	(s)	Gls
26	Tibor BARANYAI		D	22		1
29	Angouna BENJÁMIN	CIV	D	5		
8	László BOJTOR		A	1	(3)	
7	István BORGULYA		A		(1)	
23	Balázs BOZORI		A	7	(3)	1
17	Boján BOZSOVICS	SCG	A		(3)	
18	Ádám CSOBÁNKI		A	19	(2)	3
5	Roland DANCS		M	25	(2)	2
15	András DEBRECENI		D	2	(1)	
9	Attila DOBOS		M	21	(7)	5
	ERDEI		M		(1)	
16	Fredy ERIC	CMR	A	5		
23	Eugeno GENITO	MOZ	M	22	(4)	2
	Ferenc KOCSIS		A		(3)	
27	Norbert KOVÁCS		D	24	(1)	
3	Zoltán KOVÁCS		D	13	(3)	1
	István LANTOS		A	2	(5)	
12	Zsolt LÁZÁR		M	13	(3)	
14	Attila MÉSZÁROS		D	6	(3)	
2	Almiro MIRO	MOZ	M	15	(6)	4
29	Zoltán MISKI		G	3	(1)	
6	Tibor POMPER		M	7	(6)	
21	Richárd RÁTHY		G	3		
8	Balázs SCHRANCZ		M	12		2
	Levente SCHULTZ		A	1	(2)	
20	Zoltán TAKÁCS		D	25		4
16	Abdou TANGARA	FRA	A		(1)	
1	Iván TÓTH		G	24		
	János TÖKÉS		D	2	(1)	
4	Szabolcs UDVARI		D	23	(1)	
6	Krisztián VADÓCZ		M	3		1
11	Balázs VENCZEL		A	7	(7)	1
19	Andoa YANNICK	CMR	M	1	(3)	
24	Norbert ZANA		M	5	(9)	

DEBRECENI VSC
Coach – Attila Supka

2005
30/7	Zalaegerszeg	h	2-1	Sidibe, Bogdanovic
20/8	MTK Budapest	h	2-2	Bogdanovic, Sándor
28/8	Győri ETO FC	a	2-1	Bogdanovic, Brnovic
19/9	Újpest FC	h	2-2	Máté, Brnovic
24/9	Diósgyőri VTK	h	2-0	Virág, Kiss
3/10	Vasas	h	2-2	Sidibe, Brnovic
15/10	Rákospalotai EAC	a	2-1	Máté, Sándor
19/10	Kaposvári Rákóczi FC	a	2-1	og (Pintér), Sidibe
24/10	Pécsi MFC	h	3-1	Sidibe, Brnovic, Ferenczi
30/10	FC Fehérvár	h	2-0	Brnovic, Halmosi
6/11	FC Tatabánya	a	3-3	Halmosi, Ferenczi (p), Kiss
19/11	FC Sopron	h	3-1	Sidibe, Halmosi, Brnovic (p)
27/11	Ferencváros	a	0-0	
3/12	Budapest-Honvéd	h	6-1	Brnovic, og (Kovács N.), Sidibe 2 (1p), Ferenczi 2
10/12	Lombard Pápa TFC	a	3-3	Brnovic, Sidibe, Ferenczi (p)

2006
24/2	Zalaegerszeg	a	0-2	
4/3	Kaposvári Rákóczi FC	h	2-1	Bogdanovic, Éger (p)
12/3	MTK Budapest	a	4-2	Sidibe 2, Bogdanovic, Éger
19/3	Győri ETO FC	h	1-1	Sidibe (p)
26/3	Újpest FC	a	1-2	Nikolov
1/4	Diósgyőri VTK	a	3-3	Sándor, Dzsudzsák, Bogdanovic
8/4	Vasas	a	1-0	Máté
14/4	Rákospalotai EAC	h	6-1	Halmosi 2, Brnovic 3, og (Horváth G.)
22/4	Pécsi MFC	a	2-0	Sidibe 2 (1p)
30/4	FC Fehérvár	a	2-1	Sándor, Máté
6/5	FC Tatabánya	h	1-0	Bogdanovic
13/5	FC Sopron	a	2-0	Sidibe, Halmosi
21/5	Ferencváros	h	3-1	Máté, Dzsudzsák, Sidibe (p)
26/5	Budapest-Honvéd	a	1-0	Bogdanovic (p)
2/6	Lombard Pápa TFC	h	4-1	Sándor, Brnovic, Halmosi, Bogdanovic

No	Name	Nat	Pos	Aps	(s)	Gls
22	Csaba BERNÁTH		D	21	(1)	
10	Igor BOGDANOVIC	SCG	A	14	(3)	9
81	Zoltán BÖÖR		M	3	(7)	
11	Bojan BRNOVIC	CRO	A	15	(10)	12
24	Norbert CSERNYÁNSZKI		G	27		
7	Tibor DOMBI		M	22	(4)	
19	Balázs DZSUDZSÁK		M	4	(6)	2
73	László ÉGER		D	21		2
31	István FERENCZI		A	3	(8)	5
28	Péter HALMOSI		M	26		7
14	Gyula HEGEDÜS		D	1	(3)	
13	Franciel HENGEMÜHLE	BRA	A		(1)	
	Georgi HRISZTOV		A		(2)	

Hungary

No	Name		Nat	Pos	Aps	(s)	Gls
20	Gergö JEREMIÁS			M		(3)	
18	Zsombor KEREKES			A		(1)	
30	Zoltán KISS			M	14	(4)	2
16	Ádám KOMLÓSI			D	15	(2)	
8	Csaba MADAR			M	8	(16)	
2	Péter MÁTÉ			D	24	(1)	5
17	Norbert MÉSZÁROS			M	6	(3)	
25	Balázs NIKOLOV			D	5	(2)	1
9	Tamás SÁNDOR			M	27		5
26	Ibrahima SIDIBE		SEN	A	27	(1)	15
23	Ottó SZABÓ		SVK	M	5	(1)	
3	Csaba SZATMÁRI			D	20		
1	Sandro TOMIC		CRO	G	3		
6	Béla VIRÁG			M	10	(6)	1
5	Dragan VUKMIR		SCG	D	9	(3)	

DIÓSGYÖRI VTK
Coach – György Gálhidi; (23/9/05) Zoran Kuntic (SCG); (21/10/05) János Pajkos

2005
31/7	Újpest FC	h	0-1		
6/8	FC Fehérvár	h	1-0	Horváth (p)	
21/8	Vasas	a	0-2		
28/8	Rákospalotai EAC	a	2-0	Horváth, Tisza	
17/9	Pécsi MFC	a	0-5		
24/9	Debreceni VSC	a	0-2		
1/10	FC Tatabánya	a	1-2	Horváth	
15/10	FC Sopron	h	1-1	Gáspár	
21/10	Ferencváros	a	1-1	Tisza	
29/10	Budapest-Honvéd	h	1-0	Horváth	
5/11	Lombard Pápa TFC	a	3-1	Horváth, Tisza 2 (1p)	
19/11	Zalaegerszeg	h	3-0	Horváth (p), Vitelki, Sipeki	
26/11	Kaposvári Rákóczi FC	a	3-1	Horváth, Vitelki, Tisza	
3/12	MTK Budapest	h	0-0		
10/12	Györi ETO FC	a	2-1	Katona, Horváth	

2006
25/2	Újpest FC	a	2-3	Elek, Sipeki	
3/3	FC Fehérvár	a	0-5		
11/3	Vasas	h	0-2		
18/3	Rákospalotai EAC	h	1-1	Szögedi	
25/3	Pécsi MFC	h	0-0		
1/4	Debreceni VSC	h	3-3	Sipeki 2, og (Máté)	
8/4	FC Tatabánya	h	1-0	Binder	
15/4	FC Sopron	a	1-2	Binder	
23/4	Ferencváros	h	0-1		
29/4	Budapest-Honvéd	a	1-0	Binder	
6/5	Lombard Pápa TFC	h	0-1		
13/5	Zalaegerszeg	a	0-2		
19/5	Kaposvári Rákóczi FC	h	5-2	Sipeki 2, Binder 2, Jeremiás	
27/5	MTK Budapest	a	0-4		
3/6	Györi ETO FC	h	1-1	Katona	

No	Name	Nat	Pos	Aps	(s)	Gls
6	László ALMÁSI		D	3	(1)	
29	Gergely BALÁS		A	6	(2)	
1	Krisztián BERKI		G	2	(1)	
5	Ciprian BINDER	ROM	A	22	(6)	5
3	Ciprian DIANU	ROM	D	1		
3	Norbert ELEK		D	15		1
22	Milán FAGGYAS		A		(3)	
26	Norbert FARKAS		M	22	(6)	
14	Viktor FARKAS		D	27	(1)	
4	Marcell FODOR	SVK	D	2	(7)	
30	József GÁSPÁR	SVK	D	13		1
16	Tibor HALGAS		M	13	(9)	
9	Ferenc HORVÁTH		A	13		8
20	Gergö JEREMIÁS		M	11	(3)	1
81	Attila KATONA		M	22	(3)	2
66	István KÖVESFALVI		G	16		

No	Name		Nat	Pos	Aps	(s)	Gls
21	Balázs KRAJNC			M		(1)	
19	Norbert LIPUSZ			M	1	(8)	
9	László LÖRINCZ			A		(3)	
2	József MOGYORÓSI			D	15	(6)	
22	Gábor MOGYORÓSI			M	7		
67	Zoltán PINTÉR			M	9		
7	Marius SIMINIC		ROM	A	2	(6)	
7	Attila SIMON			M	3	(3)	
23	István SIPEKI			M	29		6
25	Pál SZALMA			G	12		
10	Szilárd SZÖGEDI			M	13	(1)	1
10	Tibor TISZA			A	14		5
18	Péter URBIN			A	3	(6)	
13	Csaba VÁMOSI			D	7	(4)	
8	Zoltán VITELKI			M	27		2

FC FEHÉRVÁR
Coach – Aurél Csertöi

2005
31/7	Ferencváros	a	1-0	Györök	
6/8	Diósgyöri VTK	a	0-1		
21/8	Budapest-Honvéd	h	3-0	Bozic, Disztl, Farkas	
27/8	Vasas	a	3-0	Csizmadia, Koller, Alumona	
17/9	Lombard Pápa TFC	h	2-1	Farkas, Vincze	
24/9	Rákospalotai EAC	a	2-1	Sitku 2	
1/10	Zalaegerszeg	h	1-0	Kuttor	
15/10	Pécsi MFC	a	2-0	Koller, Sitku	
22/10	Kaposvári Rákóczi FC	h	3-0	Farkas, Bozic 2	
30/10	Debreceni VSC	a	0-2		
5/11	MTK Budapest	h	1-0	Csizmadia (p)	
20/11	FC Tatabánya	a	1-0	og (Németh K.)	
26/11	Györi ETO FC	h	2-2	Sitku 2	
3/12	FC Sopron	a	1-1	Simek	
11/12	Újpest FC	h	1-1	Simek	

2006
26/2	Ferencváros	h	1-1	Lattenstein	
3/3	Diósgyöri VTK	h	5-0	Dvéri, Sitku 2 (1p), Györök, Lattenstein	
18/3	Vasas	h	1-0	Bozic	
25/3	Lombard Pápa TFC	a	2-0	Sitku 2 (1p)	
31/3	Rákospalotai EAC	h	3-1	Sitku 2, Csizmadia	
8/4	Zalaegerszeg	a	1-1	Alumona	
15/4	Pécsi MFC	h	1-0	Dvéri	
19/4	Budapest-Honvéd	a	1-1	Nagy	
22/4	Kaposvári Rákóczi FC	a	0-3		
30/4	Debreceni VSC	h	1-2	Csizmadia	
6/5	MTK Budapest	a	1-0	Horváth F.	
13/5	FC Tatabánya	h	4-1	Sitku, Kuttor, Csizmadia (p), Schwarcz	
20/5	Györi ETO FC	a	3-2	Bozic 2, Horváth F.	
27/5	FC Sopron	h	2-2	Sitku 2 (1p)	
3/6	Újpest FC	a	3-1	Csizmadia, Nagy, Horváth F.	

No	Name	Nat	Pos	Aps	(s)	Gls
11	Alex S. ALUMONA	NGA	A	15	(7)	2
21	József BARTYIK		M		(8)	
20	Mario BOZIC	SCG	M	23	(5)	6
85	Csaba CSIZMADIA		D	28		6
21	Jusuf DAJIC	BOS	A	4	(8)	
99	Dávid DISZTL		A	1	(7)	1
10	Zsolt DVÉRI		M	11	(1)	2
14	Balázs FARKAS		M	21	(3)	3
3	Zsolt FEHÉR		D	3	(3)	
5	Balázs GYÖRÖK		M	21	(2)	2
18	Ferenc HORVÁTH		A		(4)	3
33	Gábor HORVÁTH		D	12	(2)	
13	Gábor KOCSIS		A	4	(5)	
17	Ákos KOLLER		D	24	(1)	2
77	Attila KUTTOR		D	29		2

Hungary

8	Norbert LATTENSTEIN		M	18	(6)	2
7	József MAGASFÖLDI		A	1		
22	Dániel NAGY		M	4	(11)	2
6	Zoltán SCHWARCZ		M	23	(1)	1
12	Zsolt SEBÖK		G	1		
10	Péter SIMEK		M	5	(3)	2
24	Attila SIMON		M	1	(2)	
9	Illés SITKU		A	28		14
30	Daniel TUDOR	ROM	G	29		
24	Viktor VADÁSZ		D		(1)	
25	Zoltán VINCZE		D	24	(4)	1

FERENCVÁROS
Coach – Csaba László; (10/11/05) Imre Gellei

2005				
31/7	FC Fehérvár	h	0-1	
7/8	Budapest-Honvéd	a	1-3	Tímár
21/8	Lombard Pápa TFC	h	3-3	Jovánczai, og (Mutica), Rósa
27/8	Zalaegerszeg	a	2-3	Lipcsei, Budovinszky
17/9	Kaposvári Rákóczi FC	h	1-1	Laczkó
25/9	MTK Budapest	a	2-2	Tözsér, Rósa (p)
2/10	Györi ETO FC	h	2-0	Nógrádi, Laczkó
16/10	Újpest FC	a	1-2	og (Böjte)
21/10	Diósgyöri VTK	h	1-1	Jovánczai
29/10	Vasas	a	1-0	Rósa (p)
5/11	Rákospalotai EAC	h	0-2	
19/11	Pécsi MFC	a	0-0	
27/11	Debreceni VSC	h	0-0	
4/12	FC Tatabánya	a	3-2	Tímár, Jovánczai, Szalai
10/12	FC Sopron	h	1-0	Balog
2006				
26/2	FC Fehérvár	a	1-1	Tímár
10/3	Lombard Pápa TFC	a	5-1	Laczkó, Bajevski, Lipcsei (p), Jovánczai 2
17/3	Zalaegerszeg	h	2-2	Jovánczai 2 (2p)
25/3	Kaposvári Rákóczi FC	a	0-0	
2/4	MTK Budapest	h	1-0	Lipcsei (p)
9/4	Györi ETO FC	a	1-1	Tözsér (p)
12/4	Budapest-Honvéd	h	3-1	Jovánczai, Balog, Lipcsei (p)
16/4	Újpest FC	h	1-2	Lipcsei (p)
23/4	Diósgyöri VTK	a	1-0	Bajevski
29/4	Vasas	h	3-1	Bajevski, Botís, Jovánczai
6/5	Rákospalotai EAC	a	0-1	
12/5	Pécsi MFC	h	3-1	Jovánczai 2, Lipcsei
21/5	Debreceni VSC	a	1-3	Lipcsei (p)
27/5	FC Tatabánya	h	2-3	Lipcsei, Bajevski
2/6	FC Sopron	a	1-1	Bajevski

No	Name	Nat	Pos	Aps	(s)	Gls
9	Aleksandar BAJEVSKI	MAC	A	11	(9)	5
78	Zoltán BALOG		D	23		2
15	László BARTHA		A	4	(8)	
31	János BÉRESS		M		(1)	
19	Zsolt BOGNÁR		D	21	(1)	
33	Csaba BORBÉLY	ROM	M	4	(1)	
32	Sorin BOTIS	ROM	D	22	(1)	1
89	László BRETTSCHNEIDER		M		(1)	
17	Krisztián BUDOVINSZKY		D	12	(3)	1
27	Richárd CSEPREGI		M	10	(6)	
13	Zoltán CSURKA		D	3	(2)	
11	Gábor ERÖS		M	4	(9)	
87	László FITOS		M	7	(5)	
7	Dávid HORVÁTH		A		(3)	
42	Zoltán JOVÁNCZAI		A	20	(7)	11
4	József KELLER		D	1		
2	Szabolcs KEMENES		G	15		
18	Zsolt LACZKÓ		M	24	(4)	3
8	Bojan LAZIC	SCG	M	9	(1)	.

10	LEANDRO de Almeida		M	15		
6	Péter LIPCSEI		M	26		8
8	Árpád NÓGRÁDI		A	3	(4)	1
20	Dénes RÓSA		M	14		3
14	Tamás SZALAI		M	10	(7)	1
16	Zsolt SZÁLKA		D	2	(2)	
22	Lajos SZÜCS		G	15		
3	Ákos TAKÁCS		D	8	(4)	
5	Krisztián TIMÁR		D	21	(2)	3
88	Dániel TÖZSÉR		M	26		2

GYÖRI ETO FC
Coach – István Reszeli Soós; (1/1/06) János Csank

2005				
30/7	Vasas	a	2-1	Priskin 2
6/8	Rákospalotai EAC	h	2-2	Kenesei, Bajzát
20/8	Pécsi MFC	a	1-0	Vincze (p)
28/8	Debreceni VSC	h	1-2	og (Sidibe)
18/9	FC Tatabánya	a	3-3	Priskin 3
24/9	FC Sopron	h	2-1	Vincze (p), Kenesei
2/10	Ferencváros	a	0-2	
15/10	Budapest-Honvéd	h	1-2	Kenesei
22/10	Lombard Pápa TFC	a	4-1	Kenesei 2, Vincze 2
29/10	Zalaegerszeg	h	2-1	Kenesei, Priskin
5/11	Kaposvári Rákóczi FC	a	0-1	
19/11	MTK Budapest	h	1-3	Vincze (p)
26/11	FC Fehérvár	a	2-2	Kenesei 2
4/12	Újpest FC	h	1-3	Mátyus
10/12	Diósgyöri VTK	h	1-2	Granát
2006				
25/2	Vasas	h	2-1	Vincze, Mátyus
4/3	Rákospalotai EAC	a	2-1	Priskin, Vincze (p)
11/3	Pécsi MFC	h	1-1	Priskin
19/3	Debreceni VSC	a	1-1	Bajzát
24/3	FC Tatabánya	h	0-0	
1/4	FC Sopron	a	0-2	
9/4	Ferencváros	h	1-1	Bajzát
15/4	Budapest-Honvéd	a	2-3	Vincze, Priskin
22/4	Lombard Pápa TFC	a	4-0	Priskin 2, Mátyus (p), Bajzát
29/4	Zalaegerszeg	a	0-0	
6/5	Kaposvári Rákóczi FC	h	4-0	Bajzát 2, Granát 2
13/5	MTK Budapest	a	2-5	Bajzát, Granát
20/5	FC Fehérvár	h	2-3	Granát, Hanák
28/5	Újpest FC	h	2-5	Vincze, Szabó
3/6	Diósgyöri VTK	a	1-1	Szabó

No	Name	Nat	Pos	Aps	(s)	Gls
19	Péter BAJZÁT		A	16	(7)	7
5	István BANK		M	13		
23	Károly CZANIK		M	1	(8)	
16	Balázs GRANÁT		A	5	(2)	5
3	Viktor HANÁK		D	15		1
7	Tibor HEGEDÜS		M	2	(6)	
6	Róbert HORVÁTH		D	10		
12	Antal JÄKL		M	28	(1)	
9	Krisztián KENESEI		A	15		8
9	Dávid LAJTOS		M	7		
27	Miklós LENDVAI		M	12	(1)	
21	Zsolt MAKRA		D	7	(6)	
17	János MÁTYUS		D	21		3
18	Darko PERIC	CRO	A	6	(4)	
30	Tamás PRISKIN		A	22	(3)	11
14	Olivér PUSZTAI		D	7	(3)	
8	Csaba REGEDEI		D	22	(3)	
24	Csaba SOMOGYI		G		(1)	
32	Péter STARK		D	10		
25	Sasa STEVANOVIC	SCG	G	30		
25	Zsolt SZABÓ		A	3	(5)	2
15	Péter TÓTH		M	14	(4)	

Hungary

No	Name			Nat	Pos	Aps	(s)	Gls
18	Gábor VARGA				A	4	(3)	
6	Róbert VARGA				M	6	(3)	
11	Zoltán VARGA				M	9	(11)	
	Zoltán VASAS				D		(1)	
10	Ottó VINCZE				M	25	(1)	9
2	József ZSÓK				D	20	(5)	

KAPOSVÁRI RÁKÓCZI FC
Coach – László Prukner

2005
30/7	Pécsi MFC	a	1-2	Szakály P.
20/8	FC Tatabánya	a	0-1	
28/8	FC Sopron	h	2-0	Zsolnai, Máté
17/9	Ferencváros	a	1-1	Nagypál
24/9	Budapest-Honvéd	h	0-0	
1/10	Lombard Pápa TFC	a	0-0	
15/10	Zalaegerszeg	h	1-1	Zarovecz (p)
19/10	Debreceni VSC	h	1-2	Zsolnai
22/10	FC Fehérvár	a	0-3	
29/10	MTK Budapest	a	1-2	Szakály P.
5/11	Győri ETO FC	h	1-0	Kardos
19/11	Újpest FC	a	1-4	Zahorecz (p)
26/11	Diósgyőri VTK	h	1-3	Zsolnai
3/12	Vasas	a	2-0	Oláh, Zsolnai
10/12	Rákospalotai EAC	h	1-0	Oláh

2006
25/2	Pécsi MFC	h	2-2	Vasiljevic, Zsolnai
4/3	Debreceni VSC	a	1-2	Szakály P.
11/3	FC Tatabánya	h	1-1	Zsolnai
18/3	FC Sopron	a	0-2	
25/3	Ferencváros	h	0-0	
1/4	Budapest-Honvéd	a	2-0	Zsolnai, Zahorecz
8/4	Lombard Pápa TFC	h	1-0	Alves
15/4	Zalaegerszeg	a	1-0	Zahorecz (p)
22/4	FC Fehérvár	h	3-0	Alves, Zahorecz (p), Oláh
29/4	MTK Budapest	h	1-3	Oláh
6/5	Győri ETO FC	a	0-4	
14/5	Újpest FC	h	1-2	Alves
19/5	Diósgyőri VTK	a	2-5	Oláh 2
27/5	Vasas	h	4-1	Vasiljevic, Kriston 2, Alves
3/6	Rákospalotai EAC	a	3-0	Alves, Zsolnai, Pintér

No	Name	Nat	Pos	Aps	(s)	Gls
9	André ALVES	BRA	A	13	(1)	5
11	Attila ANDRUSKÓ	SCG	M	19	(7)	1
1	Szabolcs BALAJCZA		G	30		
24	István BANK		M	12		
18	Zoltán FINTA		D	5	(3)	
7	Károly GALGÓCZI		A		(1)	
19	Máté HALMOS		M		(2)	
20	Tibor HEGEDÜS		D	5	(4)	
8	Ernő KARDOS		M	6	(11)	1
21	Krisztián KOLLEGA		A		(2)	
6	Róbert KOVÁCSEVICS		D	18	(3)	
7	Ladislav KOZMÉR	SVK	D	11		
20	Attila KRISTON		M	13	(1)	2
25	Béla MARÓTI		M		(12)	
16	Péter MÁTÉ		M	27		
13	Tamás MEZÖ		D	15	(1)	
10	Tibor NAGYPÁL		M	11	(2)	1
14	Lóránt OLÁH	SCG	A	20	(3)	6
17	Viktor PETRÓK		D	28	(1)	
3	Attila PINTÉR		D	13	(5)	1
27	Dénes SZAKÁLY		M	9	(10)	
5	Péter SZAKÁLY		M	4	(2)	3
26	Péter TEREÁNSZKITÓTH		M	5	(10)	
22	Dusan VASILJEVIC	SCG	M	11	(5)	2
28	Krisztián ZAHORECZ		D	27		5
15	Róbert ZSOLNAI		A	28	(1)	8

MTK BUDAPEST
Coach – József Garami

2005
30/7	Rákospalotai EAC	a	2-1	Kanta, Czvitkovics
6/8	Pécsi MFC	h	2-0	Lambulic, Illés
20/8	Debreceni VSC	a	2-2	Kanta, Bonifert
27/8	FC Tatabánya	h	1-0	Illés
17/9	FC Sopron	a	3-0	Czvitkovics, Hrepka 2
25/9	Ferencváros	h	2-2	Hrepka, Kanta (p)
15/10	Lombard Pápa TFC	h	7-0	Kanta 2 (1p), og (Mutica), Balogh, Lambulic, Bori, Czvitkovics
24/10	Zalaegerszeg	a	4-3	Hrepka 2, Czvitkovics, Bori
29/10	Kaposvári Rákóczi FC	h	2-1	Illés, og (Petrók)
5/11	FC Fehérvár	a	0-1	
19/11	Győri ETO FC	a	3-1	Kanta 2 (1p), Balogh
26/11	Újpest FC	h	0-2	
29/11	Budapest-Honvéd	a	2-2	Kanta (p), Lambulic
3/12	Diósgyőri VTK	a	0-0	
10/12	Vasas	h	3-0	Hrepka 2, Balogh

2006
25/2	Rákospalotai EAC	h	1-0	Németh
4/3	Pécsi MFC	a	2-2	Bonifert, Balogh
12/3	Debreceni VSC	h	2-4	Hrepka, Czvitkovics
18/3	FC Tatabánya	a	1-0	Hrepka
25/3	FC Sopron	h	2-0	Zabos 2 (1p)
2/4	Ferencváros	a	0-1	
7/4	Budapest-Honvéd	h	0-0	
15/4	Lombard Pápa TFC	a	3-1	Czvitkovics, Lambulic, Hrepka
22/4	Zalaegerszeg	h	6-3	Kanta 3 (2p), Czvitkovics 2, Horváth
29/4	Kaposvári Rákóczi FC	a	3-1	Czvitkovics, Kanta, Hrepka
6/5	FC Fehérvár	h	0-1	
13/5	Győri ETO FC	h	5-2	Kanta 3, og (Regedei), Németh
20/5	Újpest FC	a	2-1	Kanta, Lambulic
27/5	Diósgyőri VTK	h	4-0	Czvitkovics, Kanta 2, Illés
3/6	Vasas	a	1-2	Hrepka

No	Name	Nat	Pos	Aps	(s)	Gls
5	Béla BALOGH		D	25		4
16	Péter BONIFERT		M	4	(6)	2
21	Gábor BORI		M	29		2
7	Péter CZVITKOVICS		M	30		10
	Dániel HAUSER		D	1	(1)	
15	Levente HORVÁTH		M	14	(9)	1
13	Ádám HREPKA		A	24	(1)	12
4	Goran JEZDIMIROVIC	SCG	M	18		
23	Roland JUHÁSZ		D	4		
10	Béla ILLÉS		A		(26)	4
19	József KANTA		A	24		18
2	Miso KOLJENOVIC	SCG	M	2		
18	Ladislav KOZMER	SVK	M		(2)	
20	Mladen LAMBULIC	SCG	D	29		5
30	Roland LIPCSEI		M	4	(5)	
18	Krisztián NÉMETH		A	4	(7)	2
9	András PÁL		A	6	(8)	
24	Zoltán POLLÁK		D	23		
22	István RODENBÜCHER		D	24		
11	András SELEI		M	1	(7)	
3	László SÜTÖ		D	1	(1)	
28	Gábor URBÁN		A		(7)	
24	Zoltán VÉGH		G	30		
25	Attila ZABOS		M	20		2
17	László ZSIDAI		M	13	(3)	

LOMBARD PÁPA TFC
Coach – Lázár Szentes; (14/11/05) Gyula Zsivóczky; (27/12/05) György

Hungary

Gálhidi; (30/3/06) Gyula Zsivóczky

2005

Date	Opponent	H/A	Score	Scorers
30/7	FC Tatabánya	a	1-1	Újhegyi
6/8	FC Sopron	h	1-2	Kovrig (p)
21/8	Ferencváros	a	3-3	Róth 3 (1p)
27/8	Budapest-Honvéd	h	2-2	Herczeg, Lipták
17/9	FC Fehérvár	a	1-2	og (Kuttor)
24/9	Zalaegerszeg	a	0-5	
1/10	Kaposvári Rákóczi FC	h	0-0	
15/10	MTK Budapest	a	0-7	
22/10	Győri ETO FC	h	1-4	og (Stark)
29/10	Újpest FC	a	1-3	Remili
5/11	Diósgyőri VTK	h	1-3	Kovrig
19/11	Vasas	a	1-1	Kovrig
26/11	Rákospalotai EAC	h	1-3	Hercegfalvi
3/12	Pécsi MFC	a	0-5	
10/12	Debreceni VSC	h	3-3	Hercegfalvi, Honma, Kovrig (p)

2006

Date	Opponent	H/A	Score	Scorers
25/2	FC Tatabánya	h	0-5	
4/3	FC Sopron	a	0-2	
11/3	Ferencváros	h	1-5	Simpson
18/3	Budapest-Honvéd	a	0-1	
25/3	FC Fehérvár	h	0-2	
1/4	Zalaegerszeg	h	2-1	Mumba, Kincses
8/4	Kaposvári Rákóczi FC	a	0-1	
15/4	MTK Budapest	h	1-3	Elder
22/4	Győri ETO FC	a	0-4	
28/4	Újpest FC	h	2-1	Fabinho, Honma
6/5	Diósgyőri VTK	a	1-0	Szabó II
13/5	Vasas	h	1-0	Szabó II
20/5	Rákospalotai EAC	a	2-2	Kozarek, Fabinho
27/5	Pécsi MFC	h	3-1	Lipták 2, Honma
2/6	Debreceni VSC	a	1-4	Fabinho

No	Name	Nat	Pos	Aps	(s)	Gls
8	Guilherme D'ARRIGO	BRA	M	7		
16	Zoltán DELI		G	2		
79	András DOMBAI		G	11		
10	Alencar ELDER	BRA	M	13	(1)	1
26	Miklós ERDÉLYI		G	2		
11	Oliveira M. FABINHO	BRA	A	6		3
3	Balázs FACSKÓ		D	5	(3)	
17	Attila FARKAS		D	25		
30	László GAÁL		D	10	(1)	
24	Tamás GERI		D	16	(5)	
22	Zoltán HERCEGFALVI		A	7	(3)	2
67	Miklós HERCZEG		A	9	(3)	1
14	Kazuo HONMA	JPN	A	8	(8)	3
	JOEVANNIE Peart	CAN	D		(1)	
23	Péter KINCSES		M	21	(2)	1
32	Ákos KOVRIG		M	11	(3)	4
5	András KOZAREK		A	8	(3)	1
20	Franco LALLI	ITA	A	3	(6)	
6	Balázs LÁSZKA		M	8	(1)	
4	Zoltán LIPTÁK		M	22	(3)	3
2	Mishek LUNGU	ZAM	M	9		
2	Lloyd MUMBA	ZAM	D	14		1
19	Dorel MUTICA	ROM	M	8		
9	Zsolt MÜLLER		M	18	(1)	
7	Marijan NIKOLIC	CRO	A	6	(1)	
31	Mohamed REMILI	ALB	M	8	(2)	1
11	Ferenc RÓTH		M	2	(1)	3
7	Dave SIMPSON	CAN	A	9	(3)	1
7	Simeon STEVICA	SLK	A	2	(1)	
5	Zoltán SZABÓ I		M	1	(2)	
18	Zoltán SZABÓ II		M	10	(3)	2
18	Krisztián SZALAI		D		(2)	
	Igor SZKUKALEK	SVK	D	13	(1)	

No	Name		Pos			
22	Lajos SZÜCS		G	14		
25	Tamás TÓTH		D		(3)	
77	Gábor ÚJHEGYI		A	4	(8)	1
21	Viktor VALENTÉNYI		D	3		
19	Dániel VARGA		D	11	(2)	
	Péter VÖRÖS		M	4	(4)	

PÉCSI MFC
Coach – József Ott; (27/9/05) Ferenc Keszei

2005

Date	Opponent	H/A	Score	Scorers
30/7	Kaposvári Rákóczi FC	h	2-1	Balaskó 2 (1p)
6/8	MTK Budapest	a	0-2	
20/8	Győri ETO FC	h	0-1	
27/8	Újpest FC	a	1-5	Balaskó (p)
17/9	Diósgyőri VTK	h	5-0	Szekeres, Schindler, Horváth G., Kulcsár, Balaskó
24/9	Vasas	a	0-3	
1/10	Rákospalotai EAC	h	4-0	Kulcsár, Tarcsa 2, Pavicevic
15/10	FC Fehérvár	h	0-2	
24/10	Debreceni VSC	a	1-3	Szögedi
29/10	FC Tatabánya	h	0-1	
5/11	FC Sopron	a	1-3	Balaskó
19/11	Ferencváros	h	0-0	
26/11	Budapest-Honvéd	a	1-1	Pavicevic
3/12	Lombard Pápa TFC	h	5-0	Kalina 4, Berdó
10/12	Zalaegerszeg	a	4-1	Szabados, Balaskó, Szekeres, Kalina

2006

Date	Opponent	H/A	Score	Scorers
25/2	Kaposvári Rákóczi FC	a	2-2	og (Zahorecz), Balaskó
4/3	MTK Budapest	h	2-2	Szekeres, Balaskó
11/3	Győri ETO FC	a	1-1	Jevdovic
18/3	Újpest FC	h	2-0	Kulcsár, Sipos N.
25/3	Diósgyőri VTK	a	0-0	
1/4	Vasas	h	0-0	
8/4	Rákospalotai EAC	a	1-1	Schindler
15/4	FC Fehérvár	a	0-1	
22/4	Debreceni VSC	h	0-2	
29/4	FC Tatabánya	a	0-2	
6/5	FC Sopron	h	2-1	Vujic, Bajúsz
12/5	Ferencváros	a	1-3	Kulcsár
20/5	Budapest-Honvéd	h	1-0	Kulcsár
27/5	Lombard Pápa TFC	a	1-3	Jevdovic
3/6	Zalaegerszeg	h	0-0	

No	Name	Nat	Pos	Aps	(s)	Gls
30	Péter ANDORKA		A	3	(7)	
19	Endre BAJÚSZ		D	16	(6)	1
7	Iván BALASKÓ		M	23		8
13	Balázs BERDÓ		M	21	(1)	1
32	Balázs BERGMANN		D	2		
5	Tamás CSEHI		M		(4)	
	Ervin DÁVID		M		(2)	
74	András DIENES		D	30		
24	Miklós GAÁL		D	4		
24	János GYŐRI		M	11	(1)	
1	Roland HERBERT		G	20		
17	Gyula HORVÁTH		A	9	(1)	1
25	Zsolt HORVÁTH		M	1	(4)	
30	Radivoje JEVDOVIC	SCG	A	5	(6)	2
22	Tibor KALINA		A	14	(8)	5
29	Zsolt KALMÁR		M	1		
11	Árpád KULCSÁR		M	20	(2)	5
18	Levente LANTOS		M	5	(7)	
10	Dávid LUCZEK		M	2		
21	Cedomir PAVICEVIC	SCG	M	24		2
36	Szabolcs SCHINDLER		D	28		2
8	János SIPOS		D	15	(5)	
4	Norbert SIPOS		M	9	(10)	1
16	Csaba SÓLYOM		G	10	(1)	

Hungary

No	Name		Nat	Pos	Aps	(s)	Gls
14	József SZABADOS			D	23		1
32	Lóránd SZATMÁRI			M		(2)	
20	Zsolt SZEKERES			D	21	(4)	3
10	Szilárd SZŐGEDI			M	3	(5)	1
9	Bence TARCSA			A	4	(8)	2
15	Zoltán TÓTH			M		(1)	
15	Roland ULRICH			M	1	(1)	
17	Goran VUJIC		SCG	A	5	(3)	1

RÁKOSPALOTAI EAC
Coach – Flórián Urbán

2005

Date	Opponent	h/a	Score	Scorers
30/7	MTK Budapest	h	1-2	og (Balogh)
6/8	Győri ETO FC	a	2-2	Török, Polonkai
20/8	Újpest FC	h	2-3	Somorjai, Földvári
28/8	Diósgyőri VTK	h	0-2	
17/9	Vasas	h	0-3	
24/9	FC Fehérvár	h	1-2	Somorjai
1/10	Pécsi MFC	a	0-4	
15/10	Debreceni VSC	h	1-2	Nyerges
22/10	FC Tatabánya	a	0-4	
29/10	FC Sopron	h	1-0	Nyerges (p)
5/11	Ferencváros	a	2-0	Török, Torma
19/11	Budapest-Honvéd	h	1-3	Nyerges (p)
26/11	Lombard Pápa TFC	a	3-1	Cseri, Nyerges, Torma
3/12	Zalaegerszeg	h	2-1	Torma, Cseri
10/12	Kaposvári Rákóczi FC	a	0-1	

2006

Date	Opponent	h/a	Score	Scorers
26/2	MTK Budapest	a	0-1	
4/3	Győri ETO FC	h	1-2	Nyerges
11/3	Újpest FC	a	0-2	
18/3	Diósgyőri VTK	a	1-1	Polonkai
25/3	Vasas	a	2-2	Torma, Polonkai
31/3	FC Fehérvár	a	1-3	Polonkai
8/4	Pécsi MFC	h	1-1	Nyerges
14/4	Debreceni VSC	a	1-6	Polonkai
22/4	FC Tatabánya	h	0-2	
29/4	FC Sopron	a	1-0	Török
6/5	Ferencváros	h	1-0	Polonkai
13/5	Budapest-Honvéd	a	3-1	Somorjai 2, Polonkai
20/5	Lombard Pápa TFC	h	2-2	Földvári, Nyerges (p)
27/5	Zalaegerszeg	a	0-3	
3/6	Kaposvári Rákóczi FC	h	0-3	

No	Name		Nat	Pos	Aps	(s)	Gls
7	Gergő CSERI			M	19	(3)	2
9	István CSOPAKI			M	12	(12)	
2	Balázs DINKA			D	9	(4)	
1	Balázs FARKAS			G	18	(1)	
4	László FEKETE			M	1	(2)	
3	Csaba FÖLDVÁRI			D	17	(2)	2
17	Gábor HORVÁTH			D	24		
16	Tamás HORVÁTH			M	5	(2)	
8	Vince KAPCSOS			D	26	(2)	
20	Tamás KOLTAI			A		(3)	
14	Balázs KOVÁCS			M	10	(8)	
6	Gábor NAGY I			D	21	(2)	
19	Gábor NAGY II			A		(6)	
13	Tamás NÉMETH			D	8	(6)	
11	Krisztián NYERGES			A	23	(5)	7
22	Attila POLONKAI			M	20	(1)	7
5	Balázs SALLAI			M	19	(3)	
23	Tamás SOMORJAI			A	21	(4)	4
12	Viktor SZENTPÉTERI			G	12		
18	Attila SZIRTESI			D	11	(5)	
9	Zoltán TAMÁSI			D	3		
10	Gábor TORMA			A	20	(5)	4
21	Sándor TÖRÖK			A	22	(6)	3
15	Tibor VIRÁGH			D	9	(5)	

FC SOPRON
Coach – János Csank; (25/9/05) Tibor Selymes (ROM); (7/2/06) (Tamás Nagy); (9/2/06) Csaba László; (17/2/06) Dario Bonetti (ITA); (5/5/06) László Vass

2005

Date	Opponent	h/a	Score	Scorers
30/7	Budapest-Honvéd	h	1-1	Lazic (p)
6/8	Lombard Pápa TFC	a	2-1	Horváth A., Ibric
20/8	Zalaegerszeg	h	0-1	
28/8	Kaposvári Rákóczi FC	a	0-2	
17/9	MTK Budapest	h	0-3	
24/9	Győri ETO FC	a	1-2	Landerl
1/10	Újpest FC	h	1-1	Landerl
15/10	Diósgyőri VTK	a	1-1	og (Gáspár)
22/10	Vasas	h	2-0	Cotan, Bagoly
29/10	Rákospalotai EAC	a	0-1	
5/11	Pécsi MFC	h	3-1	Horváth A. 2, Signori
19/11	Debreceni VSC	a	1-3	Signori (p)
26/11	FC Tatabánya	h	5-1	Bagoly 3, Horváth A., Demjén
3/12	FC Fehérvár	h	1-1	Cigan
10/12	Ferencváros	a	0-1	

2006

Date	Opponent	h/a	Score	Scorers
25/2	Budapest-Honvéd	a	3-0	Signori, Horváth A., Demjén
4/3	Lombard Pápa TFC	h	2-0	Demjén, Cigan
11/3	Zalaegerszeg	a	2-2	Sira, Horváth A.
18/3	Kaposvári Rákóczi FC	h	2-0	Bagoly, Horváth A.
25/3	MTK Budapest	a	0-2	
1/4	Győri ETO FC	h	2-0	Horváth A. (p), Radu
8/4	Újpest FC	a	1-2	Horváth A. (p)
15/4	Diósgyőri VTK	h	2-1	Cigan, Horváth A.
21/4	Vasas	a	1-1	Munteanu
29/4	Rákospalotai EAC	h	0-1	
6/5	Pécsi MFC	a	1-2	Ibric
13/5	Debreceni VSC	h	0-2	
20/5	FC Tatabánya	a	2-3	Costisor, og (Rajnay)
27/5	FC Fehérvár	a	2-2	Bagoly, Horváth A. (p)
2/6	Ferencváros	h	1-1	Bagoly

No	Name		Nat	Pos	Aps	(s)	Gls
26	Gábor BAGOLY			D	26		7
12	János BALOG			G	12		
30	Botond BIRTALAN			A		(2)	
10	Cristian CIGAN		ROM	A	20	(7)	3
15	Alexander COSTISOR		ROM	D	17	(1)	1
13	Alin COTAN		ROM	M	17	(5)	1
17	Zoltán CSONTOS			M	2	(4)	
69	Csaba CSORDÁS			A	6	(8)	
9	Gábor DEMJÉN			A	25	(3)	3
8	Róbert FECZESIN			A	8	(1)	
19	Zoltán FEHÉR			D	9	(2)	
25	Miklós FLEISCHHACKER			A		(2)	
25	Zoltán FÜLÖP			A	4	(5)	
	János GYŐRI			D	2	(4)	
14	Viktor HANÁK			D	15		
7	András HORVÁTH			A	25	(2)	11
1	Tamás HORVÁTH			G	2		
5	Ion IBRIC		ROM	D	26	(2)	2
18	Gellért IVANCSICS			M	6	(5)	
14	Zoltán KISS			D	2	(1)	
32	Tamás KOZMA			G	4		
	Rolf LANDERL		AUT	M	7	(3)	2
8	Bojan LAZIC		SCG	M	5		1
4	András LÁSZLÓ			D	10	(2)	
	LEGOZA			A		(3)	
23	Cristian MUNTEANU		ROM	M	5	(5)	1
1	Balázs RABÓCZKI			G	12		
22	Cristian Luca RADU		ROM	M	10	(3)	1
24	Luigi SARTOR		ITA	D	7		

Hungary

11	Tamás SIFTER		M	19	(3)
10	Giuseppe SIGNORI	ITA	A	7	(3) 3
19	Nicola SILVESTRI	ITA	D	10	
6	István SIRA		A	6	(3) 1
12	Tamás TAKÁCS		G	1	
21	Gábor VÉN		M	3	(2)
22	Zalán ZOMBORI		M		(2)

FC TATABÁNYA
Coach – Tibor Sisa

2005
30/7	Lombard Pápa TFC	h	1-1	Márkus
6/8	Zalaegerszeg	a	0-3	
20/8	Kaposvári Rákóczi FC	h	1-0	Márkus (p)
27/8	MTK Budapest	a	0-1	
18/9	Győri ETO FC	h	3-3	Tóth, Márkus 2
24/9	Újpest FC	a	1-5	Márkus
1/10	Diósgyőri VTK	h	2-1	Megyesi, Márkus
15/10	Vasas	a	1-1	Filó
22/10	Rákospalotai EAC	h	4-0	Márkus 2, Hajdú, Nagy
29/10	Pécsi MFC	a	1-0	Nagy
6/11	Debreceni VSC	h	3-3	Nagy, Márkus 2 (1p)
20/11	FC Fehérvár	h	0-1	
26/11	FC Sopron	a	1-5	Márkus
4/12	Ferencváros	h	2-3	Deme, Márkus
10/12	Budapest-Honvéd	a	3-1	Da Silva, Filó, Márkus

2006
25/2	Lombard Pápa TFC	a	5-0	Hajdú 2, Tóth, Kouemaha, Deme
4/3	Zalaegerszeg	h	0-1	
11/3	Kaposvári Rákóczi FC	a	1-1	Márkus
18/3	MTK Budapest	h	0-1	
24/3	Győri ETO FC	a	0-0	
1/4	Újpest FC	h	1-1	Tóth
8/4	Diósgyőri VTK	a	0-1	
15/4	Vasas	h	2-2	Kerényi 2
22/4	Rákospalotai EAC	a	2-0	Vámosi, Ngalle
29/4	Pécsi MFC	h	2-0	Márkus 2
6/5	Debreceni VSC	a	0-1	
13/5	FC Fehérvár	a	1-4	Vámosi (p)
20/5	FC Sopron	h	3-2	Márkus 2, Kouemaha
27/5	Ferencváros	a	3-2	Megyesi, Deme 2
3/6	Budapest-Honvéd	a	3-1	Filó, Márkus, Tóth

No	Name	Nat	Pos	Aps	(s)	Gls
32	Vojislav BAKRAC	SCG		4	(1)	
3	Zoltán BALOGH		M	22	(3)	
25	Jerson José DA SILVA	BRA	M	7	(12)	1
7	Imre DEME		M	24	(4)	4
9	János DUPAI		M	6	(4)	
6	Tamás FILÓ		D	26	(1)	3
19	Péter FORGÓ		M	1	(5)	
5	Norbert HAJDÚ		M	29	(1)	3
2	Norbert KERÉNYI		D	23		2
40	Dorge R. KOUEMAHA	CMR	A	5	(3)	2
18	Tibor MÁRKUS		A	25	(3)	19
79	László MEGYESI		M	13	(5)	2
16	Krisztián MILE		M	3	(3)	
11	Tamás NAGY		A	11	(4)	3
8	Ilir NALBINI	ALB	M	1	(2)	
77	Edouard NDJODO	CMR	A	5	(6)	
21	Krisztián NÉMETH	SVK	D	11	(1)	
30	Joseph M. NGALLE	CMR	A	4	(7)	1
82	Vukasin POLEKSZICS	SCG	G	14		
1	Marian POSTRK	SVK	G	1	(1)	
14	Attila RAJNAY		D	25	(1)	
23	Erin RIZVANOLLE	ALB	A	1	(4)	
35	Kálmán SZABÓ		G	1		
77	Zoltán SZABÓ		M	3	(6)	

10	Zoltán TÓTH		M	28	4
1	Géza TURI		G	14	
15	Zoltán VATI		D	11	(1)
13	Csaba VÁMOSI		A	12	(2) 2

ÚJPEST FC
Coach – Géza Mészöly

2005
31/7	Diósgyőri VTK	a	1-0	og (Mogyorósi)
6/8	Vasas	h	2-2	Kovács, Vaskó
20/8	Rákospalotai EAC	a	3-2	Kovács 2, Köhalmi
27/8	Pécsi MFC	h	5-1	Rajczi 3, Kovács 2
19/9	Debreceni VSC	a	2-2	Kovács, Tóth N. (p)
24/9	FC Tatabánya	h	5-1	Erős, Sándor, Rajczi 2, Kovács
1/10	FC Sopron	a	1-1	og (Demjén)
16/10	Ferencváros	h	2-1	Vermes, Kovács
22/10	Budapest-Honvéd	a	0-1	
29/10	Lombard Pápa TFC	h	3-1	Feczesin 2, Tóth N. (p)
6/11	Zalaegerszeg	a	3-1	Rajczi, og (Sebők), og (Csóka)
19/11	Kaposvári Rákóczi FC	h	4-1	Rajczi, Sándor, Tóth N. 2 (2p)
26/11	MTK Budapest	a	2-0	Rajczi 2
4/12	Győri ETO FC	h	3-1	Rajczi, Feczesin, og (Jäkl)
11/12	FC Fehérvár	a	1-1	Feczesin

2006
25/2	Diósgyőri VTK	h	3-2	Rajczi 2, Tisza
4/3	Vasas	a	3-2	Rajczi 2, Tóth N.
11/3	Rákospalotai EAC	h	2-0	Rajczi 2
18/3	Pécsi MFC	a	0-2	
26/3	Debreceni VSC	h	2-1	og (Máté), Kovács
1/4	FC Tatabánya	a	1-1	Tóth N.
8/4	FC Sopron	h	1-1	Tisza, Rajczi (p)
16/4	Ferencváros	a	2-1	Kovács, Rajczi (p)
22/4	Budapest-Honvéd	h	7-0	Vermes, Cariati, Füzi, Tisza, Sándor, Hullám, Vituska
28/4	Lombard Pápa TFC	a	1-2	Tóth N.
7/5	Zalaegerszeg	h	5-1	Kovács 2, Rajczi 2, Tóth N. (p)
14/5	Kaposvári Rákóczi FC	a	2-1	Kovács, Tóth N. (p)
20/5	MTK Budapest	h	1-2	Rajczi
28/5	Győri ETO FC	a	5-2	Tisza, Rajczi, Tóth N., Cariati, Vaskó
3/6	FC Fehérvár	h	1-3	Tisza

No	Name	Nat	Pos	Aps	(s)	Gls
23	Balázs BOZORI		A	1		
24	Attila BÖJTE		D	24		
9	Lucas CARIATI	ARG	A	1	(8)	2
17	Károly ERŐS		M	28		1
9	Róbert FECZESIN		A	7	(5)	4
16	Gábor FREUD		A	1	(9)	
18	Ákos FÜZI		D	14		1
4	Máté GULYÁS		M	3	(7)	
22	Attila HULLÁM		M	11	(8)	1
1	Dániel ILLYÉS		G	2	(1)	
18	Zoltán KISS		D	4	(2)	
10	Zoltán KOVÁCS		A	18	(5)	13
11	Zsolt KORCSMÁR		M		(1)	
6	András KÖHALMI		M	11	(9)	1
3	Dániel LETTRICH		D	1	(5)	
8	Péter RAJCZI		A	24		22
5	György SÁNDOR		M	25	(4)	3
13	János SZŐKE		A		(2)	
28	Tibor TISZA		A	14		5
2	Tamás TOLNAI		D		(1)	
21	Balázs TÓTH		M	27	(1)	
20	Norbert TÓTH		M	28		10

Hungary

7	Vilmos VANCZÁK		D	25		
19	Tamás VASKÓ		D	12	(3)	2
25	Krisztián VERMES		D	17	(6)	2
14	István VITUSKA		M	4	(11)	1
26	Géza VLASZÁK		G	28		

VASAS
Coach – Sándor Egervári; (5/12/05) (Péter Antal); (20/12/05) Attila Pintér

2005

Date	Opponent	H/A	Score	Scorers
30/7	Györi ETO FC	h	1-2	Gyánó (p)
6/8	Újpest FC	a	2-2	Bárányos (p), Waltner
21/8	Diósgyöri VTK	h	2-0	Elek, Bárányos
27/8	FC Fehérvár	h	0-3	
17/9	Rákospalotai EAC	a	3-0	Salamon, Gyánó, Rósa (p)
24/9	Pécsi MFC	h	3-0	Gyánó 3 (1p)
3/10	Debreceni VSC	a	2-2	Janjics, Gyánó
15/10	FC Tatabánya	h	1-1	Waltner
22/10	FC Sopron	a	0-2	
29/10	Ferencváros	h	0-1	
5/11	Budapest-Honvéd	a	2-2	Gyánó, Bárányos
19/11	Lombard Pápa TFC	h	1-1	Bárányos
26/11	Zalaegerszeg	a	0-3	
3/12	Kaposvári Rákóczi FC	h	0-2	
10/12	MTK Budapest	a	0-3	

2006

Date	Opponent	H/A	Score	Scorers
25/2	Györi ETO FC	a	1-2	Kapic
4/3	Újpest FC	h	2-3	Gyánó, Bárányos
11/3	Diósgyöri VTK	a	2-0	Rósa, Szabó
18/3	FC Fehérvár	a	0-1	
25/3	Rákospalotai EAC	h	2-2	Gyánó 2
1/4	Pécsi MFC	a	0-0	
8/4	Debreceni VSC	h	0-1	
15/4	FC Tatabánya	a	2-2	og (Filó), Waltner
21/4	FC Sopron	h	1-1	Csordás
29/4	Ferencváros	a	1-3	Rósa
5/5	Budapest-Honvéd	h	1-2	Szabó
13/5	Lombard Pápa TFC	a	0-1	
20/5	Zalaegerszeg	h	0-0	
27/5	Kaposvári Rákóczi FC	a	1-4	Gyánó
3/6	MTK Budapest	h	2-1	Balog, Molnár

No	Name	Nat	Pos	Aps	(s)	Gls
27	Zsolt BALOG		D	21	(3)	1
14	Zsolt BÁRÁNYOS		M	27		5
1	Csaba BORSZÉKI		G	6		
30	Csaba CSORDÁS		A	11	(4)	1
23	Norbert ELEK		D	14	(1)	1
25	Zoltán FEHÉR		D	8		
8	Krisztán FÜZI		M	8	(1)	
22	Szabolcs GYÁNÓ		A	19	(5)	11
13	Gyula HEGEDÜS		D	7	(1)	
29	Norbert HEGEDÜS		M	4	(1)	
7	Ivan JANJIC	SCG	M	7	(5)	1
16	Adem KAPIC	SLO	M	10	(1)	1
4	György KISS		D	1		
15	János LÁZOK		M	7	(10)	
10	Árpád MAJOROS		M	6	(17)	
2	Zoltán MOLNÁR		D	17	(1)	1
33	Gábor NÉMETH		G	24		
18	Norbert NÉMETH		M	3	(5)	
11	Zoltán PINTÉR		M	7		
20	Henrik RÓSA		M	20	(4)	3
3	Miklós SALAMON		D	12	(1)	1
19	Ottó SZABÓ	SVK	D	13	(2)	2
21	András TÓTH		D	26		
19	Dániel VARGA		D	1		
29	Dániel VÖLGYI		M	9	(2)	
9	Róbert WALTNER		A	14	(10)	3

5	Ádám WELTNER		M	4	(8)	
6	János ZOVÁTH		M	24	(1)	

ZALAEGERSZEG
Coach – László Dajka; (1/3/06) Lázár Szentes; (13/5/06) Antal Simon

2005

Date	Opponent	H/A	Score	Scorers
30/7	Debreceni VSC	a	1-2	Montvai
6/8	FC Tatabánya	h	3-0	Sebök V. 2 (2p), Józsi
20/8	FC Sopron	a	1-0	Kocsárdi
27/8	Ferencváros	h	3-2	Csóka, Koplárovics, Kriston
17/9	Budapest-Honvéd	a	0-4	
24/9	Lombard Pápa TFC	h	5-0	Sebök V. 2 (2p), Sabo, Montvai, Spasoljevic
1/10	FC Fehérvár	a	0-1	
15/10	Kaposvári Rákóczi FC	a	1-1	Sabo
24/10	MTK Budapest	h	3-4	László, Sabo, Sebök V. (p)
29/10	Györi ETO FC	a	1-2	Djorovic
6/11	Újpest FC	h	1-3	Sebök V. (p)
19/11	Diósgyöri VTK	a	0-3	
26/11	Vasas	h	3-0	Montvai, Kriston, Sebök V. (p)
3/12	Rákospalotai EAC	a	1-2	Montvai
10/12	Pécsi MFC	h	1-4	Sabo

2006

Date	Opponent	H/A	Score	Scorers
24/2	Debreceni VSC	h	2-0	Kónya, Sebök J.
4/3	FC Tatabánya	a	1-0	Nagy
11/3	FC Sopron	h	2-2	Sebök V., Sebök J.
17/3	Ferencváros	a	2-2	Sebök V. (p), Peric
25/3	Budapest-Honvéd	h	0-0	
1/4	Lombard Pápa TFC	a	1-2	Sebök J.
8/4	FC Fehérvár	h	1-1	Kónya
15/4	Kaposvári Rákóczi FC	h	0-1	
22/4	MTK Budapest	a	3-6	Sebök V. (p), og (Lambulic), Kottán
29/4	Györi ETO FC	h	0-0	
7/5	Újpest FC	a	1-5	Sebök V. (p)
13/5	Diósgyöri VTK	h	2-0	Bogunovic, Sebök J.
20/5	Vasas	a	0-0	
27/5	Rákospalotai EAC	h	3-0	Sebök J., Józsi 2
3/6	Pécsi MFC	a	0-0	

No	Name	Nat	Pos	Aps	(s)	Gls
21	Csaba BALOG		M	6	(3)	
6	Klemen BINGO		D	3	(3)	
88	Sasa BOGUNOVIC	SCG	A	7	(5)	1
14	Ivan BOJOVIC	SCG	D	7	(1)	
17	Zsolt CSÓKA		D	25		1
11	Marko DJOROVIC	SCG	A	4	(7)	1
99	András HORVÁTH		M	1	(2)	
23	György JÓZSI		M	23	(1)	3
7	András KAJ		M	11	(6)	
2	Gergely KOCSÁRDI		D	28		1
15	László KÓNYA		D	9	(3)	2
19	Béla KOPLÁROVICS		M	7	(5)	1
27	Krisztián KOTTÁN		M	1	(2)	1
18	Ladislav KOZMÉR	SLO	D	7	(2)	
27	Attila KRISTON		D	8	(1)	2
4	András LÁSZLÓ		D	15		1
13	Miklós LENDVAI		M	13		
22	Árpád MILINTE		G	4	(1)	
77	Balázs MOLNÁR		M	14		
66	Tamás MOLNÁR		A	1	(1)	
9	Tibor MONTVAI		A	13	(6)	4
16	Lajos NAGY		M	11	(11)	1
	Tibor PALKÓ		A	1		
20	Darko PERIC	CRO	A	11	(1)	1
3	István RÁCZ		D	1	(1)	
8	Radu SABO	ROM	A	9	(7)	2
14	Gábor SÁGHY		D	(1)		

Hungary

10	József SEBÖK		A	12	5
5	Vilmos SEBÖK		D	26	11
87	Gábor SIMONFALVI		D	1	(4)
99	Darko SPALEVIC		A	5	(6)
20	Bojan SPASOLJEVIC	SCG	A	10	(4)	1
1	Zoltán VARGA		G	26	
11	Zoltán VASAS		D	10	

DOMESTIC CUP 2005/06

THIRD ROUND
(20/9/05)
Baktalórántháza VSE 0, FC Fehérvár 2
(21/9/05)
Makó FC 0, Györi ETO FC 0 *(aet; 4-2 on pens)*
Felsöpakony 1, Rákospalotai EAC 3
FC Ajka 1, FC Sopron 2
Balkány SE 0, Kaposvári Rákóczi FC 5
Szentlörinc-Ormánság SE 2, Diósgyöri VTK 2 *(aet; 4-2 on pens)*
Kazincbarcikai SC 1, Vasas 2
Mosonmagyaróvári TE 2, Budapest-Honvéd 3 *(aet)*
Nyíregyháza Spartacus 1, BKV Elöre 2
Jászapáti VSE 1, MTK Budapest 3 *(aet)*
Celldömölki VSE 0, Lombard Pápa TFC 3
Gyirmót SE 0, FC Tatabánya 4
Lindab Törökbálint TC 1, Zalaegerszeg 4
Szombathelyi Haladás 2, Pécsi MFC 2 *(aet; 2-4 on pens)*
(27/9/05)
Kisbágyon 0 Újpest FC 3
Bye – Debreceni VSC

FOURTH ROUND
(26/10/05 & 9/11/05)
Zalaegerszeg v FC Sopron 1-5; 1-3 *(2-8)*
Szentlörinc-Ormánság SE v Pécsi MFC 0-2; 1-0 *(1-2)*
FC Tatabánya v Debreceni VSC 0-2; 1-2 *(1-4)*
Vasas v Lombard Pápa TFC 3-3; 2-1 *(5-4)*
Kaposvári Rákóczi FC v Rákospalotai EAC 1-1; 3-3 *(4-4; Kaposvári Rákóczi FC on away goals)*
Újpest FC v Makó FC 8-1; 1-0 *(9-1)*
(26/10/05 & 23/11/05)
Budapest-Honvéd v BKV Elöre 2-1; 3-1 *(5-2)*
(26/10/05 & 6/12/05)
FC Fehérvár v MTK Budapest 1-1; 2-1 *(3-2)*

QUARTER-FINALS
(15/3/06 & 22/3/06)
Kaposvári Rákóczi FC 1 *(Alves 17)*, FC Fehérvár 2 *(Schwarz 44, Csizmadia 78)*
FC Fehérvár 3 *(Sitku 4, Dajic 42, 62)*, Kaposvári Rákóczi FC 1 *(Oláh 87)*
(FC Fehérvár 5-2)

Pécsi MFC v, Vasas 1 *(Rósa 79)*
Vasas 1 *(Gyánó 29)*, Pécsi MFC 0
(Vasas 2-0)

(15/3/06 & 5/4/06)
Újpest FC 0, Debreceni VSC 1 *(Sidibe 69p)*
Debreceni VSC 2 *(Sidibe 24, Virág 30)*, Újpest FC 0
(Debreceni VSC 3-0)

(22/3/06 & 29/3/06)
FC Sopron 0, Budapest-Honvéd 0
Budapest-Honvéd 1 *(Schranz 83)*, Sopron FC 0
(Budapest-Honvéd 1-0)

SEMI FINALS
(25/4/06 & 3/5/06)
Debreceni VSC 0, FC Fehérvár 1 *(Dvéri 44)*

FC Fehérvár 2 *(Bogdanovics 23p, Sitku 40)*, Debreceni VSC 2 *(Csizmadia 78p, Dzsudzsák 82)*
(FC Fehérvár 3-2)

(26/4/06 & 2/5/06)
Budapest-Honvéd 1 *(Miro 47)* Vasas 3 *(Udvari 1og, Gyánó 32, Bárányos 73)*
Vasas 0, Budapest-Honvéd 1 *(Dobos 74)*
(Vasas 3-2)

FINAL
(17/5/06)
Üllöi út, Budapest
FC FEHÉRVÁR 2 *(Sitku 46, Schwarcz 57)*
VASAS 2 *(Waltner 25, Balog 84)*
(aet; 6–5 on pens)
Referee - Megyebíró
FC FEHÉRVÁR - Sebök, Csizmadia, Kuttor, Kořer, Horváth G. *(Vincze Z. 75)*, Alumona *(Dajic 79)*, Dvéri *(Horváth F. 107)*, Schwarcz, Bozic, Lattenstein, Sitku.
VASAS - Németh G., Balog, Tóth, Janjic, Molncir, Németh N. *(Gyánó 61)*, Pintér *(Kapic 46)*, Zováth, Szabó *(Csordás 69)*, Bárányos, Waltner.

SECOND LEVEL FINAL TABLES 2005/06

Eastern Group

		Pld	W	D	L	F	A	Pts
1	Dunakanyar-Vác FC	28	18	7	3	61	25	61
2	Szolnoki MÁV	28	12	13	3	45	23	49
3	Jászapáti VSE	28	15	3	10	54	34	48
4	Makó FC	28	13	8	7	44	34	47
5	Soroskári SC	28	13	6	9	44	34	45
6	Nyíregyházi Spartacus	28	12	9	7	48	30	45
7	Böcsi KSC	28	13	5	10	39	40	43
8	Kazincbarcika SC	28	12	5	11	47	42	41
9	Kecskemei TE	28	9	11	8	46	49	38
10	Orosháza FC	28	9	9	10	51	46	36
11	Baktalórántháza VSE	28	9	8	11	41	37	35
12	Vecsés FC	28	8	4	16	34	54	28
13	Karcagi SE	28	8	4	16	36	63	28
14	Budafoki LC	28	6	6	16	29	51	24
15	Erzsébeti SMTK	28	3	2	23	19	76	11

N.B. Böcsi KSC – 1 pt deducted; Szentes withdrew

Western Group

		Pld	W	D	L	F	A	Pts
1	Paksi SE	30	25	1	4	66	22	76
2	Felcsút SE	30	20	3	7	72	41	63
3	Gyirmót SE	30	15	12	3	53	25	57
4	Integrál-DAC Györ	30	15	6	9	52	38	51
5	Barcsi FC	30	13	3	14	42	47	42
6	Szombathelyi Haladás	30	12	6	12	38	37	42
7	Siófok BFC	30	11	7	12	39	40	40
8	Celldömölki VSE	30	10	8	12	31	35	38
9	Budakalász MSE	30	9	9	12	39	43	36
10	Hévíz FC	30	7	14	9	32	34	35
11	Balatonlelle SE	30	9	8	13	30	49	33
12	BKV Elöre	30	7	10	13	32	41	31
13	Dunaújvárosi Kohász	30	7	10	13	36	53	31
14	Mosonmagyaróvári TE	30	7	9	14	35	47	30
15	Kaposvölgye-Nagyberki	30	6	9	15	40	59	27
16	Ajka FC	30	5	10	15	27	53	25

Iceland

Flawless FH leave the rest standing

Having taken 75 years to win their first Icelandic title, FH, from Hafnarfjörður, were clearly in a hurry to win their second. They did so in the most comprehensive manner possible, winning every single match until it was mathematically impossible for them to be caught.

Their 15th successive victory, 2-0 at home to second-placed Valur, increased their lead at the top of the table to 14 points with three rounds left to play. It was all over. The most one-sided title race perhaps ever in European football history had run its course.

In the early weeks of the season Valur, newly promoted as First Division champions, matched FH victory for victory. Both sides had accumulated maximum points when they came face to face at Valur's Hlíðarendi stadium in round six. FH won the game 1-0 with a goal from their prolific Danish goalscorer, Allan Borgvardt, who at the end of the campaign would be crowned Player of the Season for the second time in three years. Valur also lost their next game, and from then on FH were in the clear. They just kept piling up the victories until there was no need for any more.

Impressive statistics

Completing the season with maximum points would have been nice, but once the championship trophy had been secured, FH eased off, losing two games in a row, to ÍA and Fylkir. Even so, their final statistics were pretty impressive: a 16-point winning margin; 53 goals scored in 18 games and only 11 conceded; a highest score of 8-0 (in which Borgvardt alone scored four).

In recent years the Icelandic Premier League has become more renowned for its exciting relegation fights than its title races. Incredibly, Fram, from Reykjavík, were involved in such a struggle for the seventh successive year. For the previous six seasons they had always been in the danger zone going into the final game but somehow managed to wriggle free. This time they looked safe and sound with four games remaining, but they followed three straight wins with three straight defeats, and so, once again, with one game remaining, they were threatened with the drop. Their final fixture, as fate would have it, was at home to newly-crowned champions FH.

Two other teams, ÍBV and Grindavík, looked more likely to go down with already-relegated Þróttur. The former, like Fram, were on 17 points but with an inferior goal difference, whereas the latter had only 15. Cue more amazing last-day drama.

Grindavík saved themselves with a thrilling 2-1 victory over neighbours Keflavík. ÍBV, from the volcanic Westmann Islands, lost 1-0 on the mainland to Fylkir and appeared to be going down. As full-time approached, Fram were being

NATIONAL TEAM RESULTS 2005/06

17/8/05	South Africa	H	Reykjavík	4-1	Steinsson (25), Vidarsson (42), Helguson (67), Gunnarsson V. (72)
3/9/05	Croatia (WCQ)	H	Reykjavík	1-3	Gudjohnsen (24)
7/9/05	Bulgaria (WCQ)	A	Sofia	2-3	Steinsson (9), Heidarsson (16)
7/10/05	Poland	A	Warsaw	2-3	Sigurdsson K. (15), Sigurdsson H. (38)
12/10/05	Sweden (WCQ)	A	Solna	1-3	Árnason (25)
28/2/06	Trinidad & Tobago	N	London	0-2	

Iceland

NATIONAL TEAM APPEARANCES 2005/06

Coach – Ásgeir SIGURVINSSON & Logi ÓLAFSSON /(14/10/05) Eyjólfur SVERRISSON

Name	DOB	Club	Rsa	CRO	BUL	Pol	SWE	Tri	Caps	Goals
Árni Gautur ARASON	7/5/75	Vålerenga Fotball (NOR)	G	G	G		G	G46	51	-
Kristján Örn SIGURDSSON	7/10/80	SK Brann (NOR)	D46	D	D	D	D	s79	18	2
Audun HELGASON	18/6/74	FH	D	D79	D	D75	D		35	1
Stefán GÍSLASON	15/3/80	FC Lyn Oslo (NOR)	D	M	M	M	M	M57	12	-
Indridi SIGURDSSON	12/10/81	KRC Genk (BEL)	D80	D43	D	D	D	D	31	1
Grétar Rafn STEINSSON	9/1/82	BSC Young Boys Bern (SUI) /AZ (HOL)	M64	M	M	M	M	M	11	3
Kári ÁRNASON	13/10/82	Djurgårdens IF (SWE)	M53	s79	M74	M81	M70		8	1
Eidur GUDJOHNSEN	15/9/78	Chelsea (ENG)	M	M	M			A72	40	16
Arnar Thor VIDARSSON	15/3/78	KSC Lokeren OV (BEL) /FC Twente (HOL)	M68	s43	s74	s72	s83 s57		44	1
Tryggvi GUDMUNDSSON	30/7/74	FH	M57			s81			37	10
Heidar HELGUSON	22/8/77	Fulham (ENG)	A	A24	A		A	A57	39	6
Gylfi EINARSSON	27/10/78	Leeds United (ENG)	s46	M		M73	s70	s72	24	1
Gunnar THORVALDSSON	1/4/82	Halmstads BK (SWE)	s53	s24			A74		6	1
Veigar GUNNARSSON	21/3/80	Stabaek Fotball (NOR)	s57			s73			12	2
Bjarni Ó. EIRÍKSSON	28/3/82	Valur	s64			s76			2	-
Jóhannes HARDARSON	28/7/76	IK Start (NOR)	s68						2	-
Haraldur GUDMUNDSSON	14/12/81	Aalesunds FK (NOR)	s80						2	-
Hermann HREIDARSSON	11/7/74	Charlton Athletic (ENG)		D	D			D	65	4
Brynjar GUNNARSSON	16/10/75	Reading (ENG)		M	M	M72	M83	s69	55	3
Kristján FINNBOGASON	8/5/71	KR				G86			20	-
Sölvi Geir OTTESEN	18/2/84	Djurgårdens IF (SWE)				D	D		2	-
Hannes SIGURDSSON	10/4/83	Stoke City (ENG)				A81	s74	s57	5	1
Dadi LÁRUSSON	19/6/73	FH				s86		s46	2	-
Helgi V. DANÍELSSON	13/7/81	Fylkir /Östers IF (SWE)				s81		D79	4	-
Ívar INGIMARSSON	20/8/77	Reading (ENG)					D		17	-
Jóhannes GUDJÓNSSON	25/5/80	Leicester City (ENG)						M69	25	1
Emil HALLFREDSSON	29/6/84	Malmö FF (SWE)						M	2	-

thrashed 4-1 by FH, but that result was sufficient to keep the great escape artists up. Then, in the second minute of stoppage-time, disaster struck as Fram conceded a fifth goal. It was crucial. ÍBV now had a better goal difference and Fram, at long last, were relegated. Curiously the all-important goal was scored by the league's top scorer, Tryggvi Gudmundsson, an ÍBV old boy who was born and bred in the Westmann Islands. It was his 16th goal of the season and completed his hat-trick.

Iceland

FH were on something of a revenge mission against Fram as it was they who a few weeks earlier had denied the champions a potential Double by knocking them out of the Icelandic Cup. FH were 2-0 up and cruising to the final but Fram staged an astonishing comeback and won the game after an extended penalty shoot-out.

A week after their relegation Fram thus had the chance to go down in a blaze of glory by beating their traditional foes Valur in the Cup final and qualifying for Europe. But it wasn't to be their day, and Valur won 1-0 with a quality strike from midfielder Baldur Adalsteinsson. It was the club's ninth Cup win but their first major trophy for all of 13 years.

FH also disappointed in Europe. Having performed well in 2004, much was expected of them in the Champions League qualifiers. But they fell at the first hurdle, beaten home and away by Neftçi Baku of Azerbaijan. It was a huge let-down - not just for FH's supporters but, with the club so omnipotent at home, for Icelandic football as a whole.

Keflavík partly made up for FH's early demise when they beat Etzella Ettelbruck of Luxembourg 4-0 away, with striker Hördur Steinsson scoring all four goals – an unprecedented feat for an Icelandic player. For good measure Steinsson added another goal in the 2-0 home win. Keflavík then predictably fell to German Bundesliga side Mainz, but with 2-0 defeats in each game they certainly didn't disgrace themselves. ÍBV, on the other hand, exited the same competition rather shame-faced after losing to B36 of the Faroe Islands.

Unhappy knack

The Icelandic national team had only four points to show from their World Cup qualifying campaign, but with ten goals in their last five games they seemed to be getting better. Unfortunately, they developed an unhappy knack of taking the lead then failing to hold on to it. They went in front in each of those final five qualifiers but only beat Malta (4-1). In each of the other four games they conceded three goals and lost. And to prove that it wasn't just a World Cup quirk, it also happened in a friendly against Poland.

Despite all the goals and the attractive play, it was the team's costly defensive shortcomings that led to the dismissal of joint coaches Ásgeir Sigurvinsson and Logi Ólafsson. They were replaced by ex-Stuttgart and Hertha Berlin pro Eyjólfur Sverrisson, who had impressed with the national Under-21 side. Sverrisson was given just one friendly to prepare for the Euro 2008 qualifiers, and Iceland lost it, 2-0 to World Cup-bound Trinidad & Tobago in London. The team will continue to be heavily reliant on their captain, Eidur Gudjohnsen, whose summer transfer from Chelsea to European champions Barcelona was a source of great pride for Icelandic nationals everywhere.

EUROPEAN CUPS 2005/06

UEFA CHAMPIONS LEAGUE

FH
1st qualifying round NEFTÇI BAKU (AZB)
A 0-2
Lárusson, Saevarsson, Helgason, Nielsen, Bjarnason, Vidarsson, Ásgeirsson (Gardarsson 90), Gudjónsson (Snorrason 46), Bett, Gudmundsson, Borgvardt.
H 1-2 *Borgvardt (60)*
Lárusson, Saevarsson, Helgason, Nielsen, Bjarnason (Albertsson 80), Bett (Björnsson A.V. 70), Gudjónsson, Vidarsson, Stefánsson (Snorrason 57), Borgvardt, Gudmundsson.

UEFA CUP

KEFLAVÍK
1st qualifying round ETZELLA ETTELBRUCK (LUX)
A 4-0 *Sveinsson (17, 59, 76, 80)*
Jóhannsson Ó., Abdulkadir, Johansson M., Sigurdsson, Antoníusson, Rúnarsson (Saemundsson 82), Saaevarsson, Gylfason, Kristinsson (Arnarson 69), Steinarsson, Sveinsson (Jónsson 90).
H 2-0 *Sveinsson (75), Kristinsson (88)*
Jóhannsson Ó., Antoníusson, Johansson M., Sigurdsson (Kristinsson 78), Gylfason, Rúnarsson, Saevarsson (Hólmbergsson 82), Saemundsson (Abdulkadir 58), Milicevic, Steinarsson, Sveinsson.

2nd qualifying round FSV MAINZ (GER)
A 0-2
Jóhannsson Ó., Johansson M. (Gylfason 70), Sigurdsson, Mete, Abdulkadir, Rúnarsson, Saevarsson, Gustafsson, Samuelsen, Steinarsson, Sveinsson.
H 0-2
Jóhannsson Ó., Antoníusson, Gustafsson, Mete, Abdulkadir (Milicevic 46), Sigurdsson, Rúnarsson, Saevarsson, Gylfason (Arnarson 75), Steinarsson (Samuelsen 46), Sveinsson.

ÍBV
1st qualifying round B36 (FAR)
H 1-1 *Sigurdsson P. (25)*
Kristinsson, Runólfsson, Adalsteinsson, Hjardar, Vidarsson, Platt (Sam 73), Jeffs, Gudmundsson, Jóhannsson A., Jóhannesson St. (Einarsson 60), Sigurdsson P. (Jóhannsson E. 89).
A 1-2 *Jeffs (41)*
Davídsson, Runólfsson, Adalsteinsson, Hjardar, Vidarsson (Sam 74), Ólafsson, Jeffs, Gudmundsson, Einarsson (Platt 50), Jóhannsson A., Sigurdsson P.

Iceland

TOP GOALSCORERS 2005

16	Tryggvi GUDMUNDSSON (FH)
13	Allan BORGVARDT (FH)
9	Hördur SVEINSSON (Keflavík)
8	Gardar B. GUNNLAUGSSON (Valur)
7	Gudmundur STEINARSSON (Keflavík)
	Matthías GUDMUNDSSON (Valur)
6	Hjörtur J. HJARTARSON (ÍA)
	Björgólfur TAKEFUSA (Fylkir)
	Grétar HJARTARSON (KR)
5	Sigurdur R. EYJÓLFSSON (ÍA)
	Viktor B. ARNARSSON (Fylkir)
	Steingrímur JÓHANNESSON (ÍBV)
	Andri JÚLÍUSSON (ÍA)
	Audun HELGASON (FH)
	Páll EINARSSON (Thróttur R.)

LEAGUE RESULTS/SCORERS/APPEARANCES/GOALS 2005

FH
Coach – Ólafur Jóhannesson

2005				
16/5	Keflavík	a	3-0	Gudmundsson, og (O'Callaghan), Björnsson Á.S.
22/5	Grindavík	a	5-1	Gudmundsson 3, Borgvardt, Bett
26/5	ÍBV	h	3-0	Gudmundsson, Borgvardt, Björnsson A.V.
29/5	KR	a	1-0	Stefánsson
11/6	Thróttur R.	h	3-1	Gudmundsson 2 (1p), Gardarsson
15/6	Valur	a	1-0	Borgvardt
23/6	ÍA	h	2-0	Gudmundsson, Borgvardt
26/6	Fylkir	a	5-2	Borgvardt 3, Helgason, Gudjónsson
30/6	Fram	h	3-1	Helgason, Borgvardt, Snorrason
8/7	Keflavík	h	2-0	Snorrason, Gudmundsson
24/7	ÍBV	a	1-0	Ásgeirsson
7/8	KR	h	2-0	Helgason, Bjarnason
10/8	Grindavík	h	8-0	Borgvardt 4, Gudmundsson, Ásgeirsson, Snorrason, Gardarsson
15/8	Thróttur R.	a	5-1	Gudmundsson 2 (1p), Helgason, Vidarsson, Borgvardt
21/8	Valur	h	2-0	Gudmundsson, og (Jónsson)
28/8	ÍA	a	1-2	Björnsson A.V.
11/9	Fylkir	h	1-2	Björnsson A.V.
17/9	Fram	a	5-1	Gudmundsson 3 (1p), Helgason, Björnsson Á.S.

No	Name	Nat	Pos	Aps	(s)	Gls
18	Hermann ALBERTSSON		M		(2)	
6	Ásgeir Gunnar ÁSGEIRSSON		M	14	(3)	2
8	Baldur BETT		M	7	(10)	1
5	Freyr BJARNASON		D	18		1
17	Atli Vidar BJÖRNSSON		A	5	(9)	3
15	Ármann Smári BJÖRNSSON		A	2	(7)	2
22	Allan BORGVARDT	DEN	A	15		13
7	Jónas Grani GARDARSSON		A		(6)	2
10	Heimir GUDJÓNSSON		M	13		1
9	Tryggvi GUDMUNDSSON		A	17		16
2	Audun HELGASON		D	18		5
1	Dadi LÁRUSSON		G	18		
4	Tommy NIELSEN	DEN	D	15		
14	Gudmundur SAEVARSSON		D	18		
3	Dennis SIIM	DEN	M	4	(2)	
19	Ólafur Páll SNORRASON		A	7	(5)	3
11	Jón Thorgrímur STEFÁNSSON		A	9	(4)	1
27	Davíd Thór VIDARSSON		M	18		1
29	Matthías VILHJÁLMSSON		A		(1)	

FRAM
Coach – Ólafur H. Kristjánsson

2005				
16/5	ÍBV	h	3-0	McLynn, Ottósson, Gudjónsson
22/5	KR	a	0-1	
26/5	Thróttur R.	h	3-0	Ottósson 2, Júlíusson
31/5	Valur	a	0-3	
11/6	ÍA	h	0-0	
16/6	Fylkir	a	1-1	Dadason
23/6	Grindavík	h	0-1	
26/6	Keflavík	h	2-3	og (Antoníusson), Ólason
30/6	FH	a	1-3	Dadason
10/7	ÍBV	a	0-2	
17/7	KR	h	0-4	
25/7	Thróttur R.	a	1-0	og (Einarsson)
8/8	Valur	h	2-1	Henriksen 2
14/8	ÍA	a	2-1	Henriksen, Gudjónsson
22/8	Fylkir	h	1-2	Henriksen
28/8	Grindavík	a	1-3	Mathiesen (p)
11/9	Keflavík	a	1-2	Ottósson
17/9	FH	h	1-5	Dadason

No	Name	Nat	Pos	Aps	(s)	Gls
10	Andri Steinn BIRGISSON		M	4	(3)	
22	Ívar BJÖRNSSON		M	2	(8)	
11	Ríkhardur DADASON		A	12	(2)	3
4	Vidar GUDJÓNSSON		M	10	(6)	2
7	Dadi GUDMUNDSSON		D	4	(2)	
8	Gunnar Thór GUNNARSSON		D	18		
27	Kristján HAUKSSON		D	16		
18	Ómar HÁKONARSON		M	1	(9)	
28	Bo HENRIKSEN	DEN	A	7		4
23	Thórhallur Dan JÓHANNSSON		D	16		
14	Andrés JÓNSSON		D	1		
16	Heidar Geir JÚLÍUSSON		A	3	(6)	1
24	Johan KARLEFJÄRD	SWE	D	4	(1)	
17	Vídir LEIFSSON		M	10	(3)	
15	Hans MATHIESEN	DEN	M	17		1
2	Ross McLYNN	IRL	D	7		1
20	Kim NÖRHOLT	DEN	M	5	(1)	
21	Andri Fannar OTTÓSSON		A	15		4
3	Ingvar ÓLASON		M	17		1
1	Gunnar SIGURDSSON		G	18		
9	Kristófer SIGURGEIRSSON		D	3	(9)	
5	Eggert STEFÁNSSON		D	8		
6	Thorbjörn Atli SVEINSSON		A		(4)	

Iceland

FINAL LEAGUE TABLE 2005

		Pld	Home					Away					Total					Pts
			W	D	L	F	A	W	D	L	F	A	W	D	L	F	A	
1	FH	18	8	0	1	26	4	8	0	1	27	7	16	0	2	53	11	48
2	Valur	18	5	2	2	16	6	5	0	4	13	10	10	2	6	29	16	32
3	ÍA	18	5	0	4	13	13	5	2	2	11	7	10	2	6	24	20	32
4	Keflavík	18	2	4	3	13	19	5	2	2	15	12	7	6	5	28	31	27
5	Fylkir	18	2	1	6	10	16	6	1	2	18	12	8	2	8	28	28	26
6	KR	18	5	0	4	12	12	3	1	5	10	12	8	1	9	22	24	25
7	Grindavík	18	4	2	3	13	13	1	1	7	10	28	5	3	10	23	41	18
8	ÍBV	18	5	0	4	14	11	0	2	7	4	19	5	2	11	18	30	17
9	Fram	18	3	1	5	12	16	2	1	6	7	16	5	2	11	19	32	17
10	Thróttur R.	18	2	2	5	11	15	2	2	5	10	17	4	4	10	21	32	16

FYLKIR
Coach – Thorlákur Árnason; (1/9/05) Sverrir Sverrisson & Jón Th. Sveinsson

2005

Date	Opponent	h/a	Score	Scorers
16/5	KR	h	1-2	Helgason H. (p)
22/5	Thróttur R.	a	2-1	Gíslason V., Ingason
26/5	Valur	h	1-2	Daníelsson
30/5	ÍA	a	3-0	Helgason H., Takefusa (p), Gustafsson
12/6	Grindavík	h	2-1	Hédinsson, Helgason H.
16/6	Fram	h	1-1	Takefusa
23/6	Keflavík	a	2-2	Helgason H., Christiansen
26/6	FH	h	2-5	Takefusa (p), Daníelsson
2/7	ÍBV	a	3-0	Takefusa 2, Arnarsson
11/7	KR	a	3-1	Arnarsson 2, Christiansen
17/7	Thróttur R.	h	0-1	
27/7	Valur	a	1-3	Takefusa (p)
7/8	ÍA	h	2-3	Arnarsson, Ásbjörnsson
14/8	Grindavík	a	0-3	
22/8	Fram	a	2-1	Breiddal, Arnarsson
30/8	Keflavík	h	0-1	
11/9	FH	a	2-1	Tranberg 2
17/9	ÍBV	h	1-0	Sigurdsson

No	Name	Nat	Pos	Aps	(s)	Gls
10	Viktor Bjarki ARNARSSON		M	16		5
15	Björn Vidar ÁSBJÖRNSSON		A	1	(8)	1
11	Kjartan Ágúst BREIDDAL		M	2	(9)	1
23	Christian CHRISTIANSEN	DEN	A	9	(3)	2
6	Helgi Valur DANÍELSSON		M	18		2
19	Sævar Thór GÍSLASON		A	3		
4	Valur Fannar GÍSLASON		D	16		1
14	Haukur Ingi GUDNASON		A	3	(3)	
18	Erik GUSTAFSSON	SWE	M	1	(2)	1
1	Bjarni HALLDÓRSSON		G	18		
3	Gudni Rúnar HELGASON		M	13		
7	Hrafnkell HELGASON		D	10	(4)	4
28	Jón B. HERMANNSSON		M	8	(5)	
21	Eyjólfur HÉDINSSON		M	11	(5)	1
24	Albert B. INGASON		A		(4)	1
16	Andrés JÓHANNESSON		M		(1)	
8	Finnur KOLBEINSSON		M	6		
27	Agnar Bragi MAGNÚSSON		A		(1)	
9	Gunnar Thór PÉTURSSON		D	17		
2	Ragnar SIGURDSSON		D	17		1
5	Ólafur STÍGSSON		M	2	(1)	
22	Björgólfur TAKEFUSA		A	14	(1)	6
17	Peter TRANBERG	DEN	M	3	(2)	2
20	Arnar Thór ÚLFARSSON		D	6	(2)	
25	Kristján VALDIMARSSON		D	4	(2)	

GRINDAVÍK
Coach – Milan Stefán Jankovic

2005

Date	Opponent	h/a	Score	Scorers
16/5	Valur	a	1-3	Thorsteinsson
22/5	FH	h	1-5	McShane
26/5	ÍA	a	2-3	Thorsteinsson, Ahandour
30/5	ÍBV	h	2-1	Kekic, Flóventsson (p)
12/6	Fylkir	a	1-2	Kekic
16/6	KR	h	0-0	
23/6	Fram	a	1-0	Kekic
26/6	Thróttur R.	h	1-1	Thorsteinsson
30/6	Keflavík	a	1-1	Kekic
12/7	Valur	h	0-1	
26/7	ÍA	h	1-3	Ahandour
10/8	FH	a	0-8	
14/8	Fylkir	h	3-0	Hauksson Ó., Flóventsson, og (Helgason G.)
18/8	ÍBV	a	1-5	Niestroj
21/8	KR	a	1-3	Hauksson E.
28/8	Fram	h	3-1	Flóventsson, Hauksson Ó., McShane
11/9	Thróttur R.	a	2-3	McShane, Niestroj
17/9	Keflavík	h	2-1	McShane, Flóventsson

No	Name	Nat	Pos	Aps	(s)	Gls
14	Jóhann H. ADALGEIRSSON		M	1	(1)	
11	Mounir AHANDOUR	FRA	A	14	(3)	2
28	Andri H. ALBERTSSON		D	1	(5)	
6	Ódinn ÁRNASON		D	17	(1)	
19	Gudmundur A. BJARNASON		D	5	(5)	
22	Eythór Atli EINARSSON		D	17		
7	Óli Stefán FLÓVENTSSON		D	15	(1)	4
31	Leifur GUDJÓNSSON		A		(2)	
26	Páll GUDMUNDSSON		D		(2)	
10	Eysteinn HAUKSSON		M	15	(3)	1
20	Óskar Örn HAUKSSON		M	14	(4)	2
4	Mathias JACK	GER	D	13	(1)	
25	Alfred JÓHANNSSON		A	1	(5)	

Iceland

No	Name	Nat	Pos	Aps	(s)	Gls
	Ray Anthony JÓNSSON		D	1		
	Sinisa Valdimar KEKIC		D	14		4
7	Paul McSHANE	SCO	M	17		4
	Robert NIESTROJ	GER	M	16		2
	Boban SAVIC	SCG	G	18		
	Emil Dadi SÍMONARSON		M		(2)	
8	Sveinn STEINGRÍMSSON		D	2	(1)	
3	Magnús S. THORSTEINSSON		A	15	(2)	3
6	Alexander THÓRARINSSON		M		(1)	
5	Michael ZEYER	GER	M	2	(3)	

ÍA
Coach – Ólafur Thórdarson

2005

6/5	Thróttur R.	h	1-0	Hjartarson
13/5	Valur	a	0-2	
16/5	Grindavík	h	3-2	Vilhjálmsson H., Hjartarson, Júlíusson
30/5	Fylkir	h	0-3	
1/6	Fram	a	0-0	
5/6	Keflavík	h	1-2	Hjartarson
23/6	FH	a	0-2	
29/6	ÍBV	h	2-0	Vilhjálmsson H., Júlíusson
3/7	KR	a	2-0	Vilhjálmsson H., Pesic
12/7	Thróttur R.	a	0-0	
26/7	Grindavík	a	3-1	Hjartarson, Júlíusson, Magnússon
7/8	Fylkir	a	3-2	Magnússon, Martin, Hjartarson (p)
11/8	Valur	h	1-2	Júlíusson
14/8	Fram	h	1-2	Hjartarson (p)
21/8	Keflavík	a	1-0	Eyjólfsson
28/8	FH	h	2-1	Eyjólfsson 2
11/9	ÍBV	a	2-0	Eyjólfsson, Júlíusson
17/9	KR	h	2-1	Martin, Eyjólfsson

No	Name	Nat	Pos	Aps	(s)	Gls
14	Jón Vilhelm ÁKASON		M	6	(8)	
5	Ellert Jón BJÖRNSSON		M	9	(2)	
10	Sigurdur R. EYJÓLFSSON		A	5	(10)	5
28	Thorsteinn GÍSLASON		A		(4)	
16	Bjarki GUDMUNDSSON		G	11		
8	Pálmi HARALDSSON		M	17	(1)	
9	Hjörtur J. HJARTARSON		A	14		6
26	Finnbogi LLORENS		D	9	(4)	
4	Gunnlaugur JÓNSSON		D	17		
12	Páll Gísli JÓNSSON		G	6		
20	Andri JÚLÍUSSON		A	7	(11)	5
6	Reynir LEÓSSON		D	17		
25	Helgi Pétur MAGNÚSSON		D	9	(3)	2
7	Dean E. MARTIN	ENG	M	11	(3)	2
21	Igor PESIC	SCG	M	10	(1)	1
11	Kári Steinn REYNISSON		M	14	(1)	
2	Kristinn Darri RÖDULSSON		D		(2)	
18	Gudjón H. SVEINSSON		D	18		
1	Thórdur THÓRDARSON		G	1		
17	Unnar Örn VALGEIRSSON		M	4		
23	Andrés VILHJÁLMSSON		A	2	(2)	
27	Hafthór VILHJÁLMSSON		M	11	(2)	3

ÍBV
Coach – Gudlaugur Baldursson

2005

16/5	Fram	a	0-3	
22/5	Keflavík	h	2-3	Jóhannesson St., Ólafsson
26/5	FH	a	0-3	
30/5	Grindavík	a	1-2	Platt
12/6	KR	h	2-1	Platt, Jeffs
16/6	Thróttur R.	a	0-4	
23/6	Valur	h	1-0	Jóhannesson St.
29/6	ÍA	a	0-2	
2/7	Fylkir	h	0-3	
10/7	Fram	h	2-0	Jeffs (p), Jóhannesson St.
18/7	Keflavík	a	2-2	og (Gylfason), Sigurdsson P.
24/7	FH	h	0-1	
14/8	KR	a	0-1	
18/8	Grindavík	h	5-1	Ólafsson, Runólfsson, Sigurdsson P., Jóhannesson St., Platt
21/8	Thróttur R.	h	2-0	Ólafsson, Jóhannesson St.
29/8	Valur	a	1-1	Vidarsson
11/9	ÍA	h	0-2	
17/9	Fylkir	a	0-1	

No	Name	Nat	Pos	Aps	(s)	Gls
20	Bjarni H. ADALSTEINSSON		D	13	(2)	
26	Anton BJARNASON		M	1	(1)	
12	Hrafn DAVÍDSSON		G	6	(1)	
3	Lewis DODDS	ENG	D	1	(2)	
16	Bjarni Rúnar EINARSSON		A	2	(11)	
27	Heimir S. GUDMUNDSSON		M	12		
2	Páll HJARDAR		D	16		
8	Ian JEFFS	ENG	M	17		2
13	Saethór JÓHANNESSON		M		(1)	
11	Steingrímur JÓHANNESSON		A	13	(4)	5
7	Atli JÓHANNSSON		M	16	(1)	
3	Egill JÓHANNSSON		M		(1)	
1	Birkir KRISTINSSON		G	12		
10	Rune LIND	DEN	M	5		
10	Magnús Már LÚDVÍKSSON		M	5	(1)	
6	Andri ÓLAFSSON		M	15		3
15	Matthew PLATT	ENG	M	11	(7)	3
4	James ROBINSON	ENG	M		(1)	
9	Pétur RUNÓLFSSON		D	12	(4)	1
18	Andrew SAM	ENG	A	5	(5)	
5	Einar H. SIGURDSSON		D	2	(1)	
28	Pétur Óskar SIGURDSSON		A	5	(4)	2
17	Adólf SIGURJÓNSSON		D	6		
14	Bjarni Geir VIDARSSON		D	17		1
29	Chris VORENKAMP	USA	D	6		

KEFLAVÍK
Coach – Kristján Gudmundsson

2005

16/5	FH	h	0-3	
22/5	ÍBV	a	3-2	Sveinsson, Steinarsson, Gudmundsson
26/5	KR	h	2-1	Steinarsson 2 (1p)
31/5	Thróttur R.	a	2-2	Sveinsson, Steinarsson
12/6	Valur	h	1-5	Arnarson
15/6	ÍA	a	2-1	Antoníusson, Steinarsson
23/6	Fylkir	h	2-2	og (Pétursson), Arnarson
26/6	Fram	a	3-2	Arnarson, Rúnarsson, Sveinsson
30/6	Grindavík	h	1-1	Sveinsson
8/7	FH	a	0-2	
18/7	ÍBV	h	2-2	Sveinsson (p), Jónsson
24/7	KR	a	3-1	Gustafsson, Sigurdsson, Sveinsson
7/8	Thróttur R.	h	3-3	Sveinsson 2, Samuelsen

Iceland

15/8	Valur	a	0-0		
21/8	ÍA	h	0-1		
30/8	Fylkir	a	1-0	Rúnarsson	
11/9	Fram	h	2-1	Sveinsson, Steinarsson	
17/9	Grindavík	a	1-2	Steinarsson	

No	Name	Nat	Pos	Aps	(s)	Gls
18	Issa ABDULKADIR	ENG	D	6	(4)	
17	Ásgrímur ALBERTSSON		D		(3)	
3	Gudjón Árni ANTONÍUSSON		D	16	(1)	1
29	Stefán Örn ARNARSON		A	4	(4)	3
30	Einar Orri EINARSSON		M		(2)	
8	Ingvi Rafn GUDMUNDSSON		M	2		1
21	Kenneth GUSTAFSSON	SWE	D	7		1
4	Gestur GYLFASON		D	14		
6	Atli Rúnar HÓLMBERGSSON		M		(4)	
15	Michael JOHANSSON	SWE	D	12	(2)	
1	Ómar JÓHANNSSON		G	17	(1)	
19	Ólafur Jón JÓNSSON		M		(2)	1
13	Gunnar H. KRISTINSSON		M	3	(7)	
20	Gudmundur Vidar METE		D	8		
23	Branislav MILICEVIC	SCG	D	11	(2)	
16	Brian O'CALLAGHAN	IRL	D	4		
7	Hólmar Örn RÚNARSSON		M	18		2
2	Bjarni SAEMUNDSSON		D	5	(5)	
5	Jónas Gudni SAEVARSSON		M	18		
17	Símun SAMUELSEN	FAR	A	1	(3)	1
11	Baldur SIGURDSSON		M	17	(1)	1
9	Gudmundur STEINARSSON		A	18		7
10	Hördur SVEINSSON		A	17		9
12	Magnús THORMAR		G	1	(1)	

KR
Coach – Magnús Gylfason; (26/7/05) Sigursteinn Gíslason

2005

16/5	Fylkir	a	2-1	og (Gíslason V.), Ólafsson
22/5	Fram	h	1-0	Jacobsen
26/5	Keflavík	a	1-2	Lárusson
29/5	FH	h	0-1	
12/6	ÍBV	a	1-2	og (Ólafsson A.)
16/6	Grindavík	a	0-0	
23/6	Tróttur R.	h	3-2	Jacobsen, Ólafsson, Hjartarson
27/6	Valur	a	0-3	
7/7	ÍA	h	0-2	
11/7	Fylkir	h	1-3	Bjarnason
17/7	Fram	a	4-0	Hjartarson 2, Jacobsen, Ólafsson
24/7	Keflavík	h	1-3	Gylfason
7/8	FH	a	0-2	
14/8	ÍBV	h	1-0	Kristjánsson S.
21/8	Grindavík	h	3-1	Hjartarson, Gylfason (p), Jóhannsson
28/8	Tróttur R.	a	1-0	Pauletic
11/9	Valur	h	2-0	Hjartarson 2
17/9	ÍA	a	1-2	Ólafsson

No	Name	Nat	Pos	Aps	(s)	Gls
3	Tryggvi BJARNASON		D	16		1
9	Sölvi DAVÍDSSON		M	7	(5)	
13	Gunnar EINARSSON		D	12	(1)	
23	Jökull I. ELÍSABETARSON		D	6	(5)	
1	Kristján FINNBOGASON		G	18		
15	Skúli Jón FRIDGEIRSSON		M		(2)	
26	Arnar GUNNLAUGSSON		A	5	(3)	
25	Bjarki GUNNLAUGSSON		M	3	(2)	
7	Ágúst Thór GYLFASON		D	12		2
11	Grétar HJARTARSON		A	17		6
14	Rógvi JACOBSEN	FAR	M	14	(3)	3
8	Gardar JÓHANNSSON		A	11	(3)	1
21	Vigfús A. JÓSEPSSON		D		(1)	
27	Gunnar KRISTJÁNSSON		D	8	(7)	
22	Sigmundur KRISTJÁNSSON		M	12	(2)	1
6	Bjarnólfur LÁRUSSON		M	16		1
4	Kristinn J. MAGNÚSSON		M	5	(3)	
5	Helmis MATUTE	USA	D	4	(1)	
10	Sigurvin ÓLAFSSON		M	13	(2)	4
29	Dalibor PAULETIC	CRO	D	6		1
18	Gestur PÁLSSON		M	4	(3)	
24	Sölvi STURLUSON		D	3	(2)	
2	Bjarni THORSTEINSSON		D	6	(1)	

THRÓTTUR R.
Coach – Ásgeir Elíasson; (6/7/05) Atli Edvaldsson

2005

16/5	ÍA	a	0-1	
22/5	Fylkir	h	1-2	Einarsson (p)
26/5	Fram	a	0-3	
31/5	Keflavík	h	2-2	Lárusson, Einarsson (p)
11/6	FH	a	1-3	Maruniak
16/6	ÍBV	h	4-0	Haflidason K., Jónasson, Saevarsson, Einarsson (p)
23/6	KR	a	2-3	Kristjánsson, Maruniak
26/6	Grindavík	a	1-1	Hilmisson
30/6	Valur	h	0-2	
12/7	ÍA	h	0-0	
17/7	Fylkir	a	1-0	Tryggvason
25/7	Fram	h	0-1	
7/8	Keflavík	a	3-3	Kristjánsson, Maruniak, Sigurdsson
15/8	FH	h	1-5	Einarsson (p)
21/8	ÍBV	a	0-2	
28/8	KR	h	0-1	
11/9	Grindavík	h	3-2	Hilmisson, Einarsson, Sveinsson
17/9	Valur	a	2-1	Saevarsson, Tryggvason

No	Name	Nat	Pos	Aps	(s)	Gls
8	Páll EINARSSON		M	18		5
11	Saevar EYJÓLFSSON		A	3	(5)	
5	Erlingur GUDMUNDSSON		M		(11)	
22	Davíd Logi GUNNARSSON		M		(2)	
10	Daniel HAFLIDASON		M	10	(2)	
15	Kristinn HAFLIDASON		M	7		1
3	Hallur HALLSSON		M	7	(3)	
14	Halldór A. HILMISSON		M	18		2
20	Dusan JAIC	SCG	D	5	(3)	
9	Henning E. JÓNASSON		D	4	(1)	1
7	Freyr KARLSSON		D	15	(1)	
29	Thórarinn KRISTJÁNSSON		A	14	(2)	2
6	Eysteinn P. LÁRUSSON		D	17		1
16	Magnús Már LÚDVÍKSSON		M	5	(4)	
17	Jozef MARUNIAK	SVK	A	7	(2)	3
19	Gudfinnur ÓMARSSON		A	2	(5)	
13	Jens Elvar SAEVARSSON		D	15		2
23	Haukur Páll SIGURDSSON		M	11	(2)	1
18	Ingvi SVEINSSON		M	11	(3)	1
1	Fjalar THORGEIRSSON		G	18		
4	Ólafur TRYGGVASON		D	11	(3)	2

Iceland

VALUR
Coach – Willum Thór Thórsson

2005

3/5	Grindavík	h	3-1	Hreidarsson S. (p), Benediktsson, Eiriksson
4/5	ÍA	h	2-0	Gunnlaugsson, Hreidarsson S. (p)
5/5	Fylkir	a	2-1	Gudmundsson 2
1/5	Fram	h	3-0	Gudmundsson, Júlíusson, Adalsteinsson
2/6	Keflavík	a	5-1	Adalsteinsson 2, Gudmundsson, Thórarinsson, Gunnlaugsson
5/6	FH	h	0-1	
3/6	ÍBV	a	0-1	
7/6	KR	h	3-0	Gudmundsson 2, Benediktsson
0/6	Thróttur R.	a	2-0	Gunnlaugsson, Gíslason H.
2/7	Grindavík	a	1-0	Gudmundsson
7/7	Fylkir	h	3-1	Gunnlaugsson 2, Júlíusson
/8	Fram	a	1-2	Gunnlaugsson (p)
1/8	ÍA	a	2-1	Gunnlaugsson 2
5/8	Keflavík	h	0-0	
1/8	FH	a	0-2	
9/8	ÍBV	h	1-1	Adalsteinsson
1/9	KR	a	0-2	
7/9	Thróttur R.	h	1-2	Sigurdarson

No	Name	Nat	Pos	Aps	(s)	Gls
6	Baldur I. ADALSTEINSSON		M	14	(2)	4
23	Gudmundur BENEDIKTSSON		A	18		2
21	Bjarni Ólafur EIRÍKSSON		D	18		1
10	Hálfdán GÍSLASON		A		(12)	1
3	Steinthór GÍSLASON		D	17		
11	Matthías GUDMUNDSSON		A	16	(2)	7
9	Gardar B. GUNNLAUGSSON		A	11	(6)	8
30	Bo HENRIKSEN	DEN	A		(1)	
7	Sigurbjörn HREIDARSSON		M	16	(1)	2
27	Thórdur S. HREIDARSSON		M		(1)	
4	Stefán Helgi JÓNSSON		M	15	(2)	
6	Sigthór JÚLÍUSSON		M	13	(2)	2
8	Kristinn Ingi LÁRUSSON		M	5	(11)	
20	Birkir Már SAEVARSSON		M		(1)	
2	Grétar S. SIGURDARSON		D	18		1
1	Kjartan STURLUSON		G	18		
17	Sigurdur S. THORSTEINSSON		M	2	(11)	
5	Atli Sveinn THÓRARINSSON		D	17		1

DOMESTIC CUP 2005

THIRD ROUND
(7/6/05)
Grótta 1, ÍA 2
(19/6/05)
Fjardabyggd 0, Fram 2
KS 2, Fylkir 4 (aet)
ÍR 1, Thór 2
Leiftur/Dalvík 1 ÍBV 2 (aet)
Njardvík 3, Völsungur 2 (aet)
Huginn 1, KA 4
Leiknir R. 0, KR 6
Hvíti riddarinn 1, HK 5 (aet)
Víkingur Ó. 1, Breidablik 2
(20/6/05)
Reynir Á. 0, Valur 7
Afturelding 0, Víkingur R. 1
Fjölnir 3, Keflavík 4
Vídir 0, FH 5
Haukar 1, Thróttur R. 1 *(aet; 5-4 on pens)*
Stjarnan 0, Grindavík 2

FOURTH ROUND
(4/7/05)
Víkingur R. 3, KR 3 *(aet; 5-6 on pens)*
ÍA 2, Breidablik 1 *(aet)*
Valur 5, Haukar 1
(5/7/05)
Grindavík 0, Fylkir 1
FH 3, KA 1
Thór 0, Fram 3
ÍBV 3, Njardvík 2
HK 1, Keflavík 0

QUARTER-FINALS
(16/7/05)
FH 5 *(Gudmundsson 74, Stefánsson 95, Borgvardi 108, Gardarsson 110, Björnsson A.V. 115)*, ÍA 1 *(Júlíusson 3) (aet)*
(20/7/05)
HK 0, Fylkir 2 *(Arnarsson 85, 90)*
(21/7/05)
KR 1 *(Gylfason 57)*, Valur 2 *(Hreidarsson S. 24, Gunnlaugsson 90)*
Fram 2 *(Ottósson 34, Dadason 103p)*, ÍBV 1 *(Sam 37) (aet)*

SEMI-FINALS
(3/8/05)
Fram 2 *(Ottósson 79, Henriksen 85)*, FH 2 *(Borgvardt 28, 44) (aet; 7-6 on pens)*
(4/8/05)
Valur 2 *(Gunnlaugsson 3, 84)*, Fylkir 0

FINAL
(24/9/05)
Laugardalsvöllur, Reykjavík
VALUR 1 *(Adalsteinsson 52)*
FRAM 0
Referee – Ragnarsson
VALUR – Sturluson, Gíslason S., Sigurdarson, Thórarinsson, Eiríksson, Adalsteinsson *(Gudmundsson 74)*, Jónsson, Hreidarsson S., Júlíusson, Benediktsson *(Gíslason H. 84)*, Gunnlaugsson *(Thorsteinsson 82)*.
FRAM – Sigurdsson, Karlefjärd, Jóhannsson, Hauksson, Gunnarsson, Hákonarson *(Stefánsson 77)*, Ólason, Mathiesen, Gudjónsson, Otzósson *(Sveinsson 72)*, Henriksen.

SECOND LEVEL FINAL TABLE 2005

		Pld	W	D	L	F	A	Pts
1	Breidablik	18	13	5	0	32	13	44
2	Víkingur R.	18	10	7	1	41	9	37
3	KA	18	10	4	4	40	20	34
4	Fjölnir	18	7	1	10	29	34	22
5	Víkingur Ó.	18	6	4	8	15	30	22
6	Thór	18	6	3	9	25	34	21
7	HK	18	4	8	6	18	21	20
8	Haukar	18	4	5	9	23	33	17
9	Völsungur	18	4	4	10	17	25	16
10	KS	18	2	7	9	14	35	13

Israel

Hat-trick for Maccabi Haifa

For the third year in a row Maccabi Haifa made mincemeat of the opposition and ran away with the Israeli Premier League. It was a hat-trick not just for the club but also for coach Roni Levi. Vilified at the start of his reign for being too negative, Levi has now won the title in each of his three seasons at the club, all of them in emphatic style. No Israeli team, let alone coach, had scooped three titles in succession since Hapoel Petach Tikva's five in a row from 1959-63, so it is some feat for a coach who is not yet 40.

As in the previous season, the Green Giants hit the ground running. After 11 games they had encountered every other team in the league and beaten them all. It was an imperious start and a marvellous response to the intense disappointment of being eliminated from Europe in the second qualifying round of the Champions League. A red card for striker Shlomi Arbeitman and a late goalkeeping error from Nir Davidovich in the second leg at home to Swedish champions Malmö FF meant that their European campaign was over several weeks before the domestic campaign had even begun.

The Premier League title race was also to end prematurely as Haifa kept their early momentum going into the New Year. A first defeat, 3-1 at Hapoel Petach Tikva on the last weekend of January, began a sticky patch in which they won just twice in seven matches, but they had so many points in the bank that they could almost have freewheeled to the finish without any more wins and still finished on top of the table.

There was a somewhat anti-climatic end to it all when the club's title hat-trick was sealed by proxy. A 1-1 draw in round 30 between Hapoel Tel Aviv and MS Ashdod left Haifa ten points in front with three games remaining. The following day they celebrated in front of their own fans with a thumping 4-0 victory over Hapoel Nazareth Ilit, and by the end of the campaign, despite a relatively disappointing spring that had brought a shock State Cup semi-final defeat by Bnei Yehuda Tel Aviv, their winning margin was up to 16 points – five more than in their title romp the previous season.

Mid-season move

Such was Haifa's dominance that they were able to survive the impact of star striker Yaniv Katan's mid-season move to West Ham. He was one of many Israeli internationals in the side. The others, including Arbeitman, Davidovich, winger Michael Zandberg, midfield strategist Idan Tal and defenders Alon Harazi, Arik Benado and Adoram Keissy all stayed on for the duration and made a key contribution towards the team's continued success. Davidovich set a new goalkeeping appearance record for the club during the campaign while Harazi bypassed the 400-game mark. There was also a strong South American

NATIONAL TEAM RESULTS 2005/06

15/8/05	Ukraine	A	Kiev	0-0	(5-3 on pens)
17/8/05	Poland	N	Kiev	2-3	Badir (33), Katan (47)
3/9/05	Switzerland (WCQ)	A	Basel	1-1	Keissy (20)
7/9/05	Faroe Islands (WCQ)	A	Tórshavn	2-0	Nimni (55), Katan (80)
8/10/05	Faroe Islands (WCQ)	H	Tel Aviv	2-1	Benayoun (1), Zandberg (89)
1/3/06	Denmark	H	Tel Aviv	0-2	

influence in the team, with Brazilian Gustavo Bocoli, who scored a dozen goals from midfield, being voted the Premier League player of the season and Argentine striker Roberto Colautti continuing to score at leisure, albeit not with quite the same consistency as in 2004/05 (when he was the league's top scorer).

The extent of Maccabi Haifa's achievement was put in perspective by the number of other Premier League clubs who tried to dethrone them with heavy investment.

Maccabi Tel Aviv splashed the cash in a big way in an attempt to celebrate their Centenary with a trophy or two. They were dubbed the 'Israeli galácticos' after a summer spending frenzy that brought in all sorts of big names, including two of the country's best loved veterans, Avi Nimni and Eyal Berkovic. The latter, who returned after a nine-year exile, was forthright in his ambitions, claiming that the team would win the Double. But it was soon evident that they would do no such thing. The average age of the squad was simply too high, there was no cohesion in the team, and as a result they kept losing matches – to APOEL of Cyprus in the UEFA Cup and to lowly opponents like Hapoel Kfar Saba and Hapoel Bnei Skahnin in the league.

Coach Nir Klinger was sacked in early December, but his replacement Ton Kaanen, a Dutchman who had just been controversially kicked out of Beitar Jerusalem, was unable to improve matters and after a hugely embarrassing State Cup defeat (4-0 at home to second-tier Hapoel Acco) the club's season petered out to a sorry conclusion. A disillusioned Berkovic decided to retire while owner Loni Herzikovich tried desperately to sell off his shares. It looked as if he had found a new buyer in rich French businessman Philippe Solomon, but an investigation by an Israeli newspaper uncovered all sorts of grim stories from his past, not least that he had been jailed three times for fraud. After that bombshell, the deal was naturally called off.

Russian sugar daddy

Beitar Jerusalem found themselves a genuine sugar daddy in Russian billionaire Arkady Gaydamak. He came in at the start of the season with big promises to revitalise the club. Right from the beginning, however, he wrapped himself in controversy, donating 400,000 dollars to Arab club Bnei Sakhnin as a diplomatic gesture and informing club legend Eli Ohana that his days as coach were numbered. Neither move went down well with the Beitar fans, but after just one game of the season Ohana was duly sent packing (although the official line was that he had left by mutual consent), with the coaching reins being passed on to club physiotherapist Guy Azoury.

Although Azoury did well as a stop-gap, Gaydamak brought in Dutchman Kaanen, only to change his mind soon afterwards and decide that he wanted a really well known foreigner in charge. His choice was ex-French international Luis Fernandez, who had been working on the other side of the Gulf in Qatar. Initially the ex-Paris Saint-Germain stalwart was employed as a grand overseer, but after a quarrel with Kaanen over responsibilities, Gaydamak resolved that the club wasn't big enough for the both of them and sent Kaanen on his way. Fernandez was to have an uneasy six months in charge. At times, aided by their three new foreign signings – Frenchman Jerôme Leroy and Fabrice Fernandes and Spaniard David Aganzo - Beitar played fluent, imaginative football, but on other occasions they slumped to embarrassing defeats, such as in the Cup at home to Hacoach Amidar Ramat Gan. By the end of the season Beitar had done enough to qualify for the UEFA Cup in third place but Fernandez's reign was at an end, Gaydamak opting to replace him for 2006/07 with another well-known foreigner, Argentinian World Cup winner Osvaldo Ardiles.

The man who had started the 2005/06 season as Beitar's coach, Eli Ohana, proved his credentials later on after being summoned to rescue newly promoted Hapoel Kfar Saba from an immediate relegation. The club were firmly rooted to the foot of the table when he arrived, but the former left-winger who once won the European Cup-winners Cup with Belgian club Mechelen staged a remarkable turnaround in the club's fortunes. After his arrival they lost just twice in 14 games, and although one of those defeats came on the final day, away to Maccabi Netanya, it didn't matter. Relegation rivals Hapoel Nazareth Ilit also lost 1-0 – at home to Bnei Yehuda Tel Aviv – and thus went down on goal difference.

A draw was all Nazareth Ilit needed to survive, and a draw was all Bnei Yehuda needed to qualify for the UEFA Cup, but fair play was observed and the Tel Aviv side deserved great credit for bouncing back so positively from defeat in the State Cup final to crosstown rivals Hapoel Tel Aviv four days earlier.

Israel

NATIONAL TEAM APPEARANCES 2005/06

Coach – Avraham GRANT

Player	DOB	Club	Ukr	Pol	SUI	FAR	FAR	Den	Caps	Goals
Nir DAVIDOVICH	17/12/76	Maccabi Haifa	G		G	G	G	G	40	-
Klimi SABAN	17/2/80	Maccabi Haifa	D	D90	D				10	-
Tal BEN HAIM	31/3/82	Bolton Wanderers (ENG)	D75		D	D	D	D46	26	-
Arik BENADO	5/12/73	Maccabi Haifa	D	D46	D	D	D	D	89	-
Avi YEHIEL	26/9/79	Maccabi Tel Aviv	D46	s80					3	1
Adoram KEISSY	17/6/72	Maccabi Haifa	D	D	D	D	D	D89	52	4
Idan TAL	13/9/75	Maccabi Haifa	M90	M	M	s65		M	59	5
Walid BADIR	12/3/74	Hapoel Tel Aviv	M	M	M	M	M	M	62	11
David REVIVO	5/12/77	MS Ashdod	M55						3	-
Yaniv KATAN	27/1/81	Maccabi Haifa /West Ham United (ENG)	M84	A67	A65	A86	A73	A80	24	5
Omer GOLAN	4/10/82	Maccabi Petach Tikva	A72	A73	s65		A67	s80	15	1
Abbas SOUAN	27/1/76	Hapoel Bnei Sakhnin	s46	M80	s90	M	M46	M60	12	1
Salim TUAAMA	9/8/79	Maccabi Petach Tikva	s55	s67					2	-
Moshe BITON	18/11/82	Bnei Yehuda Tel Aviv	s72	s46		s86		s75	4	-
Alon HARAZI	13/2/71	Maccabi Haifa	s75	D	D	D	D	D	89	1
Pini BALILI	18/6/79	Sivasspor (TUR)	s84	s73		A65	s73		24	7
Shimon GERSHON	6/10/77	Hapoel Tel Aviv	s90	D				s46	37	2
Dudu AWATE	17/10/77	Racing Santander (ESP)			G				18	-
Yossi SHIVHON	22/3/82	Hapoel Petach Tikva		s90				s85	2	-
Avi NIMNI	26/4/72	Maccabi Tel Aviv			M71	M	M		80	18
Yossi BENAYOUN	5/5/80	West Ham United (ENG)			M90	M	M	M85	49	11
Michael ZANDBERG	16/4/80	Maccabi Haifa			s71	s46	s60		15	4
Shlomi ARBEITMAN	14/5/85	Maccabi Haifa					s67	A75	4	3
Roni GAFNI	1/3/80	Banei Yehuda Tel Aviv						s89	1	-

Fond farewell

A 40,000-strong crowd in the Ramat Gan stadium saw Hapoel take the trophy for the first time in six years thanks to a late winning goal from Armenian striker Euguja Javrujan. The 1-0 victory was the perfect farewell present for the club's veteran coach Dror Kashtan, whose successful comeback to the club where he had won the Double in 1999/2000 was cut short by his appointment – announced in mid-season but delayed until June - as the new coach of the Israeli national side.

As Israel's most successful coach at club level (six Premier League and six State Cup wins with various teams), the 61-year-old was the logical choice to take over from Avraham Grant, who resigned from the post despite taking the team unbeaten through their ten-match World Cup qualifying group. Unfortunately, six of those games were drawn, and Israel just missed out on a play-off place because of an inferior goal difference to Switzerland.

Kashtan will have to conjure some extraordinary performances from his players if they are do equally well in a Euro 2008 qualifying group containing England, Croatia and Russia – even if all three of their chief rivals for a place in Austria and Switzerland are also in a state of transition under new coaches.

The most important concern for Israel over the summer was whether the latest military conflict in the region would force the national team and the country's European club representatives, as in the past, to play their home matches on foreign soil. If so, it would be a massive blow to Israeli football.

Israel

EUROPEAN CUPS 2005/06

UEFA CHAMPIONS LEAGUE

MACCABI HAIFA
2nd qualifying round MALMÖ FF (SWE)
A **2-3** *Harazi (2), Colautti (44)*
Davidovich, Keissy, Harazi, Benado, Saban (Olarra 75), Dirseu, Zandberg (Biruk 88), Tal, Bocoli, Katan (Arbeitman 86), Colautti.
H **2-2** *Colautti (10), Arbeitman (60)*
Davidovich, Keissy, Harazi, Benado, Olarra, Dirseu, Zandberg (Biruk 77), Tal, Bocoli, Katan (Arbeitman 56), Colautti.

UEFA CUP

MACCABI TEL AVIV
2nd qualifying round APOEL (CYP)
A **0-1**
Shtrauber, Shpungin, Yehiel, González, Abu Siam, Cohen T., Kaku, Rosso, Berkovic (Cohen L. 90), Trica, Dayan (Mesika 72).
H **2-2** *Nimni (63), Mesika (117)*
(aet)
Shtrauber, Elihav, Yehiel, González, Abu Siam, Cohen T. (Kaku 84), Cohen L., Rosso, Berkovic (Shpungin 97), Nimni, Dayan (Mesika 76).

MACCABI PETACH TIKVA
2nd qualifying round BASKIMI KUMANOVO (MAC)
A **5-0** *Magomedov (5), Toema (13), Mashiach (22p), Edrei (70), Sarsour (90)*
Cohen, Mashiach (Amar 74), Banay, Magomedov, Ganon, Tzemach, Jefisley, Toema (Sarsour 82), Edrei, Dobrovin (Janah 86), Golan.
H **6-0** *Golan (9, 39, 89), Ganon (41), Sarsour (64, 66)*
Cohen, Amar, Banay, Magomedov, Ganon (Peser 58), Mashiach, Jefisley (Janah 46), Toema (Sarsour 46), Edrei, Dobrovin, Golan.

1st round PARTIZAN BEOGRAD (SCG)
H **0-2**
Cohen, Mashiach (Amar 56), Banay, Magomedov, Ganon, Tzemach, Jefisley, Edrei (Sarsour 72), Dobrovin, Golan, Mbamba (Toema 51).
A **5-2** *Mashiach (3p), Golan (20, 44, 48), Edrei (88)*
Cohen, Amar, Banay, Magomedov, Ganon, Mashiach (Tzemach 46), Toema, Edrei, Jefisley, Dobrovin (Lokaso 80), Golan (Mbamba 58).

2nd round Group B
Match 1 PALERMO (ITA)
H **1-2** *Golan (45)*
Cohen, Amar, Lokaso, Magomedov, Ganon, Mashiach (Sarsour 81), Tzemach, Edrei (Zan 78), Jefisley, Mbamba, Golan.

Match 2 BRØNDBY IF (DEN)
A **0-2**
Cohen, Amar, Lokaso, Magomedov, Ganon, Mashiach (Dobrovin 72), Tzemach, Edrei, Jefisley, Mbamba, Golan.

Match 3 LOKOMOTIV MOSKVA (RUS)
H **0-4**
Cohen, Amar, Banay, Magomedov (Hadiya 60), Ganon, Tzemach, Edrei (Toema 46), Jefisley, Dobrovin (David 54), Mbamba, Golan.

Match 4 RCD ESPANYOL (ESP)
A **0-1**
Cohen (Mizrahi 46), Amar, Banay, Tzemach, Ganon, Peser, Jefisley, David, Toema (Edrei 70), Dobrovin, Golan (Mbamba 46).

MS ASHDOD
2nd qualifying round DOMZALE (SLO)
H **2-2** *Rajovic (18), Dika Dika (34)*
Shekel, Alfasi, Etchi, Dika Dika, Tubol, Offir, Ebiede (Peretz 64), Ohaion, Revivo, Shriki (Holtzman 64), Rajovic (Fadida 86).
A **1-1** *Ebiede (70)*
Shekel, Elkarif, Etchi, Dika Dika, Tubol (Peretz 59), Offir, Ebiede, Ohaion, Revivo, Rajovic (Shriki 59), Holtzman (Almosnino 78).

TOP GOALSCORERS 2005/06

18 Shay HOLTZMAN (MS Ashdod)

13 Roberto COLAUTTI (Maccabi Haifa)

12 Gustavo BOCOLI (Maccabi Haifa)
    Lior ASULIN (Beitar Jerusalem)

11 Toto TAMUZ (Hapoel Petach Tikva)
    Yossi SHIVHON (Hapoel Petach Tikva)

10 Omer GOLAN (Hapoel Petach Tikva)
    Avi NIMNI (Maccabi Tel Aviv)
    Papy KIMOTO (Maccabi Netanya)

9   Ibazito OGABUNA (Hapoel Tel Aviv)
    Michael ZANDBERG (Maccabi Haifa)
    Alain MASUDA (Maccabi Netanya)

LEAGUE RESULTS/ SCORERS/APPEARANCES/ GOALS 2005/06

MS ASHDOD
Coach – Yossi Mizrahi

2005
Date	Opponent	H/A	Score	Scorers
29/8	Hapoel Nazareth Ilit	a	1-2	Holtzman (p)
16/9	Hapoel Bnei Sakhnin	a	1-0	Revivo D.
24/9	Hapoel Petach Tikva	h	4-3	Shriki, Holtzman 2, Ohaion
30/9	Bnei Yehuda Tel Aviv	a	1-2	Offir
15/10	Maccabi Tel Aviv	h	0-1	
22/10	Maccabi Netanya	a	1-1	Ebiede
29/10	Maccabi Haifa	h	1-2	Holtzman
7/11	Hapoel Petach Tikva	a	2-2	Shriki, Holtzman
12/11	Beitar Jerusalem	h	2-3	Revivo D., Holtzman
19/11	Hapoel Tel Aviv	a	1-3	Offir
26/11	Hapoel Kfar Saba	h	5-0	Ebiede, Tubul, Holtzman, Ohaion (p), Revivo D.
2/12	Hapoel Nazareth Ilit	h	2-1	Ohaion, Holtzman
10/12	Hapoel Bnei Sakhnin	h	1-2	Shriki
17/12	Hapoel Petach Tikva	a	1-3	Shriki
30/12	Bnei Yehuda Tel Aviv	h	2-0	Holtzman, Ebiede

2006
Date	Opponent	H/A	Score	Scorers
7/1	Maccabi Tel Aviv	a	1-2	Offir
14/1	Maccabi Netanya	h	2-2	Kaku, Holtzman
22/1	Maccabi Haifa	a	0-4	
27/1	Maccabi Petach Tikva	h	2-0	Holtzman 2
5/2	Beitar Jerusalem	a	1-0	Holtzman
11/2	Hapoel Tel Aviv	h	1-1	Kaku
18/2	Hapoel Kfar Saba	a	2-2	Kaku, Revivo D.
25/2	Maccabi Netanya	a	1-3	Ebiede
11/3	Hapoel Kfar Saba	a	1-1	Ohaion
18/3	Hapoel Nazaret Ilit	h	0-0	
24/3	Hapoel Petach Tikva	a	2-1	Holtzman (p), Ohaion
1/4	Maccabi Petach Tikva	h	0-0	
7/4	Hapoel Bnei Sakhnin	a	3-0	Ohaion, Holtzman 2

Israel

FINAL LEAGUE TABLE 2005/06

		Pld	Home W	Home D	Home L	Home F	Home A	Away W	Away D	Away L	Away F	Away A	Total W	Total D	Total L	Total F	Total A	Pts
1	Maccabi Haifa	33	15	1	1	38	10	8	5	3	27	15	23	6	4	65	25	75
2	Hapoel Tel Aviv	33	9	7	1	30	11	7	4	5	21	14	16	11	6	51	25	59
3	Beitar Jerusalem	33	8	2	7	22	14	9	5	2	29	19	17	7	9	51	33	58
4	Bnei Yehuda Tel Aviv	33	10	2	5	23	19	4	5	7	14	22	14	7	12	37	41	49
5	Maccabi Petach Tikva	33	10	3	3	24	15	2	5	10	13	23	12	8	13	37	38	44
6	Maccabi Tel Aviv	33	9	6	2	24	14	2	5	9	11	23	11	11	11	35	37	44
7	Maccabi Netanya	33	7	5	5	22	19	4	3	9	18	26	11	8	14	40	45	41
8	MS Ashdod	33	5	7	4	25	18	4	5	8	21	29	9	12	12	46	47	39
9	Hapoel Petach Tikva	33	4	5	7	18	25	5	5	7	20	25	9	10	14	38	50	37
10	Hapoel Kfar Saba	33	4	7	5	17	17	4	3	10	13	24	8	10	15	30	41	34
11	Hapoel Nazareth Ilit	33	6	5	5	16	20	2	5	10	9	27	8	10	15	25	47	34
12	Hapoel Bnei Sakhnin	33	4	5	7	15	27	1	5	11	13	27	5	10	18	28	54	25

BEITAR JERUSALEM

Coach – Eli Ohana; (1/9/05) (Guy Azoury); (12/11/05) Ton Kaanen (HOL); (10/12/05) Luis Fernandez (FRA)

2005

Date	Opponent	H/A	Score	Scorers
28/8	Maccabi Tel Aviv	h	0-1	
17/9	Maccabi Netanya	a	3-2	N'Sumbo, Asulin 2 (1p)
25/9	Maccabi Haifa	h	0-1	
2/10	Maccabi Petach Tikva	a	2-1	Malihi, Asulin
16/10	Hapoel Bnei Sakhnin	h	3-2	Melikson, Hudeda, Ben Shushan
15/4	Maccabi Haifa	h	1-1	Holtzman
22/4	Hapoel Tel Aviv	a	1-1	Ohaion
29/4	Beitar Jerusalem	h	1-1	Shriki
5/5	Bnei Yehuda Tel Aviv	a	1-2	Holtzman
13/5	Maccabi Tel Aviv	h	1-1	Azran
23/10	Hapoel Tel Aviv	h	0-2	
29/10	Hapoel Kfar Saba	a	2-0	Totuana, Asulin
5/11	Hapoel Nazareth Ilit	h	4-0	Totuana 3, Haliba
12/11	MS Ashdod	a	3-2	Asulin 3 (1p)
19/11	Hapoel Petach Tikva	h	0-1	
27/11	Bnei Yehuda Tel Aviv	a	3-2	Asulin, Affek, Itzhaki
4/12	Maccabi Tel Aviv	a	3-2	N'Sumbo, Barochian, Itzhaki
10/12	Maccabi Netanya	h	1-1	Itzhaki
18/12	Maccabi Haifa	a	0-3	
31/12	Maccabi Petach Tikva	h	2-0	Affek, Itzhaki

2006

Date	Opponent	H/A	Score	Scorers
8/1	Hapoel Bnei Sakhnin	a	0-0	
15/1	Hapoel Tel Aviv	a	1-1	Asulin
21/1	Hapoel Kfar Saba	h	1-0	Itzhaki (p)
28/1	Hapoel Nazareth Ilit	a	1-1	Ziv
5/2	MS Ashdod	h	0-1	
11/2	Hapoel Petach Tikva	a	3-0	Barochian, Aganzo, Melikson
19/2	Bnei Yehuda Tel Aviv	h	2-2	Aganzo, Itzhaki
26/2	Maccabi Petach Tikva	h	1-0	Leroy
13/3	Hapoel Bnei Sakhnin	a	3-0	Asulin 2, Leroy
19/3	Maccabi Haifa	h	1-0	Asulin
26/3	Hapoel Tel Aviv	a	1-1	og (Gershon)
11/4	Hapoel Kfar Saba	a	0-1	
8/4	Bnei Yehuda Tel Aviv	h	3-0	Mitreski, Barochian, Itzhaki
16/4	Maccabi Tel Aviv	a	1-2	Barochian
22/4	Maccabi Netanya	h	4-0	Alberman, Aganzo, Barochian, Ziv
29/4	MS Ashdod	a	1-1	Fernandes
7/5	Hapoel Nazareth Ilit	h	0-2	
14/5	Hapoel Petach Tikva	a	2-1	Azriel, Ben Youssef (p)

No	Name	Nat	Pos	Aps	(s)	Gls
22	Sammy ADJEI	GHA	G	27		
8	Oshri ALFASI		M	7	(3)	
7	Eyal ALMOSNINO		M	25	(3)	
15	Yaniv AZRAN		A	6	(9)	1
1	Yaniv BEN ISHAY		G	5		
27	Jean DIKA-DIKA	CMR	D	2		
25	Emmanuel EBIEDE	NGA	M	24	(9)	4
3	Amir ELKARIF		D	25	(1)	
26	Roman HAUSTOV		D		(1)	
19	Shay HOLTZMAN		A	31	(1)	18
11	JAVIer GONZÁLEZ Gómez	ESP	M	7	(4)	
17	Blessing KAKU	NGA	M	18		3
28	Kobi MUSA		D	8	(2)	
16	Ernest OBEN-ETACHI	CMR	D	14		
9	Felix OBUKE		A	6	(6)	
18	Youssi OFFIR		M	32		3
9	Moshe OHAION		M	13	(20)	7
4	Maor PERETZ		M	15	(7)	
17	Zoran RAJOVIC	BOS	A		(1)	
10	David REVIVO		M	31	(1)	4
	Shay REVIVO		M		(1)	
27	Gay SHAMIR		M	7	(2)	
12	Youssi SHEKEL		G	1		
14	Idan SHRIKI		A	14	(17)	5
16	Adir TUBUL		D	31		1
5	Sheriff UCHE	NGA	D	2	(2)	
20	Maor ZOHAR		D	12	(2)	

No	Name	Nat	Pos	Aps	(s)	Gls
18	Omri AFFEK		M	9	(4)	2
27	David AGANZO	ESP	A	11	(1)	3
19	Gal ALBERMAN		M	8	(1)	1
3	David AMSALEM		D	24	(1)	
11	Lior ASULIN		A	20	(7)	12
10	Offir AZOU		M	6	(5)	
26	Chen AZRIEL		M	1		1
8	Aviram BAROCHIAN		M	8	(12)	5
12	Amir BEN SHUSHAN		A	4	(17)	1
6	Tomer BEN YOUSSEF		D	25		1
17	Eliran DANIN		M	14	(3)	
23	Youni ELIHAV		M	1	(1)	

Israel

No	Name	Nat	Pos	Aps	(s)	Gls
20	Fabrice FERNANDES	FRA	M	13	(1)	1
4	Tomer HALIBA		D	19	(4)	1
16	Eliran HUDEDA		D	9	(2)	1
9	Barak ITZHAKI		A	12	(10)	7
53	Adem KAPIC	SLO	M	6	(2)	
25	Yoni KIM		D	1		
1	Itzhak KORENFAIN		G	31		
28	Jérôme LEROY	FRA	M	15		2
26	Idan MALIHI		M	14	(6)	1
15	Maor MELIKSON		M	18	(11)	2
29	Igor MITRESKI	MAC	D	10		1
21	Kobi MOYAL		M	1	(2)	
13	Shay NISSIM		M		(1)	
24	Mazoua N'SUMBO	DRC	M	31	(3)	2
20	Eli SASSON		M	7	(2)	
22	Guy SOLOMON		G	2		
16	Jeff TOTUANA	DRC	A	16	(3)	4
14	Youav ZIV		D	27	(2)	2

BNEI YEHUDA TEL AVIV
Coach – Nitzan Shirazi

2005
27/8	Hapoel Tel Aviv	a	0-2	
17/9	Hapoel Kfar Saba	h	2-1	Baldut, Baturina
23/9	Hapoel Nazareth Ilit	a	0-0	
30/9	MS Ashdod	h	2-1	Baturina, Biton E.
15/10	Hapoel Petach Tikva	a	3-2	Biton E. 2, Biton M.
21/10	Hapoel Bnei Sakhnin	a	3-0	Biton E, Kovacevic, Badash
30/10	Maccabi Tel Aviv	h	3-1	Luz, Abarbnel, Biton E.
5/11	Maccabi Natanya	a	1-0	Baldut
14/11	Maccabi Haifa	h	0-1	
19/11	Maccabi Petach Tikva	a	0-0	
27/11	Beitar Jerusalem	h	2-3	Baldut, Biton E.
3/12	Hapoel Tel Aviv	h	0-4	
10/12	Hapoel Kfar Saba	a	1-1	Oved
16/12	Hapoel Nazareth Ilit	h	1-1	Baldut
30/12	MS Ashdod	a	0-2	

2006
6/1	Hapoel Petach Tikva	h	2-1	Biton E., Baturina
14/1	Hapoel Bnei Sakhnin	h	2-1	Baldut, Abarbnel
21/1	Maccabi Tel Aviv	a	2-2	Oved, Lukman
28/1	Maccabi Natanya	h	1-0	Biton E.
4/2	Maccabi Haifa	a	0-1	
11/2	Maccabi Petach Tikva	h	1-0	Biton M.
19/2	Beitar Jerusalem	a	2-2	Oved, Baturina
25/2	Hapoel Petach Tikva	h	2-2	Gafni, Biton M.
10/3	Maccabi Petach Tikva	a	0-1	
18/3	Hapoel Bnei Sakhnin	h	2-0	Abarbnel (p), Biton M.
25/3	Maccabi Haifa	a	0-4	
1/4	Hapoel Tel Aviv	h	0-1	
8/4	Beitar Jerusalem	a	0-3	
15/4	Hapoel Kfar Saba	h	0-1	
22/4	Maccabi Tel Aviv	h	1-0	Baldut
29/4	Maccabi Natanya	a	1-2	Biton M.
5/5	MS Ashdod	h	2-1	Abarbnel 2 (1p)
13/5	Hapoel Nazareth Ilit	a	1-0	Biton M.

No	Name	Nat	Pos	Aps	(s)	Gls
10	Eli ABARBNEL		M	29		5
11	Eliran ATAR		A	2	(4)	
15	Yair AZOULAY		D	18	(2)	
2	Yitzhak AZOUZ		M	9	(2)	
29	Barak BADASH		A	5	(18)	1
8	Assi BALDUT		D	30	(2)	6
13	Mate BATURINA	CRO	M	24	(2)	4
24	Eli BITON		A	6	(23)	8
20	Moshe BITON		A	24	(2)	6
18	Kobi DEGANI		D	11	(12)	
6	Adrian DEGMAN	ROM	D	7		
12	Yaniv ELUL		D	30		
1	Vincent ENIEMA	NGA	A	26		
4	Roni GAFNI		D	31		1
7	Hrvoje KOVACEVIC	CRO	D	30	(1)	1
21	Imoro LUKMAN	GHA	M	29	(2)	1
10	Benzion LUZ		A	10	(1)	1
16	Ernest OBEN-ETACHI	CMR	D	10	(1)	
12	Reuven OVED		M	19	(9)	3
27	Oz RALLY		M		(1)	
3	Motti SASON		M	2	(11)	
19	Kfir UDI		A	4	(4)	
22	Yahav YULZARI		G	7		

HAPOEL BNEI SAKHNIN
Coach – Momo Zafran; (28/9/05) Michael "Lupa" Kadosh; (20/3/06) Yehoshua Feigenbaum

2005
27/8	Maccabi Haifa	a	1-4	Pitu
16/9	M.S. Ashdod	h	0-1	
24/9	Maccabi Petach Tikva	a	1-2	Nicolae
1/10	Hapoel Petach Tikva	h	0-2	
16/10	Beitar Jerusalem	a	2-3	Abergil, Pitu
21/10	Bnei Yehuda Tel Aviv	h	0-3	
29/10	Hapoel Tel Aviv	a	2-2	Souan (p), Kasum
6/11	Maccabi Tel Aviv	h	1-0	Abergil
11/11	Hapoel Kfar Saba	a	0-0	
19/11	Maccabi Netanaya	h	2-2	Kasum, Souan
25/11	Hapoel Nazareth Ilit	a	2-3	og (Zoninho), Pascal
3/12	Maccabi Haifa	h	2-2	Pascal, Souan
10/12	MS Ashdod	a	2-1	og (Oben-Etachi), Kasum
19/12	Maccabi Petach Tikva	h	2-1	Kasum, Hasarma
31/12	Hapoel Petach Tikva	a	0-0	

2006
8/1	Beitar Jerusalem	h	0-0	
14/1	Bnei Yehuda Tel Aviv	a	1-2	Hasarma
21/1	Hapoel Tel Aviv	h	2-1	Pascal 2
29/1	Maccabi Tel Aviv	a	0-2	
3/2	Hapoel Kfar Saba	h	1-2	Pitu
11/2	Maccabi Netanya	a	0-0	
17/2	Hapoel Nazareth Ilit	h	1-0	og (Azoulay)
25/2	Hapoel Tel Aviv	a	0-1	
13/3	Beitar Jerusalem	h	0-3	
18/3	Bnei Yehuda Tel Aviv	a	0-2	
25/3	Maccabi Tel Aviv	h	1-1	Kasum
1/4	Maccabi Netanya	a	1-1	Souan
7/4	MS Ashdod	a	0-3	
15/4	Hapoel Nazareth Ilit	a	1-2	Pascal
21/4	Hapoel Petach Tikva	h	1-4	Pitu
29/4	Maccabi Petach Tikva	a	0-1	
7/5	Hapoel Kfar Saba	a	0-1	
12/5	Maccabi Hiafa	h	2-2	Halyla, Rabach

No	Name	Nat	Pos	Aps	(s)	Gls
9	Yaniv ABERGIL		A	21	(9)	2
23	Maharan ABU RIA		D	1	(1)	
5	Alla ABU SALLAH		D	1		
16	Yohai AHARONI		A	1		
13	Amar AWALLA		A		(1)	
24	Geva BARKAY		D	31	(1)	
1	Meir COHEN		G	32		
4	Avi DANAN		D	1	(1)	
17	Darko DJOKIC	CRO	M	2	(1)	
22	Anan FERO		G	1		
12	Bassem GANAYM		M	18	(4)	
15	Haled HALYLA		M	21	(2)	1

Israel

No	Name	Nat	Pos	Aps	(s)	Gls
17	Salah HASARMA		M	31		2
16	Eliran HUDEDA		D	10	(2)	
6	Nidal HUGIRAT		M	13	(5)	
20	Remigiusz JEZIERSKI	POL	M	8	(5)	
21	Ahmed KASUM		M	19	(5)	5
26	Islam KNA'AN		D		(1)	
5	Kfir LEIBOVITCH		D		(1)	
7	Gavriel LIMA	BRA	A	4	(2)	
20	Shuki NAGAR		D	13	(2)	
2	Gheorghe Bogdan NICOLAE	ROM	D	12	(2)	1
	Ali OTMAN		M		(2)	
13	Pascal OUE'DRAOGO	BFA	A	1	(2)	
11	PASCAL Kondafoni	NGA	M	30	(2)	5
13	Álvaro PINTOS	URU	A	2	(2)	
19	Adrian PITU	ROM	M	20	(7)	4
7	Abed RABACH		D	29	(2)	1
16	Munir SALAMI		M		(2)	
10	Nidal SHLAATA		D	9	(4)	
8	Abass SOUAN		M	26		4
20	Tomer TAYAR		M	1		
18	Nikola VALENTIC	SCG	M	2	(3)	
27	Sebastián VIERA	URU	M	2	(4)	
14	Shadi ZVIDATH		M	1	(13)	

HAPOEL KFAR SABA
Coach – Elisha Levi; (29/1/06) Eli Ohana

2005
26/8	Hapoel Petach Tikva	h	1-1	og (Heidman)
17/9	Bnei Yehuda Tel Aviv	a	1-2	Pappoe
24/9	Maccabi Tel Aviv	h	1-0	Carvalho
1/10	Maccabi Natanya	a	2-3	Menashe, Rajovic
15/10	Maccabi Haifa	h	1-2	Tchami
24/10	Maccabi Petach Tikva	a	0-0	
29/10	Beitar Jerusalem	h	0-2	
4/11	Hapoel Tel Aviv	a	1-3	Menashe
11/11	Hapoel Bnei Sakhnin	h	0-0	
18/11	Hapoel Nazareth Ilit	h	1-2	Rajovic
26/11	MS Ashdod	a	0-5	
3/12	Hapoel Petach Tikva	a	1-2	Knafo
10/12	Bnei Yehuda Tel Aviv	h	1-1	Nissim
17/12	Maccabi Tel Aviv	a	1-2	Avinu
31/12	Maccabi Natanya	h	1-2	Rajovic

2006
7/1	Maccabi Haifa	a	0-1	
14/1	Maccabi Petach Tikva	h	2-0	Knafo, Yeboah
21/1	Beitar Jerusalem	a	0-1	
28/1	Hapoel Tel Aviv	h	0-1	
3/2	Hapoel Bnei Sakhnin	a	2-1	Knafo, Yeboah
10/2	Hapoel Nazareth Ilit	a	0-1	
18/2	MS Ashdod	h	2-2	Menashe, Yeboah
25/2	Maccabi Haifa	a	1-1	Nissim
11/3	M.S. Ashdod	h	1-1	Douglas
18/3	Hapoel Tel Aviv	a	2-1	Rajovic, Menashe
25/3	Hapoel Nazareth Ilit	h	3-1	Yeboah 2, Pappoe
1/4	Beitar Jerusalem	a	1-0	Yeboah
8/4	Hapoel Petach Tikva	h	0-0	
15/4	Bnei Yehuda Tel Aviv	a	1-0	Luz (p)
22/4	Maccabi Petach Tikva	h	2-2	Abubakari, Yeboah
29/4	Maccabi Tel Aviv	a	0-0	
7/5	Hapoel Bnei Sakhnin	h	1-0	Knafo
13/5	Maccabi Netanya	a	0-1	

No	Name	Nat	Pos	Aps	(s)	Gls
19	Yahuza ABUBAKARI	GHA	M	20	(1)	1
24	Avi ALFASSI		M	1	(2)	
27	Avi AVINU		A	5	(9)	1
11	Fabrício CARVALHO	BRA	M	13		1
14	Carlos CHACANA	ARG	A	1		
21	Guy DAYAN		A	2	(9)	
5	DOUGLAS da Silva	BRA	D	33		1
4	Alon HALFON		D	23	(1)	
1	Avi IVGI		G	30		
25	Muhamad KABAHAA		D	16		
9	Avi KNAFO		A	21	(1)	4
16	Ohad LEVITE		G	3		
10	Benzion LUZ		M	16	(1)	1
7	Shalev MENASHE		M	29	(4)	4
8	Eyal MESHUMAR		M	29		
11	Oren NISSIM		A	7	(8)	2
15	Emmanuel PAPPOE	GHA	D	29		2
17	Zoran RAJOVIC	BOS	A	15	(10)	4
12	Adi SABAG		D	1	(2)	
9	Irakli SCHENGELIA	GEO	M	1	(2)	
6	Mohamad SH'HABRI		D	3	(1)	
29	Joël TCHAMI	CMR	A	4	(4)	1
19	Avraham TIKVA		M	1	(14)	
3	Valentin TUDORIKA		M	13	(8)	
30	Hector WEISHEIM	ARG	A		(3)	
26	Avihai YADIN		M	20		
29	Samuel YEBOAH	GHA	A	18		7
17	Liron ZARKO		M	9	(5)	

HAPOEL NAZARETH ILIT
Coach – Moti Iwanir

2005
29/8	MS Ashdod	h	2-1	Seslar 2 (2p)
17/9	Hapoel Petach Tikva	a	0-0	
23/9	Bnei Yehuda Tel Aviv	h	0-0	
1/10	Maccabi Tel Aviv	a	0-0	
14/10	Maccabi Netanya	h	1-3	Shechter
22/10	Maccabi Haifa	a	1-2	Elkayam
29/10	Hapoel Petach Tikva	h	2-0	Karoglan, Israilevich
5/11	Beitar Jerusalem	a	0-4	
12/11	Hapoel Tel Aviv	h	1-1	Simantov
18/11	Hapoel Kfar Saba	a	2-1	Simantov (p), Israilevich
25/11	Hapoel Bnei Sakhnin	h	3-2	Israilevich, Zoninho, Simantov
2/12	MS Ashdod	a	1-2	Shechter
9/12	Hapoel Petach Tikva	h	2-1	Shechter, Simantov (p)
16/12	Bnei Yehuda Tel Aviv	a	1-1	Elkayam
31/12	Maccabi Tel Aviv	h	0-0	

2006
7/1	Maccabi Netanya	a	0-1	
14/1	Maccabi Haifa	h	0-6	
21/1	Maccabi Petach Tikva	a	0-2	
28/1	Beitar Jerusalem	h	1-1	Simantov (p)
4/2	Hapoel Tel Aviv	a	0-4	
10/2	Hapoel Kfar Saba	h	1-0	Hristov
17/2	Hapoel Bnei Sakhnin	a	0-1	
24/2	Maccabi Tel Aviv	a	1-1	Zano
11/3	Maccabi Netanya	h	0-1	
18/3	MS Ashdod	a	0-0	
25/3	Hapoel Kfar Saba	a	1-3	Elkayam
31/3	Hapoel Petach Tikva	h	0-1	
8/4	Maccabi Petach Tikva	a	0-1	
15/4	Hapoel Bnei Sakhnin	h	2-1	Ben Ami, Banon
23/4	Maccabi Haifa	a	0-4	
29/4	Hapoel Tel Aviv	h	1-1	Hristov
7/5	Beitar Jerusalem	a	2-0	Fülöp, Hristov (p)
13/5	Bnei Yehuda Tel Aviv	h	0-1	

No	Name	Nat	Pos	Aps	(s)	Gls
23	Yohai AHARONI		A		(3)	
5	Ami AZULAY		D	26	(2)	

The Colour Section 2006/2007

Maps and Locations
Club Badges
Federation Crests
International Kits

The Colour Section

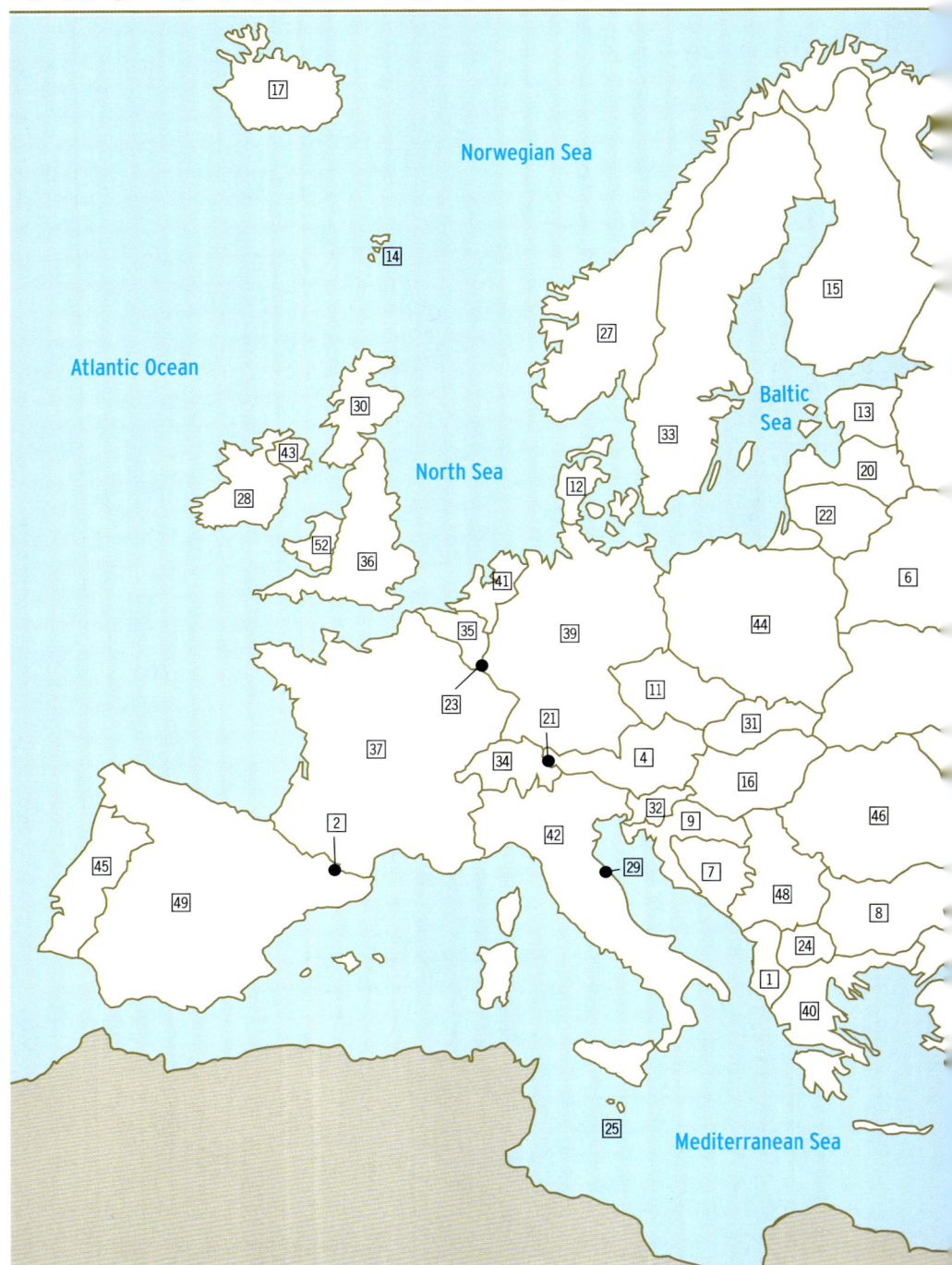

P2 - THE EUROPEAN BOOK OF FOOTBALL 2006/2007

Index

This section contains national federation crests, international kits, club badges and maps for all 52 UEFA-affiliated countries.

PLUS there are an extra six pages featuring the federation crests and kits of the non-European countries represented at the World Cup Finals in Germany

(Please note, every effort has been made to ensure the accuracy of the shirts, badges and map locations at the time of going to press.)

Country	Plate
1 **Albania**	P4
2 **Andorra**	P5
3 **Armenia**	P6
4 **Austria**	P7
5 **Azerbaijan**	P8
6 **Belarus**	P9
7 **Bosnia-Herzegovina**	P10
8 **Bulgaria**	P11
9 **Croatia**	P12
10 **Cyprus**	P13
11 **Czech Republic**	P14
12 **Denmark**	P15
13 **Estonia**	P16
14 **Faroe Islands**	P17
15 **Finland**	P18
16 **Hungary**	P19
17 **Iceland**	P20
18 **Israel**	P21
19 **Kazakhstan**	P22
20 **Latvia**	P23
21 **Liechtenstein**	P24
22 **Lithuania**	P25
23 **Luxembourg**	P26
24 **Macedonia**	P27
25 **Malta**	P28
26 **Moldova**	P29
27 **Norway**	P30
28 **Republic of Ireland**	P31
29 **San Marino**	P32
30 **Scotland**	P33
31 **Slovakia**	P34
32 **Slovenia**	P35
33 **Sweden**	P36
34 **Switzerland**	P37

WORLD CUP 2006
Non-European Nations — P38-P43

35 **Belgium**	P44
36 **England**	P46
37 **France**	P48
38 **Georgia**	P50
39 **Germany**	P52
40 **Greece**	P54
41 **Holland**	P56
42 **Italy**	P58
43 **Northern Ireland**	P60
44 **Poland**	P62
45 **Portugal**	P64
46 **Romania**	P66
47 **Russia**	P68
48 **Serbia & Montenegro**	P70
49 **Spain**	P72
50 **Turkey**	P74
51 **Ukraine**	P76
52 **Wales**	P78

Andorra

HOME INTERNATIONAL KIT

AWAY INTERNATIONAL KIT

① ATLETIC D'ESCALDES

② UE EXTREMENYA

③ INTER D'ESCALDES

④ FC LUSITANS

⑤ CE PRINCIPAT

⑥ RANGER'S FC

⑦ UE SANT JULIA

⑧ FC SANTA COLOMA

⑨ FC ENCAMP

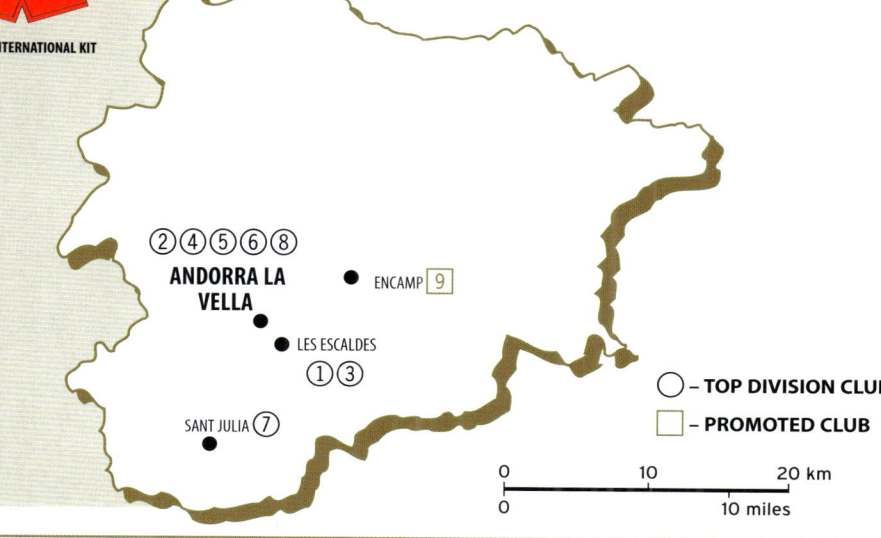

○ – TOP DIVISION CLUB
□ – PROMOTED CLUB

Armenia

Azerbaijan

HOME INTERNATIONAL KIT

AWAY INTERNATIONAL KIT

① FK BAKI

② FK GÄNCÄ

③ GÄNCLÄRBIRLIYI SUMQAYIT

④ GÖYÄZÄN QAZAX

⑤ INTER BAKI

⑥ KARVAN YEVLAX

⑦ MKT-ARAZ IMISLI

⑧ MOIK BAKI

⑨ NEFTÇI BAKI

⑩ OLIMPIK BAKI

⑪ QARABAG AGDAM

⑫ SAHDAG QUSAR

○ – TOP DIVISION CLUB
☐ – PROMOTED CLUB

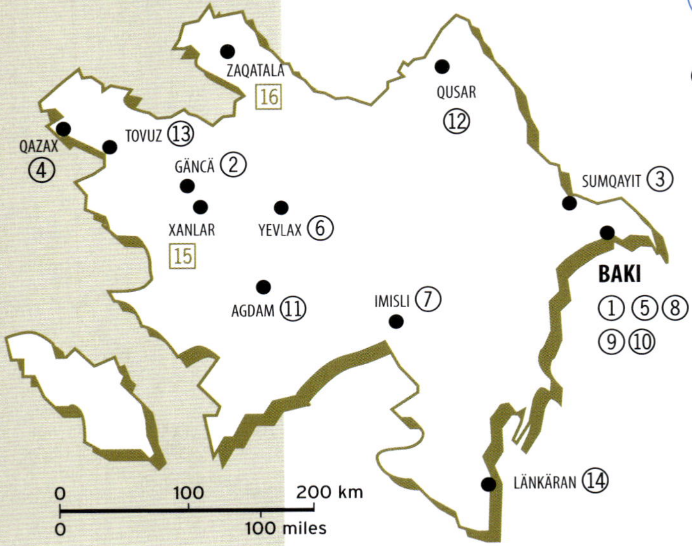

⑬ TURAN TOVUZ

⑭ XÄZÄR LÄNKÄRAN

⑮ GILAN XANLAR

⑯ SIMURQ ZAQATALA

P8 - THE EUROPEAN BOOK OF FOOTBALL 2006/2007

Belarus

HOME INTERNATIONAL KIT

AWAY INTERNATIONAL KIT

◯ – TOP DIVISION CLUB
▢ – PROMOTED CLUB

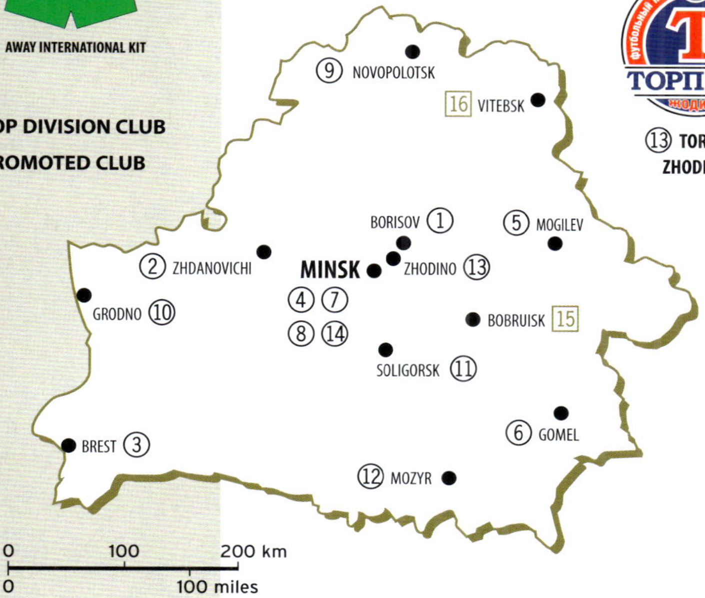

① FC BATE BORISOV
② DARIDA MIKASHEVICHI
③ DINAMO BREST
④ DINAMO MINSK
⑤ DNEPR-TRANSMASH MOGILEV
⑥ FC GOMEL
⑦ LOKOMOTIV MINSK
⑧ MTZ-RIPO MINSK
⑨ NAFTAN NOVOPOLOTSK
⑩ NEMAN GRODNO
⑪ SHAKHTER SOLIGORSK
⑫ SLAVIYA MOZYR
⑬ TORPEDO ZHODINO
⑭ ZVEZDA-VA-BGU MINSK
▢ 15 BELSHINA BOBRUISK
▢ 16 LOKOMOTIV VITEBSK

⑨ NOVOPOLOTSK
16 VITEBSK
① BORISOV
⑤ MOGILEV
② ZHDANOVICHI
MINSK ④ ⑦ ⑧ ⑭
ZHODINO ⑬
GRODNO ⑩
BOBRUISK 15
SOLIGORSK ⑪
BREST ③
⑥ GOMEL
⑫ MOZYR

0   100   200 km
0   100 miles

THE EUROPEAN BOOK OF FOOTBALL 2006/2007 - P9

Bosnia-Herzegovina

HOME INTERNATIONAL KIT

○ – TOP DIVISION CLUB
▢ – PROMOTED CLUB

① BUDUCNOST BANOVICI

② CELIK ZENICA

③ JEDINSTVO BIHAC

④ LEOTAR TREBINJE

⑤ MODRICA MAXIMA

⑥ ORASJE

⑦ POSUSJE

⑧ RADNIK BIJELJINA

⑨ SARAJEVO ⑩ SIROKI BRIJEG

⑪ SLAVIJA SARAJEVO

⑫ SLOBODA TUZLA

⑬ TRAVNIK

⑭ ZELJEZNICAR SARAJEVO

⑮ ZEPCE

⑯ ZRINJSKI MOSTAR

⑰ VELEZ MOSTAR

⑱ BORAC BANJA LUKA

AWAY INTERNATIONAL KIT

Croatia

HOME INTERNATIONAL KIT

AWAY INTERNATIONAL KIT

 ① CIBALIA VINKOVCI

 ② DINAMO ZAGREB

 ③ HAJDUK SPLIT

 ④ INTER ZAPREŠIĆ

 ⑤ KAMEN INGRAD VELIKA

 ⑥ MEĐIMURJE ČAKOVEC

 ⑦ OSIJEK

 ⑧ PULA

○ – TOP DIVISION CLUB
□ – PROMOTED CLUB

 ⑨ RIJEKA

 ⑩ SLAVEN BELUPO KOPRIVNICA

 ⑪ VARTEKS VARAŽDIN

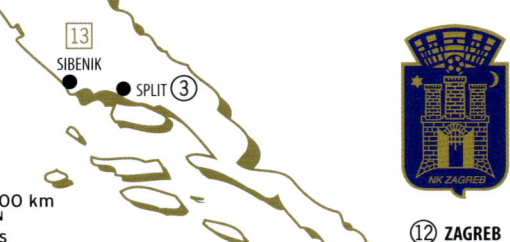

⑫ ZAGREB

 ⑬ ŠIBENIK

Cyprus

① AEK

② AEL

③ ANORTHOSIS

④ APEP

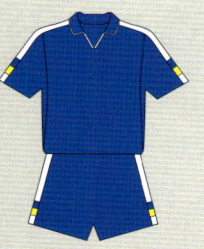
HOME INTERNATIONAL KIT

⑤ APOEL

⑥ APOLLON

⑦ APOP/KINYRAS

⑧ DIGHENIS

⑨ ENTHOI

⑩ ETHNIKOS

⑪ NEA SALAMINA

⑫ OLYMPIAKOS

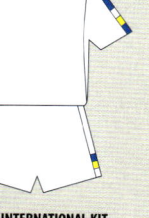
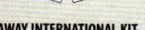
AWAY INTERNATIONAL KIT

○ – TOP DIVISION CLUB
☐ – PROMOTED CLUB

⑬ OMONIA

⑤ ⑧ ⑫ ⑬
● NICOSIA
⑭
⑨ KATO LAKATAMIA
⑩ ACHNA   ● PARALIMNI
PEYIAS ⑦
● KYPEROUNDA ④
LARNACA
PAPHOS 15
① ③
⑪   AYIA NAPA 17
LIMASSOL
② ⑥ 16

0   50   100 km
0   50 miles

⑭ PARALIMNI

15 AEP

16 ARIS

LOGO NOT AVAILABLE
17 AYIA NAPA

Czech Republic

HOME INTERNATIONAL KIT

AWAY INTERNATIONAL KIT

◯ – TOP DIVISION CLUB
▢ – PROMOTED CLUB

① FC BANÍK OSTRAVA

② 1.FC BRNO

③ FK CHMEL BLSANY

④ FK JABLONEC

⑤ FK MARILA PRÍBRAM

⑥ FK MLADÁ BOLESLAV

⑦ FK SIAD MOST

⑧ SK SIGMA OLOMOUC

⑨ SK SLAVIA PRAHA

⑩ 1.FC SLOVÁCKO

⑪ FC SLOVAN LIBEREC

⑫ AC SPARTA PRAHA

⑬ FK TEPLICE

⑭ TESCOMA ZLÍN

⑮ FC VIKTORIA PLZEN

⑯ FC VYSOCINA JIHLAVA

⑰ SK KLADNO

⑱ DYNAMO CESKE BUDEJOVICE

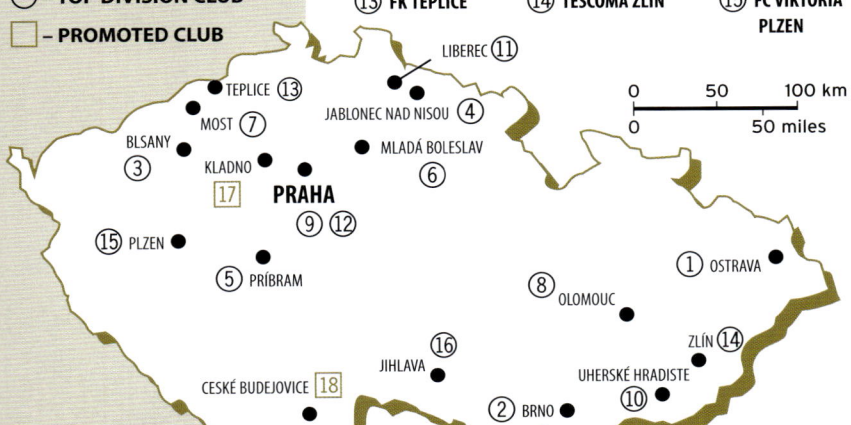

P14 – THE EUROPEAN BOOK OF FOOTBALL 2006/2007

Denmark

 ① AAB
 ② AGF
 ③ BRØNDBY IF
 ④ ESBJERG FB

 ⑤ AC HORSENS
 ⑥ FC KØBENHAVN
 ⑦ FC MIDTJYLLAND
 ⑧ FC NORDSJAELLAND

 ⑨ OB
 ⑩ SILKEBORG IF
 ⑪ SØNDERJYSKE

 ⑫ VIBORG FF
 ⑬ VEJLE BK

 ⑭ RANDERS FC

HOME INTERNATIONAL KIT

AWAY INTERNATIONAL KIT

○ – TOP DIVISION CLUB
□ – PROMOTED CLUB

Estonia

 ① JK DÜNAMO TALLINN

 ② FC FLORA TALLINN

 ③ FC KURESSAARE

 ④ FC LEVADIA TALLINN

HOME INTERNATIONAL KIT

 ⑤ JK MERKUUR TARTU

 ⑥ JK TAMMEKA TARTU

 ⑦ JK TRANS NARVA

 ⑧ JK TULEVIK VILJANDI

AWAY INTERNATIONAL KIT

 ⑨ FC TVMK TALLINN

 ⑩ FC VALGA

 ⑪ JK VAPRUS PÄRNU

 ⑫ FC AJAX LASNAMÄE

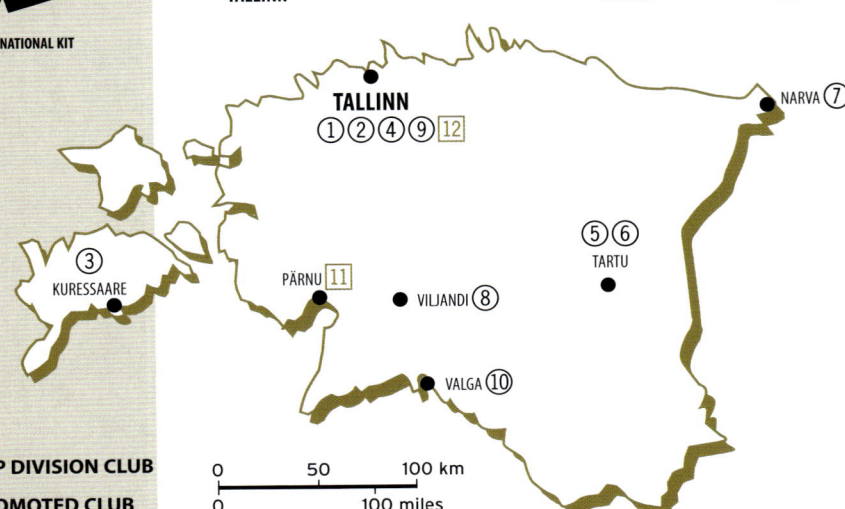

○ – TOP DIVISION CLUB
□ – PROMOTED CLUB

Faroe Islands

Finland

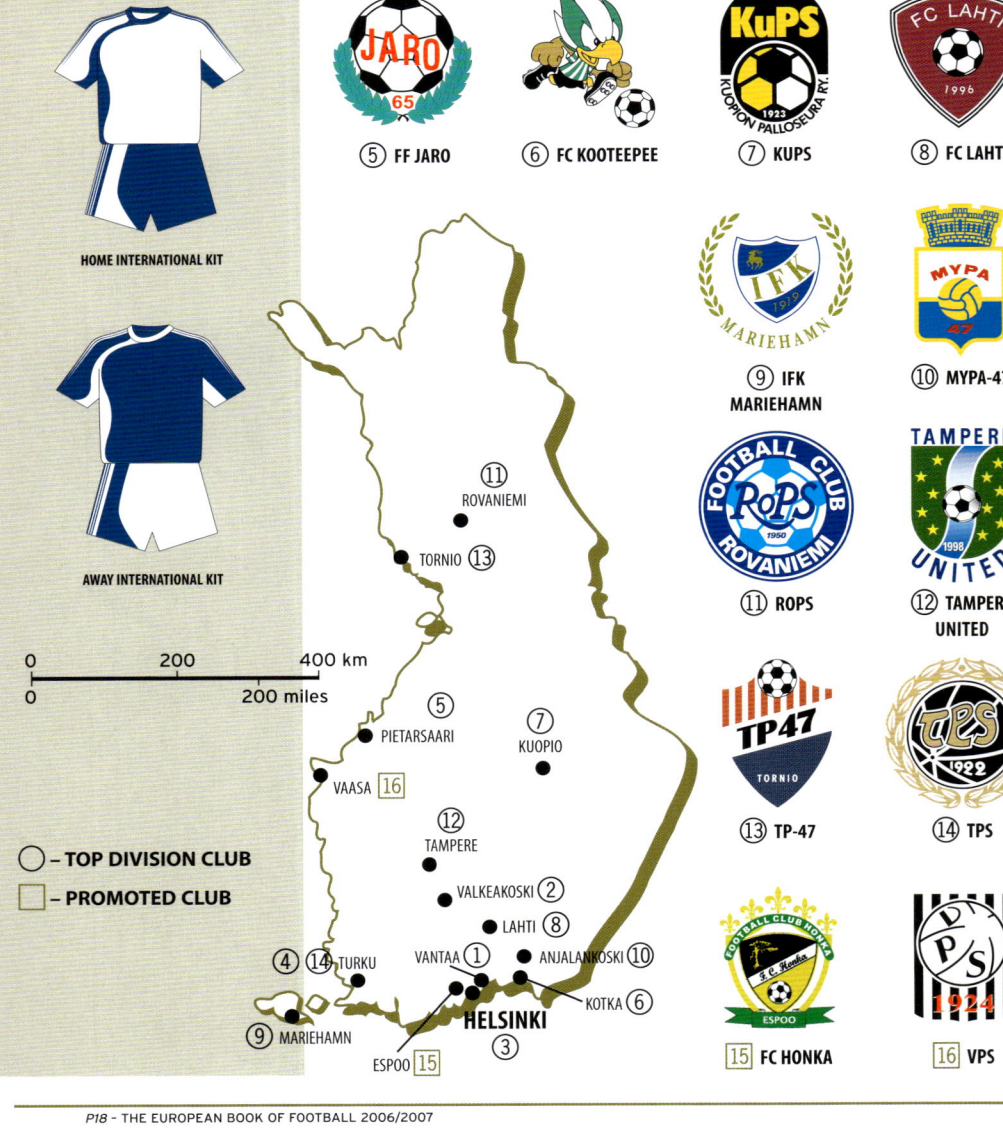

HOME INTERNATIONAL KIT

AWAY INTERNATIONAL KIT

○ – TOP DIVISION CLUB
☐ – PROMOTED CLUB

① AC ALLIANSSI
② FC HAKA
③ HJK
④ FC INTER TURKU
⑤ FF JARO
⑥ FC KOOTEEPEE
⑦ KUPS
⑧ FC LAHTI
⑨ IFK MARIEHAMN
⑩ MYPA-47
⑪ ROPS
⑫ TAMPERE UNITED
⑬ TP-47
⑭ TPS
15 FC HONKA
16 VPS

P18 - THE EUROPEAN BOOK OF FOOTBALL 2006/2007

Hungary

HOME INTERNATIONAL KIT

AWAY INTERNATIONAL KIT

① BUDAPEST-HONVÉD

② DEBRECENI VSC

③ DIÓSGYŐRI VTK

④ FC FEHÉRVÁR

⑤ FERENCVÁROS

⑥ GYŐRI ETO FC

⑦ KAPOSVÁRI RÁKÓCZI FC

⑧ MTK BUDAPEST

⑨ LOMBARD PÁPA TFC

⑩ PÉCSI MFC

⑪ RÁKOSPALOTAI EAC

⑫ FC SOPRON

⑬ FC TATABÁNYA

⑭ ÚJPEST FC

⑮ VASAS

⑯ ZALAEGERSZEG

⑰ DUNAKANYAR-VÁC FC

⑱ PAKSI SE

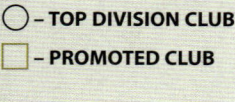

○ – TOP DIVISION CLUB
□ – PROMOTED CLUB

Iceland

HOME INTERNATIONAL KIT

AWAY INTERNATIONAL KIT

 ① FH
 ② FRAM
 ③ FYLKIR
 ④ GRINDAVÍK

 ⑤ ÍA
 ⑥ ÍBV
 ⑦ KEFLAVÍK
 ⑧ KR

 ⑨ THRÓTTUR
 ⑩ VALUR
 ⑪ BREIDABLIK
 ⑫ VÍKINGUR

 ○ – TOP DIVISION CLUB
□ – PROMOTED CLUB

① HAFNARFJÖRDUR
⑦ REYKJANESBAER
④ GRINDAVÍK
⑥ VESTMANNAEYJAR
AKRANES ⑤
REYKJAVÍK ② ③ ⑧ ⑨ ⑩ ⑫
KÓPAVOGUR ⑪

0   100   200 km
0   100 miles

Israel

HOME INTERNATIONAL KIT

AWAY INTERNATIONAL KIT

◯ – TOP DIVISION CLUB
▢ – PROMOTED CLUB

① MS ASHDOD

② BEITAR JERUSALEM

③ BNEI YEHUDA TEL AVIV

④ HAPOEL BNEI SAKHNIN

⑤ HAPOEL KFAR SABA

⑥ HAPOEL NAZARETH ILIT

⑦ HAPOEL PETACH TIKVA

⑧ HAPOEL TEL AVIV

⑨ MACCABI HAIFA

⑩ MACCABI NETANYA

⑪ MACCABI PETACH TIKVA

⑫ MACCABI TEL AVIV

⑬ MACCABI HERZLIYA

⑭ HAKOAH AMIDAR RAMAT GAN

THE EUROPEAN BOOK OF FOOTBALL 2006/2007 - P21

Kazakhstan

HOME INTERNATIONAL KIT

AWAY INTERNATIONAL KIT

○ – TOP DIVISION CLUB
☐ – PROMOTED CLUB

① **AKTOBE LENTO**

② **FK ALMATY**

③ **FK ATYRAU**

④ **BOLAT TEMIRTAU**

⑤ **EKIBASTUZETS EKIBASTUZ**

⑥ **IRTYSH PAVLODAR**

⑦ **KAIRAT ALMATY**

⑧ **OKZHETPES KOKSHETAU**

⑨ **ORDABASY SHYMKENT**

⑩ **SHAKHTYOR KARAGANDY**

⑪ **FK TARAZ**

⑫ **TOBOL KOSTANAI**

⑬ **VOSTOK OSKEMEN**

⑭ **YESIL-BOGATYR PETROPAVLOVSK**

⑮ **ZHENIS ASTANA**

⑯ **ZHETYSU TALDYKORGAN**

LOGO NOT AVAILABLE

⑰ **ENERGETIK PAVLODAR**

⑱ **KAISAR KYZYLORDA**

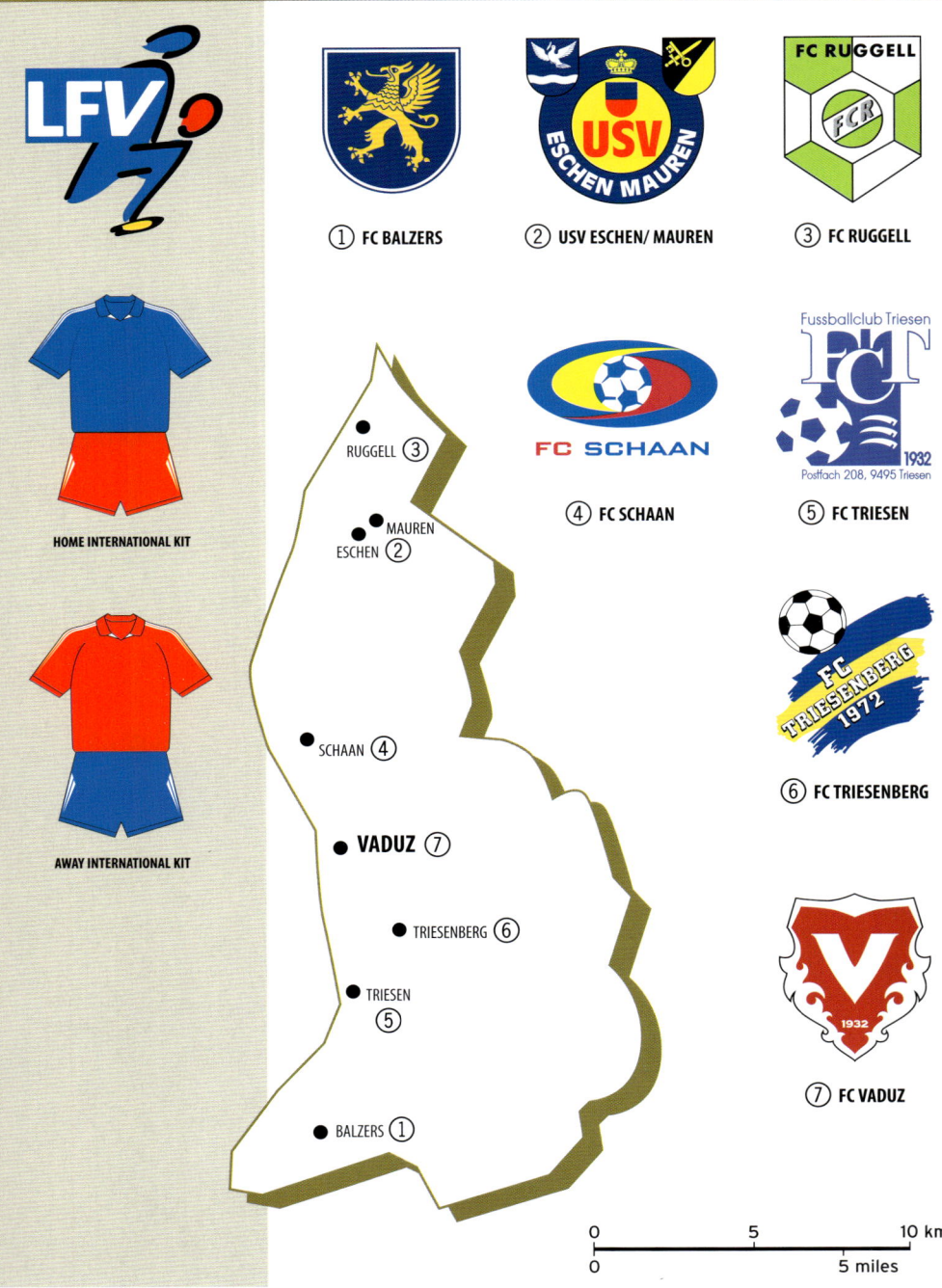

Lithuania

Luxembourg

HOME INTERNATIONAL KIT

AWAY INTERNATIONAL KIT

○ – TOP DIVISION CLUB
□ – PROMOTED CLUB

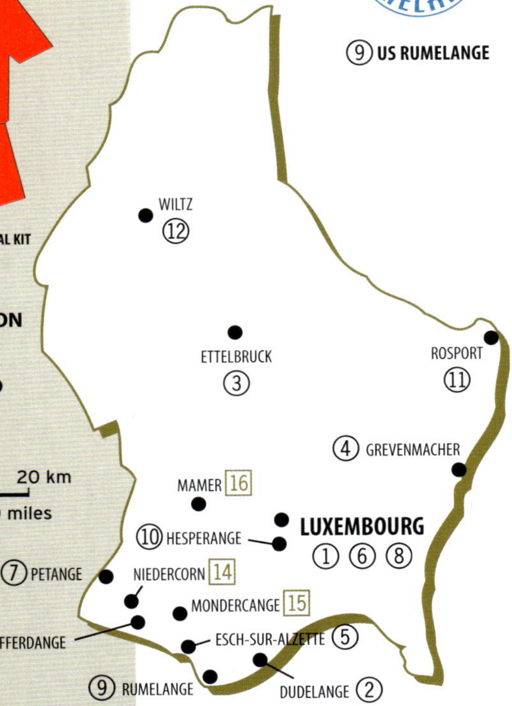

① AVENIR BEGGEN
② F91 DUDELANGE
③ ETZELLA ETTELBRUCK
④ CS GREVENMACHER
⑤ JEUNESSE ESCH
⑥ UN KÄERJÉNG 97
⑦ CS PETANGE
⑧ RFCU LËTZEBUERG
⑨ US RUMELANGE
⑩ SWIFT HESPERANGE
⑪ VICTORIA ROSPORT
⑫ FC WILTZ 71
⑬ FC DIFFERDANGE 03
⑭ PROGRES NIEDERCORN
⑮ FC MONDERCANGE
⑯ FC MAMER 32

P26 - THE EUROPEAN BOOK OF FOOTBALL 2006/2007

Macedonia

Malta

① BIRKIRKARA

② FLORIANA

③ HAMRUN SPARTANS

④ HIBERNIANS

HOME INTERNATIONAL KIT

⑤ MARSAXLOKK

⑥ MOSTA

⑦ MSIDA ST. JOSEPH

⑧ PIETA HOTSPURS

⑨ SLIEMA WANDERERS

⑩ VALLETTA

⑪ ST. GEORGE'S

AWAY INTERNATIONAL KIT

○ – TOP DIVISION CLUB
☐ – PROMOTED CLUB

⑫ MARSA

P28 – THE EUROPEAN BOOK OF FOOTBALL 2006/2007

Moldova

Norway

① AALESUNDS FK

② FK BODØ/GLIMT

③ SK BRANN

④ FREDRIKSTAD FK

⑤ HAM-KAM FOTBALL

⑥ LILLESTRØM SK

⑦ FC LYN OSLO

⑧ MOLDE FK

HOME INTERNATIONAL KIT

⑨ ODD GRENLAND

○ – TOP DIVISION CLUB
□ – PROMOTED CLUB

⑩ ROSENBORG BK

AWAY INTERNATIONAL KIT

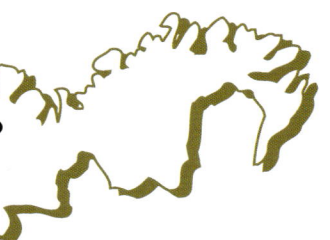

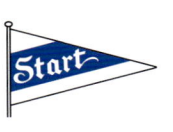
⑪ IK START

⑫ TROMSØ IL

⑬ VIKING FK

⑭ VÅLERENGA FOTBALL

⑮ STABAEK FOTBALL

⑯ SANDEFJORD FOTBALL

San Marino

① CAILUNGO

② COSMOS

③ DOMAGNANO

④ FAETANO

⑤ FIORENTINO

⑥ FOLGORE/ FALCIANO

⑦ JUVENES/ DOGANA

⑧ LA FIORITA

⑨ LIBERTAS

⑩ MURATA

⑪ PENNAROSSA

⑫ SAN GIOVANNI

HOME INTERNATIONAL KIT

⑬ TRE FIORI

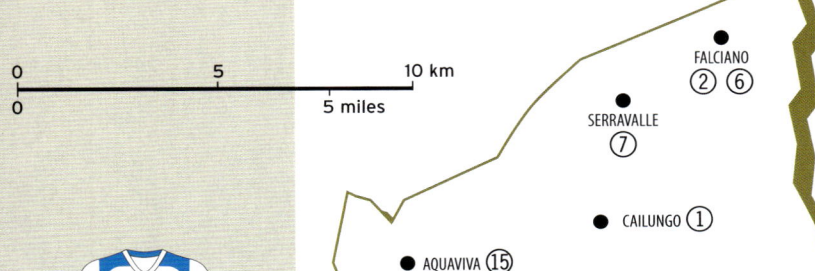

⑭ TRE PENNE

AWAY INTERNATIONAL KIT

⑮ VIRTUS

P32 - EUROPEAN BOOK OF FOOTBALL 2006/2007

Scotland

① ABERDEEN
② CELTIC
③ DUNDEE UNITED
④ DUNFERMLINE ATHLETIC
⑤ FALKIRK
⑥ HEART OF MIDLOTHIAN
⑦ HIBERNIAN
⑧ INVERNESS CALEDONIAN THISTLE
⑨ KILMARNOCK
⑩ LIVINGSTON
⑪ MOTHERWELL
⑫ RANGERS
⑬ ST. MIRREN

HOME INTERNATIONAL KIT

AWAY INTERNATIONAL KIT

◯ – TOP DIVISION CLUB
▢ – PROMOTED CLUB

100   200 km
100 miles

THE EUROPEAN BOOK OF FOOTBALL 2006/2007 - P33

Slovakia

① ARTMEDIA BRATISLAVA

② ZTS DUBNICA

③ DUKLA BANSKÁ BYSTRICA

④ INTER BRATISLAVA

⑤ MATADOR PÚCHOV

⑥ FC NITRA

⑦ MFK RUZOMBEROK

⑧ SPARTAK TRNAVA

⑨ AS TRENČÍN

⑩ MSK ZILINA

⑪ MFK KOSICE

⑫ SLOVAN BRATISLAVA

HOME INTERNATIONAL KIT

AWAY INTERNATIONAL KIT

○ – TOP DIVISION CLUB
□ – PROMOTED CLUB

⑬ FC SENEC

P34 - EUROPEAN BOOK OF FOOTBALL 2006/2007

Switzerland

① FC AARAU

② FC BASEL

③ GRASSHOPPER-CLUB ZÜRICH

④ NEUCHATEL XAMAX FC

HOME INTERNATIONAL KIT

⑤ FC ST GALLEN

⑥ FC SCHAFFHAUSEN

⑦ FC THUN

⑧ BSC YOUNG BOYS BERN

⑨ YVERDON-SPORT FC

⑩ FC ZÜRICH

⑪ FC LUZERN

⑫ FC SION

AWAY INTERNATIONAL KIT

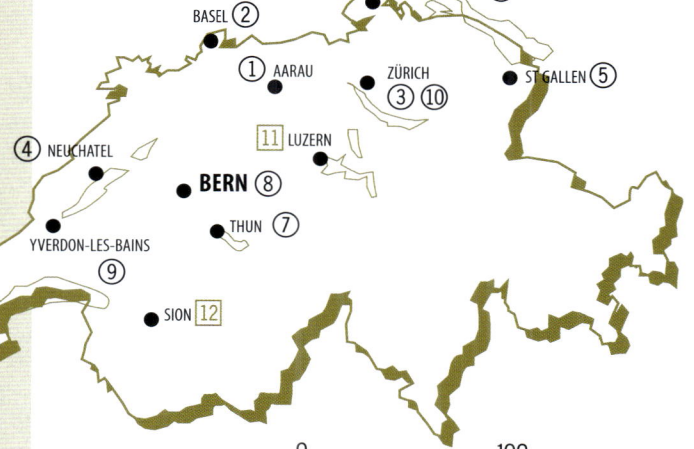

◯ – TOP DIVISION CLUB
▢ – PROMOTED CLUB

THE EUROPEAN BOOK OF FOOTBALL 2006/2007 - P37

World Cup 2006

 Angola
Group D

 Argentina
Group C

 **Australia**
Group F

HOME INTERNATIONAL KIT   **HOME INTERNATIONAL KIT**   **HOME INTERNATIONAL KIT**

AWAY INTERNATIONAL KIT   **AWAY INTERNATIONAL KIT**   **AWAY INTERNATIONAL KIT**

P38 - THE EUROPEAN BOOK OF FOOTBALL 2006/2007

Non-European Nations

 **Brazil**
Group F

 **Costa Rica**
Group A

 **Ecuador**
Group A

HOME INTERNATIONAL KIT **HOME INTERNATIONAL KIT** **HOME INTERNATIONAL KIT**

AWAY INTERNATIONAL KIT **AWAY INTERNATIONAL KIT** **AWAY INTERNATIONAL KIT**

World Cup 2006

Ghana
Group E

Iran
Group D

Ivory Coast
Group C

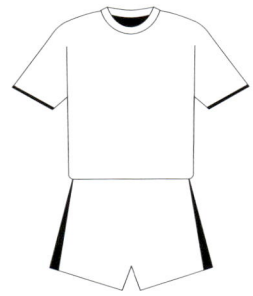  

HOME INTERNATIONAL KIT   **HOME INTERNATIONAL KIT**   **HOME INTERNATIONAL KIT**

AWAY INTERNATIONAL KIT   **AWAY INTERNATIONAL KIT**   **AWAY INTERNATIONAL KIT**

Non-European Nations

 **Japan** Group F

 **Mexico** Group D

 **Paraguay** Group B

HOME INTERNATIONAL KIT **HOME INTERNATIONAL KIT** **HOME INTERNATIONAL KIT**

AWAY INTERNATIONAL KIT **AWAY INTERNATIONAL KIT** **AWAY INTERNATIONAL KIT**

THE EUROPEAN BOOK OF FOOTBALL 2006/2007 - P41

World Cup 2006

 Saudia Arabia
Group H

 South Korea
Group G

 **Togo**
Group G

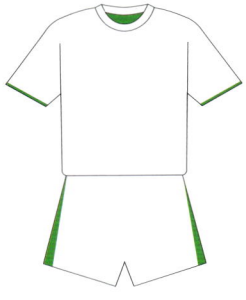

HOME INTERNATIONAL KIT

HOME INTERNATIONAL KIT

HOME INTERNATIONAL KIT

AWAY INTERNATIONAL KIT

AWAY INTERNATIONAL KIT

AWAY INTERNATIONAL KIT

Non-European Nations

 **Trinidad & Tobago** Group B

 **Tunisia** Group H

 **USA** Group D

HOME INTERNATIONAL KIT

HOME INTERNATIONAL KIT

HOME INTERNATIONAL KIT

AWAY INTERNATIONAL KIT

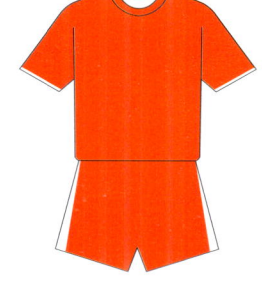

AWAY INTERNATIONAL KIT

AWAY INTERNATIONAL KIT

Belgium

HOME INTERNATIONAL KIT

AWAY INTERNATIONAL KIT

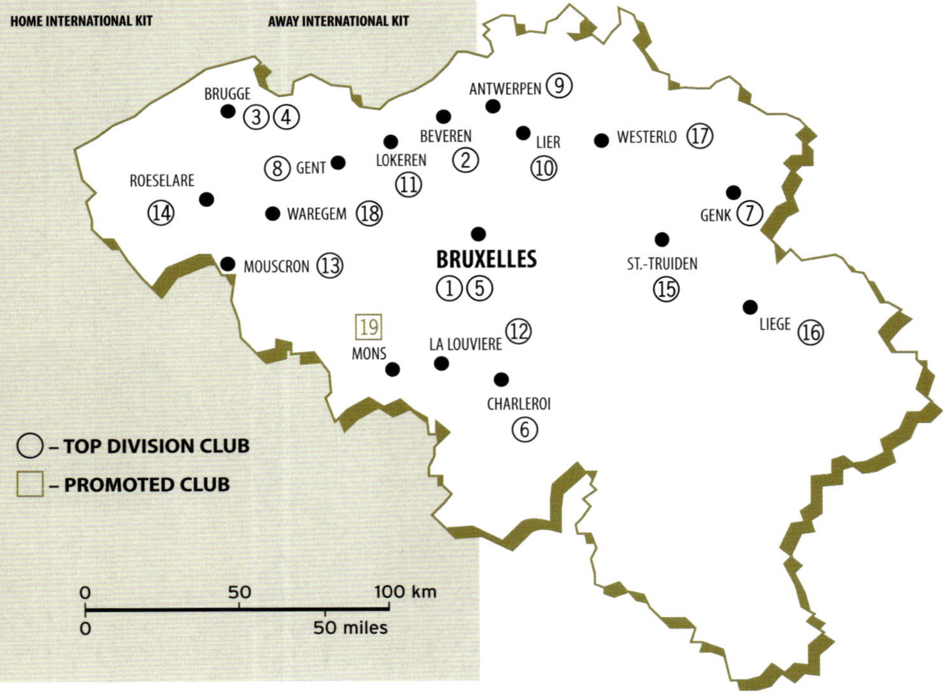

① RSC ANDERLECHT

② KSK BEVEREN

⑦ KRC GENK

⑧ KAA GENT

BRUGGE ③ ④
ANTWERPEN ⑨
BEVEREN ②
LIER ⑩
WESTERLO ⑰
⑧ GENT
LOKEREN ⑪
ROESELARE ⑭
WAREGEM ⑱
GENK ⑦
MOUSCRON ⑬
BRUXELLES ① ⑤
ST.-TRUIDEN ⑮
LIEGE ⑯
⑲ MONS
LA LOUVIERE ⑫
CHARLEROI ⑥

○ – TOP DIVISION CLUB
☐ – PROMOTED CLUB

0   50   100 km
0   50 miles

③ KSV CERCLE BRUGGE

④ CLUB BRUGGE KV

⑤ FC BRUSSELS

⑥ RSC CHARLEROI

⑨ GERMINAL BEERSCHOT ANTWERPEN

⑩ K LIERSE SK

⑪ KSC LOKEREN OV

⑫ RAA LA LOUVIERE

⑬ R EXCELSIOR MOUSCRON

⑭ KSV ROESELARE

⑮ K ST.-TRUIDENSE VV

⑯ R STANDARD LIEGE

⑰ KVC WESTERLO

⑱ SV ZULTE-WAREGEM

⑲ RAEC MONS

③ BIRMINGHAM CITY   ④ BLACKBURN ROVERS   ⑤ BOLTON WANDERERS   ⑥ CHARLTON ATHLETIC

⑧ EVERTON   ⑨ FULHAM   ⑩ LIVERPOOL   ⑪ MANCHESTER CITY

⑫ MANCHESTER UNITED   ⑬ MIDDLESBROUGH   ⑭ NEWCASTLE UNITED   ⑮ PORTSMOUTH

⑯ SUNDERLAND   ⑰ TOTTENHAM HOTSPUR   ⑱ WEST BROMWICH ALBION   ⑲ WEST HAM UNITED

⑳ WIGAN ATHLETIC   ㉑ READING   ㉒ SHEFFIELD UNITED   ㉓ WATFORD

THE EUROPEAN BOOK OF FOOTBALL 2006/2007 - P47

France

① AC AJACCIO   ② AJ AUXERRE   ③ GIRONDINS DE BORDEAUX   ④ LE MANS UC 72

⑤ RC LENS   ⑥ LILLE OSC   ⑦ OLYMPIQUE LYONNAIS   ⑧ OLYMPIQUE MARSEILLE

⑩ AS MONACO FC   ⑪ AS NANCY-LORRAINE   ⑫ FC NANTES   ⑬ OGC NICE

⑮ STADE RENNAIS FC   ⑯ AS SAINT-ETIENNE   ⑰ FC SOCHAUX   ⑱ RC STRASBOURG

⑳ ES TROYES AC   ㉑ VALENCIENNES FC   ㉒ CS SEDAN ARDENNES   ㉓ FC LORIENT

Georgia

① AMERI TBILISI

② FC BORJOMI

HOME INTERNATIONAL KIT

AWAY INTERNATIONAL KIT

⑦ KAKHETI TELAVI

⑧ KOLKHETI 1913 POTI

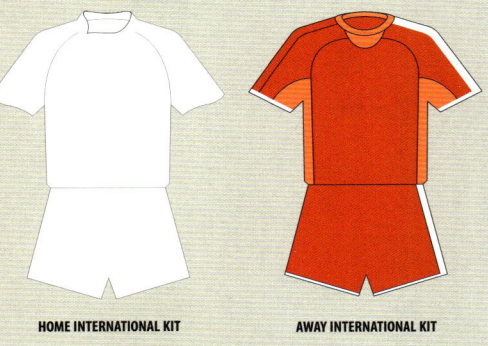

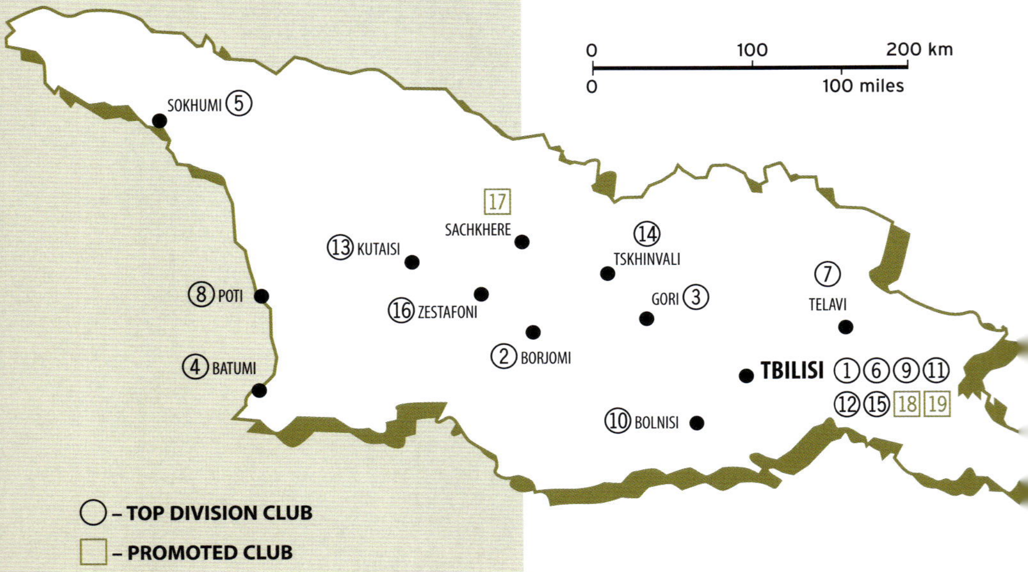

SOKHUMI ⑤

[17] SACHKHERE

⑬ KUTAISI

⑭ TSKHINVALI

⑧ POTI

⑯ ZESTAFONI

GORI ③

⑦ TELAVI

④ BATUMI

② BORJOMI

TBILISI ① ⑥ ⑨ ⑪
⑫ ⑮ [18] [19]

⑩ BOLNISI

○ – TOP DIVISION CLUB

☐ – PROMOTED CLUB

③ DILA GORI

④ DINAMO BATUMI

⑤ DINAMO SOKHUMI

⑥ DINAMO TBILISI

⑨ LOKOMOTIVI TBILISI

⑩ SIONI BOLNISI

⑪ SPARTAKI TBILISI

⑫ FC TBILISI

⑬ TORPEDO KUTAISI

⑭ FC TSKHINVALI

⑮ WIT GEORGIA TBILISI

⑯ FC ZESTAFONI

⑰ CHIKHURA SACHKHERE

⑱ MERANI TBILISI

⑲ OLIMPI RUSTAVI

Germany

① ARMINIA BIELEFELD
② BAYER 04 LEVERKUSEN

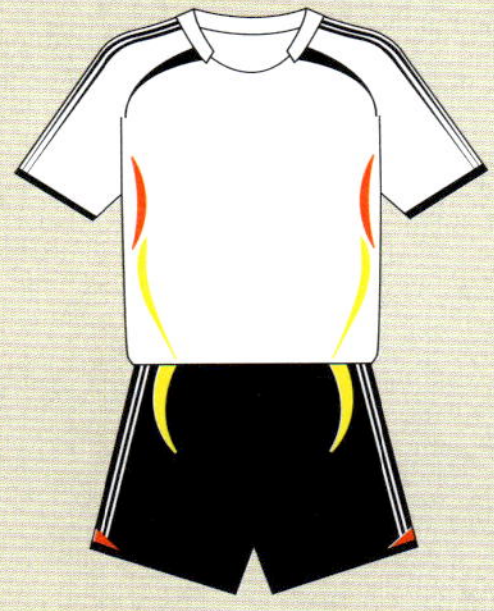

HOME INTERNATIONAL KIT

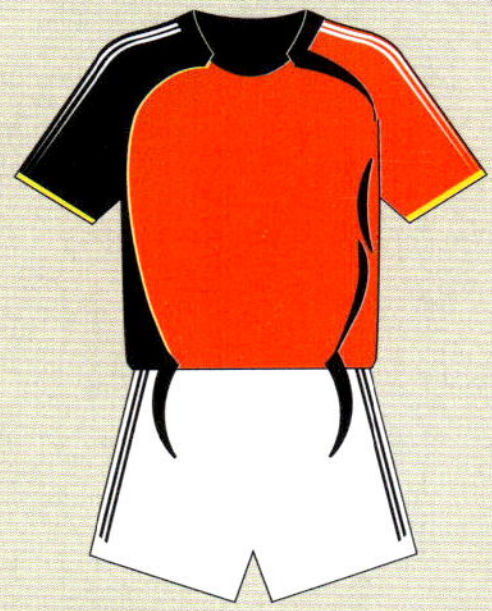

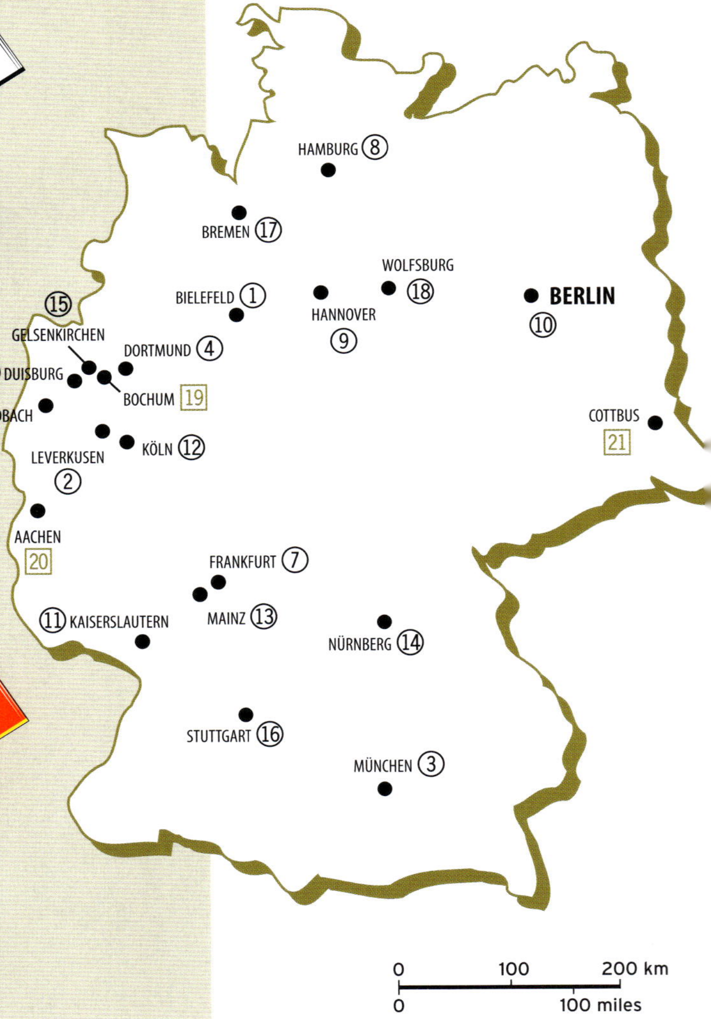

○ – TOP DIVISION CLUB
□ – PROMOTED CLUB

AWAY INTERNATIONAL KIT

- HAMBURG ⑧
- BREMEN ⑰
- BIELEFELD ① WOLFSBURG ⑱
- HANNOVER ⑨ BERLIN ⑩
- GELSENKIRCHEN ⑮
- DORTMUND ④
- DUISBURG ⑥ BOCHUM [19]
- MÖNCHENGLADBACH ⑤
- LEVERKUSEN ② KÖLN ⑫ COTTBUS [21]
- AACHEN [20]
- FRANKFURT ⑦
- KAISERSLAUTERN ⑪ MAINZ ⑬ NÜRNBERG ⑭
- STUTTGART ⑯
- MÜNCHEN ③

③ FC BAYERN MÜNCHEN

④ BORUSSIA DORTMUND

⑤ BORUSSIA MÖNCHENGLADBACH

⑥ MSV DUISBURG

⑦ EINTRACHT FRANKFURT

⑧ HAMBURGER SV

⑨ HANNOVER 96

⑩ HERTHA BSC BERLIN

⑪ 1.FC KAISERSLAUTERN

⑫ 1.FC KÖLN

⑬ FSV MAINZ 05

⑭ 1.FC NÜRNBERG

⑮ FC SCHALKE 04

⑯ VFB STUTTGART

⑰ SV WERDER BREMEN

⑱ VFL WOLFSBURG

⑲ VFL BOCHUM

⑳ ALEMANNIA AACHEN

㉑ FC ENERGIE COTTBUS

Greece

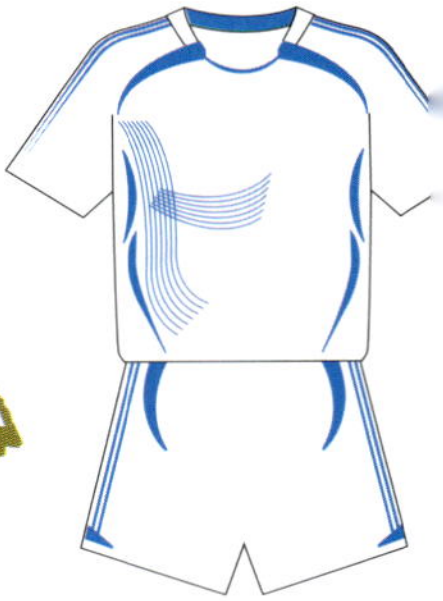

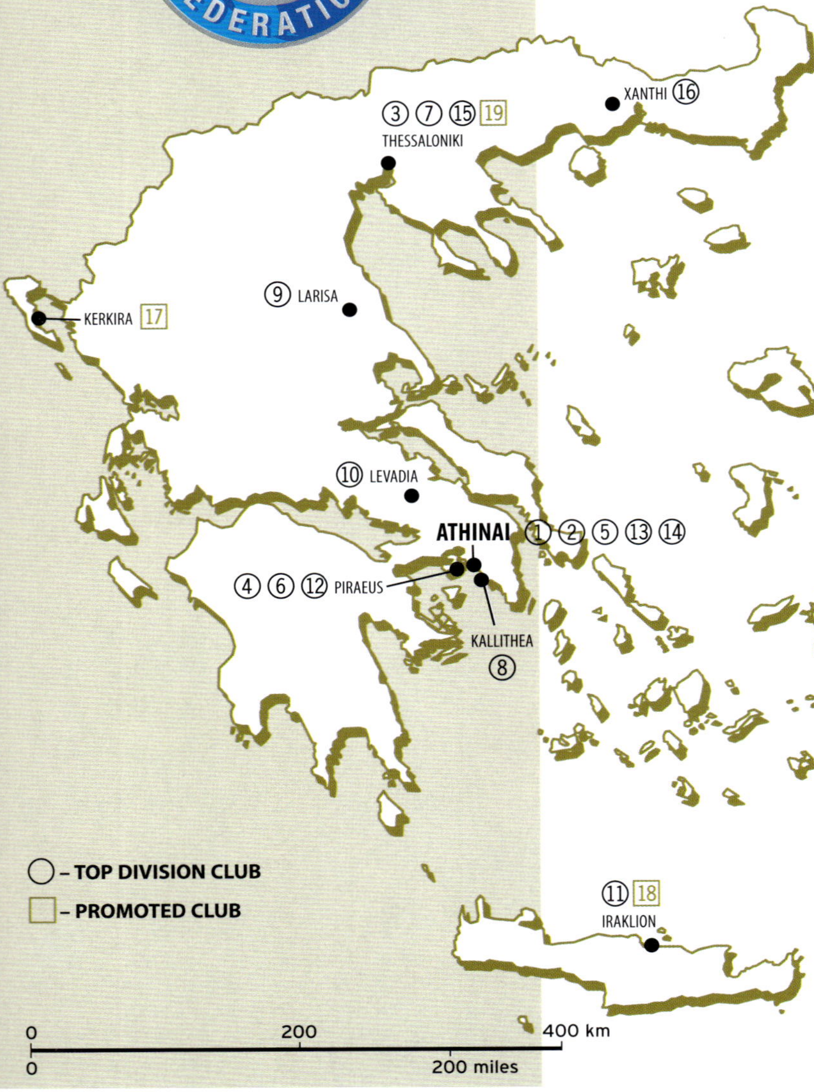

 ① AEK

 ② AKRATITOS

 ③ APOLLON KALAMARIAS

 ④ ATROMITOS-CHALKIDONA

 ⑤ EGALEO

 ⑥ IONIKOS

 ⑦ IRAKLIS

 ⑧ KALLITHEA

 ⑨ LARISA

 ⑩ LEVADIAKOS

 ⑪ OFI

 ⑫ OLYMPIAKOS

 ⑬ PANATHINAIKOS

 ⑭ PANIONIOS

 ⑮ PAOK

 ⑯ XANTHI

 ⑰ KERKIRA

 ⑱ ERGOTELIS

 ⑲ ARIS

Holland

 ① ADO DEN HAAG
 ② AJAX
 ③ AZ
 ④ FEYENOORD

 ⑥ SC HEERENVEEN
 ⑦ HERACLES ALMELO
 ⑧ NAC BREDA
 ⑨ NEC

 ⑪ RBC ROOSENDAAL
 ⑫ RKC WAALWIJK
 ⑬ RODA JC
 ⑭ SPARTA ROTTERDAM

 ⑰ VITESSE
 ⑱ WILLEM II
 ⑲ EXCESLIOR

Italy

 ③ CHIEVO
 ④ EMPOLI
 ⑤ FIORENTINA
 ⑥ INTERNAZIONALE

 ⑧ LAZIO
 ⑨ LECCE
 ⑩ LIVORNO
 ⑪ MESSINA

 ⑬ PALERMO
 ⑭ PARMA
 ⑮ REGGINA
 ⑯ ROMA

 ⑰ SAMPDORIA
 ⑱ SIENA
 ⑲ TREVISO
 ⑳ UDINESE

 21 ATALANTA
 22 CATANIA
 23 TORINO

① ARDS	② ARMAGH CITY	③ BALLYMENA UNITED	④ CLIFTONVILLE

⑤ COLERAINE	⑥ DUNGANNON SWIFTS	⑦ GLENAVON	⑧ GLENTORAN

⑨ INSTITUTE	⑩ LARNE	⑪ LIMAVADY UNITED	⑫ LINFIELD
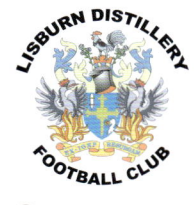			
⑬ LISBURN DISTILLERY	⑭ LOUGHGALL	⑮ NEWRY CITY	⑯ PORTADOWN

	17 CRUSADERS	18 DONEGAL CELTIC	

Poland

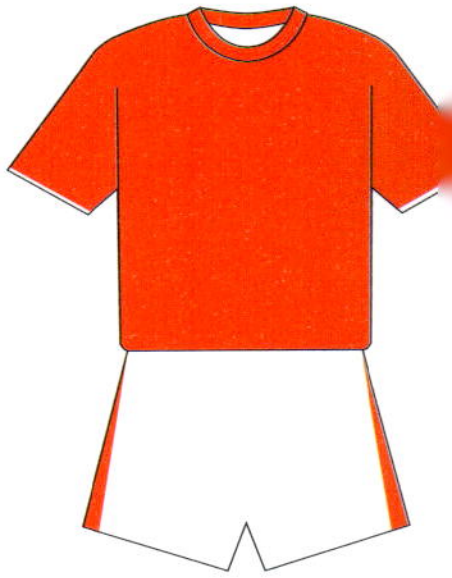

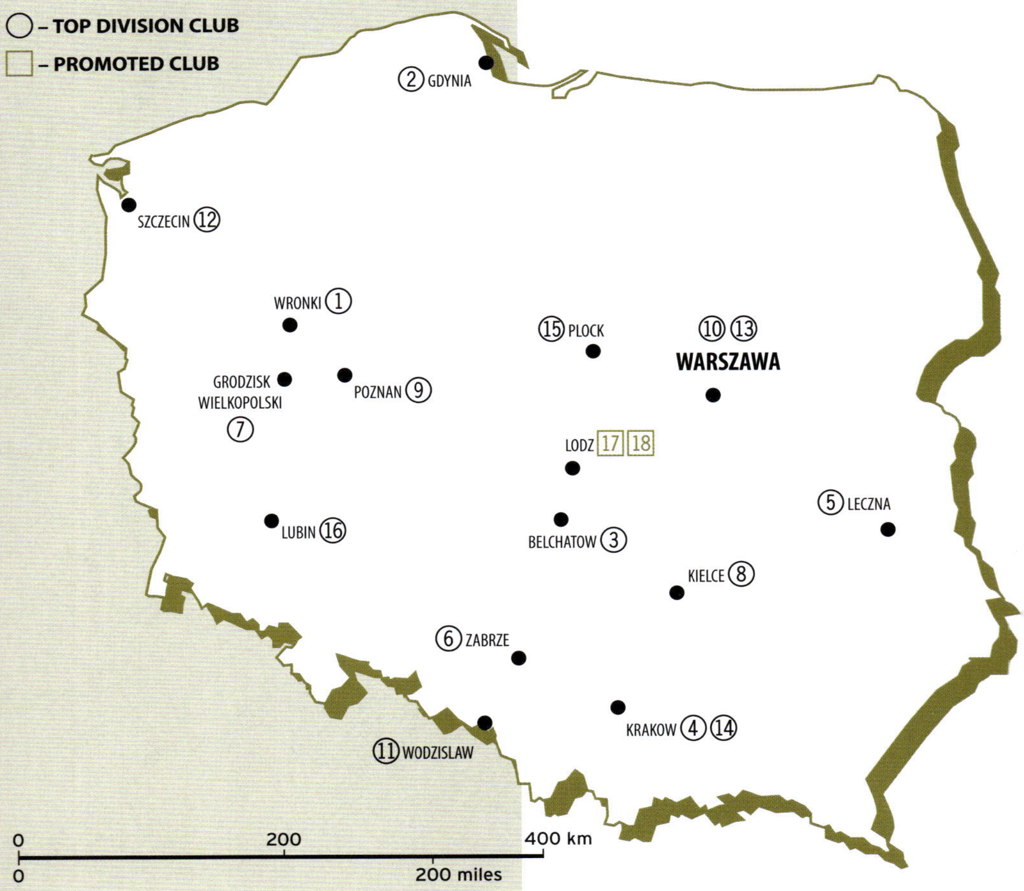

 ① AMICA WRONKI
 ② ARKA GDYNIA
 ③ GKS BELCHATOW
 ④ CRACOVIA KRAKOW

 ⑤ GORNIK LECZNA
 ⑥ GORNIK ZABRZE
 ⑦ GROCLIN DYSKOBOLIA GRODZISK
 ⑧ KORONA KIELCE

 ⑨ LECH POZNAN
 ⑩ LEGIA WARSZAWA
 ⑪ ODRA WODZISLAW
 ⑫ POGON SZCZECIN

 ⑬ POLONIA WARSZAWA
 ⑭ WISLA KRAKOW
 ⑮ WISLA PLOCK
 ⑯ ZAGLEBIE LUBIN

 ⑰ WIDZEW LODZ
 ⑱ LODZKI KS

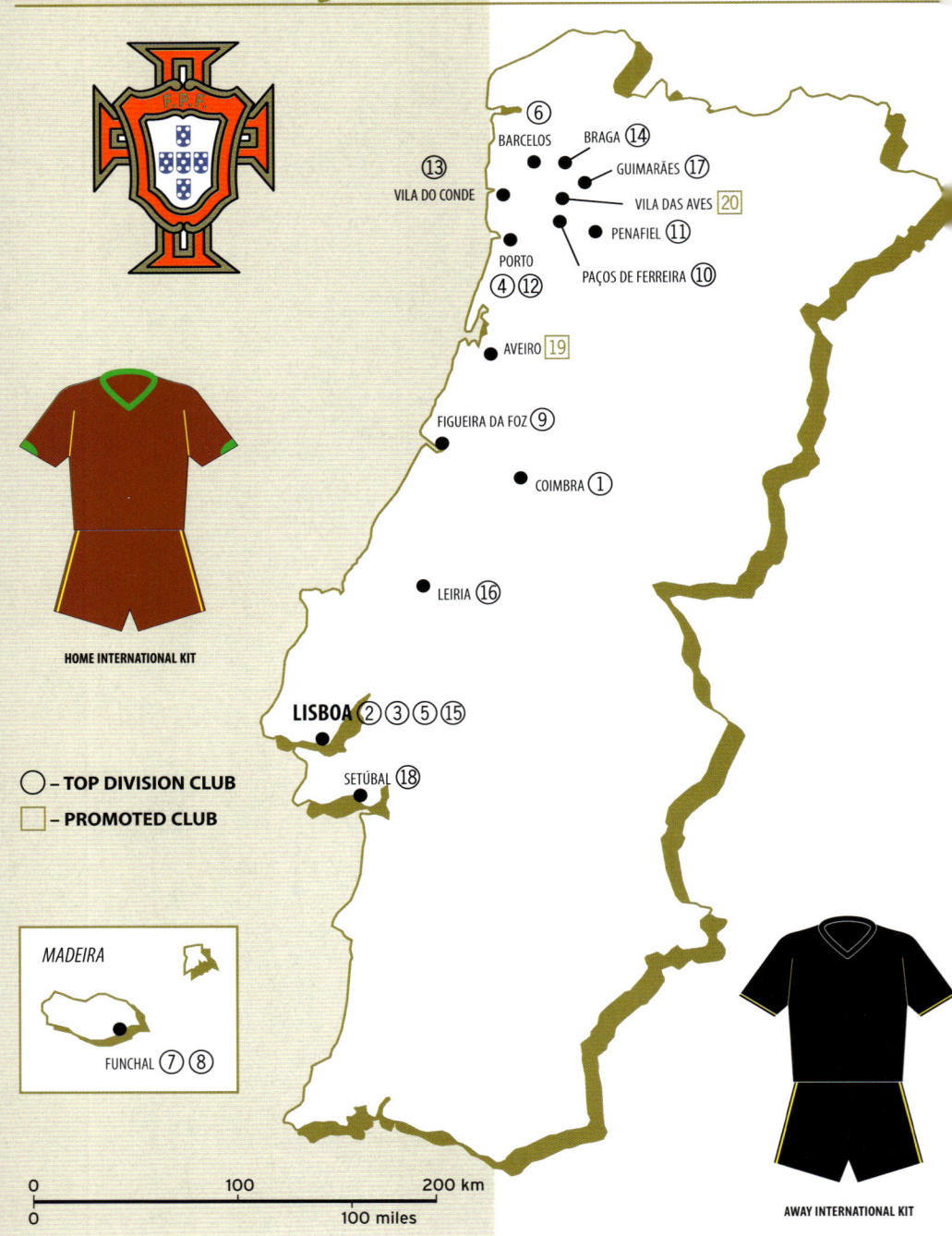

 ① ACADÉMICA COIMBRA
 ② CF OS BELENENSES
 ③ SL BENFICA
 ④ BOAVISTA FC

 ⑤ CF ESTRELA AMADORA
 ⑥ GIL VICENTE FC
 ⑦ CS MARÍTIMO
 ⑧ CD NACIONAL

 ⑨ NAVAL 1° MAIO
 ⑩ FC PAÇOS FERREIRA
 ⑪ FC PENAFIEL
 ⑫ FC PORTO

 ⑬ RIO AVE FC
 ⑭ SPORTING BRAGA
 ⑮ SPORTING CP
 ⑯ UNIÃO LEIRIA

 ⑰ VITÓRIA GUIMARÃES
 ⑱ VITÓRIA SETÚBAL
 19 SC BEIRA MAR
 20 DESPORTIVO AVES

③ CFR CLUJ

④ DINAMO BUCURESTI

⑤ FC FARUL CONSTANTA

⑥ GLORIA BISTRITA

⑨ OTELUL GALATI

⑩ PANDURII TARGU JIU

⑪ POLITEHNICA IASI

⑫ POLITEHNICA TIMISOARA

⑬ RAPID BUCURESTI

⑭ SPORTUL STUDENTESC BUCURESTI

⑮ STEAUA BUCURESTI

⑯ FC VASLUI

⑰ CEAHLAUL PIATRA NEAMT

⑱ UNIVERSITATEA CRAIOVA

⑲ UNIREA URZICENI

⑳ UTA ARAD

Russia

① **ALANIA VLADIKAVKAZ**

② **AMKAR PERM**

⑦ **FK MOSKVA**

⑧ **FK ROSTOV**

HOME INTERNATIONAL KIT

AWAY INTERNATIONAL KIT

○ – **TOP DIVISION CLUB**
□ – **PROMOTED CLUB**

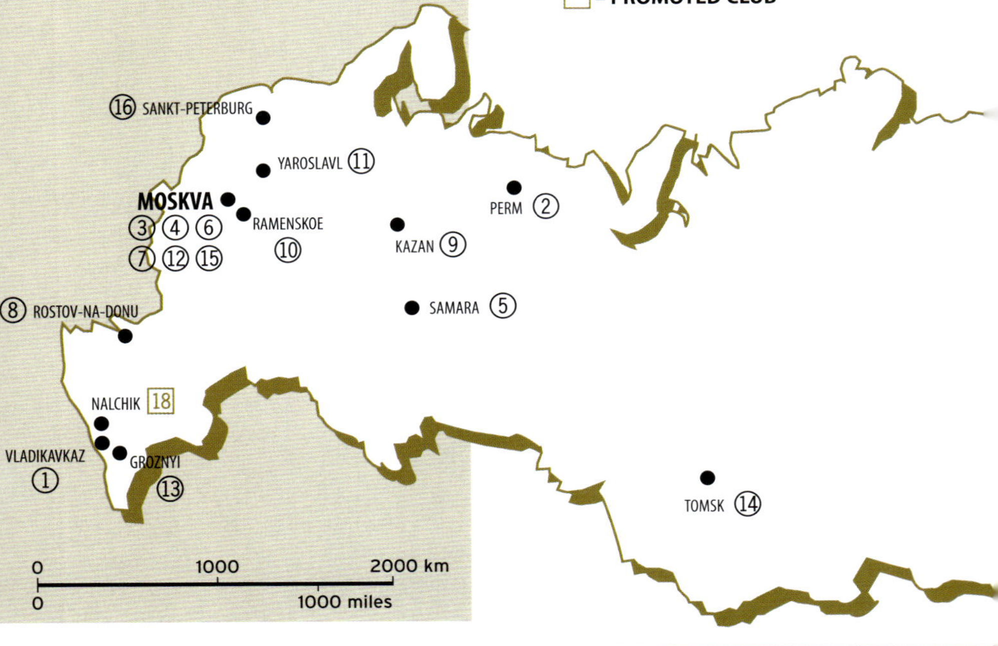

⑯ SANKT-PETERBURG

YAROSLAVL ⑪

MOSKVA
③ ④ ⑥   RAMENSKOE
⑦ ⑫ ⑮   ⑩   KAZAN ⑨   PERM ②

⑧ ROSTOV-NA-DONU

SAMARA ⑤

NALCHIK [18]

VLADIKAVKAZ
①   GROZNYI
              ⑬

TOMSK ⑭

0   1000   2000 km
0   1000 miles

③ CSKA MOSKVA

④ DINAMO MOSKVA

⑤ KRYLYA SOVETOV SAMARA

⑥ LOKOMOTIV MOSKVA

⑨ RUBIN KAZAN

⑩ SATURN RAMENSKOE

⑪ SHINNIK YAROSLAVL

⑫ SPARTAK MOSKVA

⑬ TEREK GROZNYI

⑭ TOM TOMSK

⑮ TORPEDO MOSKVA

⑯ ZENIT SANKT-PETERBURG

⑰ LUCH-ENERGIA VLADIVOSTOK

⑱ SPARTAK NALCHIK

Serbia & Montenegro

① BORAC CACAK

② BUDUCNOST BANATSKI DVOR

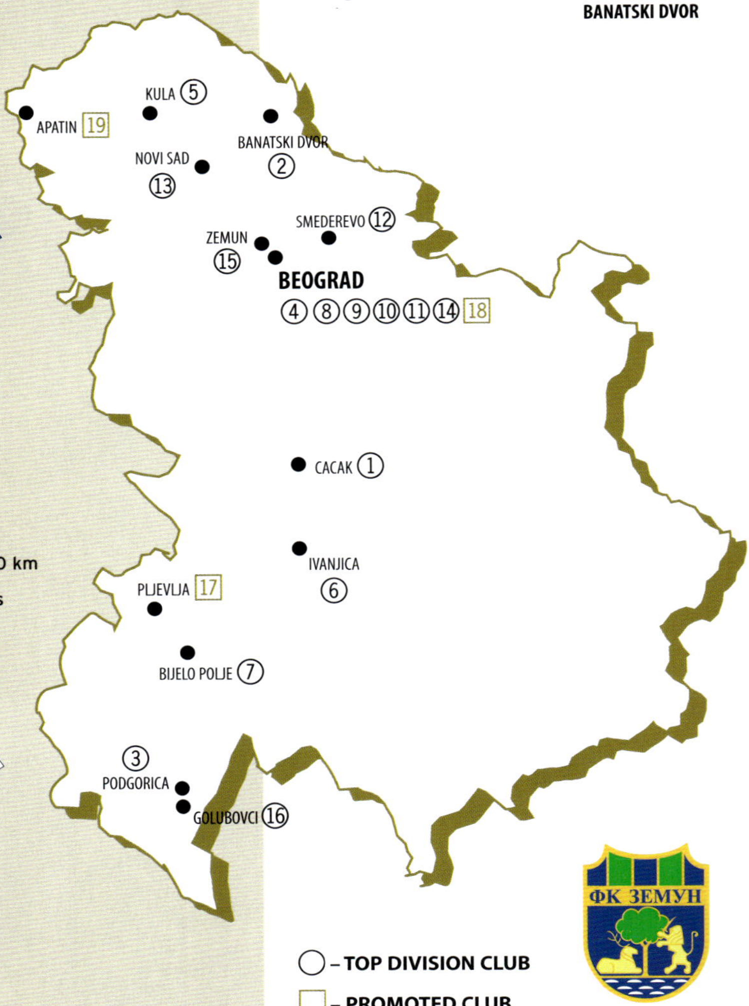

KULA ⑤
APATIN 19
BANATSKI DVOR ②
NOVI SAD ⑬
SMEDEREVO ⑫
ZEMUN ⑮
BEOGRAD
④ ⑧ ⑨ ⑩ ⑪ ⑭ 18
CACAK ①
IVANJICA ⑥
PLJEVLJA 17
BIJELO POLJE ⑦
③ PODGORICA
GOLUBOVCI ⑯

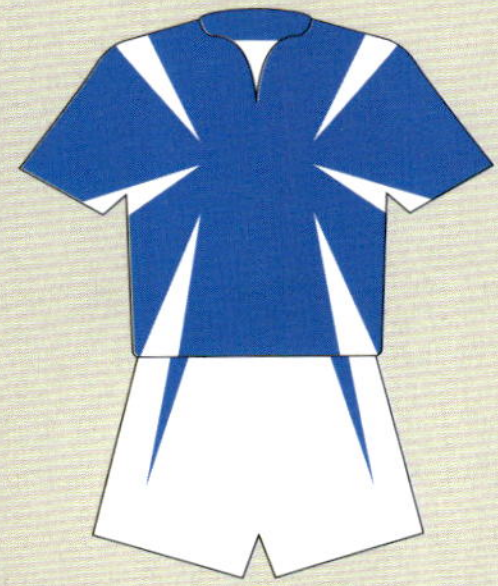

HOME INTERNATIONAL KIT

0 50 100 km
0 50 miles

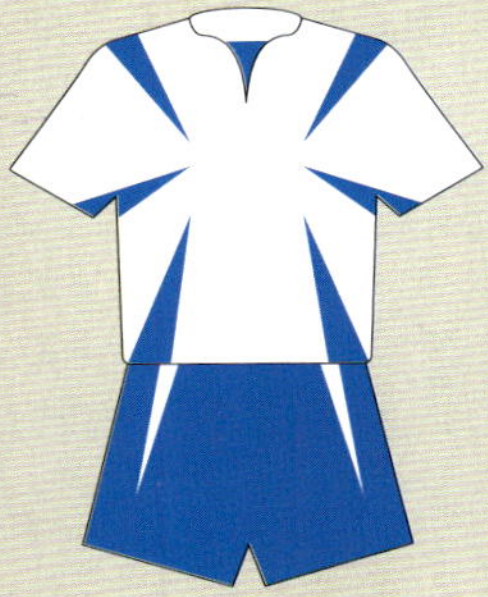

AWAY INTERNATIONAL KIT

○ – TOP DIVISION CLUB

□ – PROMOTED CLUB

⑮ ZEMUN

③ BUDUCNOST PODGORICA

④ CRVENA ZVEZDA BEOGRAD

⑤ HAJDUK RODIC MB KULA

⑥ JAVOR IVANJICA

⑦ JEDINSTVO BIJELO POLJE

⑧ OBILIC BEOGRAD

⑨ OFK BEOGRAD

⑩ PARTIZAN BEOGRAD

⑪ RAD BEOGRAD

⑫ SMEDEREVO

⑬ VOJVODINA NOVI SAD

⑭ VOZDOVAC BEOGRAD

⑯ ZETA GOLUBOVCI

⑰ RUDAR PLJEVLJA

⑱ BEZANIJA BEOGRAD

⑲ MLADOST APATIN

Spain

 ③ ATLÉTICO MADRID
 ④ FC BARCELONA
 ⑤ REAL BETIS
 ⑥ CÁDIZ CF

 ⑨ RCD ESPANYOL
 ⑩ GETAFE CF
 ⑪ MÁLAGA CF
 ⑫ RCD MALLORCA

 ⑬ CA OSASUNA
 ⑭ RACING SANTANDER
 ⑮ REAL MADRID
 ⑯ REAL SOCIEDAD

 ⑰ SEVILLA FC
 ⑱ VALENCIA CF
 ⑲ VILLARREAL CF
 ⑳ REAL ZARAGOZA

 ㉑ RC RECREATIVO
 ㉒ CLUB GIMNÀSTIC
 ㉓ LEVANTE UD

 ③ BESIKTAS

 ④ ÇAYKUR RIZESPOR

 ⑤ DENIZLISPOR

 ⑥ DIYARBAKIRSPOR

 ⑨ GAZIANTEPSPOR

 ⑩ GENÇLERBIRLIGI

 ⑪ KAYSERI ERCIYESSPOR

 ⑫ KAYSERISPOR

 ⑬ KONYASPOR

 ⑭ MALATYASPOR

 ⑮ SAMSUNSPOR

 ⑯ SIVASSPOR

 ⑱ VESTEL MANISASPOR

 ⑲ BURSASPOR

 ⑳ ANTALYASPOR

 ㉑ SAKARYASPOR

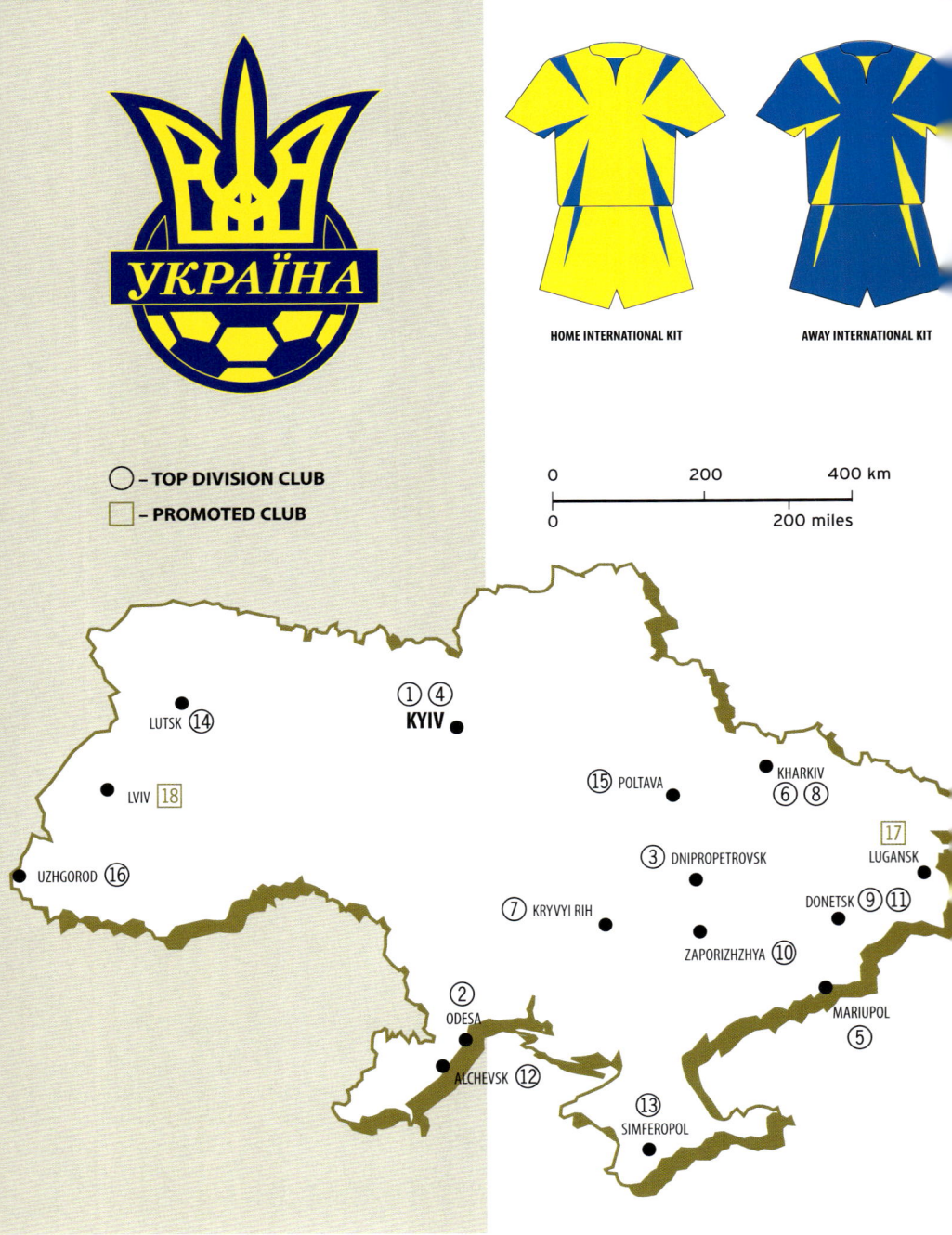

 ① ARSENAL KYIV
 ② CHORNOMORETS ODESA
 ③ DNIPRO DNIPROPETROVSK
 ④ DYNAMO KYIV

 ⑤ FC ILLICHIVETS MARIUPOL
 ⑥ FC KHARKIV
 ⑦ KRYVBAS KRYVYI RIH
 ⑧ METALIST KHARKIV

 ⑨ METALURG DONETSK
 ⑩ METALURG ZAPORIZHZHYA
 ⑪ SHAKHTAR DONETSK
 ⑫ STAL ALCHEVSK

 ⑬ TAVRIYA SIMFEROPOL
 ⑭ VOLYN LUTSK
 ⑮ VORSKLA POLTAVA
 ⑯ ZAKARPATTYA UZHGOROD

 ⑰ ZORYA LUGANSK
 ⑱ KARPATY LVIV

Wales

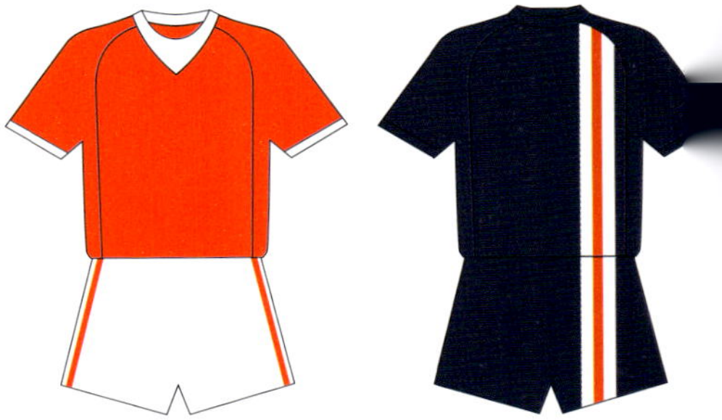

HOME INTERNATIONAL KIT

AWAY INTERNATIONAL KIT

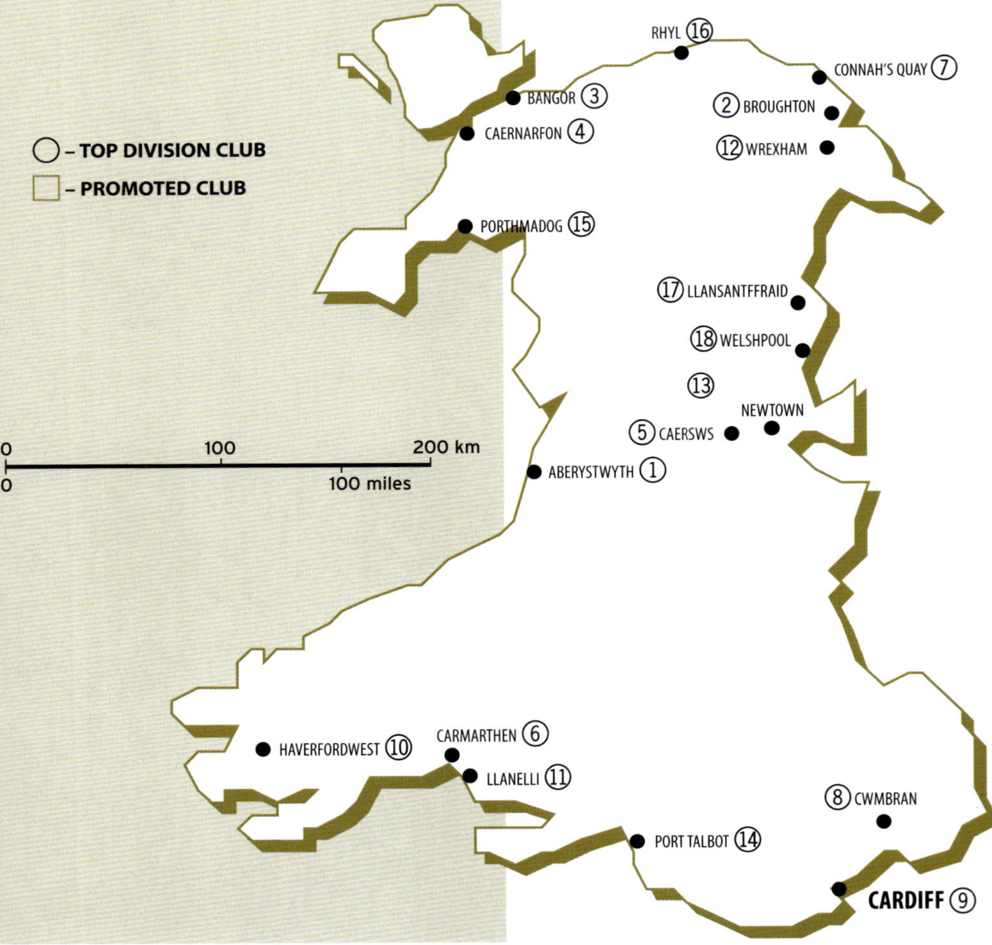

○ – TOP DIVISION CLUB
□ – PROMOTED CLUB

- RHYL ⑯
- CONNAH'S QUAY ⑦
- BANGOR ③
- ② BROUGHTON
- CAERNARFON ④
- ⑫ WREXHAM
- PORTHMADOG ⑮
- ⑰ LLANSANTFFRAID
- ⑱ WELSHPOOL
- ⑬ NEWTOWN
- ⑤ CAERSWS
- ABERYSTWYTH ①
- HAVERFORDWEST ⑩
- CARMARTHEN ⑥
- LLANELLI ⑪
- ⑧ CWMBRAN
- PORT TALBOT ⑭
- **CARDIFF** ⑨

 ① ABERYSTWYTH TOWN
 ② AIRBUS UK
 ③ BANGOR CITY
 ④ CAERNARFON TOWN

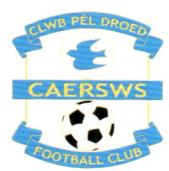 ⑤ CAERSWS
 ⑥ CARMARTHEN TOWN
 ⑦ CONNAH'S QUAY NOMADS
 ⑧ CWMBRAN TOWN

 ⑨ GRANGE HARLEQUINS
 ⑩ HAVERFORDWEST COUNTY
 ⑪ LLANELLI
 ⑫ NEWI CEFN DRUIDS

 ⑬ NEWTOWN
 ⑭ PORT TALBOT TOWN
 ⑮ CPD PORTHMADOG
 ⑯ RHYL

 ⑰ THE NEW SAINTS
 ⑱ WELSHPOOL TOWN

3 ISSUES FOR £1
SPECIAL TRIAL OFFER

World Soccer has long been hailed by players, coaches and fans as the undisputed authority on international football. Enjoy 3 trial issues for £1.

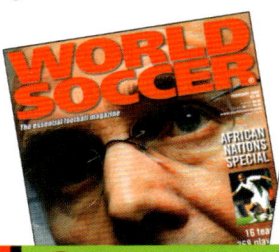

■ Don't miss out
If you enjoy the convenience of having World Soccer delivered direct to your door, you can continue by subscription and enjoy a further 15% saving!

■ What's the catch?
There isn't one – if you decide you don't like having World Soccer delivered direct, cancel your direct debit upon receipt of your second issue and £1 is all you'll have paid.

■ Next Step
Simply complete the form below, phone our order hotline or go online.

ORDER NOW

By post, simply complete the coupon below

HOTLINE 0845 676 7778
LINES OPEN 7 DAYS A WEEK, 9.00am TO 9.00pm. PLEASE HAVE PAYMENT DETAILS READY AND QUOTE CODE 551H

Order online @ www.worldsoccer.com/i026

Send coupon to: World Soccer Subscriptions, FREEPOST CY1061, Haywards Heath, West Sussex, RH16 3BR (no stamp required)

YES, PLEASE SEND ME 3 ISSUES FOR £1
After I have received my 3 issues for £1, I understand that my subscription will run at £18.23 every 6 months by Direct Debit, saving a further 15%.

I understand that I can write to cancel it upon receipt of my 2nd issue and no further money will be debited from my account.

YOUR DETAILS

Mr/Mrs/Ms/Miss: _____ Forename: _____

Surname: _____

Address: _____

Postcode: _____

Home tel. no. (inc. area code): _____

If you would like to receive emails from World Soccer and IPC containing news, special offers and product and service information and take part in our magazine research via email, please include your email below.

Email: _____

Date of birth: D D M M Y Y Y Y

INSTRUCTION TO YOUR BANK OR BUILDING SOCIETY TO PAY BY DIRECT DEBIT
For office use only. Originator's reference - 764 221

DIRECT Debit

A/C no: _____

Name of Bank _____

Address _____

Postcode _____

Account name _____

Sort Code _____ Account No. _____

Please pay IPC Media Ltd. Direct Debits from the account detailed on this instruction subject to the safeguards assured by the Direct Debit Guarantee. I understand that this instruction may remain with IPC Media Ltd. and if so, details will be passed electronically to my Bank or Building Society.

Signature _____ Date _____
(I am over 18)

This offer is only open to new UK subscribers. The closing date for this offer is **30th June 2007**. Please allow up to six weeks for your first subscription issue. **For enquiries, alternative offers and overseas orders please call +44(0)845 676 7778, or email: ipcsubs@qss-uk.com**. World Soccer, published by IPC Media Ltd (IPC), will collect your personal information to process your order. World Soccer and IPC would like to contact you by post or telephone to promote and ask your opinion on our magazines and services. Please tick here if you prefer not to hear from us. ☐ IPC may occasionally pass your details to carefully selected organisations so they can contact you by telephone or post with regards to promoting and researching their products and services. Please tick here if you prefer not to be contacted. ☐ 551H

Israel

4	Haim BANON		M	19	(1)	1
	Eyal BEN AMI		D	17	(4)	1
20	Oz BRANDWIN		M	3	(21)	
22	Ronen DAHAN		G	7		
7	Darko DJUKIC	SLO	A	1	(4)	
	Guy DROR		M		(1)	
	Israel DROR		D	3	(3)	
	Eliran ELKAYAM		D	31		3
15	Dudi FADLON		D	15	(5)	
19	Zoltán FÜLÖP	HUN	A	10	(5)	1
25	Georgi HRISTOV	MAC	A	5	(2)	3
4	Guillermo ISRAILEVICH	ARG	M	29	(3)	3
17	Igor JANCEVSKI	MAC	M	8	(4)	
23	Mislav KAROGLAN	BIH	A	19	(2)	1
11	Vladimir KOKOL	SLO	M	21	(2)	
22	Oshri LEVI		G	26		
26	Kobi NACHTYLER		D	10	(11)	
25	Miha PITAMIC	SLO	D	7		
19	Simon SESLAR	SLO	M	7	(2)	2
18	Itay SHECHTER		A	21	(5)	3
3	Rotem SHMOL		M		(3)	
24	Shachar SIMANTOV		M	25	(4)	5
21	Ashraf SULIMAN		D	12	(3)	
16	Avishay ZANO		D	26	(7)	1
8	Oren ZITUNI		M	13	(1)	
	ZONINHO	BRA	A	2	(4)	1

HAPOEL PETACH TIKVA
Coach – Rafi Cohen; (8/11/05) Nir Levin

2005
Date	Opponent	h/a	Score	Scorers
26/8	Hapoel Kfar Saba	a	1-1	Shivhon
17/9	Hapoel Nazareth Ilit	h	0-0	
24/9	MS Ashdod	a	3-4	Tamuz 2, Hassan
1/10	Hapoel Bnei Sakhnin	a	2-0	Tamuz, Shivhon
15/10	Bnei Yehuda Tel Aviv	h	2-3	Shivhon, Hassan
22/10	Maccabi Tel Aviv	a	0-3	
28/10	Maccabi Natanya	h	0-2	
5/11	Maccabi Haifa	a	0-2	
12/11	Hapoel Petach Tikva	h	2-1	Hassan (p), Shivhon
19/11	Beitar Jerusalem	a	1-0	Salmi
26/11	Hapoel Tel Aviv	h	0-3	
3/12	Hapoel Kfar Saba	h	2-1	Salmi, Elihav
9/12	Hapoel Nazareth Ilit	a	1-2	Shivhon
17/12	MS Ashdod	h	3-1	Shivhon, Gazal, Tamuz
31/12	Hapoel Bnei Sakhnin	h	0-0	

2006
Date	Opponent	h/a	Score	Scorers
6/1	Bnei Yehuda Tel Aviv	a	1-2	Tamuz
14/1	Maccabi Tel Aviv	h	2-2	Hassan, Shivhon
20/1	Maccabi Natanya	a	0-0	
28/1	Maccabi Haifa	h	3-1	Shivhon, Tamuz, Hassan
4/2	Maccabi Petach Tikva	a	0-2	
11/2	Beitar Jerusalem	h	0-3	
18/2	Hapoel Tel Aviv	a	1-1	Tamuz
25/2	Bnei Yehuda Tel Aviv	a	2-2	Tamuz 2
11/3	Maccabi Tel Aviv	h	1-1	Shivhon
17/3	Maccabi Netanya	a	3-2	Shivhon, Gazal, Tamuz
24/3	MS Ashdod	h	1-2	Sror
31/3	Hapoel Nazareth Ilit	a	1-0	Tamuz
8/4	Hapoel Kfar Saba	a	0-0	
14/4	Maccabi Petach Tikva	h	1-1	Shivhon
21/4	Hapoel Bnei Sakhnin	a	4-1	Boxenboim 2, Uzan, Slmi
29/4	Maccabi Haifa	h	0-2	
6/5	Hapoel Tel Aviv	a	0-3	
14/5	Beitar Jerusalem	h	1-2	Hassan

No	Name		Nat	Pos	Aps	(s)	Gls
11	Shimon ABU HAZEIRA			A	4	(10)	
6	Angelo ALISTER		ROM	D	17		
6	Manzour AMAR			D	1		
	Ori AVRAHAM			M			
22	Shlomi BEN HEMO			G		(1)	
2	Meir BONFITO			D	8	(2)	
19	Omer BOXENBOIM			M	19	(4)	2
31	Silvije CAVLINA		CRO	G	13		
18	Gal COHEN			D	12	(4)	
1	Rafi COHEN			G	17		
	Sagiv COHEN			D	1	(2)	
22	Maor ELBAZ			G	3		
17	Erez ELIHAV			D	15	(6)	1
29	Luís Firmino EMERSON		BRA	A	2	(3)	
24	Ravid GAZAL			M	24	(1)	2
25	Igor GJUZELOV		MAC	D	6	(1)	
4	Zeev HAIMOVICH			D	31		
10	Manor HASSAN			M	25		6
7	Daniel HEIDMAN			M	19	(2)	
14	Evyatar ILOUZ			M	6	(2)	
26	Yehuda JANASHVILI			M	2	(1)	
9	Motti KAKUN			A	1	(4)	
21	Omri KENDA			D		(1)	
23	Draziga KONE		CIV	M	3	(1)	
24	Yakir LUSKI			M		(1)	
	Rafael MALTINSKI			M			
8	Elnatan SALMI			A	14	(9)	3
5	Dorin SEMEGHIN		ROM	M	10		
27	Guy SHAMIR			M	8	(5)	
17	Eyal SHEN			M	5	(3)	
14	Yossi SHIVHON			M	33		11
25	Idan SROR			D	9	(14)	1
20	Toto TAMUZ		NGA	A	23	(5)	11
3	Dalibor TIENOVIC		BOS	M	6		
29	Uri UZAN			D	16		1
3	Dalibur VISKOVIC		CRO	M	10	(2)	
21	Ivica ZULJEVIC		CRO	A		(7)	

HAPOEL TEL AVIV
Coach – Dror Kashtan

2005
Date	Opponent	h/a	Score	Scorers
27/8	Bnei Yehuda Tel Aviv	h	2-0	Domb, Dego
18/9	Maccabi Tel Aviv	a	0-2	
24/9	Maccabi Netanaya	h	2-0	Barda, Paintsil
2/10	Maccabi Haifa	a	0-1	
15/10	Maccabi Petach Tikva	h	1-1	Paintsil
23/10	Beitar Jerusalem	a	2-0	Domb, Ogabuna
29/10	Hapoel Bnei Sachnin	h	2-2	Ogabuna, Gershon (p)
4/11	Hapoel Kfar Saba	h	3-1	Badir 2, Dego
12/11	Hapoel Nazareth Ilit	a	1-1	Gershon (p)
19/11	MS Ashdod	h	3-1	Badir, Peretz, Gershon (p)
26/11	Hapoel Petach Tikva	a	3-0	Javrujan, Peretz, Gershon (p)
3/12	Bnei Yehuda Tel Aviv	a	4-0	Vermot, Peretz, Barda, Ogabuna
11/12	Maccabi Tel Aviv	h	2-0	Badir, Ogabuna
17/12	Maccabi Netanaya	a	0-1	

2006
Date	Opponent	h/a	Score	Scorers
1/1	Maccabi Haifa	h	0-0	
7/1	Maccabi Petach Tikva	a	3-2	Javrujan, Barda 2
15/1	Beitar Jerusalem	h	1-1	Ogabuna
21/1	Hapoel Bnei Sachnin	a	1-2	Barda
28/1	Hapoel Kfar Saba	a	1-0	Javrujan
4/2	Hapoel Nazaret Ilit	h	4-0	Barda 2, Javrujan 2
11/2	MS Ashdod	a	1-1	Ogabuna
18/2	Hapoel Petach Tikva	h	1-1	Ogabuke
25/2	Hapoel Bnei Sakhnin	h	1-0	og (Barkay)
11/3	Maccabi Haifa	a	1-0	Badir

Israel

Date	Opponent	h/a	Score	Scorers
18/3	Hapoel Kfar Saba	h	1-2	Halis
26/3	Beitar Jerusalem	h	1-1	Chen
1/4	Bnei Yehuda Tel Aviv	a	1-0	Ogabuna
9/4	Maccabi Tel Aviv	h	2-0	Gershon (p), Abutbul
15/4	Maccabi Netanya	a	1-1	Javrujan
22/4	MS Ashdod	h	1-1	Javrujan
29/4	Hapoel Nazareth Ilit	h	1-1	Domb
6/5	Hapoel Petach Tikva	h	3-0	Javrujan, Ogabuna 2
13/5	Maccabi Petach Tikva	a	1-2	Abutbul

No	Name	Nat	Pos	Aps	(s)	Gls
8	Yossi ABUKSIS		M	24		
18	Shay ABUTBUL		M	10	(13)	2
4	Olabayo ADAFEMI	NGA	M	9	(1)	
20	Igal ANTEBI		D	30		
5	Walid BADIR		M	32		5
8	Elianniv BARDA		A	25	(7)	7
3	Tal CHEN		D	14	(1)	1
7	Barukh DEGO		M	26	(6)	2
55	Asi DOMB		D	22	(3)	3
1	Shavit ELIMELECH		G	32		
6	Shimon GERSHON		D	30		5
21	Rami HALIS		D	11		1
16	Euguja JAVRUJAN	ARM	A	15	(5)	8
9	Avi KNAFO		M		(4)	
12	Ognjen LAKIC	SCG	M	3	(1)	
16	Yakir LUSKI		M		(1)	
9	Felix OGABUKE	NGA	A	2	(8)	1
24	Ibazito OGABUNA	NGA	A	11	(20)	9
30	John PAINTSIL	GHA	D	27		2
32	Omer PERETZ		A	16	(8)	3
99	Nir RAHMIN		G	1		
14	Gil VERMOT		M	23	(4)	1

MACCABI HAIFA
Coach – Roni Levi

2005

Date	Opponent	h/a	Score	Scorers
27/8	Hapoel Bnei Sakhnin	h	4-1	Katan 2, Arbeitman, Zandberg
19/9	Maccabi Petach Tikva	h	3-2	Katan, Bocoli, Colautti
25/9	Beitar Jerusalem	a	1-0	Zandberg
2/10	Hapoel Tel Aviv	h	1-0	Tal
15/10	Hapoel Kfar Saba	a	2-1	Katan, Tal (p)
22/10	Hapoel Nazareth Ilit	h	2-1	Katan, Tal
29/10	MS Ashdod	a	2-1	Zandberg, Bocoli
5/11	Hapoel Petach Tikva	h	2-0	Bocoli, Zandberg
14/11	Bnei Yehuda Tel Aviv	a	1-0	Zandberg
20/11	Maccabi Tel Aviv	h	2-1	Bocoli 2
26/11	Maccabi Netanya	a	3-1	Colautti 2, Bocoli
3/12	Hapoel Bnei Sakhnin	a	2-2	Zandberg, Bocoli
10/12	Maccabi Petach Tikva	a	3-1	Keissy, Colautti, Arbeitman
18/12	Beitar Jerusalem	h	3-0	Colautti 2, Harazi

2006

Date	Opponent	h/a	Score	Scorers
1/1	Hapoel Tel Aviv	a	0-0	
7/1	Hapoel Kfar Saba	h	1-0	og (Shachbari)
14/1	Hapoel Nazareth Ilit	a	6-0	Zandberg, Arbeitman 2, Tal (p), Bocoli (p), Rafaelov
22/1	MS Ashdod	h	4-0	Bocoli, Arbeitman, Colautti 2
28/1	Hapoel Petach Tikva	a	1-3	Bocoli
4/2	Bnei Yehuda Tel Aviv	h	1-0	Arbeitman
12/2	Maccabi Tel Aviv	a	0-1	
18/2	Maccabi Netanya	h	2-1	Ben Bassat, Bocoli (p)
25/2	Hapoel Kfar Saba	h	1-1	Zandberg
11/3	Hapoel Tel Aviv	h	0-1	
19/3	Beitar Jerusalem	a	0-1	
25/3	Bnei Yehuda Tel Aviv	h	4-0	Colautti 2, Tal, Zandberg
2/4	Maccabi Tel Aviv	a	1-1	Colautti
8/4	Maccabi Netanya	h	2-1	Colautti, Bocoli
15/4	MS Ashdod	a	1-1	og (Tubol)
23/4	Hapoel Nazareth Ilit	h	4-0	Ben Bassat 2, Benado 2
29/4	Hapoel Petach Tikva	a	2-0	Arbeitman 2
6/5	Maccabi Petach Tikva	h	2-1	Harazi, Tal (p)
12/5	Hapoel Bnei Sakhnin	a	2-2	Hemed, Colautti

No	Name	Nat	Pos	Aps	(s)	Gls
22	Tom ALMADON		G	2		
11	Shlomi ARBEITMAN		A	18	(10)	8
4	Arik BENADO		D	30		2
28	Eden BEN BASSAT		A	2	(10)	3
24	Eshetu BIRUK		M		(6)	
11	Dudu BITON		A	1		
7	Gustavo BOCOLI	BRA	M	32		12
23	Maor BOZAGLO		A		(2)	
9	Roberto COLAUTTI	ARG	A	24	(4)	13
1	Nir DAVIDOVICH		G	31		
15	Xavier DIRCEU	BRA	M	30		
3	Alon HARAZI		D	28		2
16	Tommer HEMED		A	1	(2)	1
	Abed KA'ABIA		D		(1)	
20	Yaniv KATAN		A	15		5
21	Dekel KEINAN		D		(1)	
6	Adoram KEISSY		D	25		1
23	Biram KIAL		M	1	(1)	
8	Fernando LOREFICE	ARG	M	8	(10)	
18	Haim MAGRELASHVILI		D	8	(6)	
14	Shai MIMON		D	1	(1)	
19	Rafael OLARA	CHL	D	29		
26	Lior RAFAELOV		M	4	(15)	1
5	Klimi SABAN		D	13	(13)	
10	Idan TAL		M	31		6
17	Michael ZANDBERG		M	29	(2)	9

MACCABI NETANYA
Coach – Rehuven Atar

2005

Date	Opponent	h/a	Score	Scorers
28/8	Maccabi Petach Tikva	a	1-2	Vilner
17/9	Beitar Jerusalem	h	2-3	Abdul-Razak, Masudi
24/9	Hapoel Tel Aviv	a	0-2	
1/10	Hapoel Kfar Saba	h	3-2	Masudi, Kimoto, Vasihon
14/10	Hapoel Nazareth Ilit	a	3-1	og (Kokol), Masudi, Banin
22/10	MS Ashdod	h	1-1	Krupnik
28/10	Hapoel Petach Tikva	a	2-0	Masudi, Edree
5/11	Bnei Yehuda Tel Aviv	h	0-1	
12/11	Maccabi Tel Aviv	a	0-1	
19/11	Hapoel Bnei Sakhnin	a	2-2	Kimoto, Masudi
26/11	Maccabi Haifa	h	1-3	Masudi
3/12	Maccabi Petach Tikva	h	0-1	
10/12	Beitar Jerusalem	a	1-1	Kimoto
17/12	Hapoel Tel Aviv	h	1-0	Kimoto
31/12	Hapoel Kfar Saba	a	2-1	Kimoto, Zwiti

2006

Date	Opponent	h/a	Score	Scorers
7/1	Hapoel Nazaret Ilit	h	1-0	Masudi
14/1	MS Ashdod	a	2-2	Kimoto 2
20/1	Hapoel Petach Tikva	h	0-0	
28/1	Bnei Yehuda Tel Aviv	a	0-1	
4/2	Maccabi Tel Aviv	h	3-1	Edree, Masudi, Abdul-Razak
11/2	Hapoel Bnei Sakhnin	h	0-0	
18/2	Maccabi Haifa	a	1-2	Masudi
25/2	MS Ashdod	h	3-1	Hermon, Abdul-Razak 2
11/3	Hapoel Nazareth Ilit	a	1-0	Awudo
17/3	Hapoel Petach Tikva	h	2-3	Talker, Awudo
25/3	Maccabi Petach Tikva	a	1-2	Kimoto
1/4	Hapoel Bnei Sakhnin	h	1-1	Kimoto

Israel

8/4	Maccabi Haifa	a	1-2	Tega	
15/4	Hapoel Tel Aviv	h	1-1	Awudo	
22/4	Beitar Jerusalem	a	0-4		
29/4	Bnei Yehuda Tel Aviv	h	2-1	Tega, Keinan	
6/5	Maccabi Tel Aviv	a	1-3	Keinan	
13/5	Hapoel Kfar Saba	h	1-0	Kimoto	

No	Name	Nat	Pos	Aps	(s)	Gls
11	Ibrahim ABDUL-RAZAK	GHA	M	26	(3)	4
10	Samado AWUDO	GHA	A	12	3	3
32	Tal BANIN		M	26	(1)	1
19	Assaf BEN MOHA		D	3	(6)	
13	Hamude BRICK		D	17	(4)	
9	Shlomi EDREE		A	7	(21)	2
10	Kobi HASSAN		M	2	(1)	
25	Golan HERMON		D	30		1
14	Dekel KEINAN		D	21		2
17	Papy KIMOTO	DRC	M	25	(2)	10
6	Leonard KRUPNIK	USA	D	16	(8)	1
26	Mate LACIC	SCG	D	5		
27	Vitali LEDENOV	BLS	A	1		
20	Alain MASUDI	DRC	M	29	(1)	9
22	Gal NIR		G	2		
22	Avi PERETZ		G	31		
23	Rafi SAROSI		D	2	(7)	
4	Ofer TALKER		D	26	(1)	1
15	Amir TEGA		M	25	(2)	2
8	Guy TOVIAK		M	17	(11)	
21	Adam VAYER		M		(1)	
5	Assi VASIHON		D	22	(1)	1
12	Liron VILNER		A	1	(8)	1
20	Dela YAMPOLSKI	NGA	A	1	(5)	
28	Israel ZWITI		M	16	(2)	1

MACCABI PETACH TIKVA
Coach – Guy Luzon

2005

28/8	Maccabi Netanya	h	2-1	Golan, og (Lacic)
19/9	Maccabi Haifa	a	2-3	Golan, Dobrovin
24/9	Hapoel Bnei Sakhnin	h	2-1	Edree, Mbamba
2/10	Beitar Jerusalem	h	1-2	Ganon
15/10	Hapoel Tel Aviv	a	1-1	Mbamba
24/10	Hapoel Kfar Saba	h	0-0	
29/10	Hapoel Nazareth Ilit	a	0-2	
7/11	MS Ashdod	h	2-2	Golan, David
12/11	Hapoel Petach Tikva	a	1-2	Golan
19/11	Bnei Yehuda Tel Aviv	h	0-0	
26/11	Maccabi Tel Aviv	a	0-0	
3/12	Maccabi Netanya	a	1-0	Tuaama
10/12	Maccabi Haifa	h	1-3	Tzemach (p)
19/12	Hapoel Bnei Sakhnin	a	1-2	Golan
31/12	Beitar Jerusalem	a	0-2	

2006

7/1	Hapoel Tel Aviv	h	2-3	Lokembo, Golan
14/1	Hapoel Kfar Saba	a	0-0	
21/1	Hapoel Nazareth Ilit	h	2-0	Golan, Edree
27/1	MS Ashdod	a	0-2	
4/2	Hapoel Petach Tikva	h	2-0	Golan, Tzemach
11/2	Bnei Yehuda Tel Aviv	a	0-1	
18/2	Maccabi Tel Aviv	h	3-1	Dobrovin 2, Sarsur
26/2	Beitar Jerusalem	a	0-1	
10/3	Bnei Yehuda Tel Aviv	h	1-0	Dobrovin
18/3	Maccabi Tel Aviv	a	3-0	Golan, Tuaama, Suffo
25/3	Maccabi Netanya	h	2-1	Suffo, Sarsur
1/4	MS Ashdod	a	0-0	
8/4	Hapoel Nazareth Ilit	h	1-0	Golan
14/4	Hapoel Petach Tikva	a	1-1	Suffo
22/4	Hapoel Kfar Saba	a	2-2	Suffo, Sarsur
29/4	Hapoel Bnei Sakhnin	h	1-0	Suffo
6/5	Maccabi Haifa	a	1-2	Suffo
13/5	Hapoel Tel Aviv	h	2-1	Jefisley, Sarsur

No	Name	Nat	Pos	Aps	(s)	Gls
3	Ismael AMAR		D	30		
19	Shay BANAY		M	12	(3)	
20	Roee BEKEL		M		(2)	
22	Ohad COHEN		G	33		
25	Shay DAVID		D	5	(10)	1
9	Stanislav DOBROVIN	RUS	A	18	(4)	4
11	Kfir EDREE		M	17	(13)	2
7	Dovev GABAY		A		(1)	
12	Kobi GANON		D	33		1
15	Omer GOLAN		A	26	(2)	10
24	Ron GLICK		A	2	(1)	
14	Hedham HEDIA		M		(1)	
18	Ben JANAH		D	3	(1)	
8	Maor JANAH		M		(1)	
8	Andrei JEFISLEY	BRA	D	28	(2)	1
15	Udi KABUDI		A		(3)	
12	Ognjen LAKIC	SCG	A	5	(1)	
6	Fabrice LOKEMBO Lokaso	BEL	D	8	(1)	1
17	Uri LUZON		M		(2)	
6	MÁRCIO Giovanini	BRA	D	7	(1)	
7	Assi MASHIACH		M	12	(4)	
30	Emile MBAMBA	CMR	A	9	(7)	2
4	Merad MEGAMADOV	RUS	D	29	(1)	
1	Yaniv MIZRAHI		G		(1)	
20	Naor PESSER		D	15		
21	Dani PREDA		M		(1)	
16	Robil SARSUR		A	15	(7)	4
24	Patrick SUFFO	CMR	A	11	(2)	6
10	Salim TUAAMA		M	20	(6)	2
26	Soli TZEMACH		M	25	(2)	2
8	Elaad ZAN		D		(2)	

MACCABI TEL AVIV
Coach – Nir Klinger; (5/12/05) (Eli Dricks); (20/12/05) Ton Kaanen (HOL)

2005

28/8	Beitar Jerusalem	a	1-0	Nimni
18/9	Hapoel Tel Aviv	h	2-0	og (Halis), Nimni
24/9	Hapoel Kfar Saba	a	0-1	
1/10	Hapoel Nazareth Ilit	h	0-0	
15/10	MS Ashdod	a	1-0	Haim
22/10	Hapoel Petach Tikva	h	3-0	Duarte, Kaku, Nimni
30/10	Bnei Yehuda Tel Aviv	a	1-3	Nimni (p)
6/11	Hapoel Bnei Sakhnin	a	0-1	
12/11	Maccabi Netanya	h	1-0	Nimni
20/11	Maccabi Haifa	a	1-2	Nimni
26/11	Maccabi Petach Tikva	h	0-0	
4/12	Beitar Jerusalem	h	2-3	Trica, Nimni
11/12	Hapoel Tel Aviv	a	0-2	
17/12	Hapoel Kfar Saba	h	2-1	Berkovic, Dayan
31/12	Hapoel Nazareth Ilit	a	0-0	

2006

7/1	MS Ashdod	h	2-1	Mishaelof, Duarte
14/1	Hapoel Petach Tikva	a	2-2	Duarte, Nimni (p)
21/1	Bnei Yehuda Tel Aviv	h	2-0	Nimni (p), Mesika
29/1	Hapoel Bnei Sakhnin	h	2-0	Nimni, Shpungin
4/2	Maccabi Netanya	a	1-3	Haim
12/2	Maccabi Haifa	h	3-1	Haim
18/2	Maccabi Petach Tikva	a	1-3	Cohen L.
24/2	Hapoel Nazareth Ilit	h	1-1	Dayan
11/3	Hapoel Petach Tikva	a	1-1	Demetradze

Israel

18/3	Maccabi Petach Tikva	h	0-3		
25/3	Hapoel Bnei Sakhnin	a	1-1	Haim	
2/4	Maccabi Haifa	h	1-1	Berkovic (p)	
9/4	Hapoel Tel Aviv	a	0-2		
16/4	Beitar Jerusalem	h	2-1	Rosso, Demetradze	
22/4	Bnei Yehuda Tel Aviv	a	0-1		
29/4	Hapoel Kfar Saba	h	0-0		
6/5	Maccabi Netanya	h	3-1	Haim, Demetradze, Shemesh	
13/5	MS Ashdod	a	1-1	Haim	

No	Name	Nat	Pos	Aps	(s)	Gls
23	Salem ABO SIAM		D	22	(2)	
14	Elvin BEQIRI	ALB	D	10	(2)	
9	Eyal BERKOVIC		M	21	(4)	2
15	Liran COHEN		M	14	(11)	1
19	Tamir COHEN		M	10	(6)	
17	Roee DAYAN		A	10	(8)	2
26	Giorgi DEMETRADZE	GEO	A	10	(3)	3
10	José DUARTE	BRA	A	18	(5)	3
17	Erez ELIHAV		D		(2)	
6	Christian GONZÁLEZ	URU	D	21	(1)	
18	Offir HAIM		A	15	(13)	6
22	Guy HAIMOV		G	2		
17	Blessing KAKU	NGA	M	8		1
28	Henry MAKINWA	NGA	A	2	(1)	
11	Erez MESIKA		M	18	(8)	1
5	Moshe MISHAELOF		M	19	(3)	1
8	Avi NIMNI		M	21	(2)	10
11	Djovani ROSSO	CRO	M	18	(4)	1
29	Avi SHEMESH		M	1	(3)	1
30	Yakir SHINA		M	4	(2)	
4	Yuval SHPUNGIN		D	21	(1)	1
20	Ori SHTRIT		M	3		
1	Liran STRAUBER		G	31		
2	Avi STRUL		D	17	(3)	
24	Eugen TRICA	ROM	M	4	(6)	1
13	Elior VAAKNIN		A		(1)	
3	Avi YEHIEL		D	25		
21	Shiran YEINI		M	3	(1)	
16	Lior ZAN		D	15	(2)	

DOMESTIC CUP 2005/06

THIRD ROUND
(21/2/06)
Hapoel Marmorek 2, Maccabi Kiriat Gat 0
Hapoel Acco 1, Hapoel Kiriat Shmone 0
Hapoel Beer Sheva 2, Ironi Tirat H'akarmel 0 *(aet)*
Hakoah Maccabi Amidar Ramat Gan 2, Hapoel R'anana 1 *(aet)*
Maccabi Kfar Kana 1, Maccabi Or Akiva 1
Hapoel Bnei Sakhnin 4, Maccabi Beer Sheva 0
Hapoel Jerusalem 0, Maccabi Herzliya 2
Hapoel Kfar Saba 3, Maccabi Ahi Nazareth 0
Hapoel Tel Aviv 3, Irony Rishon Letzion 0
MS Ashdod 3, Hapoel Haifa 2 *(aet)*
Maccabi Haifa 1, Hapoel Petach Tikva 0
Irony Ramat H'asharon 2, Hapoel Nazareth Ilit 1 *(aet)*
(22/2/06)
Beitar Jerusalem 4, Irony Kiriat Ata 0
Maccabi Netanya 0, Maccabi Petach Tikva 2
Hapoel Ashkelon 0, Bnei Yehuda Tel Aviv 2
(28/6/05)
Bnei Lod 0, Maccabi Tel Aviv 2

FOURTH ROUND
(3/3/06)
Hapoel Marmorek 0, Hapoel Kfar Saba 1
Maccabi Herzliya 2, Maccabi Petach Tikva 2 (aet; 12-13 on pens)
(3/3/06)
Irony Ramat H'asharon 1, Hapoel Bnei Sakhnin 3
Beitar Jerusalem 0, Hakoah Maccabi Amidar Ramat Gan 1
Maccabi Tel Aviv 0, Hapoel Acco 4
MS Ashdod 0, Hapoel Tel Aviv 3
(5/3/06)
Hapoel Beer Sheva 1, Maccabi Haifa 2
(6/3/06)
Maccabi Kfar Kana 0, Bnei Yehuda Tel Aviv 1 *(aet)*

QUARTER-FINALS
(21/3/06)
Hapoel Acco 1 (Hassan 70), Bnei Yehuda Tel Aviv 2 (Badash 90, Biton M. 95) *(aet)*
Maccabi Haifa 0, Maccabi Petach Tikva 0 *(aet; 4-3 on pens)*
(22/3/06)
Hapoel Kfar Saba 1 (Abubakari 85), Hapoel Bnei Sakhnin 3 (Abergil 45, Hudeda 88, Pascal 89)
Hakoah Maccabi Amidar Ramat Gan 0, Hapoel Tel Aviv 3 (Peretz 18, Ogabuna 79, Barda 89)

SEMI-FINALS
(26/4/06)
Hapoel Tel Aviv 2 (Dego 58, Javrujan 61), Hapoel Bnei Sakhnin 0
Bnei Yehuda Tel Aviv 2 (Gafni 103, Biton E. 120), Maccabi Haifa 0 *(aet)*

FINAL
(9/5/06)
Ramat Gan Stadium, Tel Aviv
HAPOEL TEL AVIV 1 *(Javrujan 87)*
BNEI YEHUDA TEL AVIV 0
Referee - Yefet
HAPOEL TEL AVIV – Elimelech, Antebi, Gershon, Chen, Pantsil, Abuksis, Dego, Badir, Vermot (Ogabuna 62), Barda (Abutbol 88), Javrujan (Domb 90).
BNEI YEHUDA TEL AVIV – Eniema, Abarbnel, Azoulay, Etachi, Gafni, Azouz (Biton E. 70), Baldut (Baturina 90), Oved, Lukman, Kovacevic (Badash 89), Biton M.

SECOND LEVEL FINAL TABLE 2005/06

		Pld	W	D	L	F	A	Pts
1	Maccabi Herzliya	33	16	9	8	42	22	57
2	Hakoah Maccabi Amidar R G	33	15	11	7	47	31	56
3	Hapoel Kiriat Shmone	33	12	14	7	39	33	50
4	Hapoel Beer Sheva	33	11	16	6	35	25	49
5	Hapoel Jerusalem	33	13	10	10	45	40	49
6	Hapoel Haifa	33	11	14	8	40	28	47
7	Hapoel Acco	33	12	10	11	32	33	46
8	Hapoel Ashkelon	33	10	8	15	33	40	38
9	Hapoel Raanana	33	8	12	13	31	36	36
10	Nir Ramat Hasharon	33	8	13	12	30	39	35
11	Irony Rishon Letzion	33	6	13	14	24	43	31
12	Maccabi Beer Sheva	33	6	10	17	19	47	27

N.B. Nir Ramat Hasharon – 2 pts deducted; Maccabi Beer Sheva – 1 pt deducted.

Italy

The agony and the ecstasy

Italians will not forget the summer of 2006 in a hurry. The good news was provided by Marcello Lippi's Azzurri, who deservedly won the World Cup. The bad news was the worst match-fixing scandal in the history of the game, an investigation into which revealed that Italian domestic football was rotten to the core.

The sheer breadth and scale of the scam beggared belief. A series of phone taps had unearthed a vast network of corruption involving an assortment of high-profile, high-office figures, all of whom were either actively involved or passively compliant in the systematic manipulation of Serie A referees, matches and results.

At the hub of it all was the director general of Juventus, Luciano Moggi. The affair became known as Moggiopoli and its revelations were so shocking that it will probably take many years before Italian football can fully restore its credibility. In fact, in a country where conspiracy theories and paranoia are not far short of being a national obsession, the finger of suspicion might never go away. Italian football now has a dirty image, and it will take a long, long time before it can be wiped clean.

The verdicts of the investigative tribunal on the guilty men and the Serie A clubs they belonged to were delivered just five days after the World Cup final. By and large they reflected the enormity of the scandal. Moggi and his chief co-conspirator Antonio Giraudo, the former Juventus chief executive, were banned from all football activity for five years. There were long bans also for Italian federation president Franco Carraro and various referees, refereeing administrators and officials from the other three implicated clubs – Fiorentina, Lazio and Milan.

Titles stripped

The key issue concerned the punishments meted out on the clubs themselves, and these too were severe. Juventus were stripped of their 2004/05 and 2005/06 Serie A titles, and demoted to Serie B with a 30-point penalty. Fiorentina and Lazio were relegated to Serie B with respective 12-point and seven-point deductions. Milan were allowed to stay

NATIONAL TEAM RESULTS 2005/06

Date	Opponent	H/A/N	Venue	Score	Scorers
17/8/05	Republic of Ireland	A	Dublin	2-1	Pirlo (10), Gilardino (31)
3/9/05	Scotland (WCQ)	A	Glasgow	1-1	Grosso (75)
7/9/05	Belarus (WCQ)	A	Minsk	4-1	Toni (6, 14, 55), Camoranesi (45)
8/10/05	Slovenia (WCQ)	H	Palermo	1-0	Zaccardo (78)
12/10/05	Moldova (WCQ)	H	Lecce	2-1	Vieri (71), Gilardino (85)
12/11/05	Holland	A	Amsterdam	3-1	Gilardino (41), Vlaar (45og), Toni (50)
16/11/05	Ivory Coast	N	Geneva	1-1	Diana (86)
1/3/06	Germany	H	Florence	4-1	Gilardino (4), Toni (7), De Rossi (39), Del Piero (57)
31/5/06	Switzerland	A	Geneva	1-1	Gilardino (10)
2/6/06	Ukraine	N	Lausanne	0-0	
12/6/06	Ghana (WCF)	N	Hanover	2-0	Pirlo (40), Iaquinta (83)
17/6/06	United States (WCF)	N	Kaiserslautern	1-1	Gilardino (22)
22/6/06	Czech Republic (WCF)	N	Hamburg	2-0	Materazzi (26), Inzaghi (87)
26/6/06	Australia (WCF)	N	Kaiserslautern	1-0	Totti (90p)
30/6/06	Ukraine (WCF)	N	Hamburg	3-0	Zambrotta (6), Toni (59, 69)
4/7/06	Germany (WCF)	A	Dortmund	2-0	Grosso (119), Del Piero (120) (aet)
9/7/06	France (WCF)	N	Berlin	1-1	Materazzi (19) (aet; 5-3 on pens)

Italy

in Serie A but with a 15-point penalty. Additionally, all four clubs were disqualified from competing in UEFA competitions in 2006/07.

Appeals were launched by all of the guilty parties, however, and less than a fortnight later a new batch of verdicts were delivered. In just about every case the punishments were drastically reduced. While the five-year bans remained for Moggi and Giraudo, and chief referee designator Pierluigi Pairetto actually had his suspension increased by 12 months to three and a half years, the clubs all received significantly lighter sentences.

Juve's title-concession and relegation stood, but their points deduction was cut from 30 to 17, thus giving them a far better chance of returning to Serie A after just one season away. Fiorentina and Lazio were both still denied European access but retained their Serie A status, albeit with respective 19-point and 11-point deductions. Milan had their 15-point penalty reduced to eight points and, more importantly, were placed third in the 2005/06 final table (having been docked 30 points rather than the original 44), which permitted them to compete in the qualifying round of the Champions League. UEFA had the power to deny Milan entry, but with all sorts of legal threats confronting them if they did so, chose to let them back in.

Luciano Moggi – Mr Fixit no more

After the initial verdict, the reduced sentences seemed like a mere slap on the wrists for the four clubs. The message the appeals judges unwittingly sent out was that the crisis hadn't really been as serious as first thought. The only punishment that would have serious repercussions was Juventus's relegation – and the need for them to sell off most of their best players. The other three clubs, basically, could carry on as normal.

No deterrent

Appeasement has long been the Italian way of dealing with potential confrontation. Some might call it cowardice. That appears again to have been the case with Moggiopoli. The promises of harsh action proved to be empty. Worse still, there is no obvious deterrent to the same sort of thing happening again. If football is to have a future in Italy, then it has to be clean. 100 per cent clean. At the moment nobody can say with any confidence that it is, or indeed will be in the future.

For many years Juventus's meagre crowds at the Stadio delle Alpi have been a mystery. It was repeatedly claimed that the fans didn't like the stadium, or that Turin was full of Torino supporters, or that it was too expensive to get in. Now we know the truth. Spectators don't go to watch Juventus because they know they are not going to see a fair sporting contest.

The 2004/05 Serie A season – the one under investigation - was also, we now know, a complete sham. And by inference from the investigating committee's decision to take away two titles from Juventus rather than one, it can safely be deduced that the 2005/06 was utterly worthless as well. That much was confirmed when it was decided, retrospectively, to award the 2005/06 title to Inter instead.

In the real world – or in the parallel universe in which Moggi and his cronies operated – Inter finished 15 points behind Juventus. But now, and forever more, Inter will be known as the 2005/06 Serie A champions. As such, they sport the scudetto on their shirts for a year and can boast of a 17-year barren run having finally come to an end. At least, that's the official line. Most Inter fans, however, will take little or no satisfaction from their club's so-called 'achievement'. The only real bonus is direct access to the Champions League, plus the smug Schadenfreude that will stand them in good stead when they confront rival fans from Milan and – especially – Juventus.

Italy

The original final Serie A table was so completely bent out of shape by the match-fixing scenario that a more pertinent move from the league authorities might have been simply to expunge all 2005/06 records and make out that the season simply hadn't existed. Luca Toni, for example, scored 31 Serie A goals for Fiorentina – the first time anyone had passed 30 goals in Italy's top division for 47 years – but given that Fiorentina had 30 points removed from their total, what value does that record now have? Perhaps some of his goals were 'pre-arranged'. We ask and speculate only because we cannot be sure.

Worthless wins

As for the 27 victories that Juventus posted to claim what might have been their 29th national title, they now have no value at all. Officially, Juve are not placed in the 2005/06 final table, which means that those wins are no longer validated. But at the same time the teams they beat have not been awarded any of the points they 'lost' against the original champions, so the whole table is a distortion.

For the record, however, with Juve disqualified and Milan, Fiorentina and Lazio each having 30 points removed from their total, the post-season situation with regard to the key issues of European qualification and relegation stood as follows:

Inter, the new champions by default, were joined by Roma, promoted from fifth to second place, in the 2006/07 Champions League; Milan, despite their points penalty, dropped only one place to third and were put forward for Champions League qualifying, where they were joined by Chievo, who moved up from seventh to fourth; Palermo, Livorno and Parma were all given UEFA Cup places, in Parma's case only because Empoli were refused a European licence; Messina were rescued from relegation, with Juventus going down in their place alongside Lecce and Treviso.

Treviso, it is worth mentioning, were only promoted to Serie A in 2005, along with Ascoli, because of another match-rigging crime that prevented the promotion of Genoa and Torino. But as city rivals Juventus dropped out of Serie A in shame, Torino, paradoxically, returned to take their place after winning a series of promotion play-offs. The automatic promotion of the top two clubs in Serie B, Atalanta and Catania, was unaffected.

Also untouched by the scandal, one presumes, was the 2005/06 Coppa Italia. The much-decried competition was won, for the second time in as many seasons, by Inter, who beat Roma 4-2 on aggregate in the final. Nobody knew it at the time, but the final would therefore be contested by the top two teams in Serie A. Furthermore, by successfully defending the trophy Inter would claim the Double – for the very first time. Or so history will now tell us they did.

Roma's record run

It was Roma who knocked Juventus out of the competition, on away goals, in the quarter-finals (albeit after losing the home leg to a dodgy penalty). That tie came in the midst of a remarkable run of victories by Luciano Spalletti's side in the league. From late December through to the end of February, when they beat Lazio 2-0, Roma posted 11 successive wins, thus claiming a new Serie A record. The penultimate game in that sequence brought a 1-0 win over Empoli, but victory came at a price as club captain Francesco Totti broke his leg. Short of strikers in any case at the time, Roma were forced to muddle through, with Brazilian midfielders Mancini and Rodrigo Taddei taking over up front. Without the talismanic Totti, they struggled over the last three months of the season and looked to have lost their Champions League place to Fiorentina – until the match-fixing investigators had their say.

Roma were one of three Serie A clubs to drop out of the UEFA Cup simultaneously during the early spring. Udinese, who had made their Champions League debut earlier in the season, surprisingly went out to Levski Sofia while Palermo's run was ended by Schalke. As both Udinese and Palermo fielded deliberately understrength teams in the competition, they got their just desserts, but at least Roma went out with some dignity after a nail-biting tie with eventual finalists Middlesbrough.

Given all the domestic shenanigans, it was probably a good thing – from a neutral perspective at least - that Italian clubs had a poor season in the Champions League.

Juventus scraped through their last-16 game against Werder Bremen with a helping hand from…not the referee but the opposition goalkeeper, then found themselves utterly outplayed in the quarter-final by Arsenal. This time the match officials did intervene – sending off two Juve players at Highbury and another in Turin. Moggi's sphere of influence, evidently, knew some bounds.

Italy

NATIONAL TEAM APPEARANCES 2005/06

Coach – Marcello LIPPI			Irl	SCO	BLS	SLO	MOL	Hol	Civ	Ger	Sui	Ukr	GHA	USA	CZE	AUS	UKR	GER	FRA	Caps	Goals
Flavio ROMA	21/6/74	AS Monaco FC (FRA)	G																	3	-
Cristian ZACCARDO	21/12/81	Palermo	D	D46	D	s60	D		D46	D	D		D	D54		s76				15	1
Fabio CANNAVARO	13/9/73	Juventus	D63	D	D	D		D		D	D	D75	D	D	D	D	D	D	D	100	1
Alessandro NESTA	19/3/76	Milan	D46	D	D	D		D		D81		D61	D	D	D17					77	-
Gianluca ZAMBROTTA	19/2/77	Juventus	D	D		D	s62	D						D	D	D	D	D	D	57	2
Gennaro GATTUSO	9/1/78	Milan	M	M	M	M		M	s46		M			s35	M	M	M76	M	M	47	1
Andrea PIRLO	19/5/79	Milan	M76	M	M	M82		M87	M46	M73	M75	M58	M	M	M		M68	M	M	31	5
Daniele DE ROSSI	24/7/83	Roma	M46	M66	s82	M	s60	M46	M	s46	M	M	M					s61		20	3
Alessandro DEL PIERO	9/11/74	Juventus	A46			A	M	M46	A81	A46	A58	s82	s54		M75		s103	s86		79	26
Chrisian VIERI	12/7/73	Milan	A	A		s88	A													49	23
Alberto GILARDINO	5/7/82	Milan	A46		A	A60	s67	A60	A46	A64	A46		A	A64	A	A60	A46		s73	20	8
Marco MATERAZZI	19/8/78	Internazionale	s46			D		D	s81	D46	s75		s17	D			D	D		32	2
Fabio GROSSO	28/11/77	Palermo	s46	s46	D57	D	D62	D	D	D	D60	D	D		D	D	D	D	D	23	2
Aimo DIANA	2/1/78	Sampdoria	s46				M	s78	s46											12	1
Vincenzo IAQUINTA	21/1/179	Udinese	s46	A71	s67		A67	s67	A	s81	s46		s64	s62		s46		s91	s61	17	1
Andrea BARZAGLI	8/5/81	Palermo	s63		s84				D		s61				s56	D				10	-
Simone BARONE	30/4/78	Palermo	s76		s57	M	s87	M	s73		s69			s74		s68				15	1
Angelo PERUZZI	16/2/70	Lazio		G	G	G														31	-
Francesco TOTTI	27/9/76	Roma		M	M	M					M	s58	M56	M35	M	s75	A	A	A61	58	9
Mauro CAMORANESI	4/10/76	Juventus		s66	M84	M		M78	s46	M89	M46	M69	s56		M74		M68	M91	M86	26	1
Luca TONI	20/5/77	Fiorentina		s71	A67	A88		A67	s46	A	s46	A58	A82	A62		A56	A	A73	A	24	9
Morgan DE SANCTIS	26/3/77	Udinese					G													2	-
Daniele BONERA	31/5/81	Parma					D46			s60										11	-
Manuele BLASI	17/8/80	Juventus					s46													8	-
Christian ABBIATI	8/7/77	Juventus						G	G71											4	-
Massimo ODDO	14/6/76	Lazio						s46		s46	D					s68				21	-
Marco AMELIA	2/4/82	Livorno							s71											1	-
Gianluigi BUFFON	28/1/78	Juventus								G	G	G	G	G	G	G	G	G	G	67	-
Simone PERROTTA	17/9/77	Roma								s64	s75	s58	M	M	M	M	M	M103	M61	31	1
Manuel PASQUAL	13/3/82	Fiorentina								s89										1	-
Filippo INZAGHI	9/8/73	Milan									s58			s60						50	22

Italy

Milanese ousted

Inter were eliminated by competition debutants Villarreal, with Juan Román Riquelme delivering a masterclass at El Madrigal to remove the Nerazzurri from the quarter-finals for the second year running. Milan, who had dumped Inter out 12 months earlier, outlasted their city rivals again, but Barcelona proved too good for them in the semis and they were unable to make good their catastrophic defeat to Liverpool in the 2005 final. Carlo Ancelotti's men turned on the style against Bayern Munich in the last 16 but they were lucky to sneak past both Schalke and Lyon. It was a refereeing blunder in Camp Nou that helped to eliminate them, but Milan were second best to the Catalans in every respect and could have no just cause for complaint.

Milan played much of the season without their injured captain, Paolo Maldini, but the great man, now 38, did make it on to the field on a sufficient number of occasions to break Dino Zoff's all-time Serie A record of 570 appearances – having also, some years earlier, taken Zoff's title as Italy's most-capped international. Unlike the former goalkeeper, however, the Milan defender was never able to win a major international trophy with Italy. How ironic, then, that in their first World Cup without Maldini for 20 years, the Azzurri should triumph in Germany.

Cannavaro's glory

Maldini had always dreamed of lifting the World Cup, but it was his replacement as skipper, Fabio Cannavaro, who got to enjoy that moment of ecstasy on the evening of Sunday, July 9 in Berlin's Olympiastadion. No man deserved the honour more. Cannavaro had an impeccable World Cup. He was Italy's outstanding performer in at least half of their matches and should have won the Golden Ball even before its eventual winner, Zinedine Zidane, went berserk in extra-time of the final. Cannavaro made his 100th appearance for Italy in Berlin. One imagines there will be many more caps to come, perhaps enough to bypass Maldini, although he will be almost 37 when the next World Cup is played in South Africa.

There will be no more Azzurri outings, however, for Marcello Lippi. Italy's World Cup-winning coach understandably decided to bow out at the top, announcing his resignation just a couple of days after the victory over France. With almost indecent haste Roberto Donadoni, the former Italy international midfielder, was appointed to replace him. It will be a hard, perhaps impossible, act to follow.

Lippi, who had taken the job only two years previously following the team's first-round flop under Giovanni Trapattoni at Euro 2004, did just about everything right in Germany. He bonded the team well, protected them from all the scandalous goings-on back home and made shrewd selections and sound substitutions. He even, at times, made Italy enjoyable to watch. Although, as ever, the Azzurri's strength was at the back, they were surprisingly positive going forward. The reward for adventure over caution was never better illustrated than when they scored those two late goals to beat Germany in Dortmund at the end of an epic semi-final.

Every successful team needs a bit of luck here and there, and Italy certainly got their fair share. The last-minute penalty against Australia was an outrage, and other teams assisted them by having players stupidly sent off at key times – two Americans, one from the Czech Republic and, of course, one crazy Frenchman. It could be argued, in fact, that Italy were never fully at ease in any of their seven matches, but

On top of the world – Italy coach Marcello Lippi

Italy

any problems that were thrown at them were dealt with, largely through skilful defending and goalkeeping but also through sheer collective willpower.

Perfect penalties

It is unlikely that there will ever be five more perfectly struck penalties than those converted by Italy in the final shoot-out against France. Putting the ball in the net was not a problem for the Italians at any stage of the competition. Whenever they needed a goal, somebody would invariably step up and supply one. They found the net 12 times in their seven matches, and no fewer than ten players got their name on the scoresheet. That was collective responsibility on a grand scale.

If Cannavaro was the team's outstanding individual, his Juventus club colleague Gianluigi Buffon ran him a close second. The big goalkeeper was a human wall. He conceded just two goals – an own-goal and a penalty – and always came good when required to pull off an important save. Gianluca Zambrotta, another Juve player, also excelled at full-back, while Fabio Grosso and Marco Materazzi both performed beyond their wildest dreams, making decisive contributions in the semi-final and final.

Gennaro Gattuso and Andrea Pirlo were the perfect midfield pair, the former all energy and aggression, the latter all poise and precision. Simone Perrotta and Mauro Camoranesi were less prominent but both performed their duties well, and with Daniele De Rossi suspended for four games after his ugly elbow on America's Brian McBride, they had to.

It is common practice for Italy to turn to one striker for their World Cup goals (Paolo Rossi in 1982, Alessandro Altobelli in 1986, Salvatore Schillaci in 1990, Roberto Baggio in 1994 and Christian Vieri in 1998 and 2002), but nobody filled that role in Germany. Luca Toni scored twice, but so did centre-back Materazzi. Lippi persisted with the Fiorentina goal-machine but neither he nor Alberto Gilardino really rose to the occasion, while Francesco Totti, not for the first time at a major finals but perhaps not surprisingly after his long injury lay-off, made little impact.

The 2006 World Cup was not a tournament for strikers. It was a tournament for well drilled, well balanced and well equipped teams. And Italy, like it or not, were the best.

EUROPEAN CUPS 2005/06

UEFA CHAMPIONS LEAGUE

JUVENTUS

1st round Group A

Match 1 CLUB BRUGGE KV (BEL)
A 2-1 *Nedved (66), Trezeguet (75)*
Abbiati, Blasi, Kovac, Cannavaro, Zambrotta, Camoranesi (Giannichedda 88), Emerson, Vieira, Nedved, Trezeguet (Zalayeta 88), Ibrahimovic.

Match 2 SK RAPID WIEN (AUT)
H 3-0 *Trezeguet (27), Mutu (82), Ibrahimovic (85)*
Abbiati, Pessotto, Thuram, Cannavaro, Zambrotta, Camoranesi (Mutu 65), Emerson, Giannichedda (Blasi 83), Nedved, Trezeguet (Del Piero 59), Ibrahimovic.

Match 3 FC BAYERN MÜNCHEN (GER)
A 1-2 *Ibrahimovic (90)*
Abbiati, Blasi (Chiellini 46), Thuram, Cannavaro, Zambrotta, Camoranesi (Del Piero 46), Giannichedda, Emerson, Nedved, Ibrahimovic, Trezeguet (Mutu 66).

Match 4 FC BAYERN MÜNCHEN
H 2-1 *Trezeguet (61, 85)*
Abbiati, Thuram, Kovac, Camoranesi (Mutu 76), Cannavaro, Chiellini, Emerson, Vieira, Del Piero (Nedved 46), Zambrotta, Ibrahimovic, Trezeguet.

Match 5 CLUB BRUGGE KV
H 1-0 *Del Piero (80)*
Abbiati, Zambrotta, Thuram, Cannavaro, Chiellini, Camoranesi (Mutu 81), Emerson, Vieira, Nedved, Del Piero, Trezeguet (Zalayeta 84).

Match 6 SK RAPID WIEN
A 3-1 *Del Piero (35, 45), Ibrahimovic (41)*
Abbiati, Balzaretti, Kovac, Thuram, Cannavaro, Chiellini, Camoranesi (Giannichedda 78), Blasi, Vieira, Mutu (Pessotto 61), Del Piero, Ibrahimovic (Zalayeta 46).

2nd round SV WERDER BREMEN (GER)
A 2-3 *Nedved (74), Trezeguet (82)*
Buffon, Blasi, Cannavaro, Thuram, Zambrotta, Camoranesi (Zalayeta 74), Emerson, Vieira, Nedved, Ibrahimovic (Del Piero 58), Trezeguet.
H 2-1 *Trezeguet (65), Emerson (88)*
Buffon, Zebina, Thuram, Cannavaro, Zambrotta (Balzaretti 70), Camoranesi (Mutu 56), Emerson, Viera, Nedved, Ibrahimovic (Del Piero 56), Trezeguet.

Quarter-final ARSENAL (ENG)
A 0-2
Buffon, Zebina, Thuram, Cannavaro, Zambrotta, Camoranesi, Vieira, Emerson, Mutu (Chiellini 71), Ibrahimovic, Trezeguet (Zalayeta 78).
H 0-0
Buffon, Zambrotta, Kovac, Cannavaro, Chiellini (Balzaretti 66), Mutu (Zalayeta 61), Emerson, Giannichedda, Nedved, Trezeguet, Ibrahimovic.

MILAN

1st round Group E

Match 1 FENERBAHÇE (TUR)
H 3-1 *Kaká (18, 86), Shevchenko (89)*
Dida, Cafu, Nesta, Maldini, Kaladze, Gattuso (Vogel 71), Pirlo (Serginho 71), Ambrosini, Kaká, Shevchenko, Vieri (Gilardino 78).

Match 2 FC SCHALKE 04 (GER)
A 2-2 *Seedorf (1), Shevchenko (59)*
Dida, Cafu (Stam 76), Nesta, Maldini, Kaladze, Gattuso, Pirlo, Seedorf, Kaká (Rui Costa 74), Gilardino (Vieri 70), Shevchenko.

Italy

Match 3 PSV (HOL)
H 0-0
Dida, Cafu, Stam, Maldini, Kaladze, Gattuso, Pirlo, Seedorf (Serginho 75), Kaká, Shevchenko (Inzaghi 49), Vieri.

Match 4 PSV
A 0-1
Dida, Stam, Nesta, Maldini, Kaladze (Serginho 46), Seedorf, Pirlo, Gattuso (Jankulovski 46), Kaká, Vieri, Gilardino (Shevchenko 74).

Match 5 FENERBAHÇE
A 4-0 *Shevchenko (16, 52, 70, 76)*
Dida, Simic, Nesta, Maldini, Serginho, Gattuso (Vogel 80), Pirlo, Seedorf, Kaká (Rui Costa 19), Gilardino (Vieri 75), Shevchenko.

Match 6 FC SCHALKE 04
H 3-2 *Pirlo (42), Kaká (52, 60)*
Dida, Stam, Nesta, Maldini (Simic 31; Kaladze 79), Serginho, Gattuso, Pirlo, Kaká, Seedorf, Inzaghi (Gilardino 85), Shevchenko.

2nd round FC BAYERN MÜNCHEN (GER)
A 1-1 *Shevchenko (57p)*
Dida (Kalac 89), Stam, Nesta, Kaladze, Serginho, Pirlo, Gattuso (Vogel 85), Seedorf (Jankulovski 90), Kaká, Shevchenko, Gilardino.
H 4-1 *Inzaghi (8, 47), Shevchenko (25), Kaká (59)*
Dida, Stam, Nesta, Kaladze, Serginho, Vogel, Pirlo, Seedorf, Kaká (Rui Costa 86), Shevchenko (Ambrosini 76), Inzaghi (Gilardino 72).

Quarter-final OLYMPIQUE LYONNAIS (FRA)
A 0-0
Dida, Costacurta (Maldini 62), Nesta, Kaladze, Serginho, Gattuso, Pirlo (Vogel 85), Seedorf, Kaká, Gilardino (Inzaghi 62), Shevchenko.
H 3-1 *Inzaghi (25, 88), Shevchenko (90)*
Dida, Stam (Costacurta 24), Nesta, Kaladze, Serginho, Gattuso (Maldini 78), Pirlo (Ambrosini 72), Seedorf, Kaká, Inzaghi, Shevchenko.

Semi-final FC BARCELONA (ESP)
H 0-1
Dida, Stam (Cafu 75), Nesta, Kaladze, Serginho, Pirlo (Maldini 67), Gattuso (Ambrosini 72), Kaká, Seedorf, Shevchenko, Gilardino.
A 0-0
Dida, Stam, Costacurta (Cafu 63), Kaladze, Serginho, Pirlo, Kaká (Rui Costa 67), Seedorf, Kaká, Shevchenko, Inzaghi (Gilardino 79).

INTERNAZIONALE
3rd qualifying round SHAKHTAR DONETSK (UKR)
A 2-0 *Martins (68), Adriano (79)*
Júlio César, Zanetti J., Córdoba, Materazzi, Favalli, Stankovic, Cambiasso, Verón (Pizarro 77), Solari (Zé Maria 65), Adriano, Martins.
H 1-1 *Recoba (12)*
Júlio César, Zanetti J., Córdoba, Materazzi, Womé, Stankovic (Pizarro 46), Cambiasso, Verón (Zé Maria 73), Solari, Recoba, Adriano (Cruz 83).

1st round Group H
Match 1 ARTMEDIA BRATISLAVA (SVK)
A 1-0 *Cruz (17)*
Júlio César, Córdoba, Materazzi, Samuel, Womé, Figo (Martins 80), Verón, Zanetti C., Stankovic, Cruz (Pizarro 65), Adriano.

Match 2 RANGERS (SCO)
H 1-0 *Pizarro (49)*
Júlio César, Córdoba, Samuel, Materazzi, Womé, Figo (Zé Maria 75), Pizarro, Cambiasso, Solari (Kily González 84), Martins (Recoba 60), Cruz.

Match 3 FC PORTO (POR)
A 0-2
Júlio César, Córdoba, Materazzi, Samuel, Favalli, Cambiasso, Figo (Zé Maria 82), Verón, Pizarro (Recoba 53), Solari (Adriano 67), Cruz.

Match 4 FC PORTO
H 2-1 *Cruz (75p, 82)*
Júlio César, Burdisso, Materazzi, Samuel (Mihajlovic 66), Favalli, Figo, Pizarro, Verón, Womé (Cambiasso 54), Adriano (Cruz 61), Martins.

Match 5 ARTMEDIA BRATISLAVA
H 4-0 *Figo (28), Adriano (41, 59, 74)*
Júlio César, Zanetti J., Córdoba (Zanetti C. 67), Samuel, Womé, Figo (Burdisso 46), Cambiasso, Verón (Stankovic 60), Solari, Recoba, Adriano.

Match 6 RANGERS
A 1-1 *Adriano (30)*
Toldo, Andreolli (Zanetti J. 68), Mihajlovic, Materazzi (Momente 40), Burdisso, Solari, Zanetti C., Pizarro, Womé, Martins, Adriano (Boumsong 82).

2nd round AJAX (HOL)
A 2-2 *Stankovic (49), Cruz (86)*
Toldo, Zanetti J., Córdoba, Samuel, Burdisso, Figo, Cambiasso, Stankovic, César (Pizarro 46), Adriano (Martins 65), Cruz.
H 1-0 *Stankovic (57)*
Toldo, Zanetti J., Materazzi, Samuel, Womé, Figo, Verón (Zanetti C. 74), Cambiasso, Stankovic, Martins (Recoba 84), Adriano.

Quarter-final VILLARREAL CF (ESP)
H 2-1 *Adriano (7), Martins (54)*
Toldo, Zanetti J., Córdoba, Samuel, Womé, Stankovic (Kily González 82), Verón, Cambiasso, César (Materazzi 69), Recoba (Martins 28), Adriano.
A 0-1
Toldo, Córdoba, Materazzi, Samuel, Zanetti J., Figo (Mihajlovic 74), Cambiasso, Verón (Cruz 85), Stankovic, Recoba (Martins 56), Adriano.

UDINESE
3rd qualifying round SPORTING CP (POR)
A 1-0 *Iaquinta (27p)*
De Sanctis, Bertotto, Candela, Felipe, Natali, Muntari (Mauri 72), Obodo, Zenoni, Barreto (Vidigal 42), Di Natale (Rossini 81), Iaquinta.
H 3-2 *Iaquinta (23p, 90), Natali (35)*
De Sanctis, Bertotto, Natali, Felipe, Zenoni, Vidigal, Obodo, Muntari (Mauri 70), Candela, Di Natale (Barreto 82), Iaquinta.

1st round Group C
Match 1 PANATHINAIKOS (GRE)
H 3-0 *Iaquinta (28, 73, 76)*
De Sanctis, Juarez (Sensini 86), Natali, Felipe, Zenoni, Vidigal, Obodo (Pinzi 68), Muntari, Candela, Iaquinta, Di Natale (Di Michele 79).

Match 2 FC BARCELONA (ESP)
A 1-4 *Felipe (24)*
De Sanctis, Bertotto, Natali (Juarez 34), Felipe, Zenoni, Vidigal, Obodo, Muntari (Di Michele 73), Candela, Barreto, Di Natale (Mauri 52).

Match 3 SV WERDER BREMEN (GER)
H 1-1 *Di Natale (86)*
De Sanctis, Bertotto, Sensini, Felipe, Zenoni, Mauri 76), Pinzi (Di Natale 76), Obodo, Muntari, Candela, Di Michele (Barreto 58), Iaquinta.

Match 4 SV WERDER BREMEN
A 3-4 *Di Natale (54, 57), Schulz (60og)*
De Sanctis, Bertotto, Sensini, Felipe, Zenoni (Mauri 50), Pinzi, Obodo, Muntari (Di Natale 30), Candela, Iaquinta, Di Michele (Motta 73).

Italy

Match 5 PANATHINAIKOS
A 2-1 *Iaquinta (80), Candela (83)*
De Sanctis, Bertotto, Sensini, Felipe, Zenoni, Obodo, Muntari (Mauri 75), Candela, Di Natale (Barreto 62), Di Michele (Rossini 80), Iaquinta.

Match 6 FC BARCELONA
H 0-2
De Sanctis, Bertotto, Sensini, Juarez, Zenoni (Tissone 38), Vidigal, Obodo, Muntari (Mauri 64), Candela, Di Natale, Iaquinta (Di Michele 75).

UEFA CUP

ROMA

1st round ARIS (GRE)
H 5-1 *Aquilani (1), Panucci (22, 44), Montella (28), Totti (53)*
Curci, Bovo, Panucci, Kuffour, Cufré, Mancini (Alvarez 65), Aquilani, Dacourt, Taddei, Montella (Nonda 72), Totti (Kharja 79).
A 0-0
Doni, Panucci, Mexès, Chivu (Rosi 84), Bovo, Alvarez, Aquilani (Perrotta 64), Dacourt, Kharja, Taddei (De Rossi 72), Okaka Chuka.

2nd round Group E
Match 1 TROMSØ IL (NOR)
A 2-1 *Kuffour (35), Cufré (84)*
Doni, Panucci (Cufré 66), Mexès, Kuffour, Bovo, Alvarez, Dacourt (De Rossi 53), Kharja, Perrotta, Mancini (Taddei 80), Nonda.

Match 2 RC STRASBOURG (FRA)
H 1-1 *Cassano (73)*
Curci, Panucci, Mexès, Bovo, Cufré, Aquilani (Taddei 71), Dacourt, Kharja, Cassano, Totti (Alvarez 59), Nonda.

Match 3 CRVENA ZVEZDA BEOGRAD (SCG)
A 1-3 *Nonda (23)*
Curci, Panucci, Mexès, Kuffour, Cufré (Taddei 82), Alvarez (Rosi 72), Aquilani, De Rossi, Kharja, Cassano, Nonda.

Match 4 FC BASEL (SUI)
H 3-1 *Taddei (14), Totti (45), Nonda (49)*
Curci, Panucci (Chivu 40), Mexès, Bovo, Cufré, Aquilani, De Rossi, Perrotta (Rosi 74), Taddei, Totti, Nonda (Mancini 84).

3rd round CLUB BRUGGE KV (BEL)
A 2-1 *Vanaudenaerde (44og), Perrotta (74)*
Curci, Panucci, Mexès, Kuffour, Cufré, Tommasi, Dacourt, Perrotta (Kharja 88), De Rossi, Mancini (Alvarez 89), Montella (Taddei 66).
H 2-1 *Mancini (55), Bovo (71)*
Curci, Bovo, Mexès, Kuffour, Cufré, Tommasi, Alvarez (Perrotta 70), Aquilani, Kharja, Mancini (Chivu 88), Montella (Taddei 73).

4th round MIDDLESBROUGH (ENG)
A 0-1
Curci, Panucci, Mexès, Kuffour, Cufré, Dacourt (Aquilani 84), Kharja, Tommasi (Alvarez 73), Perrotta, Taddei (Okaka Chuka 61), Mancini.
H 2-1 *Mancini (43, 66p)*
Curci, Kuffour, Mexès, Chivu (Panucci 86), Bovo, De Rossi, Dacourt (Okaka Chuka 63), Alvarez (Aquilani 72), Perrotta, Taddei, Mancini.

SAMPDORIA

1st round VITÓRIA SETÚBAL (POR)
A 1-1 *Flachi (14)*
Antonioli, Castellini, Diana (Zauli 74), Pavan, Zenoni, Gasbarroni (Kutuzov 54), Palombo, Tonetto, Volpi, Bonazzoli, Flachi (Dalla Bona 61).
H 1-0 *Gasbarroni (8)*
Antonioli, Zenoni, Castellini, Pavan, Pisano, Dalla Bona, Volpi, Diana, Gasbarroni (Kutuzov 64), Zauli (Palombo 81), Bonazzoli (Flachi 56).

2nd round Group C
Match 1 STEAUA BUCURESTI (ROM)
H 0-0
Castellazzi, Castellini, Sala, Zenoni, Dalla Bona, Gasbarroni (Diana 66), Pisano, Tonetto (Kutuzov 59), Volpi, Bonazzoli, Zauli (Flachi 46).

Match 2 HALMSTADS BK (SWE)
A 3-1 *Volpi (31), Diana (67, 86)*
Castellazzi, Dalla Bona, Diana, Falcone, Sala, Zenoni, Gasbarroni (Tonetto 46), Pisano, Volpi, Bonazzoli (Borriello 87), Flachi (Kutuzov 68).

Match 3 HERTHA BSC BERLIN (GER)
H 0-0
Castellazzi, Diana (Gasbarroni 67), Falcone, Sala, Zenoni, Dalla Bona (Kutuzov 82), Pisano, Tonetto, Volpi, Bonazzoli (Zauli 90), Flachi.

Match 4 RC LENS (FRA)
A 1-2 *Flachi (23)*
Castellazzi, Diana, Falcone, Sala, Zenoni, Palombo, Pisano, Tonetto, Volpi, Bonazzoli, Flachi (Borriello 65).

PALERMO

1st round ANORTHOSIS (CYP)
H 2-1 *Corini (6), Brienza (30p)*
Santoni, Barzagli, Ferri, Santana, Bonanni (Masiello 64), Brienza (Makinwa 69), Corini, Grosso, Mutarelli, Terlizzi, Caracciolo (Pepe 84).
A 4-0 *Caracciolo (5), Makinwa (46, 68), Santana (53)*
Santoni, Zaccardo, Biava (Rinaudo 77), Terlizzi, Grosso, González, Mutarelli, Corini (Codrea 69), Santana, Caracciolo (Brienza 63), Makinwa.

2nd round Group B
Match 1 MACCABI PETACH TIKVA (ISR)
A 2-1 *Brienza (11), Terlizzi (77)*
Andujar, Ferri, Bonanni (Santana 61), Brienza (Pepe 46), Codrea (Corini 73), González, Grosso, Mutarelli, Rinaudo, Terlizzi, Caracciolo.

Match 2 LOKOMOTIV MOSKVA (RUS)
H 0-0
Andujar, Barzagli, Ferri, Codrea, González (Santana 66), Grosso, Masiello, Mutarelli (Barone 46), Terlizzi, Caracciolo (Makinwa 43), Pepe.

Match 3 RCD ESPANYOL (ESP)
A 1-1 *González (45)*
Guardalben, Accardi, Barzagli, Ferri (Ferri 88), Zaccardo, Barone, Bonanni (Grosso 52), Brienza, Codrea, González, Rinaudo, Makinwa (Caracciolo 75).

Match 4 BRØNDBY IF (DEN)
H 3-0 *Makinwa (24), Rinaudo (44, 88)*
Andujar, Barzagli, Santana, Zaccardo, Barone, Brienza, Corini, González (Bonanni 68), Grosso (Accardi 73), Rinaudo, Makinwa.

3rd round SK SLAVIA PRAHA (CZE)
A 1-2 *Conteh (40)*
Andujar, Conteh, Barzagli, Rinaudo 52), Terlizzi, Grosso, Santana, Corini, Tedesco, Mutarelli (Barone 69), Makinwa, Brienza (González 60).
H 1-0 *Godeas (51)*
Andujar, Conteh, Barzagli, Terlizzi, Grosso, Tedesco, Codrea, Santana (González 80), Brienza (Barone 59), Makinwa (Godeas 46), Mutarelli.

4th round FC SCHALKE 04 (GER)
H 1-0 *Brienza (15)*
Andujar, Conteh, Terlizzi, Barzagli, Accardi, Barone, Codrea, Tedesco (Mutarelli

Italy

61), Santana, Brienza (González 70), Godeas (Caracciolo 88).
A 0-3
Andujar, Conteh (Tedesco 50), Terlizzi, Barzagli, Zaccardo, Barone, Corini, Mutarelli, Santana (Makinwa 65), González (Brienza 76), Godeas.

UDINESE
3rd round RC LENS (FRA)
H 3-0 *Di Natale (35), Barreto (61, 82)*
De Sanctis, Zapata, Natali, Felipe, Zenoni, Muntari (Tissone 65), Baronio, Obodo, Candela, Di Natale (Barreto 55), Rossini (Iaquinta 82).
A 0-1
De Sanctis, Zapata, Felipe, Defendi, Candela, Bertotto, Vidigal, Aguilar (Obodo 58), Muntari (Baronio 90), Rossini, Iaquinta (Tissone 68).

4th round LEVSKI SOFIA (BUL)
H 0-0
De Sanctis, Bertotto, Felipe (Defendi 51), Zapata, Zenoni, Obodo, Baronio, Tissone, Candela (Muntari 60), Di Natale (Barreto 66), Rossini.
A 1-2 *Tissone (22)*
De Sanctis, Bertotto, Zapata, Juarez, Tissone, Vidigal (Barreto 73), Morosini, Baronio (Obodo 58), Pieri (Osso 90), Rossini, Lazzari.

TOP GOALSCORERS 2005/06

31	Luca TONI (Fiorentina)
23	David TREZEGUET (Juventus)
22	David SUAZO (Cagliari)
19	Cristiano LUCARELLI (Livorno)
	Andriy SHEVCHENKO (Milan)
	Francesco TAVANO (Empoli)
17	Alberto GILARDINO (Milan)
16	Tommaso ROCCHI (Lazio)
15	Julio CRUZ (Internazionale)
	Francesco TOTTI (Roma)

LEAGUE RESULTS/ SCORERS/APPEARANCES/ GOALS 2005/06

ASCOLI
Coach – Marco Giampaolo

2005
28/8	Milan	h	1-1	Cudini
11/9	Lecce	a	0-0	
18/9	Juventus	a	1-2	Cariello
21/9	Siena	h	1-1	Ferrante
25/9	Livorno	a	0-2	
2/10	Parma	h	3-1	Bjelanovic 2, Foggia
16/10	Sampdoria	h	2-1	Tosto 2
22/10	Messina	a	1-1	Comotto
26/10	Udinese	h	1-1	Fini
30/10	Roma	a	1-2	Domizzi
6/11	Fiorentina	h	0-2	
20/11	Chievo	a	1-1	og (D'Anna)
27/11	Palermo	h	1-1	Ferrante
3/12	Internazionale	a	0-1	
11/12	Reggina	h	1-1	Fini
17/12	Cagliari	a	1-2	Biso
21/12	Treviso	h	1-0	Quagliarella

2006
8/1	Lazio	a	1-4	Guana
15/1	Empoli	h	3-1	Ferrante, Bjelanovic, Domizzi
18/1	Milan	a	0-1	
22/1	Lecce	h	2-0	Ferrante, Bjelanovic
29/1	Juventus	h	1-3	Ferrante
4/2	Siena	a	1-1	Comotto
8/2	Livorno	h	0-0	
12/2	Parma	a	0-0	
19/2	Sampdoria	a	2-1	Quagliarella, Budan
26/2	Messina	h	1-0	Cariello
5/3	Udinese	a	1-1	Domizzi (p)
12/3	Roma	h	3-2	Quagliarella, Paci, Budan
19/3	Fiorentina	a	1-3	Domizzi
26/3	Chievo	h	2-2	Paci 2
2/4	Palermo	a	1-1	Foggia
8/4	Internazionale	h	1-2	Ferrante (p)
15/4	Reggina	a	0-2	
22/4	Cagliari	h	2-2	Ferrante, Domizzi (p)
30/4	Treviso	a	2-2	Foggia 2
7/5	Lazio	h	1-4	Ferrante
14/5	Empoli	a	2-1	Budan 2

No	Name	Nat	Pos	Aps	(s)	Gls
15	Daniele ADANI		D	1	(2)	
2	Mattia BISO		M	6	(1)	1
79	Sasa BJELANOVIC	CRO	A	24	(7)	4
1	Alessandro BOCCOLINI		G		(1)	
19	Igor BUDAN	CRO	A	6	(5)	4
13	Francesco CARBONE		D	7	(5)	
11	Alfredo CARIELLO		D	4	(18)	2
32	Corrado COLOMBO		A	2	(4)	
16	Gianluca COMOTTO		D	31		2
28	Fernando COPPOLA		G	38		
23	Riccardo CORALLO		D	1	(1)	
10	Nicolás Andrea CORDOVA	CHL	M	1	(3)	
55	Domenico CRISTIANO		M	11	(5)	
6	Mirko CUDINI		D	10	(1)	1
3	Cristiano DEL GROSSO		D	26	(4)	
7	Ivano DELLA MORTE		M	1	(3)	
80	Maurizio DOMIZZI		D	34		5
9	Marco FERRANTE		A	17	(9)	8
8	Michele FINI		M	35	(1)	2
17	Pasquale FOGGIA		M	30	(4)	4
22	Andrea GABRIELLI		M	1		
5	Domenico GIAMPÀ		M	3	(6)	
14	Roberto GUANA		M	30	(3)	1
53	Maurizio LAURO		D	3	(2)	
4	Alessandro MORO		M	1	(1)	
24	Massimo PACI		D	27	(4)	3
18	Andrea PAROLA		M	29	(3)	
20	Giampietro PERRULLI		M		(1)	
29	Fabio QUAGLIARELLA		A	24	(9)	3
77	Vittorio TOSTO		M	13	(2)	2
21	Nicola ZANINI		M	2	(4)	

CAGLIARI
Coach – Attilio Tesser; (29/8/05) Daniele Arrigoni; (16/9/05) Davide Ballardini; (11/11/05) Nedo Sonetti

2005
28/8	Siena	a	1-2	Esposito
11/9	Lazio	h	1-1	Suazo

Italy

FINAL LEAGUE TABLE 2005/06

		Pld	Home					Away					Total					Pts
			W	D	L	F	A	W	D	L	F	A	W	D	L	F	A	
1	Internazionale	38	16	1	2	47	13	7	6	6	21	17	23	7	8	68	30	76
2	Roma	38	11	4	4	35	21	8	8	3	35	21	19	12	7	70	42	69
3	Milan	38	18	1	0	50	13	10	3	6	35	18	28	4	6	85	31	58
4	Chievo	38	9	8	2	33	19	4	7	8	21	30	13	15	10	54	49	54
5	Palermo	38	9	5	5	31	26	4	8	7	19	26	13	13	12	50	52	52
6	Livorno	38	8	7	4	22	17	4	6	9	15	27	12	13	13	37	44	49
7	Empoli	38	9	3	7	26	26	4	3	12	21	35	13	6	19	47	61	45
8	Parma	38	7	7	5	25	22	5	2	12	21	38	12	9	17	46	60	45
9	Fiorentina	38	16	1	2	42	20	6	7	6	24	21	22	8	8	66	41	44
10	Ascoli	38	7	8	4	27	25	2	8	9	16	28	9	16	13	43	53	43
11	Udinese	38	6	5	8	19	22	5	5	9	21	32	11	10	17	40	54	43
12	Sampdoria	38	6	6	7	29	29	4	5	10	18	22	10	11	17	47	51	41
13	Reggina	38	8	4	7	25	28	3	4	12	14	37	11	8	19	39	65	41
14	Cagliari	38	6	11	2	23	17	2	4	13	19	38	8	15	15	42	55	39
15	Siena	38	5	5	9	18	27	4	7	8	24	33	9	12	17	42	60	39
16	Lazio	38	11	7	1	34	18	5	7	7	23	29	16	14	8	57	47	32
17	Messina	38	4	9	6	19	25	2	4	13	14	34	6	13	19	33	59	31
18	Lecce	38	4	7	8	16	22	3	1	15	14	35	7	8	23	30	57	29
19	Treviso	38	2	4	13	12	26	1	8	10	12	30	3	12	23	24	56	21
--	Juventus	38	14	5	0	33	9	13	5	1	38	15	27	10	1	71	24	--

N.B. After match-fixing scandal 'champions' Juventus relegated; Milan, Fiorentina and Lazio – 30 pts deducted.

Date	Opponent	H/A	Score	Scorers
18/9	Messina	h	1-1	Suazo
21/9	Empoli	a	1-3	Capone
25/9	Roma	h	0-0	
2/10	Lecce	a	0-3	
16/10	Milan	h	0-2	
23/10	Chievo	a	1-2	Suazo
26/10	Livorno	h	1-1	Suazo (p)
30/10	Fiorentina	a	1-2	Suazo
6/11	Treviso	h	0-0	
20/11	Reggina	a	1-3	Abeijón
27/11	Sampdoria	h	2-0	Suazo 2
4/12	Palermo	a	2-2	Conti, Bega
11/12	Juventus	a	0-4	
17/12	Ascoli	h	2-1	og (Del Grosso), Suazo (p)
21/12	Parma	a	0-1	
2006				
8/1	Udinese	h	2-1	Conti, Langella
15/1	Internazionale	a	2-3	Esposito, Suazo
18/1	Siena	h	1-0	Suazo
21/1	Lazio	a	1-1	Gobbi
29/1	Messina	a	0-1	
5/2	Empoli	h	4-1	Abeijón, Esposito 2, Suazo
8/2	Roma	a	3-4	Suazo, Langella, Conti
12/2	Lecce	h	0-0	
18/2	Milan	a	0-1	
26/2	Chievo	h	2-2	Suazo, Gobbi
5/3	Livorno	a	1-0	Suazo
18/3	Treviso	a	2-1	Esposito, Suazo (p)
22/3	Fiorentina	h	0-0	
26/3	Reggina	h	0-2	
2/4	Sampdoria	a	1-1	Suazo
9/4	Palermo	h	1-1	Suazo
15/4	Juventus	h	1-1	Suazo (p)
22/4	Ascoli	a	2-2	Suazo 2
30/4	Parma	h	3-1	Capone, Suazo (p), Esposito
7/5	Udinese	a	0-2	
14/5	Internazionale	h	2-2	Capone, Suazo

No	Name	Nat	Pos	Aps	(s)	Gls
18	Nélson ABEIJÓN	URU	M	25	(3)	2
31	Alessandro AGOSTINI		M	29	(6)	
4	Francesco BEGA		D	26	(3)	1
2	Joe BIZERA	URU	D	15	(1)	
16	Alessandro BUDEL		M	15	(15)	
12	Andrea CAMPAGNOLO		G	9	(2)	
3	Michele CANINI		D	30	(2)	
21	Andrea CAPONE		A	14	(14)	3
1	Fabián CARINI	URU	G	8		
25	Antonio CHIMENTI		G	21		
19	Andrea COCCO		A	2	(3)	
5	Daniele CONTI		M	29	(1)	3
24	Alessandro CONTICCHIO		M	16	(10)	
27	Andrea COSSU		A	4	(18)	
7	Mauro ESPOSITO		A	38		6
30	Claudio FERRARESE		M		(3)	
19	Michele FERRI		D	15	(1)	
8	Massimo GOBBI		D	33	(2)	2
23	Antonio LANGELLA		A	16	(8)	2
6	Diego Luis LÓPEZ	URU	D	21	(1)	
20	Claudio PANI		M		(1)	
14	Francesco PISANO		D	14	(10)	
9	David SUAZO	HON	A	37		22
13	Fabio VIGNATI		D	1		

CHIEVO
Coach – Giuseppe Pillon

2005

| 28/8 | Juventus | a | 0-1 | |

Italy

11/9	Parma	h	1-0	Mandelli
18/9	Reggina	a	3-1	Franceschini 2, Mandelli
21/9	Internazionale	h	0-1	
25/9	Sampdoria	a	2-1	Franceschini, Obinna
1/10	Treviso	h	0-0	
16/10	Palermo	a	2-2	Amauri 2 (1p)
23/10	Cagliari	h	2-1	D'Anna, Obinna
26/10	Lazio	a	2-2	D'Anna, Pellissier
30/10	Empoli	h	2-2	Semioli, Pellissier
6/11	Siena	a	1-0	Pellissier
20/11	Ascoli	h	1-1	Pellissier
26/11	Livorno	a	0-0	
3/12	Milan	h	2-1	Pellissier, Tribocchi
11/12	Messina	a	0-2	
18/12	Udinese	h	2-0	Tribocchi, Obinna
21/12	Roma	a	0-4	
2006				
8/1	Lecce	h	3-1	Pellissier 2, Zanchetta
15/1	Fiorentina	a	1-2	Zanchetta
18/1	Juventus	h	1-2	Franceschini
22/1	Parma	a	1-2	Amauri
29/1	Reggina	h	4-0	Amauri 2 (1p), Pellissier 2
5/2	Internazionale	a	0-1	
8/2	Sampdoria	h	1-1	Scurto
11/2	Treviso	a	2-1	Tribocchi 2
19/2	Palermo	h	0-0	
26/2	Cagliari	a	2-2	Tribocchi, Pellissier
5/3	Lazio	h	2-2	Tribocchi 2
12/3	Empoli	a	1-2	Brighi
19/3	Siena	h	4-1	Obinna (p), Malago, Brighi, Amauri
26/3	Ascoli	a	2-2	Amauri 2
2/4	Livorno	h	2-1	Amauri, Obinna (p)
9/4	Milan	a	1-4	Pellissier
15/4	Messina	h	2-0	og (Innocenti), Obinna
22/4	Udinese	a	1-1	Pellissier (p)
30/4	Roma	h	4-4	Amauri 2, Luciano, Pellissier (p)
7/5	Lecce	a	0-0	
14/5	Fiorentina	h	0-2	

No	Name	Nat	Pos	Aps	(s)	Gls
11	AMAURI Carvalho de Oliveira	BRA	A	32	(5)	11
13	Filippo ANTONELLI		A		(1)	
33	Matteo BRIGHI		M	22	(4)	2
24	Federico COSSATO		A	1	(3)	
3	Lorenzo D'ANNA		D	25		2
12	Alberto FONTANA		G	29		
19	Daniele FRANCESCHINI		M	36		4
17	Giuseppe GEMITI	GER	M	1	(8)	
8	Federico GIUNTI		M	27	(1)	
23	Salvatore LANNA		D	37		
5	LUCIANO Siquera de Oliveira	BRA	M	13	(6)	1
4	Marco MALAGO		D	17	(6)	1
29	Davide MANDELLI		D	32		2
20	Andrea MANTOVANI		D	3	(1)	
27	Fabio MORO		D	26	(1)	
15	Victor OBINNA	NGA	A	9	(17)	6
31	Sergio PELLISSIER		A	24	(10)	13
21	Paolo SAMMARCO		A	15	(9)	
26	Giuseppe SCURTO		D	13	(6)	1
7	Franco SEMIOLI		M	32	(3)	1
18	Lorenzo SQUIZZI		G	9	(3)	
9	Simone TRIBOCCHI		A	10	(12)	7
10	Andrea ZANCHETTA		M	5	(11)	2

EMPOLI
Coach – Mario Somma; (19/1/06) Luigi Cagni

2005				
28/8	Udinese	a	0-1	
11/9	Juventus	h	0-4	
17/9	Parma	a	0-1	
21/9	Cagliari	h	3-1	Tavano 2, Almirón
25/9	Lecce	h	1-0	Pozzi
2/10	Palermo	a	2-2	Tavano 2
16/10	Roma	h	1-0	Tavano
23/10	Treviso	a	2-1	Almirón, Tavano
26/10	Milan	h	1-3	Vannucchi
30/10	Chievo	a	2-2	Rigano, Tavano
5/11	Reggina	h	3-0	Rigano, Tavano, Vannucchi
20/11	Livorno	a	0-2	
27/11	Lazio	h	2-3	Bonetto, Tavano (p)
4/12	Sampdoria	a	0-2	
10/12	Siena	a	0-1	
18/12	Fiorentina	h	1-1	Vannucchi
21/12	Internazionale	a	1-4	Vannucchi
2006				
8/1	Messina	h	1-3	Almirón
15/1	Ascoli	a	1-3	Almirón
18/1	Udinese	h	1-1	Tavano (p)
22/1	Juventus	a	1-2	Almirón
29/1	Parma	h	1-2	Tavano (p)
5/2	Cagliari	a	1-4	Tavano
8/2	Lecce	a	2-1	Almirón, Tavano (p)
12/2	Palermo	h	0-1	
19/2	Roma	a	0-1	
26/2	Treviso	h	1-1	Rigano
4/3	Milan	a	0-3	
12/3	Chievo	h	2-1	Rigano, Tavano
19/3	Reggina	a	2-0	Pozzi, Tavano
26/3	Livorno	h	2-1	Tavano, Buscé
2/4	Lazio	a	3-3	Tosto, Tavano, og (Oddo)
9/4	Sampdoria	h	2-1	Buscé 2
15/4	Siena	h	2-1	Tosto, Tavano
22/4	Fiorentina	a	1-2	Rigano
30/4	Internazionale	h	1-0	og (Materazzi)
7/5	Messina	a	3-0	(w/o; original result 2-1 Pozzi 2)
14/5	Ascoli	h	1-2	Tavano

No	Name	Nat	Pos	Aps	(s)	Gls
4	Sergio ALMIRÓN	ARG	M	35	(2)	6
36	Nicola ASCOLI		D	4	(7)	
23	Daniele BALLI		G	13		
1	Gianluca BERTI		G	19		
8	Riccardo BONETTO		D	17		1
24	Antonio BUSCÉ		D	37		3
20	Daniele BUZZEGOLI		M		(2)	
1	Christián CEJAS	ARG	G	6		
6	Andrea CODA		D	36		
27	Fabrizio FICINI		M	28	(5)	
9	Mirco GASPARETTO		A		(5)	
21	Francesco LODI		M	4	(13)	
3	Stefano LUCCHINI		D	21	(4)	
5	Davide MORO		M	25	(7)	
7	Nicola POZZI		A	8	(16)	4
50	Francesco PRATALI		D	28		
46	Andrea RAGGI		D	21	(4)	

Italy

99	Christian RIGANO		A	27	(6)	5
13	Matteo SERAFINI		M	4	(12)	
19	Francesco TAVANO		A	34	(3)	19
9	Vittorio TOSTO		D	10		2
15	Richard VANIGLI		D	11	(6)	
80	Igli VANNUCCHI		M	26	(9)	4
33	Paolo ZANETTI		M	4	(5)	

FIORENTINA
Coach – Claudio Cesare Prandelli

2005

27/8	Sampdoria	h	2-1	Fiore, Toni (p)
11/9	Messina	a	2-2	Toni, Bojinov
18/9	Udinese	h	4-2	Fiore, Toni 2, Donadel
21/9	Lecce	a	3-1	Fiore, Bojinov, Toni
25/9	Internazionale	a	0-1	
2/10	Livorno	h	3-2	Toni, Jørgensen, Pazzini
16/10	Lazio	a	0-1	
22/10	Parma	h	4-1	Toni 3, Fiore
26/10	Siena	a	2-0	Toni 2
30/10	Cagliari	h	2-1	Toni, Jørgensen
6/11	Ascoli	a	2-0	Ujfalusi, Toni
20/11	Milan	h	3-1	Toni 2, Jørgensen
27/11	Roma	a	1-1	Toni (p)
4/12	Juventus	h	1-2	Pazzini
10/12	Treviso	h	1-0	Fiore
18/12	Empoli	a	1-1	Pazzini
21/12	Palermo	h	1-0	Jørgensen

2006

7/1	Reggina	a	1-1	Jørgensen
15/1	Chievo	h	2-1	Toni 2
18/1	Sampdoria	a	1-3	Toni
22/1	Messina	h	2-0	Toni 2
29/1	Udinese	a	0-0	
5/2	Lecce	h	1-0	Toni
8/2	Internazionale	h	2-1	Brocchi, Jiménez
12/2	Livorno	a	0-2	
19/2	Lazio	h	1-2	Bojinov
25/2	Parma	a	4-2	Bojinov 2, Jørgensen, Jiménez
5/3	Siena	h	2-1	Toni, Pazzini
19/3	Ascoli	h	3-1	Brocchi, Toni, Pazzini
22/3	Cagliari	a	0-0	
25/3	Milan	a	1-3	Toni
2/4	Roma	h	1-1	Toni
9/4	Juventus	a	1-1	Toni
15/4	Treviso	a	3-1	Toni, Brocchi, Montolivo
22/4	Empoli	h	2-1	Pasqual, Jiménez
30/4	Palermo	a	0-1	
7/5	Reggina	h	5-2	Fiore, Toni 2, Jørgensen, Bojinov
14/5	Chievo	a	2-0	Toni, Dainelli

No	Name	Nat	Pos	Aps	(s)	Gls
99	Gianluca BERTI		G	1		
8	Valeri BOJINOV	BUL	A	13	(14)	6
14	Davide BRIVIO		D		(1)	
32	Cristian BROCCHI		M	34	(1)	3
12	Christián CEJAS	ARG	G	3		
3	Dario DAINELLI		D	25	(2)	1
27	Marco DI LORETO		D	19	(1)	
4	Marco DONADEL		M	33	(1)	1
10	Stefano FIORE		M	36	(2)	6
1	Sébastien FREY		G	18		
5	Alessandro GAMBERINI		D	18	(1)	
25	Gianni GUIGOU	URU	M		(4)	
19	Luis Antonio JIMÉNEZ	CRC	M	11	(8)	3
20	Martin JØRGENSEN	DEN	M	34	(3)	7
2	Per KRØLDRUP	DEN	D	13	(1)	
22	Bogdan LOBONT	ROM	G	16	(1)	
11	Cristian MAGGIO		D		(3)	
18	Riccardo MONTOLIVO		M	8	(12)	1
26	Giuseppe PANCARO		D	12	(6)	
23	Manuel PASQUAL		D	31	(4)	1
17	Michele PAZIENZA		M	10	(13)	
29	Gianpaolo PAZZINI		A	10	(17)	5
30	Luca TONI		A	37	(1)	31
21	Tomás UJFALUSI	CZE	D	36		1

INTERNAZIONALE
Coach – Roberto Mancini

2005

28/8	Treviso	h	3-0	Adriano 3
10/9	Palermo	a	2-3	Cruz 2
17/9	Lecce	h	3-0	Martins, Stankovic, Cruz
21/9	Chievo	a	1-0	Samuel
25/9	Fiorentina	h	1-0	Martins
2/10	Juventus	a	0-2	
16/10	Livorno	h	5-0	Materazzi, Cruz, Cambiasso, Córdoba, Recoba
23/10	Udinese	a	1-0	Cruz
26/10	Roma	h	2-3	Adriano 2
29/10	Sampdoria	a	2-2	Cambiasso, Córdoba
5/11	Lazio	a	0-0	
20/11	Parma	h	2-0	Figo, Cambiasso
27/11	Messina	a	2-1	Recoba, Cambiasso
3/12	Ascoli	a	1-0	Adriano
11/12	Milan	h	3-2	Adriano 2 (1p), Martins
18/12	Reggina	a	4-0	Córdoba, Martins, Adriano, Pizarro
21/12	Empoli	h	4-1	Adriano, Cruz, Figo, Martins

2006

8/1	Siena	a	0-0	
15/1	Cagliari	h	3-2	Martins, Adriano 2 (1p)
18/1	Treviso	a	1-0	Cruz
21/1	Palermo	h	3-0	Cambiasso, Córdoba, Figo
29/1	Lecce	a	2-0	Figo, Stankovic
5/2	Chievo	h	1-0	Cruz
8/2	Fiorentina	a	1-2	Recoba
12/2	Juventus	h	1-2	Samuel
18/2	Livorno	a	0-0	
26/2	Udinese	h	3-1	Cruz 2 (1p), Martins
5/3	Roma	a	1-1	Materazzi
11/3	Sampdoria	h	1-0	Adriano
19/3	Lazio	h	3-1	Figo, Recoba 2
25/3	Parma	a	0-1	
1/4	Messina	h	3-0	Solari 2, Martins
8/4	Ascoli	a	2-1	Cruz (p), Mihajlovic
14/4	Milan	a	0-1	
22/4	Reggina	h	4-0	Cruz 2 (1p), Martins, César
30/4	Empoli	a	0-1	
7/5	Siena	h	1-1	Cruz
14/5	Cagliari	a	2-2	Cruz, Solari

No	Name	Nat	Pos	Aps	(s)	Gls
10	ADRIANO Leite Ribeiro	BRA	A	27	(3)	13
86	Ilario ALOE		M		(1)	
49	Marco ANDREOLLI		D	1	(1)	

Italy

No	Name	Nat	Pos	Aps	(s)	Gls
51	Leonardo BONUCCI		D		(1)	
55	Daniel BOUMSONG	GHA	M	1		
3	Nicolás BURDISSO	ARG	D	11	(5)	
19	Esteban CAMBIASSO	ARG	M	30	(4)	5
31	CÉSAR Rodriguez	BRA	M	5	(3)	1
2	Iván CÓRDOBA	COL	D	35		4
9	Julio CRUZ	ARG	A	17	(14)	15
16	Giuseppe FAVALLI		D	22	(1)	
7	Luís FIGO	POR	M	28	(6)	5
42	Domenico GERMINALE		A		(1)	
12	JÚLIO CÉSAR Soares	BRA	G	29		
18	Christián "KILY" GONZÁLEZ	ARG	M	10	(6)	
30	Obafemi MARTINS	NGA	A	19	(9)	9
23	Marco MATERAZZI		D	17	(5)	2
11	Sinisa MIHAJLOVIC	SCG	D	4	(1)	1
22	Paolo ORLANDONI		G	1		
8	David PIZARRO	CHL	M	15	(9)	1
20	Álvaro RECOBA	URU	A	11	(9)	5
25	Walter SAMUEL	ARG	D	26	(1)	2
89	Goran SLAVKOVSKI	SWE	A		(1)	
21	Santiago SOLARI	ARG	M	8	(5)	3
5	Dejan STANKOVIC	SCG	M	21	(2)	2
1	Francesco TOLDO		G	8		
14	Juan Sebastián VERÓN	ARG	M	24	(1)	
33	Pierre WOME	CMR	D	10	(3)	
6	Cristiano ZANETTI		M	7	(7)	
4	Javier ZANETTI	ARG	D	25		
13	José Ferreiro ZÉ MARIA	BRA	M	6	(2)	

JUVENTUS
Coach – Fabio Capello

2005
28/8	Chievo	h	1-0	Trezeguet
11/9	Empoli	a	4-0	Trezeguet 2, Vieira, Camoranesi
18/9	Ascoli	h	2-1	Del Piero 2 (1p)
21/9	Udinese	a	1-0	Vieira
24/9	Parma	a	2-1	Camoranesi, Vieira
2/10	Internazionale	h	2-0	Trezeguet, Nedved
15/10	Messina	h	1-0	Del Piero
23/10	Lecce	a	3-0	Ibrahimovic, Mutu, Zalayeta
26/10	Sampdoria	h	2-0	Trezeguet, Mutu
29/10	Milan	a	1-3	Trezeguet
6/11	Livorno	h	3-0	Ibrahimovic, Trezeguet, Del Piero
19/11	Roma	a	4-1	Nedved, Ibrahimovic, Trezeguet 2
27/11	Treviso	h	3-1	Mutu, Trezeguet, Del Piero
4/12	Fiorentina	a	2-1	Trezeguet, Camoranesi
11/12	Cagliari	h	4-0	Nedved, Trezeguet 2, og (Vignati)
17/12	Lazio	a	1-1	Trezeguet
21/12	Siena	h	2-0	Cannavaro, Trezeguet

2006
7/1	Palermo	a	2-1	Mutu 2
15/1	Reggina	h	1-0	Del Piero
18/1	Chievo	a	1-1	Vieira
22/1	Empoli	h	2-1	Cannavaro 2
29/1	Ascoli	a	3-1	Trezeguet 3
5/2	Udinese	h	1-0	Del Piero
8/2	Parma	h	1-1	Ibrahimovic
12/2	Internazionale	a	2-1	Ibrahimovic, Del Piero
18/2	Messina	a	2-2	Ibrahimovic, Mutu (p)
26/2	Lecce	h	3-1	Émerson, Kovac, Del Piero (p)
4/3	Sampdoria	a	1-0	Nedved
12/3	Milan	h	0-0	
18/3	Livorno	a	3-1	Trezeguet 2, Del Piero
25/3	Roma	h	1-1	Émerson
1/4	Treviso	a	0-0	
9/4	Fiorentina	h	1-1	Del Piero
15/4	Cagliari	a	1-1	Cannavaro
22/4	Lazio	h	1-1	Trezeguet
30/4	Siena	a	3-0	Vieira, Trezeguet, Mutu
7/5	Palermo	h	2-1	Nedved, Ibrahimovic
14/5	Reggina	a	2-0	Trezeguet, Del Piero

No	Name	Nat	Pos	Aps	(s)	Gls
32	Christian ABBIATI		G	18	(1)	
14	Federico BALZARETTI		D	13	(7)	
90	Manuele BLASI		M	6	(7)	
1	Gianluigi BUFFON		G	18		
16	Mauro CAMORANESI		M	25	(9)	3
28	Fabio CANNAVARO		D	36		4
3	Giorgio CHIELLINI		D	15	(2)	
12	Antonio CHIMENTI		G	2	(1)	
10	Alessandro DEL PIERO		A	17	(16)	12
8	ÉMERSON Ferreira	BRA	M	33	(1)	2
23	Giuliano GIANNICHEDDA		M	9	(6)	
9	Zlatan IBRAHIMOVIC	SWE	A	29	(6)	7
6	Robert KOVAC	CRO	D	15	(3)	1
18	Adrian MUTU	ROM	A	20	(12)	7
11	Pavel NEDVED	CZE	M	31	(2)	5
7	Gianluca PESSOTTO		D	6	(4)	
21	Lilian THURAM	FRA	D	25	(2)	
17	David TREZEGUET	FRA	A	28	(4)	23
4	Patrick VIEIRA	FRA	M	31		5
25	Marcelo ZALAYETA	URU	A	2	(14)	1
19	Gianluca ZAMBROTTA		D	32		
27	Jonathan ZEBINA	FRA	D	7	(3)	

LAZIO
Coach – Delio Rossi

2005
28/8	Messina	h	1-0	Pandev
11/9	Cagliari	a	1-1	Siviglia
18/9	Treviso	h	3-1	Rocchi, Pandev, Oddo (p)
21/9	Milan	a	0-2	
25/9	Palermo	h	4-2	Rocchi 2, Pandev, Manfredini
1/10	Udinese	a	0-3	
16/10	Fiorentina	h	1-0	Zauri
23/10	Roma	a	1-1	Rocchi
26/10	Chievo	h	2-2	Rocchi, Oddo (p)
30/10	Reggina	a	0-1	
5/11	Internazionale	h	0-0	
20/11	Sampdoria	a	0-2	
27/11	Empoli	a	3-2	Dabo, Tare, Liverani
4/12	Siena	h	3-2	Di Canio, César, Tare
11/12	Livorno	a	1-2	Pandev
17/12	Juventus	h	1-1	Rocchi
21/12	Lecce	a	0-0	

2006
7/1	Ascoli	h	4-1	Di Canio, Mudingayi, Pandev, Tare
15/1	Parma	a	1-1	Rocchi
18/1	Messina	a	1-1	Manfredini
21/1	Cagliari	h	1-1	Di Canio

Italy

Date	Opponent	H/A	Score	Scorers
29/1	Treviso	a	1-0	Rocchi
5/2	Milan	h	0-0	
8/2	Palermo	a	1-3	Belleri
11/2	Udinese	h	1-1	Rocchi
19/2	Fiorentina	a	2-1	Behrami, Rocchi
26/2	Roma	h	0-2	
5/3	Chievo	a	2-2	Mauri, Oddo (p)
12/3	Reggina	h	3-1	Di Canio, Rocchi, Pandev
19/3	Internazionale	a	1-3	Pandev
26/3	Sampdoria	h	2-0	Oddo 2 (1p)
2/4	Empoli	h	3-3	Pandev, Behrami, Di Canio
9/4	Siena	a	3-2	Mauri, Rocchi, Dabo
15/4	Livorno	h	3-1	Oddo (p), Pandev 2
22/4	Juventus	a	1-1	Rocchi
30/4	Lecce	h	1-0	Rocchi
7/5	Ascoli	a	4-1	Stendardo, Oddo (p), Pandev, Rocchi
14/5	Parma	h	1-0	Rocchi

No	Name	Nat	Pos	Aps	(s)	Gls
32	Marco BALLOTTA		G	6	(2)	
3	Roberto BARONIO		M	2	(5)	
85	Valon BEHRAMI	SUI	M	25	(1)	2
7	Manuel BELLERI		D	8	(8)	1
10	Massimo BONANNI		M	1	(8)	
10	CÉSAR Rodriguez	BRA	M	10	(1)	1
25	CRIBARI Emilson Sanchez	BRA	D	28		
6	Ousmane DABO	FRA	M	28	(3)	2
9	Paolo DI CANIO		A	21	(6)	5
4	Fabio FIRMANI		M	6	(1)	
16	Andrea GIALLOMBARDO		D	2	(5)	
24	Samir HANDANOVIC	SLO	G	1		
21	Simone INZAGHI		A		(7)	
31	Christian KELLER	DEN	M	3	(4)	
20	Fabio LIVERANI		M	29		1
68	Christian MANFREDINI		M	15	(11)	2
11	Stefano MAURI		M	14	(1)	2
26	Gaby MUDINGAYI	BEL	M	8	(6)	1
11	Roberto MUZZI		A		(1)	
22	Massimo ODDO		D	35		7
19	Goran PANDEV	MAC	A	22	(13)	11
1	Angelo PERUZZI		G	30		
5	Felice PICCOLO		D		(2)	
18	Tommaso ROCCHI		A	35	(2)	16
33	Matteo SERENI		G	1	(1)	
13	Sebastiano SIVIGLIA		D	31		1
2	Guglielmo STENDARDO		D	16	(2)	1
17	Igli TARE	ALB	A	4	(18)	3
8	Luciano ZAURI		D	37		1

LECCE

Coach – Angelo Gregucci; (27/9/05) Silvio Baldini; (23/1/06) Roberto Ruzzo

2005

Date	Opponent	H/A	Score	Scorers
27/8	Livorno	a	1-2	Pinardi (p)
11/9	Ascoli	h	0-0	
17/9	Internazionale	a	0-3	
21/9	Fiorentina	h	1-3	Pinardi
25/9	Empoli	a	0-1	
2/10	Cagliari	h	3-0	Konan, Pinardi (p), Ledesma
16/10	Reggina	a	0-2	
23/10	Juventus	h	0-3	
26/10	Palermo	a	0-3	
30/10	Messina	h	0-2	
6/11	Parma	a	0-2	
20/11	Siena	h	3-0	Vucinic, Konan, Cozzolino
26/11	Milan	a	1-2	Konan
4/12	Roma	h	2-2	Cozzolino, Vucinic (p)
11/12	Udinese	a	2-1	Vucinic 2
18/12	Treviso	h	1-2	Vucinic
21/12	Lazio	h	0-0	

2006

Date	Opponent	H/A	Score	Scorers
8/1	Chievo	a	1-3	Del Vecchio
14/1	Sampdoria	h	0-3	
18/1	Livorno	h	0-0	
22/1	Ascoli	a	0-2	
29/1	Internazionale	h	0-2	
5/2	Fiorentina	a	0-1	
8/2	Empoli	h	1-2	Ledesma (p)
12/2	Cagliari	a	0-0	
19/2	Reggina	h	0-0	
26/2	Juventus	a	1-3	Del Vecchio
5/3	Palermo	h	2-0	Vucinic, Giacomazzi
12/3	Messina	a	1-2	Babú
19/3	Parma	h	1-2	Vucinic (p)
26/3	Siena	a	2-1	Giacomazzi, Vucinic
1/4	Milan	h	1-0	Konan
9/4	Roma	a	1-3	Del Vecchio
15/4	Udinese	h	1-2	Giacomazzi
22/4	Treviso	h	1-1	Vucinic
30/4	Lazio	a	0-1	
7/5	Chievo	h	0-0	
14/5	Sampdoria	a	3-1	Del Vecchio, Konan 2

No	Name	Nat	Pos	Aps	(s)	Gls
5	Giuseppe ABRUZZESE		D	5		
6	ANGELO Mariano de Almeida	BRA	M	7	(5)	
13	Anderson de Oliveira BABÚ	BRA	A	8	(3)	1
99	Francesco BENUSSI		G	14	(1)	
16	Philippe BILLY	FRA	D		(2)	
30	Alessandro CAMISA		D	6	(2)	
7	Alfonso CAMORANI		M	12	(9)	
77	Marco CASSETTI		M	28	(1)	
5	Gabriel CICHERO	COL	D	1	(3)	
19	Giuseppe COZZOLINO		A	7	(17)	2
40	Gennaro DEL VECCHIO		M	28	(1)	4
2	Souleymane DIAMOUTENE	MLI	D	33		
10	Alexei EREMENKO Jr.	FIN	M	4	(4)	
15	Andrea ESPOSITO		D	2	(1)	
18	Guillermo GIACOMAZZI	URU	M	14		3
17	Davide GIORGINO		M	4	(5)	
25	Axel KONAN	CIV	A	23	(10)	6
26	Cristián LEDESMA	ARG	M	31	(2)	2
23	Francesco MARIANINI		M	11	(6)	
10	Giuseppe NEGRO		A		(1)	
4	Marco PECORARI		D	8	(2)	
90	Graziano PELLÈ		A	3	(7)	
3	Alex PINARDI		M	22	(3)	3
26	Tiziano POLENGHI		D	6	(1)	
90	Antonio ROSATI		G		(1)	
3	Erminio RULLO		D	28	(3)	
6	Karim SAIDI	TUN	D	9		
11	Luca SAUDATI		A	2	(2)	
86	Raffaele SCHIAVI		D	1		
1	Vincenzo SICIGNANO		G	24		
21	Lorenzo STOVINI		D	30	(1)	
20	Jaime Andrés VALDES	CHL	M	14	(12)	
9	Mirko VUCINIC	SCG	A	33	(1)	9

Italy

LIVORNO
Coach – Roberto Donadoni; (7/2/06) Carlo Mazzone

2005
Date	Opponent	H/A	Score	Scorers
27/8	Lecce	h	2-1	Lucarelli, Palladino
11/9	Treviso	a	1-0	Lucarelli
18/9	Roma	h	0-0	
21/9	Messina	a	0-0	
25/9	Ascoli	h	2-0	Palladino, Lucarelli (p)
2/10	Fiorentina	a	2-3	Galante, Morrone
16/10	Internazionale	a	0-5	
23/10	Reggina	h	1-0	Lucarelli
26/10	Cagliari	a	1-1	Melara
30/10	Parma	h	2-0	Lucarelli, Morrone
6/11	Juventus	a	0-3	
20/11	Empoli	h	2-0	Morrone, Lucarelli
26/11	Chievo	h	0-0	
4/12	Udinese	a	2-0	og (Obodo), Lucarelli
11/12	Lazio	h	2-1	De Ascentis, og (Peruzzi)
18/12	Palermo	a	2-0	Pfertzel, Morrone
21/12	Milan	h	0-3	

2006
Date	Opponent	H/A	Score	Scorers
8/1	Sampdoria	a	2-0	Lucarelli 2
15/1	Siena	h	2-2	Morrone, Lucarelli
18/1	Lecce	a	0-0	
22/1	Treviso	h	1-1	Galante
29/1	Roma	a	0-3	
5/2	Messina	h	2-2	Lucarelli 2
8/2	Ascoli	a	0-0	
12/2	Fiorentina	h	2-0	Lucarelli 2 (1p)
18/2	Internazionale	h	0-0	
25/2	Reggina	a	1-1	Morrone
5/3	Cagliari	h	0-1	
12/3	Parma	a	1-2	Bakayoko (p)
18/3	Juventus	h	1-3	Pfertzel
26/3	Empoli	a	1-2	Lucarelli (p)
2/4	Chievo	a	1-2	Lucarelli
8/4	Udinese	h	0-2	
15/4	Lazio	a	1-3	Colucci
22/4	Palermo	h	3-1	Lucarelli 3 (1p)
30/4	Milan	a	0-2	
7/5	Sampdoria	h	0-0	
14/5	Siena	a	0-0	

No	Name	Nat	Pos	Aps	(s)	Gls
19	Paolo ACERBIS		G	2		
1	Marco AMELIA		G	36		
5	Stefano ARGILLI		M	6	(3)	
9	Ibrahima BAKAYOKO	CIV	A	7	(14)	1
69	David BALLERI		D	14	(8)	
8	Luis Fernando CENTI		M	4	(4)	
29	CÉSAR PRATES	BRA	M	14	(15)	
23	Francesco COCO		D	27	(1)	
24	Giuseppe COLUCCI		M	18	(6)	1
15	Diego DE ASCENTIS		M	25	(4)	1
2	Stefano FANUCCI		D	4	(1)	
6	Fabio GALANTE		D	35		2
16	Luigi GIALLOMBARDO		M	1		
77	Alessandro GRANDONI		D	34		
17	Nikola LAZETIC	SCG	A	11	(5)	
99	Cristiano LUCARELLI		A	36		19
79	Matteo MELARA		D	5	(1)	1
4	Stefano MORRONE		M	35		6
20	Raffaele PALLADINO		A	14	(8)	2
28	Dario PASSONI		M	25	(5)	
21	Paulo Betanin "PAULINHO"	BRA	A	1	(10)	
7	Jean-Marc PFERTZEL	FRA	D	20	(8)	2
67	Gennaro RUOTOLO		M	13	(8)	
13	Jorge Palacios VARGAS	CHL	D	31		

MESSINA
Coach – Bortolo Mutti; (27/3/06) Giampiero Ventura

2005
Date	Opponent	H/A	Score	Scorers
28/8	Lazio	a	0-1	
11/9	Fiorentina	h	2-2	Di Napoli, Zoro
18/9	Cagliari	a	1-1	Donati
21/9	Livorno	h	0-0	
25/9	Siena	a	2-4	Zoro, Di Napoli
2/10	Sampdoria	h	1-4	D'Agostino
15/10	Juventus	a	0-1	
22/10	Ascoli	h	1-1	Zampagna
26/10	Parma	a	1-1	Muslimovic
30/10	Lecce	a	2-0	D'Agostino 2
6/11	Roma	h	0-2	
19/11	Udinese	a	0-1	
27/11	Internazionale	h	1-2	Di Napoli
4/12	Treviso	a	0-0	
11/12	Chievo	h	2-0	Di Napoli, Zampagna
18/12	Milan	a	0-4	
21/12	Reggina	h	1-1	Di Napoli

2006
Date	Opponent	H/A	Score	Scorers
8/1	Empoli	a	3-1	Muslimovic 2, Di Napoli
14/1	Palermo	h	0-0	
18/1	Lazio	h	1-1	Rafael
22/1	Fiorentina	a	0-2	
29/1	Cagliari	h	1-0	Di Napoli
5/2	Livorno	a	2-2	Di Napoli 2 (2p)
8/2	Siena	h	0-0	
12/2	Sampdoria	a	2-4	Muslimovic, Di Napoli (p)
18/2	Juventus	h	2-2	Floccari 2
26/2	Ascoli	a	0-1	
5/3	Parma	h	0-1	
12/3	Lecce	h	2-1	og (Rullo), Nanni
19/3	Roma	a	1-2	Di Napoli
26/3	Udinese	h	1-1	Di Napoli
1/4	Internazionale	a	0-3	
9/4	Treviso	h	3-1	Floccari, Sculli, Di Napoli
15/4	Chievo	a	0-2	
22/4	Milan	h	1-3	Sculli
30/4	Reggina	a	0-3	
7/5	Empoli	h	0-3	(w/o; original result 1-2 Nocerino)
14/5	Palermo	a	0-1	

No	Name	Nat	Pos	Aps	(s)	Gls
78	Filippo ANTONELLI		M	4	(8)	
6	Salvatore ARONICA		D	33	(2)	
82	Domenico BOMBARA		D	1		
10	Renato Rafael BONDI	BRA	M	6	(5)	
88	Nicolas CAGLIONI		G	3	(1)	
24	Carmine COPPOLA		M	23		
4	Filippo CRISTANTE		D	18	(4)	
7	Gaetano D'AGOSTINO		M	20	(7)	3
11	Arturo DI NAPOLI		A	28	(8)	13
5	Massimo DONATI		M	31	(2)	1
18	Sergio FLOCCARI		A	14	(4)	3
25	Luca FUSCO		D	2		
17	Domenico GIAMPÀ		M	11	(4)	

Italy

No	Name	Nat	Pos	Aps	(s)	Gls
10	Ivica ILIEV	SCG	A	5	(3)	
28	Duccio INNOCENTI		D	6	(1)	
31	José MAMEDE	POR	M	5	(6)	
20	Zlatan MUSLIMOVIC	BOS	A	15	(10)	4
9	Roberto Antonio NANNI	ARG	A	2	(7)	1
25	Antonio NOCERINO		M	7	(4)	1
3	Mathew OLORUNLEKE	NGA	D	1	(1)	
79	Andrea PANSERA		G		(1)	
19	Alessandro PARISI		D	11		
90	RAFAEL Pereira da Silva	BRA	D	7	(10)	1
2	Rahman REZAEI	IRN	D	34		
14	Giuseppe SCULLI		A	31	(3)	2
1	Marco STORARI		G	35		
41	Salvatore SULLO		M	5	(10)	
46	Andrea TUMMIOLO		D	1	(2)	
13	Atsushi YANAGISAWA	JPN	A		(7)	
9	Riccardo ZAMPAGNA		A	11		2
27	Marco ZANCHI		D	28		
8	Marc André ZORO	CIV	D	20	(2)	2

MILAN
Coach – Carlo Ancelotti

2005

28/8	Ascoli	a	1-1	Shevchenko	
10/9	Siena	h	3-1	Ambrosini, Shevchenko, Kaká	
18/9	Sampdoria	a	1-2	Gilardino	
21/9	Lazio	h	2-0	Shevchenko, Kaká	
25/9	Treviso	a	2-0	Shevchenko (p), Gilardino	
2/10	Reggina	h	2-1	Maldini 2	
16/10	Cagliari	a	2-0	Gilardino, Shevchenko	
23/10	Palermo	h	2-1	Gattuso, Inzaghi	
26/10	Empoli	a	3-1	Gilardino 2, Vieri	
29/10	Juventus	h	3-1	Seedorf, Kaká, Pirlo	
6/11	Udinese	h	5-1	Gilardino 2, Seedorf, Pirlo, Kaká	
20/11	Fiorentina	a	1-3	Gilardino	
26/11	Lecce	h	2-1	Pirlo, Inzaghi	
3/12	Chievo	a	1-2	Kaladze	
11/12	Internazionale	a	2-3	Shevchenko (p), Stam	
18/12	Messina	h	4-0	Shevchenko 2 (1p), Pirlo, Gilardino	
21/12	Livorno	a	3-0	Gilardino 2, Shevchenko	

2006

8/1	Parma	h	4-3	og (Cardone), Gilardino, Kaká, Shevchenko
15/1	Roma	a	0-1	
18/1	Ascoli	h	1-0	Inzaghi
22/1	Siena	a	3-0	Kaká 2, Shevchenko
28/1	Sampdoria	h	1-1	Shevchenko (p)
5/2	Lazio	a	0-0	
8/2	Treviso	h	5-0	Kaká, Shevchenko 2, Gilardino, Inzaghi
12/2	Reggina	a	4-1	Inzaghi 3, Gilardino
18/2	Cagliari	h	1-0	Gilardino (p)
26/2	Palermo	a	2-0	Inzaghi, Shevchenko (p)
4/3	Empoli	h	3-0	Inzaghi 2, Shevchenko
12/3	Juventus	a	0-0	
19/3	Udinese	a	4-0	Shevchenko 2, Gilardino, Seedorf
25/3	Fiorentina	h	3-1	Shevchenko, Kaká, Gattuso
1/4	Lecce	a	0-1	
9/4	Chievo	h	4-1	Nesta, Kaká 3 (1p)
14/4	Internazionale	h	1-0	Kaladze
22/4	Messina	a	3-1	Jankulovski, Gattuso, Gilardino
30/4	Livorno	h	2-0	Inzaghi 2
7/5	Parma	a	3-2	Kaká (p), Cafu, Seedorf
14/5	Roma	h	2-1	Kaká (p), Amoroso (p)

No	Name	Nat	Pos	Aps	(s)	Gls
23	Massimo AMBROSINI		M	5	(8)	1
37	Márcio AMOROSO	BRA	A	1	(3)	1
2	Marcos CAFU	BRA	D	11	(8)	1
5	Alessandro COSTACURTA		D	8	(7)	
1	Nélson de Jesus "DIDA"	BRA	G	36		
8	Gennaro GATTUSO		M	31	(4)	3
11	Alberto GILARDINO		A	29	(5)	17
9	Filippo INZAGHI		A	16	(7)	12
18	Marek JANKULOVSKI	CZE	M	7	(15)	1
22	Ricardo Izecson "KAKÁ"	BRA	M	28	(7)	14
16	Zeljko KALAC	AUS	G	2		
4	Kakhaber KALADZE	GEO	D	26	(2)	2
3	Paolo MALDINI		D	13	(1)	2
13	Alessandro NESTA		D	29	(1)	1
21	Andrea PIRLO		M	31	(2)	4
10	RUI Manuel COSTA	POR	M	12	(13)	
20	Clarence SEEDORF	HOL	M	31	(5)	4
27	Sérgio Cláudio "SERGINHO"	BRA	M	29	(4)	
7	Andriy SHEVCHENKO	UKR	A	27	(1)	19
17	Dario SIMIC	CRO	D	10	(5)	
31	Jaap STAM	HOL	D	24	(1)	1
32	Christian VIERI		A	3	(5)	1
14	Johann VOGEL	SUI	M	9	(5)	

PALERMO
Coach – Luigi Del Neri; (29/1/06) Giuseppe Papadopoulo

2005

28/8	Parma	a	1-1	Terlizzi
10/9	Internazionale	h	3-2	Corini, Terlizzi, Makinwa
18/9	Siena	a	2-1	Terlizzi, Makinwa
21/9	Reggina	h	1-0	Terlizzi
25/9	Lazio	a	2-4	Caracciolo, González
2/10	Empoli	h	2-2	Caracciolo, Makinwa
16/10	Chievo	h	2-2	Corini (p), Caracciolo
23/10	Milan	a	1-2	Caracciolo
26/10	Lecce	h	3-0	Bonanni, Mutarelli, Ferri
30/10	Udinese	a	0-0	
6/11	Sampdoria	h	0-0	
20/11	Treviso	a	2-2	Ferri, Brienza
27/11	Ascoli	a	1-1	Bonanni
4/12	Cagliari	h	2-2	Caracciolo, Makinwa
11/12	Roma	a	2-1	Biava, Caracciolo
18/12	Livorno	h	0-2	
21/12	Fiorentina	h	0-1	

2006

7/1	Juventus	h	1-2	Terlizzi
14/1	Messina	a	0-0	
18/1	Parma	h	4-2	Corini, Barzagli, Di Michele 2
21/1	Internazionale	a	0-3	
28/1	Siena	h	1-3	Godeas
5/2	Reggina	a	2-2	Barone, Caracciolo
8/2	Lazio	h	3-1	González, Tedesco, Caracciolo
12/2	Empoli	a	1-0	Barzagli
19/2	Chievo	a	0-0	
26/2	Milan	h	0-2	

Italy

5/3	Lecce	a	0-2	
12/3	Udinese	h	2-0	Di Michele, Tedesco
19/3	Sampdoria	a	2-0	Mutarelli, Di Michele
26/3	Treviso	h	1-0	Makinwa
2/4	Ascoli	h	1-1	Caracciolo
9/4	Cagliari	a	1-1	Di Michele
15/4	Roma	h	3-3	Di Michele, Barone 2
22/4	Livorno	a	1-3	Tedesco
30/4	Fiorentina	h	1-0	Di Michele
7/5	Juventus	a	1-2	Godeas
14/5	Messina	h	1-0	Godeas

No	Name	Nat	Pos	Aps	(s)	Gls
32	Pietro ACCARDI		D	4	(2)	
1	Federico AGLIARDI		G	10		
24	Mariano ANDUJAR	ARG	G	10	(1)	
8	Simone BARONE		M	35	(1)	3
43	Andrea BARZAGLI		D	35		2
21	Giuseppe BIAVA		D	15	(2)	1
6	Massimo BONANNI		M	14	(4)	2
10	Franco BRIENZA		A	11	(16)	1
29	Andrea CARACCIOLO		A	31	(4)	9
20	Paul CODREA	ROM	M	5	(7)	
25	Kewullay CONTEH	SRL	D	4	(2)	
5	Eugenio CORINI		M	27		3
17	David DI MICHELE		A	18	(1)	7
81	Michele FERRI		D	2	(5)	2
29	Denis GODEAS		A	6	(9)	3
19	Mariano GONZÁLEZ	ARG	M	19	(11)	2
11	Fabio GROSSO		M	33		
99	Matteo GUARDALBEN		G	6		
13	Cristiano LUPATELLI		G	5		
26	Stephen MAKINWA	NGA	A	17	(6)	5
7	Salvatore MASIELLO		M	1	(1)	
22	Massimo MUTARELLI		M	15	(8)	2
59	Gianluca PALMITERI		A		(1)	
9	Simone PEPE		A		(3)	
18	Leandro RINAUDO		M	7	(3)	
1	Mario Alberto SANTANA	ARG	M	20	(8)	
12	Nicola SANTONI		G	7	(1)	
4	Giovanni TEDESCO		M	6	(8)	3
23	Christian TERLIZZI		D	20	(1)	5
2	Cristian ZACCARDO		D	35	(1)	

PARMA
Coach – Mario Beretta

2005

28/8	Palermo	h	1-1	Bresciano
11/9	Chievo	a	0-1	
17/9	Empoli	h	1-0	Corradi
21/9	Roma	a	1-4	Cannavaro
24/9	Juventus	h	1-2	Delvecchio
2/10	Ascoli	a	1-3	Pisanu
16/10	Treviso	h	1-1	Simplício
22/10	Fiorentina	a	1-4	Grella
26/10	Messina	h	1-1	Simplício
30/10	Livorno	a	0-2	
6/11	Lecce	h	2-0	Marchionni, Morfeo
20/11	Internazionale	a	0-2	
27/11	Udinese	h	1-2	Corradi
4/12	Reggina	a	1-2	Cardone
11/12	Sampdoria	h	1-1	Corradi
18/12	Siena	a	2-2	Corradi, Dessena
21/12	Cagliari	h	1-0	Corradi

2006

8/1	Milan	a	3-4	Cannavaro, Marchionni 2
15/1	Lazio	h	1-1	Corradi
18/1	Palermo	a	2-4	Simplício, Cannavaro
22/1	Chievo	h	2-1	Rossi, Simplício
29/1	Empoli	a	2-1	Marchionni, Bresciano
4/2	Roma	h	0-3	
8/2	Juventus	a	1-1	Dessena
12/2	Ascoli	h	0-0	
19/2	Treviso	a	1-0	Simplício
25/2	Fiorentina	h	2-4	Simplício (p), Bresciano
5/3	Messina	a	1-0	Bresciano
12/3	Livorno	h	2-1	Simplício (p), Bresciano
19/3	Lecce	a	2-1	Bresciano, Simplício
25/3	Internazionale	h	1-0	Simplício
2/4	Udinese	a	0-2	
9/4	Reggina	h	4-0	Bresciano, Simplício, Contini (p), Dessena
15/4	Sampdoria	a	2-1	Corradi (p), Bresciano
22/4	Siena	h	1-1	Morfeo
30/4	Cagliari	a	1-3	Corradi
7/5	Milan	h	2-3	Corradi 2
14/5	Lazio	a	0-1	

No	Name	Nat	Pos	Aps	(s)	Gls
6	Jorge BOLAÑO	COL	M	14	(2)	
5	Daniele BONERA		D	22	(1)	
23	Mark BRESCIANO	AUS	M	27	(5)	8
7	Luca BUCCI		G	21	(1)	
29	Ibrahima CAMARA	GUI	D	3		
28	Paolo CANNAVARO		D	25	(4)	3
3	Giuseppe CARDONE		D	23	(1)	1
21	Luca CIGARINI		M	7	(10)	
2	Ferdinand COLY	SEN	D	7	(1)	
14	Matteo CONTINI		D	31	(1)	1
9	Bernardo CORRADI		A	35		10
1	Alfonso DE LUCIA		G	3	(1)	
18	Zlatko DEDIC	SLO	A	2	(8)	
36	Marco DELVECCHIO		A	6	(2)	1
4	Daniele DESSENA		M	7	(10)	3
24	FERNANDO COUTO	POR	D	17	(6)	
26	Damiano FERRONETTI		D	10	(2)	
13	Vincenzo GRELLA	AUS	M	34	(1)	1
99	Matteo GUARDALBEN		G	7		
22	Cristiano LUPATELLI		G	7	(1)	
27	Matteo MANDORLINI		M		(1)	
32	Marco MARCHIONNI		M	30	(1)	4
38	Filippo MATTIUZZO		D		(1)	
10	Domenico MORFEO		M	14	(9)	2
35	Daniele PAPONI		A		(5)	
33	Giovanni PASQUALE		D	16	(6)	
19	Andrea PISANU		A	6	(2)	1
17	Marco ROSSI		D	4	(6)	1
16	Francesco RUOPOLO		A	1	(5)	
15	Filippo SAVI		M	2	(6)	
30	Fábio SIMPLÍCIO	BRA	M	37		10

REGGINA
Coach – Walter Mazzarri

2005

28/8	Roma	h	0-3	
11/9	Sampdoria	a	2-3	Cozza, Missiroli
18/9	Chievo	h	1-3	Cozza
21/9	Palermo	a	0-1	

Italy

24/9	Udinese	h	2-0	Cozza, Cavalli
2/10	Milan	a	1-2	Cavalli
16/10	Lecce	h	2-0	Tedesco, Cozza
23/10	Livorno	a	0-1	
26/10	Treviso	h	1-2	Missiroli
30/10	Lazio	h	1-0	og (Zauri)
5/11	Empoli	a	0-3	
20/11	Cagliari	h	3-1	Amoruso, Cozza (p), Paredes
27/11	Siena	a	0-0	
4/12	Parma	h	2-1	Cozza, De Rosa
11/12	Ascoli	a	1-1	Paredes
18/12	Internazionale	h	0-4	
21/12	Messina	a	1-1	Cozza
2006				
7/1	Fiorentina	h	1-1	Lucarelli
15/1	Juventus	a	0-1	
18/1	Roma	a	1-3	Franceschini
22/1	Sampdoria	h	2-1	Paredes, Amoruso
29/1	Chievo	a	0-4	
5/2	Palermo	h	2-2	De Rosa, Paredes
8/2	Udinese	a	2-1	Amoruso 2
12/2	Milan	h	1-4	Paredes
19/2	Lecce	a	0-0	
25/2	Livorno	h	1-1	Cozza
5/3	Treviso	a	1-0	Amoruso
12/3	Lazio	a	1-3	Amoruso
19/3	Empoli	h	0-2	
26/3	Cagliari	a	2-0	Lucarelli, Tedesco
2/4	Siena	h	1-1	Amoruso
9/4	Parma	a	0-4	
15/4	Ascoli	h	2-0	De Rosa, Amoruso
22/4	Internazionale	a	0-4	
30/4	Messina	h	3-0	Cozza, Amoruso (p), Bianchi
7/5	Fiorentina	a	2-5	Amoruso 2 (1p)
14/5	Juventus	h	0-2	

No	Name	Nat	Pos	Aps	(s)	Gls
17	Nicola AMORUSO		A	24	(5)	11
3	Jacopo BALESTRI		D	1		
32	Antonio BARILLÀ		M		(1)	
9	Rolando BIANCHI		A	3	(6)	1
8	Davide BIONDINI		M	18	(10)	
7	BRUNO de Andrade	BRA	M		(1)	
2	Yury CANNARSA		D	7		
22	Filippo CAROBBIO		M	7	(14)	
31	Ivan CASTIGLIA		M	1	(2)	
28	Simone CAVALLI		A	6	(7)	2
32	Fabio CERAVOLO		A		(6)	
16	Lambros CHOUTOS	GRE	A	2	(7)	
10	Francesco COZZA		M	32	(1)	9
29	Gaetano DE ROSA		D	35		3
14	Ivan FRANCESCHINI		D	29	(1)	1
4	Antonio GIOSA		D	3	(3)	
55	Maurizio LANZARO		D	18	(3)	
53	Maurizio LAURO		D	2	(3)	
13	Alessandro LUCARELLI		D	32	(1)	2
20	Giandomenico MESTO		M	35		
31	Simone MISSIROLI		M	5	(20)	2
23	Francesco MODESTO		D	32	(5)	
5	Carlos PAREDES	PAR	M	28		5
99	Nicola PAVARINI		G	18	(1)	
1	Ivan PELIZZOLI		G	20		
21	Luca RIGONI		M	3	(1)	
12	Antonio SAVIANO		G		(2)	
19	Giacomo TEDESCO		M	26		2
35	Gaetano UNGARO		D		(1)	
11	Luca VIGIANI		M	30	(6)	
24	Alessandro ZOPPETTI		D	1		

ROMA
Coach – Luciano Spalletti

2005				
28/8	Reggina	a	3-0	Mancini, De Rossi, Nonda
11/9	Udinese	h	0-1	
18/9	Livorno	a	0-0	
21/9	Parma	h	4-1	Totti, Nonda 2, Panucci
25/9	Cagliari	a	0-0	
2/10	Siena	h	2-3	Taddei, Panucci
16/10	Empoli	a	0-1	
23/10	Lazio	h	1-1	Totti
26/10	Internazionale	a	3-2	Montella, Totti 2 (1p)
30/10	Ascoli	h	2-1	Panucci, Mexès
6/11	Messina	a	2-0	Mexès, Totti
19/11	Juventus	h	1-4	Totti (p)
27/11	Fiorentina	h	1-1	Tommasi
4/12	Lecce	a	2-2	Cassano, Nonda
11/12	Palermo	h	1-2	Cassano
18/12	Sampdoria	a	1-1	Totti
21/12	Chievo	h	4-0	Totti 2 (1p), Perrotta, Taddei
2006				
8/1	Treviso	a	1-0	Aquilani
15/1	Milan	h	1-0	Mancini
18/1	Reggina	h	3-1	Totti 2, Mancini
22/1	Udinese	a	4-1	Mancini 2 (1p), De Rossi, Chivu (p)
29/1	Livorno	h	3-0	Totti 2 (1p), Taddei
4/2	Parma	a	3-0	Mancini 2, Perrotta
8/2	Cagliari	h	4-3	Perrotta, De Rossi, Totti 2 (2p)
12/2	Siena	a	2-0	De Rossi, Mancini
19/2	Empoli	h	1-0	Perrotta
26/2	Lazio	a	2-0	Taddei, Aquilani
5/3	Internazionale	h	1-1	Taddei
12/3	Ascoli	a	2-3	Taddei, og (Comotto)
19/3	Messina	h	2-1	Perrotta, Aquilani
25/3	Juventus	a	1-1	Kharja
2/4	Fiorentina	a	1-1	Cufré
9/4	Lecce	h	3-1	Mancini 2 (1p), Chivu
15/4	Palermo	a	3-3	Taddei, Mancini 2 (1p)
22/4	Sampdoria	h	0-0	
30/4	Chievo	a	4-4	De Rossi 2, Taddei, Dacourt
7/5	Treviso	h	1-0	Tommasi
14/5	Milan	a	1-2	Mexès

No	Name	Nat	Pos	Aps	(s)	Gls
7	Edgar ÁLVAREZ	HON	M	3	(17)	
8	Alberto AQUILANI		M	20	(4)	3
3	Cesare BOVO		D	17	(5)	
18	Antonio CASSANO		A	4	(1)	2
26	Alessio CERCI		A		(1)	
13	Cristian CHIVU	ROM	D	27		2
25	Leandro CUFRE	ARG	D	27	(1)	1
1	Gianluca CURCI		G	10		
15	Olivier DACOURT		M	14	(12)	1
16	Daniele DE ROSSI		M	34		6
22	Alexander DONI	BRA	G	28		
29	Leandro GRECO		M		(1)	
14	Houssine KHARJA	FRA	A	2	(10)	1

Italy

4	Samuel KUFFOUR	GHA	D	19	(2)	
30	Alessandro MANCINI	BRA	A	25	(2)	12
5	Philippe MEXES	FRA	D	23	(5)	3
9	Vincenzo MONTELLA		A	9	(4)	1
40	Shabani NONDA	DRC	A	4	(11)	4
35	Stefano OKAKA CHUKA		A	1	(7)	
2	Christian PANUCCI		D	36		3
20	Simone PERROTTA		M	35		5
28	Alesandro ROSI		M	5	(12)	
11	Rodrigo TADDEI	BRA	M	38		8
17	Damiano TOMMASI		M	14	(13)	2
10	Francesco TOTTI		A	23	(1)	15

SAMPDORIA
Coach – Walter Novellino

2005

27/8	Fiorentina	a	1-2	Diana
11/9	Reggina	h	3-2	Bonazzoli, Volpi, Gasbarroni
18/9	Milan	h	2-1	Bonazzoli, Tonetto
21/9	Treviso	a	2-0	Bonazzoli 2
25/9	Chievo	h	1-2	Flachi
2/10	Messina	a	4-1	Flachi, Bonazzoli 2, Borriello
16/10	Ascoli	a	1-2	Bonazzoli
23/10	Siena	h	3-3	Flachi (p), Volpi 2
26/10	Juventus	a	0-2	
29/10	Internazionale	h	2-2	Diana 2
6/11	Palermo	a	2-0	Gasbarroni, Bonazzoli
20/11	Lazio	h	2-0	Diana, Flachi
27/11	Cagliari	a	0-2	
4/12	Empoli	h	2-0	Borriello, Flachi
11/12	Parma	a	1-1	Bonazzoli
18/12	Roma	h	1-1	Flachi (p)
21/12	Udinese	a	0-2	

2006

8/1	Livorno	h	0-2	
14/1	Lecce	a	3-0	Diana 2, Bazzani
18/1	Fiorentina	h	3-1	Palombo, Tonetto, Flachi
22/1	Reggina	a	1-2	Kutuzov
28/1	Milan	a	1-1	Gasbarroni
5/2	Treviso	h	1-1	Kutuzov
8/2	Chievo	a	1-1	Kutuzov
12/2	Messina	h	4-2	Castellini, Volpi (p), Tonetto, Foti
19/2	Ascoli	h	1-2	Volpi
26/2	Siena	a	0-1	
4/3	Juventus	h	0-1	
11/3	Internazionale	a	0-1	
19/3	Palermo	h	0-2	
26/3	Lazio	a	0-2	
2/4	Cagliari	h	1-1	Castellini
9/4	Empoli	a	1-2	Flachi (p)
15/4	Parma	h	1-2	Flachi
22/4	Roma	a	0-0	
30/4	Udinese	h	1-1	Flachi
7/5	Livorno	a	0-0	
14/5	Lecce	h	1-3	Flachi

No	Name	Nat	Pos	Aps	(s)	Gls
21	Francesco ANTONIOLI		G	35		
87	Alessandro BASTRINI		D		(1)	
9	Fabio BAZZANI		A	5	(1)	1
18	Emiliano BONAZZOLI		A	17		9
11	Marco BORRIELLO		A	1	(10)	2
1	Luca CASTELLAZZI		G	3		
14	Marcello CASTELLINI		D	33		2
27	Corrado COLOMBO		A	7	(5)	
8	Samuele DALLA BONA		M	14	(15)	
34	Aimo DIANA		M	25	(4)	6
6	Mark EDUSEI	GHA	M	1		
19	Giulio FALCONE		D	14		
10	Francesco FLACHI		A	28	(3)	11
88	Salvatore FOTI		A	4	(11)	1
7	Andrea GASBARRONI		M	18	(10)	3
28	Mark IULIANO		D	4		
13	Vitaliy KUTUZOV	BLS	A	12	(17)	3
11	Mattia MARCHESETTI		M		(8)	
29	Gionata MINGOZZI		M		(2)	
17	Angelo PALOMBO		M	28	(3)	1
32	Simone PAVAN		D	14	(5)	
26	Marco PISANO		D	32	(1)	
15	Luigi SALA		D	20	(4)	
11	Danilo SODDIMO		A		(1)	
22	Max TONETTO		D	31	(2)	3
4	Sergio VOLPI		M	35		5
3	Marco ZAMBONI		D		(1)	
20	Lamberto ZAULI		M	5	(3)	
77	Cristian ZENONI		D	32	(3)	

SIENA
Coach – Luigi De Canio

2005

28/8	Cagliari	h	2-1	Chiesa 2 (1p)
10/9	Milan	a	1-3	Tudor
18/9	Palermo	h	1-2	Locatelli
21/9	Ascoli	a	1-1	Bogdani
25/9	Messina	h	4-2	Locatelli 2, Chiesa, Colonnese
2/10	Roma	a	3-2	Negro, Chiesa, Colonnese
15/10	Udinese	h	2-3	Chiesa, og (Bertotto)
23/10	Sampdoria	a	3-3	Locatelli, Chiesa (p), Vergassola
26/10	Fiorentina	h	0-2	
30/10	Treviso	a	1-0	Chiesa
6/11	Chievo	h	0-1	
20/11	Lecce	a	0-3	
27/11	Reggina	h	0-0	
4/12	Lazio	a	2-3	Bogdani, og (Peruzzi)
10/12	Empoli	h	1-0	Bogdani
18/12	Parma	h	2-2	Locatelli, Chiesa
21/12	Juventus	a	0-2	

2006

8/1	Internazionale	h	0-0	
15/1	Livorno	a	2-2	Locatelli, Chiesa (p)
18/1	Cagliari	a	0-1	
22/1	Milan	h	0-3	
28/1	Palermo	a	3-1	Bogdani 3
4/2	Ascoli	h	1-1	Bogdani
8/2	Messina	a	0-0	
12/2	Roma	h	0-2	
19/2	Udinese	a	2-1	Volpato 2
26/2	Sampdoria	h	1-0	Vergassola
5/3	Fiorentina	a	1-2	Vergassola
11/3	Treviso	h	1-0	Bogdani
19/3	Chievo	a	1-4	Foglio (p)
26/3	Lecce	h	1-2	Bogdani
2/4	Reggina	a	1-1	Bogdani
9/4	Lazio	h	2-3	Vergassola, Chiesa
15/4	Empoli	a	1-2	Bogdani
22/4	Parma	a	1-1	Guzmán

Italy

30/4	Juventus	h	0-3	
7/5	Internazionale	a	1-1	Gastaldello
14/5	Livorno	h	0-0	

No	Name	Nat	Pos	Aps	(s)	Gls
75	ALBERTO do Carmo Neto	BRA	M	23	(8)	
26	Jonathan BACHINI		M	2	(3)	
81	Erjon BOGDANI	ALB	A	31	(3)	11
10	Enrico CHIESA		A	33	(5)	11
5	Francesco COLONNESE		D	10	(5)	1
35	Francesco COZZA		M	2		
23	Roberto D'AVERSA		M	25	(1)	
65	Gennaro ESPOSITO		M		(1)	
3	Gianluca FALSINI		D	17	(7)	
31	Paolo FOGLIO		D	15	(6)	1
14	Marco FORTIN		G	12		
46	Daniele GASTALDELLO		D	17	(8)	1
16	Tomás Andrés GUZMÁN	PAR	A	2	(8)	1
18	Pasquale IDARESTA		A		(2)	
66	Nicola LEGROTTAGLIE		D	25	(3)	
20	Tomas LOCATELLI		M	24	(4)	6
21	Massimo MARAZZINA		A	2	(6)	
4	Michele MIGNANI		D	2	(1)	
83	Antonio MIRANTE		G	26		
30	Cristian MOLINARO		D	11	(9)	
9	Roberto NANNI	ARG	A	2	(6)	
2	Paolo NEGRO		D	25	(5)	1
17	Douglas Ricaro PACKER	BRA	A		(2)	
19	Matteo PARO		M	24	(4)	
90	Daniele PORTANOVA		D	29	(2)	
7	Igor TUDOR	CRO	D	23	(1)	1
6	Simone VERGASSOLA		M	33		4
11	Rey VOLPATO		A	3	(10)	2

TREVISO
Coach – Ezio Rossi; (8/11/05) Alberto Cavasin; (21/2/06) Diego Bortoluzzi

2005

28/8	Internazionale	a	0-3	
11/9	Livorno	h	0-1	
18/9	Lazio	a	1-3	Pinga
21/9	Sampdoria	h	0-2	
25/9	Milan	h	0-2	
1/10	Chievo	a	0-0	
16/10	Parma	a	1-1	Fava
23/10	Empoli	h	1-2	Fava
26/10	Reggina	a	2-1	Beghetto, Parravicini
30/10	Siena	a	0-1	
6/11	Cagliari	a	0-0	
20/11	Palermo	h	2-2	Reginaldo 2
27/11	Juventus	a	1-3	Parravicini
4/12	Messina	h	0-0	
10/12	Fiorentina	a	0-1	
18/12	Lecce	h	2-1	Filippini E., Pinga
21/12	Ascoli	a	0-1	

2006

8/1	Roma	h	0-1	
15/1	Udinese	a	2-2	Pinga, Dellafiore
18/1	Internazionale	h	0-1	
22/1	Livorno	a	1-1	Reginaldo
29/1	Lazio	h	0-1	
5/2	Sampdoria	a	1-1	Gustavo
8/2	Milan	a	0-5	
11/2	Chievo	h	1-2	Borriello
19/2	Parma	h	0-1	
26/2	Empoli	a	1-1	Filippini E.
5/3	Reggina	h	0-1	
11/3	Siena	a	0-1	
18/3	Cagliari	h	1-2	Baseggio
26/3	Palermo	a	0-1	
_	Juventus	h	0-0	
9/4	Messina	a	1-3	Fava
15/4	Fiorentina	h	1-3	Borriello
22/4	Lecce	a	1-1	Reginaldo
30/4	Ascoli	h	2-2	Reginaldo, Borriello
7/5	Roma	a	0-1	
14/5	Udinese	h	2-1	Borriello 2 (1p)

No	Name	Nat	Pos	Aps	(s)	Gls
26	Robert ACQUAFRESCA		A	3	(5)	
17	Robert ANDERSON	BRA	M		(1)	
18	Walter BASEGGIO	BEL	M	12	(3)	1
10	Luigi BEGHETTO		A	7	(9)	1
11	Marco BORRIELLO		A	18	(2)	5
7	Roberto CHIAPPARA		A	1	(6)	
4	Marcello COTTAFAVA		D	28		
29	Raffaele DE MARTINO		M	7	(7)	
25	Hernán DELLAFIORE	ARG	D	20	(2)	1
24	Andrea DOSSENA		D	19	(2)	
31	Dino FAVA		A	15	(7)	3
14	Antonio FILIPPINI		M	26	(6)	
75	Emanuele FILIPPINI		M	28	(2)	2
22	Francesco GALEOTO		D	10	(1)	
11	Fabio GALLO		M	14		
20	Alberto GIULIATTO		D	11	(7)	
7	Gianni GUIGOU	URU	M	12	(1)	
21	GUSTAVO Lazzaretti	BRA	M	22	(4)	1
1	Samir HANDANOVIC	SLO	G	3		
35	Stefano LORENZI		D	2		
30	Christian MAGGIO		D	10	(1)	
23	Marco MALLUS		D	1	(1)	
8	Jehad MUNTASSER	LBY	M	1	(3)	
5	Francesco PARRAVICINI		M	24	(5)	2
28	André PINGA	BRA	A	19	(5)	3
27	REGINALDO Ferreira da Silva	BRA	A	20	(11)	5
16	Fabio ROSELLI		M		(1)	
33	Andrea RUSSOTTO		A		(4)	
1	Matteo SERENI		G	7		
6	Carlos VALDEZ	URU	D	15	(4)	
9	Blazej VASCÁK	SVK	M	9	(4)	
55	William VIALI		D	26		
15	WILKER Santos	BRA	M		(1)	
34	Adriano ZANCOPÉ		G	28	(1)	

UDINESE
Coach – Serse Cosmi; (11/2/06) Loris Dominissini & Roberto Néstor Sensini (ARG); (20/3/06) Giovanni Galeone

2005

28/8	Empoli	h	1-0	Muntari
11/9	Roma	a	1-0	Muntari
18/9	Fiorentina	a	2-4	Muntari, Iaquinta (p)
21/9	Juventus	h	0-0	
24/9	Reggina	a	0-2	
1/10	Lazio	h	3-0	Iaquinta (p), Di Natale, Candela
15/10	Siena	a	3-2	Di Michele 3
23/10	Internazionale	h	0-1	
26/10	Ascoli	a	1-1	Vidigal

Italy

Date	Opponent	H/A	Score	Scorers
30/10	Palermo	h	0-0	
6/11	Milan	a	1-5	Iaquinta (p)
19/11	Messina	h	1-0	Felipe
27/11	Parma	a	2-1	Barreto 2
4/12	Livorno	h	0-2	
11/12	Lecce	h	1-2	Di Natale
18/12	Chievo	a	0-2	
21/12	Sampdoria	h	2-0	Zapata, og (Castellini)
2006				
8/1	Cagliari	a	1-2	Sensini
15/1	Treviso	h	2-2	Motta, Di Natale (p)
18/1	Empoli	a	1-1	Felipe
22/1	Roma	h	1-4	Di Natale
29/1	Fiorentina	h	0-0	
5/2	Juventus	a	0-1	
8/2	Reggina	h	1-2	Iaquinta
11/2	Lazio	a	1-1	Iaquinta (p)
19/2	Siena	h	1-2	Iaquinta (p)
26/2	Internazionale	a	1-3	Iaquinta (p)
5/3	Ascoli	h	1-1	Di Natale
12/3	Palermo	a	0-2	
19/3	Milan	h	0-4	
26/3	Messina	a	1-1	Obodo
2/4	Parma	h	2-0	Di Natale, Felipe
8/4	Livorno	a	2-0	Iaquinta, Natali
15/4	Lecce	a	2-1	Barreto, og (Sicignano)
22/4	Chievo	h	1-1	Di Natale
30/4	Sampdoria	a	1-1	Di Natale
7/5	Cagliari	h	2-0	Iaquinta, Barreto
14/5	Treviso	a	1-2	Pieri

No	Name	Nat	Pos	Aps	(s)	Gls
21	Abel Enrique AGUILAR	COL	M		(2)	
88	Roberto BARONIO		M	8	(2)	
31	Paulo de Souza « BARRETO »	BRA	A	17	(10)	4
4	Valerio BERTOTTO		D	20	(6)	
32	Vincent CANDELA	FRA	M	25	(1)	1
1	Morgan DE SANCTIS		G	34		
35	Rodrigo DEFENDI	BRA	D	2		
17	David DI MICHELE		A	11	(6)	3
10	Antonio DI NATALE		A	28	(7)	8
19	FELIPE da Silva	BRA	D	35		3
11	Al Saadi GHEDDAFI	LBY	A		(1)	
9	Vincenzo IAQUINTA		A	22	(2)	9
34	« JUAREZ » Teizeira de Sousa	BRA	D	4	(1)	
33	Flavio LAZZARI		M		(2)	
17	Salvatore MASIELLO		M		(1)	
23	Stefano MAURI		M	12	(4)	
25	Piermario MOROSINI		M		(5)	
27	Marco MOTTA		D	4	(2)	1
18	Sulley Ali MUNTARI	GHA	M	29		3
14	Cesare NATALI		D	19	(1)	1
5	Chris OBODO	NGA	M	25	(3)	1
12	Gabriele PAOLETTI		G	4		
30	Simone PEPE		A	2	(4)	
26	Mirko PIERI		D	11	(3)	1
13	Giampiero PINZI		M	10	(3)	
20	Fausto ROSSINI		A	5	(9)	
6	Roberto Néstor SENSINI	ARG	D	14		1
16	Fernando TISSONE	ARG	M	12	(12)	
8	José Luís VIDIGAL	POR	M	13	(10)	1
2	Cristián ZAPATA	COL	D	21		1
7	Damiano ZENONI		M	31	(1)	

DOMESTIC CUP 2005/06

FIRST ROUND
(6/8/05)
Ascoli 2, Acireale 0
Spezia 0, Cesena 1 *(aet)*
(7/8/05)
Empoli 2, Pizzighettone 1
Sangiovannese 0, Crotone 2
Cavese 0, Parma 1
Padova 3, Triestina 0 *(w/o; original result 2-1)*
Cittadella 3, Modena 2
Lumezzane 1, Ternana 2
Livorno 3, Forlì 0
Treviso 0, Manfredonia 1
Pro Patria 0, Albinoleffe 1
San Marino 1, Cagliari 3
Grosseto 2, Mantova 0
Massese 0, Atalanta 1
Pisa 1, Catania 1 *(aet; 6-5 on pens)*
Juve Stabia 1, Siena 2
Frosinone 0, Avellino 3 *(w/o)*
Pro Sesto 0, Brescia 1
Lanciano 0, Arezzo 3
Valenzana 0, Chievo 5
Sambenedettese 2, Cremonese 4
Martina 1, Bari 2
Monza 1, Lecce 1 *(aet; 5-3 on pens)*
Pavia 2, Vicenza 1
Verona 2, Teramo 0
Lucchese 1, Piacenza 2 *(aet)*
Giugliano 1, Reggina 2 *(aet)*
Napoli 2, Pescara 0
Ravenna 0, Bologna 1
Fiorentina 4, Cisco Lodigian 0
Pistoiese 0, Rimini 1
Genoa 0, Catanzaro 3 *(w/o)*

SECOND ROUND
(13/8/05)
Manfredonia 3, Albinoleffe 2
Cesena 1, Bologna 0
(14/8/05)
Crotone 2, Empoli 3 *(aet)*
Padova 0, Parma 1
Cittadella 0, Ternana 0 *(aet; 7-6 on pens)*
Catanzaro 0, Livorno 0 *(aet; 2-4 on pens)*
Groseto 1, Cagliari 2
Pisa 0, Atalanta 1
Avellino 0, Siena 1
Arezzo 2, Brescia 2 *(aet; 6-7 on pens)*
Cremonese 0, Chievo 1
Bari 2, Ascoli 1
Monza 1, Pavia 1 *(aet; 4-5 on pens)*
Piacenza 2, Verona 1
Rimini 1, Fiorentina 2 *(aet)*
(15/8/05)
Napoli 1, Reggina 0

THIRD ROUND
(20/8/05)
Cesena 0, Fiorentina 1
(21/8/05)
Empoli 1, Parma 1 *(aet; 6-7 on pens)*

Italy

Cittadella 3, Livorno 2
Manfredonia 2, Cagliari 2 *(aet; 2-4 on pens)*
Siena 0, Atalanta 4
Pavia 0, Bari 0 *(aet; 5-6 on pens)*
Napoli 1, Piacenza 0
(22/8/05)
Brescia 1, Chievo 0

1/8 FINALS

(29/11/05 & 11/1/06)
Milan v Brescia 3-1; 4-3 *(7-4)*
(30/11/05 & 11/1/06)
Atalanta v Udinese 1-0; 1-3 *(2-3)*
(30/11/05 & 12/1/06)
Parma v Internazionale 0-1; 0-0 *(0-1)*
(1/12/05 & 10/1/06)
Fiorentina v Juventus 2-2; 1-4 *(3-6)*
(7/12/05 & 10/1/06)
Bari v Palermo 0-0 ; 4-5 *(4-5)*
(8/12/05 & 11/1/06)
Cagliari v Sampdoria 1-1; 1-2 *(2-3)*
Napoli v Roma 0-3; 1-2 *(1-5)*
(8/12/05 & 12/1/06)
Lazio v Cittadella 2-0; 0-0 *(2-0)*

QUARTER-FINALS

(24/1/06 & 2/2/06)
Lazio 1 *(Manfredini 28)*, Internazionale 1 *(Stankovic 26)*
Internazionale 1 *(Stankovic 37)*, Lazio 0
(Internazionale 2-1)

(25/1/06 & 31/1/06)
Milan 1 *(Gilardino 86)*, Palermo 0
Palermo 3 *(González 10, 49, Caracciolo 18)*, Milan 0
(Palermo 3-1)

(15/1/06 & 1/2/06)
Udinese 1 *(Di Natale 23)*, Sampdoria 1 *(Diana 76)*
Sampdoria 2 *(Foti 62, Pisano 70)*, Udinese 2 *(Di Natale 43, Pieri 59)*
(3-3; Udinese on away goals)

(26/1/06 & 1/2/06)
Juventus 2 *(Del Piero 73, 90)*, Roma 3 *(Mancini 39, Tommasi 61, Perrotta 68)*
Roma 0, Juventus 1 *(Mutu 48p)*
(3-3; Roma on away goals)

SEMI-FINALS

(22/3/06 & 12/4/06)
Internazionale 1 *(Solari 20)*, Udinese 0
Udinese 2 *(Obodo 83, Iaquinta 90p)*, Internazionale 2 *(Solari 8, Pizarro 86)*
(Internazionale 3-2)

Palermo 2 *(Brienza 4, Mutarelli 69)*, Roma 1 *(Perrotta 1)*
Roma 1 *(Tommasi 30)*, Palermo 0
(2-2; Roma on away goal)

FINAL

(3/5/06)
Stadio Olimpico, Rome
ROMA 1 *(Mancini 55)*
INTERNAZIONALE 1 *(Cruz 7)*
Referee – Trefoloni
ROMA – Doni, Panucci, Mexès, Chivu (Bovo 46), Cufré, Tommasi (Okaka Chuka 80),
De Rossi, Perrotta, Kharja, Mancini (Álvarez 85), Taddei.
INTERNAZIONALE – Júlio César, Zanetti J., Córdoba, Samuel (Burdisso 70), Favalli, Figo, Pizarro, Cambiasso, Stankovic (César 73), Adriano (Martins 80), Cruz.

(11/5/06)
Stadio Giuseppe Meazza, Milan
INTERNAZIONALE 3 *(Cambiasso 6, Cruz 45, Martins 78)*
ROMA 1 *(Nonda 80)*
Referee – Messina
INTERNAZIONALE – Júlio César, Zanetti J., Materazzi, Samuel, Favalli, Figo (Kily González 81), Pizarro, Cambiasso, Stankovic (Solari 58), Adriano (Martins 67), Cruz.
ROMA – Doni, Panucci, Chivu (Kuffour 13), Bovo, Cufré, Kharja (Nonda 76), Dacourt, Rosi, Tommasi, Mancini, Okaka Chuka (Totti 54).

(INTERNAZIONALE 4-2)

SECOND LEVEL FINAL TABLE 2005/06

		Pld	W	D	L	F	A	Pts
1	Atalanta	42	24	9	9	61	39	81
2	Catania	42	22	12	8	67	42	78
3	Torino	42	21	13	8	51	31	76
4	Mantova	42	18	15	9	46	35	69
5	Modena	42	17	16	9	59	41	67
6	Cesena	42	18	12	12	66	54	66
7	Arezzo	42	17	15	10	45	34	66
8	Bologna	42	16	16	10	55	42	64
9	Crotone	42	18	9	15	56	48	63
10	Brescia	42	15	15	12	54	44	60
11	Pescara	42	14	12	16	41	50	54
12	Piacenza	42	13	15	14	56	52	54
13	Bari	42	11	18	13	43	47	51
14	Triestina	42	12	15	15	44	51	51
15	Verona	42	10	19	13	42	41	49
16	Vicenza	42	13	10	19	38	49	49
17	Rimini	42	11	15	16	42	49	48
18	Albinoleffe	42	10	16	16	38	52	46
19	Avellino	42	11	13	18	42	62	46
20	Ternana	42	7	18	17	36	58	39
21	Cremonese	42	6	12	24	36	60	30
22	Catanzaro	42	7	7	28	26	63	28

PROMOTION/RELEGATION PLAY-OFFS

(1/6/06 & 4/6/06)
Cesena 1, Torino 1
Torino 1, Cesena 0
(Torino 2-1)

Modena 0, Mantova 0
Mantova 1, Modena 1
(1-1; Mantova on superior position in regular league)

(8/6/06 & 11/6/06)
Mantova 4, Torino 2
Torino 3, Mantova 1 *(aet)*
(5-5; Torino on superior position in regular league)

Kazakhstan

Slow progress for newcomers

Kazakhstan's integration into European football has been slow and painful.

The former Soviet republic, granted UEFA membership in time to compete in the 2006 World Cup qualifiers, found the going much tougher than in the Asian zone, collecting one solitary point from their dozen fixtures. Losing all six home games was particularly galling and it was to cost coach Sergei Timofeyev his job.

The Kazkhstan FA decided to look west for a replacement, signing up Dutchman Arno Pijpers, the former Estonian national coach, on a two-year contract to guide the team through their debut qualifying campaign in the European Championship. The new incumbent gained a measure of the task ahead when his first four friendly games, all squeezed into a fortnight in the early spring, failed to yield a goal.

Pijpers experienced another negative facet of the game in Kazakhstan when the club that he had also taken charge of, FK Astana, were denied access into the 2006/07 UEFA Cup after failing to meet the financial guarantees required to obtain a UEFA licence. The club had earned their European ticket by winning the 2005 Kazakhstan Cup – under their previous name of Zhenis Astana – but had to surrender their place to Kairat Almaty, the third-placed club in the league.

One Euro entry

Kairat had been the only club from Kazakhstan to meet the conditions of entry to Europe in 2005/06. No suitable replacements were found for FK Taraz and Irtysh Pavlodar in the UEFA Cup, so the country's European activity was limited to just one qualifying tie in the Champions League – which Kairat lost after extra-time to Slovakian champions Artmedia Bratislava.

Kairat were unable to defend their title. The 2005 championship, reduced in size and length to 16 teams and 30 matches, was won by surprise package Aktobe Lento. The club from the north-west had never finished higher than fourth in any previous season but they started strongly and kept it going right to the very end, a 3-0 victory at home to Vostok Ust-Kamenogorsk on the final day enabling them to protect a one-point advantage over Tobol Kostanai. It was Aktobe's 15th home win out of 15 and ensured that a 2-0 away defeat at Kairat four days earlier – not to mention an embarrassing mid-season 1-1 draw at bottom-placed Bolat (the only point the team from Temirtau collected all season) – had no lasting damage.

Tobol finished with five straight victories, the first of them 3-0 at home to Aktobe. They were transformed into title challengers by the arrival, in May, of coach Dmitriy Ogay, twice a champion previously with Irtysh. After just missing out on a hat-trick he consoled himself with the Coach of the Year award, while the Player of the Year prize was collected by another prominent figure in Tobol's title charge, 24-year-old national team midfielder Nurbol Zhumaskaliyev.

NATIONAL TEAM RESULTS 2005/06

Date	Opponent	H/A/N	Venue	Score	Scorers
17/8/05	Georgia (WCQ)	H	Almaty	1-2	Kenzhekhanov (23)
3/9/05	Albania (WCQ)	A	Tirana	1-2	Nizovtsev (64)
7/9/05	Greece (WCQ)	H	Almaty	1-2	Zhumaskaliyev (53)
8/10/05	Georgia (WCQ)	A	Tbilisi	0-0	
12/10/05	Denmark (WCQ)	H	Almaty	1-2	Kuchma (86)
14/2/06	Jordan	A	Amman	0-2	
24/2/06	North Korea	N	Larnaca	0-0	
28/2/06	Finland	N	Larnaca	0-0	
1/3/06	Greece	N	Nicosia	0-2	

Kazakhstan

NATIONAL TEAM APPEARANCES 2005/06

Coach – Sergei TIMOFEYEV
/(14/2/06) Arno PIJPERS (HOL)

Player	DOB	Club	GEO	ALB	GRE	GEO	DEN	Jor	Nkr	Fin	Gre	Caps	Goals
David LORIA	31/10/81	Shakhtyor Karagandy /FK Astana	G	G	G	G		G	G		G	10	-
Aleksandr KUCHMA	9/12/80	Ruch Chorzow (POL) /FK Astana	D	D	D	D50	D	D	D	D	D72	9	1
Aleksandr FAMILTSEV	3/8/75	Tom Tomsk (RUS) /Tobol Kostanai	D		D78	s50	D56		D	D	s72	33	-
Farhadbek IRISMETOV	10/8/81	Kairat Almaty	D	D		D	D66		D	D	s72	12	-
Maksat BAISHANOV	6/8/84	Irtysh Pavlodar /Kaisar Kyzylorda	M	M55							M46	7	-
Sergei LARIN	22/7/86	FK Almaty	M82	M	s52	M54	s56		M51	M69	s61	10	-
Nurbol ZHUMASKALIYEV	11/5/81	Tobol Kostanai	M	M66	M81	M	M		M78	M	s46	18	3
Maxim AZOVSKIY	4/6/86	FK Almaty /FK Astana	M58		M52	M		M			A88	6	-
Andrei TRAVIN	27/4/79	FK Almaty	M	M	s78	M	s66		s55	s79	M	10	-
Nikita KHOKHLOV	27/10/83	Zhenis Astana /FK Astana	M	D	M	s54	M		M	M	M	8	-
Daniyar KENZHEKHANOV	20/1/83	Vostok Ust-Kamenogorsk /FK Almaty	A65	A70		A64	s51		s69	A4		6	1
Maxim NIZOVTSEV	9/9/72	Tobol Kostanai	s58	s55	M							16	2
Aleksandr KROKHMAL	22/11/81	Ordabasy Shymkent	s65									3	-
Anton CHICHULIN	27/10/84	Zhenis Astana /FK Astana	s82					s59		s69	s46	11	-
Samat SMAKOV	8/12/78	Kairat Almaty		D	D	D	D					28	-
Ruslan BALTIYEV	16/9/78	Shinnik Yaroslavl (RUS) /FK Moskva (RUS)		M	s81				s62	s4 /79	M	42	7
Andrei KARPOVICH	18/1/81	Kairat Almaty		s66	M		M		M55	M		22	2
Oleg LITVINENKO	22/11/73	FK Almaty		s70	A	s64	A51	A69	A62	A65		28	6
Igor AVDEYEV	10/1/73	Shakhtyor Karagandy			D		D					27	6
Denis RODIONOV	26/7/85	FK Atyrau			M							7	-
Daniyar MUKANOV	26/9/76	Tobol Kostanai			D	D			D	D		11	1
Yuriy NOVIKOV	19/5/72	Irtysh Pavlodar				G				G		24	-
Aidar KUMISBEKOV	9/2/79	FK Astana						D			D	7	-
Egor AZOVSKIY	10/1/85	FK Astana						D			D72	3	-
Timur MOLDAGALIYEV	29/9/84	FK Astana						D				1	-
Dias KAMELOV	29/5/81	FK Astana						M59			s88	5	-
Eduard SERGIENKO	18/2/83	FK Astana						M78	s51		M61	3	-
Zhambyl KUKEYEV	20/9/88	FK Astana						M63	s78	s65	M46	4	-
Dmitriy BYAKOV	9/4/78	FK Astana						s63				10	2
Dauren KUSAINOV	10/4/84	FK Astana						s69				1	-
Murat TLESHEV	18/4/80	Irtysh Pavlodar						s78				2	-
Andrei FINONCHENKO	21/6/82	Shakhtyor Karagandy							A69			4	1
Maxim ZHALMAGAMBETOV	11/7/83	FK Astana									D	3	-

Kazakhstan

EUROPEAN CUPS 2005/06

UEFA CHAMPIONS LEAGUE

KAIRAT ALMATY
1st qualifying round ARTMEDIA BRATISLAVA (SVK)
H **2-0** *Fomenko (39), Artemov (70)*
Naboychenko, Artemov, Irismetov F., Sosnovschi, Smakov, Dicu (Bogomolov 52), Karpenko (Irismetov J. 46), Likhobabenko, Aksenov (Asanbayev 37), Lovchev, Fomenko.
A **1-4** *Bogomolov (91)*
(aet)
Naboychenko, Artemov, Abdulin, Sosnovschi, Asanbayev (Tlehugov 86), Smakov, Dicu (Bogomolov 58), Likhobabenko, Aksenov (Karpenko 60), Lovchev, Fomenko.

TOP GOALSCORERS 2005

20	Murat TLESHEV (Irtysh Pavlodar)
15	Aleksandr KROKHMAL (Ordabasy Shymkent)
	Ulugbek BAKAYEV (Tobol Kostanai)
	Kairat ASHIRBEKOV (Aktobe Lento)
14	Sergey DITKOVSKIY (Aktobe Lento)
11	Andrei FINONCHENKO (Shakhtyor Karagandy)
	Nurken MAZBAYEV (FK Taraz)
10	Jafar IRISMETOV (Kairat Almaty)
	Didarklych URAZOV (Irtysh Pavlodar)
	Maxim NIZOVTSEV (Tobol Kostanai)

LEAGUE RESULTS/SCORERS/APPEARANCES/GOALS 2005

AKTOBE LENTO
Coach – Ravil Ramazanov

2005

Date	Opponent		Score	Scorers
3/4	Vostok Ust-Kamenogorsk	a	2-0	Mytrofanov 2 (1p)
9/4	Kairat Almaty	h	2-1	Silyutin, Malkov
16/4	Ekibastuzets Ekibastuz	h	2-0	Malkov, Mytrofanov
23/4	Zhenis Astana	a	2-0	Ditkovskiy, Malkov
30/4	Tobol Kostanai	h	2-1	Ditkovskiy, Bursuc
7/5	Irtysh Pavlodar	a	0-1	
11/5	Yesil-Bogatyr Petropavlovsk	h	2-0	Ditkovskiy, Stakhiv
21/5	Shakhtyor Karagandy	a	1-1	Ditkovskiy
25/5	Okzhetpes Kokshetau	h	2-1	Ashirbekov 2 (1p)
12/6	Ordabasy Shymkent	a	0-0	
18/6	FK Taraz	h	2-0	Ashirbekov, Ditkovskiy
25/6	FK Almaty	a	1-3	Ditkovskiy
29/6	Zhetysu Taldykorgan	h	2-1	Kitsak, Loginov
3/7	FK Atyrau	a	1-0	Ditkovskiy
9/7	Bolat Temirtau	h	3-1	Ashirbekov 2, Ditkovskiy
24/7	Bolat Temirtau	a	1-0	Shoitymov
30/7	FK Atyrau	h	1-0	Ditkovskiy
7/8	Zhetysu Taldykorgan	a	1-1	Ditkovskiy
20/8	FK Almaty	h	4-3	Ashirbekov 2 (1p), Kitsak, Silyutin
23/8	FK Taraz	a	4-3	Ditkovskiy, Malkov, Mytrofanov, Bursuc
10/9	Ordabasy Shymkent	h	1-0	Ashirbekov
17/9	Okzhetpes Kokshetau	a	1-0	Malkov
23/9	Shakhtyor Karagandy	h	2-1	Kitsak, Ashirbekov (p)
27/9	Yesil-Bogatyr Petropavlovsk	a	1-0	Ashirbekov (p)
1/10	Irtysh Pavlodar	h	3-1	Ashirbekov 2 (2p), Sokolenko
16/10	Tobol Kostanai	a	0-3	
22/10	Zhenis Astana	h	2-1	Ashirbekov 2 (2p)
28/10	Ekibastuzets Ekibastuz	a	2-1	Ashirbekov, Ditkovskiy
2/11	Kairat Almaty	a	0-2	
6/11	Vostok Ust-Kamenogorsk	h	3-0	Ditkovskiy 2, Silyutin

No	Name	Nat	Pos	Aps	(s)	Gls
20	Igor ABDUSHEYEV		M	1	(3)	
18	Kairat ASHIRBEKOV		M	23	(1)	15
26	Aleksandr BESSARAB	UKR	A	2	(5)	
25	Anatoliy BOGDANOV		M	13	(8)	
3	Iulian BURSUC	MOL	M	12	(11)	2
10	Sergei DITKOVSKIY		A	28	(2)	14
6	Vitaliy KITSAK		M	30		3
23	Georgiy KOLPAKOV		D	3		
17	Vladimir LOGINOV		A	3	(13)	1
15	Anatoliy MALKOV		A	26	(3)	5
9	Oleksandr MYTROFANOV	UKR	M	19		4
1	Roman NESTERENKO	UKR	G	26		
28	Aleksei OSIPOV	UKR			(6)	
4	Boris POLYAKOV		D	27		
19	Maxim SAMCHENKO		D	26		
2	Erlan SHOITYMOV		D	11	(6)	1
8	Andrei SILYUTIN	RUS	M	21	(6)	3
5	Andrei SOKOLENKO		D	24		1
11	Aleksandr STAKHIV		A	5	(7)	1
7	Yevgeniy SVESHNIKOV		M	26	(1)	
22	Andrei ZVETKOV		G	4	(1)	

FK ALMATY
Coach – Igor Romanov; (1/6/05) Antonius Kornelis Joor (HOL)

2005

Date	Opponent		Score	Scorers
3/4	Irtysh Pavlodar	h	0-1	
9/4	Yesil-Bogatyr Petropavlovsk	h	0-1	
17/4	Shakhtyor Karagandy	h	0-2	
23/4	Okzhetpes Kokshetau	a	1-3	Ostapenko
30/4	Ordabasy Shymkent	h	2-3	Ostapenko, og (Kozulin)
7/5	FK Taraz	h	1-2	Ostapenko
14/5	Kairat Almaty	h	1-1	Litvinenko
21/5	Zhetysu Taldykorgan	h	1-2	Litvinenko
25/5	FK Atyrau	a	0-1	
12/6	Bolat Temirtau	h	3-2	Litvinenko (p), Urazayev, Travin
18/6	Vostok Ust-Kamenogorsk	a	0-2	
25/6	Aktobe Lento	h	3-1	Litvinenko 3
29/6	Ekibastuzets Ekibastuz	a	1-1	Kovalev
3/7	Zhenis Astana	h	3-2	Urazayev, Ostapenko, Litvinenko
9/7	Tobol Kostanai	a	0-5	
24/7	Tobol Kostanai	h	0-2	
30/7	Zhenis Astana	a	0-1	
7/8	Ekibastuzets Ekibastuz	h	0-0	
20/8	Aktobe Lento	a	3-4	Boicenco, Azovskiy, Urazayev
23/8	Vostok Ust-Kamenogorsk	h	2-0	Azovskiy, Boicenco
10/9	Bolat Temirtau	a	2-1	Azovskiy, Ostapenko
17/9	FK Atyrau	h	0-1	
23/9	Zhetysu Taldykorgan	a	2-0	Azovskiy 2
27/9	Kairat Almaty	h	1-0	Travin
2/10	FK Taraz	h	0-1	
16/10	Ordabasy Shymkent	a	0-1	
23/10	Okzhetpes Kokshetau	h	2-0	Ostapenko, Urazayev (p)
28/10	Shakhtyor Karagandy	a	0-1	
1/11	Yesil-Bogatyr Petropavlovsk	a	2-0	Ostapenko, Shestakov
6/11	Irtysh Pavlodar	a	0-1	

Kazakhstan

FINAL LEAGUE TABLE 2005

		Pld	Home W	D	L	F	A	Away W	D	L	F	A	Total W	D	L	F	A	Pts
1	Aktobe Lento	30	15	0	0	33	11	7	4	4	17	16	22	4	4	50	27	70
2	Tobol Kostanai	30	13	2	0	36	9	8	4	3	17	12	21	6	3	53	21	69
3	Kairat Almaty	30	11	4	0	32	6	7	4	4	24	16	18	8	4	56	22	62
4	Shakhtyor Karagandy	30	13	1	1	23	4	6	1	8	14	18	19	2	9	37	22	59
5	Irtysh Pavlodar	30	13	0	2	34	9	5	3	7	17	15	18	3	9	51	24	57
6	Ordabasy Shymkent	30	11	2	2	20	8	3	5	7	10	19	14	7	9	30	27	49
7	Yesil-Bogatyr Petropavlovsk	30	10	3	2	26	7	5	0	10	12	18	15	3	12	38	25	48
8	Zhenis Astana	30	8	4	3	23	8	3	6	6	12	15	11	10	9	35	23	43
9	Okzhetpes Kokshetau	30	7	3	5	18	14	4	1	10	8	18	11	4	15	26	32	37
10	FK Atyrau	30	8	4	3	21	10	2	3	10	11	26	10	7	13	32	36	37
11	FK Taraz	30	6	4	5	22	16	4	2	9	10	20	10	6	14	32	36	36
12	Ekibastuzets Ekibastuz	30	6	7	2	17	10	2	3	10	13	22	8	10	12	30	32	34
13	FK Almaty	30	6	1	8	17	18	3	2	10	13	25	9	3	18	30	43	30
14	Vostok Ust-Kamenogorsk	30	6	1	8	16	21	3	0	12	8	28	9	1	20	24	49	28
15	Zhetysu Taldykorgan	30	2	4	9	11	24	2	3	10	17	36	4	7	19	28	60	19
16	Bolat Temirtau	30	0	1	14	8	35	0	0	15	7	53	0	1	29	15	88	1

No	Name	Nat	Pos	Aps	(s)	Gls
19	Konstantin ALEYNIKOV		A	4	(5)	
16	Aleksandr ALIYEV		G	1		
6	Egor AZOVSKIY		D	18	(4)	
5	Maxim AZOVSKIY		M	12	(5)	5
8	Grigory BABAYAN		M	3	(1)	
18	Arman BIRKURMANOV		D		(1)	
25	Evgheni BOICENCO	MOL	M	11	(1)	2
2	Arman BOLATBEK		D	20	(2)	
13	Vadim BOROVSKOY		M	21	(7)	
14	Iosif DILMAN		M	12	(3)	
25	Konstantin GOROVENKO		D	14	(1)	
17	Tairzhan IMINOV		M		(1)	
12	Vladimir IVANOV		M	3	(3)	
17	Yevgeniy KLIMOV	RUS	D	15		
24	Viktor KOVALEV		D	24		1
7	Sergei LARIN		M	23	(2)	
16	Pavel LEUS	LIT	G	14		
10	Oleg LITVINENKO		A	15	7	7
15	Yevgeniy MALININ	KRG	M	1	(4)	
18	Bilal NASYROV		M		(5)	
23	Sergei OSTAPENKO		A	24	(4)	7
22	Yerzhan SERGAZIN		G	14		
1	Andrei SHABANOV		G	1		
20	Aleksei SHAPURIN		A		(1)	
8	Kirill SHESTAKOV	RUS	M	13		1
9	Andrei TRAVIN		M	23	(1)	2
4	Erlan URAZAYEV		M	10	(15)	4
15	Sergei VASYTIN		D	1		
21	Rustam ZHAHANOV		D	1	(3)	
3	Abzal ZHUMABAYEV		D	28		
11	Vadim ZYRYANOV		A	4	(6)	

FK ATYRAU
Coach – Aleksandr Golokolosov; (23/5/05) (Murat Mynbayev);
(12/6/05) Sergey Timofeyev

2005

3/4	Zhenis Astana	h	1-0	Gura
16/4	Irtysh Pavlodar	h	3-0	Shvydko, Kostyuk (p), Gura
23/4	Yesil-Bogatyr Petropavlovsk	a	0-0	
30/4	Shakhtyor Karagandy	h	1-1	Kirov
7/5	Okzhetpes Kokshetau	a	1-3	Mochulyak (p)
10/5	Tobol Kostanai	a	2-3	Mochulyak, Kostyuk (p)
14/5	Ordabasy Shymkent	h	1-1	Fernando
21/5	FK Taraz	a	1-6	Zaitsev
25/5	FK Almaty	h	1-0	Fernando
12/6	Zhetysu Taldykorgan	a	1-1	Kostyuk
18/6	Kairat Almaty	a	0-3	
25/6	Bolat Temirtau	h	4-0	Kostyuk 2, Oganesov, Rodionov
28/6	Vostok Ust-Kamenogorsk	a	0-1	
3/7	Aktobe Lento	h	0-1	
9/7	Ekibastuzets Ekibastuz	a	1-1	Kravchenko
24/7	Ekibastuzets Ekibastuz	h	1-0	Kozhushko
30/7	Aktobe Lento	a	0-1	
7/8	Vostok Ust-Kamenogorsk	h	2-0	Tatishev, Kostyuk
20/8	Bolat Temirtau	a	2-0	Kostyuk, Aliyev
23/8	Kairat Almaty	h	2-2	Kravchenko, Aliyev, Kozhushko
10/9	Zhetysu Taldykorgan	h	3-2	Tatishev 2, Aliyev (p)
17/9	FK Almaty	a	1-0	Kozhushko
23/9	FK Taraz	h	0-0	
27/9	Ordabasy Shymkent	a	1-2	Gura
1/10	Okzhetpes Kokshetau	h	0-1	
16/10	Shakhtyor Karagandy	a	1-2	Bitarov
22/10	Yesil-Bogatyr Petropavlovsk	h	2-1	Gura, Kirov
28/10	Irtysh Pavlodar	a	0-1	
2/11	Tobol Kostanai	h	0-1	
6/11	Zhenis Astana	a	0-2	

No	Name	Nat	Pos	Aps	(s)	Gls
11	Redzhepmurat AGABAYEV		A	2	(7)	
6	Piraly ALIYEV		M	14		3
19	Maxim BERLIZEV		M	14	(2)	
5	Robert BITAROV	RUS	M	14	(1)	1
16	David CHICHVEISHVILI	GEO	D	15		
13	Valentin CHUREYEV		A	5	(8)	
10	José da Silva FERNANDO	BRA	M	7	(9)	2
20	Aleksandr GRIGORENKO		G	25		
15	Yuriy GURA		M	26	(1)	4
8	Vasil KIROV	BUL	M	12	(10)	2
7	Sergei KOSTYUK		M	24	(1)	7
11	Viktor KOZHUSHKO		M	15		2
3	Viktor KRAVCHENKO		D	15	(3)	2

Kazakhstan

No	Name	Nat	Pos	Aps	(s)	Gls
25	Yuriy KROTOV		D	3	(2)	
18	Zhiger KUKEYEV		M	3	(2)	
23	Vasiliy LOBASHOV		M		(4)	
9	Oleg MOCHULYAK		A	13	(2)	2
17	Anton OGANESOV		A	14	(4)	1
22	Timur PRIMZHANOV		M	1	(1)	
12	Denis RODIONOV		A	22		1
23	Ruslan SAKHALBAYEV		M		(5)	
16	Igor SHVYDKO		D	13		1
9	Beybit TATISHEV		A	10	(5)	3
5	Ante VUKUSIC	CRO	M		(6)	
24	Vyacheslav YEREMEYEV		M	2		
2	Andrei YEROKHIN		D	30		
14	Kairat YERSHEYEV		M	17	(4)	
4	Sergei ZAITSEV		D	9	(2)	1
1	Jan ZOLNA	BUL	G	5	(1)	

BOLAT TEMIRTAU
Coach – Shamil Khafizov; (24/7/05) Alexandr Nesterov

2005

Date	Opponent	h/a	Score	Scorers
3/4	Ekibastuzets Ekibastuz	h	1-4	Fritz
9/4	Zhenis Astana	a	0-4	
16/4	Tobol Kostanai	h	0-1	
23/4	Irtysh Pavlodar	a	0-3	
30/4	Yesil-Bogatyr Petropavlovsk	h	0-1	
7/5	Shakhtyor Karagandy	a	0-3	
14/5	Okzhetpes Kokshetau	h	0-3	
21/5	Ordabasy Shymkent	a	0-1	
25/5	FK Taraz	h	0-2	
12/6	FK Almaty	a	2-3	Kozhushko, Volodin
18/6	Zhetysu Taldykorgan	h	1-2	Sobko
25/6	FK Atyrau	a	0-4	
29/6	Kairat Almaty	a	0-5	
5/7	Vostok Ust-Kamenogorsk	h	0-2	
9/7	Aktobe Lento	a	1-3	Fritz
24/7	Aktobe Lento	h	1-1	Karinbayev
30/7	Vostok Ust-Kamenogorsk	a	0-3	
7/8	Kairat Almaty	h	2-6	Fritz, Khomenko
20/8	FK Atyrau	h	0-2	
23/8	Zhetysu Taldykorgan	a	2-3	Khomenko, Fritz
10/9	FK Almaty	h	1-2	Khomenko
17/9	FK Taraz	a	0-3	
23/9	Ordabasy Shymkent	h	1-2	Dyakov
27/9	Okzhetpes Kokshetau	a	1-2	Igumnov
1/10	Shakhtyor Karagandy	h	0-2	
15/10	Yesil-Bogatyr Petropavlovsk	a	0-7	
22/10	Irtysh Pavlodar	h	0-3	
28/10	Tobol Kostanai	a	0-5	
2/11	Zhenis Astana	h	1-2	Volodin
6/11	Ekibastuzets Ekibastuz	a	1-4	Bolshakov

No	Name	Nat	Pos	Aps	(s)	Gls
44	Mikhail ALEKSEYEV		G	30		
1	Samir ALIYEV		G		(1)	
10	Dmitriy BOLSHAKOV		M	22	(1)	1
22	Sergei CHERKASHIN		D	3	(7)	
7	Aleksei CHOBAN		M	13		
2	Aleksei DUSEKEYEV		D	23	(4)	
24	Denis DYAKOV		M	13		1
4	Sergei ELESKIN		D	1		
9	Andrei FRITZ		M	29		4
5	Nikolai GAVRISH		D	12	(2)	
19	Amiran GIGOLAYEV		M	10	(9)	
13	Aleksandr GRICHENKO		D	4		
14	Oleg GYCHAY		D	27	(2)	
15	Aleksandr IGUMNOV		M	20	(3)	1
1	Tahir ILAYEV		G		(3)	
13	Vitaliy IVASHKIN		D	3	(4)	
8	Talgat KABDULOV		M	2	(7)	
4	Sapar KARINBAYEV		D	8	(6)	1

No	Name	Nat	Pos	Aps	(s)	Gls
6	Andrei KAZANSKY		D	1	(1)	
17	Dmitriy KHOMENKO		A	10	(3)	3
17	Viktor KOZHUSHKO		M	13		1
12	Aleksei LISITZIN		M	16	(3)	
6	Ilnur MANGUTKIN		D	12	(2)	
7	Yevgeniy NESTEROV		D	9	(1)	
11	Artem NIKITENKO	RUS	M	8	(4)	
5	Vladislav NOSENKO	UKR	M	9		
8	Aleksandr SOBKO		M	8	(3)	1
	Andrei VOLODIN		M	10	(1)	2
3	Sergei ZAGORUYKO	UKR	M	14		
5	Ivan ZAVYALOV		M		(5)	

EKIBASTUZETS EKIBASTUZ
Coach – Vitaliy Sparyshev

2005

Date	Opponent	h/a	Score	Scorers
3/4	Bolat Temirtau	a	4-1	Zvonarenko 2, Razdrogin, Yakovenko
9/4	Vostok Ust-Kamenogorsk	h	2-0	Zvonarenko 2
16/4	Aktobe Lento	a	0-2	
23/4	Kairat Almaty	h	2-2	Yakovenko, Bulgakov
30/4	Zhenis Astana	h	1-1	Danayev (p)
7/5	Tobol Kostanai	a	1-1	Gefel
14/5	Irtysh Pavlodar	h	0-0	
21/5	Yesil-Bogatyr Petropavlovsk	a	1-2	Shabayev
25/5	Shakhtyor Karagandy	h	0-1	
12/6	Okzhetpes Kokshetau	a	0-1	
18/6	Ordabasy Shymkent	h	1-0	Gefel
25/6	FK Taraz	a	0-1	
29/6	FK Almaty	h	1-1	Yakovenko
3/7	Zhetysu Taldykorgan	a	4-3	Yakovenko 3 (2p), Efymov
9/7	FK Atyrau	h	1-1	Verteletskyi
24/7	FK Atyrau	a	0-1	
30/7	Zhetysu Taldykorgan	h	1-1	Semko
7/8	FK Almaty	a	0-0	
20/8	FK Taraz	h	1-0	Voinov
23/8	Ordabasy Shymkent	a	1-2	Gefel
10/9	Okzhetpes Kokshetau	h	1-0	Gefel
17/9	Shakhtyor Karagandy	a	0-2	
23/9	Yesil-Bogatyr Petropavlovsk	h	1-0	Zavyalov
27/9	Irtysh Pavlodar	a	0-1	
1/10	Tobol Kostanai	h	0-0	
16/10	Zhenis Astana	a	0-2	
22/10	Kairat Almaty	a	1-2	Voinov
28/10	Aktobe Lento	h	1-2	Gefel (p)
2/11	Vostok Ust-Kamenogorsk	a	1-1	Nemec
6/11	Bolat Temirtau	h	4-1	Gefel 2 (2p), Nemec, Shabayev

No	Name	Nat	Pos	Aps	(s)	Gls
5	Zurab ARCHVADZE	GEO	D	19		
26	Azamat AUBAKIROV		A	1	(8)	
23	Tlektes AUBAKIROV		M	7	(14)	
10	Aleksandr BULGAKOV		D	13	(9)	1
28	Andrei BURTSEV		A		(7)	
21	Aleksei DANAYEV		D	18	(2)	1
9	Taras DANILYUK		A	1	(5)	
6	Dmytro EFYMOV	UKR	M	21	(1)	1
20	Andrei GEFEL	RUS	M	20	(1)	7
7	Denis ISAKOV		D		(1)	
14	Farkhad MIRSALIMBAYEV		D	2	(5)	
27	Miroslav NEMEC	SVK	A	14		2
3	Andriy OKSIMEC	UKR	D	12		
19	Ilian PAMUKOV	BUL	D	21		
16	Viktor RASKULOV		G	4		
11	Vitaliy RAZDROGIN		A	24	(2)	1
8	Oleg SEMKO		M	24	(2)	1
2	Nail SHABAYEV		D	29		2
22	Denis SHADROV	RUS	M	1		
13	Ruslan SHISHKIN		D		(4)	

Kazakhstan

No	Name	Nat	Pos			Gls
25	Eduard STOLBOVOY		G	26		
4	Anatoliy VERTELETSKYI	UKR	M	25	(2)	1
18	Igor VOINOV		A	3	(12)	2
24	Serhiy YAKOVENKO	UKR	M	16		6
12	Andriy ZAVYALOV	UKR	M	11		1
17	Yuriy ZVONARENKO		A	18	(7)	4

IRTYSH PAVLODAR
Coach – Sergey Volgin

2005

Date	Opponent	h/a	Score	Scorers
3/4	FK Almaty	a	1-0	Tleshev
9/4	Zhetysu Taldykorgan	a	2-0	Sofroni 2
16/4	FK Atyrau	a	0-3	
23/4	Bolat Temirtau	h	3-0	Urazov 3
30/4	Vostok Ust-Kamenogorsk	a	5-1	Agapov, Agayev, Tleshev 3
7/5	Aktobe Lento	h	1-0	Andjelkovic
14/5	Ekibastuzets Ekibastuz	a	0-0	
21/5	Zhenis Astana	h	1-0	Tleshev (p)
25/5	Tobol Kostanai	a	1-2	Urazov
12/6	Kairat Almaty	a	0-1	
18/6	Yesil-Bogatyr Petropavlovsk	h	2-1	Tleshev, Agayev
25/6	Shakhtyor Karagandy	a	0-1	
29/6	Okzhetpes Kokshetau	h	3-0	Urazov, Tleshev (p), Zheylitbayev
3/7	Ordabasy Shymkent	a	0-1	
10/7	FK Taraz	h	5-1	Tleshev 2 (1p), Urazov 2, Sofroni
25/7	FK Taraz	a	1-1	Tleshev
31/7	Ordabasy Shymkent	h	2-0	Chernyshov, Tleshev
7/8	Okzhetpes Kokshetau	a	2-0	Zarechnyi, Noskov
20/8	Shakhtyor Karagandy	h	6-1	Zheylitbayev, Tleshev 3 (1p), Sofroni, Urazov
23/8	Yesil-Bogatyr Petropavlovsk	a	0-1	
10/9	Kairat Almaty	a	0-1	
17/9	Tobol Kostanai	h	1-2	Zheylitbayev
23/9	Zhenis Astana	a	1-1	Primak
27/9	Ekibastuzets Ekibastuz	h	1-0	Urazov
1/10	Aktobe Lento	a	1-3	Sukhomlinov
16/10	Vostok Ust-Kamenogorsk	h	3-2	Zheylitbayev, Sofroni, Tleshev
22/10	Bolat Temirtau	a	3-0	Tleshev 3
28/10	FK Atyrau	h	1-0	Tleshev
2/11	Zhetysu Taldykorgan	h	4-1	Tleshev, Sofroni, Zheylitbayev, og (Seryogin)
6/11	FK Almaty	h	1-0	Urazov

No	Name	Nat	Pos	Aps	(s)	Gls
23	Yuriy AGAPOV	RUS	M	11	(1)	1
7	Muslim AGAYEV		A	15	(3)	2
99	Miodrag ANDJELOVIC	SCG	A	3	(3)	1
20	Maksat BAISHANOV		M	12	(7)	
25	Goran BOSKOVIC	SCG	D	14	(1)	
3	Vladislav CHERNYSHOV		D	26		1
6	Lyubomir KUBICA	CZE	M	4	(2)	
9	Andrei KUCHERYAVICH		M	23		
19	Yvgeniy MESHKOV		M	7	(19)	
8	Nikolai NESTERENKO		M	21	(2)	
21	Vladimir NOSKOV		A	4	(7)	1
1	Yuriy NOVIKOV		G	25		
5	Yevgeniy OVCHINOV		D	24	(1)	
14	Maxim PRIMAK		M	20	(1)	1
13	Kirill PRYADKIN		G	5		
2	Bojan SIMIC	SCG	D	22	(1)	
10	Sergei SKORYKH		M	5	(3)	
15	Vyacheslav SOFRONI	MOL	A	15	(12)	6
23	Vladislav SUKHOMLINOV	UKR	M	8		1
18	Murat TLESHEV		A	19	(4)	20
11	Didarklych URAZOV	TRK	A	12	(10)	10
4	Ilya VOROTNIKOV		D	3		
12	Konstantin ZARECHNYI		M	11	(8)	1

| 17 | Serik ZHEYLITBAYEV | | M | 21 | (4) | 5 |

KAIRAT ALMATY
Coach – Alexey Petrushin (RUS); (27/7/05) (Vladimir Gulyamkhaidarov)

2005

Date	Opponent	h/a	Score	Scorers
2/4	Okzhetpes Kokshetau	h	1-0	Lovchev
9/4	Aktobe Lento	a	1-2	Karpenko
16/4	Ordabasy Shymkent	h	3-0	Dicu, Fomenka, Buleshev
23/4	Ekibastuzets Ekibastuz	h	2-2	Sosnovschi, Smakov (p)
29/4	FK Taraz	h	4-1	Fomenka 3, Sosnovschi
7/5	Zhenis Astana	a	2-1	Karpovich, Aksenov
14/5	FK Almaty	h	1-1	Buleshev
21/5	Tobol Kostanai	a	1-2	Dicu
26/5	Zhetysu Taldykorgan	h	1-1	Buleshev
12/6	Irtysh Pavlodar	a	1-0	Smakov (p)
18/6	FK Atyrau	h	3-0	Buleshev 3
25/6	Yesil-Bogatyr Petropavlovsk	a	2-2	Irismetov J., Aksenov
29/6	Bolat Temirtau	h	5-0	Buleshev, Asanbayev, Irismetov J., Fomenka, Tlehugov
3/7	Shakhtyor Karagandy	a	0-2	
30/7	Shakhtyor Karagandy	h	2-1	Irismetov J. 2
7/8	Bolat Temirtau	a	6-2	Irismetov J., Fomenka 3, Lutu, Aliyev
20/8	Yesil-Bogatyr Petropavlovsk	h	3-0	Irismetov J., Fomenka, Tlehugov
23/8	FK Atyrau	a	2-2	Smakov (p), Tlehugov
10/9	Irtysh Pavlodar	h	1-0	Lovchev
13/9	Vostok Ust-Kamenogorsk	a	2-0	Lutu, Bogomolov
17/9	Zhetysu Taldykorgan	a	3-0	Smakov 2 (1p), Irismetov J.
23/9	Tobol Kostanai	h	0-0	
27/9	FK Almaty	a	0-1	
1/10	Zhenis Astana	h	1-1	Smakov (p)
16/10	FK Taraz	a	1-0	Irismetov J.
19/10	Vostok Ust-Kamenogorsk	h	3-0	Lutu, Karpenko 2
22/10	Ekibastuzets Ekibastuz	h	2-1	Nurdauletov, Lutu
28/10	Ordabasy Shymkent	a	1-0	Irismetov J.
2/11	Aktobe Lento	h	2-0 *	Irismetov J., Smakov
6/11	Okzhetpes Kokshetau	a	0-0	

No	Name	Nat	Pos	Aps	(s)	Gls
24	Renat ABDULIN		D	22	(1)	
23	Yuriy AKSENOV		M	10	(4)	2
22	Ali ALIYEV		M	9	(8)	1
5	Vitaliy ARTEMOV		D	9	(1)	
6	Ulugbek ASANBAYEV		M	15	(1)	1
27	Andrei BOGOMOLOV		M	8	(8)	1
29	Sergei BOICHENKO		G	9		
10	Alibek BULESHEV		A	10	(1)	7
13	Cristian DICU	ROM	M	11	(7)	2
26	Arturas FOMENKO	LIT	A	15	(3)	9
7	Farhadbek IRISMETOV		M	14	(2)	
11	Jafar IRISMETOV	UZB	A	16	(6)	10
16	Viktor KARPENKO		M	8	(6)	3
21	Andrei KARPOVICH		M	13	(3)	1
17	Valeriy LIKHOBABENKO		M	14	(3)	
28	Yevgeniy LOVCHEV		M	22	(5)	2
12	Ion Ionut LUTU	ROM	M	15		4
1	Yevgeniy NABOYCHENKO	TRK	G	6		
15	Kairat NURDAULETOV		M	11	(10)	1
3	Dmitriy PROTORCHIN		D	11	(1)	
8	Samat SMAKOV		M	27	(1)	7
25	Adrian SOSNOVSCHI	MOL	D	12	(1)	2
9	Arsen TLEHUGOV		A	8	(6)	3
4	Kairat UTABAYEV		D	20	(2)	
18	Ilya YUROV		G	15		

OKZHETPES KOKSHETAU
Coach – Vladimir Fomichev

Kazakhstan

2005

Date	Opponent	H/A	Score	Scorers
2/4	Kairat Almaty	a	0-1	
9/4	Ordabasy Shymkent	a	0-2	
16/4	FK Taraz	a	0-0	
23/4	FK Almaty	h	3-1	Barsukov, Dosmanbetov, og (Kovalev)
30/4	Zhetysu Taldykorgan	a	0-2	
7/5	FK Atyrau	h	3-1	Lashnikov, Galich, Barsukov
14/5	Bolat Temirtau	a	3-0	Barsukov, Galich, Dosmanbetov (p)
21/5	Vostok Ust-Kamenogorsk	h	1-0	Barsukov
25/5	Aktobe Lento	a	1-2	Osipenco
12/6	Ekibastuzets Ekibastuz	h	1-0	Dosmanbetov
18/6	Zhenis Astana	a	1-0	Dosmanbetov
25/6	Tobol Kostanai	h	1-2	Udalov
29/6	Irtysh Pavlodar	a	0-3	
3/7	Yesil-Bogatyr Petropavlovsk	h	1-4	Udalov
9/7	Shakhtyor Karagandy	a	0-1	
24/7	Shakhtyor Karagandy	h	0-1	
30/7	Yesil-Bogatyr Petropavlovsk	a	0-2	
7/8	Irtysh Pavlodar	h	0-2	
20/8	Tobol Kostanai	a	0-1	
23/8	Zhenis Astana	h	0-0	
10/9	Ekibastuzets Ekibastuz	a	0-1	
17/9	Aktobe Lento	h	0-1	
23/9	Vostok Ust-Kamenogorsk	a	2-1	Osipenco 2 (1p)
27/9	Bolat Temirtau	h	1-2	Lashnikov, Dosmanbetov
1/10	FK Atyrau	a	1-0	Dosmanbetov
16/10	Zhetysu Taldykorgan	h	4-0	Udalov 3, Osipenco
23/10	FK Almaty	a	0-2	
28/10	FK Taraz	h	1-0	Lashnikov
2/11	Ordabasy Shymkent	h	1-1	Dosmanbetov
6/11	Kairat Almaty	h	0-0	

No	Name	Nat	Pos	Aps	(s)	Gls
13	Artem ALEKHIN		M		(2)	
7	Andrei BARSUKOV		M	25	(4)	4
1	Arslan BEGNEPESOV	TRK	G	1	(2)	
10	Serik DOSMANBETOV		M	24	(1)	7
30	Adylet ESHENKULOV		M	1	(5)	
24	Oleg FISTICAN	MOL	D	28		
18	Ilya FOMICHEV		D	27	(1)	
23	Andrei FOSCHYI		M		(1)	
20	Dmitriy GALICH		A	13	(5)	2
14	Kirill KEKER		D	27	(1)	
27	Alik KHAIDAROV	TRK	D	22	(3)	
9	Sergei IVANOV		M	12	(7)	
3	Oleg LASHNIKOV		D	29		3
11	Maxim MIROSHNICHENKO		D	4	(9)	
16	Andrei NENASHEV		G	29		
8	Iuri OSIPENCO	MOL	M	28		4
12	Igor PAVLYUK		M	7	(9)	
4	Gennadiy PUSCA	MOL	M	24	(2)	
21	Sergei PYSHMYNZEV	RUS	A		(7)	
25	Pavel UDALOV		A	9	(13)	5
17	Yevgeniy VALENTYKEVIC		D	1	(8)	
19	Yevgeniy ZAKHARCHENKO		D	19	(7)	

ORDABASY SHYMKENT
Coach – Andrey Vaganov

2005

Date	Opponent	H/A	Score	Scorers
3/4	Shakhtyor Karagandy	h	2-0	Zhadigerov, Krokhmal
9/4	Okzhetpes Kokshetau	h	2-0	Karakulov (p), Krokhmal
16/4	Kairat Almaty	a	0-3	
23/4	FK Taraz	h	1-0	Krokhmal
30/4	FK Almaty	a	3-2	Krokhmal 3
7/5	Zhetysu Taldykorgan	h	2-1	Nazarov S., Krokhmal
14/5	FK Atyrau	a	1-1	Shapovalov
21/5	Bolat Temirtau	h	1-0	Karakulov (p)
25/5	Vostok Ust-Kamenogorsk	a	1-0	Vlasichev
12/6	Aktobe Lento	h	0-0	
18/6	Ekibastuzets Ekibastuz	a	0-1	
25/6	Zhenis Astana	h	0-0	
29/6	Tobol Kostanai	a	0-3	
3/7	Irtysh Pavlodar	h	1-0	Krokhmal (p)
9/7	Yesil-Bogatyr Petropavlovsk	a	0-1	
24/7	Yesil-Bogatyr Petropavlovsk	h	2-0	Tzhibayuli, Nazarov D.
31/7	Irtysh Pavlodar	a	0-2	
7/8	Tobol Kostanai	h	1-4	Nazarov D.
20/8	Zhenis Astana	a	1-1	Krokhmal
23/8	Ekibastuzets Ekibastuz	h	2-1	Tzhibayuli, Krokhmal
10/9	Aktobe Lento	a	0-1	
17/9	Vostok Ust-Kamenogorsk	h	3-0	Zhadigerov, Shapovalov, Krokhmal
23/9	Bolat Temirtau	a	2-1	Shapovalov, Krokhmal
27/9	FK Atyrau	h	2-1	Krokhmal 2
1/10	Zhetysu Taldykorgan	a	1-1	Krokhmal (p)
16/10	FK Almaty	h	1-0	Karakulov
22/10	FK Taraz	a	0-0	
28/10	Kairat Almaty	h	0-1	
2/11	Okzhetpes Kokshetau	a	1-1	Karakulov
6/11	Shakhtyor Karagandy	a	0-1	

No	Name	Nat	Pos	Aps	(s)	Gls
19	Zhandos AKHMETOV		M	25	(2)	
16	Bairam BERDYYEV	TRK	G	1		
34	Zhasulan DIKHANOV		G	12	(1)	
1	Oleg GORVITS		G	17		
11	Marat ISKAKOV		A	2	(3)	
7	Kuanysh KARAKULOV		M	24		4
9	Ildar KASYMOV		M	6	(5)	
22	Sergei KOZULIN		D	28	(1)	
23	Aleksandr KROKHMAL		A	26	(2)	15
15	Sergei MAKSIMOV		M	11	(7)	
25	Aleksandr MOCHINOV	UZB	A	2	(5)	
4	Mukhtar MUKHTAROV		D	19	(2)	
21	Spartak MURTAZAYEV		D	12	(2)	
8	Dilmurad NAZAROV	UZB	A	11	(2)	2
8	Sherzod NAZAROV	UZB	A	6		1
6	Yerkin NAZAROV	UZB	M	6	(1)	
20	Azat NURGALIYEV		M	13	(13)	
25	Yevhen RYMSHIN	UKR	A	3	(3)	
13	Oleg SABIROV		D	28		
3	Valeriy SHAPOVALOV	UKR	D	26		3
28	Aleksandr SOBKOVICH		M	6	(5)	
11	Aleksandr SUKHAREV		A	1	(6)	
14	Alisher TAZHIBAYULI		M	14	(8)	2
17	Andrei VLASICHEV	UZB	A	15	(6)	1
6	Volodymyr YAREMKO	UKR	M		(1)	
2	Roman YURTAYEV		A	1	(1)	
18	Askar ZHADIGEROV		M	12	(6)	2
5	Sanat ZHUMAKHANOV		M	3	(7)	

SHAKHTYOR KARAGANDY
Coach – Vakhid Masudov

2005

Date	Opponent	H/A	Score	Scorers
3/4	Ordabasy Shymkent	a	0-2	
9/4	FK Taraz	h	1-0	Kornienko
13/4	Tobol Kostanai	a	0-1	
17/4	FK Almaty	a	2-0	Peric 2
23/4	Zhetysu Taldykorgan	h	2-1	Kornienko, Finonchenko
30/4	FK Atyrau	a	1-1	Peric
7/5	Bolat Temirtau	h	3-0	Curcic, Glushko, Finonchenko
14/5	Vostok Ust-Kamenogorsk	a	0-1	
21/5	Aktobe Lento	h	1-1	Kornienko
25/5	Ekibastuzets Ekibastuz	a	1-0	Kashtanov
12/6	Zhenis Astana	h	0-1	
25/6	Irtysh Pavlodar	h	1-0	Finonchenko
29/6	Yesil-Bogatyr Petropavlovsk	a	0-1	
3/7	Kairat Almaty	h	2-0	Nasiru, Lunev
9/7	Okzhetpes Kokshetau	h	1-0	Curcic

Kazakhstan

24/7	Okzhetpes Kokshetau	a	1-0	Finonchenko
30/7	Kairat Almaty	a	1-2	Finonchenko
7/8	Yesil-Bogatyr Petropavlovsk	h	1-0	Kornienko (p)
20/8	Irtysh Pavlodar	a	1-6	Finonchenko
23/8	Tobol Kostanai	h	2-0	Finonchenko 2
10/9	Zhenis Astana	a	0-1	
17/9	Ekibastuzets Ekibastuz	h	2-0	Peric 2
23/9	Aktobe Lento	a	1-2	Nasiru
27/9	Vostok Ust-Kamenogorsk	h	3-0	Peric, Finonchenko, Kornienko
1/10	Bolat Temirtau	a	2-0	Kornienko, Imankulov
16/10	FK Atyrau	h	2-1	Finonchenko 2 (1p)
22/10	Zhetysu Taldykorgan	a	1-0	Nasiru
28/10	FK Almaty	h	1-0	Peric
2/11	FK Taraz	a	3-1	Glushko, Byakov 2
6/11	Ordabasy Shymkent	h	1-0	Kornienko

No	Name	Nat	Pos	Aps	(s)	Gls
6	Rakhman ASUHANOV		M	1	(2)	
2	Igor AVDEYEV		D	19	(2)	
9	Dmitriy BYAKOV		M	16	(3)	2
5	Vladica CURCIC	SCG	M	17	(1)	2
24	Denis DYAKOV		M	1	(1)	
14	Andrei FINONCHENKO		A	26	(2)	11
19	Mikhail GLUSHKO		A	18	(10)	2
11	Ruslan IMANKULOV		A	1	(4)	1
20	Zeljko JOKSIMOVIC	SCG	D	23		
22	Ashat KADYRKULOV		M	21	(1)	
7	Vladimir KASHTANOV		M	22	(2)	1
8	Rafael KHAMIDULOV		M	5	(8)	
3	Dmitriy KHOMENKO		A		(1)	
17	Sergei KIROV		D	9	(3)	
15	Oleg KORNIENKO		D	27	(1)	7
23	Yevgeniy KRAVCHUK		A		(4)	
99	David LORIA		G	30		
21	Yevgeniy LUNEV		A	8	(7)	1
25	Abdullah NASIRU	NGA	M	19	(5)	3
12	Ivan PERIC	SCG	A	16	(4)	7
4	Vyacheslav RUSNAK	MOL	M	22	(3)	
13	Serik SAGYNDYKOV		D	13	(6)	
1	Sergei SARANA	UKR	G		(1)	
18	Igor SHEVCHENKO		M	3	(6)	
10	Maxim SHEVCHENKO		M	10	(8)	

FK TARAZ
Coach – Yuriy Konkov; (22/8/05) Sergei Tagiyev

2005

3/4	Yesil-Bogatyr Petropavlovsk	h	1-0	Mazbayev (p)
9/4	Shakhtyor Karagandy	a	0-1	
16/4	Okzhetpes Kokshetau	h	0-0	
23/4	Ordabasy Shymkent	a	0-1	
29/4	Kairat Almaty	a	1-4	Mazbayev
7/5	FK Almaty	h	2-1	Mirzabayev (p), Niyazymbetov
14/5	Zhetysu Taldykorgan	a	2-0	Mazbayev, Gurtuyev
21/5	FK Atyrau	h	6-1	Gurtuyev 3, Mirzabayev (p), Yakovlev, Ivanov
25/5	Bolat Temirtau	a	2-0	Krendelev, Gurtuyev
12/6	Vostok Ust-Kamenogorsk	h	0-1	
18/6	Aktobe Lento	a	0-2	
25/6	Ekibastuzets Ekibastuz	h	1-0	Gurtuyev
29/6	Zhenis Astana	a	1-1	Mazbayev
3/7	Tobol Kostanai	h	0-1	
10/7	Irtysh Pavlodar	a	1-5	og (Simic)
25/7	Irtysh Pavlodar	h	1-1	Mazbayev (p)
31/7	Tobol Kostanai	a	0-1	
7/8	Zhenis Astana	h	1-1	Mazbayev (p)
20/8	Ekibastuzets Ekibastuz	a	0-1	
23/8	Aktobe Lento	h	3-4	Yurist, Krendelev, Yakovlev (p)
10/9	Vostok Ust-Kamenogorsk	a	2-0	Krendelev, Mazbayev
17/9	Bolat Temirtau	h	3-0	Mazbayev, Gurtuyev, Krendelev
23/9	FK Atyrau	a	0-0	
27/9	Zhetysu Taldykorgan	h	3-2	Mazbayev 2 (1p), Niyazymbetov
2/10	FK Almaty	a	1-0	Mazbayev
16/10	Kairat Almaty	h	0-1	
22/10	Ordabasy Shymkent	a	0-0	
28/10	Okzhetpes Kokshetau	a	0-1	
2/11	Shakhtyor Karagandy	h	1-3	Baimeshov
6/11	Yesil-Bogatyr Petropavlovsk	a	0-3	

No	Name	Nat	Pos	Aps	(s)	Gls
28	Petro ANISIM		D	21	(3)	
12	Eldar BAIMESHOV		D	3		1
23	Paata BERISHVILI	RUS	M	4		
9	Ashat BORANTAYEV		M	20	(3)	
5	Yuriy BORDOLIMOV	TRK	D	22		
25	Ruslan ESATOV		M	2	(2)	
32	Egor GLADKOV		M	4	(1)	
24	Vladimir GURTUYEV		A	26	(2)	7
20	Aleksandr IGNATIYEV		M	1	(2)	
8	Sergei IVANOV		M	9	(12)	1
11	Vyacheslav KRENDELEV	TRK	A	24	(4)	4
4	Nurtaz KURGULIN		M	7	(6)	
17	Vladimir MATSIGURA		D	4	(1)	
10	Nurken MAZBAYEV		A	22	(3)	11
1	Igor MIKHAILOV	UZB	G	12	(1)	
6	Nurmat MIRZABAYEV		M	16	(5)	2
13	Oleg NEDASHKOVSKI		A	3	(2)	
7	Azamat NIYAZYMBETOV		M	21		2
32	Vladimir PANTYSHENKO	RUS	A	1	(7)	
23	Dmitriy PAVLOV		M	2		
3	Olzhas RAKHIMULY		M	1	(1)	
14	Vyacheslav SOBOLEV		M	12	(3)	
16	Sergei STEPANENKO		G	18		
19	Kairat SULEY		A	2	(1)	
22	Vitaliy USHAKOV		M	18	(5)	
21	Vladimir YAKOVLEV		A	21	4	2
15	Erlan YELEUSINOV		D	25	(1)	
18	Vitaliy YEVSTIGNEYEV		M	3	(6)	
17	Dmitriy YURIST		A	6	(7)	1

TOBOL KOSTANAI
Coach – Vladimir Pachko; (20/5/05) Dmitriy Ogay

2005

3/4	Zhetysu Taldykorgan	a	0-0	
13/4	Shakhtyor Karagandy	h	1-0	Bakayev
16/4	Bolat Temirtau	a	1-0	Dimitrov
23/4	Vostok Ust-Kamenogorsk	h	2-1	Kharabara, Bakayev (p)
30/4	Aktobe Lento	a	1-2	Nizovtsev
7/5	Ekibastuzets Ekibastuz	h	1-1	Bakayev
10/5	FK Atyrau	h	3-2	Bakayev 2, Ryzhevskiy
14/5	Zhenis Astana	a	0-4	
21/5	Kairat Almaty	h	2-1	Strakhanovich, Yurin
25/5	Irtysh Pavlodar	a	2-1	Bakayev, Dimitrov
12/6	Yesil-Bogatyr Petropavlovsk	a	1-1	Zhumaskaliyev
25/6	Okzhetpes Kokshetau	a	2-1	Dimitrov, Nizovtsev
29/6	Ordabasy Shymkent	h	3-0	Zhumaskaliyev 3
3/7	FK Taraz	a	1-0	Kharabara
9/7	FK Almaty	h	5-0	Shkurin, Zhumaskaliyev, Nizovtsev, Yurin, Nurmagambetov
24/7	FK Almaty	a	2-0	Nizovtsev (p), Bakayev
31/7	FK Taraz	h	1-0	Nizovtsev
7/8	Ordabasy Shymkent	a	4-1	Kharabara, Nizovtsev (p), Zhumaskaliyev, Bakayev
20/8	Okzhetpes Kokshetau	h	1-0	og (Zakharchenko)
23/8	Shakhtyor Karagandy	a	0-2	

Kazakhstan

11/9	Yesil-Bogatyr Petropavlovsk	h	2-1	Zhumaskaliyev 2
17/9	Irtysh Pavlodar	a	2-1	Bakayev, Nizovtsev (p)
23/9	Kairat Almaty	a	0-0	
27/9	Zhenis Astana	h	1-1	Kharabara
1/10	Ekibastuzets Ekibastuz	a	0-0	
16/10	Aktobe Lento	h	3-0	Nizovtsev, Bakayev (p), Mukanov
23/10	Vostok Ust-Kamenogorsk	a	2-0	Nizovtsev, Garkusha
28/10	Bolat Temirtau	h	5-0	Bakayev 2 (1p), Zhumaskaliyev, Garkusha, Lotov
2/11	FK Atyrau	a	1-0	Bakayev (p)
6/11	Zhetysu Taldykorgan	h	4-1	Bakayev 2, Nizovtsev, Kotov

No	Name	Nat	Pos	Aps	(s)	Gls
21	Veselin ATANASOV	BUL	D	4	(1)	
5	Pyotr BADLO		D	23	(1)	
10	Ulugbek BAKAYEV	UZB	A	25	(3)	15
2	Aleksandr CHAYKA		M	10	(2)	
3	Stanimir DIMITROV	BUL	M	27		3
14	Valeriy GARKUSHA		A		(6)	2
77	Dias KAMELOV		M	7	(1)	
13	Andrei KHARABARA	RUS	M	22	(6)	4
6	Konstantin KOTOV		M	12	(5)	1
15	Oleg LOTOV		D	25	(5)	1
17	Denis MASHKARIN	RUS	D	5	(1)	
1	Andrei MOREV		G	24		
18	Daniyar MUKANOV		M	23	(2)	1
11	Maxim NIZOVTSEV		M	29	(1)	10
19	Vyacheslav NURMAGAMBETOV		A	7	(8)	1
17	Anatoli OSTAP	MOL	M	5	(5)	
25	Pavel RYZHEVSKIY	BLS	A	1	(5)	1
20	Levan SANIKIDZE	GEO	M		(2)	
40	Valeriy SHANTALOSOV		G	6	(1)	
12	Andrei SHKURIN		D	21	(1)	1
26	Igor SOLOSHENKO		D		(4)	
8	Oleg STRAKHANOVICH	BLS	M	9	(1)	1
7	Murat SUYMAGAMBETOV		A	2	(14)	
20	Andrei SYTCHIKHIN		D	7	(2)	
24	Igor YURIN		M	17	(5)	2
9	Nurbol ZHUMASKALIYEV		M	19	(3)	9

VOSTOK UST-KAMENOGORSK
Coach – Sergei Gorokhovodatskiy

2005

3/4	Aktobe Lento	h	0-2	
9/4	Ekibastuzets Ekibastuz	a	0-2	
16/4	Zhenis Astana	h	2-1	Shakin, Kenzhehanov
23/4	Tobol Kostanai	a	1-2	Kenzhehanov
30/4	Irtysh Pavlodar	h	1-5	Gogiashvili
7/5	Yesil-Bogatyr Petropavlovsk	a	0-1	
14/5	Shakhtyor Karagandy	h	1-0	Kenzhehanov
21/5	Okzhetpes Kokshetau	a	0-1	
25/5	Ordabasy Shymkent	h	0-1	
12/6	FK Taraz	a	1-0	Shakin
18/6	FK Almaty	h	2-0	Gogiashvili, Shakin
25/6	Zhetysu Taldykorgan	a	2-0	Meskini, Shakin
28/6	FK Atyrau	h	1-0	Shakin
5/7	Bolat Temirtau	a	2-0	Gogiashvili, Kenzhehanov
30/7	Bolat Temirtau	h	3-0	Shakin 3
7/8	FK Atyrau	a	0-2	
20/8	Zhetysu Taldykorgan	h	4-2	Meskini, Gogiashvili 2 (1p), Shakin
23/8	FK Almaty	a	0-2	
10/9	FK Taraz	h	0-2	
13/9	Kairat Almaty	a	0-2	
17/9	Ordabasy Shymkent	a	0-2	
23/9	Okzhetpes Kokshetau	h	1-2	Kenzhehanov
27/9	Shakhtyor Karagandy	a	0-3	
1/10	Yesil-Bogatyr Petropavlovsk	h	0-1	
16/10	Irtysh Pavlodar	a	2-3	Tarasov, Kenzhehanov
19/10	Kairat Almaty	a	0-3	
23/10	Tobol Kostanai	h	0-2	
28/10	Zhenis Astana	a	0-3	
2/11	Ekibastuzets Ekibastuz	h	1-1	Shatokhin
6/11	Aktobe Lento	a	0-3	

No	Name	Nat	Pos	Aps	(s)	Gls
12	Andrei ANASHKIN		M	1	(3)	
16	Sergei DYAKONU	MOL	G	5		
26	Bakhut ESHMUKHAMBETOV		M		(1)	
10	Giorgi GOGIASHVILI	RUS	A	26	(1)	5
20	Viktor GONCHAROV		M	16	(3)	
19	Denis IZMAILOV		A	2	(6)	
1	Nikolai KALYABIN		G	3		
9	Daniyar KENZHEHANOV		A	28		6
3	Aleksandr KIROV		D	18	(3)	
17	Valeriy KUZNETSOV		D		(1)	
8	Denis MAMONOV		D	14	(11)	
2	Sergei MASLENOV		D	22	(1)	
24	Bairamdyrdy MEREDOV	TRK	D	13	(1)	
7	Youssef MESKINI	MAR	M	28		2
5	Aleksandr MOSKALENKO		D	25		
18	Daulet NURASYLOV		A	1	(2)	
22	Roman PULTER		D	2		
15	Andrei PUSTOVALOV		A	1	(1)	
6	Aleksei SHAKIN		M	28		9
19	Sergei SHATOKHIN	RUS	A	5	(8)	1
4	Igor SHESNOKOV		D	11		
14	Anatoliy STAVILA	MOL	M	9	(13)	
23	Vyacheslav SUDAREV	TRK	M	8	(3)	
30	Vladimir SULEYMANOV	RUS	G	14		
21	Yevgeniy TARASOV		D	20		1
25	Yuriy TSYGALKO	BLS	G	8		
13	Pavel YAKUPOV		A	3	19	
11	Maxim ZUYEV		D	19	(3)	

YESIL-BOGATYR PETROPAVLOVSK
Coach – Oirat Saduov

2005

3/4	FK Taraz	a	0-1	
9/4	FK Almaty	a	1-0	Chukhleba
16/4	Zhetysu Taldykorgan	a	2-0	Berdyyev, Chukhleba
23/4	FK Atyrau	h	0-0	
30/4	Bolat Temirtau	a	1-0	Osadchiy
7/5	Vostok Ust-Kamenogorsk	h	1-0	Voskanyan
11/5	Aktobe Lento	a	0-2	
21/5	Ekibastuzets Ekibastuz	h	2-1	Voskanyan 2
25/5	Zhenis Astana	a	0-1	
12/6	Tobol Kostanai	h	1-1	Voskanyan
18/6	Irtysh Pavlodar	a	1-2	Voskanyan
25/6	Kairat Almaty	h	2-2	Kalyubin, og (Irismetov)
29/6	Shakhtyor Karagandy	h	1-0	Berdyyev
3/7	Okzhetpes Kokshetau	a	4-1	Lobadovskiy 2 (1p), Guzenko, Voskanyan
9/7	Ordabasy Shymkent	h	1-0	Yurevich
24/7	Ordabasy Shymkent	a	0-2	
30/7	Okzhetpes Kokshetau	h	2-0	Kishchenko, Kalyubin
7/8	Shakhtyor Karagandy	a	0-1	
20/8	Kairat Almaty	a	0-3	
23/8	Irtysh Pavlodar	h	1-0	Voskanyan
11/9	Tobol Kostanai	a	1-2	Guzenko
17/9	Zhenis Astana	h	1-0	Berdyyev
23/9	Ekibastuzets Ekibastuz	a	0-1	
27/9	Aktobe Lento	h	0-1	
1/10	Vostok Ust-Kamenogorsk	a	1-0	Grigoryan
15/10	Bolat Temirtau	h	7-0	Kalyubin 3 (1p), Agabayev 2, Yurevich, Tadzhiev (p)
22/10	FK Atyrau	a	1-2	Voskanyan
28/10	Zhetysu Taldykorgan	h	4-0	Voskanyan, Yurevich 2,

Kazakhstan

1/11	FK Almaty	h	0-2		Averchenko
6/11	FK Taraz	h	3-0		Chukhleba (p), Gevorkyan, Lobadovskiy

No	Name	Nat	Pos	Aps	(s)	Gls
11	Redzhepmurat AGABAYEV		A	5	(5)	2
17	Akhmet AKHMETZHANOV		M		(1)	
24	Yevgeniy AVERCHENKO		A		(13)	1
2	Omar BERDYYEV	TRK	D	26		3
18	Yuriy CHUKHLEBA		M	29		3
1	Sergei DAVYDENKO		G	3	(1)	
19	Artur GEVORKYAN	TRK	M	6	(5)	1
13	Igor GORYACHEV		D	12	(7)	
16	David GRIGORYAN	ARM	M	20		1
4	Andrei GUZENKO		D	26	(1)	2
15	Sergei KALYUBIN		M	22	(6)	5
25	Dmitriy KISHCHENKO		D	25	(1)	
9	Sergei LOBADOVSKIY		A	20	(10)	3
5	Sergei OSADCHIY		D	26		1
10	Konstantin PANIN	UKR	M	16	(1)	
74	Daniil RIKHARD		G	27		
3	Rustam SHAIMARDANOV		D	2	(5)	
12	Stanislav SHULYAK		M		(1)	
14	Nikolay SOLOMIN		A		(3)	
6	Tomas STASTKA	CZE	D	26		
35	Zaynitdin TADZHIYEV	UZB	A	14	(5)	1
20	Aram VOSKANYAN	ARM	A	23	(1)	9
21	Sergei YUREVICH		A	2	(15)	4

ZHENIS ASTANA
Coach – Vladimir Mukhanov; (29/6/05) (Baurzhan Baimukhamedov); (9/7/05) Vladimir Mukhanov

2005

3/4	FK Atyrau	a	0-1		
9/4	Bolat Temirtau	h	4-0		Komadina, Lunin 3
16/4	Vostok Ust-Kamenogorsk	a	1-2		Yermak
23/4	Aktobe Lento	h	0-2		
30/4	Ekibastuzets Ekibastuz	a	1-1		Nilton Mendes (p)
7/5	Kairat Almaty	h	1-2		Drozdov
14/5	Tobol Kostanai	h	4-0		Komadina, Yermak 2, Shishkin
21/5	Irtysh Pavlodar	a	0-1		
25/5	Yesil-Bogatyr Petropavlovsk	h	1-0		Nilton Mendes (p)
12/6	Shakhtyor Karagandy	a	1-0		Filippenkov
18/6	Okzhetpes Kokshetau	h	0-1		
25/6	Ordabasy Shymkent	a	0-0		
29/6	FK Taraz	h	2-3		Kumisbekov
3/7	FK Almaty	a	2-3		Nilton Mendes 2
9/7	Zhetysu Taldykorgan	h	0-0		
24/7	Zhetysu Taldykorgan	a	1-0		Voronkin
30/7	FK Almaty	h	2-0		Golovskoi 2 (1p)
7/8	FK Taraz	a	1-1		Beganskiy
20/8	Ordabasy Shymkent	h	1-1		Kosolapov
23/8	Okzhetpes Kokshetau	a	0-0		
10/9	Shakhtyor Karagandy	h	1-0		Golovskoi (p)
17/9	Yesil-Bogatyr Petropavlovsk	a	0-1		
23/9	Irtysh Pavlodar	h	1-1		Khokhlov
27/9	Tobol Kostanai	a	1-1		Sergienko
1/10	Kairat Almaty	a	1-1		Nilton Mendes
16/10	Ekibastuzets Ekibastuz	h	2-0		Nilton Mendes, Golovskoi
22/10	Aktobe Lento	a	1-2		Golovskoi
28/10	Vostok Ust-Kamenogorsk	h	3-0		Nilton Mendes (p), Beganskiy, Khokhlov
2/11	Bolat Temirtau	a	2-1		Beganskiy, Mochulyak
6/11	FK Atyrau	h	2-0		Beganskiy 2

No	Name	Nat	Pos	Aps	(s)	Gls
3	Sergei ANDREYEV		D	12	(2)	
27	Pavel BEGANSKIY	BLS	A	14	(1)	5
17	Yuriy DROZDOV	RUS	M	25	(1)	1
2	Anton CHICHULIN		D	20	(3)	
11	Sergei FILIPPENKOV		M	12	(1)	1
16	Igor GLUSHKO		G	1		
11	Konstantin GOLOVSKOI	RUS	M	10		5
20	Sergei GRISHIN	RUS	M	11		
14	Dias KAMELOV		M	4	(6)	
9	Nikita KHOKHLOV		M	25	(4)	2
26	Aleksandar KOMADINA	SCG	D	14		2
7	Aleksei KOSOLAPOV		M	25		1
23	Aleksandr KOVALEV		D	10	(1)	
5	Aidar KUMISBEKOV		D	15	(6)	1
24	Vitaliy LANKO	BLS	M	5	(2)	
20	Mikhail LUNIN		M	6	(4)	3
21	Dmitriy LYAPKIN		D	20	(1)	
26	Oleg MOCHULYAK		A	2	(8)	1
22	Aleksandr MOKIN		G	3	(1)	
10	NILTON MENDES	BRA	M	16	(10)	7
1	Yevgeniy PLOTNIKOV		G	26		
6	Eduard SERGIENKO		M	1	(12)	1
4	Mikhail SHISHKIN		D	14	(4)	1
8	Aleksandr SUCHKOV		M	19	(7)	
24	Artem VORONKIN	RUS	M	7	(1)	1
27	Maxim YERMAK	RUS	M	13	(2)	3
15	Maxim ZHALMAGAMBETOV		D		(1)	

ZHETYSU TALDYKORGAN
Coach – Boris Podkorytov; (16/5/05) Igor Svechnikov

2005

3/4	Tobol Kostanai	h	0-0		
9/4	Irtysh Pavlodar	h	0-2		
16/4	Yesil-Bogatyr Petropavlovsk	h	0-2		
23/4	Shakhtyor Karagandy	a	1-2		Urazbakhtin
30/4	Okzhetpes Kokshetau	h	2-0		Shatskikh, Kurbanov
7/5	Ordabasy Shymkent	a	1-2		Usmanov
14/5	FK Taraz	h	0-2		
21/5	FK Almaty	a	2-1		Usmanov 2
26/5	Kairat Almaty	a	1-1		Mamonov
12/6	FK Atyrau	h	1-1		Zabelin
18/6	Bolat Temirtau	a	2-1		Kurbanov, Glukhov
25/6	Vostok Ust-Kamenogorsk	h	0-2		
29/6	Aktobe Lento	h	1-1		Zabelin
3/7	Ekibastuzets Ekibastuz	h	3-4		Glukhov, Turlybayev, Kurbonov
9/7	Zhenis Astana	a	0-0		
24/7	Zhenis Astana	h	0-1		
30/7	Ekibastuzets Ekibastuz	a	1-1		Gumar
7/8	Aktobe Lento	h	1-1		Shatskikh
20/8	Vostok Ust-Kamenogorsk	a	2-4		Shatskikh, Khvostunov
23/8	Bolat Temirtau	h	3-2		Shatskikh, Urazbakhtin (p), Seregin
10/9	FK Atyrau	a	2-3		Gumar (p), Khvostunov
17/9	Kairat Almaty	h	0-3		
23/9	FK Almaty	h	0-2		
27/9	FK Taraz	a	2-3		Zabelin, Martin
1/10	Ordabasy Shymkent	h	1-1		Usmanov
16/10	Okzhetpes Kokshetau	a	0-4		
22/10	Shakhtyor Karagandy	h	0-1		
28/10	Yesil-Bogatyr Petropavlovsk	a	0-4		
2/11	Irtysh Pavlodar	a	1-4		Gumar
6/11	Tobol Kostanai	a	1-4		Turlybayev

No	Name	Nat	Pos	Aps	(s)	Gls
10	Rakhman ASUKHANOV		M	7	(1)	
6	Arman BIRKURMANOV		D	1	(3)	
16	Pavel BUGALO	UZB	G	22		
20	Fevzi DAVLETOV	UZB	D	24		
10	Bagdat DOSTAYEV		D	8	(4)	
17	Egor GLADKOV		M	6	(4)	
9	Yevgeniy GLUKHOV		A	5	(4)	2

Kazakhstan

4	Oleg GOLOVAN		M	27	(1)	
2	Ruslan GUMAR		D	19	(3)	3
17	Aleksandr KHVOSTUNOV	UZB	M	13	(1)	2
22	Yevgeniy KOSTRUB		M	9	(3)	
12	Roman KOTZ	UKR	D	21	(1)	
13	Igor KUDRENKO		D	5	(7)	
21	Mukhtar KURBANOV		M	7	(3)	3
8	Dmitriy MAMONOV		M	23		1
21	Andrei MARTIN	MOL	M	6	(3)	1
13	Serghei POGREBAN	MOL	A	12		
1	Nikolai RODIONOV		G	8	(1)	
15	Andrei SEREGIN	RUS	D	24	(1)	1
18	Aleksandr SHATSKIKH		A	15	(2)	4
6	Rustam SHAYMARDANOV		D	3	(1)	
14	Daniyar TURLYBAYEV		M	3	(17)	2
7	Rafael URAZBAKHTIN		M	16	(4)	2
11	Rustam USMANOV		A	19	(5)	4
5	Maxim ZABELIN		D	27	(1)	3

DOMESTIC CUP 2005

1/16 FINALS
(26/4/05)
FK Aktobe-Jas 0, FK Almaty 1 *(aet)*
Batyr Ekibastuz 2, Okzhetpes Kokshetau 2 *(aet; 5-6 on pens)*
Jambyl Taraz 0, FK Atyrau 6
Temirjolshy Almaty 1, Vostok Ust-Kamenogorsk 3
Munaylyl Atyrau 1, Shakhtyor Karagandy 5
Cesna Almaty 0, Zhenis Astana 4
Yesil-Bogatyr-2 Petropavlovsk 1, Tobol Kostanai 3
FK Taraz 6, Energetik Pavlodar 2
Shakhtyor-Yunost Karagandy 0, Bolat Temirtau 1
Gornyak Hromtau 1, Zhetysu Taldykorgan 2
Kaisar Kyzylorda 2, Ekibastuzets Ekibastuz 0
Irtysh-2 Pavlodar 0, Ordabasy Shymkent 3
FK Semey 2, Yesil-Bogatyr Petropavlovsk 3 *(aet)*
Eurasia Astana 1, Irtysh Pavlodar 6
Ordabasy-2 Shymkent 0, Aktobe Lento 8
Vostok-2 Ust-Kamenogorsk 0, Kairat Almaty 8

1/8 FINALS
(3/5/05)
Zhenis Astana 3, Bolat Temirtau 0
Yesil-Bogatyr Petropavlovsk 1, Aktobe Lento 0 *(aet)*
Vostok Ust-Kamenogorsk 1, Tobol Kostanai 0
Kaisar Kyzylorda 0, FK Atyrau 1
Irtysh Pavlodar 0, FK Taraz 1
Zhetysu Taldykorgan 2, Shakhtyor Karagandy 1 *(aet)*
Ordabasy Shymkent 3, FK Almaty 0
Kairat Almaty 1, Okzhetpes Kokshetau 0

QUARTER-FINALS
(17/5/05 & 21/6/05)
Yesil-Bogatyr Petropavlovsk 1 *(Berdyyev 37)*, Zhenis Astana 0
Zhenis Astana 2 *(Kosolapov 10, Nilton Mendes 105p)*, Yesil-Bogatyr Petropavlovsk 0 *(aet)*
(Zhenis Astana 2-1)

FK Atyrau 1 *(Mochulyak 10p)*, Vostok Ust-Kamenogorsk 0
Vostok Ust-Kamenogorsk 1 *(Shakin 18)*, FK Atyrau 1 *(Mochulyak 77)*
(FK Atyrau 2-1)

FK Taraz 1 *(Niyazmbetov 65)*, Zhetysu Taldykorgan 1 *(Gumar 39)*
Zhetysu Taldykorgan 2 *(Gumar 13p, Kostrub 22)*, FK Taraz 3 *(Gurtuyev 63, Krendelev 67, Mazbayev 80)*
(FK Taraz 4-3)

Ordabasy Shymkent 0, Kairat Almaty 2 *(Likhobabenko 61, Aliyev 90)*
Kairat Almaty 1 *(Lovchev 30)*, Ordabasy Shymkent 0
(Kairat Almaty 3-0)

SEMI-FINALS
(6/7/05 & 3/8/05)
Zhenis Astana 2 *(Nilton Mendes 55p, Suchkov 90)*, FK Atyrau 2 *(Oganesov 72, Rodionov 82)*
FK Atyrau 0, Zhenis Astana 2 *(Golovskoi 7p, 45p)*
(Zhenis Astana 4-2)

FK Taraz 1 *(Mirzabayev 32)*, Kairat Almaty 2 *(Karpenko 4, Fomenko 60)*
Kairat Almaty 2 *(Irismetov J. 62, 71)*, FK Taraz 1 *(Mazbayev 78)*
(Kairat Almaty 4-2)

FINAL
(11/11/05)
Qajimukan stadium, Shymkent
ZHENIS ASTANA 2 *(Beganskiy 19, Nilton Mendes 116)*
KAIRAT ALMATY 1 *(Lutu 25)*
(aet)
Referee – Holmatov
ZHENIS ASTANA – Plotnikov, Shishkin, Khokhlov, Andreyev, Golovskoi, Chichulin (Sergienko 91), Drozdov, Kosolapov, Grishin, Suchkov (Nilton Mendes 62), Beganskiy (Mochulyak 79).
KAIRAT ALMATY – Boichenko, Irismetov F., Abdulin, Smakov, Sosnovschi, Nurdauletov (Lovchev 70), Likhobabenko (Taboyev 67), Lutu, Karpovich, Asanbayev, Tlehugov.

SECOND LEVEL FINAL TABLES 2005

North-East Conference

		Pld	W	D	L	F	A	Pts
1	Energetik Pavlodar	24	21	3	0	109	7	66
2	FK Semey	24	18	5	1	76	17	59
3	Irtysh-2 Pavlodar	24	15	3	6	60	28	48
4	Shakhtyor-Yunost Karagandy	24	13	2	9	35	30	41
5	Ayat Rudniy	24	11	0	13	28	40	33
6	Asbest Jitikara	24	10	3	11	30	34	33
7	Eurasia Astana	24	9	4	11	25	34	31
8	Vostok-2 Ust-Kamenogorsk	24	8	5	11	39	43	29
9	Khimik Stepnogorsk	24	7	3	14	22	43	24
10	Batyr Ekibastuz	24	6	4	14	25	52	22
11	FK Semey-2	24	6	3	15	23	59	21
12	Yesil-Bogatyr-2 Petropavlovsk	24	5	4	15	20	73	19
13	Bolat-CSKA Temirtau	24	4	7	13	12	44	19

South-West Conference

		Pld	W	D	L	F	A	Pts
1	Kaisar Kyzylorda	22	17	4	1	51	10	55
2	Cesna Almaty	22	17	2	3	57	16	53
3	Temirjolshy Almaty	22	14	6	2	70	23	48
4	Gornyak Hromtau	22	13	3	6	30	26	42
5	Kaspiy Aktau	22	10	6	6	31	17	36
6	Ordabasy-2 Shymkent	22	9	4	9	40	48	31
7	Jambyl Taraz	22	7	3	12	24	31	24
8	Munayly Atyrau	22	7	3	12	20	38	24
9	AY Universiteti Turkistan	22	5	6	11	19	41	21
10	Jastar Oral	22	5	3	14	21	46	18
11	FK Aktobe-Jas	22	3	3	16	26	65	12
12	Zhetysu-2 Taldykorgan	22	2	3	17	14	42	9

Latvia

Metalurgs end Skonto monopoly

Skonto Riga's vice-like grip on the Virsliga championship was finally loosened in 2005 as the club from the capital, world-record winners of the title for 14 straight years following Latvia's secession from the Soviet Union, were replaced on the winners' podium by Metalurgs Liepaja.

It was an impressive seizure of power. Narrowly edged out in the 2004 title race, Metalurgs were thirsty for revenge and they dominated proceedings from start to finish. Skilfully led by former Lithuanian national team coach Benjaminas Velkevicius, they rattled off one victory after another, and as Skonto began to drop points in unexpected places, the title race soon became a private procession.

Metalurgs eventually romped home with four matches to spare, a brilliant 5-1 win at FK Ventspils lifting them into a 13-point lead that they would hold on to until the conclusion of the championship five weeks later. It was ironic that they should be crowned champions in Ventspils, because it was there, just a few miles to the north of Liepaja on the Baltic coast, that they fell to their only defeat of the season, beaten 3-0 at the end of May. Metalurgs dropped just two points at home – in a 1-1 draw against Skonto that only finished that way because of a stoppage-time penalty miss from Metalurgs captain Viktors Dobrecovs.

Despite that faux pas the Latvian international striker would finish as the Virsliga's joint-top scorer, with 18 goals – one more than his partner in attack, Alexei Katasonov, who had topped the charts (with 21 goals to Dobrecovs' 18) the previous season. Coach Velkevicius's Lithuanian influence was brought to bear by the impressive displays of his two compatriots in midfield, Mindaugas Kalonas and Darius Miceika, while Latvian international Dzintars Zirnis was the key man in defence.

Excluding the championship they had won in 1958 when Latvia was merely a regional outpost of the Soviet Union, the 2005 title was Metalurgs' first trophy success. They had hoped to win two at once, but six days before they clinched the league title at Ventspils they were beaten by their local rivals in the Latvian Cup final. It was an engaging contest, settled 2-1 in extra-time when an unforced error from Metalurgs keeper Viktors Spole gifted the winning goal to Ventspils' top scorer Igors Slesarcuks.

Cup hat-trick

It was Metalurgs' fifth Cup final defeat in as many visits but Ventspils' third victory in a row. Their previous two wins had been against Skonto, and they beat them again in 2005, at the semi-final stage, thus preventing the perennial champions

NATIONAL TEAM RESULTS 2005/06

17/8/05	Russia (WCQ)	H	Riga	1-1	Astafjevs (6)
3/9/05	Estonia (WCQ)	A	Tallinn	1-2	Laizans (90)
7/9/05	Slovakia (WCQ)	H	Riga	1-1	Laizans (74)
8/10/05	Japan	H	Riga	2-2	Rimkus (67), Rubins (89)
12/10/05	Portugal (WCQ)	A	Oporto	0-3	
12/11/05	Belarus	A	Vitebsk	1-3	Visnjakovs (25)
24/12/05	Thailand	A	Phungna	1-1	Solonicins (19)
26/12/05	North Korea	N	Phuket	1-1	Karlsons (60)
28/12/05	Oman	N	Phuket	2-1	Karlsons (52), Kalnins (90)
30/12/05	North Korea	N	Phuket	2-1	Karlsons (38), Prohorenkovs (40)
28/5/06	United States	A	Hartford	0-1	

Latvia

NATIONAL TEAM APPEARANCES 2005/06

Coach – Jurijs ANDREJEVS

Player	DOB	Club	RUS	EST	SVK	Jpn	POR	Bls	Tha	Nko	Omn	Nko	Usa	Caps	Goals
Aleksandrs KOLINKO	18/6/75	Rubin Kazan (RUS)	G	G	G	G	G						G	66	-
Dzintars ZIRNIS	25/4/77	Metalurgs Liepaja	D	D86	D	D86	D	s66	D	D	D	D	D	38	-
Maris SMIRNOVS	2/6/76	Amica Wronki (POL) /Ditton Daugavpils	D	D					D	D	D	D	D	17	-
Igors N. STEPANOVS	21/1/76	Grasshopper-Club (SUI)	D	D			D	D	D					86	3
Igors KORABLJOVS	23/11/74	Kryvbas Kryvyi Rih (UKR)	D	D	D24									20	-
Imants BLEIDELIS	16/8/75	Grazer AK (AUT)	M	M	M									94	10
Vitalijs ASTAFJEVS	3/4/71	Rubin Kazan (RUS) /Skonto Riga	M	M	M	M46	M	M	M	M85	M46	M	M	125	12
Jurijs LAIZANS	6/1/79	FK Rostov (RUS)	M	M	M	M85		M72					M70	74	11
Andrejs RUBINS	26/11/78	Spartak Moskva (RUS) /Shinnik Yaroslavl (RUS)	M	M	M	A	M	M	A90	M89	M90	M	M83	81	8
Vitas RIMKUS	21/6/73	FK Ventspils	A76	A75	A71	s46	A57							63	10
Maris VERPAKOVSKIS	15/10/79	Dynamo Kyiv (UKR)	A	A82	A	A61	A73	A70					A	53	18
Andrejs PROHORENKOVS	5/2/77	Dinamo Moskva (RUS)	s76	s75					A88	A		A77	A46	28	4
Genadijs SOLONICINS	3/1/80	Metalurgs Liepaja		s82		M34	M51	s59	M	M46	M		M46	11	1
Viktors MOROZS	30/7/80	Skonto Riga		s86	s71	M	M	M59		M	M	M	s46	17	-
Aleksandrs ISAKOVS	16/9/73	Skonto Riga			D	D	D	D87						58	-
Arturs ZAKRESEVSKIS	7/8/71	Skonto Riga			D	D	D	D						54	1
Vladimirs ZAVORONKOVS	25/11/76	FK Ventspils			s24									10	-
Mihails ZEMLINSKIS	21/12/69	Skonto Riga				s34 /46								105	12
Aleksejs VISNJAKOVS	3/2/84	Skonto Riga				s46	s51	M56	M73	s46	s46	M53	s70	13	2
Gatis KALNINS	12/8/81	Skonto Riga				s61	s57	s56	s88	s70	s80	s62	s83	15	1
Vladimirs KOLESNICENKO	4/5/80	FK Moskva (RUS)				s85	s72							31	4
Kristaps BLANKS	30/1/86	Skonto Riga				s86	s73	s70	s90	s85	s64	s53		15	-
Andrejs PIEDELS	17/9/70	Skonto Riga						G	G	G	G	G		15	-
Antons JEMELINS	19/2/84	Metalurgs Liepaja						D66						1	-
Girts KARLSONS	7/6/81	Metalurgs Liepaja						s87	s73	A70	A80	A62	s46	9	3
Kaspars GORKSS	6/11/81	Assyriska FF (SWE)							D20					1	-
Deniss IVANOVS	11/1/84	Metalurgs Liepaja							D	D	D	D	D	5	-
Viktors DOBRECOVS	1/9/77	Metalurgs Liepaja							M57	s89	M64			18	-
Oskars KLAVA	8/8/83	Metalurgs Liepaja							s20	D	D	D	D	5	-
Andrejs STOLCERS	7/7/74	FK Baki (AZB)							s57		s90	s77		81	7

Latvia

from reaching the Cup final for the 11th year running.

Skonto could hardly have imagined a more nightmarish year. They failed to win the league. They didn't reach the Cup final. And in Europe they fell at the first hurdle of Champions League qualification. Their first-leg 6-0 defeat at Macedonian champions Rabotnicki Kometal Skopje signalled the end of the road for coach Jurijs Andrejevs, the man who had replaced multi-title-winning Aleksandrs Starkovs the previous September and had also taken over from the great man as the national coach of Latvia. Andrejevs was replaced by ex-Ventspils coach Paul Ashworth, and the Englishman, to his credit, led Skonto through an unbeaten league run that ensured they at least finished runners-up.

Astafjevs allegations

Andrejevs left Skonto but carried on his work with Latvia, not only to the end of the World Cup qualifying programme but beyond. That was something of a surprise as the Latvians finished up a disheartening fifth in their group, below neighbours Estonia, who beat them 2-1 in Tallinn. It was all a far cry from the team's astonishing Euro 2004 qualification under Starkovs. The only victories came against minnows Liechtenstein and Luxemburg, and even the creditable 1-1 draw at home to former masters Russia was subsequently shrouded in controversy following newspaper claims by Latvia's record international Vitalijs Astafjevs (who scored his team's goal) that the Russians had tried to 'buy' the game. Astafjevs, an ethnic Russian who was playing in the country at the time, with Rubin Kazan, distanced himself from the article as soon as it was published, but it was no great surprise when he came home and rejoined Skonto at the end of the year.

There was better news for another of Latvia's exiled internationals, defender Igors Stepanovs, who was not only voted 2005 Latvian Player of the Year but also awarded the captaincy of Swiss club Grasshopper. None of the country's other foreign-based players excelled, however, and it was a particularly miserable 2005/06 season for star striker Maris Verpakovskis who barely played for Dynamo Kiev and failed to score for his country in seven internationals, having racked up five in the first six games of the World Cup campaign.

EUROPEAN CUPS 2005/06

UEFA CHAMPIONS LEAGUE

SKONTO RIGA
1st qualifying round RABOTNICKI KOMETAL SKOPJE (MAC)
A 0-6
Piedels, Isakovs, Zakresevskis, Nguimbat, Eliava, Menteshashvili, Zemlinskis (Ngon 75), Visnjakovs (Kalnins 58), Korgalidze (Pereplyotkin 62), Chaladze, Blanks.
H 1-0 *Pereplyotkin (90)*
Piedels, Usanov, Zakresevskis, Isakovs, Eliava, Visnjakovs, Nguimbat (Zemlinskis 76), Semjonovs (Kalnins 82), Menteshashvili, Pereplyotkin, Miholaps (Blanks 74).

UEFA CUP

FK VENTSPILS
1st qualifying round LINFIELD (NIR)
A 0-1
Romanovs, Zavoronkovs, Soleicuks, Nalivaiko (Lukasevics 40), Logins, Krohmer, Rekhviashvili, Stukalinas, Agafonov (Gruber 32), Bicka, Slesarcuks (Butriks 87).
H 2-1 *Rekhviashvili (39), Rimkus (90)*
Davidovs, Kacanovs, Lukasevics, Soleicuks, Zavoronkovs, Stukalinas, Bicka, Gruber (Rimkus 46), Krohmer, Rekhviashvili (Modebadze 77), Slesarcuks (Butriks 56).

METALURGS LIEPAJA
1st qualifying round NSÍ (FAR)
A 3-0 *Petersen (23og), Karlsons (67), Grebis (72)*
Spole, Zirnis, Ivanovs (Klava 71), Miceika, Jemelins, Kalonas, Mikadze, Solonicins, Danilovs, Dobrecovs (Karlsons 57), Katasonov (Grebis 66).
H 3-0 *Dobrecovs (4, 35), Klava (81)*
Krucs, Klava, Mikadze, Ivanovs, Surnins (Zuravljovs 75), Kalonas (Grebis 46), Zirnis, Danilovs (Karlsons 46), Solonicins, Dobrecovs, Katasonov.

2nd qualifying round KRC GENK (BEL)
H 2-3 *Kalonas (16), Dobrecovs (83p)*
Spole, Ivanovs, Mikadze, Zirnis, Jemelins, Klava, Solonicins, Danilovs (Miceika 83), Dobrecovs, Katasonov (Karlsons 84).
A 0-3
Spole, Klava (Kalonas 25), Zirnis, Mikadze, Ivanovs, Danilovs (Karlsons 64), Dobrecovs (Grebis 78), Katasonov, Solonicins, Miceika, Jemelins.

TOP GOALSCORERS 2005

18	Viktors DOBRECOVS (Metalurgs Liepaja)
	Igors SLESARCUKS (Venta Kuldiga/FK Ventspils)
17	Alexei KATASONOV (Metalurgs Liepaja)
15	Gatis KALNINS (Skonto Riga)
13	Genadijs SOLONICINS (Metalurgs Liepaja)
9	Oleksandr KRYKLYVYI (Dinaburg Daugavpils)
8	Andrejs BUTRIKS (FK Ventspils)
	Mindaugas KALONAS (Metalurgs Liepaja)
	Girts KARLSONS (Metalurgs Liepaja)
	Mihails MIHOLAPS (Skonto Riga)
	Andrei PEREPLYOTKIN (Skonto Riga)
	Mihails ZIZILEVS (Dinaburg Daugavpils)

Latvia

FINAL LEAGUE TABLE 2005

		Pld	Home					Away					Total					Pts
			W	D	L	F	A	W	D	L	F	A	W	D	L	F	A	
1	Metalurgs Liepaja	28	13	1	0	55	9	9	4	1	30	10	22	5	1	85	19	71
2	Skonto Riga	28	8	4	2	26	10	9	3	2	33	15	17	7	4	59	25	58
3	FK Ventspils	28	8	4	2	31	18	8	3	3	25	12	16	7	5	56	30	55
4	Dinaburg Daugavpils	28	5	5	4	20	16	4	3	7	17	27	9	8	11	37	43	35
5	FK Riga	28	4	3	7	16	24	5	4	5	16	22	9	7	12	32	46	34
6	FK Jurmala	28	7	2	5	20	15	2	3	9	17	23	9	5	14	37	38	32
7	Olimps Riga	28	3	2	9	12	34	2	2	10	12	34	5	4	19	24	68	19
8	Venta Kuldiga	28	1	2	11	9	33	1	1	12	9	46	2	3	23	18	79	9

LEAGUE RESULTS/SCORERS/APPEARANCES/GOALS 2005

DINABURG DAUGAVPILS
Coach – Romans Grigorcuks; (10/7/05) Dmitriy Kouzmichov; (17/9/05) Victor Demidov

2005
Date	Opponent	h/a	Score	Scorers
10/4	FK Jurmala	h	1-0	Burlakovs
16/4	Olimps Riga	a	1-2	Sokolskis
20/4	FK Riga	h	0-0	
24/4	Metalurgs Liepaja	a	2-4	Zuromskis (p), Sokolskis
30/4	FK Ventspils	h	0-1	
4/5	Venta Kuldiga	h	1-0	Kryklyvyi
8/5	Skonto Riga	a	0-3	
12/5	FK Jurmala	a	2-1	Boruns, Kryklyvyi
17/5	Olimps Riga	h	3-0	Krklyvyi, Sokolovs 2
26/5	FK Riga	a	0-3	
29/5	Metalurgs Liepaja	h	1-2	Zizilevs
13/6	FK Ventspils	a	1-1	Valjuskins
13/7	FK Jurmala	h	1-0	Zizilevs
17/7	Olimps Riga	a	1-1	Kryklyvyi
20/7	Venta Kuldiga	a	3-1	Dusins, Pucinskis (p), Kryklyvyi
24/7	FK Riga	h	2-2	Zizilevs 2 (2p)
2/8	Metalurgs Liepaja	a	0-5	
6/8	FK Ventspils	h	3-3	Zuromskis, Valjuskins 2
11/8	Skonto Riga	h	1-2	Kryklyvyi
21/8	Venta Kuldiga	h	3-0	(w/o)
28/8	Skonto Riga	a	1-1	Kryklyvyi
17/9	FK Jurmala	a	0-1	
21/9	Olimps Riga	h	1-1	Boruns (p)
1/10	FK Riga	a	2-1	Zizilevs, Kryklyvyi
16/10	Metalurgs Liepaja	h	2-2	Kryklyvyi, Pucinskis (p)
23/10	FK Ventspils	a	1-3	Zuromskis (p)
30/10	Venta Kuldiga	a	3-0	Ryzhevskiy, Zizilevs 2 (1p)
5/11	Skonto Riga	h	1-3	Zizilevs (p)

Name	Nat	Pos	Aps	(s)	Gls
Alexandr ANTTILAINEN	RUS	M		(1)	
Aleksejs BORUNS		M	20	(2)	2
Edgars BURLAKOVS		M	24	(2)	1
Dmitrijs CUGUNOVS		D	20		
Jurijs DUSINS		D	3		1
Maris ELTERMANIS		G	5		
Vadims FJODOROVS		G	22		
Tomás HEJDUSEK	CZE	D	2	(2)	
Sergey KHIMICH	RUS	D	1	(1)	
Pavels KOLCOVS		A	7	(12)	
Alexei KOSTENKO	RUS	A		(2)	
Oleksandr KRYKLYVYI	UKR	A	24	(1)	9
Marc NDIKUMADE	CMR	M	1	(1)	
Nikolai OSIPOVICH	BLS	M	4	(1)	
Tamaz PERTIA	GEO	A	9	(1)	
Jurgis PUCINSKIS		M	17	(5)	2
Marcel RESITCA	MOL	M		(1)	
Ivan RODIN	RUS	M		(6)	
Pavel RYZHEVSKIY	BLS	A	8	(2)	1
Igors SAVCENKOVS		D	10	(1)	
Nikita SHMIKOV	RUS	D	21	(2)	
Jurijs SOKOLOVS		D	24		2
Deniss SOKOLSKIS		D	11	(1)	2
Andrei STRELTSOV	RUS	M	3	(2)	
Dmitriy TIMACHOV	RUS	M	1	(1)	
Sergejs VALJUSKINS		M	3	(13)	3
Vladimirs VOLKOVS		A	5	(10)	
Mihails ZIZILEVS		M	23	(3)	8
Andrejs ZURAVLJOVS		D	4	(1)	
Andrejs ZUROMSKIS		D	25		3

FK JURMALA
Coach – Jurijs Popkovs

2005
Date	Opponent	h/a	Score	Scorers
10/4	Dinaburg Daugavpils	a	0-1	
16/4	Venta Kuldiga	h	0-0	
20/4	Skonto Riga	a	1-3	Dorosh
24/4	FK Ventspils	a	0-1	
30/4	Olimps Riga	h	1-0	Soāres
4/5	FK Riga	a	2-3	Sinicins, Torres
8/5	Metalurgs Liepaja	h	0-1	
12/5	Dinaburg Daugavpils	h	1-2	Ferreira
17/5	Venta Kuldiga	a	2-2	Ksenzovs, Malasonoks
26/5	Skonto Riga	h	3-2	Ferreira, Campora, Ksenzovs
29/5	FK Ventspils	h	2-2	Ksenzovs, Musajevs
19/6	Olimps Riga	a	3-0	Malasonoks 3
25/6	FK Riga	h	3-0	Sergejevs 2, Ksenzovs
3/7	Metalurgs Liepaja	a	1-3	Puzirevskis
13/7	Dinaburg Daugavpils	a	0-1	
17/7	Venta Kuldiga	h	4-0	Poljakovs, Soāres 2, Torres
26/7	Skonto Riga	a	1-2	Torres
2/8	FK Ventspils	a	1-2	Puzirevskis
7/8	Olimps Riga	h	4-3	Sergejevs, Zuburs, Kalns, Torres
21/8	FK Riga	a	1-1	Zuburs

Latvia

Date	Opponent	H/A	Score	Scorers
29/8	Metalurgs Liepaja	h	0-1	
17/9	Dinaburg Daugavpils	h	1-0	Kalns
21/9	Venta Kuldiga	a	4-2	Kalns, Ferreira, Sinicins, Malasonoks
1/10	Skonto Riga	h	0-3	
16/10	FK Ventspils	h	0-1	
23/10	Olimps Riga	a	1-1	Kalns
30/10	FK Riga	h	1-0	Babicevs
5/11	Metalurgs Liepaja	a	0-1	

Name	Nat	Pos	Aps	(s)	Gls
Vladimirs BABICEVS		A	6	(8)	1
Romans BEZZUBOVS		A	7	(1)	
Federico CAMPORA	ARG	M	7	(1)	1
Kaspars CINITIS		D		(3)	
Orest DOROSH	UKR	M	26		1
Antônio FERREIRA	BRA	D	22		3
Olegs FILIPOVS		M	2	(1)	
Matías GARCÍA	ARG	M	1		
Jurgis KALNS		A	10		4
Igors KORABLJOVS		D	13		
Jurijs KSENZOVS		M	14	(8)	4
Artjoms KUZNECOVS		M	8		
Andrés LEANDRO	ARG	M	2	(1)	
Vsevolods LIDAKS		D	27		
Valentins LOBANJOVS		D	6		
Olegs MALASONOKS		A	12	(10)	5
Ruslans MIHALCUKS		M	9	(2)	
Aleksandrs MUSAJEVS		M	22	(4)	1
Mihails POLJAKOVS		M	3	(12)	1
Vitalijs PUZIREVSKIS		A	1	(11)	2
Aleksandrs SERGEJEVS		A	17	(8)	3
Vadims SINICINS		D	25		2
Giovanni SOARES	BRA	A	9	(4)	3
Gintaras STAUCE	LIT	G	24		
Pavels STEINBORS		G	4		
Christián TORRES	ARG	A	20	(2)	4
Jurgis ZUBURS		D	11	(5)	2

METALURGS LIEPAJA
Coach – Benjaminas Zelkevicius (LIT)

2005

Date	Opponent	H/A	Score	Scorers
10/4	Olimps Riga	h	3-0	Dobrecovs, Katasonov, Solonicins
16/4	FK Riga	a	1-0	Solonicins
20/4	FK Ventspils	h	2-0	Katasonov, Solonicins
24/4	Dinaburg Daugavpils	h	4-2	Solonicins, Katasonov 2, Dobrecovs
30/4	Venta Kuldiga	a	0-0	
4/5	Skonto Riga	h	4-2	Solonicins, Katasonov, Kalonas, Danilovs
8/5	FK Jurmala	a	1-0	Danilovs
12/5	Olimps Riga	a	6-0	Dobrecovs 2, Kalns, Grebis 2, Kalonas
17/5	FK Riga	h	5-1	Danilovs, Katasonov 2, Dobrecovs, Grebis
25/5	FK Ventspils	a	0-3	
29/5	Dinaburg Daugavpils	a	2-1	Miceika, Grebis
19/6	Venta Kuldiga	h	5-1	Solonicins, Miceika, Katasonov 2, Dobrecovs
25/6	Skonto Riga	a	1-1	Katasonov
3/7	FK Jurmala	h	3-1	Katasonov, Kalonas 2
8/7	Olimps Riga	h	5-0	Katasonov, Grebis, Solonicins 2, Dobrecovs
19/7	FK Riga	a	3-0	Dobrecovs (p), Mikadze, Karlsons
23/7	FK Ventspils	h	2-1	Dobrecovs, Grebis
2/8	Dinaburg Daugavpils	h	5-0	Kalonas, Dobrecovs 3 (1p), Solonicins
6/8	Venta Kuldiga	a	3-1	Katasonov, Solonicins 2
21/8	Skonto Riga	h	1-1	Solonicins
29/8	FK Jurmala	a	1-0	Katasonov
17/9	Olimps Riga	h	4-0	Dobrecovs, Danilovs, Katasonov, Kalonas (p)
21/9	FK Riga	h	6-0	Danilovs 2, Dobrecovs, Kalonas, Jemelins, Katasonov
1/10	FK Ventspils	a	5-1	Miceika, Karlsons 2, og (Soleicuks), Katasonov (p)
16/10	Dinaburg Daugavpils	a	2-2	Karlsons 2
23/10	Venta Kuldiga	h	9-0	Dobrecovs 4, Karlsons 3, Kalonas, Kamess
30/10	Skonto Riga	a	1-1	Soloncins
5/11	FK Jurmala	h	1-0	Grebis

Name	Nat	Pos	Aps	(s)	Gls
Maris BRUDERS		M	1	(1)	
Edijs DANILOVS		M	24		6
Viktors DOBRECOVS		A	28		18
Kristaps GREBIS		A	2	(22)	7
Dmitrijs HALVITOVS		D	1	(3)	
Deniss IVANOVS		D	28		
Antons JEMELINS		D	15		1
Jurgis KALNS		A	1	(8)	1
Mindaugas KALONAS	LIT	M	27		8
Vladimirs KAMESS		M		(1)	1
Girts KARLSONS		A	7	(8)	8
Alexei KATASONOV	RUS	A	22	(1)	17
Intars KIRHNERS		M		(5)	
Oskars KLAVA		D	18	(7)	
Aleksejs KRUCS		G		(1)	
Darius MICEIKA	LIT	M	23	(1)	3
Lavrenti MIKADZE	GEO	D	25		1
Genadijs SOLONICINS		M	28		13
Viktors SPOLE		G	28		
Pavels SURNINS		M	1	(6)	
Dzintars ZIRNIS		D	27		
Andrejs ZURAVLJOVS		D	2		

OLIMPS RIGA
Coach – Janis Dreimanis; (1/7/05) Aleksejs Sarando

2005

Date	Opponent	H/A	Score	Scorers
10/4	Metalurgs Liepaja	a	0-3	
16/4	Dinaburg Daugavpils	h	2-1	Scanicins, Abramenko
20/4	Venta Kuldiga	a	0-3	
24/4	Skonto Riga	h	1-5	Kopca
30/4	FK Jurmala	a	0-0	
4/5	FK Ventspils	a	2-3	Muiznieks, Scanicins
8/5	FK Riga	h	0-2	
12/5	Metalurgs Liepaja	h	0-6	
17/5	Dinaburg Daugavpils	a	0-3	
26/5	Venta Kuldiga	h	2-1	Scanicins (p), Ivasko
29/5	Skonto Riga	a	2-0	Sevljakovs 2
19/6	FK Jurmala	h	0-3	
25/6	FK Ventspils	h	0-3	
3/7	FK Riga	a	0-1	
8/7	Metalurgs Liepaja	a	0-5	
17/7	Dinaburg Daugavpils	h	1-1	Ivasko

Latvia

24/7	Venta Kuldiga	a	2-0	Abramenko, Zarudnijs
31/7	Skonto Riga	h	0-1	
7/8	FK Jurmala	a	3-4	Scanicins 2, Idionovs
20/8	FK Ventspils	a	1-6	Idionovs
28/8	FK Riga	h	0-3	
17/9	Metalurgs Liepaja	h	0-4	
21/9	Dinaburg Daugavpils	a	1-1	Idionovs
1/10	Venta Kuldiga	h	5-2	Abramenko 3, Cebotarevs, Zarudnijs
16/10	Skonto Riga	a	0-3	
23/10	FK Jurmala	h	1-1	Jelisejevs
30/10	FK Ventspils	h	0-1	
5/11	FK Riga	a	1-1	Danilovs

Name	Nat	Pos	Aps	(s)	Gls
Aleksandrs ABRAMENKO		A	20	(5)	5
Olegs BAIKOVS		M	13	(6)	
Dmitrijs CEBOTAREVS		D	12	(8)	1
Aleksandrs CIKINJOVS		D	8		
Maksims DANILOVS		A	9	(5)	1
Maksims FIRSOVS		M	5		
Vladislavs GABOVS		D	26		
Sergejs GOLUBEVS		D	23		
Jurijs IDIONOVS		M	25		3
Edijs IVASKO		D	14	(3)	2
Vadims JAVOISS		M	2	(3)	
Aleksandrs JELISEJEVS		A	8	(2)	1
Aleksejs KOLESNIKOVS		M	4	(2)	
Maksims KOLOKOLENKINS		M	25		
Vladimirs KOPCA		D	2	(4)	1
Jevgenijs LAIZANS		G	22		
Raimonds LAIZANS		G	1		
Jevgenijs MAKSIMENKO		D	22		
Vladislavs MASALSKIS		G	5	(1)	
Vitalijs MELNICENKO		G		(1)	
Emils MUIZNIEKS		A	3	(6)	1
Aleksejs SARANDO Jr.		M	1		
Ilja SCANICINS		A	9	(10)	5
Jevgenijs SEMJONOVS		M	4	(1)	
Vadims SEVLJAKOVS		M	5	(7)	2
Janis SKVORCOVS		M	1	(4)	
Sergejs STARKOVS		A	2	(5)	
Vaktors TERENTJEVS		M	11	(1)	
Jevgenijs ZARUDNIJS		D	19	(3)	2
Mareks ZUNTNERS		A	7	(1)	

FK RIGA
Coach – Eriks Grigjans

2005

10/4	FK Ventspils	h	0-2	
16/4	Metalurgs Liepaja	h	0-1	
20/4	Dinaburg Daugavpils	a	0-0	
24/4	Venta Kuldiga	h	0-2	
30/4	Skonto Riga	a	2-0	Ascuks 2
4/5	FK Jurmala	h	3-2	Ascuks 2, Mezeckis
8/5	Olimps Riga	a	2-0	Mezeckis (p), Ascuks
12/5	FK Ventspils	a	0-0	
17/5	Metalurgs Liepaja	a	1-5	Matsion
26/5	Dinaburg Daugavpils	h	3-0	Kolinek 2, Mezeckis
30/5	Venta Kuldiga	a	1-0	Bonco
15/6	Skonto Riga	h	0-4	
25/6	FK Jurmala	a	0-3	
3/7	Olimps Riga	h	1-0	Zigajevs
8/7	FK Ventspils	h	1-3	Mezeckis (p)
19/7	Metalurgs Liepaja	h	0-3	
24/7	Dinaburg Daugavpils	a	2-2	Zagajevs, Kalinins
31/7	Venta Kuldiga	h	4-2	Krjauklis 2, Matsion, Ascuks
7/8	Skonto Riga	a	0-4	
21/8	FK Jurmala	h	1-1	Mezeckis
28/8	Olimps Riga	a	3-0	Zigajevs (p), Rafalskis, Kirhners
17/9	FK Ventspils	a	1-1	Kalinins
21/9	Metalurgs Liepaja	a	0-6	
1/10	Dinaburg Daugavpils	h	1-2	Zigajevs
16/10	Venta Kuldiga	a	4-0	Krjauklis 2, Bonco, Rafalskis
23/10	Skonto Riga	h	1-1	Zigajevs
30/10	FK Jurmala	a	0-1	
5/11	Olimps Riga	h	1-1	Bonco (p)

Name	Nat	Pos	Aps	(s)	Gls
Valerijs AFANASJEVS		M	19	(7)	
Deniss ASCUKS		A	13	(7)	6
Arturs BIEZAIS		G	2		
Aleksandrs BOGDANOVS		M		(2)	
Marek BONCO	SVK	A	23	(4)	3
Myroslav BUNDASH	UKR	M	9	(2)	
Vladimirs CIMANIS		D	6		
Nikolajs DJAKINS		M	1	(3)	
Jevgenijs KACANOVS		M		(1)	
Andrejs KALININS		D	21	(3)	2
Intars KIRHNERS		M	9	(1)	1
Jaroslav KOLINEK	CZE	D	12	(1)	2
Rolands KRJAUKLIS		M	10	(4)	4
Maris LESCINSKIS		D	10	(4)	
Kostyantyn MATSION	UKR	M	24	(3)	2
Roberts MEZECKIS		D	11	(10)	5
Pavels MIHADJUKS		D	28		
Alberts NIKOLSKIS		G	4	(1)	
Andrejs PAVLOVS		G	22		
Maksims RAFALSKIS		M	20	(3)	2
Antons REMENCIKS		M	6		
Andrejs SEMJONOVS		A		(1)	
Olegs SEMJONOVS		A	6	(16)	
Igors TROICKIS		D	25		
Maxim USANOV	RUS	D	12		
Jurijs ZIGAJEVS		A	15	(10)	5

SKONTO RIGA
Coach – Jurijs Andrejevs; (1/8/05) Paul Ashworth (ENG)

2005

10/4	Venta Kuldiga	a	3-0	Visnjakovs, Pereplyotkin, Kalnins
16/4	FK Ventspils	a	3-1	Visnjakovs, Pereplyotkin, Blanks
20/4	FK Jurmala	h	3-1	Blanks, Pereplyotkin, Visnjakovs
24/4	Olimps Riga	a	5-1	Kalnins 2, og (Cikinovs), Miholaps (p), Pereplyotkin
30/4	FK Riga	h	0-2	
4/5	Metalurgs Liepaja	a	2-4	Miholaps, Visnjakovs
8/5	Dinaburg Daugavpils	h	3-0	Visnjakovs, Miholaps 2
12/5	Venta Kuldiga	h	3-0	Zemlinskis (p), Zakresevskis, Kalnins
17/5	FK Ventspils	h	1-0	Zemlinskis (p)
26/5	FK Jurmala	a	2-3	Ngon-Djam, Kalnins
29/5	Olimps Riga	h	0-2	
15/6	FK Riga	a	4-0	Kalnins 3, Zemlinskis (p)
19/6	FK Ventspils	a	2-2	Visnjakovs, Kalnins

Latvia

25/6	Metalurgs Liepaja	h	1-1	*Pereplyotkin*
7/7	Venta Kuldiga	a	1-0	*Zemlinskis*
26/7	FK Jurmala	h	2-1	*Miholaps, Menteshashvili*
31/7	Olimps Riga	a	1-0	*Zemlinskis*
7/8	FK Riga	h	4-0	*Pereplyotkin 2, Morozs, Miholaps*
11/8	Dinaburg Daugavpils	a	2-1	*Menteshashvili, Pereplyotkin*
21/8	Metalurgs Liepaja	a	1-1	*Miholaps (p)*
28/8	Dinaburg Daugavpils	h	1-1	*Kalnins*
17/9	Venta Kuldiga	h	3-0	*Miholaps, Morozs, Kalnins*
21/9	FK Ventspils	h	1-1	*Kalnins*
1/10	FK Jurmala	a	3-0	*Menteshashvili (p), Chaladze, Blanks*
16/10	Olimps Riga	h	3-0	*Kalnins 2, Chaladze*
23/10	FK Riga	a	1-1	*Kalnins*
30/10	Metalurgs Liepaja	h	1-1	*Menteshashvili*
5/11	Dinaburg Daugavpils	a	3-1	*Visnjakovs, Blanks, Morozs*

Name	Nat	Pos	Aps	(s)	Gls
Olegs BLAGONADEZDINS		D	6	(1)	
Kristaps BLANKS		A	16	(8)	4
David CHALADZE	GEO	A	5	(5)	2
Pavels DOROSEVS		G	8	(1)	
Zaali ELIAVA	GEO	D	28		
David GAMEZARDASHVILI	GEO	D	1		
Aleksandrs ISAKOVS		D	26	(1)	
Gatis KALNINS		A	24	(4)	15
Levan KORGALIDZE	GEO	M	7	(8)	
Sergejs KOZANS		D	4		
Olegs LAIZANS		M		(1)	
Zurab MENTESHASHVILI	GEO	M	23	(1)	4
Mihails MIHOLAPS		A	20	(4)	8
Viktors MOROZS		D	17	(2)	3
Claude-Parfait NGON-DJAM	CMR	A	4	(6)	1
Aaron NGUIMBAT	CMR	D	15	(1)	
Andrei PEREPLYOTKIN	RUS	M	21	(6)	8
Andrejs PIEDELS		G	20		
Igors SEMJONOVS		M	10	(6)	
Marian SLUKA	SVK	M	4	(2)	
Vitalijs SMIRNOVS		D	1	(1)	
Aleksandrs SOLOVJOVS		D		(1)	
Maxim USANOV	RUS	D	8		
Aleksejs VISNJAKOVS		M	21	(5)	7
Arturs ZAKRESEVSKIS		D	10	(1)	1
Mihails ZEMLINSKIS		D	9	(2)	5

VENTA KULDIGA
Coach – Oleh Luzhnyi (UKR); Volodymyr Zhuravchak (UKR)

2005

10/4	Skonto Riga	h	0-3	
16/4	FK Jurmala	a	0-0	
20/4	Olimps Riga	h	3-0	*Krjauklis, Slesarcuks 2*
24/4	FK Riga	a	2-0	*Slesarcuks 2*
30/4	Metalurgs Liepaja	h	0-0	
4/5	Dinaburg Daugavpils	a	0-1	
8/5	FK Ventspils	h	0-1	
12/5	Skonto Riga	a	0-3	
17/5	FK Jurmala	h	2-2	*Poljakovs, Slesarcuks*
26/5	Olimps Riga	a	1-2	*Slesarcuks*
30/5	FK Riga	h	0-1	
19/6	Metalurgs Liepaja	a	1-5	*Jakovlevs*
3/7	FK Ventspils	a	1-5	*Jakovlevs*
7/7	Skonto Riga	h	0-1	
17/7	FK Jurmala	a	0-4	
20/7	Dinaburg Daugavpils	h	1-3	*Kondakovs*
24/7	Olimps Riga	h	0-2	
31/7	FK Riga	a	2-4	*Nesterenko 2*
6/8	Metalurgs Liepaja	h	1-3	*Kondakovs*
21/8	Dinaburg Daugavpils	a	0-3	*(w/o)*
28/8	FK Ventspils	h	0-6	
17/9	Skonto Riga	a	0-3	
21/9	FK Jurmala	h	2-4	*Kopca 2*
1/10	Olimps Riga	a	2-5	*Kondakovs, og (Baikovs)*
16/10	FK Riga	h	0-4	
23/10	Metalurgs Liepaja	a	0-9	
30/10	Dinaburg Daugavpils	h	0-3	
5/11	FK Ventspils	a	0-2	

Name	Nat	Pos	Aps	(s)	Gls
Yuriy BENYO	UKR	D	12		
Romans BEZZUBOVS		A	17		
Edijs BLEKTE		M		(2)	
Aleksandrs DMITRIJEVS		M		(6)	
Artjoms GONCARS		M	6		
Vadims GOSPODARS		M	12	(1)	
Andrejs FEDOTOVS		D	1	(2)	
Dmitrijs JAKOVLEVS		A	12	(6)	2
Girts KARLSONS		A	6		
Alexandr KHATSKEVICH	BLS	M	4		
Konstantins KLIMENKO		M	3	(1)	
Aleksejs KOLESNIKOVS		M	14		
Vjaceslavs KONDAKOVS		A	10	(9)	3
Vladimirs KOPCA		D	7		2
Vitalijs KOZJAIKINS		M	1	(2)	
Rolands KRJAUKLIS		M	2	(3)	1
Edgars KVASNINS		D	14	(2)	
Valentins LOBANJOVS		D	15		
Vladimirs LUKKONENS		G	1		
Oleh LUZHNYI	UKR	D	9		
Andrejs MALISS		M	7		
Dmitrijs MIHAILOVS		D	7		
Kirils MITINS		M	6		
Sergejs NAGIBINS		M	6	(2)	
Maciej NALEPA	POL	G	9		
Jean-Paul NDEKI	CMR	D	8	(1)	
Bogdans NESTERENKO		D	19	(1)	2
Nikolajs POLJAKOVS		D	17		1
Valerijs REDJKO		A	21	(1)	
Igors RINKUS		M	5	(2)	
Jevgenijs ROMANOVS		D	15	(2)	
Gatis ROZKALNS		M	2		
Jevgenijs SIROMOLOTOVS		G	4		
Janis SKABARDIS		G	6		
Igors SLESARCUKS		A	9		6
Sergejs VASILJEVS		M	1		
Viktors VILMANIS		M	2	(1)	
Aleksandrs VLASOVS		G	7		

FK VENTSPILS
Coach – Sergejs Semjonovs; (14/6/05) (Igors Stepanovs); (10/7/05)
Romans Grigorcuks

2005

10/4	FK Riga	a	2-0	*Butriks, Bicka*
16/4	Skonto Riga	h	1-3	*Butriks*
20/4	Metalurgs Liepaja	a	0-2	
24/4	FK Jurmala	h	1-0	*Modebadze*
30/4	Dinaburg Daugavpils	a	1-0	*Butriks*

Latvia

4/5	Olimps Riga	h	3-2	Krohmer, Bicka, Stukalinas
8/5	Venta Kuldiga	a	1-0	Bicka
12/5	FK Riga	h	0-0	
17/5	Skonto Riga	a	0-1	
25/5	Metalurgs Liepaja	h	3-0	og (Miceika), Zavoronkovs, Butriks
29/5	FK Jurmala	a	2-2	Zavoronkovs (p), Rekhviashvili
13/6	Dinaburg Daugavpils	h	1-1	Rekhviashvili
19/6	Skonto Riga	h	2-2	Gruber 2
25/6	Olimps Riga	a	3-0	Krohmer, Butriks, Toryan
3/7	Venta Kuldiga	h	5-1	Stukalinas 2, Zavoronkovs (p), Butriks 2
8/7	FK Riga	a	3-1	Agafonov, Slesarcuks, Zavoronkovs
23/7	Metalurgs Liepaja	a	1-2	Soleicuks
2/8	FK Jurmala	h	2-1	Slesarcuks, Zavoronkovs (p)
6/8	Dinaburg Daugavpils	a	3-3	Rimkus 2, Butriks
20/8	Olimps Riga	h	6-1	Slesarcuks 3, Gruber 2, Zavoronkovs
28/8	Venta Kuldiga	a	6-0	Rimkus 3, Bicka, Gruber, Slesarcuks
17/9	FK Riga	h	1-1	Rimkus
21/9	Skonto Riga	a	1-1	Bicka
1/10	Metalurgs Liepaja	h	1-5	Agafonov
16/10	FK Jurmala	a	1-0	Rekhviashvili
23/10	Dinaburg Daugavpils	h	3-1	Slesarcuks 3
30/10	Olimps Riga	a	1-0	Slesarcuks (p)
5/11	Venta Kuldiga	h	2-0	Slesarcuks 2 (1p)

Name	Nat	Pos	Aps	(s)	Gls
Andrei AGAFONOV	RUS	M	11	(8)	2
Deimantas BICKA	LIT	M	26	(2)	5
Andrejs BUTRIKS		A	19	(6)	8
Pavels DAVIDOVS		G	15		
Jurijs DUSINS		D	3		
Aleksandar GRUBER	SCG	M	13	(5)	5
Deniss KACANOVS		M	23	(2)	
Roman KAGAZEZHEV	RUS	A	1	(2)	
Sergey KHIMICH	RUS	D	3		
Andrejs KOZACUKS		A	2	(11)	
Jiri KROHMER	CZE	A	22	(2)	2
Andris KUVSINOVS		M		(10)	
Vadims LOGINS		D	7	(1)	
Viktors LUKASEVICS		D	12	(1)	
Ruslans MIHALCUKS		M	1	(4)	
Georgy MODEBADZE	GEO	A	7	(2)	1
Dmitrijs NALIVAIKO		D	9		
Jean-Paul NDEKI	CMR	D	8		
Aleksandr REKHVIASHVILI	GEO	M	24	(1)	3
Vitas RIMKUS		A	10	(2)	6
Deniss ROMANOVS		G	13		
Igors SLESARCUKS		A	13		12
Deniss SOKOLSKIS		D	3		
Aleksejs SOLEICUKS		D	28		1
Igoris STUKALINAS	LIT	M	21	(3)	3
Alexandr TORYAN	RUS	A	1	(8)	1
Vladimirs ZAVORONKOVS		D	13	(2)	6

DOMESTIC CUP 2005

FOURTH ROUND
(9/6/05)
JFC Skonto Riga 0, Olimps Riga 2
SC Dizvanagi Rezekne 0, FK Ventspils 0 *(aet; 1-3 on pens)*
Auda Riga 0, Metalurgs Liepaja 7
(10/6/05)
Alberts Riga 0, FK Riga 2
FK Valmiera 1, FK Jurmala 5
(11/6/05)
FK Jelgava 0, Skonto Riga 5
Ditton Daugavpils 0, Venta Kuldiga 4
FK Plavinas DM 0, Dinaburg Daugavpils 8

QUARTER-FINALS
(28/6/05)
Olimps Riga 2 *(Zarudnijs 41, Danilovs 46)*, Venta Kuldiga 0
(29/6/05)
Metalurgs Liepaja 2 *(Kalns 31, Solonicins 90)*, Dinaburg Daugavpils 1
(Kryklyvyi 10)
FK Riga 1 *(Mezeckis 57p)*, Skonto Riga 2 *(Zemlinskis 79p, Ngon-Djam 119) (aet)*
FK Jurmala 0, FK Ventspils 2 *(Agafonov 26, Gruber 53)*

SEMI-FINALS
(10/9/05)
Olimps Riga 0, Metalurgs Liepaja 1 *(Danilovs 55)*
(11/9/05)
FK Ventspils 1 *(Butriks 40)*, Skonto Riga 0

FINAL
(25/9/05)
Skonto Stadium, Riga
FK VENTSPILS 2 *(Rimkus 99, Slesarcuks 112)*
METALURGS LIEPAJA 1 *(Miceika 94)*
(aet)
Referee – Lajuks
FK VENTSPILS – Romanovs, Soleicuks, Ndeki, Kacanovs, Rekhviashvili, Stukalinas, Bicka, Krohmer, Slesarcuks (Kazacuks 117), Butriks (Kuvsinovs 120), Rimkus.
METALURGS LIEPAJA – Spole, Zirnis, Mikadze, Ivanovs (Grebis 115), Danilovs (Karlsons 46), Kalonas, Dobrecovs, Katasonov, Solonicins, Miceika, Jemelins.

SECOND LEVEL FINAL TABLE 2005

		Pld	W	D	L	F	A	Pts
1	Skonto-2 Riga	26	20	5	1	81	18	65
2	FK Ventspils-2	26	15	7	4	98	25	52
3	Dizvanagi Rezekne	26	15	3	8	68	43	48
4	Metalurgs-2 Liepaja	26	14	5	7	57	23	47
5	Ditton Daugavpils	26	14	5	7	59	28	47
6	FK Valmiera	26	9	8	9	37	39	35
7	JFC Skonto Riga	26	8	11	7	44	31	35
8	FKRiga-2	26	10	5	11	33	41	35
9	Jurmala-Flaminko	26	9	7	10	48	48	34
10	Zibens Ilukste	26	7	8	11	45	56	29
11	FK Jelgava	26	8	2	16	43	59	26
12	Auda Riga	26	8	2	16	27	46	26
13	FK Alberts Riga	26	5	3	18	39	111	18
14	OSC-FK33 Ogre	26	3	3	20	30	141	12

N.B. Second teams ineligible for promotion; Dinaburg-2 Daugavpils and Venta-2 Kuldiga withdrew.

PROMOTION/RELEGATION PLAY-OFF
Olimps Riga 0, Ditton Daugavpils 2

Liechtenstein

Euro 2008 on the doorstep

There is no way in the world that Liechtenstein will qualify for the finals of Euro 2008, but with the competition taking place in neighbouring Austria and Switzerland, it can safely be assumed that the local tourist board will make a killing from the event as swathes of visiting fans pass through from one country to the other.

Before then Liechtenstein's main objective for the tournament will be to build on what they achieved in the 2006 World Cup qualifiers and chalk up as many points as possible in a group that comprises Sweden, Spain, Denmark, Latvia, Iceland and Northern Ireland.

The team will be led by the same coach. Ex-Swiss international midfielder Martin Andermatt was rewarded for harvesting a best-ever tally of eight points in the World Cup campaign with a new two-year contract. The highlights were two wins over Luxembourg – the first time Liechtenstein had done the double over any opponent – and a couple of home draws against Portugal and Slovakia. There might have been even more to shout about against the Portuguese but for a late goal from Nuno Gomes that gave the group winners a nervy 2-1 win in Aveiro.

Andermatt's former club, FC Vaduz, continue to carry the flag for Liechtenstein in European competition, and they did the nation proud again in the summer of 2005 by winning a UEFA Cup tie for the second season running. Dacia Chisinau of Moldova were their victims, and that earned the club a prestige tie against Besiktas. Needless to say, Vaduz lost it, but not before they had given the Turkish giants a few things to think about in the first leg at the Rheinpark.

Nine in a row

Vaduz returned to the UEFA Cup in 2006/07 thanks to their ninth successive victory in the Liechtenstein Cup. It took them longer than usual before they could get their hands on the trophy. FC Balzers scored a last-minute penalty to take the match into extra-time, but Vaduz eventually won through thanks to goals from new Argentine striker Juan Sara and defender Martin Telser - one of seven Liechtenstein internationals on view.

Despite their efforts in the Cup competitions Vaduz failed in their main objective for the season – to qualify for the Swiss Super League. They had come extremely close in the previous two seasons, reaching the promotion/relegation play-off on each occasion, but there was never any likelihood of it being third time lucky. Despite a raft of new foreign signings, both at the start of the season and in mid-campaign, they ended the season halfway up the Challenge League with as many defeats as victories. As a result the club's Swedish coach, Mats Gren, was relieved of his duties and replaced by 43-year-old Swiss-Italian, Maurizio Jacobacci.

NATIONAL TEAM RESULTS 2005/06

Date	Opponent	H/A/N	Venue	Score	Scorers
17/8/05	Slovakia (WCQ)	H	Vaduz	0-0	
3/9/05	Russia (WCQ)	A	Moscow	0-2	
7/9/05	Luxembourg (WCQ)	H	Vaduz	3-0	Frick M. (38), Fischer (77), Beck T. (90)
8/10/05	Portugal (WCQ)	A	Aveiro	1-2	Fischer (32)
12/11/05	Macedonia	H	Vaduz	1-2	D'Elia (35)
2/6/06	Togo	H	Vaduz	0-1	
7/6/06	Australia	N	Ulm	1-3	Neill (80g)

Liechtenstein

NATIONAL TEAM APPEARANCES 2005/06
Coach – Martin ANDERMATT (SUI)

Name	DoB	Club	SVK	RUS	LUX	POR	Mac	Tog	Aus	Caps	Goals
Peter JEHLE	22/1/82	Grasshopper-Club Zürich (SUI)	G	G	G	G	G	G	G	48	-
Martin TELSER	16/10/78	FC Vaduz	D	D	D	D	D	D	D	61	1
Martin BÜCHEL	19/2/77	FC Ruggell	D	D	D76			s71		8	-
Mario WOLFINGER	24/3/82	FC Balzers	D							3	-
Martin STOCKLASA	29/5/79	FC Vaduz	D	D	D	D	M	M	M	58	5
Michael STOCKLASA	2/12/80	FC Vaduz	D89	D	D	D	D			47	1
Franz-Josef VOGT	30/10/85	FC Chur (SUI)	M75	M46				s46		12	-
Roger BECK	3/8/83	VfB Hohenems (AUT)	M		s83	s56	M71	M46	s87	23	1
Ronny BECK	19/3/82	USV Eschen/Mauren	M	M70	M83	M	s30	M71	M	41	-
Thomas BECK	21/2/81	FC Chiasso (SUI)	A	A85	A	M88	A	A79	A87	48	3
Raphael ROHRER	3/5/85	USV Eschen/Mauren	A65	s46	s76	s51	M78	s14	s87	17	-
Claudio ALABOR	20/1/85	USV Eschen/Mauren	s65							3	-
Daniel FRICK	19/6/78	FC Balzers	s75	s85	s89	s88		s79	s69	16	-
Marco RITZBERGER	27/12/86	FC Vaduz	s89				s50	D	D	5	-
Fabio D'ELIA	19/1/83	FC Vaduz		M	M	D	D50	D	D	30	2
Franz BURGMEIER	7/4/82	FC Aarau (SUI)		M	M	M	M30	M14		29	5
Mario FRICK	7/9/74	Ternana (ITA)		M	M89	M51			M	62	8
Benjamin FISCHER	19/10/80	FC Vaduz		s70	A	A56	A	A84	A87	6	2
Daniel HASLER	18/5/74	FC Vaduz				D	D	D	D	66	1
Wolfgang KIEBER	22/7/84	FC BW Feldkirch (AUT)					s71	s84		2	-
Stefan BÜCHEL	30/6/86	FC Vaduz					s78			1	-
Sandro MEIERHOFER	31/5/85	FC Balzers							M69	6	-

EUROPEAN CUPS 2005/06

UEFA CUP

FC VADUZ
1st qualifying round DACIA CHISINAU (MOL)
H **2-0** Gohouri (53), Gaspar de Souza (72)
Silva, Bell, Hasler (López 63), Stocklasa Ma., Telser, Burki (D'Elia 81), Pérez, Zarn, Gohouri, Gaspar de Souza, Pohja.
A **0-1**
Silva, Bell, Stocklasa Ma., Telser, Pérez (Maggetti 81), Zarn, Gerster, Gohouri, Gaspar de Souza, Pohja (Burki 72), D'Elia.

2nd qualifying round BESIKTAS (TUR)
H **0-1**
Silva, Bell, Stocklasa Ma., Telser, Zuniga, Burki (Hasler 74), Pérez, Zarn, Gohouri, Antic (Pohja 59), Gaspar de Souza.
A **1-5** Gaspar de Souza (29)
König, Bell, Stocklasa Mi. (Gohouri 79), Stocklasa Ma., López, Burki, Maggetti (Pérez 61), Gerster, Gaspar de Souza, Pohja, D'Elia (Zarn 72).

DOMESTIC CUP 2005/06

FIRST ROUND
(13/9/06)
FC Vaduz III 2, USV Eschen/Mauren II (aet)
FC Schaan II 3, FC Ruggell 4 (aet)
FC Balzers II 2, FC Triesenberg 0

(14/9/06)
FC Triesenberg II 0, USV Eschen/Mauren 6
FC Triesen Esp. 0, FC Balzers 9
FC Ruggell II 0, FC Schaan 3
FC Vaduz II 0, FC Triesen 3
FC Schaan Azz. 0, FC Vaduz 12

QUARTER-FINALS
(18/10/05)
FC Schaan 1, FC Balzers 2
FC Triesen 0, USV Eschen/Mauren 4
(19/10/05)
USV Eschen/Mauren II 1, FC Ruggell 2
FC Balzers II 0, FC Vaduz 12

SEMI-FINALS
(8/11/05)
FC Ruggell 1, FC Balzers 2
(9/11/05)
USV Eschen/Mauren 1, FC Vaduz 3

FINAL
(17/4/06)
Rheinpark Stadion, Vaduz
FC VADUZ 4 (Ritzberger 14, Antic 71, Sara 97, Telser 104)
FC BALZERS 2 (Angelov 39, Büchel M. 90p)
(aet)
Referee – Rutschi
FC VADUZ – König, Telser, Stocklasa Ma., Ritzberger, Akdemir, Zarn, Gedeon, Maggetti (Perez 46), Shala (Burki 46), Fischer (Antic 70), Sara.
FC BALZERS – Vogt R., Hämmerle, Wolfinger, Ioanna, Meierhofer, Christen (Kindle 101), Frick D., Büchel M., Wille (Pietrafasa 70), Angelov, Vogt J. (Akyer 58).

Lithuania

Ekranas come good at last

Everyone knew that one day their time would come, and in 2005 Ekranas Panevezys finally fulfilled their potential to end the six-year reign of FBK Kaunas and win the Lithuanian championship.

The two clubs had developed an intense rivalry, but it was always Kaunas who came through to win. In 2004 it had even come down to the final game of the season before the perennial champions collected the title. In 2005, with the A Lyga expanded from eight clubs to ten, Ekranas were determined to put Kaunas under pressure right from the start. The plan worked a treat.

When the two teams came face to face in early May, in round eight of the 36-match series, Ekranas had won all seven games whereas the defending champions had not only fallen six points behind but had also sacked their Double-winning coach, Valdas Ivanauskas (who would later resurface at Kaunas owner Vladimir Romanov's Scottish enterprise, Heart of Midlothian). Ekranas duly won the game 1-0, and from that moment on they were always in complete control of their destiny.

Although the season was a long one, with eight games more than in 2004, Ekranas never relaxed their grip. In fact, the longer the season went on, the bigger their lead grew. It was a slow build-up of excitement until, on October 26, a 3-1 victory away to Atlantas Klaipeda put them out of range of their pursuers. For the first time in 12 years, the title was theirs.

A nation celebrates

It was a triumph that delighted not just the Ekranas fans but also the nation in general. It was practically an all-Lithuanian squad, led by a Lithuanian coach, Virginijus Liubsys, who had also been in charge when Ekranas last won the title in 1993. The team had largely grown up together, and although three members of the group – Aurimas Kucys, Mindaugas Gardzijauskas and Donatas Petrauskas – all missed a large chunk of the season with injury, the solidarity and resolve of the others masked their absence. Captain Mantas Savenas was the star of the show. He was the A Lyga's top scorer, with 27 goals, and also scooped the Player of the Year award, with team-mate Gediminas Paulauskas finishing runner-up. Furhermore, Savenas, Paulauskas and defender Arunas Klimavicius – all 23-year-olds born within a couple of months of one another - became regulars in the Lithuanian national team.

Ekranas's title win fully compensated for the disappointment of going out of the UEFA Cup to Cork City and of losing in the semi-final of the Lithuanian Cup to Kaunas. In both instances Ekranas went out because of defeats at home. Remarkably the team would remain unbeaten away from Panevezys in all competitions during 2005 – a total of 22 matches.

NATIONAL TEAM RESULTS 2005/06

17/8/05	Belarus	H	Vilnius	1-0	Cesnauskis D. (45)
3/9/05	Serbia & Montenegro (WCQ)	A	Belgrade	0-2	
7/9/05	Bosnia-Herzegovina (WCQ)	H	Vilnius	0-1	
8/10/05	Serbia & Montenegro (WCQ)	H	Vilnius	0-2	
12/10/05	Belgium (WCQ)	H	Vilnius	1-1	Deschacht (38og)
1/3/06	Albania	A	Tirana	2-1	Savenas (34), Danilevicius (41)
2/5/06	Poland	A	Belchatow	1-0	Gedgaudas (14)

Lithuania

NATIONAL TEAM APPEARANCES 2005/06

Coach - Algimantas LIUBINSKAS

Player	DOB	Club	BIs	SCG	BOS	SCG	BEL	Alb	Pol	Caps	Goals
Zydrunas KARCEMARSKAS	24/5/83	Dinamo Moskva (RUS)	G	G	G	G	G			17	-
Nerijus BARASA	6/1/78	Krylya Sovetov Samara (RUS)	D90							24	2
Andrius SKERLA	29/4/77	Dunfermline Athletic (SCO) /Tom Tomsk (RUS)	D	D		D	D	D		46	-
Rolandas DZIAUKSTAS	1/4/78	FK Moskva (RUS) /Saturn Ramenskoe (RUS)	D	D85	D	D	D			35	-
Aurelijus SKARBALIUS	12/5/73	Brøndby IF (DEN)	D89	D	D46					65	5
Deividas CESNAUSKIS	30/6/81	Heart of Midlothian (SCO)	M81	M	M66					21	4
Deividas SEMBERAS	2/8/78	CSKA Moskva (RUS)	M	M	M	M	M			44	-
Tomas DANILEVICIUS	18/7/78	Avellino (ITA)	M46		M	A88	A	A85		28	4
Edgaras CESNAUSKIS	5/2/84	Dynamo Kyiv (UKR)	M	M	M					19	1
Robertas POSKUS	5/5/79	Zenit Sankt-Peterburg (RUS)	A46		A			A71		31	7
Edgaras JANKAUSKAS	12/3/75	Heart of Midlothian (SCO)	A62	A	A	A				45	8
Aidas PREIKSAITIS	15/7/70	Vetra Vilnius	s46	M72		M	M		M	44	3
Dimitrijus GUSCINAS	12/12/75	TuS Koblenz (GER)	s46							5	-
Saulius MIKOLIUNAS	2/5/84	Heart of Midlothian (SCO)	s62	M68	s66	M60	s83	M81		14	-
Mantas SAVENAS	27/8/82	Ekranas Panevezys	s81	s72	s46	M	M	M61	M90	8	1
Gediminas PAULAUSKAS	27/10/82	Ekranas Panevezys	s89	D		D77	D	D	D	8	-
Arunas KLIMAVICIUS	5/10/82	Ekranas Panevezys	s90						D	3	-
Tomas RADZINEVICIUS	5/6/81	Suduva Marijampole /FC Slovan Liberec (CZE)		s68		s88	s90	A		14	-
Darius ZUTAUTAS	30/9/78	Alania Vladikavkaz (RUS) /unattached /Atlantas Klaipeda		s85			D	s88	D	23	-
Marius STANKEVICIUS	15/7/81	Brescia (ITA)			D	D	D90	D		22	1
Tomas ZVIRGZDAUSKAS	18/3/75	Halmstads BK (SWE)			D			D		38	-
Igoris MORINAS	21/2/75	Zalgiris Vilnius			s60	M83			M	38	7
Aivaras LAURISAS	5/4/77	Atlantas Klaipeda			s77					3	-
Mindaugas MALINAUSKAS	11/8/83	Zalgiris Vilnius					G			1	-
Darius MICEIKA	22/2/83	Metalurgs Liepaja (LAT)					M88			1	-
Linas PILIBAITIS	5/4/85	FBK Kaunas					s61	s68		2	-
Marius ZALIUKAS	10/11/83	FBK Kaunas					s71	s90		2	-
Mindaugas KALONAS	28/2/84	Metalurgs Liepaja (LAT)					s81			1	-
Povilas LUKSYS	7/7/79	Ekranas Panevezys					s85	s79		2	-
Vaidotas ZUTAUTAS	18/7/71	Vetra Vilnius						G		9	-
Irmantas ZELMIKAS	3/1/80	FBK Kaunas						D		3	-
Andrius GEDGAUDAS	18/9/78	Atlantas Klaipeda						M74		7	2
Valdas TRAKYS	20/3/79	Atlantas Klaipeda						A79		5	2
Ricardas BENIUSIS	23/4/80	FBK Kaunas						A68		11	1
Vitalijus KAVALIAUSKAS	7/7/83	Ekranas Panevezys						s74		5	-

Lithuania

Kaunas paid the price for complacency in the league. After six titles on the trot they thought they were unbeatable, but they finished up ten full points behind Ekranas and went through three coaches. Russian Aleksandr Piskaryov had the privilege of leading Kaunas into battle against holders Liverpool in the second qualifying round of the Champions League but was sacked immediately afterwards. The man who replaced him, Igoris Pankratjevas, had his finest moment at the end of October when he steered Kaunas to a successful defence of the Lithuanian Cup with a 2-0 extra-time victory over Vetra Vilnius.

Vetra missed out on one route into the UEFA Cup by losing the Cup final and they were to surrender another opportunity by allowing Suduva Marijampole to sneak past them and take third place in the league. Vetra had held the position virtually all season but two costly away defeats in the run-in opened the door to Suduva, and the provincial side took full advantage. Earlier in the campaign, with Italian coach Rino Lavezzini at the helm, Suduva had been down in eighth place, but once Algimantas Gabrys took over, they began to fly up the table. Their star performer, as usual, was striker Tomas Radzinevicius, whose 25 goals earned him third place in the Player of the Year poll and a winter transfer to Czech league leaders Slovan Liberec.

Relegation cancelled

2005 was a wretched season for big clubs Atlantas Klaipeda and Zilgiris Vilnius, who finished seventh and eighth, respectively. It should have been worse still for the two teams below them, but as the clubs eligible for promotion – Alytis Alytus and Gelezinis Vilkas Vilnius – both declined a place in the A Lyga on financial grounds, Siauliai and Nevezis Kedainiai were allowed to stay up. In the case of Nevezis, who failed to win a game all season, salvation probably felt more like a punishment than a prize.

The Lithuanian national team's slim hopes of a World Cup play-off spot evaporated with home defeats by Bosnia-Herzegovina and Serbia & Montenegro, but two friendly victories in the spring away to Albania and Poland proved that Algimantas Liubinskas's side could play constructive and disciplined football when they wanted. They might discover that Italy, France and Ukraine prove rather tougher nuts to crack in the Euro 2008 qualifiers.

EUROPEAN CUPS 2005/06

UEFA CHAMPIONS LEAGUE

FBK KAUNAS

1st qualifying round HB (FAR)
A 4-2 *Velicka (2, 25), Klimek (35), Zelmikas (63)*
Kurskis, Kancelskis, Zelmikas, Baguzis (Kunevicius 74), Manchkhava, Kvartskhelia (Papeckys 46), Tamosauskas, Poderis, Barevicius, Klimek (Rimkevicius 74), Velicka.
H 4-0 *Velicka (44), Rimkevicius (64, 82), Zelmikas (90)*
Kurskis, Kancelskis, Zelmikas, Baguzis, Manchkhava, Papeckys, Tamosauskas, Poderis (Pacevicius 72), Barevicius (Maciulis 66), Klimek (Rimkevicius 46), Velicka.

2nd qualifying round LIVERPOOL (ENG)
H 1-3 *Barevicius (21)*
Kurskis, Kancelskis, Zelmikas, Pacevicius (Petrenka 46), Baguzis, Manchkhava, Tamosauskas, Poderis (Maciulis 88), Klimek, Barevicius (Papeckys 72), Rimkevicius.
A 0-2
Kilijonas, Kancelskis, Zelmikas, Baguzis, Manchkhava, Pehlic (Barevicius 66), Petrenko (Klimek 45), Kvartskhelia, Kunevicius, Poderis (Maciulis 87), Rimkevicius.

UEFA CUP

EKRANAS PANEVEZYS

1st qualifying round CORK CITY (IRL)
H 0-2
Skrupskis, Banevicius (Saulenas 46), Skroblas, Paulauskas, Klimavicius, Galkevicius (72 Mizigurskis), Tomkevicius, Savenas, Gardzijauskas, Luksys, Kavaliauskas.
A 1-0 *Klimavicius (60)*
Skrupskis, Skroblas, Paulauskas, Kilimavicius, Mizigurskis (Galkevicius 59), Tomkevicius, Savenas, Gardzijauskas, Saulenas (Mykolaitis 79), Luksys, Kavaliauskas.

ATLANTAS KLAIPEDA

1st qualifying round RHYL (WAL)
A 1-2 *Zvingilas (77)*
Lekevicius, Deveika, Maciulevicius, Zukauskas, Gnedojus, Bartkus, Zernys (Zvingilas 46), Petreikis, Ksanavicius (Lapeikis 73), Laurisas, Trakys.
H 3-2 *Zernys (12p), Laurisas (68), Petreikis (78)*
Valius, Deveika (Maciulevicius 53), Tolis, Navikas, Zukauskas (Sarunas 59), Ringys (Zvingilas 46), Bartkus, Zernys, Petreikis, Ksanavicius, Laurisas.

TOP GOALSCORERS 2005

27	Mantas SAVENAS (Ekranas Panevezys)
25	Tomas RADZINEVICIUS (Suduva Marijampole)
19	Povilas LUKSYS (Ekranas Panevezys)
16	Ricardas BENIUSIS (FBK Kaunas)
15	Andrius VELICKA (FBK Kaunas)
14	Vitalijus KAVALIAUSKAS (Ekranas Panevezys)
	Gvidas JUSKA (Silute)
13	Gediminas BUTAVICIUS (Siauliai)
11	Aivaras LAURISAS (Atlantas Klaipeda)
	Mindaugas PANKA (Vilnius)

Lithuania

FINAL LEAGUE TABLE 2005

		Pld	Home					Away					Total					Pts
			W	D	L	F	A	W	D	L	F	A	W	D	L	F	A	
1	Ekranas Panevezys	36	14	2	2	42	11	15	3	0	45	12	29	5	2	87	23	92
2	FBK Kaunas	36	13	2	3	47	14	13	2	3	42	11	26	4	6	89	25	82
3	Suduva Marijampole	36	9	6	3	35	18	7	5	6	32	25	16	11	9	67	43	59
4	Vetra Vilnius	36	12	2	4	30	17	5	4	9	15	28	17	6	13	45	45	57
5	Vilnius	36	6	8	4	20	10	5	6	7	16	19	11	14	11	36	29	47
6	Silute	36	9	4	5	27	24	3	4	11	17	37	12	8	16	44	61	44
7	Atlantas Klaipeda	36	6	5	7	23	27	5	3	10	17	25	11	8	17	40	52	41
8	Zalgiris Vilnius	36	5	5	8	20	23	6	3	9	20	29	11	8	17	40	52	41
9	Siauliai	36	5	3	10	24	35	3	6	9	16	26	8	9	19	40	61	33
10	Nevezis Kedainiai	36	0	2	16	6	53	0	3	15	12	62	0	5	31	18	115	5

LEAGUE RESULTS/SCORERS/APPEARANCES/GOALS 2005

ATLANTAS KLAIPEDA
Coach - Igoris Pankratjevas; (1/6/05) Vacys Lekevicius

2005

12/4	Suduva Marijampole	h	1-0	Zvingilas
16/4	Silute	a	0-3	
19/4	Vetra Vilnius	h	1-0	Zvingilas
23/4	Zalgiris Vilnius	a	2-1	Zigutis, Bartkus
26/4	Nevezis Kedainiai	h	5-1	Laurisas 2, Trakys, Zigutis, Zvingilas
30/4	Ekranas Panevezys	h	0-1	
3/5	FBK Kaunas	a	1-2	Laurisas
7/5	Siauliai	h	3-1	Navikas, Laurisas 2
14/5	Vilnius	a	0-1	
17/5	Ekranas Panevezys	a	2-1	Navikas, Veseljevas
24/5	Suduva Marijampole	a	0-1	
28/5	Silute	h	0-0	
8/6	Vetra Vilnius	a	2-0	Zvingilas, Laurisas
11/6	Zalgiris Vilnius	h	2-2	Laurisas, Zvingilas
14/6	Nevezis Kedainiai	a	0-0	
18/6	Ekranas Panevezys	a	0-0	
25/6	FBK Kaunas	a	1-3	Pioch
28/6	Siauliai	a	0-2	
2/7	Vilnius	h	0-1	
5/7	Suduva Marijampole	a	1-2	Trakys
23/7	Silute	a	0-1	
2/8	Vetra Vilnius	h	1-3	Zvingilas
7/8	Zalgiris Vilnius	a	1-0	Laurisas
20/8	Nevezis Kedainiai	h	2-2	Bezykornovas, Zernys (p)
23/8	FBK Kaunas	h	0-2	
27/8	Siauliai	h	2-0	Laurisas, Bezykornovas
10/9	Vilnius	a	1-4	Bezykornovas
17/9	Suduva Marijampole	h	1-3	Gussev
24/9	Silute	h	2-2	Zernys (p), Ksanavicius
1/10	Vetra Vilnius	a	2-3	Bezykornovas, Petreikis
15/10	Zalgiris Vilnius	h	1-1	Laurisas
18/10	Nevezis Kedainiai	a	3-0	Zvingilas, Laurisas, Gussev
26/10	Ekranas Panevezys	h	1-3	Maciulevicius
30/10	FBK Kaunas	h	0-5	
6/11	Siauliai	a	1-1	Zvingilas
12/11	Vilnius	h	1-0	Petreikis

No	Name	Nat	Pos	Aps	(s)	Gls
12	Maksimas ALILUJEVAS		A		(2)	
6	Andrius BARTKUS		M	18	(6)	1
18	Marius BEZYKORNOVAS		M	6	(2)	4
2	Kestutis DEVEIKA		D	15	(2)	
20	Kazimieras GNEDOJUS		D	14	(1)	
4	Haroldas GRACHOLSKIS		M		(1)	
16	Mantas GRIGAITIS		M	2	(4)	
15	Vitali GUSSEV	EST	A	6	(2)	2
15	Badr HAMDOUCHI	GER	A	1	(2)	
28	Audrius KSANAVICIUS		A	6	(2)	1
8	Vilius LAPEIKIS		M	5	(2)	
7	Aivaras LAURISAS		A	30		11
12	Arnas LEKEVICIUS		G	5		
3	Romas MACIULEVICIUS		D	19	(3)	1
32	Mindaugas MAKSVYTIS		G	1		
15	Audrius MIRAUSKAS		M		(3)	
13	Donatas NAVIKAS		M	24		2
18	Justas NOREIKA		D		(1)	
25	Andrius PANCEROVAS		D	6	(4)	
11	Andrius PETREIKIS		M	24	(2)	2
14	Markus PIOCH	GER	M	3	(4)	1
13	Andrius PUOTKALIS		A	6		
19	Darius RAMONAS		D	4	(2)	
4	Darius REGELSKIS		D	6		
24	Robertas RINGYS		M	6	(9)	
23	Povilas SARUNAS		D	17	(4)	
	Dmitrijus SISKINAS		M		(1)	
17	Marius SOBLINSKAS		D	1	(2)	
27	Antanas TAUTVYDAS		M	7	(13)	
4	Audrius TOLIS		D	9		
30	Valdas TRAKYS		A	16	(3)	
2	Evaldas UZKURAITIS		D	9	(1)	
1	Liudvikas VALIUS		G	30		
29	Ivan VASILYEV	RUS	A	9	(1)	
18	Aleksandras VESELJEVAS		M	8		1
17	Dainius ZERNYS		M	33		2
21	Mindaugas ZIGUTIS		D	12	(4)	2
9	Egidijus ZUKAUSKAS		D	20		
10	Rimantas ZVINGILAS		A	18	(12)	8

EKRANAS PANEVEZYS
Coach - Virginijus Liubsys

2005

Lithuania

Date	Opponent	H/A	Score	Scorers
12/4	Vilnius	h	5-1	Luksys, Paulauskas, Gardzijauskas, Savenas, Skroblas
16/4	Suduva Marijampole	h	2-0	Kucys, Gardzijauskas
19/4	Silute	h	2-1	Savenas (p), Luksys
23/4	Vetra Vilnius	a	2-0	Kucys, Luksys
26/4	Zalgiris Vilnius	h	2-0	Klimavicius, Savenas (p)
30/4	Atlantas Klaipeda	a	1-0	Paulauskas
3/5	Nevezis Kedainiai	h	1-0	Kavaliauskas
7/5	FBK Kaunas	h	1-0	Gardzijauskas
14/5	Siauliai	h	1-0	Kavaliauskas
17/5	Atlantas Klaipeda	h	1-2	Kavaliauskas
24/5	Vilnius	a	1-0	Savenas
28/5	Suduva Marijampole	a	2-2	Savenas 2 (1p)
8/6	Silute	a	5-1	Kavaliauskas 2, Kucys, og (Baguzis), Saulenas
11/6	Vetra Vilnius	h	8-0	Luksys 3, Kucys, Gardzijauskas, Kavaliauskas, Savenas, Mykolaitis
14/6	Zalgiris Vilnius	a	4-0	Kavaliauskas 2, Paulauskas, Savenas
18/6	Atlantas Klaipeda	h	0-0	
25/6	Nevezis Kedainiai	a	4-0	Luksys 2, Saulenas, Savenas
28/6	FBK Kaunas	a	2-1	Klimavicius, Savenas
2/7	Siauliai	a	2-2	Kavaliauskas, Paulauskas
5/7	Vilnius	h	2-0	Kavaliauskas, Luksys
23/7	Suduva Marijampole	a	2-1	Savenas, Kavaliauskas
2/8	Silute	h	3-0	Kavaliauskas 2, Galkevicius
6/8	Vetra Vilnius	a	1-1	Savenas
20/8	Zalgiris Vilnius	h	4-0	Savenas 3 (2p), Luksys
23/8	Nevezis Kedainiai	a	4-1	Kavolis, Klimavicius, Kavaliauskas, Savenas (p)
27/8	FBK Kaunas	h	0-0	
10/9	Siauliai	a	3-1	Savenas (p), Luksys 2
17/9	Vilnius	a	1-0	Savenas
24/9	Suduva Marijampole	h	4-1	Savenas, Galkevicius, Luksys, Mykolaitis
1/10	Silute	a	2-0	Luksys 2
15/10	Vetra Vilnius	h	1-0	Luksys
18/10	Zalgiris Vilnius	a	2-0	Savenas, Luksys
26/10	Atlantas Klaipeda	a	3-1	Paulauskas, Savenas 2
30/10	Nevezis Kedainiai	a	5-0	Savenas 3, Luksys 2
6/11	FBK Kaunas	a	3-2	Savenas 2 (1p), Saulenas
9/11	Siauliai	h	1-5	Mizigurskis

No	Name	Nat	Pos	Aps	(s)	Gls
8	Andrius ARLAUSKAS		D		(5)	
16	Audrius BANEVICIUS		D	27	(2)	
2	Giorgi BERIANIDZE	GEO	D		(3)	
18	Dominykas GALKEVICIUS		M	17	(3)	2
25	Mindaugas GARDZIJAUSKAS		M	24		4
12	Paulius GRYBAUSKAS		G	6	(2)	
3	Lauras JANUSEVICIUS		D	5	(4)	
21	Vitalijus KAVALIAUSKAS		A	33	(2)	14
24	Tomas KAVOLIS		M	5	(9)	1
4	Arunas KLIMAVICIUS		D	34		3
10	Aurimas KUCYS		M	17		4
9	Povilas LUKSYS		A	35		19
17	Valerijus MIZIGURSKIS		A	3	(19)	1
6	Kestutis MYKOLAITIS		M	3	(14)	2
13	Gediminas PAULAUSKAS		D	33		5
23	Donatas PETRAUSKAS		M	5	(9)	
31	Laurynas RIMAVICIUS		D	3	(11)	
14	Dainius SAULENAS		A	13	(18)	3
7	Mantas SAVENAS		M	36		27
20	Alfredas SKROBLAS		D	35		1
1	Arvydas SKRUPSKIS		G	30		
77	Giedrius TOMKEVICIUS		M	32	(1)	

FBK KAUNAS

Coach - Valdas Ivanauskas; (3/5/05) Aleksandr Piskaryov (RUS); (6/8/05) Igoris Pankratjevas

2005

Date	Opponent	H/A	Score	Scorers
12/4	Siauliai	h	5-1	Beniusis 3, Velicka, Barevicius
16/4	Vilnius	a	0-1	
19/4	Suduva Marijampole	h	3-0	Poderis, Velicka, Barevicius
23/4	Silute	a	4-0	Beniusis 2, Puotkalis, Barevicius
26/4	Vetra Vilnius	h	0-2	
30/4	Zalgiris Vilnius	h	4-0	Velicka, Beniusis 2, Barevicius
3/5	Atlantas Klaipeda	h	2-1	Sanajevas, Poderis
7/5	Ekranas Panevezys	a	0-1	
11/5	Zalgiris Vilnius	a	2-0	Rimkevicius 2
14/5	Nevezis Kedainiai	a	8-0	Tamosauskas 2, Sanajevas, Kunevicius, Zelmikas, Velicka 2, Rimkevicius
24/5	Siauliai	h	0-0	
28/5	Vilnius	h	0-0	
8/6	Suduva Marijampole	a	1-0	Zelmikas
11/6	Silute	h	4-1	Velicka, Barevicius 2, Rimkevicius
14/6	Vetra Vilnius	a	1-0	Barevicius
21/6	Vilnius	a	0-0	
25/6	Atlantas Klaipeda	h	3-1	Puotkalis, Beniusis 2
28/6	Ekranas Panevezys	h	1-2	Tamosauskas (p)
2/7	Nevezis Kedainiai	h	5-0	Velicka 2, Poderis, Tamosauskas, Kvartskhelia
5/7	Siauliai	a	0-1	
6/8	Silute	a	4-1	Poderis 2 (1p), Rimkevicius, Pilibaitis
12/8	Zalgiris Vilnius	a	3-2	Klimek 2, Pehlic
20/8	Vetra Vilnius	h	3-0	Rimkevicius, Klimek 2
23/8	Atlantas Klaipeda	a	2-0	Klimek 2
27/8	Ekranas Panevezys	a	0-0	
10/9	Nevezis Kedainiai	h	3-0	Kvartskhelia, Pilibaitis, Rimkevicius
17/9	Siauliai	a	3-2	Pehlic, Rimkevicius, Maciulis
20/9	Suduva Marijampole	h	3-1	Klimek, Barevicius, Pehlic
24/9	Vilnius	h	1-0	Velicka
1/10	Suduva Marijampole	a	4-3	Kvartskhelia 2, Klimek, Pilibaitis
15/10	Silute	h	5-0	Velicka 2, Beniusis 2, Pilibaitis
18/10	Vetra Vilnius	a	3-0	Kvartskhelia, Beniusis, Pehlic
26/10	Zalgiris Vilnius	h	3-2	Beniusis, Velicka, Zelmikas
30/10	Atlantas Klaipeda	a	5-0	Velicka, Rimkevicius, Beniusis 2, Papeckys
6/11	Ekranas Panevezys	h	2-3	Beniusis, Rimkevicius
9/11	Nevezis Kedainiai	a	2-0	Velicka 2

No	Name	Nat	Pos	Aps	(s)	Gls
4	Mindaugas BAGUZIS		D	10		

Lithuania

No	Name	Nat	Pos	Aps	(s)	Gls
7	Giedrius BAREVICIUS		M	25	(8)	8
8	Ricardas BENIUSIS		A	17	(11)	16
16	Andrius GEDGAUDAS		M	1	(4)	
10	Vitali GUSSEV	EST	A	1	(7)	
24	Kestutis IVASKEVICIUS		M	9	(6)	
5	Tomas KANCELSKIS		D	22	(1)	
14	Tadas KIJANSKAS		D	1	(1)	
1	Sarunas KILIJONAS		G	12		
13	Arkadiusz KLIMEK	POL	A	8	(2)	8
21	Audrius KSANAVICIUS		A	2	(3)	
23	Dainius KUNEVICIUS		D	21	(2)	1
12	Eduardas KURSKIS		G	24		
20	Givi KVARATSKHELIA	GEO	M	28		5
9	Nerijus MACIULIS		M	3	(6)	1
6	Nukri MANCHKHAVA	GEO	D	14	(1)	
4	Mindaugas PACEVICIUS		D	7	(1)	
15	Tadas PAPECKYS		M	16	(6)	1
27	Edin PEHLIC	BOS	M	11	(2)	4
21	Vadimas PETRENKA		M	6	(6)	
24	Linas PILIBAITIS		A	7	(8)	4
19	Eimantas PODERIS		A	23	(4)	5
13	Andrius PUOTKALIS		A	6	(6)	2
14	Darius REGELSKIS		D	18		
11	Arturas RIMKEVICIUS		A	13	(8)	10
2	Darius SANAJEVAS		D	17		2
	Valentinas SULKEVICIUS		M		(1)	
25	Tomas TAMOSAUSKAS		M	14	(3)	4
17	Andrius VELICKA		A	27	(3)	15
26	Marius ZALIUKAS		D	10	(2)	
3	Irmantas ZELMIKAS		D	22		3
	Vygantas ZUBAVICIUS		M	1	(1)	

NEVEZIS KEDAINIAI
Coach - Vytautas Vaskunas

2005

Date	Opponent	h/a	Score	Scorers
12/4	Vetra Vilnius	a	0-1	
16/4	Siauliai	h	0-2	
19/4	Zalgiris Vilnius	a	0-4	
23/4	Vilnius	h	0-2	
26/4	Atlantas Klaipeda	a	1-5	Juknevicius
30/4	Suduva Marijampole	a	0-5	
3/5	Ekranas Panevezys	a	0-1	
7/5	Silute	h	0-0	
14/5	FBK Kaunas	h	0-8	
24/5	Vetra Vilnius	a	0-6	
28/5	Siauliai	a	0-4	
8/6	Zalgiris Vilnius	h	0-2	
11/6	Vilnius	a	1-1	Rabikauskas
14/6	Atlantas Klaipeda	h	0-0	
18/6	Suduva Marijampole	h	1-5	Cinikas
25/6	Ekranas Panevezys	h	0-4	
2/7	FBK Kaunas	a	0-5	
5/7	Vetra Vilnius	h	1-2	Cinikas
30/7	Zalgiris Vilnius	a	2-5	Stankevicius, Kestenis
6/8	Vilnius	h	0-3	
9/8	Silute	a	2-3	Popovas, Juknevicius
12/8	Suduva Marijampole	h	1-6	Stankevicius
20/8	Atlantas Klaipeda	a	2-2	Stankevicius 2
23/8	Ekranas Panevezys	a	1-4	Popovas
27/8	Silute	h	1-3	Cinikas
10/9	FBK Kaunas	a	0-3	
14/9	Siauliai	h	1-2	Stankevicius (p)
17/9	Vetra Vilnius	h	0-2	
24/9	Siauliai	a	2-2	Stankevicius 2
1/10	Zalgiris Vilnius	h	1-2	Juknevicius
15/10	Vilnius	a	0-3	
18/10	Atlantas Klaipeda	h	0-3	
26/10	Suduva Marijampole	a	1-5	Popovas
30/10	Ekranas Panevezys	h	0-5	
6/11	Silute	a	0-3	
9/11	FBK Kaunas	h	0-2	

No	Name	Nat	Pos	Aps	(s)	Gls
8	Darius ADOMAITIS		M	31	(3)	
13	Marius CINIKAS		A	35		3
11	Oleg DOROSHCHENKO	UKR	M	9	(1)	
15	Janas JANUSEVSKIS		M	4	(10)	
12	Tautvydas JAZOKAS		G	21	(1)	
14	Donatas JODENIS		M		(4)	
22	Martynas JUKNEVICIUS		M	31		3
5	Vitalijus JUREVICIUS		D	17	(6)	
21	Nerijus KESTENIS		M	32		1
24	Akaki KHUBUTIA	GEO	D	15		
16	Andrius KLIMAKOVAS		D	26	(2)	
24	David KVITATIANI	GEO	D	6		
	Deivydas LATUSENKA		M		(3)	
7	Paulius OLISAUSKAS		M	1	(3)	
18	Modestas PETRUSEVICIUS		D	10	(15)	
	Kestutis PIKELIS		M		(1)	
9	Aleksandras POPOVAS		A	19	(7)	3
12	Marius POSKUS		G	15		
20	Valentinas RABIKAUSKAS		D	32	(1)	1
7	Karolis ROKAS		M	1	(1)	
6	Rolandas SLEPAKOVAS		M	19	(13)	
10	Kestutis SMILGINAS		M	10		
17	Kestutis SRUOGIS		M	5	(11)	
3	Aivaras STANCIUS		D	12		
11	Vitalis STANKEVICIUS		A	33		7
15	Andrius URBSYS		M		(6)	
7	Vytautas VASKUNAS		D	12	(4)	

SIAULIAI
Coach - Vytautas Janciauskas; (1/10/05) Saulius Vertelis

2005

Date	Opponent	h/a	Score	Scorers
12/4	FBK Kaunas	a	1-5	Vasilkovas
16/4	Nevezis Kedainiai	a	2-0	og (Petrusevicius), og (Khubutia)
20/4	Vilnius	a	0-0	
23/4	Suduva Marijampole	a	0-1	
27/4	Silute	h	1-4	Atigbiolaye
30/4	Vetra Vilnius	a	1-2	Butavicius (p)
4/5	Zalgiris Vilnius	h	0-0	
7/5	Atlantas Klaipeda	a	1-3	Butavicius
14/5	Ekranas Panevezys	a	0-1	
24/5	FBK Kaunas	h	0-0	
28/5	Nevezis Kedainiai	h	4-0	Lunskis 2, Butavicius 2
8/6	Vilnius	h	0-1	
11/6	Suduva Marijampole	h	1-3	Smilginas
14/6	Silute	h	2-1	Butavicius, Sidlauskas A.
28/6	Atlantas Klaipeda	h	2-0	Atigbiolaye, Siciunas
2/7	Ekranas Panevezys	a	2-2	Rukas, Krukovskis
5/7	FBK Kaunas	h	1-0	Butavicius
30/7	Vilnius	h	0-2	
4/8	Suduva Marijampole	a	0-0	
9/8	Vetra Vilnius	h	1-2	Varnas
13/8	Vetra Vilnius	a	0-2	

Lithuania

Date	Opponent	H/A	Score	Scorers
20/8	Silute	h	1-4	Varnas (p)
23/8	Zalgiris Vilnius	h	0-4	
27/8	Atlantas Klaipeda	a	0-2	
10/9	Ekranas Panevezys	h	1-3	Butavicius
14/9	Nevezis Kedainiai	a	2-1	Butavicius, Sidlauskas A.
17/9	FBK Kaunas	h	2-3	Juodeikis, Butavicius
24/9	Nevezis Kedainiai	h	2-2	og (Rabikauskas), Sidlauskas A.
1/10	Vilnius	a	1-1	Varnas
4/10	Zalgiris Vilnius	h	2-3	Biecius, Krukovskis
15/10	Suduva Marijampole	h	1-4	Varnas
18/10	Silute	a	1-2	Varnas
26/10	Vetra Vilnius	h	1-0	Sidlauskas A.
30/10	Zalgiris Vilnius	a	1-1	Sidlauskas A.
6/11	Atlantas Klaipeda	h	1-1	Lunskis
12/11	Ekranas Panevezys	a	5-1	Butavicius 4, Varnas (p)

No	Name	Nat	Pos	Aps	(s)	Gls
12	Giedrius ARLAUSKIS		G	7	(1)	
16	Amaro ATIGBIOLAYE	NGA	M	27	(2)	2
23	Laimonas BALCIUNAS		M	5	(4)	
20	Evaldas BIECIUS		M	12	(9)	1
5	Marius BUIVIDAVICIUS		D	14	(2)	
21	Gediminas BUTAVICIUS		A	32	(2)	13
0	Vitalijus DANILICEVAS		M	2	(10)	
25	Aurimas GARUCKAS		M	7	(5)	
27	Nerijus GARUCKAS		M	5	(2)	
22	Gintaras JUODEIKIS		D	34		1
14	Tomas KAVOLIS		M	6	(8)	
8	Marekas KRUKOVSKIS		D	31		2
15	Deividas LUNSKIS		D	35		3
3	Andrejus ORIOLAS		D	22	(5)	
12	Audrius PASKEVICIUS		G	5		
14	Edvardas PSELENSKIS		A		(1)	
4	Darius RUKAS		D	24		1
10	Gintaras SICIUNAS		A	2	(21)	1
9	Andrius SIDLAUSKAS		M	35		5
28	Paulius SIDLAUSKAS		M		(1)	
19	Kestutis SMILGINAS		M	16	(4)	1
27	Donatas STROCKIS		M		(2)	
17	Eduardas TUCINSKIS		D	32		
	Mindaugas VALYS		D	5		
27	Egidijus VARNAS		A	12	(3)	6
18	Denisas VASILKOVAS		A	2	(5)	1
1	Vaidas ZUTAUTAS		G	24		

SILUTE
Coach - Svajunas Cesnulis

2006

Date	Opponent	H/A	Score	Scorers
12/4	Zalgiris Vilnius	a	0-2	
16/4	Atlantas Klaipeda	h	3-0	Grigalevicius, Juska 2
19/4	Ekranas Panevezys	a	1-2	Baguzis
23/4	FBK Kaunas	h	0-4	
27/4	Siauliai	h	4-1	Sulimenko, Grigalevicius 2, Juska
30/4	Vilnius	a	1-0	Juska
3/5	Suduva Marijampole	h	1-1	Juska (p)
7/5	Nevezis Kedainiai	a	0-0	
14/5	Vetra Vilnius	h	2-0	Cesnulis, Juska
24/5	Zalgiris Vilnius	h	1-0	Juska
28/5	Atlantas Klaipeda	a	0-0	
8/6	Ekranas Panevezys	h	1-5	Maciulis
11/6	FBK Kaunas	a	1-4	Butkus
14/6	Siauliai	a	1-2	Smitas
17/6	Vilnius	h	1-1	Juska
25/6	Suduva Marijampole	a	1-4	Maciulis
2/7	Vetra Vilnius	a	0-1	
23/7	Atlantas Klaipeda	h	1-0	Ivaskevicius
2/8	Ekranas Panevezys	a	0-3	
6/8	FBK Kaunas	h	1-4	Smitas
9/8	Nevezis Kedainiai	h	3-2	Grigalevicius, Ivaskevicius 2
12/8	Vilnius	h	1-1	Vicius
20/8	Siauliai	a	4-1	Kijanskas, Khubutia, Juska (p), Vicius
23/8	Suduva Marijampole	h	0-0	
27/8	Nevezis Kedainiai	a	3-1	Juska (p), Grigalevicius, Podelis
10/9	Vetra Vilnius	h	3-1	Ivaskevicius, Vicius, Grigalevicius
17/9	Zalgiris Vilnius	h	0-1	
24/9	Atlantas Klaipeda	a	2-2	Podelis, Grigalevicius
28/9	Zalgiris Vilnius	a	0-0	
1/10	Ekranas Panevezys	h	0-2	
15/10	FBK Kaunas	a	0-5	
18/10	Siauliai	h	2-1	Grigalevicius, Juska
26/10	Vilnius	a	1-5	Juska
30/10	Suduva Marijampole	a	1-2	Ivaskevicius
6/11	Nevezis Kedainiai	h	3-0	Juska 2 (2p), Grigalevicius
12/11	Vetra Vilnius	a	1-3	Judickas

No	Name	Nat	Pos	Aps	(s)	Gls
18	Maksimas ALILUJEVAS		A	2	(4)	
6	Audrius ANDRIEKUS		M	17	(4)	
4	Mindaugas BAGUZIS		D	17		1
15	Zigmantas BUTKUS		M	27	(2)	1
7	Svajunas CESNULIS		M	15		1
21	Deividas GARLIAUSKAS		D	2	(1)	
2	Edvardas GAURILOVAS		D	32	(1)	
16	Mindaugas GRIGALEVICIUS		A	20	(2)	9
10	Kestutis IVASKEVICIUS		M	15	(1)	5
3	Tomas JEGELAVICIUS		M	3	(1)	
8	Marius JUDICKAS		M	6	(6)	1
9	Gvidas JUSKA		A	32	(2)	14
23	Robertas KAMINSKAS		M	2	(6)	
25	Tomas KAZAKEVICIUS		M		(2)	
24	Tadas KAZLAUSKAS		M	4	(3)	
5	Akaki KHUBUTIA	GEO	D	14	(1)	1
24	Tadas KIJANSKAS		D	11		1
25	Marius KIZYS		M	10	(2)	
23	Karolis LEIKUS		D	2	(2)	
10	Nerijus MACIULIS		M	16		2
11	Saulius MALINAUSKAS		A	2	(1)	
14	Tomas MIKLINEVICIUS		M	22		
4	Jaunius MOCKUS		D	18		
30	Arturas NORMANTAS		G	2	(1)	
18	Mindaugas PACEVICIUS		D	10		
20	Gintas PODELIS		A	4	(11)	2
3	Darius RAMONAS		D	3	(3)	
25	Adomas RATKEVICIUS		D		(2)	
22	Robertas SMITAS		A	6	(10)	2
1	Modestas STONYS		G	34		
8	Yuriy SULIMENKO	UKR	A	10	(1)	1
20	Elnaras TARVYDAS		D		(2)	
19	Evaldas UZKURAITIS		D	10	(2)	
17	Gediminas VICIUS		M	8	(7)	3
5	Marius ZALIUKAS		D	14	(1)	

Lithuania

26	Vygintas ZUBAVICIUS		M	6	(6)	

SUDUVA MARIJAMPOLE
Coach - Rino Lavezzini (ITA); (28/5/05) Algimantas Gabrys

2005					
12/4	Atlantas Klaipeda	a	0-1		
16/4	Ekranas Panevezys	a	0-2		
19/4	FBK Kaunas	a	0-3		
23/4	Siauliai	h	1-0	Maciulevicius	
26/4	Vilnius	a	0-0		
30/4	Nevezis Kedainiai	h	5-0	Maciulevicius 2, Radzinevicius, Slavickas V., Afanasenko	
3/5	Silute	a	1-1	Radzinevicius	
7/5	Vetra Vilnius	a	0-1		
14/5	Zalgiris Vilnius	h	1-1	Radzinevicius	
24/5	Atlantas Klaipeda	h	1-0	Uselis	
28/5	Ekranas Panevezys	h	2-2	Radzinevicius, Uselis	
8/6	FBK Kaunas	h	0-1		
11/6	Siauliai	a	3-1	Radzinevicius, og (Tucinskis), Grigas	
14/6	Vilnius	h	2-2	Braga 2	
18/6	Nevezis Kedainiai	a	5-1	Grigas, Braga 2, Maciulevicius, Uselis	
25/6	Silute	h	4-1	Braga 2, Gvildys, Chigladze D.	
29/6	Vetra Vilnius	a	2-2	Radzinevicius (p), Butkus	
5/7	Atlantas Klaipeda	h	2-1	Maciulevicius, Uselis	
23/7	Ekranas Panevezys	h	1-2	Radzinevicius	
4/8	Siauliai	h	0-0		
12/8	Nevezis Kedainiai	a	6-1	Maciulevicius, Radzinevicius 4 (1p), Uselis	
20/8	Vilnius	a	1-1	og (Artiomovas)	
23/8	Silute	a	0-0		
26/8	Vetra Vilnius	h	1-1	Maciulevicius	
10/9	Zalgiris Vilnius	h	2-0	Maciulevicius (p), Radzinevicius	
13/9	Zalgiris Vilnius	a	4-2	Braga, Radzinevicius 3	
17/9	Atlantas Klaipeda	a	3-1	Radzinevicius 2, Uselis	
20/9	FBK Kaunas	a	1-3	Radzinevicius	
24/9	Ekranas Panevezys	a	1-4	Radzinevicius	
1/10	FBK Kaunas	h	3-4	Grigas, Radzinevicius, Afanasenko	
15/10	Siauliai	a	4-1	Veikutis, Adomaitis, Uselis, Braga	
18/10	Vilnius	h	1-1	Radzinevicius	
26/10	Nevezis Kedainiai	h	5-1	Uselis, Radzinevicius 3 (1p), Veikutis	
30/10	Silute	h	2-1	og (Mockus), Maciulevicius	
6/11	Vetra Vilnius	h	2-0	Radzinevicius, Butkus	
12/11	Zalgiris Vilnius	a	1-0	Maciulevicius	

No	Name	Nat	Pos	Aps	(s)	Gls
8	Vidas ADOMAITIS		M	23	(4)	1
7	Viktor AFANASENKO	BLS	M	18	(15)	2
5	Gerdas ALEKSA		D	19	(8)	
11	Ottávio BRAGA	BRA	A	11	(12)	8
21	Saulius BUTKUS		M	23	(7)	2
24	Besik CHIGLADZE	GEO	D	12	(3)	
14	David CHIGLADZE	GEO	D	31		1
26	Jose CORDEIRO	ITA	M	11	(1)	
	Nerijus DEVETINAS		D		(2)	
6	Enzo FERRARI	CHL	D	1		

2	Gvidas GRIGAS		D	24	(1)	3
3	Darius GVILDYS		D	36		1
4	Giedrius KLEVINSKAS		D	13	(1)	
55	Saulius KLEVINSKAS		G	3		
12	Povilas LEIMONAS		D		(5)	
15	Darius MACIULEVICIUS		M	32	(2)	10
20	Gytis PADIMANSKAS		G	24		
10	Tomas RADZINEVICIUS		A	35	(1)	25
13	Christian SAGNA	SEN	A	4		
9	Giedrius SLAVICKAS		M		(1)	
19	Vaidas SLAVICKAS		A	6	(11)	1
18	Valerio SPOSATO	ITA	D	1	(1)	
17	Andrius URBSYS		M	2	(7)	
16	Mantas USELIS		M	25	(8)	8
23	Audrius VEIKUTIS		D	33		2
51	Vaidas ZUTAUTAS		G	9		

VETRA VILNIUS
Coach - Sergei Borovskiy (BLS)

2005					
12/4	Nevezis Kedainiai	h	1-0	Sivinskis	
16/4	Zalgiris Vilnius	h	2-0	Douglas, Kochanauskas	
19/4	Atlantas Klaipeda	a	0-1		
23/4	Ekranas Panevezys	h	0-2		
26/4	FBK Kaunas	a	2-0	Douglas 2	
30/4	Siauliai	h	2-1	Vaineikis, Blazys	
3/5	Vilnius	a	0-0		
7/5	Suduva Marijampole	h	1-0	Sasnauskas	
14/5	Silute	a	0-2		
24/5	Nevezis Kedainiai	h	6-0	Vasiliauskas 2, Rinkus, Vaineikis, Blazys 2	
28/5	Zalgiris Vilnius	a	0-1		
8/6	Atlantas Klaipeda	h	0-2		
11/6	Ekranas Panevezys	a	0-8		
14/6	FBK Kaunas	h	0-1		
29/6	Suduva Marijampole	h	2-2	Kochanauskas 2	
2/7	Silute	h	1-0	Litvinas	
5/7	Nevezis Kedainiai	a	2-1	Vaineikis, Kochanauskas	
26/7	Vilnius	h	2-1	Preiksaitis (p), Litvinas	
2/8	Atlantas Klaipeda	a	3-1	Butrimavicius 2, Vaineikis	
6/8	Ekranas Panevezys	h	1-1	Sasnauskas	
9/8	Siauliai	a	2-1	Litvinas, Rinkus	
13/8	Siauliai	h	2-0	Preiksaitis (p), Vasiliauskas	
20/8	FBK Kaunas	a	0-3		
23/8	Vilnius	a	1-1	Vasiliauskas	
27/8	Suduva Marijampole	a	1-1	Sasnauskas	
10/9	Silute	a	1-3	Litvinas	
17/9	Nevezis Kedainiai	a	2-0	Stesko I. (p), Litvinas	
20/9	Zalgiris Vilnius	h	2-1	Vaineikis (p), Zudys	
24/9	Zalgiris Vilnius	a	1-1	Vaineikis (p)	
1/10	Atlantas Klaipeda	h	3-2	Blazys, Sasnauskas 2	
15/10	Ekranas Panevezys	a	0-1		
18/10	FBK Kaunas	h	0-3		
26/10	Siauliai	a	0-1		
30/10	Vilnius	h	2-0	Litvinas, Sernas	
6/11	Suduva Marijampole	a	0-2		
12/11	Silute	h	3-1	Sernas, Vasiliauskas, Blazys	

No	Name	Nat	Pos	Aps	(s)	Gls
15	Marius BABRAVICIUS		D	9	(2)	
20	Edvinas BLAZYS		A	10	(9)	5
18	Aleksei BOROVSKIY	BLS	M	3		
8	Gedimins BUTRIMAVICIUS		M	23	(5)	2

Lithuania

No	Name	Nat	Pos	Aps	(s)	Gls
22	Awenayeri DOUGLAS	NGA	A	6	(2)	3
2	Zydrunas GRUDZINSKAS		D	3		
9	Saulius KIJANSKAS		M	2		
6	Andrius KOCHANAUSKAS		A	25	(7)	4
14	Sarunas LITVINAS		A	16	(9)	6
5	Edvinas LUKOSEVICIUS		D	9	(1)	
12	Ramunas MERKELIS		G	27		
1	Mirza MERLANI	GEO	G	9		
27	Kestutis NEPAS		A	1		
25	Aidas PREIKSAITIS		M	30	(1)	2
4	Julius RALIUKONIS		D	34		
26	Janis RINKUS	LAT	M	18	(6)	2
3	Nerijus SASNAUSKAS		D	24	(4)	5
10	Darvydas SERNAS		M	13	(11)	2
17	Andzejus SIVINSKIS		M	16	(6)	1
19	Arturas STESKO		M	16	(7)	
23	Igoris STESKO		M	31	(3)	1
11	Rolandas VAINEIKIS		M	19	(7)	6
21	Nerijus VASILIAUSKAS		A	16	(6)	5
24	Robertas VEZEVICIUS		M	2	(14)	
16	Zilvinas ZUDYS		D	34		1

VILNIUS
Coach - Kestutis Latoza

2005

12/4	Ekranas Panevezys	a	1-5	Panka (p)
16/4	FBK Kaunas	h	1-0	Panka (p)
20/4	Siauliai	h	0-0	
23/4	Nevezis Kedainiai	a	2-0	Radavicius, Panka
26/4	Suduva Marijampole	h	0-0	
30/4	Silute	h	0-1	
3/5	Vetra Vilnius	h	0-0	
7/5	Zalgiris Vilnius	a	0-1	
14/5	Atlantas Klaipeda	h	1-0	Astrauskas
24/5	Ekranas Panevezys	h	0-1	
28/5	FBK Kaunas	a	0-0	
8/6	Siauliai	a	1-0	Panka
11/6	Nevezis Kedainiai	h	1-1	Astrauskas
14/6	Suduva Marijampole	a	2-2	Buinickis, Radavicius
17/6	Silute	a	1-1	Panka (p)
21/6	FBK Kaunas	h	0-0	
2/7	Atlantas Klaipeda	a	1-0	Luksa
5/7	Ekranas Panevezys	a	0-2	
26/7	Vetra Vilnius	a	1-2	Panka
30/7	Siauliai	a	2-0	Panka, Brazauskas
6/8	Nevezis Kedainiai	a	3-0	Panka (p), Astrauskas, Radavicius
12/8	Silute	a	1-1	Bakalag
20/8	Suduva Marijampole	h	1-1	Jersovas
23/8	Vetra Vilnius	h	1-1	Luksa
27/8	Zalgiris Vilnius	a	0-0	
10/9	Atlantas Klaipeda	h	4-1	Buinickis, Jersovas, Luksa, Brazauskas
17/9	Ekranas Panevezys	h	0-1	
24/9	FBK Kaunas	a	0-1	
1/10	Siauliai	h	1-1	Jersovas
15/10	Nevezis Kedainiai	h	3-0	Luksa, Panka, Radavicius
18/10	Suduva Marijampole	a	1-1	Luksa
22/10	Zalgiris Vilnius	h	2-0	Radavicius (p), Luksa
26/10	Silute	h	5-1	Panka 2, Bakalag, Luksa, Radavicius
30/10	Vetra Vilnius	a	0-2	
6/11	Zalgiris Vilnius	h	0-1	
12/11	Atlantas Klaipeda	a	0-1	

No	Name	Nat	Pos	Aps	(s)	Gls
15	Darius ARTIOMOVAS		D	35		
9	Nerijus ASTRAUSKAS		A	24	(8)	3
18	Pierre-Olivier BAKALAG	CMR	A	16	(13)	2
19	Andrius BRAZAUSKAS		M	21	(5)	2
11	Arsenijus BUINICKIS		A	15	(11)	2
7	CLÁUDIO Barbosa da Silva	BRA	A		(2)	
6	GLEYTON Barbosa	BRA	M	12		
7	Aleksandras IVANOVAS		M		(1)	
31	Vikentijus IVANOVAS		D		(1)	
40	Dainius JAGMINAS		D	31	(1)	
20	Arturas JERSOVAS		A	8	(16)	3
10	Valerian KATSITADZE	GEO	M	20	(7)	
16	Marius KAZLAUSKAS		D	34		
1	Maciej KIJEWSKI	POL	G	35		
6	LEONARDO Rodrigues dos Santos	BRA	A	1	(2)	
5	Vytautas LUKSA		M	32	(4)	7
32	Aleksandras MININKOVAS		M		(2)	
17	Mindaugas PANKA		M	33		11
2	Mindaugas PUODZIUNAS		D	1		
7	Nikolajus PUPKINAS		M		(1)	
13	Ramunas RADAVICIUS		M	34	(1)	6
12	Arturas SEMEZAS		G	1		
3	Andrejus SOKOLOVAS		D	36		
21	Marius STANAITIS		M		(2)	
4	Arturas ZARNOVSKIS		D	7	(2)	

ZALGIRIS VILNIUS
Coach - Saulius Sirmelis; (16/8/05) Viaceslavas Sukristovas; (6/10/05) Vincas Kateiva

2005

12/4	Silute	h	2-0	Jasaitis, Kauspadas
16/4	Vetra Vilnius	a	0-2	
19/4	Nevezis Kedainiai	h	4-0	Bezykornovas, Morinas 2, Kauspadas
23/4	Atlantas Klaipeda	h	1-2	Bezykornovas
26/4	Ekranas Panevezys	a	0-2	
30/4	FBK Kaunas	a	0-4	
4/5	Siauliai	h	0-0	
7/5	Vilnius	h	1-0	Joksas
11/5	FBK Kaunas	h	0-2	
14/5	Suduva Marijampole	a	1-1	Osipovich
24/5	Silute	a	0-1	
28/5	Vetra Vilnius	h	1-0	Bezykornovas
8/6	Nevezis Kedainiai	a	2-0	Morinas, Lemezis
11/6	Atlantas Klaipeda	a	2-2	Joksas, og (Deveika)
14/6	Ekranas Panevezys	h	0-4	
30/7	Nevezis Kedainiai	h	5-2	Jasaitis (p), Mikuckis, Kauspadas, Graziunas, Osipovich
7/8	Atlantas Klaipeda	h	0-1	
12/8	FBK Kaunas	h	2-3	Lemezis, Kauspadas
20/8	Ekranas Panevezys	a	0-4	
23/8	Siauliai	a	4-0	Dovksa, Morinas, Graziunas, og (Oriolas)
27/8	Vilnius	h	0-0	
10/9	Suduva Marijampole	a	0-2	
13/9	Suduva Marijampole	h	2-4	Morinas, Karalius
17/9	Silute	a	1-0	Morinas
20/9	Vetra Vilnius	a	1-2	Yagodkin
24/9	Vetra Vilnius	h	1-1	Maksimovicius
28/9	Silute	h	0-0	
1/10	Nevezis Kedainiai	a	2-1	Morinas, Karalius
4/10	Siauliai	a	3-2	Morinas, Lemezis, Karalius

Lithuania

15/10	Atlantas Klaipeda	a	1-1	Dovksa	
18/10	Ekranas Panevezys	h	0-2		
22/10	Vilnius	a	0-2		
26/10	FBK Kaunas	a	2-3	Lemezis, og (Zelmikas)	
30/10	Siauliai	h	1-1	Lemezis	
6/11	Vilnius	a	1-0	Karalius	
12/11	Suduva Marijampole	h	0-1		

No	Name	Nat	Pos	Aps	(s)	Gls
26	Valentinas BARANOVSKIS		M		(3)	
7	Marius BEZYKORNOVAS		M	14		3
9	Marijanas CHORUZIJUS		M	6	(6)	
24	Jevgenijus DOVKSA		M	10	(7)	2
18	Tadas GRAZIUNAS		D	25		2
19	Karolis JASAITIS		M	15	(4)	2
21	Branislav JASUREK	SVK	A	7	(3)	
2	Andrius JOKSAS		D	18	(9)	2
10	Martynas KARALIUS		A	11	(2)	4
11	Vidas KAUSPADAS		A	10	(13)	4
4	Arturas KILIKEVICIUS		D	5	(2)	
15	Virmantas LEMEZIS		M	33	(2)	5
12	Pavelas LEUSAS		G	3		
23	Andzejus MAKSIMOVICIUS		M	18	(5)	1
1	Mindaugas MALINAUSKAS		G	23		
5	Tomas MIKUCKIS		D	23	(1)	1
20	Andrius MILISKEVICIUS		M	6	(5)	
14	Igoris MORINAS		M	29		8
16	Antonas NAUMOVAS		M	1	(3)	
13	Aleksandr OSIPOVICH	BLS	A	5	(9)	2
17	Paulius PAKNYS		D	15	(2)	
10	Vadimas PETRENKA		M	7		
12	Ernestas SETKUS		G	10	(1)	
6	Andrei SHILO	BLS	M	30	(2)	
22	Andzejus SOROKINAS		D	10	(3)	
8	Ramunas STONKUS		M	13	(6)	
3	Andrejus TERESKINAS		D	21	(3)	
22	Nerijus VALSKIS		M	7	(4)	
7	Iliya YAGODKIN	RUS	M	4	(1)	1
3	Vytautas ZABORAS		A	1	(4)	
25	Arturas ZEKONIS		D	16	(1)	

DOMESTIC CUP 2005

1/8 FINALS
(18/3/05 & 21/3/05)
Zalgiris Vilnius v Polonija Vilnius 4-0; 5-0 (9-0)
(18/3/05 & 22/3/05)
FBK Kaunas v Vetra-2 Vilnius 4-0; 8-0 (12-0)
Vetra Vilnius v Kauno Jegeriai 4-0; 0-1 (4-1)
Silute v Babrungas Plunge 5-1; 2-0 (7-1)
(18/3/05 & 23/3/05)
Suduva Marijampole v Rodovitas Klaipeda 12-0, 4-0 (16-0)
(19/3/05 & 22/3/05)
Ekranas Panevezys v Lietava Jonava 3-0; 5-0 (8-0)
Atlantas Klaipeda v Nevezis Kedainiai 6-1, 0-0 (6-1)
(22/3/05 & 26/3/05)
Vilnius v Siauliai 1-1, 0-1 (1-2)

QUARTER-FINALS
(3/4/05 & 9/4/05)
Silute 1 *(Juska 16p)*, Ekranas Panevezys 1 *(Kavaliauskas 87)*
Ekranas Panevezys 2 *(Savenas 54p, Luksys 62)*, Silute 0
(Ekranas Panevezys 3-1)

FBK Kaunas 1 *(Velicka 39p)*, Siauliai 0
Siauliai 1 *(Vasilkovas 70p)*, FBK Kaunas 1 *(Beniusis 90)*
(FBK Kaunas 2-1)

Vetra Vilnius 1 *(Litvinas 63)*, Suduva Marijampole 0
Suduva Marijampole 2 *(Uselis 52, Radzinevicius 69)*, Vetra Vilnius 1 *(Vaineikis 7)*
(2-2; Vetra Vilnius on away goal)

Zalgiris Vilnius 0, Atlantas Klaipeda 0
Atlantas Klaipeda 1 *(Laurisas 99)*, Zalgiris Vilnius 0 *(aet)*
(Atlantas Klaipeda 1-0)

SEMI-FINALS
(13/9/05 & 27/9/05)
FBK Kaunas 0, Ekranas Panevezys 0
Ekranas Panevezys 0, FBK Kaunas 1 *(Barevicius 79)*
(FBK Kaunas 1-0)

Vetra Vilnius 1 *(Blazys 16)*, Atlantas Klaipeda 1 *(Zernys 20p)*
Atlantas Klaipeda 0, Vetra Vilnius 1 *(Stesko A. 9)*
(Vetra Vilnius 2-1)

FINAL
(22/10/05)
Vetros stadionas, Vilnius
FBK KAUNAS 2 *(Beniusis 102, Poderis 118)*
VETRA VILNIUS 0
(aet)
Referee - Zuta
FBK KAUNAS - Kurskis, Kancelskis, Manchkhava, Zelmikas, Zaliukas, Kvartskhelia, Maciulis (Pehlic 66), Barevicius, Pilibaitis (Poderis 74), Rimkevicius (Beniusis 46), Velicka.
VETRA VILNIUS - Merlani, Zudys, Raliukonis, Babravicius, Sasnauskas, Stesko I., Butrimavicius, Litvinas (Sivinskis 106), Stesko A. (Vaineikis 75), Kochanauskas (Vasiliauskas 61), Blazys.

SECOND LEVEL FINAL TABLE 2005

		Pld	W	D	L	F	A	Pts
1	Alytis Alytua	34	25	6	3	92	21	81
2	Kauno Jegeriai	34	23	6	5	83	18	75
3	Vetra-2 Vilnius	34	21	8	5	70	20	71
4	Polonija Vilnius	34	21	5	8	85	33	68
5	Gelezinis Vilkas Vilnius	34	18	7	9	66	41	61
6	Siauliai-2	34	17	7	10	54	45	58
7	LKKA Kaunas	34	17	6	11	67	46	57
8	Suduva-2 Marijampole	34	16	7	11	57	38	55
9	Lietava Jonava	34	17	4	13	63	48	55
10	Kruoja Pakruojis	34	16	5	13	64	50	53
11	Atletas Kaunas	34	13	5	16	49	45	44
12	Babrungas Plunge	34	12	6	16	48	54	42
13	Kursiai Neringa	34	9	7	18	42	58	34
14	Vilkmerge Ukmerge	34	8	8	18	34	60	32
15	Vilnius-2	34	8	4	22	32	61	28
16	Utenis Utena	34	9	1	24	40	115	28
17	Tauras Taurage	34	7	6	21	45	83	27
18	Rodovitas Klaipeda	34	0	0	34	19	174	0

N.B. Alytis Alytua declined promotion; Gelezinas Vilkas Vilnius declined promotion play-off match.

Luxembourg

First Double for Dudelange

F91 Dudelange reaffirmed their position as Luxembourg's number one club in 2005/06, retaining the league title, winning the Cup and, perhaps most impressively of all, winning their opening tie in the UEFA Champions League.

Michel Leflochmoan's side could hardly have made a better start to the season than when they beat Zrinjski Mostar in Europe. It wasn't any old victory either. Beaten 1-0 at home, they snatched a dramatic last-minute leveller in the return, through French striker Thomas Gruszczynski, before adding three further goals in extra-time. It was an extraordinary performance, undoubtedly the best ever by a Luxembourg club in Europe.

No matter that Dudelange were thrashed by Rapid Vienna in the next round. By beating Zrinjski, they had not only won a European tie for the first time but also posted the first victory in UEFA's premier competition by any club from Luxembourg in 42 years. It was also the first European victory for any Luxembourg team in a decade.

Buoyed by that success, Dudelange went on to dominate the domestic scene. Their fifth league title of the 21st century was never under serious threat, especially as they won all four direct duels against their closest pursuers, Jeuensse Esch. This included an amazing 9-0 victory in the play-off series – the heaviest defeat in Jeuensse's history. With the previous season's challengers Etzella Ettelbruck proving too inconsistent to challenge, Dudelange were four points in the clear at the winter break, seven points in front at the 22-match cut-off and 11 points ahead in the final table.

Cup final comeback

Just to put the lid on a fabulous season for Leflochmoan and his players (almost all of them foreigners), they inflicted another defeat on Jeunesse to win the Cup final and thus complete the club's first Double. Their opponents put up much stiffer resistance than usual and led 2-0 at half-time, but the champions stormed back to claim the trophy for the second time with a magnificent three-goal blitz midway through the second half. Gruszczynski scored the first two goals, but it was his fellow Frenchman Joris Di Gregorio, signed the previous summer from Cherbourg, who was Dudelange's top scorer in the league (with 22 goals) and also the Luxembourg Player of the Year.

With the National Division reverting to a traditional format in 2006/07, with 14 teams involved rather than 12, four teams were promoted and two relegated. Avenir Beggen, extraordinarily, failed to win any of their first 24 games then won all of their last four before losing their play-off to Mondercange in extra-time. The former six-time champions thus dropped out of the top division for the first time in 40 years.

NATIONAL TEAM RESULTS 2005/06

Date	Opponent	H/A	Venue	Score	Scorers
3/9/05	Portugal (WCQ)	A	Faro/Loulé	0-6	
7/9/05	Liechtenstein (WCQ)	A	Vaduz	0-3	
8/10/05	Russia (WCQ)	A	Moscow	1-5	Reiter (52p)
12/10/05	Estonia (WCQ)	H	Luxembourg	0-2	
16/11/05	Canada	H	Luxembourg	0-1	
1/3/06	Belgium	H	Luxembourg	0-2	(abandoned after 64 minutes)
27/5/06	Germany	A	Freiburg	0-7	
3/6/06	Portugal	N	Metz	0-3	
8/6/06	Ukraine	H	Luxembourg	0-3	

Luxembourg

NATIONAL TEAM APPEARANCES 2005/06

Coach – Guy HELLERS

Player	DOB	Club	POR	LIE	RUS	EST	Can	Bel	Ger	Por	Ukr	Caps	Goals
Marc OBERWEIS	6/11/82	CS Grevenmacher	G	G					G			5	-
Eric HOFFMANN	21/6/84	Etzella Ettelbruck	D	D	D	D	D		D	D	D	31	-
Benoît LANG	19/12/83	CS Grevenmacher	D40									3	-
Tim HEINZ	5/2/84	Etzella Ettelbruck /CS Grevenmacher	D						D	D71		5	-
Claude REITER	2/7/81	Jeunesse Esch	D	D	D	D	D	D	D26	D	D	28	1
Jeff STRASSER	5/10/74	Borussia M'gladbach (GER)	M	M					M	M	M	70	5
Alphonse LEWECK	12/12/81	Etzella Ettelbruck	M		M	M	M		M55	s58	s62	33	1
Sébastien REMY	16/4/79	F91 Dudelange	M68	M61	M	M	M	M	M	M	M	34	-
Ben FEDERSPIEL	18/5/81	Etzella Ettelbruck	M	D	s74	s73	D		s71	s72		24	-
Dan COLLETTE	2/4/85	Swift Hesperange	A	M79	M78	M	s59					10	-
Carlo PACE	7/4/78	UN Käerjéng 97	A62	s79								4	-
Tom SCHNELL	8/10/85	RFCU Lëtzebuerg	s40	D	D		D		s26	D72	D	8	-
Chris SAGRAMOLA	25/2/88	Jeunesse Esch	s62	A68								2	-
Ernad SABOTIC	23/10/79	Jeunesse Esch	s68	s61	s78							4	-
Charles LEWECK	19/7/83	Etzella Ettelbruck		M	M74	M78			M74	M58	M62	17	-
Aurélien JOACHIM	10/8/86	Excelsior Virton (BEL)		A			A	A	s26	A88	A85	6	-
Claudio DA LUZ	27/5/79	Etzella Ettelbruck		s68	s86	s78						4	-
Stéphane GILLET	20/8/77	RFCU Lëtzebuerg		G	G	G	G					17	-
Mario MUTSCH	3/9/84	RFCU La Calamine (BEL)		D	D73	M59	M		D	D	D	7	-
René PETERS	15/6/81	Swift Hesperange		M	M	M	M		M	M90	M	38	1
Paul MANNON	21/3/84	Victoria Rosport			A86	A58	A66					14	-
Kim KINTZIGER	2/4/87	Swift Hesperange			D		D					2	-
Joël KITENGE	12/11/87	CS Obercorn			s58				s74			2	-
Gilles BETTMER	31/3/89	SC Freiburg (GER)					s66					1	-
Carlos FERREIRA	24/8/80	Etzella Ettelbruck					M			M	M	4	-
Daniel HUSS	8/10/79	CS Grevenmacher					A		A26	s88		37	2
Clayton DE SOUSA	24/2/88	Jeunesse Esch							s55		s85	2	-
Jonathan JOUBERT	12/9/79	F91 Dudelange								G	G	2	-
Claudio LOMBARDELLI	4/10/87	Jeunesse Esch								s90	M	2	-

EUROPEAN CUPS 2005/06

UEFA CHAMPIONS LEAGUE

F91 DUDELANGE

1st qualifying round ZRINJSKI MOSTAR (BOS)
H 0-1
Joubert, Kabongo, Borbiconi, Baudry, Mouny, Crapa, Mazurier (Bellini 62), Remy (Saboga 78), Martine, Gruszczynski, Di Gregorio (El Aouad 69).

A 4-0 *Gruszczynski (90, 105), Di Gregorio (96), Hug (112) (aet)*
Joubert, Borbiconi, Baudry, Mouny, Crapa (Di Gregorio 77), Kabongo, Remy, Hug, Cleiton (Bellini 65), El Aouad (Gruszczynski 49), Martine.

2nd qualifying round SK RAPID WIEN (AUT)
H 1-6 *Martine (8)*
Joubert, Kabongo, Borbiconi, Baudry, Mouny, Crapa (Bellini 73), Cleiton, Hug, Remy, Martine (El Aouad 79), Di Gregorio (Gruszczynski 58).
A 2-3 *Tosun (7og), Gruszczynski (37)*
Joubert, Kabongo, Baudry, Mouny, Kabongo (Franceschi 65), Zeghdane, Crapa, Bellini (Martine 75), Remy, El Aouad, Gruszczynski (Di Gregorio 54).

Luxembourg

UEFA CUP

CS PETANGE
1st qualifying round AC ALLIANSSI (FIN)
A 0-3
Perfetto, Marester, Maric, Michel (Sabotic 79), Soraire (Peinado 54), Sallani, Cangini, Latic (Boukellal 63), Dervisevic, Dutheil, Kefert.
H 1-1 *Kefert (55)*
Perfetto, Sabotic (Carloni 85), Marester (Boukellal 41), Maric, Cylwik, Sallani, Latic (Benchamma 66), Dervisevic, Soraire, Dutheil, Kefert.

ETZELLA ETTELBRUCK
1st qualifying round KEFLAVÍK (ISL)
H 0-4
Reuter, Plein, Ferron (Heinz 32), Leweck C., Federspiel, Ferreira, Holtz (Da Luz 75), Leweck A., Fevry (Mischo 43), Da Mota Daniel, Grettnich.
A 0-2
Diederich, Federspiel, Engeldinger, Hoffmann, Fernandes, Leweck C., Ferreira, Leweck A., Da Mota Daniel, Mischo, Grettnich.

TOP GOALSCORERS 2005/06

23	Fatih SÖZEN (CS Grevenmacher)
22	Joris DI GREGORIO (F91 Dudelange)
	Fabrizio ROSAMILIA (FC Wiltz 71)
18	Daniel HUSS (CS Grevenmacher)
17	Daniel DA MOTA (Etzella Ettelbruck)
	Rudy MARCHAL (Jeunesse Esch)
16	Stéphane MARTINE (F91 Dudelange)
15	Thomas GRUSZCZYNSKI (F91 Dudelange)
14	Sergio PUPOVAC (RFCU Lëtzebuerg)
13	Carlo PACE (UN Käerjéng 97)

LEAGUE RESULTS/SCORERS/APPEARANCES/GOALS 2005/06

AVENIR BEGGEN
Coach – Florim Alijaj; (25/9/05) Fernando Gutiérrez

2005

Date	Opponent	H/A	Score	Scorers
6/8	RFCU Lëtzebuerg	a	0-0	
10/8	Etzella Ettelbruck	h	1-3	Alijaj
14/8	Victoria Rosport	a	0-3	
20/8	CS Grevenmacher	h	0-11	
11/9	US Rumelange	h	1-2	Calvaruso
18/9	CS Pétange	a	0-2	
22/9	Swift Hesperange	h	1-5	Ayyildiz (p)
16/10	F91 Dudelange	a	1-4	Birrou
23/10	Jeunesse Esch	h	0-1	
26/10	FC Wiltz 71	a	0-4	
30/10	UN Käerjéng 97	h	0-3	
6/11	Etzella Ettelbruck	a	0-5	
12/11	Victoria Rosport	h	1-1	Ayyildiz
20/11	CS Grevenmacher	a	0-2	
4/12	CS Pétange	h	1-2	Vieira
11/12	Swift Hesperange	a	1-1	Krings
18/12	US Rumelange	a	1-4	Calvaruso

2006

Date	Opponent	H/A	Score	Scorers
19/2	F91 Dudelange	h	1-1	Lazaar
12/3	FC Wiltz 71	h	0-5	
19/3	Jeunesse Esch	a	0-8	
26/3	UN Käerjéng 97	a	0-3	
2/4	RFCU Lëtzebuerg	h	1-1	Minas
8/4	Victoria Rosport	h	1-4	Minas
22/4	CS Pétange	a	0-2	
30/4	UN Käerjéng 97	a	1-0	Ayyildiz
4/5	CS Pétange	h	1-0	Minas
7/5	UN Käerjéng 97	h	3-2	Birrou (p), Ayyildiz, Lazaar
14/5	Victoria Rosport	a	2-0	Ayyildiz 2

Name	Nat	Pos	Aps	(s)	Gls
Florim ALIJAJ	BOS	M	5		1
Patrick ALMEIDA	POR	D	12	(2)	
Bülent AYYILDIZ	FRA	A	25		6
Azouz BENLAOUIRA	FRA	D	12	(1)	
Slimane BIRROU	FRA	M	17	(3)	2
Christophe CALVARUSO	FRA	M	22		2
Philippe CHRISMOUSSE	FRA	G	26		
Lou CONSBRUCK		G		(1)	
Lionel DA SILVA		D	18	(4)	
Pascal DENIGRO		M	1	(4)	
Patrick GOMES		M	1	(1)	
Fernando GUTIERREZ	ARG	M		(1)	
Karim GROUNE	FRA	D	24		
Kevin HARTERT		G	1		
Lionel KLEIN	FRA	M	7	(3)	
Danny KRINGS		A	7	(14)	1
Frédéric LARICCIA	FRA	D	25		
Mourad LAZAAR	MAR	A	17	(1)	2
Daniel LOPES	POR	M	2	(1)	
Patrick MINAS	POR	M	10	(1)	3
Geoffrey MONIVAS	FRA	M	3	(2)	
Miguel OLIVEIRA	POR	A	3	(7)	
Andy RIPPINGER		G	1		
Anibal SANTOS	CVD	D	20	(2)	
Frédéric TAVARES	POR	M	4	(9)	
João TAVARES	CVD	M	15	(10)	
Gabriel VIEIRA	POR	M	11	(9)	1
Aldo ZAMPA	ITA	D	19		

F91 DUDELANGE
Coach – Michel Leflochmoan

2005

Date	Opponent	H/A	Score	Scorers
7/8	Jeunesse Esch	a	3-0	Baudry (p), Di Gregorio, Martine
10/8	FC Wiltz 71	h	2-0	Martine, Hug
14/8	UN Käerjéng 97	a	4-0	Martine 3, El Aouad (p)
21/8	RFCU Lëtzebuerg	h	5-0	Di Gregorio, Kabongo, El Aouad, Martine (p), Gruszczynski (p)
12/9	Etzella Ettelbruck	a	0-1	
18/9	Victoria Rosport	h	3-0	Hug, Martine 2
24/9	CS Grevenmacher	a	1-1	Di Gregorio
16/10	Avenir Beggen	h	4-1	Di Gregorio 2, Martine (p), Antonicelli
23/10	CS Pétange	a	1-0	Di Gregorio
26/10	Swift Hesperange	h	3-1	Gruszczynski, Di Gregorio 2
30/10	US Rumelange	h	6-1	Di Gregorio, Gruszczynski 4, Mazurier

Luxembourg

FINAL LEAGUE TABLES 2005/06

PLAY-OFFS

Championship Group

		Pld	Home W	D	L	F	A	Away W	D	L	F	A	Total W	D	L	F	A	Pts
1	F91 Dudelange	28	12	1	1	50	9	8	3	3	33	13	20	4	4	83	22	64
2	Jeunesse Esch	28	9	2	3	35	13	8	0	6	23	23	17	2	9	58	36	53
3	Etzella Ettelbruck	28	10	0	4	32	17	6	1	7	27	30	16	1	11	59	47	49
4	CS Grevenmacher	28	8	1	5	28	19	5	2	7	30	20	13	3	12	58	39	42

Relegation Group A

		Pld	Home W	D	L	F	A	Away W	D	L	F	A	Total W	D	L	F	A	Pts
1	FC Wiltz 71	28	8	4	2	25	12	5	4	5	24	24	13	8	7	49	36	47
2	RFCU Lëtzebuerg	28	7	2	5	22	14	5	3	6	18	25	12	5	11	40	39	41
3	Swift Hesperange	28	8	4	2	27	18	1	5	8	14	26	9	9	10	41	44	36
4	US Rumelange	28	2	4	8	15	34	2	0	12	10	36	4	4	20	25	70	16

Relegation Group B

		Pld	Home W	D	L	F	A	Away W	D	L	F	A	Total W	D	L	F	A	Pts
1	CS Pétange	28	8	2	4	22	13	4	2	8	17	27	12	4	12	39	40	40
2	UN Käerjéng 97	28	7	4	3	27	21	3	3	8	17	25	10	7	11	44	46	37
3	Victoria Rosport	28	6	3	5	20	22	2	5	7	14	28	8	8	12	34	50	32
4	Avenir Beggen	28	2	3	9	12	41	2	2	10	6	38	4	5	19	18	79	17

N.B. After 22 matches the top four play off for the title. The bottom eight are split into two relegation groups.

FIRST PHASE

		Pld	Home W	D	L	F	A	Away W	D	L	F	A	Total W	D	L	F	A	Pts
1	F91 Dudelange	22	10	0	1	38	7	6	3	2	25	8	16	3	3	63	15	51
2	Jeunesse Esch	22	7	2	2	30	8	7	0	4	19	11	14	2	6	49	19	44
3	Etzella Ettelbruck	22	8	0	3	28	14	5	1	5	20	22	13	1	8	48	36	40
4	CS Grevenmacher	22	7	1	3	21	10	5	1	5	30	17	12	2	8	51	27	38
5	FC Wiltz 71	22	6	3	2	19	10	3	4	4	17	17	9	7	6	36	27	34
6	UN Käerjéng 97	22	7	2	2	21	14	3	2	6	15	19	10	4	8	36	33	34
7	RFCU Lëtzebuerg	22	5	2	4	14	10	5	2	4	17	20	10	4	8	31	30	34
8	CS Pétange	22	6	1	4	16	12	4	1	6	13	21	10	2	10	29	33	32
9	Swift Hesperange	22	5	4	2	18	17	1	4	6	13	20	6	8	8	31	37	26
10	Victoria Rosport	22	5	2	4	18	19	1	3	7	6	23	6	5	11	24	42	23
11	US Rumelange	22	1	3	7	12	30	2	0	9	8	28	3	3	16	20	58	12
12	Avenir Beggen	22	0	3	8	7	35	0	2	9	3	36	0	5	17	10	71	5

Date	Opponent	H/A	Score	Scorers
6/11	FC Wiltz 71	a	1-1	Di Gregorio
12/11	UN Käerjéng 97	h	4-0	Mazurier, Remy, Gruszczynski, El Aouad
20/11	RFCU Lëtzebuerg	a	0-1	
10/12	CS Grevenmacher	h	1-2	Martine
14/12	Victoria Rosport	a	4-2	Di Gregorio 3, El Aouad
18/12	Etzella Ettelbruck	h	3-1	Di Gregorio 2, Martine (p)
2006				
19/2	Avenir Beggen	a	1-1	Di Gregorio
12/3	Swift Hesperange	a	6-1	Zeghdane, Gruszczynski, Di Gregorio, El Aouad, Kabongo, Cicchirillo
19/3	CS Pétange	h	5-1	Gruszczynski 2, Crapa, Di Gregorio, Antonicelli
26/3	US Rumelange	a	4-0	Gruszczynski 2, Crapa, Cicchirillo
2/4	Jeunesse Esch	h	2-0	Martine 2
8/4	CS Grevenmacher	h	0-0	
22/4	Jeunesse Esch	h	9-2	Gruszczynski 3, Martine 2, Di Gregorio 2, Crapa, Baudry
30/4	Etzella Ettelbruck	a	3-0	Martine, Di Gregorio, Cicchirillo
4/5	Jeunesse Esch	a	4-1	Mouny, Zeghdane, Crapa, Di Gregorio
7/5	Etzella Ettelbruck	h	3-2	El Aouad, Bellini, Cicchirillo
14/5	CS Grevenmacher	a	1-4	Baudry

Luxembourg

Name	Nat	Pos	Aps	(s)	Gls
Michael AFONSO	POR	A		(2)	
Pasquale ANTONICELLI	ITA	M	2	(21)	2
Olivier BAUDRY	FRA	D	13	(3)	3
Johan BELLINI	FRA	M	8	(3)	1
Ronny BODRI		D		(10)	
Christophe BORBICONI	FRA	D	21		
Gordon BRAUN		A	6	(3)	
Frédéric CICCHIRILLO	FRA	A	2	(5)	4
Luciano CRAPA	ITA	M	21	(4)	4
Christophe CUM		G	1		
Joris DI GREGORIO	FRA	A	23	(4)	22
Ahmed EL AOUAD	MAR	A	18	(6)	6
Alexandre FRANCESCHI	FRA	D	20		
Thomas GRUSZCZYNSKI	FRA	A	17	(4)	15
Gaël HUGFRA		M	24	(1)	2
Andrew JOUBERT	FRA	M		(3)	
Jonathan JOUBERT		G	27		
Evariste KABONGO	DRC	D	19		2
Stéphane MARTINE	FRA	A	20	(2)	16
Sébastien MAZURIER	FRA	M	10	(3)	2
Loïc MOUNY	FRA	D	17		1
Sébastien REMY		M	21	(3)	1
Lehit ZEGHDANE	FRA	M	18		2

ETZELLA ETTELBRUCK
Coach – Luc Holtz

2005

7/8	CS Grevenmacher	h	2-1	Da Mota Dan., Grettnich
10/8	Avenir Beggen	a	3-1	Da Luz, Hoffmann, Da Mota Dan.
14/8	CS Pétange	h	5-0	Févry, Grettnich, Mischo 3
21/8	Swift Hesperange	a	3-2	Grettnich, Da Mota Dan., Mischo
12/9	F91 Dudelange	h	1-0	Leweck C.
18/9	Jeunesse Esch	a	0-3	
25/9	FC Wiltz 71	h	1-2	Févry
17/10	UN Käerjéng 97	a	2-2	Da Mota Dan., Févry
23/10	RFCU Lëtzebuerg	h	1-3	Da Mota Dan.
26/10	US Rumelange	a	2-0	Hoffmann (p), Févry
30/10	Victoria Rosport	a	2-1	Leweck A., Da Mota Dan.
6/11	Avenir Beggen	h	5-0	Da Mota Dan. 2 (1p), Févry 2, Leweck C.
12/11	CS Pétange	a	3-1	Da Luz, Mischo, Da Mota Dan.
20/11	Swift Hesperange	h	2-1	Leweck A. 2
4/12	Jeunesse Esch	h	2-1	Da Mota Dan. 2
10/12	FC Wiltz 71	a	3-4	Mischo, Holtz, Fernandes
18/12	F91 Dudelange	a	1-3	Da Mota Dan.

2006

12/3	US Rumelange	h	4-1	Da Mota Dan. 2 (1p), Févry, Grettnich (p)
19/3	RFCU Lëtzebuerg	a	0-1	
22/3	UN Käerjéng 97	h	1-3	Da Mota Dan. (p)
26/3	Victoria Rosport	h	4-2	Da Luz 2, Févry, Leweck A.
2/4	CS Grevenmacher	a	1-4	Da Luz
8/4	Jeunesse Esch	a	1-3	Leweck C.
22/4	CS Grevenmacher	h	2-0	Da Mota Dan., Binsfeld
30/4	F91 Dudelange	h	0-3	
3/5	CS Grevenmacher	a	4-2	Hoffmann, Leweck C., Mischo, Da Mota Dan.
7/5	F91 Dudelange	a	2-3	Févry 2
14/5	Jeunesse Esch	h	2-0	Leweck C., Da Mota Dav.

Name	Nat	Pos	Aps	(s)	Gls
Marc BINSFELD		M	13	(6)	1
Claudio DA LUZ		A	19	(7)	5
Daniel DA MOTA	POR	A	25	(3)	17
David DA MOTA	POR	M	1	(2)	1
Christophe DIEDERICH		G	23	(1)	
Gilles ENGELDINGER		D	7	(4)	
Ben FEDERSPIEL		D	25	(3)	
Jorge FERNANDES		D	20		1
Carlos FERREIRA		M	20	(2)	
Ralph FERRON		D	13	(2)	
Fabian FEVRY	BEL	A	16	(11)	10
Patrick GRETTNICH		A	5	(6)	4
Tim HEINZ		D	3	(2)	
Eric HOFFMANN		D	26		3
Luc HOLTZ		M	3	(14)	1
Alphonse LEWECK		M	24		4
Charles LEWECK		M	24	(1)	5
Luc MISCHO		A	12	(11)	7
Daniel PEREIRA	POR	D		(1)	
Jacques PLEIN		D	14	(5)	
Patrick POSING		M	10	(3)	
Marc REUTER		G	5		

CS GREVENMACHER
Coach – Álvaro Da Cruz

2005

7/8	Etzella Ettelbruck	a	1-2	Huss
10/8	Victoria Rosport	h	0-1	
14/8	US Rumelange	h	4-0	Sözen, Thimmesch L., og (Muller), Huss
20/8	Avenir Beggen	a	11-0	Sözen 5, Huss 2, Martin 2, Bozic 2
12/9	CS Pétange	h	2-1	Sözen, Huss
18/9	Swift Hesperange	a	1-3	Thimmesch L.
24/9	F91 Dudelange	h	1-1	Huss
17/10	Jeunesse Esch	a	2-4	Albrecht, Sözen
23/10	FC Wiltz 71	h	3-1	Sözen, Huss 2
26/10	UN Käerjéng 97	a	1-5	Huss
30/10	RFCU Lëtzebuerg	h	0-2	
6/11	Victoria Rosport	a	4-1	Albrecht, Huss 2 (1p), Sözen
12/11	US Rumelange	a	6-0	Sözen 3, Huss 3 (1p)
20/11	Avenir Beggen	h	2-0	Huss (p), Schmitt
4/12	Swift Hesperange	h	3-0	og (Peters), Sözen, Albrecht
10/12	F91 Dudelange	a	2-1	Sözen 2
16/12	CS Pétange	a	0-1	

2006

19/2	Jeunesse Esch	h	0-2	
12/3	UN Käerjéng 97	h	2-1	Sözen, Oliveira
19/3	FC Wiltz 71	a	0-0	
26/3	RFCU Lëtzebuerg	a	2-0	og (Bigard), Huss
2/4	Etzella Ettelbruck	h	4-1	Schmitt, Huss, Sözen 2
8/4	F91 Dudelange	a	0-0	
22/4	Etzella Ettelbruck	a	0-2	
30/4	Jeunesse Esch	h	1-4	Huss
3/5	Etzella Ettelbruck	h	2-4	Sözen, Henrot
7/5	Jeunesse Esch	a	0-1	
14/5	F91 Dudelange	h	4-1	Kordian, Sözen 3

Name	Nat	Pos	Aps	(s)	Gls
Christian ALBRECHT	GER	D	26		3
Kerem ARMUT	TUR	M		(7)	
Anton BOZIC		A	4	(2)	2
Christian BRAUN		M	15	(10)	

Luxembourg

Name	Nat	Pos	Aps	(s)	Gls
Paul ENGEL		D	13	(7)	
José FERREIRA	POR	M		(1)	
Tim HEINZ		D	7	(1)	
Nino HELBIG	GER	M	25	(2)	
Jérôme HENROT	FRA	D	16	(4)	1
Daniel HUSS		A	26	(1)	18
Stefan KORDIAN	GER	D	18	(1)	1
Markus KOSTER	GER	D	21	(1)	
Benoît LANG		D	2	(1)	
Kevin MARTIN	FRA	M	26		2
Marc OBERWEIS		G	28		
Steve OLIVEIRA	POR	M	4	(9)	1
André ORIGER		G		(2)	
Jonathan PROIETTI	FRA	M	6	(10)	
Volker SCHMITT	GER	D	16		2
Fatih SÖZEN	TUR	A	28		23
Alain THIMMESCH		M	9	(1)	
Luc THIMMESCH		M	14	(1)	2
Alexander ZIEHL	GER	D	4	(1)	

JEUNESSE ESCH
Coach – Harald Kohr; (6/12/05) Romeo Codello

2005
Date	Opponent	H/A	Score	Scorers
7/8	F91 Dudelange	h	0-3	
10/8	US Rumelange	a	4-1	Stoclosa, Pouget 2, Deharchies
14/8	FC Wiltz 71	a	3-1	Reiter (p), Sagramola, Wagner N.
21/8	UN Käerjéng 97	h	2-0	Pouget, Lombardelli
12/9	RFCU Lëtzebuerg	a	1-0	Sabotic
18/9	Etzella Ettelbruck	h	3-0	Pouget, Wagner S., Marchal
22/9	Victoria Rosport	a	0-1	
1710	CS Grevenmacher	h	4-2	Pouget 2, Schauls, Sabotic
23/10	Avenir Beggen	a	1-0	Pouget
26/10	CS Pétange	h	0-1	
30/10	Swift Hesperange	a	1-2	Pouget
6/11	US Rumelange	h	5-0	Marchal 3 (1p), Wagner S. 2
12/11	FC Wiltz 71	h	1-1	Marchal
20/11	UN Käerjéng 97	a	4-1	Marchal 3 (1p), Deharchies
4/12	Etzella Ettelbruck	a	1-2	Marchal
11/12	Victoria Rosport	h	2-0	Deharchies, Reiter
17/12	RFCU Lëtzebuerg	h	4-0	Lombardelli, Sagramola, Marchal 2

2006
Date	Opponent	H/A	Score	Scorers
19/2	CS Grevenmacher	a	2-0	Morocutti (p), De Sousa Moreira
12/3	CS Pétange	a	2-1	De Sousa Moreira, Morocutti
19/3	Avenir Beggen	h	8-0	Marchal 4 (1p), Stoklosa, Sagramola, Wagner S., Reiter
26/3	Swift Hesperange	h	1-1	Stoklosa
2/4	F91 Dudelange	a	0-2	
8/4	Etzella Ettelbruck	h	3-1	Morocutti, og (Federspiel), Sagramola
22/4	F91 Dudelange	a	0-9	
30/4	CS Grevenmacher	a	4-1	Pouget, Stoklosa, og (Engel), Marchal
4/5	F91 Dudelange	h	1-4	Marchal
7/5	CS Grevenmacher	h	1-0	Reiter
14/5	Etzella Ettelbruck	a	0-2	

Name	Nat	Pos	Aps	(s)	Gls
Gordon BRAUN		A		(1)	
Manuel CARDONI		M	18	(4)	
Steve CODELLO		M	1	(5)	
Clayton DE SOUSA MOREIRA		D	15	(4)	2
Julien DEHARCHIES	FRA	A	12	(11)	3
Joé FLICK		G	26		
Tim LEHNEN		D	8	(4)	
Claudio LOMBARDELLI		M	24		2
Rudy MARCHAL	FRA	A	15	(7)	17
Gilles MEURISSE		D		(1)	
Laurent MOND		G	2		
Manuel MOROCUTTI		M	5	(5)	3
Ben PAYAL		M	8	(10)	
Laurent PELLEGRINO	FRA	D	25		
Cyrille POUGET	FRA	A	17	(2)	9
Christopher REIN		D	1	(4)	
Claude REITER		D	23		4
Ernad SABOTIC		M	21		2
Chris SAGRAMOLA		A	5	(11)	4
Manou SCHAULS		D	28		1
Damian STOKLOSA	GER	D	26		4
Nikki WAGNER	GER	M	15	(1)	1
Stefan WAGNER	GER	A	13	(10)	

UN KÄERJÉNG 97
Coach – Angelo Fiorucci

2005
Date	Opponent	H/A	Score	Scorers
7/8	CS Pétange	h	3-1	Pace 3
10/8	Swift Hesperange	a	0-0	
14/8	F91 Dudelange	h	0-4	
21/8	Jeunesse Esch	a	0-2	
12/9	FC Wiltz 71	h	2-0	Thill, Fassbender
17/9	US Rumelange	a	5-3	Fassbender, Pace 3 (2p), Mukenge
22/9	RFCU Lëtzebuerg	a	0-1	
17/10	Etzella Ettelbruck	h	2-2	Thill, Delobel
23/10	Victoria Rosport	a	1-1	Matos
26/10	CS Grevenmacher	h	5-1	Thill, Mukenge, Pires, Kivunghe, Tana
30/10	Avenir Beggen	a	3-0	Marinelli 2, Mukenge
6/11	Swift Hesperange	h	1-1	Matos
12/11	F91 Dudelange	a	0-4	
20/11	Jeunesse Esch	h	1-4	Mukenge
4/12	US Rumelange	h	1-0	Pires
9/12	RFCU Lëtzebuerg	h	2-1	Pires, Marinelli

2006
Date	Opponent	H/A	Score	Scorers
12/2	FC Wiltz 71	a	1-3	Kivunghe
12/3	CS Grevenmacher	a	1-2	Kivunghe
19/3	Victoria Rosport	h	1-0	Pace
22/3	Etzella Ettelbruck	a	3-1	Thill, Pace 2 (1p)
26/3	Avenir Beggen	h	3-0	og (Zampa), Pace (p), Delobel
2/4	CS Pétange	a	1-2	Pace (p)
8/4	CS Pétange	a	0-3	
22/4	Victoria Rosport	a	0-0	
30/4	Avenir Beggen	h	0-1	
4/5	Victoria Rosport	a	3-3	Pires, Marinelli 2
7/5	Avenir Beggen	a	2-3	Pace, Pires
14/5	CS Pétange	h	3-3	Kivunghe, Pace, Rodrigues

Name	Nat	Pos	Aps	(s)	Gls
Nicolas ALEXANDRE	FRA	D	6	(4)	
Tom BAUMERT		D	3	(3)	
Paulo DA COSTA	POR	D	19		
Laurent DE GRAEVE		D	1	(1)	

Luxembourg

Name	Nat	Pos	Aps	(s)	Gls
Eric DELOBEL	FRA	M	12	(6)	2
Luc DEMEYER		A		(4)	
Jean-Philippe FACQUES	FRA	D	26	(1)	
Frédéric FASSBENDER	FRA	A	8	(4)	2
Pit HAHN		M	1	(4)	
Mutamba KIVUNGHE	BEL	A	19	(3)	4
Jérôme MARCOLINO		D		(2)	
Vito MARINELLI		M	22	(5)	5
Gil MARTINS	POR	M	11	(4)	
Valéry MARTINS		M	2	(2)	
Telmo MATOS	POR	M	23		2
Remy MUKENGE	FRA	M	24	(1)	4
Carlo PACE		A	18	(2)	13
Marco PIRES	POR	A	10	(10)	5
Alberto RODRIGUES	POR	M		(5)	1
Sergio SILVA COSTA	POR	G	25		
Dany TANA		M	5	(10)	1
Xavier THILL	FRA	A	22	(1)	4
Damien TRIEM	FRA	D	14	(3)	
Michael WILLEMIN	FRA	M	16	(1)	
Christophe WILWERT		G	3		
Karim ZAMOUM	FRA	D	16		
Daniel ZANON		M	2	(6)	
Mathieu ZEIMET		M		(1)	

Name	Nat	Pos	Aps	(s)	Gls
Vincent CARLONI	FRA	M	2	(2)	1
Marius CYLWIK	POL	D	3	(6)	
Tun DEFAY		M	4	(10)	
Jasmin DERVISEVIC	SCG	M	15	(4)	3
Laurent DUTHEIL	FRA	A	25		11
Jérôme ELIZABETH	FRA	A	3	(1)	
Steve IHRY		D	1	(1)	
Dejan KEFERT	SLO	A	6	(2)	3
Sanel LATIC	BEL	M	4	(6)	
Miguel MACHADO	POR	M	2	(2)	1
Jeff MARESTER	FRA	D	16	(1)	
Dario MARIC		D	26	(1)	
Paulo MENDES BRITO	POR	M	2	(5)	
Christophe MICHEL	FRA	D	22	(2)	1
Douglas PEINADO	BRA	D	19	(1)	3
Adrien PERFETTO	FRA	G	13		
Almir RAMCILOVIC	SCG	A	11	(3)	3
Anis RAMDEDOVIC	SCG	A	5	(9)	1
Yuri Kaleu REBELO	POR	M		(1)	
Enver SABOTIC	SCG	M	15	(7)	3
Abderahmane SALLANI	FRA	D	21		
Dario SORAIRE	ARG	M	21	(4)	3
Faruk SULKANOVIC	SCG	D	1		
David TEIXEIRA	POR	M	12	(5)	1
Patrick WORRÉ		G	15	(1)	

CS PETANGE
Coach – Manuel Peixoto

2005
7/8	UN Käerjéng 97	a	1-3		Dervisevic
10/8	RFCU Lëtzebuerg	h	1-2		Kefert
14/8	Etzella Ettelbruck	a	0-5		
21/8	Victoria Rosport	h	2-0		Kefert, Michel
12/9	CS Grevenmacher	a	1-2		Boukellal
18/9	Avenir Beggen	h	2-0		Dutheil, Kefert
25/9	US Rumelange	h	4-2		Boukellal, Peinado, Dutheil, Sabotic
16/10	Swift Hesperange	a	1-1		Sabotic
23/10	F91 Dudelange	h	0-1		
26/10	Jeunesse Esch	a	1-0		Peinado
30/10	FC Wiltz 71	h	1-1		Soraire
6/11	RFCU Lëtzebuerg	a	3-1		Soraire, Boukellal, Teixeira
12/11	Etzella Ettelbruck	h	1-3		Dutheil
20/11	Victoria Rosport	a	0-1		
4/12	Avenir Beggen	a	2-1		Ramcilovic, Dervisevic
11/12	US Rumelange	a	3-1		Sabotic, Dutheil, Dervisevic
16/12	CS Grevenmacher	h	1-0		Dutheil

2006
19/2	Swift Hesperange	h	1-0		Dutheil
12/3	Jeunesse Esch	h	1-2		Dutheil
19/3	F91 Dudelange	a	1-5		Dutheil
26/3	FC Wiltz 71	a	0-1		
2/4	UN Käerjéng 97	h	2-1		Dutheil, Ramcilovic
8/4	UN Käerjéng 97	h	3-0		Carloni, Boukellal, Soraire
22/4	Avenir Beggen	h	2-0		Dutheil, Ramdedovic
28/4	Victoria Rosport	a	1-2		Dutheil
4/5	Avenir Beggen	a	0-1		
7/5	Victoria Rosport	h	1-1		Machado
14/5	UN Käerjén g97	a	3-3		Ramcilovic, Cangini, Peinado

Name	Nat	Pos	Aps	(s)	Gls
Abdellah BENCHAMMA	ALG	A	3	(3)	
Mourad BOUKELLAL	ALG	M	24	(3)	4
David CANGINI	FRA	M	17	(1)	1

RFCU LËTZEBUERG
Coach – Jacques Muller

2005
6/8	Avenir Beggen	h	0-0		
10/8	CS Pétange	a	2-1		Bigard, Pupovac
14/8	Swift Hesperange	h	3-0		Bigard, Pupovac, Schnell
21/8	F91 Dudelange	a	0-5		
12/9	Jeunesse Esch	h	0-1		
17/9	FC Wiltz 71	a	2-1		Pupovac, og (Sarmento)
22/9	UN Käerjéng 97	h	1-0		Belli (p)
16/10	US Rumelange	a	1-1		Muhovic
23/10	Etzella Ettelbruck	a	3-1		Belli (p), Bernard, Pupovac
26/10	Victoria Rosport	h	5-0		Pupovac 2, Enger, og (Weber), Omerovic
30/10	CS Grevenmacher	a	2-0		Pupovac 2
6/11	CS Pétange	h	1-3		Pupovac
12/11	Swift Hesperange	a	2-3		Bernard, Pupovac
20/11	F91 Dudelange	h	1-0		Pupovac
4/12	FC Wiltz 71	h	2-2		Belli (p), Mendes
9/12	UN Käerjéng 97	a	1-2		Belli
17/12	Jeunesse Esch	a	0-4		

2006
19/2	US Rumelange	h	0-2		
12/3	Victoria Rosport	a	3-1		Pupovac 2, Schnell
19/3	Etzella Ettelbruck	h	1-0		Pupovac
26/3	CS Grevenmacher	h	0-2		
2/4	Avenir Beggen	a	1-1		Bigard
8/4	FC Wiltz 71	a	1-1		De Cae
22/4	Swift Hesperange	a	0-2		
30/4	US Rumelange	h	3-1		og (Kleber), Bigard, Feller
3/5	Swift Hesperange	h	3-0		Bernard, Schnell, Mendes
7/5	US Rumelange	a	0-2		
14/5	FC Wiltz 71	h	2-3		Carvalho 2

Name	Nat	Pos	Aps	(s)	Gls
Jean-Pierre ALMEIDA		D	14	(5)	
Assim ALOMEROVIC	BOS	M	7	(5)	
Almin BABACIC	BOS	D	16		

Luxembourg

Anouar BELLI	BEL	M	17		4
Daniel BERNARD		M	19	(2)	3
Jérôme BIGARD		D	21	(1)	4
Luc BIVER		A	1	(7)	
Michael CARVALHO	POR	A	4	(6)	2
Nedin CIRIKOVIC	BOS	M		(2)	
Antonio COIMBRA	POR	D		(1)	
Chris D'EXCELLE	BEL	M		(1)	
Amer DAUTBASIC	BOS	M		(3)	
Matthew DE CAE		M	4	(2)	1
Selim DJEFAFLIA	ALG	M	2		
Mato DJURIC		A		(1)	
Patrick ENGER	FRA	A	6	(6)	1
Jeff FELLER		M	27		1
Stéphane GILLET		G	17		
René GONÇALVES		M	25	(1)	
Tomas GONZÁLEZ	ESP	M		(2)	
Ben GREIVELDINGER		D	1		
David GROSS		M		(1)	
Devid HALIMOVIC	BOS	A	1		
Kai HILLMANN	GER	G	8		
Roland ITOUA	FRA	D	2	(4)	
David MADARIAGA	POR	M	1		
Alain MENDES	FRA	A	11	(4)	2
Damir MUHOVIC		M	11	(10)	1
Adis OMEROVIC	BOS	M	22	(1)	1
Jeff OSTER		G	2		
Tiago PIGNATELLI	POR	M	1		
Lucien PINA CRUZ	POR	G	1	(1)	
Sergio PUPOVAC	FRA	A	24	(1)	14
Marc RAUS		D	1		
Donny SAPONARO		M	1		
Tom SCHNELL		D	20	(1)	3
Christophe SCHOLER		D	1	(2)	
Marco SIMÕES	POR	M	17	(2)	
Fabien SPINELLI	ITA	D	1		
Dan SPOGEN		M	1	(6)	
Valentin TUDOSE		D	1		

US RUMELANGE
Coach – Gérard Jeitz

2005
6/8	Victoria Rosport	h	0-0	
10/8	Jeunesse Esch	h	1-4	Dillmann
14/8	CS Grevenmacher	a	0-4	
20/8	FC Wiltz 71	h	1-3	Bekkadour
11/9	Avenir Beggen	a	2-1	Da Costa, Charlet
17/9	UN Käerjéng 97	h	3-5	Bekkadour, Neis (p), Lincker
25/9	CS Pétange	a	2-4	Charlet, Lahéry
16/10	RFCU Lëtzebuerg	h	1-1	Neis
23/10	Swift Hesperange	a	0-1	
26/10	Etzella Ettelbruck	h	0-2	
30/10	F91 Dudelange	a	1-6	Lahéry
6/11	Jeunesse Esch	a	0-5	
12/11	CS Grevenmacher	h	0-6	
20/11	FC Wiltz 71	a	0-1	
4/12	UN Käerjéng 97	a	0-1	
11/12	CS Pétange	h	1-3	Dillmann
18/12	Avenir Beggen	h	4-1	Lahéry, Dillmann 2, Bekkadour

2006
19/2	RFCU Lëtzebuerg	a	2-0	Dillmann 2 (1p)
12/3	Etzella Ettelbruck	a	1-4	Bekkadour
19/3	Swift Hesperange	h	1-1	Santos
26/3	F91 Dudelange	h	0-4	
2/4	Victoria Rosport	a	0-1	
8/4	Swift Hesperange	h	1-1	Mitten
22/4	FC Wiltz 71	a	1-3	Da Costa
30/4	RFCU Lëtzbuerg	a	1-3	Dillmann
4/5	FC Wiltz 71	h	0-3	
7/5	RFCU Lëtzebuerg	h	2-0	Bekkadour 2
14/5	Swift Hesperange	a	0-2	

Name	Nat	Pos	Aps	(s)	Gls
Philippe ALMEIDA	POR	M		(5)	
Cédric BASTOS		M	7	(3)	
Djillali BEKKADOUR	FRA	A	15	(7)	6
Stefano BENSI		M	9	(2)	
Ronny BODRI		M	9	(2)	
Pierre BOISSON	FRA	M		(3)	
Christophe BOULARD	FRA	D	19		
Kevin CHARLET		D	14	(4)	2
Sergio DA COSTA		M	25	(1)	2
Philippe DILLMANN	FRA	A	14	(5)	7
Daniel FABBRI		D	4	(3)	
Kevin HIRECHE		M	12	(4)	
Kim KLEBER		M	4	(7)	
David KRATZ		A		(1)	
Benoît LAHERY	FRA	A	14	(6)	3
Ludovic LARUELL	FRA	D	22	(2)	
David LINCKER	FRA	M	15	(2)	1
Romain MITTEN		D	8	(4)	1
Fabrice MULLER		A	10		
Paul NATHAN		D	8	(1)	
Ludovic NEIS	FRA	M	12	(4)	2
Cheikh NIANG	FRA	A		(2)	
Reinaldo PEREIRA	POR	D	2	(3)	
Kim ROHMANN		G	27		
Sascha ROHMANN		D	19	(1)	
Miguel SANTOS		M	21		1
Anthony SOMMEN	FRA	D	17		
Jérôme WINCKEL		G	1		

SWIFT HESPERANGE
Coach – Benny Reiter; (6/4/06) Luc Muller

2005
6/8	FC Wiltz 71	a	0-0	
10/8	UN Käerjéng 97	h	0-0	
14/8	RFCU Lëtzebuerg	a	0-3	
21/8	Etzella Ettelbruck	h	2-3	Medina, Collette
12/9	Victoria Rosport	a	3-4	De Oliveira, Collette, Di Domenico (p)
18/9	CS Grevenmacher	h	3-1	Hamdaoui, Medina 2
22/9	Avenir Beggen	a	5-1	Molitor, Cravo Roxo 2, Medina, Collette
16/10	CS Pétange	h	1-1	Di Domenico
23/10	US Rumelange	h	1-0	Cravo Roxo
26/10	F91 Dudelange	a	1-3	Cravo Roxo
30/10	Jeunesse Esch	h	2-1	Di Domenico (p), Medina
6/11	UN Käerjéng 97	a	1-1	Peters
12/11	RFCU Lëtzebuerg	h	3-2	Cravo Roxo, Medina, Collette
20/11	Etzella Ettelbruck	a	1-2	Di Domenico (p)
4/12	CS Grevenmacher	a	0-3	
11/12	Avenir Beggen	h	1-1	Di Domenico (p)

2006
14/2	Victoria Rosport	h	2-2	Collette, Di Domenico (p)
19/2	CS Pétange	a	0-1	
12/3	F91 Dudelange	h	1-6	Borges

Luxembourg

19/3	US Rumelange	a	1-1	Tavares
26/3	Jeunesse Esch	a	1-1	Peters
2/4	FC Wiltz 71	h	2-0	Ramos, Borges
8/4	US Rumelange	a	1-1	Peters
22/4	RFCU Lëtzebuerg	h	2-0	Medina 2
28/4	FC Wiltz 71	h	5-1	Di Domenico 3, Molitor, Jungbluth
3/5	RFCU Lëtzebuerg	a	0-3	
7/5	FC Wltz 71	a	0-2	
14/5	US Rumelange	h	2-0	Diakhaté, Metzger

Name	Nat	Pos	Aps	(s)	Gls
Cédric AMOLVIN	FRA	D	7		
Walter ANTUNEZ	ARG	M		(3)	
Alija BESIC		G	19	(1)	
Marco BORGES	POR	M	12	(7)	2
Alex BOUKHETAIA	FRA	G	9		
Dan COLLETTE		A	12	(8)	5
Jérémy CORREIRA	POR	M		(3)	
Jorge CRAVO ROXO	BRA	A	10		5
Adailton DE OLIVEIRA	BRA	M	22	(1)	1
Sven DI DOMENICO		M	22	(4)	9
Muhamed DIAKHATE	FRA	D	25	(1)	1
Philippe DURRER		A		(2)	
Gilles FABER		M		(1)	
Chris FELTEN		D	11	(7)	
Kim FELTEN		M	1	(1)	
Carlos FERNANDEZ	BRA	M	11	(6)	
Aissam HAMDAOUI	MAR	M	8	(3)	1
Kézi HEZOU	TOG	A		(4)	
Grimour JOHANSSON	ISL	M		(1)	
Gilles JUNGBLUTH		M	2	(1)	1
Kim KINTZIGER		D	25		
Christian LAURENBORG	DEN	D	12	(1)	
Rodrigo LUBIANA	BRA	D		(2)	
Stéphane MARQUES		M	1	(7)	
Aldino MEDINA	CVD	A	18		8
Daniel METZGER		M		(1)	1
Grégory MOLITOR		M	21	(2)	2
Christopher PASSOS	POR	M	1		
Renö PETERS		M	27		3
Guy RAMOS	POR	M	2	(1)	1
Andy REUTER		M	4	(9)	
Armando TAVARES	CVD	D	26		1

VICTORIA ROSPORT
Coach – Reiner Brinsa

2005

6/8	US Rumelange	a	0-0	
10/8	CS Grevenmacher	a	1-0	Buschmann
14/8	Avenir Beggen	h	3-0	Mannon, Schiltz, Huwer (p)
21/8	CS Pétange	a	0-2	
12/9	Swift Hesperange	h	4-3	Gaspar 2, Huwer (p), Görres
18/9	F91 Dudelange	a	0-3	
22/9	Jeunesse Esch	h	1-0	Mannon
16/10	FC Wiltz 71	a	0-3	
23/10	UN Käerjéng 97	h	1-1	Schiltz
26/10	RFCU Lëtzebuerg	a	0-5	
30/10	Etzella Ettelbruck	h	1-2	Mannon
6/11	CS Grevenmacher	h	1-4	Weber
12/11	Avenir Beggen	a	1-1	Schmidt
20/11	CS Pétange	h	1-0	Schmidt
11/12	Jeunesse Esch	a	0-2	
14/12	F91 Dudelange	h	2-4	Zöllner, Mannon

2006

14/2	Swift Hesperange	a	2-2	Gaspar, Schmidt
19/2	FC Wiltz 71	h	2-2	Noske, Schmidt
12/3	RFCU Lëtzebuerg	h	1-3	Berens
19/3	UN Käerjéng 97	a	0-1	
26/3	Etzella Ettelbruck	a	2-4	Zöllner, Noske
2/4	US Rumelange	h	1-0	Görres
8/4	Avenir Beggen	a	4-1	og (Tavares J.), Görres, Berens, Schiltz
22/4	UN Käerjéng 97	h	0-0	
28/4	CS Pétange	h	2-1	Görres, Zöllner
4/5	UN Käerjéng 97	a	3-3	Noske, Habte, Giese
7/5	CS Pétange	a	1-1	Noske
14/5	Avenir Beggen	h	0-2	

Name	Nat	Pos	Aps	(s)	Gls
Sascha APITZ	GER	G	26		
Thomas BERENS	GER	M	25		2
Frank BUSCHMANN	GER	D	24	(1)	1
Achim EBERHARD	GER	M	4	(5)	
Fabio GASPAR	POR	M	16	(8)	3
Denis GIESE	GER	D	20	(2)	1
Marc GÖRRES	GER	M	23	(4)	4
Sammy HABTE	GER	D	22	(2)	1
Markus HUWER	GER	M	17	(6)	2
Paul MANNON		M	16		4
Jérôme NEYEN		G	2		
Patrick NOSKE	GER	A	8	(3)	4
Alex PAULOS		D	21	(4)	
Alex POTT		A	1	(7)	
Laurent SCHILTZ		A	17	(1)	3
David SCHMIDT		A	21	(1)	4
Tom SCHMIT		D	4	(9)	
Steve TOLLARDO		M	3	(14)	
Frank WAGNER	GER	A	1	(4)	
Mike WEBER		D	23		1
Patrick ZÖLLNER	GER	M	14	(3)	3

FC WILTZ 71
Coach – Daniel Boccar

2005

6/8	Swift Hesperange	h	0-0	
10/8	F91 Dudelange	a	0-2	
14/8	Jeunesse Esch	h	1-3	Teixeira (p)
20/8	US Rumelange	a	3-1	Remacle 2, Ipoua
12/9	UN Käerjéng 97	a	0-2	
17/9	RFCU Lëtzebuerg	h	1-2	Kreins
25/9	Etzella Ettelbruck	a	2-1	Rosamilia, Kopecky
16/10	FC Victoria Rosport	h	3-0	Rosamilia 3
23/10	CS Grevenmacher	a	1-3	Rosamilia
26/10	Avenir Beggen	h	4-0	Pasqualino, Remacle, Rosamilia 2 (1p)
30/10	CS Pétange	a	1-1	Rosamilia
6/11	F91 Dudelange	h	1-1	Rosamilia
12/11	Jeunesse Esch	a	1-1	Remacle
20/11	US Rumelange	h	1-0	Kopecky
4/12	RFCU Lëtzebuerg	a	2-2	Rosamilia 2 (1p)
10/12	Etzella Ettelbruck	h	4-3	Rosamilia 2, Libambu, og (Ferron)

2006

12/2	UN Käerjéng 97	h	3-1	Schaack, Theissen, Rosamilia (p)
19/2	Victoria Rosport	a	2-2	Remacle, Rosamilia

Luxembourg

12/3	Avenir Beggen	a	5-0	Rosamilia 2, Schaack, Remacle 2
19/3	CS Grevenmacher	h	0-0	
26/3	CS Pétange	h	1-0	og (Sulikanovic)
2/4	Swift Hesperange	a	0-2	
8/4	RFCU Lëtzebuerg	h	1-1	Dos Santos
22/4	US Rumelange	h	3-1	Rosamilia 3
28/4	Swift Hesperange	a	1-5	Remacle
4/5	US Rumelange	a	3-0	Florkin 2, Rosamilia
7/5	Swift Hesperange	h	2-0	Rosamilia, Florkin
14/5	RFCU Lëtzebuerg	a	3-2	Dos Santos, Remacle 2

Name	Nat	Pos	Aps	(s)	Gls
Emmanuel ANDRIEN	BEL	G	6		
Sanel BADIC	BOS	A		(2)	
Moussa BAH	GUI	D	14	(3)	
Fernando BARBOSA	POR	M	5	(10)	
Manuel DOS SANTOS	POR	M	19	(2)	2
Vedad DURAKU	SCG	A	2	(1)	
Philippe FLORKIN	BEL	M	25		3
Fabian GALLEE	BEL	G	22		
Marc GIRA		A	4	(8)	
Samuel IPOUA	CMR	A	11	(2)	1
Tom KOPECKY		D	27		2
Claude KREINS		A	5	(8)	1
Guy LIBAMBU	BEL	D	25		1
LIN Yi		M		(3)	
Fabrice MAVINGA	BEL	D	12	(5)	
Asmir MUJKIC	BOS	D	2		
Mehmet MUJKIC	BOS	M	14	(8)	
Sevad MUJKIC	BOS	M	8	(2)	
Antony PASQUALINO	BEL	M	12		1
Gauthier REMACLE	BEL	M	27		10
Charles ROEMER		G		(1)	
Fabrizio ROSAMILIA	BEL	A	25		22
Sergio SARMENTO		D	17	(8)	
Steve SCHAACK		M	18	(6)	2
Carlos TEIXEIRA		M	7	(5)	1
Christian THEISSEN	BEL	A	1	(1)	1

DOMESTIC CUP 2005/06

1/16 FINALS

(25/2/06)
Orania Vianden 0, Victoria Rosport 4
Union Mertert/Wasserbillig 4, UN Käerjéng 3
Progrès Niedercorn 6, Jeunesse Biwer 1
Blue Boys Muhlenbach 1, F91 Dudelange 7
US Sandweiler 0, Jeunesse Esch 1
Jeunesse Canach 0, CS Grevenmacher 5 *(aet)*
CS Hobscheid 0, Etzella Ettelbruck 6
Marisca Mersch 1, Swift Hesperange 4
US Hostert 4, US Rumelange 2 *(aet)*
FC Mamer 1, RFCU Lëtzebuerg 3
RM Hamm 3, FC Wiltz 4 *(aet)*
Jeunesse Schieren 1, Avenir Beggen 0
CS Obercorn 0, CS Pétange 1
Daring Echternach 0, FC Mondercange 2
FC Differdange 5, FC Belvaux 1
AS Colmarberg 3, Koeppchen Wormeldange 0

1/8 FINALS

(15/3/06)
Jeunesse Schieren 2, CS Pétange 2 *(aet; 6-7 on pens)*
US Hostert 0, Victoria Rosport 2
Etzella Ettelbruck 3, CS Grevenmacher 0
RFCU Lëtzebuerg 4, FC Differdange 2 *(aet)*
Union Mertert/Wasserbillig 0, F91 Dudelange 10
Progrès Niedercorn 3, FC Mondercange 1
FC Wiltz 1, Swift Hesperange 2
(22/3/06)
AS Colmarberg 0, Jeunesse Esch 2

QUARTER-FINALS

(18/4/06)
Jeunesse Esch 2 *(Deharchies 78, Pouget 89)*, Swift Hesperange 0
Victoria Rosport 2 *(Schiltz 52, Noske 113)*, Etzella Ettelbruck 1 *(Mischo 42)* *(aet)*
F91 Dudelange 4 *(Gruszczynski 1, Di Gregorio 14, 43, Baudry 68)*, Progrès Niedercorn 4 *(Masi 33, Dos Santos R. 39, 63, Zhan 90)*
(aet; 6-5 on pens)
(19/4/06)
CS Pétange 1 *(Dutheil 3)*, RFCU Lëtzebuerg 1 *(Mendes 85)* *(aet; 4-5 on pens)*

SEMI-FINALS

(10/5/06)
Victoria Rosport 0, Jeunesse Esch 1 *(Buschmann 46og)*
RFCU Lëtzebuerg 1 *(Pupovac 68)*, F91 Dudelange 3 *(Di Gregorio 11, Martine 119, Gruszczynski 120)* *(aet)*

FINAL

(20/5/06)
Stade Josy Barthel, Luxembourg
F91 DUDELANGE 3 *(Gruszczynski 66, 68, Hug 71)*
JEUNESSE ESCH 2 *(Stoklosa 16, Pouget 29)*
Referee – Mangen
F91 DUDELANGE – Joubert, Borbiconi, Zeghdane (Cicchirillo 77), Mouny, Kabongo (Baudry 56), Remy, Hug, Antonicelli (Braun 56), Martine, Di Gregorio, Gruszczynski.
JEUNESSE ESCH – Mond, Stoklosa, Schauls, Pellegrino, Reiter (Lehnen 50), Payal (Deharchies 77), Wagner N., De Sousa, Lombardelli (Marchal 85), Cardoni, Pouget.

SECOND LEVEL FINAL TABLE 2005/06

		Pld	W	D	L	F	A	Pts
1	FC Differdange 03	26	17	5	4	52	21	56
2	Progrès Niedercorn	26	16	7	3	58	23	55
3	FC Mondercange	26	16	5	5	73	22	53
4	FC Mamer 32	26	16	2	8	50	41	50
5	FC Cebra 01	26	12	7	7	40	29	43
6	FC RM Hamm	26	13	3	10	55	40	42
7	Union Mertert/Wasserbillig	26	11	6	9	55	37	39
8	FC Erpeldange 72	26	11	4	11	46	46	37
9	Sporting Mertzig	26	8	6	12	42	62	30
10	Koeppchen Wormeldange	26	9	3	14	44	66	30
11	Jeunesse Canach	26	8	2	16	35	61	26
12	CS Obercorn	26	6	4	16	28	55	22
13	Minerva Lintgen	26	4	5	17	34	65	17
14	AS Colmarberg	26	3	5	18	28	72	14

PROMOTION/RELEGATION PLAY-OFFS

US Rumelange 0, FC Mamer 32 0 *(aet; 3-4 on pens)*
Avenir Beggen 2, FC Mondercange 3 *(aet)*

Macedonia

Rabotnicki do their duty

It is a tradition, almost an obligation, for first-time winners of Macedonia's Prva Liga to follow it up with a successful defence. Rabotnicki Kometal Skopje dutifully delivered.

It was not quite the romp of 2004/05, but there was little in the way of a consistent challenge to Gjore Jovanovski's side. Only newly promoted Makedonija GP Skopje posed any kind of threat, while the major club from the capital, Vardar, were distracted by persistent off-field rifts between club president and chief sponsor.

The generally low quality of the fare on offer, coupled with the lack of excitement in the title race, resulted in a decline in attendances, with the average gate dropping into three figures for the first time ever.

Rabotnicki set themselves up for their title defence with an eventful summer in Europe. Having thrashed Latvia's Skonto Riga 6-0 on their Champions League debut, they came close to eliminating Russian giants Lokomotiv Moscow. One-nil up in the home leg until the last minute (it ended 1-1), Jovanovski's men were level at 0-0 in Moscow with 15 minutes left when they were awarded a penalty. Alas, midfielder Pance Stojanov missed his kick and Lokomotiv recovered to score twice and take the tie. Baskimi Kumanovo and Vardar also failed at the second qualifying round stage of the UEFA Cup, with the former suffering total annihilation at the hands of Israeli side Maccabi Petach Tikva.

Start to finish

Rabotnicki led the way in the league from start to finish. Inspired from the touchline by Jovanovski (four times a previous title winner) and from central midfield by captain Stojan Ignatov (voted 2005 Macedonian Player of the Year), they lost just once in the autumn, to Skendija 79 Tetovo, and although they went down again to the same opponents in early May, a home win over Pobeda Prilep four days later wrapped up the title.

Makedonija surpassed all expectations to finish second but their best was yet to come. The 2006 Macedonian Cup final was a classic, an antidote to the meagre offerings in the league, and Makedonija won it, against Skendija, thanks to a goal that will be remembered for many a year. After a goalless hour Skendija twice took the lead, only to be pegged back soon afterwards. With extra-time looming Makedonija's leading scorer, Under-21 international striker Filip Ivanovski, collected the ball out on the right near the halfway line. He raced inside past one defender then dribbled around another into the penalty area before beating the goalkeeper with a spectacular shot, aesthetically despatched into the far corner with the outside of his right foot. As the saying

NATIONAL TEAM RESULTS 2005/06

17/8/05	Finland (WCQ)	H	Skopje	0-3	
7/9/05	Finland (WCQ)	A	Tampere	1-5	Maznov (48)
12/10/05	Holland (WCQ)	A	Amsterdam	0-0	
12/11/05	Liechtenstein	A	Vaduz	2-1	Baldovaliev (70), Ilijoski (90)
1/3/06	Bulgaria	H	Skopje	0-1	
28/5/06	Ecuador	N	Madrid	2-1	Maznov (29), Mitreski I. (73p)
4/6/06	Turkey	N	Krefeld	1-0	Maznov (81)

Macedonia

NATIONAL TEAM APPEARANCES 2005/06

Coach - Slobodan SANTRAC (SCG)
/(25/8/05) (Boban BABUNSKI)
/(1/3/06) Srecko KATANEC (SLO)

Name	DOB	Club	FIN	FIN	HOL	Lie	Bul	Ecu	Tur	Caps	Goals
Filip MADZOVSKI	1/1/84	Rabotnicki Kometal Skopje	G							3	-
Aleksandar VASOSKI	21/11/79	Eintracht Frankfurt (GER)	D64		D	D	D			28	2
Goce SEDLOSKI	10/4/74	Diyarbakirspor (TUR)	D		D	D	D46	D	D	71	4
Nikolce NOVESKI	28/4/79	FSV Mainz 05 (GER)	D	D	D	D75	s46			7	-
Robert PETROV	2/6/78	Lokomotiv Plovdiv (BUL)	D						D70	17	-
Goran POPOV	24/1/84	Egaleo (GRE)	M	s46	D54	s75	D			9	1
Aleksandar MITRESKI	5/8/80	Grasshopper-Club Zürich (SUI)	M	D						28	-
Velice SUMULIKOSKI	24/4/81	Zenit Sankt-Peterburg (RUS)	M	M46	s54	s70	M	M	M	34	1
Goran PANDEV	27/7/83	Lazio (ITA)	M31	A	A	A	A75			26	9
Ardijan NUHIJI	7/12/78	Rabotnicki Kometal Skopje	A57	s80						3	-
Goran MAZNOV	22/4/81	Diyarbakirspor (TUR)	A	A80			A	A88	A90	19	5
Ilami HALIMI	8/11/75	Lokomotiv Plovdiv (BUL)	s31							6	-
Vlatko GROZDANOSKI	30/1/83	Omonia (CYP)	s57	M58			s75	M89	s70	28	3
Robert POPOV	16/4/82	Litex Lovech (BUL)	s64	M						14	-
Gogo JOVCEV	25/3/74	Cementarnica 55 Skopje	G							6	-
Vasko BOZINOVSKI	8/8/74	Kamen Ingrad Velika (CRO) /Makedonija GP Skopje	D					s68		15	-
Vlade LAZAREVSKI	9/6/83	Groclin Grodzisk (POL)	D				D68	D	D	6	-
Nebi MUSTAFI	21/8/76	Neuchâtel Xamax FC (SUI)	M							7	-
Stojan IGNATOV	22/12/79	Rabotnicki Kometal Skopje	s58							11	-
Petar MILOSEVSKI	6/12/73	Paralimni (CYP)			G			G		46	-
Igor MITRESKI	19/2/79	Metalurg Zaporizhzhya (UKR) /Beitar Jerusalem (ISR)		D	D		D	D	D	30	1
Toni MEGLENSKI	22/5/81	Pobeda Prilep		D	M					4	-
Danco MASEV	16/12/83	Vardar Skopje		M	M64					6	-
Darko TASEVSKI	20/5/84	Metalurg Zaporizhzhya (UKR)		M71	M70	s54	s72	s46		5	-
Ilco NAUMOSKI	29/7/83	SV Mattersburg (AUT)		A89	A46			A59	A46	13	1
Aco STOJKOV	29/4/83	RAA La Louvière (BEL)		s71				s59	s46	14	3
Georgi HRISTOV	30/1/76	Debereceni VSC (HUN)		s89						48	16
Ljupco KMETOVSKI	8/7/72	Vardar Skopje			G					1	-
Artim SAKIRI	23/9/73	AaB (DEN)			M46			M72	M46	70	15
Zoran BALDOVALIEV	21/5/83	MKT-Araz Imisli (AZB)			s46					4	1
Blaze ILIJOSKI	9/8/84	Rabotnicki Kometal Skopje			s46	A66				2	1
Arben NUHIJI	27/2/72	Vardar Skopje			s64					5	2
Igor JANCEVSKI	16/9/74	Hapoel Nazareth Ilit (ISR)				M54	M		s90	23	-
Ismail ISMAILI	14/11/81	Makedonija GP Skopje				s66				2	-
Jane NIKOLOVSKI	12/12/73	Slaven Belupo Koprivnica (CRO)					G			16	-
Miroslav VAJS	27/7/79	Rabotnicki Kometal Skopje					D			7	-
Vulnet EMINI	10/9/78	Skendija 79 Tetovo					s88	M46		2	-
Daniel IVANOVSKI	27/6/83	Vardar Skopje					s89	D		2	-
Tome PACOVSKI	28/6/82	Rabotnicki Kometal Skopje						G		1	-
JILSON da Silva	12/6/77	Kastoria (GRE)						s46		1	-

Macedonia

goes, it was a goal fit to win a Cup final.

Two draws against Holland apart, the Macedonian national side suffered a fairly calamitous World Cup qualifying campaign. Three coaches were used, with the second of them, Serbian Slobodan Santrac, quitting after only a few months for family reasons. Nevertheless, the Macedonian FA decided to go for another foreign coach, Slovenian Srecko Katanec, as the man to lead them into the Euro 2008 qualifying campaign. Against all odds Katanec took his native land to the finals of Euro 2000 and the 2002 World Cup, and the Macedonian fans will be hoping for another miracle. Their optimism was enhanced when, in the late spring, Katanec led the side to a couple of confidence-boosting wins on neutral soil over Ecuador and Turkey.

EUROPEAN CUPS 2005/06

UEFA CHAMPIONS LEAGUE

RABOTNICKI KOMETAL SKOPJE
1st qualifying round SKONTO RIGA (LAT)
H 6-0 *Kralevski (30), Ignatov (57p), Nuhiji (65, 85), Trajcov (69), Maznov (76)*
Madzovski, Stojanov Ig., Karcev, Jovanoski, Kralevski, Trajcov, Stojanov P., Ignatov (Mihajlovic 85), Nuhiji, Maznov (Ilijoski 80), Pejcic (Toleski 82).
A 0-1
Madzovski, Karcev, Kralevski, Stojanov Ig., Jovanoski, Mihajlovic, Jankep, Stojanov P. (Trajcov 74), Ignatov (Pejcic 62), Toleski, Ilijoski.

2nd qualifying round LOKOMOTIV MOSKVA (RUS)
H 1-1 *Nuhiji (12)*
Madzovski, Stojanov Ig., Karcev, Kralevski, Jovanoski, Trajcov, Stojanov P. (Mihajlovic 72), Ignatov (Jankep 90), Nuhiji, Maznov (Ilijoski 75), Pejcic.
A 0-2
Madzovski, Stojanov Ig. (Stojanov II. 12), Jovanoski, Karcev, Kralevski, Stojanov P., Trajcov, Ignatov (Jankep 54), Nuhiji (Ilijoski 77), Maznov, Pejcic.

UEFA CUP

BASKIMI KUMANOVO
1st qualifying round ZEPCE (BOS)
H 3-0 *(w/o; original result 0-0)*
Ugrenovic, Elmazovski, Gorgievski, Redzep, Trenoski, Petkovski, Fatic, Gjurcevski (Kerimi 45), Presilski (Isufi 67), Da Silva, Miserdovski (Gjorgiev 60).
A 1-1 *Gjurcevski (49)*
Ugrenovic, Elmazovski, Gorgievski, Redzep, Trenoski, Petkovski, Gjurcevski (Kerimi 72), Fatic (Isufi 60), Presilski, Da Silva (Gjorgiev 65).

2nd qualifying round MACCABI PETACH TIKVA (ISR)
H 0-5
Ugrenovic, Elmazovski (Bisevac 39), Georgievski, Redzep, Trenoski, Petkovski, Gjurcevski (Aziri 71), Isufi, Presilski, Miserdovski, Da Silva (Fatic 55).
A 0-6
Ajdini, Ismaili, Bisevac, Fatic, Selimi, Petkovski, Elmazovski, Gjurcevski (Gjeorgiev 43), Isufi, Presilski, Da Silva (Miserdovski 71).

VARDAR SKOPJE
1st qualifying round ELBASANI (ALB)
A 1-1 *Trickovski (65)*
Zdravkovic, Brankovic, Markovski, Gligorov, Sekulovski (Tanevski 35), Tasevski, Gligorovski (Nedzipi 74), Masev, Serafimovski, Naumov, Trickovski.
H 0-0
Zdravkovic, Gligorov, Tanevski, Brankovic, Markovski, Serafimoski, Gligorovski (Nedzipi 59), Tasevski, Naumov, Trickovski, Masev.

2nd qualifying round RAPID BUCURESTI (ROM)
A 0-3
Kmetovski, Markovski, Gligorov, Brankovic, Tanevski, Demiri (Kostovski 72), Serafimoski, Tasevski, Ristovski, Naumov, Trickovski.
H 1-1 *Naumov (39)*
Kmetovski, Sekulovski (Medic 63), Tanevski, Brankovic, Braga, Gligorov, Gligorovski (Kostovski 58), Masev (Ristovski 53), Deilson, Trickovski, Naumov.

TOP GOALSCORERS 2005/06

27	Stevica RISTIC (Sileks Kratovo)
22	Filip IVANOVSKI (Makedonija GP Skopje)
15	Riste NAUMOV (Vardar Skopje)
14	Aleksandar TOLESKI (Cementarnica 55 Skopje)
13	Muarem BAJRAMI (Vlazrimi Kicevo)
	Vance TRAJCOV (Rabotnicki Kometal Skopje)
	Burhan EMURLAHU (Skendija 79 Tetovo)
	Blaze ILIJOSKI (Rabotnicki Kometal Skopje)
11	Saso ALEKSOVSKI (Skendija 79 Tetovo)
10	Zoran MISERDOVSKI (Baskimi Kumanovo)
	Orhan ISUFI (Baskimi Kumanovo)
	Goce TOLESKI (Renova Cepciste)

LEAGUE RESULTS/SCORERS/APPEARANCES/GOALS 2005/06

BASKIMI KUMANOVO
Coach – Burhamedin Beadini; (10/10/05) Edmond Miha; (15/12/05) Biljbilj Sokoli

2005				
8/8	Rabotnicki Kometal Skopje	a	0-2	
21/8	Sileks Kratovo	h	1-1	Gjurcevski
28/8	Skendija 79 Tetovo	a	1-0	Da Silva (p)
11/9	Vlazrimi Kicevo	h	0-1	
18/9	Cementarnica 55 Skopje	a	0-1	
25/9	Pobeda Prilep	h	2-1	Miserdovski, Redzep
1/10	Vardar Skopje	a	1-3	Da Silva
4/10	Belasica Strumica	h	2-1	Presilski, Georgievski
16/10	Renova Cepciste	a	0-1	
23/10	Bregalnica Kraun Stip	a	1-0	Miserdovski (p)
30/10	Makedonija GP Skopje	h	5-0	Miserdovski 3, Isufi, Da Silva
6/11	Rabotnicki Kometal Skopje	h	1-1	Stojkovic
9/11	Sileks Kratovo	a	1-4	Redzep
20/11	Skendija 79 Tetovo	h	4-2	Isufi 3, Miserdovski

Macedonia

FINAL LEAGUE TABLE 2005/06

		Pld	Home					Away					Total					Pts
			W	D	L	F	A	W	D	L	F	A	W	D	L	F	A	
1	Rabotnicki Kometal Skopje	33	14	2	1	38	11	7	7	2	26	15	21	9	3	64	26	72
2	Makedonija GP Skopje	33	13	3	1	33	7	8	3	5	22	16	21	6	6	55	23	69
3	Vardar Skopje	33	11	5	1	26	9	8	2	6	16	10	19	7	7	42	19	64
4	Pobeda Prilep	33	13	2	2	34	11	3	4	9	24	35	16	6	11	58	46	54
5	Skendija 79 Tetovo	33	11	1	5	33	23	4	3	9	15	24	15	4	14	48	47	49
6	Baskimi Kumanovo	33	10	4	3	38	20	3	2	11	12	29	13	6	14	50	49	45
7	Renova Cepciste	33	11	2	3	29	18	2	3	12	16	31	13	5	15	45	49	44
8	Vlazrimi Kicevo	33	10	2	4	28	17	3	2	12	16	40	13	4	16	44	57	43
9	Sileks Kratovo	33	7	6	3	31	24	3	5	9	23	34	10	11	12	54	58	41
10	Bregalnica Kraun Stip	33	6	4	6	21	19	4	2	11	23	36	10	6	17	44	55	36
11	Cementarnica 55 Skopje	33	7	5	4	26	18	1	3	13	12	33	8	8	17	38	51	32
12	Belasica Strumica	33	1	1	14	12	38	1	1	15	10	46	2	2	29	22	84	8

Date	Opponent	H/A	Score	Scorers
27/11	Vlazrimi Kicevo	a	2-2	Miserdovski, Elmazovski
4/12	Cementarnica 55 Skopje	h	3-2	Presilski, Miserdovski 2
11/12	Pobeda Prilep	a	1-3	Miserdovski
2006				
5/3	Vardar Skopje	h	0-1	
12/3	Belasica Strumica	a	2-0	Isufi, Da Silva
15/3	Renova Cepciste	h	3-2	Isufi 2, Georgiev
19/3	Bregalnica Kraun Stip	h	2-2	Gasi, Georgievski
22/3	Makedonija GP Skopje	a	0-3	
26/3	Belasica Strumica	h	6-0	Ajdini, Ali, Da Silva, Georgievski, Elmazovski, Isufi
2/4	Vlazrimi Kicevo	h	2-1	Jancevski 2
9/4	Skendija 79 Tetovo	a	0-1	
16/4	Pobeda Prilep	h	2-0	Ali, Elmazovski (p)
19/4	Makedonija GP Skopje	a	0-2	
22/4	Vardar Skopje	h	1-1	Jancevski
29/4	Rabotnicki Kometal Skopje	a	0-0	
3/5	Bregalnica Kraun Stip	h	2-3	Statovci, Gasi
7/5	Sileks Kratovo	a	0-3	
14/5	Cementarnica 55 Skopje	h	2-1	Jancevski, Isufi
21/5	Renova Cepciste	a	3-4	Arifi, Isufi, og (Redzepi)

Name	Nat	Pos	Aps	(s)	Gls
Afrim AJDINI		M	7	(5)	1
Astrit AJETI		M	1	(2)	
Ilber ALI		M	8	(3)	2
Armend ALIMI		M	1	(2)	
Baskim ARIFI		M	2	(3)	1
Avni AZIRI		A	7	(6)	
Omer BISEVAC		M	7	(7)	
Erdogan BRANDO		M	2	(2)	
Souza DA SILVA	BRA	D	24	(2)	5
Ilir ELMAZOVSKI		D	25	(2)	3
Berisa ETRIT		M	1	(3)	
Nermin FATIC	BOS	M	26		
Fisnik GASI		M	4	(6)	2
Vasko GEORGIEV		M	20	(3)	1
Dejan GEORGIEVSKI		M	23	(4)	3
Blagoja GJURCEVSKI		M	12	(1)	1
Skender ISMAILI		D	7	(4)	
Orhan ISUFI		D	26	(1)	10
Boban JANCEVSKI		A	14		4
Jeton KERIMI		M	4	(5)	
Florijan MAKSIMOVSKI		M	3	(5)	
Dardan MIFTARI		G	22		
Zoran MISERDOVSKI		A	15		10
Stefan PETKOVSKI		D	14	(5)	
Bruno PRESILSKI		M	13	(4)	2
Besim RECI		M	1	(2)	
Saban REDZEP		A	25		2
Erhan SELIMI		M	25	(6)	
Faruk STATOVCI		M	2	(5)	1
Dalibor STOJKOVIC		M	11	(6)	1
Dragan UGRENOVIC		G	11		

BELASICA STRUMICA
Coach – Miroslav Jakovlevic; (30/9/05) Sefki Arifovski; (15/12/05) Zvonko Todorov

Date	Opponent	H/A	Score	Scorers
2005				
8/8	Skendija 79 Tetovo	a	0-2	
21/8	Vlazrimi Kicevo	h	0-1	
28/8	Cementarnica 55 Skopje	a	0-3	
11/9	Pobeda Prilep	h	2-5	Pandev 2
18/9	Vardar Skopje	a	1-2	Pandev
25/9	Bregalnica Kraun Stip	a	1-3	Jakimovski
1/10	Renova Cepciste	h	2-0	Savic, Ignatovski
4/10	Baskimi Kumanovo	a	1-2	Tasev
16/10	Makedonija GP Skopje	h	0-2	
23/10	Rabotnicki Kometal Skopje	a	0-3	
30/10	Sileks Kratovo	h	1-1	Alagjozovski
6/11	Skendija 79 Tetovo	h	1-2	Alagjozovski
9/11	Vlazrimi Kicevo	a	1-3	Stojkov D.
20/11	Cementarnica 55 Skopje	h	0-2	
27/11	Pobeda Prilep	a	0-3	
4/12	Vardar Skopje	h	0-2	
11/12	Bregalnica Kraun Stip	h	0-1	
2006				
5/3	Renova Cepciste	a	3-2	Projkov, Stojkov M., Savic
12/3	Baskimi Kumanovo	h	0-2	
15/3	Makedonija GP Skopje	a	0-1	
19/3	Rabotnicki Kometal Skopje	h	1-2	Cacev
22/3	Sileks Kratovo	a	0-1	
26/3	Baskimi Kumanovo	a	0-7	

Macedonia

2/4	Skendija 79 Tetovo	h	0-3	
9/4	Pobeda Prilep	a	1-2	Tasev
16/4	Makedonija GP Skopje	h	1-4	Alagjozovski (p)
19/4	Vardar Skopje	a	0-3	
22/4	Rabotnicki Kometal Skopje	h	0-3	
30/4	Bregalnica Kraun Stip	a	1-6	Jakimovski
3/5	Sileks Kratovo	h	4-6	Savic 4
7/5	Cementarnica 55 Skopje	a	1-1	Savic
14/5	Renova Cepciste	h	0-2	
21/5	Vlazrimi Kicevo	a	0-3	

Name	Nat	Pos	Aps	(s)	Gls
Martin ALAGJOZOVSKI		A	12	(6)	3
Kire ANGELOVSKI		M		(4)	
Toni ATANASOV		M	1	(3)	
Elvis BAJRAM		M	2	(6)	
Darko BOZINOV		M	4	(5)	
Koco CACEV		M	18	(1)	1
Zlatko DELOVSKI		M	18	(4)	
Sasko DIMOV		D	29	(1)	
Toni EFTIMOV		A	4	(1)	
Marjan GROZDANOVSKI		M	12	(2)	
Davor IGNATOVSKI		M	4	(3)	1
Daniel JAKIMOVSKI		M	21		2
Dragan KARAKACANOV		M	8	(2)	
Slagan KRALEVSKI		G	3		
Elmir MANDAK		M	4	(2)	
Borce MANEVSKI		M	12	(3)	
Aleksandar MILUSEV		M	14	(4)	
Dejan MITREV		M	3	(3)	
Vasko NIKOLOV		G	28		
Jovica OBRADOVIC	SCG	M	3	(2)	
Sasko PANDEV		M	8	(1)	3
Martin PETROV		M		(3)	
Oliver POPCANOVSKI		M	12	(2)	
Goran PROJKOV		M	23	(3)	1
Riste RISTOV		M	1	(2)	
Sasko RISTOV		M	4	(4)	
Dusan SAVIC		A	25		7
Gjorgi STANKOVSKI		M		(5)	
Dragan STOJKOV		M	25	(1)	1
Miki STOJKOV		D	21	(4)	1
Jordanco STOJMENOVSKI		M	2	(2)	
Marjan TASEV		M	21	(3)	2
Mitko TIMOV		M	14	(4)	
Aleksandar VASILEV		M	4	(2)	
Toni VELJANOVSKI		M		(4)	
Gjorgi VRGOV		M	1	(3)	
Kostadin ZAHOV		G	2		
Nikola ZERDESKI		G		(1)	

BREGALNICA KRAUN STIP
Coach – Nikola Spasov (BUL); (15/12/05) Kiril Dojcinovski

2005

8/8	Makedonija GP Skopje	a	0-1	
21/8	Pobeda Prilep	h	2-0	Davitkov, Lazarevski (p)
28/8	Rabotnicki Kometal Skopje	a	2-7	Velkovski, Spasovski
11/9	Vardar Skopje	h	0-3	
18/9	Sileks Kratovo	a	3-4	Spasovski, Dimitrovski, Gjilas
25/9	Belasica Strumica	h	3-1	Spasovski 2, Pitoska
1/10	Skendija 79 Tetovo	a	4-1	Pitoska, Spasovski, Lazarevski, Alomerovic
4/10	Renova Cepciste	h	2-1	Lazarevski, Spasovski
16/10	Vlazrimi Kicevo	a	1-2	Davitkov
23/10	Baskimi Kumanovo	h	0-1	
30/10	Cementarnica 55 Skopje	a	2-1	Dimitrovski, Alomerovic
6/11	Makedonija GP Skopje	h	0-4	
9/11	Pobeda Prilep	a	0-3	
20/11	Rabotnicki Kometal Skopje	h	1-2	Spasovski
27/11	Vardar Skopje	a	0-1	
4/12	Sileks Kratovo	h	1-2	Davitkov
11/12	Belasica Strumica	a	1-0	Davitkov

2006

5/3	Skendija 79 Tetovo	h	2-0	Angelov, Stankovic
12/3	Renova Cepciste	a	1-2	Lazarov
15/3	Vlazrimi Kicevo	h	1-1	Gjilas
19/3	Baskimi Kumanovo	a	2-2	Bajlozov, Dimitrovski
22/3	Cementarnica 55 Skopje	h	2-1	Davitkov, Tonev
26/3	Vardar Skopje	a	0-1	
1/4	Rabotnicki Kometal Skopje	h	0-0	
9/4	Vlazrimi Kicevo	a	0-1	
16/4	Sileks Kratovo	a	3-3	Andonov 2, Gjilas
19/4	Cementarnica 55 Skopje	h	0-0	
22/4	Renova Cepciste	a	1-2	Manev
30/4	Belasica Strumica	h	6-1	Ademov 2, Gjilas 2, Zdravkov (p), Mandak
3/5	Baskimi Kumanovo	a	3-2	Gjilas, Lazarov, Dimitrovski
7/5	Skendija 79 Tetovo	h	0-0	
14/5	Pobeda Prilep	a	0-3	
21/5	Makedonija GP Skopje	h	1-2	Andonov

Name	Nat	Pos	Aps	(s)	Gls
Vedat ADEMOV		M	8	(6)	2
Kemal ALOMEROVIC		M	10	(2)	2
Dusko ANDONOV		M	11	(1)	3
Stojan ANGELOV		M	18		1
Sasko BAJLOZOV		M	8	(2)	1
Petar BASNARKOV		G	15		
Daniel BELCHEV	BUL	G	7		
Vladica CEKIC	SCG	M	10	(9)	
Ljubisa CVETANOVSKI		M	2	(6)	
Vlado DAVITKOV		M	23	(1)	5
Dejan DIMITROVSKI		M	24	(2)	4
Mihail DONEV		M	11	(1)	
Haris FAKIC		M	10	(6)	
Vladimir GJILAS	SCG	M	22	(5)	6
Robert HRISTOVSKI		M	7	(2)	
Dragan IVANOV		A	6	(1)	
Vladimir KASIC		M		(3)	
Miroslav LAZAREVSKI		M	23		3
Lazar LAZAROV		M	2	(5)	2
Dimitar MADZUNAROV		D	5	(4)	
Elmir MANDAK		M	15	(4)	1
Jordan MANEV		M	6	(3)	
Toni PITOSKA		A	7		2
Zoran POPPANEV		D	8	(6)	
Dejan POSTOLOVSKI		M	1	(7)	
Darko SAVEVSKI		M		(4)	
Dimitar SPASOVSKI		A	24	(1)	7
Zvonimir STANKOVIC	SCG	M	12	(2)	1
Igor TASKOVIC	SCG	D	20	(2)	
Bobi TENEV		G	11		
Nikola TONEV		D	11	(6)	1

Macedonia

Slavco VELKOVSKI		M	21	(1)	1
Goran ZDRAVKOV		A	5	(5)	1

CEMENTARNICA 55 SKOPJE
Coach – Zanko Savov; (1/11/05) Zoran Rosic; (1/4/06) Borce Hristov

2005
8/8	Pobeda Prilep	h	2-2	Spasovski, Bozinovski
21/8	Vardar Skopje	a	1-1	Spasovski (p)
28/8	Belasica Strumica	h	3-0	Mileski, Toleski, Bozinovski
11/9	Renova Cepciste	a	1-2	Toleski
18/9	Baskimi Kumanovo	h	1-0	Spasovski
25/9	Makedonija GP Skopje	a	0-4	
1/10	Rabotnicki Kometal Skopje	h	2-2	Toleski 2
4/10	Sileks Kratovo	a	2-3	Toleski 2 (1p)
16/10	Skendija 79 Tetovo	h	1-2	Bozinovski
23/10	Vlazrimi Kicevo	a	0-4	
30/10	Bregalnica Kraun Stip	h	1-2	Toleski (p)
6/11	Pobeda Prilep	a	0-3	
9/11	Vardar Skopje	h	0-1	
20/11	Belasica Strumica	a	2-0	Toleski 2
27/11	Renova Cepciste	h	2-0	Georgievski, Bozinovski
4/12	Baskimi Kumanovo	a	2-3	Milosevski D., Toleski
11/12	Makedonija GP Skopje	h	2-2	Georgievski, Musa
18/12	Rabotnicki Kometal Skopje	a	1-3	Spasovski

2006
12/3	Sileks Kratovo	h	2-0	Bozinovski, Milosevski D. (p)
15/3	Skendija 79 Tetovo	a	0-1	
19/3	Vlazrimi Kicevo	h	3-1	Kostovski 3
22/3	Bregalnica Kraun Stip	a	1-2	Jovanovski
26/3	Pobeda Prilep	h	0-1	
2/4	Makedonija GP Skopje	a	0-2	
9/4	Vardar Skopje	a	0-2	
16/4	Rabotnicki Kometal Skopje	h	0-0	
19/4	Bregalnica Kraun Stip	a	0-0	
22/4	Sileks Kratovo	h	3-2	Toleski 2 (1p), Tunevski
30/4	Vlazrimi Kicevo	a	0-0	
3/5	Renova Cepciste	a	1-2	Jovanovski
7/5	Belasica Strumica	h	1-1	Kostovski
14/5	Baskimi Kumanovo	a	1-2	Toleski
21/5	Skendija 79 Tetovo	h	3-1	Angelovski, Cvetkovski, Toleski (p)

Name	Nat	Pos	Aps	(s)	Gls
Igor ANGELOVSKI		M	14	(3)	1
Erdzan ARIF		M	23	(2)	
Alaedin BATIJAR		M	11	(4)	
Bobi BOZINOVSKI		M	14	(2)	5
Igor BRNJARCEVSKI		M	15	(3)	
Gjoko CVETANOVSKI		M	14	(2)	
Dejan CVETKOVSKI		M	21	(1)	1
Igor DIMOV		G	1	(1)	
Nedzat DRAZANIN		D	1	(7)	
Slavco GEORGIEVSKI		M	5	(1)	2
Marjan GROZDANOVSKI		M	14	(9)	
Goran HRISTOVSKI		M	16	(4)	
Saso JANEV		M	14	(2)	
Saso JOVANOVSKI		M	1	(8)	2
Gogo JOVCEV		G	13		
Jovan KOSTOVSKI		A	7	(5)	4
Blagoja MILESKI		M	25		1
Igor MILEVSKI		D	19	(2)	
Dejan MILOSEVSKI		M	12	(3)	2
Nikola MILOSEVSKI		M		(4)	
Gjorgi MOJSOV		M		(5)	
Ali MUSA NGA		M	9		1
Goran NAUMOVSKI		M		(3)	
Minas OSMANI		A	14	(2)	
Alan PRUDNIKOV	RUS	G	18		
Darko RUNTEV		G	1	(1)	
Ahil SAIT		M	18	(6)	
Vladimir SPASOVSKI		M	12	(1)	4
Aleksandar TOLESKI		A	28	(4)	14
Mihajlo TUNEVSKI		M	11	(5)	1
Goran TRPKOVSKI		A	12	(4)	
Igor ZAJKOV		M		(5)	

MAKEDONIJA GP SKOPJE
Coach – Perica Gruevski; (10/2/06) Radmilo Ivancevic (SCG)

2005
8/8	Bregalnica Kraun Stip	h	1-0	Petreski
21/8	Rabotnicki Kometal Skopje	h	0-3	
28/8	Sileks Kratovo	a	2-0	Ivanovski, Dimovski
11/9	Skendija 79 Tetovo	h	1-0	Milosevic
18/9	Vlazrimi Kicevo	a	1-0	Ivanovski
25/9	Cementarnica 55 Skopje	h	4-0	Brnjarcevski, Ivanovski, Dimovski (p), Curlinov
1/10	Pobeda Prilep	a	1-1	Ivanovski
4/10	Vardar Skopje	h	1-0	Ivanovski
16/10	Belasica Strumica	a	2-0	Manevski, Milosevic
23/10	Renova Cepciste	h	3-0	Ivanovski, Milosevic, Dzangarovski
30/10	Baskimi Kumanovo	a	0-5	
6/11	Bregalnica Kraun Stip	a	4-0	Milosevic, Ivanovski 2, Ismaili
9/11	Rabotnicki Kometal Skopje	a	0-1	
20/11	Sileks Kratovo	h	3-1	Milosevic 2, Dimovski
27/11	Skendija 79 Tetovo	a	1-2	Ivanovski
4/12	Vlazrimi Kicevo	h	3-0	Brnjarcevski, Ivanovski, Milosevic
11/12	Cementarnica 55 Skopje	a	2-2	Petreski, Ivanovski

2006
5/3	Pobeda Prilep	h	1-0	Aranitovic
12/3	Vardar Skopje	a	0-1	
15/3	Belasica Strumica	h	1-0	Manevski
19/3	Renova Cepciste	a	0-2	
22/3	Baskimi Kumanovo	h	3-0	Ivanovski, Milosevic, Dimovski
26/3	Sileks Kratovo	h	1-1	og (Sadzakov)
2/4	Cementarnica 55 Skopje	a	2-0	Brnjarcevski, Stojanovski
9/4	Renova Cepciste	h	0-0	
16/4	Belasica Strumica	a	4-1	Stojanovski, Dzangarovski, Ivanovski 2
19/4	Baskimi Kumanovo	a	2-0	Ivanovski 2 (1p)
22/4	Skendija 79 Tetovo	a	1-0	Ivanovski
29/4	Pobeda Prilep	h	3-0	Aranitovic, Brnjarcevski, Ivanovski
3/5	Vlazrimi Kicevo	h	6-2	Ivanovski 4 (1p), Dimovski 2
7/5	Vardar Skopje	a	0-0	
14/5	Rabotnicki Kometal Skopje	h	0-0	
21/5	Bregalnica Kraun Stip	a	2-1	Kirovski 2

Macedonia

Name	Nat	Pos	Aps	(s)	Gls
Vangel ALTIPARMAKOVSKI		M		(3)	
Jovo ARANITOVIC	SCG	D	15	(1)	2
Kuzman BABEU	SCG	D	3	(2)	
Okvucukvu BANI	NGA	M	4	(5)	
Marjan BELCEV		D	5	(5)	
Antonio BOGATINOV		M	1	(1)	
Vasko BOZINOVSKI		D	14	(1)	
Toni BRNJARCEVSKI		M	23	(4)	4
Cvetan CURLINOV		M	5	(4)	1
Gjoko CVETANOVSKI		D		(3)	
Goran DIMOVSKI		D	27	(5)	6
Boban DZANGAROVSKI		D	22	(5)	2
Jordan GEORGIEVSKI		G	3		
Ismail ISMAILI		A	20	(5)	1
Filip IVANOVSKI		A	27	(5)	22
Daniel JOVANOVSKI		D	20	(2)	
Hristijan KIROVSKI		A	3	(6)	2
Darko KOSTOVSKI		G	1		
Dimitar LAZAREVSKI		D	1	(2)	
Blagojce LJAMCEVSKI		D	1	(4)	
Dragan LJUBISAVLJEVIC	SCG	D	22	(3)	
Marjan MADZAROVSKI		G	1		
Gjorgi MANEVSKI		A	4	(5)	2
Vlada MILOSAVLJEVIC	SCG	D	10	(4)	
Miroslav MILOSEVIC	SCG	M	25	(2)	8
Vasko MITREV		M	22	(3)	
Goce PETRESKI		A	11	(1)	2
Mile POPOVSKI		M			
Voislav SIMONOVSKI		D	11	(4)	
Goran SIMOV	SCG	G	28		
Goranco STOJANOVSKI		M	22	(2)	2
Dragan TRENOSKI		M	8	(2)	
Nikola TRIFUNOVSKI		M	4	(5)	

POBEDA PRILEP
Coach – Petar Kurcubic (SCG); (28/9/05) Nikolce Zdraveski

2005
8/8	Cementarnica 55 Skopje	a	2-2	Zdravevski, Krstev
21/8	Bregalnica Kraun Stip	a	0-2	
28/8	Vardar Skopje	h	0-1	
11/9	Belasica Strumica	a	5-2	Bojic 2, Emerson 2, Nacev
18/9	Renova Cepciste	h	2-1	Emerson, Manevski
25/9	Baskimi Kumanovo	a	1-2	Gjorgjioski (p)
1/10	Makedonija GP Skopje	h	1-1	Manevski
4/10	Rabotnicki Kometal Skopje	a	1-1	Meglenski (p)
16/10	Sileks Kratovo	h	2-1	Gjorgjioski, Vujovic
23/10	Skendija 79 Tetovo	a	5-4	Vujovic, Dameski, Gesoski, Banduliev, Manevski
30/10	Vlazrimi Kicevo	h	1-0	Manevski
6/11	Cementarnica 55 Skopje	h	3-0	Stojkovic, Gjorgjioski, Manevski
9/11	Bregalnica Kraun Stip	a	3-0	Manevski, Nacev, Popovski
20/11	Vardar Skopje	a	1-1	Manevski
27/11	Belasica Strumica	h	3-0	Manevski, Nacev, Emerson
4/12	Renova Cepciste	a	0-2	
11/12	Baskimi Kumanovo	h	3-1	Manevski, Nacev, Gesoski

2006
5/3	Makedonija GP Skopje	a	0-1	
12/3	Rabotnicki Kometal Skopje	h	3-3	Krstev, Banduliev, Gesoski
15/3	Sileks Kratovo	a	2-2	Krstev, Stojanovic
19/3	Skendija 79 Tetovo	h	1-0	Gesoski
22/3	Vlazrimi Kicevo	a	4-2	Kapinkovski, Gjorgjioski, Ristevski, Radovic
26/3	Cementarnica 55 Skopje	h	1-0	Kapinkovski (p)
2/4	Renova Cepciste	a	0-3	
9/4	Belasica Strumica	h	2-1	Krstev 2
16/4	Baskimi Kumanovo	a	0-2	
19/4	Skendija 79 Tetovo	h	3-0	Krsteski, Emerson, Gesoski
22/4	Vlazrimi Kicevo	h	1-2	Tancevski
29/4	Makedonija GP Skopje	a	0-3	
3/5	Vardar Skopje	h	2-0	Stojkovic, Ristevski
7/5	Rabotnicki Kometal Skopje	a	1-2	Tancevski
14/5	Bregalnica Kraun Stip	h	3-0	Gesoski 2, Apostolovski
21/5	Sileks Kratovo	a	2-4	Krsteski, Stojkovic

Name	Nat	Pos	Aps	(s)	Gls
Nove ACESKI		M	1	(5)	
Oliver APOSTOLOVSKI		M	3	(8)	1
Toni BANDULIEV		M	12	(2)	2
Veselin BOJIC	SCG	M	24	(2)	2
Blagojce DAMESKI		M	21	(6)	1
Blagoj DONEV		M	2	(5)	
EMERSON de Souza Pereira	BRA	A	24	(6)	5
Blagoja GESOSKI		D	22	(3)	7
Zeljko GJOKIC	SCG	M	14	(1)	
Blaze GJORGJIOSKI		M	14	(3)	4
Miodrag JOVANOVIC	SCG	M	1		
Dimitar KAPINKOVSKI		D	21	(5)	2
Zlatko KARESKI		M	8	(3)	
Aleksandar KRSTESKI		M	23	(3)	2
Sasko KRSTEV		A	11	(7)	5
Borce MANEVSKI		A	16	(2)	9
Toni MEGLENSKI		M	23	(1)	1
Marjan NACEV		D	12	(5)	4
Edin NUREDINOVSKI		G	21		
Aleksandar POPOVSKI		D	20	(7)	1
Ivan RADOVIC		M	2	(3)	1
Pance RISTEVSKI		M	7	(4)	2
Zoran SALEVSKI		D	1	(2)	
Marko SCEPANOVIC	SCG	M	8	(1)	
Aleksandar STOJANOVIC		M	2	(2)	1
Nebojsa STOJKOVIC	SCG	M	14	(4)	3
Miodrag STOKIC	SCG	M	2	(1)	
Igor TANCEVSKI		A	7	(2)	2
Darko TOFILOSKI		G	12		
Vladimir VUJOVIC	SCG	M	12	(2)	2
Nikolce ZDRAVEVSKI		M	3	(1)	1

RABOTNICKI KOMETAL SKOPJE
Coach – Gjore Jovanovski

2005
8/8	Baskimi Kumanovo	h	2-0	Todorcev, Trajcov
21/8	Makedonija GP Skopje	a	3-0	Trajcov 2, Ilijoski
28/8	Bregalnica Kraun Stip	h	7-2	Mihajlovic, Pejcic 3, Ignatov (p), Ilijoski, Nuhiji
11/9	Sileks Kratovo	h	3-1	Mihajlovic, Ignatov, Pejcic
18/9	Skendija 79 Tetovo	a	1-2	Trajcov
25/9	Vlazrimi Kicevo	h	2-1	Ilijoski 2
1/10	Cementarnica 55 Skopje	a	2-2	Ilievski, Nuhiji
4/10	Pobeda Prilep	h	1-1	Trajcov (p)
16/10	Vardar Skopje	a	2-0	Pejcic, Nedzipi
23/10	Belasica Strumica	h	3-0	og (Stojkov), Ignatov (p), Ilievski

Macedonia

30/10	Renova Cepciste	a	1-1	Trajcov	
6/11	Baskimi Kumanovo	a	1-1	Trajcov	
9/11	Makedonija GP Skopje	h	1-0	Ignatov	
20/11	Bregalnica Kraun Stip	a	2-1	Pejcic, Ilijoski	
27/11	Sileks Kratovo	a	4-2	Nedzipi, Pejcic, Ilijoski 2	
4/12	Skendija 79 Tetovo	h	3-0	Trajcov, Ignatov 2 (1p)	
11/12	Vlazrimi Kicevo	a	1-0	Nedzipi	
18/12	Cementarnica 55 Skopje	h	3-1	Trajcov, Ilijoski, Velkovski	
2006					
12/3	Pobeda Prilep	a	3-3	Vajs, Stojanov P., Velkovski	
15/3	Vardar Skopje	h	1-0	Trajcov	
19/3	Belasica Strumica	a	2-1	Stepanovski, Trajcov	
22/3	Renova Cepciste	h	1-0	Stepanovski	
25/3	Vlazrimi Kicevo	h	4-0	Nuhiji 2, Pejcic, Stepanovski	
1/4	Bregalnica Kraun Stip	a	0-0		
8/4	Sileks Kratovo	h	1-0	Trajcov	
16/4	Cementarnica 55 Skopje	a	0-0		
19/4	Renova Cepciste	h	3-1	Ilijoski 2, Trajcov	
22/4	Belasica Strumica	h	3-0	Stojanov P., Ilijoski, Nuhiji	
29/4	Baskimi Kumanovo	h	0-0		
3/5	Skendija 79 Tetovo	a	1-2	Nedzipi	
7/5	Pobeda Prilep	h	2-1	Vajs, Ilijoski	
14/5	Makedonija GP Skopje	a	0-0		
21/5	Vardar Skopje	h	1-3	Ilijoski	

Name	Nat	Pos	Aps	(s)	Gls
Carlos ABRÍLIO	BRA	M	2	(8)	
Dragan JAKOVLEVSKI		M	1	(5)	
Armand Dubois JANKEP	CMR	M	15	(5)	
Dragoljub JEREMIC	SCG	M	9	(5)	
Zoran JOVANOVSKI		D	25	(2)	
Stojan IGNATOV		M	27	(4)	6
Milan ILIEVSKI		M	12	(3)	2
Baze ILIJOSKI		A	25	(4)	13
Nikola KARCEV		D	18	(7)	
Filip MADZOVSKI		G	15		
Goce MARKOVSKI		M		(2)	
Bojan MIHAJLOVIC	SCG	M	23	(4)	2
Nderim NEDZIPI		A	21	(4)	4
Ardijan NUHIJI		A	24	(2)	5
Tome PACOVSKI		G	18		
Ivan PEJCIC	SCG	A	26	(6)	8
Metodija STEPANOVSKI		A	5	(4)	3
Igorce STOJANOV		M	18	(5)	
Ilija STOJANOV		D	1	(6)	
Pance STOJANOV		M	20	(2)	2
Goran TODORCEV		M	6	(6)	1
Goce TOLESKI		A		(4)	
Vance TRAJCOV		M	27	(4)	13
Miroslav VAJS		D	19	(3)	2
Krste VELKOVSKI		M	6	(2)	1

RENOVA CEPCISTE
Coach – Gani Sejdiu; (7/12/05) Toni Jakimovski

2005					
8/8	Sileks Kratovo	a	1-1	Simovski	
21/8	Skendija 79 Tetovo	h	0-2		
28/8	Vlazrimi Kicevo	a	3-4	Simovski 2, Sait	
11/9	Cementarnica 55 Skopje	h	2-1	Bajlozov, Simovski	
18/9	Pobeda Prilep	a	1-2	Iseni	
25/9	Vardar Skopje	h	0-1		
1/10	Belasica Strumica	a	0-2		
4/10	Bregalnica Kraun Stip	a	1-2	Simovski	
16/10	Baskimi Kumanovo	h	1-0	Iseni	
23/10	Makedonija GP Skopje	a	0-3		
30/10	Rabotnicki Kometal Skopje	h	1-1	Lena	
6/11	Sileks Kratovo	h	1-1	Lena	
9/11	Skendija 79 Tetovo	a	1-2	Lena	
20/11	Vlazrimi Kicevo	h	4-3	Emini, Simovski, Dimitrievski, Savevski	
27/11	Cementarnica 55 Skopje	a	0-2		
4/12	Pobeda Prilep	h	2-0	Lena, Simovski	
11/12	Vardar Skopje	a	1-1	Dimitrievski	
2006					
5/3	Belasica Strumica	h	2-3	Toleski 2 (1p)	
12/3	Bregalnica Kraun Stip	h	2-1	Iseni, Petreski	
15/3	Baskimi Kumanovo	a	2-3	Toleski, Iseni	
19/3	Makedonija GP Skopje	h	2-0	Fatic, Iseni	
22/3	Rabotnicki Kometal Skopje	a	0-1		
26/3	Skendija 79 Tetovo	a	2-1	Petreski 2	
2/4	Pobeda Prilep	h	3-0	Toleski, Iseni 2	
9/4	Makedonija GP Skopje	a	0-0		
16/4	Vardar Skopje	h	1-0	Savevski	
19/4	Rabotnicki Kometal Skopje	a	1-3	Bajram	
22/4	Bregalnica Kraun Stip	a	2-1	Petreski, Toleski	
30/4	Sileks Kratovo	a	0-2		
3/5	Cementarnica 55 Skopje	h	2-1	Toleski 2 (1p)	
7/5	Vlazrimi Kicevo	a	1-2	Fatic	
14/5	Belasica Strumica	a	2-0	Petreski, Serafimovski	
21/5	Baskimi Kumanovo	h	4-3	Toleski 3 (1p), Iseni	

Name	Nat	Pos	Aps	(s)	Gls
Arsim ABAZI		M		(2)	
Ferat ABDULI		G	1	(1)	
Saban ABURAMANI		M	14	(4)	
Ilber ALIU		M	5	(5)	
Skumbin ARSLANI		M	10	(4)	
Sasko BAJLOZOV		M	17	(3)	1
Oldzaj BAJRAM		M	8	(5)	1
Bojan DIMITRIEVSKI		M	14	(4)	2
Izair EMINI		M	14	(1)	1
Robert ENDEKOVSKI		M	9	(2)	
Jahji EVZAL		M	1	(3)	
Nermin FATIC		M	4	(8)	2
Darko IGNJATOVSKI		M	22	(1)	
Genc ISENI		M	22	(2)	8
Dragan JOVANOVSKI		M	1		
Goran JOVANOVSKI		D	18	(4)	
Nijas LENA		M	18	(2)	4
M.Patrik MEVONGO		M			
Srecko MISAJLOVSKI		M	20		
Fisnik NUHIU		M	6	(7)	
Goce PETRESKI		A	10	(2)	5
Gasi RAMADAN		D	15	(5)	
Redzep SABAN		M	5	(5)	
Lirim SAIT		M	10	(5)	1
Darko SAVEVSKI		M	9	(5)	2
Rasim SELMANI		M		(2)	
Zarko SERAFIMOVSKI		M	8	(4)	1
Ljupco SIMOVSKI		A	19	(5)	7
Goce TOLESKI		A	14	(2)	10
Dragan VESELINOVSKI		D	27	(4)	
Goran ZDRAVKOV		M	10		
Muarem ZEKIR		G	32		

Macedonia

SILEKS KRATOVO
Coach – Nebojsa Petrovic (SCG); (26/9/05) Kire Trajcev; (10/1/06) Josip Pirmajer (SCG)

2005
Date	Opponent	h/a	Score	Scorers
8/8	Renova Cepciste	h	1-1	Limanov
21/8	Baskimi Kumanovo	a	1-1	Ristic
28/8	Makedonija GP Skopje	h	0-2	
11/9	Rabotnicki Kometal Skopje	a	1-3	Ristic
18/9	Bregalnica Kraun Stip	h	4-3	og (Gjilas), Brkovic, Todorovski 2
25/9	Skendija 79 Tetovo	h	1-1	Todorovski
1/10	Vlazrimi Kicevo	a	1-0	Ristic
4/10	Cementarnica 55 Skopje	h	3-2	Ristic 3
16/10	Pobeda Prilep	a	1-2	Ristic
23/10	Vardar Skopje	h	0-2	
30/10	Belasica Strumica	a	1-1	Todorovski
6/11	Renova Cepciste	a	1-1	Ristic
9/11	Baskimi Kumanovo	h	4-1	Brkovic, Ristic 2, og (Petkovski)
20/11	Makedonija GP Skopje	a	1-3	Arsovski
27/11	Rabotnicki Kometal Skopje	h	2-4	Ristic 2
4/12	Bregalnica Kraun Stip	a	2-1	Brkovic 2
11/12	Skendija 79 Tetovo	a	1-4	Ristic

2006
Date	Opponent	h/a	Score	Scorers
5/3	Vlazrimi Kicevo	h	1-1	Jablan
12/3	Cementarnica 55 Skopje	a	0-2	
15/3	Pobeda Prilep	h	2-2	Ristic, Divljak
19/3	Vardar Skopje	a	0-2	
22/3	Belasica Strumica	h	1-0	Todorovski
26/3	Makedonija GP Skopje	a	1-1	Ristic
2/4	Vardar Skopje	h	0-0	
8/4	Rabotnicki Kometal Skopje	a	0-1	
16/4	Bregalnica Kraun Stip	h	3-3	Leskaroski 2, Ristic
19/4	Vlazrimi Kicevo	a	2-3	Ristic, Todorovski
22/4	Cementarnica 55 Skopje	a	2-3	Todorovski, Leskaroski
30/4	Renova Cepciste	h	2-0	Ristic, Natkov
3/5	Belasica Strumica	a	6-4	Ristic 5, Gjorevski
7/5	Baskimi Kumanovo	h	3-0	Ristic 2, Todorovski
14/5	Skendija 79 Tetovo	a	2-2	Ristic, Gjorevski
21/5	Pobeda Prilep	h	4-2	Ristic, Brkovic, Natkov, Leskaroski

Name	Nat	Pos	Aps	(s)	Gls
Eftim AKSENTIEV		A	9	(5)	
Igor ARSOVSKI		M	19	(3)	1
Martin BOGATINOV		G	26		
Slavisa BRKOVIC	SCG	M	26	(2)	5
Bojan CVETANOVSKI		M	2	(2)	
Ognjan DAMJANOVIC		M	2	(1)	
Dejan DIMITROVSKI		M	3	(4)	
Marko DIVLJAK	SCG	M	9	(6)	1
Saso GJOREVSKI		A	28	(1)	2
Gligor GLIGOROV		A	8	(7)	
Daniel IVANOVSKI		D	13		
Miljan JABLAN		M	7	(8)	1
Branislav JANEVSKI		M	20	(1)	
Gjorgi JOVANOVSKI		M	6	(1)	
Aleksandar KIRKOV	SCG	M	7	(7)	
Dejan LESKARKOSKI		M	12	(6)	4
Gjoksen LIMANOV		M	20	(4)	1
Marjan MICKOV		D	24	(6)	
Vukomir MIJANOVIC	SCG	G	7		
Mirce NATKOV		M	14	(3)	2
Bosko PETROVIC	SCG	D	20	(1)	
Stevica RISTIC	SCG	A	31		27
Dusan SADZAKOV		M	9	(9)	
Igor SAVEVSKI		D	10	(8)	
Kiril SOTIROVSKI		M	1	(6)	
Blaze TODOROVSKI		M	29		8
Darko TRAJCEV		M		(2)	
Branko ZDRAVEVSKI		M	1	(4)	

SKENDIJA 79 TETOVO
Coach – Nedzat Husein

2005
Date	Opponent	h/a	Score	Scorers
8/8	Belasica Strumica	h	2-0	Emini, Aleksovski
21/8	Renova Cepciste	a	2-0	Emurlahu 2
28/8	Baskimi Kumanovo	h	0-1	
11/9	Makedonija GP Skopje	a	0-1	
18/9	Rabotnicki Kometal Skopje	h	2-1	Aleksovski, Emini
25/9	Sileks Kratovo	a	1-1	Aleksovski
1/10	Bregalnica Kraun Stip	h	1-4	Emini
4/10	Vlazrimi Kicevo	h	2-1	Polozani, Velija
16/10	Cementarnica 55 Skopje	a	2-1	og (Hristovski), Polozani
23/10	Pobeda Prilep	h	4-5	Aleksovski, Georgiev, Emurlahu 2 (2p)
30/10	Vardar Skopje	a	0-1	
6/11	Belasica Strumica	a	2-1	Emini, Emurlahu
9/11	Renova Cepciste	h	2-1	Aleksovski, Emini
20/11	Baskimi Kumanovo	a	2-4	Emurlahu, Georgiev
27/11	Makedonija GP Skopje	h	2-1	Aleksovski, Memedi
4/12	Rabotnicki Kometal Skopje	a	0-3	
11/12	Sileks Kratovo	h	4-1	Aleksovski, Memedi, Polozani, Emurlahu

2006
Date	Opponent	h/a	Score	Scorers
5/3	Bregalnica Kraun Stip	a	0-2	
12/3	Vlazrimi Kicevo	a	0-1	
15/3	Cementarnica 55 Skopje	h	1-0	Aleksovski
19/3	Pobeda Prilep	h	0-3	
22/3	Vardar Skopje	h	2-1	Despotovski, Emurlahu
26/3	Renova Cepciste	h	1-2	Emurlahu (p)
2/4	Belasica Strumica	a	3-0	Emurlahu 2, Ibraimi
9/4	Baskimi Kumanovo	h	1-0	Emurlahu
16/4	Vlazrimi Kicevo	h	5-1	Aleksovski 2, Emini, Mustafi, Idrizi
19/4	Pobeda Prilep	a	0-3	
22/4	Makedonija GP Skopje	h	0-1	
30/4	Vardar Skopje	a	2-2	Savevski, Emini
3/5	Rabotnicki Kometal Skopje	h	2-1	Ibraimi, Emurlahu
7/5	Bregalnica Kraun Stip	a	0-0	
14/5	Sileks Kratovo	h	2-2	Aleksovski, Emini
21/5	Cementarnica 55 Skopje	a	1-3	Jasari

Name	Nat	Pos	Aps	(s)	Gls
Festim ADEMI		M	4	(10)	
Saso ALEKSOVSKI		M	21	(4)	11
Almir BAJRAMOVSKI		D	10	(5)	
Admir DEMIRI		M	1	(8)	
Vladimir DESPOTOVSKI		A	22	(4)	1
Armend ELEZI		G	17		
Vulnet EMINI		M	24	(4)	8
Burlan EMURLAHU		M	25	(5)	13
Goranco GEORGIEV		M	26	(6)	2
Agim IBRAIMI		M	21	(5)	2

Macedonia

Mensur IDRIZI		M	17	(2)	1
Ismail ISMAILI		A	7	(4)	
Minas JASARI		A	2	(1)	1
Vance MANCEVSKI		G	16		
Agron MEMEDI		D	25	(4)	2
Nuri MUSTAFI		D	26	(2)	1
Artim POLOZANI		A	27	(4)	3
Igor SAVEVSKI		D	6	(9)	1
Vasko STEFANOV		D	22	(6)	
Ilija STOJCEVSKI		D	18	(8)	
Bilal VELIJA		M	26	(3)	1

VARDAR SKOPJE
Coach – Vujadin Stanojkovic; (28/11/05) (Petar Georgievski); (15/12/05) Dragan Kanatlarovski

2005
8/8	Vlazrimi Kicevo	a	0-1	
21/8	Cementarnica 55 Skopje	h	1-1	Serafimovski
28/8	Pobeda Prilep	a	1-0	Scepanovic
11/9	Bregalnica Kraun Stip	a	3-0	Naumov, Gligorovski, Scepanovic
18/9	Belasica Strumica	h	2-1	Ristovski, Naumov
25/9	Renova Cepciste	a	1-0	Masev
1/10	Baskimi Kumanovo	h	3-1	Masev, Scepanovic, Naumov
4/10	Makedonija GP Skopje	a	0-1	
16/10	Rabotnicki Kometal Skopje	h	0-2	
23/10	Sileks Kratovo	a	2-0	Naumov, Demiri
30/10	Skendija 79 Tetovo	h	1-0	Naumov
6/11	Vlazrimi Kicevo	h	2-0	Naumov, Nuhiji
9/11	Cementarnica 55 Skopje	a	1-0	Nuhiji
20/11	Pobeda Prilep	h	1-1	Masev
27/11	Bregalnica Kraun Stip	h	1-0	Ristovski
4/12	Belasica Strumica	a	2-0	Naumov, Nuhiji
11/12	Renova Cepciste	h	1-1	Ristovski

2006
5/3	Baskimi Kumanovo	a	1-0	Kaptiev
12/3	Makedonija GP Skopje	h	1-0	Trickovski
15/3	Rabotnicki Kometal Skopje	a	0-1	
19/3	Sileks Kratovo	h	2-0	Naumov 2
22/3	Skendija 79 Tetovo	a	1-2	Tanevski (p)
26/3	Bregalnica Kraun Stip	a	1-0	Ristovski
2/4	Sileks Kratovo	a	0-0	
9/4	Cementarnica 55 Skopje	h	2-0	Markovski, Trickovski
16/4	Renova Cepciste	a	0-1	
19/4	Belasica Strumica	h	3-0	Banduliev, Naumov 2
22/4	Baskimi Kumanovo	a	1-1	Naumov
30/4	Skendija 79 Tetovo	h	2-2	Ristovski (p), Naumov
3/5	Pobeda Prilep	a	0-2	
7/5	Makedonija GP Skopje	h	0-0	
14/5	Vlazrimi Kicevo	h	3-0	Naumov, Kaptiev, Stojanovski
21/5	Rabotnicki Kometal Skopje	a	3-1	Kaptiev, Naumov, Osmani

Name	Nat	Pos	Aps	(s)	Gls
Toni BANDULIEV		M	8	(1)	1
Aguinaldo de Jesus BRAGA	BRA	M	17	(7)	
Dejan BRANKOVIC	SCG	D	20	(6)	
DEILSON Elijas da Silva	BRA	M	16	(8)	
Ertan DEMIRI		M	10	(7)	1
Blagija GJURCEVSKI		M	14	(4)	
Nikola GLIGOROV		M	11	(4)	
Ivica GLIGOROVSKI		M	18	(2)	1
Daniel IVANOVSKI		D	27	(1)	
Rosen KAPTIEV	BUL	A	6	(5)	3
Ljupco KMETOVSKI		G	27		
Jovan KOSTOVSKI		M	1	(3)	
Bojan MARKOVSKI		D	28	(1)	1
Danco MASEV		A	9	(3)	3
Riste NAUMOV		A	27	(6)	15
Arben NUHIJI		A	22	(4)	3
Minas OSMANI		A	2		1
Dejan RISTOVSKI		M	16	(6)	5
Vucina SCEPANOVIC	SCG	M	7	(7)	3
Vladimir SEKULOVSKI		M	23	(5)	
Zarko SERAFIMOVSKI		M	13	(1)	1
Aleksandar STOJANOVSKI		M	1	(6)	1
Zlatko TANEVSKI		D	22	(2)	1
Darko TASEVSKI		M	1		
Ivan TRICKOVSKI		A	11	(4)	2
Velimir ZDRAVKOVIC	SCG	G	6	(1)	

VLAZRIMI KICEVO
Coach – Vlatko Kostov; (24/3/06) Nazmi Ajdini

2005
8/8	Vardar Skopje	h	1-0	Bajrami
21/8	Belasica Strumica	a	1-0	Bajrami
28/8	Renova Cepciste	h	4-3	Masic, Boric, Osmani, Bajrami
11/9	Baskimi Kumanovo	a	1-0	Bajrami
18/9	Makedonija GP Skopje	h	0-1	
25/9	Rabotnicki Kometal Skopje	a	1-2	Angelov
1/10	Sileks Kratovo	h	0-1	
4/10	Skendija 79 Tetovo	a	1-2	Osmani
16/10	Bregalnica Kraun Stip	h	2-1	Bajrami 2
23/10	Cementarnica 55 Skopje	h	4-0	Manev, Bajrami 3 (1p)
30/10	Pobeda Prilep	a	0-1	
6/11	Vardar Skopje	h	0-2	
9/11	Belasica Strumica	h	3-1	Krstev, Cakal, Bajrami
20/11	Renova Cepciste	a	3-4	Osmani, Bajrami 2
27/11	Baskimi Kumanovo	h	2-2	Abelunde, Krstev
4/12	Makedonija GP Skopje	a	0-3	
11/12	Rabotnicki Kometal Skopje	h	0-1	

2006
5/3	Sileks Kratovo	a	1-1	Angelov
12/3	Skendija 79 Tetovo	h	1-0	Lazarevski
15/3	Bregalnica Kraun Stip	a	1-1	Spasovski
19/3	Cementarnica 55 Skopje	a	1-3	Demiri
22/3	Pobeda Prilep	h	2-4	Bajrami, Spasovski
25/3	Rabotnicki Kometal Skopje	a	0-4	
2/4	Baskimi Kumanovo	a	1-2	Spasovski
9/4	Bregalnica Kraun Stip	h	1-0	Zulbeari
16/4	Skendija 79 Tetovo	a	1-5	Spasovski
19/4	Sileks Kratovo	h	3-2	Abelunde, Arslani, Presilski
22/4	Pobeda Prilep	a	2-1	Spasovski, Demiri
30/4	Cementarnica 55 Skopje	h	0-0	
3/5	Makedonija GP Skopje	a	2-6	Ibraimi, Ramadan
7/5	Renova Cepciste	h	2-1	Lazarevski, Spasovski
14/5	Vardar Skopje	a	0-3	
21/5	Belasica Strumica	h	3-0	Ibraimi, Demiri, Lazarevski

Name	Nat	Pos	Aps	(s)	Gls
Lukmoi ABELUNDE	NGA	M	16	(8)	2
Stojan ANGELOV		M	18	(4)	

Macedonia

Toni ANGELOV			M	12	(5)	2
Skumbin ARSLANI			D	5	(5)	1
Muarem BAJRAMI			A	24	(1)	13
Kustrim BALAZI			M	6	(3)	
Emir BORIC			M	21	(1)	1
Elvir CAKAL	BOS		M	10	(1)	1
Ardijan CUCULI			M	20	(3)	
Abil DEMIRI			M		(4)	
Agron DEMIRI			M	7	(6)	3
Edmond HODZA			M	1	(4)	
Besrat IBRAIMI			M	4	(6)	2
Armend JUSUFI			G	2		
Bekim JUSUFI			M	4	(3)	
Jetrim KADRIU			M	16	(1)	
Ljupco KOLEV			G	31		
Sasko KRSTEV			A	11		2
Sasko LAZAREVSKI			M	7	(7)	3
Jordan MANEV			M	20	(2)	1
Asmer MASIC	BOS		M	8	(4)	1
Vlatko NOVAKOV			M	25	(4)	
Minas OSMANI			A	13	(1)	3
Borce POSTOLOV			M	20	(1)	
Bruno PRESILSKI			D	12	(1)	1
Oleg SALIN			M	1	(9)	
Zekirija RAMADAN			M	20	(3)	1
Vladimir SPASOVSKI			A	10	(8)	6
Burim ZULBEARI			M	19	(1)	1

DOMESTIC CUP 2005/06

FIRST ROUND

(31/7/05)
Skopje 0, Vardar Skopje 1
Milano 4, Baskimi Kumanovo 5
Kozuv 6, Madzari Solidarnost Skopje 1
Mladost Sushica 0, Pobeda Prilep 2
Bratstvo 0, Sileks Kratovo 1
11 Oktomvri 0, Cementarnica 55 Skopje 3
Borec 0, Napredok Kicevo 3
Asimi 1, Belasica Strumica 9
Ohrid 1, Makedonija GP Skopje 1 *(4-3 on pens)*
Osogovo 2, Vlazrimi Kicevo 6
Pelister Bitola 0, Skendija 79 Tetovo 2
Teteks Tetovo 3, Turnovo 1
Tiverija 0, Renova Cepciste 5
Lokomotiva 1, Sloga Jugomagnat Skopje 0
(23/8/05)
Karaorman Struga 2, Rabotnicki Kometal Skopje 2 *(5-4 on pens)*

SECOND ROUND

(14/9/05 & 19/10/05)
Pobeda Prilep v Vlazrimi Kicevo 3-0; 2-2 *(5-2)*
Vardar Skopje v Kozuf 3-0; 2-0 *(5-0)*
Makedonija GP Skopje v Napredok Kicevo 2-0; 2-2 *(4-2)*
Belasica Strumica v Sileks Kratovo 1-2; 0-3 *(1-5)*
Cementarnica 55 Skopje v Karaorman Struga 3-2; 1-0 *(4-2)*
Teteks Tetovo v Lokomotiva 3-1; 1-2 *(4-3)*
Skendija 79 Tetovo v Renova Cepciste 4-0; 1-1 *(5-1)*
Bregalnica Kraun Stip v Baskimi Kumanovo 2-1; 2-2 *(4-3)*

QUARTER-FINALS

(2/11/05 & 30/11/05)
Makedonija GP Skopje 1 *(Brnjarcevski 87)*, Cementarnica 55 Skopje 0
Cementarnica 55 Skopje 0, Makedonija GP Skopje 1 *(Milosevic 80)*
(Makedonija GP Skopje 2-0)

Vardar Skopje 1 *(Naumov 20)*, Bregalnica Kraun Stip 3 *(Spasovski 52, Dimitrovski 67, Andonov 76)*
Bregalnica Kraun Stip 0, Vardar Skopje 0
(Bregalnica Kraun Stip 3-1)

Skendija 79 Tetovo 2 *(Emrulahu 37, Emini 90)*, Pobeda Prilep 0
Pobeda Prilep 2 *(Kapinkovski 56p, Manevski 90)*, Skendija 79 Tetovo 2 *(Aleksovski 30, Ibraimi 84)*
(Skendija 79 Tetovo 4-2)

Sileks Kratovo 3 *(Ristic 23, Todorovski 33, Janevski 42)*, Teteks Tetovo 0
Teteks Tetovo 2 *(Radovic 36, 89)*, Sileks Kratovo 3 *(Ristic 50, 58, Dimitrovski 74)*
(Sileks Kratovo 6-2)

SEMI-FINALS

(5/4/06 & 10/5/06)
Skendija 79 Tetovo 1 *(Polozani 37)*, Bregalnica Kraun Stip 1 *(Gjulas 5)*
Bregalnica Kraun Stip 0, Skendija 79 Tetovo 1 *(Polozani 77)*
(Skendija 79 Tetovo 2-1)

Makedonija GP Skopje 1 *(Milosevic 25)*, Sileks Kratovo 1 *(Brkovic 35)*
Sileks Kratovo 1 *(Divjak 13)*, Makedonija GP Skopje 2 *(Milosevic 64, Ismaili 77)*
(Makedonija GP Skopje 3-2)

FINAL

(24/5/06)
Gradski stadon, Skopje
MAKEDONIJA GP SKOPJE 3 *(Stefanov 69og, Belcev 85, Ivanovski 90)*
SKENDIJA 79 TETOVO 2 *(Polozani 61, Mustafi 80)*
Referee - Krstevski
MAKEDONIJA GP SKOPJE – Simov, Bozinovski, Ljubisavljevic, Dzangarovski, Jovanovski, Stojanovski (Belcev 80), Milosavlevic (Mitrev 60), Milosevic, Ivanovski, Brnjarcevski, Ismaili (Aranitovic 55).
SKENDIJA 79 TETOVO – Mancevski, Velija, Memedi, Stefanov, Savevski, Mustafi (Demiri 90), Polozani, Emini (Ademi 81), Georgiev, Aleksovski (Ibraimi 65), Emurlahu.

SECOND LEVEL FINAL TABLE 2005/06

		Pld	W	D	L	F	A	Pts
1	Pelister Bitola	30	19	4	7	52	22	61
2	Napredok Kicevo	30	15	7	8	44	38	52
3	Karaorman Struga	30	15	5	10	47	38	50
4	Madzari Solidarnost Skopje	30	11	8	11	33	30	41
5	Sloga Jugomagnat Skopje	30	11	7	12	35	39	40
6	Skopje	30	11	7	12	30	36	40
7	Turnovo	30	11	6	13	39	36	39
8	Metalurg Skopje	30	10	7	13	29	36	37
9	Lozar Demir Kapija	30	10	7	13	34	45	37
10	Teteks Tetovo	30	11	2	17	36	45	35
11	Novaci 2005	30	9	4	17	29	42	31

N.B. Mladost Susica withdrew during the first half of the season.

PROMOTION/RELEGATION PLAY-OFFS

(28/5/06)
Sileks Kratovo 1, Madzari Solidarnost Skopje 0

Bregalnica Kraun Stip 3, Karaorman Struga 3 *(aet; 4-3 on pens)*

Malta

Birkirkara turn the tables

After finishing as runners-up to Sliema Wanderers in each of the previous three seasons, Birkirkara swapped positions in 2005/06 to claim only the second championship title in their 56-year history.

The Stripes timed their run to perfection. Off the pace in the autumn when Sliema, with wins in their first eight games, and then Hibernians, after a 2-0 victory over the champions, ruled the roost, Birkirkara moved ahead in the New Year with a stunning surge that included victories against each of their two rivals.

As the leading six teams entered the Championship Pool, Stephen Azzopardi's side held a one-point lead. With Wanderers and, especially, Hibs struggling for form, the path to the title opened up for Birkirkara and they cruised home to victory with a decisive unbeaten run. A 3-3 draw between Sliema Wanderers and Msida St. Joseph on Saturday May 6 proved conclusive and The Stripes celebrated their title triumph the following day with a 1-0 win over Hibernians.

Birkirkara were worthy champions, not least because they played attractive football and scored lots of goals. Skipper Michael Galea bagged 19 for himself, the top tally in the league, while his young strike partner Etienne Barbara scored 14. In his fifth season at the helm coach Azzopardi claimed the most treasured of his 11 trophies. He would have liked to make it a nice round dozen by completing the Double with victory in the FA Trophy, but that dream died when Hibernians suddenly emerged from their slump to beat the champions 1-0 in the semi-final.

One-nil would also suffice for the Paolites in the final as a goal from Haruna Doda accounted for Floriana, a team that had surprisingly eclipsed Sliema 2-0 in the other semi. Such is the structure of the FA Trophy that Hibs only needed to win three games (as opposed to five for Floriana) to take the Cup. Even so, considering that they were undergoing a dreadful spell in the league when they entered the competition, goalkeeper Mario Muscat and his defence deserved credit for keeping clean sheets in every game. The Cup final was doubly crucial for Robert Gatt's side as it put them back into the UEFA Cup after they had dropped to a disappointing fourth place (behind Marsaxlokk) in the league

Cohen collects

Hibs striker Andrew Cohen was voted Malta Footballer of the Year for the second season running, just ahead of Birkirkara's Galea. Cohen's partner in the Maltese national side, Ivan Woods, scored 16 goals for Sliema Wanderers, but although his team qualified for Europe as league runners-up, there was considerable disappointment that they had missed out on an unprecedented fourth consecutive title.

Still, Wanderers were in a far better shape than their traditional rivals Valletta, who won only ten games all season, and Floriana, who dropped into the

NATIONAL TEAM RESULTS 2005/06

17/8/05	Northern Ireland	H	Ta' Qali	1-1	Woods (35)
3/9/05	Hungary (WCQ)	A	Budapest	0-4	
7/9/05	Croatia (WCQ)	H	Ta' Qali	1-1	Wellman (74)
12/10/05	Bulgaria (WCQ)	H	Ta' Qali	1-1	Barbara (78)
27/2/06	Moldova	H	Ta' Qali	0-2	
1/3/06	Georgia	H	Ta' Qali	0-2	
4/6/06	Japan	N	Düsseldorf	0-1	

Malta

Relegation Pool and only scrambled to safety on the last day after a 3-3 draw against Mosta, who went down instead. The other newly promoted club, Hamrun Spartans, were already condemned after a 0-0 draw with Mosta the previous weekend. St. George's and Marsa, the top two in the First Division, will hope for better fortunes in 2006/07.

Malta finished their World Cup qualifying programme with a pair of highly creditable 1-1 draws at home to Croatia and Bulgaria. Behind in both games, they did brilliantly to earn a point, with Stephen Wellman's thunderous free-kick equaliser against the Croatians a particularly memorable moment for the island's long-suffering fans (even if it did spark a mini-riot among the outraged visiting supporters). Despite those two results, coach Horst Heese announced that he would not be staying on as coach. The 62-year-old German was replaced in January by another foreigner, Dusan Fitzel, a Czech, who left his position as coach of his native land's Under-19 team to sign on to the Malta FA payroll as both head coach and technical director. Three defeats without a goal – the first against what was essentially a Moldovan youth team – did not exactly bode well for the Euro 2008 qualifiers.

NATIONAL TEAM APPEARANCES 2005/06

Coach – Horst HEESE (GER)
/(17/1/06) Dusan FITZEL (CZE)

Player	DOB	Club	Nir	HUN	CRO	BUL	Mol	Geo	Jpn	Caps	Goals
Justin HABER	9/6/81	US Quévillaise (FRA)	G	G	G	G		G	G	12	-
Roderick BRIFFA	4/8/81	Birkirkara	D	D	D	D	s46	D		14	-
Luke DIMECH	11/1/77	Chester City (ENG)	D62			D		D	D	41	1
Brian SAID	15/5/73	Sliema Wanderers	D	D	D	D	D			62	3
Stephen WELLMAN	31/8/82	Marsaxlokk	D	D	D	D		D	D	9	1
Peter PULLICINO	17/6/76	Hibernians	M62	M	D	M	M			12	-
Claude MATTOCKS	21/2/80	Sliema Wanderers	M79	M	M73			M46	s64	14	-
Gilbet AGIUS	21/2/74	Valletta	M74		M		s74	M	M80	91	6
Orosco ANONAM	15/7/79	Sliema Wanderers	M	M	M		M74			4	-
Ivan WOODS	31/12/76	Sliema Wanderers	A	A	A	A70	A74			18	1
Andrew COHEN	13/5/81	Hibernians	A86	A85	A89	A88	s74	s46	A88	13	-
Ian CIANTAR	19/12/75	Floriana	s62	s85	s73	M		M	D	19	-
Kenneth SCICLUNA	15/6/79	Birkirkara	s62	D55	D46		D			4	-
George MALLIA	10/10/78	Birkirkara	s74			M	M46	M	s69	44	4
Antoine ZAHRA	9/1/81	Birkirkara	s79	s55		s64				46	1
Kevin SAMMUT	26/5/81	Marsaxlokk	s86	s65	s46				M	8	-
Massimo GRIMA	5/7/79	Valletta		M65	s89	s88				11	-
Ian AZZOPARDI	12/8/82	Floriana				D64	s46	D	D	17	-
Etienne BARBARA	10/6/82	Birkirkara				s70	A	s46		12	3
Mario MUSCAT	18/8/76	Hibernians					G			57	-
Alex MUSCAT	14/12/84	Sliema Wanderers					D			2	-
Trevor CILIA	2/1/83	Floriana					D46		s88	2	-
Andrei AGIUS	12/8/86	Mascalucia (ITA)					M		s80	2	-
William CAMENZULI	11/2/79	Birkirkara						D46		14	-
Michael MIFSUD	17/4/81	Lillestrøm SK (NOR)						A		38	11
Roderick BAJADA	4/1/83	Sliema Wanderers							D69	4	-
Jamie PACE	1/1/77	Marsaxlokk							M	2	-
Andre SCHEMBRI	27/5/86	Marsaxlokk							A64	1	-

Malta

EUROPEAN CUPS 2005/06

UEFA CHAMPIONS LEAGUE

SLIEMA WANDERERS
1st qualifying round SHERIFF TIRASPOL (MOL)
H 1-4 Bogdanovic (72)
Akanji, Brincat (Muscat 64), Di Lello, Said, Turner (Farrugia 84), Bogdanovic, Doncic, Chetcuti, Woods (Mifsud 84), Anonam, Giglio.
A 0-2
Akanji, Brincat, Di Lello, Said, Turner, Bogdanovic, Doncic, Chetcuti, Woods (Mifsud 75), Anonam (Muscat 86), Giglio (Lombardi 87).

UEFA CUP

BIRKIRKARA
1st qualifying round APOEL (CYP)
H 0-2
Simon, Sammut (Calascione 65), Camenzuli, Yanchev, Scicluna, Galea L., Bonnici, Briffa (Zahra 69), Monye (Micallef 79), Ciantar, Barbara.
A 0-4
Simon, Micallef (Mallia 46), Yanchev, Camenzuli, Scicluna, Galea L. (Zahra 64), Bonnici, Briffa, Monye (Calascione 74), Ciantar, Barbara.

HIBERNIANS
1st qualifying round OMONIA (CYP)
A 0-3
Muscat, Pullicino, Pulis, Xuereb, Mintoff, Mbong, Scerri, Cohen, Baldacchino, Camilleri, Doda (Zahra 70).
H 0-3
Muscat, Pullicino, Pulis, Xuereb, Mbong, Scerri, Cohen (Zahra 75), Baldacchino (Vella 84), Camilleri, Failla (Mintoff 46), Doda.

TOP GOALSCORERS 2005/06

19	Michael GALEA (Birkirkara)
16	Daniel NWOKE (Msida St. Joseph)
	Ivan WOODS (Sliema Wanderers)
15	Adrian MIFSUD (Floriana)
14	Etienne BARBARA (Birkirkara)
	Andrew COHEN (Hibernians)
	Wendell GOMES (Marsaxlokk)
13	Danilo DONCIC (Sliema Wanderers)
12	Ikechukwu CHIBUEZE (Mosta)
	Cleaven FRENDO (Marsaxlokk)

LEAGUE RESULTS/SCORERS/APPEARANCES/GOALS 2005/06

BIRKIRKARA
Coach – Stephen Azzopardi

2005			
5/8	Valletta	4-2	Camenzuli, Briffa, Zahra, Calascione
12/8	Msida St. Joseph	5-2	Mallia 2, Calascione, Briffa, Ciantar
22/8	Marsaxlokk	1-1	Galea M.
12/9	Sliema Wanderers	1-2	Galea M. (p)
18/9	Pietà Hotspurs	4-1	Galea M. 2 (1p), Barbara, Galea L.
26/9	Hibernians	2-5	Calascione, Mifsud Triganza
1/10	Hamrun Spartans	2-1	Zahra 2
15/10	Mosta	3-2	Camenzuli, Galea M., Barbara
21/10	Floriana	1-0	Galea M.
28/10	Valletta	2-0	Galea M. 2
3/12	Msida St.Joseph	4-1	Zahra, Mifsud Triganza, Barbara, Galea M.
8/12	Marsaxlokk	0-2	
2006			
3/1	Sliema	2-1	Ciantar 2
7/1	Pietà Hotspurs	2-0	Barbara, Calascione
14/1	Hibernians	2-0	Mallia, Camenzuli
21/1	Hamrun Spartans	6-0	Barbara 3, Galea M. 2, Camenzuli
29/1	Mosta	6-0	Barbara 2, Galea M. 4 (1p)
5/2	Floriana	1-1	Barbara
4/3	Msida St.Joseph	5-0	Galea M. 2, Barbara, Ciantar, Briffa
11/3	Valletta	0-0	
18/3	Marsaxlokk	1-0	Calascione
25/3	Hibernians	3-1	Galea M. 2, Mallia
2/4	Sliema Wanderers	1-1	Mifsud Triganza
15/4	Msida St.Joseph	4-1	Barbara 2, Briffa, Mifsud Triganza
21/4	Valletta	3-0	Mifsud Triganza 2, Briffa
30/4	Marsaxlokk	1-1	Mifsud Triganza
7/5	Hibernians	1-0	Barbara
14/5	Sliema Wanderers	1-2	Mifsud Triganza

No	Name	Nat	Pos	Aps	(s)	Gls
13	Martin ANASTASI		M		(2)	
22	Etienne BARBARA		A	23	(1)	14
2	Mark Anthony BONNICI		D	15	(7)	
15	Patrick BORG		A	2		
19	Roderick BRIFFA		M	22	(1)	5
7	Matthew CALASCIONE		M	10	(14)	5
6	William CAMENZULI		D	26		4
23	Adrian CIANTAR		M	11	(2)	4
3	Lino GALEA		D	22	(2)	1
9	Michael GALEA		A	22	(4)	19
8	Jonathan HOLLAND		M	8	(5)	
21	George MALLIA		M	22		4
14	Ryan MIFSUD		D	2	(1)	
20	Jean Pierre MIFSUD TRIGANZA		A	9	(12)	8
4	Precious MONYE	NGA	D	26		
10	Chucks NWOKO	NGA	M	1	(5)	
25	Bernard PARIS		G	3	(2)	
5	Roderick SAMMUT		D	13	(4)	
17	Kenneth SCICLUNA		D	25	(1)	
1	David SIMON	CZE	G	25		
16	Luke STIVALA		A		(3)	
18	Anthony VASSALLO		D		(1)	
12	Emil YANCHEV	BUL	D	17	(4)	
11	Antoine ZAHRA		M	4	(5)	4
24	Joseph ZERAFA		A		(1)	

FLORIANA
Coach – Jimmy Briffa; (3/9/05) Jan Artz

2005			
5/8	Pietà Hotspurs	0-2	
11/8	Valletta	1-1	Cassar

Malta

Date	Opponent	Score	Scorers
20/8	Hibernians	0-3	
10/9	Msida St.Joseph	2-4	Ciantar I. 2
17/9	Hamrun Spartans	1-3	Micallef
21/9	Marsaxlokk	1-1	Baldacchino
25/9	Mosta	4-4	Mifsud 2 (1p), Azzopardi, Caruana C.
16/10	Sliema Wanderers	0-1	
21/10	Birkirkara	0-1	
30/10	Pietà Hotspurs	3-1	Mifsud 2, Cilia
3/12	Valletta	2-1	Baldacchino, Eviparker
14/12	Hibernians	1-1	Micallef
17/12	Msida St.Joseph	0-0	
2006			
7/1	Hamrun Spartans	4-2	Mifsud 3 (1p), Caruana C.
17/1	Marsaxlokk	1-2	Mifsud
24/1	Mosta	3-0	Eviparker, Mifsud, Caruana C.
28/1	Sliema Wanderers	0-0	
5/2	Birkirkara	1-1	Cilia
12/3	Hamrun Spartans	3-0	Cilia, Eviparker, Micallef
25/3	Pietà Hotspurs	1-2	Mifsud
2/4	Mosta	0-1	
21/4	Hamrun Spartans	4-2	Cilia, Mifsud 3
6/5	Pietà Hotspurs	1-1	Gango-Rtsa
12/5	Mosta	3-3	Mifsud 2, Azzopardi

No	Name	Nat	Pos	Aps	(s)	Gls
12	Simon AGIUS		G	22		
13	Ian AZZOPARDI		D	18		2
7	Nicolo BALDACCHINO		A	11	(5)	2
27	Joseph BORG		M		(3)	
4	Julian BRIFFA		D	17		
17	Jermain BRINCAT		D	1	(6)	
10	Mauro BRINCAT		M	9		
22	Angus BUHAGIAR		D		(1)	
15	Christian CARUANA		M	8	(9)	3
6	Mario CARUANA		D	14	(6)	
8	Christian CASSAR		M	15	(1)	1
3	Clifton CIANTAR		D	4		
19	Ian CIANTAR		D	16		2
16	Trevor CILIA		M	20		4
18	Ryan DARMANIN		A	2		
19	Andre Rocha DA SILVA	BRA	M	4		
24	Adama DIAO	SEN	D	3		
21	Anthony EVIPARKER	NGA	A	10	(11)	3
5	Keith FABRI		D	9		
1	David FARRUGIA		G	2	(1)	
11	Kurt FORMOSA		M	13	(3)	
2	Riad-Mynel GANGO-RTSA	CON	D	21		1
20	Mark GAUCI		M	2	(3)	
9	Manolito MICALLEF		A	19	(2)	3
23	Adrian MIFSUD		A	20	(1)	15
14	Rufin OBA	CON	M	3	(5)	
5	Joseph Craig SCHEMBRI		D	1	(1)	

FINAL LEAGUE TABLES 2005/06

Second Phase
Championship Pool

		Pld	W	D	L	F	A	Pts
1	Birkirkara	28	19	5	4	68	27	42
2	Sliema Wanderers	28	17	5	6	58	27	37
3	Marsaxlokk	28	16	5	7	52	36	36
4	Hibernians	28	14	4	10	49	37	28
5	Valletta	28	10	5	13	37	49	24
6	Msida St.Joseph	28	6	7	15	40	59	15

Relegation Pool

		Pld	W	D	L	F	A	Pts
7	Floriana	24	6	9	9	36	37	18
8	Pietà Hotspurs	24	6	6	12	31	47	17
9	Mosta	24	5	5	14	34	65	16
10	Hamrun Spartans	24	6	3	15	35	56	12

First Phase

		Pld	W	D	L	F	A	Pts
1	Birkirkara	18	13	2	3	48	21	41 (21)
2	Sliema Wanderers	18	12	3	3	37	12	39 (20)
3	Hibernians	18	12	1	5	37	19	37 (19)
4	Marsaxlokk	18	10	4	4	36	23	34 (17)
5	Valletta	18	7	2	9	22	31	23 (12)
6	Msida St.Joseph	18	6	3	9	28	33	21 (11)
7	Hamrun Spartans	18	6	1	11	29	41	19 (10)
8	Floriana	18	4	7	7	24	28	19 (10)
9	Pietà Hotspurs	18	4	3	11	22	39	15 (8)
10	Mosta	18	2	2	14	20	56	8 (4)

N.B. Figures in brackets indicate points carried forward to the Second Phase.

HAMRUN SPARTANS
Coach – Michael Degiorgio

Date	Opponent	Score	Scorers
2005			
11/8	Marsaxlokk	1-2	Sultana
20/8	Pietà Hotspurs	2-4	Spiteri, Galea D.
25/8	Sliema Wanderers	1-4	Spiteri
10/9	Hibernians	0-1	
17/9	Floriana	3-1	Okoro, Spiteri, Nwankwo
28/9	Mosta	2-1	Okoro (p), Nwankwo
1/10	Birkirkara	1-2	Spiteri
17/10	Valletta	4-2	Spiteri 2, Okoro, Mangion
23/10	Msida St.Joseph	1-2	Spiteri
30/10	Marsaxlokk	3-4	Okoro 2 (1p), Spiteri
20/11	Sliema Wanderers	1-1	Nwankwo
14/12	Pietà Hotspurs	3-2	Sultana, Mangion, Cucciardi
18/12	Hibernians	0-2	
2006			
7/1	Floriana	2-4	Fenech Ry., Okoro
17/1	Mosta	3-0	Sultana, Spiteri, Fenech Ry.
21/1	Birkirkara	0-6	
5/2	Valletta	2-1	Borg, Zammit
12/2	Msida St. Joseph	0-2	
12/3	Floriana	0-3	
19/3	Mosta	3-5	Nwankwo, Sultana 2 (1p)
16/4	Pietà Hotspurs	0-2	
21/4	Floriana	2-4	Nwankwo 2
5/5	Mosta	0-0	
13/5	Pietà Hotspurs	1-1	Cucciardi

No	Name	Nat	Pos	Aps	(s)	Gls
2	Aaron ATTARD		D	7	(2)	
20	Garreth BARTOLO		D		(1)	
7	Kevin BORG		M	19	(4)	1
18	Evano BRIFFA		D	1	(7)	
1	Jason CORDINA		G	22		
3	Diego Armando CUCCIARDI		A	1	(16)	2
13	John DEBATTISTA		D	19	(2)	

Malta

HIBERNIANS
Coach – Robert Gatt

No	Name	Nat	Pos	Aps	(s)	Gls
12	Micheal FALZON		G	2		
10	Robert FENECH		M	1	(2)	
8	Ryan FENECH		A	20		2
17	Jonathan FRANCICA		M	6	(1)	
21	David GALEA		D	9	(6)	1
22	Neville GALEA		D	1		
26	Iyiabo Mohima IYIABA	NGA	M	3		
4	Jonathan MAGRI OVERAND		D	12	(2)	
14	Rupert MANGION		M	19	(1)	2
25	Adam MANSUETO		D	8	(3)	
24	Stephen MEILAK		A		(1)	
19	Patrick NDUBISI NDAH	NGA	D	22		
16	Eric Chidi NWANWKO	NGA	A	10	(9)	6
15	Maczerob OKORO	NGA	A	19		6
5	Steve SADOWSKI		D	15	(3)	
9	Gaetan SPITERI		A	18	(1)	9
11	Stefan SULTANA		A	13	(4)	5
23	Ishaku UMORU		A	3		
6	Ivan ZAMMIT		M	14		1

2005
Date	Opponent	Score	Scorers
6/8	Sliema Wanderers	0-3	
12/8	Pietà Hotspurs	4-0	og (Deanov), Cohen, Zahra, Scerri
20/8	Floriana	3-0	Cohen, Doda, Scerri
10/9	Hamrun Spartans	1-0	Cohen
17/9	Mosta	3-0	Failla, Cohen, Scerri
26/9	Birkirkara	5-2	Mbong 2, Camilleri 3
2/10	Valletta	0-2	
15/10	Msida St.Joseph	4-2	Cohen 3 (2p), Scerri
23/10	Marsaxlokk	4-1	Scerri, Camilleri 2 (1p), Doda
29/10	Sliema Wanderers	2-0	Mbong, Doda
4/12	Pietà Hotspurs	2-1	Doda, Cohen (p)
14/12	Floriana	1-1	Cohen (p)
18/12	Hamrun Spartans	2-0	Scerri, Vella

2006
Date	Opponent	Score	Scorers
8/1	Mosta	3-2	Doda, Pulis, Baldacchino
14/1	Birkirkara	0-2	
28/1	Valletta	1-2	Cohen
4/2	Msida St.Joseph	2-0	Doda, Baldacchino
11/2	Marsaxlokk	0-1	
4/3	Valletta	1-3	Mbong
11/3	Sliema	0-3	
19/3	Msida St.Joseph	1-1	Cohen
25/3	Birkirkara	1-3	Cohen
1/4	Marsaxlokk	3-1	Cohen, Baldacchino, Doda
15/4	Valletta	2-2	Agius, Doda
22/4	Sliema Wanderers	4-3	Cohen (p), Doda 2, Scerri
30/4	Msida St.Joseph	0-0	
7/5	Birkirkara	0-1	
13/5	Marsaxlokk	0-1	Schembri

No	Name	Nat	Pos	Aps	(s)	Gls
21	Edmond AGIUS		D	18	(6)	1
17	Chris AZZOPARDI		M		(1)	
15	Roderick BALDACCHINO		M	8	(13)	3
20	Matthew BARTOLO		D		(1)	
13	Luka Desira BUTTIGIEG		D		(3)	
12	Alex CAMILLERI		G	4		
18	Ben CAMILLERI		M	4	(4)	
19	David CAMILLERI		M	27	(1)	5
22	Jonathan CARUANA		D		(1)	
10	Andrew COHEN		A	26		14
88	Haruna DODA		A	26		10
6	Clayton FAILLA		M	18	(5)	1
8	Essien MBONG		M	26		4
16	Ryan MINTOFF		D	12	(1)	
1	Mario MUSCAT		G	24		
24	Jonathan PEARSON		D	5	(4)	
4	Adrian PULIS		D	23	(1)	1
3	Peter PULLICINO		M	20	(1)	
25	Quelin REFALO		M		(1)	
9	Terence SCERRI		A	17	(2)	7
2	Kenneth SPITERI		M	8	(8)	
14	Julian VELLA		A	8	(10)	1
7	David WILLIAMSON	IRL	A	8		
5	Aaron XUEREB		D	22	(1)	
11	Antoine ZAHRA		A	4	(1)	1

MARSAXLOKK
Coach – Atanas Marinov; (6/10/05) Oliver Spiteri & Ray Farrugia

2005
Date	Opponent	Score	Scorers
11/8	Hamrun Spartans	2-1	Frendo, Licari
22/8	Birkirkara	1-1	Frendo
25/8	Mosta	5-1	Bajjada 2, Schembri, Frendo, Licari
11/9	Valletta	2-3	Schembri, Frendo
18/9	Msida St.Joseph	1-1	Frendo
21/9	Floriana	1-1	Bajada
1/10	Sliema Wanderers	1-2	Pace
16/10	Pietà Hotspurs	4-1	Gomes W. 3, Licari
23/10	Hibernians	1-4	Schembri
30/10	Hamrun Spartans	4-3	Gomes W. 2, Frendo 2
20/11	Mosta	3-1	Frendo 3
8/12	Birkirkara	2-0	Gomes W., Schembri
3/01	Valletta	4-0	Frendo, Mamo K., Schembri, Mamo C.

2006
Date	Opponent	Score	Scorers
8/1	Msida St.Joseph	1-0	Gomes W.
17/1	Floriana	2-1	Schembri 2
24/1	Sliema Wanderers	0-0	
4/2	Pietà Hotspurs	1-3	Licari
11/2	Hibernians	1-0	og (Xuereb)
5/3	Sliema Wanderers	2-1	Gomes W., Sammut
12/3	Msida St.Joseph	1-0	Schembri
18/3	Birkirkara	0-1	
26/3	Valletta	3-4	Gomes W. 2, Bajada
1/4	Hibernians	1-3	Schembri
16/4	Sliema Wanderers	1-0	Frendo
22/4	Msida St.Joseph	4-3	Gomes W. 3, Bajada
30/4	Birkirkara	1-1	Gomes W.
5/5	Valletta	2-0	Gomes N., Schembri
13/5	Hibernians	1-0	Schembri

No	Name	Nat	Pos	Aps	(s)	Gls
20	Shaun BAJADA		M	18	(9)	5
8	Chris BART-WILLIAMS	ENG	M	8		
26	Clyde CARABOTT		M	1	(2)	
25	Brian CARUANA		D		(2)	
24	Malcolm CARUANA		M		(1)	
74	Reuben DEBONO		G	9	(1)	
26	Cleaven FRENDO		A	25		12
1	Reuben GAUCI		G	19	(1)	
4	Nuno Miguel Dos Santos GOMES	POR	D	19	(2)	1
13	Wendell GOMES	BRA	A	21	(5)	14
9	Malcolm LICARI		A	13	(9)	4
14	Charlo MAGRO		D	22	(1)	
3	Carlo MAMO		D	24		1

Malta

No	Name	Nat	Pos	Aps	(s)	Gls
16	Kevin MAMO		M		(10)	1
12	Jurgen MICALLEF		G		(1)	
15	Chucks NWOKO		A	10	(3)	
18	Jamie PACE		M	22	(4)	1
6	Cesar PAIBER	ARG	D	6	(1)	
7	Kevin SAMMUT		M	23	(1)	1
10	Andre SCHEMBRI		M	24		11
11	Gareth SCIBERRAS		D	8	(4)	
27	Shaun TELLUS		D	1	(2)	
17	Trevor TEMPLEMAN		M	10	(7)	
13	Edmond THORNTON		M		(2)	
5	Stephen WELLMAN		M	25		

MOSTA
Coach – Paul Zammit; (10/11/05) Charles Agius

2005
Date	Opponent	Score	Scorers
6/8	Msida St. Joseph	2-1	Chibueze, Nwoko
21/8	Sliema Wanderers	0-6	
25/8	Marsaxlokk	1-5	Sciriha (p)
11/9	Pietà Hotspurs	3-3	Falzon, Nwoko, Borg M.
17/9	Hibernians	0-3	
25/9	Floriana	4-4	Bilocca 2, Nwoko, Chibueze
28/9	Hamrun Spartans	1-2	Chibueze
15/10	Birkirkara	2-3	Sciriha (p), Nwoko
22/10	Valletta	0-1	
29/10	Msida St.Joseph	1-4	Falzon
20/11	Marsaxlokk	1-3	Sciriha
4/12	Sliema Wanderers	0-2	
17/12	Pietà Hotspurs	3-1	Nwoko, Bilocca, Falzon

2006
Date	Opponent	Score	Scorers
8/1	Hibernians	2-3	Chibueze 2
17/1	Hamrun Spartans	0-3	
24/1	Floriana	0-3	
29/1	Birkirkara	0-6	
12/2	Valletta	0-3	
5/3	Pietà Hotspurs	3-1	Falzon, Sciriha, Camilleri
19/3	Hamrun Spartans	5-3	Okonkwo 2 (1p), Chibueze 2 (1p), Nwoko
2/4	Floriana	1-0	Chibueze
29/4	Pietà Hotspurs	2-2	Chibueze 2
5/5	Hamrun Spartans	0-0	
12/5	Floriana	3-3	Chibueze 2, Sciriha

No	Name	Nat	Pos	Aps	(s)	Gls
17	Bryan AGIUS		D	3	(1)	
16	Carl ATTARD		D	12		
7	Matthew BARTOLO		M	21		
15	Ives BILOCCA		M	13	(7)	3
8	Matthew BORG		M	1	(12)	1
13	Steve BORG		D	11	(2)	
18	Mark BRINCAT		D	1		
23	Philip CAMILLERI		A	15	(9)	1
21	Jonathan CARUANA		M	15	(2)	
14	Ikechukwu CHIBUEZE		A	23		12
19	Lydon CILIA		M		(6)	
11	Duncan CUSCHIERI		M	2	(1)	
22	Ryan DEGUARA		M	1	(10)	
20	Dyson FALZON		A	22	(1)	4
12	Matthew FARRUGIA		G	21		
24	Brian GALEA		M		(3)	
3	Jonathan GRECH		D	2	(3)	
6	Ryan NEWELL		D	19		
10	Udochukwu NWOKO	NGA	A	19	(2)	6
5	Digger OKONKWO	NGA	D	22		2
1	Charles SCIBERRAS		G	3		

No	Name					
2	Pio SCIRIHA		D	20	(1)	5
25	Mirdljub SPASIC	SCG	D	16	(1)	
4	Pio VASSALLO		M	2		

MSIDA ST. JOSEPH
Coach – Todor Stoyanov Raykov (BUL)

2005
Date	Opponent	Score	Scorers
6/8	Mosta	1-2	Nwoke
12/8	Birkirkara	2-5	Nwoke, Theuma (p)
21/8	Valletta	3-1	Babatunde, Carabott, Nwoke
10/9	Floriana	4-2	Farrugia, Bajada, Nwoke, Micallef C.
18/9	Marsaxlokk	1-1	Theuma
24/9	Sliema Wanderers	1-2	Bajada
2/10	Pietà Hotspurs	4-2	Babatunde 2, Nwoke, Theuma
15/10	Hibernians	2-4	Bajada (p), Nwoke
23/10	Hamrun Spartans	2-1	Sciberras, Fenech
29/10	Mosta	4-1	Farrugia, Bajada, Nwoke 2
3/12	Birkirkara	1-4	Theuma (p)
8/12	Valletta	0-1	
17/12	Floriana	0-0	

2006
Date	Opponent	Score	Scorers
8/1	Marsaxlokk	0-1	
14/1	Sliema Wanderers	1-4	Nwoke
29/1	Pietà Hotspurs	0-0	
4/2	Hibernians	0-2	
12/2	Hamrun Spartans	2-0	Babatunde, Nwoke
4/3	Birkirkara	0-5	
12/3	Marsaxlokk	0-1	
19/3	Hibernians	1-1	Nwoke
26/3	Sliema Wanderers	1-4	Nwoke
1/4	Valletta	2-2	Nwoke, Theuma
15/4	Birkirkara	1-4	Farrugia
22/4	Marsaxlokk	3-4	Nwoke, Zongo 2
30/4	Hibernians	0-0	
6/5	Sliema Wanderers	3-3	Babatunde, Nwoke 2
12/5	Valletta	1-2	og (Pace)

No	Name	Nat	Pos	Aps	(s)	Gls
19	Gerard ANCHILLERI		D		(1)	
14	Darren ATTARD		M		(1)	
11	Ibrahim BABATUNDE	NGA	A	26		5
5	Roderick BAJADA		M	11	(1)	4
1	Manuel BARTOLO		G	4		
22	Omar BORG		G	24		
18	Dino CACHIA		M	25		
4	David CARABOTT		D	10		1
12	Karl EBEJER		M		(6)	
10	Tyron FARRUGIA		D	25		3
6	Paul FENECH		M	24	(1)	1
21	Donald GATT		M	3	(15)	
3	Stefano GRIMA		D	12	(6)	
2	Clint MICALLEF		D	8	(4)	1
17	Lydon MICALLEF		M	12	(4)	
23	Josef MIFSUD		D	24		
16	Daniel NWOKE	NGA	A	27	(1)	16
9	Mark PULLICINO		D	14	(4)	
8	Charles SCIBERRAS		M	21	(3)	1
33	Antoine SPITERI		M		(2)	
13	Shane TAGLIAFERRO		A	4	(13)	
29	Daniel THEUMA		D	21	(1)	5
7	Micheal VALENZIA		A	1	(11)	
20	Ousseni ZONGO	BFA	A	12	(1)	2

Malta

PIETÀ HOTSPURS
Coach – George Deanov (BUL)

2005

Date	Opponent	Score	Scorers
5/8	Floriana	2-0	Sciuto (p), Deanov M.
12/8	Hibernians	0-4	
20/8	Hamrun Spartans	4-2	Sciuto 2, Deanov M., Darmanin
11/9	Mosta	3-3	Deanov I. (p), Deanov M., Hogg
18/9	Birkirkara	1-4	Deanov M.
25/9	Valletta	0-0	
2/10	Msida St.Joseph	2-4	Decesare, Camenzuli
16/10	Marsaxlokk	1-4	Deanov M. (p)
22/10	Sliema Wanderers	1-0	Deanov M.
30/10	Floriana	1-3	Sciberras
4/12	Hibernians	1-2	Camilleri R.
14/12	Hamrun Spartans	2-3	Deanov M., Camenzuli
17/12	Mosta	1-3	Calleja

2006

Date	Opponent	Score	Scorers
7/1	Birkirkara	0-2	
21/1	Valletta	0-1	
29/1	Msida St.Joseph	0-0	
4/2	Marsaxlokk	3-1	Deanov M. (p), Calleja, Galea
11/2	Sliema Wanderers	0-3	
5/3	Mosta	1-3	Okoh
25/3	Floriana	2-1	Filip, Decesare
16/4	Hamrun Spartans	2-0	Ciscaldi, Deanov M.
29/4	Mosta	2-2	Calleja 2
6/5	Floriana	1-1	Deanov M.
13/5	Hamrun Spartans	1-1	Kondev

No	Name	Nat	Pos	Aps	(s)	Gls
2	Pierre AQUILINA		D	5		
23	Eman BUGEJA		D		(1)	
27	Gary BUSUTTIL		D		(1)	
10	Claudio CALLEJA		M	17	(4)	4
4	David CAMENZULI		D	17		2
3	Elton CAMILLERI		D		(1)	
19	Ryan CAMILLERI		M	3	(5)	1
8	Silvan CISCALDI		D	19	(2)	1
25	Keith DARMANIN		M		(2)	1
6	Ilian DEANOV		M	13		1
7	Martin DEANOV		A	21		10
21	Andrew DECESARE		A	11	(4)	2
11	Marius FILIP	ROM	A	9		1
26	Mark GALEA		D	4	(2)	1
28	Daniel GATT		M		(3)	
17	Dean GERA		M	15	(4)	
22	Ryan GRECH		M	13	(4)	
1	Andrew HOGG		G	23		1
16	Svetlan KONDEV	BUL	M	9		1
29	Dylan KOVAKESSIS		M		(1)	
2	Malcolm MARMARA		D	1	(3)	
24	Dominic MIFSUD		M	5	(2)	
15	Darren O'FLAHERTY		A	1	(1)	
31	Chris OKOH		D	4	(5)	1
12	Paul PSAILA		G	1	(1)	
30	Carl PULO		A	2	(1)	
9	Quilin REFALO		A		(1)	
13	Carl SAMMUT		D	21		
32	Jean Paul SCERRI		M		(1)	
20	Heathcliff SCHEMBRI		D	6	(1)	
5	Bernard SCIBERRAS		M	21		1
18	Carmelo Angelo SCIUTO	ITA	A	6		3
14	Andrew SPITERI		M	16	(4)	
9	Stefan ZAHRA		A	1		(1)

SLIEMA WANDERERS
Coach – Edward Aquilina

2005

Date	Opponent	Score	Scorers
6/8	Hibernians	3-0	Brincat 2, Bogdanovic
21/8	Mosta	6-0	Doncic 3, Giglio, Woods (p), Bogdanovic
25/8	Hamrun	4-1	Doncic 2, Bogdanovic, Giglio
12/9	Birkirkara	2-1	Brincat, Bogdanovic
16/9	Valletta	3-1	Bogdanovic, Doncic, Woods
24/9	Msida St.Joseph	2-1	Woods 2 (1p)
1/10	Marsaxlokk	2-1	Doncic, Bogdanovic
16/10	Floriana	1-0	Bogdanovic
22/10	Pietà Hotspurs	0-1	
29/10	Hibernians	0-2	
20/11	Hamrun Spartans	1-1	Brincat
04/12	Mosta	2-0	Woods, Bogdanovic
18/12	Valletta	3-0	Giglio, Doncic, Woods

2006

Date	Opponent	Score	Scorers
3/1	Birkirkara	1-2	Doncic
14/1	Msida St.Joseph	4-1	Woods 2, Bogdanovic 2
24/1	Marsaxlokk	0-0	
28/1	Floriana	0-0	
11/2	Pietà Hotspurs	3-0	Brincat, Woods, Giglio
5/3	Marsaxlokk	1-2	Doncic
11/3	Hibernians	3-0	Giglio 2, Bajada
18/3	Valletta	2-1	Woods, Doncic
26/3	Msida St.Joseph	4-1	Woods 2, Said, Muscat
2/4	Birkirkara	1-1	Woods
16/4	Marsaxlokk	0-1	
22/4	Hibernians	3-4	Doncic, Mintoff, Turner
29/4	Valletta	2-1	Woods (p), og (Bondin)
6/5	Msida St.Joseph	3-3	Woods 2, Di Lello
14/5	Birkirkara	2-1	og (Galea), Doncic

No	Name	Nat	Pos	Aps	(s)	Gls
22	Murphy AKANJI	NGA	G	28		
18	Orosco ANONAM	NGA	A	7	(3)	
10	Roderick BAJADA		D	12	(1)	1
32	Daniel BOGDANOVIC		A	23		10
1	Joe BRINCAT		M	19	(2)	5
21	Matthew CAMILLERI		G		(4)	
3	David CARABOTT		D	2	(7)	
13	Jeffrey CHETCUTI		D	21	(2)	
5	Darren DEBONO		D	20		
12	Mauro DI LELLO		D	21		1
9	Danilo DONCIC	SCG	A	25	(1)	13
11	Joseph FARRUGIA		M	5	(12)	
26	Stefan GIGLIO		M	18	(1)	6
16	Lee GRIMA		M	2	(5)	
6	Lee LOMBARDI		D	8	(2)	
8	Claude MATTOCKS		M	3	(6)	
15	Nicholas MICALLEF		M		(2)	
10	Adrian MIFSUD		A		(1)	
17	John MINTOFF		A	3		1
2	Alex MUSCAT		D	19	(5)	1
4	Brian SAID		D	28		1
19	Mark SCERRI		D		(1)	
7	Noel TURNER		M	19	(3)	1
14	Ivan WOODS		A	28		16

VALLETTA
Coach – Joseph John Aquilina; (10/11/05) Paul Zammit

2005

Date	Opponent	Score	Scorers
5/8	Birkirkara	2-4	Galea, Nisevic

Malta

11/8	Floriana	1-1	Zammit	
21/8	Msida St. Joseph	1-3	Forace	
11/9	Marsaxlokk	3-2	Nisevic, Zammit 2	
16/9	Sliema Wanderers	1-3	Grima (p)	
25/9	Pietà Hotspurs	0-0		
2/10	Hibernians	2-0	og (Muscat), Camilleri	
17/10	Hamrun Spartans	2-4	Agius, Chukunyere	
22/10	Mosta	1-0	Zammit	
28/10	Birkirkara	0-2		
3/12	Floriana	1-2	Nisevic	
8/12	Msida St.Joseph	1-0	Ani	
18/12	Sliema Wanderers	0-3		
2006				
3/1	Marsaxlokk	0-4		
21/1	Pietà Hotspurs	1-0	Grima	
28/1	Hibernians	2-1	Monesterolo, Agius	
5/2	Hamrun Spartans	1-2	Agius	
12/2	Mosta	3-0	Mattocks 2, Monesterolo	
4/2	Hibernians	3-1	Monesterolo 3	
11/3	Birkirkara	0-0		
19/3	Sliema Wanderers	1-2	Bondin	
26/3	Marsaxlokk	4-3	Zammit, Agius, Monesterolo 2	
1/4	Msida St.Joseph	2-2	Monesterolo 2	
15/4	Hibernians	2-2	Monesterolo 2 (2p)	
21/4	Birkirkara	0-3		
29/4	Sliema Wanderers	1-2	Zammit	
5/5	Marsaxlokk	0-2		
12/5	Msida St.Joseph	2-1	Agius, Mattocks	

No	Name	Nat	Pos	Aps	(s)	Gls
7	Gilbert AGIUS		A	22	(1)	5
10	Jeremiah ANI	NGA	A	6	(1)	1
15	Mark BARBARA		M	2	(4)	
13	Steve BEZZINA		M	11	(5)	
4	Jonathan BONDIN		D	19		1
20	Roberto BRINCAT		M		(1)	
17	Chris CAMILLERI		M	6	(13)	1
22	Kevin CASSAR		D	22		
33	Ndubisi CHUKUNYERE	NGA	A	3	(1)	1
10	Craig DEAN	ENG	A	13		
19	Anatole DEBONO		M	3	(10)	
8	Keith FENECH		M	20	(2)	
3	Rennie FORACE		D	19	(3)	1
2	Jonathan FRANCICA		D		(3)	
23	Mark GALEA		A	10	(2)	1
6	Massimo GRIMA		M	16		2
35	Justin GRIOLI		D	1	(3)	
16	Kurt MAGRO		M	3	(12)	
27	Claude MATTOCKS		M	13		3
21	Omar Sebastián MONESTEROLO	ARG	A	13		11
36	Miguel MONTFORT		G	6	(1)	
5	Branko NISEVIC	SCG	D	26		3
29	Sharlon PACE		D	22	(2)	
11	Milen PENCHEV	BUL	M	2		
77	Sean SULLIVAN		G	22		
9	Ian ZAMMIT		A	19	(1)	6
14	Dylan ZARB		M	9	(15)	

DOMESTIC CUP 2005/06

FIRST ROUND
(5/11/05)
Marsaxlokk 3, Lija Athletics 0
St. George's 1, Hamrun Spartans 2
(6/11/05)
St. Patrick 3, Mosta 1
Floriana 3, Tarxien Rainbows 1
(12/11/05)
Pieta Hotspurs 0, San Gwann 5
Mqabba 1, Msida St .Joseph 0
(13/11/05)
St. Andrews 0, Marsa 1
Naxxar Lions 0, Senglea Athletics 0 (aet; 1-3 on pens)

SECOND ROUND
(18/2/06)
Marsaxlokk 2, Marsa 0
Hamrun Spartans 3, St. Patrick 2
(19/2/06)
Floriana 4, Senglea 0
Msida St. Joseph 2, San Gwann 1 (aet)

QUARTER FINALS
(8/4/06)
Hibernians 1 (Cohen 89), Hamrun Spartans 0
Marsaxlokk 0, Sliema Wanderers 2 (Di Lello 27, Lombardi 90)
(9/4/06)
Valletta 0, Birkirkara 2 (Briffa 107, Holland 119) (aet)
Floriana 2 (Mifsud 6p, 66), Msida St. Joseph 0

SEMI-FINALS
(19/5/06)
Floriana 2 (Cilia 71, 89), Sliema Wanderers 0
(20/5/06)
Hibernians 1 (Agius 69), Birkirkara 0

FINAL
(26/5/06)
National Stadium, Ta' Qali
HIBERNIANS 1 (Doda 44)
FLORIANA 0
Referee – Sammut
HIBERNIANS – Muscat, Pullicino, Pulis, Xuereb, Camilleri D., Williamson (Pearson 79), Mbong, Agius (Scerri 42), Cohen, Failla (Baldacchino 64), Doda.
FLORIANA – Agius, Gango-Rtsa, Azzopardi, Caruana M., Cassar, Micallef, Cilia, Mifsud, Ciantar E., Oba (Caruana C. 58) Eviparker.

SECOND LEVEL FINAL TABLE 2005/06

		Pld	W	D	L	F	A	Pts
1	St.George's	18	10	5	3	27	14	35
2	Marsa	18	9	6	3	33	20	33
3	Mqabba	18	9	4	5	28	18	31
4	Tarxien Rainbows	18	8	5	5	25	18	29
5	Senglea Athletics	18	8	3	7	21	23	27
6	St. Patrick	18	7	5	6	29	22	26
7	San Gwann	18	7	2	9	23	25	23
8	Naxxar Lions	18	6	2	10	32	38	20
9	Lija Athletics	18	5	3	10	20	33	18
10	St. Andrew's	18	1	5	12	13	40	8

Moldova

Small beer for Sheriff

Moldova's Divizia Nationala has to rank as one of the dullest leagues in Europe. It contains only eight clubs, most of them from just two towns, and every year it is dominated by one team – the same team, Sheriff Tiraspol.

In 2005/06 Sheriff strolled uncontested to yet another title, their sixth in a row. There was never any doubt that they would triumph. After victories in each of their first ten matches, including two against chief rivals Zimbru Chisinau, and with just one goal conceded, they had already raced into a 14-point lead. The season was over before the end of October.

To try and drum up some interest, daily newspaper Sport-Plus announced that it would give 100 litres of beer to the first team to beat the champions-in-waiting. Eventually, at the end of March, a team did manage to claim the prize when Tiligul-Tiras Tiraspol, coached by former Soviet Union maverick midfielder Igor Dobrovolsky, beat their city rivals 2-1. But by then Sheriff were about to crack open something a bit more expensive than the local brew. A few weeks later, after a 7-1 annihilation of bottom club Dinamo Bender – their biggest win of the season – Sheriff's record-breaking sixth successive title was secure.

That defeat by Tiligul-Tiras would be the only stain on the champions' record as they finished up with slightly better figures in all categories than the previous season – more points (71 to 70), more goals scored (57 to 54), fewer goals conceded (11 to 12) and a larger margin of victory (18 points to 16). As before, Sheriff's was a squad with a distinctly cosmopolitan flavour. Moldovans were fairly thin on the ground, with only goalkeeper Serghey Pascenco getting a regular gig. A couple of African imports – Ghana's Samuel Yeboah (in the autumn) and Benin's Razak Omotoiossi (in the spring) – made a positive impression, but the real stars were Razvan Cocis, who became a regular Romanian international during the season, and Belarussian striker Alexei Kuchiuk, the team's top scorer and son of coach Leonid Kuchiuk.

Zimbru, who enjoyed a period of dominance similar to Sheriff's during the 1990s, rolled home a distant second but it was a massive improvement on the previous season, when they could finish only fifth. They lost three of their four games to the champions, and the goalless draw they managed on the fourth meeting came only after Sheriff had already taken the title. Furthermore, they lost to Sheriff in the semi-finals of the Moldovan Cup, which their victors then went on to win, beating holders Nistru Otaci 2-0 in the final to complete a third Double.

Little victory

Zimbru did, however, claim one little victory over Sheriff when their second team beat their rivals' equivalent to win the second division title. Neither team could of course go up, so the two promotion

NATIONAL TEAM RESULTS 2005/06

Date	Opponent	H/A/N	Venue	Score	Scorers
3/9/05	Belarus (WCQ)	H	Chisinau	2-0	Rogaciov (15, 49)
7/9/05	Slovenia (WCQ)	H	Chisinau	1-2	Rogaciov (30)
8/10/05	Norway (WCQ)	A	Oslo	0-1	
12/10/05	Italy (WCQ)	A	Lecce	1-2	Gatcan (76)
27/2/06	Malta	A	Ta'Qali	2-0	Namascu Se. (46), Bugaev (73)
1/3/06	Georgia	N	Ta'Qali	5-1	Zislis (5, 13), Alexeev (48), Namasco Se. (54p), Golovatenco (72)
18/5/06	Azerbaijan	H	Chisinau	0-0	

Moldova

NATIONAL TEAM APPEARANCES 2005/06

Coach – Viktor PASULKO (UKR)
(Boris TROPANET)
/(1/2/06) Anatoly TESLEV

Player	DOB	Club	BLS	SLO	NOR	ITA	Mlt	Geo	Azb	Caps	Goals
Evgheny HMARUC	13/6/77	CSKA Sofia (BUL) /Tiligul-Tiras Tiraspol	G	G	G				G	30	-
Alexei SAVINOV	19/4/79	Zakarpattya Uzhgorod (UKR)	D	D	D	D				16	-
Ghenadie OLEXICI	23/8/78	Amkar Perm (RUS)	D	D	D	D				31	-
Valeriu CATINSUS	27/4/78	Tom Tomsk (RUS)	D	D	D	D			D	47	-
Iurie PRIGANIUC	23/10/78	FC Khimki (RUS)	D	D	D	D				26	-
Radu REBEJA	8/6/73	FK Moskva (RUS)	M	M					M	57	2
Serghey COVALCIUC	20/1/82	Spartak Moskva (RUS)	M87	M89	M	M				28	2
Stanislav IVANOV	7/10/80	FK Moskva (RUS)	M	M	M82				M	29	-
Vadim BORET	5/9/76	Neftçi Baki (AZB)	M46		s68	M			s54	32	1
Serghey ROGACIOV	20/5/77	Saturn Ramenskoe (RUS) /Aktobe Lento (KAZ)	A56	A90	A	A87			s46	42	7
Serghey DADU	23/1/81	Alania Vladikavkaz (RUS)	A	A83	A73	A			A46	20	6
Vitalie BORDIAN	11/8/84	Metalist Kharkiv (UKR)	s46	D	M68					3	-
Alexandr POPOVICI	9/4/77	Kryvbas Kryvyi Rih (UKR)	s56	s90	s73					11	3
Viorel FRUNZA	6/12/79	FC Vaslui (ROM)	s87	s83						11	1
Serghey IEPUREANU	12/9/76	Vorskla Poltava (UKR)		s89						42	2
Serghey LASCENCOV	24/3/80	Illichivets Mariupol (UKR)			D	D			D54	12	-
Alexandr GATCAN	27/3/84	Spartak Chelyabinsk (RUS) /Rubin Kazan (RUS)			s82	M			M	4	1
Serghey PASCENCO	18/12/82	Sheriff Tiraspol				G				1	-
Iurie MITEREV	28/2/75	Chornomorets Odesa (UKR)				s87			A46	36	8
Ilie CEBANU	29/12/86	SK Sturm Graz (AUT)					G			1	-
Semion BULGARU	26/5/85	Zimbru Chisinau					D	D		2	-
Igor SOLTANICI	4/5/84	Tiligul-Tiras Tiraspol					D	D		2	-
Victor GOLOVATENCO	28/4/84	FC Tiraspol					D	D		4	-
Vadim BOLOHAN	15/8/86	Nistru Otaci					D	D		2	1
Sergiu JAPALAU	30/4/84	MTZ-RIPO Minsk (BLS)					M46	s83		3	-
Serghey NAMASCO	19/6/84	FC Tiraspol					M	M		2	2
Alexandr SUVOROV	2/2/87	Sheriff Tiraspol					M	M	s46	3	-
Denis ZMEU	8/5/85	Zimbru Chisinau					M74	M77		2	-
Igor BUGAEV	26/6/84	Chornomorets Odesa (UKR)					A			1	1
Serghey ALEXEEV	31/5/86	Sheriff Tiraspol					A81	A		2	1
Nicolae RUDAC	23/3/86	FC Tiraspol					s46	M		2	-
Andrei BEREGHICI	9/12/86	Rapid Chisinau					s74	s77		2	-
Alexandr ZISLIS	14/3/86	Dacia Chisinau					s81	A83		2	2
Stanislav NAMASCO	10/11/86	FC Tiraspol						G		1	-
Ion TESTIMITANU	27/4/74	Sibir Novosibirsk (RUS)							D	49	6
Victor BERCO	20/4/79	FK Almaty (KAZ)							M	12	-
Vitalie MANALIU	23/3/85	Zimbru Chisinau							A46	1	-
Serghey CLESCENCO	20/5/72	Sibir Novosibirsk (RUS)							s46	64	10

Moldova

places went to the clubs in positions three and four, namely Olimpia Balti and Iskra-Stali Ribnita. As in the top division, there were few thrills and spills in the promotion race, with Iskra-Stali finishing ten points clear of fifth-placed Floreni Anenii Noi. However, that was more exciting than the battle to avoid relegation, because in the end there wasn't one. The league authorities, in their wisdom, decided, belatedly, to increase the size of the Divizia Nationala to ten clubs, which probably got a mixed reception at Dinamo Bender whose first season back at the top level had yielded just two victories and 15 points.

Another decision announced for 2006/07 was a reduction in the number of foreigners permitted to compete in any Divizia Nationala game. Clearly the Moldovan FA is beginning to get concerned by the lack of opportunities for regular top-flight football open to homegrown youngsters. Proof of the potential of some of those players came in the early spring when Moldova sent a group of Under-21 players to represent the country at the Malta International Tournament – with full caps awarded – and they not only beat their (full-strength) hosts 2-0 but thrashed Georgia 5-1 a couple of days later. (The Georgians, incidentally, refused to acknowledge the game as a full international).

Teslov takes over

Those matches were played under regular Under-21 boss Boris Tropanet even though Moldova had by then appointed a new senior coach, 58-year-old Anatoliy Teslov, to replace Viktor Pasulko, whose four-year stint ended with the World Cup qualifying campaign. Moldova finished bottom of their group and the Ukrainian's contract was not renewed.

Whether Teslov can fare any better in the Euro 2008 qualifiers remains to be seen. He has chosen Dobrovolsky, arguably Moldova's most famous footballer of all time, to assist him, but despite that popular move his prediction that the team will qualify for the European finals in Austria and Switzerland would appear to be wildly optimisitic. Although his team are placed in the easiest of the seven qualifying groups, the fact that not one Moldovan player belongs to a high-profile Western European club, nor is likely to in the foreseeable future, suggests that Teslov's words and deeds may not amount to quite the same thing. If a reality check was needed, he surely got it in his first match in charge – an insipid goalless draw at home to Azerbaijan.

EUROPEAN CUPS 2005/06

UEFA CHAMPIONS LEAGUE

SHERIFF TIRASPOL
1st qualifying round SLIEMA WANDERERS (MLT)
A 4-1 *Epureanu (21, 62), Kuchiuk (25), Florescu (51)*
Hutan, Tassembedo, Testimitanu (Dinu 59), Takhnishvili, Florescu, Derme, Ionescu (Goginashvili 58), Epureanu (Gnanu 63), Lacusta, Kuchiuk, Cocis.
H 2-0 *Derme (78), Cocis (83)*
Pascenco S., Tassembedo (Goginashvili 73), Gumeniuk, Testimitanu, Tarkhnishvili, Florescu (Dinu 67), Derme, Ionescu (Kuchiuk 59), Epureanu (Cocis), Lacusta.

2nd qualifying round PARTIZAN BEOGRAD (SCG)
A 0-1
Hutan, Tassembedo, Gumeniuk (Bichkov 84), Tarkhnishvili, Florescu, Derme, Ionescu (Goginashvili 58), Epureanu, Lacusta, Kuchiuk (Dinu 55), Cocis.
H 0-1
Hutan, Tassembedo, Gumeniuk (Bichkov 84), Testimitanu, Trakhnishvili, Florescu (Kuchiuk 83), Derme, Ionescu (Goginashvili 73), Epureanu, Lacusta, Cocis.

UEFA CUP

NISTRU OTACI
1st qualifying round XÄZÄR LÄNKÄRAN (AZB)
H 3-1 *Pancovici (12), Matiura (69p), Blajco (88)*
Leu, Lupascu, Pancovici, Atakorah, Popescu, Tcaciuc Al., Yanchuk (Blajco 86), Pogreban (Botan 90), Bolohan, Malitskyi (Lichioiu 57), Matiura.
A 2-1 *Lichioiu (19, 41)*
Leu, Lupascu, Pancovici, Atakorah, Popescu, Tcaciuc Al. (Cacican 89), Yanchuk (Malitskyi 58), Lichioiu (Blajco 86), Pogreban, Bolohan, Matiura.

2nd qualifying round GRAZER AK (AUT)
H 0-2
Leu, Lupascu, Pancovici, Popescu, Tcaciuc Al., Yanchuk (Blajco 87), Lichioiu (Marian 84), Bolohan, Malitskyi (Coltunovschi 75), Matiura, Stadiiciuc.
A 0-1
Matiughin, Lupascu, Cebotari, Popescu, Tcaciuc Al., Yanchuk (Marian 88), Bolohan, Stadiiciuc, Coltunovschi (Blajco 78), Malitskyi (Cacican 82), Matiura.

DACIA CHISINAU
1st qualifying round FC VADUZ (LIE)
A 0-2
Chirilov, Andronic (Mardari 85), Rascu, Andriuta, Potrimba, Gluhenchi (Gorobet 76), Comleonoc, Japalau V. (Chirsul 66), Orbu G., Japalau S., Boghiu.
H 1-0 *Japalau V. (64)*
Chirilov, Andronic (Orbu D. 80), Rascu, Andriuta, Potrimba, Gluhenchi, Mardari, Japalau V. (Gorobet 82), Orbu G., Japalau S., Boghiu.

LEAGUE RESULTS/SCORERS/ APPEARANCES 2005/06

DACIA CHISINAU
Coach – Emil Caras

2005				
13/8	Politechnica Chisinau	a	1-1	*Ciuico*
20/8	Zimbru Chisinau	h	0-2	

Moldova

TOP GOALSCORERS 2005/06

13	Alexei KUCHIUK (Sheriff Tiraspol)
11	Sergiu CHIRILOV (Zimbru Chisinau)
10	Razvan COCIS (Sheriff Tiraspol)
9	Maxim FRANTUZ (Zimbru Chisinau)
8	Serhiy YANCHUK (Nistru Otaci)
7	Ghenadie ORBU (Dacia Chisinau)
6	Samuel YEBOAH (Sheriff Tiraspol)
	Galust PETROSYAN (Zimbru Chisinau)
	Vitalie MANALIU (Politechnica Chisinau/Zimbru Chisinau)
5	Oleg ICHIM (Dinamo Bender)
	Wilfried Benjamin BALIMA (Sheriff Tiraspol)
	Serghey ALEXEEV (FC Tiraspol)

Date	Opponent		Score	Scorers
28/8	Tiligul-Tiras Tiraspol	a	0-0	
11/9	FC Tiraspol	h	1-2	Orbu G.
15/9	Nistru Otaci	a	2-1	Zislis, Rascu
19/9	Dinamo Bender	a	2-0	Orbu G., Druta
24/9	Sheriff Tiraspol	h	0-1	
2/10	Politechnica Chisinau	h	0-2	
15/10	Zimbru Chisinau	a	1-0	Orbu G.
23/10	Tiligul-Tiras Tiraspol	h	1-1	Orbu G.
29/10	FC Tiraspol	a	2-2	Orbu G., Chirilov
6/11	Nistru Otaci	h	0-0	
16/11	Dinamo Bender	h	2-1	Druta, Resitca
20/11	Sheriff Tiraspol	a	1-5	Druta
2006				
10/3	Politechnica Chisinau	a	0-0	
15/3	Zimbru Chisinau	h	1-1	Zislis
19/3	Tiligul-Tiras Tiraspol	a	1-3	Resitca
24/3	FC Tiraspol	h	1-2	Zislis
27/3	FC Tiraspol	a	2-2	Martin, Gritiuc
1/4	Nistru Otaci	a	0-3	
9/4	Dinamo Bender	a	0-1	
18/4	Sheriff Tiraspol	h	0-1	
22/4	Politechnica Chisinau	h	1-0	Martin
29/4	Zimbru Chisinau	a	1-2	Orbu G.
6/5	Tiligul-Tiras Tiraspol	h	2-0	Frunza 2
20/5	Nistru Otaci	h	1-1	Soimu
24/5	Dinamo Bender	h	5-2	Resitca 2, Orbu G. (p), Japalau V. 2
28/5	Sheriff Tiraspol	a	0-3	

Name	Nat	Pos	Aps	Gls
Liviu ANDRIUTA		D	18	
Maxim ANDRONIC		D	27	
Boris CEBOTARI		M	6	
Alexandru CHIRILOV		G	12	1
Andrei CHIRSUL		M	7	
Nicolae CIORBADJI		M	1	
Serghey CIUICO		A	7	1
Aurel DRUTA		A	15	3
Viorel FRUNZA		A	5	2
Vitalie GLUHENCHI		M	20	
Alexandru GOROBET		M	9	
Serghey GRITIUC		A	13	1
Vladimir JAPALAU		M	21	2
Vitalie MARDARI		D	7	
Victor MARIAN		M	1	
Andrei MARTIN		M	11	2
Nicolae MINCEV		D	8	
Mihai MORARU		G	13	
Vladimir MURA		G	6	
Igor NEGRESCU		D	18	
Valeriu ONILA		M	12	
Denis ORBU		M	8	
Ghenadie ORBU		M	26	7
Florin Daniel PANCOVICI	ROM	D	7	
Bogdan Marius PETRE	ROM	M	7	
Sergiu POTRIMBA		D	13	
Ghenadie PUSCA		D	6	
Ruslan RASCU		D	24	1
Marcel RESITCA		A	21	4
Constantin RUSU		M	1	
Iurie SOIMU		M	19	1
Adrian SOSNOVSCI		D	7	
Petru STINGA		M	6	
Alexandr ZISLIS		A	21	3

DINAMO BENDER
Coach – Iury Hodichin

Date	Opponent		Score	Scorers
2005				
13/8	Sheriff Tiraspol	a	1-3	Hodichin
22/8	FC Tiraspol	h	0-4	
29/8	Politechnica Chisinau	a	2-2	Ichim, Tuticenco
10/9	Nistru Otaci	h	2-1	Tcaciuc 2
14/9	Zimbru Chisinau	a	1-5	Lapaci
19/9	Dacia Chisinau	h	0-2	
24/9	Tiligul-Tiras Tiraspol	a	0-1	
13/8	Sheriff Tiraspol	h	0-1	
15/10	FC Tiraspol	a	0-1	
23/10	Politechnica Chisinau	h	0-0	
29/10	Nistru Otaci	a	0-1	
6/11	Zimbru Chisinau	h	0-3	
16/11	Dacia Chisinau	a	1-2	Ichim
20/11	Tiligul-Tiras Tiraspol	h	2-2	Costrov, Tofan
2006				
11/3	Sheriff Tiraspol	a	0-4	
15/3	FC Tiraspol	h	1-1	Bicov
19/3	Politechnica Chisinau	a	0-1	
24/3	Nistru Otaci	h	1-1	Tofan
27/3	Nistru Otaci	a	1-3	Ichim
1/4	Zimbru Chisinau	a	0-7	
9/4	Dacia Chisinau	h	1-0	Bicov
18/4	Tiligul-Tiras Tiraspol	a	1-1	Ichim
22/4	Sheriff Tiraspol	h	1-7	Tofan
29/4	FC Tiraspol	a	0-0	
5/5	Politechnica Chisinau	h	0-0	
9/5	Zimbru Chisinau	h	0-1	
24/5	Dacia Chisinau	a	2-5	Ichim, Tofan
28/5	Tiligul-Tiras Tiraspol	h	0-1	

Name	Nat	Pos	Aps	Gls
Veaceslav AGAFONOV		M	3	
Alexandr BICOV		A	13	2
Alexei BOBU		M	1	
Igor BARDUC		D	8	
Oleg CARACIOR		M	5	
Maxim CEBOTARI		D	27	
Vladimir CIUBCO		A	8	
Igor COSTROV		M	20	1
Vladimir DRAGAN		M	21	
Vitalie GLAVCEV		M	14	
Alexei GONCEAROV		M	5	
Alexandr HODICHIN		A	21	1
Oleg ICHIM		D	23	5

Moldova

FINAL LEAGUE TABLE 2005/06

		Pld	Home					Away					Total					Pts
			W	D	L	F	A	W	D	L	F	A	W	D	L	F	A	
1	Sheriff Tiraspol	28	13	1	0	36	5	9	4	1	21	6	22	5	1	57	11	71
2	Zimbru Chisinau	28	9	2	3	31	12	6	6	2	16	8	15	8	5	47	20	53
3	FC Tiraspol	28	4	8	2	10	9	4	5	5	14	12	8	13	7	24	21	37
4	Tiligul-Tiras Tiraspol	28	4	9	1	13	7	3	4	7	9	16	7	13	8	22	23	34
5	Nistru Otaci	28	5	6	3	15	10	1	7	6	9	17	6	13	9	24	27	31
6	Dacia Chisinau	28	4	4	6	15	16	3	5	6	13	23	7	9	12	28	39	30
7	Politechnica Chisinau	28	3	5	6	9	17	2	5	7	9	20	5	10	13	18	37	25
8	Dinamo Bender	28	2	5	7	8	24	0	4	10	9	35	2	9	17	17	59	15

Name	Nat	Pos	Aps	Gls
Alexandru JICUL		M	11	
Alexandr LAPACI		M	26	1
Dmitry MELCIACOV		M	7	
Maxim MIHAILOV		A	21	
Serghey MIHAILOV		A	14	
Alexandr NAMASCO		M	26	
Mihail PAIUS		G	28	
Eugen PATULA		M	24	
Vitalie POPOV		M	12	
Serghey SCOROMET		M	13	
Artur SPINU		M	1	
Alexandru SVET		D	10	
Andrei TCACIUC		A	14	2
Leonid TOFAN		D	26	4
Nicolae TUTICENCO		D	12	1
Sergiu VICOL		M	1	

NISTRU OTACI
Coach – Alexandr Matiura; (5/06) Nicolae Bunea

2005
15/8	Zimbru Chisinau	a	1-1	Yanchuk
20/8	Tiligul-Tiras Tiraspol	h	0-1	
29/8	FC Tiraspol	a	0-0	
10/9	Dinamo Bender	a	1-2	Yanchuk
15/9	Dacia Chisinau	h	1-2	Malitskyi
19/9	Sheriff Tiraspol	a	0-2	
24/9	Politechnica Chisinau	h	1-1	Matiura (p)
2/10	Zimbru Chisinau	h	2-1	og (Amarandei), Matiura (p)
15/10	Tiligul-Tiras Tiraspol	a	0-1	
23/10	FC Tiraspol	h	0-1	
29/10	Dinamo Bender	h	1-0	Popescu
6/11	Dacia Chisinau	a	0-0	
16/11	Sheriff Tiraspol	h	0-0	
20/11	Politechnica Chisinau	a	3-1	Popescu, Yanchuk, Magomedov

2006
11/3	Zimbru Chisinau	a	0-2	
15/3	Tiligul-Tiras Tiraspol	h	0-0	
19/3	FC Tiraspol	a	0-1	
24/3	Dinamo Bender	a	1-1	Yanchuk
27/3	Dinamo Bender	h	3-1	Matiura 2 (1p), Petrenko
1/4	Dacia Chisinau	h	3-0	Yanchuk 2, Tcaciuc An.
9/4	Sheriff Tiraspol	a	1-4	Tcaciuc An.
18/4	Politechnica Chisinau	h	2-1	Yanchuk, Taranu
22/4	Zimbru Chisinau	h	1-1	Yanchuk
29/4	Tiligul-Tiras Tiraspol	a	0-0	
5/5	FC Tiraspol	h	1-1	Taranu
20/5	Dacia Chisinau	a	1-1	Taranu
24/5	Sheriff Tiraspol	h	0-0	
28/5	Politechnica Chisinau	a	1-1	Bolohan

Name	Nat	Pos	Aps	Gls
Alexandr BLAJCO		A	12	
Oleg BLOHIN	UKR	D	9	
Vadim BOLOHAN		D	26	1
Igor BOTAN		M	1	
Andrei BURCOVSCHI		M	5	
Iulian BURSUC		M	8	
Vladimir CACICAN		M	16	
Sergiu CEBOTARI		D	15	
Oleg COLTUNOVSCHI		M	5	
Dumitru DOLGOV	UKR	D	9	
Friday ENYONG	NGA	M	4	
Denis ERSOV		G	3	
Roman EVMENEV		M	11	
Cristian Djeumakou FOKOU	NGA	M	1	
Andrei GHIRCEA		M	4	
Gocka HABIB	CMR	D	14	
Maxwell Kofi HOTOR	GHA	A	6	
Anatol LEU		G	1	
Catalin LICHIOIU	ROM	A	1	
Valentin LUPASCU		M	24	
Isref MAGOMEDOV	AZB	D	10	1
Olexandr MALITSKYI	UKR	M	13	1
Victor MARIAN		M	8	
Evgheny MATIUGHIN		G	25	
Andrei MATIURA		M	21	4
Petr PANTELEICIUC		D	1	
Arteom PETRENKO	RUS	M	5	1
Iaroslav PIKUNOV	RUS	M	11	
Lilian POPESCU		M	14	2
Pavlo RUDAI	UKR	D	1	
Vladislav SAVCIUC		M	8	
Oleg SOIMU		M	12	
Alexandr STADIICIUC		M	26	
Igor STASIUK	UKR	A	3	
Anatol STAVILA		M	9	
Evgheni SUHARI	UKR	D	7	
Alexandr TCACIUC		M	2	
Andrei TCACIUC		A	12	2
Vladimir TARANU		A	10	3
Ben TEEKLON	LIB	M	11	
Serhiy YANCHUK	UKR	A	27	8

POLITECHNICA CHISINAU
Coach – Ivan Caras

2005

Moldova

Date	Opponent	H/A	Score	Scorers
13/8	Dacia Chisinau	h	1-1	Manaliu
20/8	Sheriff Tiraspol	a	0-4	
29/8	Dinamo Bender	h	2-2	Belan, Soimu
10/9	Zimbru Chisinau	h	0-4	
14/9	Tiligul-Tiras Tiraspol	a	0-3	
18/9	FC Tiraspol	h	1-0	Baran
24/9	Nistru Otaci	a	1-1	Baran
2/10	Dacia Chisinau	a	2-0	Soimu O., Gusila
15/10	Sheriff Tiraspol	h	0-1	
23/10	Dinamo Bender	a	0-0	
29/10	Zimbru Chisinau	a	2-5	Cojusea, Donici
6/11	Tiligul-Tiras Tiraspol	h	2-1	Gusila, Baran
16/11	FC Tiraspol	a	0-1	
20/11	Nistru Otaci	h	1-3	Donici
2006				
10/3	Dacia Chisinau	h	0-0	
15/3	Sheriff Tiraspol	a	0-1	
19/3	Dinamo Bender	h	1-0	Ciuico
24/3	Zimbru Chisinau	h	0-1	
27/3	Zimbru Chisinau	a	1-1	Patras
1/4	Tiligul-Tiras Tiraspol	a	1-0	Andronic
9/4	FC Tiraspol	h	0-0	
18/4	Nistru Otaci	a	1-2	Tamascov
22/4	Dacia Chisinau	a	0-1	
29/4	Sheriff Tiraspol	h	0-2	
5/5	Dinamo Bender	a	0-0	
20/5	Tiligul-Tiras Tiraspol	h	0-1	
24/5	FC Tiraspol	a	1-1	Patras
28/5	Nistru Otaci	h	1-1	Martun

Name	Nat	Pos	Aps	Gls
Valeriu ANDRONIC		M	5	1
Ghenadie ANGHEL		M	13	
Vasile ARLET		D	18	
Serghey BARAN		A	24	3
Oleg BELAN		M	26	1
Dinu CARAS		M	2	
Dinu CARP		M	2	
Alexandru CHELTUIALA		D	9	
Eugen CHEPTENE		G	28	
Dmitry CIUMAC		A	1	
Mihai COJUSEA		A	13	1
Serghey CIUICO		A	3	1
Andrei DONICI		M	26	2
Friday ENYONG	NGA	M	12	
Maxim GAICIUC		D	11	
Eugen GILCA		D	11	
Lilian GOLBAN		M	14	
Dumitru GUSILA		A	10	2
Valentin IVAHNENCO		M	13	
Vitalie MANALIU		A	9	1
Igor MARTUN		A	21	1
Iurie MIRZA		M	24	
Ruslan MOLDOVAN		D	13	
Alexandru MORARU		D	4	
Ghenadie OCHINCA		D	21	
Artur PATRAS		M	15	2
Vladimir PETCOV		D	13	
Alexandr RAZDOROZNII		D	9	
Oleg SOIMU		M	14	2
Eduard TAMASCOV		A	21	1

SHERIFF TIRASPOL
Coach – Leonid Kuchiuk (BLS)

2005

Date	Opponent	H/A	Score	Scorers
13/8	Dinamo Bender	h	3-1	Cocis, Kuchiuk 2
20/8	Politechnica Chisinau	h	4-0	Kuchiuk, Yeboah 3
28/8	Zimbru Chisinau	a	1-0	Gnanu
10/9	Tiligul-Tiras Tiraspol	h	2-0	Cocis, Yeboah
14/9	FC Tiraspol	a	2-0	Kuchiuk, Epureanu
19/9	Nistru Otaci	h	2-0	Florescu, Yeboah
24/9	Dacia Chisinau	a	1-0	Gnanu
2/10	Dinamo Bender	a	1-0	Ionescu
15/10	Politechnica Chisinau	a	2-0	Cocis
23/10	Zimbru Chisinau	h	3-0	Cocis, Epureanu, Kuchiuk
29/10	Tiligul-Tiras Tiraspol	a	1-1	Gnanu
6/11	FC Tiraspol	h	1-0	Florescu
16/11	Nistru Otaci	a	0-0	
20/11	Dacia Chisinau	h	5-1	Ionescu, Kuchiuk, Yeboah, og (Potrimba), og (Andriuta)
2006				
11/3	Dinamo Bender	h	4-0	Cocis 2, Ruamba, Balima
15/3	Politechnica Chisinau	h	1-0	Kuchiuk
19/3	Zimbru Chisinau	a	3-2	og (Nofitovici), Cocis, Balima
24/3	Tiligul-Tiras Tiraspol	h	2-1	Kuchiuk, Omotoiossi
27/3	Tiligul-Tiras Tiraspol	a	1-2	Cocis
1/4	FC Tiraspol	a	0-0	
9/4	Nistru Otaci	h	4-1	Corneencov, Balima 2, Omotoiossi
18/4	Dacia Chisinau	a	1-0	Florescu
22/4	Dinamo Bender	a	7-1	Cocis 2, Kuchiuk 3, Namasco, Corneencov
29/4	Politechnica Chisinau	a	2-0	Suvorov, Alexeev
5/5	Zimbru Chisinau	h	0-0	
20/5	FC Tiraspol	h	2-1	Alexeev, Balima
24/5	Nistru Otaci	a	0-0	
28/5	Dacia Chisinau	h	3-0	Kuchiuk 2 (2p), Pascenco A.

Name	Nat	Pos	Aps	Gls
Serghey ALEXEEV		A	10	2
Wilfried Benjamin BALIMA	BFA	M	14	5
Alexandru BICHKOV	UKR	A	11	
Iurie BONDARCIUC		A	1	
Vitalie BULAT		M	8	
Razvan COCIS	ROM	A	22	10
Andrei CORNEENCOV		M	14	2
Ben Idrissa DERME	BFA	D	17	
Alexandru EPUREANU		D	27	2
Gheorghe FLORESCU	ROM	M	21	3
Oleg GUMENIUK	UKR	D	26	
Sergiu JURIC		G	1	
Ibrahim GNANU	BFA	D	26	3
Roman GOGINASHVILI	GEO	M	13	
Sebastian HUTAN	ROM	G	5	
Mihai IONESCU	ROM	M	14	2
Alexei KUCHIUK	BLS	A	27	13
Abdoul-Gafar MAMAH	TOG	D	7	
Razak OMOTOIOSSI	BEN	A	14	2
Alexandr PASCENCO		M	4	1
Serghey PASCENCO		G	22	
Serghey NAMASCO		M	12	1
Florent RUAMBA	BFA	M	2	1
Andrei SECRIERU		M	3	
Alexandr SUVOROV		A	21	1
Vazha TARKHNISHVILI	GEO	D	27	
Sumaila TASSEMBEDO	BFA	M	11	
Fernando Pareira WALLACE	BRA	D	12	
Vyacheslav YAROSLAVSKIY	BLS	M	6	
Samuel YEBOAH	GHA	A	13	6

Moldova

TILIGUL-TIRAS TIRASPOL
Coach – Igor Dobrovolsky

2005

Date	Opponent	H/A	Score	Scorers
13/8	FC Tiraspol	h	1-1	Taranu
20/8	Nistru Otaci	a	1-0	Croitoru
28/8	Dacia Chisinau	h	0-0	
10/9	Sheriff Tiraspol	a	0-2	
14/9	Politechnica Chisinau	h	3-0	Dindikov, Bulat, Vintila
19/9	Zimbru Chisinau	a	0-2	
24/9	Dinamo Bender	h	0-0	
2/10	FC Tiraspol	a	0-0	
15/10	Nistru Otaci	h	1-0	Bugaev
23/10	Dacia Chisinau	a	1-1	Vintila
29/10	Sheriff Tiraspol	h	1-1	Bugaev
6/11	Politechnica Chisinau	a	1-2	Dindikov (p)
16/11	Zimbru Chisinau	h	1-1	Cuznetov
20/11	Dinamo Bender	a	2-2	Dindikov, Bugaev

2006

Date	Opponent	H/A	Score	Scorers
11/3	FC Tiraspol	h	0-0	
15/3	Nistru Otaci	a	0-0	
19/3	Dacia Chisinau	h	3-1	Golban, Radcenco, Vintila (p)
24/3	Sheriff Tiraspol	a	1-2	Carabulea
27/3	Sheriff Tiraspol	h	2-1	Cojusea, Anghel
1/4	Politechnica Chisinau	h	0-1	
9/4	Zimbru Chisinau	a	0-1	
18/4	Dinamo Bender	h	1-1	Bulat
22/4	FC Tiraspol	a	1-2	Vintila
29/4	Nistru Otaci	h	0-0	
6/5	Dacia Chisinau	a	0-2	
20/5	Politechnica Chisinau	a	1-0	Bulat
24/5	Zimbru Chisinau	h	0-0	
28/5	Dinamo Bender	a	1-0	Bulat

Name	Nat	Pos	Aps	Gls
Ghenadie ANGHEL		M	11	1
Igor BUGAEV		A	13	3
Victor BULAT		M	20	4
Serghey BUTELSCHI		M	26	
Eugen CARABULEA		M	14	1
Eugen CIOBU		M	2	
Mihai COJUSEA		A	12	1
Dan Florin CROITORU	ROM	M	11	1
Serghey CUZNETOV		D	27	1
Olexandr DINDIKOV	UKR	M	14	3
Igor DOBROVOLSKI	RUS	M	5	
Marius DULCIANU	ROM	G	9	
Lilian GOLBAN		M	13	1
Evgheny GOSTEV		M	13	
Eduard GROSU		D	23	
Evgeheny HMARUC		G	8	
Oleg HROMTOV		A	7	
Vladimir LIFSIT		G	11	
Alexandr PETROV		M	8	
Dumitru POPOVICI		M	19	
Roman RADCENCO		M	10	1
Alexandr RAZDOROZNII		M	14	
Igor SOLTANICI		D	19	
Serghey STROENCO		D	27	
Vladimir TARANU		A	11	1
Marius VINTILA	ROM	A	24	4

FC TIRASPOL
Coach – Yury Kulish

2005

Date	Opponent	H/A	Score	Scorers
13/8	Tiligul-Tiras Tiraspol	a	1-1	Alexeev
22/8	Dinamo Bender	a	4-0	Picusciac, Alexeev 2, Necsulescu
29/8	Nistru Otaci	h	0-0	
11/9	Dacia Chisinau	a	2-1	Alexeev 2
14/9	Sheriff Tiraspol	h	0-2	
18/9	Politechnica Chisinau	a	0-1	
24/9	Zimbru Chisinau	h	0-1	
2/10	Tiligul-Tiras Tiraspol	h	0-0	
15/10	Dinamo Bender	h	1-0	Corneencov
23/10	Nistru Otaci	a	1-0	Namasco Se.
29/10	Dacia Chisinau	h	2-2	Corneencov, Picusciac
6/11	Sheriff Tiraspol	a	0-1	
16/11	Politechnica Chisinau	h	1-0	Corneencov (p)
20/11	Zimbru Chisinau	a	1-2	Corneencov

2006

Date	Opponent	H/A	Score	Scorers
11/3	Tiligul-Tiras Tiraspol	a	0-0	
15/3	Dinamo Bender	a	1-1	Sidorenco
19/3	Nistru Otaci	h	1-0	Rudac
24/3	Dacia Chisinau	a	2-1	Golovatenco 2
27/3	Dacia Chisinau	h	2-2	Rudac, og (Mardari)
1/4	Sheriff Tiraspol	h	0-0	
9/4	Politechnica Chisinau	a	0-0	
18/4	Zimbru Chisinau	h	0-0	
22/4	Tiligul-Tiras Tiraspol	h	2-1	og (Soltanici), Sidorenco
29/4	Dinamo Bender	a	0-0	
5/5	Nistru Otaci	a	1-1	Sidorenco
20/5	Sheriff Tiraspol	a	1-2	Sidorenco (p)
24/5	Politechnica Chisinau	h	1-1	Picusciac
28/5	Zimbru Chisinau	a	0-1	

Name	Nat	Pos	Aps	Gls
Serghey ALEXEEV		A	14	5
Alexandr BICHKOV	UKR	A	12	
Alexei CASIAN		M	22	
Vadim CEMARTAN		M	12	
Kennedy CHINWO	NGA	D	7	
Andrei CORNEENCOV		M	13	4
Mihai DODUL		D	8	
Victor GOLOVATENCO		D	26	2
Eugen GORODETCHI		M	25	
Pavel HORGUASHVILI	GEO	M	1	
Valter HORGUASHVILI	GEO	M	15	
Amiran KVELASHVILI	GEO	M	16	
Andrei MAKAROV	BLS	M	10	
Alexandru MELENCIUC		G	9	
Valentin NECSULESCU	ROM	D	21	1
Serghey NAMASCO		M	13	1
Stanislav NAMASCO		G	19	
Victor NOSENCO		M	12	
Andrei NOVICOV		D	23	
Georghy PANCENCO		A	8	
Igor PICUSCIAC		M	28	3
Andrei PORFIREANU		M	14	
Serghei RAVINA	BLS	M	13	
Nicolae RUDAC		M	23	2
Andrei SECRIERU		M	14	
Kiril SIDORENKO		D	21	4

ZIMBRU CHISINAU
Coach – Ivan Tabanov

2005

Date	Opponent	H/A	Score	Scorers
15/8	Nistru Otaci	h	1-1	Popescu F.
20/8	Dacia Chisinau	a	2-0	Petrosyan, Frantuz
28/8	Sheriff Tiraspol	h	0-1	
10/9	Politechnica Chisinau	a	4-0	Chirilov 3, Stan M.
14/9	Dinamo Bender	h	5-1	Chirilov, Pinzaru, Frantuz, Stan M. (p), Aleksanyan

Moldova

19/9	Tiligul-Tiras Tiraspol	h	2-0	Popescu, Petrosyan	
24/9	FC Tiraspol	a	1-0	Stan M.	
2/10	Nistru Otaci	a	1-2	Chirilov	
15/10	Dacia Chisinau	h	0-1		
23/10	Sheriff Tiraspol	a	0-3		
29/10	Politechnica Chisinau	h	5-2	Chirilov 3, Popescu, Frantuz	
6/11	Dinamo Bender	a	3-0	Frantuz, Chirilov, Petrosyan	
16/11	Tiligul-Tiras Tiraspol	a	1-1	Petrosyan	
20/11	FC Tiraspol	h	2-1	Frantuz, Aleksanyan	
2006					
11/3	Nistru Otaci	h	2-0	Frantuz, Chirilov	
15/3	Dacia Chisinau	a	1-1	Dobre	
19/3	Sheriff Tiraspol	h	2-3	Pinzaru, Frantuz	
24/3	Politechnica Chisinau	a	1-0	Bulgaru	
27/3	Politechnica Chisinau	h	1-1	Bulgaru	
1/4	Dinamo Bender	h	7-0	Frantuz 2 (1p), Manaliu 2, Stan M., Petrosyan 2	
9/4	Tiligul-Tiras Tiraspol	h	1-0	Manaliu	
18/4	FC Tiraspol	a	0-0		
22/4	Nistru Otaci	a	1-1	Chirilov	
29/4	Dacia Chisinau	h	2-1	Manaliu, Bulgaru	
5/5	Sheriff Tiraspol	a	0-0		
9/5	Dinamo Bender	a	1-0	Bucuroaia	
24/5	Tiligul-Tiras Tiraspol	a	0-0		
29/5	FC Tiraspol	h	1-0	Manaliu	

Name	Nat	Pos	Aps	Gls
Karen ALEXANIAN	ARM	M	22	2
Emanuel AMARANDEI	ROM	D	25	
Ilie Daniel BALASA	ROM	D	4	
Sorin Ciprian BUCOROAIA	ROM	A	12	1
Semion BULGARU		D	13	3
Andrei BURCOVSCHI		M	6	
Sergiu CHIRILOV		A	24	11
Adrian CUCOVEI		D	19	
Andrei COJOCARU		M	8	
Lucian DOBRE	ROM	D	25	1
Maxim FRANTUZ		M	26	9
Artiom GAIDUCEVICI		G	2	
Ionut IRIMIA	ROM	G	27	
Stipe LAPIC	CRO	M	16	
Iurie LIVANDOVSCHI		A	1	
Vitalie MANALIU		A	7	5
Alexandr MAXIM		M	1	
Oleg MOLLA		M	12	
Ramin NASIBOV	AZB	M	4	
Florin Fanel NOFITOVICI	ROM	D	27	
Galust PETROSYAN	ARM	A	19	6
Alin Cristinel PINZARU	ROM	M	22	2
Serghey PISNIC		A	3	
Filip POPESCU	ROM	M	26	3
Mircea STAN	ROM	D	27	4
Vali STAN	ROM	M	23	
Denis ZMEU		M	6	

DOMESTIC CUP 2005/06

QUARTER-FINALS
(3/11/05 & 10/11/05)
Zimbru Chisinau 2 *(Frantuz 2)*, FC Tiraspol 0
FC Tiraspol 0, Zimbru Chisinau 1 *(Popescu F.)*
(Zimbru Chisinau 3-0)

Nistru Otaci 4 *(Blajco 2, Yanchuk, Magomedov)*, Politechnica Chisinau 0

Politechnica Chisinau 3 *(Soimu, Gusila p, Cojusea)*, Nistru Otaci 0
(Nistru Otaci 4-3)

Dacia Chisinau 0, Tiligul-Tiras Tiraspol 0
Tiligul-Tiras Tiraspol 0, Dacia Chisinau 1 *(Resetca)*
(Dacia Chisinau 1-0)

Sheriff Tiraspol 4 *(Suvorov 2, Yeboah, Gnanu)*, Intersport-Aroma Chisinau 0
Intersport-Aroma Chisinau 0, Sheriff Tiraspol 3 *(Gumeniuk, Florescu, Tarkhnishvili)*
(Sheriff Tiraspol 7-0)

SEMI-FINALS
(5/4/06 & 13/4/06)
Sheriff Tiraspol 2 *(Balima, Omotoiossi)*, Zimbru Chisinau 1 *(Frantuz)*
Zimbru Chisinau 2 *(Popescu, Stan M.)*, Sheriff Tiraspol 2 *(Tarkhnishvili p, Cocis)* (aet)
(Sheriff Tiraspol 3-2)

Dacia Chisinau 0, Nistru Otaci 0
Nistru Otaci 1 *(Bursuc p)*, Dacia Chisinau 0
(Nistru Otaci 1-0)

FINAL
(10/5/06)
Republican stadium, Chisinau
SHERIFF TIRASPOL 2 *(Stadiiciuc 2og, Omotoiossi 58)*
NISTRU OTACI 0
Referee – Chepoi
SHERIFF TIRASPOL – Pascenco S., Mamah, Gumeniuk, Tarkhnishvili, Corneencov, Kuchiuk (Balima 56), Florescu, Omotoiossi (Alexeev 80), Namasco (Bulat 90), Cocis (Suvorov 70), Gnanu.
NISTRU OTACI – Matiughin, Lupascu, Habib, Cebotari (Tcaciuc An. 57), Yanchuk, Taranu (Soimu 65), Bolohan (Petrenko 88), Blohin, Bursuc, Matiura A., Stadiiciuc (Dolgov 81).

SECOND LEVEL FINAL TABLE 2005/06

		Pld	W	D	L	F	A	Pts
1	Zimbru-2 Chisinau	28	23	4	1	79	13	73
2	Sheriff-2 Tiraspol	28	20	5	3	71	28	65
3	Olimpia Balti	28	18	5	5	66	23	59
4	Iskra-Stali Ribnita	28	17	7	4	54	31	58
5	FC Floreni Anenii Noi	28	13	9	6	45	31	48
6	FC Rapid Ghidghici	28	12	10	6	42	23	46
7	CSCA-Agro Stauceni	28	12	7	9	46	31	43
8	Intersport-Aroma Cobusca Noua	28	10	9	9	26	25	39
9	USC Gagauziya Comrat	28	10	7	11	46	28	37
10	Energetic Dubasari	28	8	6	14	27	42	30
11	Tiligul-Tiras-2 Tiraspol	28	8	5	15	30	40	29
12	Moldova-03 Ungheni	28	6	6	16	27	66	24
13	Goliadir-SS-11 Chisinau	28	3	7	18	19	62	16
14	FC Glodeni	28	2	2	24	12	89	8
15	Avenarex Ratus	28	1	5	22	14	73	8

N.B. FC Otaci Calaraseuca withdrew at winter break; Avenarez Ratus withdrew during spring season, forfeiting all remaining matches 0-3.

Northern Ireland

Euphoric victory over England

Northern Ireland did not qualify for the 2006 World Cup. They never even come close. But to the vast majority of the team's fans, that wasn't important. The only thing that really mattered was that they beat England.

The date of September 7, 2005 will long be remembered as an historic date for football in the Province. Lawrie Sanchez's motley crew were supposed to have no chance against England's finely honed collection of Premiership superstars. Yet on a night when Sven Göan Eriksson's side did nothing right, Northern Ireland delighted the vociferous, passionate full house of 14,000 with their first victory over England at Windsor Park since 1927. David Healy's stunning 74th-minute winner was the first scored by Northern Ireland against the English since Terry Cochrane found the net in a 1-1 draw at Wembley in 1980.

It was an extraordinary result. Northern Ireland's international season had begun dismally a few weeks earlier when only a last-minute penalty save from Maik Taylor saved the team from an embarrassing defeat in Malta. The knives were out for Sanchez at this juncture, and when the manager sent home two players, Cardiff City duo Jeff Whitley and Philip Mulryne, for a breach of discipline prior to the September 3 qualifier at home to Azerbaijan, it looked as if he was preparing his own funeral pyre. But the Azeris were beaten 2-0 – Northern Ireland's first competitive win in Belfast for five years – and then, four days later, came the famous win against England. All of a sudden Sanchez could do no wrong.

The euphoria was dampened slightly the following month when Wales came to Windsor Park, took a two-goal half-time lead and won 3-2. The campaign ended on a losing note in Austria four days later when record marksman Healy had an off-night in front of goal, but Sanchez's men still finished an acceptable fourth in the group. Further confirmation of the team's progress was provided by a creditable 1-1 draw at home to Portugal and a 1-0 win over Estonia, but a ten-day trip to the United States in May – made with a depleted squad that included six uncapped players – predictably brought defeats against Uruguay and Romania.

If beating England was the undoubted high point of the season, the lowest was the premature death of the country's greatest ever footballer, George Best. He died in a London hospital at the age of 59, and the Province virtually came to a standstill for his funeral, held at Stormont, on Saturday, December 3; the service was broadcast live on television across the United Kingdom. The City Airport in Belfast has been re-named in his honour.

The domestic season was completely dominated by Linfield. The Belfast Blues made modern history by winning all four competitions – the Premier League, the Irish Cup, the CIS Cup and the County Antrim Shield. It was the first time since 1961/62 that a team had achieved a clean sweep of the domestic

NATIONAL TEAM RESULTS 2005/06

Date	Opponent	H/A	Venue	Score	Scorers
17/8/05	Malta	A	Ta'Qali	1-1	Healy (9)
3/9/05	Azerbaijan (WCQ)	H	Belfast	2-0	Elliott (60), Feeney (85p)
7/9/05	England (WCQ)	H	Belfast	1-0	Healy (74)
8/10/05	Wales (WCQ)	H	Belfast	2-3	Gillepsie (46), Davis (50)
12/10/05	Austria (WCQ)	A	Vienna	0-2	
15/11/05	Portugal	H	Belfast	1-1	Feeney (53)
1/3/06	Estonia	H	Belfast	1-0	Sproule (2)
21/5/06	Uruguay	N	New Jersey	0-1	
26/5/06	Romania	N	Chicago	0-2	

Northern Ireland

It's there! David Healy sends Northern Ireland into ecstasy

trophies. The only title Linfield failed to win was the cross-border Setanta Cup (which they had collected the previous season). And, of course, they also went out of Europe early – though not before knocking out the Latvians of FK Ventspils on away goals in the first qualifying round of the UEFA Cup (Linfield's first victory in a two-legged European tie for a decade).

Having surrendered the Premier League title to old rivals Glentoran in 2004/05, Linfield made a whirlwind start to the new campaign, bagging 18 goals in their first three matches. Although their fourth game resulted in a 1-1 draw at Cliftonville, that proved to be the trigger for a sensational run that brought David Jeffrey's side 17 consecutive victories. The title was as good as won by the turn of the year, at which point the Blues had built up a massive 13-point lead. Officially it was all over on March 18, following a 1-0 win at Armagh City.

Saving themselves

Linfield eased off in the final few weeks and actually suffered a defeat – their only one – at home to mid-table Lisburn Distillery, but they were clearly saving themselves for the final of the Irish Cup against Glentoran, victory in which would complete their momentous four-out-of-four achievement. The Blues had already hammered the Glens 3-0 in the CIS Cup final in December, with veteran striker Glenn Ferguson scoring all three goals. Ballymena had been their victims in the final of the County Antrim Shield, which they won 2-1. But the Irish Cup was the big one.

The match would be a personal triumph for Linfield's young striker Peter Thompson, who turned the game around in his team's favour after they had gone behind, scoring an equaliser in first-half stoppage time and heading home the winner midway through the second half. That lifted the 22-year-old's seasonal tally to an amazing 48 goals in 58 matches. Twenty-six of those had come in the Premier League, making him the competition's top scorer, two ahead of strike-partner 'Spike' Ferguson. It was little wonder that the young goal-machine attracted interest from mainland Britain, with Scottish Cup finalists Gretna and English Championship sides Plymouth and QPR all making offers and enquiries. In the end, he decided to stay at Linfield, agreeing full professional terms.

Glentoran, unable once again to defend their league title (a feat not accomplished since 1968) finished second to their arch-foes in three competitions and also lost their long-serving manager Roy Coyle. He departed in late January after a calamitous run of results that included just one win in eight league games. Coyle, who collected 15 trophies during his time at The Oval, was not long out of a job, stepping in at Newry City to replace Paul Millar, who resigned to take on the position left vacant by Coyle at Glentoran.

Ards were relegated automatically to the First Division after finishing last in the Premier League, and they were accompanied through the trapdoor by Institute, who lost their two-legged play-off to Belfast-based Donegal Celtic. Another club from the capital, Crusaders, ran away with the First Division, winning all but two of their 22 matches to return to the top flight in style after just a year away.

Northern Ireland

NATIONAL TEAM APPEARANCES 2005/06

Coach – Lawrie SANCHEZ

Player	DOB	Club	Mlt	AZB	ENG	WAL	AUT	Por	Est	Uru	Rom	Caps	Goals
Maik TAYLOR	4/9/71	Birmingham City (ENG)	G	G	G	G	G	G	G			52	-
Aaron HUGHES	8/11/79	Aston Villa (ENG)	D	D	D							46	-
Stephen CRAIGAN	29/10/76	Motherwell (SCO)	D	D	D	D	D	D	D46	D	D71	21	-
Colin MURDOCK	2/7/75	Rotherham United (ENG)	D			D	D	D		D82	s82	34	1
Jeff WHITLEY	28/1/79	Cardiff City (WAL)	D59									20	2
Keith GILLESPIE	18/2/75	Sheffield United (ENG)	M	M	M	M	M	M87				68	2
Damien JOHNSON	18/11/78	Birmingham City (ENG)	M	M	M	M	M					42	-
Steven DAVIS	1/1/85	Aston Villa (ENG)	M89	M	M	M	M	M	M68	M	M	13	1
Stuart ELLIOTT	23/7/78	Hull City (ENG)	M59	M89	M90	M65	s67	M46	s68			34	4
David HEALY	5/8/79	Leeds United (ENG)	A	A79	A85	A	A70		A59			49	19
James QUINN	15/12/74	Peterborough United (ENG)	A69	A72	A79	A	A57	A76	A59	A75	A	46	4
Chris BRUNT	14/12/84	Sheffield Wednesday (ENG)	s59			s65	M67	D	M68			7	-
Steve JONES	25/10/76	Crewe Alexandra (ENG) /Burnley (ENG)	s59	s79		s82	s70	M46	s46	M59	s66	24	1
Warren FEENEY	17/1/81	Luton Town (ENG)	s69	s72	s79		s57	A87	s59			11	2
Philip MULRYNE	1/1/78	Cardiff City (WAL)	s89									27	3
Chris BAIRD	25/2/82	Southampton (ENG)		D	D		D		M			20	-
Tony CAPALDI	12/8/81	Plymouth Argyle (ENG)		D	D	D		D	D	D	D57	18	-
Steve ROBINSON	10/12/74	Luton Town (ENG)		s89								6	-
Ivan SPROULE	18/2/81	Hibernian (SCO)			s85			s87	M46	A	M57	5	1
Michael DUFF	11/1/78	Burnley (ENG)			s90	D82	D		D	D82	D	10	-
Gareth McAULEY	5/12/79	Lincoln City (ENG)					s46		D	s82	D82	5	-
Grant McCANN	14/4/80	Cheltenham Town (ENG)					s46		s68			11	-
Peter THOMPSON	2/5/84	Linfield					s76		s59	s59	A66	4	-
Dean SHIELS	1/2/85	Hibernian (SCO)						s87		s75	M66	3	-
Brian McLEAN	28/2/85	Motherwell (SCO)							s46			1	-
Michael INGHAM	9/9/80	Wrexham (WAL)								G		2	-
Sammy CLINGAN	13/1/84	Nottingham Forest (ENG)								M82	M	2	-
Jeff HUGHES	29/5/85	Lincoln City (ENG)								M75	s57	2	-
Kyle LAFFERTY	16/9/87	Burnley (ENG)								s75	s66	2	-
Sean WEBB	4/1/83	Ross County (SCO)								s82	s71	2	-
Mark HUGHES	16/9/83	Oldham Athletic (ENG)								s82	s57	2	-
Alan BLAYNEY	9/10/81	Doncaster Rovers (ENG)									G	1	-

The European Book of Football 2006/2007 - 545

Northern Ireland

EUROPEAN CUPS 2005/06

UEFA CHAMPIONS LEAGUE

GLENTORAN
1st qualifying round SHELBOURNE (IRL)
H 1-2 *Ward (77)*
Morris, Nixon, Holmes, Walker, Leeman, Keegan, Ward, Tolan, Parkhouse (Morgan 68), McCallion, Lockhart.
A 1-4 *McCann (21)*
Morris, Nixon, Holmes, Walker, Leeman, Ward (Parkhouse 65), McCann (Keegan 46; Melaugh 88), McCallion, Morgan, Halliday, Lockhart.

UEFA CUP

PORTADOWN
1st qualifying round VIKING FK (NOR)
H 1-2 *Arkins (90p)*
Miskelly, Craig, O'Hara, Clarke, Convery, Kelly, McCann, Boyle (Quinn 85), Hamilton, Arkins, Neill.
A 0-1
Miskelly, Craig (Alerdice 84), O'Hara, Clarke, Convery, Kelly, Boyle (Quinn 79), Collins, Hamilton, Arkins, Neill (McCann 74).

LINFIELD
1st qualifying round FK VENTSPILS (LAT)
H 1-0 *Mouncey (6)*
Mannus, Ervin, McShane, McAreavey (Picking 68), Hunter, O'Kane (Kingsberry 64), Thompson, Mouncey, Larmour, Kearney (Gault 57), Bailie.
A 1-2 *Thompson (8)*
Mannus, Ervin, McShane, Kearney Murphy, O'Kane, Thompson (Larmour 82), Mouncey (Picking 85), Ferguson, Gault, Bailie.

2nd qualifying round HALMSTADS BK (SWE)
A 1-1 *Kearney (73)*
Mannus, Ervin, McShane, Kearney, Murphy, O'Kane (Kingsberry 71), Thompson, Mouncey, Ferguson (Larmour 90), Gault, Bailie.
H 2-4 *Mouncey (54), Ferguson (82)*
Mannus, Douglas (Kingsberry 53), McShane, Kearney, Murphy, O'Kane (McAreavey 58), Thompson, Mouncey (Mulgrew 84), Ferguson, Gault, Bailie.

TOP GOALSCORERS 2005/06

26	Peter THOMPSON (Linfield)
24	Glenn FERGUSON (Linfield)
15	Gary BROWNE (Glentoran)
	David SCULLION (Dungannon Swifts)
14	Timmy ADAMSON (Dungannon Swifts)
13	Gary McCUTCHEON (Larne)
12	Michael WARD (Dungannon Swifts)
11	Kevin KELBIE (Ballymena United)
	Marc McCANN (Portadown)
	Nathan McCONNELL (Cliftonville)
	Chris MORGAN (Glentoran)
	Marty VERNER (Glenavon)

LEAGUE RESULTS/SCORERS/APPEARANCES/GOALS 2005/06

ARDS
Manager – George Neill; (2/3/06) Gary Hillis & Raymond Morrison

2005
Date	Opponent	H/A	Score	Scorers
17/9	Cliftonville	h	0-1	
24/9	Glentoran	a	1-2	Hill J.
11/10	Institute	h	1-4	Hegan
15/10	Glenavon	a	0-1	
22/10	Linfield	a	0-2	
29/10	Armagh City	h	0-2	
5/11	Portadown	a	2-3	Hill J., Hunter
12/11	Ballymena United	h	1-3	Jephcott
19/11	Lisburn Distillery	a	0-1	
26/11	Limavady United	h	2-1	Jephcott, Hunter
2/12	Dungannon Swifts	a	2-4	Hill J. (p), Waterworth
9/12	Newry City	a	1-2	Tumilty
17/12	Loughgall	h	1-0	Waterworth
26/12	Larne	a	1-3	Jephcott
31/12	Coleraine	h	2-5	Hunter, Hill J. (p)

2006
Date	Opponent	H/A	Score	Scorers
2/1	Cliftonville	a	1-0	Waterworth
7/1	Glentoran	h	0-1	
21/1	Institute	a	1-2	Moran
28/1	Glenavon	h	1-0	(w/o)
4/2	Linfield	h	0-4	
18/2	Armagh City	a	0-3	
25/2	Portadown	h	1-2	McKee
11/3	Ballymena United	a	1-1	Hill J.
18/3	Lisburn Distillery	h	0-1	
25/3	Limavady United	a	0-1	
8/4	Dungannon Swifts	h	3-3	Campbell, Murray, Waterworth
15/12	Larne	h	1-3	Davidson
18/4	Loughgall	a	3-2	Hill J., Ward, Hunter
22/4	Newry City	h	1-3	og (Robinson)
29/4	Coleraine	a	4-2	Hill J., Sharratt, McKee, Waterworth

Name	Nat	Pos	Aps	(s)	Gls
Brian ADAIR		D	17		
John BAILIE		D	29		
Tom BATES	ENG	M	3		
Raymond CAMPBELL		M	22	(1)	1
Ryan DAVIDSON		D	20	(1)	1
Ross HEGAN		M	20		1
Jason HILL		A	27		7
Ryan HILL		A		(2)	
Gordon HILLIS		A	3	(1)	
Marty HUNTER		M	26		4
Avun JEPHCOTT	ENG	A	8		3
Robert KNOX		M	2	(10)	
Ian LESTER		G	17		
Jay MAGEE		D	11	(1)	
Paul McDOWELL		M	4	(4)	
Ian McGRATH		M	3	(5)	
Aaron McKEE		M	10	(1)	2
Ciaran McLAUGHLIN		G	11		
Tennant McVEA		D	3	(3)	
Mick MORAN	ENG	A	2		1
Alan MURRAY		M	9	(4)	1
Mark PARKER		A	3	(2)	
Johnny ROY		D	1	(3)	

Northern Ireland

FINAL LEAGUE TABLE 2005/06

		Pld	Home W	D	L	F	A	Away W	D	L	F	A	Total W	D	L	F	A	Pts
1	Linfield	30	12	2	1	43	11	11	4	0	45	12	23	6	1	88	23	75
2	Glentoran	30	10	2	3	30	14	9	4	2	30	14	19	6	5	60	28	63
3	Portadown	30	8	3	4	36	17	8	3	4	20	19	16	6	8	56	36	54
4	Dungannon Swifts	30	10	3	2	39	17	3	7	5	22	24	13	10	7	61	41	49
5	Cliftonville	30	5	5	5	21	17	8	3	4	24	18	13	8	9	45	35	47
6	Newry City	30	7	3	5	21	16	5	6	4	24	19	12	9	9	45	35	45
7	Ballymena United	30	7	2	6	20	23	6	4	5	22	25	13	6	11	42	48	45
8	Lisburn Distillery	30	6	3	6	20	23	6	5	4	24	15	12	8	10	44	38	44
9	Coleraine	30	4	3	8	16	23	7	1	7	24	34	11	4	15	40	57	37
10	Limavady United	30	3	7	5	20	24	6	2	7	22	25	9	9	12	42	49	36
11	Loughgall	30	4	4	7	18	22	5	3	7	15	16	9	7	14	33	38	34
12	Glenavon	30	2	5	8	16	34	5	4	6	19	25	7	9	14	35	59	30
13	Larne	30	4	4	7	24	30	3	5	7	18	33	7	9	14	42	63	30
14	Armagh City	30	4	3	8	22	28	5	0	10	16	41	9	3	18	38	69	30
15	Institute	30	2	5	8	18	29	4	3	8	19	29	6	8	16	37	58	26
16	Ards	30	3	1	11	14	33	3	1	11	17	29	6	2	22	31	62	20

Lee RUTHERFORD		G	2	
Gary SHARRATT		A	(1)	1
Chris TOWELL		M	6 (1)	
Ryan TUMILTY		M	10 (12)	
Brendan WARD	IRL	D	13	1
Andrew WATERWORTH		A	24	5
Gary WRAY		D	24	

ARMAGH CITY
Manager – Colin Malone

2005
17/9	Institute	h	1-2	Meehan
24/9	Larne	a	3-2	Delany, Ward, Reilly
1/10	Newry City	h	2-1	Ward, Reilly
15/10	Glentoran	a	0-2	
22/10	Ballymena United	h	0-1	
29/10	Ards	a	2-0	Reilly, Ward
5/11	Lisburn Distillery	a	1-3	Murphy
12/11	Portadown	h	2-2	Cowan, Ward (p)
19/11	Linfield	a	0-5	
25/11	Dungannon Swifts	h	0-0	
2/12	Limavady United	a	0-3	
9/12	Glenavon	a	3-1	McGeown, Ward 2
17/12	Coleraine	h	3-0	Murphy, Meehan, Lavery
26/12	Loughgall	a	1-2	Murphy
31/12	Cliftonville	h	1-3	Reilly

2006
2/1	Institute	a	0-4	
7/1	Larne	h	1-2	Coney
21/1	Newry City	a	2-1	Forker, Ward
28/1	Glentoran	h	5-2	Forker, Meehan, Reilly 2, Hawthorne
4/2	Ballymena United	a	0-3	
18/2	Ards	h	3-0	Meehan 2, Ward
25/2	Lisburn Distillery	h	1-6	Forker
11/3	Portadown	a	2-1	Forker 2
18/3	Linfield	h	0-1	
24/3	Dungannon Swifts	a	1-2	Hawthorne
8/4	Limavady United	h	3-3	Forker 3
15/4	Loughgall	h	0-1	
18/4	Coleraine	a	0-4	
22/4	Glenavon	h	0-4	
29/4	Cliftonville	a	1-8	McCann

Name	Nat	Pos	Aps	(s)	Gls
Kevin BATES	ENG	A		(6)	
Scott BEST		D	1	(4)	
Andrew BROWN		A	1	(1)	
Shea CAMPBELL		A	11		
Mark CARLISLE		D	17	(3)	
Robert CASEY		M	8	(4)	
Shane CONEY		A	10		1
Jonathan COWAN		D	24		1
Michael CROWE		M	2	(3)	
Liam CULLEN		M	15	(2)	
Derek DELANY	IRL	A	1	(1)	1
Shea DONNELLY		G	1		
David FAIRCLOUGH	IRL	M	13	(5)	
Jason FERRY		D	2		
Conor FORKER		A	12	(1)	8
David HAWTHORNE		A	29		2
Seamus KANE		D		(1)	
Martin LAVERY		M	2	(9)	1
Philip McBIRNEY		D	12	(1)	
Francis McCANN		A		(1)	1
Thomas McGAULEY		D	11		
Shane McGEOWN		M	13	(6)	1
Shea McGERRIGAN		A	2	(2)	
Johnny McSORLEY		M	8	(13)	
Barry MEEHAN		A	26	(3)	5
Alan MURPHY		D	14	(1)	3
Barry O'NEILL		D		(2)	
Anto REILLY		A	19	(4)	6
Paul RICE		G	29		
Mark TURKINGTON		D	21	(5)	
David WARD	IRL	A	26	(1)	8

Northern Ireland

BALLYMENA UNITED
Manager – Kenny Shiels

2005

17/9	Larne	h	1-0	Steele
24/9	Newry City	a	0-2	
1/10	Cliftonville	h	0-2	
15/10	Loughgall	a	0-1	
22/10	Armagh City	a	1-0	Sweeney
29/10	Linfield	h	0-2	
5/11	Dungannon Swifts	h	4-3	Smyth, Rosbotham, Charnock, Hamill
12/11	Ards	a	3-1	Youle, Haveron, Sweeney
19/11	Limavady United	h	1-3	Sweeney
26/11	Lisburn Distillery	h	1-0	Rosbotham
2/12	Portadown	a	1-6	Hamill
13/12	Glentoran	a	2-1	Sweeney, Kelbie
17/12	Glenavon	h	2-3	Sweeney (p), Kelbie
26/12	Coleraine	a	1-0	Sweeney
30/12	Institute	h	1-0	King

2006

2/1	Larne	a	2-1	Sweeney, Melly
7/1	Newry City	h	0-0	
21/1	Cliftonville	a	2-2	Scates, Kelbie
28/1	Loughgall	h	3-2	Smyth 2, Kelbie
4/2	Armagh City	h	3-0	Kelbie 2, Sweeney
18/2	Linfield	a	2-3	Smyth, Rowe
24/2	Dungannon Swifts	a	2-2	King 2
11/3	Ards	h	1-1	Brown
18/3	Limavady United	a	2-2	Hamill 2
25/3	Lisburn Distillery	a	1-2	Kelbie
8/4	Portadown	h	2-3	Hamill, Kelbie
15/4	Coleraine	h	1-0	Kelbie
18/4	Glenavon	a	2-2	Kelbie, Hamill
22/4	Glentoran	h	0-4	
29/4	Institute	a	1-0	Kelbie

Name	Nat	Pos	Aps	(s)	Gls
Stuart ADDIS		G	4		
Nigel BOYD		D	7	(5)	
Paul BROWN		A	6	(3)	1
Phil CHARNOCK	ENG	M	5	(4)	1
Stephen COLLIER		D	4	(1)	
Ciaran DONAGHY		D	24	(1)	
Rory HAMILL		A	17	(7)	6
Gary HAVERON		M	27	(3)	1
Kevin KELBIE	SCO	A	18	(5)	11
Stuart KING		M	23		3
Gerard McCABE		D	1		
Craig McCLEAN		M	24		
Paul McDOWELL		M	2	(8)	
William McFREDERICK		G	26		
Dominic MELLY		M		(4)	1
Randal REID		A		(1)	
Andrew ROSBOTHAM		M	8	(5)	2
Gerard ROWE	IRL	A	7	(6)	1
Garth SCATES		M	23	(5)	1
Gordon SIMMS		D	10	(1)	
Gary SMYTH		D	25		4
Johnny STEELE		M	2		1
Vincent SWEENEY		A	24	(5)	8
Aidan WATSON		D	15	(4)	
Albert WATSON		D	26	(2)	
Dean YOULE		D	2	(1)	1

CLIFTONVILLE
Manager – Eddie Patterson

2005

17/9	Ards	a	1-0	Kennedy
24/9	Portadown	h	0-2	
1/10	Ballymena United	a	2-0	Cleary, Holland
15/10	Linfield	h	1-1	Mulvenna
22/10	Newry City	h	0-0	
29/10	Glentoran	a	0-0	
5/11	Loughgall	a	3-2	McConnell, og (Harbinson), Telford
12/11	Glenavon	a	2-2	og (Black), Holland
19/11	Coleraine	a	2-0	Kennedy, Friars
26/11	Larne	h	2-2	McMullan G., O'Loughlin
13/12	Limavady United	h	0-1	
17/12	Dungannon Swifts	a	0-1	
20/12	Institute	a	3-2	McMullan G., McConnell, og (Harkin)
26/12	Lisburn Distillery	h	2-1	McConnell, Friars
31/12	Armagh City	a	3-1	McConnell 2, Downey

2006

2/1	Ards	h	0-1	
6/1	Portadown	a	1-3	McConnell
21/1	Ballymena United	h	2-2	Kennedy, Friars (p)
28/1	Linfield	a	0-1	
4/2	Newry City	a	1-3	Cleary
18/2	Glentoran	h	1-1	Friars
25/2	Loughgall	h	1-0	Scannell C.
11/3	Glenavon	h	2-1	McMullan G., McConnell
18/3	Coleraine	h	0-1	
25/3	Larne	a	4-2	O'Loughlin, McConnell, Downey, Scannell C.
8/4	Institute	h	2-0	Cleary, McConnell
15/4	Lisburn Distillery	a	0-0	
18/4	Dungannon Swifts	h	0-3	
22/4	Limavady United	a	2-1	Scannell C., Friars
29/4	Armagh City	h	8-1	O'Loughlin, McConnell 2, Scannell C. 2, Friars 2, Downey

Name	Nat	Pos	Aps	(s)	Gls
Sean CLEARY		M	20	(5)	3
Conor DOWNEY		M	26	(2)	3
Michael FARRELL		D		(6)	
Liam FLEMING		D	26		
Sean FRIARS		M	24	(5)	7
Mark HOLLAND		A	18	(5)	2
Barry JOHNSTON		M	6	(3)	
Gary KENNEDY		A	20	(7)	3
Willie LOUGHRAN		D		(1)	
Nathan McCONNELL		A	18	(7)	11
Paul McCREADY		A		(2)	
James McDONAGH		D	3	(1)	
Ciaran McMULLAN		A	4	(2)	
George McMULLAN		M	24	(2)	3
Ben MOANE		G	3	(1)	
Keith MULVENNA		D	22		1
Declan O'HARA		D	30		
John O'LOUGHLIN	IRL	M	22	(4)	3
Chris PATTERSON		M		(1)	
Chris SCANNELL		A	13	(1)	5
Ronan SCANNELL		D	17		
Aaron SMYTH		M	4	(1)	
Paul STRANEY		G	27		

Northern Ireland

Gareth TAYLOR		M		(3)	
Peter TELFORD		A	3	(5)	1

Bryan TOSH		M	3	(2)	
John WATT		M	9	(7)	1

COLERAINE
Manager – Marty Quinn

2005
Date	Opponent	H/A	Score	Scorers
17/9	Limavady United	a	3-3	Carson, Ferry, Spratt
24/9	Lisburn Distillery	h	1-0	McVey
1/10	Linfield	a	2-7	McVey, Ferry
15/10	Portadown	h	1-1	Gaston
22/10	Glentoran	h	0-0	
29/10	Larne	a	4-1	Carson 2, Ferry 2
5/11	Glenavon	h	0-0	
12/11	Loughgall	a	3-2	Gaston, Carson, Boyce
19/11	Cliftonville	h	0-2	
26/11	Institute	h	2-5	Ferry 2
2/12	Newry City	a	0-2	
9/12	Dungannon Swifts	h	2-0	Carson, Bratton
17/12	Armagh City	a	0-3	
26/12	Ballymena United	h	0-1	
31/12	Ards	a	5-2	Boyce, Anderson 2, Beatty, Neill

2006
Date	Opponent	H/A	Score	Scorers
2/1	Limavady United	h	0-2	
7/1	Lisburn Distillery	a	2-1	Spratt, Ferry (p)
21/1	Linfield	h	0-1	
28/1	Portadown	a	0-2	
4/2	Glentoran	a	0-3	
18/2	Larne	h	2-1	McVey, Patton G.
25/2	Glenavon	a	2-1	Boyce 2
11/3	Loughgall	h	1-3	Carson
18/3	Cliftonville	a	1-0	Boyce
25/3	Institute	a	1-0	Patton G.
8/4	Newry City	h	1-3	Patton D.
15/4	Ballymena United	a	0-1	
18/4	Armagh City	h	4-0	Boyce, Patton D., Watt, Anderson
21/4	Dungannon Swifts	a	1-6	Patton D.
29/4	Ards	h	2-4	Ferry, Anderson

Name	Nat	Pos	Aps	(s)	Gls
Noel ANDERSON		M	18	(3)	4
Stephen BEATTY		M	18	(3)	1
Darren BOYCE		A	22	(4)	6
Stuart BRATTON		A	4	(7)	1
Gareth CAMPBELL		D	2		
Stephen CARSON		M	29		6
Stuart CLANACHAN		D	13	(1)	
Ciaran FERRY		A	20	(4)	8
Paul GASTON		D	19	(2)	2
Tony GRAY		D	12	(1)	
Sean HENEGAN		M	2	(2)	
Barry JOHNSTON		M	7	(2)	
Stephen LYONS		A	3	(9)	
Patrick McALARY		M		(1)	
Stewart McCALLUM		D	18	(5)	
Paul McLAUGHLIN		A	7	(4)	
Ryan McLAUGHLIN		D	25	(2)	
Kyle McVEY		D	29		3
John NEILL		D	14	(9)	1
David O'HARE		G	30		
David PATTON		A	7	(1)	3
Gordon PATTON		A	9	(1)	2
Owen PEDEN		A		(1)	
Peter SPRATT		D	10	(6)	2

DUNGANNON SWIFTS
Manager – Joe McAree

2005
Date	Opponent	H/A	Score	Scorers
17/9	Loughgall	h	3-0	Scullion, Adamson, Keegan
24/9	Glenavon	a	2-2	Adamson, Fitzpatrick G.
30/9	Larne	h	3-0	Keegan, Scullion, Forker
15/10	Institute	a	3-3	McAree, Scullion, Adamson
22/10	Limavady United	a	1-1	Adamson
29/10	Lisburn Distillery	h	2-2	Scullion, Fitzpatrick T.
5/11	Ballymena United	a	3-4	Fitzpatrick G., Fitzpatrick T. 2
12/11	Linfield	h	2-3	Scullion, Ward
19/11	Portadown	a	3-2	Ward 3 (2p)
25/11	Armagh City	a	0-0	
2/12	Ards	h	4-2	Ward 2, Fitzpatrick T. Scullion
9/12	Coleraine	a	0-2	
17/12	Cliftonville	h	1-0	Scullion
26/12	Newry City	a	1-2	Adamson
31/12	Glentoran	h	2-1	Scullion, McCabe

2006
Date	Opponent	H/A	Score	Scorers
2/1	Loughgall	a	1-0	Keegan
7/1	Glenavon	h	6-0	Scullion (p), Ward, McAree, Adamson 3
21/1	Larne	a	0-1	
28/1	Institute	h	2-1	Ward, Adamson
4/2	Limavady United	h	3-2	Adamson, Murphy, Ward
18/2	Lisburn Distillery	a	0-0	
24/2	Ballymena United	h	2-2	Scullion, Ward
10/3	Linfield	a	1-1	Scullion
18/3	Portadown	h	0-1	
24/3	Armagh City	h	2-1	Scullion (p), Ward
8/4	Ards	a	3-3	Bulow 2, Adamson
15/4	Newry City	h	1-1	Everaldo
18/4	Cliftonville	a	3-0	Adamson 2, Fitzpatrick T.
21/4	Coleraine	h	6-1	og (Anderson), Scullion 2 (2p), Ward, Adamson, Bulow
29/4	Glentoran	a	1-3	Scullion

Name	Nat	Pos	Aps	(s)	Gls
Timmy ADAMSON		A	24	(1)	14
Stuart ADDIS		G	2		
David BULOW		A	3	(3)	3
Gavin CUSHLEY		G	20		
Pedro DELGADO	VEN	M	5	(9)	
EVERALDO	BRA	A	3	(7)	1
Seamus FANTHORPE		D	2	(1)	
Gary FITZPATRICK		D	20	(2)	2
Terry FITZPATRICK		M	17	(5)	5
Conor FORKER		A		(3)	1
John GALLAGHER		D	28	(1)	
Mark GRACEY		D	2		
Andrew HAMILTON		D	4	(1)	
Kevin KEEGAN		M	10	(8)	3
Mark McALLISTER		A	2	(4)	
Rodney McAREE		M	25		2
Shane McCABE		M	20	(2)	1
Mark McCONKEY		M	2	(1)	
Bryan McCRYSTAL	IRL	D	12	(1)	
Adam McMINN		D	13	(3)	
Johnny MONTGOMERY		D	10	(2)	
Darren MURPHY		D	18	(5)	1

Northern Ireland

Name	Pos	Aps	(s)	Gls
Kieran RAFFERTY	D	2		
David SCULLION	A	26	(3)	15
James SLATER	A		(1)	
Michael WARD	M	24	(2)	12
David WELLS	G	8		
Thomas WRAY	D	28	(1)	

GLENAVON
Manager – Jimmy Brown

2005
17/9	Linfield	a	1-2	Verner
24/9	Dungannon Swifts	h	2-2	McMahon (p), O'Connor
1/10	Lisburn Distillery	a	2-1	og (McCann), Campbell
15/10	Ards	h	1-0	O'Connor
22/10	Loughgall	h	0-4	
29/10	Newry City	a	2-1	Verner, McAlinden
5/11	Coleraine	a	0-0	
12/11	Cliftonville	h	2-2	Walsh C., McAlinden
19/11	Institute	a	2-1	Campbell (p), Black
26/11	Glentoran	h	0-3	
9/12	Armagh City	h	1-3	Campbell (p)
17/12	Ballymena United	a	3-2	McVeigh 2, Verner
22/12	Larne	a	2-2	Verner, Black
26/12	Portadown	h	0-1	
31/12	Limavady United	a	1-1	McVeigh

2006
2/1	Linfield	h	0-5	
7/1	Dungannon Swifts	a	0-6	
21/1	Lisburn Distillery	h	2-2	Verner 2 (1p)
28/1	Ards	a	0-1	(w/o)
4/2	Loughgall	a	1-1	O'Connor
18/2	Newry City	h	1-4	Verner
25/2	Coleraine	h	1-2	Black
11/3	Cliftonville	a	1-2	Verner
18/3	Institute	h	0-0	
25/3	Glentoran	a	0-1	
8/4	Larne	h	2-3	Black, Walsh C.
15/4	Portadown	a	0-4	
18/4	Ballymena United	h	2-2	Verner, McKnight
22/4	Armagh City	a	4-0	Verner, og (McGauley), Walsh C. 2
29/4	Limavady United	h	2-1	og (Ferry), Verner

Name	Nat	Pos	Aps	(s)	Gls
Carlos ÁLVAREZ	BOL	A	1		
Aaron BLACK		D	27		4
Shea CAMPBELL		A	15	(1)	3
Stephen CARROLL		G	1		
Paul CARVILLE		A		(1)	
Lee DUXBURY	ENG	D	8	(1)	
Paul EVANS		M	1		
Robbie FARRELL	IRL	A		(3)	
Neil GAWLEY		M	9	(16)	
Patrick HOPE		D	1	(2)	
Stephen HYNDES		M	7		
David McALINDEN		D	28		2
Stephen McALORUM		M	9	(4)	
Conor McANALLEN		D	6	(1)	
Andy McDONALD		G	23		
Paul McKNIGHT		A	9	(8)	1
Gerard McMAHON		M	25	(4)	1
Craig McMILLEN		D	3		
Aiden McVEIGH		A	14	(9)	3
James MILLER		G	4		
Johnny MONTGOMERY		D	11		

Name	Nat	Pos	Aps	(s)	Gls
Kyle NELSON		G	2		
Kieran O'CONNOR		A	28		3
Barry REID		D	28		
Peter TELFORD		A	1	(3)	
Andrew UPRICHARD		M		(1)	
Marty VERNER		A	25	(3)	11
Scott WALKER		D	14	(5)	
Conor WALSH		A	26		4
Gareth WALSH		A	4	(7)	

GLENTORAN
Manager – Roy Coyle; (14/2/06) Paul Millar

2005
17/9	Lisburn Distillery	a	4-1	McCann, Holmes, Morgan 2
24/9	Ards	h	2-1	Nixon, Holmes
1/10	Limavady United	a	2-0	Halliday, Browne
15/10	Armagh City	h	2-0	Browne, Holmes
22/10	Coleraine	a	0-0	
29/10	Cliftonville	h	0-0	
5/11	Institute	a	3-1	Nixon, Morgan, Browne
12/11	Larne	h	5-1	Browne 3, Holmes, Morgan
19/11	Newry City	a	3-0	Melaugh 2, Browne
26/11	Glenavon	a	3-0	McCann, Browne, Lockhart
2/12	Loughgall	h	1-0	Holmes
13/12	Ballymena United	h	1-2	Halliday
17/12	Portadown	a	0-0	
26/12	Linfield	h	1-4	McCann
31/12	Dungannon Swifts	a	1-2	Morgan

2006
2/1	Lisburn Distillery	h	0-0	
7/1	Ards	a	1-0	Browne
21/1	Limavady United	h	0-1	
28/1	Armagh City	a	2-5	Morgan 2
4/2	Coleraine	h	3-0	Halliday 2, Browne
18/2	Cliftonville	a	1-1	Browne
25/2	Institute	h	3-1	Morgan 2, Browne
10/3	Larne	a	3-1	Browne, Melaugh, Morgan
16/3	Newry City	h	3-2	McDonagh, Nixon (p), Melaugh
25/3	Glenavon	h	1-0	Melaugh
8/4	Loughgall	a	3-2	Lockhart, Nixon, Halliday
15/4	Linfield	a	0-0	
18/4	Portadown	h	5-1	Glendinning, Browne, Nixon 2 (2p), Ward
22/4	Ballymena United	a	4-0	Nixon, Ward, Glendinning, Halliday
29/4	Dungannon Swifts	h	3-1	Browne, Morgan, Tolan (p)

Name	Nat	Pos	Aps	(s)	Gls
Ryan BERRY		M	8	(1)	
Gary BROWNE		A	22	(5)	15
Daley CARNDUFF		M		(1)	
Mark GLENDINNING		D	17		2
Michael HALLIDAY		A	20	(4)	6
Shaun HOLMES		M	27	(3)	5
Paul LEEMAN		D	6		
Darren LOCKAHRT		M	14	(3)	2
Ian MANNUS		G	4		
Peter McCANN		M	20	(5)	3
Aaron McCUSKER		D	1	(1)	
Will McDONAGH	IRL	M	11	(1)	1
Pat McGIBBON		D	8	(1)	
Brendan McMENAMIN		D		(1)	
Gavin MELAUGH		M	27	(2)	5
Chris MORGAN		A	21	(8)	11

Northern Ireland

Elliott MORRIS		G	26		
Colin NIXON		D	29		7
Stephen PARKHOUSE		A	11	(2)	
Andy RAINEY		M		(2)	
Jamie REED	ENG	A	4	(3)	
Philip SIMPSON		D	24		
Jody TOLAN		A		(1)	1
Chris WALKER		D	6		
Sean WARD		D	22	(6)	2
Scott YOUNG	SCO	M	2	(5)	

INSTITUTE
Manager – Pascal Vaudequin; (21/11/05) Liam Beckett

2005

Date	Opponent	H/A	Score	Scorers
17/9	Armagh City	a	2-1	Ogilby, McCallion
24/9	Linfield	h	2-9	Ramsey K. (p), McCallion
11/10	Ards	a	4-1	McCreadie, Ramsey K. 2, McCallion
15/10	Dungannon Swifts	h	3-3	Ramsey K. 2, Ketchanke
22/10	Larne	h	1-1	N'Goma
29/10	Loughgall	a	0-2	
5/11	Glentoran	h	1-3	McCallion
12/11	Newry City	a	0-5	
19/11	Glenavon	h	1-2	Sproule A.
26/11	Coleraine	a	5-2	Mullan 3, Divin, McCallion
9/12	Portadown	h	1-2	N'Goma
17/12	Lisburn Distillery	a	1-4	McCallion
20/12	Cliftonville	h	2-3	Divin, McCreadie (p)
26/12	Limavady United	h	1-1	Divin
30/12	Ballymena United	a	0-1	

2006

Date	Opponent	H/A	Score	Scorers
2/1	Armagh City	h	4-0	N'Goma, Sproule G., Mullan 2
7/1	Linfield	a	0-2	
21/1	Ards	h	2-1	McLaughlin, Sproule G.
28/1	Dungannon Swifts	a	1-2	Divin
4/2	Larne	a	1-1	Mullan
18/2	Loughgall	h	0-0	
25/2	Glentoran	a	1-3	Sproule A.
11/3	Newry City	h	0-0	
18/3	Glenavon	a	0-0	
25/3	Coleraine	h	0-1	
8/4	Cliftonville	a	0-2	
15/4	Limavady United	a	3-3	Smith, Divin, Sproule G.
18/4	Lisburn Distillery	h	0-2	
22/4	Portadown	a	1-0	Divin
29/4	Ballymena United	h	0-1	

Name	Nat	Pos	Aps	(s)	Gls
Allan BLAIR		D	14	(2)	
Ruairi BOYLE		D	26	(1)	
Darren CASSIDY		M		(3)	
John CONNOLLY	IRL	G	16		
Declan DIVIN		A	29	(1)	6
Seamus FANTHORPE		D	9		
Gerard GILL		A	1	(5)	
Neil HARKIN		D	13	(5)	
Sullivan JOUS	FRA	G	3		
Bertrand KETCHANKE	FRA	D	5	(4)	1
Tommy McCALLION		M	21		6
Ruairi McCLEAN		M	1	(2)	
Darren McCREADIE		M	19	(8)	2
Ryan McILMOYLE		M	30		
Paddy McLAUGHLIN		D	14		1
Gareth MULLAN		A	19	(5)	6

George N'GOMA	DRC	M	19		3
David OGILBY		D	24	(2)	1
Russell PORTER		D	2	(2)	
Gary RAMSEY		G	8		
Kevin RAMSEY		A	16	(1)	5
Alan RYAN		G	3		
Eddie SEYDAK		D	1	(1)	
Martin SMITH		D	12	(5)	1
Andy SPROULE		M	6	(15)	2
Gareth SPROULE		A	19	(3)	3

LARNE
Manager - Jimmy McGeough; (19/10/05) Kenny Shiels

2005

Date	Opponent	H/A	Score	Scorers
17/9	Ballymena United	a	0-1	
24/9	Armagh City	h	2-3	Hamlin 2
30/9	Dungannon Swifts	a	0-3	
15/10	Limavady United	h	2-3	McCutcheon, Di Lella
22/10	Institute	a	1-1	Wright
29/10	Coleraine	h	1-4	Cleary
5/11	Newry City	h	1-1	Cleary
12/5	Glentoran	a	1-5	Dickson
19/11	Loughgall	h	0-0	
26/11	Cliftonville	a	2-2	Lindsay, Wilson
9/12	Lisburn Distillery	h	3-1	Dickson 2, Fulton
17/12	Linfield	a	1-8	McCutcheon
22/12	Glenavon	h	2-2	Black, Hamlin
26/12	Ards	h	3-1	McCutcheon, Wilson, Dickson (p)
29/12	Portadown	a	2-2	McCutcheon 2

2006

Date	Opponent	H/A	Score	Scorers
2/1	Ballymena United	h	1-2	Dickson (p)
7/1	Armagh City	a	2-1	McCutcheon 2
21/1	Dungannon Swifts	h	1-0	Cleary
28/1	Limavady United	a	0-1	
4/2	Institute	h	1-1	Ward
18/2	Coleraine	a	1-2	McCutcheon
25/2	Newry City	a	0-0	
10/3	Glentoran	h	1-3	Waide
18/3	Loughgall	a	1-1	Waide
25/3	Cliftonville	h	2-4	Dickson 2 (1p)
8/4	Glenavon	a	3-2	McCutcheon 2, Hamlin
15/4	Ards	a	3-1	Ward, McCutcheon, Fulton
18/4	Linfield	h	2-4	McCutcheon 2
22/4	Lisburn Distillery	a	1-3	Hamlin
29/4	Portadown	h	2-1	Dickson 2

Name	Nat	Pos	Aps	(s)	Gls
Gary BELL		M	12		
Ross BLACK		D	17	(4)	1
Gary CHISHOLM		A	7	(2)	
Andrew CLEARY		D	24	(1)	3
Jim CROSSLEY		A		(1)	
Niall CURNEEN		D		(1)	
Gustavo DI LELLA	ARG	M	5	(1)	1
Mark DICKSON		A	30		9
Bertie FULTON		A	20	(3)	2
Lewis HAMLIN	ENG	A	25		5
Ross HANDFORD		D	16		
Simon HUMPHREYS		M	6		
Kieran KANE		D	4	(5)	
Ryan KANE		M	1	(5)	
Christopher KEENAN		G	14		
Kris LINDSAY		D	20		1
Conor LYNCH		M	10	(7)	

Northern Ireland

Name	Nat	Pos	Aps	(s)	Gls
Steven McCAIN		M		(1)	
Gary McCUTCHEON	SCO	A	28	(1)	13
Jim McDONAGH		D	7	(1)	
John McELROY		D	6		
Johnny MONTGOMERY		M	3	(3)	
Neil OGDEN		M	1		
Ormond OKUNAIYA		M	3	(6)	
James QUIGLEY		M	8	(3)	
Gary RAFFERTY		A		(2)	
Alex SPACKMAN		G	16		
Andrew WAIDE		A	3	(1)	2
Julian WARD		D	13		2
William WHARRY		D	14	(2)	
Frankie WILSON		M	12	(3)	2
David WRIGHT		A	2	(9)	1
Dean YOULE		D	3		

LIMAVADY UNITED
Manager – Paul Kee

2005
Date	Opponent		Score	Scorers
17/9	Coleraine	h	3-3	Patrick 2, Bulow (p)
24/9	Loughgall	a	1-2	Cooke
1/10	Glentoran	h	0-2	
15/10	Larne	a	3-2	Magennis 2, Patton
22/10	Dungannon Swifts	h	1-1	Patton
29/10	Portadown	a	1-5	Shields (p)
5/11	Linfield	a	0-2	
12/11	Lisburn Distillery	h	1-1	Nelson
19/11	Ballymena United	a	3-1	Patrick 2, Magennis
26/11	Ards	a	1-2	Patrick
2/12	Armagh City	h	3-0	McIntyre, Patrick, Patton
13/12	Cliftonville	a	1-0	McIntyre
17/12	Newry City	h	1-4	McIntyre
26/12	Institute	a	1-1	McIntyre
31/12	Glenavon	h	1-1	Magennis

2006
Date	Opponent		Score	Scorers
2/1	Coleraine	a	2-0	Magennis, Friel
7/1	Loughgall	h	0-1	
21/1	Glentoran	a	1-0	Shields (p)
28/1	Larne	h	1-0	Magennis
4/2	Dungannon Swifts	a	2-3	Friel 2
17/2	Portadown	h	0-2	
25/2	Linfield	h	2-2	Friel, Parkhouse
11/3	Lisburn Distillery	a	2-1	Parkhouse, Friel
18/3	Ballymena United	h	2-2	Curran, Friel
25/3	Ards	h	1-0	Cooke
8/4	Armagh City	a	3-3	Friel, Parkhouse (p), Patrick
15/4	Institute	h	3-3	Patrick, Coyle, Curran
18/4	Newry City	a	0-1	
22/4	Cliftonville	h	1-2	Parkhouse
29/4	Glenavon	a	1-2	Clyde

Name	Nat	Pos	Aps	(s)	Gls
David BULOW	USA	A	4	(5)	1
Aaron CALLAGHAN		D	29		
Gareth CAMPBELL		D	3	(1)	
Brendan CANNING		M	3		
Tony CLYDE		A		(1)	1
Niall COOKE	ENG	A	16	(4)	2
Liam COOLEY		D	19	(2)	
Ryan COYLE		M	11	(3)	1
John CURRAN		D	20	(3)	2
Martin CUTMORE		D	24	(3)	
Michael DOHERTY		G	19		
Richard DUNLOP		D	2	(9)	

Name		Pos	Aps	(s)	Gls
Martin FERRY		M	13	(3)	
Austin FRIEL		A	14		7
Stephen LOWRY		A	6	(9)	
Mark MAGENNIS		A	20		6
Mark McDAID		M	6	(2)	
Eddie McINTYRE		D	8	(8)	4
Paul McLAUGHLIN		D	1	(2)	
Marty McNUTT		D		(1)	
Neil McVICAR		A		(1)	
Calvin MOONEY		A		(1)	
Neil MULLAN		D	5	(2)	
Dwayne NELSON		G	11		1
Stephen PARKHOUSE		A	10		4
Lee PATRICK		M	29		8
David PATTON		A	10	(6)	3
Graeme PHILSON		D	8		
Ryan SEMPLE		M	17	(5)	
Tony SHIELDS		M	21	(4)	2
Ryan STEWART		A	1		
Michael TWIST		M		(1)	
Shane WHORISKEY		M		(1)	

LINFIELD
Manager – David Jeffrey

2005
Date	Opponent		Score	Scorers
17/9	Glenavon	h	2-1	Thompson, Ferguson
24/9	Institute	a	9-2	Thompson 3, Kearney 2, Mouncey, Larmour, McAreavey, Kingsberry
1/10	Coleraine	h	7-2	Thompson 3 (1p), Kearney, Larmour, McAreavey, Kingsberry
15/10	Cliftonville	a	1-1	Thompson
22/10	Ards	h	2-0	Mouncey, Thompson
29/10	Ballymena United	a	2-0	McShane (p), Ferguson
5/11	Limavady United	h	2-0	Thompson 2
12/11	Dungannon Swifts	a	3-2	McAreavey, Kearney, Ferguson
19/11	Armagh City	h	5-0	Ferguson 3, Kearney, Thompson
26/11	Portadown	h	4-0	Thompson 2, Murphy, Picking
2/12	Lisburn Distillery	a	6-0	Gault 3, Thompson, Kearney, Ferguson
13/12	Loughgall	a	2-1	Thompson, Ferguson
17/12	Larne	h	8-1	Picking, Ferguson 3, McAreavey, Thompson, Larmour 2
26/12	Glentoran	a	4-1	Murphy, Ferguson 2, Thompson
31/12	Newry City	h	3-1	Murphy, Ferguson, Thompson

2006
Date	Opponent		Score	Scorers
2/1	Glenavon	a	5-0	Ferguson 4, (2p), Kearney
7/1	Institute	h	2-0	McAreavey, Ferguson
21/1	Coleraine	a	1-0	Ferguson (p)
28/1	Cliftonville	h	1-0	Thompson
4/2	Ards	a	4-0	Thompson 2, Ferguson, Jephcott
18/2	Ballymena United	h	3-2	Mouncey, og (Smyth), Ferguson
25/2	Limavady United	a	2-2	Kearney, Thompson
10/3	Dungannon Swifts	h	1-1	O'Kane
18/3	Armagh City	a	1-0	Ferguson
25/3	Portadown	a	0-0	

552 - The European Book of Football 2006/2007

Northern Ireland

8/4	Lisburn Distillery	h	1-3	Thompson
15/4	Glentoran	h	0-0	
18/4	Larne	a	4-2	Picking, Larmour, Bell, Thompson
22/4	Loughgall	h	2-0	Garrett, Thompson
29/4	Newry City	a	1-1	Ferguson

Name	Nat	Pos	Aps	(s)	Gls
Noel BAILIE		D	23		
James BELL		A	2		1
Stephen DOUGLAS		D	3		
Jim ERVIN		D	26		
Glenn FERGUSON		A	25	(2)	24
Stephen GARRETT		A	3		1
Michael GAULT		M	25	(3)	3
Paul HAMILTON		D	2		
Andy HUNTER		D	7	(1)	
Avun JEPHCOTT	ENG	A	1	(4)	1
Oran KEARNEY		M	23	(1)	8
Chris KINGSBERRY		M	11	(8)	2
David LARMOUR		A	4	(13)	5
Alan MANNUS		G	28		
Paul McAREAVEY		M	21	(3)	5
Timothy McCANN		M	3	(2)	
Pat McSHANE		D	28		1
Tim MOUNCEY		M	18	(4)	3
Jamie MULGREW		M	6	(2)	
William MURPHY		D	28		3
Aidan O'KANE		M	9	(15)	1
Mark PICKING		M	5	(13)	3
Greg SHANNON		G	2		
Peter THOMPSON		A	27	(2)	26

LISBURN DISTILLERY
Manager – Paul Kirk

2005
17/9	Glentoran	h	1-4	Muir
24/9	Coleraine	a	0-1	
1/10	Glenavon	h	1-2	Armour (p)
15/10	Newry City	a	3-0	Dickson, Armour, Kilmartin
22/10	Portadown	h	1-0	Armstrong
29/10	Dungannon Swifts	a	2-2	Armour, Martin
5/11	Armagh City	h	3-1	Muir, Murphy, Martin
12/11	Limavady United	a	1-1	og (Callaghan)
19/11	Ards	h	1-0	McLaughlin
26/11	Ballymena United	a	0-1	
2/12	Linfield	h	0-6	
9/12	Larne	a	1-3	Kilmartin
17/12	Institute	h	4-1	Martin 2, Hagan, Willis
26/12	Cliftonville	a	1-2	Murphy
31/12	Loughgall	h	2-3	Hagan, og (Pentland)

2006
2/1	Glentoran	a	0-0	
7/1	Coleraine	h	1-2	Catney
21/1	Glenavon	a	2-2	Johnston, Catney
28/1	Newry City	h	0-0	
4/2	Portadown	a	2-1	McKeown, Hagan (p)
18/2	Dungannon Swifts	h	0-0	
25/2	Armagh City	a	6-1	Murphy 2, Armour, Hagan 2, Armstrong
11/3	Limavady United	h	1-2	Johnston
18/3	Ards	a	1-0	Kilmartin (p)
25/3	Ballymena United	h	2-1	Muir, Buchanan
8/4	Linfield	a	3-1	Martin, Dickson, McKeown
15/4	Cliftonville	h	0-0	
18/4	Institute	a	2-0	Kilmartin (p), McLaughlin
22/4	Larne	h	3-1	Thompson, Martin, Hagan
29/4	Loughgall	a	0-0	

Name	Nat	Pos	Aps	(s)	Gls
Darren ARMOUR		A	16	(5)	4
Sean ARMSTRONG		A	16	(5)	2
Wayne BUCHANAN		D	23		1
Robert CASEY		M	6	(2)	
Ryan CATNEY		M	9	(4)	2
Chris COFFEY		D	7	(3)	
Andrew DICKSON		M	13	(8)	2
Michael DOUGHERTY		G	5		
Michael FERGUSON		D	13	(2)	
Conor HAGAN		M	19	(5)	6
Aaron JOHNSTON		A	3	(6)	2
Andrew KILMARTIN		M	13	(7)	4
John MARTIN		A	19	(4)	6
Philip MATTHEWS		G	25		
Ryan McCANN		M	22	(4)	
Gareth McKEOWN		D	21	(1)	2
Damien McLAUGHLIN		A	8	(10)	2
Kyle McQUILLAN		M		(1)	
Paul MUIR		D	23		3
Francis MURPHY		M	28		4
Gary SPENCE		D	11		
Stuart THOMPSON		D	24		1
Simon WEST		D	2	(2)	
James WILLIS		A	4	(2)	1

LOUGHGALL
Manager – Jimmy Gardiner

2005
17/9	Dungannon Swifts	a	0-3	
24/9	Limavady United	h	2-1	Guy 2
1/10	Portadown	a	1-2	Coulter (p)
15/10	Ballymena United	h	1-0	Guy
22/10	Glenavon	a	4-0	Percy, Topley, Emerson, Black
29/10	Institute	h	2-0	Percy, McCordick
5/11	Cliftonville	h	2-3	Emerson, McCordick
12/11	Coleraine	h	2-3	Black, Topley
19/11	Larne	a	0-0	
26/11	Newry City	h	0-3	
2/12	Glentoran	a	0-1	
13/12	Linfield	h	1-2	Sterritt
17/12	Ards	a	0-1	
26/12	Armagh City	h	2-1	Emerson, Pentland
31/12	Lisburn Distillery	a	3-2	Black, Waddell, Robinson N.

2006
2/1	Dungannon Swifts	h	0-1	
7/1	Limavady United	a	1-0	og (Cooley)
21/1	Portadown	h	0-0	
28/1	Ballymena United	a	2-3	Emerson, McCordick
4/2	Glenavon	h	1-1	Peden
18/2	Institute	a	0-0	
25/2	Cliftonville	a	0-1	
11/3	Coleraine	a	3-1	Emerson, Coulter 2
18/3	Larne	h	1-1	Coulter
24/3	Newry City	a	0-0	
8/4	Glentoran	h	2-3	Coulter 2
15/4	Armagh City	a	1-0	Emerson
18/4	Ards	h	2-3	Quilty, Coulter
22/4	Linfield	a	0-2	
29/4	Lisburn Distillery	h	0-0	

Northern Ireland

Name	Nat	Pos	Aps	(s)	Gls
Brian ADAIR		D	8	(2)	
Johnny BLACK		M	21	(4)	3
Stephen COULTER		A	28	(2)	7
Alain EMERSON		M	29		6
Chris GUINEY		D	10	(7)	
John GUY		A	10	(5)	3
Paul HARBINSON		D	7		
Willie HERRON		D	10	(4)	
Stephen HYNDES		M		(2)	
Colin KEENAN		D		(1)	
Scott McCORDICK		A	3	(13)	3
Darragh PEDEN		D	30		1
Bryan PENTLAND		D	19		1
Keith PERCY		M	27		2
Brian QUILTY		A	7	(1)	1
Marc ROBINSON		G	30		
Noel ROBINSON		D	17	(2)	1
Mark SAVAGE		D	3		
Clifford STERRITT		A	11	(7)	1
Johnny TOPLEY		M	23	(6)	2
Barry TUMILTY		M	2	(5)	
Glen WADDELL		D	23		1
Ian WALLACE		M	9	(3)	
Raymond WILKINSON		M		(1)	
Ally WILSON		A	3	(9)	

NEWRY CITY
Manager – Roy McCreadie; (29/11/05) Paul Millar; (20/2/06) Roy Coyle

2005

Date	Opponent		Score	Scorers
17/9	Portadown	a	1-5	Whitehead
24/9	Ballymena United	h	2-0	McAllister, Crawford
1/10	Armagh City	a	1-2	Curran D. (p)
15/10	Lisburn Distillery	h	0-3	
22/10	Cliftonville	a	0-0	
29/10	Glenavon	h	1-2	McAllister
5/11	Larne	a	1-1	Curran D.
12/11	Institute	h	5-0	Whitehead 3, Crawford, Curran D.
19/11	Glentoran	h	1-3	Ferguson
26/11	Loughgall	a	3-0	Crawford, Whitehead, Curran D.
2/12	Coleraine	h	2-0	Ferguson, og (McCallum)
9/12	Ards	h	2-1	Crawford, Curran D. (p)
17/12	Limavady United	a	4-1	Ferguson, Curran D. 2, Flynn
26/12	Dungannon Swifts	h	2-1	Crawford, Whitehead
31/12	Linfield	a	1-3	Crawford

2006

Date	Opponent		Score	Scorers
2/1	Portadown	h	0-2	
7/1	Ballymena United	a	0-0	
21/1	Armagh City	h	1-2	Willis
28/1	Lisburn Distillery	a	0-0	
4/2	Cliftonville	h	3-1	Curran D., Whitehead 2
18/2	Glenavon	a	4-1	Willis, Feeney 2, Clarke
25/2	Larne	h	0-0	
11/3	Institute	a	0-0	
16/3	Glentoran	a	2-3	Crawford 2
24/3	Loughgall	h	0-0	
8/4	Coleraine	a	3-1	McLaughlin, Feeney, Crawford
15/4	Dungannon Swifts	a	1-1	Willis
18/4	Limavady United	h	1-0	McCullagh
22/4	Ards	a	3-1	Willis, Feeney, Whitehead
29/4	Linfield	h	1-1	Willis

Name	Nat	Pos	Aps	(s)	Gls
Richard CLARKE		M	30		1
Daryl COLLINS		A		(4)	
James COSTELLO		M		(1)	
Andy CRAWFORD		A	19	(9)	9
Niall CRILLY		M	1	(3)	
Gavin CUMMINGS		A		(1)	
Darren CUNNINGHAM		M		(1)	
Barry CURRAN		M	16	(1)	
Damien CURRAN		M	29		8
Paul DONEGAN		D	24	(1)	
Robbie FARRELL	IRL	A		(2)	
Lee FEENEY		M	9	(2)	4
Steven FERGUSON		M	24	(1)	3
Gerry FLYNN		D	19	(3)	1
Padraig GOLLOGLEY	IRL	D	13		
Kevin KEEGAN		M	10	(1)	
Colin KEENAN		D	1	(4)	
Darren KING		D	9	(8)	
Chris LAWLESS		D		(1)	
Patrick McALLISTER		M	22		2
Colm McCULLAGH		M	14	(5)	1
Paddy McLAUGHLIN		D	24	(1)	1
Alan MURPHY	IRL	D	4		
John O'HARE		A		(1)	
Neil QUINN		A		(1)	
Robert ROBINSON		G	30		
Damien WHITEHEAD	ENG	A	20	(9)	9
James WILLIS		A	12		5

PORTADOWN
Manager – Ronnie McFall

2005

Date	Opponent		Score	Scorers
17/9	Newry City	h	5-1	Hamilton 2, Neill 3
24/9	Cliftonville	a	2-0	Kelly, McCann
1/10	Loughgall	h	2-1	Arkins, Hamilton
15/10	Coleraine	a	1-1	Kelly
22/10	Lisburn Distillery	a	0-1	
29/10	Limavady United	h	5-1	McCann 2, McStay 2, Baker
5/11	Ards	h	3-2	McCann, Arkins, Kelly
12/11	Armagh City	a	2-2	og (Murphy), Hamilton
19/11	Dungannon Swifts	h	2-3	Hamilton, Baker
26/11	Linfield	a	0-4	
2/12	Ballymena United	h	6-1	Clarke 2, Hamilton, Kelly, Craig, Boyle
9/12	Institute	a	2-1	Kelly, Convery
17/12	Glentoran	h	0-0	
26/12	Glenavon	a	1-0	Convery
29/12	Larne	h	2-2	Kelly (p), Baker

2006

Date	Opponent		Score	Scorers
2/1	Newry City	a	2-0	Kelly, Baker
6/1	Cliftonville	h	3-1	Clarke, Boyle, Baker
21/1	Loughgall	a	0-0	
28/1	Coleraine	h	2-0	McCann, Baker
4/2	Lisburn Distillery	h	1-2	Kelly
17/2	Limavady United	a	2-0	McCann, Boyle
25/2	Ards	a	2-1	McCann, Boyle
11/3	Armagh City	h	1-2	Neill
18/3	Dungannon Swifts	a	1-0	McCann
25/3	Linfield	h	0-0	
8/4	Ballymena United	a	3-2	Teggart, Baker, McCann
15/4	Glenavon	h	4-0	Convery, McCann 2 (1p), Teggart
18/4	Glentoran	a	1-5	Boyle

Northern Ireland

22/4	Institute	h	0-1		
29/4	Larne	a	1-2	Neill	

Name	Nat	Pos	Aps	(s)	Gls
Neil ALERDICE		D	5	(3)	
Vinny ARKINS	IRL	A	11	(2)	2
Aaron BAKER		A	12	(9)	7
Wesley BOYLE		M	23		5
Richard CLARKE		M	27	(1)	3
Michael COLLINS		M	16	(1)	
John CONVERY		D	27		3
Philip CRAIG		D	9	(3)	1
Gary HAMILTON		A	19	(1)	6
Darren KELLY		D	27		8
Gary LIGGETT		M	3	(6)	
Jamie MARKS		M	18	(5)	
Marc McCANN		M	24	(4)	11
David McCULLOUGH		M	1	(1)	
Henry McSTAY		D	25	(1)	2
David MISKELLY		G	23		
Paul MURPHY	IRL	G	7		
Kyle NEILL		M	21	(4)	5
Keith O'HARA		D	21		
Paddy QUINN	IRL	M	5	(14)	
Paul RICKERS	ENG	M	1		
Alan TEGGART		A	5	(5)	2

DOMESTIC CUP 2005/06

FIFTH ROUND
(14/1/06)
Ballymena United 4, Kilmore Recreation 0
Ballynure Old Boys 0, Ballyclare Comrades 4
Bangor 1, Harland & Wolff Welders 1
Carrick Rangers 2, Ballymoney United 1
Cliftonville 1, Dungannon Swifts 1
Coagh United 1, Newington Youth Club 1
Coleraine 1, Newry City 1
Crusaders 2, Portadown 2
Glenavon 2, Dundela 1
Glentoran 2, Ards 1
Institute 1, Lisburn Distillery 3
Larne 1, Donegal Celtic 1
Limavady United 5, PSNI 0
Linfield 5, Armagh City 0
Loughgall 0, Banbridge Town 0
Tobermore United 2, Portstewart 3

Replays
(17/1/06)
Bangor 3, Harland & Wolff Welders 1
Larne 3, Donegal Celtic 1
Loughgall 3, Banbridge Town 2
Newry City 0, Coleraine 0 *(aet; 3-4 on pens)*
Portadown 1, Crusaders 0
(18/1/06)
Coagh United 0, Newington Youth Club 2
Dungannon Swifts 1, Cliftonville 0

SIXTH ROUND
Dungannon Swifts 1, Portadown 1
Glenavon 3, Coleraine 0
Glentoran 1, Ballyclare Comrades 0
Larne 3, Carrick Rangers 0

Limavady United 1, Bangor 3
Linfield 1, Loughgall 1
Lisburn Distillery 0, Ballymena United 0
Portstewart 0, Newington Youth Club 1

Replays
(14/2/06)
Loughgall 1, Linfield 3
Portadown 3, Dungannon Swifts 1
(15/2/06)
Ballymena United 1, Lisburn Distillery 2

QUARTER-FINALS
(4/3/06)
Glentoran 2 *(Morgan 47, 65)*, Portadown 0
Larne 2 *(Dickson 25p, Black 90)*, Newington Youth Club 1 *(Bradley 10)*
Linfield 3 *(Ferguson 32, O'Kane 76, Jephcott 85)*, Glenavon 0
Lisburn Distillery 0, Bangor 1 *(Dunlop 6)*

SEMI-FINALS
(1/4/06)
Linfield 3 *(Kerr 4og, Thompson 7, Ferguson 53)*, Bangor 1 *(O'Kane 69og)*
Glentoran 2 *(Browne 36, Simpson 66)*, Larne 0

FINAL
(6/5/06)
Windsor Park, Belfast
LINFIELD 2 *(Thompson 45, 65)*
GLENTORAN 1 *(Halliday 44)*
Referee - Ross
GLENTORAN - Morris, Nixon, Glendinning, Berry (Tolan 77), Simpson, Ward, Browne (Morgan 69) Melaugh, McDonagh, Halliday, Lockhart.
LINFIELD - Mannus, Ervin, McShane, Gault, Murphy, McAreavey (Hunter 86), Thompson, Mouncey, Ferguson, Kearney (McCann 74), Bailie.

SECOND LEVEL FINAL TABLE 2005/06

		Pld	W	D	L	F	A	Pts
1	Crusaders	22	20	1	1	51	13	61
2	Donegal Celtic	22	13	5	4	41	25	44
3	Dundela	22	10	5	7	32	28	35
4	Bangor	22	10	3	9	42	32	33
5	Banbridge Town	22	8	6	8	29	29	30
6	Tobermore United	22	8	5	9	33	37	29
7	Carrick Rangers	22	8	4	10	25	29	28
8	Coagh United	22	8	3	11	25	26	27
9	Harland & Wolff Welders	22	7	4	11	21	31	25
10	Moyola Park	22	7	3	12	32	50	24
11	Ballyclare Comrades	22	6	5	11	32	37	23
12	Ballymoney United	22	3	4	15	18	44	13

PROMOTION/RELEGATION PLAY-OFFS
(5/5/06)
Donegal Celtic 3, Institute 1
(10/5/06)
Institute 0, Donegal Celtic 0
(Donegal Celtic 3-1)

Norway

Vålerenga stumble across finish line

Rosenborg's long monopoly of the Norwegian championship finally ended in 2005. The Trondheim club had a troubled season in which they were never in contention to prolong their record-breaking run of 13 successive titles. But the two teams that sought to topple them from their Tippeligaen throne, 2004 runners-up Vålerenga and newly promoted IK Start, seemed so paralysed by the prospect of taking the title that between them they failed to win any of their final four matches.

In the end it was Vålerenga who edged home by one point thanks to a battling 2-2 draw on the final day away to Odd Grenland. If Start had won or drawn at home to relegation-threatened Fredrikstad, they would have taken the honours, but despite the support of a bulging capacity-plus crowd (16,563), the team from Kristiansand blew their big chance, falling to a comprehensive 3-1 defeat.

Joy unrestrained

Joy was unrestrained for Vålerenga's players and fans. A year earlier they had been cruelly denied the title at the death by a late goal from Rosenborg that relegated them to runners-up on the number of goals scored. That nightmare scenario was a possibility again going into the final match, but fortunately fate dealt Kjetil Rekdal's team a kinder hand and they just hung on to win their first title since 1984 – despite picking up just three points and scoring only two goals in their final six matches.

The Red and Blues from the Ullevaal certainly started the season better than they finished it. Reinforced during the winter, notably with experienced defender Ronny Johnsen and gifted youngster Christian Grindheim, Vålerenga shrugged off an opening-day defeat to win their next five games and go top. A lull then followed before the team took on Rosenborg in late June at the Lerkendal. With revenge clearly acting as a source of inspiration, they beat the perennial champions 3-2. Morten Berre, whose injury-time miss had practically cost Vålerenga the 2004 title, maintained his excellent early-season form by scoring two of the goals.

That win injected Vålerenga with self-belief and they embarked on a stunning run of ten games without defeat. Grindheim was the outstanding performer during this period, developing a highly productive central midfield partnership with Ardian Gashi. Johnsen also excelled, as did fellow defenders Kjetil Waehler and new signing André Muri, while Icelandic international Arni Gautur Arason was a class act in goal.

During the July break the club made a strong statement of intent by signing two big names – Magne Hoseth and Tore André Flo – but neither player did himself justice, and with the club exiting the Champions League qualifying round after a penalty shoot-out defeat to Club Bruges, there was an unsettled look to the team as they travelled to Kristiansand for the potential title-decider against Start. Vålerenga went into the game with a three-point advantage but came out of it with no lead at all after a 3-0 drubbing.

Level on points with four games left, it was a time for cool heads and strong hearts. Alas, neither team possessed either. It was almost as if the responsibility of stepping into Rosenborg's shoes was too heavy to bear. Both teams lost their final two home games, with Vålerenga notably disappointing a record home crowd of 24,894 (the

Tippeligaen's biggest attendance of the season) with a 2-0 defeat by the outgoing champions. But while Start took one point from their last two away fixtures, Vålerenga, thanks to that draw at Odd Grenland, took two. Had the Tippeligaen gone on any longer, other teams would have come into the mix. Indeed, by the end Vålerenga's city rivals Lyn, who had never really threatened, were only two points in arrears of the champions.

It was Start, though, who had the greater cause for regret. Without a championship title for 25 years, it was their centenary in 2005. Freshly promoted from the Adeccoligaen, they were not expected to achieve any more than a mid-table position. But with coach Tom Nordlie fielding an attack-minded 4-3-3 formation (based on the successful Rosenborg model), the team set the league alight right from their sparkling opening-day 3-1 win over Lillestrøm. By the midpoint of the season, having faced all of the other 13 clubs, they had yet to lose.

Proud Start

Everybody wondered when the Start bubble would burst. But the team was full of confidence, symbolised by their indefatigable central midfielder Kristofer Haestad, a kind of 'Norwegian Gattuso'. Up front, Alex Valencia also played consistently well and would collect the prestigious Tippeligaen Player of the Year award from daily newspaper Verdens Gang. Start did finally hit the wall in the closing weeks, but although the end was agony, they had much to be proud of. They played fine, attractive football, the crowds flocked to see them, and several of their players caught the eye of national team boss Åge Hareide.

The collapse of Rosenborg almost overshadowed the achievements of Vålerenga and Start. Led by new coach Per Joar Hansen, the Trondheim club were a shambles from the beginning. The team looked old and de-motivated and were down in seventh place at the halfway point, with virtually no chance of winning another title. But things got even worse after the summer break and Hansen, never a popular figure, was jettisoned and replaced by Per Mathias Høgmo. The new man managed to qualify the team for another Champions League run at the expense of Steaua Bucharest but at home it was a different story as Rosenborg followed up the two defeats that had ended Hansen's reign with another four in succession for Høgmo. Now, astonishingly, they were 12th in the table and battling against relegation.

Fortunately, a strong finish lifted the club back up to seventh spot, but having exited the Norwegian Cup early, there would be no European football for the country's top team in 2006/07. Aware of that fact, Rosenborg fought hard in their Champions League group and did well to finish third in a section comprising Real Madrid, Lyon and Olympiakos. They took the UEFA Cup spot thanks to a superior head-to-head record over the Greeks. Youngster Per Ciljan Skjelbred will remember those two games well. He starred and scored in the opening 3-1 win in Piraeus but in the return at the Lerkendal he broke his leg.

Despite their domestic tribulations Rosenborg still drew a best-ever average attendance of 17,529 to the Lerkendal. Another highlight was the new Tippeligaen goalscoring record set by striker Harald Brattbakk – although it took him ten months to bypass Petter Belsvik's record mark and he left in mid-season to join Bodø/Glimt, where he increased his new record tally to 166 goals.

Brattbakk was unable to save Bodø/Glimt from relegation. The northerners finished bottom and were accompanied down by Aalesund. Fredrikstad's last-day win at Start lifted them clear of the drop zone, placing Molde in the play-off spot. That meant a busy finish to the season for Bo Johansson's team, who had also qualified for the

NATIONAL TEAM RESULTS 2005/06

17/8/05	Switzerland	H	Oslo	0-2	
3/9/05	Slovenia (WCQ)	A	Celje	3-2	Carew (3), Lundekvam (24), Gamst Pedersen (90)
7/9/05	Scotland (WCQ)	H	Oslo	1-2	Årst (89)
8/10/05	Moldova (WCQ)	H	Oslo	1-0	Rushfeldt (50)
12/10/05	Belarus (WCQ)	A	Minsk	1-0	Helstad (70)
12/11/05	Czech Republic (WCQ)	H	Oslo	0-1	
16/11/05	Czech Republic (WCQ)	A	Prague	0-1	
25/1/06	Mexico	N	San Francisco	1-2	Årst (10)
29/1/06	USA	A	Carson	0-5	
1/3/06	Senegal	A	Dakar	1-2	Hagen (41)
24/5/06	Paraguay	H	Oslo	2-2	Johnsen F. (22, 61)
1/6/06	South Korea	H	Oslo	0-0	

Norway

NATIONAL TEAM APPEARANCES 2005/06

Coach – Åge HAREIDE			Sui	SLO	SCO	MOL	BLS	CZE	CZE	Mex	Usa	Sen	Par	Kor	Caps	Goals
Thomas MYHRE	16/10/73	Charlton Athletic (ENG)	G	G	G	G	G	G	G		G		G	G	50	-
André BERGDØLMO	13/10/71	FC København (DEN)	D	D	D	D		D							63	-
Erik HAGEN	20/7/75	Zenit Sankt-Peterburg (RUS)	D70	D		D	D81	D	D		D46	D			14	1
Claus LUNDEKVAM	22/2/73	Southampton (ENG)	D	D	D										40	2
John Arne RIISE	24/9/80	Liverpool (ENG)	D		M	D	D	D	D90		M	D		D	54	5
Kristofer HAESTAD	9/12/83	IK Start	M	M	s46	M		M	M						9	-
Christian GRINDHEIM	17/7/83	Vålerenga Fotball	M46	M	M	M	M	M87				s85		s60	8	-
Alex VALENCIA	22/9/79	IK Start	M87		M46					M62	s46				5	-
Steffen IVERSEN	10/11/76	Vålerenga Fotball	M46	A11		M90	M	M79	M46						59	12
Morten GAMST PEDERSEN	8/9/81	Blackburn Rovers (ENG)	M	M		M	M	M	M				M	M	23	5
John CAREW	5/9/79	Olympique Lyonnais (FRA)	A46	A	A			A	A				A39	A71	54	13
Eirik BAKKE	13/9/77	Leeds United (ENG)	s46												26	-
Ole Martin ÅRST	19/7/74	Tromsø IL	s46	s82	s46			s79	s58	A		A	s39	s71	18	2
Thorstein HELSTAD	28/4/77	Rosenborg BK	s46			s90	s46		M58						21	8
Kjetil WAEHLER	16/3/76	Vålerenga Fotball	s70												1	-
Hassan EL-FAKIRI	18/4/77	Borussia M'gladbach (GER)	s87									M46			8	-
Jon Inge HØILAND	20/9/77	Malmö FF (SWE) /1.FC Kaiserslautern (GER)		D			D		D			D	D	D	13	-
Jan Gunnar SOLLI	19/4/81	Rosenborg BK		M66	D46	s63	M73	M46	s46			M			28	1
Daniel OMOYA BRAATEN	25/5/82	Rosenborg BK		s11/82	s46	s83		s46				A62			8	1
Martin ANDRESEN	2/2/77	SK Brann		s66	M								M	M	23	2
Vidar RISETH	21/4/72	Rosenborg BK			D										48	4
Egil ØSTENSTAD	2/1/72	Viking FK			M46										18	6
Brede PAULSEN HANGELAND	20/6/81	Viking FK /FC København (DEN)				D	D	D	D		D	D	D46	D	26	-
Marius JOHNSEN	28/8/81	IK Start				M63			s90						4	-
Sigurd RUSHFELDT	11/12/72	FK Austria Wien (AUT)				A83	A46								35	7
Fredrik STRØMSTAD	20/1/82	IK Start				M	s87	M					M85	M60	5	-
Ardian GASHI	20/6/81	Vålerenga Fotball				s73									7	-
Bård BORGERSEN	20/5/72	IK Start				s81				D		s46			10	2
Espen JOHNSEN	20/12/79	Rosenborg BK						G	G						18	-
Jarl-André STORBAEK	21/9/78	Vålerenga Fotball						D							4	-
Trond Erik BERTELSEN	5/6/84	Fredrikstad FK						D	s46	D71					3	-
Petter RUDI	17/9/73	Molde FK								M	M64	s46			46	3
Petter VAAGAN MOEN	5/2/84	Ham-Kam Fotball /SK Brann								M	M		M		3	-
Magne HOSETH	13/10/80	Vålerenga Fotball								M46	s64				20	1
Raymond KVISVIK	8/11/74	Fredrikstad FK								M	s46				11	2
Henning HAUGER	17/7/85	Stabæk Fotball								s46	M46				2	-
Espen OLSEN	13/3/79	Ham-Kam Fotball								s62	s46				2	-
Steinar PEDERSEN	6/6/75	IK Start								D					1	-
Frode KIPPE	17/1/78	Lillestrøm SK								D					5	-
Erlend HANSTVEIT	28/1/81	SK Brann								D46					5	-
Tomasz SOKOLOWSKI	25/6/85	FC Lyn Oslo								M46					1	-
Stian OHR	4/1/78	Molde FK								M46					1	-
Atle Roar HÅLAND	26/7/77	IK Start									s46				1	-
Pa-Modou KAH	30/7/80	Roda JC (HOL)									s71				9	1
Azar KARADAS	9/8/81	Portsmouth (ENG)									s62				9	1
Tommy SVINDAL LARSEN	11/8/73	Odd Grenland										M	M		21	-
Frode JOHNSEN	17/3/74	Rosenborg BK										M	M		31	10
Anders RAMBEKK	17/8/76	Lillestrøm SK												D	1	-

Norway

final of the Norgesmesterkapet, the Norwegian Cup, against Uwe Rösler's Lillestrøm.

Double celebration

Molde would end the season on a double high. Four-two victors over Lillestrøm after extra-time on a dreadful surface at the Ullevaal, they lifted the Cup for only the second time and thus qualified for the UEFA Cup. The success story continued when they won both of their play-off matches against Moss to remain in the Tippeligaen. It was the fifth year in a row that the top-flight side had triumphed in the relegation/promotion decider.

Stabaek and Sandefjord were promoted automatically, the latter having twice been play-off losers, in 2002 and 2003. Stabaek's short stay in the Adeccoligaen was largely down to their prolific Swedish striker Daniel Nannskog, who scored 27 goals in 29 games. In contrast the Tippeligaen's top marksman, Tromsø's Ole Martin Årst, netted only 16 – although that was one more than the rest of his team-mates managed in unison.

Tromsø finished mid-table in the league but the Arctic Circle team provided one of Norwegian football's greatest ever European results when they knocked Turkish giants Galatasaray out of the UEFA Cup. Tromsø went on to compete in the group phase, as did Roy Hodgson's Viking, who partly compensated for an average domestic campaign by scuttling out Austria Vienna and then winning at home to Monaco.

Neither Tromsø nor Viking made it through their groups, which left only Rosenborg in Europe after Christmas. There was no competitive football for the Norwegian national side in the first half of 2006 following their failure to qualify for the World Cup. Three wins in their last four group games, including a memorable 3-2 victory in Slovenia, carried Åge Hareide's team into the play-offs, but as in the Euro 2004 qualifiers they got a tough draw and were always second best to the Czech Republic (as they had been to Spain two years earlier). If it is to be third time lucky for Euro 2008, the team will have to make a major improvement on the form they showed in a handful of spring friendlies. A goalless draw against South Korea in Oslo made it seven matches without a win, a sequence that included a home-based XI going down 5-0 to the United States – Norway's heaviest defeat for 33 years.

EUROPEAN CUPS 2005/06

UEFA CHAMPIONS LEAGUE

ROSENBORG BK

3rd qualifying round STEAUA BUCURESTI (ROM)
A 1-1 *Helstad (85)*
Johnsen E., Basma, Riseth, Lago, Dorsin, Solli, Berg, Strand (Winsnes 79), Johnsen F., Braaten (Storflor 63), Helstad (Ødegaard 85).
H 3-2 Solli (38), Ødegaard (57), Radoi (60og)
Johnsen E., Basma, Riseth, Lago (Ødegaard 46), Dorsin, Srand, Berg, Winsnes, Helstad (Solli 15), Johnsen F., Storflor (Braaten 46).

1st round Group F
Match 1 OLYMPIAKOS (GRE)
A 3-1 *Ciljan Skjelbred (43), Mavrogenidis (48og), Storflor (90)*
Johnsen E., Strand, Kvarme, Lago, Dorsin, Ciljan Skjelbred (Riseth 85), Berg, Winsnes (Braaten 66), Solli, Helstad (Johnsen F. 80), Storflor.

Match 2 OLYMPIQUE LYONNAIS (FRA)
H 0-1
Johnsen E., Strand (Basma 66), Kvarme, Riseth, Dorsin, Ciljan Skjelbred, Berg, Solli, Braaten, Helstad (Johnsen F. 68), Storflor (Ødegaard 59).

Match 3 REAL MADRID (ESP)
A 1-4 *Strand (40)*
Johnsen E., Basma, Kvarme, Riseth, Dorsin, Braaten, Strand (Tettey 46), Ciljan Skjelbred (Winsnes 76), Solli, Storflor, Helstad (Johnsen F. 63).

Match 4 REAL MADRID
H 0-2
Johnsen E., Basma, Kvarme, Riseth, Dorsin (Stensaas 74), Strand (Ødegaard 83), Ciljan Skjelbred, Solli, Storflor (Helstad 66), Braaten, Johnsen F.

Match 5 OLYMPIAKOS
H 1-1 *Helstad (88)*
Johnsen E., Basma, Riseth, Kvarme, Dorsin, Strand (Helstad 27), Solli, Ciljan Skjelbred (Winsnes 10), Braaten (Ødegaard 63), Johnsen F., Storflor.

Match 6 OLYMPIQUE LYONNAIS
A 1-2 *Braaten (68)*
Johnsen E., Basma, Lago, Kvarme, Dorsin, Winsnes, Riseth (Tettey 81), Johnsen F., Braaten, Helstad (Ødegaard 57), Storflor (Eguren 83).

VÅLERENGA FOTBALL

2nd qualifying round FC HAKA (FIN)
H 1-0 *Dos Santos (50p)*
Arason, Brocken, Muri, Waehler, Dos Santos, Ishizaki (Berre 46), Holm, Mabizela (Grindheim 46), Hoseth (Gashi 56), Fredheim Holm, Flo.
A 4-1 *Waehler (26), Flo (28, 74), Iversen (59)*
Arason, Brocken, Johnsen, Waehler, Dos Santos, Gashi, Holm (Ishizaki 70), Grindheim (Mabizela 68), Fredheim Holm, Iversen (Hulsker 62), Flo.

3rd qualifying round CLUB BRUGGE KV (BEL)
H 1-0 *Iversen (57)*
Arason, Brocken, Johnsen, Waehler, Dos Santos, Gashi, Skiri, Holm, Grindheim, Flo (Hoseth 74), Iversen.
A 0-1
(aet; 3-4 on pens)
Arason, Waehler, Johnsen, Muri, Dos Santos, Skiri, Berre (Matthisen 61), Grindheim, Gashi, Fredheim Holm (Hulsker 77), Iversen (Brocken 87).

UEFA CUP

SK BRANN

2nd qualifying round AC ALLIANSSI (FIN)

Norway

H 0-0
Opdal, Sigurdsson (Miller 46), Bjarnason, Soma, Hanstveit, Knudsen (Macallister 82), Haugen, Scharner, Walde (Helegbe 71), Saeternes, Winters.
A 2-0 *Ludvigsen (58), Miller (88)*
Opdal, Sigurdsson (Ludvigsen 46), Scharner, Soma, Knudsen, Sanne (Walde 85), Andresen, Haugen (Klock 89), Hanstveit, Miller, Winters.

1st round LOKOMOTIV MOSKVA (RUS)
H 1-2 *Winters (44)*
Opdal, Sigurdsson, Scharner (Klock 70), Soma, Hanstveit, Sanne (Helegbe 51), Andresen, Miller, Huseklepp, Walde (Haugen 76), Winters.
A 2-3 *Macallister (47), Miller (74)*
Opdal, Sigurdsson, Scharner, Soma, Hanstveit, Knudsen (Thorbjørnsen 31), Haugen, Miller, Sanne (Huseklepp 75), Macallister (Walde 84), Winters.

TROMSØ IL
2nd qualifying round ESBJERG FB (DEN)
A 1-0 *Strand (10)*
Hirschfeld, Hafstad, Kibebe, Pedersen, Szekeres, Bernier, Johansen B. (Johansen R. 53), Essediri (Nilsen 84), Strand, Yndestad (Normann 67), Årst.
H 0-1
(aet; 3-2 on pens)
Hirschfeld, Hafstad (Nilsen 43), Kibebe, Moen, Szekeres (Normann 46), Essediri, Bernier, Johansen R. (Ademolu 84), Yndestad, Strand, Årst.

1st round GALATASARAY (TUR)
H 1-0 *Szekeres (77)*
Hirschfeld, Hafstad (Nilsen 70), Kibebe, Pedersen, Szekeres, Bernier, Christensen, Strand (Johansen R. 83), Essediri, Årst, Ademolu (Walltin 65).
A 1-1 *Ademolu (32)*
Hirschfeld, Nilsen, Kibebe, Pedersen (Szekeres 10), Yndestad, Bernier, Christensen, Strand, Essediri (Johansen B. 50), Årst, Ademolu (Walltin 74).

2nd round Group E
Match 1 ROMA (ITA)
H 1-2 *Årst (42)*
Hirschfeld, Nilsen (Hafstad 81), Kibebe, Pedersen, Yndestad (Szekeres 83), Walltin, Johansen B., Bernier, Essediri, Årst, Strand (Ademolu 69).

Match 2 RC STRASBOURG (FRA)
A 0-2
Hirschfeld, Nilsen, Kibebe, Pedersen, Yndestad, Walltin (Hafstad 70), Johansen B. (Szekeres 81), Bernier, Essediri, Strand (Normann 46), Ademolu.

Match 3 CRVENA ZVEZDA BEOGRAD (SCG)
H 3-1 *Kibebe (22), Årst (37, 74p)*
Hirschfeld, Nilsen, Pedersen, Kibebe, Yndestad (Szekeres 64), Walltin (Johansen B. 84), Christensen, Bernier, Strand, Essediri, Årst, Ademolu (Walltin 72).

Match 4 FC BASEL (SUI)
A 3-4 *Strand (1, 29), Årst (19)*
Hirschfeld, Nilsen, Kibebe, Pedersen (Normann 44), Szekeres, Bernier, Christensen (Ademolu 76), Walltin (Johansen B. 66), Essediri, Årst, Strand.

VIKING FK
1st qualifying round PORTADOWN (NIR)
A 2-1 *Østenstad (53p), Kopteff (79)*
Basso, Dahl, Deila, Eike Hansen, Pereira, Gaarde, Paulsen Hangeland, Nygaard, Kopteff (Berland 80), Østenstad (Nhleko 71), Sigurdsson.
H 1-0 *Nhleko (57)*
Basso, Dahl, Deila, Eike Hansen (Mambo-Mumba 62), Pereira, Gaarde, Nygaard, Paulsen Hangeland, Kopteff (Sørli 77), Nhleko (Sigurdsson 70), Østenstad.

2nd qualifying round RHYL (WAL)
A 1-0 *Kopteff (11)*
Basso, Dahl (Sørli 74), Paulsen Hangeland, Eike Hansen, Pereira, Kopteff, Mambo-Mumba, Nygaard, Gaarde, Østenstad, Sigurdsson (Nhleko 64).
H 2-1 *Nhleko (8, 26)*
Basso, Dahl, Deila, Eike Hansen, Pereira, Sørli (Lundqvist 79), Grande (Mambo-Mumba 67), Paulsen Hangeland, Kopteff, Nhleko, Østenstad.

1st round FK AUSTRIA WIEN (AUT)
H 1-0 *Mambo-Mumba (71)*
Basso, Dahl, Deila, Eike Hansen, Pereira, Kopteff, Paulsen Hangeland, Nygaard, Gaarde, Nhleko, Østenstad (Mambo-Mumba 46).
A 1-2 *Nygaard (12)*
Basso, Dahl, Deila, Eike Hansen, Pereira, Kopteff, Paulsen Hangeland, Nygaard, Gaarde, Nhleko, Østenstad (Mambo-Mumba 87).

2nd round Group A
Match 1 AS MONACO FC (FRA)
H 1-0 *Nhleko (18)*
Basso, Tengesdal, Paulsen Hangeland, Eike Hansen, Pereira, Kopteff, Nygaard, Grande (Mambo-Mumba 73), Gaarde, Nhleko (Svenning 89), Østenstad.

Match 2 HAMBURGER SV (GER)
A 0-2
Basso, Dahl, Paulsen Hangeland, Eike Hansen, Svenning, Kopteff, Nygaard, Grande (Mambo-Mumba 66), Gaarde (Tengesdal 72), Nhleko (Åse Lunde 76), Østenstad.

Match 3 SK SLAVIA PRAHA (CZE)
H 2-2 *Nhleko (26), Gaarde (55)*
Austbø, Dahl, Paulsen Hangeland, Eike Hansen, Pereira, Tengesdal, Gaarde, Nygaard, Kopteff, Nhleko (Berland 77), Østenstad.

Match 4 CSKA SOFIA (BUL)
A 0-2
Basso, Dahl, Paulsen Hangeland, Eike Hansen (Gabrielsen 49), Pereira, Tengesdal (Mambo-Mumba 61), Nygaard (Bjarnason 78), Gaarde, Kopteff, Østenstad, Nhleko.

VÅLERENGA FOTBALL
1st round STEAUA BUCURESTI (ROM)
H 0-3
Bolthof, Driscoll, Skiri, Muri, Brocken (Fredheim Holm 75), El-Gharbi (Ishizaki 60), Mabizela, Strømnes (Holm 44), Stenersen, Hoseth, Flo.
A 1-3 *Hulsker (56)*
Bolthof, Muri, Skiri (Gashi 67), Strømnes, Brocken (Dos Santos 59), Mabizela, Hoseth, Stenersen, Ishizaki, Flo, Hulsker (Berre 80).

ROSENBORG BK
3rd round ZENIT SANKT-PETERBURG (RUS)
H 0-2
Johnsen E., Basma, Kvarme, Riseth, Dorsin, Strand, Solli (Stensaas 82), Tettey (Berg 46), Braaten, Johnsen F., Storflor (Kone 67).
A 1-2 *Riseth (45)*
Johnsen E., Basma, Kvarme, Riseth, Dorsin, Strand (Tettey 90), Berg, Solli, Braaten, Johnsen F., Storflor (Kone 78).

TOP GOALSCORERS 2005

16	Ole Martin ÅRST (Tromsø IL)
14	Egil ØSTENSTAD (Viking FK)
13	Thorstein HELSTAD (Rosenborg BK)
11	Arild SUNDGOT (Lillestrøm SK)
10	Rob FRIEND (Molde FK)
9	Bengt SAETERNES (SK Brann)
	Morten BERRE (Vålerenga Fotball)
8	Robbie WINTERS (SK Brann)
	Espen OLSEN (Ham-Kam Fotball)
	Robert KOREN (Lillestrøm SK)
	Jo TESSEM (FC Lyn Oslo)
	Olivier OCCEAN (Odd Grenland)
	Marius JOHNSEN (IK Start)

Norway

FINAL LEAGUE TABLE 2005

		Pld	Home W	D	L	F	A	Away W	D	L	F	A	Total W	D	L	F	A	Pts
1	Vålerenga Fotball	26	6	4	3	19	12	7	3	3	21	15	13	7	6	40	27	46
2	IK Start	26	9	2	2	35	18	4	4	5	12	17	13	6	7	47	35	45
3	FC Lyn Oslo	26	7	4	2	24	10	5	4	4	13	11	12	8	6	37	21	44
4	Lillestrøm SK	26	9	2	2	23	9	3	4	6	14	22	12	6	8	37	31	42
5	Viking FK	26	7	4	2	21	14	5	1	7	16	18	12	5	9	37	32	41
6	SK Brann	26	8	3	2	29	11	2	4	7	14	21	10	7	9	43	32	37
7	Rosenborg BK	26	5	3	5	26	14	5	1	7	24	28	10	4	12	50	42	34
8	Tromsø IL	26	5	5	3	15	11	3	5	5	16	19	8	10	8	31	30	34
9	Odd Grenland	26	6	4	3	16	18	3	2	8	12	33	9	6	11	28	51	33
10	Ham-Kam Fotball	26	7	3	3	21	16	1	4	8	10	21	8	7	11	31	37	31
11	Fredrikstad FK	26	5	4	4	24	24	3	3	7	11	20	8	7	11	35	44	31
12	Molde FK	26	6	3	4	24	17	2	3	8	16	29	8	6	12	40	46	30
13	Aalesunds FK	26	4	3	6	13	19	2	6	5	17	23	6	9	11	30	42	27
14	FK Bodø/Glimt	26	5	3	5	17	15	1	3	9	12	30	6	6	14	29	45	24

LEAGUE RESULTS/SCORERS/APPEARANCES/GOALS 2005

AALESUNDS FK
Coach – Ivar Morten Normark

2005				
10/4	Rosenborg BK	a	2-2	Hoseth, Johansen (p)
16/4	Odd Grenland	h	2-1	Olsen, Hoseth
24/4	Ham-Kam Fotball	a	1-2	Aarøy
2/5	SK Brann	h	1-3	Olsen
5/5	Vålerenga Fotball	a	1-3	Gudmundsson
8/5	Tromsø IL	h	0-1	
16/5	Molde FK	a	2-2	M'Baye, Moldskred
22/5	FK Bodø/Glimt	a	0-0	
29/5	Fredrikstad FK	h	1-0	Dos Santos
12/6	Lillestrøm SK	a	0-3	
19/6	IK Start	h	1-2	Olsen
26/6	FC Lyn Oslo	a	0-0	
3/7	Viking FK	h	1-2	Gudmundsson
24/7	Rosenborg BK	h	2-1	og (Lago), Gudmundsson
31/7	Odd Grenland	a	1-2	Olsen
3/8	Ham-Kam Fotball	h	1-1	Olsen (p)
7/8	SK Brann	a	0-0	
13/8	Vålerenga Fotball	h	0-2	
28/8	Tromsø IL	a	1-1	Hoseth
13/9	Molde FK	h	1-4	Aarøy
18/9	FK Bodø/Glimt	h	1-1	Oliveira
25/9	Fredrikstad FK	a	4-1	Oliveira, Olsen, Holm, Aarøy
2/10	Lillestrøm SK	h	1-0	Olsen
15/10	IK Start	a	5-4	Holm, Oliveira 2 (2p), Aarøy, Fredriksen
23/10	FC Lyn Oslo	h	1-1	Oliveira (p)
29/10	Viking FK	a	0-3	

No	Name	Nat	Pos	Aps	(s)	Gls
2	Marius AAM		D	6		
9	Tor Hogne AARØY		A	12	(8)	4
10	Joakim Rune AUSTNES		M	8	(2)	
15	Gustave BAHOKEN	CMR	D	12		
24	Adin BROWN	USA	G	20		
1	Kim Erik DEINOFF		G	6	(2)	
14	Paulo DOS SANTOS	CVD	M	10	(4)	1
4	Herman EKEBERG		D	17	(1)	
8	Frode FAGERMO		M	3	(8)	
18	Karl Oskar FJØRTOFT		M	14	(3)	
7	Trond FREDRIKSEN		M	23	(1)	1
3	Haraldur GUDMUNDSSON	ISL	D	19	(2)	3
5	Erlend HOLM		M	14	(5)	2
22	Eirik HOSETH		M	9	(10)	3
13	Rune JOHANSEN		A	6	(2)	1
25	Stian Dagfinn JOHNSEN		M	7	(3)	
26	Abdoulaye M'BAYE	SEN	A	5	(4)	1
16	Bjørn Erik MELLAND		D	15	(2)	
11	Morten MOLDSKRED		A	17	(7)	1
13	Bechara OLIVEIRA	BRA	M	5	(2)	5
17	Lasse OLSEN		A	18	(6)	7
21	Thomas PEDERSEN		M		(3)	
20	Christian STEEN		D	15		
6	Peter WERNI		D	25		
29	Eamon ZAYED	IRL	A		(1)	

FK BODØ/GLIMT
Coach – Ola Haldorsen

2005				
10/4	Viking FK	a	1-2	Johansen
17/4	Rosenborg BK	h	0-1	
24/4	Odd Grenland	a	1-2	Theting
1/5	Ham-Kam Fotball	h	2-0	Paulsen, Berg R.
5/5	SK Brann	a	3-2	Ludvigsen, Sakariassen 2 (1p)
8/5	Vålerenga Fotball	h	0-1	
16/5	Tromsø IL	a	2-2	Halvorsen, Berg R.
22/5	Aalesunds FK	h	0-0	
29/5	Molde FK	a	1-1	Berg R.
12/6	Fredrikstad FK	a	2-3	Ludvigsen, Berg R.
19/6	Lillestrøm SK	h	1-1	Berg R.
26/6	IK Start	a	0-2	
3/7	FC Lyn Oslo	h	1-3	Theting
24/7	Viking FK	h	0-3	

Norway

Date	Opponent	H/A	Score	Scorers
31/7	Rosenborg BK	a	0-2	
3/8	Odd Grenland	h	5-1	Johansen 4 (1p), Berg R.
7/8	Ham-Kam Fotball	a	0-2	
14/8	SK Brann	h	2-1	Brattbakk, Sakariassen
28/8	Vålerenga Fotball	a	1-3	Brattbakk
11/9	Tromsø IL	h	2-1	Brattbakk, Olsen
18/9	Aalesunds FK	a	1-1	Olsen
26/9	Molde FK	h	2-0	Brattbakk, Olsen
2/10	Fredrikstad FK	h	1-2	Brattbakk
17/10	Lillestrøm SK	a	0-2	
23/10	IK Start	h	1-1	Sakariassen
29/10	FC Lyn Oslo	a	0-6	

No	Name	Nat	Pos	Aps	(s)	Gls
18	Chrisian BERG		M	25		
7	Runar BERG		M	22		6
9	Aasmund BJØRKAN		A	6	(9)	
23	Harald Martin BRATTBAKK		A	11		5
19	Jan Egil BREKKE		D		(5)	
21	Randall BRENES	CRC	A		(7)	
14	Håvard HALVORSEN		D	22	(1)	1
4	Cato André HANSEN		D	5		
3	Erik HOFTUN		D	13		
1	Tor Egil HORN		G	20		
16	Tom HØGLI		M	15	(2)	
17	Ruben IMINGEN		D	1		
10	Stig JOHANSEN		A	13	(3)	5
22	Fredrik KJØLNER		D	24	(1)	
12	Jonas UELAND KOLSTAD		G	1		
25	Ole Arvid LANGNES		G	5		
23	Trond Fredrik LUDVIGSEN		A	11		2
5	Roy MILLER	CRC	D		(1)	
20	Trond OLSEN		A	18	(6)	3
24	Kristoffer PAULSEN		D	23		1
27	Stig Arild RÅKET		A	6	(7)	
8	Olav RÅSTAD		M	11	(4)	
11	Håvard SAKARIASSEN		A	16	(9)	4
2	Vegard SANNES		D	8	(3)	
21	Per-Ivar STEINBAKK		M		(1)	
6	Stian THETING		M	10	(6)	2

SK BRANN
Coach – Mons Ivar Mjelde

2005

Date	Opponent	H/A	Score	Scorers
11/4	Molde FK	h	2-0	Scharner, Winters
17/4	Vålerenga Fotball	a	1-2	Saeternes
25/4	Tromsø IL	h	0-0	
2/5	Aalesunds FK	a	3-1	Winters, og (Dos Santos), Saeternes
5/5	FK Bodø/Glimt	h	2-3	Scharner, Winters
9/5	Fredrikstad FK	a	3-2	Kvisvik, Saeternes 2
16/5	Lillestrøm SK	h	6-2	Soma, Saeternes 3, Kvisvik, og (Wehrmann)
22/5	IK Start	a	2-3	Scharner, Andresen
29/5	FC Lyn Oslo	h	3-0	Scharner, Kvisvik (p), Saeternes
13/6	Viking FK	a	0-0	
19/6	Rosenborg BK	h	4-1	Miller 3 (1p), Kvisvik
26/6	Odd Grenland	a	0-0	
3/7	Ham-Kam Fotball	h	2-0	Winters, Scharner
23/7	Molde FK	a	1-3	Winters
30/7	Vålerenga Fotball	h	1-2	Saeternes
3/8	Tromsø IL	a	1-1	Winters
7/8	Aalesunds FK	h	0-0	
14/8	FK Bodø/Glimt	a	1-2	Knudsen
29/8	Fredrikstad FK	h	4-0	Huseklepp, Macallister, Andresen (p), Scharner
11/9	Lillestrøm SK	a	0-1	
19/9	IK Start	h	1-0	Winters
25/9	FC Lyn Oslo	a	0-1	
3/10	Viking FK	h	2-1	Miller, Hanstveit
16/10	Rosenborg BK	a	1-4	Knudsen
23/10	Odd Grenland	h	2-2	Winters, Miller
29/10	Ham-Kam Fotball	a	1-1	Macallister

No	Name	Nat	Pos	Aps	(s)	Gls
8	Martin ANDRESEN		M	16	(1)	2
18	Ólafur Örn BJARNASON	ISL	D	17		
4	Cato GUNTVEIT		M	10	(1)	
15	Erlend HANSTVEIT		D	22		1
6	Helge HAUGEN		M	8	(7)	
22	Michael HELEGBE	GHA	M	1	(1)	
13	Erik HUSEKLEPP		M	8	(1)	1
17	Christian KALVENES		D	4	(2)	
28	Fredrik KLOCK		D	1	(2)	
5	Martin KNUDSEN		M	9	(11)	2
27	Raymond KVISVIK		M	13		4
20	Trond Fredrik LUDVIGSEN		M	1		
9	Dylan MACALLISTER	AUS	A	6	(10)	2
16	Charlie MILLER	SCO	M	21	(2)	5
29	Nicolay MISJE		M		(1)	
12	Håkon André OPDAL		G	24		
19	Tom SANNE		M	9	(7)	
25	Paul SCHARNER	AUT	M	25		6
21	Kristján Örn SIGURDSSON	ISL	D	20	(4)	
3	Ragnvald SOMA		D	26		1
26	Thor Jørgen SPURKELAND		A		(1)	
13	Erlend STORESUND		M		(1)	
10	Bengt SAETERNES		A	18		9
1	Johan THORBJØRNSEN		G	2		
14	Arve WALDE		A	2	(7)	
7	Robbie WINTERS	SCO	A	23	(3)	8

FREDRIKSTAD FK
Coach – Egil Olsen; (28/9/05) Egil Olsen & Knut Torbjørn Eggen

2005

Date	Opponent	H/A	Score	Scorers
10/4	FC Lyn Oslo	a	1-1	Risholt (p)
18/4	Viking FK	h	2-1	Hoås, Brenne
24/4	Rosenborg BK	a	1-2	Blixt (p)
1/5	Odd Grenland	h	1-1	Brenne
5/5	Ham-Kam Fotball	a	1-1	Wiig
9/5	SK Brann	h	2-3	Viikmäe, Wiig
16/5	Vålerenga Fotball	a	0-0	
23/5	Tromsø IL	h	4-2	Wiig, West, Brenne 2
29/5	Aalesunds FK	a	0-1	
12/6	FK Bodø/Glimt	h	3-2	Ringberg 2, Blixt (p)
19/6	Molde FK	a	1-2	og (Mavric)
26/6	Lillestrøm SK	a	0-3	
3/7	IK Start	h	1-2	Ringberg
24/7	FC Lyn Oslo	h	2-1	Brenne, Kvisvik
31/7	Viking FK	a	1-2	Brenne
3/8	Rosenborg BK	h	5-1	Enerly, Hoås, Piiroja, Kvisvik (p), Tóth
7/8	Odd Grenland	a	1-2	West
13/8	Ham-Kam Fotball	h	1-1	West
29/8	SK Brann	a	0-4	
13/9	Vålerenga Fotball	h	0-4	
18/9	Tromsø IL	a	0-2	
25/9	Aalesunds FK	h	1-4	Kvisvik
2/10	FK Bodø/Glimt	a	2-1	Bjørkøy, Enerly (p)
16/10	Molde FK	h	1-1	Wiig
23/10	Lillestrøm SK	h	1-1	Hoås
29/10	IK Start	a	3-1	Hoås, Ramberg, Wiig

No	Name	Nat	Pos	Aps	(s)	Gls
4	Trond Erik BERTELSEN		D	25		

Norway

No	Name	Nat	Pos	Aps	(s)	Gls
24	John Anders BJØRKØY		M	12		1
16	Lars BLIXT		D	16	(2)	2
7	Simen BRENNE		A	21		6
2	Pål André CZWARTEK		D	9	(3)	
21	Tarik ELYOUNOUSSI		A	1	(2)	
8	Dagfinn ENERLY		M	22		2
5	Roger HELLAND		D	15	(1)	
10	Øyvind HOÅS		A	21	(1)	4
13	Tero KOSKELA	FIN	M		(4)	
14	Raymond KVISVIK		M	12		3
18	Mathias LINDSTRÖM	FIN	D	2	(1)	
1	Alexander LUND HANSEN		G	6	(1)	
28	Yherland MACDONALD	CRC	M	2	(5)	
17	Jørgen MAGNUSSEN		D	1		
27	Thomas MYHRE		G	3		
6	Christian PETERSEN		M	2	(5)	
9	Raio PIIROJA	EST	D	11	(1)	1
15	Hans Erik RAMBERG		M	17	(5)	1
19	Markus RINGBERG	SWE	A	13		3
3	Roger RISHOLT		M	8		1
20	Michael RØN		M	5	(4)	
25	Steinar SØRLIE		G	17		
21	Mihály TÓTH	HUN	A		(7)	1
18	Tor TRONDSEN		D	1		
23	Kristen VIIKMÄE	EST	A	3	(3)	1
11	Brian WEST	USA	M	9	(10)	3
22	Martin WIIG		A	8	(15)	5
24	Borivoje ZIVKOVIC	DEN	D	24		

HAM-KAM FOTBALL
Coach – Ståle Solbakken

2005

10/4	Vålerenga Fotball	h	3-1		Frigård, Abiodun, Ståhl
17/4	Tromsø IL	a	0-1		
24/4	Aalesunds FK	h	2-1		Michaelsen (p), Abiodun
1/5	FK Bodø/Glimt	a	0-2		
5/5	Fredrikstad FK	h	1-1		Olsen
8/5	Lillestrøm SK	a	0-1		
16/5	IK Start	h	0-2		
22/5	FC Lyn Oslo	a	0-1		
29/5	Viking FK	h	0-0		
12/6	Rosenborg BK	a	0-4		
19/6	Odd Grenland	h	2-1		Storbaek, Vaagen Moen
26/6	Molde FK	h	4-1		Michaelsen 2 (1p), Dokken, Olsen
3/7	SK Brann	a	0-2		
23/7	Vålerenga Fotball	a	1-2		Thorup
31/7	Tromsø IL	h	3-2		Vaagen Moen, Olsen, Ringberg
3/8	Aalesunds FK	a	1-1		Olsen
7/8	FK Bodø/Glimt	h	2-0		Ringberg, Olsen
13/8	Fredrikstad FK	a	1-1		Olsen
28/8	Lillestrøm SK	h	2-3		Ringberg, Haug
11/9	IK Start	a	1-2		Michaelsen (p)
18/9	FC Lyn Oslo	h	1-0		Haug
25/9	Viking FK	a	3-1		Ringberg, Olsen, Michaelsen (p)
2/10	Rosenborg BK	h	0-3		
16/10	Odd Grenland	a	2-2		Olsen, Vaagen Moen
23/10	Molde FK	a	1-1		Haug
29/10	SK Brann	h	1-1		Bjerke

No	Name	Nat	Pos	Aps	(s)	Gls
9	Oluwasegun ABIODUN	NGA	A	11	(2)	2
12	Felix ADEMOLA	NGA	A		(3)	
7	Vegar BJERKE		M	10	(8)	1
23	Ramiro CORRALES	USA	D	17	(3)	
10	Kenneth DOKKEN		M	8	(13)	1
22	Geir FRIGÅRD		A	12	(7)	1
6	Marius GULLERUD		M	10	(4)	
12	Eddie GUSTAFSSON	SWE	G	26		
14	Knut Henry HARALDSEN		D	10		
20	Espen HAUG		M	25	(1)	3
21	Truls JEVNE HAGEN		M		(1)	
17	Hai LAM		D		(1)	
19	Jan MICHAELSEN	DEN	M	22	(1)	5
11	Espen OLSEN		A	21	(5)	8
12	Markus RINGBERG	SWE	A	13		4
3	Axel SMEETS	BEL	D	19	(1)	
13	Jarl-André STORBAEK		D	26		1
2	Glenn Leif STÅHL	SWE	D	4	(3)	1
8	Peter SØRENSEN	DEN	D	12	(1)	
24	Joachim SØRUM		D	17	(6)	
15	Jess THORUP	DEN	A		(11)	1
5	Petter VAAGAN MOEN		M	23		3

LILLESTRØM SK
Coach – Uwe Rösler (GER)

2005

10/4	IK Start	a	1-3		Kippe
17/4	FC Lyn Oslo	h	1-0		Mifsud
24/4	Viking FK	a	1-3		Koren
1/5	Rosenborg BK	h	1-1		Andresen
5/5	Odd Grenland	a	2-0		Sundgot, Myklebust
8/5	Ham-Kam Fotball	h	1-0		Sundgot
16/5	SK Brann	a	2-6		Mifsud, Koren
22/5	Vålerenga Fotball	h	2-1		Sundgot, Mifsud
29/5	Tromsø IL	a	1-1		Mifsud
12/6	Aalesunds FK	h	3-0		Mifsud, Sundgot 2
19/6	FK Bodø/Glimt	h	1-1		Sundgot
26/6	Fredrikstad FK	h	3-0		Andersson, Koren, Powell
3/7	Molde FK	a	0-2		
25/7	IK Start	h	2-0		Strand, Myklebust
30/7	FC Lyn Oslo	a	0-1		
3/8	Viking FK	h	2-0		Koren, Strand
7/8	Rosenborg BK	a	2-1		Mifsud, Sundgot
13/8	Odd Grenland	h	2-3		Koren, Sundgot
28/8	Ham-Kam Fotball	a	3-2		Koren, Sundgot (p), Myklebust
11/9	SK Brann	h	1-0		og (Soma)
18/9	Vålerenga Fotball	a	0-0		
24/9	Tromsø IL	h	1-2		Powell
2/10	Aalesunds FK	a	0-1		
16/10	FK Bodø/Glimt	h	2-0		Sundgot (p), Koren (p)
23/10	Fredrikstad FK	a	1-1		Sundgot
29/10	Molde FK	h	2-2		Koren, Strand

No	Name	Nat	Pos	Aps	(s)	Gls
5	Christoffer ANDERSSON	SWE	D	26		1
23	Pål Steffen ANDRESEN		D	24	(1)	1
16	Mato GRUBISIC		A		(1)	
24	Andreas HADDAD	SWE	A		(6)	
13	Frode KIPPE		D	17	(2)	1
25	Robert KOREN	SLO	M	26		8
19	Michael MIFSUD	MLT	A	14	(1)	6
20	Per Magne MISUND		G	2		
8	Khaled MOUELHI	TUN	M	4	(2)	
1	Heinz MÜLLER	GER	G	5		
11	Magnus MYKLEBUST		A	4	(15)	3
10	Magnus POWELL	SWE	A	12	(12)	2
14	Sasa RADULOVIC	BOS	M	5	(1)	
2	Anders RAMBEKK		D	21	(2)	
41	Claus REITMAIER	GER	G	19		
12	Bjørn Helge RIISE		M	9	(4)	
3	Shane STEFANUTTO	AUS	D	9	(3)	
6	Pål STRAND		M	16	(3)	2

Norway

18	Arild SUNDGOT		A	26	11
7	Espen SØGÅRD		M	25	
17	Kasey WEHRMAN	AUS	M	22	
9	Johan Petter WINSNES		M		(16)

FC LYN OSLO
Coach – Hans Knutsen & Kaz Sokolowski; (22/4/05) Henning Berg

2005

Date	Opponent		Score	Scorers
10/4	Fredrikstad FK	h	1-1	Larsen
17/4	Lillestrøm SK	a	0-1	
24/4	IK Start	h	1-1	Tessem
1/5	Molde FK	h	6-1	Leonhardsen, Obi Mikel, Sørensen, Larsen, Tessem 2 (1p)
5/5	Viking FK	a	0-0	
8/5	Rosenborg BK	h	3-2	Sørensen, Huusko, Gíslason
16/5	Odd Grenland	a	2-0	Sørensen, Tessem
22/5	Ham-Kam Fotball	h	1-0	Tessem (p)
29/5	SK Brann	a	0-3	
12/6	Vålerenga Fotball	h	1-1	Huusko
19/6	Tromsø IL	a	0-0	
26/6	Aalesunds FK	h	0-0	
3/7	FK Bodø/Glimt	a	3-1	Ingebretsen 2, Larsen
24/7	Fredrikstad FK	a	1-2	Sørensen
30/7	Lillestrøm SK	h	1-0	Theorin
3/8	IK Start	a	1-1	og (Håland)
7/8	Molde FK	a	3-1	Huusko 2, Tessem (p)
14/8	Viking FK	h	2-1	Tessem (p), Larsen
28/8	Rosenborg BK	a	1-0	Tessem
11/9	Odd Grenland	h	1-2	Sokolowski
18/9	Ham-Kam Fotball	a	0-1	
25/9	SK Brann	h	1-0	Ogbuke
2/10	Vålerenga Fotball	a	1-0	Sokolowski
16/10	Tromsø IL	h	0-1	
23/10	Aalesunds FK	a	1-1	Sørensen
29/10	FK Bodø/Glimt	h	6-0	og (Ueland Kolstad), Sokolowski, Larsen, Sørensen 2, Ingebretsen

No	Name	Nat	Pos	Aps	(s)	Gls
26	Ali AL-HABSI	OMN	G	25		
14	Ezekiel BALA	NGA	A		(1)	
22	Tommy BERNTSEN		D	24		
17	Christoffer DAHL		M	2	(6)	
3	Henrik DAHL	SWE	D	1	(2)	
23	Lars-Kristian ERIKSEN		D	17		
8	Stefán GÍSLASON	ISL	M	25		1
2	Mounir HAMOUD		M	13	(4)	
11	Keijo HUUSKO	FIN	A	2	(14)	4
18	Bjarne K. INGEBRETSEN		A	2	(10)	3
13	Kevin LARSEN		M	15	(5)	5
15	Øyvind LEONHARDSEN		M	14	(2)	1
5	Steven LÜSTÜ	DEN	D	25		
1	NUNO MARQUES	POR	G	1		
20	John OBI MIKEL	NGA	M	6		1
19	Chinedu Obasi OGBUKE	NGA	A	5		1
4	Kristian FLITTIE ONSTAD		D	20		
9	Enrique ORTIZ	ARG	D	6	(4)	
6	Leif Gunnar SMERUD		M	2	(3)	
7	Tomasz SOKOLOWSKI		M	20	(5)	3
10	Jan Derek SØRENSEN		A	22	(1)	7
21	Jo TESSEM		A	24	(2)	8
25	Daniel THEORIN	SWE	D	15	(2)	1
27	Mads TIMM	DEN	A		(1)	

MOLDE FK
Coach – Bo Johansson (SWE)

2005

Date	Opponent		Score	Scorers
11/4	SK Brann	a	0-2	
17/4	IK Start	h	0-1	
24/4	Vålerenga Fotball	h	1-3	Kihlberg
1/5	FC Lyn Oslo	a	1-6	Kihlberg
5/5	Tromsø IL	h	2-1	Ohr, Friend
8/5	Viking FK	a	3-2	Ohr, Kihlberg, Ørsal
16/5	Aalesunds FK	h	2-2	Kallio, Husøy
22/5	Rosenborg BK	a	1-1	Friend
29/5	FK Bodø/Glimt	h	1-1	Friend
12/6	Odd Grenland	a	1-2	Kallio
19/6	Fredrikstad FK	h	2-1	Friend, Mavric (p)
26/6	Ham-Kam Fotball	a	1-4	Friend
3/7	Lillestrøm SK	h	2-0	Mavric (p), Konate
23/7	SK Brann	h	3-1	Ohr, Rudi, Kallio
31/7	IK Start	a	0-1	
7/8	FC Lyn Oslo	h	1-3	Mork
13/8	Tromsø IL	a	1-2	Ohr
28/8	Viking FK	h	1-2	Ohr
10/9	Vålerenga Fotball	a	1-3	Ohr
13/9	Aalesunds FK	a	4-1	Eide Møster, Strande, Ohr, Konate
17/9	Rosenborg BK	h	4-1	Berg Hestad, Mavric (p), Friend, Rudi
26/9	FK Bodø/Glimt	a	0-2	
2/10	Odd Grenland	a	4-0	Andreasson, Friend 2, Rudi (p)
16/10	Fredrikstad FK	a	1-1	Berg Hestad
23/10	Ham-Kam Fotball	h	1-1	Berg Hestad
29/10	Lillestrøm SK	a	2-2	Friend 2

No	Name	Nat	Pos	Aps	(s)	Gls
3	Marcus ANDREASSON	SWE	D	25		1
6	Daniel BERG HESTAD		M	14		3
25	Mitja BRULC	SLO	A		(1)	
9	Rob FRIEND	CAN	A	25		10
5	Øyvind GJERDE		D	10	(3)	
14	John Andreas HUSØY		M	13	(4)	1
2	Martin HØYEM		D	1	(2)	
4	Toni KALLIO	FIN	D	18	(4)	3
11	Magnus KIHLBERG	SWE	M	25		3
26	Madio KONATE	SEN	A		(8)	2
1	Knut DØRUM LILLEBAKK		G	11		
24	Matej MAVRIC	SLO	D	22	(2)	3
22	Lars Ivar MOLDSKRED		G	15		
7	Thomas MORK		M	13	(1)	1
18	Tommy EIDE MØSTER		A	12	(8)	1
21	Johan NÅS		A		(1)	
10	Stian OHR		A	23	(2)	7
16	Erlend ORMBOSTAD		D	1	(1)	
23	Torgeir RUUD RAMSLI		M		(2)	
19	Knut Olav RINDARØY		M	1	(3)	
15	Petter RUDI		M	16		3
20	Kai RØBERG		M	4	(7)	
33	Petter Christian SINGSAAS		D	5	(1)	
17	Trond STRANDE		D	23		1
8	Dag Roar ØRSAL		A	9	(6)	1

ODD GRENLAND
Coach – Arne Sandstø

2005

Date	Opponent		Score	Scorers
10/4	Tromsø IL	h	1-1	Flindt Bjerg (p)
16/4	Aalesunds FK	a	1-2	Occean
24/4	FK Bodø/Glimt	h	2-1	Hoff 2
1/5	Fredrikstad FK	a	1-1	Nornes
5/5	Lillestrøm SK	h	0-2	
8/5	IK Start	a	0-4	

Norway

16/5	FC Lyn Oslo	h	0-2		
22/5	Viking FK	a	0-1		
29/5	Rosenborg BK	h	0-5		
12/6	Molde FK	h	2-1	Nilsson, De Ornelas	
19/6	Ham-Kam Fotball	a	1-2	De Ornelas	
26/6	SK Brann	h	0-0		
4/7	Vålerenga Fotball	a	0-3		
24/7	Tromsø IL	a	1-0	Occean	
31/7	Aalesunds FK	h	2-1	Occean, Suffo	
3/8	FK Bodø/Glimt	a	1-5	De Ornelas	
7/8	Fredrikstad FK	h	2-1	Fevang, De Ornelas	
13/8	Lillestrøm SK	a	3-2	Suffo, Occean 2	
28/8	IK Start	h	2-0	De Ornelas, Occean	
11/9	FC Lyn Oslo	a	2-1	Suffo, Tchoyi	
18/9	Viking FK	h	1-0	Occean	
25/9	Rosenborg BK	a	0-6		
2/10	Molde FK	a	0-4		
16/10	Ham-Kam Fotball	h	2-2	Suffo, Henriksson	
23/10	SK Brann	a	2-2	Occean, Ruud	
29/10	Vålerenga Fotball	h	2-2	Svindal Larsen, Dale	

No	Name	Nat	Pos	Aps	(s)	Gls
16	Jan Tore AMUNDSEN		M	22	(2)	
22	Kim SJØBERG BENTSEN		D		(3)	
23	Brede BOMHOFF		D	1	(1)	
20	Tarjei DALE		M	3	(8)	1
2	Fernando DE ORNELAS	VEN	A	13	(7)	5
6	Morten FEVANG		M	19		1
7	Christian FLINDT BJERG	DEN	A	13	(2)	1
15	Torjus HANSÉN		D	22	(1)	
9	Sebastian HENRIKSSON	SWE	A	2	(9)	1
25	Espen HOFF		A	24		2
1	Erik HOLTAN		G	11	(1)	
12	Rune ALMENNING JARSTEIN		G	15	(1)	
8	Bent Inge JOHNSEN		D	9		
11	Morten KNUTSEN		A	3	(2)	
	Magnus LEKVEN		A		(1)	
25	Erik MIDTGARDEN		A		(3)	
3	Per NILSSON	SWE	D	22		1
17	Jan Frode NORNES		D	22	(1)	1
10	Olivier OCCEAN	CAN	A	22		8
18	Espen RUUD		D	15	(6)	1
23	Patrick SUFFO	CMR	A	11		4
24	Tommy SVINDAL LARSEN		M	11		1
4	Somen A. TCHOYI	CMR	M	18	(4)	1
5	Trond Viggo TORESEN		M	8	(7)	

ROSENBORG BK
Coach – Per Joar Hansen; (8/8/05) Per-Mathias Høgmo

2005

10/4	Aalesunds FK	h	2-2	Strand, Helstad
17/4	FK Bodø/Glimt	a	1-0	og (Råstad)
24/4	Fredrikstad FK	h	0-1	
1/5	Lillestrøm SK	a	1-1	Ødegaard
5/5	IK Start	h	3-0	Strand, Helstad 2 (1p)
8/5	FC Lyn Oslo	a	2-3	Dorsin, Johnsen F.
16/5	Viking FK	h	0-2	
22/5	Molde FK	h	1-1	Strand
29/5	Odd Grenland	a	5-0	Johnsen F., Storflor, Helstad 2, Brattbakk (p)
12/6	Ham-Kam Fotball	h	4-0	Ciljan Skjelbred 2, Hoftun, Brattbakk
19/6	SK Brann	a	1-4	Storflor
27/6	Vålerenga Fotball	h	2-3	Helstad, Winsnes
3/7	Tromsø IL	a	2-1	Helstad, Ødegaard
24/7	Aalesunds FK	a	1-2	Helstad
31/7	FK Bodø/Glimt	h	2-0	Johnsen F., Helstad
3/8	Fredrikstad FK	a	1-5	Johnsen F.
7/8	Lillestrøm SK	h	1-2	Ødegaard
13/8	IK Start	a	2-5	Storflor 2
28/8	FC Lyn Oslo	h	0-1	
10/9	Viking FK	a	2-3	Helstad 2
17/9	Molde FK	a	1-4	Stensaas
25/9	Odd Grenland	h	6-0	Riseth (p), og (Ruud), Braaten, Storflor, Ødegaard, Strand
2/10	Ham-Kam Fotball	a	3-0	Helstad, Riseth 2 (1p)
16/10	SK Brann	h	4-1	Helstad, Ciljan Skjelbred, Johnsen F. 2
23/10	Vålerenga Fotball	a	2-0	og (Holm), Johnsen F.
29/10	Tromsø IL	h	1-1	Braaten

No	Name	Nat	Pos	Aps	(s)	Gls
5	Ole Christer BASMA		D	19	(2)	
7	Ørjan BERG		M	12		
25	Daniel BRAATEN		A	13	(6)	2
22	Harald Martin BRATTBAKK		A	1	(8)	2
33	Mikael DORSIN	SWE	D	20	(1)	1
14	Sebastian EGUREN	URU	M	5	(3)	
20	Thorstein HELSTAD		A	19	(6)	13
3	Erik HOFTUN		D	8	(2)	1
1	Espen JOHNSEN		G	21		
9	Frode JOHNSEN		A	21	(2)	7
2	Miika KOPPINEN	FIN	D	6	(1)	
26	Bjørn Tore KVARME		D	10	(1)	
18	Alejandro LAGO	URU	D	7	(1)	
10	Vidar RISETH		D	20	(1)	3
8	Robbie RUSSELL	USA	D		(2)	
30	Ivar RØNNINGEN		G	5	(1)	
15	Per CILJAN SKJELBRED		A	9	(4)	3
11	Jan Gunnar SOLLI		M	24	(1)	
21	Ståle STENSAAS		D	10	(3)	1
17	Øyvind STORFLOR		A	15	(5)	5
6	Roar STRAND		M	23		4
19	Alexander TETTEY		M		(2)	
4	Fredrik WINSNES		M	11	(10)	1
13	Alexander ØDEGAARD		A	7	(10)	4

IK START
Coach – Tom Nordlie

2005

10/4	Lillestrøm SK	h	3-1	Borgersen, og (Wehrman), Hardarson
17/4	Molde FK	a	1-0	Garba
24/4	FC Lyn Oslo	a	1-1	Borgersen
1/5	Viking FK	h	5-2	Strømstad, Johnsen 2, Bärlin, Valencia
5/5	Rosenborg BK	a	0-0	
8/5	Odd Grenland	h	4-0	Valencia, Bärlin 2, Haestad
16/5	Ham-Kam Fotball	a	2-0	Valencia, Bärlin
22/5	SK Brann	h	3-2	Johnsen, Pedersen, Midttun Lie
30/5	Vålerenga Fotball	a	1-1	Johnsen
12/6	Tromsø IL	h	1-1	Garba
19/6	Aalesunds FK	a	2-1	Wright, Risholt
26/6	FK Bodø/Glimt	h	2-0	Johnsen, Borgersen
3/7	Fredrikstad FK	a	2-1	Johnsen 2
25/7	Lillestrøm SK	a	0-2	
31/7	Molde FK	h	1-0	Pedersen
3/8	FC Lyn Oslo	h	1-1	Jónsson
8/8	Viking FK	a	1-1	Haestad
13/8	Rosenborg BK	h	5-2	Haestad, Jónsson 3, Pedersen
28/8	Odd Grenland	a	0-2	

Norway

11/9	Ham-Kam Fotball	h	2-1	Bärlin, Strømstad	
19/9	SK Brann	a	0-1		
25/9	Vålerenga Fotball	h	3-0	Valencia, og (Skiri), Strømstad	
2/10	Tromsø IL	a	1-3	Johnsen	
15/10	Aalesunds FK	h	4-5	Valencia 2, Borgersen, Strømstad	
23/10	FK Bodø/Glimt	a	1-1	Bärlin	
29/10	Fredrikstad FK	h	1-3	Bärlin	

No	Name	Nat	Pos	Aps	(s)	Gls
28	Bjarte LUNDE AARSHEIM		M	10	(1)	
2	Glenn ANDERSEN		D	1	(8)	
16	Stefan BÄRLIN	SWE	A	10	(14)	7
5	Tom BERHUS		M	4	(7)	
20	Bård BORGERSEN		D	20	(1)	4
17	Lars Martin ENGEDAL		D	8	(3)	
14	Bala Ahmed GARBA	NGA	A	11	(6)	2
6	Jóhannes HARDARSON	ISL	M	17	(3)	1
23	Kristofer HAESTAD		M	23		3
10	Atle Roar HÅLAND		D	24		
15	Marius JOHNSEN		D	25		8
29	Todi JÓNSSON	FAR	A	9	(4)	4
26	Jesper MATHISEN		A		(2)	
18	Jon MIDTTUN LIE		A	21	(3)	1
1	Rune NILSSEN		G	26		
3	Alex NYARKO	GHA	M		(3)	
4	Steinar PEDERSEN		D	26		3
19	Kai RISHOLT		A		(3)	1
7	Fredrik STRØMSTAD		M	24		4
8	Alex VALENCIA		A	26		6
9	Ben WRIGHT	ENG	A	1	(8)	1

TROMSØ IL
Coach – Otto Ulseth; (2/8/05) Steinar Nilsen

2005

10/4	Odd Grenland	a	1-1	Essediri
17/4	Ham-Kam Fotball	h	1-0	Pedersen
25/4	SK Brann	a	0-0	
1/5	Vålerenga Fotball	a	0-1	
5/5	Molde FK	a	1-2	Årst
8/5	Aalesunds FK	a	1-0	Strand
16/5	FK Bodø/Glimt	h	2-2	Årst 2
23/5	Fredrikstad FK	a	2-4	Årst, Yndestad
29/5	Lillestrøm SK	h	1-1	Yndestad
12/6	IK Start	a	1-1	Strand
19/6	FC Lyn Oslo	h	0-0	
27/6	Viking FK	a	2-3	Strand, Årst
3/7	Rosenborg BK	h	1-2	Årst
24/7	Odd Grenland	h	0-1	
31/7	Ham-Kam Fotball	a	2-3	Årst 2
3/8	SK Brann	h	1-1	Årst
6/8	Vålerenga Fotball	a	1-1	Johnsen B.
13/8	Molde FK	h	2-1	Kibebe, Årst
28/8	Aalesunds FK	h	1-1	Årst (p)
11/9	FK Bodø/Glimt	a	1-2	Szekeres
18/9	Fredrikstad FK	h	2-0	Årst 2 (1p)
24/9	Lillestrøm SK	a	2-1	Strand, Christensen
2/10	IK Start	h	3-1	Årst 3
16/10	FC Lyn Oslo	a	1-0	Kibebe
23/10	Viking FK	h	1-0	og (Eike Hansen)
29/10	Rosenborg BK	a	1-1	Ademolu

No	Name	Nat	Pos	Aps	(s)	Gls
14	Stephen ADEMOLU	CAN	A	9	(3)	1
23	Bo ANDERSEN	DEN	G	9		
9	Patrice BERNIER	CAN	M	24		
1	Knut BORCH		G	6		
21	Roar CHRISTENSEN		M	8	(2)	1
22	Karim ESSEDIRI	TUN	M	18	(3)	1
8	Thomas HAFSTAD		D	11	(4)	
7	Janne HIETANEN	FIN	D	2	(9)	
23	Lars HIRSCHFELD	CAN	G	11		
17	Bjørn JOHANSEN		M	19	(3)	1
10	Jonas JOHANSEN		M	1	(9)	
19	Rune JOHANSEN		A	2	(6)	
4	Benjamin KIBEBE	SWE	D	24	(1)	2
14	Kim LARSEN		A		(5)	
5	Arne Vidar MOEN		D	16	(1)	
20	Ole Andreas NILSEN		D	16	(3)	
32	Runar NORMANN		M	1	(5)	
6	Morten PEDERSEN		D	17	(1)	1
11	Bjørn STORM		A		(1)	
18	Lars Iver STRAND		A	23	(1)	4
15	Tamás SZEKERES	HUN	D	11		1
12	Eirik SØRENSEN		G		(1)	
2	Daniel TORRES	CRC	D	7	(5)	
30	Joachim WALLTIN		M	3	(7)	
16	Hans Åge YNDESTAD		M	22	(2)	2
25	Ole Martin ÅRST		A	26		16

VIKING FK
Coach – Roy Hodgson (ENG)

2005

10/4	FK Bodø/Glimt	h	2-1	Østenstad, Kovács
18/4	Fredrikstad FK	a	1-2	Mambo-Mumba
24/4	Lillestrøm SK	h	3-1	Mambo-Mumba, Østenstad 2 (1p)
1/5	IK Start	a	2-5	Kovács, Østenstad
5/5	FC Lyn Oslo	h	0-0	
8/5	Molde FK	h	2-3	Mambo-Mumba, Kopteff
16/5	Rosenborg BK	a	2-0	Østenstad, Kopteff
22/5	Odd Grenland	h	1-0	Kovács
29/5	Ham-Kam Fotball	a	0-0	
13/6	SK Brann	h	0-0	
18/6	Vålerenga Fotball	a	2-1	Østenstad, Sigurdsson
27/6	Tromsø IL	h	3-2	Sigurdsson 2, Nygaard
3/7	Aalesunds FK	a	2-1	Nygaard, Gaarde
24/7	FK Bodø/Glimt	a	3-0	Nhleko, Østenstad, Kopteff
31/7	Fredrikstad FK	h	2-1	Østenstad 2
3/8	Lillestrøm SK	a	0-2	
8/8	IK Start	h	1-1	Gaarde
14/8	FC Lyn Oslo	a	1-2	Nhleko
28/8	Molde FK	a	2-1	Nhleko, Østenstad
10/9	Rosenborg BK	h	3-2	Østenstad, Gaarde, Nhleko
18/9	Odd Grenland	a	0-1	
25/9	Ham-Kam Fotball	h	1-3	Østenstad (p)
3/10	SK Brann	a	1-2	Østenstad
16/10	Vålerenga Fotball	h	0-0	
23/10	Tromsø IL	a	0-1	
29/10	Aalesunds FK	h	3-0	Gaarde, Mambo-Mumba, Østenstad

No	Name	Nat	Pos	Aps	(s)	Gls
6	Bjarte LUNDE AARSHEIM		M	3	(1)	
22	Iven AUSTBØ		G	1	(2)	
32	Anthony BASSO	FRA	G	25		
8	Bjørn BERLAND		A		(4)	
21	Allan BORGVARDT	DEN	A	1	(6)	
3	Bjørn DAHL		D	24		
13	André DANIELSEN		M	2		
4	Ronny DEILA		D	22	(1)	
28	Allan GAARDE	DEN	M	12	(1)	4
14	Sandro GRANDE	CAN	M	3	(3)	

Norway

15	Brede PAULSEN HANGELAND		M	26			
20	Frode EIKE HANSEN		D	26			
11	Peter KOPTEFF	FIN	M	25	(1)	3	
9	Péter KOVÁCS	HUN	A	6	(3)	3	
24	Trygve ÅSE LUNDE		M	1	(1)		
13	Fredrik LUNDQVIST	SWE	D	1			
23	Robert MAMBO-MUMBA	KEN	M	6	(7)	4	
27	Nkosinathi NHLEKO	RSA	A	11	(1)	4	
19	Trygve NYGAARD		M	19	(4)	2	
5	Thomas PEREIRA		D	24			
14	Jone SAMUELSEN		M		(1)		
21	Hannes SIGURDSSON	ISL	A	9	(5)	3	
29	Øyvind SVENNING		D	1	(3)		
17	Kristian SØRLI		M	2	(6)		
16	Jørgen TENGESDAL		D	11	(4)		
10	Egil ØSTENSTAD		A	25		14	

VÅLERENGA FOTBALL
Coach – Kjetil Rekdal

2005

Date	Opponent	h/a	Score	Scorers
10/4	Ham-Kam Fotball	a	1-3	Berre
17/4	SK Brann	h	2-1	Berre 2
24/4	Molde FK	a	3-1	Berre, Fredheim Holm, Johnsen
1/5	Tromsø IL	a	1-0	Berre
5/5	Aalesunds FK	h	3-1	Iversen (p), Berre, Ishizaki
8/5	FK Bodø/Glimt	a	1-0	Iversen
16/5	Fredrikstad FK	h	0-0	
22/5	Lillestrøm SK	a	1-2	Iversen
30/5	IK Start	h	1-1	Berre
12/6	FC Lyn Oslo	a	1-1	Grindheim
18/6	Viking FK	h	1-2	Iversen
27/6	Rosenborg BK	a	3-2	Berre 2, Gashi
4/7	Odd Grenland	h	3-0	og (De Ornelas), Gashi, Iversen (p)
23/7	Ham-Kam Fotball	h	2-1	Iversen, Ishizaki
30/7	SK Brann	a	2-1	Iversen (p), Dos Santos
6/8	Tromsø IL	h	1-1	Brocken
13/8	Aalesunds FK	a	2-0	Hoseth, Mathisen
28/8	FK Bodø/Glimt	h	3-1	Gashi, Waehler, Muri
10/9	Molde FK	h	3-1	Grindheim, Brocken, Gashi
13/9	Fredrikstad FK	a	4-0	og (Lund Hansen), Gashi, Fredheim Holm 2
18/9	Lillestrøm SK	h	0-0	
25/9	IK Start	a	0-3	
2/10	FC Lyn Oslo	h	0-1	
16/10	Viking FK	a	0-0	
23/10	Rosenborg BK	h	0-2	
29/10	Odd Grenland	a	2-2	Fredheim Holm, Muri

No	Name	Nat	Pos	Aps	(s)	Gls
1	Arni Gautur ARASON	ISL	G	26		
11	Morten BERRE		M	24	(1)	9
3	David BROCKEN	BEL	D	15	(1)	2
6	Freddy DOS SANTOS		D	15	(5)	1
23	Tore André FLO		A	2	(6)	
9	Ardian GASHI		M	19	(3)	5
19	Christian GRINDHEIM		M	23	(1)	2
4	Thomas HOLM		M	17	(4)	
7	Daniel FREDHEIM HOLM		A	19	(5)	4
8	Magne HOSETH		M	10	(2)	1
21	Tom Henning HOVI		D	14		
14	Bernt Nikolai HULSKER		A	7	(6)	
16	Steffen IVERSEN		A	19	(2)	7
10	Stefan ISHIZAKI	SWE	M	8	(6)	2
22	Ronny JOHNSEN		D	17	(6)	1
20	Mbulelo MABIZELA	RSA	M	1	(5)	

15	Alexander MATHISEN		A		(4)	1	
5	André MURI		D	19	(6)	2	
2	Amund ROBERTSON SKIRI		M	11	(6)		
18	Tommy STENERSEN		D		(2)		
24	Kjetil WAEHLER		D	20	(1)	1	

DOMESTIC CUP 2005

FIRST ROUND

(7/5/05)
Gneist IL 0, SK Brann 5
(10/5/05)
Orkla FK 0, Rosenborg BK 11
Tromsdalen UIL 3, FK Mjølner 0
(11/5/05)
Hadeland Fotball 2, Vålerenga Fotball 10
Dahle IL 0, Molde FK 8
Elverum Fotball 0, Ham-Kam Fotball 7
FK Fauske/Sprint 2, FK Bodø/Glimt 4
Hareid IL 0, Aalesunds FK 4
Lyngdal IL 1, IK Start 2
Klemetsrud IL 1, FC Lyn Oslo 3
Ishavsbyen FK 0, Tromsø IL 4
Gresvik IF 1, Fredrikstad FK 3
Vaulen IL 1, Viking FK 2
Sander IL 0, Lillestrøm SK 1
Langesund/Stathelle FK 0, Odd Grenland 4
FK Toten 0, Kongsvinger IL 10
IL Høyang 0, Sogndal IL Fotball 10
Fossum IF 0, Stbaek Fotball 7
Korsvoll IL 0, Follo Fotball 6
Råde IL 1, Moss FK 2
FK Voss 0, Bryne FK 2
Stryn TIL 2, IL Hødd Fotball 4
IL Runar 1, Sandefjord Fotball 3
Flint IL 0, FK Tønsberg 4
Jevnaker IF 0, Strømsgodset IF 4
Mjøndalen IF 1, Hønefoss BK 2 *(aet)*
Bossekop UL 1, Alta IF 2
Vindbjart 1, Mandalskameratene 3
FK Jerv 1, Pors Grenland IF 2 *(aet)*
IL Trio 0, Løv-Ham Fotball 1
Bygdø BK 0, Skeid 1
Baerum SK 5, SK Gjøvik-Lyn 1
Drobak/Frogn IL 5, Eidsvold IF 0
Eidsvold Turn 2, Ringsaker IF 1
Nybergsund IL 14, Grue IL 2
Notodden FK 9, KFUM Oslo 0
Innstrandens IL 2, Mo IL 2 *(aet)*
TIL Hovding 2, Fana Fotball 1
Levanger FK 7, Rissa IL 0
Frigg Oslo FK 2, Tollnes IL 1 *(aet)*
Strømmen IF 5, SK Sprint/Jeløy 2 *(aet)*
Lyngen/Karnes IL 4, Harstad IL 3 *(aet)*
Flekkeroy IL 4, Egersunds IK 0
Brumunddal 0, Grouradalen BK 5
Vard Haugesund 5, Randaberg 1
Fram Larvik 2, Larvik Turn IF 2 *(aet)*
Klepp IL 3, Ålgård FK 2
Kolstad Fotball 3, SK Traeff 2
Rørvik IL 2, Strindheim IL 3
FK Ørn-Horten 0, FK Oslo Øst 5
Åsane Fotball 1, Fyllingen 4
Raufoss Fotball 4, Asker Fotball 0
Kvik Halden FK 1, Kjelsås 2
Verdal IL 1, Steinkjer FK 1 *(aet; 6-5 on pens)*
Kopervik IL 0, FK Haugesund 1
Sandnes Ulf 1, FK Vidar 0 *(aet)*

Norway

Ranheim 1, NTNUI Gløshaugen 0
Stord/Moster FK 1, Askøy FK 0
Byåsen Toppfotball 1, IL Averøykameratene 1 (aet; 5-3 on pens)
Radøy/Manger FK 2, Jotun Årdalstangen FK 0
Ullensaker/Kisa IL 0, Sarpsborg FK 2
FK Lofoten 1, FK Skarp 1 (aet ; 4-2 on pens)
Sparta Sarpsborg 2, Lørenskog 1
Mercantile 1, FF Lillehammer 2

SECOND ROUND
(18/5/05)
Ranheim Fotball 1, FK Bodø/Glimt 4
Tromsdalen UIL 1, Tromsø IL 3
Drøbak/Frogn 0, Odd Grenland 5
Fram Larvik 1, IK Start 2
Levanger FK 0, Aalesunds FK 2
Sarpsborg FK 0, Vålerenga Fotball 4
Bryne FK 4, Sandnes Ulf 0
Nybergsund IL 3, Skeid 2 *(aet)*
Kjelsås Fotball 0, Hønefoss BK 2
Lyngen/Karnes IL 1, Alta IF 2
Mo IL 2, Byåsen Toppfotball 6
Strindheim IL 4, FK Lofoten 2
FK Tønsberg 4, Notodden FK 1
Moss FK 2, Raufoss Fotball 1
Sandefjord Fotball 2, Sparta Sarpsborg 1
Stord/Moster FK 0, Løv-Ham 1 *(aet)*
Haugesund 0, Vard Haugesund 1
(19/5/05)
Verdal IL 0, Rosenborg BK 7
Groruddalen BK 1, Fredrikstad FK 5
FF Lillehammer 0, Ham-Kam Fotball 4
Radøy/Manger FK 1, SK Brann 3
Klepp IL 2, Viking FK 4
Eidsvold Turn 1, FC Lyn Oslo 2
Strømmen IF 1, Lillestrøm SK 3
Kolstad Fotball 1, Molde FK 2
Fyllingen Fotball 3, Sogndal IL Fotball 5 *(aet)*
Pors Grenland IF 2, Frigg Oslo FK 0
Stabaek Fotball 6, Baerum SK 2
IL Hødd Fotball 5, TIL Hovding 1
Flekkerøy 0, Mandalskameratene 2
Follo Fotball 0, Strømsgodset IF 1
FK Oslo Øst 2, Kongsvinger IL 1 *(aet)*

THIRD ROUND
(15/6/05)
Aalesunds FK 3, IL Hødd Fotball 1
FK Bodø/Glimt 4, Strindheim IL 3 *(aet)*
Fredrikstad FK 2, Sandefjord Fotball 0
Sogndal IL Fotball 0, Ham-Kam Fotball 1
Lillestrøm SK 5, Moss FK 3 *(aet)*
Hønefoss BK 2, FC Lyn Oslo 1
Molde FK 3, Nybergsund IL 2
Odd Grenland 1, Pors Grenland IF 0
Byåsen Toppfotball 1, Rosenborg BK 8
IK Start 2, FK Mandalskameratene 1
Alta IF 2, Tromsø IL 1 *(aet)*
Vålerenga Fotball 7, FK Oslo Øst 0
Bryne FK 5, FK Tønsberg 1
Strømsgodset IF 0, Stabaek Fotball 1
(16/6/05)
Løv-Ham Fotball 0, SK Brann 1
(22/6/05)
SK Vard Haugesund 0, Viking FK 3

FOURTH ROUND
(29/6/05)
FK Bodø/Glimt 1, Molde FK 2
SK Brann 3, Aalesunds FK 2

Ham-Kam Fotball 2, Bryne FK 0
Odd Grenland 6, Alta IF 0
Stabaek Fotball 4, Fredrikstad FK 2
(30/6/05)
Rosenborg BK 1, Hønefoss BK 2
IK Start 2, Vålerenga Fotball 3 *(aet)*
Viking FK 0, Lillestrøm SK 2

QUARTER-FINALS
(20/8/05)
Molde FK 2 *(Ohr 31, 69)*, Odd Grenland 1 *(Occean 18)*
Vålerenga Fotball 2 *(Hulsker 15, 24)*, SK Brann 1 *(Miller 61)*
(21/8/05)
Hønefoss BK 4 *(Øverby 9p, Koskela 17, Lafton 81, Saaliti 90)*, Ham-Kam Fotball 0
Lillestrøm SK 3 *(Rambekk 33, Powell 54, 75)*, Stabaek Fotball 1 *(Poljac 88)*

SEMI-FINALS
(21/9/05)
Lillestrøm SK 2 *(Andresen 6, Sundgot 78)*, Vålerenga Fotball 0
(22/9/05)
Molde FK 1 *(Berg Hestad 74)*, Hønefoss BK 0

FINAL
(6/11/05)
Ullevaal stadion, Oslo
MOLDE FK 4 *(Friend 25, Konate 65, Berg Hestad 94, Husøy 108)*
LILLESTRØM SK 2 *(Mouelhi 46, Sundgot 90p)*
(aet)
Referee – Sandmoen
MOLDE FK – Lillebakk, Strande (Mavric 85), Andreasson, Singsaas, Gjerde (Kallio 70), Ohr, Berg Hestad, Kihlberg, Rudi, Konate (Husøy 81), Friend.
LILLESTRØM SK – Reitmaier, Andersson (Rambekk 86), Kippe, Andresen, Strand, Riise, Søgård (Haddad 70), Koren, Mouelhi, Powell (Myklebust 110), Sundgot.

SECOND LEVEL FINAL TABLE 2005

		Pld	W	D	L	F	A	Pts
1	Stabaek Fotball	30	20	7	3	63	23	67
2	Sandefjord Fotball	30	19	5	6	58	37	62
3	Moss FK	30	17	7	6	54	30	58
4	Hønefoss BK	30	17	5	8	52	41	56
5	Bryne FK	30	14	8	8	55	33	50
6	Pors Grenland	30	13	11	6	47	45	50
7	Sogndal IL Fotball	30	11	8	11	47	51	41
8	Strømsgodset IF	30	11	7	12	46	45	40
9	IL Hødd Fotball	30	10	7	13	53	54	37
10	Kongsvinger Toppfotball	30	11	4	15	41	48	37
11	Follo Fotball	30	8	10	12	40	47	34
12	Løv-Ham Fotball	30	9	4	17	31	47	31
13	FK Mandalskameratene	30	7	8	15	41	54	29
14	Skeid	30	8	5	17	39	58	29
15	FK Tønsberg	30	6	7	17	36	56	25
16	Alta IF	30	5	5	20	28	62	20

PROMOTION/RELEGATION PLAY-OFFS
(13/11/05)
Moss FK 2, Molde FK 3
(19/11/05)
Molde FK 2, Moss FK 0
(Molde FK 5-2)

Poland

Another early flight home

History repeated itself for Poland at the 2006 World Cup finals. As in 2002, defeats in their opening two games spelt early elimination, and although they signed off with a victory, the fate of their coach had already been sealed.

Pawel Janas's three-and-a-half-year spell in charge officially ended a few days after Poland returned from Germany, but there were some who suggested that he had unwittingly laid the ground for his own dismissal before the team set out for the tournament with some controversial, not to say illogical, squad selections.

Bizarrely there was no place in the chosen 23 for long-serving goalkeeper Jerzy Dudek. A decisive figure in Liverpool's Champions League triumph 12 months earlier, he had admittedly lost his place at Anfield, but to omit him completely seemed like an act of folly. There was no place, either, for Poland's top scorer in the qualifying campaign, Tomasz Frankowski; nor for the free-scoring Luaksz Sosin, dropped despite scoring twice on his debut.

Ironically the only player to score for Poland in Germany, defender Bartosz Bosacki, was someone who did not appear in Janas's initial squad. He only came in late after Damian Gorwaski was ruled out through illness.

Bosacki netted twice from set-pieces in Poland's 2-1 victory over Costa Rica, but it was goals in the opening game against Ecuador that the team really needed. With a meeting against the hosts (whom the Poles had never beaten) in Dortmund (where the Germans had never lost) second on their rota, the first match against the South Americans was always going to be Poland's pivotal fixture. A friendly between the two countries in neutral Barcelona the previous autumn had ended 3-0 to the Poles, but in the match that really mattered Janas's team were found wanting and fell to a 2-0 defeat. A courageous performance followed against the Germans, with goalkeeper Artur Boruc and veteran stopper Jacek Bak showing real defiance, especially after Radoslaw Sobolewski had been red-carded, but the decision to take off left-back Michal Zewlakow proved disastrous when the Germans exploited that area of the Polish defence to score their stoppage-time winner.

Hard to bear

To see their team lose so late in the game was desperately hard on the Polish fans, who had travelled west in their thousands to offer support. There had been idle talk in some quarters that the team might draw on the memories of the 1974 tournament (when Poland, led by the recently departed Kazimierz Gorski, had finished third on German soil) and achieve something similar. A more realistic objective was for the team simply to make the last 16.

Although Poland qualified for the finals in some

Not a happy bench as Poland go down to Ecuador

Poland

NATIONAL TEAM RESULTS 2005/06

Date	Opponent	H/A/N	Venue	Score	Scorers
15/8/05	Serbia & Montenegro	N	Kiev	3-2	Frankowski (30, 42p), Rasiak (37)
17/8/05	Israel	N	Kiev	3-2	Szymkowiak (19), Rasiak (77, 89)
3/9/05	Austria (WCQ)	H	Chorzow	3-2	Smolarek (12), Kosowski (22), Zurawski (68)
7/9/05	Wales (WCQ)	H	Warsaw	1-0	Zurawski (54p)
7/10/05	Iceland	H	Warsaw	3-2	Krzynowek (25), Baszczynski (57), Smolarek (64)
12/10/05	England (WCQ)	A	Manchester	1-2	Frankowski (45)
13/11/05	Ecuador	N	Barcelona	3-0	Klos (2), Smolarek (58), Mila (90)
16/1/105	Estonia	H	Ostrowiec	3-1	Lewandowski (8), Mila (57), Piechna (87)
1/3/06	United States	N	Kaiserslautern	0-1	
28/3/06	Saudi Arabia	A	Riyadh	2-1	Sosin (7, 63)
2/5/06	Lithuania	H	Belchatow	0-1	
14/5/06	Faroe Islands	H	Wronki	4-0	Mila (15), Rasiak (47, 83), Saganowski (73)
30/5/06	Colombia	H	Chorzow	1-2	Jelen (90)
3/6/06	Croatia	N	Wolfsburg	1-0	Smolarek (54)
9/6/06	Ecuador (WCF)	N	Gelenkirchen	0-2	
14/6/06	Germany (WCF)	A	Dortmund	0-1	
20/6/06	Costa Rica (WCF)	N	Hanover	2-1	Bosacki (33, 66)

In fairness, Wisla were desperately unlucky to be eliminated from the Champions League qualifiers by Panathinaikos. But when the team followed that up with two shocking performances against Vitória Guimarães, thus missing out also on the UEFA Cup group phase, the patience of club owner Boguslaw Cupial snapped and he gave coach Jerzy Engel the sack.

Engel, who took Poland to the 2002 World Cup, had been appointed by Cupial only a few months earlier, but his mission had been to bring the club European success and he had failed, so although Wisla were on course for a fourth successive domestic Ekstraklasa title, his dismissal was not unexpected. His assistant, Tomasz Kulawik, took over and by the winter break – cut short to a mere 83 days because of World Cup obligations – Wisla headed the table by a point from Legia Warsaw.

It was not the free-scoring Wisla of the previous season – hardly surprising as Maciej Zurawski and Tomas Frankowski, who scored 49 league goals between them in 2004/05, had both departed – but with just one goal conceded in the seven matches that preceded the mid-season stoppage, the team were sound defensively, with Polish internationals Tomasz Klos, Marcin Baszczynski and Dariusz Dudka all playing well.

Petrescu comes in

During the winter Wisla drafted in ex-Romanian international full-back Dan Petrescu as their new coach. He was a surprise choice to many, but Cupial was so sure Petrescu would be the man to deliver the goods in the club's centenary year that he lured him north on a three-year contract. His first objective was to retain the title. That seemed a straightforward task given the quality of personnel at his disposal, but while Wisla had pretensions on the championship, so too did Legia.

The club from the capital had started the season poorly, with a cluster of bad league results and a UEFA Cup pummelling by FC Zurich ending the brief reign as coach of Jacek Zielinski. He had not been helped by the sale of star players Artur Boruc and Marek Saganowski, but there was a noticeable improvement in Legia's fortunes following his replacement by ex-Celtic player Dariusz Wdowczyk.

Even so, nobody was quite prepared for the sensational burst of form that Wdowczyk's team

style, scoring plenty of goals, it was only as group runners-up, having been beaten twice by England. Defeats during the World Cup build-up to the United States, Lithuania and Colombia (for whom the opposition goalkeeper scored) served to puncture some of the pre-tournament optimism, but that couldn't camouflage the feeling of despondency after the decisive defeat by Germany.

With Janas gone, Poland's fortunes have been entrusted to the veteran Dutch coach, Leo Beenhakker. He is the team's first foreign coach, and his aim is to become the first man to lead the country to the European Championship. Although they are seeded second in their group, behind Portugal, there will be stiff competition from Serbia and Belgium, maybe Finland too, for a place at the finals.

While the national team blow hot and cold, Poland's clubs continue to serve up lukewarm fare in the European competitions. 2005/06 was a particularly abject season, with Wisla Krakow falling at the first hurdle in both competitions and the other three teams winning just one UEFA Cup tie between them.

Poland

would produce in the spring. Despite wintry conditions early on, the games came thick and fast, and so did the victories – nine in a row during the months of March and April. By the time Legia finally dropped some points – at newly promoted Korona Kielce, where they came from two goals down to draw 2-2 – their lead over Wisla had soared to five points with just three games remaining. With the two teams facing each other on the final day, Legia knew that if they won their next two games, at home to Amica Wronki and away to Gornik Zabrze, the title would be theirs.

Legia's title

Neither game saw Legia at their best, but they won them both, 1-0, and that was all that mattered. Their eighth Polish championship title was secure. It had been a breathtaking performance, and although Wisla muted Legia's celebrations by beating them 2-1 in Warsaw on the final day, in a way it served only to highlight the extent of their achievement.

Legia's most impressive performer was young goalkeeper Lukasz Fabianski, the only player to start every game (and the man who would replace Dudek in Poland's World Cup squad). Some wise investment in foreign players paid off, with Brazilian left-footer Roger Guerreiro proving especially effective – unlike most of his fellow countrymen who had arrived in bulk during the winter at Pogon Szczecin, turning the border club into a Brazilian enclave.

There was a large gap between the top two and the rest. Zaglebie Lubin, led by ex-Wisla Krakow coach Franciszek Smuda, headed the distant posse to claim third place and qualification for the UEFA Cup – this after they had surprisingly missed out on another avenue to Europe by losing the final of the Polish Cup to first-time winners Wisla Plock.

Level on points with Zaglebie (but with an inferior head-to-head record because of the away-goals rule) were Amica Wronki - in what was to be the club's final season before their long-anticipated merger with Lech Poznan. While Amica, Poland's leading white-goods manufacturer, had the money, hard-up Lech had the tradition and the fans. Now Lech has the name, the stadium, most of Amica's best players and the money to keep going. To football followers in Wronki, 60 km away from Poznan, it surely feels more like a takeover than a merger.

Ups and downs

The Amica-Lech fusion changed the landscape at the foot of the Ekstraklasa. The original plan for the new 16-team top division was that the bottom two clubs would be relegated automatically and the 14th-placed team sent into a play-off with the third-placed team in the second division. In the event, Gornik Zabrze, who finished 14th, stayed up, and Arka Gdynia, who finished 15th and should have gone down, rescued themselves in a play-off against Jagiellonia Bialystok. There was no respite, though, for bottom club Polonia Warsaw whose despair at relegation – just six years after winning the title – was doubtless intensified by the title celebrations of local foes Legia.

The two outright promotion places went to another pair of city rivals, Widzew Lodz and Lodzki KS. They will both hope to emulate the achievement of Korona Kielce, who finished a highly creditable fifth in their first season after promotion and also knocked holders Groclin Grodzisk and Legia out of the Polish Cup. Korona's 29-year-old striker Grzegorz Piechna scored 21 league goals to complete the incredible feat of topping the goalcharts of the fourth, third, second and first divisions in successive seasons. He also scored on his international debut for Poland.

NATIONAL TEAM APPEARANCES 2005/06

Coach – Pawel JANAS

Name	DOB	Club	Scg	Isr	AUT	WAL	Isl	ENG	Ecu	Est	Usa	Sau	Lit	Far	Col	Cro	ECU	GER	CRC	Caps	Goals
Wojciech KOWALEWSKI	11/5/77	Spartak M (RUS)	G80							s46										6	-
Marcin BASZCZYNSKI	7/6/77	Wisla Krakow	D		D	D	s46	D		D	D	s58	D85	D	D	D	D			35	1
Mariusz JOP	3/8/78	FK Moskva (RUS)	D	s46		D	D84	D		D84		D		D	D	D				13	-
Jacek BAK	24/3/73	Al Rayyan (QTR)	D46	D46	D	D	D		s46		D	D72			D	D76	D	D	D	75	2
Dariusz DUDKA	9/12/83	Amica Wronki /Wisla Krakow	D								s83		D76		s85			s83		8	-
Damian GORAWSKI	4/1/79	FK Moskva (RUS)	M75					M										14	1
Mariusz LEWANDOWSKI	18/5/79	Shakhtar D (UKR)	M	s46		s46	M		s46	D		M46			s85		s77	s64		27	1

Poland

NATIONAL TEAM APPEARANCES 2005/06 (contd.)

Name	DOB	Club	Scg	Isr	AUT	WAL	Isl	ENG	Ecu	Est	Usa	Sau	Lit	Far	Col	Cro	ECU	GER	CRC	Caps	Goals
Radoslaw SOBOLEWSKI	13/12/76	Wisla Krakow	M		M	M	M65	M80	M		s79	M62	s46		M46	M85	M67	M		21	1
Kamil KOSOWSKI	30/8/77	South'ton (ENG)	M88	s89	M87	M79	M46	M	M61		s61		M	M	M46	s74	s77			46	4
Tomasz FRANKOWSKI	16/8/74	Wisla Krakow /Elche CF (ESP) /Wolves (ENG)	A46	A34			s65		s39	A		A62		A	A24					20	10
Grzegorz RASIAK	12/1/79	Derby Co (ENG) /Tottenham (ENG) /South'ton (ENG)	A71	s73		A	A65	A	A	s61		A61		s46	s46	s46	s89		s85	31	8
Tomasz KLOS	7/3/73	Wisla Krakow	s46	D46	D		s84		D46		s84	D								69	6
Sebastian MILA	10/7/82	Austria W (AUT)	s46			s72		s65		s81	M		M	M	M		s64			27	6
Maciej ZURAWSKI	12/9/76	Celtic (SCO)	s71	A	A	A	A	A39							A82	A89	A84	A	A46	53	15
Tomasz RZASA	11/3/73	ADO (HOL)	s75	D	D	D	D46		s46		s73		M							36	1
Sebastian PRZYROWSKI	30/11/81	Groclin Dysk.	s80	s34																2	-
Michal ZEWLAKOW	22/4/76	Anderlecht (BEL)	s88	D69	s87	s86	D	D	D46		D73			D85	D	D	D	D83	D	59	1
Artur BORUC	20/2/80	Celtic (SCO)		G	G	G	G	G	G67		s46			s46	G46	G	G	G	G	20	-
Euzebiusz SMOLAREK	9/1/81	Dortmund (GER)		M73	M72	M86	s46	M46	A		M				A65	M83	M	M	M85	16	4
Arkadiusz RADOMSKI	27/6/77	Austria W (AUT)		M	s83	s79		s80	M		M79				s46	M	M	M	M64	23	-
Miroslaw SZYMKOWIAK	12/11/76	Trabzon (TUR)		M	M83	M					M		M			M	M64	M		31	3
Jacek KRZYNOWEK	15/5/76	Leverkusen (GER)		M89			M76	s46	M81		M	M			M	M74	M77	M77	M	61	9
Andrzej NIEDZIELAN	27/2/79	NEC (HOL)		s69							s62									17	5
Przemyslaw KAZMIERCZAK	5/5/82	Pogon Szczecin					M46			s73										3	-
Marcin KACZMAREK	3/12/79	Korona Kielce					s76		M46											2	-
Jerzy DUDEK	23/3/73	Liverpool (ENG)								s67	G46	G46	G84	G82						56	-
Marcin WASILEWSKI	9/6/80	Amica Wronki								D					s46					8	-
Bartosz BOSACKI	20/12/75	Nürnberg (GER) /Lech Poznan								D62	s72	s46	D		s76		D	D		13	2
Marcin ADAMSKI	20/8/75	Rapid W (AUT)								D										3	-
Piotr GIZA	28/2/80	Cracovia Krakow								M83	s62		s63							4	-
Marek SAGANOWSKI	31/10/78	Vitória G (POR)								A73			s24							16	3
Pawel BROZEK	21/4/83	Wisla Krakow								A46	s46				s82		s84	s90	s46	7	1
Ireneusz JELEN	9/4/81	Wisla Plock								s46	A		M	s65	s83	s67	M90	A		12	2
Grzegorz PIECHNA	18/9/76	Korona Kielce								s46										1	1
Arkadiusz GLOWACKI	13/3/79	Wisla Krakow								s62										18	-
Jakub BLASZCZYKOWSKI	14/12/85	Wisla Krakow									M46									1	-
Lukasz SOSIN	7/5/77	Apollon (CYP)									A	A46	A46							3	2
Marcin KUS	2/9/81	QPR (ENG)									s76	D58	s85							5	-
Lukasz FABIANSKI	18/4/85	Legia Warszawa									s84	s82								2	-
Seweryn GANCARCZYK	22/11/81	M K'kiv (UKR)									D	D46								2	-
Grzegorz BONIN	2/12/83	Korona Kielce									M46									1	-
Tomasz KUSZCZAK	20/3/82	WBA (ENG)													G46	s46				4	-
Maciej SCHERFCHEN	24/2/79	Lech Poznan													D63					2	-

Poland

EUROPEAN CUPS 2005/06

UEFA CHAMPIONS LEAGUE

WISLA KRAKOW
3rd qualifying round PANATHINAIKOS (GRE)
H 3-1 *Brozek Pa. (13), Uche (52), Frankowski (70)*
Majdan, Blaszczykowski (Stolarczyk 76), Klos, Glowacki, Dudka, Uche, Sobolewski (Paulista 67), Cantoro, Zienczuk, Frankowski, Brozek Pa. (Penksa 64).
A 1-4 *Sobolewski (78)*
(aet)
Majdan, Baszczynski, Klos, Glowacki, Dudka, Uche (Kuzba 75), Sobolewski, Cantoro, Zienczuk (Paulista 61), Brozek Pa. (Penksa 62), Frankowski.

UEFA CUP

GROCLIN DYSKOBOLIA GRODZISK
2nd qualifying round DUKLA BANSKÁ BYSTRICA (SVK)
H 4-1 *Rocki (46), Wozniak (55 og), Porázik (68), Slusarski (83)*
Przyrowski, Sokolowski, Mynar, Kumbev, Vranjes, Piechniak, Golinski (Sablík 88), Porázik (Lasocki 77), Sedlácek, Rocki (Sikora 86), Slusarski.
A 0-0
Przyrowski, Sokolowski, Mynar (Lasocki 54), Kumbev, Vranjes, Piechniak, Sablík, Porázik (Sninsky 73), Sedlácek, Rocki (Sikora 83), Slusarski.

1st round RC LENS (FRA)
A 1-1 *Lachor (14og)*
Przyrowski, Sokolowski, Sablík, Sninsky, Lasocki, Vranjes, Piechniak (Sabo 88), Kumbev, Rocki, Sedlácek (Porázik 90), Slusarski (Sikora 90).
H 2-4 *Sedlácek (57p), Sablík (79)*
Przyrowski, Sokolowski, Sablík, Kumbev (Sabo 73), Lasocki, Piechniak (Sikora 60), Vranjes, Golinski (Sninsky 63), Sedlácek, Rocki, Slusarski.

LEGIA WARSZAWA
2nd qualifying round FC ZÜRICH (SUI)
H 0-1
Fabianski, Sokolowski, Rzezniczak, Magiera, Kielbowicz, Szalachowski (Roslon 25), Surma, Vukovic, Karwan, Wlodarczyk (Chmiest 83), Klatt (Janczyk 74).
A 1-4 *Szalachowski (18)*
Fabianski, Sokolowski, Rzezniczak, Magiera, Kielbowicz, Szalachowski (Chmiest 80), Roslon, Vukovic (Lopes Cruz 46), Karwan, Wlodarczyk, Zjawinski (Janczyk 46).

WISLA PLOCK
2nd qualifying round GRASSHOPPER-CLUB ZÜRICH (SUI)
A 0-1
Wierzchowski, Zivkovic, Belada, Pekovic, Colakovic, Gevorgyan, Rachwal, Gesior, Vujovic, Mierzejewski (Peszko 67), Jelen.
H 3-2 *Gesior (35, 38), Zilic (69)*
Wierzchowski, Zivkovic, Belada, Pekovic, Kazimierczak (Romuzga 87), Peszko (Mierzejewski 70), Rachwal, Gesior, Vujovic (Gevorgyan 56), Jelen, Zilic.

WISLA KRAKOW
1st round VITÓRIA GUIMARÃES (POR)
A 0-3
Majdan, Baszczynski, Stolarczyk, Glowacki, Dudka, Paulista (Kuzba 70), Golos, Cantoro, Zienczuk (Barreto 80), Brozek Pa. (Penksa 46), Kryszalowicz.
H 0-1
Majdan, Baszczynski, Klos, Glowacki, Dudka (Stolarczyk 84), Penksa (Paulista 13), Sobolewski, Cantoro, Zienczuk, Brozek Pa., Kryszalowicz (Kuzba 50).

TOP GOALSCORERS 2005/06

21	Grzegorz PIECHNA (Korona Kielce)	
16	Michal CHALBINSKI (Zaglebie Lubin)	
13	Pawel BROZEK (Wisla Krakow)	
12	Krzysztof GAJTKOWSKI (Lech Poznan/Korona Kielce)	
	Radoslaw MATUSIAK (GKS Belchatow)	
11	Piotr REISS (Lech Poznan)	
10	EDI (Pogon Szczecin)	
	Maciej IWANSKI (Zaglebie Lubin)	
	Piotr WLODARCZYK (Legia Warszawa)	
9	Jacek DEMBINSKI (Amica Wronki)	

LEAGUE RESULTS/ SCORERS/APPEARANCES/ GOALS 2005/06

AMICA WRONKI
Coach – Maciej Skorza; (26/11/05) Krzysztof Chrobak

2005

Date	Opponent	H/A	Score	Scorers
27/7	Groclin Grodzisk	a	2-2	Grzybowski, Dembinski
31/7	Cracovia Krakow	a	0-1	
6/8	Odra Wodzislaw	a	4-0	Wasilewski, Kryszalowicz, Dembinski, Burkhardt
21/8	Pogon Szczecin	h	4-1	Kryszalowicz, Kikut, Dembinski (p), Micanski
27/8	Polonia Warszawa	a	0-0	
11/9	Lech Poznan	h	1-4	Micanski
17/9	Wisla Plock	a	1-0	Micanski
25/9	Zaglebie Lubin	h	3-1	Micanski, Grzybowski, Burkhardt
1/10	Korona Kielce	a	1-2	Wasilewski
15/10	Arka Gdynia	a	1-1	Bieniuk
22/10	Gornik Zabrze	h	3-1	Gregorek, Kikut, Micanski
30/10	Wisla Krakow	a	0-0	
5/11	Legia Warszawa	h	0-2	
19/11	Gornik Leczna	a	0-1	
26/11	GKS Belchatow	h	3-1	Grzybowski, Dembinski, Kikut
2/12	Groclin Grodzisk	h	2-0	og (Rocki), Gregorek
10/12	Cracovia Krakow	h	1-1	Dembinski (p)

2006

Date	Opponent	H/A	Score	Scorers
4/3	Odra Wodzislaw	h	4-0	Dembinski (p), Kucharski (p), og (Szary), Murawski
11/3	Pogon Szczecin	a	3-0	Wasilewski, Gregorek, Dembinski (p)
18/3	Polonia Warszawa	h	3-0	Bartczak, Micanski, Kikut
25/3	Lech Poznan	a	1-1	Murawski
1/4	Wisla Plock	h	2-0	Pitry, Burkhardt
7/4	Zaglebie Lubin	a	0-2	
11/4	Korona Kielce	h	0-3	
15/4	Arka Gdynia	h	1-1	Gregorek
22/4	Gornik Zabrze	a	2-0	Bieniuk, Gregorek
28/4	Wisla Krakow	h	0-1	
5/5	Legia Warszawa	a	0-1	
10/5	Gornik Leczna	h	6-0	Dembinski, Bieniuk, Gregorek 2, Wasilewski, Grzybowski

Poland

FINAL LEAGUE TABLE 2005/06

		Pld	Home W	D	L	F	A	Away W	D	L	F	A	Total W	D	L	F	A	Pts
1	Legia Warszawa	30	12	0	3	26	10	8	6	1	21	7	20	6	4	47	17	66
2	Wisla Krakow	30	12	3	0	32	6	7	4	4	18	14	19	7	4	50	20	64
3	Zaglebie Lubin	30	11	2	2	33	13	3	5	7	12	19	14	7	9	45	32	49
4	Amica Wronki	30	9	2	4	33	16	5	5	5	17	12	14	7	9	50	28	49
5	Korona Kielce	30	6	6	3	21	14	6	5	4	25	19	12	11	7	46	33	47
6	Lech Poznan	30	7	5	3	21	15	4	4	7	24	30	11	9	10	45	45	42
7	Odra Wodzislaw	30	6	5	4	11	13	4	5	6	12	14	10	10	10	23	27	40
8	Groclin Grodzisk	30	6	3	6	23	24	4	4	7	14	21	10	7	13	37	45	37
9	Cracovia Krakow	30	8	3	4	22	16	2	4	9	10	28	10	7	13	32	44	37
10	GKS Belchatow	30	5	6	4	19	15	4	4	7	11	17	9	10	11	30	32	37
11	Pogon Szczecin	30	6	5	4	18	16	3	5	7	11	18	9	10	11	29	34	37
12	Wisla Plock	30	8	3	4	21	10	2	1	12	9	35	10	4	16	30	45	34
13	Gornik Leczna	30	4	7	4	11	11	3	5	7	12	20	7	12	11	23	31	33
14	Gornik Zabrze	30	6	3	6	18	16	2	2	11	11	30	8	5	17	29	46	29
15	Arka Gdynia	30	3	8	4	11	11	1	7	7	10	22	4	15	11	21	33	27
16	Polonia Warszawa	30	2	6	7	11	20	4	1	10	9	25	6	7	17	20	45	25

13/5	GKS Belchatow	a	2-1	Bartczak, Dembinski	

No	Name	Nat	Pos	Aps	(s)	Gls
28	Arkadiusz BAK		M	2	(6)	
18	Mateusz BARTCZAK		M	14	(8)	2
13	Jaroslaw BIENIUK		D	28		3
25	Filip BURKHARDT		M	1	(20)	3
33	Radoslaw CIERZNIAK		G	26		
10	Jacek DEMBINSKI		A	28		9
17	Dariusz DUDKA		D	1		
5	Piotr DZIEWICKI		D	28		
11	Karol GREGOREK		A	18	(11)	7
21	Zbigniew GRZYBOWSKI		A	26	(2)	4
9	Marcin KIKUT		M	29	(1)	4
8	Pawel KRYSZALOWICZ		A	3	(1)	2
4	Dawid KUCHARSKI		D	9	(1)	1
1	Pawel LINKA		G	4		
26	Tomasz LISOWSKI		D		(6)	
14	Ilian MICANSKI	BUL	A	7	(10)	6
7	Rafal MURAWSKI		M	30		2
8	Przemyslaw PITRY		A	6	(4)	1
24	Jaromír SIMR	CZE	M	16	(6)	
2	Pawel SKRZYPEK		D	16	(2)	
16	Janusz SURDYKOWSKI		A		(5)	
23	Tomasz SZCZEPAN		M		(1)	
	Marcin TARNOWSKI		A		(2)	
6	Marcin WASILEWSKI		D	24		4
22	Grzegorz WOJTKOWIAK		D	14	(2)	
15	Hubert WOLAKIEWICZ		D		(1)	

ARKA GDYNIA
Coach – Miroslaw Dragan; (15/10/05) Wojciech Wasikiewicz; (6/5/06) Zbigniew Kaczmarek

2005
24/7	Legia Warszawa	h	0-0	
29/7	Lech Poznaf	a	1-1	Grishchenko
6/8	Gornik Leczna	h	1-1	Nicinski
20/8	Wisla Plock	a	1-1	Jakosz
27/8	GKS Belchatow	a	1-1	Grishchenko
10/9	Zaglebie Lubin	h	0-1	
18/9	Groclin Grodzisk	a	1-2	Nicinski
24/9	Korona Kielce	h	0-2	
1/10	Cracovia Krakow	a	1-2	Kubisz
15/10	Amica Wronki	h	1-1	Gorzad
22/10	Odra Wodzislaw	a	2-1	Nicinski, Lawa
29/10	Gornik Zabrze	h	3-0	Majda, Pilch, Grishchenko
6/11	Pogon Szczecin	a	0-0	
19/11	Wisla Krakow	h	1-0	Pilch
26/11	Polonia Warszawa	a	0-0	
3/12	Legia Warszawa	a	0-2	
9/12	Lech Poznan	h	0-2	

2006
18/3	GKS Belchatow	h	2-0	Parzy, Nicinski
25/3	Zaglebie Lubin	a	0-4	
29/3	Wisla Plock	h	1-1	Jakosz
1/4	Groclin Grodzisk	h	0-0	
4/4	Gornik Leczna	a	1-1	Wroblewski
7/4	Korona Kielce	a	0-1	
11/4	Cracovia Krakow	h	1-1	Moskalewicz
15/4	Amica Wronki	a	1-1	Moskalewicz
22/4	Odra Wodzislaw	h	1-1	Lawa
29/4	Gornik Zabrze	a	0-2	
6/5	Pogon Szczecin	h	0-0	
10/5	Wisla Krakow	a	1-3	Wroblewski
13/5	Polonia Warszawa	h	0-1	

No	Name	Nat	Pos	Aps	(s)	Gls
23	Radoslaw BARTOSZEWICZ		M	6	(7)	
1	Michal CHAMERA		G	9		
26	Jan CIOS		D	5		
10	Sebastian GORZAD		M	17		1
9	Andriy GRISHCHENKO	UKR	A	17	(9)	3
19	Benjamin IMEH	NGA	A	5	(2)	
13	Grzegorz JAKOSZ		D	27		2
14	Piotr JAWNY		D	27		
2	Marcin KICZYNSKI		D	1		

Poland

No	Name	Nat	Pos	Aps	(s)	Gls
21	Mateusz KOLODZIEJSKI		A		(3)	
4	Ireneusz KOSCIELNIAK		D	14	(2)	
3	Lukasz KOWALSKI		D	24		
1	Jaroslaw KRUPSKI		G	3		
6	Marek KUBISZ		M	3	(11)	1
20	Bartosz LAWA		M	12	(5)	2
22	Krzysztof MAJDA		D	19	(2)	1
78	Olgierd MOSKALEWICZ		A	16	(2)	2
17	Damian NAWROCIK		A	10	(1)	
16	Grzegorz NICINSKI		A	28		4
19	Tomasz PARZY		M	9	(2)	1
15	Grzegorz PILCH		A	14	(12)	2
11	Marcin PUDYSIAK		M	5	(8)	
5	Krzysztof SOBIERAJ		M	15	(4)	
27,7	Dariusz ULANOWSKI		M	16	(1)	
33	Norbert WITKOWSKI		G	18		
8	Radoslaw WROBLEWSKI		M	10	(3)	2

CRACOVIA KRAKOW
Coach – Wojciech Stawowy; (1/1/06) Albin Mikulski; (8/4/06) Stefan Bialas

2005
26/7	Korona Kielce	a	0-0	
31/7	Amica Wronki	h	1-0	Nowak
6/8	Gornik Zabrze	a	0-3	
28/8	Legia Warszawa	h	1-1	Nowak
10/9	Gornik Leczna	a	1-1	Moskala
17/9	GKS Belchatow	h	2-1	Wacek, Baran
24/9	Groclin Grodzisk	a	1-4	Wacek
1/10	Arka Gdynia	h	2-1	Bania, Bojarski
15/10	Odra Wodzislaw	h	1-0	Pawlusinski
21/10	Pogon Szczecin	a	2-1	Giza, Moskala
29/10	Polonia Warszawa	h	3-0	Bojarski, Bania, Pawlusinski
4/11	Lech Poznan	a	0-1	
19/11	Wisla Plock	h	3-1	Moskala, Bania, Szczoczarz
22/11	Wisla Krakow	a	0-3	
26/11	Zaglebie Lubin	a	1-3	Nowak
4/12	Korona Kielce	h	2-3	Moskala, Pawlusinski
10/12	Amica Wronki	h	1-1	Skrzynski

2006
3/3	Gornik Zabrze	h	1-2	Giza
12/3	Wisla Krakow	h	1-1	Giza
17/3	Legia Warszawa	a	0-5	
25/3	Gornik Leczna	h	0-1	
1/4	GKS Belchatow	a	0-2	
8/4	Groclin Grodzisk	h	1-3	Bania
11/4	Arka Gdynia	a	1-1	Giza
15/4	Odra Wodzislaw	a	0-1	
22/4	Pogon Szczecin	h	1-0	Bania
30/4	Polonia Warszawa	a	3-1	Bojarski, og (Lukasiewicz), João Paulo
7/5	Lech Poznan	h	3-2	Drumlak, Przytula, Bojarski (p)
10/5	Wisla Plock	a	0-1	
13/5	Zaglebie Lubin	h	0-0	

No	Name	Nat	Pos	Aps	(s)	Gls
26	Tomasz BALIGA		D		(1)	
11	Piotr BANIA		A	23	(5)	5
8	Arkadiusz BARAN		M	24		1
4	Marek BASTER		D	9	(2)	
21	Marcin BOJARSKI		M	27	(2)	4
33	Marcin CABAJ		G	23	(1)	
28	Pawel DRUMLAK		M	9	(10)	1
7	Piotr GIZA		M	23	(1)	4
12	Mateusz JELEN				(1)	
13	Michal KARWAN		D	23		
18	Tomasz MOSKALA		A	20	(9)	4
19	Pawel NOWAK		M	24	(3)	3
30	Slawomir OLSZEWSKI		G	7		
25	JOÃO PAULO	BRA	M	5	(12)	1
10	Dariusz PAWLUSINSKI		M	21	(2)	3
14	Karol PIATEK		D		(1)	
29	Krzysztof PRZYTULA		M	10	(3)	1
6	Krzysztof RADWANSKI		D	16	(1)	
2	Mateusz RZUCIDLO		D	9		
15	Lukasz SKRZYNSKI		D	26		1
16	Michal SWISTAK		D	3		
23	Lukasz SZCZOCZARZ		A	1	(13)	1
10	Kacper TATARA		A		(1)	
22	Lukasz USZALEWSKI		D	2	(4)	
5	Tomasz WACEK		D	22	(3)	2
27	Pawel WOJCIECHOWSKI		D	1		
35	Marcin ZIMON		M	2	(1)	

GKS BELCHATOW
Coach – Mariusz Kuras; (15/10/05) Orest Lenczyk

2005
26/7	Gornik Zabrze	h	0-0	
30/7	Wisla Krakow	a	0-3	
5/8	Legia Warszawa	h	0-3	
20/8	Gornik Leczna	a	2-0	Cecot, Dziedzic (p)
27/8	Arka Gdynia	h	1-1	Matusiak (p)
9/9	Groclin Grodzisk	h	2-2	Klepczarek, Matusiak
17/9	Cracovia Krakow	a	1-2	Dziedzic
24/9	Odra Wodzislaw	h	0-3	
1/10	Pogon Szczecin	a	0-0	
15/10	Polonia Warszawa	h	2-0	Dziedzic, Matusiak
22/10	Lech Poznan	a	1-1	Popek
29/10	Wisla Plock	h	3-0	Ujek, Matusiak 2
5/11	Zaglebie Lubin	a	1-2	Ujek
19/11	Korona Kielce	h	1-2	Kmiecik
26/11	Amica Wronki	a	1-3	Wiechowski
3/12	Gornik Zabrze	a	1-0	Ujek
11/12	Wisla Krakow	h	0-0	

2006
3/3	Legia Warszawa	a	0-1	
18/3	Arka Gdynia	a	0-2	
22/3	Gornik Leczna	h	1-1	Matusiak
25/3	Groclin Grodzisk	a	1-3	Matusiak (p)
1/4	Cracovia Krakow	h	2-0	Dziedzic 2
8/4	Odra Wodzislaw	a	2-0	Gargula, Matusiak
11/4	Pogon Szczecin	h	2-0	Popek, Matusiak
15/4	Polonia Warszawa	a	0-0	
22/4	Lech Poznan	h	1-1	Matusiak
29/4	Wisla Plock	a	1-0	Klepczarek
7/5	Zaglebie Lubin	h	3-0	Matusiak, Gargula, Dziedzic (p)
10/5	Korona Kielce	a	0-0	
13/5	Amica Wronki	h	1-2	Matusiak

No	Name	Nat	Pos	Aps	(s)	Gls
26	Jacek BANASZYNSKI		G	13	(1)	
17	Rafal BERLINSKI		D	7	(5)	
6	Edward CECOT		D	29		1
14	Ferdinand CHI-FON	CMR	A	12	(2)	
19	Jakub CIECIURA		D	2	(2)	
11	Janusz DZIEDZIC		M	19	(7)	6

Poland

No	Name	Nat	Pos	Aps	(s)	Gls
13	Amar FERHATOVIC	BOS	M		(2)	
22	Grzegorz FONFARA		D	23		
3	Jano FROELICH	SVK	D	12		
10	Lukasz GARGULA		M	28		2
8	Robert GORSKI		D	5	(3)	
3	Rafal GRODZICKI		D	4	(1)	
18	Bartosz HINC		M	4	(1)	
21	Goran JANKOVIC	SCG	M	7	(10)	
8	Tomasz JARZEBOWSKI		M	5	(1)	
16	Omar JOLDIC	BOS	M	3	(2)	
2	Piotr KLEPCZAREK (I)		M	12	(5)	2
23	Grzegorz KMIECIK		A	3	(6)	1
28	Marcin KOMOROWSKI		D	1		
16	Marcin KOWALCZYK		D	6		
7	Jacek KURANTY		M	23	(2)	
1	Piotr LECH		G	6		
20	Tomasz LUCZYWEK		M	2		
9	Radoslav MATUSIAK		A	27	(3)	12
17	Dawid NOWAK		A	1	(4)	
27	Kelechi OMEONU	NGA	A		(3)	
15	Dariusz PIETRASIK		A	15	(3)	
1	Krzysztof PILARZ		G	2		
4	Jacek POPEK		A	17	(3)	2
19	Milan RADULOVIC	SCG	D	5		
12	Lukasz SAPELA		G	9		
5	Pawel STRAK		D	5	(5)	
28	Damian SZCZESNY		A		(1)	
24	Jakub TOSIK		M		(1)	
23,25	Mariusz UJEK		A	16	(6)	3
5	Sergiusz WIECHOWSKI		M	1	(1)	1
23	Tomasz WROBEL		M	6	(2)	

GORNIK LECZNA
Coach – Boguslaw Kaczmarek; (29/10/05) Tadeusz Lapa; (19/11/05) Dariusz Kubicki

2005
26/7	Wisla Krakow	h	1-1	Kubica
30/7	Legia Warszawa	h	0-0	
6/8	Arka Gdynia	a	1-1	Bronowicki G.
20/8	GKS Belchatow	h	0-2	
28/8	Groclin Grodzisk	a	1-1	Wedzynski
10/9	Cracovia Krakow	h	1-1	Bykowski
17/9	Odra Wodzislaw	a	0-0	
24/9	Pogon Szczecin	h	0-1	
1/10	Polonia Warszawa	a	3-0	Nazaruk, Andruszczak, Bykowski
14/10	Lech Poznan	h	0-0	
22/10	Wisla Plock	a	1-2	Andruszczak
29/10	Zaglebie Lubin	h	1-3	Wedzynski
5/11	Korona Kielce	a	1-1	Bykowski
19/11	Amica Wronki	h	1-0	Kubica
26/11	Gornik Zabrze	a	0-2	
3/12	Wisla Krakow	a	0-1	
11/12	Legia Warszawa	a	2-0	Popiela, Oziemczuk

2006
22/3	GKS Belchatow	a	1-1	Grzegorzewski
25/3	Cracovia Krakow	a	1-0	Bykowski
1/4	Odra Wodzislaw	h	0-0	
4/4	Arka Gdynia	h	1-1	Kubica
8/4	Pogon Szczecin	a	1-2	Kubica
12/4	Polonia Warszawa	h	0-1	
15/4	Lech Poznan	a	0-1	
19/4	Groclin Grodzisk	h	0-0	
22/4	Wisla Plock	h	2-1	Sokolenko, Jurkowski (p)
29/4	Zaglebie Lubin	a	0-2	
6/5	Korona Kielce	h	3-0	Grzegorzewski 2, Oziemczuk
10/5	Amica Wronki	a	0-6	
13/5	Gornik Zabrze	h	1-0	Oziemczuk

No	Name	Nat	Pos	Aps	(s)	Gls
17	Artur ANDRUSZCZAK		M	13		2
22	Andrzej BLEDZEWSKI		G	24		
3	Artur BOZYK		D	12	(1)	
7	Grzegorz BRONOWICKI		M	14		1
27,7	Piotr BRONOWICKI		D	16	(2)	
20	Maciej BYKOWSKI		A	22	(4)	4
15	Toni GOLEM	CRO	D	12		
10	Jakub GRZEGORZEWSKI		A	9	(2)	3
24	Remigiusz JEZIERSKI		A		(8)	
14	Bartosz JURKOWSKI		D	26	(1)	1
8	Rafal KACZMARCZYK		M	9	(8)	
5	Lek KCIRA		CRO D		(4)	
9	Andrzej KUBICA		A	23	(6)	4
10	Cezary KUCHARSKI		A	5	(4)	
2	Przemyslaw KULIG		D	13		
11	Lukasz MADEJ		M	3	(5)	
21	Borce MANEVSKI	MAC	M	1	(9)	
11	Lukasz MASLOWSKI		M		(1)	
1	Robert MIODUSZEWSKI		G	1	(1)	
19	Slawomir NAZARUK		M	10	(3)	1
4	Veljko NIKITOVIC	SCG	D	21	(3)	
18	Kamil OZIEMCZUK		A	11	(6)	3
24	Mariusz PAWELEC		D	14	(5)	
2	Jaroslaw POPIELA		D	14	(1)	1
25	Ronald SIKLIC	CRO	D	4	(1)	
25	Walerij SOKOLENKO	UKR	D	8	(1)	1
23,44	Tomasz SOKOLOWSKI (I)		M	16	(6)	
16	Dawid SOLDECKI		M		(3)	
28	Lukasz STEFANIUK		M		(1)	
12	Przemyslaw TYTON		G	5		
6	Grzegorz WEDZYNSKI		M	24	(2)	2

GORNIK ZABRZE
Coach – Marek Wlecialowski; (5/11/05) Marek Motyka; (1/1/06) Ryszard Komornicki; (22/4/06) Przemyslaw Cecherz; (29/4/06) Marek Motyka

2005
26/7	GKS Belchatow	a	0-0	
30/7	Groclin Grodzisk	h	0-0	
6/8	Cracovia Krakow	h	3-0	Andraszak, João Paulo, Bukalski
20/8	Odra Wodzislaw	h	1-1	João Paulo
27/8	Pogon Szczecin	a	1-1	Aleksander
10/9	Polonia Warszawa	h	2-1	Aleksander, Liczka
17/9	Lech Poznan	a	2-3	Liczka, Bukalski
24/9	Wisla Plock	h	4-0	Aleksander 3, Radawiec
1/10	Zaglebie Lubin	a	0-3	
15/10	Korona Kielce	h	0-3	
22/10	Amica Wronki	a	1-3	Aleksander
29/10	Arka Gdynia	a	0-3	
5/11	Wisla Krakow	h	0-1	
18/11	Legia Warszawa	a	2-3	Wisniewski, Krol K.
26/11	Gornik Leczna	h	2-0	Bukalski (p), Krol K.
3/12	GKS Belchatow	h	0-1	
10/12	Groclin Grodzisk	a	1-0	Siedlarz

2006
3/3	Cracovia Krakow	a	2-1	og (Pawlusinski), Bartos
25/3	Polonia Warszawa	a	1-4	Seweryn

Poland

4	Lech Poznan	h	0-3		
4	Odra Wodzislaw	a	0-1		
4	Wisla Plock	a	0-1		
/4	Zaglebie Lubin	h	2-2	Krol K., Seweryn	
/4	Korona Kielce	a	1-4	og (Hernâni)	
/4	Pogon Szczecin	h	2-1	Krol K., Bartos	
/4	Amica Wronki	h	0-2		
/4	Arka Gdynia	h	2-0	Radler, Bukowiec	
5	Wisla Krakow	a	0-2		
/5	Legia Warszawa	h	0-1		
/5	Gornik Leczna	a	0-1		

No	Name	Nat	Pos	Aps	(s)	Gls
	Arkadiusz ALEKSANDER		A	15	(1)	6
	Rafal ANDRASZAK		A	7	(8)	1
7	Dawid BARTOS		D	11		2
4	Krzysztof BUKALSKI		M	27		3
	Mateusz BUKOWIEC		M	4	(3)	1
6	Marcin DUDZINSKI		A	8	(4)	
	Ogochukwu ENYINNAYA	NGA	A		(1)	
	FELIPE	BRA	D	9		
1	Grzegorz GONCERZ		A	4	(15)	
5	JOÃO PAULO	BRA	M	2	(3)	2
2	Lukasz JUSZKIEWICZ		M	23	(1)	
0	KLÉBER	BRA	A	1	(3)	
8	Kamil KROL		A	21	(5)	4
0	Pawel KROL		D	5	(3)	
	Piotr LECH		G	17		
7	Marcel LICZKA	CZE	M	7	(1)	2
3	Mariusz MAGIERA		D	23		
0	Spite MATIC	CRO	D	8		
	Carsten NULLE	GER	G	7		
1	Wojciech OKINCZYC		A		(16)	
	Sebastian OLSZAR		A		(3)	
4	Tomasz PRASNAL		M	4	(1)	
5	Artur PROKOP		D	26		
	Daniel RADAWIEC		A	2	(8)	1
	Blazej RADLER		D	24		1
6	RAMBO	BRA	D	2		
3	Damian SEWERYN		M	12		2
3	Marcin SIEDLARZ		M	13	(2)	1
8	Artur SKIBA		A	1	(3)	
2	Mateusz SLAWIK		G	6		
3	Ivailo STOIMENOV	BUL	M	20	(5)	
5	Jacek WISNIEWSKI		D	16	(1)	1
21	Pawel WOJCIECHOWSKI		D	1		
5	Tomasz WOJCIK		A		(5)	
20	Jacek ZIARKOWSKI		A	4	(5)	

GROCLIN DYSKOBOLIA GRODZISK
Coach – Dusan Radolsky (SVK); (28/10/05) Werner Licka (CZE)

2005

27/7	Amica Wronki	h	2-2	Golinski, Sninsky
30/7	Gornik Zabrze	a	0-0	
5/8	Wisla Krakow	h	2-4	Slusarski, Kumbev
20/8	Legia Warszawa	a	2-0	Vranjes, Slusarski
28/8	Gornik Leczna	h	1-1	Slusarski
9/9	GKS Belchatow	a	2-2	Lasocki, Rocki
18/9	Arka Gdynia	h	2-1	Rocki, Slusarski
24/9	Cracovia Krakow	a	4-1	Sedlácek, Rocki, Slusarski 2
2/10	Odra Wodzislaw	a	0-1	
15/10	Pogon Szczecin	h	1-3	Rocki
22/10	Polonia Warszawa	h	1-2	Sikora
28/10	Lech Poznan	h	3-1	Sablík, Sikora, Zajac

5/11	Wisla Plock	a	0-2		
20/11	Zaglebie Lubin	h	1-0	Piechniak	
26/11	Korona Kielce	a	0-3		
2/12	Amica Wronki	a	0-2		
10/12	Gornik Zabrze	h	0-1		

2006

4/3	Wisla Krakow	a	1-2	Zahorski	
11/3	Legia Warszawa	h	0-4		
25/3	GKS Belchatow	h	3-1	Zahorski, Gesior, Piechniak	
1/4	Arka Gdynia	a	0-0		
8/4	Cracovia Krakow	a	3-1	Gesior 2, Rocki	
11/4	Odra Wodzislaw	h	0-0		
15/4	Pogon Szczecin	a	3-1	Sikora 2, og (Zé Roberto)	
19/4	Gornik Leczna	a	0-0		
23/4	Polonia Warszawa	a	2-1	Piechniak 2	
29/4	Lech Poznan	a	1-4	Rocki	
6/5	Wisla Plock	h	3-0	Slusarski, Zajac, Sikora	
10/5	Zaglebie Lubin	a	0-2		
13/5	Korona Kielce	h	0-3		

No	Name	Nat	Pos	Aps	(s)	Gls
3	Adrian BARTKOWIAK		D	2		
8	Dariusz GESIOR		D	5	(2)	3
19	Michal GOLINSKI		M	9	(2)	1
16	Szymon KAZMIEROWSKI		A		(3)	
15	Igor KOZIOL		D	6	(8)	
3	Pance KUMBEV	MAC	D	13		1
26	Mate LACIC	CRO	D	12		
24	Rafal LASOCKI		D	23	(2)	1
20	Jaroslaw LATO		M	8	(1)	
4	Vlade LAZAREVSKI	MAC	D	17	(2)	
27	Marcel LICZKA	CZE	M	2		
2	Radek MYNAR	CZE	D	4		
18	Mariusz PAWLAK		D	11	(2)	
7	Piotr PIECHNIAK		M	28	(1)	4
8	Andrej PORAZÍK	SVK	A	3	(8)	
12	Sebastian PRZYROWSKI		G	27	(1)	
1	Aleksander PTAK		G	3		
21	Marcin RADZEWICZ		M	5	(9)	
22	Piotr ROCKI		M	23	(2)	6
14	Radim SABLÍK	CZE	D	19	(2)	1
10	Tibor SABO	SCG	M	8	(8)	
16	Lumír SEDLÁCEK	CZE	M	12	(1)	1
17	Adrian SIKORA		A	17	(9)	5
20	Dusan SNINSKY	SVK	D	12	(4)	1
23	Bartosz SLUSARSKI		A	16	(6)	7
11	Marek SOKOLOWSKI		M	25		
6	Mico VRANJES	SCG	D	10	(1)	1
19	Tomasz ZAHORSKI		A	6	(3)	2
9	Marcin ZAJAC		M	4	(8)	2

KORONA KIELCE
Coach – Ryszard Wieczorek

2005

26/7	Cracovia Krakow	h	0-0	
30/7	Odra Wodzis aw	h	0-1	
7/8	Pogon Szczecin	a	2-4	Golanski, Bonin
20/8	Polonia Warszawa	h	3-2	Piechna 3 (1p)
26/8	Lech Poznan	a	0-0	
10/9	Wisla Plock	h	2-3	Piechna, Bonin
17/9	Zaglebie Lubin	a	3-3	Piechna 2, Bilski
24/9	Arka Gdynia	a	2-0	Nowacki, Piechna (p)
1/10	Amica Wronki	h	2-1	Piechna 2 (1p)
15/10	Gornik Zabrze	a	3-0	Grzegorzewski, Bilski,

The European Book of Football 2006/2007 - 577

Poland

23/10	Wisla Krakow	a	2-2		Piechna
29/10	Legia Warszawa	a	0-1		Piechna 2
5/11	Gornik Leczna	h	1-1		Hermes
19/11	GKS Belchatow	a	2-1		Piechna, og (Fonfara)
26/11	Groclin Grodzisk	h	3-0		Piechna, Bilski, Dorosz
4/12	Cracovia Krakow	a	3-2		Piechna 2, Golanski
10/12	Odra Wodzislaw	a	1-1		Szewczuk
2006					
11/3	Polonia Warszawa	a	1-1		Sasin
25/3	Wisla Plock	a	0-1		
1/4	Zaglebie Lubin	h	1-1		Gajtkowski
4/4	Pogon Szczecin	h	0-1		
7/4	Arka Gdynia	h	1-0		Bednarek
11/4	Amica Wronki	a	3-0		Piechna 2, Hernâni
15/4	Gornik Zabrze	h	4-1		Gajtkowski, Piechna 2, Bonin
18/4	Lech Poznan	h	1-1		Piechna
21/1	Wisla Krakow	h	1-0		Gajtkowski
29/4	Legia Warszawa	h	2-2		Robak, Bonin
6/5	Gornik Leczna	a	0-3		
10/5	GKS Belchatow	h	0-0		
13/5	Groclin Grodzisk	a	3-0		Robak, Gajtkowski, Zganiacz (p)

No	Name	Nat	Pos	Aps	(s)	Gls
19	Robert BEDNAREK		M	21	(1)	1
7	Arkadiusz BILSKI		M	15	(7)	3
15	Grzegorz BONIN		M	20	(6)	4
21	Przemyslaw CICHON		M	7		
	Anatol DOROSZ	MOL	A		(1)	1
20	Marcin DRZYMONT		D	8	(2)	
18	Krzysztof GAJTKOWSKI		A	12		4
8	Pawel GOLANSKI		D	24	(2)	2
22	Jakub GRZEGORZEWSKI		A	10	(3)	1
17	HERMES	BRA	M	29		1
4	HERNÂNI	BRA	D	26		1
9	Marcin KACZMAREK		M	22	(4)	
2	Arkadiusz KALISZAN		D	1		
27	Jacek KIELB		A		(1)	
23	Robert KOLENDOWICZ		M	4	(6)	
20	Marcin KOSMICKI		D	1	(2)	
6	Dariusz KOZUBEK		M	2	(6)	
5	Aleksander KWIEK		M	6	(10)	
1	Maciej MIELCARZ		G	17		
3	Marcin NOWACKI		M	13	(1)	1
16	Jaroslaw PIATKOWSKI		M		(7)	
10	Grzegorz PIECHNA		A	26	(3)	21
11	Marcin ROBAK		A	4	(5)	2
14	Slawomir RUTKA		D	16	(1)	
6	Pawel SASIN		M	8	(4)	1
11	Tomasz SZEWCZUK		A	2	(9)	1
29	Lukasz SZYMONIAK		D	1		
24	Marek SZYNDROWSKI		D	11	(2)	
23	Cezary WILK		M	1	(3)	
12	Lukasz ZALUSKA		G	13		
22	Mariusz ZGANIACZ		M	10	(1)	1

LECH POZNAN
Coach – Czeslaw Michniewicz

2005					
26/7	Polonia Warszawa	h	1-2		Zakrzewski
29/7	Arka Gdynia	h	1-1		Gajtkowski
6/8	Wisla Plock	h	3-2		Gajtkowski, Zakrzewski, Reiss
20/8	Zaglebie Lubin	a	5-4		Zakrzewski, Reiss 3 (1p), Gajtkowski
26/8	Korona Kielce	h	0-0		
11/9	Amica Wronki	a	4-1		Telichowski, Gajtkowski 2, Nawrocik
17/9	Gornik Zabrze	h	3-2		Reiss 2 (1p), Swierczewski
24/9	Wisla Krakow	a	1-5		Gajtkowski
30/9	Legia Warszawa	h	1-0		Iwan
14/10	Gornik Leczna	a	0-0		
22/10	GKS Belchatow	h	1-1		Gajtkowski
28/10	Groclin Grodzisk	a	1-3		Mowlik
4/11	Cracovia Krakow	h	1-0		Gajtkowski
19/11	Odra Wodzislaw	a	1-2		Iwan
25/11	Pogon Szczecin	h	1-1		Iwan
2/12	Polonia Warszawa	a	1-2		Swierczewski
9/12	Arka Gdynia	a	2-0		Nawrocik, Reiss (p)
2006					
10/3	Zaglebie Lubin	h	0-1		
25/3	Amica Wronki	h	1-1		Buzala
1/4	Gornik Zabrze	a	3-0		Reiss, Wachowicz, Zakrzewski
4/4	Wisla Plock	a	1-5		Scherfchen
8/4	Wisla Krakow	h	2-1		Reiss, Mowlik (p)
12/4	Legia Warszawa	a	1-3		Reiss
15/4	Gornik Leczna	h	1-0		og (Kaczmarczyk)
18/4	Korona Kielce	a	1-1		Reiss
22/4	GKS Belchatow	a	1-1		Anderson
29/4	Groclin Grodzisk	h	4-1		Zakrzewski 2, Wachowicz 2
7/5	Cracovia Krakow	a	2-3		Zakrzewski, Swierczewski
10/5	Odra Wodzislaw	h	1-2		Telichowski
13/5	Pogon Szczecin	a	0-0		

No	Name	Nat	Pos	Aps	(s)	Gls
3	ANDERSON	BRA	D	23		1
14	Bartosz BOSACKI		D	11		
24	Pawel BUZALA		A	1	(10)	1
18	Arkadiusz CZARNECKI		D	2		
14	Krzysztof GAJTKOWSKI		A	14	(1)	8
19	Michal GOLINSKI		M	1		
8	Tomasz IWAN		M	9	(7)	3
1	Krzysztof KOTOROWSKI		G	28		
2	Marcin KUS		D	10		
30	Arkadiusz MALARZ		G	2		
23	Artur MARCINIAK		M	11	(4)	
21	Mariusz MOWLIK		D	16	(2)	2
10	Damian NAWROCIK		A	2	(12)	2
9	Piotr REISS		A	27		11
4	Pape SAMBA BA	SEN	M	11	(7)	
15	Pawel SASIN		M	12	(4)	
4	SAVANEH	GAM	A		(1)	
13	Maciej SCHERFCHEN		M	24		1
26	Krzysztof STRUGAREK		D		(3)	
7	Piotr SWIERCZEWSKI		M	27		3
10	Tomasz SZEWCZUK		A	9	(2)	
6	Blazej TELICHOWSKI		D	25	(1)	2
16	Dawid TOPOLSKI		M	9	(7)	
17	Marcin WACHOWICZ		M	16	(6)	3
23	Jakub WILK		M	1	(9)	
5	Zbigniew WOJCIK		D	16	(3)	
11	Zbigniew ZAKRZEWSKI		A	23	(1)	7

LEGIA WARSZAWA
Coach – Jacek Zielinski; (10/9/05) Dariusz Wdowczyk

Poland

2005

Date	Opponent	H/A	Score	Scorers
24/7	Arka Gdynia	a	0-0	
30/7	Gornik Leczna	a	0-0	
5/8	GKS Belchatow	a	3-0	Klatt 3
20/8	Groclin Grodzisk	h	0-2	
28/8	Cracovia Krakowa	a	1-1	Wlodarczyk
10/9	Odra Wodzislaw	h	2-1	Wlodarczyk, Szalachowski
16/9	Pogon Szczecin	a	2-2	og (Magdon), Szalachowski
23/9	Polonia Warszawa	h	1-0	Wlodarczyk (p)
30/9	Lech Poznan	a	0-1	
15/10	Wisla Plock	h	3-0	Djokovic, Klatt, Wlodarczyk
22/10	Zaglebie Lubin	a	1-0	Szalachowski
29/10	Korona Kielce	h	1-0	Wlodarczyk
5/11	Amica Wronki	a	2-0	Burkhardt, Szalachowski
18/11	Gornik Zabrze	h	3-2	Janczyk, Wlodarczyk 2 (1p)
27/11	Wisla Krakow	a	0-0	
3/12	Arka Gdynia	h	2-0	Janczyk, Sokolowski
11/12	Gornik Leczna	h	0-2	

2006

Date	Opponent	H/A	Score	Scorers
3/3	GKS Belchatow	h	1-0	Ouattara
11/3	Groclin Grodzisk	a	4-0	Janczyk 2, Roger Guerreiro, Burkhardt
17/3	Cracovia Krakow	h	5-0	Janczyk, Gottwald, Roger Guerreiro, Wlodarczyk, Szalachowski
25/3	Odra Wodzislaw	a	2-1	Kucharski, Burkhardt
31/1	Pogon Szczecin	h	2-0	Vukovic, Szalachowski
9/4	Polonia Warszawa	a	2-0	Ouattara, Edson
12/4	Lech Poznan	h	3-1	Ouattara, Edson, Szalachowski
15/4	Wisla Plock	a	1-0	Burkhardt
22/4	Zaglebie Lubin	h	1-0	Roger Guerreiro
29/4	Korona Kielce	a	2-2	Choto, Wlodarczyk
5/5	Amica Wronki	h	1-0	Edson
10/5	Gornik Zabrze	a	1-0	Wlodarczyk
13/5	Wisla Krakow	h	1-2	Vukovic

No	Name	Nat	Pos	Aps	(s)	Gls
7	Grzegorz BRONOWICKI		D	11		
10	Marcin BURKHARDT		M	22	(1)	4
21	Marcin CHMIEST		A	4	(6)	
4	Dickson CHOTO	ZIM	D	19		1
16,5	Veselin DJOKOVIC	SCG	D	7	(2)	1
27	EDSON	BRA	D	10		3
1	Lukasz FABIANSKI		G	30		
24	Ahmed GHANEM	EGY	D		(2)	
21	Michal GOTTWALD	SVK	A	1	(2)	1
15	Dawid JANCZYK		A	8	(10)	5
14,13	Bartosz KARWAN		M	17	(2)	
11	Tomasz KIELBOWICZ		D	21	(5)	
22	Marcin KLATT		A	4	(5)	4
23	Cezary KUCHARSKI		A	6	(3)	1
18	Jacek MAGIERA		M	3	(3)	
29	Moussa OUATTARA	BFA	D	18		3
4	Mirko POLEDICA	SCG	D	2	(1)	
6	ROGER GUERREIRO	BRA	M	13		3
19	Marcin ROSLON		M	12		
25	Jakub RZEZNICZAK		D	8	(7)	
13	Marcin SMOLINSKI		M	1	(2)	
7	Tomasz SOKOLOWSKI		D	10	(7)	1
8	Lukasz SURMA		M	26		
3	Wojciech SZALA		D	23	(1)	
20	Sebastian SZALACHOWSKI		M	22	(7)	7
10,14	Aleksandar VUKOVIC	SCG	M	6	(11)	2

No	Name	Nat	Pos	Aps	(s)	Gls
9	Piotr WLODARCZYK		A	26	(4)	10
17	Dariusz ZJAWINSKI		A		(2)	

ODRA WODZISLAW
Coach – Waldemar Fornalik

2005

Date	Opponent	H/A	Score	Scorers
26/7	Zaglebie Lubin	h	0-0	
30/7	Korona Kielce	a	1-0	og (Szyndrowski)
6/8	Amica Wronki	h	0-4	
20/8	Gornik Zabrze	a	1-1	og (Juszkiewicz)
27/8	Wisla Krakow	h	1-1	Maslowski
10/9	Legia Warszawa	a	1-2	Maslowski
17/9	Gornik Leczna	h	0-0	
24/9	GKS Belchatow	a	3-0	Czerkas, Maslowski, Zganiacz (p)
2/10	Groclin Grodzisk	h	1-0	Czerkas
15/10	Cracovia Krakow	a	0-1	
22/10	Arka Gdynia	h	1-2	Korzym
29/10	Pogon Szczecin	h	1-0	Czerkas
19/11	Lech Poznan	h	2-1	Czerkas 2
26/11	Wisla Plock	a	0-0	
6/12	Polonia Warszawa	a	3-0	Korzym, Wos, Maslowski
3/12	Zaglebie Lubin	a	0-2	
10/12	Korona Kielce	h	1-1	Malinowski

2006

Date	Opponent	H/A	Score	Scorers
4/3	Amica Wronki	a	0-4	
19/3	Wisla Krakow	a	0-1	
25/3	Legia Warszawa	h	1-2	Chmiest
1/4	Gornik Leczna	a	0-0	
4/4	Gornik Zabrze	h	1-0	Chmiest (p)
8/4	GKS Belchatow	h	0-2	
11/4	Groclin Grodzisk	a	0-0	
15/4	Cracovia Krakow	a	1-0	Chmiest
22/4	Arka Gdynia	a	1-1	Czerkas
29/4	Pogon Szczecin	a	0-1	
6/5	Polonia Warszawa	h	0-0	
10/5	Lech Poznan	a	2-1	Kokoszka, Wos
13/5	Wisla Plock	h	1-0	Korzym

No	Name	Nat	Pos	Aps	(s)	Gls
17	Tomasz ALBINGIER		A	1	(6)	
5	Damian AUGUSTYNIAK		D		(1)	
18	Jaroslaw BUJOK		D	7		
27	Marcin CHMIEST		A	10	(1)	3
2	Witold CICHY		D	4	(4)	
8	Sylwester CZERESZEWSKI		A	2	(5)	
11	Adam CZERKAS		A	14	(9)	6
5	Marcin DRZYMONT		D	16		
30	Dariusz DUDEK		D	11		
24	Marcin DYMKOWSKI		D	27		
15	Wojciech GRZYB		D	13	(2)	
20	Maciej KORZYM		A	12	(12)	3
25	Ireneusz KOWALSKI		M	18	(8)	
3	Marcin KRYSINSKI		D	19	(4)	
9	Marcin MALINOWSKI		M	29		1
16	Lukasz MASLOWSKI		A	13	(1)	4
6	Mariusz MUSZALIK		M	14	(8)	
27	Mariusz NOSAL		A	1	(1)	
12	Mariusz PAWELEK		G	17		
29	Krzysztof PILARZ		G	13		
10	Marcin SMOLINSKI		M	2	(3)	
19	Tomasz SWIERZYNSKI		A		(2)	
21	Slawomir SZARY		D	21	(2)	

Poland

No	Name		Nat	Pos	Aps	(s)	Gls
4	Piotr SZYMICZEK			D	17	(3)	
7	Jan WOS			M	29		2
10	Mariusz ZGANIACZ			M	16		1
8	Dariusz ZJAWINSKI			A	1	(4)	

POGON SZCZECIN
Coach – Boguslaw Pietrzak; (27/8/05) Bohumil Panik; (22/4/06) Mariusz Kuras

2005
Date	Opponent	h/a	Score	Scorers
26/7	Wisla Plock	h	2-0	Milar, Edi
30/7	Zaglebie Lubin	a	1-1	Milar
7/8	Korona Kielce	h	4-2	Elokan, Celeban, Edi 2
21/8	Amica Wronki	a	1-4	Tralka
27/8	Gornik Zabrze	h	1-1	Edi
10/9	Wisla Krakow	a	1-2	Edi
16/9	Legia Warszawa	h	2-2	Milar, Kazmierczak
24/9	Gornik Leczna	a	1-0	Edi
1/10	GKS Belchatow	h	0-0	
15/10	Groclin Grodzisk	a	3-1	Milar, Grzelak, Elokan
21/10	Cracovia Krakow	h	1-2	Milar
29/10	Odra Wodzislaw	a	0-1	
6/11	Arka Gdynia	h	0-0	
19/11	Polonia Warszawa	h	2-0	Edi 2
25/11	Lech Poznan	a	1-1	Divecky
3/12	Wisla Plock	a	0-0	

2006
Date	Opponent	h/a	Score	Scorers
11/3	Amica Wronki	h	0-3	
24/3	Wisla Krakow	h	1-2	Cleisson
28/3	Zaglebie Lubin	h	1-0	Kazmierczak
31/1	Legia Warszawa	a	0-2	
4/4	Korona Kielce	a	1-0	Edi
8/4	Gornik Leczna	h	2-1	Kazmierczak, Amaral
11/4	GKS Belchatow	a	0-2	
15/4	Groclin Grodzisk	h	1-3	William
19/4	Gornik Zabrze	a	1-2	Elton
22/4	Cracovia Krakow	a	0-1	
29/4	Odra Wodzislaw	h	1-0	Edi (p)
6/5	Arka Gdynia	a	0-0	
10/5	Polonia Warszawa	a	1-1	Matheus
13/5	Lech Poznan	h	0-0	

No	Name	Nat	Pos	Aps	(s)	Gls
7	AMARAL	BRA	M	6	(1)	1
22	ANDERSON	BRA	M	4	(3)	
10	BATATA	BRA	M	8		
4	BATATA (II)	BRA	D	4	(1)	
30	Artur BUGAJ		A		(10)	
14	Piotr CELEBAN		D	1	(5)	1
8	CLEISSON	BRA	M	5	(1)	1
26	Radek DIVECKY	CZE	A	13	(2)	1
5	EDI	BRA	A	29	(1)	10
19	Francois ELOKAN	CMR	A	6	(9)	2
18	ELTON	BRA	A	6	(2)	1
17	FABINHO	BRA	M	1		
16	Bartosz FABINIAK		G	6	(1)	
25	FÁBIO	BRA	A	1	(2)	
30	Kamil GROSICKI		A		(2)	
9	Rafal GRZELAK		M	21	(3)	1
13	JULCIMAR	BRA	D	25	(1)	
27	JÚNIOR	BRA	A	3	(3)	
20	Przemyslaw KAZMIERCZAK		M	21	(3)	3
22	Michal LABEDZKI		M	11	(5)	
14	LILO	BRA	M	8	(2)	
6	LOPES CRUZ	BRA	D	9	(2)	
17	Pawel MAGDON		D	13		
26	MATHEUS	BRA	D	8	(2)	1
11	Grzegorz MATLAK		M	15	(2)	
25	Krzysztof MICHALSKI		D	9	(2)	
6	Claudio MILAR	URU	A	13	(2)	5
1	NENECA	BRA	G	4		
4	Tomasz PARZY		M		(3)	
33	Boris PESCOVIC	SVK	G	20		
21	Cezary PRZEWOZNIAK		M		(3)	
3	Sandro ROSA	BRA		4		
2	TAVARES	BRA	D	22	(2)	
8	Lukasz TRALKA		M	11	(2)	1
3	VALDIR	BRA	D	12		
19	WAGNER	BRA	A	2	(5)	
15	WILLIAM	BRA	A	3	(2)	1
23	ZÉ ROBERTO	BRA	D	6	(2)	

POLONIA WARSZAWA
Coach – Dariusz Kubicki; (19/11/05) Cezary Moleda; (1/1/06) Jan Zurek; (30/4/06) Andrzej Wisniewski

2005
Date	Opponent	h/a	Score	Scorers
26/7	Lech Poznan	a	2-1	Dzwigala, Arifovic
30/7	Wisla Plock	h	0-1	
6/8	Zaglebie Lubin	h	1-1	Arifovic
20/8	Korona Kielce	a	2-3	Golaszewski, Szymanek
27/8	Amica Wronki	h	0-0	
10/9	Gornik Zabrze	a	1-2	Bak
18/9	Wisla Krakow	h	0-1	
23/9	Legia Warszawa	a	0-1	
1/10	Gornik Leczna	h	0-3	
15/10	GKS Belchatow	a	0-2	
22/10	Groclin Grodzisk	a	2-1	Golaszewski, Arifovic
29/10	Cracovia Krakow	a	0-3	
19/11	Pogon Szczecin	a	0-2	
26/11	Arka Gdynia	h	0-0	
6/12	Odra Wodzislaw	h	0-3	
2/12	Lech Poznan	h	2-1	Cichon, Arifovic (p)
10/12	Wisla Plock	a	0-4	

2006
Date	Opponent	h/a	Score	Scorers
11/3	Korona Kielce	h	1-1	Kowalczyk
18/3	Amica Wronki	a	0-3	
25/3	Gornik Zabrze	h	4-1	Dzwigala, Citko, Kmiecik, Arifovic
1/4	Wisla Krakow	a	0-2	
4/4	Zaglebie Lubin	a	0-1	
9/4	Legia Warszawa	h	0-2	
12/4	Gornik Leczna	a	1-0	Arifovic (p)
15/4	GKS Belchatow	h	0-0	
23/4	Groclin Grodzisk	h	1-2	Cichon
30/4	Cracovia Krakow	h	1-3	Cichon
6/5	Odra Wodzislaw	a	0-0	
10/5	Pogon Szczecin	h	1-1	Hucika
13/5	Arka Gdynia	a	1-0	Kosmalski

No	Name	Nat	Pos	Aps	(s)	Gls
7	Esnar ARIFOVIC	SCG	A	15	(9)	6
19	Krzysztof BAK		M	13	(6)	1
15	Maciej BIERNACKI		M	3	(2)	
1	Michal CHAMERA		G	2		
16	Adam CICHON		M	17	(8)	3
6	Marek CITKO		M	7	(2)	1
36	Dariusz DZWIGALA		M	26	(1)	2
18	Martins EKWUEME	NGA	M	11	(1)	
4	Matias FAVANO	ARG	M	1		

Poland

No	Name		Nat	Pos	Aps	(s)	Gls
30	Bartlomiej FOGLER			G	1		
11	Pawel GLOWACKI			M	1	(3)	
10	Igor GOLASZEWSKI			M	19	(7)	2
17	Branko HUCIKA		CRO	D	10		1
4	Massimiliano IEZZI		ITA	M	1	(2)	
27	Kelvyn IGWE		NGA	D	9		
17	Slawomir JARCZYK			D	12		
8	Lukasz JAROSIEWICZ			M		(4)	
12	Pawel KIESZEK			G	16		
27	Grzegorz KMIECIK			A	3	(3)	1
20	Jacek KOSMALSKI			A	16	(4)	1
4	Jacek KOWALCZYK			D	7		1
25	Dariusz KOZUBEK			M	10	(1)	
14	Grzegorz KROL			A	7	(4)	
31	Hubert LEWANDOWSKI			D		(1)	
3	Antoni LUKASIEWICZ			D	15	(4)	
21	Daniel MAKA			A	1		
26	Krzysztof MARKOWSKI			D	10	(3)	
24	Jacek MORYC			D	13	(1)	
5	Krzysztof NYKIEL			D	2	(4)	
6	Lukasz PAULEWICZ			M	3		
8	Lukasz PIATEK			M	1	(1)	
28	RODRIGO		BRA	A	5	(1)	
9	Damian SEWERYN			M	6	(2)	
12	Zankarlo SIMUNIC		CRO	G	10		
1	Mateusz SLAWIK			G	1		
23	Piotr STOKOWIEC			M	7	(3)	
13	Luis SWISHER		GUA	D	14		
2	Wojciech SZYMANEK			D	13	(2)	1
9	Maciej TERLECKI			M	2	(2)	
14	Mariusz ZASADA			M	10	(3)	
2	Mateusz ZYTKO			D	10	(1)	

WISLA KRAKOW
Coach – Jerzy Engel; (5/11/05) Tomasz Kulawik; (1/1/06) Dan Petrescu (ROM)

2005
Date	Opponent	H/A	Score	Scorers
26/7	Gornik Leczna	a	1-1	Uche
30/7	GKS Belchatow	h	3-0	Brozek Pa.2, Frankowski
5/8	Groclin Grodzisk	a	4-2	Brozek Pa., Frankowski 2, Zienczuk (p)
27/8	Odra Wodzislaw	a	1-1	Frankowski
10/9	Pogon Szczecin	h	2-1	Zienczuk 2
18/9	Polonia Warszawa	a	1-0	Penksa
24/9	Lech Poznan	h	5-1	Brozek Pa.3, Zienczuk, Penksa
2/10	Wisla Plock	a	2-1	Zienczuk (p), Kuzba
16/10	Zaglebie Lubin	a	1-2	Zienczuk (p)
23/10	Korona Kielce	h	2-2	Brozek Pa., Kuzba
30/10	Amica Wronki	h	0-0	
5/11	Gornik Zabrze	a	1-0	Sobolewski
19/11	Arka Gdynia	a	0-1	
22/11	Cracovia Krakow	h	3-0	Stolarczyk, Kuzba, Dudka
27/11	Legia Warszawa	h	0-0	
3/12	Gornik Leczna	h	1-0	Sobolewski
11/12	GKS Belchatow	a	0-0	

2006
Date	Opponent	H/A	Score	Scorers
4/3	Groclin Grodzisk	h	2-1	Kryszalowicz 2
12/3	Cracovia Krakow	a	1-1	Klos
19/3	Odra Wodzislaw	h	1-0	Brozek Pa.
24/3	Pogon Szczecin	a	2-1	Sobolewski, Baszczynski (p)
1/4	Polonia Warszawa	h	2-0	Brozek Pi., Brozek Pa.
8/4	Lech Poznan	a	1-2	Klos
11/4	Wisla Plock	h	4-0	Kryszalowicz 2, Brozek Pa.,

Date	Opponent	H/A	Score	Scorers
15/4	Zaglebie Lubin	h	2-0	Brozek Pa., Baszczynski
21/4	Korona Kielce	a	0-1	
28/4	Amica Wronki	a	1-0	Brozek Pa.
6/5	Gornik Zabrze	h	2-0	Zienczuk, Jean Paulista
10/5	Arka Gdynia	h	3-1	Penksa, Jean Paulista, Zienczuk
13/5	Legia Warszawa	a	2-1	Brozek Pa., Penksa

No	Name	Nat	Pos	Aps	(s)	Gls
19	ANDRÉ BARRETO	BRA	M	2	(4)	
4	Marcin BASZCZYNSKI		D	27	(1)	2
36	Rafal BOGUSKI		A		(2)	
16	Jakub BLASZCZYKOWSKI		M	16	(1)	
10,23	Pawel BROZEK		A	27	(3)	13
22	Piotr BROZEK		M	7	(11)	1
77	Jacob BURNS	AUS	M	7	(1)	
20	Mauro CANTORO	ARG	M	16	(3)	
11	Tomasz DAWIDOWSKI		A		(6)	
18	Dariusz DUDKA		D	29		1
21	Tomasz FRANKOWSKI		A	4		4
6	Arkadiusz GLOWACKI		D	11	(1)	
9	Konrad GOLOS		M	7	(11)	1
5	JEAN PAULISTA	BRA	M	8	(11)	2
30	Tomasz KLOS		D	29		2
8	Jacek KOWALCZYK		D	2		
14	Pawel KRYSZALOWICZ		A	15	(4)	4
31	Marcin KUZBA		A	10	(4)	3
33	Radoslaw MAJDAN		G	26		
10	Nikola MIJAJLOVIC	SCG	D	8	(3)	
1	Mariusz PAWELEK		G	4		
99	Marek PENKSA	SVK	M	5	14	4
7	Radoslaw SOBOLEWSKI		M	25	(2)	3
3	Maciej STOLARCZYK		D	15	(1)	1
10	Kalu UCHE	NGA	M	3	(1)	1
26	Norbert VARGA	ROM	M	2	(2)	
17	Marek ZIENCZUK		M	25	(2)	8

WISLA PLOCK
Coach – Miroslaw Jablonski; (5/11/05) Josef Csaplár (CZE)

2005
Date	Opponent	H/A	Score	Scorers
26/7	Pogon Szczecin	a	0-2	
30/7	Polonia Warszawa	a	1-0	Jelen
6/8	Lech Poznan	a	2-3	Gesior, Gevorgyan
20/8	Arka Gdynia	h	1-1	Vujovic
28/8	Zaglebie Lubin	h	3-2	Zilic, Gesior, Jelen
10/9	Korona Kielce	a	3-2	Jelen, Zilic, Belada (p)
17/9	Amica Wronki	h	0-1	
24/9	Gornik Zabrze	a	0-4	
2/10	Wisla Krakow	h	1-2	Kazimierczak
15/10	Legia Warszawa	a	0-3	
22/10	Gornik Leczna	h	2-1	Zilic 2
29/10	GKS Belchatow	a	0-3	
5/11	Groclin Grodzisk	h	2-0	Gesior, Pekovic
19/11	Cracovia Krakow	a	1-3	Jelen
26/11	Odra Wodzislaw	h	0-0	
3/12	Pogon Szczecin	h	0-0	
10/12	Polonia Warszawa	h	4-0	Zilic, Mierzejewski, Gevorgyan, Peszko

2006
Date	Opponent	H/A	Score	Scorers
25/3	Korona Kielce	h	1-0	Jelen (p)
29/3	Arka Gdynia	a	1-1	Belada
1/4	Amica Wronki	a	0-2	
4/4	Lech Poznan	h	5-1	Gevorgyan, Obajdin 2,

Poland

8/4	Gornik Zabrze	h	1-0	Jelen, Rachwal (p) Jelen
11/4	Wisla Krakow	a	0-4	
15/4	Legia Warszawa	h	0-1	
19/4	Zaglebie Lubin	a	0-2	
22/4	Gornik Leczna	a	1-2	Magdon
29/4	GKS Belchatow	h	0-1	
6/5	Groclin Grodzisk	a	0-3	
10/5	Cracovia Krakow	h	1-0	Gevorgyan
13/5	Odra Wodzislaw	a	0-1	

No	Name	Nat	Pos	Aps	(s)	Gls
18	Zarko BELADA	SCG	D	28		2
17	Marko COLAKOVIC	SCG	D	6	(1)	
3	Dariusz GESIOR		M	16	(1)	3
8	Wahan GEVORGYAN		M	20	(3)	4
11	Marco GRIZONIC	SLO	M	10		
21	Robert GUBIEC		G	7		
19	Lukasz JASINSKI		M	2	(5)	
4	Lukasz JEGLINSKI		D		(2)	
9	Ireneusz JELEN		A	24	(1)	7
7	Mamia JIKIA	GEO	D	3		
2	Krzysztof KAZIMIERCZAK		D	21	(2)	1
3	Pawel MAGDON		D	9	(1)	1
10	Adrian MIERZEJEWSKI		M	9	(11)	1
16	Damian NARODZONEK		A		(1)	
24	Josef OBAJDIN	CZE	A	8	(2)	2
15	Mitar PEKOVIC	SCG	D	23	(3)	1
14	Slawomir PESZKO		M	12	(9)	1
20	Patryk RACHWAL		M	25		1
6	Dariusz ROMUZGA		D	18	(7)	
19	Tomasz SAJDAK		A		(5)	
25	Lumír SEDLÁCEK	CZE	M	8	(2)	
26	Pawel SOBCZAK		A	1	(1)	
23	Robert STYRANOWSKI		A	5	(3)	
7	Maciej TRUSZCZYNSKI		D	5	(2)	
11	Predrag VUJOVIC	SCG	M	11	(2)	1
1	Jakub WIERZCHOWSKI		G	23		
77	Sead ZILIC	BOS	A	11	(13)	5
5	Nebojsa ZIVKOVIC	SCG	D	25	(1)	

ZAGLEBIE LUBIN
Coach – Drazen Besek (SCG); (10/9/05) Franciszek Smuda

2005
26/7	Odra Wodzislaw	a	0-0	
30/7	Pogon Szczecin	h	1-1	Iwanski
6/8	Polonia Warszawa	a	1-1	Iwanski
20/8	Lech Poznan	h	4-5	Chalbinski 2, Kristic, Iwanski
28/8	Wisla Plock	a	2-3	Iwanski, Chalbinski
10/9	Arka Gdynia	a	1-0	Pokorny
17/9	Korona Kielce	h	3-3	Chalbinski, Szczypkowski, Stasiak
25/9	Amica Wronki	a	1-3	Chalbinski
1/10	Gornik Zabrze	h	3-0	Mierzejewski, Lobodzinski, Chalbinski
16/10	Wisla Krakow	h	2-1	Chalbinski (p), Kalousek
22/10	Legia Warszawa	h	0-1	
29/10	Gornik Leczna	a	3-1	Plizga, Chalbinski, Lobodzinski
5/11	GKS Belchatow	h	2-1	Stasiak, Chalbinski
20/11	Groclin Grodzisk	a	0-1	
26/11	Cracovia Krakow	h	3-1	Kalousek, Chalbinski, Iwanski
3/12	Odra Wodzislaw	h	2-0	Plizga, Bartczak

2006
10/3	Lech Poznan	a	1-0	Chalbinski
25/3	Arka Gdynia	h	4-0	Iwanski 2, Chalbinski, Plizga
28/3	Pogon Szczecin	a	0-1	
1/4	Korona Kielce	a	1-1	Plizga
4/4	Polonia Warszawa	h	1-0	Chalbinski
7/4	Amica Wronki	h	2-0	Chalbinski, Plizga
11/4	Gornik Zabrze	a	2-2	Iwanski, Lobodzinski
15/4	Wisla Krakow	a	0-2	
19/4	Wisla Plock	h	2-0	Iwanski, Stasiak
22/4	Legia Warszawa	a	0-1	
29/4	Gornik Leczna	h	2-0	Chalbinski 2
7/5	GKS Belchatow	a	0-3	
10/5	Groclin Grodzisk	h	2-0	Piszczek, Iwanski
13/5	Cracovia Krakow	h	0-0	

No	Name	Nat	Pos	Aps	(s)	Gls
27	Vidas ALUNDRIS	LAT	D	9		
5	Manuel ARBOLEDA	COL	D	13		
23	Dawid BANACZEK		A	5	(3)	
19	Grzegorz BARTCZAK		D	8	(13)	1
25	Vladimir CAP	CZE	D	7	(2)	
11	Michal CHALBINSKI		A	27	(1)	16
16	FELIPE	BRA	D	10	(1)	
16	GILCIMAR CHAVES	BRA	A		(1)	
7	Maciej IWANSKI		M	26		10
14	Dariusz JACKIEWICZ		M	23	(1)	
15	David KALOUSEK	CZE	D	8	(1)	2
2	Robert KLOS		D	18	(1)	
24	Matija KRISTIC	CRO	D	4		1
21	Mariusz LIBERA		G	28	(1)	
9	Wojciech LOBODZINSKI		A	27	(2)	3
1	Danijel MADARIC	CRO	G	2		
22	Lukasz MIERZEJEWSKI		A	21	(2)	1
26	Lukasz PISZCZEK		A	10	(17)	1
17	Dawid PLIZGA		A	16	(8)	5
3	Petr POKORNY	CZE	D	8	(1)	1
28	Carlos SERRA	BRA	D	3		
4	Michal STASIAK		D	25	(1)	3
20	Pawel STRAK		M	2	(4)	
20	Ibrahim SUNDAY	NGA	M	2	(10)	
6	Andrzej SZCZYPKOWSKI		D	27	(1)	1
5	Mateusz ZYTKO		D	1	(1)	

DOMESTIC CUP 2005/06

1/16 FINALS
(20/9/05 & 25/10/05)
Cracovia Krakow v Kujawiak Wloclawek 0-0; 0-2 *(0-2)*
Odra Wodzislaw v Zaglebie Sosnowiec 4-1; 3-0 *(7-1)*
GKS Belchatow v Podbeskidzie Bielsko-Biala 0-1; 0-1 *(0-2)*
LKS Lodz v Pogon Szczecin 1-4: 1-2 *(2-6)*
(20/9/05 & 26/10/05)
Wierna Malogoszcz v Zaglebie Lubin 1-1; 0-3 *(1-4)*
KSZO Ostrowiec Swietokrzyski v Legia Warszawa 1-2; 0-2 *(1-4)*
Warta Sieradz v Wisla Plock 0-2; 0-5 *(0-7)*
(21/9/05 & 25/10/05)
Okocimski Brzesko v Lech Poznan 3-3; 1-4 *(4-7)*

Poland

Jagiellonia Bialystok v Gornik Leczna 1-0; 2-1 *(aet) (3-1)*
OKS 1945 Olsztyn v Groclin Dyskobolia Grodzisk 1-6; 0-5 *(1-11)*
(21/9/05 & 26/10/05)
Mazowsze Plock v Korona Kielce 0-3; 0-3 *(0-6)*
Tloki Gorzyce v Wisla Krakow 0-3; 0-3 *(0-6)*
Drweca Nowe Miasto Lubawskie v Amica Wronki 0-3; 0-3 *(0-6)*
Gornik Zabrze v Radomiak Radom 0-1; 0-3 *(0-4)*
(27/9/05 & 25/10/05)
Polonia Warszawa v Tur Turek 2-0; 0-1 *(2-1)*
Bye - Hetman Zamosc

1/8 FINALS
(8/11/05 & 23/11/05)
Wisla Plock v Podbeskidzie Bielsko-Biala 3-0; 0-0 *(3-0)*
(8/11/05 & 29/11/05)
Jagiellonia Bialystok v Polonia Warszawa 1-3; 3-2 *(4-5)*
(8/11/05 & 30/11/05)
Zaglebie Lubin v Wisla Krakow 1-1; 1-0 *(2-1)*
(9/11/05 & 15/11/05)
Amica Wronki v Odra Wodzislaw 0-0; 2-3 *(2-3)*
(9/11/05 & 16/11/05)
Lech Poznan v Radomiak Radom 2-0; 2-0 *(4-0)*
(9/11/05 & 22/11/05)
Kujawiak Wloclawek v Pogon Szczecin 1-0; 1-2 *(2-2; Kujawiak Wloclawek on away goal)*
(10/11/05 & 23/11/05)
Groclin Dyskobolia Grodzisk v Korona Kielce 2-2; 1-2 *(3-4)*
(11/11/05 & 23/11/05)
Hetman Zamosc v Legia Warszawa 0-4; 0-6 *(0-10)*

QUARTER-FINALS
(22/11/05 & 29/11/05)
Lech Poznan 1 *(Telichowski 61)*, Odra Wodzislaw 0
Odra Wodzislaw 0, Lech Poznan 0
(Lech Poznan 1-0)

(29/11/05 & 6/12/05)
Wisla Plock 1 *(Belada 12)*, Kujawiak Wloclawek 0
Kujawiak Wloclawek 1 *(Staniszewski 90)*, Wisla Plock 1 *(Pekovic 105) (aet)*
(Wisla Plock 2-1)

(30/11/05 & 7/3/06)
Legia Warszawa 2 *(Janczyk 11, Choto 57)*, Korona Kielce 0
Korona Kielce 3 *(Bilski 23, Gajtkowski 70, Piechna 95)*, Legia Warszawa 0 *(aet)*
(Korona Kielce 3-2)

(13/12/05 & 18/12/05)
Zaglebie Lubin 0, Polonia Warszawa 1 *(Dzwigala 18)*
Polonia Warszawa 0, Zaglebie Lubin 3 *(Chalbinski 9, 29, 58)*
(Zaglebie Lubin 3-1)

SEMI-FINALS
(14/3/06 & 22/3/06)
Zaglebie Lubin 2 *(Lobodzinski 42, Chalbinski 52)*, Korona Kielce 0
Korona Kielce 0, Zaglebie Lubin 0
(Zaglebie Lubin 2-0)

(15/3/06 & 22/3/06)
Wisla Plock 0, Lech Poznan 0
Lech Poznan 0, Wisla Plock 1 *(Zakrzwseki 56og)*
(Wisla Plock 1-0)

FINAL
(26/4/06)
GOS Stadium, Lubin
ZAGLEBIE LUBIN 2 *(Jackiewicz 63, Arboleda 87)*
WISLA PLOCK 3 *(Jelen 1, 56, Belada 89)*
Referee – Pacuda
ZAGLEBIE LUBIN – Liberda, Klos *(Bartczak 83)*, Stasiak, Arboleda, Mierzejewski, Lobodzinski, Szczypkowski, Jackiewicz, Iwanski, Plizga *(Piszczek 26)*, Chalbinski.
WISLA PLOCK – Gubiec, Zivkovic, Belada, Magdon, Kazimierczak, Gevorgyan *(Peszko 62)*, Rachwal, Romuzga, Obajdin *(Pekovic 82)*, Sedlacek *(Truszczynski 90)*, Jelen.

(3/5/06)
Gorski Stadium, Plock
WISLA PLOCK 3 *(Magdon 68, Gevorgyan 73, Truszczynski 86)*
ZAGLEBIE LUBIN 1 *(Piszczek 82)*
Referee – Slupik
WISLA PLOCK – Gubiec, Zivkovic, Belada, Magdon, Kazimierczak *(Pekovic 46)*, Gevorgyan, Rachwal, Romuzga, Obajdin, Sedlacek *(Truszczynski 83)*, Jelen *(Styranowski 88)*.
ZAGLEBIE LUBIN – Liberda, Filipe, Stasiak, Arboleda *(Bartczak 58)*, Mierzejewski *(Cap 64)*, Lobodzinski, Szczypkowski, Jackiewicz *(Ibrahim 70)*, Iwanski, Piszczek, Chalbinski.
(WISLA PLOCK 6-3)

SECOND LEVEL FINAL TABLE 2005/06

		Pld	W	D	L	F	A	Pts
1	Widzew Lodz	34	18	8	8	53	28	62
2	Lodzki KS	34	15	13	6	42	21	58
3	Jagiellonia Bialystok	34	15	11	8	48	30	56
4	Slask Wroclaw	34	16	8	10	38	35	56
5	Zaglebie Sosnowiec	34	15	9	10	48	34	54
6	Zawisza Bydgoszcz	34	13	14	7	38	26	53
7	Ruch Chorzow	34	14	9	11	50	36	51
8	Piast Gliwice	34	15	13	6	44	33	48
9	KSZO Ostrowiec Swietokrzyski	34	12	10	12	37	41	46
10	Lechia Gdansk	34	11	12	11	33	39	45
11	Gornik Polkowice	34	12	9	13	36	37	45
12	HEKO Czermno	34	10	13	11	40	42	43
13	Podbeskidzie Bielsko-Biala	34	9	14	11	37	38	41
14	Radomiak Radom	34	8	11	15	39	46	35
15	Polonia Bytom	34	9	8	17	32	51	35
16	Swit Nowy Dwor Mazowiecki	34	7	9	18	27	54	30
17	Szczakowianka Jaworzno	34	8	19	8	28	63	29
18	Finishparkiet Nowe Miasto	34	5	11	18	31	47	26

N.B. Piast Gliwice – 10 pts deducted; Kujawiak Wloclawek replaced at the winter break by Zawisza Bydgoszcz.

PROMOTION/RELEGATION PLAY-OFFS
(15/6/06)
Jagiellonia Bialystok 0, Arka Gdynia 2
(18/6/06)
Arka Gdynia 2, Jagiellonia Bialystok 1
(Arka Gdynia 4-1)

Portugal

Flattered by fourth place

Portugal returned home from the World Cup to a reception fit for heroes. Fourth place was the country's best performance at the tournament for 40 years, and the nation was understandably proud of the team's achievement

A more impartial observation of Portugal's month in Germany was that they were fortunate to last the distance. A team virtually unchanged from the one that had finished runners-up, on home soil, at Euro 2004, they played good football only in patches. In none of their seven matches did they ever truly dominate, and during the periods that they did, they were unable to make it count in front of goal.

For years Portugal have been a team overloaded with fine, technical midfielders at the expense of a potent attack. It is utterly paradoxical that Pauleta, the country's all-time top goalscorer (47 goals in 88 appearances place him ahead of the great Eusébio), should have looked so utterly out of his depth at both Euro 2004 and the 2006 World Cup. Granted, he scored a hat-trick in the 2002 World Cup – something no other player has managed at the finals since – but in Germany, apart from in the opening few minutes of the first game against Angola, when he scored, he never looked likely to add to his record haul. It was a wonder that coach Luiz Felipe Scolari persisted with him – even through to the third-place play-off.

Goal drought

Until substitute Nuno Gomes planted a header past Oliver Kahn in the dying moments of that game in Stuttgart, no Portuguese striker had found the target in almost 11 hours. In fact, no Portuguese player of any description scored in either the quarter-final or semi-final. That was a shame, because in Luís Figo, Deco and Cristiano Ronaldo the team had three of the most imaginative and threatening players on view. Figo rolled back the years with a sumptuous opening performance against Angola, Deco showed some delicious touches throughout and scored a great goal against Iran, while Cristiano Ronaldo was one of the few players at the tournament repeatedly prepared to take defenders on.

Unfortunately, all three sullied their reputations. Figo should have been sent off and suspended for a blatant head-butt on Holland's Khalid Boulahrouz; Deco received a red card in the same game; and Cristiano Ronaldo became the tournament's pantomime villain for his persistently unsporting behaviour, which included diving, whining and even urging the referee to send off his club colleague Wayne Rooney.

Ricardo, with his three saves, was the hero of that shoot-out success – as he had been against the same opposition at Euro 2004 – but in general play he failed to convince, making too many unforced (if mostly unexploited) errors. A much more assured figure was centre-back Fernando Meira, who deputised superbly for the injured Jorge Andrade and was the only Portuguese outfield player to start and finish all seven matches.

Tournament pedigree

Scolari once again proved his tournament pedigree, tagging four more wins plus a penalty shoot-out success on to the seven straight victories he had achieved in 2002 with Brazil. However, he got lucky at times and there was little evidence of the tactical mastery he had shown in the previous two tournaments. Worse still, he proved himself a bad loser with his undignified remonstrations after the final whistle against France. But the Portuguese love him, and he has agreed to stay on board for another two years and navigate the team through

Portugal

their arduous Euro 2008 qualifying journey – one that will take in long trips to Armenia, Azerbaijan and Kazakhstan as well as testing fixtures against Serbia, Poland, Belgium and Finland.

Figo has played his last game for Portugal and Pauleta has scored his last international goal, but otherwise Scolari can proceed with the same bunch of players. Nuno Gomes, with 24 goals in 55 games, deserves the chance to take up Pauleta's mantle, if only because there is no alternative; decent up-and-coming strikers are simply nowhere to be found.

Only two Portuguese players scored ten goals or more in the 2005/06 Superliga. One of them was Nuno Gomes, who netted 15 for Benfica. The other was 31-year-old journeyman João Tomás, who managed the same total for Sporting Braga. Unfortunately, most Superliga teams tend to fill their forward lines with imports, most of them from Brazil.

FC Porto are a case in point. They had mercurial Portuguese Under-21 striker Hugo Almeida on their books in 2005/06 but he made the starting line-up just six times. Despite the wondergoal he scored in the Champions League against Inter at the San Siro, he remained an eternal substitute. Not that the club's new coach, Co Adriaanse, had to justify leaving him on the bench. His results spoke for themselves, and at the end of his debut season the Dutchman was celebrating victory in both the Superliga and the Portuguese Cup.

Mediocre fare

The Superliga season as a whole was a poor one. The economic constraints on FC Porto and their two Lisbon rivals Benfica and Sporting precluded the arrival of any big-name acquisitions, and the fare served up by the Big Three and the other 15 teams was decidedly mediocre. The move to reduce the Superliga to a 16-club division may improve matters, but it could be a while before Portugal again boasts a team as good as the all-conquering José Mourinho-led Porto side of recent vintage.

Adriaanse's Porto were not remotely comparable. They won the league because they made fewer mistakes than their rivals and found their best form when it mattered most, reeling off nine consecutive victories in the run-in. Beaten home and away by Benfica (for the first time in 29 years), they were also held 1-1 at home by Sporting. But, thanks to the sterling efforts of consistent performers like young winger Ricardo Quaresma and Argentine midfielder Lucho González, they won most of the bread-and-butter fixtures, and in the last big league game of the season, at the Alvalade, they sneaked a 1-0 victory over Sporting. Had they lost, they would have been a point behind Sporting with four games remaining. Instead, victory hoisted them five points clear. A fortnight later, after another 1-0 win, at bottom club Penafiel, Porto's 21st Portuguese title was safely under lock and key.

The Cup arrived in the Porto trophy cabinet a few weeks later following a 1-0 win over holders Vitória Setúbal. A goal from Brazilian striker Adriano, who had also scored the winner at Penafiel, proved sufficient for Porto to complete the fifth Double in their history. As in the league, it was a win over Sporting that proved crucial, Porto overcoming their southern rivals on penalties in the semi-final after a highly controversial match in which they benefited from several contentious refereeing decisions.

NATIONAL TEAM RESULTS 2005/06

Date	Opponent	H/A/N	Venue	Score	Scorers
17/8/05	Egypt	H	Ponta Delgada	2-0	Fernando Meira (50), Hélder Postiga (69)
3/9/05	Luxembourg (WCQ)	H	Faro/Loulé	6-0	Jorge Andrade (23), Ricardo Carvalho (30), Pauleta (37, 56), Simão (79, 83)
7/9/05	Russia (WCQ)	A	Moscow	0-0	
8/10/05	Liechtenstein (WCQ)	H	Aveiro	2-1	Pauleta (49), Nuno Gomes (86)
12/10/05	Latvia (WCQ)	H	Oporto	3-0	Pauleta (19, 21), Hugo Viana (85)
12/11/05	Croatia	H	Coimbra	2-0	Petit (32), Pauleta (65)
15/11/05	Northern Ireland	A	Belfast	1-1	Craigan (41og)
1/3/06	Saudi Arabia	N	Düsseldorf	3-0	Cristiano Ronaldo (29, 84), Maniche (44)
27/5/06	Cape Verde Islands	H	Evora	4-1	Pauleta (1, 37, 82), Petit (59)
3/6/06	Luxembourg	N	Metz	3-0	Simão (46, 72p), Figo (85)
11/6/06	Angola (WCF)	N	Cologne	1-0	Pauleta (4)
17/6/06	Iran (WCF)	N	Frankfurt	2-0	Deco (63), Cristiano Ronaldo (80p)
21/6/06	Mexico (WCF)	N	Gelsenkirchen	2-1	Maniche (6), Simão (24p)
25/6/06	Holland (WCF)	N	Nuremberg	1-0	Maniche (23)
1/7/06	England (WCF)	N	Gelsenkirchen	0-0	(aet; 3-1 on pens)
5/7/06	France (WCF)	N	Munich	0-1	
8/7/06	Germany (WCF)	N	Stuttgart	1-3	Nuno Gomes (88)

Portugal

Two trophies

By and large the Porto fans found Adriaanse a difficult man to love. Although the Dutchman brought them two trophies, he enraged them with some of his team selections – notably the exclusion of goalkeeper Vítor Baía - and he was also forthright with his criticisms of the Portuguese game. Furthermore his tactics didn't go down too well, especially in the Champions League, where Porto's continuous failure to defend a lead cost them dear. The worst example came at home to Artmedia Bratislava when the team inexplicably surrendered a two-goal lead to lose 3-2.

Porto finished bottom of their Champions League group, but Benfica, also newly coached by a Dutchman, Ronald Koeman, steered their way through to the last 16 at the expense of Manchester United before knocking out holders Liverpool and then giving Barcelona a fright in the quarter-final.

It was impressive stuff from the Lisbon Eagles in their first Champions League campaign for six years, and it helped to gloss over an undistinguished domestic campaign in which the team were far too inconsistent to offer anything more than a token challenge for honours. Having won the championship for the first time in 11 years, under Giovanni Trapattoni, Benfica's title defence got off to an atrocious start when they collected just one point from their opening three matches, including a 2-1 defeat to Sporting in the Alvalade.

Before long, though, with Nuno Gomes banging in the goals at a tidy rate, they were off and running. A first victory away to Porto for 11 years (thanks to a Nuno Gomes double) was a real boon, but then came another lengthy lapse. Champions League qualification in December provided another timely lift, but just when the team appeared to be motoring back into title contention they dropped out for good after a run of three defeats in four games, the first of them at home to Sporting, who completed the double over their arch-rivals with an exhilarating 3-1 win.

Tug-o'-war

Marcello Moretto, Vitória Setúbal's highly-rated Brazilian goalkeeper, was signed up by Benfica in mid-season after an unruly tug-o'-war with Porto, and although he played brilliantly in the Champions League, especially against Barcelona, he made some basic errors in the league games. French winger Laurent Robert, another January recruit, wasn't a patch on resident flank man Simão, who, along with fellow Portuguese international Petit, was again the club's most consistent performer – despite missing a hefty chunk of the campaign in the late autumn through injury.

Benfica were still contesting the runners-up spot on the final day of the season, but a 3-1 defeat at Paços Ferreira ensured they would finish no higher than third and thus have to pre-qualify for the 2006/07 Champions League. When Koeman decided to cut short his stay and return home to take charge at PSV, the Benfica board decided it was time to go native again and brought in ex-Porto and Sporting boss Fernando Santos from AEK Athens.

Sporting changed their coach in mid-season. José Peseiro was always living on borrowed time after his rabbit-in-the-headlights performance in the previous season's UEFA Cup final, and when the Lions limped out of both European competitions in double-quick time then suffered back-to-back league defeats against makeweights Paços Ferreira and Académica, Peseiro didn't have a leg to stand on. Nobly accepting a share of the blame himself, president Dias de Cunha also stepped down. The directors he left behind decided to promote from within and appointed former midfielder Paulo Bento as the new coach.

Purring Lions

It was a wise move. The defensive howlers that had brought humiliation against both Udinese and Halmstad in Europe suddenly ceased, and as the title race entered its decisive phase the Lions began to purr. Their brilliant 3-1 win at Benfica in late January began a storming run that catapulted them back into title contention. Ten victories in a row, seven of them without conceding a goal (thanks largely to their two mid-season defensive recruits, Abel and Marco Caneira), carried Sporting into the potential title decider at home to Porto. Another win would take the Green and Whites to the top of the table, but the baggage they carried from their controversial Cup semi-final defeat a few weeks earlier weighed Sporting down. They didn't play with their usual freedom or confidence and were beaten by Jorginho's sucker punch late in the game.

Portugal

NATIONAL TEAM APPEARANCES 2005/06

Coach – Luiz Felipe SCOLARI (BRA)

Player	DoB	Club	Egy	LUX	RUS	LIE	LAT	Cro	Nir	Sau	Cvd	Lux	ANG	IRN	MEX	HOL	ENG	FRA	GER	Caps	Goals
Joaquim Silva "QUIM"	13/11/75	SL Benfica	G					G												24	-
Domingos Costa "ALEX"	6/9/79	VfL Wolfsburg (GER)	D																	3	-
RICARDO CARVALHO	18/5/78	Chelsea (ENG)	D	D	D	D		D	D		D	D	D	D	D	D	D	D		30	1
JORGE ANDRADE	9/4/78	RC Deportivo (ESP)	D46	D	D	D	D		D											44	3
PAULO FERREIRA	18/1/79	Chelsea (ENG)	D46	D	D	D		s61	D	s74	s46			s61			s62	D		33	-
Armando Teixeira "PETIT"	25/9/76	SL Benfica	M46		M		M73	M68	s46	M46	s46	M72	s66	M	s46	M		s46		42	4
Luís FIGO	4/1/72	Internazionale (ITA)	M62	M	M	M	M79		M46	M46	M	M	M88	M80	M85	M86	M	s77		127	32
TIAGO Pereira Mendes	2/5/81	Chelsea (ENG) / Olympique Lyonnais (FRA)	M			s71	M	M78	M77		s46	s68	M83	s80	M	s85	M74			27	-
HUGO VIANA	15/1/83	Newcastle United (ENG) / Valencia CF (ESP)	M62			s75	s79			s46	s46	s71	s83			s74				23	1
HÉLDER POSTIGA	2/8/82	FC Porto / AS Saint-Etienne (FRA)	A	s68	s68		s58	s78	s69	s46	s62	s46		A69		s86	s74			27	9
Pedro Resende "PAULETA"	28/4/73	Paris Saint-Germain (FRA)	A46	A	A68	A	A58	A66	A46	A46	A	A46	A	A	A46	A63	A67	A77		88	47
FERNANDO MEIRA	5/6/78	VfB Stuttgart (GER)	s46			D	D	D	D	D	D60	D	D	D	D	D	D	D		37	2
MARCO CANEIRA	9/2/79	Valencia CF (ESP) / Sporting CP	s46			D	D80	s63			s66	D46			D					15	-
JOÃO MOUTINHO	8/9/86	Sporting CP	s46	s46	s83															3	-
RICARDO QUARESMA	26/9/83	FC Porto	s46						s46											5	-
JOÃO ALVES	18/8/80	Sporting CP	s62				s76	s68												3	-
Luís BOA MORTE	4/8/77	Fulham (ENG)	s62				M	M63						s80						25	1
RICARDO Pereira	11/2/76	Sporting CP		G	G	G		G		G	G	G	G	G	G	G	G	G	G	56	-
NUNO VALENTE	12/9/74	Everton (ENG)		D	D	D				D66		D	D	D		D	D	D	D69	29	1
Francisco "COSTINHA"	1/12/74	Dinamo Moskva (RUS)		M	M			M	M	M	s46	M46	s60	M		M		M74	M46	49	2
Nuno Ribeiro MANICHE	11/11/77	Dinamo Moskva (RUS) / Chelsea (ENG)		M46	M83	M71	M			M46	M46	M68	s72	M66	M	M	M	M	M	38	6
CRISTIANO RONALDO	5/2/85	Manchester United (ENG)		M64	M	M83	M46	M76	M69	M	M62	M71	M60	M		M34	M	M	M	38	12
Anderson Souza "DECO"	27/8/77	FC Barcelona (ESP)		M68	M76		M			M46	M46	M46		M80		M	M	M	M	39	3
SIMÃO Sabrosa	31/10/79	SL Benfica		s64	s76	M75				s46	s46	M	s88	M	s34	s63	s67	M		50	10
NUNO GOMES	5/7/76	SL Benfica				s83	s46	s66	s46					s69				s69		55	24
MIGUEL Monteiro	4/1/80	Valencia CF (ESP)					D	D61		D74	D	D	D	D	D61	D	D	D62		34	1
Nuno FRECHAUT	24/9/77	Dinamo Moskva (RUS)					s73	s77												17	-
JORGE RIBEIRO	9/11/81	Dinamo Moskva (RUS)					s80	D												5	-
PAULO SANTOS	11/12/72	Sporting Braga						G												1	-
RICARDO COSTA	16/5/81	FC Porto									s60							D		4	-

Portugal

The title bid was over, but Sporting still had the runners-up spot to go for. They had blown the opportunity for automatic Champions League qualification the previous season, but after two nervy goalless draws a 3-1 win at Rio Ave put them back on course and on the final day, needing only a point to finish above Benfica, they becalmed their fans with a 1-0 victory courtesy of a splendid goal from midfield starlet João Moutinho.

For the fourth year in a row Sporting had no trophies to show for their efforts, but they appeared to have found a good coach, and with the books balanced and the prospect of a few million Swiss francs flooding into the club's coffers from the Champions League, the club's long-suffering fans retired for the summer in less despondent mood than usual.

There was plenty of cheer for the followers of Sporting Braga and Nacional, whose teams qualified for Europe. Remarkably, both clubs had topped the table in the first half of the season, but despite fading fortunes in the spring they held on to fourth and fifth place, respectively, to join Cup runners-up Setúbal in the UEFA Cup.

Going down

There was only misery for the supporters of Vitória Guimarães and Belenenses, however, as they digested the grim reality of relegation to the Liga de Honra. Guimarães, who had been the only one of four Portuguese teams to reach the group phase of the UEFA Cup, dropped out of the top division for the first time in 48 years. Belenenses, who boasted the league's top scorer in Albert Meyong, joined them on the final day after an outrageous combination of results conspired to send them down. Normally their 15th-place finish would have meant safety, but the reduction in size of the Superliga left them in the lurch. With only two teams promoted as opposed to four relegated, Leixões, third in the Liga de Honra behind Beira Mar and Aves, also missed out.

Belenenses and Leixões were given hope of a reprieve during the summer when it emerged that Gil Vicente might be in danger of ceding their Superliga place because of an administrative error they had made regarding the eligibility of mid-season recruit Mateus. The case went to arbitration, but as no decision had been made in early August, it looked as if Gil Vicente would hold on to their status.

EUROPEAN CUPS 2005/06

UEFA CHAMPIONS LEAGUE

SL BENFICA

1st round Group D
Match 1 LILLE OSC (FRA)
H 1-0 *Miccoli (90)*
Moreira, Nelson, Luisão, Ricardo Rocha (Anderson 46), Léo, Geovanni (Mantorras 80), Petit (Karagounis 67), Manuel Fernandes, Simão, Miccoli, Nuno Gomes.

Match 2 MANCHESTER UNITED (ENG)
A 1-2 *Simão (59)*
Moreira, Nélson, Luisão, Ricardo Rocha, Léo, Beto (Geovanni 86), Petit, Manuel Fernandes (Mantorras 86), Miccoli (João Pereira 79), Nuno Gomes, Simão.

Match 3 VILLARREAL CF (ESP)
A 1-1 *Manuel Fernandes (77)*
Quim (Rui Neréu 29), Nélson, Luisão, Anderson, Ricardo Rocha, Petit, Karagounis (Karyaka 65), Manuel Fernandes, Geovanni (Beto 90), Nuno Gomes, Simão.

Match 4 VILLARREAL CF
H 0-1
Rui Neréu, Nélson, Luisão, Anderson (Nuno Assis 83), Léo, Petit, Karagounis (João Pereira 70), Manuel Fernandes, Geovanni (Mantorras 70), Nuno Gomes, Simão.

Match 5 LILLE OSC
A 0-0
Quim, Alcides, Luisão, Anderson, Ricardo Rocha, Nélson, Beto, Petit, Léo, Nuno Gomes, Miccoli (Mantorras 43).

Match 6 MANCHESTER UNITED
H 2-1 *Geovanni (16), Beto (34)*
Quim, Alcides, Luisão, Anderson, Léo (Ricardo Rocha 90), Beto, Petit, Nélson, Nuno Gomes, Nuno Assis (João Pereira 73), Geovanni (Mantorras 80).

2nd round LIVERPOOL (ENG)
H 1-0 *Luisão (84)*
Moretto, Alcides, Luisão, Anderson, Léo (Ricardo Rocha 87), Manuel Fernandes, Petit, Beto (Karagounis 58), Simão, Nuno Gomes, Robert (Nélson 77).
A 2-0 *Simão (36) Miccoli (89)*
Moretto, Alcides, Luisão, Anderson, Léo, Beto, Manuel Fernandes, Robert (Ricardo Rocha 70), Nuno Gomes (Miccoli 76), Simão, Geovanni (Karagounis 60).

Quarter-final FC BARCELONA (ESP)
H 0-0
Moretto, Ricardo Rocha, Luisão, Anderson, Léo, Beto, Manuel Fernandes, Petit, Robert (Miccoli 46), Geovanni (Karagounis 68), Simão.
A 0-2
Moretto, Ricardo Rocha, Luisão, Anderson, Léo, Beto (Robert 72), Petit, Manuel Fernandes (Marcel 82), Geovanni (Karagounis 55), Miccoli, Simão.

FC PORTO

1st round Group H
Match 1 RANGERS (SCO)
A 2-3 *Pepe (47, 71)*
Vítor Baía, Pepe, Pedro Emanuel (Sonkaya 41), Ricardo Costa, César Peixoto, Alan (Hugo Almeida 64), Lucho González, Ibson, Jorginho, Sokota, Diego (Ricardo Quaresma 64).

Portugal

Match 2 ARTMEDIA BRATISLAVA (SVK)
H 2-3 *Lucho González (32), Diego (39)*
Vítor Baía, Bosingwa, Ricardo Costa (Alan 75), Bruno Alves, César Peixoto, Lucho González, Diego (Hugo Almeida 75), Ibson, Ricardo Quaresma, McCarthy, Jorginho.

Match 3 INTERNAZIONALE (ITA)
H 2-0 *Materazzi (22og), McCarthy (35)*
Vítor Baía, Bosingwa, Pepe, Pedro Emanuel, Cech, Jorginho (Ibson 90), Paulo Assunção, Lucho González, Ricardo Quaresma (Ivanildo 81), McCarthy (Alan 59), Hugo Almeida.

Match 4 INTERNAZIONALE
A 1-2 *Hugo Almeida (16)*
Vítor Baía, Bosingwa, Pepe, Pedro Emanuel, Cech, Paulo Assunção (Bruno Alves 61), Jorginho, Lucho González, Alan (Raul Meireles 46), Hugo Almeida (McCarthy 76), Ricardo Quaresma.

Match 5 RANGERS
H 1-1 *Lisandro López (60)*
Vítor Baía, Bosingwa, Pepe, Pedro Emanuel (Hugo Almeida 46), César Peixoto, Lucho González, Paulo Assunção, Diego (Bruno Alves 64), Jorginho, Lisandro López, Ricardo Quaresma.

Match 6 ARTMEDIA BRATISLAVA
A 0-0
Vítor Baía, Ricardo Costa, Pedro Emanuel (Bosingwa 59), Pepe, César Peixoto, Paulo Assunção, Lucho González, Diego (Hugo Almeida 46), Ricardo Quaresma (Jorginho 72), Lisandro López, McCarthy.

SPORTING CP
3rd qualifying round UDINESE (ITA)
H 0-1
Ricardo, Miguel Garcia (Rogério 58), Beto, Polga, Tello, Custódio (Nani 79), Moutinho, Sá Pinto, Douala, Liedson, Deivid (Silva 73).
A 2-3 *Douala (38), Pinilla (90)*
Ricardo, Rogério (Pinilla 80), Polga, Beto, Tello (Deivid 46), Rochemback, Luís Loureiro, Moutinho, Sá Pinto (Edson 46), Liedson, Douala.

UEFA CUP

VITÓRIA SETÚBAL
1st round SAMPDORIA (ITA)
H 1-1 *Fábio (46)*
Moretto, Janício, José Fonte, Auri, Nandinho, Ricardo Chaves (Franja 73), Pedro Oliveira, Dembelé, Sougou, Fábio (Bruno Ribeiro 66), Tchomogo.
A 0-1
Moretto, Janício, José Fonte, Auri, Nandinho, Dembelé, Binho, Tchomogo (Lacombe 79), Pedro Oliveira (Sougou 64), Bruno Ribeiro, Heitor (Fábio 70).

SPORTING BRAGA
1st round CRVENA ZVEZDA BEOGRAD (SCG)
A 0-0
Paulo Santos, Abel, Nunes, Nem, Jorge Luiz, Vandinho, Sidney (Paulo Jorge 87), Andrés Madrid, Luís Filipe, João Tomás (Maxi Bevacqua 81), Davide (Rossato 61).
H 1-1 *Jaime (86)*
Paulo Santos, Abel (Rossato 34), Nunes, Nem, Jorge Luiz, Hugo Leal, Vandinho (Paulo Jorge 73), Andrés Madrid, Luís Filipe (Jaime 55), Maxi Bevacqua, Davide.

VITÓRIA GUIMARÃES
1st round WISLA KRAKOW (POL)
H 3-0 *Cléber (21p), Mário Sérgio (70), Benachour (71)*
Paiva, Geromel, Flávio Meireles, Cléber, Mário Sérgio, Svard, Neca, Rogério Matias, Benachour (Moreno 86), Dário (Targino 42), Saganowski (Paulo Sérgio 85).
A 1-0 *Saganowski (82)*
Paiva, Mário Sérgio, Dragóner, Medeiros, Rogério Matias, Svard, Benachour, Moreno, Neca (Pintassilgo 56), Saganowski (Zezinho 83), Targino (Rivas 66).

2nd round Group H
Match 1 ZENIT SANKT-PETERBURG (RUS)
A 1-2 *Neca (59)*
Nilson, Mário Sérgio, Medeiros, Dragóner, Cléber, Svard, Flávio Meireles, Neca, Targino (Paulo Sérgio 79), Benachour, Saganowski.

Match 2 BOLTON WANDERERS (ENG)
H 1-1 *Saganowski (86)*
Paiva, Mário Sérgio, Dragóner, Cléber, Rogério Matias, Svard, Flávio Meireles, Neca (Paulo Sérgio 81), Dário (Targino 60), Benachour, Saganowski.

Match 3 SEVILLA FC (ESP)
A 1-3 *Benachour (44)*
Paiva, Mário Sérgio, Dragóner, Cléber, Rogério Matias, Svard, Moreno, Neca (Manoel 74), Saganowski (Dário 46), Benachour, Targino (Paulo Sérgio 62).

Match 4 BESIKTAS (TUR)
H 1-3 *Saganowski (12)*
Nilson, Mário Sérgio, Geromel, Medeiros, Rogério Matias (Hélder Cabral 79), Svard, Moreno, Clayton (Targino 46), Manoel (Paulo Sérgio 46), Neca, Saganowski.

SPORTING CP
1st round HALMSTADS BK (SWE)
A 2-1 *Wender (44), Deivid (47)*
Nélson, Miguel Garcia, Polga, Tonel, Tello, Luís Loureiro, João Alves, Moutinho, Wender (Nani 78), Silva (Varela 90), Deivid (Pinilla 70).
H 2-3 *Wender (34), Zvirgzdauskas (102og)*
(aet)
Nélson, Miguel Garcia, Polga, Beto, Paíto (Varela 115), Luís Loureiro (Custódio 46), Moutinho, João Alves, Douala, Deivid (Pinilla 74), Wender.

TOP GOALSCORERS 2005/06

17	Albert MEYONG (CF Os Belenenses)
15	JOÃO TOMÁS (Sporting Braga)
	NUNO GOMES (SL Benfica)
	LIEDSON (Sporting CP)
14	ANDRÉ PINTO (CD Nacional)
13	JOEANO (Académica Coimbra)
12	Marek SAGANOWSKI (Vitória Guimarães)
11	ALEXANDRE GOULART (CD Nacional)
10	LUCHO GONZÁLEZ (FC Porto)
	GAÚCHO (Rio Ave FC)

LEAGUE RESULTS/ SCORERS/APPEARANCES/ GOALS 2005/06

ACADÉMICA COIMBRA
Coach – Nelo Vingada

2005
20/8	SL Benfica	h	0-0

Portugal

FINAL LEAGUE TABLE 2005/06

		Pld	Home					Away					Total					Pts
			W	D	L	F	A	W	D	L	F	A	W	D	L	F	A	
1	FC Porto	34	13	3	1	32	7	11	4	2	22	9	24	7	3	54	16	79
2	Sporting CP	34	12	2	3	23	7	10	4	3	27	17	22	6	6	50	24	72
3	SL Benfica	34	11	4	2	27	10	9	3	5	24	19	20	7	7	51	29	67
4	Sporting Braga	34	12	3	2	27	10	5	4	8	11	12	17	7	10	38	22	58
5	CD Nacional	34	8	6	3	27	18	6	4	7	13	14	14	10	10	40	32	52
6	Boavista FC	34	8	6	3	24	17	4	8	5	13	12	12	14	8	37	29	50
7	União Leiria	34	6	6	5	22	17	7	2	8	22	25	13	8	13	44	42	47
8	Vitória Setúbal	34	8	1	8	15	13	6	3	8	13	20	14	4	16	28	33	46
9	CF Estrela Amadora	34	7	6	4	18	15	5	3	9	13	18	12	9	13	31	33	45
10	CS Marítimo	34	7	7	3	21	14	3	7	7	17	23	10	14	10	38	37	44
11	FC Paços Ferreira	34	8	4	5	24	17	3	5	9	14	32	11	9	14	38	49	42
12	Gil Vicente FC	34	8	4	5	26	18	3	3	11	11	24	11	7	16	37	42	40
13	Naval 1° Maio	34	7	3	7	21	22	4	3	10	14	26	11	6	17	35	48	39
14	Académica Coimbra	34	5	5	7	15	20	5	4	8	22	28	10	9	15	37	48	39
15	CF Os Belenenses	34	7	2	8	24	19	4	4	9	16	23	11	6	17	40	42	39
16	Rio Ave FC	34	6	4	7	20	23	2	6	9	14	30	8	10	16	34	53	34
17	Vitória Guimarães	34	5	5	7	17	19	3	5	9	11	22	8	10	16	28	41	34
18	FC Penafiel	34	2	5	10	10	22	0	4	13	11	39	2	9	23	21	61	15

Date	Opponent	H/A	Score	Scorers
28/8	CD Nacional	a	2-2	Marcel 2 (1p)
11/9	Vitória Setúbal	h	0-1	
18/9	FC Paços Ferreira	a	1-2	Marcel (p)
26/9	Boavista FC	a	1-2	Luciano
2/10	Gil Vicente FC	h	2-0	Fernando, Joeano
16/10	Sporting CP	a	1-0	Marcel
23/10	União Leiria	h	1-3	Marcel
30/10	FC Penafiel	a	0-1	
7/11	Vitória Guimarães	h	1-0	Marcel
19/11	FC Porto	a	1-5	Marcel
27/11	CF Estrela Amadora	h	1-0	Marcel
4/12	Naval 1° Maio	a	1-0	Hugo Alcântara
11/12	Rio Ave FC	h	2-2	Danilo, Marcel (p)
17/12	Sporting Braga	a	0-2	
21/12	CF Os Belenenses	h	0-1	
2006				
7/1	CS Marítimo	a	2-2	Joeano, Hugo Alcântara
15/1	SL Benfica	a	0-3	
21/1	CD Nacional	h	0-0	
30/1	Vitória Setúbal	a	1-0	Joeano
4/2	FC Paços Ferreira	h	3-0	Gelson, Dionattan, Serjão
11/2	Boavista FC	h	0-2	
19/2	Gil Vicente FC	a	3-4	Joeano 3 (1p)
25/2	Sporting CP	h	0-3	
5/3	União Leiria	a	2-0	Filipe Teixeira, Joeano
11/3	FC Penafiel	h	1-0	Filipe Teixeira
19/3	Vitória Guimarães	a	1-1	Joeano
26/3	FC Porto	h	0-1	
2/4	CF Estrela Amadora	a	2-3	Joeano, Filipe Teixeira
9/4	Naval 1° Maio	h	2-2	Joeano 2
15/4	Rio Ave FC	a	4-1	Gelson 2, Rui Miguel, Pedro Silva
24/4	Sporting Braga	h	0-3	
30/4	CF Os Belenenses	a	0-0	
6/5	CS Marítimo	h	2-2	Joeano 2 (1p)

No	Name	Nat	Pos	Aps	(s)	Gls
30	Luís Filipe ANDRADE		M	2	(3)	
13	José CASTRO		D	30		
12	Daniel Moreno " DANI "	ESP	G	6		
3	DANILO Ferrara	BRA	D	18	(1)	1
11	DIONATTAN Gehlen	BRA	M	10	(3)	1
4	EZEQUIAS Melo	BRA	D	21	(5)	1
20	FERNANDO Moura	BRA	M	8	(6)	1
14	FILIPE TEIXEIRA		M	29	(1)	3
9	GELSON Júnior		A	12	(10)	3
5	HUGO ALCNTARA	BRA	D	23	(4)	2
23	Carlos Francisco "ITO"		M		(1)	
9	JOEANO Chaves	BRA	A	16	(12)	13
6	Lirodiou Gonçalves " LIRA "	BRA	M	8		
7	LUCIANO Fonseca	BRA	A	18	(9)	1
10	MARCEL Ortolan	BRA	A	15	(1)	9
78	Ousmane N'DOYE	SEN	M	12	(1)	
27	NUNO LUÍS		D	17		
28	NUNO PILOTO		D	15	(10)	
19	PAULO ADRIANO		M	14	(7)	
24	PEDRO ROMA		G	28		
16	PEDRO SILVA		D	13	(8)	1
88	ROBERTO BRUM	BRA	M	33		
21	RUI MIGUEL Reis		A	3		1
22	Filipe SARMENTO		A	7	(4)	
50	Sérgio Silva "SERJÃO"		A	1	(9)	1
18	VÍTOR VINHA		D	11		
87	Leonardo Zinelli "ZADA"	BRA	A	4	(4)	

CF OS BELENENSES
Coach – Carlos Carvalhal; (28/10/05) José Couceiro

2005				
19/8	Sporting CP	a	1-2	Pinheiro
27/8	União Leiria	h	3-1	Meyong 2, José Pedro
12/9	FC Penafiel	a	3-0	Silas, José Pedro, Meyong
19/9	Vitória Guimarães	h	3-1	Meyong 2 (1p), Silas

Portugal

Date	Opponent	H/A	Score	Scorers
24/9	FC Porto	a	0-2	
3/10	CF Estrela Amadora	h	0-2	
16/10	Naval 1° Maio	a	1-2	Meyong
21/10	Rio Ave FC	h	1-2	Meyong
31/10	Sporting Braga	a	0-2	
5/11	Boavista FC	h	1-1	Meyong (p)
21/11	CS Marítimo	h	0-1	
27/11	SL Benfica	a	0-0	
3/12	CD Nacional	h	1-0	Meyong
12/12	Vitória Setúbal	a	0-1	
17/12	FC Paços Ferreira	h	2-0	Rolando, Meyong
21/12	Académica Coimbra	a	1-0	Meyong
2006				
6/1	Gil Vicente FC	h	0-2	
14/1	Sporting CP	h	0-1	
23/1	União Leiria	a	2-2	Sousa, Silas
29/1	FC Penafiel	h	5-0	Ahamada 3, Rolando, Romeu
5/2	Vitória Guimarães	a	2-2	Romeu, Ruben Amorim
11/2	FC Porto	h	0-2	
19/2	CF Estrela Amadora	a	2-1	Silas, Ruben Amorim
26/2	Naval 1° Maio	h	2-3	og (Nélson Veiga), Meyong (p)
6/3	Rio Ave FC	a	1-2	Rolando
13/3	Sporting Braga	h	2-0	Sandro, Meyong
18/3	Boavista FC	a	2-0	José Pedro, Meyong
25/3	CS Marítimo	a	0-1	
1/4	SL Benfica	h	1-2	José Pedro
7/4	CD Nacional	a	0-4	
14/4	Vitória Setúbal	h	3-1	Meyong 3 (2p)
23/4	FC Paços Ferreira	a	1-1	Ruben Amorim
30/4	Académica Coimbra	h	0-0	
6/5	Gil Vicente FC	a	0-1	

No	Name	Nat	Pos	Aps	(s)	Gls
7	Hassan AHAMADA	FRA	A	11	(9)	3
22	Pedro ALVES		G	3	(1)	
23	Andersson Conrado "AMARAL"	BRA	D	24	(1)	
28	Fabrício Bento "CEARÁ"	BRA	M	1	(1)	
30	Eduardo Gomes "DADY"		A		(9)	
25	Ivan DJURDJEVIC	SCG	M	7	(8)	
20	FÁBIO JANUÁRIO	BRA	A	12	(17)	
17	José GASPAR		D	11	(2)	
11	JOSÉ PEDRO Salazar		M	18	(7)	4
1	MARCO AURÉLIO Siqueira	BRA	G	31		
21	Albert MEYONG	CMR	A	26		17
8	PAULO SÉRGIO Gonçalves		A	19	(8)	
26	Pedro Monteiro "PELÉ"	BRA	D	32		
18	Pedro PINHEIRO		M	16	(7)	1
27	RICARDO ARAUJO	BRA	A	2	(1)	
13	ROLANDO Fonseca		D	24	(1)	3
9	ROMEU Almeida		A	7	(14)	2
5	RUBEN AMORIM		M	22	(3)	3
4	RUI FERREIRA		M	15	(5)	
23	RUI JORGE		D	15		
6	SANDRO Silva	BRA	M	22		1
10	Jorge Fernandes "SILAS"		A	24	4	4
16	José Carlos SOUSA		D	15		1
3	VASCO FAÍSCA		D	17	3	

SL BENFICA
Coach – Ronald Koeman (HOL)

Date	Opponent	H/A	Score	Scorers
2005				
20/8	Académica Coimbra	a	0-0	
27/8	Gil Vicente FC	h	0-2	
10/9	Sporting CP	a	1-2	Simão
18/9	União Leiria	h	4-0	Anderson, Nuno Gomes 3
23/9	FC Penafiel	a	3-1	Nuno Gomes 2, Simão
3/10	Vitória Guimarães	h	2-1	Miccoli, Simão
15/10	FC Porto	a	2-0	Nuno Gomes 2
22/10	CF Estrela Amadora	h	2-0	Karyaka, Nuno Gomes
29/10	Naval 1° Maio	a	1-1	Nuno Gomes
6/11	Rio Ave FC	h	2-2	Petit 2
19/11	Sporting Braga	a	2-3	Anderson, Nuno Gomes
27/11	CF Os Belenenses	h	0-0	
3/12	CS Marítimo	a	1-0	Mantorras
11/12	Boavista FC	h	1-0	Anderson
17/12	CD Nacional	h	1-0	Nuno Gomes
21/12	Vitória Setúbal	a	1-0	Nuno Gomes
2006				
8/1	FC Paços Ferreira	h	2-0	Nélson, Geovanni
15/1	Académica Coimbra	h	3-0	Simão (p), Luisão, Nuno Gomes
20/1	Gil Vicente FC	a	3-1	Simão (p), Geovanni, og (Jorge Baptista)
28/1	Sporting CP	h	1-3	Simão (p)
4/2	União Leiria	a	1-3	Manduca
12/2	FC Penafiel	h	4-0	Geovanni, og (Roberto), Nuno Gomes, Simão
18/2	Vitória Guimarães	a	0-2	
26/2	FC Porto	h	1-0	Robert
4/3	CF Estrela Amadora	a	2-1	Robert, Miccoli
12/3	Naval 1° Maio	h	0-0	
19/3	Rio Ave FC	a	1-0	Mantorras
25/3	Sporting Braga	h	1-0	Nuno Gomes
1/4	CF Os Belenenses	a	2-1	Miccoli, Karagounis
9/4	CS Marítimo	h	2-2	Petit, Simão (p)
15/4	Boavista FC	a	2-0	og (Tiago), Mantorras
23/4	CD Nacional	a	1-1	Miccoli
30/4	Vitória Setúbal	h	1-0	Anderson
6/5	FC Paços Ferreira	a	1-3	Manuel Fernandes

No	Name	Nat	Pos	Aps	(s)	Gls
13	Eduardo ALCIDES	BRA	D	10	(2)	
3	Beraldo ANDERSON	BRA	D	27	(2)	4
16	Gilberto Santos "BETO"	BRA	M	17	(7)	
7	Carlos Garcia "CARLITOS"		A		(1)	
11	GEOVANNI Maurício	BRA	M	19	(6)	3
28	HÉLIO ROQUE		A		(3)	
10	Giorgos KARAGOUNIS	GRE	M	9	(10)	1
17	Andrei KARYAKA	RUS	M	6	(3)	1
39	JOÃO COIMBRA		M		(1)	
47	JOÃO PEREIRA		A	4	(2)	
5	Leonardo Bastos "LEO"	BRA	D	26		
4	Anderson Luís "LUISÃO"	BRA	D	31		1
23	Gustavo MANDUCA	BRA	A	9	(7)	1
9	Pedro Torres "MANTORRAS"	ANG	A		(17)	3
18	MANUEL DOS SANTOS	FRA	D		(3)	
14	MANUEL FERNANDES		M	23	(5)	1
19	MARCEL Ortolan	BRA	A	3	(4)	
32	MARCO FERREIRA		M	2	(3)	
30	Fabrizio MICCOLI	ITA	A	16	(1)	4
1	José MOREIRA		G	6		
31	Marcello MORETTO	BRA	G	18		
22	NÉLSON Marcos		D	24	(1)	1
15	NUNO ASSIS		M	4	(6)	
21	NUNO GOMES		A	27	(2)	15
6	Armando Teixeira "PETIT"		M	30		3
12	Joaquim Sampaio " QUIM "		G	7		
33	RICARDO ROCHA		A	21	(5)	
34	Laurent ROBERT	FRA	A	8	(5)	2
43	RUI NEREU		G	3	(1)	
20	SIMÃO Sabrosa		A	24		8

Portugal

BOAVISTA FC
Coach – Carlos Brito

2005

Date	Opponent	H/A	Score	Scorers
20/8	Vitória Setúbal	h	0-0	
29/8	CF Estrela Amadora	a	1-1	Hélder Rosário
11/9	FC Paços Ferreira	h	4-1	Fary, Zé Manuel, Diogo Valente, Cafú
16/9	Naval 1° Maio	a	2-2	Guga, Fary
26/9	Académica Coimbra	h	2-1	Fary, João Pinto
1/10	Rio Ave FC	a	1-1	Manuel José
17/10	Gil Vicente FC	h	2-0	Fary (p), William Sousa (p)
22/10	Sporting Braga	a	0-1	
30/10	Sporting CP	h	2-2	João Pinto, William Sousa
5/11	CF Os Belenenses	a	1-1	João Pinto
20/11	União Leiria	h	2-0	João Pinto, William Sousa
26/11	CS Marítimo	a	1-1	Fary (p)
4/12	FC Penafiel	h	2-1	Diogo Valente, João Pinto
11/12	SL Benfica	a	0-1	
18/12	Vitória Guimarães	h	1-1	Cadú
22/12	CD Nacional	a	0-3	

2006

Date	Opponent	H/A	Score	Scorers
8/1	FC Porto	a	0-1	
16/1	Vitória Setúbal	a	2-0	Zé Manuel, Manuel José
21/1	CF Estrela Amadora	h	2-1	Ricardo Silva, Zé Manuel (p)
27/1	FC Paços Ferreira	a	1-0	Paulo Jorge
3/2	Naval 1° Maio	h	3-0	Figueredo, João Pinto, Lucas
11/2	Académica Coimbra	a	2-0	João Pinto 2
17/2	Rio Ave FC	h	2-1	Ricardo Silva, Manuel José
24/2	Gil Vicente FC	a	1-0	João Pinto
5/3	Sporting Braga	h	0-0	
11/3	Sporting CP	a	0-1	
18/3	CF Os Belenenses	h	0-2	
27/3	União Leiria	a	0-0	
2/4	CS Marítimo	h	1-1	Paulo Jorge
10/4	FC Penafiel	a	0-0	
15/4	SL Benfica	h	0-2	
21/4	Vitória Guimarães	a	1-1	Paulo Jorge
30/4	CD Nacional	a	0-1	
6/5	FC Porto	h	1-1	Paulo Jorge

No	Name	Nat	Pos	Aps	(s)	Gls
5	Miguel AREIAS		D	29	(1)	
20	Ricardo Sousa "CADÚ"		D	27	(1)	1
17	Arlindo Semedo "CAFÚ"		A	1	(13)	1
21	CARLOS Alberto Fernandes		G	12		
13	CARLOS Miguel FERNANDES		D	3		
4	Khalifa CISSÉ	FRA	D	6	(9)	
11	DIOGO VALENTE		A	12	(10)	2
25	Guy ESSAME	CMR	A	3		
9	FARY Faye	SEN	A	21	(5)	5
10	Diego FIGUEREDO	PAR	M	2	(5)	1
8	Jose Santos "GUGA"	BRA	A	5	(3)	1
37	HÉLDER ROSÁRIO		D	23	(1)	1
12	JOÃO Vieira PINTO		A	31		9
24	KHADIM Faye	SEN	G	1	(1)	
22	João LUCAS		M	29	(1)	1
81	MANUEL JOSÉ Vieira		D	33		3
23	Hugo MONTEIRO		D		(5)	
15	Tomás ORAVEC	SVK	A	3	(9)	
14	PAULO JORGE Alves		A	12	(12)	4
6	PAULO SOUSA		M	15	(1)	
73	Bruno PINHEIRO		M		(1)	
3	RICARDO SILVA		D	17		2
2	RUI DUARTE		D	17	(3)	
66	TIAGO Pereira		M	29		
1	WILLIAM Andem	CMR	G	21		
	WILLIAM Sousa	BRA	A	3	(11)	3

CF ESTRELA AMADORA
Coach – António Conceição "Toni"

2005

Date	Opponent	H/A	Score	Scorers
21/8	FC Porto	a	0-1	
29/8	Boavista FC	h	1-1	Maurício
11/9	Naval 1° Maio	h	2-1	Manu, Paulo Machado
18/9	Rio Ave FC	a	1-2	Manu
25/9	Sporting Braga	h	0-0	
30/9	CF Os Belenenses	a	2-0	Semedo 2
16/10	CS Marítimo	h	2-2	Maurício, Manu
22/10	SL Benfica	a	0-2	
30/10	CD Nacional	h	0-2	
6/11	Vitória Setúbal	a	0-1	
20/11	FC Paços Ferreira	h	0-0	
27/11	Académica Coimbra	a	0-1	
4/12	Gil Vicente FC	h	1-0	Pedro Simões (p)
9/12	Sporting CP	a	1-0	Manu
17/12	União Leiria	h	1-2	Anselmo
22/12	FC Penafiel	a	1-0	Semedo

2006

Date	Opponent	H/A	Score	Scorers
8/1	Vitória Guimarães	h	2-0	Manu, Semedo
15/1	FC Porto	h	2-1	Maurício, Coutinho
21/1	Boavista FC	a	1-2	Santamaria (p)
28/1	Naval 1° Maio	a	0-2	
5/2	Rio Ave FC	h	0-0	
12/2	Sporting Braga	a	1-1	André Barreto
19/2	CF Os Belenenses	h	1-2	Maurício
26/2	CS Marítimo	a	0-1	
4/3	SL Benfica	h	1-2	Paulo Machado
12/3	CD Nacional	a	2-1	Manu, Rui Duarte
19/3	Vitória Setúbal	h	1-0	Semedo
26/3	FC Paços Ferreira	a	1-2	N'Diaye
2/4	Académica Coimbra	h	3-2	Manu, Rui Borges 2
9/4	Gil Vicente FC	a	1-1	Santamaria
15/4	Sporting CP	h	0-0	
23/4	União Leiria	a	1-1	Rui Duarte
30/4	FC Penafiel	h	1-0	Nieto
6/5	Vitória Guimarães	a	1-0	Semedo

No	Name	Nat	Pos	Aps	(s)	Gls
2	Eurípides AMOREIRINHA		D	21		
31	ANDRÉ BARRETO	BRA	M	11		1
9	ANSELMO Cardoso		A	5	(14)	1
30	BRUNO SANTOS		M	1	(4)	
1	BRUNO VALE		G	30		
10	Rafael COUTINHO	BRA	M	22	(2)	1
14	EMERSON Luz	CVD	M	21	(2)	
17	EUSÉBIO Sousa		D	1	(5)	
4	HUGO CARREIRA		D	10	(2)	
19	IGOR Fonseca	BRA	A	1	(6)	
8	Claudinei Reis "IGOR SOUSA"	BRA	M		(3)	
20	Adelino Baptista "JORDÃO"		M	11	(2)	
35	Emanuel Evaristo "MANU"		A	31		7
15	MAURÍCIO Santos	BRA	D	31		4
33	Júlio Bevacqua "MAXI BEVACQUA"	ARG	A	7	(7)	
11	Carlos "MAXI" ESTEVEZ	ARG	M		(2)	
34	Deme N'DIAYE		M		(6)	1
32	Frederico NIETO	ARG	M		(7)	1
24	PAULO LOPES		G	4	(2)	
55	PAULO MACHADO		M	16	(9)	2
22	PEDRO SIMÕES		D	20	(3)	
6	Rafael Ledesma "RAFAEL GAÚCHO"	BRA	M	2	(2)	
21	RUI BORGES		A	24	(3)	2
3	RUI DUARTE		D	10	(12)	2
5	Ricardo Duarte "SANTAMARIA"		D	20	(2)	

| 7 | José Fernandes "ZÉ MANUEL" | | A | 19 | (7) | 3 |

Portugal

GIL VICENTE FC
Coach – Ulisses Morais; (8/3/06) Paulo Alves

2005

Date	Opponent	h/a	Score	Scorers
21/8	CS Marítimo	h	1-0	Marcos António
27/8	SL Benfica	a	2-0	Marcos António, og (Anderson)
11/9	CD Nacional	h	0-1	
18/9	Vitória Setúbal	a	0-1	
25/9	FC Paços Ferreira	h	2-0	Grégory, Williams
2/10	Académica Coimbra	a	0-2	
17/10	Boavista FC	a	0-2	
23/10	Sporting CP	h	2-2	Grégory, Carlos Carneiro
30/10	União Leiria	a	0-3	
6/11	FC Penafiel	h	2-2	Carlos Carneiro, Carlitos
18/11	Vitória Guimarães	a	0-2	
28/11	FC Porto	h	0-1	
4/12	CF Estrela Amadora	a	0-1	
11/12	Naval 1° Maio	h	2-0	Luís Coentrão, Nandinho (p)
17/12	Rio Ave FC	a	0-1	
21/12	Sporting Braga	h	2-1	Gouveia, Nandinho

2006

Date	Opponent	h/a	Score	Scorers
6/1	CF Os Belenenses	a	2-0	Carlitos, Bruno Tiago
15/1	CS Marítimo	a	1-1	og (Nuno Morais)
20/1	SL Benfica	h	1-3	Nandinho (p)
29/1	CD Nacional	a	0-2	
5/2	Vitória Setúbal	h	5-0	Carlitos 2, Rovérsio, Carlos Carneiro, Mateus
12/2	FC Paços Ferreira	a	0-1	
19/2	Académica Coimbra	h	4-3	João Pedro, Mateus, Grégory, Carlos Carneiro
24/2	Boavista FC	h	0-1	
5/3	Sporting CP	a	0-2	
11/3	União Leiria	h	1-2	Bruno Tiago
19/3	FC Penafiel	a	1-1	Grégory
26/3	Vitória Guimarães	h	1-1	Vilela
2/4	FC Porto	a	0-3	
9/4	CF Estrela Amadora	h	1-1	Grégory
15/4	Naval 1° Maio	a	4-1	Grégory, Nandinho 2, Carlitos
23/4	Rio Ave FC	h	1-0	Luís Coentrão
30/4	Sporting Braga	a	1-1	Grégory
6/5	CF Os Belenenses	h	1-0	Marcos António

No	Name	Nat	Pos	Aps	(s)	Gls
16	BRAIMA Injai		M	16	(9)	
6	BRUNO TIAGO		M	23	(1)	2
7	Carlos Cunha "CARLITOS"		A	28	(4)	5
14	CARLOS CARNEIRO		A	24	(7)	4
2	EDSON Reis	BRA	M	10		
8	ELIAS Silva		M	20	(5)	
21	Gilberto Fernandes "GIL"		A		(1)	
18	António GOUVEIA		M	24	(1)	1
15	GREGORY Armolin	FRA	D	29	(1)	7
20	JOÃO PEDRO Santos		M	26	(2)	1
47	JOÃO PEREIRA		D	14		
1	JORGE BATISTA		G	25	(1)	
9	LEANDRO NETTO	BRA	M	3	(12)	
27	LUÍS COENTRÃO		M	10	(18)	2
25	MARCOS ANTÓNIO	BRA	D	24	(1)	3
11	Galiano Costa "MATEUS"		A	4		2
13	Fernando Santos "NANDINHO"		A	26	(5)	5
16	António SEMEDO		A	30	(2)	6
26	TIAGO Rosa		M		(1)	
18	Anthony Silva "TONY"	FRA	D	32		
45	Hugo VALDIR		D	6	(2)	
7	Frederico Ribeiro "ZAMORANO"		M	7	(4)	
22	PAULO Arantes		D	6		
12	PAULO JORGE Nunes		G	9		
10	Rivanilton França "RIVAN"	BRA	M		(1)	
17	ROBÉLIO Lima	BRA	M	4	(1)	
19	RODOLFO LIMA		A	10	(14)	
4	ROVÉRSIO Barros	BRA	D	18	(4)	1
30	António Ferreira "TONANHA"		M		(3)	
77	João VILELA		A		(7)	1
26	WILLIAMS Mendonça	BRA	M	21	(2)	1

CS MARÍTIMO
Coach – Rui Rodrigues "Juca"; (25/9/05) Paulo Bonamigo; (15/3/06) Ulisses Morais

2005

Date	Opponent	h/a	Score	Scorers
21/8	Gil Vicente FC	a	0-1	
28/8	Sporting CP	h	1-2	Rincón
11/9	União Leiria	a	0-0	
18/9	FC Penafiel	h	2-2	Mancuso, Youssouf
24/9	Vitória Guimarães	a	0-1	
2/10	FC Porto	h	2-2	Manduca, Marcinho
16/10	CF Estrela Amadora	a	2-2	Kanu, og (Pedro Simões)
23/10	Naval 1° Maio	h	2-1	Kanu, Manduca
30/10	Rio Ave FC	a	2-2	Manduca, Mancuso
5/11	Sporting Braga	h	1-0	Kanu
21/11	CF Os Belenenses	a	1-0	Manduca (p)
26/11	Boavista FC	h	1-1	Kanu
3/12	SL Benfica	h	0-1	
10/12	CD Nacional	a	1-2	Kanu
17/12	Vitória Setúbal	h	1-0	Rincón
21/12	FC Paços Ferreira	a	2-1	Rincón 2

2006

Date	Opponent	h/a	Score	Scorers
7/1	Académica Coimbra	h	2-2	Rincón, Marcinho
15/1	Gil Vicente FC	h	1-1	Zé Carlos
21/1	Sporting CP	a	1-1	Leandro
29/1	União Leiria	h	3-0	Zé Carlos 2, Kanu (p)
5/2	FC Penafiel	a	2-3	Kanu, og (Sérgio Lomba)
13/2	Vitória Guimarães	h	0-1	
19/2	FC Porto	h	0-1	
26/2	CF Estrela Amadora	h	1-0	Kanu
4/3	Naval 1° Maio	a	0-2	
11/3	Rio Ave FC	h	0-0	
19/3	Sporting Braga	a	0-2	
25/3	CF Os Belenenses	h	1-0	Caíco
2/4	Boavista FC	a	1-1	Zé Carlos
9/4	SL Benfica	a	2-2	Valnei, Zé Carlos
16/4	CD Nacional	a	2-0	Olberdam, Marcinho
23/4	Vitória Setúbal	a	1-0	Zé Carlos
30/4	FC Paços Ferreira	h	1-1	Zé Carlos
6/5	Académica Coimbra	a	2-2	Van der Gaag, Marcinho

No	Name	Nat	Pos	Aps	(s)	Gls
78	ALI El-Omari		M	3	(2)	
23	Fábio Amaro "BALÚ"	BRA	D	2	(3)	
21	Nuno Sousa "BRIGUEL"		D	29		
77	Airton Santos "CAÍCO"	BRA	M	8	(3)	1
6	EVALDO Fabiano	BRA	M	33		
14	FERNANDO Dinarte		D	14	(2)	
2	Antonielton FERREIRA	BRA	D	4	(1)	
20	FILIPE OLIVEIRA		M	6	(17)	
3	Miklós GAAL	HUN	M	2	(1)	
65	JARDEL Sousa	BRA	A		(3)	
	Hamilton Santos "JÚNIOR BAHIA"	BRA	M	4	(6)	
7	Elias Rosa "KANU"	BRA	A	25		8
11	Andrej KOMAC	SLO	A	1	(6)	
5	LEANDRO Fahel	BRA	A	12	(4)	1
8	Gisley Farah "MANCUSO"	BRA	A	20	(5)	2
22	Gustavo MANDUCA	BRA	A	15		4

Portugal

No	Name	Nat	Pos	Aps	(s)	Gls
28	Márcio Silva " MARCINHO "	BRA	A	26	(2)	4
26	MARCOS Oliveira		G	33		
1	NÉLSON VASCO		G	1		
27	Jivanilson Santos "NILSON SERGIPANO"	BRA	M	3	(13)	
4	NUNO MORAIS		M	14	(3)	
13	OLBERDAM Serra	BRA	M	8		1
18	Luís OLIM		D	1	(1)	
44	Paulo Dinarte " PAULINHO "		M		(3)	
30	Gilvan Souza "RINCÓN"	BRA	A	9	(11)	5
13	Rodrigo SOUZA	BRA	A		(1)	
17	VALNEI Santos	BRA	D	20	(1)	1
25	Mitchell VAN DER GAAG	HOL	M	31		1
10	WALTER Júnior	BRA	A	2	(4)	
15	WÉNIO Pio	BRA	M	30		
31	WILIANS Ilson	BRA	D	2		
16	Sammy YOUSSOUF	GHA	A	2	(3)	1
99	José Carlos Silva "ZÉ CARLOS"	BRA	A	14	(2)	7

CD NACIONAL
Coach – Manuel Machado

2005
Date	Opponent	h/a	Score	Scorers
21/8	FC Paços Ferreira	a	1-0	André Pinto
28/8	Académica Coimbra	h	2-2	André Pinto 2
11/9	Gil Vicente FC	a	1-0	Alonso
19/9	Sporting CP	h	2-1	Alexandre Goulart, André Pinto
25/9	União Leiria	a	0-0	
2/10	FC Penafiel	h	2-0	Alexandre Goulart, Chilikov
15/10	Vitória Guimarães	a	0-0	
23/10	FC Porto	h	0-1	
30/10	CF Estrela Amadora	a	2-0	André Pinto, Alexandre Goulart
6/11	Naval 1° Maio	h	2-0	Anic, Alexandre Goulart (p)
20/11	Rio Ave FC	a	2-0	André Pinto, Miguelito
25/11	Sporting Braga	h	1-0	Alonso
3/12	CF Os Belenenses	a	0-1	
10/12	CS Marítimo	h	2-1	Bruno 2
17/12	SL Benfica	a	0-1	
22/12	Boavista FC	a	3-0	Alexandre Goulart, André Pinto 2

2006
Date	Opponent	h/a	Score	Scorers
6/1	Vitória Setúbal	h	2-2	André Pinto 2
15/1	FC Paços Ferreira	h	2-2	André Pinto, Alexandre Goulart (p)
21/1	Académica Coimbra	a	0-0	
29/1	Gil Vicente FC	h	2-0	André Pinto, Ávalos
4/2	Sporting CP	a	0-1	
12/2	União Leiria	h	1-4	Alexandre Goulart (p)
19/2	FC Penafiel	a	2-1	Alexandre Goulart, Chilikov
25/2	Vitória Guimarães	h	1-1	Chilikov
5/3	FC Porto	a	0-3	
12/3	CF Estrela Amadora	h	1-2	og (Maxi Bevacqua)
17/3	Naval 1° Maio	a	1-3	Chilikov
24/3	Rio Ave FC	h	1-1	Marchant
31/3	Sporting Braga	a	0-1	
7/4	CF Os Belenenses	h	4-0	Alexandre Goulart 2, André Pinto 2
16/4	CS Marítimo	a	0-2	
23/4	SL Benfica	h	1-1	Ricardo Fernandes
30/4	Boavista FC	h	1-0	Juliano
6/5	Vitória Setúbal	a	1-1	Alexandre Goulart

No	Name	Nat	Pos	Aps	(s)	Gls
11	Alexandre Terra "ALEX"	BRA	M	1	(3)	
10	ALEXANDRE GOULART	BRA	A	29	(2)	11
17	ALONSO Matos	BRA	D	19	(4)	2
19	ANDRÉ PINTO	BRA	A	23	(7)	14
8	Darko ANIC	SCG	M	1	(5)	1
4	Fernando ÁVALOS	ESP	D	32		1
24	Jose Francisco BELMAN	ESP	G		(1)	
	Diego BENAGLIO	SUI	G	23		
66	BRUNO Fernandes		M	32		2
	Carlos CHAINHO		M	31	(2)	
	Georgi CHILIKOV	BUL	A	9	(15)	4
6	CLÉBER Monteiro	BRA	D	25	(4)	
33	EMERSON Nunes	BRA	D	11	(7)	
3	FERNANDO CARDOZO	BRA	D	10	(1)	
66	GENALVO Oliveira	BRA	M		(2)	
1	HILÁRIO Sampaio		G	11		
	JULIANO Spadaci	BRA	A	13	(2)	1
80	LUÍS MANUEL Pereira		D		(1)	
22	Luís Oliveira "LUISINHO"		D		(1)	
7	Júlio MARCHANT	ARG	M	3	(7)	1
21	MIGUEL FIDALGO		A	5	(6)	
5	José Aguiar " MIGUELITO"		D	33	(1)	1
16	NUNO VIVEIROS		D	5	(12)	
22	Bruno PATACAS		D	29	(2)	
	Ricardo PATEIRO		M	1	(6)	
44	RICARDO FERNANDES		D	28	(2)	1
11	Sérgio Pinto " SERGINHO BAIANO"	BRA	A		(8)	

NAVAL 1° MAIO
Coach – Manuel Cajuda; (6/12/05) Álvaro Magalhães; (1/3/06) Rogério Gonçalves

2005
Date	Opponent	h/a	Score	Scorers
21/8	Vitória Guimarães	a	2-0	Bruno Fogaça, Lito
26/8	FC Porto	h	2-3	Bruno Fogaça, og (César Peixoto)
11/9	CF Estrela Amadora	a	1-2	Léo Guerra
16/9	Boavista FC	h	2-2	Bruno Fogaça, og (Cadú)
25/9	Rio Ave FC	h	1-0	Nélson Veiga
3/10	Sporting Braga	a	0-1	
16/10	CF Os Belenenses	h	2-1	Lito, Casarini
23/10	CS Marítimo	a	1-2	Gilmar
29/10	SL Benfica	h	1-1	Bruno Fogaça
6/11	CD Nacional	a	0-2	
20/11	Vitória Setúbal	h	0-3	
27/11	FC Paços Ferreira	a	1-3	Saúlo
4/12	Académica Coimbra	h	0-1	
11/12	Gil Vicente FC	a	0-2	
16/12	Sporting CP	h	0-2	
21/12	União Leiria	a	1-2	Glauber (p)

2006
Date	Opponent	h/a	Score	Scorers
7/1	FC Penafiel	h	4-1	Saúlo, Fernando, Lito, Franco
15/1	Vitória Guimarães	h	0-0	
21/1	FC Porto	a	0-1	
28/1	CF Estrela Amadora	h	2-0	Lito, Fajardo
3/2	Boavista FC	a	0-3	
12/2	Rio Ave FC	a	1-0	Franco
19/2	Sporting Braga	h	0-1	
26/2	CF Os Belenenses	a	3-2	Tiago, Saúlo, Lito
4/3	CS Marítimo	h	2-0	Bruno Fogaça 2
12/3	SL Benfica	a	0-0	
17/3	CD Nacional	h	3-1	Fajardo, Saúlo 2
26/3	Vitória Setúbal	a	1-4	og (Pedro Oliveira)
1/4	FC Paços Ferreira	h	1-0	Fajardo
9/4	Académica Coimbra	a	2-2	Lito, Saúlo
15/4	Gil Vicente FC	h	1-4	Fajardo
23/4	Sporting CP	a	0-0	
30/4	União Leiria	h	0-2	
6/5	FC Penafiel	a	1-0	Léo Guerra

No	Name	Nat	Pos	Aps	(s)	Gls

Portugal

No	Name	Nat	Pos	Aps	(s)	Gls
55	AURÉLIO Teixeira		M	2	(4)	
55	Adriano BESSA		D	9	(1)	
9	BRUNO FOGAÇA	BRA	A	19	(9)	6
7	Carlos Gonçalves " CARLITOS "		D	27	(1)	
21	Bruno CASARINI	BRA	A	6	(6)	1
6	João Gonçalves " CHINA"		D	28	(2)	
26	ÉDER Richartz	BRA	M	4	(7)	
18	João Paulo FAJARDO		M	28	(5)	4
5	FERNANDO Campagnolo	BRA	D	28		1
13	Pedro FRANCO		D	13		2
8	GILMAR Rocha	BRA	M	29		1
16	GLAUBER Farias	BRA	M	13	(3)	1
3	JOÃO PAULO Araújo	BRA	D	12	(2)	
90	LÉO GUERRA	BRA	A	3	(11)	2
11	Cláudio Aguiar " LITO "		A	29	(1)	6
6	MÁRCIO LUIZ	BRA	M	1	(4)	
4	NÉLSON VEIGA		D	21	(5)	1
88	PEDRO SANTOS		M	8	(8)	
24	RUI MIGUEL		M	9	(10)	
27	SAÚLO Santos		M	17	(12)	6
30	SOLIMAR Duarte	BRA	M	25	(2)	
1	Pedro TABORDA		G	22		
19	Leandro Martins "TATU"		A		(1)	
20	TIAGO Fraga	BRA	M	9	(3)	1
25	WILSON JÚNIOR	BRA	G	12	(1)	

FC PAÇOS FERREIRA
Coach – José Mota

2005

Date	Opponent	h/a	Score	Scorers
21/8	CD Nacional	h	0-1	
28/8	Vitória Setúbal	a	1-0	Fredy
11/9	Boavista FC	a	1-4	Rui Dolores
18/9	Académica Coimbra	h	2-1	Júnior, Geraldo
25/9	Gil Vicente FC	a	0-2	
2/10	Sporting CP	h	3-0	Ronny, Didi, Júnior
16/10	União Leiria	a	0-3	
23/10	FC Penafiel	h	2-2	Edinho 2
30/10	Vitória Guimarães	a	2-0	Didi, Edson
6/11	FC Porto	h	0-1	
20/11	CF Estrela Amadora	a	0-0	
27/11	Naval 1° Maio	h	3-1	Ronny 2, Júnior (p)
4/12	Rio Ave FC	a	2-2	Didi, Júnior (p)
11/12	Sporting Braga	h	1-0	Rui Dolores
17/12	CF Os Belenenses	a	0-2	
21/12	CS Marítimo	h	1-2	Júnior

2006

Date	Opponent	h/a	Score	Scorers
8/1	SL Benfica	a	0-2	
15/1	CD Nacional	a	2-2	Júnior (p), Luís Carlos
21/1	Vitória Setúbal	h	1-2	Ronny
27/1	Boavista FC	h	0-1	
4/2	Académica Coimbra	a	0-3	
12/2	Gil Vicente FC	h	1-0	Júnior Bahia
18/2	Sporting CP	a	0-3	
26/2	União Leiria	h	1-1	João Paulo
5/3	FC Penafiel	a	2-2	Pedrinha, Fonte
12/3	Vitória Guimarães	h	1-1	og (Dragóner)
18/3	FC Porto	a	0-3	
26/3	CF Estrela Amadora	h	2-1	Júnior Bahia, Didi
1/4	Naval 1° Maio	a	0-1	
9/4	Rio Ave FC	h	2-1	Rui Dolores, João Paulo
17/4	Sporting Braga	a	3-2	Didi 2, Júnior
23/4	CF Os Belenenses	h	1-1	Edson
30/4	CS Marítimo	a	1-1	Bispo
6/5	SL Benfica	h	3-1	Edson, Júnior 2

No	Name	Nat	Pos	Aps	(s)	Gls
20	ALEXANDRE Leitão		D	3	(13)	

No	Name	Nat	Pos	Aps	(s)	Gls
12	Luís BISPO		M	4		1
10	CRISTIANO Oliveira	BRA	M		(7)	
9	Cleidimar Silva "DIDI"	BRA	A	30	(1)	6
23	Arnaldo Lopes "EDINHO"		A	8	(13)	2
7	EDSON Nobre	ANG	M	23	(6)	3
15	EMERSON Figueiredo	BRA	M	20	(1)	
5	José Miguel FONTE		D	10	(1)	1
21	Frederico Martins "FREDY"		M	30		1
3	GERALDO Alves		D	25	(1)	1
	JOÃO DUARTE		D	1	(2)	
26	JOÃO PAULO Ribeiro		A	4	(5)	2
25	Manuel Silva JÚNIOR	BRA	M	32	(1)	9
29	Hamilton Santos "JÚNIOR BAHIA"	BRA	M	8	(7)	2
14	LUÍS CARLOS	BRA	D	14	(5)	1
18	Ricardo Duarte "MANGUALDE"		D	6	(1)	
6	PAULO SOUSA		M	32		
24	PEÇANHA Peterson	BRA	G	23		
8	Pedro Monteiro "PEDRINHA"		M	30	(2)	1
1	PEDRO Correia		G	11		
2	Pedro Guimarães "PRIMO"		D	28		
13	RENATO QUEIRÓS		A		(5)	
99	RONNY Silva	BRA	A	13	(10)	4
33	RUI DOLORES		A	18	(10)	3
	TIAGO Martins		M	1	(5)	

FC PENAFIEL
Coach – Luís Castro

2005

Date	Opponent	h/a	Score	Scorers
21/8	Rio Ave FC	h	0-2	
28/8	Sporting Braga	a	0-1	
12/9	CF Os Belenenses	h	0-3	
18/9	CS Marítimo	a	2-2	Roberto 2
23/9	SL Benfica	h	1-3	Marco Ferreira
2/10	CD Nacional	a	0-2	
16/10	Vitória Setúbal	h	0-1	
23/10	FC Paços Ferreira	a	2-2	N'Doye 2 (1p)
30/10	Académica Coimbra	h	1-0	Bruno Amaro
6/11	Gil Vicente FC	a	2-2	N'Doye, Bibishkov
20/11	Sporting CP	h	0-1	
27/11	União Leiria	a	1-1	Bibishkov
4/12	Boavista FC	h	1-2	Odair
10/12	Vitória Guimarães	h	0-1	
17/12	FC Porto	a	1-3	Bruno Amaro
22/12	CF Estrela Amadora	h	0-1	

2006

Date	Opponent	h/a	Score	Scorers
7/1	Naval 1° Maio	a	1-4	José Rui
15/1	Rio Ave FC	a	0-2	
19/1	Sporting Braga	h	0-0	
29/1	CF Os Belenenses	a	0-5	
5/2	CS Marítimo	h	3-2	Roberto, Dill, Bruno Amaro
12/2	SL Benfica	a	0-4	
19/2	CD Nacional	h	1-2	Orahovac
26/2	Vitória Setúbal	a	0-2	
5/3	FC Paços Ferreira	h	2-2	og (Fonte) 2
11/3	Académica Coimbra	a	0-1	
19/3	Gil Vicente FC	h	1-1	Bibishkov
26/3	Sporting CP	a	0-2	
2/4	União Leiria	h	1-1	Diallo
10/4	Boavista FC	h	0-0	
15/4	Vitória Guimarães	a	1-3	Jorginho
22/4	FC Porto	h	0-1	
30/4	CF Estrela Amadora	a	0-1	
6/5	Naval 1° Maio	h	0-1	

No	Name	Nat	Pos	Aps	(s)	Gls
25	Carlos BARRIONUEVO	ARG	M	14	(1)	
16	Krum BIBIBSHKOV	BUL	A	12	(8)	3

Portugal

No	Name		Nat	Pos	Aps	(s)	Gls
10	Guillaume BORONAD		FRA	D	3	(10)	
8	BRUNO AMARO			M	26	(3)	3
2	CELSO Mendes			D	15	(7)	
	CRISTOVÃO Ramos			D	3	(8)	
18	DIALLO Mallo		SEN	A	8	(4)	1
	Luís DIAS			A	3	(4)	
77	Elpídio Conceição "DILL"		BRA	M	8	(6)	1
	Hélder GUEDES			M		(3)	
7	Mário Magalhães "JACQUES"			M	3	(1)	
35	Jorge Araújo "JORGINHO"			M	21		1
11	JOSÉ RUI Veja			M	14	(10)	1
50	Hamilton Souza "JUNINHO PETROLINA"		BRA	M	11	(3)	
17	KELLY Berville		FRA	D	18		
99	MARCO FERREIRA			A	6	(1)	1
78	Ousmane N'DOYE		SEN	M	11	(1)	3
70	NILTON Fernandes		CVD	M	16	(10)	
1	NUNO AVELINO			G	5	(1)	
5	NUNO DIOGO			D	11	(1)	
13	NUNO SANTOS			G	21		
33	ODAÍR Borges		BRA	D	16		1
19	Sanibal ORAHOVAC		BOS	M	15	(3)	1
14	PEDRO ARAÚJO			M	14	(2)	
20	PEDRO MOREIRA			D	31		
9	ROBERTO Ballestero		BRA	A	16	(6)	3
22	SÉRGIO LOMBA			D	13	(6)	
32	VINICIUS Martinez		BRA	D	8		
4	WELINGTON Olveira		BRA	D	31		
30	Cleiton Ravera "YAN"		BRA	A	1	(1)	

FC PORTO
Coach – Co Adriaanse (HOL)

2005
21/8	CF Estrela Amadora	h	1-0	Ricardo Costa	
26/8	Naval 1° Maio	a	3-2	César Peixoto 2, Hugo Almeida	
10/9	Rio Ave FC	h	3-0	Quaresma, Alan, Hugo Almeida	
18/9	Sporting Braga	a	0-0		
24/9	CF Os Belenenses	h	2-0	McCarthy, Jorginho	
2/10	CS Marítimo	a	2-2	Lisandro López, César Peixoto	
15/10	SL Benfica	h	0-2		
23/10	CD Nacional	a	1-0	Hugo Almeida	
29/10	Vitória Setúbal	h	0-0		
6/11	FC Paços Ferreira	a	1-0	Quaresma	
19/11	Académica Coimbra	h	5-1	Lucho González 2, Lisandro López 2, César Peixoto	
28/11	Gil Vicente FC	a	1-0	Lucho González	
2/12	Sporting CP	h	1-1	og (Anderson)	
10/12	União Leiria	a	3-1	og (Laranjeiro), Lisandro López, Diego	
17/12	FC Penafiel	h	3-1	Lucho González 2 (1p), Lisandro López	
22/12	Vitória Guimarães	a	2-0	Quaresma, Jorginho	

2006
8/1	Boavista FC	h	1-0	Quaresma	
15/1	CF Estrela Amadora	a	1-2	Lucho González	
21/1	Naval 1° Maio	h	1-0	og (Fernando)	
29/1	Rio Ave FC	a	0-0		
6/2	Sporting Braga	h	1-1	Lucho González	
11/2	CF Os Belenenses	a	2-0	Adriano 2	
19/2	CS Marítimo	h	1-0	Raul Meireles	
26/2	SL Benfica	a	0-1		
5/3	CD Nacional	h	3-0	McCarthy, Pepe, Lucho González	
10/3	Vitória Setúbal	a	2-0	Adriano, Raul Meireles	
18/3	FC Paços Ferreira	h	3-0	McCarthy, Adriano, Lisandro López	
26/3	Académica Coimbra	a	1-0	Hugo Almeida	
2/4	Gil Vicente FC	h	3-0	Cech, Quaresma (p), Ibson	
8/4	Sporting CP	a	1-0	Jorginho	
14/4	União Leiria	h	1-0	Adriano	
22/4	FC Penafiel	a	1-0	Adriano (p)	
30/4	Vitória Guimarães	h	3-1	Lucho González 2 (1p), Adriano	
6/5	Boavista FC	a	1-1	Lisandro López	

No	Name	Nat	Pos	Aps	(s)	Gls
28	ADRIANO Louzada	BRA	A	26	(1)	7
27	ALAN Silva	BRA	A	10	(14)	1
30	ANDERSON Oliveira	BRA	M	2	(1)	
17	Jose BOSINGWA		D	21		
13	BRUNO ALVES		D	6	(1)	
35	Marek CECH	SVK	D	12	(2)	1
21	CÉSAR PEIXOTO		M	15	(1)	4
20	DIEGO Ribas Cunha	BRA	M	12	(7)	1
22	FATIH Sonkaya	TUR	D	5		
57	HÉLDER BARBOSA		A		(1)	
41	HÉLDER POSTIGA		A	2		
1	HELTON Arruda	BRA	G	10	(1)	
39	HUGO ALMEIDA		A	6	(21)	4
6	IBSON Silva	BRA	M	13	(5)	1
25	IVANILDO Cassama		A	6	(8)	
17	Jorge Sousa "JORGINHO"	BRA	M	16	(12)	3
11	LISANDRO LÓPEZ	ARG	A	18	(8)	7
8	Luis "LUCHO" GONZÁLEZ	ARG	M	30		10
77	Benni McCARTHY	RSA	A	22	(1)	3
18	PAULO ASSUNÇÃO	BRA	M	24	(1)	
3	PEDRO EMANUEL		D	26		
14	Kleper Ferreira " PEPE "	BRA	D	24		1
7	Ricardo QUARESMA		M	25	(4)	5
16	RAUL MEIRELES		D	3	(15)	2
5	RICARDO COSTA		D	15	(3)	1
19	Tomislav SOKOTA	CRO	A	1	(1)	
99	VÍTOR BAÍA		G	24		

RIO AVE FC
Coach – António Sousa; (1/3/06) João Eusébio

2005
21/8	FC Penafiel	a	2-0	Cleiton, Milhazes (p)	
28/8	Vitória Guimarães	h	3-1	Gaúcho, Niquinha, Marquinhos	
10/9	FC Porto	a	0-3		
18/9	CF Estrela Amadora	h	2-1	Gaúcho, Marquinhos	
25/9	Naval 1° Maio	a	0-1		
1/10	Boavista FC	h	1-1	Gaúcho	
14/10	Sporting Braga	h	1-2	og (Madrid)	
21/10	CF Os Belenenses	a	2-1	Milhazes (p), Cleiton	
30/10	CS Marítimo	h	2-2	Evandro, Chidi	
6/11	SL Benfica	a	2-2	Cleiton, Chidi	
20/11	CD Nacional	h	0-2		
27/11	Vitória Setúbal	a	0-1		
4/12	FC Paços Ferreira	h	2-2	Marquinhos, Gaúcho	
11/12	Académica Coimbra	a	2-2	Chidi, Gaúcho	
17/12	Gil Vicente FC	h	1-0	José Gomes	
20/12	Sporting CP	a	0-3		

2006
9/1	União Leiria	h	1-2	Evandro	
15/1	FC Penafiel	h	2-0	Evandro, Keita	
21/1	Vitória Guimarães	a	1-0	Gaúcho	
29/1	FC Porto	h	0-0		

Portugal

5/2	CF Estrela Amadora	a	0-0	
12/2	Naval 1° Maio	h	0-1	
17/2	Boavista FC	a	1-2	Bruno Mendes
27/2	Sporting Braga	a	0-5	
6/3	CF Os Belenenses	h	2-1	Gaúcho, Evandro
11/3	CS Marítimo	a	0-0	
19/3	SL Benfica	h	0-1	
24/3	CD Nacional	a	1-1	Gaúcho
3/4	Vitória Setúbal	h	1-0	Agostinho
9/4	FC Paços Ferreira	a	1-2	Niquinha
15/4	Académica Coimbra	h	1-4	Gaúcho
23/4	Gil Vicente FC	a	0-1	
30/4	Sporting CP	h	1-3	Milhazes
6/5	União Leiria	a	2-5	Gaúcho, Fábio Coentrão

No	Name	Nat	Pos	Aps	(s)	Gls
17	ADRIANO Moreira		G		(1)	
19	AGOSTINHO Ribeiro		M	2	(9)	1
45	Darko ANIC	SCG	A	2	(3)	
20	BRUNO MENDES		D	18	(1)	1
1	Luís Miguel CANDEIAS		G	2	(1)	
35	Philip CHIDI	NGA	A	28	(5)	3
29	CLEITON Pinto	BRA	A	20	(2)	3
26	DANIELSON Trindade	BRA	D	30		
6	DELSON Ferreira	BRA	M	15	(7)	
3	DIOGO Furlan		M		(2)	
4	EVANDRO Escardalete	BRA	M	15	(13)	4
11	FÁBIO COENTRÃO		M	2	(1)	1
22	Augusto GAMA		A		(3)	
13	Eric Gomes "GAÚCHO"	BRA	A	33		10
21	IDALÉCIO Rosa		D	20	(2)	
18	JOSÉ GOMES		D	34		1
27	Ladji KEITA	SEN	A	1	(20)	1
15	Marcos Barros "MARQUINHOS"		D	17	(4)	3
25	Carlos MILHAZES		D	32		1
74	Miguel MORA	ESP	G	32		
10	Rui Araújo "MOZER"		M	20	(6)	
5	Edson Barros "NIQUINHA"	BRA	M	29		2
7	RICARDO JORGE Miranda		M	6	(16)	
14	André VILAS BOAS		M	9	(4)	
28	VÍTOR GOMES		M	7	(1)	

SPORTING BRAGA
Coach – Jesualdo Ferreira

2005

22/8	União Leiria	a	1-0	Cesinha
28/8	FC Penafiel	h	1-0	Nem
9/9	Vitória Guimarães	a	2-0	Delibasic, João Tomás
18/9	FC Porto	h	0-0	
25/9	CF Estrela Amadora	a	0-0	
3/10	Naval 1° Maio	h	1-0	Vandinho
14/10	Rio Ave FC	a	2-1	og (Milhazes), Vandinho
22/10	Boavista FC	h	1-0	Madrid
31/10	CF Os Belenenses	h	2-0	João Tomás, og (Sandro Gaúcho)
5/11	CS Marítimo	a	0-1	
19/11	SL Benfica	h	3-2	Cesinha, Maxi Bevacqua 2
25/11	CD Nacional	a	0-1	
4/12	Vitória Setúbal	h	0-1	
11/12	FC Paços Ferreira	a	0-1	
17/12	Académica Coimbra	h	2-0	Nunes, João Tomás
21/12	Gil Vicente FC	a	1-2	João Tomás

2006

7/1	Sporting CP	h	3-2	Wender 2, João Tomás
14/1	União Leiria	h	1-0	Wender
19/1	FC Penafiel	a	0-0	
29/1	Vitória Guimarães	h	1-0	João Tomás
6/2	FC Porto	a	1-1	João Tomás (p)
12/2	CF Estrela Amadora	h	1-1	João Tomás
19/2	Naval 1° Maio	a	1-0	Cesinha
27/2	Rio Ave FC	h	5-0	João Tomás 2, Vandinho, Kim, Delibasic
5/3	Boavista FC	a	0-0	
13/3	CF Os Belenenses	a	0-2	
19/3	CS Marítimo	h	2-0	Paulo Jorge, João Tomás
25/3	SL Benfica	a	0-1	
31/3	CD Nacional	h	1-0	Delibasic
9/4	Vitória Setúbal	a	0-1	
17/4	FC Paços Ferreira	h	2-3	Delibasic, João Tomás (p)
24/4	Académica Coimbra	a	3-0	Frechaut, João Tomás 2
30/4	Gil Vicente FC	h	1-1	João Tomás (p)
6/5	Sporting CP	a	0-1	

No	Name	Nat	Pos	Aps	(s)	Gls
22	ABEL Ferreira		D	11		
30	CNDIDO COSTA		A	2	(9)	
13	CARLOS FERNANDES		D	5	(1)	
14	Vítor CASTANHEIRA		M	4	(13)	
29	Carlos Santos " CESINHA "	BRA	A	12	(6)	3
7	DAVIDE Dias		A	7	(1)	
19	Andrija DELIBASIC	SCG	A	5	(5)	4
	FILIPE Gonçalves		M	2	(4)	
17	Nuno FRECHAUT		D	9		1
6	HUGO LEAL		M	11	(1)	
10	JAIME Aquino	BRA	M	10	(3)	
18	JOÃO ALVES		M	3		
9	JOÃO TOMÁS		A	27	(2)	15
5	JORGE LUIZ	BRA	D	16		
27	KIM Dong-hyun	KOR	A	3	(10)	1
20	LUÍS FILIPE Fernandes		D	31	(1)	
23	Andrés MADRID	ARG	M	32		1
21	Carlo MARINELLI	ARG	M	3	(1)	
99	MATHEUS Nascimento	BRA	M		(4)	
8	Julio "MAXI" BEVACQUA	ARG	A	6	(7)	2
4	Rinaldo Lima "NEM"	BRA	D	31		1
28	José Carlos NUNES		D	16		1
3	PAULO JORGE Gomes		D	18	(2)	1
	PAULO MONTEIRO		D		(1)	
1	PAULO SANTOS		G	34		
2	PEDRO COSTA		D	6		
8	Adriano ROSSATO	BRA	D	16	(3)	
16	SIDNEY Almeida	BRA	M	7	(6)	
88	Vanderson Almeida " VANDINHO "	BRA	M	27	(4)	3
29	WELLINGTON Marinho	BRA	D	3	(1)	
15	Wenderson Said "WENDER"	BRA	M	17	(1)	3

SPORTING CP
Coach – José Peseiro; (21/10/05) Paulo Bento

2005

19/8	CF Os Belenenses	h	2-1	Rogério, Deivid
28/8	CS Marítimo	a	2-1	Liedson 2
10/9	SL Benfica	h	2-1	Luís Loureiro, Liedson
19/9	CD Nacional	a	1-2	Deivid
25/9	Vitória Setúbal	h	1-0	Deivid
2/10	FC Paços Ferreira	a	0-3	
16/10	Académica Coimbra	h	0-1	
23/10	Gil Vicente FC	a	2-2	Douala, Liedson
30/10	Boavista FC	a	2-2	Nani, Liedson
4/11	União Leiria	h	2-1	Beto, Rogério
20/11	FC Penafiel	a	1-0	Liedson
27/11	Vitória Guimarães	h	2-0	Deivid, Carlos Martins
2/12	FC Porto	a	1-1	Deivid
9/12	CF Estrela Amadora	h	0-1	
16/12	Naval 1° Maio	a	2-0	João Moutinho (p), og

Portugal

20/12	Rio Ave FC	h	3-0	(Fernando) Liedson 2, Tonel
2006				
7/1	Sporting Braga	a	2-3	Liedson 2
14/1	CF Os Belenenses	a	1-0	Tonel
21/1	CS Marítimo	h	1-1	Romagnoli
28/1	SL Benfica	a	3-1	Sá Pinto (p), Liedson 2
4/2	CD Nacional	h	1-0	Marco Caneira
12/2	Vitória Setúbal	a	2-1	Carlos Martins, João Moutinho
18/2	FC Paços Ferreira	h	3-0	Sá Pinto (p), Deivid, Tello
25/2	Académica Coimbra	a	3-0	João Moutinho, Liedson, Nani (p)
5/3	Gil Vicente FC	h	2-0	Koke 2
11/3	Boavista FC	h	1-0	Tonel
19/3	União Leiria	a	1-0	og (Costinha)
26/3	FC Penafiel	h	2-0	Nani, João Alves
1/4	Vitória Guimarães	a	1-0	Liedson
8/4	FC Porto	h	0-1	
15/4	CF Estrela Amadora	a	0-0	
23/4	Naval 1° Maio	h	0-0	
30/4	Rio Ave FC	a	3-1	Nani, Liedson, og (Danielson)
6/5	Sporting Braga	h	1-0	João Moutinho

No	Name	Nat	Pos	Aps	(s)	Gls
	ABEL Ferreira		D	16		
4	ANDERSON Polga	BRA	D	30		
55	ANDRÉ MARQUES		D	3		
22	Roberto Severo " BETO "		D	7	(1)	1
5	CARLOS MARTINS		M	13	(8)	2
27	CUSTÓDIO Castro		M	27		
42	DAVID CAIADO		A		(1)	
23	DEIVID Souza	BRA	A	19	(6)	6
17	Rudolph DOUALA	CMR	A	17	(8)	1
33	Luís EDSON	BRA	D	1		
6	HUGO Vieira		D	1	(4)	
34	JOÃO ALVES		M	9	(14)	1
28	JOÃO MOUTINHO		M	34		4
3	Pedro Contreras "KOKE"	ESP	A	2	(4)	2
31	LIEDSON Muniz	BRA	A	31		15
8	LUÍS LOUREIRO		M	5	(4)	1
	MARCO CANEIRA		D	15		1
15	MIGUEL GARCIA		D	8	(8)	
18	Luís Cunha "NANI"		M	16	(13)	4
1	NÉLSON Pereira		G	5		
21	Martinho Mocana "PAÍTO"	MOZ	D		(2)	
87	Mauricio PINILLA	CHL	A		(4)	
76	RICARDO Pereira		G	29	(1)	
26	Fábio ROCHEMBACK	BRA	M	2		
37	ROGÉRIO Regis		M	11	(1)	2
	Leandro ROMAGNOLI	ARG	M	5	(1)	1
10	Ricardo SÁ PINTO		A	23	(4)	2
9	Elpídio SILVA	BRA	A		(1)	
11	Rodrigo TELLO	CHL	M	17	(3)	1
41	António Ferreira "TOMANÉ"		A		(1)	
13	António Sousa "TONEL"		D	28	(2)	3
20	Silvestre VARELA		M		(2)	
51	Wenderson Said "WENDER"	BRA	M		(9)	

UNIÃO LEIRIA
Coach – José Gomes; (27/9/05) Jorge Jesus

2005

22/8	Sporting Braga	h	0-1	
27/8	CF Os Belenenses	a	1-3	Lourenço
11/9	CS Marítimo	h	0-0	
18/9	SL Benfica	a	0-4	
25/9	CD Nacional	h	0-0	
2/10	Vitória Setúbal	a	0-2	
16/10	FC Paços Ferreira	h	3-0	Renato, Ferreira, Maciel
23/10	Académica Coimbra	a	3-1	Ferreira 2, Fábio Felício
30/10	Gil Vicente FC	h	3-0	Lourenço 2, Maciel
4/11	Sporting CP	a	1-2	João Paulo
20/11	Boavista FC	a	0-2	
27/11	FC Penafiel	h	1-1	Fábio Felício
5/12	Vitória Guimarães	a	3-0	Touré, Paulo César 2
10/12	FC Porto	h	1-3	Fábio Felício
17/12	CF Estrela Amadora	a	2-1	Paulo César 2
21/12	Naval 1° Maio	h	2-1	Maciel, Harison
2006				
9/1	Rio Ave FC	a	2-1	og (Milhazes), Alhandra
14/1	Sporting Braga	a	0-1	
23/1	CF Os Belenenses	h	2-2	Paulo César, Touré
29/1	CS Marítimo	a	0-3	
4/2	SL Benfica	h	3-1	João Paulo, Fábio Felício, Maciel
12/2	CD Nacional	a	4-1	Alhandra, Paulo César, João Paulo (p), Maciel
20/2	Vitória Setúbal	h	0-2	
26/2	FC Paços Ferreira	a	1-1	Lourenço
5/3	Académica Coimbra	h	0-2	
11/3	Gil Vicente FC	a	2-1	Lourenço, Fábio Felício
19/3	Sporting CP	h	0-1	
27/3	Boavista FC	h	0-0	
2/4	FC Penafiel	a	1-1	Lourenço
8/4	Vitória Guimarães	h	1-0	Cadu Silva
14/4	FC Porto	a	0-1	
23/4	CF Estrela Amadora	h	1-1	Fábio Felício
30/4	Naval 1° Maio	a	2-0	João Paulo, Maciel
6/5	Rio Ave FC	h	5-2	Alhandra, og (Bruno Mendes), Paulo César, Cadu Silva, Hugo Costa

No	Name	Nat	Pos	Aps	(s)	Gls
14	Luis Joaquim " ALHANDRA "		D	23	(7)	3
6	ANDERSON Alves Silva	BRA	M	2		
22	Carlos Silva " CADU SILVA"	BRA	A	8	(8)	2
1	Paulo COSTINHA		G	25	(1)	
8	EDER Bonfim	BRA	D	28		
18	FÁBIO FELÍCIO		A	22	(5)	6
24	FERNANDO Prass	BRA	G	9		
30	Josiesley FERREIRA	BRA	A	8	(10)	3
31	GABRIEL Atz	BRA	D	29		
11	HARISON Nery	BRA	M	24	(1)	1
4	HUGO COSTA		D	1		
55	JAIME Aquino	BRA	M	6	(7)	
23	JOÃO PAULO Andrade		D	30	(1)	4
16	Nuno Cunha "KATA"		M	6	(7)	
25	Nuno LARANJEIRO		D	7	(3)	
20	Luís Carlos LOURENÇO		A	11	(12)	6
19	MACIEL Cunha	BRA	A	31		6
99	Matias MIRAMONTES	ARG	A	2	(10)	
21	Adriano Miranda "NÉNÉ "		M	2	(3)	
9	PAULO CÉSAR	BRA	A	23	(7)	7
5	PAULO GOMES		D	17	(4)	
17	RENATO Assunção		D	23	(3)	1
45	Damian TIXIER	FRA	D	21	(2)	
33	Alioune TOURÉ	FRA	A	16	(7)	2
7	VÍTOR PEREIRA		M		(1)	

VITÓRIA GUIMARÃES
Coach – Jaime Pacheco; (15/12/05) Vítor Pontes

2005

Portugal

21/8	Naval 1º Maio	h	0-2		
28/8	Rio Ave FC	a	1-3	Saganowski	
9/9	Sporting Braga	h	0-2		
19/9	CF Os Belenenses	a	1-3	Benachour	
24/9	CS Marítimo	h	1-0	Saganowski	
3/10	SL Benfica	a	1-2	Tiago Targino	
15/10	CD Nacional	h	0-0		
23/10	Vitória Setúbal	a	1-0	Saganowski	
30/10	FC Paços Ferreira	h	0-2		
7/11	Académica Coimbra	a	0-1		
18/11	Gil Vicente FC	h	2-0	Benachour, Paulo Sérgio	
27/11	Sporting CP	a	0-2		
5/12	União Leiria	h	0-3		
10/12	FC Penafiel	a	1-0	Benachour	
18/12	Boavista FC	a	1-1	Saganowski	
22/12	FC Porto	h	0-2		
2006					
8/1	CF Estrela Amadora	a	0-2		
15/1	Naval 1º Maio	a	0-0		
21/1	Rio Ave FC	h	1-1	Saganowski	
29/1	Sporting Braga	a	0-1		
5/2	CF Os Belenenses	h	2-2	Dário, Saganowski	
13/2	CS Marítimo	a	1-0	Saganowski	
18/2	SL Benfica	h	2-0	Svärd, Neca	
25/2	CD Nacional	a	1-1	Wesley	
3/3	Vitória Setúbal	h	4-0	Saganowski 3, Cléber (p)	
12/3	FC Paços Ferreira	a	1-1	Antchouet	
19/3	Académica Coimbra	h	1-1	Saganowski	
26/3	Gil Vicente FC	a	1-1	Cléber (p)	
1/4	Sporting CP	h	0-1		
8/4	União Leiria	a	0-1		
15/4	FC Penafiel	h	3-1	Benachour, Saganowski, Wesley	
21/4	Boavista FC	h	1-1	Paíto	
30/4	FC Porto	a	1-3	Antchouet	
6/5	CF Estrela Amadora	h	0-1		

No	Name	Nat	Pos	Aps	(s)	Gls
	Henry ANTCHOUET	GAB	A	5	(7)	2
8	Selim BENACHOUR	TUN	M	23	(2)	4
5	Hélder CABRAL		M	4		
28	CLAYTON Cruz	BRA	A	3	(3)	
50	CLÉBER Lima	BRA	D	27		2
55	DÁRIO Monteiro	MOZ	A	12	(12)	1
17	Attila DRAGÓNER	HUN	D	17	(2)	
26	FLÁVIO MEIRELES		M	24	(1)	
	Francisco GALLARDO	ESP	M	2		
19	Pedro GEROMEL	BRA	D	17		
22	MANOEL Filho	BRA	A	10	(9)	
8	MÁRIO SÉRGIO		D	14	(2)	
14	Leonel MEDEIROS		D	7	(1)	
18	João Teixeira " MORENO "		M	13	(9)	
	Vítor MORENO		D	15		
10	João Fernandes "NECA"		M	27	(2)	1
1	NILSON Júnior	BRA	G	27		
	José Lima OTACÍLIO	BRA	M	11	(2)	
	Martins Mocana "PAITO"	MOZ	D	16		1
51	Márcio PAIVA		G	7	(1)	
11	PAULO SÉRGIO Almeida		A	6	(17)	1
30	Carlos Pinto "PINTASSILGO"		D	1	(2)	
27	Emanuel RIVAS		D	1	(4)	
20	ROGÉRIO MATIAS		D	11	(1)	
9	Marek SAGANOWSKI	POL	A	31	(1)	12
4	Sebastian SVÄRD	SWE	M	26	(2)	1
77	TIAGO TARGINO		A	7	(13)	1
	WESLEY Silva	BRA	A	10	(4)	2
25	José Castro "ZEZINHO"		M		(4)	

VITÓRIA SETÚBAL
Coach – Norton de Matos; (19/12/05) Hélio Sousa

2005					
20/8	Boavista FC	a	0-0		
28/8	FC Paços Ferreira	h	0-1		
11/9	Académica Coimbra	a	1-0	Fábio	
18/9	Gil Vicente FC	h	1-0	Pedro Oliveira	
25/9	Sporting CP	a	0-1		
2/10	União Leiria	h	2-0	Ricardo Chaves, Fábio	
16/10	FC Penafiel	a	1-0	Binho	
23/10	Vitória Guimarães	h	0-1		
29/10	FC Porto	a	0-0		
6/11	CF Estrela Amadora	h	1-0	Fábio	
20/11	Naval 1º Maio	a	3-0	Pedro Oliveira, Fábio 2	
27/11	Rio Ave FC	h	1-0	Auri	
4/12	Sporting Braga	a	1-0	Fábio	
12/12	CF Os Belenenses	h	1-0	Auri	
17/12	CS Marítimo	a	0-1		
21/12	SL Benfica	h	0-1		
2006					
6/1	CD Nacional	a	2-2	Franja (p), Lacombe	
16/1	Boavista FC	h	0-2		
21/1	FC Paços Ferreira	a	2-1	Binho, Bruno Ribeiro	
30/1	Académica Coimbra	h	0-1		
5/2	Gil Vicente FC	a	0-5		
12/2	Sporting CP	h	1-2	Carlitos (p)	
20/2	União Leiria	a	2-0	Varela, Carlitos	
26/2	FC Penafiel	h	2-0	Binho, Adalto	
3/3	Vitória Guimarães	a	0-4		
10/3	FC Porto	h	0-2		
19/3	CF Estrela Amadora	a	0-1		
26/3	Naval 1º Maio	h	4-1	Pedro Oliveira, Sandro, Varela, Carlitos	
3/4	Rio Ave FC	a	0-1		
9/4	Sporting Braga	h	1-0	Carlitos	
14/4	CF Os Belenenses	a	1-3	Bruno Ribeiro	
23/4	CS Marítimo	h	0-1		
30/4	SL Benfica	a	0-1		
6/5	CD Nacional	h	1-1	Auri	

No	Name	Nat	Pos	Aps	(s)	Gls
13	ADALTO Silva	BRA	D	16	(5)	1
15	AURI Faustino	BRA	D	32		3
26	George Santos " BINHO "	BRA	M	24	(7)	3
11	BRUNO RIBEIRO		M	21	(6)	2
25	Carlos Garcia "CARLITOS"		A	13	(2)	4
2	DEMBELE Siranama	FRA	M	13		
4	Mamadou DIAKITE	FRA	M		(1)	
18	FÁBIO Hempel	BRA	A	16	(1)	6
19	FLÁVIO Cerqueira		D	2		
	Diogo FONSECA		A	2	(11)	
46	Antonijo FRANJA	CRO	M	6	(8)	1
	HEITOR Andrade	BRA	M		(4)	
	HÉLIO ROQUE		A	1	(10)	
14	JANÍCIO Martins	CVD	M	32		
	José FONTE		D	14	(1)	
55	JULIEN Souza		D		(2)	
21	Grégory LACOMBE	FRA	M	1	(11)	1
12	MARCO TABUAS		G	7	(1)	
1	Marcelo MORETTO	BRA	G	15		
7	Fernando Rodrigues " NANDINHO "		D	22	(2)	
25	Madior N'DIAYE	SEN	A	2	(1)	
8	PEDRO OLIVEIRA		A	20	(7)	3
3	RICARDO CHAVES		M	28	(4)	1
30	Rubens Moedim "RUBINHO"	BRA	G	12		
	Pedro RUSSIANO		M	2	(1)	
61	SANDRO Mendes		M	8	(3)	1

Portugal

20	Papa Mamadou SOUGOU	SCG	A	19	(8)	
	Oumar TCHOMOGO	SEN	A	13	(1)	
	Silvestre VARELA		A	13	(2)	2
23	Nélson VERISSIMO		D	20	(1)	

DOMESTIC CUP 2005/06

FOURTH ROUND
(26/10/05)
CS Maritimo 2, FC Tirsense 0
SC Leixões 1, SL Benfica 2
Caniçal 0, CD Fátima 1
AD Fafe 0, Vitória Setúbal
AD Oliveirense 2, União Lamas 0
Aljustrelense 3, SC Olhanense 0
Abrantes 3, Maria Fonte Povoa de Lanhoso 0
FC Vizela 3, CD Santa Clara 1
CD Feirense 1, Pinhalnovense 1 *(aet; 3-5 on pens)*
Vila Meã 2, Mirandela 1 *(aet)*
Sporting Covilhã 2, Lousada 0
FC Porto 1, FC Marco 0
Oeiras 1, Boavista FC 3
Desportivo Aves 1, CF Os Belenenses 0
Lixa 4, FC Penafiel 0
Camacha 0, GD Estoril Praia 1 *(aet)*
Académica Coimbra 3, Gil Vicente FC 2 *(aet)*
Portimonense SC 0, Souropires 0 *(aet; 4-5 on pens)*
Louletano DC 1, Atlético Lisboa 0
CF Estrela Amadora 2, União Micaelense 0
Lagoa 1, AD Ovarense 0
Rio Ave FC 0, Ribeirão 0 *(aet; 4-5 on pens)*
Sporting Braga 1, União Leiria 0
Portomosense 1, FC Barreirense 1 *(aet; 8-7 on pens)*
Sporting CP 2, Varzim SC 0
Imortal 1, CD Nacional 1 *(aet; 5-6 on pens)*
(30/10/05)
Paredes 2, Nelas 0
(12/11/05)
FC Paços Ferreira 0, Tourizense 1
(13/11/05)
Naval 1º de Maio 1, Pontassolense 0
bye – Vitória Guimarães

FIFTH ROUND
(11/1/06)
Paredes 3, Lagoa 1
Desportivo Aves 1, Sporting Braga 1 *(aet; 4-2 on pens)*
Vitória Guimarães 4, GD Estoril Praia 0
Louletano DC 0, Académica Coimbra 0 *(aet; 2-3 on pens)*
Pinhalnovense 0, Vitória Setúbal 0 *(aet; 4-5 on pens)*
Sporting CP 2, FC Vizela 1
Sporting Covilhã 1, Vila Meã 2
Naval 1º de Maio 1, FC Porto 2
Souropires 1, CF Estrela Amadora 3
Aljustrelense 0, AD Oliveirense 1
Tourizense 0, SL Benfica 2
Portomosense 0, CS Marítimo 2
Lixa 1, Ribeirão 0
CD Nacional 2, CD Fátima 0
Boavista FC 3, Abrantes 0

SIXTH ROUND
(8/2/06)
Vitória Guimarães 2, AD Oliveirense 0

CS Marítimo 3, Vila Meã 0
Desportivo Aves 1, Académica Coimbra 2
CF Estrela Amadora 0, Boavista FC 1
Sporting CP 2, Paredes 1
SL Benfica 0, CD Nacional 0 *(aet; 5-3 on pens)*
Lixa 0, Vitória Setúbal 2
bye – FC Porto

QUARTER-FINALS
(15/3/06)
Vitória Setúbal 2 *(Varela 39, Carlitos 108p)*, Boavista FC 1 *(João Pinto 61) (aet)*
CS Marítimo 1 *(Kanu 33)*, FC Porto 2 *(McCarthy 22, 96) (aet)*
Académica Coimbra 0, Sporting CP 2 *(Deivid 51, Nani 90)*
SL Benfica 0, Vitória Guimarães 1 *(Dário 22)*

SEMI-FINALS
(22/3/06)
FC Porto 1 *(McCarthy 114)*, Sporting CP 1 *(Liedson 108) (aet; 5-4 on pens)*
(23/3/06)
Vitória Setubal 1 *(Auri 118)*, Vitória Guimarães 1 *(Saganowski 110) (aet; 3-2 on pens)*

FINAL
(14/5/06)
Estadio Nacional Jamor, Lisbon
FC PORTO 1 *(Adriano 40)*
VITÓRIA SETÚBAL 0
Referee – *Duarte Gomes*
FC PORTO – Helton, Pedro Emanuel, Ricardo Quaresma *(Jorginho 67)*, Lucho González, McCarthy *(Ibson 85)*, Bosingwa, Pepe, Paulo Assunção, Alan, Adriano, Anderson *(Cech 75)*.
VITÓRIA SETÚBAL – Rubinho, Ricardo Chaves *(Pedro Oliveira 67)*, Binho *(Fonseca 81)*, Bruno Ribeiro, Adalto *(Sougou 57)*, Janício, Auri, Veríssimo, Silvestre Varela, Carlitos, Sandro.

SECOND LEVEL FINAL TABLE 2005/06

		Pld	W	D	L	F	A	Pts
1	SC Beira Mar	34	18	14	2	45	18	68
2	Desportivo Aves	34	18	10	6	47	30	64
3	Leixões SC	34	17	11	6	47	19	62
4	Varzim SC	34	13	13	8	47	39	52
5	SC Olhanense	34	13	13	8	41	28	52
6	CD Santa Clara	34	13	12	9	45	32	51
7	Gondomar SC	34	14	9	11	56	41	51
8	Desportivo Chaves	34	13	11	10	40	36	50
9	GD Estoril Praia	34	11	12	11	44	43	45
10	CD Feirense	34	12	8	14	44	44	44
11	FC Vizela	34	11	11	12	42	48	44
12	Portimonense SC	34	10	13	11	36	36	43
13	Moreirense FC	34	11	9	14	36	37	42
14	Sporting Covilhã	34	10	12	12	37	42	42
15	FC Barreirense	34	8	11	15	31	41	35
16	FC Marco	34	7	8	19	32	63	29
17	AD Ovarense	34	6	7	21	36	72	25
18	FC Maia	34	6	6	22	30	67	24

Republic of Ireland

Champagne climax for Cork

The 2005 Irish Premier Division, increased from ten clubs to 12 but with a slightly shorter fixture list, threw up many surprises. Almost all pre-season predictions had tipped Shelbourne – aka the Shelacticos – to complete a hat-trick of championship triumphs. But instead, while the Dubliners lay low, the race for the title developed into a fascinating north-south duel between the 'Citys' of Derry and Cork.

All good thrillers should have a gripping climax, and this one could hardly have been better scripted. It was the classic final day showdown with the home side, Cork, requiring victory and the visitors, League Cup winners Derry, needing a draw. The two teams had been involved in a nip-and-tuck chase all season, winning two games out of three and drawing most of the others. No wonder even Shelbourne struggled to keep pace.

O'Flynn on the mark

Neither team deserved to finish second, but there had to be a winner, and on judgment day it was Damien Richardson's Cork side that came good to win their first title for 12 years. Richardson, who had returned to manage the club only on the eve of the season as an emergency replacement for Pat Dolan, had been undecided prior to the game whether to risk his top-scoring striker John O'Flynn, who had missed the previous six games through injury. But the gamble of selecting him paid off when, just 18 minutes in, he put the home side ahead with his 11th goal of the campaign. Once in front, Cork's defence, which had been breached only six times at Turners Cross, stood solid and firm, with goalkeeper Michael Devine remaining largely untroubled. The killer blow was delivered just after the hour when winger Liam Kearney finished off a delightful move to make it 2-0.

The celebrations in the southern city were suitably manic. Cork's previous title, in 1993, had come after a complex series of play-offs, with victory being sealed in the incongruous setting of the Royal Dublin Showgrounds. This time it was the real deal, with the championship trophy being lifted in their home stadium. That honour went to an Englishman, captain Dan Murray, a mainstay of Cork's outstanding defence. The rest of the team were all Irish, most of them locally born in the province of Munster.

One key player missing from the celebrations was young striker Kevin Doyle, who, after netting seven goals in 11 games, was transferred across the Irish Sea to Reading. He went on to have a brilliant season in England, helping the club to a runaway victory in the Football League Championship and also earning regular international call-ups for the Republic of Ireland.

Drogheda's big day

Two weeks after collecting the title, Cork had the opportunity to make further history by completing the Double. They had reached the FAI Cup final, also at Derry's expense (with a last-minute penalty), and were heavily fancied to overcome Drogheda United, a club without a major trophy in its 42-year history. On this big day, however, Cork failed to deliver and were deservedly beaten by their success-starved opponents. A superb 52nd-minute volley from

NATIONAL TEAM RESULTS 2005/06

Date	Opponent	H/A	Venue	Score	Scorers
17/8/05	Italy	H	Dublin	1-2	Reid A. (32)
7/9/05	France (WCQ)	H	Dublin	0-1	
8/10/05	Cyprus (WCQ)	A	Nicosia	1-0	Elliott (6)
12/10/05	Switzerland (WCQ)	H	Dublin	0-0	
1/3/06	Sweden	H	Dublin	3-0	Duff (36), Keane Rob. (48), Miller (71)
24/5/06	Chile	H	Dublin	0-1	

Republic of Ireland

Gavin Whelan (nephew of former Liverpool and Ireland captain Ronnie Whelan) put Drogheda ahead, and the match was sealed late on when skipper Declan O'Brien sent the claret-and-blue half of the 25,000 Lansdowne Road crowd into raptures with a well-taken second goal.

As is often the case, when the first trophy is finally won, a second soon follows, and six months later Paul Doolin's team were celebrating again at Cork's expense as they beat them in the final of the new Setanta Cup, the cross-border competition featuring the top four clubs from the Republic and Northern Ireland. Although Cork had won the group game between the clubs 2-0, Drogheda turned the tables in the final at Tolka Park, winning 1-0 after extra-time with a goal from midfielder Mark Leech.

The regular dwellers at Tolka Park, Shelbourne, had a disappointing season on all fronts. Although they finished the Premier Division strongly, winning 11 of their last 13 matches and keeping clean sheets in ten of their last 11, third place was a grave disappointment. They were also unable to repeat their Champions League exploits of the previous season despite holding Romanian giants Steaua Bucharest to a goalless draw at home. They did, however, comfortably win the previous round's all-Ireland derby against Glentoran, with ace marksman Jason Byrne scoring twice in each leg. Byrne maintained his prolific strike-rate in the Premier Division, finishing top of the scorers' listings for the third season running. Another former Golden Boot hat-trick winner, Glen Crowe, left Bohemians to join Byrne at Shelbourne in 2005 but he took a while to settle and ended up with a disappointing final tally of just eight goals.

Rovers relegated

It was a poor season generally for Dublin clubs and a disastrous one in particular for Shamrock Rovers. The financial plight of the country's most decorated club worsened to the extent that supporters were asked to chip in and help pay the players' wages. Various financial irregularities resulted in the League docking eight points off the club's total, and when, following the enforced departure of several key players, Rovers ended their campaign with seven defeats in their last ten games, that points-deduction proved crucial as it dropped them into the relegation play-off zone. Manager Roddy Collins was suspended prior to the two big games against Dublin City that would shape Shamrock's future, and carateker Alan O'Neill was unable to prevent the unthinkable as Rovers went down 3-2 on aggregate to plummet out of Ireland's top division for the first time in their history. Ironically, the man who helped send them down, Dublin City manager Dermot Keely, was a playing member of the Rovers side that won four successive league titles in the 1980s and also later managed the club.

Sligo Rovers won the First Division to claim automatic promotion while their local rivals Finn Harps travelled in the opposite direction after finishing bottom of the heap in the Premier Division. For a long while Waterford United looked doomed, but the acquisition of ex-Cork manager Pat Dolan in an advisory capacity sparked an extraordinary turnaround, and they finished well clear of the drop zone.

The Republic of Ireland's failure to qualify for the World Cup signalled the end of Brian Kerr's three-year reign as manager. The FAI decided not to renew his contract, which, given that he had failed to take the team into even the play-offs of the two qualifying campaigns he had overseen, did not constitute a surprise. Ireland had gone into their final three World Cup games in a promising position, but it had been four years since they had taken a big scalp at Lansdowne Road in a match that mattered and yet again, not once but twice, they were found wanting as they lost 1-0 to France and, with a play-off berth still beckoning, drew 0-0 at home to Switzerland. Fourth place in the group was simply not good enough.

Staunton steps forward

If Kerr's departure was not unexpected, the appointment of Steve Staunton as his replacement brought widespread disbelief. The 37-year-old may

Steve Staunton – Ireland's fresh-faced new manager

Republic of Ireland

NATIONAL TEAM APPEARANCES 2005/06

Manager – Brian KERR
/(13/1/06) Steve STAUNTON

Player	DOB	Club	Ita	FRA	CYP	SUI	Swe	Chl	Caps	Goals
Shay GIVEN	20/4/76	Newcastle United (ENG)	G	G	G	G	G49	G53	76	-
Steve FINNAN	20/4/76	Liverpool (ENG)	D57		M46				38	1
Kenny CUNNINGHAM	28/6/71	Birmingham City (ENG)	D	D	D	D			72	-
Richard DUNNE	21/9/79	Manchester City (ENG)	D46	D	D	D	D	D	29	4
John O'SHEA	30/4/81	Manchester United (ENG)	D78	D	D	M	M49	D53	30	1
Steven REID	10/3/81	Blackburn Rovers (ENG)	M		s61	s80	M	M	18	2
Matt HOLLAND	11/4/74	Charlton Athletic (ENG)	M40		s46	M			49	5
Kevin KILBANE	1/2/77	Everton (ENG)	M	M78	M	M	s60	M	70	5
Andy REID	29/7/82	Tottenham Hotspur (ENG)	A73	M		M80		s85	20	3
Clinton MORRISON	14/5/79	Birmingham City (ENG) /Crystal Palace (ENG)	A	A78		A87	s68		34	9
Damien DUFF	2/3/79	Chelsea (ENG)	A	M	M61		M	M	59	7
Ian HARTE	31/8/77	Levante UD (ESP)	s40	s78		D	D60	s53	63	11
Andy O'BRIEN	29/6/79	Portsmouth (ENG)	s46				D		23	1
Stephen CARR	29/8/76	Newcastle United (ENG)	s57	D	D	D			41	-
Stephen ELLIOTT	6/1/84	Sunderland (ENG)	s73		A	s68	M49		7	1
Liam MILLER	13/2/81	Manchester United (ENG) /Leeds United (ENG)	s78				s60	M53	12	1
Roy KEANE	10/8/71	Manchester United (ENG)		M					67	9
Robbie KEANE	8/7/80	Tottenham Hotspur (ENG)		A	A80	A68	A	A	66	26
Gary DOHERTY	31/1/80	Norwich City (ENG)		s78		s87			34	4
Graham KAVANAGH	2/12/73	Wigan Athletic (ENG)			M		s49	s53	15	1
David CONNOLLY	6/6/77	Wigan Athletic (ENG)			s80				41	9
Joey O'BRIEN	17/2/86	Bolton Wanderers (ENG)					D60		1	-
Kevin DOYLE	18/9/83	Reading (ENG)					A68	A73	2	-
Stephen IRELAND	22/8/88	Manchester City (ENG)					s49		1	-
Wayne HENDERSON	16/9/83	Brighton & Hove Albion (ENG)					s49	s53	2	-
Stephen KELLY	6/9/83	Tottenham Hotspur (ENG)						D85	1	-
Gary BREEN	12/12/73	Sunderland (ENG)						D53	63	6
Aiden McGEADY	4/4/86	Celtic (SCO)						s53	4	-
Jason BYRNE	23/2/81	Shelbourne						s73	2	-

have won more international caps than any other Irishman (102) but his managerial experience is virtually non-existent. With that in mind, the FAI decided to flank him with veteran Englishman Sir Bobby Robson.

The odd couple got off to a great start when Ireland beat Sweden 3-0 at Lansdowne Road, a game in which new skipper Robbie Keane, replacing his newly retired namesake Roy, extended his record goal haul to 26. That win was followed by a rather low-key 1-0 defeat at home to Chile in May, but as most of the Irish players were in holiday mood at the time, it provided few pointers for the Euro 2008 qualifying campaign. Ireland are in an interesting group, headed by Germany and also featuring Wales. The likelihood is that they will have to edge out European Championship specialists the Czech Republic if they are to reach the finals for the first time in 20 years.

Republic of Ireland

EUROPEAN CUPS 2005/06

UEFA CHAMPIONS LEAGUE

SHELBOURNE
1st qualifying round GLENTORAN (NIR)
A 2-1 *Byrne J. (55, 65p)*
Delaney, Heary, Crawley (Moore 46), Rogers, Hawkins, Cahill, Byrne S., Hoolahan, Baker, Crowe (Fitzpatrick 76), Byrne J. (Crawford 79).
H 4-1 *Heary (13), Byrne J. (32p, 71), Crowe (58)*
Delaney, Heary, Crawley, Rogers, Hawkins, Cahill, Byrne S., Hoolahan (Crawford 73), Baker, Crowe (Fitzpatrick 83), Byrne J. (O'Neill 83).

2nd qualifying round STEAUA BUCURESTI (ROM)
H 0-0
Delaney, Heary, Crawley, Rogers, Hawkins, Cahill, Byrne S. (Crawford 36), Baker, Moore, Crowe (Harris 75), Byrne J. (Fleming 78).
A 1-4 *Byrne J. (38)*
Delaney, Heary, Crawley (Fleming 77), Rogers, Harris, Cahill, Byrne S., Baker (N'Do 80), Moore (Hoolahan 65), Crowe, Byrne J.

UEFA CUP

LONGFORD TOWN
1st qualifying round CARMARTHEN TOWN (WAL)
H 2-0 *Paisley (35), Ferguson (54)*
O'Brien, Murphy A., Dillon, Ferguson, Paisley, Martin, Kirby, Fitzgerald (Prunty 77), Byrne, Myler (Baker 86), Keegan.
A 1-5 *Myler (20p)*
O'Brien, Dillon, Ferguson, Paisley (Cawley 79), O'Connor, Martin, Kirby, Fitzgerald (Murphy A. 68), Byrne, Myler (Baker 69), Keegan.

CORK CITY
1st qualifying round EKRANAS PANEVEZYS (LIT)
A 2-0 *O'Donovan (25), O'Callaghan (90)*
Devine (Harrington 15), Murphy, Bennett, O'Halloran, Murray D., Horgan, O'Callaghan, Donovan, Gamble, Kearney (Woods 90), O'Flynn (Behan 89).
H 0-1
McNulty, Murphy, Bennett, O'Halloran, Murray D., Horgan, O'Callaghan, O'Donovan (O'Brien 89), Gamble, Kearney (Woods 90), O'Flynn.

2nd qualifying round DJURGÅRDENS IF (SWE)
A 1-1 *Fenn (8)*
Devine, Murphy, Bennett, O'Halloran, Murray D., Horgan, O'Donovan (Woods 86), Gamble, Kearney, Fenn (O'Brien 81), O'Flynn.
H 0-0
Devine, Murphy, Bennett (O'Donovan 56), O'Halloran, Murray D., Horgan, O'Callaghan, Gamble, Kearney, Fenn, O'Flynn (Coughlan 90).

1st round SK SLAVIA PRAHA (CZE)
A 0-2
Devine, Horgan, Bennett, Murray D., Murphy, O'Donovan, Gamble, O'Callaghan, Kearney, O'Flynn, Fenn (O'Halloran 71).
H 1-2 *O'Callaghan (73p)*
Devine, Horgan, Bennett, Murray D., Murphy, O'Halloran (Gamble 55), O'Callaghan, Kearney (Coughlan 76), O'Flynn, Fenn (Bruton 73).

LEAGUE RESULTS/ SCORERS/APPEARANCES 2005

BOHEMIANS
Manager – Gareth Farrelly

2005				
18/3	Shamrock Rovers	h	1-1	Aggrey
25/3	St. Patrick's Athletic	a	0-0	
1/4	Derry City	h	0-1	
8/4	Waterford United	a	0-2	
15/4	Cork City	h	0-2	
22/4	Finn Harps	h	1-0	og (Minnock)
29/4	Drogheda United	a	2-2	Grant, Harkin
6/5	UCD	a	1-1	Ward
13/5	Longford Town	h	2-0	Aggrey, Ward
20/5	Bray Wanderers	a	2-1	Oman, Harkin
27/5	Shelbourne	h	2-1	Farrelly, Oman
3/6	Shamrock Rovers	a	2-1	Foley, Grant
1/7	Waterford United	h	2-1	Foley (p), Ward
8/7	Cork City	a	1-2	Foley
16/7	Finn Harps	a	3-1	Harkin 2, Foley
22/7	Drogheda United	h	3-2	Foley 2, Harkin
29/7	UCD	h	1-1	Kelly
2/8	Derry City	a	1-3	og (Molloy)
6/8	Longford Town	a	0-1	
11/8	Bray Wanderers	h	1-0	Grant (p)
19/8	Shelbourne	a	1-2	Grant
2/9	Shamrock Rovers	h	1-3	Grant
9/9	St. Patrick's Athletic	a	1-0	O'Keefe
16/9	Derry City	h	2-3	Ward 2
30/9	Waterford United	a	0-2	
3/10	St. Patrick's Athletic	h	1-1	Grant (p)
14/10	Finn Harps	h	3-1	Farrelly, O'Keefe, Ward
28/10	UCD	a	3-1	Harkin 2, O'Keefe
31/10	Cork City	h	1-2	Ward
4/11	Longford Town	h	1-0	Farrelly
8/11	Drogheda United	a	2-3	Kelly, O'Keefe
11/11	Bray Wanderers	a	1-3	O'Keefe
18/11	Shelbourne	h	0-3	

Name	Nat	Pos	Aps	(s)	Gls
James AGGREY	ENG	D	9		2
David BRACKEN		A	3	(2)	
Des BYRNE		D	21	(1)	
Aidan COLLINS		D	8	(3)	

TOP GOALSCORERS 2005

22	Jason BYRNE (Shelbourne)
18	Mark FARREN (Derry City)
13	Kevin McHUGH (Finn Harps)
12	Eamon ZAYED (Bray Wanderers)
11	John O'FLYNN (Cork City)
8	Gavin WHELAN (Drogheda United)
	Glen CROWE (Shelbourne)
7	Kevin DOYLE (Cork City)
	Pat McCOURT (Shamrock Rovers)
	Pat McWALTER (UCD)
	Stephen WARD (Bohemians)
	Robbie DOYLE (St. Patrick's Athletic)
	Fergal HARKIN (Bohemians)
	Ciaran MARTYN (Derry City)
	Gary O'NEILL (Shelbourne)

Republic of Ireland

Name	Nat	Pos	Aps	(s)	Gls
Sean COONEY		D	4	(1)	
Kevin CRONIN		D		(1)	
Mark DUGGAN		M	3	(4)	
Paul DUNPHY		A		(2)	
Gareth FARRELLY		M	21		3
Shane FITZGERALD		M		(2)	
Dominic FOLEY		A	17		6
Tony GRANT		A	27	(1)	6
Matthew GREGG	ENG	G	33		
Fergal HARKIN	NIR	M	31		7
Thomas HEARY		M	1	(1)	
Kevin HUNT	ENG	M	29		
Mark KEANE		M		(1)	
James KEDDY		M	24	(2)	
John Paul KELLY		M	13	(6)	2
James LEE	AUS	D	1	(2)	
Mark O'BRIEN		M	10	(3)	
Aidan O'KEEFE		A	10	(5)	5
Ken OMAN		D	26	(1)	2
Niall O'REILLY		D	3		
Terry PALMER		D	11	(3)	
Conor POWELL		D		(5)	
Stephen RICE		D	29		
Stephen WARD		A	29		7

BRAY WANDERERS
Manager – Pat Devlin

2005

Date	Opponent	h/a	Score	Scorers
18/3	St. Patrick's Athletic	h	2-1	Zayed, Tresson
25/3	Cork City	a	1-1	Fox
1/4	UCD	h	1-0	Charles
8/4	Drogheda United	h	2-2	Lynch, Fox
16/4	Longford Town	a	1-2	Lynch
22/4	Waterford United	h	2-1	Ryan, Zayed
29/4	Shelbourne	a	1-4	Zayed
6/5	Shamrock Rovers	a	2-3	James, Keogh
13/5	Derry City	h	0-1	
20/5	Bohemians	h	1-2	Zayed
28/5	Finn Harps	a	2-1	O'Brien Ki., Keogh
3/6	St. Patrick's Athletic	a	0-2	
17/6	Cork City	h	1-2	Zayed
24/6	UCD	a	2-3	O'Brien Ki., Zayed
1/7	Drogheda United	a	0-3	
8/7	Longford Town	h	1-1	Zayed
15/7	Waterford United	a	2-1	Zayed 2
22/7	Shelbourne	h	2-2	Zayed, Tresson
31/7	Shamrock Rovers	h	2-3	Zayed, Georgescu
5/8	Derry City	a	2-2	Georgescu, Tresson
11/8	Bohemians	a	0-1	
19/8	Finn Harps	h	2-1	Georgescu, Zayed
2/9	St. Patrick's Athletic	h	1-0	O'Brien Ki.
9/9	Cork City	a	0-3	
16/9	UCD	h	0-1	
30/9	Drogheda United	h	0-2	
9/10	Longford Town	a	1-1	O'Brien Ki.
14/10	Waterford United	h	1-0	Fox
28/10	Shamrock Rovers	a	1-0	Caffrey
31/10	Shelbourne	a	0-5	
4/11	Derry City	h	0-3	
11/11	Bohemians	h	3-1	Tyrell D. 2, Ryan
18/11	Finn Harps	h	4-2	Tresson 2, Byrne (p), Fox

Name	Nat	Pos	Aps	(s)	Gls
Wayne BYRNE		M	1	(2)	1
Paul CAFFREY		M	6	(3)	1
Wesley CHARLES	STV	D	14		1
Hugh DAVEY	NIR	M	6		
Maurice DUNNE		M		(2)	
Robert DUNNE		M	8	(6)	
Stephen FOX		A	28	(1)	4
Andrei GEORGESCU	ROM	A	11	(2)	3
Stephen GIFFORD		D	14	(3)	
Eddie GORMLEY		M		(1)	
Kevin GROGAN		A		(2)	
Pat HANNIGAN	AUS	G	2		
Stuart HOLT		M		(1)	
Colm JAMES		M	14	(5)	1
Keith KELCH		M	1	(3)	
Philip KEOGH		M	32		2
Keith LONG		M	16	(2)	
Jody LYNCH		D	20		2
Brian McGOVERN		D	14		
Barry McGRORY		A	3	(5)	
Robbie McGUINNESS		M	6	(3)	
Paul MURPHY		A	3	(4)	
Kevin O'BRIEN		M	9	(1)	
Kieran O'BRIEN		A	10	(12)	4
Chris O'CONNOR	AUS	G	31		
Graham O'HANLON		D	6		
Paul O'REILLY		D	17	(6)	
Michael ROCHE		D	10		
Ciaran RYAN		M	10	(9)	2
Conor SINNOTT		A		(3)	
Colm TRESSON		D	31		5
David TYRELL		M	15		2
William TYRELL		D	3		
Ross ZAMBRA		A		(1)	
Eamon ZAYED		A	22		12

CORK CITY
Manager – Damien Richardson

2005

Date	Opponent	h/a	Score	Scorers
19/3	Finn Harps	a	2-0	O'Flynn (p), Doyle
25/3	Bray Wanderers	h	1-1	Behan
31/3	Longford Town	a	1-0	Behan
8/4	UCD	h	0-0	
15/4	Bohemians	a	2-0	Behan, Doyle
22/4	Drogheda United	h	0-1	
29/4	Shamrock Rovers	a	3-1	O'Callaghan 2, Doyle
6/5	St. Patrick's Athletic	h	3-1	Doyle, Behan, O'Donovan
13/5	Waterford United	a	2-2	Doyle, Murray
27/5	Derry City	a	2-0	O'Callaghan, O'Flynn
30/5	Shelbourne	a	2-0	O'Donovan, og (Brennan)
6/6	Finn Harps	h	2-0	Doyle 2
17/6	Bray Wanderers	a	2-1	O'Donovan, Fenn
24/6	Longford Town	h	0-0	
1/7	UCD	a	5-1	Kearney, O'Flynn 3 (1p), Fenn
8/7	Bohemians	h	2-1	O'Flynn, O'Donovan
17/7	Drogheda United	a	1-0	O'Callaghan
22/7	Shamrock Rovers	h	3-0	Gamble, O'Flynn, Fenn
31/7	St. Patrick's Athletic	a	2-0	Fenn 2
5/8	Waterford United	h	1-1	Kearney
15/8	Shelbourne	h	1-0	Horgan
19/8	Derry City	a	1-3	O'Callaghan (p)
9/9	Bray Wanderers	h	3-0	O'Flynn, Coughlan, O'Donovan
18/9	Longford Town	a	0-0	
2/10	UCD	h	1-0	O'Flynn
14/10	Drogheda United	h	1-0	O'Flynn

Republic of Ireland

FINAL LEAGUE TABLE 2005

		Pld	Home					Away					Total					Pts
			W	D	L	F	A	W	D	L	F	A	W	D	L	F	A	
1	Cork City	33	10	4	2	22	6	12	4	1	31	12	22	8	3	53	18	74
2	Derry City	33	11	3	2	32	14	11	3	3	24	11	22	6	5	56	25	72
3	Shelbourne	33	11	3	3	36	15	9	4	3	26	10	20	7	6	62	25	67
4	Drogheda United	33	6	7	4	19	16	6	5	5	21	17	12	12	9	40	33	48
5	Longford Town	33	8	4	5	15	12	4	5	7	14	20	12	9	12	29	32	45
6	Bohemians	33	8	3	6	22	22	5	3	8	20	26	13	6	14	42	47	45
7	Bray Wanderers	33	7	3	7	21	23	4	3	9	19	34	11	6	16	40	57	39
8	Waterford United	33	5	5	6	19	24	4	2	11	11	25	9	7	17	30	49	34
9	UCD	33	4	7	5	17	24	3	5	9	11	20	7	12	14	28	44	33
10	St. Patrick's Athletic	33	5	5	6	14	15	2	6	9	12	21	7	11	15	26	36	32
11	Shamrock Rovers	33	4	2	10	13	26	5	6	6	20	26	9	8	16	33	52	27
12	Finn Harps	33	4	3	10	18	24	1	3	12	12	27	5	6	22	30	51	21

N.B. Shamrock Rovers – 8 pts deducted.

18/10	Finn Harps	a	2-1	Bennett, Murray
28/10	St. Patrick's Athletic	h	0-1	
31/10	Bohemians	a	2-1	og (Oman), Murray
4/11	Waterford United	a	2-2	O'Brien, O'Callaghan
7/11	Shamrock Rovers	a	2-0	O'Donovan, Gamble
11/11	Shelbourne	a	0-0	
18/11	Derry City	h	2-0	O'Flynn, Kearney

Name	Nat	Pos	Aps	(s)	Gls
Denis BEHAN		A	11	(11)	4
Alan BENNETT		D	31		1
William BRUTON		A	1	(5)	
Derek COUGHLAN		D	3	(9)	1
Michael DEVINE		G	29		
Kevin DOYLE		A	11		7
Neale FENN		A	19	(8)	5
Joe GAMBLE		M	24	(1)	2
Phil HARRINGTON	WAL	G	1		
Neal HORGAN		D	33		1
Liam KEARNEY		M	27	(2)	3
Shane LONG		A		(1)	
Mark McNULTY		G	3		
Danny MURPHY		D	27		
Dan MURRAY	ENG	D	32		3
Kevin MURRAY		D		(1)	
Colin T. O'BRIEN		M	16	(7)	1
George O'CALLAGHAN		A	31	(1)	6
Roy O'DONOVAN		M	22	(4)	6
John O'FLYNN		A	16	(5)	11
Greg O'HALLORAN		M	10	(6)	
Billy WOODS		M	16	(9)	

DERRY CITY
Manager – Stephen Kenny

2005

18/3	Drogheda United	a	2-0	Murphy 2
1/4	Bohemians	a	1-0	Farren
8/4	Shelbourne	h	0-0	
12/4	Longford Town	h	1-0	O'Flynn
16/4	Finn Harps	a	2-0	Farren, Murphy (p)
22/4	Shamrock Rovers	h	2-3	Farren, Martyn
29/4	UCD	a	0-1	
6/5	Waterford United	h	1-0	Hargan
13/5	Bray Wanderers	a	1-0	Murphy
20/5	St. Patrick's Athletic	h	2-2	Murphy, Farren
27/5	Cork City	a	0-2	
3/6	Drogheda United	h	3-0	Hutton, Farren 2
18/6	Longford Town	a	0-0	
1/7	Shelbourne	a	2-1	Brennan K. Farren
8/7	Finn Harps	h	3-2	og (Boyle), Farren, Brennan K.
15/7	Shamrock Rovers	a	2-0	Martyn, Brennan K.
22/7	UCD	h	3-0	Farren, Martyn 2
29/7	Waterford United	a	3-1	Brennan K., Farren 2
2/8	Bohemians	h	3-1	Hutton (p), Martyn, Farren
5/8	Bray Wanderers	h	2-2	Martyn, Delaney
12/8	St. Patrick's Athletic	a	1-1	Farren
19/8	Cork City	h	3-1	Beckett, O'Flynn, Molloy
2/9	Drogheda United	a	1-0	Deery
9/9	Longford Town	h	3-1	McCourt, McGlynn 2
16/9	Bohemians	a	3-2	Farren 2, McGlynn
30/9	Shelbourne	h	2-1	Farren, O'Flynn
7/10	Finn Harps	a	1-0	Brennan K.
14/10	Shamrock Rovers	h	2-0	McGlynn, Farren (p)
28/10	Waterford United	h	0-1	
31/10	UCD	a	2-0	O'Flynn, Molloy
4/11	Bray Wanderers	a	3-0	Farren, O'Flynn, Martyn
12/11	St. Patrick's Athletic	h	2-0	Hutton, Delaney
18/11	Cork City	a	0-2	

Name	Nat	Pos	Aps	(s)	Gls
Gary BECKETT	NIR	A	26	(1)	1
Damien BRENNAN		D	7	(2)	
Killian BRENNAN		M	24	(5)	5
Brian CASH		M	15	(5)	
Kevin DEERY	NIR	M	13	(1)	1
Clive DELANEY		D	32		3
Eamon DOHERTY	NIR	D	8	(5)	
Mark FARREN		A	33		18
David FORDE		G	33		
Sean HARGAN	NIR	D	23	(2)	1
Ruaidhri HIGGINS	NIR	M	11	(5)	
Peter HUTTON	NIR	M	32		3
Ciaran MARTYN		M	24	(8)	7
Eddie McCALLION	NIR	D	19	(1)	

Republic of Ireland

Name	Nat	Pos	Aps	(s)	Gls
Mark McCHRYSTAL	NIR	D	7	(2)	
Pat McCOURT	NIR	M	10	(5)	1
Gareth McGLYNN	NIR	M	15	(14)	4
Paddy McLAUGHLIN	NIR	D		(1)	
Barry MOLLOY	NIR	M	12	(1)	2
Alan MURPHY		A	13	(14)	5
Stephen O'FLYNN		A	6	(20)	5
David SULLIVAN		D		(1)	
Patrick SULLIVAN		M	5	(1)	
Derek TYRRELL		D	3	(4)	
Simon WEBB		D	31		1
Gavin WHELAN		M	22	(4)	8

DROGHEDA UNITED
Manager – Paul Doolin

2005

Date	Opponent	H/A	Result	Scorers
18/3	Derry City	h	0-2	
25/3	UCD	a	2-0	Ristilä, Whelan
1/4	St. Patrick's Athletic	h	1-1	Reilly
8/4	Bray Wanderers	a	2-2	O'Brien 2
15/4	Shamrock Rovers	h	2-1	Reilly (p), Gartland
22/4	Cork City	a	1-0	Lynch (p)
29/4	Bohemians	h	2-2	Whelan, Robinson
7/5	Longford Town	a	1-1	Gray
13/5	Shelbourne	h	0-0	
20/5	Finn Harps	h	1-0	Sandvliet
27/5	Waterford United	a	3-0	Whelan, Malcolm, Reilly
3/6	Derry City	a	0-3	
17/6	UCD	h	1-2	Whelan
24/6	St. Patrick's Athletic	a	2-0	Leech 2
1/7	Bray Wanderers	h	3-0	Leech, Ristilä, Rooney
8/7	Shamrock Rovers	a	0-1	
17/7	Cork City	h	0-1	
22/7	Bohemians	a	2-3	O'Brien 2
31/7	Longford Town	h	1-1	Leech
8/8	Shelbourne	a	3-3	Sandvliet, Fahey, O'Brien
13/8	Finn Harps	a	0-0	
19/8	Waterford United	h	1-0	O'Brien
2/9	Derry City	h	1-1	Whelan
9/9	UCD	a	2-2	Fahey, O'Brien
16/9	St. Patrick's Athletic	h	1-1	Robinson
30/9	Bray Wanderers	a	2-0	Webb, og (Fox)
7/10	Shamrock Rovers	h	0-0	
14/10	Cork City	a	0-1	
29/10	Longford Town	a	10	og (Ferguson)
4/11	Shelbourne	h	0-2	
8/11	Bohemians	h	3-2	Lynch (p), Whelan 2
11/11	Finn Harps	h	2-0	Whelan, Ristilä
18/11	Waterford United	a	0-1	

Name	Nat	Pos	Aps	(s)	Gls
Paul BERNARD	SCO	M	5	(2)	
Stephen BRADLEY		M	14	(5)	
Dan CONNOR		G	29		
Keith FAHEY		M	11	(3)	2
David FREEMAN		A	6	(2)	
Graham GARTLAND		D	22	(2)	1
Jason GAVIN		D	10	(1)	
Steven GRAY		D	25	(2)	1
Paul KEEGAN		M	9	(2)	
Mark LEECH		M	9	(12)	4
Damian LYNCH		D	31		2
Stuart MALCOLM	SCO	D	20	(7)	1
Declan O'BRIEN		A	25	(3)	6
Alan REILLY		M	7	(4)	3
Sami RISTILÄ	FIN	A	21	(4)	3
Shane ROBINSON		M	20	(1)	2
Gary ROGERS		G	4	(2)	
Mark ROONEY		A	10	(13)	1
Jermaine SANDVLIET	HOL	M	24	(5)	2

FINN HARPS
Manager – Anthony Gorman

2005

Date	Opponent	H/A	Result	Scorers
19/3	Cork City	h	0-2	
25/3	Waterford United	a	1-2	Funston
2/4	Shamrock Rovers	h	1-1	Brown
8/4	St. Patrick's Athletic	a	0-2	
16/4	Derry City	h	0-2	
22/4	Bohemians	a	0-1	
30/4	Longford Town	h	0-0	
6/5	Shelbourne	a	0-3	
14/5	UCD	h	1-0	McHugh
20/5	Drogheda United	a	0-1	
28/5	Bray Wanderers	h	1-2	McHugh
6/6	Cork City	a	0-2	
18/6	Waterford United	h	2-0	McHugh, Asokuh
24/6	Shamrock Rovers	a	4-1	McHugh, McGrenaghan, Breen, Capper
2/7	St. Patrick's Athletic	h	0-2	
8/7	Derry City	a	2-3	McHugh 2
16/7	Bohemians	h	1-3	McHugh
23/7	Longford Town	a	0-1	
5/8	UCD	a	1-1	Capper
13/8	Drogheda United	h	0-0	
19/8	Bray Wanderers	a	1-2	Capper
9/9	Waterford United	h	2-2	Gorman, og (Finn)
17/9	Shamrock Rovers	h	3-0	McHugh (p), Bradley 2
23/9	Shelbourne	h	0-3	
30/9	St. Patrick's Athletic	a	0-0	
7/10	Derry City	h	0-1	
14/10	Bohemians	a	1-3	McHugh
18/10	Cork City	h	1-2	McHugh
22/10	Longford Town	h	5-0	McHugh 2, Gethins, Breen 2
28/10	Shelbourne	a	0-1	
5/11	UCD	h	1-2	McHugh
11/11	Drogheda United	a	0-2	
18/11	Bray Wanderers	h	2-4	Gethins, Funston

Name	Nat	Pos	Aps	(s)	Gls
Eloka ASOKUH	NGA	D	29		1
Fintan BONNAR		M	4	(3)	
Tom BONNAR		M	5		
Declan BOYLE		D	29		
Michael BOYLE		G	1	(1)	
Shane BRADLEY		D	25	(3)	2
Chris BREEN		A	22	(6)	3
Seamus BROWN	NIR	A	2	(2)	1
Stephen CAPPER		D	19	(2)	3
Ross CONNOLLY		A	4	(3)	
Keith COWAN		M		(4)	
Gary CROSSAN		M	2	(6)	
Gavin CULLEN		G	32		
Mickey FUNSTON		M	30	(1)	2
Conor GETHINS		A	7	(4)	2
Anthony GORMAN		M	28		1
Martin LAUCHLAN		M	10	(3)	
Ryan McGAVIGAN		M	1		
Darragh McGEE		D	2		

Republic of Ireland

Name	Nat	Pos	Aps	(s)	Gls
Shaun McGOWAN		M	15	(3)	
Paddy McGRENAGHAN		M	22	(6)	1
Kevin McHUGH	NIR	A	29		13
Jonathan MINNOCK		D	29	(1)	
Ian ROSSITER		D	12	(2)	
Mark SCOLTOCK	NIR	D	3	(3)	
Eamon SEYDAK	NIR	D	1	(3)	

LONGFORD TOWN
Manager – Alan Mathews

2005

Date	Opponent	H/A	Score	Scorers
19/3	Waterford United	h	1-2	Barrett
31/3	Cork City	h	0-1	
8/4	Shamrock Rovers	a	2-0	Paisley, Baker
12/4	Derry City	a	0-1	
16/4	Bray Wanderers	h	2-1	Baker, O'Connor
21/4	Shelbourne	h	0-2	
30/4	Finn Harps	a	0-0	
7/5	Drogheda United	h	1-1	Baker
13/5	Bohemians	a	0-2	
21/5	UCD	h	1-0	Myler
27/5	St. Patrick's Athletic	a	1-0	Myler
5/6	Waterford United	a	3-0	Keegan, Martin, Myler
18/6	Derry City	h	0-0	
24/6	Cork City	a	0-0	
27/6	Shelbourne	a	0-1	
2/7	Shamrock Rovers	h	2-1	Paisley, Dillon
8/7	Bray Wanderers	a	1-1	Paisley
23/7	Finn Harps	h	1-0	Cronin
31/7	Drogheda United	a	1-1	Ferguson (p)
6/8	Bohemians	h	1-0	Keegan
12/8	UCD	a	0-0	
20/8	St. Patrick's Athletic	h	1-0	Ferguson (p)
2/9	Waterford United	h	3-0	Mooney, Dillon, Martin
9/9	Derry City	a	1-3	Cawley
18/9	Cork City	h	0-0	
30/9	Shamrock Rovers	a	2-4	Mooney 2
9/10	Bray Wanderers	h	1-1	Mooney (p)
15/10	Shelbourne	h	0-2	
22/10	Finn Harps	a	0-5	
29/10	Drogheda United	h	0-1	
4/11	Bohemians	a	0-1	
12/11	UCD	h	1-0	Martin
18/11	St. Patrick's Athletic	a	3-1	Myler, Dillon, O'Connor

Name	Nat	Pos	Aps	(s)	Gls
Dessie BAKER		A	20	(8)	3
Shane BARRATT	ENG	A	15	(3)	1
Darran BYRNE		M	1		
Davy BYRNE		M	16	(3)	
Alan CAWLEY		M	5	(4)	1
Gary CRONIN		D	7	(7)	1
Michael DEMPSEY		G	1		
Sean DILLON		D	30		3
Barry FERGUSON		D	20		2
Dean FITZGERALD		M	28	(2)	
Stephen GOUGH		D	7	(3)	
Paul KEEGAN		A	19	(10)	2
Seamus KELLY		G	5		
Alan KIRBY		M	26	(3)	
Eric LAVINE	BAR	A		(4)	
John MARTIN		M	28	(4)	3
Dave MOONEY		A	9	(4)	4
Alan MURPHY		D	10		
Gary MURPHY		M		(1)	
Andy MYLER		A	17	(5)	4
Stephen O'BRIEN		G	27	(1)	
Danny O'CONNOR		D	28	(1)	2
Stephen PAISLEY		D	20		3
Sean PRUNTY		D	24	(2)	

ST. PATRICK'S ATHLETIC
Manager – John McDonnell

2005

Date	Opponent	H/A	Score	Scorers
18/3	Bray Wanderers	a	1-2	Doyle
25/3	Bohemians	h	0-0	
1/4	Drogheda United	a	1-1	Doyle
8/4	Finn Harps	h	2-0	Rowe, Foley C.
15/4	Shelbourne	a	1-3	Dunne
22/4	UCD	h	3-2	Rowe 2, Dunne
29/4	Waterford United	a	0-1	
6/5	Cork City	a	1-3	og (O'Callaghan)
13/5	Shamrock Rovers	h	1-1	Fahey
20/5	Derry City	a	2-2	Fahey (p), Doyle
27/5	Longford Town	h	0-1	
3/6	Bray Wanderers	h	2-0	Doyle, Fahey
24/6	Drogheda United	h	0-2	
2/7	Finn Harps	a	2-0	Fahey, Foley C.
8/7	Shelbourne	h	0-1	
15/7	UCD	a	0-1	
22/7	Waterford United	h	1-0	Dunne
31/7	Cork City	h	0-2	
5/8	Shamrock Rovers	a	0-0	
12/8	Derry City	h	1-1	Armstrong
20/8	Longford Town	a	0-1	
2/9	Bray Wanderers	a	0-1	
9/9	Bohemians	h	0-1	
16/9	Drogheda United	a	1-1	Doyle
30/9	Finn Harps	h	0-0	
3/10	Bohemians	a	1-1	Foley M. (p)
7/10	Shelbourne	a	0-1	
14/10	UCD	h	0-0	
21/10	Waterford United	a	1-1	Doyle
28/10	Cork City	a	1-0	Maguire
4/11	Shamrock Rovers	h	3-1	Reilly, Rowe, Doyle (p)
12/11	Derry City	a	0-2	
18/11	Longford Town	h	1-3	O'Connor

Name	Nat	Pos	Aps	(s)	Gls
Chris ARMSTRONG	ENG	A	6		1
David BELL		M	10	(2)	
Stephen BRENNAN		M	11		
Stephen CAFFREY		M	28		
Brendan CLARKE		G	3	(1)	
Paul DONNELLY		M	21	(6)	
Christy DORAN		M		(1)	
Robbie DOYLE		A	27	(3)	7
Keith DUNNE		M	15	(7)	3
Keith FAHEY		M	15		4
Luke FITZPATRICK		M		(1)	
Anthony FLOOD		A		(3)	
Colm FOLEY		D	16		2
Michael FOLEY		M	20	(4)	1
John FROST		D	16		
Stuart HOLT		M		(3)	
Glenn LARSEN	NOR	M	10	(2)	
Darragh MAGUIRE		D	29		1
Ian MAHER		M	8	(9)	
Gary McPHEE	SCO	A	1		
Sean O'CONNOR		M	9	(6)	1

Republic of Ireland

...idan O'KEEFE		A	5	(5)	
...inny PERTH		D	12	(2)	
...arry PRENERVILLE		D	26	(1)	
...tephen QUIGLEY		D	12	(11)	
...lan REILLY		M	12	(1)	1
...erard ROWE		A	21	(5)	4
...arry RYAN		G	30		
...obbie SMITH		A		(2)	

SHAMROCK ROVERS
Manager – Roddy Collins; (17/11/05) (Alan O'Neill)

2005

Date	Opponent		Score	Scorers
18/3	Bohemians	a	1-1	Feeney
25/3	Shelbourne	h	0-2	
2/4	Finn Harps	a	1-1	Caffrey
8/4	Longford Town	h	0-2	
15/4	Drogheda United	a	1-2	McCourt
22/4	Derry City	a	3-2	Mooney, McCourt 2
29/4	Cork City	h	1-3	McDonnell
6/5	Bray Wanderers	h	3-2	McCourt 3 (1p)
13/5	St. Patrick's Athletic	a	1-1	Mooney
20/5	Waterford United	h	0-0	
27/5	UCD	a	0-0	
3/6	Bohemians	h	1-2	McGuinness
17/6	Shelbourne	a	2-1	Mooney, McDonagh
24/6	Finn Harps	h	1-4	McCourt
2/7	Longford Town	a	1-2	McDonnell
8/7	Drogheda United	h	1-0	Mooney
15/7	Derry City	h	0-2	
22/7	Cork City	a	0-3	
31/7	Bray Wanderers	a	3-2	McDonagh, O'Connor, Sheridan
5/8	St. Patrick's Athletic	h	0-0	
12/8	Waterford United	a	1-0	Foley
19/8	UCD	h	1-0	McGuinness
2/9	Bohemians	a	3-1	Sheridan, Molloy, Roche L.
9/9	Shelbourne	h	0-2	
17/9	Finn Harps	a	0-3	
30/9	Longford Town	h	4-2	Molloy, McDonagh, Roche L. Quigley
7/10	Drogheda United	a	0-0	
14/10	Derry City	a	0-2	
28/10	Bray Wanderers	h	0-1	
4/11	St. Patrick's Athletic	a	1-3	Rutherford
7/11	Cork City	h	0-2	
11/11	Waterford United	h	1-2	McDonagh
18/11	UCD	a	2-2	O'Connor 2

Name	Nat	Pos	Aps	(s)	Gls
Paul CAFFREY		M	6	(4)	1
Martin CAMERON	SCO	A	2	(3)	
Bernard DANIEL	NGA	M	2	(15)	
Brendan DAWSON		D		(2)	
Jack DOUGLAS		M		(1)	
Keith DOYLE		D	18		
Lee FEENEY	NIR	A	4	(5)	1
Kieran FOLEY		D	12		1
Jason GAVIN		D	17		
Stephen GOUGH		D	14	(1)	
Marc KENNY		M	11	(1)	
Paul MALONE		D	3	(1)	
Robbie MANLEY		A	4	(7)	
Pat McCOURT	NIR	M	17		7
Will McDONAGH		M	25	(1)	4
Gavin McDONNELL		D	25		2
Brian McGOVERN		D	1	(4)	
Jason McGUINNESS		D	20		2
Trevor MOLLOY		A	28		2
Dave MOONEY		A	13	(2)	4
Barry MURPHY		G	24		
Cathal O'CONNOR		M	9	(6)	3
Keith O'HALLORAN		M	4	(4)	
Russell PAYNE	USA	G	9		
Derek PHILLIPS	TRI	D	8		
Mark QUIGLEY		M	9	(1)	1
Keith REDMOND		M	1		
Aidan ROCHE		M	1	(1)	
Lee ROCHE		A	7	(6)	2
Mark RUTHERFORD	ENG	M	26	(1)	1
Ian RYAN		M		(3)	
Brian SHELLEY		D	15		
Tony SHERIDAN		A	10	(4)	2
Cathal SWEETMAN		D	6	(2)	
Derek TRACEY		M	9	(6)	
Mickaël WOLSKI	FRA	D	3		

SHELBOURNE
Manager – Pat Fenlon

2005

Date	Opponent		Score	Scorers
16/3	UCD	h	1-1	Byrne S. (p)
25/3	Shamrock Rovers	a	2-0	Byrne S., Baker
1/4	Waterford United	h	1-0	Byrne J. (p)
8/4	Derry City	a	0-0	
15/4	St. Patrick's Athletic	h	3-1	O'Neill, Hoolahan, Byrne S.
21/4	Longford Town	a	2-0	Byrne J., Baker
29/4	Bray Wanderers	h	4-1	Baker 2, Hoolahan, Byrne J.
6/5	Finn Harps	h	3-0	Harris, Baker, Byrne J.
13/5	Drogheda United	a	0-0	
27/5	Bohemians	a	1-2	Moore
30/5	Cork City	h	0-2	
3/6	UCD	a	1-1	Crowe
17/6	Shamrock Rovers	h	1-2	Rogers
24/6	Waterford United	a	4-2	Crowe, Byrne S., Heary, Fitzpatrick
27/6	Longford Town	h	1-0	Byrne J.
1/7	Derry City	h	1-2	Byrne J.
8/7	St. Patrick's Athletic	a	1-0	Hoolahan
22/7	Bray Wanderers	a	2-2	Heary, Crowe
8/8	Drogheda United	h	3-3	Hoolahan, Byrne S., Byrne J.
15/8	Cork City	a	0-1	
19/8	Bohemians	h	2-1	Byrne J. (p), Crowe
2/9	UCD	h	4-2	Byrne J. 3 (1p), Heary
9/9	Shamrock Rovers	a	2-0	Ndo, Byrne J. (p)
16/9	Waterford United	h	5-0	O'Neill 2, Byrne J. 3
23/9	Finn Harps	a	3-0	O'Neill, Byrne J., Rogers (p)
30/9	Derry City	a	1-2	Crowe
7/10	St. Patrick's Athletic	h	1-0	O'Neill
15/10	Longford Town	a	2-0	Byrne J., O'Neill
28/10	Finn Harps	h	1-0	Byrne J.
31/10	Bray Wanderers	h	5-0	Byrne J. 3 (1p), Rogers, Crowe
4/11	Drogheda United	a	2-0	O'Neill, Crowe
11/11	Cork City	h	0-0	
18/11	Bohemians	a	3-0	Baker, Byrne J., Crowe

Name	Nat	Pos	Aps	(s)	Gls
Richie BAKER		A	14	(6)	6
Stephen BRENNAN		M	1	(2)	

Republic of Ireland

Name	Nat	Pos	Aps	(s)	Gls
Jason BYRNE		A	31		22
Stuart BYRNE		M	22	(3)	5
Ollie CAHILL		M	23	(8)	
Alan CAWLEY		D		(3)	
James CHAMBERS		M		(3)	
Jim CRAWFORD	USA	M	19	(3)	
David CRAWLEY		M	16	(1)	
Glen CROWE		A	17	(9)	8
Gary DEEGAN		G	1		
Dean DELANEY		G	19		
Glen FITZPATRICK		A		(13)	1
Curtis FLEMING		D	5	(5)	
Jamie HARRIS	WAL	D	8	(6)	1
Colin HAWKINS		D	26		
Owen HEARY		D	30		3
Wes HOOLAHAN		M	22	(7)	4
Alan MOORE		M	8	(8)	1
Joseph NDO	CMR	M	18		1
Gary O'NEILL		A	14	(4)	7
Alan REYNOLDS		A	4		
Dave ROGERS	ENG	D	31		3
Bobby RYAN		M	21	(3)	
Steve WILLIAMS	WAL	G	13		

UCD
Manager – Pete Martin

2005

16/3	Shelbourne	a	1-1	Dupuy
25/3	Drogheda United	h	0-2	
1/4	Bray Wanderers	a	0-1	
8/4	Cork City	a	0-0	
15/4	Waterford United	h	1-0	Martin
22/4	St. Patrick's Athletic	a	2-3	McNally, Byrne P.
29/4	Derry City	h	1-0	Martin
6/5	Bohemians	h	1-1	Martin
14/5	Finn Harps	a	0-1	
21/5	Longford Town	a	0-1	
27/5	Shamrock Rovers	h	0-0	
3/6	Shelbourne	h	1-1	McDonnell
17/6	Drogheda United	a	2-1	Dicker, McDonnell
24/6	Bray Wanderers	h	3-2	Hurley, McWalter 2
1/7	Cork City	h	1-5	McDonnell
9/7	Waterford United	a	0-0	
15/7	St. Patrick's Athletic	h	1-0	Hurley
22/7	Derry City	a	0-3	
29/7	Bohemians	a	1-1	Martin (p)
5/8	Finn Harps	h	1-1	Martin (p)
12/8	Longford Town	h	0-0	
19/8	Shamrock Rovers	a	0-1	
2/9	Shelbourne	a	2-4	Murphy T. McWalter
9/9	Drogheda United	h	2-2	Murphy T. Dicker
16/9	Bray Wanderers	a	1-0	McWalter
2/10	Cork City	a	0-1	
14/10	St. Patrick's Athletic	a	0-0	
17/10	Waterford United	h	2-3	McWalter, Murphy T.
28/10	Bohemians	h	1-3	McWalter
31/10	Derry City	h	0-2	
5/11	Finn Harps	a	2-1	McDonnell, Martin (p)
12/11	Longford Town	a	0-1	
18/11	Shamrock Rovers	h	2-2	McWalter, Finn

Name	Nat	Pos	Aps	(s)	Gls
Conan BYRNE		M	1	(7)	
Paul BYRNE		A	2	(3)	1
Gary DICKER		D	29	(2)	2
Derek DOYLE		A	4	(3)	
Willie DOYLE		M		(7)	
Damien DUPUY	FRA	A	20	(2)	1
Ronan FINN		M		(2)	1
Kieran FOLEY		D		(1)	
Brian GANNON		D	7	(11)	
Kieran HARTE		M	1	(4)	
Stephen HURLEY		M	28	(1)	2
Damian KELLY		D	1		
Conor KENNA		D	25	(1)	
Colm KIERANS		M	1	(5)	
Seamus LONG	NIR	D	1	(1)	
Aidan LYNCH		M	5	(4)	
Alan MAHON		D	23	(1)	
Robbie MARTIN		A	27	(1)	6
James MATTHEWS		A		(1)	
Robert McAULEY		D		(1)	
Tony McDONNELL		M	31		4
Aaron McENEFF		D	5		
Alan McNALLY		D	22		1
Pat McWALTER		M	33		7
Adrian MURPHY		A		(6)	
Tony MURPHY		M	15	(3)	3
Michael O'DONNELL		M	32		
Darren QUIGLEY		G	33		
Conor SAMMON		M		(9)	
Brian SHORTHALL		D	14	(2)	
Paul WHITMARSH	ENG	A	3		

WATERFORD UNITED
Manager – Giles Cheeves; (30/7/05) Brendan Rea

2005

19/3	Longford Town	a	2-1	Crowley (p), Murphy
25/3	Finn Harps	h	2-1	Finn (p), og (Bradley)
1/4	Shelbourne	a	0-1	
8/4	Bohemians	h	2-0	og (Byrne), Doyle
15/4	UCD	a	0-1	
22/4	Bray Wanderers	a	1-2	Purcell
29/4	St. Patrick's Athletic	h	1-0	Purcell
6/5	Derry City	a	0-1	
13/5	Cork City	h	2-2	Breen, Sullivan (p)
20/5	Shamrock Rovers	a	0-0	
27/5	Drogheda United	h	0-3	
5/6	Longford Town	h	0-3	
18/6	Finn Harps	a	0-2	
24/6	Shelbourne	h	2-4	Yelverton 2
1/7	Bohemians	a	1-2	Andrews
9/7	UCD	h	0-0	
15/7	Bray Wanderers	h	1-2	Andrews
22/7	St. Patrick's Athletic	a	0-1	
29/7	Derry City	h	1-3	Crowley
5/8	Cork City	a	1-1	Mulcahy
12/8	Shamrock Rovers	h	0-1	
19/8	Drogheda United	a	0-1	
2/9	Longford Town	a	0-3	
9/9	Finn Harps	h	2-2	Jack, Doherty
16/9	Shelbourne	a	0-5	
30/9	Bohemians	h	2-0	Sullivan, Crowley
14/10	Bray Wanderers	a	0-1	
17/10	UCD	a	3-2	Heffernan, Waters, Purcell
21/10	St. Patrick's Athletic	h	1-1	Sullivan
28/10	Derry City	a	1-0	Sullivan
4/11	Cork City	h	2-2	Crowley (p), Sullivan
11/11	Shamrock Rovers	a	2-1	Crowley, Waters

Republic of Ireland

18/11 Drogheda United h 1-0 Mulcahy

Name	Nat	Pos	Aps	(s)	Gls
Niall ANDREWS		D	20	(10)	2
P.J. BANVILLE		A	2	(2)	
David BREEN		D	20		1
Kenny BROWNE		D	12	(3)	
Willie BRUTON		A	10	(4)	
Paul CROWLEY		M	20	(4)	5
Kevin DOHERTY		D	19		1
Willie DOYLE		A	8	(6)	1
Gary DUNPHY		M		(2)	
Sean FINN		M	9	(8)	1
John FROST		D	12		
Stephen GRANT		M	20	(6)	
John HAYES		D	7	(1)	
Colm HEFFERNAN		M	29	(2)	1
Patrick HOLDEN		G	30		
Rodney JACK	STV	A	5	(3)	1
Daryl KAVANAGH		M	3	(4)	
John LESTER		M	6	(10)	
Derek McCARTHY		M	1	(1)	
Paul McCARTHY		A		(2)	
David MULCAHY		D	32		2
Daryl MURPHY		A	6		1
Pat PURCELL		D	28	(1)	3
Alan REYNOLDS		M	9	(1)	
Wayne RUSSELL	WAL	G	3		
Vinny SULLIVAN		M	21	(3)	5
Kevin WATERS		M	23	(5)	2
Steve YELVERTON		M	8	(5)	2

DOMESTIC CUP 2005

SECOND ROUND
(10/6/05)
Avondale United 0, Bray Wanderers 1
Bohemians 2, Athlone Town 0
Drogheda United 2, Limerick 0
Galway United 0, Cork City 0
Shelbourne 0, Derry City 2
UCD 2, Dublin City 0
Waterford United 0, St. Patrick's Athletic 1
(11/6/05)
Carew Park 1, Douglas Hall 3
Cobh Ramblers 0, Wayside Celtic 1
Kildare County 4, Galway Hibernians 1
Kilkenny City 0, Finn Harps 1
Lissadel United 0, Cherry Orchard 4
Longford Town 5, Waterford Crystal 0
Sligo Rovers 1, Malahide United 1
(12/6/05)
Monaghan United 1, Dundalk 7
Shamrock Rovers 2, Fanad United 0

Replays
(13/6/05)
Cork City 1, Galway United 0
(14/6/05)
Malahide United 0, Sligo Rovers 2 (aet)

THIRD ROUND
(26/8/05)
Bohemians 2, Wayside Celtic 2
Bray Wanderers 1, Cherry Orchard 0
Dundalk 0, Drogheda United 2
(27/8/05)
Derry City 3, Kildare County 1
Longford Town 1, UCD 1
Sligo Rovers 2, St. Patrick's Athletic 1
(28/8/05)
Shamrock Rovers 2, Douglas Hall 0
(29/8/05)
Cork City 0, Finn Harps 0

Replays
(30/8/05)
UCD 2, Longford Town 1
Wayside Celtic 1, Bohemians 2
(3/9/05)
Finn Harps 2, Cork City 3 (aet)

QUARTER-FINALS
(23/9/05)
Bray Wanderers 3 *(Murphy 12, Tyrell D. 43, O'Brien 61)*, UCD 2 *(Martin 64, McWalter 83)*
Cork City 3 *(Murray D. 45, O'Flynn 77, O'Callaghan 84p)*, Sligo Rovers 1 *(Low 40)*
Drogheda United 2 *(Keegan 2, Lynch 16)*, Bohemians 1 *(O'Keefe 50)*
(24/9/05)
Derry City 1 *(Beckett 67)*, Shamrock Rovers 0

SEMI-FINALS
(21/10/05)
Cork City 1 *(O'Callaghan 90p)*, Derry City 0
(23/10/05)
Drogheda United 2 *(O'Brien 29, Sandvliet 80)*, Bray Wanderers 1 *(Tresson 82)*

FINAL
(4/12/05)
Lansdowne Road, Dublin
DROGHEDA UNITED 2 *(Whelan 52, O'Brien 83)*
CORK CITY 0
Referee – Stokes
DROGHEDA UNITED – Connor, Lynch, Webb, Gartland, Gray, Whelan, Robinson, Bradley (Keegan 76), Sandvliet, Ristilä (Rooney 77), O'Brien (Bernard 90).
CORK CITY – Devine, Horgan, O'Halloran (O'Brien 84), Murray D., Bennett, Gamble, O'Callaghan, Woods. Kearney, O'Flynn, Fenn (Behan 63).

SECOND LEVEL FINAL TABLE 2005

		Pld	W	D	L	F	A	Pts
1	Sligo Rovers	36	15	16	5	45	27	61
2	Dublin City	36	15	14	7	57	34	59
3	Cobh Ramblers	36	15	11	10	49	40	56
4	Kilkenny City	36	15	8	13	46	35	53
5	Galway United	36	14	11	11	46	43	53
6	Dundalk	36	12	13	11	44	40	49
7	Limerick	36	13	9	14	44	49	48
8	Kildare County	36	10	11	15	33	42	41
9	Monaghan United	36	9	9	18	36	66	36
10	Athlone Town	36	6	10	20	28	52	28

PROMOTION/RELEGATION PLAY-OFFS
(22/11/05)
Shamrock Rovers 1, Dublin City 2
(25/11/05)
Dublin City 1, Shamrock Rovers 1
(Dublin City 3-2)

Romania

Bucharest – capital of Europe

Romania did not send a team to the World Cup, but there was plenty of foreign travel for the country's three European club representatives in 2005/06. Between them the Bucharest trio of Steaua, Rapid and Dinamo played a grand total of 42 European matches. Thirteen different countries were collectively visited, and there was even an all-Romanian European tie for the first time as Steaua and Rapid met in the quarter-final of the UEFA Cup.

Alas, there would be no Romanian finalist, but what the Bucharest grand tour of Europe did achieve was an incredible rise up the UEFA rankings. With a coefficient of 16.833, Romania topped the 2005/06 listings and surged up the five-year table from 25th place to tenth, the reward for which, in 2007/08, is two places in the Champions League, with the Romanian champions earning direct access to the group phase.

There were so many highlights for all three clubs; for all four if you include CFR Cluj, who, newly player-coached by record Romanian cap-holder Dorinel Munteanu, beat Athletic Bilbao and Saint-Etienne en route to the InterToto Cup final.

Happy return to Seville

Steaua may have missed out on the Champions League and collapsed in dramatic style in the second leg of their UEFA Cup semi-final with Middlesbrough, but those defeats were offset by some memorable displays, notably a 3-0 win away to Real Betis in Seville, where the club had won the European Cup in 1986.

Rapid won all seven home games against foreign opposition without conceding a goal. They also knocked out Feyenoord and two German sides. Most satisfying of all, though, for coach Razvan Lucescu was the 1-0 victory away to Shakhtar Donetsk – a team managed by his father Mircea. That match swiftly followed a 2-0 home win over Rennes, coached by another distinguished Romanian, Ladislau Bölöni.

Dinamo's UEFA Cup run did not stretch into the spring but would have done but for a highly contentious disallowed goal on the final whistle in Marseilles. Their best win came in the first round when they crushed Champions League outcasts Everton 5-1 in Bucharest.

Because of the extended involvement in Europe, the Romanian championship took a back seat for most of the season. It was only after Steaua's exit in late April that the Divizia A title race took off in earnest. Because of the country's non-involvement at the World Cup, the league campaign carried on into early June. The race for the title was closely contested, with the three European participants being joined by a fourth contender from the capital, Sportul Studentesc.

At halfway Dinamo led Steaua by a point, with Rapid and Sportul Studentesc seemingly out of the running down in seventh and ninth place, respectively. But during the winter both of the Big Two changed their coach.

Dinamo surprisingly fired Ioan Andone, who immediately found employment in Cyprus. Into his place came Estebán Vigo, but in late February, following the resignation of club president Ioan Becali, the Spaniard stood down himself. Ion Marin stepped into the breach, but after two wretched home displays he too chose to quit. Next up was Florin Marin (no relation), but he too struggled to restore equilibrium, and by the end of the season, after a very odd collection of results, Dinamo were lucky to hang on to third place and qualify for the UEFA Cup, which they did only by finishing above Sportul Studentesc on the head-to-head rule.

Protasov departs

Steaua, meanwhile, were forced into a mid-season

Romania

change of leadership after Ukrainian Oleh Protasov, appointed only the previous summer, let his heart rule his head and returned home to coach former club Dnipro Dnipropetrovsk. There was a ready-made replacement available to Steaua in the burly shape of Cosmin Olaroiu, not long dismissed by provincial wannabes Politehnica Timisoara (where the legendary Gheorghe Hagi took over but failed to see out the season).

Olaroiu's first priority was Europe, but with Steaua having been knocked out of the Romanian Cup early (by Rapid's second team, no less), he was under obligation to win the league as well. Battling on two fronts seemed to inspire rather than handicap Olaroiu and his players. As long as they remained in the UEFA Cup, Steaua continued to pick up points. But once the Euro adventure ended, the erosion of confidence had an impact at home. Three days after bowing out at Boro, Steaua were beaten 2-0 at home by Rapid (the team they had ousted from the UEFA Cup on the away-goals rule a few weeks earlier) and consequently knocked off the top of the table by their in-form conquerors.

However, Steaua still had two matches in hand on Rapid and they would make both of them count. Four wins in a row, including one that eliminated Sportul from contention, took Steaua into the final game with a two-point lead. As Rapid had the better head-to-head record, Steaua had to win. However, Steaua were fortunate in that their opponents, FC Vaslui, had just completed a remarkable escape from relegation a few days earlier and therefore had nothing to play for. It showed as Steaua struck two early goals and went on to win at a canter, with star player Nicolae Dica netting a hat-trick in a 4-0 win.

The news of Steaua's early lead soon reached Petrosani, and Rapid, who had not lost all spring, began to self-destruct. Frustration turned to malice as the tackles flew in. Star striker Daniel Niculae, who had scored the winning goal in the Cup final against FC National a few weeks earlier, was red-carded in the first half. Four of his team-mates would follow him off, leaving the referee with no option but to abandon the game (and later award Jiul a 3-0 win).

Strange goings-on

It was a bizarre way for the season to end, but many more weird and wonderful things were to happen during the summer as Romania prepared for its new-look, 18-club Liga I in 2006/07. Ceahlaul Piatra Neamt, Universitatea Craiova and Liberty Salonta won automatic promotion, with Unirea Urziceni joining them after the play-offs. But Liberty, a new small-town club from the Hungarian border region, decided they were not ready to make the leap and sold their place to the more established club in the region, UTA Arad. Despite the fact that sporting ethics had been seriously compromised, the league authorities decided to let it go.

Just five days before the start of the new season relegated Pandurii Târgu Jiu suddenly found themselves reinstated in the new Liga I in place of Sportul Studentesc, whose licence to compete at the top level was withdrawn because of outstanding fiscal debts.

Mircea Sandu was re-elected to the position of Romanian FA president, having defeated ex-national team player Gheorghe 'Gica' Popescu by a convincing margin. Many Romanians were dismayed as they hoped that Sandu, who has held the position since 1990, would make way for a new regime more ready and willing to cleanse Romanian football of its many ills.

The national team's failure to qualify for the World Cup was another body blow, although Victor Piturca's team almost reached the play-offs after winning their last three games, with skipper Adrian Mutu returning from his drug-taking suspension to score all five goals. Those results helped Romania secure second-seed status for the Euro 2008 draw, and although they face Holland again, Piturca and his players must quietly fancy their chances of qualifying for the finals at the expense of Bulgaria, Slovenia, Albania, Belarus and Luxembourg.

NATIONAL TEAM RESULTS 2005/06

17/8/05	Andorra (WCQ)	H	Constanta	2-0	Mutu (29, 41)
3/9/05	Czech Republic (WCQ)	H	Constanta	2-0	Mutu (28, 58)
8/10/05	Finland (WCQ)	A	Helsinki	1-0	Mutu (41p)
12/11/05	Ivory Coast	N	Le Mans	1-2	Iencsi (52)
16/11/05	Nigeria	H	Bucharest	3-0	Niculae D. (17), Petre F. (49), Rosu (90)
28/2/06	Armenia	N	Nicosia	2-0	Maftei (72), Cocis (86)
1/3/06	Slovenia	N	Larnaca	2-0	Mazilu (22), Pecnik (53og)
23/5/06	Uruguay	N	Los Angeles	0-2	
25/5/06	Northern Ireland	N	Chicago	2-0	Buga (7), Niculae D. (11)
26/5/06	Colombia	N	Chicago	0-0	

Romania

NATIONAL TEAM APPEARANCES 2005/06

Coach – Victor PITURCA

Name	DOB	Club	AND	CZE	FIN	Civ	Nga	Arm	Slo	Uru	Nir	Col	Caps	Goals
Bogdan Ionut LOBONT	18/1/78	Ajax (HOL)	G	G	G				G46	G		G	47	-
Cosmin Marius CONTRA	15/4/75	Getafe CF (ESP)	D	D	D54				D88	D		D76	52	5
Sebastian Gabriel TAMAS	5/11/83	Dinamo Bucuresti	D	D	D	D	D	s74	D	D		D	15	-
Cristian Eugen CHIVU	15/10/80	Roma (ITA)	D	D					D88				43	3
Razvan RAT	26/5/81	Shakhtar Donetsk (UKR)	D80	D	D	D80	D72	s63	D				31	1
Florentin PETRE	15/1/76	Dinamo Bucuresti	M76	M53	M		s46	s70	M74				37	4
Razvan Vasile COCIS	19/2/83	Sheriff Tiraspol (MOL)	M	M	M	M80	M	s70	M	M	s46	M73	10	1
Dorinel Ionel MUNTEANU	25/6/68	CFR Cluj	M46	M72	M	M69		s65	M74				130	16
Constantin Nicolae DICA	9/5/80	Steaua Bucuresti	M			s55	A64						12	-
Adrian MUTU	8/1/79	Juventus (ITA)	A	A88	A81	A				A	s46		45	18
Claudiu Iulian NICULESCU	23/6/76	Dinamo Bucuresti	A										5	-
Mihai Cosmin PASCOVICI	12/6/78	FC Farul Constanta	s80										1	-
Tiberiu Gabriel BALAN	17/2/81	Sportul Studentesc Bucuresti	s76						M	s86		M46	s52	6	-
Mihai TARARACHE	25/10/77	FC Zürich (SUI)	s46										4	-
Ovidiu PETRE	22/3/82	Politehnica Timisoara		M	M					M83	M61	M	13	1
Ionut MAZILU	9/2/82	Sportul Studentesc Bucuresti		A	A90	A55	s46	s58	A86				7	1
Valentin Emanoil BADOI	16/12/75	Rapid Bucuresti		s53	s54	D86	s85	D	s88		D	s76	9	-
Paul Constantin CODREA	4/4/81	Palermo (ITA)		s72									20	1
Gheorghe BUCUR	8/4/80	Politehnica Timisoara		s88									5	2
Adrian Mihai IENCSI	15/3/75	Spartak Moskva (RUS)			D	D		D	s88	D67	s56		30	1
Laurentiu ROSU	26/10/75	RC Recreativo (ESP)			s81	s80	s64						28	4
Daniel George NICULAE	6/10/82	Rapid Bucuresti			s90	s55	A46	A58	A	s46	A46	A	11	2
Mihai Mircea NESU	19/2/83	Steaua Bucuresti			s80	s72	D63						3	-
Flavius Vladimir STOICAN	24/11/76	Shakhtar Donetsk (UKR)			s86	D85							19	-
Sorin Ion PARASCHIV	17/6/81	Steaua Bucuresti				M55	s46						4	-
Costin LAZAR	24/4/81	Sportul Studentesc Bucuresti				s55	M46						2	-
Gabriel BOSTINA	22/5/77	Steaua Bucuresti				s69	M			s46	M		4	-
Banel NICOLITA	7/1/85	Steaua Bucuresti				M55	M46			s57	M65	M	5	-
Danut Dumitru COMAN	28/3/79	Rapid Bucuresti				G	G	s46		G			4	-
Dorin Nicolae GOIAN	12/12/80	Steaua Bucuresti					D			s61	D56	D	4	-
Vasile MAFTEI	1/1/81	Rapid Bucuresti					D74			D			2	1
Mirel RADOI	22/3/81	Steaua Bucuresti					M	s83	s67	M46	M		38	1
Bogdan PATRASCU	7/5/79	Piacenza (ITA)					M65	s74					2	-
Daniel OPRITA	10/8/81	Steaua Bucuresti					M70	s74	M57	s65			6	1
Ianis ZICU	23/10/83	Dinamo Bucuresti					A70						2	-
Pompiliu STOICA	24/11/76	FK Moskva (RUS)							D	s88	D		8	1
Florin SOAVA	24/7/78	Krylya Sovetov Samara (RUS)								M46	s46		21	-
Marius NICULAE	16/5/81	R Standard Liège (BEL)								A46		s73	28	12
Cristian PULHAC	17/8/84	Dinamo Bucuresti								D88			1	-
Muguler BUGA	16/12/77	Rapid Bucuresti								A	A52		2	1

Romania

EUROPEAN CUPS 2005/06

UEFA CHAMPIONS LEAGUE

STEAUA BUCURESTI
2nd qualifying round SHELBOURNE (IRL)
A 0-0
Khomutovsky, Radoi, Nesu, Ogararu, Ghionea, Nicolita (Dinita 82), Bostina, Paraschiv, Lovin, Iacob (Cristea 81), Dica (Oprita 89).
H 4-1 *Nicolita (18), Iacob (27), Dinita (61), Oprita (90p)*
Khomutovsky, Radoi, Nesu, Baciu, Ogararu, Ghionea, Nicolita (Paraschiv 89), Bostina (Oprita 75), Lovin, Iacob (Dinita 46), Dica.

3rd qualifying round ROSENBORG BK (NOR)
H 1-1 *Iacob (30)*
Khomutovsky, Ogararu, Radoi, Ghionea, Nesu (Marin 79), Nicolita, Paraschiv, Lovin, Bostina, Cristea (Oprita 54), Iacob.
A 2-3 *Radoi (74), Iacob (76)*
Khomutovsky, Marin (Dinita 85), Radoi, Ghionea, Ogararu, Nesu (Oprita 55), Paraschiv, Bostina, Nicolita, Lovin, Iacob.

UEFA CUP

DINAMO BUCURESTI
2nd qualifying round OMONIA (CYP)
H 3-1 *Munteanu V. (12 p), Zicu (25,43)*
Gaev (Guso 14), Balan (Tamas 46), Galamaz (Niculescu 67), Moti, Pulhac, Petre, Margaritescu, Zicu, Munteanu V., Baltoi, Bratu.
A 1-2 *Niculescu (55)*
Gaev, Pulhac, Daouda, Moti, Galamaz, Tamas (Grigorie 40), Petre, Munteanu V. (Baltoi 63), Margaritescu, Bratu (Plesan 78), Niculescu.

1st round EVERTON (ENG)
H 5-1 *Niculescu (27), Zicu (51), Petre (74), Bratu (76, 90)*
Gaev, Goian, Tamas, Moti, Pulhac, Petre (Galamaz 82), Margaritescu, Plesan (Munteanu V. 78), Grigorie, Zicu, Niculescu (Bratu 60).
A 0-1
Gaev, Galamaz, Tamas, Moti, Pulhac, Petre, Margaritescu, Plesan, Grigorie, Bratu (Chihaia 84), Zicu (Baltoi 75).

2nd round Group F
Match 1 SC HEERENVEEN (HOL)
H 0-0
Gaev, Galamaz, Moti, Pulhac, Tamas, Grigorie (Munteanu V. 72), Margaritescu, Petre, Plesan (Cristea 78), Bratu, Zicu (Baltoi 72).

Match 2 LEVSKI SOFIA (BUL)
A 0-1
Gaev, Galamaz, Moti, Pulhac, Tamas, Cristea, Grigorie (Bratu 70), Margaritescu, Petre, Baltoi, Zicu.

Match 3 CSKA MOSKVA (RUS)
H 1-0 *Munteanu V. (72)*
Gaev, Galamaz, Moti, Pulhac, Tamas, Cristea, Grigorie, Munteanu V. (Bratu 77), Petre (Balan 70), Niculescu (Daouda 84), Zicu.

Match 4 OLYMPIQUE MARSEILLE (FRA)
A 1-2 *Niculescu (52)*
Gaev, Daouda, Galamaz, Pulhac, Tamas, Grigorie (Baltoi 87), Margaritescu, Munteanu V., Petre, Bratu (Chihaia 84), Niculescu.

RAPID BUCURESTI
1st qualifying round UE SANT JULIÁ (AND)
A 5-0 *Niculae (10, 34, 66), Felix (62og), Vasilache (76)*
Dolha, Constantin M., Maftei, Moldovan (Rada 67), Badoi, Ilyes, Maldarasanu, Stancu I. (Ene 76), Buga (Burdujan 46), Vasilache, Niculae.
H 5-0 *Buga (1, 17, 21, 29), Maladarasanu (79)*
Dolha, Constantin M. (Rusu 71), Perja, Rada, Badoi, Maldarasanu, Ilyes, Stancu I. (Karamyan 64), Vasilache, Ene, Buga (Grigore 46).

2nd qualifying round VARDAR SKOPJE (MAC)
H 3-0 *Niculae (44, 50), Maldarasanu (67)*
Minca, Constantin M. (Perja 46), Maftei, Moldovan, Badoi, Maldarasanu, Stancu R., Stancu I., Vasilache (Ilyes 69), Buga, Niculae (Burdujan 83).
A 1-1 *Vasilache (58)*
Minca, Constantin M., Perja, Rada, Badoi (Karamyan 64), Maldarasanu (Grigore 80), Dica, Stancu I., Mara (Vasilache 55), Ilyes, Buga.

1st round FEYENOORD (HOL)
A 1-1 *Vasilache (74p)*
Coman, Constantin M., Constantin N., Maftei, Rada, Badoi, Maldarasanu, Ilyes, Karamyan (Perja 82), Buga (Dica 87), Niculae (Vasilache 68).
H 1-0 *Buga (12)*
Coman, Constantin M., Maftei, Rada, Badoi, Maldarasanu, Ilyes, Karamyan (Perja 90), Niculae, Constantin N. (Dica 69), Buga (Vasilache 84).

2nd round Group G
Match 1 STADE RENNAIS FC (FRA)
H 2-0 *Niculae (42), Buga (67)*
Coman, Constantin N. (Dica 53), Constantin M., Maftei, Rada, Badoi, Ilyes, Karamyan, Maldarasanu, Buga (Vasilache 71), Niculae (Burdujan 88).

Match 2 SHAKHTAR DONETSK (UKR)
A 1-0 *Maldarasanu (87)*
Coman, Constantin N. (Dica 51), Constantin M., Maftei, Rada, Badoi, Ilyes (Burdujan 76), Karamyan (Perja 81), Maldarasanu, Buga, Niculae.

Match 3 PAOK (GRE)
H 1-0 *Maldarasanu (45)*
Coman, Constantin M., Maftei, Rada, Badoi, Maldarasanu, Ilyes (Burdujan 76), Karamyan (Perja 86), Buga, Constantin N. (Dica 61), Niculae.

Match 4 VFB STUTTGART (GER)
A 1-2 *Burdujan (80)*
Minca, Constantin N. (Vasilache 52), Constantin M., Maftei, Rada, Badoi, Ilyes (Burdujan 76), Karamyan, Maldarasanu, Buga (Dica 63), Niculae.

3rd Round HERTHA BSC BERLIN (GER)
A 1-0 *Negru (68p)*
Coman, Constantin M., Maftei, Rada, Badoi, Dica, Karamyan (Perja 90), Maldarasanu, Buga (Vasilache 85), Burdujan (Negru 63), Niculae.
H 2-0 *Niculae (50), Buga (79)*
Coman, Constantin M., Maftei, Rada, Badoi, Dica, Karamyan, Maldarasanu (Stancu R. 86), Negru (Constantin N. 49), Buga, Niculae (Vasilache 89).

4th round HAMBURGER SV (GER)
H 2-0 *Niculae (45), Buga (88)*
Coman, Constantin M., Maftei, Rada, Badoi, Dica (Negru 13), Karamyan (Stancu I. 20), Stancu R., Buga, Burdujan (Moldovan 71), Niculae.
A 1-3 *Buga (51)*
Coman, Constantin M., Constantin N. (Moldovan 45), Perja, Rada, Badoi, Dica (Negru 44), Stancu R., Stancu I., Buga (Burdujan 70), Niculae.

Quarter-final STEAUA BUCURESTI (ROM)
H 1-1 *Moldovan (50)*
Coman, Constantin M., Maftei, Rada, Stancu (Grigore 46), Badoi, Dica (Negru 79), Stancu R., Buga, Moldovan (Burdujan 65), Niculae.
A 0-0
Coman, Constantin M., Maftei, Rada, Stancu I., Badoi, Grigore, Stancu R. (Dica 65), Buga (Vasilache 76), Moldovan (Burdujan 70), Niculae.

STEAUA BUCURESTI
1st round VÅLERENGA FOTBALL (NOR)
A 3-0 *Radoi (24), Iacob (35), Goian (74)*
Khomutovsky, Ogararu, Goian, Ghionea, Nesu, Nicolita (Cristea 66), Radoi, Paraschiv, Bostina (Simion 90), Oprita (Dumitru 83), Iacob.

Romania

H 3-1 *Dica (30), Bostina (41), Iacob (48)*
Khomutovsky, Ogararu, Goian, Ghionea, Nesu, Nicolita, Radoi, Paraschiv (Lovin 69), Bostina, Iacob (Cristea 80), Dica (Dumitru 80).

2nd round Group C
Match 1 RC LENS (FRA)
H 4-0 *Iacob (13), Goian (16), Dica (43,63)*
Khomutovsky, Ghionea, Goian, Ogararu, Radoi (Lovin 80), Bostina, Nesu, Paraschiv, Dica, Iacob (Cristea 84), Nicolita (Oprita 78).

Match 2 SAMPDORIA (ITA)
A 0-0
Khomutovsky, Ghionea, Goian, Ogararu, Bostina, Lovin, Nesu (Marin 79), Nicolita (Dinita 82), Paraschiv, Dica (Dumitru 90), Iacob.

Match 3 HALMSTADS BK (SWE)
H 3-0 *Radoi (11), Goian (63), Iacob (71)*
Khomutovsky, Ogararu, Goian, Ghionea, Nesu, Nicolita, Radoi (Lovin 84), Paraschiv, Bostina (Dumitru 82), Dica, Iacob (Cristea 74).

Match 4 HERTHA BSC BERLIN (GER)
A 0-0
Khomutovsky, Ghionea, Goian, Ogararu, Radoi, Bostina, Nesu (Marin 74), Paraschiv, Dica, Iacob (Cristea 78), Nicolita (Balan 84).

3rd round SC HEERENVEEN (HOL)
A 3-1 *Dica (29), Goian (76), Paraschiv (78)*
Carlos, Ogararu, Goian, Ogararu, Radoi, Bostina (Lovin 90), Nesu, Paraschiv (Oprita 83), Dica (Cristocea 87), Iacob, Nicolita.
H 0-1
Carlos, Baciu, Goian, Ogararu, Radoi, Bostina (Cristocea 87), Nesu, Paraschiv, Dica, Iacob (Cristea 80), Nicolita (Oprita 72).

4th round REAL BETIS (ESP)
H 0-0
Carlos, Ghionea, Goian, Ogararu, Radoi, Bostina (Oprita 70), Nesu, Paraschiv (Lovin 75), Dica, Iacob, Nicolita (Cristocea 89).
A 3-0 *Nicolita (54,82), Iacob (78)*
Carlos, Ghionea, Goian, Marin, Ogararu, Radoi (Lovin 81), Bostina (Oprita 72), Paraschiv, Dica, Iacob, Nicolita (Cristea 86).

Quarter-final RAPID BUCURESTI (ROM)
A 1-1 *Nicolita (5)*
Carlos, Ghionea, Goian, Marin, Ogararu, Radoi, Dica, Paraschiv (Cristocea 67), Cristea (Lovin 60), Nicolita (Nesu 90), Oprita.
H 0-0
Carlos, Ghionea, Goian, Marin (Lovin 78), Ogararu, Radoi, Dica, Paraschiv, Cristea (Balan 90), Nicolita, Oprita (Nesu 67).

Semi-final MIDDLESBROUGH (ENG)
H 1-0 *Dica (30)*
Carlos, Ogararu, Goian, Ghionea, Marin, Nicolita, Paraschiv (Lovin 86), Radoi, Bostina, Dica, Oprita (Cristea 89).
A 2-4 *Dica (16), Goian (24)*
Carlos, Ogararu, Goian, Gionea, Marin, Oprita (Baciu 81), Radoi, Lovin, Bostina (Nesu 86), Iacob (Balan 65), Dica.

TOP GOALSCORERS 2005/06

22	Ionut MAZILU	(Sportul Studentesc Bucuresti)
15	Nicolae DICA	(Steaua Bucuresti)
14	Dinu Viorel MOLDOVAN	(Politehnica Timisoara/Rapid Bucuresti)
12	Claudiu NICULESCU	(Dinamo Bucuresti)
	Tiberiu BALAN	(Sportul Studentesc Bucuresti)
11	Ciprian TANASA	(FC Arges Pitesti)
10	Alexandru BALTOI	(Dinamo Bucuresti/Otelul Galati)
	Stefan GRIGORIE	(Dinamo Bucuresti)
9	Ianis ZICU	(Dinamo Bucuresti)
	Ionut BALBA	(Politehnica Iasi)

LEAGUE RESULTS/ SCORERS/APPEARANCES/ GOALS 2005/06

FC ARGES PITESTI
Coach – Sorin Cirtu; (4/5/06) Vasile Stan

2005

Date	Opponent	H/A	Score	Scorers
6/8	Steaua Bucuresti	h	0-1	
14/8	Rapid Bucuresti	a	1-1	Tanasa
19/8	Gloria Bistrita	h	2-0	Tanasa (p), Nastasie
26/8	CFR Cluj	a	2-2	Negoita, Tanasa
9/9	Sportul Studentesc	h	2-2	Prepelita, Radu
17/9	Jiul Petrosani	a	1-0	Nastasie
24/9	FC Vaslui	h	1-0	Tanasa
1/10	FC Farul Constanta	a	0-2	
15/10	FC National Bucuresti	a	1-0	Tanase
23/10	Politehnica Timisoara	h	1-1	Tanasa (p)
29/10	Otelul Galati	a	1-0	Bilasco (p)
4/11	Pandurii Târgu Jiu	h	0-1	
19/11	Dinamo Bucuresti	a	2-1	og (Daouda), Nastasie
25/11	Politehnica Iasi	h	3-0	Nastasie, Tanasa, Costescu
3/12	FCM Bacau	a	2-3	Tanasa, Rohat

2006

Date	Opponent	H/A	Score	Scorers
12/3	Steaua Bucuresti	a	0-0	
19/3	Rapid Bucuresti	h	1-1	Costescu
25/3	Gloria Bistrita	a	0-1	
1/4	CFR Cluj	h	0-1	
5/4	Sportul Studentesc	a	0-1	
8/4	Jiul Petrosani	h	2-1	Tanasa 2
12/4	FC Vaslui	a	0-3	
16/4	FC Farul Constanta	h	1-2	Prepelita
22/4	FC National Bucuresti	a	2-3	Tanasa 2
28/4	Politehnica Timisoara	a	0-0	
7/5	Otelul Galati	h	0-5	
13/5	Pandurii Târgu Jiu	a	0-1	
20/5	Dinamo Bucuresti	h	0-1	
3/6	Politehnica Iasi	a	2-3	Bilasco 2 (1p)
7/6	FCM Bacau	h	0-0	

No	Name	Nat	Pos	Aps	(s)	Gls
3	Elías Iván BAZZI	ARG	D	12	(1)	
7	Marius Ioan BILASCO		A	23	(4)	3
12	Augustin CHIRITA		M	5	(6)	
5	Alin CHITA		D	27		
14	Daniel Stefan COSTESCU		A	4	(16)	2
20	Iulian CRIVAC		M	11	(9)	
8	Ciprian DANCIU		M	4		
25	Mariko DAOUDA	CIV	D	12		
19	Cornel DOBRE		D	6	(8)	
1	Adnan GUSO	BOS	G	11		
2	Ciprian IONASCU		D	2		
16	Adrian IONESCU		M	7	(10)	
21	Raul MARINCAU		D	3	(1)	
24	Madalin MURGAN		M	22		
11	Alin Cosmin NASTASIE		A	23	(6)	4

Romania

FINAL LEAGUE TABLE 2005/06

		Pld	Home W	D	L	F	A	Away W	D	L	F	A	Total W	D	L	F	A	Pts
1	Steaua Bucuresti	30	10	3	2	27	9	9	4	2	22	7	19	7	4	49	16	64
2	Rapid Bucuresti	30	10	5	0	24	3	7	3	5	23	20	17	8	5	47	23	59
3	Dinamo Bucuresti	30	7	3	5	34	20	10	2	3	22	12	17	5	8	56	32	56
4	Sportul Studentesc Bucuresti	30	11	1	3	31	11	6	4	5	23	24	17	5	8	54	35	56
5	CFR Cluj	30	6	6	3	16	8	8	2	5	20	19	14	8	8	36	27	50
6	FC National Bucuresti	30	9	3	3	18	13	4	4	7	14	24	13	7	10	32	37	46
7	FC Farul Constanta	30	9	1	5	25	15	5	2	8	14	23	14	3	13	39	38	45
8	Politehnica Timisoara	30	8	5	2	21	10	2	5	8	13	21	10	10	10	34	31	40
9	Otelul Galati	30	2	6	7	11	20	8	3	4	24	17	10	9	11	35	37	39
10	Gloria Bistrita	30	8	4	3	18	10	3	2	10	9	24	11	6	13	27	34	39
11	Politehnica Iasi	30	8	1	6	20	16	3	5	7	8	15	11	6	13	28	31	39
12	FC Arges Pitesti	30	4	4	7	15	19	4	4	7	12	18	8	8	14	27	37	32
13	Jiul Petrosani	30	5	3	7	20	20	2	6	7	8	19	7	9	14	28	39	30
14	FC Vaslui	30	3	5	7	12	21	3	6	6	11	16	6	11	13	23	37	29
15	Pandurii Târgu Jiu	30	4	5	6	14	17	2	2	11	8	27	6	7	17	22	44	25
16	FCM Bacau	30	3	2	10	11	24	0	3	12	5	31	3	5	22	16	55	14

15	Robert Gabriel NEAGOE	M		(1)	
4	Giani Liviu NEGOITA	D	23		1
13	Cristian Eugen NEGRU	M	3	(2)	
23	Ilie POENARU	D	18	(4)	
1	Stefan Gabriel PREDA	G	5		
10	Andrei PREPELITA	M	27	(1)	2
25	Marius Adrian RADU	D	12		1
6	Gheorghe ROHAT	D	23		1
18	Marius SAVA	M		(3)	
8	Bogdan STANCU	A	1	(6)	
9	Ciprian Ion TANASA	A	25	(1)	11
17	Cristian TANASE	M	7	(9)	1
72	Bogdan Arges VINTILA	G	14		

24/3	Otelul Galati	h	0-4	
1/4	Pandurii Târgu Jiu	a	1-2	Gheorghiu
5/4	Dinamo Bucuresti	h	0-1	
8/4	Politehnica Iasi	a	0-4	
12/4	FC Farul Constanta	a	0-2	
22/4	Rapid Bucuresti	a	1-2	Verdes
29/4	Gloria Bistrita	h	1-2	Verdes
05/5	CFR Cluj	a	0-4	
13/5	Sportul Studentesc	h	1-2	Verdes
17/5	Steaua Bucuresti	h	0-2	
21/5	Jiul Petrosani	a	0-2	
2/6	FC Vaslui	h	0-2	
7/6	FC Arges Pitesti	a	0-0	

FCM BACAU
Coach – Cristian Popovici

2005
6/8	FC National Bucuresti	a	0-1	
12/8	Politehnica Timisoara	h	1-0	Croitoru
21/8	Otelul Galati	a	0-0	
27/8	Pandurii Târgu Jiu	h	1-0	Croitoru
11/9	Dinamo Bucuresti	a	0-6	
16/9	Politehnica Iasi	h	0-1	
24/9	FC Farul Constanta	h	1-1	Gheorghiu
3/10	Steaua Bucuresti	a	0-1	
15/10	Rapid Bucuresti	h	0-1	
21/10	Gloria Bistrita	a	1-2	Geaman
29/10	CFR Cluj	h	0-2	
5/11	Sportul Studentesc	a	1-2	Gheorghiu
18/11	Jiul Petrosani	h	1-2	Dobos
26/11	FC Vaslui	a	1-1	Neagu
3/12	FC Arges Pitesti	h	3-2	Dobos (p), Geaman, David

2006
| 12/3 | FC National Bucuresti | h | 2-2 | Gheorghiu, Trofin |
| 18/3 | Politehnica Timisoara | a | 0-2 | |

No	Name	Nat	Pos	Aps	(s)	Gls
24	Stefan APOSTOL		D	4		
25	Daniel Nicolae BALAURU		M	4	(5)	
1	Jean Daniel BOGDAN		G	7	(1)	
3	Gabriel BOJESCU		D	23	(2)	
2	Corneliu Ioan CODREANU		D	26	(2)	
9	Marius Marian CROITORU		M	15		2
16	Daniel Alexandru DAVID		D	19	(1)	1
19	Marius DOBOS		M	21	(6)	2
8	Gabriel Catalin DOLTEA		A	10	(6)	
20	Mihai DORNESCU		M	2	(3)	
22	Florin GANEA		D	21		
27	Valentin GEAMAN		D	22		2
18	Adrian GHEORGHIU		M	27	(2)	4
12	Viorel Vasile IGNATESCU		G	3		
4	Stelian ISAC		D	9	(2)	
21	Ciprian Mircea MANEA		G	20	(1)	
15	Ionut MATEI		A	12	(7)	
6	Stefan MARDARE		D	4	(1)	
7	Sergiu Constantin MAVRICHE		M	9	(1)	
9	Razvan NEAGU		A	8	(16)	1

Romania

7	Florin Lucian PETCU		A	5	(12)	
16	Marius Daniel POTORAC		M	2		
17	Dan Octavian SPIRIDON		M	9		
14	Marian TANASA		A	15	(10)	
25	Ionel Sorin TROFIN		M	23	(2)	1
6	Constantin URECHE		D	2	(2)	
24	Bobi Gheorghita VERDES		A	8	(5)	3

CFR CLUJ
Coach – Dorinel Munteanu

2005

Date	Opponent	H/A	Score	Scorers
06/8	Sportul Studentesc	a	1-1	Oncica
13/8	Jiul Petrosani	h	0-0	
19/8	FC Vaslui	a	3-0	Tilinca, Anca, Surdu
26/8	FC Arges Pitesti	h	2-2	Tilinca, Anca
10/9	FC National Bucuresti	a	4-0	Tilinca, Anca, Surdu 2
18/9	Politehnica Timisoara	h	2-0	Tilinca, Surdu
24/9	Otelul Galati	a	1-0	Coroian
1/10	Pandurii Târgu Jiu	h	1-2	Bruncevic
15/10	Dinamo Bucuresti	a	0-5	
22/10	Politehnica Iasi	h	0-0	
29/10	FCM Bacau	a	2-0	Coroian 2
6/11	Steaua Bucuresti	h	1-0	Coroian
19/11	Rapid Bucuresti	a	0-1	
26/11	Gloria Bistrita	h	0-0	
3/12	FC Farul Constanta	a	2-1	Minteuan, Jula (p)

2006

Date	Opponent	H/A	Score	Scorers
11/3	Sportul Studentesc	h	0-0	
19/3	Jiul Petrosani	a	1-5	Minteuan
25/3	FC Vaslui	h	1-0	Roszel
1/4	FC Arges Pitesti	h	1-0	Anca (p)
4/4	FC National Bucuresti	h	0-0	
8/4	Politehnica Timisoara	a	2-2	Tilinca, Anca
12/4	Otelul Galati	h	0-1	
15/4	Pandurii Târgu Jiu	a	1-0	Minteuan
22/4	Dinamo Bucuresti	h	1-0	Jula
30/4	Politehnica Iasi	a	0-1	
5/5	FCM Bacau	h	4-0	Roszel, Coroian, Toma, Tilinca
14/5	Steaua Bucuresti	a	0-2	
21/5	Rapid Bucuresti	h	1-3	Surdu
3/6	Gloria Bistrita	a	2-1	Anca (p), Surdu
7/6	FC Farul Constanta	h	3-0	Coroian, Mitu, Roszel

No	Name	Nat	Pos	Aps	(s)	Gls
9	Adrian Gheorghe ANCA		A	27	(1)	6
2	György Laszlo BALINT		D	11	(2)	
18	Sead BRUNCEVIC	SCG	A		(8)	1
21	Ambrozie Cristian COROIAN		M	23	(5)	6
31	Bogdan Viorel COTOLAN		D	7	(2)	
10	Florin DAN		M	13	(7)	
20	Vasile Ilie JULA		D	19	(2)	2
16	Radu Leon MARGINEAN		M	1	(2)	
6	Casian Vasile MICLAUS		D	23		
17	Svetozar MIJIN	SCG	M	12	(8)	
28	Zoran MILOSEVIC	SCG	D	19	(6)	
14	Alin Ilie MINTEUAN		M	27	(1)	3
27	Dumitru MITU		A	7	(5)	1
8	Dorinel MUNTEANU		M	19	(2)	
7	Stefan Sorin ONCICA		M		(7)	1
4	Cristian Calin PANIN		D	22		
20	Robert ROSZEL		A	4	(7)	3
1	Emil Ioan STEF		G		(1)	
24	Romeo Constantin SURDU		A	18	(4)	6
3	Razvan TRLEA		D	5		

19	Cosmin TILINCA		A	24	(3)	6
25	Dorin TOMA		D	12	(6)	1
12	Martin TUDOR		G	18		
33	Petru TURCAS		G	12		
26	Cristian TURCU		A	4	(7)	
11	Cosmin Marin VASÎIE		D	3	(2)	

DINAMO BUCURESTI
Coach – Ioan Andone; (1/1/06) Estebán Vigo (ESP); (1/3/06) Ion Marin; (4/4/06) Florin Marin

2005

Date	Opponent	H/A	Score	Scorers
7/8	Otelul Galati	a	4-1	og (Munteanu), Baltoi, Zicu 2
14/8	Pandurii Târgu Jiu	h	3-0	Niculescu 2, Bratu
21/8	FC Farul Constanta	h	0-1	
28/8	Politehnica Iasi	a	2-0	Bratu, Grigorie (p)
11/9	FCM Bacau	h	6-0	Niculescu 2, Moti, Zicu 2, Munteanu V.
18/9	Steaua Bucuresti	a	2-2	Zicu, Baltoi
25/9	Rapid Bucuresti	h	5-2	Grigorie 2, Bratu, Plesan, Zicu
2/10	Gloria Bistrita	a	2-1	Tamas, Zicu
15/10	CFR Cluj	h	5-0	Grigorie, Baltoi, Zicu, Petre, Munteanu V.
23/10	Sportul Studentesc	a	2-0	Bratu, Baltoi
29/10	Jiul Petrosani	h	1-1	Grigorie
6/11	FC Vaslui	a	2-1	Plesan, Niculescu
19/11	FC Arges Pitesti	h	1-2	Grigorie
27/11	FC National Bucuresti	a	0-2	
4/12	Politehnica Timisoara	h	1-0	Bratu

2006

Date	Opponent	H/A	Score	Scorers
11/3	Otelul Galati	h	0-3	
18/3	Pandurii Târgu Jiu	a	2-0	Petre, Niculescu
25/3	FC Farul Constanta	a	1-0	Zicu
1/4	Politehnica Iasi	h	1-1	Danciulescu
5/4	FCM Bacau	a	1-0	Curt
9/4	Steaua Bucuresti	h	1-1	Niculescu
12/4	Rapid Bucuresti	a	0-3	
15/4	Gloria Bistrita	h	3-1	Niculescu 2, Grigorie
22/4	CFR Cluj	a	0-1	
29/4	Sportul Studentesc	h	4-5	Grigorie 2, Niculescu (p), Bratu
6/5	Jiul Petrosani	a	3-1	Curt, Niculescu, og (Mihart)
13/5	FC Vaslui	h	1-2	Alexa
20/5	FC Arges Pitesti	a	1-0	Danciulescu
3/6	FC National Bucuresti	h	2-1	Grigorie, Niculescu
7/6	Politehnica Timisoara	a	0-0	

No	Name	Nat	Pos	Aps	(s)	Gls
5	Dan ALEXA		M	13		1
27	Ionut BALAN		D	4	(5)	
17	Alexandru BALTOI		A	4	(8)	4
24	Cosmin BARCAUAN		D	7	(1)	
21	Florin Daniel BRATU		A	17	(6)	6
18	Octavian CHIHAIA		A		(3)	
20	Adrian CRISTEA		M	5	(10)	
2	Tiberiu CURT		D	6	(1)	2
10	Ion DANCIULESCU		A	12	(2)	2
2	Mariko DAOUDA	CIV	D	4	(1)	
14	Daniel FLOREA		D	9		
1	Vladimir GAEV	BLS	G	13		
15	George Daniel GALAMAZ		D	18		
29	Liviu GANEA		A		(1)	
14	Lucian GOIAN		D	3	(1)	
10	Stefan Costel GRIGORIE		M	26	(2)	10

Romania

12	Adnan GUSO	BOS	G	3		
6	Silviu Andrei MARGARITESCU		M	18	(2)	
23	Florin MATACHE		G		(1)	
18	Dorin Adrian MIHUT		D	6	(5)	
5	Cosmin Iosif MOTI		D	27		1
16	Catalin Constantin MUNTEANU		M	4	(6)	
23	Cristian MUNTEANU		G	14		
22	Vlad MUNTEANU		M	5	(12)	2
9	Claudiu Iulian NICULESCU		A	18	(2)	12
8	Florentin PETRE		M	25	(1)	2
19	Mihaita Paunel PLESAN		M	10	(2)	2
3	Cristian Corneliu PULHAC		D	17	(3)	
25	Stefan Daniel RADU		D	5	(3)	
25	Adrian Alexandru ROPOTAN		M		(5)	
16	Constantin Dorin SEMEGHIN		D		(1)	
4	Sebastian Gabriel TAMAS		D	14		1
7	Ianis Alin ZICU		M	23	(4)	9

FC FARUL CONSTANTA
Coach – Petre Grigoras; (5/11/05) (Marian Dinu); (10/11/05) Lucian Marinof; (5/1/06) Momcilo Vukotic (SCG)

2005
7/8	Pandurii Târgu Jiu	a	2-1	Barbu, Todoran	
13/8	Sportul Studentesc	h	2-2	Pascovici, Gurita	
21/8	Dinamo Bucuresti	a	1-0	Todoran	
26/8	Jiul Petrosani	h	1-0	Gurita	
11/9	Politehnica Iasi	a	1-3	Gurita	
16/9	FC Vaslui	h	2-1	Pascovici, Moldovan	
24/9	FCM Bacau	a	1-1	og (Ganea)	
1/10	FC Arges Pitesti	h	2-0	Barbu, Senin	
16/10	Steaua Bucuresti	h	1-4	Cristocea	
22/10	FC National Bucuresti	a	0-1		
30/10	Rapid Bucuresti	h	1-2	Lungu	
5/11	Politehnica Timisoara	a	2-3	Cristocea, Todoran	
20/11	Gloria Bistrita	h	3-0	Mihai L., Farmache, Moldovan	
27/11	Otelul Galati	a	1-0	Moldovan	
3/12	CFR Cluj	h	1-2	Voiculet	

2006
10/3	Pandurii Târgu Jiu	h	1-0	Mihai L.	
18/3	Sportul Studentesc	a	1-3	Moldovan	
25/3	Dinamo Bucuresti	h	0-1		
2/4	Jiul Petrosani	a	1-3	Gurita	
5/4	Politehnica Iasi	h	1-0	Todoran	
9/4	FC Vaslui	a	2-0	Voiculet, Gurita	
12/4	FCM Bacau	h	2-0	Apostu 2	
16/4	FC Arges Pitesti	a	2-1	Moldovan, Voiculet	
22/4	Steaua Bucuresti	a	0-3		
29/4	FC National Bucuresti	h	4-0	Moldovan, Todoran, Senin, Apostu	
7/5	Rapid Bucuresti	a	0-0		
13/5	Politehnica Timisoara	h	4-2	Moldovan, Voiculet, Gurita, Senin	
19/5	Gloria Bistrita	a	0-1		
3/6	Otelul Galati	h	0-1		
7/6	CFR Cluj	a	0-3		

No	Name	Nat	Pos	Aps	(s)	Gls
25	Iulian Catalin APOSTOL		M	11	(2)	
15	Radu Bogdan APOSTU		A	2	(19)	3
9	Mihai BAICU		A		(5)	
3	Ion BARBU		D	26		2
13	Mário CARLOS Jorge Costa	POR	M	2	(3)	
25	Vasilica CRISTOCEA		M	7	(4)	2
1	George CURCA		G	25		

2	Raz. Stefanel FARMACHE		D	20	(1)	1
20	Laurentiu FLOREA		D	23	(3)	
6	Decebal GHEARA		D	8	(4)	
19	Viorel GHEORGHE		A	1	(9)	
11	Mihai GURITA		A	26	(2)	6
15	Ionut LARIE		M	1		
8	Florin LUNGU		M	18	(3)	1
	Alexandru MATEL		D		(1)	
25	Armando MIHAI		D		(1)	
7	Liviu MIHAI		A	16	(2)	2
27	Liviu MIHAI Jr		M	1		
23	Tibor Florian MOLDOVAN		A	16	(12)	7
25	Vasile PACURARU		D	8	(2)	
4	Mihai Cosmin PASCOVICI		D	22	(1)	2
5	Cristian SCHIOPU		D	28		
27	Adrian SENIN		M	24	(2)	3
18	Marius Adrian SOARE		M	1	(2)	
12	Razvan Marian STANCA		G	4		
20	Cristian TARALUNGA		M		(1)	
17	Dinu Marius TODORAN		M	26	(1)	5
21	George Liviu USURELU		M	2		
30	Adrian VLAS		G	1		
14	Claudiu Dorian VOICULET		M	11	(8)	4

GLORIA BISTRITA
Coach – Ioan Ovidiu Sabau

2005
5/8	Jiul Petrosani	a	2-0	Paduretu, Costin	
13/8	FC Vaslui	h	1-1	Negrean	
19/8	FC Arges Pitesti	a	0-2		
26/8	FC National Bucuresti	h	0-2		
10/9	Politehnica Timisoara	a	0-4		
17/9	Otelul Galati	h	0-0		
24/9	Pandurii Târgu Jiu	a	1-2	Negrean	
2/10	Dinamo Bucuresti	h	1-2	Târnavean	
16/10	Politehnica Iasi	a	1-1	Negrean	
21/10	FCM Bacau	h	2-1	Muresan, Iftodi	
30/10	Steaua Bucuresti	a	1-0	Muresan	
6/11	Rapid Bucuresti	h	2-1	Sarmasan, Paduretu	
20/11	FC Farul Constanta	a	0-3		
26/11	CFR Cluj	h	0-0		
4/12	Sportul Studentesc	h	2-0	Muresan, Târnavean	

2006
12/3	Jiul Petrosani	h	0-0		
18/3	FC Vaslui	a	0-2		
25/3	FC Arges Pitesti	h	1-0	Negrean	
1/4	FC National Bucuresti	a	0-2		
5/4	Politehnica Timisoara	h	1-1	Iftodi	
8/4	Otelul Galati	a	0-1		
12/4	Pandurii Târgu Jiu	h	4-0	Negrean 2, Pacurar 2	
15/4	Dinamo Bucuresti	a	1-3	Târnavean	
21/4	Politehnica Iasi	h	1-0	Nalati (p)	
29/4	FCM Bacau	a	2-1	Abrudan, Paduretu	
6/5	Steaua Bucuresti	h	1-0	Matei	
12/5	Rapid Bucuresti	a	0-1		
19/5	FC Farul Constanta	h	1-0	Bruncevic	
2/6	CFR Cluj	a	1-2	Pacurar	
7/6	Sportul Studentesc	a	1-2	Nalati	

No	Name	Nat	Pos	Aps	(s)	Gls
19	Octavian ABRUDAN		D	10	(5)	1
22	Septimiu Calin ALBUT		G	23		
16	Dorin ARBANAS		M	16	(4)	
4	Laur Marian ASTILEAN		D	19		

Romania

No	Name	Nat	Pos	Aps	(s)	Gls
20	Sandu Lucian BORS		D	2	(1)	
6	Adrian BORZA		M	3	(3)	
23	Andrei Dan BOZESAN		M		(2)	
20	Sead BRUNCEVIC	SCG	A	8	(3)	1
5	Marius CRJAN		M		(1)	
29	Alin Nicu CHIBULCUTEAN		D	21	(1)	
7	Constantintin Marin CONSTANTINESCU		M	2	(2)	
6	Sergiu Ioan COSTIN		M	2	(2)	1
27	Goran CVETKOVIC	SCG	D	1	(3)	
26	Cosmin Vali FRASINESCU		D	4		
18	Dan Claudiu GAVRILESCU		A	1	(4)	
23	Daniel IFTODI		M	2	(18)	2
21	Arman KARAMYAN	ARM	A	2	(4)	
15	József LORINCZ		D	1		
2	Sergiu Sebastian MNDREAN		D	7	(5)	
24	Dan MATEI		D	23		1
18	Gabriel MURESAN		M	18		3
21	Adrian NALATI		A	15	(3)	2
9	Sandu NEGREAN		A	25		6
11	Sorin Stefan ONCICA		M	6	(2)	
10	Alexandru PACURAR		A	19	(7)	3
8	Romeo PADURET		M	7	(1)	
16	Razvan PADURETU		M	21	(3)	3
1	Sabin Ioan PGLISAN		G	7		
15	Daniel Puiu PAICA		D	1		
8	Florin PELECACI		M	2	(2)	
25	Adrian PREDICA		M		(1)	
15	Razvan RADU		A	1		
3	Alin Valer RUS		D	23		
15	Adrian Ioan SALAGEAN		M	2	(2)	
25	Dinu Daniel SNMARTEAN		D	5		
5	Claudiu Ovidiu SARMASAN		D	14	(1)	1
27	Mirel SOARE		M	1		
29	Marius SUMUDICA		A	1	(1)	
8	TRCA		A	1		
17	Andrei TRNAVEAN		A	14	(7)	3

JIUL PETROSANI
Coach – Ionut Chirila; (5/1/06) Aurel Sunda

2005
5/8	Gloria Bistrita	h	0-2	
13/8	CFR Cluj	a	0-0	
19/8	Sportul Studentesc	h	1-3	Pâclesan
26/8	FC Farul Constanta	a	0-1	
10/9	FC Vaslui	a	2-1	Dragan, Petre
17/9	FC Arges Pitesti	h	0-1	
25/9	FC National Bucuresti	a	1-1	Movila
1/10	Politehnica Timisoara	h	1-1	Gheorghe
16/10	Otelul Galati	a	0-0	
22/10	Pandurii Târgu Jiu	h	1-1	Gheorghe
29/10	Dinamo Bucuresti	a	1-1	Drida (p)
6/11	Politehnica Iasi	h	0-2	
18/11	FCM Bacau	a	2-1	Drida (p), Dragan
26/11	Steaua Bucuresti	h	1-2	Mihart
10/12	Rapid Bucuresti	a	0-3	

2006
12/3	Gloria Bistrita	a	0-0	
18/3	CFR Cluj	h	5-1	Dragan, Paleacu, Dinita, Ilin, Gheorghe
26/3	Sportul Studentesc	a	0-4	
2/4	FC Farul Constanta	h	3-1	Dinita, Drida, Petre
5/4	FC Vaslui	h	0-0	
8/4	FC Arges Pitesti	a	1-2	Dinita
11/4	FC National Bucuresti	h	2-0	Paleacu, Gheorghe
14/4	Politehnica Timisoara	a	0-1	
22/4	Otelul Galati	h	0-3	
28/4	Pandurii Târgu Jiu	a	1-1	Gheorghe
6/5	Dinamo Bucuresti	h	1-3	Petre
14/5	Politehnica Iasi	a	0-2	
21/5	FCM Bacau	h	2-0	Paleacu 2 (2p)
3/6	Steaua Bucuresti	a	0-1	
7/6	Rapid Bucuresti	h	3-0	(w/o; match abandoned, original result 1-0 Paleacu (p))

No	Name	Nat	Pos	Aps	(s)	Gls
2	Alexandru BADOIU		D	16		
31	Florian BOICIUC		D	2	(2)	
18	Constantin BORZA		A	1		
15	Alexandru Mugurel DEDU		M		(3)	
23	Laurentiu Nicolae DINITA		A	13		3
3	Ciprian DINU		D	17	(1)	
7	Claudiu DRAGAN		A	21	(2)	3
4	Constantin Virgil DRAGHICI		M	3	(4)	
19	Ioan Adrian DRIDA		M	16	(4)	3
11	Pavel Adrian DULCEA		A	4	(12)	
34	Florentin DUMITRU		M	2	(2)	
24	Irinel Claudiu DUMITRU		M		(1)	
16	Mircea GHEORGHE		M	18	(7)	5
1	Dumitru Emanoil HOTOBOC		G	14	(1)	
18	Alexandru Robert ILIESCU		D		(1)	
20	Alin Sorin ILIN		M	21	(2)	1
17	Marinica Lica IONICA		A	7	(5)	
27	Ovidiu ISTINIE		M		(5)	
22	Iosif KALAY		D	14	(5)	
21	Cornel MIHART		D	30		1
8	Damian MILITARU		M		(3)	
26	Bogdan Ionut MIRON		G	6		
9	Daniel MOVILA		M	3	(4)	1
22	Catalin Emanuel MULTESCU		G	10		
5	Marian PCLESAN		M	26	(1)	1
31	Alin Vasile PALEACU		M	14		5
14	Szabolcs Mihai PERENYI		D	22		
25	Catalin Ciprian PETRE		M	26		3
15	George SOLTUZ		D	8		
30	Ovidiu VEZAN		A	1	(8)	
33	Ion VOICU		D	13	(3)	
10	Mircea VOICU		M	2	(12)	

FC NATIONAL BUCURESTI
Coach – Roberto Landi (ITA); (17/9/05) Catalin Necula; (10/11/05) Cristiano Bergodi (ITA)

2005
6/8	FCM Bacau	h	1-0	Oprea
14/8	Steaua Bucuresti	a	0-4	
20/8	Rapid Bucuresti	h	1-0	Savu I.
27/8	Gloria Bistrita	a	2-0	Savu I., Abiodun (p)
10/9	CFR Cluj	h	0-4	
17/9	Sportul Studentesc	a	1-0	Bundea
25/9	Jiul Petrosani	h	1-1	Chiacu
1/10	FC Vaslui	a	0-0	
15/10	FC Arges Pitesti	h	0-1	
22/10	FC Farul Constanta	a	1-0	Savu I.
30/10	Politehnica Timisoara	a	1-2	Savu M. (p)
5/11	Otelul Galati	h	3-2	Savu I., Srhoj, Savu M.
19/11	Pandurii Târgu Jiu	a	1-1	Savu I. (p)
27/11	Dinamo Bucuresti	h	2-0	Griffiths 2

Romania

4/12	Politehnica Iasi	a	3-2	Oprea, Griffiths, Iancu
2006				
12/3	FCM Bacau	a	2-2	Oprea, Chihaia
19/3	Steaua Bucuresti	h	0-0	
26/3	Rapid Bucuresti	a	0-1	
1/4	Gloria Bistrita	h	2-0	Burca, Griffiths
4/4	CFR Cluj	a	0-0	
8/4	Sportul Studentesc	h	2-1	Bundea, Griffiths
11/4	Jiul Petrosani	a	0-2	
15/4	FC Vaslui	h	0-1	
22/4	FC Arges Pitesti	a	3-2	Abiodun, og (Rohat), Marin
29/4	FC Farul Constanta	a	0-4	
6/5	Politehnica Timisoara	h	1-0	Tames
14/5	Otelul Galati	a	0-2	
20/5	Pandurii Târgu Jiu	h	3-2	Sapunaru 3 (1p)
3/6	Dinamo Bucuresti	a	1-2	Griffiths
7/6	Politehnica Iasi	h	1-1	Griffiths

No	Name	Nat	Pos	Aps	(s)	Gls
23	ABIODUN Agunbiade	NGA	M	21	(2)	2
6	Elías Iván BAZZI	ARG	D	3	(1)	
25	Flavius Lucian BAD		A	4	(5)	
28	Zeno Marius BUNDEA		M	21	(7)	2
27	Ovidiu Nicusor BURCA		D	21	(1)	1
7	Hristu CHIACU		A	3	(6)	1
29	Octavian CHIHAIA		A	8	(4)	1
14	Robert GHINDEANU		D	16	(2)	
11	Ryan GRIFFITHS	AUS	A	21	(6)	7
16	Nicolae Ovidiu HEREA		M	11	(10)	
24	Robert IANCU		D	6	(12)	1
20	Nicolae Catalin LITA		M	10		
9	Petrus MANTA		A	2	(1)	
17	Alin MARCU		D	4	(2)	
6	D.aniel Catalin MARIN		A	6	(6)	1
4	Ersin MEHMEDOVIC	SCG	D	22	(1)	
8	Ciprian MOZACU		M	13	(1)	
13	Eugen Gheorghe NAE		G	19		
2	Emil Ducu NINU		D	3	(1)	
21	Mircea Vasile OPREA		A	22	(4)	3
26	Mihai PANC		D	13	(2)	
12	Florian PRUNEA		G	4		
19	Cristian Ionut SAPUNARU		D	20	(3)	3
15	Ionut Cristian SAVU		A	11	(1)	5
18	Marian SAVU		A	3	(4)	2
10	Wayne SRHOJ	AUS	M	22	(2)	1
22	Radostin STANEV	BUL	G	7		
15	Rajko STANKOVIC	SCG	A		(2)	
20	Iulian TAMES		M	5	(4)	1
3	Michael THWAITE	AUS	D	9		

OTELUL GALATI

Coach – Aurel Sunda; (19/11/05) Gigi Ion; (5/1/06) Petre Grigoras

2005				
07/8	Dinamo Bucuresti	h	1-4	Badescu
12/8	Politehnica Iasi	a	1-0	Munteanu (p)
21/8	FCM Bacau	h	0-0	
28/8	Steaua Bucuresti	a	0-4	
10/9	Rapid Bucuresti	h	3-3	Tanase, Aldea 2 (2p)
17/9	Gloria Bistrita	a	0-0	
24/9	CFR Cluj	h	0-1	
1/10	Sportul Studentesc	a	0-4	
16/10	Jiul Petrosani	h	0-0	
22/10	FC Vaslui	a	0-0	
29/10	FC Arges Pitesti	h	0-1	
5/11	FC National Bucuresti	a	2-3	Macare, Balauru
19/11	Politehnica Timisoara	h	0-2	
27/11	FC Farul Constanta	h	0-1	
2/12	Pandurii Târgu Jiu	a	2-2	Craciun, Ghidarcea
2006				
12/3	Dinamo Bucuresti	a	3-0	Stan 3 (1p)
17/3	Politehnica Iasi	h	0-0	
24/3	FCM Bacau	a	4-0	Baltoi, Tanase, Brujan, Paraschiv
2/4	Steaua Bucuresti	h	0-3	
9/4	Gloria Bistrita	h	1-0	Stan
12/4	CFR Cluj	a	1-0	Semeghin
15/4	Sportul Studentesc	h	2-3	Paraschiv, Baltoi
19/4	Rapid Bucuresti	a	0-4	
22/4	Jiul Petrosani	a	3-0	Stan 2, Baltoi
30/4	FC Vaslui	h	1-1	Tanase
7/5	FC Arges Pitesti	a	5-0	Paraschiv, Stan, Baltoi 2, Gado
14/5	FC National Bucuresti	h	2-0	Baltoi, Craciun
20/5	Politehnica Timisoara	a	2-0	Tanase (p), Elek
3/6	FC Farul Constanta	a	1-0	Tanase
7/6	Pandurii Târgu Jiu	h	1-1	Craciun

No	Name	Nat	Pos	Aps	(s)	Gls
9	Aurelian Bogdan ALDEA		A	9	(2)	2
19	Marian ALEXANDRU		A	1	(6)	
8	Gabriel APETREI		A		(3)	
10	Iulian Catalin APOSTOL		M	9	(1)	
5	Marius Achim BACIU		D	15		
11	Ionut BADESCU		M	17	(12)	1
20	Daniel Nicolae BALAURU		M	7		1
9	Alexandru BALTOI		A	11		6
33	Mihai BARBU		G	2		
20	Sergiu BRUJAN		M	9	(4)	1
18	Sergiu Ioan Viorel COSTIN		D	14		
7	Cristian CRACIUN		M	21	(7)	3
21	Cornel DOBRE		D	4	(1)	
16	Ionut Daniel DRAGOMIR		D	8		
8	Aurelian DUMITRU		D	3		
16	Robert ELEK		A		(4)	1
11	Ramses GADO		M	5	(3)	1
24	Sergiu GHIDARCEA		D	7	(2)	1
21	Silviu ILIE		M		(1)	
4	Silviu IZVOREANU		M	14		
17	Marius MACARE		M	6	(4)	1
6	Cosmin Nicolae MARGINEAN		D	14	(8)	
25	Daniel George MUNTEANU		D	13		1
20	Marius NECULAI		M	2	(2)	
3	Salif NOGO	BFA	D	9		
26	Danut Stelian OPREA		A	2	(4)	
23	Rares Tudor OPREA		A	2	(8)	
24	Gabriel PARASCHIV		M	15		3
5	A. PURGARIU		D		(1)	
4	Davi RANCAN Afonso	BRA	D	2	(3)	
25	Constantin Dorin SEMEGHIN		D	13		1
5	Danut SOMCHERECHI		D	9		
27	Paul Alexandr SOMODEAN		D	7	(5)	
19	Daniel STAN		A	12		7
33	Tudorel Daniel STANCIU		G	3		
14	Viorel TANASE		M	22	(1)	5
20	B. UNGURIANU		A		(1)	
1	Andrei URAI		G	10	(1)	
18	Alexander VALENCIA	COL	A	3	(1)	
82	Cosmin Andrei VTCA		G	15		

Romania

3	Tudor Marian ZECIU	D	15	

PANDURII TÂRGU JIU
Coach – Emil Sandoi; (8/9/05) Viorel Hizo; (18/4/06) Nicolae Ungureanu

2005
Date	Opponent	H/A	Score	Scorers
7/8	FC Farul Constanta	h	1-2	Vintilescu
14/8	Dinamo Bucuresti	a	0-3	
21/8	Politehnica Iasi	h	0-1	
27/8	FCM Bacau	a	0-1	
11/9	Steaua Bucuresti	h	1-2	Stefan
18/9	Rapid Bucuresti	a	0-3	
24/9	Gloria Bistrita	h	2-1	Armel, Vintilescu
1/10	CFR Cluj	a	2-1	Bogoi, Armel
16/10	Sportul Studentesc	h	0-1	
22/10	Jiul Petrosani	a	1-1	Nita
29/10	FC Vaslui	h	0-0	
4/11	FC Arges Pitesti	a	1-0	Armel
19/11	FC National Bucuresti	h	1-1	Keca
26/11	Politehnica Timisoara	a	0-1	
2/12	Otelul Galati	h	2-2	Armel, Glisca

2006
Date	Opponent	H/A	Score	Scorers
10/3	FC Farul Constanta	a	0-1	
18/3	Dinamo Bucuresti	h	0-2	
24/3	Politehnica Iasi	a	0-1	
1/4	FCM Bacau	h	2-1	Vranjkovic, Stefan
9/4	Rapid Bucuresti	h	0-0	
12/4	Gloria Bistrita	a	0-4	
15/4	CFR Cluj	h	0-1	
22/4	Sportul Studentesc	a	0-4	
28/4	Jiul Petrosani	h	1-1	Vintilescu
3/5	Steaua Bucuresti	a	0-1	
6/5	FC Vaslui	h	1-2	Armel
13/5	FC Arges Pitesti	h	1-0	Bogoi
20/5	FC National Bucuresti	a	2-3	Buta (p), Stefan
3/6	Politehnica Timisoara	h	3-2	Popescu A., Bogoi, og (Scutaru)
7/6	Otelul Galati	a	1-1	Naicu

No	Name	Nat	Pos	Aps	(s)	Gls
6	Aurel AMZUCU		D	8	(1)	
11	Disney ARMEL Mamouna	CON	A	25	(3)	5
12	Robert BALAET		G	2		
24	George Florian BERTEA		M	5	(3)	
16	Laurentiu Adrian BOGOI		D	19	(6)	3
20	Ionut Catalin BUCA		A		(1)	
8	Romulus Adrian BUIA		M	1	(5)	
77	Cornel BUTA		M	10	(2)	1
13	Ionut CAZACU		A	2	(6)	
15	Alexandru Dumit CRISTEA		D	3	(2)	
7	Ionut Daniel DRAGOMIR		D	4	(3)	
18	Paul GLISCA		A	5	(4)	1
26	Sandu Marius IORDACHE		D	4	(1)	
21	Boris KECA	BOS	D	16	(3)	1
1	Tiberiu Adrian LUNG		G	4		
26	Victor NAICU		D	7		1
13	Ionel Robert NITA		A	3	(3)	1
27	Marco Alberto OSORIO Pereira	URU	M	3		
25	Alexandru PNDARU		G	1		
23	Emanuel PATRASCU		M	2	(1)	
8	Dragan PERISIC		D	19	(1)	
9	Adrian POPESCU		M	6	(2)	1
3	Vasile Cristian POPESCU		D	2		
14	Laurentiu Florin POPETE		M	16	(3)	
22	Danilo PUSTINJAKOVIC		G	23		
5	Ioan Dorin RADOI		D	7	(9)	
13	Romeo Lucian RADOI		M	3		
6	Isam SAMI		D		(3)	
23	Marius SAVA		M	5	(3)	
2	Manuel Adrian SCARLATCHE		D	26	(1)	
10	Teodor Iulian STEFAN		A	23	(1)	3
4	Ioan Catalin TROFIN		D	21	(2)	
7	Cosmin Cristian URSU		M	7	(2)	
17	Robert Dumitru VANCEA		M	18	(3)	
9	Bobi Gheorghita VERDES		A	2	(3)	
19	Sorin VINTILESCU		A	17	(8)	3
20	Vojislav VRANJKOVIC	BOS	M	11	(2)	1

POLITEHNICA IASI
Coach – Ionut Popa

2005
Date	Opponent	H/A	Score	Scorers
7/8	Politehnica Timisoara	a	0-3	
12/8	Otelul Galati	h	0-1	
21/8	Pandurii Târgu Jiu	a	1-0	Bâlba
28/8	Dinamo Bucuresti	h	0-2	
11/9	FC Farul Constanta	h	3-1	Miclea 3
16/9	FCM Bacau	a	1-0	Ilie
25/9	Steaua Bucuresti	h	0-1	
3/10	Rapid Bucuresti	a	0-1	
16/10	Gloria Bistrita	h	1-1	Bâlba
22/10	CFR Cluj	a	0-0	
29/10	Sportul Studentesc	h	1-0	Rednic
6/11	Jiul Petrosani	a	2-0	Bâlba (p), Onofras
20/11	FC Vaslui	h	1-0	Pacurar
25/11	FC Arges Pitesti	a	0-3	
4/12	FC National Bucuresti	h	2-3	Vrajitoarea, Ciobanu

2006
Date	Opponent	H/A	Score	Scorers
11/3	Politehnica Timisoara	h	0-1	
17/3	Otelul Galati	a	0-0	
24/3	Pandurii Târgu Jiu	h	1-0	Cernoch
1/4	Dinamo Bucuresti	a	1-1	Rednic
5/4	FC Farul Constanta	a	0-1	
8/4	FCM Bacau	h	4-0	Cernoch 2, Bâlba 2
12/4	Steaua Bucuresti	a	0-1	
16/4	Rapid Bucuresti	h	1-4	Bâlba
21/4	Gloria Bistrita	a	0-1	
30/4	CFR Cluj	h	1-0	Bâlba
7/5	Sportul Studentesc	a	1-2	Rednic (p)
14/5	Jiul Petrosani	h	2-0	Cernoch, Rednic (p)
19/5	FC Vaslui	a	1-1	Bâlba
3/6	FC Arges Pitesti	h	3-2	Miclea 2, Bâlba
7/6	FC National Bucuresti	a	1-1	Rednic (p)

No	Name	Nat	Pos	Aps	(s)	Gls
23	Iulian ARHIRE		M	6	(1)	
9	Mihai Ionut BLBA		A	19	(5)	9
21	Tiberiu BECERU		D	5		
15	Dorel BERNARD		D	16	(1)	
10	Milos BOGDANOVIC	SCG	M	1	(1)	
4	Ionut BORDEANU		D	27		
1	Cristian Gigi BRANET		G	26		
28	Alin CTA		M		(1)	
27	Martin CERNOCH	CZE	A	13		4
30	Radu Eduard CIOBANU		D	15	(2)	1
19	Marius Adrian CIUBANCAN		M	2	(11)	
6	Ciprian Virgil DIANU		M	5	(3)	
8	Roberto GAVATORTA	ARG	M	19	(1)	
16	Adrian ILIE		D	14		1

Romania

No	Name	Nat	Pos	Aps	(s)	Gls
4	Ioan Irinel IONESCU		D	1		
25	Dan Mihai IURISNITI		M	14		
1	Alexandru Traian MARC		G	3		
18	Romulus Daniel MICLEA		M	17	(3)	5
5	Danut MITRUC		D	16	(8)	
11	Daniel Marius ONOFRAS		A	21	(7)	1
3	Mihai Bogdan ONUT		D	28		
7	Marius PACURAR		A	4	(8)	1
7	Clement PALIMARU		A	1	(4)	
13	Razvan PLESCA		G	1	(1)	
20	Daniel Eugen REDNIC		M	21	(5)	5
22	Martin SARIC	CRO	M	2	(2)	
14	Tudorel STANCIU		M	1		
24	Paul Catalin TINCU		A	7	(8)	
2	Adrian TOMA		D	22		
27	Bogdan Mihaita VRAJITOAREA		A	3	(9)	1

POLITEHNICA TIMISOARA
Coach – Cosmin Olaroiu; (10/11/05) Gheorghe Hagi; (21/5/06) Iosif Rotariu

2005
7/8	Politehnica Iasi	h	3-0	Coman, Osei, Silvasan
12/8	FCM Bacau	a	0-1	
20/8	Steaua Bucuresti	h	0-0	
28/8	Rapid Bucuresti	a	0-0	
10/9	Gloria Bistrita	h	4-0	Petre 2, Moldovan 2
18/9	CFR Cluj	a	0-2	
24/9	Sportul Studentesc	h	0-0	
1/10	Jiul Petrosani	a	1-1	Coman
14/10	FC Vaslui	h	2-0	Moldovan, Olah
23/10	FC Arges Pitesti	a	1-1	Moldovan
30/10	FC National Bucuresti	h	2-1	Moldovan, Coman
5/11	FC Farul Constanta	h	3-2	Moldovan, Caramarin, Bucur
19/11	Otelul Galati	a	2-0	Coman, Silvasan
26/11	Pandurii Târgu Jiu	h	1-0	Caramarin (p)
4/12	Dinamo Bucuresti	a	0-1	

2006
11/3	Politehnica Iasi	a	1-0	Gueye
18/3	FCM Bacau	h	2-0	Stoica, Gueye
26/3	Steaua Bucuresti	a	1-2	Balace
2/4	Rapid Bucuresti	h	1-3	Caramarin (p)
5/4	Gloria Bistrita	a	1-1	
8/4	CFR Cluj	h	2-2	Balace, Petre
11/4	Sportul Studentesc	a	1-3	Balace (p)
14/4	Jiul Petrosani	h	1-0	Gluscevic
21/4	FC Vaslui	a	1-1	Stanic
28/4	FC Arges Pitesti	h	0-0	
6/5	FC National Bucuresti	a	0-1	
13/5	FC Farul Constanta	a	2-4	Bucur, Torje
20/5	Otelul Galati	h	0-2	
4/6	Pandurii Târgu Jiu	a	2-3	Balace 2
7/6	Dinamo Bucuresti	h	0-0	

No	Name	Nat	Pos	Aps	(s)	Gls
17	Silviu Constantin BALACE		D	29		5
5	Florin BATRNU		D	8		
18	Gheorghe BUCUR		A	13	(7)	2
23	Gabriel CNU		D	20		
8	Gabriel Gheorghe CARAMARIN		M	17	(2)	3
28	Gigel COMAN		M	20	(2)	4
26	Marian Constantin CONSTANTINESCU		M	1	(3)	
7	Cristian DAMINUTA		M		(1)	
13	Ifeanyi EMEGHARA	NGA	D	14		
7	Dan Constantin GALDEAN		M	1	(4)	
9	Vladimir GLUSCEVIC	SCG	A	6	(3)	1
24	Mansour GUEYE	SEN	A	13	(8)	2
5	Adrian ILIE		D	2		
6	Silviu IZVOREANU		M	6	(4)	
27	Iasmin LATOVLEVIC		D	1	(1)	
4	Jonathan David McKAIN	AUS	D	23	(1)	
9	Dinu Viorel MOLDOVAN		A	12		6
11	Leonard Toni NAIDIN		M	10	(9)	
21	Adrian OLAH		D	20	(1)	1
25	Emmanuel OSEI	GHA	M	11	(2)	1
26	Ricardo David PAEZ	VEN	M		(3)	
16	Alin Vasile PALEACU		M	3	(3)	
30	Ovidiu PETRE		M	20	(1)	3
10	Mihaita Paunel PLESAN		M	7		
12	Marius Cornel POPA		G	29		
14	Sorin Nicusor RADOI		D	15	(2)	
3	Mircea Vasile RUS		D	3	(4)	
6	Cristian Dorel SCUTARU		D	3	(2)	
20	Cristian Radu SILVASAN		A	5	(5)	2
32	Peter SIMEK	HUN	A	3	(1)	
16	Rares SOPORAN		M	4	(3)	
15	Sreten STANIC	SCG	A	4	(7)	1
22	Alin STOICA		M	4		1
25	Gabriel TORJE		M	2	(3)	1
27	Valentin VELCEA		M		(5)	
1	Eduard Cristian ZIMMERMAN		G	1		

RAPID BUCURESTI
Coach – Razvan Lucescu

2005
6/8	FC Vaslui	a	1-0	Stancu R.
14/8	FC Arges Pitesti	h	1-1	Ilyes
20/8	FC National Bucuresti	a	0-1	
28/8	Politehnica Timisoara	h	0-0	
10/9	Otelul Galati	a	3-3	Niculae, Constantin N., Buga
18/9	Pandurii Târgu Jiu	h	3-0	Maftei, Constantin N., Maldarasanu
25/9	Dinamo Bucuresti	a	2-5	Niculae, Maldarasanu
3/10	Politehnica Iasi	h	1-0	Burdujan
15/10	FCM Bacau	a	1-0	Buga
23/10	Steaua Bucuresti	h	0-0	
30/10	FC Farul Constanta	a	2-1	Buga, Niculae
6/11	Gloria Bistrita	a	1-2	Ilyes (p)
19/11	CFR Cluj	h	1-0	Niculae
27/11	Sportul Studentesc	a	0-1	
10/12	Jiul Petrosani	h	3-0	Maldarasanu, Rada, Niculae

2006
12/3	FC Vaslui	h	1-1	Badoi
19/3	FC Arges Pitesti	a	1-1	Moldovan D.V.
26/3	FC National Bucuresti	h	1-0	Grigore
2/4	Politehnica Timisoara	a	3-1	Buga 2, Burdujan
9/4	Pandurii Târgu Jiu	a	0-0	
12/4	Dinamo Bucuresti	h	3-0	Moldovan D.V. 2, Niculae (p)
16/4	Politehnica Iasi	a	4-1	Moldovan D.V., Badoi 2, Negru
19/4	Otelul Galati	h	4-0	Niculae, Grigore, Burdujan, Moldovan D.V.
22/4	FCM Bacau	h	2-1	Negru, Rada
30/4	Steaua Bucuresti	a	2-0	Pancu, Moldovan D.V.
7/5	FC Farul Constanta	h	0-0	
12/5	Gloria Bistrita	h	1-0	Pancu

Romania

21/5	CFR Cluj	a	3-1	Moldovan D.V., Buga, Negru	
4/6	Sportul Studentesc	h	3-0	Buga, Moldovan D.V., Niculae	
7/6	Jiul Petrosani	a	0-3	(w/o; match abandoned, original result 0-1)	

No	Name	Nat	Pos	Aps	(s)	Gls
9	Valentin BADOI		M	29		3
29	Mugurel Mihai BUGA		A	20	(5)	7
20	Lucian BURDUJAN		A	6	(11)	3
1	Danut Dumitru COMAN		G	22		
23	Marius Marcel CONSTANTIN		D	26		
28	Nicolae CONSTANTIN		D	12	(5)	2
13	Emil Cosmin DICA		M	4	(13)	
77	Emilian Ioan DOLHA		G	3		
18	Nicolae GRIGORE		M	10	(3)	2
11	Robert ILYES		M	14	(1)	2
10	Artavazd KARAMYAN	ARM	M	13	(5)	
24	Vasile MAFTEI		D	29		1
17	Marius Constantin MALDARASANU		M	15		3
19	Ion Bogdan MARA		A	2	(3)	
32	Mihai Adrian MINCA		G	5	(1)	
99	Dinu Viorel MOLDOVAN		D	9	(4)	8
4	Flavius Lucian MOLDOVAN		D	4		
8	Valentin NEGRU		M	4	(9)	3
21	Daniel George NICULAE		A	25	(4)	8
19	Daniel Gabriel PANCU		M	13		2
14	Daniel PERJA		D	6	(4)	
4	Ionut Alin RADA		D	24		2
5	Ionut Cristian STANCU		D	17	(2)	
25	Romeo Constantin STANCU		M	14	(3)	1
7	Ciprian VASILACHE		M	4	(15)	

SPORTUL STUDENTESC BUCURESTI
Coach – Dan Petrescu; (5/1/06) Gheorghe Multescu

2005

6/8	CFR Cluj	h	1-1	Mazilu
13/8	FC Farul Constanta	a	2-2	Ratiu, Mazilu
19/8	Jiul Petrosani	a	3-1	Balan, Mazilu 2
27/8	FC Vaslui	h	3-0	Nae, Ratiu, og (Lacusta)
9/9	FC Arges Pitesti	a	2-2	Mazilu 2
17/9	FC National Bucuresti	h	0-1	
24/9	Politehnica Timisoara	a	0-0	
1/10	Otelul Galati	h	4-0	Lazar, Balan, Mazilu 2
16/10	Pandurii Târgu Jiu	a	1-0	Mazilu
23/10	Dinamo Bucuresti	h	0-2	
29/10	Politehnica Iasi	a	0-1	
5/11	FCM Bacau	h	2-1	Balan 2
20/11	Steaua Bucuresti	a	1-4	Balan (p)
27/11	Rapid Bucuresti	h	1-0	Mazilu
4/12	Gloria Bistrita	a	0-2	

2006

11/3	CFR Cluj	a	0-0	
18/3	FC Farul Constanta	h	3-1	Mazilu 3
26/3	Jiul Petrosani	h	4-0	Balan (p), Mazilu, Varga, Ferfelea
31/3	FC Vaslui	a	3-0	Ferfelea, Mazilu, Curelea
5/4	FC Arges Pitesti	h	1-0	Balan (p)
8/4	FC National Bucuresti	a	1-2	Lazar
11/4	Politehnica Timisoara	h	3-1	Nae, Varga (p), Mazilu (p)
15/4	Otelul Galati	a	3-2	Nae, Mazilu, Balan
22/4	Pandurii Târgu Jiu	h	4-0	Ratiu, Curelea 2, Mazilu
29/4	Dinamo Bucuresti	a	5-4	Mazilu 3, Curelea, Varga
7/5	Politehnica Iasi	h	2-1	Mazilu, Cruceru

13/5	FCM Bacau	a	2-1	Balan 2 (1p)
21/5	Steaua Bucuresti	h	1-2	Balan
4/6	Rapid Bucuresti	a	0-3	
7/6	Gloria Bistrita	h	2-1	Balan, Stancu

No	Name	Nat	Pos	Aps	(s)	Gls
10	Tiberiu Gabriel BALAN		M	28	(1)	12
21	Bogdan CISTEIAN		D	6	(4)	
8	Florentin CRUCERU		M	18	(6)	1
18	Costin CURELEA		A	14	(15)	4
3	Marian DEDU		D	1		
14	Viorel FERFELEA		M	19	(11)	2
11	Costin GHEORGHE		M		(2)	
5	Costin LAZAR		M	22	(3)	2
23	Florin Sandu MAXIM		M	5	(6)	
9	Ionut Costinel MAZILU		A	27	(1)	22
19	Florin MLADIN		M		(1)	
22	Marius NAE		M	19	(6)	3
17	Marius Madalin OAE		M	2	(12)	
24	Nichita Razvan PATRICHE		D	11	(4)	
2	Robert Alin RATIU		D	27		3
13	Liviu Nicolae RUSU		D	15		
6	Constantin SECAREANU		D	29		
33	Eduard Cornel STANCIOIU		G	30		
7	Stelian STANCU		D	29		1
3	George TOMA		D		(3)	
20	Serban Dacian VARGA		A	26	(2)	3
4	Nicola VASILE		M	2	(11)	

STEAUA BUCURESTI
Coach – Oleh Protasov (UKR); (15/12/05) Cosmin Olaroiu

2005

6/8	FC Arges Pitesti	a	1-0	Dica
14/8	FC National Bucuresti	h	4-0	Iacob, Ogararu, Dica, Paraschiv
20/8	Politehnica Timisoara	a	0-0	
28/8	Otelul Galati	h	4-0	Paraschiv, Dica, Iacob, Oprita
11/9	Pandurii Târgu Jiu	a	2-1	Nicolita, Bostina
18/9	Dinamo Bucuresti	h	2-2	Goian, Dica
25/9	Politehnica Iasi	a	1-0	Bostina (p)
3/10	FCM Bacau	h	1-0	Paraschiv
16/10	FC Farul Constanta	a	4-1	Iacob 2, Dica, Bostina
23/10	Rapid Bucuresti	a	0-0	
30/10	Gloria Bistrita	h	0-1	
6/11	CFR Cluj	a	0-1	
20/11	Sportul Studentesc	h	4-1	Radoi, Dica, Nicolita, Iacob
26/11	Jiul Petrosani	a	2-1	Nicolita, Dica
4/12	FC Vaslui	h	2-2	Dica, Bostina

2006

12/3	FC Arges Pitesti	h	0-0	
19/3	FC National Bucuresti	a	0-0	
26/3	Politehnica Timisoara	h	1-1	Dica, Nicolita
2/4	Otelul Galati	a	3-0	Cristea 2, Radoi (p)
9/4	Dinamo Bucuresti	a	1-1	Cristocea
12/4	Politehnica Iasi	h	1-0	Dica (p)
22/4	FC Farul Constanta	h	3-0	Nicolita 2, Dica
30/4	Rapid Bucuresti	h	0-2	
3/5	Pandurii Târgu Jiu	h	1-0	og (Naicu)
6/5	Gloria Bistrita	a	0-1	
14/5	CFR Cluj	h	2-0	Goian, Dica
17/5	FCM Bacau	a	2-0	Cristea, Lovin
21/5	Sportul Studentesc	a	2-1	Nicolita, Radoi (p)
3/6	Jiul Petrosani	h	1-0	Cristocea

Romania

7/6	FC Vaslui	a	4-0	Radoi (p), Dica 3	

No	Name	Nat	Pos	Aps	(s)	Gls
17	Catalin Eugen BACIU		D	8	(1)	
5	Daniel BALAN		D	5	(1)	
11	Gabriel BOSTINA		M	22	(5)	4
13	CARLOS Alberto Fernandes	POR	G	13		
12	Cornel CERNEA		G	2		
21	Andrei CRISTEA		A	5	(19)	3
14	Vasilica CRISTOCEA		M	7	(7)	2
10	Constantin Nicolae DICA		M	29		15
27	Laurentiu Nicolae DINITA		A	1	(7)	
2	Florentin DUMITRU		M		(7)	
24	Sorin GHIONEA		D	26		
3	Dorin Nicolae GOIAN		D	22	(1)	2
33	Vasiliy KHOMUTOVSKIY	BLS	G	15		
19	Victoras Constantin IACOB		A	20	(2)	5
28	Florin LOVIN		M	16	(7)	1
18	Petre MARIN		D	11	(3)	
15	Mihai Mircea NESU		D	20		
16	Banel NICOLITA		M	28	(1)	7
30	Razvan Iulian OCHIROSII		M		(1)	
20	George Cristian OGARARU		D	25	(3)	1
7	Daniel Ionel OPRITA		A	8	(16)	1
22	Sorin Ion PARASCHIV		M	23	(3)	3
6	Matei Mirel RADOI		D	24		4

FC VASLUI
Coach – Basarab Panduru; (14/9/05) Mircea Rednic

2005				
6/8	Rapid Bucuresti	h	0-1	
13/8	Gloria Bistrita	a	1-1	Badea V.
19/8	CFR Cluj	h	0-3	
27/8	Sportul Studentesc	a	0-3	
10/9	Jiul Petrosani	h	1-2	Jovanovic
16/9	FC Farul Constanta	a	1-2	Raducanu (p)
24/9	FC Arges Pitesti	a	0-1	
1/10	FC National Bucuresti	h	0-0	
14/10	Politehnica Timisoara	a	0-2	
22/10	Otelul Galati	h	0-0	
29/10	Pandurii Târgu Jiu	a	0-0	
6/11	Dinamo Bucuresti	h	1-2	Badea I.
20/11	Politehnica Iasi	a	0-1	
26/11	FCM Bacau	h	1-1	Raducanu
4/12	Steaua Bucuresti	a	2-2	Badea I. (p), Badea V.
2006				
12/3	Rapid Bucuresti	a	1-1	Badea V.
18/3	Gloria Bistrita	h	2-0	Croitoru, Bukvic
25/3	CFR Cluj	a	0-1	
31/3	Sportul Studentesc	h	0-3	
5/4	Jiul Petrosani	a	0-0	
9/4	FC Farul Constanta	h	0-2	
12/4	FC Arges Pitesti	h	3-0	Panait 2 (1p), Mihalcea (p)
15/4	FC National Bucuresti	a	1-0	Badea V.
21/4	Politehnica Timisoara	h	1-1	Badea I.
30/4	Otelul Galati	a	1-1	Sfarlea
6/5	Pandurii Târgu Jiu	h	2-1	Panait, Bukvic
13/5	Dinamo Bucuresti	a	2-1	Croitoru, Badea V.
19/5	Politehnica Iasi	h	1-1	Baicu
2/6	FCM Bacau	a	2-0	Bukvic, Panait
7/6	Steaua Bucuresti	h	0-4	

No	Name	Nat	Pos	Aps	(s)	Gls
4	Ionut BADEA		D	28		3
9	Valentin Vasile BADEA		A	19	(4)	5
18	Ilie Nicu BAICU		D	24		1
27	Vasile BUHAESCU		A	2	(13)	
15	Bogdan Constantin BUHUS		D	26		
26	Milorad BUKVIC	SCG	A	12	(3)	3
27	Dionisio Horno CABRERA	URU	A		(1)	
5	Cornel Flaviu CORNEA		M	5	(4)	
10	Marius Marian CROITORU		M	14		2
26	Catalin Marcel CURSARU		A	5	(6)	
21	Ionut Robert DANTES		M		(2)	
8	Igor DE LIMA	BRA	M	2	(2)	
10	Sorin FRUNZA		M	12	(1)	
7	Viorel FRUNZA	MOL	A	3	(2)	
22	Cristian HAISAN		G	8		
6	Mihai HAPIUC		M		(1)	
1	Sebastian Dumitru HUTAN		G	15		
7	Sabin ILIE		A	2	(2)	
16	Dan Mihai IURISNITI		M	6	(2)	
2	Petar JOVANOVIC	BOS	M	24	(2)	1
12	Gabriel KAJCSA		G	3		
24	Florian Dan LACUSTA		D	21	(1)	
19	Vladislav LUNGU	MOL	M	3		
23	Darko MALETIC	BOS	D	1	(4)	
24	Adrian Dumitru MIHALCEA		A	9	(4)	1
25	Falemi N'GASSAM	CMR	M	6		
16	Bogdan Gh. NICOLAE		D	4	(6)	
6	NIVALDO Vieira Lima	BRA	M	3		
17	Vasile Bogdan PANAIT		D	25	(1)	4
25	Daniel PSLA	MOL	M		(1)	
21	Cristian PELIN		M		(2)	
1	Dejan PESIC	SCG	G	4	(1)	
14	Claudiu Nicu RADUCANU		A	15		2
8	Sebastian SFRLEA		M	12		1
25	George SOLTUZ		D	1	(2)	
20	Tudorel STANCIU		M	1	(2)	
28	Mbemba SYLLA	GUI	M	1	(2)	
19	Lucian TARCEA		M	2	(1)	
11	Tihamer TÖRÖK		A	5	(8)	
3	Sorin Costel UNGURIANU		D	2	(2)	
5	Constantin Irinel VOICU		D	5	(1)	

DOMESTIC CUP 2005/06

FIRST ROUND
(20/9/05)
Gaz metan Medias 0, Otelul Galati 0 *(aet; 2-4 on pens)*
(21/9/05)
Cetatea Suceava 2, Sportul Studentesc Bucuresti 1
Gloria Buzau 1, FC Farul Constanta 2
CS Otopeni 2, Politehnica Timisoara 5
CFR Timisoara 1, FC National Bucuresti 3
Rapid II Bucuresti 0, Steaua Bucuresti 0 *(aet; 8-7 on pens)*
FCM Resita 0, Rapid Bucuresti 1
Dunarea Galati 0, Dinamo Bucuresti 1
Universitatea Craiova 1, CFR Cluj 0
Unirea Dej 0, Politehnica Iasi 2
FC Bihor Oradea 0, Jiul Petrosani 2
FCM Târgoviste 3, FC Arges Pitesti 2 *(aet)*
Petrolul Ploiesti 2, Gloria Bistrita 1 *(aet)*
Callatis Mangalia 0, Pandurii Târgu-Jiu 2
Gloria Bistrita II 1, FC Vaslui 2 *(aet)*
FC Brasov 2, FCM Bacau 2 *(aet; 2-4 on pens)*

Romania

SECOND ROUND
(25/10/05)
Pandurii Târgu-Jiu 0, Otelul Galati 2
(26/10/05)
Cetatea Suceava 2, Rapid Bucuresti 3
Petrolul Ploiesti 2, Dinamo Bucuresti 1
Rapid II Bucuresti 3, FC Farul Constanta 4
FCM Bacau 0, Jiul Petrosani 2
Politehnica Iasi 2, FC Vaslui 1 *(aet)*
FCM Târgoviste 1, Politehnica Timisoara 3 *(aet)*
FC National Bucuresti 0, Universitatea Craiova 0 *(aet; 4-3 on pens)*

QUARTER-FINALS
(7/12/05)
Petrolul Ploiesti 3 *(Hadnagy 14, Marinescu 70, Ilie 84)*, Politehnica Timisoara 2 *(Caramarin 25, Radoi 55)*
Politehnica Iasi 0, Rapid Bucuresti 1 *(Ilyes 90)*
Jiul Petrosani 0, FC Farul Constanta 1 *(Gheorghe 68)*
Otelul Galati 0, FC National Bucuresti 0 *(aet; 3-4 on pens)*

SEMI-FINALS
(22/3/06 & 26/4/06)
Rapid Bucuresti 4 *(Pancu 37, Niculae 65, Moldovan 66, Burdujan 70)*, Petrolul Ploiesti 1 *(Hadnagy 38)*
Petrolul Ploiesti 3 *(Niculae 22, Constantin M. 48, Pancu 53)*, Rapid Bucuresti 3 *(Stepanov 29, Donets 42, Marinescu 87p)*
(Rapid Bucuresti 7-4)

FC Farul Constanta 1 *(Mihai 47)*, FC National Bucuresti 0
FC National Bucuresti 4 *(Griffiths 11, 55, 76, Herea 15)*, FC Farul Constanta 1 *(Pascovici 28)*
(FC National Bucuresti 4-2)

FINAL
(17/5/06)
National stadion, Bucharest
RAPID BUCURESTI 1 *(Niculae 91)*
FC NATIONAL BUCURESTI 0
(aet)
Referee - Tudor
RAPID BUCURESTI - Coman, Constantin M., Maftei, Rada, Badoi, Grigore (Negru 67), Stancu R., Karamian (Stancu I. 99), Buga, Niculae, Pancu (Moldovan 55).
FC NATIONAL BUCURESTI - Nae, Sapunaru, Burca, Mehmedovic, Panc, Agunbiade, Srhoj (Ghindeanu 63), Bundea (Marin 92), Herea, Tames (32 Mozacu), Griffiths.

SECOND LEVEL FINAL TABLES 2005/06

Seria I
		Pld	W	D	L	F	A	Pts
1	Ceahlaul Piatra Neamt	30	20	6	4	59	20	66
2	Forex Brasov	30	18	5	7	55	31	59
3	FC Brasov	30	17	8	5	57	22	58
4	FC Botosani	30	15	4	11	32	29	49
5	Cetatea Suceava	30	14	4	12	43	34	46
6	Precizia Sacele	30	12	9	9	26	24	45
7	Dacia Unirea Braila	30	12	8	10	31	29	44
8	Gloria Buzau	30	12	7	11	37	29	43
9	Dunarea Galati	30	12	7	11	29	26	43
10	Altay Navodari	30	12	6	12	33	37	42
11	Callatis Mangalia	30	11	6	13	34	39	39
12	FCM Târgoviste	30	10	8	12	29	30	38
13	Petrolul Moinesti	30	8	8	14	33	44	32
14	Laminorul Roman	30	8	6	16	31	47	30
15	Portul Constanta	30	7	6	17	37	60	27
16	Midia Navodari	30	1	4	25	6	71	7

N.B. FC Brasov – 1 pt deducted; Midia Navodari withdrew after 15 matches.

Seria II
		Pld	W	D	L	F	A	Pts
1	Universitatea Craiova	30	20	4	6	43	16	62
2	Unirea Urziceni	30	18	5	7	55	24	59
3	Petrolul Ploiesti	30	17	5	8	48	29	56
4	CS Otopeni	30	15	9	6	40	20	54
5	Dunarea Giurgiu	30	16	3	11	35	33	51
6	CSM Rm Vâlcea	30	11	12	7	37	27	45
7	Poiana Câmpina	30	12	9	9	36	30	45
8	Dacia Mioveni	30	12	8	10	36	30	44
9	FC Caracal	30	13	4	13	35	38	43
10	Astra Ploiesti	30	12	4	14	45	50	40
11	Minerul Motru	30	9	10	11	32	34	37
12	Inter Gaz Bucuresti	30	9	9	12	30	40	36
13	Rapid II Bucuresti	30	10	2	18	27	57	32
14	Juventus Bucuresti	30	6	5	19	30	50	23
15	Dinamo II Bucuresti	30	4	9	17	28	45	21
16	FC Sibiu	30	3	8	19	12	46	17

N.B. Universitatea Craiova – 2 pts deducted.

Seria III
		Pld	W	D	L	F	A	Pts
1	Liberty Salonta	28	17	7	4	37	16	58
2	FC Bihor Oradea	28	17	4	7	53	27	55
3	Universitatea Cluj	28	15	9	4	44	16	54
4	Gaz Metan Medias	28	15	6	7	38	21	51
5	FCM Resita	28	11	7	10	26	29	40
6	Corvinul Hunedoara	28	10	8	10	33	35	38
7	CFR Timisoara	28	10	6	12	33	40	36
8	Gloria II Bistrita	28	10	6	12	25	34	36
9	Industria Sârmei Câmpia Turzii	28	8	10	10	30	29	34
10	Minerul Lupeni	28	9	7	12	26	31	34
11	Unirea Dej	28	9	5	14	29	37	32
12	Olimpia Satu Mare	28	9	5	14	24	36	32
13	Unirea Alba Iulia	28	6	10	12	21	31	28
14	UTA Arad	28	6	9	13	25	35	27
15	Unirea Sânnicolau Mare	28	6	5	17	21	48	23

N.B. Armatura Zalau withdrew after 4 matches; Liberty Salonta subsequently 'sold' their promotion to UTA Arad.

PROMOTION/RELEGATION PLAY-OFFS
(10/6/06)
Forex Brasov 2, FC Bihor Oradea 0
(14/6/06)
Unirea Urziceni 4, FC Bihor Oradea 2
(17/6/06)
Forex Brasov 0, Unirea Urziceni 1

		Pld	W	D	L	F	A	Pts
1	Unirea Urziceni	2	2	0	0	5	2	6
2	Forex Brasov	2	1	0	1	2	1	3
3	FC Bihor Oradea	2	0	0	2	2	6	0

Russia

Future belongs to Hiddink

As the largest country on the planet, with a population of almost 150 million, Russia should not be struggling to qualify for major tournaments, less still finishing third in a World Cup group behind Slovakia.

To avoid further such ignominies, the Russian FA have pushed the boat out and handed the coaching reins of the national team to Guus Hiddink. The Dutchman is renowned the world over. He took Holland and South Korea to World Cup semi-finals, he led Australia to the second round at the 2006 tournament (where they were eliminated by the eventual champions only by a dodgy penalty), and at club level he has won more Dutch championship titles (six) than anyone else in history.

Even so, coaching Russia probably represents Hiddink's biggest challenge. His first task is self-evident – to take his new charges to Euro 2008. To do that his team will have to split England and Croatia, two countries that, unlike Russia, were present at the World Cup finals in Germany. The matches against England, which take place in the early autumn of 2007, will be particularly interesting given that the Dutchman was earmarked as a potential successor to Sven Göran Eriksson before the Russians made him an offer he couldn't refuse.

Syomin unbeaten

Hiddink's predecessor, Yuriy Syomin, was unbeaten in seven matches, six of them World Cup qualifiers and the other a friendly away to Germany, yet he lasted less than six months. Like Hiddink, the long-time Lokomotiv Moscow boss was seen as a dream ticket when he was appointed. But the team's failure to win key games away to Latvia and Slovakia, and at home to Portugal, forced Syomin to accept his responsibilities and quit. It had been anticipated that he would return to Lokomotiv but instead, with his long-time assistant Vladimir Eshtrekov getting along just fine in his stead, he hooked up with their Muscovite rivals Dinamo. Meanwhile, the team he left behind were placed under the temporary stewardship of national youth team boss Alexandr Borodyuk while federation supremo Vitaliy Mutko sat tight, prepared to wait for several months until he got his man.

Hiddink will not have to travel far to watch his charges in action. Almost all of Russia's current internationals are based in Moscow, with a few others performing up the road in St. Petersburg. It is not because the players are of insufficient quality to earn a decent pay cheque abroad, rather that the Russian Premier League nowadays is an importer rather than exporter of talent. Hordes of foreigners now swell the ranks of the elite division's 16 clubs – to the extent that, in 2005, big-spending Dinamo Moscow actually fielded a team without a single Russian.

That may be good news for the prestige of the league, but it doesn't help the prospects of the national side, and Hiddink, for one, will be pleased that the federation has decided to impose a quota restricting the number of foreigners who can appear in any Premier League game. The plan is to reduce the numbers gradually so that by 2010 more than half of the players in any chosen XI will have to be Russian. The exact scale-down is seven foreigners in 2006, six in 2008 and five in 2010.

Where the imports do benefit Russian football is in the European club competitions, the obvious case in point being CSKA Moscow's UEFA Cup triumph in 2004/05 – the first victory by any Russian club in 50 years of European competition.

Leading the charge to follow CSKA into the history

Russia

books were Zenit St. Petersburg, who made it all the way into the quarter-finals of the same competition before falling to eventual winners Sevilla. Zenit had their fare share of foreigners, not least on the bench, where the Czech, Vlastimil Petrzela, oversaw the team's progress, but at the forefront, literally, of their European exploits were the Russian international strikeforce of Andrei Arshavin and Alexandr Kerzhakov, who shared 12 of the team's 17 UEFA Cup goals and were a constant twin menace to all the defences they encountered.

Lokomotiv Moscow's UEFA Cup challenge was also terminated by Sevilla, although the bigger disappointment for Eshtrekov's team was their failure to reach the group phase of the Champions League. Having seemingly done the hard work against Rapid Vienna in Austria, they crashed out by conceding a late goal in Moscow.

Tortuous end

CSKA's hold on the UEFA Cup also ended in tortuous circumstances. Although they could win only one group game, they were on the verge of qualification for round three when a last-gasp goal from Dutch side Heerenveen skewered their hopes.

That was the final, painful act in what had otherwise been a glorious year for the former army club. UEFA Cup and Russian Cup winners in the spring, Valeriy Gazzayev's side made it a clean sweep in the autumn by coming from behind to regain the Russian Premier League championship.

Because of their protracted European involvement, CSKA barely played any domestic football early on. That left them with a lot of matches in hand and, in consequence, a lot of ground to make up on the leaders. CSKA planned their comeback with patience and stealth, but things looked a bit ominous at the end of July when they lost 3-2 away to a Lokomotiv side that had not been beaten in Premier League combat since the previous September – a record-breaking run of 27 matches. After that defeat CSKA trailed their city rivals by a mammoth 13 points. Now, even if they won their three games in hand, they would still be well in arrears.

It was time for CSKA to kick on and apply a bit of pressure. Almost at once Lokomotiv began to stumble. A first defeat – 3-1 at provincial high fliers Rubin Kazan – immediately followed their victory over CSKA. Worse still, their Russian international striker Dmitry Sychov, who had just begun to find his best form, suffered a serious knee injury that ruled him out for the rest of the season (and beyond).

In for the kill

As Lokomotiv inevitably started to wobble without their star striker, CSKA moved ruthlessly in for the kill. Brazilian playmaker Daniel Carvalho, the star of their UEFA Cup final victory against Sporting, was the chief predator. The classy left-footer scored the winning goal at home to Spartak Moscow, then did likewise away to Amkar Perm in a victory that finally lifted CSKA to the top of the table for the first time. And to cap it all, he also grabbed the winner in the penultimate game away to Dinamo Moscow, a 2-1 victory that secured his team the Premier League title.

With those crucial late goals, Daniel Carvalho probably edged ahead of goalkeeper Igor Akinfeev (just 19 goals conceded in 29 outings) as the most valuable player in CSKA's title triumph. Twin defensive pillars Vasiliy and Aleksei Berezutskiy were also consistently excellent, while long-serving Bosnian midfielder Elver Rahimic deserved a special pat on the back for starting and finishing all 30 matches – the only outfield player in the entire league to do so.

CSKA ended the season with a flourish, beating Alania Vladikavkaz 4-3 at home, but the big game of the final day, played in front of a sell-out crowd of 28,800, saw Lokomotiv take on Spartak Moscow in the battle for second place. The match was particularly important because, thanks largely to CSKA's UEFA Cup win, Russia had now acquired a second Champions League qualifying berth, and the two combatants went into the game level on points. Although Lokomotiv had home advantage, Spartak, with more victories to their name, could afford to draw and still take the runners-up spot.

NATIONAL TEAM RESULTS 2005/06

Date	Opponent	H/A	Venue	Score	Scorers
17/8/05	Latvia (WCQ)	A	Riga	1-1	Arshavin (24)
3/9/05	Liechtenstein (WCQ)	H	Moscow	2-0	Kerzhakov (27, 65)
7/9/05	Portugal (WCQ)	H	Moscow	0-0	
8/10/05	Luxembourg (WCQ)	H	Moscow	5-1	Izmailov (7), Kerzhakov (18), Pavlyuchenko (69), Kirichenko (75, 90)
12/10/05	Slovakia (WCQ)	A	Bratislava	0-0	
1/3/06	Brazil	H	Moscow	0-1	
27/5/06	Spain	A	Albacete	0-0	

Russia

Titov strikes

Draws had been the bane of Lokomotiv's season (with goalless ones, nine in all, a particular weakness). They could not afford another, but that is what they got as Georgian midfielder Malkhaz Asatiani's late goal proved an inadequate response to an earlier header from Spartak skipper Yegor Titov.

That goal rounded off a brilliant comeback season (after a one-year drugs ban) for the Russian international midfielder, and it also ensured that Latvian coach Aleksandrs Starkovs' first full season in charge of Spartak ended on a high. Unfortunately, the man who took his country to Euro 2004 was no longer there the following spring when Spartak reached the Russian Cup final. His replacement, Vladimir Fedotov, had the task of trying to deny CSKA yet another prize, but he failed. The champions ran out 3-0 winners, with new Brazilian teenage striker Jô scoring two goals and his compatriot Vágner Love getting the other.

The 2006 season was made more arduous for all the participants by the promotion to the Premier League of Luch-Energia, from the naval port of Vladivostok located half a world – and a ten-hour flight - away from Moscow on the Sea of Japan. Spartak Nalchik, from slightly closer to home, took the other promotion place, replacing two teams from roughly the same neck of the woods, the North Ossetians of Alania Vladikavkaz and the Chechnyans of Terek Groznyi.

NATIONAL TEAM APPEARANCES 2005/06

Coach – Yuriy SYOMIN /(15/11/05) (Alexandr BORODYUK)

Player	DOB	Club	LAT	LIE	POR	LUX	SVK	Bra	Esp	Caps	Goals
Igor AKINFEEV	8/4/86	CSKA Moskva	G	G	G	G	G	G	G	10	-
Vadim YEVSEYEV	8/1/76	Lokomotiv Moskva	D							20	1
Aleksei BEREZUTSKIY	20/6/82	CSKA Moskva	D	D	D	D	D	D	D65	16	-
Sergei IGNASHEVICH	14/7/79	CSKA Moskva	D	D	D			D	D	23	3
Dmitriy SENNIKOV	24/6/76	Lokomotiv Moskva	D		D	D	D			26	-
Yevgeniy ALDONIN	22/1/80	CSKA Moskva	M	s66	M			M	M	24	-
Andrei KARYAKA	1/4/78	SL Benfica (POR)	M59							27	6
Dmitriy KHOKHLOV	22/12/75	Lokomotiv Moskva	M67							53	6
Diniyar BILYALETDINOV	27/2/85	Lokomotiv Moskva	M84	M	M		M58	s65	M90	6	-
Andrei ARSHAVIN	29/5/81	Zenit Sankt-Peterburg	A	A75	A88	A61	A	A	A46	18	7
Alexandr KERZHAKOV	27/11/82	Zenit Sankt-Peterburg	A	A82	A	A67	A67	A	A46	34	7
Vladimir BYSTROV	31/1/84	Spartak Moskva	s59							8	-
Igor SEMSHOV	6/4/78	Torpedo Moskva	s67			M				11	-
Dmitriy KIRICHENKO	17/1/77	FK Moskva	s84	s82		s67	s67		s90	12	4
Vasiliy BEREZUTSKIY	20/6/82	CSKA Moskva		D	D	D	D	D	D	12	-
Alexandr ANYUKOV	28/9/82	Zenit Sankt-Peterburg		D	s88	M	M83	D	M	15	1
Aleksei SMERTIN	1/5/75	Charlton Athletic (ENG) /Dinamo Moskva		M	M		M	M	M	54	-
Marat IZMAILOV	21/9/82	Lokomotiv Moskva		M	M73	M57	M			28	2
Roman PAVLYUCHENKO	15/12/81	Spartak Moskva		A66		s61	s83			4	1
Yegor TITOV	29/5/76	Spartak Moskva		s75					s46	38	7
Sergei SEMAK	27/2/76	Paris Saint-Germain (FRA)			s73	s57	s58			42	4
Dmitriy LOSKOV	13/2/74	Lokomotiv Moskva				M	M	M65	M	24	2
Rolan GUSEV	17/9/77	CSKA Moskva					M			31	1
Yuriy ZHIRKOV	20/8/83	CSKA Moskva						M		5	-
Dmitriy SYCHOV	26/10/83	Lokomotiv Moskva							s46	26	10
Konstantin ZYRYANOV	5/10/77	Torpedo Moskva							s65	1	-

Russia

EUROPEAN CUPS 2005/06

UEFA CHAMPIONS LEAGUE

LOKOMOTIV MOSKVA
2nd qualifying round RABOTNICKI KOMETAL SKOPJE (MAC)
A 1-1 *Sychov (90)*
Ovchinnikov, Yevseyev, Asatiani, Sennikov, Gurenko, Lima, Maminov, Khokhlov (Samedov 62), Bilyaletdinov, Kanyenda (Lebedenko 75), Sychov.
H 2-0 *Sychov (75), Asatiani (85)*
Ovchinnikov, Yevseyev, Asatiani, Pashinin, Gurenko, Samedov (Maminov 72), Lima (Sennikov 82), Bikey, Khokhlov, Bilyaletdinov (Lebedenko 89), Sychov.

3rd qualifying round SK RAPID WIEN (AUT)
A 1-1 *Samedov (10)*
Ovchinnikov, Gurenko, Asatiani, Bikey, Sennikov, Samedov (Pashinin 76), Lima, Maminov, Khokhlov (Yevseyev 90), Bilyaletdinov, Lebedenko (Ruopolo 80).
H 0-1
Ovchinnikov, Gurenko (Ruopolo 85), Pashinin, Asatiani, Sennikov, Yevseyev, Maminov, Samedov (Izmailov 57), Bilyaletdinov, Khokhlov, Lebedenko.

UEFA CUP

CSKA MOSKVA
1st round FC MIDTJYLLAND (DEN)
H 3-1 *Gusev (21), Daniel Carvalho (76, 79)*
Akinfeev, Ignashevich, Berezutskiy A., Daniel Carvalho, Gusev, Vágner Love (Aldonin 17), Odiah, Krasic, Dudu Cearense (Samodin 58; Salugin 87), Berezutskiy V., Rahimic.
A 3-1 *Daniel Carvalho (61, 77), Samodin (76)*
Akinfeev, Semberas, Ignashevich, Berezutskiy A., Daniel Carvalho (Salugin 79), Gusev, Odiah, Dudu Cearense (Taranov 84), Aldonin, Berezutskiy V. (Samodin 39), Rahimic.

2nd round Group F
Match 1 OLYMPIQUE MARSEILLE (FRA)
H 1-2 *Vágner Love (80)*
Akinfeev, Berezutskiy V. (Zhirkov 46), Berezutskiy A., Gusev, Aldonin, Ignashevich, Rahimic, Odiah, Krasic (Vágner Love 57), Rahimic, Samodin (Salugin 79).

Match 2 SC HEERENVEEN (HOL)
A 0-0
Akinfeev, Semberas, Ignashevich, Berezutskiy A., Daniel Carvalho, Gusev, Vágner Love (Samodin 80), Odiah, Zhirkov (Krasic 86), Aldonin, Rahimic.

Match 3 LEVSKI SOFIA (BUL)
H 2-1 *Vágner Love (49, 73)*
Akinfeev, Semberas, Ignashevich, Berezutskiy A., Aldonin, Rahimic, Odiah, Gusev (Krasic 87), Zhirkov (Berezutskiy V. 90), Daniel Carvalho (Dudu Cearense 79), Vágner Love.

Match 4 DINAMO BUCURESTI (ROM)
A 0-1
Akinfeev, Semberas (Krasic 75), Berezutskiy V., Berezutskiy A., Ignashevich, Odiah (Gusev 78), Aldonin, Rahimic, Daniel Carvalho, Zhirkov, Vágner Love.

KRYLYA SOVETOV SAMARA
2nd qualifying round FC BATE BORISOV (BLS)
H 2-0 *Baba Adamu (8), Husin (74p)*
Lobos, Bober, Kovba, Husin, Leilton, Temile (Skvernyuk 77), Nemov (Vinogradov 32), Bulyga, Shpakov (Bikmaev 60), Baba Adamu, Koroman.
A 2-0 *Bulyga (5), Vinogradov (50)*
Lobos, Bober, Kovba, Husin, Leilton, Solomatin, Nemov (Skvernyuk 77), Bulyga (Tetradze 66), Koroman, Shpakov (Vinogradov 46), Baba Adamu.

1st round AZ (HOL)
H 5-3 *Leilton (12), Baba Adamu (45), Kovba (50), Husin (62), Bober (90)*
Lobos, Bober, Booth, Dokhoyan, Husin, Solomatin, Kovba, Soava (Tetradze 68), Bulyga (Vinogradov 85), Leilton, Baba Adamu.
A 1-3 *Baba Adamu (16)*
Lobos, Bober, Booth, Husin, Dokhoyan, Solomatin, Kovba, Soava (Tetradze 75), Bulyga (Shpakov 87), Leilton (Temile 63), Baba Adamu.

ZENIT SANKT-PETERBURG
2nd qualifying round FC SUPERFUND PASCHING (AUT)
A 2-2 *Kerzhakov (15), Arshavin (73)*
Contofalsky, Flachbart, Hagen, Skrtel, Mares, Anyukov (Sumulikoski 88), Horshkov (Poskus 90), Radimov, Spivak (Vlasov 46), Arshavin, Kerzhakov.
H 1-1 *Spivak (12p)*
Contofalsky, Flachbart, Hagen, Skrtel, Mares, Anyukov (Vlasov 46), Horshkov, Radimov (Denisov 70), Spivak, Arshavin (Poskus 56), Kerzhakov.

1st round AEK (GRE)
H 0-0
Contofalsky, Anyukov, Vjestica, Hagen, Mares, Denisov, Horshkov (Poskus 54), Radimov, Spivak (Sirl 86), Arshavin (Vlasov 75), Kerzhakov.
A 1-0 *Arshavin (89)*
Contofalsky, Flachbart (Spivak 74), Vjestica, Hagen, Mares, Anyukov, Horshkov (Sumulikoski 90), Rdaimov (Denisov 85), Sirl, Arshavin, Kerzhakov.

2nd round Group H
Match 1 VITÓRIA GUIMARÃES (POR)
H 2-1 *Spivak (39p), Arshavin (54)*
Contofalsky, Anyukov, Hagen, Skrtel, Mares (Flachbart 40), Radimov, Denisov (Sumulikoski 78), Denisov, Spivak, Kerzhakov, Arshavin (Poskus 67).

Match 2 BOLTON WANDERERS (ENG)
A 0-1
Contofalsky, Flachbart, Hagen, Vjestica, Skrtel (Horshkov 25), Anyukov, Sumulikoski, Denisov, Vlasov (Kozlov 90), Kerzhakov, Arshavin.

Match 3 SEVILLA FC (ESP)
H 2-1 *Kerzhakov (11, 89)*
Contofalsky, Flachbart, Hagen, Krizanac, Mares, Anyukov, Horshkov, Radimov (Denisov 67), Spivak (Vlasov 88), Arshavin (Sumulikoski 90), Kerzhakov.

Match 4 BESIKTAS (TUR)
A 1-1 *Horshkov (29)*
Contofalsky, Flachbart, Hagen, Krizanac, Mares, Anyukov (Vlasov 90), Horshkov, Radimov (Denisov 64), Spivak, Arshavin (Sumulikoski 68), Kerzhakov.

3rd round ROSENBORG BK (NOR)
A 2-0 *Arshavin (22), Kerzhakov (32)*
Contofalsky, Skrtel, Hagen, Krizanac, Mares, Anyukov, Sirl, Radimov, Horshkov (Sumulikoski 84), Spivak, Arshavin, Kerzhakov (Denisov 84).
H 2-1 *Kerzhakov (55), Denisov (87)*
Contofalsky (Malefeyev 24), Rdaimov, Skrtel, Krzanac, Spivak (Hyun 66), Sirl, Arshavin, Kerzhakov, Hagen, Anyukov, Horshkov (Denisov 74).

4th round OLYMPIQUE MARSEILLE (FRA)
A 1-0 *Arshavin (51)*
Malafeyev, Skrtel, Hagen, Krizanac, Anyukov, Sirl, Radimov, Spivak (Trifonov 63), Denisov (Hyun 90), Arshavin (Poskus 90), Kerzhakov.
H 1-1 *Kerzhakov (69)*
Malafeyev, Anyukov, Vjestica, Hagen, Krizanac, Horshkov (Sumulikoski 80), Radimov, Sirl (Mares 63), Denisov, Kerzhakov, Arshavin.

Quarter-finals SEVILLA FC (ESP)
A 1-4 *Kerzhakov (45)*

Russia

LEAGUE RESULTS/SCORERS/APPEARANCES/GOALS 2005

Malafeyev, Anyukov, Hagen, Krizanac, Skrtel, Radimov, Sumulikoski (Horshkov 89), Sirl (Mares 76), Denisov (Spivak 29), Arshavin, Kerzhakov.
H 1-1 *Hyun (50)*
Malafeyev, Anyukov, Krizanac, Skrtel, Mares, Hyun (Kozhanov 58), Radimov, Vlasov, Sirl (Trifonov 79), Poskus, Kerzhakov.

LOKOMOTIV MOSKVA

1st round SK BRANN (NOR)
A 2-1 *Ruopolo (70), Lebedenko (76)*
Ovchinnikov, Yevseyev (Sennikov 31), Pashinin, Asatiani, Gurenko, Samedov, Maminov (Bikey 46), Khokhlov (Lebedenko 46), Bilyaletdinov, Izmailov, Ruopolo.
H 3-2 *Loskov (61), Asatiani (77), Bilyaletdinov (90)*
Ovchinnikov, Gurenko, Sennikov, Asatiani, Kruglov, Lima, Izmailov (Bikey 69), Maminov (Khokhlov 46), Loskov, Bilyaletdinov, Ruopolo (Lebedenko 79).

2nd round Group B
Match 1 RCD ESPANYOL (ESP)
H 0-1
Ovchinnikov, Bugayev (Ruopolo 69), Pashinin, Sennikov, Gurenko, Lima, Bikey, Bilyaletdinov, Izmailov, Asatiani, Lebedenko.

Match 2 PALERMO (ITA)
A 0-0
Ovchinnikov, Yevseyev, Bikey (Gurenko 77), Asatiani, Sennikov, Lima, Maminov, Khokhlov, Izmailov, Bilyaletdinov, Ruopolo (Lebedenko 90).

Match 3 BRØNDBY IF (DEN)
H 4-2 *Loskov (60, 64, 84), Lebedenko (63)*
Ovchinnikov, Yevseyev, Bikey, Pashinin, Sennikov, Gurenko, Samedov (Ruopolo 32), Asatiani, Loskov, Bilyaletdinov, Lebedenko (Bugayev 90).

Match 4 MACCABI PETACH TIKVA (ISR)
A 4-0 *Loskov (27), Lebedenko (47, 48), Ruopolo (52)*
Polyakov, Yevseyev, Bikey, Sennikov, Pashinin, Gurenko (Bugayev 80), Loskov, Asatiani (Omeliyanchuk 86), Bilyaletdinov (Kruglov 83), Lebedenko, Ruopolo.

3rd round SEVILLA FC (ESP)
H 0-1
Polyakov, Spahic, Pashinin, Asatiani, Gurenko, Bikey, Kingston (Maminov 60), Bilyaletdinov (Izmailov 81), Samedov, Loskov, Parks (Lebedenko 46).
A 0-2
Polyakov, Gurenko, Asatiani, Pashinin, Parks 68), Spahic, Bikey, Maminov, Samedov, Bilyaletdinov (Izmailov 61), Loskov, Lebedenko.

TOP GOALSCORERS 2005

14	Dmitriy KIRICHENKO (FC Moskva)
13	DERLEI (Dinamo Moskva)
12	Igor SEMSHOV (Torpedo Moskva)
11	Roman PAVLYUCHENKO (Spartak Moskva)
10	Ivica OLIC (CSKA Moskva)
	Alexandr PANOV (Torpedo Moskva)
9	Andrei ARSHAVIN (Zenit Sankt-Peterburg)
	Jambulad BAZAYEV (Alania Vladikavkaz)
8	Diniyar BILYALETDINOV (Lokomotiv Moskva)
7	Roman ADAMOV (Terek Groznyi)
	Tomás CÍZEK (Rubin Kazan)
	Andriy HUSIN (Krylya Sovetov Samara)
	Alexandr KERZHAKOV (Zenit Sankt-Peterburg)
	VÁGNER LOVE (CSKA Moskva)
	Maxim BUZNIKIN (FC Rostov)

ALANIA VLADIKAVKAZ

Coach – Bakhva Tedeyev; (3/4/05) Edgar Gess; (28/6/05) Itzhak Shum (ISR); (27/9/05) (Alexandr Yanovskiy)

2005

Date	Opponent		Score	Scorers
12/3	Krylya Sovetov Samara	a	0-2	
20/3	Zenit Sankt-Peterburg	h	0-3	
2/4	Torpedo Moskva	a	0-3	
10/4	Shinnik Yaroslavl	h	1-1	Dadu
16/4	Saturn Ramenskoe	a	1-3	Gogniyev
23/4	Spartak Moskva	h	2-1	Dadu, Bazayev J.
30/4	FK Moskva	a	0-1	
15/5	Rubin Kazan	h	4-3	Bazayev J. 2, Bazayev G., Tudor
22/5	Amkar Perm	a	0-0	
28/5	FK Rostov	h	0-0	
12/6	Dinamo Moskva	a	0-1	
18/6	Lokomotiv Moskva	a	0-3	
25/6	Terek Groznyi	h	1-0	Bazayev J.
2/7	Tom Tomsk	a	0-0	
9/7	CSKA Moskva	h	1-1	Daraselia
17/7	Krylya Sovetov Samara	h	2-0	Bazayev J., Dadu
23/7	Zenit Sankt-Peterburg	a	1-3	Tudor
31/7	Torpedo Moskva	h	2-2	Demetradze 2
6/8	Shinnik Yaroslavl	a	0-1	
21/8	Saturn Ramenskoe	h	1-0	Dadu
27/8	Spartak Moskva	a	1-5	Bazayev J. (p)
10/9	FK Moskva	h	0-2	
17/9	Rubin Kazan	a	2-4	Bazayev J. 2 (1p)
25/9	Amkar Perm	h	0-1	
2/10	FK Rostov	a	0-1	
16/10	Dinamo Moskva	h	2-4	Gogniyev, Dadu (p)
23/10	Lokomotiv Moskva	h	0-0	
30/10	Terek Groznyi	a	2-1	Bazayev J., Gogniyev
6/11	Tom Tomsk	h	1-2	Dadu (p)
19/11	CSKA Moskva	a	3-4	Gogniyev 3

No	Name	Nat	Pos	Aps	(s)	Gls
7	Alan AGAYEV		D	25	(1)	
14	Amzor AILAROV		A		(1)	
49	Ruslan ALBOROV		A		(1)	
6	Nerijus BARASA	LIT	D	7	(2)	
17	Giorgi BAZAYEV		M	24	(3)	1
18	Jambulat BAZAYEV		M	28		9
21	Elvin BESHIRI	ALB	D	6		
50	Alberto BLANCO	PAN	M	2		
88	Vladimir BURDULI	GEO	M	9	(5)	
15	Justice CHRISTOPHER	NGA	M	4	(3)	
11	Serghei DADU	MOL	A	16	(11)	6
10	Vitali DARASELIA	GEO	M	17	(2)	1
99	Giorgi DEMETRADZE	GEO	A	6	(5)	2
24	Slavoljub DJORDJEVIC	SCG	D	7	(1)	
4	Rakhmatullo FUZAILOV		D	12		
77	Spartak GOGNIYEV		A	21	(7)	6
60	Vladan GRUJIC	BOS	D	26		
47	Levani GVAZAVA	GEO	M		(6)	
14	Leopoldo JIMÉNEZ	VEN	D	9		
23	Jaba KANKAVA	GEO	M	6	(6)	
9	Artur KUSOV		M		(2)	
16	Daviti KVIRKVELIA	GEO	D	12	(2)	
90	Vladislav LUNGU	MOL	M	1	(1)	
30	Thiago MACIEL	BRA	D	9		
3	Isaac OKORONKWO	NGA	D	18	(2)	

Russia

FINAL LEAGUE TABLE 2005

		Pld	Home					Away					Total					Pts
			W	D	L	F	A	W	D	L	F	A	W	D	L	F	A	
1	CSKA Moskva	30	12	3	0	31	8	6	5	4	17	12	18	8	4	48	20	62
2	Spartak Moskva	30	9	3	3	28	13	7	5	3	19	13	16	8	6	47	26	56
3	Lokomotiv Moskva	30	8	6	1	25	9	6	8	1	16	9	14	14	2	41	18	56
4	Rubin Kazan	30	9	6	0	25	9	5	3	7	20	22	14	9	7	45	31	51
5	FK Moskva	30	9	2	4	20	11	5	6	4	16	15	14	8	8	36	26	50
6	Zenit Sankt-Peterburg	30	9	5	1	33	13	4	5	6	12	13	13	10	7	45	26	49
7	Torpedo Moskva	30	8	3	4	21	15	4	6	5	16	18	12	9	9	37	33	45
8	Dinamo Moskva	30	7	2	6	16	14	5	0	10	20	32	12	2	16	36	46	38
9	Shinnik Yaroslavl	30	8	3	4	19	17	1	8	6	7	14	9	11	10	26	31	38
10	Tom Tomsk	30	6	5	4	20	15	3	5	7	8	18	9	10	11	28	33	37
11	Saturn Ramenskoe	30	6	5	4	15	11	2	4	9	8	14	8	9	13	23	25	33
12	Amkar Perm	30	5	8	2	14	9	2	4	9	11	27	7	12	11	25	36	33
13	FK Rostov	30	6	4	5	13	13	2	3	10	13	28	8	7	15	26	41	31
14	Krylya Sovetov Samara	30	6	5	4	19	13	1	3	11	10	31	7	8	15	29	44	29
15	Alania Vladikavkaz	30	4	6	5	17	21	1	2	12	10	32	5	8	17	27	53	23
16	Terek Groznyi	30	3	3	9	11	21	2	2	11	9	29	5	5	20	20	50	14

N.B. Terek Groznyi – 6 pts deducted.

2	Artur PAGAYEV		D	3	
55	Ruslan PIMENOV		A	4	(2)
22	Dejan RADIC	SCG	G	26	
56	Giorgi SHASHIASHVILI	GEO	M	4	(3)
20	Iulian TAMES	ROM	M	2	(1)
8	Cristian TUDOR	ROM	A	4	(11)	2
44	Nikolai TZYGAN		G	4	(2)
13	Darius ZUTAUTAS	LIT	D	18	

AMKAR PERM
Coach – Sergei Aborin

2005
Date	Opponent	h/a	Score	Scorers
12/3	Shinnik Yaroslavl	a	1-1	Olexici
20/3	Saturn Ramenskoe	a	0-2	
3/4	Spartak Moskva	a	1-1	Shutov
10/4	FK Moskva	h	0-0	
16/4	Rubin Kazan	a	0-2	
23/4	Lokomotiv Moskva	a	1-1	Paramonov
1/5	FK Rostov	h	1-0	Pyatibratov (p)
14/5	Dinamo Moskva	a	2-1	Lincar, Pyatibratov (p)
22/5	Alania Vladikavkaz	h	0-0	
28/5	Terek Groznyi	a	2-2	Kobenko, Subasic
12/6	Tom Tomsk	h	0-0	
19/6	CSKA Moskva	a	1-3	Didenko
26/6	Krylya Sovetov Samara	h	1-1	Ziyati
2/7	Zenit Sankt-Peterburg	a	1-5	og (Horshkov)
9/7	Torpedo Moskva	h	0-0	
17/7	Shinnik Yaroslavl	h	0-0	
23/7	Saturn Ramenskoe	h	3-2	Kushev, Belorukov, Volkov
30/7	Spartak Moskva	h	0-0	
7/8	FK Moskva	a	0-1	
21/8	Rubin Kazan	h	1-0	Sargsyan
28/8	Lokomotiv Moskva	h	3-4	Kushev 2, Leonchenko (p)
10/9	FK Rostov	a	0-2	
17/9	Dinamo Moskva	h	4-1	Belorukov, Makarov, Volkov 2
25/9	Alania Vladikavkaz	a	1-0	Volkov
2/10	Terek Groznyi	h	0-0	
15/10	Tom Tomsk	a	0-3	
23/10	CSKA Moskva	h	0-1	
30/10	Krylya Sovetov Samara	a	0-1	
6/11	Zenit Sankt-Peterburg	h	1-0	Volkov
19/11	Torpedo Moskva	a	1-2	Lincar (p)

No	Name	Nat	Pos	Aps	(s)	Gls
77	Ildar AKHMETZYANOV		D	2	(1)	
33	Pavel ALIKIN		D		(1)	
6	Igor BAKHTIN		M	11	(8)	
21	Dmitriy BELORUKOV		D	18	(5)	2
32	Ivan CHERENCHIKOV		M	5		
19	Anatoliy DIDENKO	UKR	M	8	(5)	1
34	Maxim FILIPPOV		A		(1)	
15	Algis JANKAUSKAS	LIT	D	1	(2)	
10	Andrei KOBENKO		M	15	(4)	1
29	Martin KUSHEV	BUL	A	7		3
3	Andrei LAVRIK	BLS	M	24	(3)	
17	Vladimir LEONCHENKO		M	16	(5)	1
20	Ivan LEVENETS		G	14		
16	Eric LINCAR	ROM	M	17	(5)	2
11	Dmitriy MAKAROV		A	8	(6)	1
4	Ghenadie OLEXICI	MOL	D	20	(3)	1
9	Konstantin PARAMONOV		A	5		1
24	Aleksei POPOV		D	20		
2	Maxim POVOROV		D	17	(1)	
7	Dmitriy PYATIBRATOV		D	15		2
27	Albert SARGSYAN	ARM	D	14	(2)	1
18	Sergei SAVOCHKIN		M	6	(2)	
5	Oleksandr SHUTOV	UKR	M	14	(10)	1
14	Zahari SIRAKOV	BUL	D	24	(1)	
12	Aleksei STEPANOV		G	16		
26	Branimir SUBASIC	SCG	A	3	(3)	1
8	Sergei VOLKOV		A	19	(4)	5
28	Evgeni YORDANOV	BUL	A	2	(3)	
99	Noureddine ZIYATI	MAR	M	9	(14)	1

CSKA MOSKVA
Coach – Valeriy Gazzayev

2005
Date	Opponent	h/a	Score	Scorers
13/3	Terek Groznyi	h	3-0	Olic, Daniel Carvalho, Rahimic
20/3	Tom Tomsk	a	0-0	
3/4	Lokomotiv Moskva	h	0-0	

Russia

Date	Opponent	H/A	Score	Scorers
10/4	Krylya Sovetov Samara	h	5-0	Krasic, Olic 2 (1p), Pravosud, Laizans
17/4	Zenit Sankt-Peterburg	a	0-1	
22/5	Spartak Moskva	a	3-1	Aldonin, Berezutskiy V., Olic
12/6	Rubin Kazan	a	0-1	
15/6	Saturn Ramenskoe	h	1-0	Gusev
19/6	Amkar Perm	h	3-1	Krasic, Vágner Love 2
22/6	Shinnik Yaroslavl	a	1-1	Zhirkov
25/6	FK Rostov	a	2-0	Olic 2 (2p)
2/7	Dinamo Moskva	h	2-0	Dudu Cearense, Olic (p)
9/7	Alania Vladikavkaz	a	1-1	Vágner Love
17/7	Terek Groznyi	a	0-1	
20/7	Torpedo Moskva	h	2-0	Berezutskiy V., Odiah
24/7	Tom Tomsk	h	2-0	Ignashevich, Vágner Love
30/7	Lokomotiv Moskva	a	2-3	Berezutskiy A., Olic
3/8	FK Moskva	h	1-1	Olic
6/8	Krylya Sovetov Samara	a	2-2	Ignashevich, Gusev
10/8	Torpedo Moskva	a	2-0	Gusev, Olic
21/8	Zenit Sankt-Peterburg	h	1-1	Ignashevich (p)
10/9	Shinnik Yaroslavl	h	2-0	Gusev, Dudu Cearense
19/9	Saturn Ramenskoe	a	1-0	Dudu Cearense
24/9	Spartak Moskva	h	1-0	Daniel Carvalho
2/10	FK Moskva	a	0-0	
16/10	Rubin Kazan	h	2-1	Odiah, Ignashevich
23/10	Amkar Perm	a	1-0	Daniel Carvalho
30/10	FK Rostov	h	2-1	Zhirkov, Vágner Love
6/11	Dinamo Moskva	a	2-1	Berezutskiy A., Daniel Carvalho
19/11	Alania Vladikavkaz	h	4-3	Ignashevich, Salugin, Vágner Love 2
21/5	FK Rostov	a	3-0	Cicero, Derlei 2 (1p)
28/5	Lokomotiv Moskva	a	1-4	Derlei
12/6	Alania Vladikavkaz	h	1-0	Derlei
18/6	Terek Groznyi	a	1-0	Yashin
26/6	Tom Tomsk	h	0-0	
2/7	CSKA Moskva	a	0-2	
10/7	Krylya Sovetov Samara	h	3-1	Derlei 3 (1p)
17/7	Zenit Sankt-Peterburg	h	1-2	Danny Alves
24/7	Torpedo Moskva	a	1-2	og (Spahic)
31/7	Shinnik Yaroslavl	a	1-2	Derlei
6/8	Saturn Ramenskoe	a	1-0	Jorge Ribeiro
21/8	Spartak Moskva	h	0-1	
27/8	FK Moskva	a	1-2	Jorge Ribeiro
11/9	Rubin Kazan	h	3-1	Maniche, Derlei 2
17/9	Amkar Perm	a	1-4	Derlei (p)
25/9	FK Rostov	h	2-1	Enakarhire, Derlei
2/10	Lokomotiv Moskva	h	0-0	
16/10	Alania Vladikavkaz	a	4-2	Tochilin, Derlei, Jorge Ribeiro, Maniche
23/10	Terek Groznyi	h	0-1	
30/10	Tom Tomsk	a	2-3	Danny Alves, Cicero
6/11	CSKA Moskva	h	1-2	Kolodin
19/11	Krylya Sovetov Samara	a	1-0	Danny Alves

No	Name	Nat	Pos	Aps	(s)	Gls
35	Igor AKINFEEV		G	29		
22	Yevgeniy ALDONIN		M	16	(13)	1
6	Aleksei BEREZUTSKIY		D	27		2
24	Vasiliy BEREZUTSKIY		D	27		2
7	DANIEL da Silva CARVALHO	BRA	A	24	(5)	4
20	DUDU CEARENSE	BRA	M	12	(9)	3
10	Osmar Daniel FERREYRA	ARG	M		(2)	
8	Rolan GUSEV		M	17	(8)	4
4	Sergei IGNASHEVICH		D	21	(1)	5
17	Milos KRASIC	SCG	M	19	(7)	2
19	Jurijs LAIZANS	LAT	M	1	(2)	1
1	Veniamin MANDRYKIN		G	1		
15	Chidi ODIAH	NGA	D	23	(4)	2
9	Ivica OLIC	CRO	A	19	(1)	10
38	Sergei PRAVOSUD		A	4	(1)	1
25	Elver RAHIMIC	BOS	M	30		
40	Alexandr SALUGIN		A	1	(4)	1
13	Sergei SAMODIN		A	3	(9)	
2	Deividas SEMBERAS	LIT	D	23	(5)	
28	Bohdan SHERSHUN	UKR	D		(1)	
39	Ivan TARANOV		M		(1)	
11	VÁGNER "LOVE" de Sousa	BRA	A	16	(5)	7
18	Yuriy ZHIRKOV		M	17	(3)	2

DINAMO MOSKVA
Coach – Oleg Romantsev; (16/5/05) (Andrei Kobelev); (21/7/05) Ivo Wortmann (BRA); (24/10/05) (Andrei Kobelev); (7/11/05) Yuriy Syomin

2005

Date	Opponent	H/A	Score	Scorers
12/3	Zenit Sankt-Peterburg	a	1-4	Frechaut
20/3	Torpedo Moskva	h	2-1	Danny Alves, Beschastnykh
2/4	Shinnik Yaroslavl	h	1-0	Yashin
9/4	Saturn Ramenskoe	h	1-0	Beschastnykh
17/4	Spartak Moskva	a	1-5	Jorge Ribeiro
23/4	FK Moskva	h	0-2	
30/4	Rubin Kazan	a	1-2	Bulykin
14/5	Amkar Perm	h	1-2	Cicero

No	Name	Nat	Pos	Aps	(s)	Gls
5	Radoslav BATAK	SCG	D	7		
1	Roman BEREZOVSKIY	ARM	G	12		
20	Vladimir BESCHASTNYKH		A	7	(3)	2
10	Dmitriy BULYKIN		A	5	(3)	1
19	CÍCERO Sanches Semedo	BRA	M	6	(5)	3
74	Francisco Costa "COSTINHA"	POR	M	10		
2	Alexandru COVALENCO	MOL	D	7	(1)	
10	DANNY ALVES Gomes	POR	M	27		4
11	Vanderlei "DERLEI" Fernandes da Silva	BRA	A	22	(1)	13
9	Andrei DYATEL		M		(3)	
82	Joseph ENAKARHIRE	NGA	D	9		1
23	Nuno FRECHAUT Barreto	POR	D	14	(1)	1
7	Baffour GYAN	GHA	A	2	(7)	
4	Michal HANEK	SVK	D	6	(2)	
16	JORGE RIBEIRO de Oliveira Miguel	POR	D	27		4
21	Zydrunas KARCEMARSKAS	LIT	G	1		
27	Denis KOLODIN		D	11	(2)	1
39	Dmitriy KOMBAROV		M	1		
33	German KUTARBA		M		(2)	
15	Sergei KUZNETSOV		M	12	(2)	
32	Maxym LEVYTSKYI	UKR	G	6		
66	LUÍS Fernando Graça LOUREIRO	POR	M	4		
8	Nuno Ribeiro "MANICHE"	POR	M	12		2
13	Pascal MENDY	SEN	D	3	(1)	
26	Stanislav MURYGIN		A	1	(1)	
77	NUNO Simões do Espirito Santo	POR	G	11		
17	Patrick OVIE	NGA	D	5		
25	Dmitriy POLOVINCHUK		M	17	(5)	
99	Andrejs PROHORENKOVS	LAT	A	1		
22	Maxim ROMASHCHENKO	BLS	M	6		
81	Yourkas SEITARIDIS	GRE	D	8		
42	Valeriy SOROKIN		M		(2)	
6	Nenad TANASIJEVIC	SCG	M	22	(2)	
3	Aleksandr TOCHILIN		D	18	(1)	1
24	Oleg SHKABARA	BLS	M	9	(7)	
18	Sergei YASHIN		M	21	(1)	2

KRYLYA SOVETOV SAMARA
Coach – Gadzhi Gadzhiyev

2005

Date	Opponent	H/A	Score	Scorers
12/3	Alania Vladikavkaz	h	2-0	Booth, Poskus
20/3	Terek Groznyi	a	0-2	

Russia

Date	Opponent	H/A	Score	Scorers
3/4	Tom Tomsk	h	1-1	Karyaka
10/4	CSKA Moskva	a	0-5	
16/4	Lokomotiv Moskva	h	0-0	
23/4	Zenit Sankt-Peterburg	h	3-0	Kolodin, Husin, og (Mares)
30/4	Torpedo Moskva	a	0-0	
15/5	Shinnik Yaroslavl	h	1-0	Karyaka (p)
22/5	Saturn Ramenskoe	a	1-1	Bober
28/5	Spartak Moskva	h	1-3	Bober
12/6	FK Moskva	a	1-0	Husin (p)
19/6	Rubin Kazan	h	2-2	Husin, Koroman
22/6	Lokomotiv Moskva	a	0-1	
26/6	Amkar Perm	a	1-1	Husin
2/7	FK Rostov	h	1-1	Bulyga
10/7	Dinamo Moskva	a	1-3	Bulyga
17/7	Alania Vladikavkaz	a	0-2	
23/7	Terek Groznyi	h	0-1	
31/7	Tom Tomsk	a	2-4	Husin 2 (1p)
6/8	CSKA Moskva	h	2-2	Husin (p), Baba Adamu
28/8	Zenit Sankt-Peterburg	a	1-4	Baba Adamu (p)
10/9	Torpedo Moskva	a	0-1	
18/9	Shinnik Yaroslavl	a	1-3	Topic
24/9	Saturn Ramenskoe	h	1-0	Bulyga
2/10	Spartak Moskva	a	0-1	
16/10	FK Moskva	h	4-1	Topic 3 (1p), Bober
23/10	Rubin Kazan	a	1-2	Baba Adamu
30/10	Amkar Perm	h	1-0	Baba Adamu
6/11	FK Rostov	a	1-2	Topic
19/11	Dinamo Moskva	h	0-1	

No	Name	Nat	Pos	Aps	(s)	Gls
2	Alexandr ANYUKOV		D	15		
26	Baxtiyor ASHURMATOV	UZB	D		(1)	
8	Armandu BABA ADAMU	GHA	A	10	(1)	4
4	Nerijus BARASA	LIT	D		(4)	
5	Cosmin BARCAUAN	ROM	D	1	(1)	
51	Marat BIKMOYEV	UZB	M	2	(3)	
7	Anton BOBER		M	20	(4)	3
22	Matthew Paul BOOTH	RSA	D	18		1
10	Vitaliy BULYGA	BLS	A	10	(18)	3
14	Karen DOKHOYAN	ARM	A	19	(1)	
56	Mahach GADJIYEV		M		(1)	
15	Andriy HUSIN	UKR	M	22	(4)	7
8	JOSÉ de SOUSA Ivanildo	BRA	D	1	(3)	
5	Andrei KARYAKA		M	13		2
25	Laryea KINGSTON	GHA	M	12		
55	Denis KOLODIN		D	14		1
23	Ognjen KOROMAN	SCG	M	15	(3)	1
9	Denis KOVBA	BLS	M	23	(2)	
3	LEÍLTON Silva dos Santos	BRA	D	16	(5)	
1	Eduardo LOBOS Landueta	CHL	G	28		
41	Alexandr MAKAROV		G	2		
24	Pyotr NEMOV		M	4	(4)	
4	Patrick OVIE	NGA	D	12		
32	Robertas POSKUS	LIT	A	11	(1)	1
33	Ivan SHPAKOV		A	5	(9)	
19	Aleksei SKVERNYUK	BLS	M		(5)	
2	Costin Florin SOAVA	ROM	D	6		
6	Andrei SOLOMATIN		D	9		
11	Omonigho TEMILE	NGA	M	11	(6)	
31	Omari TETRADZE		D	7	(5)	
75	Marko TOPIC	BOS	A	8	(1)	5
17	Sergei VINOGRADOV		M	16	(7)	

LOKOMOTIV MOSKVA
Coach – Yuriy Syomin; (19/4/05) Vladimir Eshtrekov

2005

Date	Opponent	H/A	Score	Scorers
12/3	Tom Tomsk	h	2-0	Lebedenko, Loskov
19/3	FK Moskva	h	0-0	
3/4	CSKA Moskva	a	0-0	
10/4	Rubin Kazan	h	1-0	Sychov
16/4	Krylya Sovetov Samara	a	0-0	
23/4	Amkar Perm	h	1-1	Izmailov
30/4	Zenit Sankt-Peterburg	a	1-1	Loskov (p)
14/5	FK Rostov	h	4-0	Yevseyev, Loskov 2 (1p), Khokhlov
22/5	Torpedo Moskva	h	1-0	Izmailov
28/5	Dinamo Moskva	h	4-1	Loskov, Lebedenko 2, Izmailov
11/6	Shinnik Yaroslavl	a	2-0	og (Starostyak), Loskov
15/6	Zenit Sankt-Peterburg	h	0-0	
18/6	Alania Vladikavkaz	h	3-0	Bilyaletdinov, Lebedenko, Sychov
22/6	Krylya Sovetov Samara	h	1-0	Bilyaletdinov
26/6	Saturn Ramenskoe	a	0-0	
3/7	Terek Groznyi	h	4-0	Bilyaletdinov, Yevseyev (p), Asatiani, Sychov
9/7	Spartak Moskva	a	2-1	Sychov, Bilyaletdinov
17/7	Tom Tomsk	a	0-0	
23/7	FK Moskva	a	1-0	Sychov
30/7	CSKA Moskva	h	3-2	Khokhlov, Sychov, Pashinin
6/8	Rubin Kazan	a	1-3	Lebedenko
28/8	Amkar Perm	a	4-3	Bilyaletdinov 2 (2p), Izmailov, Lebedenko
18/9	FK Rostov	a	1-1	Sennikov
24/9	Torpedo Moskva	h	0-3	
2/10	Dinamo Moskva	a	0-0	
16/10	Shinnik Yaroslavl	h	0-0	
23/10	Alania Vladikavkaz	a	0-0	
29/10	Saturn Ramenskoe	h	1-1	Bilyaletdinov
6/11	Terek Groznyi	a	3-0	Bilyaletdinov, Khokhlov, Asatiani
19/11	Spartak Moskva	h	1-1	Asatiani

No	Name	Nat	Pos	Aps	(s)	Gls
30	Malkhaz ASATIANI	GEO	M	28		3
32	Mikheil ASHVETIA	GEO	A	1	(1)	
2	André BIKEY	CMR	D	6	(3)	
63	Diniyar BILYALETDINOV		M	24	(5)	8
9	Aleksei BUGAYEV		D	5	(3)	
15	Maxim BUZNIKIN		A		(2)	
55	Giorgi CHELIDZE	GEO	A	1	(1)	
41	Sergei GURENKO	BLS	D	26		
7	Marat IZMAILOV		M	13	(3)	4
6	Essau Boxer KANYENDA	MWI	A	2	(1)	
28	Dmitriy KHOKHLOV		M	23	(7)	3
3	Dmitri KRUGLOV	EST	D	3	(5)	
33	Igor LEBEDENKO		A	13	(10)	6
5	Francisco Gouvinho LIMA	BRA	M	26		
10	Dmitriy LOSKOV		M	20	(2)	6
8	Vladimir MAMINOV	UZB	M	10	(10)	
1	Sergei OVCHINNIKOV		G	29		
4	Sergei OMELIYANCHUK		D	9	(4)	
52	Winston PARKS	CRC	A		(5)	
14	Oleg PASHININ		D	12	(6)	1
	Ruslan PIMENOV		A		(1)	
21	Aleksei POLYAKOV		G	1		
31	Francesco RUOPOLO	ITA	A	4	(3)	
40	Alexandr SAMEDOV		M	7	(2)	
17	Dmitriy SENNIKOV		D	29		1
11	Dmitriy SYCHOV		A	21		6
16	Vadim YEVSEYEV		D	17	(4)	2

FK MOSKVA
Coach – Valeriy Petrakov; (14/7/05) Leonid Slutskiy

2005

Date	Opponent	H/A	Score	Scorers
12/3	Spartak Moskva	a	2-0	Jop, Kirichenko

Russia

19/3	Lokomotiv Moskva	a	0-0	
2/4	Rubin Kazan	h	0-1	
10/4	Amkar Perm	a	0-0	
16/4	FK Rostov	h	1-0	Melyoshin
23/4	Dinamo Moskva	a	2-0	Bracamonte, Kirichenko
30/4	Alania Vladikavkaz	h	1-0	Bracamonte
15/5	Terek Groznyi	a	0-0	
21/5	Tom Tomsk	h	4-1	Bracamonte, Kirichenko 3 (2p)
12/6	Krylya Sovetov Samara	h	0-1	
19/6	Zenit Sankt-Peterburg	a	2-2	Rebeja, Gorawski
25/6	Torpedo Moskva	h	1-1	Kirichenko
2/7	Shinnik Yaroslavl	a	1-0	Kuzmin
9/7	Saturn Ramenskoe	h	0-1	
16/7	Spartak Moskva	h	3-1	Kirichenko 2, Bracamonte
23/7	Lokomotiv Moskva	h	0-1	
30/7	Rubin Kazan	a	1-1	Kuzmin
3/8	CSKA Moskva	a	1-1	Bracamonte
7/8	Amkar Perm	h	1-0	Kirichenko (p)
21/8	FK Rostov	a	0-1	
27/8	Dinamo Moskva	h	2-1	Kirichenko 2 (1p)
10/9	Alania Vladikavkaz	a	2-0	Melyoshin, Godunok
17/9	Terek Groznyi	h	2-1	Kirichenko 2
24/9	Tom Tomsk	a	2-3	Kuzmin, Melyoshin
2/10	CSKA Moskva	h	0-0	
16/10	Krylya Sovetov Samara	a	1-4	Golubov
23/10	Zenit Sankt-Peterburg	h	2-0	Rebeja, Kirichenko
29/10	Torpedo Moskva	a	0-2	
6/11	Shinnik Yaroslavl	h	3-2	Gorawski, Melyoshin 2 (1p)
19/11	Saturn Ramenskoe	a	2-1	Golubov 2

No	Name	Nat	Pos	Aps	(s)	Gls
28	Armandu BABA ADAMU	GHA	A	1	(5)	
24	Ruslan BALTIYEV	KAZ	M	1	(2)	
13	Maxym BELETSKYI	UKR	M	9	(4)	
19	Héctor Andrés BRACAMONTE	ARG	A	24	(1)	5
11	Budun BUDUNOV		M	1	(14)	
34	Vyacheslav DANILIN		M		(7)	
3	Rolandas DZIAUKSTAS	LIT	M	3	(2)	
17	Stanton FREDERICKS	RSA	A	4	(7)	
2	Dmitriy GODUNOK		D	27		1
35	Dmitriy GOLUBOV		A	4	(1)	3
42	Pavel GOLYSHEV		M		(1)	
7	Damian GORAWSKI	POL	M	12	(7)	2
77	Stanislav IVANOV	MOL	M	22	(6)	
25	Mariusz JOP	POL	D	26	(1)	1
10	Dmitriy KIRICHENKO		A	25	(1)	14
22	Oleg KUZMIN		D	28		3
20	Aleksei MELYOSHIN		M	27		5
7	Andrei MOVSESIYAN		A	5	(9)	
32	Kirill NABABKIN		D	6	(1)	
18	Kirill ORLOV		D		(1)	
5	Radu REBEJA	MOL	M	28		2
8	Pompiliu STOICA	ROM	D	19	(8)	
99	Jerry-Christian TCHUISSE		D	28		
30	Yuriy ZHEVNOV	BLS	G	30		

FK ROSTOV
Coach – Gennadiy Styopushkin; (17/4/05) Paul Ashworth (ENG); (3/5/05) Gennadiy Styopushkin; (19/7/05) Valeriy Petrakov; (11/8/05) Sergei Balakhnin

2005

13/3	Torpedo Moskva	a	1-3	Mnguni
20/3	Shinnik Yaroslavl	h	2-2	Bidoudane, Kanyenda
3/4	Saturn Ramenskoe	a	0-2	
10/4	Spartak Moskva	h	0-1	
16/4	FK Moskva	a	0-1	
23/4	Rubin Kazan	h	1-1	Kanyenda

1/5	Amkar Perm	a	0-1	
14/5	Lokomotiv Moskva	a	0-4	
21/5	Dinamo Moskva	h	0-3	
28/5	Alania Vladikavkaz	a	0-0	
12/6	Terek Groznyi	h	1-0	Osinov (p)
18/6	Tom Tomsk	a	2-1	Pérez, Osinov (p)
25/6	CSKA Moskva	h	0-2	
2/7	Krylya Sovetov Samara	a	1-1	Alkhazov
9/7	Zenit Sankt-Peterburg	h	0-1	
17/7	Torpedo Moskva	h	1-1	Pérez
23/7	Shinnik Yaroslavl	a	1-2	Ashvetia
30/7	Saturn Ramenskoe	h	0-0	
7/8	Spartak Moskva	a	0-2	
21/8	FK Moskva	h	1-0	Buznikin
27/8	Rubin Kazan	h	0-1	
10/9	Amkar Perm	h	2-0	Buznikin 2
18/9	Lokomotiv Moskva	h	1-1	Osinov
25/9	Dinamo Moskva	a	1-2	Osinov (p)
2/10	Alania Vladikavkaz	h	1-0	Bochkov
15/10	Terek Groznyi	a	3-2	Olenikov, Kruscic, Buznikin
23/10	Tom Tomsk	h	2-0	Buznikin, Pérez
30/10	CSKA Moskva	a	1-2	Buznikin
6/11	Krylya Sovetov Samara	h	2-1	Buznikin, Horák
19/11	Zenit Sankt-Peterburg	a	2-4	Horák, Osinov

No	Name	Nat	Pos	Aps	(s)	Gls
9	Alexandr ALKHAZOV		A	1	(9)	1
99	Mikheil ASHVETIA	GEO	A	11	(2)	1
30	Abdelilah BAGUI	MAR	G	11		
23	Sergei BENDZ		D	2		
32	Mustapha BIDOUDANE	MAR	A	3	(7)	1
17	Andrei BOCHKOV		M	25	(3)	1
20	Maxim BURCHENKO		M	11	(3)	
36	Dmitriy BURMISTROV		A	1	(10)	
70	Maxim BUZNIKIN		A	12	(1)	7
19	Igor CHERNYSHOV		D	1		
1	Andrei CHICHKIN		G	19		
55	Tony David COYLE	RSA	D	1		
25	Alexander DANTSEV		M	8	(3)	
2	Carlos Eduardo GUTIÉRREZ	URU	D	28		
7	Andrei HAKOBYANTS	UZB	M	3	(3)	
17	Rowan HENDRICKS	RSA	M	12	(5)	
15	Vadim HINCHAGOV		M	1	(2)	
75	Martin HORÁK	CZE	D	9		2
12	Ilia KALASHNIKOV		M	8	(6)	
9	Essau Boxer KANYENDA	MWI	A	14		2
88	Gocha KHOJAVA	GEO	M		(1)	
3	Milos KRUSCIC	SCG	D	28		1
37	Gustavo MANCINI	URU	M	4		
19	Bennett MNGUNI	RSA			(1)	1
14	Nikolai OLENIKOV		D	29		1
83	Kirill ORLOV		D	7	(1)	
6	Mikhail OSINOV		M	26	(1)	5
21	Omar Mario PÉREZ	URU	M	14	(7)	3
5	Vitas RIMKUS	LAT	A	5	(4)	
4	Anton ROGOCHIY		D	3		
60	Mikhail SAVCHENKO		G		(1)	
22	Nikolai SHIRSHOV	UZB	M	21		
28	Giorgi SMURNOV		M		(1)	
10	Japhet ZWANE	RSA	M	12	(4)	

RUBIN KAZAN
Coach – Kurban Berdyyew (TRK)

2005

13/3	Saturn Ramenskoe	a	0-0	
20/3	Spartak Moskva	a	0-3	
2/4	FK Moskva	h	1-0	Cízek
10/4	Lokomotiv Moskva	a	0-1	

Russia

Date	Opponent	H/A	Score	Scorers
16/4	Amkar Perm	h	2-0	Bayramow, Roni
23/4	FK Rostov	h	1-1	Scotti
30/4	Dinamo Moskva	h	2-1	Roni (p), Domínguez
15/5	Alania Vladikavkaz	a	3-4	Ralph, Scotti, Roni
21/5	Terek Groznyi	h	1-1	Cízek
28/5	Tom Tomsk	a	2-1	Astafjevs, Sillah
12/6	CSKA Moskva	h	1-0	Cízek
18/6	Krylya Sovetov Samara	a	2-2	Domínguez, Konovalov
26/6	Zenit Sankt-Peterburg	h	1-0	Scotti
2/7	Torpedo Moskva	a	1-1	Buitkus
9/7	Shinnik Yaroslavl	h	2-0	Bayramow, Ayupov (p)
17/7	Saturn Ramenskoe	h	0-0	
23/7	Spartak Moskva	a	0-0	
30/7	FK Moskva	h	1-1	Bayramow
6/8	Lokomotiv Moskva	h	3-1	Ayupov (p), Domínguez, Bayramow
21/8	Amkar Perm	a	0-1	
27/8	FK Rostov	a	1-0	Astafjevs
11/9	Dinamo Moskva	a	1-3	Calisto
17/9	Alania Vladikavkaz	h	4-2	Scotti (p), Domínguez, Cízek, Calisto
25/9	Terek Groznyi	a	5-1	Domínguez 2 (1p), Kinkladze 2, Cízek
2/10	Tom Tomsk	h	0-0	
16/10	CSKA Moskva	a	1-2	Bukharov
23/10	Krylya Sovetov Samara	h	2-1	Bayramow, Bukharov
29/10	Zenit Sankt-Peterburg	a	1-0	Bayramow
6/11	Torpedo Moskva	h	5-1	Ralph, Calisto, Cízek, Scotti, Jalland
19/11	Shinnik Yaroslavl	a	2-3	Ayupov (p), Cízek

No	Name	Nat	Pos	Aps	(s)	Gls
15	Vitalijs ASTAFJEVS	LAT	M	17	(5)	2
77	Ansar AYUPOV		M	23	(1)	3
32	Vladimir BAYRAMOW	TRK	A	13	(8)	6
28	Orestas BUITKUS	LIT	M	4	(6)	1
30	Alexandr BUKHAROV		A	1	(7)	2
3	Orlando CALISTO de Sousa	BRA	D	27		3
11	Tomás CÍZEK	CZE	M	16	(5)	7
2	Oscar DÍAZ González	PAR	D	4	(1)	
18	Alejandro DOMÍNGUEZ	ARG	A	10	(12)	6
5	Andrei FYODOROV		D	14	(1)	
18	Lenar GILMULLIN		D	4		
8	Jørgen JALLAND	NOR	M	7	(5)	1
79	Pavel KHARCHIK		G	13		
25	Rustem KHUZIN		D	3	(4)	
27	Giorgi KINKLADZE	GEO	M	9		2
1	Aleksandrs KOLINKO	LAT	G	17		
14	Andrei KONOVALOV		M	19	(2)	1
4	Marat MAKHMUTOV		D	8	(2)	
10	Damani RALPH	JAM	A	20	(5)	2
17	Ronielton Perreira dos Santos "RONI"	BRA	A	8	(1)	3
9	Lasha SALUKVADZE	GEO	D	21	(1)	
19	Andrés SCOTTI	URU	M	29		5
41	Macbeth SIBAYA	RSA	M	10	(2)	
23	Ebrima SILLAH	GAM	M	11	(4)	1
20	Igor SIMUTENKOV		A		(1)	
21	Mikhail SINYOV		D	15	(2)	
98	Dmitriy VASILEV		D	7		

SATURN RAMENSKOE
Coach – Alexandr Tarkhanov; (23/6/05) Vladimir Shevchuk

2005

Date	Opponent	H/A	Score	Scorers
13/3	Rubin Kazan	h	0-0	
20/3	Amkar Perm	h	2-0	Géder, Yesipov
3/4	FK Rostov	h	2-0	Kanchelskis, Bareiro
9/4	Dinamo Moskva	a	0-1	
16/4	Alania Vladikavkaz	h	3-1	Shirokov, Géder, Pavlovich
23/4	Terek Groznyi	a	0-1	
30/4	Tom Tomsk	h	0-2	
22/5	Krylya Sovetov Samara	h	1-1	Shirokov
28/5	Zenit Sankt-Peterburg	a	0-1	
12/6	Torpedo Moskva	h	1-0	Yesipov
15/6	CSKA Moskva	a	0-1	
18/6	Shinnik Yaroslavl	a	0-1	
26/6	Lokomotiv Moskva	h	0-0	
2/7	Spartak Moskva	h	1-1	Kharitonov
9/7	FK Moskva	a	1-0	Yesipov
17/7	Rubin Kazan	a	0-0	
23/7	Amkar Perm	a	2-3	Parks, Shirokov
30/7	FK Rostov	a	0-0	
6/8	Dinamo Moskva	h	0-1	
21/8	Alania Vladikavkaz	a	1-1	Bareiro
27/8	Terek Groznyi	h	3-2	Parks, Bareiro (p), Jolovic
11/9	Tom Tomsk	a	3-0	Bareiro, Jean Carlos, Yesipov
18/9	CSKA Moskva	h	0-1	
24/9	Krylya Sovetov Samara	a	0-1	
2/10	Zenit Sankt-Peterburg	h	0-0	
15/10	Torpedo Moskva	a	0-2	
23/10	Shinnik Yaroslavl	h	1-0	Parks
29/10	Lokomotiv Moskva	a	1-1	Jean Carlos
6/11	Spartak Moskva	a	0-1	
19/11	FK Moskva	h	1-2	Bareiro

No	Name	Nat	Pos	Aps	(s)	Gls
17	Anton ARKHIPOV		A		(2)	
24	Freddy José BAREIRO Gamarra	PAR	A	21	(4)	5
7	Pyotr BYSTROV		M	26		
16	Valeriy CHIZHOV		G	1		
11	Javier Omar DELGADO	URU	M		(5)	
3	Rolandas DZIAUKSTAS	LIT	D	10		
19	António GÉDER	BRA	D	19		2
32	Andrei GORBANETS		M		(3)	
5	Aleksei IGONIN		D	14	(3)	
20	JEAN CARLOS da Silva Ferreira	BRA	A	6	(3)	2
14	JEAN Ferreira NARDE	BRA	D	25		
6	Nikola JOLOVIC	SCG	D	12		1
15	Martín Emilio HIDALGO	PER	M	3		
47	Andrei KANCHELSKIS		M	15	(5)	1
21	Alexandr KHARITONOV		M	15	(12)	1
1	Antonin KINSKY	CZE	G	29		
4	Milan LESNJAK	SCG	D	14	(4)	
39	Alexandr MAKARENKO		M	3	(3)	
10	Daniel MONTENEGRO	ARG	M	6	(1)	
77	Viktor ONOPKO		D	25		
15	Winston PARKS	CRC	A	10	(1)	3
9	Nicolás PAVLOVICH	ARG	A	5	(6)	1
11	Serghei ROGACIOV	MOL	A	3	(10)	
34	Renat SABITOV		D	16		
8	Roman SHIROKOV		M	16	(2)	3
20	Vyacheslav SVIDERSKYI	UKR	D	5		
33	Valeriy YESIPOV		A	25	(1)	4
29	Aleksei ZHITNIKOV		M	6	(2)	

SHINNIK YAROSLAVL
Coach – Oleg Dolmatov

2005

Date	Opponent	H/A	Score	Scorers
12/3	Amkar Perm	h	1-1	Kulchiy
20/3	FK Rostov	a	2-2	Korchagin, og (Bendz)
2/4	Dinamo Moskva	a	0-1	
10/4	Alania Vladikavkaz	a	1-1	Bikey
16/4	Terek Groznyi	h	2-1	Hazov, Spahic (p)
23/4	Tom Tomsk	a	0-0	
15/5	Krylya Sovetov Samara	a	0-1	
21/5	Zenit Sankt-Peterburg	h	1-0	Spahic

Russia

28/5	Torpedo Moskva	a	0-0	
11/6	Lokomotiv Moskva	h	0-2	
18/6	Saturn Ramenskoe	h	1-0	Hazov
22/6	CSKA Moskva	h	1-1	Pogrebnyak
25/6	Spartak Moskva	a	1-1	Hazov
2/7	FK Moskva	h	0-1	
9/7	Rubin Kazan	a	0-2	
17/7	Amkar Perm	a	0-0	
23/7	FK Rostov	h	2-1	Pogrebnyak, Budisa
31/7	Dinamo Moskva	h	2-1	Pogrebnyak, Baltiyev (p)
6/8	Alania Vladikavkaz	h	1-0	Pogrebnyak
21/8	Terek Groznyi	a	1-0	Hazov
27/8	Tom Tomsk	h	0-0	
10/9	CSKA Moskva	a	0-2	
18/9	Krylya Sovetov Samara	h	3-1	Lagiewka, Shtanyuk, Hazov
24/9	Zenit Sankt-Peterburg	a	0-0	
1/10	Torpedo Moskva	h	1-3	Shirko
16/10	Lokomotiv Moskva	a	0-0	
23/10	Saturn Ramenskoe	a	0-1	
29/10	Spartak Moskva	h	1-3	Chernogaev
6/11	FK Moskva	a	2-3	Shirko 2
19/11	Rubin Kazan	h	3-2	Shirko, Koshelev, Lagiewka

No	Name	Nat	Pos	Aps	(s)	Gls
25	Ruslan BALTIYEV	KAZ	M	10	(1)	1
23	André BIKEY	CMR	D	11		1
14	Serge BRANCO	CMR	D	23	(1)	
18	Igor BUDISA	CRO	D	7	(3)	1
17	Vladimir BUT	GER	M	7		
4	Sergei CHERNOGAEV		M	8		1
49	Ilia DOLMATOV		A		(3)	
15	Renat DUBINSKIY		D	1	(4)	
40	Andrei DYATEL		M	5	(5)	
16	Anton HAZOV		A	25	(4)	5
8	Mario JURIC	CRO	M	10	(5)	
40	Yaroslav KHARITONSKIY		M	1		
19	Erik KORCHAGIN		A	11	(5)	1
5	Oleg KORNAUKHOV		D	6	(6)	
45	Leonid KOSHELEV	UZB	M	5	(1)	1
4	Alexandr KULCHIY	BLS	M	6		1
21	Krzysztof LAGIEWKA	POL	D	20	(1)	2
7	Darko MALETIC	BOS	M	4	(4)	
39	Viktor MYAGKOV		M	5	(8)	
29	Anatoliy NEZHELEV		M	1	(3)	
11	Pavel POGREBNYAK		M	15	(8)	4
3	Aleksander RADOSAVLJEVIC	SLO	D	29		
1	Yevgeniy SAFONOV		G	27		
66	Yegor SHEVCHENKO		M		(1)	
24	Alexandr SHIRKO		A	9	(1)	4
13	Sergei SHTANYUK	BLS	D	27		1
18	Emir SPAHIC	CRO	D	8		2
2	Mykhailo STAROSTYAK	UKR	D	25	(1)	
9	Sergei TEREKHOV		M	4		
30	Alexandr TUMENKO		M		(2)	
52	Georgiy ULYANOV		D	1		
6	Dmitriy VASILEV Vladimirovich		D	5	(1)	
12	Dmitriy VASILEV Vyacheslavovich		A	5	(3)	
7	Vyacheslav VISHNEVSKIY		A	4	(10	
53	Platon ZAKHARCHUK		G	3		
28	Artyom ZASYADVOVK	UKR	M	2	(3)	

SPARTAK MOSKVA
Coach – Aleksandrs Starkovs (LAT)

2005

12/3	FK Moskva	h	0-2	
20/3	Rubin Kazan	h	3-0	Cavenaghi (p), Titov 2
3/4	Amkar Perm	h	1-1	Cavenaghi
10/4	FK Rostov	a	1-0	Pavlyuchenko
17/4	Dinamo Moskva	h	5-1	Cavenaghi 2, Boyarintsev 2, Rodriguez
23/4	Alania Vladikavkaz	a	1-2	Pavlyuchenko
30/4	Terek Groznyi	h	3-0	Dedura, Boyarintsev, Kalynychenko
15/5	Tom Tomsk	a	1-0	Pavlenko
22/5	CSKA Moskva	h	1-3	Boyarintsev
28/5	Krylya Sovetov Samara	a	3-1	Kalynychenko 2, Pavlyuchenko
11/6	Zenit Sankt-Peterburg	a	1-1	Pavlyuchenko
18/6	Torpedo Moskva	a	3-1	Pavlyuchenko 2, Kovác
25/6	Shinnik Yaroslavl	h	1-1	Vidic (p)
2/7	Saturn Ramenskoe	a	1-1	Pavlyuchenko
9/7	Lokomotiv Moskva	h	1-2	Cavenaghi
16/7	FK Moskva	a	1-3	Pavlenko
23/7	Rubin Kazan	a	0-0	
26/7	Amkar Perm	a	0-0	
7/8	FK Rostov	h	2-0	Pjanovic, Bazhenov
21/8	Dinamo Moskva	a	1-0	Pavlyuchenko
27/8	Alania Vladikavkaz	h	5-1	Kovác 2, Covalciuc, Bystrov, Cavenaghi
11/9	Terek Groznyi	a	2-1	Bystrov, Iencsi
17/9	Tom Tomsk	h	2-1	Covalciuc, Pavlyuchenko
24/9	CSKA Moskva	a	0-1	
2/10	Krylya Sovetov Samara	h	1-0	Kovác
16/10	Zenit Sankt-Peterburg	h	1-1	Vidic (p)
22/10	Torpedo Moskva	h	1-0	Kalynychenko
29/10	Shinnik Yaroslavl	a	3-1	Bystrov, Pavlyuchenko 2
6/11	Saturn Ramenskoe	h	1-0	Titov
19/11	Lokomotiv Moskva	a	1-1	Titov

No	Name	Nat	Pos	Aps	(s)	Gls
8	Dmitriy ALENICHEV		M	1	(7)	
32	Nikita BAZHENOV		A	4	(6)	1
7	Denis BOYARINTSEV		M	19	(8)	4
23	Vladimir BYSTROV		M	14		3
19	Fernando CAVENAGHI	ARG	A	20	(5)	6
27	Serghei COVALCIUC	MOL	M	20	(1)	2
20	Ignas DEDURA	LIT	D	18		1
5	Mihai Adrian IENCSI	ROM	D	12	(1)	1
13	Martin JIRÁNEK	CZE	D	22		
14	Maxym KALYNYCHENKO	UKR	M	10	(8)	4
15	Radoslav KOVÁC	CZE	M	27		4
30	Wojciech KOWALEWSKI	POL	G	29		
24	MOZART Santos	BRA	M	7		
18	Dmytro PARFYONOV	UKR	D		(2)	
25	Alexandr PAVLENKO		M	8	(6)	2
10	Roman PAVLYUCHENKO		A	16	(9)	11
3	Emanuel POGATETZ	AUT	D	11		
28	Mihajlo PJANOVIC	SCG	A	10	(7)	1
17	Clemente RODRÍGUEZ	ARG	D	23	(2)	1
4	Andrejs RUBINS	LAT	M		(5)	
40	Alexandr SAMEDOV		A	5	(6)	
4	Costin Florin SOAVA	ROM	M		(7)	
9	Yegor TITOV		M	26	(2)	4
26	Nemanja VIDIC	SCG	D	27		2
46	Aleksei ZUYEV		G	1		

TEREK GROZNYI
Coach – Vait Talgayev (KAZ); (23/10/05) Alexandr Tarkhanov

2005

13/3	CSKA Moskva	a	0-3	
20/3	Krylya Sovetov Samara	h	2-0	Teryokhin, Adamov
3/4	Zenit Sankt-Peterburg	a	1-5	Fedkov
10/4	Torpedo Moskva	h	0-1	

Russia

Date	Opponent	h/a	Score	Scorers
16/4	Shinnik Yaroslavl	a	1-2	Fedkov
23/4	Saturn Ramenskoe	h	1-0	Fedkov
30/4	Spartak Moskva	a	0-3	
15/5	FK Moskva	h	0-0	
21/5	Rubin Kazan	a	1-1	Fedkov
28/5	Amkar Perm	h	2-2	Bokov, Teryokhin
12/6	FK Rostov	a	0-1	
18/6	Dinamo Moskva	h	0-1	
25/6	Alania Vladikavkaz	a	0-1	
3/7	Lokomotiv Moskva	a	0-4	
9/7	Tom Tomsk	h	0-1	
17/7	CSKA Moskva	h	1-0	Adamov
23/7	Krylya Sovetov Samara	a	1-0	Adamov
30/7	Zenit Sankt-Peterburg	h	0-0	
6/8	Torpedo Moskva	a	1-2	Korytko
21/8	Shinnik Yaroslavl	h	0-1	
27/8	Saturn Ramenskoe	a	2-3	Adamov 2 (1p)
11/9	Spartak Moskva	h	1-2	Sirkhaev
17/9	FK Moskva	a	1-2	Koroman (p)
25/9	Rubin Kazan	h	1-5	Atangana
2/10	Amkar Perm	a	0-0	
15/10	FK Rostov	h	2-3	Adamov, Atangana
23/10	Dinamo Moskva	a	1-0	Adamov
30/10	Alania Vladikavkaz	h	1-2	Mazayev
6/11	Lokomotiv Moskva	h	0-3	
19/11	Tom Tomsk	a	0-2	

No	Name	Nat	Pos	Aps	(s)	Gls
20	Roman ADAMOV		A	12	(6)	7
21	Ruslan ADJINDJAL		M	29		
13	Simon-Pierre ATANGANA	CMR	A	5	(4)	2
87	Serhiy BOIKO	UKR	M	2		
5	Maxim BOKOV		D	14		1
15	Viktor BULATOV		M	17	(1)	
4	Serhiy DATSENKO	UKR	D	4		
50	ÉDER Guterres	BRA	A	6		
31	Ismail EDIEV		D	2		
9	Andrei FEDKOV		A	15	(7)	4
3	Deni GAISUMOV		D	28	(1)	
16	Dmitriy GONCHAROV		G	8		
36	Ismail HALINBEKOV		D		(1)	
18	Timur JABRAILOV		D	12	(3)	
39	Adlan KATSAEV		M		(1)	
7	Dmitriy KHOMUKHA		M	1	(1)	
26	Laryea KINGSTON	GHA	M	10	(1)	
17	Denis KLYUEV		M	3	(5)	
77	Ognjen KOROMAN	SCG	M	6		1
47	Vladimir KORYTKO	BLS	M	19	(3)	1
49	Igor LAZIC	SLO	D	4		
22	Alexandr LIPKO		D	20	(1)	
10	Musa MAZAYEV		M	5	(20)	1
27	Ruslan NIGMATULLIN		G	19		
6	Gennadiy NIZHEGORODOV		D	11	(3)	
55	Jalen POKORN	SLO	D	6	(1)	
30	Rizvan SADAEV		A		(1)	
1	Volodymyr SAVCHENKO	UKR	G	3		
28	Roman SHARONOV		D	21		
24	Alexandr SHIRKO		A	1	(2)	
2	Alexandr SHMARKO		D	7	(2)	
8	Narvik SIRKHAEV		M	18	(2)	1
14	TAMER Tuna	TUR	M	13	(7)	
11	Oleg TERYOKHIN		A	8	(5)	2
40	Rizvan UTZIEV		M		(1)	
45	Idris ZAINULABIDOV		A	1		

TOM TOMSK
Coach – Boris Stukalov; (6/8/05) Anatoliy Byshovets (UKR)

2005

Date	Opponent	h/a	Score	Scorers
12/3	Lokomotiv Moskva	a	0-2	
20/3	CSKA Moskva	h	0-0	
3/4	Krylya Sovetov Samara	a	1-1	Klimov
10/4	Zenit Sankt-Peterburg	h	2-0	Borzenkov, Medvedev
16/4	Torpedo Moskva	a	0-3	
23/4	Shinnik Yaroslavl	h	0-0	
30/4	Saturn Ramenskoe	a	2-0	Medvedev, Kaleshin
15/5	Spartak Moskva	h	0-1	
21/5	FK Moskva	a	1-4	Klimov
28/5	Rubin Kazan	h	1-2	Sischin
12/6	Amkar Perm	a	0-0	
18/6	FK Rostov	h	1-2	Dyomkin
26/6	Dinamo Moskva	a	0-0	
2/7	Alania Vladikavkaz	h	0-0	
9/7	Terek Groznyi	a	1-0	Medvedev
17/7	Lokomotiv Moskva	h	0-0	
24/7	CSKA Moskva	a	0-2	
31/7	Krylya Sovetov Samara	h	4-2	Klimov 2, Medvedev, Catinsus
6/8	Zenit Sankt-Peterburg	a	0-1	
21/8	Torpedo Moskva	h	1-1	Budunov
27/8	Shinnik Yaroslavl	a	0-0	
11/9	Saturn Ramenskoe	h	0-3	
17/9	Spartak Moskva	a	1-2	Vejic
24/9	FK Moskva	h	3-2	Sischin 2 (1p), Leonov
2/10	Rubin Kazan	a	0-0	
15/10	Amkar Perm	h	3-0	Skerla, Kaleshin, Krunic
23/10	FK Rostov	a	0-2	
30/10	Dinamo Moskva	h	3-2	Krunic, Kiselyov 2
6/11	Alania Vladikavkaz	a	2-1	Krunic (p), Medvedev
19/11	Terek Groznyi	h	2-0	Bornosuzov, Vejic

No	Name	Nat	Pos	Aps	(s)	Gls
50	Illya BLIZNYUK	UKR	G	13		
52	Atanas BORNOSUZOV	BUL	M	6	(3)	1
6	Albert BORZENKOV		D	29		1
49	Budun BUDUNOV		M	5		1
19	Rustam BULATOV		D	8		
21	Valeriu CATINSUS	MOL	M	23	(1)	1
1	Pavel DYAKONOV		G	1		
9	Andrei DYOMKIN		A	1	(2)	1
15	Alexandr FAMILTSEV		D	7	(1)	
48	Andrius GEDGAUDAS	LIT	M		(1)	
11	Yevgeniy KALESHIN		M	17	(7)	2
17	Denis KISELYOV		A	12	(9)	2
3	Valeriy KLIMOV		M	24	(3)	4
10	Branislav KRUNIC	BOS	M	11	(4)	3
77	Alexandr KULCHIY	BLS	M	10		
12	Valeriy LEONOV		M	1	(3)	1
18	Vladimir MAZOV		M		(2)	
13	Aleksei MEDVEDEV		A	27	(3)	5
27	Pavel MOGILEVSKIY		D	1	(4)	
8	Jevgeni NOVIKOV	EST	M		(1)	
25	Sergei PAREIKO	EST	G	16		
20	Sergiy REKHTIN		D	8		
5	Alexandr SHVETSOV		M	4	(7)	
14	Oleg SISCHIN	MOL	M	10	(7)	3
55	Andrius SKERLA	LIT	D	10		1
24	Dmitriy SKOBLYAKOV		A		(1)	
7	Sergei SKOBLYAKOV		M	3	(10)	
22	Konstantin SKRYLNIKOV		M	20	(5)	
30	Mikhail VANEV		M	1	(1)	
84	Hrvoje VEJIC	CRO	D	11		2
31	Tomás VYCHODIL	CZE	D	1	(1)	

Russia

TORPEDO MOSKVA
Coach – Sergei Petrenko

2005

Date	Opponent	h/a	Score	Scorers
13/3	FK Rostov	h	3-1	Panov, Volkov (p), Semshov
20/3	Dinamo Moskva	a	1-2	Oper
2/4	Alania Vladikavkaz	h	3-0	Kormyltsev, Semshov, Panov
10/4	Terek Groznyi	a	1-0	Zyryanov
16/4	Tom Tomsk	h	3-0	Panov 2, Volkov
30/4	Krylya Sovetov Samara	h	0-0	
5/5	Zenit Sankt-Peterburg	a	1-1	Semshov
22/5	Lokomotiv Moskva	h	0-1	
28/5	Shinnik Yaroslavl	h	0-0	
12/6	Saturn Ramenskoe	a	0-1	
18/6	Spartak Moskva	h	1-3	Volkov
25/6	FK Moskva	a	1-1	Semshov
2/7	Rubin Kazan	h	1-1	Stepanov
9/7	Amkar Perm	a	0-0	
17/7	FK Rostov	a	1-1	Zyryanov
20/7	CSKA Moskva	a	0-2	
24/7	Dinamo Moskva	h	2-1	Semshov, Panov
31/7	Alania Vladikavkaz	a	2-2	Laizans, Panov
6/8	Terek Groznyi	h	2-1	Semshov, Panov
10/8	CSKA Moskva	h	0-2	
21/8	Tom Tomsk	a	1-1	Semshov
10/9	Krylya Sovetov Samara	a	1-0	Semshov
18/9	Zenit Sankt-Peterburg	h	0-4	
24/9	Lokomotiv Moskva	a	3-0	Panov, Budylin, Lutsenko
1/10	Shinnik Yaroslavl	a	3-1	Semshov 2, Budylin (p)
15/10	Saturn Ramenskoe	h	2-0	Semshov, Panov
22/10	Spartak Moskva	a	0-1	
29/10	FK Moskva	h	2-0	Zyryanov, Semshov
6/11	Rubin Kazan	a	1-5	Budylin
19/11	Amkar Perm	h	2-1	Panov, og (Olexici)

No	Name	Nat	Pos	Aps	(s)	Gls
22	Dmitriy BORODIN		G	28		
21	Sergei BUDYLIN		M	21	(6)	3
33	Igor BYRLOV		M	4	(4)	
19	Sergei CHERNOGAEV		D	4	(4)	
20	Cristian DANCIA	ROM	D	9		
29	Alexandr HEINRICH	UZB	A	8	(3)	
2	Enaar JÄÄGER	EST	D	7	(6)	
15	Djordje JOKIC	SCG	D	29		
4	Nikola JOLOVIC	SCG	D	2	(1)	
16	Maxim KABANOV		G	2		
17	Dmitriy KAMAROVSKIY	BLS	A		(1)	
5	Serhiy KORMYLTSEV	UKR	M	16	(14)	1
26	Sergei KOROVUSHKIN		A	2	(5)	
6	Dmitriy KUDINOV		D	4		
33	Jurijs LAIZANS	LAT	M	5	(4)	1
48	Yevgeniy LUTSENKO		A	7	(11)	1
28	Pavel MAMAYEV		M	7	(6)	
7	Andres OPER	EST	A	9	(6)	1
27	Sergei OSIPOV		M		(3)	
15	Andrei PANFYOROV		M	12	(4)	
23	Alexandr PANOV		A	26	(2)	10
3	Mantas SAMUSEVAS	LAT	D	6	(2)	
10	Igor SEMSHOV		M	29		12
1	Emir SPAHIC	CRO	D	15		
24	Andrei STEPANOV	EST	D	24		1
19	Ruslan TARALA		A		(1)	
18	Vitaliy VOLKOV		A	25		3
8	Konstantin ZYRYANOV		M	29		3
4	Vasiliy YANOTOVSKIY		M	24	(1)	
14	Sergei YASKOVICH	BLS	D	26		
23	Ivan ZAVALIY		A		(2)	

ZENIT SANKT-PETERBURG
Coach – Vlastimil Petrzelka (CZE)

2005

Date	Opponent	h/a	Score	Scorers
12/3	Dinamo Moskva	h	4-1	Krizanac, Arshavin, Kerzhakov, Mares
20/3	Alania Vladikavkaz	a	3-0	Vjestica, Spivak (p), Kerzhakov
3/4	Terek Groznyi	h	5-1	Arshavin 3 (1p), Radimov 2
10/4	Tom Tomsk	a	0-2	
17/4	CSKA Moskva	h	1-0	Bystrov
23/4	Krylya Sovetov Samara	a	0-3	
30/4	Lokomotiv Moskva	h	1-1	Hartig
5/5	Torpedo Moskva	h	1-1	Mares
21/5	Shinnik Yaroslavl	a	0-1	
28/5	Saturn Ramenskoe	h	1-0	Denisov
11/6	Spartak Moskva	h	1-1	Kerzhakov
15/6	Lokomotiv Moskva	a	0-0	
19/6	FK Moskva	h	2-2	Denisov, Spivak (p)
26/6	Rubin Kazan	a	0-1	
2/7	Amkar Perm	h	5-1	Arshavin 3, Sirl, Kozhanov
9/7	FK Rostov	a	1-0	Mares
17/7	Dinamo Moskva	a	2-1	Spivak, Kerzhakov
23/7	Alania Vladikavkaz	h	3-1	Krizanac, Poskus, Spivak
30/7	Terek Groznyi	a	0-0	
6/8	Tom Tomsk	h	1-0	Spivak
21/8	CSKA Moskva	a	1-1	Skrtel
28/8	Krylya Sovetov Samara	h	4-1	Anyukov, Denisov, Spivak (p), Sumulikoski
18/9	Torpedo Moskva	a	4-0	Kerzhakov, Arshavin, Denisov 2
24/9	Shinnik Yaroslavl	h	0-0	
2/10	Saturn Ramenskoe	a	0-0	
16/10	Spartak Moskva	a	1-1	Arshavin
23/10	FK Moskva	a	0-2	
29/10	Rubin Kazan	h	0-1	
6/11	Amkar Perm	a	0-1	
19/11	FK Rostov	h	4-2	Kerzhakov 2 (1p), Mares, Cadikovski

No	Name	Nat	Pos	Aps	(s)	Gls
44	Alexandr ANYUKOV		D	12		1
10	Andrei ARSHAVIN		A	29		9
34	Vladimir BYSTROV		M	8	(5)	1
21	Dragan CADIKOVSKI	MAC	A	1	(3)	1
1	Kamil CONTOFALSKY	SVK	G	19		
27	Igor DENISOV		M	14	(6)	5
28	Jan FLACHBART	CZE	D	21	(1)	
14	Erik HAGEN	NOR	D	28		
15	Lukás HARTIG	CZE	A		(6)	1
88	Oleksandr HORSHKOV	UKR	M	2	(6)	
11	Alexandr KERZHAKOV		A	25		7
20	Oleg KOZHANOV		A	1	(8)	1
33	Mikhail KOZLOV		A		(3)	
4	Ivica KRIZANAC	CRO	D	10	(2)	2
16	Vyacheslav MALAFEYEV		G	11		
8	Pavel MARES	CZE	M	26		4
25	Robertas POSKUS	LIT	A	7	(4)	1
2	Vladislav RADIMOV			24		2
9	Radek SIRL	CZE	A	10	(4)	1
3	Martin SKRTEL	SVK	D	15	(3)	1
6	Oleksandr SPIVAK	UKR	M	28		6
19	Velice SUMULIKOSKI	MAC	M	6	(10)	1
22	Valeriy TSVETKOV		D	2	(1)	
7	Oleg TRIFONOV		M	2	(5)	
5	Milan VJESTICA	SCG	D	8	(4)	1
43	Oleg VLASOV		M	1	(12)	

Russia

DOMESTIC CUP 2005/06

FIFTH ROUND
(6/7/05 & 13/7/05)
CSKA Moskva v Torpedo Vladimir 2-1; 1-1 *(3-2)*
Tom Tomsk v Spartak Kostroma 3-2; 0-2 *(3-4)*
Metallurg Lipetsk v Shinnik Yarslavl 1-0; 0-4 *(1-4)*
Rubin Kazan v Vityaz Podolsk 1-0; 2-1 *(3-1)*
Lada Togliatti v Amkar Perm 1-0; 0-2 *(1-2)*
Spartak Moskva v Okean Nakhodka 6-0; 2-1 *(8-1)*
(6/7/05 & 21/8/05)
Krylya Sovetov Samara v Saturn Yegoryevsk 4-1; 0-1 *(4-2)*
(13/7/05 & 20/7/05)
Kuban Krasnodar v Zenit Sankt-Peterburg 1-1; 0-0 *(1-1; Zenit Sankt-Peterburg on away goal)*
(13/7/05 & 11/8/05)
Dinamo Bryansk v Dinamo Moskva 0-0; 0-4 *(0-4)*
Dinamo Makhachkala v FK Moskva 1-4; 2-2 *(3-6)*
(13/7/05 & 13/8/05)
Terek Groznyi v Spartak Nalchik 5-0; 1-1 *(6-1)*
(13/7/05 & 31/8/05)
Saturn Ramenskoe v Ural Yekaterinburg 1-1; 2-1 *(3-2)*
Luch-Energia Vladivostok v FK Rostov 2-1; 1-1 *(3-2)*
(13/7/05 & 21/9/05)
Alania Vladikavkaz v Lokomotiv Chita 2-0; 0-2 *(aet) (2-2; Lokomotiv Chita 5-4 on pens)*
(13/7/05 & 12/11/05)
Lokomotiv Moskva v Metallurg-Kuzbass Novokuznetsk 2-0; 1-1 *(3-1)*
(28/8/05 & 9/11/05)
Volgar GazProm Astrakhan v Torpedo Moskva 0-2; 0-2 *(0-4)*

SIXTH ROUND
(4/3/06 & 12/3/06)
Zenit Sankt-Peterburg v Terek Groznyi 2-0; 0-1 *(2-1)*
(4/3/06 & 14/3/06)
Luch-Energia Vladivostok v Spartak Moskva 0-1; 0-1 *(0-2)*
(5/3/06 & 8/3/06)
Rubin Kazan v Shinnik Yaroslavl 0-1; 2-0 *(aet) (2-1)*
(5/3/06 & 12/3/06)
Torpedo Moskva v FK Moskva 1-2; 3-1 *(4-3)*
(5/3/06 & 13/3/06)
Krylya Sovetov Samara v Dinamo Moskva 2-0; 0-2 *(aet) (Dinamo Moskva 3-1 on pens)*
Amkar Perm v Saturn Ramenskoe 0-1; 0-0 *(0-1)*
(5/3/06 & 15/3/06)
CSKA Moskva v Spartak Kostroma 5-0; 3-0 *(8-0)*
Lokomotiv Moskva w/o Lokomotiv Chita

QUARTER-FINALS
(22/3/06 & 12/4/06)
Rubin Kazan 1 *(Bukharov 71)*, CSKA Moskva 1 *(Gusev 3)*
CSKA Moskva 4 *(Jô 39, 67, Vágner Love 42, Olic 90)*, Rubin Kazan 1 *(Ghazkan 64)*
(CSKA Moskva 5-2)

Zenit Sankt-Peterburg 2 *(Kerzhakov 22, 51)*, Torpedo Moskva 0
Torpdo Moskva 2 *(Budylin 72, 76)*, Zenit Sankt-Peterburg 3 *(Kerzhakov 23, 26p, Skrtel 45)*
(Zenit Sankt-Peterburg 5-2)

Saturn Ramenskoe 3 *(Mendy 8og, Eremenko 25p, Igonin 88)*, Dinamo Moskva 0
Dinamo Moskva 3 *(Danny 45, Romashchenko 64p, 73p)*, Saturn Ramenskoe 1 *(Jakubko 21)*
(Saturn Ramenskoe 4-3)

Spartak Moskva 2 *(Kovác 65, Pjanovic 69)*, Lokomotiv Moskva 2 *(O'Connor 21, Loskov 27)*
Lokomotiv Moskva 1 *(Bilyaletdinov 10)*, Spartak Moskva 2 *(Pjanovic 15, Mozart 87p)*
(Spartak Moskva 4-3)

SEMI-FINALS
(3/5/06 & 10/5/06)
CSKA Moskva 1 *(Daniel Carvalho 60)*, Zenit Sankt-Peterburg 0
Zenit Sankt-Peterburg 0, CSKA Moskva 3 *(Vágner Love 10, Dudu Cearense 20, Ignashevich 30)*
(CSKA Moskva 4-0)

Spartak Moskva 1 *(Cavenaghi 16)*, Saturn Ramenskoe 1 *(Sabitov 84)*
Saturn Ramenskoe 1 *(Bareiro 60)*, Spartak Moskva 3 *(Cavenaghi 45, Mozart 64p, Pavlenko 83)*
(Spartak Moskva 4-2)

FINAL
(20/5/06)
Luzhniki Stadium, Moscow
CSKA MOSKVA 3 *(Jô 43, 90, Vágner Love 89)*
SPARTAK MOSKVA 0
Referee – Ivanov
CSKA MOSKVA – Akinfeev, Berezutskiy V., Ignashevich, Berezutskiy A., Semberas, Aldonin, Daniel Carvalho *(Taranov 55)*, Dudu Cearense, Zhirkov *(Tatarchuk 89)*, Jô, Vágner Love *(Grigoryev 90)*.
SPARTAK MOSKVA – Kowalewski, Tamas, Iencsi, Stranzl, Rodríguez *(Owusu-Abeyie 55)*, Mozart, Covalciuc *(Pavlenko 77)*, Titov, Bystrov, Pavlyuchenko, Cavenaghi *(Bazhenov 46)*.
Sent off: Mozart *(88)*

SECOND LEVEL FINAL TABLE 2005

		Pld	W	D	L	F	A	Pts
1	Luch-Energia Vladivostok	42	27	11	4	81	32	92
2	Spartak Nalchik	42	25	11	6	67	36	86
3	KamAZ Naberezhnye Chelny	42	26	6	10	80	32	84
4	FK Khimki	42	23	13	6	75	36	82
5	Kuban Krasnodar	42	23	12	7	55	25	81
6	Dinamo Makhachkala	42	23	7	12	64	41	76
7	Ural Yekaterinburg	42	21	10	11	51	34	73
8	FK Oryol	42	17	12	13	55	48	63
9	Spartak Chelyabinsk	42	16	13	13	60	53	61
10	Chkalovets-1936 Novosibirsk	42	15	11	16	51	53	56
11	Anzhi Makhachkala	42	14	13	15	47	48	55
12	SKA-Energie Khabarovsk	42	15	9	18	40	43	54
13	Dinamo Bryansk	42	13	13	16	44	49	52
14	Volgar-Gazprom Astrakhan	42	14	9	19	50	56	51
15	Lokomotiv Chita	42	14	8	20	57	67	50
16	Avangard Kursk	42	11	15	16	36	45	48
17	Fakel Voronezh	42	13	7	22	39	60	46
18	Metallurg-Kuzbass Novokuznetsk	42	10	15	17	48	61	45
19	Amur Blagoveshscensk	42	10	7	25	44	70	37
20	Metallurg Lipetsk	42	7	5	30	40	78	26
21	Petrotest Sankt-Peterburg	42	7	5	30	37	107	26
22	Sokol Saratov	42	7	10	25	37	84	25

N.B. Sokol Saratov – 6 pts deducted.

San Marino

No relief in sight

The quest for a first competitive victory continues. The only UEFA member without a win in World Cup or European Championship qualifying, San Marino will hope for that day of deliverance to arrive on the road to Euro 2008. Their best bet looks to be the home game against Cyprus in August 2007.

The Principality's fourth World Cup qualifying campaign ended, as expected, with three more defeats to add to the five of the previous season. There were no further goals, either – at least not from San Marino. Belgium, Bosnia-Herzegovina and Spain combined to put 17 in at the other end, swelling San Marino's 'goals against' column to 40, an average of five per game.

With no friendly internationals arranged in the first half of 2006, coach Gianpaolo Mazza was unable to prepare his players for the big Euro 2008 opener at home to Germany. Nor was there a chance for goalkeeper Federico Gasperoni and striker Paolo Montagna to add some caps to their total in their bid to become the first San Marino international to reach the half-century. Mirko Gennari, who made 48 appearances between 1992 and 2003, still holds the record.

Domagnano, the Principality's most successful club since the turn of the century, had a poor season in 2005/06. It began with an 8-0 thrashing in the UEFA Cup preliminaries and ended 11 months later with a 3-2 defeat by Tre Penne in the quarter-finals of the Coppa Titano.

There was a new name on the championship roll of honour as Murata, the previous season's beaten finalists, claimed their first title in stunning style. Play-offs included, Federico Rossini's side played 23 matches and lost only one – to a controversial stoppage-time penalty in a cross-group fixture against Faetano. Top of Group B with a seven-point lead over Pennarossa, Murata were to meet the 2004 champions in the play-off final after disposing of Libertas and Group A winners Tre Fiori en route.

Veteran Agostini

Murata's stars were top-scoring Marco De Luigi and 42-year-old ex-Serie A striker Massimo Agostini, but in the play-off final the winning goal, an 18th-minute header, came from young San Marino international midfielder Alex Gasperoni.

Having put so much effort into winning the league, Murata barely figured in the post-season Coppa Titano. Like all the championship play-off qualifiers, they did reach the quarter-finals, but the country's oldest competition was won by Libertas, who ended the season with a flourish, scoring three late goals to beat Tre Penne 4-1 in the final and take the trophy for a record tenth time.

EUROPEAN CUPS 2005/06

UEFA CUP

DOMAGNANO
1st qualifying round DOMZALE (SLO)
H 0-5
Montanari, Cicchetti (Morri 64), Bacciocchi S., Ugolini, Rossi, Zavoli, Celli, Marinelli (Palanghi 86), Casadei, Bacciocchi N. (Moretti 68), Fambri.
A 0-3
Montanari, Cicchetti, Bacciocchi S., Ranocchini (Fambri 78), Rossi, Morri, Celli, Marinelli, Palanghi, Casadei (Zanotti 90), Bacciocchi N. (Moretti 66).

NATIONAL TEAM RESULTS 2005/06

7/9/05	Belgium (WCQ)	A	Brussels	0-8
8/10/05	Bosnia-Herzegovina (WCQ)	A	Zenica	0-3
12/10/05	Spain (WCQ)	H	Serravalle	0-6

San Marino

NATIONAL TEAM APPEARANCES 2005/06

Coach – Giampaolo MAZZA			BEL	BOS	ESP	Caps	Goals
Michele CECCOLI	4/12/73	Libertas	G	G		3	-
Carlo VELENTINI	15/3/82	Virtus	D			17	-
Fedrico CRESCENTINI	13/4/82	Tre Fiori	D77	D77		6	-
Alessandro DELLA VALLE	8/6/82	Tropical Coriano (ITA)	D	D	D	12	-
Matteo ANDREINI	10/10/81	Tre Fiori	D	D	D84	6	-
Simone BACCIOCCHI	22/1/77	Marignanese (ITA)	D		D	32	-
Giacomo MAIANI	10/7/82	Tropical Corinao (ITA)	M61			4	-
Marco DOMENICONI	29/1/84	Urbino (ITA)	M	M90	M	11	-
Alex GASPERONI	30/6/84	Tolenzino (ITA)	M	M	M	13	1
Michele MORETTI	26/10/81	Sammaurese (ITA)	M70	s90		8	-
Andy SELVA	23/5/76	Padova (ITA)	A	A		29	7
Roberto SELVA	2/1/81	Juvenes/Dogana	s61			12	-
Nicola CIACCI	7/7/82	Pennarossa	s70			9	1
Luca NANNI	12/12/78	Tre Penne	s77	D	D	8	-
Damiano VANNUCCI	30/7/77	Libertas		M	M	32	-
Michele MARANI	16/11/82	Real Misano (ITA)		M	M	19	-
Manuel MARANI	7/6/84	Juvenes/Dogana		M81	M87	2	-
Mirko PALAZZI	21/3/87	Rimini (ITA)		s77	s84	2	-
Paolo MONTAGNA	28/5/76	Juvenes/Dogana		s81	A71	40	-
Federico GASPERONI	10/9/76	Cattolica (ITA)			G	41	-
Mattia MASI	4/12/84	Colligiana (ITA)			s71	1	-
Federico NANNI	22/9/81	Tre Penne			s87	1	-

DOMESTIC CUP 2006

FIRST PHASE
(Played in Groups)

Group A

(20/5/06)
Domagnano 2, Folgore/Falciano 0
Libertas 3, San Giovanni 2
(24/5/06)
Domagnano 1, Murata 0
San Giovanni 1, Folgore/Falciano 3
(27/5/06)
San Giovanni 1, Murata 4
Folgore/Falciano 0, Libertas 0
(31/5/06)
Murata 0, Libertas 2
Domagnano 3, San Giovanni 0
(5/6/06)
Libertas 1, Domagnano 2
Murata 4, Folgore/Falciano 1

Final Standings
1 Domagnano 12 pts; 2 Libertas 7 pts; 3 Murata 6 pts *(qualified)*
4 Folgore/Falciano 4 pts; 5 San Giovanni 0 pts *(eliminated)*

Group B

(19/5/06)
Pennarossa 4, Cosmos 1
(20/5/06)
Tre Fiori 1, La Fiorita 0
(23/5/06)
Cosmos 2, La Fiorita 1
(24/5/06)
Tre Fiori 4, Virtus 1
(26/5/06)
La Fiorita 0, Pennarossa 4
(27/5/06)
Cosmos 0, Virtus 0
(30/5/06)
Virtus 2, Pennarossa 4
(31/5/06)
Tre Fiori 3, Cosmos 0
(2/6/06)
Pennarossa 0, Tre Fiori 1
(5/6/06)
Virtus 4, La Fiorita 2

Final Standings
1 Tre Fiori 12 pts; 2 Pennarossa 9 pts *(qualified)*
3 Virtus 4 pts; 4 Cosmos 4 pts; 5 La Fiorita 0 pts *(eliminated)*

San Marino

Group C

(19/5/06)
Fiorentino 0, Cailungo 1
Tre Penne 2, Faetano 1
(23/5/06)
Juvenes/Dogana 3, Fiorentino 1
Cailungo 1, Faetano 1
(26/5/06)
Faetano 0, Juvenes/Dogana 3 (w/o)
Cailungo 3, Tre Penne 3
(30/5/06)
Juvenes/Dogana 3, Tre Penne 2
Fiorentino 1, Faetano 2
(2/6/06)
Juvenes/Dogana 0, Cailungo 2
Tre Penne 2, Fiorentino 1

Final Standings
1 Juvenes/Dogana 9 pts; 2 Cailungo 8 pts; 3 Tre Penne 7 pts *(qualified)*
4 Faetano 4 pts; 5 Fiorentino 0 pts *(eliminated)*

QUARTER-FINALS
(13/6/06)
Juvenes/Dogana 2, Murata 0
Domagnano 2, Tre Penne 3
(14/6/06)
Tre Fiori 1, Libertas 2
Cailungo 0, Pennarossa 2

SEMI-FINALS
(19/6/06)
Juvenes/Dogana 1, Tre Penne 3
Libertas 4, Pennarossa 3

FINAL
(23/6/06)
Stadio Serravalle
LIBERTAS 4 *(Vannucci 35, 76p, Toccaceli 87, Ghiotti 90)*
TRE PENNE 1 *(Cibelli 50)*

TOP GOALSCORERS 2005/06

Group A

17	Simon PARMA	(La Fiorita)
16	Elton SHABANI	(Faetano)
14	Marco CASADEI	(Domagnano)
	Daniele PALANGHI	(Domagnano)
11	Giacomo FAMBRI	(Domagnano)

Group B

19	Marco DE LUIGI	(Murata)
15	Andrea BARTOLI	(Virtus)
	Nicola CIACCI	(Pennarossa)
13	Steven VENERUCCI	(Fiorentino)
10	Damiano VANNUCCI	(Libertas)

FINAL LEAGUE TABLES 2005/06

FIRST PHASE

Group A		Pld	W	D	L	F	A	Pts
1	Tre Fiori	21	14	5	2	37	12	47
2	Domagnano	21	12	6	3	52	23	42
3	Tre Penne	21	11	6	4	27	15	39
4	Folgore/Falciano	21	9	4	8	22	25	31
5	La Fiorita	21	7	7	7	31	35	28
6	Faetano	21	6	3	12	32	40	21
7	Cosmos	21	5	5	11	13	22	20
8	San Giovanni	21	1	2	18	13	60	5

Group B		Pld	W	D	L	F	A	Pts
1	Murata	20	15	4	1	49	20	49
2	Pennarossa	20	12	6	2	38	19	42
3	Libertas	20	10	3	7	42	22	33
4	Virtus	20	7	4	9	23	33	25
5	Juvenes/Dogana	20	3	8	9	27	44	17
6	Cailungo	20	4	4	12	11	25	16
7	Fiorentino	20	3	3	14	30	52	12

CHAMPIONSHIP PLAY-OFFS

First Round
(19/4/06)
Domagnano 1, Libertas 4
Pennarossa 1, Tre Penne 1 *(aet; 2-3 on pens)*

Second Round
(22/4/06)
Tre Fiori 1, Tre Penne 0
Murata 3, Libertas 1

Third Round
(27/4/06)
Tre Penne 1, Domagnano 1 *(aet ; 5-3 on pens)*
Libertas 0, Pennarossa 2
(Domagnano and Libertas eliminated)

Fourth Round
(28/4/06)
Tre Fiori 0, Murata 1
(2/5/06)
Tre Penne 2, Pennarossa 3 *(aet)*
(Tre Penne eliminated)

Semi-final
Tre Fiori 1, Pennarossa 2
(Tre Fiori eliminated)

Final
(11/5/06)
Stadio Serravalle
MURATA 1 *(Gasperoni 18)*
PENNAROSSA 0

Scotland

Strachan's Celtic dig deep

The final Scottish Premier League table was pretty conclusive. Celtic, with 28 wins, 93 goals and 91 points, were way out in front. Their 40th title had been sealed a month in advance with six matches still to play. With victory in the League Cup thrown in, it was a pretty satisfactory first season in the Parkhead hot seat for new manager Gordon Strachan.

Or so it seemed. In fact, Celtic's road to victory had been littered with pot-holes. Strachan, who had come in for the highly successful Martin O'Neill, had to dig himself out of a yawning crater right at the start of his tenure when the Bhoys capitulated to the most embarrassing European defeat in their history, losing 5-0 away to Artmedia Bratislava in the first leg of their Champions League second qualifying-round tie.

Celtic won the return 4-0 – in typical Scottish 'heroic loser' fashion – but that was as far as the club's European campaign went. With millions of pounds of prospective Champions League revenue fluttering away in the breeze, the diminutive ex-Scotland midfielder was under severe pressure to turn things around quickly and get off to a good start in the SPL. A defeat in the first Old Firm game of the season, 3-1 at Ibrox, was not what the Celtic fans or the board of directors had in mind, but as the weeks went by Celtic finally began to settle. Instead of shipping goals, they started scoring them, and as a consequence the points started to accumulate.

Hearts on fire

It was not Rangers they had to catch, but Hearts. The Edinburgh club, with no European distractions from the outset, set off like a house on fire under their new manager, George Burley. Eight successive victories, the last of them at home to Rangers, launched the Tynecastle club into a commanding early lead. Naturally, because this was Hearts and not one of the Old Firm, everyone expected the bubble to burst. In fact, it was pricked from within. Although the club's wealthy Lithuanian owner, Vladimir Romanov, had appointed Burley to the job, it soon became evident that, despite the brilliant results, the two men didn't get on. Burley resented Romanov's interference in team affairs, while Romanov regarded Burley as a menace to his authority. In October, following an impressive 1-1 draw at Celtic, Burley was removed from office.

With Hearts leading the SPL at the time, it seemed like sporting suicide. The club's first defeat soon followed – 2-0 at gloating city rivals Hibernian – and although Romanov eventually found a replacement for Burley, his choice of Englishman Graham Rix was roundly condemned by the Tynecastle faithful. The stuffing had completely been knocked out of the club, all their early momentum had gone, and when, on New Year's Day, they lost 3-2 at home to Celtic

NATIONAL TEAM RESULTS 2005/06

17/8/05	Austria	A	Graz	2-2	Miller (3), O'Connor (38)
3/9/05	Italy (WCQ)	H	Glasgow	1-1	Miller (12)
7/9/05	Norway (WCQ)	A	Oslo	2-1	Miller (21, 31)
8/10/05	Belarus (WCQ)	H	Glasgow	0-1	
12/10/05	Slovenia (WCQ)	A	Celje	3-0	Fletcher (4), McFadden (47), Hartley (84)
12/11/05	United States	H	Glasgow	1-1	Webster (38)
1/3/06	Switzerland	H	Glasgow	1-3	Miller (55)
11/5/06	Bulgaria	N	Kobe	5-1	Boyd (14, 42), McFadden (69), Burke (78, 89)
13/5/06	Japan	A	Saitama	0-0	

Scotland

after going 2-0 up in the first eight minutes, Hearts' challenge for the championship was all but over.

After that victory, secured by two late goals from young defender Steven McManus, the coast was clear for Celtic. They now had a seven-point lead, and with defending champions Rangers way off the pace after an atrocious autumn during which they suffered the longest run without a victory in their 133-year history (ten matches, all competitions included), Strachan's young team had only to go through the motions during the second half of the season and the championship flag would be back in their possession.

To boost their title challenge, Strachan brought in the iconic figure of Roy Keane – former Republic of Ireland and Manchester United skipper and devout Celtic fan – but his first game ended in ignominy as Celtic were knocked out of the Scottish Cup (a trophy they held) by First Division Clyde. That was the end of Celtic's Treble hopes and of Strachan's bid to emulate O'Neill, who had won all three domestic trophies in his debut season. The Bhoys had not won the League Cup since that 2000/01 campaign, but having eliminated Rangers in the quarter-finals in early November, they beat Motherwell 2-1 in the semi-final in February and then Dunfermline Athletic 3-0 in the final, at Hampden, on March 19, to end the five-year wait.

Title pocketed

By that stage the SPL title was also virtually in Celtic's pocket. With the exception of one 3-3 draw at home to Dundee United, the Hoops had won every one of their league games since the turn of the year, even crushing Dunfermline 8-1 – a month before their League Cup final clash – thanks chiefly to four goals from Polish striker Maciej Zurawski. The ex-Wisla Krakow man also scored the only goal in a 1-0 win over Rangers at Ibrox.

On April 5 the title race was over as Celtic beat Hearts 1-0 at home to stretch their lead to an unassailable 20 points. An early goal from leading scorer John Hartson was enough to spark the championship celebrations. The Welshman enjoyed another excellent season, as did Stilian Petrov and Neil Lennon in central midfield, but the efforts of those O'Neill stalwarts were matched by those of Strachan's new signings, notably Zurawski and his goalkeeping compatriot Artur Boruc and, especially, dazzling Japanese left-footer and free-kick specialist Shunsuke Nakamura. Eclipsing all the foreign talent, though, was local lad Shaun Maloney, who recovered brilliantly from a long-term knee injury to become Celtic's most influential player, scooping both the SPFA Player of the Year and young Player of the Year awards.

Several Hearts players challenged Maloney for the

Shunsuke Nakamura, Celtic's impressive Oriental import, awaits acclaim from Scotland's Player of the Year Shaun Maloney

Scotland

main award. Goalkeeper Craig Gordon and midfielder Paul Hartley both enjoyed the best seasons of their career, while there were a couple of outstanding foreigners in top-scoring Czech Rudi Skácel and Greek European Championship-winning left-back Panagiotis 'Takis' Fyssas. At the end of the season these players were celebrating on two fronts as Hearts not only held off a resurgent Rangers to secure second place in the SPL – and with it a Champions League qualifying berth – but also made the most of the Old Firm's early exit from the Scottish Cup by taking the trophy for only the second time in 50 years. They did so with another new manager at the helm, Rix having suffered the same fate as Burley and been replaced by one of Romanov's own, ex-Lithuanian international striker Valdas Ivanauskas.

Historically Hearts were obliged to win the Cup in 2006, having also lifted the trophy in 1906 and 1956. With little Gretna, the newly crowned Second Division champions, as their opponents in the Hampden final, everything was set up for a comfortable victory. Not so. The team from the border town made famous for granting 'quickie' marriages to eloping English couples fought with grit and determination from start to finish, equalising a Skácel strike 15 minutes from time and taking the SPL side all the way to penalties before succumbing to defeat. The big consolation for Gretna was that, with Hearts in the Champions League, they had already secured a place in the 2006/07 UEFA Cup.

Historic qualification

Qualification for the UEFA Cup was the only prize Rangers collected from a season that was rescued from total failure only by their historic qualification for the knockout round of the Champions League. No Scottish team had ever successfully negotiated a group phase in a major tournament, whether in the World Cup, European Championship, UEFA Cup or Champions League. It could not be said that Rangers ended that dismal record with any great panache – they won only one of their matches, the first, 3-2 at home to FC Porto – but they doggedly fought their way through, and that was all that mattered. The team's qualification for the last 16 also kept manager Alex McLeish in his job – if only for another half a season.

In February, five days after the team crashed out of the Scottish Cup to Hibs (beaten 3-0 at home), McLeish was informed by Rangers chairman David Murray that his services would no longer be required at the end of the season. There was still a chance for further success in the Champions League, but Rangers were knocked out on away goals by Villarreal after two draws (to add to the four that had concluded their group programme).

All that remained was for Rangers to try to claw back the deficit on Hearts and re-qualify for the Champions League. They did their best, going through their last dozen SPL games undefeated, but when McLeish bowed out with a 2-0 win at Ibrox over Hearts, the victory was worthless – if not for him, then certainly for his successor, Frenchman Paul Le Guen. Back-to-back home wins for Hearts in the previous week – the first of them 3-0 against an unsurprisingly charitable Celtic – had already secured that coveted second place.

At the other end of the table Livingston succumbed to relegation with fewer points – just 18 in 38 games – than any previous SPL side. They also equalled the record for the fewest victories (four) and most defeats (28). Up to replace them came St. Mirren, comfortable winners of the First Division.

Kirin Cup success

Scotland's improvement under Walter Smith continued in the latter stages of the World Cup qualifying campaign, but an excellent performance at home to Italy and two fine wins in Norway and Slovenia were sabotaged by a dreadful home defeat by Belarus. The closing 3-0 win in Slovenia, in which the team's three brightest stars, Darren Fletcher, James McFadden and Paul Hartley, all got on the scoresheet, was Scotland's biggest away win in a dozen years. Seven months later an experimental team lacking any players from Celtic and Hearts did even better, thrashing Bulgaria 5-1 at the Kirin Cup in Japan. It was an extraordinary performance, with Kris Boyd, the SPL's runaway top scorer, and his Rangers team-mate Chris Burke both scoring twice on their international debut. A goalless draw against the hosts two days later enabled Scotland to come home with the trophy.

It was the perfect fillip for the Euro 2008 qualifying campaign, although the subsequent performances at the World Cup from Italy, France and Ukraine – three of Scotland's group opponents – suggest that the team's chances of avoiding a fifth successive qualifying failure are, at best, minimal. Roll on the 2010 World Cup…

Scotland

NATIONAL TEAM APPEARANCES 2005/06

Coach – Walter SMITH

Player	DOB	Club	Aut	ITA	NOR	BLS	SLO	Usa	Sui	Bul	Jpn	Caps	Goals
Craig GORDON	31/12/82	Heart of Midlothian	G46	G	G	G	G	G	G49			15	-
Jackie McNAMARA	24/10/73	Wolverhampton W. (ENG)	D	D	D							33	-
Graham ALEXANDER	10/10/71	Preston North End (ENG)	D	D	D	D	M	D	M			23	-
Steven PRESSLEY	11/10/73	Heart of Midlothian	D46		D	D	D46	D46				28	-
Steven CALDWELL	12/9/80	Sunderland (ENG)	D				s71	s46	s56			9	-
Andrew WEBSTER	23/4/82	Heart of Midlothian	D	D	D		D	D	D			22	1
Christian DAILLY	23/10/73	West Ham United (ENG)	M	M		M	M	D	M			61	5
Brian O'NEIL	6/9/72	Preston North End (ENG)	M46									7	-
Nigel QUASHIE	20/7/78	Southampton (ENG) /West Bromwich A. (ENG)	M73	M66			M71	M	M			12	1
Kenny MILLER	23/12/79	Wolverhampton W. (ENG)	A46	A75	A40	A	A46		A			26	7
Garry O'CONNOR	7/5/83	Hibernian	A				s46	A73				7	1
Rab DOUGLAS	24/4/72	Celtic	s46									19	-
Russell ANDERSON	25/10/78	Aberdeen	s46							D	D	9	-
Scott SEVERIN	15/2/79	Aberdeen	s46							M69	M46	13	-
Derek RIORDAN	16//83	Hibernian	s46									1	-
Richard HUGHES	25/6/79	Portsmouth (ENG)	s73									5	-
David WEIR	10/5/70	Everton (ENG)		D	D	D		D46	D56	D	D	48	1
Barry FERGUSON	2/2/78	Rangers		M	M	M			M50			33	2
Darren FLETCHER	1/2/84	Manchester United (ENG)		M	M	M	M	M	M	M	M	23	3
Paul HARTLEY	19/10/76	Heart of Midlothian		M	M	M	M					7	1
Neil McCANN	11/8/74	Southampton (ENG)		s66	s40			M62				26	3
Craig BEATTIE	16/1/84	Celtic		s75	s72							2	-
James McFADDEN	14/4/83	Everton (ENG)			M72		A	s62	A	s52	A59	27	8
Ian MURRAY	20/3/81	Rangers				D46				s78	s46	6	-
Lee McCULLOCH	14/5/78	Wigan Athletic (ENG)				M				M78	M69	7	-
Shaun MALONEY	24/1/83	Celtic				s46		s73				2	-
Gary CALDWELL	12/4/82	Hibernian					s46	s46	D	D	D	20	1
Neil ALEXANDER	10/3/78	Cardiff City (WAL)							s49	G	G	3	-
Gary TEALE	21/7/78	Wigan Athletic (ENG)							s50	M74	M59	3	-
Gary NAYSMITH	16/11/78	Everton (ENG)								D	M46	30	1
Graeme MURTY	13/11/74	Reading (ENG)								D82	D79	3	-
Kris BOYD	18/8/83	Rangers								A52	s59	2	2
Gavin RAE	28/11/77	Rangers								s69	s46	11	-
Christopher BURKE	2/12/83	Rangers								s74	s59	2	2
David McNAMEE	10/10/80	Livingston								s82	s79	4	-
Lee MILLER	18/5/83	Dundee United									s69	1	-

Scotland

EUROPEAN CUPS 2005/06

UEFA CHAMPIONS LEAGUE

RANGERS
3rd qualifying round ANORTHOSIS (CYP)
A 2-1 *Novo (64), Ricksen (71)*
Waterreus, Pierre-Fanfan, Andrews, Rodriguez, Ball, Ricksen, Ferguson, Murray, Buffel (Løvenkrands 58), Novo (Burke 79), Prso (Thompson 74).
H 2-0 *Buffel (39), Prso (58)*
Waterreus, Ricksen, Pierre-Fanfan, Rodriguez, Ball, Ferguson, Murray (Rae A. 85), Løvenkrands, Buffel (McCormack 74), Novo, Prso (Thompson 66).

1st round Group H
Match 1 FC PORTO (POR)
H 3-2 *Løvenkrands (35), Prso (59), Kyrgiakos (85)*
Waterreus, Ricksen, Rodriguez, Kyrgiakos, Bernard, Namouchi (Novo 72), Ferguson, Murray, Løvenkrands (Buffel 56), Prso, Jeffers (Thompson 84).

Match 2 INTERNAZIONALE (ITA)
A 0-1
Waterreus, Ricksen, Rodriguez, Kyrgiakos, Bernard, Namouchi (Thompson 89), Ferguson, Murray (Nieto 84), Løvenkrands, Buffel (Jeffers 78), Prso.

Match 3 ARTMEDIA BRATISLAVA (SVK)
H 0-0
Waterreus, Ricksen, Rodriguez, Kyrgiakos (Andrews 58), Bernard, Namouchi (Burke 75), Ferguson, Hemdani, Løvenkrands, Nieto (Thompson 37), Prso.

Match 4 ARTMEDIA BRATISLAVA
A 2-2 *Prso (3), Thompson (44)*
Waterreus, Hutton, Kyrgiakos, Rodriguez, Bernard (Murray 89), Ricksen, Ferguson, Hemdani, Løvenkrands, Thompson (Jeffers 70), Prso.

Match 5 FC PORTO
A 1-1 *McCormack (83)*
Waterreus, Murray, Kyrgiakos, Andrews, Ricksen, Løvenkrands (Burke 78), Ferguson, Hemdani, Rae A. (Thompson 62), Namouchi, Jeffers (McCormack 76).

Match 6 INTERNAZIONALE
H 1-1 *Løvenkrands (38)*
Waterreus, Ricksen, Andrews, Kyrgiakos, Murray, Burke, Ferguson, Malcolm, Namouchi, Buffel, Løvenkrands.

2nd round VILLARREAL CF (ESP)
H 2-2 *Løvenkrands (21), Peña (81og)*
Waterreus, Hutton, Rodriguez, Kyrgiakos, Smith, Burke, Hemdani, Ferguson, Namouchi (Buffel 69), Prso (Boyd 89), Løvenkrands (Novo 75).
A 1-1 *Løvenkrands (11)*
Waterreus, Hutton, Rodriguez, Kyrgiakos, Murray, Burke (Novo 87), Ferguson, Hemdani, Namouchi, Buffel (Boyd 64), Løvenkrands.

CELTIC
2nd qualifying round ARTMEDIA BRATISLAVA (SVK)
A 0-5
Marshall, Telfer, Varga, Baldé, Camara, Zurawski (Maloney 60), Lennon, Petrov, Thompson (Aliadière 66), Hartson, Sutton (McGeady 17).
H 4-0 *Thompson (21p), Hartson (44), McManus (54), Beattie (82)*
Boruc, Telfer, Baldé, McManus, Camara, Petrov, Lennon, Thompson (Aliadière 87), Wallace (Maloney 53), Zurawski (Beattie 63), Hartson.

UEFA CUP

DUNDEE UNITED
2nd qualifying round MYPA (FIN)
A 0-0
Stillie, Wilson, McCracken, Archibald, Duff, Crawford, Kerr, Brebner, McIntyre, Robson, Miller.
H 2-2 *Kerr (15), Samuel (29)*
Stillie, Ritchie, Archibald, Wilson, Duff, Kerr, Brebner, Robson, Samuel (Crawford 75), Miller, McIntyre.

HIBERNIAN
1st round DNIPRO DNIPROPETROVSK (UKR)
H 0-0
Malkowski, Whittaker, Hogg, Smith G. (Caldwell 45), Stewart (Sproule 52), Murphy, Brown S. (Glass 69), Beuzelin, Thomson, Shiels, O'Connor.
A 1-5 *Riordan (10)*
Malkowski, Beuzelin (Fletcher 66), Caldwell, Murphy, O'Connor (Morrow 77), Riordan, Sproule, Stewart (Shiels 72), Hogg, Thomson, Whittaker.

TOP GOALSCORERS 2005/06

32	Kris BOYD (Kilmarnock/Rangers)
18	John HARTSON (Celtic)
16	Craig DARGO (Inverness Caledonian Thistle)
	Derek RIORDAN (Hibernian)
	Rudolf SKÁCEL (Heart of Midlothian)
	Maciej ZURAWSKI (Celtic)
14	Paul HARTLEY (Heart of Midlothian)
	Peter LØVENKRANDS (Rangers)
13	Shaun MALONEY (Celtic)
	Steven NAISMITH (Kilmarnock)

LEAGUE RESULTS/SCORERS/APPEARANCES/GOALS 2005/06

ABERDEEN
Manager – Jimmy Calderwood

2005				
30/7	Dundee United	a	1-1	Nicholson
6/8	Kilmarnock	h	1-2	Anderson
14/8	Rangers	a	3-2	Anderson, Lovell, Smith
20/8	Heart of Midlothian	a	0-2	
27/8	Falkirk	h	3-0	Smith 2, Clark
10/9	Celtic	a	0-2	
17/9	Dunfermline Athletic	a	2-0	Crawford, Severin
24/9	Livingston	h	0-0	
1/10	Motherwell	h	2-2	Mackie 2 (1p)
15/10	Inverness Caledonian Thistle	a	1-1	Smith
22/10	Hibernian	h	0-1	
25/10	Dundee United	h	2-0	Smith, Crawford
29/10	Kilmarnock	a	2-4	Anderson, Crawford
5/11	Rangers	a	0-0	
20/11	Heart of Midlothian	h	1-1	Smith
26/11	Falkirk	a	2-1	og (Ireland), Anderson
4/12	Celtic	h	1-3	Winter
10/12	Dunfermline Athletic	h	0-0	
17/12	Livingston	a	0-0	
26/12	Motherwell	a	1-3	Stewart
31/12	Inverness Caledonian Thistle	h	0-0	
2006				
14/1	Hibernian	a	2-1	Crawford, Mackie
21/1	Dundee United	a	1-1	Mackie

Scotland

FINAL LEAGUE TABLE 2005/06

		Pld	Home W	D	L	F	A	Away W	D	L	F	A	Total W	D	L	F	A	Pts
1	Celtic	38	14	4	1	41	15	14	3	2	52	22	28	7	3	93	37	91
2	Heart of Midlothian	38	15	2	2	43	9	7	6	6	28	22	22	8	8	71	31	74
3	Rangers	38	13	4	2	38	11	8	6	5	29	26	21	10	7	67	37	73
4	Hibernian	38	11	1	7	39	24	6	4	9	22	32	17	5	16	61	56	56
5	Kilmarnock	38	11	3	5	39	29	4	7	8	24	35	15	10	13	63	64	55
6	Aberdeen	38	8	9	3	30	17	5	6	7	16	23	13	15	10	46	40	54
7	Inverness Caledonian Thistle	38	5	6	7	21	21	10	7	3	30	17	15	13	10	51	38	58
8	Motherwell	38	7	5	7	35	31	6	5	8	20	30	13	10	15	55	61	49
9	Dundee United	38	5	8	6	22	28	2	4	13	19	38	7	12	19	41	66	33
10	Falkirk	38	2	6	11	14	30	6	3	10	21	34	8	9	21	35	64	33
11	Dunfermline Athletic	38	3	5	11	17	39	5	4	10	16	29	8	9	21	33	68	33
12	Livingston	38	3	4	12	15	33	1	2	16	10	46	4	6	28	25	79	18

N.B. League splits into top and bottom halves after the 33rd game, with each team playing five further matches exclusively against teams from its half of the table.

Date	Opponent		Score	Scorers
28/1	Kilmarnock	h	2-2	Nicholson, Anderson
8/2	Rangers	h	2-0	Smith, Lovell
11/2	Heart of Midlothian	a	2-1	og (Pressley), Clark
18/2	Falkirk	h	1-0	Smith
4/3	Celtic	a	0-3	
11/3	Dunfermline Athletic	a	0-1	
18/3	Livingston	h	3-0	Anderson, Lovell, Snoyl
25/3	Motherwell	h	2-2	Lovell 2
1/4	Inverness Caledonian Thistle	a	1-0	Lovell
8/4	Hibernian	h	1-0	Severin
15/4	Rangers	a	1-1	Severin
22/4	Kilmarnock	a	0-0	
29/4	Hibernian	h	4-0	Crawford, Lovell 2, Foster
3/5	Heart of Midlothian	a	0-1	
7/5	Celtic	h	2-2	Stewart 2

No	Name	Nat	Pos	Aps	(s)	Gls
4	Russell ANDERSON		D	36		6
17	Richie BYRNE	IRL	D	18	(1)	
11	Christopher CLARK		M	30	(1)	2
21	Andrew CONSIDINE		D	8	(4)	
25	Steven CRAIG		A		(3)	
23	Steven CRAWFORD		A	27	(3)	5
14	Gary DEMPSEY	IRL	M	17	(7)	
5	Alexander DIAMOND		D	31	(2)	
27	David DONALD		D		(1)	
1	Ryan ESSON		G	18		
19	Richard FOSTER		M	8	(17)	1
31	Daniel GRIFFIN	NIR	D	9	(1)	
2	Michael HART		D	4		
20	Jamie LANGFIELD		G	20		
9	Steven LOVELL	ENG	A	22	(5)	8
29	Neil MACFARLANE		M	2	(4)	
22	Kyle MACAULEY		M	3	(2)	
10	Darren MACKIE		A	11	(17)	4
26	Christopher MAGUIRE		A		(1)	
3	Kevin McNAUGHTON		D	34		
18	Scott MUIRHEAD		M	10	(8)	
8	Barry NICHOLSON		M	32	(1)	2
6	Scott SEVERIN		M	28		3
7	Jamie SMITH		M	35		8
15	Ferne SNOYL	HOL	M	9	(3)	1
16	John STEWART		A	2	(15)	3
15	Jamie WINTER		M	4	(3)	1

CELTIC
Manager – Gordon Strachan

2005

Date	Opponent		Score	Scorers
30/7	Motherwell	a	4-4	Hartson 3 (1p), Beattie
6/8	Dundee United	h	2-0	Hartson, Beattie
13/8	Falkirk	h	3-1	Hartson, Thompson 2
20/8	Rangers	a	1-3	Maloney (p)
28/8	Dunfermline Athletic	a	4-0	Zurawski 2, Hartson, Nakamura
10/9	Aberdeen	h	2-0	Zurawski, Petrov
18/9	Hibernian	a	1-0	Petrov
24/9	Inverness Caledonian Thistle	h	2-1	Beattie 2
1/10	Livingston	a	5-0	McManus, Maloney, Zurawski, Sutton, Beattie
15/10	Heart of Midlothian	h	1-1	Beattie
23/10	Kilmarnock	a	1-0	Petrov
26/10	Motherwell	h	5-0	Petrov 3, Maloney, Nakamura
30/10	Dundee United	a	4-2	Hartson, Sutton, og (Archibald), Pearson
6/11	Falkirk	a	3-0	Maloney, McGeady, Hartson
19/11	Rangers	h	3-0	Hartson, Baldé, McGeady
26/11	Dunfermline Athletic	h	0-1	
4/12	Aberdeen	a	3-1	McGeady, Petrov, Telfer
10/12	Hibernian	h	3-2	Hartson 2, Maloney
18/12	Inverness Caledonian Thistle	a	1-1	Hartson
26/12	Livingston	h	2-1	Maloney (p), Nakamura

2006

Date	Opponent		Score	Scorers
1/1	Heart of Midlothian	a	3-2	Pearson, McManus 2
14/1	Kilmarnock	h	4-2	Nakamura, Maloney (p), McManus, Zurawski
22/1	Motherwell	a	3-1	Zurawski, McGeady, Hartson
28/1	Dundee United	h	3-3	Hartson, Zurawski, Petrov
8/2	Falkirk	h	2-1	Keane, McManus
12/2	Rangers	a	1-0	Zurawski
19/2	Dunfermline Athletic	a	8-1	Petrov, Hartson, Zurawski 4, Maloney, Lennon
4/3	Aberdeen	h	3-0	Petrov, Maloney, Zurawski
12/3	Hibernian	a	2-1	Maloney (p), McManus
22/3	Inverness Caledonian Thistle	h	2-1	McManus, Maloney

Scotland

Date	Opponent	h/a	Score	Scorers
26/3	Livingston	a	2-0	Zurawski, Maloney (p)
5/4	Heart of Midlothian	h	1-0	Hartson
9/4	Kilmarnock	a	4-1	Nakamura 2, Hartson, Dublin
16/4	Hibernian	h	1-1	Zurawski
23/4	Rangers	h	0-0	
30/4	Heart of Midlothian	a	0-3	
3/5	Kilmarnock	h	2-0	Zurawski, Varga
7/5	Aberdeen	a	2-2	Hartson, Maloney

No	Name	Nat	Pos	Aps	(s)	Gls
17	Didier AGATHE	FRA	M		(4)	
6	Bobo BALDE	GUI	D	28		1
37	Craig BEATTIE		A	7	(7)	6
1	Artur BORUC	POL	G	34		
3	Mohammed CAMARA	GUI	D	18		
9	Dion DUBLIN	ENG	A	3	(8)	1
10	John HARTSON	WAL	A	29	(6)	18
16	Roy KEANE	IRL	M	10		1
35	Paul LAWSON		M	1	(2)	
18	Neil LENNON	NIR	M	32		1
29	Shaun MALONEY		A	27	(9)	13
22	David MARSHALL		G	4		
46	Aiden McGEADY	IRL	A	11	(9)	4
42	Michael McGLINCHEY		A		(1)	
44	Steven McMANUS		D	36		7
25	Shunsuke NAKAMURA	JPN	M	30	(3)	6
11	Stephen PEARSON		M	2	(16)	2
19	Stilian PETROV	BUL	M	36	(1)	10
9	Chris SUTTON	ENG	A	7	(1)	2
2	Paul TELFER		D	36		1
8	Alan THOMPSON	ENG	M	11	(5)	2
23	Stanislav VARGA	SVK	D	9	(1)	1
4	Adam VIRGO	ENG	D	3	(7)	
33	Ross WALLACE		M	8	(3)	
12	Mark WILSON		D	14	(1)	
7	Maciej ZURAWSKI	POL	A	22	(2)	16

DUNDEE UNITED
Manager – Gordon Chisholm; (10/1/06) (Billy Dodds); (16/1/06) Craig Brewster

2005

Date	Opponent	h/a	Score	Scorers
30/7	Aberdeen	h	1-1	Miller
6/8	Celtic	a	0-2	
14/8	Heart of Midlothian	h	0-3	
20/8	Motherwell	a	5-4	Miller 2, Fernández, Brebner 2
28/8	Inverness Caledonian Thistle	h	1-1	Miller
10/9	Hibernian	a	1-2	Brebner
17/9	Livingston	h	2-0	Fernández, Canero
24/9	Dunfermline Athletic	a	1-2	McCracken
1/10	Kilmarnock	h	0-0	
16/10	Rangers	h	0-0	
22/10	Falkirk	a	3-1	og (Glennon), Canero, Samuel
25/10	Aberdeen	a	0-2	
30/10	Celtic	h	2-4	og (Sutton), Samuel
5/11	Heart of Midlothian	a	0-3	
19/11	Motherwell	h	1-1	McIntyre
26/11	Inverness Caledonian Thistle	a	1-1	Miller (p)
3/12	Hibernian	h	1-0	Samuel
10/12	Livingston	a	0-1	
20/12	Dunfermline Athletic	h	2-1	Samuel, Robson
26/12	Kilmarnock	a	1-2	Samuel
31/12	Rangers	a	0-3	

2006

15/1	Falkirk	h	2-1	Fernández, McInnes
21/1	Aberdeen	h	1-1	Archibald
28/1	Celtic	a	3-3	Fernández 2, Miller
7/2	Heart of Midlothian	h	1-1	Brebner
11/2	Motherwell	a	0-2	
18/2	Inverness Caledonian Thistle	h	2-4	Mulgrew 2
25/2	Dunfermline Athletic	a	1-1	Kenneth
4/3	Hibernian	a	1-3	Goodwillie
11/3	Livingston	h	3-1	Miller 2, Kerr
25/3	Kilmarnock	h	2-2	McCracken, McInnes
2/4	Rangers	h	1-4	Samuel
8/4	Falkirk	a	0-1	
15/4	Livingston	a	1-3	Robertson
22/4	Inverness Caledonian Thistle	a	0-1	
29/4	Falkirk	h	0-2	
2/5	Dunfermline Athletic	h	0-1	
6/5	Motherwell	a	1-1	Samuel

No	Name	Nat	Pos	Aps	(s)	Gls
29	Stuart ABBOT		D	2	(1)	
5	Alan ARCHIBALD		D	33		1
8	Grant BREBNER		M	26		4
16	Craig BREWSTER		A		(1)	
26	Greg CAMERON		M	2	(2)	
6	Peter CANERO		D	9	(2)	2
	Steven CRAWFORD		A	4		
12	Stuart DUFF		M	24	(5)	
30	William EASTON		D		(1)	
20	David FERNÁNDEZ	ESP	A	29	(1)	5
28	Ross GARDINER		D	4		
36	David GOODWILLIE		A		(10)	1
18	Gary KENNETH		D	12	(4)	1
7	Mark KERR		M	35		1
15	Lee MAIR		D	5	(1)	
3	David McCRACKEN		D	34		2
4	Derek McINNES		M	9	(3)	2
10	James McINTYRE		A	18	(7)	1
9	Lee MILLER		A	22	(12)	8
6	Charles MULGREW		D	13		2
23	Paul RITCHIE		A	20	(1)	
25	David ROBERTSON		M	6	(5)	1
11	Barry ROBSON		M	30	(1)	1
17	Craig SAMSON		G	8		
21	Collin SAMUEL	TRI	A	23	(12)	7
1	Derek STILLIE		G	30		
2	Mark WILSON		D	20	(1)	

DUNFERMLINE ATHLETIC
Manager – Jim Leishman

2005

Date	Opponent	h/a	Score	Scorers
30/7	Hibernian	a	1-1	Shields
6/8	Motherwell	a	0-1	
13/8	Inverness Caledonian Thistle	h	0-1	
20/8	Livingston	a	1-1	Makel
28/8	Celtic	h	0-4	
10/9	Kilmarnock	a	2-3	Burchill, Young De.
17/9	Aberdeen	h	0-2	
24/9	Dundee United	h	2-1	Tod, Ross
1/10	Rangers	a	1-5	Hunt
15/10	Falkirk	h	0-1	
22/10	Heart of Midlothian	a	0-2	
26/10	Hibernian	h	1-2	Mason
29/10	Motherwell	h	0-3	
5/11	Inverness Caledonian Thistle	a	1-2	Makel
19/11	Livingston	h	0-1	
26/11	Celtic	a	1-0	Ross

Scotland

3/12	Kilmarnock	h	0-1	
10/12	Aberdeen	a	0-0	
20/12	Dundee United	a	1-2	Wilson S.
26/12	Rangers	h	3-3	Tod, Burchill, Young Da. (p)
31/12	Falkirk	a	2-1	Burchill, Hunt
2006				
14/1	Heart of Midlothian	h	1-4	Burchill
21/1	Hibernian	a	1-3	Donnelly
28/1	Motherwell	h	1-1	Young Da.
8/2	Inverness Caledonian Thistle	h	2-2	Hunt, Burchill
11/2	Livingston	a	1-0	Burchill
19/2	Celtic	h	1-8	Tod
25/2	Dundee United	h	1-1	Burchill
4/3	Kilmarnock	a	0-1	
11/3	Aberdeen	h	1-0	Burchill
25/3	Rangers	a	0-1	
1/4	Falkirk	h	1-1	Burchill
8/4	Heart of Midlothian	a	0-4	
15/4	Dunfermline Athletic	a	0-0	
22/4	Livingston	h	3-2	Burchill 2 (1p), Hunt
29/4	Motherwell	a	3-2	Campbell I., Burchill (p), Mason
2/5	Dundee United	a	1-0	Daquin
6/5	Inverness Caledonian Thistle	h	0-1	

No	Name	Nat	Pos	Aps	(s)	Gls
9	Mark BURCHILL		A	24	(7)	12
24	Andrew CAMPBELL		A	1	(4)	
25	Iain CAMPBELL		D	14	(3)	1
26	Frédéric DAQUIN	FRA	A	2	(7)	1
14	Simon DONNELLY		M	8	(5)	1
32	John DUNN		A		(1)	
17	Gardur GUNNLAUGSSON	ISL	A		(1)	
20	Bryn HALLIWELL	ENG	G	12		
21	Liam HORSTED	ENG	M	6	(5)	
16	Noel HUNT	IRL	A	22	(10)	4
19	Aaron LABONTE	FRA	D	19	(3)	
10	Lee MAKEL	ENG	M	20		2
8	Gary MASON		M	29		2
5	Jamie McCUNNIE		M	18	(4)	
1	Alan McGREGOR		G	26		
6	Scott MORRISON		M	3		
28	Scott MUIRHEAD		M	11	(1)	
37	Nicholas PHINN		M	1	(2)	
23	Greg ROSS		D	21	(2)	2
2	Greg SHIELDS		D	33		1
27	Stephen SIMMONS		M	3	(3)	
5	Andrius SKERLA	LIT	D	1	(1)	
7	Bartosz TARACHULSKI	POL	A	12	(15)	
6	Scott THOMSON		M	23	(2)	
18	Andrew TOD		D	26	(4)	3
22	Craig WILSON		A	6	(8)	
3	Scott WILSON		D	31	(1)	1
4	Darren YOUNG		M	21		2
11	Derek YOUNG		A	12	(6)	1
15	Yannick ZAMBERNARDI	FRA	D	13	(2)	

FALKIRK
Manager – John Hughes

2005				
30/7	Inverness Caledonian Thistle	h	0-2	
6/8	Livingston	a	2-0	Latapy, Duffy
13/8	Celtic	a	1-3	Duffy (p)
20/8	Hibernian	h	0-2	
27/8	Aberdeen	a	0-3	
10/9	Rangers	h	1-1	McBreen
17/9	Motherwell	a	0-5	
24/9	Kilmarnock	a	1-1	Gow
2/10	Heart of Midlothian	h	2-2	Duffy (p), og (Pressley)
15/10	Dunfermline Athletic	a	1-0	Duffy
22/10	Dundee United	h	1-3	Duffy
26/10	Inverness Caledonian Thistle	a	3-0	Thomson S., Duffy, Moutinho
29/10	Livingston	h	1-1	og (Pinxten)
6/11	Celtic	a	0-3	
19/11	Hibernian	a	3-2	Duffy 2, Gow
26/11	Aberdeen	h	1-2	McBreen
3/12	Rangers	a	2-2	Gow, Moutinho
10/12	Motherwell	h	0-1	
17/12	Kilmarnock	h	1-2	Milne
26/12	Heart of Midlothian	a	0-5	
31/12	Dunfermline Athletic	h	1-2	Duffy
2006				
15/1	Dundee United	a	1-2	McBreen
21/1	Inverness Caledonian Thistle	h	1-4	Ireland
28/1	Livingston	a	1-0	O'Donnell
8/2	Celtic	a	1-2	Milne
11/2	Hibernian	h	0-0	
18/2	Aberdeen	a	0-1	
4/3	Rangers	h	1-2	Latapy
11/3	Motherwell	a	1-3	Cregg
18/3	Kilmarnock	a	1-2	McBreen
25/3	Heart of Midlothian	h	1-2	Gow
1/4	Dunfermline Athletic	a	1-1	Ross
8/4	Dundee United	h	1-0	Ross
15/4	Dunfermline Athletic	h	0-0	
22/4	Motherwell	h	1-1	Gow
29/4	Dundee United	a	2-0	Gow, McBreen
3/5	Inverness Caledonian Thistle	a	0-2	
6/5	Livingston	h	1-0	McBreen

No	Name	Nat	Pos	Aps	(s)	Gls
20	Darren BARR		M		(1)	
	Graeme CHURCHILL		A		(1)	
26	Liam CRAIG		M	10	(6)	
4	Patrick CREGG		M	14	(2)	1
27	Karl DODD	AUS	D	8	(1)	
11	Daryl DUFFY		A	19	(2)	9
1	Alan FERGUSON		G	9		
27	Matthew GLENNAN	NZL	G	21		
8	Alan GOW		M	30	(4)	6
13	Mark HOWARD	ENG	G	8		
24	John HUGHES		D	1		
6	Craig IRELAND		D	23		1
10	Russell LATAPY	TRI	M	24	(6)	2
2	Andrew LAWRIE		D	27	(2)	
21	Jean-François LESCINEL	FRA	D	8		
18	Vítor Manuel LIMA SANTOS	POR	D	21	(7)	
19	Daniel McBREEN		A	21	(11)	6
3	Craig McPHERSON		M	12	(6)	
14	Ryan McSTAY		M	1	(4)	
16	Ian McSWEEN		A		(1)	
15	Kenneth MILNE		D	32	(1)	2
7	Pedro MOUTINHO	POR	A	8	(20)	2
28	Stephen O'DONNELL		M	21	(6)	1
21	John O'NEIL		M	3	(5)	
25	Tiago RODRIGUES	POR	D	31	(1)	
5	Jack ROSS		M	16	(1)	2
12	Neil SCALLY		M	13	(5)	
33	Thomas SCOBIE		D	2	(1)	
9	Andrew THOMSON		A		(4)	
28	Steven THOMSON		M	30	(2)	1

Scotland

23	Mark TWADDLE		M	5	(1)	

HEART OF MIDLOTHIAN
Manager – George Burley; (22/10/05) (John McGlynn); (8/11/05) Graham Rix (ENG); (22/3/06) (Valdas Ivanauskas (LIT))

2005

Date	Opponent	H/A	Score	Scorers
30/7	Kilmarnock	a	4-2	Skácel, Bednár, Mikoliunas, Hartley (p)
7/8	Hibernian	h	4-0	Skácel, Hartley (p), Simmons, Mikoliunas
14/8	Dundee United	a	3-0	Pressley, Bednár, Skácel
20/8	Aberdeen	h	2-0	Skácel, Pospísil
27/8	Motherwell	h	2-1	Skácel, Jankauskas
11/9	Livingston	a	4-1	Skácel, Webster, Hartley 2 (1p)
17/9	Inverness Caledonian Thistle	a	1-0	Skácel
24/9	Rangers	h	1-0	Bednár
2/10	Falkirk	a	2-2	Pressley 2
15/10	Celtic	a	1-1	Skácel
22/10	Dunfermline Athletic	h	2-0	Skácel, Pospísil
26/10	Kilmarnock	h	1-0	Jankauskas
29/10	Hibernian	a	0-2	
5/11	Dundee United	h	3-0	Hartley, Skácel, Pospísil
20/11	Aberdeen	a	1-1	Skácel
26/11	Motherwell	a	1-1	Hartley (p)
3/12	Livingston	h	2-1	Skácel 2
10/12	Inverness Caledonian Thistle	h	0-0	
17/12	Rangers	a	0-1	
26/12	Falkirk	h	5-0	Hartley, Skácel, Elliot 2, Pospísil

2006

Date	Opponent	H/A	Score	Scorers
1/1	Celtic	h	2-3	Jankauskas, Pressley
14/1	Dunfermline Athletic	a	4-1	Pressley, Pospísil 2, Skácel
21/1	Kilmarnock	a	0-1	
28/1	Hibernian	h	4-1	Harley 2 (1p), Skácel, Elliot
7/2	Dundee United	a	1-1	Hartley (p)
11/2	Aberdeen	h	1-2	Elliot
18/2	Motherwell	h	3-0	Jankauskas 2, Elliot
5/3	Livingston	a	3-2	Aguiar, Jankauskas, Bednár
11/3	Inverness Caledonian Thistle	a	0-0	
19/3	Rangers	h	1-1	Jankauskas
25/3	Falkirk	a	2-1	Hartley, Jankauskas
5/4	Celtic	a	0-1	
8/4	Dunfermline Athletic	h	4-0	Pospísil, Bednár, Mikoliunas, Mäkelä
15/4	Kilmarnock	h	2-0	Hartley, Berra
22/4	Hibernian	a	1-2	Bednár
30/4	Celtic	h	3-0	og (McManus), Hartley, Bednár
3/5	Aberdeen	h	1-0	Hartley (p)
7/5	Rangers	a	0-2	

No	Name	Nat	Pos	Aps	(s)	Gls
36	Bruno AGUIAR	POR	M	10		1
13	Steven BANKS	ENG	G	2	(1)	
32	Nerijus BARASA	LIT	D	1	(3)	
12	Roman BEDNÁR	CZE	A	19	(3)	7
20	Christophe BERRA		D	10	(2)	1
11	Mirsad BESLIJA	BOS	M	2	(2)	
28	Julien BRELLIER	FRA	M	28	(2)	
5	Samuel Almeida CAMAZZOLA	BRA	M	5	(3)	
18	Deividas CESNAUSKIS	LIT	M	15	(10)	
26	Calum ELLIOT		A	17	(11)	5
3	Panagiotis FYSSAS	GRE	D	32		
34	José GONÇALVES	SUI	D	3	(1)	
1	Craig GORDON		G	36		
15	Christopher HACKETT	ENG	M	1	(1)	
10	Paul HARTLEY		M	34		14
9	Edgaras JANKAUSKAS	LIT	A	24	(1)	8
31	L JOHNSON	ENG	M	1	(3)	
11	Neil MACFARLANE		M	1	(2)	
35	Juho MÄKELÄ	FIN	A		(2)	1
14	Jamie McALLISTER		D	8	(9)	
33	Neil McCANN		M	1		
16	Saulius MIKOLIUNAS	LIT	A	16	(7)	3
2	Robert NEILSON		D	36	(1)	
38	Martin PETRÁS	SVK	D	4	(1)	
21	Michal POSPÍSIL	CZE	A	13	(11)	7
4	Stephen PRESSLEY		D	29		5
15	Stephen SIMMONS		M	1	(10)	1
8	Rudolf SKÁCEL	CZE	A	33	(2)	16
37	Ludek STRACENY	CZE	A	1	(1)	
29	Ibrahim TALL	SEN	D	3	(1)	
27	Halmar THORARINSSON	ISL	A		(1)	
22	Lee WALLACE		M	2	(11)	
6	Andrew WEBSTER		D	30		1

HIBERNIAN
Manager – Tony Mowbray (ENG)

2005

Date	Opponent	H/A	Score	Scorers
30/7	Dunfermline Athletic	h	1-1	O'Connor
7/8	Heart of Midlothian	a	0-4	
13/8	Livingston	h	3-0	Murphy, Shiels, O'Connor
20/8	Falkirk	a	2-0	Brown Sc., Riordan (p)
27/8	Rangers	a	3-0	Sproule 3
10/9	Dundee United	h	2-1	O'Connor (p), Sproule
18/9	Celtic	h	0-1	
24/9	Motherwell	a	3-1	Beuzelin, Stewart, Riordan
2/10	Inverness Caledonian Thistle	h	1-2	Fletcher
15/10	Kilmarnock	h	4-2	Caldwell, Beuzelin 2, Riordan
22/10	Aberdeen	a	1-0	Riordan
26/10	Dunfermline Athletic	a	2-1	O'Connor 2
29/10	Heart of Midlothian	h	2-0	Beuzelin, O'Connor
5/11	Livingston	a	2-1	Shiels, O'Connor
19/11	Falkirk	h	2-3	Riordan 2
27/11	Rangers	h	2-1	Riordan, O'Connor
3/12	Dundee United	a	0-1	
10/12	Celtic	a	2-3	Beuzelin, Fletcher
17/12	Motherwell	h	2-1	Fletcher, Riordan
26/12	Inverness Caledonian Thistle	a	0-2	

2006

Date	Opponent	H/A	Score	Scorers
2/1	Kilmarnock	a	2-2	Hogg, O'Connor
14/1	Aberdeen	h	1-2	Whittaker
21/1	Dunfermline Athletic	h	3-1	Riordan 2, Fletcher
28/1	Heart of Midlothian	a	1-4	O'Connor
8/2	Livingston	h	7-0	Killen, Riordan 2, O'Connor, og (Mackay), Fletcher 2
11/2	Falkirk	a	0-0	
18/2	Rangers	a	0-2	
4/3	Dundee United	h	3-1	Riordan, og (Archibald), Killen
12/3	Celtic	h	1-2	Riordan
18/3	Motherwell	a	2-2	Killen, Glass
25/3	Inverness Caledonian Thistle	h	0-2	
5/4	Kilmarnock	h	2-1	Riordan, Dalglish
8/4	Aberdeen	a	0-1	
16/4	Celtic	a	1-1	Fletcher
22/4	Heart of Midlothian	h	2-1	Riordan, Benjelloun
29/4	Aberdeen	h	0-4	
2/5	Rangers	h	1-2	og (Hemdani)
7/5	Kilmarnock	a	1-3	Fletcher

Scotland

No	Name	Nat	Pos	Aps	(s)	Gls
36	Abdessalam BENJELLOUN	MAR	A	2	(3)	1
14	Guillaume BEUZELIN	FRA	M	21		5
17	Scott BROWN		A	16	(3)	1
1	Simon BROWN		G	7	(1)	
4	Gary CALDWELL		D	34		1
27	Paul DALGLISH		A	4	(7)	1
20	Steven FLETCHER		M	16	(18)	8
11	Steven GLASS		M	23	(5)	1
15	Chris HOGG		D	21	(2)	1
33	Chris KILLEN	NZL	A	6	(1)	3
29	Oumar KONDE	SUI	D	7	(4)	
19	Amadou KONTE	MLI	A	1	(12)	
35	Sean LYNCH		A		(2)	
31	Zbigniew MALKOWSKI	POL	G	31		
18	Jamie McCLUSKEY		M		(3)	
23	Kevin McDONALD		M		(2)	
9	Samuel MORROW	NIR	A		(8)	
3	David MURPHY	ENG	D	30		1
16	Antonio MURRAY	ENG	M	1		
9	Gary O'CONNOR		A	24	(2)	11
10	Derek RIORDAN		A	32	(4)	16
25	Humphrey RUDGE	HOL	D	4	(2)	
24	James SHIELDS		M	7		
22	Dean SHIELS	NIR	A	8	(8)	2
5	Gary SMITH		D	19	(1)	
17	Ivan SPROULE	NIR	M	18	(14)	4
6	Michael STEWART		M	24	(1)	1
8	Kevin THOMSON		M	28	(3)	
2	Steven WHITTAKER		M	34		1

INVERNESS CALEDONIAN THISTLE
Manager – Craig Brewster; (12/11/05) (Charlie Christie & John Docherty); (27/1/06) Charlie Christie

2005
Date	Opponent		Score	Scorers
30/7	Falkirk	a	2-0	Brewster 2
6/8	Rangers	h	0-1	
13/8	Dunfermline Athletic	a	1-0	Fox
20/8	Kilmarnock	h	2-2	Brewster 2
28/8	Dundee United	a	1-1	Brewster
10/9	Motherwell	h	1-2	Brewster
17/9	Heart of Midlothian	h	0-1	
24/9	Celtic	a	1-2	Wyness
2/10	Hibernian	a	2-1	Proctor, Wyness
15/10	Aberdeen	h	1-1	Bayne
22/10	Livingston	a	1-1	Morgan
26/10	Falkirk	h	0-3	
29/10	Rangers	a	1-1	Dargo
5/11	Dunfermline Athletic	h	2-1	Black, Proctor
19/11	Kilmarnock	a	2-2	Bayne, Dargo
26/11	Dundee United	h	1-1	Tokely
3/12	Motherwell	a	2-0	Dargo 2
10/12	Heart of Midlothian	h	0-0	
18/12	Celtic	h	1-1	Dargo
26/12	Hibernian	h	2-0	Wilson, Dargo
31/12	Aberdeen	a	0-0	

2006
Date	Opponent		Score	Scorers
14/1	Livingston	h	3-0	Dargo 2 (1p), Wyness
21/1	Falkirk	a	4-1	Wilson, Wyness, Dargo (p), Tokely
29/1	Rangers	h	2-3	Dargo, Wyness
8/2	Dunfermline Athletic	a	2-2	Dargo (p), Wyness
11/2	Kilmarnock	h	3-3	Wyness, Dargo, Proctor
18/2	Dundee United	a	4-2	Dods, Wyness, Dargo, Morgan
4/3	Motherwell	h	0-1	
11/3	Heart of Midlothian	h	0-0	
22/3	Celtic	a	1-2	Hart
25/3	Hibernian	a	2-0	Dods, Wilson (p)
1/4	Aberdeen	h	0-1	
8/4	Livingston	a	1-2	Tokely
15/4	Motherwell	a	1-0	Dargo
22/4	Dundee United	h	1-0	Dargo
29/4	Livingston	a	1-0	Wilson
3/5	Falkirk	h	2-0	Duncan, Dargo
6/5	Dunfermline Athletic	a	1-0	Morgan

No	Name	Nat	Pos	Aps	(s)	Gls
9	Graham BAYNE		A	8	(9)	2
24	Ian BLACK		M	24	(2)	1
25	Craig BREWSTER		A	17	(1)	6
1	Mark BROWN		G	37		
17	Craig DARGO		A	30	(2)	16
4	Darren DODS		D	37		2
12	Russell DUNCAN		M	29	(2)	1
23	Liam FOX		M	9	(8)	1
21	Michael FRASER		G	1		
3	Stuart GOLABEK		D	14	(3)	
10	Richard HART		M	11	(20)	1
16	Richard HASTINGS		D	26	(1)	
8	Steven HISLOP		A		(3)	
11	JUANJO	ESP	M		(2)	
15	Liam KEOGH		A	5	(3)	
28	Rory McALLISTER		A	2	(11)	
6	Roy McBAIN		M	17	(1)	
5	Stuart McCAFFREY		D	7	(1)	
22	Alan MORGAN		M	14	(8)	3
14	Grant MUNRO		D	32		
18	David PROCTOR		D	12	(5)	3
45	Alexander SUTHERLAND		M	1		
2	Ross TOKELY		D	34		3
7	Barry WILSON		M	33	(1)	4
19	Dennis WYNESS		A	18	(9)	8

KILMARNOCK
Manager – Jim Jeffries

2005
Date	Opponent		Score	Scorers
30/7	Heart of Midlothian	h	2-4	Naismith, Greer
6/8	Aberdeen	a	2-1	Johnston, Naismith
13/8	Motherwell	h	4-1	Johnston, Boyd 2, McDonald
20/8	Inverness Caledonian Thistle	a	2-2	Nish, Boyd
27/8	Livingston	h	3-0	Nish 3
10/9	Dunfermline Athletic	h	3-2	Dodds, Boyd, Invincibile
17/9	Rangers	a	0-3	
24/9	Falkirk	h	1-1	Boyd (p)
1/10	Dundee United	a	0-0	
15/10	Hibernian	a	2-4	Ford, Fowler
23/10	Celtic	h	0-1	
26/10	Heart of Midlothian	a	0-1	
29/10	Aberdeen	h	4-2	Ford, Invincibile, Boyd 2
5/11	Motherwell	a	2-2	Boyd 2
19/11	Inverness Caledonian Thistle	h	2-2	Boyd, Naismith
26/11	Livingston	a	3-0	Boyd 2, Naismith
3/12	Dunfermline Athletic	a	1-0	Boyd
11/12	Rangers	h	2-3	McDonald, Boyd
17/12	Falkirk	a	2-1	Fowler, Boyd
26/12	Dundee United	h	2-1	McDonald, Wales

2006
Date	Opponent		Score	Scorers
2/1	Hibernian	h	2-2	Naismith, Wales
14/1	Celtic	a	2-4	Naismith (p), Invincibile

Scotland

21/1	Heart of Midlothian	h	1-0	Invincibile	
28/1	Aberdeen	a	2-2	Naismith (p), Lilley	
8/2	Motherwell	h	2-0	Wales 2	
11/2	Inverness Caledonian Thistle	a	3-3	Naismith, Wales 2	
18/2	Livingston	h	3-1	Wales, Naismith, Invincibile	
4/3	Dunfermline Athletic	h	1-0	Invincibile	
11/3	Rangers	a	0-4		
18/3	Falkirk	h	2-1	Invincibile, Naismith	
25/3	Dundee United	a	2-2	Naismith 2	
5/4	Hibernian	a	1-2	Wales	
9/4	Celtic	h	1-4	Nish	
15/4	Heart of Midlothian	a	0-2		
22/4	Aberdeen	a	0-0		
29/4	Rangers	h	1-3	Nish	
3/5	Celtic	a	0-2		
7/5	Hibernian	h	3-1	Naismith (p), Greer, Nish	

No	Name	Nat	Pos	Aps	(s)	Gls
9	Kris BOYD		A	18	(1)	15
24	Robert CAMPBELL		A		(2)	
1	Alan COMBE		G	32		
20	Paul DI GIACOMO		A	2	(10)	
16	Rhian DODDS	CAN	M	6	(5)	1
6	Simon FORD		D	32		2
2	James FOWLER		D	38		2
5	Gordon GREER		D	27		2
3	Gary HAY		D	35		
11	Danny INVINCIBILE	AUS	M	34	(3)	7
12	Alan JOHNSTON		A	36	(1)	2
22	Peter LEVEN		M	4	(2)	
4	David LILLEY		D	8	(3)	1
8	Gary LOCKE		M	10	(5)	
7	Gary McDONALD		M	16	(11)	3
19	Stephen MURRAY		A	1	(14)	
14	Steven NAISMITH		A	32	(4)	13
15	Colin NISH		A	25	(9)	7
13	Graeme SMITH		G	6	(1)	
10	Gary WALES		M	18	(12)	8
21	Lindsey WILSON		D	11	(2)	
18	Fraser WRIGHT		D	27		

LIVINGSTON
Manager – Paul Lambert; (15/2/06) John Robertson

2005

31/7	Rangers	a	0-3	
6/8	Falkirk	h	0-2	
13/8	Hibernian	a	0-3	
20/8	Dunfermline Athletic	h	1-1	Pereira
27/8	Kilmarnock	a	0-3	
11/9	Heart of Midlothian	h	1-4	Dalglish
17/9	Dundee United	a	0-2	
24/9	Aberdeen	a	0-0	
1/10	Celtic	h	0-5	
15/10	Motherwell	a	0-1	
22/10	Inverness Caledonian Thistle	h	1-1	Pinxten
26/10	Rangers	h	2-2	Snodgrass 2
29/10	Falkirk	a	1-1	Snodgrass
5/11	Hibernian	h	1-2	Strong
19/11	Dunfermline Athletic	a	1-0	Dalglish
26/11	Kilmarnock	h	0-3	
3/12	Heart of Midlothian	a	1-2	Walker
10/12	Dundee United	h	1-0	Snodgrass
17/12	Aberdeen	h	0-0	
26/12	Celtic	a	1-2	Dalglish
31/12	Motherwell	h	1-2	Pinxten

2006

14/1	Inverness Caledonian Thistle	a	0-3	
21/1	Rangers	a	1-4	Vincze
28/1	Falkirk	h	0-1	
8/2	Hibernian	a	0-7	
11/2	Dunfermline Athletic	h	0-1	
18/2	Kilmarnock	a	1-3	Hislop
5/3	Heart of Midlothian	h	2-3	Brittain, Mackay
11/3	Dundee United	a	1-3	Morrow
18/3	Aberdeen	a	0-3	
26/3	Celtic	h	0-2	
1/4	Motherwell	a	1-2	Whelan
8/4	Inverness Caledonian Thistle	h	2-1	Brittain, Healy
15/4	Dundee United	h	3-1	Morrow, Pinxten, Brittain (p)
22/4	Dunfermline Athletic	a	2-3	Brittain (p), Healy
29/4	Inverness Caledonian Thistle	h	0-1	
3/5	Motherwell	h	0-1	
7/5	Falkirk	a	0-1	

No	Name	Nat	Pos	Aps	(s)	Gls
8	Derek ADAMS		A	21	(6)	
25	Graham BARRETT	IRL	A	6		
	Neil BARRETT	ENG	M	6	(3)	
19	Scott BOYD		D	2	(2)	
7	Richard BRITTAIN		M	33	(2)	4
11	Jason DAIR		M	21	(1)	
9	Paul DALGLISH		A	15	(2)	3
6	Emmanuel DORADO	FRA	D	17	(4)	
24	Graeme DORRANS		A	4	(4)	
21	Colin HEALY	IRL	M	6	(3)	2
28	Steven HISLOP		A	7	(7)	1
10	Wesley HOOLAHAN	IRL	M	14	(2)	
35	Paul LAMBERT		M	7		
3	David MACKAY		D	38		1
1	Roderick McKENZIE		G	32		
18	Scott McLAUGHLIN		M	1	(2)	
2	David McNAMEE		D	13	(1)	
22	James McPAKE		A	5	(10)	
20	Gary MILLER		D	2	(2)	
9	Samuel MORROW	NIR	A	11		2
10	Ramón PEREIRA	ESP	A	5	(6)	1
4	Harald PINXTEN	BEL	D	26		3
17	Ludovic ROY	FRA	G	6		
14	Martin SCOTT		M	8	(11)	
12	Robert SNODGRASS		A	12	(14)	4
5	Greg STRONG	ENG	D	28	(2)	1
21	Dubravko TESEVIC	BOS	M	2	(2)	
15	Paul TIERNEY	ENG	M	25	(6)	
13	Gabor VINCZE	HUN	M	12	(6)	1
23	Allan WALKER		M	28	(5)	1
32	S WEIR		A		(1)	
18	Noel WHELAN	ENG	A	5	(3)	1

MOTHERWELL
Manager – Terry Butcher (ENG)

2005

30/7	Celtic	h	4-4	Kerr, Hamilton, McDonald Sc., Kinniburgh
6/8	Dunfermline Athletic	h	1-0	Hamilton
13/8	Kilmarnock	a	1-4	Clarkson
20/8	Dundee United	h	4-5	McCormack, McDonald Sc., Fitzpatrick, Hamilton
27/8	Heart of Midlothian	a	1-2	Foran (p)
10/9	Inverness Caledonian Thistle	a	2-1	McDonald Sc., Kinniburgh
17/9	Falkirk	h	5-0	Hamilton, Foran 2, Fagan, McDonald Sc.

Scotland

Date	Opponent	H/A	Score	Scorers
24/9	Hibernian	h	1-3	Foran (p)
1/10	Aberdeen	a	2-2	Clarkson 2
15/10	Livingston	h	1-0	Foran
22/10	Rangers	a	0-2	
26/10	Celtic	a	0-5	
29/10	Dunfermline Athletic	a	3-0	Kerr, Corrigan, Hamilton
5/11	Kilmarnock	h	2-2	McDonald Sc., Kerr
19/11	Dundee United	a	1-1	McDonald Sc.
26/11	Heart of Midlothian	h	1-1	McLean
3/12	Inverness Caledonian Thistle	h	0-2	
10/12	Falkirk	a	1-0	Hamilton
17/12	Hibernian	h	1-2	McDonald Sc.
26/12	Aberdeen	h	3-1	McDonald Sc. 2, McCormack
31/12	Livingston	a	2-1	Foran, McBride
2006				
15/1	Rangers	h	0-1	
22/1	Celtic	h	1-3	Hamilton
28/1	Dunfermline Athletic	a	1-1	Hamilton
8/2	Kilmarnock	a	0-2	
11/2	Dundee United	h	2-0	Foran 2
18/2	Heart of Midlothian	a	0-3	
4/3	Inverness Caledonian Thistle	a	1-0	Foran (p)
11/3	Falkirk	h	3-1	McDonald Sc. 2, Foran
18/3	Hibernian	h	2-2	O'Donnell, Craigan
25/3	Aberdeen	a	2-2	McLean, Foran (p)
1/4	Livingston	h	2-1	Hamilton, McLean
8/4	Rangers	a	0-1	
15/4	Inverness Caledonian Thistle	h	0-1	
22/4	Falkirk	a	1-1	O'Donnell
29/4	Dunfermline Athletic	h	2-3	Paterson, Craigan
3/5	Livingston	a	1-0	Clarkson
7/5	Dundee United	h	1-1	Hamilton

No	Name	Nat	Pos	Aps	(s)	Gls
12	David CLARKSON		A	12	(18)	4
33	Adam COAKLEY		A		(1)	
2	Martyn CORRIGAN		D	27	(2)	1
5	Stephen CRAIGAN		D	36		2
27	Robert DONNELLY		M	1	(1)	
21	Shaun FAGAN		M	11	(5)	1
24	Marc FITZPATRICK		A	1	(8)	1
9	Ritchie FORAN		A	29	(3)	11
16	James HAMILTON		A	30	(4)	10
3	Stephen HAMMELL		D	32	(1)	
23	David KEOGH		D		(1)	
4	Brian KERR		M	32	(4)	3
22	William KINNIBURGH		D	17	(4)	2
8	Scott LEITCH		M	1		
1	Gordon MARSHALL		G	1		
17	Kevin McBRIDE		M	15	(6)	1
6	Alan McCORMACK	IRL	M	24		2
7	Scott McDONALD	AUS	A	30	(4)	11
13	Steven McDONALD		M	1	(1)	
14	Steven McGARRY		M	2	(7)	
47	Brian McLEAN	NIR	D	27	(3)	3
18	Colin MELDRUM		G	7	(1)	
10	Philip O'DONNELL		M	23	(6)	2
11	James PATERSON		M	10	(9)	1
19	Paul QUINN		D	15	(3)	
39	Mark REYNOLDS		D	1		
19	Andrew SMITH	NIR	A	3	(4)	
37	Darren Lee SMITH		A		(1)	
15	Graeme SMITH		G	30		
23	Abel THERMEUS	FRA	A		(1)	
20	Kenneth WRIGHT		M		(1)	

RANGERS
Manager – Alex McLeish

Date	Opponent	H/A	Score	Scorers
2005				
31/7	Livingston	h	3-0	Prso, Pierre-Fanfan, Løvenkrands
6/8	Inverness Caledonian Thistle	a	1-0	Ferguson
14/8	Aberdeen	a	2-3	Prso, Løvenkrands
20/8	Celtic	h	3-1	Prso, Buffel, Novo (p)
27/8	Hibernian	h	0-3	
10/9	Falkirk	a	1-1	Novo (p)
17/9	Kilmarnock	h	3-0	Prso (p), Ferguson, og (Greer)
24/9	Heart of Midlothian	a	0-1	
1/10	Dunfermline Athletic	h	5-1	Buffel, Prso, Nieto, Løvenkrands, McCormack
16/10	Dundee United	a	0-0	
22/10	Motherwell	h	2-0	Burke, Løvenkrands
26/10	Livingston	a	2-2	Ferguson, Burke
29/10	Inverness Caledonian Thistle	h	1-1	Thompson
5/11	Aberdeen	h	0-0	
19/11	Celtic	a	0-3	
27/11	Hibernian	a	1-2	Ferguson
3/12	Falkirk	h	2-2	og (Ireland), Løvenkrands (p)
11/12	Kilmarnock	a	3-2	Løvenkrands 3
17/12	Heart of Midlothian	h	1-0	Løvenkrands
26/12	Dunfermline Athletic	a	3-3	Løvenkrands 2 (1p), Burke
31/12	Dundee United	h	3-0	Buffel, Thompson, Løvenkrands
2006				
15/1	Motherwell	a	1-0	Løvenkrands
21/1	Livingston	h	4-1	Boyd 2, Prso 2
29/1	Inverness Caledonian Thistle	a	3-2	Boyd 2 (1p), Andrews
8/2	Aberdeen	a	0-2	
12/2	Celtic	h	0-1	
18/2	Hibernian	h	2-0	Boyd, Ferguson
4/3	Falkirk	a	2-1	Boyd, og (Twaddle)
11/3	Kilmarnock	h	4-0	Boyd, Rodriguez, Prso (p), Løvenkrands
19/3	Heart of Midlothian	a	1-1	Buffel
25/3	Dunfermline Athletic	h	1-0	Kyrgiakos
2/4	Dundee United	a	4-1	Prso, Boyd 3
8/4	Motherwell	h	1-0	Boyd
15/4	Aberdeen	h	1-1	Boyd
23/4	Celtic	a	0-0	
29/4	Kilmarnock	a	3-1	Andrews 2, Boyd
2/5	Hibernian	a	2-1	Boyd 2
7/5	Heart of Midlothian	h	2-0	Boyd 2

No	Name	Nat	Pos	Aps	(s)	Gls
38	Charlie ADAM		M		(1)	
5	Marvin ANDREWS	TRI	D	21		3
66	Moses ASHIKODI	ENG	A		(1)	
18	Michael BALL	ENG	D	2		
3	Olivier BERNARD	FRA	D	9		
15	Kris BOYD		A	15	(2)	17
4	Thomas BUFFEL	BEL	M	25	(4)	4
17	Chris BURKE		M	25	(2)	3
6	Barry FERGUSON		M	32		5
7	Brahim HEMDANI	ALG	M	18	(1)	
8	Alan HUTTON		D	17	(2)	
21	Francis JEFFERS	ENG	A	4	(4)	
1	Stefan KLOS	GER	G	2		
14	Sotiris KYRGIAKOS	GRE	D	28		1
26	Peter LØVENKRANDS	DEN	A	23	(10)	14
51	Alan LOWING		D	1	(1)	

Scotland

12	Bob MALCOLM		M	11	(2)	
44	Ross McCORMACK		A	2	(6)	1
24	Ian MURRAY		M	26	(4)	
31	Hamed NAMOUCHI	TUN	M	6	(1)	
23	Federico NIETO	ESP	M		(3)	1
10	Nacho NOVO	ESP	A	10	(14)	2
18	José-Karl PIERRE-FANFAN	FRA	D	7		1
9	Dado PRSO	CRO	A	29	(3)	9
8	Alex RAE		M	5	(4)	
11	Gavin RAE		M	4	(4)	
2	Fernando RICKSEN	HOL	D	20	(1)	
41	Lee ROBINSON	ENG	G		(1)	
16	Julien RODRIGUEZ	FRA	D	20	(1)	1
21	Maurice ROSS		D		(1)	
34	Steven SMITH		D	16	(2)	
19	Steven THOMPSON		A	4	(1)	2
25	Ronald WATTEREUS	HOL	G	36		

DOMESTIC CUP 2005/2006

THIRD ROUND
(7/1/06)
Alloa Athletic 1, Livingston 1
Dundee United 2, Aberdeen 3
Dunfermline Athletic 3, Airdrie United 4
Falkirk 2, Brechin City 1
Heart of Midlothian 2, Kilmarnock 1
Hibernian 6, Arbroath 0
Inverness Caledonian Thistle 1, Ayr United 1
Queen of the South 1, Hamilton Academical 1
Rangers 5, Peterhead 0
Ross County 5, Forfar Athletic 0
St. Johnstone 0, Gretna 1
St. Mirren 3, Motherwell 0
The Spartans 3, Queen's Park 2
Stirling Albion 0, Partick Thistle 1
(8/1/06)
Clyde 2, Celtic 1
Dundee 2, Stranraer 0

Replays
(11/1/06)
Livingston 1, Alloa Athletic 2
(16/1/06)
Ayr United 0, Inverness Caledonian Thistle 2
(17/1/06)
Hamilton Academical 1, Queen of the South 0 (aet)

FOURTH ROUND
(4/2/06)
Airdrie United 1, Dundee 1
Clyde 0, Gretna 0
Falkirk 1, Ross County 1
Hamilton Academical 0, Alloa Athletic 0
Heart of Midlothian 3, Aberdeen 0
Inverness Caledonian Thistle 2, Partick Thistle 2
Rangers 0, Hibernian 3
(5/2/06)
The Spartans 0, St. Mirren 0

Replays
(7/2/06)
Alloa Athletic 0, Hamilton Academical 3
(14/2/06)
Dundee 2, Airdrie United 0
Gretna 4, Clyde 0
Ross County 0, Falkirk 1
St. Mirren 3, The Spartans 0
(15/2/06)
Partick Thistle 1, Inverness Caledonian Thistle 1 *(aet; 4-2 on pens)*

QUARTER-FINALS
(25/2/06)
Falkirk 1 *(McBreen 69)*, Hibernian 5 *(Riordan 8, O'Connor 66, Sproule 73, Caldwell 76, Fletcher 87)*
Gretna 1 *(Deuchar 73)*, St. Mirren 0
Hamilton Academical 0, Dundee 0
Heart of Midlothian 2 *(Jankauskas 5, Cesnauskis 62)*, Partick Thistle 1 *(Roberts 74)*

Replay
(9/3/06)
Dundee 3 *(Mann 56, Lynch 68, Craig 91)*, Hamilton Academical 2 *(Juanjo 75, Keogh 82) (aet)*

SEMI-FINALS
(1/4/06)
Hampden Park, Glasgow
Gretna 3 *(Deuchar 45, McGuffie 58p, Smith 82og)*, Dundee 0
(2/4/06)
Hampden Park, Glasgow
Hibernian 0, Heart of Midlothian 4 *(Hartley 28, 59, 88p, Jankauskas 81)*

FINAL
(13/5/06)
Hampden Park, Glasgow
HEART OF MIDLOTHIAN 1 *(Skácel 39)*
GRETNA 1 *(McGuffie 76)*
(aet; 4-2 on pens)
Referee – McDonald
HEART OF MIDLOTHIAN – Gordon, Nelson, Pressley, Tall, Fyssas, Cesnauskis (Mikoliunas 86), Aguiar (Brellier 72), Hartley, Skácel, Bednar (Pospísil 70), Jankauskas.
Sent off: Hartley (120)
GRETNA – Main, Birch, Townsley, Innes, Nicholls (Graham 55), McGuffie, Tosh, O'Neil, Skelton, Grady, Deuchar (McQuilken 103).

SECOND LEVEL FINAL TABLE 2005/06

		Pld	W	D	L	F	A	Pts
1	St. Mirren	36	23	7	6	52	28	76
2	St. Johnstone	36	18	12	6	59	34	66
3	Hamilton Academical	36	15	14	7	53	39	59
4	Ross County	36	14	14	8	47	40	56
5	Clyde	36	15	10	11	54	42	55
6	Airdrie United	36	11	12	13	57	43	45
7	Dundee	36	9	16	11	43	50	43
8	Queen of the South	36	7	12	17	31	54	33
9	Stranraer	36	5	14	17	33	53	29
10	Brechin City	36	2	11	23	28	74	17

Serbia & Montenegro

A unified nation no more

Serbia & Montenegro's appearance at the 2006 World Cup was the final act of a unified nation. The last vestiges of the former Yugoslavia were formally annulled at the end of June following the decision of the Montenegrin people to vote for independence in a national referendum held on May 21.

In footballing terms, that means the two nations now run their own separate leagues and Cup competitions. There are also two national teams, with Serbia, as the larger state, having been deemed the legal successor to Serbia & Montenegro and therefore given permission to take the former country's place in the qualifying competition for Euro 2008. Montenegro will have to make do with friendly internationals for the next two years before they gain admission to the 2010 World Cup qualifying competition. As a sweetener for their compliance, the newly formed Montenegrin FA was granted 25 per cent of the two countries' World Cup income.

The break-up should not unduly affect Serbia's chances of qualifying for the European finals in Austria and Switzerland. After all, there was only one Montenegrin in Serbia & Montenegro's World Cup squad – goalkeeper Dragoslav Jevric – and even he has declared that he would prefer to play for Serbia.

Worst team

Serbian fans will be happy to draw a line under the past after the calamitous events that unfolded in Germany. Having qualified for the World Cup in such style, top of their group (above Spain), undefeated and with just one goal conceded, there was no reason to believe that Ilija Petkovic's side would find the going so tough at the finals. But the Group of Death proved to be just that.

Defeated in all three games (and annihilated in one), Serbia & Montenegro were officially the worst of the 32 teams at the finals.

It was difficult to pinpoint exactly why the team flopped so badly, but the furore caused by the coach's decision to call up his son Dusan to the squad as a replacement for injured striker Mirko Vucinic didn't help. Petkovic junior was so embarrassed by all the criticism heaped upon his father that he pulled out, leaving Serbia & Montenegro with just 22 players. Another key factor was the injury sustained on the eve of the tournament by centre-back Nemanja Vidic – one of the mainstays of the back four that had proved so obdurate during the qualifiers. The Manchester United man would have been suspended from the Holland game anyway but without him the

NATIONAL TEAM RESULTS 2005/06

15/8/05	Poland	N	Kiev	2-3	Zigic (32), Vidic (59)
17/8/05	Ukraine	A	Kiev	1-2	Kezman (90)
3/9/05	Lithuania (WCQ)	H	Belgrade	2-0	Kezman (18), Ilic (75)
7/9/05	Spain (WCQ)	A	Madrid	1-1	Kezman (68)
8/10/05	Lithuania (WCQ)	A	Vilnius	2-0	Kezman (43), Vukic (88)
12/10/05	Bosnia-Herzegovina (WCQ)	H	Belgrade	1-0	Kezman (7)
13/11/05	China	A	Nankin	2-0	Djordjevic N. (49), Zigic (65)
16/11/05	South Korea	A	Seoul	0-2	
1/3/06	Tunisia	A	Tunis	1-0	Kezman (11)
27/5/06	Uruguay	H	Belgrade	1-1	Stankovic (17)
11/6/06	Holland (WCF)	N	Leipzig	0-1	
16/6/06	Argentina (WCF)	N	Gelsenkirchen	0-6	
21/6/06	Ivory Coast (WCF)	N	Munich	2-3	Zigic (10), Ilic (20)

Serbia & Montenegro

defence was unbalanced and disjointed. Indiscipline also assisted in the team's downfall; half of the ten goals they conceded were with ten men.

Positives were hard to find. The only inventive player was veteran midfielder Predrag Djordjevic. Dejan Stankovic was exceedingly quiet, while the team offered virtually nothing up front. Skipper Savo Milosevic became the first Serb/Yugoslav to reach 100 caps but as the milestone was reached against Argentina, he was hardly in the mood to celebrate. In fact, he announced his international retirement after the tournament, with defender Mladen Krstajic doing likewise.

Coach Petkovic inevitably called it quits too, expressing dismay at how his team had performed but also lamenting the lack of quality players at his disposal. It did not take long for the new Serbian FA to find a replacement. Three weeks later 52-year-old Spaniard Javier Clemente, who had a successful six-year spell in charge of his own country during the 1990s, was handed a two-year contract. The appointment of a foreign coach – an unprecedented move – is clear evidence that Serbia wish to wipe the slate clean. Although Clemente will take time to settle in, the likelihood is that he will draw increasingly from the Under-21 teams that finished runners-up in the European championship of 2004 and reached the semi-finals in 2006.

Easy ride

The last unified domestic championship proved to be a fairly easy ride for the country's most famous and successful club, Red Star (Crvena Zvezda) Belgrade. Their appointment of a foreign coach, ex-Italian World Cup goalkeeper Walter Zenga, proved to be an unqualified success – as did the return to the club, as president, of former golden boy Dragan "Pixie" Stojkovic.

Without a trophy in 2004/05, Red Star were a much more stable unit, both on an off the field, under their new direction. The only major setback was the team's failure, once again, to make progress in Europe. Having lost their opening two games in the group phase of the UEFA Cup, the first behind closed doors at home to FC Basel, they fought back with a thrilling 3-1 victory over Roma and were 2-0 up away to Strasbourg in a game they needed to win to reach the third round. But faced with the prospect of playing post-Christmas European football for the first time in 14 years, they collapsed under the pressure and conceded two goals, the second of them in stoppage-time.

In the league Red Star failed to win their opening game for the fifth year in a row – 2-2 at Hajduk Kula – then lost 2-1 away to Borac Cacak in their next away fixture, but these were just early jitters. Ten straight victories followed, including a 2-0 home win over eternal rivals Partizan (who were going through a terrible spell at the time), and by the winter break, despite their Euro woes, Red Star held a three-point lead.

That increased during the spring. The arrival, from new merger club Vozdovac Belgrade, of the league's leading scorer Dusan Djokic provided towering centre-forward Nikola Zigic with the perfect partner, and with classy defenders like Dusan Basta and Milan Dudic keeping things tight at the back, Red Star proved irresistible. The only team that could stop them, needless to say, was Partizan, but the big Belgrade derby game finished goalless – thus extending Red Star's remarkable unbeaten run against their arch-rivals to 12 matches – and that left Zenga's side seven points ahead with six games remaining. Three matches later Red Star's 24th national title was confirmed, a 2-0 victory over OFK Belgrade giving them an unassailable nine-point advantage (head-to-head results included) over Partizan.

Red Star also met OFK in the final of the Serbo-Montenegrin Cup. Although OFK were already certain of UEFA Cup qualification, the team that had led the league early on were determined to finish the campaign on a high and emulate the achievements of Sartid Smederevo (2003) and Zeleznik Belgrade (2005), who had both beaten Red Star in the final. Another shock loomed when OFK went 2-0 up just before the hour but, with both teams reduced to ten men, Red Star threw everything into attack and reaped their reward with goals from Zigic and substitute Milan Purovic. Zigic then completed the comeback with his second goal ten minutes into extra-time before full-back Basta finished off OFK with a breakaway fourth goal near the end.

Zenga departs

That was Zenga's final game in charge. Despite his success – and the Cup final was arguably his finest hour – his family could not settle in Belgrade. Still,

Serbia & Montenegro

NATIONAL TEAM APPEARANCES 2005/06

Coach – Ilija PETKOVIC

Player	DOB	Club	Pol	Ukr	LIT	ESP	LIT	BOS	Chn	Kor	Tun	Uru	HOL	ARG	CIV	Caps	Goals
Dragoslav JEVRIC	8/7/74	BB Ankaraspor (TUR)	G	G	G	G	G	G	G80	G83	G	G	G	G	G	43	-
Marjan MARKOVIC	28/9/81	Genoa (ITA)	D66													8	-
Nemanja VIDIC	21/10/81	Spartak Moskva (RUS) /Manchester United (ENG)	D	D46	D	D	D	D			D	s63				20	1
Goran GAVRANCIC	2/8/78	Dynamo Kyiv (UKR)	D	D	D	D	D	D			D	D	D	D	D	28	-
Aleksandar LUKOVIC	23/10/82	Crvena Zvezda Beograd	M				M	s87	M	M						5	-
Dejan STANKOVIC	11/9/78	Internazionale (ITA)	M78		M	M	M10				M	M79	M	M	M	61	11
Igor DULJAJ	29/10/79	Shakhtar Donetsk (UKR)	M	M	M	M		M			M	M	M	D	M	40	2
Zvonimir VUKIC	19/7/79	Shakhtar Donetsk (UKR) /Portsmouth (ENG) /Partizan Beograd	M62	s49		s89		M	M67	M65	M74			s70		26	6
Predrag DJORDJEVIC	4/8/72	Olympiakos (GRE)	M82	M76	M	M	M	M			M	M	M	M	M	37	1
Mateja KEZMAN	12/4/79	Atlético Madrid (ESP)	A46	s46	A75	A	A88	A87	A46	A46	A83	A75	A66	A		49	17
Nikola ZIGIC	25/9/80	Crvena Zvezda Beograd	A82	s46	s75	s46 /90	A53	A	s46	s46		s56	s46		A66	13	4
Savo MILOSEVIC	2/9/73	CA Osasuna (ESP)	s46	A46	A60		s88		A46	A46	A75	A56	A46	A70	s66	101	35
Sasa ILIC	30/12/77	Galatasaray (TUR)	s62	M49	M89	M46		s73	s75	s74		s79			M	33	6
Ognjen KOROMAN	19/9/78	Terek Groznyi (RUS) /Portsmouth (ENG)	s66	s76	s60	M83		M	M52	s46		M89	M68	s43	M49	27	1
Milos MARIC	5/3/82	Olympiakos (GRE)	s78	M		s83										7	-
Dragan MLADENOVIC	16/2/76	Crvena Zvezda Beograd	s82				s10	s67	M75	M74						17	1
Danijel LJUBOJA	4/9/78	Paris Saint-Germain (FRA) /VfB Stuttgart (GER)	s82	s76				s53		s46	s46	s83	s68	s66	s49	17	1
Mladen KRSTAJIC	4/3/74	FC Schalke 04 (GER)		D	D	D	D	D			D	D63	D		D	D16	48	2
Ivica DRAGUTINOVIC	13/11/75	Sevilla FC (ESP)		M76	D	D					D	D	D			28	-
Nenad JESTROVIC	9/5/76	RSC Anderlecht (BEL)		A46												12	5
Milan DUDIC	1/11/79	Crvena Zvezda Beograd		s46									D	D		13	-
Nenad KOVACEVIC	11/11/80	Crvena Zvezda Beograd				s90			s52	M46						8	-
Albert NADJ	29/10/74	Partizan Beograd					M	M73	M	s74	M65	M	M	M46	s16	45	3
Nenad DJORDJEVIC	7/8/79	Partizan Beograd					D	D	s89		D43		D			17	1
Marko BASA	29/12/82	OFK Beograd					D	D								3	-
Djordje JOKIC	20/1/81	Torpedo Moskva (RUS)					D	D								4	-
Branko BOSKOVIC	21/6/80	Paris Saint-Germain (FRA)							s65	s46						12	2
Oliver KOVACEVIC	29/10/74	CSKA Sofia (BUL)							s80	s83						3	-
Bojan NEZIRI	26/2/82	VfL Wolfsburg (GER)								M46						3	-
Dusan BASTA	18/8/84	Crvena Zvezda Beograd										s65				2	-
Mirko VUCINIC	1/10/83	Lecce (ITA)										s75				3	-
Ivan ERGIC	21/1/81	FC Basel (SUI)										s75		s46	M	3	-

Serbia & Montenegro

the Red Star fans were happy enough when president Stojkovic revealed that the Italian's successor was to be Dusan Bajevic, who had finally decided to return to his homeland after a decade of serial trophy-winning in Greece.

Partizan also decided to replace a foreigner with a Serb, giving the boot to German Jürgen Röber and bringing in Miodrag Jesic, latterly of CSKA Sofia, in his stead. Röber, the former Stuttgart and Hertha Berlin boss, had been recruited only the previous October following the dismissal of Vladimir Vermezovic, who had led the club to an historic undefeated championship triumph in 2004/05. Vermezovic fell on his sword after two ghastly home defeats in Europe – the first on penalties against Artmedia Bratislava in the final qualifying round of the Champions League, the second when his team suffered an incredible 5-2 reverse to Maccabi Petach Tikva in the first round of the UEFA Cup, having won the first leg 2-0 in Israel.

Röber had to pick up the pieces, but his first three matches all ended in defeat – by Red Star and Vozdovac in the league and then, most shockingly of all, with another penalty shoot-out loss at home to third division minnows Timok Zajecar. To give the German his due, Partizan would suffer no further defeats, but with the club's fans boycotting games after a long-running feud with the board of directors, the grim atmosphere demanded another change of direction for 2006/07.

Vozdovac Belgrade should have joined Partizan in the UEFA Cup but, as in their previous guise of Zeleznik 12 months earlier, they failed to obtain a licence to compete in Europe, so Hajduk Kula, who finished a place below them in fourth spot, qualified instead.

Even before Montenegrin independence, it had been decided to reduce the Prva Liga from 16 teams to 12, which meant seven teams being relegated and three promoted. But the political change led to Montenegrin club Zeta Golubovci (who finished fifth) being removed along with 'newly promoted' Rudar Pljevlja, which in turn allowed Zemun and Smederevo to retain their places. There were, however, three newcomers to the new Serbian Premier League, with First League qualifiers Bezanija Belgrade and Mladost Apatin being joined by another merger club, Banat Zrenjanin, formed from a fusion of Buducnost Banatski Dvor and Proleter Zrenjanin.

EUROPEAN CUPS 2005/06

UEFA CHAMPIONS LEAGUE

PARTIZAN BEOGRAD

2nd qualifying round SHERIFF TIRASPOL (MOL)
H 1-0 *Odita (63)*
Kralj, Vukcevic, Mirkovic, Bajic, Brnovic, Radonjic (Boya 46), Lomic, Odita (Grubjesic 82), Radovic, Rnic, Nadj (Vukajlovic 73).
A 1-0 *Odita (74)*
Kralj, Vukcevic, Mirkovic (Cirkovic 89), Bajic, Brnovic, Boya, Radovic (Babovic 82), Lomic, Odita, Djordjevic, Nadj (Marinkovic 90).

3rd qualifying round ARTMEDIA BRATISLAVA (SVK)
A 0-0
Kralj, Vukcevic, Mirkovic, Bajic (Emeghara 46), Brnovic, Boya, Lomic, Djordjevic, Odita, Tomic, Nadj.
H 0-0
(aet; 3-4 on pens)
Kralj, Vukcevic, Mirkovic, Brnovic, Boya, Djordjevic, Lomic (Bajic 110), Emeghara, Odita (Radovic 68), Nadj, Tomic (Grubjesic 76).

UEFA CUP

CRVENA ZVEZDA BEOGRAD

2nd qualifying round INTER ZAPRESIC (CRO)
A 3-1 *Zigic (20, 49), Pantelic (80)*
Randjelovic, Lukovic, Dudic, Jankovic (Miladinovic 78), Pantelic, Joksimovic, Kovacevic, Djordjevic, Trajkovic (Perovic 65), Mudrinic, Zigic (Purovic 75).
H 4-0 *Jankovic (6), Pantelic (42, 85), Zigic (44p)*
Randjelovic (Stojkovic 46), Lukovic, Miladinovic (Bisevac 78), Dudic, Jankovic, Pantelic, Perovic, Joksimovic, Kovacevic, Mudrinic (Krivokapic 67), Zigic.

1st round SPORTING BRAGA (POR)
H 0-0
Randjelovic, Lukovic, Dudic, Bisevac, Jankovic, Perovic (Basta 76), Joksimovic (Djokaj 84), Kovacevic, Purovic, Mudrinic (Stojanovic 64), Mladenovic.
A 1-1 *Purovic (10)*
Stojkovic, Lukovic, Dudic, Jankovic (Miladinovic 89), Joksimovic, Kovacevic, Purovic (Djokaj 56), Mudrinic (Miladinovic 37), Zigic, Basta, Mladenovic.

2nd round Group E
Match 1 FC BASEL (SUI)
H 1-2 *Purovic (25)*
Stojkovic, Lukovic, Dudic, Basta, Bisevac, Jankovic (Trajkovic 87), Perovic, Kovacevic, Mladenovic, Purovic (Raskovic 84), Zigic.

Match 2 TROMSØ IL (NOR)
A 1-3 *Zigic (24)*
Stojkovic, Lukovic, Dudic, Basta, Joksimovic, Djokaj (Trajkovic 77), Bisevac, Kovacevic, Mudrinic (Krivokapic 65), Zigic, Purovic.

Match 3 ROMA (ITA)
H 3-1 *Zigic (37, 86), Purovic (77)*
Stojkovic, Lukovic, Dudic, Bisevac, Basta, Djokaj (Mudrinic 76), Jankovic, Kovacevic, Miladinovic (Purovic 59; Joksimovic 87), Mladenovic, Zigic.

Match 4 RC STRASBOURG (FRA)
A 2-2 *Basta (34), Djokaj (64)*
Stojkovic, Lukovic, Dudic, Bisevac, Djokaj (Draman 77), Jankovic, Kovacevic, Basta, Miladinovic, Mladenovic (Mudrinic 70), Zigic (Purovic 88).

ZETA GOLUBOVCI
2nd qualifying round SIROKI BRIJEG (BOS)
H 0-1

Serbia & Montenegro

Radulovic, Todorovic, Zavisic, Markoski (Knezevic 60), Marijan, Milic, Nuhi, Tumbasovic (Vukovic 55), Vukomanovic, Mester (Camaj 80), Kuc.
A 2-4 *Vukovic (4, 44)*
Radulovic, Todorovic, Zavisic (Kaludjerovic M. 81), Vukovic, Markoski, Marijan, Milic, Nuhi (Camaj 67), Vukomanovic, Kaludjerovic, Mester (Knezevic 72).

OFK BEOGRAD
2nd qualifying round LOKOMOTIV PLOVDIV (BUL)
H 2-1 *Kirovski (32), Ivanovic (39)*
Eric, Ivanovic, Bajalica, Rajkovic, Tosic, Simic (Kascelan 80), Stancic, Petrovic, Bozovic (Arsenijevic 71), Bakovic (Stosic 58), Kirovski.
A 0-1
Eric, Kascelan, Ivanovic, Rajkovic, Tosic, Simic (Vusljanin 85), Stancic, Petrovic, Bozovic, Bakovic (Arsenijevic 66), Kirovski (Stosic 74).

PARTIZAN BEOGRAD
1st round MACCABI PETACH TIKVA (ISR)
A 2-0 *Vukcevic (33), Radonjic (46)*
Kralj, Vukcevic, Cirkovic (Djordjevic 60), Mirkovic (Milovic 60), Bajic, Brnovic, Radonjic, Babovic (Radovic 72), Odita, Emegharo, Nadj.
H 2-5 *Radonjic (12p, 41)*
Pantic, Vukcevic, Mirkovic, Bajic, Brnovic (Tomic 57), Radonjic, Radovic (Boya 70), Lomic, Emeghara (Grubjesic 82), Odita, Nadj.

TOP GOALSCORERS 2005/06

20	Srdjan RADONJIC (Partizan Beograd)	
19	Dusan DJOKIC (Vozdovac Beograd/Crvena Zvezda Beograd)	
12	Nikola ZIGIC (Crvena Zvezda Beograd)	
	Bosko JANKOVIC (Crvena Zvezda Beograd)	
	Nenad MILIJAS (Zemun/Crvena Zvezda Beograd)	
11	Milan PUROVIC (Crvena Zvezda Beograd)	
	Dejan OSMANOVIC (Hajduk Rodic MB Kula)	
	Drazen MILIC (Zeta Golubovci)	
9	Nebojsa MARINKOVIC (Partizan Beograd/Vozdovac Beograd)	
	Ivan VUKOVIC (Zeta Golubovci)	
	Ljubisa VUKELJA (Vojvodina Novi Sad)	
	Jovan DAMJANOVIC (Borac Cacak)	
	Nikola DRINCIC (Buducnost Banatski Dvor)	

LEAGUE RESULTS/SCORERS/APPEARANCES/GOALS 2005/06

BORAC CACAK
Coach – Miodrag Bozovic

2005
6/8	Vojvodina Novi Sad	a	1-0	Davidov
14/8	Zeta Golubovci	h	0-1	
20/8	Hajduk Rodic MB Kula	a	2-2	Kostic, Spasojevic
28/8	Crvena Zvezda Beograd	h	2-1	Kostic, Dmitrovic (p)
10/9	Vozdovac Beograd	a	0-4	
17/9	Jedinstvo Bijelo Polje	h	1-2	Spasojevic
24/9	Buducnost Banatski Dvor	h	0-1	
2/10	Rad Beograd	a	3-0	Nedeljkovic, Galic, Davidov
15/10	Obilic Beograd	h	1-3	Drinic
22/10	Buducnost Podgorica	a	1-1	Davidov
29/10	Partizan Beograd	h	0-2	
5/11	Smederevo	a	0-0	
19/11	Habitpharm Javor Ivanjica	h	0-0	
26/11	OFK Beograd	a	1-1	Damjanovic
3/12	Zemun	h	2-0	Nedeljkovic, Dmitrovic
10/12	Vojvodina Novi Sad	h	1-0	Damjanovic
15/12	Zeta Golubovci	a	1-3	Nedeljkovic

2006
18/2	Hajduk Rodic MB Kula	h	1-0	Dmitrovic (p)
25/2	Crvena Zvezda Beograd	a	0-1	
4/3	Vozdovac Beograd	h	0-1	
11/3	Jedinstvo Bijelo Polje	a	2-0	Davidov, Damjanovic
21/3	Buducnost Banatski Dvor	a	1-0	Krsteski
25/3	Rad Beograd	h	2-1	Nedeljkovic, Damjanovic
1/4	Obilic Beograd	a	0-0	
8/4	Buducnost Podgorica	h	2-0	Damjanovic 2
15/4	Partizan Beograd	a	0-1	
22/4	Smederevo	h	4-0	Nedeljkovic 2, Damjanovic 2
29/4	Habitpharm Javor Ivanjica	a	2-0	Damjanovic, Spasojevic
3/5	OFK Beograd	h	1-1	Markovic
6/5	Zemun	a	1-1	Markovic

No	Name	Nat	Pos	Aps	(s)	Gls
8	Jovan DAMJANOVIC		A	23	(2)	9
10	Milan DAVIDOV		M	28		4
16	Ivan DJOKOVIC		M	12	(5)	
6	Boban DMITROVIC		D	27		3
20	Dragan DRAGUTINOVIC		D	19	(3)	
18	Darko DRINIC		A	8	(12)	1
9	Dragan GALIC		A		(5)	1
1	Radisa ILIC		G	30		
2	Vladimir JASIC		D	17	(4)	
25	Vitomir JELIC		D		(1)	
7	Zoran KOSTIC		M	26		2
11	Sasa KOVACEVIC		A		(3)	
23	Marko KRASIC		D	12	(3)	
11	Vladimir KRNJINAC		M	11		
4	Darko KRSTESKI	MAC	D	12		1
24	Ivan MAKSIMOVIC		A		(2)	
9	Slobodan MARKOVIC		M	11	(1)	2
17	Zvonko NEDELJKOVIC		M	24	(4)	6
15	Bojan PAVLOVIC		M	10	(10)	
21	Dragisa PEJOVIC		D	23	(2)	
13	Darko RAKOCEVIC		D	2	(3)	
28	Vladan SPASOJEVIC		M	17	(8)	3
3	Ivan STEVANOVIC		D	13	(1)	
19	Dejan TARABIC		A		(1)	
5	Dusan VESKOVAC		D	4	(4)	
31	Rade VUKOTIC		A	1	(3)	

BUDUCNOST BANATSKI DVOR
Coach – Radivoje Draskovic; (22/10/05) Nikola Rakojevic

2005
6/8	Zemun	a	0-2	
13/8	Vojvodina Novi Sad	h	1-0	Micic
20/8	Zeta Golubovci	a	0-1	
27/8	Hajduk Rodic MB Kula	h	2-0	Belic, Drincic
10/9	Crvena Zvezda Beograd	a	1-5	Stojakovic I.
17/9	Vozdovac Beograd	h	0-0	
24/9	Borac Cacak	a	1-0	Belic
1/10	Jedinstvo Bijelo Polje	a	0-2	
15/10	Rad Beograd	h	1-0	
22/10	Obilic Beograd	a	0-1	
29/10	Buducnost Podgorica	h	2-1	Micic 2
5/11	Partizan Beograd	a	0-2	
19/11	Smederevo	h	2-0	Kasom 2
26/11	Habitpharm Javor Ivanjica	a	2-4	Drincic, Savic
3/12	OFK Beograd	h	1-0	Stojakovic I.
13/12	Zemun	h	3-0	Kasom, Stojakovic I., Drincic (p)

Serbia & Montenegro

FINAL LEAGUE TABLE 2005/06

		Pld	Home W	D	L	F	A	Away W	D	L	F	A	Total W	D	L	F	A	Pts
1	Crvena Zvezda Beograd	30	15	0	0	42	9	10	3	2	31	14	25	3	2	73	23	78
2	Partizan Beograd	30	10	3	2	28	7	12	2	1	25	10	22	5	3	53	17	71
3	Vozdovac Beograd	30	10	1	4	30	14	5	5	5	22	24	15	6	9	52	38	51
4	Hajduk Rodic MB Kula	30	11	4	0	28	6	2	7	6	13	20	13	11	6	41	26	50
5	Zeta Golubovci	30	11	3	1	28	11	3	2	10	14	25	14	5	11	42	36	47
6	OFK Beograd	30	8	2	5	24	12	5	3	7	11	17	13	5	12	35	29	44
7	Borac Cacak	30	8	2	5	18	11	4	6	5	14	16	12	8	10	32	27	44
8	Buducnost Banatski Dvor	30	9	3	3	24	10	4	2	9	10	21	13	5	12	34	31	44
9	Vojvodina Novi Sad	30	9	4	2	19	9	2	6	7	9	18	11	10	9	28	27	43
10	Zemun	30	7	6	2	21	14	4	2	9	13	25	11	8	11	34	39	41
11	Smederevo	30	7	4	4	20	15	4	2	9	10	22	11	6	13	30	37	39
12	Habitpharm Javor Ivanjica	30	7	4	4	14	10	1	4	10	8	25	8	8	14	22	35	32
13	Rad Beograd	30	5	3	7	17	19	4	1	10	10	16	9	4	17	27	35	31
14	Buducnost Podgorica	30	5	6	4	18	15	1	4	10	6	28	6	10	14	24	43	25
15	Obilic Beograd	30	2	4	9	10	18	1	2	12	13	35	3	6	21	23	53	15
16	Jedinstvo Bijelo Polje	30	3	2	10	15	32	0	0	15	3	40	3	2	25	18	72	11

N.B. As Montenegro is now an independent country, Zeta Golubovci (from Montenegro) are automatically 'relegated'.

17/12	Vojvodina Novi Sad	a	0-1	
2006				
18/2	Zeta Golubovci	h	3-1	Kasom, Zafirovic, Drincic
25/2	Hajduk Rodic MB Kula	a	0-1	
5/3	Crvena Zvezda Beograd	h	0-3	
11/3	Vozdovac Beograd	a	1-1	Drincic
21/3	Borac Cacak	h	0-1	
25/3	Jedinstvo Bijelo Polje	h	5-1	Baljak, Drincic 2, Stojakovic N., Zafirovic
2/4	Rad Beograd	a	1-0	Kasom
8/4	Obilic Beograd	h	3-0	Belic 3
15/4	Buducnost Podgorica	a	2-0	Drincic 2 (1p)
22/4	Partizan Beograd	h	1-1	Stojakovic I.
29/4	Smederevo	a	1-1	Baljak
3/5	Habitpharm Javor Ivanjica	h	1-1	Kasom
6/5	OFK Beograd	a	1-1	Micic

No	Name	Nat	Pos	Aps	(s)	Gls
6	Mirko ANDRIC		D	29		
24	Srdjan BALJAK		A	11		2
26	Danilo BELIC		A	10	(11)	5
25	Nikola BELJIC		D	11	(1)	
9	Nikola DRINCIC		M	28		9
17	Darko JOVANDIC		D	16	(2)	
15	Jovan JOVANOVIC		A	1	(5)	
21	Petar KASOM		A	17	(2)	6
11	Zoran KULIC		M	8	(10)	
3	Nenad KUTLACIC	BOS	D	14	(1)	
19	Dragan MICIC		A	13	(9)	4
5	Zeljko MILOSEVIC		D	29		
10	Nemanja PAVLOVIC		M	11	(6)	
22	Marinko PETKOVIC		A		(3)	
2	Srdjan PJEVAC		M	12	(6)	
12	Milos RADANOVIC		G	30		
18	Nikola RADOVANOVIC		M		(2)	
4	Branko SAVIC		D	25		1
20	Igor STOJAKOVIC		M	18	(5)	4
29	Nenad STOJAKOVIC		M	5	(3)	1
7	Milan STUPAR		M	13	(8)	
16	Zoran TOSIC		D	2	(5)	
23	Dejan VASIC		M		(2)	
8	Djordje ZAFIROVIC		M	27		2

BUDUCNOST PODGORICA
Coach – Branislav Milacic; (21/3/06) (Anto Drobnjak); (26/3/06) Bozidar Vukovic

2005				
6/8	Smederevo	a	1-1	Sekulic
13/8	Habitpharm Javor Ivanjica	h	3-1	Burzanovic, Mugosa, Sekulic
20/8	OFK Beograd	a	0-3	
28/8	Zemun	h	1-1	Usanovic
10/9	Vojvodina Novi Sad	a	0-0	
17/9	Zeta Golubovci	h	1-1	Boskovic
24/9	Hajduk Rodic MB Kula	a	0-1	
2/10	Crvena Zvezda Beograd	h	1-2	Boskovic
15/10	Vozdovac Beograd	a	1-4	Boskovic
22/10	Borac Cacak	h	1-1	Boskovic
29/10	Buducnost Banatski Dvor	a	1-2	Carapic
5/11	Rad Beograd	h	2-1	Perisic, Burzanovic
19/11	Obilic Beograd	a	0-0	
26/11	Jedinstvo Bijelo Polje	a	1-0	Burzanovic
3/12	Partizan Beograd	h	0-1	
10/12	Smederevo	h	1-2	Boskovic
15/12	Habitpharm Javor Ivanjica	a	0-0	
2006				
18/2	OFK Beograd	h	2-2	Sekulic, Burzanovic
25/2	Zemun	a	1-3	Raicevic
4/3	Vojvodina Novi Sad	h	0-0	
11/3	Zeta Golubovci	a	0-3	(w/o)
21/3	Hajduk Rodic MB Kula	h	0-0	
25/3	Crvena Zvezda Beograd	a	0-4	
1/4	Vozdovac Beograd	h	2-0	Burzanovic 2
8/4	Borac Cacak	a	0-2	
15/4	Buducnost Banatski Dvor	h	0-2	
22/4	Rad Beograd	a	1-2	Burzanovic (p)
29/4	Obilic Beograd	h	2-1	Sekulic 2
3/5	Jedinstvo Bijelo Polje	h	2-0	og (Zindovic), Lakic R.
6/5	Partizan Beograd	a	0-3	

No	Name	Nat	Pos	Aps	(s)	Gls
16	Ivan BOSKOVIC		A	14	(4)	5

Serbia & Montenegro

No	Name	Nat	Pos	Aps	(s)	Gls
40	Balsa BOZOVIC		M	3	(7)	
32	Drasko BOZOVIC		D	1		
10	Igor BURZANOVIC		M	26		7
37	Boban CABARKAPA		D	3		
7	Aleksandar CADJENOVIC		M	14	(6)	
5	Ivan CARAPIC		D	27		1
24	Ivan DELIC		M	1	(3)	
3	Nebojsa DJORDJEVIC		D		(1)	
39	Milan DJURISIC		A	10	(2)	
23	Marko DZEVARDANOVIC		D		(2)	
49	Milos LAKIC		D	8	(5)	
2	Risto LAKIC		D	27		1
3	Mirza LJUMIC		A		(4)	
9	Drazen MEDJEDOVIC		M		(5)	
35	Bogdan MILIC		A		(3)	
20	Marko MUGOSA		M	26	(1)	1
27	Goran PERISIC		D	16	(1)	1
11	Bracan POPOVIC		D	19	(1)	
6	Mirko RAICEVIC		M	27		1
4	Blazo RAJOVIC		D	15	(2)	
17	Radislav SEKULIC		A	20	(3)	5
15	Nenad SOFRANAC		M	8	(4)	
25	Vladan TATAR		D	7	(2)	
13	Bojan USANOVIC		M	11	(4)	1
21	Miroslav VUJADINOVIC		G	29		
14	Nikola VUKCEVIC		D	2	(2)	
36	Petar VUKCEVIC		M	3	(5)	
18	Nemanja VUKOVIC		M		(2)	
30	Krsto ZVICER		A	2	(7)	

CRVENA ZVEZDA BEOGRAD
Coach – Walter Zenga (ITA)

2005
6/8	Hajduk Rodic MB Kula	a	2-2	Jankovic 2
20/8	Vozdovac Beograd	h	3-1	Jankovic 2, Trajkovic
28/8	Borac Cacak	a	1-2	Zigic
10/9	Buducnost Banatski Dvor	h	5-1	Jankovic, Kovacevic (p), Zigic, Mladenovic, Raskovic
18/9	Rad Beograd	a	4-2	Purovic, Raskovic, Zigic, Draman
21/9	Jedinstvo Bijelo Polje	a	4-0	Zigic, Jankovic, Purovic, Raskovic
24/9	Obilic Beograd	h	4-2	Purovic, Zigic 2, Raskovic
2/10	Buducnost Podgorica	a	2-1	Purovic, og (Rajovic)
15/10	Partizan Beograd	h	2-0	Lukovic (p), Perovic
22/10	Smederevo	a	3-1	Purovic 2, Zigic
29/10	Habitpharm Javor Ivanjica	h	2-0	Perovic, Jankovic
6/11	OFK Beograd	a	1-0	Dudic
20/11	Zemun	h	2-1	Mladenovic, Djokaj
27/11	Vojvodina Novi Sad	a	0-1	
4/12	Zeta Golubovci	h	3-2	Jankovic, Mladenovic, Zigic
10/12	Hajduk Rodic MB Kula	h	4-1	Trajkovic, Purovic, Raskovic, Jankovic
17/12	Jedinstvo Bijelo Polje	a	4-0	Jankovic, Djokaj, Milovanovic, Purovic

2006
18/2	Vozdovac Beograd	a	2-0	Djokic, Jankovic
25/2	Borac Cacak	h	1-0	Jankovic
5/3	Buducnost Banatski Dvor	a	3-0	Milovanovic, Lukovic (p), Dudic
11/3	Rad Beograd	h	1-0	Milijas
21/3	Obilic Beograd	a	3-2	Djokic 2, Lukovic (p)
25/3	Buducnost Podgorica	h	4-0	Djokic 2, Milijas, Zigic
1/4	Partizan Beograd	a	0-0	
8/4	Smederevo	h	2-0	Milijas 2
15/4	Habitpharm Javor Ivanjica	a	2-1	Zigic 2
22/4	OFK Beograd	h	2-0	Djokic 2
29/4	Zemun	a	2-0	Purovic 2
3/5	Vojvodina Novi Sad	h	3-1	Zigic, Djokic, Dudic
6/5	Zeta Golubovci	a	2-2	Purovic, Perovic

No	Name	Nat	Pos	Aps	(s)	Gls
18	Dusan ANDJELKOVIC		D	3		
22	Zoran BANOVIC		G		(1)	
30	Dusan BASTA		D	25		
6	Milan BISEVAC		D	20		
7	Ardijan DJOKAJ		M	5	(3)	2
9	Dusan DJOKIC		A	9		8
46	Filip DJORDJEVIC		A		(1)	
18	Slavoljub DJORDJEVIC		D	1		
2	Haminu DRAMAN	GHA	D		(4)	1
5	Milan DUDIC		D	28		3
8	Bosko JANKOVIC		M	26		12
15	Nebojsa JOKSIMOVIC		D	12	(6)	
16	Nenad KOVACEVIC		M	22	(3)	1
10	Radovan KRIVOKAPIC		M	4	(5)	
3	Aleksandar LUKOVIC		D	27		3
24	Bojan MILADINOVIC		D	2	(4)	
17	Nenad MILIJAS		M	8	(2)	4
32	Dejan MILOVANOVIC		M	16	(7)	2
44	Dragan MLADENOVIC		M	14	(3)	3
33	Dragan MRDJA		A		(1)	
23	Vladimir MUDRINIC		M	12	(8)	
9	Marko PANTELIC		A	3		
11	Marko PEROVIC		M	9	(9)	3
20	Milan PUROVIC		A	17	(7)	11
1	Ivan RANDJELOVIC		G	9		
27	Milanko RASKOVIC		A	2	(11)	5
13	Boban STOJANOVIC		A	1	(3)	
34	Vladimir STOJKOVIC		G	21		
19	Takayuki SUZUKI	JPN	A	1	(5)	
40	Nenad TOMOVIC		D	1		
21	Nikola TRAJKOVIC		M	9	(4)	2
42	Jagos VUKOVIC		M		(1)	
25	Nikola ZIGIC		A	23		12

HABITPHARM JAVOR IVANJICA
Coach – Radovan Curcic

2005
6/8	Obilic Beograd	h	0-0	
13/8	Buducnost Podgorica	a	1-3	Pejic
19/8	Partizan Beograd	h	0-1	
27/8	Smederevo	h	0-1	
10/9	Jedinstvo Bijelo Polje	h	1-0	Pejic
17/9	OFK Beograd	h	1-0	Bogdanovic
24/9	Zemun	a	0-1	
1/10	Vojvodina Novi Sad	h	2-2	Nikitovic, Radosavljevic (p)
15/10	Zeta Golubovci	a	0-1	
22/10	Hajduk Rodic MB Kula	h	0-0	
29/10	Crvena Zvezda Beograd	a	0-2	
5/11	Vozdovac Beograd	a	0-1	
19/11	Borac Cacak	a	0-0	
26/11	Buducnost Banatski Dvor	h	4-2	Mutavdzic, Temwanjera, Pejic, Bogdanovic
4/12	Rad Beograd	a	0-1	
10/12	Obilic Beograd	a	0-0	
15/12	Buducnost Podgorica	h	0-0	

2006
18/2	Partizan Beograd	a	0-6	
25/2	Smederevo	h	1-0	Nikitovic
4/3	Jedinstvo Bijelo Polje	a	2-0	Milovic, Radosavljevic
11/3	OFK Beograd	a	2-3	Odita, Temwanjera
25/3	Vojvodina Novi Sad	a	1-1	Simic
29/3	Zemun	h	2-0	Odita, Cvetkovic
1/4	Zeta Golubovci	h	1-0	Odita
8/4	Hajduk Rodic MB Kula	a	0-3	

Serbia & Montenegro

Date	Opponent	H/A	Score	Scorers
15/4	Crvena Zvezda Beograd	h	1-2	Odita
22/4	Vozdovac Beograd	a	1-2	Radosavljevic
29/4	Borac Cacak	h	0-2	
3/5	Buducnost Banatski Dvor	a	1-1	Temwanjera
6/5	Rad Beograd	h	1-0	Odita

No	Name	Nat	Pos	Aps	(s)	Gls
4	Aleksandar BOGDANOVIC		D	28		2
29	Igor BONDZULIC		G	26		
16	Bojan BRAJKOVIC		A	1	(5)	
13	Ivan CVETKOVIC		D	29		1
22	Predrag DJOROVIC		M		(6)	
18	Denis FETAHOVIC		D	5	(7)	
17	Nikola IGNJATIJEVIC		D	26		
24	Ivan JESIC		M	1	(3)	
3	Nikola LISANIN		D	21	(1)	
7	Vladimir LIVAJA		M		(1)	
27	Milovan MILOVIC		D	11		1
31	Miljan MUTAVDZIC		D	6	(2)	1
8	Jovan NIKITOVIC		M	27		2
19	Nikola NOVITOVIC		A	1	(10)	
35	Bojan OBRENOVIC		A	1		
26	Obiorah Emanuel ODITA	NGA	A	12		5
9	Dragan PEJIC		A	14	(8)	3
20	Aleksandar PETAKOVIC		M	5	(9)	
6	Miljan PETROVIC		D	4	(3)	
10	Zoran RADOSAVLJEVIC		M	12	(13)	3
21	Momcilo RAMIC		D	12	(5)	
7	Nikola SIMIC		M	10		1
1	Srdjan SOLDATOVIC		G	4		
11	Michael TEMWANJERA	ZIM	A	22	(4)	3
14	Radojica VASIC		D	25		
2	Miroslav VULICEVIC		D	7	(6)	
5	Dragisa ZUNIC		D	20	(6)	

HAJDUK RODIC MB KULA
Coach – Dragobljub Bekvalac; (11/3/06) (Jovo Cuckovic); (21/3/06) Nebojsa Vucicevic

2005

Date	Opponent	H/A	Score	Scorers
6/8	Crvena Zvezda Beograd	h	2-2	Mandic, Bulatovic
13/8	Vozdovac Beograd	a	1-2	Stanic
20/8	Borac Cacak	h	2-2	Davidov, Radivojevic
27/8	Buducnost Banatski Dvor	a	0-2	
10/9	Rad Beograd	h	1-0	Cirka
17/9	Obilic Beograd	a	1-0	Cirka
24/9	Buducnost Podgorica	h	1-0	Mandic
2/10	Partizan Beograd	a	0-0	
15/10	Smederevo	h	1-0	Osmanovic
22/10	Habitpharm Javor Ivanjica	a	0-0	
29/10	OFK Beograd	h	3-0	Osmanovic 2, Stanic
5/11	Zemun	a	2-2	Osmanovic, Davidov
19/11	Vojvodina Novi Sad	h	0-0	
26/11	Zeta Golubovci	a	3-5	Osmanovic, Mandic 2
3/12	Jedinstvo Bijelo Polje	h	2-0	Djukanovic, Vasiljevic
10/12	Crvena Zvezda Beograd	a	1-4	Mandic
17/12	Vozdovac Beograd	h	2-0	Vasiljevic, Stojmirovic

2006

Date	Opponent	H/A	Score	Scorers
18/2	Borac Cacak	a	0-1	
25/2	Buducnost Banatski Dvor	h	1-0	Osmanovic
5/3	Rad Beograd	a	0-0	
11/3	Obilic Beograd	h	1-0	Radivojevic
21/3	Buducnost Podgorica	a	0-0	
25/3	Partizan Beograd	h	0-0	
1/4	Smederevo	a	1-1	Vasiljevic
8/4	Habitpharm Javor Ivanjica	h	3-0	Osmanovic 2, Djukanovic
16/4	OFK Beograd	a	1-2	Stojanovic (p)
22/4	Zemun	h	6-1	Osmanovic 2, Davidov 2, Radivojevic, Vasiljevic
29/4	Vojvodina Novi Sad	a	0-0	
3/5	Zeta Golubovci	h	3-1	Stojanovic 2, Osmanovic
6/5	Jedinstvo Bijelo Polje	a	3-1	Stanic 2, Stojanovic

No	Name	Nat	Pos	Aps	(s)	Gls
13	Zoran ANTIC		D	25	(1)	
20	Nikola BOGIC		M	27	(1)	
3	Rados BULATOVIC		D	8	(10)	1
6	Ivan CIRKA		D	28		2
8	Aleksandar DAVIDOV		M	26	(2)	4
17	Srdjan DJUKANOVIC		M	4	(14)	2
25	Andjelko DJURICIC		G	28		
15	Bojan DOJKIC		D	1		
26	Ljubomir FEJSA		M	1	(3)	
12	Goran HABENSUS		D		(3)	
21	Aleksandar JOVANOVIC		M	2	(3)	
34	Nikola KOMAZEC		A	1	(1)	
33	Milan KRALJ		A	1	(1)	
16	Zeljko LJUBENOVIC		M	7	(6)	
14	Ilija MANDIC		A	22	(1)	5
1	Nikola MILOJEVIC		G	2		
4	Dragan MOJIC		D	11		
5	Djordje MRDJANIN		D	13	(4)	
19	Dusan OBRADOVIC		M		(1)	
18	Dejan OSMANOVIC		A	20	(5)	11
35	Marko PANOVIC		A		(1)	
2	Savo PAVICEVIC		D	26		
7	Jovan RADIVOJEVIC		M	27	(2)	3
15	Igor RADOVIC		M	1	(3)	
10	Srdjan STANIC		M	25		4
16	Boban STOJANOVIC		A	7	(3)	4
11	Aleksandar STOJMIROVIC		A	8	(7)	1
32	Branislav TRAJKOVIC		M	2	(1)	
24	Nermin USENI		D	1	(4)	
9	Miodrag VASILJEVIC		A	4	(8)	4
22	Nebojsa VUKOJICIC		M	2		

JEDINSTVO BIJELO POLJE
Coach – Sava Kovacevic; (18/2/06) Fikret Kurgas; (21/3/06) Dragan Karisik; (9/4/06) Rade Vesovic

2005

Date	Opponent	H/A	Score	Scorers
6/8	Partizan Beograd	a	0-2	
20/8	Smederevo	a	0-1	
27/8	Vozdovac Beograd	h	2-2	Trifunovic, Velickovic
10/9	Habitpharm Javor Ivanjica	a	0-1	
17/9	Borac Cacak	h	2-1	Trifunovic, Drndar Ek.
21/9	Crvena Zvezda Beograd	h	0-4	
24/9	OFK Beograd	a	0-4	
1/10	Buducnost Banatski Dvor	h	2-0	Trifunovic, Savic
15/10	Zemun	a	1-2	Savic
22/10	Rad Beograd	h	1-4	Babaca
29/10	Vojvodina Novi Sad	a	0-2	
5/11	Obilic Beograd	h	2-1	Babaca, Trifunovic
19/11	Zeta Golubovci	a	0-3	
26/11	Buducnost Podgorica	h	0-1	
3/12	Hajduk Rodic MB Kula	a	0-2	
7/12	Partizan Beograd	h	2-3	Trifunovic 2
17/12	Crvena Zvezda Beograd	a	0-4	

2006

Date	Opponent	H/A	Score	Scorers
18/2	Smederevo	h	2-3	Madzgalj 2
25/2	Vozdovac Beograd	a	1-3	Madzgalj
4/3	Habitpharm Javor Ivanjica	h	0-2	
11/3	Borac Cacak	a	0-2	
21/3	OFK Beograd	h	0-1	
25/3	Buducnost Banatski Dvor	a	1-5	Drobnjak M.
1/4	Zemun	h	0-2	
9/4	Rad Beograd	a	0-2	
15/4	Vojvodina Novi Sad	h	1-1	Djalovic

Serbia & Montenegro

2/4	Obilic Beograd	a	0-5	
9/4	Zeta Golubovci	h	0-4	
/5	Buducnost Podgorica	a	0-2	
/5	Hajduk Rodic MB Kula	h	1-3	Franca

No	Name	Nat	Pos	Aps	(s)	Gls
0	Sead BABACA		M	17		2
8	Aleksandar BRDJANIN		A	2	(6)	
2	Edis CINDRAK		A	16	(5)	
3	Danilo CULAFIC		M		(1)	
0	Enes CURKIC		M	7	(5)	
0	Arslan DACIC		G	2	(1)	
9	Scepan DJALOVIC		M	9	(2)	1
5	Ljubo DJUROVIC		D	7	(1)	
2	Milanko DRASKOVIC		M	21	(2)	
	Ekrem DRNDAR		M	17	(8)	1
	Ermin DRNDAR		D	24		
	Goran DROBNJAK		D	11		
7	Ljubomir DROBNJAK		A	5	(5)	
24	Milutin DROBNJAK		A	2	(3)	1
29	Nikola DROBNJAK		M		(1)	
31	Zeljko DROBNJAK		G	8		
27	Leid FRANCA		A	3	(12)	1
2	Nemanja JOVSIC		G	17		
	Mladen KALUDJEROVIC		D	5		
11	Radojko MADZGALJ		A	15	(5)	3
17	Sladjan NIKOLIC		M	2		
34	Damir NUMANOVIC		A	7	(1)	
35	Milos PERISIC		A	2	(1)	
18	Ranko PESIC		D	18	(1)	
8	Rade PATROVIC		M	15		
26	Marko RAKONJAC		M	1	(6)	
23	Dusan SADZAKOV		D	15		
21	Zdravko SAVIC		A	4	(5)	2
25	Bojan SLJIVANCANIN		D	8		
19	Darko STOJANOVIC		D	8	(2)	
14	Milos TRIFUNOVIC		M	15		6
5	Veselin VELICKOVIC		D	11	(1)	1
4	Predrag VIDEKANIC		D	6	(3)	
9	Zlatko VUKOVIC		A	20	(8)	
16	Srdjan ZINDOVIC		D	7	(2)	
1	Bosko ZURIC		G	3		

OBILIC BEOGRAD
Coach – Zoran Djurdjevic; (10/9/05) Nebojsa Licanin; (15/10/05) Dusan Jevric; (18/2/06) Nebojsa Vucicevic; (11/3/06) Darko Vargec

2005

6/8	Habitpharm Javor Ivanjica	a	0-0	
14/8	OFK Beograd	h	0-1	
20/8	Zemun	a	0-2	
27/8	Vojvodina Novi Sad	h	0-1	
10/9	Zeta Golubovci	a	1-4	Andjelkovic
17/9	Hajduk Rodic MB Kula	a	0-2	
24/9	Crvena Zvezda Beograd	h	2-4	Ocokoljic, Tadic
1/10	Vozdovac Beograd	h	2-5	Zajic, Vanic
15/10	Borac Cacak	a	3-1	Zajic, Vranjkovic, Stankovic
22/10	Buducnost Banatski Dvor	h	1-0	Radojicic
30/10	Rad Beograd	a	1-1	Zajic
5/11	Jedinstvo Bijelo Polje	a	1-2	og (Sadzakov)
19/11	Buducnost Podgorica	h	0-0	
26/11	Partizan Beograd	a	2-4	Zajic, Petrovic
3/12	Smederevo	h	0-2	
10/12	Habitpharm Javor Ivanjica	h	0-0	
15/12	OFK Beograd	a	1-3	Stefanovic

2006

18/2	Zemun	h	0-2	
25/2	Vojvodina Novi Sad	a	0-1	
4/3	Zeta Golubovci	h	0-0	
11/3	Hajduk Rodic MB Kula	a	0-1	
21/3	Crvena Zvezda Beograd	h	2-3	Randjelovic, Tadic
25/3	Vozdovac Beograd	a	0-4	
1/4	Borac Cacak	h	0-0	
8/4	Buducnost Banatski Dvor	a	0-3	
15/4	Rad Beograd	h	0-1	
22/4	Jedinstvo Bijelo Polje	h	5-0	Randjelovic 2, Jovanovic, Popovic, Zavisic
29/4	Buducnost Podgorica	a	1-2	Nikolic S.
3/5	Partizan Beograd	h	0-2	
6/5	Smederevo	a	1-3	Knezevic

No	Name	Nat	Pos	Aps	(s)	Gls
27	Mirko ALEKSIC		M	4		
2	Marko ANDJELKOVIC		M		(2)	1
8	Ivan BABIC		D	15		
25	Aleksandar BOJANIC		A		(3)	
17	Srdjan CUBRILO		G	13	(1)	
12	Dusan DJOKIC		G	8		
5	Ivan DJUROVIC		D	8		
18	Radoje JOKANOVIC		A		(4)	
3	Aleksandar JOVANOVIC		D	15	(1)	1
23	Zeljko KLJAJEVIC		A	1	(1)	
26	Srdjan KNEZEVIC		D	20	(1)	1
32	Igor KOJIC		G		(1)	
15	Nikola LAKIC		M		(2)	
31	Veljko MARKOVIC		M	1	(2)	
14	Marko MAROVIC		D	24	(1)	
23	Aleksandar MIJATOVIC		D	15		
33	Nikola MILIC		D		(1)	
7	Vladan MILOSAVLJEVIC		D	8	(2)	
9	Dragan MILOVANOVIC		A	2	(1)	
21	Ratko NIKOLIC		D	5	(4)	
19	Srdjan NIKOLIC		A	1	(3)	1
24	Aleksandar OCOKOLJIC		M	8		1
30	Dejan OGNJANOVIC		D	13	(1)	
6	Peter OMODUEMUKE	NGA	M	8	(1)	
27	Djordje PANTIC		G	7		
5	Dejan PERIC		D	2	(1)	
11	Ivan PETROVIC		M	5	(7)	1
13	Ivan POPOVIC		D	20	(3)	1
29	Gabrijel RADOJICIC		A	4	(6)	1
9	Predrag RANDJELOVIC		A	10		3
12	Predrag RISTOVIC		G	2		
22	Ivan STANKOVIC		M	9	(2)	1
16	Jovan STEFANOVIC		A	7	(11)	1
10	Bozidar TADIC		M	19	(3)	1
8	Srdjan UROSEVIC		M	7	(1)	
4	Nenad VANIC		D	15		1
35	Nikola VASILIC		A	1		
25	Nemanja VIDAKOVIC		A	2	(2)	
1	Djordje VLAJIC		M	5	(3)	
1	Vojislav VRANJKOVIC		M	4	(4)	1
6	Bojan ZAJIC		M	14		4
7	Bojan ZAVISIC		D	12		1
28	Sasa ZIMONJIC		M	2		
20	Marko ZIVKOVIC		D	14	(3)	

OFK BEOGRAD
Coach – Branko Babic; (29/10/05) Slobodan Krcmarevic

2005

6/8	Rad Beograd	h	1-0	Rajkovic
14/8	Obilic Beograd	a	1-0	Ivanovic
20/8	Buducnost Podgorica	h	3-0	Bakovic 2, Petrovic
28/8	Partizan Beograd	a	1-0	Stosic
10/9	Smederevo	h	3-0	Stosic, Bakovic, Tosic
17/9	Habitpharm Javor Ivanjica	a	0-1	
24/9	Jedinstvo Bijelo Polje	h	4-0	Tosic, Ivanovic, Bakovic,

Serbia & Montenegro

Date	Opponent	h/a	Score	Scorers
1/10	Zemun	h	2-0	Bozovic, Bakovic, Bozovic
15/10	Vojvodina Novi Sad	a	0-1	
29/10	Hajduk Rodic MB Kula	a	0-3	
2/11	Zeta Golubovci	h	0-1	
6/11	Crvena Zvezda Beograd	h	0-1	
19/11	Vozdovac Beograd	a	1-0	Petrovic
26/11	Borac Cacak	h	1-1	Ivanovic
3/12	Buducnost Banatski Dvor	a	0-1	
10/12	Rad Beograd	a	2-1	Bozovic, Arsenijevic
15/12	Obilic Beograd	h	3-1	Bozovic, Simic, Arsenijevic
2006				
18/2	Buducnost Podgorica	a	2-2	Bozovic 2
25/2	Partizan Beograd	h	0-1	
4/3	Smederevo	a	1-2	Bakovic
11/3	Habitpharm Javor Ivanjica	h	3-2	Bakovic 2, Stosic
21/3	Jedinstvo Bijelo Polje	a	1-0	Kolarov
25/3	Zemun	a	1-3	Bozovic
1/4	Vojvodina Novi Sad	h	0-1	
8/4	Zeta Golubovci	a	0-0	
16/4	Hajduk Rodic MB Kula	h	2-1	Rakic, Petkovic
22/4	Crvena Zvezda Beograd	a	0-2	
29/4	Vozdovac Beograd	h	2-2	Petrovic, Vusljanin
3/5	Borac Cacak	a	1-1	Petrovic
6/5	Buducnost Banatski Dvor	h	0-1	

No	Name	Nat	Pos	Aps	(s)	Gls
38	Goran ANTELJ		A	1		
17	Nemanja ARSENIJEVIC		A	7	(17)	2
20	Milos BAJALICA		D	22		
10	Branko BAKOVIC		A	17	(2)	8
11	Vladimir BOZOVIC		M	27	(1)	7
30	Milan CULUM		M		(6)	
23	Igor DEVIC	CRO	M		(2)	
1	Nenad ERIC		G	23		
25	Milan ILIC		D	2	(1)	
2	Branislav IVANOVIC		D	15		3
32	Djordje IVELJA		A	4	(6)	
34	Andrija KALUDJEROVIC		A		(1)	
33	Djordje KAMBER		M	6	(2)	
4	Mladen KASCELAN		M	10	(6)	
9	Hristijan KIROVSKI	MAC	A	5	(5)	
3	Aleksandar KOLAROV		D	11		1
18	Nemanja MILISAVLJEVIC		M		(2)	
13	Dusan PETKOVIC		D	5		1
21	Ivan PETROVIC		M	24		4
5	Slobodan RAJKOVIC		D	20	1	
19	Djordje RAKIC			8	(3)	1
37	Bojan SARANOV		G	2		
36	Aleksandar SIMCEVIC		D		(1)	
7	Aleksandar SIMIC		M	28	(1)	1
28	Dragan STANCIC		M	23		
24	Ivan STEVANOVIC		D	10		
8	Stevan STOSIC		M	17	(4)	3
26	Zoran SUPIC		D	11	(4)	
3	Dusko TOSIC		D	17		2
35	Dalibor VESELINOVIC		A	2	(1)	
9	Dragan VUKOVIC		A	3	(5)	
27	Irfan VUSLJANIN		M	4	(9)	1
31	Zlatko ZECEVIC		G	5		
22	Dejan ZIVKOVIC		M	1	(1)	

PARTIZAN BEOGRAD

Coach – Vladimir Vermezovic; (2/10/05) (Blagoje Paunovic); (7/10/05) Jürgen Röber (GER)

Date	Opponent	h/a	Score	Scorers
2005				
6/8	Jedinstvo Bijelo Polje	h	2-0	Tomic, Radovic
14/8	Smederevo	h	2-1	Vukcevic, Tomic (p)
19/8	Habitpharm Javor Ivanjica	a	1-0	Tomic (p)
28/8	OFK Beograd	h	0-1	
10/9	Zemun	a	2-0	Vukcevic (p), Radonjic
18/9	Vojvodina Novi Sad	h	3-0	Bajic, Marinkovic Neb. 2
24/9	Zeta Golubovci	a	3-1	Radonjic, Vukcevic, Odita
2/10	Hajduk Rodic MB Kula	a	0-0	
15/10	Crvena Zvezda Beograd	a	0-2	
22/10	Vozdovac Beograd	h	2-3	Radonjic, Babovic
29/10	Borac Cacak	a	2-0	Nadj, Radonjic (p)
5/11	Buducnost Banatski Dvor	h	2-0	Radonjic (p), Marinkovic Neb.
20/11	Rad Beograd	a	2-1	Radonjic 2
26/11	Obilic Beograd	h	4-2	Radonjic 2 (1p), Djordjevic, Nadj
3/12	Buducnost Podgorica	a	1-0	Smiljanic
7/12	Jedinstvo Bijelo Polje	a	3-2	Lomic, Radonjic, Saveljic
15/12	Smederevo	a	1-0	Saveljic
2006				
18/2	Habitpharm Javor Ivanjica	h	6-0	Lazovic 2, Radonjic 3 (2p), Babovic
25/2	OFK Beograd	a	1-0	og (Bajalica)
5/3	Zemun	h	0-0	
11/3	Vojvodina Novi Sad	a	3-2	Radonjic 2 (1p), Sljivancanin
21/3	Zeta Golubovci	h	1-0	Babovic
25/3	Hajduk Rodic MB Kula	a	0-0	
1/4	Crvena Zvezda Beograd	h	0-0	
8/4	Vozdovac Beograd	a	3-1	Boya 2, Radonjic
15/4	Borac Cacak	h	1-0	Lazovic
22/4	Buducnost Banatski Dvor	a	1-1	Lazovic
29/4	Rad Beograd	h	2-0	Radovic, Lazovic
3/5	Obilic Beograd	a	2-0	Radonjic 2
6/5	Buducnost Podgorica	h	3-0	Boya, Radonjic 2

No	Name	Nat	Pos	Aps	(s)	Gls
30	Nikolas ASPROGENOUS	CYP	G	5		
10	Stefan BABOVIC		M	19	(4)	3
5	Branimir BAJIC	BOS	D	10	(2)	1
8	Pierre BOYA	CMR	A	22	(5)	3
7	Nenad BRNOVIC		M	21		
2	Milivoje CIRKOVIC		D	9		
14	Nenad DJORDJEVIC		D	20		1
16	Ifeany EMEGHARA	NGA	D	10	(2)	
34	Nikola GRUBJESIC		A	1	(5)	
38	Stevan JOVETIC		M		(2)	
77	Nemanja JOVSIC		G	2		
25	Ivica KRALJ		G	21		
17	Danko LAZOVIC		A	11		5
13	Marko LOMIC		D	28	(1)	1
36	Nebojsa MARINKOVIC		M		(5)	3
29	Nenad MARINKOVIC		A		(6)	
20	Milovan MILOVIC		D	1	(2)	
4	Zoran MIRKOVIC		D	13		
28	Albert NADJ		M	28		2
15	Obiorah Emanuel ODITA	NGA	A	6	(7)	1
27	Djordje PANTIC		G	2	(1)	
9	Srdjan RADONJIC		A	28		20
11	Miroslav RADOVIC		M	6	(6)	2
24	Nemanja RNIC		D	9	(1)	
3	Nisa SAVELJIC		D	19		2
6	Bojan SLJIVANCANIN		D	1		1
31	Milan SMILJANIC		M	9	(6)	1
26	Perica STANCEVSKI		D	1		
44	Miralem SULEJMANI		M		(1)	
21	Ivan TOMIC		M	12	(4)	3
35	Borko VESELINOVIC		A	3	(9)	
1	Simon VUKCEVIC		M	13		3
88	Zvonimir VUKIC		M		(2)	

Serbia & Montenegro

RAD BEOGRAD
Coach – Cedomir Djoincevic; (2/10/05) Bogdan Korak

2005
Date	Opponent	H/A	Score	Scorers
6/8	OFK Beograd	a	0-1	
14/8	Zemun	h	0-1	
20/8	Vojvodina Novi Sad	a	0-2	
28/8	Zeta Golubovci	h	3-0	Sretenovic, Gluscevic, Ljubinkovic
10/9	Hajduk Rodic MB Kula	a	0-1	
18/9	Crvena Zvezda Beograd	h	2-4	Sikimic, Tintor
24/9	Vozdovac Beograd	a	1-2	Tintor (p)
2/10	Borac Cacak	h	0-3	
15/10	Buducnost Banatski Dvor	a	1-0	Pavlovic N.
22/10	Jedinstvo Bijelo Polje	h	4-1	Sikimic 3, Novkovic
30/10	Obilic Beograd	h	1-1	Novakovic
5/11	Buducnost Podgorica	a	1-2	Novakovic
20/11	Partizan Beograd	h	1-2	Novakovic
26/11	Smederevo	a	1-0	Tintor
4/12	Habitpharm Javor Ivanjica	h	1-0	Gluscevic
10/12	OFK Beograd	h	1-2	Gluscevic
17/12	Zemun	a	0-0	

2006
Date	Opponent	H/A	Score	Scorers
19/2	Vojvodina Novi Sad	h	1-1	Sikimic
25/2	Zeta Golubovci	a	0-1	
5/3	Hajduk Rodic MB Kula	h	0-0	
11/3	Crvena Zvezda Beograd	a	0-1	
21/3	Vozdovac Beograd	h	3-1	Delic, Tintor, Bates
25/3	Borac Cacak	a	1-2	Urumov
2/4	Buducnost Banatski Dvor	h	0-1	
9/4	Jedinstvo Bijelo Polje	h	2-0	Urumov, Bogunovic
15/4	Obilic Beograd	a	1-0	Urumov (p)
22/4	Buducnost Podgorica	h	2-1	Urumov, Bates
29/4	Partizan Beograd	a	0-2	
3/5	Smederevo	h	0-2	
6/5	Habitpharm Javor Ivanjica	a	0-1	

No	Name	Nat	Pos	Aps	(s)	Gls
35	Nemanja ANDRIC		M		(4)	
4	Ivan BABIC		D	8	(1)	
29	Stevan BATES		D	23		2
19	Dejan BATROVIC		D	2	(1)	
21	Milos BOGUNOVIC		A	9	(4)	1
32	Uros DELIC		M	9	(2)	1
2	Sasa DJORDJEVIC		D	9	(1)	
21	Vladimir GLUSCEVIC		A	9	(6)	3
3	Marko GRUBELIC		D	1	(1)	
12	Bojan ISAILOVIC		G	1		
14	Marko JAKSIC		A	2	(3)	
1	Bojan JORGACEVIC		G	13	(1)	
26	Srdjan KLJAJEVIC		G	16		
30	Cvetin KRSTIC		M	2	(3)	
37	Milos KRSTIC		M	2	(2)	
7	Marko LJUBINKOVIC		M	13	(1)	1
20	Srdjan MAKSIMOVIC		M	1		
36	Rodoljub MARJANOVIC		A	5	(3)	
17	Milan MARTINOVIC		M	22	(2)	
16	Nenad MISKOVIC	BOS	D	5		
23	Dalibor MITROVIC		A	6	(5)	
30	Pavle NINKOV		A		(4)	
27	Mitar NOVAKOVIC		M	26		3
18	Rade NOVKOVIC		D	23	(2)	1
34	Aleksandar PAUNOVIC		M	2	(8)	
22	Nebojsa PAVLOVIC		A	10	(3)	1
20	Vladan PAVLOVIC		M		(1)	
33	Nemanja PEJCINOVIC		D	1		
38	Rados PROTIC		M	1		
10	Rusmir Dejan RUSMIR		M	10	(2)	

Continued:

9	Predrag SIKIMIC		A	15	(5)	5
15	Aleksandar SREDOJEVIC		M	3		
13	Sreten SRETENOVIC		D	12	(3)	1
11	Sreten STANIC		A	8	(4)	
8	Nenad STOJAKOVIC		M	14	(1)	
5	Vladimir TINTOR		M	14	(3)	4
11	Zoran URUMOV		D	19		4
25	Vladimir VUKAJLOVIC		M	6	(4)	
6	Vladan VUKOVIC		D	8	(7)	

SMEDEREVO
Coach – Tomislav Sivic; (5/11/05) (Aleksandar Pantic); (3/12/05) Jaime Coll Bauzá (ESP)

2005
Date	Opponent	H/A	Score	Scorers
6/8	Buducnost Podgorica	h	1-1	Milovanovic
14/8	Partizan Beograd	a	1-2	Kekezovic
20/8	Jedinstvo Bijelo Polje	h	1-0	Radosavljevic
27/8	Habitpharm Javor Ivanjica	h	1-0	Djuraskovic
10/9	OFK Beograd	a	0-3	
17/9	Zemun	h	3-2	Jovanovic, Zivanovic, Zecevic
25/9	Vojvodina Novi Sad	a	0-1	
1/10	Zeta Golubovci	h	4-1	Milovanovic, Djuraskovic, Cukic, Jovanovic
15/10	Hajduk Rodic MB Kula	a	0-1	
22/10	Crvena Zvezda Beograd	h	1-3	Djuraskovic
29/10	Vozdovac Beograd	a	0-3	
5/11	Borac Cacak	h	0-0	
19/11	Buducnost Banatski Dvor	a	0-2	
26/11	Rad Beograd	h	0-1	
3/12	Obilic Beograd	a	2-0	Zecevic 2
10/12	Buducnost Podgorica	a	2-1	Djuraskovic, Radosavljevic
15/12	Partizan Beograd	h	0-1	

2006
Date	Opponent	H/A	Score	Scorers
18/2	Jedinstvo Bijelo Polje	a	3-2	Zivanovic 3
25/2	Habitpharm Javor Ivanjica	a	0-1	
4/3	OFK Beograd	h	2-1	Zecevic, Kekezovic
11/3	Zemun	a	0-0	
21/3	Vojvodina Novi Sad	h	1-0	Zivanovic
25/3	Zeta Golubovci	a	0-0	
1/4	Hajduk Rodic MB Kula	h	1-1	Zivkovic
8/4	Crvena Zvezda Beograd	a	0-2	
15/4	Vozdovac Beograd	h	1-2	Nikolic
22/4	Borac Cacak	a	0-4	
29/4	Buducnost Banatski Dvor	h	1-1	Zecevic
3/5	Rad Beograd	a	2-0	Milovanovic, Zoric
6/5	Obilic Beograd	h	3-1	Zivanovic, Zecevic, Zoric

No	Name	Nat	Pos	Aps	(s)	Gls
23	Mirko ALEKSIC		M	1	(6)	
33	Dragan CERAN		A	4	(5)	
5	Vladan CUKIC		M	15	(3)	1
12	Igor DJOKIC		M	3	(3)	
21	Zoran DJURASKOVIC		A	10	(7)	4
21	Bozo DJURKOVIC		A	2	(6)	
1	Srdjan DUSIC		G	5		
20	Mario GAVRILOVIC		A		(2)	
18	Nikola JEVTIC		A		(6)	
14	Goran JOVANOVIC		M	12	(4)	2
27	Dejan KEKEZOVIC		D	24	(2)	2
10	Sasa KOCIC		M	19	(3)	
4	Zeljko KOVACEVIC		D	10	(1)	
13	Marko MILOVANOVIC		D	17	(5)	3
7	Milan NIKOLIC		M	23	(3)	1
15	Dejan NOVAKOVIC		D		(1)	
11	Dragan PAUNOVIC		D	15	(2)	
19	Igor POPOVIC		D	2	(2)	
30	Dejan RADJENOVIC		M	11		
8	Dragan RADOSAVLJEVIC		D	20	(3)	2

Serbia & Montenegro

No	Name	Nat	Pos	Aps	(s)	Gls
22	Dejan RANKOVIC		G	13		
17	Nebojsa SAVIC		D	12	(1)	
3	Marko SOCANAC		D	10	(2)	
28	Dragan TADIC		A	7	(13)	
25	Bozidar UROSEVIC		G	12		
9	Milorad ZECEVIC		A	24	(2)	6
26	Ivan ZIVANOVIC		D	24		6
19	Dejan ZIVKOVIC		M	12		1
16	Sasa ZORIC		M	16	(3)	2

VOJVODINA NOVI SAD
Coach – (Milan Djuricic); (20/8/05) Zoran Maric

2005

Date	Opponent	H/A	Score	Scorers
6/8	Borac Cacak	h	0-1	
13/8	Buducnost Banatski Dvor	a	0-1	
20/8	Rad Beograd	h	2-0	Vukelja 2
27/8	Obilic Beograd	a	1-0	Jovanovic
10/9	Buducnost Podgorica	h	0-0	
18/9	Partizan Beograd	a	0-3	
25/9	Smederevo	h	1-0	Dobric
1/10	Habitpharm Javor Ivanjica	a	2-2	Jovanovic, Buac
15/10	OFK Beograd	h	1-0	Djuric
22/10	Zemun	a	1-1	Vukelja
29/10	Jedinstvo Bijelo Polje	h	2-0	Jovanovic, Vukelja
5/11	Zeta Golubovci	h	3-1	Vukelja 2, Dobric (p)
19/11	Hajduk Rodic MB Kula	a	0-0	
27/11	Crvena Zvezda Beograd	h	1-0	Kizito
3/12	Vozdovac Beograd	a	0-2	
10/12	Borac Cacak	a	0-1	
17/12	Buducnost Banatski Dvor	h	1-0	Vukelja

2006

Date	Opponent	H/A	Score	Scorers
19/2	Rad Beograd	a	1-1	Vukelja
25/2	Obilic Beograd	h	1-0	Dobric
4/3	Buducnost Podgorica	a	0-0	
11/3	Partizan Beograd	h	2-3	Nastic, Vukelja
21/3	Smederevo	a	0-1	
25/3	Habitpharm Javor Ivanjica	h	1-1	Nastic
1/4	OFK Beograd	a	1-0	og (Bajalica)
8/4	Zemun	h	2-1	Dobric (p), Milutinovic
15/4	Jedinstvo Bijelo Polje	h	1-1	Kacar
22/4	Zeta Golubovci	a	1-2	Nastic
29/4	Hajduk Rodic MB Kula	h	0-0	
3/5	Crvena Zvezda Beograd	a	1-3	Kacar
6/5	Vozdovac Beograd	h	2-2	Buac, Petkovic

No	Name	Nat	Pos	Aps	(s)	Gls
23	Vladimir BUAC		A	7	(14)	2
22	Mladen COVIC		A		(3)	
21	Ranko DESPOTOVIC		A	1	(10)	
24	Igor DJURIC		D	12	(4)	1
37	Stefan DJUROVIC		A		(1)	
20	Sasa DOBRIC		M	24	(1)	4
19	Sasa DRAKULIC		A		(1)	
14	Ljubisa DUNDJERSKI		M	2	(4)	
10	Marko JOVANOVIC		A	22		3
4	Gojko KACAR		M	20	(6)	2
1	Damir KAHRIMAN		G	13		
2	Joseph Nesteroy KIZITO	UGA	D	22	(1)	1
3	Bojan KRASIC		D	6		
7	Branko LAZAREVIC		D	3		
15	Dragan MANDIC		D	29		
13	Uros MILOSAVLJEVIC		M	2		
8	Milan MILUTINOVIC		M	14	(9)	1
18	Nenad NASTIC		D	20	(6)	3
11	Borislav PAVLOVIC		M	5	(7)	
6	Nino PEKARIC		D	18		
5	Nikola PETKOVIC		D	5	(1)	1
17	Aleksandar POPOVIC		M	3	(6)	

No	Name	Nat	Pos	Aps	(s)	Gls
12	Borivoje RISTIC		G	1		
1	Milan STEPANOV		D	15		
16	Miodrag STOSIC		D	25		
25	Milan SUSAK		D	3	(5)	
5	Sasa TODIC		G	16		
9	Ljubisa VUKELJA		A	28		9
40	Dragomir VUKOBRATOVIC		M	14	(6)	

VOZDOVAC BEOGRAD
Coach – Mihajlo Ivanovic

2005

Date	Opponent	H/A	Score	Scorers
5/8	Zeta Golubovci	a	0-1	
13/8	Hajduk Rodic MB Kula	h	2-1	Jovanovic, Mihajlov
20/8	Crvena Zvezda Beograd	a	1-3	Jovanovic
27/8	Jedinstvo Bijelo Polje	a	2-2	Kalajdzic (p), Djokic
10/9	Borac Cacak	h	4-0	Kalajdzic (p), Jovanovic, Pavlovic, Cetkovic
17/9	Buducnost Banatski Dvor	a	0-0	
24/9	Rad Beograd	h	2-1	Djokic 2
1/10	Obilic Beograd	a	5-2	Mikic, Jovanovic 2 (1p), Djokic 2
15/10	Buducnost Podgorica	h	4-1	Djokic 3, Mikic
22/10	Partizan Beograd	a	3-2	Jovanovic, Andjelkovic, Kalajdzic
29/10	Smederevo	h	3-0	Djokic, Jovanovic, Milosevic
5/11	Habitpharm Javor Ivanjica	a	1-0	Zivkovic
19/11	OFK Beograd	h	0-1	
26/11	Zemun	a	2-2	Jovanovic, Djokic (p)
3/12	Vojvodina Novi Sad	h	2-0	Kalajdzic, Djokic
7/12	Zeta Golubovci	h	1-0	Milosevic
17/12	Hajduk Rodic MB Kula	a	0-2	

2006

Date	Opponent	H/A	Score	Scorers
18/2	Crvena Zvezda Beograd	h	0-2	
25/2	Jedinstvo Bijelo Polje	h	3-1	Stepanovic, Marinkovic, Grubjesic
4/3	Borac Cacak	a	1-0	Marinkovic
11/3	Buducnost Banatski Dvor	h	1-1	Pavlovic
21/3	Rad Beograd	a	1-3	Kalajdzic
25/3	Obilic Beograd	h	4-0	Stepanovic, og (Zavisic), Spasojevic, Marinkovic
1/4	Buducnost Podgorica	a	0-2	
8/4	Partizan Beograd	h	1-3	Stepanovic
15/4	Smederevo	a	2-1	Kalajdzic, Marinkovic
22/4	Habitpharm Javor Ivanjica	a	2-1	Grubjesic, Marinkovic
29/4	OFK Beograd	a	2-2	Grubjesic, Spasojevic
3/5	Zemun	h	1-2	Marinkovic
6/5	Vojvodina Novi Sad	a	2-2	Grubjesic 2

No	Name	Nat	Pos	Aps	(s)	Gls
22	Milos ADAMOVIC		G	30		
3	Dusan ANDJELKOVIC		D	17		1
10	Marko BASARA		M		(8)	
19	Djordjije CETKOVIC		A		(6)	1
13	Dusan DJOKIC		A	17		11
7	Nikola GRUBJESIC		A	9	(4)	5
11	Slavisa JEREMIC		A		(1)	
20	Ivan JOVANOVIC		M	17		8
8	Zeljko KALAJDZIC		M	28		6
28	Darko LOVRIC		D	6	(8)	
2	Aleksandar MADZAR		A		(1)	
9	Nebojsa MARINKOVIC		M	13		6
21	Milos MIHAJLOV		D	27		1
7	Borislav MIKIC		M	12	(2)	2
5	Milan MILIJAS		D	17	(7)	
33	Goran MILOSEVIC		D	27		2
9	Nenad MITROVIC		A		(1)	
4	Aleksandar PANTIC		D	28		
23	Milos PAVLOVIC		M	24		2

Serbia & Montenegro

No	Name	Nat	Pos	Aps	(s)	Gls
14	Dejan PERIC		D	9	(3)	
6	Aleksandar PETROVIC		D	10	(1)	
15	Nenad PETROVIC		M	3	(16)	
2	Uros SAVIC		D		(1)	
17	Bojan SPASOJEVIC		A	9	(3)	2
20	Slaven STANKOVIC		M		(7)	
24	Bojan STEPANOVIC		M	6	(9)	3
13	Igor TASEVSKI		D	6		
18	Aleksandar ZIVKOVIC		M	15		1

ZEMUN
Coach – Miodrag Martac

2005

Date	Opponent	h/a	Score	Scorers
6/8	Buducnost Banatski Dvor	h	2-0	Mijanovic, Milijas
14/8	Rad Beograd	a	1-0	Mijanovic
20/8	Obilic Beograd	h	2-0	Milijas, Vujosevic
28/8	Buducnost Podgorica	a	1-1	Vidovic
10/9	Partizan Beograd	h	0-2	
17/9	Smederevo	a	2-3	Milijas (p), Markoski
24/9	Habitpharm Javor Ivanjica	h	1-0	Milijas (p)
1/10	OFK Beograd	a	0-2	
15/10	Jedinstvo Bijelo Polje	h	2-1	Lazarevic, Milijas (p)
22/10	Vojvodina Novi Sad	h	1-1	Sandulovic
29/10	Zeta Golubovci	a	0-1	
5/11	Hajduk Rodic MB Kula	h	2-2	Veselinovic, Milijas (p)
20/11	Crvena Zvezda Beograd	a	1-2	Vujosevic
26/11	Vozdovac Beograd	h	2-2	Milijas 2 (1p)
3/12	Borac Cacak	a	0-2	
13/12	Buducnost Banatski Dvor	a	0-3	
17/12	Rad Beograd	h	0-0	

2006

Date	Opponent	h/a	Score	Scorers
18/2	Obilic Beograd	a	2-0	Markoski 2
25/2	Buducnost Podgorica	h	3-1	Vidovic, Babaca, Markoski
5/3	Partizan Beograd	a	0-0	
11/3	Smederevo	h	0-0	
25/3	OFK Beograd	h	3-1	Mester, Tucakovic, Markoski
29/3	Habitpharm Javor Ivanjica	a	0-2	
1/4	Jedinstvo Bijelo Polje	h	2-0	Markoski, Ilic
8/4	Vojvodina Novi Sad	a	1-2	Martac
15/4	Zeta Golubovci	h	2-1	Ilic, Prodanovic
22/4	Hajduk Rodic MB Kula	a	1-6	Markoski
29/4	Crvena Zvezda Beograd	h	0-2	
3/5	Vozdovac Beograd	a	2-1	Mester, Vidovic
6/5	Borac Cacak	h	1-1	Markoski (p)

No	Name	Nat	Pos	Aps	(s)	Gls
15	Sead BABACA		M	5	(5)	1
16	Zivko BAKIC		D	3	(10)	
4	Bojan COSIC		D	13	(1)	
24	Milos DAJEVIC		A		(2)	
6	Stevo GLOGOVAC		D	15		
9	Brana ILIC		A	25	(2)	2
34	Darko ISIDOROVIC		A	2	(1)	
1	Damir KAHRIMAN		G	14		
17	Slaven KOVACEVIC		M	5	(11)	
38	Nenad LALATOVIC		D	5		
23	Mladen LAZAREVIC		D	25		1
36	Dimitrija LAZAREVSKI	MAC	M	4	(5)	
16	Ivan LITERA		A		(1)	
10	Marko MARKOSKI		A	21	(3)	8
14	Nikola MARTAC		M	1	(6)	1
7	Milan MESTER		M	12		2
2	Cedomir MIJANOVIC		D	21		2
7	Nenad MILIJAS		M	15		8
31	Edvin MUJOVIC		M		(5)	
11	Aleksandar NEDELJKOVIC		A	1	(6)	
18	Nebojsa NESKOVIC		A		(3)	
37	Vasilije PRODANOVIC		M	19	(2)	1

No	Name	Nat	Pos	Aps	(s)	Gls
1	Radovan RADAKOVIC		G	12		
5	Vladimir SANDULOVIC		D	10	(1)	1
6	Uros SAVIC		D	13		
29	Sasa STOJANOVIC		A		(3)	
22	Nemanja SUPIC		G	4		
20	Mirko TEODOROVIC		M	26		
26	Kristijan TUCAKOVIC		D	14	(2)	1
21	Jovan VESELINOVIC		M	16	(6)	1
8	Sasa VIDOVIC		M	22	(6)	3
27	Nikola VUJOSEVIC		A	7	(5)	2

ZETA GOLUBOVCI
Coach – Dejan Vukicevic

2005

Date	Opponent	h/a	Score	Scorers
5/8	Vozdovac Beograd	h	1-0	Vukovic
14/8	Borac Cacak	a	1-0	Milic
20/8	Buducnost Banatski Dvor	h	1-0	Milic
28/8	Rad Beograd	a	0-3	
10/9	Obilic Beograd	h	4-1	Vukovic 2, Milic, Tumbasovic
17/9	Buducnost Podgorica	a	1-1	Milic
24/9	Partizan Beograd	h	1-3	Milic
1/10	Smederevo	a	1-4	Milic (p)
15/10	Habitpharm Javor Ivanjica	h	1-0	Nuhi
29/10	Zemun	h	1-0	Nuhi
2/11	OFK Beograd	a	1-0	Todorovic
5/11	Vojvodina Novi Sad	a	1-3	Vukovic (p)
19/11	Jedinstvo Bijelo Polje	h	3-0	Markoski, Nuhi, Milic
26/11	Hajduk Rodic MB Kula	h	5-3	Milic 2 (1p), Vukovic, Nuhi, Vukomanovic
4/12	Crvena Zvezda Beograd	a	2-3	Vukovic, Markoski
7/12	Vozdovac Beograd	a	0-1	
15/12	Borac Cacak	h	3-1	Nuhi, Milic 2 (1p)

2006

Date	Opponent	h/a	Score	Scorers
18/2	Buducnost Banatski Dvor	a	1-3	Vukovic
25/2	Rad Beograd	h	1-0	Djurovic
4/3	Obilic Beograd	a	0-0	
11/3	Buducnost Podgorica	h	3-0	(w/o)
21/3	Partizan Beograd	a	0-1	
25/3	Smederevo	h	0-0	
1/4	Habitpharm Javor Ivanjica	a	0-1	
8/4	OFK Beograd	h	0-0	
15/4	Zemun	a	1-2	Petrovic
22/4	Vojvodina Novi Sad	h	2-1	Petrovic 2
29/4	Jedinstvo Bijelo Polje	a	4-0	Vukovic 2, Stjepanovic 2
3/5	Hajduk Rodic MB Kula	a	1-3	Markoski
6/5	Crvena Zvezda Beograd	h	2-2	Petrovic, Vujadinovic

No	Name	Nat	Pos	Aps	(s)	Gls
7	Zivko BAKIC		D	6		
28	Vlado BOLJEVIC		M		(1)	
22	Djulijano CAMAJ		A		(4)	
23	Marko CETKOVIC		D	4	(6)	
39	Marko DJURETIC		M		(1)	
14	Nenad DJUROVIC		D	4	(2)	1
3	Blazo IGUMANOVIC		D	7	(4)	
1	Sasa IVANOVIC		G	1		
2	Aleksandar JOVIC		G	20		
24	Aleksandar KALUDJEROVIC		D	7	(1)	
5	Miroslav KALUDJEROVIC		M	10	(7)	
26	Ivan KNEZEVIC		A	1	(13)	
25	Zarko KORAC		A		(1)	
14	Igor KUC		D		(2)	
38	Igor LAMBULIC		M		(1)	
17	Dragan MARAS		D	1	(6)	
15	Arsen MARJAN		D	13		
10	Jovan MARKOSKI		M	21	(4)	3
8	Darko MARKOVIC		M	1	(11)	
23	Milan MESTER		M	10	(5)	

The European Book of Football 2006/2007 - 669

Serbia & Montenegro

18	Drazen MILIC	A	24		11	
19	Ajazdin NUHI	M	29		5	
22	Branimir PETROVIC	M	10	(1)	4	
12	Mileta RADULOVIC	G	8			
11	Slaven STJEPANOVIC	A		(6)	2	
6	Ivan TODOROVIC	M	25		1	
20	Janko TUMBASOVIC	M	24	(2)	1	
27	Ivan VUCKOVIC	D	1	(2)		
17	Nikola VUJADINOVIC	D	10		1	
4	Darko VUKASINOVIC	D	24			
21	Branislav VUKOMANOVIC	M	22		1	
9	Ivan VUKOVIC	A	25	(2)	9	
7	Bojan ZAVISIC	D	11			

DOMESTIC CUP 2005/06

1/16 FINALS
(20/9/05)
Mladost Podgorica 2, Vozdovac Beograd 1
(21/9/05)
Vlasina Vlasotince 1, Buducnost Podgorica 0
Mladost Lucani 0, Smederevo 0 *(6-7 on pens)*
Sutjeska Niksic 1, Macva Sabac 0
Partizan Beograd 2, Habitpharm Javor Ivanjica 0
Hajduk Beograd 0, Radnicki Nis 0 *(4-5 on pens)*
Mladost Apatin 0, Obilic Beograd 1
PSK Pancevo 0, Hajduk Rodic MB Kula 1
Zemun 1, Buducnost Banatski Dvor 0
Crvena Stijena Podgorica 2, Vojvodina Novi Sad 1
Rad Beograd 2, Cukaricki Stankom Beograd 1
Kolubara Lazarevac 0, Borac Cacak 0 *(3-2 on pens)*
Timok Zajecar 2, Radnicki Novi Beograd 0
(27/9/05)
Mokra Gora Zubin Potok 0, OFK Beograd 3
(28/9/05)
Radnicki Sombor 1, Zeta Golubovci 0
(19/10/05)
Takovo Gornji Milanovac 0, Crvena Zvezda Beograd 1

1/8 FINALS
(26/10/05)
Radnicki Nis 0, Zemun 0 *(3-1 on pens)*
Hajduk Kula 2, Sutjeska Niksic 0
Vlasina Vlasotince 2, Rad Beograd 0
Radnicki Sombor 0, Kolubara Lazarevac 1
Smederevo 4, Crvena Stijena Podgorica 1
Partizan Beograd 1, Timok Zajecar 1 *(5-6 on pens)*
OFK Beograd 2, Obilic Beograd 1
Crvena Zvezda Beograd 2, Mladost Lucani 1

QUARTER-FINALS
(7/12/05)
Kolubara Lazarevac 0, Vlasina Vlasotince 0 *(5-4 on pens)*
OFK Beograd 1 *(Simic 88)*, Hajduk Rodic MB Kula 0
Radnicki Nis 2 *(Jovanovic 15, Bogunovic 44)*, Timok Zajecar 0
Crvena Zvezda Beograd 2 *(Lukovic 37p, Milovanovic 47)*, Smederevo 0

SEMI-FINALS
(11/4/06)
Radnicki Nis 0, Crvena Zvezda Beograd 5 *(Suzuki 27, 80, Basta 29, Purovic 33, 59)*
(12/4/06)
OFK Beograd 4 *(Bakovic 21, Rankovic M. 35og,, Simic 56, Bozovic 83)*, Kolubara Lazarevac 1 *(Pavlovic 59)*

FINAL
(10/5/06)
Stadion FK Partizan, Beograd
CRVENA ZVEZDA BEOGRAD 4 *(Zigic 66, 100, Purovic 73, Basta 116)*
OFK BEOGRAD 2 *(Rakic 11, Bakovic 59)*
(aet)
Referee - Vukadinovic
CRVENA ZVEZDA BEOGRAD – Randjelovic, Basta, Bisevac, Dudic, Lukovic, Jankovic *(Purovic 63)*, Kovacevic, Milovanovic, Milijas, Djokic *(Joksimovic 105)*, Zigic *(Miladinovic 120)*.
Sent off: *Milovanovic (54)*
OFK BEOGRAD – Saranov, Ivelja *(Supic 102)*, Bajalica, Rajkovic, Kolarov, Petrovic, Petkovic, Stancic, Bozovic, Bakovic *(Kaludjerovic 110)*, Rakic *(Simic 66)*.
Sent off: *Kolarov (42)*

SECOND LEVEL FINAL TABLES 2005/06

FIRST LEAGUE SERBIA

		Pld	W	D	L	F	A	Pts
1	Bezanija Beograd	38	25	7	6	69	25	82
2	Mladost Apatin	38	23	9	6	56	18	78
3	CSK Pivara Celarevo	38	23	7	8	59	28	76
4	Cukaricki Stankom Beograd	38	22	9	7	64	29	75
5	Srem Sremska Mitrovica	38	17	8	13	46	41	59
6	Napredak Krusevac	38	17	7	14	49	43	58
7	Macva Sabac	38	14	13	11	54	55	55
8	Sevojno	38	13	13	12	44	42	52
9	Spartak Subotica	38	13	12	13	43	41	51
10	Radnicki Nis	38	14	9	15	37	40	51
11	BASK 1903 Beograd	38	14	8	16	47	54	50
12	Mladenovac	38	12	11	15	36	46	47
13	Radnicki Pirot	38	13	7	18	50	52	46
14	Vlasina Vlasotince	38	10	14	14	37	46	44
15	Novi Pazar	38	11	11	16	34	54	44
16	PSK Pancevo	38	11	7	20	47	58	40
17	Jedinstvo Ub	38	11	7	20	37	54	40
18	Radnicki Kragujevac	38	10	9	19	36	59	39
19	Novi Sad	38	9	8	21	31	53	35
20	OFK Nis	38	7	6	25	26	64	27

FIRST LEAGUE MONTENEGRO

		Pld	W	D	L	F	A	Pts
1	Rudar Pljevlja	36	22	6	8	58	34	72
2	Sutjeska Niksic	36	15	11	10	40	28	56
3	Kom Zlatica Podgorica	36	14	10	12	37	32	52
4	Grbalj Radanovici	36	14	9	13	34	34	51
5	Mogren Budva	36	12	12	12	35	31	48
6	OFK Petrovac	36	11	14	11	33	34	47
7	Decic Tuzi	36	11	14	11	32	34	47
8	Zora Spuz	36	11	14	11	34	35	47
9	Mornar Bar	36	9	7	20	23	46	33
10	Bokelj Kotor	36	7	11	18	29	47	32

N.B. Mornar Bar – 1 pt deducted; Rudar Pljevlja did not obtain promotion as a result of Montenegrin independence.

Slovakia

Happy 100th birthday for Ruzomberok

2005/06 was a positive season for Slovakian football. The national team, led by Dusan Galis, reached the World Cup qualifying play-offs then inflicted a first defeat on Raymond Domenech's France, while Artmedia Bratislava became only the second Slovakian team to compete in the UEFA Champions League. Meanwhile, on the domestic front MFK Ruzomberok caused a sensation by winning both the league and the Cup.

To add to Ruzomberok's joy, the Double came in their centenary year. For 99 years the club had won nothing. Now they scooped two trophies at once, creating arguably the biggest upset in the history of independent Slovakian football.

The mastermind behind the club's dramatic rise was Czech coach Frantisek Komnacky. A title winner across the border with Baník Ostrava in 2004, he joined Ruzomberok six months later but succeeded only in taking the club to seventh place in his first half-season. When Ruzomberok lost their opening two games of the 2005/06 campaign, it looked like business as usual for a club that had been consistent mid-table makeweights since their promotion in 1996.

Komnacky had other ideas. The ex-MSK Zilina and Matador Púchov coach brought in several Czech players, and slowly but surely the team began to gel, especially at home. Goalkeeper Lubos Hajdúch was outstanding, working his way into the Slovakian national team (and making his debut in the 2-1 victory at the Stade de France), while Jozef Dvorník (one of the Czech intake) and Martin Laurinc were peerless in defence and Erik Jendrisek a consistent marksman up front. The real revelation was 23-year-old Marek Sapara, whose skill and technique in midfield had many in the country hailing him as the 'new Lubomír Moravcík'.

Sense of unity

With Sapara making the play, Ruzomberok's football was pleasing on the eye as well as effective. There was a strong sense of unity too, with the team remaining virtually untouched throughout the 36-match campaign. The Slovakian Cup was the first of the two trophies to fall into their hands, although in truth they needed a fair degree of luck to win it, overcoming both Artmedia in the semis and Spartak Trnava in the final on penalties. That Cup win infused the team with confidence for the league run-in, however, and they turned on the style in their final few games, decisively beating title rivals Artmedia 3-0 at home before sealing the title with their biggest win of the season – 5-0 at Dukla Banská Bystrica, with Jendrisek scoring a hat-trick. There was another hat-trick, from Czech striker Jan Nezmar, on the final day as Komnacky's side signed off the season with their 17th successive home win, 3-0 against AS Trencín. The only points they had dropped at home all season were on the opening day.

NATIONAL TEAM RESULTS 2005/06

17/8/05	Liechtenstein (WCQ)	A	Vaduz	0-0	
3/9/05	Germany	H	Bratislava	2-0	Karhan (20p, 38)
7/9/05	Latvia (WCQ)	A	Riga	1-1	Vittek (35)
8/10/05	Estonia (WCQ)	H	Bratislava	1-0	Hlinka (76)
12/10/05	Russia (WCQ)	H	Bratislava	0-0	
12/11/05	Spain (WCQ)	A	Madrid	1-5	Németh (49)
16/11/05	Spain (WCQ)	H	Bratislava	1-1	Holosko (50)
1/3/06	France	A	Saint-Denis	2-1	Németh (62), Valachovic (82)
20/5/06	Belgium	H	Trnava	1-1	Holosko (65)

Slovakia

Artmedia Bratislava were unable to do what most Slovakian champions had done before and retain their title, but they made up for it with their Herculean efforts in Europe. After scraping past the champions of Kazakhstan, they produced one of the biggest European Cup shocks of all time by knocking out Scottish giants Celtic. Their 5-0 victory in Bratislava will be remembered for many a year – both by victors and vanquished. A 4-0 defeat in Glasgow did not perturb Vladimír Weiss's side, and they created a piece of history in the next round when they knocked out Partizan Belgarde on penalties after two goalless draws, thus becoming (together with holders Liverpool) the first club to pass through all three Champions League qualifying rounds.

It was widely felt that the group phase would be too much for them, but Artmedia more than held their own. There was more fantasy football from Weiss's men when they came from two goals down to win 3-2 away to FC Porto, and but for a host of clear-cut chances that went begging on a rain-sodden pitch in the return game against the Portuguese side, Slovakia's finest would have reached the last 16. Instead, they parachuted into the UEFA Cup.

By the time Artmedia came to play their tie with Levski Sofia, the club had been pillaged of its finest talents. Weiss was lured to Russia to take charge of Saturn Ramenskoe and several key players also followed him abroad - centre-back Ján Durica to the very same club, captain Balázs Borbély to Kaiserslautern, winger Blazej Vascák to Treviso and playmaker Ján Kozák to West Bromwich Albion. To make matters worse, defender Ondrej Debnár suffered a long-term injury while the team's impressive veteran goalkeeper Juraj Cobej was forced to rest after having surgery to remove a (benign) brain tumour.

Artmedia duly lost their UEFA Cup tie but, to their credit, kept things going pretty well in the league. Top of the table on goal difference at Christmas, they were expected to plummet, but new coach Ladislav Molnár managed to rebuild with some useful new signings like Marián Cisovsky, Dusan Sninsky, Michal Kubala and Lubomír Reiter, and it was only after that 3-0 defeat in Ruzomberok that their dreams of a Champions League return in 2006/07 finally evaporated.

Tears for Trnava

For much of the season Spartak Trnava harboured realistic hopes of winning their first Slovakian title. But yet again, despite having the strongest support in the land and also the wiliest (and most controversial) coach, 63-year-old ex-Czechoslovakia striker Jozef Adamec, they couldn't see their challenge through to the finish. Throughout the autumn they played to near-full houses, but an injury to their inspirational veteran midfielder Marek Ujlaky completely derailed them and they ended up 12 points adrift at the finish. Reaching the Cup final at least ensured that they qualified for the UEFA Cup.

Zilina's fourth place was also a disappointment, with disruptions to the coaching staff having an adverse affect on performance. Losing all four matches against Ruzomberok didn't help. Newcomers Nitra, on the other hand, were delighted to finish fifth. They brought a breath of fresh air to the league, with striker Róbert Rák particularly impressing. He scored precisely half of their 42 goals to share the Golden Boot with Ruzomberok's Jendrisek.

Inter Bratislava pulled off a miraculous escape from relegation under ex-national team boss Ladislav Jurkemik, sending Matador Púchov down instead. With the top flight increasing in membership to 12 teams in 2006/07, there were three teams promoted, including the most famous Slovakian club of them all, Slovan Bratislava, after two seasons in purgatory.

Victory in Paris

Former Slovan player and coach Dusan Galis has proved a big hit as the Slovakian national coach since he replaced Jurkemik in January 2004. To reach the World Cup play-offs ahead of Russia was quite a feat, even if Spain proved too good for Galis and his players in the two additional ties. Confidence for the Euro 2008 qualifiers, in which Slovakia face the Czech Republic among others, was boosted by a remarkable 2-1 win in Paris – a result that looked even better after France's performance in the World Cup.

Many Slovakian footballers are now earning a decent living abroad – not just in the Czech Republic or Russia but further afield. German club Nuremberg has become a particular favourite of Slovakian fans. After the goalscoring feats in 2003/04 and 2004/05 of Marek Mintál, it was another Slovakian, 24-year-old Róbert Vittek, who hogged the limelight (while his team-mate missed virtually the whole season with injury) by scoring 16 Bundesliga goals in the second half of the season alone.

Slovakia

NATIONAL TEAM APPEARANCES 2005/06

Coach – Dusan GALIS			LIE	Ger	LAT	EST	RUS	ESP	ESP	Fra	Bel	Caps	Goals
Kamil CONTOFALSKY	3/6/78	Zenit Sankt-Peterburg (RUS)	G	G	G	G	G	G	G		s3/46	22	-
Radoslav ZÁBAVNÍK	16/9/80	CSKA Sofia (BUL) /AC Sparta Praha (CZE)	D	D	D	D	D	M	D	D90		25	1
Roman KRATOCHVÍL	24/6/74	Denizlispor (TUR)	D	D	D	D	D	D	D			33	1
Marián HAD	16/9/82	1.FC Brno (CZE)	D	D46	D	D73	D	D				12	-
Vratislav GRESKO	24/4/77	Blackburn Rovers (ENG)	M56	M	M			s67	M78			29	2
Miroslav KARHAN	21/6/76	VfL Wolfsburg (GER)	M	M67	M		M67	M73			M	78	9
Peter HLINKA	5/12/78	SK Rapid Wien (AUT)	M46	s67	s65	M	M	M	M	M86		25	1
Karol KISEL	15/3/77	AC Sparta Praha (CZE)	M		s77	M	s67					23	1
Marek MINTÁL	2/9/77	1.FC Nürnberg (GER)	M	M46	M65							28	6
Martin JAKUBKO	26/2/80	Dukla Banská Bystrica	A46	s80						A69		8	-
Róbert VITTEK	1/4/82	1.FC Nürnberg (GER)	A	A61	A	A	A	A	A	A90	A	39	13
Dusan SNINSKY	7/7/77	Groclin Grodzisk (POL)	s46									8	-
Lubomír REITER	3/12/74	Chicago Fire (USA)	s46			s73						28	9
Samuel SLOVÁK	17/10/75	1.FC Nürnberg (GER)	s56									19	-
Martin SKRTEL	15/12/84	Zenit Sankt-Peterburg (RUS)		D	D	D	D	D	D	D	D	10	-
Jozef VALACHOVIC	12/7/75	SK Rapid Wien (AUT)		M51	M86		M			s78	s60	30	1
Filip HOLOSKO	17/1/84	FC Slovan Liberec (CZE) /Vestel Manisaspor (TUR)		A80	M77	s46	s56	A46	s46	M59	s46	8	2
Ján DURICA	10/11/81	Artmedia Bratislava /Saturn Ramenskoe (RUS)		s46			s82		D	D	D	9	-
Ján KOZÁK	22/4/80	Artmedia Bratislava		s46								2	-
Martin PETRÁS	2/11/79	AC Sparta Praha (CZE)		s51			D					23	1
Mário BRESKA	27/12/79	Panionios (GRE)		s61								8	-
Stanislav VARGA	8/10/72	Celtic (SCO)			s86							52	1
Ivan HODÚR	7/10/79	FC Slovan Liberec (CZE)				M77	M56	M67	M46	s86	s46	7	-
Szilárd NÉMETH	8/8/77	Middlesbrough (ENG) /RC Strasbourg (FRA)				A	A82	s46	A83	s59		56	22
Stanislav SESTÁK	16/12/82	MSK Zilina				A46						5	-
Marek SAPARA	31/7/82	MFK Ruzomberok				s77				M46		2	-
Vladimír JANOCKO	2/12/76	FK Austria Wien (AUT)					s73					40	3
Matej KRAJCÍK	19/3/78	FC Slovan Liberec (CZE)							M	M78	D80	3	-
Marek CECH	26/1/83	FC Porto (POR)							s78	D	D	12	-
Branislav FODREK	5/2/81	Artmedia Bratislava							s83		M46	4	-
Lubos HAJDUCH	6/3/80	MFK Ruzomberok								G	s46	2	-
Balazs BORBÉLY	2/10/79	1.FC Kaiserslautern (GER)								M	M	6	-
Mário BICAK	21/10/79	MFK Kosice								s69	s20/60	2	-
Kamil KOPUNEK	18/5/84	Spartak Trnava								s90	s80	2	-
Peter PETRÁS	7/5/79	Artmedia Bratislava								s90		1	-
Juraj COBEJ	7/8/71	Artmedia Bratislava									G3	1	-
Michal PANCÍK	18/8/82	Dukla Banská Bystrica									A20	1	-

Slovakia

EUROPEAN CUPS 2005/06

UEFA CHAMPIONS LEAGUE

ARTMEDIA BRATISLAVA
1st qualifying round KAIRAT ALMATY (KAZ)
A 0-2
Cobej, Stano, Burák, Durica, Debnár (Kotula 81), Gajdos, Borbély, Kozák (Vascák 63), Tchur (Hellebrand 72), Mikulic, Obzera.
H 4-1 *Borbély (21), Tchur (32), Kozák (94p), Stano (120)*
(aet)
Cobej, Kotula, Debnár, Durica, Hellebrand (Mikulic 72), Vascák (Gajdos 76), Kozák, Borbély, Tchur (Stano 83), Fodrek, Obzera.

2nd qualifying round CELTIC (SCO)
H 5-0 *Halenár (43, 76, 89), Vascák (57), Mikulic (78)*
Cobej, Kotula, Debnár, Durica, Tchur (Stano 84), Vascák (Mikulic 72), Kozák, Borbély, Obzera (Burák 76), Fodrek, Halenár.
A 0-4
Cobej, Burák (Stano 70), Debnár, Durica, Tchur, Vascák (Mikulic 74), Kozák, Borbély, Obzera, Fodrek, Halenár (Bukvic 88).

3rd qualifying round PARTIZAN BEOGRAD (SCG)
H 0-0
Cobej, Kotula, Borbély, Durica, Tchur, Vascák (Gomes 90), Kozák, Stano, Petrás (Obzera 58), Halenár, Fodrek.
A 0-0
(aet; 4-3 on pens)
Cobej, Burák (Mikulic 112), Debnár, Durica, Petrás, Fodrek, Kozák, Borbély, Tchur (Stano 55), Halenár, Vascák (Gomes 90).

1st round Group H
Match 1 INTERNAZIONALE (ITA)
H 0-1
Cobej, Petrás, Debnár, Durica, Urbánek (Konecny 74), Vascák, Kozák, Stano (Gomes 62), Fodrek, Hartig (Mikulic 71), Halenár.

Match 2 FC PORTO (POR)
A 3-2 *Petrás (45), Kozák (54), Borbely (74)*
Cobej, Burák (Halenár 46), Borbély, Durica, Urbánek, Vascák, Debnár, Kozák, Fodrek, Petrás (Stano 79), Hartig (Obzera 84).

Match 3 RANGERS (SCO)
A 0-0
Cobej, Petrás, Debnár, Durica, Urbánek, Vascák (Obzera 68), Borbély, Kozák, Halenár (Tchur 78), Fodrek, Hartig (Stano 83).

Match 4 RANGERS
H 2-2 *Borbély (8), Kozák (59)*
Cobej, Petrás, Debnár, Durica, Urbánek , Vascák (Tchur 83), Kozák, Borbély, Fodrek, Obzera (Stano 87), Hartig (Halenár 73).

Match 5 INTERNAZIONALE
A 0-4
Cobej, Petrás, Debnár, Durica, Urbánek (Stano 80), Vascák (Mikulic 71), Kozák (Tchur 71), Borbély, Fodrek, Halenár, Obzera.

Match 6 FC PORTO
H 0-0
Cobej, Petrás, Debnár, Durica, Urbánek, Obzera (Halenár 87), Stano, Kozák, Borbély, Fodrek, Hartig (Vascák 60).

UEFA CUP

DUKLA BANSKÁ BYSTRICA
2nd qualifying round GROCLIN DYSKOBOLIA GRODZISK (POL)
A 1-4 *Bazík (72)*
Zajac, Svintek (Bukac 69), Páleník, Wozniak, Pancík, Vyskoc, Vesely, Bazík, Pecovsky, Leitner, Jakubko.
H 0-0
Zajac, Vyskoc, Páleník, Wozniak (Fabus 56), Pancík, Vesely, Pecovsky (Libic 82), Bazík, Leitner, Semeník, Jakubko (Gibala 87).

MSK ZILINA
1st qualifying round FK BAKI (AZB)
A 0-1
König, Cisovsky, Labant, Dolezaj, Minarcík (Vomácka 85), Barcík, Jez, Strba, Belák, Bartos (Sesták 69), Gottwald.
H 3-1 *Straka (7), Cisovsky (37), Labant (85)*
König, Cisovsky (Pekárik 74), Labant, Dolezaj (Vomácka 82), Minarcík, Barcík, Jez, Strba, Sesták, Gottwald (Pecalka 70), Straka.

2nd qualifying round FK AUSTRIA WIEN (AUT)
H 1-2 *Bartos (40)*
König, Cisovsky, Labant, Svestka, Minarcík, Pekárik, Dolezaj (Gavaric 84), Strba, Gottwald (Pecalka 78), Barcík, Bartos (Vomácka 90).
A 2-2 *Cisovsky (26), Gottwald (31)*
König, Cisovsky, Labant, Svestka, Minarcík, Bartos (Pekárik 84), Dolezaj (Krsko 90), Vomácka, Barcík (Belák 68), Straka, Gottwald.

ARTMEDIA BRATISLAVA
3rd round LEVSKI SOFIA (BUL)
H 0-1
Kamenár, Burák, Stano, Tchur, Kubala (Reiter 53), Obzera (Konecny 86), Petrás, Straka, Fodrek, Halenár (Mikulic 75), Hartig.
A 0-2
Kamenár, Burák (Kubala 55), Stano, Tchur (Gajdos 83), Petras, Straka, Mikulic, Fodrek, Urbánek, Reiter (Halenár 67), Hartig.

TOP GOALSCORERS 2005/06

21	Róbert RÁK (FC Nitra)
	Erik JENDRISEK (MFK Ruzomberok)
18	Robert SEMENÍK (Dukla Banská Bystrica)
17	Jan NEZMAR (MFK Ruzomberok)
	Stanislav SESTÁK (MSK Zilina)
16	Pavol STRAKA (MSK Zilina)
12	Miroslav KRISS (Spartak Trnava)
9	Lubos BLAHA (Spartak Trnava)
	Vladimír KOZUCH (Spartak Trnava)
8	Marek BAKOS (Matador Púchov)
	Juraj HALENÁR (Inter Bratislava/Artmedia Bratislava)
	Lukás HARTIG (Artmedia Bratislava)
	Branislav FODREK (Artmedia Bratislava)
	Michal FILO (ZTS Dubnica)

Slovakia

LEAGUE RESULTS/ SCORERS/APPEARANCES/ GOALS 2005/06

ARTMEDIA BRATISLAVA
Coach - Vladimír Weiss; (15/2/06) Ladislav Molnár

2005
Date	Opponent	H/A	Score	Scorers
17/7	Spartak Trnava	h	0-2	
23/7	FC Nitra	a	0-1	
31/7	Matador Púchov	h	2-0	Debnár, Fodrek
6/8	MSK Zilina	a	2-1	Stano, Fodrek
14/8	ZTS Dubnica	h	2-2	Kozák (p), Fodrek
19/8	MFK Ruzomberok	h	2-1	Kozák (p), Mikulic
27/8	Dukla Banská Bystrica	a	0-3	
9/9	AS Trencín	h	3-0	Hartig, Halenár, Vascák
17/9	Inter Bratislava	a	2-1	Kozak (p), Hartig
20/9	Spartak Trnava	a	3-1	Halenár 2, Borbély
25/9	FC Nitra	h	1-1	Borbély
2/10	Matador Púchov	a	2-1	Kozak (p), Hartig
16/10	MSK Zilina	h	1-1	Hartig
22/10	ZTS Dubnica	a	2-0	Obzera, Vascák
28/10	MFK Ruzomberok	a	0-1	
6/11	Dukla Banská Bystrica	h	2-0	Debnár, Hartig
9/11	AS Trencín	a	1-1	Kozak (p)
19/11	Spartak Trnava	h	2-1	Obzera, Hartig
27/11	FC Nitra	a	2-0	Vascák, Stano
30/11	Inter Bratislava	h	7-1	Vascák, Borbély, Halenár 2, Fodrek 2, Kozak

2006
Date	Opponent	H/A	Score	Scorers
19/3	ZTS Dubnica	h	3-2	Reiter, Straka, Halenár
22/3	Matador Púchov	h	1-0	Fodrek
26/3	MFK Ruzomberok	h	2-0	Hartig, Stano
1/4	Dukla Banská Bystrica	a	0-0	
4/4	MSK Zilina	a	1-0	Fodrek
9/4	AS Trencín	h	3-1	Sninsky, Stano, Reiter
15/4	Inter Bratislava	a	2-1	Hartig, Stano
22/4	Spartak Trnava	a	0-1	
25/4	FC Nitra	h	2-0	Stano, Reiter
29/4	Matador Púchov	a	3-1	og (Prokes), Sninsky, Reiter
3/5	MSK Zilina	h	1-2	Reiter
13/5	ZTS Dubnica	a	1-0	Fodrek
16/5	MFK Ruzomberok	a	0-3	
23/5	Dukla Banská Bystrica	h	1-0	Cisovsky
27/5	AS Trencín	a	1-3	Kubala
31/5	Inter Bratislava	h	1-0	Sninsky

Name	Nat	Pos	Aps	(s)	Gls
Balázs BORBÉLY		M	18	(1)	3
Milorad BUKVIĖ	SCG	A		(1)	
Peter BURÁK		D	20	(3)	
Marián CISOVSKY		D	14		1
Juraj COBEJ		G	16	(1)	
Ondrej DEBNÁR		D	13	(4)	2
Tomás DOSEK	CZE	D	1	(2)	
Ján DURICA		D	20		
Branislav FODREK		M	32	(2)	8
Vratislav GAJDOS		M	4	(6)	
Luís Fábio GOMES	BRA	A		(5)	
Juraj HALENÁR		A	23	(5)	6
Andrej HANTÁK		M		(2)	
Lukás HARTIG	CZE	A	20	(1)	8
Ales HELLEBRAND	CZE	D	3		
Tomás HORVÁTH		M	1		
Andrej KALINA		M		(1)	
Lubos KAMENÁR		G	16		
Stefan KOLLÁR		G	4	(1)	
Roman KONECNY		D	6	(9)	
Jozef KOTULA		D	4	(2)	
Ján KOZÁK		M	17	(1)	6
Michal KUBALA		M	10	(2)	1
Martin MIKULIC		M	13	(16)	1
Branislav OBZERA		M	11	(4)	2
Peter PETRÁS		D	16		
Juraj PIROSKA		A		(3)	
Lubomír REITER		A	7	(4)	5
Dusan SNINSKY		D	15	(1)	3
Anton SOLTIS		A		(1)	
Pavol STANO		D	24	(7)	6
Gabriel STRAKA		M	11	(2)	1
Daniel TCHUR		D	17	(10)	
Ales URBÁNEK	CZE	M	26	(2)	
Blazej VASCÁK		M	14	(5)	4

ZTS DUBNICA
Coach - Lubos Nosicky; (20/9/05) Peter Gergely

2005
Date	Opponent	H/A	Score	Scorers
26/7	Matador Púchov	a	2-0	Novák, Drzik
31/7	MSK Zilina	a	0-3	
6/8	Inter Bratislava	h	1-1	Adam
9/8	AS Trencín	h	1-1	Drzik
14/8	Artmedia Bratislava	a	2-2	Kopacka (p), Jonás
20/8	Spartak Trnava	h	0-3	
27/8	MFK Ruzomberok	a	0-1	
10/9	FC Nitra	h	0-1	
17/9	Dukla Banská Bystrica	a	1-4	Adam
20/9	Matador Púchov	h	1-1	Brusko
24/9	AS Trencín	a	0-2	
1/10	MSK Zilina	h	2-4	Tesak, Kiska
15/10	Inter Bratislava	a	3-0	Dovicovic, Tesak, Adam
22/10	Artmedia Bratislava	h	0-2	
29/10	Spartak Trnava	a	1-2	Tesak
5/11	MFK Ruzomberok	h	3-0	Tesak 2, Dovicovic
8/11	FC Nitra	a	0-0	
19/11	Matador Púchov	a	3-1	Kiska, Filo, Dovicovic
26/11	AS Trencín	h	1-1	Kiska
30/11	Dukla Banská Bystrica	h	1-0	Brusko

2006
Date	Opponent	H/A	Score	Scorers
4/3	MSK Zilina	a	0-0	
11/3	Inter Bratislava	h	2-0	Kiska, Filo
19/3	Artmedia Bratislava	a	2-3	Adam, Kopacka (p)
25/3	Spartak Trnava	h	0-2	
1/4	MFK Ruzomberok	a	1-3	Brusko
8/4	FC Nitra	h	2-1	Filo 2
15/4	Dukla Banská Bystrica	a	3-2	Kopacka (p), Jonás, Filo
22/4	Matador Púchov	h	0-1	
25/4	AS Trencín	a	2-1	Filo 2
29/4	MSK Zilina	h	1-0	Kopacka (p)
3/5	Inter Bratislava	a	2-0	Spendla, Filo
13/5	Artmedia Bratislava	h	0-1	
16/5	Spartak Trnava	a	1-4	Brusko
23/5	MFK Ruzomberok	h	1-1	Kiska
27/5	FC Nitra	a	2-2	Kopacka (p), Kiska
31/5	Dukla Banská Bystrica	h	0-0	

Name	Nat	Pos	Aps	(s)	Gls
Marián ADAM		A	17	(10)	4

Slovakia

FINAL LEAGUE TABLE 2005/06

		Pld	Home					Away					Total					Pts
			W	D	L	F	A	W	D	L	F	A	W	D	L	F	A	
1	MFK Ruzomberok	36	17	0	1	39	9	9	2	7	26	19	26	2	8	65	28	80
2	Artmedia Bratislava	36	13	3	2	36	14	10	2	6	22	19	23	5	8	58	33	74
3	Spartak Trnava	36	14	2	2	34	10	7	3	8	23	21	21	5	10	57	31	68
4	MSK Zilina	36	9	2	7	32	21	9	4	5	37	23	18	6	12	69	44	60
5	FC Nitra	36	8	6	4	28	22	4	3	11	14	26	12	9	15	42	48	45
6	Dukla Banská Bystrica	36	9	2	7	27	22	3	4	11	10	20	12	6	18	37	42	42
7	AS Trencín	36	9	5	4	22	15	2	4	12	9	34	11	9	16	31	49	42
8	ZTS Dubnica	36	4	6	8	16	25	6	4	8	25	30	10	10	16	41	55	40
9	Inter Bratislava	36	4	6	8	15	25	3	3	12	12	37	7	9	20	27	62	30
10	Matador Púchov	36	4	1	13	13	31	3	4	11	16	33	7	5	24	29	64	26

Name	Nat	Pos	Aps	(s)	Gls
Jozef ADÁMIK		D	12		
Peter AUGUSTÍNY		M	1	(8)	
Marián BELLÁK		M		(2)	
Tomás BRUSKO		M	33	(2)	4
Juraj DOVICOVIC		M	9	(3)	3
Igor DRZÍK		M	31		2
Michal FILO		A	12	(12)	8
Erik GRENDEL		M	20	(8)	
Peter HOLEC		G	12		
Marek IGAZ		G	3		
Matej IZVOLT		M	29	(2)	
Michal JONÁS		D	18	(1)	2
Peter KISKA		A	28	(7)	6
Dusan KOLMOKOV		G	1		
Pavol KOPACKA		M	27	(1)	5
Marek KUZMA		A	4	(8)	
Matej LENDVAY		A		(1)	
Milan MUJKOS		M	3	(4)	
Róbert NOVÁK		D	27	(5)	1
Dusan PERNIS		G	18		
Dalibor PLEVA		D	31		
Marián POSTRK		G	2		
Mouhamad SEYE	SEN	A		(1)	
Roman SKULTÉTY		D	3	(2)	
Cyril SPENDLA		D	24	(3)	1
Martin STASKO		M		(1)	
Martin SVESTKA	CZE	D	3		
Ján SVIKRUHA		M	1	(6)	
Lukas TESÁK		M	15	(4)	5
Lukás ZÁPOTOKA		A		(6)	
Marián ZIMEN		D	12	(1)	

DUKLA BANSKÁ BYSTRICA
Coach - Václav Daník; (Jozef Prochotsky); (1/1/06) Dusan Radolsky

2005

16/7	AS Trencín	h	2-0	Semeník 2
23/7	Inter Bratislava	a	0-2	
30/7	Spartak Trnava	h	0-1	
6/8	FC Nitra	a	3-0	Bazík, Semeník 2
14/8	Matador Púchov	h	3-1	og (Brisuda), Semeník, Pálenik
20/8	MSK Zilina	a	0-2	
27/8	Artmedia Bratislava	h	3-0	Semeník 2, Bazík
10/9	MFK Ruzomberok	a	0-2	
17/9	ZTS Dubnica	h	4-1	Libic 2, Semeník, Gibala
20/9	AS Trencín	a	1-2	Juska
24/9	Inter Bratislava	h	1-0	Semeník
1/10	Spartak Trnava	a	0-1	
15/10	FC Nitra	h	2-0	Vesely, Semeník
22/10	Matador Púchov	a	1-0	Libic
29/10	MSK Zilina	h	0-4	
6/11	Artmedia Bratislava	a	0-2	
8/11	MFK Ruzomberok	h	0-2	
19/11	AS Trencín	h	0-1	
26/11	Inter Bratislava	a	1-1	Semeník
30/11	ZTS Dubnica	a	0-1	
2006				
11/3	FC Nitra	a	1-2	Semeník (p)
14/3	Spartak Trnava	h	1-2	Jakubko
18/3	Matador Púchov	h	2-0	Semeník, Vesely
25/3	MSK Zilina	a	0-2	
1/4	Artmedia Bratislava	h	0-0	
8/4	MFK Ruzomberok	a	0-1	
15/4	ZTS Dubnica	h	2-3	Semeník 2 (1p)
22/4	AS Trencín	a	0-0	
25/4	Inter Bratislava	h	3-0	(w/o)
29/4	Spartak Trnava	a	1-1	Semeník
3/5	FC Nitra	h	2-0	Bazík, Vyskoc
13/5	Matador Púchov	a	2-0	Vyskoc, Semeník
16/5	MSK Zilina	h	2-2	Pecovsky, Semeník
23/5	Artmedia Bratislava	a	0-1	
27/5	MFK Ruzomberok	h	0-5	
31/5	ZTS Dubnica	a	0-0	

Name	Nat	Pos	Aps	(s)	Gls
Marek BAZÍK		M	28	(3)	3
Peter BOROS		G	8	(1)	
Radek BUKAC	CZE	A	3	(5)	
Michal DURIS		M	11	(4)	
Martin FABUS		A	3	(1)	
Milos GIBALA		A	4	(14)	1
Ján HRBEK		D	3	(4)	
Martin JAKUBKO		A	8		1
Marián JARABICA		M	2	(5)	
Ján JUSKA		M	8	(3)	1
Vladimír KANDA		M	1	(8)	
Róbert KLÚCIAR		D	8		
Peter KONCEK		M	2	(3)	
Ján KOZIAK		M	4	(4)	
Radovan KULÍK		M	7	(8)	
Frantisek KUNZO		D	14		
Vladimír LEITNER		M	18		

Slovakia

Tomáš LIBIC		D	30	(3)	3
Martin MIKULANIN		D		(1)	
Peter OCOVAN		M	9	(8)	
Milan PÁLENÍK	CZE	D	27	(1)	1
Michal PANČÍK		M	28	(1)	
Viktor PECOVSKY		M	28	(1)	1
Tomáš RAPCAN		M	1	(4)	
Róbert SEMENÍK		A	29	(1)	18
Peter STUBER		M		(1)	
Martin SVINTEK		M	9	(9)	
Martin TOMÁS		A		(2)	
Stanislav VELICKY		M	7	(1)	
Vladimír VESELY		D	26	(2)	2
Lubomír VYSKOC		A	19	(4)	2
Radim WOZNIAK	CZE	D	23	(2)	
Richard ZAJAC		G	28		

INTER BRATISLAVA
Coach - Karol Brezík; (27/3/06) Ladislav Jurkemik

2005
16/7	Ruzomberok	a	2-1	Halenár 2 (1p)
23/7	Dukla Banská Bystrica	h	2-0	Petrás, Kunzo (p)
29/7	AS Trencín	a	0-2	
6/8	ZTS Dubnica	a	1-1	Baláz
13/8	Spartak Trnava	h	1-0	Brezík
20/8	FC Nitra	a	0-2	
27/8	Matador Púchov	h	1-1	Brezík
10/9	MSK Zilina	a	2-5	Brezík, Tomcák
17/9	Artmedia Bratislava	h	1-2	Kunzo (p)
20/9	MFK Ruzomberok	h	0-3	
24/9	Dukla Banská Bystrica	a	0-1	
1/10	AS Trencín	h	0-0	
15/10	ZTS Dubnica	h	0-3	
22/10	Spartak Trnava	a	0-3	
29/10	FC Nitra	h	1-2	Tomcák
5/11	Matador Púchov	a	0-3	
8/11	MSK Zilina	h	0-4	
19/11	MFK Ruzomberok	a	1-3	Tomcák
26/11	Dukla Banská Bystrica	h	1-1	Kunzo (p)
30/11	Artmedia Bratislava	a	1-7	Hodek

2006
4/3	AS Trencín	a	2-1	Slahor, Brezík
11/3	ZTS Dubnica	a	1-2	Slahor
18/3	Spartak Trnava	h	2-2	Hodek, Slahor
25/3	FC Nitra	a	0-1	
1/4	Matador Púchov	h	2-1	Dirnbach, Slahor
8/4	MSK Zilina	a	1-1	Hodek
15/4	Artmedia Bratislava	h	1-2	Sedivy
22/4	MFK Ruzomberok	h	0-1	
25/4	Dukla Banská Bystrica	a	0-3	(w/o)
29/4	AS Trencín	h	0-0	
3/5	ZTS Dubnica	h	0-2	
13/5	Spartak Trnava	a	0-0	
16/5	FC Nitra	h	2-0	Tomcák 2
23/5	Matador Púchov	a	1-0	Pecalka
27/5	MSK Zilina	h	1-1	Tomcák
31/5	Artmedia Bratislava	a	0-1	

Name	Nat	Pos	Aps	(s)	Gls
Radoslav AUGUSTÍN		A	1	(6)	
Pavol BALÁZ		M	19	(6)	1
Pavol BARMOS		D	2		
Michal BENKO		D	1		
Tomáš BERNADY	CZE	G	16		
Marek BONCO		D	12	(2)	
Peter BREZÍK		M	27		4
Andrej BURZA		D	11	(1)	
Igor CHALUPKA		M	16	(2)	
Erik CIKOS		M	1	(1)	
Marián DIRNBACH		M	12	(4)	1
Michal DRAHNO		D	25		
Ernest FULMEK		M		(1)	
Juraj HALENÁR		A	1		2
Boris HESEK		A		(3)	
Andrej HODEK		M	3	(4)	3
Vojtech HORVÁTH		M	17	(3)	
Ján JETKO		A	5	(6)	
Zdenko KAPRÁLIK		M	7	(3)	
Tomáš KOSICKY		G	6		
Martin KRNÁC		G	14		
Radoslav KUNZO		D	28		3
Tomáš MAJTÁN		M	5	(5)	
Dusan MATOVIC	SCG	D	14		
Juraj ONDRKA		M	2	(6)	
Augustín PAULÍK		M	22	(6)	
Mário PECALKA		M	12		1
Peter PETRÁN		D	23	(4)	
Peter PETRÁS		D	3		1
Radovan PISI		D	5	(1)	
Marek PLICHTA		A	4	(8)	
Peter SEDIVY		D	27	(2)	1
Ján SLAHOR		A	16		4
Róbert SZEGEDI		M		(2)	
Roman TAREK		M	5		
Pavel TOMÁSIK		M		(1)	
Marián TOMCÁK		A	25	(4)	6
Mário ZAVATERNÍK		D	9	(2)	

MATADOR PÚCHOV
Coach - Pavel Vrba; (5/4/06) Peter Ancic

2005
26/7	ZTS Dubnica	h	0-2	
23/7	MSK Zilina	h	1-5	Bakos
31/7	Artmedia Bratislava	a	0-2	
6/8	MFK Ruzomberok	h	0-2	
14/8	Dukla Banská Bystrica	a	1-3	Labun
20/8	AS Trencín	h	2-1	Bakos 2
27/8	Inter Bratislava	a	1-1	Hricko
10/9	Spartak Trnava	h	1-3	Majerník
17/9	FC Nitra	a	1-3	Bakos
20/9	ZTS Dubnica	a	1-1	Saláta
24/9	MSK Zilina	a	2-1	Bakos, Demjan
2/10	Artmedia Bratislava	h	1-2	Bakos
15/10	MFK Ruzomberok	a	1-3	Bakos (p)
22/10	Dukla Banská Bystrica	h	0-1	
29/10	AS Trencín	a	1-1	Saláta
5/11	Inter Bratislava	h	3-0	Bakos, Hlousek, Demjan
8/11	Spartak Trnava	a	0-4	
19/11	ZTS Dubnica	h	1-3	Saláta
26/11	MSK Zilina	h	0-1	
30/11	FC Nitra	h	0-0	

2006
18/3	Dukla Banská Bystrica	a	0-2	
22/3	Artmedia Bratislava	a	0-1	
25/3	AS Trencín	h	2-1	Saláta, Majerník
1/4	Inter Bratislava	a	1-2	Jelsic
4/4	MFK Ruzomberok	h	0-2	
8/4	Spartak Trnava	h	0-2	

Slovakia

15/4	FC Nitra	a	1-1	Durica (p)
22/4	ZTS Dubnica	a	1-0	Jelsic
25/4	MSK Zilina	a	1-3	Vavrik Pe.
29/4	Artmedia Bratislava	h	1-3	Németh
3/5	MFK Ruzomberok	a	1-3	Jelsic
13/5	Dukla Banská Bystrica	h	0-2	
16/5	AS Trencín	a	3-1	Jelsic 2, Náther
23/5	Inter Bratislava	h	0-1	
27/5	Spartak Trnava	a	0-1	
31/5	FC Nitra	h	1-0	Demjan

Name	Nat	Pos	Aps	(s)	Gls
Marek BAKOS		A	18	(1)	8
Ján BELIANCIN		D	11	(1)	
Tomás BERNADY	CZE	G	15		
Pavol BRISUDA		D	26	(1)	
Ján CHOVANEC		A	10	(5)	
Róbert DEMJAN		A	14	(14)	3
Lukás DENES		M		(1)	
Tomás DURICA		M	11	(1)	1
Adrián GULA		M	2		
Martin HLOUSEK		M	16	(4)	1
Igor HOLCÍK		D	5		
Peter HRICKO		D	31	(2)	1
Lubos ILIZI		G	6		
Milan JAMBOR		M	29	(1)	
Jozef JELSIC		A	14	(1)	5
Tomás LABUN		A	16	(4)	1
Peter MAJERNÍK		M	20	(6)	2
Peter MICIC		M	2		
Patrik MRÁZ		M	15	(20)	
Matej NÁTHER		M	11	(4)	1
Krisztián NÉMETH		D	16		1
Erik NOVISEDLÁK		M	8	(9)	
Miroslav PAVLOVIC		M	2	(1)	
Michal PROKES	CZE	M	23	(8)	
Kornel SALÁTA		D	26	(3)	4
Peter SNEGON		A	4	(9)	
Miroslav VALACH		G	15		
Michal VANÁK		M	1	(4)	
Pavol VAVRÍK		D	25	(1)	
Peter VAVRÍK		M	4	(6)	1
Mário ZAVATERNÍK		D		(1)	

FC NITRA
Coach - Ivan Galád

2005

17/7	MSK Zilina	a	5-2	Rák 3, Kona, Dobiás
23/7	Artmedia Bratislava	h	1-0	Dobiás
30/7	MFK Ruzomberok	a	0-2	
6/8	Dukla Banská Bystrica	h	0-3	
12/8	AS Trencín	a	1-2	Bochnovic
20/8	Inter Bratislava	h	2-0	Dobiás, Grajciar
27/8	Spartak Trnava	a	0-2	
10/9	ZTS Dubnica	a	1-0	Grajciar
17/9	Matador Púchov	h	3-1	Stajer, Kona, Hesek
20/9	MSK Zilina	h	0-2	
25/9	Artmedia Bratislava	a	1-1	Kona
1/10	MFK Ruzomberok	h	2-2	Grajciar, Hesek
15/10	Dukla Banská Bystrica	a	0-2	
22/10	AS Trencín	h	3-1	Hesek, Rák 2
29/10	Inter Bratislava	a	2-1	Rák 2
5/11	Spartak Trnava	h	3-1	Szórad, Rák, og (Poljovka)
8/11	ZTS Dubnica	h	0-0	
19/11	MSK Zilina	a	1-2	Kona
27/11	Artmedia Bratislava	h	0-2	
30/11	Matador Púchov	a	0-0	

2006

4/3	MFK Ruzomberok	a	0-2	
11/3	Dukla Banská Bystrica	h	2-1	Rák 2
18/3	AS Trencín	a	1-1	Rák
25/3	Inter Bratislava	h	1-0	Rák
1/4	Spartak Trnava	a	1-0	Rák
8/4	ZTS Dubnica	a	1-2	Rák
15/4	Matador Púchov	h	1-1	Demo
22/4	MSK Zilina	h	2-2	Rák 2 (1p)
25/4	Artmedia Bratislava	a	0-2	
29/4	MFK Ruzomberok	h	2-3	Rák 2 (1p)
3/5	Dukla Banská Bystrica	a	0-2	
13/5	AS Trencín	h	3-0	Rák, Grajciar, Glenda
16/5	Inter Bratislava	a	0-2	
23/5	Spartak Trnava	h	1-1	Rák
27/5	ZTS Dubnica	h	2-2	Rák, Grajciar
31/5	Matador Púchov	a	0-1	

Name	Nat	Pos	Aps	(s)	Gls
Martin BABIC		M	2	(6)	
Slavomír BALIS		A	15	(2)	
Marián BOCHNOVIC		M		(11)	1
Marek BUBENKO		A	15	(10)	
Tomás CABAJ		M	5	(2)	
Adrián CEMAN		D	25	(2)	
Martin CIZMÁR		A	1	(2)	
Ondrej CURGALI		M		(1)	
Marián DATKO		D	11		
Igor DEMO		M	12		1
Adrián DEVECKA		M	3	(4)	
Peter DOBIÁS		M	8	(6)	3
Michal FARKAS		M	27	(4)	
Pavol FARKAS		D	13	(12)	
Igor FERENCZY		M		(3)	
Róbert GLENDA		A	5		1
Peter GRAJCIAR		A	28	(3)	5
Andrej HESEK		A	16	(7)	3
Erik HRNCÁR		M	21	(9)	
Karol KARLÍK		D	3	(4)	
Tomás KÓNA		M	20		4
Ivan KOVÁC		D	3		
Tomás KUKOL		M	10	(2)	
Ján LESKO		D	8	(2)	
Jan NECAS	CZE	D	26	(2)	
Marián PCOLA		M		(1)	
Róbert RÁK		A	29	(2)	21
Stefan SENECKY		G	34	(1)	
Milos SIMONCIC		M	1	(3)	
Ján STAJER		M	26	(2)	1
Miroslav STOCH		A	1	(2)	
Csaba SZÓRÁD		D	26	(1)	1
Martin TÓTH		M		(1)	
Tomás TUJVEL		G	2		

MFK RUZOMBEROK
Coach - Frantisek Komnacky (CZE)

2005

16/7	Inter Bratislava	h	1-2	Nezmar
23/7	Spartak Trnava	a	0-2	
30/7	FC Nitra	h	2-0	Nezmar, Jendrisek
6/8	Matador Púchov	a	2-0	Nezmar 2

Slovakia

14/8	MSK Zilina	h	2-0	Laurinc, Sapara	
19/8	Artmedia Bratislava	a	1-2	Jendrisek	
27/8	ZTS Dubnica	h	1-0	Nezmar	
10/9	Dukla Banská Bystrica	h	2-0	Zofcák, Jendrisek	
17/9	AS Trencín	a	0-1		
20/9	Inter Bratislava	a	3-0	Dvorník, Jendrisek, Nezmar	
24/9	Spartak Trnava	h	4-1	Sapara, Jendrisek 2, Nezmar	
1/10	FC Nitra	a	2-2	Dubek, Laurinc	
15/10	Matador Púchov	h	3-1	Jendrisek 2, Nezmar	
22/10	MSK Zilina	a	1-0	Nezmar	
28/10	Artmedia Bratislava	h	1-0	Sapara	
5/11	ZTS Dubnica	a	0-3		
9/11	Dukla Banská Bystrica	a	2-0	Zofcák, Jendrisek	
19/11	Inter Bratislava	h	3-1	Pospísil, Sapara, Urban	
26/11	Spartak Trnava	a	1-2	Bozok	
30/11	AS Trencín	h	1-0	Nezmar	
2006					
4/3	FC Nitra	h	2-0	Siva, Jendrisek	
18/3	MSK Zilina	h	2-1	Dvorník, Dovicovic	
26/3	Artmedia Bratislava	a	0-2		
1/4	ZTS Dubnica	h	3-1	Nezmar, Dovicovic, Jendrisek	
4/4	Matador Púchov	a	2-0	Dvorník, Dovicovic	
8/4	Dukla Banská Bystrica	h	1-0	Jendrisek	
15/4	AS Trencín	a	0-1		
22/4	Inter Bratislava	a	1-0	Jendrisek	
25/4	Spartak Trnava	h	2-1	Nezmar 2	
29/4	FC Nitra	a	3-2	Sapara (p), Dvorník, Jendrisek	
3/5	Matador Púchov	h	3-1	Kotrys, Nezmar, Zofcák (p)	
13/5	MSK Zilina	a	2-1	Jendrisek, Laurinc	
16/5	Artmedia Bratislava	h	3-0	Jendrisek 2, Sapara	
23/5	ZTS Dubnica	a	1-1	Jendrisek	
27/5	Dukla Banská Bystrica	a	5-0	Dvorník, Jendrisek 3, Sedlák	
31/5	AS Trencín	h	3-0	Nezmar 3	

Name	Nat	Pos	Aps	(s)	Gls
Lukás BAKOS		M		(1)	
Miroslav BOZOK		M	22	(13)	1
Juraj DOVICOVIC		M	2	(10)	3
Tomás DUBEK		M	13	(11)	1
Josef DVORNÍK	CZE	D	34		5
Lubos HAJDÚCH		G	34		
Erik JENDRISEK		A	34		21
David KOTRYS	CZE	D	33		1
Martin LAURINC		D	35		3
Ján MASLO		M		(1)	
Ján MUCHA		G	2		
Jan NEZMAR	CZE	A	36		17
Pavol PILÁR		D		(8)	
Jirí POSPÍSIL	CZE	D	28	(4)	1
Marek SAPARA		M	35		6
Tomás SEDLÁK		M	29	(6)	1
Matej SIVA		D	10	(11)	1
Rudolf URBAN		M	3	(22)	1
Pavel ZBOZÍNEK	CZE	M	1	(3)	
Igor ZOFCÁK		M	34		3
Stefan ZOSÁK		M	11	(10)	

SPARTAK TRNAVA
Coach - Jozef Adamec

2005					
17/7	Artmedia Bratislava	a	2-0	Ujlaky, Kozuch	
23/7	MFK Ruzomberok	h	2-0	Kriss 2	
30/7	Dukla Banská Bystrica	a	1-0	Fall	
6/8	AS Trencín	h	1-0	Kopúnek	
13/8	Inter Bratislava	a	0-1		
20/8	ZTS Dubnica	a	3-0	Kriss, Juhász, Duris	
27/8	FC Nitra	h	2-0	Kozuch, Duris	
10/9	Matador Púchov	a	3-1	Kozuch 2, Kriss	
17/9	MSK Zilina	h	4-1	Kriss, Hrabal, Cvirik, Kozuch	
20/9	Artmedia Bratislava	h	1-3	Ujlaky	
24/9	MFK Ruzomberok	a	1-4	Kopúnek	
1/10	Dukla Banská Bystrica	h	1-0	og (Vesely)	
15/10	AS Trencín	a	0-0		
22/10	Inter Bratislava	h	3-0	Semanko, Hrabal, Cvirik (p)	
29/10	ZTS Dubnica	h	2-1	Kozuch 2	
5/11	FC Nitra	a	1-3	Kriss	
8/11	Matador Púchov	h	4-0	Duris, Kriss, og (Brisuda), Hrabal	
19/11	Artmedia Bratislava	a	1-2	Kozuch	
26/11	MFK Ruzomberok	h	2-1	Kopúnek, Kriss	
30/11	MSK Zilina	a	0-1		
2006					
11/3	AS Trencín	h	3-0	Cvirik (p), Ujlaky, Blaha	
14/3	Dukla Banská Bystrica	a	2-1	Blaha 2	
18/3	Inter Bratislava	a	2-2	Cvirik (p), Blaha	
25/3	ZTS Dubnica	a	2-0	Ujlaky, Blaha	
1/4	FC Nitra	h	0-1		
8/4	Matador Púchov	a	2-0	Kopúnek, Filip	
15/4	MSK Zilina	h	2-1	Kriss, Cvirik (p)	
22/4	Artmedia Bratislava	h	1-0	Kriss	
26/4	MFK Ruzomberok	a	1-2	Kriss	
29/4	Dukla Banská Bystrica	h	1-1	Husár	
3/5	AS Trencín	a	0-1		
13/5	Inter Bratislava	h	0-0		
16/5	ZTS Dubnica	h	4-1	Blaha 2, Filip, Kozuch	
23/5	FC Nitra	a	1-1	Blaha	
27/5	Matador Púchov	h	1-0	Kriss	
31/5	MSK Zilina	a	1-2	Blaha	

Name	Nat	Pos	Aps	(s)	Gls
Tomás BARTOS		A		(3)	
Michal BERNÁT		M		(2)	
Lubos BLAHA	CZE	A	14	(1)	9
Igor CHALUPKA		M	3	(5)	
Peter CVIRIK		D	32		5
Peter DURIS		M	36		3
Soukeymane FALL	SEN	D	12	(7)	1
Andrej FILIP		M	20	(9)	2
Michal GASPARÍK		M	2	(2)	
Tomás GERICH		D	3		
Lubos HANZEL		A		(2)	
Jaroslav HRABAL		D	25	(7)	3
Miroslav HRDINA		G	1	(1)	
Martin HUSÁR		D	18	(3)	1
Milos JUHÁSZ		M	7	(12)	1
Kamil KOPÚNEK		M	32		4
Jozef KOTULA		D	27		
Vladimír KOZUCH		A	33	(1)	9
Miroslav KRISS		A	22	(8)	12
Vladimír LABANT		M	11	(4)	
Martin LIPCÁK		G	35		
Pavol MASARYK		A		(1)	
Marián MOLNÁR		M	1	(3)	
Martin POLJOVKA		D	32		
Karol SEBÍK		M		(1)	
Dalibor SEMANKO		M	8	(20)	1
Marek UJLAKY		M	22		4
Lukás VIDO		M		(3)	

Slovakia

AS TRENCÍN
Coach - Ladislav Hudec; (13/3/06) Radúz Dorsák

2005
16/7	Dukla Banská Bystrica	a	0-2	
29/7	Inter Bratislava	h	2-0	Kamensky 2
6/8	Spartak Trnava	a	0-1	
9/8	ZTS Dubnica	a	1-1	Velicky
12/8	FC Nitra	h	2-1	Kamensky, Velicky
20/8	Matador Púchov	a	1-2	Kubala (p)
28/8	MSK Zilina	h	0-1	
9/9	Artmedia Bratislava	a	0-3	
17/9	MFK Ruzomberok	h	1-0	Fabus
20/9	Dukla Banská Bystrica	h	2-1	Baranyai, og (Wozniak)
24/9	ZTS Dubnica	h	2-0	Kamensky, Baranyai
1/10	Inter Bratislava	a	0-0	
15/10	Spartak Trnava	h	0-0	
14/10	FC Nitra	a	1-3	Kamensky
29/10	Matador Púchov	h	1-1	Prekop
5/11	MSK Zilina	a	2-1	Fabus, Baranyai
9/11	Artmedia Bratislava	h	1-1	Baranyai
19/11	Dukla Banská Bystrica	a	1-0	Fabus
26/11	ZTS Dubnica	a	1-1	Micenec
30/11	MFK Ruzomberok	a	0-1	

2006
4/3	Inter Bratislava	h	1-2	Baranyai
11/3	Spartak Trnava	a	0-3	
18/3	FC Nitra	h	1-1	Pastva
25/3	Matador Púchov	a	1-2	Prekop
1/4	MSK Zilina	h	2-1	Kamensky, Styvar
9/4	Artmedia Bratislava	a	1-3	Seman (p)
15/4	MFK Ruzomberok	h	1-0	Tárnyik
22/4	Dukla Banská Bystrica	h	0-0	
25/4	ZTS Dubnica	h	1-2	Tárnyik
29/4	Inter Bratislava	a	0-0	
3/5	Spartak Trnava	h	1-0	og (Cvirik)
13/5	FC Nitra	a	0-3	
16/5	Matador Púchov	h	1-3	Lietava
23/5	MSK Zilina	a	0-5	
27/5	Artmedia Bratislava	h	3-1	Lesták, Horváth, Rozník
31/5	MFK Ruzomberok	a	0-3	

Name	Nat	Pos	Aps	(s)	Gls
Peter AMRICH		A		(6)	
Gejza BARANYAI		A	20	(7)	5
Milos BUCHTA	CZE	G	10		
Martin FABUS		A	25	(3)	3
Roman GERCEL		M	2	(1)	
Filip HLOHOVSKY		M	3	(4)	
Roman HODÁL		G	22		
Csaba HORVÁTH		D	15		1
Jaroslav KAMENSKY		A	28		6
Peter KLESCÍK		M	3		
Antonín KONCITÍK		M	2		
Ivo KRAJCOVIC	CZE	D	10	(5)	
Michal KUBALA		M	18		1
Juraj LESTÁK		M	4	(6)	1
Ivan LIETAVA		M	12	(7)	1
Ján LINTNER		D	3	(4)	
Tomás MARCEK		M	3		
Milan MICENEC		D	27	(4)	1
Vladislav PALSA		D	30	(3)	
Milan PASTVA		M	24	(9)	1
Juraj PIROSKA		A		(3)	
Jozef POSTRK		D	3	(6)	
Jaroslav PREKOP		M	31	(1)	2
Matej ROZNÍK		A	4	(11)	1
Lukás SEBEK		M		(3)	
Marek SEMAN		M	27	(1)	1
Peter STYVAR		D	31		1
Igor SZKUKÁLEK		D	14		
Stefan TÁRNYIK		A	2	(9)	2
Stanislav VELICKY		M	19		2
Milos VOLESÁK		G	4	(1)	MSK

MSK ZILINA
Coach - Karol Pecze; (25/8/05) Milan Nemec; (1/1/06) Marijan Vlak (CRO)

2005
17/7	FC Nitra	h	2-5	Straka, Jez
23/7	Matador Púchov	a	5-1	Sesták 2, Straka 2, Dolezaj
31/7	ZTS Dubnica	h	3-0	Jez, Sesták (p), Cisovsky
6/8	Artmedia Bratislava	h	1-2	Jez
14/8	MFK Ruzomberok	a	0-2	
20/8	Dukla Banská Bystrica	h	2-0	Straka, Svestka
28/8	AS Trencin	a	1-0	Bartos
10/9	Inter Bratislava	h	5-2	Jez, Straka 2, Barcík, Vrsic
17/9	Spartak Trnava	a	1-4	Sesták
20/9	FC Nitra	a	2-0	Sesták, Svestka
24/9	Matador Púchov	h	1-2	Sesták
1/10	ZTS Dubnica	a	4-2	Bartos 2, Belak, Straka
16/10	Artmedia Bratislava	a	1-1	Sesták
22/10	MFK Ruzomberok	h	0-1	
29/10	Dukla Banská Bystrica	a	4-0	Pekárik, Bartos, Cisovsky, Straka
5/11	AS Trencin	h	1-2	Straka
8/11	Inter Bratislava	a	4-0	Cisovsky, Vrsic, Barcík, Krisko
19/11	FC Nitra	h	2-1	Straka 2
26/11	Matador Púchov	a	1-0	Vrsic
30/11	Spartak Trnava	h	1-0	Straka

2006
4/3	ZTS Dubnica	h	0-0	
18/3	MFK Ruzomberok	a	1-2	Straka
25/3	Dukla Banská Bystrica	a	2-0	Svestka, Sesták
1/4	AS Trencin	a	1-2	Straka
4/4	Artmedia Bratislava	h	0-1	
8/4	Inter Bratislava	h	1-1	Vomácka
15/4	Spartak Trnava	a	1-2	Svestka
22/4	FC Nitra	a	2-2	Sesták, Dolezaj
25/4	Matador Púchov	h	3-1	Vomácka, Strba, Sesták
29/4	ZTS Dubnica	a	4-1	Sesták, Straka 2, Jez
3/5	Artmedia Bratislava	a	2-1	Svestka, Sesták
13/5	MFK Ruzomberok	h	1-2	Strba
16/5	Dukla Banská Bystrica	a	2-2	Sesták, Labant
23/5	AS Trencin	h	5-0	Sesták, Barcík, Pekárik, Jez, Vrsic
27/5	Inter Bratislava	a	1-1	Sesták
31/5	Spartak Trnava	h	2-1	Sesták 2 (1p)

Name	Nat	Pos	Aps	(s)	Gls
Marek BAJZA		A		(8)	
Miroslav BARCÍK		M	31	(2)	3
Ivan BARTOS		A	6	(8)	4
Ivan BELÁK		M	13	(4)	1
Martin BELANÍK		D	3	(2)	
Marián CISOVSKY		D	19		3
Peter DOLEZAJ		D	19	(4)	2
Martin DURICA		M		(3)	
Stefan GAVARIC	BOS	D		(8)	

Slovakia

Michal GOTTWALD		A	3	(8)	
Róbert JEZ		M	31	(3)	6
Miroslav KÖNIG		G	9		
Milos KRISKO		D	14	(2)	1
Dusan KUCIAK		G	20	(1)	
Branislav LABANT		D	23	(4)	1
Martin MINARCÍK		D	7	(6)	
Adam NEMEC		A	10	(3)	
Mário PECALKA		M		(2)	
Peter PEKÁRIK		D	23	(4)	2
Dusan PERNIS		G	7		
Kristian POLOVANEC	CRO	A	6	(1)	
Andrej PORÁZIK		M	2	(1)	
Stanislav SESTÁK		A	28	(1)	17
Pavol STRAKA		A	26	(6)	16
Zdeno STRBA		M	26	(2)	2
Martin SVESTKA	CZE	D	25	(1)	5
Lukás TESÁK		M	7	(4)	
Benjamin VOMÁCKA	CZE	D	29		2
Dare VRSIC	SLO	A	9	(10)	4

DOMESTIC CUP 2005/06

FIRST ROUND
(2/8/05)
MFK Ruzomberok 3, HFC Humenné 0
Sport Podbrezová 1, Tatran Presov 0
Odeva Lipany 1, LAFC Lucenec 0
FC Lamac 1, FC Nitra 6
Spartak Trnava 2, DAC Dunajská Streda 1
FC Nitra 'B' 0, Inter Bratislava 6
FK Barca 0, MFK Kosice 4
(3/8/05)
FC Rimavská Sobota 1, Zemplín Michalovce 1 *(6-5 on pens)*
Turcianske Teplice 1, MSK Zilina 8
SK Mocenok 3, Zlaté Moravce 0
Slovan Duslo Sala 2, ZTS Dubnica 1
Spartak Trnava 'B' 0, AS Trencín 1
FC Bác 0, FC Senec 3
Slovan Bratislava 0, Matador Púchov 0 *(5-6 on pens)*
Byes – Artmedia Bratislava, Dukla Banská Bystrica

SECOND ROUND
(30/8/05)
Sport Podbrezová 1, FC Senec 2
Slovan Duslo Sala 3, Odeva Lipany 0
MFK Ruzomberok 1, Matador Púchov 0
Spartak Trnava 1, MFK Kosice 0
(31/8/05)
Inter Bratislava 0, Artmedia Bratislava 2
FC Nitra 1, MSK Zilina 1 *(5-3 on pens)*
AS Trencín 3, Dukla Banská Bystrica 0
SK Mocenok 3, FC Rimavská Sobota 0

QUARTER-FINALS
(5/10/05 & 25/10/05)
Artmedia Bratislava 1 *(Obzera 48)*, FC Senec 0
FC Senec 1 *(Moughfire 55)*, Artmedia Bratislava 1 *(Kozák J. 79p)*
(Artmedia Bratislava 2-1)

(18/10/05 & 25/10/05)
Slovan Duslo Sala 2 *(Vencel 10, Lancz 74)*, FC Nitra 2 *(Hrncar 86, Rák 89)*

FC Nitra 2 *(Rák 10, 20)*, Slovan Duslo Sala 1 *(Lalák 70)*
(FC Nitra 4-3)

AS Trencín 0, MFK Ruzomberok 3 *(Pospísil 56, Nezmar 89, 90)*
MFK Ruzomberok 0, AS Trencín 0
(MFK Ruzomberok 3-0)

SK Mocenok 0, Spartak Trnava 4 *(Kozuch 14, Kriss 16, Semanko 48, Filip 90)*
Spartak Trnava 1 *(Duris 27)*, SK Mocenok 0
(Spartak Trnava 5-0)

SEMI-FINALS
(28/3/06 & 11/4/06)
FC Nitra 1 *(Dobias 49)*, Spartak Trnava 3 *(Cvirik 13, Semanko 50, 75)*
Spartak Trnava 1 *(Blaha 9)*, FC Nitra 1 *(Grajciar 63)*
(Spartak Trnava 4-2)

(29/3/06 & 12/4/06)
MFK Ruzomberok 2 *(Dvorník 27, Jendrisek 86)*, Artmedia Bratislava 0
Artmedia Bratislava 2 *(Reiter 8, 35)*, MFK Ruzomberok 0
(2-2; MFK Ruzomberok 6-5 on pens)

FINAL
(8/5/06)
Inter stadion, Bratislava
MFK RUZOMBEROK 0
SPARTAK TRNAVA 0
(aet; 4-3 on pens)
Referee – Michel
MFK RUZOMBEROK – Hajdúch, Pospísil *(Urban 106)*, Dvorník, Laurinc, Kotrys, Zbozinek *(Dovicovic 64)*, Zofcák, Sapara, Bozok *(Dubek 71)*, Jendrisek, Nezmar.
SPARTAK TRNAVA – Hrdina, Fall *(Molnár 60)*, Hrabal, Poljovka, Cvirik, Semanko, Duris, Kopúnek, Husar *(Labant 82)*, Kriss *(Filip 55)*, Kozúch.

SECOND LEVEL FINAL TABLE 2005/06

		Pld	W	D	L	F	A	Pts
1	MFK Kosice	30	23	4	3	67	12	73
2	Slovan Bratislava	30	19	6	5	47	25	63
3	FC Senec	30	19	3	8	65	35	60
4	Tatran Presov	30	15	7	8	37	22	52
5	LAFC Lucenec	30	15	7	8	40	34	52
6	FC Rimavská Sobota	30	17	5	8	49	23	50
7	MFK Michalovce	30	14	6	10	38	30	48
8	VION Zlaté Moravce	30	14	6	10	33	25	48
9	Slovan Duslo Sala	30	13	6	11	42	29	45
10	Sport Podbrezová	30	12	8	10	39	30	44
11	HFC Humenné	30	10	7	13	35	45	37
12	DAC Dunajská Streda	30	7	6	17	27	51	27
13	Odeva Lipany	30	6	4	20	27	61	22
14	Spartak Trnava 'B'	30	4	5	21	17	56	17
15	FC Bác	30	3	7	20	17	63	16
16	FC Nitra 'B'	30	4	3	23	25	64	15

N.B. FC Rimavská Sobota – 6 pts deducted.

Slovenia

Gorica pushed hard by Domzale

Following the financial collapse of Olimpija Ljubljana and the enforced withdrawal of two other clubs, the Slovenian First League was obliged to change format in 2005/06.

Instead of 12 teams playing in a two-tier system, ten clubs faced each other four times over a 36-match campaign that stretched from July through to June with a four-month hibernation.

ND Gorica had won the previous two campaigns played under the old system, and the club from the Italian border town of Nova Gorica would make it a hat-trick of titles – and four championships overall – after an absorbing season-long battle with Domzale.

The latter, led by enthusiastic young coach Slavisa Stojanovic, had done brilliantly to finish second to Gorica in 2004/05 but they had never been in the title race. This time they posted an early message of intent by thrashing newly promoted Rudar Velenje 8-0 in their first away game. A long unbeaten run followed, and there was an added bonus for the club's supporters as Domzale survived two qualifying rounds in the UEFA Cup, predictably hammering San Marino's Domagnano into submission before edging past Israel's Ashdod on the away-goals rule with a last-minute 'winner'. German side VfB Stuttgart unsurprisingly ended Domzale's interest in the first round proper but not before the Slovenians had worried Giovanni Trapattoni's side with a 1-0 victory in the home leg.

New star Stevanovic

Domzale's winning goal against the Bundesliga side came from their gifted Slovenian Under-21 international forward Dalibor Stevanovic, and he would be the star of the autumn campaign, scoring nine goals in the league to help Domzale enter the long mid-season break at the top of the table. Unfortunately, word of Stevanovic's superior talent – and a growing reputation as the 'new Zlatko Zahovic' - had spread across Europe, and Domzale were powerless to turn down a lucrative offer from Real Sociedad, who offered the 21-year-old a four-and-a-half-year contract. Domzale also lost the services of their top scorer, Slovenian international striker Ermin Rakovic, who found new employers in Turkey.

Those two key departures were to be the turning point of the season. Whereas Domzale had to revamp their attack, Gorica withstood the advances of a number of foreign clubs to keep their dynamic young striking duo of Miran Burgic and Valter Birsa. In the spring these two whippersnappers proved even more irresistible than they had been during a fruitful autumn. Hardly a game passed without one or the other getting his name on the scoresheet, and by the end of the season Burgic, 21, was the league's top marksman on 24 goals, with Birsa, 19, close behind on 18.

NATIONAL TEAM RESULTS 2005/06

17/8/05	Wales	A	Swansea	0-0	
3/9/05	Norway (WCQ)	H	Celje	2-3	Cimerotic (5), Zlogar (83)
7/9/05	Moldova (WCQ)	A	Chisinau	2-1	Lavric (46), Mavric M. (57)
8/10/05	Italy (WCQ)	A	Palermo	0-1	
12/10/05	Scotland (WCQ)	H	Celje	0-3	
28/2/06	Cyprus	A	Larnaca	1-0	Ljubijankic (85)
1/3/06	Romania	N	Larnaca	0-2	
31/5/06	Trinidad & Tobago	H	Celje	3-1	Novakovic (4, 16, 77)
4/6/06	Ivory Coast	N	Paris	0-3	

Slovenia

Two of the latter's most important goals came in the head-to-head clash with Domzale at the beginning of May. The two teams had been neck and neck for weeks until the defending champions slipped to a shock 2-0 defeat at Drava four days before their summit meeting in Nova Gorica. That put Domzale four points ahead, and with each of the three previous games between the top two having ended 1-1, it was imperative for Gorica to win the game to stay in the hunt. Birsa's brace did the trick, and Domzale were so deflated that three days later they lost again – 2-0 at home to Drava – while Gorica, their confidence restored, romped to a 4-0 win over Publikum Celje to go two points clear.

A week later the two teams were level again after Gorica dropped two points at home to in-form Koper, but the champions kept their nerve down the stretch, winning all of their four remaining matches. A last-day 4-0 win at home to bottom club Rudar ended the marathon campaign on a triumphant note as long-serving coach Pavel Pinni and his players celebrated a hat-trick of championship titles. The victory kept Gorica two points above their valiant rivals, whose 2-0 home win over Maribor was in vain.

There was a huge gap between the top two and third place, but Koper, the club that filled it, would have given Gorica and Domzale a good run for their money if the title race had started at Christmas. The club from the Adriatic coast benefited from the investment of Serbian tycoon Milan Mandaric (the chairman of English Premiership club Portsmouth), and they were beaten only twice in 18 games during the second half of the campaign.

Cup for Koper

Better still, Koper won the Slovenian Cup – for the first time in 15 years – after a thrilling final in Celje against stadium dwellers and Cup holders CMC Publikum. Having deposited both Domzale and Gorica out of the competition in the previous two rounds, Koper came through to win the final on penalties after a 1-1 draw. The hero of the hour was former Slovenian international Mladen Rudonja. Recruited by the club in mid-season (alongside another Slovenia old boy Amir Karic) in a dual role as player and sports director, Rudonja not only scored the goal that gave Koper an early lead but also converted the decisive spot-kick in the shoot-out. Having been the better team throughout, Koper fully deserved the win that booked their place in the 2006/07 UEFA Cup.

One oddity of the 2005/06 season was that no First League matches took place in the capital. The promotion of Second League champions Factor Ljubljana ensured there would be no repeat in 2006/07. They took the position vacated by Rudar Velenje, whose woeful first season back among the elite brought just two wins. The other promoted club, Nafta Lendava, fared far better, finishing seventh despite the disadvantage of being refused permission to play home games in their dilapidated stadium. Second League runners-up Dravinja Duol narrowly missed promotion on two counts, finishing just a point behind Factor and then losing their play-off with Bela Krajina on away goals.

There was no near-miss for the Slovenian national team in the World Cup qualifiers. They could finish only fourth in their qualifying group, their famous 1-0 home win over Italy at the start of the campaign proving to be a mere flash in the pan. No matter that no other country subsequently beat the Azzurri during the remainder of Marcello Lippi's triumphant two-year reign. As the only other team Slovenia managed to overcome during the qualifiers was Moldova (twice), it meant that they dropped into the fourth band of seeds for the Euro 2008 qualifying draw.

Short hop

The collective talents of Holland, Romania and Bulgaria will probably prove too much too soon for Branko Oblak's young, developing team, although it goes without saying that Slovenia will be extremely keen to participate at a tournament co-hosted by neighbouring Austria. Klagenfurt, one of the finals venues, is only a short hop through the mountains from Ljubljana.

There was no indication from four friendly internationals played in the first half of 2006 that Slovenia would be fully competitive for the Euro qualifiers, although striker Milivoje Novakovic caused quite a stir when he scored a hat-trick against World Cup-bound Trinidad & Tobago on only his third appearance. Novakovic was the joint-top scorer in the Bulgarian league, with Litex Lovech, but generally Slovenia's overseas players did little of note. The best moment for a Slovenian footballer in 2005/06 was probably the winning goal scored by Milenko Acimovic for Lille against Manchester United in a Champions League group game played in front of 60,000 at the Stade de France.

Slovenia

NATIONAL TEAM APPEARANCES 2005/06

Coach – Branko OBLAK			Wal	NOR	MOL	ITA	SCO	Cyp	Rom	Tri	Civ	Caps	Goals
Borut MAVRIC	27/3/70	SpVgg Greuther Fürth (GER)	G62	G		G		G		G	G46	14	-
Matej MAVRIC	29/1/79	Molde FK (NOR)	D46	D	D	D	D26	D46	D	D		19	1
Aleksander KNAVS	5/12/75	Red Bull Salzburg (AUT)	D	D	D	D	D					63	3
Bostjan CESAR	9/7/82	Dinamo Zagreb (CRO)	D	D	D	D	D					16	1
Suad FILEKOVIC	16/9/78	R Excelsior Mouscron (BEL)	D	D60	D46	D						10	-
Andrej KOMAC	4/12/79	CS Marítimo (POR) /ND Gorica	M87	M		M	M		M	M46	M55	s46 /56	18	-
Anton ZLOGAR	24/11/77	Paralimni (CYP)	M	M	M	M	M	M	M	M82	M	18	1
Jalen POKORN	7/6/79	Terek Groznyi (RUS)	M56			M46						12	-
Nastja CEH	16/1/78	FK Austria Wien (AUT)	M	M	M		M	M57	M46	M84		39	6
Klemen LAVRIC	12/6/81	MSV Duisburg (GER)	A46	s56	s46					A52	A46	9	1
Milenko ACIMOVIC	15/2/77	Lille OSC (FRA)	M46	M56		M	M			s52	M	69	13
Goran SUKALO	24/8/81	Alemannia Aachen (GER)	s46		s89					s82	M	26	1
Aleksandar RODIC	26/12/79	Portsmouth (ENG)	s46	A	A89	A84	A54					9	1
Sebastjan CIMEROTIC	14/9/74	Incheon United (KOR)	s46	A	A46	s46	A					33	6
Branko ILIC	6/2/83	Domzale	s56				s56	D	D	D	D	11	-
Samir HANDANOVIC	14/7/84	Treviso (ITA) /Lazio (ITA)	s62		G		G			G	s46	9	-
Andrej PECNIK	27/9/81	SK Sigma Olomouc (CZE)	s87		s46		s26 /56		D57			4	-
Robert KOREN	20/9/80	Lillestrøm SK (NOR)		s60	M	M	M	M78	s46	M		17	-
Simon SESLAR	5/4/74	Hapoel Nazareth Ilit (ISR)			M							19	-
Ermin SILJAK	11/5/73	R Excelsior Mouscron (BEL)				s84	s54					48	14
Sebastjan GOBEC	6/12/79	CMC Publikum Celje						D74				2	-
Dominik BERSNJAK	15/7/81	CMC Publikum Celje						M				1	-
Bojan JOKIC	17/5/86	ND Gorica						M64	s46	s84	s46	4	-
Milivoje NOVAKOVIC	18/5/79	Litex Lovech (BUL)						A63	A71	A84	A86	4	3
Janez ZAVRL	25/12/82	Domzale /SK Brann (NOR)						s46	M	M70		3	-
Dalibor STEVANOVIC	27/9/84	Real Sociedad (ESP)						s57	s76			2	-
Zlatan LJUBIJANKIC	15/12/83	Domzale						s63	A76			2	1
Ales KOKOT	23/10/79	SpVgg Greuther Fürth (GER)						s64	s71	D	D	7	-
Valter BIRSA	7/8/86	ND Gorica						s74	A	s70	A46	4	-
Miso BRECKO	1/5/84	FC Hansa Rostock (GER)						s78	s57		s56	5	-
Borut SEMLER	25/2/85	FC Bayern München (GER)								s55	M80	5	-
Dejan RUSIC	5/12/82	CMC Publikum Celje								s84	s80	2	-
Fabijan CIPOT	25/8/76	Nafta Lendava									D	19	-
Darijan MATIC	28/5/83	Domzale									s86	1	-

Slovenia

EUROPEAN CUPS 2005/06

UEFA CHAMPIONS LEAGUE

ND GORICA
1st qualifying round SK TIRANA (ALB)
H 2-0 *Kovacevic M. (66), Birsa (82)*
Pirih, Suler, Handanagic, Srebrnic, Krsic, Zivec, Kovacevic N., Ranic (Demirovic 46), Burgic (Birsa 46), Kovacevic M., Pus.
A 0-3
Pirih, Suler, Handanagic, Srebrnic, Krsic (Sabec 70), Zivec (Demirovic 46), Kovacevic N., Ranic, Birsa (Burgic 46), Kovacevic M., Pus.

UEFA CUP

CMC PUBLIKUM CELJE
2nd qualifying round LEVSKI SOFIA (BUL)
H 1-0 *Bersnjak (68)*
Mujcinovic, Kriznik, Duro (Sulejmanovic 46), Pecnik, Budimir, Gobec, Bersnjak (Urbanc 80), Robnik (Pranjic 82), Brulc, Stajic, Snofl.
A 0-3
Mujcinovic, Snofl, Gobec, Budimir (Sulejmanovic 46), Kriznik, Pecnik, Urbanc, Bersnjak, Pranjic (Robnik 55), Stajic, Brulc.

DOMZALE
1st qualifying round DOMAGNANO (SMR)
A 5-0 *Stevanovic (14), Zavrl (47), Nikezic (63, 86), Kacicnik (82)*
Strajnar, Kline (Kacicnik 70), Zeljkovic, Zavrl, Topic, Elsner, Djuranovic, Stevanovic, Matic (Lunder 77), Nikezic, Dvorancic (Ljubijankic 58).
H 3-0 *Juninho (20), Nikezic (45), Zeljkovic (88p)*
Strajnar, Da Souza, Zeljkovic, Kacicnik, Lunder, Juninho, Djuranovic (Nikezic 46), Stevanovic (Tomazic 76), Topic, Ilic, Ljubijankic (Jesemicnik 88).

2nd qualifying round MS ASHDOD (ISR)
A 2-2 *Stevanovic (2), De Souza (27)*
Nemec, Zavrl, De Souza, Zeljkovic, Nikezic, Kacicnik, Elsner (Matic 67), Djuranovic, Stevanovic (Lunder 46), Ilic, Ljubijankic (Rajkovic 46).
H 1-1 *Nikezic (90)*
Strajnar, Da Souza, Ilic, Elsner, Kline, Zeljkovic, Zavrl (Kirm 58), Matic, Djuranovic (Juninho 46), Stevanovic, Rakovic (Nikezic 78).

1st round VFB STUTTGART (GER)
A 0-2
Nemec, Zavrl, De Souza (Topic 88), Kline, Zeljkovic, Matic, Djuranovic (Juninho 57), Stevanovic (Lunder 80), Ilic, Ljubijankic, Rakovic.
H 1-0 *Stevanovic (16)*
Nemec, De Souza, Zavrl, Ilic, Matic, Elsner, Kacicnik, Zeljkovic, Djuranovic (Ljubijankic 57), Rakovic, Stevanovic.

TOP GOALSCORERS 2005/06

24	Miran BURGIC (ND Gorica)	
18	Valter BIRSA (ND Gorica)	
	Oskar DROBNE (Koper)	
16	Viktor TRENEVSKI (Drava)	
14	Ermin RAKOVIC (Domzale)	
	Drazen ZEZELJ (Primorje Ajdovscina)	
13	Joze BENKO (Nafta Lendava)	
	Enes DEMIROVIC (ND Gorica)	
10	Rok KRONAVETER (Drava)	
	Nikola NIKEZIC (Domzale)	

LEAGUE RESULTS/SCORERS/APPEARANCES 2005/06

BELA KRAJINA CRNOMELJ
Coach - Tomaz Kavcic; (19/11/05) Ivan Buljan (CRO)

2005

Date	Opponent	H/A	Score	Scorers
24/7	ND Gorica	a	0-4	
31/7	Primorje Ajdovscina	h	1-0	Causevic
7/8	Drava	a	0-3	
14/8	Maribor	h	2-2	Causevic, Cirar
20/8	Domzale	a	0-4	
28/8	Nafta Lendava	h	1-4	Causevic
10/9	CMC Publikum Celje	a	3-0	Causevic, Zinko, Mujakovic (p)
18/9	Rudar Velenje	h	1-0	Causevic
21/9	Koper	a	1-2	Causevic
25/9	ND Gorica	h	1-1	Causevic
2/10	Primorje Ajdovscina	a	1-2	Yusuf
15/10	Drava	h	1-1	Zinko
22/10	Maribor	a	1-1	Lamesic
26/10	Domzale	h	1-1	Marinic
29/10	Nafta Lendava	a	1-1	Penica
5/11	CMC Publikum Celje	h	1-0	Grabic
19/11	Koper	h	1-3	Mujakovic
26/11	ND Gorica	a	0-5	

2006

Date	Opponent	H/A	Score	Scorers
11/3	Rudar Velenje	a	0-0	
18/3	Primorje Ajdovscina	h	0-1	
25/3	Drava	a	1-0	Grabic
29/3	Maribor	h	0-1	
1/4	Domzale	a	1-2	Grabic
8/4	Nafta Lendava	h	3-0	Andjelkovic, Grabic (p), Causevic
12/4	CMC Publikum Celje	a	0-2	
15/4	Rudar Velenje	h	1-1	Mejac
22/4	Koper	a	0-2	
26/4	ND Gorica	h	1-1	Causevic
29/4	Primorje Ajdovscina	a	2-2	Spelic, Mujakovic
2/5	Drava	h	1-5	Grabic
6/5	Maribor	a	0-0	
13/5	Domzale	h	0-1	
17/5	Nafta Lendava	a	3-3	Mujakovic (p), Mejac 2
20/5	CMC Publikum Celje	h	3-1	Mejac 3
27/5	Rudar Velenje	a	2-2	Mejac, Grabic (p)
3/6	Koper	h	0-3	

No	Name	Nat	Pos	Aps	(s)	Gls
27	Tomaz ADLESIC		M	9	(3)	
5	Milan ANDJELKOVIC		D	34		1
7	Davor BRCINA		M		(1)	
8	Dejan CAUSEVIC		A	18	(12)	9
3	Rok CIRAR		M	23	(3)	1
25	Denis DERVISEVIC		A		(1)	
30	Nikola DRKUSIC		G	17	(1)	
2	Sasa FARTEK		D	2	(7)	
33	Dejan GRABIC		M	27		6
5	Timotej KRAJNC		D	5	(1)	
15	Mario LAMESIC	CRO	M	29	(3)	1
20	Rok MARINIC		M	24		1
7	Ales MEJAC		M	12	(1)	7
10	Amel MUJAKOVIC		A	33		4
32	Ales MUSIC		M		(1)	
1	Luka PELHAN		G	11		
16	Kristjan PENICA		M	27	(4)	1

Slovenia

FINAL LEAGUE TABLE 2005/06

		Pld	Home					Away					Total					Pts
			W	D	L	F	A	W	D	L	F	A	W	D	L	F	A	
1	ND Gorica	36	14	4	0	42	5	7	6	5	33	25	21	10	5	75	30	73
2	Domzale	36	15	2	1	43	10	5	9	4	26	18	20	11	5	69	28	71
3	Koper	36	10	5	3	29	15	6	4	8	20	24	16	9	11	49	39	57
4	Maribor	36	9	4	5	25	17	7	2	9	26	25	16	6	14	51	42	54
5	Drava	36	11	4	3	30	17	4	5	9	20	29	15	9	12	50	46	54
6	CMC Publikum Celje	36	10	2	6	28	27	5	2	11	20	32	15	4	17	48	59	49
7	Nafta Lendava	36	8	5	5	22	20	5	2	11	20	32	13	7	16	42	52	46
8	Primorje Ajdovscina	36	8	7	3	34	24	3	3	12	9	26	11	10	15	43	50	43
9	Bela Krajina Crnomelj	36	5	6	7	19	26	2	7	9	16	35	7	13	16	35	61	34
10	Rudar Velenje	36	2	5	11	17	40	0	4	14	11	43	2	9	25	28	83	15

6	Matej PEZDIRC		M	8	(12)
11	Marko POKLEKA		M	14	(1)
9	Blaz PUC		A	5	
19	Jasmin RAHMANOVIC		D	16	(3)
22	Boban SAVIC	SCG	G	6	
14	Josip SPELIC		M	6	(4) 1
18	Ljubisa STRBAC		A	11	(7)
9	Tadej VENTA		A		(7)
31	Alem VEZIROVIC		G	2	
17	Tadej VRSCAJ		M	20	(3)
13	Abdulrashid YUSUF	NGA	A	3	(14) 1
23	Marko ZAGAR		A	15	(2)
20	Aleksandar ZECEVIC		M	8	(2)
10	Luka ZINKO		M	11	(1) 2

DOMZALE
Coach - Slavisa Stojanovic

2005
22/7	Nafta Lendava	h	2-0	Ljubijankic, Stevanovic
31/7	Rudar Velenje	a	8-0	Rakovic 2, Nikezic, Djuranovic (p), Zeljkovic, Ljubijankic, Stevanovic, Kline
6/8	ND Gorica	h	1-1	Stevanovic
14/8	Drava	a	1-1	Nikezic
20/8	Bela Krajina Crnomelj	h	4-0	Rakovic 3, Ljubijankic
29/8	CMC Publikum Celje	h	5-0	Stevanovic 2, Rakovic 2, Nikezic
10/9	Koper	a	2-2	Rakovic 2
18/9	Primorje Ajdovscina	h	3-0	De Souza, Rakovic, Ljubijankic
21/9	Maribor	a	0-0	
24/9	Nafta Lendava	a	1-0	De Souza
3/10	Rudar Velenje	h	4-1	Stevanovic 3, De Souza
15/10	ND Gorica	a	1-1	Rakovic
22/10	Drava	h	1-0	Ljubijankic
26/10	Bela Krajina Crnomelj	a	1-1	Rakovic
29/10	CMC Publikum Celje	a	2-3	Stevanovic, Rakovic
5/11	Koper	h	4-1	Lunder, Juninho, Rakovic, Nikezic
19/11	Maribor	h	2-1	Nikezic 2

2006
11/3	Primorje Ajdovscina	a	2-2	Ilic, LoDuca
15/3	Nafta Lendava	h	3-1	Dvorancic 3
18/3	Rudar Velenje	h	0-2	
25/3	ND Gorica	h	1-1	De Souza
29/3	Drava	a	1-1	Matic

1/4	Bela Krajina Crnomelj	h	2-1	Matic (p), LoDuca
8/4	CMC Publikum Celje	h	2-1	Ljubijankic, Matic
12/4	Koper	a	0-2	
15/4	Primorje Ajdovscina	h	2-0	Matic, Ljubijankic
22/4	Maribor	a	3-0	(w/o; match abandoned, original result 2-1 Ljubijankic, Nikezic)
26/4	Nafta Lendava	a	0-0	
29/4	Rudar Velenje	h	3-0	Karapetrovic, Zeljkovic, Lunder
3/5	ND Gorica	a	0-2	
6/5	Drava	h	0-2	
13/5	Bela Krajina Crnomelj	a	1-0	Matic
17/5	CMC Publikum Celje	a	3-1	Juninho, Nikezic, Lubijankic
20/5	Koper	h	2-0	Nikezic 2 (1p)
27/5	Primorje Ajdovscina	a	0-0	
3/6	Maribor	h	2-0	Ilic, Zinko

No	Name	Nat	Pos	Aps	(s)	Gls
4	Tadej APATIC		M	3	(1)	
19	Dzengis CAVUSEVIC		A		(2)	
11	Jhonnes DE SOUZA	BRA	A	19	(1)	4
25	Dejan DJURANOVIC		M	22		1
8	Slavisa DVORANCIC		A	5	(4)	3
29	Luka ELSNER		D	28	(2)	
14	Branko ILIC		D	34		2
3	Ales JESENICNIK		D	4	(3)	
10	Júnior Wilson JUNINHO	BRA	M	17	(16)	2
28	Ales KACICNIK		M	20	(3)	
5	Darko KARAPETROVIC		M	10	(5)	1
30	Andraz KIRM		D	17	(12)	
7	Miha KLINE		M	11	(7)	1
9	Tim LODUCA		A	5	(8)	2
27	Marko LUNDER		M	10	(10)	2
20	Zlatan LJUBIJANKIC		A	29	(1)	9
6	Darijan MATIC		M	32	(1)	5
18	Denis MESANOVIC		M	2		
1	Dejan NEMEC		G	27		
17	Nikola NIKEZIC	SCG	A	18	(5)	10
19	Zan PETERCA		M		(1)	
9	Ermin RAKOVIC		A	13	(2)	14
21	Dalibor STEVANOVIC		M	14	(1)	9
22	Janez STRAJNAR		G	9		
24	Tadej TOMAZIC		M	2		
16	Darko TOPIC		M	3	(5)	
6	Janez ZAVRL		D	14	(1)	
15	Zoran ZELJKOVIC		M	23		2

Slovenia

DRAVA
Coach - Srecko Lucic (CRO); (15/10/05) Milko Djurovski (MAC)

2005

Date	Opponent	h/a	Score	Scorers
23/7	Rudar Velenje	h	1-0	Miljatovic
30/7	ND Gorica	a	0-2	
7/8	Bela Krajina Crnomelj	h	3-0	Trenevski 2, Sladojevic
14/8	Domzale	h	1-1	Tezacki
20/8	CMC Publikum Celje	a	0-2	
27/8	Koper	h	1-0	Chietti
10/9	Primorje Ajdovscina	a	2-6	Chietti, Trenevski (p)
17/9	Maribor	h	0-3	
21/9	Nafta Lendava	a	0-1	
24/9	Rudar Velenje	a	0-0	
1/10	ND Gorica	h	1-3	Stromajer
15/10	Bela Krajina Crnomelj	a	1-1	Kronaveter
22/10	Domzale	a	0-1	
26/10	CMC Publikum Celje	h	1-0	Miljatovic
29/10	Koper	a	1-0	og (Pahor)
5/11	Primorje Ajdovscina	h	4-1	Trenevski 2, Stromajer, Ceh
19/11	Nafta Lendava	h	3-2	Chietti 2, Trenevski

2006

Date	Opponent	h/a	Score	Scorers
4/3	Rudar Velenje	h	2-1	Trenevski 2 (1p)
11/3	Maribor	a	1-2	Trenevski
18/3	ND Gorica	a	0-4	
25/3	Bela Krajina Crnomelj	h	0-1	
29/3	Domzale	h	1-1	Trenevski
1/4	CMC Publikum Celje	a	1-3	Stromajer
8/4	Koper	h	1-1	Ceh
12/4	Primorje Ajdovscina	a	2-2	Berko, Kelenc
15/4	Maribor	h	3-2	Horvat, Zajc, Trenevski
22/4	Nafta Lendava	a	0-0	
26/4	Rudar Velenje	a	3-1	Trenevski 2 (2p), Horvat
29/4	ND Gorica	h	2-0	Trenevski (p), Kronaveter
2/5	Bela Krajina Crnomelj	a	5-1	Kronaveter 4, Ceh
6/5	Domzale	a	2-0	Kronaveter 2
13/5	CMC Publikum Celje	h	4-1	Ceh, Trenevski 2, Kronaveter
17/5	Koper	a	1-1	Chietti
20/5	Primorje Ajdovscina	h	0-0	
27/5	Maribor	a	1-2	Berko
3/6	Nafta Lendava	h	2-0	Gorinsek, Kronaveter

No	Name	Nat	Pos	Aps	(s)	Gls
23	Sebastjan BERKO		A	18		2
17	Sasa BOSILJ		D	7	(6)	
29	Kliton BOZGO	ALB	A	5		
8	Ales CEH		M	18	(2)	4
27	Gennaro CHIETTI	ITA	A	14	(6)	5
22	Mladen DABANOVIC		G	35		
9	Dejan DJENIC		D		(1)	
20	Marko DREVENSEK		M	4	(14)	
39	Janez EMERSIC		D		(1)	
2	Mitja EMERSIC		D	19	(5)	
1	Dejan GERMIC		G	1		
16	Gorazd GORINSEK		A	21	(6)	1
25	Lucas Mario HORVAT		A	12	(1)	2
70	Doris KELENC		M	19	(7)	1
4	Matjaz KOREZ		M		(1)	
15	Rok KRONAVETER		M	16	(11)	10
4	Armin KRUSCICA		D		(1)	
19	Rok LETONJA		M	3	(3)	
14	Dragan LJUBANIC		A		(1)	
18	Matjaz LUNDER		M	29		
25	Matej MILJATOVIC		D	16		2
21	Herolind OSAJ		M		(2)	
26	Primoz PETEK		M	3	(2)	
23	Luka ZINKO		M	5	(4)	1
13	Andrej PREJAC		M	17	(9)	
13	Vladimir SLADOJEVIC	BOS	D	8	(1)	1
17	Ales SMON		D	7	(2)	
5	Emil STERBAL		D	31		
11	Jaka STROMAJER		A	12	(5)	3
32	Robert TEZACKI	CRO	M	7	(1)	1
6	Borut TISNIKAR		D	14	(4)	
21	Tomaz TOPLAK		D	1	(4)	
10	Viktor TRENEVSKI	MAC	A	34		16
7	Aljaz ZAJC		M	14	(4)	1
14	Aleksandar ZECEVIC		M	11	(1)	

ND GORICA
Coach - Pavel Pinni

2005

Date	Opponent	h/a	Score	Scorers
24/7	Bela Krajina Crnomelj	h	4-0	Burgic 3, Ranic
30/7	Drava	h	2-0	Demirovic, Birsa
6/8	Domzale	a	1-1	Zivec
14/8	CMC Publikum Celje	h	2-1	Demirovic 2
20/8	Koper	a	0-2	
27/8	Primorje Ajdovscina	h	2-0	Burgic, Birsa
11/9	Maribor	a	1-2	Burgic
17/9	Nafta Lendava	h	2-0	Demirovic, Zivec
21/9	Rudar Velenje	a	2-1	Burgic, Zivec
25/9	Bela Krajina Crnomelj	a	1-1	Burgic
1/10	Drava	a	3-1	Burgic 2, Kovacevic M.
15/10	Domzale	h	1-1	Nikolic
22/10	CMC Publikum Celje	a	1-2	Suler
26/10	Koper	h	3-0	Burgic 2, Demirovic
29/10	Primorje Ajdovscina	a	2-2	Birsa 2
6/11	Maribor	h	4-1	Burgic 2, Birsa 2
19/11	Rudar Velenje	h	0-0	
26/11	Bela Krajina Crnomelj	h	5-0	Zivec 2, Birsa, Burgic, Krsic

2006

Date	Opponent	h/a	Score	Scorers
11/3	Nafta Lendava	a	4-2	Birsa 2, Demirovic (p), Burgic
18/3	Drava	h	4-0	Birsa 3, Burgic
25/3	Domzale	a	1-1	Demirovic
29/3	CMC Publikum Celje	h	2-0	Burgic, Demirovic
1/4	Koper	a	1-1	Birsa
8/4	Primorje Ajdovscina	a	2-0	Birsa, Burgic
12/4	Maribor	a	1-4	Demirovic
15/4	Nafta Lendava	h	1-1	Zivec
22/4	Rudar Velenje	a	3-0	Kovacevic N., Demirovic, Jogan
26/4	Bela Krajina Crnomelj	a	1-1	Burgic
29/4	Drava	a	0-2	
3/5	Domzale	h	2-0	Birsa 2
6/5	CMC Publikum Celje	a	4-0	Burgic, Ranic (p), Kovacevic M., og (Snofl)
13/5	Koper	h	0-0	
17/5	Primorje Ajdovscina	a	3-1	Demirovic, Birsa, Pus
20/5	Maribor	h	2-1	Demirovic, Burgic
27/5	Nafta Lendava	a	4-1	Burgic 2, Jokic, Birsa
3/6	Rudar Velenje	h	4-0	Burgic, Demirovic, Srebrnic, Sturm

No	Name	Nat	Pos	Aps	(s)	Gls
33	Valter BIRSA		A	28	(6)	18
15	Danijel BLASKO		M		(1)	
28	Rok BRAJIC		M		(2)	
17	Miran BURGIC		A	33		24
27	Goran CVIJANOVIC		D		(2)	
24	Enes DEMIROVIC	BOS	M	26	(5)	13
4	Enes HANDANAGIC		D	30		
16	Alen JOGAN		M	1	(3)	1
14	Bojan JOKIC		M	27	(4)	1

Slovenia

No	Name	Nat	Pos	Aps	(s)	Gls
11	Andrej KOMAC		M	12	(3)	
21	Mladen KOVACEVIC		A	11	(13)	2
8	Nebojsa KOVACEVIC		M	23	(5)	1
10	Admir KRSIC		M	10	(9)	1
2	Dragoljub NIKOLIC		M	14	(4)	1
22	Mitja PIRIH		G	18		
3	Ales PUS		D	32	(2)	1
31	Danijel RAKUSCEK		M		(1)	
7	Sasa RANIC		M	17	(9)	2
26	Gzim REXHAJ		M		(2)	
11	Jaka SABEC		A	7	(12)	
12	Vasja SIMCIC		G	18	(1)	
6	Miran SREBRNIC		D	30		1
20	Jani STURM		D	2	(12)	1
25	Marko SULER		D	32	(1)	1
23	Simon ZIVEC		M	25	(3)	6

KOPER
Coach - Samir Zulic; (26/11/05) Milivoj Bracun (CRO)

2005

Date	Opponent	h/a	Score	Scorers
23/7	Primorje Ajdovscina	h	1-1	Drobne
30/7	Maribor	a	2-1	Jakomin, Volas
6/8	Nafta Lendava	h	0-2	
13/8	Rudar Velenje	a	1-2	Drobne
20/8	ND Gorica	h	2-0	Jakomin, Kremenovic
27/8	Drava	a	0-1	
10/9	Domzale	h	2-2	Drobne (p), Knezovic
17/9	CMC Publikum Celje	a	3-3	Knezovic, Kremenovic, Bozic
21/9	Bela Krajina Crnomelj	h	2-1	Viler, Drobne
25/9	Primorje Ajdovscina	a	0-2	
2/10	Maribor	h	2-3	Jakomin, Kuzmanovic
15/10	Nafta Lendava	a	0-1	
22/10	Rudar Velenje	h	2-1	Kremenovic, Drobne (p)
26/10	ND Gorica	a	0-3	
29/10	Drava	h	0-1	
5/11	Domzale	h	1-4	Drobne (p)
19/11	Bela Krajina Crnomelj	a	3-1	Bozic, Drobne (p), Jakomin
26/11	Primorje Ajdovscina	h	1-0	Gunjac

2006

Date	Opponent	h/a	Score	Scorers
11/3	CMC Publikum Celje	h	2-0	Drobne, Rudonja
18/3	Maribor	a	1-0	Jakomin
25/3	Nafta Lendava	h	2-0	Karic, Drobne
29/3	Rudar Velenje	a	2-2	Kremenovic, Knezovic
1/4	ND Gorica	h	1-1	Knezovic
8/4	Drava	a	1-1	Jakomin
12/4	Domzale	h	2-0	Drobne, Kremenovic
15/4	CMC Publikum Celje	a	2-0	Jakomin, Drobne
22/4	Bela Krajina Crnomelj	h	2-0	Kremenovic, Drobne
26/4	Primorje Ajdovscina	a	0-1	
29/4	Maribor	h	2-0	Drobne 2
2/5	Nafta Lendava	a	1-0	Jakomin
6/5	Rudar Velenje	h	3-0	Drobne 2, Kremenovic
13/5	ND Gorica	a	0-0	
17/5	Drava	h	1-1	Drobne
20/5	Domzale	a	0-2	
27/5	CMC Publikum Celje	h	2-2	Drobne, Bozic
3/6	Bela Krajina Crnomelj	a	3-0	Kremenovic 2, Gregoric

No	Name	Nat	Pos	Aps	(s)	Gls
16	Primoz BARUT		M	1		
15	Toni BIUK	CRO	M	3	(8)	
13	Rok BOZIC		M	17	(5)	3
7	Oskar DROBNE		A	24	(7)	18
14	Simon GREGORIC		M	25	(3)	1
27	Ivica GUBERAC		A		(1)	
23	Andrej GUDIC		M		(3)	
17	Edmond GUNJAC		M	15	(1)	1
19	Damir HADZIC		M	13		
1	Jasmin HANDANOVIC		G	36		
2	Sasa JAKOMIN		A	34		8
20	Amir KARIC		M	15		1
25	Ivan KNEZOVIC	CRO	M	30		4
18	Darko KREMENOVIC		M	30	(2)	9
16	Veselin KUZMANOVIC		M	1	(3)	1
5	Igor LAZIC		D	13		
10	Anej LOVRECIC		D	7	(6)	
33	Mitja LUZNAR		A		(1)	
17	Jan PAHOR		M	26	(3)	
31	Rok PAHOR		D		(3)	
8	Manuel PERSIC		M	22	(5)	
24	Andrej POLJASK		D	12		
4	Miroslav RADULOVIC		D	14		
26	Aleksander RAJCEVIC		A	3	(1)	
20	Elvis RIBARIC		D	1	(1)	
9	Mladen RUDONJA		A	11	(1)	1
33	Erik SALKIC		M	2	(2)	
3	Edin SECIC		M	7	(12)	
6	Luka SKRBINA		A	16	(7)	
32	Blaz VALENCIC		M	2	(8)	
23	Mitja VILER		M	16	(9)	1
19	Dalibor VOLAS		M		(10)	1

MARIBOR
Coach - Milan Djuricic (CRO); (13/5/06) Marijan Pusnik

2005

Date	Opponent	h/a	Score	Scorers
24/7	CMC Publikum Celje	a	0-0	
30/7	Koper	h	1-2	Zajc
7/8	Primorje Ajdovscina	a	1-2	Zajc
14/8	Bela Krajina Crnomelj	a	2-2	Pregelj, Siberie
20/8	Nafta Lendava	h	1-0	Pregelj
27/8	Rudar Velenje	a	1-0	Vuksanovic
11/9	ND Gorica	h	2-1	Dzinic, Oslaj
17/9	Drava	a	3-0	Siberie 2, Eterovic
21/9	Domzale	h	0-0	
24/9	CMC Publikum Celje	h	0-2	
2/10	Koper	a	3-2	Popovic, Zeba, Zajc
15/10	Primorje Ajdovscina	h	2-0	Zeba, Zajc
22/10	Bela Krajina Crnomelj	h	1-1	Pregelj
26/10	Nafta Lendava	a	4-0	Siberie 2, Rakic (p), Jelic
29/10	Rudar Velenje	h	1-1	Simic
6/11	ND Gorica	a	1-4	Simic
19/11	Domzale	a	1-2	Rakic (p)

2006

Date	Opponent	h/a	Score	Scorers
8/3	CMC Publikum Celje	a	0-1	
11/3	Drava	h	2-1	Simic, Zeba
18/3	Koper	h	0-1	
25/3	Primorje Ajdovscina	a	3-0	Jelic, Pekic (p), Pregelj
29/3	Bela Krajina Crnomelj	a	1-0	Jelic
1/4	Nafta Lendava	h	5-1	Pregelj 2, Jelic, Rakic, Mihelic
8/4	Rudar Velenje	a	3-2	Pekic 2, Jelic
12/4	ND Gorica	h	4-1	Pekic 3, Pregelj
15/4	Drava	a	2-3	Rakic, Jelic
22/4	Domzale	h	1-2	Vuksanovic
26/4	CMC Publikum Celje	a	0-3	(w/o; match abandoned, original result 1-2 Pregelj)
29/4	Koper	a	0-2	
2/5	Primorje Ajdovscina	h	2-0	Jelic, Rakic
6/5	Bela Krajina Crnomelj	h	0-0	
13/5	Nafta Lendava	a	0-1	
17/5	Rudar Velenje	h	1-0	Popovic
20/5	ND Gorica	a	1-2	Zajc
27/5	Drava	h	2-1	Rakic, Jelic
3/6	Domzale	a	0-2	

Slovenia

No	Name	Nat	Pos	Aps	(s)	Gls
23	Erdzan BECIRI		D	20		
21	Sasa BOZICIC		M	13	(2)	
3	Elvedin DZINIC		D	15	(2)	1
8	Mate ETEROVIC	CRO	A	5	(3)	1
2	Marko GASPARIC		D	11	(1)	
31	Aljaz HORVAT		M	6	(2)	
28	Dragan JELIC		M	18	(14)	8
26	Dejan KORAT		M		(1)	
36	Marko KRAMBERGER		A		(1)	
35	Mihael LAZNIK		D		(1)	
17	Klemen MEDVED		M	4	(5)	
29	Rene MIHELIC		M	9	(7)	1
1	Tomaz MURKO		G	30		
14	Damjan OSLAJ		D	23		1
13	Leon PANIKVAR		A	10	(12)	
11	Damir PEKIC		A	9	(4)	6
21	Marko POKLEKA		M	10	(4)	
27	Marko POPOVIC	SCG	M	30	(1)	2
6	Martin PREGELJ		M	22	(1)	8
34	Marko PRIDIGAR		G	5		
18	Leon RAGOLIC		M	10	(4)	
4	Milan RAKIC		D	27	(3)	6
12	Marko RANILOVIC		G	1	(1)	
24	Rok ROJ		M	2	(1)	
9	Simon Sibino SIBERIE	HOL	A	14	(2)	5
7	Jan SIMENKO		M	1	(5)	
8	Predrag SIMIC	CRO	M	27		3
16	David TOMAZIC SERUGA		M	1		
33	Zikica VUKSANOVIC		D	30		2
25	Gorazd ZAJC		A	17	(10)	5
20	Zajko ZEBA	BOS	M	26		3

NAFTA LENDAVA
Coach - Damir Rob; (8/4/06) Vojislav Simeunovic

2005
22/7	Domzale	a	0-2	
30/7	CMC Publikum Celje	h	2-1	Gerencar B., Dominko (p)
6/8	Koper	a	2-0	Benko 2
13/8	Primorje Ajdovscina	h	1-0	Dominko
20/8	Maribor	a	0-1	
28/8	Bela Krajina Crnomelj	a	4-1	Dominko, Gerencar B., Benko, Bukovec
10/9	Rudar Velenje	h	5-0	Celcar, Benko, Dominko (p), Bukovec, Srsa
17/9	ND Gorica	a	0-2	
21/9	Drava	h	1-0	Ristic
24/9	Domzale	h	0-1	
1/10	CMC Publikum Celje	a	3-1	Benko 2, Bukovec
15/10	Koper	h	1-0	Benko
22/10	Primorje Ajdovscina	a	0-2	
26/10	Maribor	h	0-4	
29/10	Bela Krajina Crnomelj	h	1-1	Srsa
5/11	Rudar Velenje	a	3-1	Kulcar, Ristic, Vogrincic
19/11	Drava	a	2-3	Ristic, Zore

2006
11/3	ND Gorica	h	2-4	Benko, og (Jokic)
15/3	Domzale	a	1-3	Benko
18/3	CMC Publikum Celje	h	0-0	
25/3	Koper	a	0-2	
29/3	Primorje Ajdovscina	h	2-0	Benko, Cipot
1/4	Maribor	a	1-5	Benko
8/4	Bela Krajina Crnomelj	a	0-3	
12/4	Rudar Velenje	h	2-1	Cipot, Zemljic (p)
15/4	ND Gorica	a	1-1	Zemljic
22/4	Drava	h	0-0	
26/4	Domzale	h	0-0	
29/4	CMC Publikum Celje	a	1-2	Benko
2/5	Koper	h	0-1	
6/5	Primorje Ajdovscina	a	0-0	
13/5	Maribor	h	1-0	Benko
17/5	Bela Krajina Crnomelj	a	3-3	Gerencar B., Ristic, Zore
20/5	Rudar Velenje	a	2-1	Kozul, Gerencar B.
27/5	ND Gorica	h	1-4	Dominko (p)
3/6	Drava	a	0-2	

No	Name	Nat	Pos	Aps	(s)	Gls
14	Joze BENKO		A	18	(9)	13
4	Mihael BUKOVEC		D	32	(1)	3
11	Gregor BUNC		A	13	(3)	
17	Tomaz CELCAR		A	13	(7)	1
2	Franc CIFER		D	2	(1)	
29	Fabijan CIPOT		M	9	(3)	2
13	Miran DOMA		A	5	(9)	
9	Marjan DOMINKO		D	26		5
15	Borut GERENCAR		M	27	(6)	4
18	Peter GERENCAR		M	7	(8)	
22	Tomaz HORVAT		M		(1)	
16	Vladimir KOZUL	SCG	D	20		1
8	Kristjan KULCAR		M	8	(6)	1
32	Stanislav KUZMA		G	14		
12	Ales LUK		G	32		
3	Bojan MATJASEC		M	11	(14)	
7	Goran RISTIC		M	35		4
5	Hrvoje SKLEPIC	CRO	M	26	(4)	
20	Denis SRSA		M	9	(17)	2
23	Admir SULJIC		A	3	(2)	
28	Arpad VAS		M		(1)	
10	Sebastjan VOGRINCIC		M	24	(5)	1
2	Bostjan ZEMLJIC		D	32	(2)	2
21	Gregor ZORE		D	30		2

PRIMORJE AJDOVSCINA
Coach - Darko Milanic; (12/4/06) Bojan Prasnikar

2005
23/7	Koper	a	1-1	Skerjanc
31/7	Bela Krajina Crnomelj	a	0-1	
7/8	Maribor	h	2-1	Medic (p), Skerjanc
13/8	Nafta Lendava	a	0-1	
24/8	Rudar Velenje	h	6-1	Zezelj 4, Arnaut, Kosmac
27/8	ND Gorica	a	0-2	
10/9	Drava	h	6-2	Arnaut 2, Ostojic, Zezelj, Cerne, Zatkovic
18/9	Domzale	a	0-3	
21/9	CMC Publikum Celje	h	1-0	Mlakar
25/9	Koper	h	2-0	Zezelj 2
2/10	Bela Krajina Crnomelj	h	2-1	Arnaut, Skerjanc
15/10	Maribor	a	0-2	
22/10	Nafta Lendava	h	2-0	Zatkovic, Ostojic
26/10	Rudar Velenje	a	4-0	Jankovic, Arnaut, Zezelj, Zatkovic
29/10	ND Gorica	h	2-2	Zezelj (p), Jankovic
5/11	Drava	a	1-4	Skerjanc
19/11	CMC Publikum Celje	a	0-2	
26/11	Koper	h	0-1	

2006
11/3	Domzale	h	2-2	Zezelj, Arnaut
18/3	Bela Krajina Crnomelj	a	1-0	Zezelj
25/3	Maribor	h	0-3	
29/3	Nafta Lendava	a	0-2	
1/4	Rudar Velenje	h	1-1	Ostojic
8/4	ND Gorica	a	0-2	
12/4	Drava	h	2-2	Jankovic, Zezelj

Slovenia

Date	Opponent	H/A	Score	Scorers
15/4	Domzale	a	0-2	
22/4	CMC Publikum Celje	h	2-4	Zatkovic, Mlakar
26/4	Koper	h	1-0	Kalin
29/4	Bela Krajina Crnomelj	h	2-2	Kalin, Mlakar
2/5	Maribor	a	0-2	
6/5	Nafta Lendava	h	0-0	
13/5	Rudar Velenje	a	1-1	Zezelj
17/5	ND Gorica	h	1-3	Ostojic
20/5	Drava	a	0-0	
27/5	Domzale	h	0-0	
3/6	CMC Publikum Celje	a	1-0	Zezelj

No	Name	Nat	Pos	Aps	(s)	Gls
28	Goran ARNAUT	SCG	M	26	(1)	6
30	Denis BALOH		G	3	(2)	
9	Andrej BASA		A	9	(7)	
29	Sasa BOZICIC		M	14	(2)	
8	Danijel CERNE		A	7	(9)	1
13	Bostjan COLJA		D	2	(1)	
21	Miroslav CVIJANOVIC		M	13	(3)	
3	Alen DZUZDANOVIC		A	22	(2)	
7	Sinisa JANKOVIC	SCG	M	27		3
25	Peter KALIN		M	11	(6)	2
24	Nace KOSMAC		M	5	(10)	1
17	Bostjan KREFT		D	17	(6)	
16	Igor KRSTIC		M	29	(1)	
20	Tim LO DUCA		M	1	(1)	
29	Rade MEDIC	SCG	M	6	(5)	1
2	Emir MEHANOVIC		D	2	(2)	
23	Matej MLAKAR		M	32		3
1	Igor NENEZIC		G	4		
4	Vladimir OSTOJIC		M	29	(1)	4
6	Andrej RASTOVAC		D	15	(1)	
22	Uros RUTAR		G	29		
20	Denis SELIMOVIC		M	9	(2)	
15	Davor SKERJANC		M	12	(20)	4
27	Luka SPETIC		M	2	(5)	
26	Jan VIDIC		M	11	(3)	
19	Mitja ZATKOVIC		A	33	(1)	4
11	Drazen ZEZELJ		A	26	(6)	14

CMC PUBLIKUM CELJE
Coach - Marko Pocrnjic; (28/8/05) Nikola Ilievski (MAC)

2005

Date	Opponent	H/A	Score	Scorers
24/7	Maribor	h	0-0	
30/7	Nafta Lendava	a	1-2	Vrsic
6/8	Rudar Velenje	h	2-1	Stajic, og (Rahmanovic)
14/8	ND Gorica	a	1-2	Gobec
20/8	Drava	h	2-0	og (Sterbal), Bersnjak
29/8	Domzale	a	0-5	
10/9	Bela Krajina Crnomelj	h	0-3	
17/9	Koper	h	3-3	Ibeji, Brulc, Kriznik
21/9	Primorje Ajdovscina	a	0-1	
24/9	Maribor	a	2-0	Pecnik, Stajic
1/10	Nafta Lendava	h	1-3	Robnik
15/10	Rudar Velenje	a	1-0	Rusic
22/10	ND Gorica	h	2-1	Stajic, Bersnjak
26/10	Drava	a	0-1	
29/10	Domzale	h	3-2	Brulc, Gobec, Ibeji
5/11	Bela Krajina Crnomelj	a	0-1	
19/11	Primorje Ajdovscina	h	2-0	Bersnjak, Robnik

2006

Date	Opponent	H/A	Score	Scorers
8/3	Maribor	h	1-0	Bersnjak (p)
11/3	Koper	a	0-2	
18/3	Nafta Lendava	a	0-0	
25/3	Rudar Velenje	h	4-2	Kriznik, Biscan, Gobec, Bakaric
29/3	ND Gorica	a	0-2	
1/4	Drava	h	3-1	Bersnjak, Kriznik, Stajic
8/4	Domzale	a	1-2	Rusic
12/4	Bela Krajina Crnomelj	h	2-0	Bersnjak, Rusic
15/4	Koper	h	0-2	
22/4	Primorje Ajdovscina	a	4-2	Bersnjak, Stajic, Rusic, Pecnik
26/4	Maribor	a	2-1	Rusic 2
29/4	Nafta Lendava	h	2-1	Brulc 2
2/5	Rudar Velenje	a	4-2	Biscan, Brezic, Stajic, Urbanc
6/5	ND Gorica	h	0-4	
13/5	Drava	a	1-4	Rusic
17/5	Domzale	h	1-3	Bakaric
20/5	Bela Krajina Crnomelj	a	1-3	Bersnjak
27/5	Koper	a	2-2	Bersnjak, Gobec
3/6	Primorje Ajdovscina	h	0-1	

No	Name	Nat	Pos	Aps	(s)	Gls
19	Sasa BAKARIC		A	2	(6)	2
20	Dominik BERSNJAK		M	32	(1)	9
20	Darijo BISCAN		A	3	(10)	2
30	Danijel BREZIC		M	31	(1)	1
25	Mitja BRULC		A	34	(1)	4
2	Primoz BRUMEN		D	1	(5)	
13	Marijan BUDIMIR	CRO	D	6	(1)	
33	Sebastjan CELOFIGA		G	3		
6	Samir DURO	BOS	M	4		
12	Gregor FINK		G	4	(1)	
18	Sebastjan GOBEC		D	32		4
17	Damir HADZIC		M	8	(4)	
23	Sunday Chibuke IBEJI	NGA	A	20	(4)	2
23	Dejan KELHAR		D	20	(3)	
17	Uros KORUN		M	2	(2)	
4	Marko KRIZNIK		D	29		3
1	Amel MUJCINOVIC		G	28		
9	Dejan NAPRUDNIK		A		(2)	
7	Andrej PECNIK		A	20	(10)	2
3	Antonio PRANJIC		M	4	(7)	
11	Dejan ROBNIK		A	7	(17)	2
8	Dejan RUSIC		A	21	(3)	7
28	Matej SNOFL		D	23	(6)	
27	Dusko STAJIC	SCG	M	23	(8)	6
5	Almir SULEJMANOVIC		D	4	(2)	
22	Jernej SUSNIK		G	1		
29	Jure TRAVNER		D	25		
27	Dejan URBANC		M	7	(10)	1
10	Dare VRSIC		A	2		1

RUDAR VELENJE
Coach - Drago Kostanjsek; (18/9/05) Borut Jarc; (26/11/05) Roman Frangez

2005

Date	Opponent	H/A	Score	Scorers
23/7	Drava	a	0-1	
31/7	Domzale	h	0-8	
6/8	CMC Publikum Celje	a	1-2	Dragic
13/8	Koper	h	2-1	Jesenicnik, Mernik
24/8	Primorje Ajdovscina	a	1-6	Jesenicnik
27/8	Maribor	h	0-1	
10/9	Nafta Lendava	a	0-5	
18/9	Bela Krajina Crnomelj	a	0-1	
21/9	ND Gorica	h	1-2	Ibrahimovic
24/9	Drava	h	0-0	
3/10	Domzale	a	1-4	Komljenovic
15/10	CMC Publikum Celje	h	0-1	
22/10	Koper	a	1-2	Dragic
26/10	Primorje Ajdovscina	h	0-4	
29/10	Maribor	a	1-1	Pavlovic (p)

Slovenia

Date	Opponent	H/A	Score	Scorers
5/11	Nafta Lendava	h	1-3	Halilovic
19/11	ND Gorica	a	0-0	
2006				
4/3	Drava	a	1-2	Grbic
11/3	Bela Krajina Crnomelj	h	0-0	
18/3	Domzale	h	2-0	Azizi, Hankic
25/3	CMC Publikum Celje	a	2-4	Pavlovic, Muharemovic
29/3	Koper	h	2-2	Pavlovic, Komar
1/4	Primorje Ajdovscina	a	1-1	Halilovic
8/4	Maribor	h	2-3	Muharemovic, Azizi
12/4	Nafta Lendava	a	1-2	Azizi
15/4	Bela Krajina Crnomelj	a	1-1	Komar
22/4	ND Gorica	h	0-3	
26/4	Drava	h	1-3	Azizi
29/4	Domzale	a	0-3	
2/5	CMC Publikum Celje	h	2-4	Mujakovic, Trifkovic
6/5	Koper	a	0-3	
13/5	Primorje Ajdovscina	h	1-1	Grbic
17/5	Maribor	a	0-1	
20/5	Nafta Lendava	h	1-2	Halilovic
27/5	Bela Krajina Crnomelj	h	2-2	Pavlovic 2
3/6	ND Gorica	a	0-4	

No	Name	Nat	Pos	Aps	(s)	Gls
7	Maksut AZIZI		A	18	(1)	4
6	Edvard BORSTNER		M	5	(3)	
1	Slobodan COSIC		G		(1)	
26	Rusmin DEDIC		D	15		
14	Goran DRAGIC		A	11	(7)	2
8	Robert FUNTEK		D		(3)	
21	Denis GRBIC		M	28	(5)	2
17	Baskim HAJDARI		M		(4)	
23	Denis HALILOVIC		M	18	(1)	3
4	Enver HANKIC		D	17	(2)	1
7	Mirnes IBRAHIMOVIC		D	7	(2)	1
1	Anel JAHIC		M	7	(4)	
2	Damjan JESENICNIK		D	13		2
22	Nemanja JOZIC		G	16		
5	Peter KLANCAR		D	16	(1)	
10	Matej KOLENC		M	7	(3)	
9	Slavko KOMAR	SCG	A	9	(8)	2
9	Dejan KOMLJENOVIC		A	9	(1)	1
24	Jovisa KRALJEVIC	SCG	D	30		
5	Peter MERNIK		D	10		1
2	Mirnes MESIC		D		(2)	
6	Elvis MUHAREMOVIC		M	11	(4)	2
10	Alem MUJAKOVIC		A	20	(2)	1
14	Nejc OMLADIC		M	11	(2)	
28	Zoran PAVLOVIC		M	27		5
23	Borut PUSNIK		D	9	(2)	
8	Almir RAHMANOVIC		M	13	(13)	
27	Alen Nikola RAJKOVIC		M		(1)	
11	Uros ROSER		A	14	(4)	
15	Ednan SOFTIC		M	16		
3	Janko SRIBAR		G	16		
20	Danijel STANKOVIC		A		(1)	
3	Damjan TRIFKOVIC		M	19		1
1	Dejan VERSOVNIK		G	4		

DOMESTIC CUP 2005/06

THIRD ROUND
(28/9/05)
ND Gorica 2, Primorje Ajdovscina 0
Bela Krajina Crnomelj 2, Koper 2 *(aet; 2-4 on pens)*
Rudar Velenje 1, Drava 1 *(aet; 5-4 on pens)*
CMC Publikum Celje 2, Brda 0
Tehnotim Pesnica 1, Maribor 8
Livar Ivancna Gorica 1, Nafta Lendava 0
Avtoplus Korte 1, Aluminij 0
(19/10/05)
Zagorje 0, Domzale 3

QUARTER-FINALS
(19/10/05)
Rudar Velenje 0, ND Gorica 1 *(Ranic 18)*
Maribor 1 *(Oslaj 18)*, Avtoplus Korte 0
CMC Publkum Celje 5 *(Bersnjak 18p, Robnik 42, Stajic 78, 85, 90)*, Livar Ivancna Gorica 1 *(Maric 48)*
(2/11/05)
Koper 2 *(Matic 60og, Kremenovic 82)*, Domzale 1 *(Rakovic 30)*

SEMI-FINALS
(19/4/06 & 9/5/06)
ND Gorica 0, Koper 2 *(Kremenovic 39, 49)*
Koper 0, ND Gorica 1 *(Demirovic 76)*
(Koper 2-1)

CMC Publikum Celje 1 *(Rusic 24)*, Maribor 0
Maribor 1 *(Pekic 8)*, CMC Publikum Celje 2 *(Rusic 52, 81)*
(CMC Publikum Celje 3-1)

FINAL
(24/5/06)
Petrol Arena, Celje
KOPER 1 *(Rudonja 4)*
CMC PUBLIKUM CELJE 1 *(Rusic 75)*
(aet; 5-3 on pens)
Referee - Ceferin
KOPER – Handanovic, Radulovic *(Secic 82)*, Knezovic, Lazic *(Lovrecic 115)*, Pahor, Persic, Karic, Kremenovic *(Gregoric 46)*, Rudonja, Drobne, Jakomin.
CMC PUBLIKUM CELJE– Mujcinovic *(Celofiga 5)*, Kriznik, Rusic, Bersnjak *(Urbanc 57)*, Kelhar, Gobec, Ibeji *(Robnik 46)*, Brulc, Stajic, Travner, Brezic.
Sent off: Kelhar *(117)*

SECOND LEVEL FINAL TABLE 2005/06

		Pld	W	D	L	F	A	Pts
1	Factor Ljubljana	27	15	5	7	37	27	50
2	Dravinja Duol	27	14	7	6	46	24	49
3	Supernova Triglav	27	13	9	5	36	18	48
4	Aluminij	27	12	7	8	27	24	43
5	Krsko	27	10	10	7	34	36	40
6	Tinex Sencur	27	8	9	10	34	43	33
7	Livar Ivancna Gorica	27	7	6	14	31	38	27
8	Zagorje	27	5	11	11	22	34	26
9	Svoboda Ljubljana	27	7	4	16	26	33	25
10	Koroska Dravograd	27	6	8	13	26	52	23

PROMOTION/RELEGATION PLAY-OFFS
Dravinja Duol 2, Bela Krajina Crnomelj 2
Bela Krajina Crnomelj 0, Dravinja Duol 0
(2-2; Bela Krajina Crnomelj on away goals)

Spain

Catalan joy, Spanish despair

It has long been a recurring theme. While the clubs of La Liga conquer Europe, the Spanish national team flatters to deceive. Some things, it seems, are destined never to change.

At the end of a season in which Barcelona returned to the summit of European club football with victory in the Champions League, and Sevilla followed proudly in their slipstream to capture the UEFA Cup, there was quiet confidence in Spain's ability to shake up the established order of international football and win the World Cup.

Unfortunately, Luis Aragonés's team of many talents did not even come close. The habitual quarter-finalists failed to get past the first knockout round, beaten in Hanover as much by their own hang-ups and the weight of history as by a revitalised French side.

The nearly men became also-rans, yet it could, should, have been so different. Spain began the tournament brilliantly, grilling Ukraine in the heat of Leipzig with a comprehensive 4-0 win. It was the most impressive opening performance from any of the 32 teams and a firm indication that two years without defeat during Aragonés's tenure – a run of 22 games – had instilled real confidence and vibrancy into Spain's game. No matter that they had required a play-off victory over Slovakia to reach their eighth successive World Cup finals. With pace, purpose, balance and a cluster of gifted players in their early-to-mid 20s (Iker Casillas, Fernando Torres, Xabi Alonso, David Villa etc), there was good reason to believe that Spain might be genuine contenders in Germany.

Flying colours

Their second game, against Tunisia in Stuttgart, revealed other qualities. Patience and perseverance were the watchwords as Spain struggled to break down a tightly packed Tunisian defence. This was a big test for Aragonés and his players, but they came through it with flying colours, eventually winning 3-1. With qualification confirmed, the coach decided to rest his entire first-choice team for the final group game against Saudi Arabia. Spain won the game 1-0 to take maximum points from their group for the second successive World Cup.

Logically, changing the team was the right thing to do. If Spain were to win the World Cup, there would be four more matches and they needed to keep their best players fresh. Unfortunately, when the regulars returned against France the momentum had gone. Conscious perhaps that they had never beaten Les Bleus in a competitive match, the Spanish players were suddenly besieged by self-doubt and anxiety. They tried to force the issue rather than allowing their natural inclinations to flow. It was a different Spain from earlier in the tournament and France took advantage, their greater experience and tactical know-how sending Spain spinning out of the tournament with their first defeat in two years.

At once, a good tournament had become a bad one. There was deep despondency as Spain became one of only two group seeds to depart before the quarter-finals. Nevertheless, after the dust had settled, it was obvious to even the most disgruntled supporter that Spain had a team young enough and talented enough to flourish in the future. In teenager Cesc Fábregas, Spain have a wonderful talent who could go on to star in another three World Cups, while Fernando Torres demonstrated enough quality in Germany to suggest that he will become one of the world's great strikers over the next decade.

At 68 years of age Aragonés may be getting on a bit, but his team are maturing nicely. Given Spain's propensity to blow a fuse in major tournaments, it

Spain

might be folly to predict that they will be up there among the favourites for Euro 2008, but assuming they can get through a qualifying section that involves awkward trips to Scandinavia to play Sweden and Denmark (two teams that outlasted them at the Euro 2004 finals), they have the players to make a deep impact in Austria and Switzerland.

"Catalonia is not Spain" is a favourite slogan at Camp Nou, but the whole nation stood to applaud Frank Rijkaard's ebullient Barcelona side during a season in which they conquered not only Spain but the whole of Europe. Even a few diehards at the Estádio Bernabéu were moved to put their hands together for the enemy when a Ronaldinho-inspired Barça ripped Real Madrid to shreds with a 3-0 victory in mid-November. The visitors had 23 shots in that game to the home side's three. When Real visited Camp Nou for the return fixture in April, they managed a 1-1 draw after battling for two thirds of the game with ten men, but again the statistics spoke of total domination for the Catalans. Shots on target: Barcelona 16, Real Madrid one.

Winning machine

Having finally won La Liga in 2004/05 after a six-year absence, Barça had no intention of relaxing their grip. Virtually unchanged from the previous season, with only Dutch midfielder Mark van Bommel added, they began the season edgily, but once they hit their stride, in mid-autumn, they became a ruthless winning machine. A 3-0 victory at home to early-season upstarts Osasuna began an extraordinary sequence of victories in all competitions that lasted all the way through to the end of January, incorporating 18 matches. Fourteen of those were in the league – a sequence in which Barça scored 38 goals (including at least two in every game) and conceded just six (never more than one at a time). The highlight, clearly, was the massacre of Real in Madrid, where Ronaldinho's two majestic goals confirmed the Brazilian as the world's number one footballer and moved Barça into first place in the table – a position from which they would not be dislodged.

By the time bogey side Atlético Madrid, and bogeyman Fernando Torres (with his sixth and seventh goals against the Catalans), brought a halt to Barcelona's winning run – one short of Real Madrid's record sequence in 1960/61 – the title race was all but over. Barcelona were so far out of reach at the top that even a second defeat a week later at Valencia

raised only the faintest of alarm bells. The team soon returned to winning ways, and the 1-1 draw at home to Real, though displeasing per se, represented a positive outcome as it kept Rijkaard's men 11 points out in front with seven games remaining. All was eventually decided on the evening of Wednesday, May 3 when Barcelona discovered at half-time during their match at Celta Vigo (which they won 1-0) that Valencia had lost at Mallorca. It wasn't the perfect climax, but the outcome had never been in any doubt.

That early conquest of La Liga allowed Barcelona to give their full attention to the final of the Champions League a fortnight later. The club's obsession with recapturing the trophy they had won only once previously – in 1992 – had so often proved counter-productive. But in 2005/06 the talent in the team was matched by a ferocious determination to succeed. That was plain for all to see against Arsenal in Paris, when, with Ronaldinho misfiring and the fates seemingly conspiring against them, they kept going till the end and were rewarded with two goals in four

NATIONAL TEAM RESULTS 2005/06

Date	Opponent	H/A	Venue	Score	Scorers
17/8/05	Uruguay	H	Gijón	2-0	García (25og), Vicente (37p)
3/9/05	Canada	H	Santander	2-1	Tamudo (7), Morientes (69)
7/9/05	Serbia & Montenegro (WCQ)	H	Madrid	1-1	Raúl (18)
8/10/05	Belgium (WCQ)	A	Brussels	2-0	Fernando Torres (56, 59)
12/10/05	San Marino (WCQ)	A	Serravalle	6-0	Antonio López (1), Fernando Torres (10, 78p, 89), Sergio Ramos (30, 38)
12/11/05	Slovakia (WCQ)	H	Madrid	5-1	Luis García (8, 16, 72), Fernando Torres (65p), Morientes (78)
16/11/05	Slovakia (WCQ)	A	Bratislava	1-1	David Villa (71)
1/3/06	Ivory Coast	H	Valladolid	3-2	David Villa (23), Reyes (72), Juanito (85)
27/5/06	Russia	H	Albacete	0-0	
3/6/06	Egypt	H	Elche	2-0	Raúl (14), Reyes (57)
7/6/06	Croatia	N	Geneva	2-1	Pernía (62), Fernando Torres (90)
14/6/06	Ukraine (WCF)	N	Leipzig	4-0	Xabi Alonso (13), David Villa (17, 48p), Fernando Torres (81)
19/6/06	Tunisia (WCF)	N	Stuttgart	3-1	Raúl (72), Fernando Torres (76, 90p)
23/6/06	Saudi Arabia (WCF)	N	Kaiserslautern	1-0	Juanito (36)
27/6/06	France (WCF)	N	Hanover	1-3	David Villa (28p)

Spain

minutes to turn the game and carry them those last few steps to the Holy Grail.

Worthy winners

Arsenal were sore losers, but nobody could seriously question Barcelona's right to the European throne. They romped through their group, giving one of the all-time great Champions League performances against Panathinaikos (5-0 at Camp Nou). Then they got their revenge on 2004/05 conquerors Chelsea, outclassing the English champions in both matches. In the quarter-finals Barça played some stunning football against Benfica, especially in Lisbon, but an inability to convert their chances led to a stressful qualification. There was a goal shortage, too, against Milan in the semis, but Ludovic Giuly got the only one of the tie, in the San Siro, and, as against Chelsea, Barcelona were the better of the two teams. Like Arsenal, they went to Paris unbeaten.

There was so much to admire about Rijkaard's all-conquering team. The calm, pleasant, unflustered manner of the coach, for one thing. Barça were a machine in which all the moving parts were beautifully synchronised. Ronaldinho, evidently, was the star attraction. He scored 17 goals in La Liga and another seven in the Champions League, and he pleased the crowds week in, week out with his wonderful array of flicks and tricks.

The emergence of Argentine whizzkid Lionel Messi gave Barça an even greater aesthetic appeal. For once the 'new Maradona' tag did not seem misplaced. It was a shame that the outrageously gifted teenager suffered a thigh injury that cut short his season by three months, because he was just coming into some serious form at the time (notably against Chelsea at Stamford Bridge). Giuly wasn't a bad replacement, though. The Frenchman assumed Messi's right-wing duties in Barça's attacking trident, with Ronaldinho on the left and the prolific Eto'o in the centre. The Cameroonian was miffed to miss out on the Pichichi award the previous season, but he made amends, clinching first place in La Liga's top-scorer listings on the final day with his 26th goal of the season.

Once again Eto'o was the only player in the team given licence to roam. Everyone else had a set position and function. There was understandable concern that the whole structure might fall apart when chief midfield pivot Xavi suffered serious knee ligament damage in November. But another young Catalan, Andrés Iniesta, was handed the chance and he seized it brilliantly. Two other local youth products, skipper Carles Puyol and goalkeeper Víctor Valdés, were again highly influential, while Mexican international Rafael Márquez played better than ever. Restored to central defence from midfield, he was the perfect partner for Puyol, his positional sense and accuracy of distribution complementing the skipper's unflagging tenacity and speed. If Barça had a weak link, it was at full-back. Neither Juliano Belletti on the right – despite his Champions League winner – nor Giovanni van Bronckhorst on the left did well enough defensively to hold down a regular place, and the man who generally stood in for both, Oleguer, was no great shakes either. Two players who did perform consistently well, however, were Deco, a perfect amalgam of skill and industry in midfield, and Henrik Larsson, who, though injured and benched for much of the season, still managed ten goals in La Liga and, also, more importantly, turned the Champions League final with his two immaculate assists. As for new boy Van Bommel, the end-of-term report read: satisfactory, could do better.

Real pain

Where there is joy for Barcelona, there is inevitably pain for Real Madrid. The arrogant aristocrats from the capital had another disastrous season on all fronts. Second place in La Liga, secured on the final day despite defeat at Sevilla, was a consolation of sorts. But the so-called galácticos were not on the same planet as Barça. They never seriously threatened to win La Liga, and for the second season

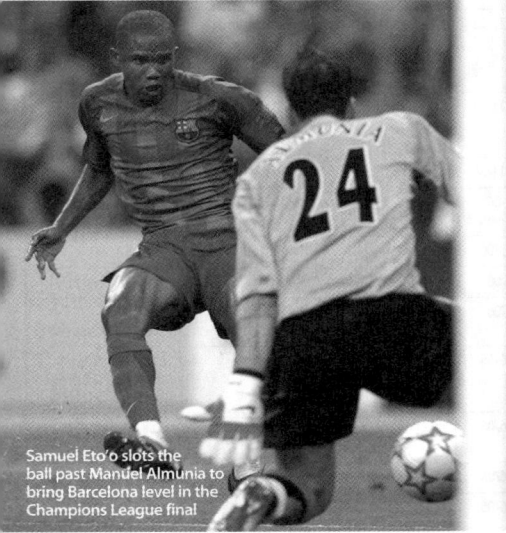

Samuel Eto'o slots the ball past Manuel Almunia to bring Barcelona level in the Champions League final

Spain

NATIONAL TEAM APPEARANCES 2005/06

Coach – Luis ARAGONÉS

Player	DOB	Club	Uru	Can	SCG	BEL	SMR	SVK	SVK	Civ	Rus	Egy	Cro	UKR	TUN	SAU	FRA	Caps	Goals
José Manuel REINA	31/8/82	Liverpool (ENG)	G	G									G46					3	-
MÍCHEL SALGADO	22/10/75	Real Madrid	D59		D	D		D	D	s46			D46			D		51	-
Carlos MARCHENA	31/7/79	Valencia CF	D		D	D											D	28	1
Carles PUYOL	13/4/78	FC Barcelona	D		D	D		D	D	D46	D	D	D	D	D		D	50	1
Asier DEL HORNO	18/1/81	Chelsea (ENG)	D71		D			D										10	2
JOAQUÍN Sánchez	21/7/81	Real Betis	M59	s55	M65	M51				s46	s72		M73		s56	A	s54	41	4
XAVI Hernández	25/1/80	FC Barcelona	M	s74	M	M		M74		s46	s46	M	M	M	s66	M72		40	1
XABIer ALONSO	25/11/81	Liverpool (ENG)	M46	s46	M			s64	M	M57	s46	s46	M	M55	M		M	29	1
VICENTE Rodríguez	16/7/81	Valencia CF	M	s67	M75	M51	s68	s54	M									38	3
RAÚL González	27/6/77	Real Madrid	A68	s55	A	A	M73	A	A65		s46	A62	A46	s55	s46	A46	M54	99	44
Fernando MORIENTES	5/4/76	Liverpool (ENG)	A46	s55				s75	s65	s67								43	26
SERGIO González	10/11/76	RC Deportivo	s46															11	-
FERNANDO TORRES	20/3/84	Atlético Madrid	s46	A55	A53	A70	A	A	A61	A68	A	A	s46	A	A	s69	A	34	13
SERGIO RAMOS	30/3/86	Sevilla FC / Real Madrid	s59	D		D		s74	D	D	D		s46	D	D		D	14	2
LUIS GARCÍA	24/6/78	Liverpool (ENG)	s59	M67	s65		M75			A46	A46	s62	s46	M77	M46		s54	13	3
Alberto LUQUE	11/3/78	RC Deportivo / Newcastle United ENG)	s68	M55	s75													17	2
ANTONIO LÓPEZ	13/9/81	Atlético Madrid	s71	D		D	D		D	D	D72	D				D		11	1
PABLO Ibáñez	3/8/81	Atlético Madrid		D			D	D	D	D79	D	D85	D	D			D	14	-
JUANITO Gutiérrez	23/7/76	Real Betis		D			D			s79		s85				D		16	2
Pablo ORBAIZ	6/2/79	Athletic Bilbao		M46														4	-
Iván DE LA PEÑA	6/5/76	RCD Espanyol		M74			M											5	-
Raúl TAMUDO	19/10/77	RCD Espanyol		A55	s53													9	4
Iker CASILLAS	20/5/81	Real Madrid			G	G	G	G	G	G	G	G		G	G		G	61	-
David ALBELDA	1/9/77	Valencia CF				M	M	M64		M67	M46	M46		s55		M		35	-
DAVID VILLA	3/12/81	Valencia CF			s51	A58		s61	A	A61	A46	A62	A55	A56	s46	A54		12	5
José Antonio REYES	1/9/83	Arsenal (ENG)			s51	M68	M54		s68	s61	s46	M46			A69			20	4
Rubén BARAJA	11/7/75	Valencia CF			s70	s58	M											43	7
Miguel A Ferrer "MISTA"	12/11/78	Valencia CF				s73												2	-
Francesc FÁBREGAS	4/5/87	Arsenal (ENG)								M	M46	M68	s73	s77	s46	M66	M	8	-
Marcos SENNA	17/7/76	Villarreal CF								s57	M46	M46		M	M46		s72	6	-
Andrés INIESTA	11/5/84	FC Barcelona								s46	s68	s62			M			4	-
Mariano PERNÍA	4/5/77	Getafe CF											D	D	D		D	4	1
Santiago CAÑIZARES	18/12/69	Valencia CF											s46			G		46	-

Spain

running they were dumped out of the Champions League at the last-16 stage, outplayed, outfought and outthought by the team that would eventually lose the final to Barcelona - Arsenal.

It was midway through that fateful European tie, after an embarrasing first-leg defeat at the Bernabéu, that club president Florentino Pérez – the high priest of the galácticos culture – decided that enough was enough and resigned. The realisation that Real would go three years without silverware for the first time in over half a century persuaded him to fall on his sword and let someone else have a go. In charge since August 2000, when he defeated Lorenzo Sanz in the presidential election, Pérez turned Real into a money-making merchandising machine with his insatiable desire to bring all of the world's glitziest names to the Bernabéu, but although there was some early success – notably Champions League victory in 2002 – the second half of Pérez's reign was characterised by grotesque decadence and, ultimately, massive underachievement.

The 2005/06 season was just like the two before – all over the place. Real Madrid needed firm leadership and direction. A touch of humility wouldn't have come amiss, either. But instead they just blundered on in the hope that suddenly everything would click into place. There were more big purchases, including the latest galáctico, Robinho, and Sevilla duo Júlio Baptista and Sergio Ramos. In the winter they drafted in youngsters Cicinho and Antonio Cassano. But with the old guard of Ronaldo, Roberto Carlos and Zidane Zidane failing to string two decent performances together, the results just wouldn't come.

Brazilian coach Vanderlei Luxemburgo was dismissed in early December after an abject performance at home to Getafe and replaced by B team coach Juan Ramón López Caro. The new man did reasonably well, but only feats of superhuman endeavour were ever going to keep him in the job beyond the end of the season. In the summer Real gained a new president, Ramón Calderón, and his first act was to re-install 1996/97 championship-winning coach Fabio Capello. With centre-back extraordinaire Fabio Cannavaro and midfield enforcer Émerson having also accompanied the Italian from Juventus, it looks as if there will at last be some substance to go with the style at the Bernabéu.

While Real's 2005/06 Champions League campaign ended early, a couple of La Liga's lesser lights strode to the fore in Europe.

Villarreal, playing in the premier European competition for the first time, lasted all the way through to the semi-finals. It was deeply ironic that their best player, midfield strategist Juan Román Riquelme, should be the fall guy for their failure to reach the final when he missed a late penalty against Arsenal at El Madrigal. Manuel Pellegrini's side paid for their European exertions, however, and could finish only seventh at home, which meant a fall from grace into the InterToto Cup.

Sevilla triumph

Sevilla went all the way in their European journey, becoming only the third Spanish club (after Real Madrid and Valencia) to have their name engraved on the UEFA Cup. New coach Juande Ramos performed wonders to lead the Andalusians to their first trophy in 58 years, and there could hardly have been a more enjoyable climax to their journey than when they thrashed Middlesbrough 4-0 in the final.

Sevilla also performed well in La Liga, only missing out on a Champions League berth when Osasuna overcame Valencia 2-1 in their final match. In contrast to Sevilla, Osasuna's UEFA Cup run had ended in the very first round, but they consolidated their good start in La Liga and boasted one of the revelations of the season in young midfield schemer Raúl García.

Valencia also returned to the Champions League (qualifiers) after a season without European football, finishing third in La Liga. A draw at Osasuna would have put them second at the expense of Real Madrid (simultaneously beaten 4-3 at Sevilla), but it was generally a rewarding first season for coach Quique Sánchez. Although new signings Patrick Kluivert and Edú were duds, ex-Zaragoza striker David Villa had a brilliant debut campaign at the Mestalla, scoring 25 goals – just one shy of Eto'o's Pichichi-winning haul.

Espanyol ensured further celebration in Catalonia by winning the Copa del Rey – they overcame Cup specialists and Barcelona/Real Madrid conquerors Real Zaragoza 4-1 in an entertaining final – and then saving themselves from relegation on the final day of the season. A last-minute goal from midfielder Ferran Corominas (who was also on target in the Cup final) gave Espanyol a 1-0 win over Real Sociedad to send Alavés down with Cádiz and Málaga. There was a Catalan club among the promoted trio, too, as Gimnàstic of Tarragona ascended alongside Recreativo of Huelva and Levante of Valencia, the latter returning to the Primera División after just a year away.

Spain

EUROPEAN CUPS 2005/06
UEFA CHAMPIONS LEAGUE

FC BARCELONA
1st round Group C
Match 1 SV WERDER BREMEN (GER)
A **2-0** *Deco (13), Ronaldinho (77p)*
Víctor Valdés, Belletti (Edmílson 46), Oleguer, Puyol, Van Bronckhorst, Xavi (Van Bommel 79), Márquez, Deco, Giuly (Messi 66), Ronaldinho, Eto'o.

Match 2 UDINESE (ITA)
H **4-1** *Ronaldinho (13, 32, 90p), Deco (41)*
Víctor Valdés, Belletti, Puyol, Oleguer, Van Bronckhorst, Xavi, Van Bommel (Iniesta 62), Deco, Messi (Ezquerro 70), Eto'o (Larsson 81), Ronaldinho.

Match 3 PANATHINAIKOS (GRE)
A **0-0**
Víctor Valdés, Belletti, Puyol, Márquez, Van Bronckhorst, Xavi (Iniesta 76), Van Bommel (Motta 56), Deco, Larsson (Messi 67), Ronaldinho, Eto'o.

Match 4 PANATHINAIKOS
H **5-0** *Van Bommel (1), Eto'o (14, 40, 65), Messi (34)*
Víctor Valdés, Oleguer, Puyol, Edmílson, Van Bronckhorst, Xavi (Ezquerro 69), Van Bommel (Gabri 60), Iniesta (Motta 50), Messi, Ronaldinho, Eto'o.

Match 5 SV WERDER BREMEN
H **3-1** *Gabri (14), Ronaldinho (26), Larsson (71)*
Víctor Valdés, Oleguer, Puyol, Márquez (Belletti 74), Van Bronckhorst, Motta, Gabri (Iniesta 77), Deco, Giuly (Ezquerro 64), Ronaldinho, Larsson.

Match 6 UDINESE
A **2-0** *Ezquerro (86), Iniesta (90)*
Jorquera, Belletti, Oleguer, Puyol, Van Bronckhorst, Gabri (Iniesta 75), Edmílson, Deco, Giuly, Larsson, Ezquerro.

2nd round CHELSEA (ENG)
A **2-1** *Terry (71og), Eto'o (80)*
Víctor Valdés, Oleguer, Puyol, Márquez, Van Bronckhorst (Sylvinho 69), Edmílson, Deco (Iniesta 85), Motta (Larsson 66), Messi, Ronaldinho, Eto'o.
H **1-1** *Ronaldinho (79)*
Víctor Valdés, Oleguer, Puyol, Márquez, Van Bronckhorst, Edmílson, Motta, Deco, Messi (Larsson 24), Ronaldinho, Eto'o.

Quarter-final SL BENFICA (POR)
A **0-0**
Víctor Valdés, Belletti, Oleguer, Motta, Puyol, Márquez, Van Bronckhorst, Deco (Gabri 76), Iniesta, Larsson (Giuly 76), Ronaldinho, Eto'o.
H **2-0** *Ronaldinho (19), Eto'o (88)*
Víctor Valdés, Belletti, Oleguer, Puyol, Van Bronckhorst, Iniesta, Van Bommel (Edmílson 84), Deco, Larsson (Giuly 85), Ronaldinho, Eto'o.

Semi-final MILAN (ITA)
A **1-0** *Giuly (58)*
Víctor Valdés, Oleguer (Motta 77), Puyol, Márquez, Van Bronckhorst, Edmílson, Van Bommel, Iniesta, Giuly (Belletti 70), Ronaldinho (Maxi López 89), Eto'o.
H **0-0**
Víctor Valdés, Belletti, Puyol, Márquez, Van Bronckhorst, Edmílson, Iniesta, Deco, Giuly (Larsson 68), Ronaldinho, Eto'o (Van Bommel 88).

Final ARSENAL (ENG)
Saint-Denis
2-1 *Eto'o (77), Belletti (81)*
Víctor Valdés, Oleguer (Belletti 71), Puyol, Márquez, Van Bronckhorst, Edmílson (Iniesta 46), Deco, Van Bommel (Larsson 61), Giuly, Ronaldinho, Eto'o.

REAL MADRID
1st round Group F
Match 1 OLYMPIQUE LYONNAIS (FRA)
A **0-3**
Casillas, Míchel Salgado, Helguera, Sergio Ramos, Roberto Carlos, Beckham, Gravesen (Guti 61), Pablo García, Júlio Baptista, Raúl, Robinho.

Match 2 OLYMPIAKOS (GRE)
H **2-1** *Raúl (9), Soldado (86)*
Casillas, Míchel Salgado (Diogo 80), Sergio Ramos, Helguera, Roberto Carlos, Beckham, Pablo García (Gravesen 84), Júlio Baptista (Soldado 78), Guti, Robinho, Raúl.

Match 3 ROSENBORG BK (NOR)
H **4-1** *Woodgate (48), Raúl (52), Helguera (68), Beckham (82)*
Casillas, Diogo, Woodgate (Mejía 83), Helguera, Roberto Carlos, Beckham, Pablo García, Zidane (Gravesen 70), Robinho, Júlio Baptista (Guti 46), Raúl.

Match 4 ROSENBORG BK
A **2-0** *Dorsin (26og), Guti (41)*
Casillas, Míchel Salgado (Mejía 46), Woodgate, Pavón, Roberto Carlos, Beckham (De la Red 90), Diogo, Sergio Ramos, Guti (Bravo 84), Robinho, Raúl.

Match 5 OLYMPIQUE LYONNAIS
H **1-1** *Guti (41)*
Casillas, Diogo, Helguera, Pavón, Roberto Carlos, Sergio Ramos, Pablo García, Beckham (Míchel Salgado 80), Zidane (Júlio Baptista 75), Guti, Robinho.

Match 6 OLYMPIAKOS
A **1-2** *Sergio Ramos (7)*
López, Diogo, Pavón, Sergio Ramos, Raúl Bravo, De la Red (Javi García 80), Gravesen, Balboa (Martín 57), Júlio Baptista, Robinho (Jurado 80), Soldado.

2nd round ARSENAL (ENG)
H **0-1**
Casillas, Cicinho, Sergio Ramos, Woodgate (Mejía 9), Roberto Carlos, Beckham, Gravesen (Júlio Baptista 75), Guti, Zidane, Robinho (Raúl 62), Ronaldo.
A **0-0**
Casillas, Míchel Salgado (Robinho 83), Sergio Ramos, Raúl Bravo, Roberto Carlos, Gravesen (Júlio Baptista 67'), Guti, Zidane, Beckham, Raúl (Cassano 72), Ronaldo.

VILLARREAL CF
3rd qualifying round EVERTON (ENG)
A **2-1** *Figueroa (27), Josico (45)*
Barbosa, Javi Venta, Quique Álvarez, Gonzalo Rodríguez, Arruabarrena, Senna, Josico, Riquelme, Sorín (Peña 89), Forlán (Guayre 85), Figueroa (Tacchinardi 64).
H **2-1** *Sorín (21), Forlán (90)*
Barbosa, Javi Venta (Kromkamp 14), Gonzalo Rodríguez, Quique Álvarez, Arruabarrena, Josico, Senna, Sorín, Riquelme, Figueroa (Tacchinardi 81), Forlán.

1st round Group D
Match 1 MANCHESTER UNITED (ENG)
H **0-0**
Viera, Kromkamp, Quique Álvarez, Gonzalo Rodríguez, Arruabarrena, Senna, Josico (Tacchinardi 46), Sorín, Font (Roger 70), Guayre (Figueroa 65), Forlán.

Match 2 LILLE OSC (FRA)
A **0-0**

Spain

Viera, Kromkamp, Quique Álvarez (Gonzalo Rodríguez 57), Peña, Arruabarrena, Riquelme, Tacchinardi, Josico, Sorín (Senna 46), Figueroa, Forlán (Guayre 85).

Match 3 SL BENFICA (POR)
H 1-1 *Riquelme (73p)*
Viera, Kromkamp, Gonzalo Rodríguez, Arzo, Arruabarrena (Josico 46), Santi Cazorla, Tacchinardi (Roger 84), Sorín, Riquelme, José Mari (Figueroa 79), Forlán.

Match 4 SL BENFICA
A 1-0 *Senna (82)*
Barbosa, Javi Venta, Gonzalo Rodríguez, Quique Álvarez, Arruabarrena, Josico, Senna (Peña 90), Sorín, Riquelme, José Mari (Guayre 69), Forlán (Figueroa 51).

Match 5 MANCHESTER UNITED
A 0-0
Barbosa, Javi Venta, Gonzalo Rodríguez, Peña, Arruabarrena, Roger (Font 65), Tacchinardi, Senna (Josico 77), Sorín, José Mari, Figueroa (Xisco 86).

Match 6 LILLE OSC
H 1-0 *Guayre (67)*
Viera, Kromkamp, Gonzalo Rodríguez, Peña, Arruabarrena, Sorín (Font 36), Senna, Josico, Riquelme, José Mari (Guayre 59), Forlán (Roger 83).

2nd round RANGERS (SCO)
A 2-2 *Riquelme (7p), Forlán (34)*
Viera, Javi Venta, Gonzalo Rodríguez, Peña, Arruabarrena (Sorín 60), Josico, Tacchinardi, Senna, Riquelme (Arzo 89), José Mari (Roger 83), Forlán.
H 1-1 *Arruabarrena (49)*
Viera, Javi Venta (Font 46), Gonzalo Rodríguez, Peña, Arruabarrena, Senna, Josico, Tacchinardi, Riquelme (Calleja 86), Forlán, José Mari (Franco 46).

Quarter-final INTERNAZIONALE (ITA)
A 1-2 *Forlán (1)*
Viera, Javi Venta, Gonzalo Rodríguez, Peña, Sorín, Senna, Arzo (Quique Álvarez 60), Riquelme, Calleja (Santi Cazorla 87), José Mari (Franco 76), Forlán.
H 1-0 *Arruabarrena (56)*
Viera, Javi Venta, Quique Álvarez, Peña, Arruabarrena, Tacchinardi, Senna, Sorín (Josico 77), Riquelme, José Mari (Franco 77), Forlán (Calleja 89).

Semi-final ARSENAL (ENG)
A 0-1
Barbosa, Javi Venta, Quique Álvarez, Arzo, Arruabarrena, Senna, Tacchinardi, Sorín (Josico 72), Riquelme, Forlán (Calleja 90), José Mari (Franco 54).
H 0-0
Barbosa, Javi Venta, Peña, Quique Álvarez, Arruabarrena (Roger 81), Josico (José Mari 63), Senna, Riquelme, Sorín, Franco, Forlán.

REAL BETIS

3rd qualifying round AS MONACO FC (FRA)
H 1-0 *Edú (90)*
Doblas, Melli, Juanito, Rivas, Luis Fernández, Joaquín, Marcos Assunção (Arzu 77), Rivera, Fernando (Denilson 55), Edú, Dani (Xisco 64).
A 2-2 *Ricardo Oliveira (17, 75)*
Doblas, Melli, Juanito, Rivas, Luis Fernández, Marcos Assunção, Joaquín (Varela 56), Rivera (Miguel Ángel 76), Xisco (Nano 56), Edú, Ricardo Oliveira.

1st round Group G
Match 1 LIVERPOOL (ENG)
H 1-2 *Arzu (51)*
Doblas, Melli, Juanito (Xisco 46), Rivas, Óscar López, Joaquín, Arzu (Capi 71), Marcos Assunção, Valera, Fernando (Dani 35), Ricardo Oliveira.

Match 2 RSC ANDERLECHT (BEL)
A 1-0 *Ricardo Oliveira (69)*
Doblas, Melli, Rivas (Nano 73), Juanito, Óscar López, Varela, Miguel Ángel, Rivera, Xisco (Fernando 76), Joaquín (Marcos Assunção 90), Ricardo Oliveira.

Match 3 CHELSEA (ENG)
A 0-4
Doblas, Melli, Juanito, Rivas, Óscar López (Xisco 46), Miguel Ángel (Marcos Assunção 56), Rivera, Varela, Joaquín, Edú, Ricardo Oliveira.

Match 4 CHELSEA
H 1-0 *Dani (28)*
Contreras, Varela, Juanito, Nano (Castellini 20), Melli, Joaquín, Rivera, Arzu, Edú, Capi (Fernando 83), Ricardo Oliveira (Dani 24).

Match 5 LIVERPOOL
A 0-0
Doblas, Melli, Juanito, Rivas, Óscar López, Joaquín, Marcos Assunção (Capi 70), Rivera, Arzu, Xisco, Fernando (Israel 78).

Match 6 RSC ANDERLECHT
H 0-1
Doblas, López, Lembo, Rivas, Castellini, Rivera, Juande (Marcos Assunção 69), Israel (Joaquín 46), Capi, Juanlu (Xisco 46), Fernando.

UEFA CUP

CA OSASUNA
1st round STADE RENNAIS FC (FRA)
A 1-3 *Milosevic (50)*
Ricardo, Izquierdo, Cruchaga, Cuéllar, Clavero, Valdo, Puñal, Raúl García (Sosa 78), Delporte (Moha 68), Romeo (Webo 46), Milosevic.
H 0-0
Ricardo, Javier Flaño, Cruchaga (Romeo 78), Cuéllar, Corrales, David López, Sosa (Valdo 46), Raúl García, Delporte (Moha 69), Webo, Milosevic.

RCD ESPANYOL
1st round FK TEPLICE (CZE)
A 1-1 *Luis García (84)*
Iraizoz, Zabaleta (Armando Sá 64), Jarque, Lopo, David García, Domi, Edú Costa, Fredson, Juanfran (De la Peña 61), Corominas (Soriano 80), Luis García.
H 2-0 *Fredson (81), Jofre (89)*
Iraizoz, Zabaleta, Lopo, Jarque, Armando Sá, Fredson, Edú Costa, Juanfran (Hurtado 87) De la Peña (Jofre 90) Riera (Ito 67), Luis García.

2nd round Group B
Match 1 LOKOMOTIV MOSKVA (RUS)
A 1-0 *Tamudo (53)*
Iraizoz, David García (Hurtado 74), Lopo, Pochettino, Jarque, Zabaleta, Ito, De la Peña, Fredson (Edú Costa 66), Luis García (Corominas 70'), Tamudo.

Match 2 PALERMO (ITA)
H 1-0 *Kami (90)*
Iraizoz, Zabaleta, Hurtado, Jarque, David García, Edú Costa, De la Peña, Armando Sá (Fredson 76), Jofre (Corominas 60), Luis García, Soriano (Tamudo 60).

Match 3 BRØNDBY IF (DEN)
A 1-1 *Tamudo (42)*
Kameni, Zabaleta, Lopo, Jarque, Domi, Hurtado, Fredson, Luis García (Ito 72), De la Peña (Jofre 83), Riera (Corominas 64), Tamudo.

Match 4 MACCABI PETACH TIKVA (ISR)
H 1-0 *Pochettino (83)*
Iraizoz, Jarque, Lopo, Pochettino, David García, Armando Sá (De la Peña 67), Ito,

Spain

Hurtado, Riera (Tamudo 67), Luis García (Corominas 57), Soriano.

3rd round FC SCHALKE 04 (GER)
A 1-2 *Luis García (34)*
Iraizoz, Armando Sá, Lopo, Jarque, David García (Armando Sánchez 81), Domi, Edú Costa, Ito (De la Peña 78), Zabaleta, Luis García (Corominas 71), Pandiani.
H 0-3
Kameni, Armando Sá (Corominas 56), Lopo, Jarque, Pochettino, Domi (Juanfran 67) Edú Costa, De la Peña, Zabaleta (Jofre 67), Luis García, Pandiani.

SEVILLA FC

1st round FSV MAINZ (GER)
H 0-0
Notario, Alves, Aitor Ocio, Dragutinovic, David, Maresca, Renato, Jesús Navas, Luís Fabiano (Kepa 63), Adriano (Jesuli 63, Jordi 82), Kanouté.
A 2-0 *Kanouté (9, 40)*
Notario, Alves, Javi Navarro, Dragutinovic, Puerta, Jesús Navas (Jordi 68), Maresca, Martí, Adriano (Alfaro 76), Kanouté, Saviola (Luís Fabiano 78).

2nd round Group H
Match 1 BESIKTAS (TUR)
H 3-0 *Saviola (64), Kanouté (65, 89)*
Notario, Alves, Javi Navarro, Aitor Ocio, David, Sales (Jordi 71), Martí, Maresca, Adriano (Puerta 77), Saviola, Luís Fabiano (Kanouté 58).

Match 2 ZENIT SANKT-PETERBURG (RUS)
A 1-2 *Saviola (90)*
Notario, David (Jesús Navas 53), Alves, Aitor Ocio, Dragutinovic, Puerta, Sales (Kanouté 63), Renato (Jordi 15), Maresca, Saviola, Kepa.

Match 3 VITÓRIA GUIMARÃES (POR)
H 3-1 *Saviola (10, 27), Adriano (39)*
Palop, Alves, Aitor Ocio, Dragutinovic, Puerta, Jesús Navas, Martí, Maresca, Adriano (Capel 72), Kanouté (Kepa 51), Saviola (Jordi 76).

Match 4 BOLTON WANDERERS (ENG)
A 1-1 *Adriano (74)*
Notario, Crespo, David Prieto, Pablo Alfaro, Dragutinovic, Jordi (Adriano 67), Martí, Ruiz (Aitor Ocio 57), Puerta, Kepa (Saviola 73), Luís Fabiano.

3rd round LOKOMOTIV MOSKVA (RUS)
A 1-0 *Jordi (74)*
Notario, Alves, Javi Navarro, Dragutinovic, David, Jesús Navas (Escudé 87), Jordi, Martí, Adriano (Puerta 78), Kanouté, Luís Fabiano (Saviola 68).
H 2-0 *Maresca (33), Puerta (89)*
Notario, Alves, Javi Navarro (Aitor Ocio 82) Dragutinovic, David, Jesús Navas, Maresca, Jordi, Puerta, Saviola (Adriano 46), Luís Fabiano (Kepa 69).

4th round LILLE OSC (FRA)
A 0-1
Notario, Alves, Javi Navarro, Dragutinovic, David, Jesús Navas, Martí (Jordi 72), Renato, Adriano (Puerta 75), Kanouté, Luís Fabiano (Saviola 55).
H 2-0 *Kanouté (29), Luís Fabiano (45)*
Palop, Alves (Jordi 66), Javi Navarro, Dragutinovic, Jesús Navas, Martí, Renato, Adriano (Escudé 90), Kanouté, Luís Fabiano (Aitor Ocio 74).

Quarter-final ZENIT SANKT-PETERBURG (RUS)
H 4-1 *Saviola (15, 80), Martí (54p) Adriano (90)*
Palop, Martí (Maresca 75), Javi Navarro, Escudé, David, Sales (Puerta 63), Renato, Jordi (Blanco 81), Adriano, Kanouté, Saviola.
A 1-1 *Kepa (63)*
Palop, Aitor Ocio, Javi Navarro, Escudé, David, Alves, Maresca (Renato 70), Martí, Adriano (Jesuli 57), Jesús Navas, Luís Fabiano (Kepa 62).

Semi-final FC SCHALKE 04 (GER)
A 0-0
Palop, Alves, Javi Navarro, Escudé, David, Jesús Navas, Maresca, Puerta (Adriano 81), Martí, Saviola (Luís Fabiano 62), Kanouté (Renato 31).
H 1-0 *Puerta (100)*
(ae)
Palop, Alves, Aitor Ocio, Escudé, David, Navas, Martí, Maresca, Adriano (Puerta 77), Saviola (Makukula 108), Luís Fabiano (Renato 98).

Final MIDDLESBROUGH (ENG)
Eindhoven
4-0 *Luís Fabiano (26), Maresca (78, 84), Kanouté (89)*
Palop, Alves, Javi Navarro, Escudé, David, Jesús Navas, Martí, Maresca, Adriano (Puerta 86), Saviola (Kanouté 46), Luís Fabiano (Renato 72).

REAL BETIS

3rd round AZ (HOL)
H 2-0 *Tardelli (70), Robert (79)*
Contreras, Varela, Melli, Juanito, Luis Fernández, Arzu, Rivera, Joaquín (Óscar López 87), Dani (Tardelli 63), Edú, Robert (Israel 79).
A 1-2 *Melli (93)*
Contreras, Óscar López (Luis Fernández 51), Juanito, Melli, Rivas, Varela (Rivera 61), Joaquín, Arzu, Capi (Dani 85), Edú, Robert.

4th round STEAUA BUCURESTI (ROM)
A 0-0
Doblas, Melli, Rivas, Juanito, Luis Fernández, Varela (Dani 85), Rivera, Capi, Joaquín (Tardelli 90), Edú, Robert (Arzu 79).
H 0-3
Contreras, Melli, Juanito, Nano, Luis Fernández, Joaquín, Rivera, Arzu (Dani 57), Tardelli (Xisco 56), Edú, Robert.

TOP GOALSCORERS 2005/06

26	Samuel ETO'O (FC Barcelona)
25	DAVID VILLA (Valencia CF)
17	RONALDINHO (FC Barcelona)
15	Diego MILITO (Real Zaragoza)
14	RONALDO (Real Madrid)
13	BAIANO (RC Celta)
	FERNANDO TORRES (Atlético Madrid)
12	EWERTHON (Real Zaragoza)
	Juan Román RIQUELME (Villarreal CF)
11	Juan Fernando ARANGO (RCD Mallorca)
	Savo MILOSEVIC (CA Osasuna)
	DIEGO TRISTÁN (RC Deportivo)

LEAGUE RESULTS/ SCORERS/APPEARANCES/ GOALS 2005/06

DEPORTIVO ALAVÉS
Coach – Jesús Gómez; (9/1/06) Juan Carlos Oliva; (17/2/06) Mario Luna (ARG)

2005				
27/8	FC Barcelona	h	0-0	
11/9	Real Sociedad	a	1-2	*De Lucas*
18/9	Getafe CF	h	3-4	*Nené 3 (2p)*

Spain

FINAL LEAGUE TABLE 2005/06

		Pld	Home					Away					Total					Pts
			W	D	L	F	A	W	D	L	F	A	W	D	L	F	A	
1	FC Barcelona	38	15	3	1	45	15	10	4	5	35	20	25	7	6	80	35	82
2	Real Madrid	38	11	4	4	40	21	9	6	4	30	19	20	10	8	70	40	70
3	Valencia CF	38	10	8	1	34	16	9	4	6	24	17	19	12	7	58	33	69
4	CA Osasuna	38	12	3	4	28	20	9	2	8	21	23	21	5	12	49	43	68
5	Sevilla FC	38	12	5	2	29	15	8	3	8	25	24	20	8	10	54	39	68
6	RC Celta	38	13	0	6	25	13	7	4	8	20	20	20	4	14	45	33	64
7	Villarreal CF	38	9	6	4	28	18	5	9	5	22	21	14	15	9	50	39	57
8	RC Deportivo	38	6	5	8	19	22	9	5	5	28	23	15	10	13	47	45	55
9	Getafe CF	38	8	7	4	32	24	7	2	10	22	25	15	9	14	54	49	54
10	Atlético Madrid	38	7	6	6	21	18	6	7	6	24	19	13	13	12	45	37	52
11	Real Zaragoza	38	6	6	7	26	26	4	10	5	20	25	10	16	12	46	51	46
12	Athletic Bilbao	38	7	6	6	19	18	4	6	9	21	28	11	12	15	40	46	45
13	RCD Mallorca	38	6	8	5	21	21	4	5	10	16	30	10	13	15	37	51	43
14	Real Betis	38	8	5	6	19	19	2	7	10	15	32	10	12	16	34	51	42
15	RCD Espanyol	38	7	4	8	26	24	3	7	9	10	32	10	11	17	36	56	41
16	Real Sociedad	38	8	4	7	31	27	3	3	13	17	38	11	7	20	48	65	40
17	Racing Santander	38	4	6	9	18	26	5	7	7	18	23	9	13	16	36	49	40
18	Deportivo Alavés	38	6	6	7	20	24	3	6	10	15	30	9	12	17	35	54	39
19	Cádiz CF	38	4	8	7	22	25	4	4	11	14	27	8	12	18	36	52	36
20	Málaga CF	38	3	5	11	16	25	2	4	13	20	43	5	9	24	36	68	24

Date	Opponent	H/A	Score	Scorers
21/9	Málaga CF	a	0-0	
25/9	Real Madrid	h	0-3	
2/10	Racing Santander	a	2-1	Wésley, Santiago Carpintero
15/10	Villarreal CF	h	1-1	Nené
22/10	Sevilla FC	a	0-2	
27/10	RCD Espanyol	h	1-1	Sarriegui
30/10	Cádiz CF	h	0-0	
6/11	RC Celta	a	1-2	Astudillo
20/11	Athletic Bilbao	h	2-0	Nené, Bodipo
27/11	CA Osasuna	a	2-3	Nené, Aloisi
4/12	RCD Mallorca	h	0-3	
11/12	Atlético Madrid	a	1-1	Sarriegui
18/12	Valencia CF	h	0-1	
21/12	Real Betis	a	0-3	
2006				
8/1	Real Zaragoza	h	0-2	
15/1	RC Deportivo	a	2-0	Aloisi, Bodipo
22/1	FC Barcelona	a	0-2	
29/1	Real Sociedad	h	3-1	Santiago Carpintero, Aloisi 2
5/2	Getafe CF	a	2-2	Aloisi, Bodipo
12/2	Málaga CF	h	3-2	Bodipo 2, Aloisi
18/2	Real Madrid	a	0-3	
26/2	Racing Santander	h	2-2	Nené (p), Aloisi
4/3	Villarreal CF	a	2-3	Aloisi, De Lucas
12/3	Sevilla FC	h	2-1	Nené, Bodipo
19/3	Cádiz CF	a	0-0	
22/3	RC Celta	h	1-0	Aloisi (p)
26/3	RCD Espanyol	a	0-0	
2/4	Athletic Bilbao	h	0-0	
9/4	CA Osasuna	h	1-2	Bodipo
15/4	RCD Mallorca	a	0-0	
22/4	Atlético Madrid	h	0-1	
30/4	Valencia CF	a	0-3	
3/5	Real Betis	h	2-0	Aloisi, Nené
7/5	Real Zaragoza	a	0-3	
13/5	RC Deportivo	h	1-0	Bodipo

No	Name	Nat	Pos	Aps	(s)	Gls
22	John ALOISI	AUS	A	25	(8)	10
14	Henri Arnaud ANTCHOUET	GAB	A		(3)	
18	Martín Mauricio ASTUDILLO	ARG	M	32	(1)	1
24	Arthuri BERNHARDT	BRA	A	1	(5)	
19	Rodolfo BODIPO		A	29	(6)	8
25	Roberto BONANO	ARG	G	7		
7	Lluís CARRERAS		D	4		
2	David COROMINA		D	23	(4)	
1	Franco COSTANZO	ARG	G	31		
10	Enrique DE LUCAS		M	18	(4)	2
17	EDU ALONSO		D	35		
14	ELTON Giovanni Machado	BRA	M		(4)	
12	GASPAR Gálvez		D	19	(2)	
7	Blagoy GEORGIEV	BUL	M	3	(7)	
6	IBÓN BEGOÑA Zubiaurre		M	3	(1)	
21	JANDRO Castro		M	18	(14)	
4	JUANITO Gutiérrez		D	34	(3)	
26	Mehdi LACEN	FRA	M	9	(10)	
20	José María MENA		A	3	(7)	
23	Anderson de Carvalho "NENÉ"	BRA	M	38		9
3	Mauricio PELLEGRINO	ARG	D	11	(2)	
16	POLI Fernández		D	8	(1)	
9	RUBÉN NAVARRO		A	10	(5)	
15	SANTIAGO CARPINTERO		M	22	(5)	2
5	Josu SARRIEGUI		D	30		2
6	Óscar TÉLLEZ		D	2	(2)	
11	Pape Bouna THIAW	SEN	A		(5)	
8	WÉSLEY Lopes da Silva	BRA	M	3	(7)	1

Spain

ATHLETIC BILBAO
Coach – José Luis Mendilíbar; (30/10/05) Javier Clemente

2005
Date	Opponent	H/A	Score	Scorers
27/8	Real Sociedad	h	3-0	Yeste, Llorente, Luis Prieto
11/9	Getafe CF	a	1-1	Casas
18/9	Málaga CF	h	1-2	Lacruz
22/9	Real Madrid	a	1-3	og (Woodgate)
25/9	Racing Santander	h	0-0	
2/10	Villarreal CF	a	1-3	Etxeberria
16/10	Sevilla FC	h	0-1	
23/10	Cádiz CF	a	0-1	
26/10	CA Osasuna	a	2-3	Gurpegui, og (Clavero)
29/10	RC Celta	h	1-1	Gurpegui
5/11	RCD Espanyol	a	1-1	Luis Prieto
20/11	Deportivo Alavés	h	0-2	
26/11	RCD Mallorca	a	1-0	Luis Prieto
3/12	Atlético Madrid	h	1-1	Orbaiz
10/12	Valencia CF	a	1-1	Etxeberria
17/12	Real Betis	h	2-0	Urzaiz, Dañobeitia
21/12	Real Zaragoza	a	2-3	Lacruz, Etxeberria

2006
Date	Opponent	H/A	Score	Scorers
7/1	RC Deportivo	h	1-2	Urzaiz
15/1	FC Barcelona	a	1-2	Llorente
22/1	Real Sociedad	a	3-3	Aduriz 2, Iraola
28/1	Getafe CF	h	1-0	Orbaiz (p)
4/2	Málaga CF	a	1-2	Aduriz
11/2	Real Madrid	h	0-2	
19/2	Racing Santander	a	1-0	Urzaiz
26/2	Villarreal CF	h	1-1	Aduriz
5/3	Sevilla FC	a	1-2	Aduriz
12/3	Cádiz CF	h	1-0	Tiko (p)
19/3	RC Celta	a	1-0	Aduriz
22/3	RCD Espanyol	h	1-1	Yeste
25/3	CA Osasuna	a	1-0	Luis Prieto
2/4	Deportivo Alavés	a	0-0	
9/4	RCD Mallorca	h	1-1	Yeste
16/4	Atlético Madrid	a	0-1	
23/4	Valencia CF	h	0-3	
29/4	Real Betis	a	1-1	Lacruz
3/5	Real Zaragoza	h	1-0	Yeste
7/5	RC Deportivo	a	2-1	Casas, Orbaiz (p)
20/5	FC Barcelona	h	3-1	Iraola, Felipe, og (Oleguer)

No	Name	Nat	Pos	Aps	(s)	Gls
23	Aritz ADURIZ		A	13	(2)	6
30	Fernando AMOREBIETA		D	15		
13	Daniel ARANZUBIA		G	18		
48	Urko ARROYO		M		(1)	
6	Endika BORDAS		M	1	(1)	
3	Javier CASAS		D	21	(3)	2
38	Mikel DAÑOBEITIA		M	8	(14)	1
27	Igor ETXEBARRIETA		M			
17	Joseba ETXEBERRIA		A	24	(5)	3
2	Unai EXPÓSITO		D	19	(5)	
5	FELIPE Guréndez		M		(1)	1
8	Julen GUERRERO		M	4	(13)	
18	Carlos GURPEGUI		M	30		2
22	Ibón GUTIÉRREZ		M	5	(1)	
15	Andoni IRAOLA		M	34	(4)	2
11	JAVI GONZÁLEZ		M	3	(2)	
12	Jesús María LACRUZ		D	25	(5)	3
1	Iñaki LAFUENTE		G	20		
9	Fernando LLORENTE		A	12	(10)	2
14	LUIS PRIETO		D	36		4
19	Ander MURILLO		D	19	(7)	
16	Pablo ORBAIZ		D	36		3
21	Francisco Javier TARANTINO		D	2	(1)	
7	Roberto Martínez "TIKO"		M	6	(22)	1
20	Ismael URZAIZ		A	16	(10)	3
29	USTARITZ Aldekoaotalora		D	17		
10	Francisco Javier YESTE		M	34	(1)	4

ATLÉTICO MADRID
Coach – Carlos Bianchi (ARG); (12/1/06) José Murcia

2005
Date	Opponent	H/A	Score	Scorers
28/8	Real Zaragoza	h	0-0	
10/9	RC Deportivo	a	0-1	
18/9	FC Barcelona	h	2-1	Fernando Torres, Kezman
21/9	Real Sociedad	a	2-3	Fernando Torres, Kezman
24/9	Getafe CF	h	0-1	
2/10	Málaga CF	a	2-0	Fernando Torres (p), Kezman
15/10	Real Madrid	h	0-3	
23/10	Racing Santander	a	1-0	Maxi
27/10	Cádiz CF	h	3-0	Maxi, Pablo, Galletti
30/10	Villarreal CF	h	1-1	Zahínos
6/11	Sevilla FC	a	0-0	
20/11	RC Celta	a	1-2	Antonio López
27/11	RCD Espanyol	h	1-1	Luccin
3/12	Athletic Bilbao	a	1-1	Kezman
11/12	Deportivo Alavés	h	1-1	Fernando Torres
18/12	RCD Mallorca	a	2-2	Petrov, Colsa
22/12	CA Osasuna	a	1-2	Petrov

2006
Date	Opponent	H/A	Score	Scorers
8/1	Valencia CF	h	0-0	
14/1	Real Betis	a	0-1	
21/1	Real Zaragoza	h	2-0	Maxi, Fernando Torres (p)
28/1	RC Deportivo	h	3-2	Maxi 2, Antonio López
5/2	FC Barcelona	a	3-1	Fernando Torres 2, Maxi
12/2	Real Sociedad	h	1-0	Kezman
19/2	Getafe CF	a	3-0	Luccin, Maxi, Fernando Torres
25/2	Málaga CF	h	5-0	Fernando Torres 2, Maxi, Valera 2
4/3	Real Madrid	a	1-2	Kezman
12/3	Racing Santander	h	2-1	Fernando Torres (p), Pablo
18/3	Villarreal CF	a	1-1	Fernando Torres
23/3	Sevilla FC	h	0-1	
26/3	Cádiz CF	a	1-1	Kezman
2/4	RC Celta	a	0-3	
9/4	RCD Espanyol	a	1-1	Gabi
16/4	Athletic Bilbao	h	1-0	Fernando Torres
22/4	Deportivo Alavés	a	1-0	Antonio López
30/4	RCD Mallorca	h	0-1	
3/5	CA Osasuna	h	0-1	
6/5	Valencia CF	a	1-1	Maxi
13/5	Real Betis	h	1-1	Kezman

No	Name	Nat	Pos	Aps	(s)	Gls
3	ANTONIO LÓPEZ Guerrero		D	36		3
14	Ángel Javier ARIZMENDI		A		(1)	
26	BRAULIO Nóbrega		A		(1)	
4	Gonzalo COLSA		M	5	(9)	1
28	Manu DEL MORAL		A	2	(3)	
30	Ismael FALCÓN		G	4	(1)	
9	FERNANDO TORRES		A	36		13
20	GABI Fernández		M	21	(11)	1
7	Luciano Martín GALLETTI	ARG	A	15	(11)	1

Spain

No	Name	Nat	Pos	Aps	(s)	Gls
5	José Antonio GARCÍA CALVO		D	6	(6)	
8	Ariel Santiago IBAGAZA	ARG	M	17	(8)	
10	Mateja KEZMAN	SCG	A	28	(2)	8
25	LEOnardo FRANCO	ARG	G	33	(1)	
23	Peter LUCCIN	FRA	M	28	(1)	2
31	MARIO Suárez		M	2	(2)	
37	José Fernando MARQUÉS		A	1	(6)	
11	MAXI Rodríguez	ARG	M	25	(4)	9
15	Francisco José MOLINERO		D	10	(1)	
36	Antonio MORENO		M		(1)	
22	PABLO Ibáñez		D	35		2
21	Luis Amaranto PEREA	COL	D	34		
17	Martin PETROV	BUL	A	31	(5)	2
33	ROBERTO Jiménez		G	1		
40	RUFINO Segovia		A		(1)	
27	Pablo SICILIA		D		(1)	
18	Juan VALERA		M	10	(7)	2
38	Julián VARA		M		(2)	
2	Juan VELASCO		D	25		
6	José Ignacio ZAHÍNOS		M	13	(4)	1

FC BARCELONA
Coach – Frank Rijkaard (HOL)

2005

Date	Opponent	H/A	Score	Scorers
27/8	Deportivo Alavés	a	0-0	
11/9	RCD Mallorca	h	2-0	Eto'o 2
18/9	Atlético Madrid	a	1-2	Eto'o
21/9	Valencia CF	h	2-2	Giuly, Deco
24/9	Real Betis	a	4-1	Van Bommel, Eto'o 2, Ezquerro
1/10	Real Zaragoza	h	2-2	Ronaldinho (p), Eto'o
15/10	RC Deportivo	a	3-3	Eto'o, Ronaldinho 2 (1p)
22/10	CA Osasuna	h	3-0	Eto'o 2, Giuly
26/10	Málaga CF	h	2-0	Ronaldinho (p), Larsson
30/10	Real Sociedad	h	5-0	Van Bommel, Ronaldinho 2, Puyol, Larsson
6/11	Getafe CF	a	3-1	Eto'o, Giuly, Motta
19/11	Real Madrid	a	3-0	Eto'o, Ronaldinho 2
27/11	Racing Santander	h	4-1	Eto'o, Messi, Ronaldinho (p), Sylvinho
4/12	Villarreal CF	a	2-0	og (Peña), Deco
11/12	Sevilla FC	h	2-1	Eto'o, Ronaldinho
17/12	Cádiz CF	a	3-1	Giuly, Eto'o 2 (1p)
20/12	RC Celta	h	2-0	Eto'o 2

2006

Date	Opponent	H/A	Score	Scorers
7/1	RCD Espanyol	a	2-1	Deco, Eto'o
15/1	Athletic Bilbao	h	2-1	Ronaldinho (p), Messi
22/1	Deportivo Alavés	h	2-0	Larsson, Messi
29/1	RCD Mallorca	a	3-0	Giuly, Messi 2
5/2	Atlético Madrid	h	1-3	Larsson
12/2	Valencia CF	a	0-1	
18/2	Real Betis	h	5-1	Larsson, og 2 (Melli 2), Ronaldinho, Messi
25/2	Real Zaragoza	a	2-0	Ronaldinho (p), Larsson
4/3	RC Deportivo	h	3-2	Ronaldinho, Larsson, Eto'o
12/3	CA Osasuna	a	1-2	Larsson
18/3	Real Sociedad	a	2-0	Larsson, Eto'o
21/3	Getafe CF	h	3-1	og (Matellan), Eto'o 2
25/3	Málaga CF	a	0-0	
1/4	Real Madrid	h	1-1	Ronaldinho (p)
9/4	Racing Santander	a	2-2	Larsson, Eto'o
14/4	Villarreal CF	h	1-0	Eto'o
29/4	Cádiz CF	h	1-0	Ronaldinho
3/5	RC Celta	a	1-0	Eto'o

6/5	RCD Espanyol	h	2-0	og (Jarque), Ronaldinho
13/5	Sevilla FC	a	2-3	Ezquerro, Sylvinho
20/5	Athletic Bilbao	a	1-3	Eto'o

No	Name	Nat	Pos	Aps	(s)	Gls
2	Juliano BELLETTI	BRA	D	20	(7)	
20	Anderson de Souza "DECO"	BRA	M	28	(1)	3
15	EDMÍLSON José Gomes	BRA	D	24	(4)	
9	Samuel ETO'O	CMR	A	34		26
14	Santiago EZQUERRO		A	3	(9)	2
18	GABRI García		M	4	(7)	
8	Ludovic GIULY	FRA	A	21	(8)	5
24	Andrés INIESTA		M	14	(19)	
25	Albert JORQUERA		G	3		
7	Henrik LARSSON	SWE	A	14	(14)	10
4	Rafael MÁRQUEZ	MEX	D	25		
40	Francisco Javier MARTOS		M		(1)	
45	Ramón MASÓ		M		(1)	
11	MAXI LÓPEZ	ARG	A	2	(4)	
19	Lionel Andrés MESSI	ARG	A	11	(6)	6
42	Francisco MONTAÑÉS		M		(1)	
3	Thiago MOTTA	BRA	D	11	(4)	1
23	OLEGUER Presas		D	31	(2)	
43	Jesús OLMO		D	1		
44	Andrea ORLANDI		D	1		
27	Josep Comadevall "PITU"		A		(1)	
5	Carles PUYOL		D	35		1
26	Sergio Rodríguez "RODRI"		D	3	(1)	
10	RONALDINHO de Assis Moreira	BRA	A	29		17
41	Ludovic SYLVESTRE	FRA	M	1	(1)	
16	SYLVINHO Mendes	BRA	D	22	(4)	2
17	Mark VAN BOMMEL	HOL	M	17	(7)	2
12	Giovanni VAN BRONCKHORST	HOL	D	15	(4)	
1	VÍCTOR VALDÉS		G	35		
6	XAVI Hernández		M	14	(2)	

REAL BETIS
Coach – Lorenzo Serra Ferrer

2005

Date	Opponent	H/A	Score	Scorers
27/8	Valencia CF	a	0-1	
10/9	CA Osasuna	h	1-0	Ricardo Oliveira (p)
18/9	Real Zaragoza	h	0-0	
21/9	RC Deportivo	a	1-1	Ricardo Oliveira
24/9	FC Barcelona	h	1-4	Juanito
2/10	Real Sociedad	a	1-1	Juanito
16/10	Getafe CF	h	1-0	Ricardo Oliveira (p)
23/10	Málaga CF	a	0-5	
26/10	Villarreal CF	h	2-3	Ricardo Oliveira, og (Javi Venta)
29/10	Real Madrid	h	0-2	
6/11	Racing Santander	a	1-1	Dani
19/11	Sevilla FC	a	0-1	
27/11	Cádiz CF	h	1-1	Marcos Assunção
3/12	RC Celta	a	1-2	Edú
11/12	RCD Espanyol	h	0-0	
17/12	Athletic Bilbao	a	0-2	
21/12	Deportivo Alavés	h	3-0	Fernando, Xisco, Joaquín

2006

Date	Opponent	H/A	Score	Scorers
8/1	RCD Mallorca	a	1-1	Robert
14/1	Atlético Madrid	h	1-0	Capi
22/01	Valencia CF	h	0-2	
29/01	CA Osasuna	a	2-0	Luis Fernández, Edú
5/2	Real Zaragoza	a	3-4	Dani 3
12/2	RC Deportivo	h	0-1	

Spain

18/2	FC Barcelona	a	1-5	Joaquín
26/2	Real Sociedad	h	2-0	Dani, Robert
5/3	Getafe CF	a	0-1	
12/3	Málaga CF	h	1-1	Rivas
19/3	Real Madrid	a	0-0	
22/3	Racing Santander	h	1-0	Edú
25/3	Villarreal CF	a	2-1	Robert 2
2/4	Sevilla FC	h	2-1	Robert (p), Varela
8/4	Cádiz CF	a	1-1	Joaquín
16/4	RC Celta	h	0-2	
23/4	RCD Espanyol	a	0-2	
29/4	Athletic Bilbao	h	1-1	Robert
3/5	Deportivo Alavés	a	0-2	
7/5	RCD Mallorca	h	2-1	og (Pereyra), Robert
13/5	Atlético Madrid	a	1-1	Arzu

No	Name	Nat	Pos	Aps	(s)	Gls
8	ARZU García		M	19	(10)	1
10	Juan José CAÑAS		M	1	(2)	
14	Jesús Capitán "CAPI"		M	14	(7)	1
22	Paolo CASTELLINI	ITA	D	6	(1)	
1	Pedro CONTRERAS		G	15	(2)	
6	DANI Martín		A	12	(13)	5
13	Antonio DOBLAS		G	23	(1)	
24	EDÚ Schmidt	BRA	A	34		3
9	FERNANDO Fernández		M	3	(10)	1
19	ISRAEL Bascón		M	1	(7)	
17	JOAQUÍN Sánchez		M	35		3
4	JUANITO Gutiérrez		D	34		2
23	JUNALU Gómez		M		(3)	
3	Daniel Alejandro LEMBO	URU	D	1	(1)	
2	LUIS FERNÁNDEZ		D	19		1
20	MARCOS ASSUNÇAO	BRA	M	21	(5)	1
27	Juan Alberto Andreu "MELLI"		D	30	(1)	
25	MIGUEL ÁNGEL Lozano		M	6	(4)	
15	NANO Rivas		D	10	(3)	
16	ÓSCAR LÓPEZ Hernández		D	18		
12	RICARDO de OLIVEIRA	BRA	A	9		4
5	David RIVAS		D	19	(2)	1
18	Alberto RIVERA		M	28	(6)	
12	ROBERT de Pinho de Souza	BRA	A	13	(6)	7
11	Diego TARDELLI	BRA	A	5	(7)	
7	Fernando VARELA		D	26	(3)	1
21	XISCO Muñoz		A	16	(9)	1

CÁDIZ CF
Coach – Víctor Espárrago (URU)

2005

28/8	Real Madrid	h	1-2	Pavoni
11/9	Racing Santander	a	1-0	Sesma
18/9	Villarreal CF	h	1-1	Oli
21/9	Sevilla FC	a	0-0	
25/9	CA Osasuna	a	0-2	
2/10	RC Celta	h	1-1	Fleurquin
16/10	RCD Espanyol	a	2-0	Pavoni, Sesma
23/10	Athletic Bilbao	h	1-0	Enrique
27/10	Atlético Madrid	a	0-3	
30/10	Deportivo Alavés	h	0-0	
6/11	RCD Mallorca	h	1-2	Enrique
20/11	Valencia CF	h	0-1	
27/11	Real Betis	a	1-1	Manolo Pérez (p)
4/12	Real Zaragoza	h	1-2	Enrique
11/12	RC Deportivo	a	0-1	
17/12	FC Barcelona	h	1-3	Mirosavljevic
21/12	Real Sociedad	a	0-2	

2006

8/1	Getafe CF	h	1-0	Mirosavljevic (p)
15/1	Málaga CF	a	2-0	Medina 2
21/1	Real Madrid	a	1-3	Medina
28/1	Racing Santander	h	1-1	Raúl López
5/2	Villarreal CF	a	1-1	Medina
11/2	Sevilla FC	h	0-4	
19/2	CA Osasuna	h	1-3	Lucas Lobos
26/2	RC Celta	a	0-2	
4/3	RCD Espanyol	h	2-0	Paz, Sesma
12/3	Athletic Bilbao	a	0-1	
19/3	Deportivo Alavés	h	0-0	
22/3	RCD Mallorca	a	0-1	
26/3	Atlético Madrid	h	1-1	Lucas Lobos (p)
2/4	Valencia CF	a	3-5	Enrique, Sesma 2
8/4	Real Betis	h	1-1	Lucas Lobos (p)
16/4	Real Zaragoza	a	2-1	Lucas Lobos (p), Pavoni
23/4	RC Deportivo	h	1-1	Lucas Lobos
29/4	FC Barcelona	a	0-1	
3/5	Real Sociedad	h	2-2	Estoyanoff, Lucas Lobos (p)
7/5	Getafe CF	a	1-3	Lucas Lobos
13/5	Málaga CF	h	5-0	Pavoni, Sesma 2, Estoyanoff, Mirosavljevic

No	Name	Nat	Pos	Aps	(s)	Gls
5	ABRAHAM PAZ Cruz		D	20	(2)	1
1	ARMANDO Ribeiro		G	25		
15	BENJAMÍN Zarandona		M	7	(7)	
7	Eduardo BERIZZO	ARG	D	13	(1)	
22	Marc BERTRÁN		D	1		
24	Juan José BEZARES		M	20	(7)	
2	Julián DE LA CUESTA	COL	D	15		
4	Ramón DE QUINTANA		D	28		
8	ENRIQUE Fernando Ortiz		A	29	(7)	4
10	Fabián Larry ESTOYANOFF	URU	A	10	(19)	2
16	Andrés José FLEURQUIN	URU	M	27	(3)	1
14	IVÁN ANIA		M	5	(4)	
25	Óscar Alejandro LIMIA	ARG	G	13		
17	LUCAS Armando LOBOS	ARG	A	14	(6)	7
23	MANOLO PÉREZ		M		(4)	1
18	MÁRIO Magalhaes da SILVA	POR	D	6	(1)	
20	Alexandre Jesús MEDINA	URU	A	13	(6)	4
12	Nenad MIROSAVLJEVIC	CRO	A	8	(4)	3
23	Fernando MORÁN		M	4	(11)	
9	OLI Álvarez		A	15	(14)	1
11	Matías Nicolás PAVONI	ARG	M	26	(3)	4
3	RAÚL LÓPEZ		D	27		1
19	Jonathan SESMA		A	29	(7)	7
6	Roberto SUÁREZ		M	21	(2)	
21	Alejandro Pablo VARELA		D	34	(1)	
22	Luciano Germán VELLA	ARG	D	8	(2)	

RC CELTA
Coach – Fernando Vázquez

2005

28/8	Málaga CF	h	2-0	Gustavo López, Baiano
10/9	Real Madrid	a	3-2	Contreras, Núñez, Canobbio
18/9	Racing Santander	h	0-1	
21/9	Villarreal CF	a	2-1	Baiano 2
25/9	Sevilla FC	h	2-1	Baiano, Oubiña
2/10	Cádiz CF	a	1-1	Baiano
16/10	CA Osasuna	a	0-2	
23/10	RCD Espanyol	h	1-0	Silva

Spain

Date	Opponent	H/A	Score	Scorers
26/10	RCD Mallorca	a	0-1	
29/10	Athletic Bilbao	a	1-1	Ángel
6/11	Deportivo Alavés	h	2-1	Canobbio, Aspas
20/11	Atlético Madrid	h	2-1	Baiano, Canobbio
26/11	Valencia CF	a	0-2	
3/12	Real Betis	h	2-1	Canobbio, Baiano
11/12	Real Zaragoza	a	0-1	
17/12	RC Deportivo	h	0-3	
20/12	FC Barcelona	a	0-2	
2006				
8/1	Real Sociedad	h	1-0	Canobbio
15/1	Getafe CF	a	1-1	Ángel
22/01	Málaga CF	a	2-0	Núñez, Silva
29/1	Real Madrid	h	1-2	Lequi
5/2	Racing Santander	a	1-0	Perera
12/2	Villarreal CF	h	1-0	Baiano (p)
18/2	Sevilla FC	a	0-1	
26/2	Cádiz CF	h	2-0	Contreras, Silva
5/3	CA Osasuna	h	2-0	Baiano, Canobbio
11/3	RCD Espanyol	a	0-2	
19/3	Athletic Bilbao	h	0-1	
22/3	Deportivo Alavés	a	0-1	
26/3	RCD Mallorca	h	2-0	Contreras, Baiano
2/4	Atlético Madrid	a	3-0	Lequi, Baiano (p), De Ridder
8/4	Valencia CF	h	0-1	
16/4	Real Betis	a	2-0	Jorge, Perera
22/4	Real Zaragoza	h	4-0	Canobbio 2, Jorge, Perera
29/4	RC Deportivo	a	2-0	Silva, Perera
3/5	FC Barcelona	h	0-1	
7/5	Real Sociedad	a	2-2	Baiano 2 (1p)
13/5	Getafe CF	h	1-0	Contreras

No	Name	Nat	Pos	Aps	(s)	Gls
8	ÁNGEL Domingo López		D	37		2
20	Jonathan ASPAS		M	5	(10)	1
18	João Fernando Nelo "BAIANO"	BRA	A	32	(1)	13
24	Néstor Fabián CANOBBIO	URU	A	32		8
15	Pablo Andrés CONTRERAS	CHL	D	23	(6)	4
22	Daniel DE RIDDER	HOL	A	9	(8)	1
1	ESTEBAN Andrés		G	1	(1)	
5	Everton GIOVANELLA	BRA	M	1	(1)	
25	IRINEY Santos da Silva	BRA	M	26	(3)	
10	Francisco JAVIer GUERRERO		A	3	(16)	
11	GUSTAVO LÓPEZ	ARG	M	6	(10)	1
21	JORGE Larena		M	19	(7)	2
2	JOSÉ ENRIQUE Sánchez		D	12	(2)	
3	Matías LEQUI	ARG	D	26	(3)	2
17	Sebastián Ariel MÉNDEZ	ARG	D	1	(9)	
7	Antonio NÚÑEZ		M	26	(6)	2
4	Borja OUBIÑA		M	36		1
14	José Jesús PERERA		A	2	(15)	4
13	José Manuel PINTO		G	37		
12	Diego PLACENTE	ARG	D	25		
9	Juan Ginés SÁNCHEZ		A	1	(2)	
23	SERGIO Fernández		D	26		
16	David Jiménez SILVA		M	31	(3)	4
6	Roberto SOUSA		A	1	(7)	

RC DEPORTIVO
Coach – Joaquín Caparrós

Date	Opponent	H/A	Score	Scorers
2005				
28/8	RCD Mallorca	a	1-0	Juanma
10/9	Atlético Madrid	h	1-0	Capdevila
17/9	Valencia CF	a	2-2	Diego Tristán, Sergio
21/9	Real Betis	h	1-1	Diego Tristán (p)
24/9	Real Zaragoza	a	1-1	Diego Tristán
2/10	CA Osasuna	h	0-1	
15/10	FC Barcelona	h	3-3	Valerón, Munitis, Rubén Castro
23/10	Real Sociedad	a	0-2	
26/10	Real Madrid	h	3-1	De Guzmán, Juanma 2
30/10	Getafe CF	h	1-0	Diego Tristán
6/11	Málaga CF	a	1-1	Valerón
20/11	Racing Santander	a	3-0	og (Neru), og (Moratón), Taborda
27/11	Villarreal CF	h	0-2	
4/12	Sevilla FC	a	2-0	Diego Tristán (p), Víctor
11/12	Cádiz CF	h	1-0	Diego Tristán
17/12	RC Celta	a	3-0	Diego Tristán (p), Valerón, Capdevila
21/12	RCD Espanyol	h	1-2	Diego Tristán
2006				
7/1	Athletic Bilbao	a	2-1	og (Lacruz), Arizmendi
15/1	Deportivo Alavés	h	0-2	
22/1	RCD Mallorca	a	2-2	Valerón, Diego Tristán (p)
28/1	Atlético Madrid	a	2-3	Rubén Castro, Capdevila
4/2	Valencia CF	h	0-1	
12/2	Real Betis	a	1-0	Rubén Castro
19/2	Real Zaragoza	a	1-1	Munitis
26/2	CA Osasuna	a	2-1	Sergio, Diego Tristán
4/3	FC Barcelona	a	2-3	Juanma, Jorge Andrade
11/3	Real Sociedad	h	0-1	
18/3	Getafe CF	a	2-1	Víctor, Xisco
22/3	Málaga CF	h	2-1	Sergio, Víctor
26/3	Real Madrid	a	0-4	
2/4	Racing Santander	h	2-0	Capdevila, Iglesias
9/4	Villarreal CF	a	1-1	Sergio
15/4	Sevilla FC	h	0-0	
23/4	Cádiz CF	a	1-1	Iglesias
29/4	RC Celta	h	0-2	
3/5	RCD Espanyol	a	2-1	Carril, Diego Tristán
7/5	Athletic Bilbao	h	1-2	Arizmendi
13/5	Deportivo Alavés	a	0-1	

No	Name	Nat	Pos	Aps	(s)	Gls
16	Roberto Miguel ACUÑA	ARG	M		(5)	
10	Ángel Javier ARIZMENDI		A	12	(5)	2
15	Juan CAPDEVILA		D	36		4
35	Iván CARRIL		M	1	(9)	1
5	CÉSAR Martín		D	2	(5)	
23	Fabricio COLOCCINI	ARG	D	23	(3)	
6	Julián DE GUZMÁN	CAN	M	17	(5)	1
9	DIEGO TRISTÁN		A	27	(9)	11
4	Aldo Pedro DUSCHER	ARG	M	31		
12	Francisco GALLARDO		M	1	(6)	
24	HÉCTOR Berenguel		D	15		
41	IAGO Iglesias		A	8	(3)	2
19	JESÚS Muñoz		M		(1)	
14	JORGE Manuel ANDRADE	POR	D	18		1
22	JUANMA Delgado		D	22	(1)	4
2	MANUEL PABLO García		D	28	(3)	
1	José Francisco MOLINA		G	38		
20	MOMO Figueroa		M	1	(4)	
11	Pedro Manuel MUNITIS		M	32	(5)	2
3	Enrique Fernández ROMERO		D	17	(3)	
17	RUBÉN CASTRO		A	13	(11)	3
12	Lionel Sebastián SCALONI	ARG	M	8	(7)	
40	SENEL Lafuente		A	1	(2)	

Spain

RCD ESPANYOL
Coach – Miguel Ángel Lotina

2005

Date	Opponent	h/a	Score	Scorers
28/8	Getafe CF	h	0-2	
11/9	Málaga CF	a	2-1	Zabaleta, Luis García
18/9	Real Madrid	h	1-0	Jarque
21/9	Racing Santander	a	0-1	
24/9	Villarreal CF	h	1-2	Luis García
2/10	Sevilla FC	a	1-1	Frédson
16/10	Cádiz CF	h	0-2	
23/10	RC Celta	a	0-1	
27/10	Deportivo Alavés	a	1-1	Luis García
30/10	CA Osasuna	a	0-2	
5/11	Athletic Bilbao	h	1-1	Corominas
20/11	RCD Mallorca	h	2-0	Tamudo (p), Luis García
27/11	Atlético Madrid	a	1-1	Jarque
4/12	Valencia CF	h	1-3	Corominas
11/12	Real Betis	a	0-0	
18/12	Real Zaragoza	h	2-2	Tamudo 2
21/12	RC Deportivo	a	2-1	Frédson, Armando Sá

2006

Date	Opponent	h/a	Score	Scorers
7/1	FC Barcelona	h	1-2	Tamudo
15/1	Real Sociedad	a	1-0	Tamudo
22/1	Getafe CF	a	0-5	
29/1	Málaga CF	h	3-1	Tamudo 2, Luis García
4/2	Real Madrid	a	0-4	
12/2	Racing Santander	h	0-2	
18/2	Villarreal CF	a	0-4	
26/2	Sevilla FC	h	5-0	Frédson, Zabaleta, Luis García 3 (1p)
4/3	Cádiz CF	a	0-2	
11/3	RC Celta	h	2-0	Tamudo, Frédson
19/3	CA Osasuna	h	2-4	Tamudo, Luis García
22/3	Athletic Bilbao	a	1-1	Juanfran
26/3	Deportivo Alavés	h	0-0	
2/4	RCD Mallorca	a	0-0	
9/4	Atlético Madrid	h	1-1	Pandiani
16/4	Valencia CF	a	0-4	
23/4	Real Betis	h	2-0	Jarque, Tamudo
30/4	Real Zaragoza	a	1-1	Jarque
3/5	RC Deportivo	h	1-2	Luis García
6/5	FC Barcelona	a	0-2	
13/5	Real Sociedad	h	1-0	Corominas

No	Name	Nat	Pos	Aps	(s)	Gls
2	ARMANDO Correia de SÁ	POR	D	11	(9)	1
20	Ferran COROMINAS		M	13	(19)	3
3	DAVID GARCÍA		D	26	(1)	
9	Iván DE LA PEÑA		M	28	(2)	
18	Didier DOMI	FRA	D	14	(3)	
6	EDUARDO COSTA	BRA	M	28	(2)	
15	FRÉDSON Cámara	BRA	M	20	(8)	4
1	Gorka IRAIZOZ		G	21		
14	Antonio Álvarez "ITO"		M	21	(5)	
21	Daniel JARQUE		D	34		4
11	JOFRE Mateu		M	1	(11)	
17	JUANFRAN Torres		M	20	(10)	1
16	Idris Carlos KAMENI	CMR	G	17		
8	SERGIO González		M	31	(5)	4
7	Sebastián TABORDA	URU	A		(9)	1
21	Juan Carlos VALERÓN		M	17	(3)	4
18	VÍCTOR Sánchez		M	18	(3)	3
36	XISCO Jiménez		A	1	(11)	1
4	Alberto LOPO		D	33		
10	LUIS GARCÍA Fernández		A	32	(4)	10
31	MIKI Martínez		M		(2)	
22	MOISÉS Hurtado		D	15	(5)	
7	Walter PANDIANI	URU	A	7	(11)	1
5	Mauricio POCHETTINO	ARG	D	11	(1)	
25	Martín Andrés POSSE	ARG	A	1	(3)	
7	Albert RIERA		M	4	(4)	
27	Sergio SÁNCHEZ		D	10	(1)	
24	Jonathan SORIANO		A		(3)	
23	Raúl TAMUDO		A	26	(3)	10
29	Albert YAGÜE		A		(1)	
8	Pablo Javier ZABALETA	ARG	M	25	(2)	2

GETAFE CF
Coach – Bernd Schuster (GER)

2005

Date	Opponent	h/a	Score	Scorers
28/8	RCD Espanyol	a	2-0	Gavilán, Riki
11/9	Athletic Bilbao	h	1-1	Güiza
18/9	Deportivo Alavés	a	4-3	Belenguer, Riki 2, Pernía
21/9	RCD Mallorca	h	1-1	Güiza
24/9	Atlético Madrid	a	1-0	Pernía
1/10	Valencia CF	h	2-1	Riki, Redondo
16/10	Real Betis	a	0-1	
23/10	Real Zaragoza	h	5-2	Paunovic, Güiza 2 (1p), Pulido, Redondo
27/10	Real Sociedad	a	0-3	
30/10	RC Deportivo	a	0-1	
6/11	FC Barcelona	h	1-3	Pernía
19/11	CA Osasuna	h	0-0	
27/11	Málaga CF	h	3-2	Paunovic 2, og (Gerardo)
3/12	Real Madrid	a	0-1	
11/12	Racing Santander	h	1-2	Pernía
18/12	Villarreal CF	a	1-2	Riki
21/12	Sevilla FC	h	1-0	Güiza

2006

Date	Opponent	h/a	Score	Scorers
8/1	Cádiz CF	a	0-1	
15/1	RC Celta	h	1-1	Gavilán
22/1	RCD Espanyol	h	5-0	Güiza 2, Pernía 2, Gavilán
28/1	Athletic Bilbao	a	0-1	
5/2	Deportivo Alavés	h	2-2	Pernía (p), Güiza
12/2	RCD Mallorca	a	1-1	Vivar Dorado
19/2	Atlético Madrid	h	0-3	
26/2	Valencia CF	a	1-1	Nano
5/3	Real Betis	h	1-0	Paunovic
12/3	Real Zaragoza	a	2-1	Paunovic 2
18/3	RC Deportivo	h	1-2	Pachón
22/3	FC Barcelona	a	1-3	Nano
26/3	Real Sociedad	h	2-1	Pernía (p), Güiza
2/4	CA Osasuna	a	4-0	Paunovic 2, Vivar Dorado, Pernía
8/4	Málaga CF	a	2-1	Paunovic 2
16/4	Real Madrid	h	1-1	Tena
23/4	Racing Santander	a	3-1	Riki 2, Pernía
30/4	Villarreal CF	h	1-1	Gavilán
3/5	Sevilla FC	a	0-3	
7/5	Cádiz CF	h	3-1	Pulido, Pachón, Riki
13/5	RC Celta	a	0-1	

No	Name	Nat	Pos	Aps	(s)	Gls
24	ALBERTO Aguilar		M	9	(7)	
4	David BELENGUER		D	28	(1)	1
13	Juan Jesús CALATAYUD		G	13		
20	Fabio CELESTINI	SUI	M	19		

Spain

No	Name	Nat	Pos	Aps	(s)	Gls
2	Cosmin CONTRA	ROM	D	24		
7	Mario Gutiérrez COTELO		M	24	(6)	
8	Gheorghe CRAIOVEANU	ROM	A		(14)	
5	David García CUBILLO		M	6	(5)	
22	Jaime GAVILÁN		M	30	(2)	4
19	Daniel González GÜIZA		A	25	(7)	9
9	JAJA Avelino Coelho	BRA	A		(2)	
1	LUIS GARCÍA Conde		G	25		
12	Aníbal MATELLÁN	ARG	D	22		
21	NANO Macedo da Silva		M	3	(5)	2
17	Valentín Sergio PACHÓN		A	2	(20)	2
15	Javier PAREDES		D	2	(5)	
14	Veljko PAUNOVIC	SCG	A	21	(9)	10
3	Mariano Andrés PERNÍA		D	36		10
10	Rubén Martín PULIDO		D	21	(4)	2
18	Pablo REDONDO		M	14	(13)	2
11	Iván Sánchez "RIKI"		A	28	(4)	8
6	Diego RIVAS		M	33		
23	Manuel TENA		D	16		1
16	Ángel VIVAR DORADO		M	17	(8)	2

MÁLAGA CF
Coach – Antonio Tapia; (30/1/06) Manuel Ruiz Hierro

2005
Date	Opponent	h/a	Score	Scorers
28/8	RC Celta	a	0-2	
11/9	RCD Espanyol	h	1-2	Gerardo (p)
18/9	Athletic Bilbao	a	2-1	Edgar, Antonio Hidalgo
21/9	Deportivo Alavés	h	0-0	
25/9	RCD Mallorca	a	4-1	Salva, Duda 2, Edgar
2/10	Atlético Madrid	h	0-2	
16/10	Valencia CF	a	1-2	Salva
23/10	Real Betis	h	5-0	Salva 2, Fernando Sanz, Couñago 2
26/10	FC Barcelona	a	0-2	
30/10	Real Zaragoza	a	1-1	Edgar
6/11	RC Deportivo	h	1-1	Nacho
20/11	Real Sociedad	h	3-1	César Navas, Antonio Hidalgo, Edgar
27/11	Getafe CF	a	2-3	Nacho, Juan Rodríguez
4/12	CA Osasuna	h	1-2	Nacho
11/12	Real Madrid	h	0-2	
18/12	Racing Santander	a	1-1	César Navas
21/12	Villarreal CF	h	0-0	

2006
Date	Opponent	h/a	Score	Scorers
8/1	Sevilla FC	a	1-3	Salva
15/1	Cádiz CF	h	0-2	
22/1	RC Celta	h	0-2	
29/1	RCD Espanyol	a	1-3	Alexis
4/2	Athletic Bilbao	h	2-1	Litos, Salva
12/2	Deportivo Alavés	a	2-3	Duda, Antonio Hidalgo
19/2	RCD Mallorca	h	0-2	
25/2	Atlético Madrid	a	0-5	
5/3	Valencia CF	h	0-0	
12/3	Real Betis	a	1-1	Antonio Hidalgo
19/3	Real Zaragoza	h	0-1	
22/3	RC Deportivo	a	1-2	Duda
25/3	FC Barcelona	h	0-0	
1/4	Real Sociedad	a	0-3	
8/4	Getafe CF	h	1-2	Couñago
16/4	CA Osasuna	a	1-1	Morales
23/4	Real Madrid	a	1-2	Bóvio
30/4	Racing Santander	h	2-3	Alexis 2
3/5	Villarreal CF	a	1-2	Gerardo (p)
6/5	Sevilla FC	h	0-2	
13/5	Cádiz CF	a	0-5	

No	Name	Nat	Pos	Aps	(s)	Gls
34	Salvador Jiménez "ADOR"		M		(2)	
6	ALEXIS Ruano		D	34		3
3	ANDERSON da Silva	BRA	M	8	(7)	
8	ANTONIO HIDALGO		M	12	(23)	4
21	ANTONIO LÓPEZ Álvarez		M	9	(4)	
1	Francesc ARNAU		G	36		
23	Ricardo BÓVIO	BRA	M	15	(2)	1
32	Diego CASTRO		A		(2)	
5	CÉSAR González NAVAS		D	26	(2)	2
18	Pablo COUÑAGO		A	17	(10)	3
20	Sergio Paulo Barbosa "DUDA"	POR	M	13	(1)	4
10	EDGAR de Carvalho	ANG	A	26	(7)	4
9	Francisco ESTEBAN		A	2	(9)	
19	FERNANDO SANZ Durán		D	29		1
2	GABRIEL Rodrigues	BRA	D	11	(6)	
7	GERARDO García		M	29		2
13	Iñaki GOITIA		G	1	(1)	
27	JESÚS Gámez		D	12	(3)	
22	JUAN RODRÍGUEZ		M	27	(2)	1
4	LITOS de Oliveira Magalhães	POR	D	7	(1)	1
15	MANU Sánchez		M	9	(3)	
16	Richard MORALES	URU	A	8	(15)	1
11	NACHO Pérez		M	31	(1)	3
33	Jorge PINA		M		(2)	
26	Manuel REINA		G	1		
24	Miguel de Oliveira RIBEIRO	POR	D	4	(1)	
14	Marcelo ROMERO	URU	M	4		
17	SALVA Ballesta		A	29	(5)	6
38	SAÚL Fernández		M	1	(1)	
31	Fernando USERO		M	1	(1)	
12	Vicente VALCARCE		D	16		

RCD MALLORCA
Coach – Héctor Cúper (ARG); (13/2/06) Gregorio Manzano

2005
Date	Opponent	h/a	Score	Scorers
28/8	RC Deportivo	h	0-1	
11/9	FC Barcelona	a	0-2	
17/9	Real Sociedad	h	5-2	Yordi, Arango 3, Choutos
21/9	Getafe CF	a	1-1	Fernando Navarro
25/9	Málaga CF	h	1-4	Choutos
2/10	Real Madrid	a	0-4	
16/10	Racing Santander	h	0-0	
23/10	Villarreal CF	a	0-3	
26/10	RC Celta	h	1-0	Doni
30/10	Sevilla FC	h	1-1	Víctor
6/11	Cádiz CF	a	2-1	Víctor, Arango
20/11	RCD Espanyol	a	0-2	
26/11	Athletic Bilbao	h	0-1	
4/12	Deportivo Alavés	a	3-0	Víctor 2, Iuliano
11/12	CA Osasuna	a	0-1	
18/12	Atlético Madrid	h	2-2	Iuliano 2
21/12	Valencia CF	a	0-3	

2006
Date	Opponent	h/a	Score	Scorers
8/1	Real Betis	h	1-1	Gutiérrez
15/1	Real Zaragoza	a	1-3	Arango
22/1	RC Deportivo	a	2-2	Okubo, Arango
29/1	FC Barcelona	h	0-3	
5/2	Real Sociedad	a	1-2	Pisculichi
12/2	Getafe CF	h	1-1	Arango
19/2	Málaga CF	a	2-0	Pisculichi, Campano
26/2	Real Madrid	h	2-1	Pisculichi (p), Arango

Spain

5/3	Racing Santander	a	0-0		
12/3	Villarreal CF	h	1-1	Pereyra	
19/3	Sevilla FC	a	1-1	Okubo	
22/3	Cádiz CF	h	1-0	Víctor	
26/3	RC Celta	a	0-2		
2/4	RCD Espanyol	h	0-0		
9/4	Athletic Bilbao	a	1-1	Arango	
15/4	Deportivo Alavés	h	0-0		
23/4	CA Osasuna	h	0-1		
30/4	Atlético Madrid	a	1-0	Gutiérrez	
3/5	Valencia CF	h	2-1	Arango, Doni	
7/5	Real Betis	a	1-2	Yordi	
13/5	Real Zaragoza	h	3-1	Arango, Farinós, Yordi	

No	Name	Nat	Pos	Aps	(s)	Gls
18	Juan Fernando ARANGO	VEN	M	36	(1)	11
22	Sergio Martínez BALLESTEROS		D	19	(1)	
2	Angelis BASINAS	GRE	M	13	(1)	
6	BORJA Fernández		D	6	(10)	
21	BRAULIO Nóbrega		A		(2)	
7	Alejandro CAMPANO		M	10	(16)	1
24	Lampros CHOUTOS	GRE	A		(9)	2
8	David CORTÉS		D	27		
5	Cristiano DONI	ITA	M	18	(6)	2
10	Francisco Javier FARINÓS		M	12	(5)	1
3	FERNANDO NAVARRO		D	33		1
11	Jonás GUTIÉRREZ	ARG	A	29	(1)	2
21	Mark IULIANO	ITA	D	13	(1)	3
14	Francisco MACIEL	ARG	D	16	(3)	
1	Miguel Ángel MOYÁ		G	8	(1)	
16	José Carlos de Araújo NUNES	POR	D	17		
17	Yoshito OKUBO	JPN	A	9	(17)	2
16	Adrián PERALTA	ARG	M	5	(2)	
4	Guillermo Ariel PEREYRA	ARG	M	27	(2)	1
12	Leonardo Nicolás PISCULICHI	ARG	M	13	(3)	3
23	Alessandro POTENZA	ITA	D	15	(2)	
25	Antonio PRATS		G	30		
27	RAFITA Ramos		D		(1)	
15	Antonio Luis Adrover "TUNI"		A	26	(8)	
20	Eduardo Nicolás TUZZIO	ARG	D	10		
19	VÍCTOR Casadesús		A	20	(8)	5
9	YORDI González		A	6	(10)	3

CA OSASUNA
Coach – Javier Aguirre (MEX)

2005
28/8	Villarreal CF	h	2-1	Romeo 2
10/9	Real Betis	a	0-1	
18/9	Sevilla FC	h	1-0	David López
21/9	Real Zaragoza	a	1-3	Delporte
25/9	Cádiz CF	h	2-0	David López, Moha
2/10	RC Deportivo	a	1-0	Muñoz
16/10	RC Celta	h	2-1	Milosevic, Webo
22/10	FC Barcelona	a	0-3	
26/10	Athletic Bilbao	h	3-2	Raúl García, Milosevic, Webo
30/10	RCD Espanyol	h	2-0	David López, Muñoz
5/11	Real Sociedad	a	2-1	Raúl García, Cuéllar
19/11	Getafe CF	a	0-0	
27/11	Deportivo Alavés	h	3-2	Milosevic, Puñal (p), Moha
4/12	Málaga CF	a	2-1	Webo, Valdo
11/12	RCD Mallorca	h	1-0	Webo
18/12	Real Madrid	a	1-1	Milosevic
22/12	Atlético Madrid	h	2-1	Raúl García, Romeo

2006
8/1	Racing Santander	h	1-1	Delporte
14/1	Valencia CF	a	0-2	
22/1	Villarreal CF	a	1-2	Raúl García
29/1	Real Betis	h	0-2	
5/2	Sevilla FC	a	1-0	Milosevic
11/2	Real Zaragoza	h	1-1	Milosevic
19/2	Cádiz CF	a	3-1	Milosevic, David López, Raúl García
26/2	RC Deportivo	h	1-2	Romeo
5/3	RC Celta	a	0-2	
12/3	FC Barcelona	h	2-1	Valdo, Puñal (p)
19/3	RCD Espanyol	a	4-2	David López, Webo, Milosevic, Muñoz
22/3	Real Sociedad	h	2-0	Muñoz, Puñal (p)
25/3	Athletic Bilbao	a	0-1	
2/4	Getafe CF	h	0-4	
9/4	Deportivo Alavés	a	2-1	Webo, Milosevic
16/4	Málaga CF	h	1-1	Puñal (p)
23/4	RCD Mallorca	a	1-0	Delporte
30/4	Real Madrid	h	0-1	
3/5	Atlético Madrid	a	1-0	Muñoz
7/5	Racing Santander	a	1-2	Milosevic
16/5	Valencia CF	h	2-1	Milosevic, David López

No	Name	Nat	Pos	Aps	(s)	Gls
24	Gorka BRIT		A		(4)	
3	Rafael CLAVERO		D	21	(1)	
19	Enrique CORRALES		D	17	(1)	
7	César CRUCHAGA		D	12	(8)	
5	Carlos Javier CUÉLLAR		D	27	(2)	1
16	DAVID LÓPEZ Moreno		M	29	(5)	6
23	Ludovic DELPORTE	FRA	M	21	(6)	3
1	Juan ELÍA		G	8		
17	Javier FLAÑO		D	31		
4	Miguel FLAÑO		D	9	(3)	
2	José IZQUIERDO		D	7		
14	JOSETXO Romero		D	28	(1)	
9	Savo MILOSEVIC	SCG	A	31	(1)	11
11	MOHA El Yaagoubi Youbi	MAR	M	15	(12)	2
12	Francisco MORENO		M	2	(5)	
22	Iñaki MUÑOZ		M	16	(14)	5
8	Juan Manuel ORTIZ		M	3	(4)	
10	Francisco PUÑAL		M	32	(2)	4
6	RAÚL GARCÍA Escudero		M	28	(5)	5
13	RICARDO López		G	30		
20	Bernardo Daniel ROMEO	ARG	A	19	(5)	4
18	Marcelo Fabián SOSA	URU	M	3	(8)	
21	VALDO Lopes Rocha		A	12	(7)	2
15	Pierre Achille WEBO	CMR	A	17	(14)	6

RACING SANTANDER
Coach – Manuel Preciado; (24/4/06) Nando Trío "Yosu"

2005
28/8	Sevilla FC	a	0-1	
11/9	Cádiz CF	h	0-1	
18/9	RC Celta	a	1-0	Casquero
21/9	RCD Espanyol	h	1-0	Antoñito
25/9	Athletic Bilbao	a	0-0	
2/10	Deportivo Alavés	h	1-2	Juanjo
16/10	RCD Mallorca	a	0-0	
23/10	Atlético Madrid	h	0-1	
27/10	Real Zaragoza	a	1-1	Aganzo
30/10	Valencia CF	a	1-1	Aganzo

Spain

Date	Opponent	H/A	Score	Scorers
6/11	Real Betis	h	1-1	Antoñito
20/11	RC Deportivo	h	0-3	
27/11	FC Barcelona	a	1-4	Casquero (p)
4/12	Real Sociedad	h	2-2	Antoñito, og (Riesgo)
11/12	Getafe CF	a	2-1	Antoñito, Aganzo
18/12	Málaga CF	h	1-1	Casquero
21/12	Real Madrid	a	2-1	Ayoze, Felipe Melo
2006				
8/1	CA Osasuna	a	1-1	Antoñito
15/1	Villarreal CF	h	1-0	Matabuena
22/1	Sevilla FC	h	2-3	Juanjo, Felipe Melo
28/1	Cádiz CF	a	1-1	Felipe Melo (p)
5/2	RC Celta	h	0-1	
12/2	RCD Espanyol	a	2-0	Damià, Casquero
19/2	Athletic Bilbao	h	0-1	
26/2	Deportivo Alavés	a	2-2	Pinilla (p), Dalmat W.
5/3	RCD Mallorca	h	0-0	
12/3	Atlético Madrid	a	1-2	Damià
19/3	Valencia CF	h	2-1	Damià, Ayoze
22/3	Real Betis	a	0-1	
26/3	Real Zaragoza	h	0-0	
2/4	RC Deportivo	a	0-2	
9/4	FC Barcelona	h	2-2	Antoñito, Serrano
15/4	Real Sociedad	a	0-1	
23/4	Getafe CF	h	1-3	Antoñito
30/4	Málaga CF	a	3-2	Casquero, Antoñito, Juanjo
4/5	Real Madrid	h	2-3	Matabuena 2
7/5	CA Osasuna	h	2-1	Pablo Alfaro, Antoñito
13/5	Villarreal CF	a	0-2	

No	Name	Nat	Pos	Aps	(s)	Gls
9	David AGANZO		A	8	(9)	3
34	ALEX García		M		(1)	
35	ANTONIO TOMÁS		M	15	(8)	
20	ANTOÑITO Ramiro		A	21	(11)	9
1	Dudu AWATE	ISR	G	37		
21	AYOZE Díaz		D	28		2
19	Francisco Javier CASQUERO		M	20	(6)	5
18	Stéphane DALMAT	FRA	M	11	(2)	
17	Wilfred DALMAT	FRA	M	4	(7)	1
2	DAMIÀ Abella		D	15	(3)	3
23	FELIPE MELO de Carvalho	BRA	M	26	(7)	3
4	Ezequiel GARAY	ARG	D	7		
32	JUANJO Expósito		A	11	(11)	3
25	LEE Ho-jin	KOR	M	1		
7	José Fernando MARQUÉS		A	2		
27	Raúl MARTÍN		A	6	(7)	
24	Sergio MATABUENA		M	16	(7)	3
22	José MORATÓN		D	23	(1)	
5	Francisco Enrique "NERU"		D	11	(4)	
3	ORIOL Lozano		D	19		
11	ÓSCAR SERRANO		A	23	(9)	1
16	PABLO ALFARO		D	16	(1)	1
15	Mauricio Ricardo PINILLA	CHL	A	8	(5)	1
14	Pablo PINILLOS		D	33		
33	Cristian PORTILLA		M	2	(1)	
8	Walid REGRAGUI	FRA	D	8	(1)	
28	SAMUEL San José		D	7		
13	Juan José VALENCIA		G	1		
10	Jonathan VALLE		A	9	(9)	
6	VITOLO Añino		M	30	(3)	

REAL MADRID
Coach – Vanderlei Luxemburgo (BRA); (5/12/05) Juan Ramón López Caro

Date	Opponent	H/A	Score	Scorers
2005				
28/8	Cádiz CF	a	2-1	Ronaldo, Raúl
10/9	RC Celta	h	2-3	Ronaldo (p), Júlio Baptista
18/9	RCD Espanyol	a	0-1	
22/9	Athletic Bilbao	h	3-1	Robinho, Raúl 2
25/9	Deportivo Alavés	a	3-0	Ronaldo 2, Guti
2/10	RCD Mallorca	h	4-0	Ronaldo, Roberto Carlos 2, Júlio Baptista
15/10	Atlético Madrid	a	3-0	Ronaldo 2 (1p), og (Perea)
23/10	Valencia CF	h	1-2	Raúl
26/10	RC Deportivo	a	1-3	Raúl
29/10	Real Betis	a	2-0	Robinho, Mejía
6/11	Real Zaragoza	h	1-0	Roberto Carlos (p)
19/11	FC Barcelona	h	0-3	
27/11	Real Sociedad	a	2-2	Raúl Bravo, Zidane
3/12	Getafe CF	h	1-0	Ronaldo
11/12	Málaga CF	a	2-0	Sergio Ramos, Robinho
18/12	CA Osasuna	h	1-1	Soldado
21/12	Racing Santander	h	1-2	Ronaldo
2006				
8/1	Villarreal CF	a	0-0	
15/1	Sevilla FC	h	4-2	Guti, Zidane 3 (1p)
21/1	Cádiz CF	h	3-1	Roberto Carlos, Beckham, Robinho
29/1	RC Celta	a	2-1	Robinho, Cicinho
4/2	RCD Espanyol	h	4-0	Guti, Zidane 2, Ronaldo
11/2	Athletic Bilbao	a	2-0	Robinho, Raúl Bravo
18/2	Deportivo Alavés	h	3-0	Guti, Robinho, Cicinho
26/2	RCD Mallorca	a	1-2	Sergio Ramos
4/3	Atlético Madrid	h	2-1	Cassano, Júlio Baptista
11/3	Valencia CF	a	0-0	
19/3	Real Betis	h	0-0	
22/3	Real Zaragoza	a	1-1	Ronaldo
26/3	RC Deportivo	h	4-0	og (Héctor), Ronaldo, Sergio Ramos, Júlio Baptista
1/4	FC Barcelona	a	1-1	Ronaldo
8/4	Real Sociedad	h	1-1	Ronaldo
16/4	Getafe CF	a	1-1	Júlio Baptista
23/4	Málaga CF	h	2-1	Zidane (p), Sergio Ramos
30/4	CA Osasuna	a	1-0	Júlio Baptista (p)
4/5	Racing Santander	a	3-2	Roberto Carlos (p), Soldado, Robinho
7/5	Villarreal CF	h	3-3	Júlio Baptista 2, Zidane
16/5	Sevilla FC	a	3-4	Beckham 2, Zidane

No	Name	Nat	Pos	Aps	(s)	Gls
35	Javier BALBOA		A		(2)	
23	David BECKHAM	ENG	M	30	(1)	3
1	Iker CASILLAS		G	37		
19	Antonio CASSANO	ITA	A	3	(9)	1
11	Cicero João de Cezare "CICINHO"	BRA	D	15	(4)	2
28	Rubén DE LA RED		M		(3)	
21	Carlos Andrés DIOGO	URU	D	7	(6)	
16	Thomas GRAVESEN	DAN	M	10	(7)	
14	José María Gutiérrez "GUTI"		M	28	(5)	4
6	Iván HELGUERA		D	18	(1)	
8	JÚLIO César BAPTISTA	BRA	M	25	(7)	8
29	José Manuel JURADO		M		(2)	
13	Diego LÓPEZ		G	1	(1)	
24	Álvaro MEJÍA		D	13	(4)	1
2	MÍCHEL SALGADO		D	26	(1)	

Spain

12	PABLO Gabriel GARCÍA	URU	M	17	(5)	
22	Francisco PAVÓN		D	9	(1)	
7	RAÚL González		A	20	(6)	5
15	RAÚL BRAVO Sanfelix		D	8	(7)	2
3	ROBERTO CARLOS da Silva	BRA	D	35		5
10	Robson de Souza "ROBINHO"	BRA	A	31	(6)	8
9	RONALDO Luiz Nazário de Lima	BRA	A	21	(2)	14
4	SERGIO RAMOS		D	32	(1)	4
27	Roberto SOLDADO		A	1	(10)	2
18	Jonathan WOODGATE	ENG	D	7	(2)	
5	Zinedine ZIDANE	FRA	M	24	(5)	9

REAL SOCIEDAD
Coach – José María Amorrortu; (30/1/06) Gonzalo Arconada; (23/3/06) José María Bakero

2005
27/8	Athletic Bilbao	a	0-3	
11/9	Deportivo Alavés	h	2-1	Barkero 2 (1p)
17/9	RCD Mallorca	a	2-5	Novo, Sabih Prieto
21/9	Atlético Madrid	h	3-2	Kovacevic 2, Nihat
24/9	Valencia CF	a	1-2	Nihat
2/10	Real Betis	h	1-1	Kovacevic
16/10	Real Zaragoza	a	1-0	Xabi Prieto (p)
23/10	RC Deportivo	h	2-0	Kovacevic, Jauregi
27/10	Getafe CF	h	3-0	Aranburu, Nihat, Sabih Prieto (p)
30/10	FC Barcelona	a	0-5	
5/11	CA Osasuna	h	1-2	Xabi Prieto (p)
20/11	Málaga CF	a	1-3	De Paula
27/11	Real Madrid	h	2-2	Xabi Prieto (p), De Paula
4/12	Racing Santander	a	2-2	Novo, De Paula
10/12	Villarreal CF	h	1-3	Nihat
18/12	Sevilla FC	a	2-3	Labaka, Garitano
21/12	Cádiz CF	h	2-0	Gabilondo, Xabi Prieto (p)

2006
8/1	RC Celta	a	0-1	
15/1	RCD Espanyol	h	0-1	
22/1	Athletic Bilbao	h	3-3	Nihat 2, Skoubo
29/1	Deportivo Alavés	a	1-3	Stevanovic
5/2	RCD Mallorca	h	2-1	Skoubo, Mark González
12/2	Atlético Madrid	a	0-1	
19/2	Valencia CF	h	1-2	Skoubo
26/2	Real Betis	a	0-2	
5/3	Real Zaragoza	h	1-3	Nihat
11/3	RC Deportivo	a	1-0	Garitano
18/3	FC Barcelona	h	0-2	
22/3	CA Osasuna	a	0-2	
26/3	Getafe CF	a	1-2	Mark González
1/4	Málaga CF	h	3-0	Ansotegui, Skoubo, Xabi Prieto
8/4	Real Madrid	a	1-1	Mark González
15/4	Racing Santander	h	1-0	Mark González
22/4	Villarreal CF	a	2-0	Alonso, Mark González
30/4	Sevilla FC	h	1-2	og (Jordi)
3/5	Cádiz CF	a	2-2	Xabi Prieto, Garitano
7/5	RC Celta	h	2-2	Xabi Prieto (p), Skoubo
13/5	RCD Espanyol	a	0-1	

No	Name	Nat	Pos	Aps	(s)	Gls
40	Imanol AGIRRETXE		M		(1)	
1	ALBERTO López		G	5		
22	Mikel ALONSO		M	34	(3)	1
31	Jon ANSOTEGUI		D	13		1
11	Mikel ARANBURU		M	13		1
20	José Javier BARKERO		M	3	(14)	2
23	BORIS González		D	1	(2)	
5	Jérémie BRÉCHET	FRA	D	3		
18	Daniel CIFUENTES		D	12	(1)	
21	Óscar DE PAULA		A	3	(3)	3
39	Iñigo DÍAZ DE CERIO		A	1	(2)	
17	Igor GABILONDO		M	6	(10)	1
8	Gaizka GARITANO		M	17	(2)	3
19	Javier GARRIDO		M	33		
3	Mark GONZÁLEZ	CHL	A	12	(4)	5
41	Mikel GONZÁLEZ		D	3		
7	Igor JAUREGI		D	23		1
9	Darko KOVACEVIC	SCG	A	9		4
6	Mikel LABAKA		D	31	(2)	1
33	Gorka LARREA		M	3	(9)	
14	Aitor LÓPEZ REKARTE		D	29	(2)	
15	NIHAT Kahveci	TUR	A	24	(8)	7
10	Álvaro NOVO		M	27	(6)	2
13	Asier RIESGO		G	33		
12	Morten SKOUBO	DAN	A	16	(2)	5
4	Dalibor STEVANOVIC	SLO	A	7	(8)	1
16	Garikoitz URANGA		M	15	(18)	
2	John Edvis VIÁFARA	COL	M	10	(1)	
24	XABIer PRIETO		M	32	(6)	9

SEVILLA FC
Coach – Juan de la Cruz Ramos

2005
28/8	Racing Santander	h	1-0	Kepa
11/9	Villarreal CF	a	1-1	Adriano
18/9	CA Osasuna	a	0-1	
21/9	Cádiz CF	h	0-0	
25/9	RC Celta	a	1-2	Maresca (p)
2/10	RCD Espanyol	h	1-1	og (Hurtado)
16/10	Athletic Bilbao	a	1-0	Alves
22/10	Deportivo Alavés	h	2-0	Adriano, Maresca (p)
27/10	Valencia CF	a	2-0	Luís Fabiano, og (Ayala)
30/10	RCD Mallorca	a	1-1	Kepa
6/11	Atlético Madrid	h	0-0	
19/11	Real Betis	h	1-0	Maresca (p)
27/11	Real Zaragoza	a	2-0	Saviola, Alves
4/12	RC Deportivo	h	0-2	
11/12	FC Barcelona	a	1-2	Kanouté
18/12	Real Sociedad	h	3-2	Kepa 2, Kanouté
21/12	Getafe CF	a	0-1	

2006
8/1	Málaga CF	h	3-1	Maresca, Adriano, Dragutinovic
15/1	Real Madrid	a	2-4	Luís Fabiano, Aitor Ocio
22/1	Racing Santander	a	3-2	Kanouté, Maresca 2 (2p)
29/1	Villarreal CF	h	2-0	Luís Fabiano, Kanouté
5/2	CA Osasuna	h	0-1	
11/2	Cádiz CF	a	4-0	Saviola, Puerta, Kepa, Kanouté
18/2	RC Celta	h	1-0	Saviola
26/2	RCD Espanyol	a	0-5	
5/3	Athletic Bilbao	h	2-1	Maresca (p), Kanouté
12/3	Deportivo Alavés	a	1-2	Saviola
19/3	RCD Mallorca	h	1-1	Saviola
23/3	Atlético Madrid	a	1-0	Puerta
26/3	Valencia CF	h	1-0	Jordi
2/4	Real Betis	a	1-2	Saviola
9/4	Real Zaragoza	h	1-1	Maresca
15/4	RC Deportivo	a	0-0	

Spain

30/4	Real Sociedad	a	2-1	Jesús Navas, Martí (p)
3/5	Getafe CF	h	3-0	og (Pulido), Saviola, Luís Fabiano
6/5	Málaga CF	a	2-0	Renato, Sales
13/5	FC Barcelona	h	3-2	Alves, Aitor Ocio (p), Kepa
16/5	Real Madrid	h	4-3	Jesús Navas, Saviola 2, Luís Fabiano

No	Name	Nat	Pos	Aps	(s)	Gls
16	ADRIANO Correia	BRA	M	30	(2)	3
20	AITOR OCIO Carrión		D	19	(4)	2
39	Alejandro ALFARO		M		(2)	
24	Pablo ALFARO		D		(4)	
4	Daniel ALVES	BRA	D	35		3
34	Diego CAPEL		M		(4)	
35	José Ángel CRESPO		D	2	(1)	
3	DAVID Castedo		D	32	(1)	
19	Ivica DRAGUTINOVIC	SCG	D	20	(1)	1
14	Julien ESCUDE	FRA	D	12	(4)	
38	Bruno HERRERA		M		(2)	
2	JAVIer NAVARRO		D	24	(1)	
17	JESULI Mora		M	2	(4)	
8	JORDI López		M	11	(8)	1
12	Frédéric KANOUTÉ	FRA	A	26	(6)	6
30	KEPA Blanco		A	9	(17)	6
21	Antonio LÓPEZ		M	1	(1)	
10	LUÍS FABIANO Clemente	BRA	A	15	(8)	5
25	Enzo MARESCA	ITA	M	25	(4)	8
18	José Luis MARTÍ		M	28	(5)	1
15	Jesús NAVAS		M	31	(3)	2
13	Antonio NOTARIO		G	2		
1	Andrés PALOP		G	36		
28	David PRIETO		D	4		
27	Antonio José PUERTA		M	8	(9)	2
5	Sergio RAMOS		D	1		
11	RENATO Dirnei Florencio	BRA	M	15	(6)	1
23	Pablo RUIZ		D		(2)	
22	Fernando SALES		M	8	(5)	1
7	Javier Pedro SAVIOLA	ARG	A	22	(7)	9

VALENCIA CF
Coach – Enrique Sánchez Flores

2005

27/8	Real Betis	h	1-0	Aimar
11/9	Real Zaragoza	a	2-2	Angulo, David Villa
17/9	RC Deportivo	h	2-2	David Villa (p), Miguel
21/9	FC Barcelona	a	2-2	David Villa 2 (1p)
24/9	Real Sociedad	h	2-1	Aimar, David Villa
1/10	Getafe CF	a	1-2	David Villa
16/10	Málaga CF	h	2-1	Ayala, Vicente
23/10	Real Madrid	a	2-1	Baraja, David Villa (p)
27/10	Sevilla FC	h	0-2	
30/10	Racing Santander	h	1-1	Albelda
5/11	Villarreal CF	a	0-1	
20/11	Cádiz CF	a	1-0	Vicente
26/11	RC Celta	h	2-0	David Villa, Fábio Aurélio
4/12	RCD Espanyol	a	3-1	Angulo, David Villa, Aimar
10/12	Athletic Bilbao	h	1-1	Vicente
18/12	Deportivo Alavés	a	1-0	Albiol
21/12	RCD Mallorca	h	3-0	Albelda, David Villa, Fábio Aurélio

2006

8/1	Atlético Madrid	a	0-0	
14/1	CA Osasuna	h	2-0	Regueiro, David Villa
22/1	Real Betis	a	2-0	David Villa 2
29/1	Real Zaragoza	h	2-2	Kluivert, Aimar
4/2	RC Deportivo	a	1-0	David Villa
12/2	FC Barcelona	h	1-0	David Villa
19/2	Real Sociedad	a	2-1	Regueiro 2
26/2	Getafe CF	h	1-1	David Navarro
5/3	Málaga CF	a	0-0	
11/3	Real Madrid	h	0-0	
19/3	Racing Santander	a	1-2	David Villa
22/3	Villarreal CF	h	1-1	Baraja
26/3	Sevilla FC	a	0-1	
2/4	Cádiz CF	h	5-3	David Villa 2, Angulo 2, David Navarro
8/4	RC Celta	a	1-0	Angulo
16/4	RCD Espanyol	h	4-0	David Villa (p), Ayala, Mista, Baraja
23/4	Athletic Bilbao	a	3-0	David Villa 3
30/4	Deportivo Alavés	h	3-0	Baraja, Aimar, David Villa (p)
3/5	RCD Mallorca	a	1-2	Angulo
6/5	Atlético Madrid	h	1-1	David Villa (p)
16/5	CA Osasuna	a	1-2	David Villa

No	Name	Nat	Pos	Aps	(s)	Gls
21	Pablo César AIMAR	ARG	A	28	(4)	5
6	David ALBELDA		M	32		2
33	Raúl ALBIOL		D	29		1
10	Miguel Ángel ANGULO		M	26	(6)	6
4	Roberto Fabián AYALA	ARG	D	23		2
8	Rubén BARAJA		M	31		4
25	Ludovic BUTELLE	FRA	G	1		
12	Marco Simoes CANEIRA	POR	D	4	(1)	
1	Santiago CAÑIZARES		G	36		
15	Amedeo CARBONI	ITA	D	3	(2)	
23	CURRO TORRES		D	1	(2)	
17	DAVID NAVARRO		D	7	(1)	2
7	DAVID VILLA		A	35	(2)	25
22	Marco DI VAIO	ITA	A	2	(3)	
22	EDÚ César Daud Gaspar	BRA	M	1	(5)	
3	FÁBIO AURÉLIO Rodrigues	BRA	D	11	(13)	2
27	Pablo HERNÁNDEZ		M		(1)	
16	HUGO Ferreira VIANA	POR	M	4	(15)	
9	Patrick KLUIVERT	HOL	A	1	(9)	1
18	Jorge LÓPEZ		M	1	(4)	
5	Carlos MARCHENA		D	21	(4)	
2	MIGUEL Brito Garcia	POR	D	31		1
20	Miguel Ángel Ferrer "MISTA"		A	10	(19)	1
13	Juan Luis MORA		G	1		
24	Emiliano MORETTI	ITA	D	33		
11	Mario Ignacio REGUEIRO	URU	M	18	(6)	3
19	Joaquín Pérez RUFETE		M	9	(10)	
14	VICENTE Rodríguez		M	19	(2)	3

VILLARREAL CF
Coach – Manuel Pellegrini (CHL)

2005

28/8	CA Osasuna	a	1-2	Forlán
11/9	Sevilla FC	h	1-1	Figueroa
18/9	Cádiz CF	a	1-1	José Mari
21/9	RC Celta	h	1-2	Riquelme
24/9	RCD Espanyol	a	2-1	Josico, Senna
2/10	Athletic Bilbao	h	3-1	Riquelme, José Mari, Senna
15/10	Deportivo Alavés	a	1-1	Roger
23/10	RCD Mallorca	h	3-0	Riquelme, José Mari, Forlán

Spain

Date	Opponent	h/a	Score	Scorers
26/10	Real Betis	a	3-2	José Mari, Sorín, Riquelme (p)
30/10	Atlético Madrid	a	1-1	Forlán
5/11	Valencia CF	h	1-0	Figueroa
19/11	Real Zaragoza	h	0-0	
27/11	RC Deportivo	a	2-0	Riquelme, Sorín
4/12	FC Barcelona	h	0-2	
10/12	Real Sociedad	a	3-1	Guayre 2, Riquelme
18/12	Getafe CF	h	2-1	Riquelme, Forlán
21/12	Málaga CF	a	0-0	
2006				
8/1	Real Madrid	h	0-0	
15/1	Racing Santander	a	0-1	
22/1	CA Osasuna	h	2-1	Riquelme 2 (2p)
29/1	Sevilla FC	a	0-2	
5/2	Cádiz CF	h	1-1	Calleja
12/2	RC Celta	a	0-1	
18/2	RCD Espanyol	h	4-0	Tacchinardi, Senna, Forlán, Font
26/2	Athletic Bilbao	a	1-1	Forlán
4/3	Deportivo Alavés	h	3-2	Riquelme 2, Franco
12/3	RCD Mallorca	a	1-1	José Mari
18/3	Atlético Madrid	h	1-1	Forlán
22/3	Valencia CF	a	1-1	Forlán
25/3	Real Betis	h	1-2	Sorín
1/4	Real Zaragoza	a	1-0	Roger
9/4	RC Deportivo	h	1-1	Franco
14/4	FC Barcelona	a	0-1	
22/4	Real Sociedad	h	0-2	
30/4	Getafe CF	a	1-1	Franco
3/5	Málaga CF	h	2-1	Franco, Tacchinardi og (Mejía), Forlán 2 (1p)
7/5	Real Madrid	a	3-3	
13/5	Racing Santander	h	2-0	Riquelme (p), Xisco

No	Name	Nat	Pos	Aps	(s)	Gls
30	Carlos ALCÁNTARA		M	3		
3	Rodolfo Martín ARRUABARRENA	ARG	D	33		
4	César ARZO		M	5	(7)	
25	Mariano Damián BARBOSA	ARG	G	9	(1)	
11	Javier CALLEJA		A	2	(11)	1
8	Luciano FIGUEROA	ARG	A	7	(5)	2
14	Héctor FONT		M	8	(13)	1
5	Diego FORLÁN	URU	A	30	(2)	10
9	Guillermo FRANCO	MEX	A	8	(4)	4
2	GONZALO RODRÍGUEZ	ARG	D	29		
7	Antonio GUAYRE Betancort		A	7	(10)	2
17	JAVIer VENTA		D	25		
23	JOSÉ MARI Romero		A	28	(4)	5
24	JOSEMI González		D	8	(1)	
6	JOSICO Moreno		M	26	(1)	1
15	Jan KROMKAMP	HOL	D	6		
36	Óscar LÓPEZ		D	1		
22	Juan Manuel PEÑA	BOL	D	23	(2)	
16	Enrique "QUIQUE" ÁLVAREZ		D	20	(1)	
8	Juan Román RIQUELME	ARG	M	25		12
10	ROGER García		M	8	(16)	2
33	José Javier RUBIO		M	1		
21	SANTIago CAZORLA		M	14	(9)	
19	Marcos António SENNA		M	29	(1)	3
12	Juan Pablo SORÍN	ARG	D	16	(4)	3
18	Alessio TACCHINARDI	ITA	M	17	(6)	2
20	Luis Antonio VALENCIA	EQU	M	1	(1)	
13	Mario Sebastián VIERA	URU	G	29		
26	XISCO Nadal		A		(4)	1

REAL ZARAGOZA
Coach – Víctor Muñoz

Date	Opponent	h/a	Score	Scorers
2005				
28/8	Atlético Madrid	a	0-0	
11/9	Valencia CF	h	2-2	Ewerthon, Cani
18/9	Real Betis	a	0-0	
21/9	CA Osasuna	h	3-1	Diego Milito, Sergio García, Sávio
24/9	RC Deportivo	h	1-1	Diego Milito
1/10	FC Barcelona	a	2-2	Gabriel Milito, Diego Milito
16/10	Real Sociedad	h	0-1	
23/10	Getafe CF	a	2-5	Movilla, og (Berenguer)
27/10	Racing Santander	h	1-1	Diego Milito
30/12	Málaga CF	h	1-1	Ewerthon
6/11	Real Madrid	a	0-1	
19/11	Villarreal CF	a	0-0	
27/11	Sevilla FC	h	0-2	
4/12	Cádiz CF	a	2-1	Cani, Ewerthon
11/12	RC Celta	h	1-0	Ewerthon
18/12	RCD Espanyol	a	2-2	Generelo, Diego Milito
21/12	Athletic Bilbao	h	3-2	Ewerthon 2 (1p), Diego Milito
2006				
8/1	Deportivo Alavés	a	2-0	Diego Milito, Ewerthon
15/1	RCD Mallorca	h	3-1	Óscar, Diego Milito 2
21/1	Atlético Madrid	h	0-2	
29/1	Valencia CF	a	2-2	Sergio García, Ewerthon
5/2	Real Betis	h	4-3	Diego Milito 2, Óscar, Sergio García
11/2	CA Osasuna	a	1-1	Ponzio
19/2	RC Deportivo	a	1-1	Diego Milito
25/2	FC Barcelona	h	0-2	
5/3	Real Sociedad	a	3-1	Ewerthon 2, Óscar
12/3	Getafe CF	h	1-2	Diego Milito
19/3	Málaga CF	a	1-0	Ewerthon
22/3	Real Madrid	h	1-1	Diego Milito
26/3	Racing Santander	a	0-0	
1/4	Villarreal CF	h	0-1	
9/4	Sevilla FC	a	1-1	Sergio García
16/4	Cádiz CF	h	1-2	Sávio
22/4	RC Celta	a	0-4	
30/4	RCD Espanyol	h	1-1	Ewerthon
3/5	Athletic Bilbao	a	0-1	
7/5	Deportivo Alavés	h	3-0	Diego Milito, Sávio, Óscar
13/5	RCD Mallorca	a	1-3	Sávio

No	Name	Nat	Pos	Aps	(s)	Gls
5	ÁLVARO Luis Maior de Aquino	BRA	D	31		
3	Agustín ARANZÁBAL		D	3	(6)	
8	Rubén Gracia "CANI"		M	24	(6)	2
24	Manuel Borja Calvar "CAPI"		D	7	(1)	
16	Alberto CELADES		M	21	(5)	
19	CÉSAR Jiménez		D		(1)	
23	Miguel Ángel García "CORONA"		M		(3)	
4	Luis Carlos CUARTERO		D	8	(7)	
17	EWERTHON Henrique	BRA	A	30	(7)	12
20	David GENERELO		M	15	(15)	1
27	Jesús María HERRERO		D	3	(2)	
15	Ángel LAFITA		M	2	(11)	
22	Diego MILITO	ARG	A	35	(1)	15
6	Gabriel MILITO	ARG	D	33	(1)	1
7	José María MOVILLA		M	16	(9)	1
18	ÓSCAR González		M	29	(7)	4
14	Leonardo Daniel PONZIO	ARG	M	35		

Spain

1	César SÁNCHEZ		G	35		
10	SÁVIO Bortolini	BRA	A	24	(6)	4
9	SERGIO GARCÍA		A	7	(12)	4
12	Delio César TOLEDO	PAR	D	30	(2)	
25	Raúl VALBUENA		G	3	(2)	
21	Alberto ZAPATER		M	27	(8)	

DOMESTIC CUP 2005/06

THIRD ROUND
(19/10/05)
SD Éibar 1, Deportivo Alavés 0
(20/10/05)
CE L'Hospitalet 4, Club Gimnàstic Tarragona 3
Burgos CF 1, Racing Santander 0
CD Baza 1, Málaga CF 1 *(aet; 5-4 on pens)*
Xerez CD 3, CD Numancia 2
SD Tenisca 1, RC Celta 3
Rayo Vallecano Madrid 1, Getafe CF 2
CD Alcoyano 4, RCD Mallorca 1
Real Unión Irún 0, Athletic Bilbao 1
Logroñés CF 0, UE Lleida 1 *(aet)*
Albacete Balompié 1, Cádiz CF 3 *(aet)*
Zamora CF 1, Real Sociedad 1 *(aet; 2-0 on pens)*
UD Las Palmas 0, Atlético Madrid 1
Alicante CF 1, Real Zaragoza 1 *(aet; 5-6 on pens)*

FOURTH ROUND
(9/11/05)
UE Lleida 2, Getafe CF 4 *(aet)*
CE L'Hospitalet 1, Athletic Bilbao 3
Burgos CF 0, Cádiz CF 2
Zamora CF 1, SD Éibar 1 *(aet; 5-4 on pens)*
CD Baza 0, RC Celta 1 *(aet)*
(30/11/05)
Xerez CD 2, Real Zaragoza 2 *(aet; 6-7 on pens)*
CD Alcoyano 0, Atlético Madrid 1

1/8 FINALS
(3/1/06 & 11/1/06)
Zamora CF v FC Barcelona 1-3; 0-6 *(1-9)*
(3/1/06 & 12/1/06)
Athletic Bilbao v Real Madrid 0-1; 0-4 *(0-5)*
(4/1/06 & 11/1/06)
RC Celta v Real Betis 1-1; 0-0 *(1-1; Real Betis on away goal)*
Cádiz CF v Sevilla FC 3-2; 0-0 *(3-2)*
RC Deportivo v CA Osasuna 3-0; 1-2 *(4-2)*
Villarreal CF v Valencia CF 0-2; 0-1 *(0-3)*
Getafe CF v RCD Espanyol 0-1; 3-3 *(3-4)*
(11/1/06 & 18/1/06)
Atlético Madrid v Real Zaragoza 0-1; 2-2 *(2-3)*

QUARTER-FINALS
(18/1/06 & 25/1/06)
Real Betis 0, Real Madrid 1 *(Cassano 65)*
Real Madrid 1 *(Robinho 44)*, Real Betis 0
(Real Madrid 2-0)

Cádiz CF 0, RCD Espanyol 2 *(Pandiani 50, Frédson 88)*
RCD Espanyol 2 *(Jofre 73, 76p)*, Cádiz CF 0
(RCD Espanyol 4-0)

(19/1/06 & 1/2/06)
RC Deportivo 1 *(Sergio 78p)*, Valencia CF 0
Valencia CF 1 *(David Villa 44)*, RC Deportivo 1 *(Víctor 69p)*
(RC Deportivo 2-1)

(26/1/06 & 1/2/06)
Real Zaragoza 4 *(Diego Milito 23, 90p, Ewerthon 25, 27)*, FC Barcelona 2 *(Larsson 37, Ronaldinho 61p)*
FC Barcelona 2 *(Messi 42, Larsson 90)*, Real Zaragoza 1 *(Óscar 66)*
(Real Zaragoza 5-4)

SEMI-FINALS
(8/2/06 & 14/2/06)
Real Zaragoza 6 *(Diego Milito 15, 22, 34, 56, Ewerthon 60, 83)*, Real Madrid 1 *(Júlio Baptista 38)*
Real Madrid 4 *(Cicinho 1, Robinho 5, Ronaldo 10, Roberto Carlos 60)*, Real Zaragoza 0
(Real Zaragoza 6-5)

(9/2/06 & 15/3/06)
RCD Espanyol 2 *(Luis García 56p, Pandiani 90)*, RC Deportivo 1 *(Rubén 14p)*
RC Deportivo 0, RCD Espanyol 0
(RCD Espanyol 2-1)

FINAL
(12/4/06)
RCD ESPANYOL 4 *(Tamudo 2, Luis García 33, 86, Corominas 71)*
REAL ZARAGOZA 1 *(Ewerthon 28)*
Referee – Medina Cantalejo
RCD ESPANYOL – Kameni, Zabaleta, Lopo, Jarque, David García, Ito (Corominas 60), Frédson (Moisés 60), Eduardo Costa, De la Peña, Luis García, Tamudo (Pandiani 76).
REAL ZARAGOZA – César, Ponzio, Álvaro, Gabriel Milito, Toledo (Valbuena 75), Óscar (Sávio 50), Zapater, Celades (Movilla 65), Cani, Ewerthon, Diego Milito.
Sent off: César (74).

SECOND LEVEL FINAL TABLE 2005/06

		Pld	W	D	L	F	A	Pts
1	RC Recreativo	42	22	12	8	67	32	78
2	Club Gimnàstic Tarragona	42	23	7	12	48	38	76
3	Levante UD	42	20	14	8	53	39	74
4	Ciudad Murcia CF	42	20	12	10	53	42	72
5	Lorca DCF	42	19	12	11	56	39	69
6	Almería CF	42	20	7	15	54	43	67
7	Xerez CD	42	18	13	11	60	46	67
8	CD Numancia	42	18	9	15	50	55	63
9	Real Sporting Gijón	42	13	17	12	41	34	56
10	Real Valladolid	42	14	13	15	54	54	55
11	Real Madrid Castilla	42	16	7	19	55	50	55
12	CD Castellón	42	14	12	16	46	50	54
13	Albacete Balompié	42	14	12	16	44	57	54
14	Elche CF	42	13	14	15	47	54	53
15	CP Ejido	42	15	8	19	43	50	53
16	Real Murcia	42	13	13	16	41	40	52
17	Hércules CF	42	13	13	16	39	49	52
18	CD Tenerife	42	13	12	17	53	60	51
19	UE Lleida	42	12	10	20	43	53	46
20	RC Ferrol	42	7	16	19	44	63	37
21	Málaga CF /B	42	8	12	22	42	68	36
22	SD Éibar	42	6	17	19	28	45	35

Sweden

Nothing ventured, nothing gained

As in 2002, Sweden were eliminated from the World Cup in the second round. But whereas the team had flown home from Japan content that they had done their best, the same couldn't be said about the class of 2006 in Germany.

Lars Lagerbäck's team were unimpressive. Had it not been for Freddie Ljungberg's late winning goal against Paraguay, the Swedes would probably have returned home after three games. Had it not been for the outstanding goalkeeping of Andreas Isaksson against Germany, they might have suffered the heaviest World Cup defeat in their history.

In fairness, Sweden did not go into the tournament with high expectations. Although they had qualified for Germany without recourse to the play-offs, it was only as a 'best runner-up'. A first qualifying defeat away from home in eight years enabled Croatia to do the double over them and top the group. Subsequently Sweden played half a dozen friendly games in the build-up to the finals (albeit two of them with a B team) and failed to win any. Alarming deficiencies in defence were noted in a 3-0 defeat by Ireland, while goals proved hard to come by at the other end, with 2005 Swedish Footballer of the Year Zlatan Ibrahimovic, the team's eight-goal top scorer in qualifying, looking totally out of sorts.

Goal drought

Given the goal drought and the fact that Sweden hadn't won an opening World Cup game since 1958, it was perhaps unsurprising that they failed to beat Trinidad & Tobago – even with the opposition down to ten men for the entire second half. That goalless draw looked like being repeated after another scruffy performance against Paraguay. But just when the massed ranks of yellow-clad fans in Berlin's Olympiastadion appeared to have given up hope of ever seeing their team score, up popped Ljungberg to bring joy and relief with his 89th-minute header.

Now Sweden only needed a draw against England to reach the second phase, but a win would enable them to avoid hosts Germany. Outplayed in the first half, they came alive after the interval, with Marcus Allbäck scoring the 2,000th goal in World Cup history to equalise. The game eventually ended 2-2, thus enabling the Swedes to maintain their 38-year

NATIONAL TEAM RESULTS 2005/06

Date	Opponent	H/A/N	Venue	Score	Scorers
17/8/05	Czech Republic	H	Gothenburg	2-1	Larsson (19), Rosenberg (26)
3/9/05	Bulgaria (WCQ)	H	Solna	3-0	Ljungberg (60), Mellberg (75), Ibrahimovic (90)
7/9/05	Hungary (WCQ)	A	Budapest	1-0	Ibrahimovic (90)
8/10/05	Croatia (WCQ)	A	Zagreb	0-1	
12/10/05	Iceland (WCQ)	H	Solna	3-1	Ibrahimovic (29), Larsson (42), Källström 90)
12/11/05	South Korea	A	Seoul	2-2	Elmander (9), Rosenberg (57)
18/1/06	Saudi Arabia	A	Riyadh	1-1	Svensson (32)
23/1/06	Jordan	A	Abu Dhabi	0-0	
1/3/06	Republic of Ireland	A	Dublin	0-3	
25/5/06	Finland	H	Gothenburg	0-0	
2/6/06	Chile	H	Solna	1-1	Larsson (32)
10/6/06	Trinidad & Tobago (WCF)	N	Dortmund	0-0	
15/6/06	Paraguay (WCF)	N	Berlin	1-0	Ljungberg (89)
20/6/06	England (WCF)	N	Cologne	2-2	Allbäck (51), Larsson (90)
24/6/06	Germany (WCF)	A	Münich	0-2	

Sweden

unbeaten record against England and clinch qualification, but it was perverse that Henrik Larsson should milk the celebrations after his late equaliser rather than rushing back to the centre circle and making the most of the remaining minutes of stoppage-time to try to get a winner against a reeling English defence.

In retrospect, Larsson and his team-mates would surely have reacted differently, because against Germany in Munich they were torn to shreds. With two early goals conceded and Teddy Lucic sent off, a rout looked on the cards. Isaksson, brilliantly, kept his team in the game, but when Larsson skied over a penalty, Sweden's last chance had gone.

It was not the best way for Larsson, a Champions League final hero with Barcelona, to end his international career – which he confirmed a couple of weeks later as he returned home to play for Helsingborg – but at least he had made some impact on the tournament, unlike the completely ineffective Ibrahimovic. It was coach Lagerbäck, inevitably, who came in for the heaviest criticism. Operating at a major tournament for the first time without co-coach Tommy Söderberg, he was accused of being too cautious in his approach and too loyal to several underperforming stalwarts. Nevertheless, the Swedish FA did not punish him with dismissal. Preferring continuity to upheaval, they confirmed him as the coach for Euro 2008 – a tournament for which Sweden will need freshening up in several areas, not least up front where, with Larsson retired, the opportunity knocks for young guns Markus Rosenberg and Johan Elmander.

Rosenberg, the Ajax striker, did not see a minute of action in Germany, and Elmander, who made an immediate impression when he came on against Paraguay, was also underused. As for the young star of the 2005 Allsvenskan, Djurgårdens IF winger Tobias Hysén, he couldn't even find a place in Lagerbäck's squad.

Djurgården Double

Hysén, the son of former Liverpool, Fiorentina and Sweden defender Glenn Hysén, was the dominant figure in a Djurgården side that returned to the pinnacle of the domestic game by winning both the Allsvenskan and the Svenska Cupen. It was the Stockholm side's second Double in four seasons and their third championship win over the same stretch.

There were only seven survivors in the squad from the 2003 title-winning side. Previous big hitters like Isaksson, Elmander and Kim Källström had all moved abroad, and there was also a new coach in former technical director Kjell Jonevret. Djurgården were not considered among the pre-season favourites, but with giant Danish striker Søren Larsen banging in the goals at a healthy rate, they soon became involved in the race for honours. Unfortunately, Larsen's prowess attracted interest from abroad, and he moved to Schalke in July (after netting ten goals in 12 games). A dip in form – which included a shock UEFA Cup elimination by Cork City - immediately followed Larsen's departure, but the team came on strong again and eventually held off the challenge of IFK Gothenburg to take the title with a game to spare.

They key fixture over the closing stretch was the game away to Gothenburg in round 22, in which Hysén scored twice as Djurgården pulled off a stunning 3-1 win to go six points clear. A 1-0 defeat to Häcken on their return to Gothenburg the following week re-opened the race, and it looked as if nothing would be settled until the final day when Djurgården drew their penultimate game 0-0 – also in Gothenburg – to Örgryte. But IFK conceded two late goals in Stockholm against Djurgården's rivals Hammarby to turn a 2-1 win into a 3-2 defeat, and that was that.

Djurgården celebrated with a thumping 8-1 win at home to Elfsborg the following weekend. It took their final goal haul to 60 and also put Jonevret's men in the right frame of mind for the Swedish Cup final six days later.

Elfsborg had been Djurgården's victims in the semi-final, but they were the only other Allsvenskan side they had been obliged to face in a competition full of upsets. Second level outfit Åtvidabergs FF reached the final without encountering any top-division opponents, so it was no surprise when they went down to the champions in the Råsunda. They put up spirited resistance, though, and it was only when Hysén scored a second goal late on that Djurgården's successful defence of the trophy was complete.

Tax scandal

Åtvidaberg qualified for the UEFA Cup, where they were joined by IFK Gothenburg. That was scant reward for the league runners-up as they contemplated a ninth successive season without a title. But with new Norwegian coach Arne Erlandsen

Sweden

NATIONAL TEAM APPEARANCES 2005/06

Coach – Lars LAGERBÄCK

Player	DOB	Club	Cze	BUL	HUN	CRO	ISL	Kor	Sau	Jor	Irl	Fin	Chl	TRI	PAR	ENG	GER	Caps	Goals
Andreas ISAKSSON	3/10/81	Stade Rennais FC (FRA)	G	G	G	G	G				G		G		G	G	G	42	-
Alexander ÖSTLUND	2/11/78	Feyenoord (HOL) /Southampton (ENG)	D	D	D	D	D	D				D74						22	-
Olof MELLBERG	3/9/77	Aston Villa (ENG)	D46	D	D	D	D				D	D	D	D	D	D	D	68	2
Petter HANSSON	14/12/76	SC Heerenveen (HOL)	D								D	D					s39	14	-
Erik EDMAN	11/11/78	Tottenham Hotspur (ENG) /Stade Rennais (FRA)	D46	D		D	D				D	D85	D	D	D	D	D	41	1
Tobias LINDEROTH	21/4/79	FC København (DEN)	M77	M	M	M66	M	M			M70	M46	M	M79	M	M90	M	62	1
Niclas ALEXANDERSSON	29/12/71	IFK Göteborg	M	s72	M	M	s66	M	M	M		D	D46	D	D	D	D	91	7
Kim KÄLLSTRÖM	24/8/82	Stade Rennais FC (FRA)	M	M72		s71	s74				M61	M	s46	s79	M86	M	M39	38	4
Christian WILHELMSSON	8/12/79	RSC Anderlecht (BEL)	M	M80	M	s66	M66				M	M	M46	M79	M68	s52	s52	33	2
Markus ROSENBERG	27/9/82	Ajax (HOL)	A67					s44			s38	A69						8	3
Henrik LARSSON	20/9/71	FC Barcelona (ESP)	A84	A	A82	A	A				A80		A	A	A	A	A	93	36
Johan ELMANDER	27/5/81	Brøndby IF (DEN)	s46			s66		A78			M61	A			s86	s74		20	7
Olof PERSSON	5/5/78	Malmö FF	s46							D54								4	-
Marcus ALLBÄCK	5/7/73	FC Hansa Rostock (GER) /FC København (DEN)	s67		s90		s74	A44			s80	s69		s62	s46	A74	s72	60	24
Daniel ANDERSSON	28/8/77	Malmö FF	s77	s90			s72				s70	s46				s90		48	1
Johan ARNENG	14/6/79	Djurgårdens IF	s84															2	-
Teddy LUCIC	15/4/73	BK Häcken		D	D	D	D	D	D			D	D	D	D	D		85	-
Fredrik LJUNGBERG	16/4/77	Arsenal (ENG)		M90	M	M	M					M46	M	M	M	M		61	13
Zlatan IBRAHIMOVIC	3/10/81	Juventus (ITA)		A	A90		A74				A38		A	A	A46		A72	41	18
Mattias JONSON	16/1/74	Djurgårdens IF		s80	s82	A66		A85	A73		s61		s46	s79	s68	M52	M52	57	9
Christoffer ANDERSSON	22/10/78	Lillestrøm SK (NOR)		D					D		s46	s74						24	-
Anders SVENSSON	17/7/76	IF Elfsborg			M71	M74	M72	M	s58		s61		M	M62				67	13
Eddie GUSTAFSSON	31/1/77	Ham-Kam Fotball (NOR)					G	G										8	-
Fredrik RISP	15/12/80	Gençlerbirliği (TUR)					D60											3	-
Mikael DORSIN	6/10/81	Rosenborg BK (NOR)					D											9	-
Tobias HYSÉN	9/3/82	Djurgårdens IF						M	M79	s58								5	-
Daniel MAJSTOROVIC	5/4/77	FC Twente (HOL)						s60										5	1
Fredrik BERGLUND	21/3/79	Esbjerg FB (DEN)						s78	A71	s73								10	2
Karl SVENSSON	21/3/84	IFK Göteborg						D										1	-
Max VON SCHLEEBRÜGGE	1/2/77	Hammarby IF						D	D46									4	-
Martin ERICSSON	4/9/80	AaB (DEN)							M71									3	-
Jeffrey AUBYNN	12/5/77	Hammarby IF							s71	M58								4	-
Yksel OSMANOVSKI	24/2/77	Malmö FF							s79									15	2
Stefan SELAKOVIC	9/1/77	IFK Göteborg							s71	A58								12	4
Dusan DJURIC	16/9/84	Halmstads BK							s85	M								3	-
John ALVBÅGE	10/8/82	Viborg FF (DEN)								G		G46	G76					2	-
Matias CONCHA	31/3/80	Djurgårdens IF								D								1	-
Stefan ISHIZAKI	15/5/82	IF Elfsborg								M								7	-
Andreas GRANQVIST	16/4/85	Helsingborgs IF								s54								1	-
Mikael NILSSON	24/6/78	Panathinaikos (GRE)										M	s46					27	3
Rami SHAABAN	30/6/75	Fredrikstad FK (NOR)										s46		G				2	-
Fredrik STENMAN	2/6/83	Bayer Leverkusen (GER)										s85						1	-

Sweden

in charge, the team appeared to be moving in the right direction. His blend of experience (Bengt Andersson, Niclas Alexandersson, Håkan Mild) and youth (Oscar Wendt, Mattias Bjärsmyr) largely paid dividends. Swedish international striker Stefan Selakovic also proved a useful addition, but it later emerged that his transfer from Heerenveen had involved financial irregularities, and before long the club were immersed in a major tax-fraud scandal.

Malmö FF were the major disappointment of the season, finishing a mere fifth, which meant that they failed even to qualify for the Scandinavian Royal League (Kalmar and Hammarby, placed third and fourth respectively, joined Djurgården and Gothenburg in that winter competition). The defending champions failed on all fronts, with a crushing Champions League qualifying defeat to Swiss underdogs FC Thun representing the nadir of their year. Serious injuries to key players like Patrik Andersson and Niklas Skoog, plus the mid-season departure to Ajax of Markus Rosenberg, made life difficult for coach Tom Prahl, and even the move to revive the team's fortunes with the introduction of Finnish legend Jari Litmanen proved ill-starred as he was also struck down after only two games. The only real positive was the consistent marksmanship of Brazilian striker Afonso Alves, whose tally of 14 goals put him in double figures for the fourth year running.

The Allsvenskan's leading marksman was Halmstad's Icelandic hotshot Gunnar Heidar Thorvaldsson, with 16 goals. He also scored in each leg of the team's astonishing UEFA Cup victory over Sporting of Portugal. Halmstad went on to lose all their group games and finished only tenth in the Allsvenskan (eight places lower than in 2004), but Thorvaldsson's goals provided plenty of light relief.

Allsvenskan newcomers Assyriska struggled to compete at the higher level. An early 3-0 win in Gothenberg proved to be an illusion and they finished bottom by some distance after losing each of their last eight games while conceding 30 goals. The other two promoted clubs, Häcken and Gefle, both survived, with the latter even gaining UEFA Cup qualification via the Fair Play route. GIF Sundsvall and Landskrona were relegated, the latter after a play-off defeat against GAIS. As expected, AIK raced to victory in the Superettan (second level) and they were accompanied up automatically by Östers IF, the club that had been refused a licence to compete in the 2005 Allsvenskan for financial reasons.

EUROPEAN CUPS 2005/06

UEFA CHAMPIONS LEAGUE

MALMÖ FF
2nd qualifying round MACCABI HAIFA (ISR)
H 3-2 *Osmanovski (33), Andersson D. (48p), Mattisson (68)*
Asper, Høiland, Andersson P., Persson, Elanga, Andersson A. (Abelsson 89), Mattisson, Andersson D., Bech (Olsson 86), Osmanovski, Afonso.
A 2-2 *Afonso (21), Abelsson (88)*
Asper, Høiland, Andersson P. (Abelsson 82), Persson, Elanga, Andersson A. (Litmanen 60), Andersson D., Olsson, Bech, Osmanovski, Afonso.

3rd qualifying round FC THUN (SUI)
H 0-1
Asper, Høiland, Andersson P. (Holgersson 85), Abelsson, Elanga, Andersson A., Litmanen (Lawan 88), Andersson D., Osmanovski, Afonso, Pode.
A 0-3
Asper, Høiland, Mattisson, Abelsson, Elanga, Bech, Olsson, Andersson D., Osmanovski, Afonso, Pode.

UEFA CUP

DJURGÅRDENS IF
2nd qualifying round CORK CITY (IRL)
H 1-1 *Amoah (80)*
Tourray, Concha, Kuivasto, Johannesson, Stenman, Arneng, Hysén, Barsom (Árnason, 71), Sjölund (Amoah, 67), Jonson (Ba, 45), Kusi Asare.
A 0-0
Tourray, Concha, Kuivasto, Johannesson, Stenman, Arneng, Rasck (Árnason 60), Sjölund (Amoah 90), Jonson, Kusi Asare (Barsom 46), Hysén.

HALMSTADS BK
2nd qualifying round LINFIELD (NIR)
H 1-1 *Johansson A. (32)*
Johansson C., Larsson, Zvirgzdauskas, Jönsson, Johansson P., Johansson A., Svensson, Djuric (Sashcheka 86), Jensen (Ingelsten 76), Preko (Johansson J. 63), Thorvaldsson.
A 4-2 *Thorvaldsson (10), Jönsson (33), Preko (45), Djuric (74)*
Johansson C., Larsson, Zvirgzdauskas, Jönsson, Johansson P., Djuric, Johansson A., Svensson (Sashcheka 79), Jensen (Ingelsten 67), Preko, Thorvaldsson (Anklev 85).

1st round SPORTING CP (POR)
H 1-2 *Thorvaldsson (43p)*
Johansson C., Jensen, Zvirgzdauskas, Jönsson, Johansson P., Anklev, Djuric, Johansson A. (Johansson J. 69), Svensson, Preko (Ingelsten 77), Thorvaldsson.
A 3-2 *Thorvaldsson (15), Zvirgzdauskas (89), Ingelsten (113)* (aet)
Johansson C., Jensen, Zvirgzdauskas, Jönsson, Johansson P. (Delani 82), Anklev (Ingelsten 78), Djuric, Johansson A. (Johansson J. 74), Svensson, Preko, Thorvaldsson.

2nd round Group C
Match 1 HERTHA BSC BERLIN (GER)
H 0-1
Johansson C., Jensen, Zvirgzdauskas, Jönsson, Johansson P. (Delani 86), Anklev (Ingelsten 75), Djuric, Johansson A., Svensson, Preko (Johansson J. 75), Thorvaldsson.

Match 2 RC LENS (FRA)
A 0-5

Sweden

Johansson C., Larsson (Preko 74), Zvirgzdauskas, Jönsson, Johansson P., Johansson A., (Johanson J. 74), Djuric, Svensson, Ingelsten, Jensen, Thorvaldsson.

Match 3 SAMPDORIA (ITA)
H 1-3 *Djuric (18)*
Johansson C., Jensen, Zvirgzdauskas, Jönsson, Johansson P. (Johansson J. 78), Anklev, Djuric, Svensson, Ingelsten, Preko (Fribrock 68), Delani (Larsson 85).

Match 4 STEAUA BUCURESTI (ROM)
A 0-3
Sahlman, Jensen, Zvirgzdauskas, Jönsson, Johansson P., Anklev, Djuric, Svensson, Ingelsten, Fribrock (Larsson 46), Delani (Johansson J. 82).

MALMÖ FF
1st round BESIKTAS (TUR)
A 1-0 *Afonso (71)*
Asper, Høiland, Persson, Abelsson, Holgersson (Kouakou 80), Elanga, Mattisson, Olsson (Safari 89), Osmanovski, Afonso, Pode (Bech 68).

H 1-4 *Afonso (61)*
Asper, Høiland, Persson, Abelsson, Elanga, Bech, Olsson (Andersson A. 56), Andersson D., Osmanovski, Afonso, Pode.

TOP GOALSCORERS 2005
16	Gunnar Heidar THORVALDSSON (Halmstads BK)
14	AFONSO Alves (Malmö FF)
13	Hans BERGGREN (IF Elfsborg)
	AÍLTON Almeida (Örgryte IS)
12	Jones KUSI ASARE (Djurgårdens IF)
10	Søren LARSEN (Djurgårdens IF)
9	Tobias HYSÉN (Djurgårdens IF)
	Björn RUNSTRÖM (Hammarby IF)
	Stefan SELAKOVIC (Halmstads BK)
8	Jonas HENRIKSSON (BK Häcken)
	Dioh WILLIAMS (BK Häcken)
	Daniel BERNHARDSSON (Gefle IF)

LEAGUE RESULTS/SCORERS/APPEARANCES/GOALS 2005

ASSYRISKA FF
Coach – José Morais (POR)

2005
12/4	Hammarby IF	h	1-2	Hamzo
17/4	IFK Göteborg	a	3-0	Haddad 2, Lukanovic
24/4	Halmstads BK	h	0-0	
1/5	Gefle IF	a	0-1	
8/5	Malmö FF	h	0-2	
15/5	Landskrona BoIS	a	1-2	Haddad
23/5	Djurgårdens IF	a	1-3	Hamzo
29/5	GIF Sundsvall	h	1-0	Atiku
13/6	Kalmar FF	a	0-1	
16/6	Helsingborgs IF	h	0-1	
19/6	Örgryte IS	a	0-2	
26/6	IF Elfsborg	h	1-2	Nordbeck
3/7	BK Häcken	a	2-0	Samura, Batan
18/7	BK Häcken	h	0-1	
25/7	IF Elfsborg	a	3-1	Cetinkaya 2, Samura
31/7	Örgryte IS	h	0-1	
7/8	Landskrona BoIS	h	0-1	
14/8	Malmö FF	a	2-2	Samura, Nordbeck
22/8	GIF Sundsvall	a	0-5	
28/8	Djurgårdens IF	h	0-2	
11/9	Helsingborgs IF	a	0-2	
18/9	Kalmar FF	h	0-7	
26/9	Hammarby IF	a	0-3	
2/10	IFK Göteborg	h	2-3	Isakovic, Batan
16/10	Halmstads BK	a	0-5	
23/10	Gefle IF	h	0-3	

No	Name	Nat	Pos	Aps	(s)	Gls
12	ADELINO Lopes	POR	M	3		
15	Ibrahim ATIKU	GHA	M	19	(2)	1
19	Naramsin AWROHUM		M		(1)	
20	Stefan BATAN		M	22		2
4	Pierre BENGTSSON		D	10	(1)	
33	Hasan CETINKAYA		M	12		2
10	Melke DEMIR		M	8	(7)	
5	David DURMAZ		D	17	(4)	
13	Kaspars GORKSS	LAT	D	23		
9	Andreas HADDAD		A	11	(2)	3
8	Ghassan HAMED	IRQ	D	4	(4)	
11	Dani HAMZO		A	13	(10)	2
1	Erland HELLSTRÖM		G	25		
7	Ivan ISAKOVIC	SCG	M	10	(8)	1
25	Mattias KESENCI		M		(1)	
22	Darko LUKANOVIC		A	1	(12)	1
6	Johan LÄNDIN		D	21	(2)	
2	Zoran MANOVIC	SCG	D	23		
17	MATEUS Lopes	POR	A	2	(2)	
26	Eliyas MERKEZ		M		(1)	
18	Eddie MOUSSA		M		(1)	
3	David NORDBECK		M	22	(2)	2
12	Michel NOYAN		M		(1)	
14	Charles SAMPSON	GHA	M	18	(5)	
16	Kabba SAMURA	SRL	A	15	(7)	3
24	Thomas THUDIN		G	1		
23	Gabriel UCAR		D	6		

DJURGÅRDENS IF
Coach – Kjell Jonevret

2005
11/4	BK Häcken	h	2-1	Hysén, Stenman
18/4	Halmstads BK	a	1-3	Larsen
25/4	Örgryte IS	h	2-2	Larsen (p), Arneng
2/5	IF Elfsborg	a	2-1	Arneng, Larsen
9/5	Gefle IF	h	3-1	Kusi Asare, Ba, Larsen
18/5	Hammarby IF	a	1-2	Kusi Asare
23/5	Assyriska FF	h	3-1	Larsen 2, Barsom
29/5	Kalmar FF	a	2-0	Kusi Asare 2
13/6	IFK Göteborg	h	0-0	
16/6	Malmö FF	a	3-1	Kusi Asare, Larsen, Sjölund
20/6	Helsingborgs IF	h	5-2	Kuivasto, Hysén 2, Barsom, Larsen
27/6	Landskrona BoIS	a	2-0	Larsen 2
11/7	GIF Sundsvall	a	1-1	Hysén
18/7	GIF Sundsvall	h	4-0	Sjölund 2, Magro, Kusi Asare
27/7	Landskrona BoIS	h	0-1	
1/8	Helsingborgs IF	h	0-2	
4/8	Hammarby IF	h	2-2	Kusi Asare, Stenman
14/8	Gefle IF	a	3-1	Sjölund 2 (1p), Kusi Asare
21/8	Kalmar FF	h	3-1	Kuivasto 2, Kusi Asare

Sweden

FINAL LEAGUE TABLE 2005

		Pld	Home					Away					Total					Pts
			W	D	L	F	A	W	D	L	F	A	W	D	L	F	A	
1	Djurgårdens IF	26	9	3	1	40	13	7	2	4	20	13	16	5	5	60	26	53
2	IFK Göteborg	26	7	3	3	19	11	7	4	2	19	11	14	7	5	38	22	49
3	Kalmar FF	26	7	4	2	16	8	4	6	3	20	13	11	10	5	36	21	43
4	Hammarby IF	26	7	5	1	24	9	5	2	6	19	21	12	7	7	43	30	43
5	Malmö FF	26	8	2	3	27	13	4	3	6	11	14	12	5	9	38	27	41
6	Helsingborgs IF	26	9	1	3	19	9	3	2	8	13	29	12	3	11	32	28	39
7	IF Elfsborg	26	8	1	4	20	13	2	6	5	15	30	10	7	9	35	43	37
8	BK Häcken	26	7	2	4	19	13	4	1	8	10	16	11	3	12	29	29	36
9	Örgryte IS	26	7	3	3	25	19	3	2	8	12	19	10	5	11	37	38	35
10	Halmstads BK	26	7	2	4	29	14	2	3	8	9	24	9	5	12	38	38	32
11	Gefle IF	26	4	3	6	12	16	5	1	7	15	17	9	4	13	27	33	31
12	Landskrona BoIS	26	5	3	5	14	15	3	3	7	12	29	8	6	12	26	44	30
13	GIF Sundsvall	26	6	5	2	25	15	0	2	11	6	31	6	7	13	31	46	25
14	Assyriska FF	26	1	1	11	5	25	3	1	9	12	27	4	2	20	17	52	14

28/8	Assyriska FF	a	2-0	Hysén 2
12/9	Malmö FF	h	2-0	Jonson, Stenman
19/9	IFK Göteborg	a	3-1	Hysén 2, Nomvethe
25/9	BK Häcken	a	0-1	
3/10	Halmstads BK	h	6-1	Jonson 2, Hysén, Kusi Asare, Stenman, Arneng
17/10	Örgryte IS	a	0-0	
23/10	IF Elfsborg	h	8-1	Kusi Asare 2, Sjölund 2, Stenman, Tourray (p), Jonson, Amoah

No	Name	Nat	Pos	Aps	(s)	Gls
25	Patrick AMOAH		A		(17)	1
14	Kari ÁRNASON	ISL	M	15	(6)	
7	Johan ARNENG		M	24		3
23	Ibrahim BA	FRA	M	6	(8)	1
77	Abgar BARSOM		M	13	(8)	2
13	Stefan BERGTOFT		M		(2)	
2	Matias CONCHA		D	23		
8	Tobias HYSÉN		M	24	(1)	9
21	Jesper HÅKANSSON	DEN	M		(1)	
16	Markus JOHANNESSON		M	24		
12	Mattias JONSON		A	9	(1)	4
6	Toni KUIVASTO	FIN	D	26		3
9	Jones KUSI ASARE		A	20	(4)	12
17	Søren LARSEN	DEN	A	12		10
10	Feliciano MAGRO	SUI	M	8	(5)	1
19	Siyabonga NOMVETHE	RSA	A	1	(4)	1
5	Sölvi OTTESEN	ISL	D	2		
18	Niclas RASCK		D	7	(11)	
11	Daniel SJÖLUND	FIN	A	16	(6)	7
3	Fredrik STENMAN		D	26		5
4	Elias STORM		D	4	(1)	
15	Pa Dembo TOURRAY	GAM	G	26		1

IF ELFSBORG
Coach – Magnus Haglund

2005

11/4	GIF Sundsvall	a	1-3	Berggren (p)
17/4	Örgryte IS	h	1-0	Mobaeck
25/4	Helsingborgs IF	a	0-3	
2/5	Djurgårdens IF	h	1-2	Holmén
8/5	Landskrona BoIS	h	1-2	Alexandersson D.
15/5	BK Häcken	a	2-2	Alexandersson D., Berggren
23/5	Hammarby IF	h	4-1	Holmén, Berggren 2, Alexandersson D.
30/5	IFK Göteborg	a	1-1	Alexandersson D.
12/6	Halmstads BK	h	1-1	Berggren
15/6	Gefle IF	a	2-1	Alexandersson D., Sjöhage
20/6	Malmö FF	h	3-1	Berggren 2 (1p), Sjöhage
26/6	Assyriska FF	a	2-1	Sjöhage, Berggren
4/7	Kalmar FF	h	1-0	Svensson M.
18/7	Kalmar FF	a	1-1	Berggren
25/7	Assyriska FF	h	1-3	Berggren (p)
30/7	Malmö FF	a	1-1	Klarström
8/8	BK Häcken	h	2-0	Sjöhage, Klarström
13/8	Landskrona BoIS	a	1-4	Klarström
25/8	IFK Göteborg	h	0-2	
29/8	Hammarby IF	a	0-0	
12/9	Gefle IF	h	1-0	Berggren
19/9	Halmstads BK	a	1-1	Klarström
27/9	GIF Sundsvall	h	2-1	Berggren, Alexandersson D.
2/10	Örgryte IS	a	2-4	Berggren, Alexandersson D.
17/10	Helsingborgs IF	h	2-0	Sjöhage 2
23/10	Djurgårdens IF	a	1-8	Holmén

No	Name	Nat	Pos	Aps	(s)	Gls
6	Daniel ALEXANDERSSON		A	18	(7)	7
14	Joakim ALEXANDERSSON		D	19		
5	Martin ANDERSSON		D	19		
17	Jesper ARVIDSSON		A	1	(3)	
13	Hans BERGGREN		A	23		13
20	Andreas DRUGGE		A		(4)	
28	Marcus FALK OLANDER		D		(1)	
1	Abbas HASSAN		G	8	(2)	
10	Samuel HOLMÉN		M	24		3
7	Jari ILOLA	FIN	M	11	(4)	
4	Johan KARLSSON		M	25		
15	Andreas KLARSTRÖM		M	15	(6)	4
2	Jonas LUNDÉN		M	2	(7)	
11	Daniel MOBAECK		A	13	(9)	1
25	Andreas NILSSON		D	1	(1)	
16	Magnus SAMUELSSON		M	22	(2)	

Sweden

18	Eder SARKIS	A		(1)	
3	Johan SJÖBERG	D	21		
12	Joakim SJÖHAGE	A	14	(9)	6
23	Martin STRÖMBERG	M	16	(6)	
8	Anders SVENSSON	M	9		
35	Håkan SVENSSON	G	7		
9	Mathias SVENSSON	A	7	(6)	1
30	Johan WILAND	G	11		

GEFLE IF
Coach – Per Olsson

2005

9/4	Kalmar FF	a	0-1	
19/4	Helsingborgs IF	h	1-2	Westlin
24/4	Malmö FF	a	0-3	
1/5	Assyriska FF	h	1-0	Claesson
9/5	Djurgårdens IF	a	1-3	Ytterbom
16/5	GIF Sundsvall	h	2-1	Bernhardsson, Westlin
22/5	BK Häcken	a	1-2	Westlin
29/5	Halmstads BK	h	2-0	Bernhardsson, Woxlin
12/6	Örgryte IS	a	0-2	
15/6	IF Elfsborg	h	1-2	Woxlin
20/6	Landskrona BoIS	h	0-0	
26/6	Hammarby IF	a	1-0	Mattsson
6/7	IFK Göteborg	h	0-2	
20/7	IFK Göteborg	a	1-0	Bernhardsson
25/7	Hammarby IF	h	1-1	Bernhardsson
2/8	Landskrona BoIS	a	1-0	Bernhardsson
8/8	GIF Sundsvall	a	2-2	Woxlin (p), Ericsson Joh.
14/8	Djurgårdens IF	h	1-3	Mattsson
21/8	Halmstads BK	a	4-1	Makondele, Mattsson, Woxlin (p), Bernhardsson
28/8	BK Häcken	h	0-0	
12/9	IF Elfsborg	a	0-1	
18/9	Örgryte IS	h	0-2	
25/9	Kalmar FF	h	1-2	Woxlin
2/10	Helsingborgs IF	a	1-2	Wikström M.
16/10	Malmö FF	h	2-1	Ytterbom, Makondele
23/10	Assyriska FF	a	3-0	Woxlin (p), Bernhardsson 2

No	Name	Nat	Pos	Aps	(s)	Gls
12	Daniel BERNHARDSSON		M	23	(2)	8
11	Johan CLAESSON		M	12	(11)	1
8	Johannes ERICSSON		M	22		1
19	Jon ERICSSON		M	5	(12)	
2	Thomas HEDLUND		D	26		
1	Mattias HUGOSSON		G	26		
18	Antouman JALLOW		A	1	(2)	
7	Patrik KARLSSON		D	26		
10	René MAKONDELE	DRC	A	17	(3)	2
21	Benny MATTSSON		A	10	(7)	3
15	Joseph NGUIJOL	CMR	M	1	(1)	
5	Andreas REVAHL		D	25		
4	Mikael THURESSON		D	2	(5)	
20	Daniel WESTLIN		A	14	(6)	3
6	Anders WIKSTRÖM		D	2	(3)	
16	Magnus WIKSTRÖM		D	24		1
14	Mathias WOXLIN		M	24		6
9	Daniel YTTERBOM		A	26		2

IFK GÖTEBORG
Coach – Arne Erlandsen (NOR)

2005

10/4	Malmö FF	a	2-1	Selakovic, Mild
17/4	Assyriska FF	h	0-3	
26/4	Hammarby IF	h	1-0	Ijeh
2/5	Landskrona BoIS	a	1-1	Alexandersson
9/5	Kalmar FF	a	0-0	
16/5	Helsingborgs IF	h	0-0	
24/5	Örgryte IS	h	3-0	Risp, Wowoah, Selakovic
30/5	IF Elfsborg	h	1-1	Ijeh
13/6	Djurgårdens IF	a	0-0	
16/6	GIF Sundsvall	h	2-0	Johansson M. (p), Svensson
22/6	BK Häcken	a	1-3	Risp
29/6	Halmstads BK	h	4-0	Alexandersson, Selakovic, Mild, Mourad
6/7	Gefle IF	a	2-0	Ijeh, Selakovic
20/7	Gefle IF	h	0-1	
28/7	Halmstads BK	a	2-0	og (Johansson C.), Selakovic
1/8	BK Häcken	h	1-0	Selakovic
8/8	Helsingborgs IF	a	2-0	Berg M., Alexandersson
13/8	Kalmar FF	h	0-0	
25/8	IF Elfsborg	a	2-0	Mourad, Wowoah
29/8	Örgryte IS	a	2-1	Wendt, Mourad
12/9	GIF Sundsvall	a	0-0	
19/9	Djurgårdens IF	h	1-3	Selakovic
26/9	Malmö FF	h	2-1	Berg M., Alexandersson
2/10	Assyriska FF	a	3-2	Selakovic 2, Johansson M. (p)
17/10	Hammarby IF	a	2-3	Alexandersson 2
23/10	Landskrona BoIS	h	4-2	Wowoah, Berg M., Berg J., Wernbloom

No	Name	Nat	Pos	Aps	(s)	Gls
10	Niclas ALEXANDERSSON		M	26		6
1	Bengt ANDERSSON		G	26		
24	Jonatan BERG		A		(9)	1
21	Marcus BERG		A	8	(6)	3
5	Mattias BJÄRSMYR		D	15	(4)	
19	Peter IJEH	NGA	A	11	(1)	3
6	Adam JOHANSSON		D	11	(2)	
16	Magnus JOHANSSON		D	24		2
4	Sebastian JOHANSSON		M	15	(1)	
20	Dennis JONSSON		D		(1)	
14	Hjálmar JÓNSSON	ISL	D	8		
13	Tommy LYCÉN		M		(1)	
7	Håkan MILD		M	18		2
17	George MOURAD		A	20	(3)	3
3	Fredrik RISP		D	11		2
3	Erkan SAGLIK		D		(1)	
15	Mikael SANDKLEF		D		(6)	
9	Stefan SELAKOVIC		A	24	(1)	9
18	Martin SMEDBERG		M	3	(3)	
2	Karl SVENSSON		D	16		1
8	Martin ULANDER		M	4		
23	Andrés VÁSQUES		M		(3)	
22	Oscar WENDT		M	19	(2)	1
19	Pontus WERNBLOOM		M	6	(1)	1
11	Samuel WOWOAH		A	21	(3)	2

HALMSTADS BK
Coach – Jan Andersson

2005

9/4	Helsingborgs IF	a	0-2	
18/4	Djurgårdens IF	h	3-1	Preko, Djuric, Ingelsten
24/4	Assyriska FF	a	0-0	
1/5	Kalmar FF	h	0-1	
10/5	GIF Sundsvall	a	3-1	Preko, Larsson, Ingelsten
15/5	Örgryte IS	h	4-2	Larsson, Jensen, Ingelsten 2
23/5	Landskrona BoIS	h	5-1	Larsson, Thorvaldsson 3, Djuric
29/5	Gefle IF	a	0-2	

Sweden

12/6	IF Elfsborg	a	1-1	Jönsson	
15/6	BK Häcken	h	1-0	Djuric	
19/6	Hammarby IF	h	1-2	Jensen	
29/6	IFK Göteborg	a	0-4		
4/7	Malmö FF	h	0-0		
17/7	Malmö FF	a	1-2	Thorvaldsson	
28/7	IFK Göteborg	h	0-2		
1/8	Hammarby IF	a	1-2	Thorvaldsson	
7/8	Örgryte IS	a	1-2	Thorvaldsson	
14/8	GIF Sundsvall	h	6-0	Johansson A., Preko, Thorvaldsson 3 (1p), Ingelsten	
21/8	Gefle IF	h	1-4	Preko	
29/8	Landskrona BoIS	a	0-0		
11/9	BK Häcken	a	1-0	Thorvaldsson	
19/9	IF Elfsborg	h	1-1	Thorvaldsson	
25/9	Helsingborgs IF	h	2-0	Thorvaldsson 2	
3/10	Djurgårdens IF	a	1-6	Thorvaldsson	
16/10	Assyriska FF	h	5-0	Thorvaldsson 2, Johansson A., Anklev, Delani	
23/10	Kalmar FF	a	0-2		

No	Name	Nat	Pos	Aps	(s)	Gls
16	Magnus ANDERSSON		A	12	(2)	
18	Björn ANKLEV		A	9	(14)	1
8	Alphajor Mamadu BAH	SRL	M	8	(1)	
8	Eduardo DELANI	BRA	M		(6)	1
14	Dusan DJURIC		M	25		3
25	Kristoffer FAGERCRANTZ		M		(5)	
17	Patrik INGELSTEN		A	19	(7)	5
23	Emil JENSEN		D	23		2
13	Andreas JOHANSSON		M	14	(4)	2
1	Conny JOHANSSON		G	26		
24	Joel JOHANSSON		M	4	(12)	
2	Per JOHANSSON		D	22	(1)	
4	Tommy JÖNSSON		D	15	(1)	1
15	Peter LARSSON		D	19		3
19	Johan MANGFORS		M		(1)	
6	Yaw PREKO	GHA	A	22	(1)	4
11	Dzianis SASHCHEKA	BLS	M	2	(9)	
9	Magnus SVENSSON		M	25		
10	Gunnar Heidar THORVALDSSON	ISL	A	17	(6)	16
12	Tomas ZVIRGZDAUSKAS	LIT	D	24		

HAMMARBY IF
Coach – Anders Linderoth

2005

12/4	Assyriska FF	a	2-1	Aubynn, Furuseth Olsen	
18/4	Kalmar FF	h	0-0		
26/4	IFK Göteborg	a	0-1		
3/5	Malmö FF	h	1-1	Aubynn	
9/5	Helsingborgs IF	a	1-2	Andersson M.	
18/5	Djurgårdens IF	a	2-1	Marteinsson, Andersson M.	
23/5	IF Elfsborg	a	1-4	Piñones-Arce	
30/5	BK Häcken	h	3-1	Runström, Furuseth Olsen, Andersson M.	
12/6	GIF Sundsvall	a	1-2	Aubynn	
15/6	Örgryte IS	h	0-0		
19/6	Halmstads BK	a	2-1	Andersson P., Piñones-Arce	
26/6	Gefle IF	h	0-1		
3/7	Landskrona BoIS	a	3-0	Piñones-Arce (p), Johansson D., Runström	
17/7	Landskrona BoIS	h	4-0	Stoor, Andersson P. 2, Runström	
25/7	Gefle IF	a	1-1	Aubynn	
1/8	Halmstads BK	h	2-1	Runström, Furuseth Olsen	
4/8	Djurgårdens IF	a	2-2	Andersson M., Runström	
13/8	Helsingborgs IF	h	6-2	Runström 2, Andersson P., Zengin 2, Johansson E.	
22/8	BK Häcken	a	3-1	Johansson D., Runström, Fischbein	
29/8	IF Elfsborg	h	0-0		
12/9	Örgryte IS	a	2-3	Runström, Andersson P.	
19/9	GIF Sundsvall	h	0-0		
26/9	Assyriska FF	h	3-0	Paulinho 2, Johansson D.	
2/10	Kalmar FF	a	0-3		
17/10	IFK Göteborg	h	3-2	Von Schleebrügge, Andersson P., Johansson E.	
23/10	Malmö FF	a	1-0	Furuseth Olsen	

No	Name	Nat	Pos	Aps	(s)	Gls
16	Mikael ANDERSSON		M	9	(10)	4
22	Petter ANDERSSON		M	24	(1)	6
21	Jeffrey AUBYNN		M	14	(3)	4
1	Ante COVIC	AUS	G	26		
5	Eric FISCHBEIN		M	11	(1)	1
15	Petter FURUSETH OLSEN	NOR	M	25		4
8	Patrik GERRBRAND		D	13		
6	Nichlas HINDSBERG	DEN	M		(4)	
23	Joakim JENSEN		D	2	(2)	
14	Mikkel JENSEN	DEN	M	23		
2	David JOHANSSON		D	24	(1)	3
10	Erik JOHANSSON		M	3	(13)	2
18	Haris LAITINEN		M	1	(6)	
3	Pétur MARTEINSSON	ISL	D	8		1
19	PAULINHO Guará	BRA	A	4	(3)	2
11	Pablo PIÑONES-ARCE		A	11	(6)	3
20	Björn RUNSTRÖM		A	19	(4)	9
25	Kleber SAARENPÄÄ		D	1		
7	Süleyman SLEYMAN		D	18	(3)	
4	Fredrik STOOR		D	18	(2)	1
13	Max VON SCHLEBRÜGGE		D	20	(2)	1
17	Erkan ZENGIN		M	12	(10)	2

HELSINGBORGS IF
Coach – Peter Swärdh

2005

9/4	Halmstads BK	h	2-0	Graulund 2	
19/4	Gefle IF	a	2-1	Hutchinson, Graulund	
25/4	IF Elfsborg	h	3-0	Järdler, Granqvist, Wahlstedt	
2/5	BK Häcken	a	0-3		
9/5	Hammarby IF	h	2-1	Karisik E., Hutchinson	
16/5	IFK Göteborg	a	0-0		
22/5	Kalmar FF	h	2-2	Hutchinson, Karekezi	
30/5	Landskrona BoIS	a	3-4	Järdler, Hutchinson, Graulund	
13/6	Malmö FF	h	0-1		
16/6	Assyriska FF	a	1-0	Mngomeni	
20/6	Djurgårdens IF	a	2-5	Graulund, Karisik E.	
28/6	GIF Sundsvall	h	2-1	Karekezi, Karisik E.	
4/7	Örgryte IS	a	2-1	Graulund, Karisik E.	
17/7	Örgryte IS	h	1-0	Graulund	
24/7	GIF Sundsvall	a	1-1	Karisik E.	
1/8	Djurgårdens IF	h	2-0	Karisik E., Karekezi	
8/8	IFK Göteborg	h	0-2		
13/8	Hammarby IF	a	2-6	Andersson G, Hutchinson	
22/8	Landskrona BoIS	h	1-0	Hutchinson	
29/8	Kalmar FF	a	0-2		
11/9	Assyriska FF	h	2-0	Karekezi, Khalili	
20/9	Malmö FF	a	0-2		
25/9	Halmstads BK	a	0-2		

Sweden

2/10	Gefle IF	h	2-1	Karekezi, Dahl
17/10	IF Elfsborg	a	0-2	
23/10	BK Häcken	h	0-1	

No	Name	Nat	Pos	Aps	(s)	Gls
1	Daniel ANDERSSON		G	26		
7	Gustaf ANDERSSON		A	8	(10)	1
4	Jakob AUGUSTSSON		D	4	(5)	
3	Fredrik BJÖRCK		D	14	(4)	
17	Peter CHRISTIANSEN	DEN	D	11		
9	Andreas DAHL		M	20	(2)	1
14	Andreas GRANQVIST		D	25	(1)	1
11	Peter GRAULUND	DEN	A	18	(3)	7
13	Atiba HUTCHINSON	CAN	M	24	(1)	6
16	Andreas JAKOBSSON		D	11		
16	Christian JÄRDLER		D	11		2
15	Olivier KAREKEZI	RWA	M	12	(6)	5
20	Eldin KARISIK		M	20	(5)	6
21	Fahrudin KARISIK		M	1	(4)	
6	Imad KHALILI		M	2	(13)	1
5	David LJUNG		D	14	(3)	
10	Thando MNGOMENI	RSA	A	10	(4)	1
19	Babis STEFANIDIS		M	10	(3)	
8	Fredrik SVANBÄCK	FIN	M	20	(4)	
23	Erik WAHLSTEDT		M	25		1
18	Björn WESTERBLAD		A		(2)	

BK HÄCKEN
Coach – Stefan Lundin

2005

11/4	Djurgårdens IF	a	1-2	Andersson P.
18/4	GIF Sundsvall	h	1-0	Lucic
25/4	Kalmar FF	a	0-2	
2/5	Helsingborgs IF	h	3-0	Marek, Williams, Henriksson
8/5	Örgryte IS	a	4-0	Marek, Williams, Johnson, Töfting
15/5	IF Elfsborg	h	2-2	Williams 2
22/5	Gefle IF	h	2-1	Henriksson, Marek
30/5	Hammarby IF	a	1-3	Henriksson
12/6	Landskrona BoIS	h	3-0	Henriksson 2, Williams
15/6	Halmstads BK	a	0-1	
22/6	IFK Göteborg	h	3-1	Dybendal, Henriksson, Johnson
27/6	Malmö FF	a	1-2	Henriksson
3/7	Assyriska FF	h	0-2	
18/7	Assyriska FF	a	1-0	Töfting
21/7	Malmö FF	h	1-0	Williams
1/8	IFK Göteborg	a	0-1	
8/8	IF Elfsborg	a	0-2	
14/8	Örgryte IS	h	1-2	Henriksson
22/8	Hammarby IF	h	1-3	Ljung
28/8	Gefle IF	a	0-0	
9/11	Halmstads BK	h	0-1	
19/9	Landskrona BoIS	a	1-0	Williams
25/9	Djurgårdens IF	h	1-0	Williams
3/10	GIF Sundsvall	a	0-3	
16/10	Kalmar FF	h	1-1	Töfting (p)
23/10	Helsingborgs IF	a	1-0	Ljung

No	Name	Nat	Pos	Aps	(s)	Gls
12	Mattias ANDERSSON		A		(11)	
14	Patric ANDERSSON		A	3		1
5	Jimmy DIXON	LIB	D	23		
11	Eirik DYBENDAL	NOR	A	6	(6)	1
18	Tom EKLIDEN		A	2	(7)	
22	Daniel FORSELL		D	11	(2)	
8	Mats HAGLUND		A		(2)	
3	Mats HEDÉN		D	25		
21	Jonas HENRIKSSON		A	26		8
16	Marcus JARLEGREN		D	14	(9)	
10	Dulee JOHNSON	LIB	M	20		2
20	Magnus JONSSON		G	8		
23	Yazid KAISSI	FRA	M	6	(2)	
17	Rikard KAPELLA-KARLSSON		M	3	(4)	
1	Christoffer KÄLLQVIST		G	18		
15	Daniel LARSSON		A	1	(4)	
2	Johan LIND		D	16	(4)	
7	Jesper LJUNG		M	17	(1)	2
4	Teddy LUCIC		D	21		1
6	David MAREK		D	18	(1)	3
99	Stig TØFTING	DEN	M	23		3
9	Dioh WILLIAMS	LIB	A	25		8

KALMAR FF
Coach – Nanne Bergstrand

2005

10/4	Gefle IF	h	1-0	Fábio Augusto
18/4	Hammarby IF	a	0-0	
25/4	BK Häcken	h	2-0	Carlsson, César Santín
1/5	Halmstads BK	a	1-0	Carlsson
9/5	IFK Göteborg	h	0-0	
16/5	Malmö FF	a	0-1	
22/5	Helsingborgs IF	a	2-2	César Santín 2
29/5	Djurgårdens IF	h	0-2	
13/6	Assyriska FF	h	1-0	Dede Anderson
16/6	Landskrona BoIS	a	1-1	Dede Anderson
21/6	GIF Sundsvall	a	2-0	og (Lundqvist), Koroma
27/6	Örgryte IS	h	2-1	og (Prytz), Dede Anderson
4/7	IF Elfsborg	a	0-1	
18/7	IF Elfsborg	h	1-1	Ponomarev
25/7	Örgryte IS	a	3-3	Carlsson, César Santín, Dede Anderson
31/7	GIF Sundsvall	h	0-0	
6/8	Malmö FF	h	0-2	
13/8	IFK Göteborg	a	0-0	
21/8	Djurgårdens IF	a	1-3	Johansson
29/8	Helsingborgs IF	h	2-0	Petersson, Blomberg (p)
11/9	Landskrona BoIS	h	2-2	Petersson, Blomberg
18/9	Assyriska FF	a	7-0	Rosengren, Blomberg (p), Rydström, Johansson, Ponomarev, Fábio Augusto, og (Nordbeck)
25/9	Gefle IF	a	2-1	Fábio Augusto, Rosengren
2/10	Hammarby IF	h	3-0	Blomberg, Fábio Augusto, Dede Anderson
16/10	BK Häcken	a	1-1	Dede Anderson
23/10	Halmstads BK	h	2-0	Rosengren, Ponomarev

No	Name	Nat	Pos	Aps	(s)	Gls
7	Mikael BLOMBERG		M	23	(1)	4
5	Tobias CARLSSON		D	21	(3)	3
25	CÉSAR SANTÍN	BRA	A	17	(5)	4
9	DEDE ANDERSON	BRA	A	14	(2)	6
18	Rasmus ELM		M	1	(6)	
11	FÁBIO AUGUSTO	BRA	M	23		4
24	Jonas FRIED		D		(1)	
21	Lasse JOHANSSON		M	23	(1)	2
2	Niklas KALDNER		D	8	(7)	
19	Brima KOROMA	SRL	A	3	(8)	1
3	Joachim LANTZ		D	26		
16	Xhevdet LLUMNICA	ALB	A		(3)	
12	Filip NEKMOUCHE		M		(2)	

Sweden

23	Fredrik PETERSSON		M	8	(5)	2
10	Daniel PETTERSSON		D	1	(3)	
13	Anatoli PONOMAREV	AZB	A	6	(7)	3
14	Patrik ROSENGREN		D	25		3
8	Henrik RYDSTRÖM		M	26		1
17	Svante SAMUELSSON		M	10	(11)	
20	Robert STOLTZ		D	25		
1	Petter WASTÅ		G	26		

12	Mikael RYNELL		M	4	(10)	
22	Jonas SANDQVIST		G	23		
6	Pontus SEGERSTRÖM		D	24		2
1	Mats SVENSSON		G	3	(1)	
9	Håkan SÖDERSTJERNA		M	3	(3)	1
24	Måns SÖRENSSON		A	1	(7)	
13	Robin WIKMAN		A		(3)	
21	Andreas YNGVESSON		A	10	(1)	1

LANDSKRONA BOIS
Coach – Mats Jingblad

2005

11/4	Örgryte IS	a	1-2	Oneykachi Amuneke
17/4	Malmö FF	h	0-1	
24/4	GIF Sundsvall	a	2-2	Jönsson, Oneykachi Amuneke
2/5	IFK Göteborg	h	1-1	Oneykachi Amuneke
8/5	IF Elfsborg	a	2-1	Eklund, Segerström
15/5	Assyriska FF	h	2-1	Pettersson, Segerström
23/5	Halmstads BK	a	1-5	Jönsson
30/5	Helsingborgs IF	h	4-3	Oneykachi Amuneke, Okkonen, Jönsson (p), Andersson G.
12/6	BK Häcken	a	0-3	
16/6	Kalmar FF	h	1-1	og (Carlsson)
20/6	Gefle IF	a	0-0	
27/6	Djurgårdens IF	h	0-2	
3/7	Hammarby IF	h	0-3	
17/7	Hammarby IF	a	0-4	
27/7	Djurgårdens IF	a	1-0	Yngvesson
2/8	Gefle IF	h	0-1	
7/8	Assyriska FF	a	1-0	Pettersson
13/8	IF Elfsborg	h	4-1	Pettersson (p), Oneykachi Amuneke, Bola, Söderstjerna
22/8	Helsingborgs IF	a	0-1	
29/8	Halmstads BK	h	0-0	
11/9	Kalmar FF	a	2-2	Pettersson, Corneliusson
19/9	BK Häcken	h	0-1	
26/9	Örgryte IS	h	1-0	Pettersson
3/10	Malmö FF	a	0-5	
17/10	GIF Sundsvall	h	1-0	Oneykachi Amuneke
23/10	IFK Göteborg	a	2-4	Schei Lindbaek, Oneykachi Amuneke

No	Name	Nat	Pos	Aps	(s)	Gls
14	Kevin ONEYKACHI AMUNEKE	NGA	A	22	(1)	7
5	Kingsley AMUNEKE	NGA	D	8	(3)	
8	Gustaf ANDERSSON		D	18	(2)	1
25	Johan ANDERSSON		A	4	(5)	
26	Morten AVNSKJOLD	DEN	M	10	(1)	
18	BoBo BOLA	RWA	A	1	(6)	1
3	Karl CORNELIUSSON		D	7		1
13	Matthias EKLUND		A	3	(1)	1
17	Anders FRIBERG		D	24		
3	Patrik HOLMGREN		M		(2)	
10	Jon JÖNSSON		M	21		3
	Andrew KELLY	ENG	D		(1)	
10	Valentino LAI		M	1	(3)	
15	André SCHEI LINDBÆK	NOR	A	3	(6)	1
16	Jonas LINDH		M	1	(3)	
4	Johnny LUNDBERG		D	24		
2	Johan NORELL		D	17	(2)	
7	Antti OKKONEN	FIN	M	20	(3)	1
3	Jonas OLSSON		D	12		
11	Jörgen PETTERSSON		A	22		5

MALMÖ FF
Coach – Tom Prahl

2005

10/4	IFK Göteborg	h	1-2	Afonso
17/4	Landskrona BoIS	a	1-0	Rosenberg
24/4	Gefle IF	h	3-0	Høiland, Skoog, Olsson
3/5	Hammarby IF	a	1-1	Osmanovski
8/5	Assyriska FF	a	2-0	Afonso 2
16/5	Kalmar FF	h	1-0	Afonso
22/5	GIF Sundsvall	a	0-2	
29/5	Örgryte IS	h	1-0	Afonso
13/6	Helsingborgs IF	a	1-0	Afonso
16/6	Djurgårdens IF	h	1-3	Rosenberg
20/6	IF Elfsborg	a	1-3	Rosenberg
27/6	BK Häcken	h	2-1	Rosenberg, Afonso
4/7	Halmstads BK	a	0-0	
17/7	Halmstads BK	h	2-1	Mattisson 2
21/7	BK Häcken	a	0-1	
30/7	IF Elfsborg	h	1-1	Afonso
6/8	Kalmar FF	a	2-0	Osmanovski, Afonso
14/8	Assyriska FF	h	2-2	Litmanen, Afonso
20/8	Örgryte IS	a	1-1	Osmanovski
28/8	GIF Sundsvall	h	6-2	Afonso 2, Pode, Abelsson, Høiland, Holgersson
12/9	Djurgårdens IF	a	0-2	
20/9	Helsingborgs IF	h	2-0	Andersson D., Osmanovski
26/9	IFK Göteborg	a	1-2	Afonso
3/10	Landskrona BoIS	h	5-0	Andersson D. (p), Bech, Ofere, Kouakou, Afonso
16/10	Gefle IF	a	1-2	Pode
23/10	Hammarby IF	h	0-1	

No	Name	Nat	Pos	Aps	(s)	Gls
4	Peter ABELSSON		D	15	(7)	1
8	AFONSO Alves	BRA	A	24		14
2	Anders ANDERSSON		M	11		
30	Daniel ANDERSSON		M	25		2
18	Patrik ANDERSSON		D	9		
1	Mattias ASPER		G	26		
15	Samuel BARLAY	SRL	M		(4)	
22	Jesper BECH	DEN	A	13		1
10	Louay CHANKO		M	8	(5)	
7	Joseph ELANGA	CMR	M	25	(1)	
19	Glenn HOLGERSSON		M	3	(4)	1
14	Jon Inge HØILAND	NOR	D	22	(1)	2
21	Raoul KOUAKOU	CIV	D	3	(1)	1
28	Rawez LAWAN		M	1	(4)	
23	Jari LITMANEN	FIN	M	2		1
6	Hans MATTISSON		M	18	(3)	2
17	Joakim NILSSON		M		(1)	
19	Edward OFERE	NGA	A	2	(4)	1
5	Thomas OLSSON		M	11	(8)	1
11	Yksel OSMANOVSKI		A	16	(5)	4
3	Olof PERSSON		D	24		
26	Marcus PODE		A	9	(6)	2
23	Markus ROSENBERG		A	12		4
25	Behrang SAFARI		M	1	(2)	

Sweden

9	Niklas SKOOG		A	4	1
28	Daniel SLIPER		M		(1)
21	Andreas YNGVESSON		A	2	(8)

GIF SUNDSVALL
Coach – Jan Halvor Halvorsen (NOR); (16/8/05) Anders Högman

2005

11/4	IF Elfsborg	h	3-1		Olofsson, Wallerstedt, Dahlberg
18/4	BK Häcken	a	0-1		
24/4	Landskrona BoIS	h	2-2		Hermansson, Bergersen
1/5	Örgryte IS	a	1-4		Lundqvist (p)
10/5	Halmstads BK	h	1-3		og (Zvirgzdauskas)
16/5	Gefle IF	a	1-2		Lundqvist (p)
22/5	Malmö FF	h	2-0		Hermansson 2
29/5	Assyriska FF	a	0-1		
12/6	Hammarby IF	h	2-1		Ålander, Dahlberg
16/6	IFK Göteborg	a	0-2		
21/6	Kalmar FF	h	0-2		
28/6	Helsingborgs IF	a	1-2		Eriksson
11/7	Djurgårdens IF	h	1-1		Eriksson
18/7	Djurgårdens IF	a	0-4		
24/7	Helsingborgs IF	h	1-1		Eriksson
31/7	Kalmar FF	a	0-0		
8/8	Gefle IF	h	2-2		Olofsson 2
14/8	Halmstads BK	a	0-6		
22/8	Assyriska FF	h	5-0		Eriksson-Ohlsson, Olofsson 2, Gerba 2
28/8	Malmö FF	a	2-6		Olofsson, Gerba
12/9	IFK Göteborg	h	0-0		
19/9	Hammarby IF	a	0-0		
27/9	IF Elfsborg	a	1-2		Gerba
3/10	BK Häcken	h	3-0		Gerba, Dahlberg, Lustig
17/10	Landskrona BoIS	a	0-1		
23/10	Örgryte IS	h	3-2		Dahlberg, Lustig, Eriksson

No	Name	Nat	Pos	Aps	(s)	Gls
13	Michael ADEYINKA	NGA	M		(1)	
2	Johan ANDERSSON		D	9	(1)	
29	Tomas BACKMAN		D		(3)	
11	Tommy BERGERSEN	NOR	M	14	(5)	1
9	Hans BERGH		M	18	(4)	
21	Christoffer BRÄNNSTRÖM		M		(1)	
16	Mikael DAHLBERG		A	23	(3)	4
18	Tobias ERIKSSON		M	17	(2)	4
4	Patrik ERIKSSON-OHLSSON		D	23		1
27	Ali GERBA	CAN	A	11		5
14	Andreas HERMANSSON		A	17	(7)	3
24	Linus JOHANSSON		A	5	(2)	
26	Naim KHREIS		A		(1)	
17	Edib KURTOVIC		A		(9)	
3	Fredric LUNDQVIST		M	11		2
28	Mikael LUSTIG		A	8		2
5	Mattias NYLUND		D	24		
8	Daniel NÄSHOLM		M	4	(4)	
23	Peter OLOFSSON		A	23	(1)	6
30	Elias STORM		D	10		
1	Fredrik SUNDFORS		G	26		
7	Øyvind SVENNING	NOR	A	4	(8)	
19	Jonas WALLERSTEDT		A	1	(2)	1
10	Donatas VENCEVICIUS	LIT	M	6	(7)	
6	Stefan ÅLANDER		D	25		1
15	Mikael ÅSKOOGH		M	7	(11)	

ÖRGRYTE IS
Coach – Zoran Lukic

2005

11/4	Landskrona BoIS	h	2-1		Källander, Ganemyr
17/4	IF Elfsborg	a	0-1		
25/4	Djurgårdens IF	a	2-2		Paulinho 2
1/5	GIF Sundsvall	h	4-1		Ganemyr, Källander, Aílton 2
8/5	BK Häcken	h	0-4		
15/5	Halmstads BK	a	2-4		Uusimäki, Johannesen
24/5	IFK Göteborg	a	0-3		
29/5	Malmö FF	a	0-1		
12/6	Gefle IF	h	2-0		Paulinho 2
15/6	Hammarby IF	a	0-0		
19/6	Assyriska FF	h	2-0		Uusimäki, Aílton
27/6	Kalmar FF	a	1-2		Mwila
4/7	Helsingborgs IF	h	1-2		Källander
17/7	Helsingborgs IF	a	0-1		
25/7	Kalmar FF	h	3-3		Sauso, Paulinho, Aílton
31/7	Assyriska FF	a	1-0		Anegrund
7/8	Halmstads BK	h	2-1		Yobe, Anegrund
14/8	BK Häcken	a	2-1		Paulinho, Mellqvist
20/8	Malmö FF	h	1-1		Aílton
29/8	IFK Göteborg	h	1-2		Källander
12/9	Hammarby IF	h	3-2		Aílton 2, Mwila
18/9	Gefle IF	a	2-0		Aílton, Mwila
26/9	Landskrona BoIS	a	0-1		
2/10	IF Elfsborg	h	4-2		Aílton 4
17/10	Djurgårdens IF	h	0-0		
23/10	GIF Sundsvall	a	2-3		Johannesen, Aílton

No	Name	Nat	Pos	Aps	(s)	Gls
10	AÍLTON Almeida	BRA	A	23		13
21	Johan ANEGRUND		D	14		2
17	Nadir BENCHENAA		M	5	(5)	
3	Marcus DAHLIN		D	11	(4)	
23	Robin GANEMYR		M	14	(8)	2
15	Jóhann GUDMUNDSSON	ISL	M	7	(11)	
11	Christian HEMBERG		A	5	(4)	
24	Erik JOHANNESEN		M	5	(11)	2
8	Dejan JURKIC	SLO	D		(1)	
20	Johan KARLEFJÄRD		M	3	(1)	
36	Magnus KÄLLANDER		M	23		4
1	Dick LAST		G	25		
26	Alexander MELLQVIST		M		(4)	1
19	Clifford MULENGA	ZAM	A	2	(5)	
22	Boyd MWILA	ZAM	A	16	(5)	3
19	PAULINHO Guará	BRA	A	18		6
14	Edwin PHIRI	ZAM	D	7	(2)	
5	Anders PRYTZ		D	24		
2	Jukka SAUSO	FIN	D	20	(1)	1
16	Henri SCHEWELEFF	FIN	A	4		
18	VALTER TOMAZ Jr	BRA	D	22		
9	Tuomas UUSIMÄKI	FIN	A	23		2
6	Angelo VEGA		M	3	(6)	
30	Axel WIBRÅN		G	1		
7	Dominic YOBE	ZAM	A	11	(6)	1

DOMESTIC CUP 2005

SECOND ROUND
(19/4/05)
Bara GoIF 0, IK Sleipner 6
Bureå IF 0, Trelleborgs FF 2
FC Trollhättan 0, Väsby United 0 *(aet; 6-7 on pens)*
(20/4/05)
Forssa BK 3, Tenhults IF 4 *(aet)*
Visby IF Gute FK 2, Friska Viljor FC 0
Skövde AIK 0, Östersunds FK 1

Sweden

Husqvarna FF 0, IF Elfsborg 7
IFK Ölme 1, IK Brage 1 *(aet; 4-1 on pens)*
Ystads IF FF 0, Halmstads BK 2
Kalmar AIK 1, IFK Göteborg 7
Kinna IF 1, Åtvidabergs FF 2 *(aet)*
Melleruds IF 0, GAIS 3 *(aet)*
Topkapi IK 0, Landskrona BoIS 3
Anundsjö IF 1, IFK Norrköping 5
Lunds BK 2, Västra Frölunda IF 2 *(aet; 5-3 on pens)*
Sandvikens IF 1, Östers IF 2
Skellefteå AIK FK 1, IF Brommapojkarna 1 *(aet, 4-2 on pens)*
Spårvägens FF 0, Assyriska FF 2
Tidaholms GoIF 0, Bodens BK 4
Vallentuna BK 1, Malmö FF 3
Vasalunds/Essinge IF 1, Örebro SK FK 1 *(aet; 4-3 on pens)*
(21/4/05)
IFK Värnamo 0, Hammarby IF 2
Bunkeflo IF 1, Västerås SK FK 0
Enskede IK 2, Helsingborgs IF 0 *(aet)*
Limhamns IF 0, BK Häcken 0 *(aet; 4-5 on pens)*
Lärje/Angereds IF 0, Kalmar FF 0 *(aet; 4-5 on pens)*
Rynninge IK 1, Djurgårdens IF 3
Valsta Syrianska IK 4, Falkenbergs FF 3 *(aet)*
Carlstad United 0, AIK 3
Svenljunga IK 0, Gefle IF 2
Degerfors IF 1, Örgryte IS 3
Malmö Anadolu BI 0, GIF Sundsvall 1 *(aet)*

THIRD ROUND
(4/5/05)
Valsta Syrianska IK 0, Örgryte IS 4
Östersunds FK 2, Åtvidabergs FF 3
Assyriska FF 2, Gefle IF 1
(5/5/05)
Bunkeflo IF 0, GIF Sundsvall 3
Enskede IK 3, Visby IF Gute FK 1
Halmstads BK 3, Bodens BK 2 *(aet)*
IK Sleipner 1, GAIS 2 *(aet)*
Kalmar FF 3, Hammarby IF 1
Lunds BK 1, IFK Norrköping 4
Skellefteå AIK FK 2, IFK Göteborg 11
Tenhults IF 0, IFK Ölme 1
Trelleborgs FF 1, AIK 0
Vasalunds/Essinge IF 0, IF Elfsborg 1
Väsby United 0, Djurgårdens IF 2
Östers IF 0, BK Häcken 1
(19/5/05)
Landskrona BoIS 1, Malmö FF 3

FOURTH ROUND
(1/6/05)
IFK Ölme 1, Kalmar FF 1 *(aet; 5-4 on pens)*
(7/6/05)
Örgryte IS 1, Assyriska FF 1 *(aet; 2-4 on pens)*
(9/6/05)
IFK Göteborg 1, IF Elfsborg 2
(10/6/05)
Enskede IK 1, Djurgårdens IF 5
(30/6/05)
BK Häcken 0, Malmö FF 0 *(aet; 4-3 on pens)*
Åtvidabergs FF 1, Trelleborgs FF 0
(7/7/05)
IFK Norrköping 2, GIF Sundsvall 0

(13/7/05)
GAIS 2, Halmstads BK 1

QUARTER-FINALS
(22/6/05)
IFK Ölme 0, Djurgårdens IF 6 *(Hysén 28, Sjölund 30p, 33, 79, Árnason 51, Amoah 78)*
(3/8/05)
Assyriska FF 2 *(Samura 33, Lukanovic 117)*, IFK Norrköping 2 *(Alm 82, Thordarsson 112)* *(aet; 10-11 on pens)*
(4/8/05)
IF Elfsborg 4 *(Sjöhage 25, 52, Strömberg 56, Holmén 93)*, BK Häcken 3 *(Williams 58, Johnson 77, Töfting 79)* *(aet)*
Åtvidabergs FF 1 *(Bergström 104)*, GAIS 1 *(Lundgren 105)* *(aet; 5-4 on pens)*

SEMI-FINALS
(8/9/05)
Åtvidabergs FF 1 *(Bapupa 57)*, IFK Norrköping 0
(22/9/05)
Djurgårdens IF 2 *(Sjölund 7, 18)*, IF Elfsborg 1 *(Sjöhage 43)*

FINAL
(29/10/05)
Råsunda, Solna
DJURGÅRDENS IF 2 *(Kuivasto 36, Hysén 89)*
ÅTVIDABERGS FF 0
Referee – Hansson
DJURGÅRDENS IF – Wahlström, Concha, Kuivasto, Johannesson, Stenman, Arneng, Sjölund *(Árnason 71)*, Barsom, Jonson *(Amoah 77)*, Kusi Asare, Hysén.
ÅTVIDABERGS FF – Gustavsson, Åhman, Johansson, Ekunde, Elgström *(Gashi 87)*, Jönsson, Bergström, Shhadeh, Bapupa, Suma *(Thelin 80)*, Karlsson.

SECOND LEVEL FINAL TABLE 2005

		Pld	W	D	L	F	A	Pts
1	AIK	30	19	7	4	56	27	64
2	Östers IF	30	17	4	9	48	36	55
3	GAIS	30	14	10	6	52	35	52
4	Ljungskile SK	30	13	11	6	41	29	50
5	Örebro SK FK	30	12	9	9	40	32	45
6	IF Brommapojkarna	30	13	5	12	48	42	44
7	IFK Norrköping	30	12	8	10	44	40	44
8	Falkenbergs FF	30	11	8	11	38	43	41
9	Väsby United	30	11	6	13	32	40	39
10	Åtvidabergs FF	30	9	11	10	36	32	38
11	Trelleborgs FF	30	9	9	12	34	34	36
12	Mjällby AIF	30	9	8	13	44	49	35
13	Degerfors IF	30	9	7	14	31	36	34
14	Bodens BK	30	9	5	16	28	48	32
15	Västerås SK FK	30	7	6	17	35	62	27
16	Västra Frölunda IF	30	7	4	19	32	54	25

PROMOTION/RELEGATION PLAY-OFFS
(26/10/05)
GAIS 2, Landskrona BoIS 1
(30/10/05)
Landskrona BoIS 0, GAIS 0
(GAIS 2-1)

Switzerland

On track for Euro 2008

Switzerland's first World Cup appearance in 12 years ended in the heartbreak of a penalty shoot-out defeat, but on the whole the tournament was a positive experience for coach Köbi Kuhn and his young team.

The World Cup is football's pinnacle and can never be regarded as preparation for something bigger, but, as the co-hosts of the next European Championship, Switzerland could be excused for using the event in Germany as a soundcheck before they walk out in front of their own fans in 2008.

The Swiss appear to be building up nicely for that Alpine summer. Some observers found their style of play in Germany dull and unappealing, but there was a sense of purpose and co-ordination about the team's performances. They won their first-round group – the only non-seeds other than Portugal to do so – and became the first team ever to be eliminated from the World Cup without conceding a goal.

Four clean sheets

Switzerland defended so well as a team that goalkeeper Pascal Zuberbühler, the only regular member of the side over 30, was seldom extended. He proved himself up to the task when called upon, but credit for the four clean sheets the Swiss kept was as much due to the team's unbreakable tactical discipline. The back four of Philipp Degen, Patrick Müller, Philippe Senderos and Ludovic Magnin were solid as a rock, and there was also strong support from midfield, at the centre of which captain Johann Vogel directed operations with his usual economy and discretion.

Going forward, Switzerland might have offered more. Alexander Frei, who had missed much of the season through injury, did well to score two goals, especially as he lacked support. The mercurial Hakan Yakin, a late replacement in the squad for Johan Vonlanthen, provided the odd moment of skill and ingenuity and Tranquillo Barnetta was a bundle of youthful enthusiasm, but generally Switzerland's pragmatic progress came from playing to their (defensive) strengths.

Penalty-taking was certainly an area of weakness. To go out in a shoot-out is bad enough, but to miss every kick – as Switzerland did against Ukraine – is a sin that begs no pardon. Marco Streller, Barnetta and Ricardo Cabanas, the guilty parties, will doubtless have endured many sleepless nights of painful reflection, but all three players should get the opportunity to redeem themselves – if not directly from the penalty spot – as Switzerland go for glory in 2008.

Kuhn, whose contract runs to the end of those European finals, has the luxury of being able to keep his World Cup team largely intact over the next two years. He will want to improve the team's midfield creativity and sharpness up front, but otherwise everything is in good order. Careful nurturing is all that is required, and if Zuberbühler, who will be 37 in 2008, lasts the pace, there is every chance that Switzerland will field a virtually unchanged line-up at the European Championship.

An indication of Switzerland's recent rise to prominence is that almost all of the national team players are now affiliated to clubs in the major European leagues. Zuberbühler was the only regular member of the World Cup team belonging to a Swiss club, and even he departed in the summer, leaving FC Basel for West Bromwich Albion.

Zubi's last European game for Basel took place in England and is one he will want to erase from memory. The Swiss club looked to be cruising towards a UEFA Cup semi-final when they led 3-0 on aggregate midway through the first half of their quarter-final second leg in Middlesbrough. But Boro came storming

Switzerland

back, scoring their decisive fourth goal in the final minute with a shot that beat Zuberbühler at his near post.

Title thriller

If that Euro exit was hard to take, Zubi and his Basel team-mates would endure even greater suffering a few weeks later as the unthinkable happened and they failed to win a Swiss title race they had led practically all season. The climax could not have been crueller. Requiring one point from their last two games to complete a hat-trick of championship wins, Christian Gross's team lost the first, a game in hand at Young Boys Berne, going down 4-2. That set the scene for a last-day thriller at the St. Jakob Park against an FC Zurich side that had won their previous six matches. Another victory for Lucien Favre's in-form young team would give them the title at Basel's expense on goal difference.

Despite the defeat in Berne, Basel were confident of completing the job in a home stadium where they had not lost a league game since December 2002 – a record-breaking run of 59 matches. However, Zurich had beaten Basel there just before Christmas in a Swiss Cup game (4-3), and as they hadn't lost in the league for 23 matches (since a 4-2 defeat by Basel in October), they were not short of self-belief either.

After 30 minutes a goal from the Super League's top scorer, Alhassane Keita, put the visitors ahead. But with 18 minutes remaining Basel were back on top of the table after an equalising free-kick from Croatian striker Mladen Petric. The stadium was gripped by tension in the closing minutes. The Basel fans tried to sing their team across the finish line, but in the third minute of stoppage-time they were struck dumb when Zurich's veteran Romanian defender Iulian Filipescu pounced to score a momentous winning goal.

There was barely time for Basel to kick off before the referee signalled the end of the match. The home fans were so enraged that many of them invaded the pitch and tried to assault the jubilant Zurich players. There was bedlam also in the stands and outside the stadium. Basel were subsequently handed a two-match spectator ban and a heavy fine, but the most painful punishment was Filipescu's goal.

FC Zurich had literally won the title in the last second of the season. They had topped the table only once previously – in mid-August – but now, right at the death, they had overhauled Basel and become champions of Switzerland again for the first time in 25 years. That Filipescu should be their match-winner was astonishing as the Romanian had never previously scored for the club in 64 matches.

Recurring theme

Zurich's refusal to give up a lost cause was a recurring theme. Within their 24-match unbeaten run were two extraordinary comebacks – turning a three-goal deficit into a 5-3 victory away to Neuchâtel, and coming from 3-0 down again to draw 3-3 with Young Boys. FCZ were the masters at grabbing late goals. Filipescu's was the seventh they registered in additional time, while 32 of their 87 goals were scored in the last 15 minutes (with just six conceded in the same time-frame).

Zurich had been steered to their 1981 title by Daniel Jeandupeux, and now they triumphed under another francophone coach. Favre might one day emulate Jeandupeux by taking charge of the Swiss national team, but, for now, having signed a contract extension with FCZ to 2008, he remains the hottest property on the Swiss club scene. His faith in youth underpinned Zurich's victory. With the exception of 32-year-old Filipescu, almost all the other regulars were 23 or younger, including midfielders Xavier Margairaz and Blerim Dzemaili, both called up to Switzerland's World

NATIONAL TEAM RESULTS 2005/06

Date	Opponent	H/A/N	Venue	Score	Scorers
17/8/05	Norway	A	Oslo	2-0	Frei (50), Bergdølmo (59og)
3/9/05	Israel (WCQ)	H	Basle	1-1	Frei (5)
7/9/05	Cyprus (WCQ)	A	Nicosia	3-1	Frei (15), Senderos (70), Gygax (86)
8/10/05	France (WCQ)	H	Berne	1-1	Magnin (79)
12/10/05	Republic of Ireland (WCQ)	A	Dublin	0-0	
12/11/05	Turkey (WCQ)	H	Berne	2-0	Senderos (41), Behrami (86)
16/11/05	Turkey (WCQ)	A	Istanbul	2-4	Frei (2p), Streller (84)
1/3/06	Scotland	A	Glasgow	3-1	Barnetta (21), Gygax (42), Cabanas (69)
27/5/06	Ivory Coast	H	Basle	1-1	Barnetta (32)
31/5/06	Italy	H	Geneva	1-1	Gygax (32)
3/6/06	China	H	Zurich	4-1	Frei (40, 49p), Streller (47, 73)
13/6/06	France (WCF)	N	Stuttgart	0-0	
19/6/06	Togo (WCF)	N	Dortmund	2-0	Frei (17), Barnetta (88)
23/6/06	South Korea (WCF)	N	Hanover	2-0	Senderos (23), Frei (77)
26/6/06	Ukraine (WCF)	N	Cologne	0-0	(aet; 0-3 on pens)

Switzerland

NATIONAL TEAM APPEARANCES 2005/06

Coach – Jakob "Köbi" KUHN

Player	DOB	Club	Nor	ISR	CYP	FRA	IRL	TUR	TUR	Sco	Civ	Ita	Chn	FRA	TOG	KOR	UKR	Caps	Goals
Pascal ZUBERBÜHLER	8/1/71	FC Basel	G	G	G	G	G	G	G	G46	G	G46	G46	G	G	G	G	44	-
Philipp DEGEN	15/2/83	Dortmund (GER)	D	D	D	D	D	D	D46	D	s46	D	s42	D56	D	D	D	19	-
Patrick MÜLLER	17/12/76	FC Basel /Lyon (FRA)	D	D	D	D	D	D	D	D30		D70	D75	D	D	D	D	68	3
Philippe SENDEROS	14/2/85	Arsenal (ENG)	D87	D	D	D	D	D	D	D74	D	D70		D	D	D53		15	3
Ludovic MAGNIN	20/4/79	Stuttgart (GER)	D80	D89		D	D	D			D	D46	D	D	D		D	33	2
Ricardo CABANAS	17/1/79	Grasshopper-Club /1.FC Köln (GER)	M46	s65		M	M	M	M	M	M	M46	M63	M	M77	M	M	41	4
Johann VOGEL	8/3/77	Milan (ITA)	M	M	M	M	M	M	M	M82	M67	M	M46	M	M	M	M	89	2
Hakan YAKIN	22/2/77	BSC Young Boys	M	M65	s73						s46	s70		s46	M71	M64		49	14
Tranquillo BARNETTA	22/5/85	Leverkusen (GER)	M	M	M89	M90	M89	M83	M	M	M46	M		M	M	M	M	17	3
Alexander FREI	15/7/79	Rennes (FRA)	A80	A	A73	A	A	A	A		A	A	A	A	A88	A	A116	49	27
Marco STRELLER	18/6/81	Stuttgart (GER) /1.FC Köln (GER)	A46			s54	A77	s33 /87		A74	A		A	A	s77		s64	13	3
Daniel GYGAX	28/8/81	Lille OSC (FRA)	s46	M	M	s60	s89	M	M33	M	M46	M90		s56	A46			24	5
Johan VONLANTHEN	1/2/86	NAC Breda (HOL)	s46	A82	A81	A60	A54	s77		s46								17	5
Christoph SPYCHER	30/3/78	Frankfurt (GER)	s80	s89	D			D			s46	s46			D			22	-
Mauro LUSTRINELLI	26/2/76	FC Thun /Sparta Praha (CZE)	s80	s82	s81	s83				s74				s88		s116		7	-
Boris SMILJANIC	28/9/76	FC Basel	s87							s74								3	-
Raphaël WICKY	26/4/77	Hamburg (GER)			M	M83	M		M	M46	s46	M46	M46	M82	M	M88	M	71	1
Benjamin HUGGEL	7/7/77	Frankfurt (GER)		s89				s87										16	-
Valon BEHRAMI	19/4/85	Lazio (ITA)			s90		s83	s46	D46	D76		D42			s88			7	1
Stéphane GRICHTING	30/3/79	AJ Auxerre (FRA)								D	s30	s70	D			s33		7	-
Fabio COLTORTI	3/12/80	Grasshopper-Club								s46		s46						2	-
Johan DJOUROU	18/1/87	Arsenal (ENG)								s46		D		s75		s53	D33	5	-
Blerim DZEMAILI	12/4/86	FC Zürich								s82	s67		s63					3	-
David DEGEN	15/2/83	FC Basel								s76	s90	M						3	-
Xavier MARGAIRAZ	7/1/84	FC Zürich									s46	s46	s82		s71			5	-
Diego BENAGLIO	8/9/83	CD Nacional (POR)									s46							1	-

Switzerland

Cup squad, and sharpshooting strikers Keita (from Guinea) and Rafael (from Brazil).

Zurich's hopes of doing the Double were torpedoed by a brilliant performance in the semi-final by Young Boys, who ousted the holders with a 4-1 win. But the team from the capital could not repeat the trick in the final, played in their new home, the Stade de Suisse. An eventful game against FC Sion ended 1-1, and the underdogs from the Challenge League came through to win 5-3 on penalties. In taking the trophy, Sion prolonged their extraordinary record of winning every Cup final they had played in – this victory made it a nice round ten out of ten – and they also became the first team from outside the top flight to win the competition in its 81-year history.

Suitably buoyed, Sion went on to claim promotion back to the Super League with a play-off victory over Neuchâtel Xamax. The lakeside club, coached by Croatian veteran Miroslav Blazevic, thus dropped out of the elite for the first time in 40 years. Despite his double success, Sion coach Christophe Moulin chose to leave and was replaced by ex-Argentine international Néstor Clausen, a Sion player from 1988-94.

FC Luzern won the Challenge League to gain automatic promotion (at the expense of Yverdon) and they too entered the Super League with a new coach as ex-Swiss international midfielder Ciriaco Sforza took over from René van Eck after the Dutchman failed to agree new contract terms.

Thun sensation

Seven of the ten Super League clubs changed coach during the course of the season, with Aarau doing so twice. They were belatedly rescued from the drop by Urs 'Longo' Schönenberger, the man who had caused a sensation the previous summer by leading little FC Thun past Dynamo Kiev and Malmö FF into the UEFA Champions League. Thun did not disgrace themselves among Europe's elite, losing to Arsenal away and Ajax at home only through last-minute goals and even stretching their debut European adventure beyond Christmas after finishing above Sparta Prague to qualify for the UEFA Cup. But whereas Thun had done better than Basel in the Champions League, Basel would outlast Thun in the UEFA Cup, knocking out French clubs Monaco and Strasbourg - and supplying the competition's top scorer in seven-goal Argentine playmaker Matías Delgado - before their hopes of becoming the first Swiss club to win a European trophy bit the dust in that epic quarter-final against Middlesbrough.

EUROPEAN CUPS 2005/06

UEFA CHAMPIONS LEAGUE

FC BASEL
3rd qualifying round SV WERDER BREMEN (GER)
H 2-1 *Degen (27), Rossi (52)*
Zuberbühler, Zanni, Quennoz, Smiljanic, Kléber, Degen, Ba, Chipperfield (Rossi 46), Delgado (Ergic 65), Petric, Sterjovski (Baykal 71).
A 0-3
Zuberbühler, Zanni, Quennoz (Sterjovski 69), Smiljanic, Kléber, Degen, Ba, Chipperfield, Delgado, Eduardo, Rossi (Ergic 81).

FC THUN
2nd qualifying round DYNAMO KYIV (UKR)
A 2-2 *Rodolfo (38og), Aegerter (66)*
Jakupovic, Pallas, Hodzic, Deumi, Leandro (Bernardi 87), Ferreira, Aegerter, Milicevic, Adriano (Gonçalves 29), Gerber (Gelson 85), Lustrinelli.
H 1-0 *Bernardi (90)*
Jakupovic, Pallas, Hodzic, Deumi, Gonçalves, Gerber, Milicevic, Aegerter, Ferreira (Leandro 76), Adriano (Bernardi 87), Lustrinelli (Gelson 90).

3rd qualifying round MALMÖ FF (SWE)
A 1-0 *Adriano (34)*
Jakupovic, Pallas, Hodzic, Deumi (Leandro 16), Gonçalves, Gerber (Gelson 84), Milicevic, Bernardi, Ferreira (Sen 77), Adriano, Lustrinelli.
H 3-0 *Bernardi (26), Lustrinelli (40, 66)*
Jakupovic, Pallas, Hodzic, Milicevic, Gonçalves, Gerber (Leandro 70), Aegerter, Bernardi, Ferreira, Adriano (Gelson 79), Lustrinelli (Sen 85).

1st round Group B
Match 1 ARSENAL (ENG)
A 1-2 *Ferreira (53)*
Jakupovic, Orman, Hodzic, Milicecic, Gonçalves, Gerber (Leandro 72), Bernardi, Aegerter, Ferreira, Adriano (Gelson 57), Lustrinelli (Omar 87).

Match 2 AC SPARTA PRAHA (CZE)
A 1-0 *Hodzic (89)*
Jakupovic, Orman (Gerber 46), Milicevic, Deumi, Gonçalves, Hodzic, Ferreira, Aegerter, Adriano (Gelson 83), Leandro, Lustrinelli (Sen 79).

Match 3 AJAX (HOL)
A 0-2
Jakupovic, Orman, Milicevic, Deumi, Gonçalves, Ferreira, Aegerter, Adriano (Sen 74), Leandro, Gelson (Duruz 85), Lustrinelli (Omar 85).

Match 4 AJAX
H 2-4 *Lustrinelli (56), Adriano (74)*
Jakupovic, Orman (Gerber 67), Milicevic (Adriano 42), Deumi, Gonçalves, Hodzic, Ferreira, Bernardi, Aegerter, Leandro (Sen 81), Lustrinelli.

Match 5 ARSENAL
H 0-1
Jakupovic, Orman, Hodzic, Deumi, Gonçalves (Bernardi 90), Ferreira, Milicevic, Aegerter, Leandro, Adriano, Lustrinelli (Sen 84).

Match 6 AC SPARTA PRAHA
A 0-0
Jakupovic, Orman, Hodzic, Gonçalves, Duruz, Spadoto (Sen 56), Bernardi (Savic 70), Aegerter, Leandro, Adriano (Gelson 89), Lustrinelli.

UEFA CUP

FC ZÜRICH
2nd qualifying round LEGIA WARSZAWA (POL)

Switzerland

A 1-0 *Rafael (90)*
Leoni, Nef, Von Bergen, Filipescu, Schneider, Dzemaili, Tararache, Di Jorio, Margairaz, César (Rafael 86), Keita.
H 4-1 *Keita (35, 65), Dzemaili (30), César (78p)*
Leoni, Nef (Stahel 19), Filipescu, Von Bergen, Stucki, Di Jorio (Abdi 83), Dzemaili, Tararache (Rapisarda 82), César, Rafael, Keita.

1st round BRØNDBY IF (DEN)
A 0-2
Leoni, Stahel, Filipescu, Von Bergen, Stucki, Tararache, Dzemaili, Di Jorio (Akhalaia 90), Margairaz (Rafael 72), César, Keita.
H 2-1 *Rafael (14, 80)*
Leoni, Stahel (Nef 68), Filipescu, Von Bergen, Stucki (Margairaz 68), Di Jorio (Abdi 85), Dzemaili, Tararache, César, Rafael, Keita.

GRASSHOPPER-CLUB ZÜRICH
2nd qualifiying round WISLA PLOCK (POL)
H 1-0 *Eduardo (68)*
Coltorti, Schwegler R., Mitreski, Stepanovs, Jaggy, Chihab, Renggli, Eduardo (Touré 89), Cabanas (Salatic 84), Dos Santos (Pavlovic 46), Rogério.
A 2-3 *Dos Santos (30), Eduardo (83)*
Coltorti, Chihab, Mitreski, Stepanovs, Jaggy (Sutter 87), Pavlovic, Renggli, Cabanas, Dos Santos (Touré 79), Eduardo, Rogério.

1st round MYPA (FIN)
H 1-1 *Rogério (1)*
Coltorti, Sutter, Denicolà, Stepanovs, Jaggy, Salatic, Schwegler R. (Touré 46), Renggli, Dos Santos (Lütolf 46), Eduardo (Peralta 81), Rogério.
A 3-0 *Touré (74), Salatic (80), Rogério (86)*
Coltorti, Sutter, Mitreski, Stepanovs, Jaggy, Chihab, Salatic (Denicolà 90), Cabanas, Dos Santos (Hürlimann 83), Rogério, Touré (Schwegler R. 78).

2nd round Group D
Match 1 MIDDLESBROUGH (ENG)
H 0-1
Coltorti, Sutter, Mitreski, Stepanovs, Jaggy, Renggli (Salatic 87), Chihab (Touré 82), Cabanas, Dos Santos, Eduardo, Rogério.

Match 2 LITEX LOVECH (BUL)
A 1-2 *Dos Santos (90)*
Coltorti, Sutter, Mitreski, Stepanovs, Jaggy, Chihab (Hürlimann 9; Salatic 76), Renggli, Dos Santos, Cabanas, Eduardo, Rogério.

Match 3 DNIPRO DNIPROPETROVSK (UKR)
H 2-3 *Touré (85), Renggli (90)*
Coltorti, Sutter (Chihab 59), Mitreski, Stepanovs, Jaggy, Salatic (Pavlovic 63), Cabanas, Dos Santos, Touré, Rogério.

Match 4 AZ (HOL)
A 0-1
Coltorti, Sutter, Mitreski, Denicolà, Jaggy, Schwegler R. (Salatic 17), Renggli, Touré, Cabanas, Dos Santos, Rogério (Chihab 88).

FC BASEL
1st round SIROKI BRIJEG (BOS)
H 5-0 *Delgado (10, 79, 88), Ergic (70), Eduardo (85)*
Zuberbühler, Zanni, Müller, Smiljanic, Chipperfield, Ba, Degen (Ergic 64), Delgado, Rossi (Sterjovski 77), Eduardo, Petric (Baykal 90).
A 1-0 *Petric (7)*
Zuberbühler, Zanni, Müller, Smiljanic, Chipperfield, Ba (Baykal 57), Degen, Delgado (Rakitic 76), Ergic, Petric, Eduardo (Sterjovski 46).

2nd round Group E
Match 1 RC STRASBOURG (FRA)
H 0-2
Zuberbühler, Zanni, Müller, Smiljanic, Chipperfield, Degen, Ba, Rossi (Sterjovski 70), Delgado, Petric (Baykal 64), Eduardo.

Match 2 CRVENA ZVEZDA BEOGRAD (SCG)
A 2-1 *Delgado (30p), Rossi (88)*
Zuberbühler, Zanni, Quennoz, Smiljanic, Chipperfield, Degen (Sterjovski 84), Ergic (Petric 58), Ba, Rossi, Delgado, Eduardo.

Match 3 TROMSØ IL (NOR)
H 4-3 *Petric (17), Delgado (61), Chipperfield (67), Degen (75)*
Zuberbühler, Zanni, Müller, Smiljanic, Chipperfield, Ba (Ergic 60), Degen, Delgado (Baykal 81), Rossi, Eduardo, Petric.

Match 4 ROMA (ITA)
A 1-3 *Petric (78)*
Zuberbühler, Zanni, Müller, Smiljanic, Chipperfield (Sterjovski 65), Ba (Petric 46), Ergic (Baykal 72), Degen, Delgado, Rossi, Eduardo.

3rd round AS MONACO FC (FRA)
H 1-0 *Degen (78)*
Zuberbühler, Zanni, Majstorovic, Smiljanic, Berner, Degen, Delgado (Ergic 77), Ba, Petric (Baykal 70), Sterjovski (Kuzmanovic 90), Eduardo.
A 1-1 *Majstorovic (56)*
Zuberbühler, Zanni, Majstorovic, Smiljanic, Berner, Ba, Degen, Delgado (Ergic 82), Petric, Sterjovski (Baykal 80), Eduardo.

4th round RC STRASBOURG (FRA)
H 2-0 *Delgado (8), Kuzmanovic (88)*
Zuberbühler, Zanni, Majstorovic, Smiljanic, Berner, Ba (Ergic 83), Degen (Kuzmanovic 77), Petric, Delgado, Sterjovski, Eduardo.
A 2-2 *Eduardo (3, 26)*
Zuberbühler, Zanni, Majstorovic, Smiljanic, Berner (Chipperfield 79), Ba, Degen, Delgado (Ergic 66), Petric, Sterjovski, Eduardo (Baykal 86).

Quarter-final MIDDLESBROUGH (ENG)
H 2-0 *Delgado (43), Degen (45)*
Zuberbühler, Zanni, Majstorovic, Smiljanic, Berner, Ba, Degen, Delgado, Petric (Ergic 85), Sterjovski (Chipperfield 64), Eduardo.
A 1-4 *Eduardo (22)*
Zuberbühler, Zanni, Majstorovic, Smiljanic, Berner, Ba, Degen (Chipperfield 61), Delgado (Ergic 70), Petric, Sterjovski (Quennoz 85), Eduardo.

FC THUN
3rd round HAMBURGER SV (GER)
H 1-0 *Adriano (30)*
Jakupovic, Hodzic, Milicevic, Deumi, Duruz, Orman (Leandro 62), Friedli, Aegerter, Ferreira, Adriano, Faye (Gelson 90).
A 0-2
Jakupovic, Hodzic, Deumi, Milicevic, Duruz, Ferreira (Bernardi 84), Friedli, Aegerter, Leandro (Sen 53), Adriano (Cengel 78), Faye.

TOP GOALSCORERS 2005/06

20	Alhassane KEITA (FC Zürich)
18	Matías Emilio DELGADO (FC Basel)
	JOÃO PAULO (BSC Young Boys Bern)
14	Mladen PETRIC (FC Basel)
	RAFAEL (FC Zürich)
13	António DOS SANTOS (Grasshopper-Club Zürich)
	Eric HASSLI (FC St. Gallen)
	Francisco AGUIRRE (Yverdon-Sport FC)
12	Alex TACHIE-MENSAH (FC St. Gallen)
	CÉSAR (FC Zürich)

Switzerland

FINAL LEAGUE TABLE 2005/06

		Pld	Home					Away					Total					Pts
			W	D	L	F	A	W	D	L	F	A	W	D	L	F	A	
1	FC Zürich	36	11	6	1	46	18	12	3	3	40	18	23	9	4	86	36	78
2	FC Basel	36	14	3	1	40	14	9	6	3	47	28	23	9	4	87	42	78
3	BSC Young Boys Bern	36	10	4	4	28	25	7	7	4	32	21	17	11	8	60	46	62
4	Grasshopper-Club Zürich	36	8	9	1	27	15	6	4	8	17	18	14	13	9	44	33	55
5	FC Thun	36	9	4	5	32	24	5	3	10	18	29	14	7	15	50	53	49
6	FC St. Gallen	36	8	5	5	34	23	3	2	13	17	33	11	7	18	51	56	40
7	FC Aarau	36	7	4	7	18	26	1	7	10	11	37	8	11	17	29	63	35
8	FC Schaffhausen	36	1	7	10	14	34	6	5	7	18	21	7	12	17	32	55	33
9	Neuchâtel Xamax FC	36	8	3	7	25	24	1	3	14	16	46	9	6	21	41	70	33
10	Yverdon-Sport FC	36	8	0	10	23	28	1	5	12	15	36	9	5	22	38	64	32

LEAGUE RESULTS/SCORERS/APPEARANCES/GOALS 2005/06

FC AARAU
Coach - Andy Egli; (13/12/05) Alain Geiger; (30/4/06) Urs Schönenberger

2005
Date	Opponent	H/A	Score	Scorers
16/7	FC Thun	a	0-2	
23/7	FC St. Gallen	h	1-4	Burgmeier
6/8	Neuchâtel Xamax FC	h	2-0	Giallanza (p), Bieli
10/8	BSC Young Boys Bern	a	0-0	
13/8	Yverdon-Sport FC	h	1-1	Berisha
20/8	FC Basel	a	2-7	Giallanza, Bieli
28/8	Grasshopper-Club Zürich	h	0-1	
11/9	FC Schaffhausen	a	1-0	Giallanza
21/9	FC Zürich	h	1-1	Giallanza
24/9	FC Thun	h	2-1	Bieli, Tcheutchoua
1/10	FC St. Gallen	a	1-2	Bieli
16/10	BSC Young Boys Bern	h	1-0	Bieli
30/10	Neuchâtel Xamax FC	a	0-2	
6/11	Yverdon-Sport FC	a	1-4	Giallanza (p)
20/11	FC Basel	h	0-2	
26/11	Grasshopper-Club Zürich	a	1-1	Giallanza
4/12	FC Schaffhausen	h	0-2	
11/12	FC Zürich	a	0-3	

2006
Date	Opponent	H/A	Score	Scorers
12/2	Grasshopper-Club Zürich	h	1-0	Neri
19/2	FC St. Gallen	a	1-1	Bättig
26/2	FC Schaffhausen	a	0-0	
11/3	BSC Young Boys Bern	a	1-2	Baning
19/3	FC Zürich	h	1-1	Giallanza
22/3	FC Basel	a	1-1	Bieli
26/3	Yverdon-Sport FC	h	1-0	Carreño
29/3	Neuchâtel Xamax FC	h	3-1	Giallanza 2, Baning
2/4	FC Thun	a	1-1	Berisha
6/4	FC Thun	h	0-1	
9/4	Yverdon-Sport FC	a	1-3	Bieli
12/4	FC Basel	h	1-5	Bieli
20/4	FC Zürich	a	0-6	
23/4	BSC Young Boys Bern	h	1-5	Tcheutchoua
30/4	Neuchâtel Xamax FC	a	0-2	
3/5	FC Schaffhausen	h	1-1	Baning
6/5	FC St. Gallen	h	1-0	Giallanza
14/5	Grasshopper-Club Zürich	a	0-0	

No	Name	Nat	Pos	Aps	(s)	Gls
30	Albert BANING	CMR	M	17		3
6	Roland BÄTTIG		M	20		1
8	Argiend BEKIRI	MAC	A	15	(11)	
11	Johan BERISHA		A	6	(13)	2
9	Rainer BIELI		A	25	(8)	8
21	Admir BILIBANI	BOS	D	28	(4)	
15	Franz BURGMEIER	LIE	A	33	(2)	1
16	Fernando CARREÑO	URU	D	18	(4)	1
5	Sven CHRIST		D	26		
23	Massimo COLOMBA		G	34		
24	Vojan CVIJANOVIC		M		(1)	
28	Fabrice EHRET	FRA	M	11	(1)	
27	Adrian EUGSTER		D	11	(2)	
26	Sehar FEJZULAHI	SCG	A	14	(15)	
7	Gaetano GIALLANZA		A	24	(6)	10
20	Gökhan INLER	TUR	M	7	(4)	
12	Paulo MENEZES	BRA	M	6	(8)	
3	Davide MORETTO	ITA	D		(2)	
22	Francisco Valmerino NERI	BRA	A	9	(1)	1
14	David OPANGO	BUR	D	14	(5)	
17	Manuel SCHENKER		D	6	(5)	
2	Flavio SCHMID		D	13		
10	Augustine SIMO	CMR	M	21	(5)	
1	Oliver STÖCKLI		G	2		
19	Jean-Pierre TCHEUTCHOUA	CMR	D	18	(1)	2
4	Harutyun VARDANYAN	ARM	D	18	(3)	

FC BASEL
Coach - Christian Gross

2005
Date	Opponent	H/A	Score	Scorers
16/7	FC Schaffhausen	h	1-0	Ergic
22/7	FC Thun	a	0-3	
30/7	FC Zürich	h	2-1	Degen, Delgado
6/8	Yverdon-Sport FC	a	2-1	Sterjovski 2
14/8	FC St. Gallen	a	3-3	Petric, Giménez 2
20/8	FC Aarau	h	7-2	Giménez 3, Delgado 2, Petric, Sterjovski
27/8	Neuchâtel Xamax FC	h	3-0	Delgado 2, Eduardo
11/9	Grasshopper-Club Zürich	a	2-2	Delgado (p), Rossi

Switzerland

22/9	BSC Young Boys Bern	h	1-1	Rossi	
25/9	FC Schaffhausen	a	2-1	Delgado, Eduardo	
2/10	FC Thun	h	5-1	Degen, Petric 3, Ba	
16/10	FC Zürich	a	4-2	Degen, Delgado 2, Eduardo	
29/10	Yverdon-Sport FC	h	3-1	Degen, Chipperfield, Delgado	
6/11	FC St. Gallen	h	1-0	Zanni	
20/11	FC Aarau	a	2-0	Ba, Rossi	
4/12	Grasshopper-Club Zürich	h	1-0	Delgado (p)	
7/12	Neuchâtel Xamax FC	a	2-3	Smiljanic, Petric	
11/12	BSC Young Boys Bern	a	6-1	Degen, Smiljanic, Ergic, Eduardo, Delgado, Sterjovski	
2006					
12/2	FC Zürich	a	1-1	Petric	
19/2	FC Schaffhausen	h	1-1	Majstorovic	
26/2	Yverdon-Sport FC	h	2-1	Nakata, Sterjovski	
4/3	FC Thun	a	1-1	Eduardo	
12/3	Grasshopper-Club Zürich	h	2-1	Eduardo, Kavelashvili	
19/3	FC St. Gallen	a	2-2	Ergic, Smiljanic	
22/3	FC Aarau	h	1-1	Kavelashvili	
2/4	BSC Young Boys Bern	h	2-0	Petric, Majstorovic (p)	
9/4	Neuchâtel Xamax FC	h	2-1	Chipperfield, Majstorovic	
12/4	FC Aarau	a	5-1	Chipperfield 2, og (Carreño), Ergic, Kavelashvili	
15/4	Neuchâtel Xamax FC	a	5-1	Petric, Chipperfield, Delgado, Sterjovski, Degen	
20/4	FC St. Gallen	h	3-1	Majstorovic, Delgado, Petric	
23/4	Grasshopper-Club Zürich	a	1-1	og (Mitreski)	
29/4	FC Thun	h	2-0	Delgado, Petric	
3/5	Yverdon-Sport FC	a	3-1	Majstorovic, Petric, Sterjovski	
6/5	FC Schaffhausen	a	4-0	Delgado 2, Kuzmanovic, Kavelashvili	
10/5	BSC Young Boys Bern	a	2-4	Petric, Delgado	
13/5	FC Zürich	h	1-2	Petric	

No	Name	Nat	Pos	Aps	(s)	Gls
12	Papa Malick BA	SEN	M	26	(4)	2
29	Kulagsizoglou BAYKAL		M	4	(11)	
24	Bruno BERNER		D	16	(1)	
9	César Andrés CARIGNANO	ARG	A		(3)	
11	Scott CHIPPERFIELD	AUS	M	26	(2)	5
21	David DEGEN		M	30	(4)	6
20	Matías Emilio DELGADO	ARG	M	33		18
3	Damir DZOMBIC		D	2	(2)	
23	EDUARDO Adelino da Silva	BRA	A	28	(1)	6
22	Ivan ERGIC	AUS	M	16	(15)	4
13	Christian GIMÉNEZ	ARG	A	5		5
26	Mikheil KAVELASHVILI	GEO	M		(10)	4
19	Correa de Carvalho KLÉBER	BRA	D	6		
27	Zdravko KUZMANOVIC		A	5	(12)	1
5	Daniel MAJSTOROVIC	SWE	D	18		5
14	Djamel MESBAH	ALG	A		(2)	
16	Patrick MÜLLER		D	13		
6	Koji NAKATA	JPN	D	9	(1)	1
10	Mladen PETRIC	CRO	A	26	(5)	14
4	Alexandre QUENNOZ		D	5	(2)	
17	Ivan RAKITIC	CRO	A		(1)	
33	Julio Hernán ROSSI	ARG	A	15	(3)	3
30	Boris SMILJANIC		D	29	(2)	3
8	Mile STERJOVSKI	AUS	M	11	(20)	7
15	Murat YAKIN		D	1		
32	Reto ZANNI		D	36		1
1	Pascal ZUBERBÜHLER		G	36		

GRASSHOPPER-CLUB ZÜRICH
Coach - Hanspeter Latour ; (Piet Hamberg); (16/1/06)
Krasimir Balakov (BUL)

2005					
16/7	Yverdon-Sport FC	h	3-2	Salatic, Pavlovic, Eduardo	
24/7	FC Zürich	a	2-4	Dos Santos, Cabanas Ri. (p)	
30/7	FC Schaffhausen	h	1-1	Renggli	
6/8	BSC Young Boys Bern	a	3-0	Eduardo, Rogério 2	
14/8	FC Thun	a	1-2	Rogério	
20/8	FC St. Gallen	h	3-1	Dos Santos 2 (1p), Renggli	
28/8	FC Aarau	a	1-0	Cabanas Ri.	
11/9	FC Basel	h	2-2	Cabanas Ri., Rogério	
21/9	Neuchâtel Xamax FC	h	3-0	Rogério, Dos Santos (p), Chihab	
25/9	Yverdon-Sport FC	a	0-2		
2/10	FC Zürich	h	1-0	Dos Santos	
16/10	FC Schaffhausen	a	2-0	Eduardo, Dos Santos	
30/10	BSC Young Boys Bern	h	1-1	Dos Santos	
6/11	FC Thun	h	2-0	Cabanas Ri., Eduardo	
20/11	FC St. Gallen	a	1-1	Eduardo	
26/11	FC Aarau	h	1-1	Eduardo	
4/12	FC Basel	a	0-1		
11/12	Neuchâtel Xamax FC	a	0-0		
2006					
12/2	FC Aarau	a	0-1		
19/2	Neuchâtel Xamax FC	h	2-2	Muff, Seoane	
26/2	BSC Young Boys Bern	a	1-1	Rogério	
12/3	FC Basel	h	1-2	Dos Santos	
18/3	Yverdon-Sport FC	h	1-1	Seoane	
22/3	FC Thun	a	1-0	Pavlovic	
26/3	FC Schaffhausen	h	0-1		
29/3	FC Zürich	h	0-0		
2/4	FC St. Gallen	h	2-1	Renggli 2	
6/4	FC St. Gallen	a	2-0	Dos Santos 2	
12/4	FC Thun	h	3-1	Dos Santos 2, Touré	
15/4	FC Schaffhausen	a	1-1	Pavlovic	
20/4	Yverdon-Sport FC	a	1-0	Dos Santos (p)	
23/4	FC Basel	h	1-1	Touré	
30/4	FC Zürich	a	0-2		
3/5	BSC Young Boys Bern	h	1-0	Touré	
6/5	Neuchâtel Xamax FC	a	0-1		
14/5	FC Aarau	h	0-0		

No	Name	Nat	Pos	Aps	(s)	Gls
34	Antonio AIELLO		M		(1)	
31	David BLUMER		A	2	(3)	
23	Raul CABANAS		M	8	(4)	
15	Ricardo CABANAS		M	15		4
5	Tariq CHIHAB	MAR	M	16	(3)	1
1	Fabio COLTORTI		G	35		
13	Luca DENICOLA		D	19	(4)	
30	António DOS SANTOS	BRA	M	34	(1)	13
10	EDUARDO Ribeiro	BRA	A	9	(5)	6
3	Igor HÜRLIMANN		D	2	(7)	
24	Kim JAGGY		D	32		
18	Peter JEHLE	LIE	G	1	(1)	
20	Fonseca LEANDRO	BRA	A	5	(6)	
29	Marc LÜTOLF		D		(3)	
26	Aleksandar MITRESKI	MAC	M	24		
9	André MUFF		A	5	(1)	1
14	Dusan PAVLOVIC		M	19	(5)	3
16	Walter Horacio PERALTA	URU	A		(2)	
17	Vladimir PERALTA	ITA	M		(1)	
8	Michel RENGGLI		M	33	(2)	4
11	ROGÉRIO Luiz da Silva	BRA	A	21	(5)	6

Switzerland

No	Name	Nat	Pos	Aps	(s)	Gls
33	Leonel Medina ROMERO		M	1		
35	Veroljub SALATIC		M	19	(11)	1
4	Roland SCHWEGLER		D	4	(9)	
6	Gerardo SEOANE		M	13	(2)	2
2	Igors STEPANOVS	LAT	D	27		
32	Scott Lee SUTTER		D	27		
7	Demba TOURE	SEN	A	20	(13)	3
19	Alexander VIVEROS	COL	M	3	(2)	
27	Kay Fabian VOSER		D	2	(1)	

NEUCHATEL XAMAX FC
Coach - Alain Geiger; (27/9/05) Miroslav Blazevic (CRO)

2005
13/7	BSC Young Boys Bern	h	1-3	Agolli
23/7	FC Schaffhausen	a	1-1	Agolli
30/7	Yverdon-Sport FC	h	4-0	Griffiths, Coly (p), Mangane, Maraninchi (p)
6/8	FC Aarau	a	0-2	
14/8	FC Zürich	a	2-3	Xhafa, Rey
19/8	FC Thun	h	0-2	
27/8	FC Basel	a	0-3	
11/9	FC St. Gallen	h	0-1	
21/9	Grasshopper-Club Zürich	a	0-3	
25/9	BSC Young Boys Bern	a	2-3	Rey, Mangane
2/10	FC Schaffhausen	h	1-0	Mangane
16/10	Yverdon-Sport FC	a	1-4	Xhafa
30/10	FC Aarau	h	2-0	Rey, Xhafa
6/11	FC Zürich	h	3-5	Rey 2, og (Stahel)
18/11	FC Thun	a	3-2	Besle, Agolli, Rey
4/12	FC St. Gallen	a	1-7	Coly
7/12	FC Basel	h	3-2	Lubamba (p), Rey, Coly
11/12	Grasshopper-Club Zürich	h	0-0	

2006
12/2	FC Thun	h	0-0	
19/2	Grasshopper-Club Zürich	a	2-2	Nuzzolo, Rey
26/2	FC St. Gallen	h	2-2	Coly, Cordonnier
12/3	FC Schaffhausen	a	0-0	
19/3	BSC Young Boys Bern	a	0-1	
22/3	FC Zürich	a	1-4	Coly
29/3	FC Aarau	a	1-3	Sehic
2/4	Yverdon-Sport FC	a	1-2	Coly
6/4	Yverdon-Sport FC	h	2-0	Sehic, Nuzzolo
9/4	FC Basel	a	1-2	Sehic
15/4	FC Basel	h	1-5	Coly
20/4	BSC Young Boys Bern	h	1-3	Coly (p)
23/4	FC Schaffhausen	h	2-0	Nuzzolo, Lombardo
26/4	FC Zürich	h	0-1	
30/4	FC Aarau	h	2-0	og (Vardanyan), Coly
3/5	FC St. Gallen	a	0-1	
6/5	Grasshopper-Club Zürich	h	1-0	Coly
14/5	FC Thun	a	0-3	

No	Name	Nat	Pos	Aps	(s)	Gls
3	Ansi AGOLLI	ALB	D	22	(7)	3
12	Eugène Hervé AKA'A	CMR	D	7	(9)	
14	Eddy BAREA		D	19		
20	Patrick BAUMANN		M	16	(10)	
1	Jean François BEDENIK	FRA	G	26		
4	Stéphane BESLE	FRA	D	23	(1)	1
21	Matar COLY	SEN	A	30	(2)	10
19	Julien CORDONNIER	FRA	M	26	(4)	1
25	Charles DOUDIN		A		(3)	
13	Bastien GEIGER		D	17	(1)	
9	Joel GRIFFITHS	AUS	A	11	(2)	1
26	Igor HÜRLIMANN		D	3		
18	Tvrtko KALE	CRO	G	10	(1)	
5	Vik LALIC	CRO	D	10	(1)	
7	Massimo LOMBARDO		M	32	(3)	1
2	Badile LUBAMBA		D	11	(1)	1
6	Abdou Kader MANGANE	SEN	D	25		3
15	Christophe MARANINCHI	FRA	M	14	(7)	1
17	Juan MUÑOZ	ESP	M		(5)	
10	Nebi MUSTAFI	MAC	M	9	(2)	
24	Raphaël NUZZOLO		M	21	(9)	3
8	Pascal OPPLIGER		M	11	(5)	
11	Alexandre REY		A	17	(4)	8
22	Asim SEHIC	CRO	A	12	(4)	3
22	Mounir SOUFIANI	MAR	D	16	(2)	
16	Daniel XHAFA	ALB	A	8	(13)	3

FC ST. GALLEN
Coach - Ralf Loose (GER); (14/4/06) Rolf Fringer

2005
16/7	FC Zürich	h	1-3	Marazzi
23/7	FC Aarau	a	4-1	Hassli, Tachie-Mensah 3
30/7	FC Thun	h	5-1	Tachie-Mensah, Hassli 2 (1p), Zellweger, Leonardo
6/8	FC Schaffhausen	a	1-1	Gjasula
14/8	FC Basel	h	3-3	Hassli 2 (1p), Koubsky
20/8	Grasshopper-Club Zürich	a	1-3	Callà
28/8	BSC Young Boys Bern	h	0-1	
11/9	Neuchâtel Xamax FC	a	1-0	Zellweger
21/9	Yverdon-Sport FC	h	2-1	Koubsky, Agouda
25/9	FC Zürich	a	0-3	
1/10	FC Aarau	h	2-1	Marazzi, Tachie-Mensah
14/10	FC Thun	a	1-5	Hassli
29/10	FC Schaffhausen	h	0-0	
6/11	FC Basel	a	0-1	
20/11	Grasshopper-Club Zürich	h	1-1	Tachie-Mensah
26/11	BSC Young Boys Bern	a	0-1	
4/12	Neuchâtel Xamax FC	h	7-1	Hassli 2, Koubsky 2, og (Lubamba), og (Bedenik), Merenda
11/12	Yverdon-Sport FC	a	0-1	

2006
12/2	FC Schaffhausen	a	3-1	Tachie-Mensah 2, Ljubojevic
19/2	FC Aarau	h	1-1	Ljubojevic
26/2	Neuchâtel Xamax FC	a	2-2	Tachie-Mensah, Ljubojevic
11/3	FC Zürich	a	0-1	
19/3	FC Basel	h	2-2	Callà, Tachie-Mensah
22/3	Yverdon-Sport FC	a	1-2	Zellweger
26/3	FC Thun	h	1-0	Tachie-Mensah
29/3	BSC Young Boys Bern	h	1-3	Koubsky
2/4	Grasshopper-Club Zürich	a	1-2	Zellweger
6/4	Grasshopper-Club Zürich	h	0-2	
9/4	FC Aarau	a	1-3	Hassli
15/4	Yverdon-Sport FC	h	2-0	Callà, Tachie-Mensah
20/4	FC Basel	a	1-3	Ljubojevic
23/4	FC Zürich	h	2-3	Hassli 2
29/4	BSC Young Boys Bern	a	0-2	
3/5	Neuchâtel Xamax FC	h	1-0	Callà
6/5	FC Aarau	a	0-1	
14/5	FC Schaffhausen	h	3-0	Hassli 2, Ljubojevic

No	Name	Nat	Pos	Aps	(s)	Gls
20	Kwabena AGOUDA	GHA	A		(14)	1
13	Davide CALLÀ		M	32		4
7	Pascal CERRONE		D	25	(5)	
25	Fábio de Souza FABINHO	BRA	M	14	(7)	
6	Juan Pablo GARAT	ARG	D	13	(7)	

Switzerland

No	Name	Nat	Pos	Aps	(s)	Gls
9	Jürgen GJASULA	GER	M	21	(7)	1
29	Eric HASSLI	FRA	A	35		13
19	Jiri KOUBSKY	CZE	D	31		5
8	LEONARDO Pereira	BRA	M	7	(8)	1
27	Goran LJUBOJEVIC	CRO	A	10	(7)	5
12	David MARAZZI		M	28	(4)	2
5	Mijat MARIC		D	22	(6)	
22	Moreno MERENDA		A	1	(16)	1
3	Philippe MONTANDON		D	30		
15	Philipp MUNTWILER		D	1	(2)	
1	Stefano RAZZETTI	ITA	G	33		
10	Bruno SUTTER		M	5	(9)	
11	Alex TACHIE-MENSAH	GHA	A	32	(3)	12
21	Frank WIBLISHAUSER	GER	M	19	(4)	
18	Gabriel WÜTHRICH		G	3	(1)	
17	Marc ZELLWEGER		D	34	(1)	4

FC SCHAFFHAUSEN
Coach - Jürgen Seeberger (GER)

2005
16/7	FC Basel	a	0-1	
23/7	Neuchâtel Xamax FC	h	1-1	Weller
30/7	Grasshopper-Club Zürich	a	1-1	Rama
6/8	FC St. Gallen	h	1-1	Rama
13/8	BSC Young Boys Bern	h	3-2	Todisco, Rama, Da Silva
20/8	Yverdon-Sport FC	a	1-0	Todisco
28/8	FC Zürich	a	0-5	
11/9	FC Aarau	h	0-1	
21/9	FC Thun	h	0-4	
25/9	FC Basel	h	1-2	Bunjaku
2/10	Neuchâtel Xamax FC	a	0-1	
16/10	Grasshopper-Club Zürich	h	0-2	
29/10	FC St. Gallen	a	0-0	
6/11	BSC Young Boys Bern	a	1-3	Rama (p)
20/11	Yverdon-Sport FC	h	1-2	Tarone
27/11	FC Zürich	h	0-2	
4/12	FC Aarau	a	2-0	Todisco, Tarone (p)
11/12	FC Thun	a	3-0	Sereinig 2, Todisco

2006
12/2	FC St. Gallen	h	1-3	Todisco
19/2	FC Basel	a	1-1	Pires
26/2	FC Aarau	h	0-0	
12/3	Neuchâtel Xamax FC	h	0-0	
18/3	FC Thun	a	1-2	Sereinig
22/3	BSC Young Boys Bern	h	1-1	Merenda
26/3	Grasshopper-Club Zürich	a	1-0	Da Silva
29/3	Yverdon-Sport FC	a	4-0	Pesenti, Merenda, Diogo, Ademi
2/4	FC Zürich	h	1-4	Weller
6/4	FC Zürich	a	0-0	
12/4	BSC Young Boys Bern	a	2-1	Todisco, Rama
15/4	Grasshopper-Club Zürich	h	1-1	Maric
20/4	FC Thun	h	2-3	Weller, Tsawa
23/4	Neuchâtel Xamax FC	a	0-2	
29/4	Yverdon-Sport FC	h	1-1	Tsawa
3/5	FC Aarau	a	1-1	Merenda
6/5	FC Basel	h	0-4	
14/5	FC St. Gallen	a	0-3	

No	Name	Nat	Pos	Aps	(s)	Gls
17	Almir ADEMI	SCG	M	8	(13)	1
18	Flavio AGOSTI		G	5		
9	Albert BUNJAKU		A	6	(9)	1
12	Carlos DA SILVA	POR	M	13	(20)	2
25	César de Souza FERNANDO	BRA	D	31	(2)	
24	Paulo da Cruz DIOGO	POR	M	17	(2)	1
5	Mark DISLER		D	13		
15	Gennaro FRONTINO	ITA	A		(1)	
9	Gilberlándio Rolin GIL	BRA	A		(10)	
1	Marcel HERZOG		G	31		
16	Simon LEU		D	6	(2)	
20	Oliver MARIC		D	18	(5)	1
24	Elvir MELUNOVIC		M	1	(4)	
28	Moreno MERENDA		A	18		3
24	Tobias MÜLLER	GER	M		(1)	
10	Remo PESENTI		M	10		1
13	Rosemir PIRES	BRA	A	14	(1)	1
7	Milaim RAMA		A	23	(3)	5
23	Daniel SENN		M	9	(11)	
19	Daniel SEREINIG		D	34		3
22	Mounir SOUFIANI	FRA	D	11	(1)	
14	Daniel TARONE		M	29	(2)	2
3	Enzo TODISCO	ITA	A	23	(6)	6
21	Jens TRUCKENBROD	GER	A	31	(2)	
4	Dorjee TSAWA		M	30		2
8	Thomas WELLER	GER	M	15	(6)	3
11	Ursal YASAR		A		(4)	

FC THUN
Coach - Urs Schönenberger; (14/2/06) Heinz Peischl

2005
16/7	FC Aarau	h	2-0	Gerber, Deumi (p)
22/7	FC Basel	h	3-0	Lustrinelli 2, Leandro
30/7	FC St. Gallen	a	1-5	Adriano
6/8	FC Zürich	a	2-2	Ferreira, Adriano
14/8	Grasshopper-Club Zürich	h	2-1	Lustrinelli, Bernardi
19/8	Neuchâtel Xamax FC	a	2-0	Gelson, Lustrinelli (p)
28/8	Yverdon-Sport FC	a	0-2	
10/9	BSC Young Boys Bern	a	0-0	
21/9	FC Schaffhausen	a	4-0	Ferreira 2, Sen, Bernardi
24/9	FC Aarau	a	1-2	Lustrinelli
2/10	FC Basel	a	1-5	Sen
14/10	FC St. Gallen	h	5-1	Ferreira 2, Gelson 2, Lustrinelli
29/10	FC Zürich	h	1-6	Deumi (p)
6/11	Grasshopper-Club Zürich	a	0-2	
18/11	Neuchâtel Xamax FC	h	2-3	Lustrinelli 2
27/11	Yverdon-Sport FC	h	3-0	Ferreira, Sen, Lustrinelli
2/12	BSC Young Boys Bern	h	1-1	Lustrinelli (p)
11/12	FC Schaffhausen	h	0-3	

2006
12/2	Neuchâtel Xamax FC	a	0-0	
19/2	BSC Young Boys Bern	h	1-1	Faye
26/2	FC Zürich	a	0-1	
4/3	FC Basel	h	1-1	Gelson
12/3	Yverdon-Sport FC	a	1-0	Milicevic
18/3	FC Schaffhausen	h	2-1	Cengel 2
22/3	Grasshopper-Club Zürich	h	0-1	
26/3	FC St. Gallen	a	0-1	
2/4	FC Aarau	h	1-1	Adriano
6/4	FC Aarau	a	1-0	Deumi (p)
9/4	FC St. Gallen	h	3-1	og (Razzetti), Cengel, Gelson
12/4	Grasshopper-Club Zürich	a	1-3	Faye
20/4	FC Schaffhausen	a	3-2	Cengel, Faye, Friedli
23/4	Yverdon-Sport FC	h	1-0	Deumi (p)
29/4	FC Basel	a	0-2	
3/5	FC Zürich	h	1-3	Faye
7/5	BSC Young Boys Bern	a	1-2	Sen
14/5	Neuchâtel Xamax FC	h	3-0	Savic, Cengel, Ba

Switzerland

No	Name	Nat	Pos	Aps	(s)	Gls
9	Faria Pimenta ADRIANO	BRA	M	25	(7)	3
19	Silvan AEGERTER		M	24		
24	Ibrahima BA	SEN	M	6	(4)	1
6	Tiago BERNARDI	BRA	M	5	(9)	2
23	Önder CENGEL		A	7	(8)	5
12	Armand DEUMI	CMR	M	29		4
25	João Paulo DI FABIO	ITA	D	4	(2)	
7	Grégory DURUZ		D	15	(8)	
13	Pape Omar FAYE	SEN	M	10	(13)	4
21	Nelson FERREIRA	POR	M	36		6
16	Roman FRIEDLI		M	18		1
8	Rodrigues GELSON	BRA	M	16	(12)	5
11	Andres GERBER		M	9	(5)	1
33	Stefan GLARNER		M		(2)	
2	José GONÇALVES	POR	D	15	(1)	
26	Selver HODZIC		M	31		
1	Eldin JAKUPOVIC	BOS	G	22		
2	LEANDRO Vieira	BRA	D	17	(4)	1
28	Daniel LOPAR		G	4		
20	Mauro LUSTRINELLI		A	18		10
5	Ljubo MILICEVIC	AUS	D	25	(1)	1
17	Alen ORMAN	AUT	D	18	(1)	
22	David PALLAS	ESP	M	6		
18	Alain PORTMANN		G	10		
14	Nenad SAVIC		M	9	(4)	1
23	Lukas SCHENKEL		D		(1)	
15	Eren SEN	GER	A	7	(14)	4
4	Sehid SINANI	SCG	D	10	(2)	
10	Adriano Luís SPADOTO	BRA	M		(2)	

BSC YOUNG BOYS BERN
Coach - Hans-Peter Zaugg; (17/10/05) Gernot Rohr (GER)

2005
13/7	Neuchâtel Xamax FC	a	3-1	Sermeter (p), Neri 2
20/7	Yverdon-Sport FC	a	3-0	Yakin, Magnin, Schneuwly
6/8	Grasshopper-Club Zürich	h	0-3	
10/8	FC Aarau	h	0-0	
13/8	FC Schaffhausen	a	2-3	Schwegler P, Neri
21/8	FC Zürich	h	3-1	Varela, Raimondi, Yakin
28/8	FC St. Gallen	a	1-0	Yakin
10/9	FC Thun	h	0-0	
22/9	FC Basel	a	1-1	João Paulo
25/9	Neuchâtel Xamax FC	h	3-2	João Paulo 2, Sermeter (p)
2/10	Yverdon-Sport FC	h	2-2	Raimondi 2
16/10	FC Aarau	a	0-1	
30/10	Grasshopper-Club Zürich	a	1-1	João Paulo
6/11	FC Schaffhausen	h	3-1	Gohouri, Varela, João Paulo
20/11	FC Zürich	a	1-1	João Paulo
26/11	FC St. Gallen	h	1-0	Varela
2/12	FC Thun	a	1-1	Gohouri
11/12	FC Basel	h	1-6	Raimondi

2006
12/2	Yverdon-Sport FC	h	2-1	João Paulo, Everson
19/2	FC Thun	h	1-1	Everson
26/2	Grasshopper-Club Zürich	h	1-1	João Paulo
11/3	FC Aarau	h	2-1	João Paulo 2
19/3	Neuchâtel Xamax FC	h	1-0	Gohouri
22/3	FC Schaffhausen	a	1-1	og (Da Silva)
26/3	FC Zürich	h	0-2	
29/3	FC St. Gallen	a	3-1	Raimondi, og (Koubsky), João Paulo
2/4	FC Basel	a	0-2	
9/4	FC Zürich	a	3-3	Gohouri, João Paulo, Tiago
12/4	FC Schaffhausen	h	1-2	João Paulo
20/4	Neuchâtel Xamax FC	a	3-1	João Paulo, Raimondi, Häberli
23/4	FC Aarau	a	5-1	Häberli 3, Yakin, Yapi Yapo
29/4	FC St. Gallen	h	2-0	Häberli, Magnin
3/5	Grasshopper-Club Zürich	a	0-1	
7/5	FC Thun	h	2-1	Gohouri, Yakin
10/5	FC Basel	h	4-2	Yapi Yapo, Yakin, Tiago, João Paulo
14/5	Yverdon-Sport FC	a	3-1	João Paulo 3

No	Name	Nat	Pos	Aps	(s)	Gls
24	Yao AZIAWONOU	TOG	M	10	(12)	
18	Patrick BETTONI		G	1		
27	Ferhat CÖKMÜS		D	1		
17	Patrick DE NAPOLI		M		(1)	
5	Mark DISLER		D	1		
3	Adrian EUGSTER		D	15	(3)	
22	Pereira EVERSON	BRA	M	9		2
23	Patrick GERHARDT NYEMA		D		(1)	
25	Steve Lohoré GOHOURI	CIV	D	20		5
15	Thomas HÄBERLI		M	17	(10)	5
29	Matthias HADORN		M		(1)	
2	Ronny HODEL		D	30		
9	Daniel JOÃO PAULO	BRA	A	23	(5)	18
14	Joël MAGNIN		M	20	(9)	2
7	Francisco NERI	BRA	A	5	(6)	3
12	Miguel PORTILLO	ARG	D	27	(3)	
16	Mario RAIMONDI		A	31	(4)	6
26	Marco SCHNEUWLY		A	3	(8)	1
13	Christian SCHWEGLER		M	12	(4)	
20	Pirmin SCHWEGLER		M	27	(5)	1
8	Gürkan SERMETER		M	19	(8)	2
21	Jun SHI	CHN	A	1	(12)	
23	Grétar STEINSSON	ISL	D	7		
4	Calvano TIAGO	ITA	D	28	(2)	2
11	Gabriel URDANETA	VEN	A	2	(5)	
19	Carlos VARELA	ESP	M	30	(3)	3
1	Marco WÖLFLI		G	35		
10	Hakan YAKIN		M	11	(13)	6
30	Gilles YAPI YAPO	CIV	M	11	(5)	2

YVERDON-SPORT FC
Coach - Radu Nunweiler; (24/8/05) Roberto Morinini

2005
16/7	Grasshopper-Club Zürich	a	2-3	Gomes, Aguirre
20/7	BSC Young Boys Bern	h	0-3	
30/7	Neuchâtel Xamax FC	a	0-4	
6/8	FC Basel	h	1-2	Gomes
13/8	FC Aarau	a	1-1	Aguirre
20/8	FC Schaffhausen	h	0-1	
28/8	FC Thun	h	2-0	Aguirre, Biscotte
10/9	FC Zürich	h	0-2	
21/9	FC St. Gallen	a	1-2	Aguirre
25/9	Grasshopper-Club Zürich	h	2-0	Aguirre, Biscotte
2/10	BSC Young Boys Bern	a	2-2	Aguirre, Biscotte
16/10	Neuchâtel Xamax FC	h	4-1	Biscotte, Aguirre 2, El Haimour
29/10	FC Basel	a	1-3	Aguirre
6/11	FC Aarau	h	4-1	Marazzi, Biscotte, Aguirre (p), Alexandre
20/11	FC Schaffhausen	a	2-1	Darbellay, Aguirre
27/11	FC Thun	a	0-3	
4/12	FC Zürich	a	1-1	Aguirre
11/12	FC St. Gallen	h	1-0	Aguirre

Switzerland

2006

Date	Opponent	H/A	Score	Scorers
12/2	BSC Young Boys Bern	a	1-2	Milicevic
19/2	FC Zürich	h	0-3	
26/2	FC Basel	a	1-2	og (Smiljanic)
12/3	FC Thun	h	0-1	
18/3	Grasshopper-Club Zürich	a	1-1	Milicevic
22/3	FC St. Gallen	h	2-1	Marcão, Milicevic
26/3	FC Aarau	a	0-1	
29/3	FC Schaffhausen	h	0-4	
2/4	Neuchâtel Xamax FC	h	2-1	Biscotte, Gomes
6/4	Neuchâtel Xamax FC	a	0-2	
9/4	FC Aarau	h	3-1	Biscotte 2, Dugic
15/4	FC St. Gallen	a	0-2	
20/4	Grasshopper-Club Zürich	h	0-1	
23/4	FC Thun	a	0-1	
29/4	FC Schaffhausen	a	1-1	Cerino
3/5	FC Basel	h	1-3	Cerino
6/5	FC Zürich	a	1-4	Moser
14/5	BSC Young Boys Bern	h	1-3	Biscotte

No	Name	Nat	Pos	Aps	(s)	Gls
11	Francisco AGUIRRE	ARG	A	17		13
6	ALEXANDRE de Oliveira	BRA	D	22	(7)	1
18	Nicolas BENEY		G	9		
25	Mbala Mbuta BISCOTTE	DRC	A	27	(6)	9
16	Rogerio Barbosa CERINO	BRA	A	9	(1)	2
24	Marek CITKO	POL	M	4	(2)	
12	Raphaël DARBELLAY		D	19	(8)	1
11	Slavisa DUGIC		A	3	(6)	1
3	Mounir EL HAIMOUR	MAR	D	26		1
1	Claudio GENTILE		G	23		
10	Vaca GETULIO	BOL	M	8	(5)	
8	Vagner GOMES	POR	M	31	(2)	3
15	Fabio GROSSO	ITA	A	1	(2)	
19	Goran GRUBESIC		A		(4)	
5	Christophe JAQUET		D	34		
21	Pascal JENNY		M	32		
14	Diango MALACARNE		D	22	(1)	
7	Nicolas MARAZZI		M	19	(6)	1
17	Marcos António Aparecido MARCÃO	BRA	A	13	(4)	1
20	Mickaël MARSIGLIA	FRA	M	18	(6)	
22	Danijel MILICEVIC		A	12	(5)	3
24	Adrian MOSER		A	3	(7)	1
13	Makhtar Amadou N'DIAYE	SEN	M	14	(7)	
2	Nicola NOSEDA		M	12	(5)	
30	Sébastien ROTH		G	4		
17	Mustafa SEJMENOVIC	BOS	M	3	(2)	
4	Jauregui SERGIO	BOL	M	3		
9	Vladimir TANURCOV	ROM	M	5	(7)	
23	Julien TOURNUT	FRA	A	1	(3)	
22	Sebahattin YOKSUZOGLU	TUR	M	2	(4)	

FC ZÜRICH
Coach - Lucien Favre

2005

Date	Opponent	H/A	Score	Scorers
16/7	FC St. Gallen	a	3-1	César, Tararache, Keita
24/7	Grasshopper-Club Zürich	h	4-2	Rafael 2, Nef, Keita
30/7	FC Basel	a	1-2	Tararache
6/8	FC Thun	h	2-2	Di Jorio, Nef
14/8	Neuchâtel Xamax FC	h	3-2	César (p), Keita, og (Oppliger)
21/8	BSC Young Boys Bern	a	1-3	Rafael
28/8	FC Schaffhausen	h	5-0	Keita 2, César, Di Jorio, Akhalaia
10/9	Yverdon-Sport FC	a	2-0	César 2
21/9	FC Aarau	a	1-1	Schneider
25/9	FC St. Gallen	h	3-0	Rafael, César (p), Keita
2/10	Grasshopper-Club Zürich	a	0-1	
16/10	FC Basel	h	2-4	Margairaz, Rafael
29/10	FC Thun	a	6-1	Rafael 2, Nef 2, Keita, Alphonse
6/11	Neuchâtel Xamax FC	a	5-3	og (Agolli), Rafael 2, César, Keita
20/11	BSC Young Boys Bern	h	1-1	Dzemaili
27/11	FC Schaffhausen	a	2-0	Keita 2
4/12	Yverdon-Sport FC	h	1-1	Margairaz
11/12	FC Aarau	h	3-0	César (p), Rafael, Alphonse

2006

Date	Opponent	H/A	Score	Scorers
12/2	FC Basel	h	1-1	Dzemaili
19/2	Yverdon-Sport FC	a	3-0	Rafael, Margairaz, Stanic
26/2	FC Thun	h	1-0	Stahel
11/3	FC St. Gallen	h	1-0	Keita
19/3	FC Aarau	a	1-1	Stahel
22/3	Neuchâtel Xamax FC	h	4-1	César 2 (1p), Margairaz, Rafael
26/3	BSC Young Boys Bern	a	2-0	Stanic, Alphonse
29/3	Grasshopper-Club Zürich	a	0-0	
2/4	FC Schaffhausen	a	4-1	César (p), Keita, Alphonse, Margairaz
6/4	FC Schaffhausen	h	0-0	
9/4	BSC Young Boys Bern	h	3-3	Keita 2 (1p), Inler
20/4	FC Aarau	h	6-0	Alphonse 3, Keita 2, Inler
23/4	FC St. Gallen	a	3-2	Keita, Schneider 2
26/4	Neuchâtel Xamax FC	a	1-0	Alphonse
30/4	Grasshopper-Club Zürich	h	2-0	César, Keita
3/5	FC Thun	a	3-1	Margairaz, Rafael, Stanic
6/5	Yverdon-Sport FC	h	4-1	Keita, Rafael, Dzemaili, Schneider
13/5	FC Basel	a	2-1	Keita, Filipescu

No	Name	Nat	Pos	Aps	(s)	Gls
19	Almen ABDI		M	1	(9)	
9	Lado AKHALAIA	GEO	A		(5)	1
12	Alexandre ALPHONSE	FRA	A	8	(13)	8
20	Clederson CESAR	BRA	M	27	(2)	12
16	Francesco DI JORIO		M	27	(2)	2
7	Blerim DZEMAILI		M	32		3
25	Iulian FILIPESCU	ROM	D	28	(2)	1
8	Gökhan INLER	TUR	M	16	(1)	2
21	Alhassane KEITA	GUI	A	31	(1)	20
18	Johnny LEONI		G	32		
5	Xavier MARGAIRAZ		M	25	(4)	6
3	Alain NEF		D	20	(12)	4
14	RAFAEL de Araújo	BRA	A	28	(3)	14
26	Giuseppe RAPISARDA		D		(9)	
24	Marc SCHNEIDER		D	18	(5)	4
13	Florian STAHEL		D	27	(4)	2
11	Kresimir STANIC		A		(13)	3
15	Daniel STUCKI		D	21	(8)	
1	Davide TAINI		G	4		
8	Mihai TARARACHE	ROM	M	15		2
4	Steve VON BERGEN		D	36		

DOMESTIC CUP 2005/06

1/32 FINALS

(16/9/05)
SC Derendingen 1, FC Concordia Basel 3
SC Zofingen 2, FC Wohlen 0
(17/9/05)
FC Giffers-Tentlingen 1, FC Sion 8

Switzerland

FC Orpund 0, BSC Young Boys Bern 8
SC Cham 0, FC Winterthur 1
FC Bülach 0, FC Zürich 8
FC Lanquart-Herrschaft 1, FC Locarno 2
FC Arbon 05 1, AC Lugano 3
FC Echallens 1, FC La Chaux-de-Fonds 3
Losone Sportiva 3, FC Wil 3 *(aet; 5-6 on pens)*
FC Breitenrain 1, SC Kriens 6
FC Le Mont-sur-Lausanne 2, FC Monthey 0 *(aet)*
FC Schattdorf 1, SC YF Juventus 5
FC Thalwil 0, AC Bellinzona 1
FC Wittenbach 0, SV Schaffhausen 0 *(aet; 4-5 on pens)*
US Collombey-Muraz 4, Lausanne-Sport FC 2
FC Kölliken 3, BSC Old Boys Basel 4
AC Taverne 1, FC Chiasso 2 *(aet)*
FC Meilen 0, FC Küssnacht a. R. 2
FC Sursee 1, FC Baden 3
FC Perly-Certoux 1, Etoile-Carouge FC 0
Stade Payerne 1, FC Luzern 5
SV Lyss 0, FC Baulmes 4
FC Ascona 1, FC Schaffhausen 3
(18/9/05)
SC Düdingen 0, FC Thun 1
FC Bex 0, Neuchâtel Xamax FC 4
Servette FC Genève 4, FC Meyrin 2 *(aet)*
FC Cortaillod 0, Yverdon-Sport FC 2
Zug 94 2, Grasshopper-Club Zürich 6
GC Biaschesi 1, FC St. Gallen 5
SR Delémont 2, FC Aarau 3
(19/9/05)
FC Solothurn 1, FC Basel 4

1/16 FINALS
(22/10/05)
FC Le Mont-sur-Lausanne 2, FC Sion 3 *(aet)*
SC YF Juventus 0, FC Zürich 2
AC Lugano 2, Neuchâtel Xamax FC 1
FC Küssnacht a. R. 2, FC St. Gallen 1
SC Zofingen 0, FC Wil 2
BSC Old Boys Basel 1, FC Basel 6
FC Baden 0, FC Schaffhausen 2
FC Luzern 0, FC Concordia Basel 0 *(aet; 4-2 on pens)*
(23/10/05)
FC La Chaux-de-Fonds 0, BSC Young Boys Bern 4
FC Winterthur 4, Grasshopper-Club Zürich 2
US Collombey-Muraz 0, Servette FC Genève 3
SV Schaffhausen 1, SC Kriens 3
FC Baulmes 1, FC Aarau 4
FC Locarno 3, Yverdon-Sport FC 2 *(aet)*
FC Perly-Certoux 1, FC Thun 7
FC Chiasso 0, AC Bellinzona 2

1/8 FINALS
(10/12/05)
FC Küssnacht a. R. 1, FC Locarno 2
(11/12/05)
FC Winterthur 2, FC Luzern 0 *(aet)*
AC Lugano 2, FC Wil 1
FC Sion 1, AC Bellinzona 0
(17/12/05)
SC Kriens 1, BSC Young Boys Bern 2
FC Basel 3, FC Zürich 4
Servette FC Genève 1, FC Thun 1 *(aet; 5-4 on pens)*
(18/12/05)
FC Schaffhausen 0, FC Aarau 0 *(aet; 4-5 on pens)*

QUARTER-FINALS
(5/2/06)
FC Locarno 0, FC Sion 1 *(Vogt 78)*
AC Lugano 1 *(Rodrigues 90)*, BSC Young Boys Bern 2 *(Varela 50, 57)*
Servette FC Genève 1 *(Tréand 119)*, FC Winterthur 3 *(Kozarac 106, Mikari 112, Renfer 120) (aet)*
FC Aarau 1 *(Baning 35)*, FC Zürich 1 *(Cesar 34p) (aet; 2-3 on pens)*

SEMI-FINALS
(15/3/06)
FC Winterthur 0, FC Sion 1 *(Vogt 81)*
FC Zürich 1 *(Dzemaili 66)*, BSC Young Boys Bern 4 *(Everson 23, João Paulo 31, 67, Raimondi 90)*

FINAL
(17/4/06)
Stade de Suisse, Berne
FC SION 1 *(Obradovic 55)*
BSC YOUNG BOYS BERN 1 *(Varela 16)*
(aet; 5-3 on pens)
Referee – Rutz
FC SION – Vailati, Gaspoz, Sarni, João Pinto, Meoli, Luiz Carlos (Regazzoni 46), Gelson, Di Zenzo, Obradovic, Thurre (Crettenand 119), Vogt (Leandro 107).
Sent off: João Paulo (120)
BSC YOUNG BOYS BERN – Wölfli, Schwegler Ch., Tiago, Gohouri, Hodel (Aziawonou 90), Magnin J., Everson (Yakin 106), Varela, Yapi (Portillo 35), Raimondi, João Paulo.
Sent off: Gohouri (31)

SECOND LEVEL FINAL TABLE 2005/06

		Pld	W	D	L	F	A	Pts
1	FC Luzern	34	24	7	3	69	33	79
2	FC Sion	34	22	6	6	61	24	72
3	FC Lausanne-Sport	34	20	8	6	64	42	68
4	FC Chiasso	34	17	8	9	51	31	59
5	FC La Chaux-de-Fonds	34	15	13	6	60	44	58
6	FC Wil 1900	34	14	9	11	61	55	51
7	FC Wohlen	34	14	8	12	48	41	50
8	FC Vaduz	34	13	8	13	58	52	47
9	AC Bellinzona	34	12	10	12	43	45	46
10	AC Lugano	34	10	11	13	41	52	41
11	FC Baulmes	34	9	13	12	36	45	40
12	FC Concordia Basel	34	10	9	15	44	57	39
13	SC Kriens	34	9	12	13	42	56	39
14	FC Winterthur	34	10	7	17	62	53	37
15	SC YF Juventus	34	8	14	12	39	53	35
16	FC Locarno	34	7	7	20	35	60	28
17	FC Baden	34	6	9	19	30	59	27
18	FC Meyrin	34	1	11	22	26	68	14

N.B. SC YF Juventus – 3 pts deducted.

PROMOTION/RELEGATION PLAY-OFF
(18/5/06)
FC Sion 0, Neuchâtel Xamax FC 0
(21/5/06)
Neuchâtel Xamax FC 0, FC Sion 3
(FC Sion 3-0)

Turkey

Tunnel brawl brings ban

There is never a dull moment in Turkish football. Controversy and scandal stalk the game from all directions, and violence is never far away. But the post-match fracas that followed the team's World Cup elimination by Switzerland was probably the worst incident of its kind.

Just after the final whistle in the Sükrü Saracoglu Stadium, after Turkey had beaten Switzerland 4-2 in the second leg of the qualifying play-off but lost the tie on away goals, bedlam broke out on the touchline and in the tunnel as players and officials of both teams physically assaulted each other. The Turks were the chief aggressors, with several of their players and coaching staff caught on camera aiming kicks and punches at their opponents. One Swiss player needed hospital treatment while another later claimed that the atmosphere was so poisonous he genuinely feared for his life.

Behind closed doors

FIFA launched a full investigation. Turkey were concerned they might be banned from the 2010 World Cup, but instead they were ordered to play their next six competitive internationals abroad behind closed doors. On appeal, this was reduced to three. There were also suspensions for some Turkish players and officials, while federation president Levent Bicakci was forced to resign.

It could have been worse. There were no repercussions for the next World Cup, and only half of their six home Euro 2008 qualifiers would be affected – the first three, against Malta, Moldova and Norway. Their other three opponents – Hungary, Greece and Bosnia-Herzegovina – would have to face the intimidating Turkish crowds in the autumn of 2007, although further trouble will almost certainly lead to exclusion from World Cup 2010.

The 2006 campaign ended in disgrace, but Turkey had done well to reach the play-offs, with reinstalled coach Fatih Terim leading the team to 1-0 wins away to Ukraine (in which Hakan Sükür won his 100th cap) and Albania. Even after losing the first leg of the play-off 2-0 in Berne and then conceding a first-minute penalty in Istanbul, the Turks refused to give up. But local hero Tuncay Sanli's hat-trick proved to be in vain.

Although Turkey didn't go to the World Cup, they did travel to Germany and the surrounding area for a series of friendlies. Many new players were tried out, and the only defeat in six came at the end of the tour, against Macedonia. It was deemed a worthwhile exercise – especially as Turkey seemed likely to use German stadiums for those first three home qualifiers.

World Cup failure and the ensuing scandal capped a miserable autumn for Turkish football. The European club competitions brought a succession of setbacks. Trabzonspor's international activity was ended in mid-summer by Cypriot champions Anorthosis. Galatasaray returned to Europe after a year's sabbatical and were eliminated by Tromsø. Besiktas reached the UEFA Cup group phase but went no further. Fenerbahçe gained automatic admission to the Champions League, but three closing defeats left them bottom of the group.

Absorbing battle

With all international participation over by Christmas, the spotlight switched to the battle for the domestic title between Fenerbahçe and Galatasaray. It was an absorbing confrontation that would hold everyone's interest right through to the very end.

Besiktas threw the towel in early after a bad start that saw popular ex-player Riza Çambilay reluctantly jettisoned in October. A couple of unlikely upstarts enjoyed some early glory but before long the Super

Turkey

Lig title race was confined to just two runners.

Fenerbahçe were strongly tipped to complete a hat-trick of championship wins – a feat they had never achieved. Their strong, Brazilian-influenced squad was supplemented by the arrival, from Juventus, of Ghanaian international Stephen Appiah, and although they began their title defence with two draws, once they had shaken off the cobwebs they were nigh-on unstoppable, reeling off 12 straight victories, including a 1-0 win at Galatasaray, to enter the winter break with a record 45 points and a four-point lead.

Despite the excellent results, many neutrals were unconvinced, claiming that Fener were unfairly assisted by referees. The most glaring example came at Konya. Two-nil down with 20 minutes remaining, Fener reduced the deficit with a blatantly illegal goal from Nicolas Anelka and went on to win 4-2.

During the mid-season shutdown Fenerbahçe's odds shortened as a result of a player revolt at Galatasaray because of unpaid wages. New coach Eric Gerets did his best to douse the flames, but the crisis would rumble on.

While everyone expected Fenerbahçe to exploit their rivals' problems, they started to drop points in surprising places, losing back-to-back fixtures in Ankara and Kayseri. Galatasaray also struggled away from home but with stalwarts Hakan Sükür and Hasan Sas driving the team on, it was the Yellow and Reds rather than the Yellow and Blues who boasted a three-point lead going into the head-to-head at the Sükrü Saracoglu.

Fenerbahçe had knocked Galatasaray out of the Turkish Cup on away goals a few weeks earlier but this time there was a clear gulf in class between the two as Fener routed their rivals 4-0. Coach Christoph Daum rated it as the club's best performance during his three-year tenure. Now, although the two teams were level on points, Fenerbahçe, with two victories in the direct meetings, topped the table.

Neck and neck

By the final game both clubs were still separated only by Fener's head-to-head advantage. Galatasaray were at home, to Kayserispor, but Fenerbahçe faced an awkward trip to Denizlispor, who were fighting against relegation. No matter that Fener had thrashed their opponents 6-2 at home and blitzed them in the Cup. The pressure-cooker atmosphere and the prizes at stake made all previous contests irrelevant.

Galatsaaray easily won 3-0, but there was high drama in Denizli. The unruly home crowd continuously interrupted the match by throwing objects on to the field. It was a deliberate ploy to delay the game so that it finished later than the other relegation-affected matches. They succeeded. Although the news for Denizlispor from elsewhere was good, there were 16 minutes of stoppage-time to play. Galatasaray, their game completed, could only sit, wait and hope. Relief seemed at hand when Denizlispor scored in the 89th minute but three minutes later Tuncay equalised. For the next 14 minutes Fenerbahçe tried everything to score, but Denizlispor, their own safety assured, valiantly kept them out. In the last second Appiah fired a shot against the post. But it remained 1-1. Galatasaray were the champions.

The ecstasy and the agony in the two camps was intense. Gala's 16th title brought them level in the all-time listings with Fener, whereas Daum's team had nothing to show for their season's efforts. They had also finished a close second in the Turkish Cup, losing the final to Besiktas 3-2 after extra-time. Seeking to win the trophy for the first time in 23 years, Fener came from behind to send the game into the extra period, but a second strike on the night from Turkish international Tümer Metin brought victory for Besiktas and their new French coach Jean Tigana. Tümer would subsequently leave Besiktas for Fenerbahçe, who then replaced Daum with Brazilian legend Zico.

NATIONAL TEAM RESULTS 2005/06

Date	Opponent	H/A/N	Venue	Score	Scorers
17/8/05	Bulgaria	A	Sofia	1-3	Fatih Tekke (21)
3/9/05	Denmark (WCQ)	H	Istanbul	2-2	Okan Buruk (48), Tümer (81)
7/9/05	Ukraine (WCQ)	A	Kiev	1-0	Tümer (55)
8/10/05	Germany	H	Istanbul	2-1	Halil (25), Nuri (89)
12/10/05	Albania (WCQ)	A	Tirana	1-0	Tümer (57)
12/11/05	Switzerland (WCQ)	A	Berne	0-2	
16/11/05	Switzerland (WCQ)	H	Istanbul	4-2	Tuncay (24, 38, 89), Necati (52p)
1/3/06	Czech Republic	H	Izmir	2-2	Ümit Karan (89, 90)
12/4/06	Azerbaijan	A	Baku	1-1	Hasan Kabze (78)
24/5/06	Belgium	A	Genk	3-3	Necati (2), Hasan Kabze (26), Tuncay (76)
26/5/06	Ghana	N	Bochum	1-1	Nihat (17)
28/5/06	Estonia	N	Hamburg	1-1	Gökhan Ünal (53)
31/5/06	Saudi Arabia	N	Offenbach	1-0	Necati (59)
2/6/06	Angola	N	Arnhem	3-2	Necati (53), Nihat (71), Halil (84)
4/6/06	Macedonia	N	Krefeld	0-1	

Turkey

NATIONAL TEAM APPEARANCES 2005/06
Coach – FATIH Terim

Player	DOB	Club	Bul	DEN	UKR	Ger	ALB	SUI	SUI	Cze	Azb	Bel	Gha	Est	Sau	Ang	Mac	Caps	Goals
RÜSTÜ Reçber	10/5/73	Fenerbahçe	G					G		G	G		G			G	G46	108	-
BÜLENT Korkmaz	24/11/68	Galatasaray	D10															102	3
TOLGA Seyhan	17/1/77	Shakhtar D (UKR)	D	s85				D	D									18	2
ÜMIT Özat	30/10/76	Fenerbahçe	D83	D	D	D79	D	D77										41	1
HAMIT Altintop	8/12/82	FC Schalke 04 (GER)	D	D	D	D	D	D		D	D		s46	D	D89	M46		22	-
SELÇUK Sahin	31/1/81	Fenerbahçe	M78	M	M	M86	M	M	M		M70							15	-
GÖKDENIZ Karadeniz	11/1/80	Trabzonspor	M69		M46							s64	M46			s76	s46	31	5
EMRE Belözoglu	7/9/80	Newcastle Utd (ENG)	M27			s46		M82										43	3
HASAN Sas	1/8/76	Galatasaray	M	M46	s83				M46									40	2
SERHAT Akin	5/6/81	Anderlecht (BEL)	A		s90	s84		A70										16	3
FATIH Tekke	9/9/77	Trabzonspor	A46	A	A83			s81			s46	s72						21	8
IBRAHIM Toraman	20/11/81	Besiktas	s10	D	D	D	D			D	D							25	1
KORAY Avci	19/5/78	Besiktas	s27															6	1
HAKAN Sükür	1/9/71	Galatasaray	s46	A	A			A	A									102	46
SERKAN Balci	22/8/83	Fenerbahçe	s69		s46		D											21	-
HÜSEYIN Çimsir	26/5/79	Trabzonspor	s78	s46	s46	M	M	M			M80		M	M72		M80	M46 s46	20	-
DENIZ Baris	2/7/77	Fenerbahçe	s83															20	-
VOLKAN Demirel	27/10/81	Fenerbahçe		G	G	G	G		G				G		G			11	-
ALPAY Özalay	29/5/73	1.FC Köln (GER)		D	D	D	D	D										90	4
YILDIRAY Bastürk	24/12/78	Hertha BSC (GER)		M46		M46	M46		s82	s46								43	2
TÜMER Metin	14/10/74	Besiktas		M85	M	M67	M	M	s70									12	4
OKAN Buruk	19/10/73	Besiktas		s46	M90		M46	s46										54	8
NIHAT Kahveci	23/11/79	Real Sociedad (ESP)			M84	s46	M46				A82	A46	M72	A72	A46			44	11
HALIL Altintop	8/12/82	Kaiserslautern (GER)			A46	A90	s77		s61		A68		A72	s72	s72	A		11	3
ERGÜN Penbe	17/5/72	Galatasaray			s46		s83	D										47	-
NECATI Ates	3/1/80	Galatasaray			s67	s90		A81	M		A46	A64		A83	A76			18	5
IBRAHIM Akin	4/1/84	Besiktas				s79			s75	A46		M46						4	-
NURI Sahin	5/9/88	Bor Dortmund (GER)				s86			s46		M46	M64	s46	s80		s46	M80	8	1
TUNCAY Sanli	16/1/82	Fenerbahçe					A83	A	M75		M	A64		M88	A46	s46		34	10
GÖKHAN Zan	7/9/81	Besiktas							D				D	D	D	D		5	-
UGUR Boral	14/4/82	Gençlerbirligi							D46	D68	s46	s46				s46	M46	6	-
MEHMET Topuz	7/9/83	Kayserispor							M	D	s61	M	M	M		M	D	8	-
GÖKHAN Ünal	23/7/82	Kayserispor							A61	A77			s46	A46				4	1
ERSEN Martin	23/5/79	BB Ankaraspor							A46	A83								3	-
ORHAN Ak	29/9/79	Galatasaray							s46									2	-
ÜMIT Karan	1/10/76	Galatasaray							s80									7	2
TOLGA Zengin	10/10/83	Trabzonspor								G								1	-
CAN Arat	21/1/84	Fenerbahçe								D			D	D	D	D		5	-
BAKI Mercimek	17/9/82	Gençlerbirligi								D								1	-
VOLKAN Arslan	29/8/78	Galatasaray									M46	s68	s64					11	-
HASAN Kabze	26/5/82	Galatasaray									A	A61	s64	s46	s46	A46	s80	7	2
HAKAN Balta	23/3/83	Vestel Manisaspor									s46							1	-
FAHRI Tatan	30/5/83	Çaykur Rizespor									s46		s82	M	s83	s46	M88	6	-
YASIN Çakmak	6/1/85	Çaykur Rizespor									s68							1	-
BURAK Yilmaz	15/7/85	Antalyaspor									s70	s46		M46		s88		4	-
SINAN Kaloglu	10/6/81	Vestel Manisaspor									s77							1	-
EMRE Toraman	5/1/79	Kayseri Erciyespor									s83							1	-
SERVET Çetin	17/3/81	Fenerbahçe									D	D		s88	s89			13	-
VOLKAN Yaman	27/8/82	Antalyaspor										D46						1	-
CANER Erkin	4/10/88	Vestel Manisaspor										D46			D			2	-
MURAT Ocak	1/1/82	Istanbul Belediyespor											D	D	D			3	-
BILAL Kisa	22/6/83	Malatyaspor											s72					1	-
ORKUN Usak	5/11/80	Ankaragücü														s46		1	-

Turkey

EUROPEAN CUPS 2005/06

UEFA CHAMPIONS LEAGUE

FENERBAHÇE
1st round Group E
Match 1 MILAN (ITA)
A 1-3 *Alex (63p)*
Volkan, Serkan, Önder, Luciano, Ümit, Selçuk, Appiah (Kemal 53; Márcio Nobre 90), Marco Aurélio, Tuncay, Alex, Anelka.

Match 2 PSV (HOL)
H 3-0 *Alex (40p, 68), Appiah (90)*
Volkan, Serkan, Luciano, Önder, Ümit, Selçuk, Appiah, Marco Aurélio, Alex (Kemal 90), Anelka, Márcio Nobre (Mehmet 90).

Match 3 FC SCHALKE 04 (GER)
H 3-3 *Luciano (14), Márcio Nobre (73), Appiah (79)*
Volkan, Serkan, Luciano, Önder, Ümit, Selçuk, Appiah, Marco Aurélio (Tuncay 67), Alex, Anelka, Márcio Nobre.

Match 4 FC SCHALKE 04
A 0-2
Volkan, Serkan, Luciano, Önder, Ümit, Selçuk, Appiah, Marco Aurélio, Tuncay, Anelka, Márcio Nobre (Mehmet 46).

Match 5 MILAN
H 0-4
Volkan, Serkan, Servet, Önder, Ümit, Selçuk (Kemal 28), Appiah, Deniz, Mehmet (Márcio Nobre 56), Tuncay, Anelka.

Match 6 PSV
A 0-2
Volkan, Serkan, Luciano, Önder, Ümit, Appiah, Marco Aurélio, Tuncay, Alex, Anelka (Mehmet 65), Márcio Nobre (Semih 79).

TRABZONSPOR
2nd qualifying round ANORTHOSIS (CYP)
A 1-3 *Fatih Tekke (75)*
Jefferson, Emrah, Erdinç, Eller (Tayfun 81), Celaleddin (Lee 88), Hüseyin, Volkan, Szymkowiak, Yattara, Gökdeniz, Mehmet (Fatih 65).

H 1-0 *Fatih Tekke (40)*
Jefferson, Emrah, Erdinç (Özgür 69), Eller, Celaleddin, Hüseyin, Volkan (Lee 59), Szymkowiak, Adem (Mehmet 46), Gökdeniz, Fatih.

UEFA CUP

GALATASARAY
1st round TROMSØ IL (NOR)
A 0-1
Mondragón, Ugur (Hakan 61), Tomas, Song, Orhan, Saidou, Cihan, Hasan Sas, Heinz, Ümit (Hasan Kabze 87), Necati.

H 1-1 *Hakan (78)*
Mondragón, Ugur (Zafer 75), Tomas, Song, Ergün (Sabri 46), Saidou, Volkan (Hakan 38), Hasan Sas, Heinz, Ümit, Necati.

BESIKTAS
2nd qualifying round FC VADUZ (LIE)
A 1-0 *Okan (12)*
Córdoba, Ali Tandogan (Ali Günes 46), Gökhan Zan, Ibrahim Toraman, Adem, Koray, Pancu (Sergen 70), Okan, Ahmed Hassan, Youla (Ahmet Dursun 83), Veysel.

H 5-1 *Aîlton (35), Ahmed Hassan (61), Ahmet (83), Adem (89), Pancu (90)*
Córdoba, Ali Günes, Gökhan Zan, Adem, Koray, Pancu, Sergen (Mustafa 46), Okan, Ahmed Hassan, Youla (Veysel 79), Aîlton (Ahmet Dursun 76).

1st round MALMÖ FF (SWE)
H 0-1
Córdoba, Ali Tandogan, Mustafa (Youla 38), Ibrahim Toraman, Ibrahim Üzülmez (Ibrahim Akin 76), Koray, Pancu, Kléberson, Tümer, Ahmed Hassan, Ahmet Dursun (Veysel 71).

A 4-1 *Youla (28, 34, 52), Tümer (90)*
Córdoba, Ali Günes (Adem 77), Gökhan Zan, Koray, Ibrahim Toraman, Çagdas, Kléberson, Okan, Sergen (Tayfur 61), Ahmed Hassan (Tümer 73), Youla.

2nd round Group H
Match 1 BOLTON WANDERERS (ENG)
H 1-1 *Aîlton (7)*
Córdoba, Adem, Koray, Çagdas, Ibrahim Toraman (Gökhan Zan 45; Mustafa 70), Tayfur, Kléberson, Ibrahim Akin, Ahmed Hassan, Tümer (Ibrahim Üzülmez 36), Aîlton.

Match 2 SEVILLA FC (ESP)
A 0-3
Córdoba, Ali Tandogan, Ibrahim Toraman, Çagdas, Adem, Koray, Kléberson (Pancu 75), Okan (Ahmed Hassan 68), Ibrahim Akin (Youla 65), Tümer, Aîlton.

Match 3 ZENIT SANKT-PETERBURG (RUS)
H 1-1 *Ibrahim Akin (23)*
Córdoba, Ali Tandogan, Ibrahim Toraman, Mustafa, Ibrahim Üzülmez, Çagdas, Adem (Aîlton 66), Okan (Veysel 80), Ahmed Hassan, Sergen (Kléberson 59), Ibrahim Akin.

Match 4 VITÓRIA GUIMARÃES (POR)
A 3-1 *Ibrahim Toraman (9, 60), Youla (18)*
Córdoba, Ali Tandogan, Adem, Çagdas, Ibrahim Üzülmez, Ibrahim Toraman, Koray, Kléberson, Sergen (Tümer 63), Ahmed Hassan (Veysel 57), Youla (Pancu 83).

TOP GOALSCORERS 2005/06

25	GÖKHAN Ünal (Kayserispor)
22	FATIH Tekke (Trabzonspor)
20	CENK Isler (Kayseri Erciyesspor)
18	NECATI Ates (Galatasaray)
	MÁRCIO NOBRE (Fenerbahçe)
17	ÜMIT Karan (Galatasaray)
16	UMUT Bulut (Ankaragücü)
15	TUNCAY Sanli (Fenerbahçe)
14	ALEX de Souza (Fenerbahçe)
	MEHMET Çakir (Gençlerbirligi)

LEAGUE RESULTS/ SCORERS/APPEARANCES/ GOALS 2005/06

ANKARAGÜCÜ
Coach - Adnan Sentürk; (18/9/05) Safet Susic (BOS); (6/2/06) Hikmet Karaman

2005
7/8	Vestel Manisaspor	a	2-2	Umut, Ismet
12/8	Galatasaray	h	0-1	

Turkey

FINAL LEAGUE TABLE 2005/06

		Pld	Home W	D	L	F	A	Away W	D	L	F	A	Total W	D	L	F	A	Pts
1	Galatasaray	34	15	1	1	52	16	11	4	2	30	18	26	5	3	82	34	83
2	Fenerbahçe	34	13	4	0	49	16	12	2	3	41	18	25	6	3	90	34	81
3	Besiktas	34	6	4	7	24	20	9	5	3	28	19	15	9	10	52	39	54
4	Trabzonspor	34	8	4	5	27	18	7	3	7	24	24	15	7	12	51	42	52
5	Kayserispor	34	10	2	5	38	22	5	4	8	21	20	15	6	13	59	42	51
6	Gençlerbirligi	34	9	4	4	28	18	5	5	7	19	21	14	9	11	47	39	51
7	Konyaspor	34	9	3	5	26	19	3	7	7	13	24	12	10	12	39	43	46
8	Sivasspor	34	7	5	5	24	24	3	8	6	10	20	10	13	11	34	44	43
9	Çaykur Rizespor	34	6	6	5	19	21	4	5	8	16	23	10	11	13	35	44	41
10	Kayseri Erciyesspor	34	5	6	6	14	17	4	7	6	22	30	9	13	12	36	47	40
11	Gaziantepspor	34	4	8	5	19	22	6	2	9	15	28	10	10	14	34	50	40
12	Vestel Manisaspor	34	7	3	7	27	29	4	4	9	25	32	11	7	16	52	61	40
13	Ankaragücü	34	6	4	7	24	22	4	5	8	19	26	10	9	15	43	48	39
14	BB Ankaraspor	34	4	7	6	23	24	5	5	7	21	27	9	12	13	44	51	39
15	Denizlispor	34	5	6	6	22	19	4	4	9	19	31	9	10	15	41	50	37
16	Malatyaspor	34	5	6	6	16	22	4	3	10	18	28	9	9	16	34	50	36
17	Samsunspor	34	4	5	8	18	25	5	4	8	27	37	9	9	16	45	62	36
18	Diyarbakirspor	34	5	2	10	15	30	3	3	11	16	39	8	5	21	31	69	29

Date	Opponent	h/a	Score	Scorers
20/8	Trabzonspor	a	1-3	Umut
28/8	Kayseri Erciyesspor	h	1-2	Heverton
11/9	Denizlispor	a	0-0	
17/9	Gençlerbirligi	h	1-1	Ilhan
25/9	Diyarbakirsporspor	a	3-0	Coridon, Batista, Evren Turhan
2/10	Çaykur Rizespor	h	1-0	Ilhan
15/10	Fenerbahçe	a	1-2	Umut
22/10	Ankaraspor	h	3-2	Umut 2, Ilhan
30/10	Besiktas	a	2-4	Ilhan, Umut
6/11	Kayserispor	h	2-0	Umut, Deniz
20/11	Konyaspor	a	0-2	
27/11	Samsunspor	h	1-1	Abdurrahman
5/12	Malatyaspor	a	0-0	
10/12	Gaziantepsor	a	1-1	Umut
17/12	Sivasspor	h	0-0	
2006				
21/1	Vestel Manisaspor	h	0-2	
5/2	Trabzonspor	h	1-2	Niyazi
11/2	Kayseri Erciyesspor	a	2-1	Umut, Niyazi
19/2	Denizlispor	h	1-1	Petkov
26/2	Gençlerbirligi	a	1-1	Baljic
5/3	Diyarbakirsporspor	h	5-1	og (Stavrevski), Umut 2 (1p), Coridon, Abdurrahman
11/3	Çaykur Rizespor	a	0-1	
18/3	Fenerbahçe	h	1-4	Fehmi Emre
26/3	Ankaraspor	a	2-1	Petkov, Baljic
29/3	Galatasaray	a	0-2	
1/4	Besiktas	h	2-3	Umut, Ahmed Belal
9/4	Kayserispor	a	2-1	Umut 2
16/4	Konyaspor	h	3-0	Okan, Umut, Ahmed Belal
23/4	Samsunspor	a	1-2	Fehmi Emre
29/4	Malatyaspor	h	0-1	
7/5	Gaziantepsorspor	h	2-1	Ahmed Belal, Umut
13/5	Sivasspor	a	1-3	Ali

No	Name	Nat	Pos	Aps	(s)	Gls
61	ABDURRAHMAN Dereli		D	23	(4)	2
99	AHMED Belal	EGY	A	9	(4)	3
35	ALI Ölmez		M	1	(2)	1
14	AYHAN Evren		M	8	(5)	
19	AYTEKIN Viduslu		M	14	(1)	
25	Elvir BALJIC	BOS	M	14	(1)	2
6	Jean BATISTA	BRA	M	7	(4)	1
9	BIROL Aksancak		A	7	(6)	
38	BURAK Karaduman		M	18	(2)	
32	Charles-Edouard CORIDON	FRA	M	14	(3)	2
11	DENIZ Kolgu		M	5	(6)	1
28	ERMAN Güracar		D	3	(4)	
53	EVREN Erdeniz		M	4	(3)	
7	EVREN Turhan		M	5	(9)	1
39	FARUK Namdar		A	2	(2)	
2	FEHMI EMRE Güngör		D	23	(4)	2
30	Mohamed Ali GHERIENI	TUN	M	2	(3)	
4	HAKAN Kutlu		D	26		
90	HEVERTON Alves	BRA	M	7	(8)	1
17	IBRAHIM Yavuz		D	13	(1)	
26	ILHAN Mansiz		A	8	(1)	4
76	ISMET Tasdemir		M	4	(2)	1
50	MURAT Duruer		M		(1)	
12	NIYAZI Güney		D	20	(5)	2
77	OKAN Koç		M	3	(2)	1
21	ONUR Acar		M	13	(7)	
34	ORKUN Usak		G	24		
16	Ivailo PETKOV	BUL	D	15		2
88	ROBSON Assis	BRA	M		(1)	
3	SEDAT Bayrak		D	25	(1)	
1	SERKAN Kirintili		G	10		
5	TOLGA Dogantez		D		(1)	
10	UMUT Bulut		A	33		16
20	Xavier ZENGUE	CMR	D	14	(2)	

Turkey

BB ANKARASPOR
Coach - Samet Aybaba; (6/11/05) Riza Çalimbay; (23/1/06) Giray Bulak

2005
Date	Opponent	H/A	Score	Scorers
7/8	Denizlispor	a	1-1	Jaba
14/8	Gençlerbirligi	h	0-0	
21/8	Diyarbakirsporspor	a	2-1	Murat, Jaba (p)
27/8	Çaykur Rizespor	h	0-0	
10/9	Fenerbahçe	a	1-2	Tita
18/9	Samsunspor	h	3-3	Hürriyet, Jaba, Tita
25/9	Besiktas	h	2-0	Jaba, Molnár
2/10	Kayserispor	a	1-2	Jaba
15/10	Konyaspor	h	0-0	
22/10	Ankaragücü	a	2-3	Tita, Jaba
29/10	Malatyaspor	h	1-2	Jaba (p)
5/11	Gaziantepspor	a	3-3	Jaba 2 (1p), Mustafa Sarp
20/11	Sivasspor	h	1-1	Emre Aktas
26/11	Vestel Manisaspor	a	0-1	
3/12	Galatasaray	h	1-2	Murat
11/12	Trabzonspor	a	3-2	Musa, Ersen, Emre Aktas
18/12	Kayseri Erciyespor	h	1-1	Jaba

2006
Date	Opponent	H/A	Score	Scorers
22/1	Denizlispor	h	1-3	Ersen
4/2	Diyarbakirsporspor	h	3-3	Musa, Ersen, Wederson
12/2	Çaykur Rizespor	a	1-1	Özgür
18/2	Fenerbahçe	h	2-1	Mustafa Sarp, Petrous
26/2	Samsunspor	a	1-0	Tita
5/3	Besiktas	a	0-3	
12/3	Kayserispor	h	1-3	og (Yordanov)
19/3	Konyaspor	a	0-0	
26/3	Ankaragücü	h	1-2	Musa
29/3	Gençlerbirligi	a	1-2	Ramazan
2/4	Malatyaspor	a	2-0	Erman, Ersen
8/4	Gaziantepspor	h	3-0	Jaba 2, Ersen
16/4	Sivasspor	a	2-2	Tita, Ramazan
22/4	Vestel Manisaspor	h	3-1	Ersen, Petrous 2 (2p)
29/4	Galatasaray	a	0-4	
6/5	Trabzonspor	h	0-2	
14/5	Kayseri Erciyespor	a	1-0	Kürsat

No	Name	Nat	Pos	Aps	(s)	Gls
4	AHMET Yildirim		D	17	(3)	
3	Radoslav BATAK	SCG	D	22	(4)	
13	CEM Yanik		A	9	(3)	
21	EMRE Aktas		M	3	(11)	2
7	ERMAN Özgür		M	19	(10)	1
9	ERSEN Martin		A	21	(8)	6
22	HASAN Yigit		D	18	(5)	
50	HÜRRIYET Güçer		M	30		1
20	JABA de Carvalho	BRA	A	22	(1)	12
1	Dragoslav JEVRIC	SCG	G	33		
78	Richard KINGSTON	GHA	G	1		
49	KÜRSAT Duymus		D	4	(3)	1
77	Balázs MOLNÁR	HUN	M	9	(2)	1
10	MURAT Erdogan		M	17	(7)	2
6	MUSA Büyük		M	26	(5)	3
8	MUSTAFA Sarp		M	18	(6)	2
23	MUSTAFA Yalçinkaya		M	1	(4)	
17	ÖZGÜR Bayer		D	7	(9)	1
2	Adam PETROUS	CZE	D	17		3
5	RAMAZAN Tunç		D	20	(3)	2
15	SAVAS Bahadir		D	6		
35	SENOL Yavas		D	7	(1)	
11	TITA dos Santos	BRA	A	22	(7)	5
14	ÜMIT Aydin		M	2	(2)	
30	WEDERSON da Silva	BRA	M	23		1

BESIKTAS
Coach - Riza Çalimbay; (17/10/05) (Mehmet Eksi); (1/11/05) Jean Tigana (FRA)

2005
Date	Opponent	H/A	Score	Scorers
6/8	Kayseri Erciyespor	a	1-1	Sergen
14/8	Denizlispor	h	2-0	Ailton, Ahmed Hassan
20/8	Gençlerbirligi	a	2-0	Ailton, Tümer
28/8	Diyarbakirsporspor	h	1-1	Ibrahim Toraman
10/9	Çaykur Rizespor	a	0-1	
18/9	Fenerbahçe	h	1-2	Kléberson
25/9	Ankaraspor	a	0-2	
2/10	Samsunspor	h	3-2	Sergen, Youla, Ailton
16/10	Kayserispor	h	0-0	
23/10	Konyaspor	a	1-0	Ahmed Hassan
30/10	Ankaragücü	h	4-2	Sergen, Çagdas, Ailton, Ahmed Hassan
6/11	Malatyaspor	a	1-1	Youla
20/11	Gaziantepspor	h	0-1	
26/11	Sivasspor	a	3-1	Ali Tandogan, Ibrahim Akin, Tümer
4/12	Vestel Manisaspor	h	3-1	Ibrahim Akin, Ahmed Hassan, Kléberson
10/12	Galatasaray	a	2-3	Ibrahim Toraman 2
18/12	Trabzonspor	h	0-1	

2006
Date	Opponent	H/A	Score	Scorers
21/1	Kayseri Erciyespor	h	2-2	Ailton, Sergen
4/2	Gençlerbirligi	h	2-1	Ali Günes, Tümer (p)
10/2	Diyarbakirspor	a	3-1	Bobo, Gökhan Güleç, Jun
17/2	Çaykur Rizespor	h	0-1	
26/2	Fenerbahçe	a	2-2	Sergen 2
5/3	Ankaraspor	h	3-0	Tümer, Gökhan Güleç, Ibrahim Akin
12/3	Samsunspor	a	3-1	Okan, Gökhan Güleç 2
17/3	Kayserispor	h	1-0	Bobo
24/3	Konyaspor	h	0-1	
29/3	Denizlispor	a	1-1	Kléberson
1/4	Ankaragücü	a	3-2	Gökhan Güleç, Ibrahim Üzülmez, Tümer
8/4	Malatyaspor	h	2-2	Ahmed Hassan, Gökhan Güleç
16/4	Gaziantepspor	a	2-2	Gökhan Güleç, Bobo (p)
23/4	Sivasspor	h	0-1	
28/4	Vestel Manisaspor	a	1-0	Bobo
7/5	Galatasaray	h	1-2	Tümer
14/5	Trabzonspor	a	2-1	Bobo, Ibrahim Akin

No	Name	Nat	Pos	Aps	(s)	Gls
2	ADEM Dursun		D	10		
17	AHMED HASSAN	EGY	M	21	(3)	5
60	AHMET Dursun		A	3	(8)	
9	AILTON Gonçalves	BRA	A	13	(1)	5
30	ALI Günes		M	14	(9)	1
22	ALI Tandogan		D	14	(4)	1
13	Rogério BOBO	BRA	A	12	(2)	5
35	Óscar CÓRDOBA	COL	G	28		
6	ÇAGDAS Atan		D	20		1
88	EMRE Özkan		D		(1)	
24	GÖKHAN Güleç		A	13		7
5	GÖKHAN Zan		D	10	(1)	
70	GÜVEN Kocabal		M		(1)	
55	IBRAHIM Akin		A	12	(13)	4
58	IBRAHIM Toraman		D	28		3
19	IBRAHIM Üzülmez		M	24	(2)	1
28	Tomás JUN	CZE	A	2	(4)	1
80	KENAN Özer		A		(1)	

Turkey

No	Name	Nat	Pos	Aps	(s)	Gls
15	José KLÉBERSON	BRA	M	31		3
41	KORAY Avci		D	29		
49	KÜRSAT Duymus		D	1		
87	MEHMET Sedef		M	9		
29	MURAT Sahin		G	6		
4	MUSTAFA Dogan		D	14	(3)	
8	NAIL Tilbaç		A		(2)	
7	OKAN Buruk		M	16	(5)	1
1	Daniel PANCU	ROM	M	3	(3)	
23	RIZA Sen		A		(2)	
10	SERGEN Yalçin		M	9	(9)	6
3	TAYFUR Havutçu		M	4		
11	TÜMER Metin		M	19	(6)	6
50	VEYSEL Cihan		A	1	(10)	
25	Souleymane YOULA	GUI	A	8	(4)	2

ÇAYKUR RIZESPOR
Coach - Metin Yildiz; (3/10/05) Sakip Özberk; (11/12/05) Güvenç Kurtar

2005
Date	Opponent	H/A	Score	Scorers
6/8	Diyarbakirspor	a	0-1	
13/8	Samsunspor	h	1-2	Okan
21/8	Fenerbahçe	h	1-2	Okan (p)
27/8	Ankaraspor	a	0-0	
10/9	Besiktas	h	1-0	Cire
17/9	Kayserispor	a	1-3	Okan
25/9	Konyaspor	h	1-1	Cire
2/10	Ankaragücü	a	0-1	
16/10	Malatyaspor	h	1-0	Cire
23/10	Gaziantepspor	a	1-1	Okan (p)
30/10	Sivasspor	h	1-0	Okan
6/11	Vestel Manisaspor	a	1-1	Cem
20/11	Galatasaray	h	0-3	
25/11	Trabzonspor	a	1-3	og (Ufukhan)
3/12	Kayseri Erciyesspor	h	2-2	Evren, Ünal
10/12	Denizlispor	a	0-2	
18/12	Gençlerbirligi	h	1-1	Okan (p)

2006
Date	Opponent	H/A	Score	Scorers
22/1	Diyarbakirspor	h	2-0	Ferdi, Altan
3/2	Fenerbahçe	a	1-1	Serkan
12/2	Ankaraspor	h	1-1	Gökhan
17/2	Besiktas	a	1-0	Ünal
26/2	Kayserispor	h	0-0	
5/3	Konyaspor	a	1-3	Ferdi
11/3	Ankaragücü	h	1-0	Cem
19/3	Malatyaspor	a	0-1	
26/3	Gaziantepspor	h	0-0	
29/3	Samsunspor	a	0-0	
2/4	Sivasspor	a	2-1	Cem, Ferdi
9/4	Vestel Manisaspor	h	4-1	Fahri 2, Altan, Hasan
16/4	Galatasaray	a	2-4	Okan, og (Cihan)
23/4	Trabzonspor	h	1-6	Cire
29/4	Kayseri Erciyesspor	a	2-0	Cem, Fahri
6/5	Denizlispor	h	1-2	Ünal
14/5	Gençlerbirligi	a	3-1	Cire, Douglas, Aydin

No	Name	Nat	Pos	Aps	(s)	Gls
21	ALLYSON Santos	BRA	D	10	(3)	
13	ALTAN Aksoy		M	15		2
29	ATILLA Koca		G	4	(1)	
26	AYDIN Kuzu		M		(4)	1
15	BASHIR El Tabei	EGY	D	29	(1)	
77	CAFERCAN Aksu		M		(2)	
7	CEM Baki		M	28	(2)	4
5	Dia CIRE	SEN	A	5	(12)	5
8	DOUGLAS dos Santos	BRA	M	15		1
22	ERAY Açikgöz		M		(3)	
6	ERGIN Yücetas		M	16	(7)	
53	EVREN Kürkçü		D	8	(4)	1
3	FAHRI Tatan		M	31	(1)	3
87	FATIH Gültekin		M	1		
35	FERDI Elmas		M	5	(16)	3
54	GÖKHAN Kaba		A	7	(11)	1
57	HAKAN Ünsal		D	3	(1)	
2	HASAN Ugur		M	16		1
28	HÜSEYIN Bak		A		(1)	
4	MEHMET Polat		D	2		
23	MURAT Salar		M	2	(2)	
9	OKAN Öztürk		A	29	(2)	7
10	SAFFET Akyüz		A	4	(4)	
14	SERHAT Akyüz		D	11	(6)	
11	SERKAN Özdemir		M	20	(2)	1
43	SENER Askaroglu		M	13	(6)	
74	ÜNAL Alpugan		M	23	(6)	3
17	Gustavo VICTORIA	COL	D	17		
5	YASIN Çakmak		D	29	(1)	
48	YÜKSEL Babayigit		M		(1)	
1	Zdravko ZDRAVKOV	BUL	G	30		

DENIZLISPOR
Coach - Giray Bulak; (25/9/05) Kenan Atay; (2/10/05) Nurullah Saglam

2005
Date	Opponent	H/A	Score	Scorers
7/8	Ankaraspor	h	1-1	Mustafa
14/8	Besiktas	a	0-2	
20/8	Kayserispor	h	1-3	Yusuf
27/8	Konyaspor	a	0-1	
11/9	Ankaragücü	h	0-0	
17/9	Malatyaspor	a	1-0	Ömer Riza
24/9	Gaziantepsorspor	h	1-2	Fatih
1/10	Sivasspor	a	0-1	
16/10	Vestel Manisaspor	h	1-1	Hüseyin
22/10	Galatasaray	a	1-1	Multaharju
28/10	Trabzonspor	h	0-1	
5/11	Kayseri Erciyesspor	a	0-2	
19/11	Samsunspor	h	2-1	Ömer Riza, Multaharju
27/11	Gençlerbirligi	h	0-2	
4/12	Diyarbakirspor	a	0-1	
10/12	Çaykur Rizespor	h	2-0	Yusuf, Bülent
17/12	Fenerbahçe	a	2-6	Serhat, Kratochvil (p)

2006
Date	Opponent	H/A	Score	Scorers
22/1	Ankaraspor	a	3-1	Kratochvil, Serhat 2
4/2	Kayserispor	a	2-2	Mehmet, Selahattin
12/2	Konyaspor	h	5-2	Burak, Yusuf, Selahattin, Serhat, Abraham
19/2	Ankaragücü	a	1-1	Mehmet
26/2	Malatyaspor	h	1-0	Mehmet
5/3	Gaziantepsor	a	0-1	
12/3	Sivasspor	h	4-0	Kratochvil, Serhat, Oliveira, Alex Alves
18/3	Vestel Manisaspor	a	2-4	Oliveira, Selahattin
25/3	Galatasaray	h	1-2	Mehmet
29/3	Besiktas	h	1-1	Oliveira
2/4	Trabzonspor	a	0-3	
9/4	Kayseri Erciyesspor	h	1-1	Fatih
15/4	Samsunspor	h	1-2	Serhat
23/4	Gençlerbirligi	a	3-3	Selahattin 2, Ibrahim Ege
29/4	Diyarbakirspor	h	1-0	Kratochvil (p)
6/5	Çaykur Rizespor	a	2-1	Mehmet, Kratochvil (p)
14/5	Fenerbahçe	h	1-1	Mustafa

Turkey

No	Name	Nat	Pos	Aps	(s)	Gls
4	Tomás ABRAHAM	CZE	M	33		1
70	AHMET Çagiran		D		(3)	
99	ALEX ALVES	BRA	A		(10)	1
3	BURAK Özsaraç		D	33		1
25	BÜLENT Ertugrul		D	23	(3)	1
27	Radek DOSOUDIL	CZE	D	4	(3)	
23	ENDER Alkan		M	1	(8)	
30	EYÜP Kaymakçi		A	2	(6)	
8	FATIH Yigen		M	7	(17)	2
13	GÜVEN Varol		M	9		
9	HÜSEYIN Ates		A	6	(3)	1
21	IBRAHIM Çelik		D	10	(8)	
77	IBRAHIM Ege		M	7	(2)	1
7	Roman KRATOCHVIL	SVK	D	34		5
33	LEVENT Kartop		M	12	(3)	
61	MEHMET Yilmaz		A	15		5
22	Miikka MULTAHARJU	FIN	M	12	(10)	2
11	MUSTAFA Keçeli		M	31		2
19	Alessandro OLIVEIRA	BRA	A	7	(5)	3
10	ÖMER RIZA		A	16		2
35	SELAHATTIN Kinali		A	14	(2)	5
14	SELIM Teber		M	1	(3)	
20	SERDAL Boyraz		M		(2)	
6	SERHAT Gülpinar		M	33		6
16	SOULEYMANOU Hamidou	CMR	G	26	(1)	
1	SÜLEYMAN Küçük		G	8		
15	TAYLAN Uzunoglu		M	3	(6)	
2	VOLKAN Al		M		(1)	
5	YUSUF Simsek		M	27	(5)	3

DIYARBAKIRSPOR
Coach - Hüseyin Kalpar; (26/9/05) Mehmet Budakin; (3/10/05) Nejat Bijedic (CRO); (27/2/06) Mehmet Budakin; (6/3/06) Faruk Hadzibegic (BOS)

2005
6/8	Çaykur Rizespor	h	1-0	Ilyas
13/8	Fenerbahçe	a	2-2	Ilyas, Maznov
21/8	Ankaraspor	h	1-2	Sedloski
28/8	Besiktas	a	1-1	Ilyas
10/9	Kayserispor	h	0-2	
17/9	Konyaspor	a	1-5	Serdar
25/9	Ankaragücü	h	0-3	
2/10	Malatyaspor	a	2-1	Ilyas, Hasan (p)
15/10	Gaziantepspor	h	1-2	Cem
23/10	Sivasspor	a	1-4	Serdar
30/10	Vestel Manisaspor	h	0-2	
4/11	Galatasaray	a	0-2	
19/11	Trabzonspor	h	3-0	Sedloski 2, Burhan
27/11	Kayseri Erciyesspor	a	2-0	Maznov, Ilyas
4/12	Denizlispor	h	1-0	Maznov
11/12	Gençlerbirligi	a	0-4	
18/12	Samsunspor	h	0-0	

2006
22/1	Çaykur Rizespor	a	0-2	
4/2	Ankaraspor	a	3-3	Mohamed Ali 2, Ilyas
10/2	Besiktas	h	1-3	Rakovic
19/2	Kayserispor	a	0-3	
26/2	Konyaspor	h	0-3	(w/o; match abandoned, original result 0-1)
5/3	Ankaragücü	a	1-5	Mikic
12/3	Malatyaspor	h	3-2	Cumhur 2, Ilyas
19/3	Gaziantepspor	a	0-2	
25/3	Sivasspor	h	1-1	Rakovic
30/3	Fenerbahçe	h	0-4	
2/4	Vestel Manisaspor	a	3-0	Ilyas 2, Mikic
7/4	Galatasaray	h	1-3	Mikic
15/4	Trabzonspor	a	0-3	
23/4	Kayseri Erciyesspor	h	2-1	Burhan, Mohamed Ali
29/4	Denizlispor	a	0-1	
6/5	Gençlerbirligi	h	0-2	
14/5	Samsunspor	a	0-1	

No	Name	Nat	Pos	Aps	(s)	Gls
5	AHMET Çagiran		D	4	(4)	
28	ALI Sakal		M	4		
7	ATILLA Birlik		A	7	(7)	
87	BARIS Atas		M	7	(2)	
27	BURHAN Eser		M	18	(9)	2
13	CEM Yanik		M	12	(1)	1
53	CUMHUR Bozaci		M	31	(2)	2
20	ELYASA Süme		M	1	(1)	
16	ENDER Alkan		M	1	(4)	
91	ERHAN Ölker		M		(2)	
77	GÖKSEL Akinci		D	32		
93	Sammy GTARI	FRA	A	1		
9	HASAN Özer		A	8	(3)	1
10	ILYAS Kahraman		M	31		9
8	Redi JUPI	ALB	M	29	(1)	
17	Goran MAZNOV	MAC	A	22	(7)	3
33	METIN Aktas		G	9		
25	Borislav MIKIC	BOS	M	13	(1)	3
22	MOHAMED ALI Kurtulus		M	9	(6)	3
21	MURAT Yigiter		G	15		
1	OGUZ Daglaroglu		G	2		
29	OKTAY Derelioglu		A		(2)	
49	ÖZCAN Turan		G	1	(1)	
90	Ermin RAKOVIC	SLO	A	7	(6)	2
35	RAMAZAN Kursunlu		G	7	(2)	
19	SALIM Ayan		M	1	(4)	
4	Goce SEDLOSKI	MAC	D	25	(2)	3
11	SERDAR Samatyali		M	3	(10)	2
18	SERKAN Aslan		M	1	(2)	
61	SINAN Demircioglu		D	26	(3)	
32	SINAN Turan		M	4	(2)	
2	Goran STAVREVSKI	MAC	D	20	(5)	
3	TALIP Toprak		D	17	(1)	
14	TOLGA Dogantez		D	6	(1)	

FENERBAHÇE
Coach - Christoph Daum (GER)

2005
5/8	Gençlerbirligi	a	0-0	
13/8	Diyarbakirspor	h	2-2	Alex, Tuncay
21/8	Çaykur Rizespor	a	2-1	Márcio Nobre, Semih
27/8	Samsunspor	h	5-2	Alex 2, Anelka, Márcio Nobre, Semih
10/9	Ankaraspor	h	2-1	Alex, Marco Aurélio
18/9	Besiktas	a	2-1	Anelka, Tuncay
24/9	Kayserispor	h	3-0	Alex, Márcio Nobre, Anelka
1/10	Konyaspor	a	4-2	Anelka 2, Márcio Nobre 2
15/10	Ankaragücü	h	2-1	Luciano, Alex (p)
23/10	Malatyaspor	a	3-0	Mehmet 2, Tuncay
29/10	Gaziantepspor	h	1-0	Alex (p)
6/11	Sivasspor	a	3-2	Marco Aurélio, Alex, Tuncay
19/11	Vestel Manisaspor	h	2-1	Tuncay, Semih
27/11	Galatasaray	a	1-0	Márcio Nobre
2/12	Trabzonspor	h	2-2	Márcio Nobre 2
11/12	Kayseri Erciyesspor	a	3-0	Önder, Alex (p), Tuncay
17/12	Denizlispor	h	6-2	Semih 4, Appiah, Marco Aurélio

Turkey

2006

Date	Opponent	H/A	Score	Scorers
20/1	Gençlerbirligi	h	3-0	Önder, Márcio Nobre 2
3/2	Çaykur Rizespor	h	1-1	Tuncay
11/2	Samsunspor	a	5-0	Appiah, Tuncay 2, Marco Aurélio, Anelka
18/2	Ankaraspor	a	1-2	Anelka
26/2	Besiktas	h	2-2	Tuncay, Márcio Nobre
5/3	Kayserispor	a	0-1	
11/3	Konyaspor	h	5-0	Anelka, Márcio Nobre 2, Önder, Appiah
18/3	Ankaragücü	a	4-1	og (Ibrahim), Tuncay, Appiah, Alex
26/3	Malatyaspor	h	2-0	Mehmet, og (Johansson)
30/3	Diyarbakirspor	a	4-0	Luciano, Appiah, Márcio Nobre 2
2/4	Gaziantepspor	a	2-0	Tuncay, Márcio Nobre
9/4	Sivasspor	h	3-0	Alex 2 (1p), Tuncay
15/4	Vestel Manisaspor	a	3-5	Anelka, Márcio Nobre, og (Caner)
22/4	Galatasaray	h	4-0	Appiah, Luciano, Alex, Anelka
29/4	Trabzonspor	a	3-2	Tuncay, Márcio Nobre, Semih
7/5	Kayseri Erciyesspor	h	4-2	Alex, Appiah 2, Selçuk
14/5	Denizlispor	a	1-1	Tuncay

No	Name	Nat	Pos	Aps	(s)	Gls
20	ALEX de Souza	BRA	M	31		14
39	Nicolas ANELKA	FRA	A	23	(2)	10
4	Stephen APPIAH	GHA	M	32		8
17	CAN Arat		D		(2)	
24	DENIZ Baris		D	11	(6)	
18	GÜRHAN Gürsoy		M		(1)	
27	KEMAL Aslan		M	2	(10)	
2	Fábio LUCIANO	BRA	D	32		3
6	MAHMUT HANEFI Erdogdu		D		(1)	
11	MÁRCIO NOBRE	BRA	A	25	(4)	18
15	MARCO AURÉLIO	BRA	M	31		4
7	MEHMET Yozgatli		M	13	(14)	3
29	OLCAN Adin		M		(3)	
19	ÖNDER Turaci		D	30		3
34	RÜSTÜ Reçber		G	17		
21	SELÇUK Sahin		M	10	(7)	1
23	SEMIH Sentürk		A	4	(18)	8
30	SERKAN Balci		D	26	(6)	
3	SERVET Çetin		D	8	(3)	
10	TUNCAY Sanli		M	28	(2)	15
5	ÜMIT Özat		D	34		
1	VOLKAN Demirel		G	17	(1)	
8	ZAFER Biryol		A		(2)	

GALATASARAY
Coach - Eric Gerets (BEL)

2005

Date	Opponent	H/A	Score	Scorers
7/8	Konyaspor	h	2-1	Ilic 2
12/8	Ankaragücü	a	1-0	Ümit
21/8	Malatyaspor	h	5-2	Ümit 3 (1p), Altan, Hasan Sas
26/8	Gaziantepspor	a	2-2	Ümit, Hasan Kabze
11/9	Sivasspor	h	2-0	Ümit 2 (1p)
18/9	Vestel Manisaspor	a	4-1	Necati 2, Ümit 2
25/9	Samsunspor	a	2-1	Necati 2
2/10	Trabzonspor	a	4-1	Hakan, Heinz, Ümit, Necati
15/10	Kayseri Erciyesspor	a	2-1	Hakan 2
22/10	Denizlispor	h	1-1	Hasan Sas
30/10	Gençlerbirligi	a	1-2	Ilic
4/11	Diyarbakirsporspor	h	2-0	Ümit, Ilic
20/11	Çaykur Rizespor	a	3-0	Cihan, Necati, Hasan Kabze
27/11	Fenerbahçe	h	0-1	
3/12	Ankaraspor	a	2-1	Ümit, Necati
10/12	Besiktas	h	3-2	Necati, Ilic 2
16/12	Kayserispor	h	3-1	Necati, Ümit, Cihan

2006

Date	Opponent	H/A	Score	Scorers
22/1	Konyaspor	a	1-0	Aydin
5/2	Malatyaspor	a	1-1	Volkan
12/2	Gaziantepspor	h	6-0	Ümit 3, Hakan, Heinz, Necati
19/2	Sivasspor	a	0-0	
25/2	Vestel Manisaspor	h	4-2	Necati, Volkan, Song, Sabri
4/3	Samsunspor	h	3-2	Necati 2, Ilic
12/3	Trabzonspor	a	1-1	Necati
19/3	Kayseri Erciyesspor	h	4-2	Ayhan, Necati, Ümit, Hasan Kabze
25/3	Denizlispor	a	2-1	og (Bülent), Heinz
29/3	Ankaragücü	h	2-0	Hakan, Cihan
1/4	Gençlerbirligi	h	3-0	Necati 2 (2p), Ilic
7/4	Diyarbakirsporspor	a	3-1	Hakan 2, Necati
16/4	Çaykur Rizespor	h	4-2	Ilic, Hakan 2, og (Allyson)
22/4	Fenerbahçe	a	0-4	
29/4	Ankaraspor	h	4-0	Ilic 2, Hakan, Hasan Kabze
7/5	Besiktas	a	2-1	Hasan Kabze 2
14/5	Kayserispor	h	3-0	Ilic, Sabri 2

No	Name	Nat	Pos	Aps	(s)	Gls
14	ALTAN Aksoy		M	4	(5)	1
26	AYDIN Yilmaz		M	3	(9)	1
18	AYHAN Akman		M	13	(4)	1
19	CIHAN Haspolatli		D	27		3
21	EMRE Asik		D	2	(1)	
67	ERGÜN Penbe		M	11	(4)	
25	FERHAT Öztorun		D	8	(1)	
9	HAKAN Sükür		A	23	(8)	10
58	HASAN Kabze		A	2	(16)	6
11	HASAN Sas		M	26		2
8	Marek HEINZ	CZE	M	10	(8)	3
22	Sasa ILIC	SCG	M	26	(4)	12
24	MEHMET Güven		M		(1)	
1	Faryd MONDRAGÓN	COL	G	34		
10	NECATI Ates		A	30	(2)	18
5	ORHAN Ak		D	22		
27	ÖZGÜRCAN Özcan		A		(1)	
55	SABRI Sarioglu		M	9	(12)	3
7	Allioum SAIDOU	CMR	M	23		
4	Rigobert SONG	CMR	D	28	(1)	1
2	Stjepan TOMAS	CRO	D	32		
50	UGUR Demirok		D		(1)	
33	UGUR Uçar		D	10	(7)	
99	ÜMIT Karan		A	19	(5)	17
20	VOLKAN Arslan		M	9	(7)	2
6	YALÇIN Ayhan		D	3	(1)	
23	ZAFER Sakar		M		(2)	

GAZIANTEPSPOR
Coach - Faruk Hadzibegic (BOS); (11/12/05) Hüseyin Kalpar; (20/2/06) Samet Aybaba

2005

Date	Opponent	H/A	Score	Scorers
7/8	Samsunspor	a	3-2	Erdal, Ilhan, Lazarov
13/8	Sivasspor	h	0-0	
21/8	Vestel Manisaspor	a	2-1	Erdal, Lazarov
26/8	Galatasaray	h	2-2	Lazarov, Ilhan

Turkey

11/9	Trabzonspor	a	0-2	
18/9	Kayseri Erciyesspor	h	1-2	Erdal
24/9	Denizlispor	a	2-1	El Taib, Lazarov
30/9	Gençlerbirligi	h	1-1	Aytek
15/10	Diyarbakirspor	a	2-1	Ivanov, Sedat
23/10	Çaykur Rizespor	h	1-1	Ekrem
29/10	Fenerbahçe	a	0-1	
5/11	Ankaraspor	h	3-3	Lazarov 2 (1p), Ilhan
20/11	Besiktas	a	1-0	Erman
27/11	Kayserispor	h	1-4	Lazarov (p)
3/12	Konyaspor	a	2-3	Lazarov, Gökhan
10/12	Ankaragücü	h	1-1	Fahmi
17/12	Malatyaspor	a	0-2	
2006				
22/1	Samsunspor	h	0-1	
5/2	Vestel Manisaspor	h	1-1	Özgür
12/2	Galatasaray	a	0-6	
19/2	Trabzonspor	h	0-2	
25/2	Kayseri Erciyesspor	a	0-1	
5/3	Denizlispor	h	1-0	Lazarov
11/3	Gençlerbirligi	a	1-3	Ali
19/3	Diyarbakirspor	h	2-0	Lazarov, Sedat
26/3	Çaykur Rizespor	a	0-0	
29/3	Sivasspor	a	0-0	
2/4	Fenerbahçe	h	0-2	
8/4	Ankaraspor	a	0-3	
16/4	Besiktas	h	2-2	Mehmet, Ekrem
23/4	Kayserispor	a	1-0	Kirita
29/4	Konyaspor	h	2-0	Lazarov (p), Kirita
7/5	Ankaragücü	a	1-2	Ali
14/5	Malatyaspor	h	1-0	og (Ömer)

No	Name	Nat	Pos	Aps	(s)	Gls
58	ADEM Dursun		D	14		
10	ALI Bayraktar		A		(8)	2
34	AYTEK Asikoglu		D	4	(3)	1
45	BARIS Durmaz		D	13	(1)	
4	BEKIR Irtegun		D	29	(2)	
47	BURAK Solakel		M	5	(5)	
23	EKREM Dag		M	13	(9)	2
14	Tarik EL TAIB	LBY	M	14	(4)	1
41	ENGIN Öztonga		M	5	(15)	
15	ERDAL Günes		M	11	(1)	3
99	ERMAN Güracar		D	14		1
2	Abdelilah FAHMI	EGY	D	9	(2)	1
26	FARUK Bayar		M	24	(3)	
9	GÖKHAN Güleç		A	4	(4)	1
27	HAKAN Korkmaz		D	5	(5)	
1	Kenan HASAGIC	BOS	G	31		
38	HASAN Yurt		M	13	(5)	
66	ILHAN Özbay		M	9	(4)	3
69	Georgi IVANOV	BUL	A	13		1
25	Shingayl KAONDERA	ZIM	A	1	(5)	
22	KAYA Tarakçi		G	3	(1)	
3	Giani KIRITA	ROM	M	22	(1)	2
11	Zdravko LAZAROV	BUL	A	27	(1)	11
6	MEHMET Çogum		D	22		1
18	Sofiene MELLITI	TUN	M	10	(4)	
36	ÖZGÜR Yildirim		M	23	(3)	1
7	SEDAT Agçay		M	23	(2)	2
8	SERKAN Atak		M	1	(4)	
52	SERKAN Özsoy		D		(1)	
17	SEVKI Koç		M	2	(3)	
50	VEYSEL Cihan		A	10	(2)	

GENÇLERBIRLIGI
Coach - Ziya Dogan; (29/8/05) Mesut Bakkal

2005				
5/8	Fenerbahçe	h	0-0	
14/8	Ankaraspor	a	0-0	
20/8	Besiktas	h	0-2	
28/8	Kayserispor	a	0-2	
11/9	Konyaspor	h	1-1	Bogdanovic
17/9	Ankaragücü	a	1-1	Promise
24/9	Malatyaspor	h	2-0	Mehmet Çakir, Promise
30/9	Gaziantepsor	a	1-1	Promise
16/10	Sivasspor	h	0-1	
23/10	Vestel Manisaspor	a	3-0	Mehmet Çakir, Erhan, Bogdanovic
30/10	Galatasaray	h	2-1	Promise, Ugur
5/11	Trabzonspor	a	1-1	Mehmet Çakir
19/11	Kayseri Erciyesspor	h	3-0	Baki 2, Mehmet Çakir
27/11	Denizlispor	a	2-0	Mehmet Çakir 2
4/12	Samsunspor	h	0-1	
11/12	Diyarbakirspor	h	4-0	Ayhan, Promise, Ugur 2
18/12	Çaykur Rizespor	a	1-1	Mehmet Çakir
2006				
20/1	Fenerbahçe	a	0-3	
4/2	Besiktas	a	1-2	Mehmet Çakir
12/2	Kayserispor	h	3-2	Promise, Ali Cansun, Ismail
19/2	Konyaspor	a	3-0	og (El Saka), Promise, Ugur (p)
26/2	Ankaragücü	h	1-1	Promise
5/3	Malatyaspor	a	3-1	Promise, Mehmet Nas, Ali Cansun
11/3	Gaziantepsor	h	3-1	Ugur, Promise, Mehmet Çakir
19/3	Sivasspor	a	1-2	Tayfun
25/3	Vestel Manisaspor	h	2-1	Ugur (p), Mehmet Çakir
29/3	Ankaraspor	a	2-1	Ali Cansun, Ayhan
1/4	Galatasaray	a	0-3	
9/4	Trabzonspor	h	1-0	Mehmet Çakir
16/4	Kayseri Erciyesspor	a	0-2	
23/4	Denizlispor	h	3-3	Mehmet Çakir 2, Ugur
29/4	Samsunspor	a	0-2	
6/5	Diyarbakirspor	a	2-0	Ali Cansun, Mehmet Nas
14/5	Çaykur Rizespor	h	1-3	Mehmet Çakir

No	Name	Nat	Pos	Aps	(s)	Gls
45	Solomon ABWO	NGA	A		(6)	
77	ALI CANSUN Begeçarslan		A	8	(12)	4
35	AYHAN Tuna		D	22	(2)	2
12	AYMAN Abdelaziz	EGY	M	27	(2)	
23	BAKI Mercimek		D	10	(4)	2
19	Igor BOGDANOVIC	SCG	A	2	(2)	2
21	DOGA Kaya		M	1	(5)	
54	ENGIN Baytar		M		(4)	
34	EREN Aydin		D	11	(3)	
44	ERHAN Güven		D	22	(1)	1
6	ERKAN Özbey		D	15	(2)	
99	GÖKHAN Tokgöz		G	17	(1)	
18	HASAN Ugur		M	6	(6)	
2	ISMAIL Güldüren		D	31		1
16	Christian JÄRDLER	SWE	M	7	(3)	
61	KEREM Seras		M	19	(6)	
69	Christophe LEPOINT	BEL	A		(4)	
8	MEHMET Çakir		A	32	(1)	14
9	MEHMET Nas		M	17	(9)	2
10	José OLIVIERA	BRA	A	1	(5)	
1	ÖMER Çatkiç		G	17		

Turkey

14	Isaac PROMISE	NGA	A	33	(1)	10
3	Fredrik RISP	SWE	D	28		
5	SEDAT Yesilkaya		M	7	(11)	
11	SERTAN Eser		M	4	(2)	
4	TAYFUN Korkut		M	11	(2)	1
20	UGUR Boral		M	26	(2)	7
7	YERTEK Basaran		A		(1)	

KAYSERISPOR
Coach - Ertugrul Saglam

2005

6/8	Trabzonspor	a	1-2	Bülent Karaman
14/8	Kayseri Erciyesspor	h	1-2	Muhammet Hanifi
20/8	Denizlispor	a	3-1	Yordanov, Mehmet Topuz, Gökhan
28/8	Gençlerbirligi	h	2-0	Gökhan, Rodic
10/9	Diyarbakirspor	a	2-0	Gökhan, Bülent Bölükbasi
17/9	Çaykur Rizespor	h	3-1	Gökhan, Bülent Karaman 2
24/9	Fenerbahçe	a	0-3	
2/10	Ankaraspor	h	2-1	Gökhan 2
16/10	Besiktas	a	0-0	
22/10	Samsunspor	h	6-3	Fatih, Rodic 2, Gökhan, Mehmet Topuz, Bülent Bölükbasi
30/10	Konyaspor	h	1-0	Gökhan
6/11	Ankaragücü	a	0-2	
20/11	Malatyaspor	h	2-0	Gökhan, Rodic
27/11	Gaziantepspor	a	4-1	Yordanov, Gökhan 2, Bülent Bölükbasi
4/12	Sivasspor	h	2-2	Rodic, Gökhan
9/12	Vestel Manisaspor	a	0-1	
16/12	Galatasaray	h	1-3	Gökhan

2006

22/1	Trabzonspor	h	4-2	Yordanov (p), Gökhan 2, Mehmet Topuz
4/2	Denizlispor	h	2-2	Rodic, Bülent Bölükbasi
12/2	Gençlerbirligi	a	2-3	Bayram, Gökhan
19/2	Diyarbakirspor	h	3-0	Gökhan, Yordanov (p), Enver
26/2	Çaykur Rizespor	a	0-0	
5/3	Fenerbahçe	h	1-0	Gökhan
12/3	Ankaraspor	a	3-1	Gökhan, Rodic, Bülent Bölükbasi
17/3	Besiktas	h	0-1	
26/3	Samsunspor	a	0-0	
29/3	Kayseri Erciyesspor	a	0-0	
2/4	Konyaspor	a	0-1	
9/4	Ankaragücü	h	1-2	Gökhan
15/4	Malatyaspor	a	1-2	Yordanov
23/4	Gaziantepspor	h	0-1	
30/4	Sivasspor	a	5-0	Ilhan, Yordanov, Bülent Bölükbasi 2, Gökhan
6/5	Vestel Manisaspor	h	7-2	Gökhan 4 (1p), Ilhan, Bülent Bölükbasi, Mehmet Topuz
14/5	Galatasaray	a	0-3	

No	Name	Nat	Pos	Aps	(s)	Gls
16	ALI Üçkulak		G	1	(1)	
6	ALTAN Günes		M		(1)	
25	AYDIN Toscali		D	22		
26	BAYRAM Toysal		M	3	(8)	1
3	BÜLENT Bölükbasi		M	28	(1)	8
79	BÜLENT Karaman		A	1	(5)	3
30	CEM Kargin		D	1		
45	ENGIN Cicem		A		(6)	
35	ENVER Isik		A		(3)	1
41	ERGÜN Teber		D	23	(5)	
81	FATIH Ceylan		M	26		1
9	GÖKHAN Ünal		A	32		25
17	ILHAN Parlak		A	9	(9)	2
27	Dimitar IVANKOV	BUL	G	31		
15	Samuel JOHNSON	GHA	D	32		
38	KAMBER Arslan		M	24	(5)	
19	KEMAL Okyay		M		(17)	
11	KÖKSAL Yedek		M	1	(9)	
66	MEHMET Topuz		M	31	(1)	4
1	METIN Aktas		G	2		
4	MUHAMMET HANIFI Yoldas		D	30		1
8	RAGIP Basdag		M	25	(7)	
32	Aleksandar RODIC	BOS	A	14	(2)	7
14	Rashad SADIGOV	AZB	D	8	(1)	
21	VEYSEL Aksu		D	4	(6)	
10	Aleksandar YORDANOV	BUL	M	26	(5)	6

KAYSERI ERCIYESSPOR
Coach - Mustafa Ugur

2005

6/8	Besiktas	h	1-1	Cenk
14/8	Kayseraspor	a	2-1	Cenk, Burak
21/8	Konyaspor	h	0-0	
28/8	Ankaragücü	a	2-1	Agali, Cenk
10/9	Malatyaspor	h	1-1	Cenk
18/9	Gaziantepspor	a	2-1	Cenk, Timuçin
25/9	Sivasspor	h	0-0	
1/10	Vestel Manisaspor	a	2-0	Burhan, Mutlu
15/10	Galatasaray	h	1-2	Cenk
21/10	Trabzonspor	a	0-0	
30/10	Samsunspor	h	1-1	Dié
5/11	Denizlispor	h	2-0	Cenk, Agali
19/11	Gençlerbirligi	a	0-3	
27/11	Diyarbakirspor	h	0-2	
3/12	Çaykur Rizespor	a	2-2	Agali, Ömer Közen
11/12	Fenerbahçe	h	0-3	
18/12	Ankaraspor	a	1-1	Cenk

2006

21/1	Besiktas	a	2-2	Cenk, Agali (p)
5/2	Konyaspor	a	0-2	
11/2	Ankaragücü	h	1-2	Ilhan
19/2	Malatyaspor	a	2-2	Cenk 2
25/2	Gaziantepspor	h	1-0	Cenk (p)
5/3	Sivasspor	a	0-3	
10/3	Vestel Manisaspor	h	2-1	Cenk 2
19/3	Galatasaray	a	2-4	Cenk 2
26/3	Trabzonspor	h	1-0	Ilkem
29/3	Kayserispor	h	0-0	
2/4	Samsunspor	h	2-2	Cenk, Agali
9/4	Denizlispor	a	1-1	Ilhan
16/4	Gençlerbirligi	h	2-0	Cenk, Ilhan
23/4	Diyarbakirspor	a	1-2	Cenk
29/4	Çaykur Rizespor	h	0-2	
7/5	Fenerbahçe	a	2-4	Devran, Cenk
14/5	Ankaraspor	h	0-1	

No	Name	Nat	Pos	Aps	(s)	Gls
22	Victor AGALI	NGA	A	25	(2)	5
17	ALI Akdeniz		D	4	(1)	
58	AYDIN Yildirim		D	3	(2)	
13	Riadh BOUAZIZI	TUN	D	32		
54	BURAK Akdis		A	1	(10)	1
9	BURHAN Coskun		A	2	(11)	1

Turkey

No	Name	Nat	Pos	Aps	(s)	Gls
45	CEM Kargin		D	10	(2)	
21	CENK Isler		A	34		20
77	Junivan DE MELO	BRA	M		(2)	
72	DEVRAN Ayhan		M	32	(1)	1
6	Serge DIE	CIV	M	23	(4)	1
5	EMRE Toraman		M	26		
1	Khaled FADHEL	TUN	G	31		
19	GÖKHAN Kök		D	26		
70	GÜVEN Kocabal		M	1	(5)	
66	ILHAN Özbay		M	16	(1)	3
39	ILKEM Özkaynak		D	13	(1)	1
11	JÚLIO CÉSAR	BRA	M	6	(5)	
20	KAZIM Seker		M	2	(1)	
12	Seck MAMADOU	SEN	D	5	(2)	
61	MEHMET Ayaz		M		(4)	
38	MURAT Akyüz		D	9	(8)	
35	MUTLU Kiziltan		M	2	(16)	1
3	ÖMER Ates		D	17	(1)	
7	ÖMER Közen		M	7	(15)	1
27	SENOL Yavas		D	14	(3)	
10	TIMUÇIN Bayazit		M	30	(1)	1
64	YUSUF Soysal		G	2		
14	ZAFER Özgültekin		G	1	(1)	

KONYASPOR
Coach - Aykut Kocaman

2005
7/8	Galatasaray	a	1-2	Levent (p)
14/8	Trabzonspor	h	0-0	
21/8	Kayseri Erciyesspor	a	0-0	
27/8	Denizlispor	h	1-0	El Saka
11/9	Gençlerbirligi	a	1-1	Erhan
17/9	Diyarbakirspor	h	5-1	El Saka 2, Ahmed Belal, Ceyhun, Murat
25/9	Çaykur Rizespor	a	1-1	og (Yasin)
1/10	Fenerbahçe	h	2-4	Ceyhun, Murat
15/10	Ankaraspor	a	0-0	
23/10	Besiktas	h	0-1	
30/10	Kayserispor	a	0-1	
6/11	Samsunspor	h	4-2	Ceyhun 2, Ahmed Belal, Murat
20/11	Ankaragücü	h	2-0	El Saka, Volkan
26/11	Malatyaspor	a	0-1	
3/12	Gaziantepspor	h	3-2	og (Fahmi), Tayfun Türkmen, Ahmed Belal
11/12	Sivasspor	a	1-1	Bebbe
18/12	Vestel Manisaspor	h	1-1	Yasin

2006
22/1	Galatasaray	h	0-1	
5/2	Kayseri Erciyesspor	h	2-0	Tayfun Türkmen, Okan
12/2	Denizlispor	a	2-5	Okan, Erhan
19/2	Gençlerbirligi	h	0-3	
26/2	Diyarbakirspor	a	3-0	(w/o; match abandoned, original result 1-0 Bebbe)
5/3	Çaykur Rizespor	h	3-1	Okan 2, Murat (p)
11/3	Fenerbahçe	a	0-5	
19/3	Ankaraspor	h	0-0	
24/3	Besiktas	a	1-0	og (Ibrahim Toraman)
30/3	Trabzonspor	a	2-1	Murat, Tayfun Seven
2/4	Kayserispor	h	1-0	Murat
9/4	Samsunspor	a	1-1	Ghodhbane
16/4	Ankaragücü	a	0-3	
23/4	Malatyaspor	h	0-2	
29/4	Gaziantepspor	a	0-2	
7/5	Sivasspor	h	2-1	Murat, Volkan

| 13/5 | Vestel Manisaspor | a | 0-0 | | | |

No	Name	Nat	Pos	Aps	(s)	Gls
11	AHMED BELAL	EGY	A	9	(5)	3
2	João BATISTA	BRA	M	12	(2)	
20	Anilet BEBBE	CMR	A	13	(7)	2
10	CEYHUN Eris		M	10		4
5	Abdelzaher EL SAKA	EGY	D	23	(3)	4
34	ERAY Birniçan		G	1		
60	ERAY Er		M		(13)	
77	ERHAN Öztürk		D	33		2
21	ERMAN Ergin		M	18	(13)	
38	FIRAT Akkoyun		M	3	(4)	
17	Kais GHODHBANE	TUN	M	8	(1)	1
37	GÖKHAN Çakir		M	1		
22	HALUK Tanriseven		G	2		
6	LEVENT Kartop		M	6	(3)	1
53	MURAT Hacioglu		M	32	(1)	7
13	MUSTAFA Er		M	20	(9)	
32	OKAN Yilmaz		A	11	(3)	4
48	OZAN Özkan		M		(1)	
4	ÖMER Gündostu		D	25	(3)	
1	ÖZDEN Öngün		G	29		
41	Jobanny RIVERO	COL	M	5	(1)	
18	TAYFUN Seven		M	8	(1)	1
33	TAYFUN Türkmen		D	21	(12)	2
14	ÜMIT Bozkurt		D	20	(1)	
40	Vladimir VASILJ	CRO	G	2		
9	VOLKAN Çekiç		A	5	(15)	2
42	YASIN Çelik		D	31	(1)	1
8	ZAFER Biryol		A	3	(1)	
25	ZAFER Demir		M	23		

MALATYASPOR
Coach - Feyyaz Uçar; (29/8/05) Ziya Dogan; (13/3/06) Ümit Kayihan

2005
6/8	Sivasspor	a	1-1	Mert
13/8	Vestel Manisaspor	h	0-5	
21/8	Galatasaray	a	2-5	Mert (p), Mustafa
28/8	Trabzonspor	h	1-1	Mert (p)
10/9	Kayseri Erciyesspor	a	1-1	Homola
17/9	Denizlispor	h	0-1	
24/9	Gençlerbirligi	a	0-2	
2/10	Diyarbakirspor	h	1-2	Effa
16/10	Çaykur Rizespor	a	0-1	
23/10	Fenerbahçe	h	0-3	
29/10	Ankaraspor	a	2-1	Effa, Okan
6/11	Besiktas	h	1-1	Effa
20/11	Kayserispor	a	0-2	
26/11	Konyaspor	h	1-0	Johansson
5/12	Ankaragücü	h	0-0	
11/12	Samsunspor	a	2-1	Bülent, Okan
17/12	Gaziantepspor	h	2-0	Okan 2

2006
22/1	Sivasspor	h	0-0	
5/2	Galatasaray	h	1-1	Tóth
12/2	Trabzonspor	a	0-1	
19/2	Kayseri Erciyesspor	h	2-2	Senkerik, Mustafa
26/2	Denizlispor	a	0-1	
5/3	Gençlerbirligi	h	1-3	Bilal
12/3	Diyarbakirspor	a	2-3	Senkerik, Ömer
19/3	Çaykur Rizespor	h	1-0	Senkerik
26/3	Fenerbahçe	a	0-2	
29/3	Vestel Manisaspor	a	3-4	Volkan, Evren, Mert
2/4	Ankaraspor	h	0-2	

Turkey

8/4	Besiktas	a	2-2	Evren, Mert (p)	
15/4	Kayserispor	h	2-1	Ömer, Homola	
23/4	Konyaspor	a	2-0	Ömer, Sertan	
29/4	Ankaragücü	a	1-0	og (Sedat)	
6/5	Samsunspor	h	3-0	Evren 2, Senkerík	
14/5	Gaziantepsor	a	0-1		

No	Name	Nat	Pos	Aps	(s)	Gls
54	AYTAÇ Ak		D	4		
19	BILAL Kisa		M	25	(4)	1
35	BORA Körk		G	13	(1)	
6	BÜLENT Akin		M	8	(2)	1
5	EFFA Owosu	CMR	A	8	(4)	3
41	EMRAH Eren		D	16	(1)	
34	EREN Aydin		D	5	(4)	
98	ERGUN Cengiz		A		(1)	
7	EVREN Turhan		M	14	(2)	4
82	FEHMI Berk		D		(1)	
48	FEVZI Tuncay		G	21		
4	Cristiano GRIGULO	BRA	D	3	(2)	
25	GÜNGÖR Tugcu		M	2	(2)	
61	HAKAN Aslantas		D	14	(3)	
68	HAKAN Söyler		M	14	(4)	
33	Jiri HOMOLA	CZE	D	21	(1)	2
24	Hans JOHANSSON	SWE	M	14	(2)	1
15	Ibrahim KARGBO	SRL	D	1		
30	KATATAU de Toledo	BRA	A	5	(1)	
66	Jiri MASEK	CZE	A	9	(6)	
20	MEHMET Albayrak		A		(5)	
22	MEHMET Budak		M	5	(2)	
44	MERT Korkmaz		D	31		5
17	Tomás MICHÁLEK	CZE	M	6	(1)	
11	MUSTAFA Özkan		A	18	(10)	2
10	OKAN Yilmaz		A	7	(10)	4
3	ÖMER Erdogan		D	28	(2)	3
8	RAMAZAN Kahya		M	5	(1)	
14	Zdenek SENKERÍK	CZE	A	12	(4)	4
28	SERDAL Boyraz		M		(2)	
99	SERKAN Bensol		D	23	(3)	
70	SERTAN Eser		A	2	(8)	1
9	TANER Demirbas		A	1	(7)	
26	Balázs TÓTH	HUN	M	29	(2)	1
47	VOLKAN Bekiroglu		M	10	(4)	1

SAMSUNSPOR
Coach - Saban Yildirim; (12/9/05) Erdogan Arica; (20/3/06) Hasan Sengün

2005

7/8	Gaziantepsor	h	2-3	Serkan, Ivanov
13/8	Çaykur Rizespor	a	2-1	Ghodhbane, Celil
20/8	Sivasspor	h	1-2	Serkan (p)
27/8	Fenerbahçe	a	2-5	Ghodhbane, Serkan
11/9	Vestel Manisaspor	h	1-1	Serkan (p)
18/9	Ankaraspor	a	3-3	Musa 2, Serkan
25/9	Galatasaray	h	1-2	Rafael
2/10	Besiktas	a	2-3	Adnan, Ghodhbane
16/10	Trabzonspor	h	3-1	Ghodhbane (p), Rafael, Muhammet
22/10	Kayserispor	a	3-6	Ghodhbane, Celil, Rafael
30/10	Kayseri Erciyesspor	h	1-1	Serkan
6/11	Konyaspor	a	2-4	Rafael, Serkan
19/11	Denizlispor	h	1-2	Serkan
27/11	Ankaragücü	a	1-1	Ghodhbane
4/12	Gençlerbirligi	a	1-0	Ghodhbane
11/12	Malatyaspor	h	1-2	Ghodhbane
18/12	Diyarbakirspor	a	0-0	

2006

22/1	Gaziantepsor	a	1-0	Serkan
5/2	Sivasspor	a	3-0	Rafael, Ceyhun, Tamer
11/2	Fenerbahçe	h	0-5	
19/2	Vestel Manisaspor	a	0-3	
26/2	Ankaraspor	h	0-1	
4/3	Galatasaray	a	2-3	Tamer 2
12/3	Besiktas	h	1-3	og (Mustafa)
19/3	Trabzonspor	a	1-2	Serkan
26/3	Kayserispor	h	0-0	
29/3	Çaykur Rizespor	a	0-0	
2/4	Kayseri Erciyesspor	a	2-2	Caner, Ceyhun
9/4	Konyaspor	h	1-1	Tamer
15/4	Denizlispor	a	2-1	Ceyhun, Caner
23/4	Ankaragücü	a	2-1	Rafael 2
29/4	Gençlerbirligi	h	2-0	Adnan, Caner
6/5	Malatyaspor	a	0-3	
14/5	Diyarbakirspor	h	1-0	Celil

No	Name	Nat	Pos	Aps	(s)	Gls
13	ADNAN Güngör		M	31		2
11	ALI Akdeniz		D	11	(1)	
2	ALPER Akici		D	3	(8)	
5	Anis AYARI	TUN	D	20	(5)	
1	Alioum BOUKAR	CMR	G	10		
20	CANER Altin		A	9	(8)	3
55	CELIL Sagir		M	31	(2)	3
77	CEYHUN Eris		M	9	(6)	3
3	ELYASA Süme		D	6	(3)	
14	ERTAN Aktepe		M		(4)	
27	FATIH Özer		M		(5)	
6	Kais GHODHBANE	TUN	M	17		8
42	Ibrahima GUEYE	SEN	D	9		
9	Georgi IVANOV	BUL	A	2	(1)	1
28	KENAN Yelek		D	29		
16	KEREM Inan		G	21		
12	Dejan MAKSIC	SCG	G	3	(1)	
32	MARCIEL Back	BRA	M	3		
33	MEHMET Polat		D	9	(2)	
22	MUHAMMET Seker		D	16	(5)	1
7	MUSA Aydin		M	13	(18)	2
23	MUSTAFA Çlçek		M	21	(5)	
4	MUZAFFER Taskin		M		(2)	
30	Ivailo PETKOV	BUL	D	15		
8	Dejan RADJENOVIC	SCG	A	1	(1)	
19	RAFAEL Marques	BRA	A	25	(4)	7
36	SAMET Kiliç		M		(1)	
37	SEFA Aksoy		M		(2)	
10	SERKAN Aykut		A	17	(4)	10
75	TAMER Tuna		M	14	(2)	4
35	TOLGA Dogantez		D	16		

SIVASSPOR
Coach - Werner Lorant (GER)

2005

6/8	Malatyaspor	h	1-1	Hakki
13/8	Gaziantepsor	a	0-0	
20/8	Samsunspor	a	2-1	Anderson, Hakki
27/8	Vestel Manisaspor	h	1-2	Anderson
11/9	Galatasaray	a	0-2	
16/9	Trabzonspor	h	2-1	Sérgio, Balili
25/9	Kayseri Erciyesspor	a	0-0	

Turkey

Date	Opponent	H/A	Score	Scorers
1/10	Denizlispor	h	1-0	Anderson
15/10	Gençlerbirligi	a	1-0	Mehmet
23/10	Diyarbakirspor	h	4-1	Anderson, Hayrettin, Mohamed Ali 2 (1p)
30/10	Çaykur Rizespor	a	0-1	
6/11	Fenerbahçe	h	2-3	Sérgio, Anderson
20/11	Ankaraspor	a	1-1	Gökhan
26/11	Besiktas	h	1-3	Hakki
4/12	Kayserispor	a	2-2	Balili, Musa
11/12	Konyaspor	h	1-1	Mehmet
17/12	Ankaragücü	a	0-0	
2006				
22/1	Malatyaspor	a	0-0	
5/2	Samsunspor	h	0-3	
11/2	Vestel Manisaspor	a	1-3	og (Johana)
19/2	Galatasaray	h	0-0	
26/2	Trabzonspor	a	0-0	
5/3	Kayseri Erciyesspor	h	3-0	Hakki, Anderson 2
12/3	Denizlispor	a	0-4	
19/3	Gençlerbirligi	h	2-1	Hakki, Yasir
25/3	Diyarbakirspor	a	1-1	Musa
29/3	Gaziantepspor	h	0-0	
2/4	Çaykur Rizespor	h	1-2	Hakan Bayraktar
9/4	Fenerbahçe	a	0-3	
16/4	Ankaraspor	h	2-2	Gökhan, Anderson
23/4	Besiktas	a	1-0	Balili
30/4	Kayserispor	h	0-5	
7/5	Konyaspor	a	1-2	Balili
13/5	Ankaragücü	h	3-1	Balili, Anderson, Gökhan

No	Name	Nat	Pos	Aps	(s)	Gls
35	AKIN Vardar		G	2		
7	ANDERSON dos Santos	BRA	A	23	(3)	9
9	ATILLA Birlik		A	5	(2)	
17	Pini BALILI	ISR	A	18	(6)	5
40	CEM Can		M	15	(1)	
20	CEM Karaca		M	23	(6)	
99	DENNYS Lamego	BRA	M		(1)	
10	EDSON da Silva	BRA	A	2	(3)	
8	ERTUGRUL Arslan		M		(1)	
41	FATIH Tutar		M		(1)	
11	GÖKHAN Bozkaya		M	14	(8)	3
6	HAKAN Bayraktar		D	32	(1)	1
49	HAKAN Turan		M	1	(6)	
4	HAKKI Hocaoglu		D	32		5
58	HAYRETTIN Yerlikaya		D	32		1
22	IBRAHIM Aydemir		M	12	(10)	
33	ILHAN Ummak		M	1	(2)	
5	Raymond KALLA	CMR	D	18	(8)	
9	MEHMET Yildiz		A	4	(10)	2
10	MOHAMED ALI Kurtulus		A	7	(3)	2
51	MURAT Duman		D	31		
55	MURAT Sözgelmez		D	6	(1)	
36	MUSA Kus		M	24	(8)	2
26	OGUZ Daglaroglu		G	2		
1	Michael PETKOVIC	AUS	G	28		
30	Fran SÉRGIO	BRA	D	24	(1)	2
57	ÜNAL Demirkiran		M	1	(2)	
15	VEDAT Kaburtu		G	2	(1)	
42	YASIR Elmaci		M	13	(8)	1
64	YUSUF Akbel		M	1	(1)	
61	YUSUF Peken		M	1	(1)	

TRABZONSPOR
Coach - Senol Günes; (24/9/05) Orhan Çikrikçi; (3/10/05) Vahid Halilhodzic (BOS)

Date	Opponent	H/A	Score	Scorers
2005				
6/8	Kayserispor	h	2-1	Szymkowiak, Yattara
14/8	Konyaspor	a	0-0	
20/8	Ankaragücü	h	3-1	Fatih Tekke 2, Yattara
28/8	Malatyaspor	a	1-1	Fatih Tekke
11/9	Gaziantepspor	h	2-0	Yattara (p), Fatih Tekke
16/9	Sivasspor	a	1-2	Kürsat
23/9	Vestel Manisaspor	h	0-2	
2/10	Galatasaray	a	1-4	Mehmet
16/10	Samsunspor	a	1-3	Mehmet
21/10	Kayseri Erciyesspor	h	0-0	
28/10	Denizlispor	a	1-0	Kürsat
5/11	Gençlerbirligi	h	1-1	Fatih Tekke
19/11	Diyarbakirspor	a	0-3	
25/11	Çaykur Rizespor	h	3-1	Yattara, Fatih Tekke, Erdinç
2/12	Fenerbahçe	a	2-2	Lee, Fatih Tekke
11/12	Ankaraspor	h	2-3	Yattara, Szymkowiak
18/12	Besiktas	a	1-0	og (Adem)
2006				
22/1	Kayserispor	a	2-4	Fatih Tekke, Szymkowiak (p)
5/2	Ankaragücü	a	2-1	Fatih Tekke 2
12/2	Malatyaspor	h	1-0	Ali
19/2	Gaziantepspor	a	2-0	Szymkowiak, Djokaj
26/2	Sivasspor	h	0-0	
4/3	Vestel Manisaspor	a	2-1	Ömer Riza, Ferhat
12/3	Galatasaray	h	1-1	Gökdeniz
19/3	Samsunspor	h	2-1	og (Kenan), Fatih Tekke
26/3	Kayseri Erciyesspor	a	0-1	
30/3	Konyaspor	h	1-2	Fatih Tekke
2/4	Denizlispor	h	3-0	Fatih Tekke 2, Szymkowiak
9/4	Gençlerbirligi	a	0-1	
15/4	Diyarbakirspor	h	3-0	Yattara, Fatih Tekke, Gökdeniz
23/4	Çaykur Rizespor	a	6-1	Fatih Tekke 3, Gökdeniz 3
29/4	Fenerbahçe	h	2-3	Fatih Tekke 2
6/5	Ankaraspor	a	2-0	Fatih Tekke 2
14/5	Besiktas	h	1-2	Gökdeniz

No	Name	Nat	Pos	Aps	(s)	Gls
66	ADEM Koçak		M	17	(9)	
77	AHMET Sahin		G	1		
23	ALI Güzeldal		A	1	(5)	1
99	CELALEDDIN Koçak		D	19	(3)	
17	Ardian DJOKAJ	SCG	M	5	(4)	1
4	Fabiano ELLER	BRA	D	9	(2)	
34	EMRAH Eren		D	13		
38	ERDINÇ Yavuz		D	19	(1)	1
27	ERGIN Keles		M		(3)	
3	FATIH Akyel		D	14	(1)	
9	FATIH Tekke		A	28		22
85	FERHAT Çökmüs		M	6	(5)	1
2	FERIDUN Sungur		D		(2)	
61	GÖKDENIZ Karadeniz		M	14	(1)	6
22	HASAN Sönmez		G		(1)	
6	HASAN Üçüncü		M	11	(12)	
5	HÜSEYIN Çimsir		M	33		
25	IBRAHIM Ege		M	2	(6)	
1	JEFFERSON Galvão	BRA	G	26		
21	Tomás JUN	CZE	A	4	(12)	
49	KÜRSAT Duymus		D	9	(1)	2
19	LEE Eul-yong	KOR	M	27	(2)	1
10	MEHMET Yilmaz		A	7	(2)	2

Turkey

No	Name	Nat	Pos	Aps	(s)	Gls
88	ÖMER RIZA		A	7	(7)	1
14	ÖZGÜR Bayer		D	1	(2)	
55	Milan STEPANOV	SCG	D	15	(1)	
7	Miroslaw SZYMKOWIAK	POL	M	23	(2)	5
18	TAYFUN Cora		D	16	(2)	
29	TOLGA Zengin		G	7		
20	UFUKHAN Bayraktar		D	10	(3)	
8	VOLKAN Bekiroglu		M	4	(4)	
11	Ibrahima YATTARA	GUI	A	26	(6)	6

VESTEL MANISASPOR
Coach - Levent Eris; (2/10/05) Ersun Yanal

2005
Date	Opponent	h/a	Score	Scorers
7/8	Ankaragücü	h	2-2	og (Onur), Sinan
13/8	Malatyaspor	a	5-0	Serkan Dökme, Duarte, Sinan, Ugur (p), Meduna
21/8	Gaziantepsor	h	1-2	Meduna
27/8	Sivasspor	a	0-1	
11/9	Samsunspor	a	1-1	Mehmet Akdemir
18/9	Galatasaray	h	1-4	Böör
23/9	Trabzonspor	a	2-0	Meduna 2
1/10	Kayseri Erciyesspor	h	0-2	
16/10	Denizlispor	a	1-1	Ugur
23/10	Gençlerbirligi	h	0-3	
30/10	Diyarbakirspor	a	2-0	Johana, Mithat
6/11	Çaykur Rizespor	h	1-1	Hakan
19/11	Fenerbahçe	a	1-2	Johana
26/11	Ankaraspor	h	1-0	Meduna
4/12	Besiktas	a	1-3	Sinan
9/12	Kayserispor	h	1-0	D'Haene
18/12	Konyaspor	a	1-1	Zafer Demiray

2006
Date	Opponent	h/a	Score	Scorers
21/1	Ankaragücü	a	2-0	D'Haene, Arda
5/2	Gaziantepsor	a	1-1	Zelenka
11/2	Sivasspor	h	3-1	Selçuk, Hakan, Zelenka
19/2	Samsunspor	h	3-0	og (Ayari), Hakan (p), Zafer Demiray
25/2	Galatasaray	a	2-4	Holosko 2
4/3	Trabzonspor	h	1-2	Selçuk
10/3	Kayseri Erciyesspor	a	1-2	Zelenka
18/3	Denizlispor	h	4-2	Yilmaz, Holosko, Arda, Meduna
25/3	Gençlerbirligi	a	1-2	Yilmaz
29/3	Malatyaspor	h	4-3	Caner, Meduna 2, Tufan
2/4	Diyarbakirspor	h	0-3	
9/4	Çaykur Rizespor	a	1-4	Meduna
15/4	Fenerbahçe	h	5-3	Holosko, Caner, Sinan 3 (1p)
22/4	Ankaraspor	a	1-3	Sinan
28/4	Besiktas	h	0-1	
6/5	Kayserispor	a	2-7	Tufan, Selçuk
13/5	Konyaspor	h	0-0	

No	Name	Nat	Pos	Aps	(s)	Gls
23	AHMET Kolcu		M		(2)	
99	ARDA Turan		D	13	(2)	2
32	Zoltán BÖÖR	HUN	M	7		1
61	BÜLENT Ataman		G	26		
88	CANER Erkin		M	21	(3)	2
24	Karel D'HAENE	BEL	D	25	(1)	2
45	Fábio DUARTE	BRA	M	4	(6)	1
22	GÖKSEL Gencer		G	6		
81	GÜROL Azer		D	11	(6)	
16	HAKAN Balta		M	29	(2)	3
13	Filip HOLOSKO	SVK	A	17		4
7	INANÇ Gültekin		D	4	(2)	
19	Petr JOHANA	CZE	D	28		2
54	KENAN Aslanoglu		M	2		
17	MAHMUT Yilmaz		A		(1)	
26	Michal MEDUNA	CZE	A	22	(2)	9
9	MEHMET Akdemir		A	5	(10)	1
14	MEHMET AKIF Kengel		A		(3)	
66	Miguel MENDES	POR	M	2	(2)	
20	MITHAT Yavas		M	2	(7)	1
8	MURAT Özkan		A		(1)	
4	ÖZGÜR Vurur		D	2		
18	SELÇUK Inan		M	12	(1)	3
6	SERKAN Dökme		M	26	(4)	1
34	SERKAN Özsoy		D	6		
21	SINAN Kaloglu		A	13	(12)	7
33	TUFAN Esin		D	15	(5)	2
86	UFUK Ceylan		G	2		
10	UGUR Inceman		M	9		2
5	YILMAZ Özlem		M	15	(4)	2
2	YUNUS Ceylan		D	10	(8)	
11	ZAFER Demiray		A	20	(9)	2
25	ZAFER Sakar		M	4	(5)	
77	Lukás ZELENKA	CZE	M	16		3

DOMESTIC CUP 2005/06

GROUP PHASE
(Top two teams from each group qualify)

Group A
(26/10/05)
Diyarbakirspor 0 Malatyaspor 1
(27/10/05)
Galatasaray 4 Mersin Idmanyurdu 0
(20/12/05)
Malatyaspor 1 Galatasaray 1
(21/12/05)
Giresunspor 1 Diyarbakirspor 2
(31/1/06)
Mersin Idmanyurdu 0 Malatyaspor 1
(2/2/06)
Galatasaray 5 Giresunspor 0
(15/2/06)
Diyarbakirspor 0 Galatasaray 1
Giresunspor 2 Mersin Idmanyurdu 1
(22/2/06)
Malatyaspor 2 Giresunspor 0
Mersin Idmanyurdu 1 Diyarbakirspor 4
Positions: 1 Galatasaray 10pts; 2 Malatyaspor 10pts; 3 Diyarbakirspor 6pts; 4 Giresunspor 3pts; 5 Mersin Idmanyurdu 0pts

Group B
(26/10/05)
Gaziantepspor 2 Kayseri Erciyesspor 0
Ankaragücü 2 Fenerbahçe 3
(21/12/05)
Tarsus Idmanyurdu 3 Ankaragücü 4
Fenerbahçe 0 Gaziantepspor 2
(31/1/06)
Kayseri Erciyesspor 0 Fenerbahçe 0
(1/2/06)
Gaziantepspor 1 Tarsus Idmanyurdu 0
(15/2/06)
Ankaragücü 1 Gaziantepspor 1

Turkey

Tarsus Idmanyurdu 1 Kayseri Erciyesspor 1
(22/2/06)
Fenerbahçe 4 Tarsus Idmanyurdu 0
Kayseri Erciyesspor 2 Ankaragücü 1
Positions: 1 Gaziantepspor 10pts; 2 Fenerbahçe 7pts; 3 Kayseri Erciyesspor 5pts; 4 Ankaragücü 4pts; 5 Tarsus Idmanyurdu 1pt

Group C
(25/10/05)
Denizlispor 2 Altay 0
Trabzonspor 0 Kayserispor 3
(20/12/05)
Kayserispor 2 Denizlispor 3
(21/12/05)
Karagümrük 1 Trabzonspor 2
(1/2/06)
Altay 0 Kayserispor 4
Denizlispor 2 Karagümrük 0
(15/206)
Karagümrük 0 Altay 2
(16/2/06)
Trabzonspor 3 Denizlispor 1
(23/2/06)
Altay 0 Trabzonspor 1
Kayserispor 2, Karagümrük 0
Positions: 1 Kayserispor 9pts; 2 Denizlispor 9 pts; 3 Trabzonspor 9pts; 4 Altay 3pts; 5 Karagümrük 0pts

Group D
(26/10/05)
Konyaspor 1 Besiktas 1
Sariyer 2 Samsunspor 3
(21/12/05)
Inegölspor 1 Sariyer 1
Samsunspor 5 Konyaspor 3
(1/2/06)
Besiktas 3 Samsunspor 0
Konyaspor 2 Inegölspor 0
(14/2/06)
Inegölspor 1 Besiktas 0
(15/2/06)
Sariyer 1 Konyaspor 2
(21/2/06)
Besiktas 3 Sariyer 0
Samsunspor 2 Inegölspor 1
Positions: 1 Samsunspor 9pts; 2 Besiktas 7pts; 3 Konyaspor 7pts; 4 Inegölspor 4pts; 5 Sariyer 1pt

QUARTER-FINALS
(8/3/06 & 23/3/06)
Malatyaspor 1 *(Senkerik 35)*, Gaziantepspor 0
Gaziantepspor 2 *(Ekrem 52, Kirita 86)*, Malatyaspor 0
(Gaziantepspor 2-1)

(8/3/06 & 22/3/06)
Fenerbahçe 2 *(Luciano 24, Alex 86)*, Galatasaray 1 *(Ümit 56)*
Galatasaray 3 *(Ayhan 11, Necati 35, Hakan 76)*, Fenerbahçe 2 *(Tuncay 7, Appiah 72)*
(4-4; Fenerbahçe on away goals)

(9/3/06 & 21/3/06)
Besiktas 2 *(Gökhan Güleç 65, Bobo 76)*, Kayserispor 0
Kayserispor 1*(Muhammet Hanifi 68)* Besiktas 0
(Besiktas 2-1)

(9/3/06 & 22/3/06)
Denizlispor 1 *(De Oliveria 18)*, Samsunspor 0
Samsunspor 1 *(Multaharju 50og)*, Denizlispor 1 *(Burak 43)*
(Denizlispor 2-1)

SEMI-FINALS
(5/4/06 & 19/4/06)
Gaziantepspor 1 *(Veysel 15)*, Besiktas 3 *(Tümer 56, Bobo 63, 76)*
Besiktas 2 *(Gökhan Güleç 44, Bobo 64)*, Gaziantepspor 0
(Besiktas 5-1)

(6/4/06 & 18/4/06)
Denizlispor 0, Fenerbahçe 4 *(Deniz 24, Márcio Nobre 36, Semih 63, Marco Aurélio 73)*
Fenerbahçe 3 *(Mehmet 16, Semih 52, 73)*, Denizlispor 0
(Fenerbahçe 7-0)

FINAL
(3/5/06)
Atatürk Stadium, Izmir
BESIKTAS 3 *(Tümer 31, 115, Gökhan Güleç 35)*
FENERBAHÇE 2 *(Alex 54, Mehmet 80)*
(aet)
Referee - Bülent Demirlek
BESIKTAS : Córdoba, Ibrahim Toraman (Sergen 86), Gökhan Zan, Koray, Ibrahim Üzülmez, Okan (Ali Günes 73), Kléberson, Tümer, Mehmet (Ali Tandogan 80), Gökhna Güleç, Bobo.
FENERBAHÇE: Volkan, Deniz, Önder, Luciano, Ümit, Appiah, Marco Aurélio, Selçuk (Semih 46), Tuncay (Mehmet 46), Alex (Serkan 102), Anelka.
Sent off: Marco Aurélio (110)

SECOND LEVEL FINAL TABLE 2005/06

		Pld	W	D	L	F	A	Pts
1	Bursaspor	34	21	8	5	56	26	71
2	Antalyaspor	34	20	7	7	68	34	67
3	Altay	34	18	10	6	54	39	64
4	Sakaryaspor	34	17	9	8	54	36	60
5	Istanbulspor	34	16	6	12	58	35	54
6	Orduspor	34	14	12	8	53	42	54
7	Istanbul Belediye	34	13	13	8	43	31	52
8	Türk Telecom	34	11	12	11	40	40	45
9	Kocaelispor	34	11	12	11	41	41	45
10	Elazigspor	34	11	12	11	40	45	45
11	Mardinspor	34	11	10	13	38	41	43
12	Gaziantep Belediye	34	12	5	17	47	52	41
13	Karsiyaka	34	10	11	13	47	49	41
14	Usakspor	34	11	7	16	40	54	40
15	Akçaabat Sebatspor	34	7	13	14	37	54	34
16	Mersin Idmanyurdu	34	6	11	17	30	54	29
17	Yozgatspor	34	6	10	18	32	55	28
18	Çanakkale Dardanelspor	34	5	4	25	23	73	19

PROMOTION PLAY-OFFS
Altay 1, Orduspor 0
Sakaryaspor 2, Istanbulspor 2 (5-3 on pens)
Sakaryaspor 4, Altay 1

Ukraine

Quarter-finals at first attempt

The 2006 World Cup will go down as a watershed in the history of Ukrainian football. Not content with becoming the first European nation to qualify for the tournament, Ukraine overachieved in Germany, marking their major-tournament debut by reaching the quarter-finals.

Oleh Blokhin's team were the only one of five representatives from Eastern Europe to survive the opening round. While Poland, Croatia, the Czech Republic and Serbia & Montenegro all bit the dust early, Ukraine remained in Germany until the last day in June, when they were knocked out by eventual winners Italy.

Unlike Argentina, Brazil and England, the other three beaten quarter-finalists, Ukraine never had serious pretensions of winning the trophy, so their elimination brought no great pain. Blokhin had made a few vainglorious battle-cries about winning the trophy immediately after qualification, but those were mostly in jest. In fact, star striker Andriy Shevchenko was decidedly unamused, suggesting that the comments only heaped unnecessary pressure on the team.

Four-nil, four-nil

Against Spain in their opening game, Ukraine looked like a team under pressure. Overawed by the occasion, outplayed by their opponents and seemingly over-reliant on Shevchenko, who was only just recovering from a knee injury, they were thrashed 4-0 and looked destined for an early flight home. Luckily, though, the draw had been kind to them. Next up were Saudi Arabia, and Ukraine thoroughly enjoyed their first competitive international against non-European opposition, hammering their hapless opponents 4-0 in Hamburg.

Needing only a draw against Tunisia to reach the last 16, Ukraine edged home in Berlin with a fortuitous Shevchenko penalty. It was a desperately poor game, and so was their next one, against Switzerland in Cologne, but after two hours of goalless tedium Ukraine prevailed on penalties to earn themselves a quarter-final date with Italy. The Azzurri predictably sent them home, winning 3-0.

To reach the last eight was a major achievement, but Ukraine won few admirers. Much was expected of Shevchenko, but, perhaps because of his injury, he looked a pale shadow of the Milan superstriker and former European Footballer of the Year. Ukraine's best performer was blond midfielder and set-piece taker Maxym Kalynychenko, but, like the team in general, he caught the eye in one match only – against the Saudis. Oleh Gusev was energetic on the right touchline, while midfielder Anatoliy Tymoshchuk commanded the team tactically and diligently from his base camp in front of the defence. But otherwise none of the men in the bright yellow really stood out.

Monstrous task

Having broken their World Cup duck, Ukraine will hope to do likewise in the European Championship. But, grouped as they are with the two teams that contested the World Cup final, France and Italy, their task of reaching the 2008 finals will be monstrously difficult. Even though Blokhin and his players will have gained invaluable experience from their World Cup adventure, and are young enough to stay together for at least another two years, a trip to the Alps in 2008 has to be considered unlikely, if not impossible.

With the odd exception (Shevchenko, Kalynychenko, Andriy Gusin, Andriy Voronin), the

Ukraine

Ukrainian World Cup squad was full of Ukrainian league players, with a predictably sizeable percentage belonging to the nation's top two clubs, Dynamo Kiev and Shakhtar Donetsk.

There was no evidence of any cliques or warring factions between Dynamo and Shakhtar players in Germany, but for the whole of the season leading up to the World Cup the two clubs were engaged in a high-octane duel for supremacy in the Ukrainian Premier League. In fact, the battle was so intense and closely fought that the winner could only be determined after a championship play-off on neutral terrain.

The quest for domestic silverware became even more important after both Dynamo and Shakhtar failed to qualify for the UEFA Champions League. Dynamo's run of seven successive appearances in the group phase was brutally ended by Swiss upstarts FC Thun, who eliminated them in the second qualifying round, thus ending the club's interest in all European competition in one fell swoop. Shakhtar, as reigning Ukrainian champions, entered a round later, but the Italians of Inter proved too smart and street-wise for their former coach, Mircea Lucescu, and Shakhtar had to earn their Euro corn in the UEFA Cup instead. They did well in the group phase, winning three out of four matches, but were eliminated by French club Lille in February after a frustrating 0-0 draw in Donetsk.

Dynamo's early European eclipse proved fatal for new coach Leonid Buryak. The former Ukraine national team boss (Blokhin's predecessor) and Dynamo legend was moved 'upstairs' after the defeat by Thun and replaced by loyal coaching staff member Anatoliy Demyanenko. It was meant to be a temporary move while Dynamo president Ihor Surkis went shopping for a big-name foreign coach, but Demyanenko did so well that by Christmas, following a run of ten successive victories that included a vital 1-0 win at Shakhtar, he was given the job for the remainder of the season.

Strong start

Shakhtar made their usual strong start, winning their first seven matches (it had been ten and nine, respectively, in the previous two seasons), but their extra-curricular activity in Europe proved burdensome. Lucescu's men were surprisingly knocked out of the Ukrainian Cup by First Division leaders Karpaty Lviv, and it was immediately after a 2-0 victory in Stuttgart that they lost at home to Dynamo – a result that enabled their rivals to leapfrog into top spot and thereby claim the notional title of 'winter champions' – even if it was only early November.

Because of the World Cup, an additional four rounds of the championship had been brought forward from spring to late autumn. By the time of the actual winter break, Dynamo had extended their lead to three points.

With Serhiy Rebrov, back from a long spell abroad, proving inspirational in a new withdrawn striker role, the club from the capital kept their noses in front for several weeks after the spring resumption. It even looked as if they might complete the 30-match campaign undefeated. But on April 17, in round 26, those hopes were shattered when they lost 2-0 at home to a Dnipro Dnipropetrovsk side that had been revitalised by

NATIONAL TEAM RESULTS 2005/06

15/8/05	Israel	H	Kiev	0-0	(aet; 3-5 on pens)
17/8/05	Serbia & Montenegro	H	Kiev	2-1	Rebrov (62), Nazarenko (71)
3/9/05	Georgia (WCQ)	A	Tbilisi	1-1	Rotan (44)
7/9/05	Turkey (WCQ)	H	Kiev	0-1	
8/10/05	Albania (WCQ)	H	Dnipropetrovsk	2-2	Shevchenko (45), Rotan (86)
12/10/05	Japan	H	Kiev	1-0	Gusin (89p)
28/2/06	Azerbaijan	A	Baku	0-0	
28/5/06	Costa Rica	H	Kiev	4-0	Nazarenko (29), Vorobei (35), Kalynychenko (40), Belik (56)
2/6/06	Italy	N	Lausanne	0-0	
5/6/06	Libya	N	Gossau	3-0	Yezerskyi (50), Belik (87), Vorobei (89)
8/6/06	Luxembourg	A	Luxembourg	3-0	Voronin (55), Shevchenko (83), Kalynychenko (84)
14/6/06	Spain (WCF)	N	Leipzig	0-4	
19/6/06	Saudi Arabia (WCF)	N	Hamburg	4-0	Rusol (4), Rebrov (36), Shevchenko (46), Kalynychenko (84)
23/6/06	Tunisia (WCF)	N	Berlin	1-0	Shevchenko (70p)
26/6/06	Switzerland (WCF)	N	Cologne	0-0	(aet; 3-0 on pens)
30/6/06	Italy (WCF)	N	Hamburg	0-3	

Ukraine

Serhiy Rebrov – a new role proved productive at Dynamo Kiev

after 20 minutes. But Shakhtar fought back to score twice themselves, through defender Dmytro Chyhrynskyi and Brazilian import Jadson, early in the second half. The two clubs could not be separated, and the game finished 2-2. The World Cup preparations would have to be put on hold. It was time for the Golden Game.

Death or glory

Four days later the two gladiators reconvened in neutral Kryvyi Rih. This time it was a fight to the death, with penalty-kicks required if necessary. A crowd of nearly 30,000 came to watch two teams that had not lost a league game away from home all season. The first half was predictably cagey, but on the hour mark Shakhtar went ahead when Romanian striker Ciprian Marica converted from close range at the second attempt. Dynamo battled back to equalise, through Brazilian substitute Rodolfo, ten minutes from time to send the game into extra-time, but it was Shakhtar substitute Julius Aghahowa who had the final say, powerfully heading home the winning – and title-clinching – goal with 100 minutes on the clock.

Remarkably, it was the Nigerian striker's only goal of the league campaign. But it was a golden goal in every sense. With Shakhtar owner Rinat Akhmetov having spent a fortune on the team, a trophyless season would have been considered disastrous. But now, thanks to Aghahowa's timely strike, all the investment was worthwhile. No fewer than 18 foreigners donned the Shakhtar orange and black during the course of the season. The large Brazilian contingent was hugely influential, collectively scoring 38 of the team's 64 goals during the regular league campaign. Striker Brandão's individual haul of 15 put him level with Arsenal Kiev's Nigerian striker Emmanuel Okoduwa at the head of the Premier League standings.

Arsenal needed all of Okoduwa's goals, including seven in the last four games, to avoid relegation. More than half the teams in the division were embroiled in the relegation scrap. While the gap between the top two clubs and third-placed Chornomorets Odesa was a massive 30 points, only 12 points separated Chornomorets and 15th-placed Volyn Lutsk, the team that eventually lost their place (on goal difference) to join stranded Zakarpattya Uzhgorod (60 points behind Shakhtar and Dynamo) in the First Division. Up in their place, a few weeks later, came two famous names from the Soviet era, Zorya Lugansk and Karpaty Lviv.

the arrival in mid-season of club icon (and Dynamo old boy) Oleh Protasov as coach.

That defeat let Shakhtar back in, and although they ceded two points four days later with a goalless draw at home to lowly Vorskla Poltava, when Dynamo did likewise away to Tavriya Simferopol in round 29, it left the two title-chasers level on points with just their summit meeting in Kiev to come. It was a classic winner-takes-all scenario, but, as in Russia, the regulation was that if the top two teams ended the season with the same number of points, goal difference and head-to-head records were irrelevant. Instead, there would be a play-off – a Golden Game.

Dynamo, with home advantage, were expected to regain the title. They were on for a Double, having beaten Metalurg Zaporizhzhya 1-0 in the Cup final eight days earlier. Everything looked to be going to plan when regular hitman Maxim Shatskikh and young gun Artem Milevskyi put Dynamo 2-0 up

Ukraine

NATIONAL TEAM APPEARANCES 2005/06

Coach – Oleh BLOKHIN

Player	DOB	Club	Isr	Scg	GEO	TUR	ALB	Jpn	Azb	Crc	Ita	Lby	Lux	ESP	SAU	TUN	SUI	ITA	Caps	Goals
Olexandr SHOVKOVSKYI	2/1/75	Dynamo Kyiv	G		G	G	G			G46	G	G46	G	G	G	G	G	G	73	-
Andriy NESMACHNYI	28/2/79	Dynamo Kyiv	D	D67	D	D		D	D	D46	D	D	D46	D	D	D	D	D	54	-
Vladyslav VASHCHUK	2/1/75	Chornomrets Odesa /Dynamo Kyiv	D	D			D		D	s46	D	D	D46	D			D	s45	61	1
Vyacheslav SVIDERSKYI	1/1/79	Saturn Ram. (RUS) /Arsenal Kyiv	D59							D46	s90	s46	s46		D	D		D20	9	-
Volodymyr YEZERSKYI	15/11/76	Dnipro Dniprop'vsk	D	D55	D				D	s46	D	D	D46	D					25	1
Anatoliy TYMOSHCHUK	30/3/79	Shakhtar Donetsk	M	s55	M	M	D	D65		M46	M87	s46		M	M	M	M	M	60	1
Ruslan ROTAN	29/10/81	Dynamo Kyiv	M		M	M68	M	s46	M56	M46	M74	s46	s46	M64	s71		s75		22	3
Maxym KALYNYCHENKO	26/1/79	Spartak M (RUS)	M55						M77	M	M56	M	s63		M	M75	M75	M	25	3
Serhiy NAZARENKO	16/2/80	Dnipro Dniprop'vsk	A63	s59	s73		A70	s46 /90	s77	A62	s74	A46	s46						15	2
Serhiy REBROV	3/6/74	Dynamo Kyiv	A56	s61	s66				s46			M58	s64	M71	M54	s93			74	15
Oleh VENHLYNSKYI	21/3/78	AEK (GRE)	A77	s46		s68	s46												10	1
Oleh GUSEV	25/4/83	Dynamo Kyiv	s55	M		M	M		M46	s46		M46	M	M46	M		D	D	M	30	1
Olexiy BELIK	15/2/81	Shakhtar Donetsk	s56		A	s58	A46	A		A	s56	A	A46					s72	16	4
Olexandr RADCHENKO	19/7/76	Dnipro Dniprop'vsk	s59	s67			s46												17	-
Andriy GUSIN	11/12/72	Krylyla Sovetov (RUS)	s63	M	M	s84		M	M67	s46	M90	s46	M46	M46	s78	s75	D	D	69	9
Olexandr KOSYRIN	18/8/82	Chornomorets Odesa	s77																7	-
Maxym STARTSEV	20/1/80	Kryvbas Kryvyi Rih		G			G												2	-
Andriy RUSOL	16/1/83	Dnipro Dniprop'vsk	D	D	D	D	s90	D46	D	D	D46	D	D	D	D		D45		27	2
Oleh SHELAYEV	5/11/76	Dnipro Dniprop'vsk	M		M80	M	M46	s67	s62	M87	M	M	s46	M	M	M	M		24	-
Olexandr RYKUN	6/5/78	Dnipro Dniprop'vsk		M59			M46												7	-
Andriy VORONIN	21/7/79	B Leverkusen (GER)	A61	A73	A84	A		A46	s46	A	A46	s46	A	A78	A	A110			36	4
Andriy SHEVCHENKO	29/9/76	Milan (ITA)	A46	A		A58						s58	A	A85	A88	A	A		69	31
Serhiy FEDOROV	18/2/75	Dynamo Kyiv		D	D	D		D											28	1
Serhiy SHYSHCHENKO	13/1/76	Metalurg Donetsk			M66	s80		M46											14	1
Vyacheslav SHEVCHUK	13/5/79	Shakhtar Donetsk					M												4	-
Andriy VOROBEI	29/11/78	Shakhtar Donetsk					s70	A	s46	A	A	s46	A63	s46		s54	M93	s20	57	7
Olexandr YATSENKO	24/2/85	FC Kharkiv					D												1	-
Olexandr MAXYMOV	13/2/85	FC Kharkiv						s65											1	-
Bohdan SHUST	4/3/86	Shakhtar Donetsk								G	s46		s46						3	-
Serhiy SEREBRENNIKOV	1/9/76	RSC Charleroi (BEL)						s56											12	1
Artem MILEVSKYI	12/1/85	Dynamo Kyiv												s85	s88	s110	A72		4	-

Ukraine

EUROPEAN CUPS 2005/06

UEFA CHAMPIONS LEAGUE

SHAKHTAR DONETSK
3rd qualifying round INTERNAZIONALE (ITA)
H 0-2
Lastuvka, Hübschman, Rat, Barcauan, Tymoshchuk, Duljaj (Fernandinho 69), Srna, Matuzalem, Elano (Jadson 58), Belik (Marica 72), Brandão.
A 1-1 *Elano (24)*
Lastuvka, Hübschman, Rat, Lewandowski, Duljaj (Fernandinho 86), Tymoshchuk, Srna, Matuzalem, Elano (Jadson 65), Brandão, Marica (Belik 71).

DYNAMO KYIV
2nd qualifying round FC THUN (SUI)
H 2-2 *Gusev (20), Shatskikh (45)*
Shovkovskyi, Rodolfo, Yussuf, Gavrancic, Nesmachnyi, Leko (Aliyev 68), Gusev, Rotan, Belkevich (Diogo RIncón 58), Rebrov, Shatskikh (Verpakovskis 58).
A 0-1
Shovkovskyi, Rodolfo, Rodrigo, Yussuf, Gavrancic, Nesmachnyi, Cernat, Gusev, Rotan (Belkevich 69), Shatskikh (Cleber 62), Cesnauskis (Diogo Rincon 56).

UEFA CUP

METALURG DONETSK
2nd qualifying round FC SOPRON (HUN)
A 3-0 *Shyshchenko (53), Oleksiyenko (85, 90)*
Virt, Grncarov, Florea, Checher, Aliuta (Kondrashchenko 89), Zakarluyka (Melikyan 75), Zotov, Polyanskyi, Ristic, Tkachenko, Shyshchenko (Olexiyenko 79).
H 2-1 *Zotov (56), Oleksiyenko (89p)*
Virt, Grncarov, Florea, Checher, Busaidi, Aliuta (Tkachenko 70), Zotov, Polyanskyi, Ristic (Olexiyenko 81), Zakarluyka, Shyshchenko (Melikyan 85).

1st round PAOK (GRE)
A 1-1 *Shyshchenko (68)*
Virt, Gjuzelov, Né, Florea, Aliuta (Melikyan 92), Zotov, Zakarluyka, Ristic (Olexiyenko 83), Shyshchenko, Tkachenko, Kosyrin (Priyomov 89).
H 2-2 *Kosyrin (39), Shyshchenko (57)*
Virt, Gjuzelov (Grncarov 90), Checher, Florea, Aliuta, Zotov, Zakarluyka, Ristic (Priyomov 84), Shyshchenko, Tkachenko, Kosyrin.

DNIPRO DNIPROPETROVSK
2nd qualifying round BANANTS YEREVAN (ARM)
A 4-2 *Yezerskyi (49), Kornilenko (82 83), Balabanov (85)*
Medin, Hrytsai, Yezerskyi, Rusol, Radchenko (Kornilenko 75), Shelayev, Lysytskyi (Rykun 46), Kostyshyn, Semochko, Nazarenko, Melashchenko (Balabanov 67).
H 4-0 *Shelayev (10p 45), Rykun (32), Balabanov (70)*
Kernozenko, Yezerskyi, Kornilenko, Radchenko (Kostyshyn 46), Shelayev, Rusol, Rykun, Semochko, Kravchenko (Balabanov 52), Shershun, Nazarenko (Hrytsai 46).

1st round HIBERNIAN (SCO)
A 0-0
Kusliy, Hrytsai, Kotenko, Radchenko, Shershun, Shelayev, Rusol, Semochko, Andriyenko (Motuz 78), Kornilenko (Balabanov 67), Kravchenko (Kostyshyn 81).
H 5-1 *Nazarenko (1), Shershun (26), Shelayev (39p), Melashchenko (87, 90)*
Kusliy, Hrytsai, Shelayev, Kotenko (Kravchenko 62), Radchenko, Shershun, Rusol, Semochko, Andriyenko (Lysytskyi 46), Kornilenko (Melashchenko 68), Nazarenko.

2nd round Group D
Match 1 AZ (HOL)
H 1-2 *Matyukhin (67)*
Kusliy, Yezerskyi, Shelayev, Radchenko, Shershun (Motuz 64), Matyukhin, Rusol, Semochko (Kornilenko 60), Andriyenko (Kravchenko 43), Nazarenko, Melashchenko.

Match 2 MIDDLESBROUGH (ENG)
A 0-3
Kusliy, Yezerskyi, Shershun, Shelayev, Radchenko, Rusol (Lysytskyi 58), Semochko, Rykun, Mykhailenko (Motuz 66), Nazarenko, Kostyshyn (Melashchenko 52).

Match 3 LITEX LOVECH (BUL)
H 0-2
Kernozenko, Yezerskyi, Radchenko, Rusol, Lysytskyi, Shelayev (Kornilenko 56), Balabanov (Hrytsa 65), Rykun, Semochko, Kravchenko (Kostyshyn 72), Nazarenko.

Match 4 GRASSHOPPER-CLUB ZÜRICH (SUI)
A 3-2 *Nazarenko (39), Kravchenko (62), Mykhailenko (83)*
Kernozenko, Hrytsai, Yezerskyi (Matyukhin 22), Shelayev, Rusol, Lysytskyi (Mykhailenko 45), Kostyshyn, Semochko, Kravchenko (Kornilenko 75), Balabanov, Nazarenko.

SHAKHTAR DONETSK
1st round DEBRECENI VSC (HUN)
H 4-1 *Elano (1), Brandão (34, 45p), Vorobei (73)*
Lastuvka, Srna, Tolga, Lewandowski, Rat, Duljaj, Matuzalem (Jadson 75), Elano, Brandão (Belik 84), Fernandinho, Marica (Vorobei 46).
A 2-0 *Brandão (20), Elano (24)*
Lastuvka, Srna, Rat, Tymoshchuk, Matuzalem, Elano, Brandão, Marica (Aghahowa 60), Tolga, Lewandowski (Hübschman 46), Duljaj (Fernandinho 69).

2nd round Group G
Match 1 PAOK (GRE)
H 1-0 *Brandão (68p)*
Shutkov, Srna, Lewandowski, Tolga, Rat, Tymoshchuk, Matuzalem, Elano, Duljaj, Brandão, Marica (Aghahowa 59).

Match 2 VFB STUTTGART (GER)
A 2-0 *Fernandinho (31), Marica (88)*
Shutkov, Srna, Lewandowski, Tolga, Rat, Tymoshchuk, Matuzalem (Marica 84), Duljaj, Fernandinho (Vorobei 75), Elano, Brandão (Belik 90).

Match 3 RAPID BUCURESTI (ROM)
H 0-1
Lastuvka, Lewandowski, Huubschman, Rat, Tymoshchuk, Matuzalem, Duljaj, Elano (Jadson 75), Belik, Stoican (Srna 46), Aghahowa (Fernandinho 55).

Match 4 STADE RENNAIS FC (FRA)
A 1-0 *Elano (38p)*
Shutkov, Srna, Lewandowski, Hübschman, Rat, Tymoshchuk, Matuzalem, Duljaj, Elano (Brandão 70), Fernandinho (Fomin 90), Aghahowa (Marica 79).

3rd round LILLE OSC (FRA)
A 2-3 *Brandão (89), Marica (90)*
Shust, Srna, Chyhrynskyi, Lewandowski (Tymoshchuk 60), Hübschman, Rat, Duljaj (Marica 69), Matuzalem, Elano (Jadson 75), Fernandinho, Brandão.
H 0-0
Shust, Srna, Chyhrynskyi, Tolga, Rat, Duljaj, Matuzalem, Elano (Jadson 72), Fernandinho (Vorobei 63), Marica, Brandão (Aghahowa 81).

Ukraine

TOP GOALSCORERS 2005/06

15	BRANDÃO (Shakhtar Donetsk)	
	Emmanuel OKODUWA (Arsenal Kyiv)	
13	Olexandr KOSYRIN (Metalurg Donetsk/Chornomorets Odesa)	
	Serhiy REBROV (Dynamo Kyiv)	
	Vasyl SACHKO (Volyn Lutsk)	
11	CLÉBER (Dynamo Kyiv)	
10	Ara AKOBYAN (Stal Alchevsk)	
	MATUZALEM (Shakhtar Donetsk)	
	DIOGO RINCÓN (Dynamo Kyiv)	
9	Vasil GIGIADZE (Kryvbas Kryvyi Rih)	

LEAGUE RESULTS/SCORERS/APPEARANCES/GOALS 2005/06

ARSENAL KYIV
Coach – Olexandr Baranov; (31/10/05) Olexandr Zavarov

2005

Date	Opponent	H/A	Score	Scorers
12/7	Chornomorets Odesa	a	1-1	Gancarczyk
17/7	Dynamo Kyiv	h	0-2	
23/7	Volyn Lutsk	a	1-2	Okoduwa
31/7	Dnipro Dnipropetrovsk	h	1-0	Okoduwa
7/8	FC Kharkiv	a	1-3	Okoduwa
21/8	Kryvbas Kryvyi Rih	h	1-1	Kostyuk (p)
28/8	Tavriya Simferopol	a	1-0	Okoduwa
11/9	Shakhtar Donetsk	h	0-0	
18/9	Metalurg Zaporizhzhya	a	2-2	Okoduwa, Mizin
25/9	Metalist Kharkiv	a	2-1	Mizin, Kowalczyk
2/10	Stal Alchevsk	h	1-1	Kowalczyk
16/10	Zakarpattya Uzhgorod	a	1-2	Okoduwa
23/10	FC Illichivets Mariupol	h	0-2	
30/10	Vorskla Poltava	a	0-2	
6/11	Metalurg Donetsk	h	0-2	
20/11	Chornomorets Odesa	h	0-1	
27/11	Dynamo Kyiv	a	1-3	Kowalczyk
4/12	Volyn Lutsk	h	2-1	Babych, Okoduwa
10/12	Dnipro Dnipropetrovsk	a	0-1	

2006

Date	Opponent	H/A	Score	Scorers
5/3	FC Kharkiv	h	0-0	
12/3	Kryvbas Kryvyi Rih	a	2-1	Peric, Pershin
19/3	Tavriya Simferopol	h	1-0	Peric
25/3	Shakhtar Donetsk	a	0-1	
1/4	Metalurg Zaporizhzhya	h	1-2	Okoduwa
9/4	Metalist Kharkiv	h	1-1	Pershin
15/4	Stal Alchevsk	a	0-1	
22/4	Zakarpattya Uzhgorod	h	2-1	Okoduwa, Mizin
28/4	FC Illichivets Mariupol	a	5-3	Kowalczyk, Romanchuk, Okoduwa 2, Mizin (p)
6/5	Vorskla Poltava	h	2-0	Okoduwa 2
10/5	Metalurg Donetsk	a	2-2	Okoduwa 2

No	Name	Nat	Pos	Aps	(s)	Gls
26	Volodymyr ANIKEYEV		D	3	(1)	
7	Kostyantyn BABYCH		A	6	(8)	1
43	Roman BAIRASHEVSKYI		G	9		
23	Ivan BARANOV		M	1	(2)	
7	Andriy BASHLAI		D		(2)	
19	Olexandr BATALSKYI		A	1	(10)	
1	Ihor BAZHAN		G	18		
33	Yuriy BENIO		D	19		
32	Dario BRGELES	CRO	M	8	(3)	
4	Mirko BUNJEVCEVIC	SCG	D	15	(3)	
24	Volodymyr CHERNIKOV		M	1	(1)	
12	Vadym DEONAS		G	2		
15	Patrick Guyome EBANDA	CMR	M	19	(1)	
2	Seweryn GANCARCZYK	POL	D	4		1
9	Olexiy IVANOV		M	20	(5)	
22	Jaba KANKAVA	GEO	M	7	(3)	
18	Vasyl KARDASH		M	3	(1)	
8	Serhiy KONOVALOV		M	2	(4)	
55	Ihor KOSTYUK		M	9	(3)	1
6	Maciej KOWALCZYK	POL	M	13	(9)	4
30	Sergei KRYUCHIKHIN	RUS	D		(1)	
21	Serhiy MIZIN		M	23	(3)	4
20	Emmanuel Oseyi OKODUWA	NGA	A	29		15
39	Ivan PERIC	SCG	M	6	(1)	2
5	Olexandr PERSHIN		D	22	(2)	2
17	Ivica PIRIC	CRO	D	15	(4)	
16	Vladimir RIBIC	SCG	A	2	(5)	
2	Olexandr ROMANCHUK		M	9		1
25	Vitaliy ROZGON		D	16	(4)	
22	Andrei RYABYKH	RUS	A		(1)	
26	Oleh SHANDRUK		D	8		
14	Ihor SKOBA		M	18	(2)	
4	Vyacheslav SVIDERSKYI		D	10		
33	Olexandr SYTNYK		M		(1)	
24	Alexei UVAROV	RUS	M	8	(4)	
41	Serhiy VOKALCHUK		G	1		
28	Dmytro VOROBEI		M		(2)	
10	Kostyantyn YAROSHENKO		D	3	(3)	

CHORNOMORETS ODESA
Coach – Semen Altman

2005

Date	Opponent	H/A	Score	Scorers
12/7	Arsenal Kyiv	h	1-1	Kosyrin
17/7	Stal Alchevsk	a	1-0	Kosyrin (p)
23/7	Zakarpattya Uzhgorod	h	2-0	Nagy, Kosyrin
31/7	FC Illichivets Mariupol	a	1-0	Kyrlyk
7/8	Vorskla Poltava	h	1-2	Kosyrin
21/8	Metalurg Donetsk	a	2-3	og (Checher), Kosyrin
28/8	Metalist Kharkiv	h	5-2	Bilozor, Loshankov 2, Kosyrin 2
11/9	Dynamo Kyiv	h	0-1	
18/9	Volyn Lutsk	a	3-0	Loshankov, Tereshchenko, Miterev
25/9	Dnipro Dnipropetrovsk	h	0-0	
2/10	FC Kharkiv	a	1-0	Poltavets
16/10	Kryvbas Kryvyi Rih	h	2-1	Miterev 2
23/10	Tavriya Simferopol	a	1-1	Lutsenko
30/10	Shakhtar Donetsk	h	0-1	
5/11	Metalurg Zaporizhzhya	a	0-1	
20/11	Arsenal Kyiv	a	1-0	Poltavets
27/11	Stal Alchevsk	h	2-2	Miterev 2
4/12	Zakarpattya Uzhgorod	a	1-2	Miterev (p)
8/12	FC Illichivets Mariupol	h	1-2	Kyrlyk (p)

2006

Date	Opponent	H/A	Score	Scorers
5/3	Vorskla Poltava	a	2-1	Kirilchik, Bugaev
12/3	Metalurg Donetsk	h	1-0	og (Busaidi)
18/3	Metalist Kharkiv	a	1-1	Kyrlyk (p)
26/3	Dynamo Kyiv	a	1-4	Poltavets
2/4	Volyn Lutsk	h	2-0	Poltavets (p), Bugaev
9/4	Dnipro Dnipropetrovsk	a	2-1	Osipov, Kyrlyk
16/4	FC Kharkiv	h	1-0	Kyrlyk (p)
22/4	Kryvbas Kryvyi Rih	a	0-1	
29/4	Tavriya Simferopol	h	1-2	Kyrlyk (p)
6/5	Shakhtar Donetsk	a	0-2	

Ukraine

FINAL LEAGUE TABLE 2005/06

		Pld	Home					Away					Total					Pts
			W	D	L	F	A	W	D	L	F	A	W	D	L	F	A	
1	Shakhtar Donetsk	30	11	3	1	29	4	12	3	0	35	10	23	6	1	64	14	75
2	Dynamo Kyiv	30	9	5	1	37	14	14	1	0	31	6	23	6	1	68	20	75
3	Chornomorets Odesa	30	6	4	5	19	14	7	2	6	17	17	13	6	11	36	31	45
4	FC Illichivets Mariupol	30	7	2	6	19	17	5	5	5	11	17	12	7	11	30	34	43
5	Metalist Kharkiv	30	8	2	5	20	20	4	5	6	15	22	12	7	11	35	42	43
6	Dnipro Dnipropetrovsk	30	6	4	5	16	12	5	6	4	17	11	11	10	9	33	23	43
7	Tavriya Simferopol	30	6	2	7	17	16	5	4	6	12	15	11	6	13	29	31	39
8	Metalurg Zaporizhzhya	30	8	2	5	22	21	3	4	8	10	19	11	6	13	32	40	39
9	Metalurg Donetsk	30	7	6	2	26	15	3	3	9	9	20	10	9	11	35	35	39
10	Vorskla Poltava	30	5	5	5	14	15	4	5	6	14	19	9	10	11	28	34	37
11	Stal Alchevsk	30	5	6	4	13	12	4	3	8	13	27	9	9	12	26	39	36
12	Arsenal Kyiv	30	5	5	5	12	14	4	3	8	19	25	9	8	13	31	39	35
13	FC Kharkiv	30	8	2	5	18	13	1	4	10	11	23	9	6	15	29	36	33
14	Kryvbas Kryvyi Rih	30	8	2	5	19	15	1	4	10	8	20	9	6	15	27	35	33
15	Volyn Lutsk	30	7	2	6	19	15	2	4	9	12	30	9	6	15	31	45	33
16	Zakarpattya Uzhgorod	30	3	5	7	13	21	0	1	14	4	32	3	6	21	17	53	15

Championship Play-off: Shakhtar Donetsk 2, Dynamo Kyiv 1 (aet)

DNIPRO DNIPROPETROVSK
Coach – Yevhen Kucherevskyi; (20/10/05) Vadym Tyshchenko; (19/12/05) Oleh Protasov

2005

12/7	Tavriya Simferopol	h	1-3	Kornilenko
17/7	Shakhtar Donetsk	a	0-2	
10/5	Metalurg Zaporizhzhya	h	0-0	

No	Name	Nat	Pos	Aps	(s)	Gls
22	Hennadiy ALTMAN		G	8		
5	Serhiy BILOZOR		D	28		1
10	Igor BUGAEV	MOL	M	11		2
33	Serhiy DANYLOVSKYI		M	4		
15	Viktor DOTSENKO		M	5	(10)	
11	Ruslan GILAZEV		M	30		
37	Dmytro HRYSHKO		M	16	(1)	
35	Ilia KANDELAKI	GEO	M	22		
23	Pavel KIRILCHIK	BLS	M	9		1
6	Olexandr KLYMENKO		D	6	(1)	
10	Olexandr KOSYRIN		A	7		7
8	Andriy KYRLYK		M	26		6
14	Yevgeniy LOSHANKOV	BLS	M	8	(5)	3
7	Roman LUTSENKO		M	1		
7	Yevhen LUTSENKO		M	8	(13)	1
24	Iurie MITEREV	MOL	A	10	(11)	6
28	Kakhaber MJAVANADZE	GEO	D	10		
20	Zoltán NAGY	HUN	A	3	(6)	1
27	Sergei OSIPOV	RUS	M	10		1
9	Volodymyr OSTROUSHKO		M	5	(3)	
21	Andrei OSTROVSKIY	BLS	D	20		
32	Valentyn POLTAVETS		M	25	(3)	4
34	Oleh PTACHYK		D	2	(2)	
1	Vataliy RUDENKO		G	22		
4	Serhiy SYMONENKO		D	13	(5)	
19	Vyacheslav TERESHCHENKO		A	9	(6)	1
3	Vladyslav VASHCHUK		D	6		
30	Artem YASHKIN		M		(6)	
17	Olexandr ZGURA		M	2	(5)	
13	Serhiy ZGURA		M	4	(5)	

23/7	Metalurg Zaporizhzhya	h	3-0	Nazarenko, Melashchenko 2
31/7	Arsenal Kyiv	a	0-1	
6/8	Stal Alchevsk	h	0-1	
21/8	Zakarpattya Uzhgorod	a	2-1	Shershun, Nazarenko
29/8	FC Illichivets Mariupol	h	0-1	
11/9	Vorskla Poltava	a	1-1	Kornilenko
19/9	Metalurg Donetsk	h	1-0	Shelayev
25/9	Chornomorets Odesa	a	0-0	
3/10	Dynamo Kyiv	h	0-3	
16/10	Volyn Lutsk	a	1-2	Melashchenko
23/10	Metalist Kharkiv	h	0-0	
30/10	FC Kharkiv	h	2-0	Kostyshyn, Semochko
7/11	Kryvbas Kryvyi Rih	a	2-2	Rusol, Mykhailenko
19/11	Tavriya Simferopol	a	1-0	Kravchenko
27/11	Shakhtar Donetsk	h	2-2	Shelayev, Radchenko
5/12	Metalurg Zaporizhzhya	a	0-1	
10/12	Arsenal Kyiv	h	1-0	Shelayev

2006

12/3	Zakarpattya Uzhgorod	h	4-0	Melashchenko, Rusol, Kotenko, Nazarenko
19/3	FC Illichivets Mariupol	a	0-0	
26/3	Vorskla Poltava	h	0-0	
2/4	Metalurg Donetsk	a	1-1	Nazarenko
9/4	Chornomorets Odesa	h	2-0	Kornilenko
17/4	Dynamo Kyiv	a	2-0	Balabanov 2
22/4	Volyn Lutsk	h	0-0	
26/4	Stal Alchevsk	a	0-0	
30/4	Metalist Kharkiv	a	6-0	Kravchenko 2, Balabanov, og (Ganczarczyk), og (Danilov), Kornilenko
6/5	FC Kharkiv	a	1-0	Rusol
10/5	Kryvbas Kryvyi Rih	h	1-0	Kornilenko

No	Name	Nat	Pos	Aps	(s)	Gls
22	Denys ANDRIYENKO		M	5	(6)	
9	Kostyantyn BALABANOV		A	10	(8)	3
17	Ruslan BIDNENKO		M	1	(2)	
3	Olexandr HRYTSAI		D	23	(2)	
23	Vyacheslav KERNOZENKO		G	17		
8	Sergei KORNILENKO	BLS	A	12	(15)	5

Ukraine

No	Name		Nat	Pos	Aps	(s)	Gls
10	Ruslan KOSTYSHYN			A	9	(11)	1
11	Ivan KOTENKO			A	6	(8)	1
24	Kostyantyn KRAVCHENKO			M	14	(9)	3
77	Artem KUSLIY			G	12		
4	Vitaliy LYSYTSKYI			M	6	(6)	
15	Serhiy MATYUKHIN			D	4		
1	Mykola MEDIN			G	1		
7	Olexandr MELASHCHENKO			A	14	(6)	4
2	Serhiy MOTUZ			M		(4)	
19	Dmytro MYKHAILENKO			M	6	(6)	1
28	Serhiy NAZARENKO			M	28		4
13	Georgi Ivanov PEEV		BUL	M	10		
14	Olexandr RADCHENKO			D	26		1
16	Andriy RUSOL			A	30		3
20	Olexandr RYKUN			M	9	(2)	
21	Dmytro SEMOCHKO			A	16		1
27	Vyacheslav SERDYUK			M	6	(1)	
6	Oleh SHELAYEV			M	26		3
25	Bohdan SHERSHUN			D	22	(1)	1
5	Volodymyr YEZERSKYI			D	17		

DYNAMO KYIV
Coach – Leonid Buryak; (8/8/05) Anatoliy Demyanenko

2005
13/7	Metalurg Zaporizhzhya	h	1-1	Byalkevich
17/7	Arsenal Kyiv	a	2-0	Rotan, Aliyev (p)
22/7	Stal Alchevsk	h	4-0	Rodolfo 2, Diogo Rincón, Rebrov
30/7	Zakarpattya Uzhgorod	a	2-1	Rotan, Cernat
7/8	FC Illichivets Mariupol	h	1-1	Yussuf
21/8	Vorskla Poltava	a	4-0	Cléber 2, Shatskikh, Gavrancic
29/8	Metalurg Donetsk	h	3-1	Diogo Rincón (p), Rotan, Rebrov
11/9	Chornomorets Odesa	a	1-0	Diogo Rincón
18/9	Metalist Kharkiv	h	2-2	Rebrov, Diogo Rincón
25/9	Volyn Lutsk	h	7-1	Rotan, Shatskikh 2, Gavrancic 2, Diogo Rincón, Rebrov
3/10	Dnipro Dnipropetrovsk	a	3-0	Gusev, Cléber, Diogo Rincón
16/10	FC Kharkiv	h	1-0	Diogo Rincón (p)
23/10	Kryvbas Kryvyi Rih	a	1-0	Vashchuk
30/10	Tavriya Simferopol	h	2-0	Cléber, Diogo Rincón
7/11	Shakhtar Donetsk	a	1-0	Rebrov
20/11	Metalurg Zaporizhzhya	a	2-1	Gusev, Rebrov
27/11	Arsenal Kyiv	h	3-1	Cléber, Yussuf, Byalkevich
4/12	Stal Alchevsk	a	2-1	Cléber, Gusev
7/12	Zakarpattya Uzhgorod	h	4-1	Verpakovskis, Yussuf, Shatskikh, Peev

2006
5/3	FC Illichivets Mariupol	a	2-1	Diogo Rincón, Rebrov
11/3	Vorskla Poltava	h	0-0	
18/3	Metalurg Donetsk	a	3-0	Rebrov 2, Cléber
26/3	Chornomorets Odesa	h	4-1	Cléber 3, Diogo Rincón (p)
2/4	Metalist Kharkiv	a	2-1	Milevskyi, Yeshchenko
8/4	Volyn Lutsk	a	3-1	Gusev, Milevskyi, Rebrov
17/4	Dnipro Dnipropetrovsk	h	0-2	
22/4	FC Kharkiv	a	3-0	Rebrov, Gavrancic, Byalkevich
28/4	Kryvbas Kryvyi Rih	h	3-1	Cléber, Rebrov 2 (1p)
6/5	Tavriya Simferopol	a	0-0	
10/5	Shakhtar Donetsk	h	2-2	Shatskikh, Milevskyi

Play-off
14/5	Shakhtar Donetsk	n	1-2	Rodolfo

No	Name	Nat	Pos	Aps	(s)	Gls
88	Olexandr ALIYEV		M	1	(4)	1
8	Valentin BYALKEVICH	BLS	M	15	(10)	3
10	Florin Lucian CERNAT	ROM	M	4	(9)	1
84	Edgaras CESNAUSKIS	LIT	M	2	(1)	
9	CLÉBER de Souza Freitas	BRA	A	22	(1)	11
15	DIOGO Pacheco RINCÓN	BRA	A	19	(4)	10
30	Badr EL-KADDURI	MAR	M	15	(1)	
3	Serhiy FEDOROV		D	21		
32	Goran GAVRANCIC	SCG	D	14	(1)	4
17	Tiberiu GHIOANE	ROM	D	1	(1)	
20	Oleh GUSEV		M	23	(1)	4
7	Jerko LEKO	CRO	M	6		
12	Taras LUTSENKO		G	1		
81	Marjan MARKOVIC	SCG	D	1		
6	Otar MARTSVELADZE	GEO	M		(4)	
25	Artem MILEVSKYI		A	9	(7)	3
17	Taras MYKHALYK		M	2	(3)	
26	Andriy NESMACHNYI		D	17	(2)	
36	Milos NINKOVIC	SCG	M	2	(1)	
11	Georgi Ivanov PEEV	BUL	M	1	(3)	1
5	Serhiy REBROV		A	24	(3)	13
4	Dantas Bispo RODOLFO	BRA	D	15	(10)	3
44	RODRIGO da Costa Baldasso	BRA	D	7		
14	Ruslan ROTAN		M	20	(8)	4
55	Olexandr RYBKA		G	6		
13	Goran SABLIC	CRO	D	1	(2)	
16	Maxim SHATSKIKH	UZB	A	18	(4)	5
1	Olexandr SHOVKOVSKYI		G	24		
27	Vladyslav VASHCHUK		D	24		1
23	Maris VERPAKOVSKIS	LAT	A	3	(6)	1
33	Andrei YESHCHENKO	RUS	D	9	(1)	1
37	Atanda Aila YUSSUF	NGA	M	14		3

FC ILLICHIVETS MARIUPOL
Coach – Ivan Balan

2005
12/7	Metalist Kharkiv	h	0-2	
17/7	Vorskla Poltava	h	3-2	Konyushenko, Gribanov, Hai (p)
23/7	Metalurg Donetsk	a	0-0	
31/7	Chornomorets Odesa	h	0-1	
7/8	Dynamo Kyiv	a	1-1	Gribanov
21/8	Volyn Lutsk	h	1-1	Hai
29/8	Dnipro Dnipropetrovsk	a	1-0	Konyushenko
11/9	FC Kharkiv	h	2-1	Konyushenko, Mazurenko
18/9	Kryvbas Kryvyi Rih	a	1-0	Leviha
25/9	Tavriya Simferopol	h	0-1	
3/10	Shakhtar Donetsk	a	0-6	
16/10	Metalurg Zaporizhzhya	h	1-0	Kryvosheyenko
23/10	Arsenal Kyiv	a	2-0	Tsykhmeistruk, Hai
30/10	Stal Alchevsk	h	3-0	Platonov, Hai, Konyushenko (p)
5/11	Zakarpattya Uzhgorod	a	1-1	Hai
20/11	Metalist Kharkiv	a	1-1	Kryvosheyenko
27/11	Vorskla Poltava	a	0-1	
4/12	Metalurg Donetsk	h	1-0	Hai
8/12	Chornomorets Odesa	a	2-1	Leviha, Konyushenko

2006
5/3	Dynamo Kyiv	h	1-2	Tsykhmeistruk
11/3	Volyn Lutsk	a	0-0	
19/3	Dnipro Dnipropetrovsk	h	0-0	
26/3	FC Kharkiv	a	0-3	
2/4	Kryvbas Kryvyi Rih	h	1-0	Yaksmanytskyi
8/4	Tavriya Simferopol	a	1-0	Platonov
16/4	Shakhtar Donetsk	h	1-2	Hai
22/4	Metalurg Zaporizhzhya	a	1-2	Kryvosheyenko
28/4	Arsenal Kyiv	h	3-5	Lashchenkov, Kryvosheyenko, Hai
6/5	Stal Alchevsk	a	0-1	
10/5	Zararpattya Uzhgorod	h	2-0	Konyushenko, Hai (p)

Ukraine

No	Name	Nat	Pos	Aps	(s)	Gls
24	Olexandr ANTONENKO		M		(2)	
9	Kostyantyn BABYCH		A	3	(4)	
20	Andriy BOIKO		D	3	(4)	
4	Leonid BOYARINTSEV		D	18	(1)	
15	Serhiy GRIBANOV		A	12	(1)	2
19	Olexiy HAI		D	29		8
13	Mykola HYBALYUK		M	4	(10)	
22	Andriy KONYUSHENKO		M	28		6
6	Oleh KRASNOPEROV		M	29		
11	Ivan KRYVOSHEYENKO		A	6	(21)	4
15	Denys KULAKOV		D	4	(2)	
14	Serhiy LASHCHENKOV		M	3	(4)	1
21	Ruslan LEVIHA		A	18	(5)	3
17	Olexandr MALTSEV		D	24		
8	Oleh MAZURENKO		M	20		1
1	Andriy NIKITIN		G	12	(1)	
39	Olexandr PAPUSH		M		(1)	
27	Serhiy PIVNENKO		M		(5)	
16	Valentyn PLATONOV		M	15	(1)	2
25	Adrian PUKANYCH		M	8	(9)	
99	Ihor SHUKHOVTSEV		G	18	(2)	
55	Eduard TSYKHMEISTRUK		M	28		2
18	Volodymyr YAKSMANYTSKYI		D	23		1
7	Dmytro YESIN		M	24	(2)	
14	Serhiy ZAKARLYUKA		M	1		

FC KHARKIV
Coach – Hennadiy Lytovchenko

2005
12/7	Kryvbas Kryvyi Rih	h	1-1	Samborskyi
17/7	Tavriya Simferopol	a	1-2	Shopin
23/7	Shakhtar Donetsk	h	2-3	Tselykh, Ribeiro (p)
31/7	Metalurg Zaporizhzhya	a	6-3	Tselykh 3 (1p), Ibragimov 2, Shopin
7/8	Arsenal Kyiv	h	3-1	Cheberyachko, Tselykh, Ibragimov
21/8	Stal Alchevsk	a	0-0	
28/8	Zakarpattya Uzhgorod	h	1-0	Yatsenko
11/9	FC Illichivets Mariupol	a	1-2	Ribeiro
18/9	Vorskla Poltava	h	2-0	Maximov, Ribeiro (p)
25/9	Metalurg Donetsk	a	1-1	Koval
2/10	Chornomorets Odesa	h	0-1	
16/10	Dynamo Kyiv	a	0-1	
23/10	Volyn Lutsk	h	3-2	Oprya, Ribeiro (p), Koval
30/10	Dnipro Dnipropetrovsk	a	0-2	
5/11	Metalist Kharkiv	h	1-0	Berezovchuk
20/11	Kryvbas Kryvyi Rih	a	1-3	Hunchak
27/11	Tavriya Simferopol	h	0-0	
5/12	Shakhtar Donetsk	a	0-3	
10/12	Metalurg Zaporizhzhya	h	1-0	Ribeiro

2006
5/3	Arsenal Kyiv	a	0-0	
12/3	Stal Alchevsk	h	0-1	
19/3	Zakarpattya Uzhgorod	a	1-2	og (Kravchenko)
26/3	FC Illichivets Mariupol	h	3-0	Ribeiro 2 (p), Hladkyi
2/4	Vorskla Poltava	a	0-0	
8/4	Metalurg Donetsk	h	1-0	Shopin
16/4	Chornomorets Odesa	a	0-1	
22/4	Dynamo Kyiv	h	0-3	
29/4	Volyn Lutsk	a	0-2	
6/5	Dnipro Dnipropetrovsk	h	0-1	
10/5	Metalist Kharkiv	a	0-1	

Name	Nat	Pos	Aps	(s)	Gls
9 Victor BARISEV	MOL	M	1		
7 Andriy BEREZOVCHUK		M	29		1
14 Yevhen CHEBERYACHKO		M	23		1
3 Dmytro GOLOLOBOV		D	1	(4)	
4 Olexandr GRANOVSKYI		D	17	(1)	
20 Olexandr HLADKYI		A	9	(16)	1
26 Ruslan HUNCHAK		M	13	(6)	1
22 Eldar IBRAGIMOV		M	10	(11)	3
12 Rustam KHUDZHAMOV		G	7		
5 Vitaliy KOMARNYTSKYI		D	29		
21 Andriy KOVAL		M		(6)	2
8 Olexandr MAXIMOV		M	17	(1)	1
77 Andriy OBEREMKO		M	25	(2)	
99 Andriy ONIKIYENKO		G	4		
25 Anatoliy OPRYA		M	24	(1)	1
19 Ihor PRODAN		A		(1)	
10 RIBEIRO Anderson	BRA	A	19	(3)	7
18 Volodymyr SAMBORSKYI		M	4		1
11 Ihor SHOPIN		M	27		3
32 Dmytro STOIKO		G	19		
33 Yuriy TSELYKH		A	16	(6)	5
27 Igor TSYGIRLASH	MOL	M		(8)	
30 Serhiy VETRENNIKOV		M	8	(5)	
32 Mykola VOLOSHYN		D		(1)	
24 Olexandr YATSENKO		D	27		1
23 Vladyslav ZAICHUK		M	1	(1)	

KRYVBAS KRYVYI RIH
Coach – Olexandr Kosevych

2005
12/7	FC Kharkiv	a	1-1	Gigiadze
17/7	Metalist Kharkiv	a	0-1	
23/7	Tavriya Simferopol	h	2-0	Popovici 2
30/7	Shakhtar Donetsk	a	0-1	
7/8	Metalurg Zaporizhzhya	h	1-0	Kashevskiy
21/8	Arsenal Kyiv	a	1-1	Gigiadze
28/8	Stal Alchevsk	h	2-1	Kashevskiy, Gigiadze (p)
11/9	Zakarpattya Uzhgorod	a	0-0	
18/9	FC Illichivets Mariupol	h	0-1	
25/9	Vorskla Poltava	a	0-0	
3/10	Metalurg Donetsk	h	0-1	
16/10	Chornomorets Odesa	a	1-2	Popovici
23/10	Dynamo Kyiv	h	0-1	
30/10	Volyn Lutsk	a	0-3	
7/11	Dnipro Dnipropetrovsk	h	2-2	Gigiadze, Adiyev
20/11	FC Kharkiv	h	3-1	Gigiadze (p), Kabanov 2
27/11	Metalist Kharkiv	h	2-1	Gigiadze (p), Dunjic
4/12	Tavriya Simferopol	a	0-1	
10/12	Shakhtar Donetsk	h	0-2	

2006
5/3	Metalurg Zaporizhzhya	a	1-2	Kabanov
12/3	Arsenal Kyiv	h	1-2	Panferov
19/3	Stal Alchevsk	a	1-0	Gigiadze
26/3	Zakarpattya Uzhgorod	h	1-0	Gigiadze (p)
2/4	FC Illichivets Mariupol	a	0-1	
9/4	Vorskla Poltava	h	2-2	Panferov, Kashevskiy
16/4	Metalurg Donetsk	a	2-3	og (Né), Ivashchenko
22/4	Chornomorets Odesa	h	1-0	Shevelyukhin
28/4	Dynamo Kyiv	a	1-3	Alegbe
6/5	Volyn Lutsk	h	2-1	Gigiadze, Trisovic
10/5	Dnipro Dnipropetrovsk	a	0-1	

Name	Nat	Pos	Aps	(s)	Gls
24 Mahomed ADIYEV	RUS	A	11	(7)	1
8 Antoni "Toni" ALEGBE	NGA	M	22	(1)	1
23 Illya BLYZNYUK		G	6		
17 Andriy BOIKO		D	1	(3)	
4 Serhiy DMITRIYEV		D	2	(1)	
9 Pavel DOVGULEVETS	BLS	D	9	(1)	
5 Darko DUNJIC	SCG	M	18	(1)	1

Ukraine

No	Name	Nat	Pos	Aps	(s)	Gls
20	Vasil GIGIADZE	GEO	A	27	(2)	9
19	Yuriy GROSHEV		M	16		
16	Olexandr IVASHCHENKO		M	2	(6)	1
10	Taras KABANOV		A	9	(14)	3
7	Nikolai KASHEVSKIY	BLS	M	24	(4)	3
17	Pavel KIRILCHIK	BLS	D	1	(1)	
21	Denys KOLCHIN		D	11		
11	Igors KORABLJOVS	LAT	D	17	(1)	
2	Oleh KOTELYUKH		D	24	(2)	
40	Ivan KUCHERENKO		M		(1)	
23	Andriy KURAYEV		G	1		
6	Zeljko LJUBENOVIC	SCG	M	7	(2)	
6	Sergei NIKITENKO	BLS	M	8	(2)	
3	Vyacheslav NYVYNSKYI		D	17	(2)	
4	Andrei PANFEROV	RUS	D	5	(1)	2
24	Olexandr POKLONSKIY		D	4	(1)	
36	Alexandru POPOVICI	MOL	A	11	(11)	3
13	Murad RAMAZANOV	RUS	A	3	(3)	
15	Serhiy SHCHEGLOV		D	16	(6)	
18	Olexandr SHEVELYUKHIN		D	4		1
13	Mykhailo STAROSTYAK		D	8		
1	Maxym STARTSEV		G	23	(1)	
22	Alexandar TRISOVIC	SCG	M	16	(7)	1
32	Serhiy ZGURA		M	7	(3)	

METALIST KHARKIV
Coach – Myron Markevych

2005
12/7	FC Illichivets Mariupol	a	2-0	Jakobia, Yarosh
17/7	Kryvbas Kryvyi Rih	h	1-0	Jakobia
23/7	Vorskla Poltava	a	1-0	Bordian
31/7	Tavriya Simferopol	h	2-0	Mrdakovic 2
6/8	Metalurg Donetsk	a	1-3	Jakobia
20/8	Shakhtar Donetsk	h	1-5	Jakobia (p)
28/8	Chornomorets Odesa	a	2-5	Kucher 2
11/9	Metalurg Zaporizhzhya	h	3-1	Valyayev 2, Jakobia (p)
18/9	Dynamo Kyiv	a	2-2	Yarosh, Jakobia
25/9	Arsenal Kyiv	h	1-2	Varlamov
2/10	Volyn Lutsk	a	0-3	
16/10	Stal Alchevsk	h	1-0	Oliynyk
23/10	Dnipro Dnipropetrovsk	a	0-0	
30/10	Zakarpattya Uzhgorod	a	4-1	Bordian, Slyusar, Valyayev, Mrdakovic
5/11	FC Kharkiv	a	0-1	
20/11	FC Illichivets Mariupol	h	1-1	Mrdakovic
27/11	Kryvbas Kryvyi Rih	a	1-2	Mrdakovic
4/12	Vorskla Poltava	h	0-1	
10/12	Tavriya Simferopol	a	1-0	Yarosh

2006
5/3	Metalurg Donetsk	h	2-0	Ganczarczyk, Slyusar
12/3	Shakhtar Donetsk	a	0-2	
18/3	Chornomorets Odesa	h	1-1	Kuznetsov
26/3	Metalurg Zaporizhzhya	a	0-0	
2/4	Dynamo Kyiv	h	1-2	Fomin
9/4	Arsenal Kyiv	a	1-1	Yarosh
16/4	Volyn Lutsk	h	1-0	Slyusar
22/4	Stal Alchevsk	a	1-1	Danilov
30/4	Dnipro Dnipropetrovsk	h	0-6	
6/5	Zakarpattya Uzhgorod	h	3-2	Mrdakovic 2, Kuznetsov
10/5	FC Kharkiv	h	1-0	Babych

No	Name	Nat	Pos	Aps	(s)	Gls
5	Marco ALVES	BRA	M		(1)	
21	Olexandr BABYCH		D	23		1
37	Vitali BORDIAN	MOL	M	28	(1)	2
23	Alexandr DANILOV	BLS	M	27	(2)	1
16	Serhiy DAVYDOV		A		(4)	
8	Anatoliy DIDENKO		M	2	(5)	
24	Ruslan FOMIN		A	8	(1)	1
6	Seweryn GANCZARCZYK	POL	D	9		1
29	Olexandr GORYAINOV		G	23		
4	Oleh HLUSHOK		D	6	(7)	
6	élexandr HONCHAR		M	7	(3)	
22	élexandr HUMENYUK		G	7		
47	JADER da Silva	BRA	M	1	(5)	
10	Lasha JAKOBIA	GEO	A	22	(1)	6
24	Andriy KHANAS		D	1		
2	Andriy KHOMYN		D	10	(4)	
51	Serhiy KOSTYUK		M		(4)	
35	Olexiy KRIVOSHEYEV		D	4	(1)	
3	Olexandr KUCHER		D	23		2
15	Sergei KUZNETSOV	BLS	M	18	(3)	2
8	Viktor MELNYK		M	6	(1)	
19	Milan MRDAKOVIC	SCG	M	20	(5)	7
33	Karen OGANYAN	RUS	A	3	(1)	
18	Olexiy OLIYNYK		M	3	(7)	1
1	Oleh OSTAPENKO		G		(1)	
17	Yuriy PETROV		A	1	(11)	
9	Valentyn SLYUSAR		M	25	(1)	3
25	Andriy SPIVAK		M	1	(3)	
7	Serhiy VALYAYEV		M	13	(5)	3
5	Yevgeniy VARLAMOV	RUS	D	8		1
14	Ruslan YAROSH		M	30		4
39	Kostyantyn YAROSHENKO		M	1	(12)	

METALURG DONETSK
Coach – Olexandr Sevidov; (15/3/06) Stepan Matviiv

2005
12/7	Stal Alchevsk	h	5-0	Demetradze 2 (1p), Ristic, Shyshchenko 2
17/7	Zakarpattya Uzhgorod	a	0-0	
23/7	FC Illichivets Mariupol	h	0-0	
31/7	Vorskla Poltava	a	1-1	Olexiyenko
7/8	Metalist Kharkiv	h	3-1	Shyshchenko 3
21/8	Chornomorets Odesa	h	3-2	Shyshchenko 3
29/8	Dynamo Kyiv	a	1-3	Aliuta
10/9	Volyn Lutsk	h	4-0	Kosyrin 2, Zakarlyuka, Aliuta
19/9	Dnipro Dnipropetrovsk	a	0-1	
25/9	FC Kharkiv	h	1-1	Zotov
3/10	Kryvbas Kryvyi Rih	a	1-0	Priyomov
16/10	Tavriya Simferopol	h	0-0	
23/10	Shakhtar Donetsk	a	0-2	
30/10	Metalurg Zaporizhzhya	h	0-0	
6/11	Arsenal Kyiv	a	2-0	og (Bunjevcevic), Kosyrin
20/11	Stal Alchevsk	a	1-1	Gjuzelov
27/11	Zakarpattya Uzhgorod	h	1-0	Kosyrin
4/12	FC Illichivets Mariupol	a	0-1	
8/12	Vorskla Poltava	h	2-0	Polyanskyi, Zakarlyuka

2006
5/3	Metalist Kharkiv	a	0-2	
12/3	Chornomorets Odesa	a	0-1	
18/3	Dynamo Kyiv	h	0-3	
25/3	Volyn Lutsk	a	2-1	Kosyrin (p), Checher
2/4	Dnipro Dnipropetrovsk	h	1-1	Busaidi
8/4	FC Kharkiv	a	0-1	
16/4	Kryvbas Kryvyi Rih	h	3-2	Zeze, Melnyk, Checher
22/4	Tavriya Simferopol	a	0-3	
30/4	Shakhtar Donetsk	h	1-3	Checher
6/5	Metalurg Zaporizhzhya	a	1-3	Checher
10/5	Arsenal Kyiv	h	2-2	og (Chernikov), Kosyrin

No	Name	Nat	Pos	Aps	(s)	Gls
14	Ara AKOBYAN	ARM	A	2	(6)	
5	Armen AKOPYAN		M	6	(2)	
16	Marian ALIUTA	ROM	M	13	(10)	2

Ukraine

No	Name	Nat	Pos	Aps	(s)	Gls
14	Aruna BABANGIDA	NGA	M		(2)	
3	Elvin BEQIRI	ALB	D	4		
12	Anis BUSAIDI	TUN	M	19	(1)	1
4	Vyacheslav CHECHER		D	29		4
99	Giorgi DEMETRADZE	GEO	A	3		2
66	Vladimir DISLJENKOVIC	SCG	G	12		
3	Joseph EIMOFE	NGA	M	2		
55	Daniel FLOREA	ROM	D	13		
33	Igor GJUZELOV	MAC	D	10		1
27	García GOMES	ARG	M	3	(4)	
6	Boban GRNCAROV	MAC	D	5	(2)	
11	Marko GRUBELIC	SCG	M	8		
28	Olexandr KOSYRIN		A	19	(1)	6
10	Egishe MELIKYAN	ARM	M	10	(11)	
9	Vadym MELNYK		A	8	(5)	1
99	Don Marius MITU	ROM	A	3	(1)	
18	Arsène NE	CIV	D	11		
40	Odgobe OCHUKO	NGA	M		(1)	
22	Samuel OKUNOWO	NGA	M	2		
11	Olexandr OLEXIYENKO		M	5	(6)	1
3	Artem PIDHAINYI		M	1		
2	Olexiy POLYANSKYI		D	12	(8)	1
15	Volodymyr PRIYOMOV		A	5	(8)	1
23	Bratislav RISTIC	SCG	M	20	(5)	1
88	Serhiy SHYSHCHENKO		M	17	(2)	8
5	Andriy SKARLOSH		M		(1)	
8	Serhiy TKACHENKO		M	27	(1)	
20	Levan TSKITISHVILI	GEO	M	3		
1	Yuriy VIRT		G	13	(1)	
31	Dmitriy VOROBYOV	RUS	G	5	(1)	
17	Serhiy ZAKARLYUKA		M	20	(2)	2
26	Venanc ZEZE	CIV	A	3		1
7	Olexandr ZOTOV		M	17		1
30	Ivica ZULJEVIC	CRO	A		(1)	

METALURG ZAPORIZHZHYA
Coach – Valeriy Yaremchenko; (23/7/05) Anatoliy Chantsev; (20/10/05) Vyacheslav Hroznyi

2005
13/7	Dynamo Kyiv	a	1-1	Bredun
17/7	Volyn Lutsk	h	0-1	
23/7	Dnipro Dnipropetrovsk	a	0-3	
31/7	FC Kharkiv	h	3-6	Arzhanov, Selak 2
7/8	Kryvbas Kryvyi Rih	a	0-1	
21/8	Tavriya Simferopol	h	2-1	Kutarba, Selak
28/8	Shakhtar Donetsk	a	1-3	Demchenko
11/9	Metalist Kharkiv	a	1-3	Andjelkovic
18/9	Arsenal Kyiv	h	2-2	Kriventsov, Andjelkovic
25/9	Stal Alchevsk	a	1-1	Nahornyak (p)
2/10	Zakarpattya Uzhgorod	h	3-0	Chyhrynskyi, Akopyan, Lyubarskyi
16/10	FC Illichivets Mariupol	a	0-1	
23/10	Vorskla Poltava	h	0-2	
30/10	Metalurg Donetsk	a	0-0	
5/11	Chornomorets Odesa	h	1-0	Modebadze
20/11	Dynamo Kyiv	h	1-2	Aristarkhov
27/11	Volyn Lutsk	a	1-0	Modebadze
5/12	Dnipro Dnipropetrovsk	h	1-0	Chyhrynskyi
10/12	FC Kharkiv	a	0-1	

2006
5/3	Kryvbas Kryvyi Rih	h	2-1	Tasevski, Nahornyak
12/3	Tavriya Simferopol	a	0-1	
19/3	Shakhtar Donetsk	h	0-3	
26/3	Metalist Kharkiv	h	0-0	
1/4	Arsenal Kyiv	a	2-1	Nahornyak, Kutarba (p)
8/4	Stal Alchevsk	h	2-1	Kutarba 2 (1p)
16/4	Zakarpattya Uzhgorod	a	2-0	Lyubarskyi, Shyshchenko
22/4	FC Illichivets Mariupol	h	2-1	Korytko, Aristarkhov
28/4	Vorskla Poltava	a	1-3	Aliyev
6/5	Metalurg Donetsk	h	3-1	Korytko 2, Kutarba (p)
10/5	Chornomorets Odesa	a	0-0	

No	Name	Nat	Pos	Aps	(s)	Gls
21	Armen AKOPYAN		M	16		1
9	Olexandr ALIYEV		M	6	(2)	1
49	Miodrag ANDJELKOVIC	SCG	A	8	(2)	2
56	Maxim ARISTARKHOV	RUS	A	11	(5)	2
17	Volodymyr ARZHANOV		M	1	(4)	1
13	Spomenko BOSNJAK	CRO	D	1	(1)	
14	Yevhen BREDUN		M	9	(6)	1
28	Artem CHELYADINSKIY	BLS	D	14	(2)	
27	Dmytro CHYHRYNSKYI		D	15		2
8	Andriy DEMCHENKO		M	6	(5)	1
23	Olexiy GODIN		M	1	(2)	
1	Andriy HLUSHCHENKO		G	16		
32	Roman KARAKEVYCH		A	2	(3)	
23	Oleh KARAMUSHKA		D	5	(2)	
	Yuriy KHRIYENKO		G	1		
30	Vladimir KORYTKO	BLS	M	8		3
21	Dmytro KOVALENKO		M	1	(1)	
4	Valeriy KRIVENTSOV		M	2		1
	Andriy KRUHLYAK		A		(1)	
28	German KUTARBA	RUS	M	12	(2)	5
16	Dato KVIRKVELIA	GEO	M	10		
20	Yevhen LOZYNSKYI		M	5	(2)	
77	Ihor LUCHKEVYCH		M	11		
46	Ruslan LYUBARSKYI		M	24	(1)	2
18	Danco MASEV	MAC	A	1	(2)	
48	Igor MITERSKI	MAC	D	12		
15	Irakli MODEBADZE	GEO	A	8	(5)	2
55	Serhiy MOROZOV		M		(1)	
50	Serhiy NAHORNYAK		M	24		3
43	Dmytro NEVMYVAKA		D	7	(3)	
19	Tefik OSMANI	ALB	D	4	(1)	
46	Volodymyr POLYOVYI		M	8	(4)	
5	Serhiy POPOV		D	9	(2)	
12	Vitaliy POSTRANSKYI		G	2		
58	Ljubisa RANKOVIC	SCG	M	4	(1)	
55	Mirko SELAK	CRO	A	5	(6)	3
10	Bledi SHKEMBI	ALB	M	6	(2)	
5	Sergei SHTANYUK	BLS	D	10		
8	Serhiy SHYSHCHENKO		M	5	(3)	1
44	Serhiy SYLYUK		M	5	(6)	
7	Darko TASEVSKI	MAC	M	15	(3)	1
51	Andriy TLUMAK		G	10		
6	Aleksandar TOMOVSKI	BUL	D	3		
4	Maxym TRUSEVYCH		D	1	(3)	
53	Dmitriy VOROBYOV	RUS	G	1		
39	Yaroslav VYSHNYAK		D	5		

SHAKHTAR DONETSK
Coach – Mircea Lucescu (ROM)

2005
13/7	Volyn Lutsk	a	1-0	Elano
17/7	Dnipro Dnipropetrovsk	h	2-0	Vorobei, Jadson
23/7	FC Kharkiv	a	3-2	Belik, Tymoshchuk, Matuzalem
30/7	Kryvbas Kryvyi Rih	h	1-0	Brandão
6/8	Tavriya Simferopol	a	3-0	Brandão, Belik, Elano
20/8	Metalist Kharkiv	a	5-1	Brandão 4, Fomin
28/8	Metalurg Zaporizhzhya	h	3-1	Belik 2, Elano (p)
11/9	Arsenal Kyiv	a	0-0	
18/9	Stal Alchevsk	h	1-1	Belik
24/9	Zakarpattya Uzhgorod	a	3-0	Elano 2, og (Lozynskyi)
3/10	FC Illichivets Mariupol	h	6-0	Jadson 2, Matuzalem 2, Brandão 2

Ukraine

Date	Opponent	H/A	Score	Scorers
16/10	Vorskla Poltava	a	2-0	Tymoshchuk, Brandão
23/10	Metalurg Donetsk	h	2-0	Jadson, Matuzalem
30/10	Chornomorets Odesa	a	1-0	Brandão
7/11	Dynamo Kyiv	h	0-1	
20/11	Volyn Lutsk	h	2-0	Belik, Matuzalem
27/11	Dnipro Dnipropetrovsk	a	2-2	Fernandinho, Matuzalem
5/12	FC Kharkiv	h	3-0	Brandão 2, Tymoshchuk
10/12	Kryvbas Kryvyi Rih	a	2-0	Belik, Matuzalem
2006				
5/3	Tavriya Simferopol	h	1-1	Lewandowski
12/3	Metalist Kharkiv	a	2-0	Brandão, Srna
19/3	Metalurg Zaporizhzhya	a	3-0	Matuzalem, Marica, Jadson
25/3	Arsenal Kyiv	h	1-0	Brandão
1/4	Stal Alchevsk	a	3-1	Tymoshchuk, Jadson, Srna
9/4	Zakarpattya Uzhgorod	h	3-0	og (Chuchman), Matuzalem, Chyhrynskyi
16/4	FC Illichivets Mariupol	a	2-1	Marica, Matuzalem (p)
21/4	Vorskla Poltava	h	0-0	
30/4	Metalurg Donetsk	a	3-1	Brandão, Chyhrynskyi, Marica
6/5	Chornomorets Odesa	h	2-0	Tymoshchuk, Marica
10/5	Dynamo Kyiv	a	2-2	Chyhrynskyi, Jadson
Play-off				
14/5	Dynamo Kyiv	n	2-1	Marica, Aghahowa

No	Name	Nat	Pos	Aps	(s)	Gls
17	Julius AGHAHOWA	NIG	A	5	(9)	1
2	Cosmin BARCAUAN	ROM	D	2		
20	Olexiy BELIK		A	17	(6)	7
25	BRANDÃO Lemos da Silva	BRA	A	21	(5)	15
27	Dmytro CHYHRYNSKYI		D	11		3
6	Igor DULJAJ	SCG	M	20	(4)	
36	ELANO Blumer	BRA	M	15	(10)	5
7	FERNANDINHO Luís Roza	BRA	M	14	(9)	1
24	Ruslan FOMIN		A	1	(5)	1
3	Tomás HÜBSCHMAN	CZE	D	16		
38	JADSON Rodrigues da Silva	BRA	M	15	(8)	7
23	Ihor KOROTETSKYI		D		(2)	
16	Jan LASTUVKA	CZE	G	13		
8	LEONARDO Jose Aparecido	BRA	D	4	(1)	
18	Mariusz LEWANDOWSKI	POL	M	20	(1)	1
29	Ciprian Andrei MARICA	ROM	A	9	(13)	5
9	MATUZALEM da Silva	BRA	M	28		10
26	Razvan Dinca RAT	ROM	D	16	(2)	
13	Vyacheslav SHEVCHUK		M	15	(5)	
35	Bohdan SHUST		G	9		
12	Dmytro SHUTKOV		G	9		
33	Darijo SRNA	CRO	M	18	(3)	2
14	Flavius Vladimir STOICAN	ROM	M	12	(1)	
28	Seyhan TOLGA	TUR	D	15		
4	Anatoliy TYMOSHCHUK		M	27		5
11	Andriy VOROBEI		A	9	(7)	1
10	Zvonimir VUKIC	SCG	M		(2)	

STAL ALCHEVSK
Coach – Anatoliy Volobuyev

2005

Date	Opponent	H/A	Score	Scorers
12/7	Metalurg Donetsk	a	0-5	
17/7	Chornomorets Odesa	h	0-1	
22/7	Dynamo Kyiv	a	0-4	
31/7	Volyn Lutsk	h	2-2	Akobyan, Khramtsov
6/8	Dnipro Dnipropetrovsk	a	1-0	Akobyan
21/8	FC Kharkiv	h	0-0	
28/8	Kryvbas Kryvyi Rih	a	1-2	Akobyan
11/9	Tavriya Simferopol	h	1-0	Akobyan (p)
18/9	Shakhtar Donetsk	a	1-1	Tsimakuridze
25/9	Metalurg Zaporizhzhya	h	1-1	Akobyan (p)
2/10	Arsenal Kyiv	a	1-1	Gomes
16/10	Metalist Kharkiv	a	0-1	
23/10	Zakarpattya Uzhgorod	h	1-0	Akobyan
30/10	FC Illichivets Mariupol	a	0-3	
6/11	Vorskla Poltava	h	2-0	Akobyan 2
20/11	Metalurg Donetsk	h	1-1	Sernetskyi
27/11	Chornomorets Odesa	a	2-2	Sernetskyi, Okana-Stazi
1/12	Dynamo Kyiv	h	1-2	Akobyan (p)
10/12	Volyn Lutsk	a	1-0	Akobyan
2006				
12/3	FC Kharkiv	a	1-0	Danayev
19/3	Kryvbas Kryvyi Rih	h	0-1	
26/3	Tavriya Simferopol	a	2-5	Okana-Stazi, Sernetskyi
1/4	Shakhtar Donetsk	h	1-3	Okana-Stazi
8/4	Metalurg Zaporizhzhya	a	1-2	Tsimakuridze
15/4	Arsenal Kyiv	h	1-0	Shuha
22/4	Metalist Kharkiv	h	1-1	Nesteruk
26/4	Dnipro Dnipropetrovsk	h	0-0	
29/4	Zakarpattya Uzhgorod	a	2-0	Mara, Nesteruk
6/5	FC Illichivets Mariupol	h	1-0	Mara (p)
10/5	Vorskla Poltava	a	0-1	

No	Name	Nat	Pos	Aps	(s)	Gls
7	Ara AKOBYAN	ARM	A	18	(1)	10
33	Olexandr AKYMENKO		A	1	(3)	
17	Serhiy ARTEMOV		M	1		
14	Dmytro BOIKO		A	1	(1)	
31	Daniel CIRITA	ROM	D	21	(1)	
8	Andriy DANAYEV		M	5	(2)	1
2	Andriy GAVRYUSHOV		D	29		
27	Ruben GOMES	ARG	M	15	(3)	1
16	Dmytro GORBUSHIN		M	7	(7)	
15	Artem KASIYANOV		M	5	(10)	
32	Olexiy KHRAMTSOV		D	16		1
1	Andriy KOMARNYTSKYI		G	30		
29	Yuriy KONDAKOV		D	5		
25	Petro KONDRATYUK		M	16	(5)	
20	Ioan Bogdan MARA	ROM	M	11		2
27	Florinel Cristi MIREA	ROM	M	1		
23	Pavlo NESTERUK		A	2	(4)	2
24	Burnel OKANA-STAZI	CON	M	16	(11)	3
26	Florin Cristian PARVU	ROM	M	23		
3	Olexandr POLOVKOV		D	22	(5)	
13	Olexandr SAVANCHUK		A	2	(10)	
10	Serhiy SERNETSKYI		A	21	(2)	3
4	Ivan SHUHA		D	28		1
19	Olexandr STASOVSKYI		M	2	(2)	
24	Serhiy TRETYAK		A		(13)	
9	Georgi TSIMAKURIDZE	GEO	D	29		2
6	Ruslan YERMOLENKO		M	3	(4)	
7	Hennadiy ZUBOV		M		(5)	

TAVRIYA SIMFEROPOL
Coach – Oleh Fedorchuk; (5/1/06) Mykhailo Fomenko

2005

Date	Opponent	H/A	Score	Scorers
12/7	Dnipro Dnipropetrovsk	a	3-1	Kovpak, Kornev, Homenyuk
17/7	FC Kharkiv	h	2-1	Nesteruk 2
23/7	Kryvbas Kryvyi Rih	a	0-2	
31/7	Metalist Kharkiv	a	0-2	
6/8	Shakhtar Donetsk	h	0-3	
21/8	Metalurg Zaporizhzhya	a	1-2	Júnior
28/8	Arsenal Kyiv	h	0-1	
11/9	Stal Alchevsk	a	0-1	
18/9	Zakarpattya Uzhgorod	h	1-0	Homenyuk
25/9	FC Illichivets Mariupol	h	1-0	Melnyk
2/10	Vorskla Poltava	h	2-3	Edmar, Júnior
16/10	Metalurg Donetsk	a	0-0	
23/10	Chornomorets Odesa	h	1-1	Júnior
30/10	Dynamo Kyiv	a	0-2	

Ukraine

Date	Opponent	H/A	Score	Scorers
6/11	Volyn Lutsk	h	1-2	Júnior (p)
19/11	Dnipro Dnipropetrovsk	h	0-1	
27/11	FC Kharkiv	a	0-0	
4/12	Kryvbas Kryvyi Rih	h	1-0	Júnior
10/12	Metalist Kharkiv	h	0-1	
2006				
5/3	Shakhtar Donetsk	a	1-1	Vasiliauskas
12/3	Metalurg Zaporizhzhya	h	1-0	Joksas
19/3	Arsenal Kyiv	a	0-1	
26/3	Stal Alchevsk	h	5-2	Vasiliauskas, Kovpak 2, Edmar 2
2/4	Zakarpattya Uzhgorod	a	1-0	Vishnevskiy (p)
8/4	FC Illichivets Mariupol	h	0-1	
16/4	Vorskla Poltava	a	3-2	Vishnevskiy, Godin, Edmar
22/4	Metalurg Donetsk	h	3-0	Kornev, Kovpak, Vishnevskiy
29/4	Chornomorets Odesa	a	2-1	Vasiliauskas, Kovpak
6/5	Dynamo Kyiv	h	0-0	
10/5	Volyn Lutsk	a	0-0	

No	Name	Nat	Pos	Aps	(s)	Gls
15	Aleksandre AMISUASHVILI	GEO	D	10		
6	Sasa CILINSEK	SCG	G	1		
3	Olexandr CHYZHEVSKYI		D	19	(1)	
1	Vadym DEONAS		G	6		
17	Yuriy DMITRULIN		D	11	(1)	
8	EDMAR de Lacerda	BRA	A	25	(1)	4
27	Olexiy GODIN		M	3	(2)	1
25	Serhiy GRIBANOV		A	1		
28	Olexandr HOLOVKO		D	16	(1)	
40	Volodymyr HOMENYUK		M	7	(10)	2
18	Audrius JOKSAS	LIT	M	7	(1)	1
11	JÚNIOR Luís António	BRA	A	18	(5)	5
10	Yevhen KARMALITA		M		(6)	
7	Andriy KORNEV		M	27	(2)	2
9	Olexandr KOVPAK		A	17	(5)	5
22	Ivan KOZORIZ		M	16	(1)	
4	Serhiy LYTOVCHENKO		D	16	(1)	
38	Vadym MELNYK		A	9	(1)	1
23	Anton MONAKHOV		D	8	(4)	
18	Andriy NESTERUK		A	1	(7)	2
99	Harrison Orowianor OMOKO	NGA	D	11		
13	Olexiy OSIPOV		M		(2)	
5	Oleh PESTRYAKOV		M	4	(2)	
2	Olexandr POKLONSKYI		D	7		
20	Volodymyr POSTOLATIYEV		A	6	(3)	
36	Fedir PROKHOROV		D	3		
33	Vitaliy REVA		G	13		
6	Yuriy SELEZNEV		M	3	(4)	
14	Serhiy SIBIRYAKOV		M	3	(12)	
27	Andriy SMALKO		M	1	(1)	
17	Serhiy SNYTKO		D	11		
20	Ruslan SOLYANYK		M		(3)	
13	Artem STARHORODSKYI		M	12	(4)	
1	Sasa TODIC	SCG	G	11		
77	Nerijus VASILIAUSKAS	LIT	A	11		3
23	Audrius VEIKUTIS	LIT	M	9	(1)	
21	Vyacheslav VISHNEVSKYI	RUS	M	7	(3)	3

VOLYN LUTSK
Coach – Vitaliy Kvartsyanyi

Date	Opponent	H/A	Score	Scorers
2005				
13/7	Shakhtar Donetsk	h	0-1	
17/7	Metalurg Zaporizhzhya	a	1-0	Sachko
23/7	Arsenal Kyiv	h	2-1	Tovkatskyi, Sachko
31/7	Stal Alchevsk	a	2-2	Sachko, Aloizi
7/8	Zakarpattya Uzhgorod	h	3-1	og (Kobin), Mitic, Buta
21/8	FC Illichivets Mariupol	a	1-1	Sachko
28/8	Vorskla Poltava	h	2-1	Sachko, Tovkatskyi
10/9	Metalurg Donetsk	a	0-4	
18/9	Chornomorets Odesa	h	0-3	
25/9	Dynamo Kyiv	a	1-7	Stepanov
2/10	Metalist Kharkiv	h	3-0	Maxymyuk, Buta (p), Sachko
16/10	Dnipro Dnipropetrovsk	h	2-1	Rähn, Tovkatskyi
23/10	FC Kharkiv	a	2-3	Cebotari, Sachko (p)
30/10	Kryvbas Kryvyi Rih	h	3-0	Sachko 2, Pishchur
6/11	Tavriya Simferopol	a	2-1	Schumacher, Sachko
20/11	Shakhtar Donetsk	a	0-2	
27/11	Metalurg Zaporizhzhya	h	0-1	
4/12	Arsenal Kyiv	a	1-2	Aloizi
10/12	Stal Alchevsk	h	0-1	
2006				
5/3	Zakarpattya Uzhgorod	a	1-1	Sokolenko
11/3	FC Illichivets Mariupol	h	0-0	
19/3	Vorskla Poltava	a	0-2	
25/3	Metalurg Donetsk	h	1-2	Sachko (p)
2/4	Chornomorets Odesa	a	0-2	
8/4	Dynamo Kyiv	h	1-3	Sachko
16/4	Metalist Kharkiv	a	0-1	
22/4	Dnipro Dnipropetrovsk	a	0-0	
29/4	FC Kharkiv	h	2-0	Devic 2
6/5	Kryvbas Kryvyi Rih	a	1-2	Sachko
10/5	Tavriya Simferopol	h	0-0	

No	Name	Nat	Pos	Aps	(s)	Gls
16	Michael ALOIZI Chidi	NGA	A	7	(9)	2
3	Milan BOZIC	SCG	D	2		
77	Cornel BUTA	ROM	M	19		2
33	Boris CEBOTARI	MOL	D	17	(4)	1
19	Marko DEVIC	SCG	M	15	(3)	2
4	Miodrag DJUDOVIC	SCG	D	1		
45	Slavoljub DJORDJEVIC	SCG	M	6		
5	Andriy DONETS		D	5	(2)	
8	Volodymyr GASHCHIN		M	18	(4)	
31	Oleh HERASYMYUK		A	13	(6)	
20	Serhiy HONCHARENKO		M	1		
15	Yaroslav KHOMA		M	7	(1)	
3	Roman KOTS		M		(1)	
2	Volodymyr KOVALYUK		D	14	(3)	
10	Branislav KRUNIC	BOS	M	1		
18	Olexandr LUZHANKOV		M	1	(2)	
35	Ruslan MAIDAN		M		(1)	
11	Roman MAXYMYUK		M	22	(3)	1
9	Sasa MITIC	SCG	A	1	(4)	1
24	Vitaliy NEDILKO		G	1		
44	Falemi Nana N'GHASSAN	CMR	M	7		
4	Harrison Orowianor OMOKO	NGA	D	17	(1)	
21	Giue PAPA	SEN	M	15		
43	Olexandr PISHCHUR		A	13	(4)	1
4	Borys POLYAKOV		D	4		
1	Vitaliy POSTRANSKYI		G	19		
9	Oleh RATIY		A	3		
6	Taavi RÄHN	EST	D	19		1
1	Vsevolod ROMANENKO		G	10		
26	Pavlo RYBKOVSKYI		D	1	(1)	
7	Vasyl SACHKO		A	30		13
14	Zdravko SARABA	BOS	D	3		
10	Alexei SAVINOV	MOL	M	1		
10	Constantin SCHUMACHER	ROM	M	10	(7)	1
25	Ivan SEMYRYAK		M		(1)	
32	Serhiy SHPAK		D		(1)	
5	Pavlo SOKOLENKO		M	10		1
27	Andriy STEPANOV		A	6	(3)	1
13	Vasyl TOVKATSKYI		A	4	(21)	3
20	Alexander TRISOVIC	SCG	M	3		
17	Roman ZHERSH		M	4	(3)	

Ukraine

VORSKLA POLTAVA
Coach – Viktor Nosov

2005
Date	Opponent	H/A	Score	Scorers
12/7	Zakarpattya Uzhgorod	h	0-0	
17/7	FC Illichivets Mariupol	a	2-3	Popov, Curri
23/7	Metalist Kharkiv	h	0-1	
31/7	Metalurg Donetsk	h	1-1	Epureanu
7/8	Chornomorets Odesa	a	2-1	Onyshchenko, Epureanu (p)
20/8	Dynamo Kyiv	h	0-4	
28/8	Volyn Lutsk	a	1-2	Medvedev
11/9	Dnipro Dnipropetrovsk	h	1-1	Epureanu
18/9	FC Kharkiv	a	0-2	
25/9	Kryvbas Kryvyi Rih	h	0-0	
2/10	Tavriya Simferopol	a	3-2	Epureanu (p), Brovkin, Melliti
16/10	Shakhtar Donetsk	h	0-2	
23/10	Metalurg Zaporizhzhya	a	2-0	Hlavyna, Brovkin
30/10	Arsenal Kyiv	h	2-0	Hlavyna, Curri
6/11	Stal Alchevsk	a	0-2	
20/11	Zakarpattya Uzhgorod	a	1-1	Epureanu (p)
27/11	FC Illichivets Mariupol	h	1-0	Curri
4/12	Metalist Kharkiv	a	1-0	Epureanu
8/12	Metalurg Donetsk	a	0-2	

2006
Date	Opponent	H/A	Score	Scorers
5/3	Chornomorets Odesa	h	1-2	Hlavyna
11/3	Dynamo Kyiv	a	0-0	
19/3	Volyn Lutsk	h	2-0	Hlavyna, Lita
26/3	Dnipro Dnipropetrovsk	a	0-0	
2/4	FC Kharkiv	h	0-0	
9/4	Kryvbas Kryvyi Rih	a	2-2	Hlavyna, Chizhov
16/4	Tavriya Simferopol	h	2-3	Hlavyna, og (Vasiliauskas)
21/4	Shakhtar Donetsk	a	0-0	
28/4	Metalurg Zaporizhzhya	h	3-1	Kravchenko, Popov, Djuricic
6/5	Arsenal Kyiv	a	0-2	
10/5	Stal Alchevsk	h	1-0	Lita

No	Name	Nat	Pos	Aps	(s)	Gls
31	Mykhailo BONDARENKO		A		(1)	
10	Dmytro BROVKIN		A	29		2
36	Olexandr CHIZHOV		A	3	(7)	1
20	Debatik CURRI	ALB	M	28		3
38	Armend DAPLKU	ALB	D	25		
32	Sasa DJURICIC	CRO	D	24		1
1	Serhiy DOLHANSKYI		G	19		
43	Serghei EPUREANU	MOL	M	28		6
11	Denys HLAVYNA		A	27	(2)	6
35	Maxym KARPENKO		A		(8)	
16	Anton KOVALEVSKYI		M		(1)	
14	Serhiy KRAVCHENKO		M	11		1
9	Nicolae Catalin LITA	ROM	M	1	(10)	2
25	Hennadiy MEDVEDEV		D	23	(3)	1
9	Sofien MELLITI	TUN	M	12	(5)	1
27	Volodymyr OLEFIR		D	3	(1)	
7	Denys ONYSHCHENKO		M	17	(6)	1
24	Anatoliy PODROBAKHA		A		(1)	
29	Volodymyr POPOV		M	23	(5)	2
21	Andriy PYATOV		G	11		
23	Serhiy RADEVYCH		M	2	(3)	
26	Pavlo REBENOK		M	3	(21)	
8	Ihor SHVETS		M		(1)	
4	Denys STOYAN		D	25		
37	Hryhoriy YARMASH		D	16	(8)	

ZAKARPATTYA UZHGOROD
Coach – Viktor Ryashko; (22/8/05) Volodymyr Vasyutyk; (6/9/05) Petro Kushlyk

2005
Date	Opponent	H/A	Score
12/7	Vorskla Poltava	a	0-0
17/7	Metalurg Donetsk	h	0-0
23/7	Chornomorets Odesa	a	0-2
30/7	Dynamo Kyiv	h	1-2
7/8	Volyn Lutsk	a	1-3
21/8	Dnipro Dnipropetrovsk	h	1-2
28/8	FC Kharkiv	a	0-1
11/9	Kryvbas Kryvyi Rih	h	0-0
18/9	Tavriya Simferopol	a	0-1
24/9	Shakhtar Donetsk	h	0-3
2/10	Metalurg Zaporizhzhya	a	0-3
16/10	Arsenal Kyiv	h	2-1
23/10	Stal Alchevsk	a	0-1
30/10	Metalist Kharkiv	a	1-4
5/11	FC Illichivets Mariupol	h	1-1
20/11	Vorskla Poltava	h	1-1
27/11	Metalurg Donetsk	a	0-1
4/12	Chornomorets Odesa	h	2-1
7/12	Dynamo Kyiv	a	1-4

Scorers: 30/7 Mykhalyk; 7/8 Mykhalyk; 21/8 Smirnov (p); 16/10 Pikhur 2; 30/10 Ryzhykh; 5/11 Mykhalyk; 20/11 Smirnov (p); 4/12 Pikhur, Ryzhykh; 7/12 Mykulyak

2006
Date	Opponent	H/A	Score	Scorers
5/3	Volyn Lutsk	h	1-1	Seleznev (p)
12/3	Dnipro Dnipropetrovsk	a	0-4	
19/3	FC Kharkiv	h	2-1	Malytskyi, Prodan
26/3	Kryvbas Kryvyi Rih	a	0-1	
2/4	Tavriya Simferopol	h	0-1	
9/4	Shakhtar Donetsk	a	0-3	
16/4	Metalurg Zaporizhzhya	h	0-2	
22/4	Arsenal Kyiv	a	1-2	Prodan
29/4	Stal Alchevsk	h	0-2	
6/5	Metalist Kharkiv	h	2-3	Chuchman, Dombraye
10/5	FC Illichivets Mariupol	a	0-2	

No	Name	Nat	Pos	Aps	(s)	Gls
4	Olexandr ANTONYUK		D	12	(7)	
33	Dmytro BABENKO		G	7		
11	Olexandr BURYI		A	9		
24	Ihor CHUCHMAN		D	23		1
20	Eddy Lord DOMBRAYE	NGA	M	9	(5)	1
26	Yuriy DUDNYK		M	9		
27	Denys HOLAIDO		M	21	(3)	
30	Olexandr HREBENOZHKO		M	1	(1)	
7	Mykhailo HURKA		M	26	(1)	
2	Taras ILNYTSKYI		D	21	(3)	
28	Igor JOKSIMOVIC	SCG	M	1	(3)	
	Vasyl KAMINSKIY		A		(2)	
12	Ruslan KHUDZHAMOV		G	10		
19	Vasyl KOBIN		M	13	(7)	
15	Mykhailo KOPOLOVETS		M	3	(7)	
5	Volodymyr KRAVCHENKO		M	6	(1)	
14	Anatoliy KYTSUTA		M	9	(2)	
77	Yevhen LOZYNSKYI		M	14		
6	Olexandr MALYTSKYI		M	7	(3)	1
99	Maryan MARUSHCHAK		G		(1)	
17	Taras MYKHALYK		A	14	(4)	3
23	Vladyslav MYKULYAK		M	7	(7)	1
2	Olexandr NAGY		G	2		
1	Volodymyr OVSIYENKO		G	9		
32	Olexandr PISHCHUR		M	3	(3)	
10	Olexandr PIKHUR		M	11	(6)	3
10	Ihor PRODAN		A	6	(4)	2
6	Serhiy ROZHOK		D	7	(3)	
8	Serhiy RYZHYKH		A	8	(2)	2
5	Andriy SAPUHA		D	10	(2)	
25	Alexei SAVINOV	MOL	M	18		
2	Serhiy SELEZNEV		D	10		1
18	Denys SMIRNOV		M	15	(2)	
9	Vyacheslav TERESHCHENKO		A	2	(1)	
1	Serhiy VELYCHKO		G	2		
2	Artem YEVLANOV		M		(2)	
9	Vadym ZAYATS		M	5	(3)	

Ukraine

DOMESTIC CUP 2005/06

SECOND ROUND
(13/8/05)
FC Rawa Rawa-Ruska 1, Gelios Kharkiv 0
Desna Chernihiv 2, Shakhtar Donetsk 5
Fakel Ivano-Frankivsk 0, Spartak Sumy 1
Nyva Teropil 1, Chornomorets Odesa 3
Osvita Borodyanka 0, FC Kharkiv 3
Veres Rivne 2, Energetyk Burshtyn 1
Chornohora Ivano-Frankivsk 1, Volyn Lutsk 4
Naftovyk Dolyna 1, Borysfen Boryspil 0 *(aet)*
Zhytychi Zhytomyr 0, Stal Dniprodzerzhynsk 1
MFC Mykolaiv 1, Metalurg Zaporizhzhya 2
Krystal Kherson 0, Dynamo Kyiv 5
Hirnyk Kryvyi Rih 2, Karpaty Lviv 3
Tytan Armyansk 1, FC Illichivets Mariupol 2
Ros Bila Tserkva 0, Kryvbas Kryvyi Rih 2
Olkom Melitopol 0, Zakarpattya Uzhgorod 1
Dnidter Ovisiopol 2, Metalist Kharkiv 3
Zirka Kirovohrad 0, Spartak Ivano-Frankivsk 2
Energiya Yuzhnoukrainsk 1, Stal Alchevsk 5
Yednist Plysky 0, Vorskla Poltava 3
Khimik Krasnoperekopsk 3, FC Bershad 2
Yalos Yalta 1, Podillya Khmelnytkyi 0
Nafkom Brovary 3, Nartovyk-Ukrnafta Okhtyrka 3 *(aet; 2-4 on pens)*
Dnipro Cherkasy 0, Obolon Kyiv 0 *(aet; 6-7 on pens)*
Gazovyk-GKhV Kharkiv 0, Tavriya Simferopol 4
MFC Oleksandriya 0, Arsenal Kyiv 6
Hirnyk-Sport Komsomolsk 2, Dynamo IgroServis Simferopol 1
Yavir Krasnopillua 0, Gazovyk-Skala Stryi 3
Olimpik Donetsk 2, Krymteplytsya Molodizhne 3
Bukovyna Chernivtsi w/o Zorya Lugansk
Metalurg Donetsk w/o Blyskavka Severodonetsk
(14/8/05)
PFC Oleksandriya 1, Dnipro Dnipropetrovsk 2

THIRD ROUND
(21/9/05)
Karpaty Lviv 1, Chornomorets Odesa 0
CSCA Kyiv 0, Metalurg Donetsk 1
Spartak Ivano-Frankivsk 0, Dynamo Kyiv 7
Stal Dniproderzhynsk 3, Volyn Lutsk 1
Naftovyk-Ukrnafta Okhtyrka 2, Stal Alchevsk 3
Hazovyk-Skala Stryi 0, FC Kharkiv 1
Spartak Sumy 1, Metalurg Zaporizhzhya 4
Krymteplytsya Molodizhne 1, Shakhtar Donetsk 3
FC Rawa Rawa-Ruska 0, Dnipro Dnipropetrovsk 2
Dnipro Cherkasy 1, Metalist Kharkiv 2
Bukovyna Chernivtsi 0, Arsenal Kyiv 1
Veres Rivne 2, Zakarpattya Uzhgorod 2 *(aet; 5-3 on pens)*
Hirnyk-Sport Komsomolsk 0, Vorskla Poltava 2
Naftovyk Dolyna 0, Tavriya Simferopol 4
Khimik Krasnoperekopsk 2, Kryvbas Kryvyi Rih 3
Yalos Yalta 0, FC Illichivets Mariupol 1 *(aet)*

FOURTH ROUND
(26/10/05)
Karpaty Lviv 1, Shakhtar Donetsk 0
Dynamo Kyiv 1, Metalist Kharkiv 0
Stal Alchevsk 1, Metalurg Donetsk 2
Vorskla Poltava 1, Dnipro Dnipropetrovsk 0
Hazovyk-Skala Stryi 0, FC Illichivets Mariupol 1
Kryvbas Kryvyi Rih 2, Tavriya Simferopol 0
Stal Dniproderzhynsk 0, Arsenal Kyiv 2
Veres Rivne 2, Metalurg Zaporizhzhya 4

QUARTER-FINALS
(13/11/05)
Dynamo Kyiv 2 *(Rotan 18, Gusev 34)*, Metalurg Donetsk 0
(23/11/05)
Karpaty Lviv 1 *(Batista 25)*, Vorskla Poltava 0
(13/12/05)
FC Illichivets Mariupol 2 *(Hai 7, 47)*, Arsenal Kyiv 0
(14/12/05)
Metalurg Zaporizhzhya 3 *(Kutarba 11, Poliovyi 50, Nahornyak 84)*, Kryvbas Kryvyi Rih 0

SEMI-FINALS
(22/3/06 & 12/4/06)
Metalurg Zaporizhzhya 2 *(Aliyev 61, Lyubarskyi 73)*, FC Illichivets Mariupol 1 *(Konyushenko 53)*
FC Illichivets Mariupol 1 *(Hai 67)*, Metalurg Zaporizhzhya 1 *(Modebadze 31)*
(Metalurg Zaporizhzhya 3-2)

Karpaty Lviv 0, Dynamo Kyiv 2 *(Gusev 32, Milevskyi 57)*
Dynamo Kyiv 1 *(Cléber 6)*, Karpaty Lviv 0
(Dynamo Kyiv 3-0)

FINAL
(2/5/06)
NSK Olimpiyskyi Stadium, Kiev
DYNAMO KYIV 1 *(Cléber 48)*
METALURG ZAPORIZHZHYA 0
Referee – *Lucílio Batista (POR)*
DYNAMO KYIV – Shovkovskyi, Fedorov, Nesmachnyi, Vashchuk, Gavrancic, Belkevich (Rodolfo 82), Cléber, Gusev, Diogo Rincón (Milevskyi 86), Rebrov, Shatskikh (Rotan 89).
METALURG ZAPORIZHZHYA – Hlushchenko, Chelyadinskiy, Shtanyuk, Shyshchenko (Aliyev 69), Bredun (Poliovyí 62), Modebadze (Aristarkhov 78), Kvirkvelia, Nahornyak, Kutarba, Korytko, Lyubarskyi.

SECOND LEVEL FINAL TABLE 2005/06

		Pld	W	D	L	F	A	Pts
1	Zorya Lugansk	34	27	6	1	74	13	87
2	Karpaty Lviv	34	26	5	3	53	14	80
3	Obolon Kyiv	34	22	6	6	51	19	72
4	Naftovyk-Ukrnafta Okhtyrka	34	17	7	10	50	35	58
5	Dynamo-2 Kyiv	34	15	7	12	51	36	52
6	Gazovyk-Skala Stryi	34	14	10	10	35	33	52
7	Podillya Khmelnytskyi	34	14	7	13	39	37	49
8	Stal Dniprodzerzhynsk	34	13	9	12	34	29	48
9	Krymteplytsya Molodizhne	34	12	11	11	35	34	47
10	Spartak Ivano-Frankivsk	34	10	15	9	33	31	45
11	Shakhtar-2 Donetsk	34	12	8	14	37	42	44
12	Gelioc Kharkiv	34	12	8	14	26	35	44
13	Dynamo-IgroServis Simferopol	34	10	8	16	40	51	38
14	Enerhetyk Burshtyn	34	8	12	14	31	44	36
15	CSKA Kyiv	34	8	8	18	25	52	32
16	Borysfen Boryspil	34	3	14	17	23	46	23
17	Spartak Sumy	34	5	5	24	28	68	20
18	FC Bershad	34	3	4	27	14	60	4

N.B. FC Bershad – 9 pts deducted; Karpaty Lviv – 3 pts deducted.

Wales

New Saints go marching on

They began the season as Total Network Solutions FC with a Champions League qualifier against the mighty Liverpool and ended it as The New Saints with a second successive League of Wales title.

TNS were not displeased with their two 3-0 defeats against the European champions. Just to play competitively against the big boys from 'up the road' was a dream come true for the village team from Llansantffraid. A goal would have been nice, but they would get enough of those in the domestic league – 87 in all – over the course of the next few months as they romped to another championship triumph.

Ken McKenna's side cleaned up the opposition. Victories were easy to come by for the men in green and white hoops, and the only disappointment was that they couldn't go through the entire season without a defeat. That said, they had gone a whole year unbeaten before a late penalty from Carmarthen Town's Nathan Cotterrall ended the run in round 28 of the 34-match campaign. TNS lost again on the final day, to Aberystwyth, but still ended up with 86 points – eight more than in 2004/05 and 18 more than second-placed Llanelli.

Rhyl's Cup

The runners-up, from the South Wales rugby union stronghold, followed TNS into full-time professionalism thanks to major new investment and enjoyed their best ever season. Rhyl joined Llanelli in the UEFA Cup by winning the Welsh Cup. They beat Bangor City 2-0 at the Racecourse Ground in Wrexham (where TNS had entertained Liverpool) to regain the trophy they had won two years earlier. TNS were ousted early by Llanelli but did complete a Double of sorts by winning the League Cup, trouncing Port Talbot Town 4-0 in the final. Their opponents gained some consolation by having striker Rhys Griffiths voted Player of the Year. With 28 goals, Griffiths was also the Premier League's top marksman, finishing just ahead of TNS's ever-prolific Marc Lloyd-Williams.

Tradition defeated progress as the Premier League clubs voted to reject a switch to summer football. Although Rhyl and Carmarthen Town both passed the first qualifying round of the 2005/06 UEFA Cup, the move effectively condemns Welsh clubs to an annual struggle in Europe. UEFA's decision to regionalise the UEFA Cup qualifying rounds means that most of the Welsh clubs' potential opponents play spring-to-autumn domestic football and are therefore in mid-season when the games take place.

Wales ended their World Cup qualifying campaign on a bright note with wins against Northern Ireland and Azerbaijan, thus ending a miserable 14-match run without a competitive victory. Ryan Giggs was the star of the show in both games and has blossomed since manager John Toshack gave him the captaincy. Robbie Savage, on the other hand, has burned his bridges with Toshack after a bitter feud and will no longer be considered for selection. John Hartson initially announced his retirement from international football, but his subsequent decision to make himself available again came as a boost ahead of Wales' daunting Euro 2008 qualifying challenge.

NATIONAL TEAM RESULTS 2005/06

Date	Opponent	H/A	Venue	Score	Scorers
17/8/05	Slovenia	H	Swansea	0-0	
3/9/05	England (WCQ)	H	Cardiff	0-1	
7/9/05	Poland (WCQ)	A	Warsaw	0-1	
8/10/05	Northern Ireland (WCQ)	A	Belfast	3-2	Davies (27), Robinson (38), Giggs (61)
12/10/05	Azerbaijan (WCQ)	H	Cardiff	2-0	Giggs (3, 51)
16/11/05	Cyprus	A	Limassol	0-1	
1/3/06	Paraguay	H	Cardiff	0-0	
27/5/06	Trinidad & Tobago	N	Graz	2-1	Earnshaw (38, 87)

Wales

NATIONAL TEAM APPEARANCES 2005/06

Coach – John TOSHACK

Player	DOB	Club	Slo	ENG	POL	NIR	AZB	Cyp	Par	Tri	Caps	Goals
Danny COYNE	27/8/73	Burnley (ENG)	G	G	G						11	-
Richard DUFFY	30/8/85	Coventry City (ENG)	D73	D	s46	s51	D	D76			6	-
Robert PAGE	3/9/74	Coventry City (ENG)	D	D64				D			41	-
Danny GABBIDON	8/8/79	West Ham United (ENG)	D	D	D		D	D	D	D	26	-
David PARTRIDGE	26/11/78	Bristol City (ENG)	D89	D	D	D				D46	7	-
Sam RICKETTS	11/10/81	Swansea City	D	D	D	D87	s53	D	D		10	-
Carl ROBINSON	13/10/76	Sunderland (ENG) /Norwich City (ENG)	M85	M54		M	M	M	s75	D	29	1
Carl FLETCHER	7/5/80	West Ham United (ENG)	M	M	M	M	M69	M	M75	M46	15	-
David VAUGHAN	18/2/83	Crewe Alexandra (ENG)	M68			s76	M	M66		M55	7	-
Robert EARNSHAW	6/4/81	West Bromwich Albion (ENG) /Norwich City (ENG)	A61	s69	A81	A76		s66	s78	A	26	11
John HARTSON	5/4/75	Celtic (SCO)	A	A		A	A	A			51	14
Gavin WILLIAMS	20/6/80	West Ham United (ENG) /Ipswich Town (ENG)	s61						s46		2	-
Paul PARRY	19/8/80	Cardiff City	s68								6	1
Rob EDWARDS	25/12/82	Wolverhampton Wanderers (ENG)	s73		D46			s76	D		11	-
Craig DAVIES	9/1/86	Oxford United (ENG)	s85		s69						2	-
Gareth ROBERTS	6/2/78	Tranmere Rovers (ENG)	s89							s46	10	-
Simon DAVIES	23/10/79	Everton (ENG)		M69	M	M	M		M76	M79	30	5
Ryan GIGGS	29/11/73	Manchester United (ENG)		A	M	M	M73		M86		56	11
Jason KOUMAS	25/9/79	Cardiff City		s54	M69				M70		17	1
James COLLINS	23/8/83	West Ham United (ENG)		s64	D	D51	D		D	D	12	-
Joe LEDLEY	23/1/87	Cardiff City			s81				s70	D	3	-
Paul JONES	18/4/67	Wolverhampton Wanderers (ENG) /Queens Park Rangers (ENG)				G	G		G63		46	-
Mark DELANEY	13/5/76	Aston Villa (ENG)				D					34	-
Danny COLLINS	6/8/80	Sunderland (ENG)				s87	D53	M46			4	-
Andrew CROFTS	29/5/84	Gillingham (ENG)					s69		s76	s46	3	-
David COTTERILL	4/12/87	Bristol City (ENG)					s73		s86	A46	3	-
Lewis PRICE	19/7/84	Ipswich Town (ENG)						G	s63		2	-
Craig BELLAMY	13/7/79	Blackburn Rovers (ENG)						A	A78		35	9
Lewin NYATANGA	18/8/88	Derby County (ENG)							D	s46	2	-
Jason BROWN	18/5/82	Gillingham (ENG)								G46	1	-
Glyn GARNER	9/12/76	Leyton Orient (ENG)								s46	1	-
Gareth BALE	16/7/89	Southampton (ENG)								s55	1	-
Arron DAVIES	22/6/84	Yeovil Town (ENG)								s79	1	-

Wales

EUROPEAN CUPS 2005/06

UEFA CHAMPIONS LEAGUE

TOTAL NETWORK SOLUTIONS
1st qualifying round LIVERPOOL (ENG)
A 0-3
Doherty, Naylor, King, Baker, Evans, Holmes (Lawless 72), Jackson, Ruscoe, Wood, Ward (Leah 82), Wilde (Beck 59).
H 0-3
Doherty, Naylor, King, Baker, Evans (Jackson 78), Holmes, Ruscoe, Beck (Ward 68), Hogan, Toner, Wood (Lloyd-Williams 58).

UEFA CUP

CARMARTHEN TOWN
1st qualifying round LONGFORD TOWN (IRL)
A 0-2
Pennock, Carter, Lloyd, Giles, Cochlin, Jones (James 90), Aherne Evans, Kennedy, Dodds, Thomas, Smothers (Hardy 63).
H 5-1 *Thomas (16, 75), Lloyd (49, 65p), Cotterrall (80)*
Pennock, Hardy, Lloyd, Giles, Carter, Jones, Aherne Evans, Kennedy, Dodds, Thomas (Walters 84), Smothers (Cotterrall 59).

2nd qualifying round FC KØBENHAVN (DEN)
A 0-2
Pennock, Carter, Hardy, Lloyd, Aherne Evans, Giles, Jones, Kennedy (Walters 69), Smothers (Burke 76), Dodds, Thomas (Cotterrall 57).
H 0-2
Pennock, Carter, Hardy, Giles, Lloyd, Cotterrall (Smothers 67), Jones, Kennedy, Aherne Evans, Dodds (James 84), Thomas (Hughes 46).

RHYL
1st qualifying round ATLANTAS KLAIPEDA (LIT)
H 2-1 *Hunt (11, 70)*
McGuigan, Adamson, Powell M., Horan, Stones, Brewerton, Wilson (Powell G. 86), Hunt (Morgan 86), Graves, Limbert, Moran (Thompson 89).
A 2-3 *Stones (33), Powell (62)*
McGuigan, Adamson, Powell M., Horan, Stones, Brewerton, Graves (Connolly 90), Limbert, Morgan (Mutton 46), Powell G., Moran.

2nd qualifying round VIKING FK (NOR)
H 0-1
McGuigan, Powell M., Horan, Stones, Brewerton, Graves, Limbert, Adamson, Wilson, Hunt, Moran (Mutton 77).
A 1-2 *Adamson (35)*
McGuigan, Powell M., Horan, Stones, Brewerton, Graves, Connolly (Mutton 77), Adamson, Wilson, Hunt (Powell G. 83), Moran.

TOP GOALSCORERS 2005/06

28	Rhys GRIFFITHS (Port Talbot Town)
26	Marc LLOYD-WILLIAMS (Total Network Solutions)
22	Paul ROBERTS (Bangor City)
20	Lee HUNT (Rhyl)
19	Steve ROGERS (Welshpool Town)
18	Mike WILDE (Total Network Solutions)
16	Andy MORAN (Rhyl)
	Carl OWEN (CPD Porthmadog)
15	Danny BARTON (Newtown)
	Iván NOFUENTES (Llanelli)

LEAGUE RESULTS/SCORERS/APPEARANCES/GOALS 2005/06

ABERYSTWYTH TOWN
Manager - David Burrows (ENG); (29/10/05) (Martin Griffiths); (14/11/05) Brian Coyne (SCO)

2005

Date	Opponent	H/A	Score	Scorers
27/8	NEWI Cefn Druids	a	2-2	Meredith, Roberts S.
30/8	Grange Harlequins	h	0-0	
4/9	Rhyl	a	1-4	Sherbon
9/9	Haverfordwest County	h	1-1	Coates
17/9	Newtown	a	3-1	Evans N., Rees, Sherbon
24/9	Caernarfon Town	h	1-1	Meredith, Roberts S.
7/10	Llanelli	a	1-2	Thomas A.
14/10	Welshpool Town	h	6-2	Sherbon 3, Roberts S. 2, Coates
22/10	Total Network Solutions	a	0-5	
29/10	Port Talbot Town	h	0-3	
12/11	Bangor City	a	1-3	Hicks
18/11	Caersws FC	h	0-0	
3/12	Connah's Quay Nomads	h	1-2	Hughes
9/12	Cwmbran Town	a	3-1	Hughes, og (Price), Roberts S.
17/12	Airbus UK	h	2-2	Billing, Lloyd
26/12	CPD Porthmadog	h	4-1	Evans N. 2, Sherbon, Roberts S.

2006

Date	Opponent	H/A	Score	Scorers
2/1	CPD Porthmadog	a	2-0	Hughes 2
7/1	NEWI Cefn Druids	h	2-1	Hicks, Sherbon
14/1	Grange Harlequins	a	5-2	Billing 2, Roberts M., og (Sheppard), Lloyd
22/1	Rhyl	h	1-2	Thomas A.
27/1	Haverfordwest County	a	1-1	Hicks
11/2	Caernarfon Town	a	2-4	Hughes, Roberts M.
18/2	Llanelli	h	4-1	Hughes 3, Billing
28/2	Carmarthen Town	a	0-1	
10/3	Port Talbot Town	a	0-0	
14/3	Newtown	h	3-1	Sherbon, Morgan B., Hughes
18/3	Bangor City	h	1-0	Evans N.
24/3	Caersws FC	a	1-1	Billing
31/3	Carmarthen Town	h	1-1	Hughes
8/4	Connah's Quay Nomads	a	0-1	
14/4	Cwmbran Town	h	3-1	Hughes, Evans N., Jones
18/4	Welshpool Town	a	4-1	Hughes 3, Sherbon
22/4	Airbus UK	a	1-0	Watkins
25/4	Total Network Solutions	h	2-0	Sherbon 2 (1p)

Name	Nat	Pos	Aps	(s)	Gls
Tom BILLING		M	15	(2)	5
David BURROWS		D	17	(1)	
Jonathan COATES		M	14	(2)	2
Matthew DRISCOLL		D	3	(1)	
Eilian EVANS		D		(1)	
Nick EVANS		D	33		5
Jon FOLIGNO		M	4	(2)	
Geraint GOODRIDGE		M	3	(3)	
Tim HICKS		M	10	(3)	3
Glyndwr HUGHES		M	27		14
Llyr HUGHES		M		(1)	
Dan JAMES		M		(1)	
Sion JAMES		D	30	(1)	
Huw JONES		M	4	(2)	1

Wales

FINAL LEAGUE TABLE 2005/06

		Pld	Home					Away					Total					Pts
			W	D	L	F	A	W	D	L	F	A	W	D	L	F	A	
1	Total Network Solutions	34	15	2	0	47	5	12	3	2	40	12	27	5	2	87	17	86
2	Llanelli	34	9	4	4	30	14	12	1	4	34	14	21	5	8	64	28	68
3	Rhyl	34	10	5	2	34	13	8	5	4	31	17	18	10	6	65	30	64
4	Carmarthen Town	34	8	5	4	35	17	9	1	7	27	25	17	6	11	62	42	57
5	Port Talbot Town	34	7	7	3	20	12	8	4	5	27	18	15	11	8	47	30	56
6	Welshpool Town	34	10	4	3	37	23	5	5	7	22	25	15	9	10	59	48	54
7	Aberystwyth Town	34	8	6	3	32	19	6	4	7	27	29	14	10	10	59	48	52
8	Haverfordwest County	34	4	9	4	25	18	8	5	4	24	18	12	14	8	49	36	50
9	Bangor City	34	6	0	11	26	30	8	3	6	25	24	14	3	17	51	54	45
10	Caersws FC	34	6	4	7	21	30	5	8	4	23	26	11	12	11	44	56	45
11	CPD Porthmadog	34	7	5	5	38	25	5	3	9	19	34	12	8	14	57	59	44
12	Connah's Quay Nomads	34	7	2	8	15	17	3	6	8	21	29	10	8	16	36	46	38
13	Caernarfon Town	34	4	5	8	23	26	5	5	7	24	29	9	10	15	47	55	37
14	NEWI Cefn Druids	34	5	8	4	27	24	2	3	12	15	34	7	11	16	42	58	32
15	Airbus UK	34	4	2	11	17	30	4	6	7	18	30	8	8	18	35	60	32
16	Newtown	34	4	2	11	23	33	6	4	7	19	28	10	6	18	42	61	31
17	Cwmbran Town	34	4	3	10	23	38	4	5	8	19	35	8	8	18	42	73	19
18	Grange Harlequins	34	3	1	13	14	50	1	3	13	9	60	4	4	26	23	110	15

N.B. Cwmbran Town - 13 pts deducted; Newtown – 5 pts deducted; Grange Harlequins - 1 pt deducted.

Name		Pos	Aps	(s)	Gls
Geoff KELLAWAY		M		(1)	
Rob KING		D	5		
Gari LEWIS		D	6		
Ross LLOYD		D	22		2
Sion MEREDITH		M	11	(6)	2
Bari MORGAN		M	23	(1)	1
Richard MORGAN		G	34		
Jamie MORRIS		A		(4)	
Martin NAUGHTON		D		(1)	
Jason REES		A	3	(5)	1
Matthew ROBERTS		M	14	(7)	2
Stuart ROBERTS		A	30		6
Luke SHERBON		M	28	(1)	11
Jamie SHIELD		M		(2)	
Aneurin THOMAS		D	32	(1)	2
Gareth WATKINS		M	6		1
Chris WILKINS		M		(2)	

AIRBUS UK
Manager - Gareth Owen

2005
27/8	Grange Harlequins	h	3-0	McIntosh J., Husband, Leech
30/8	Rhyl	h	1-2	McIntosh J.
4/9	Haverfordwest County	a	1-1	Hopkins
17/9	Caernarfon Town	a	1-0	Hughes
20/9	Newtown	h	0-2	
24/9	Llanelli	h	1-0	Hughes
7/10	Welshpool Town	a	3-3	Sudlow, Hughes, Owen (p)
14/10	Total Network Solutions	h	0-5	
22/10	Port Talbot Town	a	0-4	
28/10	Bangor City	h	2-1	Leech, Hughes
12/11	Caersws FC	a	1-3	Jones
19/11	Carmarthen Town	h	1-3	Jones
25/11	Connah's Quay Nomads	a	0-3	
10/12	CPD Porthmadog	a	1-3	Hussaney
17/12	Aberystwyth Town	a	2-2	Hussaney, McIntosh J.
26/12	NEWI Cefn Druids	h	3-2	Hughes 2, Owen

2006
2/1	NEWI Cefn Druids	a	0-0	
7/1	Grange Harlequins	a	1-0	Jones
13/1	Rhyl	h	1-1	Jones
21/1	Haverfordwest County	h	1-2	McIntosh J.
28/1	Newtown	a	3-0	Hussaney, McIntosh J., Moores
7/2	Caernarfon Town	h	1-2	Hopkins
11/2	Llanelli	a	0-3	
17/2	Welshpool Town	h	0-2	
26/2	Total Network Solutions	a	0-3	
14/3	Bangor City	a	2-1	Jones, Moores
17/3	Caersws FC	h	1-1	Hughes
25/3	Carmarthen Town	a	1-2	Jones
31/3	Connah's Quay Nomads	h	2-2	Owen, White
8/4	Cwmbran Town	a	1-1	Owen
11/4	CPD Porthmadog	h	0-1	
17/4	Port Talbot Town	h	0-1	
22/4	Aberystwyth Town	h	0-1	
29/4	Cwmbran Town	h	1-3	Moores

Name	Nat	Pos	Aps	(s)	Gls
Asa BEARD	ENG	A		(2)	
Paul CONNOLLY	ENG	M	20	(4)	
John DAVIES		D	33		
Richard DORMAN		M	9	(4)	
Steve FUTCHER	ENG	M	13		
Steve HOPKINS		D	26		2
David HUGHES		M	32	(2)	7
James HUSBAND	ENG	M	3		1
James HUSSANEY		A	11	(8)	3
Pat JENNINGS		M		(3)	
Craig JONES		M	32		6

Wales

Name	Nat	Pos	Aps	(s)	Gls
Kevin LEECH	ENG	A	7	(6)	2
Adam McGHEE	ENG	G	24		
James McINTOSH	ENG	A	21	(1)	5
Stuart McINTOSH	ENG	G	2		
Chris MOORES	ENG	A	13	(1)	3
Gareth OWEN		M	32	(1)	4
Simon PEERS	ENG	M	4		
Dave PURCELL	ENG	D	8	(6)	
Neil RIGBY	ENG	D	3		
Richard SMART	ENG	M	5	(3)	
Gareth SUDLOW		D	24	(1)	1
Andy THOMAS		D	7	(8)	
Andrew WATKIN		M		(2)	
Stewart WHITE	ENG	A	7	(3)	1
Paul WHITFIELD		G	8		
Anthony WILLIAMS		M	3	(6)	
Leigh WILLIAMS	ENG	M	27		

BANGOR CITY
Manager - Peter Davenport (ENG); (4/12/05) (Mel Jones); (3/1/06) Clayton Blackmore

2005
Date	Opponent		Score	Scorers
27/8	Llanelli	a	0-5	
30/8	Welshpool Town	h	2-4	Maxwell, Roberts P.
4/9	Total Network Solutions	a	0-2	
17/9	CPD Porthmadog	a	2-1	Roberts P. 2
24/9	Caersws FC	a	6-0	Maxwell 3 (1p), Hay 2, Walsh
8/10	Carmarthen Town	h	1-2	Martin
14/10	Connah's Quay Nomads	a	1-0	Roberts P.
22/10	Cwmbran Town	h	3-0	Hay 2, Roberts P.
28/10	Airbus UK	a	1-2	Hay
12/11	Aberystwyth Town	h	3-1	Burke 2, Hay
18/11	NEWI Cefn Druids	a	2-2	Lamb, Roberts P.
26/11	Grange Harlequins	h	5-1	Roberts P. 3, Lamb, Priest
4/12	Rhyl	a	1-4	Hay
10/12	Haverfordwest County	h	0-1	
17/12	Newtown	a	1-0	Walsh
26/12	Caernarfon Town	h	1-0	Walsh

2006
Date	Opponent		Score	Scorers
2/1	Caernarfon Town	a	1-1	O'Neill
7/1	Llanelli	h	1-3	Roberts P. (p)
14/1	Welshpool Town	a	0-2	
22/1	Total Network Solutions	h	2-3	Lamb, Roberts P.
28/1	Port Talbot Town	a	2-0	Roberts P., Killackey
11/2	Caersws FC	h	1-2	Roberts P.
19/2	Carmarthen Town	a	2-0	Roberts P. 2
24/2	Connah's Quay Nomads	h	0-2	
14/3	Airbus UK	h	1-2	Linnacre
18/3	Aberystwyth Town	a	0-1	
21/3	NEWI Cefn Druids	h	2-1	Roberts P., O'Neill
25/3	Port Talbot Town	h	3-2	Lamb, Roberts P., Jones C.
4/4	CPD Porthmadog	h	1-2	Roberts P.
11/4	Rhyl	h	0-3	
15/4	Haverfordwest County	a	1-1	Jones K.
17/4	Cwmbran Town	a	2-1	Roberts P., O'Neill
22/4	Newtown	h	0-1	
30/4	Grange Harlequins	a	3-2	Roberts P. 3

Name	Nat	Pos	Aps	(s)	Gls
Lee ATHERTON	ENG	D	3		
Kwame BARNETT	ENG	M		(1)	
Martin BEATTIE	ENG	M	23	(2)	
Clayton BLACKMORE		D	28	(2)	
Liam BROWNHILL	ENG	D	1	(1)	
Kenny BURGESS	ENG	M	11	(1)	
Michael BURKE	ENG	M		(19)	2
Darren COWANS		M		(1)	
Phil CROSS	ENG	G	2		
Adam DOCKER	ENG	M	3	(1)	
Paul FRIEL	IRL	M	10	(1)	
Tommy HARRISON	ENG	D	10	(1)	
Ian HAVARD	ENG	G	4		
Alex HAY	ENG	M	15	(3)	7
Carl JONES		M	8	(1)	1
Eifion JONES		D	3		
Kyle JONES	ENG	D	23	(5)	1
Kieran KILLACKEY	ENG	D	12		1
Carl LAMB	ENG	A	25	(5)	4
Michael LINNACRE	ENG	A	10	(1)	1
Chris McGINN	ENG	A	1	(6)	
Lee MARTIN	ENG	D	8		1
Leighton MAXWELL		M	24	(7)	4
Ben OGILVEY		M	9	(9)	
Paul O'NEILL	ENG	D	29		3
Chris PREIST	ENG	M	29		1
Andrew PRICE	ENG	G	28	(1)	
Kevin ROBERTS		M		(1)	
Paul ROBERTS		A	33		22
Kevin SCOTT		M	5		
Michael WALSH	ENG	M	17	(4)	3

CAERNARFON TOWN
Manager - Mark Jones

2005
Date	Opponent		Score	Scorers
27/8	Caersws FC	h	6-0	Jones L. 3 (1p) Allen, Irons, Orlik
4/9	Carmarthen Town	a	1-1	Orlik
7/9	Connah's Quay Nomads	h	4-2	og (Williams), Watkin, Jones L., Irons
17/9	Airbus UK	h	0-1	
24/9	Aberystwyth Town	a	1-1	Irons
7/10	NEWI Cefn Druids	h	1-1	Owen D.
15/10	Grange Harlequins	a	1-4	Owen D.
21/10	Rhyl	h	0-2	
29/10	Haverfordwest County	a	2-2	McNulty, Jones L.
12/11	Newtown	h	0-0	
18/11	CPD Porthmadog	h	1-2	Evans
10/12	Total Network Solutions	a	1-2	Watkin
17/12	Port Talbot Town	h	0-1	
26/12	Bangor City	a	0-1	

2006
Date	Opponent		Score	Scorers
2/1	Bangor City	h	1-1	Sadler
7/1	Caersws FC	a	4-3	Jones E. 2, Sadler, Garside
14/1	Carmarthen Town	h	0-2	
20/1	Connah's Quay Nomads	a	1-2	Jones L.
28/1	Cwmbran Town	h	2-2	Garside, Jones L.
7/2	Airbus UK	a	2-1	Jones L. 2
11/2	Aberystwyth Town	h	4-2	March, Rowley, McNulty, Watkin
17/2	NEWI Cefn Druids	a	2-3	Watkin, Rowley
25/2	Grange Harlequins	h	2-1	Rowley, Orlik
11/3	Haverfordwest County	h	0-2	
17/3	Newtown	a	1-2	Jones L., Orlik
19/3	Cwmbran Town	a	1-0	Watkin
25/3	CPD Porthmadog	a	3-2	Maloney, Watkin, Owen D.
29/3	Rhyl	a	1-2	Orlik
5/4	Llanelli	h	0-3	
8/4	Welshpool Town	a	0-0	
14/4	Total Network Solutions	h	1-3	Jones L. (p)

Wales

17/4	Llanelli	a	1-3	Rowley
22/4	Port Talbot Town	a	1-1	Maloney (p)
29/4	Welshpool Town	h	1-1	Maloney

Name	Nat	Pos	Aps	(s)	Gls
Gavin ALLEN		A	6	(1)	1
Mark EVANS		D	11		1
Jon FOLIGNO		M	2	(2)	
Carl FURLONG	ENG	A	10	(1)	
Craig GARSIDE	ENG	M	16	(6)	2
Kenny IRONS	ENG	M	21		3
Eifion JONES		D	18		2
Lee JONES		A	28		11
Kevin LLOYD		M	1	(4)	
Jimmy McNULTY	SCO	D	34		2
Gerrard MALONEY	ENG	M	7	(1)	3
Dan MARCH		D	24		1
Marcus ORLIK		M	18	(7)	5
Dylan OWEN		M	17	(8)	3
Ian OWEN		M	5	(1)	
Richie OWEN		M	10		
Mike PARRY		D		(1)	
Gwyn PETERS		A	12	(14)	
Wayne PHILLIPS		M	22	(2)	
Paul PRITCHARD		G	34		
Kieran QUINN	ENG	M	11	(3)	
John ROWLEY		A	16	(4)	4
Jason SADLER		A	11	(3)	2
Kevin SCOTT		D	1		
Aaron THOMAS		A	1	(3)	
Darren THOMAS		M		(1)	
Steve WATKIN		A	18	(12)	6
Robbie WILLIAMS		M	20	(6)	

CAERSWS
Manager - Mickey Evans

2005

27/8	Caernarfon Town	a	0-6	
30/8	Llanelli	h	1-4	Evans
4/9	Welshpool Town	a	2-2	Roberts, Mitchell
10/9	Total Network Solutions	h	0-2	
17/9	Port Talbot Town	a	0-0	
24/9	Bangor City	h	0-6	
8/10	CPD Porthmadog	a	3-3	Stephens, Venables, Thompson
15/10	Carmarthen Town	a	3-1	Lewis G., Stephens, Thompson
22/10	Connah's Quay Nomads	h	1-0	Davies J.
29/10	Cwmbran Town	a	2-2	Stephens (p) Lewis G.
12/11	Airbus UK	h	3-1	Thompson 2, og (Futcher)
18/11	Aberystwyth Town	a	0-0	
3/12	Grange Harlequins	a	5-0	Jones G. Davies A. 2, Stephens
10/12	Rhyl	h	1-1	Jehu
17/12	Haverfordwest County	a	0-0	
26/12	Newtown	h	2-1	Clarke, Mitchell

2006

2/1	Newtown	a	2-0	Mitchell, Williams
7/1	Caernarfon Town	h	3-4	Stephens (p), Reynolds, Davies J.
14/1	Llanelli	a	0-5	
21/1	Welshpool Town	h	0-2	
27/1	Total Network Solutions	a	0-2	
7/2	Port Talbot Town	h	1-1	Griffiths A.
11/2	Bangor City	a	2-1	Stephens 2
18/2	CPD Porthmadog	h	2-1	Venables, Grist
25/2	Carmarthen Town	h	1-2	Williams
17/3	Airbus UK	a	1-1	Clarke
24/3	Aberystwyth Town	h	1-1	Stephens
28/3	Connah's Quay Nomads	a	3-1	Mitchell 2, Stephens (p)
1/4	NEWI Cefn Druids	a	0-2	
4/4	Cwmbran Town	h	1-2	Clarke
8/4	Grange Harlequins	h	2-2	Jones G., Stephens (p)
15/4	Rhyl	a	0-0	
22/4	Haverfordwest County	h	1-0	Venables
25/4	NEWI Cefn Druids	h	1-0	Stephens

Name	Nat	Pos	Aps	(s)	Gls
Jack BERMINGHAM	ENG	M	19	(8)	
Hugh CLARKE		D	29		3
Andy DAVIES		M	3		2
Jamie DAVIES		A	4	(9)	2
Ricky EVANS		M	6		1
Antony GRIFFITHS		D	12		1
Craig GRIFFITHS		M	1	(1)	
Lloyd GRIST		M	18		1
Sean JEHU		M	14		1
David JONES		G	2		
Graham JONES		M	29		3
Simon JONES		D	1	(1)	
Geraint LEWIS		M	29		2
Mark LEWIS		M		(3)	
Neil MITCHELL	ENG	A	26	(6)	5
Andy MULLINER		G	32		
Ian PROBERT	ENG	M		(10)	
Mark PROBERT		D	6	(6)	
Colin REYNOLDS		D	32		1
Ben RICHARDS		M	1	(3)	
Gareth ROBERTS		A	4	(1)	1
Tom SPAREY	ENG	D		(3)	
Ross STEPHENS		M	29	(1)	11
Andy THOMAS		D	33		
Neville THOMPSON	ENG	M	13		4
Chris VENABLES		M	17	(2)	3
Mark WILLIAMS		A	14	(9)	2

CARMARTHEN TOWN
Manager - Wayne Davies

2005

27/8	Newtown	a	1-2	Thomas D.
4/9	Caernarfon Town	h	1-1	Jones R.
7/9	Llanelli	a	2-0	Thomas D., Davies
10/9	Welshpool Town	h	2-0	Dodds, Giles
17/9	Total Network Solutions	a	1-4	Davies
24/9	Port Talbot Town	h	1-1	Davies
8/10	Bangor City	a	2-1	Jones R., Lloyd
15/10	Caersws FC	h	1-3	Lloyd (p)
29/10	Connah's Quay Nomads	a	1-0	Jones R.
12/11	Cwmbran Town	h	1-1	Aherne-Evans
19/11	Airbus UK	a	3-1	Cotterrall, Thomas D., Dodds
10/12	Grange Harlequins	h	8-0	Thomas D. 3, Walters, Lloyd (p), Dodds, og (Elliott), Davies
17/12	Rhyl	a	0-1	
26/12	Haverfordwest County	h	2-3	Jones R., Aherne-Evans

2006

2/1	Haverfordwest County	a	2-1	Aherne-Evans 2
7/1	Newtown	h	6-0	Thomas D. 2, Walters, Lloyd, Dodds, Davies
14/1	Caernarfon Town	a	2-0	Dodds, Aherne-Evans

The European Book of Football 2006/2007 - 773

Wales

Date	Opponent	H/A	Score	Scorers
20/1	Llanelli	h	0-1	
28/1	Welshpool Town	a	0-3	
11/2	Port Talbot Town	a	0-3	
19/2	Bangor City	h	0-2	
25/2	Caersws FC	a	2-1	Cotterrall, Jones W.
28/2	Aberystwyth Town	h	1-0	Cotterrall
14/3	CPD Porthmadog	a	0-3	
17/3	Cwmbran Town	a	2-3	Loss, Aherne-Evans
25/3	Airbus UK	h	2-1	Davies, Cotterrall
31/3	Aberystwyth Town	a	1-1	Thomas K.
4/4	Total Network Solutions	h	2-1	Cotterrall 2 (1p)
8/4	NEWI Cefn Druids	h	3-0	Cotterrall, Mohamed, Davies
11/4	Grange Harlequins	a	6-0	Mohamed 3, Davies 2, Thomas D.
15/4	CPD Porthmadog	h	3-1	Thomas D. 2, Dodds
17/4	NEWI Cefn Druids	a	2-1	Davies, Walters
22/4	Rhyl	h	1-1	Thomas D.
29/4	Connah's Quay Nomads	h	1-1	Davies

Name	Nat	Pos	Aps	(s)	Gls
Kevin AHERNE-EVANS		M	29	(2)	6
Richard CARTER		M	14	(4)	
Nathan COTTERRALL		M	27		7
Mattie DAVIES		A	2	(25)	11
Andrew DELVE		G	24		
Mark DODDS		A	27	(4)	6
Saad ESSA	SOM	D	2		
James FLEIG	ENG	A		(1)	
Hayden FLEMING		D	7	(1)	
Martyn GILES		D	29		1
Luke HARDY	ENG	D	32	(1)	
Craig HUGHES		A	2		
Stefan HUGHES		M	1	(6)	
Jimmy JAMES		A		(1)	
Rhodri JONES		D	18		4
Wayne JONES		D	10	(2)	1
Richard KENNEDY	IRL	D	12	(5)	
Craig LIMA		D	6	(7)	
Gary LLOYD		M	15	(7)	4
Colin LOSS		M	10	(1)	1
Kaid MOHAMED		M	14		4
Scott MORRIS		M		(2)	
Tony PENNOCK		G	8		
Neil SMOTHERS		D	26	(4)	
Danny THOMAS		A	23	(7)	12
Kris THOMAS		M	8		1
Robert THOMAS		G	2		
Sacha WALTERS		M	26	(6)	3
Gareth WARTON		D		(2)	

CONNAH'S QUAY NOMADS
Manager - Neville Powell

2005

Date	Opponent	H/A	Score	Scorers
27/8	Haverfordwest County	a	0-2	
30/8	Newtown	h	0-2	
7/9	Caernarfon Town	a	2-4	Reay, Rain
16/9	Welshpool Town	a	1-4	Williams (p)
23/9	Total Network Solutions	h	0-2	
8/10	Port Talbot Town	a	0-0	
14/10	Bangor City	h	0-1	
22/10	Caersws FC	a	0-1	
29/10	Carmarthen Town	h	0-1	
12/11	CPD Porthmadog	a	2-2	Molyneux, Hutchinson
19/11	Cwmbran Town	a	1-2	Robinson
25/11	Airbus UK	h	3-0	Pinch 2, O'Toole
3/12	Aberystwyth Town	a	2-1	Molyneux, Williams (p)
9/12	NEWI Cefn Druids	h	1-0	Robinson
17/12	Grange Harlequins	a	4-1	Molyneux 2, Murtagh, Rain
26/12	Rhyl	h	0-1	

2006

Date	Opponent	H/A	Score	Scorers
2/1	Rhyl	a	1-2	Crawford
7/1	Haverfordwest County	h	1-1	Murtagh
20/1	Caernarfon Town	h	2-1	Molyneux, Murtagh
28/1	Llanelli	a	0-2	
3/2	Welshpool Town	h	2-0	Mutton 2
10/2	Total Network Solutions	a	0-2	
24/2	Bangor City	a	2-0	og (O'Neil), Williams (p)
17/3	CPD Porthmadog	a	0-2	
25/3	Cwmbran Town	h	2-2	Cook, Mutton
28/3	Caersws FC	h	1-3	O'Toole
31/3	Airbus UK	a	2-2	Williams, Rain
4/4	Port Talbot Town	h	0-1	
8/4	Aberystwyth Town	h	1-0	O'Toole
11/4	Newtown	a	1-1	Jellicoe
14/4	NEWI Cefn Druids	h	2-2	Williams (p), Molyneux
22/4	Grange Harlequins	h	1-0	Molyneux
25/4	Llanelli	h	1-0	Molyneux
29/4	Carmarthen Town	a	1-1	Molyneux

Name	Nat	Pos	Aps	(s)	Gls
David BANFORD	ENG	M		(1)	
Liam BROWNHILL	ENG	D	7		
Anthony CANN	ENG	M		(1)	
Stuart COOK	ENG	M	9	(20)	1
Ryan CRAWFORD	ENG	A	20	(5)	1
Ryan DOHERTY	NIR	A	6	(1)	
James GAMBINO		A		(2)	
Andy GRIFFITHS	ENG	M	3		
Ben HEATH	ENG	D	24	(3)	
Ashley HENNESSEY	ENG	M		(1)	
Dean HUGHES		D	3		
Jamie HUGHES		A	1	(1)	
Jay HUGHES		M	4	(1)	
James HUSSANNEY		A	1	(4)	
Craig HUTCHINSON	ENG	M	28		1
Daniel JELLICOE	ENG	D	31		1
Liam JONES		D	7		
Jon KENWORTHY		M	4	(3)	
Gary LINNARD	ENG	M	4	(1)	
Paul McDONNELL	ENG	M	5	(2)	
Phil MOLYNEUX	ENG	M	24	(3)	9
Alan MORGAN		M	23	(1)	
Connall MURTAGH	NIR	M	27		3
Tommy MUTTON		A	13	(1)	3
Gary O'TOOLE	ENG	A	20	(1)	3
Matthew PEARSON	ENG	G	1		
Matthew PHILLIPS	ENG	A	2	(9)	
Gary PINCH	ENG	D	15	(1)	2
Stuart RAIN	CYP	A	14	(13)	3
Gary REAY	ENG	M	6	(1)	1
Martin ROBINSON	NIR	A	5	(1)	2
Andrew RUSSELL	ENG	D	7		
Paul SMITH		G	33		
Daniel STANTON		G		(1)	
Jamie WALLER	ENG	M	1	(2)	
Chris WILLIAMS		D	26		5

CWMBRAN TOWN
Manager - Brian Coyne (SCO); (22/10/05) Sean Wharton

2005

Date	Opponent	H/A	Score	Scorers
31/8	Haverfordwest County	h	3-2	Mohamed 2, Edwards

Wales

Date	Opponent	H/A	Score	Scorers
4/9	Newtown	a	1-4	Carpenter
10/9	Rhyl	a	2-1	Mohamed, Dimond
16/9	Llanelli	a	1-0	Mohamed
24/9	Welshpool Town	h	1-2	Dimond
9/10	Total Network Solutions	a	0-1	
15/10	Port Talbot Town	h	2-5	Dimond, Mohamed
22/10	Bangor City	a	0-3	
29/10	Caersws FC	h	2-2	Mohamed, Edwards
12/11	Carmarthen Town	a	1-1	Hanbury
19/11	Connah's Quay Nomads	h	2-1	Hanbury, Mohamed
26/11	CPD Porthmadog	a	1-5	Heal
9/12	Aberystwyth Town	h	1-3	Pearce
17/12	NEWI Cefn Druids	a	0-0	
2006				
4/1	Grange Harlequins	h	1-1	Hanbury
7/1	Rhyl	h	1-7	Sommers
21/1	Newtown	h	0-1	
28/1	Caernarfon Town	a	2-2	Pearce, Green
8/2	Llanelli	h	0-1	
11/2	Welshpool Town	a	1-5	Edwards (p)
17/2	Total Network Solutions	h	1-4	og (Evans)
21/2	Haverfordwest County	a	0-3	
24/2	Port Talbot Town	a	1-2	Collins
28/2	Grange Harlequins	a	1-1	Heal (p)
17/3	Carmarthen Town	h	3-2	Hanbury 2, Carpenter
19/3	Caernarfon Town	h	0-1	
25/3	Connah's Quay Nomads	a	2-2	Collins, Pearce
4/4	Caersws FC	a	2-1	Pearce 2
8/4	Airbus UK	h	1-1	Green
14/4	Aberystwyth Town	a	1-3	Loverso
17/4	Bangor City	h	1-2	Loverso
19/4	CPD Porthmadog	h	3-1	Collins, Carpenter, Ward
22/4	NEWI Cefn Druids	h	1-2	Heal
29/4	Airbus UK	a	3-1	Green, Hanbury, Misbah Z.

Name	Nat	Pos	Aps	(s)	Gls
Kyle ALLCOCK		M	2		
Tom BILLING		A	1	(1)	
Mike BINNING		M	9	(2)	
Paul BONAR	ENG	D	3	(2)	
Joseph CARLESS		M		(2)	
Rhys CARPENTER		M	23	(9)	3
Nicholas CHURCH		G	1		
Daniel CLARE		M	13	(9)	
Josh COLLINS		A	15	(1)	3
David DAVIES		M		(2)	
Jason DAVIES		D	6	(1)	
Kristian DIMOND		M	11		3
Jamie EDWARDS		A	31	(2)	3
Luke FERNQUEST		M	2	(2)	
Geraint GOODRIDGE		M	13	(5)	
Terry GREEN	ENG	M	31	(1)	3
Kristian HANBURY		D	20	(5)	6
Simon HEAL		M	33	(1)	3
Fitzroy HUTCHINSON	ENG	G	2		
Richard INGHAM		M	1		
Kristian JAMES		D	8		
Richard JEFFRIES		G	1		
Richard LANCASTER		G	15		
Ross LLOYD		D	7		
Steven LOVERSO	USA	A	7		2
Andy MAINWARING		A	1	(2)	
Samir MISBAH		M		(3)	
Zaki MISBAH		A	9	(11)	1
Kaid MOHAMED		M	11		7
Chris PEARCE		M	11	(3)	5
Jason PERRY		D	8		
Martyn PHILLIPS		M	12	(6)	
Marcus POWER		M		(1)	
Jason PRICE		D	2		
Chris ROGERS		M		(7)	
Lewis SOMMERS		A	2		1
Kris THOMAS		M	7		
Darryl TIPPINS		M	1	(3)	
Nicky WARD	ENG	M	24		1
Gareth WESSON		G	15		
Gareth WYSOME		D	16		

GRANGE HARLEQUINS
Manager - Paul Giles; (15/10/05) (Mal Camillieri); (14/11/05) Steve May

Date	Opponent	H/A	Score	Scorers
2005				
27/8	Airbus UK	a	0-3	
30/8	Aberystwyth Town	a	0-0	
4/9	NEWI Cefn Druids	h	3-1	Summers 3 (1p)
17/9	Rhyl	a	2-5	Summers 2 (1p)
24/9	Haverfordwest County	h	1-0	Ryan
8/10	Newtown	a	0-5	
15/10	Caernarfon Town	h	4-1	Rose 3, Raven
29/10	Welshpool Town	h	0-5	
12/11	Total Network Solutions	a	0-7	
18/11	Port Talbot Town	a	1-0	Summers
26/11	Bangor City	a	1-5	Showdery
3/12	Caersws FC	h	0-5	
10/12	Carmarthen Town	a	0-8	
17/12	Connah's Quay Nomads	h	1-4	Abdillahi (p)
21/12	Llanelli	a	0-1	
2006				
4/1	Cwmbran Town	a	1-1	Raven (p)
7/1	Airbus UK	h	0-5	
14/1	Aberystwyth Town	h	2-5	Baah, Abdillahi (p)
22/1	NEWI Cefn Druids	a	0-7	
28/1	CPD Porthmadog	a	0-4	
4/2	CPD Porthmadog	h	0-2	
10/2	Haverfordwest County	a	0-7	
18/2	Newtown	h	0-1	
25/2	Caernarfon Town	a	1-2	Bashir
28/2	Cwmbran Town	h	1-1	Baah
11/3	Welshpool Town	a	1-2	Karvouniaris
19/3	Total Network Solutions	h	0-3	
21/3	Llanelli	h	0-5	
28/3	Port Talbot Town	h	0-5	
8/4	Caersws FC	a	2-2	Nsowah, White
11/4	Carmarthen Town	h	0-6	
17/4	Rhyl	h	0-2	
22/4	Connah's Quay Nomads	a	0-1	
30/4	Bangor City	h	2-3	White 2

Name	Nat	Pos	Aps	(s)	Gls
Omar ABDILLAHI		M	14	(2)	2
Rasul ABDUL		A	10	(2)	
Craig ATTARD		G	1		
Nana BAAH		A	5	(1)	2
Ryan BARRY		A	1		
Atif BASHIR		D	8		1
Tony BIRD		A	1		
Lee BISHOP		M	8	(6)	
Jamie BRAND	ENG	M		(2)	
Dominic BROAD		M		(1)	
Rhys CARR		D		(1)	

Wales

Name	Nat	Pos	Aps	(s)	Gls
Danny CARTER	ENG	M	7		(1)
Eston CHIVERTON	ENG	M	9		(1)
Gareth ELLIOTT		D	9		
Saad ESSA	SOM	M	16		
Terry EVANS		D	14		
Joe FINLAYSON		M	7		(1)
Liam FISH		M	8	(5)	
Paul GILES		A			(1)
Chris GOLTON		G	6		
Stephen HEALEY		D	1		
Scott HILLMAN		D	2		(2)
Matthew HOPKINS		D	18		(3)
Phil JAMES		M	1		
Carl JENKINS		M	5		
Ramos KARVOUNIARIS		D	15	(1)	1
Robert KING		M	6		
Adam LEWIS		D	5	(4)	
Craig LIMA		M	6		
Tomás LUBUSKY	SVK	M	4	(2)	
James LYON		M	5	(5)	
David McCILROY		M	10	(2)	
Paul MICHAEL		A	3	(2)	
Gareth MORGAN		D	1		
Daniel NASH		M	3	(8)	
Ahmed NOOR		M	1	(4)	
Nelson NSOWAH	GER	A	3	(1)	1
Frank OPPONG	GHA	M	7	(1)	
Michael PARKINS		M	2		
Allan PERKINS		A	6	(3)	
Jonathan PHILLIPS		D	1		
Dale RAVEN		M	10		2
Anthony REDWOOD		M	5	(2)	
Michael REGAN		D	2	(5)	
Craig RISEBOROUGH		D	1		
Martin ROSE	ENG	M	5		3
Darren RYAN	ENG	M	3	(1)	1
Kyle SHEPPARD		M	15	(1)	
Brian SHOWDERY		M	15		1
Jamie STACEY		D	19	(2)	
Chris SUMMERS		A	6	(1)	6
Matthew TANETTA		M	15	(3)	
Daniel TANHAI		M	1	(1)	
Grant THOMAS		M		(2)	
Neil THOMAS		G	9		
Ben TINGLEY		M	16	(2)	
Nathan WHITE		A	6	(4)	3
Gareth WILLIAMS		G	17		

HAVERFORDWEST COUNTY
Manager - Deryn Brace

2005
27/8	Connah's Quay Nomads	h	2-0	Adams, Hicks
31/8	Cwmbran Town	a	2-3	Thomas W. 2
4/9	Airbus UK	h	1-1	Thomas W.
9/9	Aberystwyth Town	a	1-1	Thomas W.
17/9	NEWI Cefn Druids	h	0-0	
24/9	Grange Harlequins	a	0-1	
8/10	Rhyl	h	2-2	Hicks, Adams
15/10	CPD Porthmadog	h	1-1	Rossiter
22/10	Newtown	a	3-2	Adams 2, Rossiter
29/10	Caernarfon Town	a	2-2	Hudgell, Thomas W. (p)
12/11	Llanelli	a	1-0	Blain D.
19/11	Welshpool Town	h	2-1	Rossiter, Adams
2/12	Port Talbot Town	h	1-3	O'Sullivan
10/12	Bangor City	a	1-0	Cattlin
17/12	Caersws FC	h	0-0	
26/12	Carmarthen Town	a	3-2	Adams, Palmer N., Hudgell

2006
2/1	Carmarthen Town	h	1-2	Jones R.
7/1	Connah's Quay Nomads	a	1-1	Hudgell
21/1	Airbus UK	a	2-1	Jones R., Thomas O.
27/1	Aberystwyth Town	h	1-1	og (Hicks)
10/2	Grange Harlequins	h	7-0	Thomas W. 2 (2p), Adams, Jones R., McNabney, O'Sullivan, Hudgell
18/2	Rhyl	a	1-1	Hicks
21/2	Cwmbran Town	h	3-0	og (Wysome), Jones R., Hicks
25/2	CPD Porthmadog	a	4-1	Adams 3, Hicks
4/3	Newtown	h	1-1	Hicks
11/3	Caernarfon Town	a	2-0	Adams, Hudgell
17/3	Llanelli	h	0-2	
25/3	Welshpool Town	a	1-1	Hicks
31/3	Total Network Solutions	h	0-1	
11/4	Total Network Solutions	a	0-2	
15/4	Bangor City	h	1-1	Jones R.
20/4	Port Talbot Town	a	1-1	Hicks
22/4	Caersws FC	a	0-1	
29/4	NEWI Cefn Druids	a	1-0	Hicks

Name	Nat	Pos	Aps	(s)	Gls
Richard ADAMS	ENG	A	31	(1)	11
Dylan BLAIN		M	24	(5)	1
Peter BLAIN		G	2		
Deryn BRACE		D	28		
Lee BROWN		A	2		
Phil CATTLIN		D	21	(4)	1
Jack CHRISTOPHER		A	1	(6)	
Gareth ELLIOTT		D	4		
Tim HICKS		M	16	(2)	9
Lee HUDGELL	GER	M	29	(4)	5
Richard HUGHES		D	5		
Lee JOHN		A	6		
Robat JONES		D	31		5
Wayne JONES		D	16		
Lee KENDALL		G	32		
Colin LOSS	ENG	M	5	(1)	
Steve McNABNEY		A	2	(6)	1
Chris MILLER		A	2	(2)	
Chris O'SULLIVAN		M	23	(7)	2
Lee PALMER		D		(1)	
Nicky PALMER		M	32		1
Adam RAYMOND		M		(5)	
Dean ROSSITER		M	22	(4)	3
Brett SHAKIR		M		(9)	
Owen THOMAS		A	8	(8)	1
Wyn THOMAS		D	31		7
Nick WOODROW		A	1	(6)	

LLANELLI
Manager - Lucas Cazorla Luque (ESP); (29/1/06) Peter Nicholas

2005
27/8	Bangor City	h	5-0	Cheesman 2, Torres 2, Fernández
30/8	Caersws FC	a	4-1	Mingorance 2, Torres, Williams
7/9	Carmarthen Town	h	0-2	
16/9	Cwmbran Town	h	0-1	
24/9	Airbus UK	a	0-1	
7/10	Aberystwyth Town	h	2-1	Mingorance, Williams

Wales

Date	Opponent	H/A	Score	Scorers
16/10	NEWI Cefn Druids	a	5-2	Williams 2, Nofuentes 2, Rodríguez
29/10	Rhyl	a	1-0	Mingorance
12/11	Haverfordwest County	h	0-1	
19/11	Newtown	a	3-0	Harrhy 2, Nofuentes
10/12	Welshpool Town	a	2-3	Nofuentes, Williams
17/12	Total Network Solutions	h	0-2	
21/12	Grange Harlequins	h	1-0	Corbisiero
26/12	Port Talbot Town	a	1-0	Huggins
2006				
2/1	Port Talbot Town	h	3-1	Harrhy, Corbisiero, Thomas N.
7/1	Bangor City	a	3-1	Belle 2, Harrhy
14/1	Caersws FC	h	5-0	Jones 2, Williams, Mingorance, Nofuentes
20/1	Carmarthen Town	a	1-0	Harrhy
28/1	Connah's Quay Nomads	h	2-0	Belle, Nofuentes
8/2	Cwmbran Town	a	1-0	Thomas N.
11/2	Airbus UK	h	3-0	Nofuentes 2, Thomas N.
18/2	Aberystwyth Town	a	1-4	Lloyd
25/2	NEWI Cefn Druids	h	1-0	Belle
17/3	Haverfordwest County	a	2-0	Edwards, Williams
21/3	Grange Harlequins	a	5-0	Nofuentes 3, Williams, Belle
28/3	CPD Porthmadog	a	2-1	Nofuentes, Williams
5/4	Caernarfon Town	a	3-0	Nofuentes, Belle, Harris
8/4	CPD Porthmadog	h	2-2	Nofuentes 2
15/4	Welshpool Town	h	0-0	
17/4	Caernarfon Town	h	3-1	Belle 2, Harrhy
19/4	Newtown	h	2-2	Lloyd, Williams
22/4	Total Network Solutions	a	0-0	
25/4	Connah's Quay Nomads	a	0-1	
29/4	Rhyl	h	1-1	Harrhy

Name	Nat	Pos	Aps	(s)	Gls
Richard APPLEBY	ENG	M	3	(5)	
Cortez BELLE	ENG	A	18		8
Peter CHEESMAN		M	3		2
Craig CONNOR		M		(1)	
Antonio CORBISIERO	ENG	D	25	(2)	2
Stuart EDWARDS		A	8	(5)	1
Efren FERNÁNDEZ	ESP	D	8	(2)	
Nick HARRHY		A	15	(10)	7
Richard HARRIS	ENG	A	1	(8)	1
Kirk HUGGINS		D	15	(4)	1
Gethin JONES		D		(1)	
Stuart JONES		D	33		2
Gary LLOYD		D	14		2
Jacob MINGORANCE	ESP	M	24	(7)	5
Kaid MOHAMED		A	2	(3)	
Iván NOFUENTES	ESP	A	29		15
John PHILLIPS		D	4	(6)	
Lee PHILLIPS		D	31		
Dyfan PIERCE		D	24		
Daniel PURZYCKI	POL	A		(1)	
Iain RAMSAY	AUS	M		(1)	
Jamie REWBURY		D	20	(6)	
Duncan ROBERTS	ENG	G	34		
Francisco RODRÍGUEZ	ESP	A	5	(1)	1
Kris THOMAS		M	12	(3)	
Neil THOMAS		M	15	(4)	3
Rudi TORRES	ESP	A	9	(1)	3
Craig WILLIAMS		M	21	(12)	10
Anthony WRIGHT		M	1	(6)	

NEWI CEFN DRUIDS
Manager - Dixie McNeil & Ossie Jones

2005

Date	Opponent	H/A	Score	Scorers
27/8	Aberystwyth Town	h	2-2	Andrews (p), Coulson
30/8	CPD Porthmadog	h	1-1	Williams D.
4/9	Grange Harlequins	a	1-3	Williams D.
17/9	Haverfordwest County	a	0-0	
20/9	Rhyl	h	1-1	Edgar
23/9	Newtown	h	3-0	Griffiths 2, Williams D.
7/10	Caernarfon Town	a	1-1	Andrews (p)
16/10	Llanelli	h	2-5	Andrews (p) Williams D.
21/10	Welshpool Town	a	2-3	Andrews, Jones
28/10	Total Network Solutions	h	0-6	
12/11	Port Talbot Town	a	0-1	
18/11	Bangor City	h	2-2	Andrews, Hobson
9/12	Connah's Quay Nomads	a	0-1	
17/12	Cwmbran Town	h	0-0	
26/12	Airbus UK	a	2-3	Andrews, Leech
2006				
2/1	Airbus UK	h	0-0	
7/1	Aberystwyth Town	a	1-2	Heverin
14/1	CPD Porthmadog	a	0-5	
22/1	Grange Harlequins	h	7-0	Heverin 2, Jones 2, Cook 2, Williams D.
27/1	Rhyl	a	1-1	Barton
11/2	Newtown	a	3-2	Heverin 2 (2p), Leech
17/2	Caernarfon Town	h	3-2	Williams D. 2, McDonnell
25/2	Llanelli	a	0-1	
18/3	Port Talbot Town	h	0-0	
21/3	Bangor City	a	1-2	Heverin
28/3	Welshpool Town	h	1-0	Heverin
1/4	Caersws FC	h	2-0	Heverin, Evans
8/4	Carmarthen Town	a	0-3	
14/4	Connah's Quay Nomads	h	2-2	Jones, Williams D.
17/4	Carmarthen Town	h	1-2	Cook
19/4	Total Network Solutions	a	1-4	Kehinde
22/4	Cwmbran Town	a	2-1	Mazzarella, Cook
25/4	Caersws FC	a	0-1	
29/4	Haverfordwest County	h	0-1	

Name	Nat	Pos	Aps	(s)	Gls
Ian ANDREWS	ENG	A	12	(2)	6
Gareth BARTON		D	25	(2)	1
Martin CHALK	ENG	D	5	(1)	
Matthew COOK		M	32		4
Thomas COULSON	ENG	D	6	(3)	1
Phil CROSS	ENG	G	4		
Matthew DABBS	ENG	D	1		
Kieron DURKIN	ENG	M	3		
Andrew EDGAR	ENG	M	15	(8)	1
Alan EVANS		M	7	(2)	1
Marc GRIFFITHS		A	6	(4)	2
Troy HAYDER	ENG	M		(1)	
Mike HEVERIN	ENG	A	19		8
Paul HIVES		M		(1)	
Mark HOBSON	ENG	D	28	(4)	1
Osian JONES		M	32	(1)	4
Samuel KEHINDE	NGA	M		(5)	1
Kevin LEECH	ENG	A	8	(4)	2
Chris LIGHTFOOT	ENG	M	2		
Paul McDONNELL	ENG	M	9	(4)	1
Louis MACKIN	ENG	G	6		
Lee MARTIN	ENG	D	8		
Paul MAZZARELLA		M	24	(3)	1
Peter PAHULYI	SVK	G	24		

Wales

Name	Nat	Pos	Aps	(s)	Gls
Rhys ROBBINS		D	11	(4)	
Chris ROBERTS		D	13	(2)	
Gareth ROBERTS		D	13		
Aled ROWLANDS		D	32	(1)	
Kevin SCOTT		M	2		
Liam SWEENEY	ENG	M	2	(1)	
Darren WILLIAMS		A	20	(3)	8
Ian WILLIAMS		M	5	(7)	

NEWTOWN
Manager - Roger Preece (ENG)

2005

Date	Opponent	h/a	Score	Scorers
27/8	Carmarthen Town	h	2-1	Hughes, Smith
30/8	Connah's Quay Nomads	a	2-0	Barton 2 (1p)
4/9	Cwmbran Town	h	4-1	Barton 2 (1p), Desormeaux, Hughes
17/9	Aberystwyth Town	h	1-3	Barton (p)
20/9	Airbus UK	a	2-0	Barton, og (Purcell)
23/9	NEWI Cefn Druids	a	0-3	
8/10	Grange Harlequins	h	5-0	Moody, Barton, Lewis, Smith, Selients
15/10	Rhyl	a	1-3	Barton
22/10	Haverfordwest County	h	2-3	Smith, Barton
29/10	CPD Porthmadog	h	3-1	Barton 2, Desormeaux
12/11	Caernarfon Town	a	0-0	
19/11	Llanelli	h	0-3	
26/11	Welshpool Town	a	2-1	Hughes, Barton
3/12	Total Network Solutions	h	0-3	
10/12	Port Talbot Town	a	2-3	Lewis 2
17/12	Bangor City	h	0-1	
26/12	Caersws FC	a	1-2	Smith

2006

Date	Opponent	h/a	Score	Scorers
2/1	Caersws FC	h	0-2	
7/1	Carmarthen Town	a	0-6	
21/1	Cwmbran Town	a	1-0	Desormeaux
28/1	Airbus UK	h	0-3	
11/2	NEWI Cefn Druids	h	2-3	Daniels, Desormeaux
18/2	Grange Harlequins	a	1-0	Lewis
4/3	Haverfordwest County	a	1-1	Hooley
11/3	CPD Porthmadog	h	1-1	Barton
14/3	Aberystwyth Town	a	1-3	Hughes
17/3	Caernarfon Town	h	1-2	Hughes
4/4	Rhyl	h	1-4	Ryan
7/4	Total Network Solutions	a	1-3	Barton
11/4	Connah's Quay Nomads	h	1-1	Desormeaux
15/4	Port Talbot Town	h	0-1	
19/4	Llanelli	a	2-2	Barton (p), Hughes
22/4	Bangor City	a	1-0	Hughes
25/4	Welshpool Town	h	1-1	Hooley

Name	Nat	Pos	Aps	(s)	Gls
Mark ALLEN	ENG	D	30		
Danny BARTON	ENG	A	27	(1)	15
Mike BROWN	ENG	D		(3)	
Damien DANIELS	NIR	M	15	(2)	1
Lee DAVIES	ENG	M	4	(1)	
Danny DESORMEAUX	ENG	M	30	(3)	5
Glenn EVANS		D	4	(2)	
Martyn GILES	ENG	M	23		
Alan HOOLEY	ENG	D	24		2
Gareth HUGHES		M	28	(2)	7
Steve JONES	ENG	G	2		
Shane KIRKHAM	ENG	M		(2)	
Matthew LEWIS		M	27	(1)	4
Dylan McPHEE		M	6		
Adrian MOODY	ENG	D	31		1
Nick PARRY		D	6	(1)	
Sam PICKUP	ENG	M	5	(9)	
Jonathan ROWLEY		G	32		
Darren RYAN	ENG	A	14	(4)	1
Karl SELIENTS	ENG	A		(1)	1
Peter SMITH		A	21		4
David WATKINS		A	7	(4)	
Paul WATSON	ENG	A		(1)	
Andrew WEBB	ENG	M	1	(3)	
Craig WILLIAMS		M	28		
Oliver WILLIAMS	ENG	D	9	(1)	
Radek WOSZCZYNA	POL	A		(1)	

CPD PORTHMADOG
Manager - Viv Williams

2005

Date	Opponent	h/a	Score	Scorers
27/8	Total Network Solutions	h	2-2	Owen C., Davies L.
30/8	NEWI Cefn Druids	a	1-1	Owen R.
4/9	Port Talbot Town	h	1-1	Davies R.
17/9	Bangor City	h	1-2	Owen C.
25/9	Rhyl	h	2-1	Owen C., Foster (p)
8/10	Caersws FC	h	3-3	Foster (p), Thomas N., Davies L.
15/10	Haverfordwest County	a	1-1	Harvey J.
29/10	Newtown	a	1-3	Davies L.
12/11	Connah's Quay Nomads	h	2-2	Owen C., Roberts
18/11	Caernarfon Town	a	2-1	Owen C. 2
26/11	Cwmbran Town	h	5-1	Parry G. 2, Owen C., Foster (p), Davies L.
10/12	Airbus UK	h	3-1	Owen C. 2, Davies L.
17/12	Welshpool Town	a	0-1	
26/12	Aberystwyth Town	a	1-4	Caughter

2006

Date	Opponent	h/a	Score	Scorers
2/1	Aberystwyth Town	h	0-2	
7/1	Total Network Solutions	a	0-7	
14/1	NEWI Cefn Druids	h	5-0	Caughter, og (Roberts G.), Webber L., Roberts, Owen C.
21/1	Port Talbot Town	a	1-2	Owen C.
28/1	Grange Harlequins	h	4-0	Parry G., Owen C., Owen R., Davies L.
4/2	Grange Harlequins	a	2-0	Parry G., Caughter
11/2	Rhyl	a	0-3	
18/2	Caersws FC	a	1-2	Sadler
25/2	Haverfordwest County	h	1-4	Owen C.
11/3	Newtown	h	1-1	Davies L.
14/3	Carmarthen Town	h	3-0	Owen C. 2, Sadler
17/3	Connah's Quay Nomads	a	2-0	Sadler 2
25/3	Caernarfon Town	h	2-3	Davies L., Owen C.
28/3	Llanelli	h	1-2	Sadler
4/4	Bangor City	a	2-1	Davies L. 2
8/4	Llanelli	a	2-2	Sadler 2
11/4	Airbus UK	a	1-0	Hughes R.
15/4	Carmarthen Town	a	1-3	Sadler
19/4	Cwmbran Town	a	1-3	og (Clare)
22/4	Welshpool Town	h	2-0	Sadler, Davies L.

Name	Nat	Pos	Aps	(s)	Gls
Gareth CAUGHTER		M	23	(4)	3
Mark COOK		D		(1)	
Les DAVIES		M	32		11
Ryan DAVIES		D	11	(3)	1
Mike FOSTER		D	32		3
Paul FRIEL	IRL	M	15		
Ywain GWYNEDD		M	10	(14)	

Wales

Name		Pos	Aps	(s)	Gls
Jason HARVEY		M		(5)	1
Richard HARVEY		G	34		
Danny HUGHES		D	28	(1)	
Richard HUGHES		M	3		1
John Gwynfor JONES		D	11	(2)	
John Peris JONES		D	4	(4)	
Cai LLOYD-WILLIAMS		A		(1)	
Geraint MITCHELL		D	13	(4)	
Carl OWEN		A	25		16
Richie OWEN		M	15	(4)	2
Gareth PARRY		M	21		4
James PARRY		D	1		
Rhys ROBERTS		M	30	(1)	2
Jason SADLER		A	13	(2)	9
Iwan THOMAS		M	7	(4)	
Neil THOMAS		M	5		1
Lee WEBBER	ENG	D	34		1
Matthew WEBBER		M		(4)	
Curt WILLIAMS		M		(2)	
Ian WILLIAMS		M	1	(2)	
Iwan WILLIAMS		M		(1)	
Mark WILLIAMS		A		(2)	
Tony WILLIAMS		A	6	(14)	

PORT TALBOT TOWN
Manager - Wayne Davies

2005
27/8	Welshpool Town	h	1-1	Pridham
30/8	Total Network Solutions	h	1-1	Griffiths
4/9	CPD Porthmadog	a	1-1	Griffiths
17/9	Caersws FC	h	0-0	
24/9	Carmarthen Town	a	1-1	Johnston
8/10	Connah's Quay Nomads	h	0-0	
15/10	Cwmbran Town	a	5-2	Johnston 2, Griffiths 2 (1p), Jones
22/10	Airbus UK	h	4-0	Griffiths 4 (1p)
29/10	Aberystwyth Town	a	3-0	Griffiths 3
12/11	NEWI Cefn Druids	h	1-0	Pearson
18/11	Grange Harlequins	h	0-1	
26/11	Rhyl	h	1-0	Griffiths (p)
2/12	Haverfordwest County	a	3-1	Griffiths 2, John
10/12	Newtown	h	3-2	James 2, Griffiths
17/12	Caernarfon Town	a	1-0	Griffiths
26/12	Llanelli	h	0-1	

2006
2/1	Llanelli	a	1-3	Surman
7/1	Welshpool Town	a	1-2	Bowen
14/1	Total Network Solutions	a	0-1	
21/1	CPD Porthmadog	h	2-1	Griffiths 2
28/1	Bangor City	h	0-2	
7/2	Caersws FC	a	1-1	Griffiths
11/2	Carmarthen Town	h	3-0	John, Johnston, Griffiths
24/2	Cwmbran Town	h	2-1	Griffiths (p), John
10/3	Aberystwyth Town	h	0-0	
18/3	NEWI Cefn Druids	a	0-0	
25/3	Bangor City	a	2-3	Pridham, Griffiths
28/3	Grange Harlequins	a	5-0	Griffiths 2, John, Bowen, Pearson
4/4	Connah's Quay Nomads	a	1-0	Bowen
15/4	Newtown	a	1-0	Griffiths
17/4	Airbus UK	a	1-0	Griffiths
20/4	Haverfordwest County	h	1-1	Griffiths (p)
22/4	Caernarfon Town	h	1-1	Griffiths
25/4	Rhyl	a	0-3	

Name	Nat	Pos	Aps	(s)	Gls
Chris ASHLEY		D	3	(1)	
Luke BOWEN		A	6	(16)	3
Carl CLEMENTS		M		(1)	
Jonathan COATES		M	3		
Robert COCKINGS		D	20	(6)	
Michael DAVIES		M		(2)	
Leigh DE VULGT		D	26	(5)	
Steve DEVONALD		M	1	(2)	
Kristian DIMOND		M	9	(2)	
Marty ELLACOTT		G	4		
Rhys GRIFFITHS		A	32		28
Craig HANFORD		D	32	(1)	
Tom HOOPER		D	13	(6)	
Dave HUGHES		A		(1)	
Kristian JAMES		M	7		2
Lee JOHN		A	23	(2)	4
Dean JOHNSTON		M	15	(4)	4
Nicky JONES		M	25	(5)	1
Kyle LETHEREN		G	1		
Andrew PEARSON		A	8	(13)	2
Gareth PHILLIPS		M	27	(1)	
Chris PRIDHAM		M	28		2
Matthew REES		D	33		
Lee SURMAN		D	29	(1)	1
Neil THOMAS		G	22		
Gareth WILLIAMS		G	7		

RHYL
Manager - John Hulse (ENG)

2005
30/8	Airbus UK	a	2-1	Mutton, Moran
4/9	Aberystwyth Town	h	4-1	Moran, Brewerton, Adamson, Mutton
10/9	Cwmbran Town	h	1-2	Mutton
17/9	Grange Harlequins	h	5-2	Hunt 3, Adamson, Brewerton
20/9	NEWI Cefn Druids	a	1-1	Hunt
25/9	CPD Porthmadog	a	1-2	Stones
8/10	Haverfordwest County	a	2-2	Hunt, Mutton
15/10	Newtown	h	3-1	Mutton 2, Taylor
21/10	Caernarfon Town	a	2-0	Moran, Mutton
29/10	Llanelli	h	0-1	
12/11	Welshpool Town	a	1-3	Hunt
18/11	Total Network Solutions	h	0-0	
26/11	Port Talbot Town	a	0-1	
4/12	Bangor City	h	4-1	Moran 2, Hunt, Stones
10/12	Caersws FC	a	1-1	Hunt
17/12	Carmarthen Town	h	1-0	Adamson
26/12	Connah's Quay Nomads	a	1-0	Hunt

2006
2/1	Connah's Quay Nomads	h	2-1	Hunt, Mutton
7/1	Cwmbran Town	a	7-1	Moran 3 (2p), Wilson 2, Hunt, Taylor
13/1	Airbus UK	h	1-1	Moran
22/1	Aberystwyth Town	a	2-1	Moran, Hunt
27/1	NEWI Cefn Druids	h	1-1	Powell G.
11/2	CPD Porthmadog	h	3-0	Moran 2, Hunt
18/2	Haverfordwest County	h	1-1	Hunt
17/3	Welshpool Town	h	3-0	Horan, Moran (p), Sharp
26/3	Total Network Solutions	a	0-1	
29/3	Caernarfon Town	h	2-1	Edwards, Moran (p)
4/4	Newtown	a	4-1	Hunt 2, Edwards, Connolly
11/4	Bangor City	a	3-0	Hunt, Moran 2
15/4	Caersws FC	h	0-0	

Wales

17/4	Grange Harlequins	a	2-0	Hunt, Powell M. (p)
22/4	Carmarthen Town	a	1-1	Hunt
25/4	Port Talbot Town	h	3-0	Powell G., Adamson, Sharp
29/4	Llanelli	a	1-1	Hunt

Name	Nat	Pos	Aps	(s)	Gls
Chris ADAMSON	ENG	M	26	(7)	4
James BREWERTON		D	22	(4)	2
Mark CONNOLLY	ENG	M	21	(8)	1
Tim EDWARDS		D	10		2
Ricky EVANS		M	13	(1)	
John GANN	ENG	G	9		
Stuart GRAVES	ENG	D	28	(2)	
George HORAN	ENG	D	34		1
Peter HOY	ENG	D		(8)	
Lee HUNT	ENG	A	28	(1)	20
Marc LIMBERT		M	14	(8)	
Gerard McGUIGAN		G	10		
Andy MORAN	ENG	A	25	(4)	16
Tommy MUTTON		A	9	(10)	8
Gary POWELL	ENG	M	4	(11)	2
Mark POWELL	ENG	D	25	(4)	1
Chris SHARP	SCO	A	6	(9)	2
Greg STONES	ENG	D	33	(1)	2
Chris TAYLOR	ENG	D	15	(2)	2
Paul WHITFIELD		G	15		
Gareth WILSON		M	27		2

TOTAL NETWORK SOLUTIONS
Manager - Ken McKenna (ENG)

2005

27/8	CPD Porthmadog	a	2-2	Wilde, Lloyd-Williams
30/8	Port Talbot Town	a	1-1	Wilde
4/9	Bangor City	h	2-0	Beck, Lloyd-Williams
10/9	Caersws FC	a	2-0	Lawless, Lloyd-Williams
17/9	Carmarthen Town	h	4-1	Lloyd-Williams 3, Toner
23/9	Connah's Quay Nomads	a	2-0	Ward, Evans S.
9/10	Cwmbran Town	h	1-0	Beck
14/10	Airbus UK	a	5-0	Lloyd-Williams 3, King, Beck
22/10	Aberystwyth Town	h	5-0	Beck 2, Ruscoe, Ward, Wilde
28/10	NEWI Cefn Druids	a	6-0	Lloyd-Williams 3, Wilde 2, Ruscoe
12/11	Grange Harlequins	h	7-0	Lloyd-Williams 4, Wilde 2, Ward
18/11	Rhyl	a	0-0	
3/12	Newtown	a	3-0	Ward, Wood, og (Allen)
10/12	Caernarfon Town	h	2-1	Lloyd-Williams (p), Naylor
17/12	Llanelli	a	2-0	Ward, Beck
26/12	Welshpool Town	a	2-1	Wilde, Evans S.

2006

2/1	Welshpool Town	h	1-1	Lloyd-Williams
7/1	CPD Porthmadog	h	7-0	Lloyd-Williams 3, Beck, Evans S., Wilde, Jackson
14/1	Port Talbot Town	h	1-0	King
22/1	Bangor City	a	3-2	Wood, Beck, Lloyd-Williams
27/1	Caersws FC	h	2-0	Wilde 2
10/2	Connah's Quay Nomads	h	2-0	Evans G., Ward
17/2	Cwmbran Town	a	4-1	Ward 3 (1p), Ruscoe
26/2	Airbus UK	h	3-0	Wilde 3
19/3	Grange Harlequins	a	3-0	Holmes, Wilde, Lloyd-Williams
26/3	Rhyl	h	1-0	Wilde
31/3	Haverfordwest County	a	1-0	Lloyd-Williams
4/4	Carmarthen Town	a	1-2	Holmes
7/4	Newtown	h	3-1	Wilde 2, Ward
11/4	Haverfordwest County	h	2-0	Toner, Ward
14/4	Caernarfon Town	a	3-1	Toner, og (Rowley), Ward
19/4	NEWI Cefn Druids	h	4-1	Lloyd-Williams 2, Brown, Toner
22/4	Llanelli	h	0-0	
25/4	Aberystwyth Town	a	0-2	

Name	Nat	Pos	Aps	(s)	Gls
Phil BAKER	ENG	D	16	(8)	
Steven BECK		M	23	(2)	8
Nathan BROWN	ENG	A		(1)	1
Alfie CARTER	ENG	A	8		
Mark DAVIES		D	1	(1)	
Gerard DOHERTY	NIR	G	34		
Graham EVANS		A	3	(1)	1
Steve EVANS		D	32	(1)	3
Tyson EYO	ENG	M	1		
Adam HOBSON	ENG	A	1		
Barry HOGAN	ENG	M	27	(2)	
Tommy HOLMES	ENG	D	26	(2)	2
Michael JACKSON	ENG	D	18	(9)	1
Chris KING	ENG	M	32	(1)	2
John LAWLESS	ENG	M		(2)	1
John LEAH	ENG	M	10	(10)	
Marc LLOYD-WILLIAMS		A	24	(9)	26
Martin NAYLOR	ENG	D	16	(5)	1
Nick PUGH		M		(1)	
Scott RUSCOE	ENG	M	29	(1)	3
John TONER	ENG	A	13	(15)	4
Nicky WARD		M	17	(9)	12
Craig WHITFIELD	ENG	M		(1)	
Mike WILDE	ENG	A	24	(6)	18
Rob WILLIAMS	ENG	M		(3)	
Jamie WOOD	CAY	M	19	(3)	2

WELSHPOOL TOWN
Manager - Tomi Morgan

2005

27/8	Port Talbot Town	a	1-1	Davies
30/8	Bangor City	a	4-2	Davies 2, Lloyd, Rogers
4/9	Caersws FC	h	2-2	Rogers (p), Davies
10/9	Carmarthen Town	a	0-2	
16/9	Connah's Quay Nomads	h	4-1	Jefferies R. 2, Davies, Windsor
24/9	Cwmbran Town	a	2-1	Rogers 2
7/10	Airbus UK	h	3-3	Davies, Thomas, Rogers
14/10	Aberystwyth Town	a	2-6	Windsor, Rogers (p)
21/10	NEWI Cefn Druids	h	3-2	Wilkinson 2, Windsor
29/10	Grange Harlequins	a	5-0	Rogers 3 (1p), James, Davies
12/11	Rhyl	h	3-1	Shannon 2, Davies
19/11	Haverfordwest County	a	1-2	Davies
26/11	Newtown	h	1-2	Jefferies R.
10/12	Llanelli	h	3-2	Rogers 2, Windsor
17/12	CPD Porthmadog	h	1-0	Wickham
26/12	Total Network Solutions	h	1-2	Rogers

2006

2/1	Total Network Solutions	a	1-1	Shannon
7/1	Port Talbot Town	h	2-1	Windsor, Shannon
14/1	Bangor City	h	2-0	Rogers, Shannon
21/1	Caersws FC	a	2-0	Jefferies R., Thompson
28/1	Carmarthen Town	h	3-0	Rogers 2 (1p) Thompson
3/2	Connah's Quay Nomads	a	0-2	
11/2	Cwmbran Town	h	5-1	Shannon 3, Rogers 2 (1p)
17/2	Airbus UK	a	2-0	Wickham, Davies

Wales

11/3	Grange Harlequins	h	2-1	Lloyd, Wickham	
17/3	Rhyl	a	0-3		
25/3	Haverfordwest County	h	1-1	Rogers	
28/3	NEWI Cefn Druids	a	0-1		
8/4	Caernarfon Town	h	0-0		
15/4	Llanelli	a	0-0		
18/4	Aberystwyth Town	h	1-4	Rogers (p)	
22/4	CPD Porthmadog	a	0-2		
25/4	Newtown	a	1-1	Shannon	
29/4	Caernarfon Town	a	1-1	Thompson	

Name	Nat	Pos	Aps	(s)	Gls
Rob BLOOR		G	1		
Mark BRIGGS	ENG	M	3		
Kenny BURGESS	ENG	M	8	(3)	
Dave CUNNAH		M	21	(2)	
Calvin DAVIES		A	23	(3)	10
John ELLIOTT	ENG	D	1		
David GLEAVE	ENG	M		(1)	
Steve GOODWIN		G	5		
Tommy HARRISON	ENG	D	2	(1)	
Ceri JAMES		M	7	(11)	1
Brett JEFFERIES		D	23	(1)	
Ross JEFFERIES		A	27	(2)	4
Danny JONES	ENG	G	8		
Jonathan JONES		M	7	(7)	
John KEEGAN	ENG	M	21	(2)	
Gethin LLOYD		M	33		2
Gerard McGUIGAN		G	20		
Dan MARCH		D	5		
Tomi MORGAN		A		(1)	
Nick PARRY		D	5		
Mark ROBERTS		M	16	(9)	
Steve ROGERS	ENG	A	34		19
Aden SHANNON	ENG	A	11	(10)	9
Andy SMITH		A		(3)	
Gerrard SMITH	ENG	M	3	(3)	
Mark THOMAS		D	10		1
Mike THOMPSON	ENG	A	23	(1)	3
Justin WICKHAM	ENG	M	29	(6)	3
Craig WILKINSON	ENG	M	4	(1)	2
Geraint WINDSOR		M	24		5

DOMESTIC CUP 2005/06

FIRST ROUND

(9/9/05)
Afan Lido 0, West End 3
(10/9/05)
AFC Llwydcoed 5, Blaenrhondda 0
AFC Porth 0, Pontyclun 1
Bethesda Athletic 1, Mynydd Isa 5
Bridgend Town 1, UWIC Inter Cardiff 4
Briton Ferry Athletic 5, Llantwit Fadre 2
Buckley Town 4, Flint Town United 2
Caerleon 5, Bettws 6 *(aet)*
Caerwys 0, Llanrwst United 2
Caldicot Town 4, Porthcawl Town 0
Cefn United 0, Connah's Quay Nomads 2
Coedpoeth United 0, Caernarfon Town 3
Conwy United w/o Y Felinheli
Corwen 0, Glantraeth 6
Croesyceiliog 2, Garden Village 1
Cwmbran Celtic 2, Ystradgynlais 4
Denbigh Town 1, Prestatyn Town 4
Dinas Powys 0, Port Talbot Town 2
Ely Rangers 4, Cambrian/Clydach B&G Club 2 *(aet)*
Ento Aberaman 2, Barry Town 0
Garw Athletic 1, Taffs Well 7
Glan Conwy 0, Bala Town 3
Goytre United 7, Llanwern 1
Grange Harlequins 2, Penrhiwceiber Rangers 0
Hawarden Rangers 2, Mold Alexandra 3
Holywell Town 0, NEWI Cefn Druids 1
Knighton Town 0, Penrhyncoch 4
Llandudno Junction 0, Airbus UK 3
Llandyrnog United 2, Llanrhaeadr ym Mochnant 3
Llanfairpwll 1, Llangefni Town 3
Llanfyllin Town 2, Carno 1
Llangollen Town 0, Llanberis 2
Llanidloes Town 0, Guilsfield 7
Llanrug United 2, Llandudno 6
Maesteg Park Athletic 7, Ammanford 0
Morriston Town 0, Bryntirion Athletic 1
Neath Athletic 0, Llanelli 1
Nefyn United 1, Halkyn United 0
Newcastle Emlyn 1, Cardiff Corinthians 6
Newport YMCA 2, Caerau Ely 1
Penmaenmawr Pheonix 1, Summerhill Brymbo 1 *(aet; 4-5 on pens)*
Penrhiwfer 2, Risca United 4
Pontypridd Town 3, Pontardawe Town 2
Presteigne St Andrews w/o Meifod Meifod
Rhydymwyn 0, Holyhead Hotspur 6
Ruthin Town 3, Lex XI 4
Sealand Rovers 3, Rhos Aelwyd 2,
Tredegar Town 0, Ton Pentre 4,
Treharris Athletic 4, Goytre FC 2
Troedyrhiw 3, Treowen Stars 0 *(aet)*
(17/9/05)
Chirk AAA 3, Brynteg Village 2
Gresford Athletic 2, Bodedern 1
(21/9/05)
Rhayader Town 5, Four Crosses 1

SECOND ROUND

(1/10/05)
Aberystwyth Town 2, Bettws 0
Airbus UK 4, Conwy United 1
Bangor City 4, Llanberis 0
Caersws 5, Grange Harlequins 3
Caldicot Town 1, Cwmbran Town 3,
Cardiff Corinthians 0, Carmarthen Town 11
Gresford Athletic 1, CPD Porthmadog 2
Haverfordwest County 1, Goytre Unted 2
Holyhead Hotspur 1, Caernarfon Town 3
Lex XI 4, Connah's Quay Nomads 2 *(aet)*
Llanelli 8, Risca United 2
Newtown 5, Llandyrnog United 1
Port Talbot Town 3, Newport YMCA 2
Rhyl 4, Sealand Rovers 0
Summerhill Brymbo 2, NEWI Cefn Druids 3 *(aet)*
Total Network Solutions 4, Welshpool Town 1
Bala Town 3, Penrhyncoch FC 2 *(aet)*
Chirk AAA 1, Nefyn United 2
Croesyceiliog 3, West End 2
Ento Aberaman 0, Briton Ferry Athletic 1
Glantraeth 6, Guilsfield 1
Llanfyllin Town 1, Buckley Town 3
Llanrwst United 3, Llandudno 2
Mold Alexandra 4, Myndd Isa 3
Pontyclun 2, Maesteg Park Athletic 1 *(aet)*

Wales

Pontypridd Town 2, Ton Pentre 2 *(aet; 7-6 on pens)*
Rhayader Town 2, Llangefni Town 4
Presteigne St Andrews 2, Prestatyn Town 4 *(aet)*
Treharris Athletic 1, Ely Rangers 3
Troedyrhiw 3, Taffs Well 2 *(aet)*
UWIC Inter Cardiff 2, AFC Llwydcoed 1
Ystradgynlais 2, Bryntirion Athletic 3

THIRD ROUND

(1/11/05)
Bangor City 4, Airbus UK 2
(4/11/05)
Port Talbot Town 3, Bryntirion Athletic 0
(5/11/05)
Bala Town 4, Buckley Town 3 *(aet)*
Caersws 3, Croesyceiliog 1
Carmarthen Town 4, Briton Ferry Athletic 0
Ely Rangers 1, Cwmbran Town 4
CPD Glantraeth 2, Rhyl 5
Goytre United 6, Troedyrhiw 3
Llangefni Town 3, Llanrwst United 0
Mold Alexandra 0, Prestatyn Town 5
NEWI Cefn Druids 4, Nefyn United 1
Newtown 6, Pontyclun 0
CPD Porthmadog 0, Caernarfon Town 3
Pontypridd Town 1, Aberystwyth Town 0 *(aet)*
Total Network Solutions 4, Lex XI 0
UWIC Inter Cardiff 1, Llanelli 3

FOURTH ROUND

(4/2/06)
Bangor City 2, Newtown 1
Caernarfon Town 4, Bala Town 0
Caersws 1, Llangefni Town 3
Cwmbran Town 1, Port Talbot Town 3
Llanelli 1, Total Network Solutions 0
NEWI Cefn Druids 4, Rhyl 5
Pontypridd Town 0, Goytre United 5
Prestatyn Town 1, Carmarthen Town 2

QUARTER FINALS

(4/3/06)
Llanelli 3 *(Nofuentes 72, 90, Harrhy 60)*, Caernarfon Town 0
Port Talbot Town 3 *(John 27, Rees 67, Pearson 89)*, Llangefni Town 0
(11/3/06)
Bangor City 1 *(Roberts 88)*, Carmarthen Town 0
Rhyl 5 *(Moran 54, 65p, Sharp 73, 82, Stones 51)*, Goytre United 2 *(Davies 7, Penney 21)*

SEMI-FINALS

(1/4/06)
Bangor City 1 *(O'Neil 5)*, Llanelli 0
(8/4/06)
Rhyl 2 *(Sharp 68, Hunt 70)*, Port Talbot Town 2 *(Griffiths 45, Pridham 90) (aet; 5-4 on pens)*

FINAL

(7/5/06)
Racecourse Ground, Wrexham
RHYL 2 *(Moran 48p, Wilson 78)*
BANGOR CITY 0
Referee – *Whitby*
RHYL – Gann, Connolly (Limbert 88), Graves (Adamson 82), Stones, Horan, Edwards, Wilson, Moran, Hunt (Sharp 84), Powell M., Brewerton.
BANGOR CITY – Havard, Blackmore, O'Neil, Jones K., Beattie, Jones C., Killackey, Priest, Linnacre, Roberts, Lamb.
Sent off: Priest (48)

SECOND LEVEL FINAL TABLES 2005/06

NORTH

		Pld	W	D	L	F	A	Pts
1	CPD Glantraeth	34	21	7	6	83	36	70
2	Buckley Town	34	20	7	7	85	52	67
3	Fflint Town United	34	19	12	3	77	40	66
4	Guilsfield	34	16	12	6	73	44	60
5	Llangefni Town	34	17	7	10	68	46	58
6	Llandudno	34	17	8	9	64	42	56
7	Bala Town	34	14	9	11	63	52	51
8	Lex XI Wrexham	34	13	9	12	72	75	48
9	CPD Bodedern	34	13	6	15	40	58	45
10	CPD Penrhyncoch	34	13	4	17	62	78	43
11	Queens Park	34	11	8	15	36	59	41
12	Llanfairpwll	34	11	6	17	58	73	39
13	Llandrynog United	34	10	8	16	51	64	38
14	Gresford Athletic	34	9	9	16	45	64	36
15	Ruthin Town	34	7	13	14	43	55	34
16	Holyhead Hotspur	34	8	9	17	44	67	33
17	Holywell Town	34	5	12	17	49	72	24
18	Halkyn United	34	5	8	21	47	83	23

N.B. CPD Glantraeth and Buckley Town did not apply for promotion; Fflint Town United, Llandudno and Holywell Town – 3 pts deducted.

SOUTH

		Pld	W	D	L	F	A	Pts
1	Goytre United	34	22	9	3	82	42	75
2	Neath Athletic	34	22	7	5	76	32	73
3	Pontardawe Town	34	18	9	7	57	35	63
4	Maesteg Park	34	18	9	7	61	40	63
5	UWIC Inter Cardiff	34	16	6	12	61	52	54
6	Bridgend Town	34	16	6	12	55	47	54
7	Afan Lido	34	13	8	13	46	41	47
8	Dinas Powys	34	13	8	13	42	44	47
9	Bryntirion Athletic	34	13	6	15	62	58	45
10	Newport YMCA	34	11	11	12	48	54	44
11	Barry Town	34	11	10	13	39	50	43
12	Ely Rangers	34	12	5	17	47	59	41
13	Ton Pentre	34	11	5	18	51	60	38
14	Caerleon	34	11	4	19	33	58	37
15	Taffs Well	34	9	9	16	46	62	36
16	Bettws	34	10	5	19	46	63	35
17	Briton Ferry Athletic	34	9	6	19	43	64	33
18	Llwydcoed	34	8	3	23	35	69	27

Section 3

The Directory

ALBANIA

Federata Shqiptarë e Futbollit
Rruga Dervish Hima nr. 31, Tiranë
tel – (00355 42) 50275/6/7
fax – (00355 42) 27877
website – www.fshf.org

Year of Formation – 1930
President – Armando Duka
Secretary – Sulejman Starova
Stadium – Qemal Stafa, Tirana (18,000)

Klubi I Futbollit Apolonia
Lagjja 1 maj
Fier
tel – (34) 22364
Year of Formation – 1925
President – Koço Kokëdhima
Coach – Silviu Dumitrescu
Stadium – Loni Papuçiu (8,0000)
Colours – Green & white stripes/white/white
MAJOR HONOURS
Domestic Cup – (1) 1998.

Klubi Sportiv Besa
Rruga Vangjell Thanasi, nr.7
Kavajë
tel – (554) 2617
Year of Formation – 1925
President – Nexhat Bizhdili
Coach – Hasan Lika
Stadium – Besa (8,000)
Colours – Yellow (black trim) /black/yellow

Klubi Sportiv Dinamo
Kompleksi sportiv Dinamo
Tiranë
tel – (4) 230336
Year of Formation – 1950
President – Besnik Sulaj
Coach – Faruk Sejdini

Stadium – Qemal Stafa (18,000)
Colours – Blue (white trim)/white/white
MAJOR HONOURS
League Championship – (16) 1950, 1951, 1952, 1953, 1955, 1956, 1960, 1967, 1973, 1975, 1976, 1977, 1980, 1986, 1990, 2002.
Domestic Cup – (13) 1950, 1951, 1952, 1953, 1954, 1960, 1971, 1974, 1978, 1982, 1989, 1990, 2003.

Klubi Futbollit Elbasani
Rruga Kongresi i Elbasanit
Elbasan
Tel – (54) 53253
Year of Formation – 1923
President – Arben Laze
Coach – Nikola Ilievski
Stadium – Ruzhdi Bizhuta (8,000)
Colours – Yellow (blue trim)/blue/yellow
MAJOR HONOURS
League Championship – (2) 1984, 2006.
Domestic Cup – (2) 1975, 1992.

Klubi Sportiv Flamurtari
Lagja e Pavaresisë
Vlorë
tel – (33) 24563
Year of Formation – 1923
Coach – Agim Canaj
Stadium – Flamurtari (9,000)
Colours – Red & black stripes/white/red
MAJOR HONOURS
League Championship – (1) 1991.
Domestic Cup – (2) 1985, 1988.

Klubi sportive Kastrioti
Prane Bashkise
Krujë
Year of Formation – 1946
President – Shkëlzen Zhili
Coach – Ramazan Ndreu
Stadium – Kastrioti (5,000)
Colours – Red (black trim)/black/red
MAJOR HONOURS

Klubi sportive Luftëtari
Lagja 18 Shtatori
Gjirokastër
tel – (84) 3647
Year of Formation – 1929
Coach – Mustafa Hysi
Stadium – Gjirokastra (8,000)
Colours – Black & blue stripes/black/blue

Klubi Sportiv Partizani
Rruga Frosina Plaku, nr.31
Tiranë
tel – (4) 231582
Year of Formation – 1945
President – Albert Xhani
Coach – Neptun Bajko
Stadium – Qemal Stafa (18,000)
Colours – Red/red/red
MAJOR HONOURS
League Championship – (15) 1947, 1948, 1949, 1954, 1957, 1958, 1959, 1961, 1963, 1964, 1971, 1979, 1981, 1987, 1993.
Domestic Cup – (15)
1948, 1949, 1957, 1958, 1961, 1964, 1966, 1968, 1970, 1973, 1980, 1991, 1993, 1997, 2004.

Klubi Sportiv Shkumbini
Pranë Bashkisë
Peqin
tel – (512) 2382
Year of Formation – 1924
Coach – Vasil Bici
Stadium – Fusha Sportive (5,000)
Colours – Pale blue (white trim)/pale blue/pale blue

Klubi Sportiv Teuta
Rruga K. Kazanxhi
Durrës
tel – (5) 22215
Year of Formation – 1922
President – Edmond Hasanbelliu
Coach – Sulejman Starova

The Directory

Stadium – Niko Dovana (12,000)
Colours – Blue (white trim)/white/blue
MAJOR HONOURS
League Championship – (1) 1994.
Domestic Cup – (3) 1995, 2000, 2005.

Klubi Sportiv Tirana
c/o Stadiumi Selman Stërmasi
Rruga Muhamet Gjollesha
Tiranë
tel – (4) 26899
Year of Formation – 1920
Coach – Mirel Josa
Stadium – Selman Stërmasi (12,000)
Colours – Blue & white stripes/white/white
MAJOR HONOURS
League Championship – (22) 1930, 1931, 1932, 1934, 1936, 1965, 1966, 1967, 1968, 1970, 1982, 1985, 1988, 1989, 1995, 1996, 1997, 1999, 2000, 2003, 2004, 2005.
Domestic Cup – (12) 1963, 1976, 1977, 1983, 1984, 1986, 1994, 1996, 1999, 2001, 2002, 2006.

Klubi Sportiv Vllaznia
Rruga Vasil Shanto 13
Shkodër
tel – (22) 42045
Year of Formation – 1919
President – Valter Fushaj
Coach – Ulrich Schulze
Stadium – Loro Boriçi (15,000)
Colours – Red & blue stripes/red/red
MAJOR HONOURS
League Championship – (9) 1945, 1946, 1972, 1974, 1978, 1983, 1992, 1998, 2001.
Domestic Cup – (5) 1965, 1972, 1979, 1981, 1987.

ANDORRA

Federació Andorrana de Futbol
Avinguda Carlemany, 67 3° pis,
BP 65, Escaldes-Engordany
tel – (00376) 805830
fax – (00376) 862000
website – www.fedandfut.com
email – info@fedandfut.com

Year of Formation – 1994
President – Francesc Amat Escobar
Secretary – Tomás Gea
Stadium – Comunal (1,604)

ARMENIA

Football Federation of Armenia
Khanjyan Street 27, 375010
Yerevan
tel – (00374 10) 568883
fax – (00374 10) 539517
website – www.armenia.fifa.com
email – ffarm@arminco.com

Year of Formation – 1992
President – Ruben Hayrapetyan
Secretary – Armen Minasyan
Stadium – Razdan, Yerevan
(48,250)

FC Ararat Yerevan
Charents 1 str.
Hainakhagits Institute
Floor 4
375025 Yerevan
tel – (10) 239013
fax – (10) 239029
website – www.fcararat.am
Year of Formation – 1935
President – Hrach Kaprielyan
Coach – Abraham Khashmanyan
Stadium – Razdan (48,250)
Colours – Red (white trim)/blue/red
MAJOR HONOURS
League Championship – (1) 1993.
Domestic Cup – (4) 1993, 1994, 1995, 1997.

FC Banants Yerevan
2 Djivanu str
375032 Yerevan
tel – (10) 747868
fax – (10) 747745
website – www.fcbanants.com
Year of Formation – 1992
President – Sargis Israelyan
Coach – Nikolai Kiselev
Stadium – Kotayk, Abovyan (5,500)
Colours – White (blue trim)/white/white
MAJOR HONOURS
Domestic Cup – (1) 1992.

Gandzasar Kapan
Davit Bek st. 22/6
377810 Kapan
tel – (10) 63140
President – Maxim Hakobyan
Coach – Albert Sargsyan
Colours – Blue (white trim)/white/white

FC Kilikia
Hrazdan canyon 4
375082 Yerevan
tel – (1) 521941
fax – (1) 542161
President – Sergey Agababyan
Coach – Ashot Barsegyan
Stadium – Razdan (48,250).

FC Mika Ashtarak
H. Manandyan 41
375070 Yerevan
tel – (10) 559808
fax – (10) 564781
President – Carlos Gazaryan
Coach – Armen Adamyan
Stadium – Vardanank (1,200)
Colours – Yellow & blue stripes/blue/yellow
MAJOR HONOURS
Domestic Cup – (5) 2000, 2001, 2003, 2005, 2006.

FC Pyunik
7 Masisi str.
375100 Yerevan
tel – (01) 545973
fax – (01) 545976
President – Karen Harutyunyan
Coach – Samvel Petrosyan
Stadium – Razdan (48,250)
Colours – Blue/white/blue
MAJOR HONOURS
League Championship – (5) 2001, 2002, 2003, 2004, 2005.
Domestic Cup – (2) 2002, 2004.

FC Shirak Gyumri
Ozanyan Street 6
377500 Gyumri
tel – (41) 22589
fax – (41) 33634
website – www.fcshirak.8m.net
President – Garnik Khachatryan
Coach – Zhora Barsegyan
Stadium – Ozanyan (3,020)
Colours – Blue & white stripes/blue/blue
MAJOR HONOURS
League Championship – (3) 1994, 1995, 1999.

FC Ulis Yerevan
Vardanants Street 69
375070 Yerevan
tel – (01) 61 75 40
fax – (01) 53 40 17
President – Garnik Hayrapetyan
Coach – Arsen Chilingaryan
Stadium – Kasakh, Ashtarak (3,000)

AUSTRIA

Österreichischer Fussball-Bund
Ernst Happel Stadion,
Meiereistrasse 7, 1020 Wien
tel – (0043 1) 72718-0
fax – (0043 1) 72816-32

The Directory

website – www.oefb.at
email – oefb@asn.or.at

Year of Formation – 1904
President – Friedrich Stickler
Secretary – Alfred Ludwig
Stadium – Ernst-Happel-Stadion, Vienna (47,500)

INTERNATIONAL TOURNAMENT APPEARANCES
World Cup Finals – (7) 1934 (4th), 1954 (3rd), 1958, 1978 (2nd phase), 1982 (2nd phase), 1990, 1998.

FK Austria-Memphis Magna Wien
Franz Horr-Stadion
Matthias Sindelar-Tribüne
Fischhofgasse 12
1100 Wien
tel – (01) 68801500
fax – (01) 6880150380
website – www.fk-austria.at
Year of Formation – 1911
President – Dr. Peter Langer
Coach – Frenk Schinkels
Stadium – Franz Horr-Stadion (11,800)
Colours – Violet/violet/violet
MAJOR HONOURS
League Championship – (23) 1924, 1926, 1949, 1950, 1953, 1961, 1962, 1963, 1969, 1970, 1976, 1978, 1979, 1980, 1981, 1984, 1985, 1986, 1991, 1992, 1993, 2003, 2006.
Domestic Cup – (25) 1921, 1924, 1925, 1926, 1933, 1935, 1936, 1948, 1949, 1960, 1962, 1963, 1967, 1971, 1974, 1977, 1980, 1982, 1986, 1990, 1992, 1994, 2003, 2005, 2006.

Liebherr Grazer Athletik-Klub
Stadionplatz 1
8040 Graz
tel – (0316) 4830300
fax – (0316) 4830309
website – www.gak.at
Year of Formation – 1902
President – Stefan Sticher
Coach – Lars Søndergaard
Stadium – UPC-Arena (15,428)
Colours – Red (white trim)/red/red
MAJOR HONOURS
League Championship – (1) 2004.
Domestic Cup – (4) 1981, 2000, 2002, 2004.

SV Bauwelt Koch Mattersburg
Michael Koch-Strasse 50
7210 Mattersburg
tel – (02626) 62510
fax – (02626) 62721
website – www.svm.at
Year of Formation – 1922

President – Martin Pucher
Coach – Franz Lederer
Stadium – Pappelstadion (18,000)
Colours – Green/green/green

Sportklub Rapid Wien
Keisslergasse 6
1140 Wien
tel – (01) 91001
fax – (01) 9111906
website – www.skrapid.at
Year of Formation – 1899
President – Rudolf Edlinger
Coach – Georg Zellhofer
Stadium – Gerhard-Hanappi (19,600)
Colours – Greene & white stripes/white/white
MAJOR HONOURS
League Championship – (31) 1912, 1913, 1916, 1917, 1919, 1920, 1921, 1923, 1929, 1930, 1935, 1938, 1940, 1941, 1946, 1948, 1951, 1952, 1954, 1956, 1957, 1960, 1964, 1967, 1968, 1982, 1983, 1987, 1988, 1996, 2005.
Domestic Cup – (14) 1919, 1920, 1927, 1946, 1961, 1968, 1969, 1972, 1976, 1983, 1984, 1985, 1987, 1995.

Red Bull Salzburg
Stadion Wals-Siezenheim
Stadionstrasse 1/3
5075 Salzburg
tel – (0662) 433332-32
fax – (0662) 433332-20
website – www.austria-salzburg.at
Year of Formation – 1933
President – Rudi Theirl
Coach – Giovanni Trapattoni & Lothar Matthäus
Stadium – Wals-Siezenheim (18,812)
Colours – Violet (white trim)/violet/violet
MAJOR HONOURS
League Championship – (3) 1994, 1995, 1997.

Cashpoint SC Rheindorf Altach
Schweizer Strasse 8
6844 Altach
tel – (05576) 79911-11
fax – (05576) 79911-14
website – www.scra.at
Year of Formation – 1929
President – Werner Gunz
Coach – Michael Streiter
Stadium – Schnabelholz (10,000)
Colours – White (black trim)/black/yellow

SV Josko Fenster Ried
Volksfestplatz 2
4910 Ried im Innkreis
tel – (07752) 81100

fax – (07752) 81100-33
website – www.svried.at
Year of Formation – 1912
President – Peter Vogl
Coach – Helmut Kraft
Stadium – Fill Metallbau Stadion (7,000)
Colours – Green/black/black

SK Puntigamer Sturm Graz
Eggenberger Gürtel 9/i
8020 Graz
tel – (0316) 771771
fax – (0316) 724811
website – www.sksturm.at
Year of Formation – 1909
President – Hannes Kartnig
Coach – Franco Foda
Stadium – UPC-Arena (15,428)
Colours – Black & white checks/white/white
MAJOR HONOURS
League Championship – (2) 1998, 1999.
Domestic Cup – (3) 1996, 1997, 1999.

FC Superfund Pasching
Pluskaufstr. 11
4061 Pasching
tel – (07229) 62390
fax – (07229) 62390-20
website – www.fcsuperfund.at
Year of Formation – 1946
President – Franz Grad
Coach – Milan Djuricic
Stadium – Waldstadion (7,870)
Colours – White/white/white

FC Wacker Tirol
Feldstrasse 9
6020 Innsbruck
tel – (0512) 5888770
fax – (0512) 5888774686
website – www.fc-wacker-tirol.com
Year of Formation – 2002
President – Gerhard Stocker
Coach – Frantisek Straka
Stadium – Tivoli neu (17,400)
Colours – Green (black sleeves)/black/green

AZERBAIJAN

**Azärbaycan Futbol
Federasiyalari Assosiasiyasi
37 Xocali Prospekti, Silk Way
Business Centre, 5th floor, AZ-
1025 Baki
tel – (00994 12) 908308
fax – (00994 12) 989393
website – www.affa-az**

The Directory

email – info@affa.az

Year of Formation – 1992
President – Ramiz Mirzäyev
Secretary – Fuad Äsädov
Stadium – Tofiq Bähramov Adina Respublika Stadionu, Baki (29,850)

FK Baki
24 Häsän Äliyev Str.
370000 Baki
tel – (12) 4978866
fax – (12) 4971005
website – www.bakifc.com
Year of Formation – 1997
President – Hafiz Mämmädov
Coach – Böyükaga Haciyev
Stadium – Tofiq Bähramov (29,850)
Colours – Blue & white hoops/blue/white
MAJOR HONOURS
League Championship – (1) 2006.
Domestic Cup – (1) 2005.

PFK Gäncä
92a Atatürk Str. 92A
374712 Gäncä
tel – (22) 579360
fax – (22) 579360
Year of Formation – 1959
President – Ruslan Mämmädov
Coach – Shakhin Diniyev
Stadium – Gäncä Märkäzi Sähär Stadionu (25,000)
Colours – Black (green trim)/black/black
MAJOR HONOURS
League Championship – (3) 1995, 1998, 1999.
Domestic Cup – (4) 1994, 1997, 1998, 2000.

FK Gänclärbirliyi Sumqayit
112, Samad Vurgun Str.
1025 Sumqayit
tel – (16) 420101
fax – (12) 976032
Year of Formation – 2003
President – Ilgar Nuriyev
Coach – Äfqan Talibov
Stadium – Mehdi Hüseynzadä Adina Sumqayit Sähär Syadionu (15,350)
Colours – Blue & navy blue stripes/navy blue/blue

Gilan Xanlar
President – Cämil Muradov
Coach – Faiq Cabbarov
Stadium – Qäbälä Sähär Stadionu

PIK Inter Baki
539-40 Bäsir Säfäroglu Str.
370096 Baki
tel – (12) 4984976
fax – (12) 4215260
website – www.inter-baku.com
Year of Formation – 1997
President – Rauf Mämmädov
Coach – Valentyn Khodukin
Stadium – Tofiq Bähramov (29,850)
Colours – White/white/white

FK Karvan Yevlax
115 Ceyhun Mustafayev Str.
Yevlax
tel – (166) 60132
fax – (166) 63792
website – www.karvan.az
Year of Formation – 2004
President – Cavansir Siräliyev
Coach – Yunis Hüseynov
Stadium – Yevlax Sähär Stadionu (5,000)
Colours – Red/red/black

MKT-Araz Imisli
121 H.Äliyev Str.
Imisli
tel – (154) 56223
fax – (0154) 56223
website – www.mktaraz.com
Year of Formation – 2004
President – Ikram Kärimli
Coach – Ihor Nakonechnyi
Stadium – MKT-Araz (8,500)
Colours – Green/green/green

PFC Neftçi Baki
64 Nobel Prospekti
370000 Baki
tel – (12) 4965782
fax – (12) 4965782
website – www.neftchipfc.com
Year of Formation – 1937
President – Rövnäq Abdullayev
Coach – Qurban Qurbanov
Stadium – Tofiq Bähramov (29,850)
Colours – White & black stripes/black/black
MAJOR HONOURS
League Championship – (5) 1992, 1996, 1997, 2004, 2005.
Domestic Cup – (5) 1995, 1996, 1999, 2002, 2004.

FK Olimpik Baki
2/5 N.Räfibäyli Str.
Baki
tel – (12) 4982437
fax – (12) 4925364

Year of Formation – 1996
President – Räsul Räsulov
Coach – Äsgär Abdullayev
Stadium – Säfa (7,852)
Colours – Blue/white/blue

FK Qarabag Agdam
90 Heydar Älyev Prospekti
Baki
tel – (12) 4966001
fax – (12) 4966479
website – www.qarabagh.com
Year of Formation – 1950
President – Abdulbari Gözel
Coach – Böyükaga Agayev
Stadium – Tofiq Ismayilov Adina Suraxani Qäsäbä Stadionu (2,800)
Colours – Dark blue & white stripes/white/white
MAJOR HONOURS
League Championship – (2) 1993, 1997.
Domestic Cup – (2) 1993, 2006.

FK Sahdag Qusar
136 H.Äliyev Str.
370311 Qusar
tel – (138) 52823
fax – (12) 952615
Year of Formation – 1992
President – Bäybala Mämmädov
Coach – Sabir Äliyev
Stadium – Quba Olimpiya Idman Kompleksinn Stadionu (3,000)
Colours – Blue/blue/blue

Simurq Zaqatala
Coach – Roman Pokora
Stadium – Zaqatala Sähär Stadionu

PFK Turan Tovuz
34/1 Sämäd Vurgun str.
374809 Tovuz
tel – (231) 50304
fax – (231) 50305
website – www.turanfc.com
President – Tahir Yusifov
Coach – Sakit Aliyev
Stadium – Tovuz Sähär Stadionu (15,000)
Colours – White/red/red
MAJOR HONOURS
League Championship – (1) 1994.

FK Xäzär Länkäran
20 Füzuli Str.
Länkäran
tel – (12) 4982667
fax – (12) 4981092
website – www.lankaranfc.com

The Directory

Year of Formation – 1993
President – Mübariz Mänsimov
Coach – Agasälim Mircavadov
Stadium – Länkäran Sähär Stadionu (13,000)
Colours – White (green & black trim)/black/white

BELARUS

The Belarussian Football Federation
ul. Sergei Kirov 8/2, 220060
Minsk
tel – (00375 17) 2204540
fax – (00375 17) 2272920
website – www.belarussianfootball.by
email – gambler@belpak.minsk.by

Year of Formation – 1992
President – Gennadiy Nevyglas
Secretary – Vadim Zhuk
Stadium – Dinamo, Minsk (42,375)

FC BATE Borisov
Boulevard Revolyutsii 16
222120 Borisov
tel – (177) 32046
fax – (177) 34123
website – www.fcbate.by
Year of Formation – 1996
President – Anatoliy Kapskiy
Coach – Igor Kriushenko
Stadium – City (5,500)
Colours – Yellow/blue/yellow
MAJOR HONOURS
League Championship – (2) 1999, 2002.
Domestic Cup – (1) 2006.

Belshina Bobruisk
Ul. 50-let VLKSM 26
Bobruisk
tel – (225) 440056/442151
fax – (225) 431178
Year of Formation – 1977
President – Vladimir Bubnovskiy
Coach – Oleg Volokh
Stadium – Spartak (3,700)
Colours – Red/black/white
MAJOR HONOURS
League Championship – (1) 2001.
Domestic Cup – (3) 1997, 1999, 2001.

Darida Zhdanovichi
ul. Lineinaya 1 A
223033 Zhdanovichi
tel – (17) 5089150
fax – (17) 5088599
Year of Formation – 2000
President – Vladimir Delendik
Coach – Ludas Rumbutis
Stadium – Darida (1,500)
Colours – Blue/green/red

Dinamo Brest
ul. Vladimir Lenin 23
224075 Brest
tel – (162) 265221/265932
fax – (162) 264283
website – www.dynamo.brest.by
Year of Formation – 1960
President – Vitaliy Belinskiy
Coach – Sergei Borovskiy
Stadium – Sportkomplex Brestskiy (10,080)
Colours – White/blue/blue

Dinamo Minsk
ul. Vitebskaya 11
220004 Minsk
tel – (17) 2064821/2064823/2064395
fax – (17) 2064824
website – www.dinamo-minsk.com
Year of Formation – 1927
President – Yuriy Chizh
Coach – Olexandr Ryabokon
Stadium – Dinamo (42,375)
Colours – White/white/blue
MAJOR HONOURS
League Championship (USSR) – (1) 1982.
League Championship – (7) 1992, 1993, 1994, 1995 (spring), 1995 (autumn), 1997, 2004.
Domestic Cup – (3) 1992, 1994, 2003.

Dnepr Mogilev
Zadorozhnoye shosse 21
212026 Mogilev
tel – (222) 263485
fax – (222) 263009
website – www.fcdnepr.com
Year of Formation – 1960
President – Valeriy Streltsov
Coach – Vladimir Kostyukhov
Stadium – Spartak (6,800)
Colours – Blue/white/blue
MAJOR HONOURS
League Championship – (1) 1998.

FC Gomel
Sq. Vosstaniya 1
246000 Gomel
tel – (232) 551170/555489
fax – (232) 550044
website – www.fcgomel.by
Year of Formation – 1995
President – Semen Voronchuk
Coach – Nikolai Goryunov
Stadium – Centralnyi (15,000)
Colours – Green/yellow/white
MAJOR HONOURS
League Championship – (1) 2003.
Domestic Cup – (1) 2002.

Lokomotiv Minsk
ul. Surganova 23-1
220012 Minsk
tel – (17) 2315057/2316003
fax – (17) 2320289
website – www.skvich.com
Year of Formation – 2000
President – Yevgeniy Shabunya
Coach – Anatoliy Yurevich
Stadium – Lokomotiv (2,000)
Colours – White/red/white

Lokomotiv Vitebsk
Sq. Ludnikova 12
Vitebsk
tel – (212) 248920
fax – (212) 248920
website – www.lokomotiv-vitebsk.com
Year of Formation – 1960
President – Yuriy Kovba
Coach – Sergei Yasinskiy
Stadium – Central Sport Komplex (8,350)
Colours – White/red/black
MAJOR HONOURS
Domestic Cup – (1) 1998.

MTZ-RIPO Minsk
ul. Vaneyeva 3
220070 Minsk
tel – (017) 2307176/2308897
fax – (017) 2303393
President – Viktor Korol
Coach – Yuriy Puntus
Stadium – Traktor (17,600)
Colours – Red/green/red
MAJOR HONOURS
Domestic Cup – (1) 2005.

Naftan Novopolotsk
ul. Molodezhnaya 49A
211440 Novopolotsk
tel – (2145) 57740/50605
fax – (2145) 54377
Year of Formation – 1995
President – Leonid Podlipskiy
Coach – Vyacheslav Akshayev
Stadium – Atlant (4,500)
Colours – Blue/yellow/blue

The Directory

Neman Grodno
ul. Kommunalnaya 3
230023 Grodno
tel – (152) 723799
fax – (152) 723799
website – www.neman.boom.ru
Year of Formation – 1999
President – Sergei Koroza
Coach – Vladimir Kurnev
Stadium – Neman (6,300)
Colours – Yellow/green/yellow
MAJOR HONOURS
Domestic Cup – (1) 1993

Shakhter Soligorsk
ul. Maxim Gorkiy 5
223710 Soligorsk
tel – (1710) 20621
website – www.fcshakhter.by
Year of Formation – 1963
President – Petr Kulagin
Coach – Yuriy Vergeichik
Stadium – Stroitel (5,000)
Colours – Yellow/yellow/yellow
MAJOR HONOURS
League Championship – (1) 2005.
Domestic Cup – (1) 2004.

Torpedo Zhodino
Boulevard Mira 5/24
222160 Zhodino
tel – (01775) 71579
fax – (01775) 71579
website – www.torpedo.zhodino.by
Year of Formation – 1961
President – Alexandr Pugach
Coach – Yuriy Maleyev
Stadium – Torpedo (3,200)
Colours – Red/blue/red

BELGIUM

Union Royale des Sociétés de Football Association
Houba de Strooperlaan 145,
1020 Bruxelles
tel – (0032 2) 4771211
fax – (0032 2) 4782391
website – www.footbel.com
email –
urbsfa.kbvb@footbel.com

Year of Formation – 1895
President – François De Keersmaecker
Secretary – Jean-Paul Houben

Stadium – Roi Baudouin,
Brussels (50,000)

INTERNATIONAL TOURNAMENT APPEARANCES
World Cup – (11) 1930, 1934, 1938, 1954, 1970, 1982 (2nd phase). 1986 (4th), 1990 (2nd round), 1994 (2nd round), 1998, 2002 (2nd round).
European Championship – (3) 1972 (3rd), 1980 (runners-up). 2000.

MAJOR EUROPEAN CLUB HONOURS
Cup-winners Cup – (3) RSC Anderlecht (1976, 1978); KV Mechelen (1988).
UEFA Cup – (1) RSC Anderlecht (1983).

RSC Anderlecht
Avenue Théo Verbeeck 2
Anderlecht
1070 Bruxelles
tel – (02) 5229400/5221539
fax – (02) 5200740
website – www.rsca.be
Year of Formation – 1908
President – Roger Vanden Stock
Coach – Frankie Vercauteren
Stadium – Constant Vanden Stock (28,063)
Colours – White (mauve trim)/mauve/white
MAJOR HONOURS
League Championship – (28) 1947, 1949, 1950, 1951, 1954, 1955, 1956, 1959, 1962, 1964, 1965, 1966, 1967, 1968, 1972, 1974, 1981, 1985, 1986, 1987, 1991, 1993, 1994, 1995, 2000, 2001, 2004, 2006.
Domestic Cup – (8) 1965, 1972, 1973, 1975, 1976, 1988, 1989, 1994.
European Cup-winners Cup – (2) 1976, 1978.
UEFA Cup – (1) 1983.
European Super Cup – (2) 1976, 1978.

KSK Beveren
Klapperstraat 151 bis
9120 Beveren-Waas
tel – (03) 7502501
fax – (03) 7550800
website – www.kskbeveren.be
President – Frans Van Hoof
Coach – Walter Meeuws
Stadium – Freethiel (13,290)
Colours – Yellow & blue stripes/blue/yellow
MAJOR HONOURS
League Championship – (2) 1979, 1984.
Domestic Cup – (2) 1978, 1983.

KSV Cercle Brugge
Olympialaan 74
8200 Brugge
tel – (050) 389193

fax – (050) 391141
website – www.cerclebrugge.be
Year of Formation – 1899
President – Frans Schotte
Coach – Harm van Veldhoven
Stadium – Jan Breydel (29,042)
Colours – Green (black trim)/black/green
MAJOR HONOURS
League Championship – (3) 1911, 1927, 1930.
Domestic Cup – (2) 1927, 1985.

Club Brugge KV
Olympialaan 74
8200 Brugge
tel – (050) 402121
fax – (050) 381023
website – www.clubbrugge.be
Year of Formation – 1894
President – Michel D'Hooghe
Coach – Emilio Ferrera
Stadium – Jan Breydel (29,042)
Colours – Black & blue stripes/black/black & blue
MAJOR HONOURS
League Championship – (13) 1920, 1973, 1976, 1977, 1978, 1980, 1988, 1990, 1992, 1996, 1998, 2003, 2005.
Domestic Cup – (9) 1968, 1970, 1977, 1986, 1991, 1995, 1996, 2002, 2004.

FC Molenbeek Brussels Strombeek
Charles Malisstraat 61
tel – (02) 4127173
fax – (02) 41127177
website – www.fc-brussels.be
Year of Formation – 2003
President – Johan Vermeersch
Coach – Albert Cartier
Stadium – Edmond Machtensstadion (15,340)
Colours – Red/black/black

Royal Charleroi Sporting Club
Stade Communal du Pays de Charleroi
Boulevard Zoë Drion 19
6000 Charleroi
tel – (071) 239750
fax – (071) 239772
website – www.rcsc.be
Year of Formation – 1904
President – Abbas Bayat
Coach – Jacky Matthijssen
Stadium – Pays de Charleroi (23,186)
Colours – Black & white stripes/white/white

KRC Genk
Stadionplein 4
3600 Genk
tel – (089) 841608

The Directory

fax – (089) 841708
website – www.krcgenk.be
Year of Formation – 1988
President – Harry Lemmens
Coach – Hugo Broos
Stadium – Feniksstadion (24,738)
Colours – White/white/white
MAJOR HONOURS
League Championship – (2) 1999, 2002.
Domestic Cup – (2) 1998, 2000.

KAA Gent
Bruiloftstraat 42
9050 Gentbrugge-Gent
tel – (09) 2306610
fax – (09) 2302010
website – www.kaagent.be
Year of Formation – 1898
President – Ivan De Witte
Coach – Georges Leekens
Stadium – Jules Ottenstadion (13,265)
Colours – Light blue/white/blue
MAJOR HONOURS
Domestic Cup – (2) 1964, 1984.

Germinal Beerschot Antwerpen
Atletenstraat 80
2020 Antwerpen
tel – (03) 2484845
fax – (03) 2484846
website – www.germinal-beerschot.be
Year of Formation – 1999
President – Jos Verhaegen
Coach – Aimé Anthuenis
Stadium – Olympic Stadion (12,148)
Colours – Mauve/mauve/white & mauve
MAJOR HONOURS
Domestic Cup – (1) 2005.

K Lierse SK
Voetbalstraat 4
2500 Lier
tel – (03) 4801370
fax – (03) 4880659
website – www.lierse.com
Year of Formation – 1906
President – Leo Theyskens
Coach – René Trost
Stadium – Herman Vanderpoorten (14,538)
Colours – Yellow/black/black
MAJOR HONOURS
League Championship – (4) 1932, 1942, 1960, 1997.
Domestic Cup – (2) 1969, 1999.

KSC Lokeren Oost-Vlaanderen
Daknamstraat 91
9160 Lokeren

tel – (09) 3483905
fax – (09) 3491243
website – www.sporting.be
Year of Formation – 1970
President – Roger Lambrecht
Coach – Ariel Jacobs
Stadium – Daknam (11,260)
Colours – White (black trim)/black/yellow

RAEC Mons
Avenue du Tir 80
7000 Mons
tel – (065) 221111
fax – (065) 221138
website – www.raec-mons.be
Year of Formation – 1910
President – Dominique Leone
Coach – José Riga
Stadium – Charles Tondreau (9,000)
Colours – White (red trim)/red/red

Royal Excelsior Mouscron
Rue du Stade 33
7700 Mouscron
tel – (056) 860600
fax – (056) 860570
website – www.excelsior.be
Year of Formation – 1964
President – Edward Van Daele
Coach – Gil Vandenbrouck
Stadium – Le Canonnier (10,571)
Colours – White/red/red

KSV Roeselare
Diksmuidsesteenweg, 374
8800 Roeselare
tel – (051) 229922
fax – (051) 205002
website – www.ksvr.be
Year of Formation – 1999
President – Luc Espeel
Coach – Dick Geeraerd
Stadium – Schiervelde (8,836)
Colours – White (black trim)/black/white

K Sint-Truidense VV
Tiensesteenweg 170
3800 Sint-Truiden
tel – (011) 683829
fax – (011) 692380
website – www.stvv.com
Year of Formation – 1924
President – Roland Duchatelet
Coach – Thomas Caers
Stadium – Staaien (12,389)
Colours – Yellow (blue trim)/blue/yellow

Royal Standard de Liège
Rue de la Centrale 2
4000 Sclessin-Liège
tel – (04) 2522122
fax – (04) 2521469
website – www.standard.be
Year of Formation – 1900
President – Reto Stiffler
Coach – Johan Boskamp
Stadium – Sclessin (30,035)
Colours – Red (white trim)/white/white
MAJOR HONOURS
League Championship – (8) 1958, 1961, 1963, 1969, 1970, 1971, 1982, 1983.
Domestic Cup – (5) 1954, 1966, 1967, 1981, 1993.

KVC Westerlo
De Merodedreef 189
2260 Westerlo
tel – (014) 545288
fax – (014) 542321
website – www.kvcwesterlo.be
Year of Formation – 1933
Coach – Herman Helleputte
Stadium – 't Kuipje (8,103)
Colours – Dark blue (yellow sleeves)/yellow/dark blue
MAJOR HONOURS
Domestic Cup – (1) 2001.

SV Zulte-Waregem
Zuiderlaan 17
8790 Waregem
tel – (056) 440042
fax – (056) 440342
website – www.svzw.be
Year of Formation – 2001
President – Willy Naessens
Coach – Francky Dury
Stadium – Regenboog (8,500)
Colours – Green (red & yellow trim)/green/green
MAJOR HONOURS
Domestic Cup – (1) 2006.

BOSNIA-HERZEGOVINA

Nogometni Savez Bosne i Hercegovine
Ulica Ferhadija 30, 71000
Sarajevo
tel – (00387 33) 276676
fax – (00387 33) 444332
website – www.nsbih.ba
email – nsbih@bih.net.ba

Year of Formation – 1992
President – Iljo Dominkovic

The Directory

Secretary – Munib Usanovic
Stadium – Olympic Asim
Ferhatovic Hase Kosevo,
Sarajevo (34,600)

FK Borac
Vladike Platona 6
78000 Banja Luka
tel – (51) 312455
fax – (51) 301793
website – sfpborac@inecco.net
Year of Formation – 1926
President – Ljubomir Cubic
Coach – Mihajlo Bosnjak
Stadium – Gradski stadion (15,000)
Colours – Blue (red band)/red/blue
MAJOR HONOURS
Domestic Cup (Yugoslavia) – (1) 1988.

NK Celik
Bulevar Kulina Bana bb
72000 Zenica
tel – (32) 405812
fax – (32) 414622
Year of Formation – 1945
Chairman – Mirsad Ibrakovic
Coach – Vjeran Simunic
Stadium – Bilino Polje (13,000)
Colours – Red (black band & trim)/black/black
MAJOR HONOURS
League Championship – (3) 1994, 1996, 1997.
Domestic Cup – (2) 1995, 1996.

NK Jedinstvo
Aleja bb
7700 Bihac
tel – (37) 220548
fax – (37) 220548
Year of Formation – 1919
Chairman – Hamdija Abdic
Coach – Miralem Ibrahimovic
Stadium – NK Jedinstvo (10,000)
Colours – Red/red/red

FK Leotar
Police bb
89101 Trebinje
tel – (59) 224911
fax – (59) 224911
Year of Formation – 1925
Chairman – Zeljko Bjelica
Coach – Vladimir Pecelj
Stadium – Police (8,500)
Colours – Blue/blue/blue
MAJOR HONOURS
League Championship – (1) 2003.

FK Modrica Maxima
Berlinska bb
74480 Modrica
tel – (53) 812478
fax – (53) 812478
Year of Formation – 1974
Chairman – Zarko Vujnic
Coach – Mitar Lukic
Stadium – FK Modrica Maxima (2,500)
Colours – Yellow/blue/yellow
MAJOR HONOURS
Domestic Cup – (1) 2004.

NK Orasje
Zaobilaznica bb
76270 Orasje
tel – (31) 717123
fax – (31) 717123
Year of Formation – 1996
Chairman – Joso Markovic
Coach – Anton Jovanovac
Stadium – NC Goal (3,000)
Colours – Red/red/red
MAJOR HONOURS
Domestic Cup – (1) 2006.

NK Posusje
Batinski put bb
88240 Posusje
tel – (39) 682199
fax – (39) 682199
website – www.nkposusje.com
Year of Formation – 1950
Chairman – Ante Bosnjak
Coach – Dragan Jovic
Stadium – Mokri Dolac (4,000)
Colours – Blue & white stripes/black/black

FK Radnik
Balkanska bb
76330 Bijeljina
tel – (55) 201338
fax – (55) 201338
website – www.fcradnikbn.com
Year of Formation – 1945
Chairman – Mihajlo Vidic
Coach – Zoran Jagodic
Stadium – Gradski stadion (5,000)
Colours – Blue/blue/blue

FK Sarajevo
Marsala Tita 38/b
71000 Sarajevo
tel – (33) 442333
fax – (36) 664262
website – www.fcsarajevo.com
Year of Formation – 1946
Chairman – Hajrudin Suman
Coach – Husref Musemic
Stadium – Olympic Asim Ferhatovic Hase Kosevo (34,600)
Colours – Maroon (white trim)/maroon/maroon
MAJOR HONOURS
League Championship (Yugoslavia) – (2) 1967, 1985.
Domestic Cup – (4) 1997, 1998, 2002, 2005.

NK Siroki Brijeg
Fra Dudaka Buntica bb
88220 Siroki Brijeg
tel – (39) 705095
fax – (39) 705095
website – www.nk-siroki.brijeg.com
Year of Formation – 1948
Chairman – Zlatan Mijo Jelic
Coach – Ivica Barbaric
Stadium – Pecara (6,000)
Colours – Blue & white stripes/blue/blue
MAJOR HONOURS
League Championship – (2) 2004, 2006.

FK Slavija
Jovana Raskovica 3
71123 Sarajevo-Lukavica
tel – (57) 342343
fax – (57) 342343
Year of Formation – 1908
Chairman – Slavko Tosovic
Coach – Milomir Odovic
Stadium – SRC Slavija Lukavica (5,000)
Colours – Blue/blue/blue

FK Sloboda
Rudarska 2
75000 Tuzla
tel – (35) 283490
fax – (35) 264505
website – www.fcsloboda.com
Year of Formation – 1919
Chairman – Enver Bijedic
Coach – Ibrahim Crnkic
Stadium – Tusanj (7,000)
Colours – Red & black stripes/black/red

FK Velez
Marsala Tita 87
88000 Mostar
tel – (36) 550431
fax – (36) 550431
Year of Formation – 1922
President – Ahmed Dzubur
Coach – Milomir Seslija
Stadium – Bijeli brijeg (15,000) or Vrapcici (5,000)

The Directory

Colours – Red/red/red
MAJOR HONOURS
Domestic Cup (Yugoslavia) – (2) 1981, 1986.

FK Zeljeznicar
Zvornicka 27
71000 Sarajevo
tel – (33) 660133
fax – (33) 660134
website – www.nk.zeljeznicar.co.ba
Year of Formation – 1921
Chairman – Samir Landzo
Coach – Almir Memic
Stadium – Grbavica (15,000)
Colours – Light blue (white trim)/light blue/light blue
MAJOR HONOURS
League Championship (Yugoslavia) – (1) 1972.
League Championship – (3) 1998, 2001, 2002.
Domestic Cup – (3) 2000, 2001, 2003.

NK Zepce
Omladinska bb
72230 Zepce
tel – (32) 881189
fax – (32) 881189
website – www.nk_zepce.com
Year of Formation – 1919
Chairman – Marko Lovric
Coach – Omer Kopic
Stadium – NK Zepce (2,000)
Colours – Blue/blue/blue

NK Zrinjski
Stjepana Radica 45
88000 Mostar
tel – (36) 321507
fax – (36) 321507
website – www.zrinjski.max.net.ba
Year of Formation – 1912
Chairman – Ivan Beus
Coach – Blaz Sliskovic
Stadium – Bijeli brijeg (15,000)
Colours – White/white/white
MAJOR HONOURS
League Championship – (1) 2005.

BULGARIA

Bulgarski Futbolen Soius
26 Tzar Ivan Assen II Street
1124 Sofia
tel – (00359 2) 9426202
fax – (00359 2) 9426200
website – www.bfunion.bg
email – bfu@bfunion.bg

Year of Formation – 1923
President – Borislav Mihailov
Secretary – Stefan Kapralov
Stadium – Vasil Levski, Sofia (54,000)

INTERNATIONAL TOURNAMENT APPEARANCES
World Cup – (7) 1962, 1966, 1970, 1974, 1986 (2nd round), 1994 (4th), 1998.
European Championship – (2) 1996, 2004.

Belasitsa FC
ul. Stadionska 2
2850 Petrich
tel – (0745) 23554
fax – (0745) 23554
website – www.rondia-bg.com
Year of Formation – 1923
President – Kostadin Hadzhivanov
Coach – Stevica Kuzmanovski
Stadium – Tsar Samuil (12,000)
Colours – White/red/white

FC Beroe Stara Zagora
ul. Georgi Kiumiurev 10
6000 Stara Zagora
tel – (042) 603492
fax – (042) 603492
Year of Formation – 1916
President – Nikolai Banev
Coach – Ilian Iliev
Stadium – Beroe (22,300)
Colours – Green (white trim)/white/red
MAJOR HONOURS
League Championship – (1) 1986.

FC Botev
Bul. Istochen 10
4000 Plovdiv
tel – (032) 633375
fax – (032) 626388
website – www.botev1912.com
Year of Formation – 1912
President – Dimitar Hristolov
Coach – Svetoslav Gurkov
Stadium – Hristo Botev (21,000)
Colours – Yellow & black stripes/black/black
MAJOR HONOURS
League Championship – (2) 1929, 1967.

FC Cherno More
Nikola Vaptzarov St. 9
Ticha Stadium
9000 Varna
tel – (052) 302243
fax – (052) 302243
Year of Formation – 1913

President – Krasen Kralev
Coach – Yassen Petrov
Stadium – Ticha (12,000)
Colours – Green/white/green
MAJOR HONOURS
League Championship – (4) 1925, 1926, 1934, 1938.

FC Conegliano German
40 Iskar St.
German
Sofia
tel – (02) 9962857
fax – (02) 9962858
Year of Formation – 2001
President – Georgi Krastev
Coach – Ivailo Drazhev
Stadium – Akademik (4,000)
Colours – Black/black/black

FC CSKA Sofia
Stadion Bulgarska Armia
Bul. Dragan Tsankov 3
1504 Sofia
tel – (02) 9633477
fax – (02) 9633902
Year of Formation – 1948
President – Vasil Bozhkov
Coach – Plamen Markov
Stadium – Bulgarska Armia (24,000)
Colours – Red (white trim)/white/red
MAJOR HONOURS
League Championship – (30) 1948, 1951, 1952, 1954, 1955, 1956, 1957, 1958, 1959, 1960, 1961, 1962, 1966, 1969, 1971, 1972, 1973, 1975, 1976, 1980, 1981, 1982, 1983, 1987, 1989, 1990, 1992, 1997, 2003, 2005.
Domestic Cup – (10) 1981, 1983, 1985, 1987, 1988, 1989, 1993, 1997, 1999, 2006.

FC Levski
Ul. Todorini Kukli 47
Kvartal Podouene
1517 Sofia
tel – (02) 9892152
fax – (02) 9454227
website – www.levski.bg
Year of Formation – 1914
President – Michael Chorbi
Coach – Stanimir Stoilov
Stadium – Georgi Asparuhkov (29,698)
Colours – Blue/blue/blue
MAJOR HONOURS
League Championship – (24) 1933, 1937, 1942, 1946, 1947, 1949, 1950, 1953, 1965, 1968, 1970, 1974, 1977, 1979, 1984, 1985, 1988, 1993, 1994, 1995, 2000, 2001, 2002, 2006.

The Directory

Domestic Cup – (12) 1942, 1982, 1984, 1986, 1991, 1992, 1994, 1998, 2000, 2002, 2003, 2005.

FC Litex Lovech
PO Box 75
Han Koubrat St. 5
5500 Lovech
tel – (068) 68601092
fax – (068) 68601091
website – www.pfclitex.com/bg
Year of Formation – 1921
President – Angel Bonchev
Coach – Ljupko Petrovic
Stadium – Lovech (7,000)
Colours – Orange/black/black
MAJOR HONOURS
League Championship – (2) 1998, 1999.
Domestic Cup – (2) 2001, 2004.

FC Lokomotiv Plovdiv
Stadion Lokomotiv
Kvartal Lauta
4000 Plovdiv
tel – (032) 627373
fax – (032) 622889
website – www.lokopd.com
Year of Formation – 1936
President – Georgi Iliev
Coach – Ayan Sadakov
Stadium – Lokomotiv (18,600)
Colours – Black & white stripes/black/white
MAJOR HONOURS
League Championship – (1) 2004.

FC Lokomotiv
Bul. Rozhen 23
1220 Sofia
tel – (02) 8378479
fax – (02) 9360341
Year of Formation – 1929
President – Nikolai Gigov
Coach – Stefan Grozdanov
Stadium – Lokomotiv (25,000)
Colours – White & black stripes/black/white
MAJOR HONOURS
League Championship – (4)
1940, 1945, 1964, 1978.
Domestic Cup – (1) 1995.

FC Marek
Samoransko chaussee
Stadion Bonchuk
2600 Dupnitsa
tel – (02) 9810404
fax – (02) 9810404
Year of Formation – 1919
President – Yordan Andreev
Coach – Stoyan Kostev
Stadium – Bonchuk (12,500)
Colours – Red/red/red

FC Rilski sportist Samokov
Stadion Rilski
2000 Samokov
tel – (0888) 776431
Year of Formation – 1924
President – Yuri Galev
Coach – Ivan Mironov
Stadium – Iskar (7,000)
Colours – Blue/white/blue

FC Rodopa
Stadion Septemvri
Kvartal Raikovo
4700 Smolyan
tel – (0301) 36108
Year of Formation – 1927
President – Petar Finadov
Coach – Pavel Panov
Stadium – Septemvri (6,000)
Colours – Green/black/black

FC Slavia
ul. Koloman 1
Kvartal Ovcha Kupel
1618 Sofia
tel – (02) 8569197
fax – (02) 8552137
website – www.pfcslavia.com
Year of Formation – 1913
President – Ventsislav Stefanov
Coach – Ratko Dostanic
Stadium – Slavia (32,000)
Colours – White (black trim)/white/white
MAJOR HONOURS
League Championship – (7) 1928, 1930, 1936, 1939, 1941, 1943, 1996.
Domestic Cup – (1) 1996.

Spartak Varna
Seliolo St. 39
Spartak Stadium
9000 Varna
tel – (052) 613810
Year of Formation – 1918
President – Ivan Slavkov
Coach – Miroslav Mironov
Stadium – Spartacus (12,000)
Colours – White (blue trim)/white/white
MAJOR HONOURS
League Championship – (1) 1932.

FC Vihren Sandanski
City Park Area
Vihren
Tel – (746) 30766
Fax – (746) 30766
website – www.vihren.com
Year of Formation – 1957
President – Kostadin Dinev
Coach – Petar Zhekov
Stadium – FC Vihren (10,000)
Colours – Green (white trim)/green/green

CROATIA

Hrvatski Nogometni Savez
Rusanova, 10000 Zagreb
tel – (00385 1) 2361555
fax – (00385 1) 2441500
website – www.hns-cff.hr
email – hns-cff@zg.hinet.hr

Year of Formation – 1991
President – Vlatko Markovic
Secretary – Zorislav Srebric
Stadium – Maksimir, Zagreb (38,000)

INTERNATIONAL TOURNAMENT APPEARANCES
World Cup – (3) 1998 (3rd), 2002, 2006.
European Championship – (2) 1996 (qtr-finals), 2004.

MAJOR EUROPEAN CLUB HONOURS
Fairs Cup – (1) Dinamo Zagreb (1967)

HNK Cibalia
Ruzina 13
32100 Vinkovci
tel – (032) 306086/306088
fax – (032) 306085
Year of Formation – 1947
President – Zeljko Culo
Coach – Sinisa Jalic
Stadium – Cibalia (12,000)
Colours – Light blue (white & light blue trim)/light blue/blue

NK Dinamo
Maksimirska 128
10000 Zagreb
tel – (01) 2386111/2323234
fax – (01) 2312316
website – www.nk-dinamo.hr
Year of Formation – 1945
President – Mirko Barisic
Coach – Josip Kuze
Stadium – Maksimir (38,000)
Colours – Blue (white trim)/blue/blue
MAJOR HONOURS

The Directory

League Championship – (8) 1993, 1996, 1997, 1998, 1999, 2000, 2003, 2006.
League Championship (Yugoslavia) – (4) 1948, 1954, 1958, 1982.
Domestic Cup – (7) 1994, 1996, 1997, 1998, 2001, 2002, 2004.
Domestic Cup (Yugoslavia) – (8) 1951, 1960, 1963, 1965, 1969, 1973, 1980, 1983.
Fairs Cup – (1) 1967.

HNK Hajduk
Osmih mediteranskih igara 2
21000 Split
tel – (021) 323650/323651
fax – (021) 381241
website – www.hnkhajduk.hr
Year of Formation – 1911
President – Branko Grgic
Coach – Zoran Vulic
Stadium – Poljud (35,000)
Colours – White/blue/blue
MAJOR HONOURS
League Championship – (6) 1992, 1994, 1995, 2001, 2004, 2005.
League Championship (Yugoslavia) – (9) 1927, 1929, 1950, 1952, 1955, 1971, 1974, 1975, 1979.
Domestic Cup – (4) 1993, 1995, 2000, 2003.
Domestic Cup (Yugoslavia) – (9) 1967, 1972, 1973, 1974, 1976, 1977, 1984, 1987, 1991.

NK Kamen Ingrad
Zvonimirova bb
34330 Velika
tel – (034) 230122/230123
fax – (034) 230132
website – www.nk-kamen-ingrad.hr
Year of Formation – 1929
President – Vlado Zec
Coach – Ante Cacic
Stadium – Kamen Ingrad (4,000)

NK Medjimurje
Sportska 2
40000 Cakovec
tel – (040) 329209
fax – (040) 329208
Year of Formation – 2003
President – Josip Posavec
Coach – Stanko Mrsic
Stadium – Mladost (10,000)
Colours – Red & black stripes/black/red & black

NK Osijek
Wilsonova bb
31 000 Osijek
tel – (031) 570300/570400
fax – (031) 570400

Year of Formation – 1946
President – Branimir Glavas
Coach – Ivo Susak
Stadium – Gradski vrt (19,200)
Colours – White (blue trim)/blue/white
MAJOR HONOURS
Domestic Cup – (1) 1999.

NK Pula
Veli Joze 3
52100 Pula
tel – (052) 210496
fax – (052) 380863
Year of Formation – 2003
President – Korado Soldatic
Coach – Branko Tucak
Stadium – SRC Veruda (2,700)

NK Rijeka
Portic 3
51 000 Rijeka
tel – (051) 612030/612031
fax – (051) 261174
website – www.nk-rijeka.hr
Year of Formation – 1946
President – Robert Jezic
Coach – Dragan Skocic
Stadium – Kantrida (10,155)
Colours – White (blue trim)/white/white
MAJOR HONOURS
Domestic Cup (Yugoslavia) – (2) 1978, 1979.
Domestic Cup – (2) 2005, 2006.

HNK Sibenik
Bana Jelacica bb
22000 Sibenik
tel – (022) 212963
fax – (022) 212963
Year of Formation – 1933
President – Goran Pauk
Coach – Ivan Pudar
Stadium – Subicevac (8,000)
Colours – Blue/blue/blue

NK Slaven Belupo
Ante Starcevica 29
48 000 Koprivnica
tel – (048) 220033
fax – (048) 623960
website – www.nk-slaven-belupo.hr
Year of Formation – 1912
President – Mirsolav Vitkovic
Coach – Elvis Scoria
Stadium – Gradski (3,059)
Colours – Blue/blue/blue

NK Varteks

Zagrebacka 94
42 000 Varazdin
tel – (042) 241332/240250
fax – (042) 204260
website – www.nk-varteks.hr
Year of Formation – 1931
President – Tomislav Kezelj
Coach – Zlatko Dalic
Stadium – Gradski (8,970)
Colours – Blue/white/blue

NK Zagreb
Kranjceviceva 4
10 000 Zagreb
tel – (01) 3668111
fax – (01) 3668344
Year of Formation – 1949
President – Drazen Medic
Coach – Miroslav Blazevic
Stadium – NK Zagreb (8,000)
Colours – White/white/white
MAJOR HONOURS
League Championship – (1) 2002.

CYPRUS

Cyprus Football Association
Stasinos Street 1, PO Box 25071,
2404 Nicosia
tel – (00357 22) 352341
fax – (00357 22) 590544
email – cfa@logos.cy.net

Year of Formation – 1934
President – Costakis Koutsokoumnis
Secretary – Chris Georgiades

AEK FC
24 Kilkis str.
PO Box
46300 Larnaca
tel – (24) 653615
fax – (24) 652464
website – www.aekition.com
Year of Formation – 1994
President – Thomas Kyriakou
Coach – Marios Constandinou
Stadium – Zenon (16,000)
Colours – Green/yellow/white
MAJOR HONOURS
Domestic Cup – (1) 2004.

AEL FC
3 Grobious str.
3032 Limassol
tel – (25) 737555

The Directory

fax – (25) 737540
website – www.ael.limassol.com.cy
Year of Formation – 1930
President – Akis Agapiou
Coach – Panicos Orphanides
Stadium – Tsirion (20,000)
Colours – Yellow & blue stripes/blue/blue
MAJOR HONOURS
League Championship – (5) 1941, 1953, 1955, 1956, 1968.
Domestic Cup – (6) 1939, 1940, 1948, 1985, 1987, 1989.

AEP
25th March Street
PO Box
60425 Paphos
tel – (26) 822087
fax – (26) 222068
website – www.pafosfc.com
Year of Formation – 1953
President – Evripides Loizides
Coach – Nikos Andronikou
Stadium – Pafiakos (6000)
Colours – Blue/blue/white

Anorthosis FC Famagusta
Andonis Papadopoulos Stadium
PO Box 40756
6307 Larnaca
tel – (24) 635835
fax – (24) 635833
website – www.anorthosis.net
Year of Formation – 1911
President – Kyriakos Theocharous
Coach – Temuri Ketsbaia
Stadium – Andonis Papadopoulos (9,500)
Colours – Blue & white stripes/blue/blue
MAJOR HONOURS
League Championship – (12) 1950, 1957, 1958, 1960, 1962, 1963, 1995, 1997, 1998, 1999, 2000, 2005.
Domestic Cup – (8) 1949, 1962, 1963, 1971, 1975, 1998, 2002, 2003.

APOEL Football Co.
2 Lemesos Av.
1686 Nicosia
tel – (22) 340200
fax – (22) 379789
website – www.apoel.com.cy
Year of Formation – 1926
President – Kyriakos Zivanaris
Coach – Marinos Ouzounidis
Stadium – Pancypria (23,000)
Colours – Yellow (two blue bands)/blue/yellow
MAJOR HONOURS
League Championship – (18) 1936, 1937, 1938, 1939, 1940, 1947, 1948, 1949, 1952, 1965, 1973, 1980, 1986, 1990, 1992, 1996, 2002, 2004.
Domestic Cup – (18) 1937, 1941, 1947, 1951, 1963, 1968, 1969, 1973, 1976, 1978, 1979, 1984, 1993, 1995, 1996, 1997, 1999, 2006.

Apollon Football Co.
1 Mesologiou str.
3301 Limassol
tel – (25) 363702
fax – (25) 746808
website – www.apollon-fc.com
Year of Formation – 1954
President – George Papas
Coach – Bernd Stange
Stadium – Tsirion (20,000)
Colours – White (blue trim)/white/white
MAJOR HONOURS
League Championship – (3) 1991, 1994, 2006.
Domestic Cup – (5) 1966, 1967, 1986, 1992, 2001.

Aris
Heroes Square
PO Box
50579 Limassol
tel – (25) 349050
fax – (25) 359167
Year of Formation – 1930
President – Charistakis Athanassios
Coach – Nicos Andronikou
Stadium – Tsirion (15,000)
Colours – Green (white trim)/green/green

Ayia Napa
Kryou Nerou 18
5330 Ayia Napa
tel – (23) 816111
fax – (23) 816208
Year of Formation – 1990
President – Christakis Antoniou
Coach – Adamos Adamou
Stadium – Municipal (2,000)
Colours – Orange/black/black

Dighenis Morphou FC
38 K. Matsi
PO Box 23548
1684 Nicosia
tel – (22) 316800
fax – (22) 455598
website – www.dighenismorfeou.com
Year of Formation – 1931
President – Aris Stephanou
Coach – Aris Tirkas
Stadium – Makarion (20,000)
Colours – Green/white/green

Ethnikos Akhna FC
Dasaki Akhna
5523 Famagusta
tel – (23) 722333
fax – (23) 722060
Year of Formation – 1968
President – Kikis Philippou
Coach – Toza Sapuric
Stadium – Dasaki (8,000)
Colours – Blue (white trim)/blue/blue

Nea Salamina FC
4 Rangavi str.
6047 Larnaca
tel – (24) 663090
fax – (24) 663228
website – www.neasalamis.com.cy
Year of Formation – 1948
President – George Alexandrou
Coach – Andreas Michaelides
Stadium – Ammochostos (8,000)
Colours – Red & white stripes/white/white

Olympiakos FC
6A Athinas str.
1021 Nicosia
tel – (22) 344080
fax – (22) 344090
Year of Formation – 1931
President – Christophoros Tornarides
Coach – Nikolai Kostov
Stadium – Pancypria (23,000)
Colours – Green (black trim)/black/green & black
MAJOR HONOURS
League Championship – (3) 1967, 1969, 1971.
Domestic Cup – (1) 1977.

Omonia FC
5 Papanicoli str.
PO Box 29617
1661 Nicosia
tel – (22) 875874
fax – (22) 377496
website – www.omonoia.com.cy
Year of Formation – 1948
President – Doros Seraphim
Coach – Ioan Andone
Stadium – Pancypria (23,000)
Colours – Green & white stripes/white/white
MAJOR HONOURS
League Championship – (19) 1961, 1966, 1972, 1974, 1975, 1976, 1977, 1978, 1979, 1981, 1982, 1983, 1984, 1985, 1987, 1989, 1993, 2001, 2003.
Domestic Cup – (12) 1965, 1972, 1974, 1980, 1981, 1982, 1983, 1988, 1991, 1994, 2000, 2005.

Union of Paralimni FC

The Directory

17 A, Papadopoulos str.
PO Box 33020
5310 Paralimni
tel – (23) 827329
fax – (23) 825658
Year of Formation – 1936
President – Dimitris Tsishios
Coach – Nir Klinger
Stadium – Municipal (8,000)
Colours – Claret (blue V)/blue/white

CZECH REPUBLIC

Ceskomoravsky Fotbalovy Svaz
Diskarská 100, PO Box 11, 160 17
Praha 6 – Strahov
tel – (00420 2) 33029111
20513394
fax – (00420 2) 33353107
website – www.fotbal.cz
email – cmfs@fotbal.cz

Year of Formation – 1990
President – Ing. Pavel Mokry
Secretary – Petr Fousek
Stadium – Evzena Rosického,
Praha (19,336)

INTERNATIONAL HONOURS*
European Championship – (1) 1976.

INTERNATIONAL TOURNAMENT APPEARANCES*
World Cup – (9) 1934 (runners-up), 1938 (qtr-finals), 1954, 1958, 1962 (runners-up), 1970, 1982, 1990 (qtr-finals), 2006.
European Championship – (6) 1960 (3rd), 1976 (Winners), 1980 (3rd), 1996 (runners-up), 2000, 2004 (semi-finals).

(* before 1996 as Czechoslovakia)

FC Baník Ostrava
Bukovanského 4/1028
710 00 Ostrava 2
tel – (59) 6241687
fax – (59) 6241827
website – www.fcb.cz
Year of Formation – 1922
President – Jakub Kahoun
Coach – Karel Vecera
Stadium – Bazaly (17,372)
Colours – Blue (orange trim)/orange/blue
MAJOR HONOURS
League Championship – (4) 1976, 1980, 1981, 2004.
Domestic Cup – (4) 1973, 1978, 1991, 2005.

1. FC Brno
Srbská 47a
612 00 Brno
tel – (5) 41233582-5
fax – (5) 41233581
website – www.1fcbrno.cz
Year of Formation – 1913
President – Karel Jarusek
Coach – Josef Mazura
Stadium – Mestsky stadion (8,065)
Colours – Red/red/red
MAJOR HONOURS
League Championship – (1) 1978.

Dynamo Ceské Budejovice
Strelecky ostrov 3
370 21 Ceské Budejovice
tel – (387) 312502
fax – (387) 312503
website – www.dynamocb.cz
Year of Formation – 1905
President – Karel Poborsky
Coach – Frantisek Cipro
Stadium – E-on Stadion (4,000)
Colours – Purple/black/white

FK Jablonec 97
U stadionu 1348/5
466 01 Jablonec nad Nisou
tel – (483) 312139
fax – (483) 312140
website – www.fkjablonec.cz
Year of Formation – 1945
President – Petr Flodrman
Coach – Petr Rada
Stadium – Strelnice (6,426)
Colours – Green (white/black trim)/white/white
MAJOR HONOURS
Domestic Cup – (1) 1998.

SK Kladno
Stadion Fr. Kloze 2628
272 01 Kladno
tel – (312) 247147
fax – (312) 247147
website – www.skkladno.cz
Year of Formation – 1903
President – Ing. Michal Kraus
Coach – Miroslav Koubek
Stadium – Stadium Fr. Kloze (4,000)
Colours – White/blue/white

FK Marila Príbram
Lazec 60
261 01 Príbram
tel – (318) 620321
fax – (318) 626173

website – www.fkmarila.cz
Year of Formation – 1948
President – Jaroslav Starka
Coach – Pavel Tobiás
Stadium – FK Marila Pribram (9,100)
Colours – Yellow/yellow/yellow
MAJOR HONOURS
League Championship – (11) 1953, 1956, 1958, 1961, 1962, 1963, 1964, 1966, 1977, 1979, 1982.
Domestic Cup – (8) 1961, 1965, 1966, 1969, 1981, 1983, 1985, 1990.

FK Mladá Boleslav
U stadionu 1118/II
293 01 Mladá Boleslav
tel – (326) 719041
fax – (326) 719044
website – www.fkmb.cz
Year of Formation – 1902
President – Josef Dufek
Coach – Dusan Uhrin jr.
Stadium – Mestsky stadion (5,000)
Colours – White/blue/white

FK SIAD Most
Svatopluka Cecha 275
434 01 Most
tel – (476) 102731
fax – (476) 703975
website – www.fksiadmost.cz
Year of Formation – 1909
President – Ing. Petr Kabícek
Coach – Zdenek Scasny
Stadium – Letní stadion (7,500)
Colours – White/white/white

SK Sigma Olomouc
Legionarská 12
771 00 Olomouc
tel – (58) 5223380/5222956
fax – (58) 5220953/5222656
website – www.sigmafotbal.cz
Year of Formation – 1919
President – Ing. Josef Lébr
Coach – Vlastimil Palicka
Stadium – Andruv stadion (12,072)
Colours – Blue/blue/blue

SK Slavia Praha
Zátopkova 2
169 00 Praha 6 – Strahov
tel – (2) 33081751
fax – (2) 33081760
website – www.slavia.cz
Year of Formation – 1893
President – Ing. Vladimír Leska
Coach – Karel Jarolím

The Directory

Stadium – Stadion Evzena Rosického (19,336)
Colours – Red & white halves/white/white
MAJOR HONOURS
League Championship – (10) 1925, 1929, 1930, 1931, 1933, 1934, 1935, 1937, 1947, 1996.
Domestic Cup – (3) 1997, 1999, 2002.

1.FC Slovácko Uherské Hradiste
Stonky 635
686 01 Uherské Hradiste
tel – (572) 551801
fax – (572) 541202
website – www.fc.slovacko.cz
Year of Formation – 1927
President – Jan Rezník
Coach – Jirí Plísek
Stadium – Mestsky stadion Stonky (8,121)
Colours – White/white/white

FC Slovan Liberec
Na Hradbách 1300
460 01 Liberec 1
tel – (48) 5103714
fax – (48) 5103715
website – www.fcslovanliberec.cz
Year of Formation – 1958
President – Ing. Zbynek Stiller
Coach – Vítezslav Lavicka
Stadium – Stadion "U Nisy" (9,900)
Colours – White/white/white
MAJOR HONOURS
League Championship – (2) 2002, 2006.
Domestic Cup – (1) 2000.

AC Sparta Praha
Milady Horákové 98
170 82 Praha 7 – Letná
tel – (2) 20570323
fax – (2) 20571660
website – www.sparta.cz
Year of Formation – 1893
President – Jozef Chovanec
Coach – Stanislav Griga
Stadium – Toyota Arena (20,565)
Colours – Dark red (white trim)/dark red/dark red
MAJOR HONOURS
League Championship – (28) 1926, 1927, 1932, 1936, 1938, 1946, 1948, 1952, 1954, 1965, 1967, 1984, 1985, 1987, 1988, 1989, 1990, 1991, 1993, 1994, 1995, 1997, 1998, 1999, 2000, 2001, 2003, 2005.
Domestic Cup – (11) 1964, 1972, 1976, 1980, 1984, 1988, 1989, 1992, 1996, 2004, 2006.

FK Teplice
Na Stínadlech 2796
415 01 Teplice
tel – (417) 507401
fax – (417) 539517
website – www.fkteplice.cz
Year of Formation – 1945
President – Frantisek Hrdlicka
Coach – Vlastislav Marecek
Stadium – Stadion Na Stínadlech (18,221)
Colours – Yellow (blue trim)/blue/white
MAJOR HONOURS
Domestic Cup – (1) 2003.

FC Tescoma Zlín
Tyrsovo nábrezí 4381
760 01 Zlín
tel – (57) 7210506
fax – (57) 7430023
website – www.fctescomazlin.cz
Year of Formation – 1919
President – Ing. Zdenek Cervenka
Coach – Petr Ulicny
Stadium – Stadion Letná (6,375)
Colours – White (red trim)/white/white
MAJOR HONOURS
Domestic Cup – (1) 1970.

FC Viktoria Plzen
Struncovy sady 3
301 12 Plzen
tel – (377) 221515
fax – (377) 221543
website – www.fcviktoria.cz
Year of Formation – 1911
President – JUDr. Ladislav Valásek
Coach – Michal Bílek
Stadium – Stadion mesta Plzne (7,554)
Colours – Red/blue/blue

DENMARK

**Dansk Boldspil Union
Fodboldens Hus, DBU Allé 1,
2605 Brøndby
tel – (0045 43) 262222
fax – (0045 43) 262245
website – www.dbu.dk
email – dbu@dbu.dk**

**Year of Formation – 1889
President – Allan Hansen
Secretary – Jim Stjerne Hansen
Stadium – Parken, København
(42,305)**

INTERNATIONAL HONOURS
European Championship – (1) 1992.

INTERNATIONAL TOURNAMENT APPEARANCES
World Cup – (3) 1986 (2nd round), 1998 (qtr-finals), 2002 (2nd round).
European Championship – (7) 1964 (4th), 1984 (semi-finals), 1988, 1992 (Winners), 1996, 2000, 2004 (qtr-finals).

Aalborg Boldspilklub A/S
Hornevej 2
9220 Aalborg Øst
tel – (96) 355900
fax – (96) 355910
website – www.aabsport.dk/fodbold
Year of Formation – 1885
Chairman – Per Søndergaard Pedersen
Coach – Erik Hamrén
Stadium – Aalborg Stadion (16,000)
Colours – Red & white broad stripes/white/white
MAJOR HONOURS
League Championship – (2) 1995, 1999.
Domestic Cup – (2) 1966, 1970.

Brøndbyernes Idraets Forening
Brøndby Stadion 30
2605 Brøndby
tel – (43) 630810
fax – (43) 432627
website – www.brondby.com
Year of Formation – 1964
Chairman – Ejvind Sandal
Coach – René Meulensteen
Stadium – Brøndby Stadion (29,000)
Colours – Yellow (blue band)/blue/blue
MAJOR HONOURS
League Championship – (10) 1985, 1987, 1988, 1990, 1991, 1996, 1997, 1998, 2002, 2005.
Domestic Cup – (5) 1989, 1994, 1998, 2003, 2005.

Esbjerg Forenede Boldklubber
Gl. Vardevej 88
6700 Esbjerg
tel – (75) 453355
fax – (75) 122833
website – www.efb.dk/fodbold
Year of Formation – 1924
Chairman – Jørgen L. Jensen
Coach – Troels Bech
Stadium – Esbjerg Idraetspark (13,282)
Colours – Blue & white stripes/blue/blue
MAJOR HONOURS
League Championship – (5) 1961, 1962, 1963, 1965, 1979.
Domestic Cup – (2) 1964, 1976.

Alliance Club Horsens
Langmarksvej 65
8700 Horsens
tel – (75) 626020

The Directory

fax – (75) 626241
website – www.achorsens.dk
Year of Formation – 1994
Chairman – Ole W. Rasmussen
Coach – Kent Nielsen
Stadium – Forum, Horsens (6,000)
Colours – Yellow (black trim)/yellow/yellow

FC København
Øster Allé 50
2100 København Ø
tel – (35) 437400
fax – (35) 437422
website – www.fck.dk
Year of Formation – 1992
Chairman – Flemming Østergaard
Coach – Ståle Solbakken
Stadium – Parken (42,305)
Colours – White/white/white
MAJOR HONOURS
League Championship – (5) 1993, 2001, 2003, 2004, 2006.
Domestic Cup – (3) 1995, 1997, 2004.
Royal League – (2) 2005, 2006.

FC Midtjylland
Kaj Zartows Vej
Postboks 287
7400 Herning
tel – (96) 271040
fax – (96) 271041
website – www.fcm.dk
Year of Formation – 1999
Chairman – Anker Stensig Andersen
Coach – Erik Rasmussen
Stadium – SAS Arena, Herning (11,809)
Colours – Black (red trim)/black/white

FC Nordsjaelland
Farum Park
3520 Farum
tel – (44) 342500
fax – (44) 342510
website – www.fcnfodbold.dk
Year of Formation – 2003
Chairman – Allan K. Pedersen
Coach – Morten Wieghorst
Stadium – Farum Park (10,000)
Colours – Red (yellow trim)/red/red

Odense Boldklub
Fionia Park
Højstrupvej 7 B
5200 Odense V
tel – (63) 119090
fax – (63) 119080
website – www.ob.dk
Year of Formation – 1887

Chairman – Niels Thorborg
Coach – Bruce Rioch
Stadium – Fionia Paek, Odense (15,761)
Colours – Blue & white stripes/blue/white
MAJOR HONOURS
League Championship – (3) 1977, 1982, 1989.
Domestic Cup – (4) 1983, 1991, 1993, 2002.

Randers FC
Niels Brocks Gade 16
8900 Randers
tel – (86) 415122
fax – (86) 415150
website – www.randersfc.dk
Year of Formation – 1898
Chairman – Torben Nordbjerg Hansen
Coach – Lars Olsen
Stadium – Essex Park (12,000)
Colours – Light blue/dark blue/dark blue
MAJOR HONOURS
Domestic Cup – (4) 1967, 1968, 1973, 2006.

Silkeborg Idraets Forening
Ansvej 110
8600 Silkeborg
tel – (86) 804477
fax – (86) 804647
website – www.sif-support.dk
Year of Formation – 1917
Chairman – Kent Madsen
Coach – Viggo Jensen
Stadium – Silkeborg Stadion (9,200)
Colours – Red (white trim)/white/red
MAJOR HONOURS
League Championship – (1) 1994.
Domestic Cup – (1) 2001.

Vejle Boldklub
Postboks 444
Helligkildevej 2
7100 Vejle
tel – (75) 727500
fax – (75) 823680
website – www.vejle-boldklub.dk
Year of Formation – 1891
Chairman – Lars Skou
Coach – Kim Poulsen
Stadium – Vejle Stadion (15,000)
Colours – Red (white trim)/white/red
MAJOR HONOURS
League Championship – (5) 1958, 1971, 1972, 1978, 1984.
Domestic Cup – (6) 1958, 1959, 1972, 1975, 1977, 1981.

Viborg Fodsports Forening
Postboks 214

8800 Viborg
tel – (86) 601066
fax – (86) 601046
website – www.vff.dk
Year of Formation – 1896
Chairman – Poul Arne Jensen
Coach – Tommy Møller Nielsen
Stadium – Viborg Stadion (9,566)
Colours – Green (white trim)/white/white
MAJOR HONOURS
Domestic Cup – (1) 2000.

ENGLAND

The Football Association
25 Soho Square, London W1D 4FA
tel – (020) 77454545
fax – (020) 77454546
website – www.the-fa.org
email – info@the-fa.org

Year of Formation – 1863
Chairman – Geoff Thompson
Chief Executive – Brian Barwick

INTERNATIONAL HONOURS
World Cup – (1) 1966.

INTERNATIONAL TOURNAMENT APPEARANCES
World Cup – (12) 1950, 1954 (qtr-finals), 1958, 1962 (qtr-finals), 1966 (Winners), 1970 (qtr-finals), 1982 (2nd phase), 1986 (qtr-finals), 1990 (4th), 1998 (2nd round), 2002 (qtr-finals), 2006 (qtr-finals).
European Championship – (7) 1968 (3rd), 1980, 1988, 1992, 1996 (semi-finals), 2000, 2004 (qtr-finals).

MAJOR EUROPEAN CLUB HONOURS
Champions Cup/League – (10) Manchester United (1968, 1999), Liverpool (1977, 1978, 1981, 1984, 2005), Nottingham Forest (1979, 1980), Aston Villa (1982).
Cup-winners Cup – (8) Tottenham Hotspur (1963), West Ham United (1965), Manchester City (1970), Chelsea (1971, 1998), Everton (1985), Manchester United (1991), Arsenal (1994).
UEFA Cup – (6) Tottenham Hotspur (1972, 1984), Liverpool (1973, 1976, 2001), Ipswich Town (1981).
Fairs Cup – (4) Leeds United (1968, 1971), Newcastle United (1969), Arsenal (1970).

Arsenal FC
75 Drayton Park
London N5 1BU
tel – (020) 77044000
fax – (020) 77044001

The Directory

website – www.arsenal.com
Year of Formation – 1886
Chairman – Peter Hill-Wood
Manager – Arsène Wenger
Stadium – Emirates Stadium (60,000)
Colours – Red (white sleeves)/white/red & white
MAJOR HONOURS
League Championship – (13) 1931, 1933, 1934, 1935, 1938, 1948, 1953, 1971, 1989, 1991, 1998, 2002, 2004.
FA Cup – (10) 1930, 1936, 1950, 1971, 1979, 1993, 1998, 2002, 2003, 2005.
League Cup – (2) 1987, 1993.
European Cup-winners Cup – (1) 1994.
Fairs Cup – (1) 1970.

Aston Villa FC
Villa Park
Trinity Road
Birmingham B6 6HE
tel – (0121) 3272299
fax – (0121) 3222107
website – www.avfc.co.uk
Year of Formation – 1874
Chairman – Doug Ellis
Manager – Martin O'Neill
Stadium – Villa Park (42,700)
Colours – Claret (sky blue sleeves)/white/sky blue
MAJOR HONOURS
League Championship – (7) 1894, 1896, 1897, 1899, 1900, 1910, 1981.
FA Cup – (7) 1887, 1895, 1897, 1905, 1913, 1920, 1957.
League Cup – (5) 1961, 1975, 1977, 1994, 1996.
European Champions Cup – (1) 1982.
European Super Cup – (1) 1982.

Blackburn Rovers FC
Ewood Park
Blackburn BB2 4JF
tel – (01254) 698888
fax – (01254) 671042
website – www.rovers.co.uk
Year of Formation – 1875
Chairman – John Williams
Manager – Mark Hughes
Stadium – Ewood Park (31,367)
Colours – Blue & white halves/white/blue
MAJOR HONOURS
League Championship – (3) 1912, 1914, 1995.
FA Cup – (6) 1884, 1885, 1886, 1890, 1891, 1928.
League Cup – (1) 2002.

Bolton Wanderers FC
Reebok Stadium
Burnden Way
Lostock
Bolton BL6 6JW
tel – (01204) 673673
fax – (01204) 673773
website – www.bwfc.co.uk
Year of Formation – 1874
Chairman – Phil Gartside
Manager – Sam Allardyce
Stadium – Reebok (28,723)
Colours – White/white/white
MAJOR HONOURS
FA Cup – (4) 1923, 1926, 1929, 1958.

Charlton Athletic FC
The Valley
Floyd Road
Charlton
London SE7 8BL
tel – (020) 83334000
fax – (020) 83334001
website – www.cafc.co.uk
Year of Formation – 1905
Chairman – Martin Simons
Manager – Iain Dowie
Stadium – The Valley (27,116)
Colours – Red/white/red & white
MAJOR HONOURS
FA Cup – (1) 1947.

Chelsea FC
Stamford Bridge
Fulham Road
London SW6 1HS
tel – (0870) 3001212
fax – (020) 73814831
website – www.chelseafc.com
Year of Formation – 1905
Chairman – Bruce Buck
Manager – José Mourinho
Stadium – Stamford Bridge (42,360)
Colours – Blue/blue/white
MAJOR HONOURS
League Championship – (3) 1955, 2005, 2006.
FA Cup – (3) 1970, 1997, 2000.
League Cup – (3) 1965, 1998, 2005.
European Cup-winners Cup – (2) 1971, 1998.
European Super Cup – (1) 1998.

Everton FC
Goodison Park
Liverpool L4 4EL
tel – (0151) 3302200
fax – (0151) 2869112
website – www.evertonfc.com
Year of Formation – 1878
Chairman – Bill Kenwright
Manager – David Moyes
Stadium – Goodison Park (40,170)
Colours – Blue/white/blue
MAJOR HONOURS
League Championship – (9) 1891, 1915, 1928, 1932, 1939, 1963, 1970, 1985, 1987.
FA Cup – (5) 1906, 1933, 1966, 1984, 1995.
European Cup-winners Cup – (1) 1985.

Fulham FC
Craven Cottage
Stevenage Road
London SW6 6HH
tel – (0870) 4421222
fax – (020) 83360514
website – www.fulhamfc.co.uk
Year of Formation – 1879
Chairman – Mohamed Al Fayed
Manager – Chris Coleman
Stadium – Craven Cottage (22,400)
Colours – White/black/white

Liverpool FC
Anfield Road
Liverpool L4 0TH
tel – (0151) 2632361
fax – (0151) 2608813
website – www.liverpoolfc.tv
Year of Formation – 1892
Chairman – David Moores
Manager – Rafael Benítez
Stadium – Anfield (45,362)
Colours – Red/red/red
MAJOR HONOURS
League Championship – (18) 1901, 1906, 1922, 1923, 1947, 1964, 1966, 1973, 1976, 1977, 1979, 1980, 1982, 1983, 1984, 1986, 1988, 1990.
FA Cup – (7) 1965, 1974, 1986, 1989, 1992, 2001, 2006.
League Cup – (7) 1981, 1982, 1983, 1984, 1995, 2001, 2003.
European Champions Cup – (5) 1977, 1978, 1981, 1984, 2005.
UEFA Cup – (3) 1973, 1976, 2001.
European Super Cup – (3) 1977, 2001, 2005.

Manchester City FC
City of Manchester Stadium
SportCity
Manchester M11 3FF
tel – (0161) 2323000
fax – (0161) 4387999
website – www.mcfc.co.uk
Year of Formation – 1887
Chairman – John Wardle
Manager – Stuart Pearce
Stadium – City of Manchester Stadium (47,736)
Colours – Sky blue/white/sky blue
MAJOR HONOURS

The Directory

League Championship – (2) 1937, 1968.
FA Cup – (4) 1904, 1934, 1956, 1969.
League Cup – (2) 1970, 1976.
European Cup-winners Cup – (1) 1970.

Manchester United FC
Old Trafford
Sir Matt Busby Way
Manchester M16 0RA
tel – (0161) 8688000
fax – (0161) 8688804
website – www.manutd.com
Year of Formation – 1878
Chief Executive – David Gill
Manager – Sir Alex Ferguson
Stadium – Old Trafford (73,006)
Colours – Red/white/black
MAJOR HONOURS
League Championship – (15) 1908, 1911, 1952, 1956, 1957, 1965, 1967, 1993, 1994, 1996, 1997, 1999, 2000, 2001, 2003.
FA Cup – (11) 1909, 1948, 1963, 1977, 1983, 1985, 1990, 1994, 1996, 1999, 2004.
League Cup – (2) 1992, 2006.
European Champions Cup – (2) 1968, 1999.
European Cup-winners Cup – (1) 1991.
European Super Cup – (1) 1991.
World Club Cup – (1) 1999.

Middlesbrough FC
Riverside Stadium
Middlesbrough
Cleveland TS3 6RS
tel – (01642) 877700
fax – (01642) 877840
website – www.mfc.co.uk
Year of Formation – 1876
Chairman – Steve Gibson
Manager – Gareth Southgate
Stadium – Riverside (35,049)
Colours – Red (white horizontal band)/red/red
MAJOR HONOURS
League Cup – (1) 2004.

Newcastle United FC
St. James' Park
Newcastle-upon-Tyne NE1 4ST
tel – (0191) 2018400
fax – (0191) 2018600
website – www.nufc.co.uk
Year of Formation – 1881
Chairman – Freddy Shepherd
Manager – Glenn Roeder
Stadium – St. James' Park (52,387)
Colours – Black & white stripes/black/black
MAJOR HONOURS
League Championship – (4) 1905, 1907, 1909, 1927.
FA Cup – (6) 1910, 1924, 1932, 1951, 1952, 1955.
Fairs Cup – (1) 1969.

Portsmouth FC
Fratton Park
Frogmore Road
Portsmouth PO4 8RA
tel – (02392) 731204
fax – (02392) 734129
website – www.pompeyfc.co.uk
Year of Formation – 1898
Chairman – Milan Mandaric
Manager – Harry Redknapp
Stadium – Fratton Park (20,308)
Colours – Blue/white/red
MAJOR HONOURS
League Championship – (2) 1949, 1950.
FA Cup – (1) 1939.

Reading FC
Madejski Stadium
Bennet Road
Reading
Berkshire
RG2 0FL
tel – (0118) 9681100
fax – (0118) 9681101
website – www.readingfc.co.uk
Year of Formation – 1871
Chairman – John Madejski
Manager – Steve Coppell
Stadium – Madejski Stadium (24,200)
Colours – Blue & white hoops/white/white

Sheffield United FC
Bramall Lane
Sheffield S2 4SU
tel – (0870) 7871960
fax – (0870) 7873345
website – www.sufc.co.uk
Year of Formation – 1889
Chairman – Terry Robinson
Manager – Neil Warnock
Stadium – Bramall Lane (28,000)
Colours – Red & white stripes/black/black
MAJOR HONOURS
League Championship – (1) 1898.
FA Cup – (4) 1899, 1902, 1915, 1925.

Tottenham Hotspur FC
Bill Nicholson Way
748 High Road
Tottenham
London N17 0AP
tel – (020) 83655000
fax – (020) 83655175
website – www.spurs.co.uk
Year of Formation – 1882
Chairman – Daniel Levy
Manager – Martin Jol
Stadium – White Hart Lane (36,240)
Colours – White/navy blue/white
MAJOR HONOURS
League Championship – (2) 1951, 1961.
FA Cup – (8) 1901, 1921, 1961, 1962, 1967, 1981, 1982, 1991.
League Cup – (3) 1971, 1973, 1999.
European Cup-winners Cup – (1) 1963.
UEFA Cup – (2) 1972, 1984.

Watford FC
Vicarage Road Stadium
Watford
Herts
WD18 0ER
tel – (01923) 496000
fax – (01923) 496001
website – www.watfordfc.com
Year of Formation – 1881
Chairman – Graham Simpson
Coach – Adrian Boothroyd
Stadium – Vicarage Road (22,000)
Colours – Yellow/red/black

West Ham United FC
The Boleyn Ground
Green Street
Upton Park
London E13 9AZ
tel – (020) 85482748
fax – (020) 85482758
website – www.whufc.com
Year of Formation – 1900
Chairman – Terence Brown
Manager – Alan Pardew
Stadium – Upton Park (35,146)
Colours – Claret (sky blue sleeves)/white/white
MAJOR HONOURS
FA Cup – (3) 1964, 1975, 1980.
European Cup-winners Cup – (1) 1965.

Wigan Athletic FC
Loire Drive
Wigan WN5 0UH
tel – (01942) 774000
fax – (01942) 770477
website – www.wiganlatics.co.uk
Year of Formation – 1932
Chairman – David Whelan
Manager – Paul Jewell
Stadium – JJB Stadium (25,000)
Colours – Blue & white stripes/blue/white

ESTONIA

The Directory

Eesti Jalgpalli Liit
Rapia 8/10, 11312 Tallinn
tel – (00372 6) 512720
fax – (00372 6) 512729
website – www.jalgpall.ee
email – efa@jalgpall.ee

Year of Formation – 1921
President – Peeter Kütis
Secretary – Tõnu Sirel
Stadium – A. le Coq Arena (9,300)

FC Ajax Lasnamäe
Uuslinna 10
11415 Tallinn
tel – (6) 011229
fax – (6) 011229
website – www.fcajax.ee
Year of Formation – 1993
President – Boriss Dugan
Coach – Aleksandr Pushtov
Stadium – Ajax (500)
Colours – Blue/blue/blue

FC Flora Tallinn
Asula 4c
11312 Tallinn
tel – (6) 279940
fax – (6) 418021
website – www.fcflora.ee
Year of Formation – 1990
President – Aivar Pohlak
Coach – Pasi Rautiainen
Stadium – A. le Coq Arena (9,300)
Colours – Green (white trim)/white/green
MAJOR HONOURS
League Championship – (7) 1994, 1995, 1998, 1998, 2001, 2002, 2003.
Domestic Cup – (2) 1995, 1998.

FC Levadia Tallinn
Vana-Narva mnt. 24a
74114 Maardu
tel – (6) 379147
fax – (6) 379139
website – www.fclevadia.ee
Year of Formation – 1999
President – Viktor Levada
Coach – Tarmo Rüütli
Stadium – Kadriorg (4,700)
Colours – White (green trim)/green/ white
MAJOR HONOURS
League Championship – (3) 1999, 2000, 2004.
Domestic Cup – (4) 1999, 2000, 2004, 2005.

JK Maag Tartu
Sepa 26
51013 Tartu
tel – (7) 366913
fax – (7) 366901
Year of Formation – 1990
President – Aleksander Semjonov
Coach – Sergei Zamogilnõi
Stadium – Tamme (700)
Colours – Red/black/red

JK Tammeka Tartu
Kungla 1
50403 Tartu
tel – (7) 428038
fax – (7) 428038
website – www.jktammeka.ee
Year of Formation – 1989
President – Priit Tiru
Coach – Sergei Ratnikov
Stadium – Tamme (700)
Colours – White (black trim)/white/white

JK Trans Narva
Tiimani 3
21004 Narva
tel – (35) 73300
fax – (35) 73304
website – www.fctrans.ee
Year of Formation – 1979
President – Nikolai Burdakov
Coach – Valeri Bondarenko
Stadium – Kreenholm (2,000)
Colours – Red/black/red & orange
MAJOR HONOURS
Domestic Cup – (1) 2001.

JK Tulevik Viljandi
Ranna pst 6
71003 Viljandi
tel – (43) 48015
fax – (43) 48016
website – www.jktulevik.ee
Year of Formation – 1992
Coach – Marko Lelov
Stadium – Viljandi City Stadium (1,000)
Colours – Yellow/black/yellow

FC TVMK
Pärnu mnt 69
10134 Tallinn
tel – (6) 261501
fax – (6) 261622
website – www.fctvmk.ee
Year of Formation – 1951
President – Pjotr Sedin
Coach – Sergei Yuran
Stadium – Kadriorg (4,700)
Colours – White (blue trim)/blue/white
MAJOR HONOURS
League Championship – (1) 2005.
Domestic Cup – (3) 1993, 2003, 2006.

JK Vaprus Pärnu
Mai 18-76
80025 Pärnu
tel – (52) 71763
fax – (44) 24371
website – www.vaprus.ee
Year of Formation – 1999
President – Vello Järvesalu
Coach – Kalev Pajula
Stadium – Kalev (1,000)
Colours – Yellow (black trim)/black/yellow

FC Warrior Valga
E. Enno 15
68204 Valga
tel – (76) 61762
fax – (76) 61759
website – www.zone.ee/fcv
Year of Formation – 1997
President – Eduard Koger
Coach – Ivo Lehtmets
Stadium – Valga Keskstaadion (1,100)
Colours – White (black sleeves)/white/white & grey

FAROE ISLANDS

Fotboltssamband Føroya
Postboks 3028, Gundadalur, 110 Tórshavn
tel – (00298) 316707
fax – (00298) 319079
website – www.football.fo
email – fsf@football.fo

Year of Formation – 1979
President – Óli Holm
Secretary – Ísak Mikladal
Stadium – Svangaskard, Toftir (8,020)

Boltfelagid 36 (B 36)
Postrum 1136
110 Tórshavn
tel – 311936
fax – 318036
website – www.fcb36.org
Year of Formation – 1936
President – Sjúrdur Nordbúd
Coach – Sigfridur Clementsen
Stadium – Gundadalur (6,000)
Colours – White (black trim)/white/white
MAJOR HONOURS

The Directory

League Championship – (8) 1936, 1948, 1950, 1959, 1962, 1997, 2001, 2005.
Domestic Cup – (4) 1965, 1991, 2001, 2003.

Tofta Ítrottarfelag B68
Svangaskard
650 Toftir
tel – 449068
fax – 449050
website – www.b68.fo
Year of Formation – 1962
President – Niclas Davidsen
Coach – Joánnes Jacobsen
Stadium – Svangaskard (8,020)
Colours – Red/black/red
MAJOR HONOURS
League Championship – (3) 1984, 1985, 1992.

EB/Streymur
PO Box 7
450 Oyarabakki
tel – 508090
fax – 423072
website – www.eb-streymur.fo
Year of Formation – 1993
President – Rólant Højsted
Coach – Piotr Krakowski
Stadium – Molini (1,000)
Colours – Blue & black stripes/black/blue

Gøtu Ítrottarfelag (GÍ)
Postrum 4
510 Gøta
tel – 442024
fax – 441673
website – www.gigotu.fo
Year of Formation – 1926
President – Janus Rasmussen
Coach – Petur Mohr
Stadium – Gøtu (3,000)
Colours – Yellow (blue trim)/blue/yellow
MAJOR HONOURS
League Championship – (6) 1983, 1986, 1993, 1994, 1995, 1996.
Domestic Cup – (6) 1983, 1985, 1996, 1997, 2000, 2005.

Havnar Boltfelag (HB)
Gundadalur
Postrum 3046
110 Tórshavn
tel – 314046
fax – 318502
website – www.hb.fo
Year of Formation – 1904
President – Finn Ludvig
Coach – Krzysztof Popczynski
Stadium – Gundadalur (8,000)
Colours – Red & black stripes/black/black
MAJOR HONOURS
League Championship – (18) 1955, 1960, 1963, 1964, 1965, 1971, 1973, 1974, 1975, 1978, 1981, 1982, 1988, 1990, 1998, 2002, 2003, 2004.
Domestic Cup – (26) 1955, 1957, 1959, 1962, 1963, 1964, 1968, 1969, 1971, 1972, 1973, 1975, 1976, 1978, 1979, 1980, 1981, 1982, 1984, 1987, 1988, 1989, 1992, 1995, 1998, 2004.

Ítrottarfelag Fuglafjardar (ÍF)
Postrum 94
530 Fuglafjørdur
tel – 444636
fax – 444634
website – www.if.fo
Year of Formation – 1946
President – Mortan Thomsen
Coach – Petur Simonsen
Stadium – Fuglafjørdur (3,000)
Colours – White/white/white
MAJOR HONOURS
League Championship – (1) 1979.

Klaksvíkar Ítrottarfelag (KÍ)
Postrum 54
700 Klaksvík
tel – 456184
fax – 456167
website – www.ki-klaksvik.fo
Year of Formation – 1904
President – Torleif Sigurdsson
Coach – Tony Paris
Stadium – Klaksvík (4,000)
Colours – Blue (white trim)/white/blue
MAJOR HONOURS
League Championship – (17) 1942, 1945, 1952, 1953, 1954, 1956, 1957, 1958, 1961, 1966, 1967, 1968, 1969, 1970, 1972, 1991, 1999.
Domestic Cup – (5) 1966, 1967, 1990, 1994, 1999.

Nes Soknar Íttrotarfelag (NSÍ)
Postrum 173
620 Runavík
tel – 449909
fax – 449919
website – www.nsi.fo
Year of Formation – 1957
President – Andrias Lamhauge
Coach – Trygvi Mortensen
Stadium – Runavík (2,000)
Colours – Yellow (black trim)/black/yellow
MAJOR HONOURS
Domestic Cup – (2) 1986, 2002.

Skála Ítróttarfelag
Ítróttarhøllin
480 Skáli
tel – 441574
fax – 441576
website – www.skalaif.fo
Year of Formation – 1965
President – Hans Jákup Andreasen
Coach – Jóhan Nielsen
Stadium – Skáli (1,000)
Colours – Orange/black/orange

VB/Sumba
Postrum 127
900 Vagur
tel – 373679
fax – 373771
website – www.vb1905.fo
Year of Formation – 2006
President – Gudfinn Olsen
Coach – Ole Andersen
Stadium – Vestri a Eidinum (3,000)
Colours – Red & blue stripes/blue/blue
MAJOR HONOURS (as VB)
League Championship – (1) 2000.
Domestic Cup – (1) 1974.

FINLAND

Suomen Palloliitto
Finnair Stadium, Urheilukatu 5,
00250 Helsinki
tel – (00358 9) 742151
fax – (00358 9) 74215200
website – www.palloliitto.fi
email – tiedotus@palloliitto.fi

Year of Formation – 1907
President – Pekka Hämäläinen
Secretary – Teuvo Holopainen
Stadium – Olympiastadion,
Helsinki (40,000)

FC Haka
Kirjaskatu 1
37600 Valkeakoski
tel – (03) 5845364
fax – 0204163629
website – www.fchaka.fi
Year of Formation – 1934
President – Veikko Sievänen
Coach – Olli Huttunen
Stadium – Tehtaan kenttä (5,000)
Colours – White/black/white
MAJOR HONOURS
League Championship – (9) 1960, 1962, 1965, 1977, 1995, 1998, 1999, 2000, 2004.
Domestic Cup – (12) 1955, 1959, 1960, 1963, 1969, 1977, 1982, 1985, 1988, 1997, 2002, 2005.

The Directory

Helsingin Jalkapalloklubi (HJK)
Finnair Stadium
Urheilukatu 5
00250 Helsinki
tel – (09) 74216600
fax – (09) 74216666
website – www.hjk.fi
Year of Formation – 1907
President – Olli-Pekka Lyytikäinen
Coach – Keith Armstrong
Stadium – Finnair Stadium (11,000)
Colours – Blue & white stripes (white sleeves)/blue/blue
MAJOR HONOURS
League Championship – (21) 1911, 1912, 1917, 1918, 1919, 1923, 1925, 1936, 1938, 1964, 1973, 1978, 1981, 1985, 1987, 1988, 1990, 1992, 1997, 2002, 2003.
Domestic Cup – (8) 1966, 1981, 1984, 1993, 1996, 1998, 2000, 2003.

FC Honka
Esport Areena
Koivu-Mankkaantie 5
02200 Espoo
tel – (09) 2561600
website – www.honka.fi
Year of Formation – 1957
Co-Presidents – Jouko Harjunpää & Jouko Pakarinen
Coach – Mika Lehkosuo
Stadium – Tapiolan urheliupuisto (3,000)
Colours – Yellow & black stripes (yellow sleeves)/black/black

FC International Turku
Hippoksentie 21
20720 Turku
tel – (02) 2792700
fax – (02) 2792710
website – www.fcinter.com
Year of Formation – 1990
President – Stefan Håkans
Coach – Kari Virtanen
Stadium – Veritas Stadium (6,400)
Colours – Blue & black stripes/black/black

FF Jaro JS
Etelänummenkatu 20
68600 Pietarsaari
tel – (06) 7247936
fax – (06) 7230220
website – www.ffjaro.fi
Year of Formation – 1965
President – Timo Kuusisto
Coach – Keijo Paananen
Stadium – Keskuskenttä (4,000)

Colours – Red (white trim)/red/white

FC KooTeePee
Korkeavuorenkatu 2
48100 Kotka
tel – (05) 217044
fax – (05) 217099
website – www.fckooteepee.fi
Year of Formation – 1999
President – Matti Koski
Coach – Janne Hyppönen
Stadium – Arto Tolsa Areena (4,780)
Colours – Green & white stripes/black/white

Kuopion Palloseura (KuPS)
Kaartokatu 6
70620 Kuopio
tel – (017) 2668560
fax – (017) 2619598
website – www.kups.fi
Year of Formation – 1923
President – Manu Vesalo
Coach – Juha Malinen
Stadium – Magnum Areena (2,700)
Colours – Yellow (black trim)/black/yellow
MAJOR HONOURS
League Championship – (4) 1956, 1966, 1974, 1976.
Domestic Cup – (2) 1968, 1989

FC Lahti
Rautatienkatu 26 E
15110 Lahti
tel – (03) 880810
fax – (03) 8808131
website – www.fclahti.fi
Year of Formation – 1996
President – Risto Saloranta
Coach – Antti Muurinen
Stadium – Lahden Stadion (15,000)
Colours – Black/black/maroon

IFK Mariehamn
Ålandsvägen 17 B
22100 Mariehamn
tel – (018) 16345
fax – (018) 23715
website – www.ifkmariehamn.com/fotboll
Year of Formation – 1919
President – Mikael Granskog
Coach – Pekka Lyyski
Stadium – Wiklöf Holding Arena (1,600)
Colours – White (green trim)/green/white

Myllykosken Pallo-47 (MyPa)
Koulutie 1
46800 Anjalankoski

tel – (05) 3656686
fax – (05) 3255292
website – www.mypa.fi
Year of Formation – 1947
President – Matti Tiihonen
Coach – Ilkka Mäkelä
Stadium – Anjalankosken Jalkapallostadion (4,100)
Colours – Red (white sleeves)/white/white
MAJOR HONOURS
League Championship – (1) 2005.
Domestic Cup – (3) 1992, 1995, 2004.

Tampere United
Ratinan Rantatie 1
33100 Tampere
tel – (010) 6171500
fax – (03) 3469140
website – www.tampereunited.com
Year of Formation – 1998
President – Jari Viita
Coach – Ari Hjelm
Stadium – Ratinan Stadion (17,000)
Colours – White (blue trim)/blue/blue
MAJOR HONOURS
League Championship – (1) 2001.

Turun Palloseura (TPS)
Ruissalon puistotie 85
20100 Turku
tel – (02) 2500000
fax – (02) 2731130
website – www.tps.fi
Year of Formation – 1922
President – Jyrki Kurokallio
Coach – Kari Ukkonen
Stadium – Veritas Stadion (6,400)
Colours – Black & white stripes (white sleeves)/black/white
MAJOR HONOURS
League Championship – (8) 1928, 1939, 1941, 1949, 1968, 1971, 1972, 1975.
Domestic Cup – (2) 1991, 1994.

Vaasan Palloseura (VPS)
Reininkatu 3
65170 Vaasa
tel – (06) 3182970
fax – (06) 3182971
website – www.vps-vaasa.fi
Year of Formation – 1924
President – Veli-Matti Ristiluoma
Coach – Jari Pyykölä
Stadium – Hietalahti (4,600)
Colours – White/black/black
MAJOR HONOURS
League Championship – (2) 1945, 1948.

The Directory

FRANCE

Fédération Française de Football
60 bis Avenue d'Iena, 75783
Paris cedex 16
tel – (0033 1) 44 317300
fax – (0033 1) 47 208296
website – www.fff.fr
email – webmaster@fff.fr

Year of formation – 1919
President – Jean-Pierre Escalettes
Secretary – Jacques Lambert
Statium – Stade de France, Saint-Denis (80,000)

INTERNATIONAL HONOURS
World Cup – (1) 1998.
European Championship – (2) 1984, 2000.

INTERNATIONAL TOURNAMENT APPEARANCES
World Cup – (10) 1930, 1938 (2nd round), 1954, 1958 (3rd), 1966, 1978, 1982 (4th), 1986 (3rd), 1998 (Winners), 2002, 2006 (runners-up).
European Championship – (6) 1960 (4th), 1984 (Winners), 1992, 1996 (semi-finals), 2000 (Winners), 2004 (qtr-finals).

MAJOR EUROPEAN CLUB HONOURS
Champions Cup/League – (1) Olympique Marseille (1993).
Cup-winners Cup – (1) Paris Saint-Germain (1996).

Association de la Jeunesse Auxerroise
Route de Vaux
BP 349
89006 Auxerre Cédex
tel – (0386) 723232
fax – (0386) 522087
website – www.aja.fr
Year of Formation – 1905
President – Jean-Claude Hamel
Coach – Jean Fernandez
Stadium – Abbé-Deschamps (23,467)
Colours – White/white/white
MAJOR HONOURS
League Championship – (1) 1996.
French Cup – (4) 1994, 1996, 2003, 2005.

Football Club des Girondins de Bordeaux
Rue Juliot-Curie
33186 Le Haillan Cedex
tel – (0892) 683433
fax – (0556) 575446
website – www.girondins.com
Year of Formation – 1881
President – Jean-Louis Triaud
Coach – Ricardo Gomes
Stadium – Jacques-Chaban-Delmas (34,198)
Colours – Dark blue (with white V)/dark blue/dark blue
MAJOR HONOURS
League Championship – (5) 1950, 1984, 1985, 1987, 1999.
French Cup – (3) 1941, 1986, 1987.
League Cup – (1) 2002.

Le Mans Union Club 72
La Pincenardière
72230 Mulsanne
tel – (0243) 844600
fax – (0243) 840625
website – www.muc72.fr
Year of Formation – 1985
President – Henri Legarda
Coach – Frédéric Hantz
Stadium – Léon-Bollée (17,500)
Colours – Red/red/red

Racing Club de Lens
La Gaillette
33 rue Arthur-Lamendin
BP 23
62210 Avion Cédex
tel – (0321) 132132
fax – (0321) 132133
website – www.rclens.fr
Year of Formation – 1906
President – Gervais Martel
Coach – Francis Gillot
Stadium – Félix-Bollaert (41,809)
Colours – Yellow & red stripes/black/red
MAJOR HONOURS
League Championship – (1) 1998.
League Cup – (1) 1999.

Lille Olympique Sporting Club
Domaine de Luchin Grand Rue
BP 79
59780 Camphin en Pevele
tel – (0892) 685672
website – www.losc.fr
Year of Formation – 1944
President – Michel Seydoux
Coach – Claude Puel
Stadium – Lille Métropole de Villeneuve (18,100)
Colours – Red/black/black
MAJOR HONOURS
League Championship – (2) 1946, 1954.
French Cup – (5) 1946, 1947, 1948, 1953, 1955.

FC Lorient
Stade du Moustoir
Yves Allainmat BP 404
56104 Lorient cedex
tel – (0297) 351500
fax – (0297) 351502
website – www.fcl-lorient.com
Year of Formation – 1926
President – Alain Le Roch
Coach – Christian Gourcuff
Stadium – Le Moustoir (16,910)
Colours – Tangerine & black stripes/tangerine/white
MAJOR HONOURS
French Cup – (1) 2002.

Olympique Lyonnais
350 avenue Jean-Jaurès
69007 Lyon
tel – (0472) 767604
fax – (0478) 720399
website – www.olweb.fr
Year of Formation – 1950
President – Jean-Michel Aulas
Coach – Gérard Houllier
Stadium – Gerland (42,000)
Colours – White (blue/red left-hand stripe)/white/white
MAJOR HONOURS
League Championship – (5) 2002, 2003, 2004, 2005, 2006.
French Cup – (3) 1964, 1967, 1973.
League Cup – (1) 2001.

Olympique de Marseille
La Commanderie
33 traverse de la Martine
BP 13425
Marseille Cedex 08
tel – (0491) 765609
fax – (0491) 760777
website – www.om.net
Year of Formation – 1899
President – Pape Diouf
Coach – Albert Emon
Stadium – Vélodrome (60,000)
Colours – White (light blue trim)/white/white
MAJOR HONOURS
League Championship – (8) 1937, 1948, 1971, 1972, 1989, 1990, 1991, 1992.
French Cup – (10) 1924, 1926, 1927, 1935, 1938, 1943, 1969, 1972, 1976, 1989.
European Champions Cup – (1) 1993.

Association Sportive de Monaco Football Club
7 avenue des Castelans

The Directory

98000 Monaco
tel – (37792) 057473
fax – (37792) 053688
website – www.asm-fc.com
Year of Formation – 1924
President – Michel Pastor
Coach – Ladislau Bölöni
Stadium – Louis II (18,524)
Colours – Red & white diagonal halves/red/white
MAJOR HONOURS
League Championship – (7) 1961, 1963, 1978, 1982, 1988, 1997, 2000.
French Cup – (5) 1960, 1963, 1980, 1985, 1991.
League Cup – (1) 2003.

Association Sportive Nancy-Lorraine
90 boulevard Jean-Jaurès
54510 Tomblaine
tel – (0383) 183090
fax – (0383) 183092
website – www.asnl.net
Year of Formation – 1966
President – Jacques Rousselot
Coach – Pablo Correa
Stadium – Marcel-Picot (20,085)
Colours – White (red trim)/white/white
MAJOR HONOURS
French Cup – (1) 1978.
League Cup – (1) 2006.

Football Club Nantes Atlantique
Centre Sportif José-Arribas-la Jonelière
44240 La Chappelle-sur-Erdre
tel – (0892) 707937
fax – (0240) 372921
website – www.fcna.fr
Year of Formation – 1943
President – Rudi Roussillon
Coach – Serge Le Dizet
Stadium – La Beaujoire-Louis-Fonteneau (39,000)
Colours – Yellow (green trim)/yellow/yellow
MAJOR HONOURS
League Championship – (8) 1965, 1966, 1973, 1977, 1980, 1983, 1995, 2001.
French Cup – (3) 1979, 1999, 2000.

Olympique Gymnaste Club de Nice Côte d'Azur
Parc des Sports Charles-Ehrmann
177 Route de Grenoble
06200 Nice
tel – (0493) 180679
fax – (0493) 180679
website – www.ogcnice.com
Year of Formation – 1904
President – Maurice Cohen
Coach – Frédéric Antonetti
Stadium – Municipal du Ray (18,500)
Colours – Red & black stripes/black/black
MAJOR HONOURS
League Championship – (4) 1951, 1952, 1956, 1959.
French Cup – (3) 1952, 1954, 1997.

Paris Saint-Germain Football Club
24 rue du Commandant-Guilbaud
75781 Paris Cedex 16
tel – (0825) 075078
fax – (0141) 107100
website – www.psg.fr
Year of Formation – 1970
President – Pierre Blayau
Coach – Guy Lacombe
Stadium – Parc des Princes (48,527)
Colours – Dark blue (broad red/white central stripe)/dark blue/dark blue
MAJOR HONOURS
League Championship – (2) 1986, 1994.
French Cup – (7) 1982, 1983, 1993, 1995, 1998, 2004, 2006.
League Cup – (2) 1995, 1998.
European Cup-winners Cup – (1) 1996.

Stade Rennais Football Club
111 route de Lorient
35000 Rennes
tel – (0820) 000035
fax – (0299) 143577
website – www.staderennais.fr
Year of Formation – 1901
President – Emmanuel Cueff
Coach – Pierre Dréossi
Stadium – Route de Lorient (31,200)
Colours – Red (black trim)/black/black
MAJOR HONOURS
French Cup – (2) 1965, 1971.

Association Sportive de Saint-Etienne Loire
14 Rue Paul-et-Pierre-Guichard
42028 Saint-Etienne Cedex 01
tel – (0477) 923170
fax – (0477) 799522
website – www.asse.fr
Year of Formation – 1920
President – Bernard Caïazzo
Coach – Ivan Hasek
Stadium – Geoffroy-Guichard (36,600)
Colours – Green/white/green
MAJOR HONOURS
League Championship – (10) 1957, 1964, 1967, 1968, 1969, 1970, 1974, 1975, 1976, 1981.
French Cup – (6) 1962, 1968, 1970, 1974, 1975, 1977.

CS Sedan Ardennes
Château de Montvillers
BP 40
01840 Bazeilles
tel – (0324) 270059
fax – (0324) 270841
website – www.cssedan.com
Year of Formation – 1919
President – Pascal Urano
Coach – Serge Romano
Stadium – Louis Dugauguez (23,107)
Colours – Green (white sleeves)/white/green
MAJOR HONOURS
French Cup – (2) 1956, 1961.

Football Club Sochaux-Montbéliard
Impasse des Forges
25200 Montbéliard
tel – (0381) 997000
fax – (0381) 997001
website – www.fcsochaux.fr
Year of Formation – 1930
President – Jean-Claude Plessis
Coach – Alain Perrin
Stadium – Auguste-Bonal (20,000)
Colours – Yellow/dark blue/dark blue
MAJOR HONOURS
League Championship – (2) 1935, 1938.
French Cup – (1) 1937.
League Cup – (1) 2004.

Toulouse Football Club
1 Allée Gabriel-Biènes
BP 4023
31028 Toulouse Cedex 4
tel – (0892) 700831
fax – (0561) 535567
website – www.tfc.info
Year of Formation – 1937
President – Olivier Sadran
Coach – Elie Baup
Stadium – Stadium Municipal (38,650)
Colours – Lilac/lilac/lilac
MAJOR HONOURS
French Cup – (1) 1957.

Espérance Sportive Troyes Aube Champagne
29 bis rue St.-Exupéry
BP 801
10158 Pont Ste Marie Cedex
tel – (0892) 707926
fax – (0325) 704833
website – www.estac.fr
Year of Formation – 1986
President – Thierry Gomez
Coach – Jean-Marc Furlan

The Directory

Stadium – Stade de l'Aube (18,231)
Colours – Blue (white trim)/white/blue

Valenciennes FC
43 bis Avenue de Reims
BP 136
59300 Valenciennes
tel – (0327) 461910
fax – (0327) 360278
website – www.va-fc.com
Year of Formation – 1913
President – Francis Decourrière
Coach – Antoine Kombouaré
Stadium – Nungesser (11,316)
Colours – Red (white trim)/red/red

GEORGIA

Football Federation of Georgia
76a Ilia Chavchavadze Str., Tbilisi
0162
tel – (00995 32) 912610, 912650
fax – (00995 32) 001128
website – www.gff.ge
email – gff@gff.ge

Year of Formation – 1990
President – Nodar Akhalkatsi
Secretary – Ucha Ugulava
Stadium – Boris Paichadze,
Tbilisi (20,500)

MAJOR EUROPEAN CLUB HONOURS
Cup-winners Cup – (1) Dinamo Tbilisi (1981)

FC Ameri Tbilisi
Kazbegi Ave. 42a
0171 Tbilisi
tel – (32) 390098
fax – (32) 943380
Year of Formation – 2003
President – Zurab Potskhveria
Coach – Giorgi Chikhradze
Stadium – Ameri (1,000)
MAJOR HONOURS
Domestic Cup – (1) 2006.

FC Borjomi
Rustaveli Str. 102
1200 Borjomi
tel – (267) 21179
fax – (267) 21366
Year of Formation – 1936
President – David Gelashvili
Coach – Vladimer Khachidze
Stadium – J. Zeinklishvili (5,000)

Chikhura Sachkhere
Tavisuplebis Str. 4
4000 Sachkhere
tel – (235) 21700
Year of Formation – 1936
President – Nodar Megrelishvili
Coach – Khvicha Kasrashvili
Stadium – Central (5,000)
Colours – Purple/black/white

FC Dila Gori
Guramishvili Str. 5
1400 Gori
tel – (270) 73961
fax – (270) 73170
Year of Formation – 1949
Director – Archil Begiashvili
Coach – Otar Korgalidze
Stadium – T. Burjanadze (8,230)

Dinamo Batumi
Barbiusi Str. 32
6000 Batumi
tel – (222) 76771
fax – (222) 76770
Year of Formation – 1923
President – Tamaz Tsinaridze
Coach – Amiran Gogitidze
Stadium – Central (19,600)
Colours – Blue/blue/white
MAJOR HONOURS
Domestic Cup – (1) 1998.

Dinamo Tbilisi
Digomi Township
3rd Block
0159 Tbilisi
tel – (32) 531932/516688
fax – (32) 502037
website – www.fcdinamotbilisi.ge
Year of Formation – 1925
President – Badri Patarkatsishvili
Coach – Kakhi Kacharava
Stadium – Boris Paichadze (20,500)
Colours – White/light blue/light blue
MAJOR HONOURS
League Championship (USSR) – (2) 1964, 1978.
League Championship – (12) 1990, 1991, 1992, 1993, 1994, 1995, 1996, 1997, 1998, 1999, 2003, 2005.
Domestic Cup (USSR) – (2) 1976, 1979.
Domestic Cup – (8) 1992, 1993, 1994, 1995, 1996, 1997, 2003, 2004.
European Cup-winners Cup – (1) 1981.

FC Kakheti Telavi
Tsabadze Str. 5

3330 Telavi
tel – (250) 73101
fax – (250) 70017
Year of Formation – 1936
President – Gocha Mamatsashvili
Coach – Jemal Makharashvili
Stadium – Givi Chokheli (17,000)

Lokomotivi Tbilisi
Chavchavadze Ave. 74
0162 Tbilisi
tel – (32) 293966/253968
fax – (32) 294895
Year of Formation – 1936
President – Aleksandre Menabde
Coach – Amiran Minashvili
Stadium – Lokomotivi (24,500)
MAJOR HONOURS
Domestic Cup – (3) 2000, 2002, 2005.

Merani Tbilisi
B. Khmelnitsky Str. 48
Tbilisi
Year of Formation – 1998
President – Genadi Kikava
Coach – David Ejibashvili
Stadium – Shevardeni (3,000)

FC Olimpi Rustavi
Jikia Str. 5
0186 Tbilisi
tel – (32) 913543
fax – (32) 537945
Year of Formation – 1991
President – Badri Karkashadze
Coach – Giorgi Kiknadze
Stadium – Poladi (6,000)
Colours – White/red/white

Sioni Bolnisi
Orbeliani street 120
1100 Bolnisi
tel – (258) 22918
fax – (32) 922493
Year of Formation – 1936
President – Giorgi Arevadze
Coach – Kakhaber Tskhadadze
Stadium – Temur Stepania (3,000)
MAJOR HONOURS
League Championship – (1) 2006.

Torpedo Kutaisi
Akhalgazrdobis Shesakhvevi 3
4600 Kutaisi
tel – (231) 22495
fax – (231) 21255
Year of Formation – 1949

The Directory

President – Giorgi Khurtsidze
Coach – Mikheil Kvernadze
Stadium – Torpedo (19,400)
MAJOR HONOURS
League Championship – (3) 2000, 2001, 2002.
Domestic Cup – (2) 1999, 2001.

FC WIT Georgia Tbilisi
Tamarashvili Str.19
0117 Tbilisi
tel – (32) 311489/253748
fax – (32) 990743
website – www.wit-georgia.ge
Year of Formation – 1968
President – Guram Rukhadze
Coach – Nestor Mumladze
Stadium – Mtskheta Central (2,000)
MAJOR HONOURS
League Championship – (1) 2004.

FC Zestafoni
Sakarkhnos Str. 9
2000 Zestaphoni
tel – (32) 212908
fax – (32) 940047
Year of Formation – 1999
President – Ilia Kokaia
Coach – Merab Kochlashvili
Stadium – Central (5,000)

GERMANY

Deutscher Fussball-Bund
Otto-Fleck-Schneise 6, Postfach
710265, 60492 Frankfurt am Main
tel – (0049 69) 67880
fax – (0049 69) 6788266
website – www.dfb.de
email – info@dfb.de

Year of Formation – 1900
President – Gerhard Mayer-Vorfelder
Secretary – Horst R. Schmidt

INTERNATIONAL HONOURS*
World Cup – (3) 1954, 1974, 1990.
European Championship – (3) 1972, 1980, 1996.

INTERNATIONAL TOURNAMENT APPEARANCES*
World Cup – (16) 1934 (3rd), 1938, 1954 (Winners), 1958 (4th), 1962 (qtr-finals), 1966 (runners-up), 1970 (3rd), 1974 (Winners), 1978 (2nd phase), 1982 (runners-up), 1986 (runners-up), 1990 (Winners), 1994 (qtr-finals), 1998 (qtr-finals), 2002 (runners-up), 2006 (3rd).
European Championship – (9) 1972 (Winners), 1976 (runners-up), 1980 (Winners), 1984, 1988 (semi-finals), 1992 (runners-up), 1996 (Winners), 2000, 2004.

(* before 1992 as West Germany)

MAJOR EUROPEAN CLUB HONOURS
Champions Cup/League – (6) FC Bayern München (1974, 1975, 1976, 2001), Hamburger SV (1983), Borussia Dortmund (1997).
Cup-winners Cup – (4) Borussia Dortmund (1966), FC Bayern München (1967), Hamburger SV (1977), SV Werder Bremen (1992).
UEFA Cup – (6) Borussia Mönchengladbach (1975, 1979), Eintracht Frankfurt (1980), Bayer 04 Leverkusen (1988), FC Bayern München (1996), FC Schalke 04 (1997).

Alemannia Aachen
Sonnenweg 11
52070 Aachen
tel – (01805) 018011
fax – (0241) 9384010
website – www.alemannia-aachen.de
Year of Formation – 1900
President – Horst Heinrichs
Coach – Dieter Hecking
Stadium – Tivoli (21,000)
Colours – Yellow (black trim)/black/black

Arminia Bielefeld
Melanchthonstrasse 31a
33 615 Bielefeld
tel – (0521) 966110
fax – (0521) 9661111
website – www.arminia-bielefeld.de
Year of Formation – 1905
President – Hans-Hermann Schwick
Coach – Thomas von Heesen
Stadium – Schüco-Arena (26,601)
Colours – Blue (black trim)/black/white

TSV Bayer 04 Leverkusen
Bismarckstrasse 122-124
51373 Leverkusen
tel – (0214) 86600
fax – (0214) 62709
website – www.bayer04.de
Year of Formation – 1904
President – Klaus Beck
Coach – Michael Skibbe
Stadium – BayArena (22,500)
Colours – Red (black trim)/black/red
MAJOR HONOURS
Domestic Cup – (1) 1993.
UEFA Cup – (1) 1988.

FC Bayern München
Säbener Strasse 51
Postfach 90 04 51
81547 München
tel – (089) 699310
fax – (089) 644165
website – www.fcbayern.de
Year of Formation – 1900
President – Franz Beckenbauer
Coach – Felix Magath
Stadium – Allianz-Arena (69,000)
Colours – Red (white & dark blue trim)/red/red
MAJOR HONOURS
League Championship – (20) 1932, 1969, 1972, 1973, 1974, 1980, 1981, 1985, 1986, 1987, 1989, 1990, 1994, 1997, 1999, 2000, 2001, 2003, 2005, 2006.
Domestic Cup – (13) 1957, 1966, 1967, 1969, 1971, 1982, 1984, 1986, 1998, 2000, 2003, 2005, 2006.
European Champions Cup – (4) 1974, 1975, 1976, 2001.
European Cup-winners Cup – (1) 1967.
UEFA Cup – (1) 1996.
World Club Cup – (2) 1976, 2001.

VfL Bochum
Castroper Strasse 145
44791 Bochum
tel – (0234) 951848
fax – (0234) 951895
website – www.vfl-bochum.de
Year of Formation – 1848
President – Werner Altegoer
Coach – Marcel Koller
Stadium – Ruhrstadion (31.328)
Colours – Blue (white trim)/white/blue

BV 09 Borussia Dortmund
Rheinlanddamm 207-209
44139 Dortmund
tel – (0231) 90200
fax – (0231) 9020105
website – www.bvb.de
Year of Formation – 1909
President – Dr. Reinhard Rauball
Coach – Bert van Marwijk
Stadium – Westfalenstadion (80,700)
Colours – Yellow & white stripes/black/yellow & black
MAJOR HONOURS
League Championship – (6) 1956, 1957, 1963, 1995, 1996, 2002.
Domestic Cup – (2) 1965, 1989.
European Champions Cup – (1) 1997.
European Cup-winners Cup – (1) 1966.
World Club Cup – (1) 1997.

The Directory

Borussia Mönchengladbach
Hennes-Weisweiler-Allee 1
41179 Mönchengladbach
tel – (02161) 92930
fax – (02161) 92931009
website – www.borussia.de
Year of Formation – 1900
President – Rolf Königs
Coach – Jupp Heynckes
Stadium – Borussia-Park (54,019)
Colours – White & black stripes/white/white
MAJOR HONOURS
League Championship – (5) 1970, 1971, 1975, 1976, 1977.
Domestic Cup – (3) 1960, 1973, 1995.
UEFA Cup – (2) 1975, 1979.

SG Eintracht Frankfurt
Mörfelder Landstrasse 362
60528 Frankfurt
tel – (069) 955030
fax – (069) 95503110
website – www.eintracht.de
Year of Formation – 1899
President – Heribert Bruchhagen
Coach – Friedhelm Funkel
Stadium – Commerzbank-Arena (51,052)
Colours – Red & black broad stripes/black/red
MAJOR HONOURS
League Championship – (1) 1959.
Domestic Cup – (4) 1974, 1975, 1981, 1988.
UEFA Cup – (1) 1980.

FC Energie Cottbus
Am Eliaspark 1
03042 Cottbus
tel – (0355) 756950
fax – (0355) 713026
website – www.fcenergie.de
Year of Formation – 1966
President – Ulrich Lepsch
Coach – Petrik Sander
Stadium – Stadion der Freundschaft (22,450)
Colours – White (broad red stripe)/red/red & white

Hamburger Sport-Verein
Sylvesterallee 7
22525 Hamburg
tel – (040) 415501
fax – (040) 41551060
website – www.hsv.de
Year of Formation – 1887
President – Bernd Hoffmann
Coach – Thomas Doll
Stadium – AOL-Arena (55,000)
Colours – White (blue trim)/red/blue

MAJOR HONOURS
League Championship – (6) 1923, 1928, 1960, 1979, 1982, 1983.
Domestic Cup – (3) 1963, 1976, 1987.
European Champions Cup – (1) 1983.
European Cup-winners Cup – (1) 1977.

Hannover 96
Arthur-Menge-Ufer 5
30169 Hannover
tel – (05131) 9690096
fax – (0511) 96900796
website – www.hannover96.de
Year of Formation – 1896
President – Martin Kind
Coach – Peter Neururer
Stadium – AWD-Arena (49,000)
Colours – Red/black/black
MAJOR HONOURS
League Championship – (2) 1938, 1954.
Domestic Cup – (2) 1992.

Hertha BSC Berlin
Hanns-Braun-Strasse
Friesenhaus 2
14053 Berlin
tel – (030) 3009280
fax – (030) 30092894
website – www.herthabsc.de
Year of Formation – 1892
President – Bernd Schiphorst
Coach – Falko Götz
Stadium – Olympiastadion (74,400)
Colours – Blue & white stripes/blue/blue
MAJOR HONOURS
League Championship – (2) 1930, 1931.

FSV Mainz 05
Dr.-Martin-Luther-King-Weg
55 122 Mainz
tel – (06131) 375500
fax – (06131) 3755033
website – www.mainz05.de
Year of Formation – 1905
President – Harald Strutz
Coach – Jürgen Klopp
Stadium – Stadion am Bruchweg (20,300)
Colours – Red & white stripes/red/red

1.FC Nürnberg
Valznerweiherstrasse 200
90 480 Nürnberg
tel – (0911) 940790
fax – (0911) 9407977
website – www.fcn.de
Year of Formation – 1900
President – Michael A. Roth

Coach – Hans Meyer
Stadium – Frankenstadion (46,780)
Colours – Red (black sleeves)/black/black
MAJOR HONOURS
League Championship – (9) 1920, 1921, 1924, 1925, 1927, 1936, 1948, 1961, 1968.
Domestic Cup – (3) 1935, 1939, 1962.

FC Schalke 04
Ernst-Kuzorra-Weg 1
45891 Gelsenkirchen
tel – (0209) 36180
fax – (0209) 3618109
website – www.schalke04.de
Year of Formation – 1904
President – Gerd Rehberg
Coach – Mirko Slomka
Stadium – Veltins-Arena (61,524)
Colours – Blue/white/blue
MAJOR HONOURS
League Championship – (7) 1934, 1935, 1937, 1939, 1940, 1942, 1958.
Domestic Cup – (4) 1937, 1972, 2001, 2002.
UEFA Cup – (1) 1997.

VfB Stuttgart
Mercedesstrasse 109
70372 Stuttgart
tel – (01805) 8325463
fax – (0711) 5500733
website – www.vfb.de
Year of Formation – 1893
President – Erwin Staudt
Coach – Armin Veh
Stadium – Gottlieb-Daimler-Stadion (55,875)
Colours – White (red band)/white/white
MAJOR HONOURS
League Championship – (4) 1950, 1952, 1984, 1992.
Domestic Cup – (3) 1954, 1958, 1997.

SV Werder Bremen
Franz-Böhmert-Strasse 1c
28205 Bremen
tel – (01805) 937337
fax – (0421) 493555
website – www.werder.de
Year of Formation – 1899
President – Jürgen L. Born
Coach – Thomas Schaaf
Stadium – Weserstadion (42,500)
Colours – Green & white halves/white/green & white
MAJOR HONOURS
League Championship – (4) 1965, 1988, 1993, 2004.
Domestic Cup – (5) 1961, 1991, 1994, 1999, 2004.
European Cup-winners Cup – (1) 1992.

The Directory

VfL Wolfsburg
Zu den Allerwiesen 1
38446 Wolfsburg
tel – (05361) 89030
fax – (05361) 8903150
website – www.vfl-wolfsburg.de
Year of Formation – 1945
President – Lothar Sander
Coach – Klaus Augenthaler
Stadium – Volkswagen-Arena (30,000)
Colours – Green & white broad stripes/green/white

GREECE

Elliniki Podosfairiki Omospondia
Leoforos Singrou 137, Athens
17121
tel – (0030) 2109306000
fax – (0030) 2109359666
website – www.epo.gr
email – info@epo.gr

Year of Formation – 1926
President – Vassilis Gagatsis
Secretary – Ioannis Ikonomides
Stadium – Olympic Stadium, Athens (72,000)

INTERNATIONAL HONOURS
European Championship – (1) 2004.

INTERNATIONAL TOURNAMENT APPEARANCES
World Cup – (1) 1994.
European Championship – (2) 1980, 2004 (Winners).

Athlitiki Enosi Konstantinoupoleos (AEK)
Gramou 69-71
15124 Marousi, Athens
tel – (01) 2106121317
fax – (01) 2108234454
website – www.aekfc.gr
Year of Formation – 1924
President – Demis Nikolaidis
Coach – Lorenzo Serra Ferrer
Stadium – Olympic Stadium (72,000)
Colours – Yellow & black stripes/black/yellow
MAJOR HONOURS
League Championship – (11) 1939, 1940, 1963, 1968, 1971, 1978, 1979, 1989, 1992, 1993, 1994.
Domestic Cup – (12) 1932, 1939, 1949, 1950, 1956, 1966, 1978, 1983, 1996, 1997, 2000, 2002.

Apollon Kalamarias
Papagou & Sourmenon
Kalamaria
55131 Thessaloniki
tel – (0231) 0425533-4
fax – (0231) 0412777
website – www.apollonkalamariasfc.gr
Year of Formation – 1926
President – Elias Damilos
Coach – Thomas Katsavakis
Stadium – Kalamarias (7,000)
Colours – Red & black stripes/black/red

Aris FC
Alkminis 69
54249 Thessaloniki
tel – (2310) 325001
fax – (2310) 309035
website – www.arisfc.gr
Year of Formation – 1914
President – Haralambos Skondras
Coach – Angel Guillermo Ojios
Stadium – Kleantis Vikelidis (18,300)
Colours – Yellow (two black stripes)/yellow/black
MAJOR HONOURS
Domestic Cup – (1) 1970.

FC Atromitos-Chalkidona Near East
Knosou 49 B
18451 Piraeus
tel – (021) 04925536
fax – (021) 04921871
website – www.atromitosfc.gr
Year of Formation – 1930
President – Giorgos Spanos
Coach – Giorgos Parashos
Stadium – Peristeri (8,000)
Colours – Blue/white/blue

Egaleo FC
Smirnis 33
12243 Athens
tel – (021) 05316883
fax – (021) 05316883
website – www.egaleofc.gr
Year of Formation – 1931
President – Dimitris Koukis
Coach – Giorgos Hatzaras
Stadium – Stavros Mavrothalasitis (3,500)
Colours – Pale blue/dark blue/pale blue

Ergotelis
Leoforos N. Plastira 1
71003 Iraklio
Crete
tel – (2810) 222246
fax – (2810) 222246
website – www.ergotelis.gr
Year of Formation – 1929
President – Giorgos Soultatos
Coach – Nikos Karageorgiou
Stadium – Pagkritio (25,600)
Colours – Yellow (black trim)/black/yellow

Ionikos FC
Dafni 5 & Vournova
18122 Piraeus
tel – (021) 04945000
fax – (021) 04971490
website – www.ionikos-fc.gr
Year of Formation – 1965
President – Christos Kanellakis
Coach – Sakis Tsiolis
Stadium – Neapoli (5,850)
Colours – Light blue (white trim)/light blue/white & blue

Iraklis FC
Markou Botsari 66
54644 Thessaloniki
tel – (031) 0478800
fax – (031) 0478820
website – www.iraklis-fc.gr
Year of Formation – 1908
President – Giorgos Spanoudakis
Coach – Savvas Kofidis
Stadium – Kaftatzoglio (28,200)
Colours – Blue & white stripes/blue/white
MAJOR HONOURS
Domestic Cup – (1) 1976.

Kerkira
Samara 22
49100 Kerkira
tel – (26610) 37770
fax – (2661) 81430
website – aokerkyra.gr
Year of Formation – 1969
President – Nikos Priftis
Coach – Babis Tennes
Stadium – EAK Kerkiras (6,150)
Colours – Red & blue stripes/blue/blue

Larisa FC
Erithrou Stavrou 1-3
Larisa
tel – (0030) 2410535508
fax – (0030) 2410535505
website – www.ael.gr
Year of Formation – 1964
President – Kostas Piladakis
Coach – Giorgos Donis
Stadium – Alkazar (13,108)
Colours – White (maroon trim)/white/white
MAJOR HONOURS
League Championship – (1) 1988

The Directory

Domestic Cup – (1) 1985

Omilos Filathlon Irakliou (OFI) FC
Vardinoyanio Athlitiko Kentro
Skafidaras Gazi
71500 Iraklio
tel – (0281) 0823651
fax – (0281) 0823660
website – www.ofi.gr
Year of Formation – 1925
President – Fanouris Vatsinas
Coach – Mauer Reiner
Stadium – Pagkritio (25,600)
Colours – Black & white broad stripes/black/black
MAJOR HONOURS
Domestic Cup – (1) 1987.

Olympiakos FC
Alexandras Square
Zea
18534 Piraeus
tel – (021) 04143000
fax – (021) 04143113
website – www.olimpiakos.gr
Year of Formation – 1925
President – Sokratis Kokalis
Coach – Trond Sollied
Stadium – New Karaiskaki (33,000)
Colours – Red & white stripes/white/red
MAJOR HONOURS
League Championship – (34) 1931, 1933, 1934, 1936, 1937, 1938, 1947, 1948, 1951, 1954, 1955, 1956, 1957, 1958, 1959, 1966, 1967, 1973, 1974, 1975, 1980, 1981, 1982, 1983, 1987, 1997, 1998, 1999, 2000, 2001, 2002, 2003, 2005, 2006.
Domestic Cup – (22) 1947, 1951, 1952, 1953, 1954, 1957, 1958, 1959, 1960, 1961, 1963, 1965, 1968, 1971, 1973, 1975, 1981, 1990, 1992, 1999, 2005, 2006.

Panathinaikos FC
Irodou Attikou 12A
15121 Marousi, Athens
tel – (021) 08093630
fax – (021) 08093644
website – www.pao.gr
Year of Formation – 1908
President – Argiris Mitsou
Coach – Hans Backe
Stadium – Olympic Stadium (72,000)
Colours – Green (white trim)/green/green
MAJOR HONOURS
League Championship – (22) 1911, 1912, 1916, 1930, 1949, 1953, 1960, 1961, 1962, 1964, 1965, 1969, 1970, 1972, 1977, 1984, 1986, 1990, 1991, 1995, 1996, 2004.
Domestic Cup – (16) 1940, 1948, 1955, 1967,
1969, 1977, 1982, 1984, 1986, 1988, 1989, 1991, 1993, 1994, 1995, 2004.

Panionios FC
I. Chrisostomou 1
Nea Smirni
17121 Athens
tel – (021) 09311189
fax – (021) 09332036
website – www.panionios.gr
Year of Formation – 1890
President – Kostas Tsakiris
Coach – Ewald Lienen
Stadium – Nea Smirni (12,000)
Colours – Red & blue broad stripes (red sleeves)/blue/red
MAJOR HONOURS
Domestic Cup – (2) 1979, 1998.

Panthesalonikios Athlitikos Omilos Konstantinoupolis (PAOK) FC
Mikras Asias
Toumba Stadium
54351 Thessaloniki
tel – (031) 0950950
fax – (031) 0951000
website – www.paok-hellas.gr
Year of Formation – 1926
President – Giannis Goumenos
Coach – Ilie Dumitrescu
Stadium – Toumba (28,700)
Colours – Black & white stripes/black/black
MAJOR HONOURS
League Championship – (2) 1976, 1985.
Domestic Cup – (4) 1972, 1974, 2001, 2003.

Skoda Xanthi FC
Athletic Center Skoda Xanthi
67100 Xanthi
tel – (0541) 024466
fax – (0541) 025825
website – www.skodaxanthifc.gr
Year of Formation – 1967
President – Giorgos Gitzikis
Coach – Giannis Mantzourakis
Stadium – Pigadia Xanthis (6,200)
Colours – Dark blue (white trim)/dark blue/red

HOLLAND

Koninklijke Nederlandsche Voetbalbond
Woudenbergseweg 56-58, PO
Box 515, 3700 AM Zeist
tel – (0031 343) 499211
fax – (0031 343) 499189
website – www.knvb.nl
email – publiekinfo@knvb.nl

Year of Formation – 1889
President – Mathieu Sprengers
Secretary – Harry Been
Stadium – Feyenoord, Rotterdam (51,180)

INTERNATIONAL HONOURS
European Championship – (1) 1988.

INTERNATIONAL TOURNAMENT APPEARANCES
World Cup – (8) 1934, 1938, 1974 (runners-up), 1978 (runners-up), 1990 (2nd round), 1994 (qtr-finals), 1998 (4th), 2006 (2nd round).
European Championship – (7) 1976 (3rd), 1980, 1988 (Winners), 1992 (semi-finals), 1996 (qtr-finals), 2000 (semi-finals), 2004 (semi-finals).

MAJOR EUROPEAN CLUB HONOURS
Champions Cup – (6) Feyenoord (1970), Ajax (1971, 1972, 1973, 1995), PSV (1988).
Cup-winners Cup – (1) Ajax (1987).
UEFA Cup – (4) Feyenoord (1974, 2002), PSV (1978), Ajax (1992).

ADO Den Haag
Mr. P. Droogleever Fortuynweg 26
Postbus 32400
2503 AC Den Haag
tel – (070) 3054500
fax – (070) 3054599
website – www.adodenhaag.nl
Year of Formation – 1971
President – Ruud de Boer
Coach – Frans Adelaar
Stadium – Zuiderpark (11,000)
Colours – Green & yellow broad stripes (black sleeves)/dark green/green & yellow
MAJOR HONOURS
Domestic Cup – (1) 1975.

Ajax Amsterdam NV
Postbus 12522
1100 AM Amsterdam
tel – (020) 3111444
fax – (020) 3111480
website – www.ajax.nl
Year of Formation – 1900
President – John Jaakke
Coach – Henk ten Cate
Stadium – Amsterdam ArenA (51,859)
Colours – White (broad red central stripe)/white/white
MAJOR HONOURS
League Championship – (29) 1918, 1919, 1931, 1932, 1934, 1937, 1939, 1947, 1957, 1960, 1966, 1967, 1968, 1970, 1972, 1973, 1977, 1979, 1980,

The Directory

1982, 1983, 1985, 1990, 1994, 1995, 1996, 1998, 2002, 2004.
Domestic Cup – (16) 1917, 1943, 1961, 1967, 1970, 1971, 1972, 1979, 1983, 1986, 1987, 1993, 1998, 1999, 2002, 2006.
European Champions Cup – (4) 1971, 1972, 1973, 1995.
European Cup-winners Cup – (1) 1987.
UEFA Cup – (1) 1992.
European Super Cup – (3) 1972, 1973, 1995.
World Club Cup – (2) 1972, 1995.

AZ
Postbus 1010
1810 KA Alkmaar
tel – (072) 5478000
fax – (072) 5478080
website – www.az.nl
Year of Formation – 1967
President – Dirk Scheringa
Coach – Louis van Gaal
Stadium – DSB (16,000)
Colours – Red/white/red
MAJOR HONOURS
League Championship – (1) 1981.
Domestic Cup – (3) 1978, 1981, 1982.

Excelsior
Postbus 4369
3006 AJ Rotterdam
tel – (010) 4046041
fax – (010) 4114161
website – www.sc-excelsior.nl
Year of Formation – 1902
President – Nico Janssens
Coach – Ton Lokhoff
Stadium – Woudestein (3,527)
Colours – Black/red/red

Feyenoord
Postbus 9635
3007 AP Rotterdam
tel – (010) 2926888
fax – (010) 4325819
website – www.feyenoord.nl
Year of Formation – 1908
President – Jorien van den Herik
Coach – Erwin Koeman
Stadium – Feyenoord (51,180)
Colours – Red & white halves/black/black
MAJOR HONOURS
League Championship – (14) 1924, 1928, 1936, 1938, 1940, 1961, 1962, 1965, 1969, 1971, 1974, 1984, 1993, 1999.
Domestic Cup – (10) 1930, 1935, 1965, 1969, 1980, 1984, 1991, 1992, 1994, 1995.
European Champions Cup – (1) 1970.

UEFA Cup – (2) 1974, 2002.
World Club Cup – (1) 1970.

FC Groningen
Postbus 1399
9701 BJ Groningen
tel – (050) 5878787
fax – (050) 3125194
website – www.fcgroningen.nl
Year of Formation – 1926
President – Ed Zijp
Coach – Ron Jans
Stadium – Euroborg (20,000)
Colours – White (two broad green stripes)/white/white

SC Heerenveen
Postbus 513
8440 AM Heerenveen
tel – (0513) 612100
fax – (0513) 615061
website – www.sc-heerenveen.nl
Year of Formation – 1920
President – Koos Formsma
Coach – Gert-Jan Verbeek
Stadium – Abe Lenstra (21,000)
Colours – Blue & white stripes (with red lilies)/white/black

Heracles Almelo
Stadionlaan 1
Postbus 157
7600 AD Almelo
tel – (0546) 817070
fax – (0546) 811184
website – www.heracles.nl
Year of Formation – 1903
President – Jan Smit
Coach – Ruud Brood
Stadium – Polman (6,500)
Colours – Black & white stripes/black/black & white

NAC Breda
Postbus 3356
4800 DJ Breda
tel – (076) 5214500
fax – (076) 5211975
website – www.nac.nl
Year of Formation – 1912
President – Willem van der Hoeven
Coach – Ernie Brandts
Stadium – Rat Verlegh (16,522)
Colours – Yellow (black sash & trim)/black/white
MAJOR HONOURS
League Championship – (1) 1921.
Domestic Cup – (1) 1973.

NEC
Stadionplein 1
Postbus 6562
6503 GB Nijmegen
tel – (024) 3590360
fax – (024) 3567475
website – www.nec-nijmegen.nl
Year of Formation – 1900
President – Vincent Paes
Coach – Mario Been
Stadium – Mc DOS-Goffert (12,500)
Colours – Red & green quarters (black sleeves)/black/black

PSV
Frederiklaan 10 A
5616 NH Eindhoven
tel – (040) 2505505
fax – (040) 2505696
website – www.psv.nl
Year of Formation – 1913
President – Rob Westerhof
Coach – Ronald Koeman
Stadium – Philips (36,000)
Colours – Red & white stripes (red sleeves)/black/white
MAJOR HONOURS
League Championship – (19) 1929, 1935, 1951, 1963, 1975, 1976, 1978, 1986, 1987, 1988, 1989, 1991, 1992, 1997, 2000, 2001, 2003, 2005, 2006.
Domestic Cup – (8) 1950, 1974, 1976, 1988, 1989, 1990, 1996, 2005.
European Champions Cup – (1) 1988.
UEFA Cup – (1) 1978.

RKC Waalwijk
Postbus 4
5140 AA Waalwijk
tel – (0416) 334356
fax – (0416) 342310
website – www.rkcwaalwijk.nl
Year of Formation – 1940
President – Ad Passier
Coach – Adrie Koster
Stadium – Mandemakers (7,500)
Colours – Yellow/blue/white

Roda JC
Postbus 1156
6460 BD Kerkrade
tel – (045) 6317000
fax – (045) 6317100
website – www.rodajc.nl
Year of Formation – 1962
President – Serve Kuijer
Coach – Huub Stevens

The Directory

Stadium – Parkstad Limburg (19,500)
Colours – Yellow (black trim)/black/yellow
MAJOR HONOURS
Domestic Cup – (2) 1997, 2000.

Sparta Rotterdam
Postbus 1802
3000 BV Rotterdam
tel – (010) 8909210
fax – (010) 8909225
website – www.sparta-rotterdam.nl
Year of Formation – 1888
General Director – Peter Bonthuis
Coach – Wiljan Vloet
Stadium – Spangen ("Het Kasteel") (11,500)
Colours – Red & white stripes/black/red & white
MAJOR HONOURS
League Championship – (6) 1909, 1911, 1912, 1913, 1915, 1959.
Domestic Cup – (3) 1958, 1962, 1966.

FC Twente
Postbus 564
7500 AN Enschede
tel – (053) 8525525
fax – (053) 8525555
website – www.fctwente.nl
Year of Formation – 1965
President – Joop Munsterman
Coach – Fred Rutten
Stadium – Arke (13,500)
Colours – Red/red/red
MAJOR HONOURS
Domestic Cup – (2) 1977, 2001.

FC Utrecht
Postbus 85159
3508 AD Utrecht
tel – (030) 8885555
fax – (030) 8885559
website – www.fcutrecht.nl
Year of Formation – 1970
General Director – Jan-Willem van Dop
Coach – Foeke Booy
Stadium – Nieuw Galgenwaard (24,800)
Colours – Red (white trim)/white/white
MAJOR HONOURS
Domestic Cup – (3) 1985, 2003, 2004.

Vitesse
Postbus 366
6800 AJ Arnhem
tel – (026) 8807888
fax – (026) 8807009
website – www.vitesse.nl
Year of Formation – 1892
President – Kees Bakker

Coach – Aad de Mos
Stadium – Gelredome (26,400)
Colours – Yellow & black stripes/white/white

Willem II
Postbus 235
5000 AE Tilburg
tel – (013) 5490590
fax – (013) 5490500
website – www.willem-ii.nl
Year of Formation – 1896
President – Hans Verbun
Coach – Dennis van Wijk
Stadium – Willem II (14,700)
Colours – White, dark blue & red stripes/white/white
MAJOR HONOURS
League Championship – (3) 1916, 1952, 1955.
Domestic Cup – (2) 1944, 1963.

HUNGARY

Magyar Labdarúgó Szövetség
Köérberek-Továrós Kánai út
314/24 hrsz., 1112 Budapest
tel – (0036 1) 5779500
fax – (0036 1) 5779503
website – www.mlsz.hu
email – mlsz@mlsz.hu

Year of Formation – 1901
President – István Kisteleki
Secretary – Ildikó Kmety
Stadium – Puskás Ferenc Stadion, Budapest (35,817)

INTERNATIONAL TOURNAMENT APPEARANCES
World Cup – (9) 1934 (2nd round), 1938 (runners-up), 1954 (runners-up), 1958, 1962 (qtr-finals), 1966 (qtr finals), 1978, 1982, 1986.
European Championship – (2) 1964 (3rd), 1972 (4th).

MAJOR EUROPEAN CLUB HONOURS
Fairs Cup – (1) Ferencváros (1965).

Budapest Honvéd FC
Újtemető u. 1-3
1194 Budapest
tel – (1) 3576738
fax – (1) 3576737
website – www.honvedfc.hu
Year of Formation – 1909
Chairman – Pál Gács
Coach – Aldo Dolcetti
Stadium – József Bozsik (15,000)
Colours – Red & black stripes/black/red

MAJOR HONOURS
League Championship – (13) 1950, 1950 (autumn), 1952, 1954, 1955, 1980, 1984, 1985, 1986, 1988, 1989, 1991, 1993.
Domestic Cup – (5) 1926, 1964, 1985, 1989, 1996.

Debreceni Vasutas Sport Club-TEVA
Oláh Gábor utca 5
4028 Debrecen
tel – (52) 535409
fax – (52) 535409
website – www.dvsc.hu
Year of Formation – 1902
Chairman – Gábor Szima
Coach – Attila Supka
Stadium – Oláh Gábor utcai (10,200)
Colours – Red/white/red
MAJOR HONOURS
League Championship – (2) 2005, 2006.
Domestic Cup – (2) 1999, 2001.

Diósgyöri VTK
Andrássy u. 61
3533 Miskolc
tel – (46) 530440
fax – (46) 530440
Year of Formation – 1910
Chairman – István Sallói
Coach – János Csank
Stadium – DVTK (17,000)
Colours – Red/white/red
MAJOR HONOURS
Domestic Cup – (2) 1977, 1980.

Dunakanyar-Vác FC
Stadion út 2
2600 Vác
tel – (27) 303178
Year of Formation – 1899
Chairman – Zoltán Ofella
Coach – Károly Gergely
Stadium – Városi stadion (12,000)
Colours – Red/blue/red
MAJOR HONOURS
League Championship – (1) 1994.

FC Fehérvár
Csíkvári u.10
8000 Székesfehérvár
tel – (22) 379493
fax – (22) 500009
website – www.fcfehervar.com
Year of Formation – 1941
Chairman – László Gál
Coach – Aurél Csertöi
Stadium – Sóstói stadion (20,000)
Colours – Red & blue halves/blue/red

The Directory

MAJOR HONOURS
Domestic Cup – (1) 2006.

Györi ETO FC
Nagysándor József u. 31
9027 Györ
tel – (96) 529005
fax – (96) 529008
website – www.eto.hu
Year of Formation – 1904
Chairman – Csaba Tarsoly
Coach – János Pajkos
Stadium – ETO (22,000)
Colours – Green/white/green
MAJOR HONOURS
League Championship – (3) 1963 (autumn), 1982, 1983.
Domestic Cup – (4) 1965, 1966, 1967, 1979.

Kaposvári Rákóczi FC
Pécsi út 4
7400 Kaposvár
tel – (82) 319650
fax – (82) 319650
Year of Formation – 1923
Chairman – Kálmán Torma
Coach – László Prukner
Stadium – Rákóczi-stadion (8,000)
Colours – Green (white trim)/green/green

MTK Budapest
Salgótarjáni út 12-14
1087 Budapest
tel – (1) 3330590
fax – (1) 3338368
website – www.mtkhungaria.hu
Year of Formation – 1888
Chairman – László Domonyai
Coach – József Garami
Stadium – Hidegkuti Nándor (7,702)
Colours – White (blue sash)/blue/white
MAJOR HONOURS
League Championship – (22) 1904, 1908, 1914, 1917, 1918, 1919, 1920, 1921, 1922, 1923, 1924, 1925, 1929, 1936, 1937, 1951, 1953, 1958, 1987, 1997, 1999, 2003.
Domestic Cup – (12) 1910, 1911, 1912, 1914, 1923, 1925, 1932, 1952, 1968, 1997, 1998, 2000.

Paksi SE
Fehérvári utca
7030 Paks
tel – (75) 510618
fax – (75) 510618
website – www.paksise.hu
Year of Formation – 1952
Chairman – Judit Balog
Coach – Ferenc Lengyel
Stadium – Paksi (4,000)
Colours – Green & white stripes/green/green

PMFC-Pécs Plaza
Stadion u.2
7633 Pécs
tel – (72) 552880
fax – (72) 552881
website – www.pmfc.hu
Year of Formation – 1973
Chairman – László Toller
Coach – Ferenc Keszei
Stadium – PMFC (7,160)
Colours – Red/black/red
MAJOR HONOURS
Domestic Cup – (1) 1990.

Rákospalotai EAC
Széchenyi tér 8-10.
1152 Budapest
tel – (1) 3064015
fax – (1) 3070452
website – www.reacfoci.hu
Year of Formation – 1912
Chairman – Róbert Kutasi
Coach – Flórián Urbán
Stadium – László Budai II (7,500)
Colours – Yellow (blue trim)/blue/yellow

FC Sopron
Káposztás utca 4
9400 Sopron
tel – (99) 505470
fax – (99) 505471
website – www.fcsopron.hu
Year of Formation – 1945
Chairman – Zsolt Köteles
Coach – Tibor Selymes
Stadium – Káposztás utcai stadion (5,500)
Colours – White (red trim)/red/white
MAJOR HONOURS
Domestic Cup – (1) 2005.

FC Tatabánya
Ságvári Endre út
2800 Tatabánya
website – www.tatabanyafc.hu
Year of Formation – 1910
Chairman – József Török
Coach – Tibor Sisa
Stadium – Bányász-stadion (10,000)
Colours – Blue & white stripes/white/white

Újpest FC
Megyeri út 13
1044 Budapest
tel – (1) 2310088
fax – (1) 2310088
website – www.ujpestfc.hu
Year of Formation – 1885
Chairman – Szilárd Dányi
Coach – Valere Billen
Stadium – Szusza Ferenc stadion (13,500)
Colours – Lilac & white stripes (white sleeves)/lilac/lilac
MAJOR HONOURS
League Championship – (20) 1930, 1931, 1933, 1935, 1939, 1945, 1946, 1947, 1960, 1969, 1970, 1971, 1972, 1973, 1974, 1975, 1978, 1979, 1990, 1998.
Domestic Cup – (8) 1969, 1970, 1975, 1982, 1983, 1987, 1992, 2002.

Vasas
Fáy utca 58
1139 Budapest
tel – (1) 3296073
fax – (1) 3296073
website – www.vasasbp.hu
Year of Formation – 1911
Chairman – Miklós Vancsa
Coach – Géza Mészöly
Stadium – Illovszky Rudolf stadion (18,000)
MAJOR HONOURS
League Championship – (6) 1957 (spring), 1961, 1962, 1965, 1966, 1977.
Domestic Cup – (8) 1969, 1970, 1975, 1982, 1983, 1987, 1992, 2002.

Zalaegerszegi TE
Október 6. tér 16
8900 Zalaegerszeg
tel – (92) 596302
fax – (92) 314093
website – www.ztefc.hu
Year of Formation – 1920
Chairman – Ferenc Nagy
Coach – Antal Simon
Stadium – ZTE-stadion (15,000)
Colours – White/white/white
MAJOR HONOURS
League Championship – (1) 2002.

ICELAND

The Football Association of Iceland
Laugardalur, 104 Reykjavík
tel – (00354) 510 2900
fax – (00354) 568 9793
website – www.ksi.is
email – ksi@ksi.is

The Directory

Year of Formation – 1947
President – Eggert Magnússon
Secretary – Geir Thorsteinsson
Stadium – Laugardalsvöllur, Reykjavík (14,785)

Ungmennafélagid Breidablik
Dalsmári 5
201 Kópavogur
tel – 5106404
fax – 5540050
website – www.breidablik.is
Year of Formation – 1950
President – Einar Kristján Jónsson
Coach – Ólafur H. Kristjánsson
Stadium – Kópavogsvöllur (5,501)
Colours – Green (white trim)/white/white

Fimleikafélag Hafnarfjardar
Kaplakriki
220 Hafnarfjördur
tel – 5650711
fax – 5684222
website – www.fhingar.is
Year of Formation – 1929
President – Jón Rúnar Halldórsson
Coach – Ólafur Jóhannesson
Stadium – Kaplakriki (6,738)
Colours – White (black trim)/black/white
MAJOR HONOURS
League Championship – (2) 2004, 2005.

Knattspyrnufélagid Fylkir
Fylkisvegur 6
110 Reykjavík
tel – 5676467
fax – 5676091
website – www.fylkir.com
Year of Formation – 1967
President – Sigrún Alda Jónsdóttir
Coach – Leifur Gardarsson
Stadium – Fylkisvöllur (2,872)
Colours – Orange (black trim)/black/black
MAJOR HONOURS
Domestic Cup – (2) 2001, 2002.

Ungmennafélag Grindavíkur
Austurvegur 3
240 Grindavík
tel – 4268605
fax – 4267605
website – www.umfg.is
Year of Formation – 1935
President – Jónas Thórhallsson
Coach – Sigurdur Jónsson
Stadium – Grindavíkurvöllur (1,750)
Colours – Yellow/blue/blue

Knattspyrnufélag ÍA
Jadarsbakkar
300 Akranes
tel – 4313311
fax – 4313012
website – www.ia.is
Year of Formation – 1946
President – Sigrún Ríkhardsdóttir
Coach – Árnar Gunnlaugsson & Bjarki Gunnlaugsson
Stadium – Akranesvöllur (2,780)
Colours – Yellow (black trim)/black/black
MAJOR HONOURS
League Championship – (18) 1951, 1953, 1954, 1957, 1958, 1960, 1970, 1974, 1975, 1977, 1983, 1984, 1992, 1993, 1994, 1995, 1996, 2001.
Domestic Cup – (9) 1978, 1982, 1983, 1984, 1986, 1993, 1996, 2000, 2003.

ÍBV – Íthróttafélag
Thórsheimilid v/Hamarsveg
900 Vestmannaeyjar
tel – 4812060
fax – 4811260
website – www.ibv.is
Year of Formation – 1945
President – Vidar Elíasson
Coach – Gudlaugur Baldursson
Stadium – Hásteinsvöllur (2,384)
Colours – White (black trim)/white/white
MAJOR HONOURS
League Championship – (3) 1979, 1997, 1998.
Domestic Cup – (4) 1968, 1972, 1981, 1998.

Keflavík-Ungmenna-og íthróttafélag
Keflavíkurvöllur
230 Reykjanesbaer
tel – 4215188
fax – 4214137
website – www.keflavik.is/knattspyrna
Year of Formation – 1929
President – Rúnar Arnarson
Coach – Kristján Gudmundsson
Stadium – Keflavíkvöllur (4,957)
Colours – Dark blue/dark blue/red
MAJOR HONOURS
League Championship – (4) 1964, 1969, 1971, 1973.
Domestic Cup – (3) 1975, 1997, 2004.

Knattspyrnufélag Reykjavíkur
Frostaskjól 2
107 Reykjavík
tel – 5105310
fax – 5105309
website – www.kr.is/knattspyrna

Year of Formation – 1899
President – Magnús Ingimundarson
Coach – Teitur Thórdarson
Stadium – KR-völlur (2,781)
Colours – Black & white stripes/black/white
MAJOR HONOURS
League Championship – (24) 1912, 1919, 1926, 1927, 1928, 1929, 1931, 1932, 1934, 1941, 1948, 1949, 1950, 1952, 1955, 1959, 1961, 1963, 1965, 1968, 1999, 2000, 2002, 2003.
Domestic Cup – (10) 1960, 1961, 1962, 1963, 1964, 1966, 1967, 1994, 1995, 1999.

Knattspyrnufélagid Valur
Hlídarendi v/Laufásveg
101 Reykjavík
tel – 4148000
fax – 4148010
website – www.valur.is
Year of Formation – 1911
President – Edvard Börkur Edvardsson
Coach – Willum Thór Thórsson
Stadium – Hlídarendi (4,590)
Colours – Red (white trim)/white/white
MAJOR HONOURS
League Championship – (19) 1930, 1933, 1935, 1936, 1937, 1938, 1940, 1942, 1943, 1944, 1945, 1956, 1966, 1967, 1976, 1978, 1980, 1985, 1987.
Domestic Cup – (9) 1965, 1974, 1976, 1977, 1988, 1990, 1991, 1992, 2005.

Knattspyrnufélagid Víkingur
Tradarland 1
108 Reykjavík
tel – 5813245
fax – 5887845
website – www.vikingur.is
Year of Formation – 1908
President – Róbert Agnarsson
Coach – Magnús Gylfason
Stadium – Víkin (1,249)
Colours – Red & black stripes/black/white

ISRAEL

Israel Football Association
Ramat Gan Stadium, 299 Aba Hilell Street, 52134 Ramat Gan
tel – (00972 3) 6171503/4
fax – (00972 3) 5702044
website – www.israel-football.org.il
email – info@israel-football.org.il

Year of Formation – 1928
President – Itzhak Menachem

The Directory

Secretary – Haim Zimmer
Stadium – Ramat Gan, Tel Aviv (41,583)

INTERNATIONAL TOURNAMENT APPEARANCES
World Cup – (1) 1970.

MS Ashdod
Zabotinski St.
PO Box 3565
Ashdod 77130
tel – (08) 531240
fax – (08) 531236
website – www.fcashdod.com
Year of Formation – 1999
Chairman – Mendel Davidovic
Secretary – Itzhak Turgeman
Coach – Yossi Mizrahi
Stadium – Yud Alef (8,000)
Colours – Yellow/red/yellow

Beitar Jerusalem
Kanfei Nesharim 15
Givat Shaul
Jerusalem 95464
tel – (02) 65581333
fax – (02) 6515419
website – www.bjerusalem.co.il
Year of Formation – 1939
President – Arkady Gaydamak
Coach – Osvaldo Ardiles
Stadium – "Teddi" Malcha (18,500)
Colours – Yellow/black/black
MAJOR HONOURS
League Championship – (4) 1987, 1993, 1997, 1998.
Domestic Cup – (5) 1976, 1979, 1985, 1986, 1989.

Bnei Yehuda Tel Aviv
Simtat Kabir St. 20
Shchonat H'atikva,
PO Box 19069
Tel Aviv 61190
tel – (03) 6876445
fax – (03) 5377877
website – www.bnei-yehuda.co.il
Year of Formation – 1935
Chairman – Hezi Magen
Coach – Nitzan Shirazi
Stadium – Shchonat H'atikva (8,000)
Colours – Orange/black/black
MAJOR HONOURS
League Championship – (1) 1990.
Domestic Cup – (2) 1968, 1981.

Hakoah Amidar Ramat Gan
PO Box 8402
61084 Ramat Gan

tel – (03) 6827711
fax – (03) 6827722
website – www.hakoach.co.il
Year of Formation – 1961
President – Nimrod Vered
Coach – Uri Malmilian
Stadium – Winter (8,000)
Colours – Violet/yellow/violet
MAJOR HONOURS
League Championship – (2) 1965, 1973.
Domestic Cup – (2) 1969, 1971.

Hapoel Kfar Saba
PO Box 13
Kfar Saba
tel – (09) 7660373
fax – (09) 7660373
website – www.hapoel-kfs.org
Year of Formation – 1936
President – Eli Tabib
Chairman – Gabi Katzra
Coach – Eli Ohana
Stadium – Levita (4,500)
Colours – White/green/green
MAJOR HONOURS
League Championship – (1) 1982.
Domestic Cup – (3) 1975, 1980, 1990.

Hapoel Petach Tikva
Gisin St. 9
PO Box 2108
Petach Tikva 49120
tel – (03) 9214981
fax – (03) 9218352
website – www.hapoel-pt.co.il
Year of Formation – 1935
Chairman – Tzion Dalal
Coach – Eyal Lachman
Stadium – Petach Tikva (8,000)
Colours – Blue (white & black trim)/blue/blue
MAJOR HONOURS
League Championship – (6) 1955, 1959, 1960, 1961, 1962, 1963.
Domestic Cup – (2) 1957, 1992.

Hapoel Tel Aviv
Ha'tchia St. 1
PO Box 8402
Tel Aviv – Jaffa 61084
tel – (03) 6827711
fax – (03) 6827722
website – www.hapoelta.com
Year of Formation – 1928
President – Sami Segol
Chairman – Moni Ha'rel
Coach – Itzhak Shum
Stadium – Bloomfield (15,400)

Colours – Red/red/red
MAJOR HONOURS
League Championship – (11) 1934, 1935, 1940, 1943, 1957, 1966, 1969, 1981, 1986, 1988, 2000.
Domestic Cup – (10) 1928, 1934, 1937, 1938, 1940, 1960, 1972, 1999, 2000, 2006.

Maccabi Haifa
Heinrich Heina St. 14
Haifa 34485
tel – (04) 8380620
fax – (04) 8371540
website – www.maccabi-haifafc.walla.co.il
Year of Formation – 1913
Chairman – Jacob Shahar
Coach – Roni Levi
Stadium – Kiriat Eliezer (17,000)
Colours – Green/green/white
MAJOR HONOURS
League Championship – (10) 1984, 1985, 1989, 1991, 1994, 2001, 2002, 2004, 2005, 2006.
Domestic Cup – (5) 1962, 1991, 1993, 1995, 1998.

Maccabi Herzliya
Yossef Nevo St. 6
Herzliya
tel – (09) 95774774
fax – (09) 9509865
website – www.maccabiherzliya.com
Year of Formation – 1926
President – Ariel Shayman
Coach – Reuven Atar
Stadium – Maccabi Herzliya (8,300)
Colours – Yellow/blue/yellow

Maccabi Netanya
Zangvil St. 44
PO Box 2242
Netanya 42112
tel – (09) 8620503
fax – (09) 8334726
website – www.fanzine.co.il
Year of Formation – 1942
President – Daniel Jammer
Coach – Eli Gutman
Stadium – Maccabi Netanya (6,500)
Colours – Yellow (black trim)/black/yellow
MAJOR HONOURS
League Championship – (5) 1971, 1974, 1978, 1980, 1983.
Domestic Cup – (1) 1978.

Maccabi Petach Tikva
Finstein Corner of Ben Dror St.
PO Box 67
Petach Tikva
tel – (03) 934879

The Directory

fax – (03) 9347560
website – www.mpt-mib.com
Year of Formation – 1912
Chairman – Moshe Zuaretz
Coach – Guy Luzon
Stadium – Petach Tikva (8,000)
Colours – Blue (white/black trim)/blue/blue
MAJOR HONOURS
Domestic Cup – (2) 1935, 1952.

Maccabi Tel Aviv
Maccabi St. 4
Tel Aviv 63293
tel – (03) 5250712
fax – (03) 5288503
website – www.maccabi-tlv.nana.co.il
Year of Formation – 1906
President – Eilon Herzikovich
Coach – Eli Cohen
Stadium – Bloomfield (15,400)
Colours – Yellow/blue/blue
MAJOR HONOURS
League Championship – (19) 1937, 1939, 1941, 1947, 1949, 1950, 1951, 1952, 1954, 1956, 1968, 1970, 1972, 1977, 1979, 1992, 1995, 1996, 2003.
Domestic Cup – (22) 1929, 1930, 1933, 1941, 1946, 1947, 1954, 1955, 1958, 1959, 1964, 1965, 1967, 1970, 1977, 1987, 1988, 1994, 1996, 2001, 2002, 2005.

ITALY

Federazione Italiana Giuoco Calcio
Via Gregorio Allegri 14, CP 2450,
00198 Roma
tel – (0039 06) 84911
fax – (0039 06) 84912526
website – www.figc.it
email – figc.nazionali@figc.it

Year of Formation – 1898
Secretary – Antonio Di Sebastiano

INTERNATIONAL HONOURS
World Cup – (4) 1934, 1938, 1982, 2006.
European Championship – (1) 1968.

INTERNATIONAL TOURNAMENT APPEARANCES
World Cup – (15) 1934 (Winners), 1938 (Winners), 1950, 1958, 1962, 1966, 1970 (runners-up), 1974, 1978 (4th), 1982 (Winners), 1986 (2nd round), 1990 (3rd), 1994 (runners-up), 1998 (qtr-finals), 2002 (2nd round), 2006 (Winners).
European Championship – (6) 1968 (Winners),

1980 (4th), 1988 (semi-finals), 1996, 2000 (runners-up), 2004.

MAJOR EUROPEAN CLUB HONOURS
Champions Cup/League – (10) Milan (1963, 1969, 1989, 1990, 1994, 2003), Inter (1964, 1965), Juventus (1985, 1996).
Cup-winners Cup – (7) Fiorentina (1961), Milan (1968, 1973), Juventus (1984), Sampdoria (1990), Parma (1993), Lazio (1999).
UEFA Cup – (9) Juventus (1977, 1990, 1993), Napoli (1989), Inter (1991, 1994, 1998), Parma (1995, 1999).
Fars Cup – (1) Roma (1961).

Associazione Calcio Ascoli
Corso Vittorio Emanuele 21
63100 Ascoli Piceno
tel – (0736) 258521
fax – (0736) 255751
website – www.ascalcio.net
Year of Formation – 1898
President – Roberto Benigni
Coach – Attilio Tesser
Stadium – Lillo e Cino del Duca (20,000)
Colours – Black & white stripes/white/white

Atalanta Bergamasca Calcio
Via Pitentino 14/a
24124 Bergamo
tel – (035) 242555
fax – (035) 239677
website – www.atalanta.it
Year of Formation – 1907
President – Ivan Ruggeri
Coach – Stefano Colantuono
Stadium – Atleti Azzurri d'Italia (28,430)
Colours – Blue & black stripes/black/black
MAJOR HONOURS
Domestic Cup – (1) 1963.

Cagliari Calcio
Viale La Playa 15
09123 Cagliari
tel – (070) 604201
fax – (070) 6042029
website – www.cagliaricalcio.it
Year of Formation – 1920
President – Bruno Ghirardi
Coach – Marco Giampaolo
Stadium – Sant'Elia (24,000)
Colours – Red & dark blue halves/dark blue/dark blue
MAJOR HONOURS
League Championship – (1) 1970.

Calcio Catania
Piazza Giovanni Verga 16
95129 Catania
tel – (095) 7530811
fax – (095) 7225478
website – www.calciocatania.it
Year of Formation – 1946
President – Antonio Pulvirenti
Coach – Pasquale Marino
Stadium – Angelo Massimino (30,000)
Colours – Red & blue stripes/blue/black

AC Chievo Verona
Via Galvani 3
37138 Verona
tel – (045) 575779
fax – (045) 562298
website – www.chievoverona.it
Year of Formation – 1929
President – Luca Campedelli
Coach – Giuseppe Pillon
Stadium – Marc'Antonio Bentegodi (42,160)
Colours – Yellow (blue trim)/yellow/yellow

Empoli Football Club
Piazza Matteotti 29
50053 Empoli
tel – (0571) 72212
fax – (0571) 79606
website – www.empolifc.com
Year of Formation – 1921
President – Fabrizio Corsi
Coach – Luigi Cagni
Stadium – Carlo Castellani (19,873)
Colours – Blue/blue/blue

ACF Fiorentina
Viale Manfredo Fanti 4
50137 Firenze
tel – (055) 5030190
fax – (055) 579572
website – www.florentiaviola.it
Year of Formation – 1926
President – Andrea Della Valle
Coach – Claudio Cesare Prandelli
Stadium – Artemio Franchi (44,781)
Colours – Violet/violet/violet
MAJOR HONOURS
League Championship – (2) 1956, 1969.
Domestic Cup – (6) 1940, 1961, 1966, 1975, 1996, 2001.
European Cup-winners Cup – (1) 1961.

Internazionale Milano Football Club
Via Durini 24
20122 Milano
tel – (02) 77151
fax – (02) 781514

The Directory

website – www.inter.it
Year of Formation – 1908
President – Giacinto Facchetti
Coach – Roberto Mancini
Stadium – Giuseppe Meazza (85,700)
Colours – Black & blue stripes/black/black
MAJOR HONOURS
League Championship – (14) 1910, 1920, 1930, 1938, 1940, 1953, 1954, 1963, 1965, 1966, 1971, 1980, 1989, 2006.
Domestic Cup – (5) 1939, 1978, 1982, 2005, 2006.
European Champions Cup – (2) 1964, 1965.
UEFA Cup – (3) 1991, 1994, 1998.
World Club Cup – (2) 1964, 1965.

Società Sportiva Lazio
Via di Santa Cornelia 1000
000 60 Formello
tel – (06) 97607111
fax – (06) 90400127
website – www.sslazio.it
Year of Formation – 1900
President – Claudio Lotito
Coach – Delio Rossi
Stadium – Olimpico (82,307)
Colours – Sky blue (white trim)/white/white
MAJOR HONOURS
League Championship – (2) 1974, 2000.
Domestic Cup – (4) 1958, 1998, 2000, 2004.
European Cup-winners Cup – (1) 1999.
European Super Cup – (1) 1999.

AS Livorno Calcio
Via Indipendenza 16
57126 Livorno
tel – (0586) 219295
fax – (0586) 213552
website – www.livornocalcio.it
Year of Formation – 1915
President – Aldo Spinelli
Coach – Daniele Arrigoni
Stadium – Armando Picchi (18,200)
Colours – Maroon/maroon/maroon

Messina Peloro Football Club
Via Acireale Zona Zir
98124 Messina
tel – (090) 2282300
fax – (090) 2282390
website – www.mondomessina.it
Year of Formation – 1912
President – Pietro Franza
Coach – Bruno Giordano
Stadium – San Filippo (40,200)
Colours – White (red & yellow trim)/black/black

Milan Associazione Calcio
Via Filippo Turati 3
20121 Milano
tel – (02) 62281
fax – (02) 6598876
website – www.acmilan.com
Year of Formation – 1899
President – Silvio Berlusconi
Coach – Carlo Ancelotti
Stadium – Giuseppe Meazza (85,700)
Colours – Red & black stripes/white/black
MAJOR HONOURS
League Championship – (17) 1901, 1906, 1907, 1951, 1955, 1957, 1959, 1962, 1968, 1979, 1988, 1992, 1993, 1994, 1996, 1999, 2004.
Domestic Cup – (5) 1967, 1972, 1973, 1977, 2003.
European Champions Cup – (6) 1963, 1969, 1989, 1990, 1994, 2003.
European Cup-winners Cup – (2) 1968, 1973.
European Super Cup – (4) 1989, 1990, 1995, 2003.
World Club Cup – (3) 1969, 1989, 1990.

US Città di Palermo
Viale del Fante 11
90146 Palermo
tel – (091) 6901211
fax – (091) 6700263
website – www.ilpalermocalcio.it
Year of Formation – 1900
President – Maurizio Zamparini
Coach – Francesco Guidolin
Stadium – Renzo Barbera (38,000)
Colours – Pink (black trim)/black/black

Parma Football Club
Viale Partigiani d'Italia 1
43100 Parma
tel – (0521) 505111
fax – (0521) 505100
website – www.fcparma.com
Year of Formation – 1913
President – Guido Angiolini
Coach – Stefano Pioli
Stadium – Ennio Tardini (28,783)
Colours – Dark blue & yellow hoops/dark blue/dark blue
MAJOR HONOURS
Domestic Cup – (3) 1992, 1999, 2002.
European Cup-winners Cup – (1) 1993.
UEFA Cup – (2) 1995, 1999.
European Super Cup – (1) 1994.

Reggina Calcio
Via Tommaso Gulli 1
89127 Reggio Calabria
tel – (0965) 385711
fax – (0965) 26343
website – www.regginacalcio.it
Year of Formation – 1914
President – Pasquale Foti
Coach – Walter Mazzarri
Stadium – Oreste Granillo (28,000)
Colours – Dark red/dark red/dark red

Associazione Sportiva Roma
Via di Trigoria km. 3.600
00128 Roma
tel – (06) 501911
fax – (06) 5061736
website – www.asromacalcio.it
Year of Formation – 1927
President – Franco Sensi
Coach – Luciano Spalletti
Stadium – Olimpico (82,307)
Colours – Dark red (gold trim)/white/black
MAJOR HONOURS
League Championship – (3) 1942, 1983, 2001.
Domestic Cup – (7) 1964, 1969, 1980, 1981, 1984, 1986, 1991.
Fairs Cup – (1) 1961.

Sampdoria Unione Calcio
Piazza Borgo Pila 39
16129 Genova
tel – (010) 5316711
fax – (010) 5316777
website – www.sampdoria.it
Year of Formation – 1946
President – Riccardo Garrone
Coach – Walter Novellino
Stadium – Luigi Ferraris (40,117)
Colours – Blue (red/black/white band)/white/white
MAJOR HONOURS
League Championship – (1) 1991.
Domestic Cup – (4) 1985, 1988, 1989, 1994.
European Cup-winners Cup – (1) 1990.

Siena Associazione Calcio
Via Peruzzi 18
53100 Siena
tel – (0577) 281084
fax – (0577) 281083
website – www.acsiena.it
Year of Formation – 1904
President – Paolo De Luca
Coach – Mario Beretta
Stadium – Artemio Franchi (10,156)
Colours – Black & white stripes/white/white

Torino Calcio
Via dell'Arcivescovado 1
10100 Torino
tel – (011) 19700348
fax – (011) 19700349

The Directory

website – www.toro.it
Year of Formation – 1906
President – Urbano Cairo
Coach – Gianni De Biasi
Stadium – Stadio delle Alpi (69,041)
Colours – Grenadine/white/black
MAJOR HONOURS
League Championship – (7) 1928, 1943, 1946, 1947, 1948, 1949, 1976.
Domestic Cup – (5) 1936, 1943, 1968, 1971, 1993.

Udinese Calcio
Via A. Candolini 2
33100 Udine
tel – (0432) 544911
fax – (0432) 544933
website – www.udinese.it
Year of Formation – 1896
President – Franco Soldati
Coach – Giovanni Galeone
Stadium – Friuli (41,652)
Colours – Black & white broad stripes/black/black

KAZAKHSTAN

The Football Union of Kazakhstan
Satpayev Street 29/3, 480 072
Almaty
tel – (0073272) 924492
fax – (0073272) 921885
website – www.fsk.kz
email – kfo@mailonline.kz

Year of Formation – 1992
President – Rakhat Aliyev
Secretary – Askar Akhmetov
Stadium – Centralny, Almaty (26,500)

FK Aktobe
Maresiyev Str. 2
Aktobe
tel – (3132) 577559
fax – (3132) 504889
Coach – Vladimir Muhanov
Stadium – Centralny (13,500)
Colours – White & blue
MAJOR HONOURS
League Championship – (1) 2005.

FK Almaty
Magnitnaya Str. 13 A
Almaty
tel – (3272) 579581
fax – (3272) 510051
President – Sayan Khamitzhanov
Coach – Antonius Joor
Stadium – Centralny (26,500)
Colours – Red & white

FK Astana
Manas Str. 6
Astana
tel – (3172) 352803
fax – (3172) 352767
website – www.zhenis.kz
Coach – Arno Pijpers
Stadium – K. Munaitpasov (12,343)
Colours – Blue (yellow trim)/blue/blue
MAJOR HONOURS
League Championship – (2) 2000, 2001.
Domestic Cup – (3) 2000, 2002, 2005.

FK Atyrau
Auezov Ave 28 A
Atyrau
tel – (3122) 453255
fax – (3122) 453255
Year of Formation – 1896
Coach – Alexandr Averianov
Stadium – Munaishi (8,660)
Colours – Blue & white

FK Ekibastuzets
Stroitelnaya Str. 96 A
Ekibastuz
tel – (31835) 64958
fax – (31835) 49948
President – Rais Gainullin
Coach – Vitaliy Sparyshev
Stadium – Shakhtyor (6,300)
Colours – Orange & white

FK Energetik
Krivenki 27
140000 Pavlodar
tel – (3182) 399583
fax – (3182) 399884
President – Anatoliy Duka
Coach – Yury Konkov
Stadium – Energetik (3,000)
Colours – Red

FK Irtysh
Lunacharskiy Str. 50
Pavlodar
tel – (3182) 323129
fax – (3182) 323280
President – Nassipola Sulemenov
Coach – Sergey Volgin
Stadium – Centralny (12,000)
MAJOR HONOURS
League Championship – (5) 1993, 1997, 1999, 2002, 2003.
Domestic Cup – (1) 1997.

Kairat-Almaty KTZH
Kablukov Str. 30
Almaty
tel – (3272) 480889
fax – (3272) 484712
website – www.kairat.kz
President – Kuralbek Ordabayev
Coach – Tachmurad Agamuradov
Stadium – Centralny (26,500)
Colours – White & blue
MAJOR HONOURS
League Championship – (2) 1992, 2004.
Domestic Cup – (5) 1992, 1996, 1999, 2001, 2003.

FK Kaisar
Zheltoksan street
467021 Kyzylorda
tel – (3242) 270619
fax – (3242) 270619
Year of Formation – 1968
President – Nurlan Aubov
Coach – Teleuhan Tourmagambetov
Stadium – G. Muratbaev (5,000)
Colours – White & blue

FK Okzhetpes
Abay Str. 116
Kokshetau
tel – (3162) 230697
fax – (3162) 230697
President – Abdygakar Abdrahmanov
Coach – Sergei Gerasimets
Stadium – Okzhetpes (4,200)
Colours – White & blue

FK Ordabasy
Madeli-Kozha Str. 1
Shymkent
tel – (3252) 222389
fax – (3252) 224490
President – Ermek Darmenov
Coach – Andrey Vaganov
Stadium – Kazhimukan (30,000)
Colours – White

FK Shakhtyor
Kazakhstanskaya Str. 1
Karagandy
tel – (3212) 411800
fax – (3212) 411831
website – www.shahter.kz
President – Grigoriy Loria
Coach – Vakhid Masudov
Stadium – Shakhtyor (19,500)

The Directory

Colours – Red, black & white

FK Taraz
Abay Str. 113
Taraz
tel – (3262) 431092
fax – (3262) 457146
President – Murat Omarov
Coach – Sergey Tagiyev
Stadium – Centralny (12,000)
Colours – Green & blue
MAJOR HONOURS
League Championship – (1) 1996.
Domestic Cup – (1) 2004.

FK Tobol
1st May Str. 153
Kostanai
tel – (3142) 543182
fax – (3142) 543182
website – www.fctobol.kostanay.net
President – Khalimzhan Erzhanov
Coach – Dmitriy Ogay
Stadium – Centralny (8,000)
Colours – Yellow & black

FK Vostok
Gagarin Ave 1
Ust-Kamenogorsk
tel – (3132) 422841
fax – (3132) 426051
Year of Formation – 1906
President – Mikhail Labukov
Coach – Sergey Gorokhovodatskiy
Stadium – Vostok (8,500)
Colours – Blue, red & white
MAJOR HONOURS
Domestic Cup – (1) 1994.

FK Yesil-Bogatyr
Tchaikovskiy Str. 2 A
Petropavlovsk
Tel – (3152) 365630
Fax – (3152) 365939
President – Roman Arakelov
Coach – Oirat Saduov
Stadium – Avangard (11,000)
Colours – Blue & white

LATVIA

Latvijas Futbola Federacija
1 Augsiela, LV-1009 Riga
tel – (00371) 7292988
fax – (00371) 7315604
website – www.lff.lv
email – futbols@latnet.lv

Year of Formation – 1921
President – Guntis Indricksons
Secretary – Janis Mezeckis
Stadium – Daugava, Riga (5,800)

INTERNATIONAL TOURNAMENT APPEARANCES
European Championship – (1) 2004.

Dinaburg Daugavpils
Rigas iela 42-3
5403 Daugavpils
tel – 5439235
fax – 5439235
Year of Formation – 1996
President – Olegs Gavrilovs
Coach – Sergei Popkov
Stadium – Celtnieks (3,000)
Colours – Yellow (black trim)/black/yellow

Ditton Daugavpils
Jelgavas Str. 1R
5420 Daugavpils
tel – 5440233
fax – 5445101
website – www.dittonfc.lv
Year of Formation – 2001
President – Vladislavs Driksna
Coach – Sergei Kiryakov
Stadium – Celtnieks (3,000)
Colours – Yellow/black/yellow

Dizvanagi Rezekne
Rezekne
tel – 4622055
fax – 4622055
website – www.dizvanagi.lv
Year of Formation – 2000
President – Ivans Ribakovs
Coach – Zanis Armanis
Stadium – Town (500)
Colours – Red/red/red

FK Jurmala
Slokas 3
2016 Jurmala
tel – 7811156
fax – 7811157
Year of Formation – 2003
President – Aleksandrs Basarins
Coach – Vladimirs Babicevs
Stadium – Sloka (1,500)
Colours – Light blue & white hoops/white/white

Metalurgs Liepaja
Brivibas str. 93
3401 Liepaja

tel – 3481840
fax – 3481841
Year of Formation – 1996
President – Sergejs Zaharjins
Coach – Benjaminas Velkevicius
Stadium – Daugava Liepaya (6,000)
MAJOR HONOURS
League Championship – (1) 2005.

FK Riga
Kr. Barona Str. 116a
1012 Riga
tel – 7291933
fax – 7291933
Year of Formation – 1999
President – Pavels Lihacevs
Coach – Sergejs Semjonovs
Stadium – LU (5,000)
MAJOR HONOURS
Domestic Cup – (1) 1999.

Skonto Riga
Elizabetes str. 75
1050 Riga
tel – 7282669
fax – 7284390
Year of Formation – 1991
President – Guntis Indricksons
Coach – Paul Ashworth
Stadium – Skonto (8,500)
Colours – Red (white trim)/red/red
MAJOR HONOURS
League Championship – (14) 1991, 1992, 1993, 1994, 1995, 1996, 1997, 1998, 1999, 2000, 2001, 2002, 2003, 2004.
Domestic Cup – (7) 1992, 1995, 1997, 1998, 2000, 2001, 2002.

FK Ventspils
Dzintaru Str. 20a
3602 Ventspils
tel – 3681354
fax – 3681354
Year of Formation – 1997
President – Jurijs Bespalovs
Coach – Roman Grigorchuk
Stadium – OSC Ventspils (3,200)
Colours – Yellow (blue trim)/blue/yellow
MAJOR HONOURS
Domestic Cup – (3) 2003, 2004, 2005.

LIECHTENSTEIN

Liechtensteiner Fussball-Verband
Malbuner Huus, Altenbach 11,
Postfach 165, 9490 Vaduz

The Directory

tel – (75) 2374747
fax – (75) 2374748
website – www.lfv.li
email – info@lfv.li

Year of Formation – 1934
President – Reinhard Walser
Secretary – Roland Ospelt
Stadium – Rheinpark, Vaduz (4,548)

LITHUANIA

Lietuvos Futbolo Federacija
Seimyniskiu 15, 09312 Vilnius
tel – (00370 5) 2638741
fax – (00370 5) 2638740
website – www.futbolas.lt
email – lsff@lsff.lt

Year of Formation – 1922
President – Liutauras Varanavicius
Secretary – Julius Kvedaras
Stadium – Zalgiris, Vilnius (10,000)

FK Atlantas Klaipeda
Zveju 2
91248 Klaipeda
tel – (46) 312616
fax – (46) 312616
website – www.atlantas.lt
Year of Formation – 1960
President – Vacys Lekevicius
Coach – Vacys Lekevicius
Stadium – Klaipeda Central (10,000)
Colours – Yellow (blue band & trim)/blue/yellow
MAJOR HONOURS
Domestic Cup – (2) 2001, 2003 (spring).

FK Ekranas Panevezys
Elektronikos 1
35116 Panevezys
tel – (45) 435515
fax – (45) 581085
website – www.fkekranas.lt
Year of Formation – 1964
President – Tomas Sitnikovas
Coach – Virginijus Liubsys
Stadium – Aukstaitijos (3,000)
Colours – Red/red/red
MAJOR HONOURS
League Championship – (2) 1993, 2005.
Domestic Cup – (2) 1998, 2000.

FBK Kaunas
Raudondvario 93
44001 Kaunas
tel – (37) 361613
fax – (37) 361513
website – www.fbk.lt
Year of Formation – 1960
President – Gintaras Ugianskis
Coach – Eugenijus Riabovas
Stadium – Dariaus ir Gireno (7,432)
Colours – Yellow (green trim)/green/yellow
MAJOR HONOURS
League Championship – (6) 1999 (autumn), 2000, 2001, 2002, 2003, 2004.
Domestic Cup – (3) 2002, 2004, 2005.

FK Nevezis Kedainiai
Jaugelio-Telegos 2
57268 Kedainiai
tel – (347) 50669
fax – (347) 50669
website – www.fknevezis.lt
Year of Formation – 1962
President – Saulius Skibiniauskas
Coach – Vitalijus Stankevicius
Stadium – Dariaus ir Gireno, Kaunas (7,432)
Colours – Blue (white trim)/blue/blue

KFK Siauliai
Daukanto 23
76331 Siauliai
tel – (41) 422829
fax – (41) 422829
website – www.fcsiauliai.lt
Year of Formation – 1995
President – Alfonsas Armalas
Coach – Saulius Vertelis
Stadium – Municipal (3,517)
Colours – Yellow (black trim)/black/yellow

FK Silute
Stadiono 10
99162 Silute
tel – (441) 51133
fax – (441) 51133
Year of Formation – 2002
President – Dainius Gricevicius
Coach – Svajunas Cesnulis
Stadium – Silute (3,000)
Colours – Green/green/green

FK Suduva Marijampole
Armino 27
68290 Marijampole
tel – (343) 71178
fax – (343) 71178
website – www.fksuduva.lt
Year of Formation – 1942
President – Vidmantas Murauskas
Coach – Algimantas Gabrys
Stadium – Suduva (3,100)
Colours – Red (white trim)/red/red

FK Vetra Vilnius
Liepkalnio 13/2
02105 Vilnius
tel – (5) 2639270
fax – (5) 2639271
website – www.fkvetra.lt
Year of Formation – 1996
President – Romas Stasauskas
Coach – Aleksandr Kartanov
Stadium – Vetra (5,300)
Colours – Yellow (black trim)/yellow/yellow

FC Vilnius
Gostauto 12a
01108 Vilnius
tel – (5) 2683637
fax – (5) 2683636
website – www.fcvilnius.lt
Year of Formation – 2003
President – Algimantas Breikstas
Coach – Caio Zanardi
Stadium – Zalgiris (10,000)
Colours – Deep red/deep red/white

FK Zalgiris Vilnius
Zolyno 29
10209 Vilnius
tel – (5) 2342360
fax – (5) 2342360
website – www.vfk-zalgiris.lt
Year of Formation – 1947
President – Arminas Narbekovas
Coach – Igoris Pankratjevas
Stadium – Zalgiris (10,000)
Colours – Green & white stripes/white/white
MAJOR HONOURS
League Championship – (3) 1991, 1992, 1999.
Domestic Cup – (5) 1991, 1993, 1994, 1997, 2003 (autumn).

LUXEMBOURG

Fédération Luxembourgeoise de Football
BP5, 3901 Mondercange
tel – (00352) 488665-1
fax – (00352) 488665-82
website – www.football.lu
email – flf@football.lu

Year of Formation – 1908
President – Paul Philipp

The Directory

Secretary – Joël Wolff
Stadium – Josy Barthel, Luxembourg (8,250)

FC Differdange 03
BP 38
4501 Differdange
tel – 584710
fax – 585128
Year of Formation – 2003
President – Erny Muller
Coach – Maurice Spitoni & Emilio Lobo
Stadium – Thillenberg (6,000)
Colours – Red (white sleeves)/white/white

F91 Dudelange
BP 287
3403 Dudelange
tel – 514287
fax – 26511144
website – www.f91.lu
Year of Formation – 1991
President – Théo Fellerich
Coach – Michel Leflochmoan
Stadium – Jos Nosbaum (5,000)
Colours – Yellow & red stripes/red/red
MAJOR HONOURS
League Championship – (5) 2000, 2001, 2002, 2005, 2006.
Domestic Cup – (2) 2004, 2006.

FC Etzella Ettelbruck
BP 183
9002 Ettelbruck
tel – 26441793
fax – 26259544
website – www.fc-etzella.lu
Year of Formation – 1917
President – Jean-Pierre Gauthier
Coach – Luc Holtz
Stadium – Deich (4,500)
Colours – White/blue/blue
MAJOR HONOURS
Domestic Cup – (1) 2001.

Club Sportif Grevenmacher
67 op der Gell
5754 Frisange
tel – 4782636
fax – 758326
website – www.csg.lu
Year of Formation – 1909
President – Fernand Zanen
Coach – Álvaro Da Cruz
Stadium – Op Flohr (4,500)
Colours – Blue (white trim)/blue/blue
MAJOR HONOURS
League Championship – (1) 2003.
Domestic Cup – (3) 1995, 1998, 2003.

AS La Jeunesse d'Esch
BP 45
4001 Esch-sur-Alzette
tel – 021731823
fax – 532596
website – www.jeunesse-esch.lu
Year of Formation – 1907
President – Jean Cazzaro
Coach – Romeo Codello
Stadium – Stade de la Frontière (7,500)
Colours – Black & white stripes (white sleeves)/black/black
MAJOR HONOURS
League Championship – (27) 1921, 1937, 1951, 1954, 1958, 1959, 1960, 1963, 1967, 1968, 1970, 1973, 1974, 1975, 1976, 1977, 1980, 1983, 1985, 1987, 1988, 1995, 1996, 1997, 1998, 1999, 2004.
Domestic Cup – (12) 1935, 1937, 1946, 1954, 1973, 1974, 1976, 1981, 1988, 1997, 1999, 2000.

UN Käerjéng 97
BP 94
4901 Bascharage
tel – 26581962
fax – 26583767
website – www.un-kaerjeng.lu
Year of Formation – 1997
President – Nico Zenner
Coach – Angelo Fiorucci
Stadium – Bechel (3,000)
Colours – Red/dark blue/dark blue

FC Mamer 32
9 rue de la Libération
8245 Mamer
tel – 021195765
fax – 312095
Year of Formation – 1932
President – Romain Schumacher
Coach – Luc Olinger
Stadium – François Trausch (3,000)
Colours – Red/red/red

FC Mondercange
BP 69
3901 Mondercange
tel – 26554444
fax – 26554433
website – www.fcmondercange.lu
Year of Formation – 1933
President – Georges Zorn
Coach – Vinicio Monacelli
Stadium – Communal (4,500)
Colours – Red & black stripes/black/red & black

CS Pétange
BP 63
4701 Pétange
tel – 5046991
fax – 507385
website – www.cspetange.lu
Year of Formation – 1909
President – Pascal Wagner
Coach – Manuel Peixoto
Stadium – Municipal (3,000)
Colours – Blue (black & white trim)/blue/white
MAJOR HONOURS
Domestic Cup – (1) 2005.

Progrès Niedercorn
BP 161
4502 Differdange
tel – 583635
fax – 583635
Year of Formation – 1919
President – Roger Sosson
Coach – Olivier Ciancanelli
Stadium – Jos Haupert (4,000)
Colours – Yellow (black trim)/black/yellow
MAJOR HONOURS
League Championship – (3) 1953, 1978, 1981.
Domestic Cup – (4) 1933, 1945, 1977, 1978.

Racing Football Club Union Luxembourg
Boîte Postale 1614
1016 Luxembourg
tel – 463498
fax – 404747
website – www.racing-fc.lu
Year of Formation – 2005
President – Jean-Marc Faber
Coach – Jacques Muller
Stadium – Achille Hammerel (6,000)
Colours – Sky blue/white/white

FC Swift Hesperange
19 rue Gruewereck
6734 Grevenmacher
tel – 758893
fax – 26360341
Year of Formation – 1916
President – Fernand Laroche
Coach – Luc Muller
Stadium – Alphonse Theis (5,000)
Colours – Red/white/red
MAJOR HONOURS
Domestic Cup – (1) 1990.

FC Victoria Rosport
11 rue Giesenbour

The Directory

6583 Rosport
tel – 730280
fax – 26743279
website – www.fcvictoriarosport.lu
Year of Formation – 1928
President – Jean Dondelinger
Coach – Reiner Brinsa
Stadium – Um Camping (2,500)
Colours – Red/red/red

FC Wiltz 71
BP 47
9501 Wiltz
tel – 9595432
fax – 957710
website – www.fcwiltz.lu
Year of Formation – 1971
President – Romain Schneider
Coach – Daniel Boccar
Stadium – Gëtzt (3,000)
Colours – Red (white trim)/red/red

MACEDONIA

Macedonian Football Federation
8-ma Udarna Brigada 31a, 1000 Skopje
tel – (00389 2) 3229042
fax – (00389 2) 3235448
website – www.fmm.com.mk
email – ffm@ffm.com.mk

Year of Formation – 1909
President – Haralampie Hadziristeski
Secretary – Lazar Mitrovski
Stadium – Gradski, Skopje (20,000)

FK Baskimi Kumanovo
11 Noemvri 44
1300 Kumanovo
tel – (31) 412748
Year of Formation – 1947
President – Kjani Aliu
Coach – Hisni Madzuni
Stadium – Gradski (5,000)
Colours – Green (black trim)/black/green
MAJOR HONOURS
Domestic Cup – (1) 2005.

Bregalnica Kraun Stip
Gradski Stadion bb
92000 Stip
tel – (92) 389500
fax – (92) 396587
Year of Formation – 1921

President – Blaze Panev
Coach – Nikola Spasov
Stadium – Gradski (10,000)
Colours – Blue/blue/blue

Makedonija GP Skopje
Ul. Mice Kozar bb
1000 Skopje
tel – (2) 3044444
fax – (2) 3044444
Year of Formation – 1934
President – Jovica Nikolovski
Coach – Radmilo Ivancevic
Stadium – Gradski (2,000)
Colours – Red (yellow trim)/red/red
MAJOR HONOURS
Domestic Cup – (1) 2006.

Napredak Kicevo
Alekandar Makedonski bb.
6.250 Kicevo
tel – (45) 223 823
fax – (45) 220 210
Year of Formation – 1924
President – Vanko Stojanovski
Coach – Dragan Bocevski
Stadium – Gradski (5,000)
Colours – Blue/white/blue

Pelister Bitola
Gradski stadion "Tumbe Kafe" b.b.
7.000 Bitola
tel – (47) 227 878
fax – (47) 242 692
Year of Formation – 1945
President – Cele Vidanovski
Coach – Marjan Sekulovski
Stadium – Pod Timbe kafe (9,000)
Colours – Green (white trim)/white/green
MAJOR HONOURS
Domestic Cup – (1) 2001.

FK Pobeda
Aleksandar Makedonski bb
7500 Prilep
tel – (48) 426991
fax – (48) 423380
Year of Formation – 1941
President – Aleksandar Zabrcanec
Coach – Nikolce Zdraveski
Stadium – Goce Delcev (10,000)
Colours – Red/red/red
MAJOR HONOURS
League Championship – (1) 2004.
Domestic Cup – (1) 2002.

FK Rabotnicki Kometal

Gradski Park bb
PO Box 424
1000 Skopje
tel – (2) 3164044
fax – (2) 3164044
website – www.fcrabotnicki.com.mk
Year of Formation – 1937
President – Kosta Kostovski
Coach – Gjore Jovanovski
Stadium – Gradski (20,000)
Colours – Red (white trim)/red/white
MAJOR HONOURS
League Championship – (2) 2005, 2006.

Renova Cepciste
Stadion Cepciste
1220 Tetovo
tel – (44) 487300
fax – (44) 487300
Year of Formation – 1991
President – Tahir Abdulahi
Coach – Toni Jakimovski
Stadium – Stadion Cepciste (15,000)
Colours – Blue/white/blue

FK Sileks
Goce Delcev bb
1320 Kratovo
tell – (31) 481830/481481
fax – (31) 481876
Year of Formation – 1965
President – Vlasto Savevski
Coach – Slavko Jovic
Stadium – RIK "Sileks" (3,000)
Colours – Red (blue trim)/blue/red
MAJOR HONOURS
League Championship – (3) 1996, 1997, 1998.
Domestic Cup – (2) 1994, 1997.

Skendija 79 Tetovo
Todor Cipovski bb
1200 Tetovo
tel – (44) 341812
fax – (44) 341812
Year of Formation – 1979
President – Muhamed Idrizi
Coach – Nedzat Husein
Stadium – Gradski (15,000)
Colours – Red (black trim)/black/red

FK Vardar
Gradski park bb
1000 Skopje
tel – (2) 3217329
fax – (2) 3217329
website – www.fkvardar.com.mk
Year of Formation – 1947

The Directory

President – Dragan Zivkovic
Coach – Dragan Kanatlarovski
Stadium – Gradski (20,000)
Colours – Red (black trim)/black/red
MAJOR HONOURS
League Championship (Yugoslavia) – (1) 1987.
League Championship – (5) 1993, 1994, 1995, 2002, 2003.
Domestic Cup (Yugoslavia) – (1) 1961.
Domestic Cup – (4) 1993, 1995, 1998, 1999.

Vlazrimi Kicevo
Ul. Ohridska 18
6250 Kicevo
tel – (45) 223910
fax – (45) 221105
Year of Formation – 1980
President – Osman Cuculi
Coach – Nedzat Sabani
Stadium – Kicevo (2,000)
Colours – Blue/white/blue

MALTA

Malta Football Association
280 St. Paul's Street, Valletta, VLT 07
tel – (00356) 21 222697/232581
fax – (00356) 21 245136
website – www.mfa.com.mt
email – info@mfa.com.mt

Year of Formation – 1900
President – Joseph Mifsud
Secretary – Joe Gauci
Stadium – National, Ta' Qali (18,000)

Birkirkara FC
3 Old Church Street
Birkirkara BKR 10
tel – (21) 447005/489214
fax – (21) 489214
website – www.birkirkarafc.com
Year of Formation – 1950
President – Victor Zammit
Coach – Stephen Azzopardi
Stadium – National, Ta' Qali (18,000)
Colours – Yellow & red stripes/red/yellow
MAJOR HONOURS
League Championship – (2) 2000, 2006.
Domestic Cup – (3) 2002, 2003, 2005.

Floriana FC
28 St. Anne Street
Floriana VLT 15
tel – (21) 238664
fax – (21) 233498
website – www.florianafc.com
Year of Formation – 1894
President – Tony Zahra
Coach – Jan Artz
Stadium – National, Ta' Qali (18,000)
Colours – Green & white stripes/green/white
MAJOR HONOURS
League Championship – (25) 1910, 1912, 1913, 1921, 1922, 1925, 1927, 1928, 1929, 1931, 1935, 1937, 1950, 1951, 1952, 1953, 1955, 1958, 1962, 1968, 1970, 1973, 1975, 1977, 1993.
Domestic Cup – (18) 1938, 1945, 1947, 1949, 1950, 1953, 1954, 1955, 1957, 1958, 1961, 1966, 1967, 1972, 1976, 1981, 1993, 1994.

Hibernians FC
114 Paola Square
Paola PLA 02
tel – (21) 677764
fax – (21) 677764/240887
website – www.hibernians.com.mt
Year of Formation – 1931
President – Tony Bezzina
Coach – Robert Gatt
Stadium – Hibernians Ground, Corradino (8,000)
Colours – White & black stripes/black/white
MAJOR HONOURS
League Championship – (9) 1961, 1967, 1969, 1979, 1981, 1982, 1994, 1995, 2002.
Domestic Cup – (7) 1962, 1970, 1971, 1980, 1982, 1998, 2006.

Marsa FC
54 Balbi Street
Marsa HMR 14
tel – 21238654/377512
website – www.marsafc.com
Year of Formation – 1920
President – Twanny Mercieca
Coach – Michael Molzahn
Stadium – National, Ta' Qali (18,000)
Colours – Red & blue stripes/white/white

Marsaxlokk FC
Vendome Tower
Kavallerizza Road
Marsaxlokk ZTN 10
tel – (21) 682966
website – www.marsaxlokkfc.com
Year of Formation – 1944
President – Mark Sciriha
Coach – Oliver Spiteri & Ray Farrugia
Stadium – National, Ta' Qali (18,000)
Colours – Blue/white/blue

Msida St. Joseph FC
4 Church Street
Msida MSD 05
tel – (21) 340443
website – www.msidastjoseph.com
Year of Formation – 1906
President – Dr. Kevin Deguara
Coach – Todor Stoyanov Raykov
Stadium – National, Ta' Qali (18,000)
Colours – Red/white/white

Pietà Hotspurs FC
Our Lady of Sorrows Street
Pietà
tel – (21) 231336
fax – (21) 234150
website – www.pietahotspursfc.com
Year of Formation – 1968
President – Edward Schembri
Coach – George Deanov
Stadium – National, Ta' Qali (18,000)
Colours – Sky blue & white quarters/sky blue/sky blue

St. George's FC
12 'Centru 1890'
Pilgrimage Street Cospicua
tel – 21826971
website – www.stgeorgesfc.com
Year of Formation – 1890
President – Christopher Agius
Coach – Marco Gerada
Stadium – National, Ta' Qali (18,000)
Colours – Blue & white stripes/white/white
MAJOR HONOURS
League Championship – (1) 1917.

Sliema Wanderers FC
21 Tower Road
Sliema
tel – (21) 332033
fax – (21) 23285131
website – www.eswfc.com
Year of Formation – 1909
President – Robert Arrigo
Coach – Edward Aquilina
Stadium – National, Ta' Qali (18,000)
Colours – Dark blue & sky blue stripes/black/dark blue
MAJOR HONOURS
League Championship – (26) 1920, 1923, 1924, 1926, 1930, 1933, 1934, 1936, 1938, 1939, 1940, 1949, 1954, 1956, 1957, 1964, 1965, 1966, 1971, 1972, 1976, 1989, 1996, 2003, 2004, 2005.
Domestic Cup – (19) 1935, 1936, 1937, 1940, 1946, 1948, 1951, 1952, 1956, 1959, 1963, 1965, 1968, 1969, 1974, 1979, 1990, 2000, 2004.

Valletta FC

The Directory

126 St. Lucia Street
Valletta VLT 08
tel – (21) 224939
fax – (21) 238083
website – www.vallettafcofficial.net
Year of Formation – 1943
President – Charles Camilleri
Coach – Paul Zammit
Stadium – National, Ta' Qali (18,000)
Colours – White/white/white
MAJOR HONOURS
League Championship – (18) 1915, 1932, 1945, 1946, 1948, 1959, 1960, 1963, 1974, 1978, 1980, 1984, 1990, 1992, 1997, 1998, 1999, 2001.
Domestic Cup – (11) 1960, 1964, 1975, 1977, 1978, 1991, 1995, 1996, 1997, 1999, 2001.

MOLDOVA

Federatia Moloveneasca de Futbol
str. Tricolorului 39, 2012 Chisinau
tel – (00373 22) 210413
fax – (00373 22) 210432
website – www.fmf.md
email – fmf@mfotbal.mldnet.com

Year of Formation – 1990
President – Pavel Ciobanu
Secretary – Nicolae Cibotari
Stadium – Republican, Chisinau (8,084)

FC Dacia Chisinau
bd. Renasterii 22/2
2005 Chisinau
tel – (22) 225536
fax – (22) 213993
website – www.fcdacia.com
Year of Formation – 2000
President – Victor Terente
Coach – Emil Caras
Stadium – Republican (8,009)
Colours – Blue (yellow trim)/yellow/yellow

Dinamo Bender
Dzerjinski str. 53
3200 Bender
tel – (552) 23559/49004/ 24129
fax – (552) 23559/24129
President – Alexandr Corolev
Coach – Iury Hodichin
Stadium – Dinamo (2,000)
Colours – Blue/black/blue

Iskra-Stali Ribnita

Str. Industriala 1
5500 Ribnita
tel – (55) 77867
fax – (55) 540658
website – www.aommz.com
President – Ilia Freidchin
Coach – Serghei Sirbu
Stadium – Municipal (3,000)
Colours – Blue (red trim)/blue/blue

FC Nistru Otaci
str. Libertatii 50
7100 Otaci
tel – (271) 24510
fax – (271) 24510
website – www.fcnistru.com
Year of formation – 1953
President – Vasile Traghira
Coach – Nicolae Bunea
Stadium – Calaraseuca (1,000)
Colours – Pale blue & white stripes/white/pale blue
MAJOR HONOURS
Domestic Cup – (1) 2005.

Olimpia Balti
Str. Kiev 115
3100 Balti
tel – (231) 20314
fax – (231) 20314
Year of Formation – 1984
President – Valentin Guznac
Coach – Serghei Cebotari
Stadium – Municipal (5,000)
Colours – Red (white trim)/black/red

FC Politechnica Chisinau
Str. Studentilor 3/2 hostel N 11 office 8
2068 Chisinau
tel – (22) 319003
fax – (22) 319003
website – www.fcpolitechnica.narod.ru
President – Anatol Turcan
Coach – Ivan Caras
Stadium – Dinamo (2,962)
Colours – Black & white stripes/black/black

FC Sheriff Tiraspol
str. K. Libnekhta 1/2
3300 Tiraspol
tel – (533) 63500
fax – (533) 63510
website – www.fc.sheriff.md
Year of Formation – 1997
President – Victor Gusan
Coach – Leonid Kuchiuk

Stadium – FC Sheriff (13,460)
Colours – Yellow (black trim)/black/yellow
MAJOR HONOURS
League Championship – (6) 2001, 2002, 2003, 2004, 2005, 2006.
Domestic Cup – (4) 1999, 2001, 2002, 2006.

SC Tiligul-Tiras Tiraspol
str. Makarenko 14
3300 Tiraspol
tel – (533) 68284
fax – (533) 80481
Year of Formation – 1961
President – Petr Reih
Coach – Alexandr Vereovkin
Stadium – Municipal (3,525)
Colours – Red/red/red
MAJOR HONOURS
Domestic Cup – (3) 1993, 1994, 1995.

FC Tiraspol
str. Lenin 7, ap.60
3300 Tiraspol
tel – (533) 63691
fax – (533) 63691
Year of Formation – 1993
President – Victor Tulbea
Coach – Yury Kulish
Stadium – FC Sheriff (13,460)
Colours – Red/green/red
MAJOR HONOURS (as Constructorul Chisinau)
League Championship – (1) 1997.
Domestic Cup – (2) 1996, 2000.

CSF Zimbru Chisinau
str. Butucului 1
2060 Chisinau
tel – (22) 77 24 00
fax – (22) 771553
website – www.zimbru.md
Year of Formation – 1947
President – Andrey Chechetov
Coach – Ivan Tabanov
Stadium – CSF Zimbru (10,500)
Colours – Yellow/yellow/yellow
MAJOR HONOURS
League Championship – (8) 1992, 1993, 1994, 1995, 1996, 1998, 1999, 2000.
Domestic Cup – (4) 1997, 1998, 2003, 2004.

MONTENEGRO

Fudbalski Savez Crne Gore
19. decembra 21, 81000
Podgorica
tel – (00381 81) 664288
fax – (00381 81) 664259

The Directory

Year of Formation – 1931
President – Dejan Savicevic
Secretary – Momir Djurdjevac

FK Berane
Gradski stadion
84300 Berane
tel – (069) 085197
fax – (087) 233337
Year of Formation – 1945
President – Sasa Pesic
Coach – Slobodan Djukic
Stadium – Gradski (3,000)
Colours – Blue/blue/blue

FK Buducnost Podgorica
Vaka Djurovica bb
81000 Podgorica
tel – (081) 667 080
fax – (081) 664 304
website – www.fkbuducnost.cg.yu
Year of Formation – 1925
President – Vladan Vucelic
Coach – Miodrag Bozovic
Stadium – Gradski Pod Goricom (15,300)
Colours – Blue & white stripes/blue/blue

FK Decic Tuzi
Tuzi bb
81000 Podgorica
Year of Formation – 1926
President – Halil Dukovic
Coach – Vojislav Pejovic
Stadium – FK Decic (2,000)
Colours – Blue/white/blue

OFK Grbalj Radanovici
Radanovici bb
85320 Tivat
Year of Formation – 1995
President – Milivoje Latkovic
Coach – Milorad Malovrazic
Stadium – OFK Grbalj (2,000)
Colours – Red/white/red

FK Jedinstvo Bijelo Polje
Gradski stadion
84000 Bijelo Polje
tel – (084) 432710/(069) 498338
fax – (084) 432630
Year of Formation – 1922
President – Branislav Drobnjak
Coach – Rade Vesovic
Stadium – Gradski (7,500)
Colours – White/blue/white

FK Kom Zlatica Podgorica
Zlatica bb
81000 Podgorica
tel – (081) 652148
fax – (081) 652383
Year of Formation – 1935
President – Milutin Simovic
Coach – Sasa Petrovic
Stadium – Zlatica (7,200)
Colours – White/blue/blue

FK Mladost Podgorica
Cvijetin brijeg bb
81000 Podgorica
Year of Formation – 1930
President – Veljko Djurovic
Coach – Dimitrije Mitrovic
Stadium – Na Cvijetinom brijegu (5,000)
Colours – Red/white/white

FK Mogren Budva
Jadranski put bb
85310 Budva
tel – (086) 451647
fax – (086) 452487
Year of Formation – 1945
President – Rajko Kuljaca
Coach – Dragan Djukanovic
Stadium – Lugovi (4,000)
Colours – Yellow/blue/blue

OFK Petrovac
Brezine 4
85300 Petrovac
Year of Formation – 1969
President – Jovo Zenovic
Coach – Aleksandar Miljenovic
Stadium – Pod Malim Brdom (5,000)
Colours – Blue/white/white

FK Rudar Pljevlja
Gradski Stadion pod Golubinjom
84210 Pljevlja
tel – (087) 281033
fax – (087) 285606
Year of Formation – 1920
President – Radovan Klacar
Coach – Mirko Maric
Stadium – Pod Golubinjom (7,000)
Colours – Blue/white/blue

FK Sutjeska Niksic
Dragova luka bb
81400 Niksic
tel – (083) 246425
fax – (083) 246425
Year of Formation – 1927
President – Ratko Vukotic
Coach – Brajan Nenezic
Stadium – FK Sutjeska (10,800)
Colours – Blue/blue/blue

FK Zeta Golubovci
Golubovci bb
81000 Podgorica – Golubovci
tel – (081) 8731412
fax – (081) 873142
website – www.fkzeta.com
Year of Formation – 1927
President – Radojica Bozovic
Coach – Dejan Vukicevic
Stadium – FK Zeta (8,000)
Colours – Blue/blue/blue

NORTHERN IRELAND

The Irish Football Association
20 Windsor Avenue, Belfast BT9 6EE
tel – (0044 28) 90669458
fax – (0044 28) 90667620
website – www.irishfa.com
email – enquiries@irishfa.com

Year of Formation – 1880
President – Jim Boyce
Chief Executive – Howard J.C. Wells
Stadium – Windsor Park, Belfast (14,063)

INTERNATIONAL TOURNAMENT APPEARANCES
World Cup – (3) 1958 (qtr-finals), 1982 (2nd phase), 1986.

Armagh City FC
Holm Park
Ardmore
Newry Road
Armagh
Tel – (028) 37511560
Year of Formation – 1964
Chairman – Nigel Cooke
Manager – Gary McKinstry
Stadium – Holm Park (2,800)
Colours – Sky blue & black broad stripes/black/black

Ballymena United FC
The Showgrounds
Warden Street
Ballymena
BT43 7DR
tel – (028) 25652049
website – www.ballymenaunitedfc.com

The Directory

Year of Formation – 1928
Chairman – Robert Cupples
Manager – Tommy Wright
Stadium – The Showgrounds (3,800)
Colours – Sky blue/white/sky blue
MAJOR HONOURS
Domestic Cup – (6) 1929, 1940, 1958, 1981, 1984, 1989.

Cliftonville FC

Solitude
Cliftonville Street
Belfast BT14 6LP
tel – (028) 90754628
fax – (028) 90729011
website – www.cliftonvillefc.net
Year of Formation – 1879
Chairman – Hugh McCartan
Manager – Eddie Patterson
Stadium – Solitude (5,000)
Colours – Red/white/red
MAJOR HONOURS
League Championship – (3) 1906, 1910, 1998.
Domestic Cup – (8) 1883, 1888, 1897, 1900, 1901, 1907, 1909, 1979.

Coleraine FC

The Showgrounds
Ballycastle Road
Coleraine
tel – (028) 70353655
fax – (028) 70329188
website – www.colerainefc.com
Year of Formation – 1927
Manager – Marty Quinn
Stadium – The Showgrounds (4,900)
Colours – White (two blue hoops)/blue/blue
MAJOR HONOURS
League Championship – (1) 1974.
Domestic Cup – (5) 1965, 1972, 1975, 1977, 2003.

Crusaders FC

Seaview
Shore Road
Belfast BT 15 3PL
tel – (028) 90370777
fax – (028) 90771049
website – www.crusadersfc.com
Year of Formation – 1898
Chairman – Jim Semple
Manager – Stephen Baxter
Stadium – Seaview (9,000)
Colours – Red & black stripes/white/white
MAJOR HONOURS
League Championship – (4) 1973, 1976, 1995, 1997
Domestic Cup – (2) 1967, 1968

Donegal Celtic FC

32 Suffolk Road
Belfast
BT 17
tel – (028) 9062 9810
Year of Formation – 1970
Chairman – Raymond Bonner
Manager – Paddy Kelly
Stadium – Suffolk Road (1,500)
Colours – Green & white hoops/white/white

Dungannon Swifts FC

Stangmore Park
Dungannon
tel – (028) 87723257
website – www.dungannonswiftsfc.co.uk
Year of Formation – 1949
Chairman – David Holmes
Manager – Harry Fay
Stadium – Stangmore Park (5,000)
Colours – Blue (white trim)/blue/blue & white

Glenavon FC

Mourneview Park
Lurgan BT66 8EW
tel – (028) 38322472
website – www.glenavonfc.com
Year of Formation – 1889
Chairman – Ronnie Ferguson
Manager – Colin Malone
Stadium – Mourneview Park (5,000)
Colours – Blue/white/blue
MAJOR HONOURS
League Championship – (3) 1952, 1957, 1960.
Domestic Cup – (5) 1957, 1959, 1961, 1992, 1997.

Glentoran FC

The Oval
Mersey Street
Belfast BT4 1FG
tel – (028) 90457670
fax – (028) 90732956
website – www.glentoran.net
Year of Formation – 1882
Chairman – Stafford Reynolds
Manager – Paul Millar
Stadium – The Oval (10,000)
Colours – Green/white/white, red, green & black
MAJOR HONOURS
League Championship – (22) 1894, 1897, 1905, 1912, 1913, 1921, 1925, 1931, 1951, 1953, 1964, 1967, 1968, 1970, 1972, 1977, 1981, 1988, 1992, 1999, 2003, 2005.
Domestic Cup – (20) 1914, 1917, 1921, 1932, 1933, 1935, 1951, 1966, 1973, 1983, 1985, 1986, 1987, 1988, 1990, 1996, 1998, 2000, 2001, 2004.

Larne FC

Inver Park
Inver Road
Larne
BT40 3BW
tel – (028) 28774292
website – www.larnefc.co.uk
Year of Formation – 1890
Chairman – Sam McCready
Manager – Jim Hagan
Stadium – Inver Park (3,000)
Colours – Red (white trim)/white/red

Limavady United FC

The Showgrounds
Rathmore Road
Limavady
BT49 0DF
tel – (028) 77764351
website – www.limavadyunited.com
Year of Formation – 1876
Chairman – Liam Kelly
Manager – John Cunningham
Stadium – The Showgrounds (2,500)
Colours – Blue (white trim)/white/blue

Linfield FC

Windsor Park
Donegal Ave
Belfast BT12 6LW
tel – (028) 90244198
fax – (028) 90244691
website – www.linfield-fc.com
Year of Formation – 1886
Manager – David Jeffrey
Stadium – Windsor Park (20,000)
Colours – Blue/white/blue & red
MAJOR HONOURS
League Championship – (46) 1891, 1892, 1893, 1895, 1898, 1902, 1904, 1907, 1908, 1909, 1911, 1914, 1922, 1923, 1930, 1932, 1934, 1935, 1949, 1950, 1954, 1955, 1956, 1959, 1961, 1962, 1966, 1969, 1971, 1975, 1978, 1979, 1980, 1982, 1983, 1984, 1985, 1986, 1987, 1989, 1993, 1994, 2000, 2001, 2004, 2006.
Domestic Cup – (37) 1891, 1892, 1893, 1895, 1898, 1899, 1902, 1904, 1912, 1913, 1915, 1916, 1919, 1922, 1923, 1930, 1931, 1934, 1936, 1939, 1942, 1945, 1946, 1948, 1950, 1953, 1960, 1962, 1963, 1970, 1978, 1980, 1982, 1994, 1995, 2002, 2006.

Lisburn Distillery FC

New Grosvenor Stadium
Ballyskeagh Road
Lambeg
Lisburn

The Directory

tel – (028) 90301148
website – www.lisburn-distillery.net
Year of Formation – 1879
Chairman – Jim McGrory
Manager – Paul Kirk
Stadium – New Grosvenor (7,000)
Colours – White (navy blue trim)/navy blue/white
MAJOR HONOURS
League Championship – (6) 1896, 1899, 1901, 1903, 1906, 1963.
Domestic Cup – (12) 1884, 1885, 1886, 1889, 1894, 1896, 1903, 1905, 1910, 1925, 1956, 1971.

Loughgall FC
Lakeview Park
Ballygasey Road
Loughgall
tel – (028) 38891400
website – www.loughgallfc.org
Year of Formation – 1967
Chairman – Alan Davison
Manager – Jimmy Gardiner
Stadium – Lakeview Park (3,000)
Colours – Blue/blue/blue

Newry City FC
The Showgrounds
Newry
tel – (028) 30252581
Year of Formation – 1923
Chairman – Bernie Keenan
Manager – Roy Coyle
Stadium – The Showgrounds (5,000)
Colours – Blue & white stripes/blue/blue

Portadown FC
Shamrock Park
Brownstown Road
Portadown
tel – (028) 38332726
fax – (028) 38334907
website – www.portadownfc.co.uk
Year of Formation – 1924
Chairman – Roy McMahon
Manager – Ronnie McFall
Stadium – Shamrock Park (15,000)
Colours – Red (white trim)/red/red
MAJOR HONOURS
League Championship – (4) 1990, 1991, 1996, 2002.
Domestic Cup – (3) 1991, 1999, 2005.

NORWAY

Norges Fotballforbund

Serviceboks 1, Ullevaal stadion,
0840 Oslo
tel – (0047) 21 029300
fax – (0047) 21 029301
website – www.fotbal.no
email – nff@fotball.no

Year of Formation – 1902
President – Sondre Kåfjord
Secretary – Karen Espelund
Stadium – Ullevaal, Oslo (25,572)

INTERNATIONAL TOURNAMENT APPEARANCES
World Cup – (3) 1938, 1994, 1998 (2nd round).
European Championship – (1) 2000.

Sportsklubben Brann
Postboks 8
Minde
5821 Bergen
tel – 55 598500
fax – 55 598525
website – www.brann.no
Year of Formation – 1908
Chairman – Magne Revheim
Coach – Mons Ivar Mjelde
Stadium – Brann (19,400)
Colours – Red (white trim)/red/red
MAJOR HONOURS
League Championship – (2) 1962, 1963.
Domestic Cup – (6) 1923, 1925, 1972, 1976, 1982, 2004.

Fredrikstad Fotballklubb
Postboks 300
1610 Fredrikstad
tel – 69 301720
fax – 69 301721
website – www.fredrikstadfk.no
Year of Formation – 1903
Chairman – Bjørn Jensen
Coach – Knut Torbjørn Eggen
Stadium – Fredrikstad stadium (10,000)
Colours – White (red trim)/red/white
MAJOR HONOURS
League Championship – (9) 1938, 1939, 1949, 1951, 1952, 1954, 1957, 1960, 1961.
Domestic Cup – (10) 1932, 1935, 1936, 1938, 1940, 1950, 1957, 1961, 1966, 1984.

Ham-Kam Fotball
Arenavegen 2
2321 Hamar
tel – 62 553080
fax – 62 553081
website – www.hamkam.no
Year of Formation – 1918
Chairman – Erik Stensrud

Coach – Frode Grodås
Stadium – Briskeby Gressbane (11,000)
Colours – White (green trim)/green/white

Lillestrøm Sportsklubb
C.J. Hansensvej 3B
2007 Kjeller
tel – 63 805660
fax – 63 805670
website – www.lsk.no
Year of Formation – 1917
Chairman – Per Mathisen
Coach – Uwe Rösler
Stadium – Åråsen (12,000)
Colours – Yellow (black trim)/black/yellow
MAJOR HONOURS
League Championship (5) 1959, 1976, 1977, 1986, 1989.
Domestic Cup – (4) 1977, 1978, 1981, 1985.

FC Lyn Oslo
Postboks 3928
Ullevaal stadion
0805 Oslo
tel – 23 005190
fax – 23 005191
website – www.lyn.no
Year of Formation – 1896
Chairman – Sveinung Lunde
Coach – Henning Berg
Stadium – Ullevaal (25,572)
Colours – Red (broad white central stripe)/blue/white
MAJOR HONOURS
League Championship – (2) 1964, 1968.
Domestic Cup – (8) 1908, 1909, 1910, 1911, 1945, 1946, 1967, 1968.

Molde Fotballklubb
Julsundveien 14
6412 Molde
tel – 71 202500
fax – 71 202501
website – www.moldefk.no
Year of Formation – 1911
Chairman – Oddne Hansen
Coach – Arild Stavrum
Stadium – Aker (11,167)
Colours – Blue (white trim)/white/blue
MAJOR HONOURS
Domestic Cup – (2) 1994, 2005.

Odd Grenland
Postboks 1605 Falkum
3705 Skien
tel – 35 900150
fax – 35 900159

The Directory

website – www.oddgrenland.no
Year of Formation – 1894
Chairman – Tore Andersen
Coach – Arne Sandstø & Gaute Larsen
Stadium – Odd stadium (10,000)
Colours – White (black trim)/black/white
MAJOR HONOURS
Domestic Cup – (12) 1903, 1904, 1905, 1906, 1913, 1915, 1919, 1922, 1924, 1926, 1931, 2000.

Rosenborg Ballklub
7492 Trondheim
tel – 73 822100
fax – 73 944070
website – www.rbk.no
Year of Formation – 1917
Chairman – Terje Svendsen
Coach – Per-Mathias Høgmo
Stadium – Lerkendal (21,166)
Colours – White/black/white
MAJOR HONOURS
League Championship – (19) 1967, 1969, 1971, 1985, 1988, 1990, 1992, 1993, 1994, 1995, 1996, 1997, 1998, 1999, 2000, 2001, 2002, 2003, 2004.
Domestic Cup – (9) 1960, 1964, 1971, 1988, 1990, 1992, 1995, 1999, 2003.

Sandefjord Fotball
Postboks 1302
3205 Sandefjord
tel – 33 423010
fax – 33 423011
website – www.sandefjordfotball.no
Year of Formation – 1998
Chairman – Roger Gulliksen
Coach – Tor Thodesen
Stadium – Storstadion (7,000)
Colours – Blue/blue/white

Stabaek Fotball
Gamle Ringeriksvei 61
1357 Bekkestua
tel – 67 121212
fax – 67 582610
website – www.stabak.no
Year of Formation – 1912
Chairman – Mimi Berdal
Coach – Jan Jönsson
Stadium – Nadderud (7,200)
Colours – Dark blue (three light blue stripes)/light blue/dark blue
MAJOR HONOURS
Domestic Cup – (1) 1998.

Idrettsklubben Start
Postboks 1533 Valhalla
4688 Kristiansand
tel – 38 106666
fax – 38 097535
website – www.ikstart.no
Year of Formation – 1905
Chairman – Odd Skuggen
Coach – Stig Inge Bjørnebye
Stadium – Kristiansand stadium (15,000)
Colours – Yellow (black trim)/black/yellow
MAJOR HONOURS
League Championship – (2) 1978, 1980.

Tromsø Idrettslag
Postboks 5
9251 Tromsø
tel – 77 602600
fax – 77 602601
website – www.til.no
Year of Formation – 1920
Chairman – Trygve Myrvang
Coach – Ivar Morten Normark
Stadium – Alfheim (8,000)
Colours – Red & white stripes/white/white
MAJOR HONOURS
Domestic Cup – (2) 1986, 1996.

Viking Fotballklubb
Postboks 4051
4092 Stavanger
tel – 51 329700
fax – 51 329701
website – www.viking-fk.no
Year of Formation – 1899
Chairman – Ole Rugland
Coach – Tom Prahl
Stadium – Viking (15,300)
Colours – Dark blue (white trim)/white/dark blue
MAJOR HONOURS
League Championship – (8) 1958, 1972, 1973, 1974, 1975, 1979, 1982, 1991.
Domestic Cup – (5) 1953, 1959, 1979, 1989, 2001.

Vålerenga Fotball
Postboks 6064 Etterstad
0601 Oslo
tel – 23 247820
fax – 23 247801
website – www.vif.no
Year of Formation – 1913
Chairman – Odd Skarheim
Coach – Kjetil Rekdal
Stadium – Ullevaal (25,572)
Colours – Blue/white/red
MAJOR HONOURS
League Championship – (5) 1965, 1981, 1983, 1984, 2005.
Domestic Cup – (3) 1980, 1997, 2002.

POLAND

Polski Zwiazek Pilki Noznej
Miodowa 1, 00-080 Warszawa
tel – (0048 22) 55512200
fax – (0048 22) 5512300
website – www.pzpn.pl
email – pzpn@pzpn.pl

Year of Formation – 1919
President – Michal Listkiewicz
Secretary – Zdzislaw Krecina
Stadium – Slaski, Chorzow (47,000)

INTERNATIONAL TOURNAMENT APPEARANCES
World Cup – (7) 1938, 1974 (3rd), 1978 (2nd phase), 1982 (3rd), 1986 (2nd round), 2002, 2006.

Arka Gdynia
Ul. Olimpijska 5/9
81-538 Gdynia
tel – (058) 6623936
fax – (058) 6906016
website – www.arka.gdynia.pl
Year of formation – 1929
President – Jacek Milewski
Coach – Wojciech Stawowy
Stadium – Arka (12,000)
Colours – Yellow & blue stripes (yellow sleeves)/yellow/yellow
MAJOR HONOURS
Domestic Cup – (1) 1979

Cracovia Krakow
Ul. Wielicka 101
30-552 Kraków
website- www.cracovia.pl
Year of Formation – 1906
President – Janusz Filipiak
Coach – Stefan Bialas
Stadium – Cracovia (10,000)
Colours – Red & white stripes (black trim)/white/white
MAJOR HONOURS
League Championship – (5) 1921, 1930, 1932, 1937, 1948.

GKS Belchatow
Ul. Sportowa 3
97-400 Belchatow
tel – (044) 6350355
fax – (044) 6350791
website – www.gksbelchatow.pl
Year of formation – 1977
President – Janusz Paduch
Coach – Orest Lenczyk

The Directory

Stadium – GKS (7,000)
Colours – Yellow (black trim)/black/white

Gornik Leczna
Al. Jana Pawla II 13
21-010 Leczna
tel – (081) 7521740
website – www.gornik.leczna.pl
Year of Formation – 1979
President – Wieslaw Sikora
Coach – Dariusz Kubicki
Stadium – Gornik (6,500)
Colours – Dark green & white diagonal halves/white/white

Klub Sportowy Gornik Zabrze
Ul. Roosevelta 81
41-800 Zabrze
tel – (032) 2714926/2710941
fax – (032) 2710530
website – www.gornikzabrze.com.pl
Year of Formation – 1948
President – Eugeniusz Postlski
Coach – Marek Motyka
Stadium – Gornik (18,000)
Colours – Red (blue sleeves)/red/red
MAJOR HONOURS
League Championship – (14) 1957, 1959, 1961, 1963, 1964, 1965, 1966, 1967, 1971, 1972, 1985, 1986, 1987, 1988.
Domestic Cup – (6) 1965, 1968, 1969, 1970, 1971, 1972.

Klub Sportowy Groclin Dyskobolia Grodzisk Wielkopolski
Ul. Sportowa 2
62-065 Grodzisk Wielokpolski
tel – (061) 4436250
fax – (061) 4446249
website – www.dyskobolia.com.pl
Year of Formation – 1922
President – Zbigniew Drzymala
Coach – Werner Licka
Stadium – Dyskobolia (6,000)
Colours – White (green candy stripes & white sleeves)/white/white
MAJOR HONOURS
Domestic Cup – (1) 2005.

Kolporter Korona Kielce
Ul. Stachyrska 6
25-659 Kielce
tel – (041) 3613640
fax – (041) 3613640
website – www.korona-kielce.pl
Year of formation – 1973
President – Krzysztof Klicki
Coach – Ryszard Wieczorek
Stadium – Korona (7,000)
Colours – Yellow & red stripes/yellow/yellow

Lech Poznan
Ul. Bulgarska 5/7
60-320 Poznan
tel – (061) 8673061
fax – (061) 8672661
website – www.lech.poznan.pl
Year of Formation – 1922
President – Andrzej Kadzinski
Coach – Franciszek Smuda
Stadium – Lech (26,500)
Colours – Blue & white stripes/white/white
MAJOR HONOURS
League Championship – (5) 1983, 1984, 1990, 1992, 1993.
Domestic Cup – (4) 1982, 1984, 1988, 2004.

Legia Warszawa
Ul. Lazienkowska 3
00-449 Warszawa
tel – (022) 6210896/6281360
fax – (022) 6218261
website – www.legia.pl
Year of Formation – 1916
President – Piotr Zygo
Coach – Dariusz Wdowczyk
Stadium – Wojska Polskiego (13,662)
Colours – White/black/white
MAJOR HONOURS
League Championship – (8) 1955, 1956, 1969, 1970, 1994, 1995, 2002, 2006.
Domestic Cup – (12) 1955, 1956, 1964, 1966, 1973, 1980, 1981, 1989, 1990, 1994, 1995, 1997.

Lodzki KS
Al. Unii Lubelskiej 2
94-020 Lodz
tel –(042) 6860668
fax –(042) 6873497
website –www.lkslodz.pl
Year of Formation –1908
President –Roman Stepien
Coach –Marek Chojnacki
Stadium –LKS (18,000)
Colours – Red/white/white
MAJOR HONOURS
League Championship – (2) 1958, 1998.
Domestic Cup – (1) 1957.

Miejski Klub Sportowy Odra Wodzislaw
Ul. Boguminska 8
44-300 Wodzislaw Slaski
tel – (032) 4551394
fax – (032) 4554435
website – www.odra.wodzislaw.pl
Year of Formation – 1922
President – Ireneusz Serwotka
Coach – Waldemar Fornalik
Stadium – Odra (8,000)
Colours – White (red trim)/dark blue/dark blue

MKS Pogon Szczecin
ul. Karlowicza 28
71-102 Szczecin
tel – (091) 4860099
fax – (091) 4877969
website – www.pogonszczecin.pl
Year of Formation – 1948
President – Antoni Ptak
Coach – Mariusz Kuras
Stadium – Pogon (17,500)
Colours – Claret & dark blue diagonal halves/dark blue/dark blue

TS Wisla Krakow
Ul. Reymonta 22
30-059 Krakow
tel – (012) 6377120
fax – (012) 6307692
website – www.wisla.krakow.pl
Year of Formation – 1906
President – Boguslaw Cupial
Coach – Dan Petrescu
Stadium – Wisla (9,500)
Colours – Red (white trim)/white/white
MAJOR HONOURS
League Championship – (10) 1927, 1928, 1949, 1950, 1978, 1999, 2001, 2003, 2004, 2005.
Domestic Cup – (4) 1926, 1967, 2002, 2003.

Widzew Lodz
Al. Marszalka Pilsudskiego 138
92-300 Lodz
tel –(042) 2505178
fax –(048) 6740175
website –www.widzew.lodz.pl
Year of Formation –1922
President – Władysław Puchalski
Coach – Michal Probierz
Stadium – Widzew (9,882)
Colours – Red (white trim)/red/red
MAJOR HONOURS
League Championship – (4) 1981, 1982, 1996, 1997.
Domestic Cup – (1) 1985.

Wisla Plock
Ul. Lukasiewicza 34
09-400 Plock
tel – (024) 2622555/2624638

fax – (024) 3655220
website – www.wisla.plock.pl
Year of Formation – 1947
President – Krzysztof Dmoszynski
Coach – Josef Csaplár
Stadium – Wisla (12,800)
Colours – Blue (broad white central stripe)/blue/blue
MAJOR HONOURS
Domestic Cup – (1) 2006.

SSA Zaglebie Lubin
ul. Marii Sklodowskiej-Curie 98
59-300 Lubin
tel – (076) 8478642
fax – (076) 8478565
website – www.zaglebie-lubin.com.pl
Year of Formation – 1946
President – Miroslaw Jablonski
Coach – Edward Klejndinst
Stadium – GOS (27,300)
Colours – Orange (black trim)/white/black

PORTUGAL

Federação Portuguesa de Futebol
Praça de Alegria 25, Apartado 21 100, 1250-004 Lisboa
tel – (00351 213) 252700
fax – (00351 213) 252780
website – www.fpf.pt
email – info@fpf.pt

Year of Formation – 1914
President – Gilberto Madaíl
Secretary – Manuel Mourato Quaresma
Stadium – Nacional, Lisbon (48,000)

INTERNATIONAL TOURNAMENT APPEARANCES
World Cup – (4) 1966 (3rd), 1986, 2002, 2006 (4th).
European Championship – (4) 1984 (semi-finals), 1996 (qtr-finals), 2000 (semi-finals), 2004 (runners-up).

MAJOR EUROPEAN CLUB HONOURS
Champions Cup/League – (4) SL Benfica (1961, 1962), FC Porto (1987, 2004).
Cup-winners Cup – (1) Sporting CP (1964).
UEFA Cup – (1) FC Porto (2003).

Associação Académica da Coimbra
Rua Infante D. Maria 23
3030-330 Coimbra
tel – (239) 793890
fax – (239) 793893
website – www.academica-oaf.pt
Year of Formation – 1887
President – José Eduardo Cruz Simões
Coach – Manuel Machado
Stadium – Municipal de Coimbra (30,000)
Colours – Black/black/black

Clube Desportivo das Aves
Rua Luís Gonzaga Mendes de Carvalho 265
4795-080 Vila das Aves
tel – (252) 941816
fax – (252) 873267
website – www.cdaves.pt
Year of Formation – 1930
President – Joaquim Eduardo Pereira
Coach – Manuel Gonçalves Gomes "Prof. Neca"
Stadium – Desportivo das Aves (9,000)
Colours – Red & white broad stripes/red/red

SC Beira Mar
Estádio Municipal de Aveiro
Aveiro
tel – (234) 377420
fax – (234) 377429
website – www.beiramar.pt
Year of Formation – 1922
President – Artur Valente Filipe
Coach – Augusto Inácio
Stadium – Municipal de Aveiro (30,000)
Colours – Yellow & black stripes (yellow sleeves)/black/yellow
MAJOR HONOURS
Domestic Cup – (1) 1999.

Sport Lisboa e Benfica
Complexo Desportivo SL Benfica
Avenida General Norton de Matos
Estádio da Luz
1501-805 Lisboa
tel – (217) 219500
fax – (217) 264781
website – www.slbenfica.pt
Year of Formation – 1904
President – Luís Filipe Vieira
Coach – Fernando Santos
Stadium – Luz (65,000)
Colours – Red (white trim)/white/red
MAJOR HONOURS
League Championship – (31) 1936, 1937, 1938, 1942, 1943, 1945, 1950, 1955, 1957, 1960, 1961, 1963, 1964, 1965, 1967, 1968, 1969, 1971, 1972, 1973, 1975, 1976, 1977, 1981, 1983, 1984, 1987, 1989, 1991, 1994, 2005.
Domestic Cup – (27) 1930, 1931, 1935, 1940, 1943, 1944, 1949, 1951, 1952, 1953, 1955, 1957, 1959, 1962, 1964, 1969, 1970, 1972, 1980, 1981, 1983, 1985, 1986, 1987, 1993, 1996, 2004.
European Champions Cup – (2) 1961, 1962.

Boavista Futebol Clube
Rua O Primeiro de Janeiro
4100-365 Porto
tel – (226) 071030
fax – (226) 071031
website – www.boavistafc.pt
Year of Formation – 1903
President – João Eduardo Pinto Loureiro
Coach – Jesualdo Ferreira
Stadium – Bessa (30,000)
Colours – Black & white checks (yellow trim)/black/white
MAJOR HONOURS
League Championship – (1) 2001.
Domestic Cup – (5) 1975, 1976, 1979, 1992, 1997.

Clube de Futebol Estrela da Amadora
Rua Gomes Freire 27
2700-428 Amadora
tel – (214) 999110/930601
website – www.brigadatricolor.pt
Year of Formation – 1932
President – António Oliveira
Coach – Daúto Faquirá
Stadium – José Gomes (25,000)
Colours – Green, white & red broad stripes (white sleeves)/white/white
MAJOR HONOURS
Domestic Cup – (1) 1990.

Gil Vicente Futebol Clube
Rua Diogo Pinheiro 25
Apartado 197
4750-282 Barcelos
tel – (253) 811523
fax – (253) 823102
website – www.gilvicente.bcl.pt
Year of Formation – 1924
President – Abílio Martins Gomes
Coach – Paulo Alves
Stadium – Municipal de Barceloa (12,500)
Colours – Red (blue trim)/white/red

Clube Sport Marítimo
Rua D. Carlos I 17
9050-041 Funchal
tel – (291) 205000
fax – (291) 222939
website – www.csmaritimo-madeira.pt
Year of Formation – 1910
President – João Carlos Rodrigues Pereira
Coach – Ulisses Morais
Stadium – Barreiros (10,000)

The Directory

Colours – Green & red broad stripes/white/red
MAJOR HONOURS
Domestic Cup – (1) 1926.

Clube Desportivo Nacional
Rua do Esmeraldo 46
9050-052 Funchal
tel – (291) 227335
fax – (291) 225590
website – www.nacional-da-madeira.com
Year of Formation – 1910
President – Rui António Macedo Alves
Coach – Carlos Brito
Stadium – Engenheiro Rui Alves (3,000)
Colours – Black & white broad stripes/black/white

Associação Naval 1° Maio
Estádio Municipal José Bento Pessoa
Apartado 2053
3081-801 Figueira da Foz
tel – (233) 428939
fax – (233) 411065
website – www.figueira.net/naval
Year of Formation – 1893
President – Aprígio Santos
Coach – Rogério Gonçalves
Stadium – Municipal José Bento Pessoa (10,000)
Colours – Green & white hoops/green/white

Futebol Clube Paços de Ferreira
Rua do Estádio
Apartado 26
4590-909 Paços de Ferreira
tel – (255) 965230
fax – (255) 866149
website – www.fcpf.com.pt
Year of Formation – 1950
President – Fernando Sequeira
Coach – José Mota
Stadium – Mata Real (15,000)
Colours – Yellow (green trim)/green/yellow

Futebol Clube do Porto
Estádio do Dragão
Via Futebol Clube do Porto
4350-415 Porto
tel – (22) 5570500 / fax – (22) 5070522
website – www.fcporto.pt
Year of Formation – 1893
President – Jorge Nuno Pinto da Costa
Coach – Co Adriaanse
Stadium – Dragão (52,000)
Colours – Blue & white stripes (blue sleeves)/blue/white
MAJOR HONOURS
League Championship – (21) 1935, 1939, 1940, 1956, 1959, 1978, 1979, 1985, 1986, 1988, 1990, 1992, 1993, 1995, 1996, 1997, 1998, 1999, 2003, 2004, 2006.
Domestic Cup – (17) 1922, 1925, 1932, 1937, 1956, 1958, 1968, 1977, 1984, 1988, 1991, 1994, 1998, 2000, 2001, 2003, 2006.
European Champions Cup – (2) 1987, 2004.
UEFA Cup – (1) 2003.
European Super Cup – (1) 1987.
World Club Cup – (1) 1987.

Sporting Clube de Braga
Estádio 1° de Maio – Parque da Ponte
Apartado 12
4711-909 Braga
tel – (253) 205150
fax – (253) 611686
website – www.scbraga.pt
Year of Formation – 1921
President – António Salvador Rodrigues
Coach – Carls Faria "Carvalhal"
Stadium – Municipal (30,000)
Colours – Red (white sleeves)/white/red & white
MAJOR HONOURS
Domestic Cup – (2) 1966, 1992.

Sporting Clube de Portugal
Rua Prof. Fernando da Fonseca
Edificio Visconde de Alvalade 1600-616 Lisboa
tel – (217) 516000
fax – (217) 516685
website – www.sporting.pt
Year of Formation – 1906
President – Dr. Filipe Soãres Franco
Coach – Paulo Bento
Stadium – José Alvalade XXI (54,000)
Colours – Green & white hoops/black/green & white
MAJOR HONOURS
League Championship – (18) 1941, 1944, 1947, 1948, 1949, 1951, 1952, 1953, 1954, 1958, 1962, 1966, 1970, 1974, 1980, 1982, 2000, 2002.
Domestic Cup – (17) 1923, 1934, 1936, 1938, 1941, 1945, 1946, 1948, 1954, 1963, 1971, 1973, 1974, 1978, 1982, 1995, 2002.
European Cup-winners Cup – (1) 1964.

União Desportiva de Leiria
Av. Heróis de Angola – Galerias Alcrima – 2°
Apartado 3074
2400-154 Leiria
tel – (244) 823532
fax – (244) 827987
website – www.udl.leirianet.pt
Year of Formation – 1966
President – João Alberto Amado Bartolomeu
Coach – Domingos Paciencia

Stadium – Municipal Magalhães Pessoa (30,000)
Colours – White (red trim)/white/white

Vitória Futebol Clube Setúbal
Palácio Salema
Rua do Bocage 4
2901-901 Setúbal
tel – (265) 526959/522880
fax – (265) 553496/221746
website – www.vitoriafutebolclub.pt
Year of Formation – 1910
President – Rui João Soeiro Chumbita Nunes
Coach – Hélio Sousa
Stadium – Bonfim (35,000)
Colours – Green & white stripes/white/white
MAJOR HONOURS
Domestic Cup – (1) 2005.

REPUBLIC OF IRELAND

The Football Association of Ireland
80 Merrion Square, Dublin 2
tel – (00353 1) 7037500
fax – (00353 1) 6610931
website – www.fai.ie
email – info@fai.ie

Year of Formation – 1921
Honorary Secretary – Michael Cody
Chairman – Milo Corcoran
Stadium – Lansdowne Road, Dublin (33,000)

INTERNATIONAL TOURNAMENT APPEARANCES
World Cup – (3) 1990 (qtr-finals), 1994 (2nd round), 2002 (2nd round).
European Championship – (1) 1988.

Bohemian FC
Dalymount Park
Phibsborough
Dublin 7
tel – (01) 8680923/8681034
fax – (01) 8686460
website – www.bohemians.ie
Year of Formation – 1890
Chairman – Felim O'Reilly
Manager – Gareth Farrelly
Stadium – Dalymount Park (14,800)
Colours – Red & black stripes/black/red
MAJOR HONOURS
League Championship – (9) 1924, 1928, 1930, 1934, 1936, 1975, 1978, 2001, 2003 (interim).
Domestic Cup – (6) 1928, 1935, 1970, 1976, 1992, 2001.

The Directory

Bray Wanderers
Carlisle Grounds
Quinsboro Road
Bray
County Wicklow
tel – (01) 2828214/2863552
fax – (01) 2828684
website – www.braywanderers.ie
Year of Formation – 1942
Chairman – Eddie Slevin
Manager – Pat Devlin
Stadium – Carlisle Grounds (5,300)
Colours – Green (white trim)/white/green
MAJOR HONOURS
Domestic Cup – (2) 1990, 1999

Cork City FC
Turners Cross Stadium
Curragh Road
Turners Cross
Cork
tel – (021) 4321958
fax – (021) 4321958
website – www.corkcityfc.ie
Year of Formation – 1984
Chairman – Brian Lennox
Manager – Damien Richardson
Stadium – Turners Cross (7,085)
Colours – Green & white stripes (red trim)/white/white
MAJOR HONOURS
League Championship – (2) 1993, 2005.
Domestic Cup – (1) 1998.

Derry City FC
Brandywell Stadium
Lone Moor Road
Derry
Northern Ireland BT48 9HZ
tel – (028) 71281333
fax – (028) 71281334
website – www.derrycityfc.net
Year of Formation – 1928
Chairman – Jim Roddy
Manager – Stephen Kenny
Stadium – Brandywell (2,500)
Colours – Red & white stripes/black/white
MAJOR HONOURS
League Championship – (2) 1989, 1997.
Domestic Cup – (3) 1989, 1995, 2002 (interim).

Drogheda United FC
United Park
Windmill Road
Drogheda
Co Louth
tel – (041) 9830190
fax – (041) 9830195
website – www.droghedaunited.ie
Year of Formation – 1919
Chairman – Vincent Hoey
Manager – Paul Doolin
Stadium – United Park (6,000)
Colours – Maroon (sky blue trim)/sky blue/sky blue
MAJOR HONOURS
Domestic Cup – (1) 2005.

Longford Town FC
Flancare Park
Strokestown Road
Longford
tel – (0906) 494555
fax – (0906) 493311
website – www.longfordtownfc.com
Year of Formation – 1924
Chairman – Jim Hanley
Manager – Alan Matthews
Stadium – Flancare Park (5,700)
Colours – Red & black broad stripes/black/black
MAJOR HONOURS
Domestic Cup – (2) 2003, 2004.

St. Patrick's Athletic FC
Stadium of Light
Richmond Park
125 Emmet Road
Inchicore
Dublin 8
tel – (01) 4546332
fax – (01) 4546211
website – www.stpatsfc.com
Year of Formation – 1929
Chairman – Andy O'Callaghan
Manager – John McDonnell
Stadium – Richmond Park (7,000)
Colours – Red (white sleeves)/white/white
MAJOR HONOURS
League Championship – (7) 1952, 1955, 1956, 1990, 1996, 1998, 1999.
Domestic Cup – (2) 1959, 1961.

Shelbourne FC
Tolka Park
Richmond Road
Drumcondra
Dublin 3
tel – (01) 8375536/8375754
fax – (01) 8375588
website – www.shelbournefc.ie
Year of Formation – 1895
Chairman – Finbarr Flood
Manager – Pat Fenlon
Stadium – Tolka Park (9,681)
Colours – Red/white/red
MAJOR HONOURS
League Championship – (12) 1926, 1929, 1931, 1944, 1947, 1953, 1962, 1992, 2000, 2002, 2003, 2004.
Domestic Cup – (7) 1939, 1960, 1963, 1993, 1996, 1997, 2000.

Sligo Rovers FC
PO Box 275
Sligo
tel – (071) 9171212
fax – (071) 9171331
website – www.sligorovers.com
Year of Formation – 1928
Chairman – Michael Toolan
Manager – Sean Connor
Stadium – The Showgrounds (6,000)
Colours – Red & white stripes/white/red
MAJOR HONOURS
League Championship – (2) 1937, 1977.
Domestic Cup – (2) 1983, 1994.

University College Dublin AFC
Sports Centre
UCD
Belfield
Dublin 4
tel – (01) 7162142
fax – (01) 2698099
website – www.ucdsoccer.com
Year of Formation – 1895
Chairman – Gerry Horkan
Manager – Pete Mahon
Stadium – Belfield Park (4,750)
Colours – Light blue/dark blue/dark blue
MAJOR HONOURS
Domestic Cup – (1) 1984.

Waterford United FC
Top Floor
15 Parnell Street
Waterford
tel – (051) 853222
fax – (051) 853226
website – www.waterford-united.ie
Year of Formation – 1930
Manager – Mike Kerley
Stadium – Regional Sports Centre (5,000)
Colours – Light blue/light blue/white
MAJOR HONOURS
League Championship – (6) 1966, 1968, 1969, 1970, 1972, 1973.
Domestic Cup – (2) 1937, 1980.

The Directory

ROMANIA

Federatia Româna de Fotbal
Casa Fotbalului, Str. Serg.
Serbanica Vasile 12, 73412
Bucuresti
tel – (0040 21) 3250678
fax – (0040 21) 3250679
website – www.frf.ro
email – frf@frf.ro

Year of Formation – 1909
President – Mircea Sandu
Secretary – Adalbert Kassai
Stadium – Lia Manoliu,
Bucharest (61,000)

INTERNATIONAL TOURNAMENT APPEARANCES
World Cup – (7) 1930, 1934, 1938, 1970, 1990 (2nd round), 1994 (qtr-finals), 1998 (2nd round).
European Championship – (3) 1984, 1996, 2000 (qtr-finals).

MAJOR EUROPEAN CLUB HONOURS
Champions Cup/League – (1) Steaua Bucuresti (1986).

Fotbal Club Ceahlaul Piatra Neamt
Str. Eroilor nr.18
610 053 Piatra Neamt
tel – (233) 212702
website – www.fcceahlaul.ro
Year of Formation – 1919
President – Dan Petrescu
Coach – Mihai Stoica
Stadium – Ceahlaul (15,000)
Colours – Yellow & black stripes/black/black

CFR Ecomax Cluj
Str. Republicii nr. 109
400489 Cluj
tel – (0264) 598833
fax – (0264) 406327
website – www.cfr-ecomax.ro
Year of Formation – 1907
President – Arpad Paszkany
Coach – Dorinel Munteanu
Stadium – CFR (10,000)
Colours – Maroon (white trim)/maroon/maroon

Fotbal Club Dinamo Bucuresti
Calea Floreasca 18-20
014461 Bucuresti
tel – (21) 2106974
fax – (21) 2303485
website – www.fcdinamo.ro
Year of Formation – 1948

President – Nicolae Badea
Coach – Mircea Rednic
Stadium – Dinamo (15,300)
Colours – White (red trim)/red/white
MAJOR HONOURS
League Championship – (17) 1955, 1962, 1963, 1964, 1965, 1971, 1973, 1975, 1977, 1982, 1983, 1984, 1990, 1992, 2000, 2002, 2004.
Domestic Cup – (12) 1959, 1964, 1968, 1982, 1984, 1986, 1990, 2000, 2001, 2003, 2004, 2005.

FC Farul Constanta
Str. Primaverii 2
900635 Constanta
tel – (241) 616142
fax – (241) 665891
website – www.fcfarul.ro
Year of Formation – 1949
President – Gheorghe Bosânceanu
Coach – Momcilo Vukotic
Stadium – Stadiu Farul (15,500)
Colours – Blue & white stripes/white/white

CF Gloria-1922 Bistrita
Str. Parcului 3
420035 Bistrita
tel – (263) 212998
fax – (263) 217437
website – www.gloriabistrita.ro
Year of Formation – 1922
President – Jean Padureanu
Coach – Ioan Ovidiu Sabau
Stadium – Gloria (14,500)
Colours – White/blue/white

Sport Club Jiul Petrosani
Str. Lunca nr.100
332061 Petrosani
tel – (0254) 545472
website – www.jiul.home.ro
Year of Formation: 1919
President – Alin Simota
Coach – Florin Marin
Stadium – Jiul (25,000)
Colours – White/black/white
MAJOR HONOURS
Domestic Cup – (1) 1974

Fotbal Club National Bucuresti
Str. Dr. Lister 37
05041 Bucuresti
tel – (21) 4109220
fax – (21) 4106606
website – www.nationalfc.ro
Year of Formation – 1944
President – Constantin Iacov
Coach – Marin Duna

Stadium – Cotroceni (14,542)
Colours – Sky blue (white trim)/white/white
MAJOR HONOURS
Domestic Cup – (1) 1960.

Fotbal Club Otelul Galati
Str. Anghel Saligny 2
800686 Galati
tel – (236) 464677
fax – (236) 463898
Year of Formation – 1964
President – Marius Stan
Coach – Petre Grigoras
Stadaium – Otelul (13,500)
Colours – Red & blue stripes/blue/red

Pandurii Târgu Jiu
Str. Victorei nr. 22
210165 Târgu Jiu
tel – (0253) 223588
website – www.pandurii-tg-jiu.ro
Year of Formation – 1974
President – Marin Condescu
Coach – Eugen Neagoe
Stadium – Municipal (15,000)
Colours – Light blue/white/light blue

Fotbal Club 2005 Pitesti
Str. Armand Calinescu 15
110047 Pitesti
tel – (248) 217214
fax – (248) 214350
website – www.fcarges.net
Year of Formation – 1953
President – Cornel Penescu
Coach – Giuseppe Giannini
Stadium – Nicolae Dobrin (15,500)
Colours – Violet (white trim)/violet/violet
MAJOR HONOURS
League Championship – (2) 1972, 1979.

Fotbal Club Politehnica Iasi
Aleea Grigore Ghica Voda nr.12-24
700506 Iasi
tel – (0232) 213018
fax – (0232) 213796
Year of Formation – 1945
President – Sorin Boca
Coach – Ionut Popa
Stadium – Emil Alexandrescu (12,500)
Colours – Light blue & white stripes/light blue/light blue

FC Universitar Politehnica Timisoara
bd. Regele Ferdinand I nr.2
300006 Timisoara
tel – (256) 309852

The Directory

fax – (256) 309852
website – www.politimisoara.com
Year of Formation – 2002
President – Marian Iancu
Coach – Sorin Cîrtu
Stadium – Dan Paltinisanu (40,000)
Colours – Violet (white trim)/white/violet

Fotbal Club Rapid Bucuresti

Calea Bd. Bucurestii Noi 170
012369 Bucuresti
tel – (21) 2234490
fax – (21) 2203125
website – www.rapid.pcnet.ro
Year of Formation – 1923
President – Dinu Gheorghe
Coach – Razvan Lucescu
Stadium – Valentin Stanescu (19,100)
Colours – Maroon/white/white
MAJOR HONOURS
League Championship – (3) 1967, 1999, 2003.
Domestic Cup – (12) 1935, 1937, 1938, 1939, 1940, 1941, 1942, 1972, 1975, 1998, 2002, 2006.

Fotbal Club Steaua Bucuresti

B-dul Ghencea nr. 45
050726 Bucuresti
tel – (21) 4114656
fax – (21) 4034252
website – www.steauafc.ro
Year of Formation – 1947
President – Mihai Stoica
Coach – Cosmin Olaroiu
Stadium – Steaua (27,063)
Colours – Red (blue trim)/red/red
MAJOR HONOURS
League Championship – (23) 1951, 1952, 1953, 1956, 1960, 1961, 1968, 1976, 1978, 1985, 1986, 1987, 1988, 1989, 1993, 1994, 1995, 1996, 1997, 1998, 2001, 2005, 2006.
Domestic Cup – (21) 1949, 1950, 1951, 1952, 1955, 1962, 1966, 1967, 1969, 1970, 1971, 1976, 1979, 1985, 1987, 1988, 1989, 1992, 1996, 1997, 1999.
European Champions Cup – (1) 1986.
European Super Cup – (1) 1986.

FC Unirea Urziceni

Str. Buzaului nr.50
Urziceni
tel – (243) 255925
website – www.fcunirea.ro
President – Adrian Alexandrescu
Coach – Costel Orac
Stadium – Tineretului (7,000)
Colours – White (light blue sleeves)/white/white

FC Universitatea Craiova

Str. Sfântul Dumitru nr.1
Craiova
tel – (251) 414726
website – fcuniversitatea.ro
Year of Formation – 1948
President – Adrian Mititelu
Coach – Ovidiu Stînga
Stadium – Ion Oblemenco (28,000)
Colours – White (blue trim)/blue/white
MAJOR HONOURS
League Championship – (4) 1974, 1980, 1981, 1991.
Domestic Cup – (6) 1977, 1978, 1981, 1983, 1991, 1993.

UTA Arad

Calea Aurel Vlaicu nr.39
Arad
tel – (257) 289204
website – www.uta-arad.ro
Year of Formation – 1945
Coach – Marius Lacatus
Stadium – UTA (12,500)
Colours – Red/white/red
MAJOR HONOURS
League Championship – (6) 1947, 1948, 1950, 1954, 1969, 1970.
Domestic Cup – (2) 1948, 1953.

Fotbal Club Vaslui

Str. Decebal nr.1
730227 Vaslui
tel – (0235) 316097
fax – (0235) 316097
website – www.fcvaslui.ro
Year of Formation – 2002
President – Octavian Apetrei
Coach – Gheorghe Multescu
Stadium – Municipal (11,000)
Colours – Green/yellow/green

RUSSIA

Russian Football Union
Luzhnetskaja Naberezhnaja 8,
119 871 Moskva
tel – (007 495) 2010834
fax – (007 495) 2011303
website – www.rfs.ru
email – rfs@rinet.ru

Year of Formation – 1992
President – Vitaliy Mutko
Secretary – Vladimir Radionov
Stadium – Luzhniki, Moscow (84,745)

INTERNATIONAL HONOURS*
European Championship – (1) 1960.

INTERNATIONAL TOURNAMENT APPEARANCES*
World Cup – (9) 1958 (qtr-finals), 1962 (qtr-finals), 1966 (4th), 1970 (qtr-finals), 1982 (2nd phase), 1986 (2nd round), 1990, 1994, 2002.
European Championship – (8) 1960 (Winners), 1964 (runners-up), 1968 (4th), 1972 (runners-up), 1988 (runners-up), 1992, 1996, 2004.

(* before 1992 as USSR; 1992 as CIS)

MAJOR EUROPEAN CLUB HONOURS
UEFA Cup – (1) CSKA Moskva (2005).

Amkar Perm

Kuibysheva Str. 95
614010 Perm
tel – (3222) 440281/457769
fax – (3222) 440281
website – www.amkar.ru
Year of Formation – 1994
President – Valeriy Chuprakov
Coach – Sergei Oborin
Stadium – Zvezda (12,500)
Colours – Red/black/white

CSKA (Centralnyi Sportivnyi Klub Armii) Moskva

Leningradskiy prospekt 39 A
125167 Moskva
tel – (495) 6120780/6132538
fax – (495) 6132809
website – www.cska-football.ru
Year of Formation – 1923
President – Yevgeniy Giner
Coach – Valeriy Gazzayev
Stadium – Dinamo (36,800)
Colours – Red/blue/blue
MAJOR HONOURS
League Championship – (2) 2003, 2005.
League Championship (USSR) – (7) 1946, 1947, 1948, 1950, 1951, 1970, 1991.
Domestic Cup – (3) 2002, 2005, 2006.
Domestic Cup (USSR) – (5) 1945, 1948, 1951, 1955, 1991.
UEFA Cup – (1) 2005.

Dinamo Moskva

Leningradskiy prospekt 36
125167 Moskva
tel – (495) 6127172
fax – (495) 6131612
website – www.fcdynamo.ru
Year of Formation – 1923

The Directory

General Director – Vladimir Zavarzin
Coach – Yuriy Syomin
Stadium – Dinamo (36,800)
Colours – White (blue trim)/blue/white
MAJOR HONOURS
League Championship (USSR) – (11) 1936, 1937, 1940, 1945, 1949, 1954, 1955, 1957, 1959, 1963, 1976 (spring).
Domestic Cup – (1) 1995.
Domestic Cup (USSR) – (6) 1937, 1953, 1967, 1970, 1977, 1984.

Krylya Sovetov Samara
Shushenskaya Str. 50A
443 011 Samara
tel – (846) 3351635/3355441
fax – (846) 22219840
website – www.kc-camara.ru
Year of Formation – 1942
President – Alexandr Baranovskiy
Coach – Gadzhi Gadzhiyev
Stadium – Metallurg (24,325)
Colours – Blue/blue/blue

Lokomotiv Moskva
B. Cherkizovskaya Str. 125A
107553 Moskva
tel – (495) 5003102
fax – (495) 5003070
website – www.fclm.ru
Year of Formation – 1923
President – Valeriy Filatov
Coach – Slavoljub Muslin
Stadium – Lokomotiv (29,300)
Colours – Red & green stripes/red/red
MAJOR HONOURS
League Championship – (2) 2002, 2004.
Domestic Cup – (4) 1996, 1997, 2000, 2001.
Domestic Cup (USSR) – (2) 1936, 1957.

Luch-Energia Vladivostok
Ovchinnikova Str. 26a
690048 Vladivostok
tel – (4232) 335095
fax – (4232) 332808
website – www.luch-vlad.ru
Year of Formation – 1958
General Director – Alexandr Kostenko
Coach – Sergei Pavlov
Stadium – Dinamo (10,200)
Colours – Yellow/blue/yellow

FK Moskva
Tatarskiy per. 4a
113184 Moskva
tel – (095) 5444366
fax – (095) 5444367

website – www.fcmoscow.ru
Year of Formation – 1997
General Director – Yuriy Belous
Coach – Leonid Slutskiy
Stadium – Eduard Streltsov (13,200)
Colours – Black (white & red trim)/white/white

FK Rostov-na-Donu
Sholokhava Str. 31
344029 Rostov-na-Donu
tel – (8632) 519539
fax – (8632) 519539
website – www.fc-rostov.ru
Year of Formation – 1930
General Director – Rokhus Shokh
Coach – Sergei Balakhnin
Stadium – Olimp-XXI vek (18,500)
Colours – Blue/yellow/yellow

Rubin Kazan
Krylova Str. 2
420036 Kazan
tel – (843) 5711724
fax – (843) 5711424
website – www.rubin-kazan.ru
Year of Formation – 1936
President – Alexandr Gusev
Coach – Kurban Berdyyev
Stadium – Centralnyi (25,000)
Colours – Red/red/red

Saturn Ramenskoe
Gorodskoi park
Stadium Saturn
140103 Ramenskoe
Moskovskaya obl.
tel – (49646) 79372
fax – (49646) 79595
website – www.saturn-fc.ru
Year of Formation – 1946
General Director – Mikhail Vorontsov
Coach – Vladimír Weiss
Stadium – Saturn (16,500)
Colours – Blue (white trim)/blue/blue

Shinnik Yaroslavl
Sovetskaya Str. 69
150003 Yaroslavl
tel – (4852) 720566
fax – (4852) 720626
website – www.shinnik.yar.ru
Year of Formation – 1957
President – Anatoliy Lsitsyn
Coach – Oleg Dolmatov
Stadium – Shinnik (22,984)
Colours – Black/blue/blue

Spartak Moskva
Pokrovsky bul'var, dom 3, str. 1
109028 Moskva
tel – (095) 9808640
fax – (095) 9808641
website – www.spartak.com
Year of Formation – 1922
General Director – Sergei Shavlo
Coach – Vladimir Fedotov
Stadium – Luzhniki (84,745) or Eduard Streltsov (13,200)
Colours – Red (white trim)/white/red
MAJOR HONOURS
League Championship – (9) 1992, 1993, 1994, 1996, 1997, 1998, 1999, 2000, 2001.
League Championship (USSR) – (12) 1936, 1938, 1939, 1952, 1953, 1956, 1958, 1962, 1969, 1979, 1987, 1989.
Domestic Cup – (3) 1994, 1998, 2003.
Domestic Cup (USSR) – (10) 1938, 1939, 1946, 1947, 1950, 1958, 1963, 1965, 1971, 1992.

Spartak Nalchik
Shogenzukova Str. 1
360051 Nalchik
tel – (8662) 425267
fax – (8662) 473520
website – www.spartak-nalchik.ru
Year of Formation – 1935
President – Khazratali Berdov
Coach – Yuriy Krasnozhan
Stadium – Spartak (15,500)
Colours – White (red trim)/red/white

Tom Tomsk
Belinskogo Str. 15/1
634050 Tomsk
tel – (3822) 527967
fax – (3812) 528010
website – www.football.tomsk.ru
Year of Formation – 1957
General Director – Yuriy Stepanov
Coach – Valeriy Petrakov
Stadium – Trud (7000)
Colours – White (green trim)/white/white

Torpedo Moskva
Luzhniki 24
119048 Moskva
tel – (495) 6370501
fax – (495) 2460105
website – www.torpedo.ru
Year of Formation – 1924
General Director – Yuriy Mishin
Coach – Sergei Petrenko
Stadium – Luzhniki (84,745)
Colours – White (black trim)/black/white

The Directory

MAJOR HONOURS
League Championship (USSR) – (3) 1960, 1965, 1976 (autumn).
Domestic Cup – (1) 1993.
Domestic Cup (USSR) – (6) 1949, 1952, 1960, 1968, 1972, 1986.

Zenit Sankt-Peterburg
Nekrasova Str. 3/5
191104 Sankt Peterburg
tel – (812) 2750330
fax – (812) 2750333
website – www.fc-zenit.ru
Year of Formation – 1925
President – Sergei Fursenko
Coach – Dick Advocaat
Stadium – Petrovskiy (21,838)
Colours – Blue/blue/blue
MAJOR HONOURS
League Championship (USSR) – (1) 1984.
Domestic Cup – (1) 1999.
Domestic Cup (USSR) – (1) 1944.

SAN MARINO

Federazione Sammarinese Giuoco Calcio
Via Campo dei Giudei 14, 47899 San Marino
tel – (00378 054) 990515
fax – (00378 054) 992348
website – www.fsgc.sm
email – fsgc@omniway.sm

Year of Formation – 1931
President – Giorgio Crescentini
Secretary – Luciano Casadei
Stadium – Olimpico, Serravalle (5,387)

SCOTLAND

The Scottish Football Association
Hampden Park, Glasgow G42 9AY
tel – (0044 141) 6166000
fax – (0044 141) 6166001
website – www.scottishfa.co.uk
email – info@scottishfa.co.uk

Year of Formation – 1873
Chairman – John McGinn
Secretary – David Taylor
Stadium – Hampden Park, Glasgow (52,046)

INTERNATIONAL TOURNAMENT APPEARANCES
World Cup – (8) 1954, 1958, 1974, 1978, 1982, 1986, 1990, 1998.
European Championship – (2) 1992, 1996.

MAJOR EUROPEAN CLUB HONOURS
Champions Cup/League – (1) Celtic (1967)
Cup-winners Cup – (2) Rangers (1972), Aberdeen (1983).

Aberdeen FC
Pittodrie Stadium
Pittodrie Street
Aberdeen AB24 5QH
tel – (01224) 650400
fax – (01224) 644173
website – www.afc.co.uk
Year of Formation – 1903
Chairman – Stewart Milne
Manager – Jimmy Calderwood
Stadium – Pittodrie Stadium (22,199)
Colours – Red/red/red
MAJOR HONOURS
League Championship – (4) 1955, 1980, 1984, 1985.
Scottish Cup – (7) 1947, 1970, 1982, 1983, 1984, 1986, 1990.
League Cup – (5) 1956, 1977, 1986, 1990, 1996.
European Cup-winners Cup – (1) 1983
European Super Cup – (1) 1983.

Celtic FC
Celtic Park
Glasgow G40 3RE
tel – (0871) 2261888
fax – (0141) 5518106
website – www.celticfc.net
Year of Formation – 1888
Chairman – Brian Quinn
Manager – Gordon Strachan
Stadium – Celtic Park (60,832)
Colours – Green & white hoops/white/white
MAJOR HONOURS
League Championship – (40) 1893, 1894, 1896, 1898, 1905, 1906, 1907, 1908, 1909, 1910, 1914, 1915, 1916, 1917, 1919, 1922, 1926, 1936, 1938, 1954, 1966, 1967, 1968, 1969, 1970, 1971, 1972, 1973, 1974, 1977, 1979, 1981, 1982, 1986, 1988, 1998, 2001, 2002, 2004, 2006.
Scottish Cup – (33) 1892, 1899, 1900, 1904, 1907, 1908, 1911, 1912, 1914, 1923, 1925, 1927, 1931, 1933, 1937, 1951, 1954, 1965, 1967, 1969, 1971, 1972, 1974, 1975, 1977, 1980, 1985, 1988, 1989, 1995, 2001, 2004, 2005.
League Cup – (13) 1957, 1958, 1966, 1967, 1968, 1969, 1970, 1975, 1983, 1998, 2000, 2001, 2006.
European Champions Cup – (1) 1967.

Dundee United FC
Tannadice Park
Tannadice Street
Dundee DD3 7JW
tel – (01382) 833166
fax – (01382) 889398
website – www.dundeeunitedfc.co.uk
Year of Formation – 1909
Chairman – Eddie Thompson
Manager – Craig Brewster
Stadium – Tannadice Park (14,209)
Colours – Tangerine/black/tangerine
MAJOR HONOURS
League Championship – (1) 1983.
Scottish Cup – (1) 1994.
League Cup – (2) 1980, 1981.

Dunfermline Athletic FC
East End Park
Halbeath Road
Dunfermline
Fife KY12 7RB
tel – (01383) 724295
fax – (01383) 723468
website – www.dafc.co.uk
Year of Formation – 1885
Chairman – John Yorkston
Manager – Jim Leishman
Stadium – East End Park (11,998)
Colours – Black (white candy stripes & trim)/white/white
MAJOR HONOURS
Scottish Cup – (2) 1961, 1968.

Falkirk FC
The Falkirk Stadium
Westfield
Falkirk FK2 9DX
tel – (01324) 624121
fax – (01324) 612418
website – www.falkirkfc.co.uk
Year of Formation – 1876
Chairman – Campbell Christie
Manager – John Hughes
Stadium – The Falkirk Stadium (6,122)
Colours – Dark blue (red trim)/white/red
MAJOR HONOURS
Scottish Cup – (2) 1913, 1957.

Heart of Midlothian FC
Tynecastle Stadium
Gorgie Road
Edinburgh EH11 2NL
tel – (0131) 2007200
fax – (0131) 2007222
website – www.heartsfc.co.uk

The Directory

Year of Formation – 1874
Chairman – Roman Romanov
Manager – Valdas Ivanauskas
Stadium – Tynecastle Stadium (18,000)
Colours – Maroon (white trim)/white/maroon
MAJOR HONOURS
League Championship – (4) 1895, 1897, 1958, 1960.
Scottish Cup – (7) 1891, 1896, 1901, 1906, 1956, 1998, 2006.
League Cup – (4) 1955, 1959, 1960, 1963.

Hibernian FC
Easter Road Stadium
12 Albion Road
Edinburgh EH7 5QG
tel – (0131) 6612159
fax – (0131) 6596488
website – www.hibernianfc.co.uk
Year of Formation – 1875
Chairman – Rod Petrie
Manager – Tony Mowbray
Stadium – Easter Road (17,400)
Colours – Green (white sleeves)/green/green
MAJOR HONOURS
League Championship – (4) 1903, 1948, 1951, 1952.
Scottish Cup – (2) 1887, 1902.
League Cup – (2) 1973, 1992.

Inverness Caledonian Thistle FC
Caledonian Stadium
East Longman
Inverness IV1 1FF
tel – (01463) 222880
fax – (01463) 715816
Year of Formation – 1994
Chairman – Alan Savage
Manager – Charlie Christie
Coach – Malcolm Thomson
Stadium – Tulloch Caledonian Stadium (7,500)
Colours – Red & blue stripes (blue sleeves)/blue/blue

Kilmarnock FC
Rugby Park
Rugby Road
Kilmarnock KA1 2DP
tel – (01563) 545300
fax – (01563) 522181
website – www.kilmarnockfc.co.uk
Year of Formation – 1869
Chairman – Michael Johnston
Manager – Jim Jefferies
Stadium – Rugby Park (18,128)
Colours – Blue & white stripes/blue/blue
MAJOR HONOURS
League Championship – (1) 1965.
Scottish Cup – (3) 1920, 1929, 1997.

Motherwell FC
Fir Park
Fir Park Street
Motherwell ML1 2QN
tel – (01698) 333333
fax – (01698) 338001
website – www.motherwellfc.co.uk
Year of Formation – 1886
Chairman – John Boyle
Manager – Maurice Malpas
Stadium – Fir Park (13,742)
Colours – Amber (claret band)/white/claret
MAJOR HONOURS
League Championship – (1) 1932.
Scottish Cup – (2) 1952, 1991.
League Cup – (1) 1951.

Rangers FC
Ibrox Stadium
150 Edmiston Drive
Glasgow G51 2XD
tel – (0870) 6001972
fax – (0870) 6001978
website – www.rangers.co.uk
Year of Formation – 1872
Chairman – David E. Murray
Manager – Paul Le Guen
Stadium – Ibrox Stadium (50,444)
Colours – Blue/white/black
MAJOR HONOURS
League Championship – (51) 1891, 1899, 1900, 1901, 1902, 1911, 1912, 1913, 1918, 1920, 1921, 1923, 1924, 1925, 1927, 1928, 1929, 1930, 1931, 1933, 1934, 1935, 1937, 1939, 1947, 1949, 1950, 1953, 1956, 1957, 1959, 1961, 1963, 1964, 1975, 1976, 1978, 1987, 1989, 1990, 1991, 1992, 1993, 1994, 1995, 1996, 1997, 1999, 2000, 2003, 2005.
Scottish Cup – (31) 1894, 1897, 1898, 1903, 1928, 1930, 1932, 1934, 1935, 1936, 1948, 1949, 1950, 1953, 1960, 1962, 1963, 1964, 1966, 1973, 1976, 1978, 1979, 1981, 1992, 1993, 1996, 1999, 2000, 2002, 2003.
League Cup – (24) 1947, 1949, 1961, 1962, 1964, 1965, 1971, 1976, 1978, 1979, 1982, 1984, 1985, 1987, 1988, 1989, 1991, 1993, 1994, 1997, 1999, 2002, 2003, 2005.
European Cup-winners Cup – (1) 1972.

St. Mirren FC
St. Mirren Park
Love Street
Paisley PA3 2EA
tel – (0141) 8892558
fax – (0141) 8486444
website – www.saintmirren.net
Year of Formation – 1877
Chairman – Stewart Gilmour
Manager – Gus MacPherson
Stadium – St. Mirren Park (10,752)
Colours – Black & white stripes/white/white
MAJOR HONOURS
Scottish Cup – (3) 1926, 1959, 1987.

SERBIA

Fudbalski Savez Srbije
Terazije 35, 11000 Beograd
tel – (00381 11) 3221443
fax – (00381 11) 3222162
website – www.fss.org.yu
email – office@fss.org.yu

Year of Formation – 1919
President – Zvezdan Terzic
Secretary – Miroljub Rajic

INTERNATIONAL TOURNAMENT APPEARANCES*
World Cup – (10) 1930 (semi-finals), 1950, 1954 (qtr-finals), 1958 (qtr-finals), 1962 (4th), 1974 (2nd phase), 1982, 1990 (qtr-finals), 1998 (2nd round), 2006.
European Championship – (5) 1960 (runners-up), 1968 (runners-up), 1976 (4th), 1984, 2000 (qtr-finals).

(*before 2006 as Yugoslavia; 2006 as Serbia & Montenegro)

MAJOR EUROPEAN CLUB HONOURS
Champions Cup/League – (1) Crvena Zvezda Beograd (1991).

FK Banat Zrenjanin
Karadjordjev trg 100
23000 Zrenjanin
tel – (023) 511595
fax – (023) 511595
Year of Formation – 1938
President – Mirko Vucurevic
Coach – Nikola Rakojevic
Stadium – Karadjordjev park (16,000)
Colours – Red/red/red

FK Bezanija Beograd
Vojvodanska 68
11000 Novi Beograd
tel – (011) 2278644
fax – (011) 2278644
Year of Formation – 1921
President – Goran Mijatovic
Coach – Dragoljub Bekvalac

The Directory

Stadium – Kraj bezanijske crkve (5,500)
Colours – Blue & red stripes/blue/blue

FK Borac Cacak
Gradski Bedem 6
32000 Cacak
tel – (032) 222481
fax – (032) 225458
Year of Formation – 1926
President – Predrag Teofilovic
Coach – Radovan Curcic
Stadium – Gradski kraj Morave (6,000)
Colours – Red & white hoops/white/red

FK Crvena Zvezda
Ljutice Bogdana 1a
11000 Beograd
tel – (011) 3672060
fax – (011) 3672070
website – www.fc-redstar.net
Year of Formation – 1945
President – Dragan Stojkovic
Coach – Dusan Bajevic
Stadium – Crvena Zvezde (51,398)
Colours – Red & white stripes/white/red
MAJOR HONOURS
League Championship – (24) 1951, 1953, 1956, 1957, 1959, 1960, 1964, 1968, 1969, 1970, 1973, 1977, 1980, 1981, 1984, 1988, 1990, 1991, 1992, 1995, 2000, 2001, 2004, 2006.
Domestic Cup – (21) 1948, 1949, 1950, 1958, 1959, 1964, 1968, 1970, 1971, 1982, 1985, 1990, 1993, 1995, 1996, 1997, 1999, 2000, 2002, 2004, 2006.
European Champions Cup – (1) 1991.
World Club Cup – (1) 1991.

FK Hajduk Rodic MB
Svetozara Markovica 8
25230 Kula
tel – (025) 722812
fax – (025) 722814
website – www.fkhajduk.com
Year of Formation – 1925
President – Stevan Milisavljevic
Coach – Nebojsa Vucicevic
Stadium – Hajduk (11,000)
Colours – White/white/white

FK Mladost Apatin
Dunavska obala bb
25260 Apatin
tel – (025) 773994
fax – (025) 773685
Year of Formation – 1928
President – Milan Trtica
Coach – Dragi Bogic

Stadium – SC Rade Svilar (5,000)
Colours – Red/red/red

OFK Beograd
Mije Kovacevica 10
11000 Beograd
tel – (011) 2765425/2767045
fax – (011) 2762364
website – www.ofkbeograd.co.yu
Year of Formation – 1945
President – Vladimir Bulatovic
Coach – Slobodan Krcmarevic
Stadium – Omladinski (13,912)
Colours – Pale blue & white stripes/pale blue/pale blue
MAJOR HONOURS
Domestic Cup – (4) 1953, 1958, 1962, 1966.

FK Partizan
Humska 1
11000 Beograd
tel – (011) 3227181/3229793
fax – (011) 3229906
website – www.partizan.co.yu
Year of Formation – 1945
President – Ivan Curkovic
Coach – Miodrag Jesic
Stadium – Partizan (30,176)
Colours – Black & white stripes/black/black
MAJOR HONOURS
League Championship – (19) 1947, 1949, 1961, 1962, 1963, 1965, 1976, 1978, 1983, 1986, 1987, 1993, 1994, 1996, 1997, 1999, 2002, 2003, 2005.
Domestic Cup – (9) 1947, 1952, 1954, 1957, 1989, 1992, 1994, 1998, 2001.

FK Smederevo
Goranska 55
11300 Smederevo
tel – (026) 223319/224509
fax – (026) 223030
website – www.fksmederevo.com
Year of Formation – 1924
President – Bojan Bojkovic
Coach – Mihajlo Ivanovic
Stadium – Gradski (16,700)
Colours – Light blue/light blue/light blue
MAJOR HONOURS
Domestic Cup – (1) 2003.

FK Vojvodina
Ignjata Pavlasa 8
21000 Novi Sad
tel – (021) 421687/8
fax – (021) 429270
website – www.fcvojvodina.co.yu
Year of Formation – 1914

President – Aleksandar Jevtic
Coach – Zoran Maric
Stadium – Gradski stadion Karadjorde (15,800)
Colours – Red & white halves/white/white
MAJOR HONOURS
League Championship – (2) 1968, 1989.

FK Vozdovac Beograd
Zaplanjaska 32
11000 Beograd
tel – (011) 2491045
fax – (011) 2491045
Year of Formation – 1912
President – Branislav Pavlovic
Coach – Tomislav Sivic
Stadium – Vozdovac (5,000)
Colours – White/white/white

FK Zemun
Ugrinovacka 80
11080 Zemun
tel – (011) 612949/618889
fax – (011) 666197
website – www.fkzemun.co.yu
Year of Formation – 1946
President – Sreten Karic
Coach – Miodrag Martac
Stadium – Gradski (15,000)
Colours – Blue & green stripes/blue/blue

SLOVAKIA

Slovensky Futbalovy Zvaz
Junácka 6, 83280 Bratislava
tel – (00421 2) 49249151
fax – (00421 2) 49249554
website – www.futbalsfz.sk
email – sfzsec@sztk.sk

Year of Formation – 1990
President – Frantisek Laurinec
Secretary – Dusan Tittel
Stadium – Tehelne pole, Bratislava (30,087)

MAJOR EUROPEAN CLUB HONOURS
Cup-winners Cup – (1) Slovan Bratislava (1969).

FC Artmedia Bratislava
Krasovského 1
851 01 Bratislava
tel – (02) 62250115
fax – (02) 62250043
Year of Formation – 1898
President – Vladimír Bajan
Coach – Jozef Adamec
Stadium – Za starym mostom (10,500)

The Directory

Colours — Black & white broad stripes/white/white
MAJOR HONOURS
League Championship — (1) 2005.
Domestic Cup — (1) 2004.

FK ZTS Dubnica
Sportovcov 655
018 41 Dubnica nad Váhom
tel — (042) 4420025/4421906
fax — (042) 4420033
Year of Formation — 1926
President — Ivan Nemeckay
Coach — Peter Gergely
Stadium — ZTS (10,000)
Colours — Blue (white sleeves)/blue/blue

FK Dukla Banská Bystrica
Stadion SNP
Stiavnicky
974 01 Banská Bystrica
tel — (048) 4230444
fax — (048) 4230444
Year of Formation — 1965
President — Ján Kovácik
Coach — Dusan Radolsky
Stadium — SNP (11,500)
Colours — Red (two white hoops & trim)/red/red
MAJOR HONOURS
Domestic Cup — (1) 2005.

ASK Inter Slovnaft Bratislava
Junácka 10
832 84 Bratislava
tel — (02) 44371007
fax — (02) 44451341
Year of Formation — 1940
President — Jaroslav Linkes
Coach — Ladislav Jurkemik
Stadium — Inter (15,000)
Colours — Yellow (black trim)/black/black
MAJOR HONOURS
League Championship (Czechoslovakia) — (1) 1959.
League Championship — (2) 2000, 2001.
Domestic Cup — (4) 1984, 1995, 2000, 2001.

MFK Kosice
Cermelská 1
040 01 Kosice
tel — (055) 7994788
fax — (055) 7994788
website — www.fcsteeltrans.sk
Year of Formation — 2005
President — Blazej Podolak
Coach — Ján Kozák
Stadium — MFK Kosice (9,200)

Colours — Blue (yellow sleeves)/blue/blue

FC Nitra
Jesenského 4
949 01 Nitra
tel — (037) 7414958
fax — (037) 7414959
Year of Formation — 1919
President — Vladimir Vikor
Coach — Ivan Galád
Stadium — FC Nitra (11,384)
Colours — Blue/blue/blue

MFK SCP Ruzomberok
Zilinská cesta 21
034 01 Ruzomberok
tel — (044) 4322506
fax — (044) 4323589
Year of Formation — 1906
President — Vladimír Lajciak
Coach — Frantisek Komnacky
Stadium — SCP (5,000)
Colours — Orange/black/black
MAJOR HONOURS
League Championship — (1) 2006.
Domestic Cup — (1) 2006.

FC Senec
Rybárska 29
903 01 Senec
tel — (02) 45650079
fax — (02) 45650081
website — www.fcsenec.sk
Year of Formation — 1991
President — Daniel Jammer
Coach — Jozef Valovic
Stadium — FC Senec (3,264)
Colours — Orange/white/orange

SK Slovan Bratislava
Viktora Tegelhoffa 4
831 04 Bratislava
tel — (02) 44636363
fax — (02) 44636365
website — www.skslovan.com
Year of Formation — 1919
President — Ludovit Cernak
Coach — Jozef Jankech
Stadium — SK Slovan (30,000)
Colours — Blue/blue/blue
MAJOR HONOURS
European Cup-winners Cup — (1) 1969.
League Championship (Czechoslovakia) — (8) 1949, 1950, 1951, 1955, 1970, 1974, 1975, 1992.
League Championship — (7) 1940, 1941, 1942, 1944, 1994, 1995, 1996.
Domestic Cup (Czechoslovakia) — (5) 1962, 1963, 1968, 1974, 1982.
Domestic Cup — (9) 1970, 1972, 1974, 1976, 1982, 1983, 1989, 1994, 1997.

FC Spartak Trnava
Sportova 1
917 60 Trnava
tel — (033) 5503804
fax — (033) 5503806
Year of Formation — 1923
President — Jozef Bachraty
Coach — Jozef Bubenko
Stadium — Anton Malatinsky (18,500)
Colours — Red & black stripes/black/black
MAJOR HONOURS
League Championship (Czechoslovakia) — (5) 1968, 1969, 1971, 1972, 1973.
Domestic Cup (Czechoslovakia) — (4) 1967, 1971, 1975, 1986.
Domestic Cup — (5) 1971, 1975, 1986, 1991, 1998.

AS Trencín
Mládeznicka 1
911 01 Trencín
tel — (032) 7441137
fax — (032) 7441137
Year of Formation — 1992
President — Robert Rybnicek
Coach — Ladislav Hudec
Stadium — Na Sihoti (16,000)
Colours — Red (white trim)/red/red

MSK Zilina
Sportova 9
010 01 Zilina
tel — (041) 5626955
fax — (041) 5626955
Year of Formation — 1908
President — Jozef Michalko
Coach — Pavel Vrba
Stadium — Pod Dubnom (12,500)
Colours — Yellow/green/yellow
MAJOR HONOURS
League Championship — (3) 2002, 2003, 2004.

SLOVENIA

Nogometna zveza Slovenija
Cerinova 4, PP 3986, 1001 Ljubljana
tel — (00386 1) 5300400
fax — (003861) 5300410
website — www.nzs.si
email — nzs@nzs.si

Year of Formation — 1920
President — Rudolf Zavrl

The Directory

Secretary – Dane Jost
Stadium – Petrol Arena, Celje (12,000)

INTERNATIONAL TOURNAMENT APPEARANCES
World Cup – (1) 2002.
European Championship – (1) 2000.

NK Bela Krajina
Pri stadionu 2
8340 Crnomelj
tel – (07) 3052500
fax – (07) 3052500
Year of Formation – 1965
President – Andrej Fabjan
Coach – Ivan Buljan
Stadium – Crnomelj (3,000)
Colours – White (blue trim)/white/white

NK Domzale
Kopaliska 4
1230 Domzale
tel – (01) 7226550
fax – (01) 7210373
website – www.nogometniklub-domzale.si
Year of Formation – 1948
President – Stane Orazem
Coach – Slavisa Stojanovic
Stadium – Mestni stadion (3,000)
Colours – Yellow/yellow/yellow

NK Drava
Cuckova ulica 7
2250 Ptuj
tel – (02) 7797431
fax – (02) 7797431
website – www.nkptuj-klub.si
Year of Formation – 1933
President – Robert Furjan
Coach – Milko Djurovski
Stadium – Ptuj (4,000)
Colours – Blue/blue/blue

NK Factor
Tesovnikova 54
1000 Ljubljana
tel – (31) 648388
fax – (01) 5683831
Year of Formation – 1985
President – Lado Kreft
Coach – Tomaz Kavcic
Stadium – Jezica (2,000)
Colours – White/white/white

ND Gorica
Bazoviska 4
pp 183
5000 Nova Gorica
tel – (05) 3334086
fax – (05) 3334087
website – www.nd-gorica.com
Year of Formation – 1938
President – Viliam Brea
Coach – Pavel Pinni
Stadium – Nova Gorica (5,000)
Colours – Blue & white stripes/blue/blue
MAJOR HONOURS
League Championship – (4) 1996, 2004, 2005, 2006.
Domestic Cup – (2) 2001, 2002.

NK Koper
Ljubijanska cesta 2
6000 Koper
tel – (05) 6395050
fax – (05) 6313101
website – www.nkkoper.net
Year of Formation – 1950
President – Bojan Aver
Coach – Borut Jarc
Stadium – Bonifika (10,000)
Colours – Yellow/blue/blue
MAJOR HONOURS
League Championship – (2) 1985, 1988.
Domestic Cup – (2) 1991, 2006.

NK Maribor
Mladinska 29
2000 Maribor
tel – (02) 2284700
fax – (02) 2284720
website – www.nkmaribor.com
Year of Formation – 1958
President – Rudi Turk
Coach – Marijan Pusnik
Stadium – Ljudski vrt (15,000)
Colours – Purple/purple/purple & yellow
MAJOR HONOURS
League Championship – (12) 1961, 1976, 1982, 1984, 1986, 1997, 1998, 1999, 2000, 2001, 2002, 2003.
Domestic Cup – (18) 1965, 1966, 1968, 1973, 1974, 1978, 1980, 1982, 1984, 1986, 1987, 1989, 1990, 1992, 1994, 1997, 1999, 2004.

NK Nafta
Kolodvorska 7
Pp 46
9220 Lendava
tel – (02) 5772288
fax – (02) 5772289
website – www.nogometniklub-lendava.si
Year of Formation – 1945
President – Mirko Horvat
Coach – Vojislav Simeunovic
Stadium – Nafta (5,000)
Colours – Blue/blue/white

NK Primorje
Goriska cesta 44
pp 3
5270 Ajdovscina
tel – (05) 3689254
fax – (05) 3661042
Year of Formation – 1924
President – Dusan Cernigoj
Coach – Bojan Prasnikar
Stadium – Primorje (5,000)
Colours – Red & black stripes/black/black
MAJOR HONOURS
Domestic Cup – (1) 1976.

NK CMC Publikum
Cesta na grad 12
3000 Celje
tel – (03) 5482250
fax – (03) 5482251
website – www.publikum.com
Year of Formation – 1946
President – Marjan Vengust
Coach – Jani Zilnik
Stadium – Petrol Arena (12,000)
Colours – Yellow/blue/blue
MAJOR HONOURS
League Championship – (1) 1964.
Domestic Cup – (2) 1964, 2005.

SPAIN

Real Federación Española de Fútbol
Av Ramón y Cajal s/n, 28230 Las Rozas (Madrid)
tel – (0034 914) 959800
fax – (0034 914) 959801
website – www.rfef.es
email – rfef@tsai.es

Year of Formation – 1913
President – Angel María Villar

INTERNATIONAL HONOURS
European Championship – (1) 1964.

INTERNATIONAL TOURNAMENT APPEARANCES
World Cup – (12) 1934, 1950 (4th), 1962, 1966, 1978, 1982 (2nd phase), 1986 (qtr-finals), 1990 (2nd round), 1994 (qtr-finals), 1998, 2002 (qtr-finals), 2006 (2nd round).
European Championship – (7) 1964 (Winners), 1980, 1984 (runners-up), 1988, 1996 (qtr-finals),

The Directory

2000 (qtr-finals), 2004.

MAJOR EUROPEAN CLUB HONOURS
Champions Cup/League – (11) Real Madrid (1956, 1957, 1958, 1959, 1960, 1966, 1998, 2000, 2002), FC Barcelona (1992, 2006).
Cup-winners Cup – (7) Atlético Madrid (1962), FC Barcelona (1979, 1982, 1989, 1997), Valencia CF (1980), Real Zaragoza (1995).
UEFA Cup – (4) Real Madrid (1985, 1986), Valencia CF (2004), Sevilla FC (2006).
Fairs Cup – (6) FC Barcelona (1958, 1960, 1966), Valencia CF (1962, 1963), Real Zaragoza (1964).

Athletic Club
Alameda Mazarredo 23
48009 Bilbao
tel – (944) 240877
fax – (944) 263324
website – www.athletic-club.net
Year of Formation – 1898
President – Fernando Lamikiz
Coach – Félix Sarriugarte
Stadium – San Mamés (39,750)
Colours – Red & white stripes/black/black
MAJOR HONOURS
League Championship – (8) 1930, 1931, 1934, 1936, 1943, 1956, 1983, 1984.
Domestic Cup – (23) 1903, 1904, 1910, 1911, 1914, 1915, 1916, 1921, 1923, 1930, 1931, 1932, 1933, 1943, 1944, 1945, 1950, 1955, 1956, 1958, 1969, 1973, 1984.

Club Atlético de Madrid
Paseo Virgen del Puerto 67
28005 Madrid
tel – (913) 664707
fax – (913) 669811
website – www.clubatleticodemadrid.com
Year of Formation – 1903
President – Enrique Cerezo
Coach – Javier Aguirre
Stadium – Vicente Calderón (54,851)
Colours – Red & white stripes/blue/red
MAJOR HONOURS
League Championship – (9) 1940, 1941, 1950, 1951, 1966, 1970, 1973, 1977, 1996.
Domestic Cup – (9) 1960, 1961, 1965, 1972, 1976, 1985, 1991, 1992, 1996.
European Cup-Winners' Cup – (1) 1962.
World Club Cup – (1) 1974.

Fútbol Club Barcelona
Arístides Maillol s/n
08028 Barcelona
tel – (902) 189900
fax – (934) 112219
website – www.fcbarcelona.com
Year of Formation – 1899
President – Joan Laporta
Coach – Frank Rijkaard
Stadium – Camp Nou (98,260)
Colours – Blue (two broad scarlet stripes)/blue/blue
MAJOR HONOURS
League Championship – (18) 1929, 1945, 1948, 1949, 1952, 1953, 1959, 1960, 1974, 1985, 1991, 1992, 1993, 1994, 1998, 1999, 2005, 2006.
Domestic Cup – (24) 1910, 1912, 1913, 1920, 1922, 1925, 1926, 1928, 1942, 1951, 1952, 1953, 1957, 1959, 1963, 1968, 1971, 1978, 1981, 1983, 1988, 1990, 1997, 1998.
European Champions Cup – (2) 1992, 2006.
European Cup-winners Cup – (4) 1979, 1982, 1989, 1997.
Fairs Cup – (3) 1958, 1960, 1966.
European Super Cup – (2) 1992, 1998.

Real Betis Balompié
Avenida de Heliópolis s/n
41012 Sevilla
tel – (954) 610340
fax – (954) 614774
website – www.realbetisbalompie.es
Year of Formation – 1907
President – Manuel Ruiz de Lopera
Coach – Javier Irureta
Stadium – Manuel Ruiz de Lopera (52,500)
Colours – Green & white stripes/white/green
MAJOR HONOURS
League Championship – (1) 1935.
Domestic Cup – (2) 1977, 2005.

Real Club Celta de Vigo
Avenida de Balaídos s/n
36210 Vigo (Pontevedra)
tel – (986) 110900
fax – (986) 292040
website – www.celtavigo.net
Year of Formation – 1923
President – Horacio Gómez Araujo
Coach – Fernando Vázquez
Stadium – Balaídos (31,800)
Colours – Sky blue/white/sky blue

Real Club Deportivo La Coruña
Plaza de Pontevedra 19
15003 A Coruña
tel – (981) 259500
fax – (981) 265919
website – www.canaldeportivo.com
Year of Formation – 1906
President – Augusto Joaquín César Lendoiro
Coach – Joaquín Caparrós

Stadium – Riazor (34,178)
Colours – Blue & white stripes/blue/blue
MAJOR HONOURS
League Championship – (1) 2000.
Domestic Cup – (2) 1995, 2002.

Reial Club Deportiu Espanyol de Barcelona
Paseo Olímpico 17-19
08038 Barcelona
tel – (932) 927700
fax – (934) 254552
website – www.rcdespanyol.com
Year of Formation – 1900
President – Daniel Sánchez Llibre
Coach – Ernesto Valverde
Stadium – Montjuïc (55,000)
Colours – Blue (two broad white stripes)/blue/white
MAJOR HONOURS
Domestic Cup – (4) 1929, 1940, 2000, 2006.

Getafe Club de Fútbol
Avda Teresa de Calcuta s/n
28903 Getafe (Madrid)
tel – (916) 959771
fax – (916) 811212
website – www.getafecf.com
Year of Formation – 1983
President – Angel Torres
Coach – Bernd Schuster
Stadium – Coliseum Alfonso Pérez (14,400)
Colours – Blue/blue/blue

Club Gimnàstic de Tarragona
Partida Budellera s/n
43007 Tarragona
tel – (977) 215103
fax – (977) 244125
website – www.gimnasticdetarragona.com
Year of Formation – 1914
President – Josep Maria Andreu
Coach – Luis Ángel César
Stadium – Nou Estadi (12,000)
Colours – Red (white trim)/white/black

Levante UD
Paseo de la Alameda 34-7°-A
46023 Valencia
tel – (963) 379530
fax – (963) 379531
website – www.levanteud.com
Year of Formation – 1939
President – Pedro Villarroel
Coach – Juan Ramón López Caro
Stadium – Ciudad de Valencia (25,534)
Colours – Scarlet & blue stripes/blue/scarlet

The Directory

Real Club Deportivo Mallorca
Camí del Rei s/n
07011 Palma de Mallorca
tel – (971) 221221
fax – (971) 220388
website – www.rcdmallorca.es
Year of Formation – 1916
President – Vicenç Grande
Coach – Gregorio Manzano
Stadium – ONO (24,142)
Colours – Red/black/black
MAJOR HONOURS
Domestic Cup – (1) 2003.

Club Atlético Osasuna
Estadio El Sadar
c/ El Sadar s/n
31006 Pamplona
tel – (948) 152636
fax – (948) 151655
website – www.osasuna.es
Year of Formation – 1920
President – Francisco Izco
Coach – José Ángel Ciganda
Stadium – Reyno dee Navarra (19,980)
Colours – Red/dark blue/dark blue

Real Racing Club de Santander
Calle Real Racing Club s/n
39005 Santander
tel – (942) 282828
fax – (942) 280724
website – www.realracingclub.es
Year of Formation – 1913
President – Francisco Pernía
Coach – Miguel Ángel Portugal
Stadium – El Sardinero (22,500)
Colours – White/black/green

Real Madrid Club de Fútbol
Concha Espina 1
28036 Madrid
tel – (913) 984300
fax – (913) 984382
website – www.realmadrid.es
Year of Formation – 1902
President – Ramón Calderón
Coach – Fabio Capello
Stadium – Santiago Bernabéu (80,000)
Colours – White/white/white
MAJOR HONOURS
League Championship – (29) 1932, 1933, 1954, 1955, 1957, 1958, 1961, 1962, 1963, 1964, 1965, 1967, 1968, 1969, 1972, 1975, 1976, 1978, 1979, 1980, 1986, 1987, 1988, 1989, 1990, 1995, 1997, 2001, 2003.
Domestic Cup – (17) 1905, 1906, 1907, 1908, 1917, 1934, 1936, 1946, 1947, 1962, 1970, 1974, 1975, 1980, 1982, 1989, 1993.
European Champions Cup – (9) 1956, 1957, 1958, 1959, 1960, 1966, 1998, 2000, 2002.
UEFA Cup – (2) 1985, 1986.
European Super Cup – (1) 2002.
World Club Cup – (3) 1960, 1998, 2002.

Real Sociedad de Fútbol
Paseo de Anoeta 1
20014 San Sebastián
tel – (943) 462833
fax – (943) 458941
website – www.realsociedad.com
Year of Formation – 1909
President – Miguel Fuentes
Coach – José María Bakero
Stadium – Anoeta (32,082)
Colours – Blue & white stripes/white/blue & white
MAJOR HONOURS
League Championship – (2) 1981, 1982.
Domestic Cup – (2) 1909, 1987.

RC Recreativo de Huelva
Avda. Del Decano s/n
21001 Huelva
tel – (959) 270208
fax – (959) 271222
website – www.recreativohuelva.com
Year of Formation – 1889
President – Francisco Mendoza
Coach – Marcelino García Toral
Stadium – Nuevo Colombino (19,860)
Colours – Blue & white stripes/white/white

Sevilla Fútbol Club
Estadio Sánchez Pizjuán
Avda Eduardo Dato s/n
41005 Sevilla
tel – (954) 535353
fax – (954) 536061
website – www.sevillafc.es
Year of Formation – 1905
President – José María del Nido
Coach – Juande Ramos
Stadium – Sánchez Pizjuán (43,000)
Colours – White (red trim)/white/white
MAJOR HONOURS
UEFA Cup – (1) 2006.
League Championship – (1) 1946.
Domestic Cup – (3) 1935, 1939, 1948.

Valencia Club de Fútbol
Antigua Senda de Senent 11-9
46010 Valencia
tel – (963) 372626
fax – (963) 375093
website – www.valenciacf.es
Year of Formation – 1919
President – Juan Bautista Soler
Coach – Enrique "Quique" Sánchez Flores
Stadium – Mestalla (55,000)
Colours – White/black/white
MAJOR HONOURS
League Championship – (6) 1942, 1944, 1947, 1971, 2002, 2004.
Domestic Cup – (6) 1941, 1949, 1954, 1967, 1979, 1999.
European Cup-winners Cup – (1) 1980.
UEFA Cup – (1) 2004.
Fairs Cup – (2) 1962, 1963.
European Super Cup – (2) 1980, 2004.

Villarreal Club de Fútbol
Avda Blasco Ibáñez 2
12540 Villarreal (Castellón)
tel – (964) 500250
fax – (964) 500167
website – www.villarrealcf.com
Year of Formation – 1923
President – Fernando Roig Alfonso
Coach – Manuel Pellegrini
Stadium – El Madrigal (23,500)
Colours – Yellow/yellow/yellow

Real Zaragoza
Eduardo Ibarra 6
50009 Zaragoza
tel – (976) 567777
fax – (976) 568863
website – www.realzaragoza.com
Year of Formation – 1932
President – Eduardo Bandrés
Coach – Víctor Muñoz
Stadium – La Romareda (34,596)
Colours – White/blue/white
MAJOR HONOURS
Domestic Cup – (6) 1964, 1966, 1986, 1994, 2001, 2004.
European Cup-winners Cup – (1) 1995.
Fairs Cup – (1) 1964.

SWEDEN

Svenska Fotbollförbundet
P.O. Box 1216, 171 23 Solna
tel – (08) 7350900
fax – (08) 7350901
website – www.svenskfotboll.se
email – svff@svenskfotboll.se

Year of Formation – 1904
President – Lars-Åke Lagrell
Secretary – Sune Hellströmer

The Directory

Stadium – Råsunda Stadion, Solna (36,800)

INTERNATIONAL TOURNAMENT APPEARANCES
World Cup – (11) 1934 (2nd round), 1938 (4th), 1950 (3rd), 1958 (runners-up), 1970, 1974 (2nd phase), 1978, 1990, 1994 (3rd), 2002 (2nd round), 2006 (2nd round).
European Championship – (3) 1992 (semi-finals), 2000, 2004 (qtr-finals).

MAJOR EUROPEAN CLUB HONOURS
UEFA Cup – (2) IFK Göteborg (1982, 1987).

AIK
Box 1257
17124 Solna
tel – (08) 7359671
fax – (08) 735 96 96
website – www.aik.se
Year of Formation – 1891
President – Per Bystedt
Coach – Rikard Norling
Stadium – Råsunda Stadion (36,800)
Colours – Black (yellow trim)/white/black & yellow
MAJOR HONOURS
League Championship – (10) 1900, 1901, 1911, 1914, 1916, 1923, 1932, 1937, 1992, 1998.
Domestic Cup – (7) 1949, 1950, 1976, 1985, 1996, 1997, 1999.

Djurgårdens Idrottsförening
Box 1257
114 33 Stockholm
tel – (08) 54515800
fax – (08) 54515801
website – www.dif.se
Year of Formation – 1891
President – Bo Lundquist
Coach – Kjell Jonevret
Stadium – Stockholms Stadion (14,417)
Colours – Light blue & dark blue stripes/dark blue/dark blue
MAJOR HONOURS
League Championship – (11) 1912, 1915, 1917, 1920, 1955, 1959, 1964, 1966, 2002, 2003, 2005.
Domestic Cup – (4) 1990, 2002, 2004, 2005.

Idrottsföreningen Elfsborg
Ålgårdsvägen 32
506 30 Borås
tel – (033) 139191
fax – (033) 129191
website – www.elfsborg.se
Year of Formation – 1904
President – Bo Johansson
Coach – Magnus Haglund
Stadium – Borås Arena (18,500)
Colours – Yellow/black/yellow
MAJOR HONOURS
League Championship – (4) 1936, 1939, 1940, 1961.
Domestic Cup – (2) 2001, 2003.

GAIS
Gamla Boråsvägen
41276 Göteborg
tel – (031) 403690
fax – (031) 406685
website – www.gais.se
Year of Formation – 1894
President – Christer Wallin
Coach – Roland Nilsson
Stadium – Gamla Ullevi (16,500)
Colours – Green & black stripes/white/green
MAJOR HONOURS
League Championship – (4) 1919, 1922, 1931, 1954.
Domestic Cup – (1) 1942.

Gefle IF
Box 857
801 31 Gävle
tel – (026) 652233
fax – (026) 610240
website – www.geflefotboll.com
Year of Formation – 1882
President – Leif Lindstrand
Coach – Per Olsson
Stadium – Strömvallen (7,500)
Colours – Sky blue/white/white

Idrottsföreningen Kamraterna Göteborg
Alfreds Gärdes Väg
416 55 Göteborg
tel – (031) 7037300
fax – (031) 404121
website – www.ifkgoteborg.se
Year of Formation – 1904
President – Bengt Halse
Coach – Arne Erlandsson
Stadium – Gamla Ullevi (16,500)
Colours – Blue & white stripes/blue/blue
MAJOR HONOURS
League Championship – (17) 1908, 1910, 1918, 1935, 1942, 1958, 1969, 1982, 1983, 1984, 1987, 1990, 1991, 1993, 1994, 1995, 1996.
Domestic Cup – (4) 1979, 1982, 1983, 1991.
UEFA Cup – (2) 1982, 1987.

Halmstads Bollklubb
Box 223
301 06 Halmstad
tel – (035) 171880
fax – (035) 103436
website – www.hbk.se
Year of Formation – 1914
President – Bengt Sjöholm
Coach – Jan Andersson
Stadium – Örjans vall (15,500)
Colours – Blue/black/blue
MAJOR HONOURS
League Championship – (4) 1976, 1979, 1997, 2000.
Domestic Cup – (1) 1995.

Hammarby Fotboll AB
Veterinärgränd 6
12163 Johanneshov
tel – (08) 4628810
fax – (08) 4629320
website – www.hammarbyfotboll.se
Year of Formation – 1897
President – Jan Friedman
Coach – Anders Linderoth
Stadium – Söderstadion (16,187)
Colours – Green & white broad stripes/green/white
MAJOR HONOURS
League Championship – (1) 2001.

Helsingborgs Idrottsförening
Box 2074
250 02 Helsingborg
tel – (042) 377000
fax – (042) 377027
website – www.hif.se
Year of Formation – 1907
President – Stein-Inge Fredin
Coach – Stuart Baxter
Stadium – Olympia (16,802)
Colours – Red/blue/red
MAJOR HONOURS
League Championship – (6) 1929, 1930, 1933, 1934, 1941, 1999.
Domestic Cup – (2) 1941, 1998.

BK Häcken
Box 220 51
400 72 Göteborg
tel – (031) 506790
fax – (031) 506799
website – www.bkhacken.se
Year of Formation – 1940
President – Åke Nilsson
Coach – Stefan Lundin
Stadium – Rambergsvallen (7,000)
Colours – Yellow & black broad stripes/black/yellow

The Directory

Kalmar FF
Box 169
391 22 Kalmar
tel – (0480) 444430
fax – (0480) 88720
website – www.kalmarff.se
Year of Formation – 1910
President – Ronny Nilsson
Coach – Nanne Bergstrand
Stadium – Fredriksskans (9,689)
Colours – Red (white trim)/red/red
MAJOR HONOURS
Domestic Cup – (2) 1981, 1987.

Malmö Fotbollförening
Box 19067
200 73 Malmö
tel – (040) 326600
fax – (040) 326601
website – www.mff.se
Year of Formation – 1910
President – Bengt Madsen
Coach – Sören Åkeby
Stadium – Malmö Stadion (27,500)
Colours – Sky blue/white/sky blue
MAJOR HONOURS
League Championship – (15) 1944, 1949, 1950, 1951, 1953, 1965, 1967, 1970, 1971, 1974, 1975, 1977, 1986, 1988, 2004.
Domestic Cup – (14) 1944, 1946, 1947, 1951, 1953, 1967, 1973, 1974, 1975, 1977, 1980, 1984, 1986, 1989.

Örgryte Idrottssällskap
Box 52025
400 25 Göteborg
tel – (031) 866770
fax – (031) 866781
website – www.ois.se
Year of Formation – 1887
President – Anders Lundberg
Coach – Sören Börjesson
Stadium – Gamla Ullevi (16,500)
Colours – Red/blue/red
MAJOR HONOURS
League Championship – (14) 1896, 1897, 1898, 1899, 1902, 1904, 1905, 1906, 1907, 1909, 1913, 1926, 1928, 1985.
Domestic Cup – (1) 2000.

Östers IF
Tipshallen Hejaregatan
35246 VÄXJÖ
tel – (0470) 724050
fax – (0470) 724059
website – www.osterfotboll.se
Year of Formation – 1930
President – Curt Persson
Coach – Lasse Jacobsson
Stadium – Värendsvallen (15,000)
Colours – Red (blue trim)/blue/red
MAJOR HONOURS
League Championship – (4) 1968, 1978, 1980, 1981.
Domestic Cup – (1) 1977.

SWITZERLAND

Schweizerischer Fussballverband
Haus des Fussballs, Postfach,
3000 Bern 15
tel – (0041 31) 9508111
fax – (0041 31) 9508181
website – www.football.ch
email – sfv.asf@football.ch

Year of Formation – 1895
President – Ralph Zloczower
Secretary – Peter Gilliéron

INTERNATIONAL TOURNAMENT APPEARANCES
World Cup – (8) 1934, 1938 (qtr-finals), 1950, 1954 (qtr-finals), 1962, 1966, 1994 (2nd round), 2006 (2nd round).
European Championship – (2) 1996, 2004.

FC Aarau
Postfach
5001 Aarau
tel – (062) 8362082
fax – (062) 8362081
website – www.fcaarau.ch
Year of Formation – 1902
President – Michael Hunziker
Coach – Urs Schönenberger
Stadium – Brügglifeld (13,232)
Colours – Red (white trim)/red/red
MAJOR HONOURS
League Championship – (3) 1912, 1914, 1993.
Domestic Cup – (1) 1985.

FC Basel
Postfach 114
4028 Basel
tel – (061) 3751010
fax – (061) 3751011
website – www.fcb.ch
Year of Formation – 1893
President – Frau Gigi Oeri
Coach – Christian Gross
Stadium – St. Jakob-Park (33,010)
Colours – Red & blue halves/blue/blue
MAJOR HONOURS
League Championship – (11) 1953, 1967, 1969, 1970, 1972, 1973, 1977, 1980, 2002, 2004, 2005.
Domestic Cup – (7) 1933, 1947, 1963, 1967, 1975, 2002, 2003.

Grasshopper-Club Zürich
Hardturmstrasse 321
8037 Zürich
tel – (044) 4474646
fax – (044) 4474690
website – www.gcz.ch
Year of Formation – 1886
President – Walter Brunner
Coach – Krasimir Balakov
Stadium – Hardturm (20,079)
Colours – Blue & white halves/white/white
MAJOR HONOURS
League Championship – (27) 1898, 1900, 1901, 1905, 1921, 1927, 1928, 1931, 1937, 1939, 1942, 1943, 1945, 1952, 1956, 1971, 1978, 1982, 1983, 1984, 1990, 1991, 1995, 1996, 1998, 2001, 2003.
Domestic Cup – (18) 1926, 1927, 1932, 1934, 1937, 1938, 1940, 1941, 1942, 1943, 1946, 1952, 1956, 1983, 1988, 1989, 1990, 1994.

FC Luzern
Postfach 2918
6002 Luzern
tel – (041) 3170080
fax – (041) 3170099
website – www.fcl.ch
Year of Formation – 1901
President – Walter Stierli
Coach – Ciriaco Sforza
Stadium – Allmend (18,400)
Colours – White (blue trim)/blue/blue
MAJOR HONOURS
League Championship – (1) 1989.
Domestic Cup – (2) 1960, 1992.

FC St. Gallen
Postfach 14
9009 St. Gallen
tel – (071) 2430909
fax – (071) 2430900
website – www.fcsg.ch
Year of Formation – 1879
President – Dieter Froehlich
Coach – Rolf Fringer
Stadium – Espenmoos (13,000)
Colours – Deep green (white trim)/white/deep green
MAJOR HONOURS
League Championship – (2) 1904, 2000.
Domestic Cup – (1) 1969.

The Directory

FC Schaffhausen
Postfach 479
8201 Schaffhausen
tel – (052) 6321480
fax – (052) 6321400
website – www.fcschaffhausen.ch
Year of Formation – 1896
President – Aniello Fontana
Coach – Jürgen Seeberger
Stadium – Breite (7,500)
Colours – Black (yellow trim)/black/black

FC Sion
Case postale 32
1921 Martigny
tel – (027) 7471313
fax – (027) 7471314
website – www.fc-sion.ch
Year of Formation – 1909
President – Christian Constantin
Coach – Néstor Clausen
Stadium – Tourbillon (16,000)
Colours – White (red trim)/white/white
MAJOR HONOURS
League Championship – (2) 1992, 1997.
Domestic Cup – (10) 1965, 1974, 1980, 1982, 1986, 1991, 1995, 1996, 1997, 2006.

FC Thun 1898
Postfach 2151
3601 Thun
tel (033) 2251898
fax – (033) 2251899
website – www.fcthun.ch
Year of Formation – 1898
President – Dr. Kurt Weder
Coach – Heinz Peischl
Stadium – Lachen (10,800)
Colours – Red (white trim)/red/red

BSC Young Boys Bern
Postfach 61
3000 Bern 22
tel – (031) 3448000
fax – (031) 3448089
website – www.bscyb.ch
Year of Formation – 1898
President – Peter Mast
Coach – Gernot Rohr
Stadium – Stade de Suisse (32,000)
Colours – Yellow & black halves/black/black
MAJOR HONOURS
League Championship – (11) 1903, 1909, 1910, 1911, 1920, 1927, 1957, 1958, 1959, 1960, 1986.
Domestic Cup – (6) 1930, 1945, 1953, 1958, 1977, 1987.

FC Zürich
Postfach 3375
8021 Zürich
tel – (044) 5211212
fax – (044) 5211213
website – www.fcz.ch
Year of Formation – 1896
President – Sven Hotz
Coach – Lucien Favre
Stadium – Letzigrund (23,000); 2006/07 – Hardturm (20,079)
Colours – White (blue trim)/white/white
MAJOR HONOURS
League Championship – (10) 1902, 1924, 1963, 1966, 1968, 1974, 1975, 1976, 1981, 2006.
Domestic Cup – (7) 1966, 1970, 1972, 1973, 1976, 2000, 2005.

TURKEY

Türkiye Futbol Federasyönü
Konaklar Mahallesi, Ihlamurlu
Sokak 9, 4 Levent, 80620
Istanbul
tel – (0090 212) 2827010
fax – (0090 212) 2827016
website – www.tff.org
email – tff@tff.org

Year of Formation – 1923
President – Haluk Ülüsoy
Secretary – Lutfi Aribogan

INTERNATIONAL TOURNAMENT APPEARANCES
World Cup – (2) 1954, 2002 (3rd)
European Championship – (2) 1996, 2000 (qtr-finals).

MAJOR EUROPEAN CLUB HONOURS
UEFA Cup – (1) Galatasaray (2000).

Makina Kimya Endüstrisi Ankaragücü Kulübü
GMK Bulvari
Tandogan Meydani
06570 Ankara
tel – (312) 2220175
fax – (312) 2312772
website – www.ankaragucu.org.tr
Year of Formation – 1910
President – Cemal Aydin
Coach – Vlado Bozinoski
Stadium – 19 Mayis (24,000)
Colours – Yellow (dark blue trim)/dark blue/yellow
MAJOR HONOURS
Domestic Cup – (2) 1972, 1981.

Büyüksehir Belediyesi Ankaraspor
Kecioren Aktepe Spor
Tesisleri Kecioren
Ankara
tel – (312) 3574770
fax – (312) 3570500
Year of Formation – 1978
President – Hilmi Gökçinar
Coach – Aykut Kocaman
Stadium – 19 Mayis (24,000)
Colours – Blue (white trim)/blue/blue

Antalyaspor
Meltem Mahallesi Hasan Subasi Spor Tesisleri
07050 Antalya
tel – (242) 2370881
fax – (242) 2374951
website – www.antalyaspor.com.tr
Year of Formation – 1966
President – Sedat Peker
Coach – Yilmaz Vural
Stadium – Atatürk (20,000)
Colours – Red (white trim)/red/red

Besiktas Jimnastik Kulübü
Süleyman Seba Caddesi 92
Akraetler
Besiktas
86090 Istanbul
tel – (212) 3101000
fax – (212) 2588194
website – www.besiktasjk.com.tr
Year of Formation – 1903
President – Yildirim Demiroren
Coach – Jean Tigana
Stadium – Inönü (20,700)
Colours – White (black trim)/white/white
MAJOR HONOURS
League Championship – (12) 1957, 1958, 1960, 1966, 1967, 1982, 1986, 1990, 1991, 1992, 1995, 2003.
Domestic Cup – (6) 1975, 1989, 1990, 1994, 1998, 2006.

Bursaspor
Orhan Özselek Tesisleri Vakif Mahalelsi Yildirim
16375 Bursa
tel – (224) 3530092
fax – (224) 3530099
website – www.bursaspor.org
Year of Formation – 1963
President – Levent Kizil
Coach – Rasit Cetiner
Stadium – Atatürk (20,000)
Colours – Green & white stripes/white/green
MAJOR HONOURS
Domestic Cup – (1) 1986.

The Directory

Çaykur Rizespor Kulübü
Mehmet Cengiz Sosyal Tesisleri
Islampasa Mahallesi Karayollari Ici
53020 Rize
tel – (464) 2121012
fax – (464) 2141911
website – www.rizespor.cjb.net
President – Ekrem Cengiz
Coach – Güvenç Kurtar
Stadium – Atatürk (20,000)
Colours – Blue & green stripes/blu/white

Denizlispor Kulübü
Kenan Evren Bulvari 9
Merkez
Denizli
tel – (258) 2659861
fax – (258) 2659014
website – www.denizlispor.com
Year of Formation – 1966
President – Ali Ipek
Coach – Faruk Hadzibegic
Stadium – Denizli Sehir (15,000)
Colours – Green & black stripes/black/black

Fenerbahçe Spor Kulübü
Fenerbahçe Tesisleri
Kiziltoprak
Kadiköy
81030 Istanbul
tel – (216) 4146464
fax – (216) 3483060
website – www.fenerbahce.org.tr
Year of Formation – 1907
President – Aziz Yildirim
Coach – Zico
Stadium – Fenerbahçe Sükrü Saracoglu (42,000)
Colours – Yellow & dark blue stripes/white/white
MAJOR HONOURS
League Championship – (16) 1959, 1961, 1964, 1965, 1968, 1970, 1974, 1975, 1978, 1983, 1985, 1989, 1996, 2001, 2004, 2005.
Domestic Cup – (4) 1968, 1974, 1979, 1983.

Galatasaray Spor Kulübü
Hasnun Galip Sok 7-9-11
Beyoglu
80700 Istanbul
tel – (212) 2515707
fax – (212) 2511212
website – www.galatasaray.org.tr
Year of Formation – 1905
President – Özhan Canaydin
Coach – Eric Gerets
Stadium – Ali Sami Yen (40,000)
Colours – Yellow & red halves/red/red
MAJOR HONOURS
League Championship – (16) 1962, 1963, 1969, 1971, 1972, 1973, 1987, 1988, 1993, 1994, 1997, 1998, 1999, 2000, 2002, 2006.
Domestic Cup – (14) 1963, 1964, 1965, 1966, 1973, 1976, 1982, 1985, 1991, 1993, 1996, 1999, 2000, 2005.
UEFA Cup – (1) 2000.
European Super Cup – (1) 2000.

Gaziantepspor Kulübü
Celal Dogan Tesisleri
E24 Darayolu uzeri
PK 149 Merkez
27010 Gaziantep
tel – (342) 3222000
fax – (342) 3222069
website – www.gaziantepspor.org.tr
Year of Formation – 1969
President – Ibrahim Kizil
Coach – Walter Zenga
Stadium – Kamil Ocak (20,000)
Colours – Red (black trim)/red/red

Gençlerbirligi Spor Kulübü
Gazi Mustafa Kemal Bulvari 75/B
Maltepe
06570 Ankara
tel – (312) 2153000
fax – (312) 2212125
Year of Formation – 1923
President – Ilhan Cavcav
Coach – Mesut Bakkal
Stadium – 19 Mayis (25,000)
Colours – White (red sleeves & black trim)/black/red
MAJOR HONOURS
Domestic Cup – (2) 1987, 2001.

Kayserispor
Erkilet Yolu Üzeri Karputazan Tesisleri Kocasinan
38080 Kayseri
tel – (352) 3512727
fax – (352) 3512219
Year of Formation – 1966
President – Recep Mamur
Coach – Ertugrul Saglam
Stadium – Atatürk (20,000)
Colours – White (red & yellow trim)/white/white

Kayseri Erciyesspor
Yeniköy Mahallesi Bülbül Caddesi
Haci Boydak Tesisleri
Melikgazi 38110
tel – (352) 3553000
fax – (352) 3552998
Year of Formation – 1975
President – Enver Kemaloglu
Coach – Mustafa Ugur
Stadium – Kayseri Atatürk (25,000)
Colours – Blue/black/white

Konyaspor Kulübü
Zafer Meydani Zafer Carsisi Kat:3 Meram
42200 Konya
tel – (332) 3531522
fax – (332) 3536863
Year of Formation – 1981
President – Ahmet San
Coach – Nurullah Saglam
Stadium – Atatürk (20,000)
Colours – Light green/light green/light green

Sakaryaspor AS
Atatürk Stadi Arkasi
Alt Yapi Tesisler
Adapazari (Sakarya)
tel – (264) 2818155
fax – (264) 2818158
website – www.sakaryasporas.com.tr
Year of Formation – 1965
President – Ömer Yazici
Coach – Nejat Biyedic
Stadium – Atatürk (20,000)
Colours – Green & black stripes/black/green
MAJOR HONOURS
Domestic Cup – (1) 1988.

Sivasspor
Tesisleri Ankara Yolu 3.KM
Sivas
tel – (346) 2264180-3
fax – (346) 2262458
Year of Formation – 1967
President – Mecnun Odyakmaz
Coach – Karol Pecze
Stadium – Sivas 4 Eylül (20,000)
Colours – White (red trim)/dark blue/white

Trabzonspor Kulübü
Mehmet Ali Yilmaz Tesisleri
PK 27
61000 Trabzon
tel – (462) 3250967
fax – (462) 3255514
website – www.trabzonspor.org.tr
Year of Formation – 1967
President – Nuri Albayrak
Coach – Sebastião Lazaroni
Stadium – Avni Aker (30,000)
Colours – Claret & sky blue stripes (sky blue sleeves)/sky blue/sky blue
MAJOR HONOURS
League Championship – (6) 1976, 1977, 1979, 1980, 1981, 1984.
Domestic Cup – (7) 1977, 1978, 1984, 1992, 1995,

The Directory

2003, 2004.

Vestel Manisaspor
Tarik Almis Spor Tesisleri Laleli
45000 Manisa
tel – (236) 2333767
fax – (236) 2339202
Year of Formation – 1965
President – Haluk Çubukçu
Coach – Erun Yanal
Stadium – Manisa 19 Mayis (15,000)
Colours – White (red trim)/black/white

UKRAINE

Football Federation of Ukraine
vul. Labolatorna1, PO Box 293,
03150 Kyiv
tel – (00380 44) 2528498
fax – (00380 44) 2528513
website – www.ffu.org.ua
email – info@ffu.kiev.ua

Year of Formation – 1991
President – Hryhoriy Surkis
Secretary – Anatoliy Popov
Stadium – National Sport
Komplex Olimpiyskyi, Kyiv
(83,160)

INTERNATIONAL TOURNAMENT APPEARANCES
World Cup – (1) 2006 (qtr-finals).

MAJOR EUROPEAN CLUB HONOURS
Cup-winners Cup – (2) Dynamo Kyiv (1975, 1986).

Arsenal Kyiv
vul. Turgenivska 21
01054 Kyiv
tel – (044) 2468504/2284565
fax – (044) 2169401
website – www.arsenal-kiev.com
Year of Formation – 2003
President – Valeriy Borisov
Coach - Olexandr Zavarov
Stadium – CSK ZSU (12,000)
Colours – Blue (white trim)/blue/blue

Chornomorets Odesa
Av. Taras Shevchenko 8 A
65058 Odesa
tel – (0482) 684894/250411
fax – (0482) 680415
website – www.chernomorets.odessa.ua
Year of Formation – 1958
President – Leonid Klimov
Coach – Semen Altman
Stadium – Chornomorets (35,000)
Colours – Blue (white trim)/white/blue
MAJOR HONOURS
Domestic Cup – (2) 1992, 1994.

Dnipro Dnipropetrovsk
vul. Bilshovytska 1
49008 Dnipropetrovsk
tel – (0562) 344379/283381/283384
fax – (0562) 342990/342989
website – www.fcdnipro.dp.ua
Year of Formation – 1962
President – Yuriy Alexeyev
Coach – Oleh Protasov
Stadium – Meteor (30,352)
Colours – Light blue/dark blue/dark blue
MAJOR HONOURS
League Championship (USSR) – (2) 1983, 1988.
Domestic Cup (USSR) – (1) 1989.

Dynamo Kyiv
vul. Mykhailo Hrushevskyi 3
01101 Kyiv
tel – (044) 5360003
fax – (044) 2284135
website – www.fcdynamo.kiev.ua
Year of Formation – 1927
President – Ihor Surkis
Coach – Anatoliy Demyanenko
Stadium – National Sport Komplex Olimpiyskyi (83,160) or Dynamo im. V. Lobanovskyi (16,873)
Colours – White (dark blue sash)/white/white & dark blue
MAJOR HONOURS
League Championship (USSR) – (13) 1961, 1966, 1967, 1968, 1971, 1974, 1975, 1977, 1980, 1981, 1985, 1986, 1990.
League Championship – (11) 1993, 1994, 1995, 1996, 1997, 1998, 1999, 2000, 2001, 2003, 2004.
Domestic Cup (USSR) – (9) 1954, 1964, 1966, 1974, 1978, 1982, 1985, 1987, 1990.
Domestic Cup – (8) 1993, 1996, 1998, 1999, 2000, 2003, 2005, 2006.
European Cup-winners Cup – (2) 1975, 1986.
European Super Cup – (1) 1975.

FC Illichivets Mariupol
vul. Yevpatoriyska 45A
87515 Mariupol
tel – (0629) 534486
fax – (0629) 534486
website – www.fcilyich.com.ua
Year of Formation – 2003
President – Volodymyr Boiko
Coach – Ivan Balan
Stadium – Illichivets (12,673)
Colours – Red (white sleeves)/red/red

Karpaty Lviv
Sq. Adam Mickiewicz 6/7
79005 Lviv
tel – (322) 727744
fax – (322) 724072
website – www.fckarpaty.lviv.ua
Year of Formation – 1963
President – Petro Dyminskyi
Coach – Olexandrlshchenko
Stadium – Ukraina (28,058)
Colours – Green (white trim)/green/green
MAJOR HONOURS
Domestic Cup (USSR) – (1) 1969.

FC Kharkiv
Av. Lenin 27A ap. 323
61072 Kharkiv
tel – (057) 7578453
fax – (057) 7578453
Year of Formation – 1998
Website – www.arsenal.kharkov.ua
Chairman – Yevhen Krasnikov
President – Vitaliy Danilov
Coach – Hennadiy Lytovchenko
Stadium – Metalist (28,313)
Colours – Red (white trim)/white/red

Kryvbas Kryvyi Rih
vul. Metalurgiv 5
50 070 Kryvyi Rih
tel – (0564) 283019/284011/400835/716488
fax – (0564) 400836
website – www.fckrivbass.dp.ua
Year of Formation – 1959
President – Serhiy Polishchuk
Coach – Olexandr Kosevych
Stadium – Metalurg (29,830)
Colours – Red (black trim)/red/red

Metalist Kharkiv
vul. Plekhanivska 65
61101 Kharkiv
tel – (0572) 194271/277646
fax – (0572) 277936/194284
website – www.metallist.kharkov.com
Year of Formation – 1925
President – Olexandr Yaroslavskyi
Coach – Myron Markevych
Stadium – Metalist (28,313)
Colours – White (blue trim)/white/white
MAJOR HONOURS
Domestic Cup (USSR) – (1) 1988.

Metalurg Donetsk
vul. Kuibysheva 26 A
83 062 Donetsk

The Directory

tel – (062) 3850486/2616094
fax – (062) 3850486/3830488
website – www.metalurg.donetsk.ua
Year of Formation – 1995
President – Serhiy Taruta
Coach – "Pichi" Alonso Herrera
Stadium – Lokomotiv (24,510)

Metalurg Zaporizhzhya
vul. 12 April 2
69037 Zaporizhzhya
tel – (0612) 240656/326672/571433
fax – (0612) 326672
website – www.fcmetalurg.com.ua
Year of Formation – 1949
President – Andriy Kurhanskyi
Coach – Vyacheslav Hroznyi
Stadium – AutoZaZ-Daewoo (6,619)
Colours – Red/red/red

Shakhtar Donetsk
Boulevard A. Pushkin 20A
83050 Donetsk
tel – (0622) 33499406/33533191
fax – (0622) 3349908
website – www.shakhtar.com
Year of Formation – 1936
President – Rinat Akhmetov
Coach – Mircea Lucescu
Stadium – Central (31,547)
Colours – Orange & black broad stripes/black/black
MAJOR HONOURS
League Championship – (3) 2002, 2005, 2006.
Domestic Cup (USSR) – (4) 1961, 1962, 1980, 1983.
Domestic Cup – (5) 1995, 1997, 2001, 2002, 2004.

Stal Alchevsk
vul. Leningradska 41
Alchevsk
tel – (06442) 23487/35256
fax – (06442) 23485
Year of Formation – 1935
website – www.fcstal.lg.ua
Chairman – Valeriy Stoyan
President – Kostyantyn Petrov
Coach – Anatoliy Volobuyev
Stadium – Stal (10,500)
Colours – Red/red/red

Tavriya Simferopol
vul. Alexandr Pushkin 46
95001 Simferopol
tel – (0652) 255383/276543
fax – (0652) 270147
website – www.fctavria.crimea.ua
Year of Formation – 1958

President – Serhiy Kunitsyn
Coach – Mykhailo Fomenko
Stadium – Tavriya (19,978)
Colours – Dark blue/dark blue/dark blue
MAJOR HONOURS
League Championship – (1) 1992.

Vorskla Poltava
Nezalezhnosti square 16
36 000 Poltava
tel – (05322) 221670/229623/229598
fax – (05322) 224833
website – www.fcvorskla.com.ua
Year of Formation – 1984
President – Valentyn Ulyanov
Coach – Viktor Nosov
Stadium – Vorskla (24,850)
Colours – Green (white trim)/green/green

Zorya Lugansk
Vul. Oboronna 4 W
91011 Lugansk
tel – (642) 536345
fax – (642) 530708
website – www.fczarya.lugansk.ua
Year of Formation – 1923
President – Valeriy Shpychka
Coach – Yuriy Koval
Stadium – Avangard (32,000)
Colours – Red (white trim)/black/red
MAJOR HONOURS
League Championship (USSR) – (1) 1972.

WALES

The Football Association of Wales
11/12 Neptune Court, Vanguard Way, Cardiff CF24 5PJ
tel – (0044 2920) 435830
fax – (0044 2920) 496953
website – www.faw.org.uk
email – info@faw.org.uk

Year of Formation – 1876
President – Tegwyn Evans
Secretary – David Collins
Stadium – Millennium Stadium, Cardiff (72,000)

INTERNATIONAL TOURNAMENT APPEARANCES
World Cup – (1) 1958 (qtr-finals).

Aberystwyth Town FC
Park Avenue
Aberystwyth
SY23 1PG

tel – (01970) 612122
website – www.atfc.org.uk
Year of Formation – 1888
Chairman – Donald Kane
Manager – Brian Coyne
Stadium – Park Avenue (5,000)
Colours – Green & black stripes/black/green
MAJOR HONOURS
Domestic Cup – (1) 1900.

Airbus UK
Broughton Wings Sports & Social Club
Chester Road
Broughton
CH4 0DR
tel – (01244) 537107
fax – (01244) 537107
website – www.airbusfc.co.uk
Year of Formation – 1946
Chairman – John Sutton
Manager – Gareth Owen
Stadium – The Airfield (2,000)
Colours – Blue/white/blue

Bangor City FC
Farrar Road
Bangor
Gwynedd LL57 1LJ
tel – (01248) 355852
fax – (01248) 355852
website – www.bangorcityfc.com
Year of Formation – 1893
Chairman – Ken Jones
Manager – Clayton Blackmore
Stadium – Farrar Road (3,200)
Colours – Blue (white trim)/white/white
MAJOR HONOURS
League Championship – (2) 1994, 1995.
Domestic Cup – (5) 1889, 1896, 1962, 1998, 2000.

Caernarfon Town FC
The Oval
Marcus Street
Caernarfon LL55 2HT
tel – (01766) 810391
fax – (01286) 676885
website – www.caernarfontown.net
Year of Formation – 1937
Chairman – George Denham
Manager – Wayne Phillips
Stadium – The Oval (2,500)
Colours – Yellow/green/yellow

Caersws FC
Dolhafren
Caersws SY17 5SF
tel – (01686) 688258

The Directory

website – www.caersws-fc.com
Year of Formation – 1887
Chairman – Garth Williams
Manager – Mickey Evans
Stadium – Recreation Ground (2,500)
Colours – Blue (white trim)/white/blue

Carmarthen Town FC
Richmond Park
Priory Street
Carmarthen
SA31 1LR
tel – (01267) 232101
fax – (01267) 222851
website – www.carmarthentownafc.net
Year of Formation – 1948
Chairman – Jeff Thomas
Manager – Mark Jones
Stadium – Richmond Park (3,000)
Colours – Old gold (black trim)/old gold/old gold & black

Connah's Quay Nomads FC
40 Brookdale Avenue
Connah's Quay
Deeside
CH5 4LU
tel – (01244) 831212
fax – (01244) 831212
Year of Formation – 1947
Chairman – John Gray
Manager – Neville Powell
Stadium – Deeside Stadium (3,500)
Colours – White (blue trim)/blue/white

Haverfordwest County AFC
Bridge Meadow Stadium
Bridge Meadow Lane
Haverfordwest
SA61 2EX
tel – (01437) 769048
fax – (01437) 769048
website – www.haverfordwestcounty.com
Year of Formation – 1900
Chairman – Rob Summons
Manager – Deryn Brace
Stadium – Bridge Meadow (2,000)
Colours – Blue/blue/blue

Llanelli AFC
Stebonheath Park
Llanelli
SA15 1HF
tel – (01554) 758018
fax – (01554) 758018
Year of Formation – 1896
website – www.llanelliafc.co.uk
Chairman – Nitin Parekh
Manager – Peter Nicholas
Stadium – Stebonheath Park (3,700)
Colours – Red/red/red

NEWI (North East Wales Institute) Cefn Druids FC
Plaskynaston Lane
Cefn Mawr
LL14 3AT
tel – (01978) 824332
fax – (01978) 824332
website – www.cefndruidsafc.co.uk
Year of Formation – 1876
Chairman – Ian Parry
Managers – Dixie McNeill & Ossie Jones
Stadium – Plaskynaston Lane (2,000)
Colours – Black & white stripes/black/black & white
MAJOR HONOURS
Domestic Cup – (8) 1880, 1881, 1882, 1885, 1886, 1898, 1899, 1904.

Newtown AFC
Graham Grigg Latham Park
Newtown
SY16 1EN
tel – (01686) 623120
fax – (01686) 623120
website – www.newtownafc.co.uk
Year of Formation – 1875
Chairman – Alwyn Preece
Manager – Roger Preece
Stadium – Graham Grigg Latham Park (5,000)
Colours – Red/red/red
MAJOR HONOURS
Domestic Cup – (2) 1879, 1895.

CPD Porthmadog
Y Traeth
Porthmadog
LL49 9PP
tel – (01766) 514687/512991
fax – (01766) 514687
website – www.porthmadogfc.com
Chairman – Phil Jones
Manager – Viv Williams & Osian Jones
Stadium – Y Traeth (2,500)
Colours – Red & black quarters/black/red

Port Talbot Town FC
Victoria Road
Port Talbot
SA12 6AD
tel – (01639) 791172
fax – (01639) 886991
website – www.porttalbottown.com
Year of Formation – 1901

Chairman – Andrew Edwards
Manager – Wayne Davies
Stadium – Victoria Road (2,000)
Colours – Blue/blue/blue

Rhyl FC
Belle Vue Stadium
Grange Road
Rhyl
LL18 4BV
tel – (01745) 338327
fax – (01745) 338327
website – www.rhylfc.com
Year of Formation – 1883
Chairman – Paul Higginson
Manager – John Hulse
Stadium – Belle Vue (3,800)
Colours – White/navy blue/navy blue
MAJOR HONOURS
League Championship – (1) 2004.
Domestic Cup – (4) 1952, 1953, 2004, 2006.

The New Saints FC
Enterprise House
Mile Oak
Oswestry SY10 8NS
tel – (01691) 664053
fax – (01691) 663601
website – www.saints-alive.co.uk
Year of Formation – 1959
Chairman – Edgar Jones
Manager – Ken McKenna
Stadium – Treflan (2,000)
Colours – Green & white hoops/white/white
MAJOR HONOURS
League Championship – (3) 2000, 2005, 2006.
Domestic Cup – (2) 1996, 2005.

Welshpool Town FC
Farhing Gates
Severn Lane
Welshpool SY21 7BB
tel – (01978) 552260
fax – (01978) 553614
Year of Formation – 1878
Chairman – Steve Hughes
Manager – Tomi Morgan
Stadium – Maes-y-Dre (7,000)
Colours – White (black trim)/black/white

N.B. Deadline for updates – August 7, 2006

Section 4

The European Book of Football 2006/07
Top 100 Players of the Season

This section of the Book profiles, in words, pictures and statistics, the 100 Players who, in the considered opinion of the *European Book of Football* team, had a particularly profound impact on the 2005/06 season.

There are no specific conditions of entry other than merit. However, in order to give the list a reasonable balance, the final selection process was influenced by a number of factors, such as geographical spread, age mix, nationality…and the 2006 World Cup finals.

There is no ranking within the 100. The only classification is by alphabetical order. Like last year, to encourage you to thumb through the pages and see which players made the final cut, there is no Index. Unlike last year, the statistics should be self-explanatory so there is no Key either.

Happy browsing…

MIKE HAMMOND
Editor

N.B. The cut-off date for International Caps and Goals is July 31, 2006.

Daniel ALVES da Silva
Right-Back
Born 6/5/83, Juazeiro, Brazil
Height 171cm, Weight 64kg

The star of the 2006 UEFA Cup final with his driving runs down the right touchline and pin-point crosses (one of which led to the opening goal), Sevilla full-back Daniel Alves did enough in that one game to attract the attention of a number of the Continent's leading clubs. Liverpool, in particular, were keen to lure him to Anfield, but the Andalusians slapped a prohibitive bid price on his head and negotiations broke down. The 23-year-old's fourth season at Sevilla was unquestionably his best. He started 13 of the team's 15 UEFA Cup games and was absent only three times in La Liga. His combination play down the right with the equally sprightly Jesús Navas was not only pleasing on the eye but also a fertile source of many of the team's goals. A World Youth Cup winner with Brazil in 2003, it was suggested by some that Alves might earn a late call-up to the senior squad in Germany, but that was already a closed shop. Maybe in 2010.

International Career
BRAZIL
uncapped
Club Career
Major Honours – UEFA Cup (2006)
Clubs: 01-02 FC Bahia; 02- Sevilla FC (ESP)

Stephen APPIAH
Midfielder
Born 24/12/80, Accra, Ghana
Height 178cm, Weight 77kg

He cost Fenerbahçe eight million euros from Juventus, and he was well worth the price. Stephen Appiah had a terrific debut season in Turkey. Alas, there were no medals for him to hang around his neck at the end of it as his new club finished runners-up in both the Super Lig and the Turkish Cup, but he succeeded in replacing the departed Pierre van Hooijdonk as the new darling of the Fener fans with a succession of top-notch performances. A born leader, he linked superbly with Brazilians Marco Aurélio and Alex and stamped his authority and class on just about every game. It was a great pity that he missed a late chance to win the title in Fener's final game at Denizlispor, but the supporters soon forgave him. At the World Cup his dynamic form continued as he skippered Ghana into the last 16. It was his man-of-the-match display – and winning penalty – against the USA that booked the Black Stars their last-16 date with Brazil, thus preventing an African whitewash in the first round.

International Career
GHANA
Major Honours – none
Debut – 24/12/96 v Benin (a, Cotonou, friendly) (sub), drew 1-1
First Goal – 8/10/00 v Zimbabwe (h, Accra, ANQ), won 4-1
Caps 46 **Goals** 12
Major Tournaments – African Nations Cup 2000; African Nations Cup 2006; World Cup 2006

Top 100 players of the season

Club Career
Major Honours – Italian Cup (2002)
Clubs: 96-97 Hearts of Oak; 97-00 Udinese (ITA); 00-02 Parma (ITA); 02-03 Brescia (ITA); 03-05 Juventus (ITA); 05- Fenerbahçe (TUR)

Andrei ARSHAVIN
Striker/Winger
Born 29/5/81, St. Petersburg, Russia
Height 172cm, Weight 69kg

A graduate of the renowned Smena soccer school in St. Petersburg, Andrei Arshavin has steadily moved up through the gears at local club Zenit and is now regarded as not only one of the most accomplished forwards in the Russian Premier League but also a key member of the Russian national team, where he also links up with his regular club strike-partner Alexandr Kerzhakov. A winger-cum-support striker, he gave a captivating display of skill and speed for his country against Brazil on a freezing Moscow night in March then repeated the trick for Zenit against Marseille a week later in the UEFA Cup, capping a superb display with the winning goal at the Stade Vélodrome. He scored a goal in every round of Zenit's UEFA Cup run – up until the quarter-final against Sevilla. Harshly sent off in the last minute of the first leg, he was therefore suspended for the second game in St. Petersburg, and without him Zenit exited the competition.

International Career
RUSSIA
Major Honours – none
Debut – 17/5/02 v Belarus (h, Moscow, friendly), drew 1-1
First Goal – 13/2/03 v Romania (n, Limassol, friendly), won 4-2
Caps 18 **Goals** 7
Major Tournaments – none
Club Career
Major Honours – none
Clubs: 00- Zenit Sankt-Peterburg

Shota ARVELADZE
Striker
Born 22/2/73, Tbilisi, Georgia
Height 180cm, Weight 72kg

Now 33, Shota Arveladze has enjoyed a long and distinguished career. A natural finisher, he has found goals easy to come by wherever he has played. There was a suggestion that the ex-Ajax striker might find it difficult readjusting to the Dutch Eredivisie when he moved to AZ in the summer of 2005 after four years in the Scottish Premier League with Rangers. Not a bit of it. He was up and running immediately, scoring nine goals in his first five matches for Louis van Gaal's attack-oriented team and eventually going on to score 22 for the season – second only in the Eredivisie listings to Klaas-Jan Huntelaar. A sharpshooter with both feet, Arveladze has been a Georgian international almost from day one (independence from the Soviet Union came in 1991) and has been earmarked by his country's new German coach Klaus Toppmöller as a key man in the Euro 2008 qualifying campaign.

International Career
GEORGIA
Major Honours – none
Debut – 17/9/92 v Azerbaijan (h, Tbilisi, friendly), won 6-3
First Goal – 17/9/92 v Azerbaijan (h, Tbilisi, friendly), won 6-3
Caps 57 **Goals** 21
Major Tournaments – none
Club Career
Major Honours – Dutch Championship (1998); Scottish Championship (2003, 2005); Georgian Championship (1991, 1992, 1993, 1995); Dutch Cup (1998, 1999); Scottish Cup (2002, 2003); Scottish League Cup (2002, 2003, 2005); Georgian Cup (1992, 1993, 1995)
Clubs: 90- Martve Tbilisi; 91-92 Iberia Tbilisi; 92-93 Dinamo Tbilisi; 93-94 Trabzonspor (TUR); 94-95 Dinamo Tbilisi; 95-97 Trabzonspor (TUR); 97-01 Ajax (HOL); 01-05 Rangers (SCO); 05- AZ (HOL)

Michael BALLACK
Midfielder
Born 26/9/76, Chemnitz, Germany
Height 189cm, Weight 80kg

The ultimate dream of lifting the World Cup in Berlin eluded him, but Michael Ballack played his part in taking Germany further than most people expected at the World Cup. Although he was injured and ineffective in the semi-final against Italy, he played a captain's role in each of the previous two rounds against Sweden and Argentina. Undoubtedly the finest German player of his generation, Ballack has left a gaping hole in the Bundesliga following his summer switch to Chelsea. He was the competition's leading attraction bar none for several years, and although the last of his four seasons at Bayern Munich wasn't his very best, he still contributed 14 goals in 26 league games as Bayern retained the league title (and the Cup). The second half of the season was dominated by talk of his future whereabouts, but once Chelsea offered him a king's ransom, there was never much doubt that he would pursue his career at Stamford Bridge rather than the Allianz-Arena or the Bernabéu. It remains to be seen whether he can prove as dominant in the Premiership as he was back home. That is a challenge every bit as daunting as the one he faced as captain of his country last summer.

International Career
GERMANY
Major Honours – none
Debut – 28/4/99 v Scotland (h, Bremen, friendly) (sub), lost 0-1
First Goal – 28/3/01 v Greece (a, Athens, WCQ), won 4-2
Caps 70 **Goals** 31
Major Tournaments – Confederations Cup 1999; Euro 2000; World Cup 2002; Euro 2004; Confederations Cup 2005; World Cup 2006
Club Career
Major Honours – German Championship (1998, 2003, 2005, 2006); German Cup (2003, 2005, 2006)
Clubs: 95-97 Chemnitzer FC; 97-99 1.FC Kaiserslautern; 99-02 Bayer 04

Top 100 players of the season

Leverkusen; 02-06 FC Bayern München; 06- Chelsea (ENG)

Sergej BARBAREZ
Attacking Midfielder
Born 17/9/71, Mostar, Bosnia-Herzegovina
Height 188cm, Weight 82kg

Some players get better with age, and on the evidence of Sergej Barbarez's form for club and country over the past couple of years, the final curtain is still a long way off. The classy Bosnian veteran initially retired from playing for his country at the end of the World Cup qualifiers, but a few weeks later, realising that he still had much to offer, he changed his mind. Coach Blaz Sliskovic immediately confirmed that Barbarez would captain the side in the Euro 2008 qualifiers. A refugee to Germany during the Balkan conflict of the early 1990s, Barbarez has spent his entire career in the country. The 2005/06 season was among his very best. He remained fit throughout and scored 10 goals in 33 Bundesliga appearances for Hamburg, his last goal coming on what was to be a disappointing farewell appearance as HSV lost 2-1 at home to Hanseatic rivals Werder Bremen in the battle to finish runners-up. Shortly afterwards Barbarez decided to join Bayer Leverkusen – his sixth German club.

International Career
BOSNIA-HERZEGOVINA
Major Honours – none
Debut – 14/5/98 v Argentina (a, Córdoba, friendly), lost 0-5
First Goal – 5/9/98 v Estonia (h, Sarajevo, ECQ), drew 1-1
Caps 46 Goals 15
Major Tournaments – none
Club Career
Major Honours – none
Clubs: 91-93 Hannover 96 (GER); 93-96 1.FC Union Berlin (GER); 96-98 FC Hansa Rostock (GER); 98-00 Borussia Dortmund (GER); 00-06 Hamburger SV (GER); 06- Bayer 04 Leverkusen (GER)

Yossi BENAYOUN
Attacking Midfielder
Born 5/5/80, Dimona, Israel
Height 178cm, Weight 70kg

Many foreign players need a year or more to adapt to the rigours of the English Premiership. Yossi Benayoun took to it like a duck to water. His debut season with West Ham almost ended with an FA Cup winner's medal. He had a superb game against Liverpool in the Millennium Stadium, which wasn't surprising as six days earlier he had scored a wonderful goal to beat Tottenham in the last Premiership game of the season – and prevent their local rivals from qualifying for the Champions League. It was the Israeli international's fifth goal of a highly impressive debut Premiership campaign. Many Hammers fans had not forgiven Benayoun when he spurned Bolton at the last minute to join the east Londoners from Racing Santander, but his skills, dribbles and inch-perfect passes – not to mention his never-say-die attitude – soon had the Upton Park faithful drooling. The 26-year-old is the stand-out player in the current Israeli national side and he could cause big problems for England when the two nations meet in the Euro 2008 qualifying competition.

International Career
ISRAEL
Major Honours – none
Debut – 18/11/98 v Portugal (a, Setúbal, friendly), lost 0-2
First Goal – 5/9/99 v Cyprus (a, Limassol, ECQ), lost 2-3
Caps 49 Goals 11
Major Tournaments – none
Club Career
Major Honours – Israeli Championship (2001, 2002)
Clubs: 97-98 Hapoel Beer Sheva; 98-02 Maccabi Haifa; 02-05 Racing Santander (ESP); 05- West Ham United (ENG)

Darren BENT
Striker
Born 6/2/84, London, England
Height 180cm, Weight 73kg

The general consensus was that Jermain Defoe was the unluckiest player to miss out on a place in England's World Cup squad. Darren Bent had good reason to feel equally aggrieved. The top-scoring Englishman in the Premiership, with 18 goals, he enjoyed a magnificent first season of top-flight football following a £2.7m move from his boyhood club Ipswich Town. Two goals on his Premiership debut at Sunderland and another in each of his next three games caught the eye of England coach Sven Göran Eriksson and he was drafted into the squad for the closing games of the World Cup qualifying campaign. It would be six months before he made his debut – against Uruguay at Anfield – but one disappointing performance led to his exclusion not just from the final 23 but also from the standby list. At 22, though, he is young enough to come again. A second Premiership season like his first, in which his pace and cool finishing were a lethal combination, should cement his place in new England boss Steve McClaren's plans

International Career
ENGLAND
Major Honours – none
Debut – 1/3/06 v Uruguay (h, Liverpool, friendly), won 2-1
Caps 1 Goals 0
Major Tournaments – none
Club Career
Major Honours – none
Clubs: 01-05 Ipswich Town; 05- Charlton Athletic

Dimitar BERBATOV
Striker
Born 30/1/81, Blagoevgrad, Bulgaria
Height 188cm, Weight 79kg

Dimitar Berbatov is the new pin-up boy of Bulgarian

Top 100 players of the season

football. He scored seven goals in as many matches for his country during the 2006/07 season to lift his cumulative tally to 32 in 49 internationals – just five in arrears of his national team coach, the great Hristo Stoichkov. In July, Tottenham Hotspur paid Bayer Leverkusen £10.9m – a record fee for a Bulgarian footballer – to add him to their strikeforce. The 25-year-old target man would appear to have all the necessary attributes to make his mark in the Premiership; he is tall, powerful and ruthless in front of goal. The last of his six seasons at Leverkusen was probably his best as he rattled in 21 goals in 34 Bundesliga appearances. Only Miroslav Klose, the World Cup's Golden Boot winner, scored more. Fifteen of Berbatov's tally came during the spring and he departed the Rhineland club in style with five in his last three games.

International Career
BULGARIA
Major Honours – none
Debut – 17/11/99 v Greece (a, Kozani, friendly) (sub), lost 0-1
First Goal – 12/2/00 v Chile (a, Valparaíso, friendly), lost 2-3
Caps 49 **Goals** 32
Major Tournaments – Euro 2004
Club Career
Major Honours – Bulgarian Cup (1999)
Clubs: 92-97 Pirin Blagoevgrad; 97-00 CSKA Sofia; 01-06 Bayer 04 Leverkusen (GER); 06- Tottenham Hotspur (ENG)

Diniyar BILYALETDINOV
Midfielder
Born 27/2/85, Moscow, Russia
Height 185cm, Weight 79kg

Lokomotiv Moscow changed their coach midway through the 2005 season, with long-serving Yuriy Syomin being seconded to the Russian national side. It was a big blow to the club but not, it seemed, to the career advancement of young midfielder Diniyar Bilyaletdinov. No sooner had Syomin left than the 20-year-old suddenly embarked on a majestic spell of form that not only brought him a glut of goals and assists for Lokomotiv but also persuaded Syomin to give him his first senior caps for Russia. The son of Rinat Bilyaletdinov, who played for Lokomotiv in the early-to-mid 1980s, Diniyar was unable to succeed in either of his 2005 missions – i.e. to retain the Russian title with Lokomotiv and qualify for the World Cup with Russia – but the young left-footer provided enough glimpses of his exceptional talent to suggest that he will become a big star both at club and international level in the coming years.

International Career
RUSSIA
Major Honours – none
Debut – 17/8/05 v Latvia (a, Riga, WCQ), drew 1-1
Caps 6 **Goals** 0
Major Tournaments – none
Club Career
Major Honours – Russian Championship (2004)
Clubs: 04- Lokomotiv Moskva

Erjon BOGDANI
Striker
Born 14/4/77, Tirana, Albania
Height 191cm, Weight 87kg

Erjon Bogdani has been playing in Italy since the turn of the century, but nobody really took much notice of him until he started banging in the goals for Serie B side Verona in 2004/05. His 17-goal tally – three shy of the best in the division – earned him a move to Serie A club Siena, where it was expected that he would have to live in the shadow of established names like Enrico Chiesa and Tomas Locatelli. But the Albanian international was far from overawed by his new surroundings and soon found his place in an attacking trident, his height and power proving the perfect complement to Chiesa's sharp movement and Locatelli's craft. By the end of the season Bogdani had scored 11 goals, including a memorable hat-trick at Palermo, and played such a huge part in keeping Siena out of relegation trouble that the club's Ultras voted him their Player of the Season. There was also a positive return to the international fold for the strapping striker as he scored three goals in back-to-back World Cup qualifiers, including a brilliant brace in a 2-2 draw away to group winners Ukraine.

International Career
ALBANIA
Major Honours – none
Debut – 24/4/96 v Bosnia-Herzegovina (a, Zenica, friendly) (sub), drew 0-0
First Goal – 10/2/99 v Macedonia (h, Tirana, friendly) (sub), won 2-0
Caps 30 **Goals** 5
Major Tournaments – none
Club Career
Major Honours – Albanian Cup (1997)
Clubs: 94-97 Partizani Tiranë; 98- Gençlerbirliği (TUR); 98- Dinamo Tiranë; 99- Zagreb (CRO); 00-03 Reggina (ITA); 03-04 Salernitana (ITA); 04-05 Verona (ITA); 05- Siena (ITA)

Mbark BOUSSOUFA
Midfielder
Born 15/8/84, Amsterdam, Holland
Height 167cm, Weight 59kg

Overlooked for first-team action during spells in the youth sides at Ajax and Chelsea, Mbark Boussoufa decided to try his luck in Belgium, with Gent. Highly promising in his first season at the club, he was exceptional during the second, heading the Eerste Klasse ranking for assists (with 17) and capturing the attention of the whole country with a marvellous hat-trick against defending champions Club Bruges. At the season's end he was rewarded with the Ebbenhouten Schoen (Ebony Shoe) – the prize given to the best player in the league of African origin – and a fortnight later he had another award to celebrate as he was voted by his fellow professionals as the best player in

Top 100 players of the season

the Eerste Klasse full stop. Although born in Holland, the diminutive midfielder's roots are Moroccan, and he made his international debut for the North African country in May – just before he became the most expensive footballer in Belgian football history with a 3.5 million euro transfer to champions Anderlecht. An excellent reader of the game with a keen eye for the killer pass, Boussoufa could go on to make Ajax and Chelsea regret their lack of faith in his talent.

International Career
MOROCCO
Major Honours – none
Debut – 23/5/06 v United States (a, Nashville, friendly), drew 1-1
Caps 3 **Goals** 0
Major Tournaments – none
Club Career
Major Honours – none
Clubs: 01-04 Chelsea (ENG); 04-06 KAA Gent (BEL); 06- RSC Anderlecht (BEL)

Kris BOYD
Striker
Born 18/8/83, Irvine, Scotland
Height 184cm, Weight 83kg

Since making his debut for Kilmarnock in 2001, striker Kris Boyd has increased his goal output with each successive season. He netted 15 goals in 18 SPL starts during the first half of the 2005/06 season – a sufficient haul to earn him a £500,000 mid-term transfer to Rangers. Having arrived at Ibrox during a time of fading fortunes for the club, Boyd faced a major examination of his credentials. Inevitably there were many who doubted that he could cut it in the big time, but the youngster simply carried on where he had left off, scoring a further 17 league goals (plus two in the Scottish Cup) for his new club and ending the season as the SPL's runaway leading marksman with 32 goals. A first full Scotland cap was the least he deserved for his efforts, and Boyd's dream season ended on perhaps the biggest high of all when he scored twice on his international debut as the Scots routed Bulgaria 5-1 in Japan at the Kirin Cup. Scotland have been looking for a top-class striker for years. Who knows? Maybe, in Boyd, they have finally found one.

International Career
SCOTLAND
Major Honours – none
Debut – 11/5/06 v Bulgaria (n, Kobe, Kirin Cup), won 5-1
First Goal – 11/5/06 v Bulgaria (n, Kobe, Kirin Cup), won 5-1
Caps 2 **Goals** 2
Major Tournaments – none
Club Career
Major Honours – none
Clubs: 00-06 Kilmarnock; 06- Rangers

Gianluigi BUFFON
Goalkeeper
Born 28/1/78, Carrara, Italy
Height 190cm, Weight 88kg

Gianluigi Buffon became the world's most expensive goalkeeper when he joined Juventus from Parma in 2001. Now, five years later, there is no argument whatsoever that he is also the world's best. His performances during the World Cup were immense. No opposition player put the ball past him in open play, and even the penalty with which Zinedine Zidane deceived him in the final barely made it over the line. Brave, agile and thoroughly dependable, he is young enough, at 28, to remain the Azzurri no.1 for many, many years to come. Dino Zoff was 40 when he became a world champion in 1982. Will we see Buffon at the 2018 World Cup? You never know. Although Juventus were stripped of their 2005/06 title for match-fixing, their goalkeeper was the usual model of consistency – although only for half a season; he missed the first four months of the campaign with a shoulder injury. Not that the lay-off did him any harm. In Germany he was fit, fresh and in fantastic form. The only surprise was that he didn't save any of France's penalties. Fortunately, he didn't need to.

International Career
ITALY
Major Honours – World Cup (2006)
Debut – 29/10/97 v Russia (a, Moscow, WCQ) (sub), drew 1-1
Caps 67 **Goals** 0
Major Tournaments – World Cup 1998; World Cup 2002; Euro 2004; World Cup 2006
Club Career
Major Honours – UEFA Cup (1999); Italian Championship (2002, 2003); Italian Cup (1999)
Clubs: 95-01 Parma; 01- Juventus

Fabio CANNAVARO
Central Defender
Born 13/9/73, Naples, Italy
Height 176cm, Weight 75kg

If Fabio Cannavaro had been commissioned to provide the script for the 2006 World Cup, he could not have written in a better role for himself. He was Italy's number one hero, consistently their best player, and on the occasion of his 100th cap he got to lift the most famous trophy in sport. In Germany, the Italy skipper wrote himself into the World Cup Hall of Fame. It was his third stab at the tournament. The other two, in France and the Far East, had not gone to plan. But in 2006, his first World Cup as captain, Cannavaro proudly led the Azzurri by example, and the rest of the team followed. The fact that he was deprived of his regular central defensive partner Alessandro Nesta in the knockout rounds only added to his achievement. That Zinedine Zidane, not he, was awarded the Golden Ball as the player of the tournament will always be a huge embarrassment to FIFA – not to mention to those journalists who cast their vote for the Frenchman. It was also a monstrous injustice. Irrespective of Zidane's headbutt, he played only fitfully throughout the tournament and

Top 100 players of the season

brilliantly just once (against Brazil). Cannavaro was exceptional in every game. In one of those supreme ironies that sport throws up every so often, Cannavaro left Juventus in the summer to join Real Madrid, where he was given the no.5 shirt previously worn by...Zidane.

International Career
ITALY
Major Honours – World Cup (2006)
Debut – 22/1/97 v Northern Ireland (h, Palermo, friendly) (sub), won 2-0
First Goal – 30/5/04 v Tunisia (a, Tunis, friendly), won 4-0
Caps 100 **Goals** 1
Major Tournaments – World Cup 1998; Euro 2000; World Cup 2002; Euro 2004; World Cup 2006
Club Career
Major Honours – UEFA Cup (1999); Italian Cup (1999, 2002)
Clubs: 92-95 Napoli; 95-02 Parma; 02-04 Internazionale; 04-06 Juventus; 06- Real Madrid (ESP)

Petr CECH
Goalkeeper
Born 20/5/82, Plzen, Czech Republic
Height 197cm, Weight 87kg

Petr Cech will have to accept that he is not, as many have claimed, the best goalkeeper in the world. Gianluigi Buffon outpointed him by some distance at the World Cup, although it was the Czech who probably provided the best individual goalkeeping performance of the tournament with his octopus-arm heroics in the group game against Ghana. At club level Cech had another masterful season with Chelsea. It was every bit as good as his debut season and once again resulted in a Premiership winner's medal and an open-top bus ride around west London. The giant keeper played in 34 of the club's league games and conceded only 20 goals. He was on the losing side only three times, and if he made any bad unforced errors, then nobody picked up on them. No goalkeeper is flawless, but Cech, who, at just 24, has youth as well as a vast amount of top-level experience on his side, is about as close to perfection as it gets.

International Career
CZECH REPUBLIC
Major Honours – none
Debut – 12/2/02 v Hungary (n, Larnaca, friendly), won 2-0
Caps 44 **Goals** 0
Major Tournaments – Euro 2004; World Cup 2006
Club Career
Major Honours – English Premiership (2005, 2006); English League Cup (2005)
Clubs: 99-01 FK Chmel Blsany; 01-02 AC Sparta Praha; 02-04 Stade Rennais FC (FRA); 04- Chelsea (ENG)

Joe COLE
Attacking Midfielder
Born 8/11/81, London, England
Height 175cm, Weight 74kg

For years England had a big, seemingly unsolvable problem on the left-hand side of midfield. Not any more. Joe Cole is not naturally left-footed, but he knows how to play in that position. He was one of the team's most productive players in the qualifying stages for the 2006 World Cup and, buoyed by a wonderful virtuoso display in a friendly against Uruguay, he was also one of the few England players who lived up to the billing at the finals. His goal against Sweden was possibly the most spectacular of the tournament, and his skill on the ball and willingness to take on defenders made him the pick of England's attacking players. Cole went to Germany on the back of a brilliant season for Chelsea. Finally free of the bench-warming duties that had marked his first two years at Stamford Bridge, he became a fully-fledged first-team regular, contributing eight goals to Chelsea's second successive Premiership title. Arguably the best of the lot came against Manchester United on the day Chelsea sealed the title – brilliant footwork on the edge of the area followed by a glorious shot into the top corner. Cole's ability has never been in question; nor his enthusiasm. But under José Mourinho he has learnt to channel his exquisite natural talent to the benefit of the team. His club, and his country, should continue to reap the benefit of his growing maturity for many years to come.

International Career
ENGLAND
Major Honours – none
Debut – 25/5/01 v Mexico (h, Derby, friendly), won 4-0
First Goal – 3/6/03 v Serbia & Montenegro (h, Leicester, friendly), won 2-1
Caps 37 **Goals** 6
Major Tournaments – World Cup 2002; Euro 2004; World Cup 2006
Club Career
Major Honours – English Premiership (2005, 2006); English League Cup (2005)
Clubs: 98-03 West Ham United; 03- Chelsea

Grégory COUPET
Goalkeeper
Born 31/12/72, Le Puy-en-Velay, France
Height 181cm, Weight 80kg

France coach Raymond Domenech's decision to choose Fabien Barthez as his World Cup goalkeeper did not go down too well with the French public. Grégory Coupet was the preferred candidate in every poll – and by some distance, too. As Les Bleus went all the way to the final, and conceded only two goals en route, it could of course be argued that Domenech made the right choice. An alternative viewpoint is that France went as far as they did in spite of Barthez rather than because of him. Whatever, Coupet, who stood in superbly during the qualifying tournament while his rival was serving a long suspension for spitting at a referee, is entitled to feel aggrieved that he has now gone to three major tournaments and failed to get a single minute of action. The 33-year-old, who is 18 months Barthez's junior, had another outstanding season for his club, Olympique Lyonnais,

Top 100 players of the season

winning his fifth successive Ligue 1 title. He started all but one of the club's league matches and was once again a fundamental cornerstone of their success.

International Career
FRANCE
Major Honours – Confederations Cup (2001, 2003)
Debut – 1/6/01 v Australia (n, Suwon, CC), lost 0-1
Caps 18 **Goals** 0
Major Tournaments – Confederations Cup 2001; World Cup 2002; Confederations Cup 2003; Euro 2004; World Cup 2006

Club Career
Major Honours – French Championship (2002, 2003, 2004, 2005, 2006); French League Cup (2001)
Clubs: 93-96 AS Saint-Etienne; 96- Olympique Lyonnais

DAVID VILLA Sánchez
Striker
Born 3/12/81, Langreo, Spain
Height 175cm, **Weight** 69kg

It takes someone special to shift a legend like Raúl, but David Villa managed it at the World Cup, receiving the nod of approval from Spain coach Luis Aragonés to start up front alongside Fernando Torres in place of the country's all-time record scorer. With three goals at the finals, the 24-year-old striker did not let his coach down. Uncapped until the closing stages of the qualifying campaign, he earned his elevation with a brilliant first season at Valencia. Transferred from Real Zaragoza, where he had established his reputation as a nifty, aggressive striker with an eye for goal, Villa upped the ante at Valencia and pressed Barcelona's Samuel Eto'o all the way for the coveted Pichichi trophy, scoring 25 goals, including two nerveless spot-kicks in Camp Nou and the Bernabéu. Valencia's new coach Quique Sánchez took a chance on the young striker and, unlike his acquisition of Dutchman Patrick Kluivert, the gamble paid off handsomely as Villa's goals propelled the club into third place in La Liga.

International Career
SPAIN
Major Honours – none
Debut – 8/10/05 v Belgium (a, Brussels, WCQ) (sub), won 2-0
First Goal – 16/11/05 v Slovakia (a, Bratislava, WCQ) (sub), drew 1-1
Caps 12 **Goals** 5
Major Tournaments – World Cup 2006

Club Career
Major Honours – Spanish Cup (2004)
Clubs: 00-03 Sporting Gijón; 03-05 Real Zaragoza; 05- Valencia CF

Steven DAVIS
Midfielder
Born 1/1/85, Ballymena, Northern Ireland
Height 170cm, **Weight** 60kg

Aston Villa are one of English football's sleeping giants. Without a major trophy for a decade, they underwent major surgery during the summer with the arrival of the highly respected Martin O'Neill as manager followed by a takeover from an American billionaire. One of the team's greatest assets on the pitch is O'Neill's fellow Northern Irishman Steven Davis. The gifted young midfielder was a shining light in the gloom for the club during the 2005/06 season, providing skill and industry in equal measure and making a clean sweep of all the club's player awards at the end of the campaign. He also enjoyed himself at international level, setting up David Healy's historic winner against England and scoring his first international goal in the following match against Wales. Although he is only 21, Davis has the proverbial 'old head on young shoulders' and has been widely touted to captain his country in the not too distant future.

International Career
NORTHERN IRELAND
Major Honours – none
Debut – 9/2/05 v Canada (h, Belfast, friendly), lost 0-1
First Goal – 8/10/05 v Wales (h, Belfast, WCQ), lost 2-3
Caps 13 **Goals** 1
Major Tournaments – none

Club Career
Major Honours – none
Clubs: 04- Aston Villa (ENG)

Anderson Luís de Souza "DECO"
Midfielder
Born 17/8/77, São Bernardo do Campo (São Paulo), Brazil
Height 174cm, **Weight** 75kg

When FC Porto beat Celtic in the 2003 UEFA Cup final, Deco was so good he looked like a right-footed Maradona. There were times during the World Cup when the little midfielder promised more of the same. Promised, but didn't quite deliver. Stupidly sent off in the Battle of Nuremberg against Holland, it seemed that his first World Cup might end there and then, but Portugal defeated England without him and when he returned, against France, he ran the show in the early stages. It was a similar story in the third-place match against Germany, but of course Portugal lost both games. Deco had more joy with Barcelona, winning his second Spanish title in as many seasons and also a second Champions League (following his success with Porto in 2004). As in the previous campaign, he impressed as much with his selfless endeavour and tactical discipline as with his exuberant skills. But in a team with Ronaldinho, Samuel Eto'o and Lionel Messi, it is not easy to stand out through skill alone.

International Career
PORTUGAL
Major Honours – none
Debut – 29/3/03 v Brazil (h, Oporto, friendly) (sub), won 2-1
First Goal – 29/3/03 v Brazil (h, Oporto, friendly) (sub), won 2-1
Caps 39 **Goals** 3
Major Tournaments – Euro 2004; World Cup 2006

Top 100 players of the season

Club Career
Major Honours – UEFA Champions League (2004, 2006); UEFA Cup (2003); Spanish Championship (2005, 2006); Portuguese Championship (1999, 2003, 2004); Portuguese Cup (2000, 2001, 2003)
Clubs: 97- Corinthians (BRA); 97-98 FC Alverca; 98 SC Salgueiros; 99-04 FC Porto; 04- FC Barcelona (ESP)

Daniele DE ROSSI
Midfielder
Born 24/7/83, Rome, Italy
Height 184cm, **Weight** 83kg

Of all Italy's World Cup winners, Daniele De Rossi probably has the least happy memory of his month in Germany. He spent most of it regretting the red card and four-game ban he received for planting his right elbow in the face of USA striker Brian McBride (a violent act for which he profusely apologised). He was eligible again for the final and, after appearing as a substitute, made a vital contribution to the Azzurri's success by striking home the third of their five successful penalty-kicks (the crucial one immediately after David Trezeguet had missed for France). The young midfielder, who also won the European Under-21 championship with Italy in 2004, had a fabulous season at club level with Roma. He played a major part in helping the Giallorossi set a new Serie A record of 11 successive victories, scoring three goals and setting up many others during that fabulous run. He also demonstrated his sense of fair play in a later game against Messina when he scored a goal with his hand and admitted as much to the referee, who therefore disallowed it.

International Career
ITALY
Major Honours – World Cup (2006)
Debut – 4/9/04 v Norway (h, Palermo, WCQ), won 2-1
First Goal – 4/9/04 v Norway (h, Palermo, WCQ), won 2-1
Caps 20 **Goals** 3
Major Tournaments – World Cup 2006
Club Career
Major Honours – none
Clubs: 01- Roma

Matías Emilio DELGADO
Attacking Midfielder
Born 15/12/82, Rosario, Argentina
Height 181cm, **Weight** 77kg

With Christian Giménez departing for Marseille in the late summer and Julio Hernán Rossi joining Nantes in the winter, Matías Delgado was the only one of FC Basel's illustrious Argentine trio to complete the season. It ended traumatically with a last-minute goal conceded to FC Zurich in the Swiss title decider, but up to that moment Delgado had enjoyed a fabulous run, both in the Super League and the UEFA Cup. He scored 18 goals in the league and seven more in Europe – a tally that made him the UEFA Cup's top scorer. A dead ringer for Argentine legend Gabriel Batistuta, he has yet to be capped at full international level by his country. As the Biancoceleste showed at the World Cup, they are not exactly short of skilful attacking midfielders and set-piece specialists. But at 23, Delgado still has strong international ambitions, and having left Basel to join Besiktas, the higher profile he is likely to get in Turkey should improve his chances of international recognition.

International Career
ARGENTINA
uncapped
Club Career
Major Honours – Swiss Championship (2004, 2005)
Clubs: 98-99 River Plate; 99-00 Argentinos Juniors; 00-03 Chacarita Juniors; 03-06 FC Basel (SUI); 06- Besiktas (TUR)

Nicolae Marius DICA
Attacking Midfielder
Born 9/5/80, Pitesti, Romania
Height 181cm, **Weight** 73kg

Had Steaua Bucharest withstood Middlesbrough's astonishing fightback to reach the UEFA Cup final, they would have had to face Sevilla in Eindhoven without their best player. Nicolae Dica received a yellow card at the Riverside that would have ruled him out of the final. His other contributions to the tie were a goal in each game, bringing his total in the competition to six. Sharp, skilful and clever on the ball, Dica showed all those qualities with a superb spin and strike to win the first leg in Bucharest, and there was further evidence of his talent throughout the season, especially on the home front where he was Steaua's top scorer for the second year running. His 15 goals included a hat-trick on the last day in a 4-0 win at Vaslui – a result that ensured a successful title defence for the former army club. A Romanian international, Dica didn't score for his country in his first dozen outings, but the 26-year-old is sure to be heavily involved as Romania seek to end their major tournament drought by qualifying for Euro 2008.

International Career
ROMANIA
Major Honours – none
Debut – 11/10/03 v Japan (h, Bucharest, friendly), drew 1-1
Caps 12 **Goals** 0
Major Tournaments – none
Club Career
Major Honours – Romanian Championship (2005, 2006)
Clubs: 98-00 Dacia Pitesti; 00-03 FC Arges Pitesti; 04- Steaua Bucuresti

Predrag DJORDJEVIC
Attacking Midfielder
Born 4/8/72, Kragujevac, Serbia
Height 182cm, **Weight** 75kg

It was difficult for any Serbia & Montenegro international to shine amidst the chaos of their World Cup adventure in Germany, but if anyone did, it was the oldest player in their party, left-footed schemer

Top 100 players of the season

Predrag Djordjevic. It was the veteran's first major tournament, and almost certainly his last. He went to Germany in good heart after completing his tenth successive season at Greek club Olympiakos with another domestic Double. He not only captained the team to glory but also scored more goals than anyone else in the team, albeit 60 per cent of them from the penalty spot. With nine championship-winning medals in his ten seasons, it is little wonder that Djordjevic is now regarded as the greatest player in Olympiakos's history. He has spent virtually his entire career in Greece and has Greek citizenship through marriage, but he still considers himself a proud Serb, and although it was expected that he would retire from international football after the World Cup, he expressed a desire to bow out with at least one appearance in the new Serbian national team.

International Career
SERBIA
Major Honours – none
Debut – 2/9/98 v Switzerland (h, Nis, friendly) (sub), drew 1-1
First Goal – 5/9/01 v Slovenia (h, Belgrade, WCQ), drew 1-1
Caps 37 **Goals** 1
Major Tournaments – World Cup 2006
Club Career
Major Honours – Greek Championship (1997, 1998, 1999, 2000, 2001, 2002, 2003, 2005, 2006); Greek Cup (1999, 2005, 2006)
Clubs: 91-92 Spartak Subotica; 92-96 Panilikaos (GRE); 96- Olympiakos (GRE)

Valeri DOMOVCHIYSKI
Striker
Born 10/5/86, Plovdiv, Bulgaria
Height 178cm, Weight 74kg

It can only be a matter of time before Valeri Domovchiyski lands himself a juicy fat contract with one of Europe's top clubs. Levski Sofia know they have a special talent on their hands, however, and will not allow him to be sold for a pittance. The young striker has been introduced gradually to the side by coach Stanimir Stoilov, but although ten of his 24 league appearances in 2005/06 were as a substitute, he still weighed in with 11 goals, many of them crucial in Levski's Bulgarian championship triumph. Though less prominent in the club's run to the UEFA Cup quarter-final, the youngster had his moments. Clever on the ball and ice-cool in front of goal, Domovschiyski was called up to the Bulgarian national squad for the Kirin Cup and made his debut on his last day as a teenager in a 2-1 victory over Japan. Like his illustrious national team coach, Domovchiyski hails from the city of Plovdiv, and even started out at the same club, Maritsa. The 'new Hristo Stoichkov' perchance?

International Career
BULGARIA
Major Honours – none
Debut – 9/5/06 v Japan (a, Osaka, Kirin Cup) (sub), won 2-1
Caps 2 **Goals** 0
Major Tournaments – none
Club Career
Major Honours – Bulgarian Championship (2006); Bulgarian Cup (2005)
Clubs: 04- Levski Sofia

Emmanuel EBOUE
Right-Back
Born 4/6/83, Abidjan, Ivory Coast
Height 178cm, Weight 72kg

Emmanuel Eboué has emerged from nowhere to become a major star for both Arsenal and the Ivory Coast. It was not until the 26th match of the 2005/06 season that the young full-back made his first Premiership start for the Gunners. His Champions League bow came earlier, in the autumn, but nobody could have imagined that he would rise to such extraordinary heights in such a short space of time. He became a pivotal member of Arsenal's unbreachable defence in the Champions League. With Lauren injured, Eboué stepped into the right-back role full of confidence and added a new dimension to Arsenal's play with his swashbuckling runs and energetic tackling. He took his lead from fellow Ivorian Kolo Touré and played out of his skin in the big Champions League ties against Real Madrid and Juventus. The two men were together also for the Ivory Coast at the African Nations Cup and the World Cup, where Eboué further enhanced his growing reputation.

International Career
IVORY COAST
Major Honours – none
Debut – 5/9/04 v Sudan (h, Abidjan, WCQ), won 5-0
Caps 14 **Goals** 0
Major Tournaments – African Nations Cup 2006; World Cup 2006
Club Career
Major Honours – none
Clubs: 02-04 KSK Beveren (BEL); 05- Arsenal (ENG)

Urby EMANUELSON
Left-Back
Born 16/6/86, Amsterdam, Holland
Height 176cm, Weight 66kg

Left-back has been a problem position at Ajax for many years, so the sudden emergence during the 2005/06 season of youngster Urby Emanuelson was a real bonus. The recruitment on a season-long loan of Spanish international Juanfran from Besiktas was originally intended to allow Emanuelson to develop gradually in the reserves, but the youngster had other ideas, playing with such fluency and confidence in his early games that coach Danny Blind, a former full-back himself, had no reservations about selecting him week in, week out, both in the Eredivisie and the Champions League. Given the speed with which talented young Ajax players traditionally gain senior international recognition, it was widely speculated that Emanuelson might get a surprise World Cup call-

Top 100 players of the season

up. Instead, he went on to star for the successful Dutch Under-21 side at the European championship in Portugal.

International Career
HOLLAND
uncapped

Club Career
Major Honours – Dutch Cup (2006)
Clubs: 04- Ajax (HOL)

Samuel ETO'O Fils
Striker
Born 10/3/81, Nkon, Cameroon
Height 180cm, Weight 75kg

Most of the best strikers in the game went to the World Cup. With the exception of Miroslav Klose, none emerged with their reputations enhanced. Maybe Samuel Eto'o would have challenged the German for the Golden Shoe if Cameroon had made it to the finals. He was probably the best player not to take part in Germany. His 2005/06 campaign at club level was sensational. It ended with the ultimate prize of the UEFA Champions League to add to his, and Barcelona's, second successive Spanish championship title. Eto'o was a major factor in both triumphs. He scored six goals in Europe, including the winner at Chelsea and the equaliser in the final against Arsenal, and fulfilled a personal ambition, some might say obsession, by winning the Pichichi award as La Liga's top marksman. Having been edged out the previous season by Diego Forlán, Eto'o took first place ahead of David Villa with the help of Barça's postponed last fixture against Athletic Bilbao, in which he scored the all-important 26th goal.

International Career
CAMEROON
Major Honours – African Nations Cup (2000, 2002)
Debut – 9/3/97 v Costa Rica (a, San José, friendly) (sub), lost 0-5
First Goal – 28/1/00 v Ivory Coast (n, Accra, ANF), won 3-0
Caps 64 Goals 24
Major Tournaments – World Cup 1998; African Nations Cup 2000; Confederations Cup 2001; African Nations Cup 2002; World Cup 2002; Confederations Cup 2003; African Nations Cup 2004; African Nations Cup 2006

Club Career
Major Honours – UEFA Champions League (2006); Spanish Championship (2005, 2006); Spanish Cup (2003)
Clubs: 97-98 CD Leganés (ESP); 98 Real Madrid (ESP); 99 RCD Espanyol (ESP); 99 Real Madrid (ESP); 00-04 RCD Mallorca (ESP); 04- FC Barcelona (ESP)

Francesc FÁBREGAS
Midfielder
Born 4/5/87, Arenys de Mar, Spain
Height 175cm, Weight 67kg

When Arsenal allowed Patrick Vieira to leave for Juventus, there were fears that their central midfield would be critically underpowered in his absence. Arsène Wenger knew different. He placed his trust in a teenager, and Francesc 'Cesc' Fábregas did not let him down. The young Spaniard had an awesome season, especially in the Champions League. Outstanding against Real Madrid, he was even better against Juventus, his world-class display in the home leg utterly eclipsing that of Highbury homecomer Patrick Vieira. His brilliance did not go unnoticed by Spanish national team coach Luis Aragonés, who handed Fábregas his debut in March and was so enthralled that he found a place for him in his World Cup squad. With Xavi recovered from a long-standing knee injury, Fábregas was not given a starting place initially, but a brilliant, match-turning performance as a substitute against Tunisia – which drew warm praise from, among others, Diego Maradona – changed that and he was selected from the start against France.

International Career
SPAIN
Major Honours – none
Debut – 1/3/06 v Ivory Coast (h, Valladolid, friendly), won 3-2
Caps 8 Goals 0
Major Tournaments – World Cup 2006

Club Career
Major Honours – FA Cup (2005)
Clubs: 03- Arsenal (ENG)

Jefferson Agustín FARFÁN Guadelupe
Striker
Born 26/10/84, Lima, Peru
Height 180cm, Weight 82kg

PSV took a shot in the dark when they bought Jefferson Farfán from Peruvian club Alianza Lima in 2004. Although he was a big hit in his homeland, he was barely known anywhere else. Also, with so few Peruvians plying their trade in Europe – the exceptions being Nolberto Solano and Claudio Pizarro – there was a strong likelihood that he would fail to adapt to life in Holland. But if Farfán took a year to settle, his second campaign in Eindhoven brought a dramatic explosion of form. The lively winger scored 21 Eredivisie goals to help PSV to a second straight championship triumph and also netted some useful ones in the Dutch Cup. The highlight, though, was his winning goal in the Champions League against Milan, the team that had unjustly eliminated PSV in the previous season's semi-final. There was a black side to Farfán's game, however, when he dived his way to a match-winning penalty in the league game at home to Ajax.

International Career
PERU
Major Honours – none
Debut – 23/2/03 v Haiti (h, Lima, friendly), won 5-1
First Goal – 23/2/03 v Haiti (h, Lima, friendly), won 5-1
Caps 28 Goals 12
Major Tournaments – Copa América (2004)

Club Career
Major Honours – Dutch Championship (2005, 2006); Peruvian Championship

Top 100 players of the season

(2003, 2004); Dutch Cup (2005)
Clubs: 01-04 Alianza Lima; 04- PSV (HOL)

Gennaro Ivan GATTUSO
Midfielder
Born 9/1/78, Corigliano Schiavone, Italy
Height 177cm, **Weight** 77kg

Gennaro Gattuso is a symbol of hope for honest midfield grafters everywhere. He was one of Italy's best and most consistent performers at the World Cup. Officially selected as man of the match for the quarter-final victory over Ukraine, he was also a prime candidate for the honour in the final, when his dogged resistance and energy enabled Italy to survive a strong French rally. Every successful team needs a Gattuso in their ranks. The playmakers cannot perform unless they have someone to win the ball and give it to them, and Gattuso does this task better than anyone. Although there is an aggressive streak to his game, that is part of the qualification for the job. The 28-year-old's style of play may not widely appeal to spectators, but he is a coach's dream. Many top English managers have talked glowingly of Gattuso's qualities, and the man who joined Scottish giants Rangers as a teenager would certainly be a hit in the Premiership. But the past seven years have brought him glory and recognition with Milan and, for now, that is where he is happy to stay.

International Career
ITALY
Major Honours – World Cup (2006)
Debut – 23/2/00 v Sweden (h, Palermo, friendly) (sub), won 1-0
First Goal – 15/11/00 v England (h, Turin, friendly), won 1-0
Caps 47 **Goals** 1
Major Tournaments – World Cup 2002; Euro 2004; World Cup 2006

Club Career
Major Honours – UEFA Champions League (2003); Italian Championship (2004); Italian Cup (2003); European Super Cup (2003)
Clubs: 94-97 Perugia; 97-98 Rangers (SCO); 98-99 Salernitana; 99- Milan

Steven GERRARD
Midfielder
Born 30/5/80, Liverpool, England
Height 187cm, **Weight** 78kg

If lifting the Champions League trophy as the captain of Liverpool was the highlight of Steven Gerrard's career, the low point must surely be the penalty that he put too close to Ricardo in England's World Cup quarter-final defeat by Portugal. It was his last act of a season that began almost a full year earlier in the first qualifying round of the Champions League. So much was expected of Gerrard in Germany, yet that one crucial missed penalty effectively branded him a World Cup flop. Given that he scored two fine goals in the group phase, that was an unfair assessment, but he certainly didn't impose himself on the tournament as many England fans had hoped. Sven Göran Eriksson's muddled tactics didn't help, of course, but Gerrard, who missed the 2002 tournament with injury, will know that, at 26, his big chance of World Cup glory may now have passed. Liverpool supporters, on the other hand, could not have been happier with their captain's contributions in 2005/06. The season climaxed perfectly as two brilliant goals from Gerrard in the FA Cup final against West Ham enabled Liverpool to come back and draw 3-3 before winning the trophy on penalties. It was Istanbul all over again, only this time Gerrard took one of the spot-kicks...and scored.

International Career
ENGLAND
Major Honours – none
Debut – 31/5/00 v Ukraine (h, Wembley, friendly), won 2-0
First Goal – 1/9/01 v Germany (a, Munich, WCQ), won 5-1
Caps 47 **Goals** 9
Major Tournaments – Euro 2000; Euro 2004; World Cup 2006

Club Career
Major Honours – UEFA Champions League (2005); UEFA Cup (2001); FA Cup (2001, 2006); English League Cup (2001, 2003); European Super Cup (2001, 2005)
Clubs: 98- Liverpool

Craig GORDON
Goalkeeper
Born 31/12/82, Edinburgh, Scotland
Height 193cm, **Weight** 77kg

Scottish goalkeepers don't enjoy the best of reputations – especially in England – but there is mounting evidence that the best of the current bunch could turn out to be a bit special. Craig Gordon was voted Scottish Football Writers' Footballer of the Year at the end of an excellent season that also saw the young keeper rewarded with a first trophy – the Scottish Cup – and permanent residence in Walter Smith's national team. Despite the turbulent series of events at Hearts that saw two managers dismissed, the Edinburgh-born keeper played with confidence and skill throughout. Celtic eventually ran away with the SPL, but Hearts stalked them for a long time and the end-of-season accounts showed that the runners-up conceded six goals fewer than the champions. Gordon was the man chiefly responsible for that, standing tall, defiant and undefeated in a number of big games.

International Career
SCOTLAND
Major Honours – none
Debut – 30/5/04 v Trinidad & Tobago (h, Edinburgh), won 4-1
Caps 15 **Goals** 0
Major Tournaments – none

Club Career
Major Honours – Scottish Cup (2006)
Clubs: 99- Heart of Midlothian

Michael GRAVGAARD
Central Defender
Born 3/4/78, Randers, Denmark
Height 187cm, **Weight** 88kg

Top 100 players of the season

When Michael Gravgaard made his national team debut, at the age of 27, in a friendly at home to England in August 2005, it marked the start of a year that the big Danish centre-back will never forget. He had just joined Denmark's biggest club, FC København, after an outstanding season for Viborg in which he was often required to deputise as an emergency striker. Lo and behold, after coming on as a half-time sub against England, he marked his first international with a goal – Denmark's third in a handsome 4-1 win – and then added another couple in the World Cup qualifiers against Greece and Kazakhstan. There was joy too at club level – although not many goals – as Gravgaard played an important part in helping FCK to victory in both the Danish championship and the Scandinavian Royal League. He missed the closing weeks of the campaign through injury but that could not mar an extraordinarily successful season for the late-developing defender.

International Career
DENMARK
Major Honours – none
Debut – 17/8/05 v England (h, Copenhagen, friendly) (sub), won 4-1
First Goal – 17/8/05 v England (h, Copenhagen, friendly) (sub), won 4-1
Caps 6 **Goals** 3
Major Tournaments – none
Club Career
Major Honours – Danish Championship (2006)
Clubs: 98-02 Randers FC; 02-05 Viborg FF; 05- FC København

Christian GRINDHEIM
Midfielder
Born 17/7/83, Haugesund, Norway
Height 179cm, **Weight** 76kg

Christian Grindheim is the rising star of Norwegian football. The young midfielder was playing second-level football for hometown club Haugesund in 2004, but despite the team's relegation he exhibited enough quality to earn himself a transfer to top Tippeligaen side Vålerenga. He hit it off straight away with coach Kjetil Rekdal and began to play in a similar manner to the former Norwegian international midfielder – all energy, aggression and powerful long-range shooting. A particularly impressive mid-season run earned Grindheim a call-up to the Norwegian national side, and again he took the move to a higher level in his stride, forming a youthful new midfield combination with Kristofer Haestad of Vålerenga's title rivals IK Start. Grindheim ended his dream year with a Norwegian championship winner's medal as Vålerenga scraped home ahead of Start, but there would be disappointment on the international front as Norway lost their World Cup qualifying play-off to the Czech Republic.

International Career
NORWAY
Major Honours – none
Debut – 17/8/05 v Switzerland (h, Oslo, friendly), lost 0-2
Caps 8 **Goals** 0
Major Tournaments – none
Club Career
Major Honours – Norwegian Championship (2005)
Clubs: 02-05 FK Haugesund; 05- Vålerenga Fotball

Fabio GROSSO
Left-Back
Born 28/11/77, Chieti, Italy
Height 185cm, **Weight** 74kg

He went to the World Cup as a journeyman full-back and returned home as a national hero. Fabio Grosso was the man who shrugged off unimaginable pressure to smash home the winning penalty in the final shoot-out against France. He was also the man who scored the winning goal, late in extra-time, to beat hosts Germany in the semi-final. And it was he, too, who 'won' the stoppage-time penalty for the Azzurri in their last-16 encounter against Australia. Grosso might not even have been in the side during the latter stages had it not been for regular right-back Cristian Zaccardo's howler of an own-goal against the USA in the second group game. Grosso had been left out of that fixture to make way for Gianluca Zambrotta, who was fit again from a thigh injury, but that faux pas from Zaccardo (Grosso's team-mate at Palermo) persuaded coach Marcello Lippi to switch Zambrotta to the right and restore Grosso at left-back. The 28-year-old would not miss a minute of play thereafter. Shortly after returning to Italy, Grosso was transferred from Palermo (where, intriguingly, he had not scored all season) to Internazionale.

International Career
ITALY
Major Honours – World Cup (2006)
Debut – 30/4/03 v Switzerland (a, Geneva, friendly), won 2-1
First Goal – 3/9/05 v Scotland (a, Glasgow, WCQ) (sub), drew 1-1
Caps 23 **Goals** 2
Major Tournaments – World Cup 2006
Club Career
Major Honours – none
Clubs: 99-01 Chieti; 01-04 Perugia; 04-06 Palermo; 06- Internazionale

Paul HARTLEY
Attacking Midfielder
Born 19/10/76, Glasgow, Scotland
Height 173cm, **Weight** 67kg

Reaching the summit of Scottish football has been a long and winding journey for Paul Hartley, but he finally got there, at the age of 29, in 2005/06. His third season at Heart of Midlothian saw him cement his place both at the Tynecastle club and in the Scotland national side. He contributed 17 goals in all competitions for Hearts, including a hat-trick in the 4-0 mauling of Edinburgh rivals Hibernian in the semi-final of the Scottish Cup. Hartley's build-up play in midfield proved to be just as useful as his goalscoring

Top 100 players of the season

prowess – a fact not lost on Scotland manager Walter Smith who added Hartley to his list of midfield indispensables alongside Darren Fletcher and Barry Ferguson. The 29-year-old has done the rounds of the Scottish game and might have added Celtic to his ports of call when the Glasgow giants made a bid for him in January 2005, but Hearts rejected the offer and both club and player have since gone from strength to strength.

International Career
SCOTLAND
Major Honours – none
Debut – 26/3/05 v Italy (a, Milan, WCQ), lost 0-2
First Goal – 12/10/05 v Slovenia (a, Celje, WCQ), won 3-0
Caps 7 **Goals** 1
Major Tournaments – none
Club Career
Major Honours – Scottish Cup (2006)
Clubs: 94-96 Hamilton Academical; 96-97 Millwall (ENG); 97-98 Raith Rovers; 99-00 Hibernian; 00-03 St. Johnstone; 03- Heart of Midlothian

HASAN Sas
Attacking Midfielder
Born 1/8/76, Adana, Turkey
Height 177cm, Weight 74kg

Hasan Sas rocked the world in 2002 when he played a leading role in Turkey's run to the semi-finals of the World Cup in Korea/Japan. It was the pinnacle of a career that has frequently wavered from one extreme to the other. He was unable to take his country back to the global stage in 2006 but he returned to prominence in a big way at club level with Galatasaray. Little had been seen of the fiery left-footer since those heady days in the Far East, but in the second half of the 2005/06 campaign he became a real team leader for Galatasaray both on and off the pitch. He used his experience and influence to help quell a players' mutiny over unpaid wages and led the club's charge to the Turkish title with a steady supply of valuable crosses and passes for front men Hakan Sükür, Ümit Karan and Necati Ates. When Gala edged out arch-rivals Fenerbahçe to win the Super Lig on the final day, Hasan Sas broke down in tears. It was a side of the 'bald angry guy' that few had seen before and made for one of the most memorable, and symbolic, images of the Turkish season.

International Career
TURKEY
Major Honours – none
Debut – 22/4/98 v Russia (a, Moscow, friendly), lost 0-1
First Goal – 3/6/02 v Brazil (n, Ulsan, WCF), lost 1-2
Caps 40 **Goals** 2
Major Tournaments – World Cup 2002
Club Career
Major Honours – UEFA Cup (2000); Turkish Championship (1999, 2000, 2002, 2006); Turkish Cup (1999, 2000, 2005)
Clubs: 94-95 Adana Demirspor; 95-98 Ankaragücü; 98- Galatasaray

Thierry HENRY
Striker
Born 17/8/77, Paris, France
Height 187cm, Weight 81kg

Thierry Henry ended a long and historic season with the double disappointment of losing both the Champions League final with Arsenal and the World Cup final with France. Needless to say, he would have swapped two silvers for one gold. Judging by his heated reaction after the game against Barcelona in (his home town of) Paris, that was the defeat that hurt more. A couple of days later he signed a new contract for Arsenal, having looked set to join Barça. Events in the Stade de France (where he played uncharacteristically poorly and missed two big chances) seemingly persuaded him to change his mind. That was a very tasty sweetener for the Arsenal fans, who would have been heartbroken to lose a player who had become the club's all-time record goalscorer during the season and once again – for the fourth time in five seasons – finished up as the Premiership's top marksman, completing his 27-goal haul with a hat-trick on the final day of the season in the last game ever staged at Highbury. Henry was not quite in the same majestic form for France at the World Cup, but he still managed three goals (only one other player scored more) and that included a famous winner against Brazil.

International Career
FRANCE
Major Honours – World Cup (1998); European Championship (2000); Confederations Cup (2003)
Debut – 11/10/97 v South Africa (h, Lens, friendly), won 2-1
First Goal – 12/6/98 v South Africa (h, Marseilles, WCF), won 3-0
Caps 85 **Goals** 36
Major Tournaments – World Cup 1998; Euro 2000; World Cup 2002; Confederations Cup 2003; Euro 2004; World Cup 2006
Club Career
Major Honours – English Premiership (2002, 2004); French Championship (1997); FA Cup (2002, 2003, 2005)
Clubs: 94-98 AS Monaco; 99 Juventus (ITA); 99- Arsenal (ENG)

Klaas-Jan HUNTELAAR
Striker
Born 12/8/83, Drempt, Holland
Height 186cm, Weight 80kg

His exclusion from Holland's World Cup squad was deemed highly controversial, yet Klaas-Jan Huntelaar had never played a senior match for his country when Marco van Basten revealed his list of 23. What the young striker had done, though, was score a vast number of goals in the Eredivisie – 17 in the first half of the season for Heerenveen and, after his record Dutch transfer in January, 16 for Ajax – and then win the Dutch Cup for his new club with two goals in the final against former club PSV (the second with the last kick of the game). If that was the icing on the cake of an unforgettable season, the cherry came soon

Top 100 players of the season

afterwards as Huntelaar went to the European Under-21 championship in Portugal and became the top scorer of the tournament, scoring four goals, including two in the final, which Holland won 3-0 against Ukraine. A veritable goal-machine, Huntelaar may well have kept his prolific run going at the World Cup, but Van Basten was not prepared to give him the chance. After the team's struggles in front of goal in Germany, it is a decision the Bondscoach must now surely regret.

International Career
HOLLAND
uncapped
Club Career
Major Honours – Dutch Cup (2006)
Clubs: 02 PSV; 03 De Graafschap; 03-04 AGOVV Apeldoorn; 04-06 SC Heerenveen; 06- Ajax

Tobias HYSÉN
Winger
Born 9/3/82, Gothenburg, Sweden
Height 179cm, Weight 79kg

His father, Glenn Hysén, was one of Sweden's most celebrated defenders, winning 68 international caps, lifting two UEFA Cups with IFK Gothenburg and playing for major European clubs PSV, Fiorentina and Liverpool. Tobias has a long way to go to match that record but he was the dominant figure in the 2005 domestic season in Sweden, carrying Stockholm club Djurgårdens IF to victory in both the Allsvenskan and the Svenska Cupen. His father might have had divided loyalties as it was his beloved Gothenburg that Djurgården defeated to win the league title, but Hysén junior surely did his Dad proud with his sustained excellence in the Djurgården midfield. He supplied nine goals and ten assists in the league and terrorised defences all season with his speed, technical ability and lethal left foot. There was disappointment for the 24-year-old, however, when he was omitted from Sweden's World Cup squad.

International Career
SWEDEN
Major Honours – none
Debut – 22/1/05 v South Korea (n, Los Angeles, friendly), drew 1-1
Caps 5 Goals 0
Major Tournaments – none
Club Career
Major Honours – Swedish Championship (2005); Swedish Cup (2004, 2005)
Clubs: 98 Lundby IF; 99-03 BK Häcken; 04- Djurgårdens IF

Andrés INIESTA
Midfielder
Born 11/5/85, Fuentealbilla, Spain
Height 170cm, Weight 67kg

It is often the case in football that one player's misfortune leads to the making of another. Andrés Iniesta benefited hugely from the long-term knee injury sustained by his Barcelona team-mate Xavi in November 2005. No longer was he the utility substitute that Frank Rijkaard threw on when others got tired. Now Iniesta's energetic midfield play was regularly on view from the start. The responsibility of dictating the tempo of Barça's play was huge, but Iniesta fully justified his promotion. Although similar in physique to Xavi, Iniesta prefers to operate in a more advanced position closer to the attackers. He is also more daring in his choice of pass and rarely shirks the opportunity to shoot on goal. Iniesta started all four matches for Barça in the Champions League quarter- and semi-finals, so it was a disappointment for him to be benched again for the final. But he came on at half-time and helped to turn the game. Called up to Spain's World Cup squad, the Under-21 captain played just once, against Saudi Arabia, but seems sure to figure more prominently in the future.

International Career
SPAIN
Major Honours – none
Debut – 27/5/06 v Russia (h, Albacete, friendly), drew 0-0
Caps 4 Goals 0
Major Tournaments – World Cup 2006
Club Career
Major Honours – UEFA Champions League (2006); Spanish Championship (2005, 2006)
Clubs: 00- FC Barcelona

Jussi JÄÄSKELÄINEN
Goalkeeper
Born 19/4/75, Mikkeli, Finland
Height 191cm, Weight 81kg

With Antti Niemi retired from international football, Juusi Jääskeläinen's patience has finally been rewarded with a regular place in the Finnish national team. The 31-year-old impressed new head coach Roy Hodgson by keeping a clean sheet in a 0-0 draw against neighbours Sweden in May. That was hardly a surprise given the excellence of the big keeper's displays all season long in the English Premiership with Bolton Wanderers. Jääskeläinen was occasionally excused from duty during Bolton's UEFA Cup run in order to give his deputy, ex-England international Ian Walker, a run-out, but in the Premiership the popular Finn was an ever-present. Bought for a mere £100,000 in November 1997, he completed his 500th match for Bolton in March and helped to steer the unfashionable northern club to their third top-ten finish in a row.

International Career
FINLAND
Major Honours – none
Debut – 25/3/98 v Malta (a, Ta' Qali, friendly), won 2-0
Caps 27 Goals 0
Major Tournaments – none
Club Career
Major Honours – none
Clubs: 92-95 MP; 96-97 VPS; 97- Bolton Wanderers (ENG)

Top 100 players of the season

JUNINHO Pernambucano
Attacking Midfielder
Born 30/1/75, Recife, Brazil
Height 179cm, Weight 74kg

When Olympique Lyonnais bought Juninho from Vasco da Gama in 2001, they had never won the French championship. Now, five years later, they have won it five times. To say that they would not have done so without the Brazilian can never be proved, but equally it would be hard to argue with the notion that Juninho is the greatest player in Lyon's history. Three others have taken part in all five triumphs – Grégory Coupet, Cláudio Caçapa and Sidney Govou – but Juninho has consistently been the outstanding performer, none more so than in 2005/06 when he was rewarded for his efforts with the French Player of the Year award. As ever, Juninho bamboozled goalkeepers and defensive walls with his stunning array of free-kicks. He has now scored enough goals from free-kicks for Lyon to warrant a best-selling DVD. Arguably the best of all came away to Ajaccio on March 4 when he found the top corner from all of 40 metres. He went to the World Cup with Brazil but only as a fringe player and announced his international retirement after the quarter-final defeat to France.

International Career
BRAZIL
Major Honours – Confederations Cup (2005)
Debut – 7/9/99 v Argentina (h, Porto Alegre, friendly), won 4-2
First Goal – 16/6/05 v Greece (n, Leipzig, CC) (sub), won 3-0
Caps 40 **Goals** 6
Major Tournaments – Copa América 2001; Confederations Cup 2005; World Cup 2006
Club Career
Major Honours – Brazilian Championship (1997, 2001); French Championship (2002, 2003, 2004, 2005, 2006)
Clubs: 93-94 Sport Recife; 95-01 Vasco da Gama; 01- Olympique Lyonnais (FRA)

Ricardo Izecson dos Santos Leite "KAKÁ"
Attacking Midfielder
Born 22/4/82, Brasília, Brazil
Height 183cm, Weight 73kg

He was the best of Brazil's so-called Magic Quartet in Germany, but not even Kaká could honestly claim that he had a good World Cup. His winning goal against Croatia in the Seleção's opening game was a gem, but thereafter the lithe schemer never really stamped his class on the tournament. To be rated better than Ronaldinho would normally count as a glowing reference, but not in Germany. However, like the Barcelona megastar, Kaká had an excellent season on the club front. He carried on his Champions League form from the previous season, scoring five goals at the San Siro, and he was also Milan's best player in Serie A. Among his 14 league goals was the winner in the home game over Juventus – the only league defeat the Turin giants would suffer all season...until the book was thrown at them by the investigators of the Moggiopoli match-fixing scandal.

International Career
BRAZIL
Major Honours – World Cup (2002); Copa América (2004); Confederations Cup (2005)
Debut – 31/1/02 v Bolivia (h, Goiánia, friendly) (sub), won 6-0
First Goal – 7/3/02 v Iceland (h, Cuiaba, friendly), won 6-1
Caps 44 **Goals** 15
Major Tournaments – World Cup 2002; Copa América 2004; Confederations Cup 2005; World Cup 2006
Club Career
Major Honours – Italian Championship (2004)
Clubs: 00-03 FC São Paulo; 03- Milan (ITA)

Robbie KEANE
Striker
Born 8/7/80, Dublin, Republic of Ireland
Height 176cm, Weight 73kg

March 2006 was a memorable month for Robbie Keane. It started with him celebrating his first match as the new captain of the Republic of Ireland – an honour bestowed on him by new manager Steve Staunton – with his record-extending 26th international goal. Two days later it was announced that he had signed a lucrative new four-year contract with Tottenham Hotspur, and to celebrate he scored five goals in three Premiership matches, all of them won, as Spurs closed in on what they hoped would be a Champions League place. Unfortunately, Keane was one of several Tottenham players struck down with food poisoning on the day of their final Premiership game at West Ham and they lost the match 2-1 to allow bitter rivals Arsenal to leapfrog over them into that coveted fourth spot. Keane had scored his 16th league goal of the campaign a fortnight earlier in the 1-1 draw at Highbury. It was one of the most controversial goals of the entire Premiership season, with Arsenal claiming that Spurs should have put the ball into touch to allow treatment to an injured Arsenal player rather than play on to the whistle.

International Career
REPUBLIC OF IRELAND
Major Honours – none
Debut – 25/3/98 v Czech Republic (a, Olomouc, friendly) (sub), lost 1-2
First Goal – 14/10/98 v Malta (h, Dublin, ECQ), won 5-0
Caps 66 **Goals** 26
Major Tournaments – World Cup 2002
Club Career
Major Honours – none
Clubs: 97-99 Wolverhampton Wanderers (ENG); 99-00 Coventry City (ENG); 00-01 Internazionale (ITA); 01-02 Leeds United (ENG); 02- Tottenham Hotspur (ENG)

Alexandr KERZHAKOV
Striker
Born 27/11/82, Kingisepp, Russia
Height 175cm, Weight 67kg

Having been the top scorer in the Russian Premier

Top 100 players of the season

League with 18 goals for Zenit St. Petersburg in 2004, Alexandr Kerzhakov managed a mere seven in 2005, but that didn't stop the managers of the division's 16 clubs from voting him as their Player of the Year. The young striker is more than just a goalscorer. Strong, two-footed and skilful, he also has exceptional acceleration from a standing start and can leave defenders for dead when placed in a one-on-one situation. Kerzhakov's partnership with Andrei Arshavin has flourished both at Zenit and in the Russian national team. It has been especially prolific in the UEFA Cup, where Kerzhakov has scored 16 goals in 23 games, qualifying rounds included. He netted six goals in the competition proper in 2005/06, including a brace in a 2-1 win over eventual winners Sevilla during the group phase.

International Career
RUSSIA
Major Honours – none
Debut – 27/3/02 v Estonia (a, Tallinn, friendly) (sub), lost 1-2
First Goal – 21/8/02 v Sweden (h, Moscow, friendly) (sub), drew 1-1
Caps 34 **Goals** 7
Major Tournaments – World Cup 2002; Euro 2004
Club Career
Major Honours – none
Clubs: 00 Svetogorets Svetogorsk; 01- Zenit Sankt-Peterburg

Miroslav KLOSE
Striker
Born 9/6/78, Opole, Poland
Height 182cm, Weight 81kg

Five goals, all against Latin American opposition, were enough to win Miroslav Klose the FIFA Golden Shoe as the 2006 World Cup's top goalscorer. No other player scored more than three, so although it was the lowest winning total since six players scored four goals apiece at the 1962 tournament in Chile, Klose still won it by the proverbial landslide. Furthermore the 28-year-old striker claimed a World Cup scoring record all of his own when he became the first man ever to score five or more goals in successive finals, having also claimed that number in 2002. It was no surprise that Klose had such a good tournament. He went into the World Cup bursting with confidence after a brilliant Bundesliga season with Werder Bremen. Despite being laid low three times during the season, with injuries to his knee, shoulder and face, he still managed to score a league-best 25 goals (and provide a further 14 assists) as he spearheaded Bremen's charge to second place behind Bayern Munich. Fittingly, it was his late header away to Hamburg on the final day that booked Bremen an automatic Champions League berth at their northern rivals' expense.

International Career
GERMANY
Major Honours – none
Debut – 24/3/01 v Albania (h, Leverkusen, WCQ) (sub), won 2-1
First Goal – 24/3/01 v Albania (h, Leverkusen, WCQ) (sub), won 2-1
Caps 62 **Goals** 29
Major Tournaments – World Cup 2002; Euro 2004; World Cup 2006
Club Career
Major Honours – none
Clubs: 98-99 FC Homburg; 99-04 1.FC Kaiserslautern; 04- SV Werder Bremen

Philipp LAHM
Full-Back
Born 11/11/83, Munich, Germany
Height 170cm, Weight 62kg

Technically, and visually, the most perfectly struck goal of the World Cup was the very first of the tournament, curled into the top corner from the left angle of the penalty area by German left-back Philipp Lahm in the sixth minute of the Opening Game against Costa Rica. The 22-year-old would not score again but he would play every minute of every game – the only German to do so – and earn most people's vote as the best left-back in the competition. Lahm, who had hinted at his potential at Euro 2004, was as fresh as a daisy for the World Cup, having missed the first half of the season while recovering from a serious knee injury sustained just after he had returned to his boyhood club Bayern Munich after a two-year loan at VfB Stuttgart. He finally made his Bundesliga debut for Bayern in December 2005 and helped the club to the league and Cup Double, but it was at the World Cup, with his novel interpretation of full-back play (i.e. as a right-footer playing on the left), that he really made his mark.

International Career
GERMANY
Major Honours – none
Debut – 18/2/04 v Croatia (a, Split, friendly), won 2-1
First Goal – 28/4/04 v Romania (a, Bucharest, friendly), lost 1-5
Caps 25 **Goals** 2
Major Tournaments – Euro 2004; World Cup 2006
Club Career
Major Honours – German Championship (2006); German Cup (2006)
Clubs: 03-05 VfB Stuttgart; 05- FC Bayern München

Frank LAMPARD
Midfielder
Born 20/6/78, Romford, England
Height 183cm, Weight 79kg

The less said about Frank Lampard's World Cup, the better. England's leading goalscorer in the qualifying competition never looked like finding the net in Germany – despite FIFA's statistical division informing everybody that he had more efforts on goal than any other player at the tournament. Even his penalty against Portugal in the quarter-final shoot-out was saved. It was a different story altogether for the midfielder on the home front, where once again he was a central figure in Chelsea's domination of the Premiership under José Mourinho. Lampard scored 16 league goals – three more than in 2004/05 – to become Chelsea's top scorer once again. He had

Top 100 players of the season

reached double figures by the end of October after a scintillating start and would be rewarded for his exceptional form throughout 2005 with second place to Ronaldinho in the voting both for the Ballon d'Or and the FIFA World Player of the Year award.

International Career
ENGLAND
Major Honours – none
Debut – 10/10/99 v Belgium (h, Sunderland, friendly), won 2-1
First Goal – 20/8/03 v Croatia (h, Ipswich, friendly), won 3-1
Caps 45 **Goals** 11
Major Tournaments – Euro 2004; World Cup 2006
Club Career
Major Honours – English Premiership (2005, 2006); English League Cup (2005)
Clubs: 95-01 West Ham United (96 Swansea City); 01- Chelsea

Søren LARSEN
Striker
Born 6/9/81, Copenhagen, Denmark
Height 193cm, Weight 86kg

For two decades the Danish national side has been looking for the 'new Preben Elkjaer'. Ebbe Sand had a go but never quite filled the 1980s superstar's boots. Now it is Søren Larsen's turn. The big striker has energetically pressed his claims since making his Denmark debut in June 2005, scoring six goals in his first nine international appearances (seven as a substitute), but it might take a change of tactics from national team boss Morten Olsen, or an injury to Jon Dahl Tomasson, for Larsen to become a regular starter during the Euro 2008 qualifying campaign. Until 2005 few Danish fans knew who Søren Larsen was. A move to Sweden provided the breakthrough. He rifled in ten goals in the first half of the 2005 Allsvenskan season for Djurgårdens IF – a contribution that would help the Stockholm club to regain the Swedish title. The big Dane would not be there to collect his medal at the finish, though, having been snapped up by German heavyweights Schalke. Another ten goals in the Bundesliga would make him Schalke's joint-top scorer, although, as with Denmark, his greatest impact was as a supersub.

International Career
DENMARK
Major Honours – none
Debut – 2/6/05 v Finland (a, Tampere, friendly) (sub), won 1-0
First Goal – 8/6/05 v Albania (h, Copenhagen, friendly), won 3-1
Caps 9 **Goals** 6
Major Tournaments – none
Club Career
Major Honours – Swedish Championship (2005)
Clubs: 00-01 Køge BK; 01-02 Brøndby IF; 02-04 BK Frem; 04-05 Djurgårdens IF (SWE); 05- FC Schalke 04 (GER)

Jens LEHMANN
Goalkeeper
Born 10/11/69, Essen, Germany
Height 187cm, Weight 80kg

When Jürgen Klinsmann announced that Jens Lehmann would be his number one goalkeeper at the World Cup instead of 2002 saviour Oliver Kahn, most Germans were shocked. But the 36-year-old keeper's outstanding form for Arsenal demanded his elevation. Although his season ended with a controversial red card in the Champions League final, the good news was that his early dismissal guaranteed he went through the entire European campaign without conceding a goal. His best moment was the penalty save from Villarreal's Juan Román Riquelme late in the semi-final, and at the World Cup he would become a hero once again with his spot-kick stops from Roberto Ayala and Esteban Cambiasso in the quarter-final against Argentina. Having never played in a World Cup match before, not even a qualifier, Lehmann fully justified Klinsmann's faith in him. With Kahn now retired from international football, it looks as if Lehmann has the job for keeps. An immensely fit athlete, he could even turn up for the 2010 World Cup at the age of 40.

International Career
GERMANY
Major Honours – none
Debut – 28/4/99 v Scotland (h, Bremen, friendly) (sub), lost 0-1
First Goal – 28/3/01 v Greece (a, Athens, WCQ), won 4-2
Caps 70 **Goals** 31
Major Tournaments – World Cup 1998; Confederations Cup 1999; Euro 2000; World Cup 2002; Euro 2004; Confederations Cup 2005; World Cup 2006
Club Career
Major Honours – UEFA Cup (1997); Italian Championship (1999); German Championship (2002); English Premiership (2004); FA Cup (2005)
Clubs: 89-98 FC Schalke 04; 98 Milan (ITA); 99-03 Borussia Dortmund; 03- Arsenal (ENG)

Aaron LENNON
Right-Winger
Born 16/4/87, Leeds, England
Height 168cm, Weight 65kg

Unlike Theo Walcott, the 'unknown' 17-year-old nonsensically taken to the World Cup by England coach Sven Göran Eriksson, Aaron Lennon was a gamble that paid off. In fact, had Eriksson been braver and used the jet-heeled young winger more often – as opposed to persisting with the pedestrian David Beckham – the chances are that England would have had a brighter tournament. Lennon was uncapped when he was named in the World Cup squad. He owed his place largely to a wretched first season at Chelsea for ex-Manchester City winger Shaun Wright-Phillips, but there was clear evidence of his international potential during a domestic campaign in which his form systematically improved as the months went by. Tottenham had bought him from Leeds for a knockdown fee of £1m. He had to bide his time, but in the second half of the season he was sensational, roasting a succession of Premiership full-backs with his trickery and searing pace. The lad from Leeds has a dazzling future ahead of him.

Top 100 players of the season

International Career
ENGLAND
Major Honours – none
Debut – 3/6/06 v Jamaica (h, Manchester, friendly) (sub), won 6-0
Caps 4 **Goals** 0
Major Tournaments – World Cup 2006
Club Career
Major Honours – none
Clubs: 03-05 Leeds United; 05- Tottenham Hotspur

Roland LINZ
Striker
Born 9/8/81, Leoben, Austria
Height 185cm, Weight 73kg

He is still only 25, but Roland Linz has already added a catalogue of clubs to his CV, the latest being Boavista, whom he joined in the summer after coming to the end of a one-year contract with Austria Vienna. The Violetten were sad to see him go, because Linz was one of the chief contributors to the club's Austrian championship triumph. He scored 15 league goals, all but one of them leading to victories (the exception was a bizarre 4-4 draw at home to bottom club Admira Wacker Mödling on April Fool's Day). That tally was enough to earn him a joint share of the Bundesliga's top-scorer prize. It also pushed him to the head of the queue to lead Austria's attack at Euro 2008. The pacy striker gave an incredible second-half performance as a substitute in Austria's World Cup qualifier away to Poland, scoring two fine goals, missing a couple of chances, then heading against the bar in the last minute.

International Career
AUSTRIA
Major Honours – none
Debut – 27/3/02 v Slovakia (h, Graz, friendly), won 2-0
First Goal – 3/9/05 v Poland (a, Chorzow, WCQ) (sub), lost 2-3
Caps 15 **Goals** 2
Major Tournaments – none
Club Career
Major Honours – Austrian Championship (2003, 2006); Austrian Cup (2003, 2006)
Clubs: 97-99 TSV 1860 München (GER); 99-01 DSV Leoben; 01-03 FK Austria Wien; 03-04 VfB Admira Wacker Mödling; 04 OGC Nice (FRA); 05 SK Sturm Graz; 05-06 FK Austria Wien; 06- Boavista FC (POR)

LÚCIO Ferreira da Silva
Central Defender
Born 8/5/78, Brasília, Brazil
Height 188cm, Weight 80kg

The 2006 World Cup was not a happy experience for any Brazilian, but according to the statisticians at FIFA centre-back Lúcio set a new tournament record for a defender by going 386 minutes without conceding a foul. He has always been renowned for his class and elegance, and he showed plenty of those qualities during his five appearances in Germany. An ever-present now for the Seleção in two successive World Cups, Lúcio is young enough to complete the hat-trick in South Africa in 2010, but before then he has other objectives, the first of which will be to win a third successive German league and Cup Double with Bayern Munich. Since his transfer from Bayer Leverkusen in 2004, Lúcio has known only success with the Bavarian club. In 2005/06 he frequently played alongside three Frenchmen in the Bayern back four – Willy Sagnol, Valerien Ismaël and Bixente Lizarazu – so Brazil's World Cup quarter-final defeat to Les Bleus will probably have hurt him a little bit more than most.

International Career
BRAZIL
Major Honours – World Cup (2002); Confederations Cup (2005)
Debut – 15/11/00 v Colombia (h, São Paulo, WCQ), won 1-0
First Goal – 9/2/05 v Hong Kong (a, Hong Kong, friendly), won 7-1
Caps 56 **Goals** 2
Major Tournaments – Confederations Cup 2001; World Cup 2002; Confederations Cup 2003; Confederations Cup 2005; World Cup 2006
Club Career
Major Honours – German Championship (2005, 2006); German Cup (2005, 2006)
Clubs: 97-00 Internacional Porto Alegre; 01-04 Bayer 04 Leverkusen (GER); 04- FC Bayern München (GER)

Ludovic MAGNIN
Left-Back
Born 20/4/79, Sion, Switzerland
Height 185cm, Weight 76kg

Switzerland were castigated by many for their negative play at the World Cup, but much of the criticism was unjustified. One player who certainly didn't deserve any flak was left-back Ludovic Magnin. He impressed in the opening game against France – played on the home ground of his club, VfB Stuttgart – and maintained his form in the subsequent matches against Togo and Ukraine (he was injured for the final group game against South Korea). Forceful and dynamic going forward, he sent in some exquisite crosses and also showed that he could defend, too, frequently keeping a cool head under pressure. Magnin will almost certainly be active for his country again at Euro 2008, but in the meantime he needs to improve his consistency at club level. Less than a success at Werder Bremen (he barely played in their Double-winning campaign of 2003/04), his first season at Stuttgart was better, but generally it was in the red and white of his country rather than his club that he excelled.

International Career
SWITZERLAND
Major Honours – none
Debut – 16/8/00 v Greece (h, St. Gallen, friendly) (sub), drew 2-2
First Goal – 13/2/02 v Hungary (n, Limassol, friendly), won 2-1
Caps 33 **Goals** 2
Major Tournaments – Euro 2004; World Cup 2006
Club Career
Major Honours – German Championship (2004); German Cup (2004)
Clubs: 96-97 Lausanne-Sports; 98-00 Yverdon-Sport FC; 00-01 FC Lugano; 02-05 SV Werder Bremen (GER); 05- VfB Stuttgart (GER)

Top 100 players of the season

Claude MAKELELE
Defensive Midfielder
Born 18/2/73, Kinshaha, Zaire
Height 170cm, Weight 65kg

The prototype of the modern holding midfielder, Claude Makelele is so adept at the position that commentators and fans in England, where he has played for the past three years with Chelsea, have taken to speaking of the "Makelele role". The Frenchman rarely ventures outside his own half, screening the defence with timely challenges and interceptions before invariably relaying the ball a short distance to the closest team-mate. Chelsea manager José Mourinho was effusive in his praise for Makelele after his debut Premiership success in 2004/05, and there was no need for him to repeat himself a year later after another virtually fault-free campaign from the little anchorman. A relative latecomer to the French national side, Makelele decided to retire from international football after Euro 2004 but returned a year later in Zinedine Zidane's wake and prospered at the World Cup finals. He was on the field for every minute of Les Bleus' roller-coaster ride in Germany, doing what he does best. After winning his 50th cap in the final, he decided to call it quits again…but then backtracked once more and declared himself available if needed.

International Career
FRANCE
Major Honours – none
Debut – 22/7/95 v Norway (a, Oslo, friendly), drew 0-0
Caps 50 **Goals** 0
Major Tournaments – World Cup 2002; Euro 2004; World Cup 2006
Club Career
Major Honours – UEFA Champions League (2002); Spanish Championship (2001, 2003); English Premiership (2005, 2006); French Championship (1995); English League Cup (2005)
Clubs: 92-97 FC Nantes; 97-98 Olympique Marseille; 98-00 RC Celta (ESP); 00-03 Real Madrid (ESP); 03- Chelsea (ENG)

Shaun MALONEY
Striker
Born 24/1/83, Kuala Lumpur, Malaysia
Height 168cm, Weight 69kg

Injury comebacks don't get much better than this: 13 league goals, 11 assists (the joint-highest total in the SPL), an international debut and two prestigious awards. Not a bad haul for a 23-year-old who barely played at all during the previous season after suffering a complicated cruciate ligament injury in January 2004. The pressure on Shaun Maloney following his long lay-off was intense, but he quickly impressed new Celtic manager Gordon Strachan with his skill and drive and went on to deliver a succession of top-quality performances as the Bhoys won the SPL title. The youngster built up momentum as the season progressed, scoring in six consecutive matches in the early spring, including a magnificent goal from a curling free-kick to set Celtic on the road to victory against Dunfermline in the League Cup final. Maloney capped a marvellous season by winning both the SPFA Player and Young Player of the Year awards. It was the first time anyone had scooped both awards simultaneously.

International Career
SCOTLAND
Major Honours – none
Debut – 8/10/05 v Belarus (h, Glasgow, WCQ) (sub), lost 0-1
Caps 2 **Goals** 0
Major Tournaments – none
Club Career
Major Honours – Scottish Championship (2002, 2004, 2006); Scottish Cup (2004, 2006); Scottish League Cup (2006)
Clubs: 00- Celtic

Rafael MÁRQUEZ
Central Defender/Midfielder
Born 13/2/79, Zamora, Mexico
Height 182cm, Weight 75kg

Take the Italians out of the equation and Rafael Márquez was probably the outstanding defender at the World Cup. The captain of Mexico was also their best player. Brilliant in the opening game against Iran, when he popped up all over the field, he was every bit as impressive in the epic last-16 encounter against Argentina, putting his team into the lead with a smartly-taken volley and then masterminding a brilliant defensive performance from the Mexican back three. Márquez had an unlucky loser that evening in Leipzig but he came to the World Cup as a serial winner, having helped Barcelona to victory in both the Spanish championship and the Champions League. His third season in Catalonia was unquestionably his best. More comfortable in central defence than in midfield, he worked superbly in tandem with Carles Puyol. Commanding in the air and tough in the tackle, Márquez was equally impressive with his rhythmic distribution from the back. His strong, physical performance in the Champions League final irked Thierry Henry so much that it probably put paid to the chances of the French flyer becoming the Mexican's team-mate in 2006/07.

International Career
MEXICO
Major Honours – Confederations Cup (1999)
Debut – 5/2/97 v Ecuador (h, Mexico City, friendly) (sub), won 3-1
First Goal – 19/2/99 v Egypt (n, Hong Kong, friendly), won 3-0
Caps 70 **Goals** 9
Major Tournaments – Copa América 1999; Confederations Cup 1999; Gold Cup 2000; Copa América 2001; World Cup 2002; Gold Cup 2003; Copa América 2004; Confederations Cup 2005; World Cup 2006
Club Career
Major Honours – UEFA Champions League (2006); Spanish Championship (2005, 2006); French Championship (2000); French League Cup (2003)
Clubs: 96-99 Atlas; 99-03 AS Monaco FC (FRA); 03- FC Barcelona (ESP)

Top 100 players of the season

Lionel MESSI
Winger/Striker
Born 24/6/87, Rosario, Argentina
Height 166cm, Weight 60kg

It would have been nice to see a bit more of Lionel Messi at the World Cup. Whenever the youngster came on to the field, the crowd was lifted in anticipation of what he might do. The 'new Maradona' is a label that has been attached to many gifted young Argentine footballers over the years, but Messi could be the real thing. Argentina's star turn at the 2005 World Youth Cup in Holland, when he inspired his country to victory with some dazzling performances and a top-scoring tally of six goals, the multi-talented 18-year-old made massive strides forward for Barcelona during the 2005/06 season. His performance against Chelsea at Stamford Bridge took the breath away, so it was a great shame that he picked up a thigh injury in the return leg that would rule him out for the rest of the season...until his reappearance for Argentina in Germany. Although stocky and unathletic in stature, he is living proof that appearances can be deceptive. When in possession, Messi has the speed and guile to glide past opponents at will, and although much stronger on his left side, he can go past defenders both ways. Maradona himself has given the 19-year-old his stamp of approval. The football world awaits his further development with eager anticipation.

International Career
ARGENTINA
Major Honours – none
Debut – 17/8/05 v Hungary (a, Budapest, friendly) (sub), won 2-1
First Goal – 1/3/06 v Croatia (n, Basle, friendly), lost 2-3
Caps 10 **Goals** 2
Major Tournaments – World Cup 2006
Club Career
Major Honours – UEFA Champions League (2006); Spanish Championship (2005, 2006)
Clubs: 04- FC Barcelona (ESP)

Philippe MEXES
Central Defender
Born 30/3/82, Toulouse, France
Height 187cm, Weight 82kg

According to insider information Marcello Lippi, the coach of Italy, was so impressed with the form of Philippe Mexès for Roma that he would gladly have included him in his World Cup squad. He couldn't, of course, because Mexès is French, so imagine the Azzurri boss's surprise when the 24-year-old stopper failed to make the cut for Les Bleus. Raymond Domenech preferred experience to youth in his World Cup backline, and it largely paid off, but there is no doubt that Mexès will be part of his plans on the road to Euro 2008. A huge prospect in his teens, when his calm air of authority brought comparisons with World Cup winner Laurent Blanc, he made 133 appearances in the French First Division for Auxerre before moving to Roma in 2004. He suffered something of a form crisis following the switch – largely because of a red card on his Champions League debut in the infamous abandoned game against Dynamo Kiev – but he returned to his very best in 2005/06.

International Career
FRANCE
Major Honours – Confederations Cup (2003)
Debut – 16/10/02 v Malta (a, Ta' Qali, ECQ) (sub), won 4-0
Caps 6 **Goals** 0
Major Tournaments – Confederations Cup 2003
Club Career
Major Honours – French Cup (2003)
Clubs: 99-04 AJ Auxerre; 04- Roma (ITA)

Luka MODRIC
Attacking Midfielder
Born 9/9/85, Zadar, Croatia
Height 173cm, Weight 65kg

Luka Modric played so well in his first season at Dinamo Zagreb that Croatia's top club tied him to a ten-year contract. The 21-year-old has been hailed as Croatian football's next big thing, and it is easy to understand why. The diminutive, floppy-haired youngster has all the tricks in the book. He passes the ball beautifully and is alive to everything around him. A natural midfield orchestrator, his only defect is a lack of physical strength, but he makes up for that with his high energy levels and never-say-die spirit. He was a pivotal figure in Dinamo's return to the Croatian league summit in 2005/06, starting all 32 matches, scoring eight goals and feeding the likes of Eduardo and Ivan Bosnjak with a copious supply of inch-perfect through-balls. He had a tremendous national team debut for Croatia against Argentina, but Zlatko Kranjcar saw fit to give him only a couple of late run-outs from the bench at the World Cup. New Croatia coach Slaven Bilic may well rebuild the team around him.

International Career
CROATIA
Major Honours – none
Debut – 1/3/06 v Argentina (n, Basle, friendly), won 3-2
Caps 7 **Goals** 0
Major Tournaments – World Cup 2006
Club Career
Major Honours – Croatian Championship (2006)
Clubs: 03-04 Zrinjski Mostar (BOS); 04-05 Inter Zapresic; 05- Dinamo Zagreb

Lucas NEILL
Right-Back/Central Defender
Born 9/3/78, Sydney, Australia
Height 185cm, Weight 76kg

Up until the 2006 World Cup, Lucas Neill was regarded as nothing more than a tough, uncompromising, sometimes over-aggressive right-back, whose main claim to fame was breaking the leg of Liverpool

Top 100 players of the season

defender Jamie Carragher with a violent challenge at the start of the 2003/04 season. But four superb performances for Australia in Germany altered many people's perceptions of his ability. Deployed by coach Guus Hiddink in an unfamiliar central defensive role, Neill was the Socceroos' most consistent performer. It was a desperately cruel twist of fate that he should be the player responsible for the team's exit, conceding the highly contentious last-minute penalty with which Italy won an evenly contested last-16 clash in Kaiserslautern. That glitch, however, could not cloud what had gone before, and there was even talk after the tournament that European champions Barcelona might be interested in making an offer to Blackburn for his services.

International Career
AUSTRALIA
Major Honours – none
Debut – 9/10/96 v Saudi Arabia (a, Riyadh, friendly), drew 0-0
Caps 29 **Goals** 0
Major Tournaments – Confederations Cup 2005; World Cup 2006
Club Career
Major Honours – English League Cup (2002)
Clubs: 95-01 Millwall (ENG); 01- Blackburn Rovers (ENG)

Pedro Miguel Carreiro Resendes "PAULETA"
Striker
Born 28/4/73, Ponta del Gada, Azores, Portugal
Height 180cm, **Weight** 78kg

Pauleta's confidence going into the World Cup finals could not have been higher. He had finished as the leading scorer in the European qualifying zone, with 11 goals, overtaking the legendary Eusébio as Portugal's all-time record marksman in the process. He had also topped the scoring charts in France's Ligue 1 with 21 goals for Paris Saint-Germain. Furthermore, he had won the Coupe de France, scoring some brilliant, and crucial, goals en route to the final against Marseille. In short, the 33-year-old had enjoyed arguably the finest season of his career. Yet in Germany, perplexingly, he was more of a liability to his country than an asset. As at Euro 2004, stage fright appeared to take hold and his usual predatory sharpness vanished. As with Turkey and their underperforming star striker Hakan Sükür in 2002, Portugal reached the semi-finals in spite of Pauleta rather than because of him. He had hoped to bow out of the international arena with 50 goals but will remain stuck forever on 47.

International Career
PORTUGAL
Major Honours – none
Debut – 20/8/97 v Armenia (h, Setúbal, WCQ) (sub), won 3-1
First Goal – 26/3/99 v Azerbaijan (h, Guimarães, ECQ) (sub), won 7-0
Caps 88 **Goals** 47
Major Tournaments – Euro 2000; World Cup 2002; Euro 2004; World Cup 2006
Club Career

Major Honours – Spanish Championship (2000); French Cup (2004, 2006); French League Cup (2002)
Clubs: 95-96 GD Estoril Praia; 96-98 UD Salamanca (ESP); 98-00 RC Deportivo (ESP); 00-03 Girondins de Bordeaux (FRA); 03- Paris Saint-Germain (FRA)

Mariano PERNÍA
Left-Back
Born 4/5/77, Tandil, Argentina
Height 177cm, **Weight** 81kg

Mariano Pernía could not have imagined at the start of the 2005/06 season that he would end it playing for Spain at the World Cup finals. For one thing, he is Argentinian. For another, he was playing for Getafe, a pint-sized club from the Madrid suburbs. But as the season progressed, he drew attention to himself with his fabulous long-range shooting. By the end of the season, his lethal left foot had brought him 10 goals – the highest number recorded by a defender in La Liga for 20 years. Having applied for, and received, Spanish citizenship, Pernía became available for selection to Spain, but Luis Aragonés originally left him out of his World Cup squad and it was only after an ankle injury to Asier Del Horno that Pernía was drafted in. He had a perfect debut, scoring against Croatia, and that won him a starting place in Germany. There were some who suggested that he was too slow and at fault for France's first goal in the last-16 clash in Hanover, but soon after his return to Spain, Atlético Madrid fended off interest from Valencia to sign up the 29-year-old on a four-year contract.

International Career
SPAIN
Major Honours – none
Debut – 7/6/06 v Croatia (n, Geneva, friendly), won 2-1
First Goal – 7/6/06 v Croatia (n, Geneva, friendly), won 2-1
Caps 4 **Goals** 1
Major Tournaments – World Cup 2006
Club Career
Major Honours – none
Clubs: 00-02 Independiente (ARG); 02-04 RC Recreativo; 04-06 Getafe CF; 06- Atlético Madrid

Andrea PIRLO
Midfielder
Born 19/5/79, Brescia, Italy
Height 177cm, **Weight** 68kg

Andrea Pirlo had never played at the World Cup finals prior to 2006 but he was no stranger to major tournaments, having donned the blue of Italy at each of the last two Olympic Games as well as Euro 2004. A former Under-21 star (he won the European title with the Azzurrini in 2000), he took a while to make the grade at senior level, but since his conversion to a deep-lying regista role at Milan, his career has soared to new heights. The World Cup saw him at the peak of his powers. He scored Italy's first goal of the tournament, against Ghana, and his form never wavered thereafter. His cunningly disguised through-

The European Book of Football 2006/2007 - 869

Top 100 players of the season

ball to Fabio Grosso for the winning goal against Germany was probably the pass of the tournament. As the team's midfield pivot, many of the Azzurri's attacking manoeuvres were channelled through Pirlo, and his partnership with Gennaro Gattuso was every bit as effective as it has been for many years with Milan.

International Career
ITALY
Major Honours – World Cup (2006)
Debut – 7/9/02 v Azerbaijan (a, Baku, ECQ) (sub), won 2-0
First Goal – 30/5/04 v Tunisia (a, Tunis, friendly) (sub), won 4-0
Caps 31 Goals 5
Major Tournaments – Euro 2004; World Cup 2006
Club Career
Major Honours – UEFA Champions League (2003); Italian Championship (2004); Italian Cup (2003); European Super Cup (2003)
Clubs: 94-98 Brescia; 98-99 Internazionale; 99-00 Reggina; 00 Internazionale; 01 Brescia; 01- Milan

Karel PITÁK
Midfielder
Born 28/1/80, Hradec Králové, Czech Republic
Height 181cm, Weight 75kg

Karel Piták did not win any trophies in 2005/06, but the Slavia Prague captain was the outstanding player in the Czech league bar none. Deemed unlucky by many not to be included in Karel Brückner's World Cup squad, the forceful 26-year-old midfielder had to content himself with a summer transfer to new Austrian superteam Red Bull Salzburg and the prospect of competing in the UEFA Champions League. Piták was a European Under-21 champion with the Czech Republic in 2002 but he had to wait almost four years for his first senior international appearance. He earned that distinction with some tremendous performances for Slavia. A skilful ball-carrier who likes to break from midfield as often as possible and support the attack, he scored four goals in successive games to steer the club from the Czech capital into the group phase of the UEFA Cup and he also found the net ten times in the Gambrinus Liga.

International Career
CZECH REPUBLIC
Major Honours – none
Debut – 1/3/06 v Turkey (a, Izmir, friendly) (sub), drew 2-2
Caps 1 Goals 0
Major Tournaments – none
Club Career
Major Honours – Czech Cup (2002)
Clubs: 99-01 SK Hradec Králové; 01-06 SK Slavia Praha; 06- Red Bull Salzburg (AUT)

Claudio PIZARRO
Striker
Born 3/10/78, Callao, Peru
Height 186cm, Weight 80kg

The Peruvian international with an Italian passport overcame an early-season injury to become one of the stars of Bayern Munich's all-conquering team. Pizarro's fifth season in Munich continued his year-by-year improvement, and there was a perfect conclusion to it when he scored the winning goal in the Cup final against Eintracht Frankfurt. The 27-year-old striker had already been the goalscoring hero of both the quarter-final and semi-final victories, and his header in Berlin ensured a second successive domestic Double for Felix Magath's side. Pizarro also made his presence felt repeatedly in the Bundesliga as he took his cumulative tally in that competition to 92 goals in 197 matches. He must have been concerned at the end of the season when Bayern signed up new German sensation Lukas Podolski to their attack, but Pizarro is a born fighter and will not surrender his place easily.

International Career
PERU
Major Honours – none
Debut – 10/2/99 v Ecuador (h, Lima, friendly), lost 1-2
First Goal – 17/2/99 v Ecuador (a, Guayaquil, friendly), won 2-1
Caps 43 Goals 10
Major Tournaments – Copa América 1999; Copa América 2004
Club Career
Major Honours – German Championship (2003, 2005, 2006); German Cup (2003, 2005, 2006); World Club Cup (2001)
Clubs: 96-97 Deportivo Pesquero; 97-99 Alianza Lima; 99-01 SV Werder Bremen (GER); 01- FC Bayern München (GER)

Carles PUYOL
Central Defender
Born 13/4/78, Pobla de Segur, Spain
Height 180cm, Weight 79kg

Fittingly it was a Catalan who lifted the European Cup for Barcelona. Carles Puyol is Barça through and through. He has known no other club and perhaps, like Paolo Maldini at Milan, never will. The 28-year-old defender has lived through the dark days at Camp Nou. His first six years failed to bring a single piece of silverware. But now he has two Spanish championship winner's medals and become only the second Barcelona captain, after José Alexanko in 1992, to lift European football's most prestigious trophy. Puyol played in all but one of Barça's 13 Champions League matches and was a man of steel at the back throughout. He got lucky in the semi-final when he slipped, allowed Andriy Shevchenko to score but was rescued by the referee who wrongly ruled for a foul. Other than that he was utterly dependable. The shaggy-haired stopper reached 50 caps for Spain at the World Cup and raised more than a few eyebrows when he ventured forward spectacularly to set up Fernando Torres's goal against Ukraine. Normally the only time this tough, disciplined warrior ventures over the halfway line is to shake hands at the final whistle.

International Career
SPAIN

Top 100 players of the season

Major Honours – none
Debut – 15/11/00 v Holland (h, Seville, friendly), lost 1-2
First Goal – 17/4/02 v Northern Ireland (a, Belfast, friendly), won 5-0
Caps 50 **Goals** 1
Major Tournaments – World Cup 2002; Euro 2004; World Cup 2006

Club Career
Major Honours – UEFA Champions League (2006); Spanish Championship (2005, 2006)
Clubs: 99- FC Barcelona

Franck RIBERY
Attacking Midfielder
Born 1/4/83, Boulogne-sur-Mer, France
Height 170cm, Weight 62kg

The calls for France coach Raymond Domenech to include Ligue 1 showstopper Franck Ribéry in his World Cup squad were deafening. Although Domenech's previous selections had indicated an over-reliance on experience and a suspicion of youth, he eventually bowed to the pressure and invited the talented Marseille tearaway into his chosen 23 for Germany. The pre-tournament training must have been instructive because when Les Bleus opened their campaign against Switzerland, Ribéry was in the team. It was his first ever international start. Things didn't go too well for the busy attacking midfielder that day and he was dropped for the next game, but he returned for the crucial clash against Togo and after opening his international goalscoring account with the equaliser against Spain, Ribéry became a permanent fixture on the right flank, going on to win his 10th cap in the World Cup final. He ended up on the losing side – as he had done in the final of the French Cup for Marseille a couple of months earlier – but a new French star was born.

International Career
FRANCE
Major Honours – none
Debut – 27/5/06 v Mexico (h, Saint-Denis, friendly) (sub), won 1-0
First Goal – 27/6/06 v Spain (n, Hanover, WCF), won 3-1
Caps 10 **Goals** 1
Major Tournaments – World Cup 2006

Club Career
Major Honours – Turkish Cup (2005)
Clubs: 01-02 US Boulogne; 02-03 Olympique Alès; 03-04 Stade Brestois 29; 04-05 FC Metz; 05 Galatasaray (TUR); 05- Olympique Marseille

RICARDO Andrade QUARESMA Bernardo
Right-Winger
Born 26/9/83, Lisbon, Portugal
Height 173cm, Weight 67kg

Luiz Felipe Scolari's argument was that he had enough wingers in his squad already. Nevertheless it was a shock to some that the Portugal coach decided to leave Ricardo Quaresma at home for the World Cup, preferring to let him continue his international football education with the Under-21s at the European championship. Long regarded as the heir apparent to Luís Figo, the young right-winger began his career, like Figo, at Sporting before moving on, like Figo again, to Barcelona. Things didn't work out for him at Camp Nou, so he returned home to join FC Porto. His first season back was so-so, but his second brought high praise from all quarters as his youthful endeavour sparked the club to a surprise Portuguese league and Cup Double under new Dutch coach Co Adriaanse. A classic right-winger, Quaresma crosses the ball brilliantly and is always willing to have a go at the full-back. He may have missed the 2006 World Cup but he could be a major star in the next one.

International Career
PORTUGAL
Major Honours – none
Debut – 10/6/03 v Bolivia (h, Lisbon, friendly) (sub), won 4-0
Caps 5 **Goals** 0
Major Tournaments – none

Club Career
Major Honours – Portuguese Championship (2002, 2006); Portuguese Cup (2002, 2006); World Club Cup (2004)
Clubs: 00-03 Sporting CP; 03-04 FC Barcelona (ESP); 04- FC Porto

Juan Román RIQUELME
Attacking Midfielder
Born 24/6/78, San Fernando (Buenos Aires), Argentina
Height 180cm, Weight 76kg

2005/06 was a season of highs and lows for Juan Román Riquelme, but it was another in which he reaffirmed his status as one of the classiest, most visually appealing midfield schemers in the game. The season began with his decision to reject the overtures of Atlético Madrid and remain at Villarreal. It ended with him watching helplessly from the sidelines as Argentina went out of the World Cup on penalties to Germany. The decision to withdraw Riquelme from the fray while Argentina were 1-0 up proved calamitous for coach José Pekerman, who offered his resignation immediately after the defeat. Riquelme's form had been so impressive in the earlier games that he was an early candidate for the Golden Ball. But Pekerman, who, unlike his predecessors, had shown admirable faith in Riquelme's glorious talent, unwittingly pulled the plug on that possibility with his infamous substitution. Riquelme was the linchpin of Villarreal's extraordinary run to the semi-finals of the Champions League. He played the match of his life at home to Inter in the quarter-final but then missed the late penalty against Arsenal in the semi that would have taken the tie into extra-time. Some you win, some you lose.

International Career
ARGENTINA
Major Honours – none
Debut – 16/11/97 v Colombia (h, Buenos Aires, WCQ) (sub), drew 1-1
First Goal – 30/4/03 v Libya (a, Tripoli, friendly) (sub), won 3-1

Top 100 players of the season

Caps 36 **Goals** 8
Major Tournaments – Copa América 1999; Confederations Cup 2005; World Cup 2006
Club Career
Major Honours – Libertadores Cup (2000, 2001); World Club Cup (2000); Argentine Championship (Ap. 1998, Cl. 1999, Ap. 2000)
Clubs: 96-02 Boca Juniors; 02-03 FC Barcelona (ESP); 03- Villarreal CF (ESP)

Paul ROBINSON
Goalkeeper
Born 15/10/79, Beverley, England
Height 192cm, **Weight** 91kg

He had the chance to become a national hero but, like so many England goalkeepers before him, Paul Robinson was unable to impose himself in a big penalty shoot-out. In fairness, it wasn't Robinson's fault that England went out of the World Cup to Portugal. The Tottenham keeper had a reasonably good tournament, keeping four clean sheets out of five. It was just that when England needed something special from him, he wasn't able to deliver. Even so, it can be safely assumed that the big Yorkshireman will be minding England's net for a number of years to come. At 26 years of age and with no apparent rivals to his position (just about all of the best keepers in the Premiership are imports), a long international career lies in front of him. Robinson enjoyed a fine season for Tottenham, marred only by the club's last-day defeat at West Ham that prevented them from taking fourth spot (which they had held virtually all season) and qualifying for a shot at the Champions League.

International Career
ENGLAND
Major Honours – none
Debut – 12/2/03 v Australia (h, London, friendly) (sub), lost 1-3
Caps 26 **Goals** 0
Major Tournaments – Euro 2004; World Cup 2006
Club Career
Major Honours – none
Clubs: 98-04 Leeds United; 04- Tottenham Hotspur

RONALDINHO de Assis Moreira
Attacking Midfielder
Born 21/3/80, Porto Alegre, Brazil
Height 180cm, **Weight** 76kg

Brilliant for Barcelona, bafflingly bad for Brazil. That is a fairly accurate résumé of Ronaldinho's season. So much was expected of him in Germany, yet he offered so very little. He went into the tournament buoyed by a magnificent nine-month campaign for Barcelona, during which he was voted as the world's best player – officially by FIFA and unofficially by everybody else. It seemed that Ronaldinho was poised to claim a place in the pantheon of sporting gods in Germany. It was widely anticipated that he might dominate the 2006 World Cup in the way that Diego Maradona lit up Mexico 86 or Johan Cruyff dazzled in 1974. In the event, there was barely a trace of the outrageous 'joga bonita' for which he had become famous the world over. The toothy smile was replaced by pursed lips and empty stares as his passes went astray and his free-kicks sailed harmlessly over the bar. It was a massive let-down, not just for Brazil but for the football-loving public in general. Still, at least the memories of his glorious season with Barça were still fresh. There were too many magical moments to mention, but as a highlight his majestic Champions League hat-trick against Udinese took some beating.

International Career
BRAZIL
Major Honours – World Cup (2002); Copa América (1999); Confederations Cup (2005)
Debut – 26/6/99 v Latvia (h, Curitiba, friendly), won 3-0
First Goal – 30/6/99 v Venezuela (n, Ciudad del Este, CA) (sub), won 7-0
Caps 68 **Goals** 27
Major Tournaments – Copa América 1999; Confederations Cup 1999; World Cup 2002; Confederations Cup 2003; Confederations Cup 2005; World Cup 2006
Club Career
Major Honours – UEFA Champions League (2006); Spanish Championship (2005, 2006)
Clubs: 98-01 Grêmio; 01-03 Paris Saint-Germain (FRA); 03- FC Barcelona (ESP)

Wayne ROONEY
Striker
Born 24/10/85, Liverpool, England
Height 180cm, **Weight** 76kg

Fortunately there will be other World Cups for Wayne Rooney. The 2006 tournament was like a bad dream for the young Englishman. For a long time it looked as if the bone he broke in his right foot at the end of April would prevent him from playing. Then, after a miraculous recovery, he got himself fit enough to play but was foolishly asked to lead the England attack on his own. And, just to cap everything, when his country needed him most, in the quarter-final against Portugal, he got himself sent off. Perhaps the expectations on him were too high. No 20-year-old had ever dominated a World Cup, yet the fans and the media in England virtually pinned all their hopes on him. In part that was understandable. Sven Göran Eriksson's team had often struggled to function properly without him, and Rooney, until his unfortunate injury at Stamford Bridge, had enjoyed a brilliant Premiership campaign for Manchester United. His first trophy as a professional may only have been the League Cup (he scored twice in the final in a 4-0 victory over Wigan), but without his fierce commitment, energy and sublime skill, not to mention 16 goals, United would have fallen apart and Chelsea would have wrapped up the title long before that fateful day when the young striker's metatarsal went snap.

International Career
ENGLAND
Major Honours – none

Top 100 players of the season

Andriy SHEVCHENKO
Striker
Born 29/9/76, Dvirkvshchyna, Ukraine
Height 183cm, **Weight** 73kg

With nine goals in the Champions League, including all four in a group game away to Fenerbahçe, Andriy Shevchenko lifted his all-time tally to a remarkable 43. The Ukrainian stamped his class all over the competition in the season after his fateful final against Liverpool in Istanbul, and he was also on fire in Serie A, scoring 19 goals to take his all-time league total for the Rossoneri to 127 in 208 games. The World Cup awaited his pleasure, but unfortunately a knee injury sustained at the end of the Italian season meant that he was still working his way back to full fitness when the tournament began. He scored two goals and helped Ukraine to reach the quarter-finals, but, like most of the big-name strikers on view, 'Sheva' didn't really come to the party. Chelsea will expect a lot more from the Ukrainian having spent £30m to lure him away from his beloved Milan. His arrival is a major coup for the Premiership, but it remains to be seen whether, at 30, his best days are behind him. Another glut of Champions League goals would certainly help to pay off a slice of that exorbitant fee.

International Career
UKRAINE
Major Honours – none
Debut – 25/3/95 v Croatia (a, Zagreb, ECQ), lost 0-4
First Goal – 1/5/96 v Turkey (a, Samsun, friendly), lost 2-3
Caps 69 **Goals** 31
Major Tournaments – World Cup 2006
Club Career
Major Honours – UEFA Champions League (2003); Italian Championship (2004); Ukrainian Championship (1995, 1996, 1997, 1998, 1999); Italian Cup (2003); Ukrainian Cup (1996, 1998, 1999); European Super Cup (2003)
Clubs: 94-99 Dynamo Kyiv; 99-06 Milan (ITA); 06- Chelsea (ENG)

Rudolf SKÁCEL
Attacking Midfielder
Born 17/7/79, Ústí nad Orlici, Czech Republic
Height 178cm, **Weight** 77kg

The accusation against Czech coach Karel Brückner that he chose his World Cup squad on reputation rather than form had substance in the case of Rudolf 'Rudi' Skácel. The former Slavia Prague and Under-21 star played better than ever before in 2005/06. Although his stay in Scotland with Hearts proved to be brief, he left a lasting impression. In fact, it was his first impression that alerted everyone in Scotland – and beyond – to his talent. The left-sided midfielder set a new SPL record by scoring in each of the first seven games of the season, all of which Hearts won. He would go on to score 16 SPL goals and also find the net in the final of the Scottish Cup, in which Hearts triumphed on penalties against Gretna. Skácel's best form had come while George Burley was the manager so it was no great surprise when he decided to rejoin his ex-boss at Southampton in the summer – even though the Czech's decision to choose second-tier football in England rather than possible top-level football in Europe seemed illogical for a player with international aspirations.

International Career
CZECH REPUBLIC
Major Honours – none
Debut – 15/11/03 v Canada (h, Teplice, friendly) (sub), won 5-1
First Goal – 15/11/03 v Canada (h, Teplice, friendly) (sub), won 5-1
Caps 3 **Goals** 1
Major Tournaments – none
Club Career
Major Honours – Czech Cup (2002); Scottish Cup (2006)
Clubs: 99-01 SK Hradec Králové; 02-03 SK Slavia Praha; 03-04 Olympique Marseille (FRA); 04-05 Panathinaikos (GRE); 05-06 Heart of Midlothian (SCO); 06- Southampton (ENG)

Euzebiusz SMOLAREK
Winger/Striker
Born 9/1/81, Lodz, Poland
Height 178cm, **Weight** 68kg

Named after legendary Portuguese striker Eusébio by his father Wlodzimierz Smolarek, a pretty decent player in his own right, Euzebiusz 'Ebi' Smolarek had hoped to follow in the footsteps of both his Dad and his Dad's idol by making a big impression on the World Cup. Having missed the 2002 tournament through injury, he was hyper-keen to get involved for Poland in 2006, especially as it was in Germany, where he had just enjoyed an excellent debut season for Borussia Dortmund. In truth, Smolarek's best form had come in the autumn, shortly after being switched from the right wing to the centre of attack to cover for the injured Jan Koller. With 11 goals in 13 games, the young Pole was the talk of the Bundesliga. He was also big news back home, and at the end of 2005 he was voted Polish Player of the Year by influential magazine Pilka Nozna. The spring season brought a drastic reduction in his goal output but his speed, stamina and intelligence persuaded coach Bert van Marwijk to select him continuously and by the end of the season he had started all 34 league games – the only Dortmund player to do so. He also started all of Poland's World Cup games – in midfield rather than attack – but could do nothing to prevent their early exit. Going out to a late goal from Germany in the Westfalenstadion, his home stadium, merely compounded Smolarek's misery

---

Debut – 12/2/03 v Australia (h, London, friendly) (sub), lost 1-3
First Goal – 6/9/03 v Macedonia (a, Skopje, ECQ), won 2-1
Caps 33 **Goals** 11
Major Tournaments – Euro 2004; World Cup 2006
Club Career
Major Honours – English League Cup (2006)
Clubs: 02-04 Everton; 04- Manchester United

Top 100 players of the season

International Career
POLAND
Major Honours – none
Debut – 13/2/02 v Northern Ireland (n, Limassol, friendly) (sub), won 4-1
First Goal – 3/9/05 v Austria (h, Chorzow, WCQ), won 3-2
Caps 16 Goals 4
Major Tournaments – World Cup 2006
Club Career
Major Honours – UEFA Cup (2002)
Clubs: 00-05 Feyenoord (HOL); 05- Borussia Dortmund (GER)

Lukasz SOSIN
Striker
Born 7/5/77, Krakow, Poland
Height 190cm, Weight 84kg

Scoring goals consistently in Cyprus may not qualify as the ideal reference for World Cup involvement, but Lukasz Sosin was entitled to feel a bit upset when, after being invited to play for Poland for the first time and scoring two goals on his debut, he was overlooked by coach Pawel Janas for the trip to Germany. Nobody can be sure whether Sosin would have made a difference to Poland's fortunes had he been included, but the 29-year-old ex-Wisla Krakow striker could hardly have been more goal-shy than the strikers who did make the cut. For the third season running Sosin topped the goal charts in the Cypriot top flight. Better still, he increased his tally from 21 to 28 goals and the last two came on the final day of the season as his club Apollon beat outgoing champions Anorthosis to clinch the Cypriot title for the first time in a dozen years. Sosin was already regarded as a hero at the Limassol club; now he qualifies as a living legend.

International Career
POLAND
Major Honours – none
Debut – 28/3/06 v Saudi Arabia (a, Riyadh, friendly), won 2-1
First Goal – 28/3/06 v Saudi Arabia (a, Riyadh, friendly), won 2-1
Caps 3 Goals 2
Major Tournaments – none
Club Career
Major Honours – Polish Championship (2001); Cypriot Championship (2006)
Clubs: 96-97 Cracovia Krakow; 97-99 Hutnik Krakow; 99-00 Odra Wodzislaw; 00-01 Wisla Krakow; 01-02 Odra Wodzislaw; 02- Apollon (CYP)

Darijo SRNA
Right Wing-Back/Midfielder
Born 1/5/82, Metkovic, Croatia
Height 182cm, Weight 78kg

Croatia went out of the World Cup after three games but Darijo Srna deserved to be around for longer. Although he had a penalty brilliantly saved in the team's second game, against Japan, the 24-year-old wing-back redeemed himself in the next match against Australia by scoring a fabulous free-kick. It wasn't sufficient to win the game, but Srna departed the competition with his reputation enhanced. It had been his winning goals in both qualifiers against Sweden that had enabled Croatia to win their qualifying group, and his all-round energy and set-piece play in Germany confirmed him to be not only a wing-back of the highest class but also a fundamental cog in the Croatian machine. Srna has also proved his worth repeatedly for Shakhtar Donetsk over the past three years and won his second successive Ukrainian title in 2005/06. The big Western clubs have now been alerted to his talents, and it can only be a matter of time before Shakhtar receive an offer they can't refuse.

International Career
CROATIA
Major Honours – none
Debut – 20/11/02 v Romania (a, Timisoara, friendly), won 1-0
First Goal – 29/3/03 v Belgium (h, Zagreb, ECQ), won 4-0
Caps 39 Goals 10
Major Tournaments – Euro 2004; World Cup 2006
Club Career
Major Honours – Croatian Championship (2001); Ukrainian Championship (2005, 2006); Croatian Cup (2003); Ukrainian Cup (2004)
Clubs: 99-03 Hajduk Split; 03- Shakhtar Donetsk (UKR)

John TERRY
Central Defender
Born 7/12/80, Barking, England
Height 182cm, Weight 78kg

He was the only Englishman to be included in FIFA's all-star World Cup squad, but that was scant consolation to John Terry after his team's miserable showing in Germany. His central defensive partnership with Rio Ferdinand worked well – only one goal was conceded while the pair were together on the field – but the Chelsea captain is such a born winner that he will not care to reflect too much on his first World Cup. He will already be thinking forward to the next one, which, all being well, he will go to as the England captain, having been handed the armband by new boss Steve McClaren in preference to the other prime candidate, Steven Gerrard, following David Beckham's post-World Cup abdication. Terry is a central defender of traditional English stock – all brawn, commitment and unbreakable spirit – and he also regularly makes a nuisance of himself in the air at the other end of the pitch at corners and free-kicks. His commanding leadership at Chelsea, in a team full of foreigners, has helped to bring two successive Premiership titles to Stamford Bridge. Now he eyes the hat-trick...while also dreaming of lifting the Champions League trophy in Athens next May.

International Career
ENGLAND
Major Honours – none
Debut – 3/6/03 v Serbia & Montenegro (h, Leicester, friendly) (sub), won 2-1
First Goal – 30/5/06 v Hungary (h, Manchester, friendly), won 3-1
Caps 29 Goals 1
Major Tournaments – Euro 2004; World Cup 2006

Top 100 players of the season

Lilian THURAM
Central Defender
Born 1/1/72, Pointe-à-Pitre, Guadeloupe
Height 185cm, Weight 79kg

It was all planned. After the World Cup Lilian Thuram would retire from international football as France's most capped player of all time and return to Turin to play out the remainder of his club career at Juventus. But events in Germany and Italy rather changed things. Thuram had a brilliant World Cup. In fact, he played so well that he surprised himself. He played every minute of France's adventure and enjoyed it so much that, even with that record tally of 121 caps (he broke Marcel Desailly's record against Togo), he couldn't bring himself to say adieu to Les Bleus. Then came the bombshell in Italy – Juventus, the team he had just helped to two successive Serie A titles, were guilty of match-fixing and would not only be forced to surrender those two titles but also be relegated to Serie B. That was no place for Thuram to end his career. Fortunately Barcelona, the European champions, swiftly came to his rescue, luring him to Camp Nou on a generous two-year contract. Even at 34 going on 35, there could be a lot more to come from this giant of European football.

International Career
FRANCE
Major Honours – World Cup (1998); European Championship (2000)
Debut – 17/8/94 v Czech Republic (h, Bordeaux, friendly), drew 2-2
First Goal – 8/7/98 v Croatia (h, Saint-Denis, WCF), won 2-1
Caps 121 **Goals** 2
Major Tournaments – Euro 96; World Cup 1998; Euro 2000; World Cup 2002; Euro 2004; World Cup 2006

Club Career
Major Honours – UEFA Cup (1999); Italian Championship (2002, 2003); Italian Cup (1999)
Clubs: 91-96 AS Monaco; 96-01 Parma (ITA); 01-06 Juventus (ITA); 06- FC Barcelona (ESP)

Luca TONI
Forward
Born 26/5/77, Pavullo nel Frignano, Italy
Height 193cm, Weight 88kg

Fiorentina's implication in the Great Italian Match-Fixing Scandal rather soured the achievement of Luca Toni in becoming the first player to score more than 30 goals in a Serie A season for nearly half a century. Apparently, though, the record still stands. It was some feat – especially for a long-time journeyman of the Italian scene whose first season it was at a big club. His towering presence and sharpness in the box unnerved every Serie A defence and there were only four clubs he failed to score against, one of them being Palermo, the Sicilian club with whom he had made such a huge impact in the previous two seasons. As if his club exploits were not enough, Toni went to Germany with Italy and won the World Cup. He was Marcello Lippi's first-choice striker, starting every game bar one, and although he had his moments, his tally of two goals – both scored in quick succession against Ukraine – was rather meagre. His best moment was the fantastic header he powered past Fabien Barthez in the final. Unfortunately, it was ruled out (correctly) for offside.

International Career
ITALY
Major Honours – World Cup (2006)
Debut – 18/8/04 v Iceland (a, Reykjavík, friendly) (sub), lost 0-2
First Goal – 4/9/04 v Norway (h, Palermo, WCQ) (sub), won 2-1
Caps 24 **Goals** 9
Major Tournaments – World Cup 2006

Club Career
Major Honours – none
Clubs: 94-96 Modena; 96-97 Empoli; 97-98 Fiorenzuola; 98-99 Lodigiani; 99-00 Treviso; 00-01 Vicenza; 02-03 Brescia; 03-05 Palermo; 05- Fiorentina

Kolo TOURE
Central Defender
Born 19/3/81, Sokoura Bouake, Ivory Coast
Height 177cm, Weight 74kg

For someone who started his Arsenal career as a utility player-cum-full-back, Kolo Touré has developed into a mightily impressive central defender. Following Sol Campbell's transfer to Portsmouth, the 25-year-old from the Ivory Coast is now the linchpin of the Gunners' defence. He was the senior figure in a makeshift back four that defied predictions by keeping a succession of clean sheets on Arsenal's journey to the Champions League final. Furthermore, Touré scored the only goal of the semi-final against Villarreal. He also took time out from his club duties in mid-season to play for his country at the African Nations Cup. In Egypt, Touré was one of the classiest players on view as he helped the Elephants into the final against the host nation. There was an even bigger stage for Touré and his younger brother Yaya (of Olympiakos) to perform on at the end of the season as the Ivory Coast travelled to Germany for their first appearance at the World Cup finals. Drawn in an extremely difficult group, the West Africans failed to qualify but, like his team, the Arsenal defender performed with distinction.

International Career
IVORY COAST
Major Honours – none
Debut – 9/4/00 v Rwanda (a, Kigali, WCQ), drew 2-2
First Goal – 28/4/04 v Guinea (n, Aix-les-Bains, friendly), won 4-2
Caps 44 **Goals** 1
Major Tournaments – African Nations Cup 2002; African Nations Cup 2006; World Cup 2006

Club Career
Major Honours – English Premiership (2004); FA Cup (2003, 2005)
Clubs: 00-02 ASEC Mimosas; 02- Arsenal (ENG)

Top 100 players of the season

David TREZEGUET
Striker
Born 15/10/77, Rouen, France
Height 187cm, Weight 75kg

David Trezeguet missed the vital penalty in the World Cup final shoot-out, and that stigma will stay with him forever. But to most people watching the real villain of the piece was his captain, Zinedine Zidane, who was not there when France needed him most. Trezeguet's World Cup was largely forgettable. With coach Raymond Domenech favouring a lone striker – Thierry Henry – backed by three attacking midfielders – Franck Ribéry, Zidane and Florent Malouda – there was no place for the 32-goal striker apart from the substitute's bench. Most other teams, though, would have found room for a player who, free of injury for the first time in a while, had banged in 23 Serie A goals for Juventus. Whether they were all legitimate or not it was hard to know after the match-rigging revelations, but another half a dozen goals in the Champions League, including two at home in the 2-1 victory over Bayern Munich, provided more credible proof of the Frenchman's awesome goalscoring pedigree.

International Career
FRANCE
Major Honours – World Cup (1998); European Championship (2000)
Debut – 28/1/98 v Spain (h, Saint-Denis, friendly) (sub), won 1-0
First Goal – 5/6/98 v Finland (a, Helsinki, friendly) (sub), won 1-0
Caps 66 Goals 32
Major Tournaments – World Cup 1998; Euro 2000; World Cup 2002; Euro 2004; World Cup 2006
Club Career
Major Honours – Italian Championship (2002, 2003); French Championship (1997, 2000)
Clubs: 93-95 Platense (ARG); 95-00 AS Monaco; 00- Juventus (ITA)

TUNCAY Sanli
Striker/Winger
Born 16/1/82, Adapazari, Turkey
Height 182cm, Weight 70kg

The best young forward in Turkey is also one of the most controversial. After his beloved Fenerbahçe had knocked Galatasaray out of the Turkish Cup, Tuncay Sanli was caught on camera singing indecent songs about Galatasaray and Besiktas. Unfortunately for him, those two teams would have the last laugh – Besiktas by beating Fenerbahçe in the Cup final and Galatasaray by edging out Fener in the Super Lig title race. Although he won no trophies and was submerged in criticism, Tuncay was one of the Super Lig's leading attractions. He scored 15 goals in the league, most of them at crucial times, and, unlike some of his Brazilian colleagues, played well consistently. Although sometimes accused of squandering possession too easily, he is a born fighter and never gives up. That was never more clearly illustrated than in the infamous second leg of Turkey's World Cup qualifying play-off against Switzerland when, with all hope seemingly lost after an early Swiss penalty, he rallied his side with a brilliant hat-trick. It wasn't quite enough, but on that dreadful night in the Sükrü Saracoglu stadium at least one Turk emerged with some credit.

International Career
TURKEY
Major Honours – none
Debut – 20/11/02 v Italy (a, Pescara, friendly) (sub), drew 1-1
First Goal – 19/6/03 v United States (n, Saint-Etienne, CC), won 2-1
Caps 34 Goals 10
Major Tournaments – Confederations Cup 2003
Club Career
Major Honours – Turkish Championship (2004, 2005)
Clubs: 01-02 Sakaryaspor; 02- Fenerbahçe

Tomás UJFALUSI
Central Defender
Born 24/3/78, Rymarov, Czech Republic
Height 183cm, Weight 78kg

One of the Czech Republic's most dependable and impressive performers at Euro 2004, headband-wearing centre-back Tomás Ujfalusi was expected to repeat the trick at the World Cup. The only player to start all 14 of the team's qualifying matches, he went to Germany in excellent shape after an inspired season in Italy with Fiorentina, which ended – or so he thought at the time – with the Tuscan club finishing fourth behind the big three of Juventus, Milan and Inter. But after a good opening performance against the USA, Ujfalusi's World Cup ended early when he was sent off midway through the second half of the second group game against Ghana – a match in which he was collecting his 50th cap. Once he was off the field, the Czech defence disintegrated, and in the next game, against Italy, his sturdy presence was again sorely missed as the team lost 2-0 and were eliminated. Although Ujfalusi has always been a central defender for his country, he was used almost exclusively as a right-back by Fiorentina in 2005/06.

International Career
CZECH REPUBLIC
Major Honours – none
Debut – 28/2/01 v Macedonia (a, Skopje, friendly), drew 1-1
First Goal – 6/9/02 v Yugoslavia (h, Prague, friendly), won 5-0
Caps 50 Goals 2
Major Tournaments – Euro 2004; World Cup 2006
Club Career
Major Honours – none
Clubs: 96-00 SK Sigma Olomouc; 01-04 Hamburger SV (GER); 04- Fiorentina (ITA)

Daniel VAN BUYTEN
Central Defender
Born 7/2/78, Chimay, Belgium
Height 196cm, Weight 96kg

Top-class Belgian footballers are hard to find these days, but Daniel Van Buyten flew the flag for his country with pride, passion and no little success during an outstanding season in the German Bundesliga with Hamburg. The giant, muscular defender was an inspiration for HSV as Thomas Doll's side surprisingly challenged Bayern Munich for the title. Thanks to the big Belgian's solidity at the back, Hamburg had the best defensive figures in the league, conceding just 30 goals in 34 matches. The impact made by Van Buyten was not lost on champions Bayern Munich, who forked out 10 million euros to bring him to Bavaria on a three-year contract. At the time he packed his bags for the long journey south, Van Buyten was unsure as to his role in the Belgian national team under new head coach René Vandereycken, but by mid-summer, with the Euro 2008 campaign approaching, it was clear that the 28-year-old would play a major part in the team's bid to qualify for the finals in Austria and Switzerland.

International Career
BELGIUM
Major Honours – none
Debut – 28/2/01 v San Marino (h, Brussels, WCQ), won 10-1
First Goal – 24/3/01 v Scotland (a, Glasgow, WCQ) (sub), drew 2-2
Caps 31 **Goals** 3
Major Tournaments – World Cup 2002
Club Career
Major Honours – none
Clubs: 97-99 RSC Charleroi; 99-01 R Standard Liège; 01-03 Olympique Marseille (FRA); 04 Manchester City (ENG); 04-06 Hamburger SV (GER); 06- FC Bayern München (GER)

Edwin VAN DER SAR
Goalkeeper
Born 29/10/70, Voorhout, Holland
Height 196cm, Weight 85kg

The Dutch national appearance record of 112 caps, previously held by Frank de Boer, was broken by Edwin van der Sar during the first round of the World Cup. He may be getting on a bit, but the lanky keeper, who has been Holland's first choice for over a decade and also set a new Dutch record when he played 38 internationals in a row from April 2003 to May 2006, is not past his sell-by date yet. An excellent World Cup qualifying campaign, in which he started all 12 games and was unbeaten in the last nine, was matched by a peerless first season at Manchester United, where he finally became the reliable, world-class custodian that the Old Trafford club had been hunting down since the departure, six years earlier, of Peter Schmeichel. Coach Marco van Basten handed Van der Sar the responsibility of captaining the side in Germany, and although the 35-year-old doubtless had dreams of becoming the first goalkeeper to lift the World Cup since Italy's Dino Zoff in 1982, it wasn't to be. He'll just have to try again in 2010.

International Career
HOLLAND
Major Honours – none
Debut – 7/6/95 v Belarus (a, Minsk, ECQ), lost 0-1
Caps 113 **Goals** 0

Major Tournaments – World Cup 1994; Euro 96; World Cup 1998; Euro 2000; Euro 2004; World Cup 2006
Club Career
Major Honours – UEFA Champions League (1995); Dutch Championship (1994, 1995, 1996, 1998); Dutch Cup (1993, 1998); English League Cup (2006)
Clubs: 90-98 Ajax; 98-01 Juventus (ITA); 01-05 Fulham (ENG); 05- Manchester United (ENG)

Rafael VAN DER VAART
Attacking Midfielder
Born 11/2/83, Heemskerk, Holland
Height 175cm, Weight 74kg

Many Dutch fans were bemused when Rafael van der Vaart decided to quit Ajax for Hamburg in the summer of 2005. It had been widely predicted that the youngster would follow the well-trodden path from Amsterdam to Barcelona – or at least to a club of Ajax's equivalent standing in England, Italy or Spain. But the north German port club welcomed him with open arms and he responded with a scintillating burst of form in the first few weeks, scoring goals galore and wooing the crowds at the AOL-Arena with his deftness of touch and left-footed trickery. He even showed nerves of steel to convert a vital last-minute penalty against FC København in the UEFA Cup. Alas, not for the first time in his career, injury would intervene just when he was at the top of his game, and although he returned to good effect in the spring, Hamburg's hopes of challenging Bayern Munich for the title effectively followed the Dutchman to the treatment table. Still not fully fit, he was only a bit-part player for Holland at the World Cup, but Van der Vaart's time will definitely come again.

International Career
HOLLAND
Major Honours – none
Debut – 6/10/01 v Andorra (h, Arnhem, WCQ) (sub), won 4-0
First Goal – 6/9/03 v Austria (h, Rotterdam, ECQ), won 3-1
Caps 38 **Goals** 6
Major Tournaments – Euro 2004; World Cup 2006
Club Career
Major Honours – Dutch Championship (2002, 2004); Dutch Cup (2002)
Clubs: 99-05 Ajax; 05- Hamburger SV (GER)

Aleksandar VASOSKI
Central Defender
Born 21/11/79, Skopje, Macedonia
Height 180cm, Weight 70kg

While Lazio striker Goran Pandev is regarded as Macedonia's most illustrious football export, Aleksandar Vasoski is not far behind. The gifted centre-back joined German club Eintracht Frankfurt midway through the 2004/05 season and helped steer them to promotion. In 2005/06 he was one of the main reasons why Friedhelm Funkel's side retained their place in the Bundesliga. Vasoski missed just one league game all season and he also played a

Top 100 players of the season

starring role as Frankfurt finished runners-up to Bayern Munich in the German Cup, conceding just four goals in their six matches. With Bayern also winning the league, Eintracht qualified for the UEFA Cup. Won over by the Macedonian's contributions, the club extended his contract to 2009. At international level Vasoski furthered his reputation for taut, disciplined defending as he helped Macedonia to an unexpected 0-0 draw against Holland at the Amsterdam ArenA in the last of their World Cup qualifiers. The 26-year-old is sure to be a key figure in the plans of new national coach Srecko Katanec.

International Career
MACEDONIA
Major Honours – none
Debut – 26/7/00 v Azerbaijan (n, Varna, friendly) (sub), won 2-1
First Goal – 20/11/02 v Israel (h, Skopje, friendly), lost 2-3
Caps 28 **Goals** 2
Major Tournaments – none
Club Career
Major Honours – Macedonian Championship (2002, 2003)
Clubs: 99-01 Cementarnica 55 Skopje; 01-04 Vardar Skopje; 05- Eintracht Frankfurt (GER)

Nemanja VIDIC
Central Defender
Born 21/10/81, Uzice, Serbia
Height 188cm, Weight 84kg

Was it mere coincidence that when Nemanja Vidic stood in the heart of the Serbia & Montenegro defence during the World Cup qualifying series the team conceded just one goal, but when they were without him at the finals they let in ten in three matches? Injured in training on the eve of the tournament and then more seriously just after it had started, Vidic's absence wrecked the plans of coach Ilija Petkovic to reinstate his defensive Famous Four – as Vidic and his fellow defenders Mladen Krstajic, Goran Gavrancic and Ivica Dragutinovic had become known during the qualifiers – and the result was too much tampering and tinkering and, ultimately, total chaos. Vidic made big waves in his homeland when he moved from Spartak Moscow to Manchester United in January. The £7m fee was the highest paid for a Serbian player, and although the 24-year-old centre-back knew that he would have his work cut out to gain a regular place in the team, it was a testimony to the excellent marking and tackling ability he had shown during a superb season in Russia that he found himself in the employ of one of the world's biggest clubs.

International Career
SERBIA
Major Honours – none
Debut – 12/10/02 v Italy (a, Naples, ECQ), drew 1-1
First Goal – 15/8/05 v Poland (n, Kiev, friendly), lost 2-3
Caps 20 **Goals** 1
Major Tournaments – World Cup 2006
Club Career
Major Honours – Serbo-Montenegrin Championship (2004); Yugoslav Cup (2002); Serbo-Montenegrin Cup (2004); English League Cup (2006)
Clubs: 00-01 Spartak Subotica; 01-04 Crvena Zvezda Beograd; 04-05 Spartak Moskva (RUS); 06- Manchester United (ENG)

Mark VIDUKA
Striker
Born 9/10/75, Melbourne, Australia
Height 188cm, Weight 93kg

There were no goals for Mark Viduka at the World Cup but he captained his country well, especially in the heated final group encounter against Croatia, the country of his roots. After a dozen years of intermittent international activity for the Socceroos, the big striker with the deft touch deserved his opportunity to appear on the biggest stage of them all. He went to Germany frustrated that his club, Middlesbrough, had been beaten in the UEFA Cup final by Sevilla but proud nonetheless that the unfashionable team from the north-east of England had made it that far in only their second season of Continental involvement. Viduka was Boro's leading scorer in the competition, netting six goals, three of which came in the momentous comebacks at the Riverside Stadium against FC Basel and Steaua Bucharest. He had a big chance in the final (with the score at 1-0) but put his shot too close to the keeper. He also had a decent penalty shout that went unanswered. It was not the Aussie's night in Eindhoven, but it was a memorable season for him all the same.

International Career
AUSTRALIA
Major Honours – none
Debut – 8/6/94 v South Africa (h, Adelaide, friendly), won 1-0
First Goal – 1/10/97 v Tunisia (a, Tunis, friendly), won 3-0
Caps 37 **Goals** 6
Major Tournaments – Confederations Cup 2005; World Cup 2006
Club Career
Major Honours – Croatian Championship (1996, 1997, 1998); Scottish League Cup (2000)
Clubs: 92-95 Melbourne Knights; 95-98 Croatia Zagreb (CRO); 98-00 Celtic (SCO); 00-04 Leeds United (ENG); 04- Middlesbrough (ENG)

Róbert VITTEK
Striker
Born 1/4/82, Bratislava, Slovakia
Height 187cm, Weight 82kg

Slovakian international striker Róbert Vittek had German statisticians scouring the archives as he struck 16 goals in the Bundesliga for Nuremberg, every single one of them after Christmas. A change of coach at the Frankenstadion worked wonders for both him and the club. Ex-Wolfsburg boss Wolfgang Wolf tried to turn the young striker into an attacking midfielder in order to compensate for the long-term injury to his compatriot Marek Mintál, who had

Top 100 players of the season

topped the Bundesliga goal charts, with 24 goals, the previous season. Vittek wanted none of it and was set to leave in the winter, but after Wolf's dismissal, a new coach, Hans Mayer, arrived and he restored Vittek to his proper position. The dividends during the spring were astonishing as Nuremberg rose from 15th at the winter break to a final position of eighth. Half of Vittek's goals came in an incredible three-match spell in March, when the feisty two-footed striker scored successive hat-tricks against fellow strugglers Duisburg and Cologne and a brace in a resounding 3-1 win over high-flying Werder Bremen.

International Career
SLOVAKIA
Major Honours – none
Debut – 29/5/01 v Germany (a, Bremen, friendly) (sub), lost 0-2
First Goal – 15/8/01 v Iran (h, Bratislava, friendly), lost 3-4
Caps 39 **Goals** 13
Major Tournaments – none
Club Career
Major Honours – none
Clubs: 99-03 SK Slovan Bratislava; 03- 1.FC Nürnberg (GER)

Davor VUGRINEC
Attacking Midfielder/Striker
Born 24/3/75, Varazdin, Croatia
Height 189cm, **Weight** 80kg

For reasons best known to himself Zlatko Kranjcar did not include Davor Vugrinec in his 2006 World Cup squad. The 31-year-old forward returned to the Croatian league after an eight-year exile (most of it across the Adriatic in Italy) and outshone everybody else during the 2005/06 campaign. Rijeka were the beneficiaries of his return. He scored 15 goals in the league, including a sensational hat-trick away to defending champions Hajduk Split, and powered his new club to their second Croatian Cup win in a row. The final, against his hometown and former club Varteks Varazdin, was a bizarre affair. Vugrinec scored twice in the first leg to give Rijeka a seemingly insurmountable lead, but Varteks scored three late goals in the return leg to win 5-1. Fortunately Vugrinec's third goal of the tie – the precious away goal – was enough to earn his club the Cup and give him the first major silverware in his long and winding career. Unwanted at the World Cup, Vugrinec was much in demand from other clubs, but rather than go abroad again he chose to fulfil a personal ambition and join newly crowned Croatian champions Dinamo Zagreb.

International Career
CROATIA
Major Honours – none
Debut – 10/4/96 v Hungary (h, Osijek, friendly) (sub), won 4-1
First Goal – 10/10/98 v Malta (a, Ta' Qali, ECQ) (sub), won 4-1
Caps 27 **Goals** 7
Major Tournaments – World Cup 2002
Club Career

Major Honours – Croatian Cup (2006)
Clubs: 92-97 Varteks Varazdin; 97-00 Trabzonspor (TUR); 00-02 Lecce (ITA); 03-04 Atalanta (ITA); 04-05 Catania (ITA); 05-06 Rijeka; 06- Dinamo Zagreb

Gianluca ZAMBROTTA
Full-Back
Born 19/2/77, Como, Italy
Height 181cm, **Weight** 76kg

Gianluca Zambrotta is not the sort of player to attract attention, either on or off the pitch, but his performances in Italy's World Cup triumph were so consistently impressive that he has now gained superstar status in his homeland. Not that he will be living there for a while. After his jamboree in Germany and the enforced relegation of Juventus, his club for the past seven years, he was signed up on a four-year contract by Champions League winners Barcelona in a joint £13m transfer with French veteran Lilian Thuram. Zambrotta missed Italy's first game at the World Cup with a thigh injury but was on the field for every minute thereafter. Having played as a right-sided midfielder for the Azzurri at the 2002 tournament and at Euro 2004, he was all set to play left-back in Germany, but the emergence of Fabio Grosso saw him return to the right. Although Zambrotta is right-footed, he is happy to play on either side of the pitch. Versatile and disciplined are the two adjectives that best describe him. He should fit in well at Camp Nou.

International Career
ITALY
Major Honours – World Cup (2006)
Debut – 10/2/99 v Norway (h, Pisa, friendly), drew 0-0
First Goal – 30/5/04 v Tunisia (a, Tunisia, friendly), won 4-0
Caps 57 **Goals** 2
Major Tournaments – Euro 2000; World Cup 2002; Euro 2004; World Cup 2006
Club Career
Major Honours – Italian Championship (2002, 2003)
Clubs: 94-97 Como; 97-99 Bari; 99-06 Juventus; 06- FC Barcelona (ESP)

Nikola ZIGIC
Striker
Born 25/9/80, Backa Topola, Serbia
Height 202cm, **Weight** 90kg

The Czech Republic had Jan Koller, England had Peter Crouch, and Serbia & Montenegro had Nikola Zigic. Like those other two giant centre-forwards, the Red Star Belgrade striker stamped his mark on the tournament with a goal, but whereas Koller and Crouch scored with their head in matches their teams won, Zigic found the net with his foot, against the Ivory Coast, and Serbia & Montenegro went on to lose the match, 3-2. The best of Zigic in 2005/06 was not seen in the blue and white of his country but in the red and white of his club. He scored 20 goals in all competitions for 'Crvena Zvezda', including one absolute beauty from long range against Roma in the UEFA Cup. Red Star won both domestic trophies, and

Top 100 players of the season

Zigic set up almost as many goals with his tidy knockdowns and lay-offs as he netted himself. Despite his moderate World Cup foreign clubs were queueing up to add him to their 2006/07 squads, but he preferred to wait and see if he could help Red Star into the Champions League before making any move.

International Career
SERBIA
Major Honours – none
Debut – 31/3/04 v Norway (h, Belgrade, friendly) (sub), lost 0-1
First Goal – 8/6/05 v Italy (n, Toronto, friendly), drew 1-1
Caps 13 **Goals** 4
Major Tournaments – World Cup 2006
Club Career
Major Honours – Serbo-Montenegrin Championship (2004, 2006); Serbo-Montenegrin Cup (2004, 2006)
Clubs: 98-01 AIK Backa Topola; 02 Mornar Bar; 02-03 Kolubar Lazarevac; 03 Spartak Subotica; 03- Crvena Zvezda Beograd

Pascal ZUBERBÜHLER
Goalkeeper
Born 8/1/71, Frauenfeld, Switzerland
Height 197cm, **Weight** 98kg

The pre-tournament talk suggested that Pascal Zuberbühler might inherit the 'El Loco' tag normally attached to madcap World Cup goalkeepers from Latin America. As it turned out, the veteran Swiss keeper was nothing of the sort. The only goals he conceded in Switzerland's four matches in Germany were in the penalty shoot-out that followed the goalless snore draw against Ukraine in Cologne. Otherwise he was flawless. Zubi's reputation, suitably enhanced during a hit-and-miss qualifying campaign, was that of a man who could occasionally be world-class but at other times look hopelessly at sea, flapping at crosses, spilling shots and generally spreading unease. At the World Cup he was neither – just a calm, confident goalkeeper who did all he could to prevent the ball entering his net. He suffered a nightmare end to the Swiss domestic campaign with FC Basel as FC Zurich claimed the title in the St. Jakob Park with the last kick of the season. That would be his final game for the club as he moved to England after the World Cup to join Championship side West Bromwich Albion.

International Career
SWITZERLAND
Major Honours – none
Debut – 9/9/94 v United Arab Emirates (h, Sion, friendly) (sub), won 1-0
Caps 44 **Goals** 0
Major Tournaments – Euro 2004; World Cup 2006
Club Career
Major Honours – Swiss Championship (1995, 1996, 1998, 2002, 2004, 2005); Swiss Cup (1994, 2002, 2003)
Clubs: 91-99 Grasshopper-Club Zürich; 99-00 FC Basel; 00 Bayer 04 Leverkusen (GER); 01 FC Aarau; 01-06 FC Basel; 06- West Bromwich Albion (ENG)

Maciej ZURAWSKI
Striker
Born 12/9/76, Poznan, Poland
Height 180cm, **Weight** 74kg

Maciej Zurawski scored sackloads of goals in the Polish league – 120 in 230 matches, a figure that included two Golden Boot-winning tallies for Wisla Krakow – so it was inevitable that he would leave for foreign fields at some stage of his career. In the summer of 2005, despite pleas from the Wisla faithful for him to stay, he decided that the time was right to depart. Trabzonspor and Austria Vienna made an approach but it was Celtic, with a little help from their former Polish left-back Dariusz Wdowczyk, who proved more decisive in contract negotiations and persuaded him to move to Glasgow for £2m on a three-year deal. Before long the Pole had been christened 'Magic' Zurawski by the Celtic fans. He ended the season with 20 goals in all competitions, including 16 in the SPL. Four of those came in one game – a record 8-1 win at Dunfermline – and he also scored a memorable winner against Rangers at Ibrox. He went to the World Cup as a Polish celebrity but, starved of service and support, never looked like adding to the seven goals he had struck in the qualifying campaign.

International Career
POLAND
Major Honours – none
Debut – 10/11/98 v Slovakia (a, Bratislava, friendly) (sub), won 3-1
First Goal – 10/2/02 v Faroe Islands (n, Limassol, friendly), won 2-1
Caps 53 **Goals** 15
Major Tournaments – World Cup 2002; World Cup 2006
Club Career
Major Honours – Scottish Championship (2006); Polish Championship (2001, 2003, 2004, 2005); Polish Cup (2002, 2003); Scottish League Cup (2006)
Clubs: 94-97 Warta Poznan; 98-99 Lech Poznan; 99-05 Wisla Krakow; 05- Celtic (SCO)

…and the ten players who didn't quite make it:

Valter BIRSA

Tim BOROWSKI

Khalid BOULAHROUZ

Pascal CHIMBONDA

Torsten FRINGS

LUCHO GONZÁLEZ

Tarmo NEEMELO

Willy SAGNOL

Dimitris SALPIGIDIS

Zinedine ZIDANE